# NETWORK ANALYSIS and SYNTHESIS

**Second Edition**

# About the Author

**Ravish R Singh** is presently Director at Thakur Ramnarayan College of Arts and Commerce, Mumbai. He obtained a BE degree from University of Mumbai in 1991, an MTech degree from IIT Bombay in 2001, and a PhD degree from Faculty of Technology, University of Mumbai, in 2013. He has published several books with McGraw Hill Education (India) on varied subjects like *Engineering Mathematics, Applied Mathematics, Electrical Networks, Network Analysis and Synthesis, Electrical Engineering, Basic Electrical and Electronics Engineering*, etc., for all-India curricula as well as regional curricula of some universities like Gujarat Technological University, Mumbai University, Pune University, Jawaharlal Nehru Technological University, Anna University, Uttarakhand Technical University, and Dr A P J Abdul Kalam Technical University. Dr Singh is a member of IEEE, ISTE, and IETE, and has published research papers in national and international journals. His fields of interest include Circuits, Signals and Systems, and Engineering Mathematics.

# NETWORK ANALYSIS and SYNTHESIS

## Second Edition

**Ravish R Singh**
*Director*
*Thakur Ramnarayan College of Arts & Commerce*
*Mumbai, Maharashtra*

**McGraw Hill Education (India) Private Limited**

Published by McGraw Hill Education (India) Private Limited,
Anjana Complex No: 5/90 A, Butt Road, St. Thomas Mount, Chennai – 600016, Tamil Nadu, India.

**Network Analysis and Synthesis, 2e**



Second reprint 2024



**Print Edition**
ISBN-13: 978-93-5316-672-4
ISBN-10: 93-5316-672-1

**E-Book Edition**
ISBN-13: 978-93-5316-673-1
ISBN-10: 93-5316-673-X

**03 04 05 06 07 SDR 28 27 26 25 24**



Typeset at APS Compugraphics, 4G, PKT 2, Mayur Vihar, Phase – III, Delhi 110096, and Printed and bound in India at SDR Printers, A-7, Sector-B-3, Tronica City, Ghaziabad, (U.P.) 201103

Cover Image Source: Design Pics / Corey Hochachka
Cover Designer: APS Compugraphics

Visit us at: www.mheducation.co.in
Toll free in India: 1800 103 5875
Write to us at: support.india@mheducation.com
CIN: U80302TN2010PTC111532

**Dedicated to**

***My Father***

*Late Shri Ramsagar Singh*

*and*

***My Mother***

*Late Shrimati Premsheela Singh*

# Contents

# Preface

## Overview

Network Analysis and Synthesis is one of the core subjects for students of Electrical Engineering, Electronics Engineering, Electronics and Telecommunication Engineering, Instrumentation Engineering, Biomedical Engineering and related branches of engineering in the third/fourth semester course of almost all universities in India. This subject is also one of the important topics of competitive examinations such as GATE, IAS, IES, etc. and examinations conducted by various public-sector undertakings in this field.

## About the Book

*Network Analysis and Synthesis* is a complete solution for the undergraduate student who wishes to prepare for university and competitive examinations. This highly illustrative text makes the subject matter interesting and easy for students.

As per the course requirement, five major topics that are mandatory to be covered by any book on the subject are dc and ac circuits, transient analysis, network functions, two-port networks and network synthesis. Generally, numerical problems are expected in university examinations in this subject. The weightage given to problems is more than 70-80% in examinations. This book attempts to cover almost all the topics and solved problems on these important topics. The simplistic presentation style sequentially takes the readers from basic to advance concepts and the crisp theory helps in ready understanding. Numerous solved examples and graded problems have been provided in this book, especially in important chapters from the examination viewpoint. Objective-type questions from various papers of competitive examinations like GATE are included in each chapter. This will help students in sharpening their knowledge about core concepts. Covering both analysis and synthesis of networks, the text provides a simple explanation about the concepts of electrical networks with brief theory and a large number of problems. Numerous examples and exercise problems have been included to help the reader develop an intuitive grasp of the contents.

## Salient Features

- Span of coverage meets curriculum requirements
- Simplistic presentation and logical sequencing of topics
- Graded problem-solving approach

- Numerous solved examples from frequently asked examination questions
- Rich pedagogy
  - Illustrations: 2306
  - Solved Examples: 896
  - LTspice Solved Examples: 38
  - Practice Problems: 309
  - Objective Type Questions: 373

## New in the Edition

The entire content is modified as per AICTE syllabus. Complete pedagogy is refreshed and many important topics like Routh Hurwitz Criterion, Bode diagrams, locus diagrams has been added. Separate section on LTspice is given with each chapter which will help students to hone their skills and applications of the concept.

## Chapter Organisation

The entire text is organised into 15 chapters, primarily based on the electrical and electronics engineering syllabi in BE/B.Tech undergraduate courses of universities around the country. The summary of the book can be organised in the following major parts:

- Circuit Elements and Network Analysis
- Network Theorems for dc and ac Circuits
- Resonance and Coupled Circuits
- Network Topology/Graph Theory
- Transient Analysis and Laplace Transforms
- Two-Port Networks
- Network Functions

Within this structure, a more in-depth and detailed breakdown can be obtained from the table of contents. The fluid flow of text dealing with different topics as well as illustrations, examples, questions and numerical problems are extremely relevant and appropriate for students as well as instructors. The main strength of the book thus is its strong focus towards students' readability and understanding with the scope for independent study and problem-solving skill development. I am confident that the depth of this book has been judiciously developed so that students not only treat this as a textbook, but, in addition, can also gather enough practical and theoretical knowledge to appear in national-level competitive examinations and interviews.

## Web Supplements

The text is supplemented with an exhaustive Online Learning Center, which can be accessed at https://connect.mheducation.com.

## Acknowledgements

I would like to thank all the staff at McGraw Hill Education (India), especially Shalini Jha, Vaishali Thapliyal, Satinder Singh Baveja and Anuj Kr. Shrivastava for coordinating with me during the editorial, copyediting and production stages of this book. My acknowledgements would be incomplete without a mention of the contribution of my family members. I feel indebted to my father and mother for their lifelong inspiration.

I also send a heartfelt thanks to my wife, Nitu; son, Aman; and daughter, Aditri, for always motivating and supporting me during the preparation of the project. Finally, I would like to appreciate the role of all the reviewers for providing valuable inputs on the subject of *Network Analysis and Synthesis* which have significantly enriched this text.

**Ravish R. Singh**

## Publisher's Note

McGraw Hill Education (India) invites suggestions and comments from you, all of which can be sent to info.india@mheducation.com (Kindly mention the title and author name in the subject line).
Piracy-related issues may also be reported.

CHAPTER 1

# Basic Network Concepts

## LEARNING OBJECTIVES

**After studying this chapter, you should be able to:**

- **LO 1.1** Explain the concepts of resistance, inductance, and capacitance
- **LO 1.2** Discuss sources and their types
- **LO 1.3** Define network and circuit, linear and non-linear elements, active and passive elements, unilateral and bilateral elements, lumped and distributed elements, active and passive networks, time-invarient and time-varient networks
- **LO 1.4** Analyse series and parallel combination of resistors, inductors, and capacitors
- **LO 1.5** Simplify the networks using star-to-delta and delta-to-star transformations
- **LO 1.6** Discuss source transformation and source-shifting techniques
- **LO 1.7** Use Kirchhoff's laws in solving the networks

## INTRODUCTION

We know that like charges repel each other whereas unlike charges attract each other. To overcome this force of attraction, a certain amount of work or energy is required. When the charges are separated, it is said that a potential difference exists and the work or energy per unit charge utilised in this process is known as voltage or potential difference.

The phenomenon of transfer of charge from one point to another is termed current. Current ($I$) is defined as the rate of flow of electrons in a conductor. It is measured by the number of electrons that flow in unit time.

Energy is the total work done in the electric circuit. The rate at which the work is done in an electric circuit is called electric power. Energy is measured in joules (J) and power in watts (W).

## 1.1 RESISTANCE

LO 1.1

Explain the concepts of resistance, inductance, and capacitance

Resistance is the property of a material due to which it opposes the flow of electric current through it.

Certain materials offer very little opposition to the flow of electric current and are called conductors, e.g., metals, acids and salt solutions. Certain materials offer very high resistance to the flow of electric current and are called insulators, e.g., mica, glass, rubber, Bakelite, etc.

The practical unit of resistance is **ohm** and is represented by the symbol Ω. A conductor is said to have resistance of one ohm if a potential difference of one volt across its terminals causes a current of one ampere to flow through it.

The resistance of a conductor depends on the following factors.

(i) It is directly proportional to its length.
(ii) It is inversely proportional to the area of cross-section of the conductor.
(iii) It depends on the nature of the material.
(iv) It also depends on the temperature of the conductor.

Hence,

$$R \propto \frac{l}{A}$$

$$R = \rho \frac{l}{A}$$

where $l$ is length of the conductor, $A$ is the cross-sectional area and $\rho$ is a constant known as specific resistance or resistivity of the material.

**1. *Current-Voltage Relationship in a Resistor*** $v = R\,i$

**2. *Power Dissipated in a Resistor*** When current flows through any resistor, power is absorbed by the resistor, which is given by

$$p = v\,i$$

The power dissipated in the resistor is converted to heat which is given by

$$E = \int_0^t v\,i\,dt = \int_0^t R\,i\,i\,dt = i^2\,Rt$$

**EXAMPLE 1.1** ●○○

*A 25 Ω resistor has a voltage of 150 sin 377t. Find the corresponding current i and power p.*

**Note** Difficulty Level ●○○— Easy; ○●○— Medium; ○○●— Difficult

**Solution**

$$R = 25\ \Omega$$
$$v = 150 \sin 377t$$
$$i = \frac{v}{R} = \frac{150 \sin 377t}{25} = 6 \sin 377t$$
$$p = vi = (150 \sin 377t)(6 \sin 377t) = 900 \sin^2 337t$$

**EXAMPLE 1.2**

*A current waveform shown in Fig. 1.1 is applied to a 2 Ω resistor. Draw the voltage waveform.*

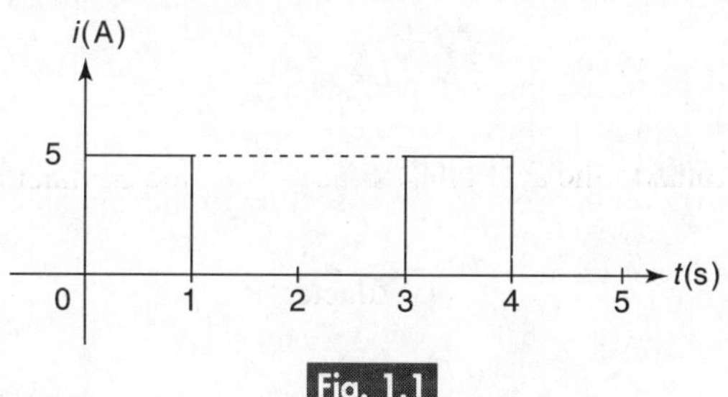


Fig. 1.1

**Solution**

For the resistor, $v = Ri$

(a) For $0 < t < 1$, $v = Ri = 2 \times 5 = 10$ V

(b) For $1 < t < 3$, $v = Ri = 2 \times 0 = 0$

(c) For $3 < t < 4$, $v = Ri = 2 \times 5 = 10$ V

The voltage waveform is shown in Fig. 1.2.

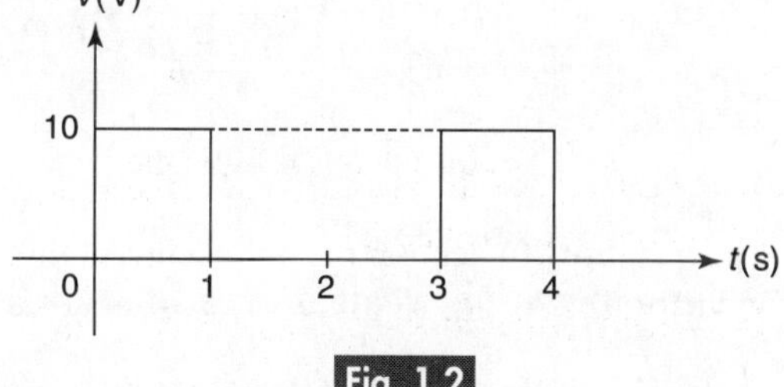


Fig. 1.2

## 1.2 INDUCTANCE

LO 1.1

Inductance is the property of a coil that opposes any change in the amount of current flowing through it. If the current in the coil is increasing, the self-induced emf is set up in such a direction so as to oppose the rise of current. Similarly, if the current in the coil is decreasing, the self-induced emf will be in the same direction as the applied voltage.

Inductance is defined as the ratio of flux linkage to the current flowing through the coil. The practical unit of inductance is **henry** and is represented by the symbol H. A coil is said to have an inductance of one henry if a current of one ampere, when flowing through it, produces flux linkages of one weber-turn in it.

The inductance of an inductor depends on the following factors.

(i) It is directly proportional to the square of the number of turns.
(ii) It is directly proportional to the area of cross-section.
(iii) It is inversely proportional to the length.
(iv) It depends on the absolute permeability of the magnetic material.

Hence,

$$L \propto \frac{N^2 A}{l}$$

$$L = \mu \frac{N^2 A}{l}$$

where $l$ is the mean length, $A$ is the cross-sectional area and $\mu$ is the absolute permeability of the magnetic material.

***1. Current–Voltage Relationships in an Inductor*** We know that

$$v = L\frac{di}{dt}$$

Expressing inductor current as a function of voltage,

$$di = \frac{1}{L} v\, dt$$

Integrating both the sides,

$$\int_{i(0)}^{i(t)} di = \frac{l}{L}\int_0^t v\, dt$$

$$i(t) = \frac{1}{L}\int_0^t v\, dt + i(0)$$

The quantity $i(0)$ denotes the initial current through the inductor. When there is no initial current through the inductor,

$$i(t) = \frac{1}{L}\int_0^t v\, dt$$

***2. Energy Stored in an Inductor*** Consider a coil of inductance $L$ carrying a changing current $I$. When the current is changed from zero to a maximum value $I$, every change is opposed by the self-induced emf produced. To overcome this opposition, some energy is needed and this energy is stored in the magnetic field. The voltage $v$ is given by

$$v = L\frac{di}{dt}$$

Energy supplied to the inductor during interval $dt$ is given by

$$dE = v\, i\, dt = L\frac{di}{dt} i\, dt = L\, i\, dt$$

Hence, total energy supplied to the inductor when current is increased from 0 to $I$ amperes is

$$E = \int_0^I dE = \int_0^I L\, i\, di = \frac{1}{2} L I^2$$

**EXAMPLE 1.3**

*An inductance of 3 mH has a current $i = 5(1 - e^{-5000t})$. Find the corresponding voltage and the maximum stored energy.*

**Solution**

$$L = 3 \text{ mH}$$

$$i = 5(1 - e^{-5000t})$$

$$v = L\frac{di}{dt} = 3\times10^{-3}\frac{d}{dt}\left[5(1-e^{-5000t})\right] = 3\times10^{-3}(5\times5000\, e^{-5000t}) = 75\, e^{-5000t}$$

$$I_{\max} = i(\infty) = 5(1 - e^{-\infty}) = 5 \text{ A}$$

$$E_{\max} = \frac{1}{2}LI_{\max}^2 = \frac{1}{2}\times3\times10^{-3}\times(5)^2 = 37.5 \text{ mJ}$$

**EXAMPLE 1.4**

*A current waveform is applied to a 2 H inductor. Draw the voltage waveform for Fig. 1.3.*

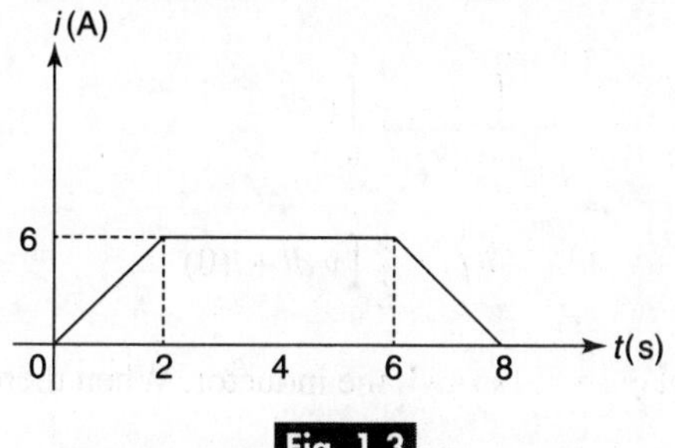


Fig. 1.3

**Solution**

$$v = L\frac{di}{dt}$$

(a) For $0 < t < 2$,

$$v = 2\times\frac{(6-0)}{(2-0)} = 6 \text{ V}$$

(b) For $2 < t < 6$,

$$v = 2\times\frac{(6-6)}{(6-2)} = 0$$

(c) For $6 < t < 8$,

$$v = 2\times\frac{(0-6)}{(8-6)} = -6 \text{ V}$$

The voltage waveform is shown in Fig. 1.4.

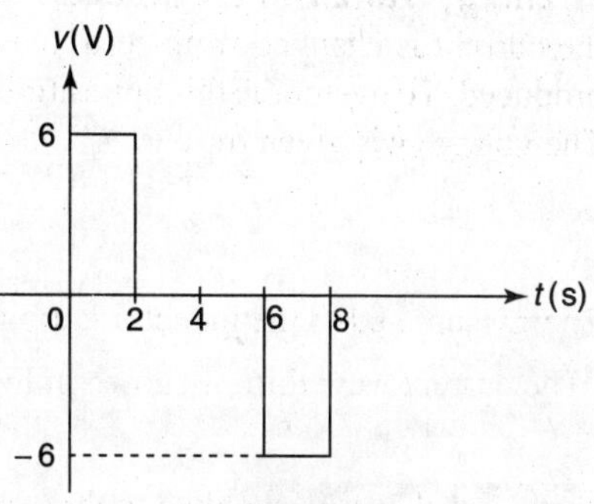


Fig. 1.4

## EXAMPLE 1.5

*A voltage waveform shown in Fig. 1.5 is applied across a 1 H inductor. Draw the current waveform.*

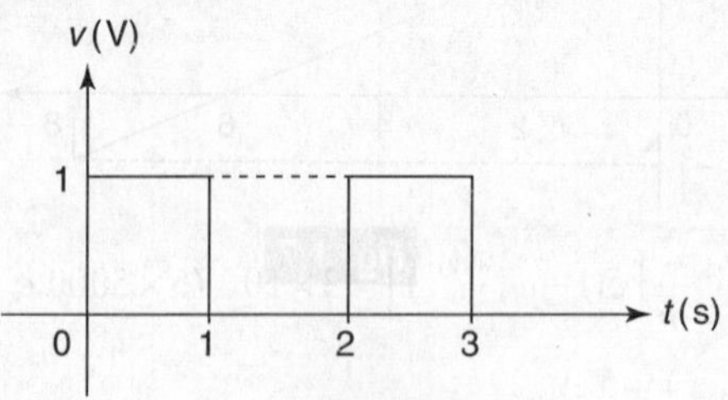


Fig. 1.5

**Solution** $i = \frac{1}{L}\int_0^t v\,dt + i(0)$

(a) For $0 < t < 1$,

$$v = 1$$

$$i = \frac{1}{1}\int_0^t 1\,dt + i(0) = [t]_0^t + 0 = t$$

$$i(1) = 1 \text{ A}$$

(b) For $1 < t < 2$,

$$v = 0$$

$$i = \frac{1}{1}\int_1^t 0 \cdot dt + i(1) = 0 + 1 = 1 \text{ A}$$

$$i(2) = 1 \text{ A}$$

(c) For $2 < t < 3$,

$$v = 1$$

$$i = \frac{1}{1}\int_2^t 1\,dt + i(2) = [t]_2^t + 1 = t - 2 + 1 = t - 1$$

$$i(3) = 3 - 1 = 2 \text{ A}$$

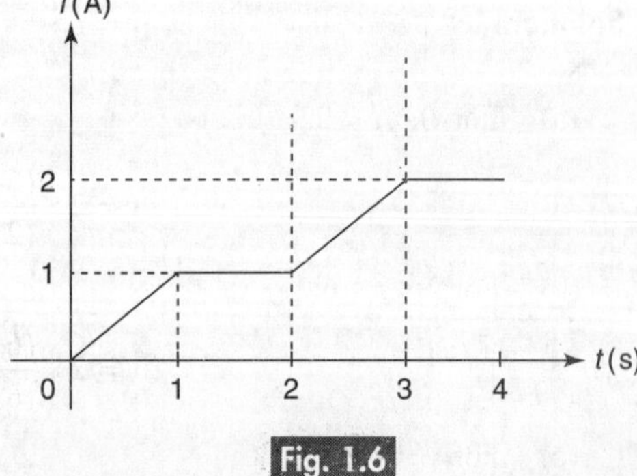


Fig. 1.6

The current waveform is shown in Fig. 1.6.

## EXAMPLE 1.6

*A voltage waveform shown in Fig. 1.7 is applied across a 2 H inductor. Draw the current waveform.*

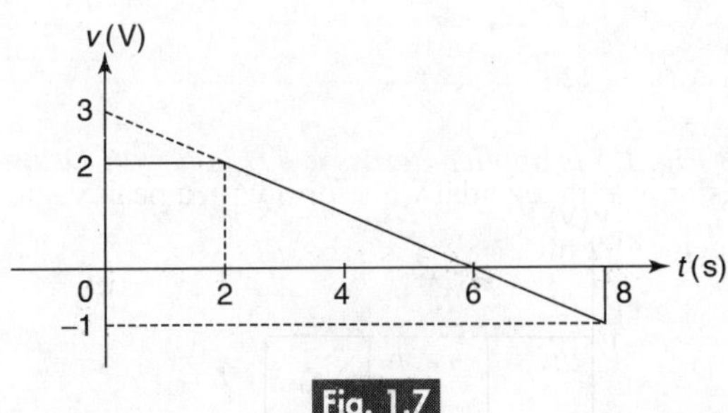


Fig. 1.7

**Solution** $i = \frac{1}{L}\int_0^t v(t) + i(0)$

(a) For $0 < t < 2$,

$$v = 2$$

$$i = \frac{1}{2}\int_0^t 2\,dt + i(0) = 0.5[2t]_0^t + 0 = t$$

$$i(2) = 2\text{ A}$$

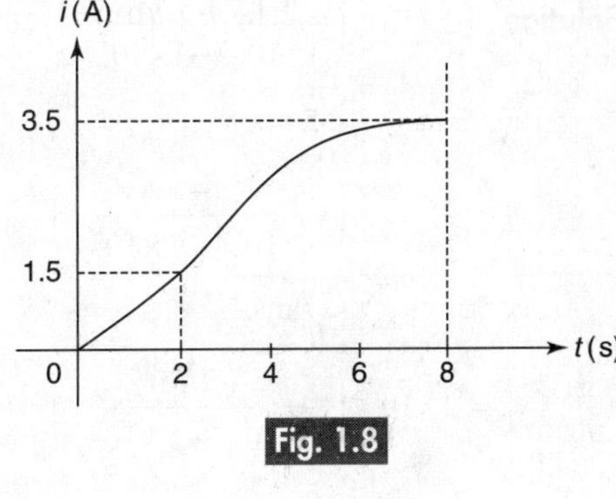


Fig. 1.8

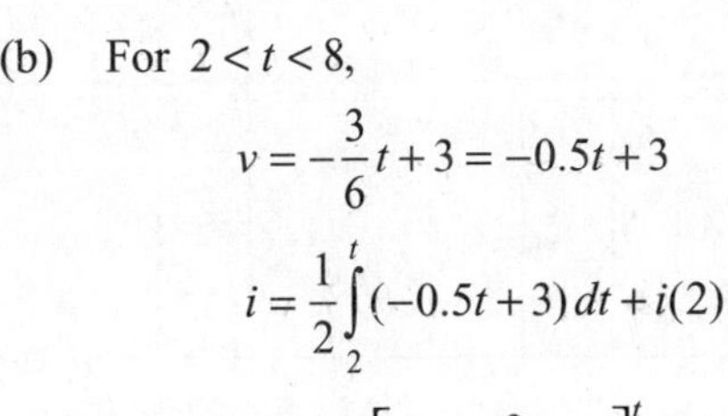

(b) For $2 < t < 8$,

$$v = -\frac{3}{6}t + 3 = -0.5t + 3$$

$$i = \frac{1}{2}\int_2^t (-0.5t + 3)\,dt + i(2)$$

$$= 0.5\left[-0.5\frac{t^2}{2} + 3t\right]_2^t + 2 = 0.5[-0.25t^2 + 3t + 0.5\times 2 - 3\times 2] + 2 = 0.5[-0.25t^2 + 3t - 5] + 2$$

$$i(8) = 0.5[-0.25(64) + 3(8) - 5] + 2 = 3.5\text{ A}$$

The current waveform is shown in Fig. 1.8.

## EXAMPLE 1.7

*The following current waveform i(t) is passed through a series RL circuit with $R = 2\ \Omega$ and $L = 2\ mH$. Find the voltage across each element and sketch the same.*

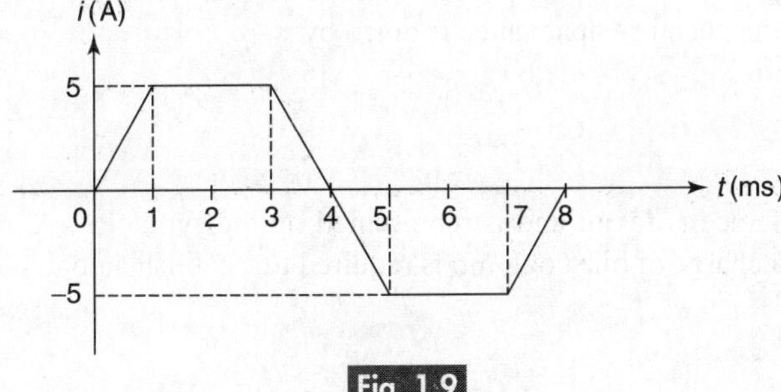


Fig. 1.9

**Solution**

(a) Voltage across the resistor of 2 Ω

$$v_R = Ri$$

Voltage across the resistor is a trapezoidal waveform with a peak value of 10 V.

(b) Voltage across the inductor of 2 mH

$$v_L = L\frac{di}{dt}$$

For $0 < t < 1$ ms,

$$v_L = 2\times10^{-3}\left(\frac{5-0}{1\times10^{-3}-0}\right) = 10 \text{ V}$$

For 1 ms $< t <$ 3 ms,

$$v_L = 2\times10^{-3}\left(\frac{-5-5}{3\times10^{-3}-1\times10^{-3}}\right) = 0$$

For 3 ms $< t <$ 5 ms,

$$v_L = 2\times10^{-3}\left(\frac{5-5}{5\times10^{-3}-3\times10^{-3}}\right) = -10 \text{ V}$$

For 5 ms $< t <$ 7 ms,

$$v_L = 2\times10^{-3}\left(\frac{-5+5}{7\times10^{-3}-5\times10^{-3}}\right) = 0$$

For 7 ms $< t <$ 8 ms,

$$v_L = 2\times10^{-3}\left(\frac{0+5}{8\times10^{-3}-7\times10^{-3}}\right) = 10 \text{ V}$$

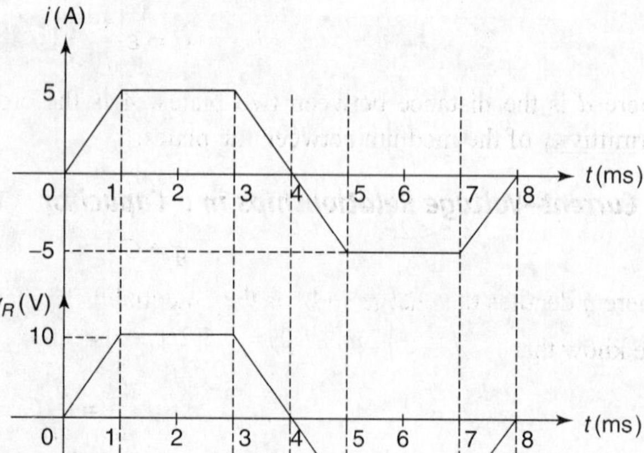


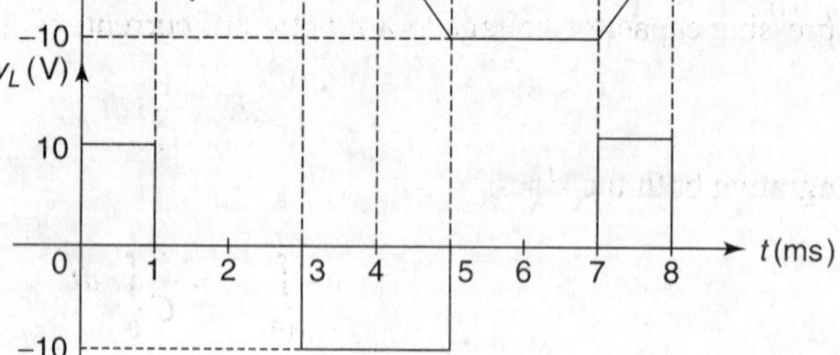


The voltage waveforms are shown in Fig. 1.10.

**Fig. 1.10**

## 1.3 CAPACITANCE

LO 1.1

Capacitance is the property of a capacitor to store an electric charge when its plates are at different potentials. If $Q$ coulombs of charge is given to one of the plates of a capacitor and if a potential difference of $V$ volts is applied between the two plates then its capacitance is given by

$$C = \frac{Q}{V}$$

The practical unit of capacitance is **farad** and is represented by the symbol F. A capacitor is said to have capacitance of one farad if a charge of one coulomb is required to establish a potential difference of one volt between its plates.

The capacitance of a capacitor depends on the following factors.

(i) It is directly proportional to the area of the plates.
(ii) It is inversely proportional to the distance between two plates.
(iii) It depends on the absolute permittivity of the medium between the plates.

Hence,

$$C \propto \frac{A}{d}$$

$$C = \varepsilon \frac{A}{d}$$

where $d$ is the distance between two plates, $A$ is the cross-sectional area of the plates and $\varepsilon$ is absolute permittivity of the medium between the plates.

**1. Current–Voltage Relationships in a Capacitor** The charge on a capacitor is given by

$$q = Cv$$

where $q$ denotes the charge and $v$ is the potential difference across the plates at any instant.

We know that

$$i = \frac{dq}{dt} = \frac{d}{dt}Cv = C\frac{dv}{dt}$$

Expressing capacitor voltage as a function of current,

$$dv = \frac{1}{C} i\, dt$$

Integrating both the sides,

$$\int_{v(0)}^{v(t)} dv = \frac{1}{C}\int_0^t i\, dt$$

$$v(t) = \frac{1}{C}\int_0^t i\, dt + v(0)$$

The quantity $v$ (0) denotes the initial voltage across the capacitor. When there is no initial voltage on the capacitor,

$$v(t) = \frac{1}{C}\int_0^t i\, dt$$

**2. Energy Stored in a Capacitor** Let a capacitor of capacitance $C$ farads be charged from a source of $V$ volts. Then current $i$ is given by

$$i = C\frac{dv}{dt}$$

Energy supplied to the capacitor during interval $dt$ is given by

$$dE = v\, i\, dt = v\, C\frac{dv}{dt} dt$$

Hence, total energy supplied to the capacitor when potential difference is increased from 0 to $V$ volts is

$$E = \int_0^V dE = \int_0^V C\,v\,dv = \frac{1}{2}CV^2$$

## EXAMPLE 1.8

*A voltage is defined by*

$$v(t) = \begin{cases} 0 & t < 0 \\ 2t & 0 < t < 2\,s \\ 4\,e^{-(t-2)} & t > 2\,s \end{cases}$$

*and is applied to the 10 μF capacitor. Find i(t).*

**Solution**

$$i = C\frac{dv}{dt}$$

For $t < 0$,

$$i = 0$$

For $0 < t < 2\,s$,

$$v = 2t$$

$$i = 10 \times 10^{-6}\frac{d}{dt}(2t) = 20\ \mu\text{A}$$

For $t > 2\,s$,

$$v = 4\,e^{-(t-2)}$$

$$i = 10 \times 10^{-6}\frac{d}{dt}[4e^{-(t-2)}] = 10 \times 10^{-6}[-4e^{-(t-2)}] = -40\,e^{-(t-2)}\ \mu\text{A}$$

## EXAMPLE 1.9

*A voltage waveform shown in Fig. 1.11 is applied to the capacitor. Draw the current waveform.*

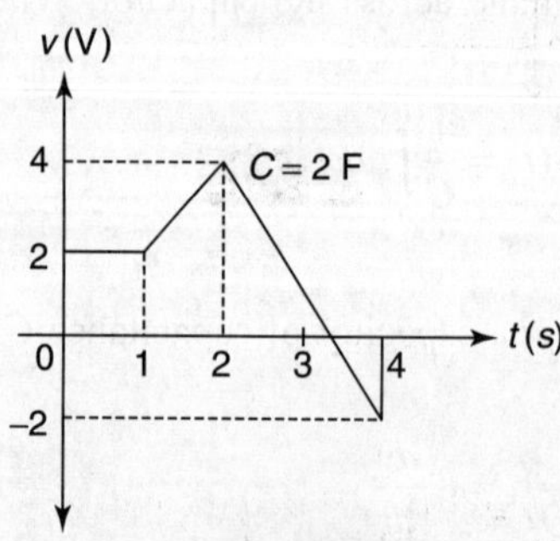


Fig. 1.11

**Solution**

$$i = C\frac{dv}{dt}$$

(a) $0 < t < 1$

At $t = 0$, $v = 2$ V

At $t = 1$, $v = 2$ V

$$i = C\frac{dv}{dt} = 2\left(\frac{2-2}{1-0}\right) = 0$$

(b) $1 < t < 2$

At $t = 1$, $v = 2$ V

At $t = 2$, $v = 4$ V

$$i = C\frac{dv}{dt} = 2\left(\frac{4-2}{2-1}\right) = 4 \text{ A}$$

(c) $2 < t < 4$

At $t = 2$, $v = 4$ V

At $t = 4$, $v = -2$ V

$$i = C\frac{dv}{dt} = 2\left(\frac{-2-4}{4-2}\right) = 2\left(\frac{-6}{2}\right) = -6 \text{ A}$$

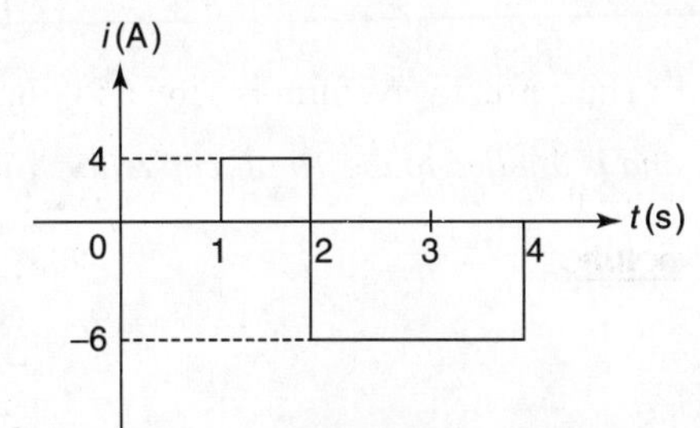


Fig. 1.12

The current waveform is shown in Fig. 1.12.

## EXAMPLE 1.10

*A voltage waveform shown in Fig. 1.13 is applied to the capacitor. Draw the current waveform.*

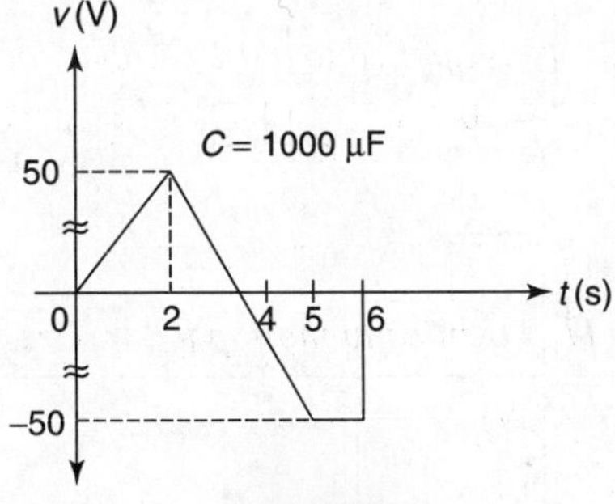


Fig. 1.13

**Solution**

(a) $0 < t < 2$

At $t = 0$, $v = 0$ V

At $t = 2$, $v = 50$ V

$$i = C\frac{dv}{dt} = 10^{-3}\left(\frac{50-0}{2-0}\right) = 10^{-3}\left(\frac{50}{2}\right) = 25\times10^{-3} \text{ A}$$

(b) $2 < t < 5$

At $t = 2$, $v = 50$ V

At $t = 5$, $v = -50$ V

$$i = C\frac{dv}{dt} = 10^{-3}\left(\frac{-50-50}{5-2}\right) = 10^{-3}\left(\frac{-100}{3}\right) = -33.33\times10^{-3}\ \text{A}$$

(c) $5 < t < 6$

At $t = 5$, $v = -50$ V

At $t = 6$, $v = -50$ V

$$i = C\frac{dv}{dt} = 10^{-3}\left(\frac{-50+50}{6-5}\right) = 0$$

The current waveform is shown in Fig. 1.14.

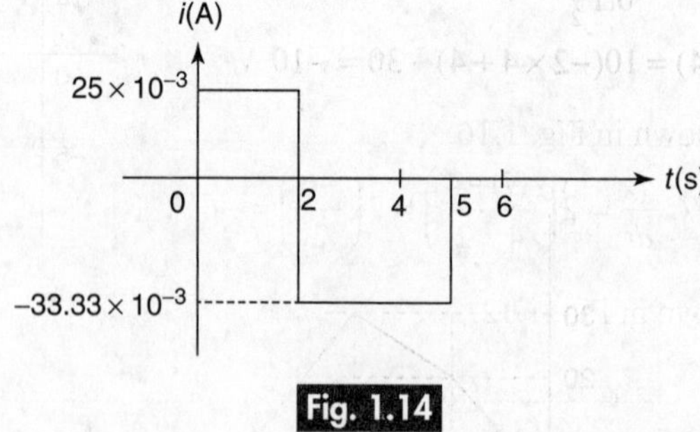


Fig. 1.14

**EXAMPLE 1.11**

*A current waveform shown in Fig. 1.15 is applied to a 0.1 F capacitor. Draw the voltage waveform.*

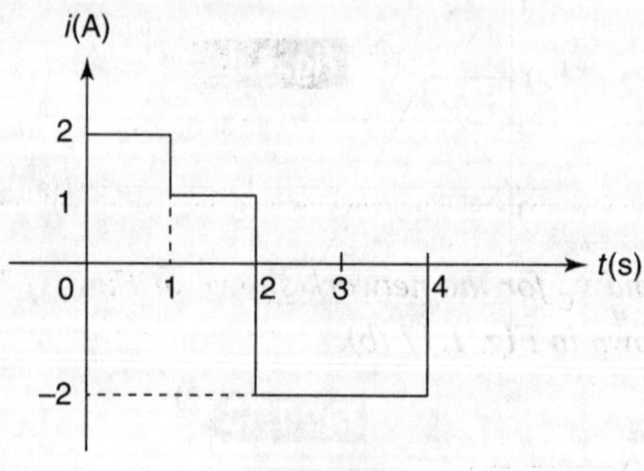


Fig. 1.15

**Solution**

$$v = \frac{1}{C}\int_0^t i\,dt + v(0)$$

(a) For $0 < t < 1$,

$$i = 2$$

$$v = \frac{1}{0.1}\int_0^t 2\,dt + v(0) = 10[2t]_0^t + 0 = 20\,t$$

$$v(1) = 20\ \text{V}$$

(b) For $1 < t < 2$,

$$i = 1$$

$$v = \frac{1}{0.1}\int_1^t 1\,dt + v(1) = 10[t]_1^t + 20 = 10(t-1) + 20$$

$$v(2) = 10(2-1) + 20 = 30 \text{ V}$$

(c) For $2 < t < 4$,

$$i = -2$$

$$v = \frac{1}{0.1}\int_2^t -2\,dt + v(2) = 10[-2t]_2^t + 30 = 10(-2t+4) + 30$$

$$v(4) = 10(-2\times 4 + 4) + 30 = -10 \text{ V}$$

The voltage waveform is shown in Fig. 1.16.

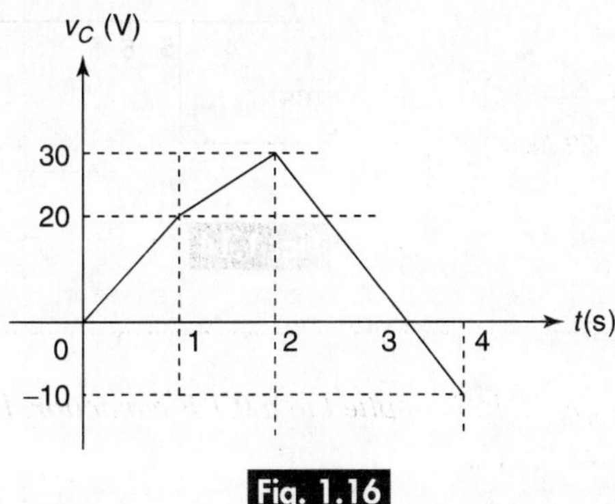


Fig. 1.16

## EXAMPLE 1.12

*Draw the waveforms for $v_R$ and $v_C$ for the network shown in Fig. 1.17 (a) when it is excited by a current source having a waveform shown in Fig. 1.17 (b).*

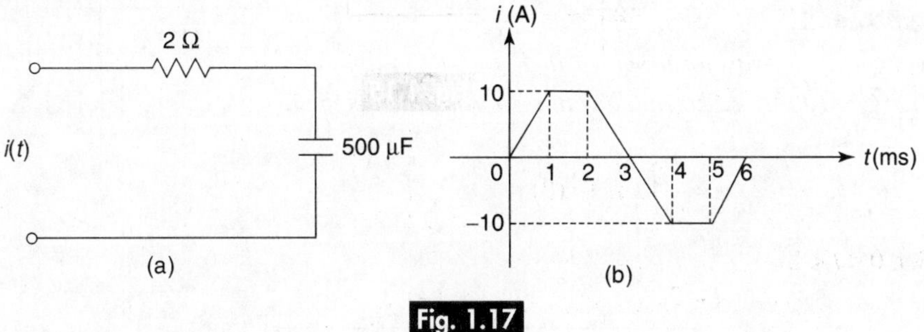


Fig. 1.17

**Solution**

(a) Voltage across the resistor of 2 Ω

$$v_R = Ri$$

Voltage across the resistor is a trapezoidal waveform with a peak value of 20 V.

(b) Voltage across capacitor of 500 μF

$$v_C = \frac{1}{C}\int_0^t i\,dt + v(0)$$

For $0 < t < 1$ ms,

$$i = \frac{10}{10^{-3}}t = 10000t$$

$$v_C = \frac{1}{500\times10^{-6}}\int_0^t 10000t\,dt + 0 = 10^7 t^2$$

$$v_C(1\text{ ms}) = 10^7\times(10^{-3})^2 = 10\text{ V}$$

For 1 ms $< t <$ 2 ms,

$$i = 10$$

$$v_C = \frac{1}{500\times10^{-6}}\int_{1\text{ ms}}^t 10\,dt + v_c(1\text{ ms})$$

$$= 2000[10t]_{1\text{ ms}}^t + 10$$

$$= 2000(10t - 10\times10^{-3}) + 10$$

$$= 20000t - 20 + 10 = 20000t - 10$$

$$v_C(2\text{ ms}) = 20000(2\times10^{-3}) - 10 = 30\text{ V}$$

Similarly it can be found that

$v_C(3\text{ ms}) = 40$ V

$v_C(4\text{ ms}) = 30$ V

$v_C(5\text{ ms}) = 10$ V

$v_C(6\text{ ms}) = 0$ V

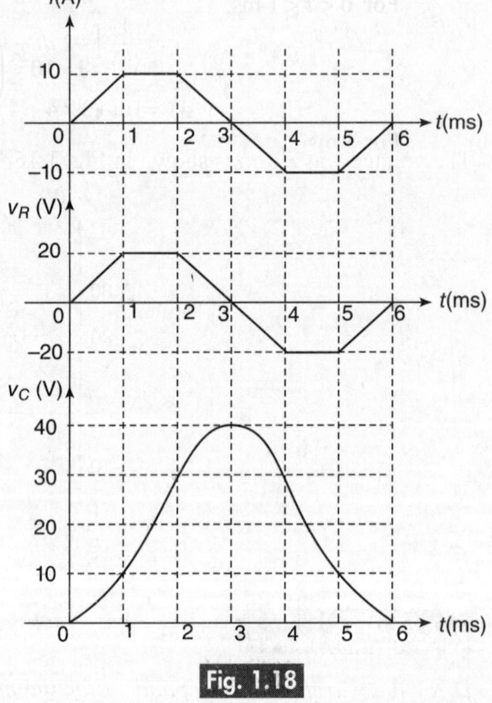


Fig. 1.18

The voltage waveforms are shown in Fig. 1.18.

## EXAMPLE 1.13

*A current with periodic waveform shown in Fig. 1.19 is applied to a series RLC circuit with R = 1 Ω, L = 1 mH and C = 100 μF. Sketch the voltage across each element.*

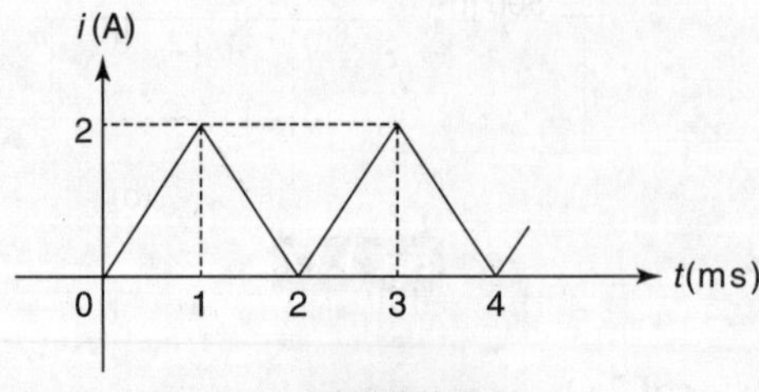


Fig. 1.19

**Solution**

(a) Voltage across the resistor of 1 Ω

$$v_R = R\,i$$

Voltage across the resistor is a triangular waveform with peak value of 2 V.

(b) Voltage across inductor of 1 mH

$$v_L = L\frac{di}{dt}$$

For $0 < t < 1$ ms,

$$v_L = 1\times10^{-3}\left(\frac{2-0}{1\times10^{-3}-0}\right) = 2\text{ V}$$

For 1 ms $< t <$ 2 ms,

$$v_L = 1\times10^{-3}\left(\frac{0-2}{2\times10^{-3}-1\times10^{-3}}\right) = -2\text{ V}$$

Voltage across the inductor is a square waveform.

(c) Voltage across capacitor of 100 μF

$$v_C = \frac{1}{C}\int_0^t i\,dt + v(0)$$

For $0 < t < 1$ ms,

$$i = \frac{2}{10^{-3}}t = 2000t$$

$$v_C = \frac{1}{100\times10^{-6}}\int_0^t 2000t\,dt + 0 = 10^4\left(\frac{2000t^2}{2}\right) = 10^7\,t^2$$

$$v_C(1\text{ ms}) = 10^7(10^{-3})^2 = 10\text{ V}$$

For 1 ms $< t <$ 2 ms,

$$i = -\frac{2}{10^{-3}}t + 4 = -2000t + 4$$

$$v_C = \frac{1}{100\times10^{-6}}\int_{1\text{ ms}}^t (-2000t+4)dt + v(1\text{ ms}) = 10^4(-1000t^2 + 4t - 3\times10^{-3}) + 10$$

$$= 10^4(-1000t^2 + 4t) - 20$$

$$v_C(2\text{ ms}) = 10^4\left[-1000(2\times10^{-3})^2 + 4(2\times10^{-3})\right] - 20 = 20\text{ V}$$

Similarly it can be found that

$$v_C\,(3\text{ ms}) = 30\text{ V}$$

$$v_C\,(4\text{ ms}) = 40\text{ V}$$

Voltage across the capacitor keeps rising continuously. The voltage waveforms are shown in Fig. 1.20.

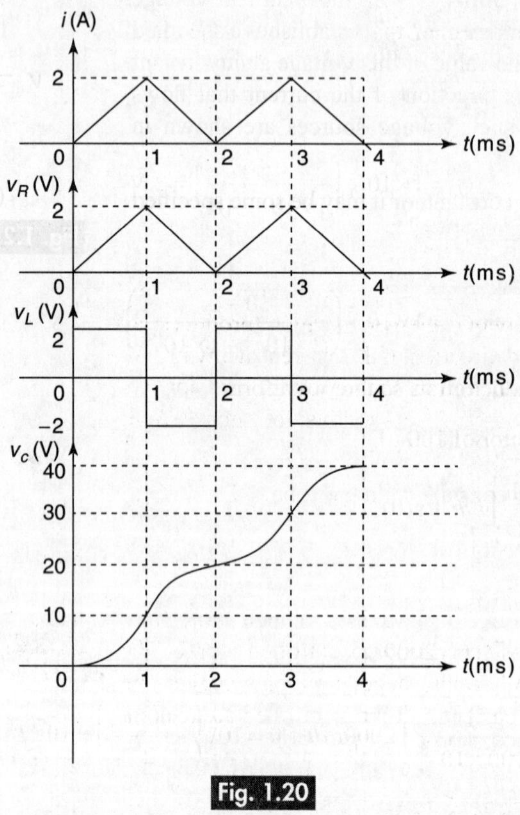


Fig. 1.20

## 1.4 SOURCES

LO 1.2

Discuss sources and their types

Source is a basic network element which supplies energy to the networks. There are two classes of sources, namely,

1. Independent sources
2. Dependent sources

### 1.4.1 Independent Sources

Output characteristics of an independent source are not dependent on any network variable such as a current or voltage. Its characteristics, however, may be time-varying. There are two types of independent sources:

1. Independent voltage source
2. Independent current source

***1. Independent Voltage Source*** An independent voltage source is a two-terminal network element that establishes a specified voltage across its terminals. The value of this voltage at any instant is independent of the value or direction of the current that flows through it. The symbols for such voltage sources are shown in Fig. 1.21.

The terminal voltage may be a constant, or it may be some specified function of time.

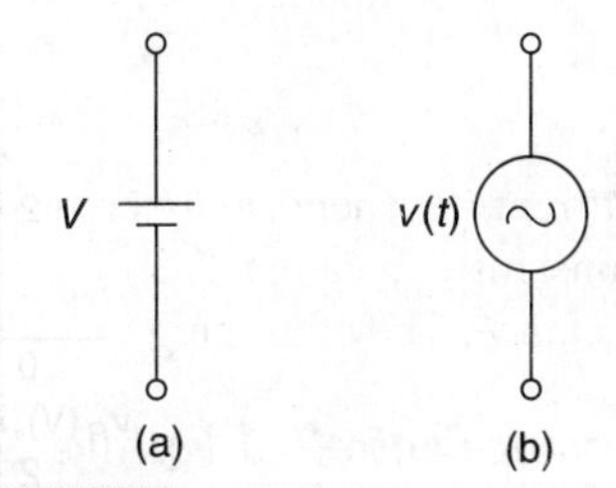


**Fig. 1.21** *Symbols for independent voltage source*

***2. Independent Current Source*** An independent current source is a two-terminal network element, which produces a specified current. The value and direction of this current at any instant is independent of the value or direction of the voltage that appears across the terminals of the source. The symbols for such current sources are shown in Fig. 1.22.

The output current may be a constant or it may be a function of time.

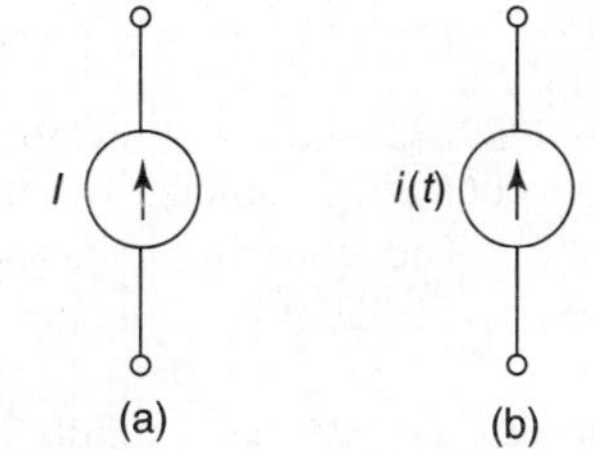


**Fig. 1.22** *Symbols for independent current source*

### 1.4.2 Dependent Sources

If the voltage or current of a source depends in turn upon some other voltage or current, it is called as dependent or controlled source. The dependent sources are of four kinds, depending on whether the control variable is voltage or current and the controlled source is a voltage source or current source.

***1. Voltage-Controlled Voltage Source (VCVS)*** A voltage-controlled voltage source is a four-terminal network component that establishes a voltage $v_{cd}$ between two points $c$ and $d$ in the circuit that is proportional to a voltage $v_{ab}$ between two points $a$ and $b$.

The symbol for such a source is shown in Fig. 1.23.

The (+) and (–) sign inside the diamond of the component symbol identifies the component as a voltage source.

$$v_{cd} = \mu\, v_{ab}$$

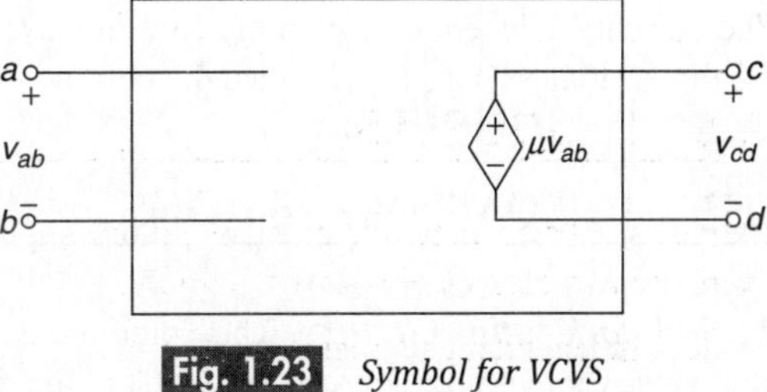


**Fig. 1.23** *Symbol for VCVS*

The voltage $v_{cd}$ depends upon the control voltage $v_{ab}$ and the constant $\mu$, a dimensionless constant called voltage gain.

**2. *Voltage-Controlled Current Source (VCCS)*** A voltage-controlled current source is a four-terminal network component that establishes a current $i_{cd}$ in a branch of the circuit that is proportional to the voltage $v_{ab}$ between two points *a* and *b*.

The symbol for such a source is shown in Fig. 1.24.

The arrow inside the diamond of the component symbol identifies the component as a current source.

$$i_{cd} = g_m\, v_{ab}$$

The current $i_{cd}$ depends only on the control voltage $v_{ab}$ and the constant $g_m$, called the transconductance or mutual conductance. The constant $g_m$ has dimension of ampere per volt or siemens (S).

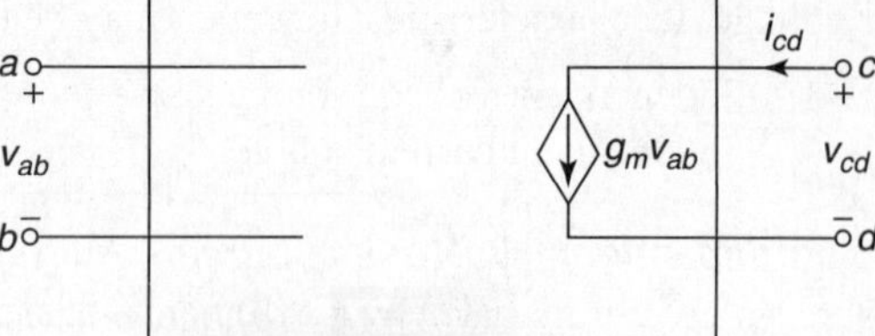


**Fig. 1.24** *Symbol for VCCS*

**3. *Current-Controlled Voltage Source (CCVS)*** A current-controlled voltage source is a four-terminal network component that establishes a voltage $v_{cd}$ between two points *c* and *d* in the circuit that is proportional to the current $i_{ab}$ in some branch of the circuit.

The symbol for such a source is shown in Fig. 1.25.

$$v_{cd} = r\, i_{ab}$$

The voltage $v_{cd}$ depends only on the control current $i_{ab}$ and the constant *r* called the transresistance or mutual resistance. The constant *r* has dimension of volt per ampere or ohm (Ω).

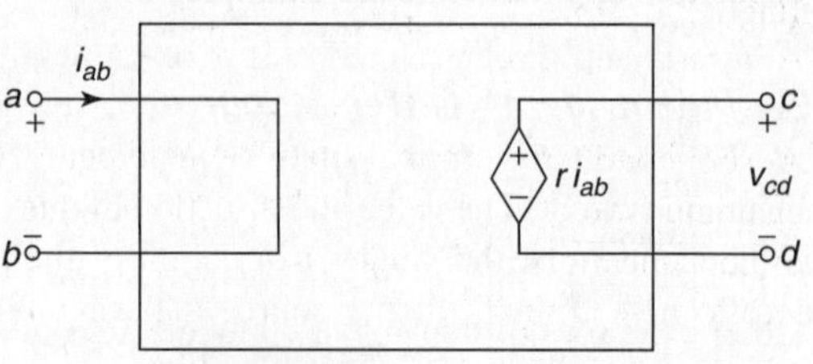


**Fig. 1.25** *Symbol for CCVS*

**4. *Current-Controlled Current Source (CCCS)*** A current-controlled current source is a four-terminal network component that establishes a current $i_{cd}$ in one branch of a circuit that is proportional to the current $i_{ab}$ in some branch of the network.

The symbol for such a source is shown in Fig. 1.26.

$$i_{cd} = \beta\, i_{ab}$$

The current $i_{cd}$ depends only on the control current $i_{ab}$ and the dimensionless constant *β*, called the current gain.

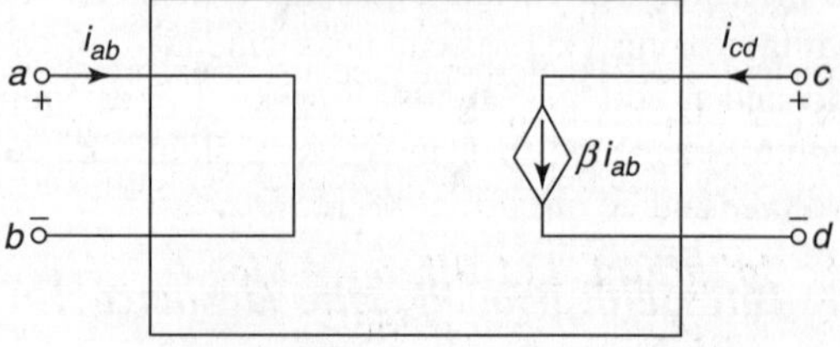


**Fig. 1.26** *Symbol for CCCS*

## 1.5 SOME DEFINITIONS

LO 1.3

Define network and circuit, linear and non-linear elements, active and passive elements, unilateral and bilateral elements, lumped and distributed elements, active and passive networks, time-invarient and time-varient networks

**1. *Network and Circuit*** The interconnection of two or more circuit elements (viz., voltage sources, resistors, inductors and capacitors) is called an *electric network*. If the network contains at least one closed path, it is called an electric circuit. Every circuit is a network, but all networks are not circuits. Figure 1.27(a) shows a network which is not a circuit and Fig. 1.27(b) shows a network which is a circuit.

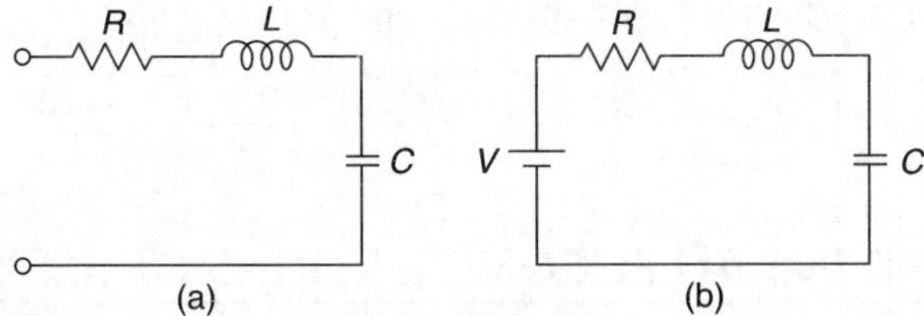


**Fig. 1.27** *(a) Network which is not a circuit (b) Network which is a circuit*

***2. Linear and Non-linear Elements*** If the resistance, inductance or capacitance offered by an element does not change linearly with the change in applied voltage or circuit current, the element is termed as *linear element*. Such an element shows a linear relation between voltage and current, as shown in Fig. 1.28. Ordinary resistors, capacitors and inductors are examples of linear elements.

A non-linear circuit element is one in which the current does not change linearly with the change in applied voltage. A semiconductor diode operating in the curved region of characteristics, as shown in Fig. 1.28, is a common example of non-linear element.

Other examples of non-linear elements are voltage-dependent resistor (VDR), voltage-dependent capacitor (varactor), temperature-dependent resistor (thermistor), light-dependent resistor (LDR), etc. Linear elements obey Ohm's law whereas non-linear elements do not obey Ohm's law.

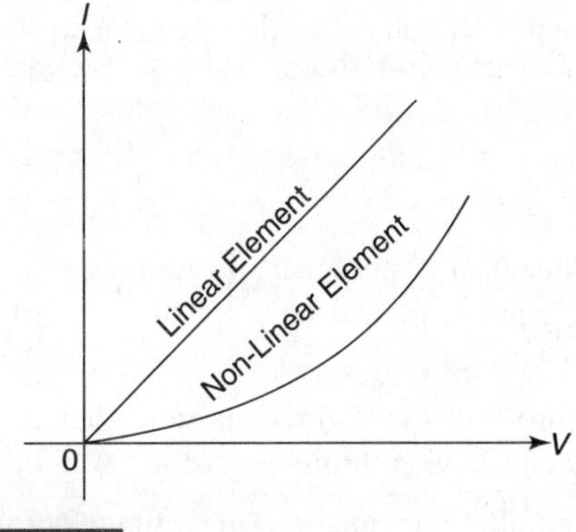


**Fig. 1.28** *V-I characteristics of linear and non-linear elements*

***3. Active and Passive Elements*** An element which is a source of electrical signal or which is capable of increasing the level of signal energy is termed as *active element*. Batteries, BJTs, FETs or OP-AMPs are treated as active elements because these can be used for the amplification or generation of signals. All other circuit elements, such as resistors, capacitors, inductors, VDR, LDR, thermistors, etc., are termed *passive elements.* The behaviour of active elements cannot be described by Ohm's law.

***4. Unilateral and Bilateral Elements*** If the magnitude of current flowing through a circuit element is affected when the polarity of the applied voltage is changed, the element is termed *unilateral element.* Consider the example of a semiconductor diode. Current flows through the diode only in one direction. Hence, it is called an unilateral element. Next, consider the example of a resistor. When the voltage is applied, current starts to flow. If we change the polarity of the applied voltage, the direction of the current is changed but its magnitude is not affected. Such an element is called a *bilateral element.*

***5. Lumped and Distributed Elements*** A lumped element is the element which is separated physically, like resistors, inductors and capacitors. Distributed elements are those which are not separable for analysis purposes. Examples of distributed elements are transmission lines in which the resistance, inductance and capacitance are distributed along its length.

***6. Active and Passive Networks*** A network which contains at least one active element such as an independent voltage or current source is an active network. A network which does not contain any active element is a passive network.

***7. Time-invariant and Time-variant Networks*** A network is said to be time-invariant or fixed if its input–output relationship does not change with time. In other words, a network is said to time-invariant, if for any time shift in input, an identical time-shift occurs for output. In time-variant networks, the input–output relationship changes with time.

## 1.6 SERIES AND PARALLEL COMBINATIONS OF RESISTORS

LO 1.4

Analyse series and parallel combination of resistors, inductors, and capacitors

Let $R_1, R_2$ and $R_3$ be the resistances of three resistors connected in series across a dc voltage source $V$, as shown in Fig. 1.29. Let $V_1, V_2$ and $V_3$ be the voltages across resistances $R_1$, $R_2$ and $R_3$ respectively.

In series combination, the same current flows through each resistor but voltage across each resistor is different.

$$V = V_1 + V_2 + V_3$$

$$R_T I = R_1 I + R_2 I + R_3 I$$

$$R_T = R_1 + R_2 + R_3$$

Hence, when a number of resistors are connected in series, the equivalent resistance is the sum of all the individual resistance.

**Fig. 1.29** *Series combination of resistors*

Figure 1.30 shows three resistors connected in parallel across a dc voltage source $V$. Let $I_1, I_2$ and $I_3$ be the current flowing through resistors $R_1, R_2$ and $R_3$ respectively.

In parallel combination, the voltage across each resistor is same but current through each resistor is different.

$$I = I_1 + I_2 + I_3$$

$$\frac{V}{R_T} = \frac{V}{R_1} + \frac{V}{R_2} + \frac{V}{R_3}$$

$$\frac{1}{R_T} = \frac{1}{R_1} + \frac{1}{R_2} + \frac{1}{R_3}$$

$$R_T = \frac{R_1 R_2 R_3}{R_2 R_3 + R_3 R_1 + R_1 R_2}$$

**Fig. 1.30** *Parallel combination of resistors*

Hence, when a number of resistors are connected in parallel, the reciprocal of the equivalent resistance is equal to the sum of reciprocals of individual resistances.

**EXAMPLE 1.14** ●○○

*Find an equivalent resistance between A and B in the network of Fig. 1.31.*

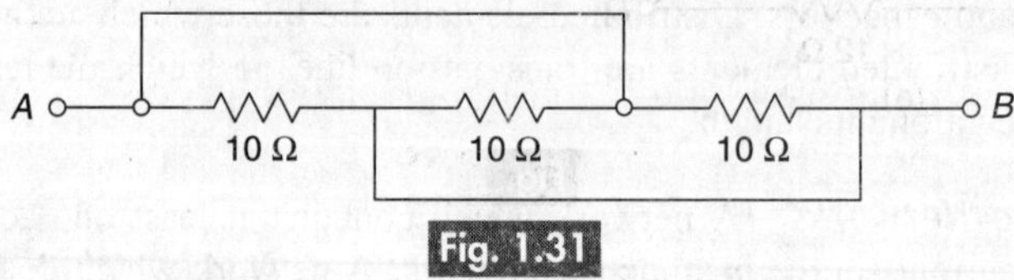


**Fig. 1.31**

**Solution** Marking all the junctions and redrawing the network (Fig. 1.32),

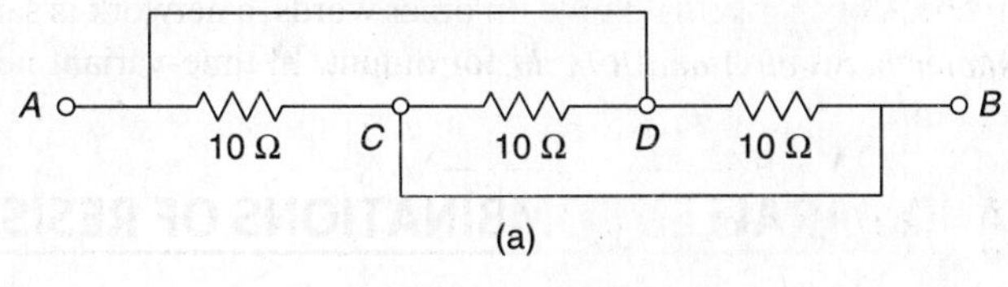


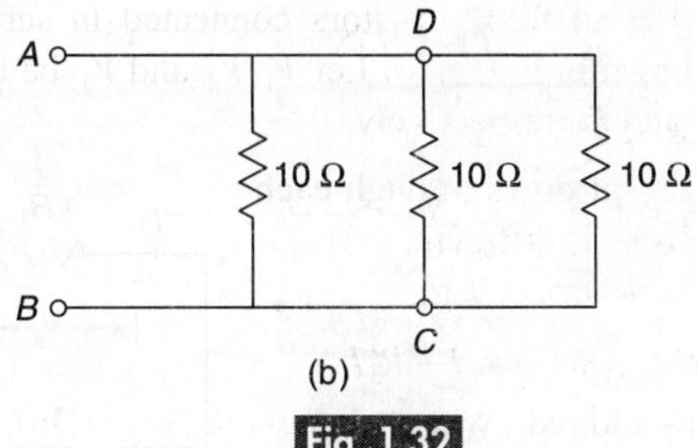


Fig. 1.32

$$R_{AB} = 10 \parallel 10 \parallel 10 = 3.33\ \Omega$$

**EXAMPLE 1.15**

*Find an equivalent resistance between A and B in the network of Fig. 1.33.*

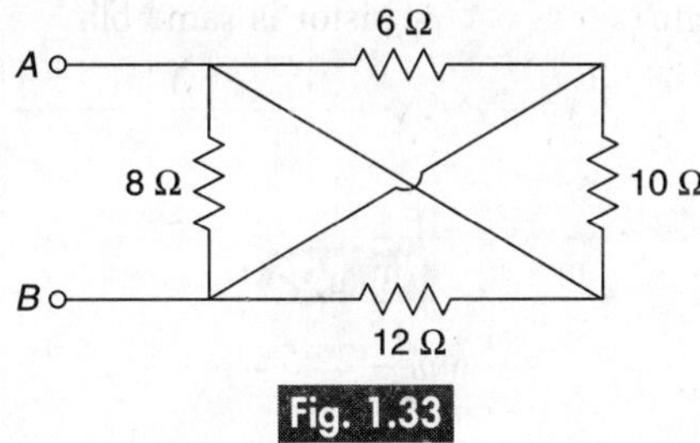


Fig. 1.33

**Solution** Marking all the junctions and redrawing the network (Fig. 1.34),

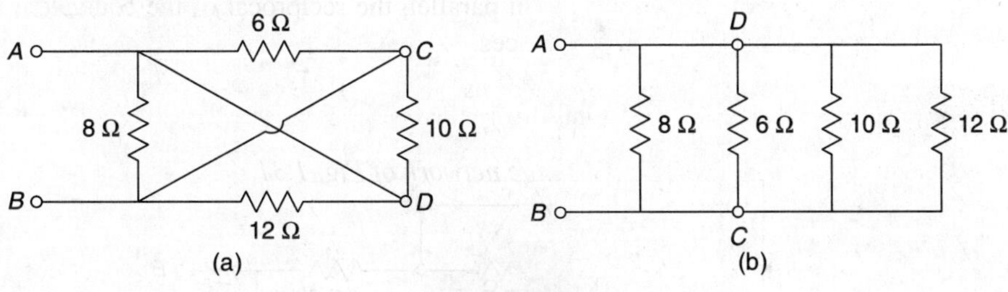


Fig. 1.34

$$R_{AB} = 8 \parallel 6 \parallel 10 \parallel 12 = 2.11\ \Omega$$

## EXAMPLE 1.16

*Find the equivalent resistance between A and B in the network of Fig. 1.35.*

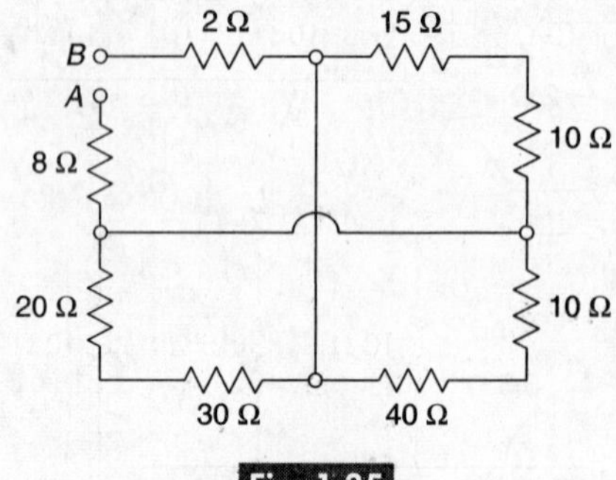


Fig. 1.35

**Solution** Marking all the junctions and redrawing the network (Fig. 1.36),

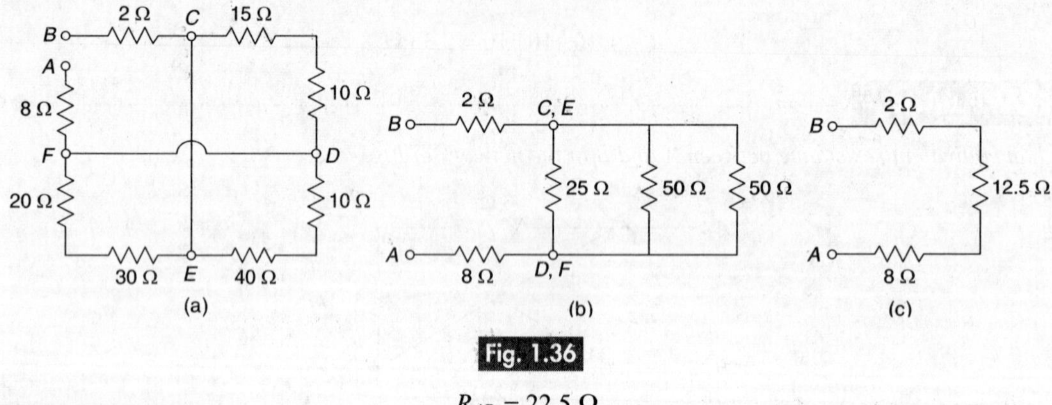


Fig. 1.36

$$R_{AB} = 22.5\ \Omega$$

## EXAMPLE 1.17

*Determine the current delivered by the source in the network of Fig. 1.37.*

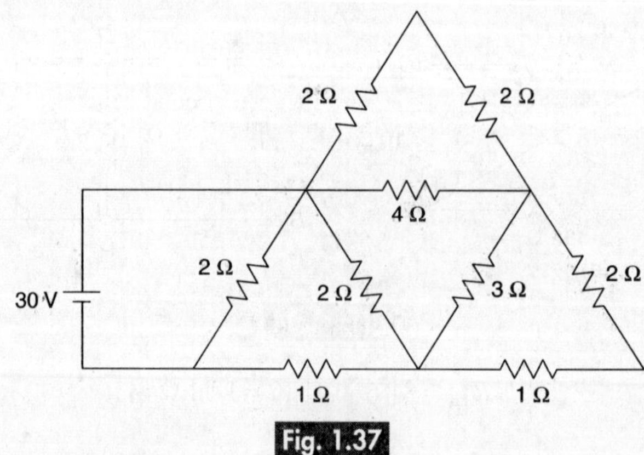


Fig. 1.37

**Solution** The network can be simplified by series–parallel reduction technique (Fig. 1.38).

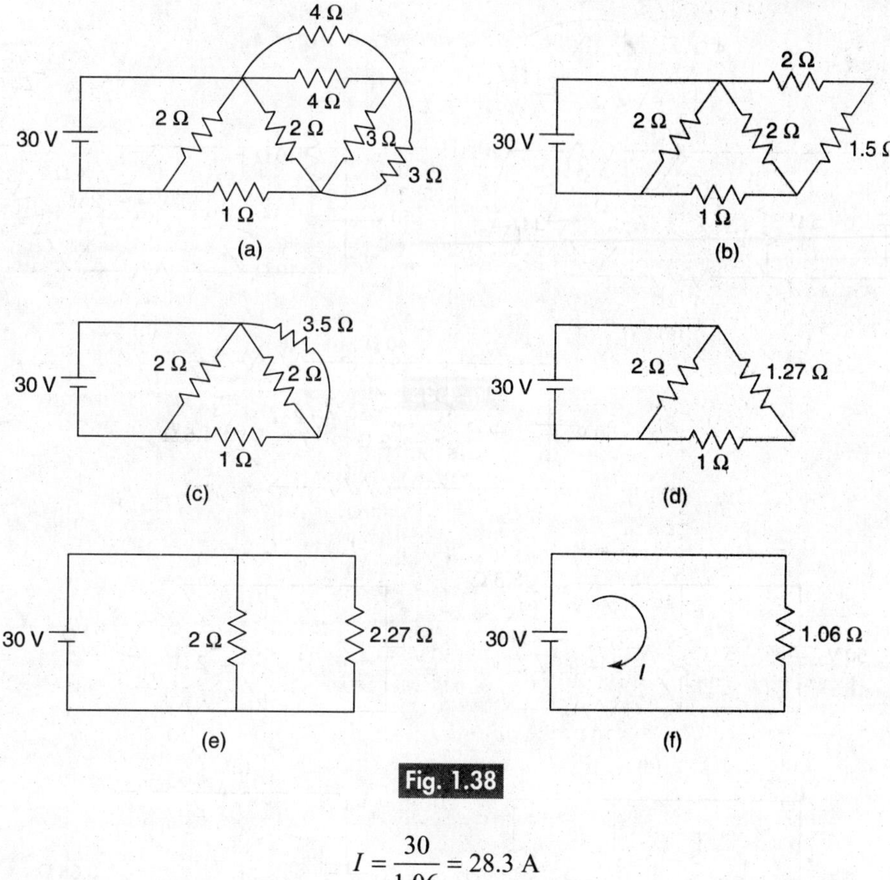


Fig. 1.38

$$I = \frac{30}{1.06} = 28.3 \text{ A}$$

## EXAMPLE 1.18

*Find the current delivered by the source in the network of Fig. 1.39.*

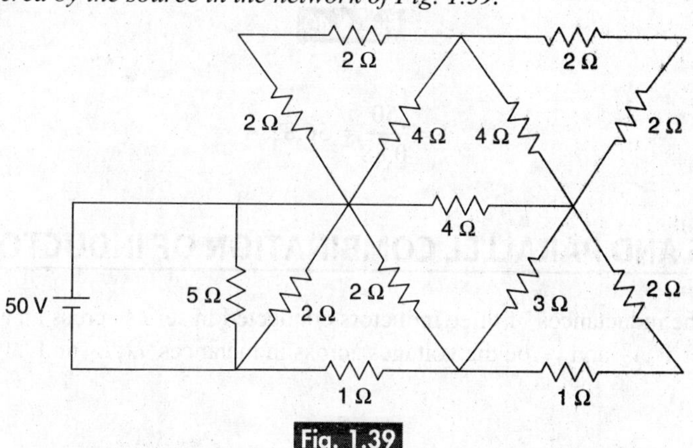


Fig. 1.39

**Solution** The network can be simplified by series–parallel reduction technique (Fig. 1.40).

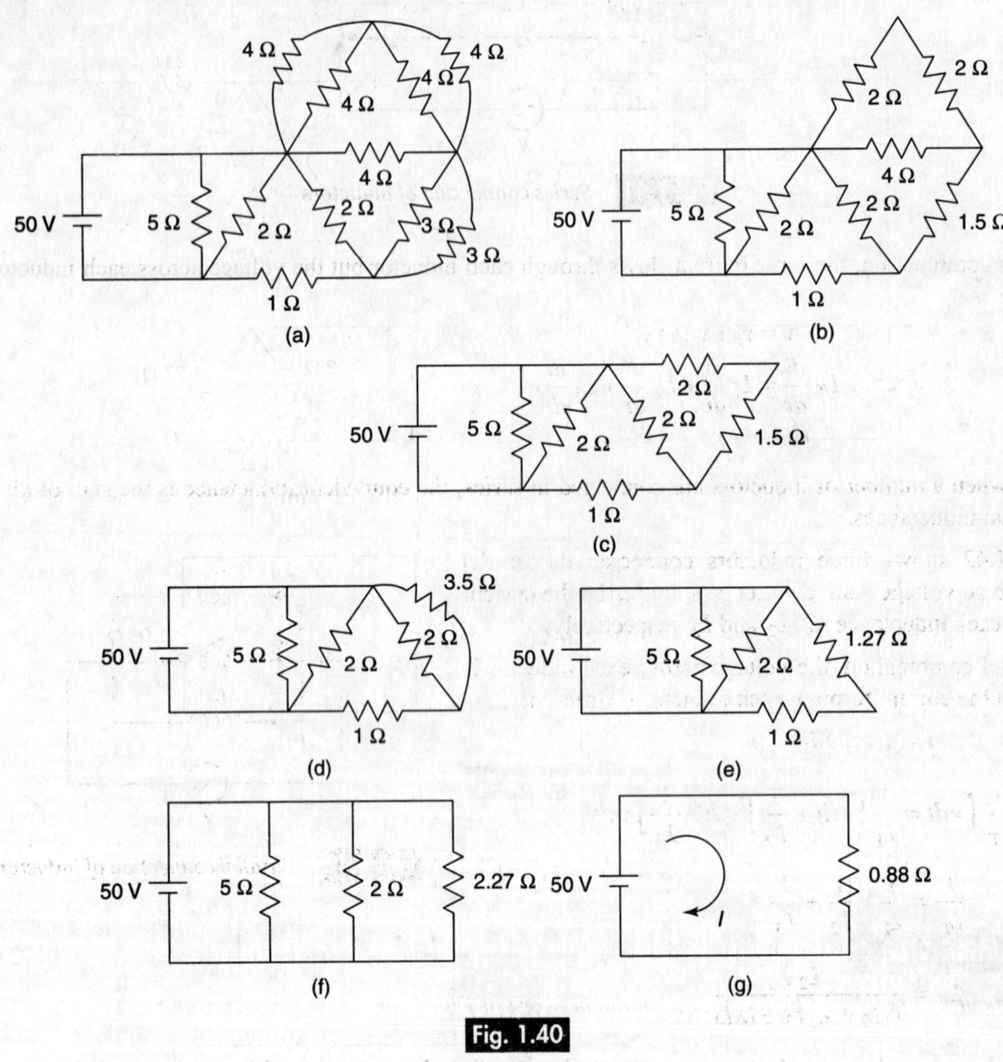


Fig. 1.40

$$I = \frac{50}{0.88} = 56.82 \text{ A}$$

## 1.7 SERIES AND PARALLEL COMBINATION OF INDUCTORS

LO 1.4

Let $L_1, L_2$ and $L_3$ be the inductances of three inductors connected in series across an ac voltage source $v$, as shown in Fig. 1.41. Let $v_1, v_2$ and $v_3$ be the voltages across inductances $L_1, L_2$ and $L_3$ respectively.

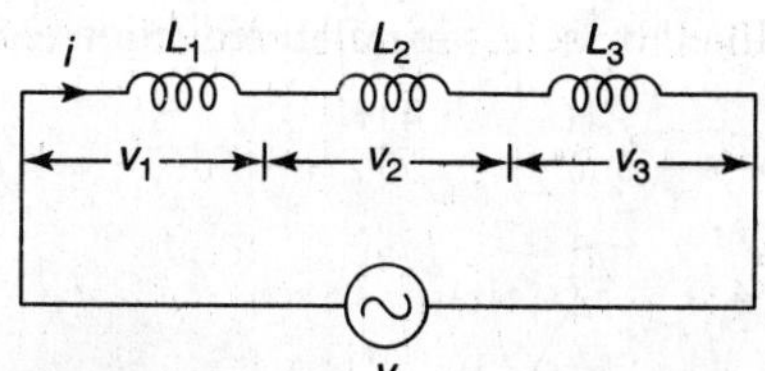


Fig. 1.41 *Series connection of inductors*

In series combination, the same current flows through each inductor but the voltage across each inductor is different.

$$v = v_1 + v_1 + v_3$$

$$L_T \frac{di}{dt} = L_1 \frac{di}{dt} + L_2 \frac{di}{dt} + L_3 \frac{di}{dt}$$

$$L_T = L_1 + L_2 + L_3$$

Hence, when a number of inductors are connected in series, the equivalent inductance is the sum of all the individual inductances.

Figure 1.42 shows three inductors connected in parallel across an ac voltage source $v$. Let $i_1, i_2$ and $i_3$ be the current through each inductance $L_1, L_2$ and $L_3$ respectively.

In parallel combination, the voltage across each inductor is same but the current through each inductor is different.

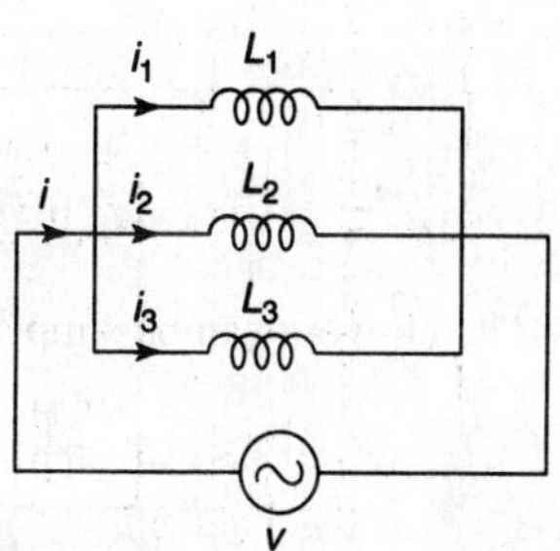


Fig. 1.42 *Parallel connection of inductors*

$$i = i_1 + i_2 + i_3$$

$$\frac{1}{L_T} \int v\,dt = \frac{1}{L_1} \int v\,dt + \frac{1}{L_2} \int v\,dt + \frac{1}{L_3} \int v\,dt$$

$$\frac{1}{L_T} = \frac{1}{L_1} + \frac{1}{L_2} + \frac{1}{L_3}$$

$$L_T = \frac{L_1 L_2 L_3}{L_1 L_2 + L_2 L_3 + L_3 L_1}$$

Hence, when a number of inductors are connected in parallel, the reciprocal of the equivalent inductance is equal to the sum of reciprocals of individual inductances.

**EXAMPLE 1.19** ●○○

*Find an equivalent inductance between terminals A and B in the network of Fig. 1.43.*

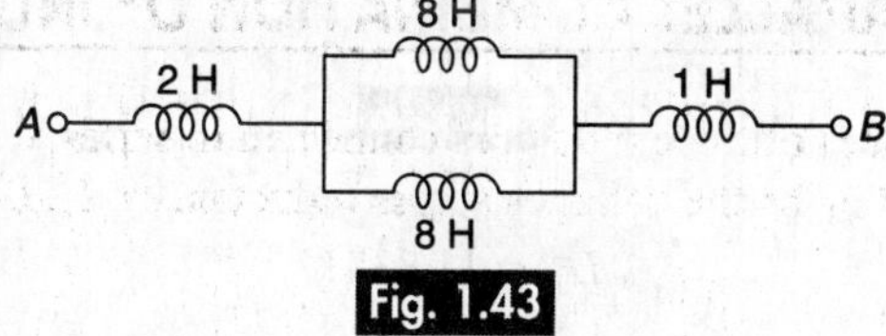


Fig. 1.43

**Solution** The network can be simplified by series–parallel reduction technique (Fig. 1.44).

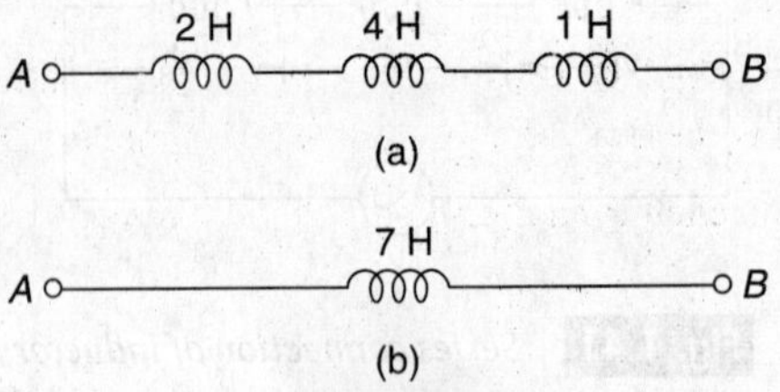

(a)

(b)

Fig. 1.44

$$L_{AB} = 7\text{ H}$$

**EXAMPLE 1.20**

*Find an equivalent inductance of the network shown in Fig. 1.45.*

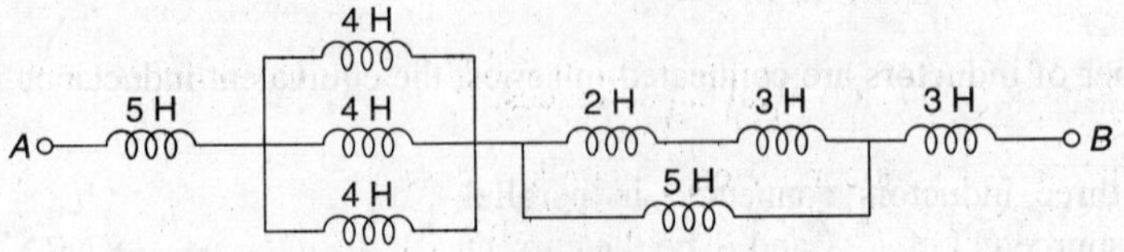

Fig. 1.45

**Solution** The network can be simplified by series–parallel reduction technique (Fig. 1.46).

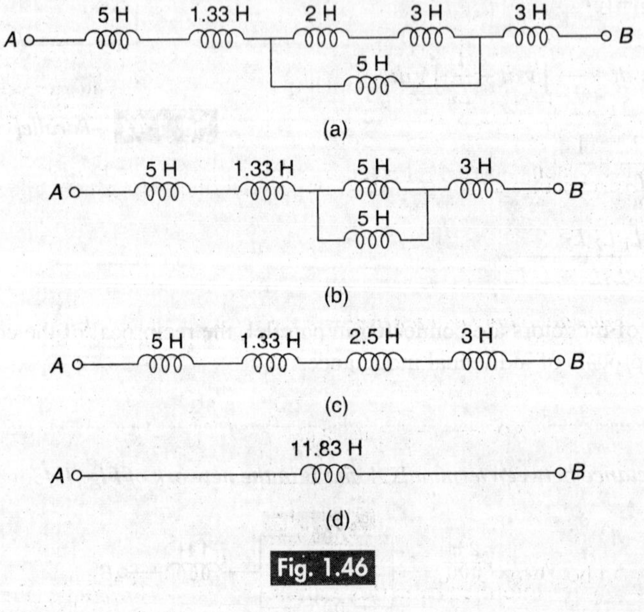

(a)

(b)

(c)

(d)

Fig. 1.46

$$L_{AB} = 11.83\text{ H}$$

## 1.8 SERIES AND PARALLEL COMBINATION OF CAPACITORS

LO 1.4

Let $C_1, C_2$ and $C_3$ be the capacitances of three capacitors connected in series across an ac voltage source $v$, as shown in Fig. 1.47. Let $v_1, v_2$ and $v_3$ be the voltages across capacitances $C_1, C_2$ and $C_3$ respectively.

In series combination, the charge on each capacitor is same but voltage across each capacitor is different.

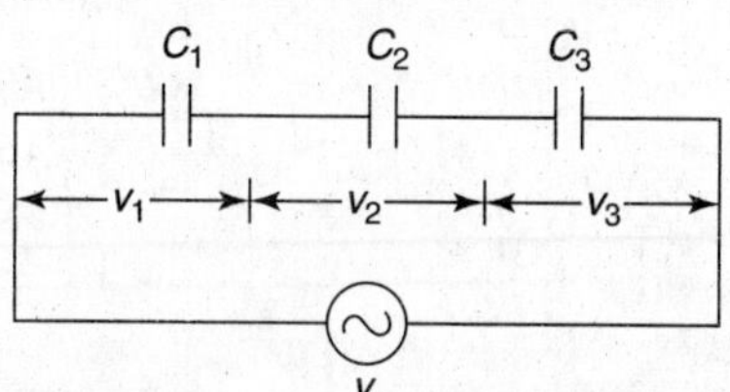


Fig. 1.47 *Series combination of capacitors*

$$v = v_1 + v_2 + v_3$$

$$\frac{1}{C_T}\int i\,dt = \frac{1}{C_1}\int i\,dt + \frac{1}{C_2}\int i\,dt + \frac{1}{C_3}\int i\,dt$$

$$\frac{1}{C_T} = \frac{1}{C_1} + \frac{1}{C_2} + \frac{1}{C_3}$$

$$C_T = \frac{C_1C_2C_3}{C_1C_2 + C_2C_3 + C_3C_1}$$

Hence, when a number of capacitors are connected in series, the reciprocal of the equivalent capacitance is equal to the sum of reciprocals of individual capacitances.

Figure 1.48 shows three capacitors connected in parallel across an ac voltage source $v$. Let $i_1, i_2$ and $i_3$ be the current through each capacitance $C_1, C_2$ and $C_3$ respectively.

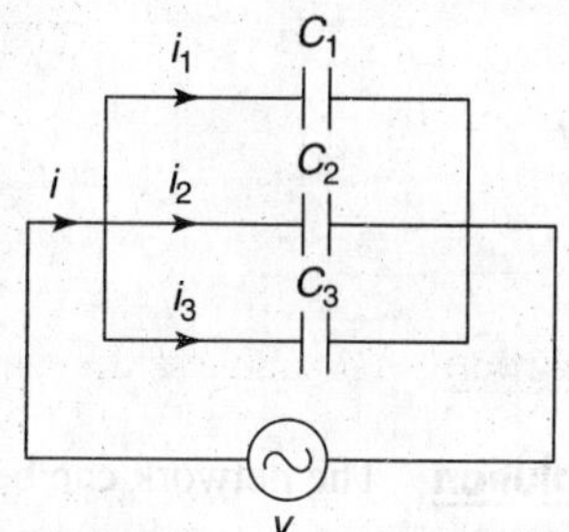


Fig. 1.48 *Parallel combination of capacitors*

In parallel combination, the voltage across each capacitor is same but current through each capacitor is different.

$$i = i_1 + i_2 + i_3$$

$$C_T\frac{dv}{dt} = C_1\frac{dv}{dt} + C_2\frac{dv}{dt} + C_3\frac{dv}{dt}$$

$$C_T = C_1 + C_2 + C_3$$

Hence, when a number of capacitors are connected in parallel, the equivalent capacitance is the sum of all the individual capacitance.

### EXAMPLE 1.21

*What is the equivalent capacitance between terminals A and B in the network of Fig. 1.49.*

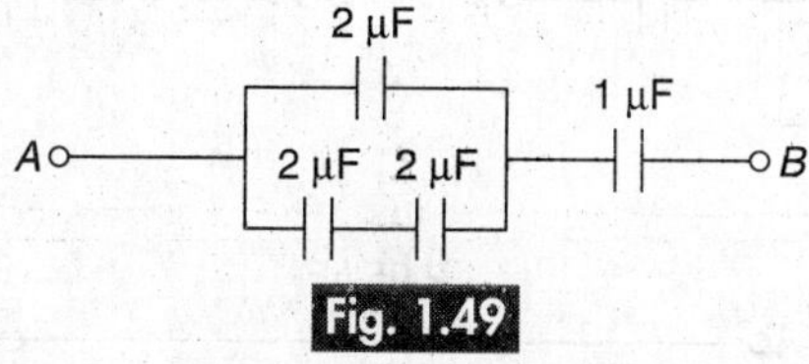


Fig. 1.49

**Solution** The network can be simplified by series–parallel reduction technique (Fig. 1.50).

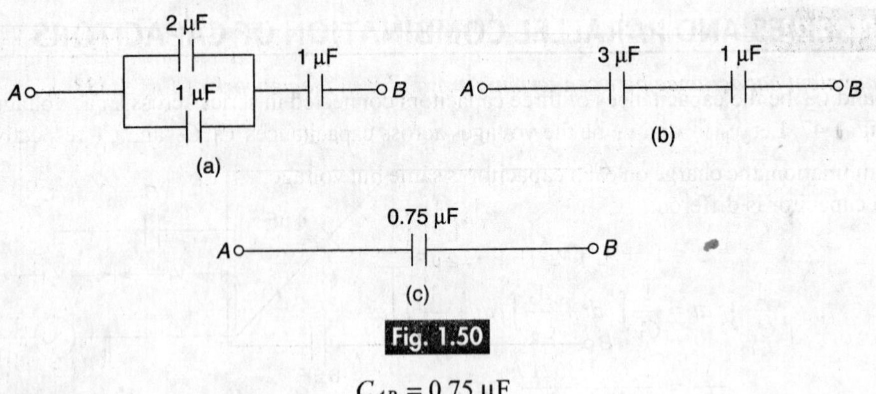


Fig. 1.50

$$C_{AB} = 0.75\ \mu\text{F}$$

## EXAMPLE 1.22

*Find the equivalent capacitance for the network of Fig. 1.51.*

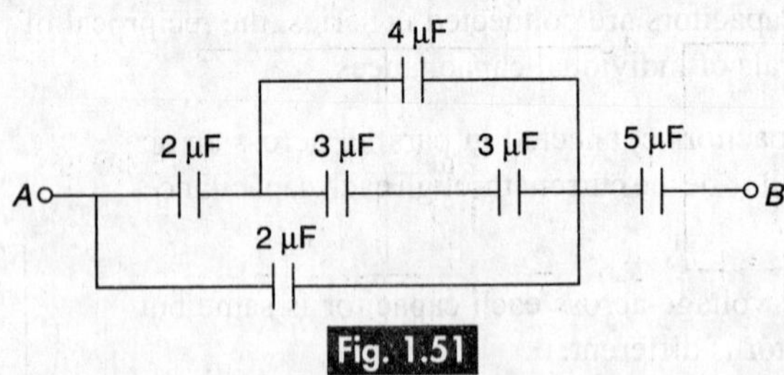


Fig. 1.51

**Solution** The network can be simplified by series–parallel reduction technique (Fig. 1.52).

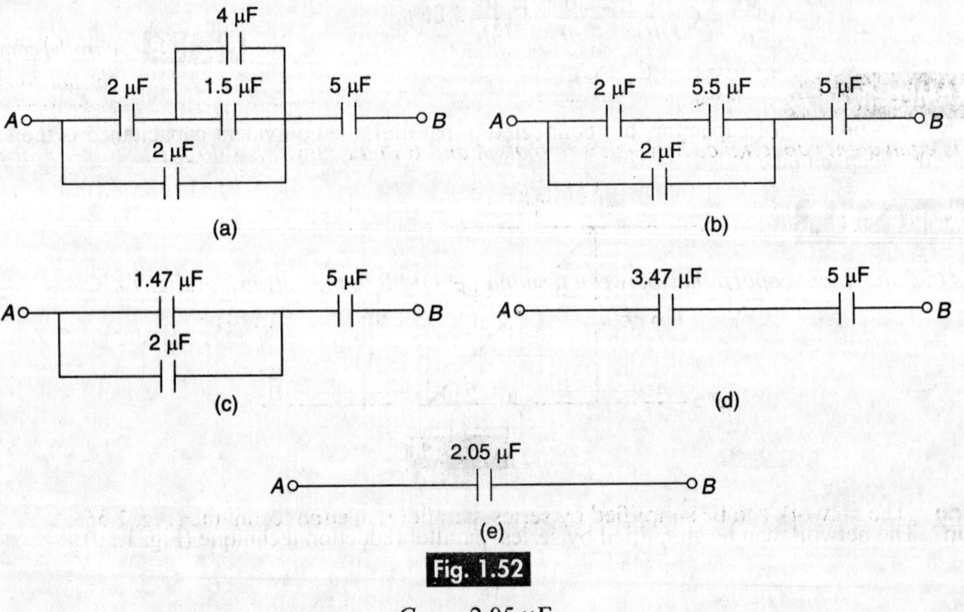


Fig. 1.52

$$C_{AB} = 2.05\ \mu\text{F}$$

## EXAMPLE 1.23

*What is equivalent capacitance between terminals A and B in the network of Fig. 1.53?*

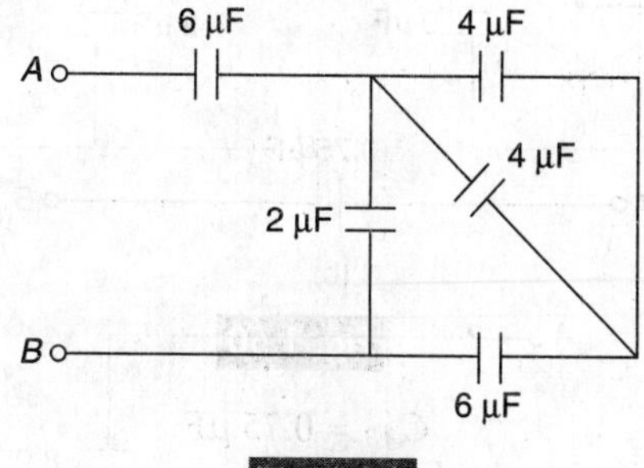


Fig. 1.53

**Solution** The network can be simplified by series–parallel reduction technique (Fig. 1.54).

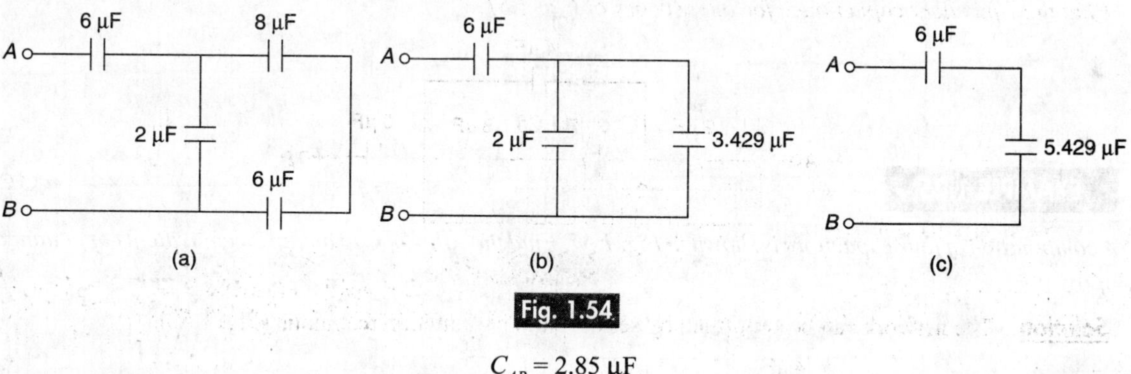


Fig. 1.54

$$C_{AB} = 2.85\ \mu\text{F}$$

## EXAMPLE 1.24

*What is equivalent capacitance between terminals A and B in the network of Fig. 1.55?*

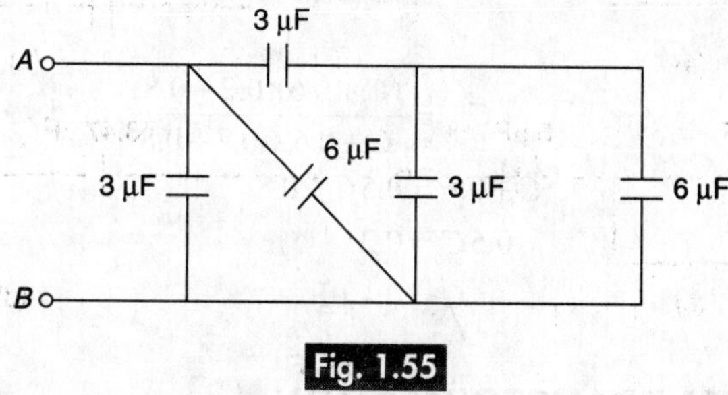


Fig. 1.55

**Solution** The network can be simplified by series–parallel reduction technique (Fig. 1.56).

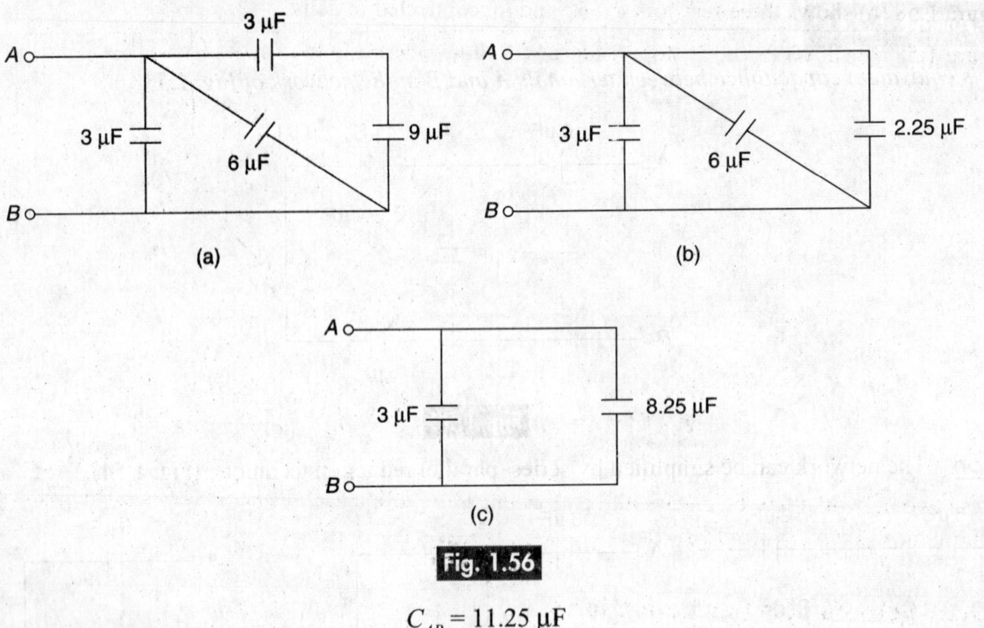


Fig. 1.56

$$C_{AB} = 11.25\ \mu\text{F}$$

**EXAMPLE 1.25**

*A combination of four capacitors is shown in Fig. 1.57. Find the value of C to obtain an equivalent capacitance of 0.5 μF.*

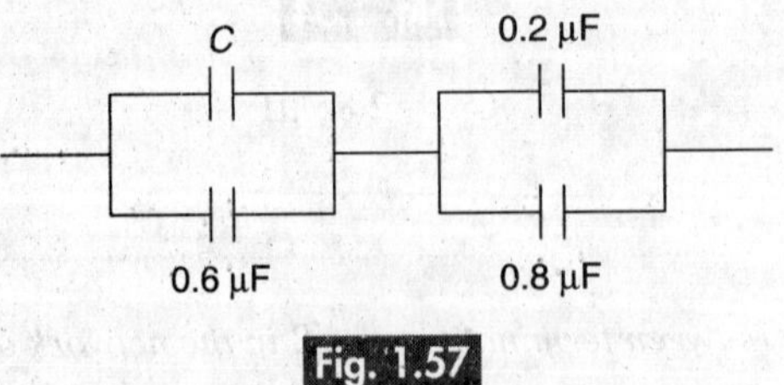


Fig. 1.57

**Solution**

$$C_{\text{eq}} = \frac{(C+0.6)(0.2+0.8)}{C+0.6+0.2+0.8} = 0.5$$

$$C+0.6 = 0.5C+0.8$$

$$0.5C = 0.2$$

$$C = 0.4\ \mu\text{F}$$

## 1.9 STAR–DELTA TRANSFORMATION

LO 1.5

When a circuit cannot be simplified by normal series–parallel reduction technique, the star–delta transformation can be used.

Simplify the networks using star-to-delta and delta-to-star transformations

Figure 1.58 (a) shows three resistors $R_A$, $R_B$ and $R_C$ connected in delta.

Figure 1.58 (b) shows three resistors $R_1$, $R_2$ and $R_3$ connected in star.

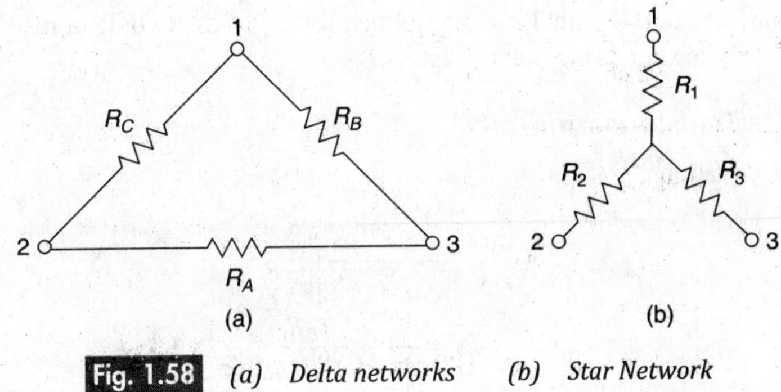


Fig. 1.58 *(a) Delta networks (b) Star Network*

These two networks will be electrically equivalent if the resistance measured between any pair of terminals is the same in both the arrangements.

### 1.9.1 Delta to Star Transformation

Referring to delta network shown in Fig. 1.58 (a),

the resistance between terminals 1 and 2 = $R_C \parallel (R_A + R_B) = \dfrac{R_C(R_A + R_B)}{R_A + R_B + R_C}$

Referring to the star network shown in Fig. 1.58 (b), the resistance between terminals 1 and 2 = $R_1 + R_2$.

Since the two networks are electrically equivalent,

$$R_1 + R_2 = \frac{R_C(R_A + R_B)}{R_A + R_B + R_C} \quad \text{...(1.1)}$$

Similarly,

$$R_2 + R_3 = \frac{R_A(R_B + R_C)}{R_A + R_B + R_C} \quad \text{...(1.2)}$$

and

$$R_3 + R_1 = \frac{R_B(R_A + R_C)}{R_A + R_B + R_C} \quad \text{...(1.3)}$$

Subtracting Eq. (1.2) from Eq. (1.1),

$$R_1 - R_3 = \frac{R_B R_C - R_A R_B}{R_A + R_B + R_C} \quad \text{...(1.4)}$$

Adding Eq. (1.4) and Eq. (1.3),

$$R_1 = \frac{R_B R_C}{R_A + R_B + R_C}$$

Similarly,

$$R_2 = \frac{R_A R_C}{R_A + R_B + R_C}$$

$$R_3 = \frac{R_A R_B}{R_A + R_B + R_C}$$

Thus, star resistor connected to a terminal is equal to the product of the two delta resistors connected to the same terminal divided by the sum of the delta resistors.

### 1.9.2 Star to Delta Transformation

Multiplying the above equations,

$$R_1 R_2 = \frac{R_A R_B R_C^2}{(R_A + R_B + R_C)^2} \quad \text{...(1.5)}$$

$$R_2 R_3 = \frac{R_A^2 R_B R_C}{(R_A + R_B + R_C)^2} \quad \text{...(1.6)}$$

$$R_3 R_1 = \frac{R_A R_B^2 R_C}{(R_A + R_B + R_C)^2} \quad \text{...(1.7)}$$

Adding Eqs (1.5), (1.6) and (1.7),

$$R_1 R_2 + R_2 R_3 + R_3 R_1 = \frac{R_A R_B R_C (R_A + R_B + R_C)}{(R_A + R_B + R_C)^2} = \frac{R_A R_B R_C}{R_A + R_B + R_C}$$

$$= R_A R_1 = R_B R_2 = R_C R_3$$

Hence,

$$R_A = \frac{R_1 R_2 + R_2 R_3 + R_3 R_1}{R_1} = R_2 + R_3 + \frac{R_2 R_3}{R_1}$$

$$R_B = \frac{R_1 R_2 + R_2 R_3 + R_3 R_1}{R_2} = R_1 + R_3 + \frac{R_3 R_1}{R_2}$$

$$R_C = \frac{R_1 R_2 + R_2 R_3 + R_3 R_1}{R_3} = R_1 + R_2 + \frac{R_1 R_2}{R_3}$$

Thus, delta resistor connected between the two terminals is the sum of two star resistors connected to the same terminals plus the product of the two resistors divided by the remaining third star resistor.

**Note** (1) When three equal resistors are connected in delta (Fig. 1.59), the equivalent star resistance is given by

$$R_Y = \frac{R_\Delta R_\Delta}{R_\Delta + R_\Delta + R_\Delta} = \frac{R_\Delta}{3}$$

$$R_\Delta = 3R_Y$$

(2) Star–delta transformation can also be applied to network containing inductors and capacitors.

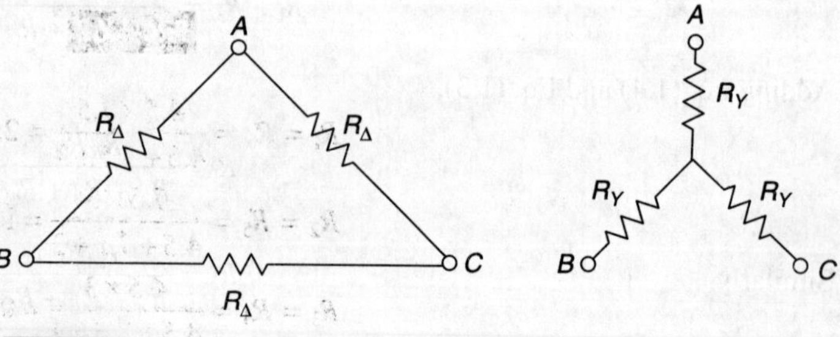


**Fig. 1.59** *Equivalent star resistance for three equal delta resistors*

## EXAMPLE 1.26

*Find an equivalent resistance between A and B in the network of Fig. 1.60.*

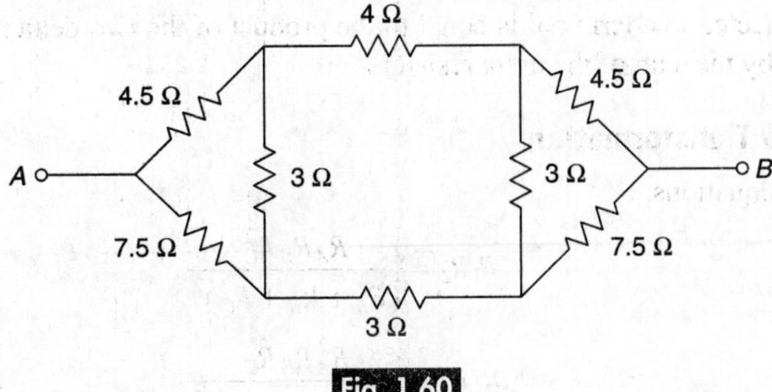


Fig. 1.60

**Solution** Converting the two delta networks formed by resistors of 4.5 Ω, 3 Ω and 7.5 Ω into equivalent star networks (Fig. 1.61 and Fig. 1.62),

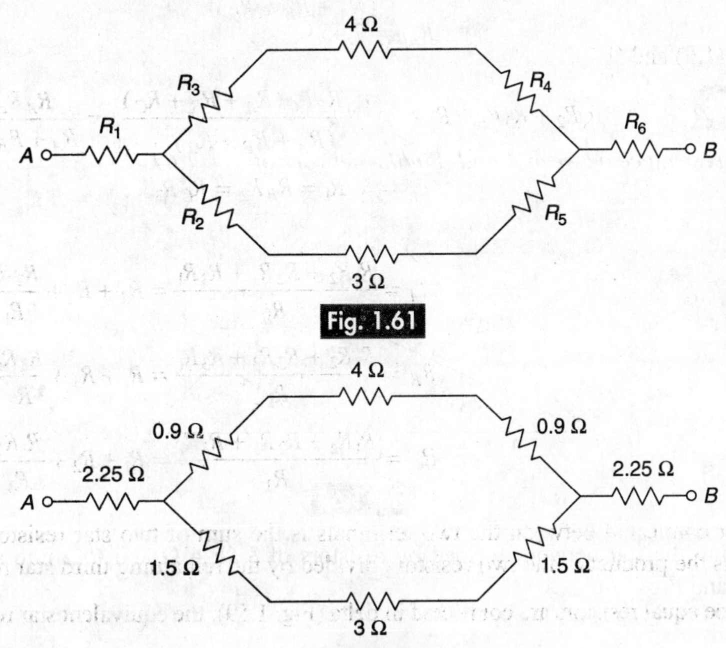


Fig. 1.61

Fig. 1.62

$$R_1 = R_6 = \frac{4.5 \times 7.5}{4.5 + 7.5 + 3} = 2.25\ \Omega$$

$$R_2 = R_5 = \frac{7.5 \times 3}{4.5 + 7.5 + 3} = 1.5\ \Omega$$

$$R_3 = R_4 = \frac{4.5 \times 3}{4.5 + 7.5 + 3} = 0.9\ \Omega$$

Simplifying the network (Fig. 1.63),

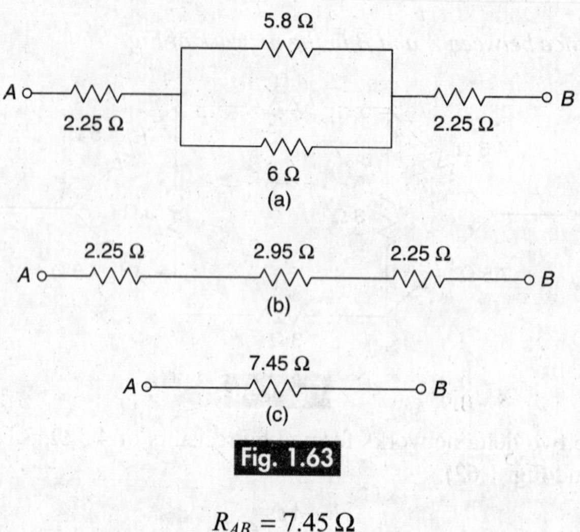


Fig. 1.63

$$R_{AB} = 7.45\ \Omega$$

## EXAMPLE 1.27

*Find an equivalent resistance between A and B in the network of Fig. 1.64.*

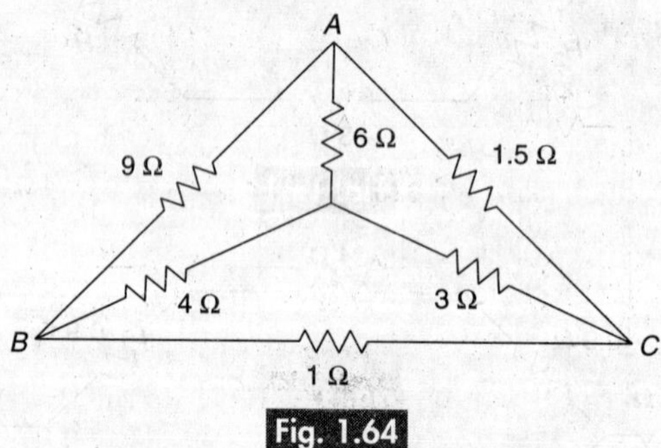


Fig. 1.64

**Solution** Converting the star network formed by resistors of 3 Ω, 4 Ω and 6 Ω into an equivalent delta network (Fig. 1.65 and Fig. 1.66),

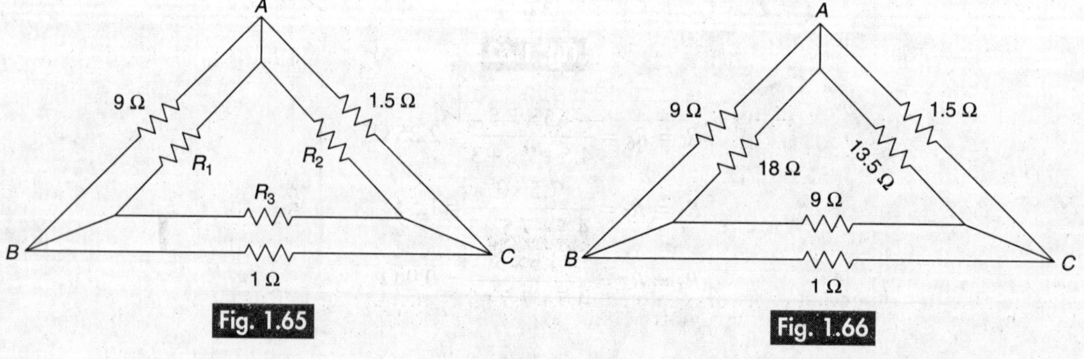


Fig. 1.65

Fig. 1.66

$$R_1 = 6 + 4 + \frac{6 \times 4}{3} = 18\ \Omega$$

$$R_2 = 6 + 3 + \frac{6 \times 3}{4} = 13.5\ \Omega$$

$$R_3 = 4 + 3 + \frac{4 \times 3}{6} = 9\ \Omega$$

Simplifying the network (Fig. 1.67),

$$R_{AB} = 6 \,||\, (1.35 + 0.9)$$

$$= 6 \,||\, 2.25$$

$$= 1.64\ \Omega$$

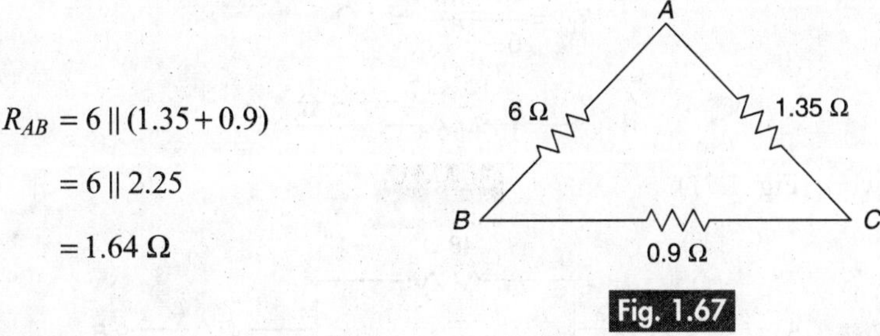


Fig. 1.67

## EXAMPLE 1.28

*Find an equivalent resistance between A and B in the network of Fig. 1.68.*

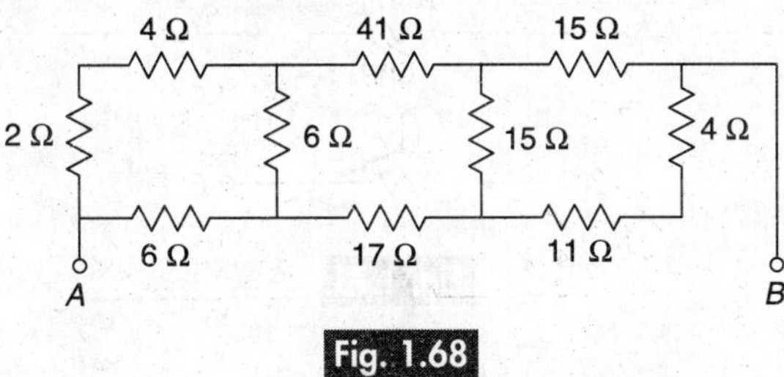


Fig. 1.68

**Solution** The resistors of 2 Ω and 4 Ω and the resistors of 4 Ω and 11 Ω are connected in series (Fig. 1.69).

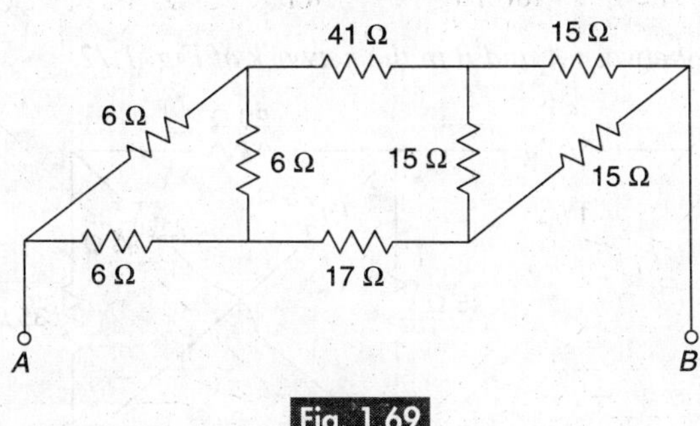


Fig. 1.69

Converting the two outer delta networks into equivalent star networks (Fig. 1.70),

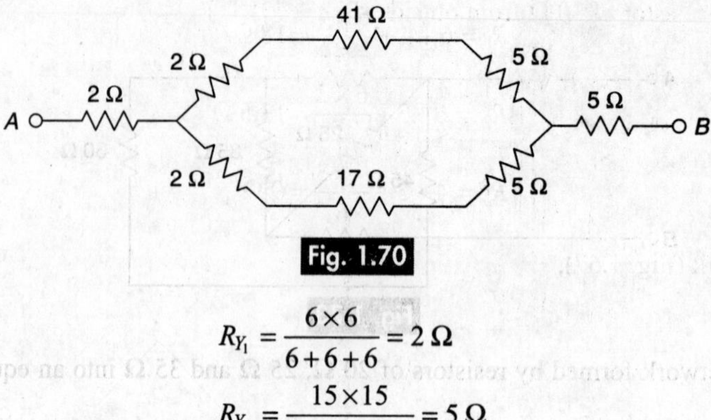


Fig. 1.70

$$R_{Y_1} = \frac{6 \times 6}{6+6+6} = 2\ \Omega$$

$$R_{Y_2} = \frac{15 \times 15}{15+15+15} = 5\ \Omega$$

Simplifying the network (Fig. 1.71),

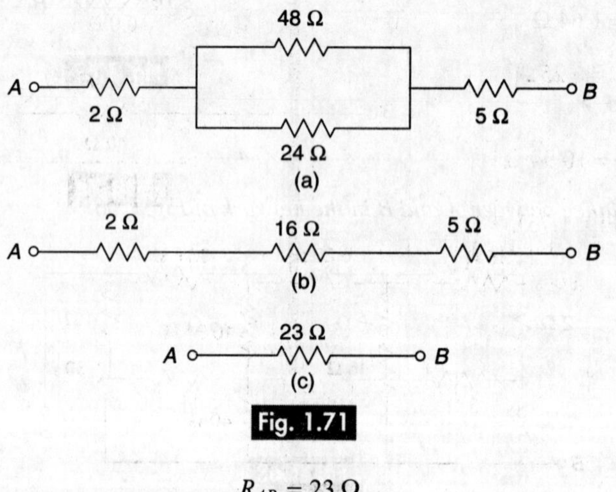


Fig. 1.71

$$R_{AB} = 23\ \Omega$$

## EXAMPLE 1.29

*Find an equivalent resistance between A and B in the network of Fig. 1.72.*

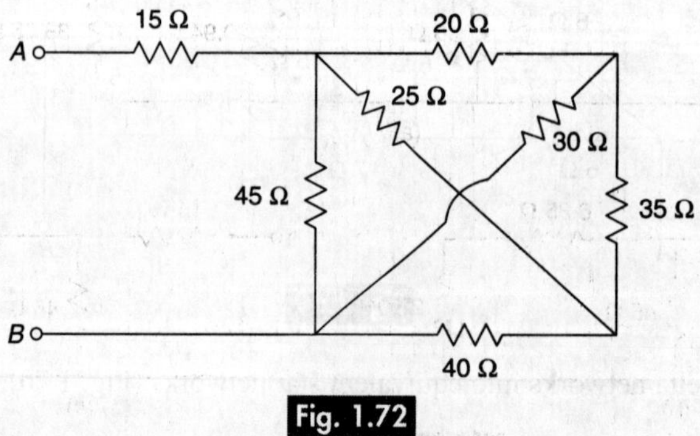


Fig. 1.72

**Solution** Drawing the resistor of 30 Ω from outside (Fig. 1.73),

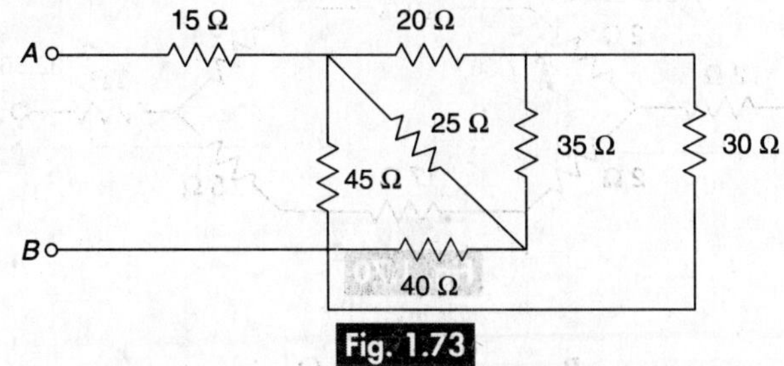


Fig. 1.73

Converting the delta network formed by resistors of 20 Ω, 25 Ω and 35 Ω into an equivalent star network (Fig. 1.74),

$$R_1 = \frac{20 \times 35}{20+35+25} = 8.75\ \Omega$$

$$R_2 = \frac{20 \times 25}{20+35+25} = 6.25\ \Omega$$

$$R_3 = \frac{35 \times 25}{20+35+25} = 10.94\ \Omega$$

Fig. 1.74

Redrawing the network (Fig. 1.75),

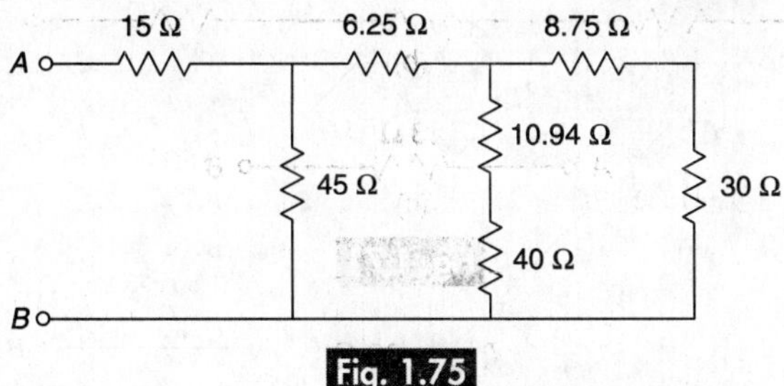


Fig. 1.75

Simplifying the network (Fig. 1.76),

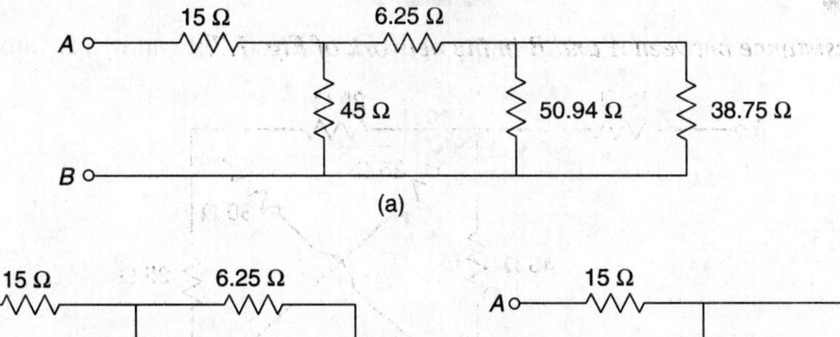


(b)

(c)

Fig. 1.76 *Continued*

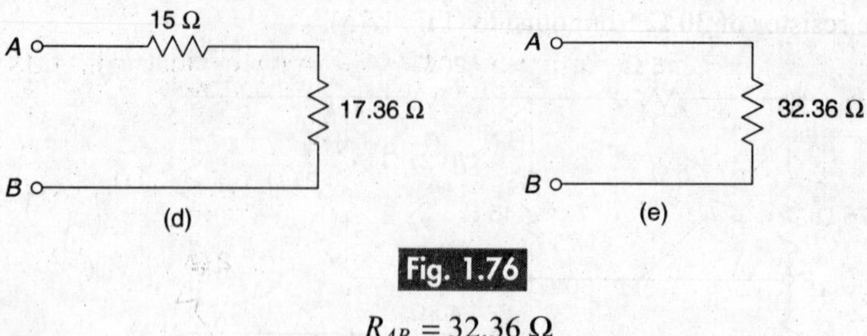


Fig. 1.76

$$R_{AB} = 32.36\ \Omega$$

## EXAMPLE 1.30

*Find an equivalent resistance between A and B in the network of Fig. 1.77.*

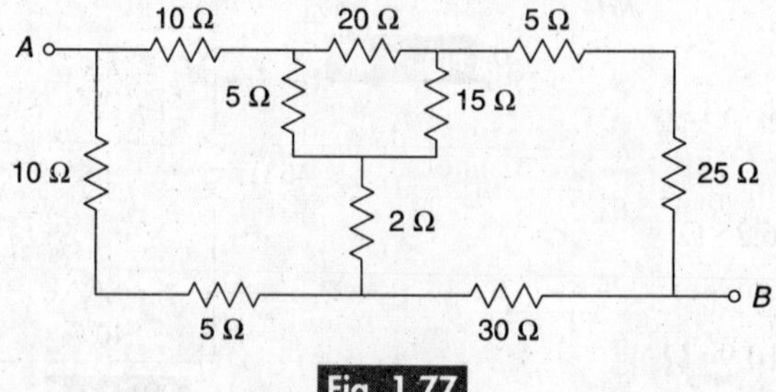


Fig. 1.77

**Solution** The resistors of 5 Ω and 25 Ω and the resistors of 10 Ω and 5 Ω are connected in series (Fig. 1.78).

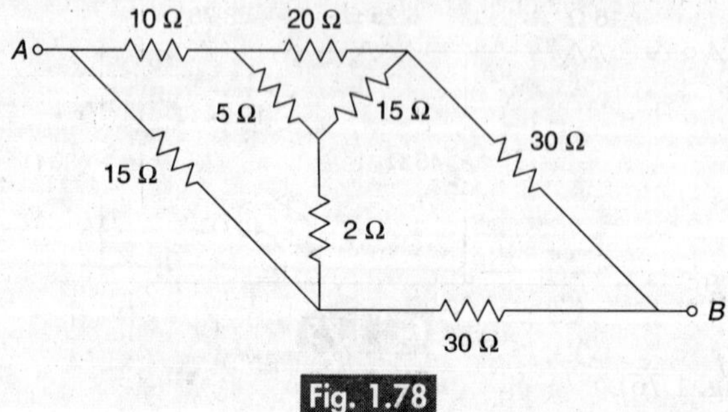


Fig. 1.78

Converting the delta network formed by the resistors of 20 Ω, 5 Ω and 15 Ω and 15 Ω into an equivalent star network (Fig. 1.79),

$$R_1 = \frac{20 \times 5}{20+5+15} = 2.5\ \Omega$$

$$R_2 = \frac{20 \times 15}{20+5+15} = 7.5\ \Omega$$

$$R_3 = \frac{5 \times 15}{20+5+15} = 1.875\ \Omega$$

10 Ω

A

$R_1$ $R_2$

30 Ω

15 Ω

$R_3$

2 Ω

B

30 Ω

Fig. 1.79

Redrawing the network (Fig. 1.80),

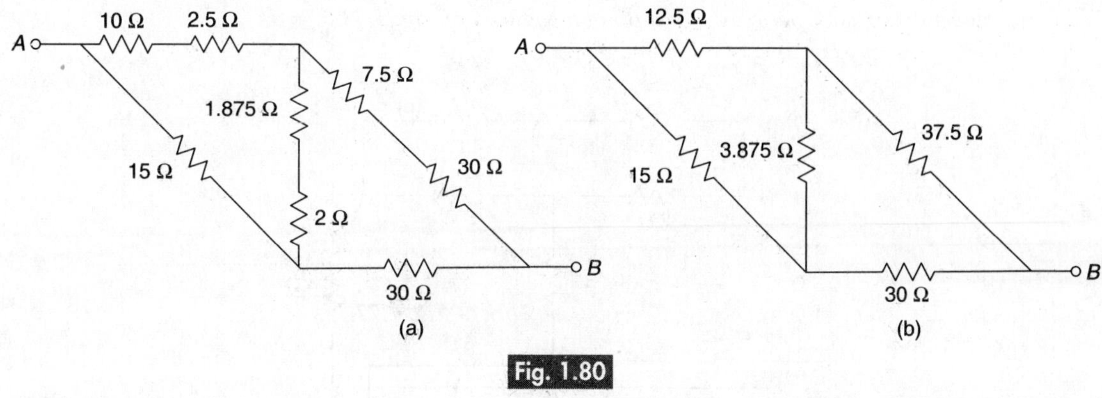


Fig. 1.80

Converting the delta network formed by the resistors of 3.875 Ω, 37.5 Ω and 30 Ω into an equivalent star network (Fig. 1.81),

$$R_4 = \frac{3.875 \times 37.5}{3.875 + 37.5 + 30} = 2.04\ \Omega$$

$$R_5 = \frac{3.875 \times 30}{3.875 + 37.5 + 30} = 1.63\ \Omega$$

$$R_6 = \frac{37.5 \times 30}{3.875 + 37.5 + 30} = 15.76\ \Omega$$

Fig. 1.81

Simplifying the network (Fig. 1.82),

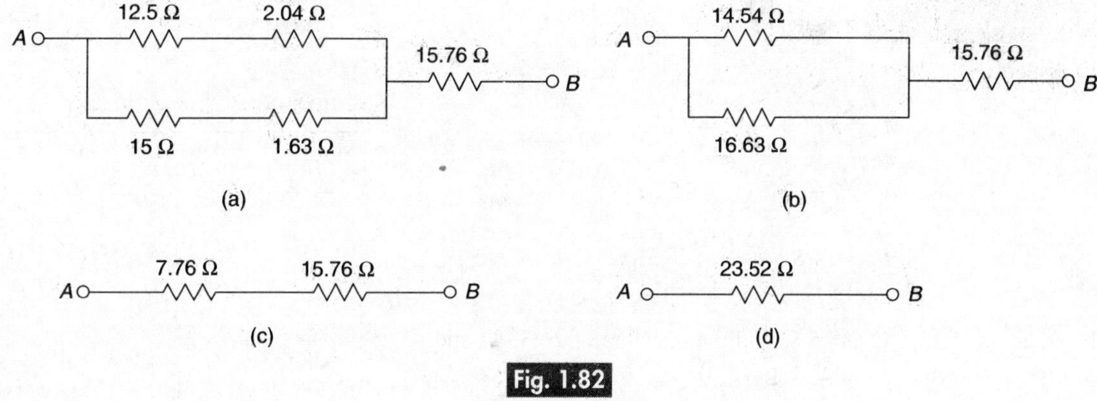


Fig. 1.82

$$R_{AB} = 23.52\ \Omega$$

EXAMPLE 1.31

*Find an equivalent resistance between A and B in the network of Fig. 1.83.*

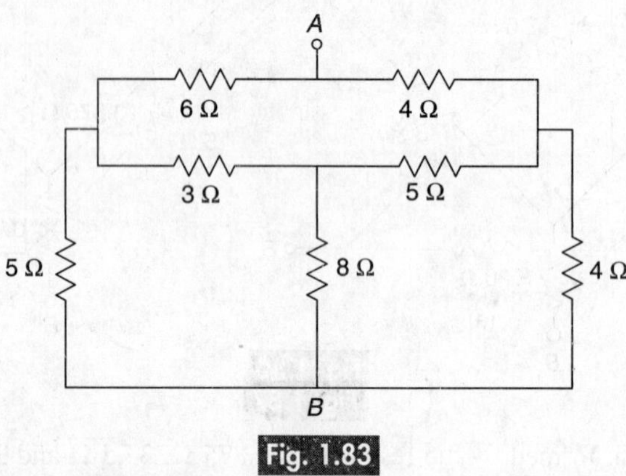


Fig. 1.83

**Solution** Converting the star network formed by the resistors of 3 Ω, 5 Ω and 8 Ω into an equivalent delta network (Fig. 1.84 and Fig. 1.85),

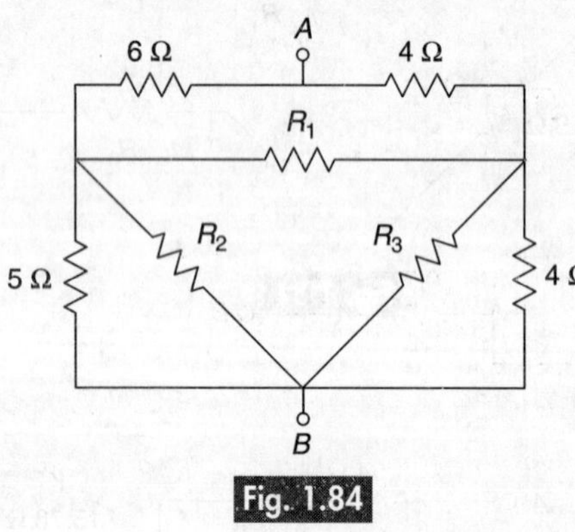


Fig. 1.84

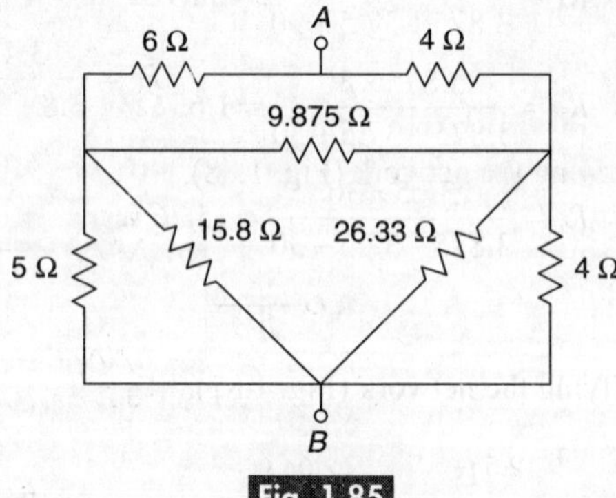


Fig. 1.85

$$R_1 = 3+5+\frac{3\times 5}{8} = 9.875\ \Omega$$

$$R_2 = 3+8+\frac{3\times 8}{5} = 15.8\ \Omega$$

$$R_3 = 5+8+\frac{5\times 8}{3} = 26.33\ \Omega$$

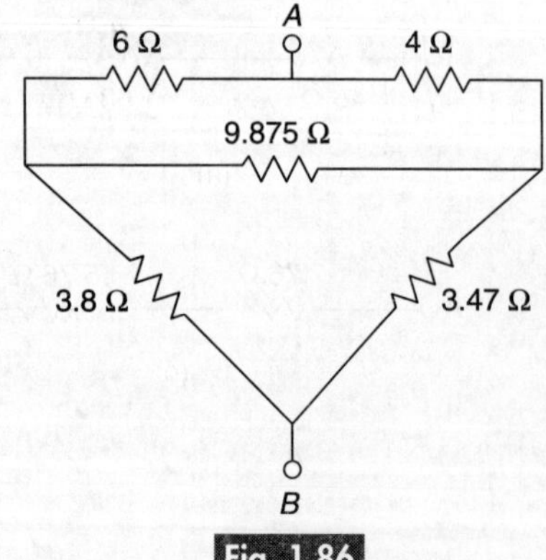


Fig. 1.86

The resistors of 15.8 Ω and 5 Ω and the resistors of 26.33 Ω and 4 Ω are connected in parallel (Fig. 1.86),

Converting the delta network into a star network (Fig. 1.87),

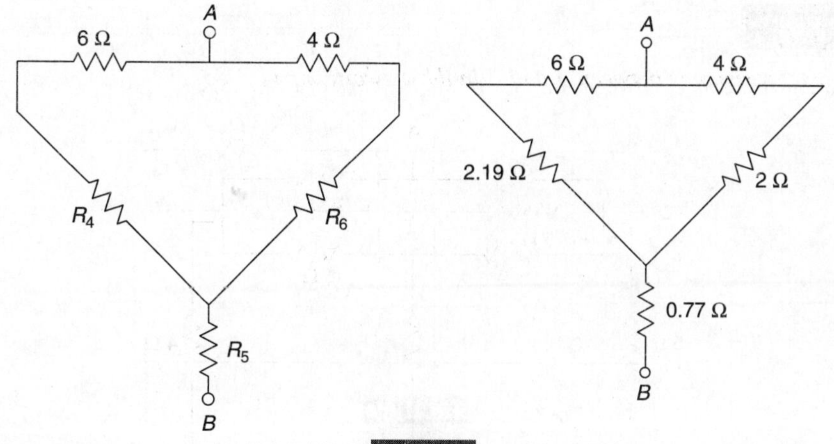


Fig. 1.87

$$R_4 = \frac{3.8 \times 9.875}{3.8 + 9.875 + 3.47} = 2.19\ \Omega$$

$$R_5 = \frac{3.8 \times 3.47}{3.8 + 9.875 + 3.47} = 0.77\ \Omega$$

$$R_6 = \frac{3.47 \times 9.875}{3.8 + 9.875 + 3.47} = 2\ \Omega$$

Simplifying the network (Fig. 1.88),

(a)

(b)

(c)

(d)

Fig. 1.88

$$R_{AB} = 4.23\ \Omega$$

## EXAMPLE 1.32

*Find an equivalent resistance between A and B in the network of Fig. 1.89.*

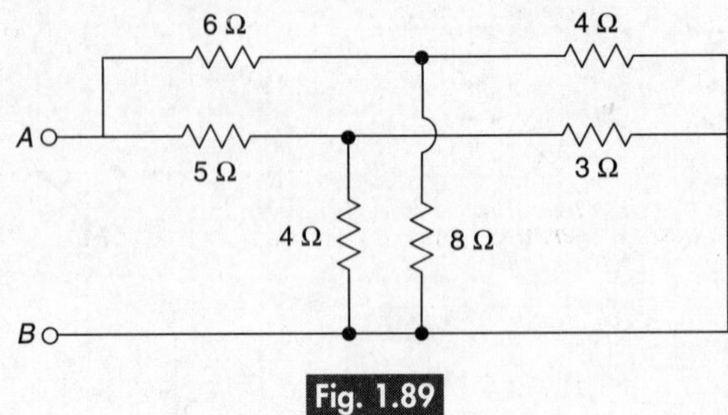


Fig. 1.89

**Solution** Converting the star network formed by the resistors of 3 Ω, 4 Ω and 5 Ω into an equivalent delta network (Fig. 1.90),

$$R_1 = 5 + 4 + \frac{5 \times 4}{3} = 15.67\ \Omega$$

$$R_2 = 3 + 4 + \frac{3 \times 4}{5} = 9.4\ \Omega$$

$$R_3 = 5 + 3 + \frac{5 \times 3}{4} = 11.75\ \Omega$$

5 Ω 3 Ω 4 Ω (a) ⇒ $R_3$ $R_1$ $R_2$ (b)

Fig. 1.90

Similarly, converting the star network formed by the resistors of 4 Ω, 6 Ω and 8 Ω into an equivalent delta network (Fig. 1.91),

$$R_4 = 6 + 8 + \frac{6 \times 8}{4} = 26\ \Omega$$

$$R_5 = 4 + 8 + \frac{4 \times 8}{6} = 17.33\ \Omega$$

$$R_6 = 6 + 4 + \frac{6 \times 4}{8} = 13\ \Omega$$

6 Ω 4 Ω 8 Ω (a) ⇒ $R_6$ $R_4$ $R_5$ (b)

Fig. 1.91

These two delta networks are connected in parallel between points *A* and *B* (Fig. 1.92).

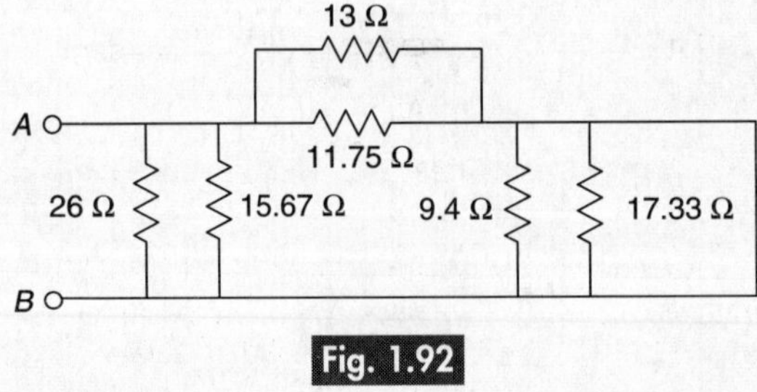


Fig. 1.92

The resistors of 9.4 Ω and 17.33 Ω are in parallel with a short. Hence, the equivalent resistance of this combination becomes zero.

Simplifying the parallel networks (Fig. 1.93),

$$R_{AB} = 6.17 \,||\, 9.78 = 3.78\ \Omega$$

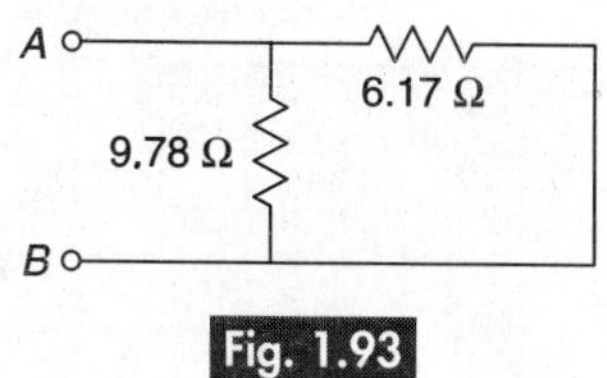


Fig. 1.93

## EXAMPLE 1.33

*Find an equivalent inductance between terminals A and B in the network of Fig. 1.94.*

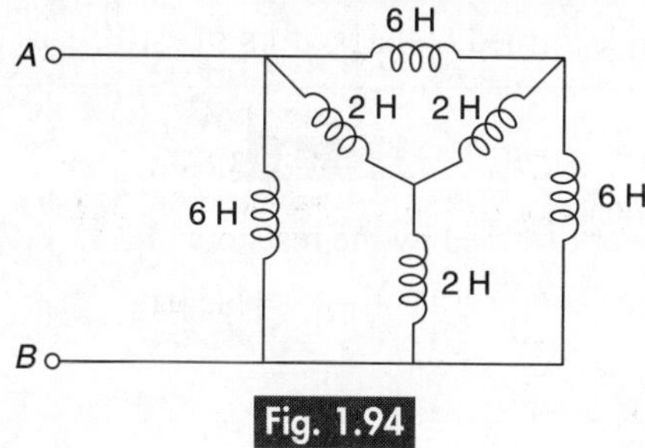


Fig. 1.94

**Solution** Converting the star network formed by inductors of 2 H, 2 H and 2 H into an equivalent delta network (Fig. 1.95),

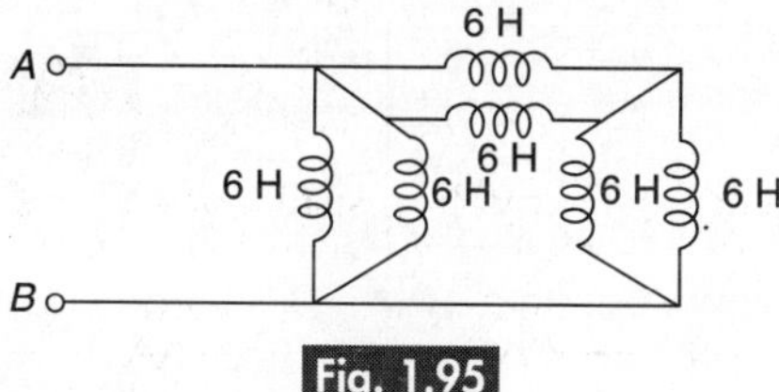


Fig. 1.95

Simplifying the network (Fig. 1.96),

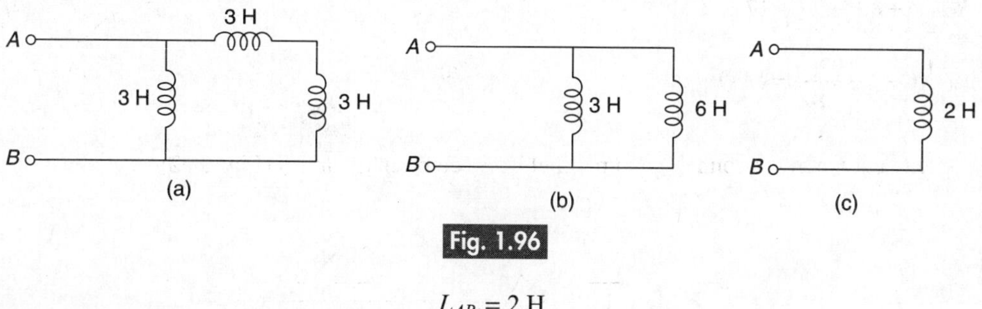


Fig. 1.96

$$L_{AB} = 2\text{ H}$$

## EXAMPLE 1.34

*Determine the capacitance between terminals A and B in the network of Fig. 1.97.*

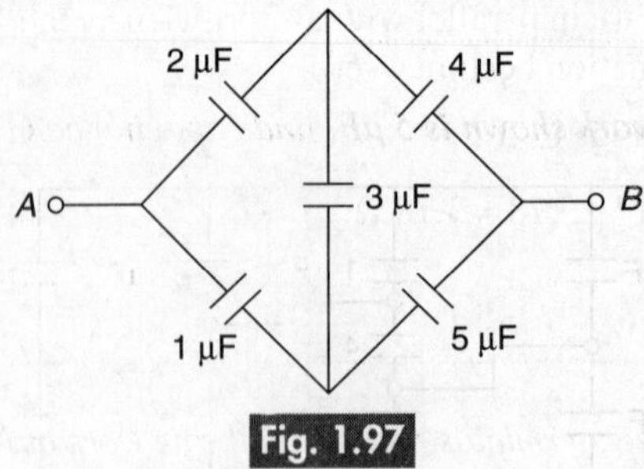


Fig. 1.97

**Solution** Converting delta network formed by capacitors of 2 μF, 1 μF and 3 μF into an equivalent star network [Fig. 1.98 (a)],

$$C_1 = 1 + 2 + \frac{1 \times 2}{3} = 3.67\ \mu\text{F}$$

$$C_2 = 1 + 3 + \frac{1 \times 3}{2} = 5.5\ \mu\text{F}$$

$$C_3 = 2 + 3 + \frac{2 \times 3}{1} = 11\ \mu\text{F}$$

Simplifying the network (Fig. 1.98),

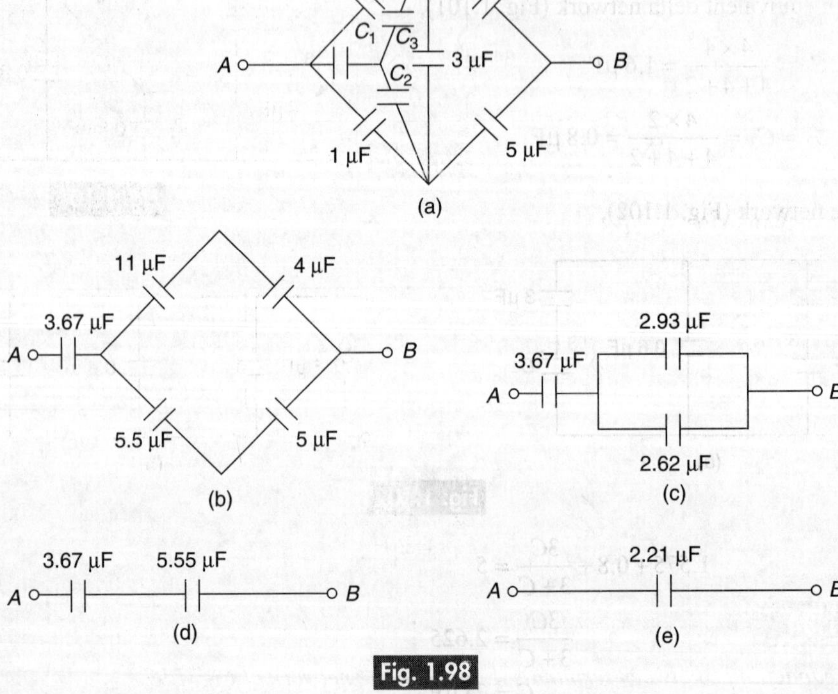


Fig. 1.98

$$C_{AB} = 2.21\ \mu\text{F}$$

**EXAMPLE 1.35**

*If the combined capacitance of network shown is 5 μF, find capacitance C in the network of Fig. 1.99.*

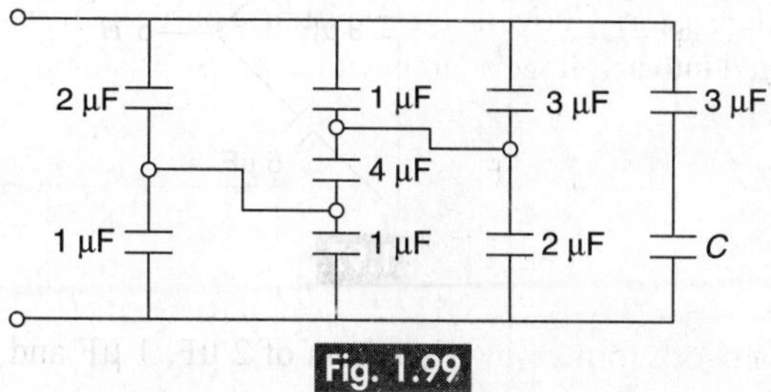


Fig. 1.99

**Solution** The capacitors of 1 μF and 1 μF and the capacitors of 1 μF and 3 μF are in parallel (Fig. 1.100),

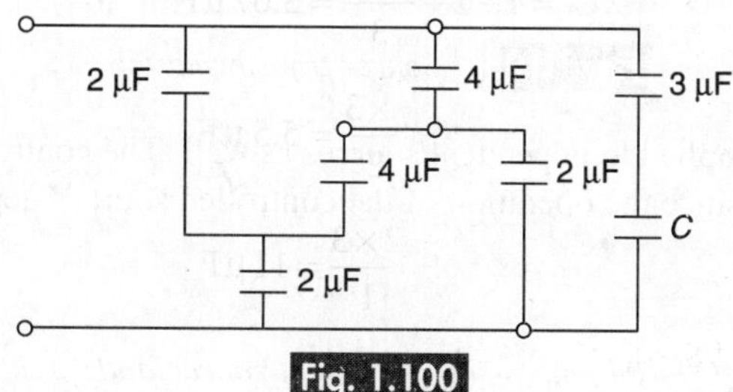


Fig. 1.100

Replacing star network formed by capacitors of 4 μF, 4 μF and 2 μF into an equivalent delta network (Fig. 1.101),

$$C_1 = \frac{4 \times 4}{4+4+2} = 1.6\ \mu\text{F}$$

$$C_2 = C_3 = \frac{4 \times 2}{4+4+2} = 0.8\ \mu\text{F}$$

Fig. 1.101

Simplifying the network (Fig. 1.102),

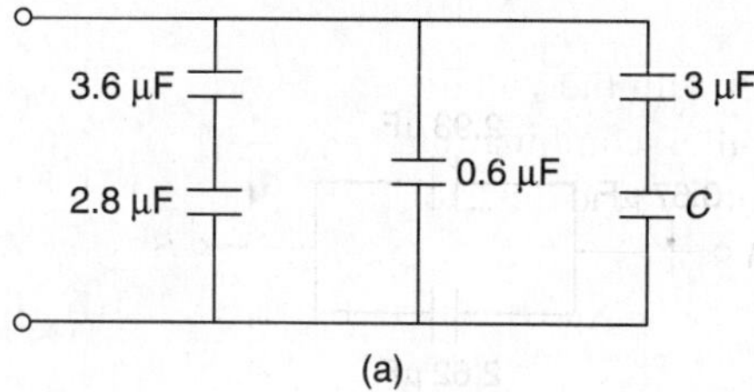


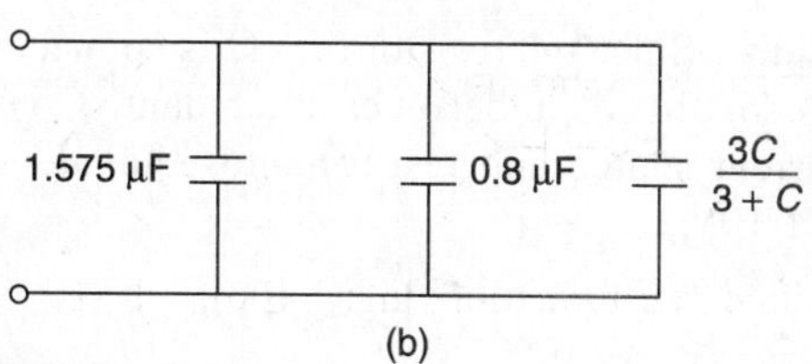


Fig. 1.102

$$1.575 + 0.8 + \frac{3C}{3+C} = 5$$

$$\frac{3C}{3+C} = 2.625$$

$$C = 21\ \mu\text{F}$$

## 1.10 SOURCE TRANSFORMATION

LO 1.6

Discuss source transformation and source-shifting techniques

A voltage source with a series resistor can be converted into a equivalent current source with a parallel resistor. Conversely, a current source with a parallel resistor can be converted into a voltage source with a series resistor, as shown in Fig. 1.103.

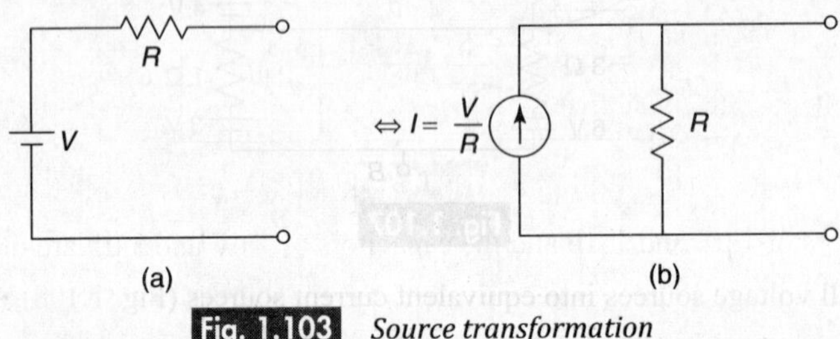


Fig. 1.103 *Source transformation*

Source transformation can be applied to dependent sources as well. The controlling variable, however, must not be tampered with any way since the operation of the controlled sources depends on it.

### EXAMPLE 1.36

*Replace the given network of Fig. 1.104 with a single current source and a resistor.*

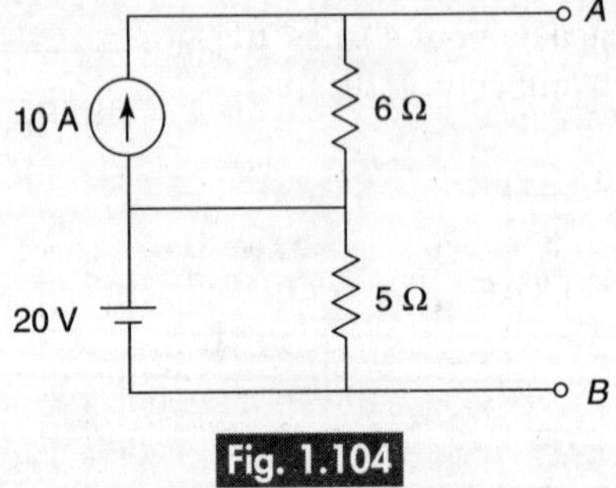


Fig. 1.104

**Solution** Since the resistor of 5 Ω is connected in parallel with the voltage source of 20 V, it becomes redundant. Converting parallel combination of current source and resistor into equivalent voltage source and resistor (Fig. 1.105),

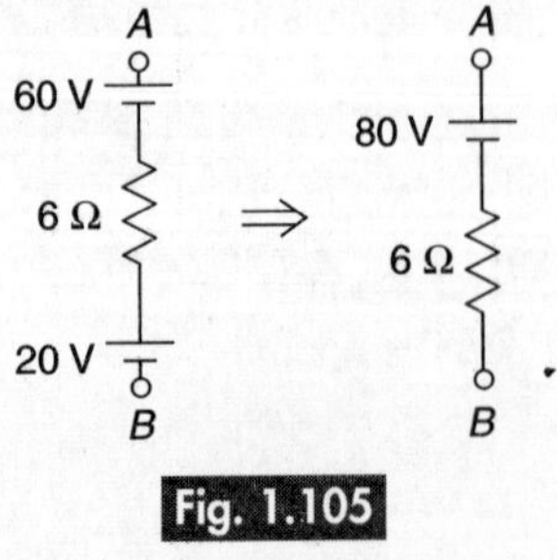


Fig. 1.105

By source transformation (Fig. 1.106),

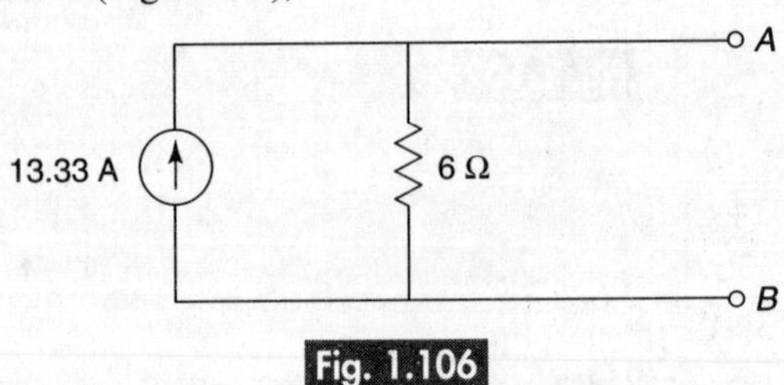


Fig. 1.106

## EXAMPLE 1.37

*Reduce the network shown in Fig. 1.107 into a single source and a single resistor between terminals A and B.*

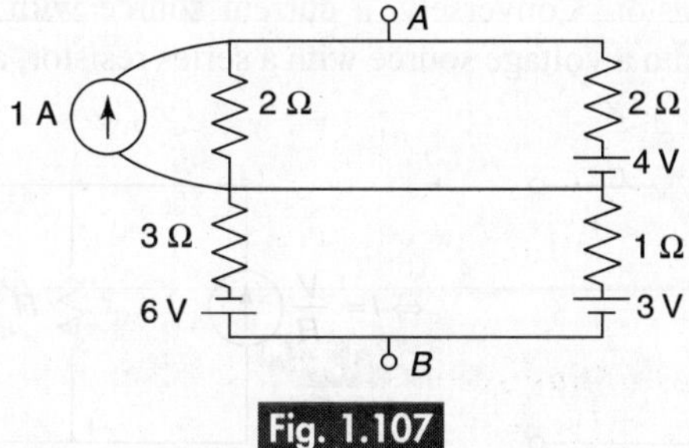


Fig. 1.107

**Solution** Converting all voltage sources into equivalent current sources (Fig. 1.108),

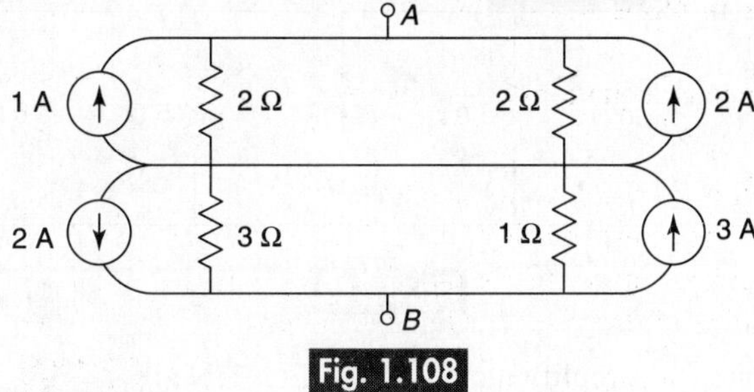


Fig. 1.108

Adding the current sources and simplifying the network (Fig. 1.109),

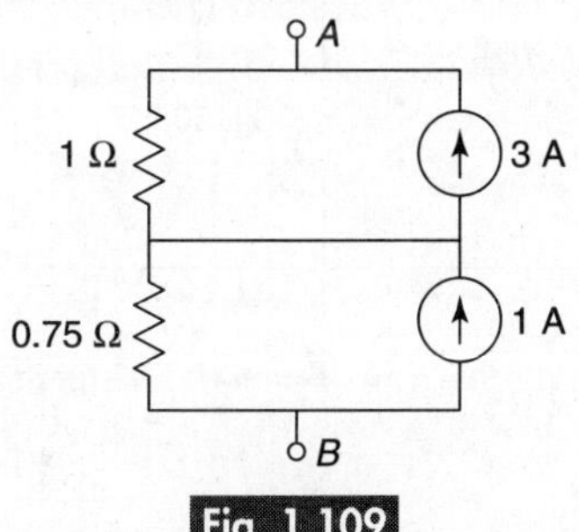


Fig. 1.109

Converting the current sources into equivalent voltage sources (Fig. 1.110),

Fig. 1.110

## EXAMPLE 1.38

*Replace the circuit between A and B in Fig. 1.111 with a voltage source in series with a single resistor.*

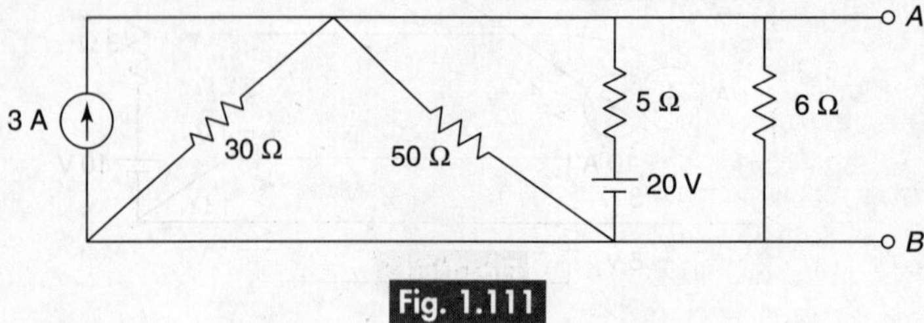


Fig. 1.111

**Solution** Converting the series combination of voltage source of 20 V and a resistor of 5 Ω into equivalent parallel combination of current source and resistor (Fig. 1.112),

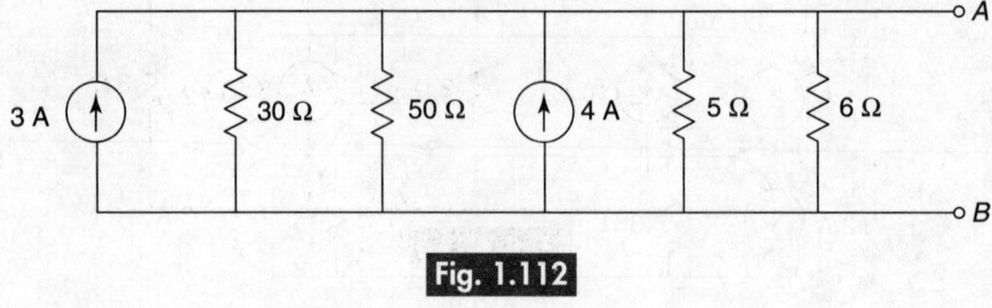


Fig. 1.112

Adding the two current sources and simplifying the circuit (Fig. 1.113),

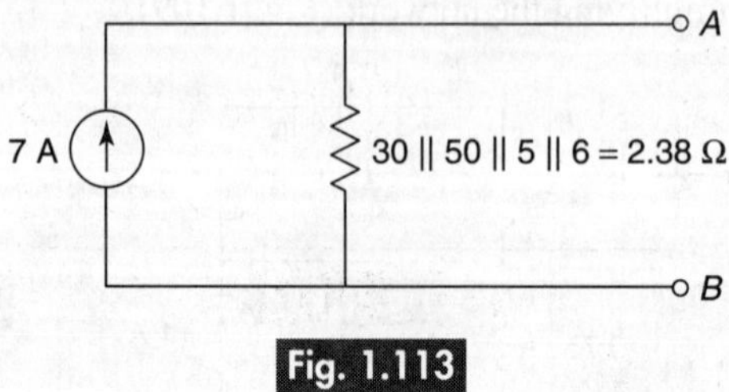


Fig. 1.113

By source transformation (Fig. 1.114),

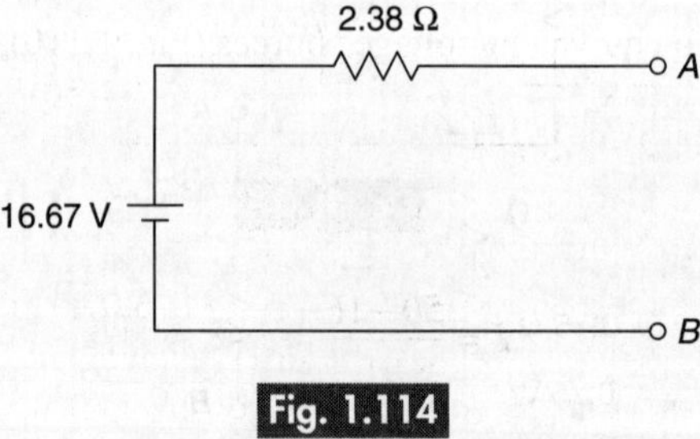


Fig. 1.114

## EXAMPLE 1.39

*Find the power delivered by the 50 V source in the network of Fig. 1.115.*

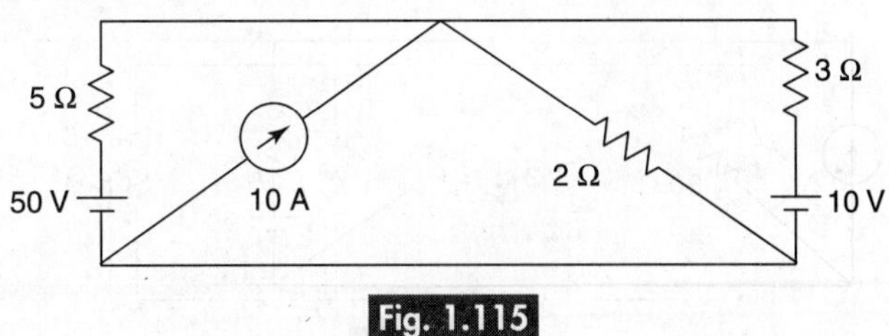


Fig. 1.115

**Solution** Converting the series combination of voltage source of 10 V and resistor of 3 Ω into equivalent current source and resistor (Fig. 1.116),

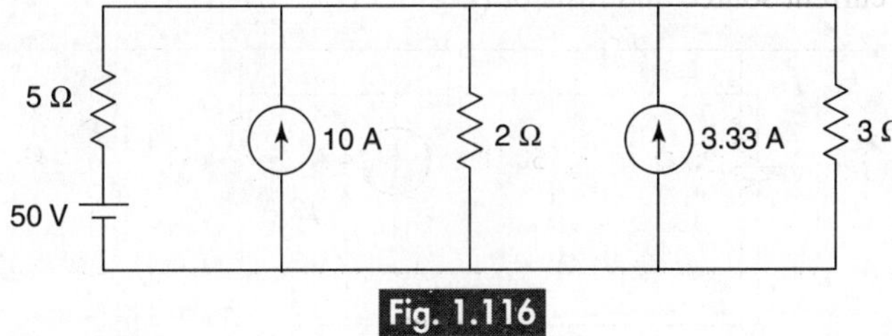


Fig. 1.116

Adding the two current sources and simplifying the network (Fig. 1.117),

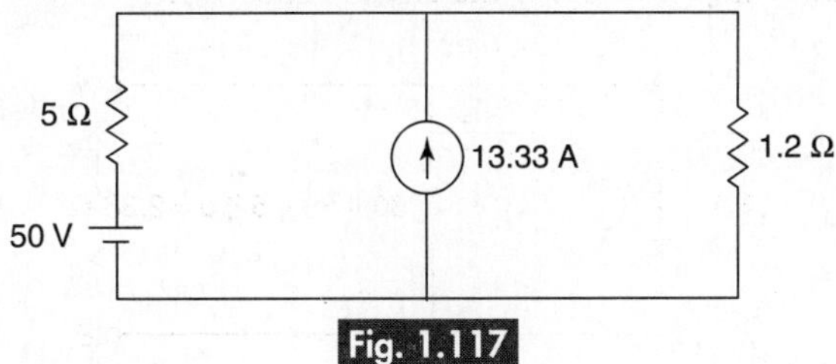


Fig. 1.117

By source transformation (Fig. 1.118),

Fig. 1.118

$$I = \frac{50-16}{5+1.2} = 5.48 \text{ A}$$

Power delivered by the 50 V source = 50 × 5.48 = 274 W

## EXAMPLE 1.40

*Find the current in the 4 Ω resistor shown in network of Fig. 1.119.*

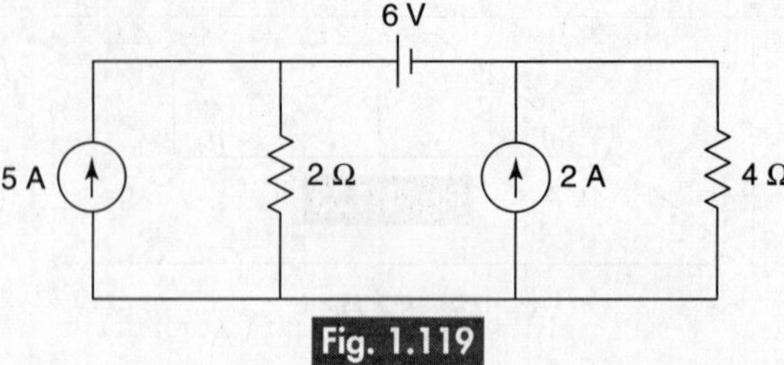


Fig. 1.119

**Solution** Converting the parallel combination of the current source of 5 A and the resistor of 2 Ω into an equivalent series combination of voltage source and resistor (Fig. 1.120),

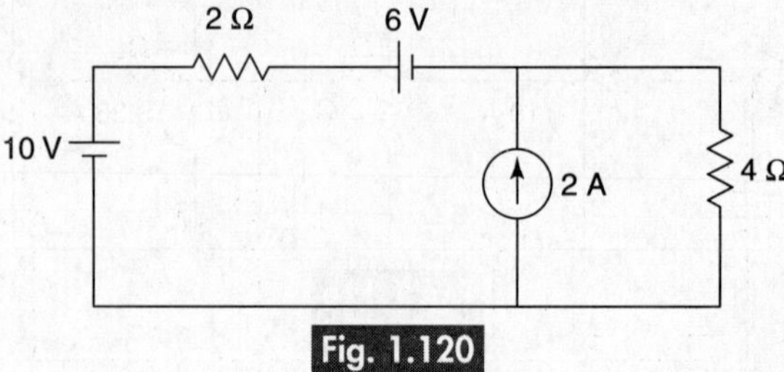


Fig. 1.120

Adding two voltage sources (Fig. 1.121),

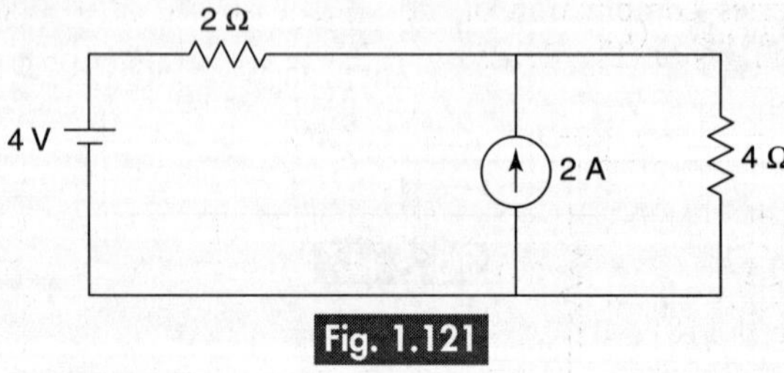


Fig. 1.121

Again by source transformation (Fig. 1.122),

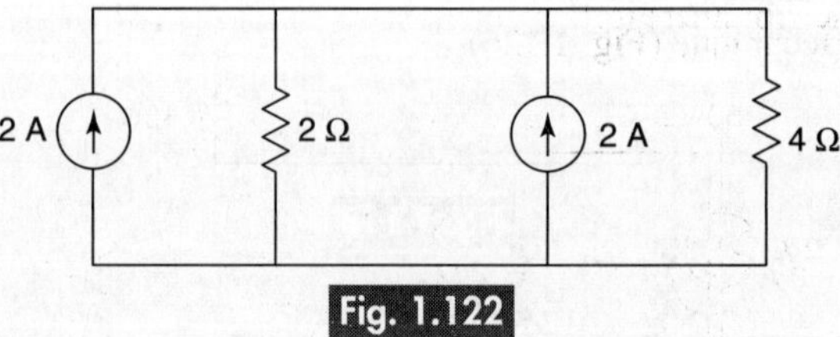


Fig. 1.122

Adding two current sources (Fig. 1.123),

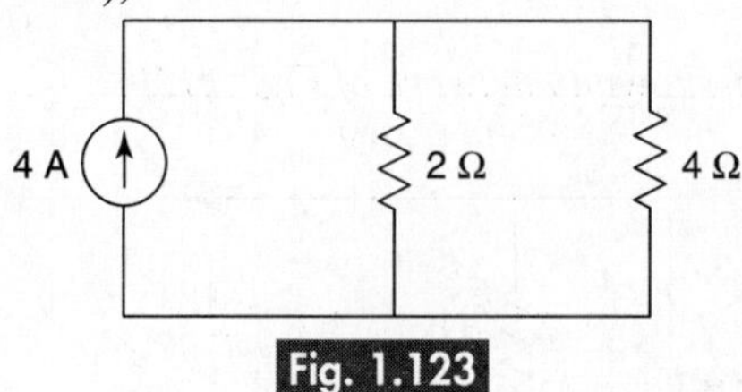


Fig. 1.123

By current-division rule,

$$I_{4\Omega} = 4 \times \frac{2}{2+4} = 1.33 \text{ A}$$

**EXAMPLE 1.41**

*Find the voltage across the 4 Ω resistor shown in network of Fig. 1.124.*

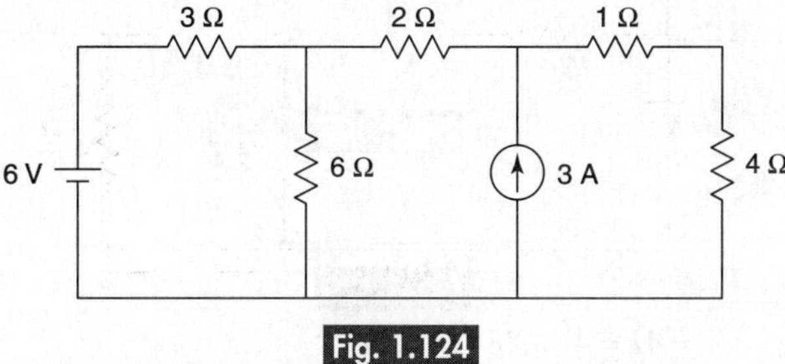


Fig. 1.124

**Solution** Converting the series combination of the voltage source of 6 V and the resistor of 3 Ω into equivalent current source and resistor (Fig. 1.125),

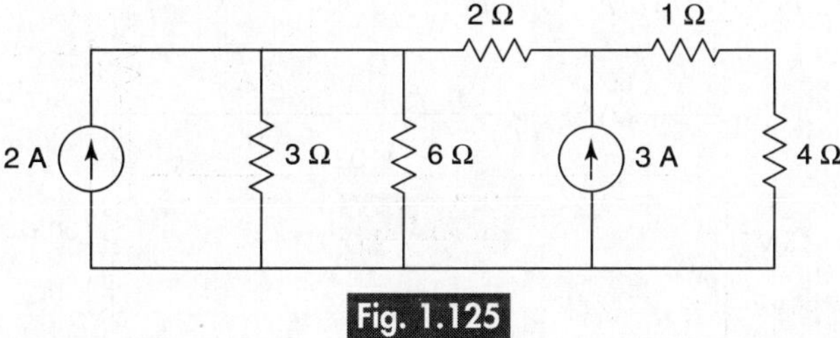


Fig. 1.125

By series–parallel reduction technique (Fig. 1.126),

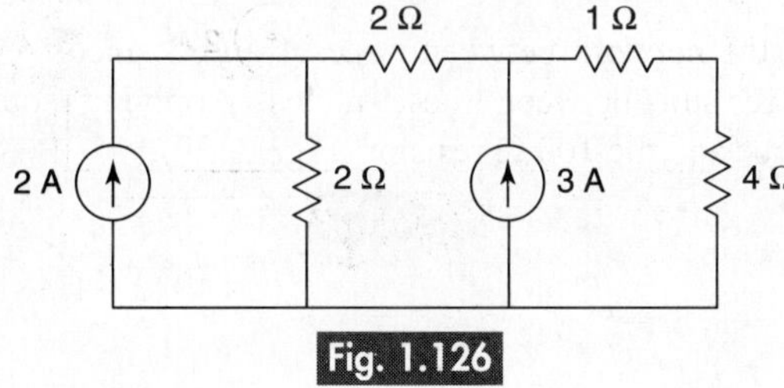


Fig. 1.126

By source transformation (Fig. 1.127),

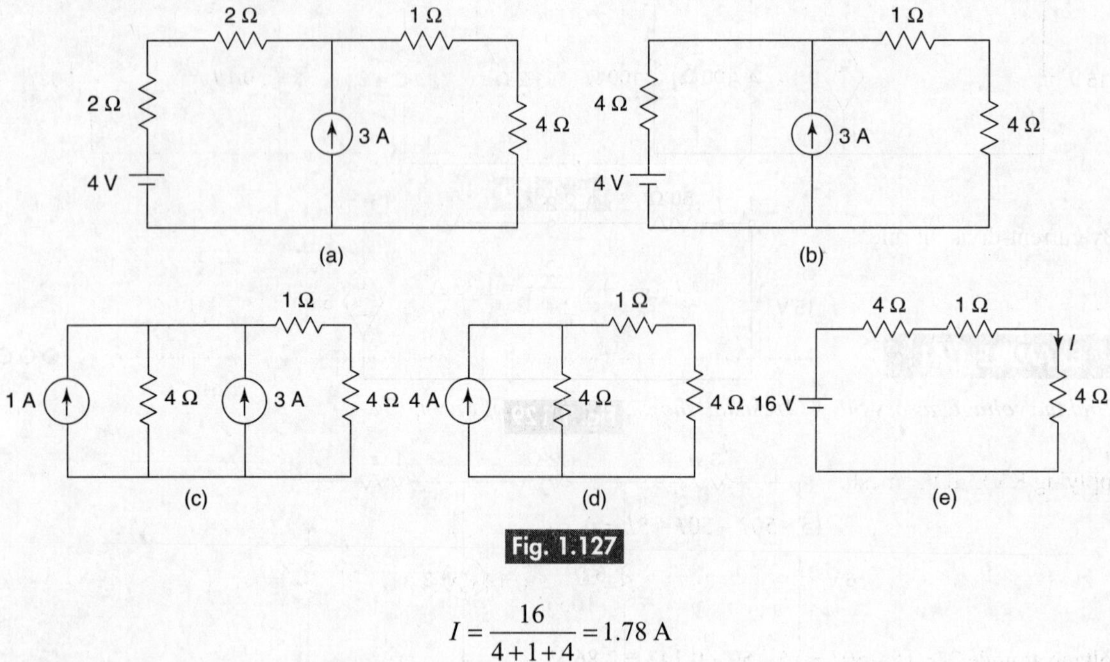


Fig. 1.127

$$I = \frac{16}{4+1+4} = 1.78 \text{ A}$$

Voltage across the 4 Ω resistor $= 4I = 4 \times 1.78 = 7.12$ V

## EXAMPLE 1.42

*Find the voltage at node 2 of the network shown in Fig. 1.128.*

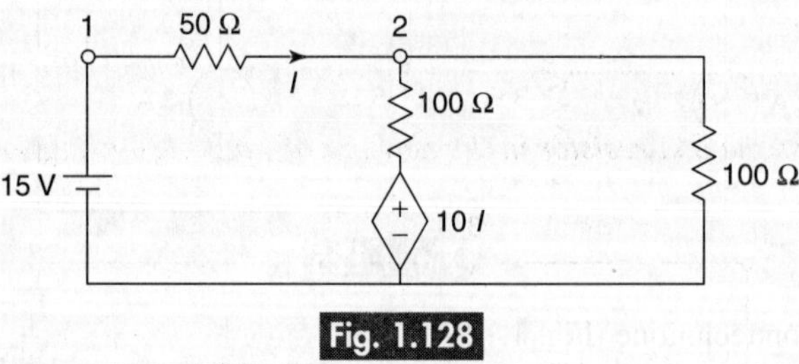


Fig. 1.128

**Solution** We cannot change the network between nodes 1 and 2 since the controlling current $I$, for the controlled source is in the resistor between these nodes. Applying source transformation to series combination of controlled source and the 100 Ω resistor (Fig. 1.129),

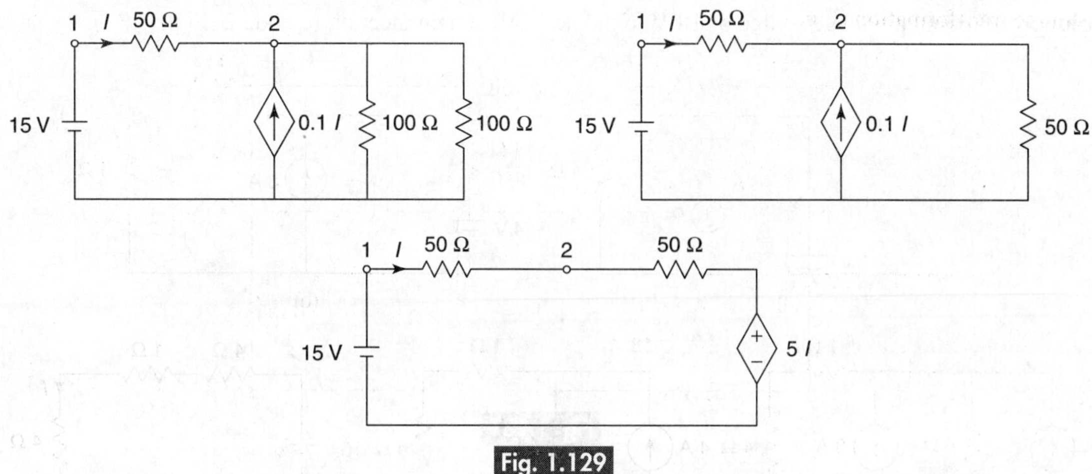


Fig. 1.129

Applying KVL to the mesh,

$$15 - 50I - 50I - 5I = 0$$

$$I = \frac{15}{105} = 0.143 \text{ A}$$

Voltage at node 2 $= 15 - 50I = 15 - 50 \times 0.143 = 7.86$ V

## 1.11 SOURCE SHIFTING

LO 1.6

Source shifting is the simplification technique used when there is no resistor in series with a voltage source or a resistor in parallel with a current source.

### EXAMPLE 1.43

*Calculate the voltage across the 6 Ω resistor in the network of Fig. 1.130 using source-shifting technique.*

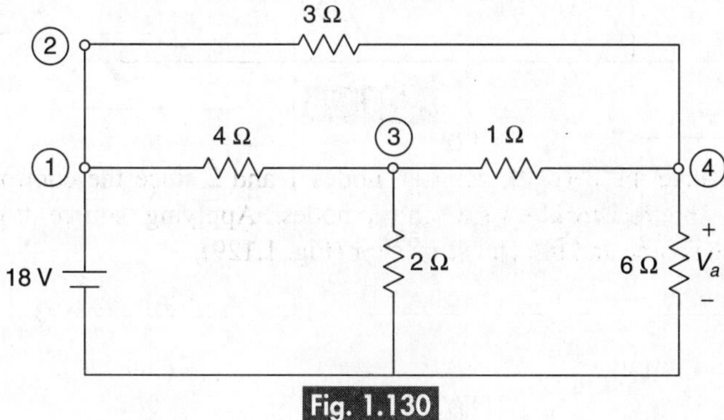


Fig. 1.130

**Solution** Adding a voltage source of 18 V to the network and connecting to node 2 (Fig. 1.131), we have

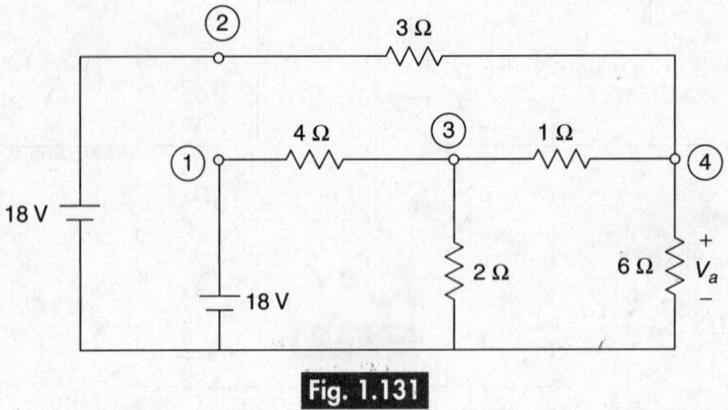


Fig. 1.131

Since nodes 1 and 2 are maintained at the same voltage by the sources, the connection between nodes 1 and 2 is removed. Now, the two voltage sources have resistors in series and source transformation can be applied (Fig. 1.132).

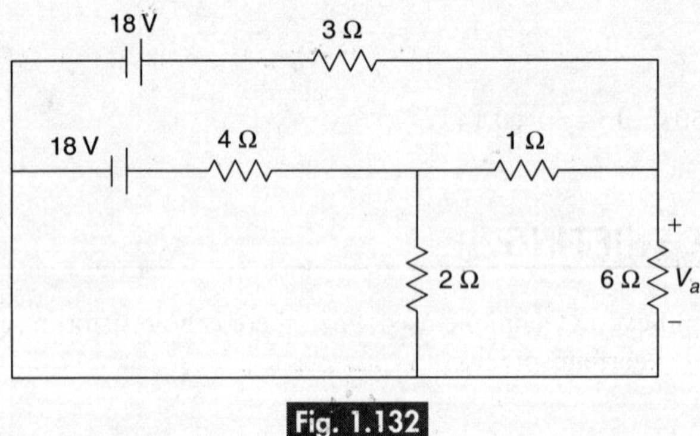


Fig. 1.132

Simplifying the network (Fig. 1.133),

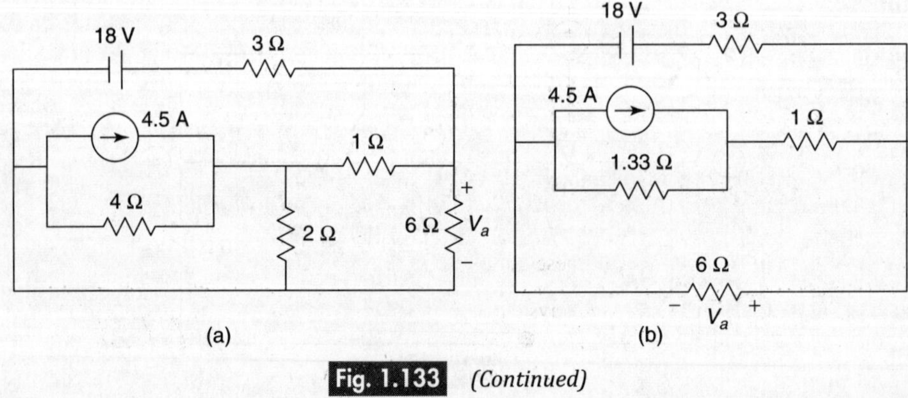


Fig. 1.133 *(Continued)*

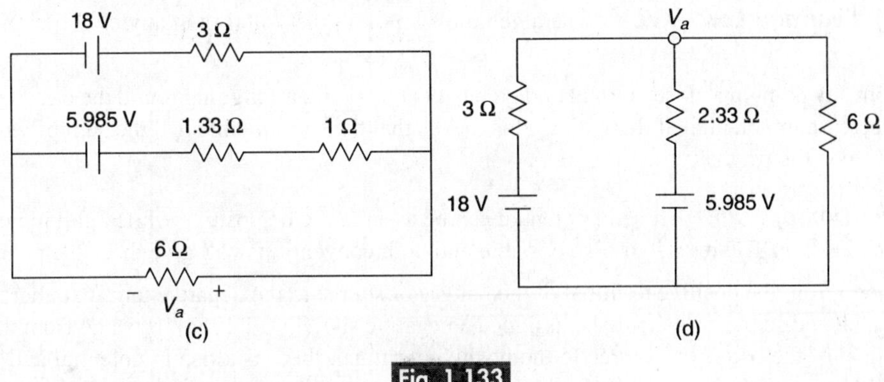


Fig. 1.133

Applying KCL at the node,

$$\frac{V_a - 18}{3} + \frac{V_a - 5.985}{2.33} + \frac{V_a}{6} = 0$$

$$V_a = 9.23 \text{ V}$$

## 1.12 KIRCHHOFF'S LAWS

LO 1.7

Use Kirchhoff's laws in solving the networks

The entire study of electric network analysis is based mainly on Kirchhoff's laws. But before discussing this, it is essential to familiarise ourselves with the following terms:

*Node* A node is a junction where two or more network elements are connected together.

*Branch* An element or number of elements connected between two nodes constitute a branch.

*Loop* A loop is any closed part of the circuit.

*Mesh* A mesh is the most elementary form of a loop and cannot be further divided into other loops. All meshes are loops but all loops are not meshes.

***1. Kirchhoff's Current Law (KCL)*** The algebraic sum of currents meeting at a junction or node in an electric circuit is zero.

Consider five conductors, carrying currents $I_1$, $I_2$, $I_3$, $I_4$ and $I_5$, meeting at a point $O$, as shown in Fig. 1.134. Assuming the incoming currents to be positive and outgoing currents negative, we have

$$I_1 + (-I_2) + I_3 + (-I_4) + I_5 = 0$$

$$I_1 - I_2 + I_3 - I_4 + I_5 = 0$$

$$I_1 + I_3 + I_5 = I_2 + I_4$$

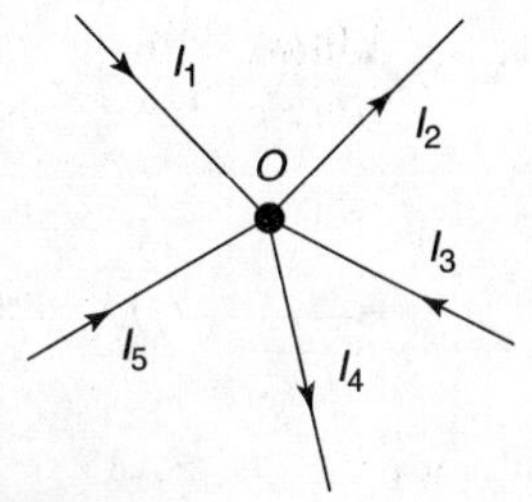


Fig. 1.134 *Kirchhoff's current law*

Thus, the above law can also be stated as the sum of currents flowing towards any junction in an electric circuit is equal to the sum of the currents flowing away from that junction.

**2. Kirchhoff's Voltage Law (KVL)** The algebraic sum of all the voltages in any closed circuit or mesh or loop is zero.

If we start from any point in a closed circuit and go back to that point, after going round the circuit, there is no increase or decrease in potential at that point. This means that the sum of emfs and the sum of voltage drops or rises meeting on the way is zero.

**3. Determination of Sign** A rise in potential can be assumed to be positive while a fall in potential can be considered negative. The reverse is also possible and both conventions will give the same result.

(i) If we go from the positive terminal of the battery or source to the negative terminal, there is a fall in potential and so the emf should be assigned a negative sign (Fig. 1.135a). If we go from the negative terminal of the battery or source to the positive terminal, there is a rise in potential and so the emf should be given a positive sign (Fig. 1.135b).

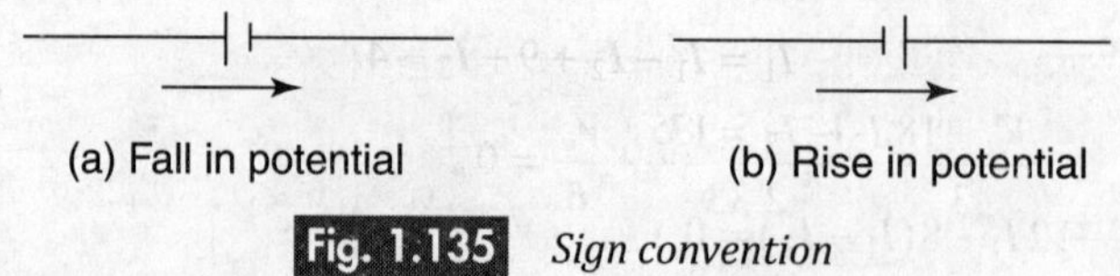


**Fig. 1.135** *Sign convention*

(ii) When current flows through a resistor, there is a voltage drop across it. If we go through the resistor in the same direction as the current, there is a fall in the potential and so the sign of this voltage drop is negative (Fig. 1.136a). If we go opposite to the direction of the current flow, there is a rise in potential and hence, this voltage drop should be given a positive sign (Fig. 1.136b).

**Fig. 1.136** *Sign convention*

## EXAMPLE 1.44

*Determine the currents $I_1$, $I_2$ and $I_3$ in Fig. 1.137.*

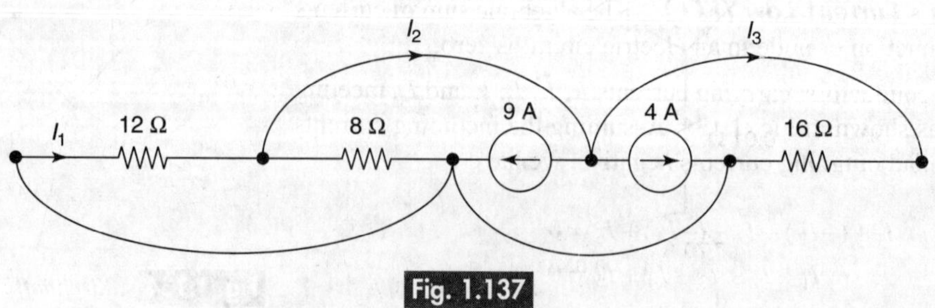


**Fig. 1.137**

**Solution** Assigning currents to all the branches (Fig. 1.138),

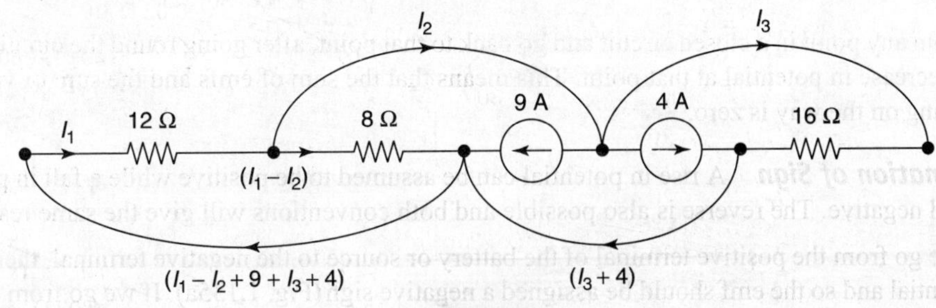


Fig. 1.138

From Fig. 1.138,

$$I_1 = I_1 - I_2 + 9 + I_3 + 4$$

$$I_2 - I_3 = 13 \qquad \text{...(i)}$$

Also,

$$-12 I_1 - 8(I_1 - I_2) = 0$$

$$-20 I_1 + 8 I_2 = 0 \qquad \text{...(ii)}$$

and

$$-12 I_1 - 16 I_3 = 0 \qquad \text{...(iii)}$$

Solving Eqs (i), (ii) and (iii),

$$I_1 = 4 \text{ A}$$

$$I_2 = 10 \text{ A}$$

$$I_3 = -3 \text{ A}$$

## EXAMPLE 1.45

*Find currents in all the branches of the network shown in Fig. 1.139.*

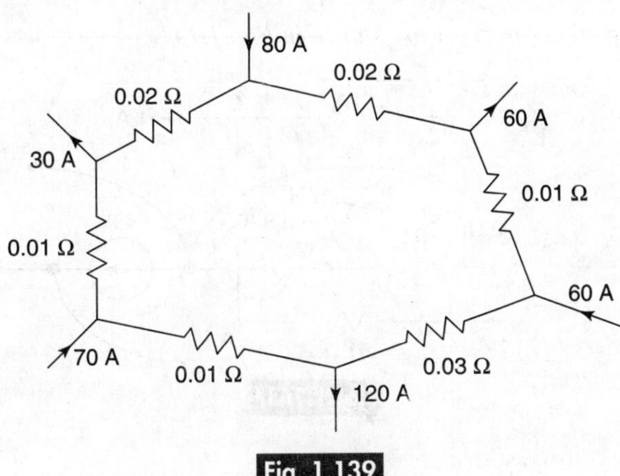


Fig. 1.139

**Solution** Let $I_{AF} = x$

Then

$$I_{FE} = x - 30$$

$$I_{ED} = x + 40$$

$$I_{DC} = x - 80$$

$$I_{CB} = x - 20$$

$$I_{BA} = x - 80$$

Applying KVL to the closed path *AFEDCBA* (Fig. 1.140),

Fig. 1.140

$$-0.02x - 0.01(x-30) - 0.01(x+40) - 0.03(x-80) - 0.01(x-20) - 0.02(x-80) = 0$$

$$x = 41 \text{ A}$$

$$I_{AF} = 41 \text{ A}$$

$$I_{FE} = 41 - 30 = 11 \text{ A}$$

$$I_{ED} = 41 + 40 = 81 \text{ A}$$

$$I_{DC} = 41 - 80 = -39 \text{ A}$$

$$I_{CD} = 39 \text{ A}$$

$$I_{CB} = 41 - 20 = 21 \text{ A}$$

$$I_{BA} = 41 - 80 = -39 \text{ A}$$

$$I_{AB} = 39 \text{ A}$$

## EXAMPLE 1.46

*Find currents in all the branches of the network shown in Fig. 1.141.*

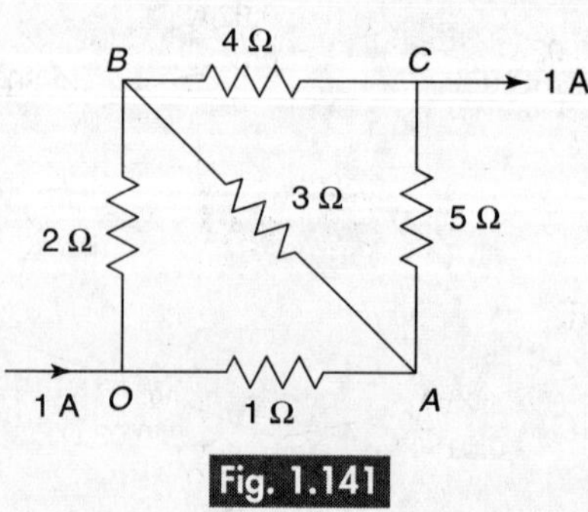


Fig. 1.141

**Solution** Assigning currents to all the branches (Fig. 1.142).

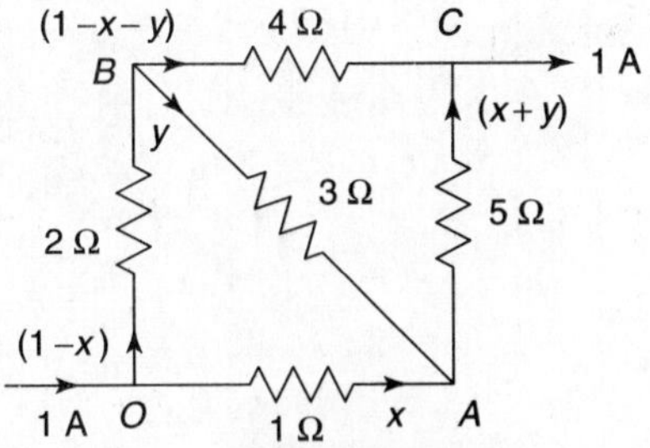

Applying KVL to the closed path *OBAO*,

$$-2(1-x)-3y+1(x)=0$$
$$3x-3y=2 \quad \ldots\text{(i)}$$

Applying KVL to the closed path *ABCA*,

$$3y-4(1-x-y)+5(x+y)=0$$
$$9x+12y=4 \quad \ldots\text{(ii)}$$


Fig. 1.142

Solving Eqs (i) and (ii),

$$x = 0.57\text{ A}$$
$$y = -0.095\text{ A}$$
$$I_{OA} = 0.57\text{ A}$$
$$I_{OB} = 1-0.57 = 0.43\text{ A}$$
$$I_{AB} = 0.095\text{ A}$$
$$I_{AC} = 0.57-0.095 = 0.475\text{ A}$$
$$I_{BC} = 1-0.57+0.095 = 0.525\text{ A}$$

## Examples with Dependent Sources

**EXAMPLE 1.47** ●○○

*In the network of Fig. 1.143, find $I_1$, $I_2$ and V.*

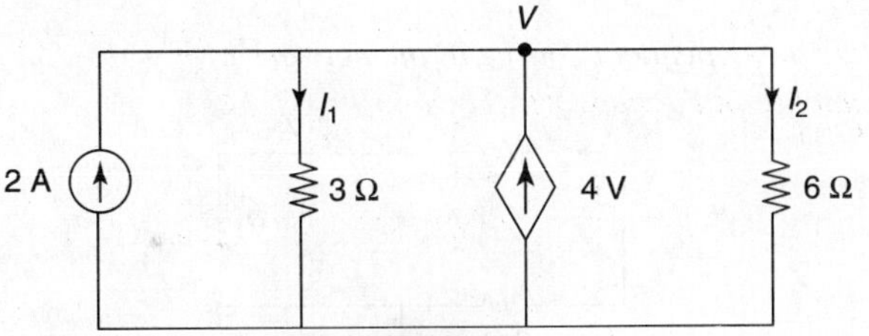

Fig. 1.143

**Solution** Applying KCL at the node,

$$2+4V = \frac{V}{3}+\frac{V}{6}$$
$$\frac{V}{3}+\frac{V}{6}-4V = 2$$

$$-\frac{7}{2}V = 2$$

$$V = -\frac{4}{7}\text{ V}$$

$$I_1 = \frac{V}{3} = -\frac{4}{21}\text{ A}$$

$$I_2 = \frac{V}{6} = -\frac{2}{21}\text{ A}$$

**EXAMPLE 1.48**

*Find voltages $V_1$ and $V_2$ in the network of Fig. 1.144.*

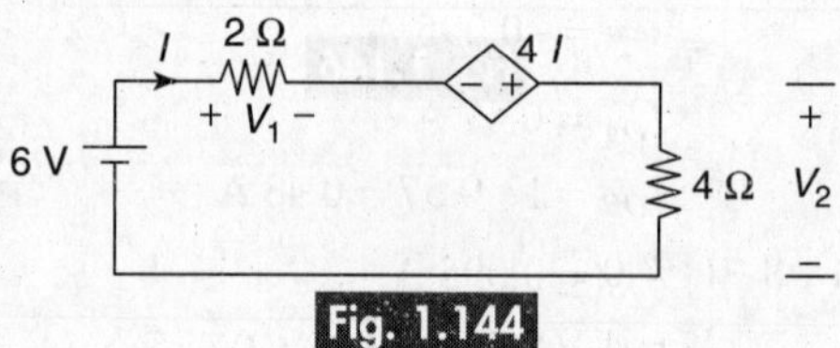


Fig. 1.144

**Solution** Applying KVL to the loop,

$$6 - 2I + 4I - 4I = 0$$

$$I = 3\text{ A}$$

From Fig. 1.144,

$$V_1 = 2I = 2(3) = 6\text{ V}$$

$$V_2 = 4I = 4(3) = 12\text{ V}$$

**EXAMPLE 1.49**

*Find the power delivered by the dependent source in the network of Fig. 1.145.*

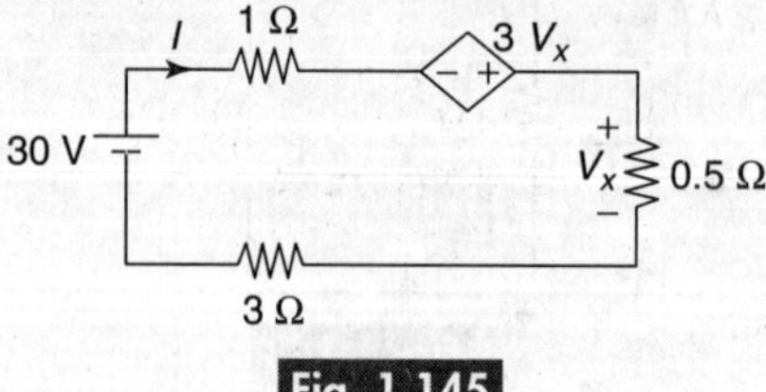


Fig. 1.145

**Solution** From Fig. 1.145,

$$V_x = 0.5I$$

Applying KVL to the loop,

$$30 - 1I + 3V_x - 0.5I - 3I = 0$$

$$30 - I + 3(0.5I) - 0.5I - 3I = 0$$

$$30 - 3I = 0$$

$$I = 10 \text{ A}$$

$$V_x = 0.5(10) = 5 \text{ V}$$

Power supplied by the dependent source $= (3V_x)(I) = 3 \times 5 \times 10 = 150$ W

## EXAMPLE 1.50

*Find the current $I_2$ in the network of Fig. 1.146.*

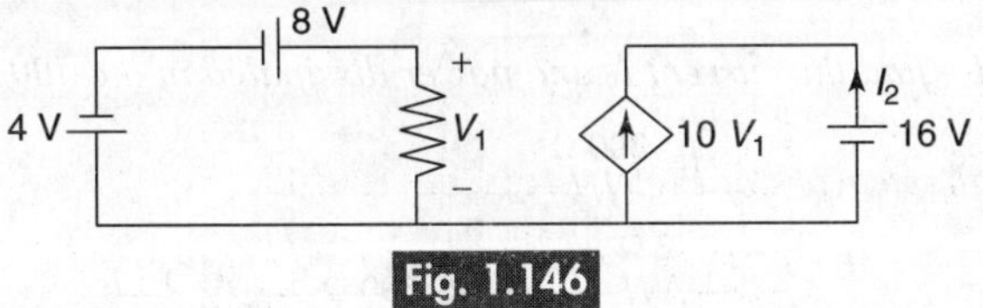


Fig. 1.146

**Solution** Applying KVL to the left loop,

$$-4 + 8 - V_1 = 0$$

$$V_1 = 4 \text{ V}$$

Applying KCL to the right part,

$$10\,V_1 + I_2 = 0$$

$$10(4) + I_2 = 0$$

$$I_2 = -40 \text{ A}$$

## EXAMPLE 1.51

*Find the voltage $V_x$ in the network of Fig. 1.147.*

Fig. 1.147

**Solution** Applying KCL at the node,

$$2 + \frac{1}{6}V_y = \frac{V_x}{9} \quad \ldots\text{(i)}$$

From Fig. 1.147,

$$V_y = 3\left(\frac{V_x}{9}\right) = \frac{V_x}{3} \quad \ldots\text{(ii)}$$

Substituting Eq. (ii) in Eq. (i),

$$2+\frac{1}{6}\left(\frac{V_x}{3}\right)=\frac{V_x}{9}$$

$$2+\frac{V_x}{18}-\frac{V_x}{9}=0$$

$$V_x = 36 \text{ V}$$

## EXAMPLE 1.52

*In the network of Fig. 1.148, find the current $I_1$ and power dissipated in the 500 Ω resistor.*

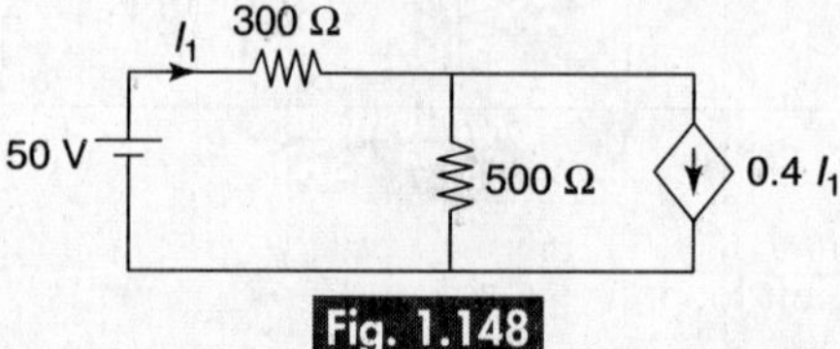


Fig. 1.148

**Solution** Assigning currents to all the branches, as shown in Fig. 1.149,

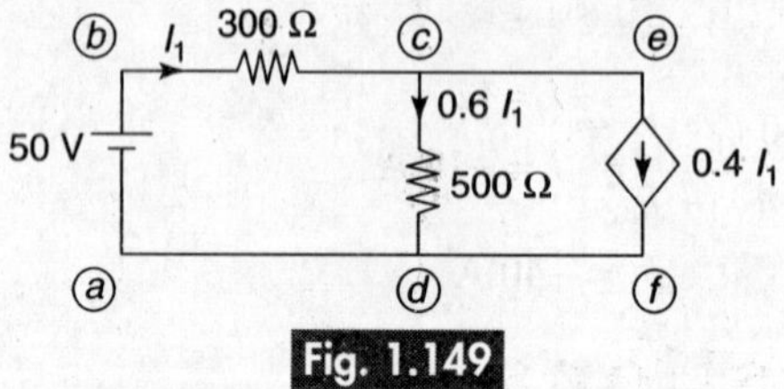


Fig. 1.149

Applying KVL to the closed loop *abcda*,

$$50-300\,I_1-500(0.6\,I_1)=0$$

$$I_1 = 0.083 \text{ A}$$

Power dissipated in the 500 Ω resistor = $500\,(0.6I_1)^2$ = $500\,(0.6 \times 0.083)^2$ = 1.24 W

## EXAMPLE 1.53

*Find the current I in the network shown in Fig. 1.150.*

Fig. 1.150

**Solution** Assigning currents in all the branches, as shown in Fig. 1.151,

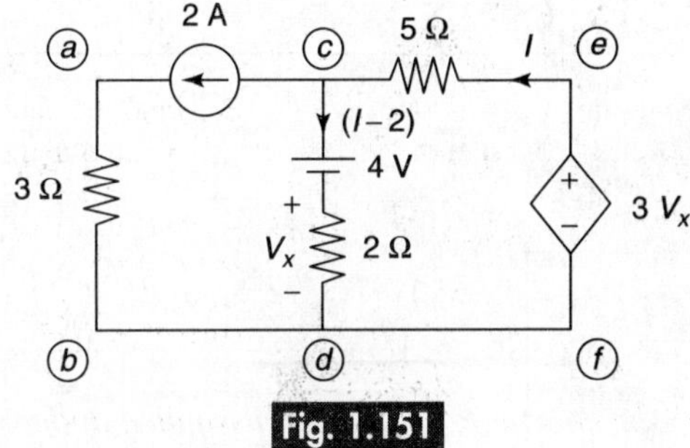


Fig. 1.151

From Fig. 1.151,

$$V_x = 2(I-2) \quad \text{...(i)}$$

Applying KVL to the closed loop *fecdf*,

$$3V_x - 5I - 4 - 2(I-2) = 0$$

$$3[2(I-2)] - 5I - 4 - 2(I-2) = 0$$

$$6I - 12 - 5I - 4 - 2I + 4 = 0$$

$$-I = 12$$

$$I = -12 \text{ A}$$

## Theory Questions

**1.1** What is resistance and explain the factors on which resistance of conductor depends? **[LO 1.1]** ●○○

**1.2** What is inductance and explain the factors on which inductance of a coil depends? **[LO 1.1]** ●○○

**1.3** Derive the expression for energy stored in inductor. **[LO 1.1]** ○●○

**1.4** What is capacitance and explain the factors on which capacitor of a capacitive depends. **[LO 1.1]** ●○○

**1.5** Derive the expression for energy stored in capacitor. **[LO 1.1]** ○●○

**1.6** Define independent and dependent sources. **[LO 1.2]** ●○○

**1.7** What are different types of dependent sources? **[LO 1.2]** ●○○

**1.8** Define following terms: **[LO 1.3]** ●○○

(i) Network and circuit (ii) Linear and non-linear elements

(iii) Active and passive elements (iv) Unilateral and bilateral elements

(v) Lumped and distributed elements (vi) Active and passive networks

(vii) Time-variant and time-invariant networks

**1.9** Write the expressions for series and parallel combinations of (i) resistors (ii) inductors (iii) capacitors. **[LO 1.4]** ●○○

**1.10** Derive the expressions for delta-to-star and star-to-delta transfer functions. **[LO 1.5]** ●○○

**1.11** State and explain Kirchhoff's laws. **[LO 1.7]** ○●○

# Practice Problems

**1.1** Find the resistance between terminals *A* and *B* in the network of Fig. 1.152. ●○○

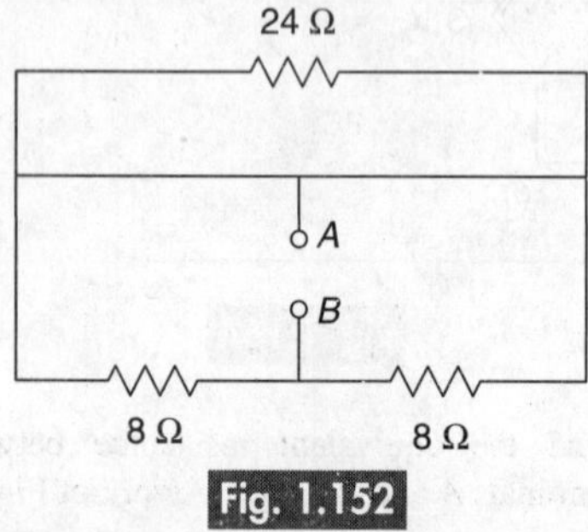


Fig. 1.152

**1.2** Find the resistance between terminals *A* and *B* in the network of Fig. 1.153. ●○○

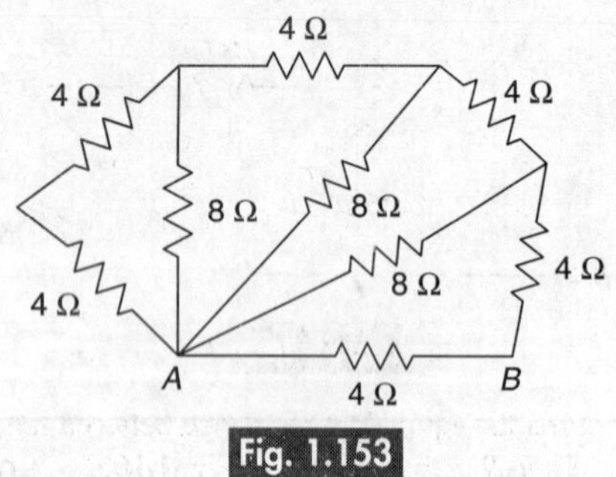


Fig. 1.153

**1.3** Find the equivalent resistance between terminals *A* and *B* in the network of Fig. 1.154. ●○○

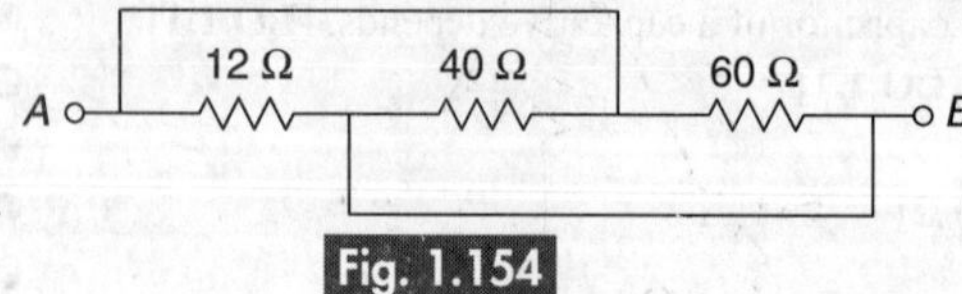


Fig. 1.154

**1.4** What is the equivalent resistance between terminals *A* and *B* of the networks shown in Fig. 1.155? ●○○

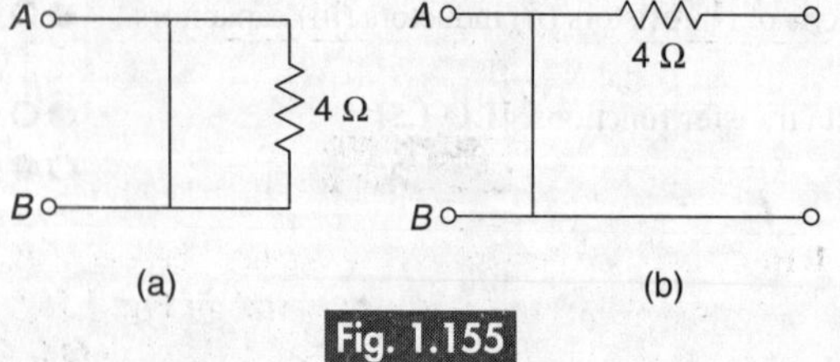


Fig. 1.155

**1.5** Find the equivalent resistance between terminals *A* and *B* in the network of Fig. 1.156. ●○○

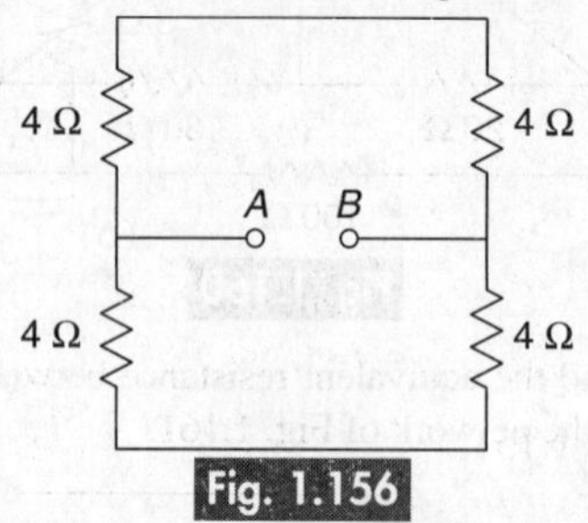


Fig. 1.156

**1.6** Find the equivalent resistance between terminals *A* and *B* in the network of Fig. 1.157. ○●○

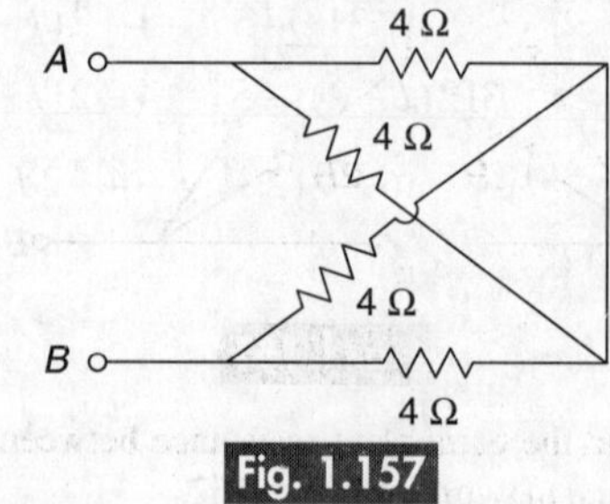


Fig. 1.157

**1.7** Find the equivalent resistance between terminals *A* and *B* in the network of Fig. 1.158. ●○○

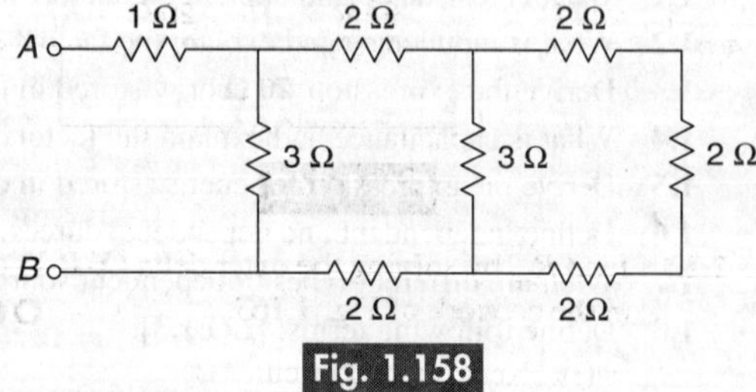


Fig. 1.158

**1.8** Find the equivalent resistance between *A* and *B* in the network of Fig. 1.159. ●○○

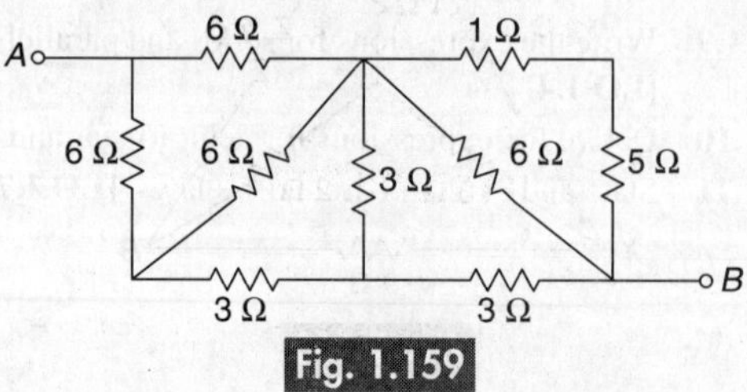


Fig. 1.159

**1.9** Find the equivalent resistance between $A$ and $B$ in the network of Fig. 1.160. ●○○

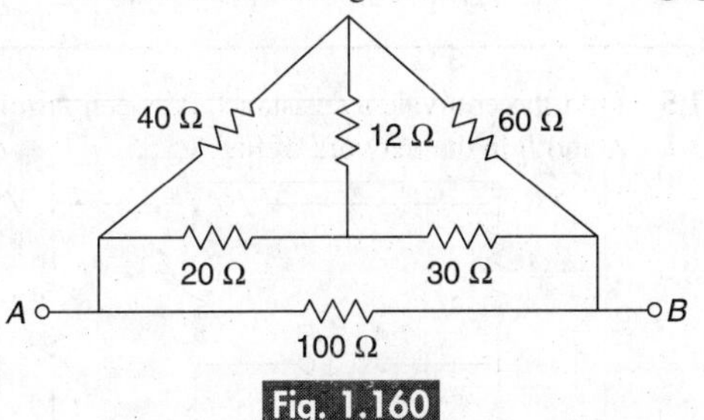


Fig. 1.160

**1.10** Find the equivalent resistance between $A$ and $B$ in the network of Fig. 1.161. ●○○

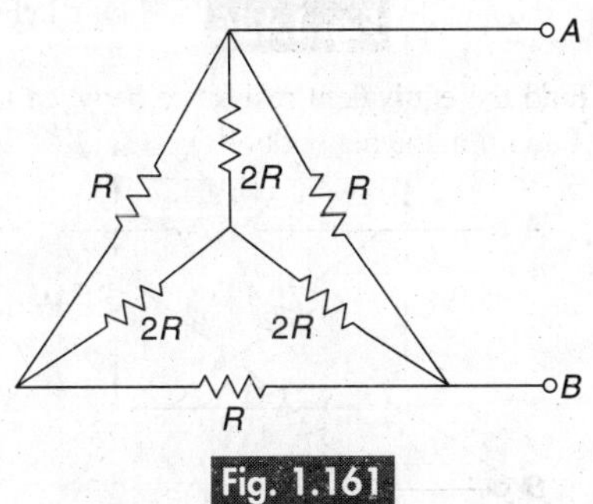


Fig. 1.161

**1.11** Find the equivalent resistance between $A$ and $B$ in the network of Fig. 1.162. ●○○

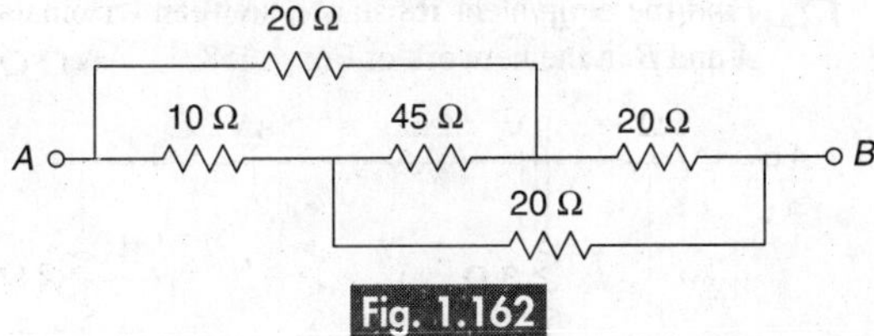


Fig. 1.162

**1.12** Find $R_{AB}$ by solving the outer delta ($X$-$B$-$Y$) only in the network of Fig. 1.163. ○●○

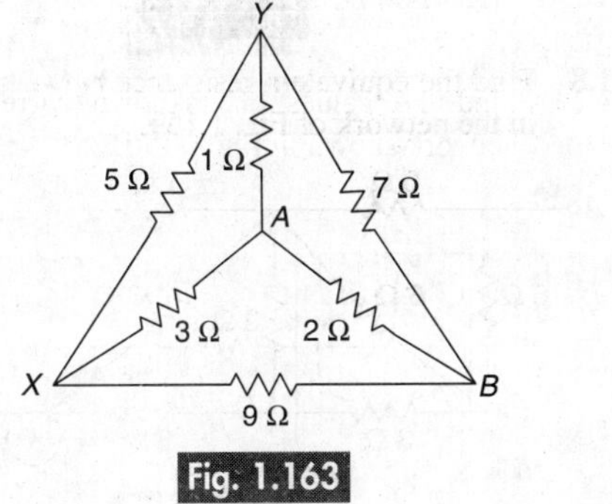


Fig. 1.163

**1.13** Find the equivalent resistance between $A$ and $B$ in the network of Fig. 1.164. ●○○

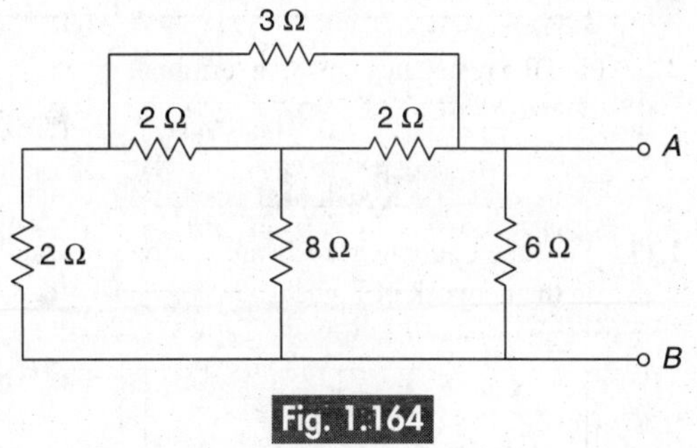


Fig. 1.164

**1.14** Find the equivalent resistance between the terminals $A$ and $B$ in the network of Fig. 1.165. ●○○

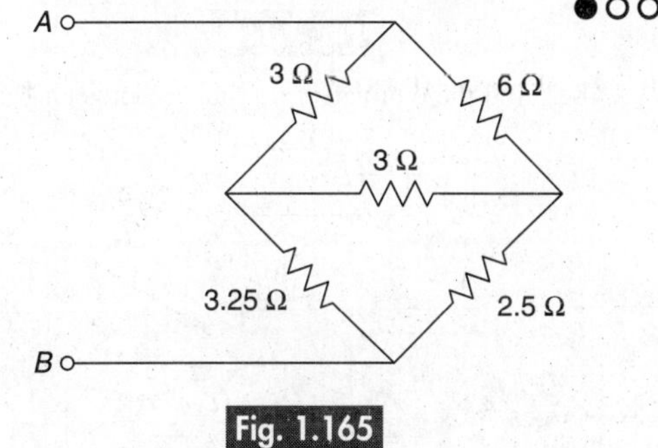


Fig. 1.165

**1.15** Find the equivalent resistance between terminals $A$ and $B$ in the network of Fig. 1.166. ○●○

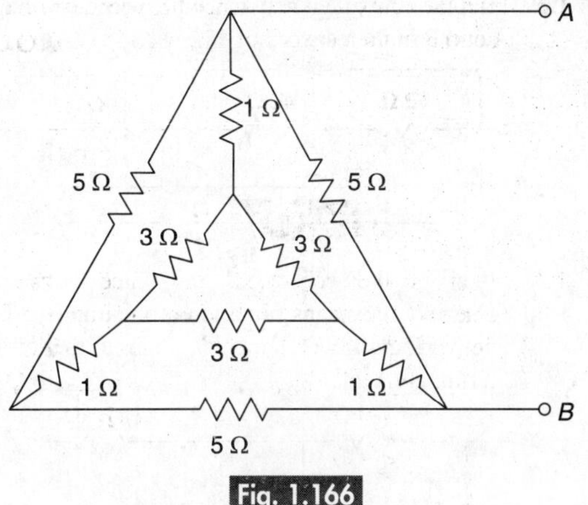


Fig. 1.166

**1.16** Find the equivalent resistance between the terminals $A$ and $B$ in the network of Fig. 1.167. ●○○

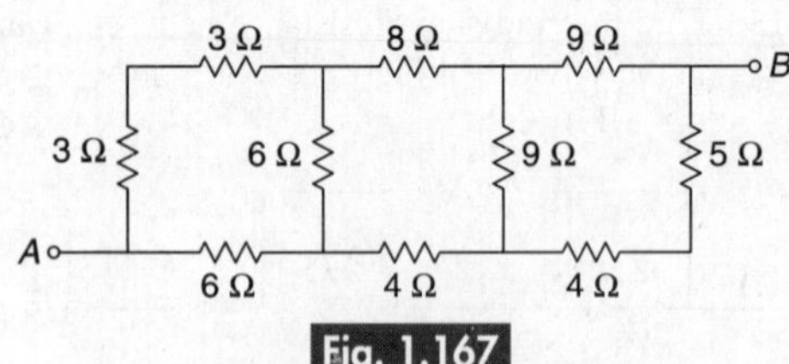


Fig. 1.167

**1.17** Find the equivalent resistance between $A$ and $B$ in the network of Fig. 1.168. ●○○

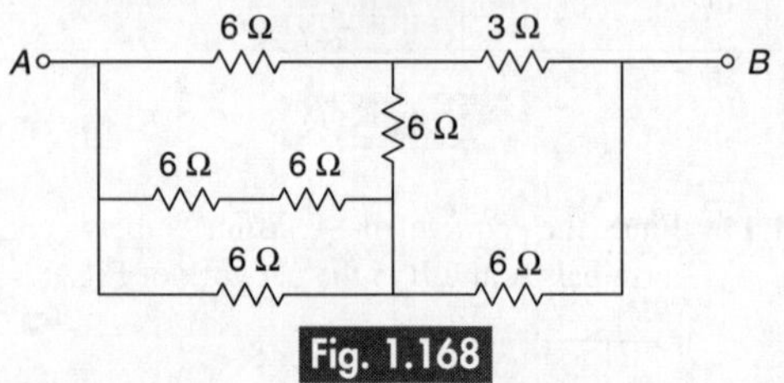


Fig. 1.168

**1.18** Find the equivalent resistance between $A$ and $B$ in the network of Fig. 1.169. ○●○

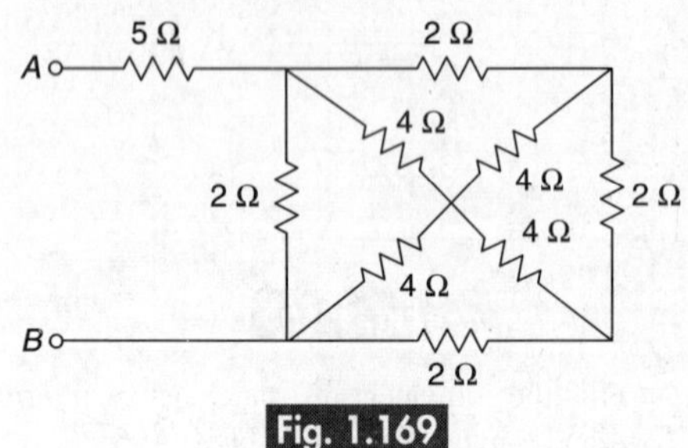


Fig. 1.169

**1.19** Replace the given network with a single voltage source and a resistor. ●○○

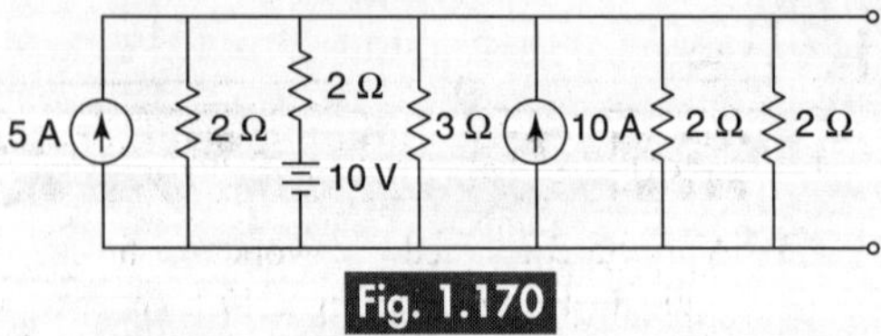


Fig. 1.170

**1.20** Use source transformation to simplify the network until two elements remain to the left of terminals $A$ and $B$. ●○○

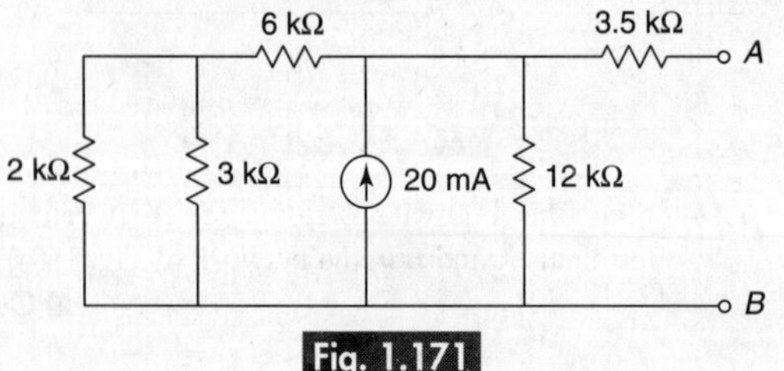


Fig. 1.171

**1.21** Determine the voltage $V_x$ in the network of Fig. 1.172 by source-shifting technique. ○●○

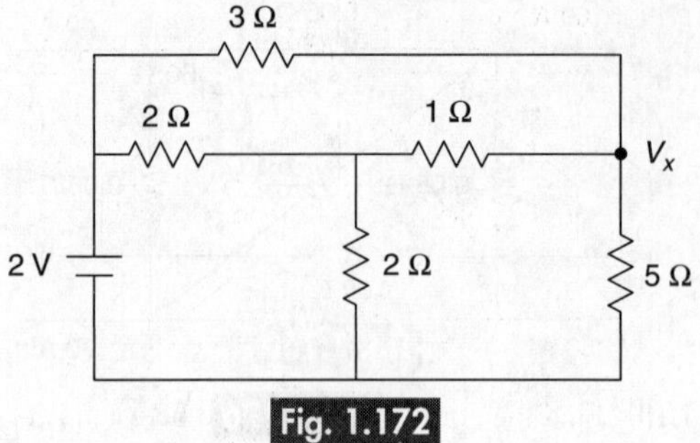


Fig. 1.172

**1.22** Find $I_x$ and $V_x$ in the network shown in Fig. 1.173. ●○○

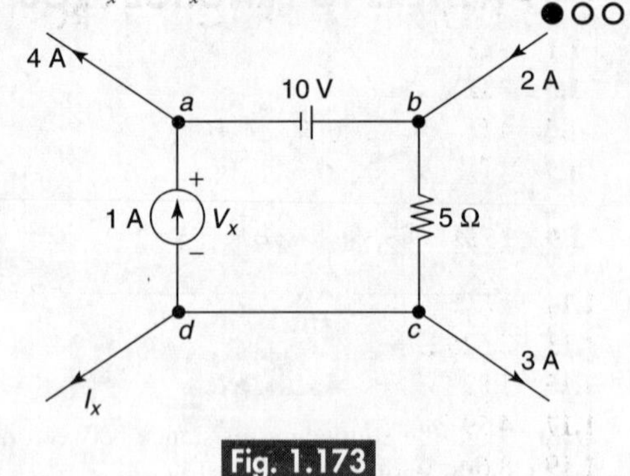


Fig. 1.173

**1.23** Find $V_1$ and $V_2$ in the network shown in Fig. 1.174. ●○○

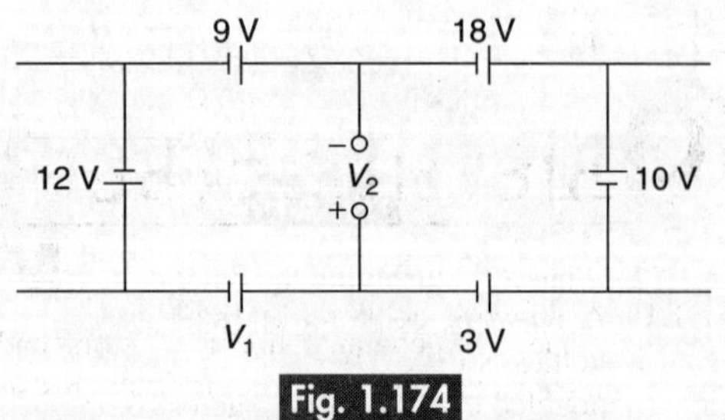


Fig. 1.174

**1.24** Find the values of unknown currents in the network shown in Fig. 1.175. ●○○

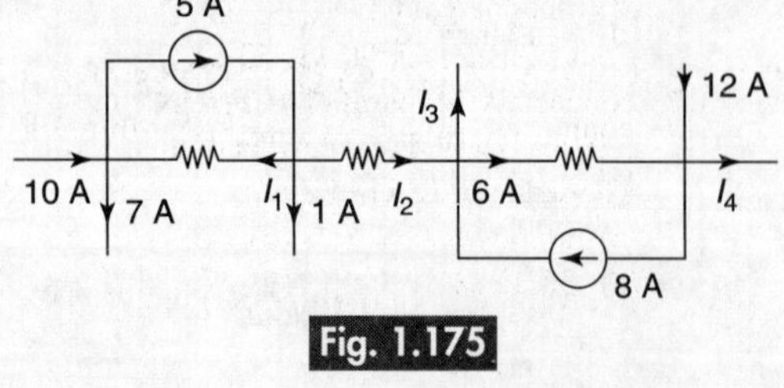


Fig. 1.175

**1.25** Find the current in the branch *XY*, as shown in Fig. 1.176. ●○○

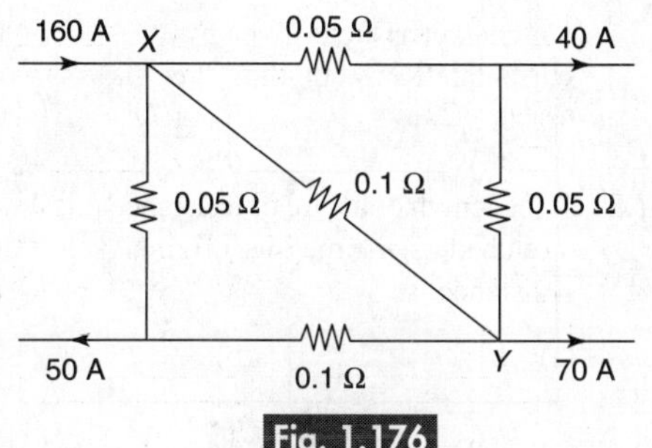


Fig. 1.176

**1.26** Find $I$ and $V_{AB}$ for the network, as shown in Fig. 1.177. ●○○

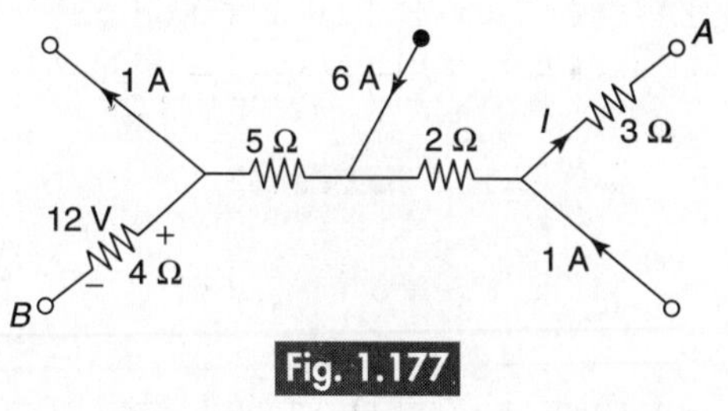


Fig. 1.177

## ANSWERS TO PRACTICE PROBLEMS

| | | | |
|---|---|---|---|
| **1.1** | 4 Ω | **1.2** | 2.67 Ω |
| **1.3** | 8 Ω | **1.4** | (a) 0 (b) 0 |
| **1.5** | 4 Ω | **1.6** | 4 Ω |
| **1.7** | 3 Ω | **1.8** | 5 Ω |
| **1.9** | 25 Ω | **1.10** | $\frac{4}{7}R$ |
| **1.11** | 17 Ω | **1.12** | 1.41 Ω |
| **1.13** | 2.625 Ω | **1.14** | 3.5 Ω |
| **1.15** | 1.82 Ω | **1.16** | 10.32 Ω |
| **1.17** | 4.59 Ω | **1.18** | 6.24 Ω |
| **1.19** | 8.6 V, 0.43 Ω | **1.20** | 88.42 V, 7.92 k Ω |
| **1.21** | 1.129 V | **1.22** | –5 A, –15 V |
| **1.23** | 2 V, 5 V | **1.24** | $I_1 = 2\text{ A}, I_2 = 2\text{ A}, I_3 = 4\text{ A}, I_4 = 10\text{ A}$ |
| **1.25** | 40 A | **1.26** | 3A, 19 V |

# Objective-Type Questions

## From GATE and Other Competitive Examinations

**1.1** A network contains linear resistors and ideal voltage sources. If values of all the resistors are doubled then the voltage across each resistor is ○●○

(a) halved
(b) doubled
(c) increased by four times
(d) not changed

**1.2** Four resistances 80 Ω, 50 Ω, 25 Ω, and R are connected in parallel. Current through 25 Ω resistor is 4 A. Total current of the supply is 10 A. The value of R will be ○●○

(a) 66.66 Ω (b) 40.25 Ω
(c) 36.36 Ω (d) 76.56 Ω

**1.3** A delta-connected network with its wye-equivalent is shown in Fig. 1.178. The resistances $R_1$, $R_2$ and $R_3$ (in ohms) are respectively. ●○○

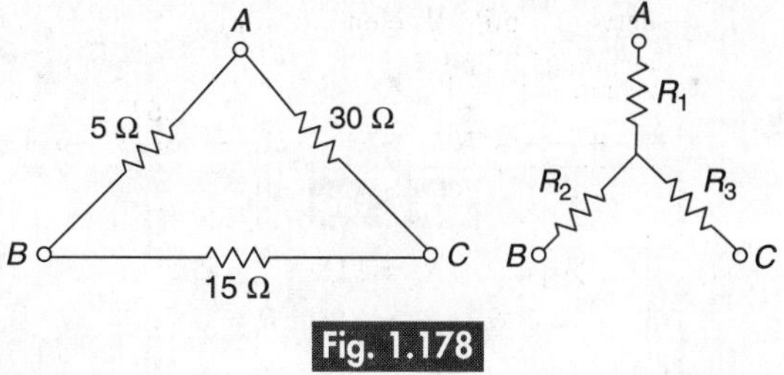


Fig. 1.178

(a) 1.5, 3, 9 (b) 3, 9, 1.5
(c) 9, 3, 1.5 (d) 3, 1.5, 9

**1.4** If each branch of a delta network has resistance $\sqrt{3}\,R$, then each branch of the equivalent wye network has resistance ●○○

(a) $\dfrac{R}{\sqrt{3}}$ (b) $3\,R$

(c) $3\sqrt{3}\,R$ (d) $\dfrac{R}{3}$

**1.5** Viewed from the terminal AB, the network of Fig. 1.179 can be reduced to an equivalent network of a single voltage source in series with a single resistor with the following parameters ●○○

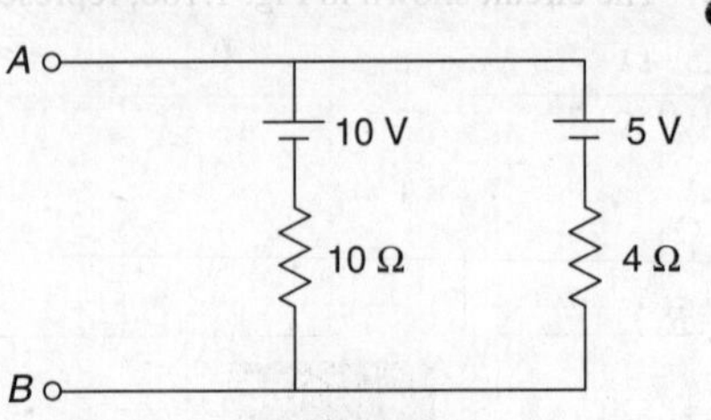


Fig. 1.179

(a) 5 V source in series with a 10 Ω resistor
(b) 1 V source in series with a 2.4 Ω resistor
(c) 15 V source in series with a 2.4 Ω resistor
(d) 1 V source in series with a 10 Ω resistor

**1.6** Consider the star network shown in Fig. 1.180. The resistance between terminals A and B with C open is 6 Ω, between terminals B and C with A open is 11 Ω and between terminals C and A with B open is 9 Ω, then resistance $R_A$, $R_B$ and $R_C$ will be ○●○

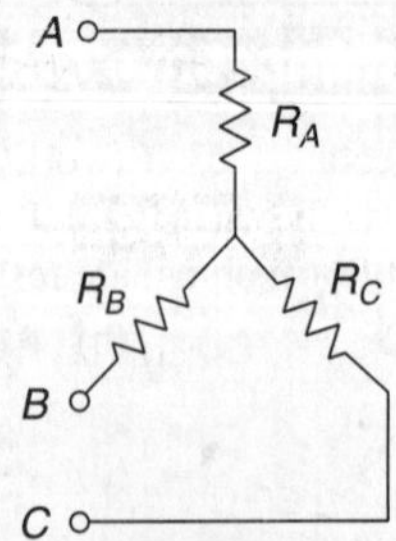


Fig. 1.180

(a) $R_A = 4\,\Omega$, $R_B = 2\,\Omega$, $R_C = 5\,\Omega$
(b) $R_A = 2\,\Omega$, $R_B = 4\,\Omega$, $R_C = 7\,\Omega$
(c) $R_A = 3\,\Omega$, $R_B = 3\,\Omega$, $R_C = 4\,\Omega$
(d) $R_A = 5\,\Omega$, $R_B = 1\,\Omega$, $R_C = 10\,\Omega$

**1.7** A 10 V battery with an internal resistance of 1 Ω is connected across a non-linear load whose *V-I* characteristic is given by $7I = V^2 + 2V$. The current delivered by the battery is ○●○

(a) 0 (b) 10 A
(c) 5 A (d) 8 A

**1.8** If the length of a wire of resistance *R* is uniformly stretched to *n* times its original value, its new resistance is ●○○

(a) $nR$ (b) $\dfrac{R}{n}$

(c) $n^2R$ (d) $\dfrac{R}{n^2}$

**1.9** All the resistances in Fig. 1.181 are 1 Ω each. The value of *I* will be ●○○

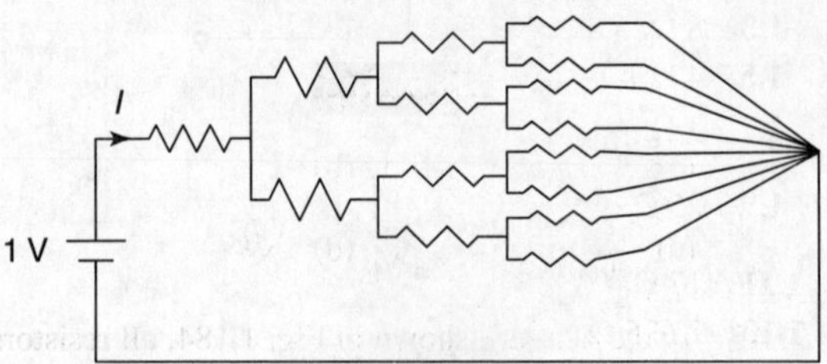


Fig. 1.181

(a) $\dfrac{1}{15}$ A (b) $\dfrac{2}{15}$ A

(c) $\dfrac{4}{15}$ A (d) $\dfrac{8}{15}$ A

**1.10** The current waveform in a pure resistor at 10 Ω is shown in Fig. 1.182. Power dissipated in the resistor is ○●○

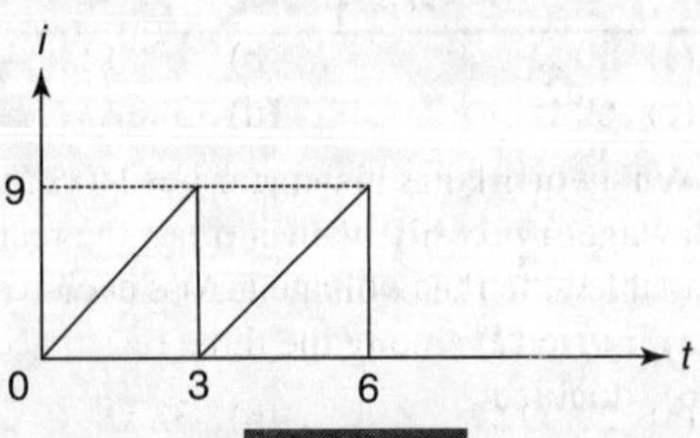


Fig. 1.182

(a) 7.29 W (b) 52.4 W
(c) 135 W (d) 270 W

**1.11** Two wires *A* and *B* of the same material and length *L* and 2*L* have radius *r* and 2*r* respectively. The ratio of their specific resistance will be ●○○

(a) 1 : 1 (b) 1 : 2
(c) 1 : 4 (d) 1 : 8

**1.12** Consider a delta connection of resistors and its equivalent star connection, as shown in Fig. 1.183. If all the elements of the delta connection are scaled by a factor $k$, $k > 0$, the elements of the corresponding star equivalent will be scaled by a factor of ●○○

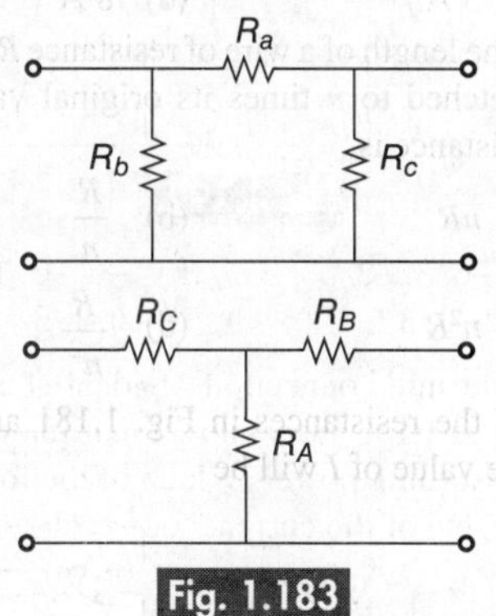


Fig. 1.183

(a) $k^2$ (b) $k$

(c) $\frac{1}{k}$ (d) $\sqrt{k}$

**1.13** In the network shown in Fig. 1.184, all resistors are identical with $R = 300\ \Omega$. The resistance $R_{ab}$ (in Ω) of the network is ○●○

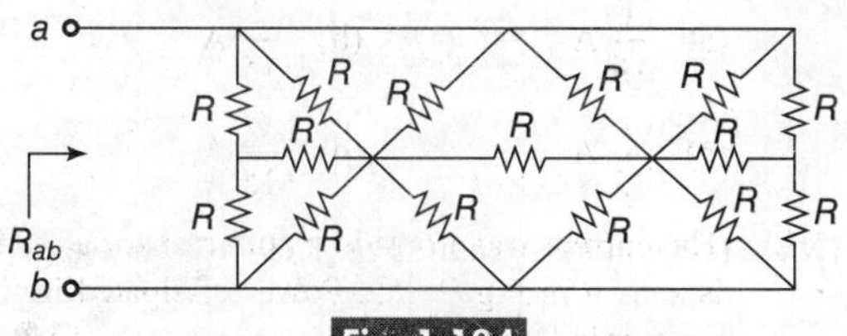


Fig. 1.184

(a) 30 Ω (b) 100 Ω
(c) 60 Ω (d) 300 Ω

**1.14** A $Y$-network has resistances of 10 Ω each in two of its arms, while the third arm has a resistance of 11 Ω. In the equivalent Δ-network, the lowest value (in Ω) among the three resistances is ●○○

(a) 29.09 Ω (b) 32 Ω
(c) 22 Ω (d) 21 Ω

**1.15** For the $Y$-network shown in the Fig. 1.185, the value of $R_1$ (in Ω) in the equivalent Δ-network is ●○○

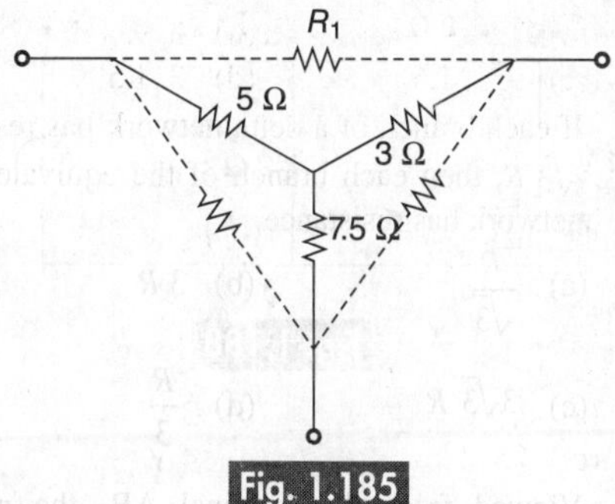


Fig. 1.185

(a) 5 (b) 10
(c) 15.5 (d) 2

**1.16** The circuit shown in Fig. 1.186, represents a ●○○

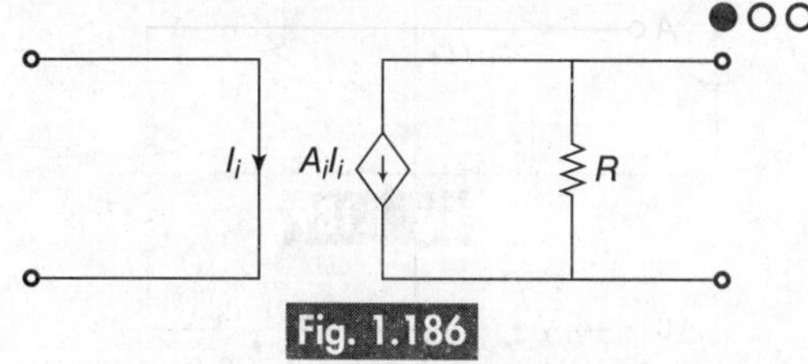


Fig. 1.186

(a) voltage-controlled voltage source
(b) voltage-controlled current source
(c) current-controlled current source
(d) current-controlled voltage source

**1.17** In the circuit shown in Fig. 1.187, each resistor has a value equal to 1 Ω. The equivalent resistance across the terminals $a$ and $b$ is ●○○

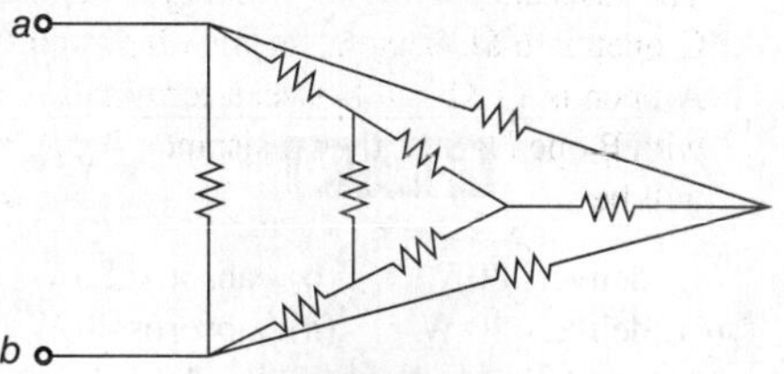


Fig. 1.187

(a) $\frac{1}{6}$ Ω (b) $\frac{1}{3}$ Ω

(c) $\frac{9}{20}$ Ω (d) $\frac{8}{15}$ Ω

**1.18** The voltage across terminals $a$ and $b$ in Fig. 1.188 is ●○○

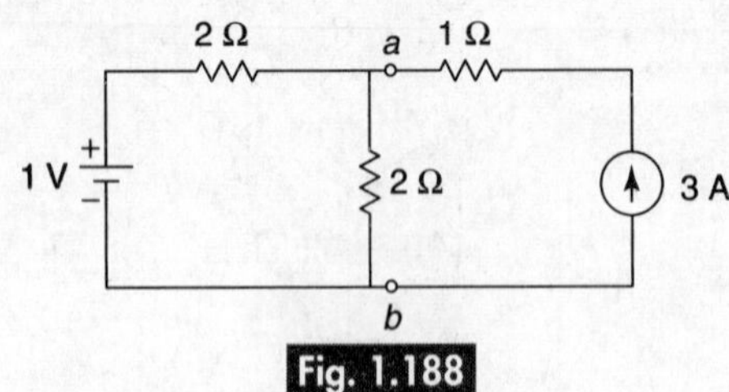

Fig. 1.188

(a) 0.5 V (b) 3 V
(c) 3.5 V (d) 4 V

**1.19** The voltage $V_0$ in Fig. 1.189 is ●○○

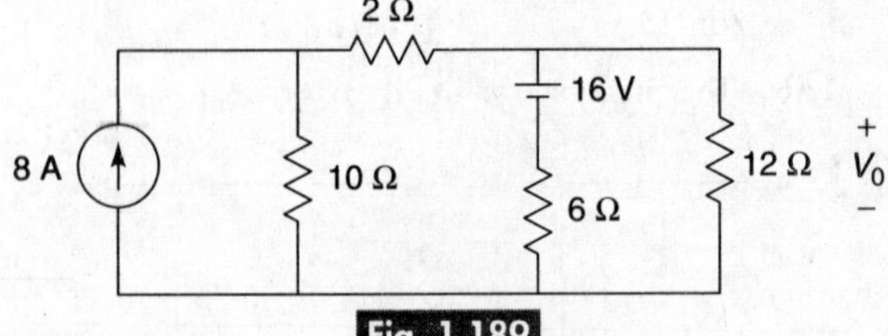

Fig. 1.189

(a) 48 V (b) 24 V
(c) 36 V (d) 28 V

**1.20** The dependent current source shown in Fig. 1.190. ○●○

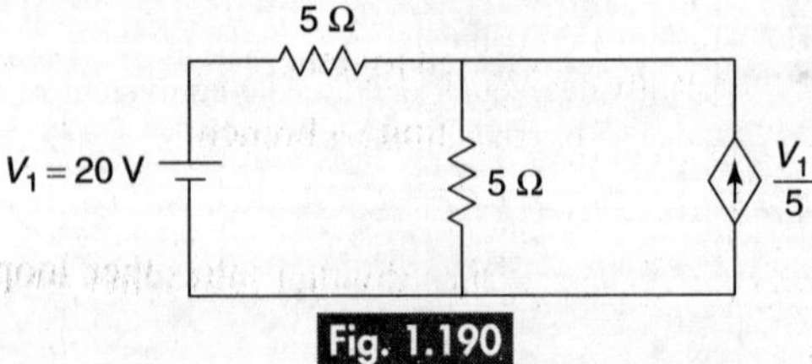

Fig. 1.190

(a) delivers 80 W (b) absorbs 80 W
(c) delivers 40 W (d) absorbs 40 W

**1.21** If $V = 4$ V in Fig. 1.191, the value of $I_s$ is given by ○●○

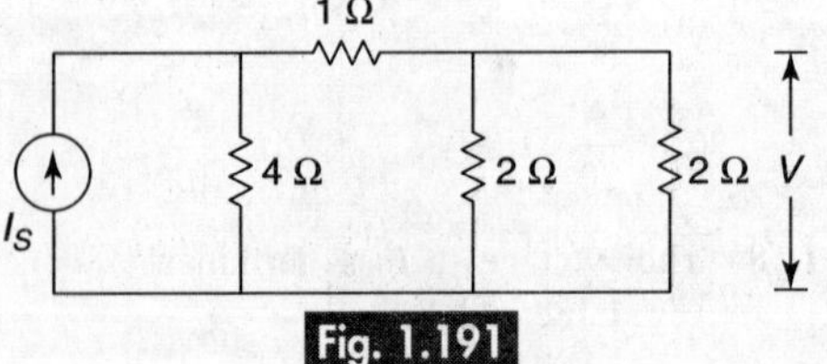

Fig. 1.191

(a) 6 A (b) 2.5 A
(c) 12 A (d) none of these

**1.22** The values of $V_x$, $V_y$ and $V_z$ in Fig. 1.192 shown are ●○○

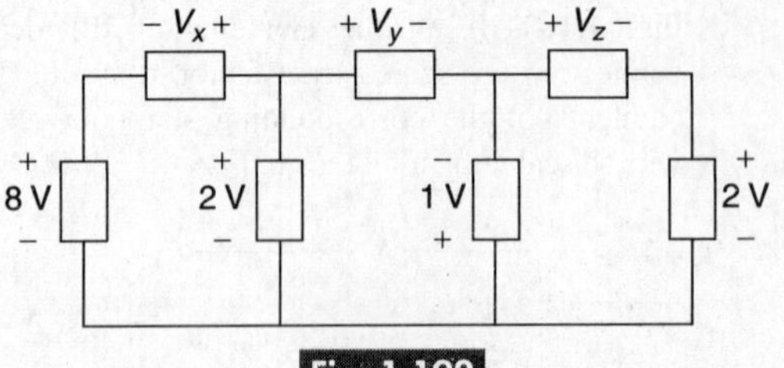

Fig. 1.192

(a) −6, 3, −3 (b) −6, −3, 1
(c) 6, 3, 3 (d) 6, 1, 3

**1.23** In the interconnection of ideal sources shown in Fig. 1.193, it is known that the 60 V source is absorbing power. Which of the following can be value of the current source $I$? ○●○

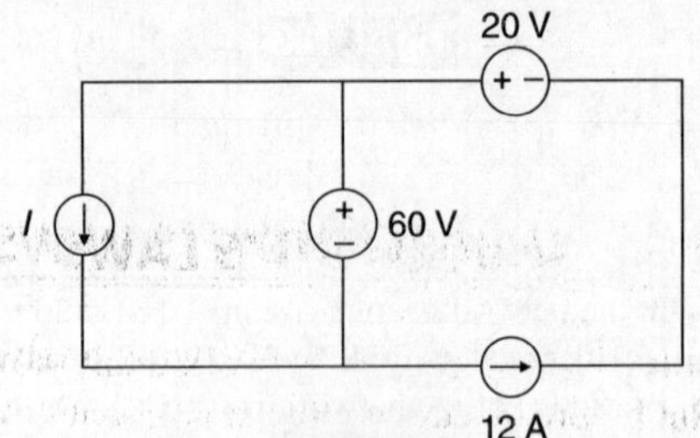

Fig. 1.193

(a) 10 A (b) 13 A
(c) 15 A (d) 18 A

**1.24** The voltage $e_0$ in the Fig. 1.194 is ●○○

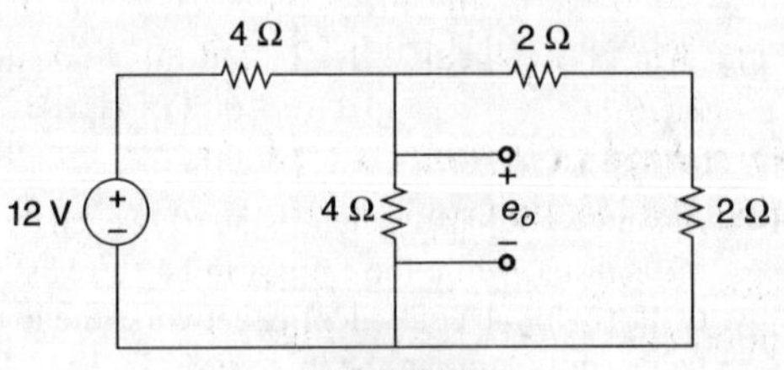

Fig. 1.194

(a) 2 V (b) $\frac{4}{3}$ V
(c) 4 V (d) 8 V

**1.25** In the circuit of Fig. 1.195, the value of the voltage source $E$ is ○●○

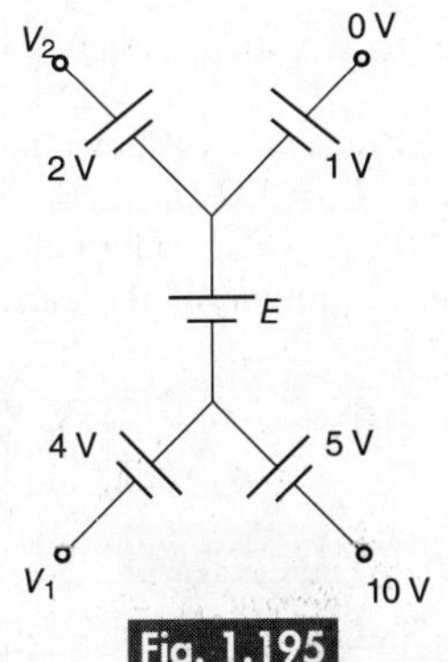


Fig. 1.195

(a) –16 V (b) 4 V
(c) –6 V (d) 16 V

**1.26** The current $i_4$ in the circuit of the Fig. 1.196 is equal to ●○○

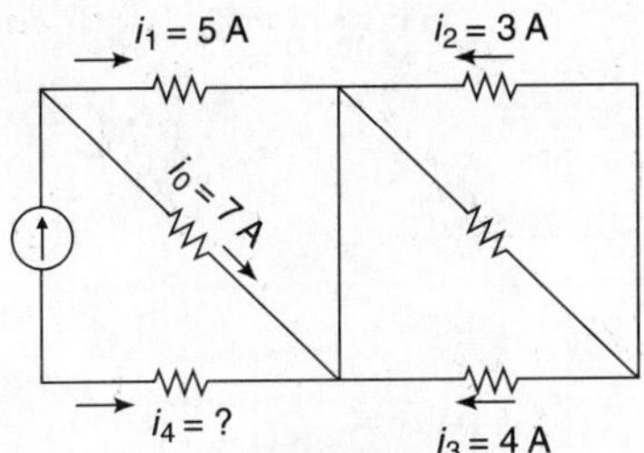


Fig. 1.196

(a) 12 A (b) –12 A
(c) 4 A (d) none of these

**1.27** The voltage $V$ in the Fig. 1.197 is equal to ●○○

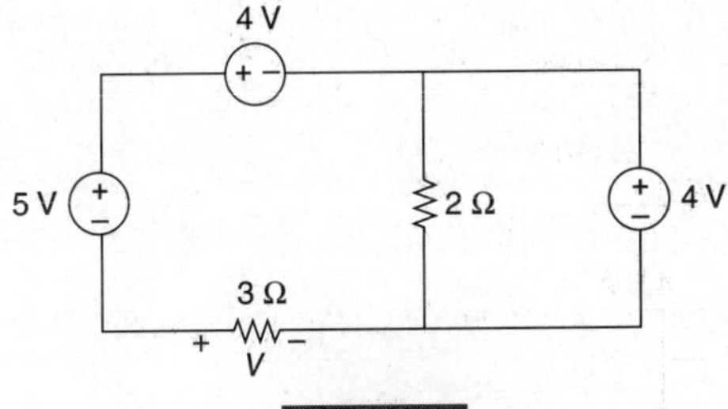


Fig. 1.197

(a) 3 V (b) –3 V
(c) 5 V (d) none of these

**1.28** The voltage $V$ in the Fig. 1.198 is always equal to ●○○

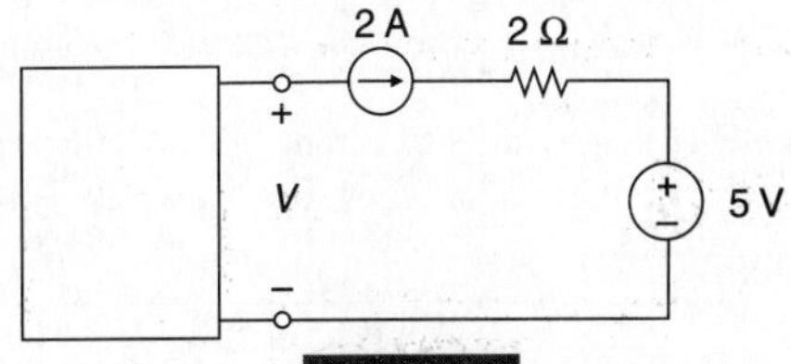


Fig. 1.198

(a) 9 V (b) 5 V
(c) 1 V (d) none of these

**1.29** The voltage $V$ in the Fig. 1.199 is ●○○

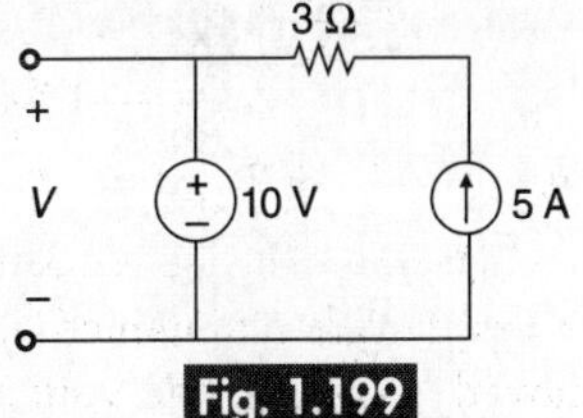


Fig. 1.199

(a) 10 V (b) 15 V
(c) 5 V (d) none of these

**1.30** For the circuit shown in Fig. 1.200, $i_6$ is equal to ●○○

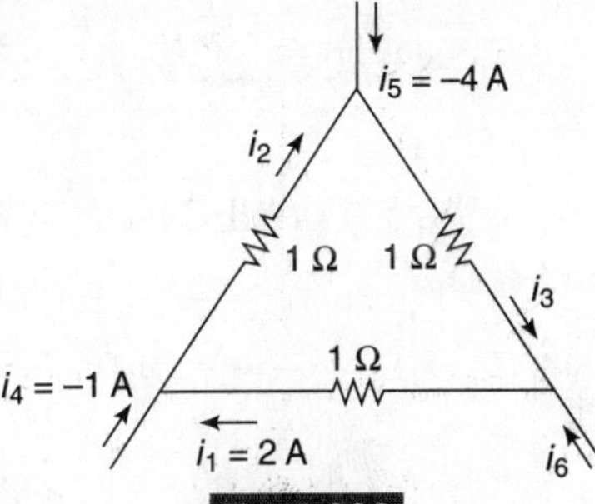


Fig. 1.200

(a) 5 A (b) –5A
(c) 3 A (d) 1 A

**1.31** In the Fig. 1.201, the value of the current $I$ (in amperes) is ●○○

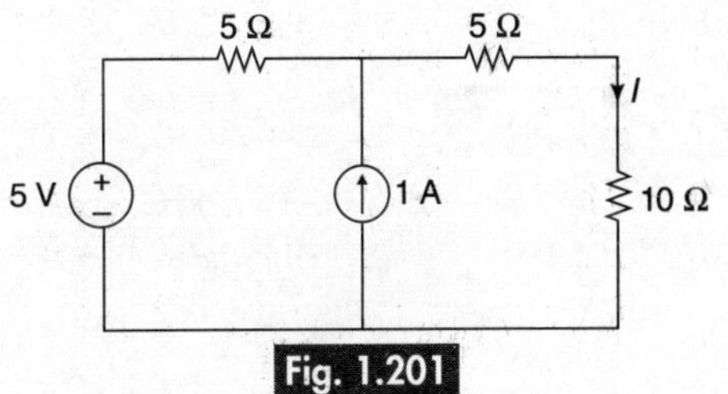


Fig. 1.201

(a) 0.5 (b) 0.8
(c) 1 (d) 0.2

**1.32** The magnitude of current (in mA) through the resistor $R_2$ in the Fig. 1.202 shown is ●○○

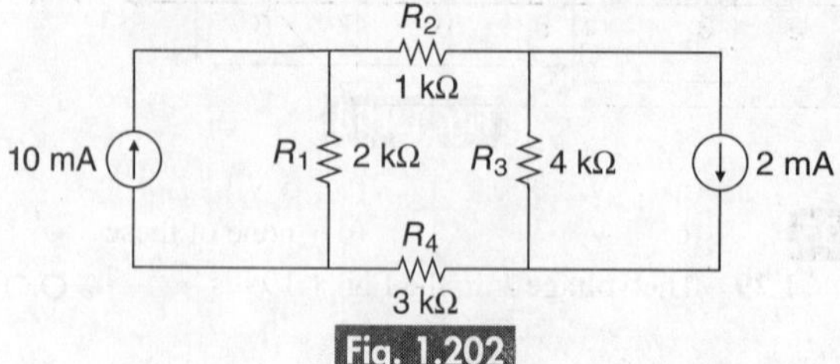


Fig. 1.202

(a) 2.8 (b) 3
(c) 4 (d) 5

**1.33** In the circuit shown in Fig. 1.203, the magnitude of the current (in amperes) through $R_2$ is ●○○

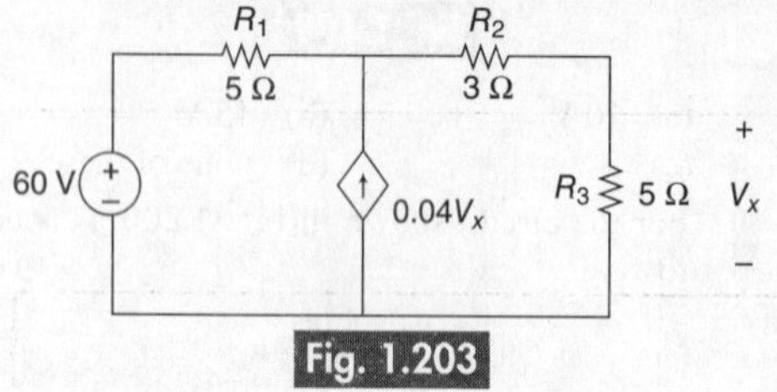


Fig. 1.203

(a) 2 (b) 3
(c) 5 (d) 4

**1.34** Consider the network shown in Fig. 1.204 with $R_1 = 1\ \Omega$, $R_2 = 2\ \Omega$ and $R_3 = 3\ \Omega$. The network is connected to a constant voltage source of 11 V. The magnitude of the current (in ampere) through the source is ○●○

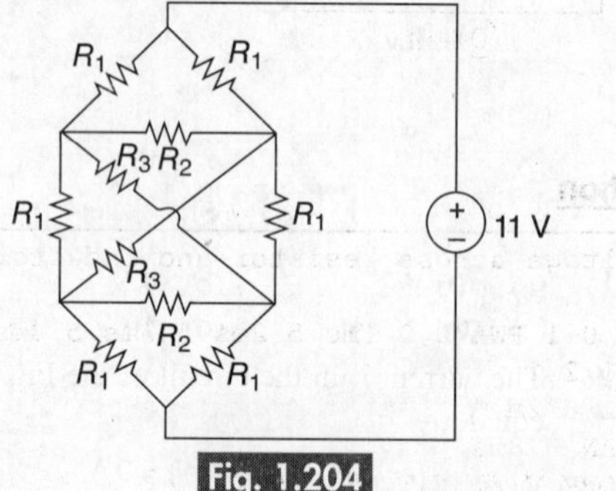


Fig. 1.204

(a) 8 A (b) 10 A
(c) 5 A (d) 11 A

## ANSWERS TO OBJECTIVE-TYPE QUESTIONS

| | | | | | | |
|---|---|---|---|---|---|---|
| **1.1.** (d) | **1.2.** (c) | **1.3.** (d) | **1.4.** (a) | **1.5.** (b) | **1.6.** (b) | **1.7.** (c) |
| **1.8.** (c) | **1.9.** (d) | **1.10.** (d) | **1.11.** (b) | **1.12** (b) | **1.13** (b) | **1.14** (a) |
| **1.15** (b) | **1.16** (c) | **1.17** (d) | **1.18** (c) | **1.19** (d) | **1.20** (a) | **1.21** (d) |
| **1.22** (a) | **1.23** (a) | **1.24** (c) | **1.25** (a) | **1.26** (b) | **1.27** (a) | **1.28** (d) |
| **1.29** (a) | **1.30** (a) | **1.31** (a) | **1.32** (a) | **1.33** (c) | **1.34** (a) | |

# LTspice Section

## EXAMPLE 1.1 ○●○

*The following current waveform i(t) is passed through a series RL circuit with R = 2 Ω and L = 2 mH. Find the voltage across each element and sketch the same.*

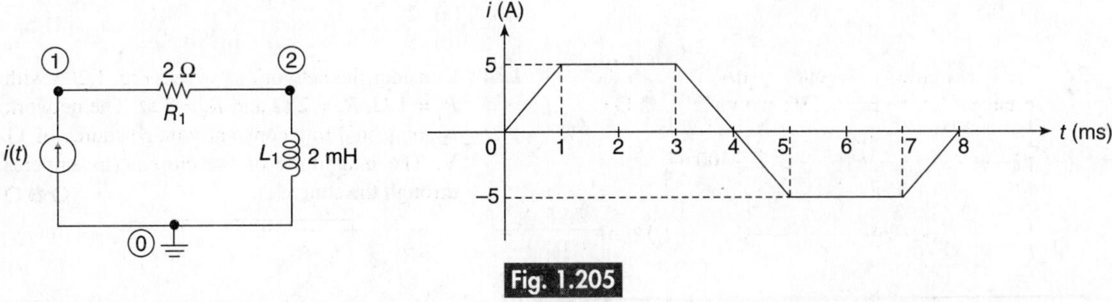


Fig. 1.205

## Solution

```
*Voltage across resistor and inductor

IIN 0 1 PWL(0 0 1ms 5 2ms 5 3ms 5 4ms 0 5ms -5 6ms -5 7ms -5 8ms 0)
R1 1 2 2
L1 2 0 2M
.TRAN 0 8ms
.PROBE V(2) V(1,2)
.END
```

**Voltage across resistor**

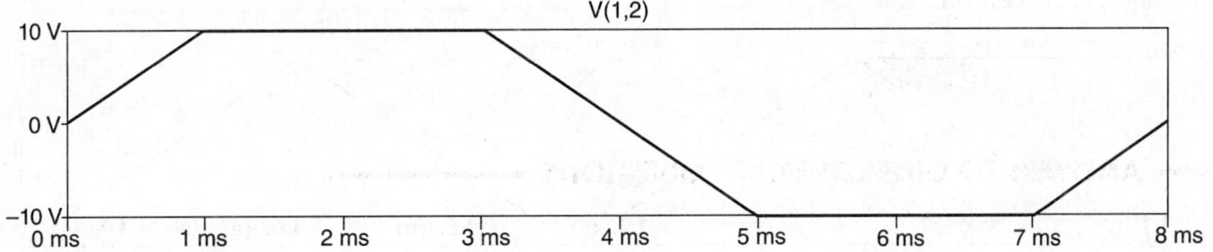


**Voltage across inductor**

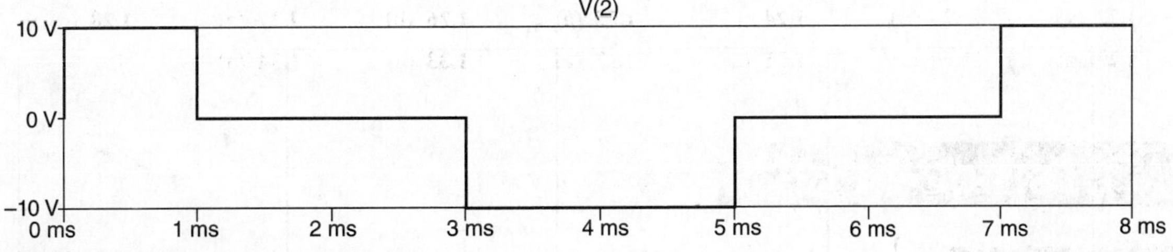


**EXAMPLE 1.2**

*A current with periodic waveform shown in Fig. 1.206 is applied to a series RLC circuit with $R = 1\ \Omega$, $L = 1$ mH and $C = 100\ \mu F$. Sketch the voltage across each element.*

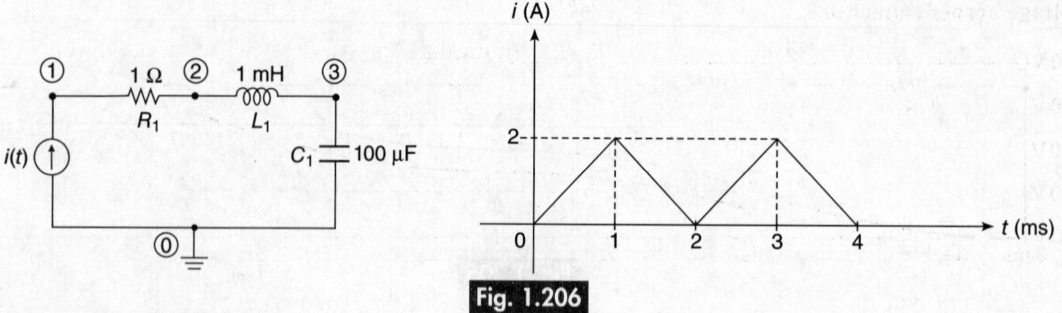


Fig. 1.206

## Solution

```
*Voltage across resistor, inductor and capacitor

IIN 0 1 PWL(0 0 1ms 2 2ms 0 3ms 2 4ms 0)
R1 1 2 1
L1 2 3 1M
C1 3 0 100U
.TRAN 0 4ms
.PROBE V(1,2) V(2,3) V(3)
.END
```

**Voltage across resistor**

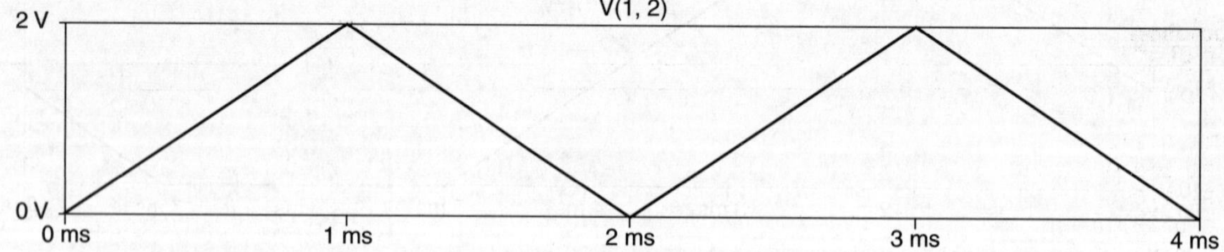


**Voltage across inductor**

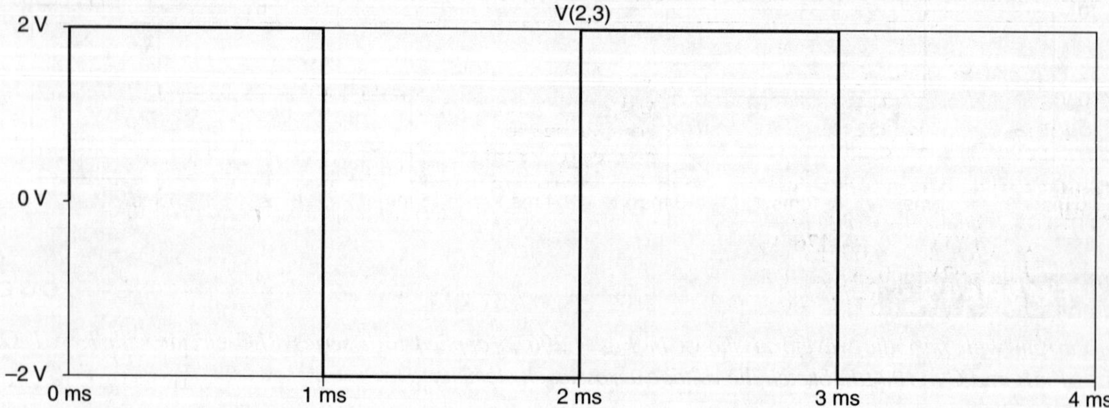

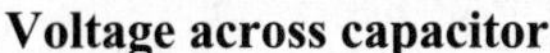

**Voltage across capacitor**

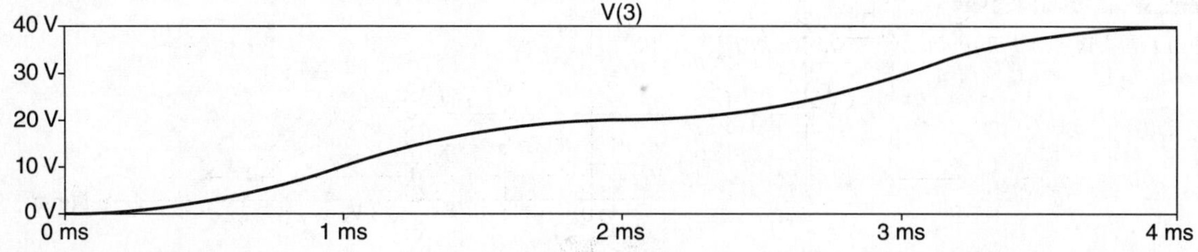


## EXAMPLE 1.3

*In the network of Fig. 1.207, find $I_1$, $I_2$ and V.*

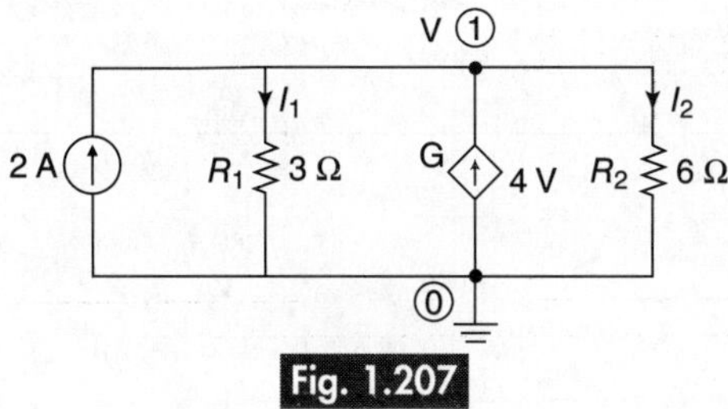


Fig. 1.207

### Solution

```
*Calculation of I1,I2 and V

I1 0 1 2
R1 1 0 3
R2 1 0 6
G 0 1 1 0 4
.PRINT DC I(R1) I(R2) V(1)
.OP
.END
```

```
          Operating Point

V(1):         -0.571429            voltage
I(R2):        -0.0952381           device_current
I(R1):        -0.190476            device_current
```

**Result**

$$I_1 = I(R1) = -0.190476 \text{ A}$$
$$I_2 = I(R2) = -0.0952381 \text{ A}$$
$$V = V(1) = -0.571429 \text{ V}$$

## EXAMPLE 1.4

*Find the current I in the network shown in Fig. 1.208.*

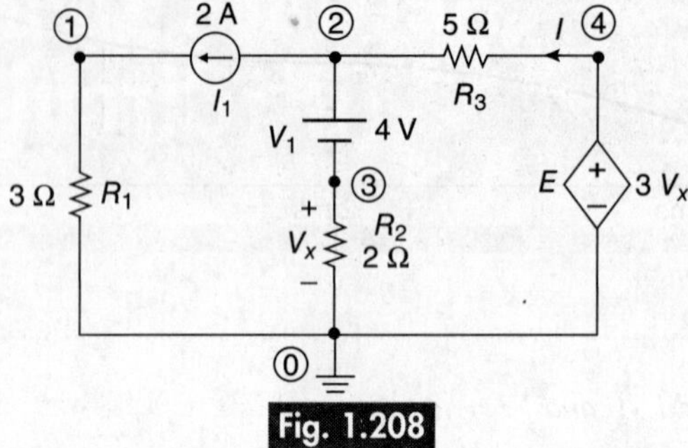


Fig. 1.208

### Solution

```
*Calculation of I

I1 2 1 2
V1 2 3 4
R1 1 0 3
R2 3 0 2
R3 2 4 5
E 4 0 3 0 3
.PRINT DC I(R3)
.OP
.END
```

```
            Operating Point
 I(R3):        12                         device_current
```

**Result**

$$I = -I(R3) = -12 \text{ A}$$

CHAPTER 2

# Network Theorems (dc Circuits)

## LEARNING OBJECTIVES

**After studying this chapter, you should be able to:**

- **LO 2.1** Explain the concepts of mesh and supermesh analysis
- **LO 2.2** Explain the concepts of node and supernode analysis
- **LO 2.3** Analyse the networks using superposition theorem
- **LO 2.4** Analyse the networks using Thevenin's theorem
- **LO 2.5** Analyse the networks using Norton's theorem
- **LO 2.6** Analyse the networks using maximum power transfer theorem
- **LO 2.7** Explain reciprocity theorem
- **LO 2.8** Explain Millman's theorem
- **LO 2.9** Explain Tellegen's theorem
- **LO 2.10** Explain substitution and compensation theorems

## INTRODUCTION

In Chapter 1, we have studied basic circuit concepts. In network analysis, we have to find currents and voltages in various parts of networks. In this chapter, we will study elementary network theorems like mesh analysis and node analysis. These methods are applicable to all types of networks. The first step in analysing networks is to apply Ohm's law and Kirchhoff's laws. The second step is the solving of these equations by mathematical tools. There are some other methods also to analyse circuits. We will also study superposition theorem, Thevenin's theorem, Norton's theorem, maximum power transfer theorem, reciprocity theorem, Millman's theorem, Tellegen's theorem, substitution theorem and compensation theorem. We can find currents and voltages in various parts of the circuits with these methods.

## 2.1 MESH ANALYSIS

LO 2.1

Explain the concepts of mesh and supermesh analysis

A mesh is defined as a loop which does not contain any other loops within it. Mesh analysis is applicable only for planar networks. A network is said to be planar if it can be drawn on a plane surface without crossovers. In this method, the currents in different meshes are assigned continuous paths so that they do not split at a junction into branch currents. If a network has a large number of voltage sources, it is useful to use mesh analysis. Basically, this analysis consists of writing mesh equations by Kirchhoff's voltage law in terms of unknown mesh currents.

### ➤ Steps to be followed in Mesh Analysis

1. Identify the mesh, assign a direction to it and assign an unknown current in each mesh.
2. Assign the polarities for voltage across the branches.
3. Apply KVL around the mesh and use Ohm's law to express the branch voltages in terms of unknown mesh currents and the resistance.
4. Solve the simultaneous equations for unknown mesh currents.

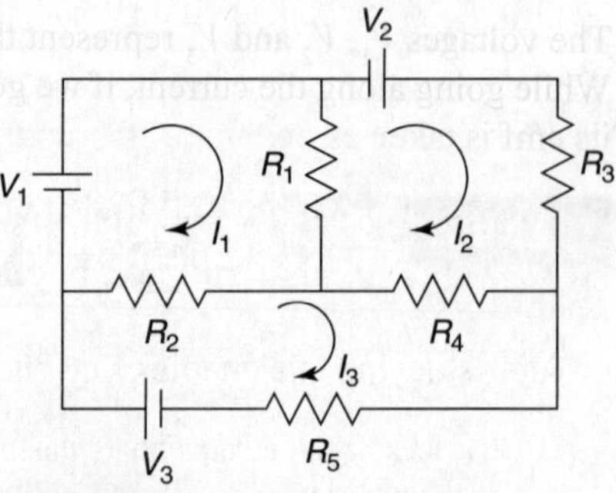


Fig. 2.1 *Circuit for mesh analysis*

Consider the network shown in Fig. 2.1 which has three meshes. Let the mesh currents for the three meshes be $I_1$, $I_2$, and $I_3$ and all the three mesh currents may be assumed to flow in clockwise direction. The choice of direction for any mesh current is arbitrary.

Applying KVL to mesh 1,

$$V_1 - R_1(I_1 - I_2) - R_2(I_1 - I_3) = 0$$

$$(R_1 + R_2)I_1 - R_1 I_2 - R_2 I_3 = V_1 \qquad \dots(2.1)$$

Applying KVL to mesh 2,

$$V_2 - R_3 I_2 - R_4(I_2 - I_3) - R_1(I_2 - I_1) = 0$$

$$-R_1 I_1 + (R_1 + R_3 + R_4) I_2 - R_4 I_3 = V_2 \qquad \dots(2.2)$$

Applying KVL to mesh 3,

$$-R_2(I_3 - I_1) - R_4(I_3 - I_2) - R_5 I_3 + V_3 = 0$$

$$-R_2 I_1 - R_4 I_2 + (R_2 + R_4 + R_5) I_3 = V_3 \qquad \dots(2.3)$$

Writing Eqs (2.1), (2.2), and (2.3) in matrix form,

$$\begin{bmatrix} R_1 + R_2 & -R_1 & -R_2 \\ -R_1 & R_1 + R_3 + R_4 & -R_4 \\ -R_2 & -R_4 & R_2 + R_4 + R_5 \end{bmatrix} \begin{bmatrix} I_1 \\ I_2 \\ I_3 \end{bmatrix} = \begin{bmatrix} V_1 \\ V_2 \\ V_3 \end{bmatrix}$$

In general,

$$\begin{bmatrix} R_{11} & R_{12} & R_{13} \\ R_{21} & R_{22} & R_{23} \\ R_{31} & R_{32} & R_{33} \end{bmatrix} \begin{bmatrix} I_1 \\ I_2 \\ I_3 \end{bmatrix} = \begin{bmatrix} V_1 \\ V_2 \\ V_3 \end{bmatrix}$$

where $R_{11}$ = Self-resistance or sum of all the resistance of mesh 1

$R_{12} = R_{21}$ = Mutual resistance or sum of all the resistances common to meshes 1 and 2

$R_{13} = R_{31}$ = Mutual resistance or sum of all the resistances common to meshes 1 and 3

$R_{22}$ = Self-resistance or sum of all the resistance of mesh 2

$R_{23} = R_{32}$ = Mutual resistance or sum of all the resistances common to meshes 2 and 3

$R_{33}$ = Self-resistance or sum of all the resistance of mesh 3

If the directions of the currents passing through the common resistance are the same, the mutual resistance will have a positive sign, and if the direction of the currents passing through common resistance are opposite then the mutual resistance will have a negative sign. If each mesh current is assumed to flow in the clockwise direction then all self-resistances will always be positive and all mutual resistances will always be negative.

The voltages $V_1$, $V_2$ and $V_3$ represent the algebraic sum of all the voltages in meshes 1, 2 and 3 respectively. While going along the current, if we go from the negative terminal of the battery to the positive terminal then its emf is taken as positive. Otherwise, it is taken as negative.

## EXAMPLE 2.1 ●○○

*Find the current through the 5 Ω resistor shown in Fig. 2.2.*

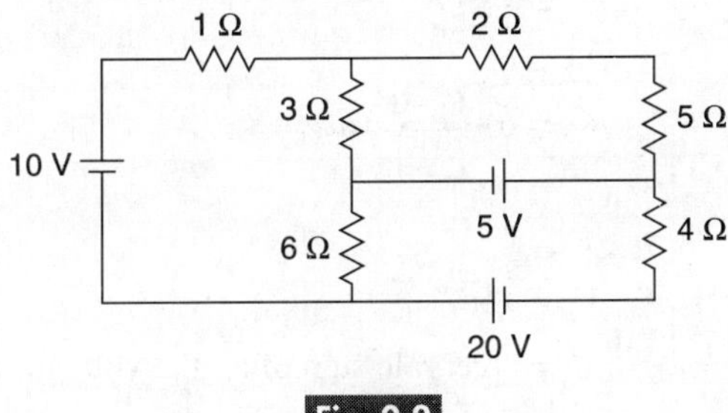


Fig. 2.2

**Solution** Assign clockwise currents in three meshes, as shown in Fig. 2.3.

Applying KVL to mesh 1,

$$10 - 1I_1 - 3(I_1 - I_2) - 6(I_1 - I_3) = 0$$

$$10\,I_1 - 3\,I_2 - 6\,I_3 = 10 \qquad \text{...(i)}$$

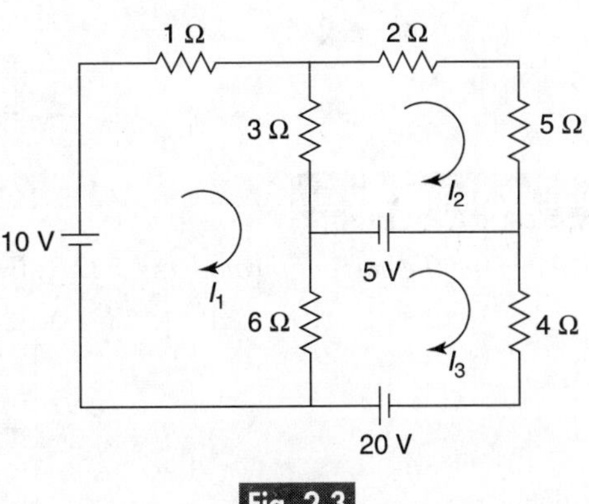


Fig. 2.3

Applying KVL to mesh 2,

$$-3(I_2 - I_1) - 2\,I_2 - 5\,I_2 - 5 = 0$$

$$-3\,I_1 + 10\,I_2 = -5 \qquad \text{...(ii)}$$

Applying KVL to mesh 3,

$$-6(I_3 - I_1) + 5 - 4\,I_3 + 20 = 0$$

$$-6\,I_1 + 10\,I_3 = 25 \qquad \text{...(iii)}$$

**Note** Difficulty Level ●○○— Easy; ○●○— Medium; ○○●— Difficult

Writing Eqs (i), (ii) and (iii) in matrix form,

$$\begin{bmatrix} 10 & -3 & -6 \\ -3 & 10 & 0 \\ -6 & 0 & 10 \end{bmatrix}\begin{bmatrix} I_1 \\ I_2 \\ I_3 \end{bmatrix} = \begin{bmatrix} 10 \\ -5 \\ 25 \end{bmatrix}$$

We can write matrix equation directly from Fig. 2.3,

$$\begin{bmatrix} R_{11} & R_{12} & R_{13} \\ R_{21} & R_{22} & R_{23} \\ R_{31} & R_{32} & R_{33} \end{bmatrix}\begin{bmatrix} I_1 \\ I_2 \\ I_3 \end{bmatrix} = \begin{bmatrix} V_1 \\ V_2 \\ V_3 \end{bmatrix}$$

where $R_{11}$ = Self-resistance of mesh 1 = 1 + 3 + 6 = 10 Ω

$R_{12}$ = Mutual resistance common to meshes 1 and 2 = –3 Ω

Here, negative sign indicates that the currents through common resistance are in opposite direction.

$R_{13}$ = Mutual resistance common to meshes 1 and 3 = –6 Ω

Similarly,

$$R_{21} = -3\ \Omega$$
$$R_{22} = 3+2+5 = 10\ \Omega$$
$$R_{23} = 0$$
$$R_{31} = -6\ \Omega$$
$$R_{32} = 0$$
$$R_{33} = 6+4 = 10\ \Omega$$

For voltage matrix,

$$V_1 = 10\ \text{V}$$
$$V_2 = -5\ \text{V}$$

$V_3$ = algebraic sum of all the voltages in mesh 3 = 5 + 20 = 25 V

Solving Eqs (i), (ii) and (iii),

$$I_1 = 4.27\ \text{A}$$
$$I_2 = 0.78\ \text{A}$$
$$I_3 = 5.06\ \text{A}$$
$$I_{5\Omega} = I_2 = 0.78\ \text{A}$$

**EXAMPLE 2.2**

*Determine the current through the 5 Ω resistor of the network shown in Fig. 2.4.*

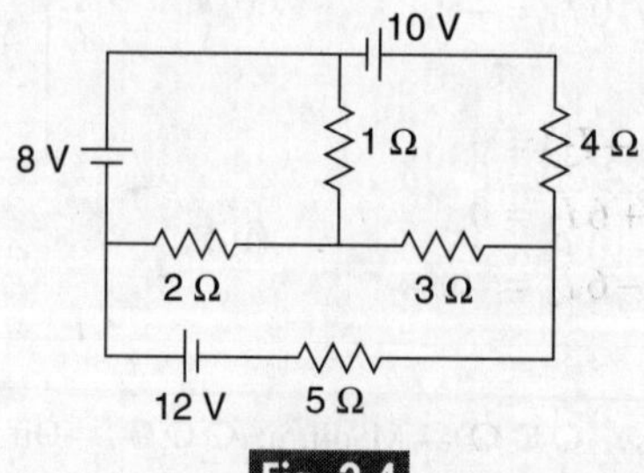


Fig. 2.4

**Solution** Assign clockwise currents in three meshes, as shown in Fig. 2.5.

Applying KVL to mesh 1,

$$8-1(I_1-I_2)-2(I_1-I_3)=0$$

$$3I_1-I_2-2I_3=8 \quad \ldots\text{(i)}$$

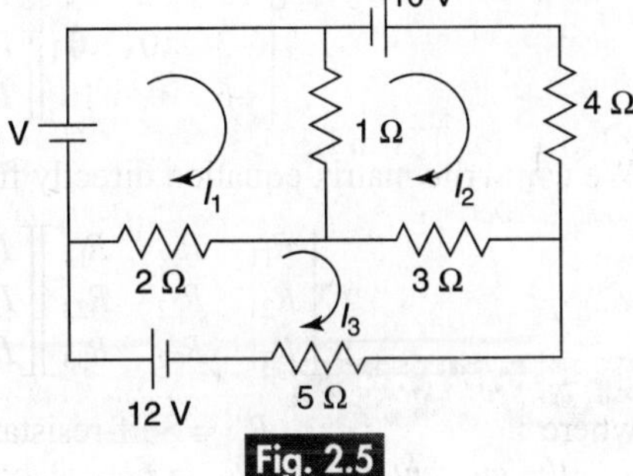

Fig. 2.5

Applying KVL to mesh 2,

$$10-4I_2-3(I_2-I_3)-1(I_2-I_1)=0$$

$$-I_1+8I_2-3I_3=10 \quad \ldots\text{(ii)}$$

Applying KVL to mesh 3,

$$-2(I_3-I_1)-3(I_3-I_2)-5I_3+12=0$$

$$-2I_1-3I_2+10I_3=12 \quad \ldots\text{(iii)}$$

Solving Eqs (i), (ii), and (iii),

$$I_1=6.01\text{ A}$$

$$I_2=3.27\text{ A}$$

$$I_3=3.38\text{ A}$$

$$I_{5\Omega}=I_3=3.38\text{ A}$$

## EXAMPLE 2.3

*Find the current through the 2 Ω resistor in the network of Fig. 2.6.*

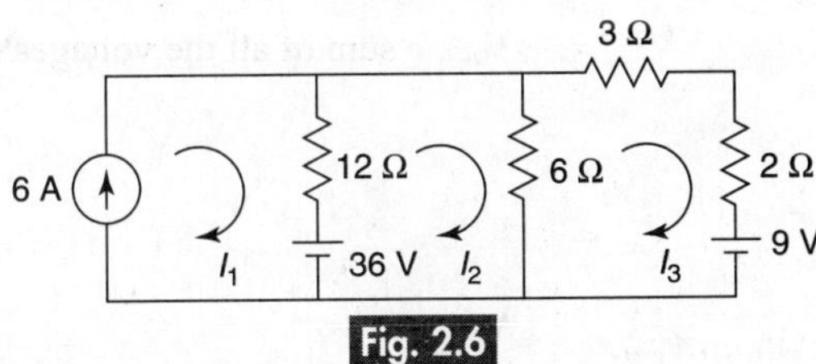

Fig. 2.6

**Solution** Mesh 1 contains a current source of 6 A. Hence, we can write current equation for mesh 1. Since direction of current source and mesh current $I_1$ are same,

$$I_1=6 \quad \ldots\text{(i)}$$

Applying KVL to mesh 2,

$$36-12(I_2-I_1)-6(I_2-I_3)=0$$

$$36-12(I_2-6)-6I_2+6I_3=0$$

$$18I_2-6I_3=108 \quad \ldots\text{(ii)}$$

Applying KVL to mesh 3,

$$-6(I_3 - I_2) - 3I_3 - 2I_3 - 9 = 0$$

$$6I_2 - 11I_3 = 9 \quad \text{...(iii)}$$

Solving Eqs (ii) and (iii),

$$I_3 = 3\text{ A}$$

$$I_{2\Omega} = I_3 = 3\text{ A}$$

**EXAMPLE 2.4**

*Find the current through the 5 Ω resistor in the network of Fig. 2.7.*

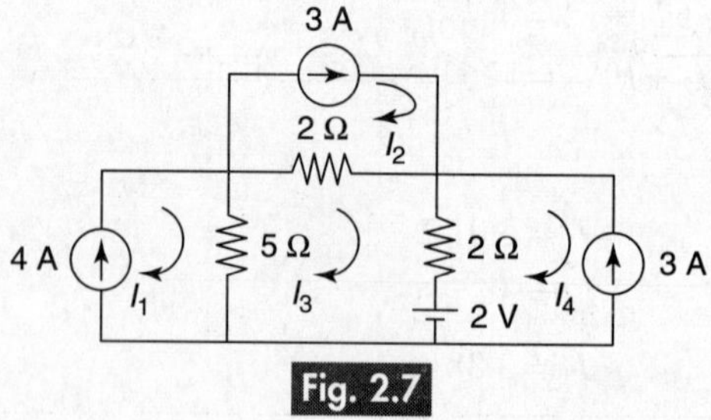


Fig. 2.7

**Solution** Writing current equations for meshes 1, 2 and 4,

$$I_1 = 4 \quad \text{...(i)}$$

$$I_2 = 3 \quad \text{...(ii)}$$

$$I_4 = -3 \quad \text{...(iii)}$$

Applying KVL to mesh 3,

$$-5(I_3 - I_1) - 2(I_3 - I_2) - 2(I_3 - I_4) - 2 = 0 \quad \text{...(iv)}$$

Substituting Eqs (i), (ii) and (iii) in Eq. (iv),

$$-5(I_3 - 4) - 2(I_3 - 3) - 2(I_3 + 3) - 2 = 0$$

$$I_3 = 2\text{ A}$$

$$I_{5\Omega} = I_1 - I_3 = 4 - 2 = 2\text{ A}$$

## Examples with Dependent Sources

**EXAMPLE 2.5**

*Obtain the branch currents in the network shown in Fig. 2.8.*

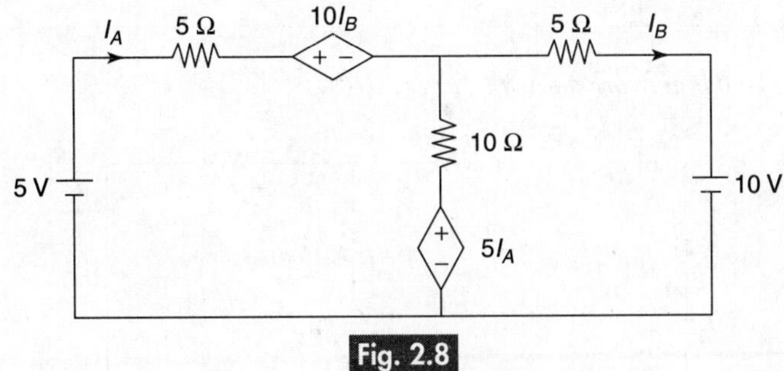


Fig. 2.8

**Solution** Assign clockwise currents in two meshes, as shown in Fig. 2.9.

From Fig. 2.9,

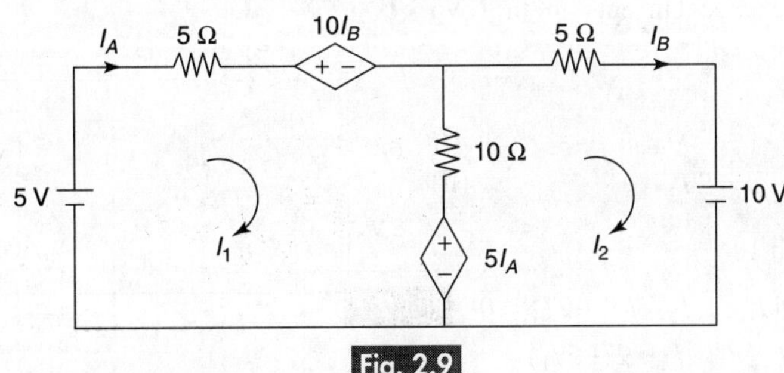


Fig. 2.9

$$I_A = I_1 \quad \text{...(i)}$$

$$I_B = I_2 \quad \text{...(ii)}$$

Applying KVL to mesh 1,

$$5 - 5I_1 - 10I_B - 10(I_1 - I_2) - 5I_A = 0$$

$$5 - 5I_1 - 10I_2 - 10I_1 + 10I_2 - 5I_1 = 0$$

$$-20I_1 = -5$$

$$I_1 = \frac{1}{4} = 0.25\text{ A} \quad \text{...(iii)}$$

Applying KVL to mesh 2,

$$5I_A - 10(I_2 - I_1) - 5I_2 - 10 = 0$$

$$5I_1 - 10I_2 + 10I_1 - 5I_2 = 10$$

$$15I_1 - 15I_2 = 10 \quad \text{...(iv)}$$

Putting $I_1 = 0.25$ A in Eq. (iv),

$$15(0.25) - 15I_2 = 10$$

$$I_2 = -0.416\text{ A}$$

## EXAMPLE 2.6

*Find the mesh currents in the network shown in Fig. 2.10.*

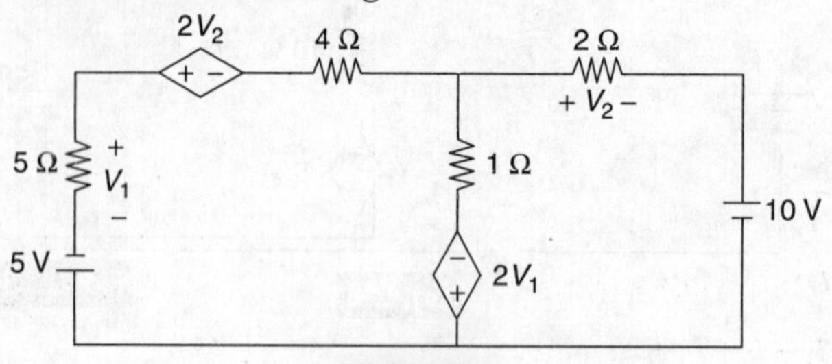


Fig. 2.10

**Solution** Assign clockwise currents in the two meshes, as shown in Fig. 2.11.

Fig. 2.11

From Fig. 2.11,

$$V_1 = -5I_1 \qquad \text{...(i)}$$

$$V_2 = 2I_2 \qquad \text{...(ii)}$$

Applying KVL to mesh 1,

$$-5 - 5I_1 - 2V_2 - 4I_1 - 1(I_1 - I_2) + 2V_1 = 0$$

$$-5 - 5I_1 - 2(2I_2) - 4I_1 - I_1 + I_2 + 2(-5I_1) = 0$$

$$20I_1 + 3I_2 = -5 \qquad \text{...(iii)}$$

Applying KVL to mesh 2,

$$-2V_1 - 1(I_2 - I_1) - 2I_2 - 10 = 0$$

$$-2(-5I_1) - I_2 + I_1 - 2I_2 = 10$$

$$11I_1 - 3I_2 = 10 \qquad \text{...(iv)}$$

Solving Eqs (iii) and (iv),

$$I_1 = 0.161 \text{ A}$$

$$I_2 = -2.742 \text{ A}$$

## EXAMPLE 2.7

*Find currents $I_x$ and $I_y$ of the network shown in Fig. 2.12.*

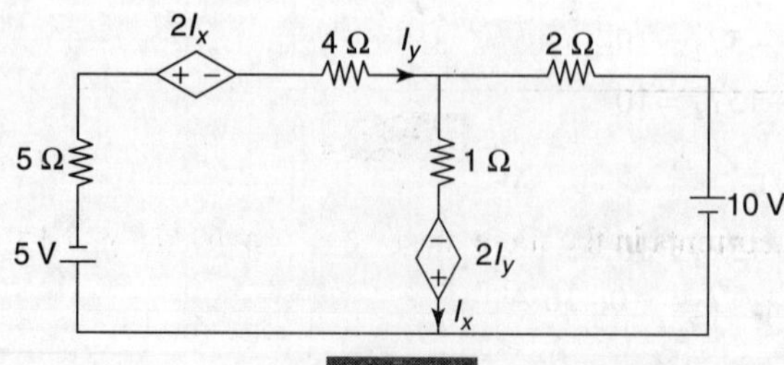


Fig. 2.12

**Solution** Assign clockwise currents in the two meshes, as shown in Fig. 2.13.

From Fig. 2.13,

$$I_y = I_1 \quad \text{...(i)}$$

$$I_x = I_1 - I_2 \quad \text{...(ii)}$$

Fig. 2.13

Applying KVL to mesh 1,

$$-5 - 5I_1 - 2I_x - 4I_1 - 1(I_1 - I_2) + 2I_y = 0$$

$$-5 - 5I_1 - 2(I_1 - I_2) - 4I_1 - I_1 + I_2 + 2I_1 = 0$$

$$-5 - 5I_1 - 2I_1 + 2I_2 - 4I_1 - I_1 + I_2 + 2I_1 = 0$$

$$-10I_1 + 3I_2 = 5 \quad \text{...(iii)}$$

Applying KVL to mesh 2,

$$-2I_y - 1(I_2 - I_1) - 2I_2 - 10 = 0$$

$$-2I_1 - I_2 + I_1 - 2I_2 = 10$$

$$-I_1 - 3I_2 = 10 \quad \text{...(iv)}$$

Solving Eqs (iii) and (iv),

$$I_1 = -\frac{15}{11} = -1.364 \text{ A}$$

$$I_2 = -2.878 \text{ A}$$

$$I_y = -1.364 \text{ A}$$

$$I_x = I_1 - I_2 = -1.364 + 2.878 = 1.514 \text{ A}$$

## EXAMPLE 2.8

*Find the currents in the three meshes of the network shown in Fig. 2.14.*

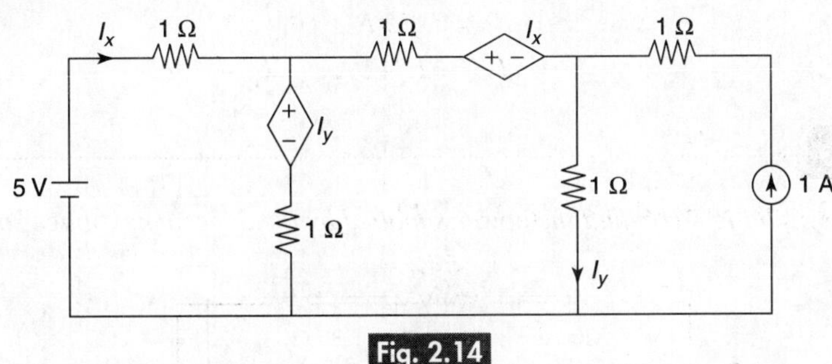


Fig. 2.14

**Solution** Assign clockwise currents in the three meshes, as shown in Fig. 2.15.

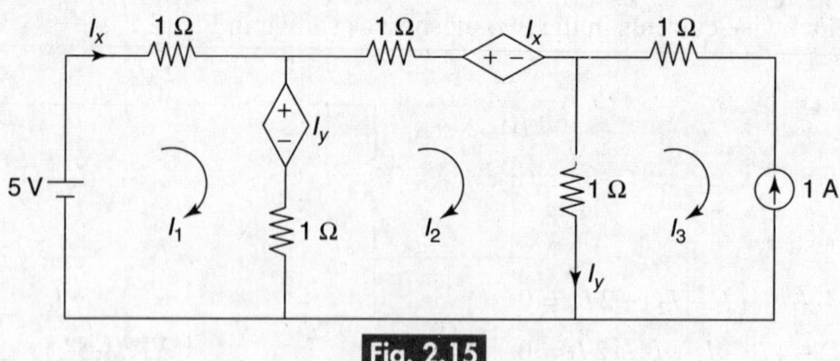

Fig. 2.15

From Fig. 2.15,

$$I_x = I_1 \quad \text{...(i)}$$

$$I_y = I_2 - I_3 \quad \text{...(ii)}$$

Applying KVL to mesh 1,

$$5 - 1I_1 - I_y - 1(I_1 - I_2) = 0$$

$$5 - I_1 - (I_2 - I_3) - (I_1 - I_2) = 0$$

$$-2I_1 + I_3 = -5 \quad \text{...(iii)}$$

Applying KVL to mesh 2,

$$-1(I_2 - I_1) + I_y - 1I_2 - I_x - 1(I_2 - I_3) = 0$$

$$-(I_2 - I_1) + (I_2 - I_3) - I_2 - I_1 - (I_2 - I_3) = 0$$

$$-2I_2 = 0 \quad \text{...(iv)}$$

For mesh 3,

$$I_3 = -1 \quad \text{...(v)}$$

Solving Eqs (iii), (iv) and (v),

$$I_1 = 2\text{ A}$$

$$I_2 = 0$$

$$I_3 = -1\text{ A}$$

## EXAMPLE 2.9

*For the network shown in Fig. 2.16, find the power supplied by the dependent voltage source.*

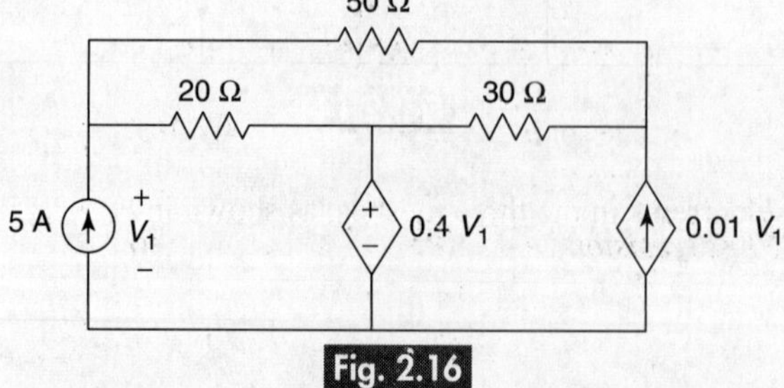

Fig. 2.16

**Solution** Assign clockwise currents in three meshes, as shown in Fig. 2.17.

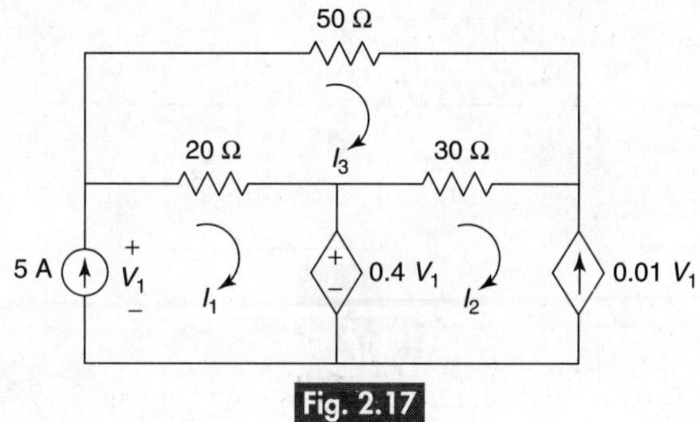


Fig. 2.17

From Fig. 2.17,

$$V_1 - 20(I_1 - I_3) - 0.4\,V_1 = 0$$

$$0.6\,V_1 = 20\,I_1 - 20\,I_3$$

$$V_1 = 33.33\,I_1 - 33.33\,I_3 \qquad \text{...(i)}$$

For mesh 1,

$$I_1 = 5 \qquad \text{...(ii)}$$

For mesh 2,

$$I_2 = -0.01\,V_1 = -0.01(33.33\,I_1 - 33.33\,I_3)$$

$$0.33\,I_1 + I_2 - 0.33\,I_3 = 0 \qquad \text{...(iii)}$$

Applying KVL to mesh 3,

$$-50\,I_3 - 30(I_3 - I_2) - 20(I_3 - I_1) = 0$$

$$-20\,I_1 - 30\,I_2 + 100\,I_3 = 0 \qquad \text{...(iv)}$$

Solving Eqs (ii), (iii) and (iv),

$$I_1 = 5 \text{ A}$$

$$I_2 = -1.47 \text{ A}$$

$$I_3 = 0.56 \text{ A}$$

$$V_1 = 33.33\,I_1 - 33.33\,I_3 = 33.33(5) - 33.33(0.56) = 148 \text{ V}$$

Power supplied by the dependent voltage source = $0.4\;V_1(I_1 - I_2) = 0.4\,(148)(5 + 1.47) = 383.02$ W

## EXAMPLE 2.10

*Find the voltage $V_x$ in the network shown in Fig. 2.18.*

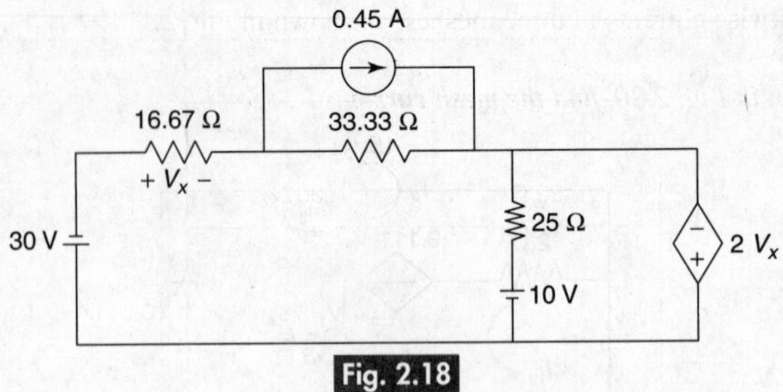


Fig. 2.18

**Solution** Assign clockwise currents in the three meshes, as shown in Fig. 2.19.

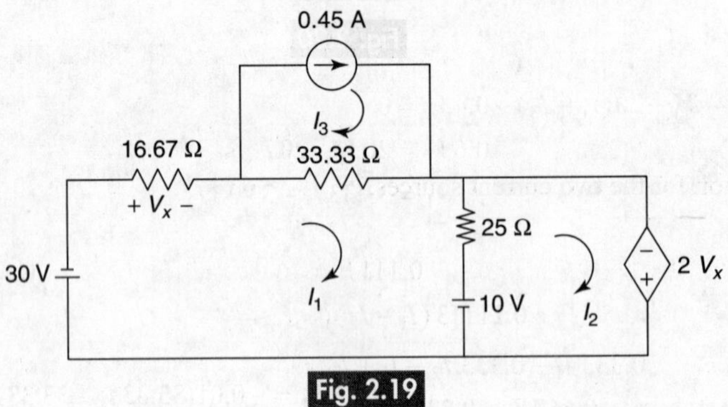


Fig. 2.19

From Fig. 2.19,

$$V_x = 16.67\, I_1 \quad \text{...(i)}$$

Applying KVL to mesh 1,

$$-30 - 16.67\, I_1 - 33.33(I_1 - I_3) - 25(I_1 - I_2) - 10 = 0$$

$$-30 - 16.67\, I_1 - 33.33\, I_1 + 33.33\, I_3 - 25\, I_1 + 25\, I_2 - 10 = 0$$

$$-75\, I_1 + 25\, I_2 + 33.33\, I_3 = 40 \quad \text{...(ii)}$$

Applying KVL to mesh 2,

$$10 - 25(I_2 - I_1) + 2\, V_x = 0$$

$$10 - 25(I_2 - I_1) + 2(16.67\, I_1) = 0$$

$$10 - 25\, I_2 + 25\, I_1 + 33.34\, I_1 = 0$$

$$58.34\, I_1 - 25\, I_2 = -10 \quad \text{...(iii)}$$

For mesh 3,

$$I_3 = 0.45 \quad \text{...(iv)}$$

Solving Eqs (ii), (iii) and (iv),

$$I_1 = -0.9 \text{ A}$$

$$I_2 = -1.7 \text{ A}$$

$$I_3 = 0.45 \text{ A}$$

$$V_x = 16.67\, I_1 = 16.67\,(-0.9) = -15 \text{ V} \quad \text{...(v)}$$

## EXAMPLE 2.11

*For the network shown in Fig. 2.20, find the mesh currents $I_1$, $I_2$ and $I_3$.*

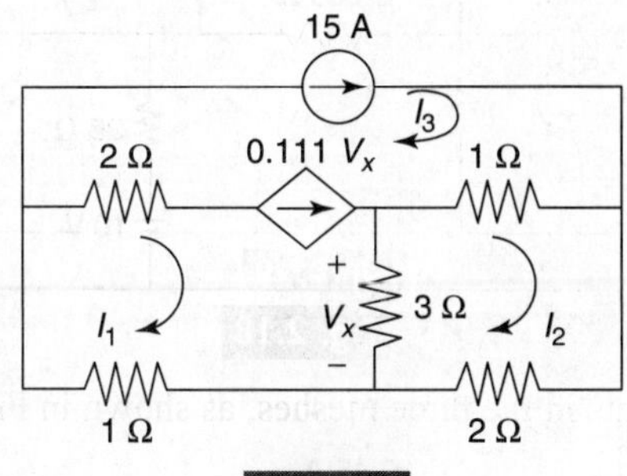


Fig. 2.20

**Solution** From Fig. 2.20,

$$V_x = 3(I_1 - I_2) \quad \text{...(i)}$$

Writing current equation for the two current sources,

$$I_3 = 15 \quad \text{...(ii)}$$

and

$$0.111\,V_x = I_1 - I_3$$

$$0.111\,[3\,(I_1 - I_2)] = I_1 - I_3$$

$$0.333\,I_1 - 0.333\,I_2 - I_1 + I_3 = 0$$

$$-0.667\,I_1 - 0.333\,I_2 + I_3 = 0 \quad \text{...(iii)}$$

Applying KVL to mesh 2,

$$-3\,(I_2 - I_1) - 1(I_2 - I_3) - 2\,I_2 = 0$$

$$-3\,I_1 + 6\,I_2 - I_3 = 0 \quad \text{...(iv)}$$

Solving Eqs (ii), (iii) and (iv),

$$I_1 = 17\text{ A}$$

$$I_2 = 11\text{ A}$$

$$I_3 = 15\text{ A}$$

## EXAMPLE 2.12

*For the network shown in Fig. 2.21, find the magnitude of $V_0$ and the current supplied by it, given that power loss in $R_L = 2\ \Omega$ resistor is 18 W.*

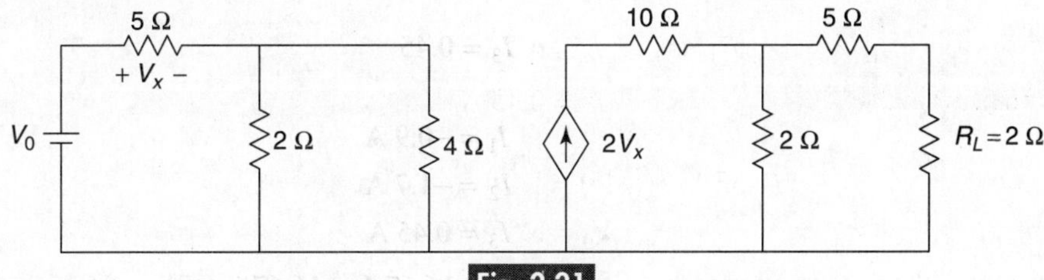


Fig. 2.21

**Solution** Assign clockwise currents in meshes, as shown in Fig. 2.22.

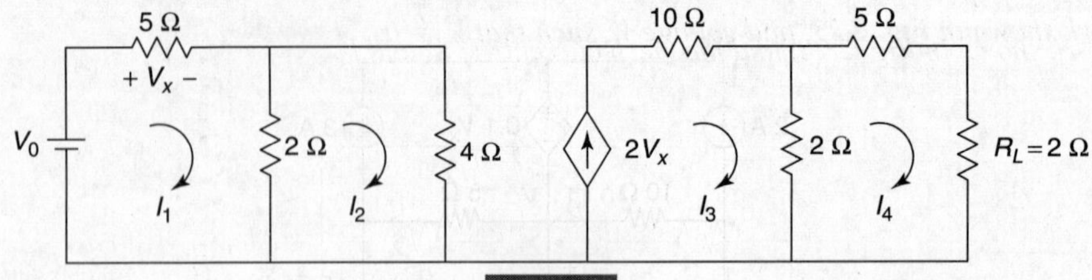


Fig. 2.22

From Fig. 2.22,

$$V_x = 5I_1 \quad \text{...(i)}$$

Also,

$$I_4^2 R_L = 18$$
$$I_4^2(2) = 18$$
$$I_4 = 3 \text{ A} \quad \text{...(ii)}$$

Applying KVL to mesh 1,

$$V_0 - 5I_1 - 2(I_1 - I_2) = 0$$
$$7I_1 - 2I_2 = V_0 \quad \text{...(iii)}$$

Applying KVL to mesh 2,

$$-2(I_2 - I_1) - 4I_2 = 0$$
$$-2I_1 + 6I_2 = 0 \quad \text{...(iv)}$$

For mesh 3,

$$I_3 = 2V_x = 2(5I_1) = 10I_1$$
$$10I_1 - I_3 = 0 \quad \text{...(v)}$$

Applying KVL to mesh 4,

$$-2(I_4 - I_3) - 5I_4 - 2I_4 = 0$$
$$-2I_3 + 9I_4 = 0$$
$$-2I_3 + 9(3) = 0$$
$$I_3 = 13.5 \text{ A}$$

From Eq. (v),

$$I_1 = \frac{I_3}{10} = \frac{13.5}{10} = 1.35 \text{ A}$$

From Eq. (iv),

$$-2(1.35) + 6I_2 = 0$$
$$I_2 = 0.45 \text{ A}$$

From Eq. (iii),

$$7(1.35) - 2(0.45) = V_0$$
$$V_0 = 8.55 \text{ V}$$

Current supplied by voltage source $V_0 = I_1 = 1.35$ A

## EXAMPLE 2.13

*In the network shown in Fig. 2.23, find voltage $V_2$ such that $V_x = 0$.*

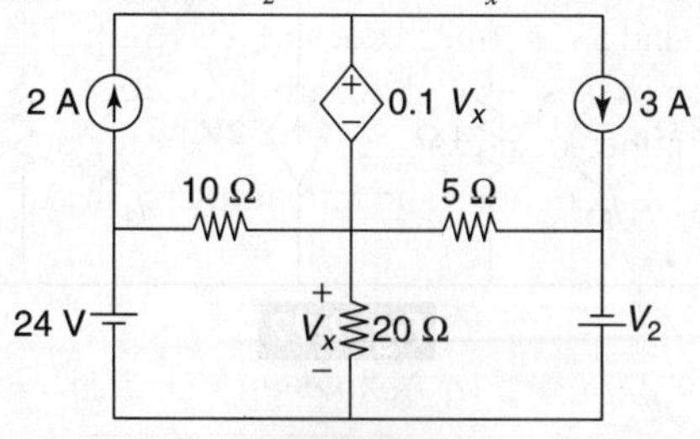


Fig. 2.23

**Solution** Assign clockwise currents in four meshes, as shown in Fig. 2.24.

Fig. 2.24

From Fig. 2.24,

$$V_x = 20\,(I_3 - I_4) \qquad \ldots\text{(i)}$$

Writing current equations for meshes 1 and 2,

$$I_1 = 2 \qquad \ldots\text{(ii)}$$

$$I_2 = 3 \qquad \ldots\text{(iii)}$$

Applying KVL to mesh 3,

$$24 - 10(I_3 - I_1) - 20(I_3 - I_4) = 0$$

$$24 - 10(I_3 - 2) - 20(I_3 - I_4) = 0$$

$$-30\,I_3 + 20\,I_4 = -44 \qquad \ldots\text{(iv)}$$

Applying KVL to mesh 4,

$$-20(I_4 - I_3) - 5(I_4 - I_2) + V_2 = 0$$

$$-20(I_4 - I_3) - 5(I_4 - 3) + V_2 = 0$$

$$20\,I_3 - 25\,I_4 = -V_2 - 15 \qquad \ldots\text{(v)}$$

But

$$V_x = 0$$

$$20(I_3 - I_4) = 0$$

$$I_3 = I_4$$

From Eq. (iv),

$$-30\,I_3 + 20\,I_3 = -44$$

$$I_3 = 4.4 \text{ A}$$

$$I_4 = 4.4 \text{ A}$$

From Eq. (v),

$$20\,(4.4) - 25\,(4.4) = -V_2 - 15$$

$$V_2 = 7 \text{ V}$$

## 2.2 SUPERMESH ANALYSIS

LO 2.1

Meshes that share a current source with other meshes, none of which contains a current source in the outer loop, form a supermesh. A path around a supermesh doesn't pass through a current source. A path around each mesh contained within a supermesh passes through a current source. The total number of equations required for a supermesh is equal to the number of meshes contained in the supermesh. A supermesh requires one mesh current equation, that is, a KVL equation. The remaining mesh current equations are KCL equations.

**EXAMPLE 2.14**

*Find the current in the 3 Ω resistor of the network shown in Fig. 2.25.*

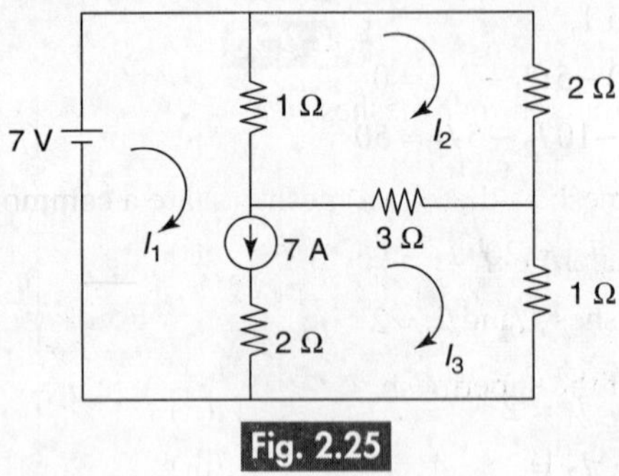


Fig. 2.25

**Solution** Meshes 1 and 3 will form a supermesh.

Writing current equation for the supermesh,

$$I_1 - I_3 = 7 \qquad \text{...(i)}$$

Applying KVL to the outer path of the supermesh,

$$7 - 1(I_1 - I_2) - 3(I_3 - I_2) - 1I_3 = 0$$

$$-I_1 + 4I_2 - 4I_3 = -7 \qquad \text{...(ii)}$$

Applying KVL to mesh 2,

$$-1(I_2 - I_1) - 2I_2 - 3(I_2 - I_3) = 0$$

$$I_1 - 6I_2 + 3I_3 = 0 \qquad \text{...(iii)}$$

Solving Eqs (i), (ii) and (iii),

$$I_1 = 9 \text{ A}$$

$$I_2 = 2.5 \text{ A}$$

$$I_3 = 2 \text{ A}$$

Current through the 3 Ω resistor $= I_2 - I_3 = 2.5 - 2 = 0.5$ A

**EXAMPLE 2.15**

*Find the current in the 5 Ω resistor of the network shown in Fig. 2.26.*

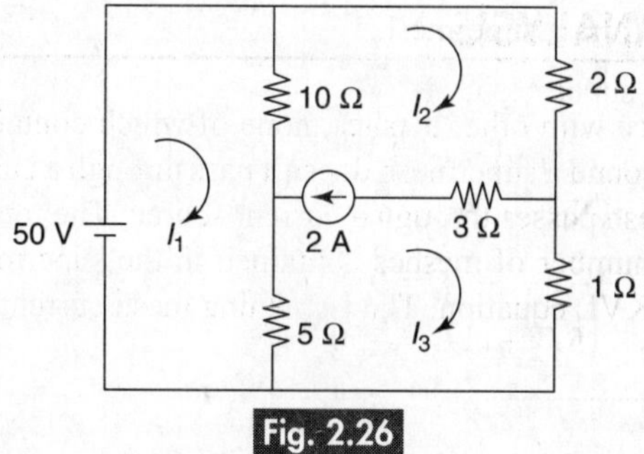


Fig. 2.26

**Solution** Applying KVL to mesh 1,

$$50-10(I_1-I_2)-5(I_1-I_3)=0$$

$$15I_1-10I_2-5I_3=50 \quad \text{...(i)}$$

Meshes 2 and 3 will form a supermesh as these two meshes share a common current source of 2 A. Writing current equation for the supermesh,

$$I_2-I_3=2 \quad \text{...(ii)}$$

Applying KVL to the outer path of the supermesh,

$$-10(I_2-I_1)-2I_2-1I_3-5(I_3-I_1)=0$$

$$-15I_1+12I_2+6I_3=0 \quad \text{...(iii)}$$

Solving Eqs (i), (ii) and (iii),

$$I_1=20\text{ A}$$

$$I_2=17.33\text{ A}$$

$$I_3=15.33\text{ A}$$

Current through the 5 Ω resistor $= I_1 - I_3 = 20 - 15.33 = 4.67$ A

## EXAMPLE 2.16

*Determine the power delivered by the voltage source and the current in the 10 Ω resistor of the network shown in Fig. 2.27.*

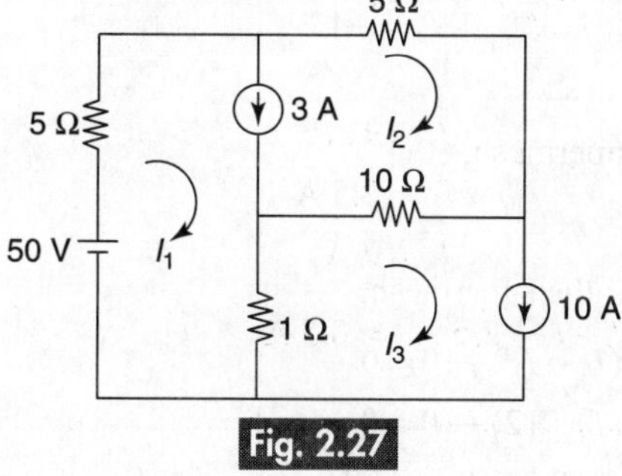


Fig. 2.27

**Solution** Meshes 1 and 2 will form a supermesh.

Writing current equation for the supermesh,

$$I_1 - I_2 = 3 \quad \text{...(i)}$$

Applying KVL to the outer path of the supermesh,

$$50 - 5I_1 - 5I_2 - 10(I_2 - I_3) - 1(I_1 - I_3) = 0$$

$$-6I_1 - 15I_2 + 11I_3 = -50 \quad \text{...(ii)}$$

For mesh 3,

$$I_3 = 10 \quad \text{...(iii)}$$

Solving Eqs (i), (ii) and (iii),

$$I_1 = 9.76 \text{ A}$$

$$I_2 = 6.76 \text{ A}$$

$$I_3 = 10 \text{ A}$$

Power delivered by the voltage source = $50\,I_1 = 50 \times 9.76 = 488$ W

$$I_{10\,\Omega} = I_3 - I_2 = 10 - 6.76 = 3.24 \text{ A}$$

## EXAMPLE 2.17

*For the network shown in Fig. 2.28, find current through the 8 Ω resistor.*

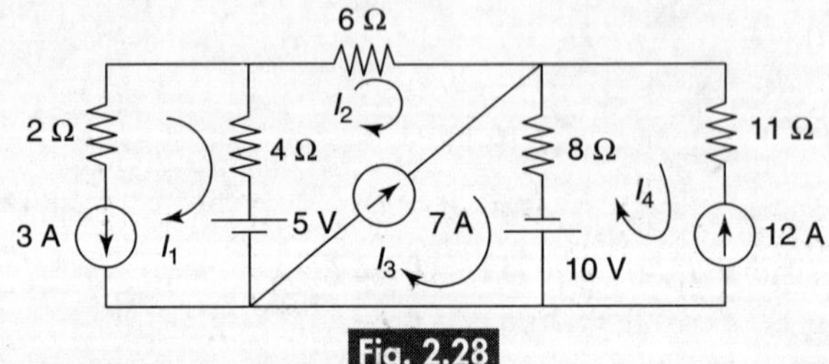


Fig. 2.28

**Solution** Writing current equations for meshes 1 and 4,

$$I_1 = -3 \quad \text{...(i)}$$

$$I_4 = -12 \quad \text{...(ii)}$$

Meshes 2 and 3 will form a supermesh.

Writing current equation for the supermesh,

$$I_3 - I_2 = 7 \quad \text{...(iii)}$$

Applying KVL to the outer path of the supermesh,

$$5 - 4(I_2 - I_1) - 6I_2 - 8(I_3 - I_4) + 10 = 0$$

$$5 - 4(I_2 + 3) - 6I_2 - 8(I_3 + 12) + 10 = 0$$

$$-10I_2 - 8I_3 = 93 \quad \text{...(iv)}$$

Solving Eqs (iii) and (iv),

$$I_2 = -8.28 \text{ A}$$
$$I_3 = -1.28 \text{ A}$$
$$I_{8\,\Omega} = I_3 - I_4 = -1.28 + 12 = 10.72 \text{ A}$$

## Examples with Dependent Sources

### EXAMPLE 2.18

*In the network of Fig. 2.29, find currents $I_1$ and $I_2$.*

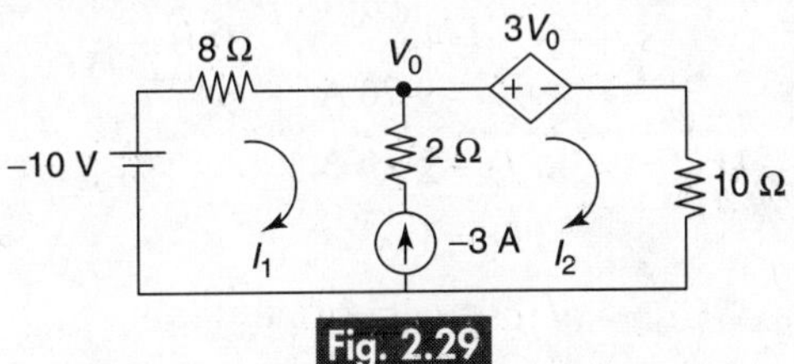


Fig. 2.29

**Solution** From Fig. 2.29,

$$-10 - 8I_1 - V_0 = 0$$
$$V_0 = -10 - 8I_1 \quad \text{...(i)}$$

Meshes 1 and 2 will form a supermesh.

Writing current equations for the supermesh,

$$I_2 - I_1 = -3 \quad \text{...(ii)}$$

Applying KVL to the outer path of the supermesh,

$$-10 - 8I_1 - 3V_0 - 10I_2 = 0$$
$$-10 - 8I_1 - 3(-10 - 8I_1) - 10I_2 = 0$$
$$16I_1 - 10I_2 = -20 \quad \text{...(iii)}$$

Solving Eqs (ii) and (iii),

$$I_1 = -8.33 \text{ A}$$
$$I_2 = -11.33 \text{ A}$$

### EXAMPLE 2.19

*In the network of Fig. 2.30, find the current through the 3 Ω resistor.*

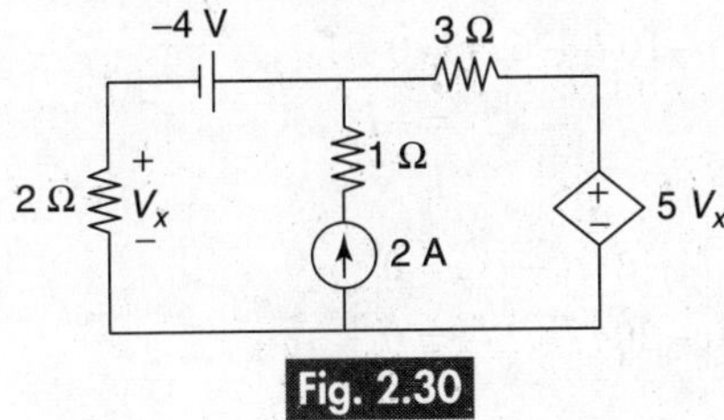


Fig. 2.30

**Solution** Assign clockwise currents in two meshes, as shown in Fig. 2.31.

From Fig. 2.31,

$$V_x = -2\,I_1 \quad \text{...(i)}$$

Fig. 2.31

Meshes 1 and 2 will form a supermesh.

Writing current equations for the supermesh,

$$I_2 - I_1 = 2 \quad \text{...(ii)}$$

Applying KVL to the outer path of the supermesh,

$$-2\,I_1 - 4 - 3\,I_2 - 5V_x = 0$$

$$-2\,I_1 - 4 - 3\,I_2 - 5(-2\,I_1) = 0$$

$$8\,I_1 - 3\,I_2 = 4 \quad \text{...(iii)}$$

Solving Eqs (ii) and (iii),

$$I_1 = 2\text{ A}$$

$$I_2 = 4\text{ A}$$

$$I_{3\Omega} = I_2 = 4\text{ A}$$

## EXAMPLE 2.20

*Find the currents $I_1$ and $I_2$ at the network shown in Fig. 2.32.*

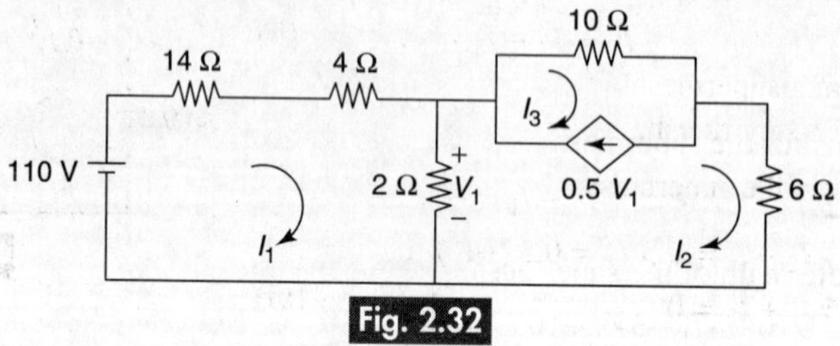


Fig. 2.32

**Solution** From Fig. 2.32,

$$V_1 = 2(I_1 - I_2)$$

Meshes 2 and 3 will form a supermesh.

Writing current equation for the supermesh,

$$I_3 - I_2 = 0.5\,\text{V}_1 = 0.5\times 2(I_1 - I_2) = I_1 - I_2$$

$$I_3 = I_1$$

Applying KVL to outer path of the supermesh,

$$-2(I_2 - I_1) - 10\,I_3 - 6\,I_2 = 0$$

$$-2\,I_2 + 2\,I_1 - 10\,I_1 - 6\,I_2 = 0$$

$$I_1 = -I_2$$

Applying KVL to mesh 1,

$$110 - 14\,I_1 - 4\,I_1 - 2(I_1 - I_2) = 0$$

$$110 - 20\,I_1 + 2\,I_2 = 0$$

$$110 + 20I_1 + 2I_2 = 0$$
$$I_2 = -5 \text{ A}$$
$$I_1 = -I_2 = 5 \text{ A}$$

## EXAMPLE 2.21

*For the network of Fig. 2.33, find current through the 8 Ω resistor.*

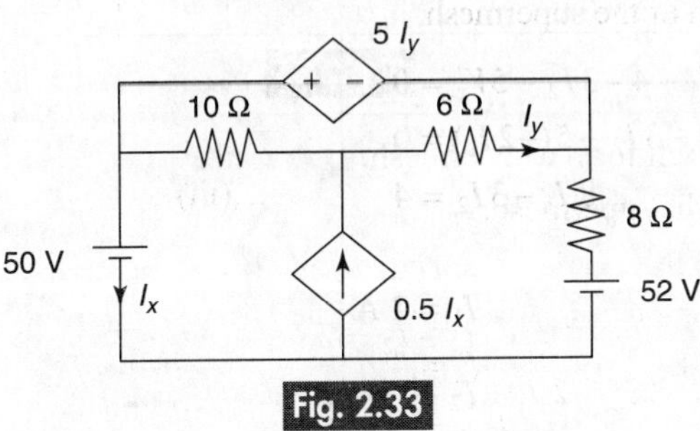

Fig. 2.33

**Solution** Assign clockwise currents to the three meshes, as shown in Fig. 2.34.

From Fig. 2.34,

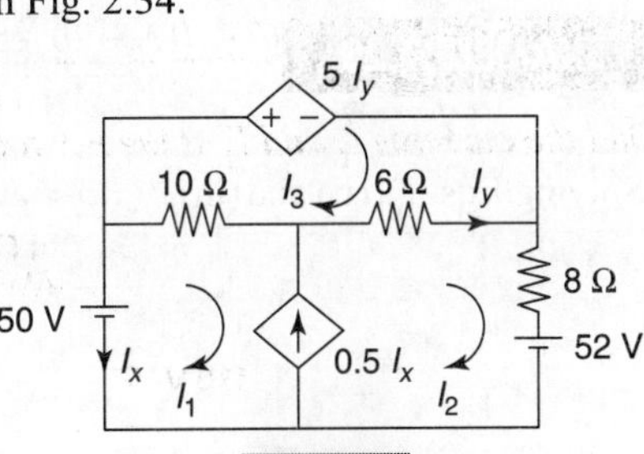

Fig. 2.34

$$I_x = -I_1 \qquad \ldots\text{(i)}$$
$$I_y = I_2 - I_3 \qquad \ldots\text{(ii)}$$

Meshes 1 and 2 will form a supermesh.

Writing current equation for the supermesh,

$$I_2 - I_1 = 0.5\, I_x = 0.5\,(-I_1)$$
$$-0.5\, I_1 + I_2 = 0 \qquad \ldots\text{(iii)}$$

Applying KVL to the outer path of the supermesh,

$$50 - 10(I_1 - I_3) - 6(I_2 - I_3) - 8I_2 - 52 = 0$$
$$-10I_1 - 14I_2 + 16I_3 = 2 \qquad \ldots\text{(iv)}$$

Applying KVL to mesh 3,

$$-5\, I_y - 6\,(I_3 - I_2) - 10\,(I_3 - I_1) = 0$$
$$-5\,(I_2 - I_3) - 6\,(I_3 - I_2) - 10\,(I_3 - I_1) = 0$$
$$10\, I_1 + I_2 - 11\, I_3 = 0 \qquad \ldots\text{(v)}$$

Solving Eqs (iii), (iv) and (v),

$$I_1 = -1.56 \text{ A}$$
$$I_2 = -0.58 \text{ A}$$
$$I_3 = -1.11 \text{ A}$$
$$I_{8\Omega} = I_2 = -0.58 \text{ A}$$

## EXAMPLE 2.22

*For the network shown in Fig. 2.35, find the current through the 10 Ω resistor.*

Fig. 2.35

**Solution** Meshes 1, 2 and 3 will form a supermesh.
Writing current equations for the supermesh,

$$I_1 - I_2 = 2 \quad \text{...(i)}$$

$$I_3 - I_2 = 2\,I_1$$

and

$$2\,I_1 + I_2 - I_3 = 0 \quad \text{...(ii)}$$

Applying KVL to the outer path of the supermesh,

$$15 - 10\,I_1 - 20 - 5\,I_2 - 4I_3 + 40 = 0$$

$$10\,I_1 + 5\,I_2 + 4\,I_3 = 35 \quad \text{...(iii)}$$

Solving Eqs (i), (ii) and (iii),

$$I_1 = 1.96 \text{ A}$$

$$I_2 = -0.04 \text{ A}$$

$$I_3 = 3.89 \text{ A}$$

$$I_{10\,\Omega} = I_1 = 1.96 \text{ A}$$

## EXAMPLE 2.23

*In the network shown in Fig. 2.36, find the power delivered by the 4 V source and voltage across the 2 Ω resistor.*

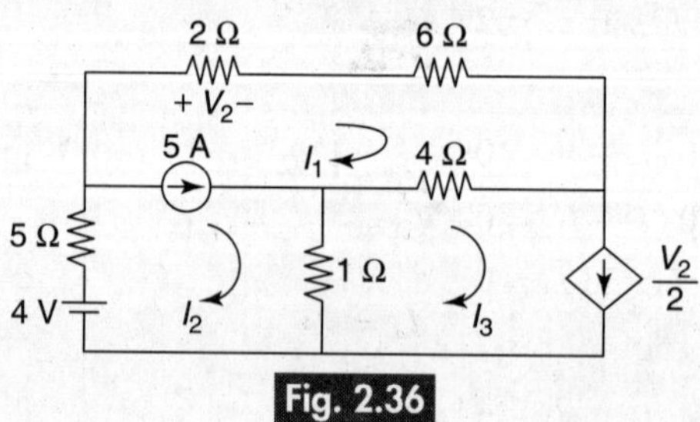


Fig. 2.36

**Solution** From Fig. 2.36,

$$V_2 = 2\,I_1 \quad \text{...(i)}$$

Meshes 1 and 2 will form a supermesh.

Writing current equation for the supermesh,

$$I_2 - I_1 = 5 \quad \text{...(ii)}$$

Applying KVL to the outer path of the supermesh,

$$4 - 5I_2 - 2I_1 - 6I_1 - 4(I_1 - I_3) - 1(I_2 - I_3) = 0$$

$$-12I_1 - 6I_2 + 5I_3 = -4 \quad \text{...(iii)}$$

For mesh 3,

$$I_3 = \frac{V_2}{2} = \frac{2I_1}{2} = I_1$$

$$I_1 - I_3 = 0 \quad \text{...(iv)}$$

Solving Eqs (ii), (iii) and (iv),

$$I_1 = -2 \text{ A}$$

$$I_2 = 3 \text{ A}$$

$$I_3 = -2 \text{ A}$$

Power delivered by the 4 V source $= 4I_2 = 4(3) = 12$ W

$$V_{2\Omega} = 2I_1 = 2(-2) = -4 \text{ V}$$

## EXAMPLE 2.24

*Find currents $I_1$, $I_2$, $I_3$, $I_4$ of the network shown in Fig. 2.37.*

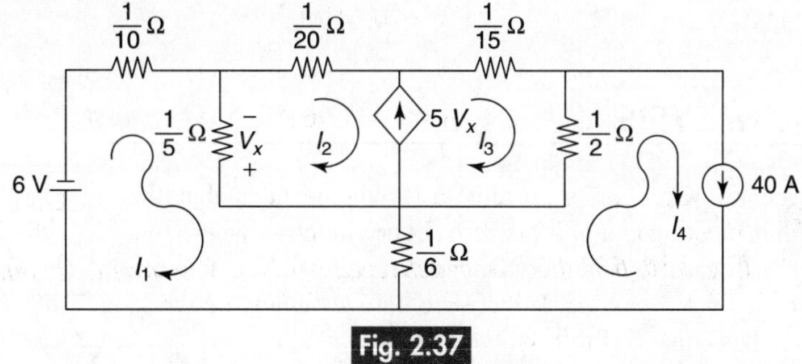


Fig. 2.37

**Solution** From Fig. 2.37,

$$V_x = \frac{1}{5}(I_2 - I_1) \quad \text{...(i)}$$

For mesh 4,

$$I_4 = 40 \quad \text{...(ii)}$$

Applying KVL to mesh 1,

$$-6 - \frac{1}{10}I_1 - \frac{1}{5}(I_1 - I_2) - \frac{1}{6}(I_1 - I_4) = 0$$

$$-6 - \frac{1}{10}I_1 - \frac{1}{5}I_1 + \frac{1}{5}I_2 - \frac{1}{6}I_1 + \frac{1}{6}(40) = 0$$

$$-\frac{7}{15}I_1 + \frac{1}{5}I_2 = -\frac{2}{3} \quad \text{...(iii)}$$

Mesh 2 and 3 will form a supermesh.

Writing current equation for the supermesh,

$$I_3 - I_2 = 5\,V_x = 5\left[\frac{1}{5}(I_2 - I_1)\right] = I_2 - I_1$$

$$I_1 - 2I_2 + I_3 = 0 \qquad \text{...(iv)}$$

Applying KVL to the outer path of the supermesh,

$$-\frac{1}{5}(I_2 - I_1) - \frac{1}{20}I_2 - \frac{1}{15}I_3 - \frac{1}{2}(I_3 - I_4) = 0$$

$$-\frac{1}{5}I_2 + \frac{1}{5}I_1 - \frac{1}{20}I_2 - \frac{1}{15}I_3 - \frac{1}{2}I_3 + \frac{1}{2}(40) = 0$$

$$\frac{1}{5}I_1 - \frac{1}{4}I_2 - \frac{17}{30}I_3 = -20 \qquad \text{...(v)}$$

Solving Eqs (iii), (iv) and (v),

$$I_1 = 10 \text{ A}$$

$$I_2 = 20 \text{ A}$$

$$I_3 = 30 \text{ A}$$

$$I_4 = 40 \text{ A}$$

## 2.3 NODE ANALYSIS

LO 2.2

Explain the concepts of node and supernode analysis

Node analysis is based on Kirchhoff's current law, which states that the algebraic sum of currents meeting at a point is zero. Every junction where two or more branches meet is regarded as a node. One of the nodes in the network is taken as *reference node* or *datum node*. If there are *n* nodes in any network, the number of simultaneous equations to be solved will be $(n - 1)$.

### ➤ *Steps to be followed in Node Analysis*

1. Assuming that a network has n nodes, assign a reference node and the reference directions, and assign a current and a voltage name for each branch and node respectively.
2. Apply KCL at each node except for the reference node and apply Ohm's law to the branch currents.
3. Solve the simultaneous equations for the unknown node voltages.
4. Using these voltages, find any branch currents required.

**EXAMPLE 2.25**

*Determine the current through the 5 Ω resistor for the network shown in Fig. 2.38.*

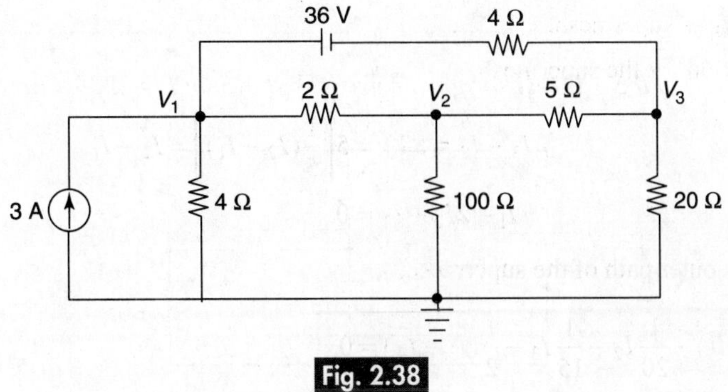


Fig. 2.38

**Solution** Assume that the currents are moving away from the nodes.
Applying KCL at node 1,

$$\frac{V_1}{4}+\frac{V_1-V_2}{2}+\frac{V_1-36-V_3}{4}=3$$

$$\left(\frac{1}{4}+\frac{1}{2}+\frac{1}{4}\right)V_1-\frac{1}{2}V_2-\frac{1}{4}V_3=3+\frac{36}{4}$$

$$V_1-0.5\,V_2-0.25\,V_3=12 \qquad \text{...(i)}$$

Applying KCL at node 2,

$$\frac{V_2-V_1}{2}+\frac{V_2}{100}+\frac{V_2-V_3}{5}=0$$

$$-\frac{1}{2}V_1+\left(\frac{1}{2}+\frac{1}{100}+\frac{1}{5}\right)V_2-\frac{1}{5}V_3=0$$

$$-0.5\,V_1+0.71\,V_2-0.2\,V_3=0 \qquad \text{...(ii)}$$

Applying KCL at node 3,

$$\frac{V_3-V_2}{5}+\frac{V_3}{20}+\frac{V_3-(-36)-V_1}{4}=0$$

$$-\frac{1}{4}V_1-\frac{1}{5}V_2+\left(\frac{1}{5}+\frac{1}{20}+\frac{1}{4}\right)V_3=-9$$

$$-0.25\,V_1-0.2\,V_2+0.5\,V_3=-9 \qquad \text{...(iii)}$$

Solving Eqs (i), (ii) and (iii),

$$V_1=13.41\text{ V}$$

$$V_2=7.06\text{ V}$$

$$V_3=-8.47\text{ V}$$

Current through the 5 Ω resistor $=\dfrac{V_2-V_3}{5}=\dfrac{7.06-(-8.47)}{5}=3.11\text{ A}$

## EXAMPLE 2.26

*Find the power dissipated in the 6 Ω resistor for the network shown in Fig. 2.39.*

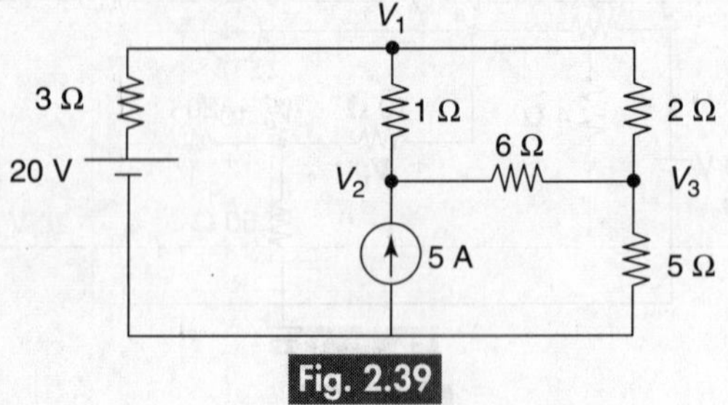


Fig. 2.39

**Solution** Assume that the currents are moving away from the nodes.
Applying KCL at node 1,

$$\frac{V_1-20}{3}+\frac{V_1-V_2}{1}+\frac{V_1-V_3}{2}=0$$

$$\left(\frac{1}{3}+1+\frac{1}{2}\right)V_1-V_2-\frac{1}{2}V_3=\frac{20}{3}$$

$$1.83\,V_1-V_2-0.5\,V_3=6.67 \qquad \text{...(i)}$$

Applying KCL at node 2,

$$\frac{V_2-V_1}{1}+\frac{V_2-V_3}{6}=5$$

$$-V_1+\left(1+\frac{1}{6}\right)V_2-\frac{1}{6}V_3=5$$

$$-V_1+1.17\,V_2-0.17\,V_3=5 \qquad \text{...(ii)}$$

Applying KCL at node 3,

$$\frac{V_3-V_1}{2}+\frac{V_3}{5}+\frac{V_3-V_2}{6}=0$$

$$-\frac{1}{2}V_1-\frac{1}{6}V_2+\left(\frac{1}{2}+\frac{1}{5}+\frac{1}{6}\right)V_3=0$$

$$-0.5\,V_1-0.17\,V_2+0.87\,V_3=0 \qquad \text{...(iii)}$$

Solving Eqs (i), (ii) and (iii),

$$V_1=23.82\text{ V}$$

$$V_2=27.4\text{ V}$$

$$V_3=19.04\text{ V}$$

$$I_{6\Omega}=\frac{V_2-V_3}{6}=\frac{27.4-19.04}{6}=1.39\text{ A}$$

Power dissipated in the 6 Ω resistor $=(1.39)^2\times 6=11.59$ W

## EXAMPLE 2.27

*Find $V_1$ and $V_2$ for the network shown in Fig. 2.40.*

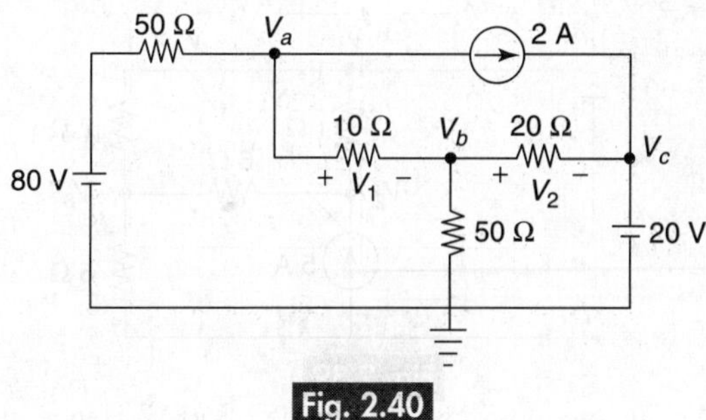


Fig. 2.40

**Solution** Assume that the currents are moving away from the nodes.

Applying KCL at node *a*,

$$\frac{V_a - 80}{50} + \frac{V_a - V_b}{10} + 2 = 0$$

$$\left(\frac{1}{50} + \frac{1}{10}\right)V_a - \frac{1}{10}V_b = \frac{80}{50} - 2$$

$$0.12\,V_a - 0.1\,V_b = -0.4 \qquad \text{...(i)}$$

Applying KCL at node *b*,

$$\frac{V_b - V_a}{10} + \frac{V_b}{50} + \frac{V_b - V_c}{20} = 0$$

$$-\frac{1}{10}V_a + \left(\frac{1}{10} + \frac{1}{50} + \frac{1}{20}\right)V_b - \frac{1}{20}V_c = 0$$

$$-0.1\,V_a + 0.17\,V_b - 0.05\,V_c = 0 \qquad \text{...(ii)}$$

Node *c* is directly connected to a voltage source of 20 V. Hence, we can write voltage equation at node *c*.

$$V_c = 20 \qquad \text{...(iii)}$$

Solving Eqs (i), (ii), and (iii),

$$V_a = 3.08 \text{ V}$$

$$V_b = 7.69 \text{ V}$$

$$V_1 = V_a - V_b = 3.08 - 7.69 = -4.61 \text{ V}$$

$$V_2 = V_b - V_c = 7.69 - 20 = -12.31 \text{ V}$$

## EXAMPLE 2.28

*Find the voltage across the 100 Ω resistor for the network shown in Fig. 2.41.*

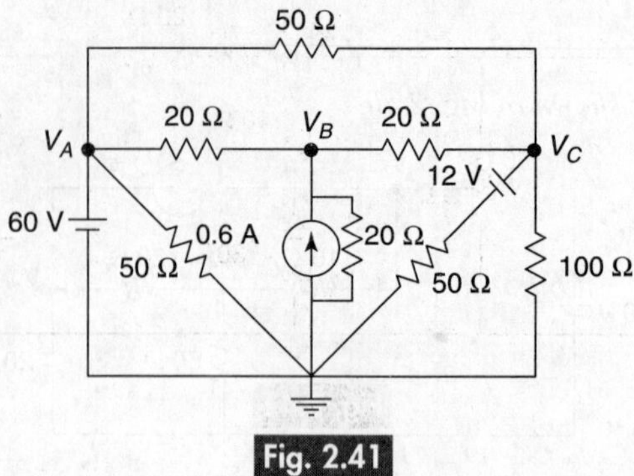


Fig. 2.41

**Solution** Node $A$ is directly connected to a voltage source of 60 V. Hence, we can write voltage equation at node $A$.

$$V_A = 60 \qquad \text{...(i)}$$

Assume that the currents are moving away from the nodes.

Applying KCL at node $B$,

$$\frac{V_B - V_A}{20} + \frac{V_B - V_C}{20} + \frac{V_B}{20} = 0.6$$

$$-\frac{1}{20}V_A + \left(\frac{1}{20} + \frac{1}{20} + \frac{1}{20}\right)V_B - \frac{1}{20}V_C = 0.6$$

$$-0.05\,V_A + 0.15\,V_B - 0.05\,V_C = 0.6 \qquad \text{...(ii)}$$

Applying KCL at node $C$,

$$\frac{V_C - V_A}{50} + \frac{V_C - V_B}{20} + \frac{V_C - 12}{50} + \frac{V_C}{100} = 0$$

$$-\frac{1}{50}V_A - \frac{1}{20}V_B + \left(\frac{1}{50} + \frac{1}{20} + \frac{1}{50} + \frac{1}{100}\right)V_C = \frac{12}{50}$$

$$-0.02\,V_A - 0.05\,V_B + 0.1\,V_C = 0.24 \qquad \text{...(iii)}$$

Solving Eqs (i), (ii), and (iii),

$$V_C = 31.68 \text{ V}$$

$$\text{Voltages across the } 100\ \Omega \text{ resistor} = 31.68 \text{ V}$$

## Examples with Dependent Sources

**EXAMPLE 2.29**

*Find the voltage across the 5 Ω resistor in the network shown in Fig. 2.42.*

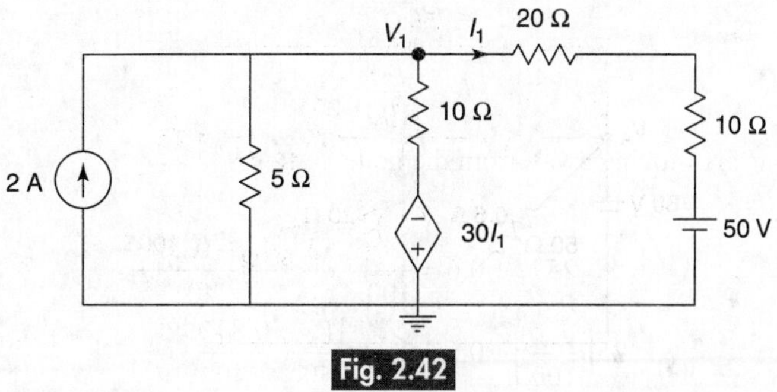


Fig. 2.42

**Solution** From Fig. 2.42,

$$I_1 = \frac{V_1 - 50}{20+10} = \frac{V_1 - 50}{30} \quad \ldots\text{(i)}$$

Assume that the currents are moving away from the node.
Applying KCL at node 1,

$$2 = \frac{V_1}{5} + \frac{V_1 + 30\,I_1}{10} + \frac{V_1 - 50}{30}$$

$$2 = \frac{V_1}{5} + \frac{V_1 + 30\left(\frac{V_1 - 50}{30}\right)}{10} + \frac{V_1 - 50}{30}$$

$$2 = \frac{V_1}{5} + \frac{2V_1 - 50}{10} + \frac{V_1 - 50}{30} \quad \ldots\text{(ii)}$$

Solving Eq. (ii),

$$V_1 = 20 \text{ V}$$

Voltage across the 5 Ω resistor = 20 V

## EXAMPLE 2.30

*For the network shown in Fig. 2.43, find the voltage $V_x$.*

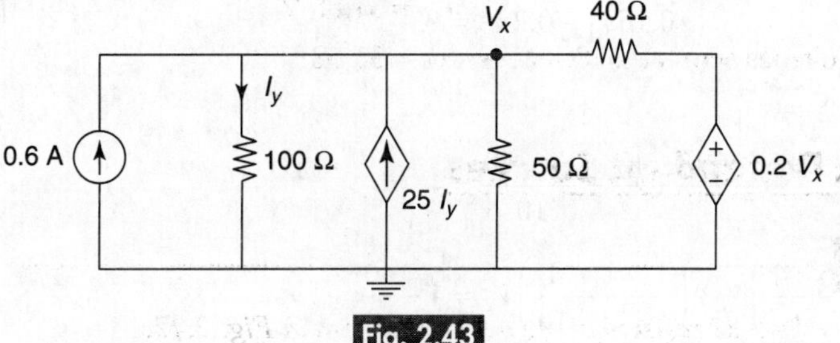


Fig. 2.43

**Solution** From Fig. 2.43,

$$I_y = \frac{V_x}{100} \qquad \text{...(i)}$$

Assume that the currents are moving away from the node.

Applying KCL at node $x$,

$$25 I_y + 0.6 = \frac{V_x}{100} + \frac{V_x}{50} + \frac{V_x - 0.2 V_x}{40}$$

$$25\left(\frac{V_x}{100}\right) + 0.6 = \frac{V_x}{100} + \frac{V_x}{50} + \frac{0.8 V_x}{40}$$

$$\left(\frac{1}{4} - \frac{1}{100} - \frac{1}{50} - \frac{0.8}{40}\right) V_x = -0.6$$

$$0.2 V_x = -0.6$$

$$V_x = -3 \text{ V}$$

## EXAMPLE 2.31

*For the network shown in Fig. 2.44, find voltages $V_1$ and $V_2$.*

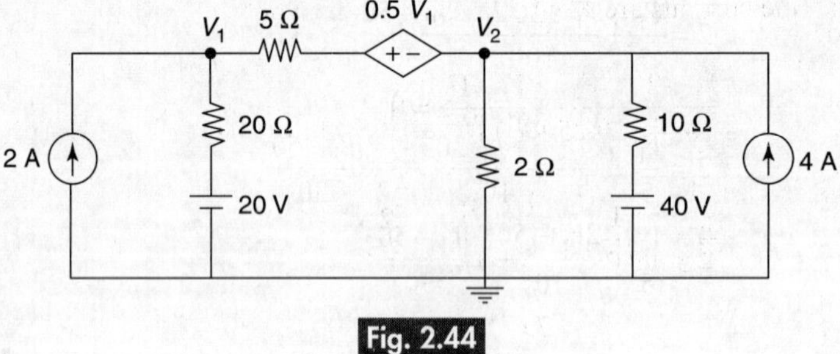


Fig. 2.44

**Solution** Assume that the currents are moving away from the nodes.
Applying KCL at node 1,

$$2 = \frac{V_1 - 20}{20} + \frac{V_1 - 0.5 V_1 - V_2}{5}$$

$$\left(\frac{1}{20} + \frac{1}{5} - \frac{0.5}{5}\right) V_1 - \frac{1}{5} V_2 = 3$$

$$0.15 V_1 - 0.2 V_2 = 3 \qquad \text{...(i)}$$

Applying KCL at node 2,

$$\frac{V_2 + 0.5 V_1 - V_1}{5} + \frac{V_2}{2} + \frac{V_2 - 40}{10} = 4$$

$$\left(\frac{0.5}{5} - \frac{1}{5}\right) V_1 + \left(\frac{1}{5} + \frac{1}{2} + \frac{1}{10}\right) V_2 = 4 + \frac{40}{10}$$

$$-0.1 V_1 + 0.8 V_2 = 8 \qquad \text{...(ii)}$$

Solving Eqs (i) and (ii),

$$V_1 = 40 \text{ V}$$

$$V_2 = 15 \text{ V}$$

## EXAMPLE 2.32

*Determine the voltages $V_1$ and $V_2$ in the network of Fig. 2.45.*

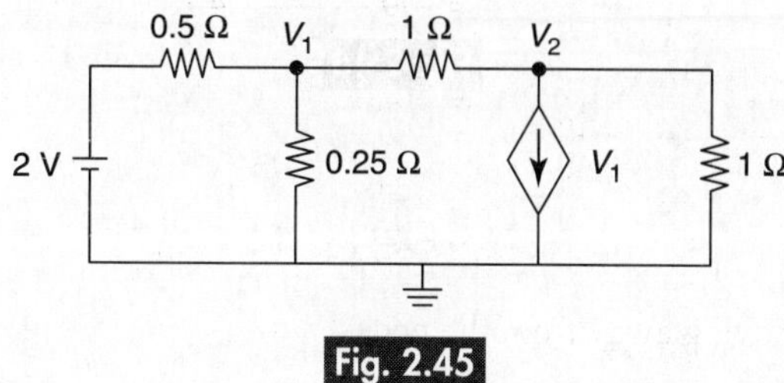


Fig. 2.45

**Solution** Assume that the currents are moving away from the nodes.

Applying KCL at node 1,

$$\frac{V_1 - 2}{0.5} + \frac{V_1}{0.25} + \frac{V_1 - V_2}{1} = 0$$

$$\left(\frac{1}{0.5} + \frac{1}{0.25} + 1\right) V_1 - V_2 = \frac{2}{0.5}$$

$$7 V_7 - V_2 = 4 \qquad \text{...(i)}$$

Applying KCL at node 2,

$$\frac{V_2 - V_1}{1} + \frac{V_2}{1} + V_1 = 0$$

$$2 V_2 = 0$$

$$V_2 = 0 \qquad \text{...(ii)}$$

From Eq. (i),

$$V_1 = \frac{4}{7} \text{ V}$$

## EXAMPLE 2.33

*In the network of Fig. 2.46, find the node voltages $V_1$, $V_2$ and $V_3$.*

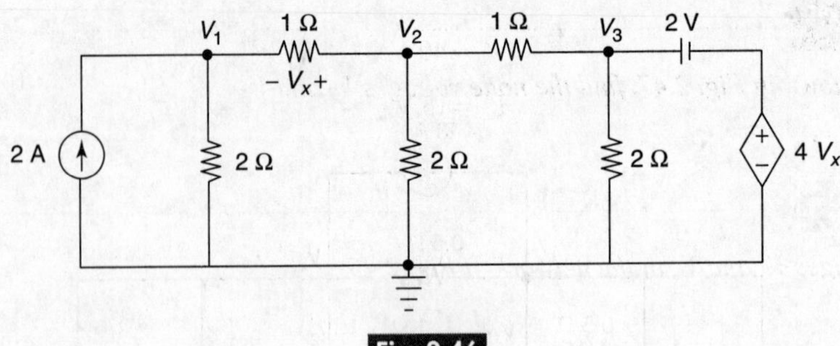


Fig. 2.46

**Solution** From Fig. 2.46,

$$V_x = V_2 - V_1 \qquad \text{...(i)}$$

Assume that the currents are moving away from the nodes.

Applying KCL at node 1,

$$2 = \frac{V_1}{2} + \frac{V_1 - V_2}{1}$$

$$\left(\frac{1}{2}+1\right)V_1 - V_2 = 2$$

$$1.5\,V_1 - V_2 = 2 \qquad \text{...(ii)}$$

Applying KCL at node 2,

$$\frac{V_2 - V_1}{1} + \frac{V_2}{2} + \frac{V_2 - V_3}{1} = 0$$

$$-V_1 + \left(1+\frac{1}{2}+1\right)V_2 - V_3 = 0$$

$$-V_1 + 2.5\,V_2 - V_3 = 0 \qquad \text{...(iii)}$$

At node 3,

$$V_3 - 4\,V_x = 2$$

$$V_3 - 4(V_2 - V_1) = 2$$

$$4\,V_1 - 4\,V_2 + V_3 = 2 \qquad \text{...(iv)}$$

Solving Eqs (ii), (iii) and (iv),

$$V_1 = -1.33\text{ V}$$

$$V_2 = -4\text{ V}$$

$$V_3 = -8.67\text{ V}$$

## EXAMPLE 2.34

*For the network shown in Fig. 2.47, find the node voltages $V_1$ and $V_2$.*

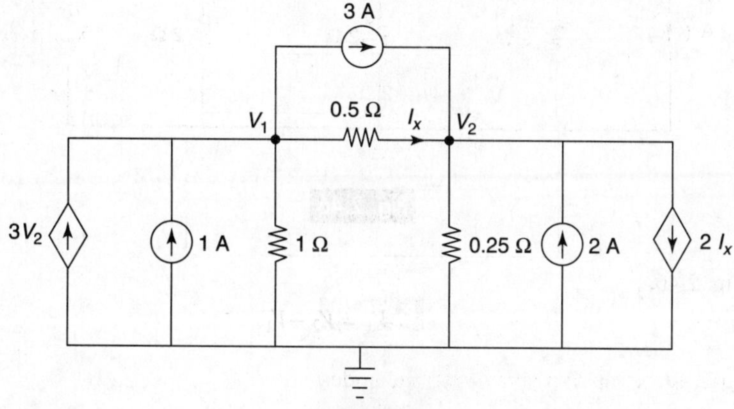


Fig. 2.47

**Solution** From Fig. 2.47,

$$I_x = \frac{V_1 - V_2}{0.5} \qquad \text{...(i)}$$

Assume that the currents are moving away from the nodes.

Applying KCL at node 1,

$$3V_2 + 1 = \frac{V_1}{1} + \frac{V_1 - V_2}{0.5} + 3$$

$$\left(1 + \frac{1}{0.5}\right)V_1 - \left(3 + \frac{1}{0.5}\right)V_2 = -2$$

$$3V_1 - 5V_2 = -2 \qquad \text{...(ii)}$$

Applying KCL at node 2,

$$3 + 2 = \frac{V_2 - V_1}{0.5} + \frac{V_2}{0.25} + 2I_x$$

$$5 = \frac{V_2 - V_1}{0.5} + \frac{V_2}{0.25} + 2\left(\frac{V_1 - V_2}{0.5}\right)$$

$$\left(-\frac{1}{0.5} + \frac{2}{0.5}\right)V_1 + \left(\frac{1}{0.5} + \frac{1}{0.25} - \frac{2}{0.5}\right)V_2 = 5$$

$$2V_1 + 2V_2 = 5 \qquad \text{...(iii)}$$

Solving Eqs (ii) and (iii),

$$V_1 = 1.31 \text{ V}$$

$$V_2 = 1.19 \text{ V}$$

## EXAMPLE 2.35

*Find voltages $V_1$ and $V_2$ in the network shown in Fig. 2.48.*

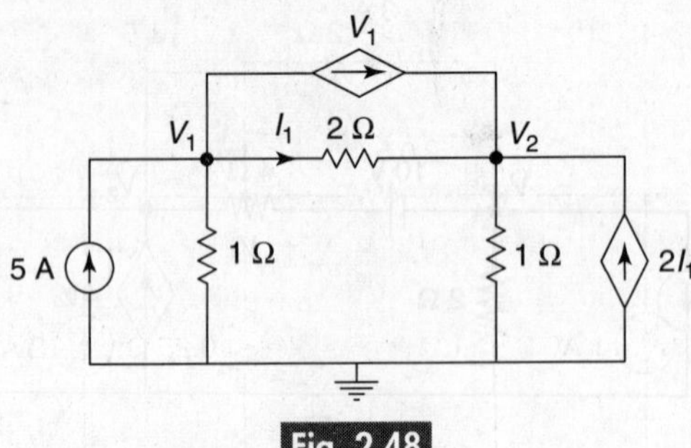


Fig. 2.48

**Solution** From Fig. 2.48,

$$I_1 = \frac{V_1 - V_2}{2} \qquad \ldots\text{(i)}$$

Assume that the currents are moving away from the nodes.

Applying KCL at node 1,

$$5 = \frac{V_1}{1} + \frac{V_1 - V_2}{2} + V_1$$

$$\left(1 + \frac{1}{2} + 1\right)V_1 - \frac{1}{2}V_2 = 5$$

$$2.5\,V_1 - 0.5\,V_2 = 5 \qquad \ldots\text{(ii)}$$

Applying KCL at node 2,

$$\frac{V_2 - V_1}{1} + \frac{V_2}{1} = 2I_1 + V_1$$

$$V_2 - V_1 + V_2 = 2\left(\frac{V_1 - V_2}{2}\right) + V_1$$

$$3\,V_1 = 3\,V_2$$

$$V_1 = V_2 \qquad \ldots\text{(iii)}$$

Solving Eqs (ii) and (iii),

$$V_1 = 2.5 \text{ V}$$

$$V_2 = 2.5 \text{ V}$$

## EXAMPLE 2.36

*Find the power supplied by the 10 V source in the network shown in Fig. 2.49.*

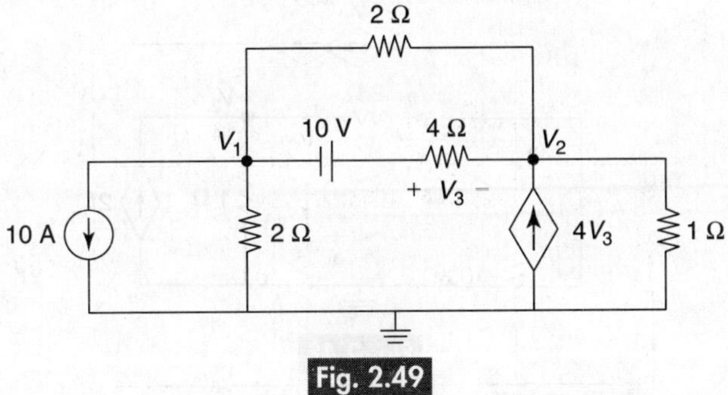


Fig. 2.49

**Solution** From Fig. 2.49,

$$V_3 = V_1 + 10 - V_2 \quad \text{...(i)}$$

Assume that the currents are moving away from the nodes.

Applying KCL at node 1,

$$10 + \frac{V_1}{2} + \frac{V_1 + 10 - V_2}{4} + \frac{V_1 - V_2}{2} = 0$$

$$\left(\frac{1}{2} + \frac{1}{4} + \frac{1}{2}\right)V_1 - \left(\frac{1}{4} + \frac{1}{2}\right)V_2 = -10 - \frac{10}{4}$$

$$1.25\,V_1 - 0.75\,V_2 = -12.5 \quad \text{...(ii)}$$

Applying KCL at node 2,

$$\frac{V_2 - 10 - V_1}{4} + \frac{V_2 - V_1}{2} + \frac{V_2}{1} = 4\,V_3$$

$$\frac{V_2 - 10 - V_1}{4} + \frac{V_2 - V_1}{2} + \frac{V_2}{1} = 4(V_1 + 10 - V_2)$$

$$\left(-\frac{1}{4} - \frac{1}{2} - 4\right)V_1 + \left(\frac{1}{4} + \frac{1}{2} + 1 + 4\right)V_2 = \frac{10}{4} + 40$$

$$-4.75\,V_1 + 5.75\,V_2 = 42.5 \quad \text{...(iii)}$$

Solving Eqs (ii) and (iii),

$$V_1 = -11.03 \text{ V}$$

$$V_2 = -1.72 \text{ V}$$

$$I_{10\text{ V}} = \frac{V_1 + 10 - V_2}{4} = \frac{-11.03 + 10 - (-1.72)}{4} = 0.173 \text{ A}$$

Power supplied by the 10 V source $= 10 \times 0.173 = 1.73$ W

## EXAMPLE 2.37

*For the network shown in Fig. 2.50, find voltages $V_1$ and $V_2$.*

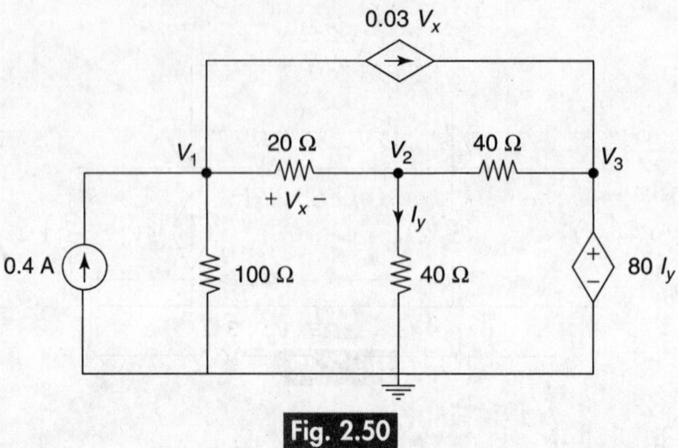


Fig. 2.50

**Solution** From Fig. 2.50,

$$V_x = V_1 - V_2 \quad \ldots\text{(i)}$$

$$I_y = \frac{V_2}{40} \quad \ldots\text{(ii)}$$

Assume that the currents are moving away from the nodes.

Applying KCL at node 1,

$$0.4 = \frac{V_1}{100} + \frac{V_1 - V_2}{20} + 0.03\,V_x$$

$$0.4 = \frac{V_1}{100} + \frac{V_1 - V_2}{20} + 0.03(V_1 - V_2)$$

$$\left(\frac{1}{100} + \frac{1}{20} + 0.03\right)V_1 - \left(\frac{1}{20} + 0.03\right)V_2 = 0.4$$

$$0.09\,V_1 - 0.08\,V_2 = 0.4 \quad \ldots\text{(iii)}$$

Applying KCL at node 2,

$$\frac{V_2 - V_1}{20} + \frac{V_2}{40} + \frac{V_2 - V_3}{40} = 0$$

$$-\frac{1}{20}V_1 + \left(\frac{1}{20} + \frac{1}{40} + \frac{1}{40}\right)V_2 - \frac{1}{40}V_3 = 0$$

$$-0.05\,V_1 + 0.1\,V_2 - 0.025\,V_3 = 0 \quad \ldots\text{(iv)}$$

For node 3,

$$V_3 = 80\,I_y = 80\left(\frac{V_2}{40}\right) = 2\,V_2$$

$$2\,V_2 - V_3 = 0 \quad \ldots\text{(v)}$$

Solving Eqs (iii), (iv) and (v),

$$V_1 = 40 \text{ V}$$
$$V_2 = 40 \text{ V}$$
$$V_3 = 80 \text{ V}$$

## EXAMPLE 2.38

*Find voltages $V_a$, $V_b$ and $V_c$ in the network shown in Fig. 2.51.*

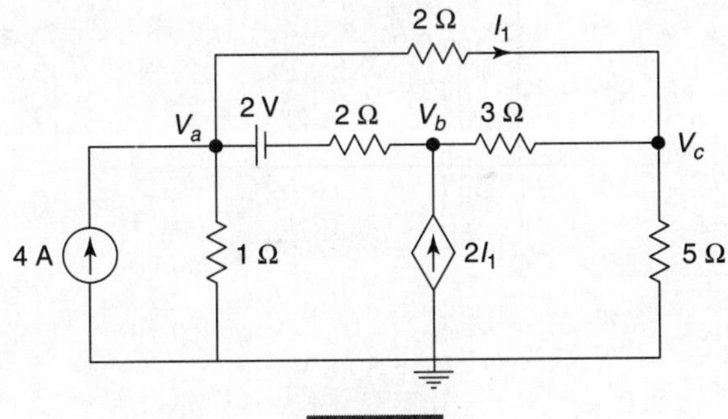


Fig. 2.51

**Solution** From Fig. 2.51,

$$I_1 = \frac{V_a - V_c}{2}$$

Assume that the currents are moving away from the nodes.

Applying KCL at node *a*,

$$4 = \frac{V_a}{1} + \frac{V_a - V_c}{2} + \frac{V_a - 2 - V_b}{2}$$

$$\left(1 + \frac{1}{2} + \frac{1}{2}\right) V_a - \frac{1}{2} V_b - \frac{1}{2} V_c = 5$$

$$2\, V_a - 0.5\, V_b - 0.5\, V_c = 5 \quad \text{...(i)}$$

Applying KCL at node *b*,

$$\frac{V_b + 2 - V_a}{2} + \frac{V_b - V_c}{3} = 2I_1$$

$$\frac{V_b + 2 - V_a}{2} + \frac{V_b - V_c}{3} = 2\left(\frac{V_a - V_c}{2}\right)$$

$$\frac{V_b + 2 - V_a}{2} + \frac{V_b - V_c}{3} = V_a - V_c$$

$$\left(-\frac{1}{2}-1\right)V_a+\left(\frac{1}{2}+\frac{1}{3}\right)V_b+\left(1-\frac{1}{3}\right)V_c=-1$$

$$-1.5\,V_a+0.83\,V_b+0.67\,V_c=-1 \qquad \text{...(ii)}$$

Applying KCL at node $c$,

$$\frac{V_c-V_b}{3}+\frac{V_c}{5}=I_1$$

$$\frac{V_c-V_b}{3}+\frac{V_c}{5}=\frac{V_a-V_c}{2}$$

$$-\frac{1}{2}V_a-\frac{1}{3}V_b+\left(\frac{1}{3}+\frac{1}{5}+\frac{1}{2}\right)V_c=0$$

$$-0.5\,V_a-0.33\,V_b+1.033\,V_c=0 \qquad \text{...(iii)}$$

Solving Eqs (i), (ii), and (iii),

$$V_a=4.303\text{ V}$$

$$V_b=3.88\text{ V}$$

$$V_c=3.33\text{ V}$$

## 2.4 SUPERNODE ANALYSIS

LO 2.2

Nodes that are connected to each other by voltage sources, but not to the reference node by a path of voltage sources, form a *supernode*. A supernode requires one node voltage equation, that is, a KCL equation. The remaining node voltage equations are KVL equations.

**EXAMPLE 2.39**

*Determine the current in the 5 Ω resistor for the network shown in Fig. 2.52.*

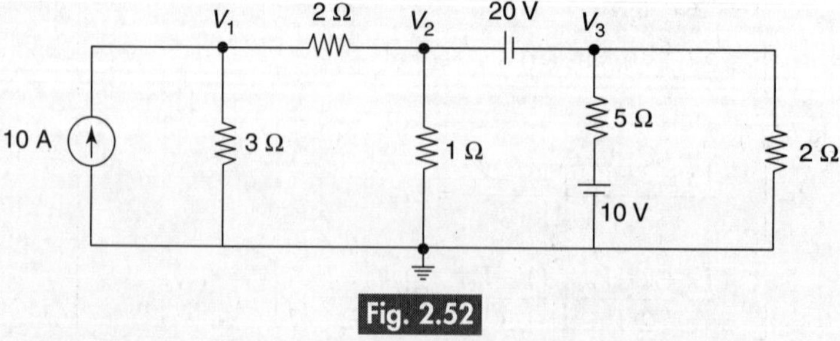


Fig. 2.52

**Solution** Assume that the currents are moving away from the nodes.

Applying KCL at node 1,

$$10 = \frac{V_1}{3} + \frac{V_1 - V_2}{2}$$

$$\left(\frac{1}{3} + \frac{1}{2}\right)V_1 - \frac{1}{2}V_2 = 10$$

$$0.83\,V_1 - 0.5\,V_2 = 10 \qquad \text{...(i)}$$

Nodes 2 and 3 will form a supernode.

Writing voltage equation for the supernode,

$$V_2 - V_3 = 20 \qquad \text{...(ii)}$$

Applying KCL at the supernode,

$$\frac{V_2 - V_1}{2} + \frac{V_2}{1} + \frac{V_3 - 10}{5} + \frac{V_3}{2} = 0$$

$$-\frac{1}{2}V_1 + \left(\frac{1}{2} + 1\right)V_2 + \left(\frac{1}{5} + \frac{1}{2}\right)V_3 = 2$$

$$-0.5\,V_1 + 1.5\,V_2 + 0.7\,V_3 = 2 \qquad \text{...(iii)}$$

Solving Eqs (i), (ii) and (iii),

$$V_1 = 19.04 \text{ V}$$

$$V_2 = 11.6 \text{ V}$$

$$V_3 = -8.4 \text{ V}$$

$$I_{5\Omega} = \frac{V_3 - 10}{5} = \frac{-8.4 - 10}{5} = -3.68 \text{ A}$$

## EXAMPLE 2.40

*Find the power delivered by the 5 A current source in the network shown in Fig. 2.53.*

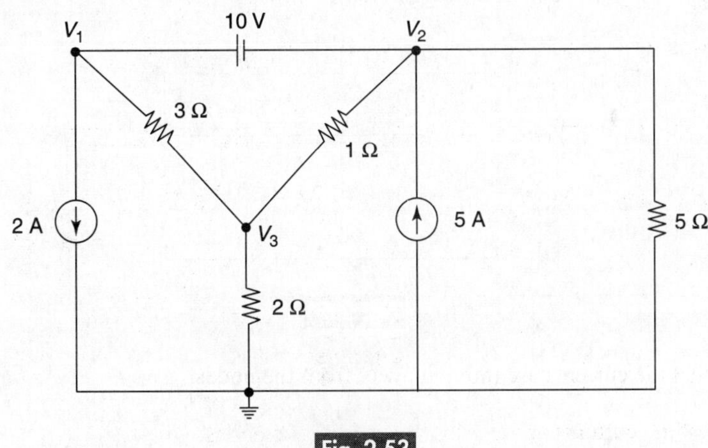


Fig. 2.53

**Solution** Assume that the currents are moving away from the nodes.

Nodes 1 and 2 will form a supernode.

Writing voltage equation for the supernode,

$$V_1 - V_2 = 10 \qquad \ldots\text{(i)}$$

Applying KCL at the supernode,

$$2 + \frac{V_1 - V_3}{3} + \frac{V_2}{5} + \frac{V_2 - V_3}{1} = 5$$

$$\frac{1}{3}V_1 + \left(\frac{1}{5}+1\right)V_2 - \left(\frac{1}{3}+1\right)V_3 = 3$$

$$0.33\,V_1 + 1.2\,V_2 - 1.33\,V_3 = 3 \qquad \ldots\text{(ii)}$$

Applying KCL at node 3,

$$\frac{V_3 - V_1}{3} + \frac{V_3 - V_2}{1} + \frac{V_3}{2} = 0$$

$$-\frac{1}{3}V_1 - V_2 + \left(\frac{1}{3}+1+\frac{1}{2}\right)V_3 = 0$$

$$-0.33\,V_1 - V_2 + 1.83\,V_3 = 0 \qquad \ldots\text{(iii)}$$

Solving Eqs (i), (ii) and (iii),

$$V_1 = 13.72 \text{ V}$$

$$V_2 = 3.72 \text{ V}$$

$$V_3 = 4.51 \text{ V}$$

Power delivered by the 5 A source = 5 $V_2$ = 5 × 3.72 = 18.6 W

**EXAMPLE 2.41**

*In the network of Fig. 2.54, find the node voltages $V_1$, $V_2$ and $V_3$.*

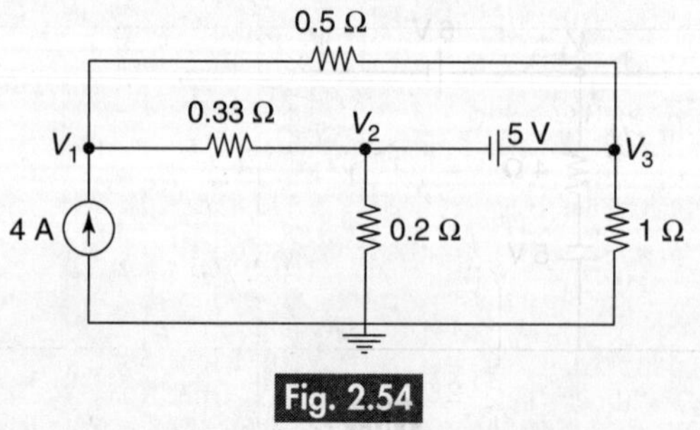


Fig. 2.54

**Solution** Assume that the currents are moving away from the nodes.

Applying KCL at node 1,

$$4 = \frac{V_1 - V_2}{0.33} + \frac{V_1 - V_3}{0.5}$$

$$\left(\frac{1}{0.33} + \frac{1}{0.5}\right) V_1 - \frac{1}{0.33} V_2 - \frac{1}{0.5} V_3 = 4$$

$$5.03\, V_1 - 3.03\, V_2 - 2\, V_3 = 4 \quad \text{...(i)}$$

Nodes 2 and 3 will form a supernode.

Writing voltage equation for the supernode,

$$V_3 - V_2 = 5 \quad \text{...(ii)}$$

Applying KCL at the supernode,

$$\frac{V_2 - V_1}{0.33} + \frac{V_2}{0.2} + \frac{V_3}{1} + \frac{V_3 - V_1}{0.5} = 0$$

$$\left(-\frac{1}{0.33} - \frac{1}{0.5}\right) V_1 + \left(\frac{1}{0.33} + \frac{1}{0.2}\right) V_2 + \left(1 + \frac{1}{0.5}\right) V_3 = 0$$

$$-5.03\, V_1 + 8.03\, V_2 + 3\, V_3 = 0 \quad \text{...(iii)}$$

Solving Eqs (i), (ii) and (iii),

$$V_1 = 2.62 \text{ V}$$
$$V_2 = -0.17 \text{ V}$$
$$V_3 = 4.83 \text{ V}$$

## Examples with Dependent Sources

**EXAMPLE 2.42**

*For the network shown in Fig. 2.55, determine the voltage $V_x$.*

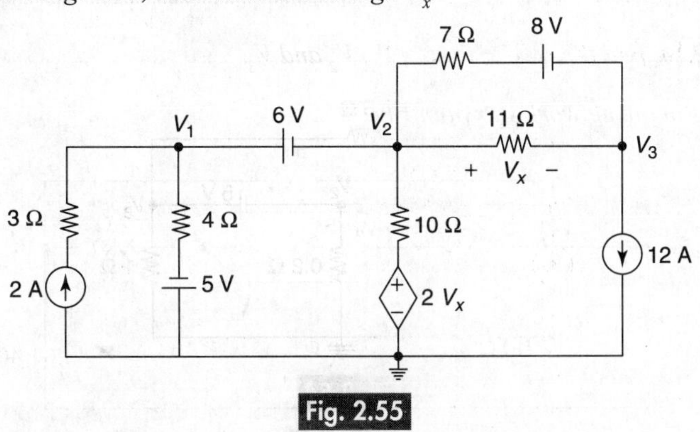


Fig. 2.55

**Solution** From Fig. 2.55,

$$V_x = V_2 - V_3$$

Assume that the currents are moving away from the nodes.

Node 1 and 2 will form a supernode.

Writing voltage equations for the supernode,

$$V_1 - V_2 = 6 \qquad \text{...(i)}$$

Applying KCL at the supernode,

$$2 = \frac{V_1+5}{4} + \frac{V_2-2V_x}{10} + \frac{V_2-8-V_3}{7} + \frac{V_2-V_3}{11}$$

$$2 = \frac{V_1+5}{4} + \frac{V_2-2(V_2-V_3)}{10} + \frac{V_2-8-V_3}{7} + \frac{V_2-V_3}{11}$$

$$\frac{1}{4}V_1 + \left(\frac{1}{10} - \frac{1}{5} + \frac{1}{7} + \frac{1}{11}\right)V_2 + \left(\frac{1}{5} - \frac{1}{7} - \frac{1}{11}\right)V_3 = 2 - \frac{5}{4} + \frac{8}{7}$$

$$0.25\,V_1 + 0.133\,V_2 - 0.033\,V_3 = 1.89 \qquad \text{...(ii)}$$

Applying KCL at node 3,

$$\frac{V_3-V_2}{11} + \frac{V_3+8-V_2}{7} + 12 = 0$$

$$\left(-\frac{1}{11} - \frac{1}{7}\right)V_2 + \left(\frac{1}{11} + \frac{1}{7}\right)V_3 = -12 - \frac{8}{7}$$

$$-0.233\,V_2 + 0.233\,V_3 = -13.14 \qquad \text{...(iii)}$$

Solving Eqs (i), (ii) and (iii),

$$V_1 = 1.8 \text{ V}$$

$$V_2 = -4.2 \text{ V}$$

$$V_3 = -60.6 \text{ V}$$

$$V_x = V_2 - V_3 = -4.2 - (-60.6) = 56.4 \text{ V}$$

**EXAMPLE 2.43**

*Find the node voltages in the network shown in Fig. 2.56.*

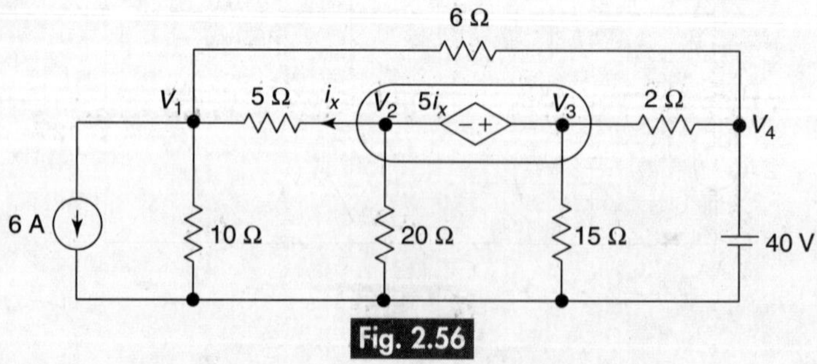


Fig. 2.56

**Solution** From Fig. 2.56,

$$I_x = \frac{V_2 - V_1}{5} \quad \ldots\text{(i)}$$

For node 4,

$$V_4 = 40 \quad \ldots\text{(ii)}$$

Applying KCL at node 1,

$$6 + \frac{V_1}{10} + \frac{V_1 - V_2}{5} + \frac{V_1 - V_4}{6} = 0$$

$$6 + \frac{V_1}{10} + \frac{V_1 - V_2}{5} + \frac{V_1 - 40}{6} = 0$$

$$\left(\frac{1}{10} + \frac{1}{5} + \frac{1}{6}\right)V_1 - \frac{1}{5}V_2 = \frac{40}{6} - 6$$

$$\frac{7}{15}V_1 - \frac{1}{5}V_2 = \frac{2}{3} \quad \ldots\text{(iii)}$$

Nodes 2 and 3 will form a supernode,
Writing voltage equation for the supernode,

$$V_3 - V_2 = 5\,I_x = 5\left(\frac{V_2 - V_1}{5}\right) = V_2 - V_1$$

$$V_1 - 2V_2 + V_3 = 0 \quad \ldots\text{(iv)}$$

Applying KCL to the supernode,

$$\frac{V_2 - V_1}{5} + \frac{V_2}{20} + \frac{V_3}{15} + \frac{V_3 - V_4}{2} = 0$$

$$\frac{V_2 - V_1}{5} + \frac{V_2}{20} + \frac{V_3}{15} + \frac{V_3 - 40}{2} = 0$$

$$-\frac{1}{5}V_1 + \left(\frac{1}{5} + \frac{1}{20}\right)V_2 + \left(\frac{1}{15} + \frac{1}{2}\right)V_3 = 20$$

$$-\frac{1}{5}V_1 + \frac{1}{4}V_2 + \frac{17}{30}V_3 = 20 \quad \ldots\text{(v)}$$

Solving Eqs (iii), (iv) and (v),

$$V_1 = 10\text{ V}$$

$$V_2 = 20\text{ V}$$

$$V_3 = 30\text{ V}$$

$$V_4 = 40\text{ V}$$

## EXAMPLE 2.44

*Find the node voltages in the network shown in Fig. 2.57.*

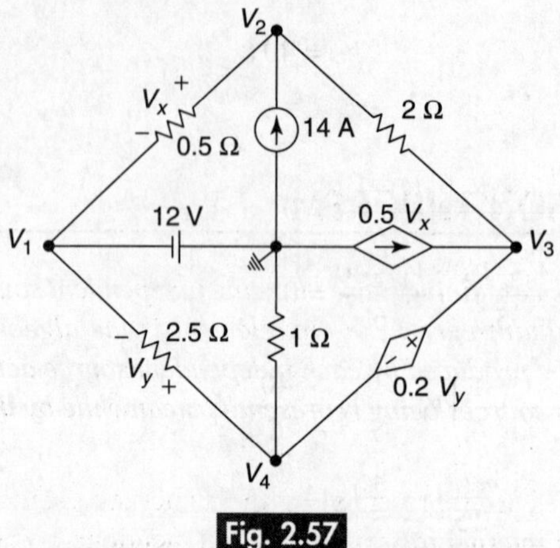


Fig. 2.57

**Solution** Selecting the central node as reference node,

$$V_1 = -12\,\text{V} \quad \ldots\text{(i)}$$

Applying KCL at node 2,

$$\frac{V_2 - V_1}{0.5} + \frac{V_2 - V_3}{2} = 14$$

$$-\frac{1}{0.5}V_1 + \left(\frac{1}{0.5} + \frac{1}{2}\right)V_2 - \frac{1}{2}V_3 = 14$$

$$-2\,V_1 + 2.5\,V_2 - 0.5\,V_3 = 14 \quad \ldots\text{(ii)}$$

Nodes 3 and 4 will form a supernode,

Writing voltage equation for the supernode,

$$V_3 - V_4 = 0.2V_y = 0.2(V_4 - V_1)$$

$$0.2V_1 + V_3 - 1.2V_4 = 0 \quad \ldots\text{(iii)}$$

Applying KCL to the supernode,

$$\frac{V_3 - V_2}{2} - 0.5V_x + \frac{V_4}{1} + \frac{V_4 - V_1}{2.5} = 0$$

$$\frac{V_3 - V_2}{2} - 0.5(V_2 - V_1) + V_4 + \frac{V_4 - V_1}{2.5} = 0$$

$$\left(0.5 - \frac{1}{2.5}\right)V_1 - \left(\frac{1}{2} + 0.5\right)V_2 + \frac{1}{2}V_3 + \left(1 + \frac{1}{2.5}\right)V_4 = 0$$

$$0.1\,V_1 - V_2 + 0.5\,V_3 + 1.4\,V_3 = 0 \quad \ldots\text{(iv)}$$

Solving Eqs (i), (ii), (iii) and (iv),

$$V_1 = -12 \text{ V}$$
$$V_2 = -4 \text{ V}$$
$$V_3 = 0$$
$$V_4 = -2 \text{ V}$$

## 2.5 SUPERPOSITION THEOREM

LO 2.3

Analyse the networks using superposition theorem

It states that '*in a linear network containing more than one independent source and dependent source, the resultant current in any element is the algebraic sum of the currents that would be produced by each independent source acting alone, all the other independent sources being represented meanwhile by their respective internal resistances.*'

The independent voltage sources are represented by their internal resistances if given or simply with zero resistances, i.e., short circuits if internal resistances are not mentioned. The independent current sources are represented by infinite resistances, i.e., open circuits.

The dependent sources are not sources but dissipative components—hence, they are active at all times. A dependent source has zero value only when its control voltage or current is zero.

A linear network is one whose parameters are constant, i.e., they do not change with voltage and current.

➤ ***Explanation*** Consider the network shown in Fig. 2.58. Suppose we have to find current $I_4$ through resistor $R_4$.

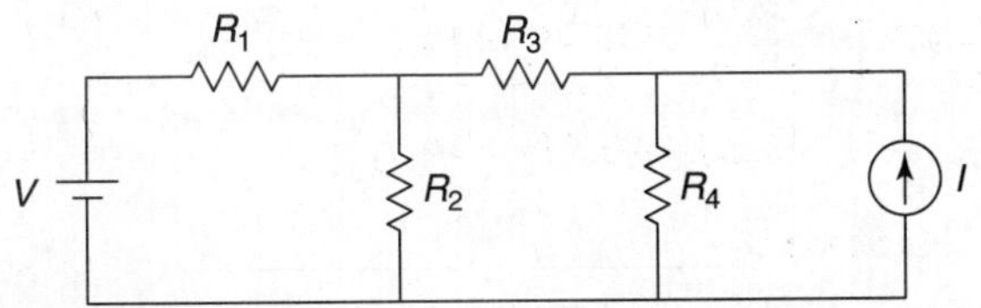


**Fig. 2.58** *Network to illustrate superposition theorem*

The current flowing through resistor $R_4$ due to constant voltage source $V$ is found to be, say, $I_4'$ (with proper direction), representing constant current source with infinite resistance, i.e., open circuit.

The current flowing through resistor $R_4$ due to constant current source $I$ is found to be, say, $I_4''$ (with proper direction), representing the constant voltage source with zero resistance or short circuit.

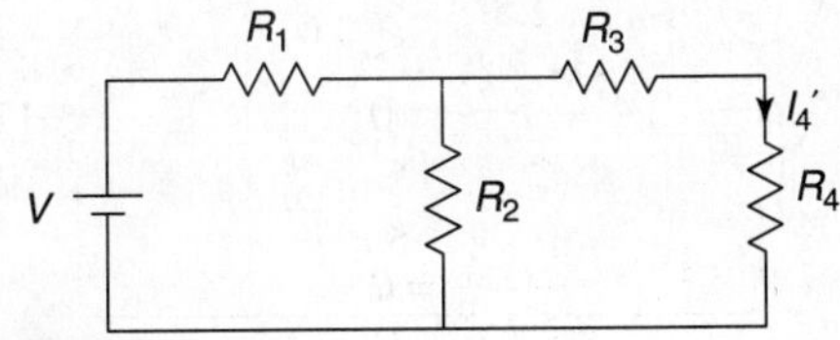


**Fig. 2.59** *When voltage source V is acting alone*

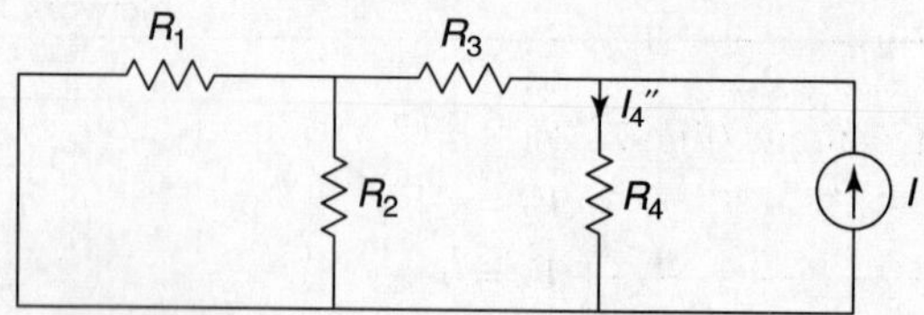


Fig. 2.60 *When current source I is acting alone*

The resultant current $I_4$ through resistor $R_4$ is found by superposition theorem.

$$I_4 = I_4' + I_4''$$

### ➤ Steps to be followed in Superposition Theorem

1. Find the current through the resistance when only one independent source is acting, replacing all other independent sources by respective internal resistances.
2. Find the current through the resistance for each of the independent sources.
3. Find the resultant current through the resistance by the superposition theorem considering magnitude and direction of each current.

## EXAMPLE 2.45

*Find the current through the 4 Ω resistor in Fig. 2.61.*

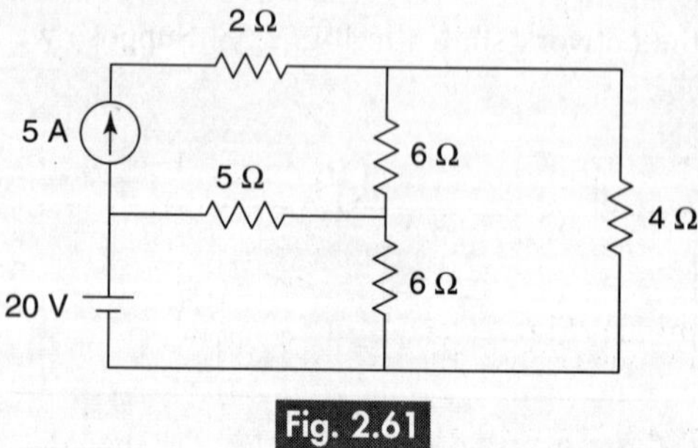


Fig. 2.61

**Solution**

***Step I*** When the 5 A source is acting alone (Fig. 2.62)

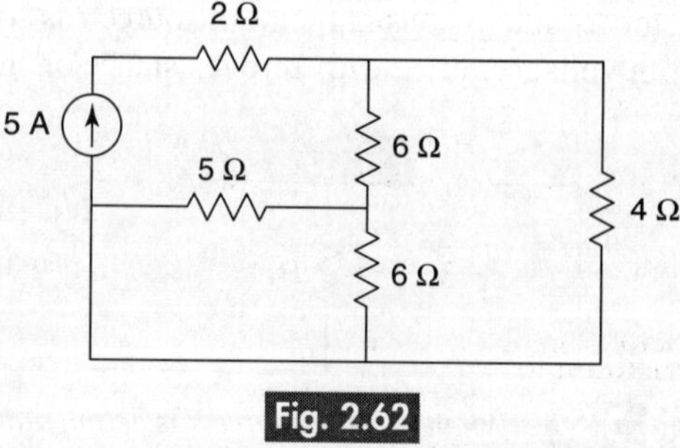


Fig. 2.62

By series–parallel reduction technique (Fig. 2.63),

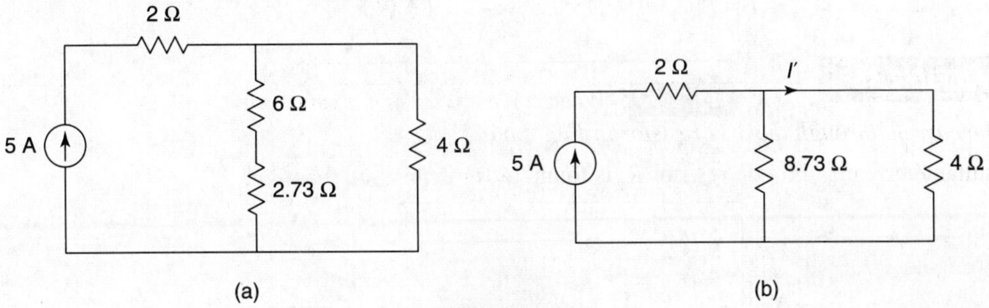


Fig. 2.63

$$I' = 5 \times \frac{8.73}{8.73+4} = 3.43 \text{ A}(\downarrow)$$

***Step II*** When the 20 V source is acting alone (Fig. 2.64)

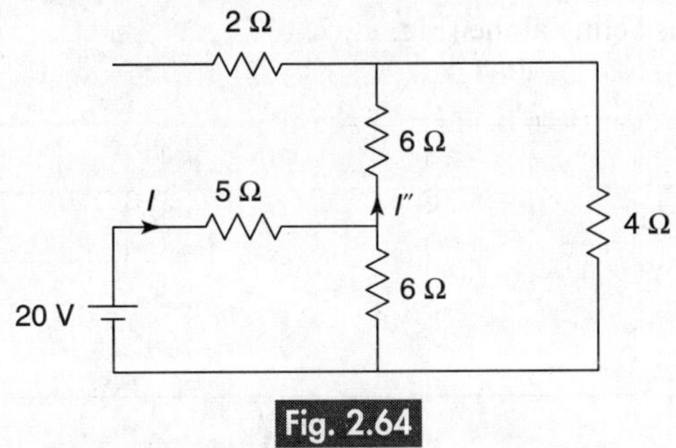


Fig. 2.64

By series–parallel reduction technique (Fig. 2.65),

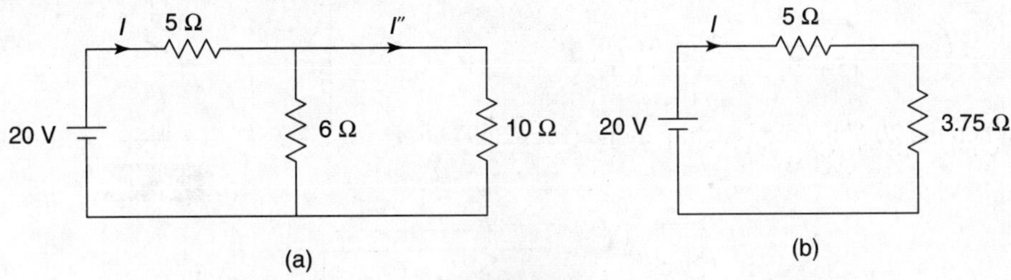


Fig. 2.65

$$I = \frac{20}{5+3.75} = 2.29 \text{ A}$$

From Fig. 2.65(a), by current-division rule,

$$I'' = 2.29 \times \frac{6}{6+10} = 0.86 \text{ A}(\downarrow)$$

***Step III*** By superposition theorem,

$$I = I' + I'' = 3.43 + 0.86 = 4.29 \text{ A} (\downarrow)$$

## EXAMPLE 2.46

*Find the current through the 3 Ω resistor in Fig. 2.66.*

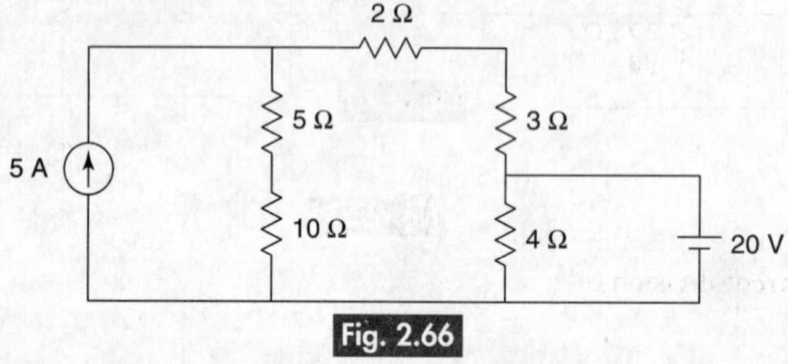


Fig. 2.66

**Solution**

***Step I*** When the 5 A source is acting alone (Fig. 2.67)

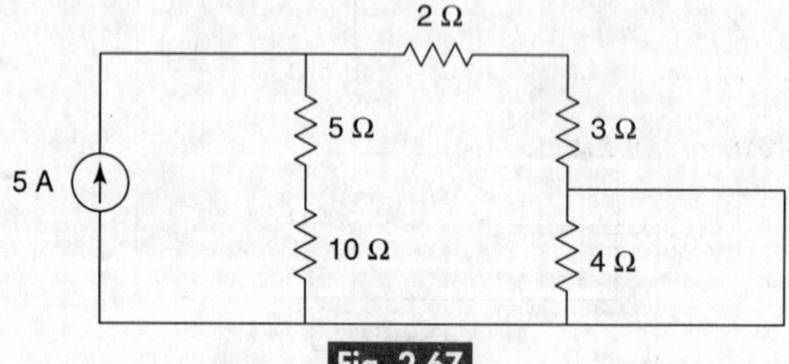


Fig. 2.67

By series–parallel reduction technique (Fig. 2.68),

$$I' = 5 \times \frac{15}{15 + 2 + 3} = 3.75 \text{ A}(\downarrow)$$

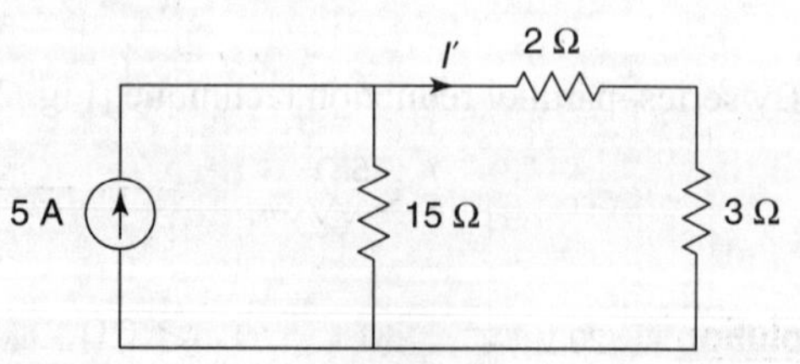


Fig. 2.68

***Step II*** When the 20 V source is acting alone (Fig. 2.69)

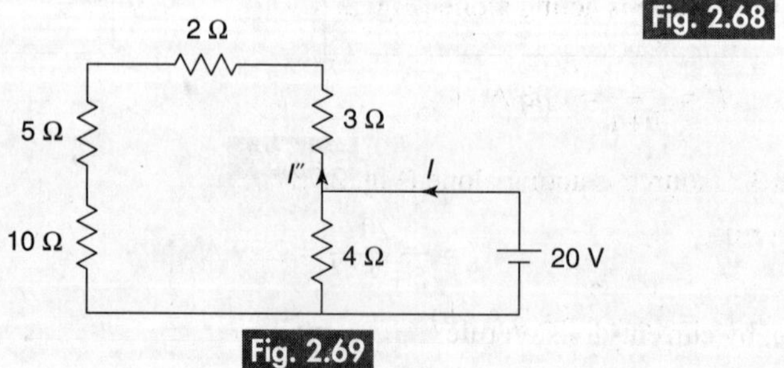


Fig. 2.69

By series–parallel reduction technique (Fig. 2.70),

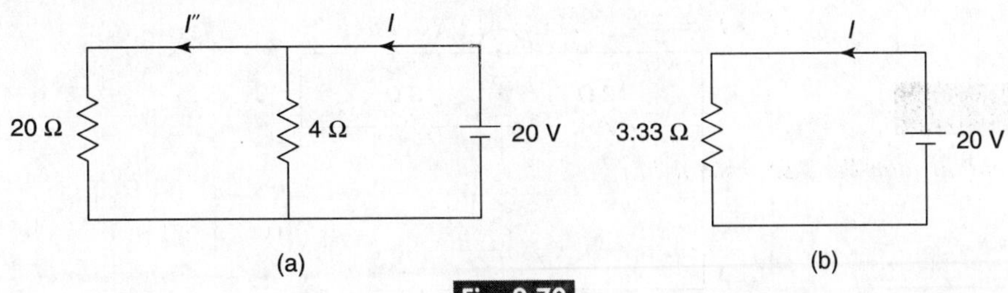


Fig. 2.70

$$I = \frac{20}{3.33} = 6 \text{ A}$$

From Fig. 2.70(a), by current-division rule,

$$I'' = 6 \times \frac{4}{20+4} = 1 \text{ A}(\uparrow) = -1 \text{ A}(\downarrow)$$

***Step III*** By superposition theorem,

$$I = I' + I'' = 3.75 - 1 = 2.75 \text{ A } (\downarrow)$$

## EXAMPLE 2.47

*Find the current in the 1 Ω resistors in Fig. 2.71.*

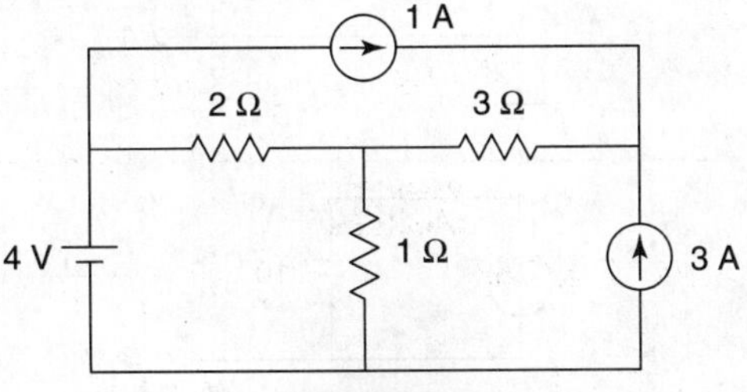


Fig. 2.71

**Solution**

***Step I*** When the 4 V source is acting alone (Fig. 2.72)

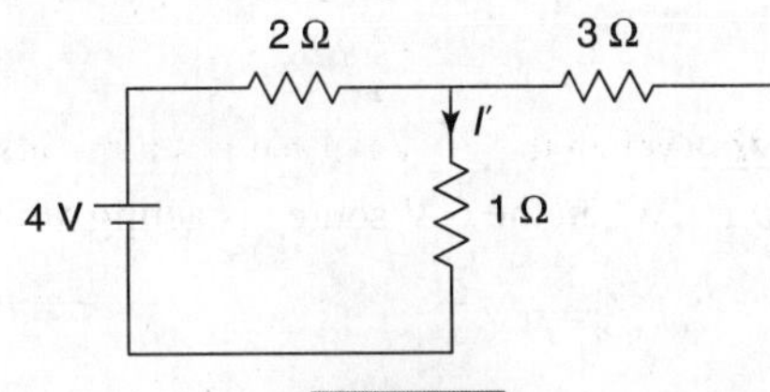


Fig. 2.72

$$I' = \frac{4}{2+1} = 1.33 \text{ A}(\downarrow)$$

***Step II*** When the 3 A source is acting alone (Fig. 2.73)

By current-division rule,

$$I'' = 3 \times \frac{2}{1+2} = 2 \text{ A } (\downarrow)$$

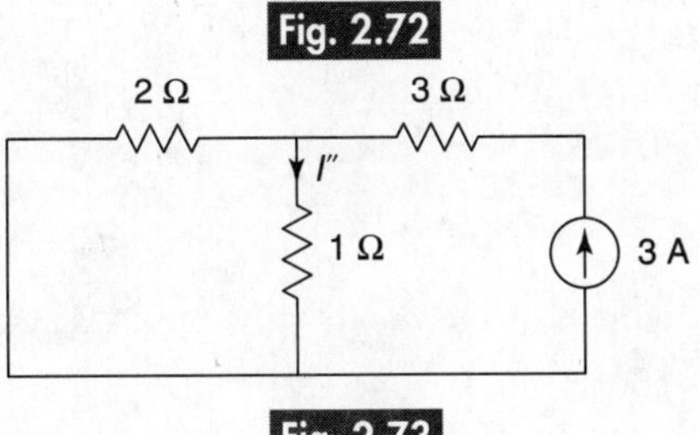


Fig. 2.73

***Step III*** When the 1 A source is acting alone (Fig. 2.74)

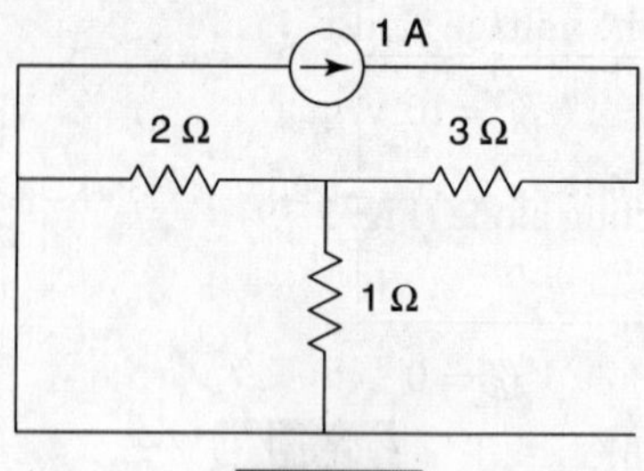


Fig. 2.74

Redrawing the network (Fig. 2.75),

By current-division rule,

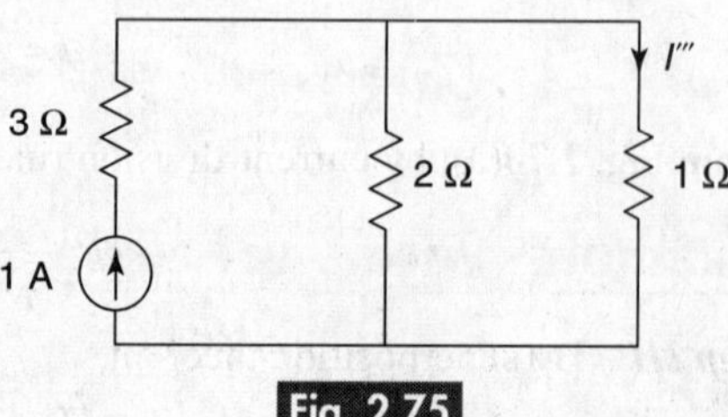


Fig. 2.75

$$I''' = 1 \times \frac{2}{2+1} = 0.66 \text{ A}(\downarrow)$$

***Step IV*** By superposition theorem,

$$I = I' + I'' + I''' = 1.33 + 2 + 0.66 = 4 \text{ A} (\downarrow)$$

## EXAMPLE 2.48

*Find the voltage $V_{AB}$ in Fig. 2.76.*

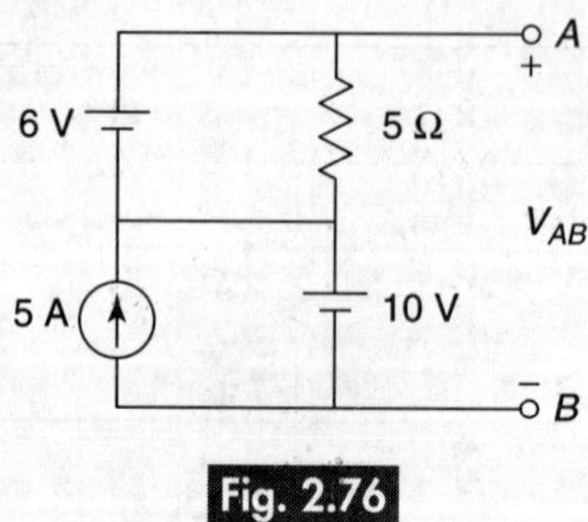


Fig. 2.76

**Solution**

***Step I*** When the 6 V source is acting alone (Fig. 2.77)

$$V'_{AB} = 6 \text{ V}$$

Fig. 2.77

***Step II*** When the 10 V source is acting alone (Fig. 2.78)

Since the resistor of 5 Ω is shorted, the voltage across it is zero.

$$V''_{AB} = 10 \text{ V}$$

***Step III*** When the 5 A source is acting alone (Fig. 2.79)

Due to short circuit in both the parts,

$$V'''_{AB} = 0$$

***Step IV*** By superposition theorem,

$$V_{AB} = V'_{AB} + V''_{AB} + V'''_{AB} = 6 + 10 + 0 = 16 \text{ V}$$

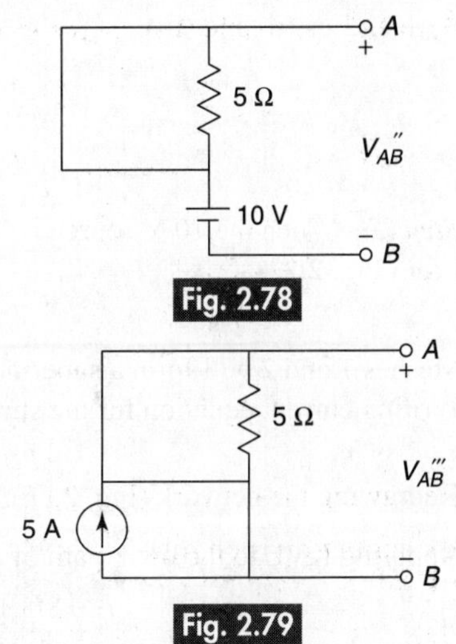


Fig. 2.78

Fig. 2.79

## Examples with Dependent Sources

**EXAMPLE 2.49**

*Find the current through the 6 Ω resistor in Fig. 2.80.*

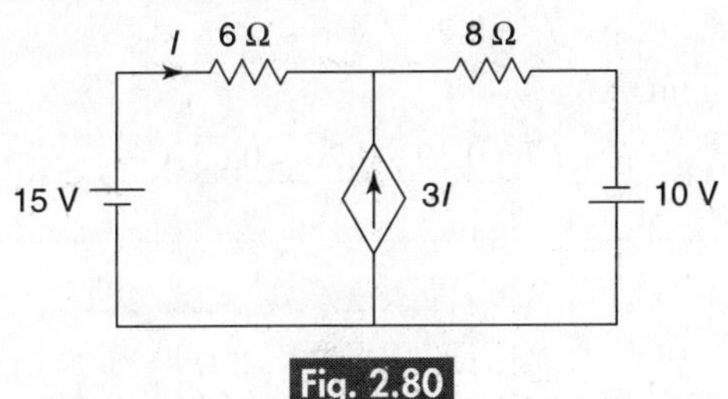


Fig. 2.80

**Solution**

***Step I*** When the 15 V source is acting alone (Fig. 2.81)

From Fig. 2.81,

$$I' = I_1 \qquad \text{...(i)}$$

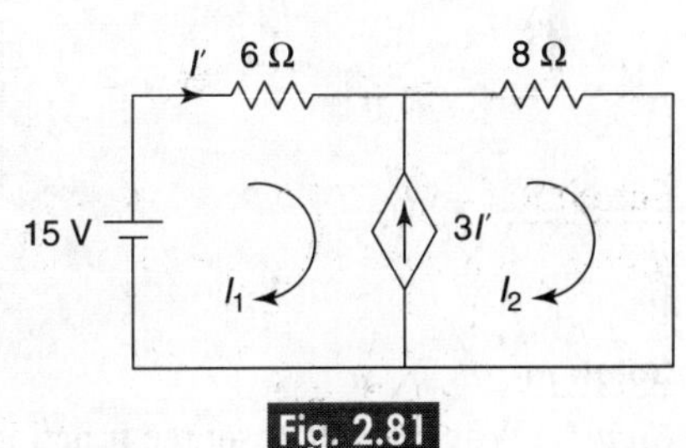


Fig. 2.81

Meshes 1 and 2 will form a supermesh.

Writing current equation for the supermesh,

$$I_2 - I_1 = 3I' = 3I_1$$

$$4I_1 - I_2 = 0 \qquad \text{...(ii)}$$

Applying KVL to the outer path of the supermesh,

$$15 - 6I_1 - 8I_2 = 0$$

$$6I_1 + 8I_2 = 15 \qquad \text{...(iii)}$$

Solving Eqs (ii) and (iii),

$$I_1 = 0.39\text{A}$$
$$I_2 = 1.57\text{A}$$
$$I' = I_1 = 0.39 \text{ A } (\rightarrow)$$

***Step II*** When the 10 V source is acting alone (Fig. 2.82)

From Fig. 2.82,

$$I'' = I_1 \quad \text{...(i)}$$

Meshes 1 and 2 will form a supermesh.

Writing current equation for the supermesh,

$$I_2 - I_1 = 3I'' = 3I_1$$
$$4I_1 - I_2 = 0 \quad \text{...(ii)}$$

Fig. 2.82

Applying KVL to the outer path of the supermesh,

$$-6I_1 - 8I_2 + 10 = 0$$
$$6I_1 + 8I_2 = 10 \quad \text{...(iii)}$$

Solving Eqs (ii) and (iii),

$$I_1 = 0.26 \text{ A}$$
$$I_2 = 1.05 \text{ A}$$
$$I'' = I_1 = 0.26 \text{ A} \quad (\rightarrow)$$

***Step III*** By superposition theorem,

$$I = I' + I'' = 0.39 + 0.26 = 0.65 \text{ A } (\rightarrow)$$

**EXAMPLE 2.50**

*Find the current $I_x$ in Fig. 2.83.*

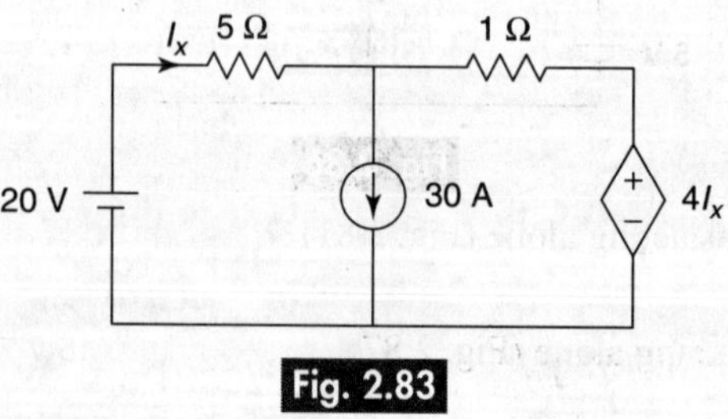


Fig. 2.83

**Solution**

***Step I*** When the 30 A source is acting alone (Fig. 2.84)

From Fig. 2.84,

$$I'_x = I_1 \quad \text{...(i)}$$

Meshes 1 and 2 will form a supermesh.

Writing current equation for the supermesh,

$$I_1 - I_2 = 30 \quad \text{...(ii)}$$

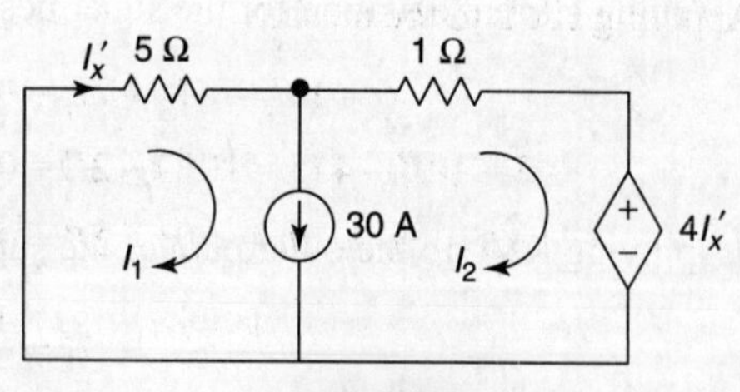


Fig. 2.84

Applying KVL to the outer path of the supermesh,

$$-5I_1 - 1I_2 - 4I_x' = 0$$
$$-5I_1 - I_2 - 4I_1 = 0$$
$$9I_1 + I_2 = 0 \qquad \text{...(iii)}$$

Solving Eqs (ii) and (iii),

$$I_1 = 3 \text{ A}$$
$$I_2 = -27 \text{ A}$$
$$I_x' = I_1 = 3 \text{ A } (\rightarrow)$$

***Step II*** When the 20 V source is acting alone (Fig. 2.85)
Applying KVL to the mesh,

$$20 - 5I_x'' - 1I_x'' - 4I_x'' = 0$$
$$I_x'' = 2 \text{ A}(\rightarrow)$$

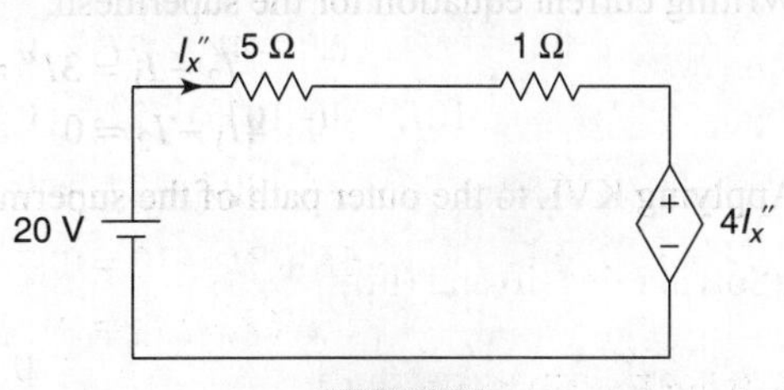


Fig. 2.85

***Step III*** By superposition theorem,

$$I_x = I_x' + I_x'' = 3 + 2 = 5 \text{ A}(\rightarrow)$$

**EXAMPLE 2.51**

*Find the current $I_1$ in Fig. 2.86.*

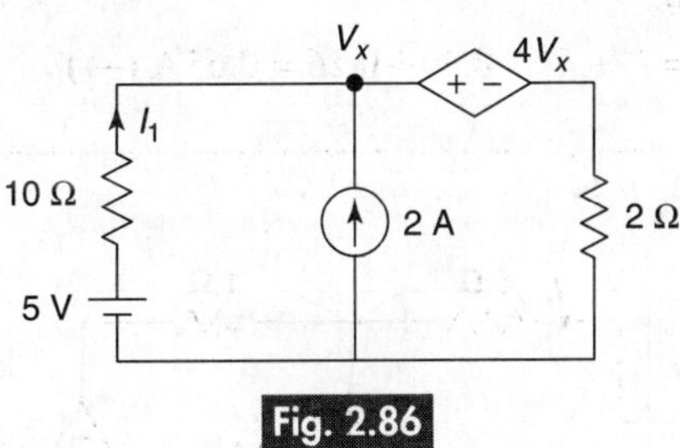


Fig. 2.86

## Solution

***Step I*** When the 5 V source is acting alone (Fig. 2.87)
From Fig. 2.87,

$$V_x = 5 - 10I_1'$$

Applying KVL to the mesh,

$$5 - 10I_1' - 4V_x - 2I_1' = 0$$
$$5 - 10I_1' - 4(5 - 10I_1') - 2I_1' = 0$$
$$5 - 10I_1' - 20 + 40I_1' - 2I_1' = 0$$
$$I_1' = \frac{15}{28} = 0.54 \text{ A}(\uparrow)$$

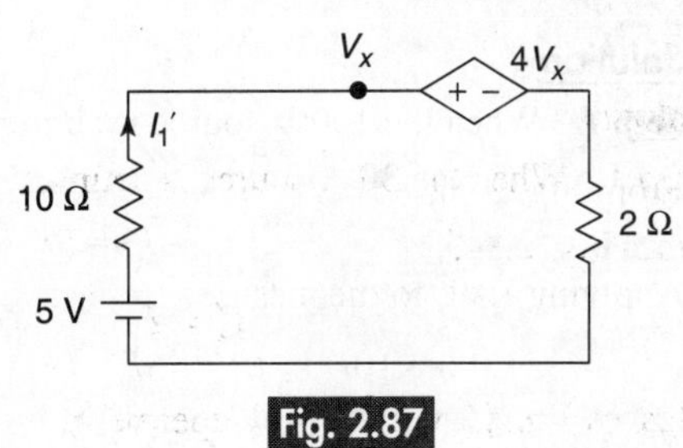


Fig. 2.87

***Step II*** When the 2 A source is acting alone (Fig. 2.88)

From Fig. 2.88,

$$V_x = -10I_1' \qquad \text{...(i)}$$

Meshes 1 and 2 will form a supermesh.

Writing current equation for the supermesh,

$$I_2 - I_1' = 2 \qquad \text{...(ii)}$$

Fig. 2.88

Applying KVL to the outer path of the supermesh,

$$-10I_1' - 4V_x - 2I_2 = 0$$

$$-10I_1' - 4(-10I_1') - 2I_2 = 0$$

$$30I_1' - 2I_2 = 0 \qquad \text{...(iii)}$$

Solving Eqs (ii) and (iii),

$$I_1 = 0.14 \text{ A } (\uparrow)$$

$$I_2 = 2.14 \text{ A}$$

***Step III*** By superposition theorem,

$$I_1 = I_1' + I_1'' = 0.54 + 0.14 = 0.68 \text{ A } (\uparrow)$$

## EXAMPLE 2.52

*Determine the current through the 10 Ω resistor in Fig. 2.89.*

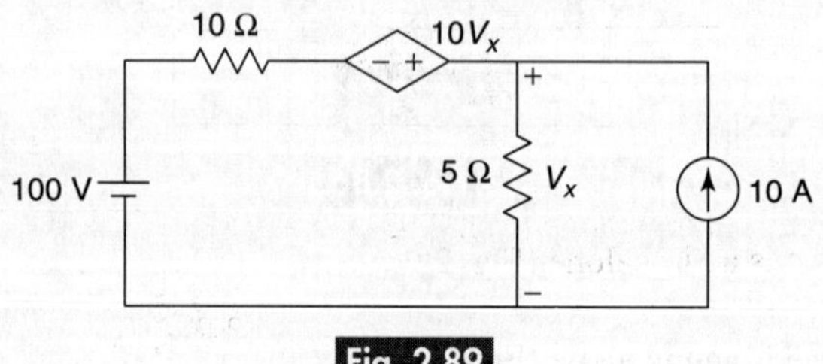


Fig. 2.89

## Solution

***Step I*** When the 100 V source is acting alone (Fig. 2.90)

From Fig. 2.90,

$$V_x = 5I'$$

Applying KVL to the mesh,

$$100 - 10I' + 10V_x - 5I' = 0$$

$$100 - 10I' + 10(5I') - 5I' = 0$$

$$I' = -2.86 \text{ A } (\rightarrow)$$

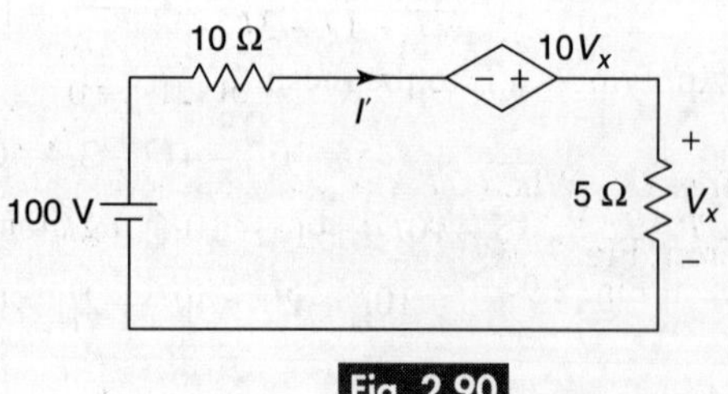


Fig. 2.90

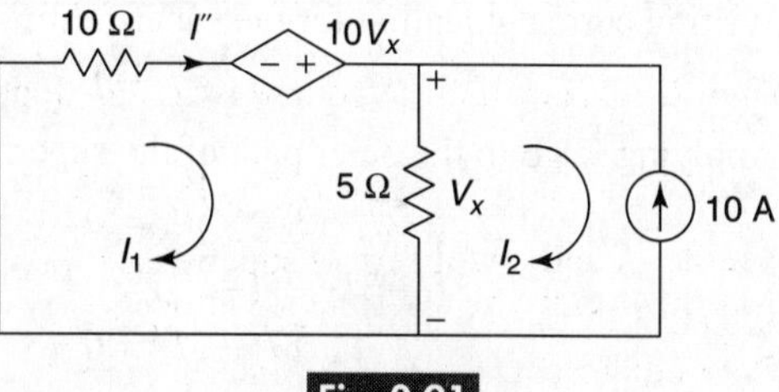


Fig. 2.91

***Step II*** When the 10 A source is acting alone (Fig. 2.91)

From Fig. 2.91,

$$V_x = 5(I_1 - I_2) \quad \text{...(i)}$$

Applying KVL to mesh 1,

$$-10I_1 + 10V_x - 5(I_1 - I_2) = 0$$

$$-10I_1 + 10\{5(I_1 - I_2)\} - 5(I_1 - I_2) = 0$$

$$35I_1 - 45I_2 = 0 \quad \text{...(ii)}$$

For mesh 2,

$$I_2 = -10 \quad \text{...(iii)}$$

Solving Eqs (ii) and (iii),

$$I_1 = -12.86 \text{ A}$$

$$I_2 = -10 \text{ A}$$

$$I'' = I_1 = -12.86 \text{ A } (\rightarrow)$$

***Step III*** By superposition theorem,

$$I = I' + I'' = -2.86 - 12.86 = -15.72 \text{ A } (\rightarrow)$$

## EXAMPLE 2.53

*Find the current I in the network of Fig. 2.92.*

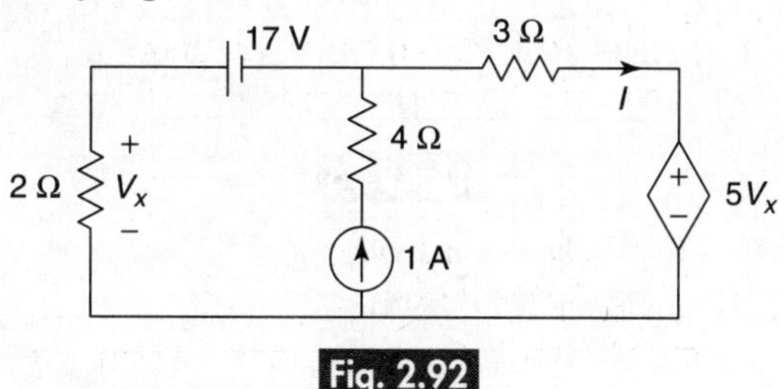


Fig. 2.92

**Solution**

***Step I*** When the 17 V source is acting alone (Fig. 2.93)

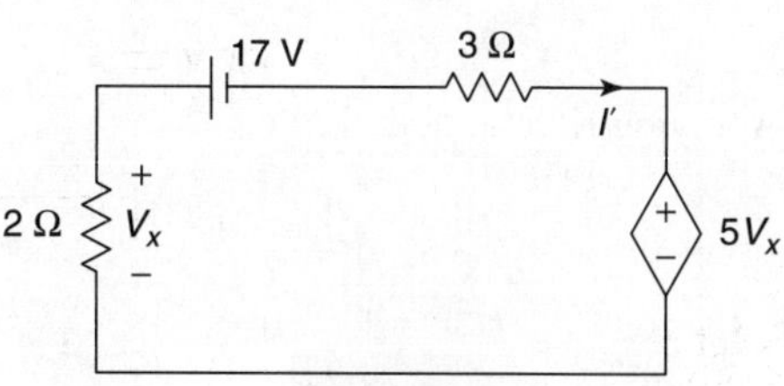


Fig. 2.93

From Fig. 2.93,

$$V_x = -2I'$$

Applying KVL to the mesh,

$$-2I' - 17 - 3I' - 5V_x = 0$$

$$-2I' - 17 - 3I' - 5(-2I') = 0$$

$$I' = 3.4 \text{ A } (\rightarrow)$$

***Step II*** When the 1 A source is acting alone (Fig. 2.94)

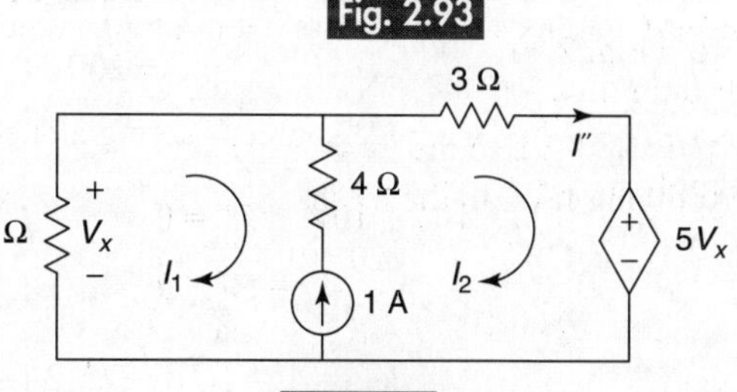


Fig. 2.94

From Fig. 2.94,

$$V_x = -2I_1 \quad \text{...(i)}$$

Meshes 1 and 2 will form a supermesh.

Writing current equation for the supermesh,

$$I_2 - I_1 = 1 \quad \text{...(ii)}$$

Applying KVL to the outer path of the supermesh,

$$-2I_1 - 3I_2 - 5V_x = 0$$

$$-2I_1 - 3I_2 - 5(-2I_1) = 0$$

$$8I_1 - 3I_2 = 0 \quad \text{...(iii)}$$

Solving Eqs (ii) and (iii),

$$I_1 = 0.6 \text{ A}$$

$$I_2 = 1.6 \text{ A}$$

$$I'' = I_2 = 1.6 \text{ A} (\rightarrow)$$

***Step III*** By superposition theorem,

$$I = I' + I'' = 3.4 + 1.6 = 5 \text{ A} (\rightarrow)$$

## EXAMPLE 2.54

*Find the voltage $V_1$ in Fig. 2.95.*

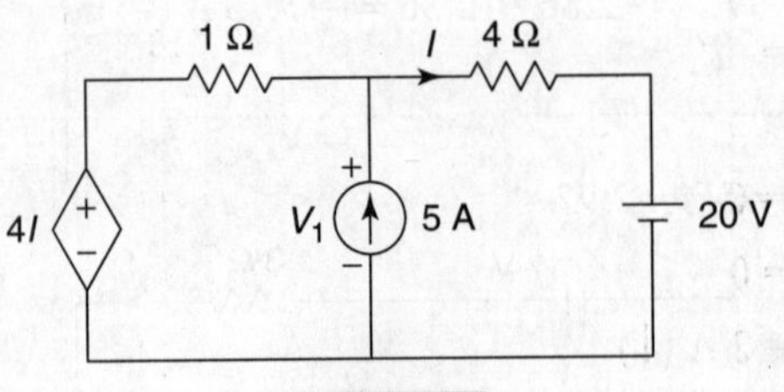


Fig. 2.95

**Solution**

***Step I*** When the 5 A source is acting alone (Fig. 2.96)

From Fig. 2.96,

$$I = \frac{V_1'}{4}$$

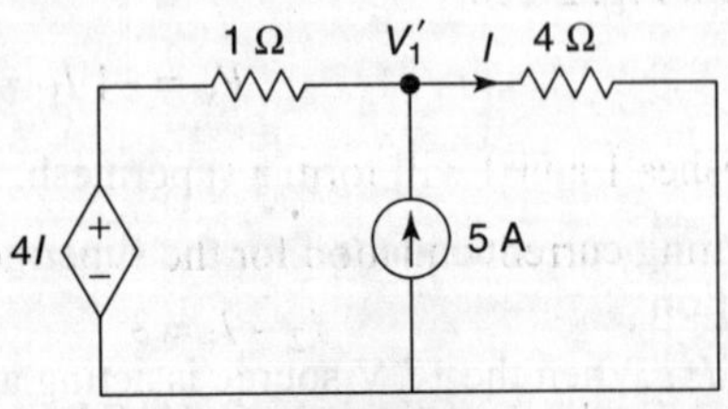


Fig. 2.96

Applying KCL at node 1,

$$\frac{V_1' - 4I}{1} + \frac{V_1'}{4} = 5$$

$$V_1' - 4\left(\frac{V_1'}{4}\right) + \frac{V_1'}{4} = 5$$

$$V_1' = 20 \text{ V}$$

***Step II*** When the 20 V source is acting alone (Fig. 2.97)

Applying KVL to the mesh,

$$4I - I - 4I - 20 = 0$$

$$I = -20 \text{ A}$$

$$V_1'' = 4I - 1(I) = 3I = 3(-20) = -60 \text{ V}$$

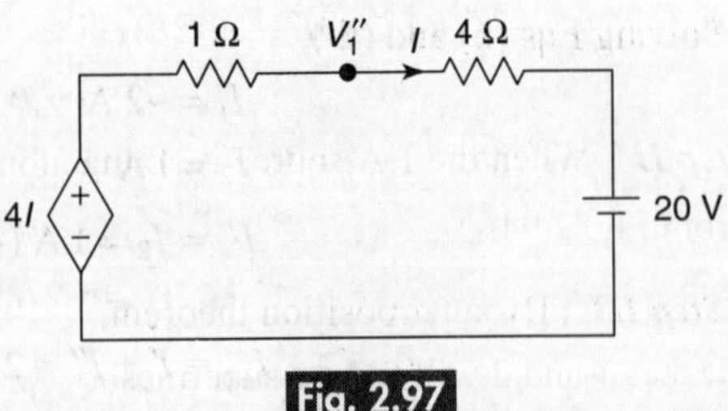


Fig. 2.97

***Step III*** By superposition theorem,

$$V_1 = V_1' + V_1'' = 20 - 60 = -40 \text{ V}$$

**EXAMPLE 2.55**

*Find the current in the 6 Ω resistor in Fig. 2.98.*

Fig. 2.98

**Solution**

***Step I*** When the 18 V source is acting alone (Fig. 2.99)

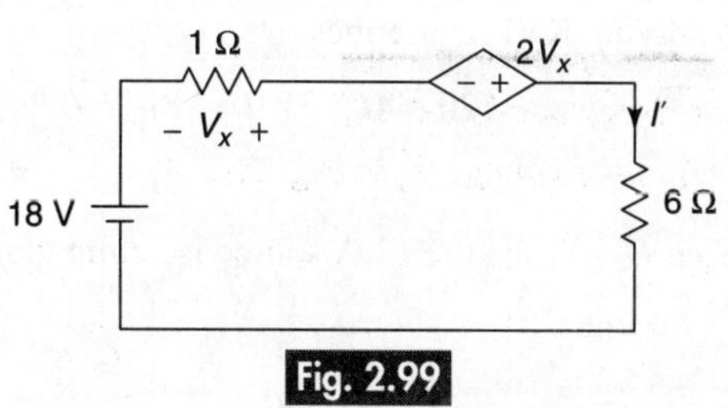

Fig. 2.99

From Fig. 2.99,

$$V_x = -I'$$

Applying KVL to the mesh,

$$18 - I' + 2V_x - 6I' = 0$$

$$18 - I' - 2I' - 6I' = 0$$

$$I' = 2 \text{ A} (\downarrow)$$

***Step II*** When the 3 A source is acting alone (Fig. 2.100)

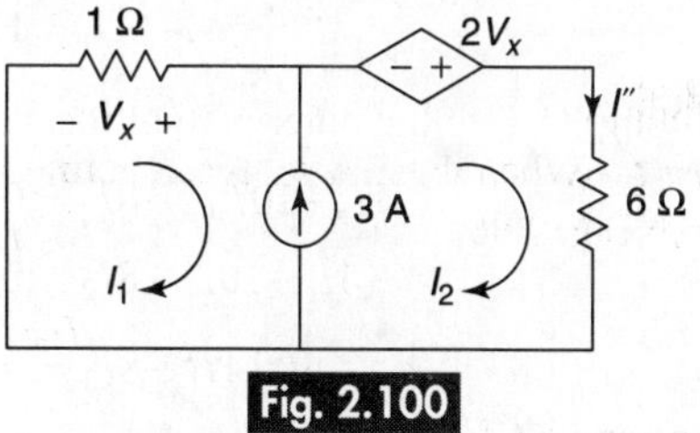

Fig. 2.100

From Fig. 2.100,

$$V_x = -1\, I_1 = -I_1 \qquad \text{...(i)}$$

Meshes 1 and 2 will form a supermesh.

Writing current equation for the supermesh,

$$I_2 - I_1 = 3 \qquad \text{...(ii)}$$

Applying KVL to the outerpath of the supermesh,

$$-1I_1 + 2V_x - 6I_2 = 0$$

$$-I_1 + 2(-I_1) - 6I_2 = 0$$

$$3I_1 + 6I_2 = 0 \qquad \text{...(iii)}$$

Solving Eqs (ii) and (iii),

$$I_1 = -2 \text{ A}$$

$$I_2 = 1 \text{ A}$$

$$I'' = I_2 = 1 \text{ A} (\downarrow)$$

***Step III*** By superposition theorem,

$$I_{6\,\Omega} = I' + I'' = 2 + 1 = 3 \text{ A} (\downarrow)$$

**EXAMPLE 2.56**

*Find the current $I_y$ in Fig. 2.101.*

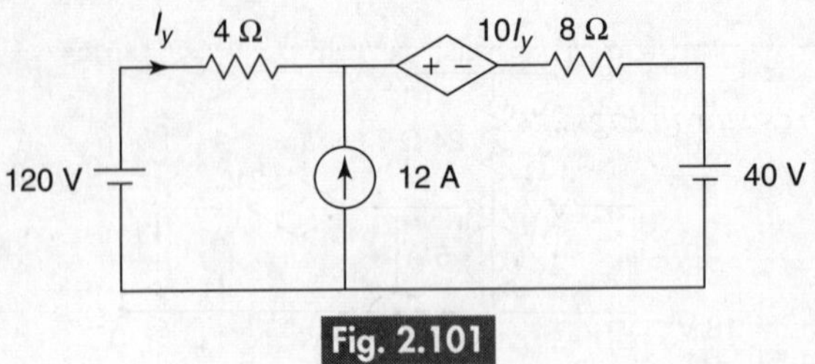


Fig. 2.101

## Solution

***Step I*** When the 120 V source is acting alone (Fig. 2.102)

Applying KVL to the mesh,

$$120 - 4I_y' - 10I_y' - 8I_y' = 0$$

$$I_y' = 5.45 \text{ A } (\rightarrow)$$

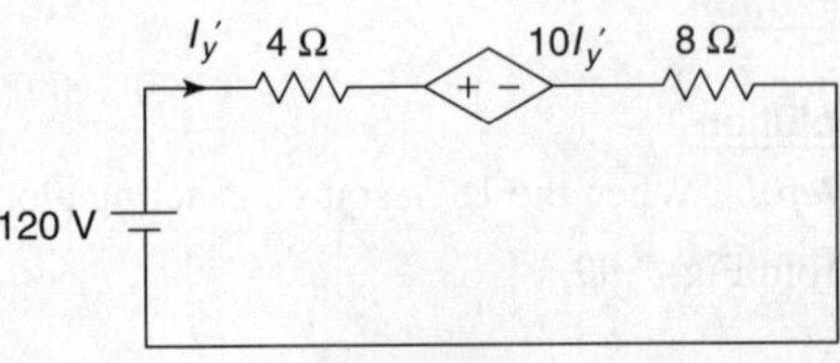


Fig. 2.102

***Step II*** When the 12 A source is acting alone (Fig. 2.103)

From Fig. 2.103,

$$I_y'' = I_1 \quad \text{...(i)}$$

Meshes 1 and 2 will form a supermesh.

Writing current equation for the supermesh,

$$I_2 - I_1 = 12 \quad \text{...(ii)}$$

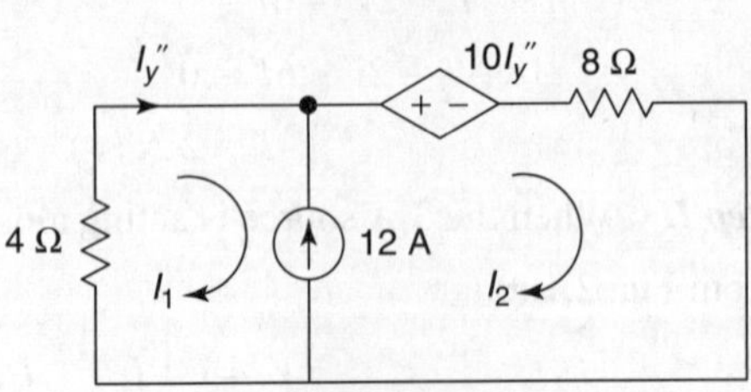


Fig. 2.103

Applying KVL to the outer path of the supermesh,

$$-4I_1 - 10I_y'' - 8I_2 = 0$$

$$-4I_1 - 10I_1 - 8I_2 = 0$$

$$14I_1 + 8I_2 = 0 \quad \text{...(iii)}$$

Solving Eqs (ii) and (iii),

$$I_1 = -4.36 \text{ A}$$

$$I_2 = 7.64 \text{ A}$$

$$Iy'' = I_1 = -4.36 \text{ A } (\rightarrow)$$

***Step III*** When the 40 V source is acting alone (Fig. 2.104)

Applying KVL to the mesh,

$$-4I_y''' - 10I_y''' - 8I_y''' - 40 = 0$$

$$I_y''' = -\frac{40}{22} = -1.82 \text{ A } (\rightarrow)$$

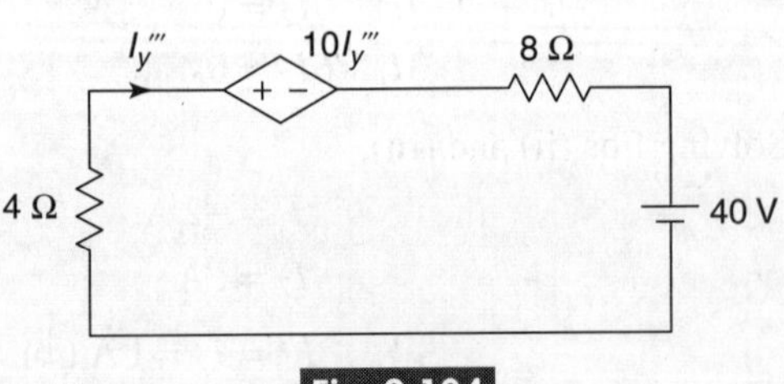


Fig. 2.104

***Step IV*** By superposition theorem,

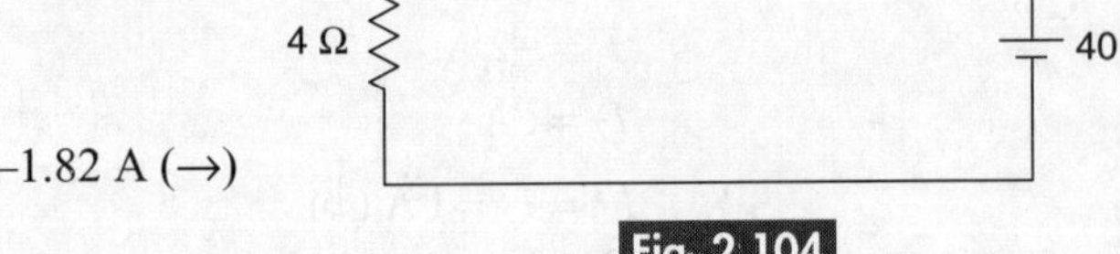

$$I_y = I_y' + I_y'' + I_y''' = 5.45 - 4.36 - 1.82 = -0.73 \text{ A } (\rightarrow)$$

## EXAMPLE 2.57

*Find the voltage $V_x$ in Fig. 2.105.*

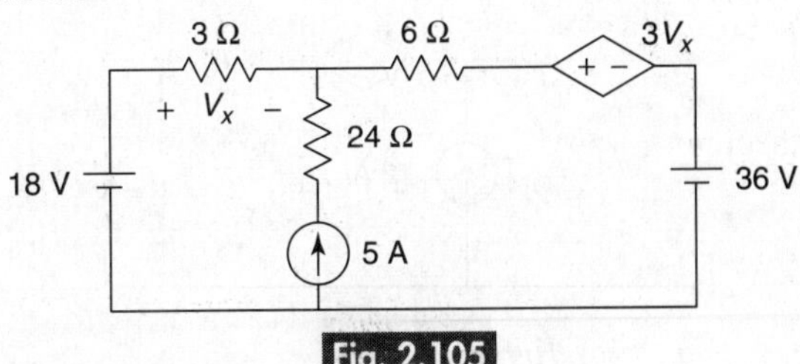


Fig. 2.105

### Solution

***Step I*** When the 18 V source is acting alone (Fig. 2.106)

From Fig. 2.106,

$$V_x' = 3I$$

Applying KVL to the mesh,

$$18 - 3I - 6I - 3V_x' = 0$$
$$18 - 3I - 6I - 3(3I) = 0$$
$$I = 1\text{ A}$$
$$V_x' = 3\text{ V}$$

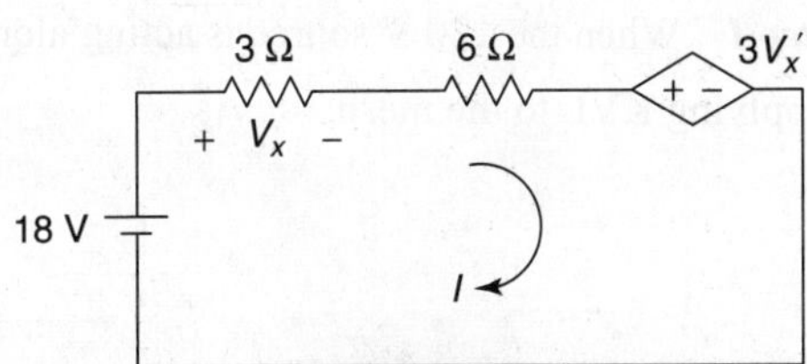


Fig. 2.106

***Step II*** When the 5 A source is acting alone (Fig. 2.107)

From Fig. 2.107,

$$V_x'' = -3I_1 \qquad \text{...(i)}$$

Meshes 1 and 2 will form a supermesh.

Writing current equation for the supermesh,

$$I_2 - I_1 = 5 \qquad \text{...(ii)}$$

Applying KVL to the outer path of the supermesh,

$$-3I_1 - 6I_2 - 3V_x'' = 0$$
$$-3I_1 - 6I_2 - 3(3I_1) = 0$$
$$12I_1 + 6I_2 = 0 \qquad \text{...(iii)}$$

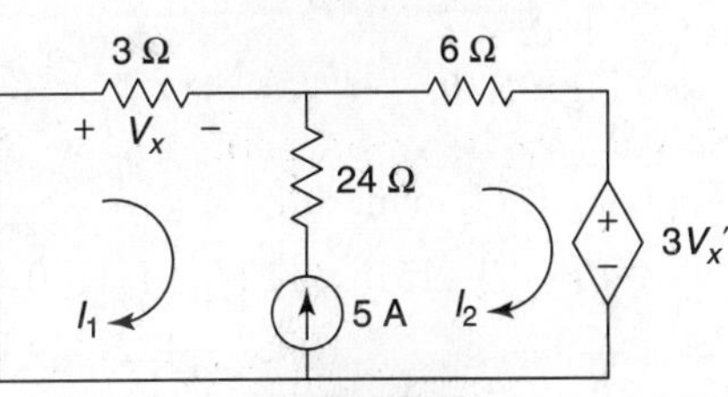


Fig. 2.107

Solving Eqs (ii) and (iii),

$$I_1 = -1.67\text{A}$$
$$I_2 = 3.33\text{ A}$$
$$V_x'' = 3I_1 = 3(-1.67) = -5\text{ V}$$

***Step III*** When the 36 V source is acting alone (Fig. 2.108)

From Fig. 2.108,

$$V_x''' = -3I$$

Applying KVL to the mesh,

$$36 + 3V_x''' - 6I - 3I = 0$$

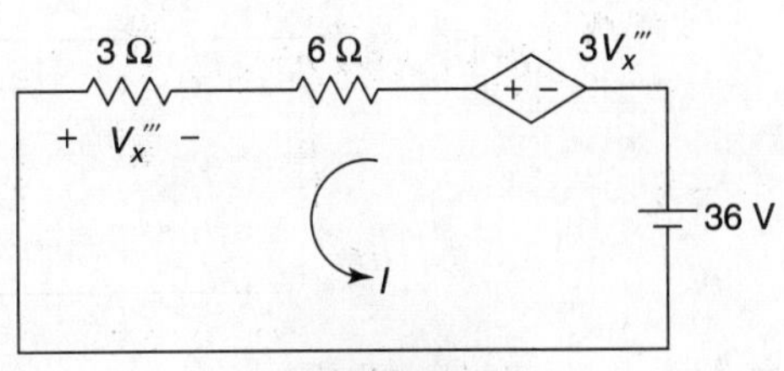


Fig. 2.108

$$36+3V_x'''-6\left(\frac{-V_x'''}{3}\right)-3\left(\frac{-V_x'''}{3}\right)=0$$

$$36+3V_x'''+2V_x'''+V_x'''=0$$

$$V_x'''=-6\text{ V}$$

***Step IV*** By superposition theorem,

$$V_x = V_x' + V_x'' + V_x''' = 3-5-6 = -8\text{ V}$$

**EXAMPLE 2.58**

*Find the voltage V in the network of Fig. 2.109.*

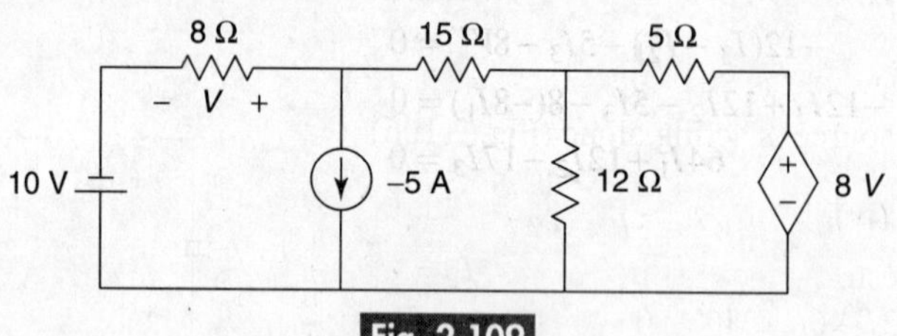


Fig. 2.109

## Solution

***Step I*** When the 10 V source is acting alone (Fig. 2.110)

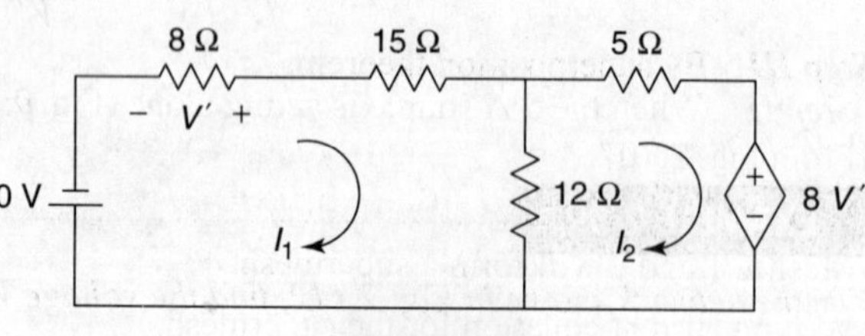


Fig. 2.110

From Fig. 2.110,

$$V' = -8I_1 \qquad \text{...(i)}$$

Applying KVL to mesh 1,

$$-10-8I_1-15\,I_1-12\,(I_1-I_2)=0$$

$$35I_1-12I_2=-10 \qquad \text{...(ii)}$$

Applying KVL to mesh 2,

$$-12(I_2-I_1)-5I_2-8V'=0$$

$$-12I_2+12I_1-5I_2-8(-8I_1)=0$$

$$76I_1-17I_2=0 \qquad \text{...(iii)}$$

Solving Eqs (ii) and (iii),

$$I_1 = 0.54\text{ A}$$

$$I_2 = 2.4\text{ A}$$

$$V' = -8I_1 = -8(0.54) = -4.32\text{ V}$$

***Step II*** When the –5 A source is acting alone (Fig. 2.111)

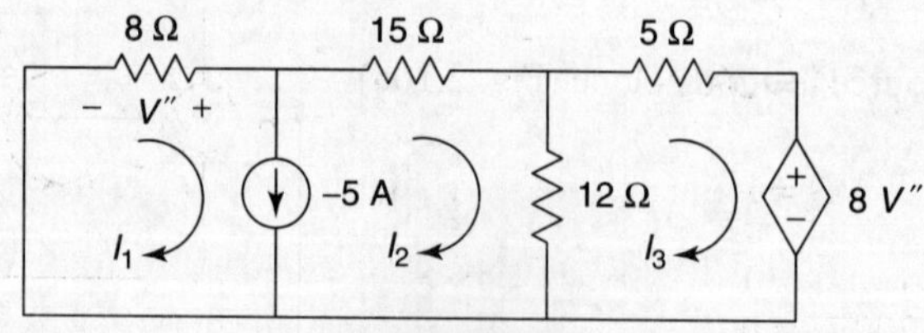


Fig. 2.111

From Fig. 2.111,

$$V'' = -8I_1 \quad \text{...(i)}$$

Meshes 1 and 2 will form a supermesh.

Writing current equation for the supermesh,

$$I_1 - I_2 = -5 \quad \text{...(ii)}$$

Applying KVL to the outer path of the supermesh,

$$-8I_1 - 15I_2 - 12(I_2 - I_3) = 0$$

$$-8I_1 - 27I_2 + 12I_3 = 0 \quad \text{...(iii)}$$

Applying KVL to mesh 3,

$$-12(I_3 - I_2) - 5I_3 - 8V'' = 0$$

$$-12I_3 + 12I_2 - 5I_3 - 8(-8I_1) = 0$$

$$64I_1 + 12I_2 - 17I_3 = 0 \quad \text{...(iv)}$$

Solving Eqs (ii), (iii) and (iv),

$$I_1 = 4.97 \text{ A}$$

$$I_2 = 9.97 \text{ A}$$

$$I_3 = 25.74 \text{ A}$$

$$V'' = -8I_1 = -8(-4.97) = -39.76 \text{ V}$$

***Step III*** By superposition theorem,

$$V = V' + V'' = -4.32 - 39.76 = -44.08 \text{ V}$$

**EXAMPLE 2.59**

*For the network shown in Fig. 2.112, find the voltage $V_0$.*

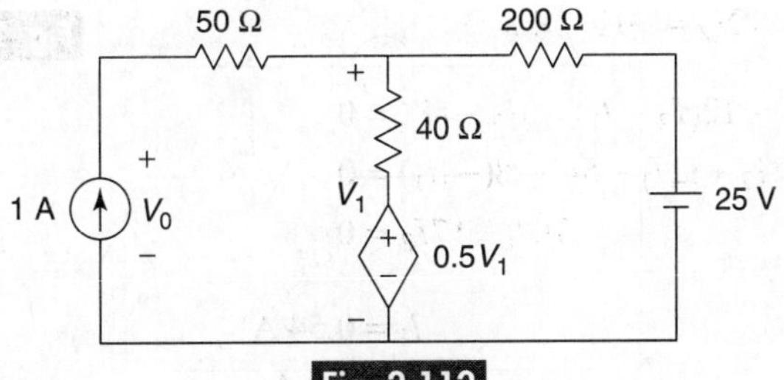


Fig. 2.112

## Solution

***Step I*** When the 1 A source is acting alone (Fig. 2.113)

From Fig. 2.113,

$$V_1 = 200\, I_2 \quad \text{...(i)}$$

For mesh 1,

$$I_1 = 1 \quad \text{...(ii)}$$

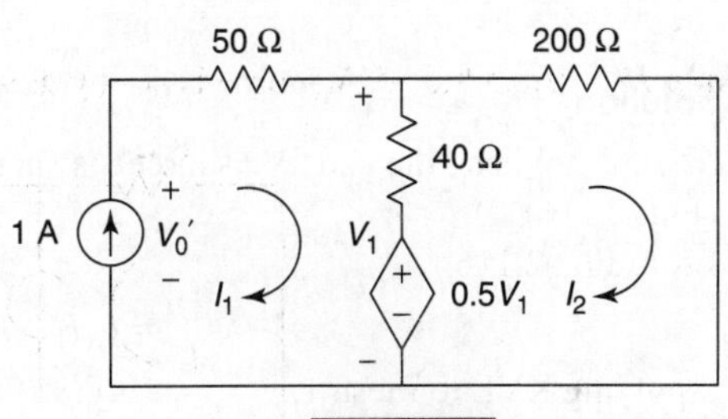


Fig. 2.113

Applying KVL to mesh 2,

$$0.5V_1 - 40(I_2 - I_1) - 200\, I_2 = 0$$

$$0.5(200I_2) - 40I_2 + 40I_1 - 200I_2 = 0$$

$$40I_1 - 140 I_2 = 0 \qquad \text{...(iii)}$$

Solving Eqs (ii) and (iii),

$$I_1 = 1 \text{ A}$$

$$I_2 = 0.29 \text{ A}$$

$$V_0' - 50\, I_1 - 200 I_2 = 0$$

$$V_0' - 50(1) - 200(0.29) = 0$$

$$V_0' = 108 \text{ V}$$

***Step II*** When the 25 V source is acting alone (Fig. 2.114)

From Fig. 2.114,

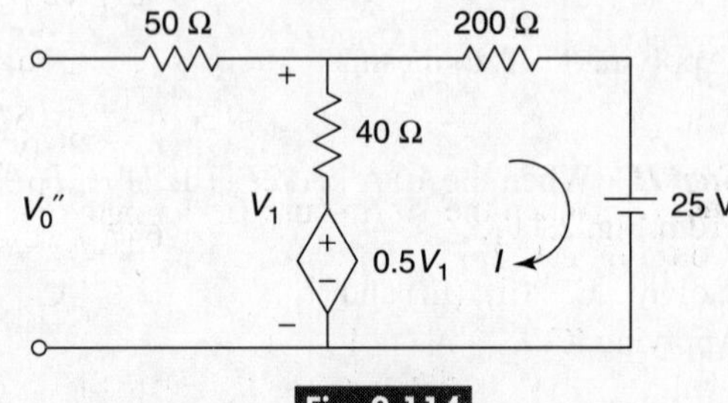


Fig. 2.114

$$V_1 - 200\, I - 25 = 0$$

$$V_1 = 200I + 25 \qquad \text{...(i)}$$

Applying KVL to mesh 1,

$$0.5V_1 - 40\, I - 200\, I - 25 = 0$$

$$0.5(200\, I + 25) - 40\, I - 200\, I - 25 = 0$$

$$I = -0.09 \text{ A}$$

$$V_0'' = V_1 = 200\, I + 25 = 200(-0.09) + 25 = 7 \text{ V}$$

***Step III*** By superposition theorem,

$$V_0 = V_0' + V_0'' = 108 + 7 = 115 \text{ V}$$

## EXAMPLE 2.60

*For the network shown in Fig. 2.115, find the voltage $V_x$.*

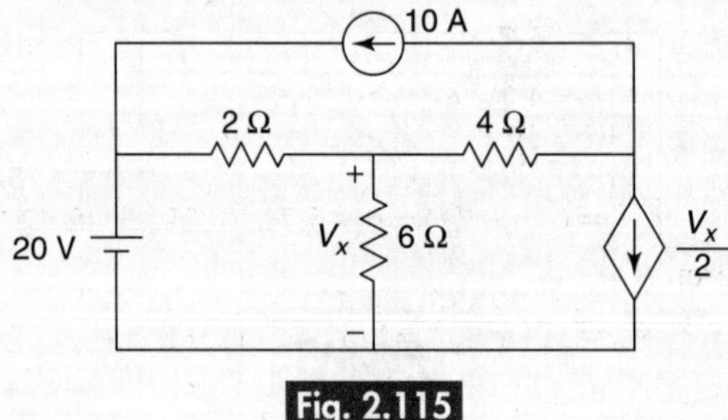


Fig. 2.115

### Solution

***Step I*** When the 20 V source is acting alone (Fig. 2.116)

From Fig. 2.116,

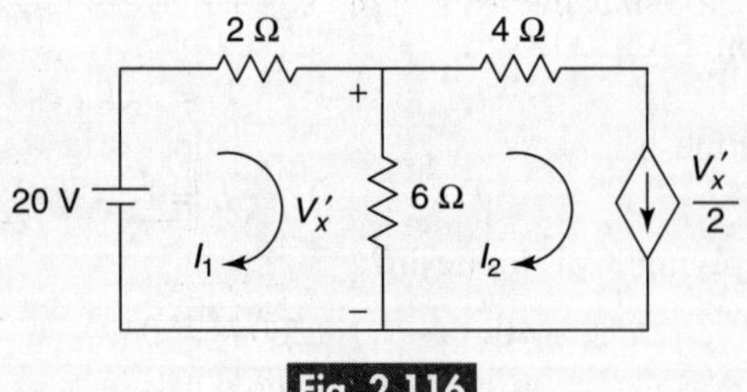


Fig. 2.116

$$V_x' = 6(I_1 - I_2) \qquad \text{...(i)}$$

Applying KVL to mesh 1,

$$20 - 2I_1 - 6(I_1 - I_2) = 0$$

$$8I_1 - 6I_2 = 20 \qquad \text{...(ii)}$$

For mesh 2,

$$I_2 = \frac{V_x'}{2} = \frac{6(I_1 - I_2)}{2} = 3I_1 - 3I_2$$

$$3I_1 - 4I_2 = 0 \qquad \text{...(iii)}$$

Solving Eqs (ii) and (iii),

$$I_1 = 5.71 \text{ A}$$

$$I_2 = 4.29 \text{ A}$$

$$V_x' = 6(I_1 - I_2) = 6(5.71 - 4.29) = 8.52 \text{ V}$$

***Step II*** When the 10 A source is acting alone (Fig. 2.117)
From Fig. 2.117,

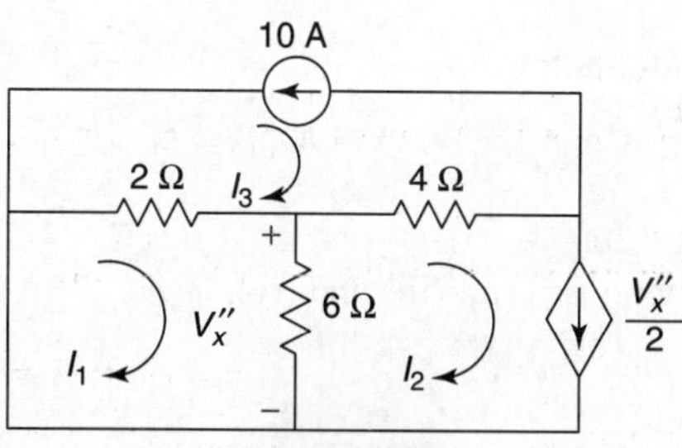

Fig. 2.117

$$V_x'' = 6(I_1 - I_2) \qquad \text{...(i)}$$

Applying KVL to mesh 1,

$$-2(I_1 - I_3) - 6(I_1 - I_2) = 0$$

$$8I_1 - 6I_2 - 2I_3 = 0 \qquad \text{...(ii)}$$

For mesh 2,

$$I_2 = \frac{V_x''}{2} = \frac{6(I_1 - I_2)}{2} = 3I_1 - 3I_2$$

$$3I_1 - 4I_2 = 0 \qquad \text{...(iii)}$$

For mesh 3,

$$I_3 = -10 \qquad \text{...(iv)}$$

Solving Eqs (ii), (iii) and (iv),

$$I_1 = -5.71 \text{ A}$$

$$I_2 = -4.29 \text{ A}$$

$$I_3 = -10 \text{ A}$$

$$V_x'' = 6(I_1 - I_2) = 6(-5.71 + 4.29) = -8.52 \text{ V}$$

***Step III*** By superposition theorem,

$$V_x = V_x' + V_x'' = 8.52 - 8.52 = 0$$

## EXAMPLE 2.61

*Calculate the current I in the network shown in Fig. 2.118.*

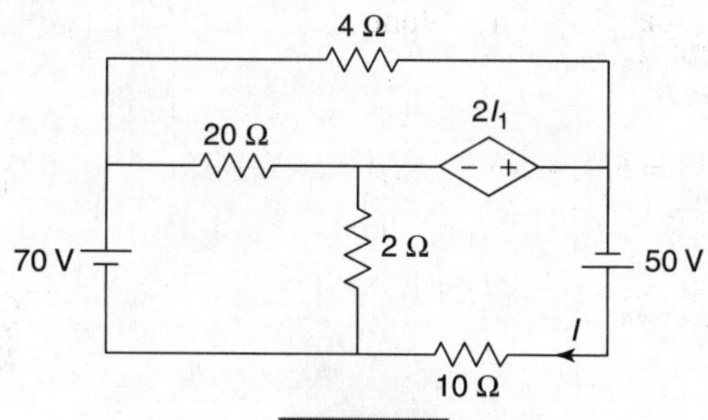

Fig. 2.118

**Solution**

***Step I*** When the 70 V source is acting alone (Fig. 2.119)

From Fig. 2.119,

$$I' = I_3 \quad \text{...(i)}$$

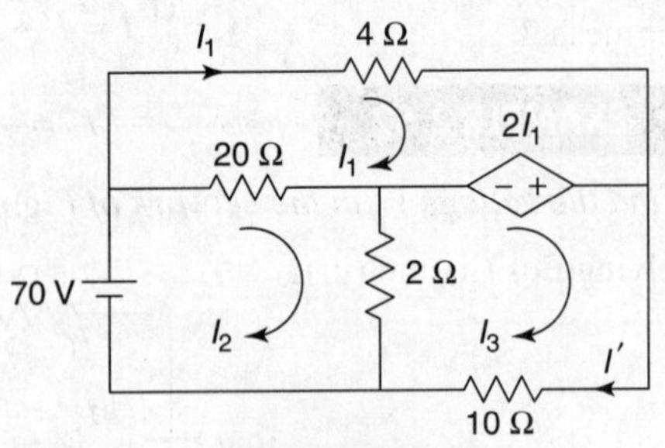


Fig. 2.119

Applying KVL to mesh 1,

$$-4I_1 - 2I_1 - 20(I_1 - I_2) = 0$$
$$26I_1 - 20I_2 = 0 \quad \text{...(ii)}$$

Applying KVL to mesh 2,

$$70 - 20(I_2 - I_1) - 2(I_2 - I_3) = 0$$
$$-20I_1 + 22I_2 - 2I_3 = 70 \quad \text{...(iii)}$$

Applying KVL to mesh 3,

$$-2(I_3 - I_2) + 2I_1 - 10I_3 = 0$$
$$2I_1 + 2I_2 - 12I_3 = 0 \quad \text{...(iv)}$$

Solving Eqs (ii), (iii) and (iv),

$$I_1 = 8.94 \text{ A}$$
$$I_2 = 11.62 \text{ A}$$
$$I_3 = 3.43 \text{ A}$$
$$I' = I_3 = 3.43 \text{ A} (\leftarrow)$$

***Step II*** When the 50 V source is acting alone (Fig. 2.120)

From Fig. 2.120,

$$I'' = I_3 \quad \text{...(i)}$$

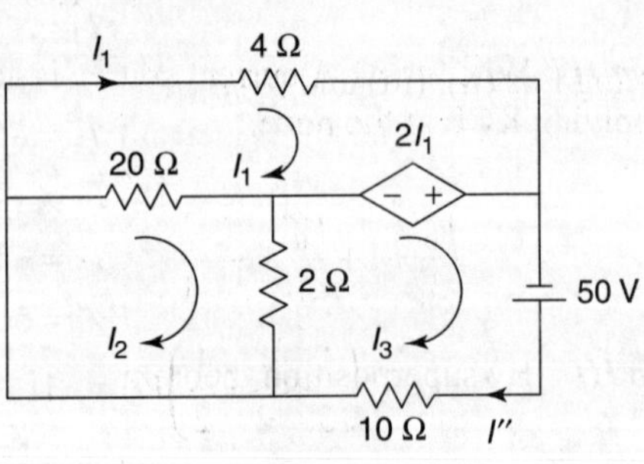


Fig. 2.120

Applying KVL to mesh 1,

$$-4I_1 - 2I_1 - 20(I_1 - I_2) = 0$$
$$26I_1 - 20I_2 = 0 \quad \text{...(ii)}$$

Applying KVL to mesh 2,

$$-20(I_2 - I_1) - 2(I_2 - I_3) = 0$$
$$-20I_1 + 22I_2 - 2I_3 = 0 \quad \text{...(iii)}$$

Applying KVL to mesh 3,

$$-2(I_3 - I_2) + 2I_1 + 50 - 10I_3 = 0$$
$$2I_1 + 2I_2 - 12I_3 = -50 \quad \text{...(iv)}$$

Solving Eqs (ii), (iii), and (iv),

$$I_1 = 1.06 \text{ A}$$
$$I_2 = 1.38 \text{ A}$$
$$I_3 = 4.57 \text{ A}$$
$$I'' = I_3 = 4.57 \text{ A} (\leftarrow)$$

***Step III*** By superposition theorem,

$$I = I' + I'' = 3.43 + 4.57 = 8 \text{ A } (\leftarrow)$$

## EXAMPLE 2.62

*Find the voltage $V_0$ in the network of Fig. 2.121.*

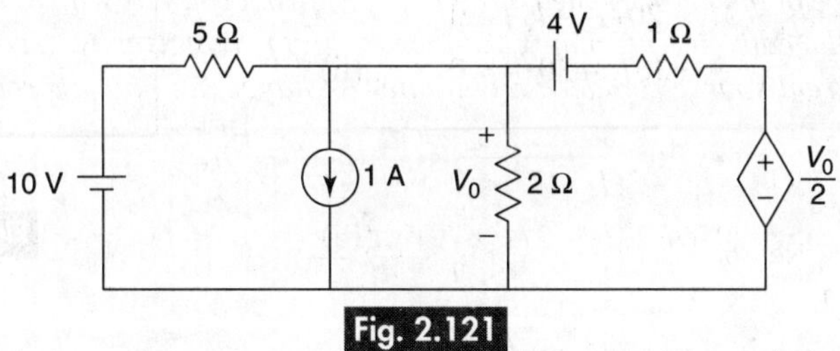


Fig. 2.121

**Solution**

***Step I*** When the 10 V source is acting alone (Fig. 2.122)

Applying KCL at the node,

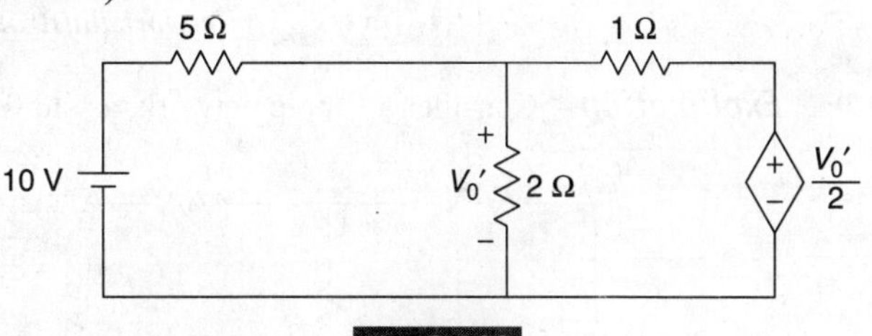


Fig. 2.122

$$\frac{V_0' - 10}{5} + \frac{V_0'}{2} + \frac{V_0' - \frac{V_0'}{2}}{1} = 0$$

$$\left(\frac{1}{5} + \frac{1}{2} + \frac{1}{2}\right) V_0' = 2$$

$$V_0' = 1.67 \text{ V}$$

***Step II*** When the 1 A current source is acting alone (Fig. 2.123)

Applying KCL at the node,

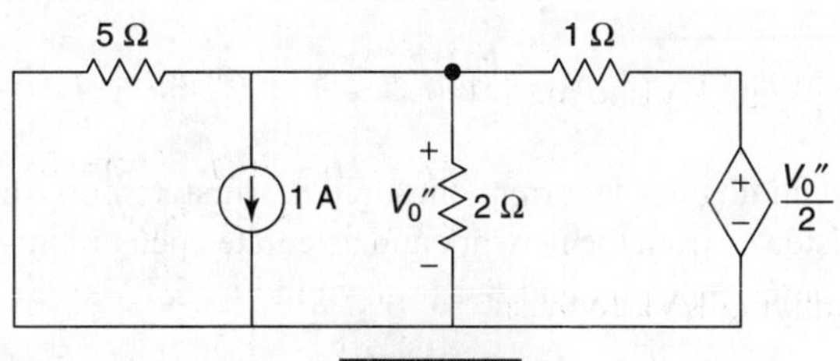


Fig. 2.123

$$\frac{V_0''}{5} + 1 + \frac{V_0''}{2} + \frac{V_0'' - \frac{V_0''}{2}}{1}$$

$$\left(\frac{1}{5} + \frac{1}{2} + \frac{1}{2}\right) V_0'' = -1$$

$$V_0'' = -0.83 \text{ V}$$

***Step III*** When the 4 V source is acting alone (Fig. 2.124)

Applying KCL at the node,

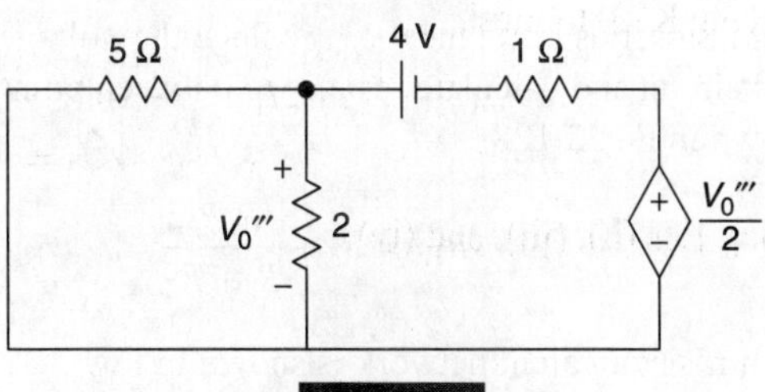


Fig. 2.124

$$\frac{V_0'''}{5} + \frac{V_0'''}{2} + \frac{V_0''' - 4 - \frac{V_0'''}{2}}{1} = 0$$

$$\left(\frac{1}{5} + \frac{1}{2} + \frac{1}{2}\right) V_0''' = 4$$

$$V_0''' = 3.33 \text{ V}$$

***Step IV*** By superposition theorem,

$$V_0 = V_0' + V_0'' + V_0''' = 1.67 - 0.83 + 3.33 = 4.17 \text{ V}$$

## 2.6 THEVENIN'S THEOREM

LO 2.4

Analyse the networks using Thevenin's theorem

It states that '*any two terminals of a network can be replaced by an equivalent voltage source and an equivalent series resistance. The voltage source is the voltage across the two terminals with load, if any, removed. The series resistance is the resistance of the network measured between two terminals with load removed and constant voltage source being replaced by its internal resistance (or if it is not given with zero resistance, i.e., short circuit) and constant current source replaced by infinite resistance, i.e., open circuit.*'

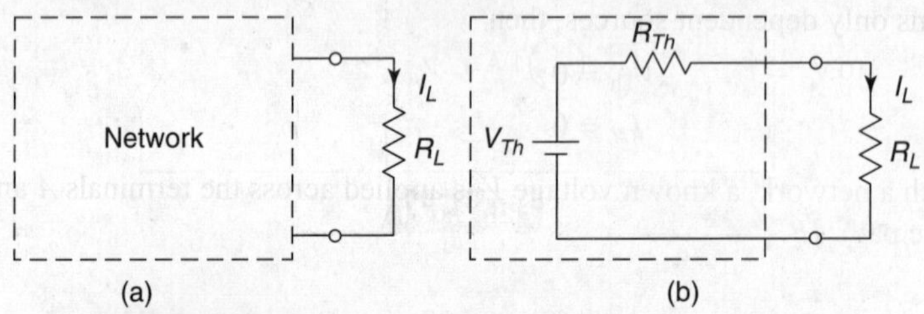


**Fig. 2.125** *Network illustrating Thevenin's theorem*

➤ ***Explanation*** Consider a simple network, as shown in Fig. 2.126.

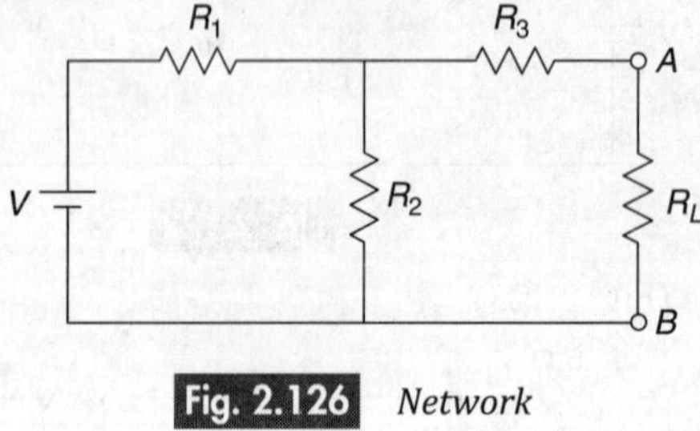


**Fig. 2.126** *Network*

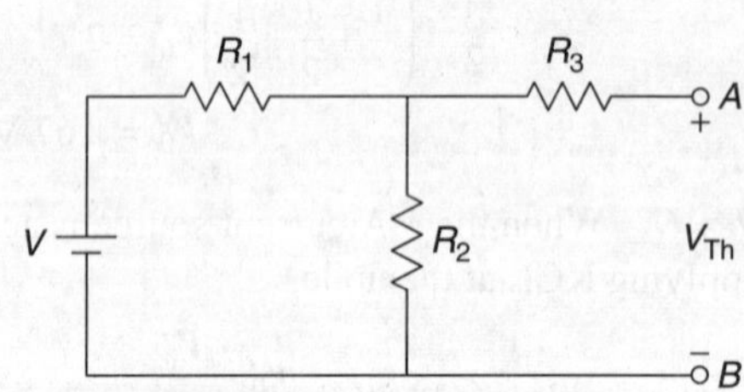


**Fig. 2.127** *Calculation of $V_{Th}$*

For finding load current through $R_L$, first remove the load resistor $R_L$ from the network and calculate open circuit-voltage $V_{Th}$ across points $A$ and $B$, as shown in Fig. 2.127.

$$V_{Th} = \frac{R_2}{R_1 + R_2} V$$

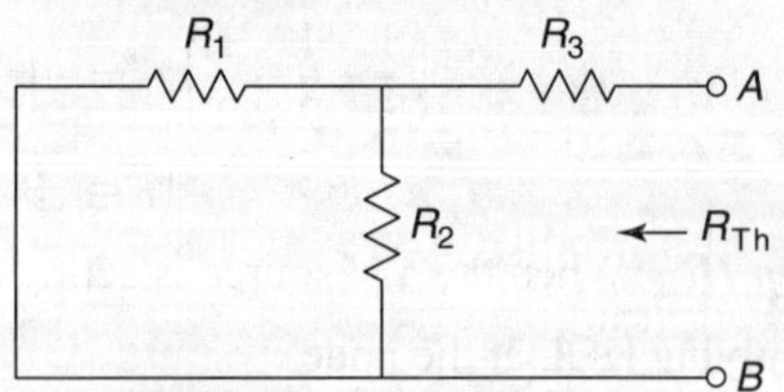


**Fig. 2.128** *Calculation of $R_{Th}$*

For finding series resistance $R_{Th}$, replace the voltage source by a short circuit and calculate resistance between points $A$ and $B$, as shown in Fig. 2.128.

$$R_{Th} = R_3 + \frac{R_1 R_2}{R_1 + R_2}$$

Thevenin's equivalent network is shown in Fig. 2.129.

$$I_L = \frac{V_{Th}}{R_{Th} + R_L}$$

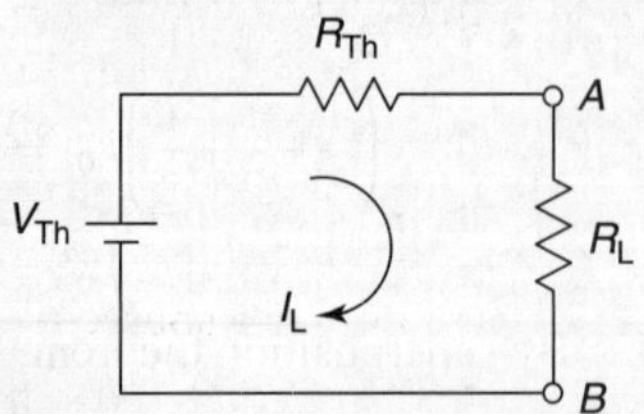


**Fig. 2.129** *Thevenin's equivalent network*

If the network contains both independent and dependent sources, Thevenin's resistance $R_{Th}$ is calculated as,

$$R_{Th} = \frac{V_{Th}}{I_N}$$

where $I_N$ is the short-circuit current, which would flow in a short circuit placed across the terminals $A$ and $B$. Dependent sources are active at all times. They have zero values only when the control voltage or current is zero. $R_{Th}$ may be negative in some cases, which indicates negative resistance region of the device, i.e., as voltage increases, current decreases in the region and vice-versa.

If the network contains only dependent sources, then

$$V_{Th} = 0$$

$$I_N = 0$$

For finding $R_{Th}$ in such a network, a known voltage $V$ is applied across the terminals $A$ and $B$ and current $I$ is calculated through the path $AB$.

$$R_{Th} = \frac{V}{I}$$

or a known current source $I$ is connected across the terminals $A$ and $B$ and voltage $V$ is calculated across the terminals $A$ and $B$.

$$R_{Th} = \frac{V}{I}$$

Thevenin's equivalent network for such a network is shown in Fig. 2.130.

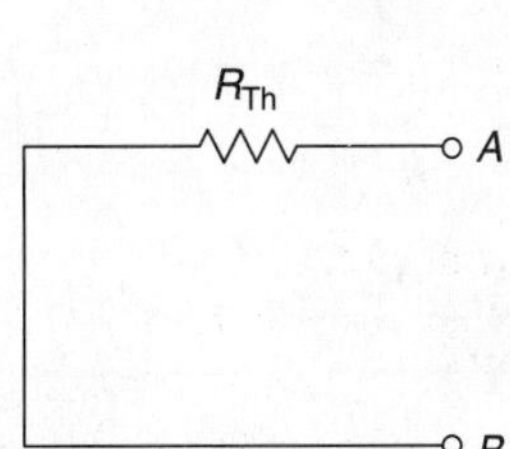


Fig. 2.130 *Thevenin's equivalent network*

### ➤ *Steps to be followed in Thevenin's Theorem*

1. Remove the load resistance $R_L$.
2. Find the open-circuit voltage $V_{Th}$ across points $A$ and $B$.
3. Find the resistance $R_{Th}$ as seen from points $A$ and $B$.
4. Replace the network by a voltage source $V_{Th}$ in series with resistance $R_{Th}$.
5. Find the current through $R_L$ using Ohm's law.

$$I_L = \frac{V_{Th}}{R_{Th} + R_L}$$

**EXAMPLE 2.63** ●○○

*Determine the current through the 24 Ω resistor in Fig. 2.131.*

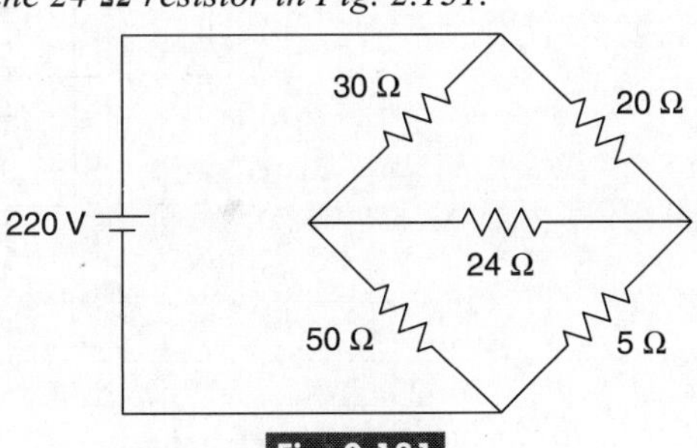


Fig. 2.131

**Solution**

***Step I*** Calculation of $V_{Th}$ (Fig. 2.132)

$$I_1 = \frac{220}{30+50} = 2.75 \text{ A}$$

$$I_2 = \frac{220}{20+5} = 8.8 \text{ A}$$

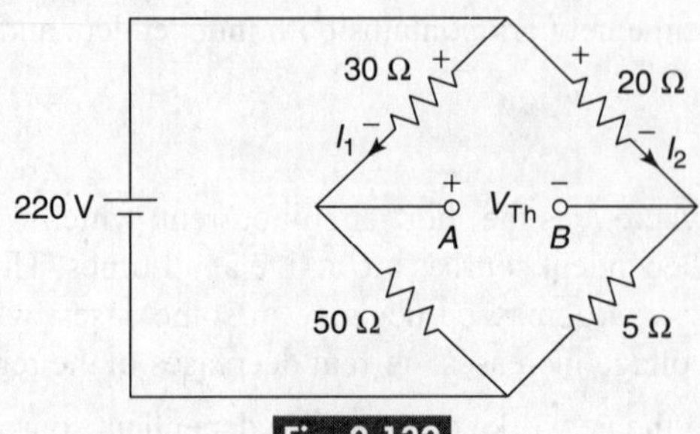

Fig. 2.132

Writing the $V_{Th}$ equation,

$$V_{Th} + 30I_1 - 20I_2 = 0$$

$$V_{Th} = 20I_2 - 30I_1 = 20(8.8) - 30(2.75) = 93.5 \text{ V}$$

***Step II*** Calculation of $R_{Th}$ (Fig. 2.133)

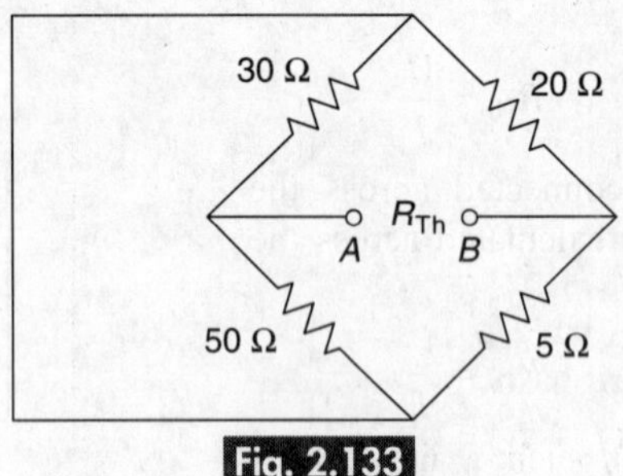

Fig. 2.133

Redrawing the circuit (Fig. 2.134),

$$R_{Th} = (30 \parallel 50) + (20 \parallel 5) = 22.75 \ \Omega$$

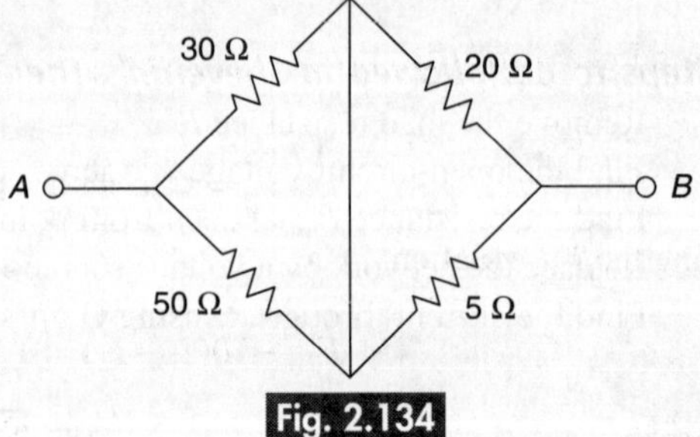

Fig. 2.134

***Step III*** Calculation of $I_L$ (Fig. 2.135)

$$I_L = \frac{93.5}{22.75+24} = 2 \text{ A}$$

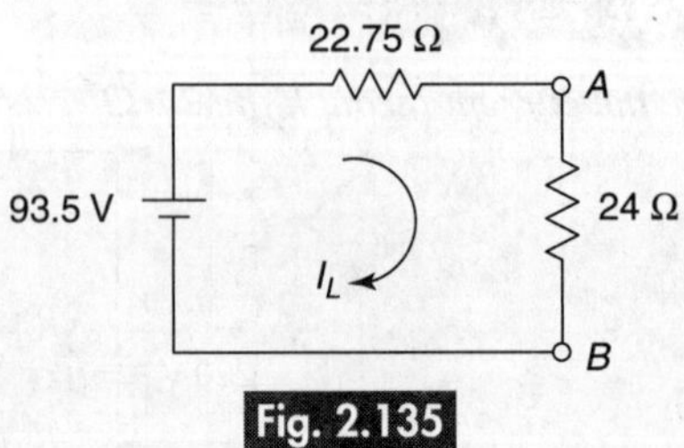

Fig. 2.135

**EXAMPLE 2.64**

*Find the current through the 20 Ω resistor in Fig. 2.136.*

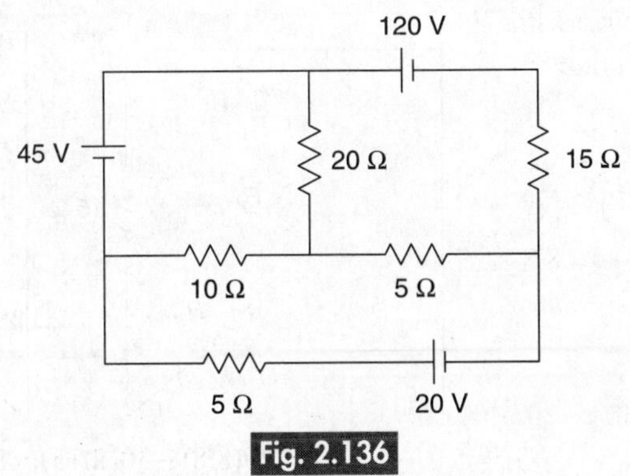

Fig. 2.136

**Solution**

***Step I*** Calculation of $V_{Th}$ (Fig. 2.137)

Applying KVL to mesh 1,

$$45 - 120 - 15I_1 - 5(I_1 - I_2) - 10(I_1 - I_2) = 0$$
$$30I_1 - 15I_2 = -75 \qquad \text{...(i)}$$

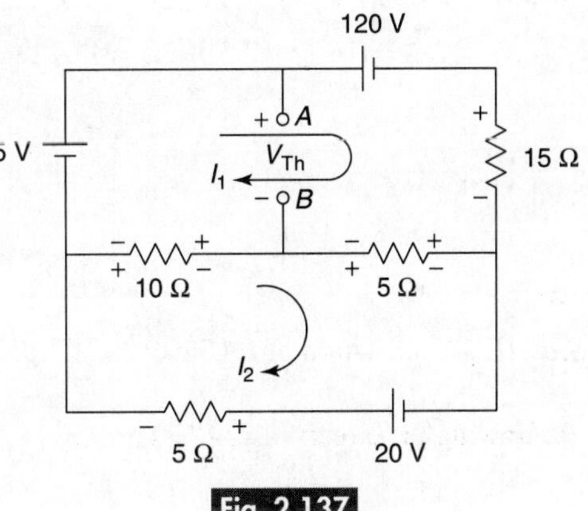

Fig. 2.137

Applying KVL to mesh 2,

$$20 - 5I_2 - 10(I_2 - I_1) - 5(I_2 - I_1) = 0$$
$$-15I_1 + 20I_2 = 20 \qquad \text{...(ii)}$$

Solving Eqs (i) and (ii),

$$I_1 = -3.2 \text{ A}$$
$$I_2 = -1.4 \text{ A}$$

Writing the $V_{Th}$ equation,

$$45 - V_{Th} - 10(I_1 - I_2) = 0$$
$$V_{Th} = 45 - 10(I_1 - I_2) = 45 - 10[-3.2 - (-1.4)] = 63 \text{ V}$$

***Step II*** Calculation of $R_{Th}$ (Fig. 2.138)

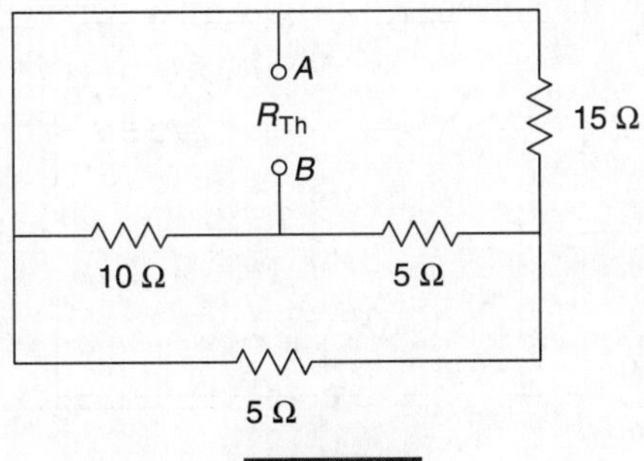

Fig. 2.138

Converting the delta formed by resistors of 10 Ω, 5 Ω and 5 Ω into an equivalent star network (Fig. 2.139),

$$R_1 = \frac{10 \times 5}{20} = 2.5\ \Omega$$

$$R_2 = \frac{10 \times 5}{20} = 2.5\ \Omega$$

$$R_3 = \frac{5 \times 5}{20} = 1.25\ \Omega$$

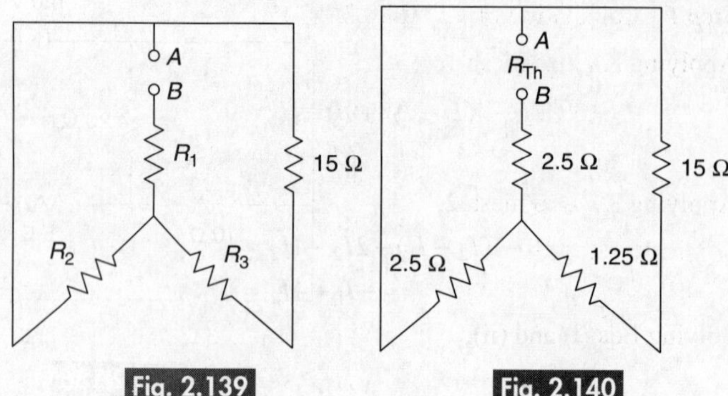


Fig. 2.139

Fig. 2.140

Simplifying the network (Fig. 2.140 and Fig. 2.141),

$$R_{Th} = (16.25 \,||\, 2.5) + 2.5 = 4.67\ \Omega$$

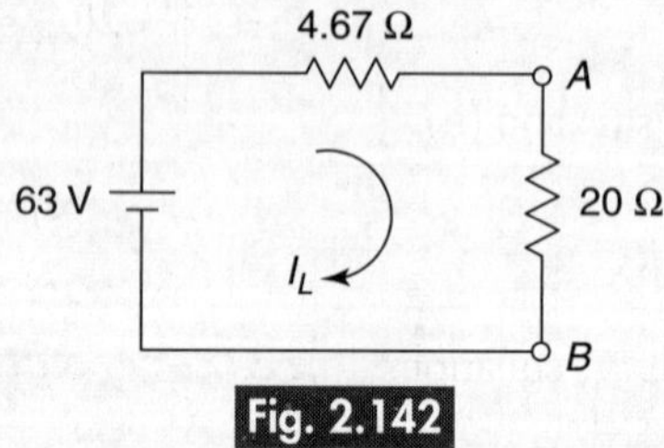


Fig. 2.141

***Step III*** Calculation of $I_L$ (Fig. 2.142)

$$I_L = \frac{63}{4.67 + 20} = 2.55\ \text{A}$$

4.67 Ω

A

63 V

20 Ω

$I_L$

B

Fig. 2.142

**EXAMPLE 2.65**

*Find the current through the 10 Ω resister in Fig. 2.143.*

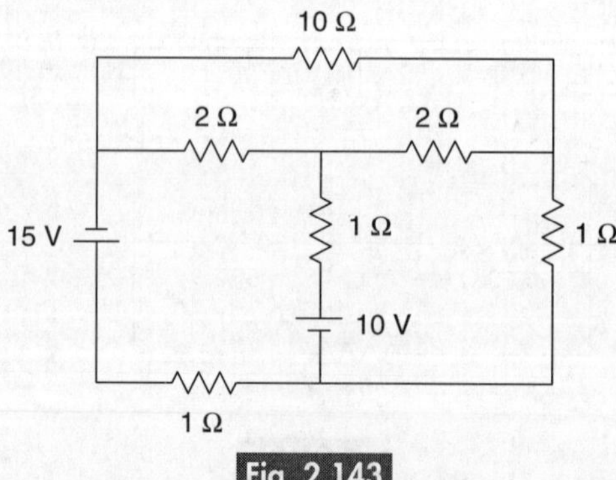


Fig. 2.143

## Solution

***Step I*** Calculation of $V_{Th}$ (Fig. 2.144)

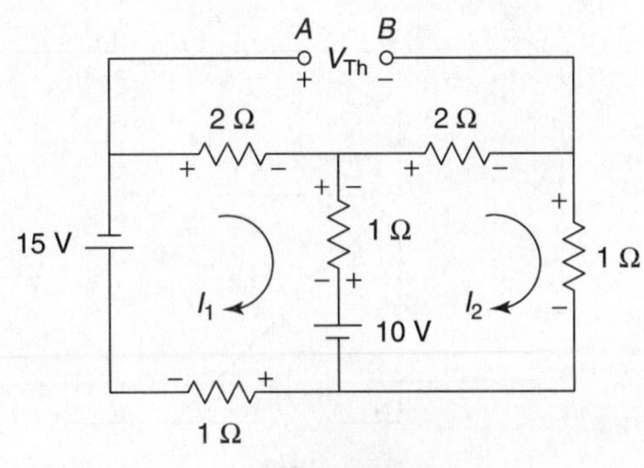

Fig. 2.144

Applying KVL to mesh 1,

$$-15-2I_1-1(I_1-I_2)-10-1I_1=0$$
$$4I_1-I_2=-25 \quad \text{...(i)}$$

Applying KVL to mesh 2,

$$10-1(I_2-I_1)-2I_2-1I_2=0$$
$$-I_1+4I_2=10 \quad \text{...(ii)}$$

Solving Eqs (i) and (ii),

$$I_1=-6\text{ A}$$
$$I_2=1\text{ A}$$

Writing the $V_{Th}$ equation,

$$-V_{Th}+2I_2+2I_1=0$$
$$V_{Th}=2I_1+2I_2=2(-6)+2(1)=-10\text{ V}$$
$$=10\text{ V (the terminal } B \text{ is positive w.r.t. } A)$$

***Step II*** Calculation of $R_{Th}$ (Fig. 2.145)

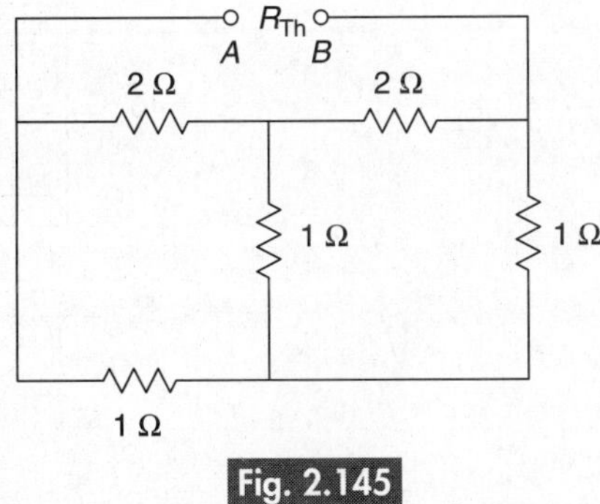

Fig. 2.145

Converting the star network formed by resistors of 2 Ω, 2 Ω and 1 Ω into an equivalent delta network (Fig. 2.146),

$$R_1=2+2+\frac{2\times 2}{1}=8\ \Omega$$
$$R_2=2+1+\frac{2\times 1}{2}=4\ \Omega$$
$$R_3=2+1+\frac{2\times 1}{2}=4\ \Omega$$

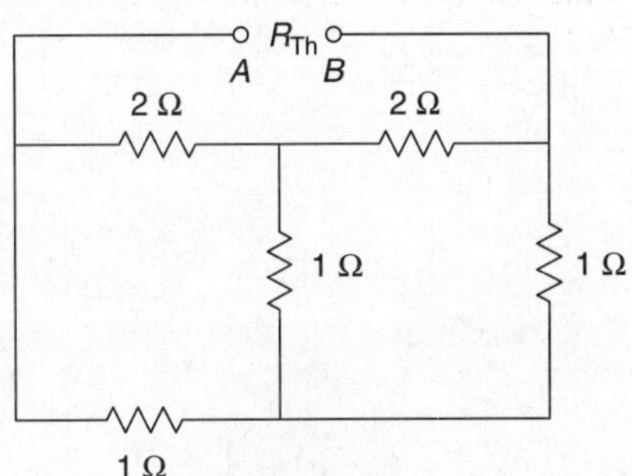

Fig. 2.146

Simplifying the network (Fig. 2.147),

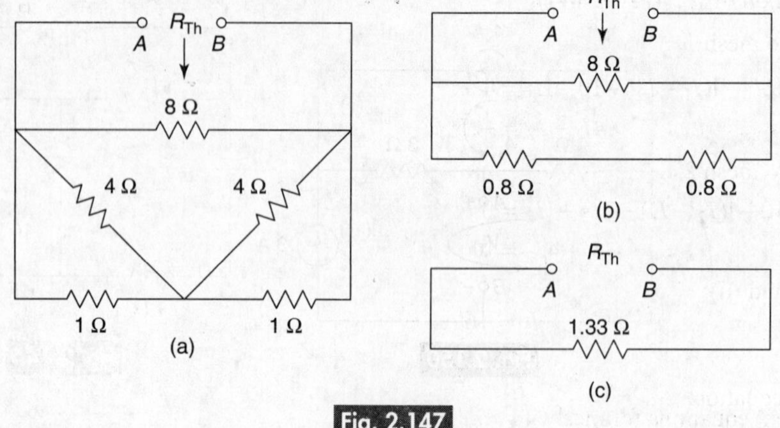


Fig. 2.147

$$R_{Th} = 1.33\ \Omega$$

***Step III*** Calculation of $I_L$ (Fig. 2.148)

$$I_L = \frac{10}{1.33+10} = 0.88\text{ A }(\uparrow)$$

Fig. 2.148

## EXAMPLE 2.66

*Find the current through the 1 Ω resistor in Fig. 2.149.*

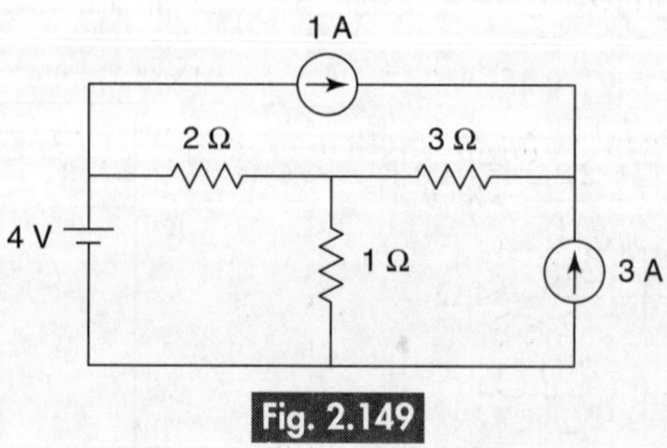


Fig. 2.149

**Solution**

***Step I*** Calculation of $V_{Th}$ (Fig. 2.150)

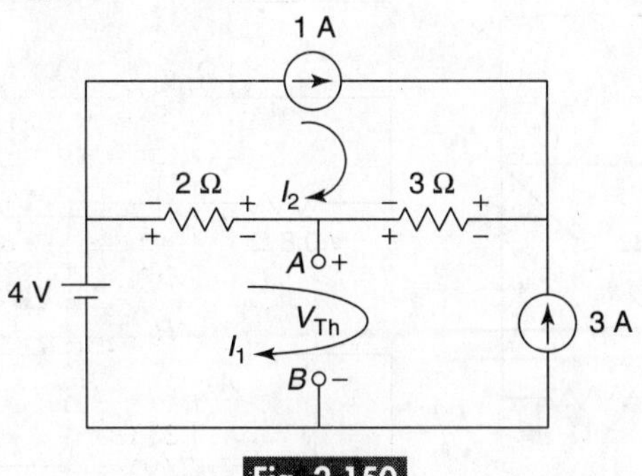


Fig. 2.150

Writing the current equations for meshes 1 and 2,

$$I_1 = -3$$

$$I_2 = 1$$

Writing the $V_{Th}$ equation,

$$4 - 2(I_1 - I_2) - V_{Th} = 0$$

$$V_{Th} = 4 - 2(I_1 - I_2) = 4 - 2(-4) = 12\text{ V}$$

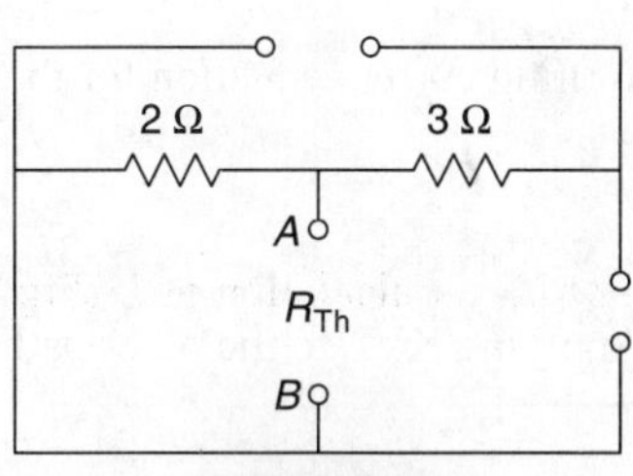


Fig. 2.151

***Step II*** Calculation of $R_{Th}$ (Fig. 2.151)

$$R_{Th} = 2\ \Omega$$

***Step III*** Calculation of $I_L$ (Fig. 2.152)

$$I_L = \frac{12}{2+1} = 4\text{ A}$$

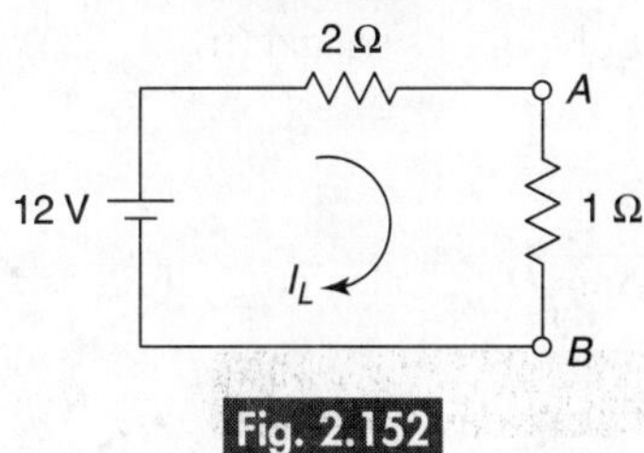


Fig. 2.152

## Examples with Dependent Sources

**EXAMPLE 2.67**

*Obtain the Thevenin equivalent network for the given network of Fig. 2.153 at terminals A and B.*

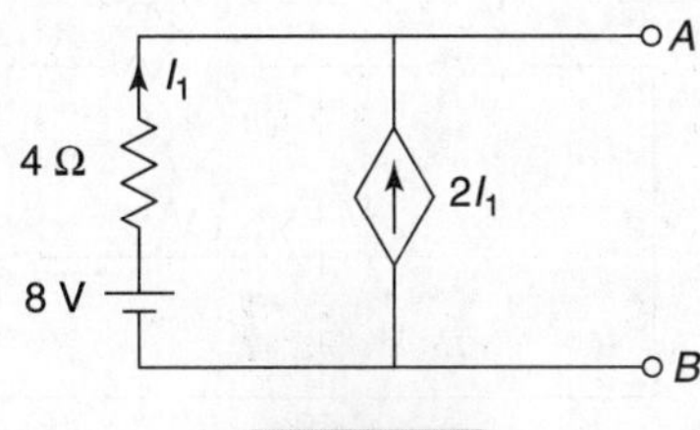


Fig. 2.153

## Solution

***Step I*** Calculation of $V_{Th}$ (Fig. 2.154)

From Fig. 2.154,

$$I_1 = -2I_1$$
$$3I_1 = 0$$
$$I_1 = 0$$

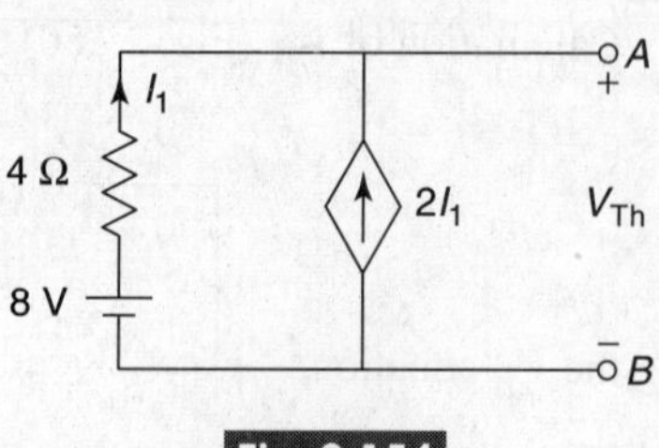

Fig. 2.154

Writing the $V_{Th}$ equation,

$$8 - 0 - V_{Th} = 0$$
$$V_{Th} = 8 \text{ V}$$

***Step II*** Calculation of $I_N$ (Fig. 2.155),

Meshes 1 and 2 will form a supermesh.

Writing current equation for the supermesh,

$$I_2 - I_1 = 2I_1$$
$$3I_1 - I_2 = 0 \qquad \text{...(i)}$$

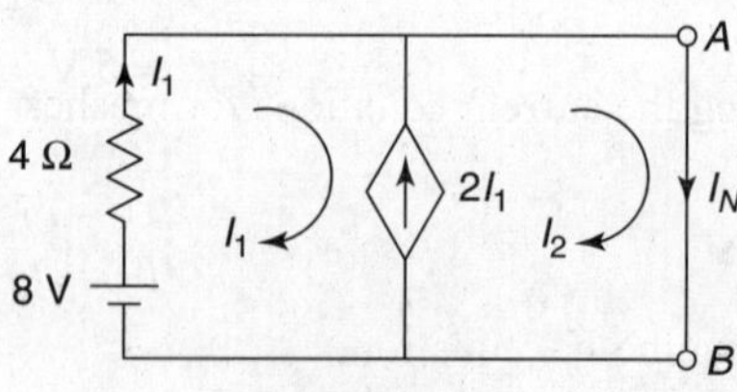

Fig. 2.155

Applying KVL to the outer path of the supermesh,

$$8 - 4I_1 = 0$$
$$I_1 = 2 \qquad \text{...(ii)}$$

Solving Eqs (i) and (ii),

$$I_2 = 6 \text{ A}$$
$$I_N = I_2 = 6 \text{ A}$$

***Step III*** Calculation of $R_{Th}$

$$R_{Th} = \frac{V_{Th}}{I_N} = \frac{8}{6} = 1.33\ \Omega$$

***Step IV*** Thevenin's Equivalent Network (Fig. 2.156)

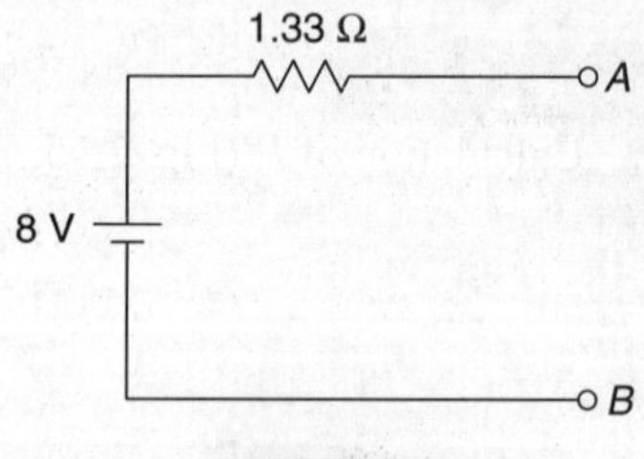

Fig. 2.156

**EXAMPLE 2.68**

*Find Thevenin's equivalent network of Fig. 2.157.*

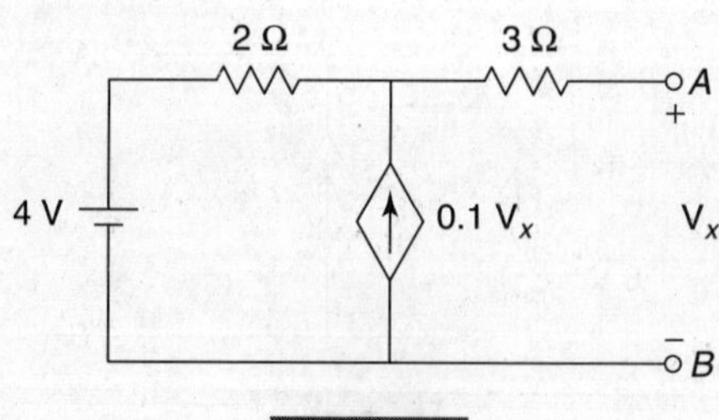

Fig. 2.157

**Solution**

***Step I*** Calculation of $V_{Th}$ (Fig. 2.158)

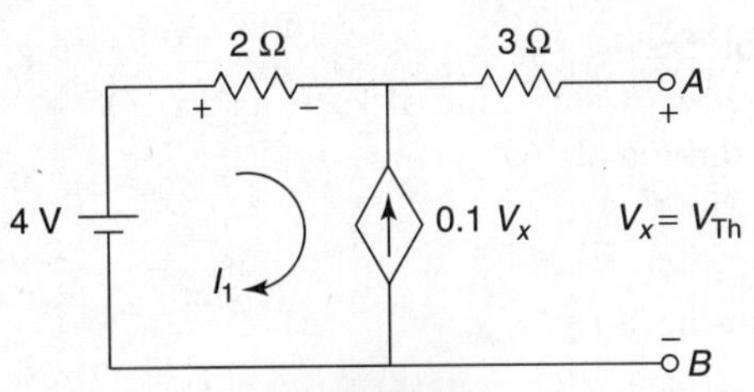

Fig. 2.158

$$V_x = V_{Th}$$

$$I_1 = -0.1 V_x$$

Writing the $V_{Th}$ equation,

$$4 - 2I_1 - V_x = 0$$

$$4 - 2(-0.1V_x) - V_x = 0$$

$$4 - 0.8V_x = 0$$

$$V_x = 5 \text{ V}$$

$$V_x = V_{Th} = 5 \text{ V}$$

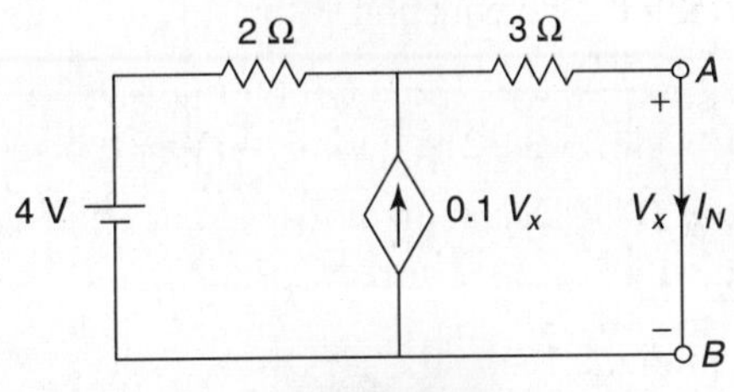

Fig. 2.159

***Step II*** Calculation of $I_N$ (Fig. 2.159)

From Fig. 2.159,

$$V_x = 0$$

The dependent source 0.1 $V_x$ depends on the controlling variable $V_x$. When $V_x = 0$, the dependent source vanishes, i.e., 0.1 $V_x = 0$, as shown in Fig. 2.160.

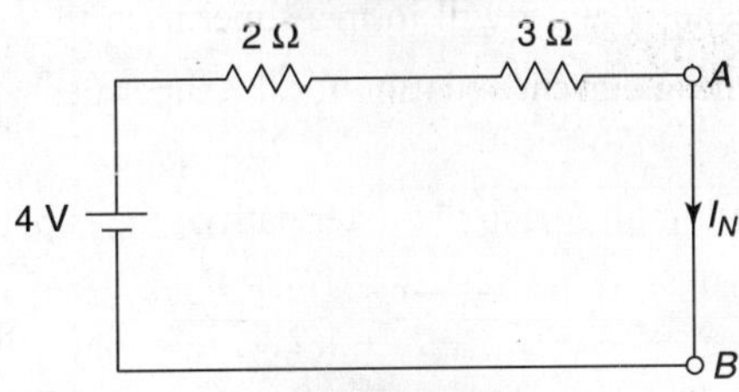

Fig. 2.160

$$I_N = \frac{4}{2+3} = 0.8 \text{ A}$$

***Step III*** Calculation of $R_{Th}$

$$R_{Th} = \frac{V_{Th}}{I_N} = \frac{5}{0.8} = 6.25\ \Omega$$

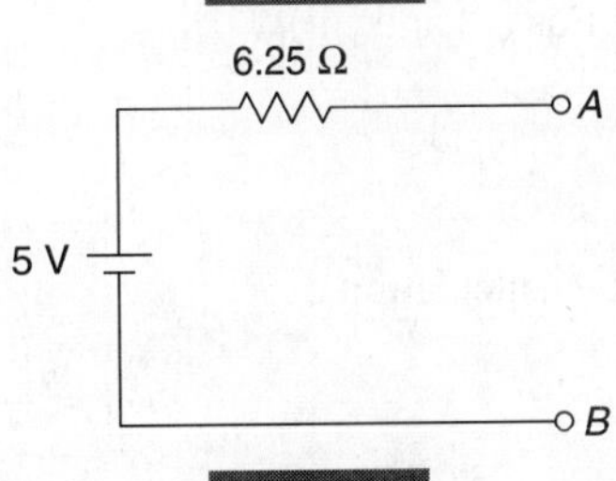

Fig. 2.161

***Step IV*** Thevenin's Equivalent Network (Fig. 2.161)

**EXAMPLE 2.69**

*Obtain the Thevenin equivalent network of Fig. 2.162 for the terminals A and B.*

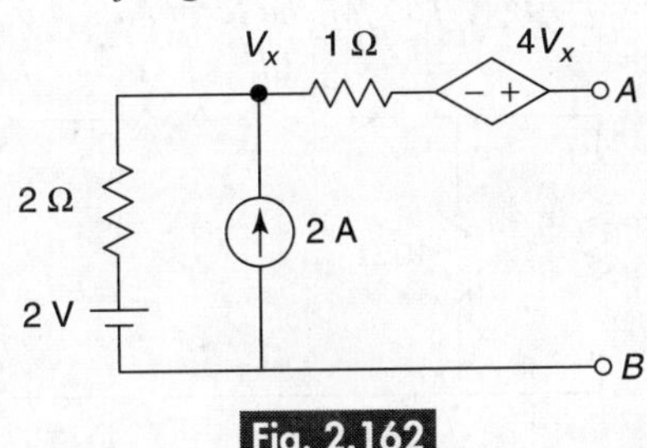

Fig. 2.162

**Solution**

***Step I*** Calculation of $V_{Th}$ (Fig. 2.163)

From Fig. 2.163,

$$2 - 2I_1 - V_x = 0$$
$$V_x = 2 - 2I_1$$

For mesh 1,

$$I_1 = -2 \text{ A}$$
$$V_x = 2 - 2(-2) = 6 \text{ V}$$

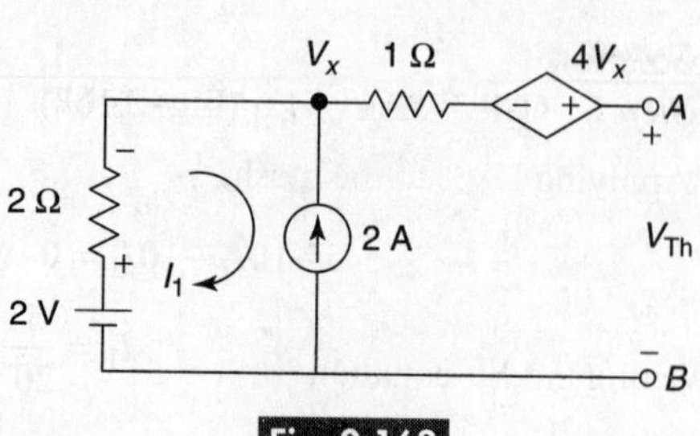

Fig. 2.163

Writing the $V_{Th}$ equation,

$$2 - 2I_1 - 0 + 4V_x - V_{Th} = 0$$
$$2 - 2(-2) - 0 + 4(6) - V_{Th} = 0$$
$$V_{Th} = 30 \text{ V}$$

***Step II*** Calculation of $I_N$ (Fig. 2.164)

From Fig. 2.164,

$$V_x = 2 - 2I_1 \qquad \text{...(i)}$$

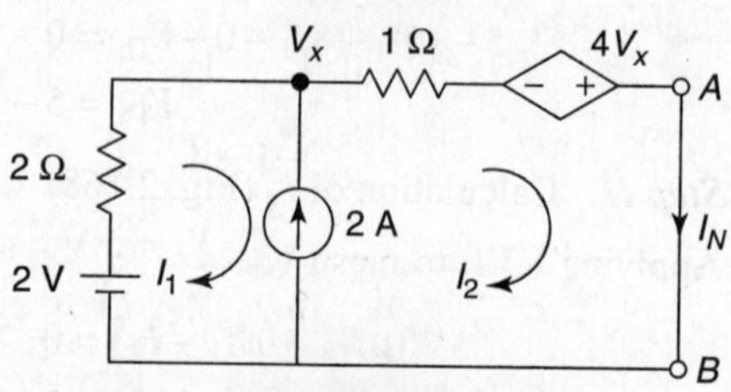

Fig. 2.164

Meshes 1 and 2 will form a supermesh.

Writing current equation for the supermesh,

$$I_2 - I_1 = 2 \qquad \text{...(ii)}$$

Applying KVL to the outer path of the supermesh,

$$2 - 2I_1 - 1I_2 + 4V_x = 0$$
$$2 - 2I_1 - I_2 + 4(2 - 2I_1) = 0$$
$$10I_1 + I_2 = 10 \qquad \text{...(iii)}$$

Solving Eqs (ii) and (iii),

$$I_1 = 0.73 \text{ A}$$
$$I_2 = 2.73 \text{ A}$$
$$I_N = I_2 = 2.73 \text{ A}$$

***Step III*** Calculation of $R_{Th}$

$$R_{Th} = \frac{V_{Th}}{I_N} = \frac{30}{2.73} = 10.98 \ \Omega$$

***Step IV*** Thevenin's Equivalent Network (Fig. 2.165)

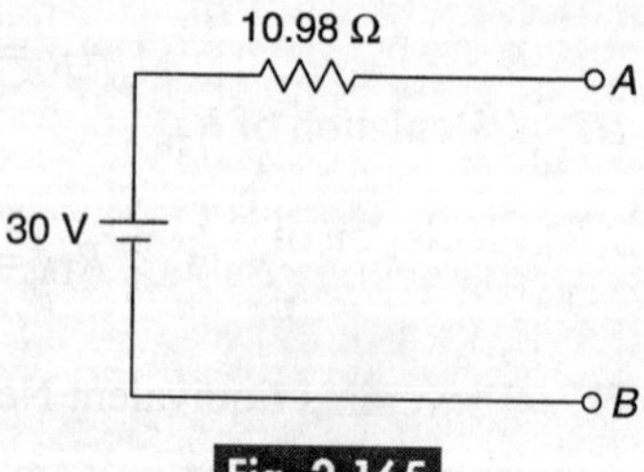

Fig. 2.165

**EXAMPLE 2.70**

*Find the Thevenin equivalent network of Fig. 2.166 for the terminals A and B.*

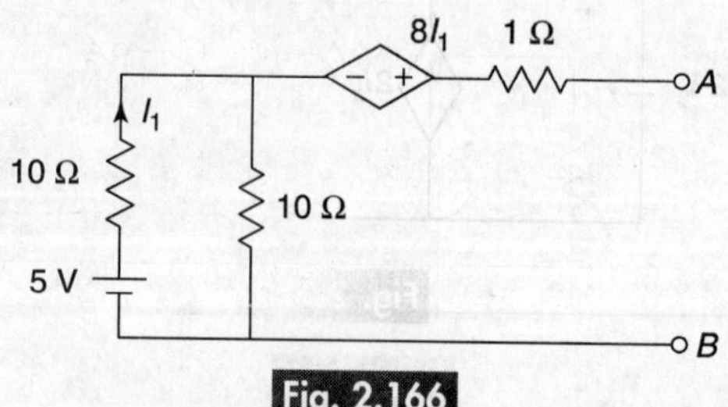

Fig. 2.166

**Solution**

***Step I*** Calculation of $V_{Th}$ (Fig. 2.167)

Applying KVL to the mesh,

$$5 - 10I_1 - 10I_1 = 0$$

$$I_1 = \frac{5}{20} = 0.25 \text{ A}$$

Fig. 2.167

Writing the $V_{Th}$ equation,

$$5 - 10I_1 + 8I_1 - 0 - V_{Th} = 0$$

$$V_{Th} = 5 - 2I_1 = 5 - 2(0.25) = 4.5 \text{ V}$$

***Step II*** Calculation of $I_N$ (Fig. 2.168)

Applying KVL to mesh 1,

$$5 - 10I_1 - 10(I_1 - I_2) = 0$$

$$20I_1 - 10I_2 = 5 \qquad \text{...(i)}$$

Fig. 2.168

Applying KVL to mesh 2,

$$-10(I_2 - I_1) + 8I_1 - 1I_2 = 0$$

$$18I_1 - 11I_2 = 0 \qquad \text{...(ii)}$$

Solving Eqs (i) and (ii),

$$I_1 = 1.375 \text{ A}$$

$$I_2 = 2.25 \text{ A}$$

$$I_N = I_2 = 2.25 \text{ A}$$

***Step III*** Calculation of $R_{Th}$

$$R_{Th} = \frac{V_{Th}}{I_N} = \frac{4.5}{2.25} = 2\ \Omega$$

***Step IV*** Thevenin's Equivalent Network (Fig. 2.169)

Fig. 2.169

**EXAMPLE 2.71**

*Find $V_{Th}$ and $R_{Th}$ between terminals A and B of the network shown in Fig. 2.170.*

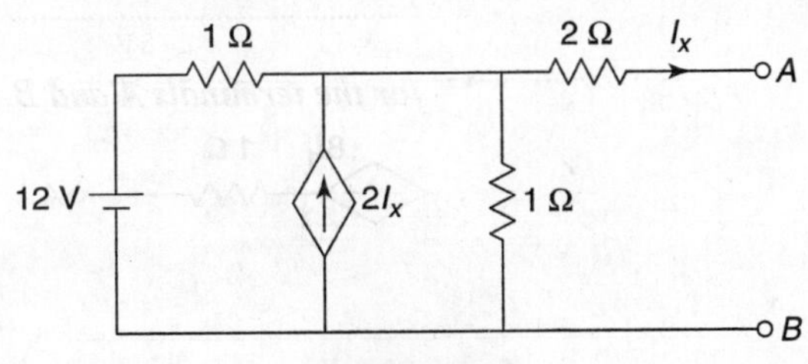


Fig. 2.170

**Solution**

***Step I*** Calculation of $V_{Th}$ (Fig. 2.171)

$$I_x = 0$$

The dependent source $2I_x$ depends on the controlling variable $I_x$. When $I_x = 0$, the dependent source vanishes, i.e., $2I_x = 0$, as shown in Fig. 2.171.

Fig. 2.171

Writing the $V_{Th}$ equation,

$$V_{Th} = 12 \times \frac{1}{1+1} = 6 \text{ V}$$

***Step II*** Calculation of $I_N$ (Fig. 2.172)

From Fig. 2.172,

$$I_x = \frac{V_1}{2}$$

Fig. 2.172

Applying KCL at node 1,

$$\frac{V_1 - 12}{1} + \frac{V_1}{1} + \frac{V_1}{2} = 2I_x$$

$$V_1 + V_1 + \frac{V_1}{2} - 12 = 2\left(\frac{V_1}{2}\right)$$

$$V_1 = 8 \text{ V}$$

$$I_N = \frac{V_1}{2} = \frac{8}{2} = 4 \text{ A}$$

***Step III*** Calculation of $R_{Th}$

$$R_{Th} = \frac{V_{Th}}{I_N} = \frac{6}{4} = 1.5\ \Omega$$

**EXAMPLE 2.72**

*Obtain the Thevenin equivalent network of Fig. 2.173 for the given network at terminals a and b.*

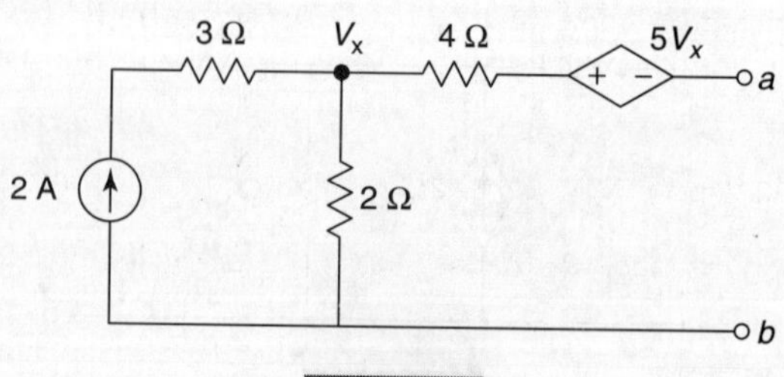


Fig. 2.173

**Solution**

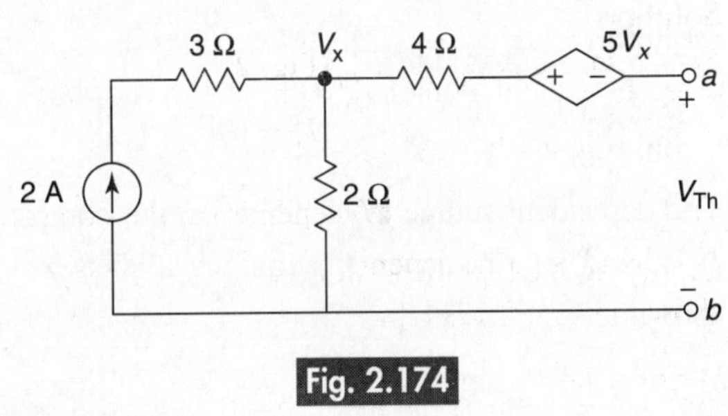

Fig. 2.174

***Step I*** Calculation of $V_{Th}$ (Fig. 2.174)

Applying KCL at node $x$,

$$2 = \frac{V_x}{2}$$

$$V_x = 4 \text{ V}$$

Writing the $V_{Th}$ equation,

$$V_{Th} = V_x - 5V_x = -4V_x$$

$$= -16 \text{ V} \quad (\text{the terminal } a \text{ is negative w.r.t. } b)$$

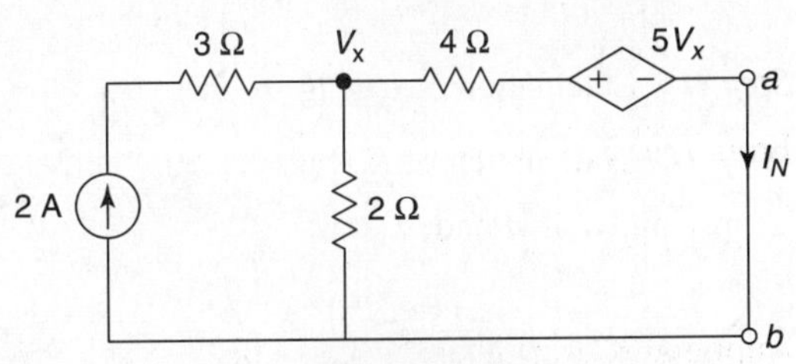

Fig. 2.175

***Step II*** Calculation of $I_N$ (Fig. 2.175)

Applying KCL at node $x$,

$$2 = \frac{V_x}{2} + \frac{V_x - 5V_x}{4}$$

$$2 = \frac{V_x}{2} - V_x = -\frac{V_x}{2}$$

$$V_x = -4 \text{ V}$$

$$I_N = \frac{V_x - 5V_x}{4} = -V_x = 4 \text{ A}$$

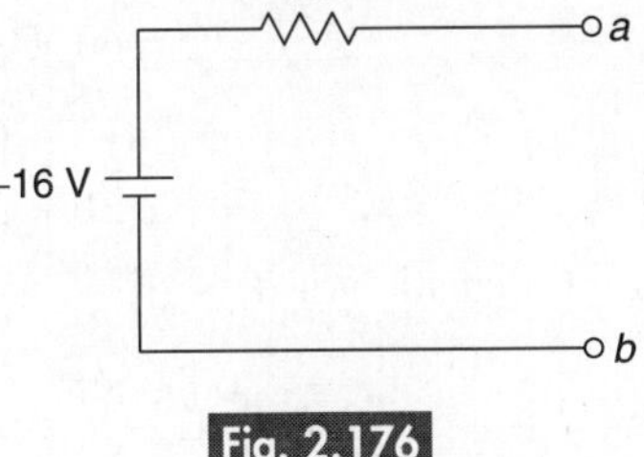

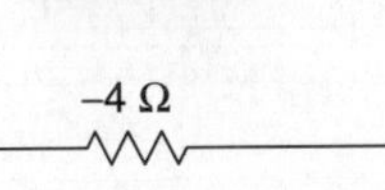
Fig. 2.176

***Step III*** Calculation of $R_{Th}$

$$R_{Th} = \frac{V_{Th}}{I_N} = \frac{-16}{4} = -4 \; \Omega$$

***Step IV*** Thevenin's Equivalent Network (Fig. 2.176)

## EXAMPLE 2.73

*Obtain the Thevenin equivalent network of Fig. 2.177 for the given network.*

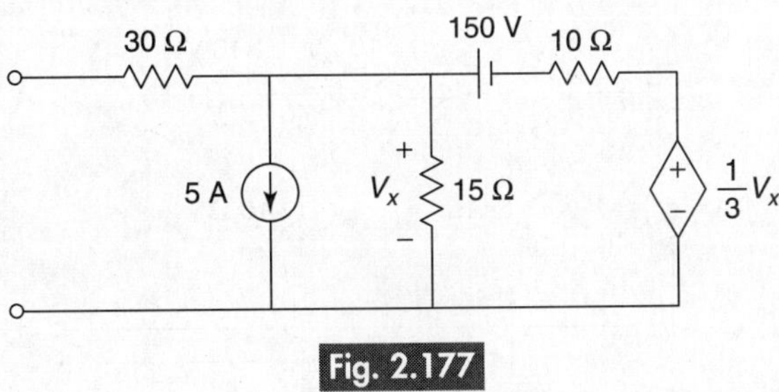

Fig. 2.177

**Solution**

***Step I*** Calculation of $V_{Th}$ (Fig. 2.178)

From Fig. 2.178,

$$V_x = V_{Th}$$

Applying KCL at the node,

$$\frac{V_x - 150 - \frac{1}{3}V_x}{10} + \frac{V_x}{15} + 5 = 0$$

$$V_x = 75 \text{ V}$$

$$V_{Th} = 75 \text{ V}$$

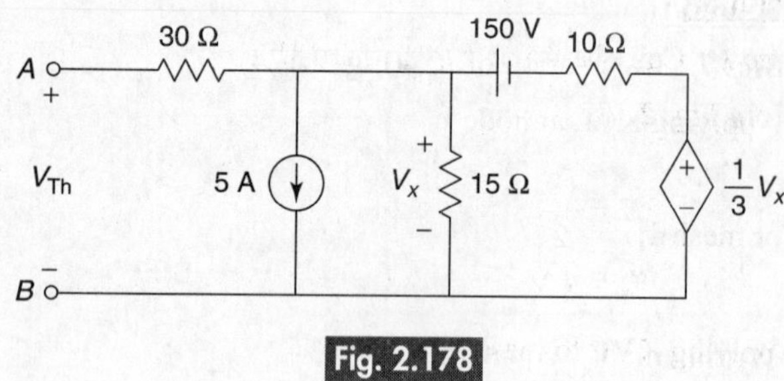


Fig. 2.178

***Step II*** Calculation of $I_N$ (Fig. 2.179)

Applying KCL at node $x$,

$$\frac{V_x}{30} + 5 + \frac{V_x}{15} + \frac{V_x - 150 - \frac{1}{3}V_x}{10} = 0$$

$$\frac{V_x}{30} + \frac{V_x}{15} + \frac{V_x}{10} - \frac{V_x}{30} = 15 - 5$$

$$V_x = 60 \text{ V}$$

$$I_N = \frac{V_x}{30} = \frac{60}{30} = 2 \text{ A}$$

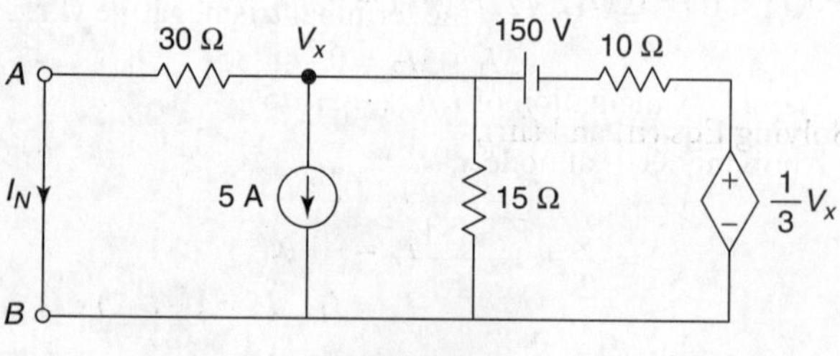


Fig. 2.179

***Step III*** Calculation of $R_{Th}$

$$R_{Th} = \frac{V_{Th}}{I_N} = \frac{75}{2} = 37.5\ \Omega$$

***Step IV*** Thevenin's Equivalent Network (Fig. 2.180)

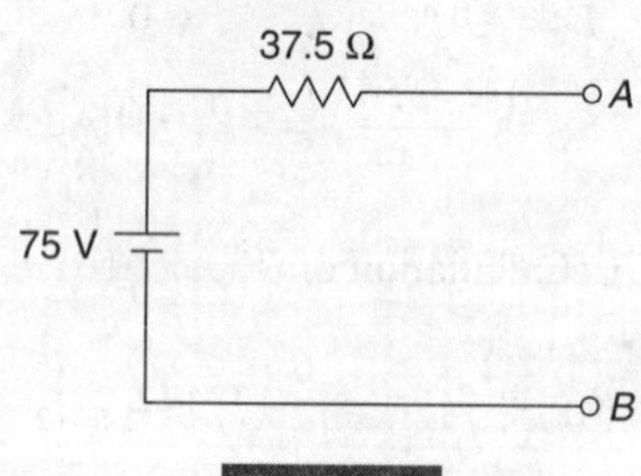


Fig. 2.180

**EXAMPLE 2.74**

*Find the Thevenin's equivalent network of the network to the left of A-B in the Fig. 2.181.*

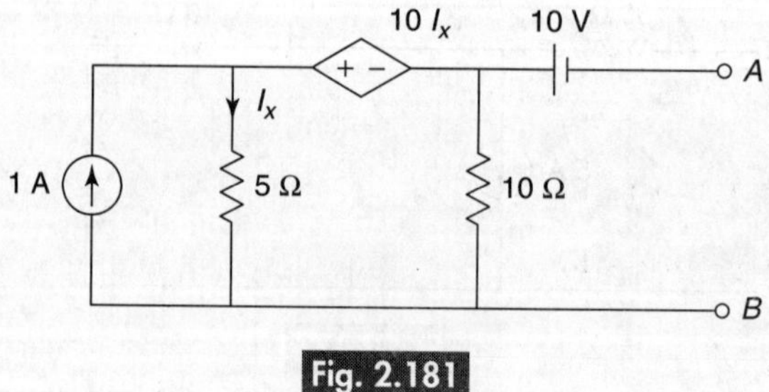


Fig. 2.181

**Solution**

***Step I*** Calculation of $V_{Th}$ (Fig. 2.182)

From Fig. 2.182,

$$I_x = I_1 - I_2 \quad \ldots\text{(i)}$$

Fig. 2.182

For mesh 1,

$$I_1 = 1 \quad \ldots\text{(ii)}$$

Applying KVL to mesh 2,

$$-5(I_2 - I_1) - 10I_x - 10I_2 = 0$$

$$-5(I_2 - I_1) - 10(I_1 - I_2) - 10I_2 = 0$$

$$5I_1 + 5I_2 = 0 \quad \ldots\text{(iii)}$$

Solving Eqs (ii) and (iii),

$$I_1 = 1 \text{ A}$$

$$I_2 = -1 \text{ A}$$

$$I_x = I_1 - I_2 = 1 - (-1) = 2 \text{ A}$$

Writing the $V_{Th}$ equation,

$$10I_2 - 10 - V_{Th} = 0$$

$$10(-1) - 10 - V_{Th} = 0$$

$$V_{Th} = -20 \text{ V}$$

***Step II*** Calculation of $I_N$ (Fig. 2.183)

From Fig. 2.183,

$$I_x = I_1 - I_2 \quad \ldots\text{(i)}$$

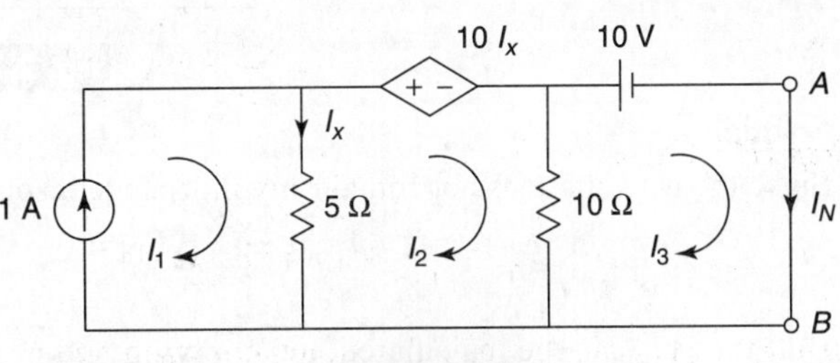

Fig. 2.183

For mesh 1,

$$I_1 = 1 \quad \ldots\text{(ii)}$$

Applying KVL to mesh 2,

$$-5(I_2 - I_1) - 10I_x - 10(I_2 - I_3) = 0$$

$$-5(I_2 - I_1) - 10(I_1 - I_2) - 10(I_2 - I_3) = 0$$

$$-5I_1 - 5I_2 + 10I_3 = 0 \quad \ldots\text{(iii)}$$

Applying KVL to mesh 3,

$$-10(I_3 - I_2) - 10 = 0$$

$$10I_2 - 10I_3 = 10 \quad \ldots\text{(iv)}$$

Solving Eqs (ii), (iii) and (iv),

$$I_1 = 1\text{ A}$$
$$I_2 = 3\text{ A}$$
$$I_3 = 2\text{ A}$$
$$I_N = I_3 = 2\text{ A}$$

***Step III*** Calculation of $R_{\text{Th}}$

$$R_{\text{Th}} = \frac{V_{\text{Th}}}{I_N} = \frac{-20}{2} = -10\ \Omega$$

***Step IV*** Thevenin's Equivalent Network (Fig. 2.184).

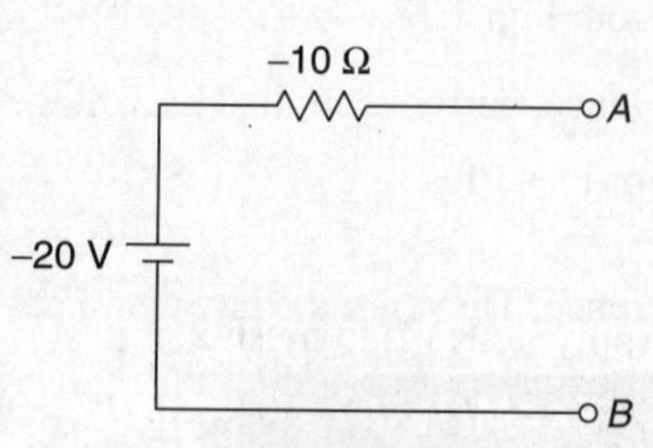


Fig. 2.184

**EXAMPLE 2.75**

*Find Thevenin's equivalent network at terminals A and B in the network of Fig. 2.185.*

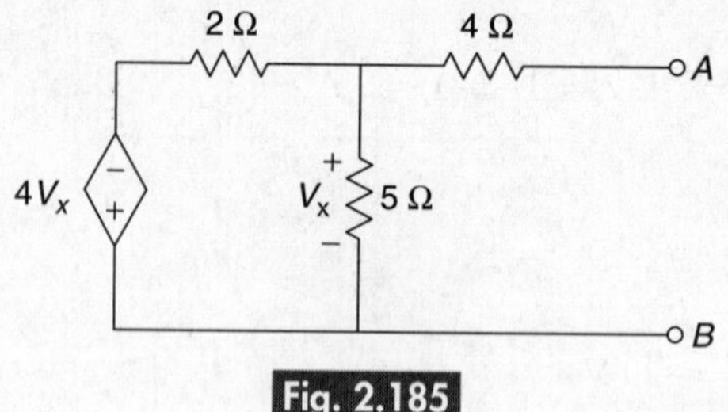


Fig. 2.185

**Solution**

Since the network does not contain any independent source,

$$V_{\text{Th}} = 0$$
$$I_N = 0$$

But the $R_{\text{Th}}$ can be calculated by applying a known voltage source of 1 V at the terminals $A$ and $B$, as shown in Fig. 2.186.

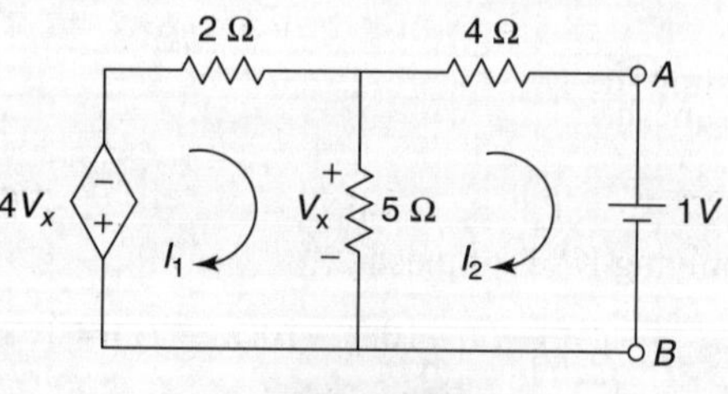


Fig. 2.186

$$R_{\text{Th}} = \frac{V}{I} = \frac{1}{I}$$

From Fig. 2.186,

$$V_x = 5(I_1 - I_2) \qquad \text{...(i)}$$

Applying KVL to mesh 1,

$$-4V_x - 2I_1 - 5(I_1 - I_2) = 0$$
$$-4[5(I_1 - I_2] - 2I_1 - 5I_1 + 5I_2 = 0$$
$$-27I_1 + 25I_2 = 0 \qquad \text{...(ii)}$$

Applying KVL to mesh 2,

$$-5(I_2 - I_1) - 4I_2 - 1 = 0$$
$$5I_1 - 9I_2 = 1 \qquad \text{...(iii)}$$

Solving Eqs (ii) and (iii),

$$I_1 = -0.21 \text{ A}$$

$$I_2 = -0.23 \text{ A}$$

Hence, current supplied by voltage source of 1 V is 0.23 A.

$$R_{\text{Th}} = \frac{1}{0.23} = 4.35\ \Omega$$

Hence, Thevenin's equivalent network is, as shown in Fig. 2.187.

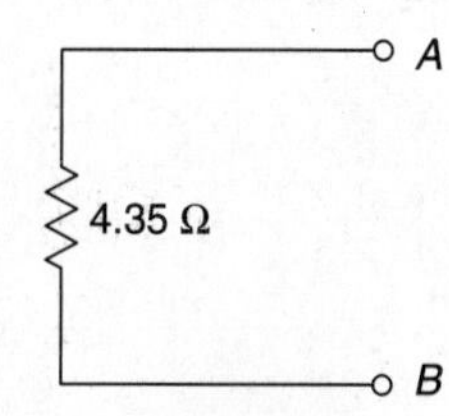

Fig. 2.187

## EXAMPLE 2.76

*Find the current in the 9 Ω resistor in Fig. 2.188.*

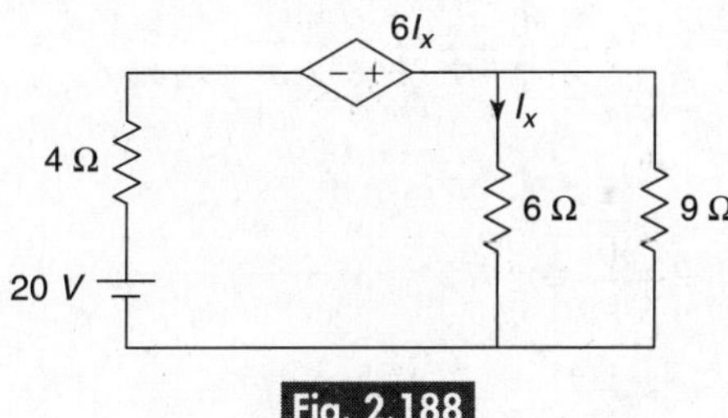

Fig. 2.188

**Solution**

***Step I*** Calculation of $V_{\text{Th}}$ (Fig. 2.189)

Applying KVL to the mesh,

$$20 - 4I_x + 6I_x - 6I_x = 0$$

$$I_x = 5 \text{ A}$$

Writing the $V_{\text{Th}}$ equation,

$$6I_x - V_{\text{Th}} = 0$$

$$6(5) - V_{\text{Th}} = 0$$

$$V_{\text{Th}} = 30 \text{ V}$$

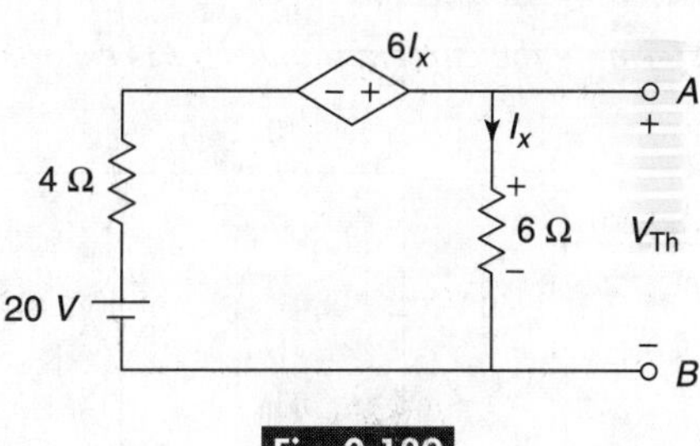

Fig. 2.189

***Step II*** Calculation of $I_N$ (Fig. 2.190).

From Fig. 2.190,

$$I_x = 0$$

The dependent source $6I_x$ depends on the controlling variable $I_x$. When $I_x = 0$, the dependent source vanishes, i.e., $6I_x = 0$, as shown in Fig. 2.191.

$$I_N = \frac{20}{4} = 5 \text{ A}$$

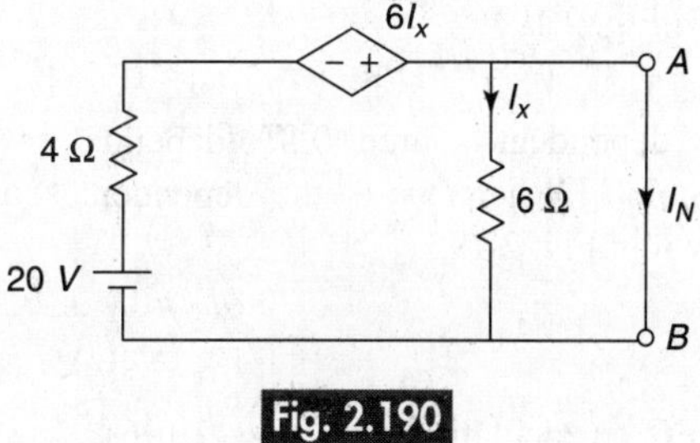

Fig. 2.190

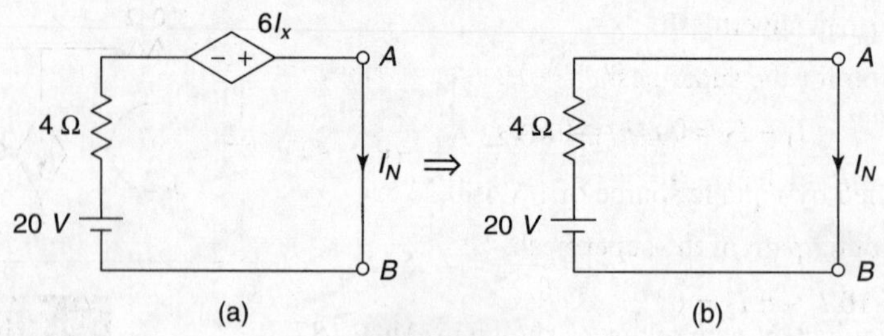


Fig. 2.191

***Step III*** Calculation of $R_{\text{Th}}$

$$R_{\text{Th}} = \frac{V_{\text{Th}}}{I_N} = \frac{30}{5} = 6\ \Omega$$

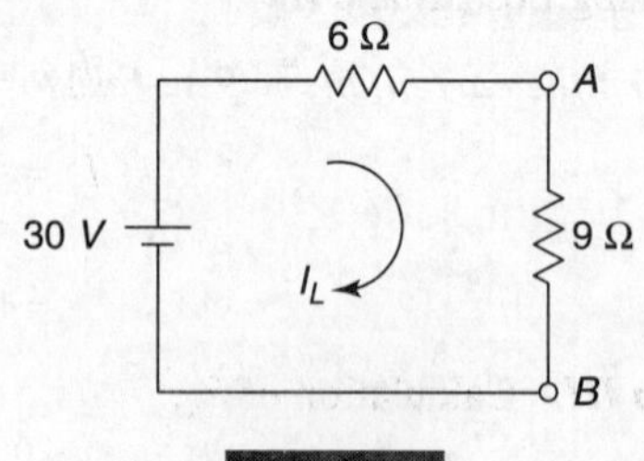


Fig. 2.192

***Step IV*** Calculation of $I_L$ (Fig. 2.192)

$$I_L = \frac{30}{6+9} = 2\ \text{A}$$

## EXAMPLE 2.77

*Determine the current in the 16 Ω resistor in Fig. 2.193.*

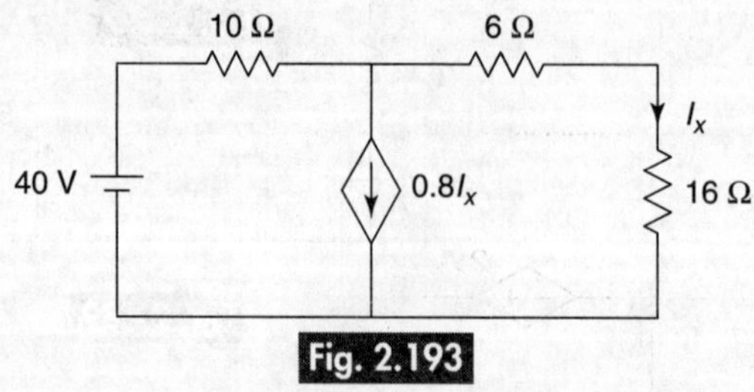


Fig. 2.193

### Solution

***Step I*** Calculation of $V_{\text{Th}}$ (Fig. 2.194)

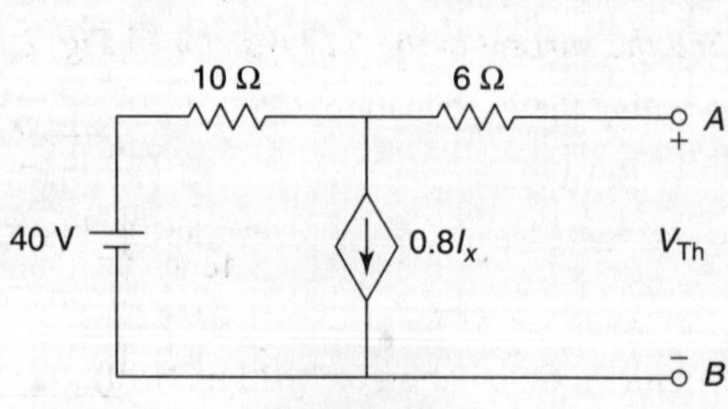


Fig. 2.194

From Fig. 2.194,

$$I_x = 0$$

The dependent source $0.8I_x$ depends on the controlling variable $I_x$. When $I_x = 0$, the dependent source vanishes, as shown in Fig. 2.195.

i.e.,
$$0.8I_x = 0$$

$$V_{\text{Th}} = 40\ \text{V}$$

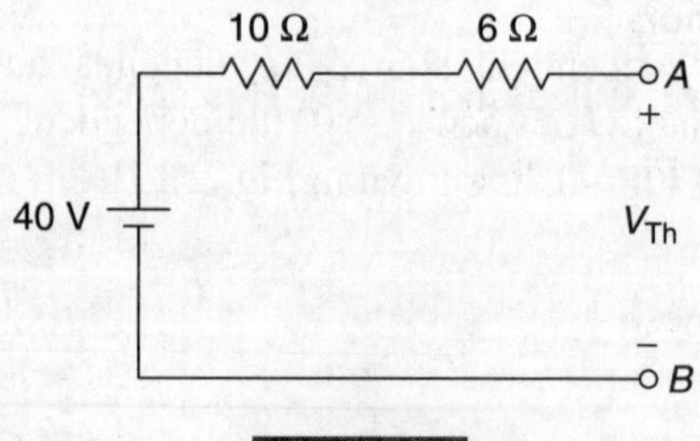


Fig. 2.195

***Step II*** Calculation of $I_N$ (Fig. 2.196)

From Fig. 2.196,

$$I_x = I_2 \qquad \ldots\text{(i)}$$

Meshes 1 and 2 will form a supermesh,

Writing current equation for the supermesh,

$$I_1 - I_2 = 0.8\, I_x = 0.8\, I_2$$

$$I_1 - 1.8\, I_2 = 0 \quad \ldots\text{(ii)}$$

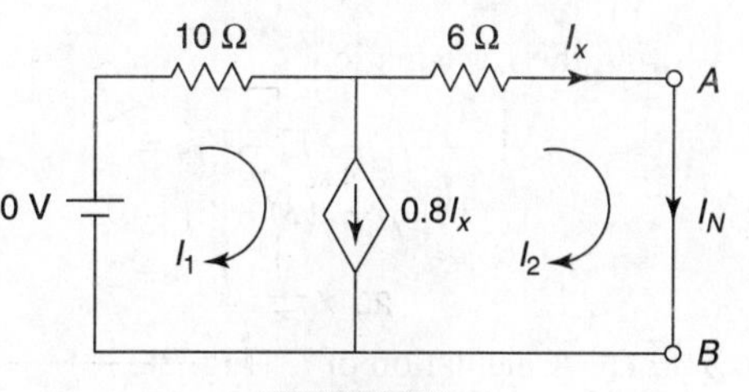

Fig. 2.196

Applying KVL to the outer path of the supermesh,

$$40 - 10\, I_1 - 6\, I_2 = 0$$

$$10\, I_1 + 6\, I_2 = 40 \quad \ldots\text{(iii)}$$

Solving Eqs (ii) and (iii),

$$I_1 = 3 \text{ A}$$

$$I_2 = \frac{5}{3} \text{ A}$$

$$I_N = I_2 = \frac{5}{3} \text{ A}$$

***Step III*** Calculation of $R_{\text{Th}}$

$$R_{\text{Th}} = \frac{V_{\text{Th}}}{I_N} = \frac{40}{\frac{5}{3}} = 24\ \Omega$$

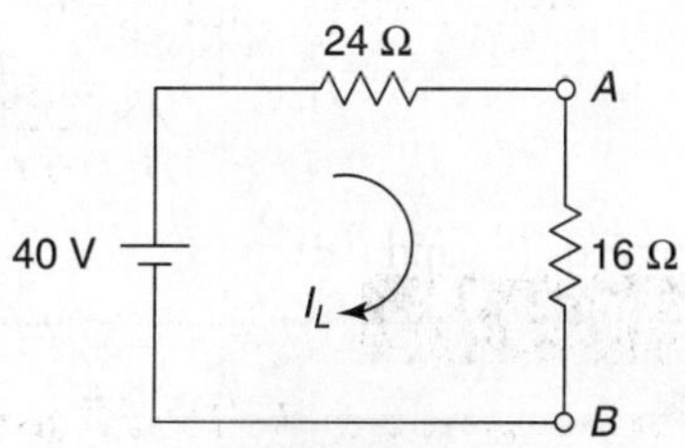

Fig. 2.197

***Step IV*** Calculation of $I_L$ (Fig. 2.197)

$$I_L = \frac{40}{24 + 16} = 1 \text{ A}$$

## EXAMPLE 2.78

*Find the current in the 6 Ω resistor in Fig. 2.198.*

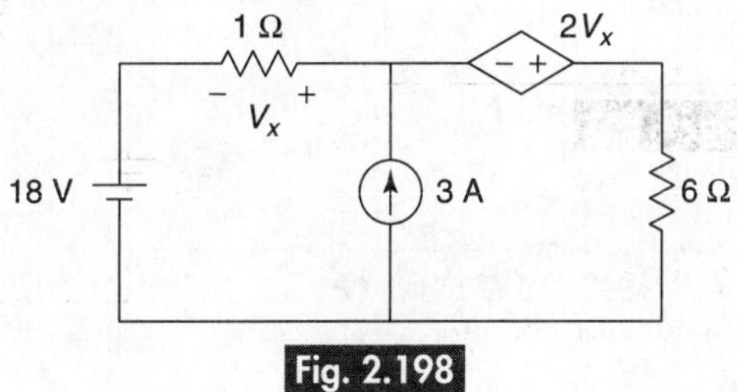

Fig. 2.198

**Solution**

***Step I*** Calculation of $V_{\text{Th}}$ (Fig. 2.199)

From Fig. 2.199,

$$V_x = -1 I_1 = -I_1 \quad \ldots\text{(i)}$$

For mesh 1,

$$I_1 = -3 \text{ A} \quad \ldots\text{(ii)}$$

$$V_x = 3 \text{ V}$$

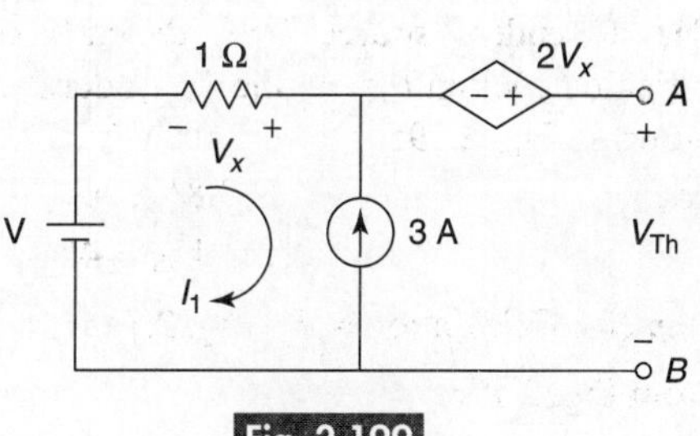

Fig. 2.199

Writing the $V_{Th}$ equation,

$$18 - 1\,I_1 + 2\,V_x - V_{Th} = 0$$
$$18 + 3 + 2(3) - V_{Th} = 0$$
$$V_{Th} = 27\text{ V}$$

***Step II*** Calculation of $I_N$ (Fig. 2.200)

From Fig. 2.200,

$$V_x = -I_1 \qquad \text{...(i)}$$

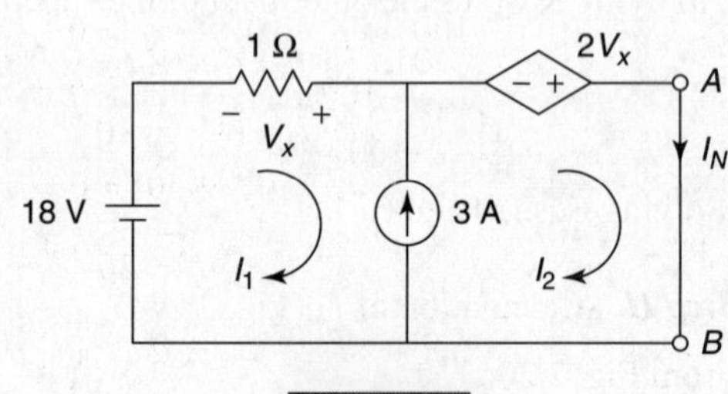

Fig. 2.200

Meshes 1 and 2 will form a supermesh.

Writing current equation for supermesh,

$$I_2 - I_1 = 3 \qquad \text{...(ii)}$$

Applying KVL to the outer path of the supermesh,

$$18 - 1I_1 + 2\,V_x = 0$$
$$18 - I_1 + 2(-I_1) = 0 \qquad \text{...(iii)}$$
$$I_1 = 6\text{ A}$$

Solving Eqs (ii) and (iii),

$$I_2 = 9\text{ A}$$
$$I_N = I_2 = 9\text{ A}$$

***Step III*** Calculation of $R_{Th}$

$$R_{Th} = \frac{V_{Th}}{I_N} = \frac{27}{9} = 3\ \Omega$$

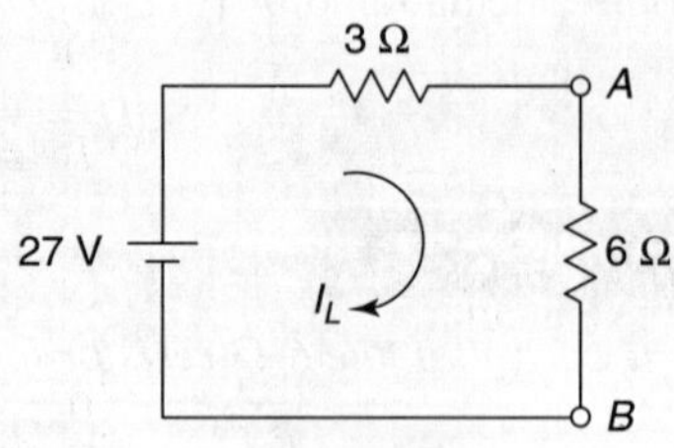

Fig. 2.201

***Step IV*** Calculation of $I_L$ (Fig. 2.201)

$$I_L = \frac{27}{3+6} = 3\text{ A}$$

**EXAMPLE 2.79**

*Find the current in the 10 Ω resistor in Fig.2.202.*

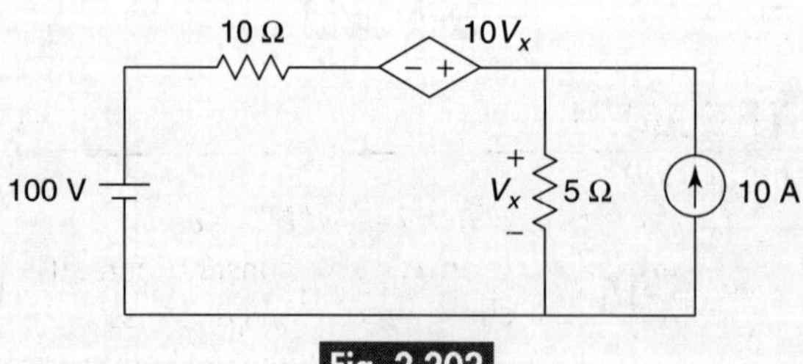

Fig. 2.202

**Solution**

***Step I*** Calculation of $V_{Th}$ (Fig. 2.203)

From Fig. 2.203,

$$V_x = 10 \times 5 = 50\text{ V}$$

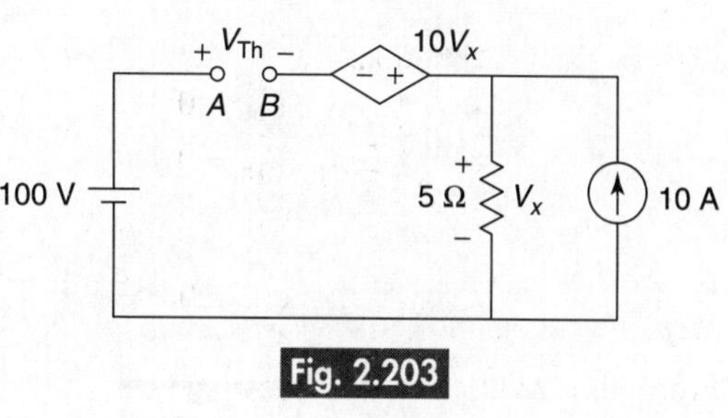


Fig. 2.203

Writing the $V_{Th}$ equation,

$$100 - V_{Th} + 10V_x - V_x = 0$$
$$100 - V_{Th} + 9V_x = 0$$
$$100 - V_{Th} + 9(50) = 0$$
$$V_{Th} = 550\text{ V}$$

***Step II*** Calculation of $I_N$ (Fig. 2.204)

From Fig. 2.204,

$$V_x = 5(I_N + 10)$$

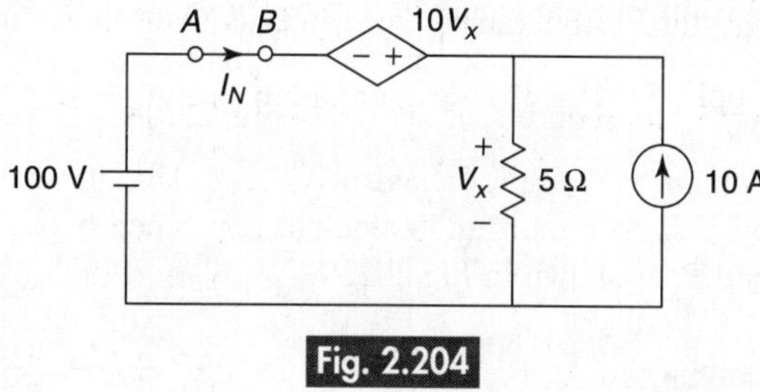


Fig. 2.204

Applying KVL to mesh 1,

$$100 + 10V_x - V_x = 0$$
$$V_x = -\frac{100}{9}$$
$$-\frac{100}{9} = 5I_N + 50$$
$$I_N = -\frac{550}{45}\text{ A}$$

***Step III*** Calculation of $R_{Th}$

$$R_{Th} = \frac{550}{-\frac{550}{45}} = -45\ \Omega$$

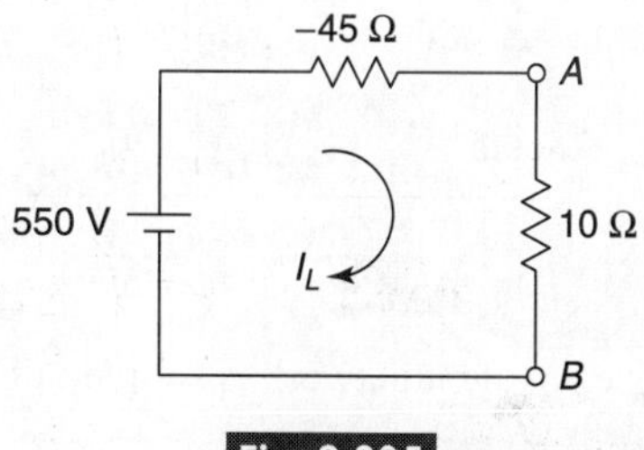


Fig. 2.205

***Step IV*** Calculation of $I_L$ (Fig. 2.205)

$$I_L = \frac{550}{-45 + 10} = -\frac{110}{7}\text{ A}$$

## 2.7 NORTON'S THEOREM

LO 2.5

Analyse the networks using Norton's theorem

It states that '*any two terminals of a network can be replaced by an equivalent current source and an equivalent parallel resistance.*' The constant current is equal to the current which would flow in a short circuit placed across the terminals. The parallel resistance is the resistance of the network when viewed from these open-circuited terminals after all voltage and current sources have been removed and replaced by internal resistances.

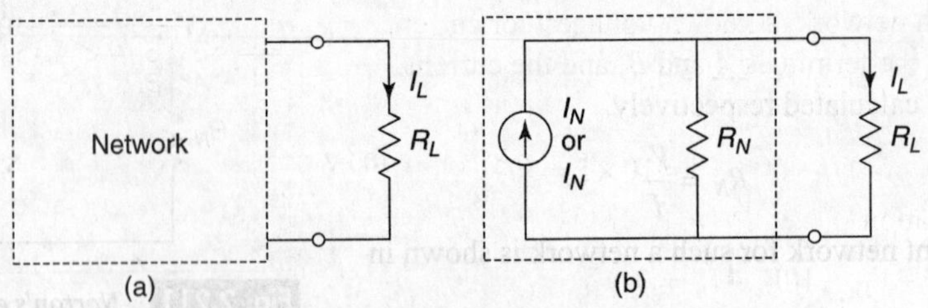


**Fig. 2.206** *Network illustrating Norton's theorem*

➤ ***Explanation*** Consider a simple network, as shown in Fig. 2.207.

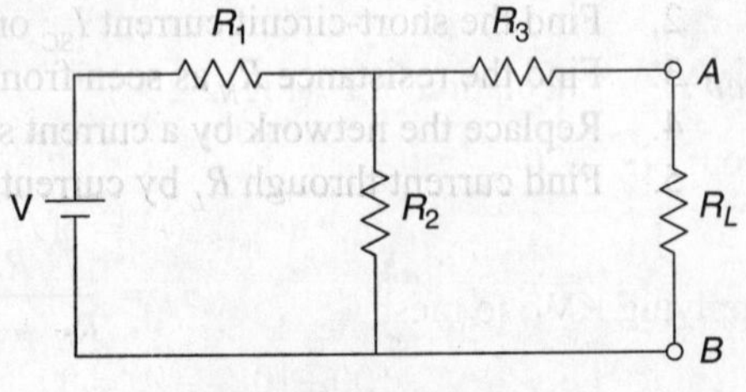


**Fig. 2.207** *Network*

For finding load current through $R_L$, first remove the load resistor $R_L$ from the network and calculate short-circuit current $I_{SC}$ or $I_N$, which would flow in a short circuit placed across terminals A and B, as shown in Fig. 2.208.

For finding parallel resistance $R_N$, replace the voltage source by a short circuit and calculate resistance between points $A$ and $B$, as shown in Fig. 2.209.

$$R_N = R_3 + \frac{R_1 R_2}{R_1 + R_2}$$

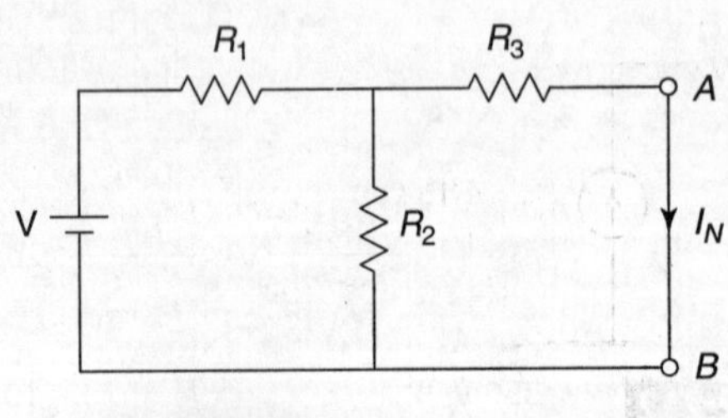


**Fig. 2.208** *Calculation of $I_N$*

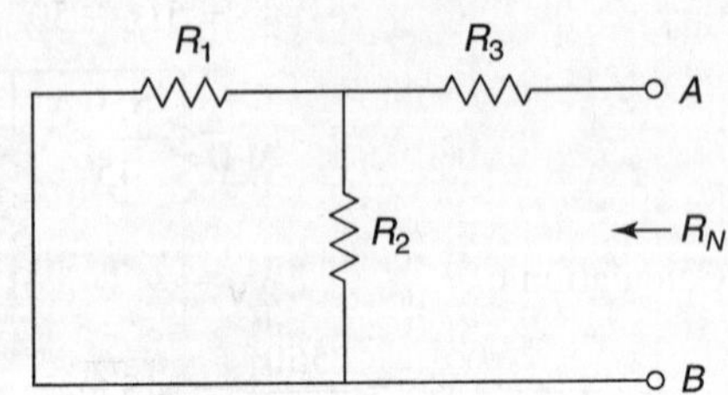


**Fig. 2.209** *Calculation of $R_N$*

Norton's equivalent network is shown in Fig. 2.210.

$$I_L = I_N \frac{R_N}{R_N + R_L}$$

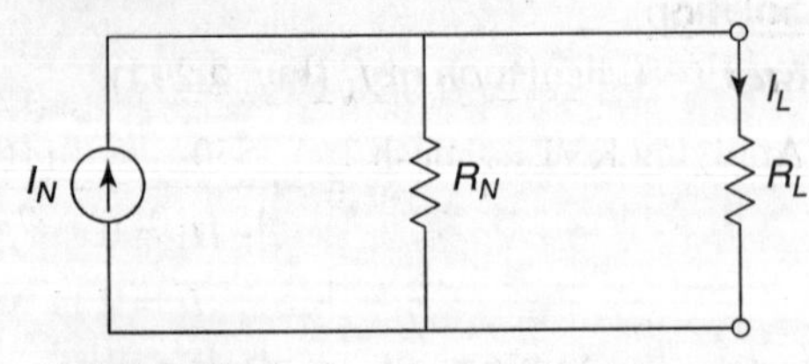


**Fig. 2.210** *Norton's equivalent network*

If the network contains both independent and dependent sources, Norton's resistances $R_N$ is calculated as

$$R_N = \frac{V_{Th}}{I_N}$$

where $V_{Th}$ is the open-circuit voltage across terminals $A$ and $B$. If the network contains only dependent sources, then

$$V_{Th} = 0$$

$$I_N = 0$$

To find $R_{Th}$ in such network, a known voltage $V$ or current $I$ is applied across the terminals $A$ and $B$, and the current $I$ or the voltage $V$ is calculated respectively.

$$R_N = \frac{V}{I}$$

Norton's equivalent network for such a network is shown in Fig. 2.211.

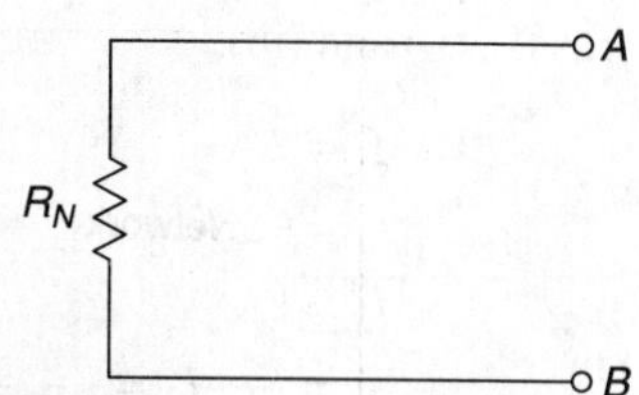


**Fig. 2.211** *Norton's equivalent network*

## ➤ Steps to be followed in Norton's Theorem

1. Remove the load resistance $R_L$ and put a short circuit across the terminals.
2. Find the short-circuit current $I_{SC}$ or $I_N$.
3. Find the resistance $R_N$ as seen from points $A$ and $B$.
4. Replace the network by a current source $I_N$ in parallel with resistance $R_N$.
5. Find current through $R_L$ by current-division rule.

$$I_L = \frac{I_N R_N}{R_N + R_L}$$

**EXAMPLE 2.80** ●○○

*Find the current through the 10 Ω resistor in Fig. 2.212.*

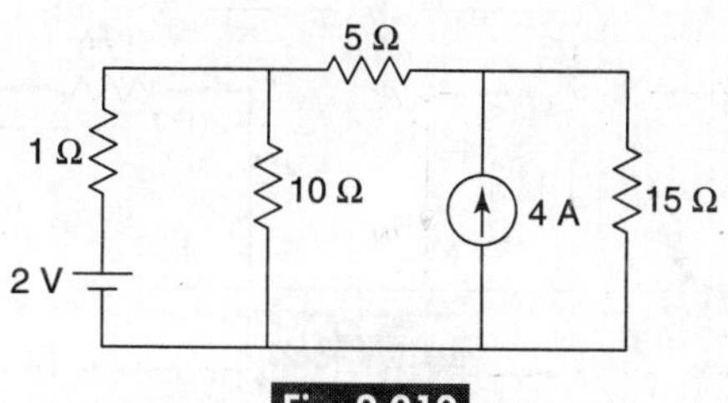


**Fig. 2.212**

**Solution**

***Step I*** Calculation of $I_N$ (Fig. 2.213)

Applying KVL to mesh 1,

$$2 - 1I_1 = 0$$

$$I_1 = 2 \quad \text{...(i)}$$

**Fig. 2.213**

Meshes 2 and 3 will form a supermesh.

Writing the current equation for the supermesh,

$$I_3 - I_2 = 4 \quad \text{...(ii)}$$

Applying KVL to the supermesh,

$$-5I_2 - 15I_3 = 0 \quad \text{...(iii)}$$

Solving Eqs (i), (ii) and (iii),

$$I_1 = 2\text{ A}$$
$$I_2 = -3\text{ A}$$
$$I_3 = 1\text{A}$$
$$I_N = I_1 - I_2 = 2 - (-3) = 5\text{ A}$$

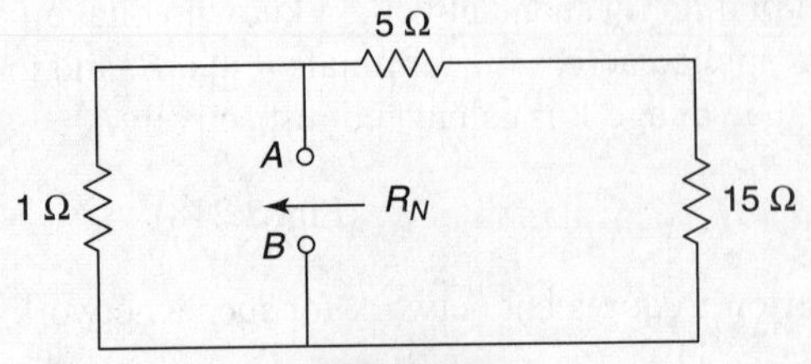

Fig. 2.214

***Step II*** Calculation of $R_N$ (Fig. 2.214)

$$R_N = 1 \,\|\, (5+15) = 0.95\ \Omega$$

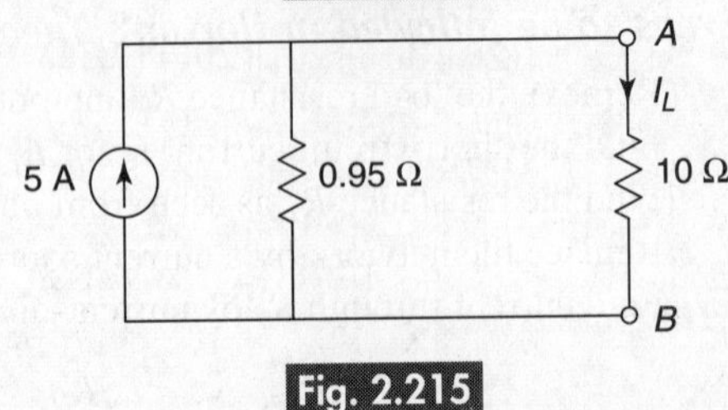

Fig. 2.215

***Step III*** Calculation of $I_L$ (Fig. 2.215)

$$I_L = 5 \times \frac{0.95}{0.95+10} = 0.43\text{ A}$$

## EXAMPLE 2.81

*Find the current through the 10 Ω resistor in Fig. 2.216.*

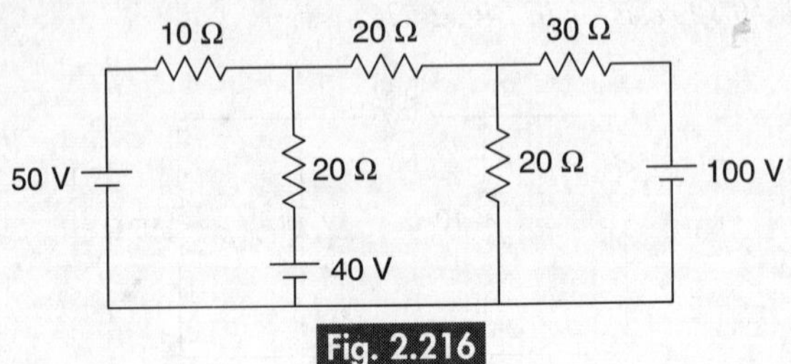

Fig. 2.216

**Solution**

***Step I*** Calculation of $I_N$ (Fig. 2.217)

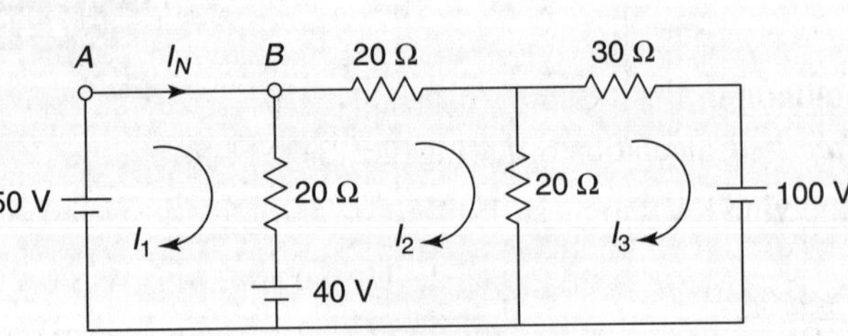

Fig. 2.217

Applying KVL to mesh 1,

$$50 - 20(I_1 - I_2) - 40 = 0$$
$$20I_1 - 20I_2 = 10 \qquad \text{...(i)}$$

Applying KVL to mesh 2,

$$40 - 20(I_2 - I_1) - 20I_2 - 20(I_2 - I_3) = 0$$
$$-20I_1 + 60I_2 - 20I_3 = 40 \qquad \text{...(ii)}$$

Applying KVL to mesh 3,

$$-20(I_3 - I_2) - 30I_3 - 100 = 0$$
$$-20I_2 + 50I_3 = -100 \qquad \text{...(iii)}$$

Solving Eqs (i), (ii) and (iii),

$$I_1 = 0.81\,\text{A}$$
$$I_N = I_1 = 0.81\,\text{A}$$

***Step II*** Calculation of $R_N$ (Fig. 2.218)

$$R_N = [(20 \,||\, 30) + 20] \,||\, 20 = 12.3\,\Omega$$

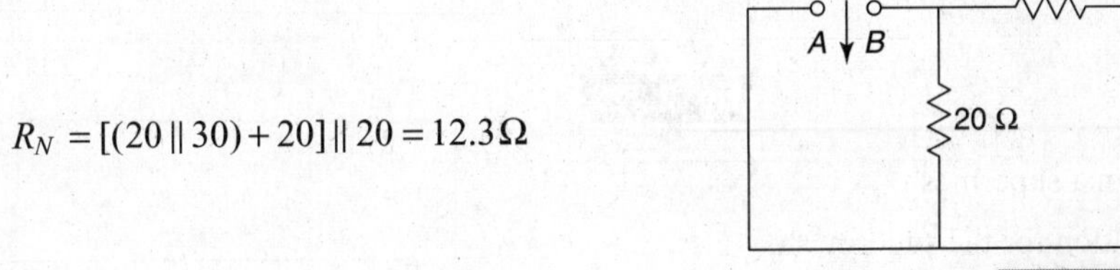

Fig. 2.218

***Step III*** Calculation of $I_L$ (Fig. 2.219)

$$I_L = 0.81 \times \frac{12.3}{12.3 + 10} = 0.45\,\text{A}$$

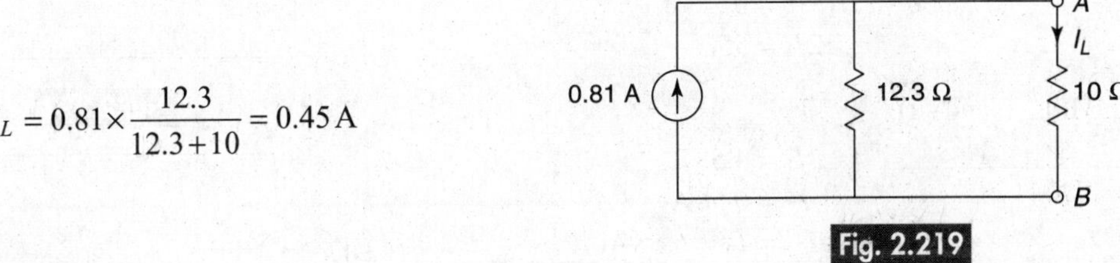

Fig. 2.219

## EXAMPLE 2.82

*Find the current through the 8 Ω resistor in Fig. 2.220.*

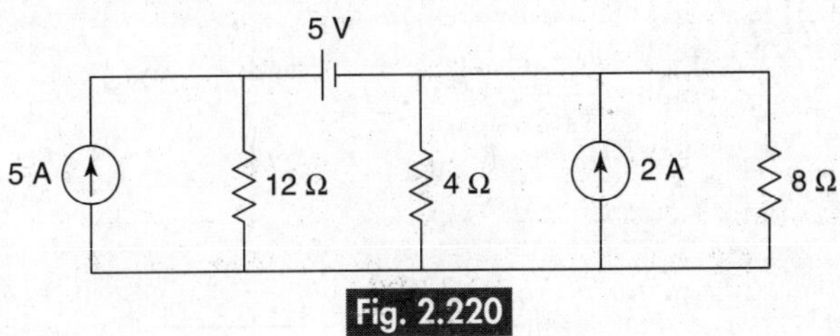

Fig. 2.220

**Solution**

***Step I*** Calculation of $I_N$ (Fig. 2.221)

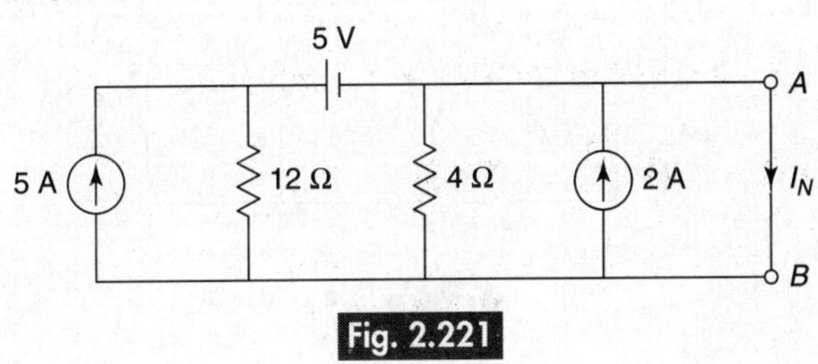

Fig. 2.221

The resistor of the 4 Ω gets shorted as it is in parallel with the short circuit. Simplifying the network by source transformation (Fig. 2.222),

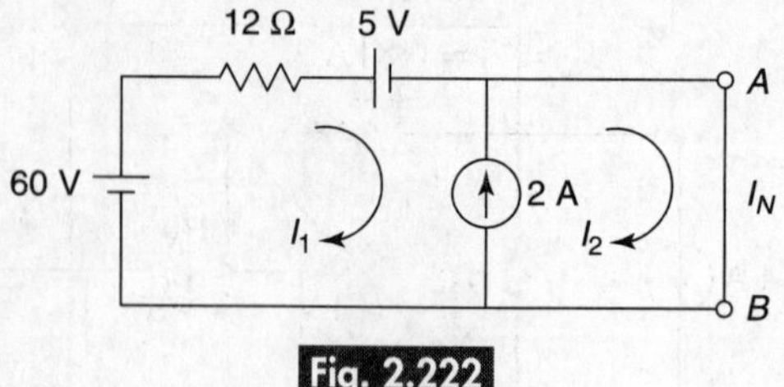


Fig. 2.222

Meshes 1 and 2 will form a supermesh.

Writing the current equation for the supermesh,

$$I_2 - I_1 = 2 \quad \text{...(i)}$$

Applying KVL to the supermesh,

$$60 - 12I_1 - 5 = 0$$
$$12I_1 = 55 \quad \text{...(ii)}$$

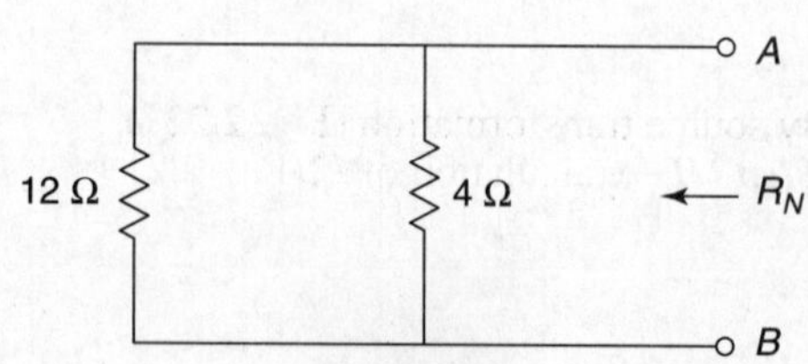


Fig. 2.223

Solving Eqs (i) and (ii),

$$I_1 = 4.58\text{ A}$$
$$I_2 = 6.58\text{ A}$$
$$I_N = I_2 = 6.58\text{ A}$$

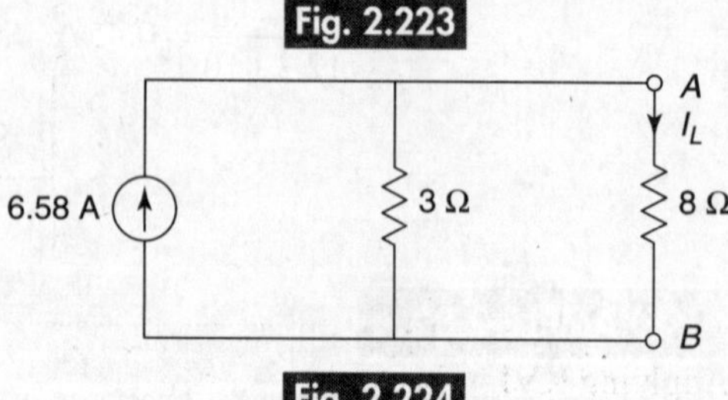


Fig. 2.224

***Step II*** Calculation of $R_N$ (Fig. 2.223)

$$R_N = 12 \parallel 4 = 3\,\Omega$$

***Step III*** Calculation of $I_L$ (Fig. 2.224)

$$I_L = 6.58 \times \frac{3}{3+8} = 1.79\text{ A}$$

**EXAMPLE 2.83**

*Find the current through the 1 Ω resistor in Fig. 2.225.*

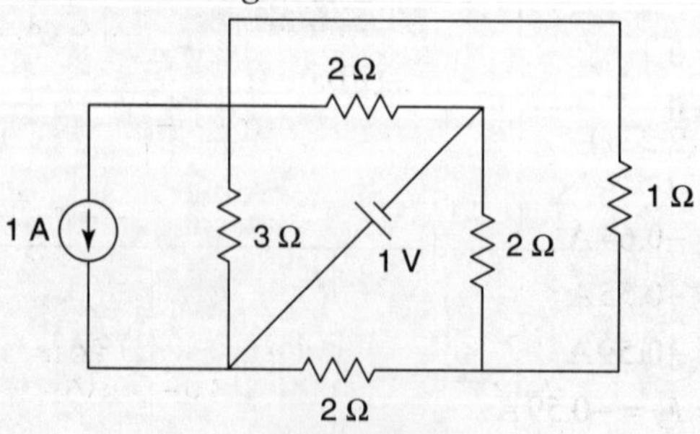


Fig. 2.225

## Solution

***Step I*** Calculation of $I_N$ (Fig. 2.226)

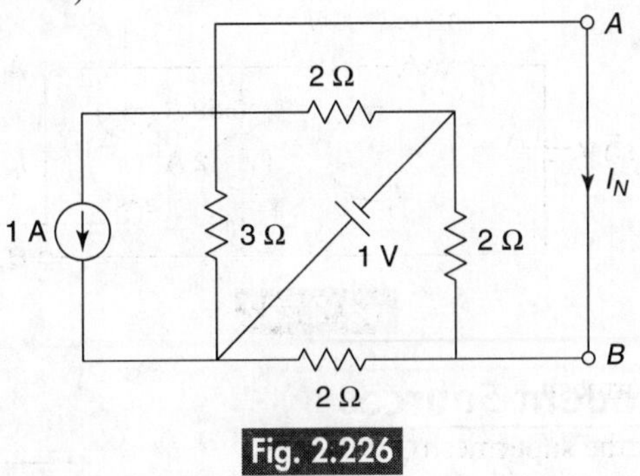


Fig. 2.226

By source transformation (Fig. 2.227),

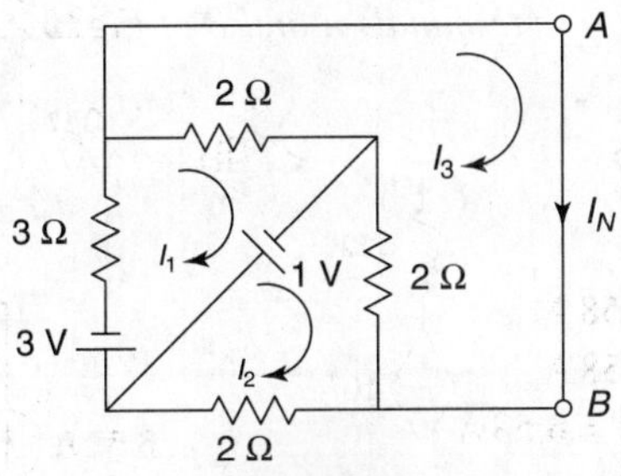


Fig. 2.227

Applying KVL to mesh 1,

$$-3-3I_1-2(I_1-I_3)+1=0$$

$$5I_1-2I_3=-2 \quad \text{...(i)}$$

Applying KVL to mesh 2,

$$-1-2(I_2-I_3)-2I_2=0$$

$$4I_2-2I_3=-1 \quad \text{...(ii)}$$

Applying KVL to mesh 3,

$$-2(I_3-I_1)-2(I_3-I_2)=0$$

$$-2I_1-2I_2+4I_3=0 \quad \text{...(iii)}$$

Solving Eqs (i), (ii) and (iii),

$$I_1=-0.64\text{ A}$$

$$I_2=-0.55\text{ A}$$

$$I_3=-0.59\text{ A}$$

$$I_N=I_3=-0.59\text{ A}$$

***Step II*** Calculation of $R_N$ (Fig. 2.228)

$$R_N=2.2\ \Omega$$

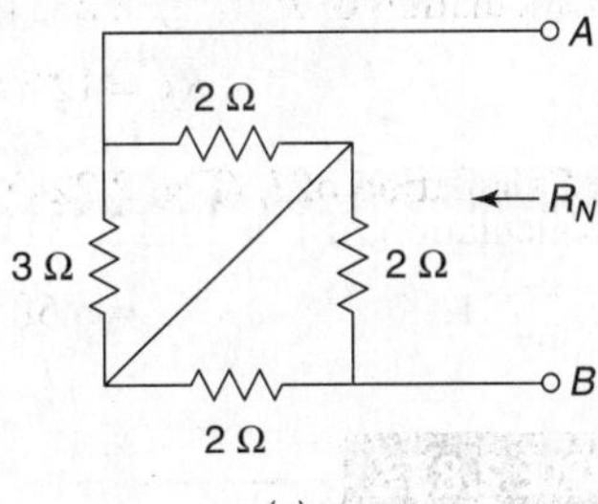


(a)

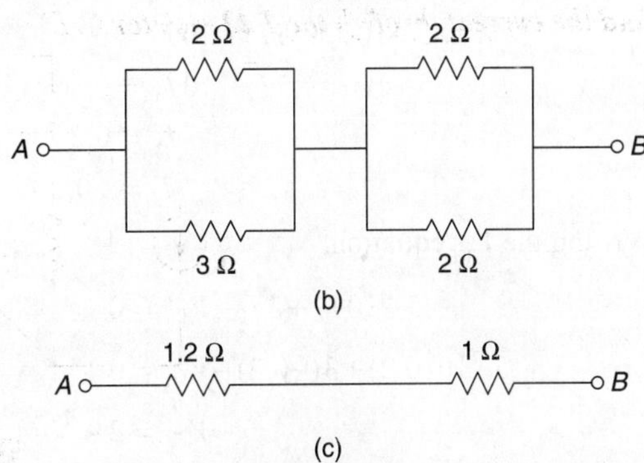


Fig. 2.228

***Step III*** Calculation of $I_L$ (Fig. 2.229)

$$I_L = 0.59 \times \frac{2.2}{2.2+1} = 0.41\,\text{A}$$

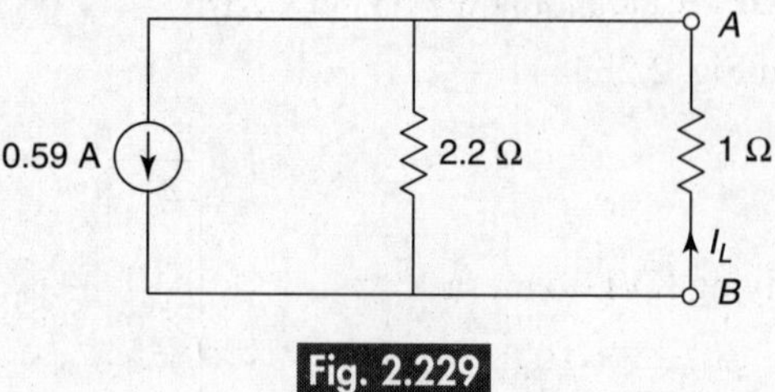


Fig. 2.229

## Examples with Dependent Sources

**EXAMPLE 2.84**

*Find Norton's equivalent network across terminals A and B of Fig. 2.230.*

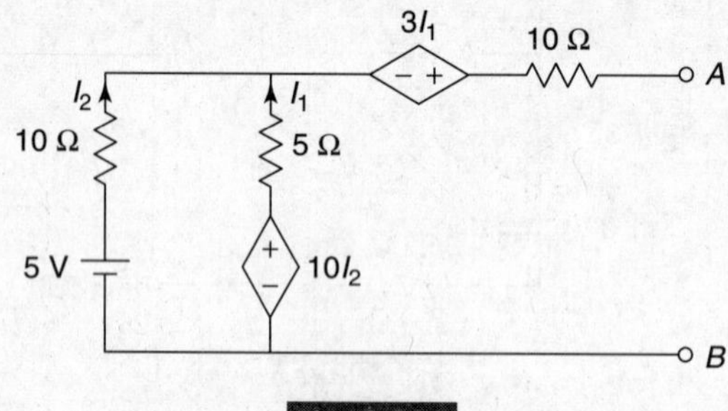


Fig. 2.230

**Solution**

***Step I*** Calculation of $V_{Th}$ (Fig. 2.231)

From Fig. 2.231,

$$I_2 = I_x$$
$$I_1 = -I_x$$

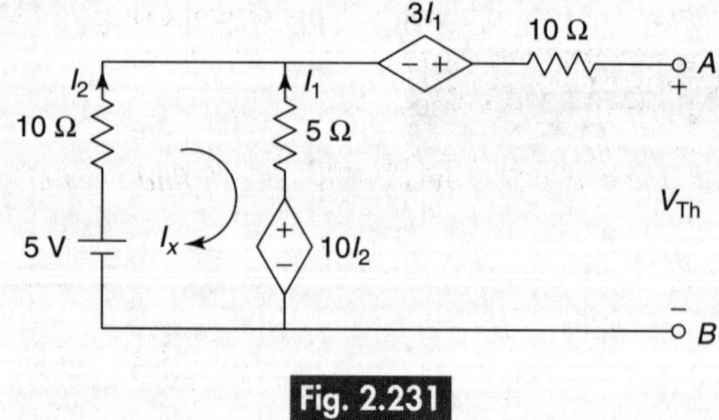


Fig. 2.231

Applying KVL to the mesh,

$$5 - 10I_x - 5I_x - 10I_2 = 0$$
$$5 - 10I_x - 5I_x - 10I_x = 0$$
$$I_x = 0.2\text{ A}$$
$$I_1 = -0.2\text{ A}$$

Writing the $V_{Th}$ equation,

$$5 - 10I_x + 3I_1 - V_{Th} = 0$$
$$5 - 10(0.2) + 3(-0.2) - V_{Th} = 0$$
$$V_{Th} = 2.4\text{ V}$$

***Step II*** Calculation of $I_N$ (Fig. 2.232)

From Fig. 2.232,

$$I_2 = I_x \quad \text{...(i)}$$

$$I_1 = I_y - I_x \quad \text{...(ii)}$$

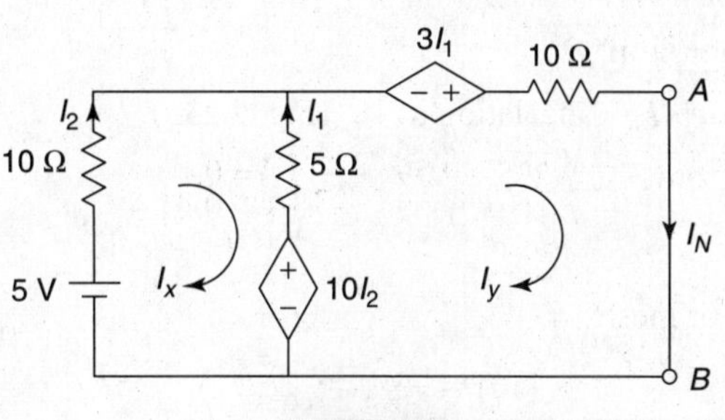

Fig. 2.232

Applying KVL to mesh 1,

$$5 - 10I_x - 5(I_x - I_y) - 10I_2 = 0$$

$$5 - 10I_x - 5I_x + 5I_y - 10I_x = 0$$

$$25I_x - 5I_y = 5 \quad \text{...(iii)}$$

Applying KVL to mesh 2,

$$10I_2 - 5(I_y - I_x) + 3I_1 - 10I_y = 0$$

$$10I_x - 5I_y + 5I_x + 3(I_y - I_x) - 10I_y = 0$$

$$12I_x - 12I_y = 0 \quad \text{...(iv)}$$

Solving Eqs (iii) and (iv),

$$I_x = 0.25 \text{ A}$$

$$I_y = 0.25 \text{ A}$$

$$I_N = I_y = 0.25 \text{ A}$$

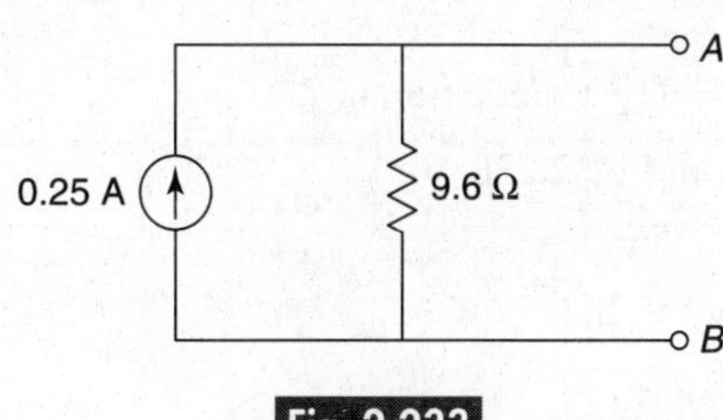

Fig. 2.233

***Step III*** Calculation of $R_N$

$$R_N = \frac{V_{\text{Th}}}{I_N} = \frac{2.4}{0.25} = 9.6\ \Omega$$

***Step IV*** Norton's Equivalent Network (Fig. 2.233)

## EXAMPLE 2.85

*For the network shown in Fig. 2.234, find Norton's equivalent network.*

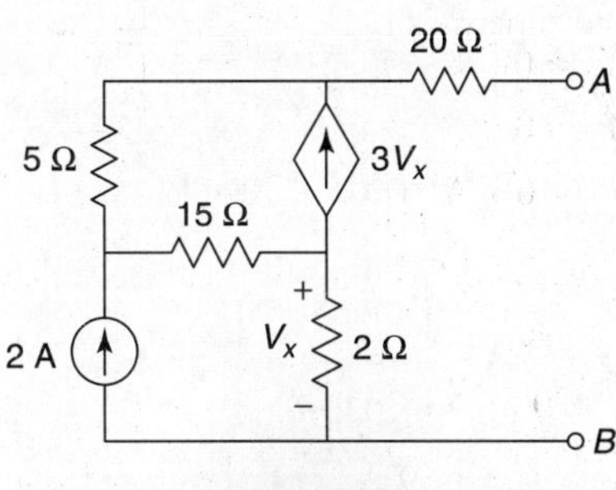

Fig. 2.234

**Solution**

***Step I*** Calculation of $V_{\text{Th}}$ (Fig. 2.235)

From Fig. 2.235,

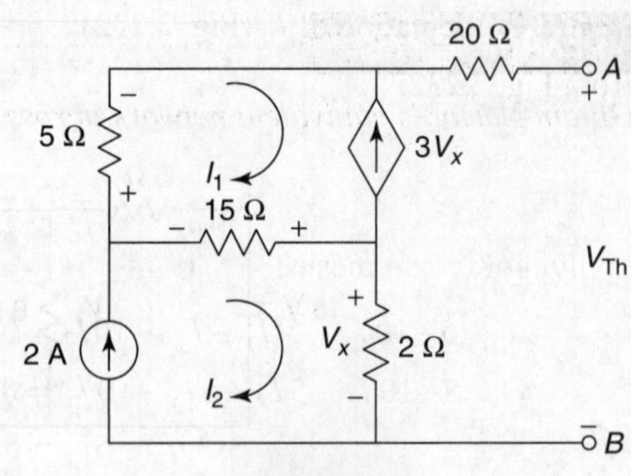

Fig. 2.235

$$V_x = 2I_2 \qquad \ldots\text{(i)}$$

For mesh 1,

$$I_1 = -3V_x = -3(2I_2) = -6I_2 \qquad \ldots\text{(ii)}$$

For mesh 2,

$$I_2 = 2 \qquad \ldots\text{(iii)}$$

$$I_1 = -6I_2 = -6(2) = -12 \text{ A}$$

Writing the $V_{\text{Th}}$ equation,

$$V_{\text{Th}} - 0 + 5I_1 + 15(I_1 - I_2) - 2I_2 = 0$$

$$V_{\text{Th}} + 5(-12) + 15(-12 - 2) - 2(2) = 0$$

$$V_{\text{Th}} = 274 \text{ V}$$

***Step II*** Calculation of $I_N$ (Fig. 2.236)

From Fig. 2.236,

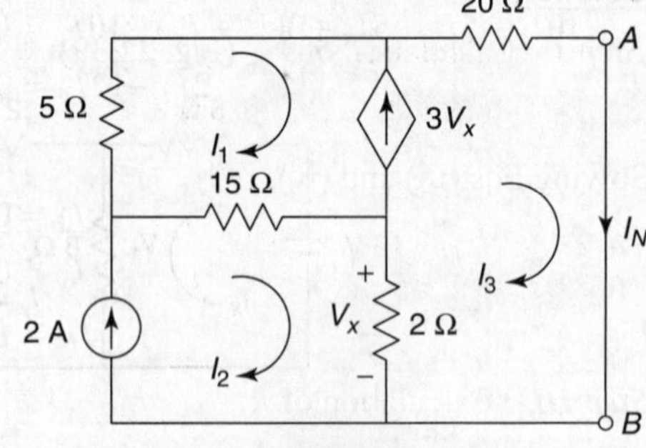

Fig. 2.236

$$V_x = 2(I_2 - I_3) \qquad \ldots\text{(i)}$$

For mesh 2,

$$I_2 = 2 \qquad \ldots\text{(ii)}$$

Meshes 1 and 3 will form a supermesh.

Writing the current equation for the supermesh,

$$I_3 - I_1 = 3V_x = 3\left[2(I_2 - I_3)\right] = 6I_2 - 6I_3$$

$$I_1 + 6I_2 - 7I_3 = 0 \qquad \ldots\text{(iii)}$$

Applying KVL to the outer path of the supermesh,

$$-5I_1 - 20I_3 - 2(I_3 - I_2) - 15(I_1 - I_2) = 0$$

$$-20I_1 + 17I_2 - 22I_3 = 0 \qquad \ldots\text{(iv)}$$

Solving Eqs (ii), (iii) and (iv),

$$I_1 = -0.16 \text{ A}$$

$$I_2 = 2 \text{ A}$$

$$I_3 = 1.69 \text{ A}$$

$$I_N = I_3 = 1.69 \text{ A}$$

***Step III*** Calculation of $R_N$

$$R_N = \frac{V_{\text{Th}}}{I_N} = \frac{274}{1.69} = 162.13\ \Omega$$

***Step IV*** Norton's Equivalent Network (Fig. 2.237)

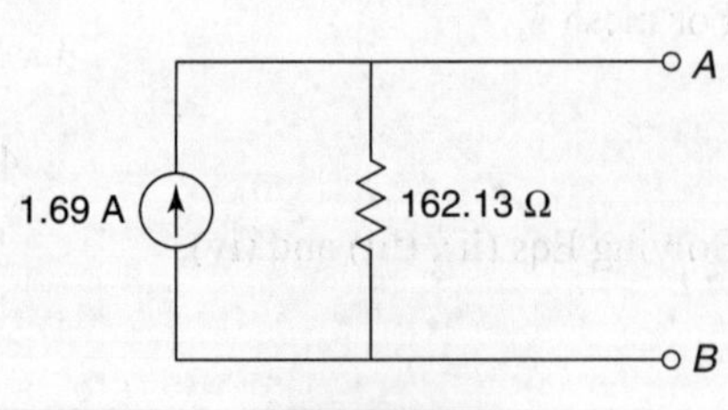

Fig. 2.237

## EXAMPLE 2.86

*Obtain Norton's equivalent network across A-B in the network of Fig. 2.238.*

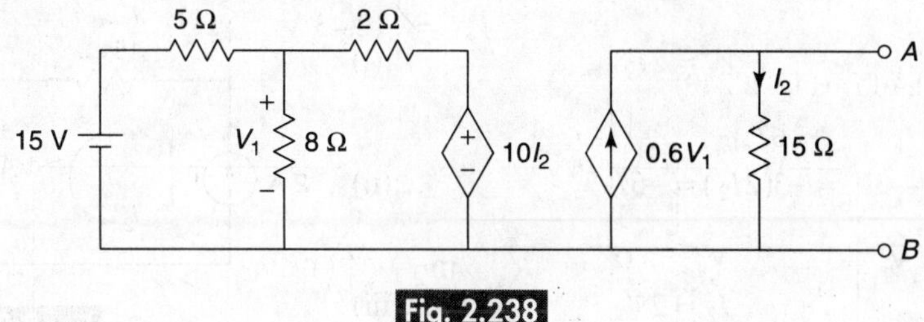


Fig. 2.238

**Solution**

***Step I*** Calculation of $V_{Th}$ (Fig. 2.239)

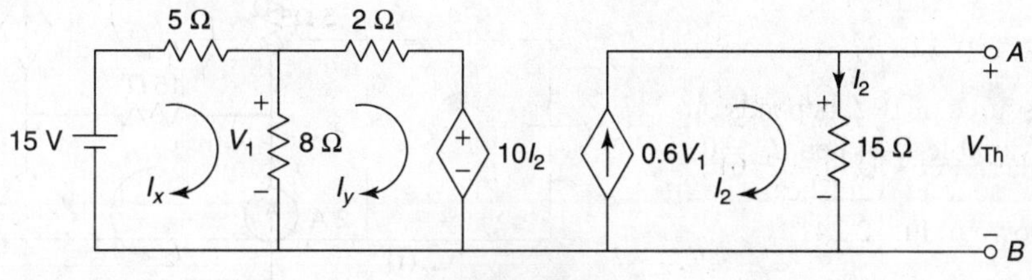


Fig. 2.239

From Fig. 2.239,

$$V_1 = 8(I_x - I_y) \qquad \text{...(i)}$$

Applying KVL to mesh 1,

$$15 - 5I_x - 8(I_x - I_y) = 0$$

$$13I_x - 8I_y = 15 \qquad \text{...(ii)}$$

Applying KVL to mesh 2,

$$-8(I_y - I_x) - 2I_y - 10I_2 = 0$$

$$8I_x - 10I_y - 10I_2 = 0 \qquad \text{...(iii)}$$

For mesh 3,

$$I_2 = 0.6V_1 = 0.6\left[8(I_x - I_y)\right]$$

$$4.8I_x - 4.8I_y - I_2 = 0 \qquad \text{...(iv)}$$

Solving Eqs (ii), (iii) and (iv),

$$I_x = 3.28 \text{ A}$$

$$I_y = 3.45 \text{ A}$$

$$I_2 = -0.83 \text{ A}$$

Writing the $V_{Th}$ equation,

$$15I_2 - V_{Th} = 0$$

$$15(-0.83) - V_{Th} = 0$$

$$V_{Th} = -12.45 \text{ V}$$

***Step II*** Calculation of $I_N$ (Fig. 2.240)

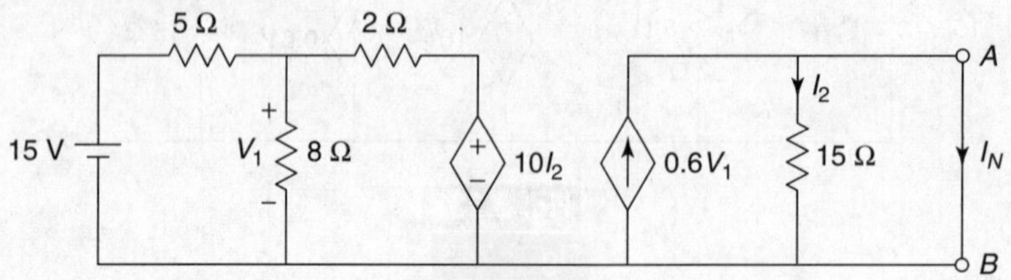


Fig. 2.240

From Fig. 2.240,

$$I_2 = 0$$

The dependent source of $10\,I_2$ depends on the controlling variable $I_2$. When $I_2 = 0$, the dependent source vanishes, i.e., $10I_2 = 0$, as shown in Fig. 2.241.

Fig. 2.241

From Fig. 2.241,

$$V_1 = 8(I_x - I_y) \qquad \text{...(i)}$$

Applying KVL to mesh 1,

$$15 - 5I_x - 8(I_x - I_y) = 0$$

$$13I_x - 8I_y = 15 \qquad \text{...(ii)}$$

Applying KVL to mesh 2,

$$-8(I_y - I_x) - 2I_y = 0$$

$$-8I_x + 10I_y = 0 \qquad \text{...(iii)}$$

Solving Eqs (ii) and (iii),

$$I_x = 2.27 \text{ A}$$

$$I_y = 1.82 \text{ A}$$

$$V_1 = 8(I_x - I_y) = 8(2.27 - 1.82) = 3.6 \text{ V}$$

For mesh 3,

$$I_N = 0.6V_1 = 0.6(3.6) = 2.16 \text{ A}$$

***Step III*** Calculation of $R_N$

$$R_N = \frac{V_{Th}}{I_N} = \frac{-12.45}{2.16} = -5.76\ \Omega$$

***Step IV*** Norton's Equivalent Network (Fig. 2.242)

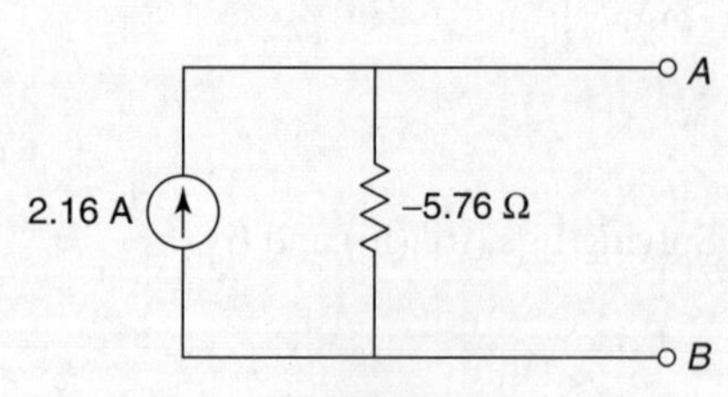


Fig. 2.242

## EXAMPLE 2.87

*Find Norton's equivalent network of Fig. 2.243.*

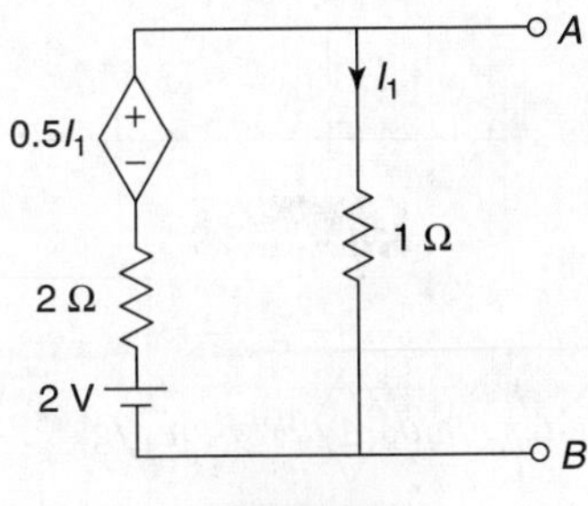


Fig. 2.243

### Solution

***Step I*** Calculation of $V_{Th}$ (Fig. 2.244)

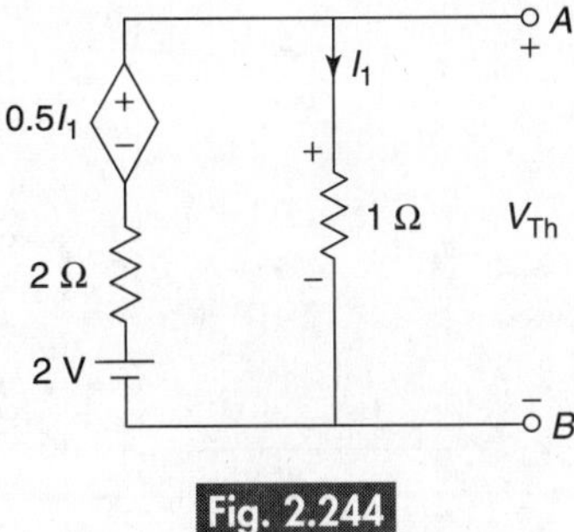


Fig. 2.244

Applying KVL to the mesh,

$$2 - 2I_1 + 0.5I_1 - 1I_1 = 0$$

$$2 - 2.5I_1 = 0$$

$$I_1 = 0.8 \text{ A}$$

Writing the $V_{Th}$ equation,

$$1I_1 - V_{Th} = 0$$

$$1(0.8) - V_{Th} = 0$$

$$V_{Th} = 0.8 \text{ V}$$

***Step II*** Calculation of $I_N$ (Fig. 2.245)

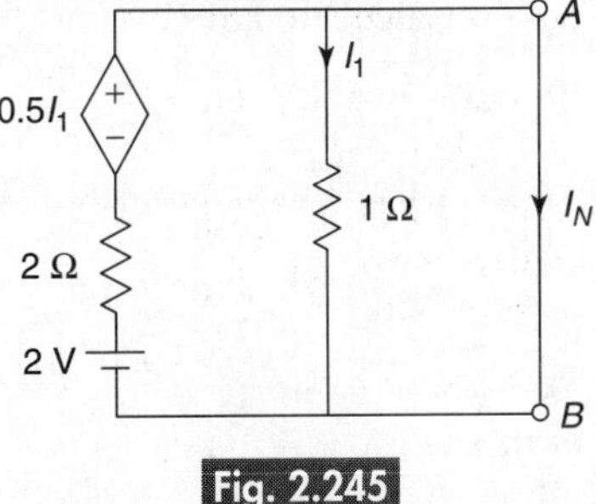


Fig. 2.245

When a short circuit is placed across the 1 Ω resistor, it gets shorted.

$$I_1 = 0$$

The dependent source of $0.5I_1$ depends on the controlling variable $I_1$. When $I_1 = 0$, the dependent source vanishes, i.e., $0.5\,I_1 = 0$, as shown in Fig. 2.246.

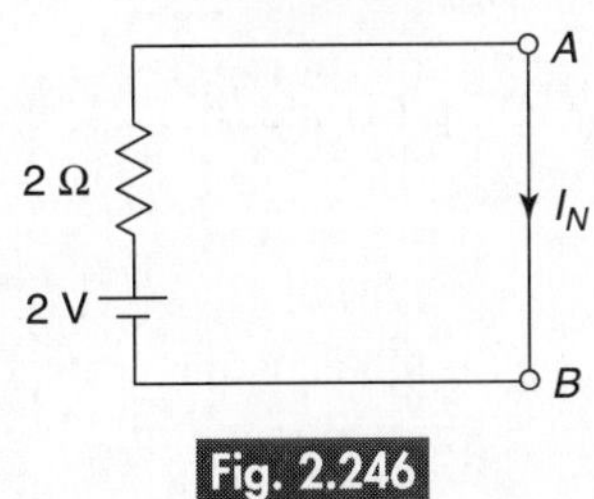


Fig. 2.246

$$I_N = \frac{2}{2} = 1 \text{ A}$$

***Step III*** Calculation of $R_N$

$$R_N = \frac{V_{Th}}{I_N} = \frac{0.8}{1} = 0.8\ \Omega$$

***Step IV*** Norton's Equivalent Network (Fig. 2.247)

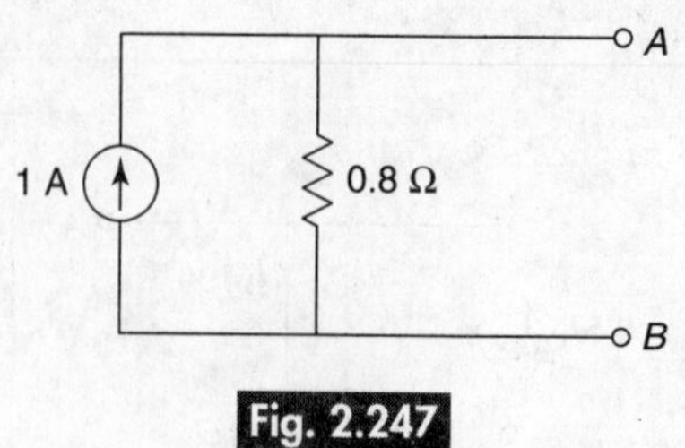


Fig. 2.247

## EXAMPLE 2.88

*Find Norton's equivalent network at the terminals A and B of Fig. 2.248.*

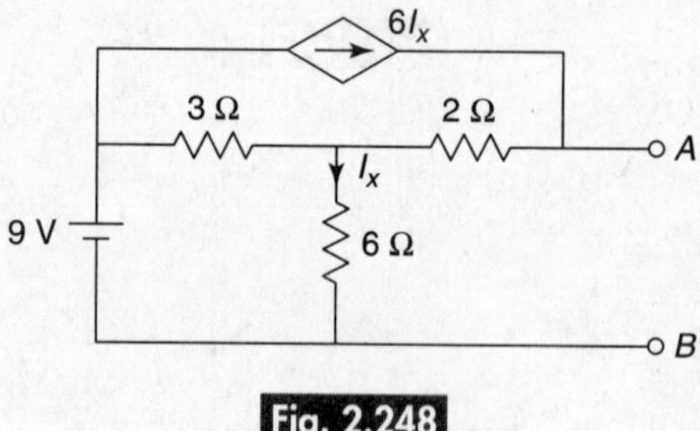


Fig. 2.248

### Solution

***Step I*** Calculation of $V_{Th}$ (Fig. 2.249)

From Fig. 2.249,

$$I_x = I_1 \qquad \text{...(i)}$$

Fig. 2.249

Applying KVL to mesh 1,

$$9 - 3(I_1 - I_2) - 6I_1 = 0$$

$$9I_1 - 3I_2 = 9 \qquad \text{...(ii)}$$

For mesh 2,

$$I_2 = 6I_x = 6I_1$$

$$6I_1 - I_2 = 0 \qquad \text{...(iii)}$$

Solving Eqs (ii) and (iii),

$$I_1 = -1 \text{ A}$$

$$I_2 = -6 \text{ A}$$

Writing the $V_{Th}$ equation,

$$9 - 3(I_1 - I_2) + 2I_2 - V_{Th} = 0$$

$$9 - 3(-1+6) + 2(-6) - V_{Th} = 0$$

$$V_{Th} = -18 \text{ V}$$

***Step II*** Calculation of $I_N$ (Fig. 2.250)

From Fig. 2.250,

$$I_x = I_1 - I_3 \qquad \text{...(i)}$$

Applying KVL to mesh 1,

$$9 - 3(I_1 - I_2) - 6(I_1 - I_3) = 0$$

$$9I_1 - 3I_2 - 6I_3 = 9 \qquad \text{...(ii)}$$

Fig. 2.250

For mesh 2,

$$I_2 = 6I_x = 6(I_1 - I_3)$$

$$6I_1 - I_2 - 6I_3 = 0 \qquad \text{...(iii)}$$

Applying KVL to mesh 3,

$$-6(I_3 - I_1) - 2(I_3 - I_2) = 0$$

$$-6I_1 - 2I_2 + 8I_3 = 0 \qquad \text{...(iv)}$$

Solving Eqs (ii), (iii) and (iv),

$$I_1 = 5 \text{ A}$$
$$I_2 = 3 \text{ A}$$
$$I_3 = 4.5 \text{ A}$$
$$I_N = I_3 = 4.5 \text{ A}$$

***Step III*** Calculation of $R_N$

$$R_N = \frac{V_{\text{Th}}}{I_N} = \frac{-18}{4.5} = -4\ \Omega$$

***Step IV*** Norton's Equivalent Network (Fig. 2.251)

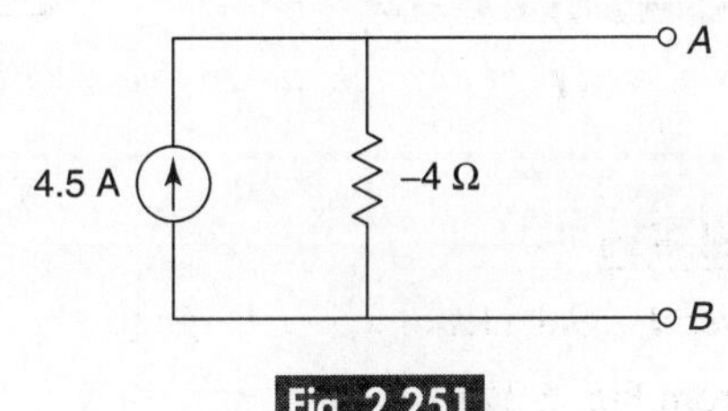


Fig. 2.251

## EXAMPLE 2.89

*Find Norton's equivalent network to the left of terminal A-B in Fig. 2.252.*

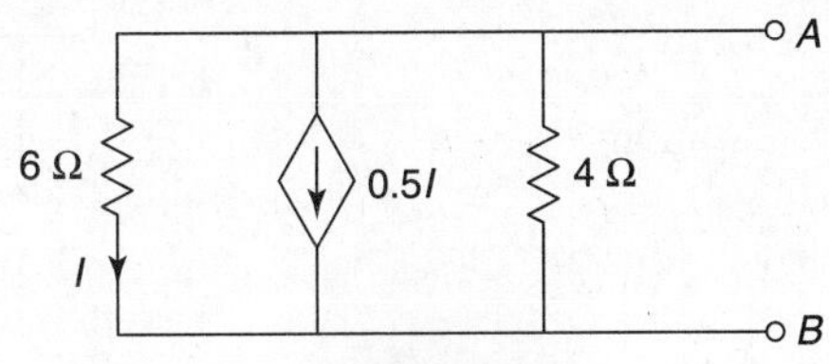


Fig. 2.252

**Solution** Since the network does not contain any independent source,

$$V_{\text{Th}} = 0$$
$$I_N = 0$$

But $R_N$ can be calculated by applying a known current source of 1 A at the terminals *A* and *B*, as shown in Fig. 2.253.

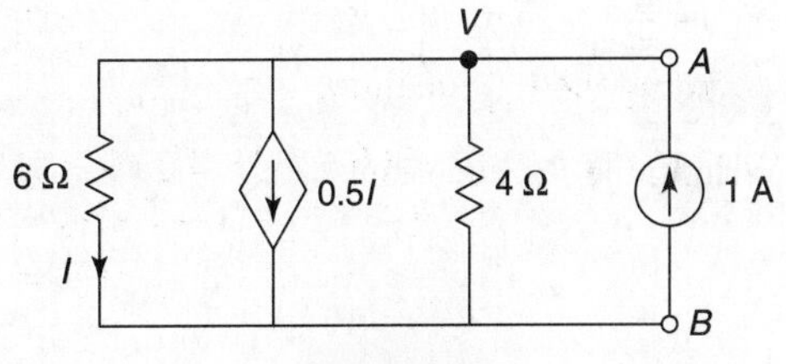


Fig. 2.253

From Fig. 2.253,

$$I = \frac{V}{6}$$

Applying KCL at the node,

$$\frac{V}{6} + 0.5I + \frac{V}{4} = 1$$

$$\frac{V}{6} + 0.5\left(\frac{V}{6}\right) + \frac{V}{4} = 1$$

$$\left(\frac{1}{6} + \frac{0.5}{6} + \frac{1}{4}\right)V = 1$$

$$V = 2$$

$$R_N = \frac{V}{1} = \frac{2}{1} = 2\ \Omega$$

Hence, Norton's equivalent network is, as shown in Fig. 2.254.

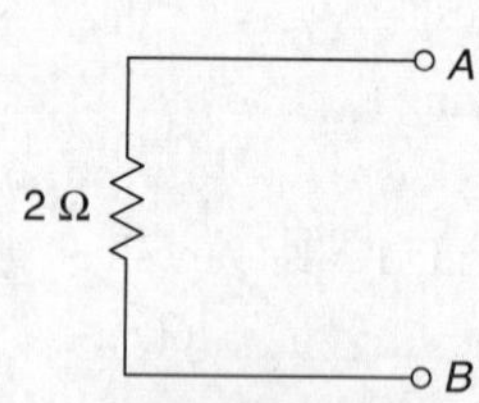


Fig. 2.254

## EXAMPLE 2.90

*Find the current through the 2 Ω resistor in the network shown in Fig. 2.255.*

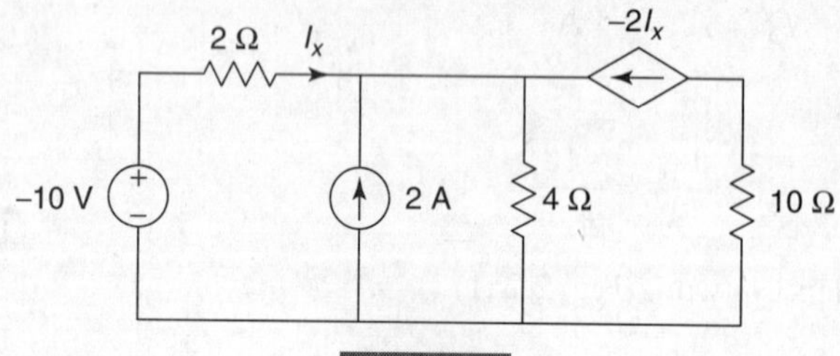


Fig. 2.255

**Solution**

***Step I*** Calculation of $V_{Th}$ (Fig. 2.256)

From Fig. 2.256,

$$I_x = 0$$

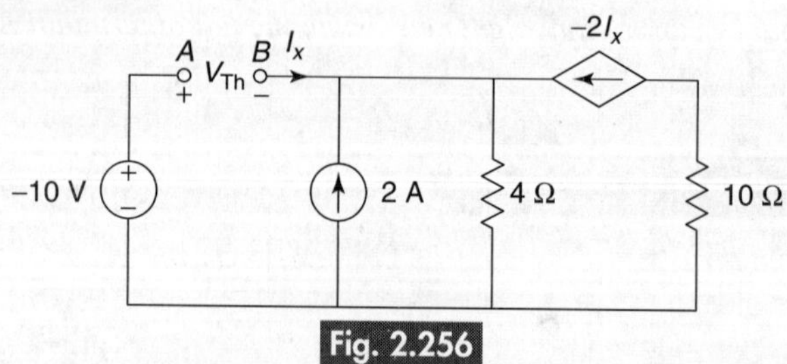


Fig. 2.256

The dependent source of $-2\,I_x$ depends on the controlling variable $I_x$. When $I_x = 0$, the dependent source vanishes, i.e., $-2I_x = 0$, as shown in Fig. 2.257.

$$I_1 = 2$$

Writing the $V_{Th}$ equation,

$$-10 - V_{Th} - 4I_1 = 0$$

$$-10 - V_{Th} - 4(2) = 0$$

$$V_{Th} = -18\ \text{V}$$

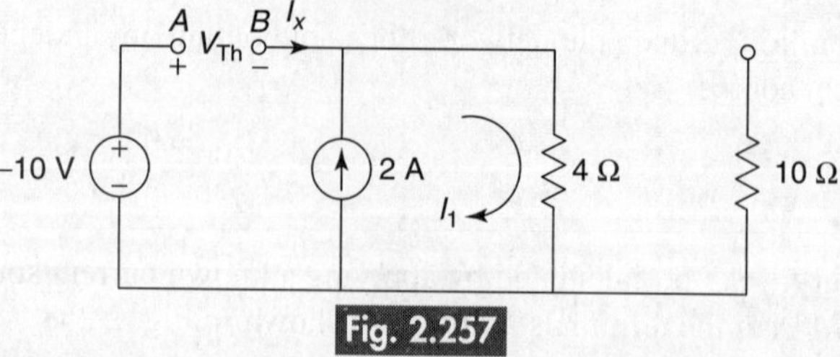


Fig. 2.257

***Step II*** Calculation of $I_N$ (Fig. 2.258)

From Fig. 2.258,

$$I_x = I_1 \quad \text{...(i)}$$

Mesh 1 and 2 will form a supermesh.

Writing the current equation for the supermesh,

$$I_2 - I_1 = 2 \quad \text{...(ii)}$$

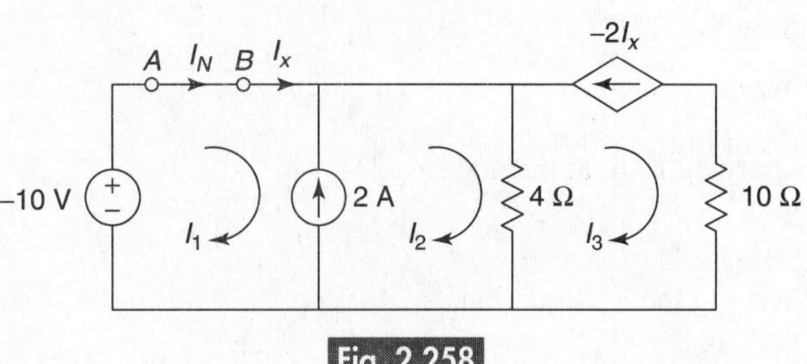

Fig. 2.258

Applying KVL to the outer path of the supermesh,

$$-10 - 4(I_2 - I_3) = 0$$

$$-4I_2 + 4I_3 = 10 \quad \text{...(iii)}$$

For mesh 3,

$$I_3 = -(-2I_x) = 2I_x = 2I_1$$

$$2I_1 - I_3 = 0 \quad \text{...(iv)}$$

Solving Eqs (ii), (iii) and (iv),

$$I_1 = 4.5 \text{ A}$$
$$I_2 = 6.5 \text{ A}$$
$$I_3 = 9 \text{ A}$$
$$I_N = I_1 = 4.5 \text{ A}$$

***Step III*** Calculation of $R_N$

$$R_N = \frac{V_{\text{Th}}}{I_N} = \frac{-18}{4.5} = -4\ \Omega$$

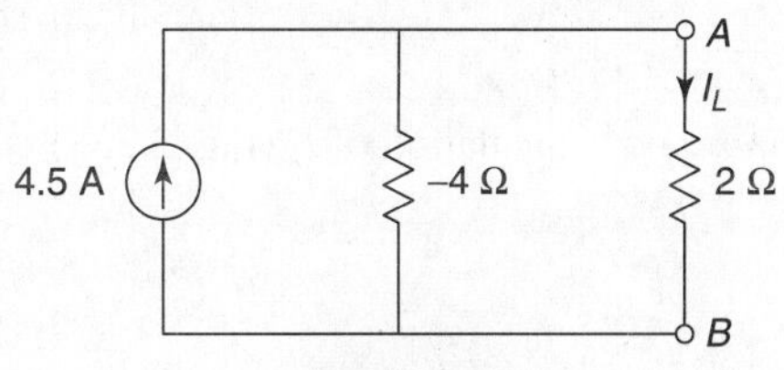

Fig. 2.259

***Step IV*** Calculation of $I_L$ (Fig. 2.259)

$$I_L = 4.5 \times \frac{-4}{-4+2} = 9 \text{ A}$$

## EXAMPLE 2.91

*Find the current through the 2Ω resistor in the network of Fig. 2.260.*

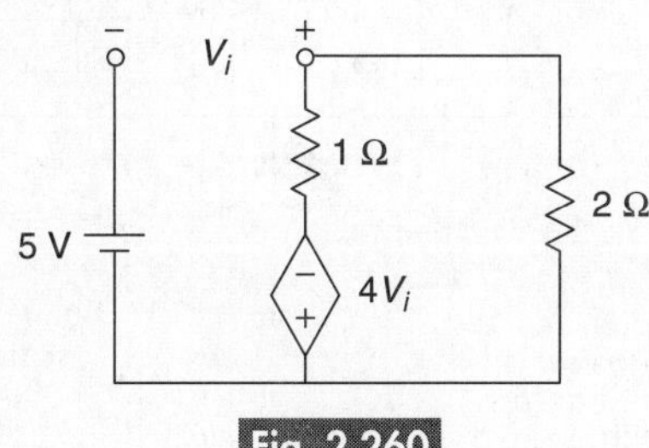

Fig. 2.260

**Solution**

***Step I*** Calculation of $V_{Th}$ (Fig. 2.261)

From Fig. 2.261,

$$5 + V_i + 4V_i = 0$$

$$V_i = -1 \text{ V}$$

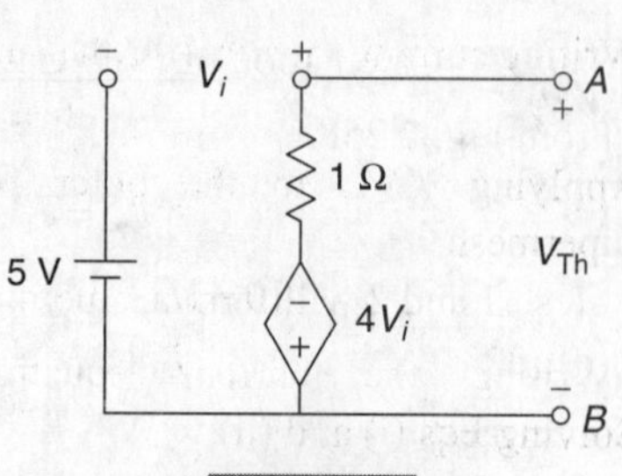

Fig. 2.261

Writing the $V_{Th}$ equation,

$$-4V_i - V_{Th} = 0$$

$$V_{Th} = -4V_i = -4(-1) = 4 \text{ V}$$

***Step II*** Calculation of $I_N$ (Fig. 2.262)

From Fig. 2.262,

$$5 + V_i = 0$$

$$V_i = -5 \text{ V}$$

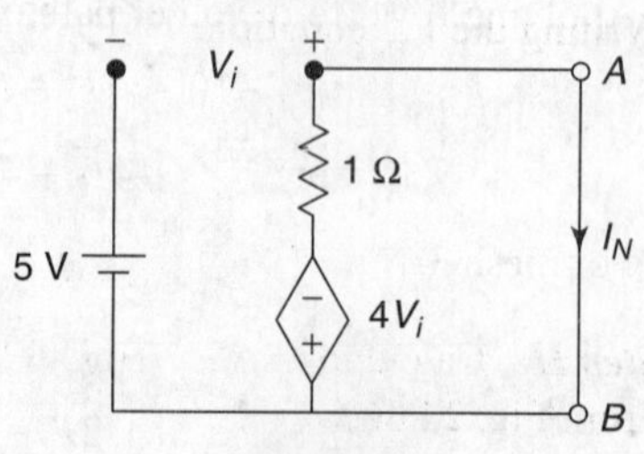

Fig. 2.262

Applying KVL to the mesh,

$$-4V_i - 1I_N = 0$$

$$I_N = -4V_i = -4(-5) = 20 \text{ A}$$

***Step III*** Calculation of $R_N$

$$R_N = \frac{V_{Th}}{I_N} = \frac{4}{20} = 0.2\ \Omega$$

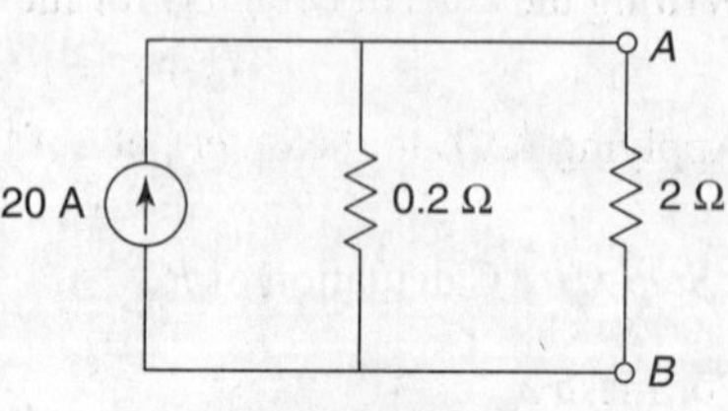

Fig. 2.263

***Step IV*** Calculation of $I_L$ (Fig. 2.263)

$$I_L = 20 \times \frac{0.2}{0.2 + 2} = 1.82 \text{ A}$$

**EXAMPLE 2.92**

*Find the current in the 2 Ω resistor in the network of Fig. 2.264.*

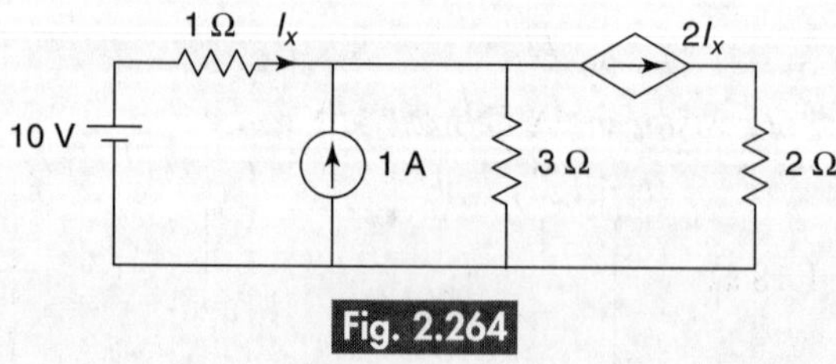

Fig. 2.264

**Solution**

***Step I*** Calculation of $V_{Th}$ (Fig. 2.265)

Meshes 1 and 2 will form a supermesh.

Writing current equation for the supermesh,

$$I_2 - I_1 = 1 \qquad \ldots\text{(i)}$$

Applying KVL to the outer path of the supermesh,

$$10 - 1I_1 - 3I_2 = 0$$

$$I_1 + 3I_2 = 10 \qquad \ldots\text{(ii)}$$

Fig. 2.265

Solving Eqs (i) and (ii),

$$I_1 = 1.75 \text{ A}$$

$$I_2 = 2.75 \text{ A}$$

Writing the $V_{Th}$ equation,

$$3I_2 - V_{Th} = 0$$

$$3(2.75) - V_{Th} = 0$$

$$V_{Th} = 8.25 \text{ V}$$

***Step II*** Calculation of $I_N$ (Fig. 2.266)

From Fig. 2.266,

$$I_x = I_1 \qquad \ldots\text{(i)}$$

Meshes 1 and 2 will form a supermesh.

Writing the current equation for the supermesh,

$$I_2 - I_1 = 1 \qquad \ldots\text{(ii)}$$

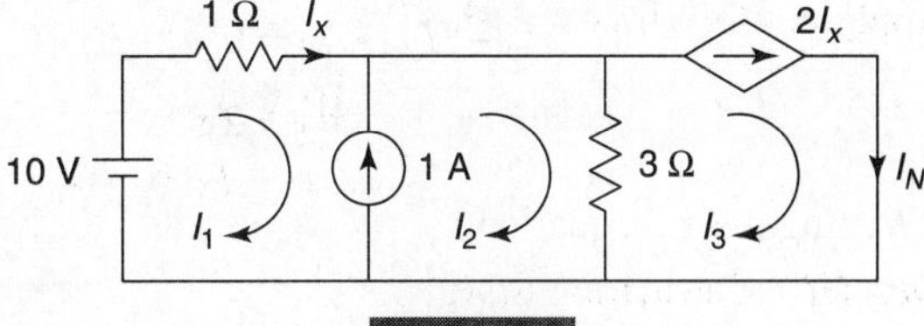

Fig. 2.266

Applying KVL to the outer path of the supermesh,

$$10 - 1I_1 - 3(I_2 - I_3) = 0$$

$$I_1 + 3I_2 - 3I_3 = 10 \qquad \ldots\text{(iii)}$$

For mesh 3,

$$I_3 = 2I_x = 2I_1$$

$$2I_1 - I_3 = 0 \qquad \ldots\text{(iv)}$$

Solving Eqs (ii), (iii) and (iv),

$$I_1 = -3.5 \text{ A}$$

$$I_2 = -2.5 \text{ A}$$

$$I_3 = -7 \text{ A}$$

$$I_N = I_3 = -7 \text{ A}$$

***Step III*** Calculation of $R_N$

$$R_N = \frac{V_{Th}}{I_N} = \frac{8.25}{-7} = -1.18\ \Omega$$

***Step IV*** Calculation of $I_L$ (Fig. 2.267)

$$I_L = -7 \times \frac{-1.18}{-1.18 + 2} = 10.07 \text{ A}$$

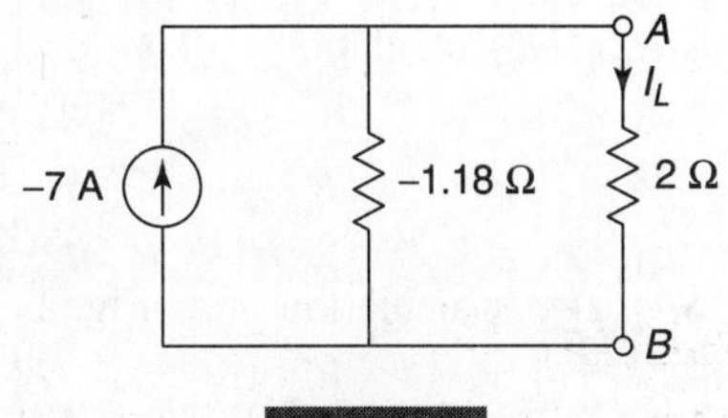

Fig. 2.267

## EXAMPLE 2.93

*Find the current through the 10 Ω resistor for the network of Fig. 2.268.*

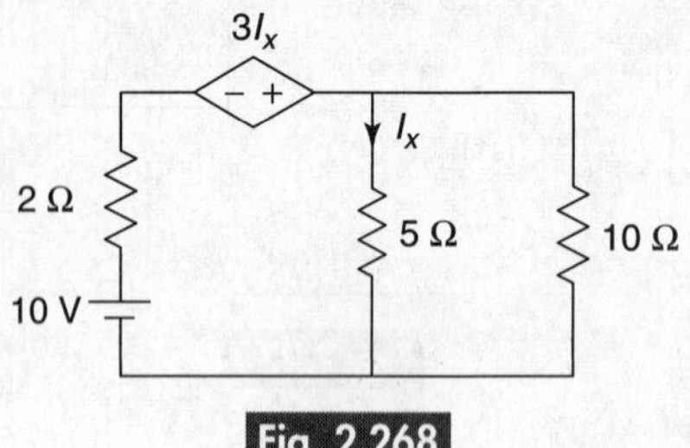


Fig. 2.268

### Solution

***Step I*** Calculation of $V_{Th}$ (Fig. 2.269)

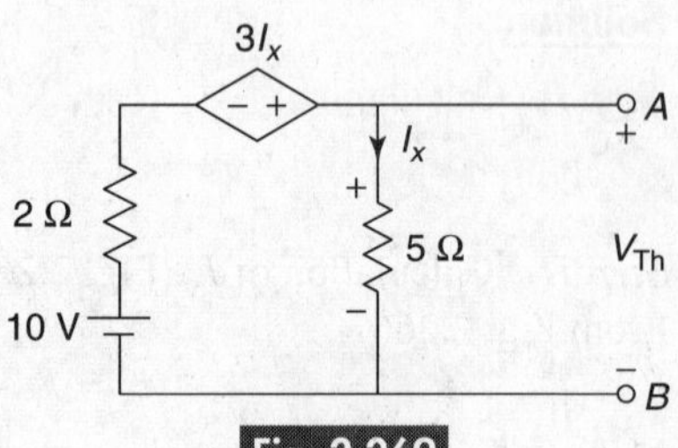


Fig. 2.269

Applying KVL to the mesh,

$$10 - 2I_x + 3I_x - 5I_x = 0$$

$$I_x = 2.5 \text{ A}$$

Writing the $V_{Th}$ equation,

$$5I_x - V_{Th} = 0$$

$$5(2.5) - V_{Th} = 0$$

$$V_{Th} = 12.5 \text{ V}$$

***Step II*** Calculation of $I_N$ (Fig. 2.270)

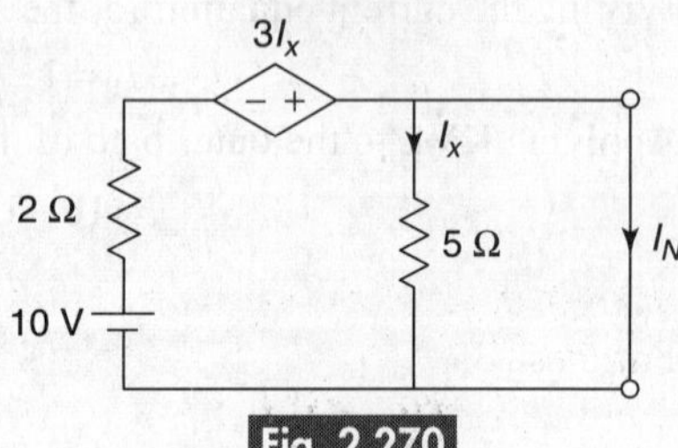


Fig. 2.270

From Fig. 2.270,

$$I_x = 0$$

The dependent source of 3 $I_x$ depends on the controlling variable $I_x$. When $I_x = 0$, the dependent source 3 $I_x$ vanishes, i.e., 3 $I_x = 0$, as shown in Fig. 2.271.

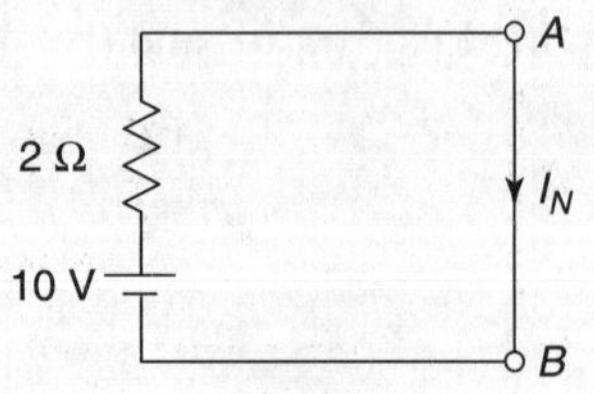


Fig. 2.271

$$I_N = \frac{10}{2} = 5 \text{ A}$$

***Step III*** Calculation of $R_N$

$$R_N = \frac{V_{Th}}{I_N} = \frac{12.5}{5} = 2.5 \ \Omega$$

***Step IV*** Calculation of $I_L$ (Fig. 2.272)

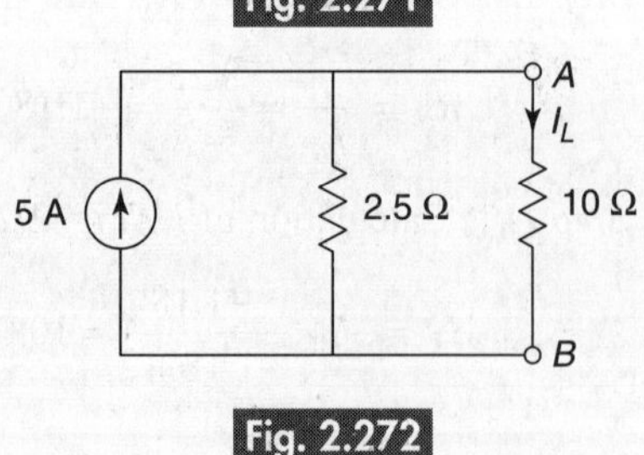


Fig. 2.272

$$I_L = 5 \times \frac{2.5}{2.5 + 10} = 1 \text{ A}$$

## EXAMPLE 2.94

*Find the current through the 5 Ω resistor in the network of Fig. 2.273.*

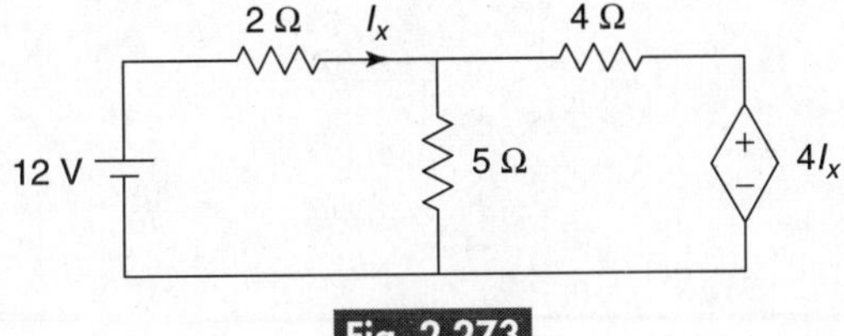


Fig. 2.273

**Solution**

***Step I*** Calculation of $V_{Th}$ (Fig. 2.274)

Applying KVL to the mesh,

$$12 - 2I_x - 4I_x - 4I_x = 0$$
$$12 - 10I_x = 0$$
$$I_x = 1.2 \text{ A}$$

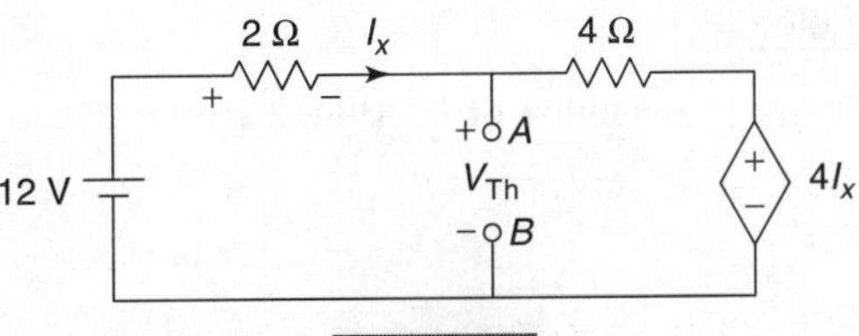


Fig. 2.274

Writing the $V_{Th}$ equation,

$$12 - 2I_x - V_{Th} = 0$$
$$12 - 2(1.2) - V_{Th} = 0$$
$$V_{Th} = 9.6 \text{ V}$$

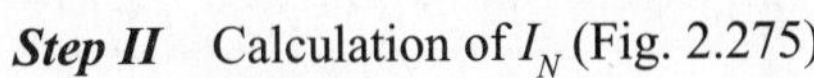

***Step II*** Calculation of $I_N$ (Fig. 2.275)

From Fig. 2.275,

$$I_x = I_1 \qquad \text{...(i)}$$

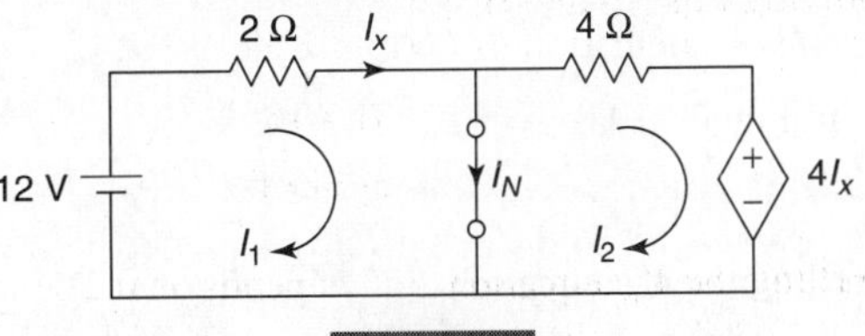


Fig. 2.275

Applying KVL to mesh 1,

$$12 - 2I_1 = 0$$
$$I_1 = 6 \text{ A} \qquad \text{...(ii)}$$

Applying KVL to mesh 2,

$$-4I_2 - 4I_x = 0$$
$$-4I_2 - 4I_1 = 0 \qquad \text{...(iii)}$$

Solving Eqs (ii) and (iii),

$$I_2 = -6 \text{ A}$$
$$I_N = I_1 - I_2 = 6 - (-6) = 12 \text{ A}$$

***Step III*** Calculation of $R_N$

$$R_N = \frac{V_{Th}}{I_N} = \frac{9.6}{12} = 0.8\ \Omega$$

***Step IV*** Calculation of $I_L$ (Fig. 2.276)

$$I_L = 12 \times \frac{0.8}{0.8 + 5} = 1.66 \text{ A}$$

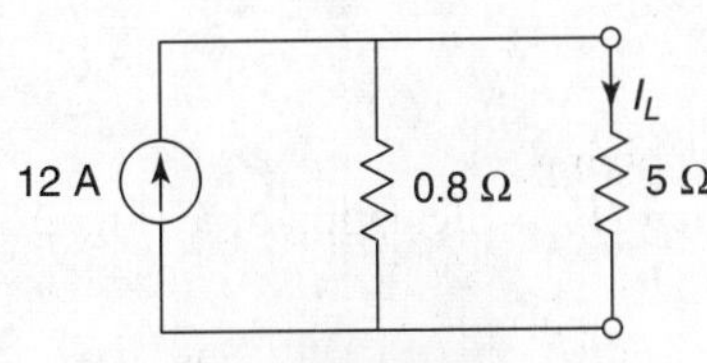


Fig. 2.276

## EXAMPLE 2.95

*Find the current through the 10 Ω resistor for the network of Fig. 2.277.*

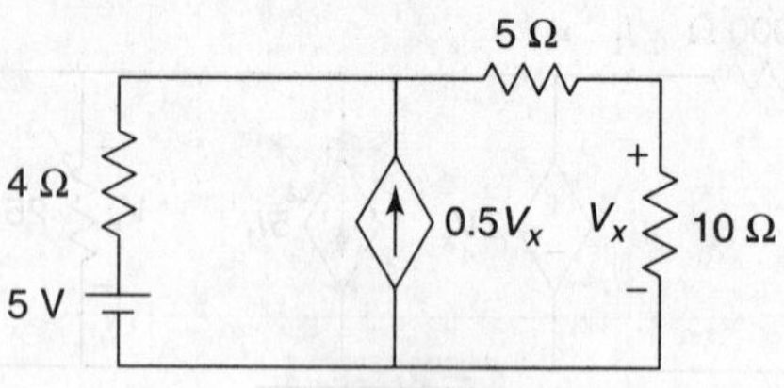


Fig. 2.277

### Solution

***Step I*** Calculation of $V_{Th}$ (Fig. 2.278)

For the mesh,

$$I = -0.5V_x = -0.5V_{Th}$$

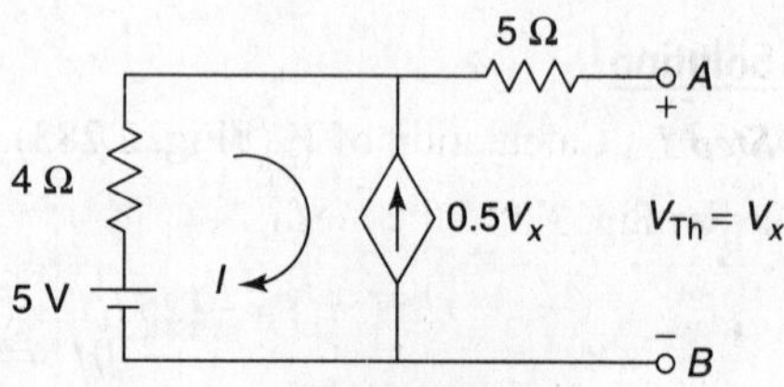


Fig. 2.278

Writing the $V_{Th}$ equation,

$$5 - 4I - 0 - V_{Th} = 0$$

$$5 - 4(-0.5V_{Th}) - V_{Th} = 0$$

$$V_{Th} = -5 \text{ V}$$

***Step II*** Calculation of $I_N$ (Fig. 2.279)

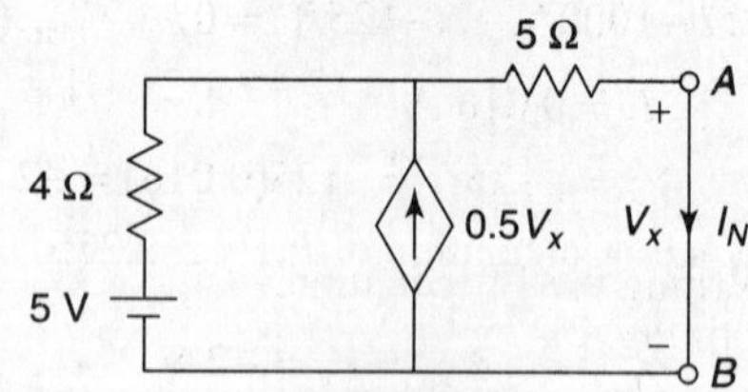


Fig. 2.279

From Fig. 2.279,

$$V_x = 0$$

The dependent source of 0.5 $V_x$ depends on the controlling variable $V_x$. When $V_x = 0$, the dependent source vanishes, i.e., 0.5 $V_x = 0$, as shown in Fig. 2.280.

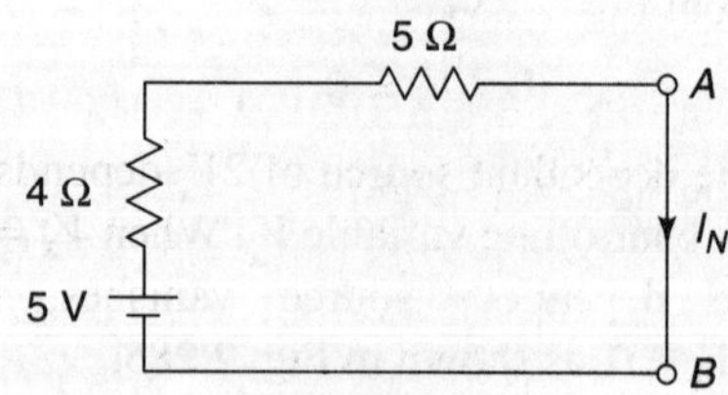


Fig. 2.280

$$I_N = \frac{5}{4+5} = \frac{5}{9} \text{ A}$$

***Step III*** Calculation of $R_N$

$$R_N = \frac{V_{Th}}{I_N} = \frac{-5}{\frac{5}{9}} = -9\ \Omega$$

***Step IV*** Calculation of $I_L$ (Fig. 2.281)

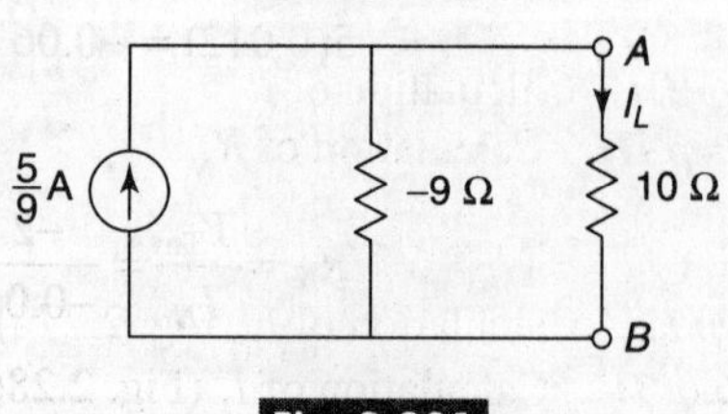


Fig. 2.281

$$I_L = \frac{5}{9} \times \frac{-9}{-9+10} = -5 \text{ A}$$

## EXAMPLE 2.96

*Find the current through the 10 Ω resistor in the network shown in Fig. 2.282.*

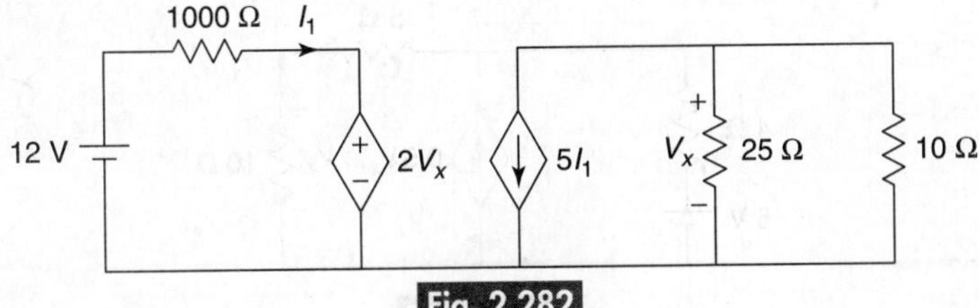


Fig. 2.282

### Solution

***Step I*** Calculation of $V_{Th}$ (Fig. 2.283)

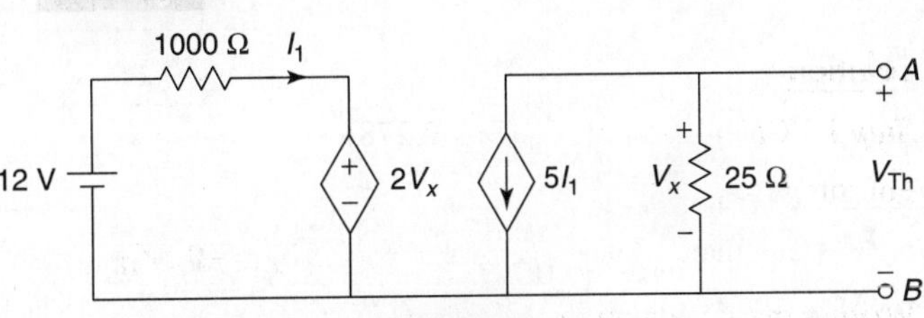


Fig. 2.283

From Fig. 2.283,

$$V_x = -25(5I_1) = -125\,I_1 \quad \ldots\text{(i)}$$

Applying KVL to mesh 1,

$$12 - 1000I_1 - 2V_x = 0$$

$$12 - 1000I_1 - 2(-125I_1) = 0 \quad \ldots\text{(ii)}$$

$$I_1 = 0.016 \text{ A}$$

$$V_x = -125I_1 = -125(0.016) = -2 \text{ V}$$

Writing the $V_{Th}$ equation,

$$V_{Th} = V_x = -2 \text{ V}$$

***Step II*** Calculation of $I_N$ (Fig. 2.284)

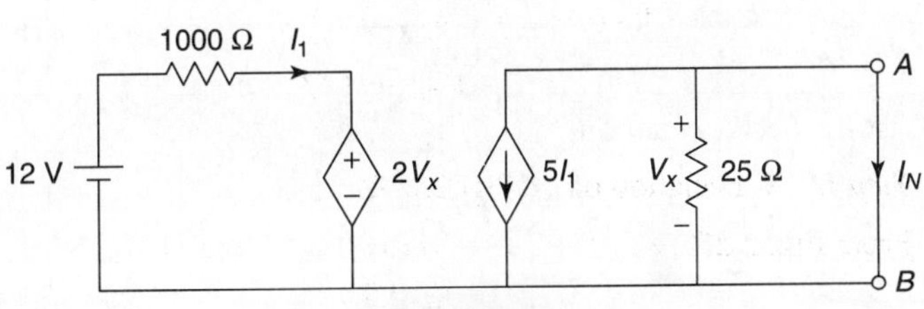


Fig. 2.284

From Fig. 2.284,

$$V_x = 0$$

The dependent source of $2V_x$ depends on the controlling variable $V_x$. When $V_x = 0$, the dependent source vanishes, i.e., $2\,V_x = 0$, as shown in Fig. 2.285.

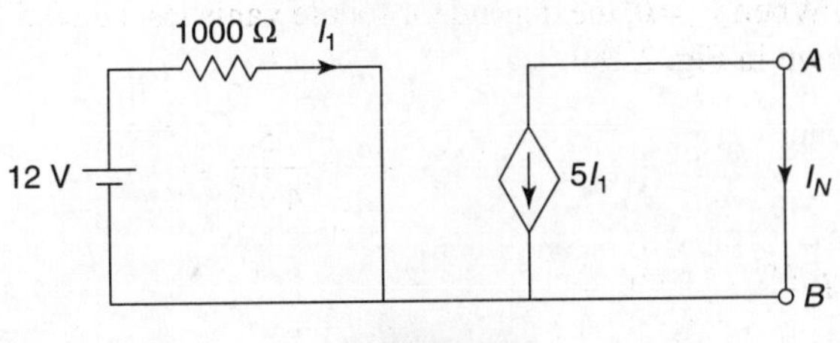


Fig. 2.285

$$I_1 = \frac{12}{1000} = 0.012 \text{ A}$$

$$I_N = -5I_1 = -5(0.012) = -0.06 \text{ A}$$

***Step III*** Calculation of $R_N$

$$R_N = \frac{V_{Th}}{I_N} = \frac{-2}{-0.06} = 33.33\ \Omega$$

***Step IV*** Calculation of $I_L$ (Fig. 2.286)

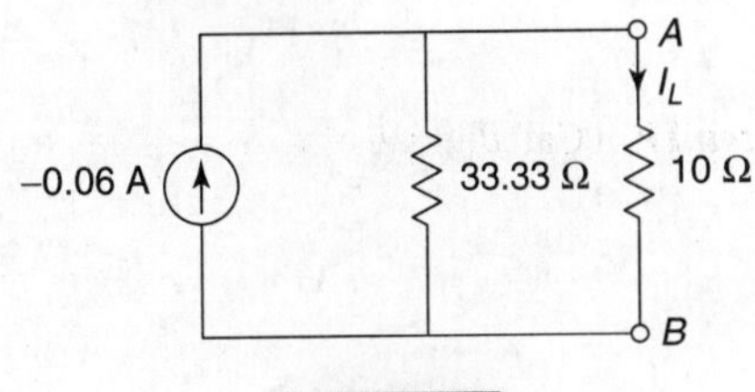


Fig. 2.286

$$I_L = -0.06 \times \frac{33.33}{33.33 + 10} = -0.046 \text{ A}$$

## EXAMPLE 2.97

*Find the current through the 5 Ω resistor for the network of Fig. 2.287.*

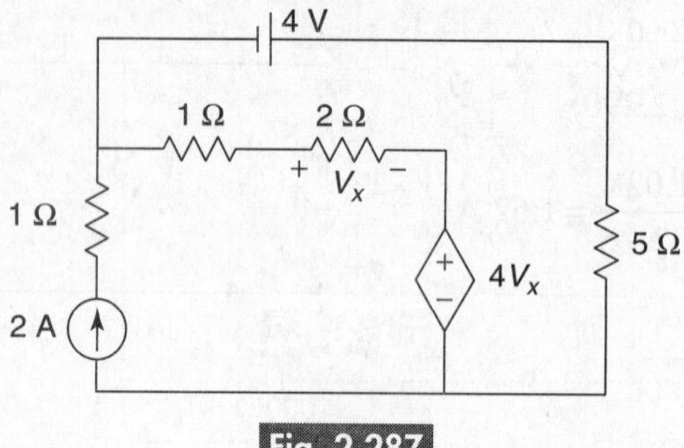


Fig. 2.287

**Solution**

***Step I*** Calculation of $V_{\text{Th}}$ (Fig. 2.288)

From Fig. 2.288,

$$V_x = 2I \qquad \ldots\text{(i)}$$

For the mesh,

$$I = 2 \qquad \ldots\text{(ii)}$$

$$V_x = 2(2) = 4 \text{ V}$$

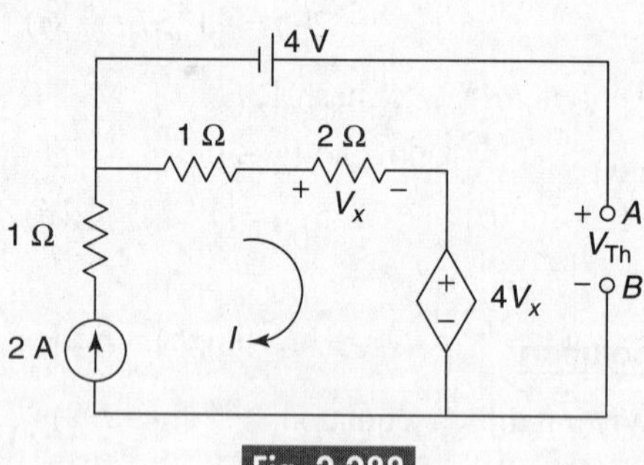


Fig. 2.288

Writing the $V_{\text{Th}}$ equation,

$$4V_x + 2I + 1I + 4 - V_{\text{Th}} = 0$$

$$4(4) + 2(2) + 2 + 4 - V_{\text{Th}} = 0$$

$$V_{\text{Th}} = 26 \text{ V}$$

***Step II*** Calculation of $I_N$ (Fig. 2.289)

From Fig. 2.289,

$$V_x = 2(I_1 - I_2) \qquad \ldots\text{(i)}$$

For mesh 1,

$$I_1 = 2 \qquad \ldots\text{(ii)}$$

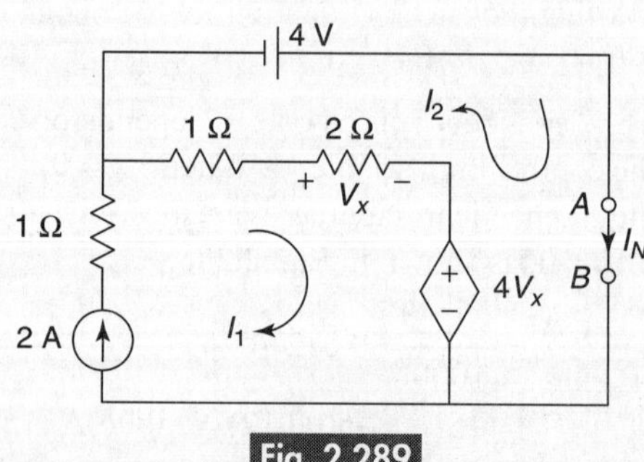


Fig. 2.289

Applying KVL to mesh 2,

$$4V_x - 2(I_2 - I_1) - 1(I_2 - I_1) + 4 = 0$$

$$4[2(I_1 - I_2)] - 2I_2 + 2I_1 - I_2 + I_1 + 4 = 0$$

$$11I_1 - 11I_2 = -4 \qquad \ldots\text{(iii)}$$

Solving Eqs (ii) and (iii),

$$I_1 = 2 \text{ A}$$

$$I_2 = 2.36 \text{ A}$$

$$I_N = I_2 = 2.36 \text{ A}$$

***Step III*** Calculation of $R_N$

$$R_N = \frac{V_{\text{Th}}}{I_N} = \frac{26}{2.36} = 11.02\ \Omega$$

***Step IV*** Calculation of $I_L$ (Fig. 2.290)

$$I_L = 2.36 \times \frac{11.02}{11.02 + 5} = 1.62\ \text{A}$$

Fig. 2.290

## EXAMPLE 2.98

*Find the current through the 1 Ω resistor in the network of Fig. 2.291.*

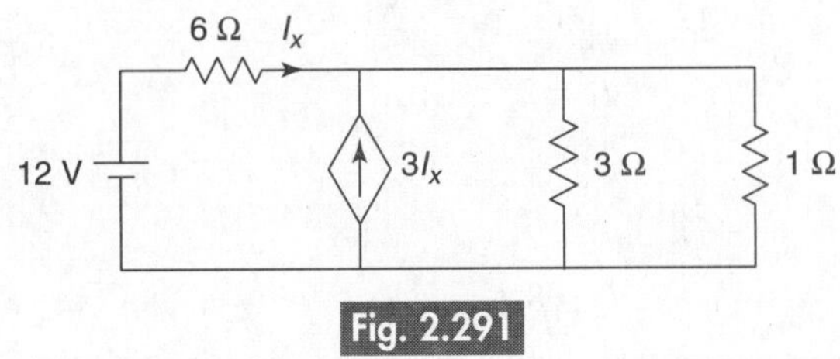


Fig. 2.291

**Solution**

***Step I*** Calculation of $V_{\text{Th}}$ (Fig. 2.292)

From Fig. 2.292,

$$I_x = I_1 \quad \ldots\text{(i)}$$

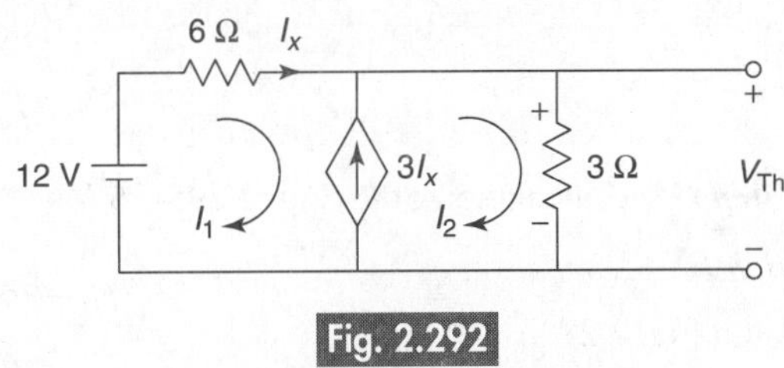


Fig. 2.292

Meshes 1 and 2 will form a supermesh.

Writing the current equation for the supermesh,

$$I_2 - I_1 = 3I_x = 3I_1$$

$$4I_1 - I_2 = 0 \quad \ldots\text{(ii)}$$

Applying KVL to the outer path of the supermesh,

$$12 - 6I_1 - 3I_2 = 0$$

$$6I_1 + 3I_2 = 12 \quad \ldots\text{(iii)}$$

Solving Eqs (ii) and (iii),

$$I_1 = 0.67\ \text{A}$$

$$I_2 = 2.67\ \text{A}$$

Writing the $V_{\text{Th}}$ equation,

$$3I_2 - V_{\text{Th}} = 0$$

$$3(2.67) - V_{\text{Th}} = 0$$

$$V_{\text{Th}} = 8\ \text{V}$$

***Step II*** Calculation of $I_N$ (Fig. 2.293)

When a short circuit is placed across a 3 Ω resistor, it gets shorted, as shown in Fig. 2.293.

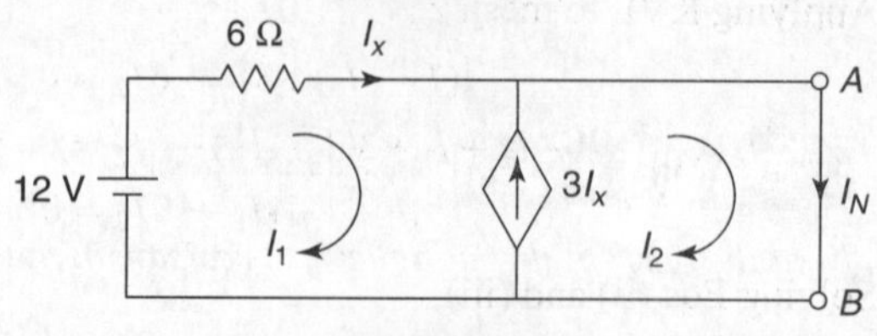


Fig. 2.293

From Fig. 2.294,

$$I_x = I_1 \quad \ldots\text{(i)}$$

Meshes 1 and 2 will form a supermesh.

Writing the current equation for the supermesh,

$$I_2 - I_1 = 3I_x = 3I_1$$

$$4I_1 - I_2 = 0 \quad \ldots\text{(ii)}$$

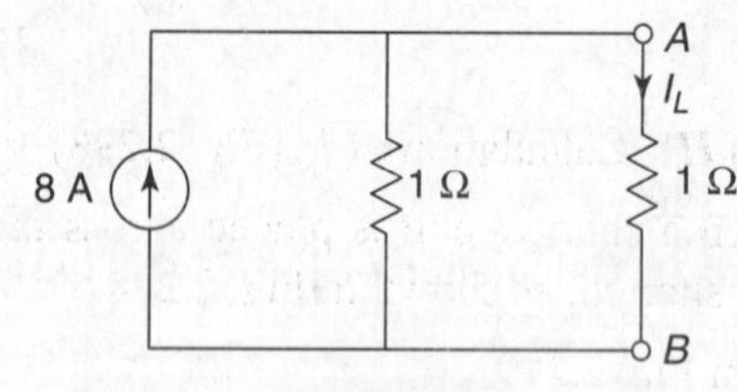


Fig. 2.294

Applying KVL to the outer path of the supermesh,

$$12 - 6I_1 = 0$$

$$I_1 = 2 \quad \ldots\text{(iii)}$$

Solving Eqs (ii) and (iii),

$$I_1 = 2\text{ A}$$

$$I_2 = 8\text{ A}$$

$$I_N = I_2 = 8\text{ A}$$

***Step III*** Calculation of $R_N$

$$R_N = \frac{V_{\text{Th}}}{I_N} = \frac{8}{8} = 1\ \Omega$$

***Step IV*** Calculation of $I_L$ (Fig. 2.295)

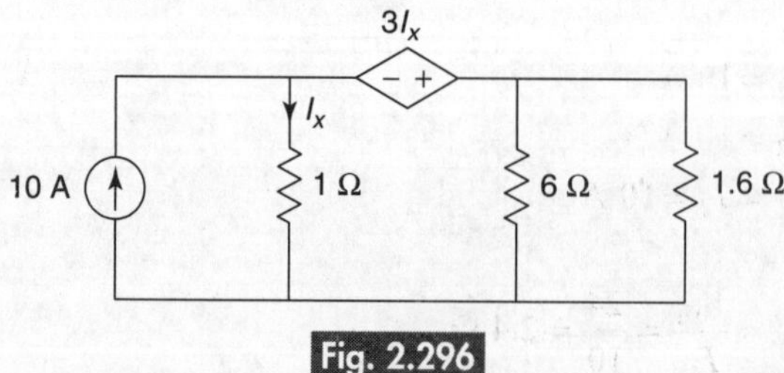


Fig. 2.295

$$I_L = 8 \times \frac{1}{1+1} = 4\text{ A}$$

**EXAMPLE 2.99**

*Find the current through the 1.6 Ω resistor in the network of Fig. 2.296.*



Fig. 2.296

**Solution**

***Step I*** Calculation of $V_{Th}$ (Fig. 2.297)

From Fig. 2.297,

$$I_x = I_1 - I_2 \quad \ldots\text{(i)}$$

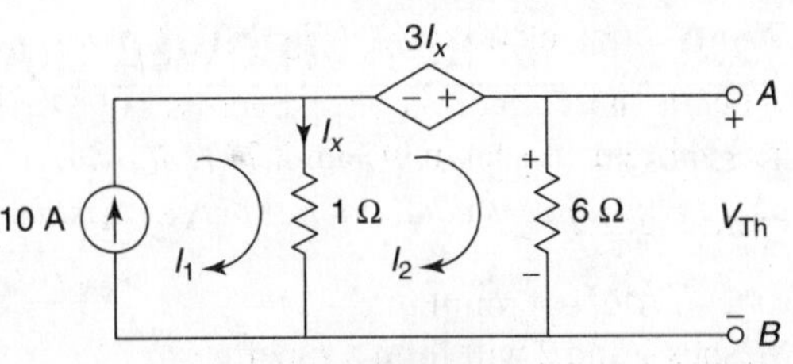

Fig. 2.297

For mesh 1,

$$I_1 = 10 \quad \ldots\text{(ii)}$$

Applying KVL to mesh 2,

$$-1(I_2 - I_1) + 3I_x - 6I_2 = 0$$

$$-I_2 + I_1 + 3(I_1 - I_2) - 6I_2 = 0$$

$$4I_1 - 10I_2 = 0 \quad \ldots\text{(iii)}$$

Solving Eqs (ii) and (iii),

$$I_1 = 10 \text{ A}$$

$$I_2 = 4 \text{ A}$$

Writing the $V_{Th}$ equation,

$$6I_2 - V_{Th} = 0$$

$$6(4) - V_{Th} = 0$$

$$V_{Th} = 24 \text{ V}$$

***Step II*** Calculation of $I_N$ (Fig. 2.298)

When a short circuit is placed across the 3 Ω resistor, it gets shorted, as shown in Fig. 2.298.

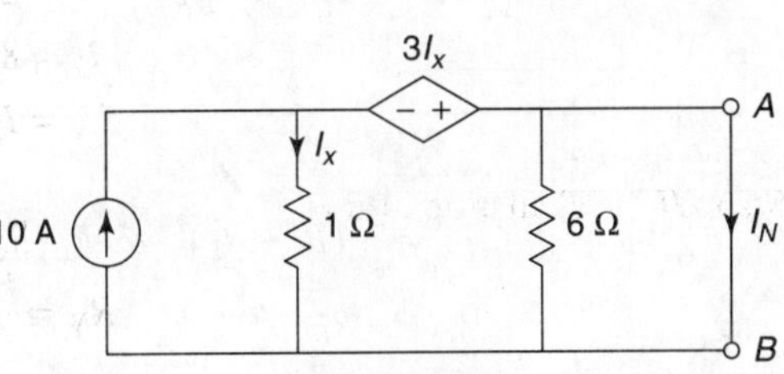

Fig. 2.298

From Fig. 2.299,

$$I_x = I_1 - I_2 \quad \ldots\text{(i)}$$

For mesh 1,

$$I_1 = 10 \quad \ldots\text{(ii)}$$

Applying KVL to mesh 2,

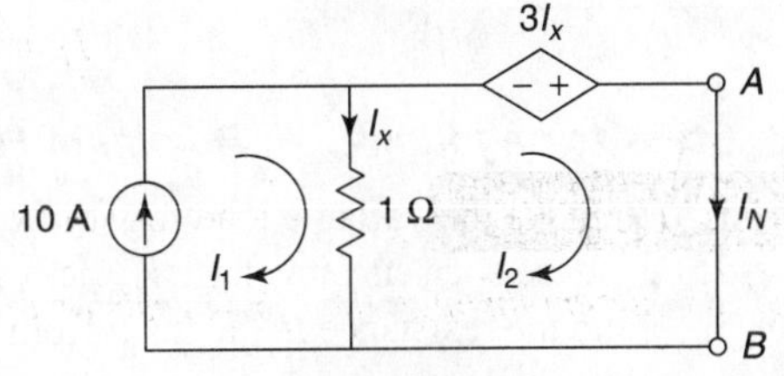

Fig. 2.299

$$-1(I_2 - I_1) + 3I_x = 0$$

$$-I_2 + I_1 + 3(I_1 - I_2) = 0$$

$$4I_1 - 4I_2 = 0 \quad \ldots\text{(iii)}$$

Solving Eqs (ii) and (iii),

$$I_1 = 10 \text{ A}$$

$$I_2 = 10 \text{ A}$$

$$I_N = I_2 = 10 \text{ A}$$

***Step III*** Calculation of $R_N$

$$R_N = \frac{V_{Th}}{I_N} = \frac{24}{10} = 2.4\ \Omega$$

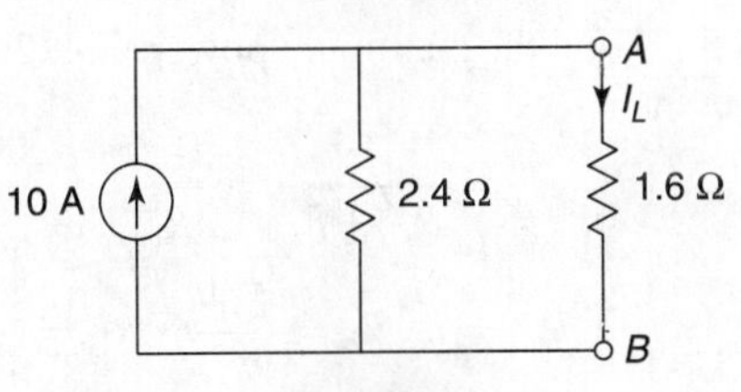

Fig. 2.300

***Step IV*** Calculation of $I_L$ (Fig. 2.300)

$$I_L = 10 \times \frac{2.4}{2.4 + 1.6} = 6 \text{ A}$$

## 2.8 MAXIMUM POWER TRANSFER THEOREM

LO 2.6

Analyse the networks using maximum power transfer theorem

It states that '*the maximum power is delivered from a source to a load when the load resistance is equal to the source resistance.*'

➤ ***Proof*** From Fig. 2.301,

$$I = \frac{V}{R_s + R_L}$$

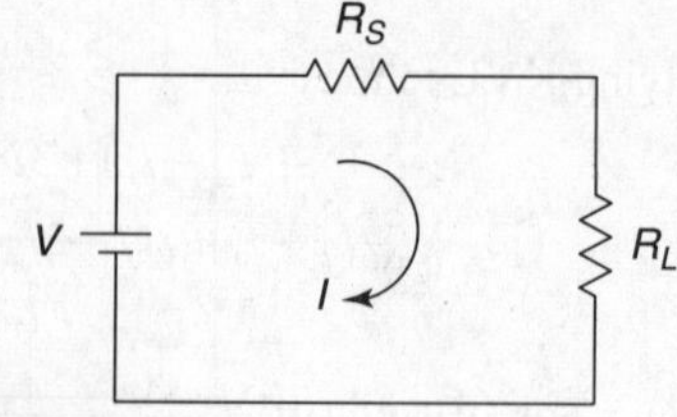


Fig. 2.301 *Network illustrating maximum power transfer theorem*

Power delivered to the load $R_L = P = I^2\ R_L = \dfrac{V^2 R_L}{(R_s + R_L)^2}$

To determine the value of $R_L$ for maximum power to be transferred to the load,

$$\frac{dP}{dR_L} = 0$$

$$\frac{dP}{dR_L} = \frac{d}{dR_L} \frac{V^2}{(R_s + R_L)^2} R_L$$

$$= \frac{V^2[(R_s + R_L)^2 - (2R_L)(R_s + R_L)]}{(R_s + R_L)^4}$$

$$(R_s + R_L)^2 - 2\,R_L(R_s + R_L) = 0$$

$$R_s^{\ 2} + R_L^{\ 2} + 2R_s R_L - 2R_L R_s - 2R_L^2 = 0$$

$$R_s = R_L$$

Hence, the maximum power will be transferred to the load when load resistance is equal to the source resistance.

### ➤ Steps to be followed in Maximum Power Transfer Theorem

1. Remove the variable load resistor $R_L$.
2. Find the open circuit voltage $V_{\text{Th}}$ across points $A$ and $B$.
3. Find the resistance $R_{\text{Th}}$ as seen from points $A$ and $B$.
4. Find the resistance $R_L$ for maximum power transfer.

$$R_L = R_{\text{Th}}$$

5. Find the maximum power (Fig. 2.302).

$$I_L = \frac{V_{\text{Th}}}{R_{\text{Th}} + R_L} = \frac{V_{\text{Th}}}{2R_{\text{Th}}}$$

$$P_{\max} = I_L^2\ R_L = \frac{V_{\text{Th}}^2}{4R_{\text{Th}}^2} \times R_{\text{Th}} = \frac{V_{\text{Th}}^2}{4R_{\text{Th}}}$$

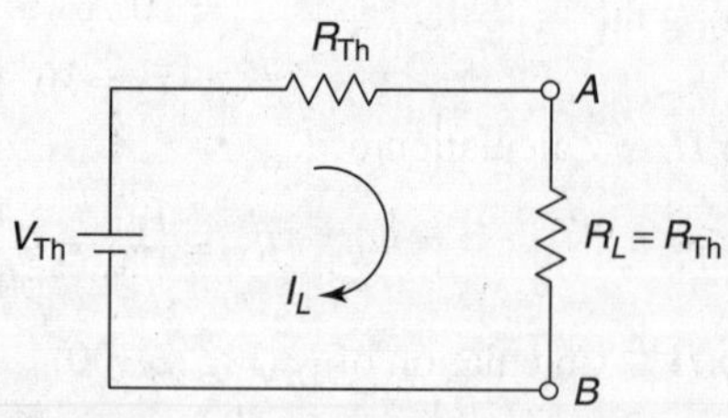


Fig. 2.302 *Thevenin's equivalent network*

## EXAMPLE 2.100

*For the value of resistance $R_L$ in Fig. 2.303 for maximum power transfer and calculate the maximum power.*

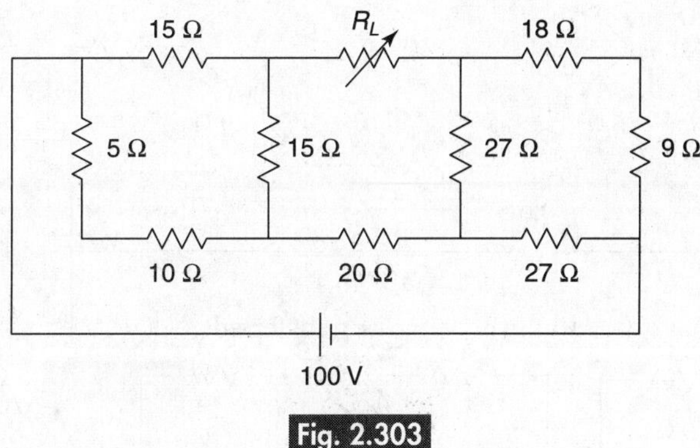


Fig. 2.303

### Solution

***Step I*** Calculation of $V_{Th}$ (Fig. 2.304)

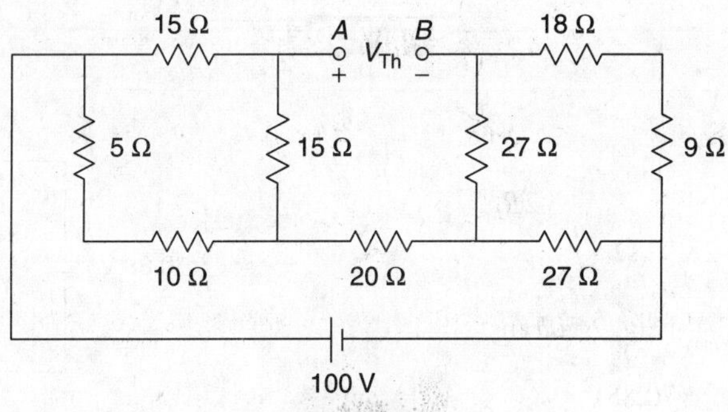


Fig. 2.304

By star–delta transformation (Fig. 2.305),

$$I = \frac{100}{5+5+20+9+9} = 2.08 \text{ A}$$

Writing the $V_{Th}$ equation,

$$100 - 5I - V_{Th} - 9I = 0$$

$$V_{Th} = 100 - 14I$$

$$= 100 - 14(2.08)$$

$$= 70.88 \text{ V}$$

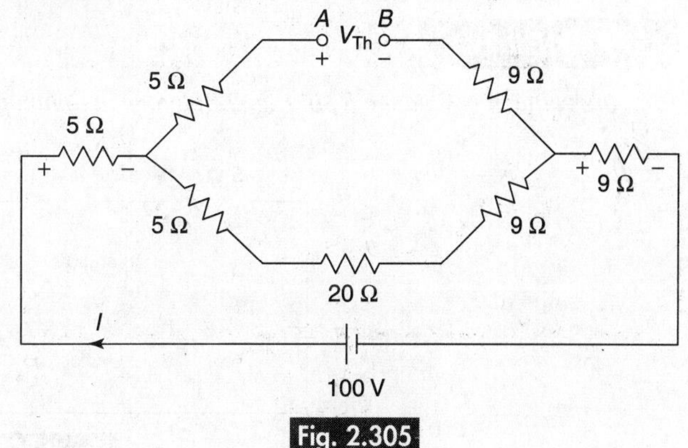


Fig. 2.305

***Step II*** Calculation of $R_{Th}$ (Fig. 2.306)

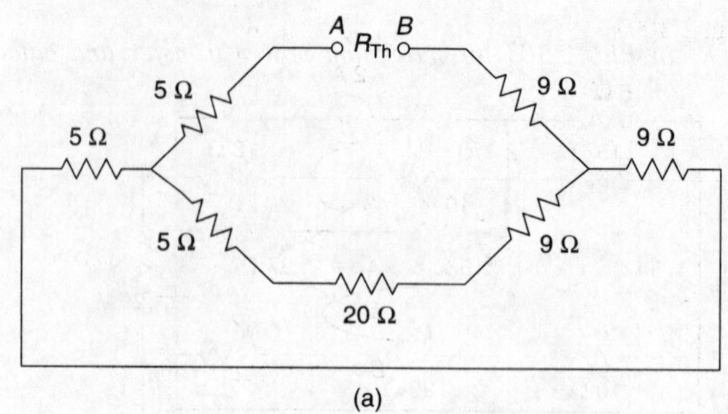

(a)

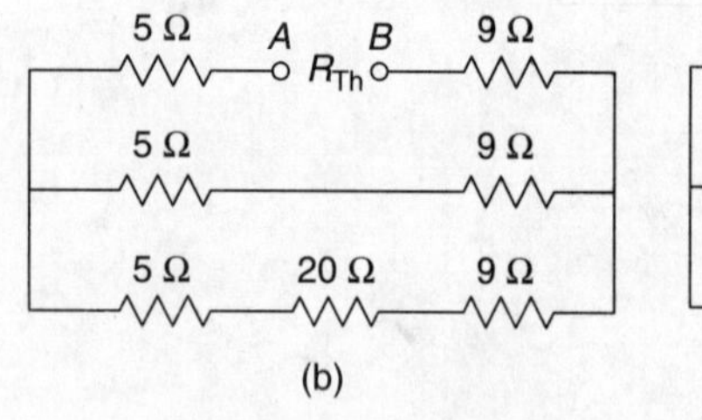

(b)

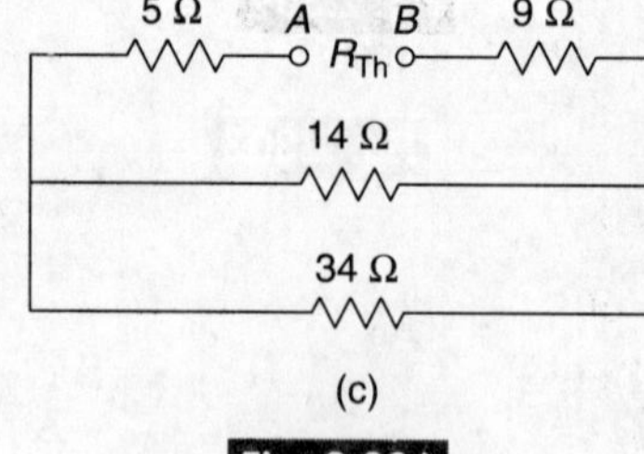

(c)

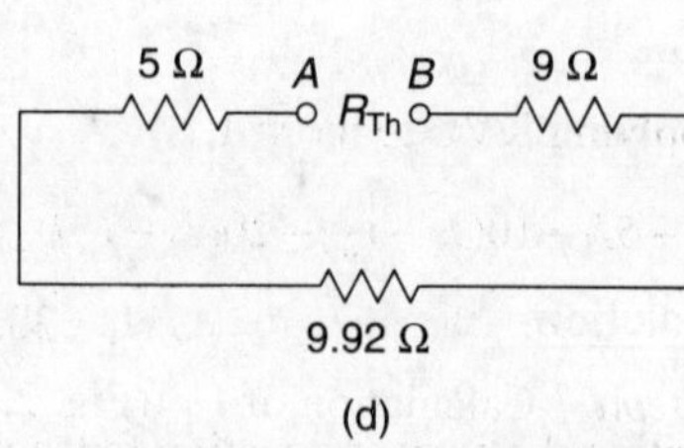

(d)

Fig. 2.306

$$R_{Th} = 23.92\ \Omega$$

***Step III*** Calculation of $R_L$

For maximum power transfer,

$$R_L = R_{Th} = 23.92\ \Omega$$

***Step IV*** Calculation of $P_{max}$ (Fig. 2.307)

$$P_{max} = \frac{V_{Th}^2}{4R_{Th}} = \frac{(70.88)^2}{4 \times 23.92} = 52.51\ \text{W}$$

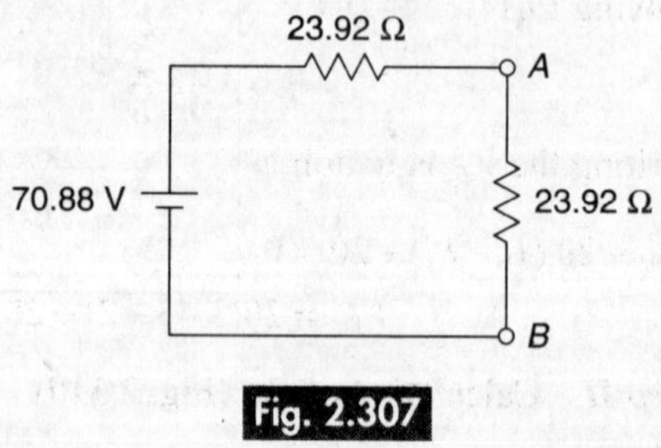

Fig. 2.307

## EXAMPLE 2.101

*Find the value of resistance $R_L$ in Fig. 2.308 for maximum power transfer and calculate the maximum power.*

Fig. 2.308

## Solution

***Step I*** Calculation of $V_{Th}$ (Fig. 2.309)

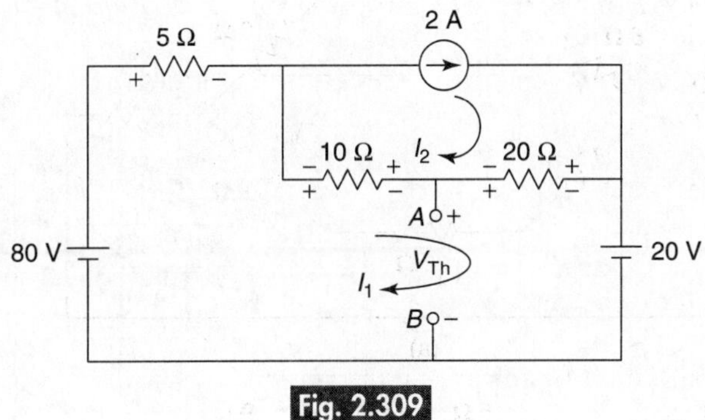


Fig. 2.309

Applying KVL to mesh 1,

$$80 - 5I_1 - 10(I_1 - I_2) - 20(I_1 - I_2) - 20 = 0$$

$$35I_1 - 30I_2 = 60 \quad \text{...(i)}$$

Writing the current equation for mesh 2,

$$I_2 = 2 \quad \text{...(ii)}$$

Solving Eqs (i) and (ii),

$$I_1 = 3.43 \text{ A}$$

Writing the $V_{Th}$ equation,

$$V_{Th} - 20\,(I_1 - I_2) - 20 = 0$$

$$V_{Th} = 20(3.43 - 2) + 20 = 48.6 \text{ V}$$

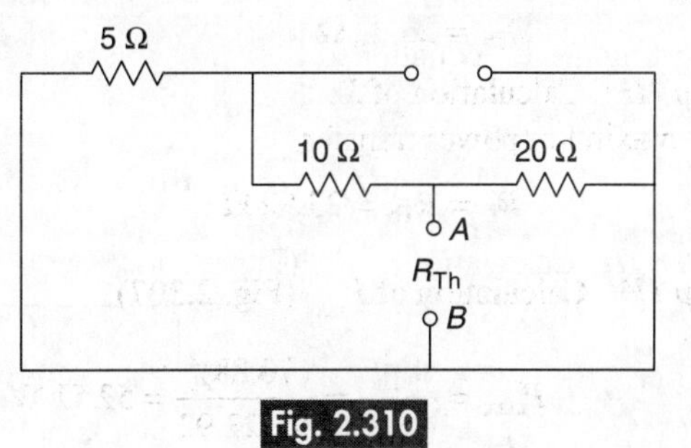


Fig. 2.310

***Step II*** Calculation of $R_{Th}$ (Fig. 2.310)

$$R_{Th} = 15 \,||\, 20 = 8.57 \ \Omega$$

***Step III*** Calculation of $R_L$

For maximum power transfer,

$$R_L = R_{Th} = 8.57 \ \Omega$$

***Step IV*** Calculation of $P_{max}$ (Fig. 2.311)

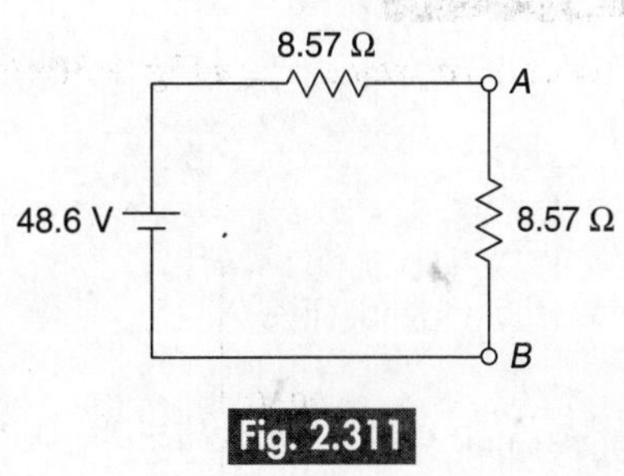


Fig. 2.311

$$P_{max} = \frac{V_{Th}^2}{4R_{Th}} = \frac{(48.6)^2}{4 \times 8.57} = 68.9 \text{ W}$$

## EXAMPLE 2.102

*Find the value of resistance $R_L$ in Fig. 2.312 for maximum power transfer and calculate the maximum power.*

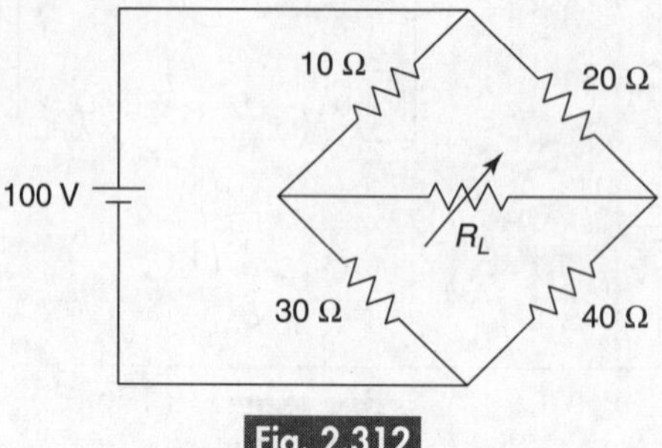


Fig. 2.312

**Solution**

***Step I*** Calculation of $V_{Th}$ (Fig. 2.313)

$$I_1 = \frac{100}{10+30} = 2.5 \text{ A}$$

$$I_2 = \frac{100}{20+40} = 1.66 \text{ A}$$

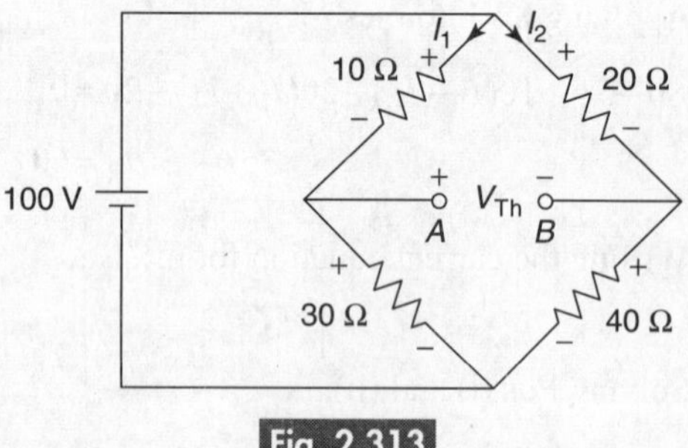


Fig. 2.313

Writing the $V_{Th}$ equation,

$$V_{Th} + 10\, I_1 - 20 I_2 = 0$$

$$V_{Th} = 20 I_2 - 10 I_1 = 20(1.66) - 10(2.5) = 8.2 \text{ V}$$

***Step II*** Calculation of $R_{Th}$ (Fig. 2.314)

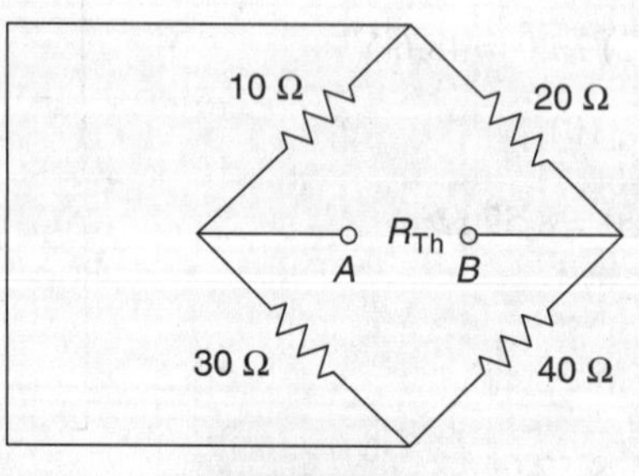


Fig. 2.314

Redrawing the network (Fig. 2.315),

$$R_{Th} = (10 \,\|\, 30) + (20 \,\|\, 40) = 20.83 \, \Omega$$

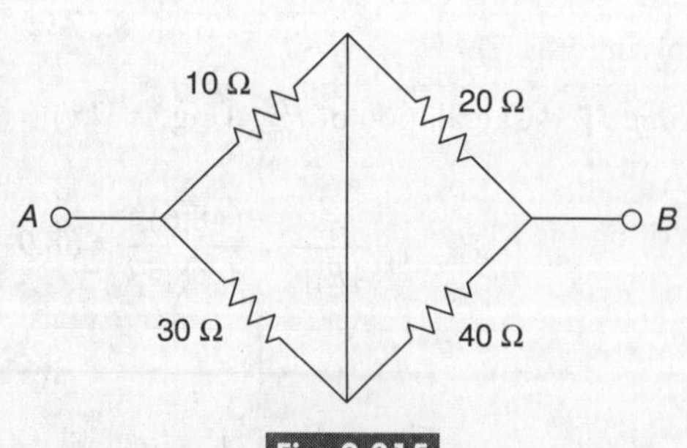


Fig. 2.315

*Step III* Value of $R_L$

For maximum power transfer,

$$R_L = R_{Th} = 20.83\ \Omega$$

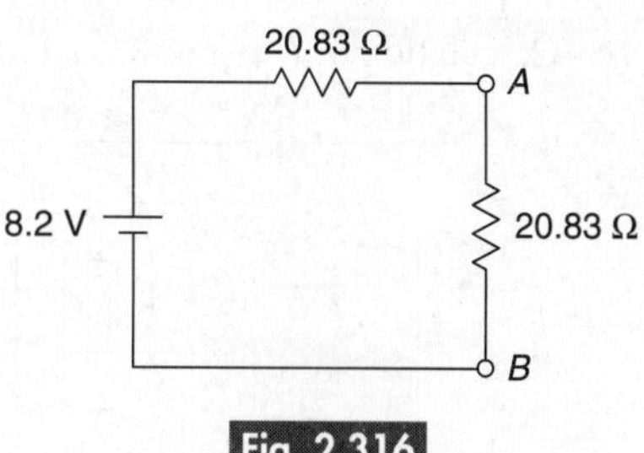


Fig. 2.316

*Step IV* Calculation of $P_{max}$ (Fig. 2.316)

$$P_{max} = \frac{V_{Th}^2}{4R_{Th}} = \frac{(8.2)^2}{4 \times 20.83} = 0.81\ \text{W}$$

## EXAMPLE 2.103

*Find the value of resistance $R_L$ in Fig. 2.317 for maximum power transfer and calculate the maximum power.*

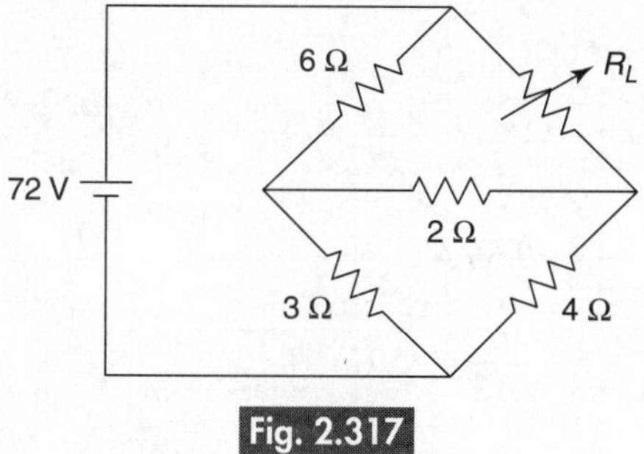


Fig. 2.317

**Solution**

*Step I* Calculation of $V_{Th}$ (Fig. 2.318)

Applying KVL to mesh 1,

$$72 - 6I_1 - 3(I_1 - I_2) = 0$$

$$9I_1 - 3I_2 = 72 \quad \ldots\text{(i)}$$

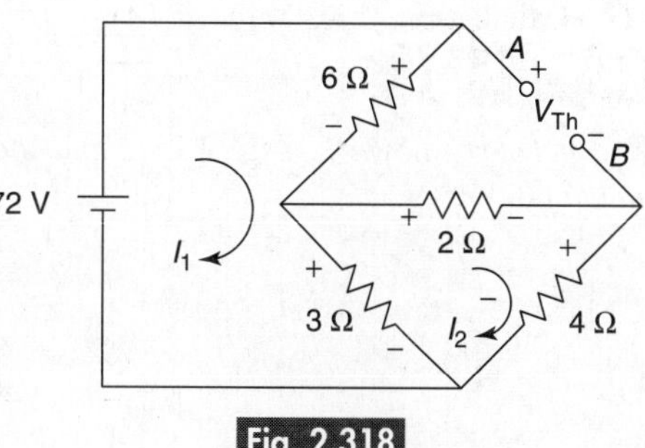


Fig. 2.318

Applying KVL to mesh 2,

$$-3(I_2 - I_1) - 2I_2 - 4I_2 = 0$$

$$-3I_1 + 9I_2 = 0 \quad \ldots\text{(ii)}$$

Solving Eqs (i) and (ii),

$$I_1 = 9\ \text{A}$$

$$I_2 = 3\ \text{A}$$

Writing the $V_{Th}$ equation,

$$V_{Th} - 6I_1 - 2I_2 = 0$$

$$V_{Th} = 6I_1 + 2I_2 = 6(9) + 2(3) = 60\ \text{V}$$

***Step II*** Calculation of $R_{Th}$ (Fig. 2.319)

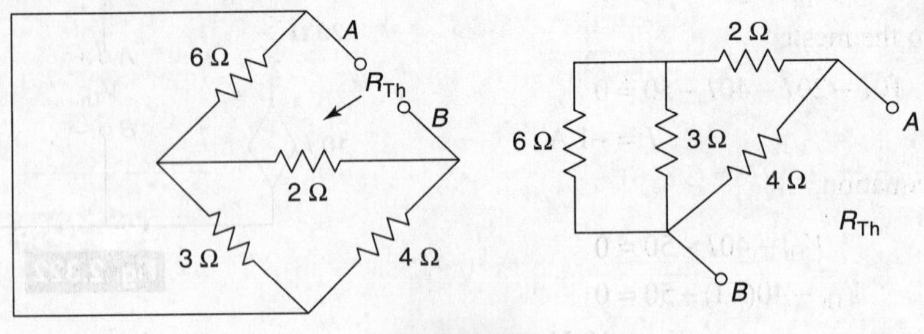


Fig. 2.319

$$R_{Th} = [(6 \parallel 3) + 2] \parallel 4 = 2\ \Omega$$

***Step III*** Calculation of $R_L$

For maximum power transfer,

$$R_L = R_{Th} = 2\ \Omega$$

***Step IV*** Calculation of $P_{max}$ (Fig. 2.320)

$$P_{max} = \frac{V_{Th}^2}{4R_{Th}} = \frac{(60)^2}{4 \times 2} = 450\ \text{W}$$

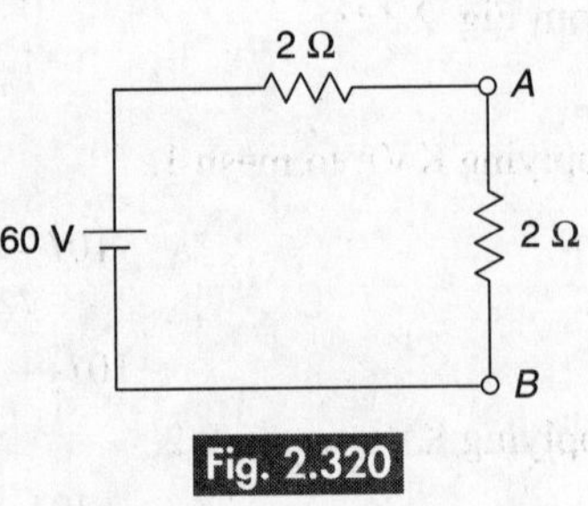


Fig. 2.320

## Examples with Dependent Sources

**EXAMPLE 2.104**

*For the network shown in Fig. 2.321, find the value of $R_L$ for maximum power transfer. Also, calculate maximum power.*

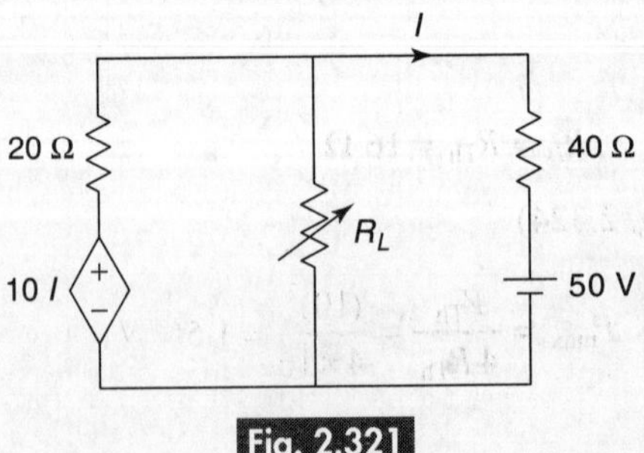


Fig. 2.321

## Solution

***Step I*** Calculation of $V_{Th}$ (Fig. 2.322)

Applying KVL to the mesh,

$$10I - 20I - 40I - 50 = 0$$

$$I = -1\text{ A}$$

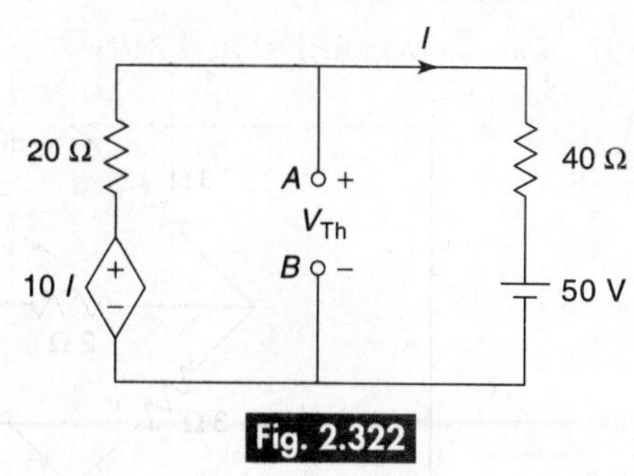


Fig. 2.322

Writing the $V_{Th}$ equation,

$$V_{Th} - 40I - 50 = 0$$

$$V_{Th} - 40(-1) - 50 = 0$$

$$V_{Th} = 10\text{ V}$$

***Step II*** Calculation of $I_N$ (Fig. 2.323)

From Fig. 2.323,

$$I = I_2 \qquad \ldots\text{(i)}$$

Applying KVL to mesh 1,

$$10I - 20I_1 = 0$$

$$10I_2 - 20I_1 = 0 \qquad \ldots\text{(ii)}$$

Fig. 2.323

Applying KVL to mesh 2,

$$-40I_2 - 50 = 0$$

$$I_2 = -1.25\text{ A} \qquad \ldots\text{(iii)}$$

Solving Eqs (i), (ii) and (iii),

$$I_1 = -0.625\text{ A}$$

$$I_N = I_1 - I_2 = -0.625 + 1.25 = 0.625\text{ A}$$

***Step III*** Calculation of $R_N$

$$R_{Th} = \frac{V_{Th}}{I_N} = \frac{10}{0.625} = 16\ \Omega$$

***Step IV*** Calculation of $R_L$

For maximum power transfer,

$$R_L = R_{Th} = 16\ \Omega$$

***Step V*** Calculation of $P_{max}$ (Fig. 2.324)

$$P_{max} = \frac{V_{Th}}{4R_{Th}} = \frac{(10)^2}{4\times16} = 1.56\text{ W}$$

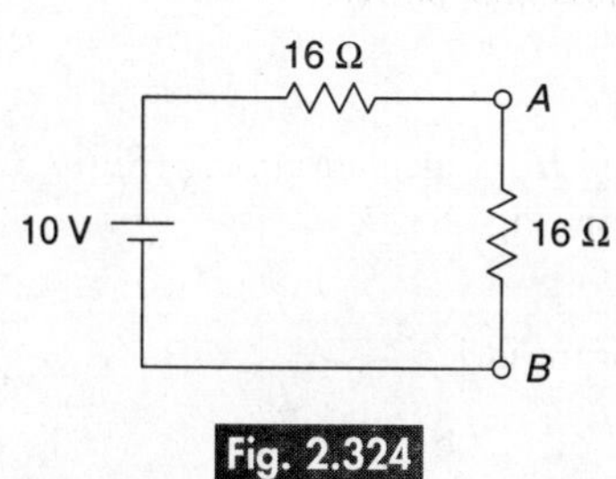


Fig. 2.324

**EXAMPLE 2.105**

*For the network shown in Fig. 2.325, calculate the maximum power that may be dissipated in the load resistor $R_L$.*

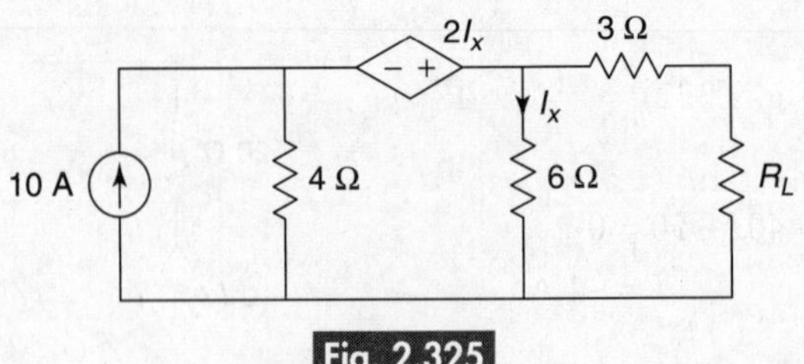


Fig. 2.325

## Solution

***Step I*** Calculation of $V_{Th}$ (Fig. 2.326)

From Fig. 2.326,

$$I_x = I_2 \qquad \ldots\text{(i)}$$

Fig. 2.326

For mesh 1,

$$I_1 = 10 \qquad \ldots\text{(ii)}$$

Applying KVL to mesh 2,

$$-4(I_2 - I_1) + 2I_x - 6I_2 = 0$$
$$-4I_2 + 4I_1 + 2I_2 - 6I_2 = 0$$
$$4I_1 - 8I_2 = 0 \qquad \ldots\text{(iii)}$$

Solving Eqs (ii) and (iii),

$$I_1 = 10 \text{ A}$$
$$I_2 = 5 \text{ A}$$

Writing the $V_{Th}$ equation,

$$6I_2 - 0 - V_{Th} = 0$$
$$V_{Th} = 6I_2 = 6(5) = 30 \text{ V}$$

***Step II*** Calculation of $I_N$ (Fig. 2.327)

From Fig. 2.327,

$$I_x = I_2 - I_3 \qquad \ldots\text{(i)}$$

For mesh 1,

$$I_1 = 10 \qquad \ldots\text{(ii)}$$

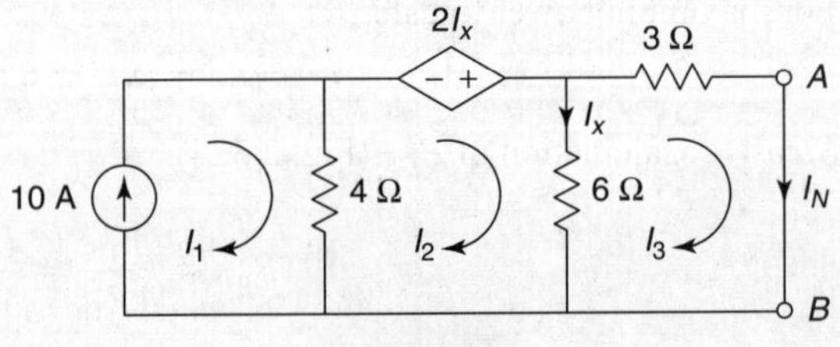


Fig. 2.327

Applying KVL to mesh 2,

$$-4(I_2 - I_1) + 2I_x - 6(I_2 - I_3) = 0$$
$$-4I_2 + 4I_1 + 2(I_2 - I_3) - 6I_2 + 6I_3 = 0$$
$$4I_1 - 8I_2 + 4I_3 = 0 \qquad \ldots\text{(iii)}$$

Applying KVL to mesh 3,

$$-6(I_3 - I_2) - 3I_3 = 0$$

$$6I_2 - 9I_3 = 0 \qquad \text{...(iv)}$$

Solving Eqs (ii), (iii) and (iv),

$$I_1 = 10 \text{ A}$$

$$I_2 = 7.5 \text{ A}$$

$$I_3 = 5 \text{ A}$$

$$I_N = I_3 = 5 \text{ A}$$

***Step III*** Calculation of $R_{Th}$

$$R_{Th} = \frac{V_{Th}}{I_N} = \frac{30}{5} = 6\ \Omega$$

***Step IV*** Calculation of $R_L$

For maximum power transfer,

$$R_L = R_{Th} = 6\ \Omega$$

***Step V*** Calculation of $P_{max}$ (Fig. 2.328)

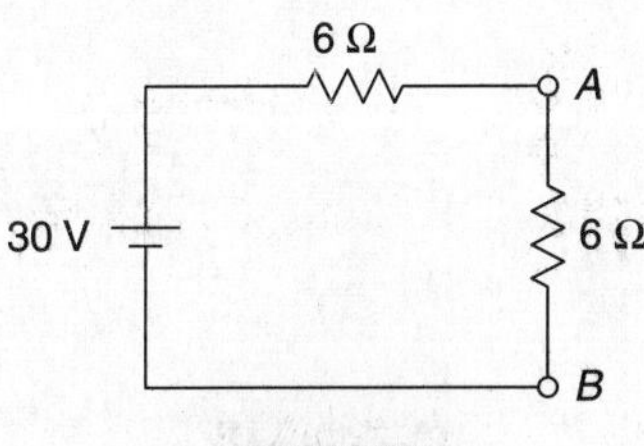

Fig. 2.328

$$P_{max} = \frac{V_{Th}^2}{4R_{Th}} = \frac{(30)^2}{4 \times 16} = 37.5 \text{ W}$$

## EXAMPLE 2.106

*For the network shown in Fig. 2.329, find the value of $R_L$ for maximum power transfer. Also, find maximum power.*

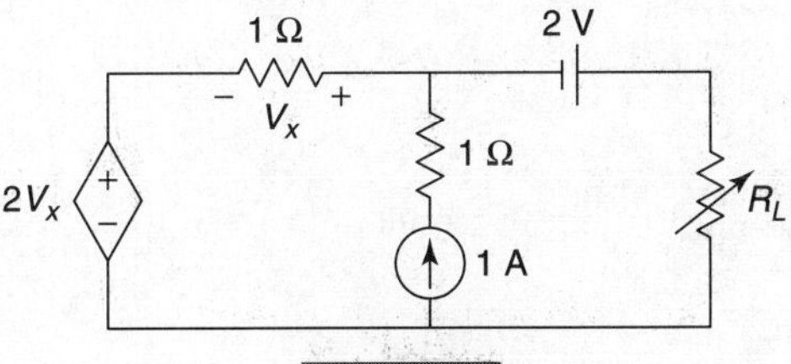

Fig. 2.329

**Solution**

***Step I*** Calculation of $V_{Th}$ (Fig. 2.330)

From Fig. 2.330,

$$V_x = -1I = -I \qquad \text{...(i)}$$

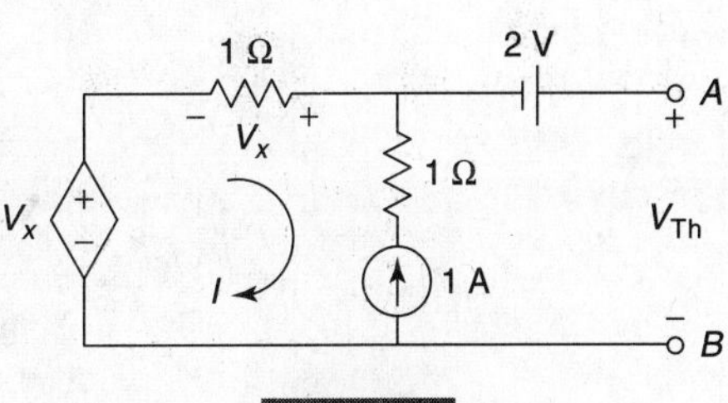

Fig. 2.330

For mesh 1,

$$I = -1 \qquad \text{...(ii)}$$

$$V_x = 1 \text{ V}$$

Writing the $V_{Th}$ equation,

$$2V_x - 1I + 2 - V_{Th} = 0$$
$$2(1) - (-1) + 2 - V_{Th} = 0$$
$$V_{Th} = 5 \text{ V}$$

***Step II*** Calculation of $I_N$ (Fig. 2.331)

From Fig. 2.331,

$$V_x = -1I_1 = -I_1 \qquad \text{...(i)}$$

Fig. 2.331

Meshes 1 and 2 will form a supermesh.

Writing the current equation for the supermesh,

$$I_2 - I_1 = 1 \qquad \text{...(ii)}$$

Applying KVL to the outer path of the supermesh,

$$2V_x - 1I_1 + 2 = 0$$
$$2(-I_1) - I_1 + 2 = 0$$
$$3I_1 = 0 \qquad \text{...(iii)}$$

Solving Eqs (ii) and (iii),

$$I_1 = 0.67 \text{ A}$$
$$I_2 = 1.67 \text{ A}$$
$$I_N = I_2 = 1.67 \text{ A}$$

***Step III*** Calculation of $R_{Th}$

$$R_{Th} = \frac{V_{Th}}{I_N} = \frac{5}{1.67} = 3\ \Omega$$

***Step IV*** Calculation of $R_L$

For maximum power transfer,

$$R_L = R_{Th} = 3\ \Omega$$

***Step V*** Calculation of $P_{max}$ (Fig. 2.332)

$$P_{max} = \frac{V_{Th}^2}{4R_{Th}} = \frac{(5)^2}{4 \times 3} = 2.08 \text{ W}$$

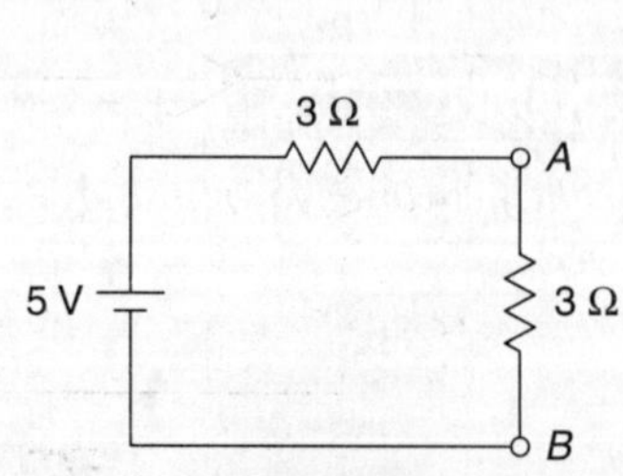

Fig. 2.332

**EXAMPLE 2.107**

*What will be the value of RL in Fig. 2.333 to get maximum power delivered to it? What is the value of this power?*

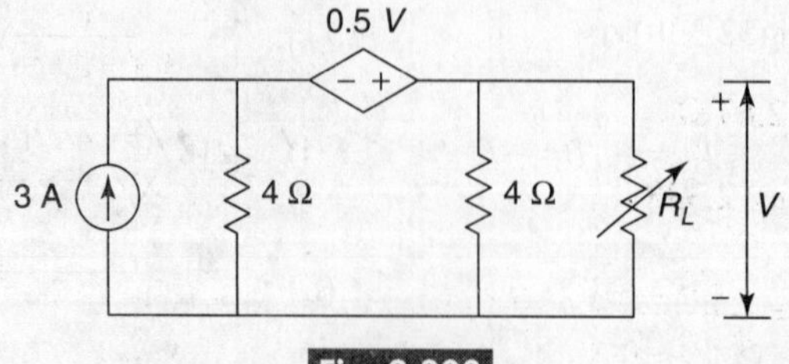

Fig. 2.333

## Solution

***Step I*** Calculation of $V_{Th}$ (Fig. 2.334)

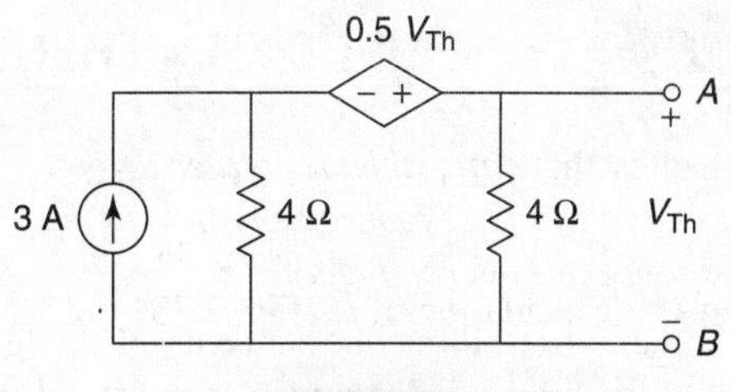


Fig. 2.334

By source transformation,

From Fig. 2.335,

$$V_{Th} = 4I$$

Applying KVL to the mesh,

$$12 - 4I + 0.5\,V_{Th} - 4I = 0$$

$$12 - V_{Th} + 0.5\,V_{Th} - V_{Th} = 0$$

$$V_{Th} = 8 \text{ V}$$

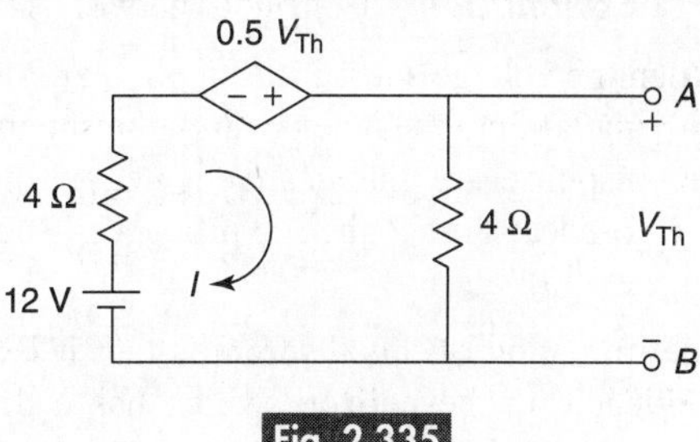


Fig. 2.335

***Step II*** Calculation of $I_N$ (Fig. 2.335)

If two terminals $A$ and $B$ are shorted, the 4 Ω resistor gets shorted.

$$V = 0$$

Dependent source 0.5 $V$ depends on the controlling variable $V$. When $V = 0$, the dependent source vanishes, i.e., 0.5 $V = 0$, as shown in Fig. 2.336 and Fig. 2.337.

$$I_N = \frac{12}{4} = 3 \text{ A}$$

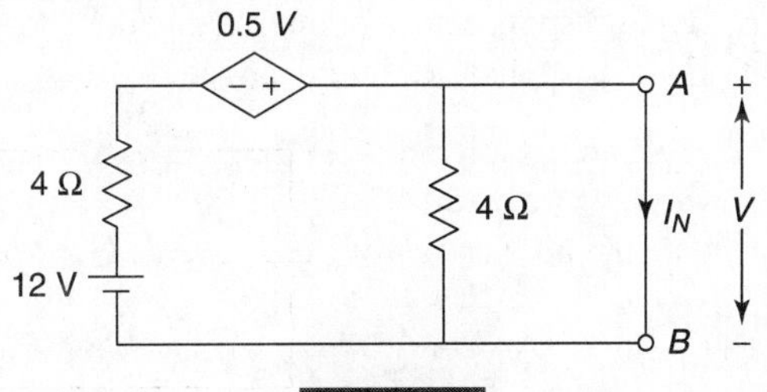


Fig. 2.336

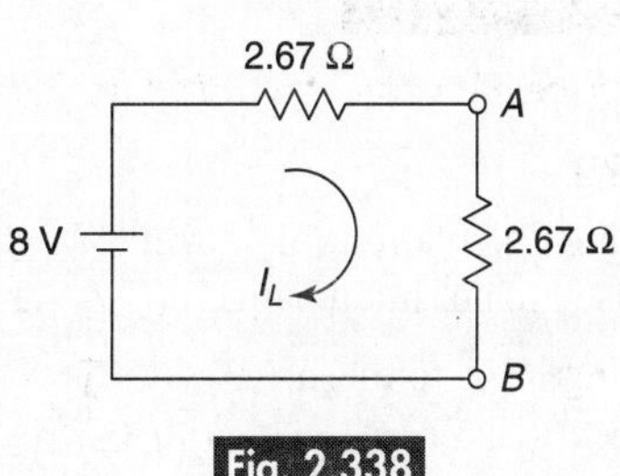


Fig. 2.337

***Step III*** Calculation of $R_{Th}$

$$R_{Th} = \frac{V_{Th}}{I_N} = \frac{8}{3} = 2.67\ \Omega$$

***Step IV*** *Calculation of $R_L$*

For maximum power transfer,

$$R_L = R_{Th} = 2.67\ \Omega$$

***Step V*** Calculation of $P_{max}$ (Fig. 2.338)

$$P_{max} = \frac{V_{Th}^2}{4R_{Th}} = \frac{(8)^2}{4 \times 2.67} = 6 \text{ W}$$

2.67 Ω

A

8 V

$I_L$

2.67 Ω

B

Fig. 2.338

## 2.9 RECIPROCITY THEOREM

LO 2.7

Explain reciprocity theorem

It states that '*in a linear, bilateral, active, single-source network, the ratio of excitation to response remains same when the positions of excitation and response are interchanged.*'

In other words, it may be stated as 'if a single voltage source $V_a$ in the branch '*a*' produces a current $I_b$ in the branch '*b*' then if the voltage source $V_a$ is removed and inserted in the branch '*b*', it will produce a current $I_b$ in branch '*a*''.

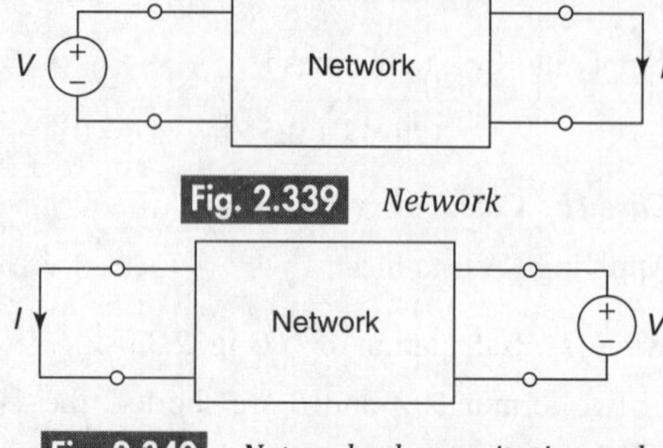


Fig. 2.339 *Network*

Fig. 2.340 *Network when excitation and response are interchanged*

➤ ***Explanation*** Consider a network shown in Fig. 2.339. When the voltage source $V$ is applied at Port 1, it produces a current $I$ at Port 2. If the positions of the excitation (source) and response are interchanged, i.e., if the voltage source is applied at Port 2 then it produces a current $I$ at Port 1 (Fig. 2.340).

The limitation of this theorem is that it is applicable only to a single-source network. This theorem is not applicable in the network which has a dependent source. This is applicable only in linear and bilateral networks. In the reciprocity theorem, the position of any passive element (R, L, C) does not change; only the excitation and response are interchanged.

➤ ***Steps to be followed in Reciprocity Theorem***

1. Identify the branches between which reciprocity is to be established.
2. Find the current in the branch when excitation and response are not interchanged.
3. Find the current in the branch when excitation and response are interchanged.

**EXAMPLE 2.108**

*Calculate current I and verify the reciprocity theorem for the network shown in Fig. 2.341.*

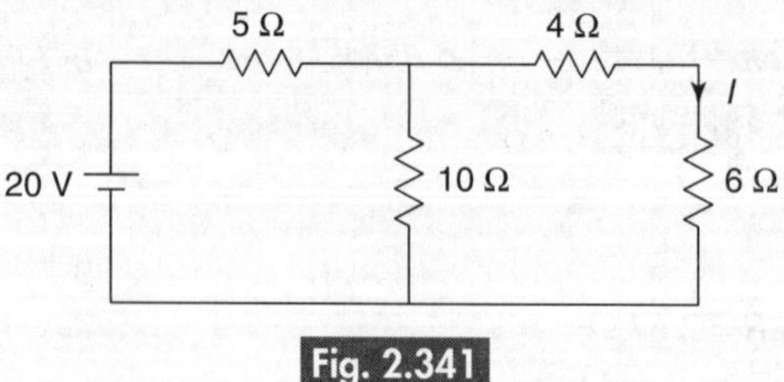


Fig. 2.341

**Solution**

***Case I*** Calculation of current $I$ when excitation and response are not interchanged (Fig. 2.342)

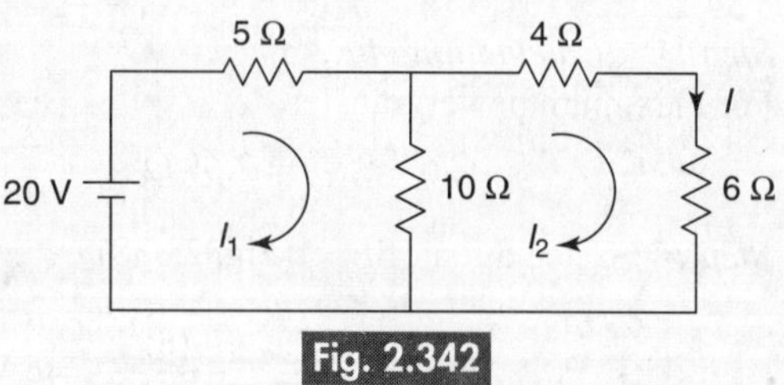


Fig. 2.342

Applying KVL to mesh 1,

$$20 - 5I_1 - 10(I_1 - I_2) = 0$$

$$15I_1 - 10I_2 = 20 \qquad \ldots\text{(i)}$$

Applying KVL to mesh 2,

$$-10(I_2 - I_1) - 4I_2 - 6I_2 = 0$$

$$-10I_1 + 20I_2 = 0 \qquad \text{...(ii)}$$

Solving. Eqs (i) and (ii),

$$I_1 = 2\text{ A}$$

$$I_2 = 1\text{ A}$$

$$I = I_2 = 1\text{ A}$$

***Case II*** Calculation of current *I* when excitation and response are interchanged (Fig. 2.343).

Applying KVL to mesh 1,

$$-5I_1 - 10(I_1 - I_2) = 0$$

$$15I_1 - 10I_2 = 0 \qquad \text{...(i)}$$

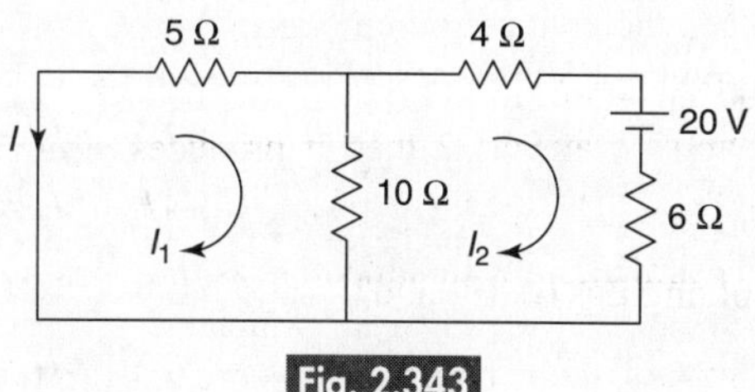

Fig. 2.343

Applying KVL to mesh 2,

$$-10(I_2 - I_1) - 4I_2 - 20 - 6I_2 = 0$$

$$-10I_1 + 20I_2 = -20 \qquad \text{...(ii)}$$

Solving Eqs (i) and (ii),

$$I_1 = -1\text{ A}$$

$$I_2 = -1.5\text{ A}$$

$$I = -I_1 = 1\text{ A}$$

Since the current *I* remains the same in both the cases, reciprocity theorem is verified.

## EXAMPLE 2.109

*Find the current I and verify reciprocity theorem for the network shown in Fig. 2.344.*

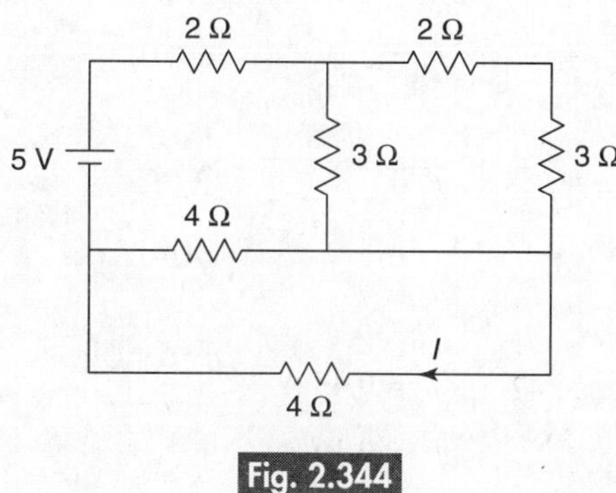

Fig. 2.344

**Solution**

***Case I*** Calculation of the current *I* when excitation and response are not interchanged (Fig. 2.345)

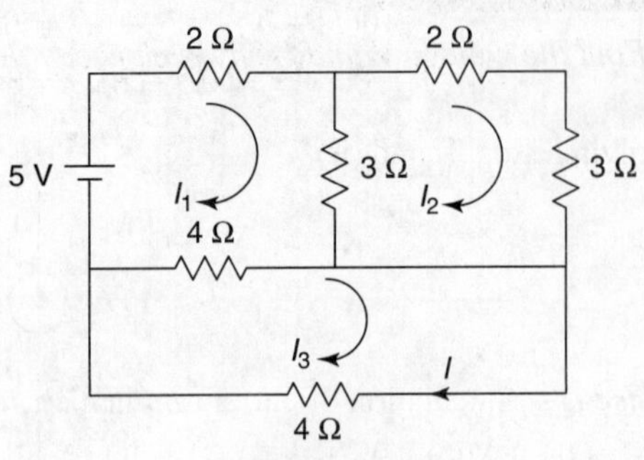

Fig. 2.345

Applying KVL to mesh 1,

$$5-2I_1-3(I_1-I_2)-4(I_1-I_3)=0$$

$$9I_1-3I_2-4I_3=5 \qquad \text{...(i)}$$

Applying KVL to mesh 2,

$$-3(I_2-I_1)-2I_2-3I_2=0$$

$$-3I_1+8I_2=0 \qquad \text{...(ii)}$$

Applying KVL to mesh 3,

$$-4(I_3-I_1)-4I_3=0$$

$$-4I_1+8I_3=0 \qquad \text{...(iii)}$$

Solving Eqs (i), (ii) and (iii),

$$I_1=0.85\text{ A}$$

$$I_2=0.32\text{ A}$$

$$I_3=0.43\text{ A}$$

$$I=I_3=0.43\text{ A}$$

***Case II*** Calculation of current *I* when excitation and response are interchanged (Fig. 2.346).

Applying KVL to mesh 1,

$$-2I_1-3(I_1-I_2)-4(I_1-I_3)=0$$

$$9I_1-3I_2-4I_3=0 \qquad \text{...(i)}$$

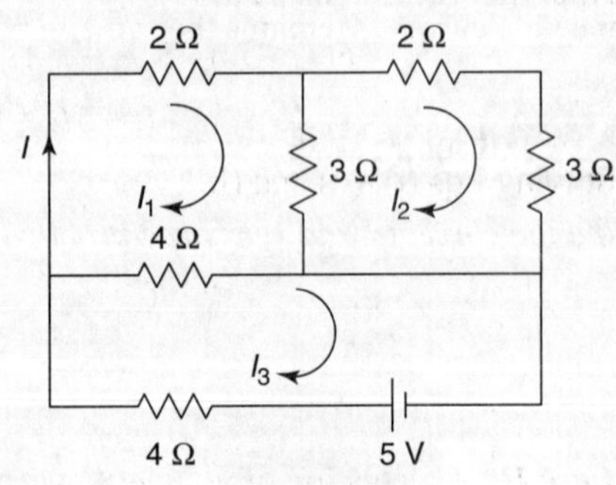

Fig. 2.346

Applying KVL to mesh 2,

$$-3(I_2-I_1)-2I_2-3I_2=0$$

$$-3I_1+8I_2=0 \qquad \text{...(ii)}$$

Applying KVL to mesh 3,

$$-4(I_3-I_1)+5-4I_3=0$$

$$-4I_1+8I_3=5 \qquad \text{...(iii)}$$

Solving Eqs (i), (ii) and (iii),

$$I_1=0.43\text{ A}$$

$$I_2=0.16\text{ A}$$

$$I_3=0.84\text{ A}$$

$$I=I_1=0.43\text{ A}$$

Since the current *I* remains the same in both the cases, reciprocity theorem is verified.

**EXAMPLE 2.110**

*Find the voltage V and verify reciprocity theorem for the network shown in Fig. 2.347.*

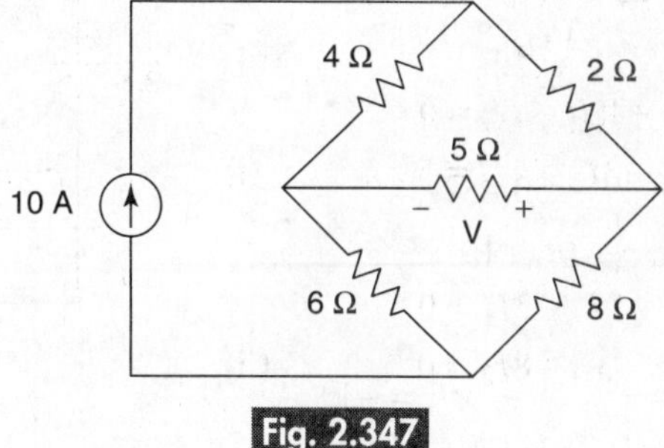


Fig. 2.347

**Solution**

***Case I*** Calculation of the voltage $V$ when excitation and response are not interchanged (Fig. 2.348)

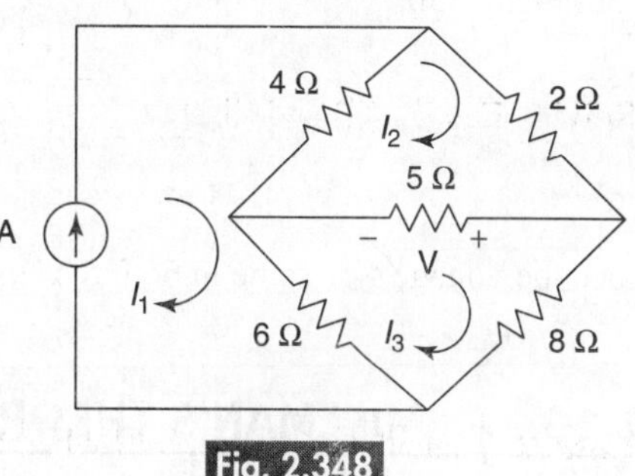


Fig. 2.348

For mesh 1,

$$I_1 = 10 \quad \ldots\text{(i)}$$

Applying KVL to mesh 2,

$$-4(I_2 - I_1) - 2I_2 - 5(I_2 - I_3) = 0$$

$$-4I_1 + 11I_2 - 5I_3 = 0 \quad \ldots\text{(ii)}$$

Applying KVL to mesh 3,

$$-6(I_3 - I_1) - 5(I_3 - I_2) - 8I_3 = 0$$

$$-6I_1 - 5I_2 + 19I_3 = 0 \quad \ldots\text{(iii)}$$

Solving Eqs (i), (ii) and (iii),

$$I_1 = 10 \text{ A}$$

$$I_2 = 5.76 \text{ A}$$

$$I_3 = 4.67 \text{ A}$$

$$V = 5(I_2 - I_3) = 5(5.76 - 4.67) = 5.45 \text{ V}$$

***Case II*** Calculation of voltage $V$ when excitation and response are interchanged (Fig. 2.349).

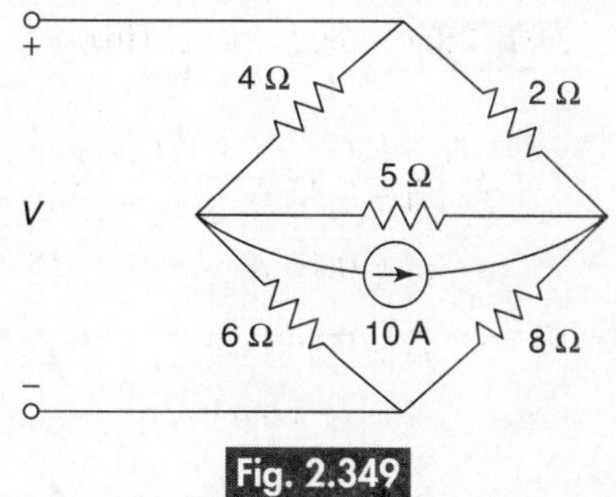


Fig. 2.349

By source transformation (Fig. 2.350),

Applying KVL to mesh 1,

$$-4I_1 - 2I_1 - 50 - 5(I_1 - I_2) = 0$$

$$11I_1 - 5I_2 = -50 \quad \text{...(i)}$$

Applying KVL to mesh 2,

$$-6I_2 - 5(I_2 - I_1) + 50 - 8I_2 = 0$$

$$-5I_1 + 19I_2 = 50 \quad \text{...(ii)}$$

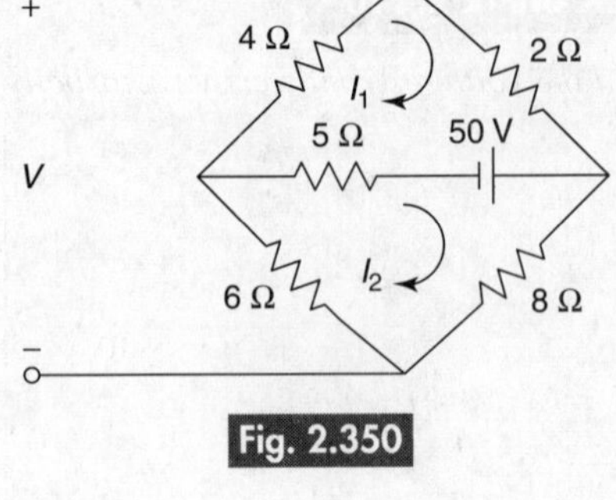


Fig. 2.350

Solving Eqs (i) and (ii),

$$I_1 = -3.8 \text{ A}$$

$$I_2 = 1.63 \text{ A}$$

From Fig. 2.350,

$$V + 4I_1 + 6I_2 = 0$$

$$V + 4(-3.8) + 6(1.63) = 0$$

$$V = 5.42 \text{ V}$$

Since the voltage $V$ is same in both the cases, the reciprocity theorem is verified.

## 2.10 MILLMAN'S THEOREM

LO 2.8

Explain Millman's theorem

It states that '*if there are n voltage sources $V_1, V_2, \ldots, V_n$ with internal resistances $R_1, R_2, \ldots, R_n$ respectively connected in parallel then these voltage sources can be replaced by a single voltage source $V_m$ and a single series resistance $R_m$*,' (Fig. 2.351).

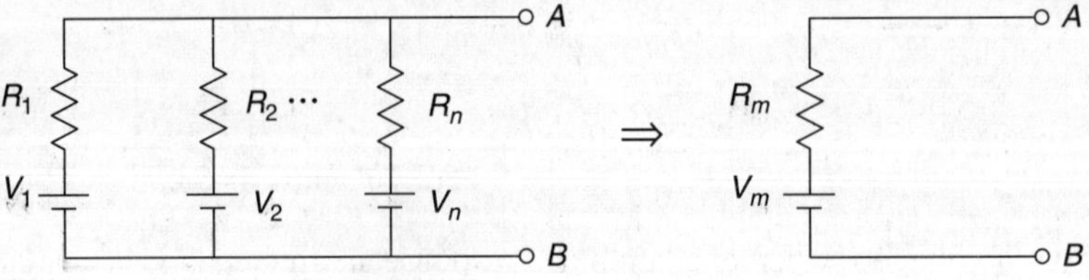


Fig. 2.351 Millman's network

where
$$V_m = \frac{V_1G_1 + V_2G_2 + \ldots + V_nG_n}{G_1 + G_2 + \ldots + G_n}$$

and
$$R_m = \frac{1}{G_m} = \frac{1}{G_1 + G_2 + \ldots + G_n}$$

➤ ***Explanation*** By source transformation, each voltage source in series with a resistance can be converted to a current source in parallel with a resistance, as shown in Fig. 2.352.

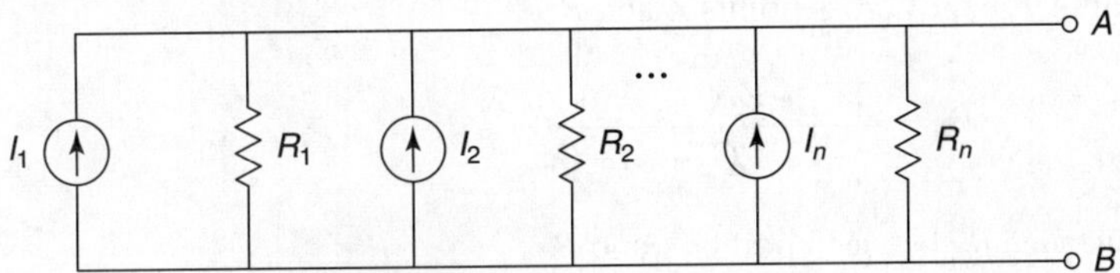


**Fig. 2.352** *Equivalent network*

Let $I_m$ be the resultant current of the parallel current sources and $R_m$ be the equivalent resistance, as shown in Fig. 2.353.

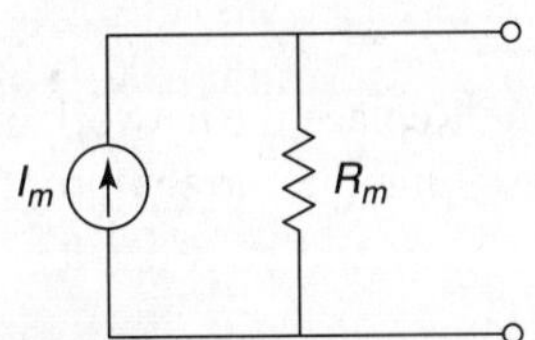


**Fig. 2.353** *Equivalent network*

$$I_m = I_1 + I_2 + \ldots + I_n = \frac{V_1}{R_1} + \frac{V_2}{R_2} + \ldots + \frac{V_n}{R_n} = V_1 G_1 + V_2 G_2 + \ldots V_n G_n$$

$$\frac{1}{R_m} = \frac{1}{R_1} + \frac{1}{R_2} + \ldots + \frac{1}{R_n}$$

$$G_m = G_1 + G_2 + \ldots + G_n$$

By source transformation, the parallel circuit can be converted into a series circuit, as shown in Fig. 2.354.

$$V_m = I_m R_m = \frac{I_m}{G_m} = \frac{V_1 G_1 + V_2 G_2 + \ldots + V_n G_n}{G_1 + G_2 + \ldots + G_n}$$

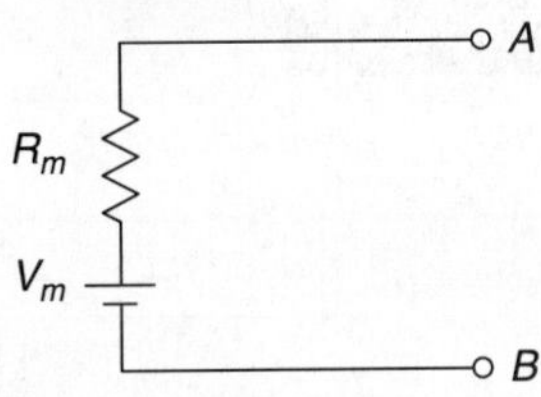


**Fig. 2.354** *Millman's equivalent network*

## Dual of Millman's Theorem

It states that '*if there are n current sources $I_1, I_2, \ldots, I_n$ with internal resistances $R_1, R_2, \ldots, R_n$ respectively, connected in series then these current sources can be replaced by a single current source $I_m$ and a single parallel resistance $R_m$*' (Fig. 2.355).

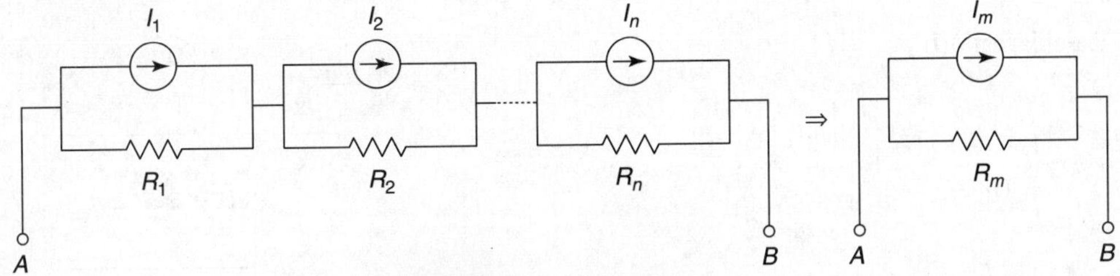


**Fig. 2.355** *Millman's network*

where
$$I_m = \frac{I_1 R_1 + I_2 R_2 + \ldots + I_n R_n}{R_1 + R_2 + \ldots + R_n}$$

$$R_m = R_1 + R_2 + \ldots + R_n$$

### ➤ Steps to be followed in Millman's Theorem

1. Remove the load resistance $R_L$.
2. Find Millman's voltage across points $A$ and $B$.

$$V_m = \frac{V_1 G_1 + V_2 G_2 + \ldots + V_n G_n}{G_1 + G_2 + \ldots + G_n}$$

3. Find the resistance $R_m$ between points $A$ and $B$.

$$R_m = \frac{1}{G_1 + G_2 + \ldots + G_n}$$

4. Replace the network by a voltage source $V_m$ in series with the resistance $R_m$.
5. Find the current through $R_L$ using Ohm's law.

$$I_L = \frac{V_m}{R_m + R_L}$$

**EXAMPLE 2.111**

*Find Millman's equivalent for the left of the terminals A-B in Fig. 2.356.*

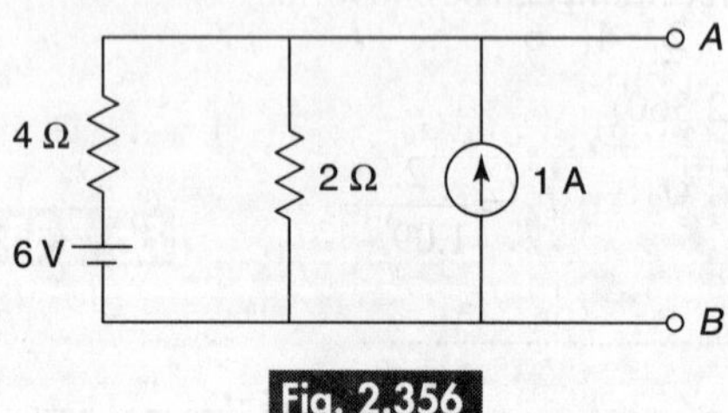


Fig. 2.356

**Solution** By source transformation, the network is redrawn, as shown in Fig. 2.357.

***Step I*** Calculation of $V_m$

$$V_m = \frac{V_1 G_1 + V_2 G_2}{G_1 + G_2} = \frac{6\left(\frac{1}{4}\right) + 2\left(\frac{1}{2}\right)}{\frac{1}{4} + \frac{1}{2}} = 3.33 \text{ V}$$

***Step II*** Calculation of $R_m$

$$R_m = \frac{1}{G_m} = \frac{1}{G_1 + G_2} = \frac{1}{\frac{1}{4} + \frac{1}{2}} = 1.33\ \Omega$$

***Step III*** Millman's Equivalent Network (Fig. 2.358)

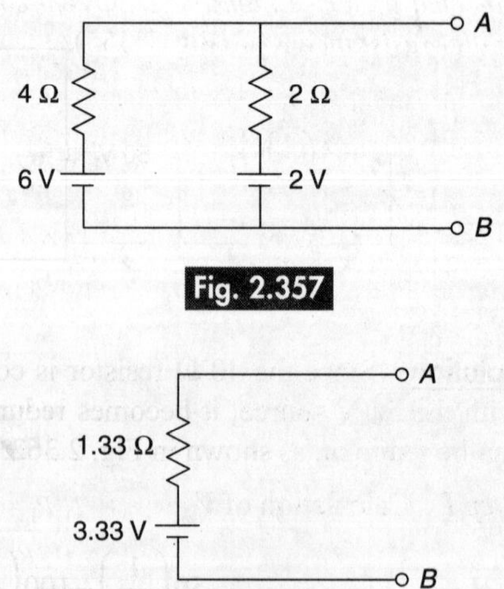


Fig. 2.357

Fig. 2.358

## EXAMPLE 2.112

*Find the current through the 10 Ω resistor in the network of Fig. 2.359.*

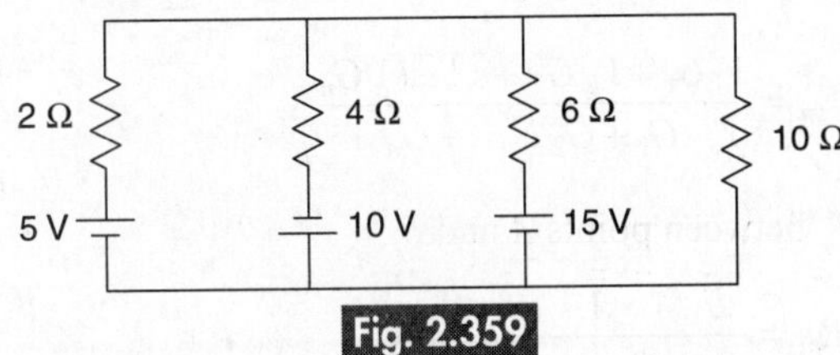


Fig. 2.359

**Solution**

***Step I*** Calculation of $V_m$

$$V_m = \frac{V_1 G_1 + V_2 G_2 + V_3 G_3}{G_1 + G_2 + G_3} = \frac{5\left(\frac{1}{2}\right) - 10\left(\frac{1}{4}\right) + 15\left(\frac{1}{6}\right)}{\frac{1}{2} + \frac{1}{4} + \frac{1}{6}} = 2.73 \text{ V}$$

***Step II*** Calculation of $R_m$

$$R_m = \frac{1}{G_m} = \frac{1}{\frac{1}{2} + \frac{1}{4} + \frac{1}{6}} = 1.09\ \Omega$$

Fig. 2.360

***Step III*** Calculation of $I_L$ (Fig. 2.360)

$$I_L = \frac{2.73}{1.09 + 10} = 0.25 \text{ A}$$

## EXAMPLE 2.113

*Find the current through the 10 Ω resistor in the network of Fig. 2.361.*

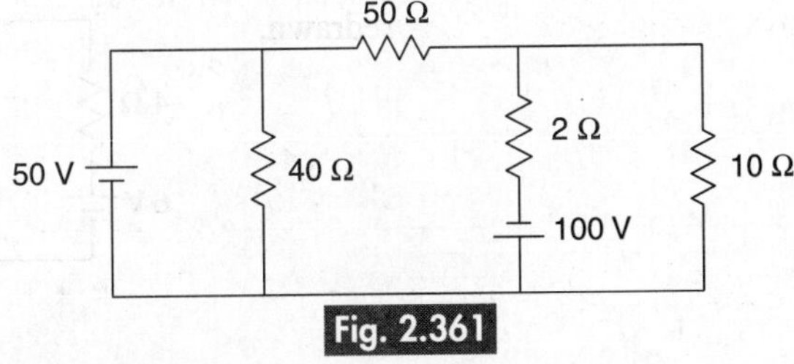


Fig. 2.361

**Solution** Since the 40 Ω resistor is connected in parallel with the 50 V source, it becomes redundant. The network can be redrawn, as shown in Fig. 2.362.

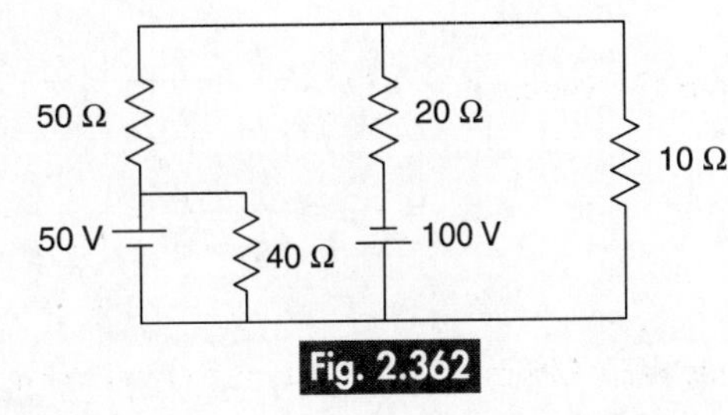


Fig. 2.362

***Step I*** Calculation of $V_m$

$$V_m = \frac{V_1 G_1 + V_2 G_2}{G_1 + G_2} = \frac{50\left(\frac{1}{50}\right) - 100\left(\frac{1}{20}\right)}{\frac{1}{50} + \frac{1}{20}} = -57.15 \text{ V}$$

***Step II*** Calculation of $R_m$

$$R_m = \frac{1}{G_m} = \frac{1}{G_1 + G_2} = \frac{1}{\dfrac{1}{50}+\dfrac{1}{20}} = 14.29\ \Omega$$

***Step III*** Calculation of $I_L$ (Fig. 2.363)

$$I_L = \frac{57.15}{14.29+10} = 2.35\text{ A}$$

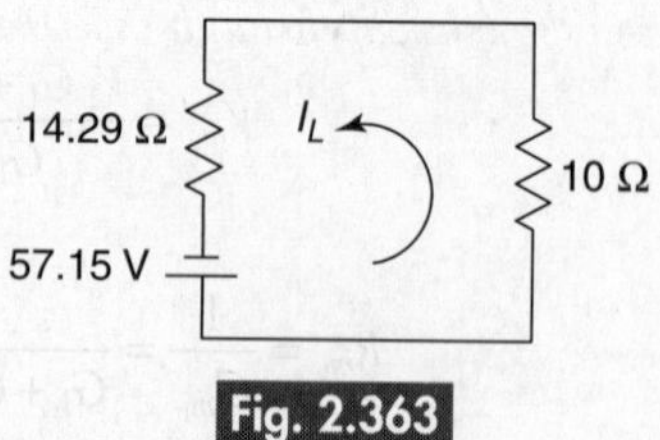

Fig. 2.363

## EXAMPLE 2.114

*Draw Millman's equivalent network across terminals AB in the network of Fig. 2.364.*

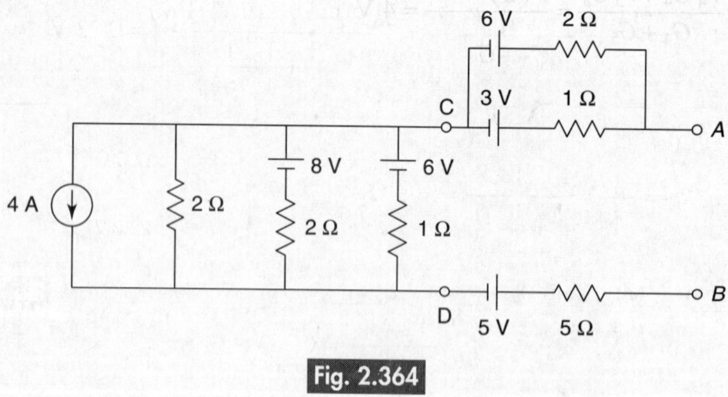

Fig. 2.364

**Solution**

***Step I*** By source transformation, the network is redrawn, as shown in Fig. 2.365.

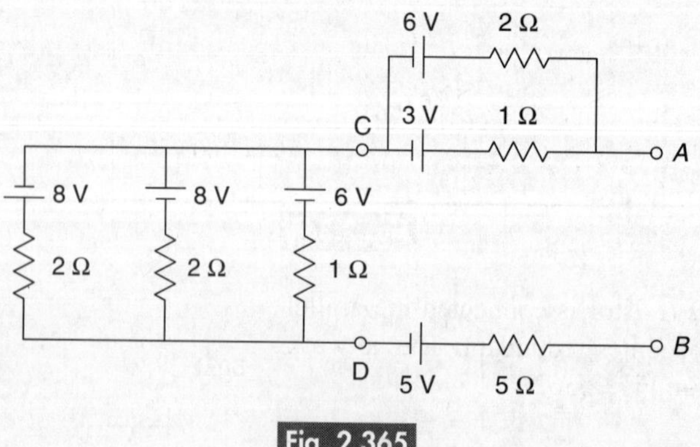

Fig. 2.365

***Step II*** Applying Millman's theorem at terminals *CD*,

$$V_{m_1} = \frac{V_1 G_1 + V_2 G_2 + V_3 G_3}{G_1 + G_2 + G_3} = \frac{-8\left(\frac{1}{2}\right) + 8\left(\frac{1}{2}\right) + 6(1)}{\frac{1}{2} + \frac{1}{2} + 1} = 3 \text{ V}$$

$$R_{m_1} = \frac{1}{G_{m_1}} = \frac{1}{G_1 + G_2 + G_3} = \frac{1}{\frac{1}{2} + \frac{1}{2} + 1} = 0.5\ \Omega$$

***Step III*** Applying Millman's theorem at terminals *CA*,

$$V_{m_2} = \frac{V_4 G_4 + V_5 G_5}{G_4 + G_5} = \frac{6\left(\frac{1}{2}\right) + 3(1)}{\frac{1}{2} + 1} = 4 \text{ V}$$

$$R_{m_2} = \frac{1}{G_{m_2}} = \frac{1}{G_4 + G_4} = \frac{1}{\frac{1}{2} + 1} = 0.67\ \Omega$$

***Step IV*** Millman's Equivalent Network (Fig. 2.366)

Simplifying Fig. 2.366 further, the Millman's equivalent network is shown in Fig. 2.367.

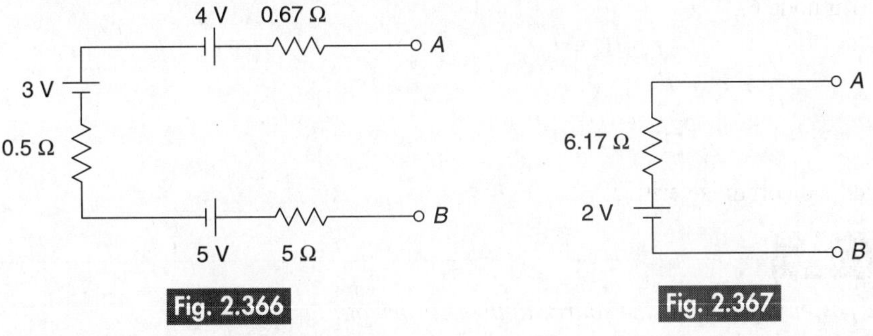


Fig. 2.366

Fig. 2.367

## 2.11 TELLEGEN'S THEOREM

LO 2.9

Explain Tellegen's theorem

It states that '*the algebraic sum of the powers in all branches of the network at any instant is zero*'.

$$\sum_{k=1}^{n} V_k\, I_k = 0$$

This condition is valid for the network which obeys Kirchhoff's voltage and current laws.

➤ ***Explanation*** Consider a network shown in Fig. 2.368.

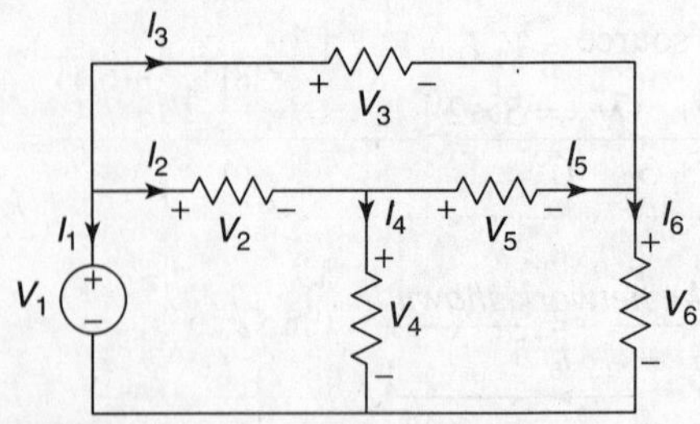


**Fig. 2.368** *Network illustrating Tellegen's theorem*

According to Tellegen's theorem,

$$\sum_{k=1}^{6} V_k\, I_k = V_1 I_1 + V_2 I_2 + V_3 I_3 + V_4 I_4 + V_5 I_5 + V_6 I_6$$

$$= V_1 I_1 + (V_1 - V_4) I_2 + (V_1 - V_6) I_3 + V_4 I_4 + (V_4 - V_6) I_5 + V_6 I_6$$

$$= V_1 (I_1 + I_2 + I_3) + V_4(-I_2 + I_4 + I_5) + V_6(-I_3 - I_5 + I_6)$$

Applying KCL at node 1,

$$I_1 + I_2 + I_3 = 0$$

Applying KCL at node 4,

$$I_2 = I_4 + I_5$$

Applying KCL at node 6,

$$I_5 + I_3 = I_6$$

$$\sum_{k=1}^{6} V_k\, I_k = V_1(0) + V_4(0) + V_6(0) = 0$$

Hence, Tellegen's theorem is verified.

**EXAMPLE 2.115**

*Determine the power supplied by the source in the network of Fig. 2.369.*

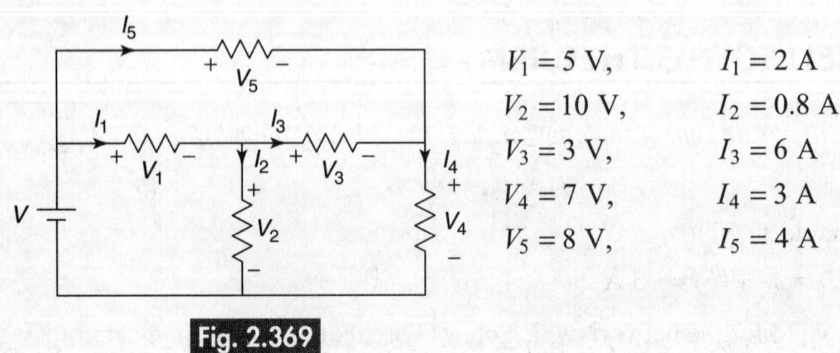


**Fig. 2.369**

**Solution** By Tellegen's theorem,

$$\text{Power supplied by the source} = V_1 I_1 + V_2 I_2 + V_3 I_3 + V_4 I_4 + V_5 I_5$$
$$= 5\times 2 + 10\times 0.8 + 3\times 6 + 7\times 3 + 8\times 4 = 89 \text{ W}$$

## EXAMPLE 2.116

*Prove the Tellegen's theorem for the network shown in Fig. 2.370.*

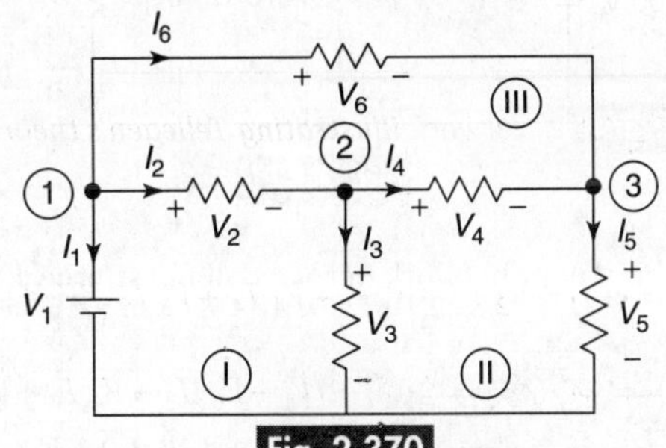


Fig. 2.370

$$V_1 = 8 \text{ V}, \quad V_2 = 4 \text{ V}, \quad V_4 = 2 \text{ V}$$
$$I_1 = 4 \text{ A}, \quad I_2 = 2 \text{ A}, \quad I_3 = 1 \text{ A}$$

**Solution** Applying KVL to mesh 1,

$$V_1 - V_2 - V_3 = 0$$
$$V_3 = V_1 - V_2 = 8 - 4 = 4 \text{ V}$$

Applying KVL to mesh 2,

$$V_3 - V_4 - V_5 = 0$$
$$V_5 = V_3 - V_4 = 4 - 2 = 2 \text{ V}$$

Applying KVL to mesh 3,

$$-V_6 + V_4 + V_2 = 0$$
$$V_6 = V_2 + V_4 = 4 + 2 = 6 \text{ V}$$

Applying KCL at node 1,

$$I_1 + I_2 + I_6 = 0$$
$$I_6 = -I_1 - I_2 = -4 - 2 = -6 \text{ A}$$

Applying KCL at node 2,

$$I_2 = I_3 + I_4$$
$$I_4 = I_2 - I_3 = 2 - 1 = 1 \text{ A}$$

Applying KCL at node 3,

$$I_5 = I_4 + I_6 = 1 + (-6) = -5 \text{ A}$$

$$\sum_{b=1}^{6} V_b I_b = V_1 I_1 + V_2 I_2 + V_3 I_3 + V_4 I_4 + V_5 I_5 + V_6 I_6 = 8\times 4 + 4\times 2 + 4\times 1 + 2\times 1 + 2\times(-5) + 6\times(-6) = 0$$

Hence, Tellegen's theorem is verified.

## EXAMPLE 2.117

*Find the value of source $V_2$ in Fig. 2.371, using Tellegen's theorem if the power absorbed by $V_2$ is 20 W.*

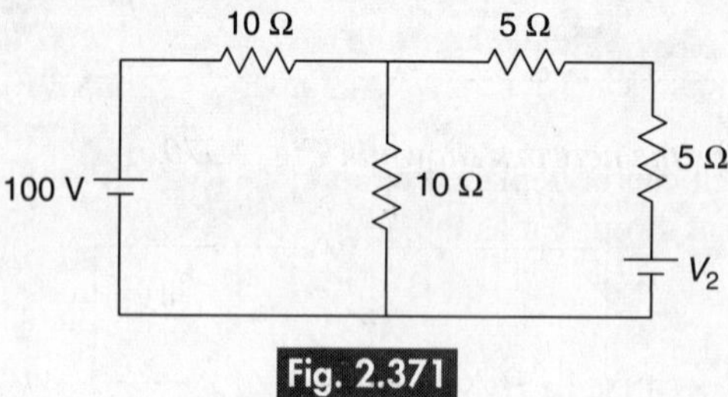


Fig. 2.371

**Solution** Finding Thevenin's equivalent network across voltage source $V_2$ (Fig. 2.372).

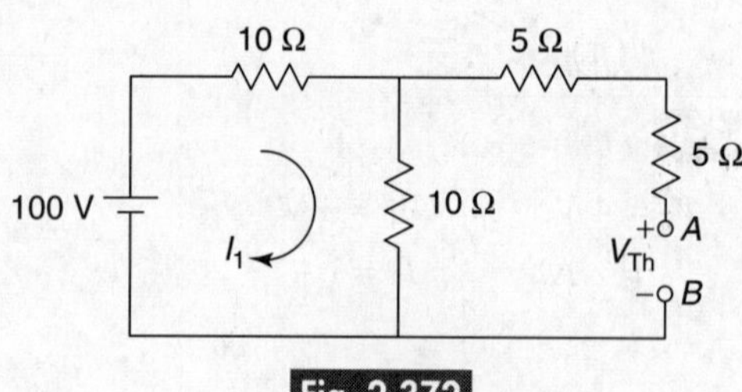


Fig. 2.372

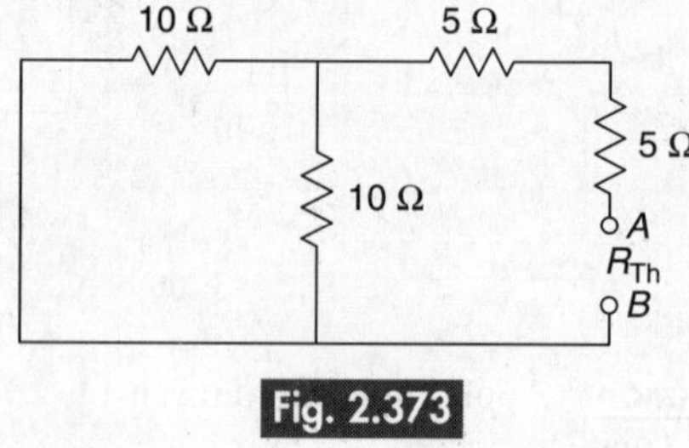


Fig. 2.373

$$I_1 = \frac{100}{10+10} = 5 \text{ A}$$

$$V_{Th} = 10I_1 = 10(5) = 50 \text{ V}$$

$$R_{Th} = (10 \,||\, 10) + 5 + 5 = 15\ \Omega$$

Thevenin's equivalent network is shown in Fig. 2.374.

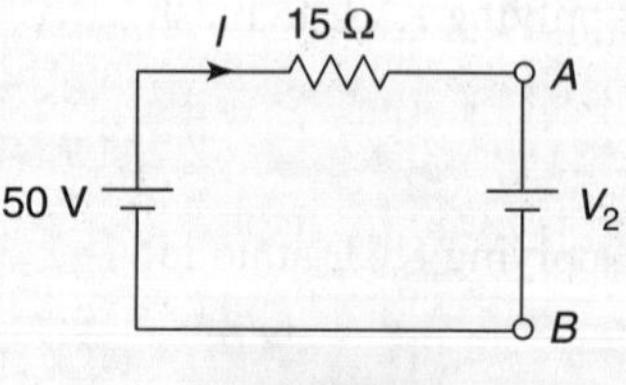


Fig. 2.374

$$V_2 I = 20$$

Applying Tellegen's theorem,

$$-50I + 15I^2 + V_2 I = 0$$

$$15I^2 - 50I + 20 = 0$$

$$I = 2.87 \text{ or } 0.46 \text{ A}$$

$$V_2 = \frac{20}{I} = \frac{20}{2.87} = 6.97 \text{ V}$$

or

$$V_2 = \frac{20}{0.46} = 43.48 \text{ V}$$

## 2.12 SUBSTITUTION THEOREM

LO 2.10

Explain substitution and compensation theorems

It states that '*any branch in a network can be substituted by a different branch without disturbing the voltages and currents in the entire network, provided the new branch has the same set of terminal voltage and current as the original network.*'

➤ ***Explanation*** Any branch can be replaced by any combination of elements that will have the same voltage across it and same current through it as the original branch (Fig. 2.375).

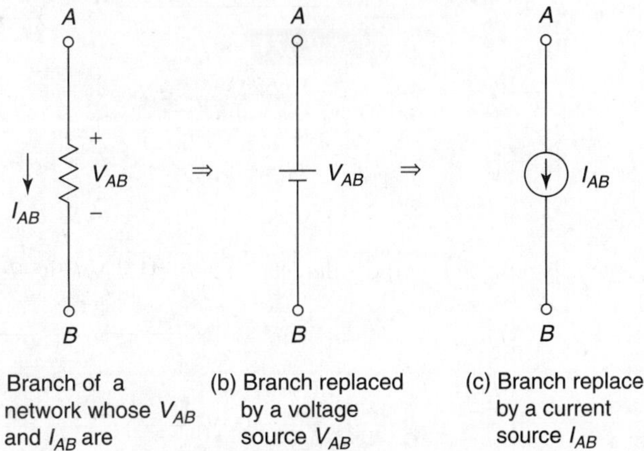


**Fig. 2.375** *Substitution theorem*

➤ ***Steps to be followed in Substitution Theorem***

1. Find the branch voltage and branch current in the network.
2. Replace the branch by an independent voltage source and find the voltage and current in the network.
3. Replace the branch by an independent current source and find the voltage and current in the network.

**EXAMPLE 2.118**

*In the network of Fig. 2.376, verify substitution theorem by replacing the 6 Ω resistor by (a) a voltage source, and (b) a current source.*

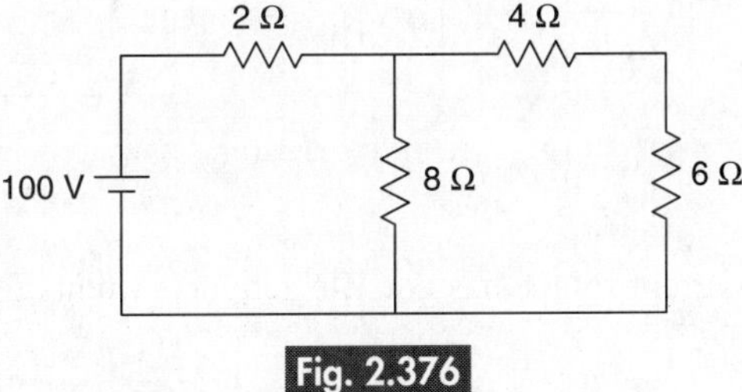


**Fig. 2.376**

## Solution

***Step I*** Calculation of current through 6 Ω resistor (Fig. 2.377)

Applying KVL to mesh 1,

$$100 - 2I_1 - 8(I_1 - I_2) = 0$$

$$10I_1 - 8I_2 = 100 \qquad \ldots\text{(i)}$$

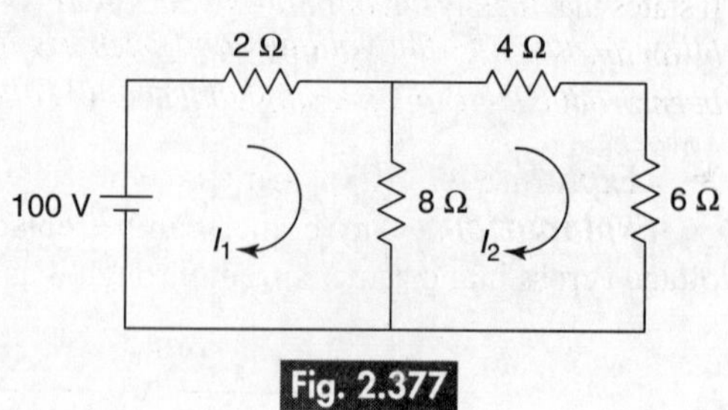


Fig. 2.377

Applying KVL to mesh 2,

$$-8(I_2 - I_1) - 4I_2 - 6I_2 = 0$$

$$-8I_1 + 18I_2 = 0 \qquad \ldots\text{(ii)}$$

Solving Eqs (i) and (ii),

$$I_1 = 15.52 \text{ A}$$

$$I_2 = 6.9 \text{ A}$$

$$I_{6\,\Omega} = I_2 = 6.9 \text{ A}$$

$$V_{6\,\Omega} = 6I_2 = 6(6.9) = 41.4 \text{ V}$$

***Step II*** When the 6 Ω resistor is replaced by the voltage source of 41.4 V (Fig. 2.378)

Applying KVL to mesh 1,

$$100 - 2I_1 - 8(I_1 - I_2) = 0$$

$$10I_1 - 8I_2 = 100 \qquad \ldots\text{(i)}$$

Applying KVL to mesh 2,

$$-8(I_2 - I_1) - 4I_2 - 41.4 = 0$$

$$-8I_1 + 12I_2 = -41.4 \qquad \ldots\text{(ii)}$$

Fig. 2.378

Solving Eqs (i) and (ii),

$$I_1 = 51.51 \text{ A}$$

$$I_2 = 6.9 \text{ A}$$

Replacing the 6 Ω resistor by a voltage source has not affected the currents $I_1$ and $I_2$. Hence, the substitution theorem is verified.

***Step III*** When the 6 Ω resistor is replaced by current source of 6.9 A (Fig. 2.379)

Applying KVL to mesh 1,

$$100 - 2I_1 - 8(I_1 - I_2) = 0$$

$$10I_1 - 8I_2 = 100 \qquad \ldots\text{(i)}$$

For mesh 2,

$$I_2 = 6.9 \qquad \ldots\text{(ii)}$$

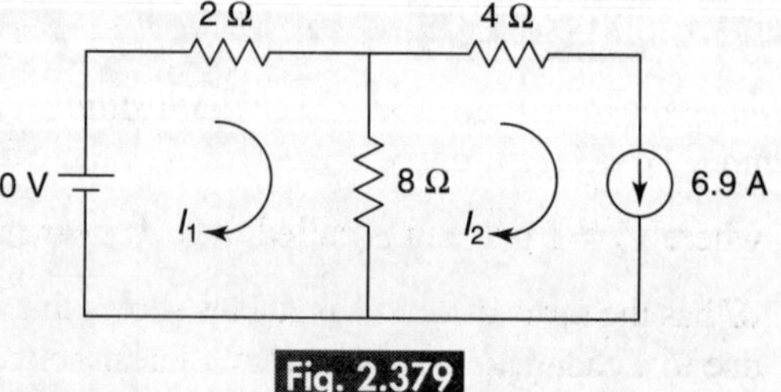


Fig. 2.379

Solving Eqs (i) and (ii),

$$I_1 = 15.52 \text{ A}$$

$$I_2 = 6.9 \text{ A}$$

Replacing the 6 Ω resistor by a current source has not affected the currents $I_1$ and $I_2$. Hence, the substitution theorem is verified.

## 2.13 | COMPENSATION THEOREM

LO 2.10

It states that '*in any linear bilateral active network, if any branch carrying a current I has its resistance R changed by an amount $\delta R$, the resulting changes that occur in the other branches are the same as those which would have been produced by an opposing voltage source of value $V_c$ ($I\delta R$) introduced into the modified branch.*'

➤ ***Explanation*** Consider a network shown in Fig. 2.380(a), having load resistance *R*.

$$I = \frac{V_{Th}}{R_{Th} + R}$$

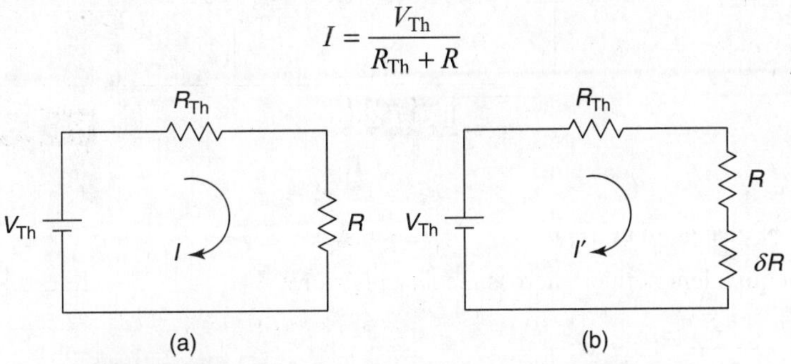


**Fig. 2.380** *Network illustrating compensation theorem*

If the load resistance *R* be changed to $R + \delta R$, as shown in Fig. 2.380(b), then the current flowing in the circuit is

$$I' = \frac{V_{Th}}{R_{Th} + R + \delta R}$$

The change in the current is

$$\delta I = I' - I = \frac{V_{Th}}{R_{Th} + R + \delta R} - \frac{V_{Th}}{R_{Th} + R}$$

$$= -\frac{V_{Th}\ \delta R}{(R_{Th} + R + \delta R)\,(R_{Th} + R)}$$

$$= -\frac{V_{Th}}{R_{Th} + R}\ \frac{\delta R}{R_{Th} + R + \delta R}$$

$$= -\frac{I\ \delta R}{R_{Th} + R + \delta R}$$

$$= -\frac{V_c}{R_{Th} + R + \delta R}$$

where $V_c = I\ \delta R$ and is called the *compensation voltage*.

$\delta I$ has the same direction as *I*. This shows that the change in current $\delta I$ due to a change in any branch in a linear network can be calculated by determining the current in that branch in a network obtained from the original network by removing all the independent sources and placing a voltage source called compensation source in series with the branch whose value is $V_c = I\ \delta R$, whose *I* is the current through the branch before its resistance is changed and $\delta R$ is the change in resistance (Fig. 2.381).

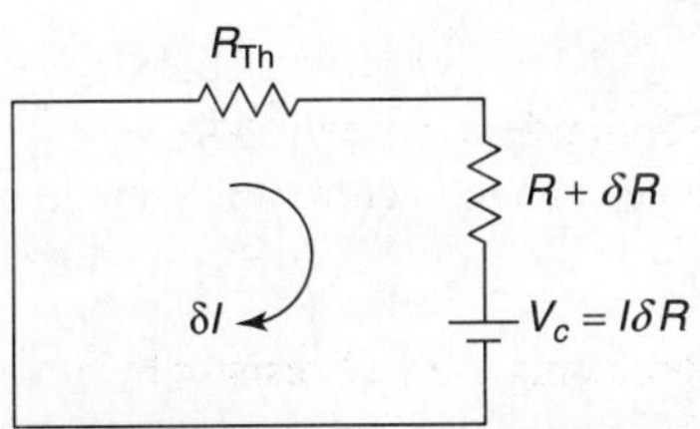


**Fig. 2.381** *Compensation network*

**EXAMPLE 2.119**

*In the network of Fig. 2.382, the resistance of 4 Ω is changed to 2 Ω. Verify the compensation theorem.*

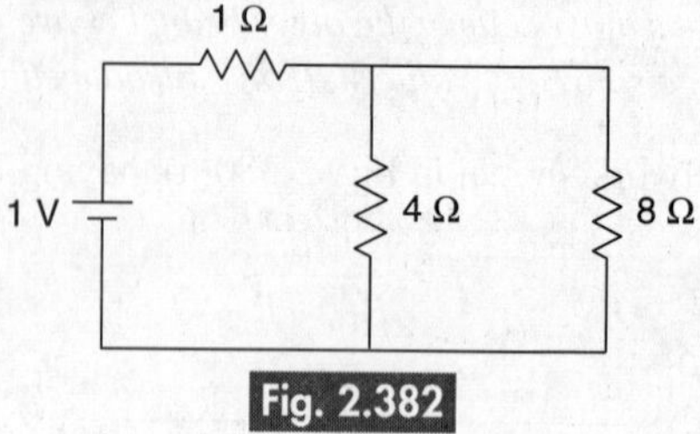


Fig. 2.382

**Solution**

***Step I*** Calculation of change in current

Finding Thevenin's equivalent network across the 4 Ω resistor,

$$V_{\text{Th}} = 1 \times \frac{8}{8+1} = 0.89 \text{ V}$$

$$R_{\text{Th}} = \frac{1 \times 8}{1+8} = 0.89 \ \Omega$$

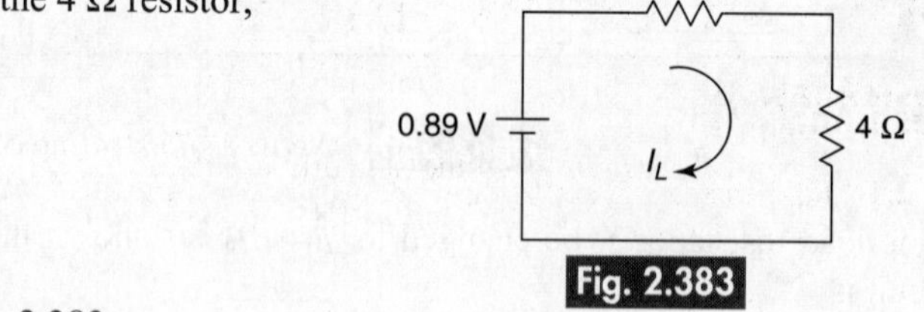


Fig. 2.383

Thevenin's equivalent network is shown in Fig. 2.383.

$$I_L = \frac{0.89}{0.89+4} = 0.18 \text{ A}$$

When resistor of 4 Ω is changed to 2 Ω (Fig.2.384),

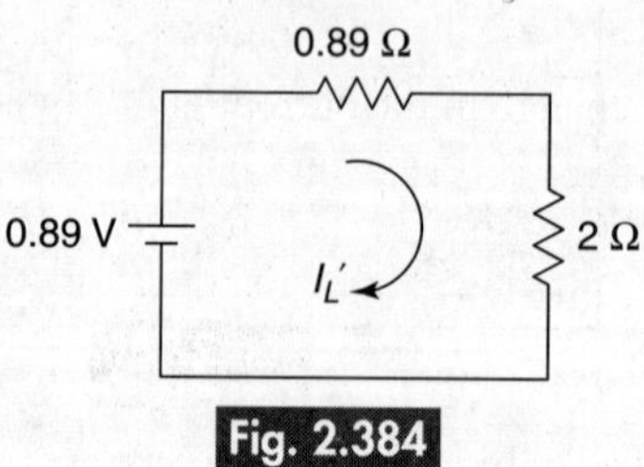


Fig. 2.384

$$I_L' = \frac{0.89}{0.89+2} = 0.31 \text{ A}$$

$$\delta I_L = I_L' - I_L = 0.31 - 0.18 = 0.13 \text{ A}$$

***Step II*** Calculation of change of current by compensation theorem

$$\delta R = 2 - 4 = -2 \ \Omega$$

$$R + \delta R = 4 - 2 = 2 \ \Omega$$

$$V_c = I_L \delta R = 0.18 \times (-2) = -0.36 \text{ V}$$

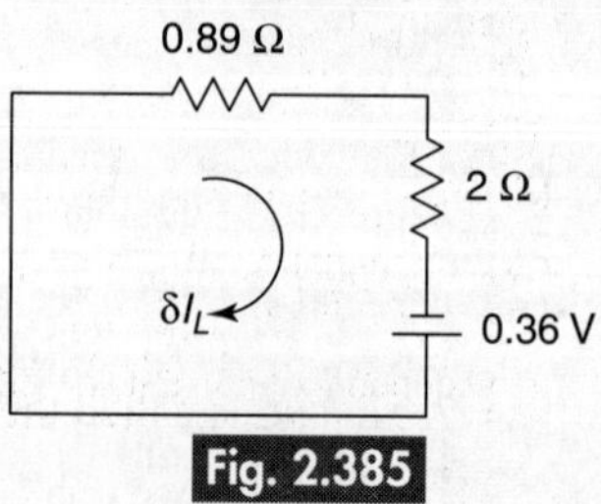


Fig. 2.385

The compensating network is shown in Fig. 2.385.

$$\delta I_L = \frac{0.36}{0.89+2} = 0.12 \text{ A}$$

Since change in current is same in both the steps, the compensation theorem is verified.

# Theory Questions

**2.1** State and explain superposition theorem. **[LO 2.3]** ○●○
**2.2** State and explain Thevenin's theorem. **[LO 2.4]** ○●○
**2.3** State and explain Norton's theorem. **[LO 2.5]** ○●○
**2.4** State and explain maximum power transfer theorem. **[LO 2.6]** ○●○
**2.5** State and explain reciprocity theorem. **[LO 2.7]** ○●○
**2.6** State and explain Millman's theorem. **[LO 2.8]** ○●○
**2.7** State and explain Tellegen's theorem. **[LO 2.9]** ○●○
**2.8** State and explain substitution theorem. **[LO 2.10]** ○●○
**2.9** State and explain compensation theorem. **[LO 2.10]** ○●○

# Practice Problems

## Mesh Analysis

**2.1** Find currents $I_x$ and $I_y$ in the network shown in Fig. 2.386. ○●○

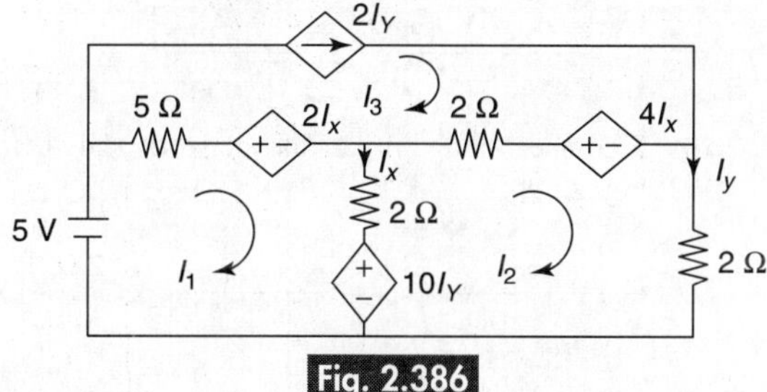


Fig. 2.386

**2.2** In the network shown in Fig. 2.387, find $V_3$ if element $A$ is a

(i) short circuit
(ii) 5 Ω resistor
(iii) 20 V independent voltage source, positive reference on the right
(iv) dependent voltage source of 1.5 $i_1$, with positive reference on the right
(v) dependent current source 5 $i_1$, arrow directed to the right ○○●

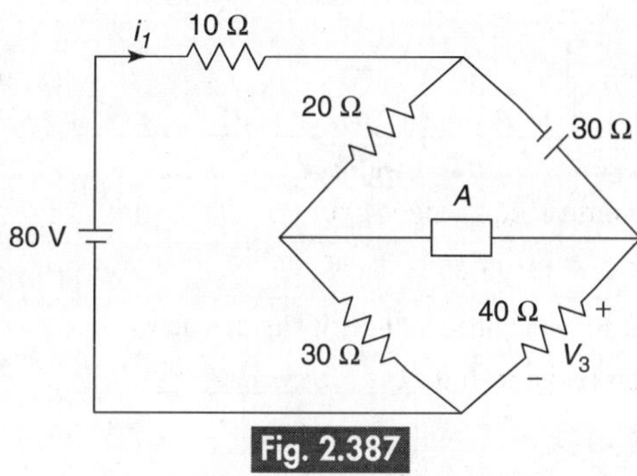


Fig. 2.387

**2.3** Find currents $I_1$, $I_2$, and $I_3$ in the network shown in Fig. 2.388. ○●○

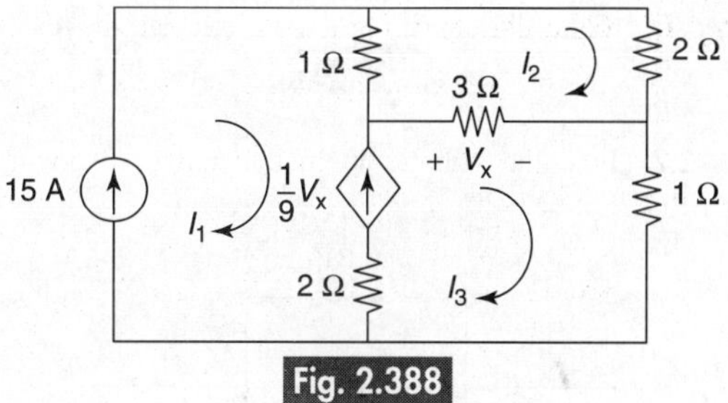


Fig. 2.388

**2.4** Find currents $I_x$ in the network shown in Fig. 2.389. ○●○

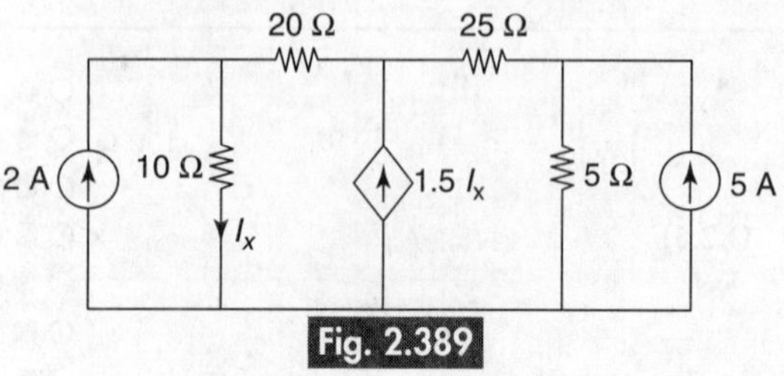


Fig. 2.389

**2.5** Find currents $I_1$ in the network shown in Fig. 2.390. ○●○

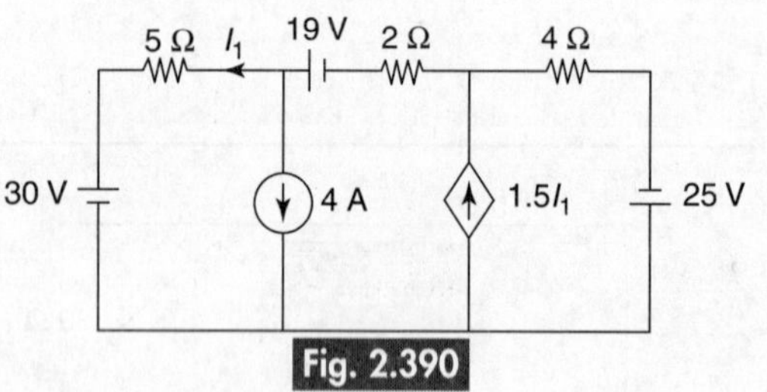


Fig. 2.390

## Node Analysis

**2.6** Find the voltage $V_x$ in the network shown in Fig. 2.391. ○●○

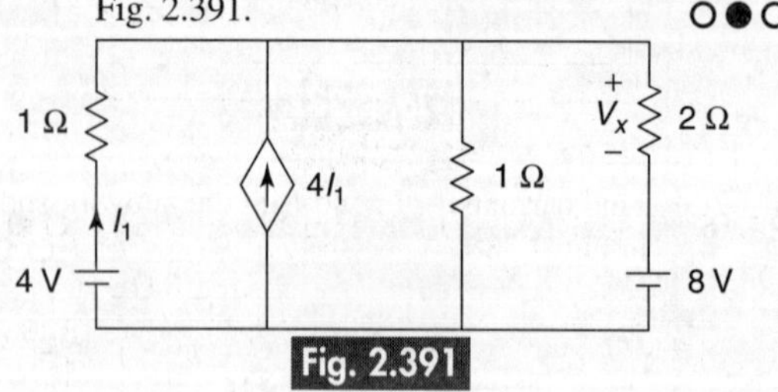


Fig. 2.391

**2.7** Find the voltage $V_x$ in the network shown in Fig. 2.392.

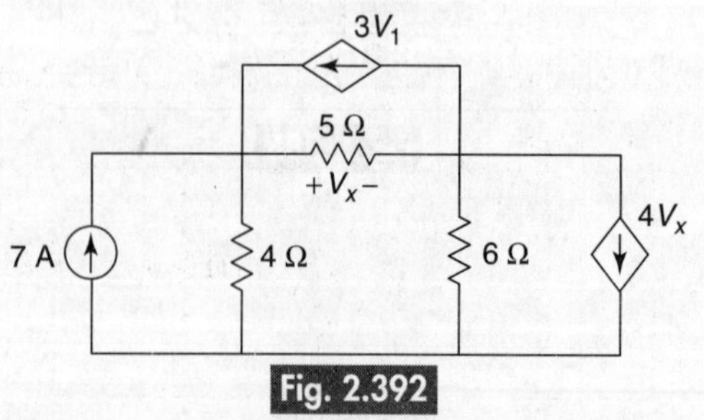


Fig. 2.392

**2.8** Find the voltage $V_x$ in the network shown in Fig. 2.393. ○●○

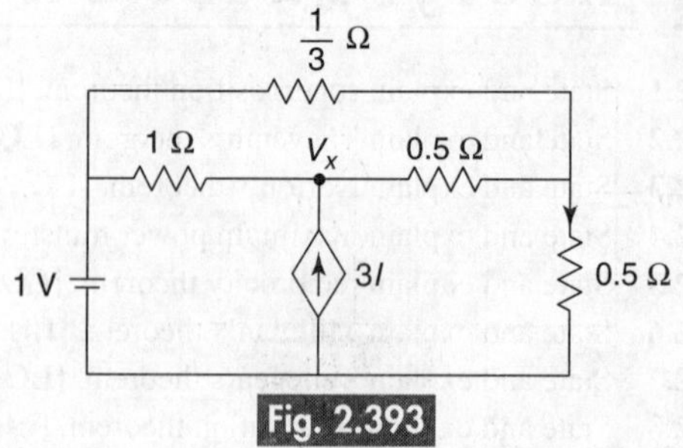


Fig. 2.393

**2.9** Determine $V_1$ in the network shown in Fig. 2.394. ○●○

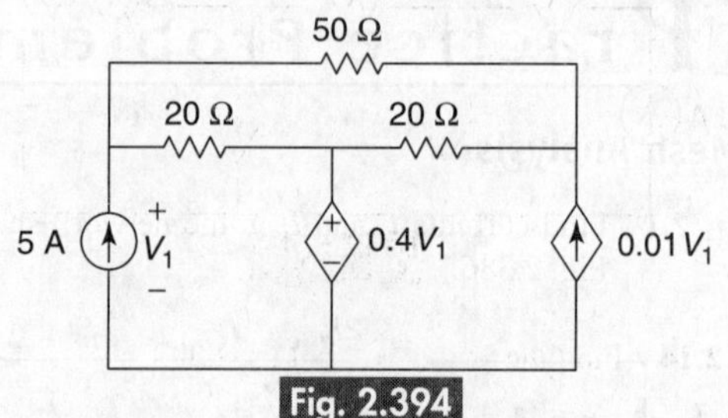


Fig. 2.394

**2.10** Find the voltage $V_y$ in the network shown in Fig. 2.395. ○●○

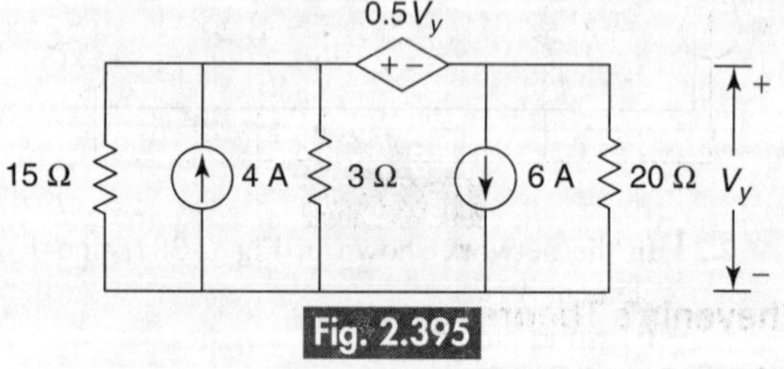


Fig. 2.395

**2.11** Find the voltage $V_2$ in the network shown in Fig. 2.396. ○●○

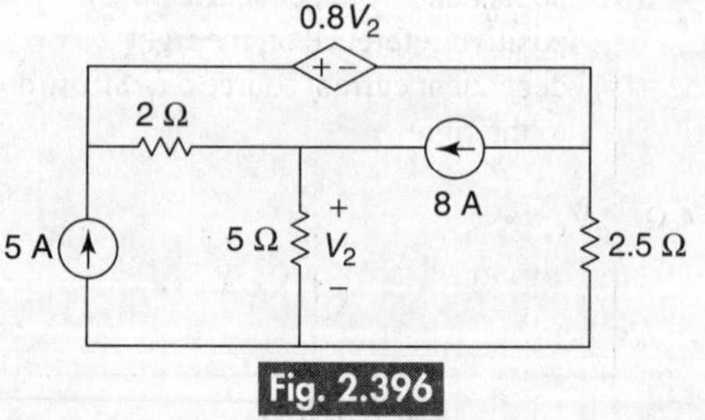


Fig. 2.396

## Superposition Theorem

**2.12** Find the voltage $V_x$ in Fig. 2.397. ○●○

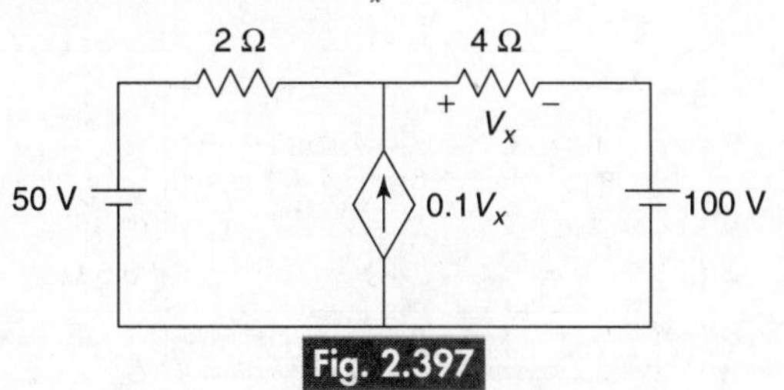


Fig. 2.397

**2.13** Determine the voltages $V_1$ and $V_2$ in Fig. 2.398. ○●○

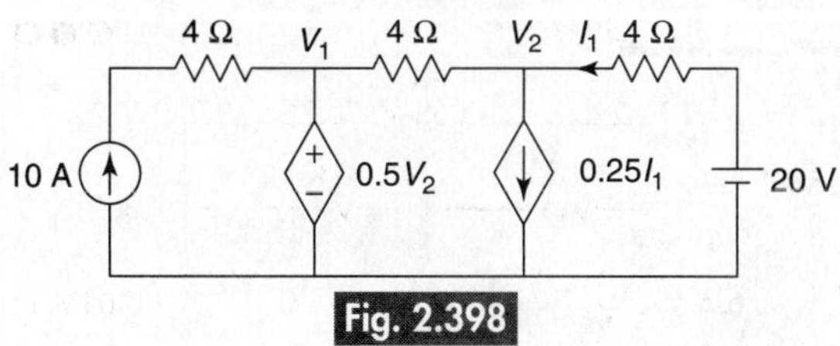


Fig. 2.398

**2.14** Find the voltage $V_x$ in Fig. 2.399. ○●○

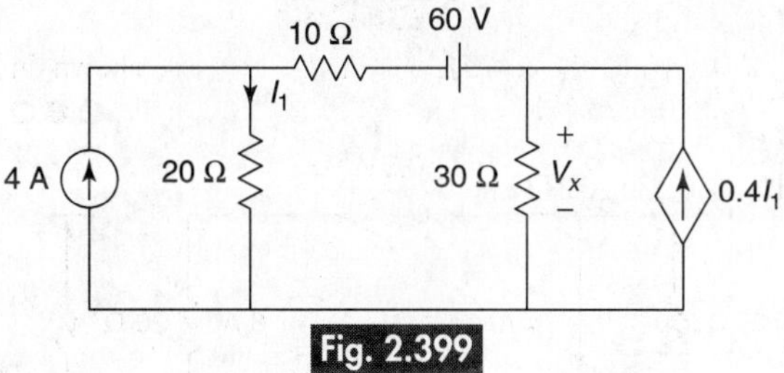


Fig. 2.399

## Thevenin's Theorem

**2.15** Determine Thevenin's equivalent network for figures 2.400 to 2.403 shown below. ○●○

(i)

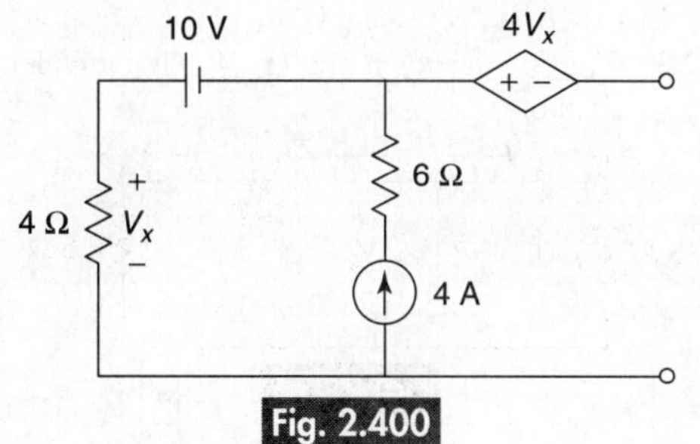


Fig. 2.400

(ii)

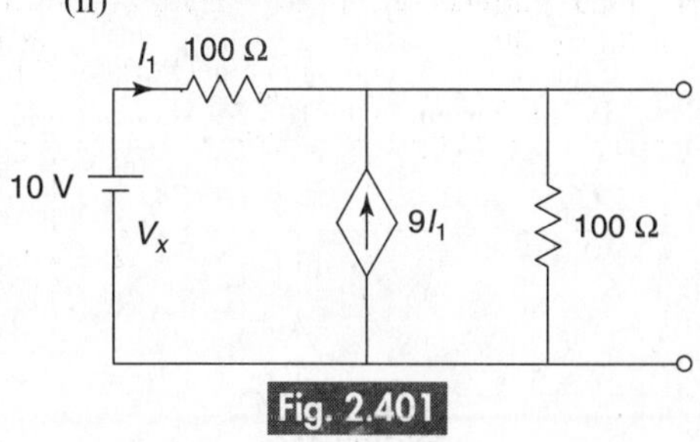


Fig. 2.401

(iii)

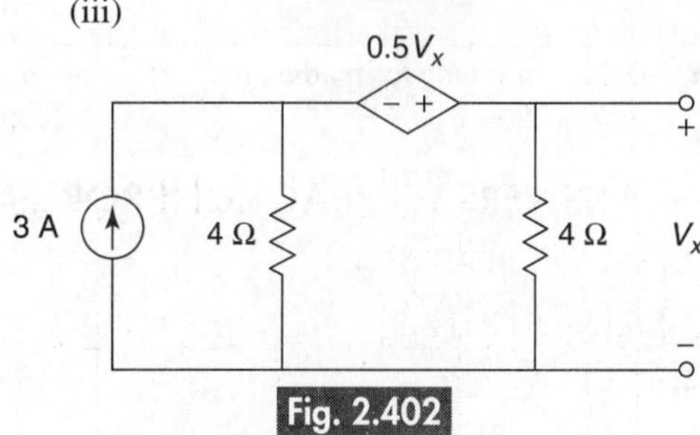


Fig. 2.402

(iv)

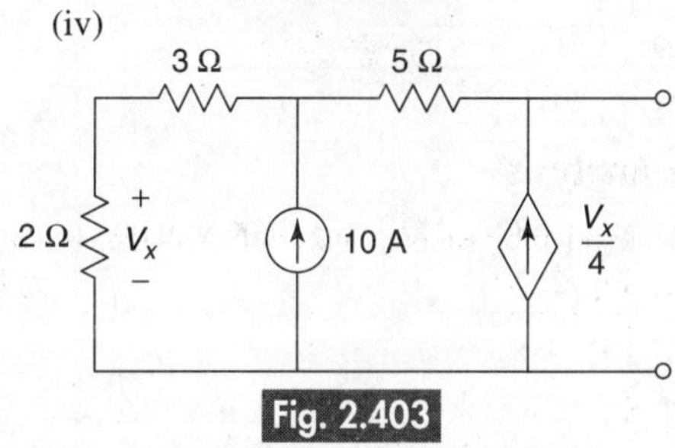


Fig. 2.403

**2.16** Find the current $I_x$ in Fig. 2.404. ○●○

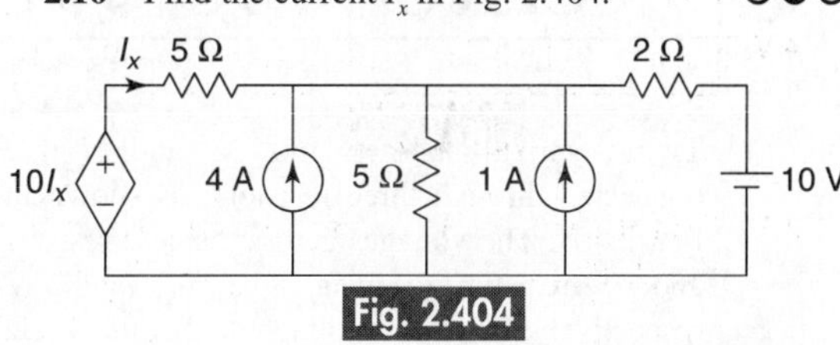


Fig. 2.404

**2.17** Find the current in the 24 Ω resistor in Fig. 2.405. ○●○

$I_x$ 1000 Ω

48 V  3$V_x$  10$I_x$  13 Ω  $V_x$  24 Ω

Fig. 2.405

## Norton's Theorem

**2.18** Find Norton's equivalent network and hence, find the current in the 10 Ω resistor in Fig. 2.406. ○●○

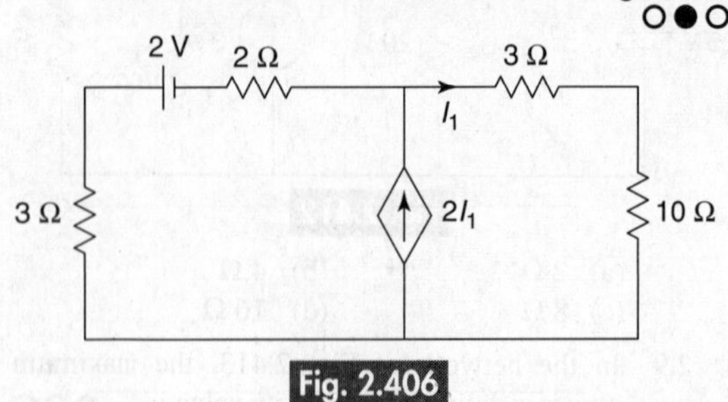


Fig. 2.406

**2.19** Find Norton's equivalent network in Fig. 2.407. ○●○

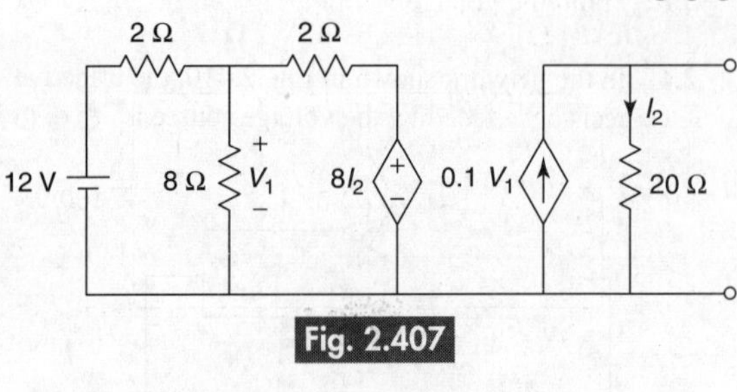


Fig. 2.407

## ANSWERS TO PRACTICE PROBLEMS

**2.1** 0.5 A, 0.1 A
**2.2** 69.4 V, 72.38 V, 73.68 V, 70.71 V, 97.39 V
**2.3** 15 A, 11 A, 17 A
**2.4** 8.33 A
**2.5** –12 A
**2.6** –4.31 V
**2.7** 2.09 V
**2.8** 6.2 V
**2.9** 140 V
**2.10** –10 V
**2.11** 25.9 V
**2.12** –38.5 V
**2.13** 6 V, 12 V
**2.14** 7.5 V
**2.15** (i) –58 V, 12 Ω (ii) 9.09 V, 9.09 Ω (iii) 8 V, 2.66 Ω (iv) 150 V, 20 Ω
**2.16** 4 A
**2.17** 0.225 A
**2.18** 0.25 A
**2.19** 0.533 A, 31 Ω

# Objective-Type Questions

### From GATE and Other Competitive Examinations

**2.1** Two electrical sub-networks $N_1$ and $N_2$ are connected through three resistors, as shown in Fig. 2.408. The voltages across the 5 Ω resistor and 1 Ω resistor are given to be 10 V and 5 V respectively. Then the voltage across the 15 Ω resistor is ○○●

(a) –105 V (b) 105 V
(c) –15 V (d) 15 V

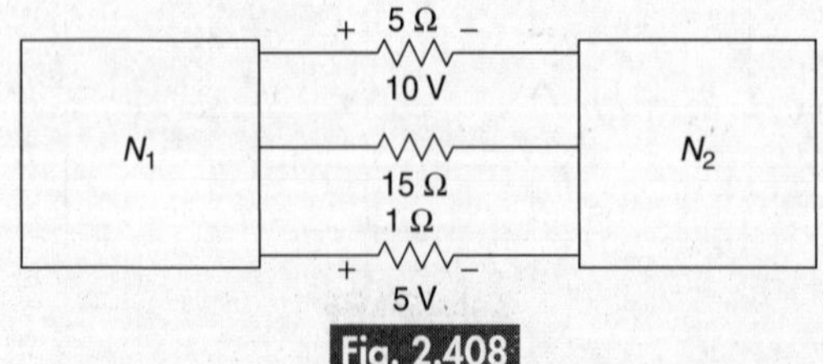


Fig. 2.408

**2.2** The nodal method of circuit analysis is based on ●○○

(a) KVL and Ohm's law
(b) KCL and Ohm's law
(c) KCL and KVL
(d) KCL, KVL and Ohm's law

**2.3** The circuit shown in Fig. 2.409 is equivalent to a load of ○●○

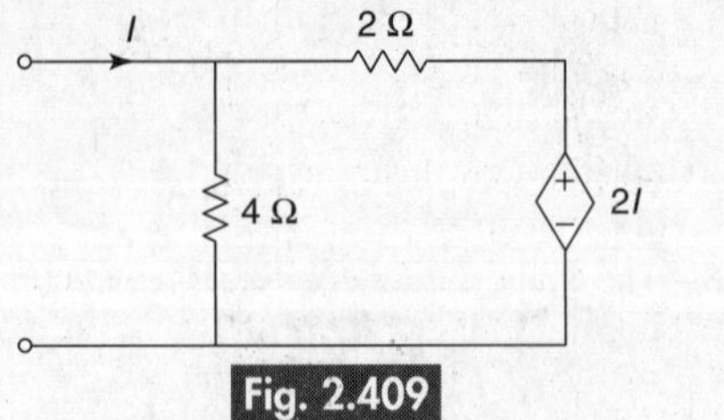


Fig. 2.409

(a) $\frac{4}{3}\,\Omega$ (b) $\frac{8}{3}\,\Omega$

(c) 4 Ω (d) 2 Ω

**2.4** In the network shown in Fig. 2.410, the effective resistance faced by the voltage source is ○●○

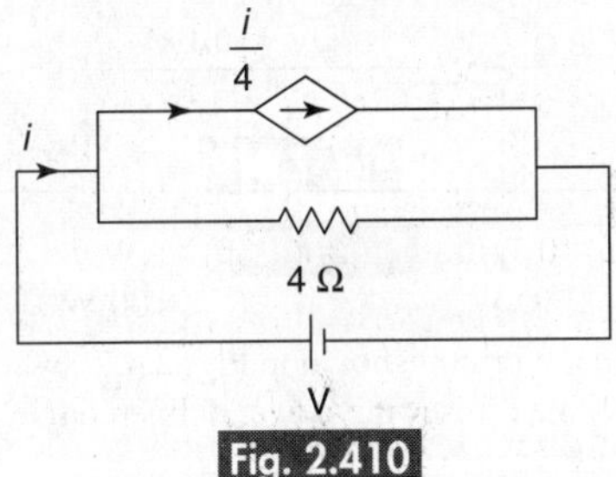


Fig. 2.410

(a) 4 Ω (b) 3 Ω

(c) 2 Ω (d) 1 Ω

**2.5** A network contains only an independent current source and resistors. If the values of all resistors are doubled, the value of the node voltages will ○●○

(a) become half (b) remain unchanged

(c) become double (d) none of these

**2.6** The value of the resistance $R$ connected across the terminals $A$ and $B$ in Fig. 2.411, which will absorb the maximum power is ●○○

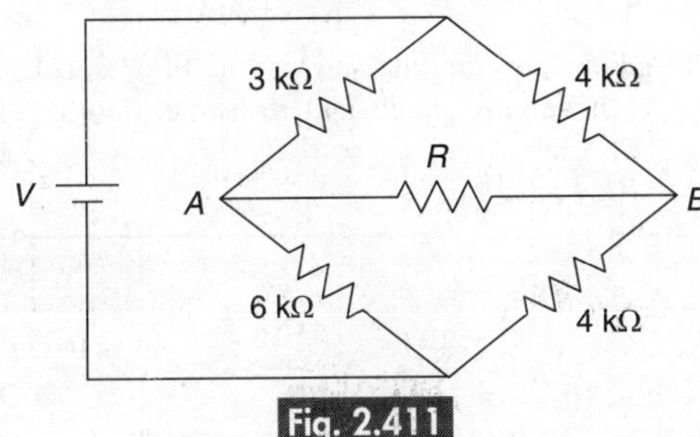


Fig. 2.411

(a) 4 kΩ (b) 4.11 kΩ

(c) 8 kΩ (d) 9 k Ω

**2.7** Superposition theorem is not applicable to networks containing ●○○

(a) non-linear elements

(b) dependent voltage source

(c) dependent current source

(d) transformers

**2.8** The value of $R$ required for maximum power transfer in the network shown in Fig. 2.412 is ●○○

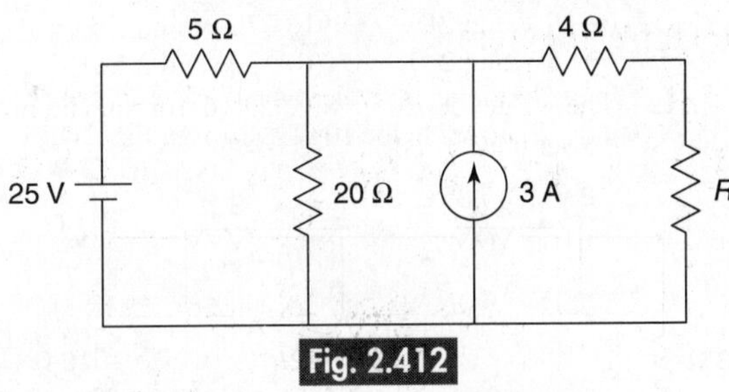


Fig. 2.412

(a) 2 Ω (b) 4 Ω

(c) 8 Ω (d) 16 Ω

**2.9** In the network of Fig. 2.413, the maximum power is delivered to $R_L$ if its value is ●○○

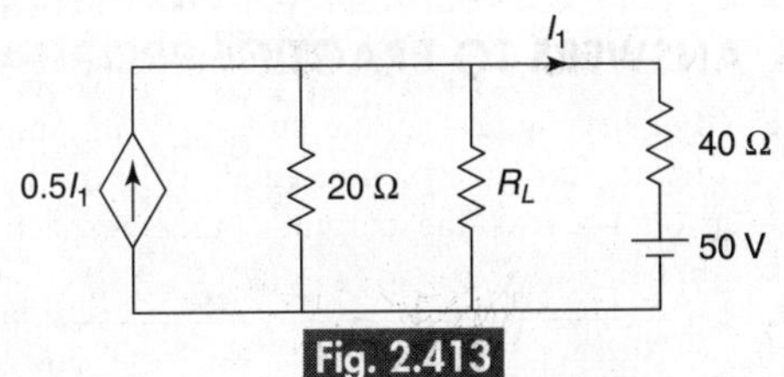


Fig. 2.413

(a) 16 Ω (b) $\frac{40}{3}\,\Omega$

(c) 60 Ω (d) 20 Ω

**2.10** The maximum power that can be transferred to the load $R_L$ from the voltage source in Fig. 2.414 is ●○○

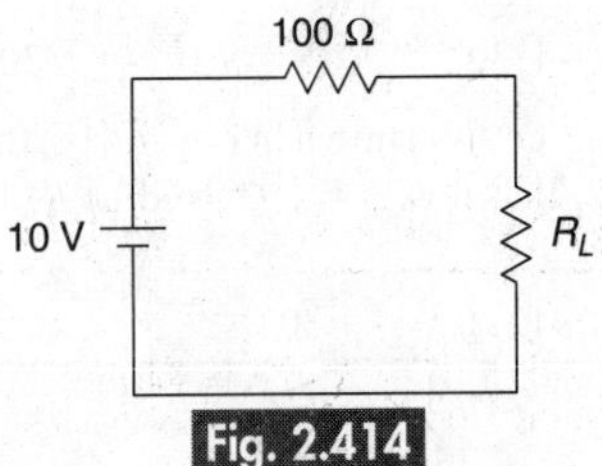


Fig. 2.414

(a) 1 W (b) 10 W

(c) 0.25 W (d) 0.5 W

**2.11** For the circuit shown in Fig. 2.415, Thevenin's voltage and Thevenin's equivalent resistance at terminals $a$-$b$ is ○●○

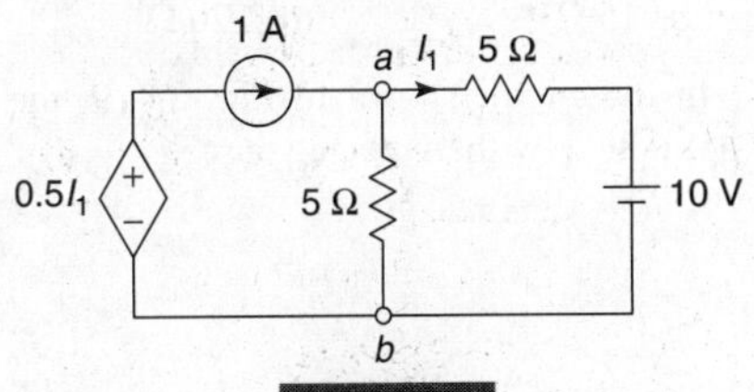


Fig. 2.415

(a) 5 V and 2 Ω (b) 7.5 V and 2.5 Ω
(c) 4 V and 2 Ω (d) 3 V and 2.5 Ω

**2.12** The value of $R_L$ in Fig. 2.416 for maximum power transfer is ○●○

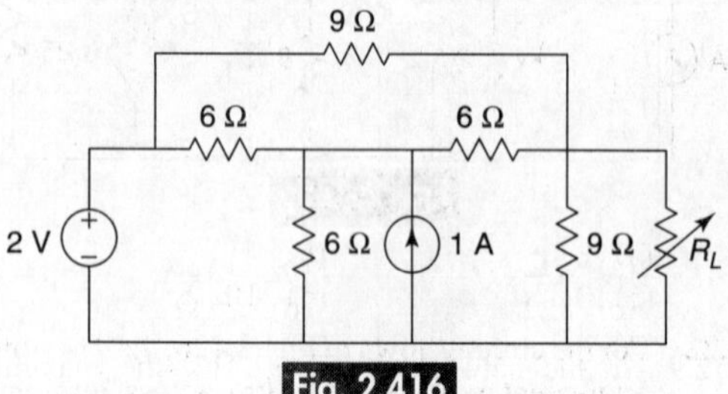


Fig. 2.416

(a) 3 Ω (b) 1.125 Ω
(c) 4.1785 Ω (d) none of these

**2.13** For the Fig. 2.417, the current $I_s$ (in Ampere) in the voltage source and voltage $V_s$ (in volts) across the current source respectively are ○●○

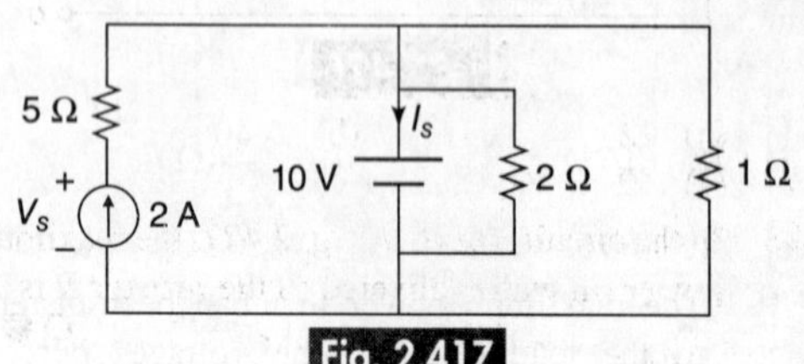


Fig. 2.417

(a) 13, –20 (b) 8, –10
(c) –8, 20 (d) –13, 20

**2.14** In the circuit shown in Fig. 2.418, the value of $R_L$ such that power transferred to $R_L$ is maximum, is ○●○

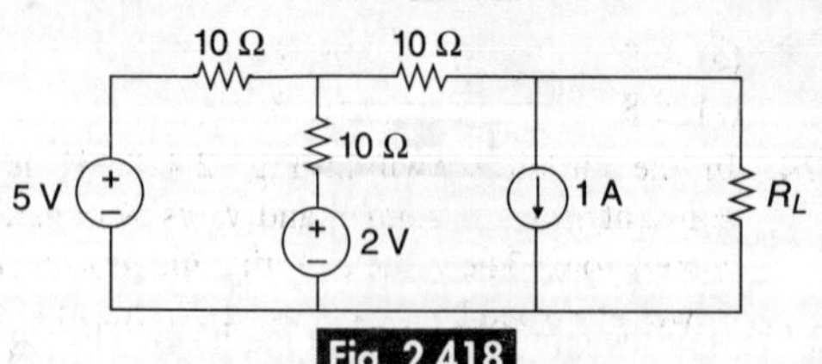


Fig. 2.418

(a) 5 Ω (b) 10 Ω
(c) 15 Ω (d) 20 Ω

**2.15** In the circuit shown in Fig. 2.419, the power supplied by the voltage source is ○●○

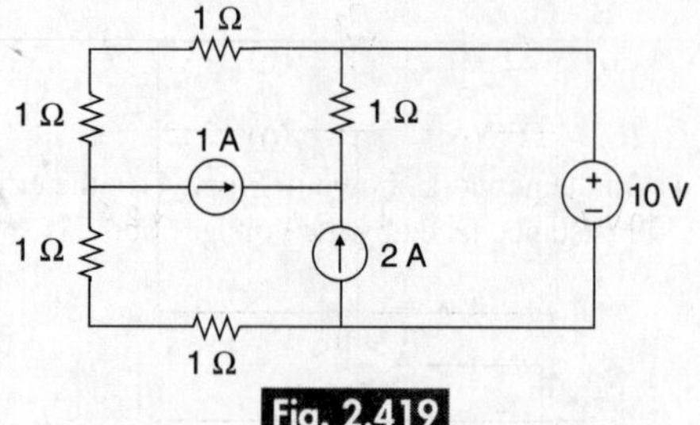


Fig. 2.419

(a) 0 W (b) 5 W
(c) 10 W (d) 100 W

**2.16** In the circuit shown in Fig. 2.420, what value of $R_L$ maximises the power delivered to $R_L$? ○●○

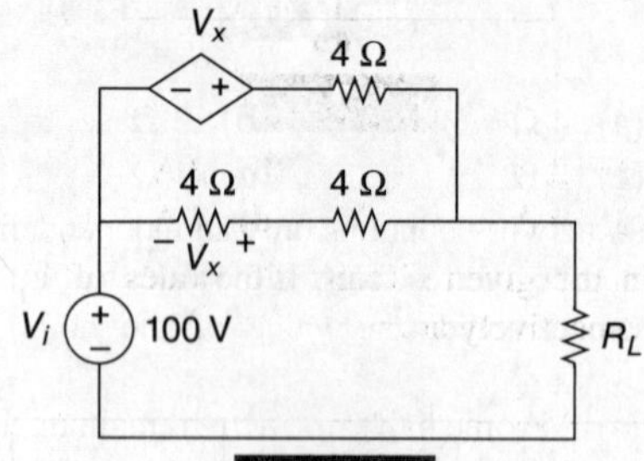


Fig. 2.420

(a) 2.4 Ω (b) $\frac{8}{3}$ Ω
(c) 4 Ω (d) 6 Ω

**2.17** For the circuit shown in Fig. 2.421, the Thevenin voltage and resistance looking into X-Y are ○●○

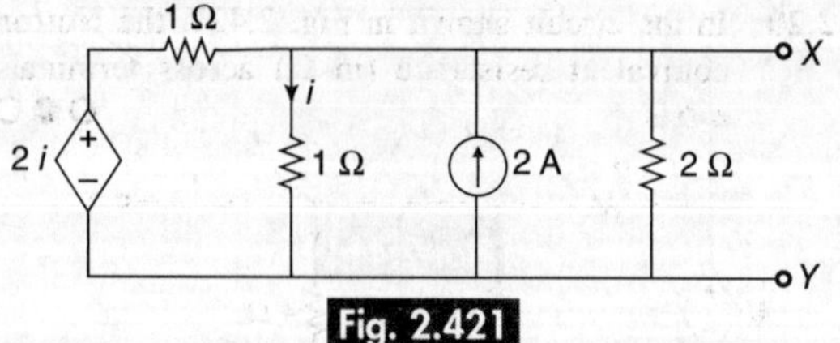


Fig. 2.421

(a) $\frac{4}{3}$ V, 2 Ω (b) 4 V, $\frac{2}{3}$ Ω
(c) $\frac{4}{3}$ V, $\frac{2}{3}$ Ω (d) 4 V, 2 Ω

**2.18** Use the data of the Fig. 2.422(a). The current $i$ in the circuit of Fig. 2.422(b) is ○●○

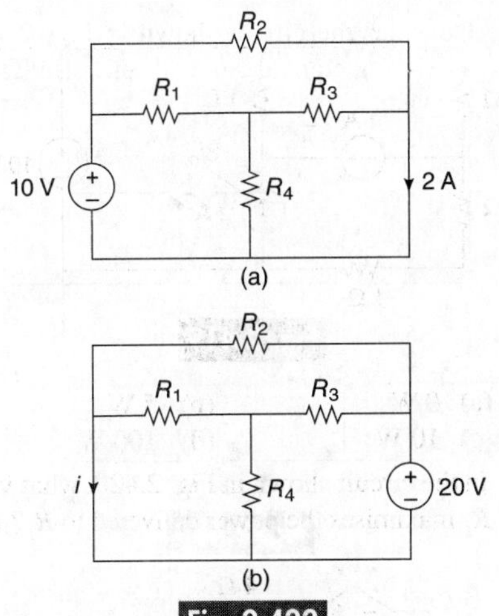


Fig. 2.422

(a) –2 A (b) 2 A
(c) –4 A (d) 4 A

**2.19** In the given circuit, the values of $V_1$ and $V_2$ respectively are ○●○

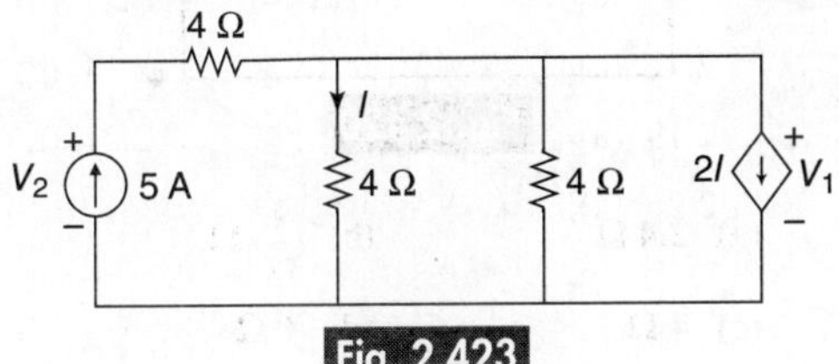


Fig. 2.423

(a) 5 V, 25 V (b) 10 V, 30 V
(c) 15 V, 35 V (d) 0 V, 20 V

**2.20** In the circuit shown in Fig. 2.424, the Norton equivalent resistance (in Ω) across terminals *a-b* is ○●○

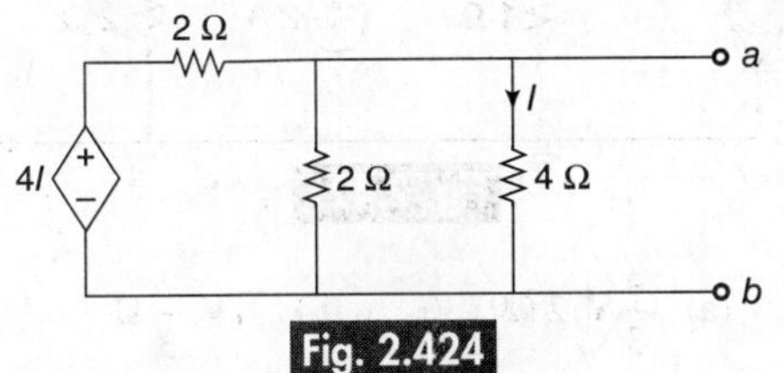


Fig. 2.424

(a) 1 (b) 1.33
(c) 2 Ω (d) 3

**2.21** In the circuit shown in Fig. 2.425, the voltage $V_x$ (in volts) is ○●○

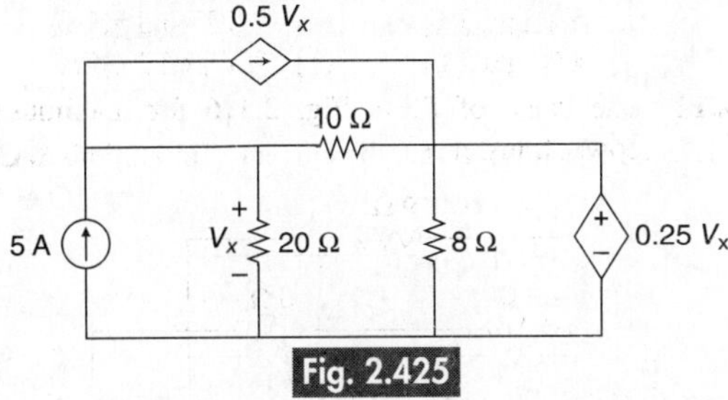


Fig. 2.425

(a) 8 (b) 4
(c) 2 (d) 10

**2.22** For the circuit shown in Fig. 2.426, the Thevenin equivalent voltage (in volts) across terminals *a-b* is ●○○

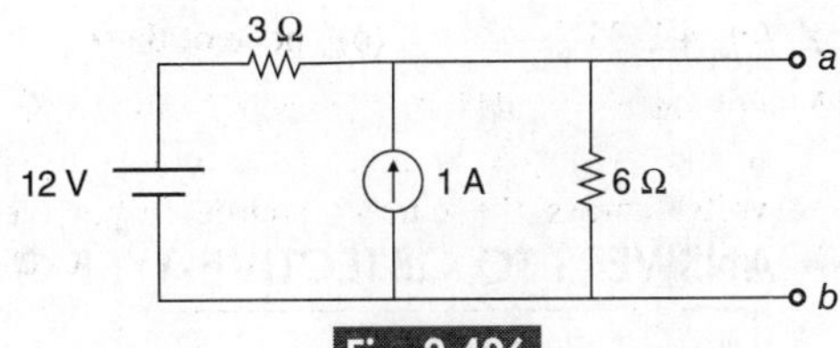


Fig. 2.426

(a) 12 (b) 6
(c) 10 (d) 4

**2.23** In the circuit shown in Fig. 2.427, the maximum power (in watt) delivered to the resistor *R* is ○●○

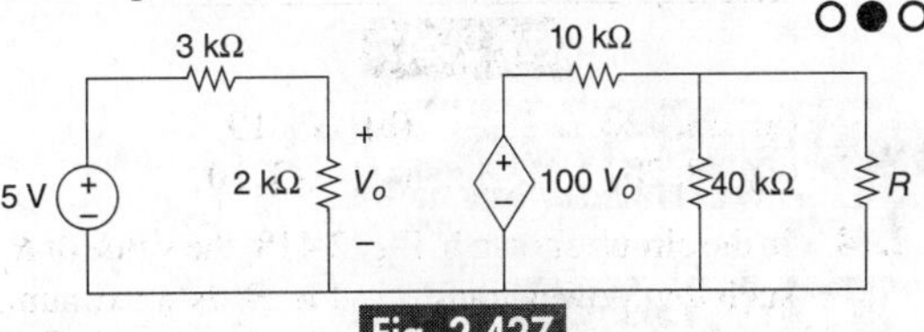


Fig. 2.427

(a) 0.5 (b) 1
(c) 0.8 (d) 2

**2.24** In the circuit shown in Fig. 2.428, $V_s$ is a constant voltage source and $I_L$ is a constant current load. The value of $I_L$ that maximizes the power absorbed by the constant current load is ○●○

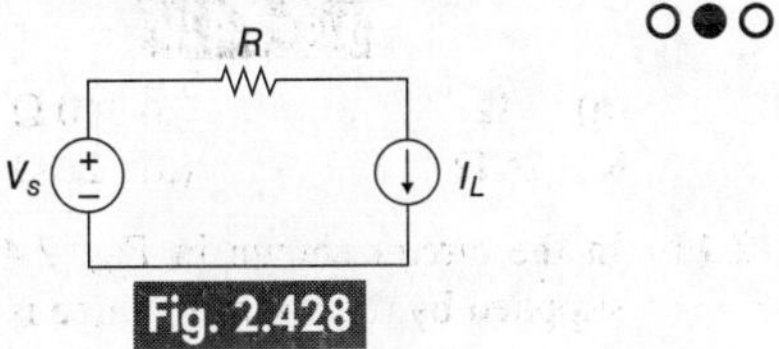


Fig. 2.428

(a) $\frac{V_s}{4R}$ (b) $\frac{V_s}{R}$

(c) $\dfrac{V_s}{2R}$ (d) $\infty$

**2.25** In the Fig. 2.429, the current $i$ (in amperes) is

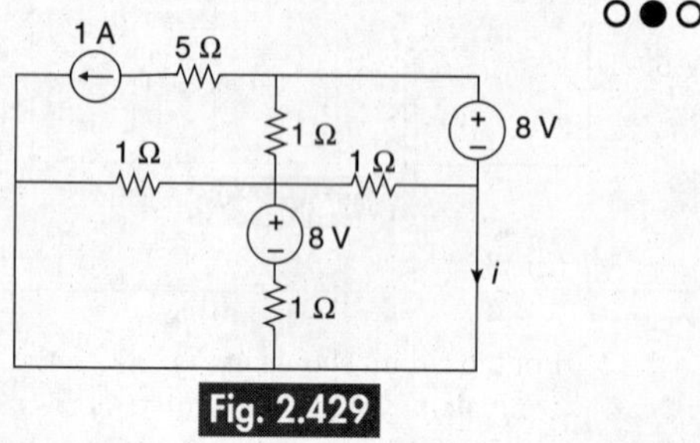

Fig. 2.429

(a) 2 A (b) 1 A
(c) –1 A (d) –2 A

**2.26** Consider the circuit shown in Fig. 2.430. The Thevenin equivalent resistance (in Ω) across $P$-$Q$ is

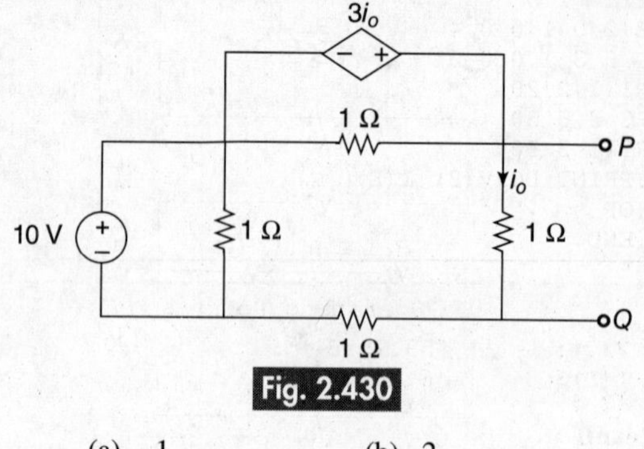

Fig. 2.430

(a) –1 (b) 2
(c) 1 (d) 10

## ANSWERS TO OBJECTIVE-TYPE QUESTIONS

| | | | | | | |
|---|---|---|---|---|---|---|
| 2.1 (a) | 2.2 (b) | 2.3 (a) | 2.4 (d) | 2.5 (b) | 2.6 (a) | 2.7 (a) |
| 2.8 (c) | 2.9 (a) | 2.10 (c) | 2.11 (b) | 2.12 (a) | 2.13 (d) | 2.14 (c) |
| 2.15 (a) | 2.16 (c) | 2.17 (d) | 2.18 (d) | 2.19 (a) | 2.20 (b) | 2.21 (a) |
| 2.22 (c) | 2.23 (c) | 2.24 (b) | 2.25 (c) | 2.26 (a) | | |

# LTspice Section

## EXAMPLE 2.1

*For the network shown in Fig. 2.431, find the power supplied by the dependent voltage source.*

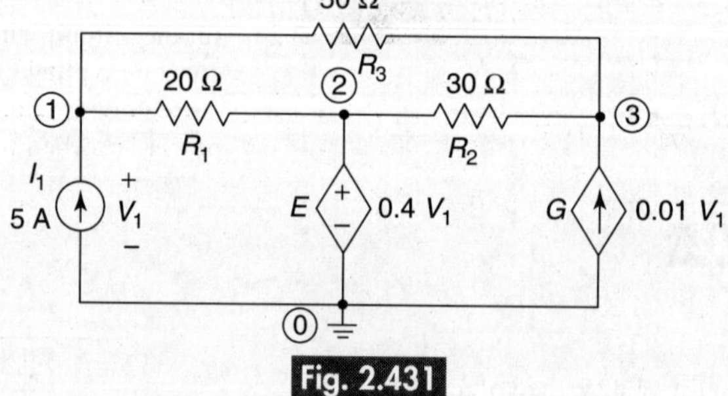

Fig. 2.431

## Solution

```
*Calculation of power supplied by the dependent voltage source

I1 0 1 5
E 2 0 1 0 0.4
G 0 3 1 0 0.01
R1 1 2 20
R2 2 3 30
R3 1 3 50
.PRINT DC V(2) I(E)
.OP
.END
```

```
              Operating Point
V(2):         59.2593                voltage
I(E):         6.48148                device_current
```

**Result**

Current supplied by dependent voltage source = $I(E) = 6.48148$ A

$$V_2 = 0.4V_1 = V(2) = 59.2593 \text{ V}$$

Power supplied by dependent voltage source = $0.4\ V_1 I(E) = 59.2593 \times 6.48148 = 384.0879$ W

## EXAMPLE 2.2

*For the network shown in Fig. 2.432, find voltages $V_1$ and $V_2$.*

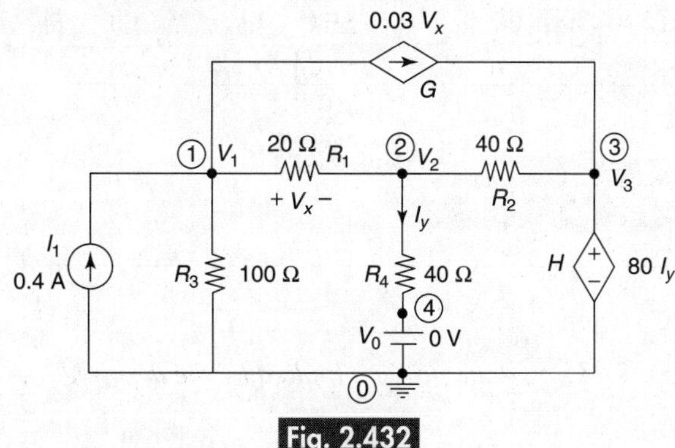


Fig. 2.432

## Solution

```
*Calculation of voltages V1 and V2

I1 0 1 0.4
V0 4 0 0
H 3 0 V0 80
G 1 3 1 2 0.03
R1 1 2 20
R2 2 3 40
R3 1 0 100
R4 2 4 40
.PRINT DC V(1) V(2) V(3)
.OP
.END
```

```
            Operating Point
V(1):                40                voltage
V(3):                80                voltage
V(2):                40                voltage
```

**Result**

$V_1 = V(1) = 40$ V
$V_2 = V(2) = 40$ V
$V_3 = V(3) = 80$ V

## EXAMPLE 2.3

*For the network shown in Fig. 2.433, determine the voltage $V_x$.*

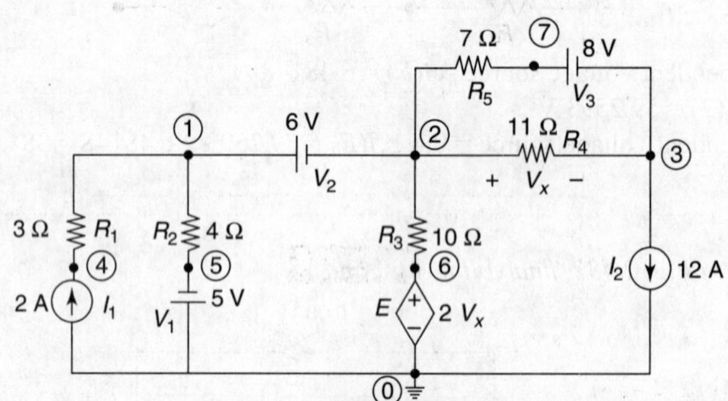


Fig. 2.433

## Solution

```
*Calculation of voltage Vx

I1 0 4 2
I2 3 0 12
V1 0 5 5
V2 1 2 6
V3 7 3 8
E 6 0 2 3 2
R1 1 4 3
R2 1 5 4
R3 2 6 10
R4 2 3 11
R5 2 7 7
.PRINT DC V(2) V(3)
.OP
.END
```

```
                 Operating Point
V(3):              -60.5238            voltage
V(2):              -4.30159            voltage
```

**Result**

$V_2 = V(2) = -4.30159$ V
$V_3 = V(3) = -60.5238$ V
$V_x = V_2 - V_3 = -4.30159 - (-60.5238) = 56.222$ V

## EXAMPLE 2.4

*Obtain the Thevenin's equivalent network of Fig. 2.434 for the given network at terminals a and b.*

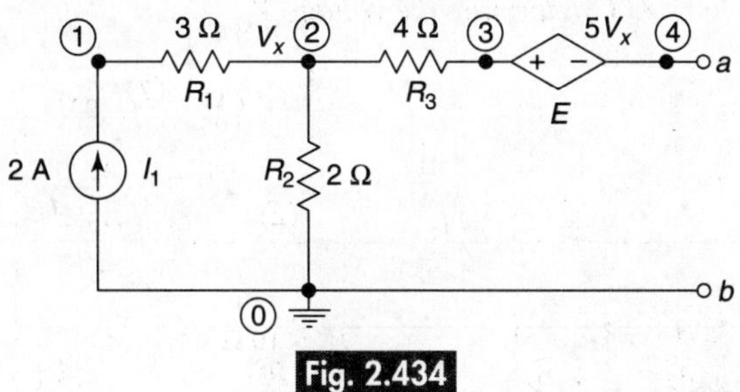


Fig. 2.434

## Solution

(a) Calculation of $V_{Th}$ (Fig. 2.434)

```
*Calculation of VTh

I1 0 1 2
E 3 4 2 0 5
R1 1 2 3
R2 2 0 2
R3 2 3 4
.PRINT DC V(4)
.OP
.END
```

```
                 Operating Point
V(4):              -16                 voltage
```

**Result**

$$V_{Th} = V(4) = -16 \text{ V}$$

(b) Calculation of $I_N$ (Fig. 2.435)

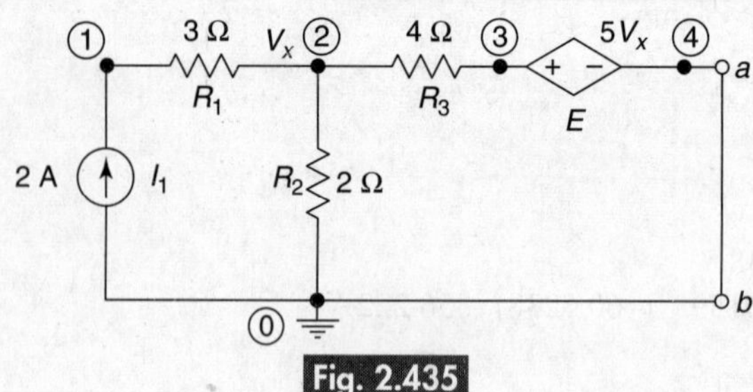


Fig. 2.435

```
*Calculation of IN

I1 0 1 2
E 3 0 2 0 5
R1 1 2 3
R2 2 0 2
R3 2 3 4
.PRINT DC I(R3)
.OP
.END
```

```
            Operating Point
  I(R3):           4                  device_current
```

**Result**

$$I_N = I(R3) = 4 \text{ A}$$

$$R_{Th} = \frac{V_{Th}}{I_N} = \frac{-16}{4} = -4\ \Omega$$

Thevenin's Equivalent Network (Fig. 2.436)

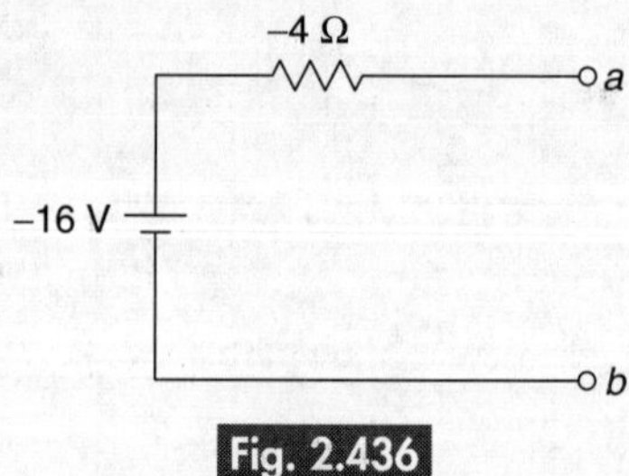


Fig. 2.436

## EXAMPLE 2.5

*For the network shown in Fig 2.437, find Norton's equivalent network.*

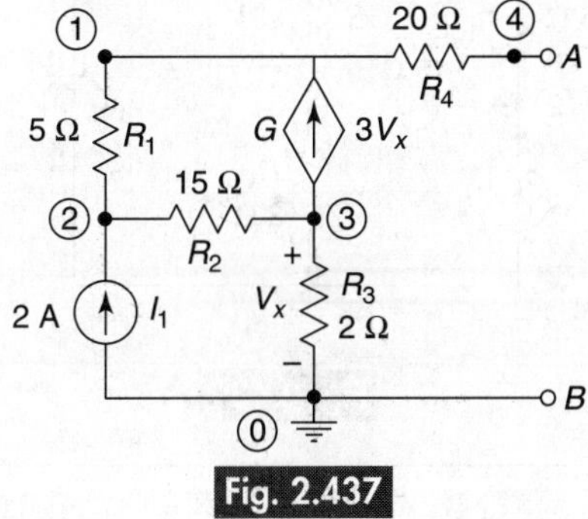


Fig. 2.437

## Solution

(a) Calculation of $I_N$ (Fig. 2.438)

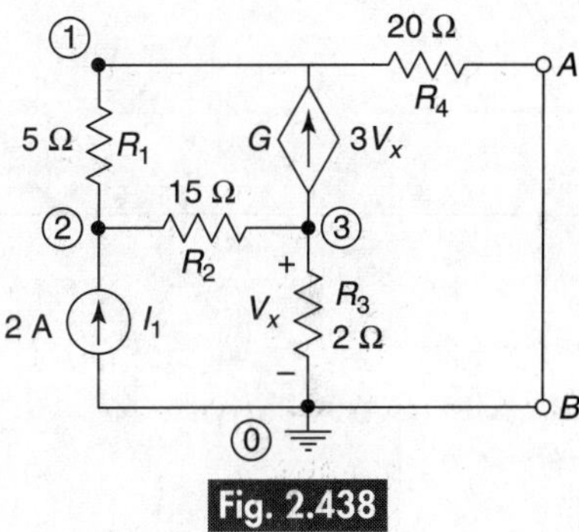


Fig. 2.438

```
*Calculation of IN

I1 0 2 2
G 3 1 3 0 3
R1 1 2 5
R2 2 3 15
R3 3 0 2
R4 1 0 20
.PRINT DC I(R4)
.OP
.END
```

```
            Operating Point
I(R4):         1.69136          device_current
```

**Result**

$$I_N = I(R4) = 1.69136 \text{ A}$$

(b) Calculation of $R_N$ (Fig. 2.439)

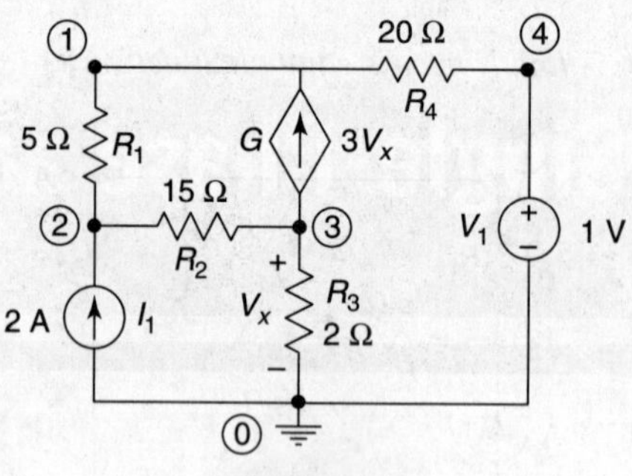


Fig. 2.439

```
Calculation of RN

I1 0 2 0
V1 4 0 1
G 3 1 3 0 3
R1 1 2 5
R2 2 3 15
R3 3 0 2
R4 1 4 20
.PRINT DC V(4) I(V1)
.OP
.END
```

```
            Operating Point

 V(4):      1                   voltage
 I(V1):     -0.00617284         device_current
```

**Result**

$$V_{AB} = V(4) = 1 \text{ V}$$

$$I(V1) = -0.00617284 \text{ A}$$

Current supplied by voltage source of 1 V is 0.00617284 A.

$$R_N = \frac{1}{0.00617284} = 162 \ \Omega$$

Norton's Equivalent Network

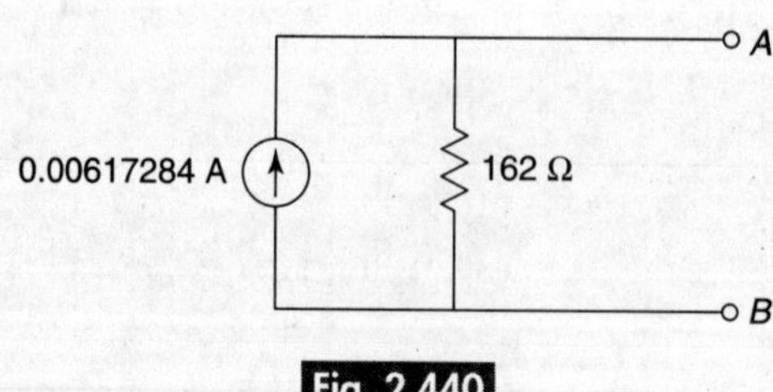


Fig. 2.440

CHAPTER 3

# Single-Phase ac Circuits

## LEARNING OBJECTIVES

**After studying this chapter, you should be able to:**

**LO 3.1** Discuss the generation of alternating voltages

**LO 3.2** Define waveform, cycle, frequency, time period, amplitude, phase and phase difference

**LO 3.3** Calculate root mean square (rms) or effective value and average value of waveforms

**LO 3.4** Discuss phasor representations of alternating quantities

**LO 3.5** Discuss mathematical representation of phasors

**LO 3.6** Explain the behaviour of a pure resistor, a pure inductor, and a pure capacitor in an ac circuit

**LO 3.7** Analyse series *RL* circuits, series *RC* circuits, and series *RLC* circuits

**LO 3.8** Analyse parallel ac circuits

**LO 3.9** Explain locus diagrams

## INTRODUCTION

An alternating waveform changes its magnitude and direction periodically. Many times, alternating voltages and currents are represented by a sinusoidal waveform. A sinusoidal waveform is more useful than other waveforms, like square, triangular, sawtooth, etc. Any waveform can be written in terms of sinusoidal function with the help of Fourier series. The sinusoidal waveform can be easily analysed and generated. A sinusoidal voltage can be represented as

$$v = V_m \sin \omega t$$

where $V_m$ is the amplitude of sinusoidal voltage.

## 3.1 GENERATION OF ALTERNATING VOLTAGES

LO 3.1

Discuss the generation of alternating voltages

An alternating voltage can be generated either by rotating a coil in a stationary magnetic field or by a rotating magnetic field within a stationary coil. In both the cases, the magnetic field is cut by the conductors or coils and an emf is induced in the coil according to Faraday's laws of electromagnetic induction. The magnitude of the induced emf depends upon the number of turns of the coil, the strength of the magnetic field and the speed at which the coil or magnetic field rotates.

Consider a rectangular coil of $N$ turns of area $A$ m$^2$ and rotating in anti-clockwise direction with angular velocity of $\omega$ radians per second in a uniform magnetic field, as shown in Fig. 3.1.

Let $\phi_m$ be the maximum flux cutting the coil when its axis coincides with $XX'$ axis (reference position of the coil). Thus, when the coil is along $XX'$, the flux linking with it is maximum, i.e., $\phi_m$. When the coil is along $YY'$, i.e., parallel to the lines of flux, the flux linking with it is zero.

The coil rotates through an angle $\theta = \omega t$ at any instant $t$. At this instant, the flux linking with the coil is

$$\phi = \phi_m \cos \omega t$$

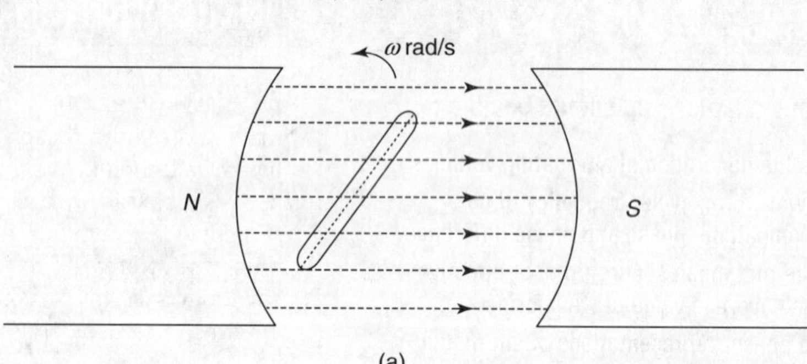


(a)

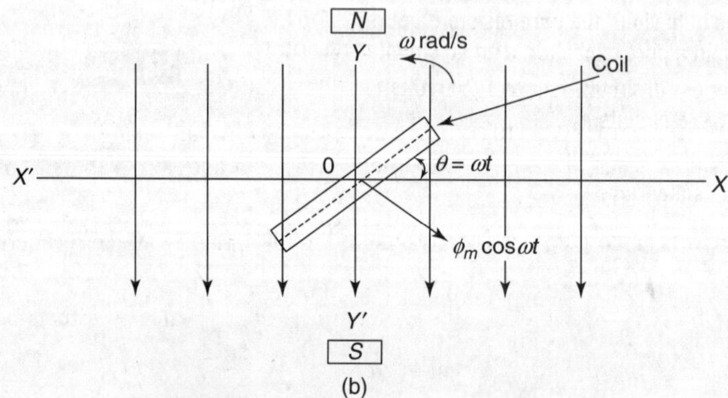


(b)

**Fig. 3.1** *Generation of alternating voltage*

According to Faraday's laws of electromagnetic induction,

$$e = -N\frac{d\phi}{dt} = -N\frac{d}{dt}(\phi_m \cos \omega t) = N\,\phi_m\,\omega \sin \omega t = E_m \sin \omega t$$

where $E_m = N\phi_m\omega$

$= \text{maximum value of induced emf}$

When $\omega t = 0, \quad \sin\omega t = 0, \quad e = 0$

When $\omega t = \frac{\pi}{2}, \quad \sin\frac{\pi}{2} = 1 \quad e = E_m$

If the induced emf is plotted against time, a sinusoidal waveform is obtained, as shown in Fig. 3.2.

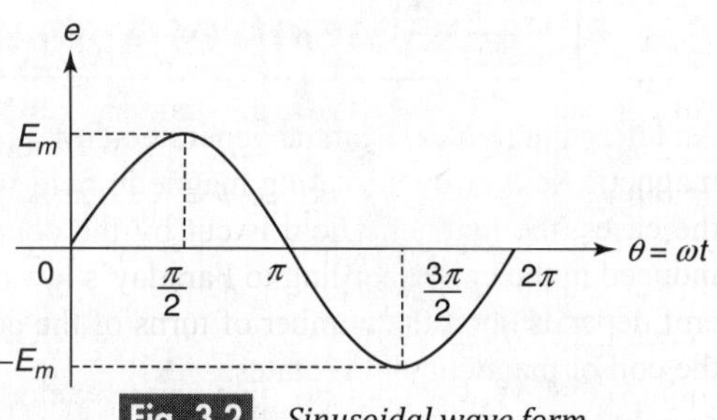


Fig. 3.2 *Sinusoidal wave form*

## 3.2 TERMS RELATED TO ALTERNATING QUANTITIES

LO 3.2

Define waveform, cycle, frequency, time period, amplitude, phase and phase difference

***1. Waveform*** A waveform is a graph in which the instantaneous value of any quantity is plotted against time. Figure 3.3 shows a few waveforms.

***2. Cycle*** One complete set of positive and negative values of an alternating quantity is termed a cycle.

***3. Frequency*** The number of cycles per second of an alternating quantity is known as its frequency. It is denoted by $f$ and is measured in hertz (Hz) or cycles per second (c/s).

***4. Time Period*** The time taken by an alternating quantity to complete one cycle is called its time period. It is denoted by $T$ and is measured in seconds.

$$T = \frac{1}{f}$$

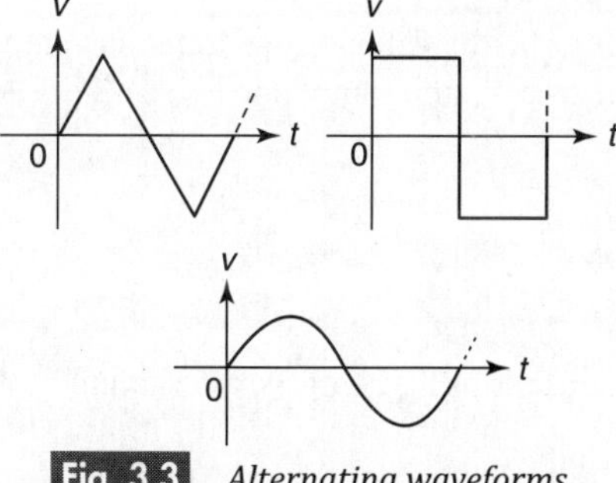


Fig. 3.3 *Alternating waveforms*

***5. Amplitude*** The maximum positive or negative value of an alternating quantity is called the amplitude.

***6. Phase*** The phase of an alternating quantity is the time that has elapsed since the quantity has last passed through zero point of reference.

***7. Phase Difference*** This term is used to compare the phases of two alternating quantities. Two alternating quantities are said to be in phase when they reach their maximum and zero values at the same time. Their maximum value may be different in magnitude.

A leading alternating quantity is one which reaches its maximum or zero value earlier compared to the other quantity.

A lagging alternating quantity is one which attains its maximum or zero value later than the other quantity.

A plus (+) sign, when used in connection with the phase difference, denotes 'lead' whereas a minus (–) sign denotes 'lag'.

$$v_A = V_m \sin\omega t$$

$$v_B = V_m \sin(\omega t + \phi)$$

Here, the quantity $B$ leads $A$ by a phase angle $\phi$, as shown in Fig. 3.4.

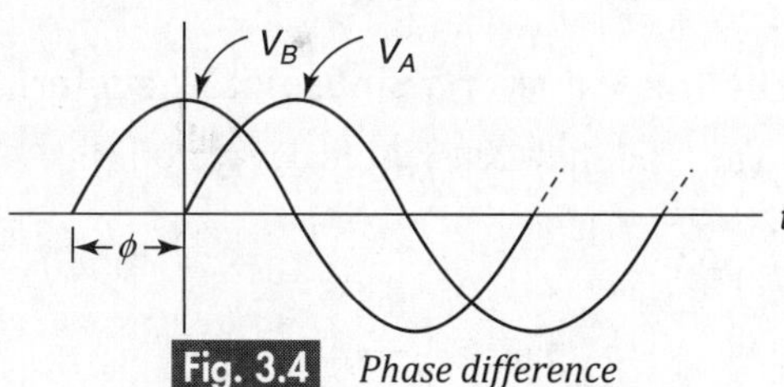


Fig. 3.4 *Phase difference*

## 3.3 ROOT MEAN SQUARE (RMS) OR EFFECTIVE VALUE

LO 3.3

Calculate root mean square (rms) or effective value and average value of waveforms

Normally, the current is measured by the amount of work it will do or the amount of heat it will produce. Hence, rms or effective value of alternating current is defined as that value of steady current (direct current) which will do the same amount of work in the same time or would produce the same heating effect as when the alternating current is applied for the same time.

Figure 3.5 shows the positive half cycle of a non-sinusoidal alternating current waveform. The waveform is divided in $m$ equal intervals of time each of duration $\frac{t}{m}$. Let the average values of instantaneous currents during these intervals be respectively $i_1$, $i_2$, ..., $i_m$. This waveform is applied to a circuit consisting of a resistance of $R$ ohms. The work done in different intervals will be $\left(i_1^2 R \times \frac{t}{m}\right), \left(i_2^2 R \times \frac{t}{m}\right), \ldots, \left(i_m^2 R \times \frac{t}{m}\right)$ joules.

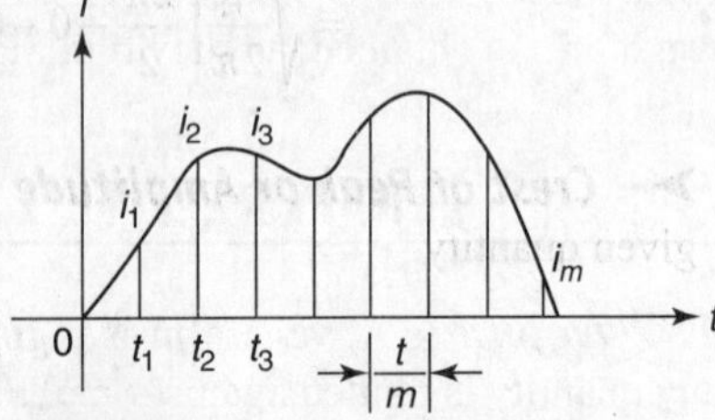


Fig. 3.5 *Non-sinusoidal alternating current waveform*

Thus, the total work done in $t$ seconds on applying an alternating current waveform to a resistance $R = \frac{i_1^2 + i_2^2 + \ldots + i_m^2}{m} \times Rt$ joules

Let $I$ be the value of the direct current that while flowing through the same resistance does the same amount of work in the same time $t$.

$$I^2 Rt = \frac{i_1^2 + i_2^2 + \ldots i_m^2}{m} \times Rt$$

$$I^2 = \frac{i_1^2 + i_2^2 + \ldots + i_m^2}{m}$$

Hence, rms value of the alternating current is given by

$$I_{\text{rms}} = \sqrt{\frac{i_1^2 + i_2^2 + \ldots + i_m^2}{m}} = \sqrt{\text{Mean value of}(i)^2}$$

The rms value of any current $i(t)$ over the specified interval $t_1$ to $t_2$ is expressed mathematically as

$$I_{\text{rms}} = \sqrt{\frac{1}{t_2 - t_1} \int_{t_1}^{t_2} i^2(t)\,dt}$$

The rms value of an alternating current is of considerable importance in practice because the ammeters and voltmeters record the rms value of alternating current and voltage respectively.

### The rms Value of a Sinusoidal Waveform

Figure 3.6 shows a sinusoidal waveform.

$$v = V_m \sin\theta \qquad 0 < \theta < 2\pi$$

$$V_{\text{rms}} = \sqrt{\frac{1}{2\pi} \int_0^{2\pi} v^2(\theta)\,d\theta}$$

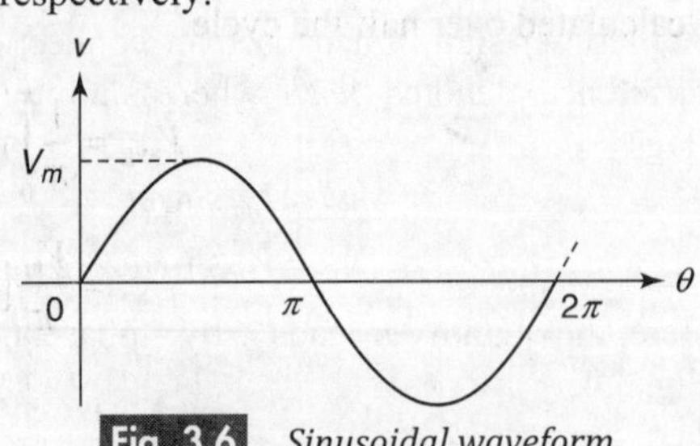


Fig. 3.6 *Sinusoidal waveform*

$$= \sqrt{\frac{1}{2\pi}\int_0^{2\pi} V_m^2 \sin^2\theta \, d\theta}$$

$$= \sqrt{\frac{V_m^2}{2\pi}\int_0^{2\pi} \sin^2\theta \, d\theta} = \sqrt{\frac{V_m^2}{2\pi}\int_0^{2\pi}\left(\frac{1-\cos 2\theta}{2}\right)d\theta} = \sqrt{\frac{V_m^2}{2\pi}\left[\frac{\theta}{2}-\frac{\sin 2\theta}{4}\right]_0^{2\pi}}$$

$$= \sqrt{\frac{V_m^2}{2\pi}\left[\frac{2\pi}{2}-0-0+0\right]} = \frac{V_m}{\sqrt{2}} = 0.707\, V_m$$

➤ ***Crest or Peak or Amplitude Factor*** It is defined as the ratio of maximum value to rms value of the given quantity.

$$\text{Peak factor } (k_p) = \frac{\text{Maximum value}}{\text{rms value}}$$

## 3.4 AVERAGE VALUE

LO 3.3

The average value of an alternating quantity is defined as the arithmetic mean of all the values over one complete cycle.

In case of a symmetrical alternating waveform (whether sinusoidal or non-sinusoidal), the average value over a complete cycle is zero. Hence, in such a case, the average value is obtained over half the cycle only.

Referring to Fig. 3.5, the average value of the current is given by

$$I_{\text{avg}} = \frac{i_1 + i_2 + \ldots + i_m}{m}$$

The average value of any current $i(t)$ over the specified interval $t_1$ to $t_2$ is expressed mathematically as

$$I_{\text{avg}} = \frac{1}{t_2 - t_1}\int_{t_1}^{t_2} i(t)\, dt$$

### Average Value of a Sinusoidal Waveform

Figure 3.7 shows a sinusoidal waveform.

$$v = V_m \sin\theta \qquad 0 < \theta < 2\pi$$

Since this is a symmetrical waveform, the average value is calculated over half the cycle.

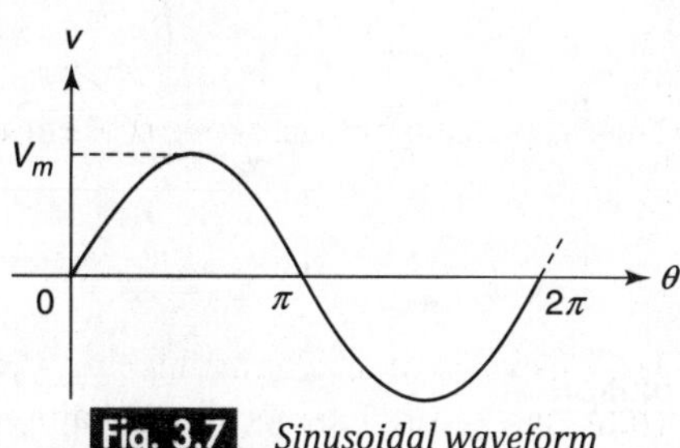


**Fig. 3.7** *Sinusoidal waveform*

$$V_{\text{avg}} = \frac{1}{\pi}\int_0^{\pi} v(\theta)\, d\theta = \frac{1}{\pi}\int_0^{\pi} V_m \sin\theta\, d\theta = \frac{V_m}{\pi}\int_0^{\pi}\sin\theta\, d\theta = \frac{V_m}{\pi}[-\cos\theta]_0^{\pi}$$

$$= \frac{V_m}{\pi}[1+1] = \frac{2V_m}{\pi} = 0.637\, V_m$$

➤ ***Form Factor*** It is defined as the ratio of rms value to the average value of the given quantity.

$$\text{Form factor}\,(k_f) = \frac{\text{rms value}}{\text{Average value}}$$

**EXAMPLE 3.1** ●○○

*A non-sinusoidal voltage has a form factor of 1.2 and peak factor of 1.5. If the average value of the voltage is 10 V, calculate (a) rms value, and (b) maximum value.*

**Solution** $k_f = 1.2, \quad k_p = 1.5, \quad V_{avg} = 10\text{ V}$

(a) rms value

$$k_f = \frac{V_{rms}}{V_{avg}}$$

$$1.2 = \frac{V_{rms}}{10}$$

$$V_{rms} = 12\text{ V}$$

(b) Maximum value

$$k_p = \frac{V_m}{V_{rms}}$$

$$1.5 = \frac{V_m}{12}$$

$$V_m = 18\text{ V}$$

**EXAMPLE 3.2** ●○○

*Find the average value and rms value of the waveform shown in Fig. 3.8.*

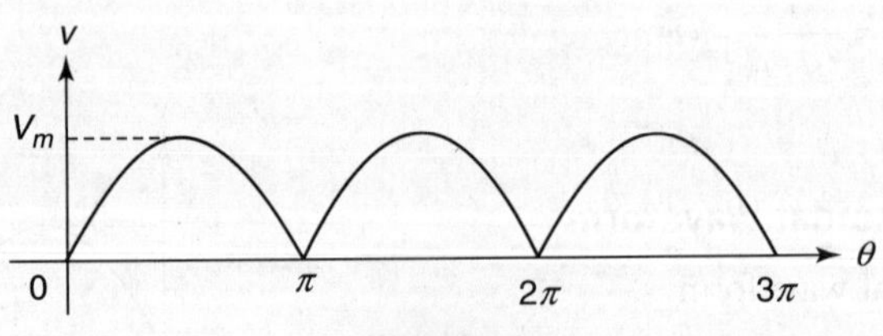


Fig. 3.8

**Solution** $v = V_m \sin\theta \qquad 0 < \theta < \pi$

(a) Average value of the waveform

$$V_{avg} = \frac{1}{\pi}\int_0^{\pi} v(\theta)\, d\theta = \frac{1}{\pi}\int_0^{\pi} V_m \sin\theta\, d\theta = \frac{V_m}{\pi}\left[-\cos\theta\right]_0^{\pi}$$

---

**Note** Difficulty Level ●○○— Easy; ○●○— Medium; ○○●— Difficult

$$= \frac{V_m}{\pi}[1+1] = 0.637\, V_m$$

(b) rms value of the waveform

$$V_{\text{rms}} = \sqrt{\frac{1}{\pi}\int_0^{\pi} v^2(\theta)\, d\theta} = \sqrt{\frac{1}{\pi}\int_0^{\pi} V_m^2 \sin^2\theta\, d\theta} = \sqrt{\frac{V_m^2}{\pi}\int_0^{\pi} \sin^2\theta\, d\theta}$$

$$= \sqrt{\frac{V_m^2}{\pi}\int_0^{\pi}\left(\frac{1-\cos 2\theta}{2}\right) d\theta} = \sqrt{\frac{V_m^2}{\pi}\left[\frac{\theta}{2} - \frac{\sin 2\theta}{4}\right]_0^{\pi}} = \sqrt{\frac{V_m^2}{\pi}\left[\frac{\pi}{2} - \frac{\sin 2\pi}{4} - 0 + \frac{\sin 0}{4}\right]} = 0.707\, V_m$$

## EXAMPLE 3.3

*Find the average and rms values of the waveform shown in Fig. 3.9.*

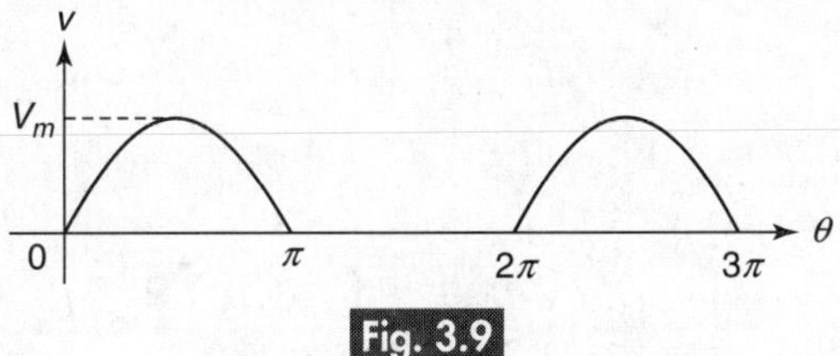


Fig. 3.9

**Solution**

$$v = V_m \sin\theta \qquad 0 < \theta < \pi$$
$$= 0 \qquad \pi < \theta < 2\pi$$

(a) Average value of the waveform

$$V_{\text{avg}} = \frac{1}{2\pi}\int_0^{2\pi} v(\theta)\, d\theta = \frac{1}{2\pi}\left[\int_0^{\pi} V_m \sin\theta\, d\theta + \int_{\pi}^{2\pi} 0\, d\theta\right]$$

$$= \frac{1}{2\pi}\int_0^{\pi} V_m \sin\theta\, d\theta = \frac{V_m}{2\pi}[-\cos\theta]_0^{\pi} = \frac{V_m}{2\pi}[1+1] = 0.318\, V_m$$

(b) rms value of the waveform

$$V_{\text{rms}} = \sqrt{\frac{1}{2\pi}\int_0^{2\pi} v^2(\theta)\, d\theta} = \sqrt{\frac{1}{2\pi}\left[\int_0^{\pi} V_m^2 \sin^2\theta\, d\theta + \int_{\pi}^{2\pi} 0\, d\theta\right]}$$

$$= \sqrt{\frac{1}{2\pi}\int_0^{\pi} V_m^2 \sin^2\theta\, d\theta} = \sqrt{\frac{V_m^2}{2\pi}\int_0^{\pi} \sin^2\theta\, d\theta} = \sqrt{\frac{V_m^2}{2\pi}\int_0^{\pi}\left(\frac{1-\cos 2\theta}{2}\right) d\theta}$$

$$= \sqrt{\frac{V_m^2}{2\pi}\left[\frac{\theta}{2} - \frac{\sin 2\theta}{4}\right]_0^{\pi}} = \sqrt{\frac{V_m^2}{2\pi}\left[\frac{\pi}{2} - \frac{\sin 2\pi}{4} - 0 + \frac{\sin 0}{4}\right]} = 0.5\, V_m$$

**EXAMPLE 3.4**

*Find the average value and rms value of the waveform shown in Fig. 3.10.*

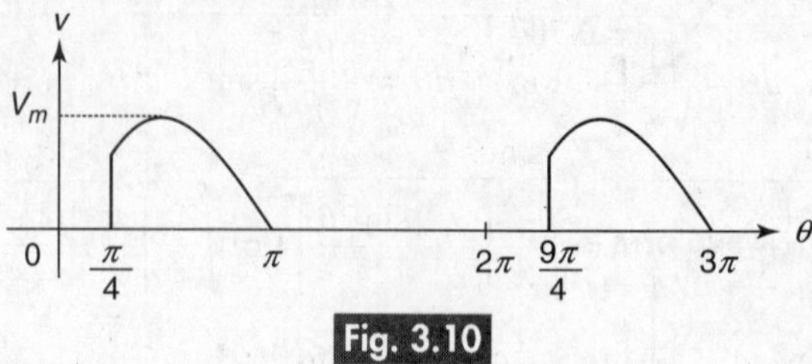


Fig. 3.10

**Solution**

$$v = 0 \qquad 0 < \theta < \frac{\pi}{4}$$

$$= V_m \sin\theta \qquad \frac{\pi}{4} < \theta < \pi$$

$$= 0 \qquad \pi < \theta < 2\pi$$

(a) Average value of the waveform

$$V_{\text{avg}} = \frac{1}{2\pi}\int_0^{2\pi} v(\theta)\, d\theta = \frac{1}{2\pi}\int_{\frac{\pi}{4}}^{\pi} V_m \sin\theta\, d\theta = \frac{V_m}{2\pi}[-\cos\theta]_{\frac{\pi}{4}}^{\pi} = \frac{V_m}{2\pi}[1+0.707] = 0.272 \text{ Vm}$$

(b) rms value of the waveform

$$V_{\text{rms}} = \sqrt{\frac{1}{2\pi}\int_0^{2\pi} v^2(\theta)\, d\theta} = \sqrt{\frac{1}{2\pi}\int_{\frac{\pi}{4}}^{\pi} V_m^2 \sin^2\theta\, d\theta} = \sqrt{\frac{V_m^2}{2\pi}\int_{\frac{\pi}{4}}^{\pi} \sin^2\theta\, d\theta} = \sqrt{\frac{V_m^2}{2\pi}\int_{\frac{\pi}{4}}^{\pi}\left(\frac{1-\cos 2\theta}{2}\right) d\theta}$$

$$= \sqrt{\frac{V_m^2}{2\pi}\left[\frac{\theta}{2} - \frac{\sin 2\theta}{4}\right]_{\frac{\pi}{4}}^{\pi}} = \sqrt{\frac{V_m^2}{2\pi}\left[\frac{\pi}{2} - \frac{\sin 2\pi}{4} - \frac{\pi}{8} + \frac{\sin\frac{\pi}{2}}{4}\right]} = 0.476\, V_m$$

**EXAMPLE 3.5**

*A full-wave rectified wave is clipped at 70.7% of its maximum value, as shown in Fig. 3.11. Find its average and rms values.*

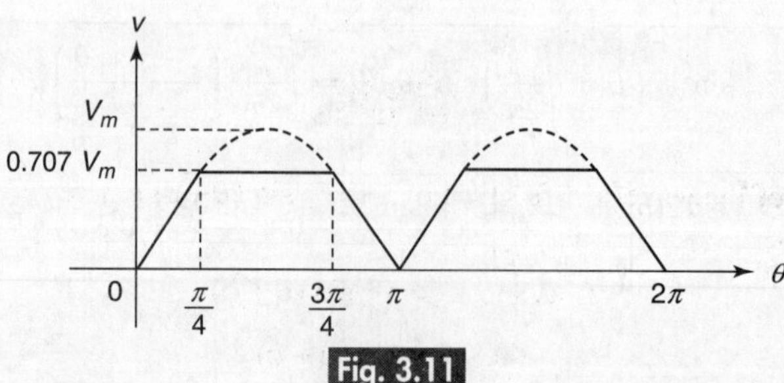


Fig. 3.11

**Solution**

$$v = V_m \sin\theta \qquad 0 < \theta < \frac{\pi}{4}$$

$$= 0.707\, V_m \qquad \frac{\pi}{4} < \theta < \frac{3\pi}{4}$$

$$= V_m \sin\theta \qquad \frac{3\pi}{4} < \theta < \pi$$

(a) Average value of the waveform

$$V_{\text{avg}} = \frac{1}{\pi}\int_0^{\pi} v(\theta)\, d\theta = \frac{1}{\pi}\left[\int_0^{\frac{\pi}{4}} V_m \sin\theta\, d\theta + \int_{\frac{\pi}{4}}^{\frac{3\pi}{4}} 0.707\, V_m\, d\theta + \int_{\frac{3\pi}{4}}^{\pi} V_m \sin\theta\, d\theta\right]$$

$$= \frac{V_m}{\pi}\left\{[-\cos\theta]_0^{\frac{\pi}{4}} + 0.707[\theta]_{\frac{\pi}{4}}^{\frac{3\pi}{4}} + [-\cos\theta]_{\frac{3\pi}{4}}^{\pi}\right\} = \frac{V_m}{\pi}(0.293 + 1.11 + 0.293) = 0.54\, V_m$$

(b) rms value of the waveform

$$V_{\text{avg}} = \sqrt{\frac{1}{\pi}\int_0^{\pi} v^2(\theta)\, d\theta} = \sqrt{\frac{1}{\pi}\left[\int_0^{\frac{\pi}{4}} V_m^2 \sin^2\theta\, d\theta + \int_{\frac{\pi}{4}}^{\frac{3\pi}{4}} (0.707 V_m)^2\, d\theta + \int_{\frac{3\pi}{4}}^{\pi} V_m^2 \sin^2\theta\, d\theta\right]}$$

$$= \sqrt{\frac{V_m^2}{\pi}\left\{\left[\frac{\theta}{2} - \frac{\sin 2\theta}{4}\right]_0^{\frac{\pi}{4}} + 0.499[\theta]_{\frac{\pi}{4}}^{\frac{3\pi}{4}} + \left[\frac{\theta}{2} - \frac{\sin 2\theta}{4}\right]_{\frac{3\pi}{4}}^{\pi}\right\}} = 0.584\, V_m$$

## EXAMPLE 3.6

*Find the rms value of the waveform shown in Fig. 3.12.*

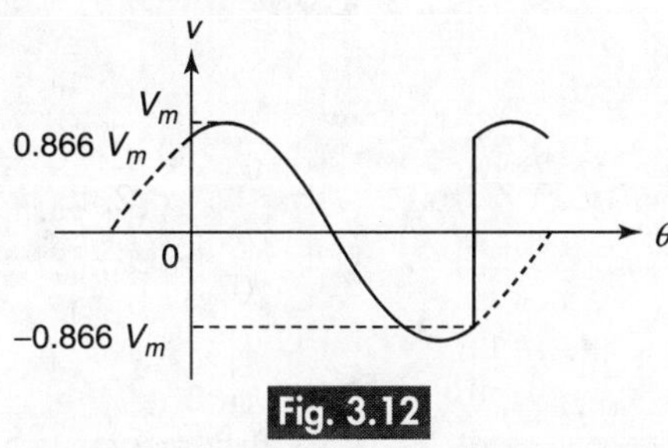


**Fig. 3.12**

**Solution** The equation of the waveform is given by $v = V_m \sin(\theta + \phi)$ where $\phi$ is the phase difference. When $\theta = 0$, $v = 0.866\, V_m$.

$$0.866\, V_m = V_m \sin(\theta + \phi)$$

$$0.866 = \sin(0 + \phi)$$

$$\phi = \sin^{-1}(0.866) = \frac{\pi}{3}$$

$$v = V_m \sin\left(\theta + \frac{\pi}{3}\right)$$

The time period of a complete sine wave is always $2\pi$. Since some part of the waveform is chopped from both the sides,

$$\text{Time period} = 2\pi - \frac{\pi}{3} - \frac{\pi}{3} = \frac{4\pi}{3}$$

$$V_{\text{rms}} = \sqrt{\frac{1}{\frac{4\pi}{3}} \int_0^{\frac{4\pi}{3}} V_m^2 \sin^2\left(\theta + \frac{\pi}{3}\right) d\theta} = \sqrt{\frac{3}{4\pi} \int_0^{\frac{4\pi}{3}} V_m^2 \sin^2\left(\theta + \frac{\pi}{3}\right) d\theta}$$

$$= \sqrt{\frac{3V_m^2}{4\pi} \int_0^{\frac{4\pi}{3}} \left[\frac{1 - \cos 2\left(\theta + \frac{\pi}{3}\right)}{2}\right] d\theta} = \sqrt{\frac{3V_m^2}{4\pi} \left[\frac{\theta}{2} - \frac{\sin 2\left(\theta + \frac{\pi}{3}\right)}{4}\right]_0^{\frac{4\pi}{3}}} = 0.776\ V_m$$

**EXAMPLE 3.7**

*Find the average and rms values of the waveform shown in Fig. 3.13.*

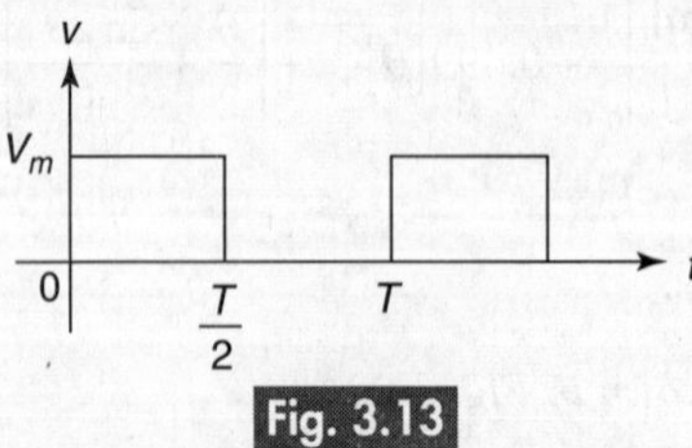


Fig. 3.13

**Solution**

$$v = V_m \qquad 0 < t < \frac{T}{2}$$

$$= 0 \qquad \frac{T}{2} < t < T$$

(a) Average value of the waveform

$$V_{\text{avg}} = \frac{1}{T}\int_0^T v(t)\, dt = \frac{1}{T}\left[\int_0^{\frac{T}{2}} V_m\, dt + \int_{\frac{T}{2}}^{T} 0\, dt\right] = \frac{1}{T}\int_0^{\frac{T}{2}} V_m\, dt$$

$$= \frac{V_m}{T}[t]_0^{\frac{T}{2}} = \frac{V_m}{T} \cdot \frac{T}{2} = 0.5\ V_m$$

(b) rms value of the waveform

$$V_{\text{rms}} = \sqrt{\frac{1}{T}\int_0^T v^2(t)\, dt} = \sqrt{\frac{1}{T}\int_0^{\frac{T}{2}} V_m^2\, dt} = \sqrt{\frac{V_m^2}{T}[t]_0^{\frac{T}{2}}}$$

$$= \sqrt{\frac{V_m^2}{T} \cdot \frac{T}{2}} = 0.707\ V_m$$

**EXAMPLE 3.8**

*Find the average and rms values of the waveform shown in Fig. 3.14.*

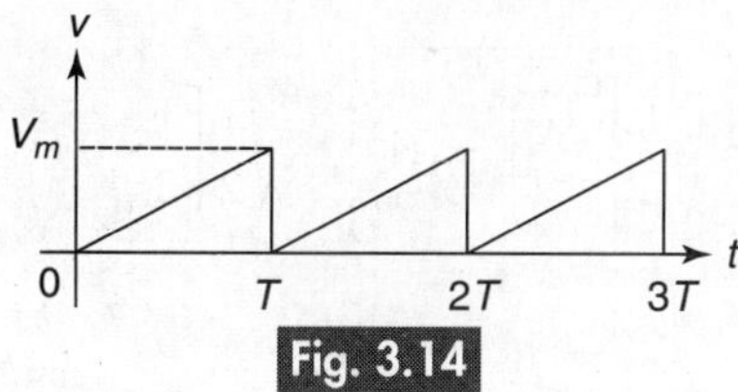


Fig. 3.14

**Solution** $v = \frac{V_m}{T} t \qquad 0 < t < T$

(a) Average value of the waveform

$$V_{\text{avg}} = \frac{1}{T}\int_0^T v(t)\, dt = \frac{1}{T}\int_0^T \frac{V_m}{T} t\, dt = \frac{V_m}{T^2}\left[\frac{t^2}{2}\right]_0^T = \frac{V_m}{T^2} \cdot \frac{T^2}{2} = 0.5\ V_m$$

(b) rms value of the waveform

$$V_{\text{rms}} = \sqrt{\frac{1}{T}\int_0^T v^2(t)\, dt} = \sqrt{\frac{1}{T}\int_0^T \frac{V_m^2}{T^2} \cdot t^2\, dt} = \sqrt{\frac{V_m^2}{T^3}\left[\frac{t^3}{3}\right]_0^T} = \sqrt{\frac{V_m^2}{T^3}\left[\frac{T^3}{3}\right]} = 0.577\ V_m$$

**·EXAMPLE 3.9**

*Find the average and rms values of the waveform shown in Fig. 3.15.*

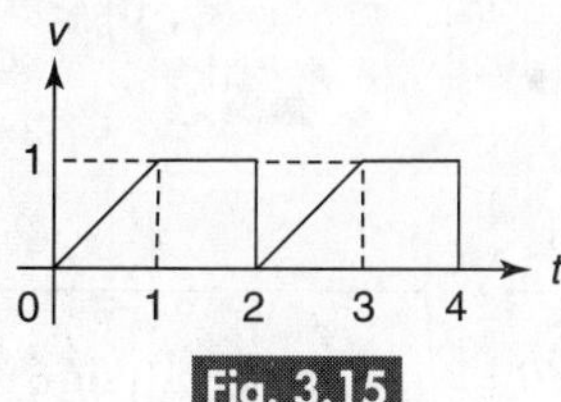


Fig. 3.15

**Solution**
$$v = t \qquad 0 < t < 1$$
$$= 1 \qquad 1 < t < 2$$

(a) Average value of the waveform

$$V_{avg} = \frac{1}{T}\int_0^T v(t)\,dt = \frac{1}{2}\left[\int_0^1 t\,dt + \int_1^2 1\,dt\right]$$

$$= \frac{1}{2}\left\{\left[\frac{t^2}{2}\right]_0^1 + [t]_1^2\right\} = \frac{1}{2}\left[\frac{1}{2} - 0 + 2 - 1\right] = 0.75 \text{ V}$$

(b) rms value of the waveform

$$V_{rms} = \sqrt{\frac{1}{T}\int_0^T v^2(t)\,dt} = \sqrt{\frac{1}{2}\left[\int_0^1 t^2\,dt + \int_1^2 (1)^2\,dt\right]}$$

$$= \sqrt{\frac{1}{2}\left\{\left[\frac{t^3}{3}\right]_0^1 + [t]_1^2\right\}} = \sqrt{\frac{1}{2}\left[\frac{1}{3} - 0 + 2 - 1\right]} = 0.816 \text{ V}$$

**EXAMPLE 3.10**

*Find the effective value of the resultant current which carries simultaneously a direct current of 10 A and a sinusoidally alternating current with a peak value of 10 A.*

**Solution** Figure 3.16 shows the current waveforms.

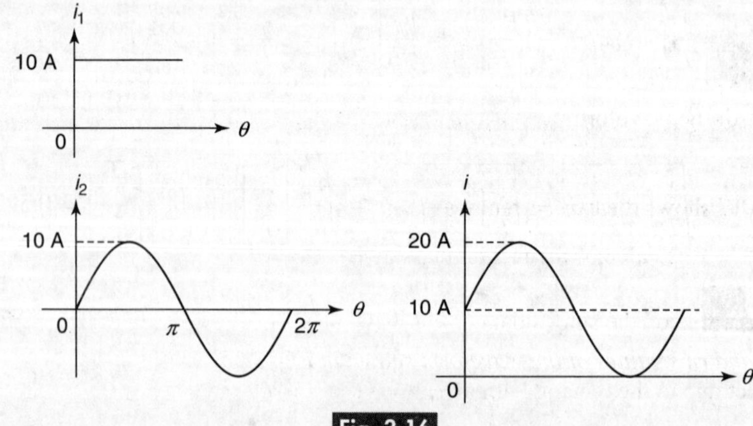


Fig. 3.16

$$i = i_1 + i_2 = 10 + 10\sin\theta$$

$$I_{eff} = I_{rms} = \sqrt{\frac{1}{2\pi}\int_0^{2\pi} i^2(\theta)\,d\theta} = \sqrt{\frac{1}{2\pi}\int_0^{2\pi} (10 + 10\sin\theta)^2\,d\theta}$$

$$= \sqrt{\frac{1}{2\pi}\int_0^{2\pi}(100+200\sin\theta+100\sin^2\theta)\,d\theta} = \sqrt{\frac{100}{2\pi}\int_0^{2\pi}(1+2\sin\theta+\sin^2\theta)\,d\theta}$$

$$= \sqrt{\frac{100}{2\pi}\int_0^{2\pi}\left[1+2\sin\theta+\left(\frac{1-\cos 2\theta}{2}\right)\right]d\theta} = \sqrt{\frac{100}{2\pi}\left[\theta-2\cos\theta+\frac{\theta}{2}-\frac{\sin 2\theta}{4}\right]_0^{2\pi}}$$

$$= \sqrt{\frac{100}{2\pi}\left[2\pi-2\cos 2\pi+\frac{2\pi}{2}-\frac{\sin 4\pi}{4}-0+2\cos 0-0+\frac{\sin 0}{4}\right]} = \sqrt{\frac{100}{2\pi}\left[2\pi-2+\frac{2\pi}{2}+2\right]}$$

$$= 12.25\text{ A}$$

## EXAMPLE 3.11

*Find the effective value of a resultant current in a wire which carries simultaneously a direct current of $i_1 = 10\,A$ and alternating current given by $i_2 = 12\sin\omega t + 6\sin\left(3\omega t - \frac{\pi}{6}\right) + 4\sin\left(5\omega t + \frac{\pi}{3}\right)$.*

**Solution**

$$i_1 = 10\text{ A}$$

$$i_2 = 12\sin\omega t + 6\sin\left(3\omega t - \frac{\pi}{6}\right) + 4\sin\left(5\omega t + \frac{\pi}{3}\right)$$

$$i = i_1 + i_2 = 10 + 12\sin\omega t + 6\sin\left(3\omega t - \frac{\pi}{6}\right) + 4\sin\left(5\omega t + \frac{\pi}{3}\right)$$

$$= 10 + 12\sin\theta + 6\sin(3\theta - 30^\circ) + 4\sin(5\theta + 60^\circ)$$

$$I_{\text{eff}} = \sqrt{\frac{1}{2\pi}\int_0^{2\pi} i^2(\theta)\,d\theta} = \sqrt{\frac{1}{2\pi}\int_0^{2\pi}[10+12\sin\theta+6\sin(3\theta-30^\circ)+4\sin(5\theta+60^\circ)]^2\,d\theta} = 14.07\text{ A}$$

## EXAMPLE 3.12

*Find the relative heating effects of two current waves of equal peak value, one sinusoidal and the other, rectangular in shape.*

**Solution** Figure 3.17 shows the two current waves.

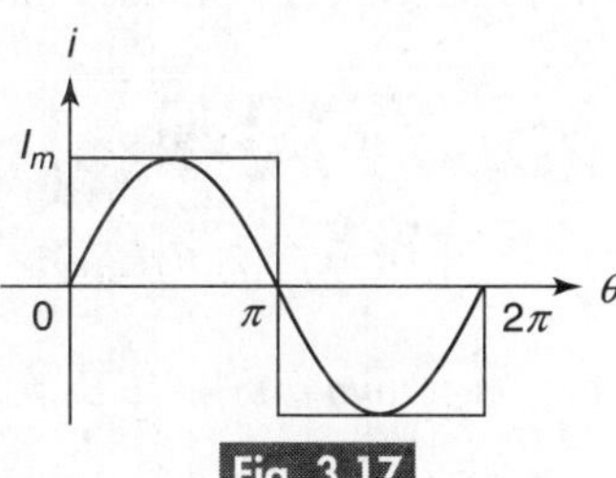

Fig. 3.17

$$\text{rms value of the rectangular wave} = I_m$$

$$\text{rms value of the sinusoidal current wave} = \frac{I_m}{\sqrt{2}}$$

$$\text{Heating effect due to the rectangular current wave} = (I_m)^2 RT$$

$$\text{Heating effect due to the sinusoidal current wave} = \left(\frac{I_m}{\sqrt{2}}\right)^2 RT = \frac{(I_m)^2}{2}RT$$

$$\text{Relative heating effects} = \frac{(I_m)^2}{2}RT : (I_m)^2 RT = \frac{1}{2} : 1 = 1 : 2$$

## 3.5 PHASOR REPRESENTATIONS OF ALTERNATING QUANTITIES

LO 3.4

Discuss phasor representations of alternating quantities

The alternating quantities are represented by phasors. A phasor is a line of definite length rotating in an anticlockwise direction at a constant angular velocity $\omega$. The length of a phasor is equal to the maximum value of the alternating quantity, and the angular velocity is equal to the angular velocity of alternating quantity.

As shown in Fig. 3.18, consider a phasor $OP = I_m$, where $I_m$ is the maximum value of the alternating current. Let this phasor rotate in an anticlockwise direction at a uniform angular velocity of $\omega$ radians/second. The projection of the phasor $OP$ on the $Y$-axis at any instant gives the instantaneous value of that alternating current.

$$OM = OP \sin \omega t = I_m \sin \omega t = i$$

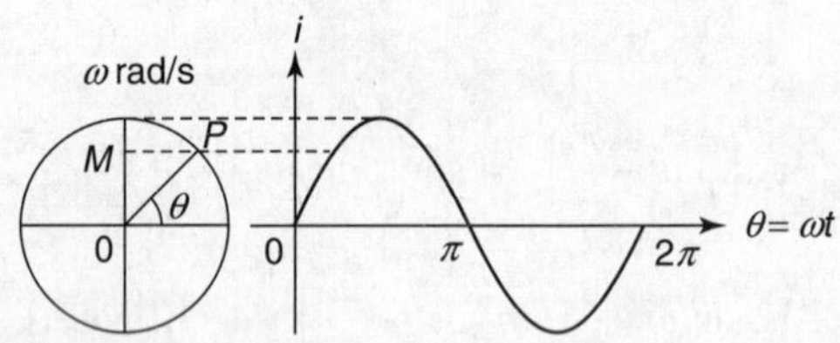


Fig. 3.18 *Representation of alternating quantities in terms of phasors*

Thus, if we plot the projections of the phasor on the $Y$-axis versus its angular position point by point, a sinusoidal alternating current waveform is obtained.

➤ ***Phasor Diagram Using rms Values*** Sinusoidal alternating currents and voltages can be represented by phasors. Electrical measuring instruments like ammeters and voltmeters are calibrated to read the rms values of ac quantities. Hence, instead of using maximum values, it is more convenient to draw phasor diagrams using rms values of alternating quantities. However, such a phasor diagram will not generate a sine wave of proper amplitude unless the length of the phasor is multiplied by $\sqrt{2}$.

### EXAMPLE 3.13

*Two currents $i_1$ and $i_2$ are given by the expressions $i_1 = 10 \sin\left(\omega t + \frac{\pi}{4}\right)$ and $i_2 = 8 \sin\left(\omega t - \frac{\pi}{3}\right)$. Find (a) $i_1 + i_2$, and (b) $i_1 - i_2$. Express the answers in the form $i = I_m \sin(\omega t \pm \phi)$.*

**Solution**

$$i_1 = 10 \sin\left(\omega t + \frac{\pi}{4}\right)$$

$$i_2 = 8 \sin\left(\omega t - \frac{\pi}{3}\right)$$

(a) Let phasors $\mathbf{I}_1$ and $\mathbf{I}_2$ represent the alternating currents $i_1$ and $i_2$ respectively in terms of their maximum values.

(i) *Analytical method*: From Fig. 3.19,

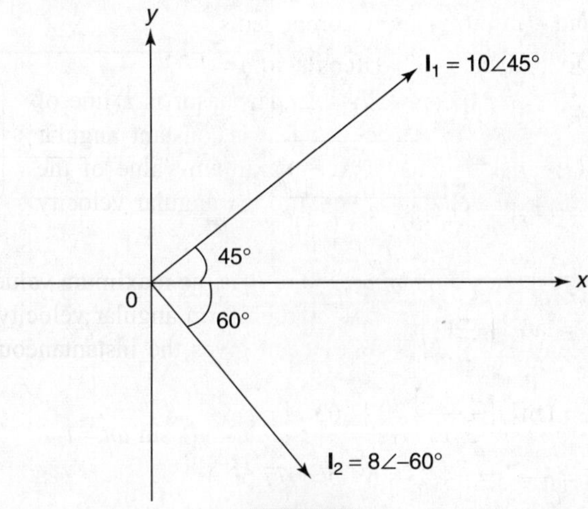


Fig. 3.19

Resolving $\mathbf{I}_1$ and $\mathbf{I}_2$ into *x*- and *y*- components,

$$\Sigma x = 10 \cos(45°) + 8 \cos(-60°) = 11.07$$

$$\Sigma y = 10 \sin(45°) + 8 \sin(-60°) = 0.14$$

$$\text{Magnitude of } (\mathbf{I}_1 + \mathbf{I}_2) = \sqrt{(\Sigma x)^2 + (\Sigma y)^2}$$

$$= \sqrt{(11.07)^2 + (0.14)^2}$$

$$= 11.07$$

$$\text{Phase angle } \phi = \tan^{-1}\left(\frac{\Sigma y}{\Sigma x}\right) = \tan^{-1}\left(\frac{0.14}{11.07}\right) = 0.72°$$

$$i = i_1 + i_2 = 11.07\ (\omega t + 0.72°)$$

(ii) *Graphical method*: The phasor sum $\mathbf{I}_1 + \mathbf{I}_2$ is obtained by adding phasors $\mathbf{I}_1$ and $\mathbf{I}_2$ by the parallelogram law, as shown in Fig. 3.20.

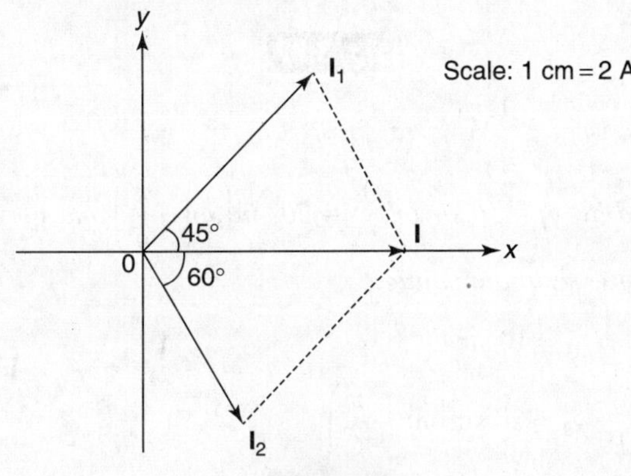


Fig. 3.20

(b) (i) *Analytical method*: From Fig. 3.21,

Resolving $\mathbf{I}_1$ and $-\mathbf{I}_2$ into $x$- and $y$-components,

$$\Sigma x = 10\cos(45°) - 8\cos(-60°) = 3.07$$
$$\Sigma y = 10\sin(45°) - 8\sin(-60°) = 14$$

Magnitude of $(\mathbf{I}_1 - \mathbf{I}_2) = \sqrt{(\Sigma x)^2 + (\Sigma y)^2}$

$$= \sqrt{(3.07)^2 + (14)^2}$$
$$= 14.33 \text{ A}$$

Phase angle $\phi = \tan^{-1}\left(\dfrac{\Sigma y}{\Sigma x}\right)$

$$= \tan^{-1}\left(\frac{14}{3.07}\right) = 77.63$$

$$i = i_1 - i_2 = 14.33 \sin(\omega t + 77.63\ )$$

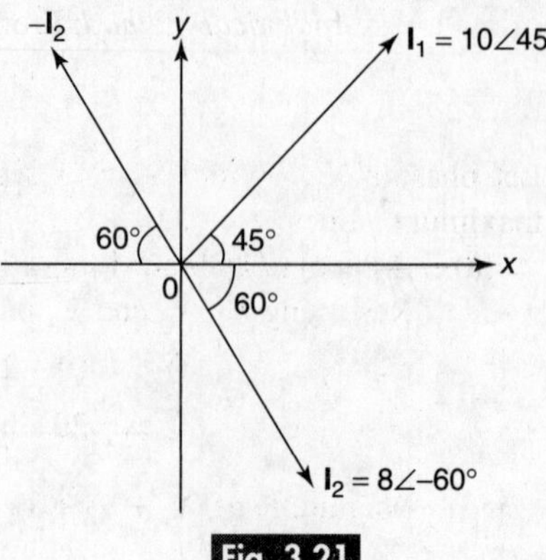

Fig. 3.21

(ii) *Graphical method*: The phasor sum $\mathbf{I}_1 - \mathbf{I}_2$ is obtained by adding phasors $\mathbf{I}_1$ and $-\mathbf{I}_2$ by the parallelogram law, as shown in Fig. 3.22.

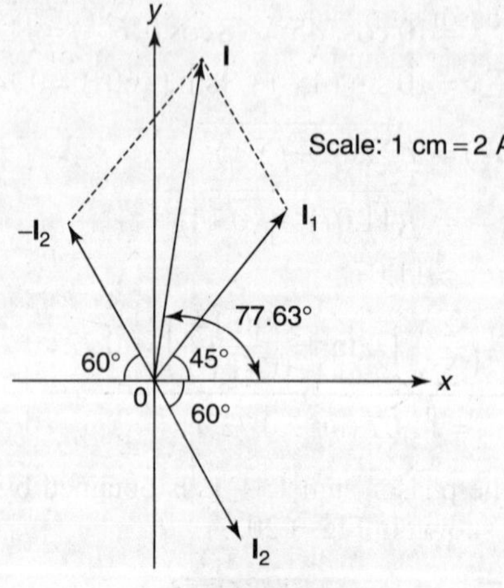

Fig. 3.22

## EXAMPLE 3.14

*Three voltages are represented by* $v_1 = 10 \sin \omega t$, $v_2 = 20 \sin\left(\omega t - \dfrac{\pi}{6}\right)$ *and* $v_3 = 30 \sin\left(\omega t + \dfrac{\pi}{4}\right)$. *Find the magnitude and phase angle of the resultant voltage.*

**Solution**

$$v_1 = 10 \sin \omega t$$
$$v_2 = 20 \sin\left(\omega t - \frac{\pi}{6}\right)$$

$$v_3 = 30 \sin\left(\omega t + \frac{\pi}{4}\right)$$

Let phasors $\mathbf{V}_1$, $\mathbf{V}_2$ and $\mathbf{V}_3$ represent the alternating voltages $v_1$, $v_2$ and $v_3$ respectively in terms of their maximum values.

(a) *Analytical method*: From Fig. 3.23,

Resolving $\mathbf{V}_1$, $\mathbf{V}_2$ and $\mathbf{V}_3$ into *x*- and *y*-components,

$$\sum x = 10 + 20\cos(-30°) + 30\cos(45°) = 48.53$$

$$\sum y = 20\sin(-30°) + 30\sin(45°) = 11.21$$

$$\text{Magnitude of } (\mathbf{V}_1 + \mathbf{V}_2 + \mathbf{V}_3) = \sqrt{(\sum x)^2 + (\sum y)^2}$$

$$= \sqrt{(48.53)^2 + (11.21)^2}$$

$$= 49.81 \text{ V}$$

$$\text{Phase angle } \phi = \tan^{-1}\left(\frac{\sum y}{\sum x}\right) = \tan^{-1}\left(\frac{11.21}{48.53}\right) = 13°$$

$$v = 49.81 \sin(\omega t + 13°)$$

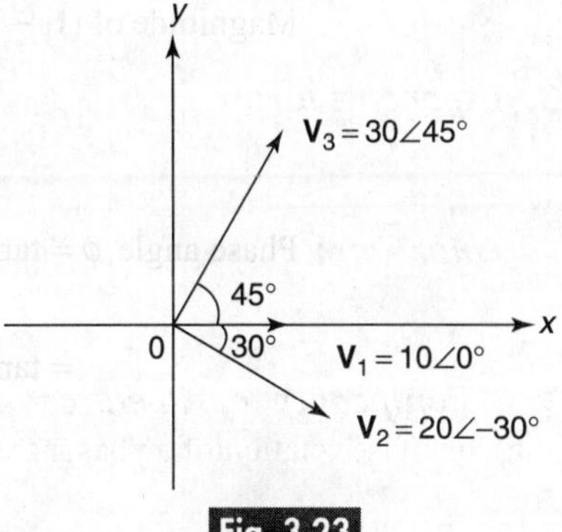


Fig. 3.23

(b) *Graphical method*: The phasor sum $\mathbf{V}_1 + \mathbf{V}_2 + \mathbf{V}_3$ is obtained by first adding phasors $\mathbf{V}_1$ and $\mathbf{V}_2$ by the parallelogram law and then adding $\mathbf{V}_3$ to the resultant of $\mathbf{V}_1$ and $\mathbf{V}_2$ by the parallelogram law, as shown in Fig. 3.24.

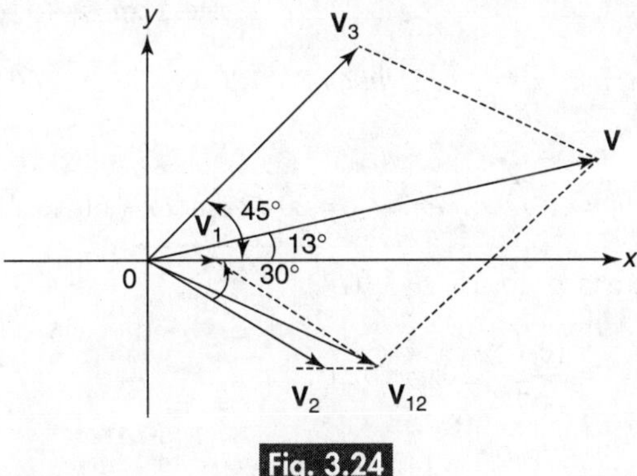


Fig. 3.24

## 3.6 MATHEMATICAL REPRESENTATIONS OF PHASORS

LO 3.5

Discuss mathematical representation of phasors

A phasor can be represented in four forms.

### 1. Rectangular Form

$$\mathbf{V} = X \pm jY$$

$$\text{Magnitude of phasor, } V = \sqrt{X^2 + Y^2}$$

$$\text{Phase angle } \phi = \tan^{-1}\left(\frac{Y}{X}\right)$$

**2. Trigonometric Form**

$$\mathbf{V} = V(\cos\phi \pm j\sin\phi)$$

**3. Exponential Form**

$$\mathbf{V} = Ve^{\pm j\phi}$$

**4. Polar Form**

$$\mathbf{V} = V\angle \pm \phi$$

➤ ***Significance of Operator j*** The operator $j$ is used in rectangular form. It is used to indicate anticlockwise rotation of a phasor through 90°. Mathematically,

$$j = \sqrt{-1}$$

Whenever a phasor is multiplied by $j$, the phasor is rotated once in the anticlockwise direction through 90°. The power of $j$ represents the number of times the phasor should be rotated through 90° in the anticlockwise direction.

**EXAMPLE 3.15**

*Two sinusoidal currents are given as $i_1 = 10\sqrt{2}\sin\omega t$, $i_2 = 20\sqrt{2}\sin(\omega t + 60°)$. Find the expression for the sum of these currents.*

**Solution**

$$i_1 = 10\sqrt{2}\sin\omega t, \quad i_2 = 20\sqrt{2}\sin(\omega t + 60°)$$

Writing currents $i_1$ and $i_2$ in the phasor form,

$$\mathbf{I}_1 = \frac{10\sqrt{2}}{\sqrt{2}}\angle 0° = 10\angle 0°$$

$$\mathbf{I}_2 = \frac{20\sqrt{2}}{\sqrt{2}}\angle 60° = 20\angle 60°$$

$$\mathbf{I} = \mathbf{I}_1 + \mathbf{I}_2 = 10\angle 0° + 20\angle 60° = 26.46\angle 40.89$$

$$i = 26.46\sqrt{2}\sin(\omega t + 40.89°) = 37.42\sin(\omega t + 40.89)$$

**EXAMPLE 3.16**

*In a circuit, four currents as indicated below, are meeting at a point. Find the resultant current.*

$$i_1 = 5\sin\omega t, \qquad i_2 = 10\sin(\omega t - 30°)$$

$$i_3 = 5\cos(\omega t - 30°) \qquad i_4 = -10\sin(\omega t + 45°)$$

**Solution**

$$i_1 = 5 \sin \omega t, \quad i_2 = 10 \sin(\omega t - 30°),$$
$$i_3 = 5 \cos(\omega t - 30°) = 5 \sin(\omega t + 60°)$$
$$i_4 = -10 \sin(\omega t + 45°) = 10 \sin(\omega t + 225°)$$

Writing currents $i_1$, $i_2$, $i_3$, and $i_4$ in the phasor form,

$$\mathbf{I}_1 = \frac{5}{\sqrt{2}} \angle 0° = 3.54 \angle 0°$$
$$\mathbf{I}_2 = \frac{10}{\sqrt{2}} \angle -30° = 7.07 \angle -30°$$
$$\mathbf{I}_3 = \frac{5}{\sqrt{2}} \angle 60° = 3.54 \angle 60°$$
$$\mathbf{I}_4 = \frac{10}{\sqrt{2}} \angle 225° = 7.07 \angle 225°$$

$$\text{Resultant current } \mathbf{I} = \mathbf{I}_1 + \mathbf{I}_2 + \mathbf{I}_3 + \mathbf{I}_4 = 3.54 \angle 0° + 7.07 \angle -30° + 3.54 \angle 60° + 7.07 \angle 225°$$
$$= 8.44 \angle -40.36°$$
$$i = 8.44\sqrt{2} \sin(\omega t - 40.36°) = 11.94 \sin(\omega t - 40.36°)$$

## EXAMPLE 3.17

*Obtain the sum of the three voltages.*

$$v_1 = 147.3 \cos(\omega t + 98.1°), \quad v_2 = 294.6 \cos(\omega t - 45°), \quad v_3 = 88.4 \sin(\omega t + 135°)$$

**Solution**

$$v_1 = 147.3 \cos(\omega t + 98.1°) = 147.3 \sin(\omega t + 188.1°)$$
$$v_2 = 294.6 \cos(\omega t - 45°) = 294.6 \sin(\omega t + 45°), \quad v_3 = 88.4 \sin(\omega t + 135°)$$

Writing voltages $v_1$, $v_2$ and $v_3$ in the phasor form,

$$\mathbf{V}_1 = \frac{147.3}{\sqrt{2}} \angle 188.1° = 104.16 \angle 188.1°$$
$$\mathbf{V}_2 = \frac{294.6}{\sqrt{2}} \angle 45° = 208.31 \angle 45°$$
$$\mathbf{V}_3 = \frac{88.4}{\sqrt{2}} \angle 135° = 62.51 \angle 135°$$

$$\text{Resultant voltage } \mathbf{V} = \mathbf{V}_1 + \mathbf{V}_2 + \mathbf{V}_3 = 104.16 \angle 188.1° + 208.31 \angle 45° + 62.51 \angle 135° = 176.82 \angle 90°$$
$$v = 176.82\sqrt{2} \sin(\omega t + 90°) = 250.06 \sin(\omega t + 90°)$$

## EXAMPLE 3.18

*Two currents are represented by* $i_1 = 15 \sin\left(\omega t + \frac{\pi}{3}\right)$ *and* $i_2 = 25 \sin\left(\omega t + \frac{\pi}{4}\right)$*. These currents are fed into a common conductor. Find the total current in the form* $i = I_m \sin(\omega t + \phi)$*. If the conductor has a resistance of 10 Ω, what will be the energy loss in 24 hours?*

**Solution** $$i_1 = 15\sin\left(\omega t + \frac{\pi}{3}\right), \quad i_2 = 25\sin\left(\omega t + \frac{\pi}{4}\right)$$

$$R = 10\ \Omega, \quad t = 24 \text{ hours} = 86400 \text{ seconds}$$

Writing currents $i_1$ and $i_2$ in the phasor form,

$$\mathbf{I}_1 = \frac{15}{\sqrt{2}}\angle 60° = 10.61\angle 60°$$

$$\mathbf{I}_2 = \frac{25}{\sqrt{2}}\angle 45° = 17.68\angle 45°$$

$$\text{Total current } \mathbf{I} = \mathbf{I}_1 + \mathbf{I}_2 = 10.61\ \angle 60° + 17.68\ \angle 45° = 28.06\ \angle 50.62°$$

$$i = 28.06\sqrt{2}\sin(\omega t + 50.62°) = 39.68\sin(\omega t + 50.62°)$$

Energy loss in 24 hours, $E = I^2Rt$ where $I$ is the rms value of the current

$$E = (28.06)^2 \times 10 \times 86400 = 6.8 \times 10^8 \text{ J}$$

## EXAMPLE 3.19

*Two voltage sources have equal emfs and a phase difference α. When they are connected in series, the voltage is 200 V. When one source is reversed, the voltage is 15 V. Find their emfs and phase angle α.*

**Solution** $$\mathbf{E}_1 = E\angle 0°, \quad \mathbf{E}_2 = E\angle \alpha°, \quad E_1 = E_2 = E$$

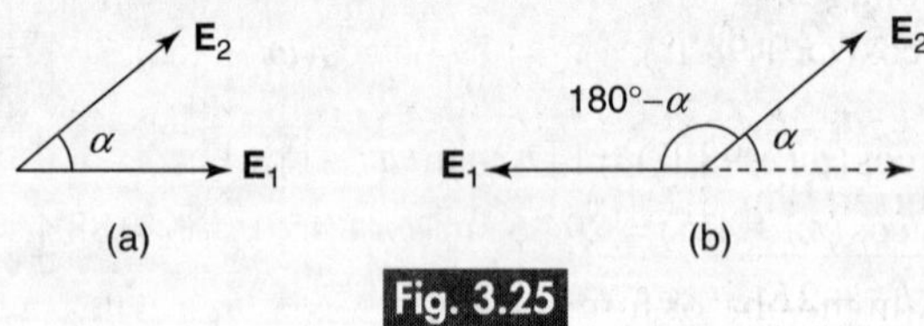


Fig. 3.25

When two sources are connected in series [Fig. 3.25(a)],

$$\sqrt{E_1^2 + E_2^2 + 2E_1E_2\cos\alpha} = 200$$

$$\sqrt{E^2 + E^2 + 2E^2\cos\alpha} = 200$$

$$2E^2 + 2E^2\cos\alpha = 40000 \qquad \text{...(i)}$$

When one source is reversed [Fig. 3.25(b)],

$$\sqrt{E_1^2 + E_2^2 - 2E_1E_2\cos\alpha} = 15$$

$$\sqrt{E^2 + E^2 - 2E^2\cos\alpha} = 15$$

$$2E^2 - 2E^2\cos\alpha = 225 \qquad \text{...(ii)}$$

Adding Eqs (i) and (ii),

$$4E^2 = 40225$$

$$E^2 = 10056.25$$

$$E = 100.28 \text{ V}$$

From Eq. (i),

$$2E^2 + 2E^2 \cos\alpha = 40000$$
$$20112.5 + 20112.5\cos\alpha = 40000$$
$$\cos\alpha = 0.988$$
$$\alpha = 8.58°$$

## EXAMPLE 3.20

*Two sinusoidal sources of emf have rms values of $E_1$ and $E_2$ and a phase difference of $\alpha$. When connected in series, the resultant voltage is 41.1 V. When one of the sources is reversed, the resultant emf is 17.52 V. When phase displacement is made zero, the resultant emf is 42.5 V. Calculate $E_1$, $E_2$ and $\alpha$.*

**Solution** $\mathbf{E}_1 = E_1\angle 0°$, $\mathbf{E}_2 = E_2\angle \alpha°$

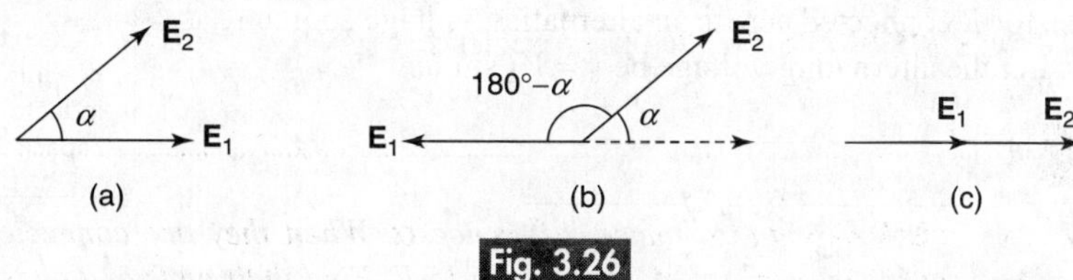


Fig. 3.26

When two sources are connected in series [Fig. 3.26(a)],

$$\sqrt{E_1^2 + E_2^2 + 2E_1E_2\cos\alpha} = 41.1$$
$$E_1^2 + E_2^2 + 2E_1E_2\cos\alpha = 1689.21 \quad \text{...(i)}$$

When one of the sources is reversed [Fig. 3.26(b)],

$$\sqrt{E_1^2 + E_2^2 - 2E_1E_2\cos\alpha} = 17.52$$
$$E_1^2 + E_2^2 - 2E_1E_2\cos\alpha = 306.95 \quad \text{...(ii)}$$

When phase displacement is made zero [Fig. 3.26(c)],

$$\sqrt{E_1^2 + E_2^2 + 2E_1E_2\cos 0°} = 42.5$$
$$E_1 + E_2 = 42.5$$
$$E_1 = 42.5 - E_2 \quad \text{...(iii)}$$

Adding Eqs (i) and (ii),

$$2(E_1^2 + E_2^2) = 1996.16$$
$$E_1^2 + E_2^2 = 998.08$$

From Eq. (iii),

$$(42.5 - E_2)^2 + E_2^2 = 998.08$$
$$1806.25 - 85E_2 + E_2^2 + E_2^2 = 998.08$$
$$E_2^2 - 42.5E_2 + 404.09 = 0 \quad \text{...(iv)}$$

Solving Eq. (iv),

$$E_2 = 28.14 \text{ V or } E_2 = 14.36 \text{ V}$$
$$E_1 = 14.36 \text{ V or } E_1 = 28.14 \text{ V}$$

Subtracting Eq. (ii) from Eq. (i),

$$4E_1E_2 \cos\alpha = 1382.26$$
$$4 \times 14.36 \times 28.14 \cos\alpha = 1382.26$$
$$\cos\alpha = 0.855$$
$$\alpha = 31.24°$$

## 3.7 BEHAVIOUR OF A PURE RESISTOR IN AN ac CIRCUIT

LO 3.6

Explain the behaviour of a pure resistor, a pure inductor, and a pure capacitor in an ac circuit

Consider a pure resistor $R$ connected across an alternating voltage source $v$, as shown in Fig. 3.27. Let the alternating voltage be $v = V_m \sin \omega t$.

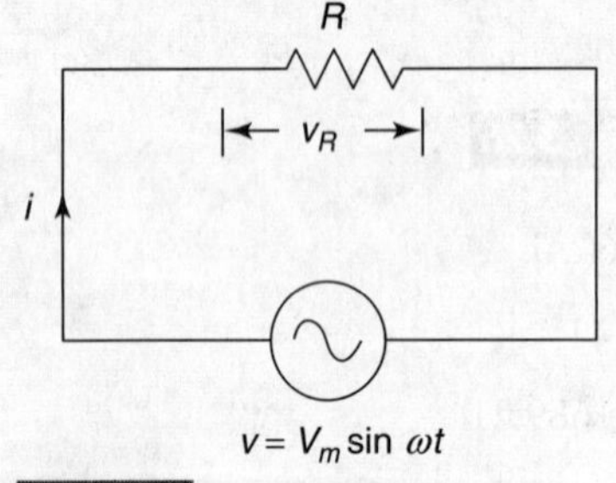


**Fig. 3.27** *Purely resistive circuit*

**1. *Current*** The alternating current $i$ is given by

$$i = \frac{v}{R} = \frac{V_m}{R} \sin \omega t = I_m \sin \omega t \qquad \ldots\left(I_m = \frac{V_m}{R}\right)$$

where $I_m$ is the maximum value of the alternating current. From the voltage and current equation, it is clear that the current is in phase with the voltage in a purely resistive circuit.

**2. *Waveforms*** Figure 3.28 shows the voltage and current waveforms.

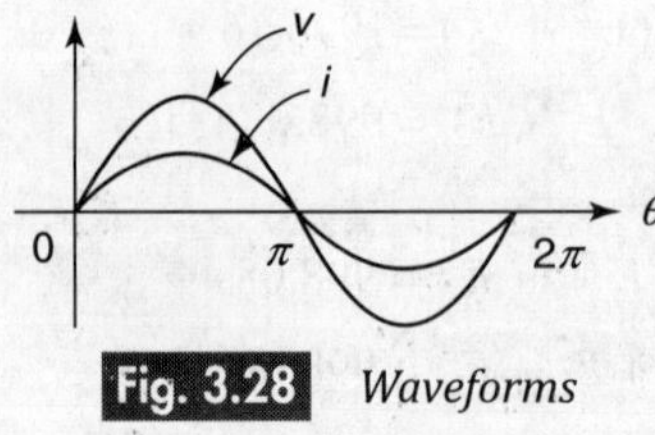


**Fig. 3.28** *Waveforms*

**3. *Phasor Diagram*** Figure 3.29 shows the phasor diagram.

I V

Fig. 3.29 *Phasor diagram*

**4. *Impedance*** It is the resistance offered to the flow of current in an ac circuit. In a purely resistive circuit,

$$Z = \frac{V}{I} = \frac{V_m}{I_m} = \frac{V_m}{\frac{V_m}{R}} = R$$

**5. *Phase Difference*** Since the voltage and current are in phase with each other, the phase difference is zero.

$$\phi = 0°$$

**6. *Power Factor*** It is defined as the cosine of the angle between the voltage and current phasors.

$$\text{Power factor} = \cos\phi = \cos(0°) = 1$$

**7. Power** Instantaneous power $p$ is given by

$$\begin{aligned} p &= vi \\ &= V_m \sin\omega t \, I_m \sin\omega t \\ &= V_m I_m \sin^2 \omega t \\ &= \frac{V_m I_m}{2}(1 - \cos 2\omega t) \\ &= \frac{V_m I_m}{2} - \frac{V_m I_m}{2}\cos 2\omega t \end{aligned}$$

The power waveform is shown in Fig. 3.30. The power consists of a constant part $\frac{V_m I_m}{2}$ and a fluctuating part $\frac{V_m I_m}{2}$ cos $2\omega t$. The frequency of the fluctuating power is twice the applied voltage frequency and its average value over one complete cycle is zero.

$$\text{Average power } P = \frac{V_m I_m}{2} = \frac{V_m}{\sqrt{2}}\frac{I_m}{\sqrt{2}} = VI$$

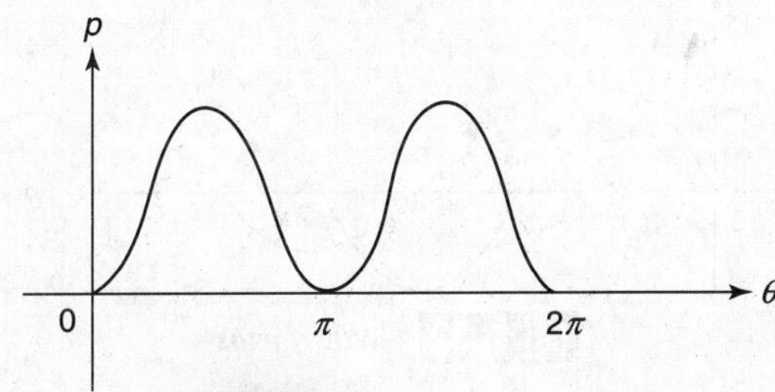


Fig. 3.30 *Power waveform*

Thus, power in a purely resistive circuit is equal to the product of rms values of voltage and current.

## 3.8 BEHAVIOUR OF A PURE INDUCTOR IN AN ac CIRCUIT

LO 3.6

Consider a pure inductor $L$ connected across an alternating voltage $v$, as shown in Fig. 3.31. Let the alternating voltage be $v = V_m \sin \omega t$.

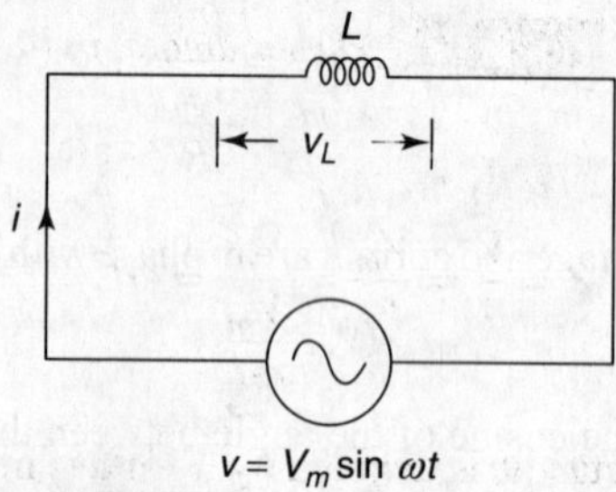


Fig. 3.31 Purely inductive circuit

***1. Current*** The alternating current $i$ is given by

$$\begin{aligned} i &= \frac{1}{L}\int v\, dt \\ &= \frac{1}{L}\int V_m \sin \omega t\, dt \\ &= \frac{V_m}{\omega L}(-\cos \omega t) \\ &= \frac{V_m}{\omega L}\sin\left(\omega t - \frac{\pi}{2}\right) \\ &= I_m \sin\left(\omega t - \frac{\pi}{2}\right) \qquad \cdots \left(I_m = \frac{V_m}{\omega L}\right) \end{aligned}$$

where $I_m$ is the maximum value of the alternating current. From the voltage and current equation, it is clear that the current lags behind the voltage by 90° in a purely inductive circuit.

***2. Waveforms*** Figure 3.32 shows the voltage and current waveforms.

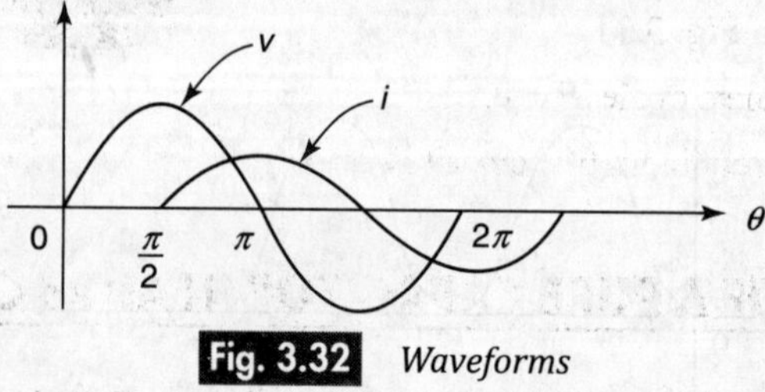


Fig. 3.32 Waveforms

***3. Phasor Diagram*** Figure 3.33 shows the phasor diagram.

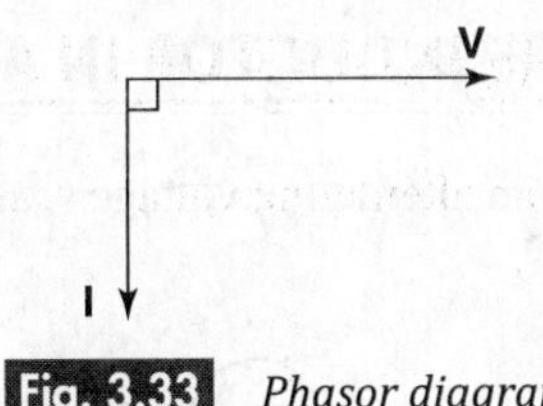


**Fig. 3.33** *Phasor diagram*

***4. Impedance*** In a purely inductive circuit,

$$Z = \frac{V}{I} = \frac{V_m}{I_m} = \frac{V_m}{\frac{V_m}{\omega L}} = \omega L$$

The quantity $\omega L$ is called inductive reactance, is denoted by $X_L$ and is measured in ohms.

For a dc supply, $f = 0$ $\therefore$ $X_L = 0$

Thus, an inductor acts as a short circuit for a dc supply.

***5. Phase Difference*** It is the angle between the voltage and current phasors.

$$\phi = 90°$$

***6. Power Factor*** It is defined as the cosine of the angle between the voltage and current phasors.

$$\text{pf} = \cos\phi = \cos(90°) = 0$$

***7. Power*** Instantaneous powers $p$ is given by

$$\begin{aligned} p &= vi \\ &= V_m \sin \omega t \, I_m \sin\left(\omega t - \frac{\pi}{2}\right) \\ &= -V_m I_m \sin \omega t \cos \omega t \\ &= -\frac{V_m I_m}{2} \sin 2\,\omega t \end{aligned}$$

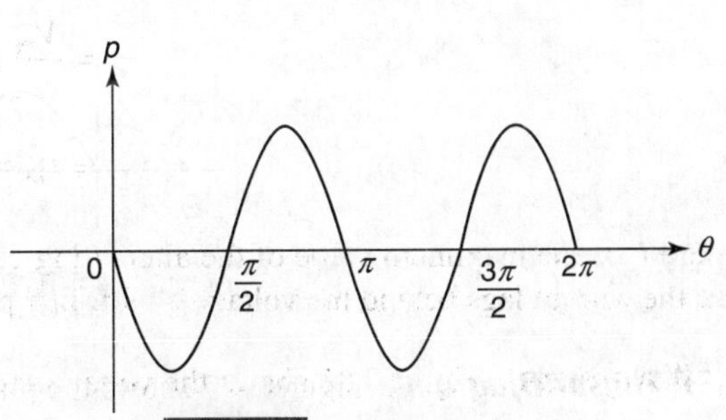


**Fig. 3.34** *Power waveform*

The power waveform is shown in Fig. 3.34

The average power for one complete cycle, $P = 0$.

Hence, power consumed by a purely inductive circuit is zero.

## 3.9 BEHAVIOUR OF A PURE CAPACITOR IN AN ac CIRCUIT

LO 3.6

Consider a pure capacitor $C$ connected across an alternating voltage $v$, as shown in Fig. 3.35.

Let the alternating voltage be $v = V_m \sin \omega t$.

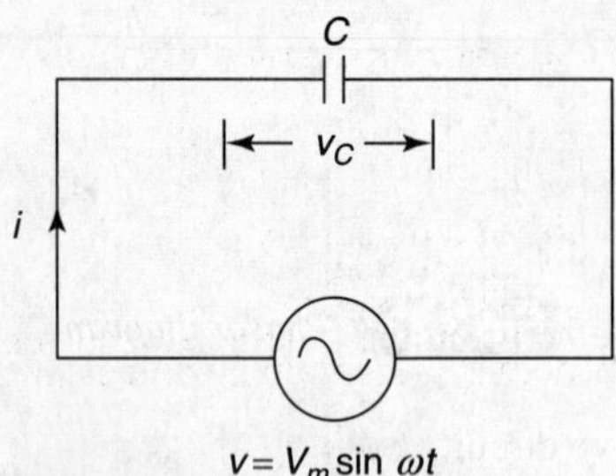


Fig. 3.35 *Purely capacitive circuit*

**1. Current** The alternating current $i$ is given by

$$i = C\frac{dv}{dt}$$
$$= C\frac{d}{dt}(V_m \sin \omega t)$$
$$= \omega C\ V_m \cos \omega t$$
$$= \omega C\ V_m \sin(\omega t + 90°)$$
$$= I_m \sin(\omega t + 90°) \qquad \ldots(I_m = \omega C\ V_m)$$

where $I_m$ is the maximum value of the alternating current. From the voltage and current equation, it is clear that the current leads the voltage by 90° in a purely capacitive circuit.

**2. Waveforms** Figure 3.36 shows the voltage and current waveforms.

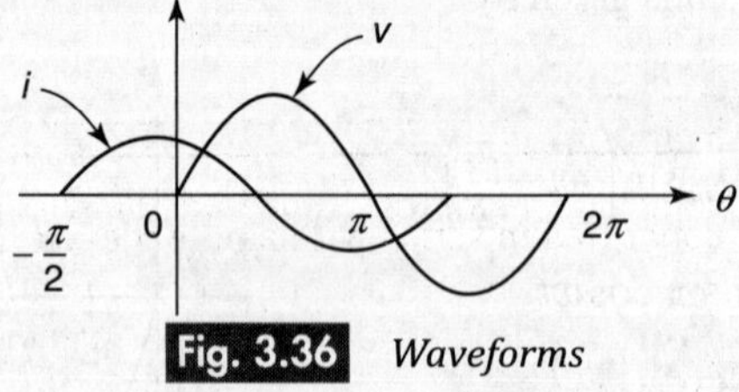


Fig. 3.36 *Waveforms*

**3. Phasor Diagram** Figure 3.37 shows the phasor diagram.

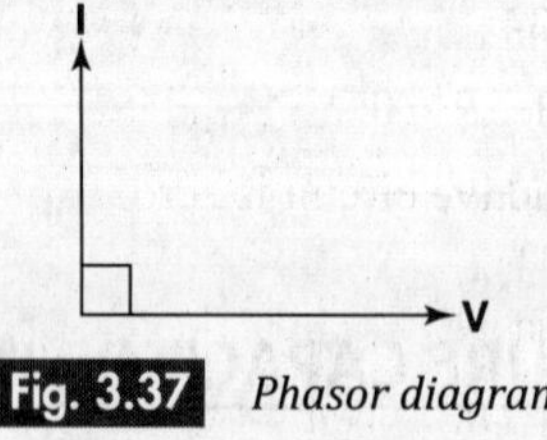


Fig. 3.37 *Phasor diagram*

**4. Impedance** In a purely capacitive circuit,

$$Z = \frac{V}{I} = \frac{V_m}{I_m} = \frac{V_m}{\omega C\ V_m} = \frac{1}{\omega C}$$

The quantity $\dfrac{1}{\omega C}$ is called capacitive reactance, is denoted by $X_C$ and is measured in ohms.

For a dc supply, $f = 0 \therefore X_C = \infty$

Thus, the capacitor acts as an open circuit for a dc supply.

***5. Phase Difference*** It is the angle between the voltage and current phasors.

$$\phi = 90°$$

***6. Power Factor*** It is defined as the cosine of the angle between the voltage and current phasors.

$$\text{pf} = \cos\phi = \cos(90°) = 0$$

***7. Power*** Instantaneous power $p$ is given by

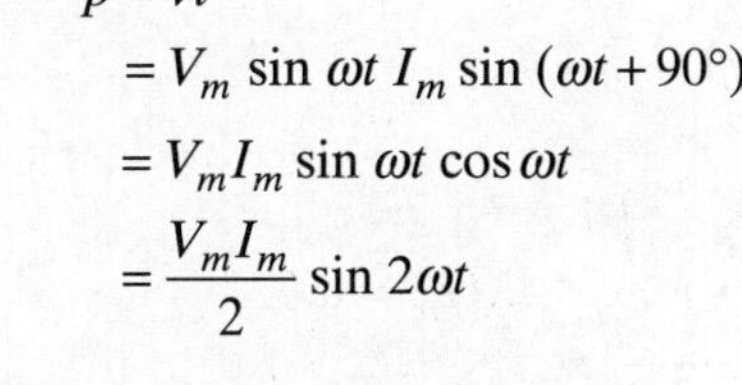

$$\begin{aligned} p &= vi \\ &= V_m \sin\omega t \, I_m \sin(\omega t + 90°) \\ &= V_m I_m \sin\omega t \cos\omega t \\ &= \frac{V_m I_m}{2} \sin 2\omega t \end{aligned}$$

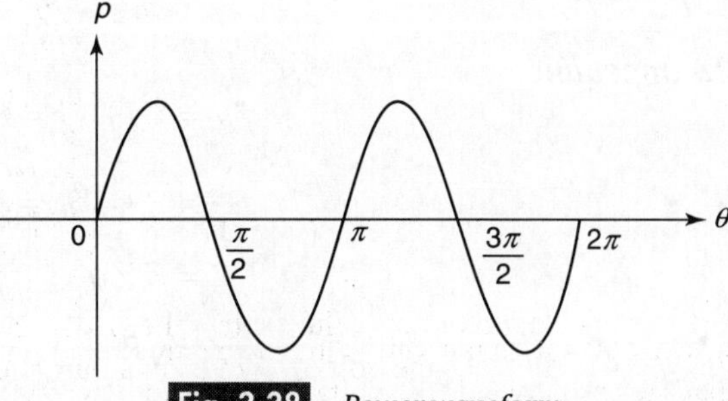


**Fig. 3.38** *Power waveform*

The power waveform is shown in Fig. 3.38.

The average power for one complete cycle, $P = 0$.

Hence, power consumed by a purely capacitive circuit is zero.

## 3.10 SERIES *RL* CIRCUIT

LO 3.7

Analyse series *RL* circuits, series *RC* circuits, and series *RLC* circuits

Figure 3.39 shows a pure resistor $R$ connected in series with a pure inductor $L$ across an alternating voltage $v = V_m \sin \omega t$

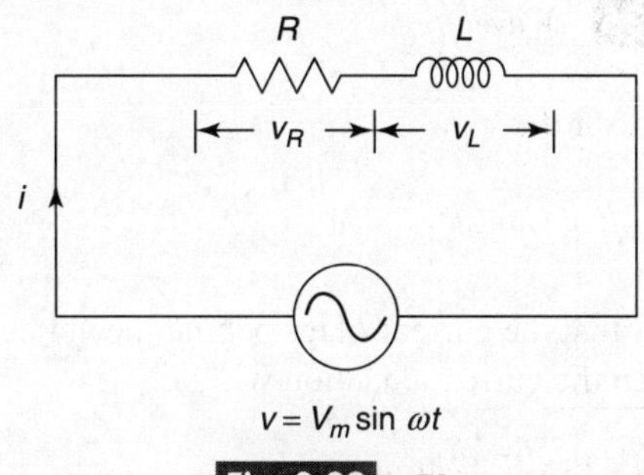


**Fig. 3.39** *RL circuit*

Let $V$ and $I$ be the rms values of applied voltage and current.

Potential difference across the resistor $= V_R = R\,I$

Potential difference across the inductor $= V_L = X_L I$

The voltage $\mathbf{V}_R$ is in phase with the current $\mathbf{I}$ whereas the voltage $\mathbf{V}_L$ leads the current $\mathbf{I}$ by 90°.

***1. Phase Diagram*** Figure 3.40 shows the phasor diagram of series *RL* circuit.

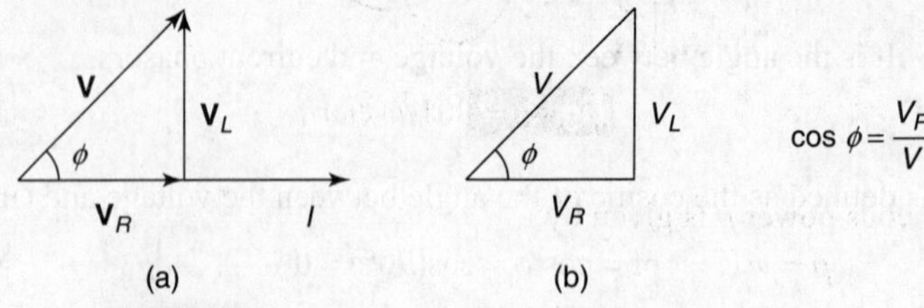


**Fig. 3.40** *(a) Phasor diagram, (b) Voltage triangle*

***2. Impedance***

$$\mathbf{V} = \mathbf{V}_R + \mathbf{V}_L = R\mathbf{I} + jX_L\mathbf{I} = (R + jX_L)\,\mathbf{I}$$

$$\frac{\mathbf{V}}{\mathbf{I}} = R + jX_L = \mathbf{Z}$$

$$\mathbf{Z} = Z\,\angle\phi$$

$$Z = \sqrt{R^2 + X_L^2} = \sqrt{R^2 + \omega^2 L^2}$$

$$\phi = \tan^{-1}\left(\frac{X_L}{R}\right) = \tan^{-1}\left(\frac{\omega L}{R}\right)$$

The quantity *Z* is called the *complex impedance* of the series *RL* circuit.

***3. Impedance Triangle*** Figure 3.41 shows the impedance triangle of series *RL* circuit.

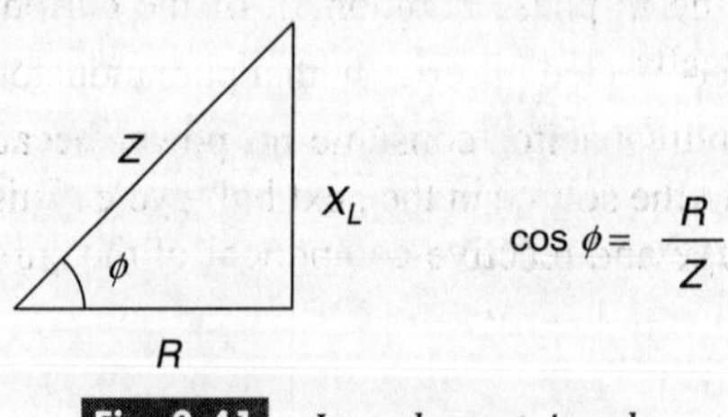


**Fig. 3.41** *Impedance triangle*

***4. Current*** From the phasor diagram, it is clear that the current *I* lags behind the voltage *V* by an angle $\phi$. If the applied voltage is given by $v = V_m \sin \omega t$ then the current equation will be

$$i = I_m \sin(\omega t - \phi)$$

where

$$I_m = \frac{V_m}{Z}$$

and

$$\phi = \tan^{-1}\left(\frac{\omega L}{R}\right)$$

**5. *Waveforms*** Figure 3.42 shows the voltage and current waveforms.

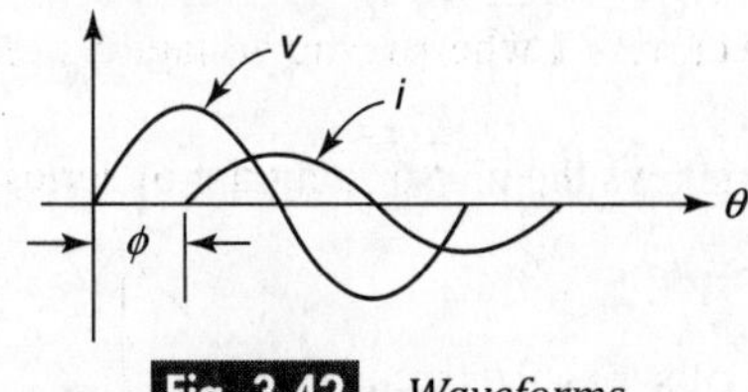


Fig. 3.42 *Waveforms*

**6. *Power*** Instantaneous power $p$ is given by

$$
\begin{aligned}
p &= vi \\
&= V_m \sin \omega t \, I_m \sin (\omega t - \phi) \\
&= V_m I_m \sin \omega t \sin (\omega t - \phi) \\
&= V_m I_m \left[ \frac{\cos \phi - \cos (2\omega t - \phi)}{20} \right] \\
&= \frac{V_m I_m}{2} \cos \phi - \frac{V_m I_m}{2} \cos (2\omega t - \phi)
\end{aligned}
$$

Thus, power consists of a constant part $\frac{V_m I_m}{2} \cos \phi$ and a fluctuating part $\frac{V_m I_m}{2} \cos (2\omega t - \phi)$. The frequency of the fluctuating part is twice the applied voltage frequency and its average value over one complete cycle is zero.

$$\text{Average power } P = \frac{V_m I_m}{2} \cos \phi = \frac{V_m}{\sqrt{2}} \frac{I_m}{\sqrt{2}} \cos \phi = VI \cos \phi$$

Thus, power is dependent upon the in-phase component of the current. The average power is also called *active power* and is measured in watts.

We know that a pure inductor and capacitor consume no power because all the power received from the source in a half cycle is returned to the source in the next half cycle. This circulating power is called *reactive power*. It is a product of the voltage and reactive component of the current, i.e., $I \sin \phi$ and is measured in VAR (volt-ampere-reactive).

Reactive power $Q = VI \sin \phi$.

The product of voltage and current is known as *apparent power* ($S$) and is measured in volt-ampere (VA).

$$S = VI = \sqrt{P^2 + Q^2}$$

**7. *Power Triangle*** In terms of circuit components,

$$\cos \phi = \frac{R}{Z}$$

and $$V = ZI$$

$$P = VI\cos\phi = ZII\frac{R}{Z} = I^2R$$

$$Q = VI\sin\phi = ZII\frac{X_L}{Z} = I^2X_L$$

$$S = VI = ZII = I^2Z$$

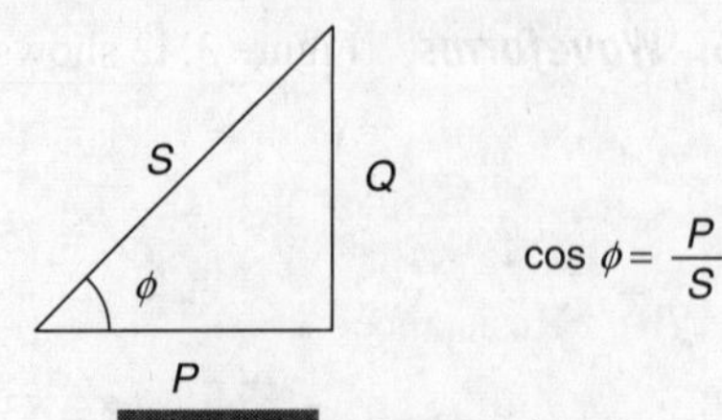

Fig. 3.43 Power triangle

Figure 3.43 shows the power triangle of series *RL* circuit.

**8. *Power Factor*** It is defined as the cosine of the angle between the voltage and current phasors.

$$\text{pf} = \cos\phi$$

From voltage triangle, $\text{pf} = \dfrac{V_R}{V}$

From impedance triangle, $\text{pf} = \dfrac{R}{Z}$

From power triangle, $\text{pf} = \dfrac{P}{S}$

In case of series *RL* circuit, the power factor is lagging in nature.

## EXAMPLE 3.21

*An alternating voltage of 80 + j60 V is applied to a circuit and the current flowing is 4 – j2 A. Find the (a) impedance, (b) phase angle, (c) power factor, and (d) power consumed.*

**Solution** $\mathbf{V} = 80 + j\,60\text{ V},\quad \mathbf{I} = 4 - j\,2\text{ A}$

(a) Impedance

$$\mathbf{Z} = \frac{\mathbf{V}}{\mathbf{I}} = \frac{80 + j60}{4 - j2} = \frac{100\angle 36.87^\circ}{4.47\angle -26.56^\circ} = 22.37\angle 63.43^\circ\ \Omega$$

$$Z = 22.37\ \Omega$$

(b) Phase angle

$$\phi = 63.43^\circ$$

(c) Power factor

$$\text{pf} = \cos\phi = \cos(63.43^\circ) = 0.447\ \text{(lagging)}$$

(d) Power consumed

$$P = VI\cos\phi = 100 \times 4.47 \times 0.447 = 199.81\text{ W}$$

## EXAMPLE 3.22

*The voltage and current in a circuit are given by **V** = 150 ∠30° V and **I** = 2 ∠–15° A. If the circuit works on a 50 Hz supply, determine impedance, resistance, reactance, power factor and power loss, considering the circuit as a simple series circuit.*

**Solution** $\mathbf{V} = 150\angle 30^\circ\text{ V},\quad \mathbf{I} = 2\angle -15^\circ\text{ A},\quad f = 50\text{ Hz}$

(a) Impedance

$$\mathbf{Z} = \frac{\mathbf{V}}{\mathbf{I}} = \frac{150\angle 30^\circ}{2\angle -15^\circ} = 75\ \angle 45^\circ\ \Omega = 53.03 + j53.03\ \Omega$$

$$Z = 75\ \Omega$$

(b) Resistance

$$R = 53.03\ \Omega$$

(c) Reactance

$$X = 53.03\ \Omega$$

(d) Power factor

$$\phi = 45^\circ$$

$$\text{pf} = \cos\phi = \cos(45^\circ) = 0.707\ \text{(lagging)}$$

(e) Power loss

$$P = VI\cos\phi = 150 \times 2 \times 0.707 = 212.1\ \text{W}$$

**EXAMPLE 3.23**

*An rms voltage of 100 ∠0° V is applied to a series combination of $Z_1$ and $Z_2$ when $\mathbf{Z}_1 = 20\ \angle 30^\circ\ \Omega$. The effective voltage drop across $\mathbf{Z}_1$ is known to be 40 ∠–30° V. Find the reactive component of $\mathbf{Z}_2$.*

**Solution**

$$\mathbf{V} = 100\ \angle 0^\circ\,\text{V}, \quad \mathbf{Z}_1 = 20\ \angle 30^\circ\Omega, \quad \mathbf{V}_1 = 40\ \angle -30^\circ\ \text{V}$$

$$\mathbf{I} = \frac{\mathbf{V}_1}{\mathbf{Z}_1} = \frac{40\ \angle -30^\circ}{20\angle\ 30^\circ} = 2\ \angle -60^\circ\text{A}$$

$$\mathbf{Z} = \frac{\mathbf{V}_1}{\mathbf{I}} = \frac{100\ \angle 0^\circ}{2\ \angle -60^\circ} = 50\ \angle 60^\circ = 25 + j43.3\ \Omega$$

$$\mathbf{Z}_1 = 20\angle 30^\circ = 17.32 + j10\ \Omega$$

$$\mathbf{Z} = \mathbf{Z}_1 + \mathbf{Z}_2$$

$$\mathbf{Z}_2 = \mathbf{Z} - \mathbf{Z}_1 = 25 + j43.3 - 17.32 - j10 = 7.68 + j33.3\ \Omega$$

Reactive component of $\mathbf{Z}_2 = 33.3\ \Omega$

**EXAMPLE 3.24**

*When an inductive coil is connected to a dc supply at 240 V, the current in it is 16 A. When the same coil is connected to an ac supply at 240 V, 50 Hz, the current is 12.27 A. Calculate (a) resistance, (b) impedance, (c) reactance, and (d) inductance of the coil.*

**Solution**

For dc : $V = 240$ V, $I = 16$ A

For ac : $V = 240$ V, $I = 12.27$ A

(a) Resistance

When an inductive coil is connected to a dc supply,

$$f = 0$$
$$X_L = 2\pi f L = 0$$

The coil behaves like a pure resistor.

$$R = \frac{V}{I} = \frac{240}{16} = 15\ \Omega$$

(b) Impedance

When the coil is connected to an ac supply,

$$Z = \frac{V}{I} = \frac{240}{12.27} = 19.56\ \Omega$$

(c) Reactance

$$X_L = \sqrt{Z^2 - R^2} = \sqrt{(19.56)^2 - (15)^2} = 12.55\ \Omega$$

(d) Inductance

$$X_L = 2\pi f L$$
$$12.55 = 2\pi \times 50 \times L$$
$$L = 0.04\ \text{H}$$

**EXAMPLE 3.25**

*An inductive coil draws 10 A current and consumes 1 kW power from a 200 V, 50 Hz ac supply. Determine (a) impedance in Cartesian and polar forms, (b) power factor, and (c) reactive and apparent power.*

**Solution**

$$I = 10\ \text{A}, \quad P = 1\ \text{kW}, \quad V = 200\ \text{V}, \quad f = 50\ \text{Hz}$$

(a) Impedance in Cartesian and polar forms

$$Z = \frac{V}{I} = \frac{200}{10} = 20\ \Omega$$
$$P = VI\cos\phi$$
$$1000 = 200 \times 10 \times \cos\phi$$
$$\cos\phi = 0.5$$
$$\phi = 60°$$

Expressing **Z** in polar form,

$$\mathbf{Z} = Z\angle\phi° = 20\ \angle 60°\ \Omega$$

Expressing **Z** in Cartesian form,

$$\mathbf{Z} = 10 + j17.32\ \Omega$$

(b) Power factor

$$\text{pf} = \cos\phi = \cos(60°) = 0.5\ \text{(lagging)}$$

(c) Reactive and apparent power

$$Q = VI \sin\phi = 200 \times 10 \times \sin(60°) = 1.73 \text{ kVAR}$$

$$S = VI = 200 \times 10 = 2 \text{ kVA}$$

**EXAMPLE 3.26**

*In the circuit of Fig. 3.44, a coil connected across a 250 V, 50 Hz supply takes a current of 10 A at 0.8 lagging power factor. What will be the power taken by the choke coil when connected across a 200 V, 25 Hz supply? Also, calculate resistance and inductance of the coil.*

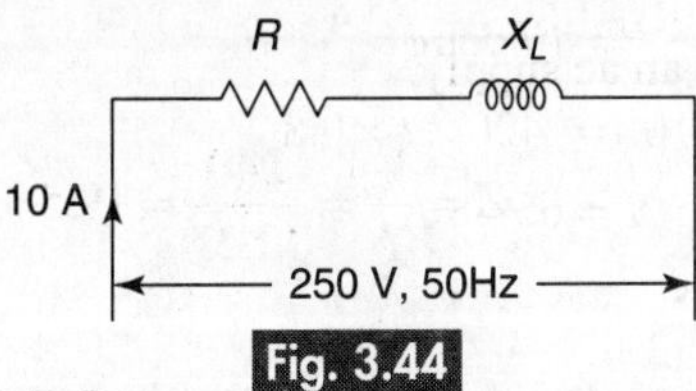


Fig. 3.44

**Solution**

$$V_1 = 250 \text{ V}, \quad f_1 = 50 \text{ Hz}, \quad I_1 = 10 \text{ A}, \quad \text{pf} = 0.8 \text{ (lagging)}$$

$$V_2 = 200\text{V}, \quad f_2 = 25 \text{ Hz}$$

(a) Resistance and inductance of the coil

$$Z_1 = \frac{V_1}{I_1} = \frac{250}{10} = 25\ \Omega$$

$$\phi_1 = \cos^{-1}(0.8) = 36.87°$$

$$\mathbf{Z}_1 = Z_1 \angle \phi_1 = 25\angle 36.87° = 20 + j15\ \Omega$$

$$R = 20\ \Omega$$

$$X_{L_1} = 15\ \Omega$$

$$X_{L_1} = 2\pi f_1\ L$$

$$15 = 2\pi \times 50 \times L$$

$$L = 0.0477 \text{ H}$$

(b) Power taken by the choke coil when connected across a 200 V, 50 Hz supply.

$$X_{L_2} = 2\pi f_2 L = 2\pi \times 25 \times 0.0477 = 7.49\ \Omega$$

$$\mathbf{Z}_2 = R + jX_{L_2} = 20 + j7.49 = 21.36\ \angle 20.53°\ \Omega$$

$$Z_2 = 21.36\ \Omega$$

$$\phi_2 = 20.53^{\circ}$$

$$I_2 = \frac{V_2}{Z_2} = \frac{200}{21.36} = 9.36 \text{ A}$$

$$P = V_2\ I_2\ \cos\phi_2 = 200 \times 9.36 \times \cos\ (20.53°) = 1.753 \text{ kW}$$

## EXAMPLE 3.27

*A load of 22 kW operates at 0.8 lagging power factor when connected to a 420 V, single-phase, 50 Hz source. Find (a) current in the load, (b) power factor angle, (c) impedance, (d) resistance of load, (e) reactance of load, (f) voltage and current equations.*

**Solution** $P = 22$ kW, pf = 0.8 (lagging), $V = 420$ V, $f = 50$ Hz

(a) Current in the load

$$P = VI\cos\phi$$

$$22\times10^3 = 420\times I\times0.8$$

$$I = 65.48 \text{ A}$$

(b) Power-factor angle

$$\phi = \cos^{-1}(0.8) = 36.87°$$

(c) Impedance

$$Z = \frac{V}{I} = \frac{420}{65.48} = 6.41\ \Omega$$

(d) Resistance of load

$$R = Z\cos\phi = 6.41\times0.8 = 5.13\ \Omega$$

(e) Reactance of load

$$X_L = Z\sin\phi = 6.41\times\sin(36.87°) = 3.85\ \Omega$$

(f) Voltage and current equations

$$v = V_m\sin 2\pi ft = 420\sqrt{2}\sin(2\pi\times50)\,t = 593.97\sin 100\,\pi t$$

The current lags behind the voltage by 36.87°.

$$i = I_m\sin(2\pi ft - \phi) = 65.48\sqrt{2}\sin(2\pi\times50t - 36.87°)$$
$$= 92.6\sin(100\,\pi t - 36.87°)$$

## EXAMPLE 3.28

*A choke coil is connected in series with fixed resistor, as shown in Fig. 3.45. A 240 V, 50 Hz supply is applied and a current of 2.5 A flows. If the voltage drops across the coil and fixed resistor are 140 V and 160 V respectively, calculate the value of the fixed resistance, the resistance and inductance of the coil, and power drawn by the coil.*

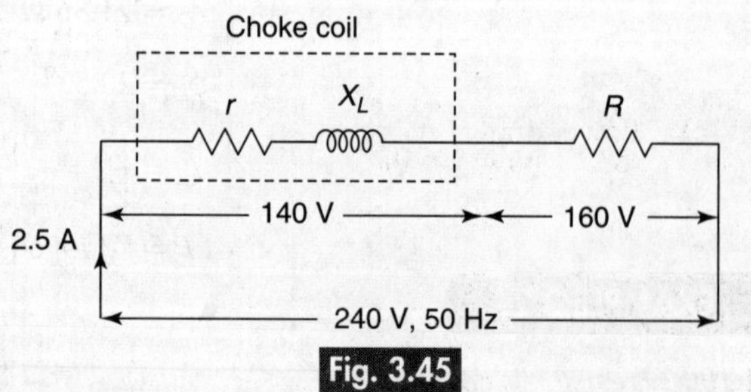


Fig. 3.45

**Solution** $V = 240$ V, $f = 50$ Hz, $I = 2.5$ A, $V_{coil} = 140$ V, $V_R = 160$ V

(a) Resistance of fixed resistor

$$R = \frac{V_R}{I} = \frac{160}{2.5} = 64\ \Omega$$

(b) Resistance and inductance of the coil

$$Z_{coil} = \frac{V_{coil}}{I} = \frac{140}{2.5} = 56\ \Omega$$

$$Z_{coil} = \sqrt{r^2 + X_L^2} = 56$$

$$r^2 + X_L^2 = 3136 \qquad \text{...(i)}$$

$$Z = \frac{V}{I} = \frac{240}{2.5} = 96\ \Omega$$

$$\mathbf{Z} = (R + r) + jX_L$$

$$Z = \sqrt{(R + r)^2 + X_L^2}$$

$$96 = \sqrt{(64 + r)^2 + X_L^2}$$

$$(64 + r)^2 + X_L^2 = 9216 \qquad \text{...(ii)}$$

Subtracting Eq. (i) from Eq. (ii),

$$(64 + r)^2 - r^2 = 6080$$

$$4096 + 128r + r^2 - r^2 = 6080$$

$$128r = 1984$$

$$r = 15.5\ \Omega$$

Substituting the value of $r$ in Eq. (i),

$$(15.5)^2 + X_L^2 = 3136$$

$$X_L^2 = 2895.75$$

$$X_L = 53.81\ \Omega$$

$$X_L = 2\pi fL$$

$$53.81 = 2\pi \times 50 \times L$$

$$L = 0.17\ \text{H}$$

(c) Power drawn by the coil

$$P_{coil} = I^2 r = (2.5)^2 \times 15.5 = 96.875\ \text{W}$$

**EXAMPLE 3.29**

*A 100 Ω resistor is connected in series with a choke coil, as shown in Fig. 3.46. When a 400 V, 50 Hz supply is applied to this combination, the voltages across the resistance and the choke coil are 200 V and 300 V respectively. Find the power consumed by the choke coil. Also, calculate the power factor of the choke coil and the power factor of the circuit.*

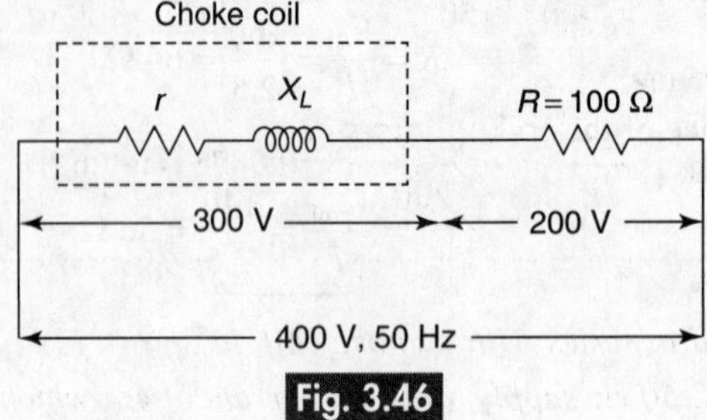


Fig. 3.46

**Solution** $R = 100\ \Omega,\quad V = 400\text{ V},\quad f = 50\text{ Hz},\quad V_R = 200\text{ V},\quad V_{coil} = 300\text{ V}$

(a) Power consumed by choke coil

$$I = \frac{V_R}{R} = \frac{200}{100} = 2\text{ A}$$

$$Z_{coil} = \frac{V_{coil}}{I} = \frac{300}{2} = 150\ \Omega$$

$$\sqrt{r^2 + X_L^2} = 150$$

$$r^2 + X_L^2 = 22500 \qquad \text{...(i)}$$

$$Z = \frac{V}{I} = \frac{400}{2} = 200\ \Omega$$

$$\mathbf{Z} = (R + r) + jX_L$$

$$Z = \sqrt{(R + r)^2 + X_L^2} = 200$$

$$(100 + r)^2 + X_L^2 = 40000 \qquad \text{...(ii)}$$

Subtracting Eq. (i) from Eq. (ii),

$$(100 + r)^2 - r^2 = 17500$$

$$10000 + 200r + r^2 - r^2 = 17500$$

$$200r = 7500$$

$$r = 37.5\ \Omega$$

Substituting the value of $r$ in Eq. (i),

$$(37.5)^2 + X_L^2 = 22500$$

$$X_L^2 = 21093.75$$

$$X_L = 145.24\ \Omega$$

$$P_{coil} = I^2 r = (2)^2 \times 37.5 = 50\text{ W}$$

(b) Power factor of the choke coil

$$\text{pf}_{\text{coil}} = \frac{r}{Z_{\text{coil}}} = \frac{37.5}{150} = 0.25 \text{ (lagging)}$$

(c) Power factor of the circuit

$$\text{pf}_{\text{circuit}} = \frac{R+r}{Z} = \frac{100+37.5}{200} = 0.6875 \text{ (lagging)}$$

## EXAMPLE 3.30

*A resistor of 25 Ω is connected in series with a choke coil, as shown in Fig. 3.47. The series combination, when connected across a 250 V, 50 Hz supply, draws a current of 4 A which lags behind the voltage by 65°. Calculate (a) resistance and inductance of the coil, (b) total power, (c) power consumed by resistance, and (d) power consumed by choke coil.*

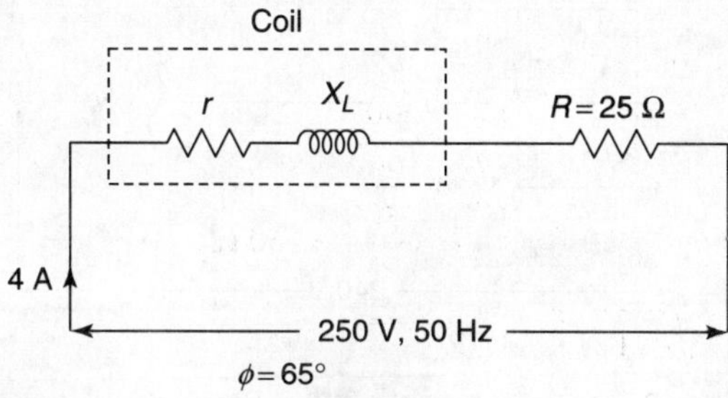


Fig. 3.47

**Solution** $R = 25\ \Omega,\quad V = 250\text{ V},\quad f = 50\text{ Hz},\quad I = 4\text{ A},\quad \phi = 65°$

(a) Resistance and inductance of the coil

$$Z = \frac{V}{I} = \frac{250}{4} = 62.5\ \Omega$$

$$\mathbf{Z} = Z\angle\phi = 62.5\angle 65° = 26.41 + j56.64\ \Omega$$

But $\mathbf{Z} = (R+r) + jX_L$

$$X_L = 56.64\ \Omega$$

$$R + r = 26.41$$

$$r = 26.41 - 25 = 1.41\ \Omega$$

$$X_L = 2\pi fL$$

$$56.64 = 2\pi \times 50 \times L$$

$$L = 0.18\text{ H}$$

(b) Total power

$$P = I^2(R+r) = (4)^2 \times 26.41 = 422.56\text{ W}$$

(c) Power consumed by resistance

$$P_R = I^2 R = (4)^2 \times 25 = 400 \text{ W}$$

(d) Power consumed by choke coil

$$P_{\text{coil}} = I^2 r = (4)^2 \times 1.41 = 22.56 \text{ W}$$

## EXAMPLE 3.31

*When a resistor and a coil in series are connected to a 240 V supply, as shown in Fig. 3.48, a current of 3 A flows, lagging 37° behind the supply voltage. The voltage across the coil is 171 volts. Find the resistance and reactance of the coil, and the resistance of the resistor.*

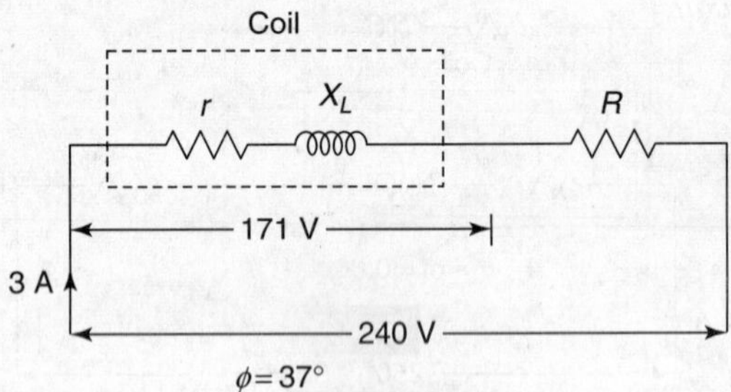


Fig. 3.48

**Solution** $V = 240 \text{ V}, \quad I = 3 \text{ A}, \quad \phi = 37°, \quad V_{\text{coil}} = 171 \text{ V}$

(a) Resistance and reactance of the coil

$$Z_{\text{coil}} = \frac{V_{\text{coil}}}{I} = \frac{171}{3} = 57 \, \Omega$$

$$\sqrt{r^2 + X_L^2} = 57$$

$$r^2 + X_L^2 = 3249$$

$$Z = \frac{V}{I} = \frac{240}{3} = 80 \, \Omega$$

$$\mathbf{Z} = Z\angle\phi = 80\angle 37° = 63.89 + j48.15 \, \Omega$$

But $$\mathbf{Z} = (R + r) + jX_L$$

$$X_L = 48.15 \, \Omega$$

$$r^2 + X_L^2 = 3249$$

$$r^2 + (48.15)^2 = 3249$$

$$r^2 = 931.04$$

$$r = 30.51 \, \Omega$$

(b) Resistance of the resistor

$$R + r = 63.89$$

$$R + 30.51 = 63.89$$

$$R = 33.38\ \Omega$$

## EXAMPLE 3.32

*A choke coil and a resistor are connected in series across a 230 V, 50 Hz ac supply, as shown in Fig. 3.49. The circuit draws a current of 2 A at 0.866 lagging pf. The voltage drop across the resistor is 100 V. Calculate the power factor of the choke coil.*

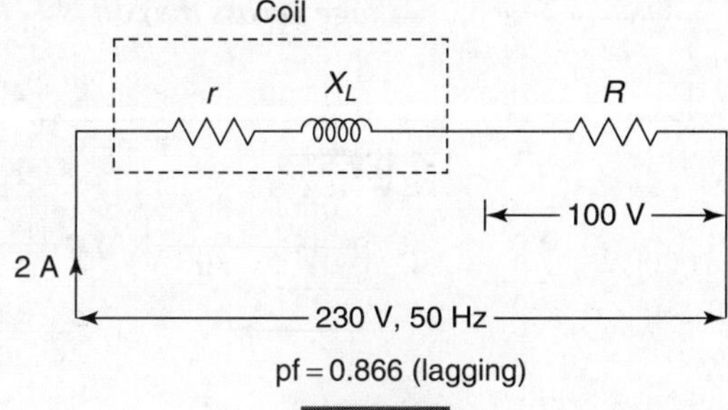


Fig. 3.49

**Solution** $V = 230$ V, $f = 50$ Hz, $I = 2$ A, pf = 0.866 (lagging), $V_R = 100$ V

$$R = \frac{V_R}{I} = \frac{100}{2} = 50\ \Omega$$

$$Z = \frac{V}{I} = \frac{230}{2} = 115\ \Omega$$

$$\text{pf} = 0.866 \text{ (lagging)}$$

$$\phi = \cos^{-1}(0.866) = 30°$$

$$\mathbf{Z} = Z\angle\phi = 115\angle 30° = 99.59 + j57.5\ \Omega$$

$$R + r = 99.59$$

$$50 + r = 99.59$$

$$r = 49.59\ \Omega$$

$$X_L = 57.5\ \Omega$$

$$Z_{\text{coil}} = \sqrt{r^2 + X_L^2} = \sqrt{(49.59)^2 + (57.5)^2} = 75.93\ \Omega$$

$$\text{pf}_{\text{coil}} = \frac{r}{Z_{\text{coil}}} = \frac{49.59}{75.93} = 0.653 \text{ (lagging)}$$

## EXAMPLE 3.33

*A circuit consists of a pure resistor and coil in series, as shown in Fig. 3.50. Power dissipated in the resistor and in the coil are 1000 W and 250 W respectively. The voltage drops across the resistor and the coil are 200 V and 300 V respectively. Determine (a) value of pure resistance, (b) resistance and reactance of the coil, (c) combined resistance of the circuit, (d) combined impedance, and (e) supply voltage.*

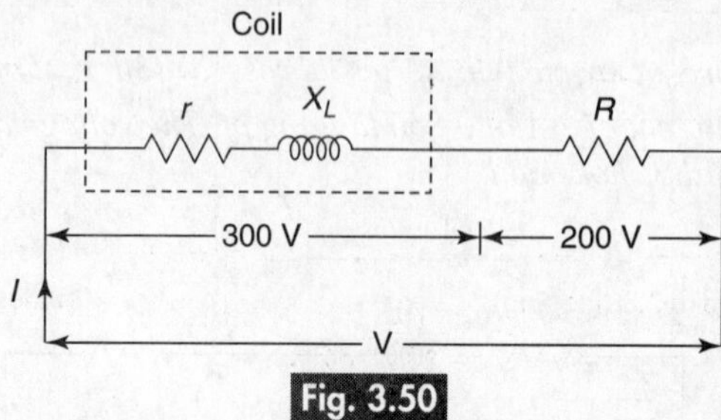


**Fig. 3.50**

**Solution** $P_R = 1000\text{ W},\quad P_{\text{coil}} = 250\text{ W},\quad V_R = 200\text{ V},\quad V_{\text{coil}} = 300\text{ V}$

(a) Value of pure resistance

$$P_R = \frac{V_R^2}{R}$$

$$1000 = \frac{(200)^2}{R}$$

$$R = 40\ \Omega$$

(b) Resistance and reactance of the coil

$$V_R = RI$$

$$200 = 40I$$

$$I = 5\text{A}$$

$$P_{\text{coil}} = I^2 r$$

$$250 = (5)^2 \times r$$

$$r = 10\ \Omega$$

$$Z_{\text{coil}} = \frac{V_{\text{coil}}}{I} = \frac{300}{5} = 60\ \Omega$$

$$X_L = \sqrt{Z_{\text{coil}}^2 - r^2} = \sqrt{(60)^2 - (10)^2} = 59.2\ \Omega$$

(c) Combined resistance of the circuit

$$R_T = R + r = 40 + 10 = 50\ \Omega$$

(d) Combined impedance

$$Z = \sqrt{(R+r)^2 + X_L^2} = \sqrt{(50)^2 + (59.2)^2} = 77.5\ \Omega$$

(e) Supply voltage

$$V = ZI = 77.5 \times 5 = 387.5\text{ V}$$

## EXAMPLE 3.34

*In the circuits of Fig. 3.51, a coil A takes 2 A at a power factor of 0.8 lagging with an applied p.d. of 10 V. A second coil B takes 2 A with a power of 0.7 lagging with an applied voltage of 5 V. What voltage will be required to produce a total current of 2 A with coils A and B in series? Find the power factor in this case.*

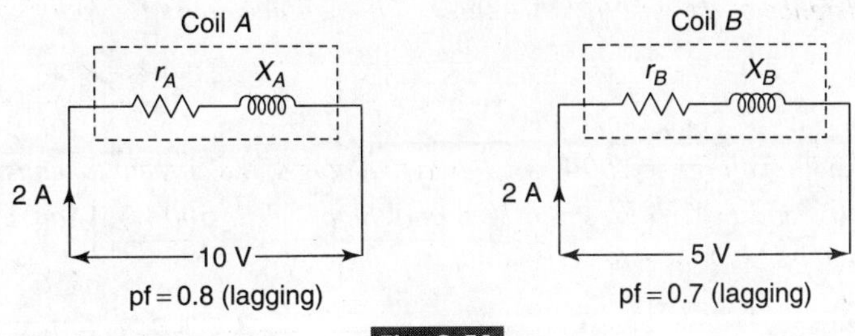


Fig. 3.51

**Solution**

| | | | |
|---|---|---|---|
| Coil *A*: | $I_A = 2$ A, | $\text{pf}_A = 0.8$ (lagging), | $V_A = 10$ V |
| Coil *B*: | $I_B = 2$ A, | $\text{pf}_B = 0.7$ (lagging), | $V_B = 5$ V |

For Coil *A*,

$$\phi_A = \cos^{-1}(0.8) = 36.87°$$

$$Z_A = \frac{V_A}{I_A} = \frac{10}{2} = 5\ \Omega$$

$$\mathbf{Z}_A = Z_A \angle\phi_A = 5\angle 36.87° = 4 + j3\ \Omega$$

$$r_A = 4\ \Omega$$

$$X_A = 3\ \Omega$$

For Coil *B*,

$$\phi_B = \cos^{-1}(0.7) = 45.57°$$

$$Z_B = \frac{V_B}{I_B} = \frac{5}{2} = 2.5\ \Omega$$

$$\mathbf{Z}_B = Z_B \angle\phi_B = 2.5\angle 45.57° = 1.75 + j1.78\ \Omega$$

$$r_B = 1.75\ \Omega$$

$$X_B = 1.78\ \Omega$$

When coils *A* and *B* are connected in series, as shown in Fig. 3.52,

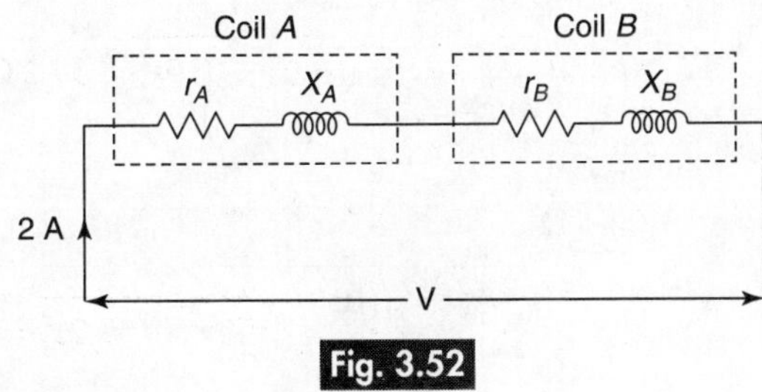


Fig. 3.52

$$\mathbf{Z} = r_A + jX_A + r_B + jX_B = 4 + j3 + 1.75 + j1.78 = 5.75 + j4.78 = 7.48\angle 39.74°\ \Omega$$
$$Z = 7.48\ \Omega$$
$$\phi = 39.74°$$
$$V = ZI = 7.48 \times 2 = 14.96\ \text{V}$$
$$\text{pf} = \cos\phi = \cos(39.74°) = 0.77\ \text{(lagging)}$$

## EXAMPLE 3.35

*In the circuits of Fig. 3.53, a voltage of 100 V is applied to a coil A, the current taken is 8 A and the power is 120 W. When applied to a coil B, the current is 10 A and the power is 500 W. What current and power will be taken when 100 V is applied to the two coils connected in series?*

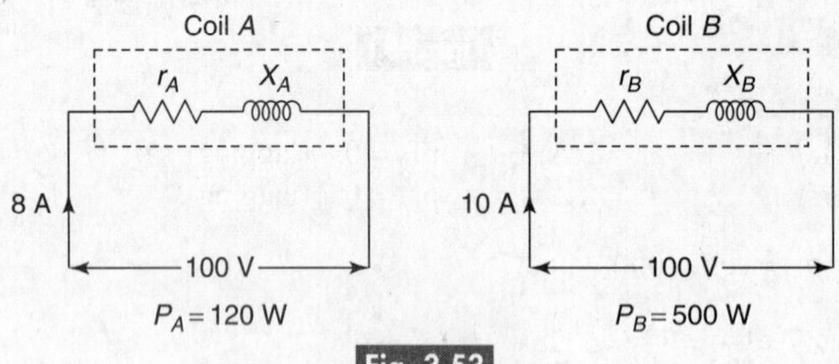


Fig. 3.53

**Solution**

Coil $A$: $V_A = 100$ V, $I_A = 8$ A, $P_A = 120$ W
Coil $B$: $V_B = 100$ V, $I_B = 10$ A, $P_B = 500$ W

For Coil $A$,
$$Z_A = \frac{V_A}{I_A} = \frac{100}{8} = 12.5\ \Omega$$
$$P_A = I_A^2 r_A$$
$$120 = (8)^2 \times r_A$$
$$r_A = 1.875\ \Omega$$
$$X_A = \sqrt{Z_A^2 - r_A^2} = \sqrt{(12.5)^2 - (1.875)^2} = 12.36\ \Omega$$

For Coil $B$,
$$Z_B = \frac{V_B}{I_B} = \frac{100}{10} = 10\ \Omega$$
$$P_B = I_B^2 r_B$$
$$500 = (10)^2 \times r_B$$
$$r_B = 5\ \Omega$$
$$X_B = \sqrt{Z_B^2 - r_B^2} = \sqrt{(10)^2 - (5)^2} = 8.66\ \Omega$$

When coils $A$ and $B$ are connected in series, as shown in Fig. 3.54,

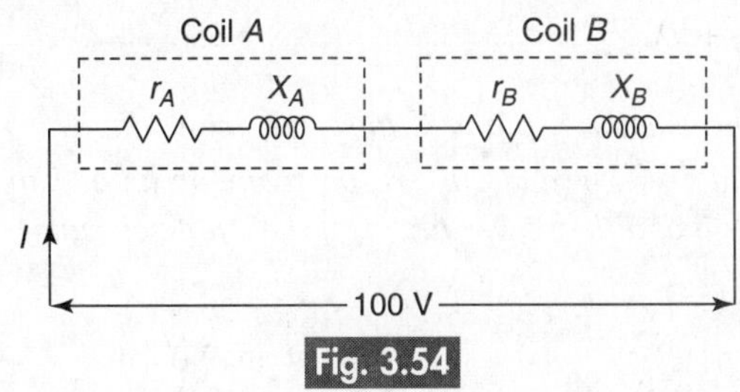


Fig. 3.54

$$\mathbf{Z} = r_A + jX_A + r_B + jX_B = 1.875 + j12.36 + 5 + j8.66 = 6.875 + j21.02 = 22.11\angle 71.89^\circ\ \Omega$$

$$Z = 22.11\ \Omega$$

$$\phi = 71.89^\circ$$

$$I = \frac{V}{Z} = \frac{100}{22.11} = 4.52\ \text{A}$$

$$P = I^2(r_A + r_B) = (4.52)^2 \times (6.875) = 140.64\ \text{W}$$

## EXAMPLE 3.36

*In a particular circuit, a voltage of 10 V at 25 Hz produces 100 mA, while the same voltage at 75 Hz produces 60 mA. Find the values of components of the circuit.*

**Solution** $V_1 = 10$ V, $f_1 = 25$ Hz, $I_1 = 100$ mA

$V_2 = 10$ V, $f_2 = 75$ Hz, $I_2 = 60$ mA

***Case (a)***

$$Z_1 = \frac{V_1}{I_1} = \frac{100}{100\times 10^{-3}} = 100\ \Omega$$

***Case (b)***

$$Z_2 = \frac{V_2}{I_2} = \frac{10}{60\times 10^{-3}} = 166.67\ \Omega$$

As frequency increases, impedance of the circuit increases. In a series *RL* circuit, inductive reactance $X_L$ increases with frequency. Hence, impedance increases. The circuit consists of a resistance *R* and an inductance *L*.

$$Z_1 = \sqrt{R^2 + X_{L_1}^2} = \sqrt{R^2 + (2\pi \times 25 \times L)^2} = 100\ \Omega$$

$$R^2 + (50\pi L)^2 = 10000 \qquad \text{...(i)}$$

$$Z_2 = \sqrt{R^2 + X_{L_2}^2} = \sqrt{R^2 + (2\pi \times 75 \times L)^2} = 166.67\ \Omega$$

$$R^2 + (150\pi L)^2 = 27778.89 \qquad \text{...(ii)}$$

Solving Eqs (i) and (ii),

$$R = 88.1\ \Omega$$

$$L = 0.3\ \text{H}$$

**EXAMPLE 3.37**

*When 1 A is passed through three coils A, B and C in series, the voltages across them are 6 V, 3 V and 8 V respectively on a dc supply and 7 V, 5 V and 10 V respectively on an ac supply. Find the power factor and the power dissipated in each coil and the power factor of the whole circuit.*

**Solution**

$I = 1$ A

On dc supply, $V_A = 6$ V, $V_B = 3$ V, $V_C = 8$ V

On dc supply, $V_A = 7$ V, $V_B = 5$ V, $V_C = 10$ V

For dc supply, $f = 0$

$$X_L = 2\pi f L = 0$$

The coils behave like pure resistors.

$$R_A = \frac{V_A}{I} = \frac{6}{1} = 6\ \Omega$$

$$R_B = \frac{V_B}{I} = \frac{3}{1} = 3\ \Omega$$

$$R_C = \frac{V_C}{I} = \frac{8}{1} = 8\ \Omega$$

For ac supply,

$$Z_A = \frac{V_A}{I} = \frac{7}{1} = 7\ \Omega$$

$$Z_B = \frac{V_B}{I} = \frac{5}{1} = 5\ \Omega$$

$$Z_C = \frac{V_C}{I} = \frac{10}{1} = 10\ \Omega$$

$$X_A = \sqrt{Z_A^2 - R_A^2} = \sqrt{(7)^2 - (6)^2} = 3.6\ \Omega$$

$$X_B = \sqrt{Z_B^2 - R_B^2} = \sqrt{(5)^2 - (3)^2} = 4\ \Omega$$

$$X_C = \sqrt{Z_C^2 - R_C^2} = \sqrt{(10)^2 - (8)^2} = 6\ \Omega$$

(a) Power factor of Coil *A*

$$\text{pf}_A = \frac{R_A}{Z_A} = \frac{6}{7} = 0.857 \text{ (lagging)}$$

(b) Power factor of Coil *B*

$$\text{pf}_B = \frac{R_B}{Z_B} = \frac{3}{5} = 0.6 \text{ (lagging)}$$

(c) Power factor of Coil *C*

$$\text{pf}_C = \frac{R_C}{Z_C} = \frac{8}{10} = 0.8 \text{ (lagging)}$$

(d) Power dissipated in Coil *A*

$$P_A = I^2 R_A = (1)^2 \times 6 = 6\text{ W}$$

(e) Power dissipated in Coil *B*

$$P_B = I^2 R_B = (1)^2 \times 3 = 3\,\text{W}$$

(f) Power dissipated in Coil *C*

$$P_C = I^2 R_C = (1)^2 \times 8 = 8\,\text{W}$$

(g) Power factor of the whole circuit

$$\mathbf{Z} = R_A + jX_A + R_B + jX_B + R_C + jX_C = 6 + j3.6 + 3 + j4 + 8 + j6 = 17 + j13.6 = 21.77\angle 38.68°\ \Omega$$

$$\text{pf}_T = \cos(38.68°) = 0.78 \text{ (lagging)}$$

## 3.11 SERIES *RC* CIRCUIT

LO 3.7

Figure 3.55 shows a pure resistor *R* connected in series with a pure capacitor *C* across an alternating voltage $v = V_m \sin \omega t$.

Let *V* and *I* be the rms values of applied voltage and current.

Potential difference across the resistor = $V_R = RI$

Potential difference across the capacitor = $V_C = X_C I$

The voltage $\mathbf{V}_R$ is in phase with the current **I** whereas voltage $\mathbf{V}_C$ lags behind the current **I** by 90°.

$$\mathbf{V} = \mathbf{V}_R + \mathbf{V}_C$$

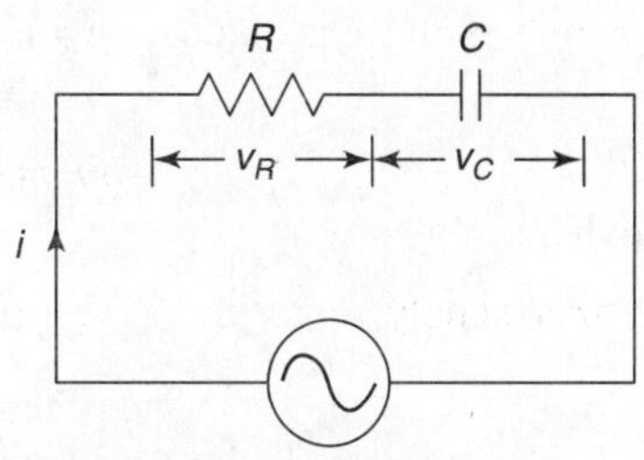


Fig. 3.55 *Series RC circuit*

**1. *Phasor Diagram*** Since the same current flows through *R* and *C*, the current *I* is taken as a reference phasor. Figure 3.56 shows the phasor diagram of series *RC* circuit.

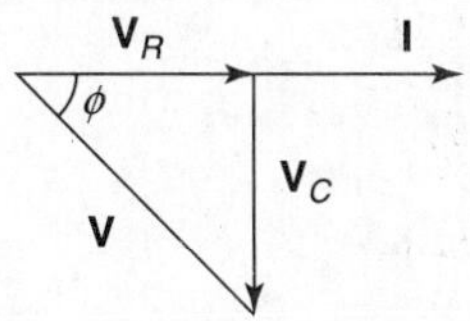


(a) Phasor diagram

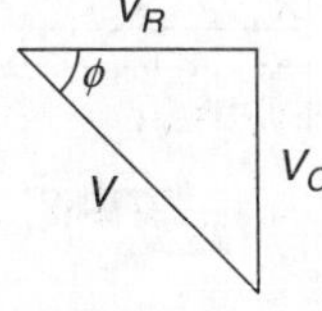


(b) Voltage triangle

$$\cos\phi = \frac{V_R}{V}$$

Fig. 3.56

**2. *Impedance***

$$\mathbf{V} = \mathbf{V}_R + \mathbf{V}_C = R\mathbf{I} - jX_C\mathbf{I} = (R - jX_C)\mathbf{I}$$

$$\frac{\mathbf{V}}{\mathbf{I}} = R - jX_C = \mathbf{Z}$$

$$\mathbf{Z} = Z\angle -\phi$$

$$Z = \sqrt{R^2 + X_C^2} = \sqrt{R^2 + \frac{1}{\omega^2 C^2}}$$

$$\phi = \tan^{-1}\left(\frac{X_C}{R}\right) = \tan^{-1}\left(\frac{1}{\omega RC}\right)$$

The quantity **Z** is called the *complex impedance* of the series *RC* circuit.

**3. *Impedance Triangle*** Figure 3.57 shows the impedance triangle of series *RC* circuit.

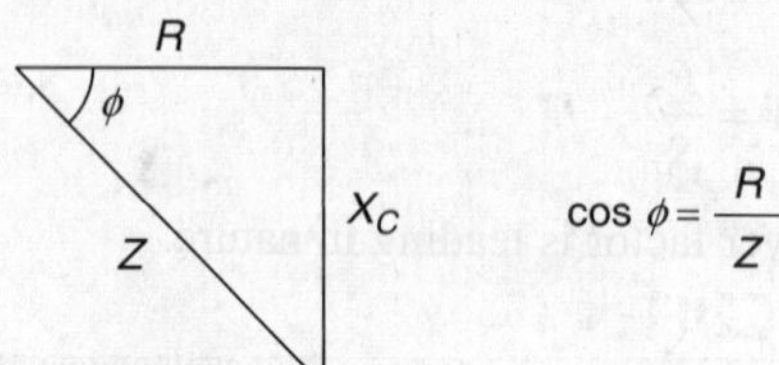


**Fig. 3.57** *Impedance triangle*

**4. *Current*** From the phasor diagram, it is clear that the current *I* leads the voltage *V* by an angle $\phi$. If the applied voltage is given by $v = V_m \sin \omega t$ then the current equation will be

$$i = I_m \sin(\omega t + \phi)$$

where
$$I_m = \frac{V_m}{Z}$$

and
$$\phi = \tan^{-1}\left(\frac{X_C}{R}\right) = \tan^{-1}\left(\frac{1}{\omega RC}\right)$$

**5. *Waveforms*** Figure 3.58 shows the voltage and current waveforms.

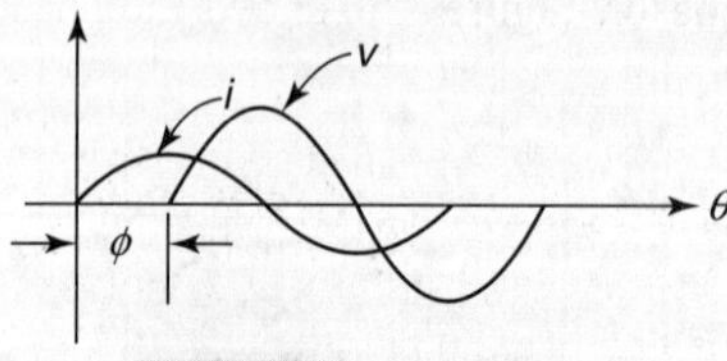


**Fig. 3.58** *Waveforms*

**6. *Power***

Active power $P = VI\cos\phi = I^2 R$

Reactive power $Q = VI\sin\phi = I^2 X_C$

Apparent power $S = VI = I^2 Z$

**7. *Power Triangle*** Figure 3.59 shows the power triangle of series *RC* circuit.

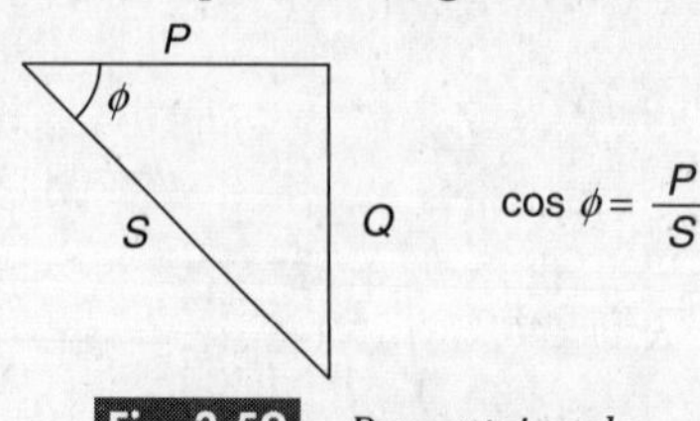


**Fig. 3.59** *Power triangle*

**8. *Power Factor*** It is defined as the cosine of the angle between voltage and current phasors.

$$\text{pf} = \cos\phi$$

From voltage triangle, $\text{pf} = \dfrac{V_R}{V}$

From impedance triangle $\text{pf} = \dfrac{R}{Z}$

From power triangle, $\text{pf} = \dfrac{P}{S}$

In case of series $RC$ circuit, the power factor is leading in nature.

## EXAMPLE 3.38

*The voltage applied to a circuit is $e = 100 \sin(\omega t + 30°)$ and the current flowing in the circuit is $i = 15 \sin(\omega t + 60°)$. Determine impedance, resistance, reactance, power factor and power.*

**Solution**

(a) Impedance

$$e = 100\sin(\omega t + 30°), \quad i = 15\sin(\omega t + 60°)$$

$$\mathbf{E} = \frac{100}{\sqrt{2}}\angle 30° \text{ V}$$

$$\mathbf{I} = \frac{15}{\sqrt{2}}\angle 60° \text{ A}$$

$$\mathbf{I} = \frac{\mathbf{E}}{\mathbf{I}} = \frac{\frac{100}{\sqrt{2}}\angle 30°}{\frac{15}{\sqrt{2}}\angle 60°} = 6.67\angle -30° = 5.77 - j3.33 = R - jX_C$$

$$Z = 6.67\ \Omega$$

(b) Resistance

$$R = 5.77\ \Omega$$

(c) Reactance

$$X_C = 3.33\ \Omega$$

(d) Power factor

$$\text{pf} = \cos\phi = \cos(30)° = 0.866 \text{ (leading)}$$

(e) Power

$$P = EI\cos\phi = \frac{100}{\sqrt{2}} \times \frac{15}{\sqrt{2}} \times 0.866 = 649.5\text{ W}$$

## EXAMPLE 3.39

*A series circuit consumes 2000 W at 0.5 leading power factor, when connected to 230 V, 50 Hz ac supply. Calculate (a) current, (b) kVA, and (c) kVAR.*

**Solution** $P = 2000$ W, $\text{pf} = 0.5$ (leading), $V = 230$ V

(a) Current

$$P = VI\cos\phi$$
$$2000 = 230 \times I \times 0.5$$
$$I = 17.39\text{ A}$$

(b) Apparent power

$$S = VI = \frac{P}{\cos\phi} = \frac{2000}{0.5} = 4\text{kVA}$$

(c) Reactive power

$$\phi = \cos^{-1}(0.5) = 60°$$
$$Q = VI\sin\phi = 230 \times 17.39 \times \sin(60°) = 3.464\text{ kVAR}$$

## EXAMPLE 3.40

*A resistor R in series with a capacitor C is connected to a 240 V, 50 Hz ac supply. Find the value of C so that R absorbs 300 W at 100 V. Find also the maximum charge and maximum stored energy in C.*

**Solution** $V = 240$ V, $f = 50$ Hz, $P = 300$ W, $V_R = 100$ V

(a) Value of $C$

$$P = \frac{V_R^2}{R}$$
$$300 = \frac{(100)^2}{R}$$
$$R = 33.33\ \Omega$$
$$P = I^2R$$
$$300 = I^2 \times 33.33$$
$$I = 3\text{A}$$
$$Z = \frac{V}{I} = \frac{240}{3} = 80\ \Omega$$
$$X_C = \sqrt{Z^2 - R^2} = \sqrt{(80)^2 - (33.33)^2} = 72.72\ \Omega$$
$$X_C = \frac{1}{2\pi fC}$$
$$72.72 = \frac{1}{2\pi \times 50 \times C}$$
$$C = 43.77\mu\text{F}$$

(b) Maximum charge

$$V_C = \sqrt{V^2 - V_R^2} = \sqrt{(240)^2 - (100)^2} = 218.17\text{ V}$$
$$V_{C\max} = 218.17 \times \sqrt{2} = 308.54\text{ V}$$
$$Q_{\max} = CV_{C\max} = 43.77 \times 10^{-6} \times 308.54 = 0.0135\text{ C}$$

(c) Maximum stored energy

$$E_{max} = \frac{1}{2} C\,(V_{Cmax})^2 = \frac{1}{2} \times 43.77 \times 10^{-6} \times (308.54)^2 = 2.08 \text{ J}$$

## EXAMPLE 3.41

*A capacitor of 35 μF is connected in series with a variable resistor. The circuit is connected across 50 Hz mains. Find the value of the resistor for a condition when the voltage across the capacitor is half the supply voltage.*

**Solution**

$$C = 35\ \mu\text{F}, \quad f = 50 \text{ Hz}, \quad V_C = \frac{1}{2}\text{V}$$

$$X_C = \frac{1}{2\pi fC} = \frac{1}{2\pi \times 50 \times 35 \times 10^{-6}} = 90.946\ \Omega$$

$$V_C = \frac{1}{2}\text{V}$$

$$X_C I = \frac{1}{2} ZI$$

$$X_C = \frac{1}{2} Z$$

$$Z = 2X_C$$

$$Z = \sqrt{R^2 + X_C^2}$$

$$(2X_C)^2 = R^2 + X_C^2$$

$$R^2 = 3X_C^2 = 3 \times (90.946)^2 = 24813.35$$

$$R = 157.5\ \Omega$$

## EXAMPLE 3.42

*A voltage of 125 V at 50 Hz is applied across a non-inductive resistor connected in series with a capacitor. The current is 2.2 A. The power loss in the resistor is 96.8 W. Calculate the resistance and capacitance.*

**Solution**

$$V = 125 \text{ V}, \quad f = 50 \text{ Hz}, \quad I = 2.2 \text{ A}, \quad P = 96.8 \text{ W}$$

(a) Resistance

$$Z = \frac{V}{I} = \frac{125}{2.2} = 56.82 \text{ A}$$

$$P = I^2 R$$

$$96.8 = (2.2)^2 \times R$$

$$R = 20\ \Omega$$

(b) Capacitance

$$X_C = \sqrt{Z^2 - R^2} = \sqrt{(56.82)^2 - (20)^2} = 53.18\ \Omega$$

$$X_C = \frac{1}{2\pi fC}$$

$$53.18 = \frac{1}{2\pi \times 50 \times C}$$

$$C = 59.85\ \mu\text{F}$$

**EXAMPLE 3.43**

*A resistor and a capacitor are connected across a 250 V supply. When the supply frequency is 50 Hz, the current drawn is 5 A. When the frequency is increased to 60 Hz, it draws 5.8 A. Find the values of R and C and the power drawn in the second case.*

**Solution** $V = 250$ V, $f_1 = 50$ Hz, $I_1 = 5$ A, $f_2 = 60$ Hz, $I_2 = 5.8$ A

(a) Values of $R$ and $C$

For $f_1 = 50$ Hz,

$$Z_1 = \frac{V}{I_1} = \frac{250}{5} = 50\ \Omega$$

$$Z_1 = \sqrt{R^2 + \left(\frac{1}{2\pi f_1 C}\right)^2} = \sqrt{R^2 + \left(\frac{1}{100\pi C}\right)^2}$$

$$R^2 + \left(\frac{1}{100\pi C}\right)^2 = 2500 \qquad \text{...(i)}$$

For $f_2 = 60$ Hz,

$$Z_2 = \frac{V}{I_2} = \frac{250}{5.8} = 43.1\ \Omega$$

$$Z_2 = \sqrt{R^2 + \left(\frac{1}{2\pi f_2 C}\right)^2} = \sqrt{R^2 + \left(\frac{1}{120\pi C}\right)^2}$$

$$R^2 + \left(\frac{1}{120\pi C}\right)^2 = 1857.9\ \Omega \qquad \text{...(ii)}$$

Solving Eqs (i) and (ii),

$$R = 19.96\ \Omega$$

$$C = 69.4\ \mu\text{F}$$

(b) Power drawn in the second case

$$P_2 = I_2^2 R = (5.8)^2 \times 19.96 = 671.45\ \text{W}$$

**TABLE 3.1 Table showing various relationships for *R*, *L*, and *C***

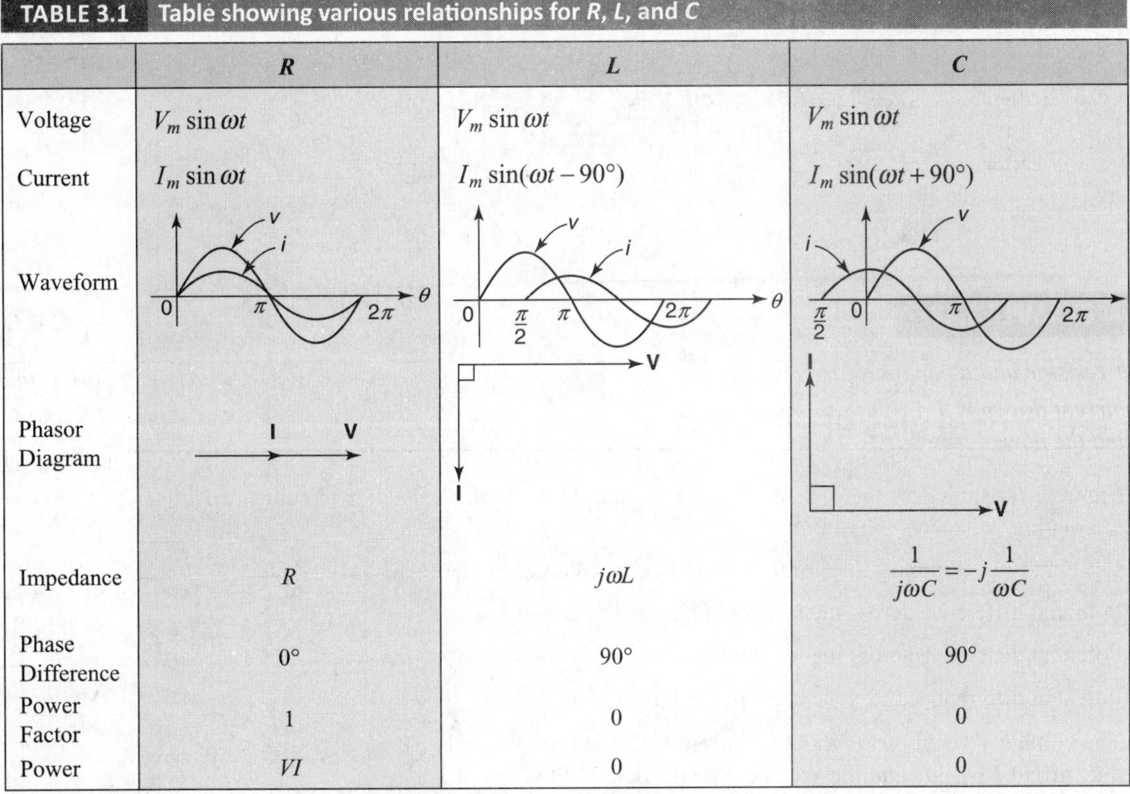

| | *R* | *L* | *C* |
|---|---|---|---|
| Voltage | $V_m \sin \omega t$ | $V_m \sin \omega t$ | $V_m \sin \omega t$ |
| Current | $I_m \sin \omega t$ | $I_m \sin(\omega t - 90°)$ | $I_m \sin(\omega t + 90°)$ |
| Waveform | | | |
| Phasor Diagram | | | |
| Impedance | $R$ | $j\omega L$ | $\frac{1}{j\omega C} = -j\frac{1}{\omega C}$ |
| Phase Difference | 0° | 90° | 90° |
| Power Factor | 1 | 0 | 0 |
| Power | $VI$ | 0 | 0 |

**TABLE 3.2 Table showing various relationships for series *RL* and series *RC* circuits**

| | *Series RL Circuit* | *Series RC Circuit* |
|---|---|---|
| Voltage | $V_m \sin \omega t$ | $V_m \sin \omega t$ |
| Current | $I_m \sin(\omega t - \phi)$ | $I_m \sin(\omega t + \phi)$ |
| Waveform | | |
| Phasor Diagram | | |

(*Contd.*)

| | *Series RL Circuit* | *Series RC Circuit* |
|---|---|---|
| Impedance | $R + jX_L,\ \ Z\angle\phi$ | $R - jX_C, Z\angle -\phi$ |
| Phase Difference | $0° < \phi < 90°$ | $0° < \phi < 90°$ |
| Power Factor | $\frac{V_R}{V} = \frac{R}{Z} = \frac{P}{S}$ | $\frac{V_R}{V} = \frac{R}{Z} = \frac{P}{S}$ |
| Power | $P = VI\cos\phi = I^2R$<br>$Q = VI\sin\phi = I^2X_L$<br>$S = VI = I^2Z$ | $P = VI\cos\phi = I^2R$<br>$Q = VI\sin\phi = I^2X_C$<br>$S = VI = I^2Z$ |

## 3.12 SERIES *RLC* CIRCUIT

LO 3.7

Figure 3.60 shows a pure resistor $R$, pure inductor $L$ and pure capacitor $C$ connected in series across an alternating voltage $v = V_m \sin \omega t$.

Let $V$ and $I$ be the rms values of the applied voltage and current.

Potential difference across the resistor $= V_R = R\,I$

Potential difference across the inductor $= V_L = X_L I$

Potential difference across the capacitor $= V_C = X_C I$

The voltage $\mathbf{V}_R$ is in phase with the current $\mathbf{I}$, the voltage $\mathbf{V}_L$ leads the current $\mathbf{I}$ by 90° and the voltage $\mathbf{V}_C$ lags behind the current $\mathbf{I}$ by 90°.

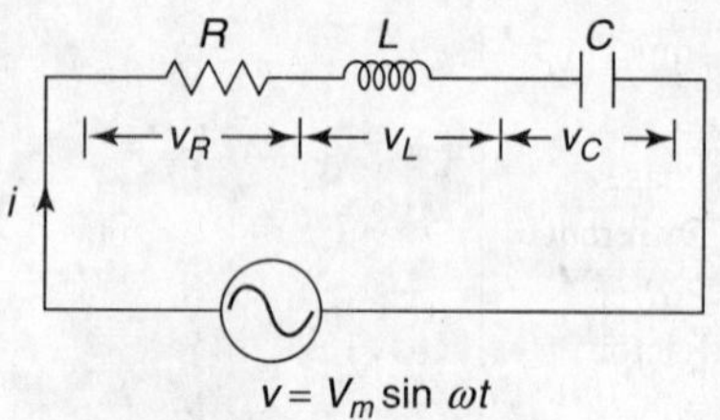


**Fig. 3.60** *Series RLC circuit*

$$\mathbf{V} = \mathbf{V}_R + \mathbf{V}_L + \mathbf{V}_C$$

***1. Phasor Diagram*** Since the same current flows through $R$, $L$ and $C$, the current $I$ is taken as a reference phasor.

***Case (i)*** $X_L > X_C$ (Fig. 3.61)

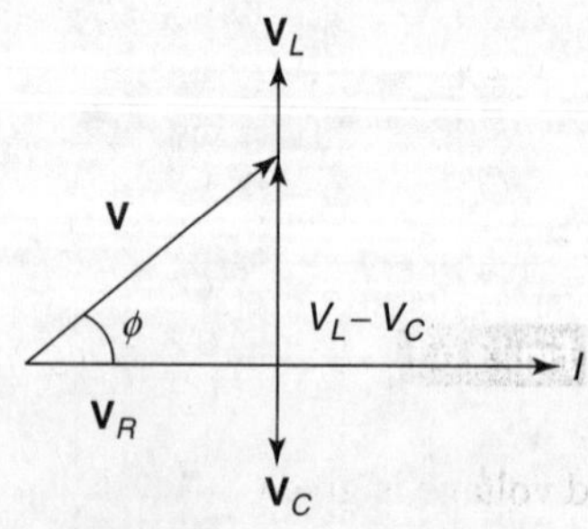


**Fig. 3.61** *Phasor diagram*

The reactance $X$ will be inductive in nature and the circuit will behave like a series $RL$ circuit.

***Case (ii)*** $X_C > X_L$ (Fig. 3.62)

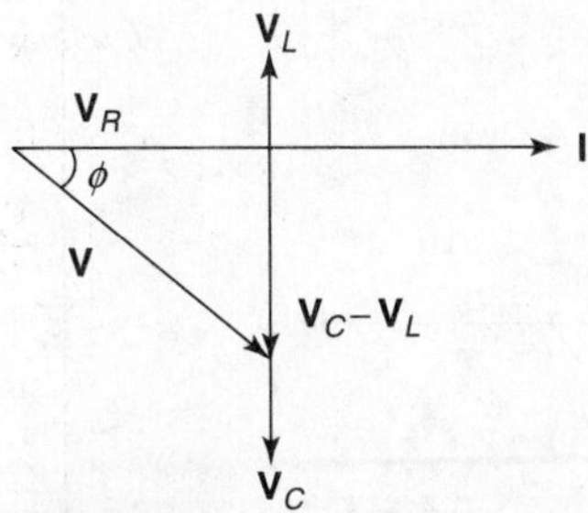


**Fig. 3.62** *Phasor diagram*

The reactance $X$ will be capacitive in nature and the circuit will behave like a series $RC$ circuit.

### 2. Impedance

$$\mathbf{V} = \mathbf{V}_R + \mathbf{V}_L + \mathbf{V}_C = R\mathbf{I} + jX_L I - jX_C \mathbf{I} = [R + j(X_L - X_C)]\mathbf{I}$$

$$\frac{\mathbf{V}}{\mathbf{I}} = R + j(X_L - X_C) = \mathbf{Z}$$

$$\mathbf{Z} = Z\angle\phi$$

$$Z = \sqrt{R^2 + (X_L - X_C)^2}$$

$$\phi = \tan^{-1}\left(\frac{X_L - X_C}{R}\right)$$

**3. Impedance Triangles** Figure 3.63 shows the impedance triangles of series $RLC$ circuit for two cases.

***Case (i)*** $X_L > X_C$ ***Case (ii)*** $X_C > X_L$

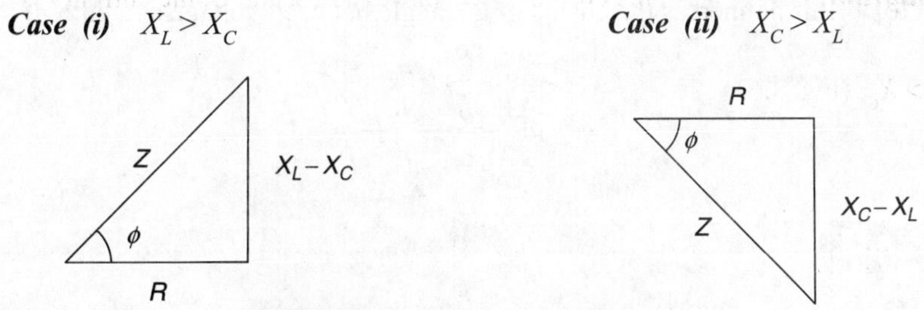


**Fig. 3.63** *Impedance triangles*

**4. Current Equation** If the applied voltage is given by $v = V_m \sin \omega t$ then current equation will be

$$i = I_m \sin(\omega t \pm \phi)$$

'–' sign is used when $X_L > X_C$.

'+' sign is used when $X_C > X_L$.

**5. Waveforms** Figure 3.64 shows the voltage and current waveforms.

***Case (i)*** $X_L > X_C$ ***Case (ii)*** $X_C > X_L$

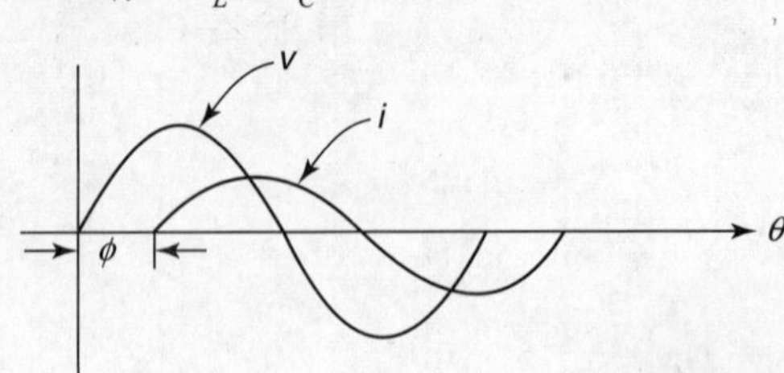


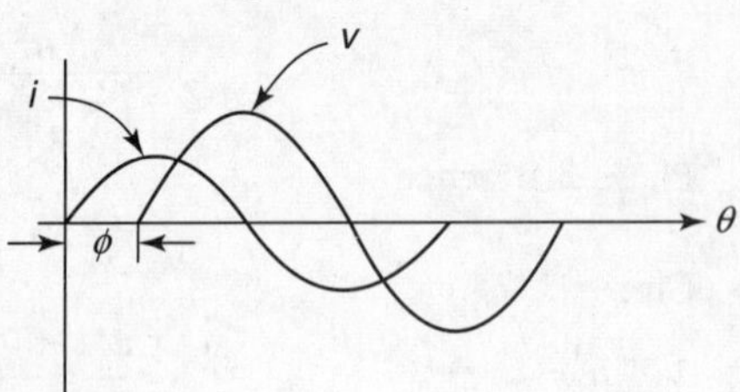


**Fig. 3.64** *Waveforms*

**6. Power**

Average power $P = VI\cos\phi = I^2R$

Reactive power $Q = VI\sin\phi = I^2X$

Apparent power $S = VI = I^2Z$

**7. Power Triangles** Figure 3.65 shows the power triangles of series *RLC* circuit.

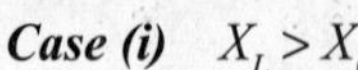

***Case (i)*** $X_L > X_C$ ***Case (ii)*** $X_C > X_L$

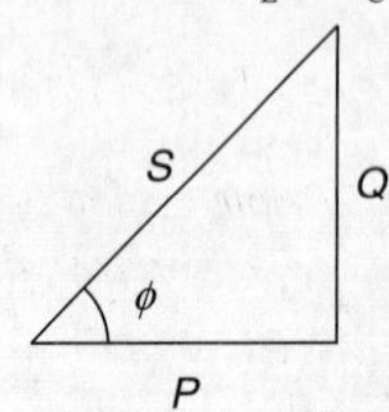


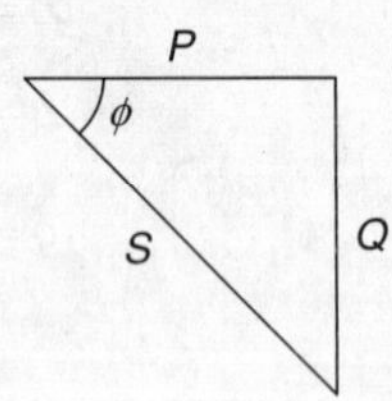


**Fig. 3.65** *Power triangles*

**8. Power Factor** It is defined as the cosine of the angle between voltage and current phasors.

$$\text{pf} = \cos\phi$$

$$\text{pf} = \frac{V_R}{V} = \frac{R}{Z} = \frac{P}{S}$$

**EXAMPLE 3.44**

*A resistor of 20 Ω, inductor of 0.05 H and a capacitor of 50 μF are connected in series, as shown in Fig. 3.66. A supply voltage 230 V, 50 Hz is connected across the series combination. Calculate the following: (a) impedance, (b) current drawn by the circuit, (c) phase difference and power factor, and (d) active and reactive power consumed by the circuit.*

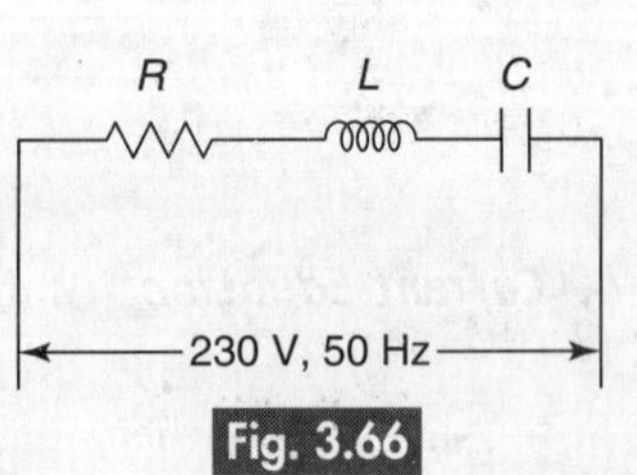


**Fig. 3.66**

**Solution** $R = 20\ \Omega,\quad L = 0.05\ \text{H},\quad C = 50\ \mu\text{F},\quad V = 230\ \text{V},\quad f = 50\ \text{Hz}$

(a) Impedance

$$X_L = 2\pi fL = 2\pi \times 50 \times 0.05 = 15.71\ \Omega$$

$$X_C = \frac{1}{2\pi fC} = \frac{1}{2\pi \times 50 \times 50 \times 10^{-6}} = 63.66\ \Omega$$

$$\mathbf{Z} = R + jX_L - jX_C = 20 + j15.71 - j63.66 = 51.95\ \angle{-67.36°}\ \Omega$$

$$Z = 51.95\ \Omega$$

(b) Phase difference

$$\phi = 67.36°$$

(c) Current

$$I = \frac{V}{Z} = \frac{230}{51.95} = 4.43\ \text{A}$$

(d) Power factor

$$\text{pf} = \cos\phi = \cos(67.36°) = 0.385\ \text{(leading)}$$

(e) Active power

$$P = VI\cos\phi = 230 \times 4.43 \times 0.385 = 392.28\ \text{W}$$

(f) Reactive power

$$Q = VI\sin\phi = 230 \times 4.43 \times \sin(67.36°) = 940.39\ \text{VAR}$$

## EXAMPLE 3.45

*A circuit consists of a pure resistor, a pure inductor, and a capacitor connected in series, as shown in Fig. 3.67. When the circuit is supplied with 100 V, 50 Hz supply, the voltages across inductor and resistor are 240 V and 90 V respectively. If the circuit takes a 10 A leading current, calculate (a) value of inductance, resistance and capacitance, (b) power factor of the circuit, and (c) voltage across the capacitor.*

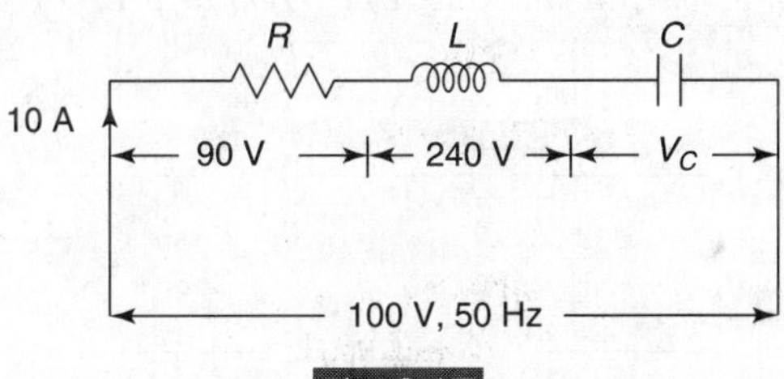


Fig. 3.67

**Solution** $V = 100$ V, $f = 50$ Hz, $V_L = 240$ V, $V_R = 90$ V, $I = 10$ A

(a) Value of inductance, resistance and capacitance

$$R = \frac{V_R}{I} = \frac{90}{10} = 9\ \Omega$$

$$X_L = \frac{V_L}{I} = \frac{240}{10} = 24\ \Omega$$

$$Z = \frac{V}{I} = \frac{100}{10} = 10\ \Omega$$

$$\mathbf{Z} = R + jX_L - jX_C = R - j(X_C - X_L)$$

$$Z = \sqrt{R^2 + (X_C - X_L)^2}$$

$$10 = \sqrt{(9)^2 + (X_C - 24)^2}$$

$$X_C = 28.36\ \Omega$$

$$X_L = 2\pi fL$$

$$24 = 2\pi \times 50 \times L$$

$$L = 0.076\ H$$

$$X_C = \frac{1}{2\pi fC}$$

$$28.36 = \frac{1}{2\pi \times 50 \times C}$$

$$C = 112.24\ \mu\text{F}$$

(b) Power factor of the circuit

$$\text{pf} = \frac{R}{Z} = \frac{9}{10} = 0.9 \text{ (leading)}$$

(c) Voltage across the capacitor

$$V_C = X_C I = 28.36 \times 10 = 283.6 \text{ V}$$

**EXAMPLE 3.46**

*Two impedances $\mathbf{Z}_1 = 40\angle 30°\ \Omega$ and $\mathbf{Z}_2 = 30\angle 60°\ \Omega$ are connected in series across a single-phase 230 V, 50 Hz supply, as shown in Fig. 3.68. Calculate the (a) current drawn, (b) pf, and (c) power consumed by the circuit.*

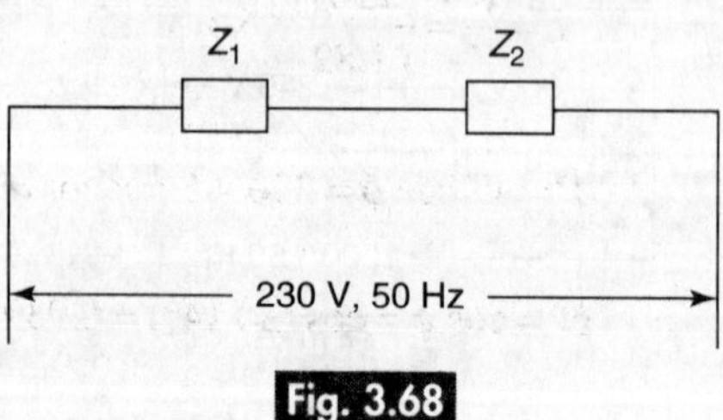


Fig. 3.68

**Solution** $\mathbf{Z}_1 = 40\angle 30°\ \Omega, \quad \mathbf{Z}_2 = 30\angle 60°\ \Omega, \quad V = 230$ V

(a) Current drawn

$$\mathbf{Z} = \mathbf{Z}_1 + \mathbf{Z}_2 = 40\ \angle 30° + 30\ \angle 60° = 67.66\ \angle 42.81°\ \Omega$$

$$I = \frac{V}{Z} = \frac{230}{67.66} = 3.4 \text{ A}$$

(b) Power factor

$$\text{pf} = \cos\phi = \cos(42.81°) = 0.734 \text{ (lagging)}$$

(c) Power consumed

$$P = VI\cos\phi = 230 \times 3.4 \times 0.734 = 573.99 \text{ W}$$

## EXAMPLE 3.47

*A circuit takes a current of 3 A at a power factor of 0.6 lagging when connected to 115 V, 50 Hz supply. Another circuit takes a current of 5 A at a power factor of 0.707 leading when connected to the same supply. If the two circuits are connected in series across a 230 V, 50 Hz supply, calculate (a) current, (b) power consumed, and (c) power factor.*

**Solution**

Circuit 1: $I_1 = 3$ A, $\text{pf}_1 = 0.6$ (lagging), $V_1 = 115$ V

Circuit 2: $I_2 = 5$ A, $\text{pf}_2 = 0.707$ (leading), $V_2 = 115$ V

$$V = 230 \text{ V}$$

For Circuit 1,

$$\phi_1 = \cos^{-1}(0.6) = 53.13°$$

$$Z_1 = \frac{V_1}{I_1} = \frac{115}{3} = 38.33\ \Omega$$

$$\mathbf{Z}_1 = Z_1 \angle \phi_1 = 38.33\angle 53.13°\ \Omega$$

For Circuit 2,

$$\phi_2 = \cos^{-1}(0.707) = 45°$$

$$Z_2 = \frac{V_2}{I_2} = \frac{115}{5} = 23\ \Omega$$

$$\mathbf{Z}_2 = Z_2 \angle \phi_2 = 23\angle -45°\ \Omega$$

When the two circuits are connected in series,

$$\mathbf{Z} = \mathbf{Z}_1 + \mathbf{Z}_2 = 38.33\angle 53.13° + 23\angle -45° = 41.82\angle 20.14°\ \Omega$$

(a) Current

$$I = \frac{V}{Z} = \frac{230}{41.82} = 5.5 \text{ A}$$

(b) Power consumed

$$P = VI\cos\phi = 230 \times 5.5 \times \cos(20.14°) = 1.187 \text{ kW}$$

(c) Power factor

$$\text{pf} = \cos\phi = \cos(20.14°) = 0.939 \text{ (lagging)}$$

## EXAMPLE 3.48

*Two impedances $Z_1$ and $Z_2$, having the same numerical value, are connected in series. If $Z_1$ has a pf of 0.866 lagging and $Z_2$ has a pf of 0.8 leading, calculate the pf of the series combination.*

**Solution**

$\text{pf}_1 = 0.866$ (lagging), $\text{pf}_2 = 0.8$ (leading), $Z_1 = Z_2 = Z$

$$\phi_1 = \cos^{-1}(0.866) = 30°$$

$$\phi_2 = \cos^{-1}(0.8) = 36.87°$$

$$\mathbf{Z}_1 = Z\angle \phi_1 = Z\angle 30° = 0.866\,Z + j0.5\,Z\ \Omega$$

$$\mathbf{Z}_2 = Z\angle -\phi_2 = Z\angle -36.87° = 0.8\,Z - j0.6\,Z\ \Omega$$

For a series combination,

$$\mathbf{Z} = \mathbf{Z}_1 + \mathbf{Z}_2 = 0.866\,Z + j0.5\,Z + 0.8\,Z - j0.6\,Z = 1.66\,Z - j0.1\,Z = Z(1.666 - j0.1) = 1.668\,Z\angle{-3.43^\circ}\ \Omega$$

$$\text{pf} = \cos(3.43^\circ) = 0.9982$$

## EXAMPLE 3.49

*A coil of 3 Ω resistance and an inductance of 0.22 H is connected in series with an imperfect capacitor, as shown in Fig. 3.69. When such a series circuit is connected across a 200 V, 50 Hz supply, it has been observed that their combined impedance is (3.8 + j6.4) Ω. Calculate the resistance and capacitance of the imperfect capacitor.*

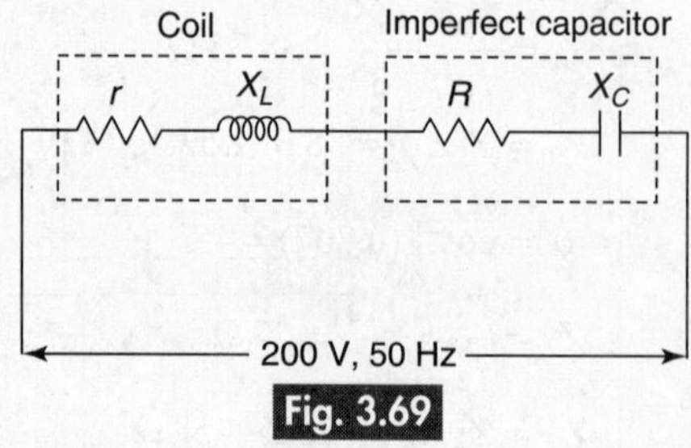


Fig. 3.69

**Solution** $r = 3\ \Omega,\quad L = 0.22\ \text{H},\quad V = 200\ \text{V},\quad f = 50\ \text{Hz},\quad Z = 3.8 + j6.4\ \Omega$

(a) Resistance of the imperfect capacitor

$$\mathbf{Z} = 3.8 + j6.4\ \Omega$$

$$X_L = 2\pi fL = 2\pi \times 50 \times 0.22 = 69.12\ \Omega$$

$$\mathbf{Z} = 3 + j69.12 + R - jX_C = (3 + R) + j(69.12 - X_C)$$

$$3 + R = 3.8$$

$$R = 0.8\ \Omega$$

(b) Capacitance of the imperfect capacitor

$$69.12 - X_C = 6.4$$

$$X_C = 62.72\ \Omega$$

$$X_C = \frac{1}{2\pi fC}$$

$$62.72 = \frac{1}{2\pi \times 50 \times C}$$

$$C = 50.75\ \mu\text{F}$$

## EXAMPLE 3.50

*An RLC series circuit has a current which lags the applied voltage by 45°. The voltage across the inductance has a maximum value equal to twice the maximum value of voltage across the capacitor. Voltage across the inductance is 300 sin (1000t) and R = 20 Ω. Find the value of inductance and capacitance.*

**Solution** $\phi = 45°, \quad v_L = 300 \sin(1000t), \quad R = 20\ \Omega$

(a) Value of inductance

$$V_{L(\max)} = 2V_{C(\max)}$$
$$V_L = 2V_C$$
$$IX_L = 2I X_C$$
$$X_L = 2X_C$$
$$\cos\phi = \frac{R}{Z}$$
$$\cos(45°) = \frac{20}{Z}$$
$$Z = 28.28\ \Omega$$

For a series *RLC* circuit,

$$Z = \sqrt{R^2 + (X_L - X_C)^2}$$
$$28.28 = \sqrt{(20)^2 + (2X_C - X_C)^2} = \sqrt{400 + X_C^2}$$
$$X_C = 20\ \Omega$$
$$X_L = 2X_C = 40\ \Omega$$
$$X_L = \omega L$$
$$40 = 1000 \times L$$
$$L = 0.04\ \text{H}$$

(b) Value of capacitance

$$X_C = \frac{1}{\omega C}$$
$$20 = \frac{1}{1000 \times C}$$
$$C = 50\ \mu\text{F}$$

**EXAMPLE 3.51**

*A coil having a power factor of 0.5 is in series with a 79.57 μF capacitor and when connected across a 50 Hz supply, the p.d. across the coil is equal to the p.d. across the capacitor. Find the resistance and inductance of the coil.*

**Solution** $\text{pf}_{\text{coil}} = 0.5, \quad C = 79.57\ \mu\text{F}, \quad f = 50\ \text{Hz}, \quad V_{\text{coil}} = V_C$

(a) Resistance of the coil

$$X_C = \frac{1}{2\pi fC} = \frac{1}{2\pi \times 50 \times 79.57 \times 10^{-6}} = 40\ \Omega$$
$$V_{\text{coil}} = V_C$$
$$IZ_{\text{coil}} = IX_C$$

$$Z_{\text{coil}} = X_C = 40\ \Omega$$

$$\text{pf}_{\text{coil}} = \cos\phi = \frac{R}{Z_{\text{coil}}}$$

$$0.5 = \frac{R}{40}$$

$$R = 20\ \Omega$$

(b) Inductance of the coil

$$X_L = \sqrt{Z_{\text{coil}}^2 - R^2} = \sqrt{(40)^2 - (20)^2} = 34.64\ \Omega$$

$$X_L = 2\pi fL$$

$$34.64 = 2\pi \times 50 \times L$$

$$L = 0.11\ \text{H}$$

## EXAMPLE 3.52

*A 250 V, 50 Hz voltage is applied to a coil having a resistance of 5 Ω and an inductance of 9.55 H in series with a capacitor C. If the voltage across the coil is 300 V, find the value of C.*

**Solution**

$$V = 250\ \text{V},\quad f = 50\ \text{Hz},\quad R = 5\ \Omega,\quad L = 9.55\ \text{H},\quad V_{\text{coil}} = 300\ \text{V}$$

$$X_L = 2\pi fL = 2\pi \times 50 \times 9.55 = 3000\ \Omega$$

$$Z_{\text{coil}} = \sqrt{R^2 + X_L^2} = \sqrt{(5)^2 + (3000)^2} = 3000\ \Omega$$

$$I = \frac{V_{\text{coil}}}{Z_{\text{coil}}} = \frac{300}{3000} = 0.1\ \text{A}$$

$$Z = \frac{V}{I} = \frac{250}{0.1} = 2500\ \Omega$$

When $X_L > X_C$,

$$Z = \sqrt{R^2 + (X_L - X_C)^2}$$

$$2500 = \sqrt{(5)^2 + (3000 - X_C)^2}$$

$$X_C = 500\ \Omega$$

$$X_C = \frac{1}{2\pi fC}$$

$$500 = \frac{2}{2\pi \times 50 \times C}$$

$$C = 6.37\ \mu\text{F}$$

When $X_C > X_L$,

$$Z = \sqrt{R^2 + (X_C - X_L)^2}$$

$$2500 = \sqrt{(5)^2 + (X_C - 300)^2}$$

$$X_C = 5500\ \Omega$$

$$X_C = \frac{1}{2\pi fC}$$

$$5500 = \frac{1}{2\pi \times 50 \times C}$$
$$C = 0.58\ \mu\text{F}$$

## EXAMPLE 3.53

*Draw the phasor diagram for the series circuit shown in Fig. 3.70 when the current in the circuit is 2 A. Find the values of $V_1$ and $V_2$ and show these voltages on the phasor diagram.*

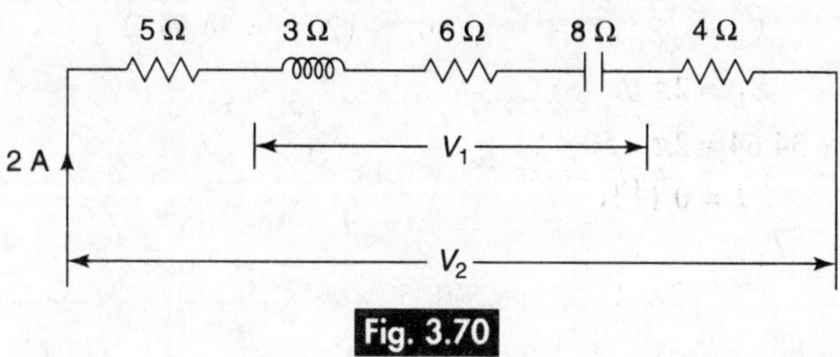


Fig. 3.70

**Solution**

$$\mathbf{Z}_1 = j3 + 6 - j8 = 6 - j5 = 7.81\ \angle{-39.8°}\ \Omega$$
$$\mathbf{Z}_2 = 5 + j3 + 6 - j8 + 4 = 15 - j5 = 15.81\ \angle{-18.43°}\ \Omega$$
$$I = 2\text{ A}$$

(a) Values of $V_1$ and $V_2$

Let
$$\mathbf{I} = 2\angle 0°\text{ A}$$
$$\mathbf{V}_1 = \mathbf{Z}_1\mathbf{I} = (7.81\ \angle{-39.8°})(2\ \angle 0°) = 15.62\ \angle{-39.8°}\text{ V}$$
$$\mathbf{V}_2 = \mathbf{Z}_2\mathbf{I} = (15.81\ \angle{-18.43°})(2\ \angle 0°) = 31.62\ \angle{-18.43°}\text{ V}$$

(b) Phasor diagram

The phasor diagram is shown in Fig. 3.71.

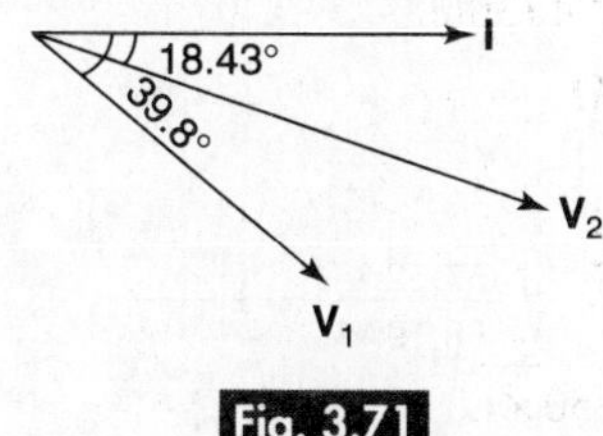


Fig. 3.71

## EXAMPLE 3.54

*Draw a vector diagram for the circuit shown in Fig. 3.72 indicating terminal voltages $V_1$ and $V_2$ and the current. Find the value of (a) current, (b) $V_1$ and $V_2$, and (c) power factor.*

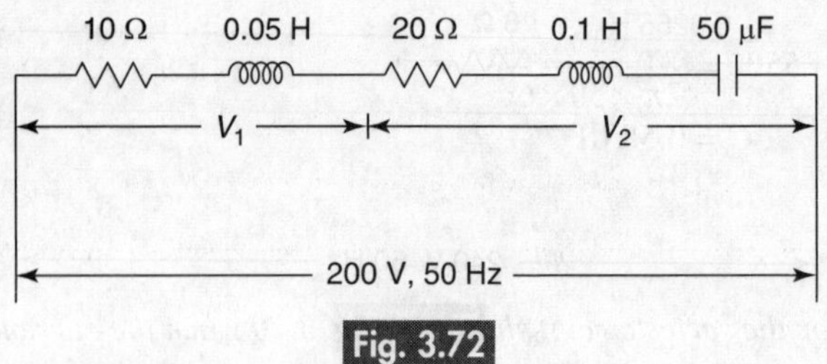

Fig. 3.72

**Solution**

(a) Current

$$X_{L_1} = 2\pi f L_1 = 2\pi \times 50 \times 0.05 = 15.71\ \Omega$$

$$X_{L_2} = 2\pi f L_2 = 2\pi \times 50 \times 0.1 = 31.42\ \Omega$$

$$X_C = \frac{1}{2\pi fC} = \frac{1}{2\pi \times 50 \times 50 \times 10^{-6}} = 63.66\ \Omega$$

$$\mathbf{Z} = 10 + j15.71 + 20 + j31.42 - j63.66 = 30 - j16.53 = 34.25\angle -28.85°\ \Omega$$

$$I = \frac{V}{Z} = \frac{200}{34.25} = 5.84\ \text{A}$$

(b) $V_1$ and $V_2$

Let

$$\mathbf{I} = 5.84\angle 0°\ \text{A}$$

$$\mathbf{Z}_1 = 10 + j15.71 = 18.62\ \angle 57.52\ \Omega$$

$$\mathbf{V}_1 = \mathbf{Z}_1\mathbf{I} = (18.62\angle 57.52°)(5.84\ \angle 0°) = 108.74\angle 57.52°\ \text{V}$$

$$\mathbf{Z}_2 = 20 + j31.42 - j63.66 = 20 - j32.24 = 37.94\angle -58.19°\ \Omega$$

$$\mathbf{V}_2 = \mathbf{Z}_2\mathbf{I} = (37.94\angle -58.19°)(5.84\ \angle 0°) = 221.57\angle -58.19°\ \text{V}$$

(c) Power factor

$$\text{pf} = \cos\phi = \cos(28.85°) = 0.875\ \text{(leading)}$$

(d) Vector diagram

The vector diagram is shown in Fig. 3.73.

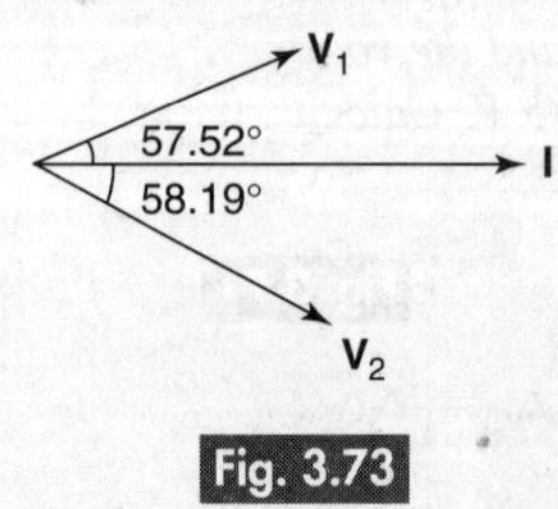

Fig. 3.73

**EXAMPLE 3.55**

*Find the values of R and C so that $V_x = 3V_y$, $V_x$ and $V_y$ are in quadrature in the circuit of Fig. 3.74.*

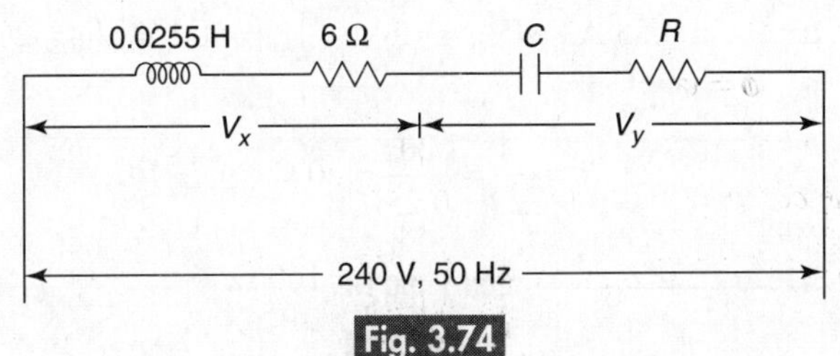


Fig. 3.74

**Solution**

$$X_L = 2\pi fL = 2\pi \times 50 \times 0.0255 = 8\ \Omega$$

$$\mathbf{Z}_x = 6 + j8 = 10\ \angle 53.13^\circ\ \Omega$$

$$V_x = 3V_y$$

$$IZ_x = 3IZ_y$$

$$Z_x = 3Z_y$$

$V_x$ and $V_y$ are in quadrature, i.e., phase angle between $V_x$ and $V_y$ is 90°. Hence, the angle between $Z_x$ and $Z_y$ will be 90°. The impedance $Z_y$ is capacitive in nature.

$$\mathbf{Z}_y = Z_y \angle -\phi$$

$$\mathbf{Z}_y = \frac{10}{3} \angle (53.13 - 90)^\circ = 3.33 \angle -36.87^\circ = 2.66 - j2\ \Omega$$

$$R = 2.66\ \Omega$$

$$X_C = 2\ \Omega$$

$$X_C = \frac{1}{2\pi fC}$$

$$2 = \frac{1}{2\pi \times 50 \times C}$$

$$C = 1.59\ \text{mF}$$

## EXAMPLE 3.56

*In the circuit of Fig. 3.75, a pure resistor R, a choke coil and a pure capacitor of 15.91 μF are connected in series across a supply of V volts and carries a current of 0.25 A. The voltage across the choke coil is 40 V, the voltage across the capacitor is 50 V and the voltage across the resistor is 20 V. The voltage across the combination of R and the choke coil is 45 V. Calculate (a) supply voltage, (b) frequency, and (c) power loss in the choke coil.*

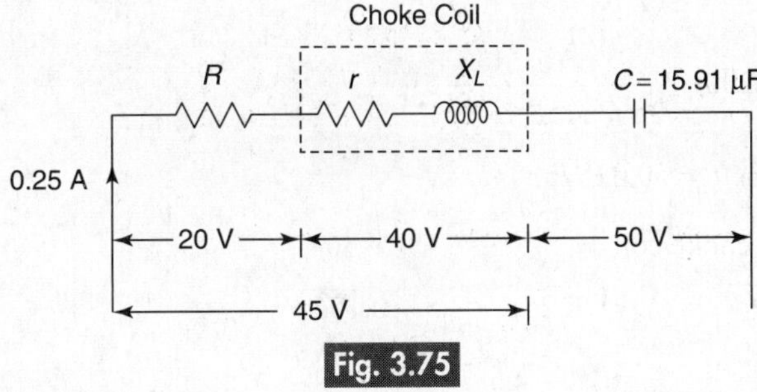


Fig. 3.75

**Solution** $C = 15.91\ \mu F,\quad I = 0.25\ A,\quad V_{coil} = 40\ V,\quad V_C = 50\ V,\quad V_R = 20\ V,\quad V_{R\text{-coil}} = 45\ V$

(a) Supply voltage

$$R = \frac{V_R}{I} = \frac{20}{0.25} = 80\ \Omega$$

$$Z_{coil} = \frac{V_{coil}}{I} = \frac{40}{0.25} = 160\ \Omega$$

$$X_C = \frac{V_C}{I} = \frac{50}{0.25} = 200\ \Omega$$

$$Z_{R\text{-coil}} = \frac{V_{R\text{-coil}}}{I} = \frac{45}{0.25} = 180\ \Omega$$

$$Z_{coil} = \sqrt{r^2 + X_L^2} = 160$$

$$r^2 + X_L^2 = 25600 \qquad \text{...(i)}$$

$$\mathbf{Z}_{R\text{-coil}} = (R + r) + j\,X_L$$

$$Z_{R\text{-coil}} = \sqrt{(R+r)^2 + X_L^2}$$

$$180 = \sqrt{(80+r)^2 + X_L^2}$$

$$(80+r)^2 + X_L^2 = 32400 \qquad \text{...(ii)}$$

Subtracting Eq. (i) from Eq. (ii),

$$(80 + r)^2 - r^2 = 6800$$

$$6400 + 160\,r + r^2 - r^2 = 6800$$

$$160\,r = 400$$

$$r = 2.5\ \Omega$$

Substituting the value of $r$ in Eq. (i),

$$(2.5)^2 + X_L^2 = 25600$$

$$X_L^2 = 25593.75$$

$$X_L = 159.98\ \Omega$$

$$Z = R + r + jX_L - jX_C = 80 + 2.5 + j\,159.98 - j200 = 82.5 - j40.02 = 91.69\angle -25.88°\ \Omega$$

$$V = ZI = 91.69 \times 0.25 = 22.92\ V$$

(b) Frequency

$$X_C = \frac{1}{2\pi fC}$$

$$200 = \frac{1}{2\pi f \times 15.91 \times 10^{-6}}$$

$$f = 50.02\ Hz$$

(c) Power loss in the choke coil

$$P_{coil} = I^2\,r = (0.25)^2 \times 2.5 = 0.156\ W$$

## EXAMPLE 3.57

*Two impedances, one inductive and the other capacitive, are connected in series across the voltage of $120\angle 30°$ V and a frequency of 50 Hz, as shown in Fig. 3.76. The current flowing in the circuit is $3\angle -15°$ A. If one of the impedances is $(10 + j48.3)\ \Omega$, find the other. Also, calculate the values of L and C in the impedances.*

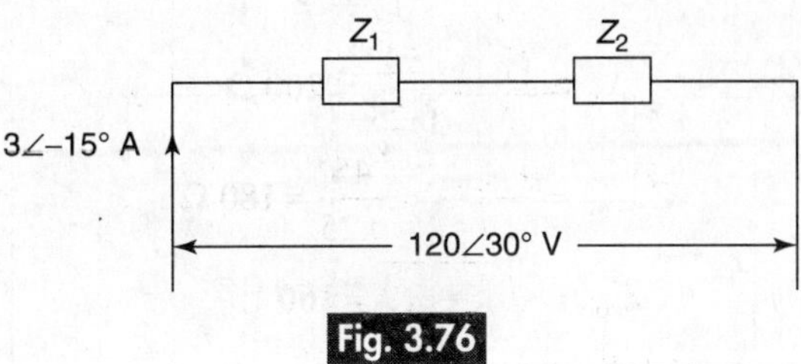


Fig. 3.76

**Solution** $\mathbf{V} = 120\angle 30°$ V, $f = 50$ Hz, $\mathbf{I} = 3\angle -15°$ A, $\mathbf{Z}_1 = 10 + j48.3\ \Omega$

(a) Impedance $Z_2$

$$\mathbf{Z} = \frac{\mathbf{V}}{\mathbf{I}} = \frac{120\angle 30°}{3\angle -15°} = 40\angle 45° = 28.28 + j28.28\ \Omega$$

$$\mathbf{Z} = \mathbf{Z}_1 + \mathbf{Z}_2$$

$$\mathbf{Z}_2 = \mathbf{Z} - \mathbf{Z}_1 = 28.28 + j28.28 - 10 - j48.3 = 18.28 - j20.02\ \Omega$$

(b) Value of $L$

$$\mathbf{Z}_1 = 10 + j48.3 = R_1 + jX_L$$

$$X_L = 48.3\ \Omega$$

$$X_L = 2\pi fL$$

$$48.3 = 2\pi \times 50 \times L$$

$$L = 0.1537\ \text{H}$$

(c) Value of $C$

$$\mathbf{Z}_2 = 18.28 - j20.02 = R_2 - jX_C$$

$$X_C = 20.02\ \Omega$$

$$X_C = \frac{1}{2\pi fC}$$

$$20.02 = \frac{1}{2\pi \times 50 \times C}$$

$$C = 159\ \mu\text{F}$$

## 3.13 PARALLEL ac CIRCUITS

LO 3.8

Analyse parallel ac circuits

In parallel circuits, resistor, inductor and capacitor or any combination of these elements are connected across same supply. Hence, the voltage is same across each branch of the parallel ac circuit. The total current supplied to the circuit is equal to the phasor sum of the branch currents.

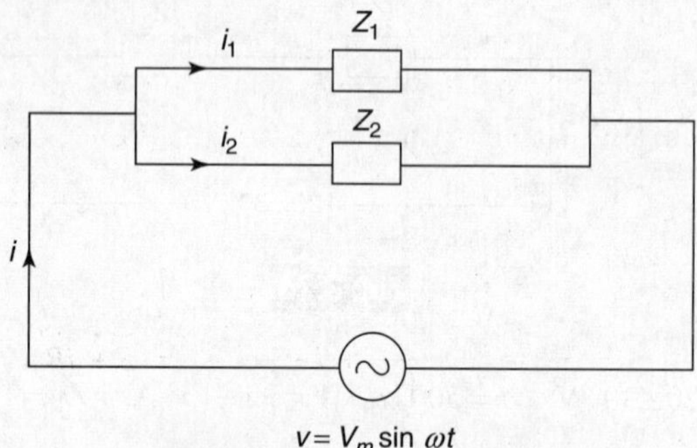


Fig. 3.77 Parallel ac circuit

For the parallel ac circuit shown in Fig. 3.77,

$$\frac{1}{\mathbf{Z}} = \frac{1}{\mathbf{Z}_1} + \frac{1}{\mathbf{Z}_2}$$

$$\mathbf{Y} = \mathbf{Y}_1 + \mathbf{Y}_2$$

where $Y$ represents the admittance of the circuit and is defined as the reciprocal of impedance. The real part of admittance is called conductance ($G$) and the imaginary part is called susceptance ($B$) and these are measured in mhos (℧) or siemens ($S$).

If $\mathbf{Z}_1 = R + jX_L$, and $\mathbf{Z}_2 = -jX_C$,

$$\frac{1}{\mathbf{Z}} = \frac{1}{R + jX_L} + \frac{1}{-jX_C}$$

$$= \frac{R - jX_L}{R^2 + X_L^2} + j\frac{1}{X_C}$$

$$= \frac{R}{R^2 + X_L^2} + j\left(\frac{1}{X_C} - \frac{X_L}{R^2 + X_L^2}\right)$$

$$= G + jB$$

where

$$G = \frac{R}{R^2 + X_L^2}$$

$$B = \frac{1}{X_C} - \frac{X_L}{R^2 + X_L^2}$$

The current in the parallel ac circuit can be found as the phasor sum of the branch currents, i.e., $\mathbf{I} = \mathbf{I}_1 + \mathbf{I}_2$

**Note** 1. For a series *RL* circuit,

$$\mathbf{Z} = R + jX_L$$

$$\mathbf{Y} = \frac{1}{\mathbf{Z}} = \frac{1}{R + jX_L} = \frac{R - jX_L}{R^2 + X_L^2} = \frac{R}{R^2 + X_L^2} - j\frac{X_L}{R^2 + X_L^2} = G - jB_L$$

where $G = \dfrac{R}{R^2 + X^2}$ and $B_L = \dfrac{X_L}{R^2 + X_L^2}$

The admittance triangle for series *RL* circuit is shown in Fig. 3.78.

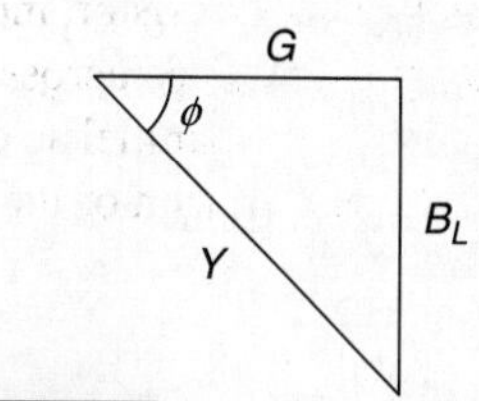


Fig. 3.78 *Admittance triangle*

2. For a series *RC* circuit,

$$\mathbf{Z} = R - jX_C$$

$$\mathbf{Y} = \frac{1}{\mathbf{Z}} = \frac{1}{R - jX_C} = \frac{R + jX_C}{R^2 + X_C^2} = \frac{R}{R^2 + X_C^2} + j\frac{X_C}{R^2 + X_C^2} = G + jB_C$$

where $G = \dfrac{R}{R^2 + X_C^2}$ and $B_C = \dfrac{X_C}{R^2 + X_C^2}$

The admittance triangle for series *RC* circuit is shown in Fig. 3.79.

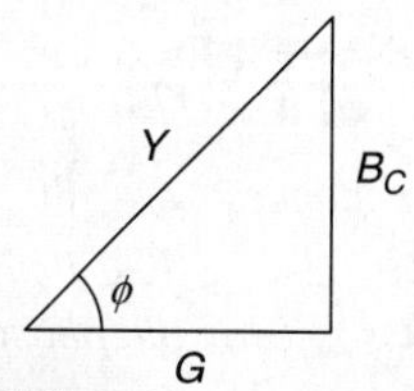


Fig. 3.79 *Admittance triangle*

## EXAMPLE 3.58

*A coil having a resistance of 50 Ω and an inductance of 0.02 H is connected in parallel with a capacitor of 25 μF across a single-phase 200 V, 50 Hz supply, as shown in Fig. 3.80. Calculate the current in coil and capacitance. Calculate also the total current drawn, total pf and total power consumed by the circuit.*

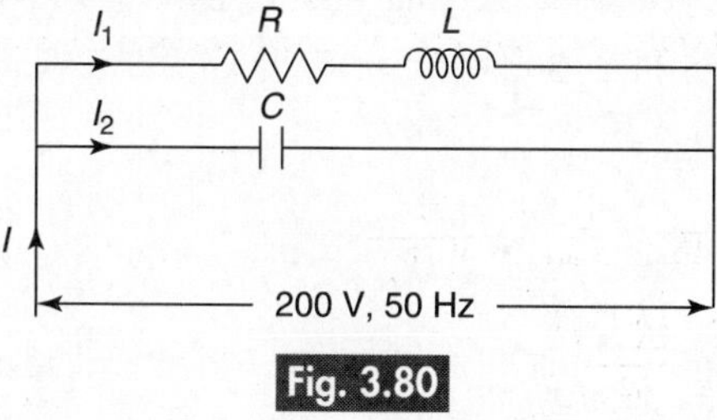


Fig. 3.80

**Solution** $R = 50\ \Omega,\quad L = 0.02\ \text{H},\quad C = 25\ \mu\text{F},\quad V = 200\ \text{V},\quad f = 50\ \text{Hz}$

(a) Current in coil and capacitance

$$X_L = 2\pi fL = 2\pi \times 50 \times 0.02 = 6.28\ \Omega$$

$$X_C = \frac{1}{2\pi fC} = \frac{1}{2\pi \times 50 \times 25 \times 10^{-6}} = 127.32\ \Omega$$

$$\mathbf{Z}_2 = R + jX_L = 50 + j6.28 = 50.39\angle 7.16°\ \Omega$$

$$\mathbf{Z}_2 = -jX_C = -j127.32 = 127.32\angle -90°\ \Omega$$

$$\mathbf{V} = 200\angle 0° = 200\ \text{V}$$

$$\mathbf{I}_1 = \frac{\mathbf{V}}{\mathbf{Z}_1} = \frac{200}{50.39\angle 7.16^\circ} = 3.97\angle -7.16^\circ \text{A}$$

$$\mathbf{I}_2 = \frac{\mathbf{V}}{\mathbf{Z}_2} = \frac{200}{127.32\angle -90^\circ} = 1.57\angle 90^\circ \text{A}$$

(b) Total current

$$\mathbf{I} = \mathbf{I}_1 + \mathbf{I}_2 = 3.97\angle -7.16^\circ + 1.57\angle 90^\circ = 4.08\angle 15.27^\circ \text{A}$$

(c) Total pf

$$\text{pf} = \cos\phi = \cos(15.27^\circ) = 0.965 \text{ (lagging)}$$

(d) Total power consumed

$$P = VI\cos\phi = 200 \times 4.08 \times 0.965 = 787.44 \text{ W}$$

## EXAMPLE 3.59

*Two impedances $\mathbf{Z}_1 = 30\angle 45^\circ\ \Omega$ and $\mathbf{Z}_2 = 45\angle 30^\circ\ \Omega$ are connected in parallel across a single-phase 230 V, 50 Hz supply. Calculate (a) current drawn by each branch, (b) total current, and (c) overall power factor. Also, draw the phasor diagram indicating the current drawn by each branch and the total current, taking the supply voltage as reference.*

**Solution** $\mathbf{Z}_1 = 30\angle 45^\circ\ \Omega$, $\mathbf{Z}_2 = 45\angle 30^\circ\ \Omega$, $V = 230$ V

(a) Current drawn by each branch

Let $\mathbf{V} = 230\angle 0^\circ = 230$ V

$$\mathbf{I}_1 = \frac{\mathbf{V}}{\mathbf{Z}_1} = \frac{230}{30\angle 45^\circ} = 7.67\angle -45^\circ \text{ A}$$

$$\mathbf{I}_2 = \frac{\mathbf{V}}{\mathbf{Z}_2} = \frac{230}{45\angle 30^\circ} = 5.11\angle -30^\circ \text{ A}$$

(b) Total current

$$\mathbf{I} = \mathbf{I}_1 + \mathbf{I}_2 = 7.67\angle -45^\circ + 5.11\angle -30^\circ$$
$$= 12.67\angle -39.01^\circ \text{ A}$$

(c) Overall power factor

$$\text{pf} = \cos\phi = \cos(39.01^\circ) = 0.777 \text{ (lagging)}$$

(d) Phasor diagram

The phasor diagram is shown in Fig. 3.81.

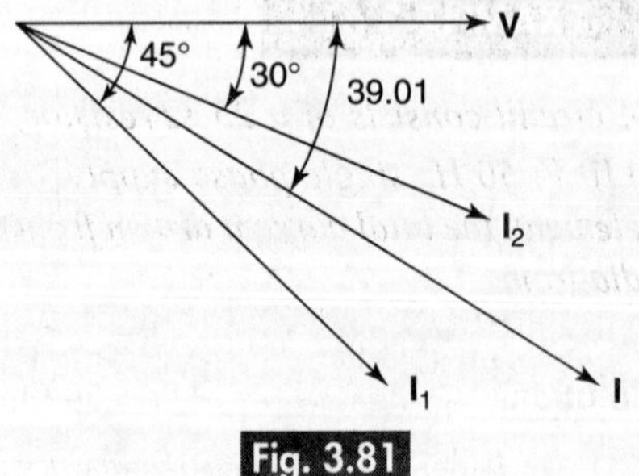


Fig. 3.81

## EXAMPLE 3.60

*Two circuits, the impedances of which are given by $\mathbf{Z}_1 = (10 + j15)$ ohms and $\mathbf{Z}_2 = (6 - j8)$ ohms, are connected in parallel across an ac supply, as shown in Fig. 3.82. If the total current supplied is 15 A, what is the power taken by each branch?*

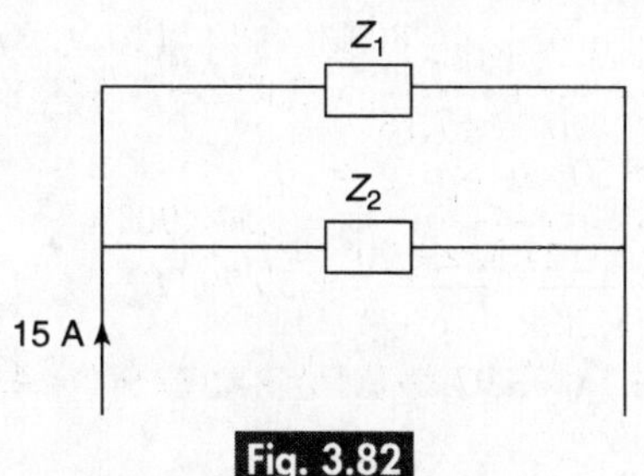


Fig. 3.82

**Solution**

$$\mathbf{Z}_1 = 10 + j15\ \Omega, \quad \mathbf{Z}_2 = 6 - j8\ \Omega, \quad I = 15\ \text{A}$$

$$\mathbf{Z} = \frac{\mathbf{Z}_1\mathbf{Z}_2}{\mathbf{Z}_1 + \mathbf{Z}_2} = \frac{(10 + j\,15)(6 - j8)}{10 + j\,15 + 6 - j8} = 10.32\angle -20.45°\ \Omega$$

$$V = ZI = 10.32 \times 15 = 154.8\ \text{V}$$

Let

$$\mathbf{V} = 154.8\angle\ 0° = 154.8\ \text{V}$$

$$\mathbf{I}_1 = \frac{\mathbf{V}}{\mathbf{Z}_1} = \frac{154.8}{10 + j\,15} = 8.59\angle -56.31°\ \text{A}$$

$$\mathbf{I}_2 = \frac{\mathbf{V}}{\mathbf{Z}_2} = \frac{154.8}{6 - j8} = 15.48\ \angle\ 53.13°\text{A}$$

$$P_1 = I_1^2 R_1 = (8.59)^2 \times 10 = 737.88\ \text{W}$$

$$P_2 = I_2^2 R_2 = (15.48)^2 \times 6 = 1437.78\ \text{W}$$

## EXAMPLE 3.61

*A circuit consists of a 25 Ω resistor, 64 mH inductor and 80 μF capacitor connected in parallel across a 110 V, 50 Hz single-phase supply, as shown in Fig. 3.83. Calculate the individual currents drawn by each element, the total current drawn from the supply and the overall power factor of the circuit. Draw the phasor diagram.*

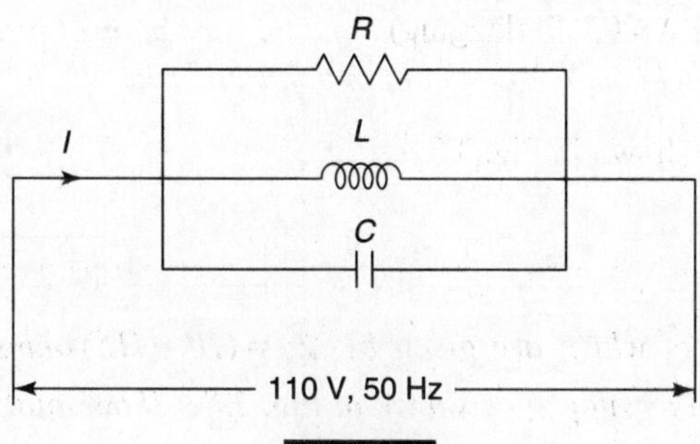


Fig. 3.83

**Solution** $R = 25\ \Omega,\quad L = 64\ \text{mH},\quad C = 80\ \mu\text{F},\quad V = 110\ \text{V},\quad f = 50\ \text{Hz}$

(a) Individual currents

$$X_L = 2\pi fL = 2\pi \times 50 \times 64 \times 10^{-3} = 20.11\ \Omega$$

$$X_C = \frac{1}{2\pi fC} = \frac{1}{2\pi \times 50 \times 80 \times 10^{-6}} = 39.79\ \Omega$$

$$\mathbf{Z}_1 = R = 25\ \Omega$$

$$\mathbf{Z}_2 = jX_L = j\,20.11\ \Omega$$

$$\mathbf{Z}_3 = -jX_C = -j\,39.79\ \Omega$$

Let

$$\mathbf{V} = 110\angle 0^\circ = 110\ \text{V}$$

$$\mathbf{I}_1 = \frac{\mathbf{V}}{\mathbf{Z}_1} = \frac{110}{25} = 4.4\angle 0^\circ\text{A}$$

$$\mathbf{I}_2 = \frac{\mathbf{V}}{\mathbf{Z}_2} = \frac{110}{j20.11} = 5.47\angle -90^\circ\ \text{A}$$

$$\mathbf{I}_3 = \frac{\mathbf{V}}{\mathbf{Z}_3} = \frac{110}{-j39.79} = 2.76\angle 90^\circ\ \text{A}$$

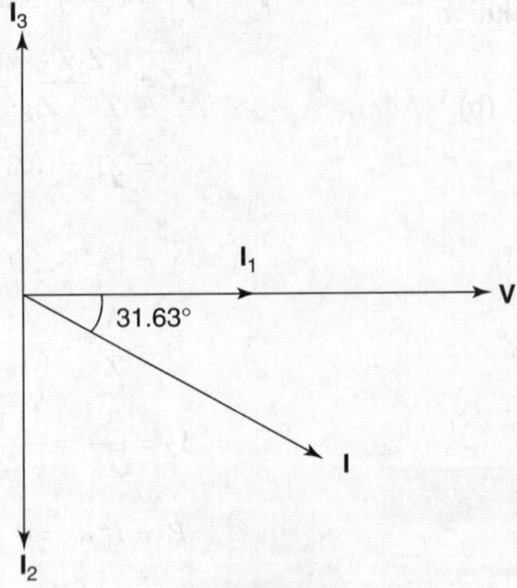


Fig. 3.84

(b) Total current

$$\mathbf{I} = \mathbf{I}_1 + \mathbf{I}_2 + \mathbf{I}_3$$
$$= 4.4\angle 0^\circ + 5.47\angle -90^\circ + 2.76\angle 90^\circ$$
$$= 5.17\angle -31.63^\circ\ \text{A}$$

(c) Overall power factor

$$\text{pf} = \cos\phi = \cos(31.63^\circ) = 0.851\ \text{(lagging)}$$

(d) Phasor diagram

The phasor diagram is shown in Fig. 3.84.

## EXAMPLE 3.62

*An ac circuit connected across a 200 V, 50 Hz, supply has two branches A and B. Branch A draws a current of 4 A at 0.8 lagging power factor, while the total current drawn by the parallel combination is 5 A at unity power factor, as shown in Fig. 3.85, Find (a) current and power factor of branch B, and (b) admittances of branch A and B, and their parallel combination both in polar and rectangular forms.*

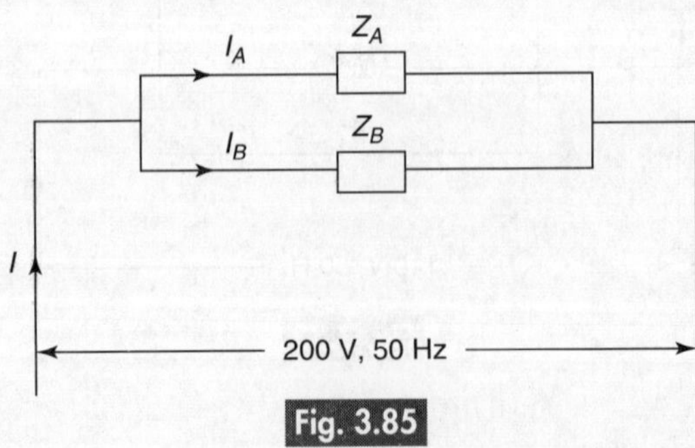


Fig. 3.85

**Solution** $V = 200$ V, $f = 50$ Hz, $I_A = 4\ A$, $\text{pf}_A = 0.8$ (lagging), $I = 5$ A, pf = 1

(a) Current and power factor of Branch *B*

$$\phi_A = \cos^{-1}(0.8) = 36.87°$$

$$\phi = \cos^{-1}(1) = 0°$$

$$\mathbf{I}_A = I_A \angle -\phi_A = 4 \angle -36.87° \text{ A}$$

$$\mathbf{I} = I \angle \phi = 5 \angle 0° \text{ A}$$

$$\mathbf{I} = \mathbf{I}_A + \mathbf{I}_B$$

$$\mathbf{I}_B = \mathbf{I} - \mathbf{I}_A = 5 \angle 0° - 4 \angle -36.87° = 3 \angle 53.13° \text{ A}$$

$$\text{pf}_B = \cos(53.13°) = 0.6 \text{ (leading)}$$

(b) Admittances of branches *A* and *B* and their parallel combination

Let $\mathbf{V} = 200 \angle 0° = 200$ V

$$\mathbf{Y}_A = \frac{\mathbf{I}_A}{\mathbf{V}} = \frac{4 \angle -36.87°}{200 \angle 0°} = 0.02 \angle -36.87° \text{ ℧}$$

$$\mathbf{Y}_B = \frac{\mathbf{I}_B}{\mathbf{V}} = \frac{3 \angle 53.13°}{200 \angle 0°} = 0.015 \angle 53.13° \text{ ℧}$$

$$\mathbf{Y} = \mathbf{Y}_A + \mathbf{Y}_B = 0.02 \angle -36.87° + 0.015 \angle 53.13° \text{ ℧} = 0.025 \angle 0° \text{ ℧}$$

## EXAMPLE 3.63

*Two circuits A and B are connected in parallel to a 115 V, 50 Hz supply, as shown in Fig. 3.86. The total current taken by the combination is 10 A at unity power factor. Circuit A consists of a 10 Ω resistor and 200 μF capacitor connected in series. Circuit B consists of a resistor and an inductor in series. Determine (a) current, (b) power factor, (c) impedance, (d) resistance, and (e) reactance of the circuit B.*

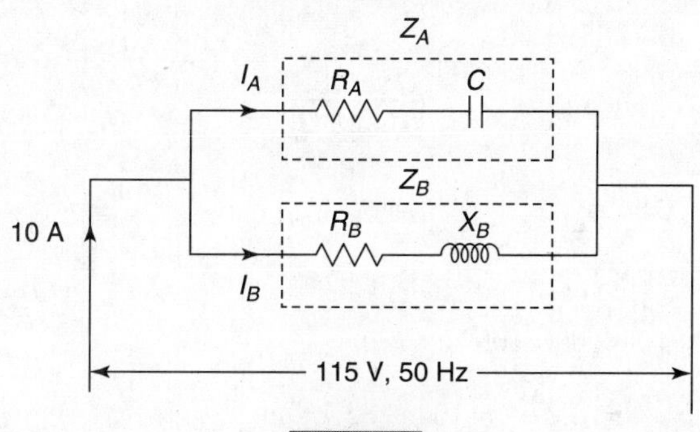


Fig. 3.86

**Solution** $V = 115$ V, $f = 50$ Hz, $I = 10$ A, pf = 1, $R_A = 10\ \Omega$, $C = 200\ \mu$F

(a) Current $I_B$

$$X_C = \frac{1}{2\pi fC} = \frac{1}{2\pi \times 50 \times 200 \times 10^{-6}} = 15.92\ \Omega$$

$$\mathbf{Z}_A = 10 - j\,15.92 = 18.8 \angle -57.87°\ \Omega$$

$$\mathbf{I}_A = \frac{\mathbf{V}}{\mathbf{Z}_A} = \frac{115}{18.8\ \angle -57.87^\circ} = 6.12\ \angle 57.87^\circ\ \text{A}$$

$$\mathbf{I} = 10\ \angle 0^\circ\ \text{A}$$

$$\mathbf{I}_B = \mathbf{I} - \mathbf{I}_A = 10\ \angle 0^\circ - 6.12\ \ \angle 57.87^\circ = 8.5\ \angle -37.54^\circ\ \text{A}$$

(b) Power factor of Circuit $B$

$$\text{pf}_B = \cos(37.54^\circ) = 0.79\ \text{(lagging)}$$

(c) Impedance of Circuit $B$

$$Z_B = \frac{\mathbf{V}}{\mathbf{I_B}} = \frac{115}{8.5\ \angle -37.54^\circ} = 13.53\ \angle 37.54^\circ\ \Omega = 10.73 + j\,8.24\ \Omega$$

(d) Resistance of Circuit $B$

$$R_B = 10.73\ \Omega$$

(e) Reactance of Circuit $B$

$$X_B = 8.24\ \Omega$$

**EXAMPLE 3.64**

*Two circuits, the impedances of which are given by $\mathbf{Z}_1 = (6 + j8)\ \Omega$ and $\mathbf{Z}_2 = (8 - j6)\ \Omega$, and are connected in parallel, as shown in Fig. 3.87. If the applied voltage to the combination is 100 V, find (a) current and pf of each branch, (b) overall current and pf of the combination, and (c) power consumed by each impedance.*

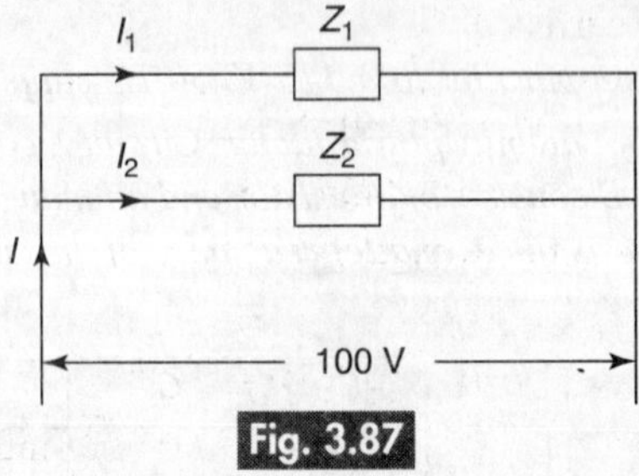


Fig. 3.87

**Solution** $\mathbf{Z}_1 = 6 + j8\ \Omega,\ \ \mathbf{Z}_2 = 8 - j6\ \Omega,\ \ V = 100\ \text{V}$

(a) Current and pf of each branch

$$\mathbf{V} = 100\ \angle 0^\circ = 100\ \text{V}$$

$$\mathbf{I}_1 = \frac{\mathbf{V}}{\mathbf{Z}_1} = \frac{100}{6 + j8} = 10\ \angle -53.13^\circ \text{A}$$

$$\mathbf{I}_2 = \frac{\mathbf{V}}{\mathbf{Z}_2} = \frac{100}{8 - j6} = 10\ \angle 36.9^\circ \text{A}$$

$$\cos\phi_1 = \cos(53.13^\circ) = 0.6\ \text{(lagging)}$$
$$\cos\phi_2 = \cos(36.9^\circ) = 0.8\ \text{(leading)}$$

(b) Overall current and pf of the combination

$$\mathbf{I} = \mathbf{I}_1 + \mathbf{I}_2 = 10\ \angle -53.13° + 10\ \angle 36.9° = 14.14\ \angle -8.13°\ \text{A}$$

$$\text{pf} = \cos\phi = \cos(8.13°) = 0.989\ \text{(lagging)}$$

(c) Power consumed by each impedance

$$P_1 = I_1^2 R_1 = (10)^2 \times (6) = 600\ \text{W}$$

$$P_2 = I^2 R_2 = (10)^2 \times (8) = 800\ \text{W}$$

## EXAMPLE 3.65

*Two impedances $R_1 - jX_{C_1}$ and $R_2 + jX_{L_2}$ are connected in parallel across a supply voltage $v = 100\sqrt{2}\sin 314\,t$. The current flowing through two impedances are $i_1 = 10\sqrt{2}\sin\left(314\,t + \frac{\pi}{4}\right)$ and $i_2 = 10\sqrt{2}\sin\left(314\,t - \frac{\pi}{4}\right)$ respectively. Find the equation for instantaneous value of total current drawn from the supply. Also, find values of $R_1$, $R_2$, $X_{C_1}$ and $X_{L_2}$.*

**Solution**

$$\mathbf{Z}_1 = R_1 - jX_{C_1}, \quad \mathbf{Z}_2 = R_2 + jX_{L_2}, \quad v = 100\sqrt{2}\sin 314\,t$$

$$i_1 = 10\sqrt{2}\sin\left(314t + \frac{\pi}{4}\right), \quad i_2 = 10\sqrt{2}\sin\left(314t - \frac{\pi}{4}\right)$$

(a) Instantaneous value of total current
Writing $v$, $i_1$ and $i_2$ in polar form,

$$\mathbf{V} = 100\ \angle 0°\ \text{V}$$

$$\mathbf{I}_1 = 10\ \angle 45°\text{A}$$

$$\mathbf{I}_2 = 10\ \angle -45°\text{A}$$

$$\mathbf{I} = \mathbf{I}_1 + \mathbf{I}_2 = 10\ \angle 45° + 10\ \angle -45° = 14.14\ \angle 0°\ \text{A}$$

$$i = I_m \sin 2\pi f t = 14.14\sqrt{2}\sin 314\,t = 20\sin 314\,t$$

(b) Values of $R_1$, $R_2$, $X_{C_1}$ and $X_{L_2}$.

$$\mathbf{Z}_1 = \frac{\mathbf{V}}{\mathbf{I}_1} = \frac{100\ \angle 0°}{10\ \angle 45°} = 10\ \angle -45° = 7.07 - j7.07\ \Omega$$

$$R_1 = 7.07\ \Omega$$

$$X_{C_1} = 7.07\ \Omega$$

$$\mathbf{Z}_2 = \frac{\mathbf{V}}{\mathbf{I}_2} = \frac{100\ \angle 0°}{10\ \angle -45°} = 10\ \angle 45° = 7.07 + j7.07\ \Omega$$

$$R_2 = 7.07\ \Omega$$

$$X_{L_2} = 7.07\ \Omega$$

### EXAMPLE 3.66

*An impedance of (7 + j5) Ω is connected in parallel with another impedance of (10 – j8) Ω across a 230 V, 50 Hz supply, as shown in Fig. 3.88. Calculate (a) admittance, conductance and susceptance of the combined circuit, and (b) total current and power factor.*

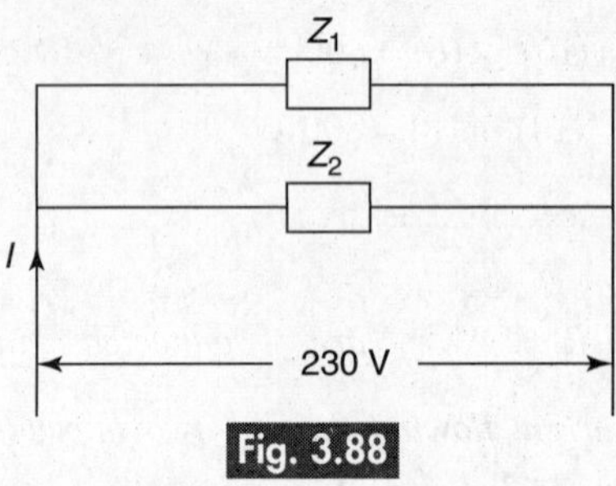


Fig. 3.88

**Solution** $\mathbf{Z}_1 = 7 + j5\,\Omega,\quad \mathbf{Z}_2 = 10 - j8\,\Omega,\quad V = 230\text{ V}$

(a) Admittance, conductance and susceptance of the combined circuit

$$\mathbf{Y}_1 = \frac{1}{\mathbf{Z}_1} = \frac{1}{7 + j5} = 0.12\angle{-35.54^\circ}\ \mho$$

$$\mathbf{Y}_2 = \frac{1}{\mathbf{Z}_2} = \frac{1}{10 - j8} = 0.08\angle 38.66^\circ\ \mho$$

$$\mathbf{Y} = \mathbf{Y}_1 + \mathbf{Y}_2 = 0.12\angle{-35.54^\circ} + 0.08\angle 38.66^\circ$$

$$= 0.16\angle{-7.04^\circ}\ \mho = 0.16 - j0.02\ \mho$$

$$Y = 0.16\ \mho$$

$$G = 0.16\ \mho$$

$$B = 0.02\ \mho$$

(b) Total current and power factor

$$\mathbf{I} = \mathbf{V}\,\mathbf{Y} = (230\angle 0^\circ)(0.16\angle{-7.04^\circ}) = 36.8\angle{-7.04^\circ}\text{ A}$$

$$I = 36.8\text{ A}$$

$$\text{pf} = \cos\phi = \cos(7.04^\circ) = 0.99\ \text{(lagging)}$$

### EXAMPLE 3.67

*Two impedances $Z_1$ and $Z_2$ are connected in parallel across a 200 V, 50 Hz ac supply. The current drawn by the impedance $Z_1$ is 4 A at 0.8 lagging pf. The total current drawn from the supply is 5 A at unity pf. Calculate the impedance $Z_2$.*

**Solution** $V = 200\text{ V},\quad I_1 = 4\text{ A at 0.8 lagging pf},\quad I = 5\text{ A at unity pf}$

$$\mathbf{I}_1 = 4\angle -\cos^{-1}(0.8) = 4\angle -36.87^\circ \text{ A}$$

$$\mathbf{I} = 5\angle\cos^{-1}(1) = 5\angle 0^\circ \text{ A}$$

$$\mathbf{I} = \mathbf{I}_1 + \mathbf{I}_2$$

$$\mathbf{I}_2 = \mathbf{I} - \mathbf{I}_1 = 5\angle 0^\circ - 4\angle -36.87^\circ = 3\angle 53.13^\circ \text{ A}$$

$$\mathbf{Z}_2 = \frac{\mathbf{V}}{\mathbf{I}_2} = \frac{200\angle 0^\circ}{3\angle 53.13^\circ} = 66.67\angle -53.13^\circ\ \Omega$$

## EXAMPLE 3.68

*Compute $Z_{eq}$ and $Y_{eq}$ for the circuit, as shown in Fig. 3.89.*

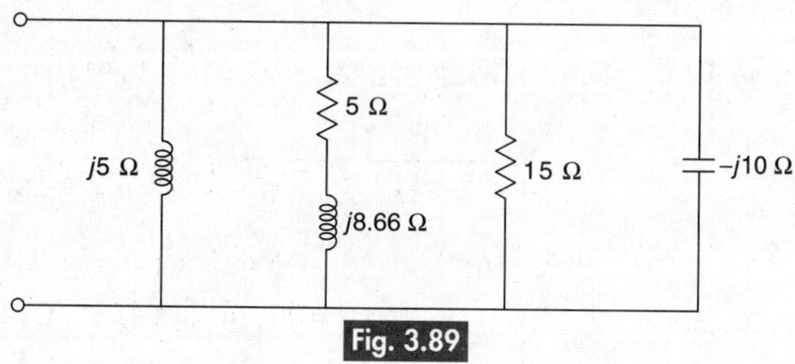


Fig. 3.89

**Solution**

$$\mathbf{Z}_1 = j5\ \Omega,\quad \mathbf{Z}_2 = 5 + j8.66\ \Omega,\quad \mathbf{Z}_3 = 15\ \Omega,\quad \mathbf{Z}_4 = -j10\ \Omega$$

$$\mathbf{Y}_{eq} = \mathbf{Y}_1 + \mathbf{Y}_2 + \mathbf{Y}_3 + \mathbf{Y}_4 = \frac{1}{\mathbf{Z}_1} + \frac{1}{\mathbf{Z}_2} + \frac{1}{\mathbf{Z}_3} + \frac{1}{\mathbf{Z}_4}$$

$$= \frac{1}{j5} + \frac{1}{5 + j8.66} + \frac{1}{15} + \frac{1}{-j10} = 0.22\ \angle -57.99^\circ\ \mho$$

$$\mathbf{Z}_{eq} = \frac{1}{\mathbf{Y}_{eq}} = \frac{1}{0.22\ \angle -57.99^\circ} = 4.54\ \angle 57.99^\circ\ \Omega$$

## EXAMPLE 3.69

*Find currents $I_1$ and $I_2$ in Fig. 3.90.*

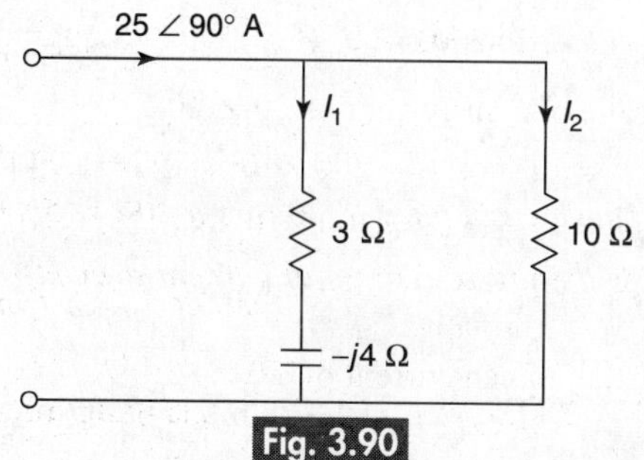


Fig. 3.90

**Solution** $\mathbf{Z}_1 = 3 - j4\ \Omega,\quad \mathbf{Z}_2 = 10\ \Omega,\quad \mathbf{I} = 25\angle 90°\text{A}$

By current-division rule,

$$\mathbf{I}_1 = \mathbf{I}\frac{\mathbf{Z}_2}{\mathbf{Z}_1+\mathbf{Z}_2} = (25\angle 90°)\frac{10}{3-j4+10} = 18.38\angle 107.1°\ \text{A}$$

$$\mathbf{I}_2 = \mathbf{I} - \mathbf{I}_1 = 25\angle 90° - 18.38\angle 107.1° = 9.19\angle 54°\ \text{A}$$

## EXAMPLE 3.70

*Three impedances of $25\angle 53.1°\Omega$, $5\angle -53.1°\Omega$ and $10\angle 36.9°\Omega$ are connected in parallel. The combination is in series with another impedance of $14.14\angle 45°\Omega$. Calculate the equivalent impedance of the circuit.*

**Solution** $\mathbf{Z}_1 = 25\angle 53.1°\ \Omega,\quad \mathbf{Z}_2 = 5\angle -53.1°\ \Omega,\quad \mathbf{Z}_3 = 10\angle 36.9°\ \Omega,\quad \mathbf{Z}_4 = 14.14\angle 45°\ \Omega$

$$\mathbf{Y} = \frac{1}{\mathbf{Z}} = \frac{1}{\mathbf{Z}_1} + \frac{1}{\mathbf{Z}_2} + \frac{1}{\mathbf{Z}_3} = \frac{1}{25\angle 53.1°} + \frac{1}{5\angle -53.1°} + \frac{1}{10\angle 36.9°} = 0.23\angle 16.86\ °\mho$$

$$\mathbf{Z} = \frac{1}{\mathbf{Y}} = 4.27\angle -16.86\ °\ \Omega$$

$$\mathbf{Z}_{eq} = \mathbf{Z} + \mathbf{Z}_4 = 4.27\angle -16.86° + 14.14\angle 45° = 16.58\angle 31.87°\ \Omega$$

## EXAMPLE 3.71

*A voltage of $200\angle 25°\ V$ is applied to a circuit composed of two parallel branches. If the branch currents are $10\angle 40°\ A$ and $20\angle -30°\ A$, determine the kVA, kVAR and kW in each branch. Also, calculate the pf of the combined load.*

**Solution** $\mathbf{V} = 200\angle 25°\ \text{V},\quad \mathbf{I}_1 = 10\angle 40°\ \text{A},\quad \mathbf{I}_2 = 20\angle -30°\text{A}$

Phase difference between $V$ and $I_1$

$$\phi_1 = 40° - 25° = 15°$$

Phase difference between $V$ and $I_2$

$$\phi_2 = 25° - (-30°) = 55°$$

$$\cos\phi_1 = \cos(15°) = 0.97\ \text{(leading)}$$

$$\cos\phi_2 = \cos(55°) = 0.57\ \text{(lagging)}$$

(a) kVA, kVAR and kW for the branch current of $10\angle 40°$ A

$$P_1 = VI_1\cos\phi_1 = 200\times 10\times 0.97 = 1.94\ \text{kW}$$

$$Q_1 = VI_1\sin\phi_1 = 200\times 10\times \sin(15°) = 0.52\ \text{kVAR}$$

$$S_1 = VI_1 = 200\times 10 = 2\ \text{kVA}$$

(b) kVA, kVAR and kW for the branch current of $20\angle -30°$ A

$$P_2 = VI_2 \cos\phi_2 = 200 \times 20 \times 0.57 = 2.28 \text{ kW}$$
$$Q_2 = VI_2 \sin\phi_2 = 200 \times 20 \times \sin(55°) = 3.28 \text{ kVAR}$$
$$S_2 = VI_2 = 200 \times 20 = 4 \text{ kVA}$$

(c) Power factor of the combined load

$$I_1 = 10 \angle 40° \text{ A}$$
$$I_2 = 20 \angle -30° \text{ A}$$
$$\mathbf{I} = \mathbf{I}_1 + \mathbf{I}_2 = 10 \angle 40° + 20 \angle -30° = 25.24 \angle -8.14° \text{A}$$
$$\phi = 25° - (-8.14°) = 33.14°$$
$$\text{pf} = \cos(33.14) = 0.84 \text{ (lagging)}$$

## EXAMPLE 3.72

*Two circuits have the same numerical value of impedances. The pf of one is 0.8 lagging and that of the other is 0.6 lagging. What is the pf of combination if they are connected in parallel?*

**Solution**

$$\text{pf}_1 = 0.8 \text{ (lagging)}, \quad \text{pf}_2 = 0.6 \text{ (lagging)}$$
$$\mathbf{Z}_1 = Z \angle \cos^{-1}(0.8) = Z \angle 36.87° \ \Omega$$
$$\mathbf{Z}_2 = Z \angle \cos^{-1}(0.6) = Z \angle 53.13° \ \Omega$$

For parallel combination,

$$\mathbf{Z} = \frac{\mathbf{Z}_1 \mathbf{Z}_2}{\mathbf{Z}_1 + \mathbf{Z}_2} = \frac{(Z \angle 36.87°)(Z \angle 53.13°)}{Z \angle 36.87° + Z \angle 53.13°}$$
$$= \frac{Z^2 \angle 90°}{Z(1.4 + j1.4)} = \frac{Z^2 \angle 90°}{1.98Z \angle 45°} = 0.505\, Z \angle 45° \ \Omega$$
$$\text{pf} = \cos(45°) = 0.707 \text{ (lagging)}$$

## EXAMPLE 3.73

*When a 240 V, 50 Hz supply is fed to a 15 Ω resistor in parallel with an inductor, the total current is 22.1 A, as shown in Fig. 3.91. What value must the frequency have for the total current to be 34 A?*

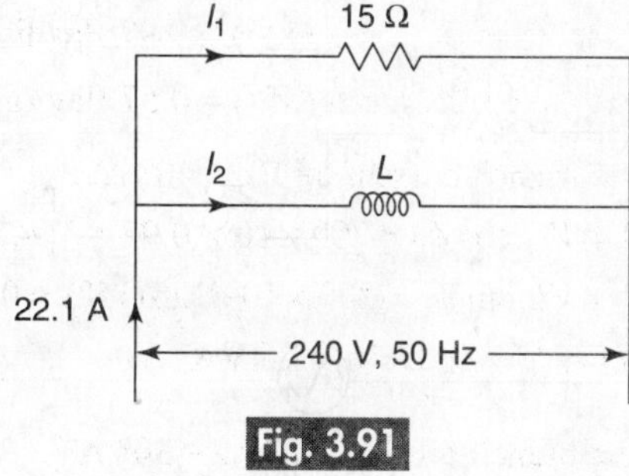


Fig. 3.91

**Solution** $V = 240\text{ V},\quad R = 15\ \Omega,\quad I = 22.1\text{ A}$

Let

$$\mathbf{V} = 240\angle 0°\text{ V}$$

$$\mathbf{I}_1 = \frac{\mathbf{V}}{R} = \frac{240\angle 0°}{15\angle 0°} = 16\angle 0° = 16\text{ A}$$

$$\mathbf{I}_2 = \frac{\mathbf{V}}{jX_L} = \frac{240\angle 0°}{X_L\angle 90°} = \frac{240}{X_L}\angle -90° = -j\frac{240}{X_L}\text{ A}$$

$$\mathbf{I} = 16 - j\frac{240}{X_L}$$

$$\sqrt{(16)^2 + \left(\frac{240}{X_L}\right)^2} = 22.1$$

$$256 + \frac{57600}{X_L^2} = 488.41$$

$$X_L = 15.74\ \Omega$$

$$X_L = 2\pi fL$$

$$15.74 = 2\pi \times 50 \times L$$

$$L = 0.05\text{ H}$$

Let the new frequency be $f$ for the total current of 34 A.

$$\sqrt{(16)^2 + \left(\frac{240}{2\pi f \times 0.05}\right)^2} = 34$$

$$256 + \frac{57600}{0.0987 f^2} = 1156$$

$$f = 25.47\text{ Hz}$$

## EXAMPLE 3.74

*Determine the current in the circuit of Fig. 3.92. Also, find the power consumed as well as pf.*

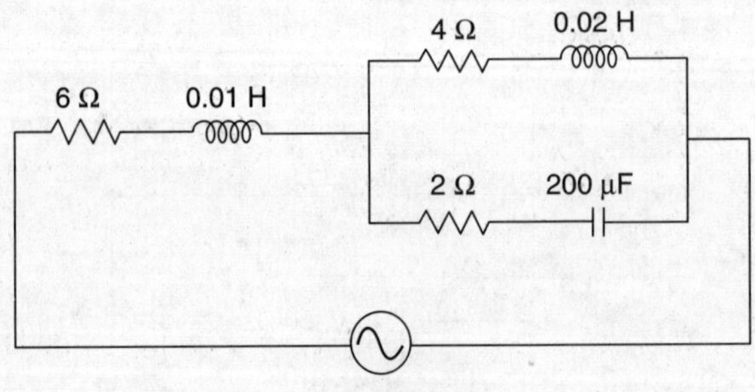


Fig. 3.92

**Solution**

$$X_{L_1} = 2\pi fL_1 = 2\pi \times 50 \times 0.01 = 3.14\ \Omega$$

$$X_{L_2} = 2\pi fL_2 = 2\pi \times 50 \times 0.02 = 6.28\ \Omega$$

$$X_C = \frac{1}{2\pi fC} = \frac{1}{2\pi \times 50 \times 200 \times 10^{-6}} = 15.92\ \Omega$$

$$\mathbf{Z}_1 = 6 + j3.14\ \Omega$$

$$\mathbf{Z}_2 = 4 + j6.28\ \Omega$$

$$\mathbf{Z}_3 = 2 - j15.92\ \Omega$$

$$\mathbf{Z} = \mathbf{Z}_1 + \frac{\mathbf{Z}_2\mathbf{Z}_3}{\mathbf{Z}_2 + \mathbf{Z}_3} = (6 + j3.14) + \frac{(4 + j6.28)(2 - j15.92)}{(4 + j6.28) + (2 - j15.92)} = 17.27\ \angle 30.75°\ \Omega$$

$$\mathbf{I} = \frac{\mathbf{V}}{\mathbf{Z}} = \frac{100\ \angle 0°}{17.27\angle 30.75°} = 5.79\ \angle -30.75°\ \text{A}$$

$$P = VI\cos\phi = 100 \times 5.79 \times \cos(30.75°) = 497.94\ \text{W}$$

$$\text{pf} = \cos\phi = \cos(30.75°) = 0.86\ \text{(lagging)}$$

## EXAMPLE 3.75

*Two impedances $\mathbf{Z}_A = (4 + j3)\ \Omega$ and $\mathbf{Z}_B = (10 - j7)\ \Omega$ are connected in parallel and impedance $\mathbf{Z}_C = (6 + j5)\ \Omega$ is connected in series with parallel combination of $\mathbf{Z}_A$ and $\mathbf{Z}_B$, as shown in Fig. 3.93. If the voltage applied across the circuit is 200 V at 59 Hz, calculate (a) currents flowing in $Z_A$, $Z_B$ and $Z_C$, and (b) total power factor of the circuit.*

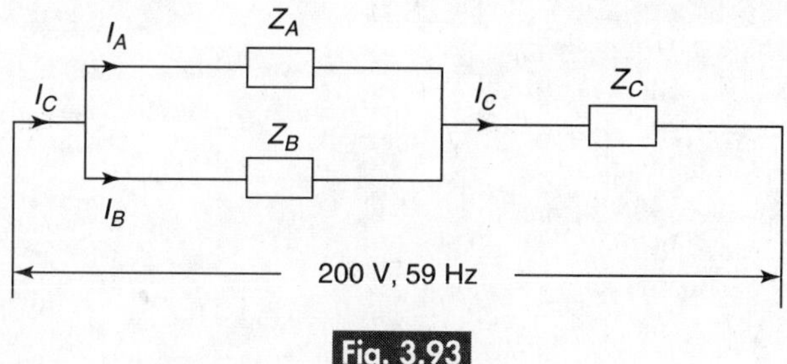


Fig. 3.93

**Solution** $\mathbf{Z}_A = 4 + j3\ \Omega$, $\mathbf{Z}_B = 10 - j7\ \Omega$, $\mathbf{Z}_C = 6 + j5\ \Omega$, $V = 200$ V, $f = 59$ Hz

(a) Currents flowing in $Z_A, Z_B$ and $Z_C$

$$\mathbf{Z}_A = 4 + j3 = 5\ \angle 36.87°\ \Omega$$

$$\mathbf{Z}_B = 10 - j7 = 12.21\ \angle -35°\ \Omega$$

$$\mathbf{Z}_C = 6 + j5\ \Omega = 7.81\ \angle 39.81°\ \Omega$$

$$\mathbf{Z} = \frac{\mathbf{Z}_A\mathbf{Z}_B}{\mathbf{Z}_A + \mathbf{Z}_B} + \mathbf{Z}_C = \frac{(5\ \angle 36.87°)(12.21\ \angle -35°)}{5\ \angle 36.87° + 12.21\ \angle -35°} + 7.81\ \angle 39.81° = 11.8\ \angle 32.17°\ \Omega$$

$$I_C = \frac{V}{Z} = \frac{200\,\angle 0°}{11.8\,\angle 32.17°} = 16.95\ \angle -32.17°\text{A}$$

$$I_A = I_C\frac{Z_B}{Z_A + Z_B} = (16.95\,\angle -32.17°)\frac{(12.21\,\angle -35°)}{5\,\angle 36.87° + 12.21\,\angle -35°} = 14.21\,\angle -51.21°\text{A}$$

$$\mathbf{I}_B = \mathbf{I}_C - \mathbf{I}_A = 16.95\,\angle -32.17° - 14.21\,\angle -51.21° = 5.82\,\angle 20.64°\ \text{A}$$

(b) Total power factor of the circuit

$$\text{pf} = \cos(32.17°) = 0.85\ \text{(lagging)}$$

## EXAMPLE 3.76

*In a series–parallel circuit, the parallel branches A and B are in series with Branch C, as shown in Fig. 3.94. The impedances are* $\mathbf{Z}_A = (4 + j3)\ \Omega$, $\mathbf{Z}_B = (4 - j\frac{16}{3})\ \Omega$ *and* $\mathbf{Z}_C = (2 + j8)\ \Omega$. *If the current* $I_c = (25 + j0)$ *A, determine the branch currents, voltages and the total voltage. Hence, calculate active and reactive powers for each branch and the whole circuit.*

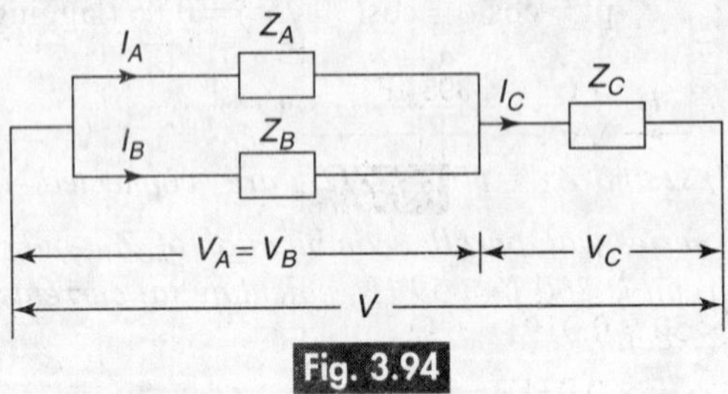


Fig. 3.94

**Solution**

$$\mathbf{Z}_A = 4 + j3\,\Omega,\quad \mathbf{Z}_B = 4 - j\frac{16}{3}\,\Omega,\quad \mathbf{Z}_C = 2 + j8\,\Omega,\quad \mathbf{I}_C = 25 + j0 = 25\,\angle\,0°\ \text{A}$$

(a) Branch currents

By current-division rule,

$$\mathbf{I}_A = \mathbf{I}_C\frac{\mathbf{Z}_B}{\mathbf{Z}_A + \mathbf{Z}_B} = (25 + j0)\frac{\left(4 - j\frac{16}{3}\right)}{4 + j3 + 4 - j\frac{16}{3}} = 20\,\angle -36.87°\ \text{A}$$

$$\mathbf{I}_B = \mathbf{I}_C - \mathbf{I}_A = 25\,\angle\,0° - 20\,\angle -36.87° = 15\,\angle\,53.13°\ \text{A}$$

(b) Branch voltages and total voltage

$$\mathbf{V}_A = \mathbf{V}_B = \mathbf{Z}_A I_A = (4 + j3)\,(20\,\angle -36.87°) = 100\,\angle -1.02°\ \text{V}$$

$$\mathbf{V}_C = \mathbf{Z}_C\mathbf{I}_C = (2 + j8)\,(25\,\angle\,0°) = 206.16\,\angle\,75.96°\ \text{V}$$

$$\mathbf{V} = \mathbf{V}_A + \mathbf{V}_C = 100\,\angle -1.02° + 206.16\,\angle\,75.16° = 249.7\,\angle\,52.27°\ \text{V}$$

(c) Active and reactive powers for each branch and the whole circuit

$$P_A = I_A^2\,R_A = (20)^2 \times 4 = 1600\ \text{W}$$

$$P_B = I_B^2\,R_B = (15)^2 \times 4 = 900\ \text{W}$$

$$P_C = I_C^2 R_C = (25)^2 \times 2 = 1250 \text{ W}$$
$$P = P_A + P_B + P_C = 1600 + 900 + 1250 = 3750 \text{ W}$$
$$Q_A = I_A^2 X_A = (20)^2 \times 3 = 1200 \text{ VAR}$$
$$Q_B = I_B^2 X_B = (15)^2 \times \frac{16}{3} = 1200 \text{ VAR}$$
$$Q_C = I_C^2 X_C = (25)^2 \times 8 = 5000 \text{ VAR}$$
$$Q = Q_A + Q_B + Q_C = 1200 + 1200 + 5000 = 7400 \text{ VAR}$$

## EXAMPLE 3.77

*Find the applied voltage $V_{AB}$ so that a 10 A current may flow through the capacitor in Fig. 3.95.*

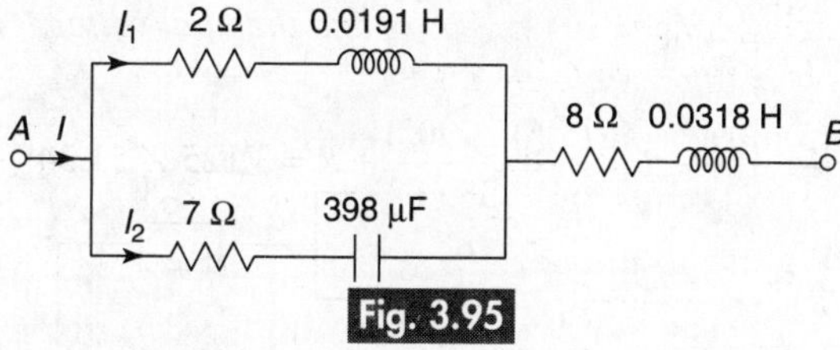


Fig. 3.95

**Solution**

$$X_{L_1} = 2\pi f L_1 = 2\pi \times 50 \times 0.0191 = 6\ \Omega$$
$$X_{L_2} = 2\pi f L_2 = 2\pi \times 50 \times 0.0318 = 10\ \Omega$$
$$X_C = \frac{1}{2\pi f C} = \frac{1}{2\pi \times 50 \times 398 \times 10^{-6}} = 8\ \Omega$$
$$\mathbf{Z}_1 = 2 + j6 = 6.32\ \angle 71.56°\ \Omega$$
$$\mathbf{Z}_2 = 7 - j8 = 10.63\ \angle -48.8°\ \Omega$$
$$\mathbf{Z}_3 = 8 + j10 = 12.8\ \angle 51.34°\ \Omega$$
$$\mathbf{Z} = \frac{\mathbf{Z}_1\mathbf{Z}_2}{\mathbf{Z}_1 + \mathbf{Z}_2} + \mathbf{Z}_3 = \frac{(2 + j6)(7 - j8)}{(2 + j6 + 7 - j8)} + (8 + j10) = 19.91\ \angle 45.53°\ \Omega$$

Let $\mathbf{I}_2 = 10\ \angle\ 0°\text{A}$

$$\mathbf{V}_2 = \mathbf{Z}_2\mathbf{I}_2 = (10.63\ \angle -48.8°)\ (10\ \angle\ 0°) = 106.3\ \angle -48.8°\ \text{V}$$
$$\mathbf{V}_1 = \mathbf{V}_2 = 106.3\ \angle -48.8°\ \text{V}$$
$$\mathbf{I}_1 = \frac{\mathbf{V}_1}{\mathbf{Z}_1} = \frac{106.3\ \angle -48.8°}{6.32\ \angle\ 71.56°} = 16.82\ \angle -120.36°\ \text{A}$$
$$\mathbf{I} = \mathbf{I}_1 + \mathbf{I}_2 = 16.82\ \angle -120.36° + 10\ \angle\ 0° = 14.58\ \angle -84.09°\ \text{A}$$
$$\mathbf{V}_{AB} = \mathbf{Z}\,\mathbf{I} = (19.91\ \angle\ 45.53°)\ (14.58\ \angle -84.09°) = 290.28\ \angle -38.56°\ \text{V}$$

## EXAMPLE 3.78

*If a voltage of 150 V applied between terminals A and B produces a current of 32 A for the circuit shown in Fig. 3.96, calculate the value of the resistance R and pf of the circuit.*

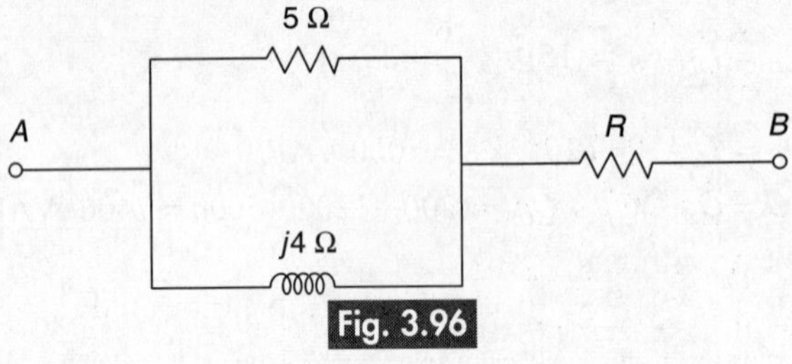


Fig. 3.96

**Solution**

$$V = 150 \text{ V}, \quad I = 32 \text{ A}$$

$$Z = \frac{150}{32} = 4.687\ \Omega$$

$$\mathbf{Z} = \frac{(5)(j4)}{5+j4} + R = \frac{(5)(4\angle 90^\circ)}{64\angle 38.66^\circ} + R = 3.125\angle 51.34^\circ + R = 1.95 + j2.44 + R$$

$$\sqrt{(1.95+R)^2 + (2.44)^2} = 4.687$$

$$(1.95+R)^2 + (2.44)^2 = (4.687)^2$$

$$(1.95+R^2) = (4.687)^2 - (244)^2$$

$$1.95 + R = 4$$

$$R = 2.05\ \Omega$$

$$\text{pf} = \frac{\text{Total resistance}}{\text{Total impedance}} = \frac{1.95+2.05}{4.687} = 0.853 \text{ (lagging)}$$

## EXAMPLE 3.79

*An impedance of R + jX ohms is connected in parallel with another impedance of –j5 ohms, as shown in Fig. 3.97. The combination is then connected in series with a pure resistance of 2 Ω. When connected across a 100 V, 50 Hz ac supply, the total current drawn by the circuit is 20 A and the total power consumed by the circuit is 2 kW. Calculate (a) currents through parallel branches, and (b) R and L.*

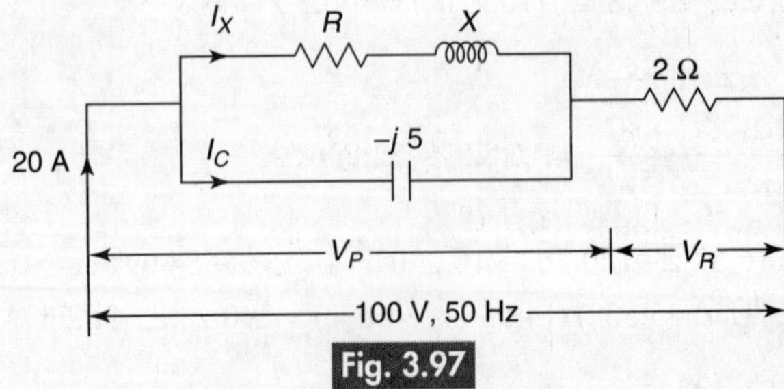


Fig. 3.97

**Solution** $P = 2\text{ kW},\quad V = 100\text{ V},\quad I = 20\text{ A}$

(a) Currents through parallel branches

$$P = VI\cos\phi$$
$$2000 = 100 \times 20 \times \cos\phi$$
$$\cos\phi = 1$$
$$\phi = 0°$$
$$\mathbf{V} = 100\angle 0°\text{ V}$$
$$\mathbf{I} = 20\angle 0°\text{ A}$$
$$\mathbf{V}_R = 2 \times 20°\angle 0° = 40\angle 0°\text{ V}$$
$$\mathbf{V}_P = \mathbf{V} - \mathbf{V}_R = 100\angle 0° - 40\angle 0° = 60\angle 0°\text{ V}$$
$$\mathbf{I}_C = \frac{\mathbf{V}_P}{\mathbf{Z}_C} = \frac{60\angle 0°}{5\angle -90°} = 12\angle 90°\text{ A}$$
$$\mathbf{I}_X = \mathbf{I} - \mathbf{I}_C = 20\angle 0° - 12\angle 90° = 23.32\angle -30.96°\text{ A}$$

(b) Resistance and inductance

$$\mathbf{Z}_X = \frac{60\angle 0°}{23.32\angle -30.96°} = 2.57\angle 30.96° = 2.2 + j1.32\ \Omega$$
$$R = 2.2\ \Omega$$
$$X_L = 1.32\ \Omega$$
$$X_L = 2\pi fL$$
$$1.32 = 2\pi \times 50 \times L$$
$$L = 4.2\text{ mH}$$

## EXAMPLE 3.80

*The circuit of Fig. 3.98 takes 12 A at a lagging power factor and dissipates 1800 W. The reading of the voltmeter is 200 V. Find $R_1$, $X_1$ and $X_2$.*

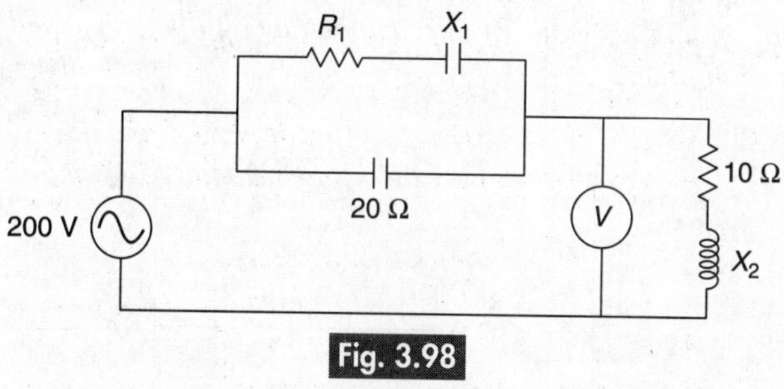


Fig. 3.98

**Solution** $I = 12\text{ A},\quad P = 1800\text{ W}$

Let $\mathbf{I} = 12 \angle 0° \text{ A}$

$$Z_2 = \frac{200}{12} = 16.67\ \Omega$$

$$Z_2 = \sqrt{R_2^2 + X_2^2}$$

$$16.67 = \sqrt{(10)^2 + X_2^2}$$

$$277.88 = 100 + X_2^2$$

$$X_2 = 13.33\ \Omega$$

$$\mathbf{V}_2 = (12 \angle 0°)(10 + j13.33) = (12 \angle 0°)(16.67 \angle 53.13°) = 200 \angle 53.13° \text{ V}$$

$$P = VI \cos \phi$$

$$1800 = 200 \times 12 \times \cos \phi$$

$$\cos \phi = 0.75$$

$$\phi = 41.41°$$

Applied voltage $\mathbf{V}_{req} = 200 \angle 41.41° \text{ V}$

Voltage across parallel branches $= 200 \angle 41.41° - 200 \angle 53.13° = 40.84 \angle -42.73° \text{ V}$

Current through capacitor $= \dfrac{40.84 \angle -42.73°}{20 \angle -90°} = 2.04 \angle 47.27° \text{A}$

Current through $R_1$ and $X_1 = 12 \angle 0° - 2.04 \angle 47.27° = 10.72 \angle -8.03° \text{ A}$

$$\mathbf{Z}_1 = \frac{40.84 \angle -42.73°}{10.72 \angle -8.03°} = 3.81 \angle -34.7° = 3.13 - j2.17$$

$$R_1 = 3.13\ \Omega$$

$$X_1 = 2.17\ \Omega$$

**EXAMPLE 3.81**

*For the circuit shown in Fig. 3.99, calculate (a) total admittance, total conductance and total susceptance, (b) total current and total pf, and (c) value of pure capacitance to be connected in parallel with the above combination to make the total pf unity.*

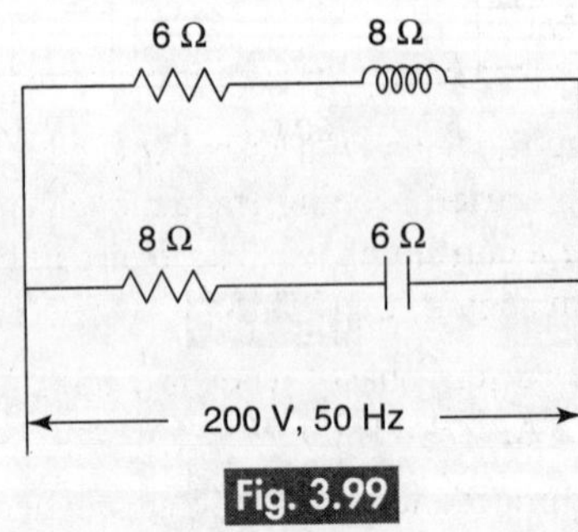


Fig. 3.99

**Solution**

(a) Total admittance, total conductance and total susceptance

$$\mathbf{Z}_1 = 6 + j8 = 10\angle 53.13°\ \Omega$$

$$\mathbf{Z}_2 = 8 - j6 = 10\angle -36.87°\ \Omega$$

$$\mathbf{Y}_1 = \frac{1}{\mathbf{Z}_1} = \frac{1}{10\angle 53.13°} = 0.1\angle -53.13°\ \mho$$

$$\mathbf{Y}_2 = \frac{1}{\mathbf{Z}_2} = \frac{1}{10\angle -36.87°} = 0.1\angle 36.87°\ \mho$$

$$\mathbf{Y} = \mathbf{Y}_1 + \mathbf{Y}_2 = 0.1\angle -53.13° + 0.1\angle 36.87° = 0.14 - j0.02\ \mho = 0.14\angle -8.13°\ \mho$$

$$Y = 0.14\ \mho$$

$$G = 0.14\ \mho$$

$$B = 0.02\ \mho$$

(b) Total current and total pf

Let $\mathbf{V} = 200\angle 0°\ \text{V}$

$$\mathbf{I} = \mathbf{V}\,\mathbf{Y} = (200\angle 0°)(0.14\angle -8.13°) = 28\angle -8.13°\ \text{A}$$

$$\text{pf} = \cos(8.13°) = 0.989\ \text{(lagging)}$$

(c) Value of pure capacitance to make total pf unity

Since the current lags behind voltage, the circuit is inductive in nature. In order to make the total pf unity, a pure capacitor is connected in parallel so that pf becomes unity and imaginary part of $\mathbf{Y}_{req}$ becomes zero.

$$\mathbf{Y}_{req} = \mathbf{Y}_1 + \mathbf{Y}_2 + \mathbf{Y}_3$$

$$\mathbf{Y}_{req} = 0.14 - j0.02 + j0.02 = 0.14$$

$$Y_3 = Y_C = \frac{1}{X_C} = 0.02\ \mho$$

$$X_C = 50\ \Omega$$

$$C = \frac{1}{2\pi \times 50 \times 50} = 63.66\ \mu\text{F}$$

## 3.14 LOCUS DIAGRAM

LO 3.9

Explain locus diagrams

Locus diagrams are useful in analysing the behaviour of an *RLC* circuit when one of its parameters, i.e., *R*, *L* or *C* is varied keeping frequency and voltage constant. The magnitude and phase of a current phasor in the circuit depends upon the values of *R*, *L* and *C* and frequency of the supply.

The path traced by the terminus of the current phasor when any one parameter *R*, *L* or *C* is varied keeping *f* and *V* constant is called *current locus*.

Locus diagrams can also be drawn for impedance and admittance when frequency is varied.

### 3.14.1 Locus Diagram of a Series RL Circuit

Figure 3.100 shows a series *RL* circuit with variable resistance and constant reactance.

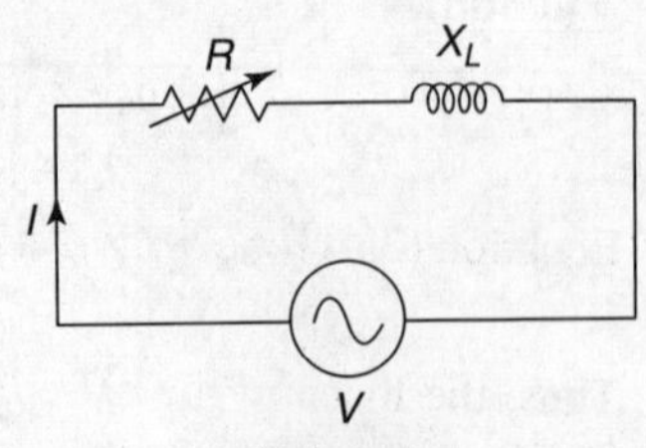

Fig. 3.100

$$I = \frac{V}{Z} = \frac{V}{\sqrt{R^2 + X_L^2}}$$

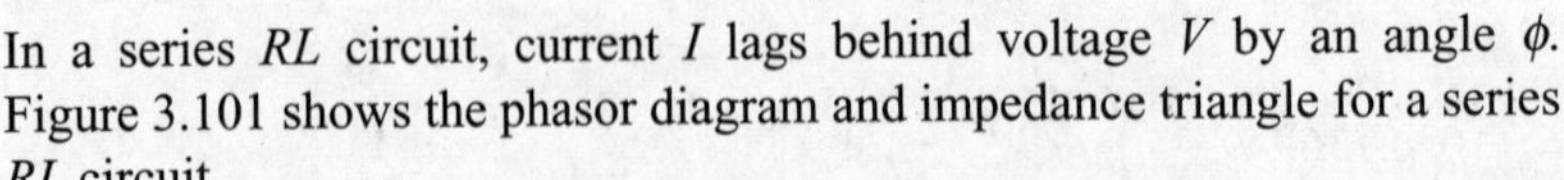

In a series *RL* circuit, current *I* lags behind voltage *V* by an angle $\phi$. Figure 3.101 shows the phasor diagram and impedance triangle for a series *RL* circuit.

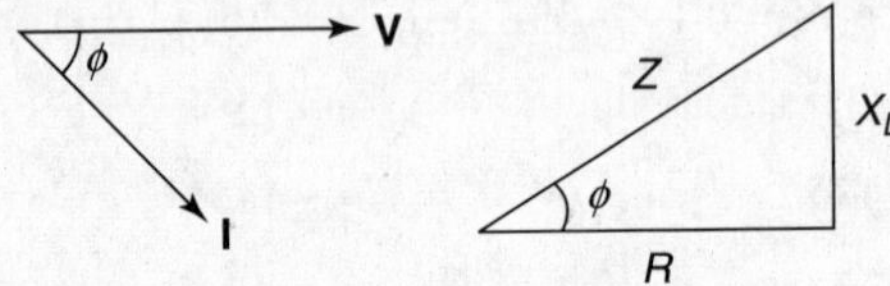

Fig. 3.101 *Phasor diagram and impedance triangle of a series RL circuit*

$$\cos\phi = \frac{R}{Z}$$

$$\sin\phi = \frac{X_L}{Z} \qquad \ldots(3.1)$$

The current *I* has two components, $I_x$ and $I_y$,

$$I_x = I\cos\phi = \frac{V}{Z}\frac{R}{Z} = \frac{VR}{Z^2} = \frac{VR}{R^2 + X_L{}^2} \qquad \ldots(3.2)$$

$$I_y = -I\sin\phi = -\frac{V}{Z}\cdot\frac{X_L}{Z} = -\frac{VX_L}{Z^2} = -\frac{VX_L}{R^2 + X_L{}^2} \qquad \ldots(3.3)$$

Squaring and adding Eqs (3.2) and (3.3),

$$I_x{}^2 + I_y{}^2 = \frac{V^2R^2}{(R^2 + X_L{}^2)^2} + \frac{V^2X_L{}^2}{(R^2 + X_L)^2}, = \frac{V^2(R^2 + X_L^2)}{(R^2 + X_L{}^2)^2}, = \frac{V^2}{R^2 + X_L^2}$$

From Eq. (3.3),

$$R^2 + X_L^2 = -\frac{VX_L}{I_y}$$

$$I_x{}^2 + I_y{}^2 = -\frac{VI_y}{X_L}$$

$$I_x{}^2 + I_y{}^2 + \frac{VI_y}{X_L} = 0$$

Adding $\left(\frac{V}{2X_L}\right)^2$ to both the sides,

$$I_x^2 + (I_y + \frac{V}{2X_L})^2 = \left(\frac{V}{2X_L}\right)^2 \quad \ldots(3.4)$$

Equation (3.4) represents a circle with radius $\frac{V}{2X_L}$ and centre $\left(0, -\frac{V}{2X_L}\right)$.

Thus, the locus of the extremity of a current phasor is a circle. But the maximum possible value for $\phi$ is 90°. When $R = 0$, the locus will be a semicircle. Hence, the locus diagram for a series *RL* circuit with variable resistance is a semicircle of radius $\frac{V}{2X_L}$ and centre $\left(0, -\frac{V}{2X_L}\right)$. The locus diagram is shown in Fig. 3.102.

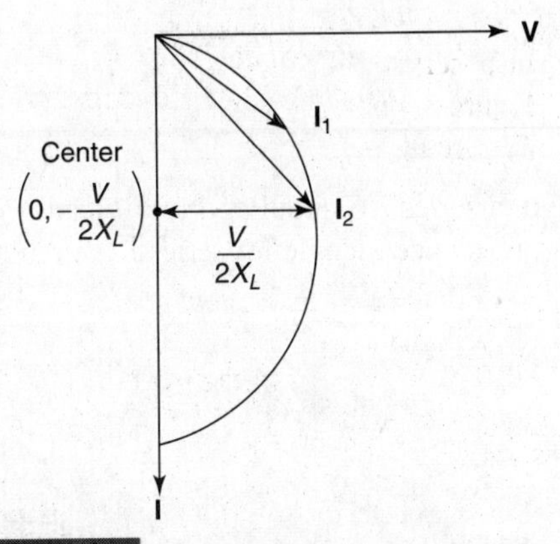


Fig. 3.102 *Locus diagram of a series RL circuit for variable R*

Similarly, the locus diagram of a series *RL* circuit with variable reactance and constant resistance can be drawn. From Eq. (3.3),

$$R^2 + X_L^2 = \frac{VR}{I_x}$$

$$I_x^2 + I_y^2 = \frac{V}{R} I_x$$

$$I_x^2 + I_y^2 - \frac{V}{R} I_x = 0$$

Adding $\left(\frac{V}{2R}\right)^2$ on both the sides,

$$\left(I_x - \frac{V}{2R}\right)^2 + I_y^2 = \left(\frac{V}{2R}\right)^2 \quad \ldots(3.5)$$

Equation (3.5) represents a circle with radius $\frac{V}{2R}$ and centre $\left(\frac{V}{2R}, 0\right)$. Thus, the locus of the extremity of a current phasor is a semicircle of radius $\frac{V}{2R}$ and centre $\left(\frac{V}{2R}, 0\right)$. The locus diagram is shown in Fig. 3.103.

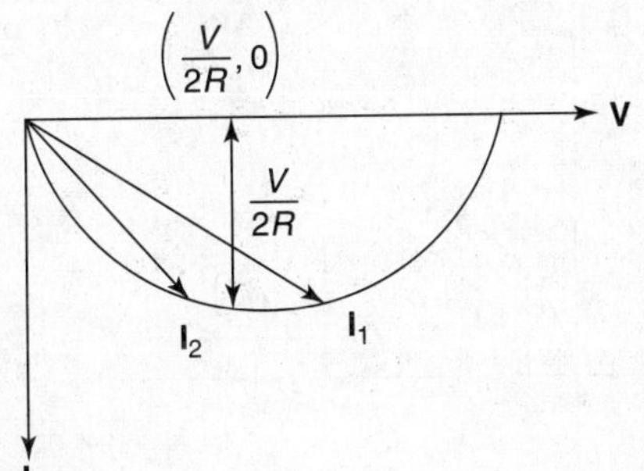


Fig. 3.103 *Locus diagram of a series RL circuit for variable $X_L$*

### 3.14.2 Locus Diagram of a Series *RC* Circuit

Figure 3.104 shows a series *RC* circuit with variable resistance and constant reactance.

$$I = \frac{V}{Z} = \frac{V}{\sqrt{R^2 + X_C^2}}$$

**Fig. 3.104** *Series RC circuit*

In a series *RC* circuit, current *I* leads voltage *V* by an angle $\phi$. Figure 3.105 shows the phasor diagram and impedance triangle for series *RC* circuit.

$$\cos\phi = \frac{R}{Z}$$

$$\sin\phi = \frac{X_C}{Z}$$

**Fig. 3.105** *Phasor diagram and impedance triangle of a series RC circuit*

It can be similarly proved that the locus of the extremity of a current phasor is a semicircle with radius $\frac{V}{2X_C}$ and centre $\left(0, \frac{V}{2X_C}\right)$. The locus diagram is shown in Fig. 3.106.

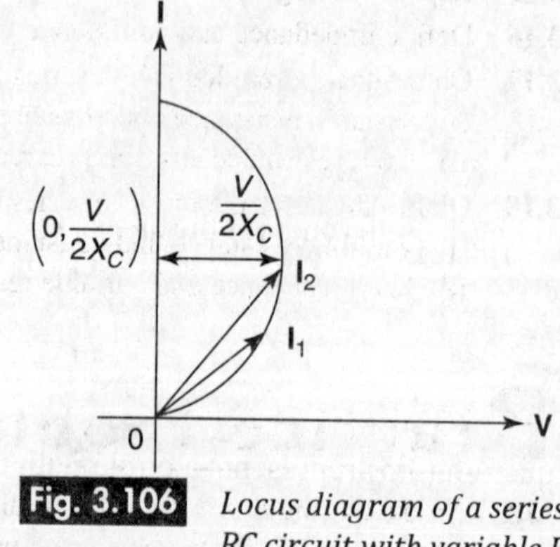


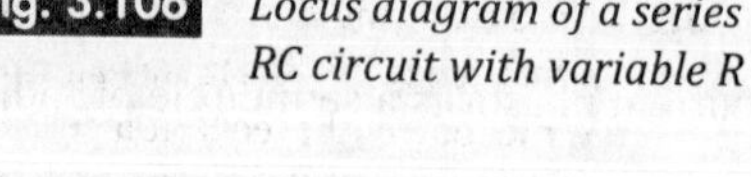

**Fig. 3.106** *Locus diagram of a series RC circuit with variable R*

For a series *RC* circuit with variable reactance and constant resistance, the locus of the extremity of a current phasor is a semicircle with radius $\frac{V}{2R}$ and centre $\left(\frac{V}{2R}, 0\right)$. The locus diagram is shown in Figure 3.107.

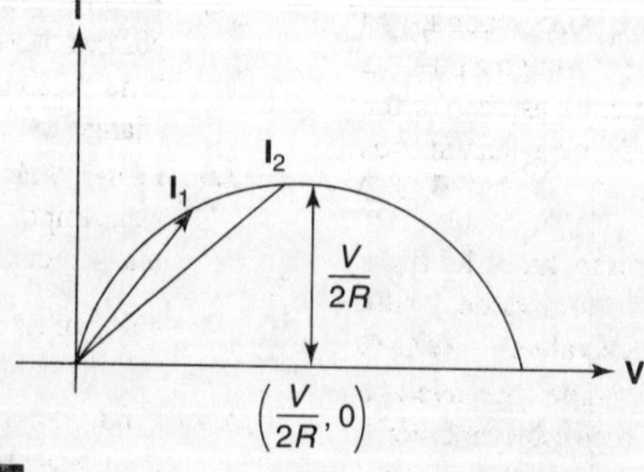


**Fig. 3.107** *Locus diagram of a series RC circuit with variable $X_C$*

# Theory Questions

3.1 Explain the concept of generation of alternating voltages. **[LO 3.1]** ●○○

3.2 Define the following terms related to alternating quantities: **[LO 3.2]** ●○○
(i) Waveform (ii) Cycle (iii) Frequency (iv) Time period
(v) Amplitude (vi) Phase (vii) Phase difference

3.3 Define RMS value and average value. **[LO 3.3]** ●○○

3.4 Define relation between RMS and maximum value of a sinusoidal waveform. **[LO 3.3]** ●○○

3.5 Derive expression for average value and form factor of a sinusoidal waveform. **[LO 3.3]** ○●○

3.6 Define form factor and peak factor. **[LO 3.3]** ●○○

3.7 Explain the method of representing sinusoidal quantities by phasors. **[LO 3.5]** ○●○

3.8 Explain the physical significance of operator *j*. **[LO 3.5]** ●○○

3.9 Explain behaviour of pure resistor in ac circuit. **[LO 3.6]** ○●○

3.10 Explain behaviour of pure inductor in ac circuit. **[LO 3.6]** ○●○

3.11 Explain behaviour of pure capacitor in ac circuit. **[LO 3.6]** ○●○

3.12 What is significance of power factor? **[LO 3.6]** ●○○

3.13 Draw the power triangles, impedance triangles and voltage triangles for series RL and series RC circuits. **[LO 3.7]** ●○○

3.14 Derive the expression for complex impedance of series RL and series RC circuits. **[LO 3.7]** ●○○

3.15 Explain average power, reactive power and apparent power related to ac circuit. **[LO 3.7]** ○●○

3.16 Define impedance and admittance of ac circuits. **[LO 3.8]** ●○○

3.17 Obtain the current locus of a series RL circuit with **[LO 3.9]** ○○●
(i) variable resistance and constant reactance
(ii) fixed resistance and variable reactance

3.18 Obtain the current locus of a series RC circuit with **[LO 3.9]** ○○●
(i) variable resistance and constant reactance
(ii) fixed resistance and variable reactance

# Practice Problems

3.1 An alternating current varying sinusoidally with a frequency of 50 Hz has an rms value of 20 A. Write down the equation for the instantaneous value and find this value (i) 0.0025 second, and (ii) 0.0125 second after passing through a positive maximum value. At what time, measured from a positive maximum value, will the instantaneous current be 14.14 A? ●○○

3.2 A certain waveform has a form factor of 1.2 and a peak factor of 1.5. If the maximum value is 100, find the rms value and average value. ●○○

3.3 Find the root mean square value, the average value and the form factor of the resultant current in a wire that carries simultaneously a direct current of 5 A and a sinusoidal alternating current with an amplitude of 5 A. ●○○

3.4 Find the relative heating effects of two in-phase current waveform of equal peak values and time periods, but one sinusoidal and the other triangular. ●○○

3.5 Prove that if a dc current of *I* amperes is superimposed in a conductor by an ac current of maximum value *I* amperes, the root mean square value of its resultant is $\sqrt{\frac{3}{2}}I$. ●○○

3.6 Find the average values and rms values of the waveforms shown in Fig. 3.108 to Fig. 3.111. ●○○

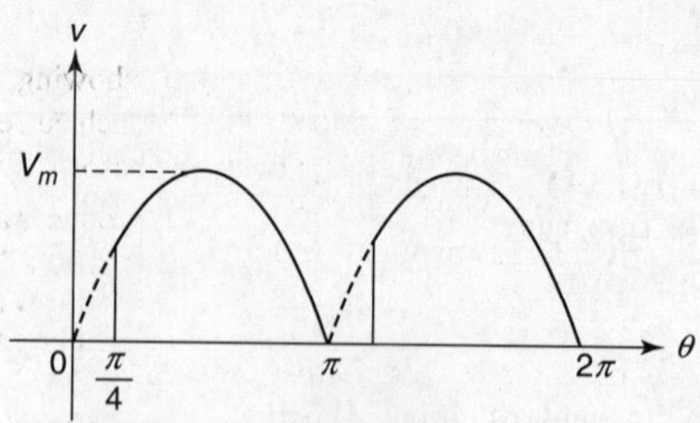

Fig. 3.108

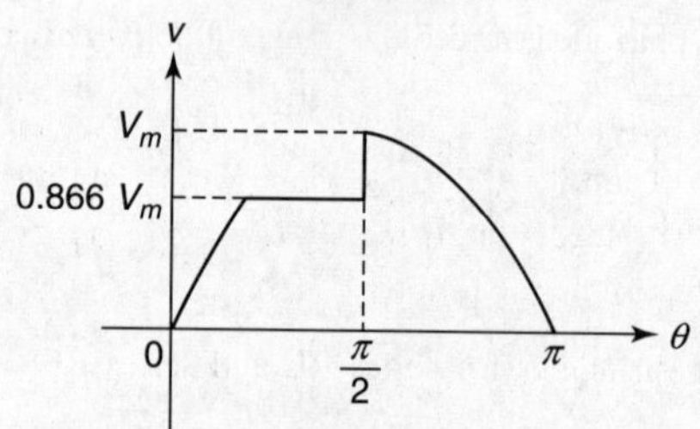

Fig. 3.109

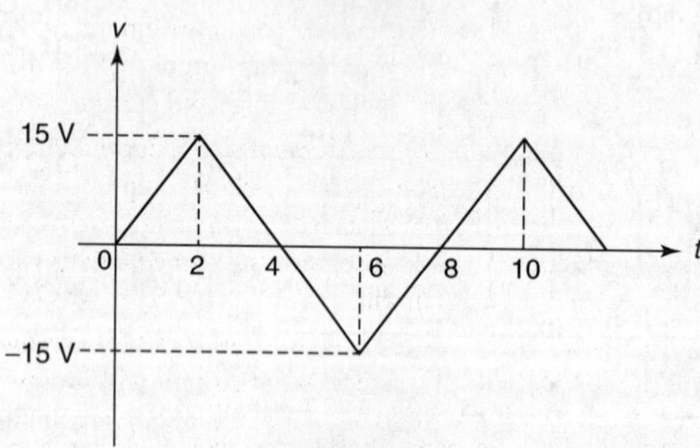

Fig. 3.110

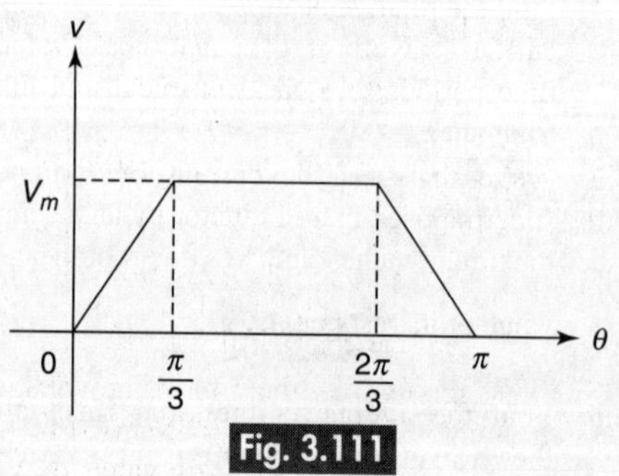

Fig. 3.111

**3.7** Find the rms value of the periodic waveform with time period $T$ given in Fig. 3.112. ○●○

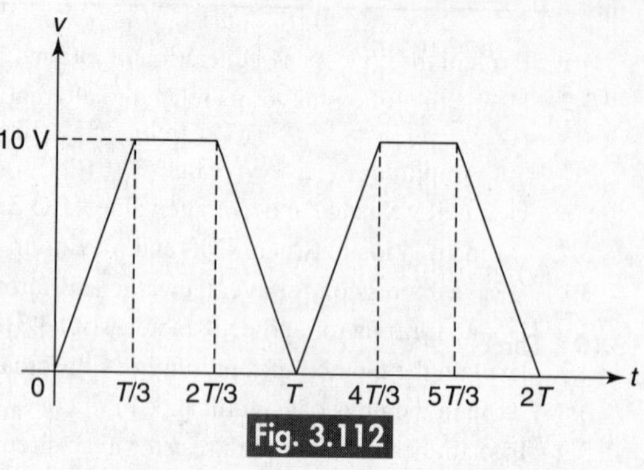

Fig. 3.112

**3.8** A voltage wave has the variation shown in Fig. 3.113. ○●○

(i) Find the average and effective values of the voltage.

(ii) If this voltage is applied to a 10 Ω resistance, find the dissipated power.

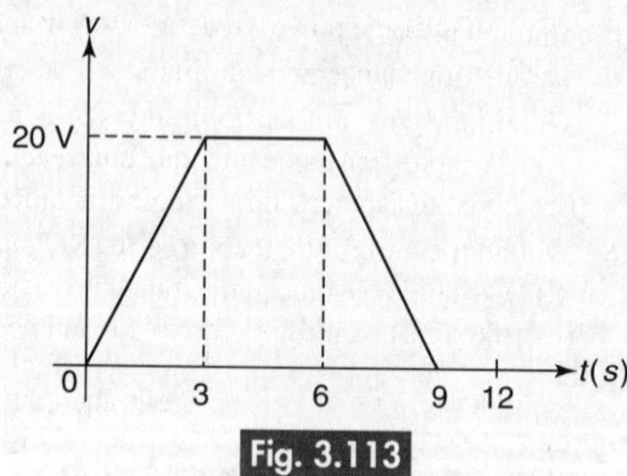

Fig. 3.113

**3.9** Find the resultants of the following voltages: ●○○

(i) $v_1 = 60 \cos\theta,$

$v_2 = 40 \sin\left(\theta - \frac{\pi}{3}\right),$

$v_3 = 15 \sin\theta$

(ii) $e_1 = 50 \sin \omega t,$

$e_2 = 100 \sin (\omega t + 120°)$

$e_3 = 120 \sin (\omega t - 30°)$

(iii) $v_1 = 4\sqrt{2} \sin (\omega t + 135°),$

$v_2 = -4\sqrt{3} \sin (\omega t + 60°),$

$v_3 = 4 \cos (\omega t - 150°)$

(iv) $e_1 = 25 \sin \omega t$,

$e_2 = 10 \sin\left(\omega t + \frac{\pi}{6}\right)$,

$e_3 = 30 \cos \omega t$,

$e_4 = 20 \sin\left(\omega t - \frac{\pi}{4}\right)$

(v) $v_1 = 10 \sin \omega t, \quad v_2 = -10 \cos \omega t$

**3.10** Three alternating currents $i_1 = 141 \sin\left(\omega t + \frac{\pi}{4}\right), i_2 = 30 \sin\left(\omega t + \frac{\pi}{2}\right)$ and $i_3 = 20 \sin\left(\omega t + \frac{\pi}{6}\right)$ are fed into a common conductor. Find graphically or otherwise the equation of the resultant current and its rms value. ●○○

**3.11** Four wires, *p*, *q*, *r*, *s* are connected to a common point. The currents in lines *p*, *q* and *r* are $6 \sin\left(\omega t + \frac{\pi}{3}\right)$, $5 \cos\left(\omega t + \frac{\pi}{3}\right)$ and $3 \cos\left(\omega t + \frac{\pi}{3}\right)$ respectively. Find the current in the wire *s*. ●○○

**3.12** A sinusoidal voltage $V_m \sin \omega t$ is applied to three parallel branches yielding branch currents as follows: ●○○

$i_1 = 14.14 \sin(\omega t - 45°)$

$i_2 = 28.3 \cos(\omega t - 60°)$

$i_3 = 7.07 \sin(\omega t + 60°)$

Find the complete expression for the source current. Draw the phasor diagram in terms of effective values. Use the voltage as reference.

**3.13** A sinusoidal voltage $V_m \sin \omega t$ is applied to three parallel branches. Two of the branch currents are given by ○●○

$i_1 = 14.14 \sin(\omega t - 37°)$

$i_2 = 28.28 \cos(\omega t - 143°)$

The source current is found to be $i = 63.8 \sin(\omega t + 12.8°)$.

(i) Find the effective value of the current in the third branch.

(ii) Write the complete time expression for the instantaneous value of the current in part (i).

(iii) Draw the phasor diagram showing the source current and the three branch currents. Use voltage as the reference phasor.

**3.14** A voltage wave $e(t) = 170 \sin 120\,t$ produces a net current of $14.14 \sin 120\,t + 7.07 \cos(120\,t + 30°)$. ●○○

(i) Express the effective value of the current as a single phasor quantity.

(ii) Draw the phasor diagram. Show the components of the current as well as the resultant.

(iii) Determine the power delivered by the source.

**3.15** The instantaneous values of two alternating voltages are represented by $v_1 = 60 \sin \theta$ and $v_2 = 40 \sin(\theta - \pi/3)$. Derive an expression for the instantaneous value of ●○○

(i) the sum, and

(ii) the difference of these voltages.

**3.16** A 250 V, 50 Hz voltage is applied across a circuit consisting of a pure resistance of 20 Ω. Determine ●○○

(i) the current flowing through the circuit, and

(ii) power absorbed by the circuit. Give the expressions for the voltage and current.

**3.17** A purely inductive circuit allows a current 20 A to flow through a 230 V, 50 Hz supply. Find (i) inductive reactance, (ii) inductance of the coil, (iii) power absorbed, and (iv) equations for voltage and current. ●○○

**3.18** A capacitor connected to a 230 V, 50 Hz supply draws a 15 A current. What current will it draw when the capacitance and frequency are both reduced to half? ●○○

**3.19** Calculate the impedance of the circuit shown in Fig. 3.114. ●○○

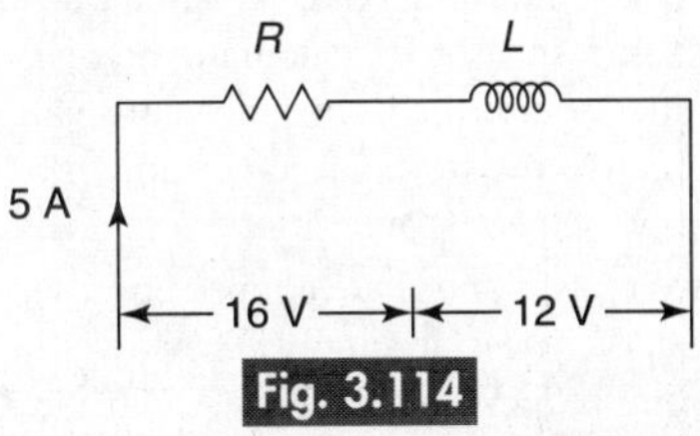


Fig. 3.114

**3.20** An ac circuit has the following voltage and current: $v = 325 \sin 314\,t$, $i = 65 \sin(314\,t - 1.57)$. Find (i) frequency, (ii) rms value of voltage and current, (iii) impedance, and (iv) power factor. ●○○

**3.21** Two sources of an electromotive force represented respectively by 200 sin $\omega t$ and 200 sin ($\omega t$ + $\pi$/6) are in series. Express the resultant in vector notation with reference to 200 sin $\omega t$ and calculate the rms current and power supplied to a circuit of 8 + $j$6 Ω impedance. ●○○

**3.22** The voltage applied to a series circuit consisting of two pure elements is given by $v$ = 180 sin $\omega t$ and the resulting current is given by $i$ = 2.5 sin ($\omega t$ – 45°). Find the average power taken by the circuit and the values of the elements. ●○○

**3.23** Find an expression for the current and calculate the power when a voltage represented by $v$ = 283 sin 100 $\pi t$ is applied to a coil having $R$ = 50 Ω and $L$ = 0.159 H. ●○○

**3.24** A voltage $V$ = (150 + $j$180) $V$ is applied across an impedance and the current is found to be $I$ = (5 – $j$4) A. Determine (i) scalar impedance, (ii) reactance, and (iii) power consumed. ●○○

**3.25** The current in a series circuit of $R$ = 5 Ω and $L$ = 30 mH lags the applied voltage by 72°. Determine the source frequency and the impedance $Z$. ●○○

**3.26** Current flowing through an inductive circuit is 15 sin ($\omega t$ + $\pi$/4). When the voltage applied across it is 30 cos $\omega t$, find the pf of the circuit. ●○○

**3.27** Voltage and current in an ac circuit are given by

$v$ = 200 sin 377$t$ $\quad$ $i$ = 8 sin (377$t$ – $\pi$/6)

Determine true power, reactive power and apparent power drawn by the circuit. ●○○

**3.28** A current of 5 A flows through a non-inductive resistor in series with a choke coil when supplied at 250 V, 50 Hz. If the voltage drops across the coil and non-inductive resistor are 200 V and 125 V respectively, calculate the resistance and inductance of the impedance coil, value of non-inductive resistor and power drawn by the coil. Draw the vector diagram. ○●○

**3.29** Two coils $A$ and $B$ are connected in series across a 200 V, 50 Hz ac supply. The power input to the circuit is 2 kW and 1.15 kVAR. If the resistance and reactance of the coil $A$ are 5 Ω and 8 Ω respectively, calculate resistance and reactance of the coil $B$. Also, calculate the active power consumed by coils $A$ and $B$. ○●○

**3.30** A choking coil and a pure resistor are connected in series across a supply of 230 V, 50 Hz. The voltage drop across the resistor is 100 V and that across the chocking coil is 150 V. Find the voltage drop across the inductance and resistance of the choking coil. Hence, find their values if the current is 1 A. ○●○

**3.31** For Fig. 3.115, find $R$ and $L$. ○●○

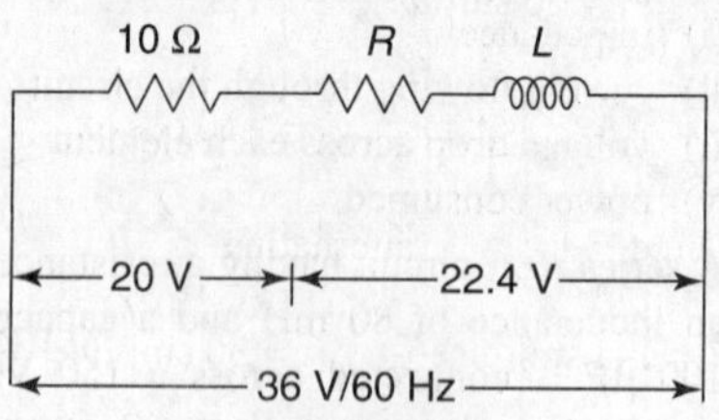


Fig. 3.115

**3.32** Voltage and current for a circuit with two pure elements in series are expressed as follows:

$$v(t) = 170\sin\left(6280t + \frac{\pi}{3}\right) \text{ volts}$$

$$i(t) = 8.5\sin\left(6280t + \frac{\pi}{2}\right) \text{ amperes}$$

Sketch the two waveforms. Determine (i) frequency, (ii) power stating its nature, and (iii) values of the elements. ●○○

**3.33** A load consisting of a capacitor in series with a resistor has an impedance of 50 Ω and a pf of 0.707 leading. The load is connected in series with a 40 Ω resistor across an ac supply and the resulting current is of 3 A. Determine the supply voltage and overall phase angle. ●○○

**3.34** A capacitive load takes 10 kVA and 5 kVAR, when connected to a 200 V, 50 Hz ac supply. Calculate (i) resistance, (ii) capacitance, (iii) active power, and (iv) pf. ○●○

**3.35** A resistor of 100 Ω is connected in series with a 50 μF capacitor to a 50 Hz, 200 V supply. Find: ●○○

(i) impedance (ii) current

(iii) power factor (iv) phase angle

(v) voltage across the resistor and across the capacitor.

**3.36** In an $RLC$ series circuit, the voltage across the resistor, inductor and capacitor are 10 V, 15 V and 10 V respectively. What is the supply voltage? ●○○

**3.37** A resistor $R$, inductor $L$ = 0.01 H and capacitor $C$ are connected in series. When a voltage of 400 sin (3000 $t$ − 10°) is applied to a series combination, the current flowing is $10\sqrt{2}$ cos (3000 $t$ − 55°). Find $R$ and $C$. ●○○

**3.38** A resistor of 20 Ω, an inductor of 0.2 H and a capacitor of 100 μF are connected in series across a 220 V, 50 Hz supply. Determine ●○○
(i) impedance
(ii) current flowing through the circuit
(iii) voltage drop across each element
(iv) power consumed

**3.39** A series $RLC$ circuit having a resistance of 8 Ω, an inductance of 80 mH and a capacitance of 100 μF is connected across a 150 V, 50 Hz supply. Calculate (i) current, (ii) power factor, and (iii) voltage across the inductance and capacitance. ●○○

**3.40** An emf of 100 V, 50 Hz is applied to an impedance $\mathbf{Z}_1 = 8 + j6$ Ω. An impedance $\mathbf{Z}_2$ is added in series with $\mathbf{Z}_1$. The current becomes half of the original and leads it by 20°. Determine $\mathbf{Z}_2$. ●○○

**3.41** In a series $RLC$ circuit, the inductor is imperfect and the capacitor has no leakage but has a lead resistance. When the circuit is connected to a 50 Hz supply, the voltage drop across the resistor and the inductor is 200 V. The voltage drop across the resistor and the capacitor is 250 V. The voltage drop across the resistor alone is 150 V. The voltage drop across the capacitor and inductor are 125 V and 100 V respectively. If the current flowing through the circuit is 1 A, find graphically ○●○
(i) capacitance
(ii) lead resistance of the capacitor
(iii) inductance
(iv) resistance of the inductor
(v) applied voltage

**3.42** Two impedances of 10 ∠ 30° Ω and 20 ∠−45° Ω are connected in series. Calculate the power factor of the series combination. ●○○

**3.43** Two impedances $Z_1$ and $Z_2$ are connected in series across a 230 V, 50 Hz ac supply. The total current drawn by the series combination in 2.3 A. The pf of $Z_1$ is 0.8 lagging. The voltage drop across $Z_1$ is twice the voltage drop across $Z_2$ and it is 90° out of phase with it. Determine the value of $Z_2$. ○●○

**3.44** In the arrangement shown in Fig. 3.116, $C = 20$ microfarads and the current flowing through the circuit is 0.345 A. If the voltages are as indicated, find the applied voltage, frequency and loss in the iron-cored inductor. Draw the phasor diagram. ○●○

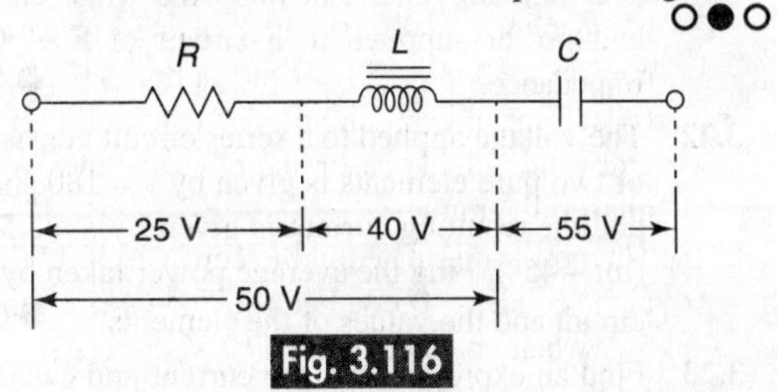


Fig. 3.116

**3.45** Two impedances of 14 + $j$5 Ω and 18 + $j$10 Ω are connected in parallel across a 200 V, 50 Hz supply, Determine (i) admittance of each branch and the entire circuit, (ii) current in each branch and total current, (iii) power and power factor of each branch, (iv) total power factor, and (v) draw phasor diagram. ●○○

**3.46** In a parallel $RC$ circuit shown in Fig. 3.117, $i_R$ = 15 cos (5000 $t$ −30°) amperes. Obtain the current in capacitance. ●○○

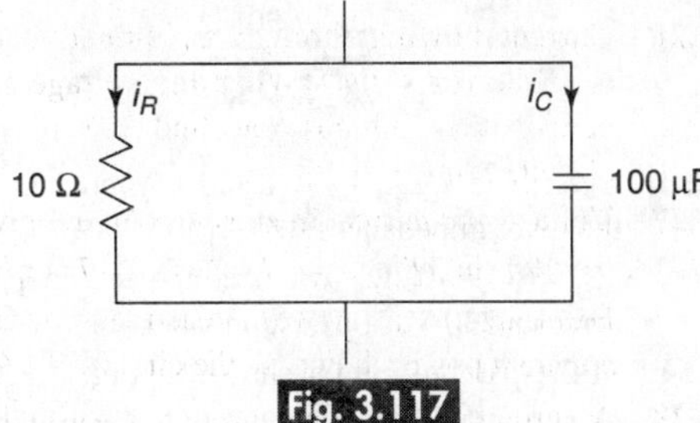


Fig. 3.117

**3.47** A voltage $v$ = 100 sin (5000 $t$ + $\pi/4$) is applied across a three-branch circuit, as shown in Fig. 3.118. Find the rms value of the current in the inductor. ●○○

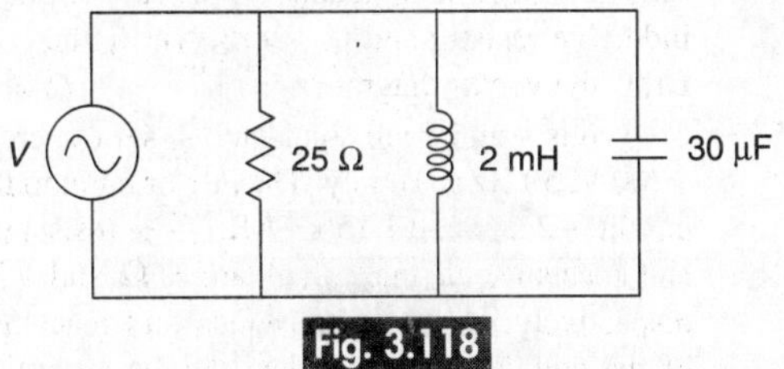


Fig. 3.118

**3.48** A circuit comprises a conductance $G$ in parallel with a susceptance $B$. Calculate the admittance $G + jB$ if the impedance is $10 + j5$ Ω. ●○○

**3.49** If an admittance of a circuit is $(8 + j6)$ ℧ and the circuit current is $2\angle 30°$A, find the pf of the circuit. Also, calculate the apparent power in the circuit. ●○○

**3.50** A resistor of 50 Ω, and inductor of 0.15 H and a capacitor of 100 μF are connected in parallel across a 100 V, 50 Hz ac supply. Calculate (i) current in each circuit, (ii) resultant current. Draw individual phasor diagrams and the overall phasor diagram. ●○○

**3.51** The power dissipated in the coil A is 300 W and in the coil B is 400 W. Each coil takes a current of 5 A when connected to a 110 V, 50 Hz supply. Find the current drawn when the coils are connected in parallel. ○●○

**3.52** Find the total impedance, supply current and pf of the entire circuit. ○●○

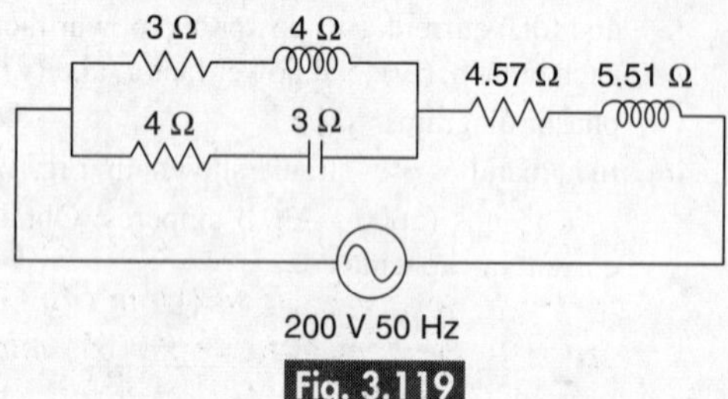


Fig. 3.119

**3.53** Determine kVA, kVAR and kW consumed by the two impedances $\mathbf{Z}_1 = (20 + j37.7)\ \Omega$ and $\mathbf{Z}_2 = (50 + j0)\ \Omega$, when connected in parallel across a 230 V, 50 Hz supply. ○●○

**3.54** In the parallel circuit shown in Fig. 3.120, the power in the 3 Ω resistor is 666 W and the total volt-amperes taken by the circuit is 3370 VA. The power factor of the whole circuit is 0.937 leading. Find *Z*. ○●○

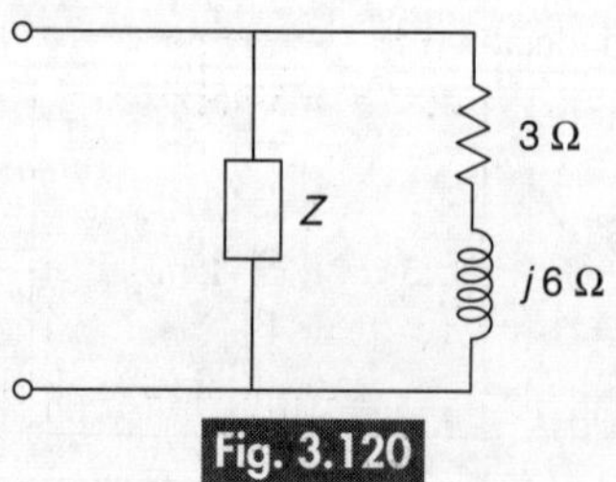


Fig. 3.120

**3.55** A coil is connected across a non-inductive resistor of 120 Ω. When a 240 V, 50 Hz supply is applied to this circuit, the coil draws a current of 5 A and the total current is 6 A. Determine the power and the power factor of (i) the coil, and (ii) the whole circuit. ○●○

**3.56** A coil takes a current of 10 A and dissipates 1410 W when connected to 220 V, 50 Hz supply. If another coil is connected in parallel with it, the total current taken from the supply is 20 A at a power factor of 0.868. Determine the current and the overall power factor when the coils are connected in series across the same supply. ○●○

**3.57** Draw an impedance triangle between terminals *AB* in Fig. 3.121, labelling its sides with appropriate values and units. ●○○

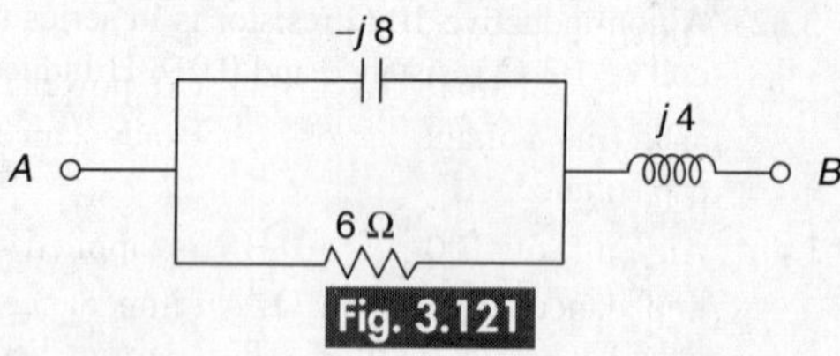


Fig. 3.121

**3.58** Draw the impedance triangle between terminals *AB* in Fig. 3.122, for the following conditions:
(i) $-X_C = 8\ \Omega$, $R = 6\ \Omega$, $X_L = 4\ \Omega$ ●○○
(ii) $X_C = 4\ \Omega$, $R = 6\ \Omega$, $X_L = 6\ \Omega$
Label its side with appropriate values and units.

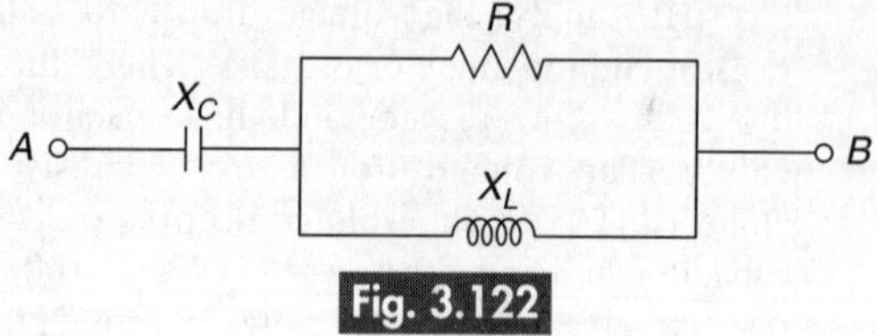


Fig. 3.122

**3.59** Draw an admittance triangle between terminals *AB* in Fig. 3.123, labelling its sides with appropriate values and units in case of ●○○
(i) $X_L = 4\ \Omega$, and $X_C = 8\ \Omega$
(ii) $X_L = 10\ \Omega$, and $X_C = 5\ \Omega$

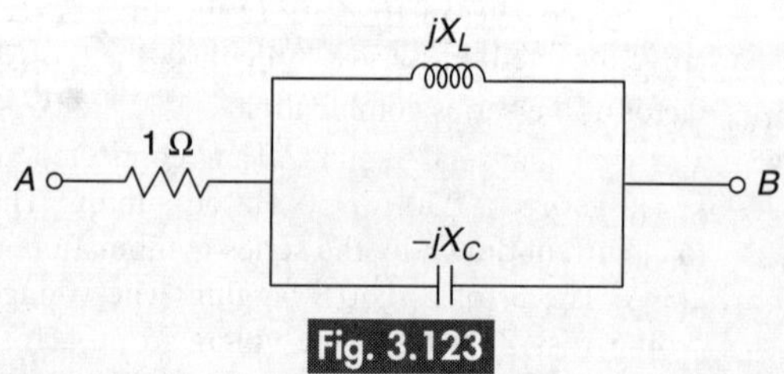


Fig. 3.123

**3.60** An inductive impedance *BC* is connected in series with a parallel combination *AB*, consisting of a capacitor and a non-inductive resistor. The circuit constants are so adjusted that the current in the parallel branches $AB$ are equal, and that the voltage across $AB$ is equal to and in quadrature with the voltage across $BC$. When a voltage of 200 V is applied to $AC$, the total power absorbed is 1200 W. Calculate the circuit constants and draw a vector diagram. ○●○

**3.61** A 100 Ω resistor, shunted by a 0.4 H inductor is in series with a capacitor $C$. A voltage of 250 V at 50 Hz is applied to the circuit. Find ○●○
(i) the value of $C$ to give unity power factor
(ii) the total current
(iii) current in the inductive branch

**3.62** A non-inductive 10 Ω resistor is in series with a coil of 1.3 Ω resistance and 0.018 H inductance. If a voltage of maximum value of 100 V at a frequency of 100 Hz is applied to this circuit, what will be the voltage across the resistor? ○●○

**3.63** Two impedances $\mathbf{Z}_1 = 10 - j15\ \Omega$ and $\mathbf{Z}_2 = 4 + j8\ \Omega$ are connected in parallel. The supply voltage is 100 V, 25 Hz. Calculate (i) the admittance, conductance and susceptance of the combined circuit, and (ii) total current drawn and pf. ●○○

**3.64** A voltage of $200\angle 53.13°$ V is applied across two impedances in parallel. The values of the impedances are $(12 + j16)\ \Omega$ and $(10 - j20)\ \Omega$. Determine kVA, kVAR and kW in each branch and the pf of the whole circuit. ●○○

**3.65** For the circuit shown in Fig. 3.124, evaluate the current through and voltage across each element. ●○○

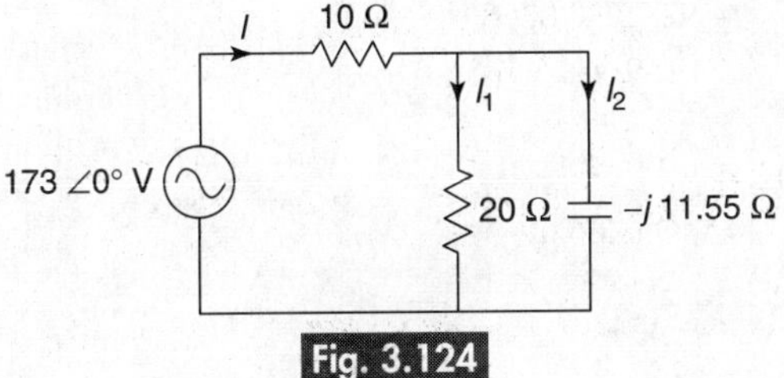


Fig. 3.124

**3.66** Two impedances $Z_1$ and $Z_2$ are connected in parallel. The first branch takes a leading current of 16 A and has a resistance of 5 Ω, while the second branch takes a lagging current at a pf of 0.8. The total power supplied is 5 kW, the applied voltage being $(100 + j200)$ V. Determine branch currents and total current. ○●○

**3.67** For the parallel branch shown in Fig. 3.125, find the value of $R_2$ when the overall power factor is 0.92 lag. ○○●

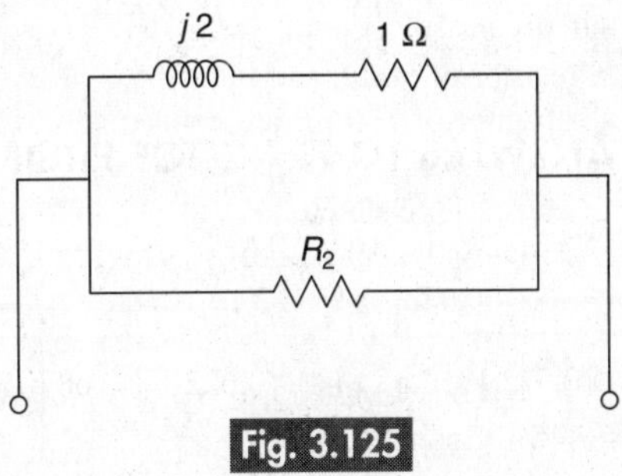


Fig. 3.125

**3.68** In a series–parallel circuit, two parallel branches $A$ and $B$ are in series with $C$. The impedances are $\mathbf{Z}_A = (10 + j8)\ \Omega$, and $\mathbf{Z}_B = (9 - j6)\ \Omega$ and $\mathbf{Z}_C(3+j2)\ \Omega$. If the voltage across $Z_C$ is $100\angle 0°$ V, determine the values $I_A$ and $I_B$. ●○○

**3.69** A capacitor is placed in parallel with two inductive loads. The current through the first inductor is 20 A at 30° lag and the current through the second is 40 A at 60° lag. What must be the current in the capacitor so that the current in the external circuit is of unity power factor? ○●○

**3.70** A circuit of 15 Ω resistance and 12 Ω inductive reactance is connected in parallel with another circuit consisting of a resistor of 25 Ω in series with a capacitive reactance of 17 Ω. This combination is energised from a 200 V, 40 Hz mains. Find the branch currents, total current and power factor of the circuit. It is desired to raise the power factor of this circuit to unity by connecting a capacitor in parallel. Determine the value of the capacitance of the capacitor. ○●○

**3.71** A resistor of 30 Ω and a capacitor of unknown value are connected in parallel across a 110 V, 50 Hz supply. The combination draws a current of 5 A from the supply. Find the value of the unknown capacitance of the capacitor. This combination is again connected across a 110 V supply of unknown frequency. It is observed that the total current drawn from the mains falls to 4 A. Determine the frequency of the supply. ○●○

**3.72** Two reactive circuits have an impedance of 20 Ω each. One of them has a lagging power factor of 0.8 and the other has a leading power factor of 0.6. Find (i) voltage necessary to send a current of 10 A through the two in series, and (ii) current drawn from 200 V supply if the two are connected in parallel. Draw a phasor diagram in each case. ○●○

**3.73** Inductor loads of 0.8 kW and 1.2 kW at lagging power factors of 0.8 and 0.6 respectively are connected across a 200 V, 50 Hz supply. Find the total current, power factor and the value of the capacitor to be put in parallel to both to raise the overall power factor to 0.9 lagging. ○●○

## ANSWERS TO PRACTICE PROBLEMS

**3.1** $i = 28.28 \sin 100\,\pi t$, 20 A, – 20 A, $\frac{1}{300}$ s

**3.2** 66.67 V, 55.67 V

**3.3** 6.12 A, 5 A, 1.224

**3.4** 3:2

**3.6** (0.543 $V_m$, 0.674 $V_m$), (0.622 $V_m$, 0.687 $V_m$), (7.5 V, 8.666 V), (0.67 $V_m$, 0.745 $V_m$)

**3.7** 7.45 V

**3.8** 10 V, 12.91 V, 16.67 W

**3.9** (i) $43.22 \sin(\theta + 35.92°)$, (ii) $107.27 \sin(\omega t + 14.35°)$, (iii) $7.73 \sin(\omega t - 135°)$
(iv) $52.14 \sin(\omega t + 23.57°)$, (v) $14.14 \sin(\omega t - 45°)$

**3.10** $167.5 \sin(\omega t + 45.6°)$, 118.54

**3.11** $9.99 \sin(\omega t - 66.84°)$

**3.12** $39.4 \sin(\omega t + 15.1°)$

**3.13** 39.95 A, $56.51 \sin(\omega t + 53.12°)$

**3.14** 8.66 ∠30° A, 901.7 W

**3.15** $87.17 \sin(\theta - 23.41°)$, $52.91 \sin(\theta + 40.89°)$

**3.16** (i) 12.5 A, (ii) 3.125 kW, (iii) $v = 353.6 \sin 314\,t$, $i = 17.68 \sin 314\,t$

**3.17** (i) 11.5 Ω, (ii) 36.62 mH, (iii) 0, (iv) $v = 325.27 \sin 314\,t$, $i = 28.28 \sin\left(314t - \frac{\pi}{2}\right)$

**3.18** 3.75 A

**3.19** 4 Ω

**3.20** 50 Hz, 229.81 V, 45.96 *A*, 5 Ω 0.99 (lagging)

**3.21** 273.2 ∠15° V, 27.32 ∠–21.87° A, 5971 W

**3.22** 159 W, 50.91 Ω, 50.91 Ω

**3.23** $4 \sin(100\pi t - \pi/4)$, 400 W

**3.24** 36.6 Ω, 36.6 Ω, 30 W

**3.25** 81.63 Hz, 16.18 Ω

**3.26** 0.707 (lagging)

**3.27** 692.82 W, 400 VAR, 800 VA

**3.28** 5.5 Ω, 0.126 H, 25 Ω, 137.5 W

**3.29** 10.3 Ω, 0.642 Ω, 665.3 W, 1334.7 W

**3.30** 109.98 V, 102 V, 0.366 H, 102 Ω

**3.31** 4.928 Ω, 0.0266 H

**3.32** (ii) 0.866 (leading) (iii) 17.32 Ω, 16 μF

**3.33** 249.69 V, 25.135°

**3.34** 3.464 Ω, $1.59 \times 10^{-3}$ F, 8.66 kW, 0.866 (leading)

**3.35** 118.6 Ω, 1.69 A,0.845 (leading), 32.48°, 168.712 V, 107.42 V

**3.36** 11.18 V

**3.37** 20 Ω, 6.66 μF

**3.38** 36.9 Ω, 5.96 A, 119.2 V, 374.52 V, 189.64 V, 710.43 W

**3.39** (i) 14.35 A (ii) 0.766 (leading) (iii) 360.47 V, 457.04 V

**3.40** $(11.14 - j0.2)$ Ω

**3.41** 33.5 μF, 81.25 Ω, 0.3 H, 25 Ω, 256.26 V

**3.42** 0.9281 (lagging)

**3.43** 44.719 Ω

**3.44** 34.2 V, 50 Hz, 1.89 W

**3.45** 0.067∠–19.6° ℧, 0.048 ∠–29.05°℧, 0.115∠–23.75° ℧, 13.45∠–19.65°A,
9.6 ∠–29.05°A, 22.91∠–23.75° A, 2532.64 W, 1658.8 W, 0.94 (lagging), 0.874 (lagging), 0.916 (lagging)

**3.46** $74.95 \sin(5000\,t + 150°)$

**3.47** 7.07 A

**3.48** 0.08 S, 0.04 S

**3.49** 0.8 (leading), 0.2 VA

**3.50** 2 ∠0° A, 2.12 ∠–90°A, 3.14 ∠90° A, 2.25 ∠27.02° A

**3.51** 9.93 ∠–50.11°A

**3.52** 10.06 $\angle 36.68°$ Ω, 19.88 $\angle -36.68°$ A,0.8 (lagging)

**3.53** 1.971 kVA, 1.095 kVAR, 1.64 kW **3.54** $(2 - j2)\ \Omega$

**3.55** 420 W, 0.35 (lagging), 900 W, 0.625 (lagging) **3.56** 5.55 A, 0.8499 (lagging)

**3.57** $R = 3.84\ \Omega$, $X = 1.12\ \Omega$ (inductive), $Z = 4\ \Omega$

**3.58** (i) $R = 1.8461\ \Omega$, $X = 5.2308\ \Omega$, (capacitive), $Z = 5.547\ \Omega$, (ii) $R = 3\ \Omega$, $X = 1\ \Omega$, (capacitive), $Z = 3.1623\ \Omega$

**3.59** (i) $G = 0.015$ ℧, $B_L = 0.123$ ℧, $Y = 0.124$ ℧, (ii) $G = 0.0098$ ℧, $B_C = 0.099$ ℧, $Y = 0.1$ ℧

**3.60** $AB = R = 33.32\ \Omega$ in parallel with $X_C = 33.32\ \Omega$, $BC = (16.66 + j16.66)\ \Omega$

**3.61** 65.4 μF, 4.08 A, 2.55 A **3.62** 62.54 V

**3.63** 0.097 ℧, 0.081 ℧, 0.054 ℧, 9.7 A, 0.83 (lagging)

**3.64** 2 kVA, 1.2 kW, 1.6 kVAR, 1.788 kVA, 0.8 kW, 1.6 kVAR, unity pf

**3.65** $\mathbf{I}_1 = 5\angle -30°$ A, $\mathbf{I}_2 = 8.66\angle 60°$ A, $\mathbf{V}_1 = 100\angle -30°$ V, $\mathbf{V}_2 = 100\angle -30°$ V, $\mathbf{V}_{10\Omega} = 100\angle -30°$ V

**3.66** $16\angle 132.46°$ A, $20.8\angle 26.57°$ A, 22.49 A **3.67** 1.35 Ω

**3.68** $15.7\angle -73.39°$ A, $18.59\angle -1.04°$ A **3.69** $44.64\angle 90°$ A

**3.70** $10.42\angle -38.56°$ A, $6.61\angle 34.21°$ A, $13.95\angle -11.56°$ A, 0.98 (lagging), 54.9 μF

**3.71** 98.58 μF, 23.68 Hz **3.72** 282.8 V, 14.14 A

**3.73** 14.87 A, 0.673 (lagging), 98 μF

# Objective-Type Questions

## From GATE and Other Competitive Examinations

**3.1** A current is said to be alternating when it changes in ●○○
(a) magnitude only
(b) direction only
(c) both magnitude and direction
(d) neither magnitude nor direction

**3.2** An alternating current of 50 Hz frequency and 100 A maximum value is given as ●○○
(a) $i = 200 \sin 628\, t$
(b) $i = 100 \sin 314\, t$
(c) $i = 100\sqrt{2} \sin 314\, t$
(d) $i = 100\sqrt{2} \sin 157\, t$

**3.3** An alternating current of 50 Hz frequency has a maximum value of 100 A. Its value $\frac{1}{600}$ second after the instant the current is zero will be ●○○
(a) 25 A (b) 12.5 A
(c) 50 A (d) 75 A

**3.4** A sinusoidal voltage varies from zero to a maximum of 250 V. The voltage at the instant of 60° of the cycle will be ●○○
(a) 150 V (b) 216.5 V
(c) 125 V (d) 108.25 V

**3.5** An alternating current is given by the expression $i = 200 \sin\left(314t + \frac{\pi}{3}\right)$ amperes. The maximum value and frequency of the current are ●○○
(a) 200 A, 50 Hz (b) $100\sqrt{2}$, 50 Hz
(c) 200 A, 100 Hz (d) 200 A, 25 Hz

**3.6** The average value of the current $i = 200 \sin t$ from $t = 0$ to $t = \frac{\pi}{2}$ is ●○○
(a) $400\, \pi$ (b) $\frac{400}{\pi}$
(c) $\frac{1}{400}$ (d) $\frac{\pi}{400}$

**3.7** The rms value of half-wave rectified current is 50 A. Its rms value for full-wave rectification would be ○●○
(a) 100 A (b) 70.7 A
(c) $\frac{50}{\pi}$ A (d) $\frac{100}{\pi}$ A

**3.8** When the two quantities are in quadrature, the phase angle between them will be ●○○
(a) 45° (b) 90°
(c) 135° (d) 60°

**3.9** The phase difference between the two waveforms can be compared when they ●○○
(a) have the same frequency
(b) have the same peak value
(c) have the same effective value
(d) are sinusoidal

**3.10** If two sinusoids of the same frequency but of different amplitude and phase difference are added, the resultant is a ●○○
(a) sinusoid of the same frequency
(b) sinusoid of double the original frequency
(c) sinusoid of half the original frequency
(d) non-sinusoid

**3.11** Two alternating currents represented as $i_1 = 4 \sin \omega t$ and $i_2 = 10 \sin\left(\omega t + \frac{\pi}{3}\right)$ are fed into a common conductor. The rms value of the resultant current is ●○○
(a) 9.62 A (b) 8.83 A
(c) 12.48 A (d) 13.6 A

**3.12** A constant current of 2.8 A exists in a resistor. The rms value of the current is ●○○
(a) 2.8 A (b) 2 A
(c) 1.4 A (d) undefined

**3.13** The current through a resistor has a waveform, as shown in Fig. 3.126. The reading shown by a moving-coil ammeter will be ●○○

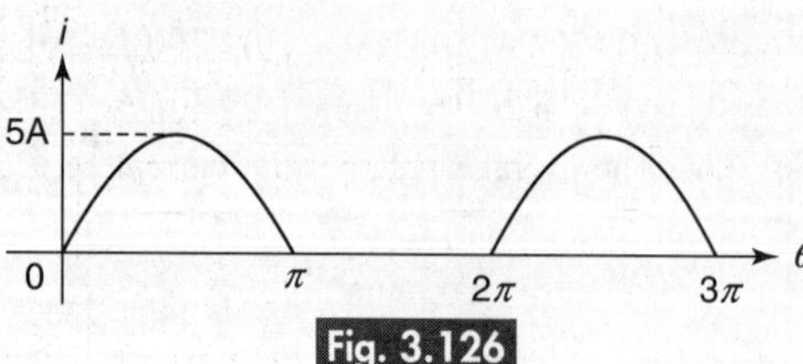

Fig. 3.126

(a) $\frac{5}{\sqrt{2}}$ A (b) $\frac{2.5}{\sqrt{2}}$ A
(c) $\frac{5}{\pi}$ A (d) 0

**3.14** Which of the following statements about the two alternating currents shown in Fig. 3.127 is correct? ●○○

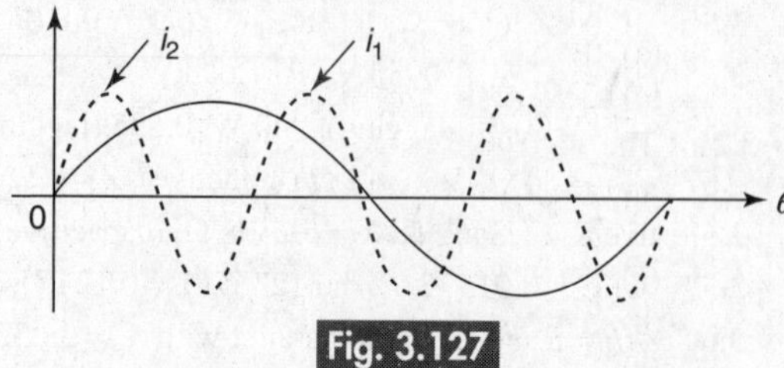


Fig. 3.127

(a) The peak values of $i_1$ and $i_2$ are different.
(b) The rms values of $i_1$ and $i_2$ are different.
(c) The time period of current $i_1$ is more than that of the current $i_2$.
(d) The frequency of current $i_1$ is more than that of the current $i_2$.

**3.15** The alternating voltage $e = 200 \sin 314\, t$ is applied to a device which offers an ohmic resistance of 20 Ω to the flow of current in one direction while entirely preventing the flow in the opposite direction. The overage value of the current will be ●○○
(a) 5 A (b) 3.18 A
(c) 1.57 A (d) 1.10 A

**3.16** A 10 mH inductor carries a sinusoidal current of 1 A rms at a frequency of 50 Hz. The average power dissipated by the inductor is ●○○
(a) 0 (b) 0.25 W
(c) 0.5 W (d) 1 W

**3.17** The power factor of an ordinary bulb is ●○○
(a) zero
(b) unity
(c) slightly more than unity
(d) slightly less than unity

**3.18** When a sinusoidal voltage is applied across *RL* series circuit having $R = X_L$, the phase angle will be ●○○
(a) 90° (b) 45°lag
(c) 45° lead (d) 90° lead

**3.19** An ac source having voltage $e = 110 \sin\left(\omega t + \frac{\pi}{3}\right)$ is connected in an ac circuit. If the current drawn from the circuit varies as $i = 5 \sin\left(\omega t - \frac{\pi}{3}\right)$, the impedance of the circuit will be ●○○
(a) 22 Ω (b) 16 Ω
(c) 30.8 Ω (d) none of these

**3.20** An ac source of 200 V rms supplies active power of 600 W and reactive power of 800 VAR. The rms current drawn from the source is ●○○

(a) 10 A (b) 5 A
(c) 3.75 A (d) 2.5 A

**3.21** The voltage phasor of a circuit is $10\angle 15°$ V and the current phasor is $2\angle -45°$ A. The active and reactive powers in the circuit are ●○○
(a) 10 W and 17.32 VAR
(b) 5 W and 8.66 VAR
(c) 20 W and 60 VAR
(d) $20\sqrt{2}$ and $10\sqrt{2}$ VAR

**3.22** In a two-element series circuit, the applied voltage and resultant current are respectively $v(t) = 50 + 50 \sin(5 \times 10^3 t)$ and $i(t) = 11.2 \sin(5 \times 10^3 t + 63.4°)$. The nature of the elements would be ●○○
(a) *RL* (b) *RC*
(c) *LC* (d) neither *R*, nor *L*, nor *C*

**3.23** A boiler at home is switched on to the ac mains supplying power at 230 V, 50 Hz. The frequency of instantaneous power consumed is ●○○
(a) 0 (b) 50 Hz
(c) 100 Hz (d) 150 Hz

**3.24** In a series *RLC* circuit, $V_R = 3$ V, $V_L = 14$ V, $V_C = 10$ V. The input voltage to the circuit is ●○○
(a) 10 V (b) 5 V
(c) 27 V (d) 24 V

**3.25** $A_1$, $A_2$ and $A_3$ are ideal ammeters, shown in Fig. 3.128. If $A_1$ reads 5 *A*, $A_2$ reads 12 A then $A_3$ should read ○●○

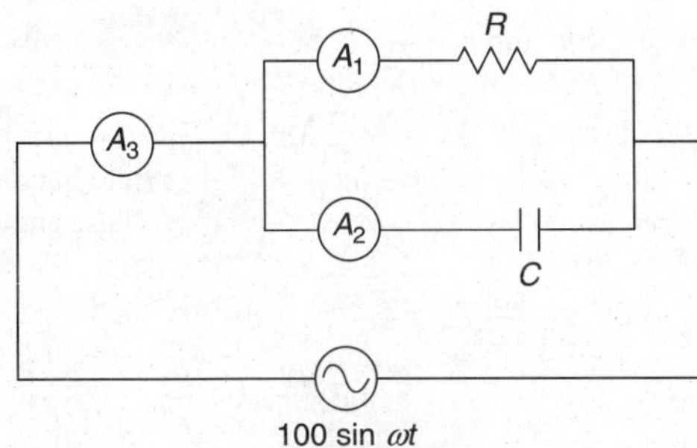


Fig. 3.128

(a) 7 A (b) 12 A
(c) 13 A (d) 17 A

**3.26** A series *RLC* circuit consisting of $R = 10\ \Omega$, $X_L = 20\ \Omega$ and $X_C = 20\ \Omega$ is connected across an ac supply of 200 V rms. The rms voltage across the capacitor is ●○○
(a) $200\angle -90°$ V (b) $200\angle 90°$ V
(c) $400\angle -90°$ V (d) $400\angle 90°$ V

**3.27** In Fig. 3.129, $A_1$, $A_2$, and $A_3$, are ideal ammeters. If $A_1$ and $A_3$ read 5 A and 13 A respectively, the reading of $A_2$ will be ○●○

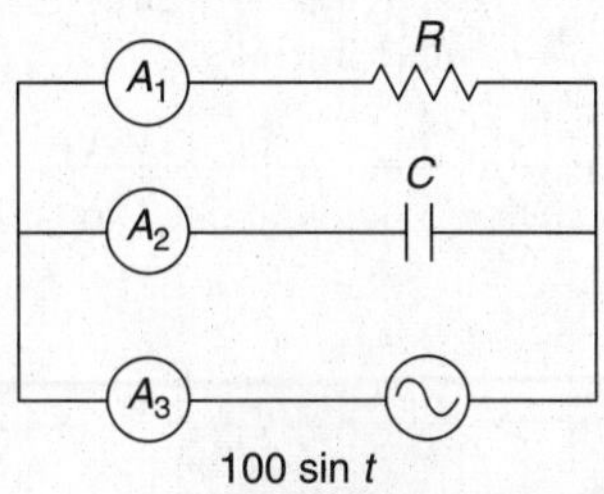


Fig. 3.129

(a) 8 A (b) 12 A
(c) 18 A (d) 10 A

**3.28** In Fig. 3.130, $i(t)$ under steady state is ○●○

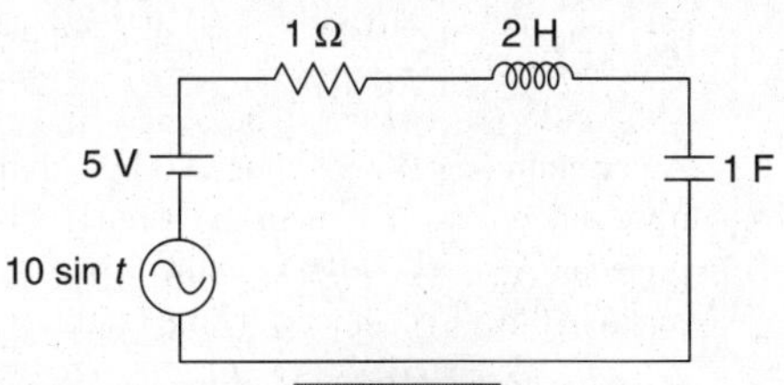


Fig. 3.130

(a) zero (b) 5
(c) 7.07 sin *t* (d) 7.07 sin$(t - 45°)$

**3.29** The circuit shown with $R = \frac{1}{3}\Omega$, $L = \frac{1}{4}$H, $C = 3$ F in Fig. 3.131 has input voltage $v(t) = \sin 2t$. The resulting current $i(t)$ is ●○○

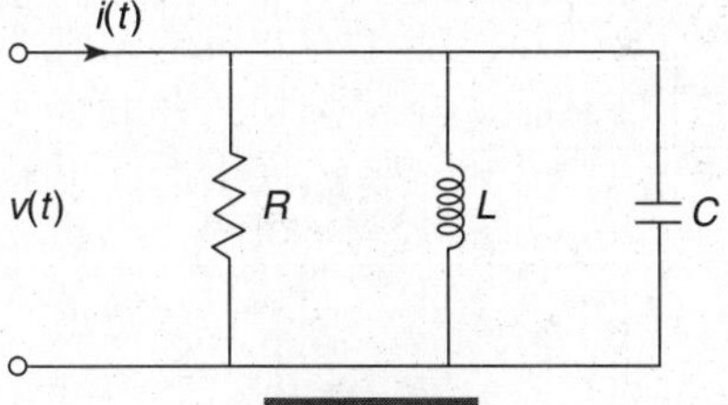


Fig. 3.131

(a) $5 \sin(2t + 53.1°)$ (b) $5 \sin(2t - 53.1°)$
(c) $25 \sin(2t + 53.1°)$ (d) $25 \sin(2t - 53.1°)$

**3.30** The average power delivered to an impedance $(4 - j3)\ \Omega$ by a current $5 \cos(100\pi t + 100°)$ A is ●○○
(a) 44.2 W (b) 50 W
(c) 62.5 W (d) 125 W

**3.31** The circuit shown in Fig. 3.132 is driven by a sinusoidal input $v_i = V_p \cos\left(\frac{t}{RC}\right)$. The steady state output is ○○●

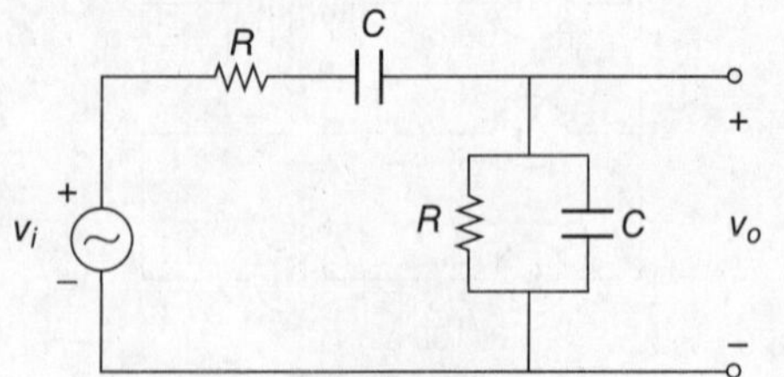


Fig. 3.132

(a) $\left(\frac{V_P}{3}\right)\cos\left(\frac{t}{RC}\right)$ (b) $\left(\frac{V_P}{3}\right)\sin\left(\frac{t}{RC}\right)$

(c) $\left(\frac{V_P}{2}\right)\cos\left(\frac{t}{RC}\right)$ (d) $\left(\frac{V_P}{2}\right)\sin\left(\frac{t}{RC}\right)$

**3.32** An ac source of RMS voltage 20 V with internal impedance $\mathbf{Z}_S = (1 + 2j)\ \Omega$ feeds a load of impedance $\mathbf{Z}_L = (7 + 4j)\ \Omega$ in the Fig. 3.133. The reactive power consumed by the load is ○○●

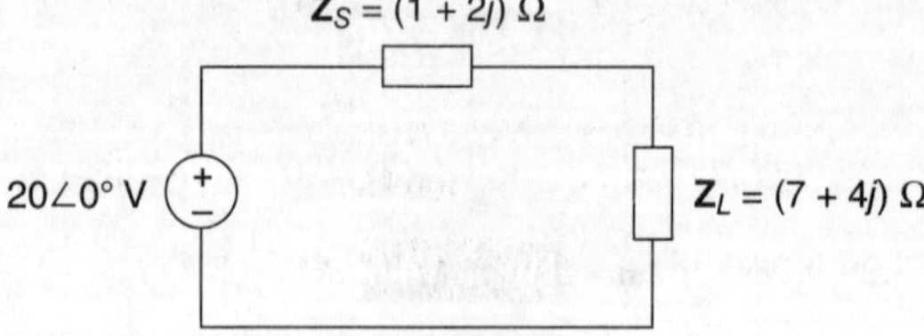


Fig. 3.133

(a) 8 VAR (b) 16 VAR
(c) 28 VAR (d) 32 VAR

**3.33** In the ac network shown in Fig. 3.134, the phasor voltage $\mathbf{V}_{AB}$ (in volts) is ○●○

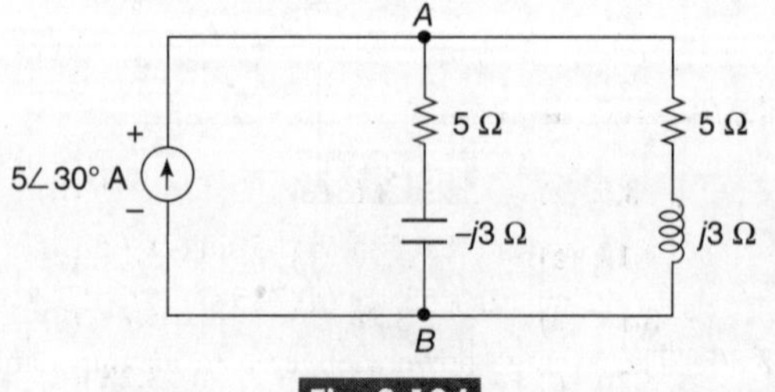


Fig. 3.134

(a) 0 (b) 5 ∠ 30°
(c) 12.5 ∠ 30° (d) 17 ∠ 30°

**3.34** For the circuit shown in Fig. 3.135, the time constant RC = 1 ms. The input voltage $v_i(t) = \sqrt{2}\ \sin^3 t$. The output voltage $v_o(t)$ is equal to ○●○

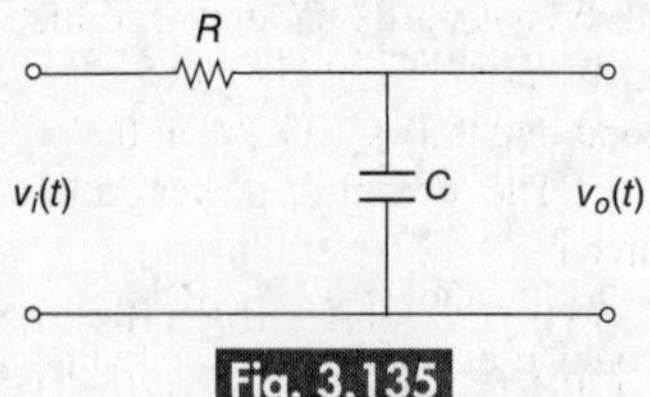


Fig. 3.135

(a) $\sin(10^3t - 45°)$ (b) $\sin(10^3t + 45°)$
(c) $\sin(10^3t - 53°)$ (d) $\sin(10^3t + 53°)$

**3.35** The voltage $V_C$ across the capacitor (in volts) in the network shown in Fig. 3.136 is ●○○

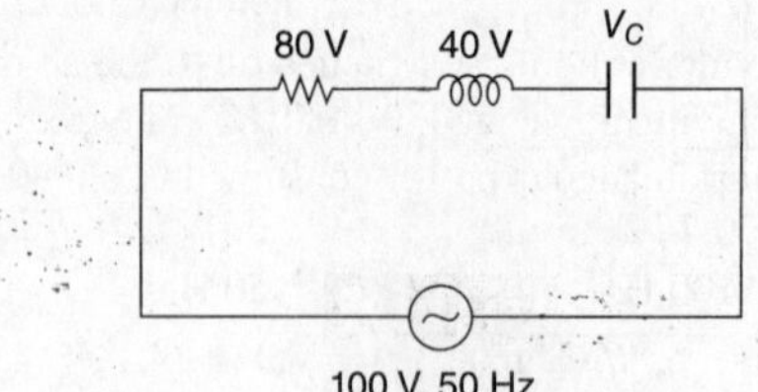


Fig. 3.136

(a) 10 (b) 40
(c) 100 (d) 50

**3.36** In the circuit shown in Fig. 3.137, the average value of the voltage $V_{ab}$ (in volts) in steady state condition is ○●○

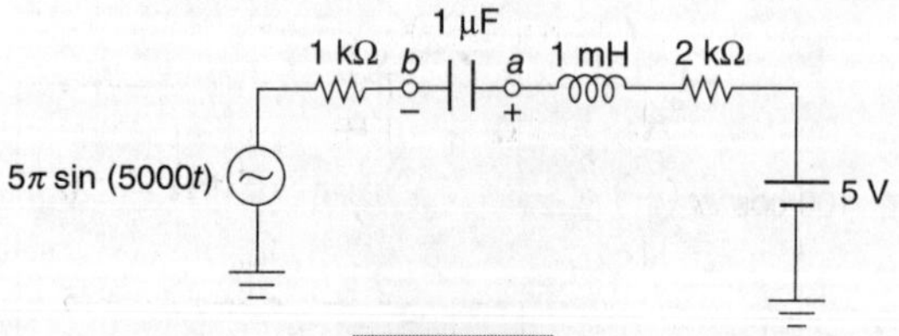


Fig. 3.137

(a) 10 (b) 5
(c) 15 (d) 0

**3.37** At very high frequencies, the peak output voltage $V_0$ (in volts) is ○○●

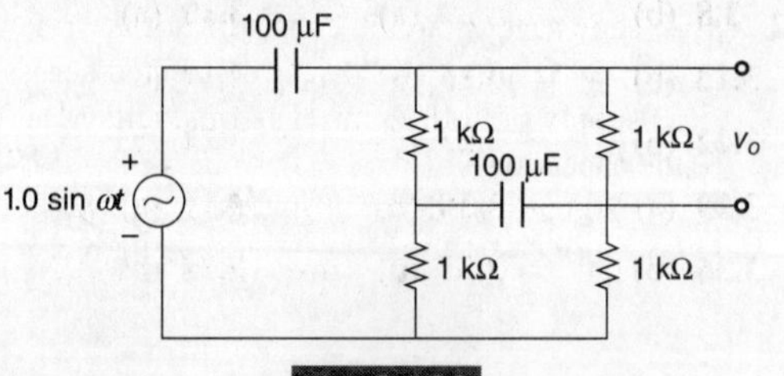


Fig. 3.138

(a) 1 (b) 2
(c) 0.5 (d) 10

**3.38** A 230 V rms source supplies power to two loads connected in parallel. The first load draws 10 kW at 0.8 leading power factor and the second one draws 10 kVA at 0.8 lagging power factor. The complex power delivered by the source is ○●○

(a) $(18 + j1.5)$ kVA (b) $(18 - j1.5)$ kVA
(c) $(20 + j1.5)$ kVA (d) $(20 - j1.5)$ kVA

**3.39** A periodic wave $x$ is shown in Fig. 3.139 as a function of time. The root-mean-square (rms) value of $x$ is ○●○

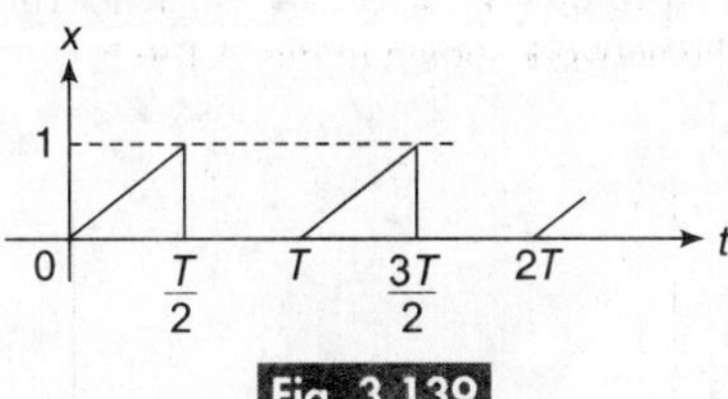


Fig. 3.139

(a) 0.707 (b) 0.5
(c) 0.638 (d) 0.4083

**3.40** In the circuit shown in Fig. 3.140, the positive angular frequency $\omega$ (in rad/s) at which magnitude of the phase difference between the voltages $V_1$ and $V_2$ equals $\frac{\pi}{4}$ radians is ○○●

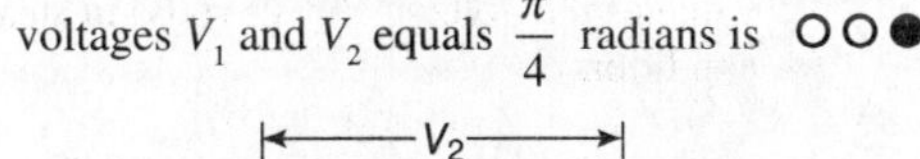

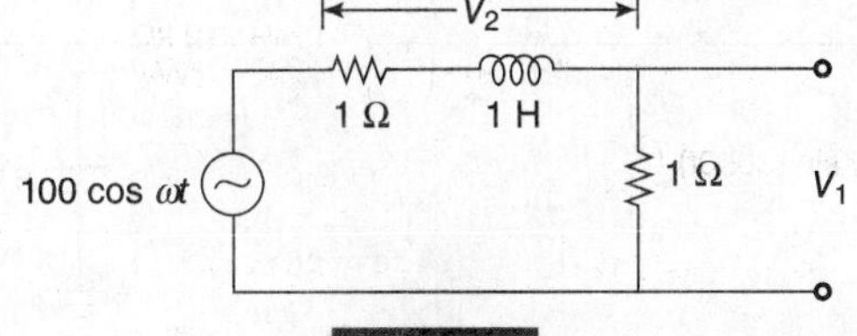


Fig. 3.140

(a) 4 (b) 3
(c) 2 (d) 1

**3.41** The Fig. 3.141 shows an RLC circuit excited by the sinusoidal voltage 100 cos 3$t$ volts, where $t$ is in seconds. The ratio $\frac{\text{amplitude of } V_2}{\text{amplitude of } V_1}$ is ○○●

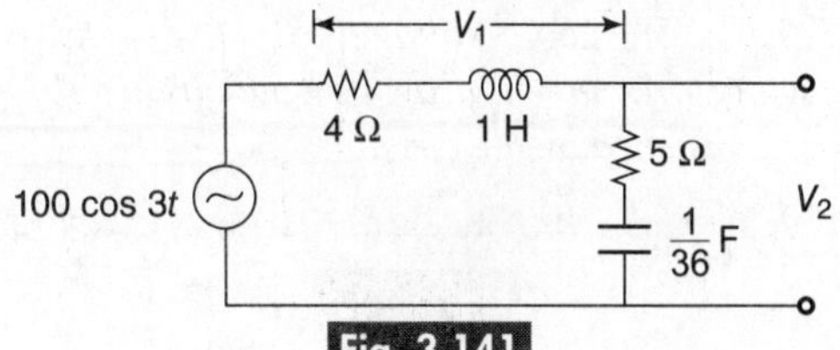


Fig. 3.141

(a) 2.6 (b) 3.6
(c) 3 (d) 1.6

**3.42** For the circuit shown in Fig. 1.142, the voltage $V_C$ (in volts) across the capacitor is ○●○

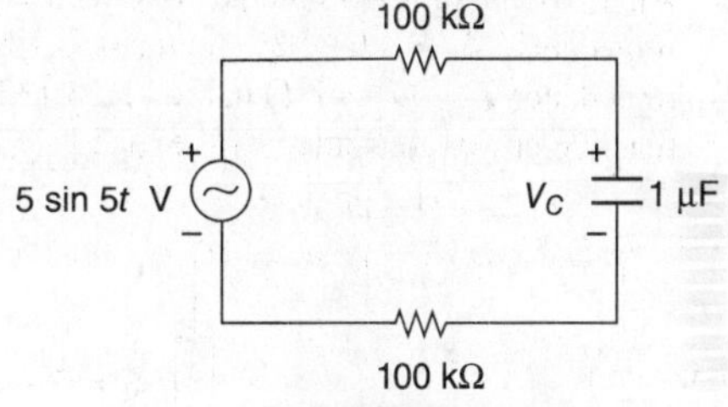


Fig. 3.142

(a) $1.25\sqrt{2}\sin(5t - 0.25\pi)$
(b) $1.25\sqrt{2}\sin(5t - 0.125\pi)$
(c) $2.5\sqrt{2}\sin(5t - 0.25\pi)$
(d) $2.5\sqrt{2}\sin(5t - 0.125\pi)$

## ANSWERS TO OBJECTIVE-TYPE QUESTIONS

| | | | | | | |
|---|---|---|---|---|---|---|
| **3.1** (c) | **3.2** (b) | **3.3** (c) | **3.4** (b) | **3.5** (a) | **3.6** (b) | **3.7** (b) |
| **3.8** (b) | **3.9** (a) | **3.10** (a) | **3.11** (c) | **3.12** (a) | **3.13** (c) | **3.14** (c) |
| **3.15** (b) | **3.16** (a) | **3.17** (d) | **3.18** (b) | **3.19** (a) | **3.20** (b) | **3.21** (a) |
| **3.22** (b) | **3.23** (c) | **3.24** (b) | **3.25** (c) | **3.26** (c) | **3.27** (b) | **3.28** (d) |
| **3.29** (a) | **3.30** (b) | **3.31** (a) | **3.32** (b) | **3.33** (d) | **3.34** (a) | **3.35** (c) |
| **3.36** (b) | **3.37** (c) | **3.38** (b) | **3.39** (d) | **3.40** (d) | **3.41** (a) | **3.42** (c) |

# LTspice Section

## EXAMPLE 3.1

*A resistor of 20 Ω, inductor of 0.05 H and a capacitor of 50 μF are connected in series, as shown in Fig. 3.143. A supply voltage 230 V, 50 Hz is connected across the series combination. Calculate the following: (a) current drawn by the circuit, (b) phase difference and power factor (d) active and reactive power consumed by the circuit.*

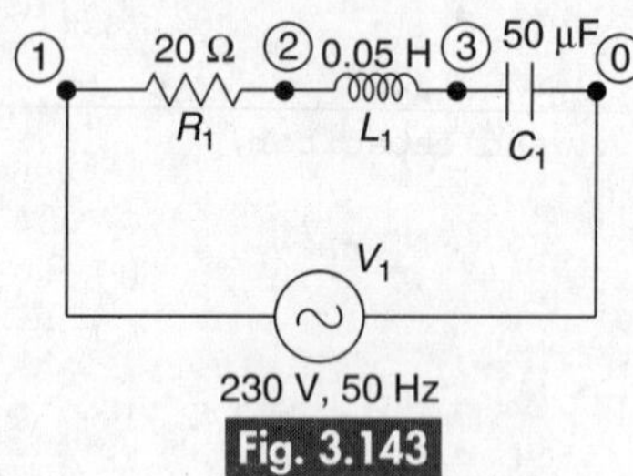


Fig. 3.143

**Solution**

```
*Calculation of current, phase di erence, power factor, active power and reactive power

V1 1 0  AC 230 0
R1 1 2 20
L1 2 3 0.05
C1 3 0 50U
.AC LIN 1 50 50
.PRINT AC I(R1)
.END
```

```
                              AC Analysis
frequency:        50                  Hz
I(R1):            mag:          4.42666   phase:  67.3596°        device_current
```

**Result**

(a) $\mathbf{I} = 4.2666 \angle 67.3596° \text{ A}$

(b) $\phi = 67.3596°$

$\text{pf} = \cos\phi = \cos(67.3596°) = 0.3849 \text{ (lagging)}$

(c) $P = VI\cos\phi = 230 \times 4.42666 \times 0.3849 = 391.8789 \text{ W}$

$Q = VI\sin\phi = 230 \times 4.42666 \times \sin(67.3596°) = 939.6736 \text{ VAR}$

## EXAMPLE 3.2

*A coil having a resistance of 50 Ω and an inductance of 0.02 H is connected in parallel with a capacitor of 25 μF across a single-phase 200 V, 50 Hz supply, as shown in Fig. 3.144. Calculate current in coil and capacitor.*

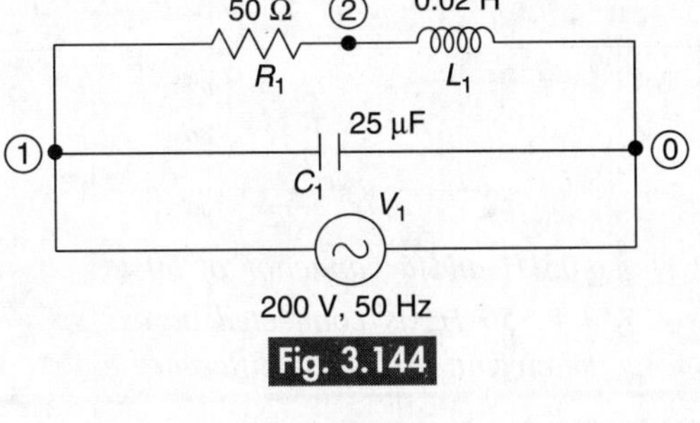


Fig. 3.144

## Solution

```
*Calculation of current in coil and capacitor

V1 1 0 AC 200 0
R1 1 2 50
L1 2 0 0.02
C1 1 0 25U
.AC LIN 1 50 50
.PRINT AC I(R1) I(C1)
.END
```

```
                              AC Analysis
frequency:          50                 Hz
I(C1):              mag:           1.5708  phase:         90°       device_current
I(R1):              mag:          3.96871  phase:  -7.16231°       device_current
```

**Result**

$$\mathbf{I}_{coil} = I(R1) = 3.96871 \angle -7.16231° \text{ A}$$

$$\mathbf{I} = I(C1) = 1.5708 \angle 90° \text{ A}$$

## EXAMPLE 3.3

*Determine the current in the circuit of Fig. 3.145. Also, find the power consumed as well as pf.*

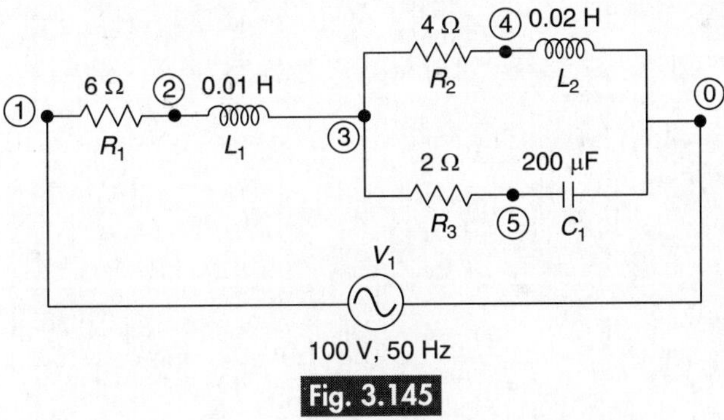


Fig. 3.145

## Solution

```
*Calculation of current, power factor and power consumed

V1 1 0 AC 100 0
R1 1 2 6
L1 2 3 0.01
R2 3 4 4
L2 4 0 0.02
R3 3 5 2
C1 5 0 200U
.AC LIN 1 50 50
.PRINT AC I(R1)
.END
```

```
                                  AC Analysis
frequency:          50                  Hz
I(R1):              mag:           5.78512   phase:  -30.7476°       device_current
```

**Result**

$$\mathbf{I} = I(R1) = 5.78512 \angle -30.7476° \text{ A}$$

$$P = VI \cos \phi = 100 \times 5.78512 \times \cos (30.7476°) = 497.1893 \text{ W}$$

$$\text{pf} = \cos \phi = \cos(30.7476°) = 0.8594 \text{ (lagging)}$$

CHAPTER 4

# Resonance

## LEARNING OBJECTIVES

**After studying this chapter, you should be able to:**

LO 4.1 Explain series resonance and its characteristics such as power factor, current, voltage, phasor diagram, behaviour of *R*, *L* and *C* with change in frequency, bandwidth and quality factor

LO 4.2 Explain parallel resonance and its characteristics such as dynamic impedance of a parallel circuit, current, phasor diagram, behaviour of conductance *G*, inductive susceptance $B_L$ and capacitive susceptance with change in frequency, bandwidth and quality factor

LO 4.3 Compare series and parallel resonant circuits

## INTRODUCTION

Resonance is a very important phenomenon in many electrical applications. At resonance, the inductive reactance and the capacitive reactance are of equal magnitude, causing electrical energy to oscillate between the magnetic field of the inductor and the electric field of the capacitor. Resonance occurs because the collapsing magnetic field of the inductor generates an electric current in its windings that charges the capacitor, and then the discharging capacitor provides an electric current that builds the magnetic field in the inductor. This process is repeated continually. Resonance is used for tuning and filtering, because it occurs at a particular frequency for given values of inductance and capacitance.

## 4.1 SERIES RESONANCE

LO 4.1

Explain series resonance and its characteristics such as power factor, current, voltage, phasor diagram, behaviour of $R$, $L$ and $C$ with change in frequency, bandwidth and quality factor

A circuit containing reactance is said to be in resonance if the voltage across the circuit is in phase with the current through it. At resonance, the circuit thus behaves as a pure resistor and the net reactance is zero.

Consider the series *RLC* circuit, as shown in Fig. 4.1. The impedance of the circuit is

$$\mathbf{Z} = R + jX_L - jX_C = R + j(X_L - X_C)$$

At resonance, the circuit is purely resistive.

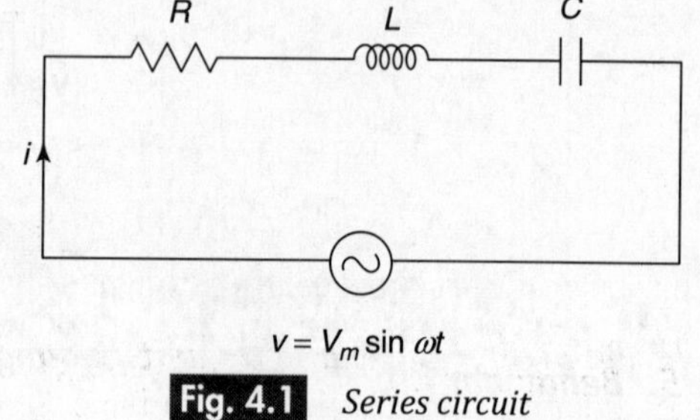


Fig. 4.1 *Series circuit*

$$X_L - X_C = 0$$

$$X_L = X_C$$

$$\omega_0 L = \frac{1}{\omega_0 C}$$

$$\omega_0^2 = \frac{1}{LC}$$

$$\omega_0 = \frac{1}{\sqrt{LC}}$$

$$f_0 = \frac{1}{2\pi\sqrt{LC}}$$

where $f_0$ is called the resonant frequency of the circuit.

**1. *Power Factor***

$$\text{Power factor} = \cos\phi = \frac{R}{Z}$$

At resonance $Z = R$

$$\text{Power factor} = \frac{R}{R} = 1$$

**2. *Current*** Since impedance is minimum, the current is maximum at resonance. Thus, the circuit accepts more current and as such, an *RLC* circuit under resonance is called an *acceptor circuit.*

$$I_0 = \frac{V}{Z} = \frac{V}{R}$$

**3. *Voltage*** At resonance,

$$\omega_0 L = \frac{1}{\omega_0 C}$$

$$\omega_0 L I_0 = \frac{1}{\omega_0 C} I_0$$

$$V_{L_0} = V_{C_0}$$

Thus, potential difference across inductor equal to potential difference across capacitor being equal and opposite cancel each other. Also, since $I_0$ is maximum, $V_{L_0}$ and $V_{C_0}$ will also be maximum. Thus, voltage magnification takes place during resonance. Hence, it is also referred to as voltage magnification circuit.

**4. *Phasor Diagram*** Figure 4.2 shows the phasor diagram of a series resonant circuit.

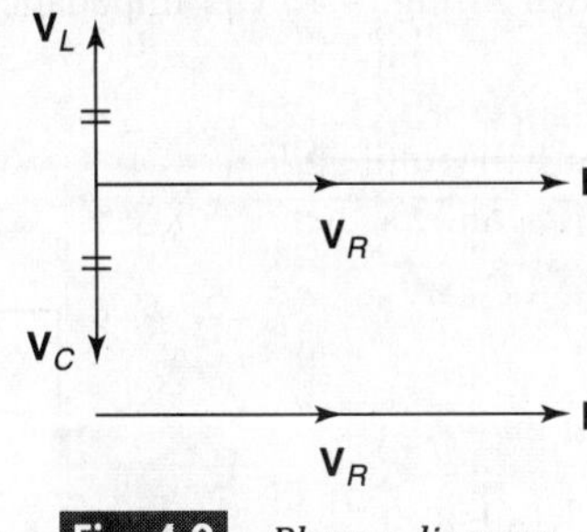


**Fig. 4.2** *Phasor diagram*

**5. *Behaviour of R, L and C with Change in Frequency*** Resistance remains constant with the change in frequencies. Inductive reactance $X_L$ is directly proportional to frequency *f*. It can be drawn as a straight line passing through the origin. Capacitive reactance $X_C$ is inversely proportional to the frequency *f*. It can be drawn as a rectangular hyperbola in the fourth quadrant. Figure 4.3 shows the behaviour of *R*, *L* and *C* with change in frequency.

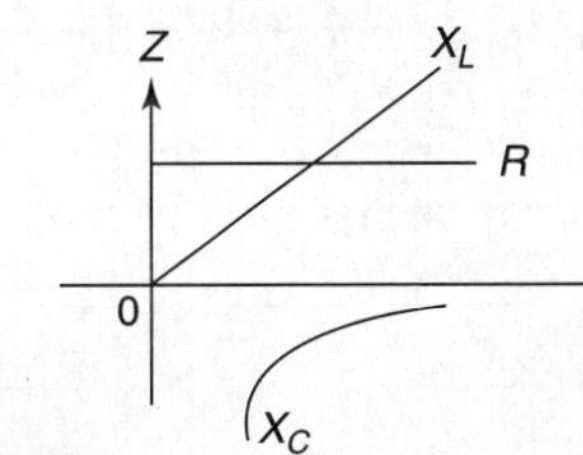


**Fig. 4.3** *Behaviour of R, L and C with change in frequency*

$$\text{Total impedance } \mathbf{Z} = R + j(X_L - X_C)$$

(a) When $f > f_0$, impedance is capacitive and decreases up to $f_0$. The power factor is leading in nature.
(b) At $f = f_0$, impedance is resistive. The power factor is unity.
(c) When $f > f_0$, impedance is inductive and goes on increasing beyond $f_0$. The power factor is lagging in nature. Figure 4.4 shows the impedance curve of series resonant circuit.

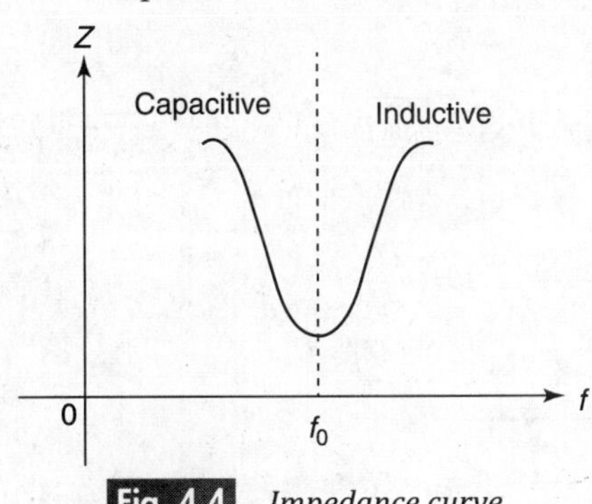


**Fig. 4.4** *Impedance curve*

***6. Bandwidth*** For the series *RLC* circuit, bandwidth is defined as the range of frequencies for which the power delivered to $R$ is greater than or equal to $\frac{P_0}{2}$ where $P_0$ is the power delivered to $R$ at resonance. From the shape of the resonance curve shown in Fig. 4.5, it is clear that there are two frequencies for which the power delivered to $R$ is half the power at resonance. For this reason, these frequencies are referred as those corresponding to the half-power points. The magnitude of the current at each half-power point is the same.

Hence, $$I_1^2 R = \frac{1}{2} I_0^2 R = I_2^2 R$$

where the subscript 1 denotes the lower half-point and the subscript 2, the higher half-point. It follows then that

$$I_1 = I_2 = \frac{I_0}{\sqrt{2}} = 0.707 I_0$$

Accordingly, the bandwidth may be identified on the resonance curve as the range of frequencies over which the magnitude of the current is equal to or greater than 0.707 of the current at resonance. In Fig. 4.5, the bandwidth is $\omega_2 - \omega_1$.

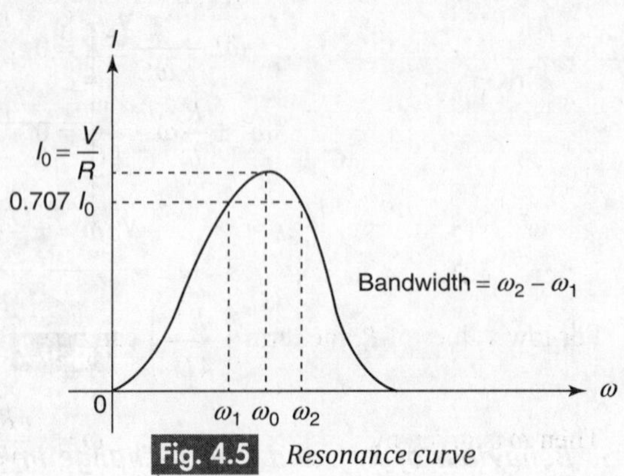


**Fig. 4.5** *Resonance curve*

➤ ***Expression for Bandwidth*** Generally, at any frequency $\omega$,

$$I = \frac{V}{Z} = \frac{V}{\sqrt{R^2 + (X_L - X_C)^2}} = \frac{V}{\sqrt{R^2 + \left(\omega L - \frac{1}{\omega C}\right)^2}} \quad \text{...(i)}$$

At half-power points,

$$I = \frac{I_0}{\sqrt{2}}$$

But $$I_0 = \frac{V}{R}$$

$$I = \frac{V}{\sqrt{2}R} \quad \text{...(ii)}$$

From Eqs (i) and (ii),

$$\frac{V}{\sqrt{R^2 + \left(\omega L - \frac{1}{\omega C}\right)^2}} = \frac{V}{\sqrt{2}R}$$

$$\sqrt{R^2 + \left(\omega L - \frac{1}{\omega C}\right)^2} = \sqrt{2}R$$

Squaring both the sides,

$$R^2 + \left(\omega L - \frac{1}{\omega C}\right)^2 = 2R^2$$

$$\left(\omega L - \frac{1}{\omega C}\right)^2 = R^2$$

$$\omega L - \frac{1}{\omega C} \pm R = 0$$

$$\omega^2 \pm \frac{R}{L}\omega - \frac{1}{LC} = 0$$

$$\omega = \pm\frac{R}{2L} \pm \sqrt{\frac{R^2}{4L^2} + \frac{1}{LC}}$$

For low values of $R$, the term $\left(\frac{R^2}{4L^2}\right)$ can be neglected in comparison with the term $\frac{1}{LC}$.

Then $\omega$ is given by $\quad \omega = \pm\frac{R}{2L} \pm \sqrt{\frac{1}{LC}} = \pm\frac{R}{2L} \pm \frac{1}{\sqrt{LC}}$

The resonant frequency for this circuit is given by

$$\omega_0 = \frac{1}{\sqrt{LC}}$$

$$\omega = \pm\frac{R}{2L} + \omega_0 \qquad \text{(considering only positive sign of } \omega_0\text{)}$$

$$\omega_1 = \omega_0 - \frac{R}{2L}$$

and
$$\omega_2 = \omega_0 + \frac{R}{2L}$$

$$f_1 = f_0 - \frac{R}{4\pi L}$$

and
$$f_2 = f_0 + \frac{R}{4\pi L}$$

$$\text{Bandwidth} = \omega_2 - \omega_1 = \frac{R}{L}$$

or
$$\text{Bandwidth} = f_2 - f_1 = \frac{R}{2\pi L}$$

***7. Quality Factor*** It is the measure of voltage magnification in the series resonant circuit. It is also a measure of selectivity or sharpness of the series resonant circuit.

$$Q_0 = \frac{\text{Voltage across inductor or capacitor}}{\text{Voltage at resonance}} = \frac{V_{L_0}}{V} = \frac{V_{C_0}}{V}$$

Substituting values of $V_{L_0}$ and $V$,

$$Q_0 = \frac{I_0 X_{L_0}}{I_0 R} = \frac{X_{L_0}}{R} = \frac{\omega_0 L}{R} = \frac{1}{\omega_0 CR}$$

Substituting values of $\omega_0$,

$$Q_0 = \frac{\left(\frac{1}{\sqrt{LC}}\right)L}{R} = \frac{1}{R}\sqrt{\frac{L}{C}}$$

**EXAMPLE 4.1** ●○○

*A series RLC circuit has the following parameter values: R = 10 Ω, L = 0.01 H, C = 100 μF. Compute the resonant frequency, bandwidth, and lower and upper frequencies of the bandwidth.*

**Solution** $R = 10\ \Omega,\quad L = 0.01\ \text{H},\quad C = 100\ \mu\text{F}$

(a) Resonant frequency

$$f_0 = \frac{1}{2\pi\sqrt{LC}} = \frac{1}{2\pi\sqrt{0.01\times 100\times 10^{-6}}} = 159.15\ \text{Hz}$$

(b) Bandwidth

$$BW = \frac{R}{2\pi L} = \frac{10}{2\pi\times 0.01} = 159.15\ \text{Hz}$$

(c) Lower frequency of bandwidth

$$f_1 = f_0 - \frac{BW}{2} = 159.15 - \frac{159.15}{2} = 79.58\ \text{Hz}$$

(d) Upper frequency of bandwidth

$$f_2 = f_0 + \frac{BW}{2} = 159.15 + \frac{159.15}{2} = 238.73\ \text{Hz}$$

**EXAMPLE 4.2** ●○○

*An RLC series circuit with a resistance of 10 Ω, inductance of 0.2 H and a capacitance of 40 μF is supplied with a 100 V supply at variable frequency. Find the following w.r.t. the series resonant circuit:*

*(a) frequency of which resonance takes place*
*(b) current*
*(c) power*

**Note** Difficulty Level ●○○ — Easy; ○●○ — Medium; ○○● — Difficult

*(d) power factor*
*(e) voltage across RLC at that time*
*(f) quality factor*
*(g) half-power points*
*(h) resonance and phasor diagrams*

**Solution** $R = 10\ \Omega, \quad L = 0.2\text{ H}, \quad C = 40\ \mu\text{F}, \quad V = 100\text{ V}$

(a) Resonant frequency

$$f_0 = \frac{1}{2\pi\sqrt{LC}} = \frac{1}{2\pi\sqrt{0.2 \times 40 \times 10^{-6}}} = 56.3\text{ Hz}$$

(b) Current

$$I_0 = \frac{V}{R} = \frac{100}{10} = 10\text{ A}$$

(c) Power

$$P_0 = I_0^2 R = (10)^2 \times 10 = 1000\text{ W}$$

(d) Power factor

$$\text{pf} = 1$$

(e) Voltage across $R, L, C$

$$V_{R_0} = R\,I_0 = 10 \times 10 = 100\text{ V}$$
$$V_{L_0} = X_{L_0}\,I_0 = 2\pi f_0 L I_0 = 2\pi \times 56.3 \times 0.2 \times 10 = 707.5\text{ V}$$
$$V_{C_0} = X_{C_0}\,I_0 = \frac{1}{2\pi f_0 C} I_0 = \frac{1}{2\pi \times 56.3 \times 40 \times 10^{-6}} \times 10 = 707.5\text{ V}$$

(f) Quality factor

$$Q = \frac{1}{R}\sqrt{\frac{L}{C}} = \frac{1}{10}\sqrt{\frac{0.2}{40 \times 10^{-6}}} = 7.07$$

(g) Half-power points

$$f_1 = f_0 - \frac{R}{4\pi L} = 56.3 - \frac{10}{4\pi \times 0.2} = 52.32\text{ Hz}$$
$$f_2 = f_0 + \frac{R}{4\pi L} = 56.3 + \frac{10}{4\pi \times 0.2} = 60.3\text{ Hz}$$

(h) Resonance and phasor diagrams are shown in Fig. 4.6.

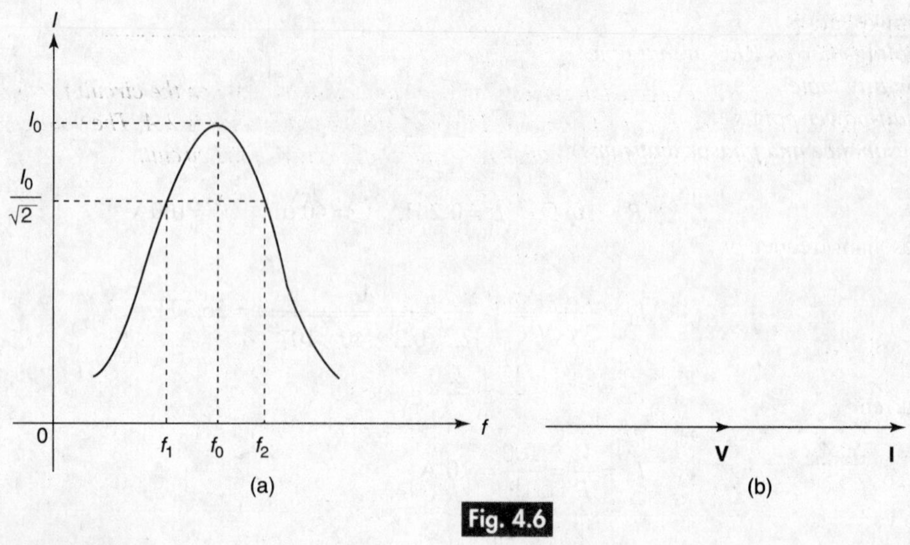


Fig. 4.6

## EXAMPLE 4.3

*A series RLC circuit is connected to a 200 V ac supply. The current drawn by the circuit at resonance is 20 A. The voltage drop across the capacitor is 5000 V at series resonance. Calculate resistance and inductance if capacitance is 4 μF. Also, calculate the resonant frequency.*

**Solution** $V = 200\text{ V},\quad I_0 = 20\text{ A},\quad V_{C_0} = 5000\text{ V},\quad C = 4\ \mu\text{F}$

(a) Resistance

$$R = \frac{V}{I_0} = \frac{200}{20} = 10\ \Omega$$

(b) Resonant frequency

$$X_{C_0} = \frac{V_{C_0}}{I_0} = \frac{5000}{20} = 250\ \Omega$$

$$X_{C_0} = \frac{1}{2\pi f_0 C}$$

$$250 = \frac{1}{2\pi \times f_0 \times 4 \times 10^{-6}}$$

$$f_0 = 159.15\text{ Hz}$$

(c) Inductance

At resonance

$$X_{C_0} = X_{L_0} = 250\ \Omega$$

$$X_{L_0} = 2\pi f_0 L$$

$$250 = 2\pi \times 159.15 \times L$$

$$L = 0.25\text{ H}$$

**EXAMPLE 4.4**

*A resistor and a capacitor are connected in series with a variable inductor. When the circuit is connected to a 230 V, 50 Hz supply, the maximum current obtained by varying the inductance is 2 A. The voltage across the capacitor is 500 V. Calculate the resistance, inductance and capacitance of the circuit.*

**Solution** $V = 230\text{ V},\quad f_0 = 50\text{ Hz},\quad I_0 = 2\text{ A},\quad V_{C_0} = 500\text{ V}$

$$I_0 = 2\text{ A}$$

$$V_{C_0} = 500\text{ V}$$

(a) Resistance

$$R = \frac{V}{I_0} = \frac{230}{2} = 115\ \Omega$$

(b) Capacitance

$$X_{C_0} = \frac{V_{C_0}}{I_0} = \frac{500}{2} = 250\ \Omega$$

$$X_{C_0} = \frac{1}{2\pi f_0 C}$$

$$250 = \frac{1}{2\pi \times 50 \times C}$$

$$C = 12.73\ \mu\text{F}$$

(c) Inductance
At resonance

$$X_{C_0} = X_{L_0} = 250\ \Omega$$

$$X_{L_0} = 2\pi f_0 L$$

$$250 = 2\pi \times 50 \times L$$

$$L = 0.795\text{ H}$$

**EXAMPLE 4.5**

*A coil of 2 Ω resistance and 0.01 H inductance is connected in series with a capacitor across 200 V mains. What must be the capacitance in order that maximum current occurs at a frequency of 50 Hz? Find also the current and the voltage across the capacitor.*

**Solution** $R = 2\ \Omega,\quad L = 0.01\text{ H},\quad V = 200\text{ V},\quad f_0 = 50\text{ Hz}$

(a) Capacitance

$$f_0 = \frac{1}{2\pi\sqrt{LC}}$$

$$50 = \frac{1}{2\pi\sqrt{0.01 \times C}}$$

$$C = 1013.2\ \mu\text{F}$$

(b) Current

$$I_0 = \frac{V}{R} = \frac{200}{2} = 100 \text{ A}$$

(c) Voltage across capacitor

$$V_{C_0} = I_0 X_{C_0} = I_0 \frac{1}{2\pi f_0 C} = 100 \times \frac{1}{2\pi \times 50 \times 1013.2 \times 10^{-6}} = 314.16 \text{ V}$$

## EXAMPLE 4.6

*A series RLC circuit has a quality factor of 5 at 50 rad/s. The current flowing through the circuit at resonance is 10 A and the supply voltage is 100 V. Find the circuit constants.*

**Solution**

$$Q_0 = 5, \quad \omega_0 = 50 \text{ rad/s}, \quad I_0 = 10 \text{ A}, \quad V = 100 \text{ V}$$

$$I_0 = \frac{V}{R}$$

$$10 = \frac{100}{R}$$

$$R = 10\ \Omega$$

$$Q_0 = \frac{\omega_0 L}{R}$$

$$5 = \frac{50 \times L}{10}$$

$$L = 1 \text{ H}$$

$$Q_0 = \frac{1}{R}\sqrt{\frac{L}{C}}$$

$$5 = \frac{1}{10}\sqrt{\frac{1}{C}}$$

$$C = 400\ \mu\text{F}$$

## EXAMPLE 4.7

*A series RLC circuit has R = 2.5 Ω, C = 100 μF and a variable inductance. The applied voltage is 50 V at 800 rad/s. The inductance is varied till the voltage across the resistance is maximum. Find (a) value of inductance under this condition, (b) Q, (c) current, and (d) voltage across resistance, capacitance and inductance.*

**Solution**

$$R = 2.5\ \Omega, \quad C = 100\ \mu\text{F}, \quad V = 50 \text{ V}, \quad \omega = 800 \text{ rad/s}$$

(a) Value of inductance

$$\omega_0 = \frac{1}{\sqrt{LC}}$$

$$800 = \frac{1}{\sqrt{L \times 100 \times 10^{-6}}}$$

$$L = 0.0156 \text{ H}$$

(b) Quality factor

$$Q_0 = \frac{\omega_0 L}{R} = \frac{800 \times 0.0156}{2.5} = 5$$

(c) Current

$$I_0 = \frac{V}{R} = \frac{50}{2.5} = 20 \text{ A}$$

(d) Voltage across resistance, capacitance and inductance

$$V_{R_0} = I_0 \ R = 20 \times 2.5 = 50 \text{ V}$$
$$V_{L_0} = Q_0 \ V = 5 \times 50 = 250 \text{ V}$$
$$V_{C_0} = Q_0 \ V = 5 \times 50 = 250 \text{ V}$$

**EXAMPLE 4.8** ●○○

*A series RLC circuit which resonates at 500 kHz has $R = 25\ \Omega$, $L = 100\ \mu H$ and $C = 1000\ pF$. Determine the quality factor, new value of C required to resonate at 500 kHz when the value of L is doubled, and the new quality factor.*

**Solution**

$$f_0 = 500 \text{ kHz}, \quad R = 25\ \Omega, \quad L = 100\ \mu\text{H}, \quad C = 1000 \text{ pF}$$

(a) Quality factor

$$Q_0 = \frac{1}{R}\sqrt{\frac{L}{C}} = \frac{1}{25}\sqrt{\frac{100 \times 10^{-6}}{1000 \times 10^{-12}}} = 12.65$$

(b) New value of $C$ when $L = 200\ \mu\text{H}$

$$f_0 = \frac{1}{2\pi\sqrt{LC}}$$

$$500 \times 10^3 = \frac{1}{2\pi\sqrt{200 \times 10^{-6} \times C}}$$

$$C = 506.61 \text{ pF}$$

(c) New $Q$ factor

$$Q_0 = \frac{1}{R}\sqrt{\frac{L}{C}} = \frac{1}{25}\sqrt{\frac{200 \times 10^{-6}}{506.61 \times 10^{-12}}} = 25.13$$

**EXAMPLE 4.9** ●○○

*Find the values of R,L and C in a series RLC circuit that resonates at 1.5 kHz and consumes 50 W from a 50 V ac source operating at the resonant frequency. The bandwidth is 0.75 kHz.*

**Solution** $f_0 = 1.5 \text{ kHz}, \quad P = 50 \text{ W}, \quad V = 50 \text{ V}, \quad BW = 0.75 \text{ kHz}$

$$P = \frac{V^2}{R}$$

$$50 = \frac{(50)^2}{R}$$

$$R = 50\ \Omega$$

$$BW = \frac{R}{2\pi L}$$

$$0.75\times10^3 = \frac{50}{2\pi\times L}$$

$$L = 0.011 \text{ H}$$

$$f_0 = \frac{1}{2\pi\sqrt{LC}}$$

$$1.5\times10^3 = \frac{1}{2\pi\sqrt{0.011\times C}}$$

$$C = 1.023\ \mu\text{F}$$

**EXAMPLE 4.10**

*A 50 Ω resistor is connected in series with an inductor having internal resistance, a capacitor and 100 V variable frequency supply, as shown in Fig. 4.7. At a frequency of 200 Hz, a maximum current of 0.7 A flows through the circuit and voltage across the capacitor is 200 V. Determine the circuit constants.*

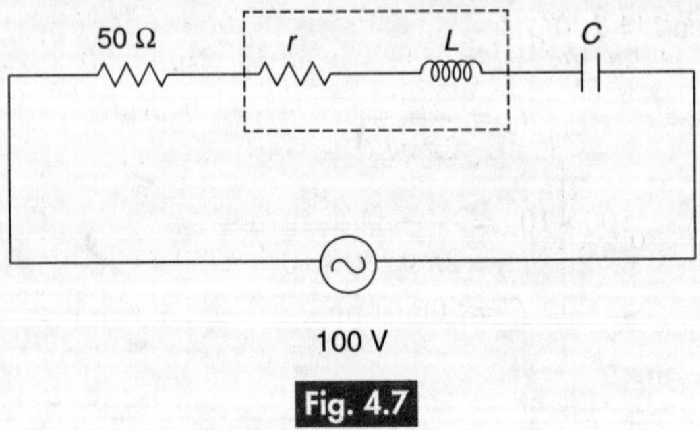


**Fig. 4.7**

**Solution** $V = 100 \text{ V}, \quad R = 50\ \Omega, \quad f_0 = 200 \text{ Hz}, \quad I_0 = 0.7 \text{ A}$

$$V_{C_0} = 200 \text{ V}$$

$$V_{C_0} = I_0 X_{C_0}$$

$$200 = 0.7 X_{C_0}$$

$$X_{C_0} = 285.71\,\Omega$$

$$X_{C_0} = \frac{1}{2\pi f_0 C}$$

$$285.71 = \frac{1}{2\pi \times 200 \times C}$$

$$C = 2.79\ \mu\text{F}$$

$$f_0 = \frac{1}{2\pi\sqrt{LC}}$$

$$200 = \frac{1}{2\pi\sqrt{L \times 2.79 \times 10^{-6}}}$$

$$L = 0.23\ \text{H}$$

At resonance, total resistance is

$$R_T = \frac{V}{I} = \frac{100}{0.7} = 142.86\ \Omega$$

$$R_T = R + r$$

$$142.86 = 50 + r$$

$$r = 92.86\ \Omega$$

**EXAMPLE 4.11**

*In the circuit shown in Fig. 4.8, a maximum current of 0.1 A flows through the circuit when the capacitor is at 5 μF with a fixed frequency and a voltage of 5 V. Determine the frequency at which the circuit resonates, the bandwidth, quality factor Q and the value of resistance at resonant frequency.*

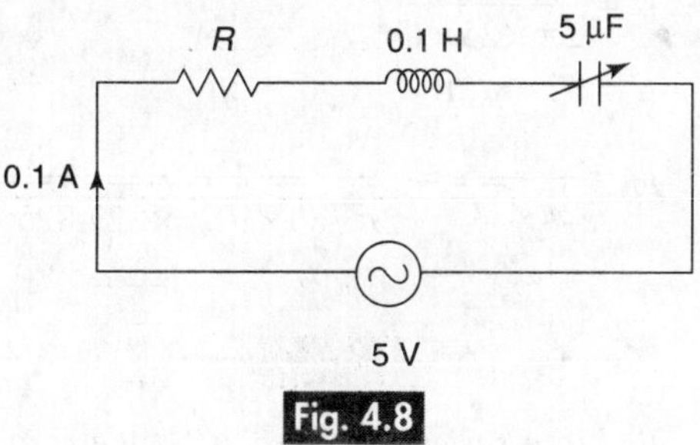


Fig. 4.8

**Solution**

$$I_0 = 0.1\ \text{A},\quad C = 5\ \mu\text{F},\quad V = 5\ \text{V},\quad L = 0.1\ \text{H}$$

$$R = \frac{V}{I_0} = \frac{5}{0.1} = 50\ \Omega$$

$$f_0 = \frac{1}{2\pi\sqrt{LC}} = \frac{1}{2\pi\sqrt{0.1\times 5\times 10^{-6}}} = 225.08 \text{ Hz}$$

$$Q_0 = \frac{1}{R}\sqrt{\frac{L}{C}} = \frac{1}{50}\sqrt{\frac{0.1}{5\times 10^{-6}}} = 2.83$$

$$BW = \frac{R}{2\pi L} = \frac{50}{2\pi \times 0.1} = 79.58 \text{ Hz}$$

## EXAMPLE 4.12

*A series RLC circuit has R = 10 Ω and L = 60 mH. At a frequency of 25 Hz, the pf of the circuit is 45° lead. At what frequency will the circuit be resonant?*

**Solution**

$$R = 10\ \Omega, \quad L = 60 \text{ mH}$$

$$X_L = 2\pi f L = 2\pi \times 25 \times 60 \times 10^{-3} = 9.42\ \Omega$$

For a series *RLC* circuit,

$$\tan\phi = \frac{X_C - X_L}{R}$$

$$\tan 45° = \frac{X_C - 9.42}{10}$$

$$1 = \frac{X_C - 9.42}{10}$$

$$X_C = 19.42\ \Omega$$

$$X_C = \frac{1}{2\pi f C}$$

$$19.42 = \frac{1}{2\pi \times 25 \times C}$$

$$C = 327.82\ \mu\text{F}$$

$$f_0 = \frac{1}{2\pi\sqrt{LC}} = \frac{1}{2\pi\sqrt{60\times 10^{-3}\times 327.82\times 10^{-6}}} = 35.89 \text{ Hz}$$

## EXAMPLE 4.13

*A voltage $v(t) = 10 \sin \omega t$ is applied to a series RLC circuit. At the resonant frequency of the circuit, the voltage across the capacitor is found to be 500 V. The bandwidth of the circuit is known to be 400 rad/s and the impedance of the circuit at resonance is 100 Ω. Determine inductance and capacitance, resonant frequency, upper and lower cut-off frequencies.*

**Solution**

$$v(t) = 10 \sin \omega t, \quad V_{C_0} = 500 \text{ V}, \quad BW = 400 \text{ rad/s}, \quad R = 100\ \Omega$$

(a) Inductance and capacitance

$$V = \frac{V_m}{\sqrt{2}} = \frac{10}{\sqrt{2}} = 7.07 \text{ V}$$

$$I_0 = \frac{V}{R} = \frac{7.07}{100} = 0.0707 \text{ A}$$

$$BW = \frac{R}{L}$$

$$400 = \frac{100}{L}$$

$$L = 0.25 \text{ H}$$

$$Q_0 = \frac{V_{C_0}}{V} = \frac{500}{7.07} = 70.72$$

$$Q_0 = \frac{1}{R}\sqrt{\frac{L}{C}}$$

$$70.72 = \frac{1}{100}\sqrt{\frac{0.25}{C}}$$

$$C = 4.99 \text{ nF}$$

(b) Resonant frequency

$$f_0 = \frac{1}{2\pi\sqrt{LC}} = \frac{1}{2\pi \times \sqrt{0.25 \times 4.99 \times 10^{-9}}} = 4506.09 \text{ Hz}$$

(c) Lower cut-off frequency

$$f_1 = f_0 - \frac{R}{4\pi L} = 4506.09 - \frac{100}{4\pi \times 0.25} = 4474.26 \text{ Hz}$$

(d) Upper cut-off frequency

$$f_2 = f_0 + \frac{R}{4\pi L} = 4506.09 + \frac{100}{4\pi \times 0.25} = 4537.92 \text{ Hz}$$

**EXAMPLE 4.14**

*A series resonant circuit has an impedance of 500 Ω at resonant frequency. Cut-off frequencies are 10 kHz and 100 Hz. Determine (a) resonant frequency, (b) value of L, C, and (c) quality factor at resonant frequency.*

**Solution**

$$R = 500\ \Omega, \quad f_1 = 100 \text{ Hz}, \quad f_2 = 10 \text{ kHz}$$

(a) Resonant frequency

$$BW = f_2 - f_1 = 10000 - 100 = 9900 \text{ Hz}$$

$$f_1 = f_0 - \frac{R}{4\pi L} \qquad \ldots\text{(i)}$$

$$f_2 = f_0 + \frac{R}{4\pi L} \qquad \ldots\text{(ii)}$$

Adding Eqs (i) and (ii),

$$f_1 + f_2 = 2f_0$$

$$f_0 = \frac{f_1 + f_2}{2} = \frac{100 + 10000}{2} = 5050 \text{ Hz}$$

(b) Values of $L$ and $C$

$$BW = \frac{R}{2\pi L}$$

$$9900 = \frac{500}{2\pi L}$$

$$L = 8.038 \text{ mH}$$

$$X_{L_0} = 2\pi f_0 L = 2\pi \times 5050 \times 8.038 \times 10^{-3} = 255.05\ \Omega$$

At resonance,

$$X_{L_0} = X_{C_0} = 255.05\ \Omega$$

$$X_{C_0} = \frac{1}{2\pi f_0 C}$$

$$255.05 = \frac{1}{2\pi \times 5050 \times C}$$

$$C = 0.12\ \mu\text{F}$$

(c) Quality factor

$$Q_0 = \frac{1}{R}\sqrt{\frac{L}{C}} = \frac{1}{500}\sqrt{\frac{8.038 \times 10^{-3}}{0.12 \times 10^{-6}}} = 0.5176$$

**EXAMPLE 4.15**

*Impedance of a circuit is observed to be capacitive and decreasing from 1 Hz to 100 Hz. Beyond 100 Hz, the impedance starts increasing. Find the values of circuit elements if the power drawn by this circuit is 100 W at 100 Hz, when the current is 1 A. The power factor of the circuit at 70 Hz is 0.707.*

**Solution** $f_0 = 100 \text{ Hz}, \quad P_0 = 100 \text{ W}, \quad I_0 = 1 \text{ A}, \quad (\text{pf})_{70 \text{ Hz}} = 0.707$

The impedance of the circuit is capacitive and decreasing from 1 Hz to 100 Hz. Beyond 100 Hz, the impedance starts increasing.

$$f_0 = 100 \text{ Hz}$$

$$P_0 = I_0^2 R$$

$$100 = (1)^2 \times R$$

$$R = 100\ \Omega$$

$$f_0 = \frac{1}{2\pi\sqrt{LC}}$$

$$100 = \frac{1}{2\pi\sqrt{LC}}$$

$$LC = 2.53\times10^{-6} \quad \ldots\text{(i)}$$

Power factor at 70 Hz is 0.707.

$$\frac{R}{Z} = 0.707$$

$$\frac{100}{Z} = 0.707$$

$$Z = 141.44\ \Omega$$

$$\text{Impedance at 70 Hz} = Z_{70} = \sqrt{R^2 + (X_C - X_L)^2}$$

$$141.44 = \sqrt{(100)^2 + \left(\frac{1}{2\pi\times70\times C} - 2\pi\times70\times L\right)^2}$$

$$\frac{2.27\times10^{-3}}{C} - 439.82\,L = 100.02 \quad \ldots\text{(ii)}$$

Solving Eqs (i) and (ii),

$$L = 0.2187\ \text{H}$$

$$C = 11.58\ \mu\text{F}$$

## EXAMPLE 4.16

*A constant voltage at a frequency of 1 MHz is applied to an inductor in series with a variable capacitor. When the capacitor is set to 500 pF, the current has its maximum value while it is reduced to one-half when the capacitance is 600 pF. Find resistance, inductance and Q-factor of inductor.*

**Solution**

$$f_0 = 1\ \text{MHz}, \quad C_1 = 500\ \text{pF}, \quad C_2 = 600\ \text{pF}$$

(a) Resistance and inductance of inductor

At resonance,

$$C = 500\ \text{pF}$$

$$f_0 = \frac{1}{2\pi\sqrt{LC}}$$

$$10^6 = \frac{1}{2\pi\sqrt{L\times500\times10^{-12}}}$$

$$L = 0.05\ \text{mH}$$

$$X_L = 2\pi f_0 L = 2\pi\times10^6\times0.05\times10^{-3} = 314.16\ \Omega$$

When capacitance is 600 pF, the current reduces to one-half of the current at resonance.

$$X_C = \frac{1}{2\pi fC} = \frac{1}{2\pi \times 10^6 \times 600 \times 10^{-12}} = 265.26\ \Omega$$

$$I = \frac{1}{2} I_0$$

$$\frac{V}{Z} = \frac{1}{2}\frac{V}{R}$$

$$Z = 2R$$

$$\sqrt{R^2 + (X_L - X_C)^2} = 2R$$

$$R^2 + (314.16 - 265.26)^2 = 4R^2$$

$$3R^2 = 2391.21$$

$$R = 28.23\ \Omega$$

(b) Quality factor

$$Q_0 = \frac{1}{R}\sqrt{\frac{L}{C}} = \frac{1}{28.23}\sqrt{\frac{0.05 \times 10^{-3}}{500 \times 10^{-12}}} = 11.2$$

## EXAMPLE 4.17

*In the circuit shown in Fig. 4.9, determine the circuit constants when the circuit draws a maximum current at 10 μF with a 10 V, 100 Hz supply. When the capacitance is changed to 12 μF, the current that flows through the circuit becomes 0.707 times its maximum value. Determine Q of the coil at 900 rad/s. Also, find the maximum current that flows through the circuit.*

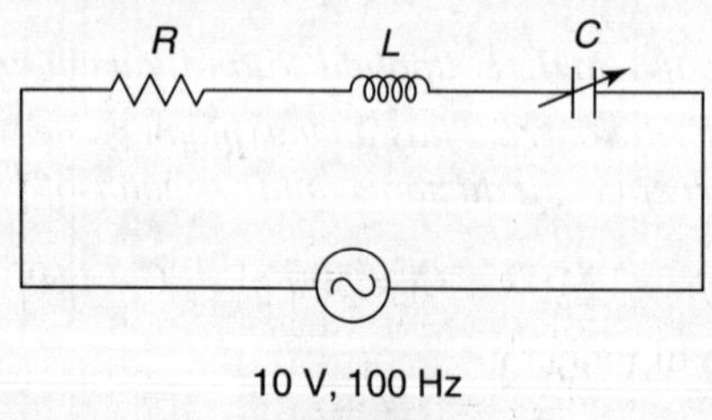


Fig. 4.9

**Solution**

$$C = 10\ \mu\text{F}, \quad V = 10\ \text{V}, \quad f_0 = 100\ \text{Hz}$$

$$f_0 = \frac{1}{2\pi\sqrt{LC}}$$

$$100 = \frac{1}{2\pi\sqrt{L \times 10 \times 10^{-6}}}$$

$$L = 0.25\ \text{H}$$

When $C = 12\ \mu F$, $\omega = 900$ rad/s

$$I = 0.707\, I_0$$

$$\frac{V}{Z} = 0.707\frac{V}{R}$$

$$Z = \frac{R}{0.707}$$

$$\sqrt{R^2 + (X_L - X_C)^2} = \frac{R}{0.707}$$

$$\sqrt{R^2 + \left(900\times 0.25 - \frac{1}{900\times 12\times 10^{-6}}\right)^2} = \frac{R}{0.707}$$

$$R = 132.37\ \Omega$$

$$Q_0 = \frac{\omega L}{R} = \frac{900\times 0.25}{132.37} = 1.7$$

$$I_0 = \frac{V}{R} = \frac{10}{132.37} = 0.076\text{ A}$$

## EXAMPLE 4.18

*A series RLC circuit is excited from a constant voltage variable frequency source. The current in the circuit becomes maximum at a frequency of $\frac{600}{2\pi}$ Hz and falls to half the maximum value at $\frac{400}{2\pi}$ Hz. If the resistance in the circuit is 3Ω, find L and C.*

**Solution**

$$f_0 = \frac{600}{2\pi}\text{ Hz},\quad R = 3\ \Omega$$

$$f_0 = \frac{1}{2\pi\sqrt{LC}}$$

$$\frac{600}{2\pi} = \frac{1}{2\pi\sqrt{LC}}$$

$$LC = 2.78\times 10^{-6} \qquad \ldots\text{(i)}$$

At $f = \frac{400}{2\pi}$ Hz,

$$I = \frac{I_0}{2}$$

$$\frac{V}{Z} = \frac{V}{2R}$$

$$Z = 2R$$

$$\sqrt{R^2 + (X_L - X_C)^2} = 2R$$

$$R^2 + (X_L - X_C)^2 = 4R^2$$

$$(X_L - X_C)^2 = 3R^2 = 3(3)^2 = 27$$

$$\left(2\pi \times \frac{400}{2\pi} \times L - \frac{1}{2\pi \times \frac{400}{2\pi} \times C}\right)^2 = 27$$

$$\left(400\,L - \frac{1}{400C}\right)^2 = 27 \qquad \ldots\text{(ii)}$$

$$\left(400 \times \frac{2.78 \times 10^{-6}}{C} - \frac{1}{400\,C}\right)^2 = 27$$

$$C = 267.12\ \mu\text{F}$$

$$L = \frac{2.78 \times 10^{-6}}{C} = \frac{2.78 \times 10^{-6}}{267.12 \times 10^{-6}} = 10.41\ \text{mH}$$

## 4.2 PARALLEL RESONANCE

LO 4.2

Explain parallel resonance and its characteristics such as dynamic impedance of a parallel circuit, current, phasor diagram, behaviour of conductance $G$, inductive susceptance $B_L$ and capacitive susceptance with change in frequency, bandwidth and quality factor

Consider a parallel circuit consisting of a coil and a capacitor, as shown in Fig. 4.10. The impedances of two branches are

$$\mathbf{Z}_1 = R + jX_L$$

$$\mathbf{Z}_2 = -jX_C$$

$$\mathbf{Y}_1 = \frac{1}{\mathbf{Z}_1} = \frac{1}{R + jX_L} = \frac{R - jX_L}{R^2 + X_L^2}$$

$$\mathbf{Y}_2 = \frac{1}{\mathbf{Z}_2} = \frac{1}{-jX_C} = \frac{j}{X_C}$$

Admittance of the circuit

$$\mathbf{Y} = \mathbf{Y}_1 + \mathbf{Y}_2 = \frac{R - jX_L}{R^2 + X_L^2} + \frac{j}{X_C} = \frac{R}{R^2 + X_L^2} - j\left(\frac{X_L}{R^2 + X_L^2} - \frac{1}{X_C}\right)$$

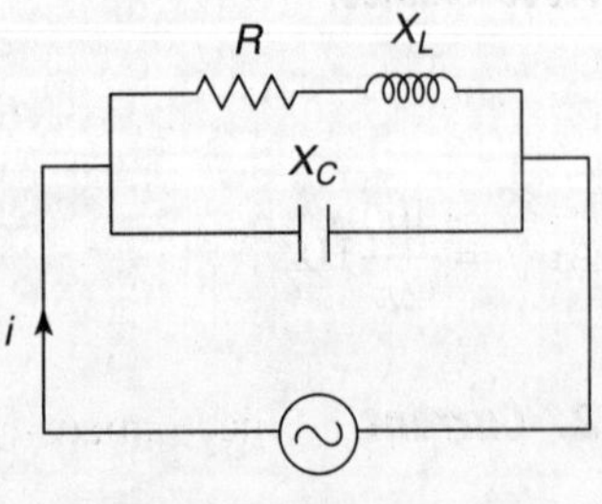


Fig. 4.10 Parallel circuit

At resonance, the circuit is purely resistive. Hence, the condition for resonance is

$$\frac{X_L}{R^2 + X_L^2} - \frac{1}{X_C} = 0$$

$$\frac{X_L}{R^2 + X_L^2} = \frac{1}{X_C}$$

$$X_L X_C = R^2 + X_L^2$$

$$\omega_0 L \frac{1}{\omega_0 c} = R^2 + \omega_0^2 L^2$$

$$\frac{L}{C} = R^2 + \omega_0^2 L^2$$

$$\omega_0^2 L^2 = \frac{L}{C} - R^2$$

$$\omega_0{}^2 = \frac{1}{LC} - \frac{R^2}{L^2}$$

$$\omega_0 = \sqrt{\frac{1}{LC} - \frac{R^2}{L^2}}$$

$$f_0 = \frac{1}{2\pi}\sqrt{\frac{1}{LC} - \frac{R^2}{L^2}}$$

where $f_0$ is called the resonant frequency of the circuit.
If $R$ is very small as compared to $L$ then

$$\omega_0 = \frac{1}{\sqrt{LC}}$$

$$f_0 = \frac{1}{2\pi\sqrt{LC}}$$

**1. *Dynamic Impedance of a Parallel Circuit*** At resonance, the circuit is purely resistive. The real part of admittance is $\dfrac{R}{R^2 + X_L^2}$. Hence, the dynamic impedance at resonance is given by

$$Z_D = \frac{R^2 + X_L^2}{R}$$

At resonance,

$$R^2 + X_L^2 = X_L X_C = \frac{L}{C}$$

$$Z_D = \frac{L}{CR}$$

**2. *Current*** Since impedance is maximum at resonance, the current is minimum at resonance.

$$I_0 = \frac{V}{Z_D} = \frac{V}{\frac{L}{CR}} = \frac{VCR}{L}$$

***3. Phasor Diagram*** At resonance, power factor of the circuit is unity and the total current drawn by the circuit is in phase with the voltage. This will happen only when the current $I_C$ is equal to the reactive component of the current in the inductive branch, i.e., $I_C = I_L \sin\phi$

Hence, at resonance

$$I_C = I_L \sin\phi$$

and $$I = I_L \cos\phi$$

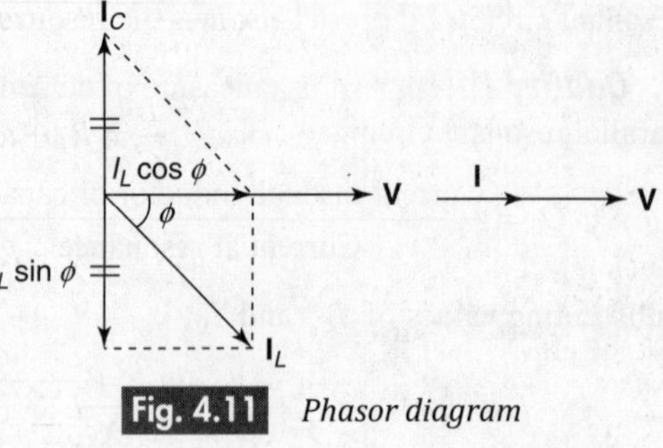


**Fig. 4.11** *Phasor diagram*

The phasor diagram of parallel resonant circuit is shown in Fig. 4.11.

***4. Behaviour of Conductance G, Inductive Susceptance $B_L$ and Capacitive Susceptance with Change in Frequency*** Conductance remains constant with the change in frequencies.

Inductive susceptance $B_L$ is

$$B_L = \frac{1}{jX_L} = -j\frac{1}{X_L} = -j\frac{1}{2\pi fL}$$

It is inversely proportional to the frequency. Thus, it decreases with the increase in the frequency. Hence, it can be drawn as a rectangular hyperbola in the fourth quadrant.

Capacitive susceptance $B_C$ is

$$B_C = \frac{1}{-jX_C} = -j\frac{1}{X_C} = j2\pi fC$$

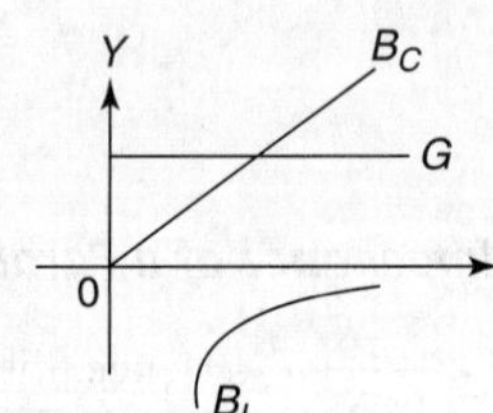


**Fig. 4.12** *Behaviour of G, $B_L$ and $B_c$ with change in frequency*

It is directly proportional to the frequency. It can be drawn as a straight line passing through the origin. Figure 4.12 shows the behaviour of $G$, $B_L$ and $B_C$ with change in frequency.

(a) When $f < f_0$, inductive susceptance predominates. Hence, the current lags behind the voltage and the power factor is lagging in nature.

(b) When $f = f_0$, net susceptance is zero. Hence, the admittance is minimum and impedance is maximum. At $f_0$, the current is in phase with the voltage and the power factor is unity.

(c) When $f > f_0$, capacitive susceptance predominates. Hence, the current leads the voltage and power factor is leading in nature.

Figure 4.13 shows the impedance curve of a parallel resonant circuit.

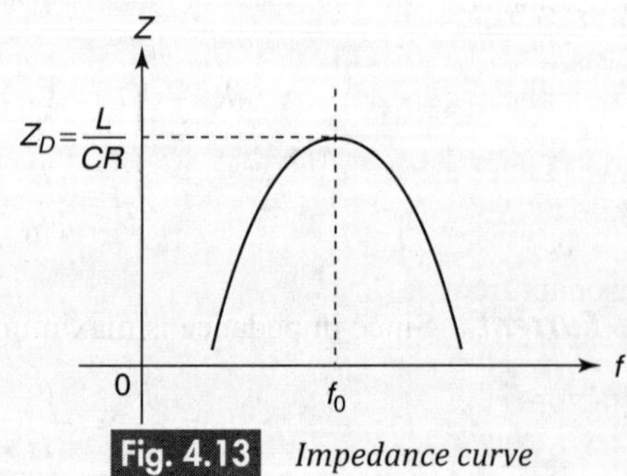


**Fig. 4.13** *Impedance curve*

***5. Bandwidth*** The bandwidth of a parallel resonant circuit is defined in the same way as that for a series resonant circuit. Figure 4.14 shows the resonance curve of a parallel resonant circuit.

***6. Quality Factor*** It is a measure of current magnification in a parallel resonant circuit.

$$Q_0 = \frac{\text{Current through inductor or capacitor}}{\text{Current at resonance}} = \frac{I_{C_0}}{I_0}$$

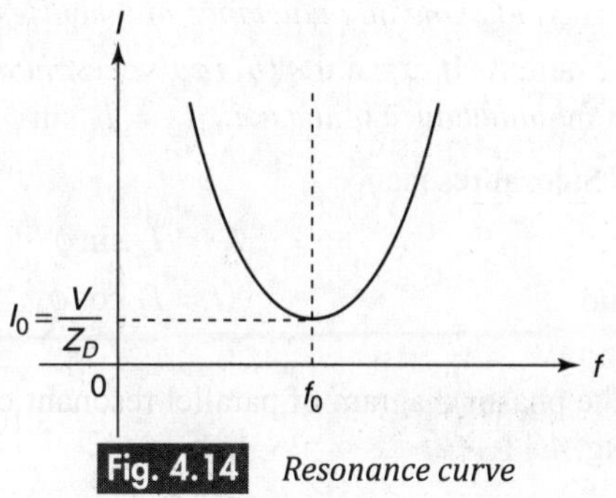


**Fig. 4.14** *Resonance curve*

Substituting values of $I_{C_0}$ and $I_0$,

$$Q_0 = \frac{\frac{V}{X_{C_0}}}{\frac{VCR}{L}} = \frac{\frac{1}{X_{C_0}}}{\frac{CR}{L}} = \frac{\omega_0 C}{\frac{CR}{L}} = \frac{\omega_0 L}{R}$$

Neglecting the resistance $R$, the resonant frequency $\omega_0$ is given by

$$\omega_0 = \frac{1}{\sqrt{LC}}$$

$$Q_0 = \frac{\left(\frac{1}{\sqrt{LC}}\right)L}{R} = \frac{1}{R}\sqrt{\frac{L}{C}}$$

## 4.3 COMPARISON OF SERIES AND PARALLEL RESONANT CIRCUITS

LO 4.3

Compare series and parallel resonant circuits

| *Parameter* | *Series Circuit* | *Parallel Circuit* |
|---|---|---|
| Current at resonance | $I = \frac{V}{R}$ and is maximum | $I = \frac{VCR}{L}$ and is minimum |
| Impedance at resonance | $Z = R$ and is minimum | $Z = \frac{L}{CR}$ and is maximum |
| Power factor at resonance | Unity | Unity |
| Resonant frequency | $f_0 = \frac{1}{2\pi\sqrt{LC}}$ | $f_0 = \frac{1}{2\pi}\sqrt{\frac{1}{LC} - \frac{R^2}{L^2}}$ |
| $Q$-factor | $Q = \frac{2\pi f_0 L}{R}$ | $Q = \frac{2\pi f_0 L}{R}$ |
| It magnifies | Voltage across $L$ and $C$ | Current through $L$ and $C$ |

## EXAMPLE 4.19

*A coil having an inductance of L henries and a resistance of 12 Ω is connected in parallel with a variable capacitor. At $\omega = 2.3\times10^6$ rad/s, resonance is achieved and at this instant, capacitance $C = 0.021\ \mu F$. Find the inductance of the coil.*

**Solution**

$$R = 12\ \Omega,\quad \omega_0 = 2.3\times10^6\ \text{rad/s},\quad C = 0.021\ \mu\text{F}$$

$$\omega_0 = \sqrt{\frac{1}{LC} - \frac{R^2}{L^2}}$$

$$2.3\times10^6 = \sqrt{\frac{1}{L\times0.021\times10^{-6}} - \frac{(12)^2}{L^2}}$$

$$L = 89.7\ \mu\text{H}$$

## EXAMPLE 4.20

*A coil of 20 Ω resistance has an inductance of 0.2 H and is connected in parallel with a condenser of 100 μF capacitance. Calculate the frequency at which this circuit will behave as a non-inductive resistance. Also, find the value of dynamic resistance.*

**Solution**

$$R = 20\ \Omega,\quad L = 0.2\ \text{H},\quad C = 100\ \mu\text{F}$$

(a) Resonant frequency

$$f_0 = \frac{1}{2\pi}\sqrt{\frac{1}{LC} - \frac{R^2}{L^2}} = \frac{1}{2\pi}\sqrt{\frac{1}{0.2\times100\times10^{-6}} - \left(\frac{20}{0.2}\right)^2} = 31.83\ \text{Hz}$$

(b) Dynamic resistance

$$Z_D = \frac{L}{CR} = \frac{0.2}{100\times10^{-6}\times20} = 100\ \Omega$$

## EXAMPLE 4.21

*In the circuit shown in Fig. 4.15, an inductance at 0.1 H having a $Q_0$ of 5 is in parallel with a capacitor. Determine the value of capacitance and coil resistance at a resonant frequency of 500 rad/s.*

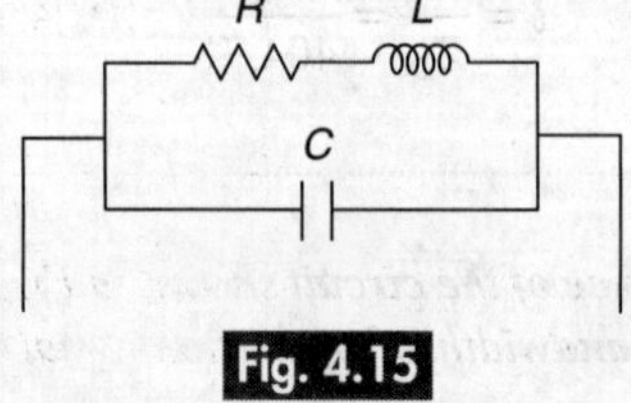


Fig. 4.15

**Solution**

$$L = 0.1\ \text{H},\quad Q_0 = 5,\quad \omega_0 = 500\ \text{rad/s}$$

$$Q_0 = \frac{\omega_0 L}{R}$$

$$5 = \frac{500 \times 0.1}{R}$$

$$R = 10\ \Omega$$

$$\omega_0 = \sqrt{\frac{1}{LC} - \frac{R^2}{L^2}}$$

$$500 = \sqrt{\frac{1}{0.1 \times C} - \frac{(10)^2}{(0.1)^2}}$$

$$C = 38.46\ \mu\text{F}$$

## EXAMPLE 4.22

*A coil of 10 Ω resistance and 0.2 H inductance is connected in parallel with a variable capacitor across a 220 V, 50 Hz supply. Calculate (a) the capacitance of the capacitor for resonance, (b) the dynamic impedance of the circuit, and (c) supply current.*

**Solution**

$$R = 10\ \Omega, \quad L = 0.2\ \text{H}, \quad V = 220\ \text{V}, \quad f_0 = 50\ \text{Hz}$$

(a) Capacitance of the capacitor

$$f_0 = \frac{1}{2\pi}\sqrt{\frac{1}{LC} - \frac{R^2}{L^2}}$$

$$50 = \frac{1}{2\pi}\sqrt{\frac{1}{0.2 \times C} - \frac{(10)^2}{(0.2)^2}}$$

$$C = 49.41\ \mu\text{F}$$

(b) Dynamic impedance of the circuit

$$Z_D = \frac{L}{CR} = \frac{0.2}{49.41 \times 10^{-6} \times 10} = 404.78\ \Omega$$

(c) Supply current

$$I = \frac{V}{Z_D} = \frac{220}{404.78} = 0.543\ \text{A}$$

## EXAMPLE 4.23

*Find the value of the dynamic impedance of the circuit shown in Fig. 4.16 at a frequency of 500 kHz and for bandwidth of operation equal to 20 kHz. The resistance of the coil is 5 Ω.*

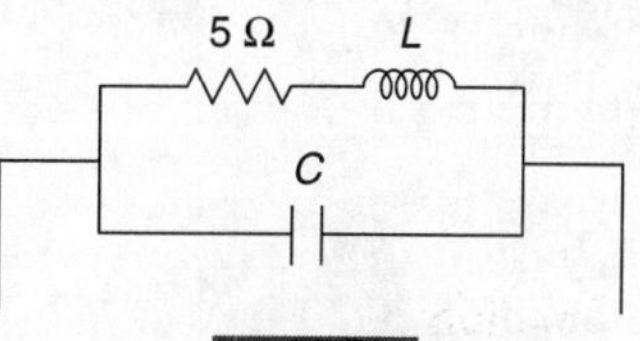

Fig. 4.16

**Solution**

$$f_0 = 500\ \text{kHz}, \quad BW = 20\ \text{kHz}, \quad R = 5\ \Omega$$

$$BW = \frac{R}{2\pi L}$$

$$20 \times 10^3 = \frac{5}{2\pi L}$$

$$L = 39.79 \text{ μH}$$

$$f_0 = \frac{1}{2\pi}\sqrt{\frac{1}{LC} - \frac{R^2}{L^2}}$$

$$500 \times 10^3 = \frac{1}{2\pi}\sqrt{\frac{1}{39.79 \times 10^{-6} \times C} - \frac{(5)^2}{(39.79 \times 10^{-6})^2}}$$

$$C = 2.54 \text{ nF}$$

$$Z_D = \frac{L}{CR} = \frac{39.79 \times 10^{-6}}{2.54 \times 10^{-9} \times 5} = 3.13 \text{ k}\Omega$$

## EXAMPLE 4.24

*A coil having a resistance of 20 Ω and an inductance of 200 μH is connected in parallel with a variable capacitor. This parallel combination is connected in series with a resistance of 8000 Ω. A voltage of 230 V at a frequency of $10^6$ Hz is applied across the circuit, as shown in Fig. 4.17. Calculate (a) the value of capacitance at resonance, (b) Q factor of the circuit, (c) dynamic impedance of the circuit, and (d) total circuit current.*

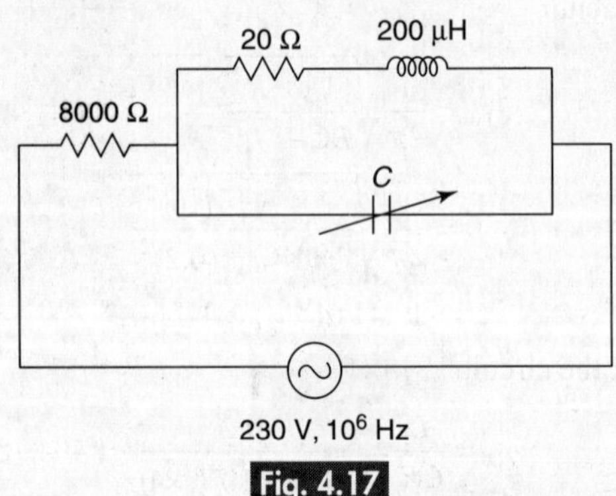


Fig. 4.17

**Solution** $R = 20\ \Omega,\quad L = 200\ \mu\text{H},\quad f_0 = 10^6\ \text{Hz},\quad V = 230\ \text{V},\quad R_S = 8000\ \Omega$

(a) Value of capacitance

$$f_0 = \frac{1}{2\pi}\sqrt{\frac{1}{LC} - \frac{R^2}{L^2}}$$

$$10^6 = \frac{1}{2\pi}\sqrt{\frac{1}{200 \times 10^{-6} \times C} - \frac{(20)^2}{(200 \times 10^{-6})^2}}$$

$$C = 126.65 \text{ pF}$$

(b) Quality factor

$$Q_0 = \frac{2\pi f_0 L}{R} = \frac{2\pi \times 10^6 \times 200 \times 10^{-6}}{20} = 62.83$$

(c) Dynamic impedance

$$Z_D = \frac{L}{CR} = \frac{200 \times 10^{-6}}{126.65 \times 10^{-12} \times 20} = 78958\ \Omega$$

(d) Current

Total impedance of the circuit at resonance $= Z_D + R_S = 78958 + 8000 = 86958\ \Omega$

$$I = \frac{230}{86958} = 2.65 \text{ mA}$$

## EXAMPLE 4.25

*Derive the expression for resonant frequency for the parallel circuit shown in Fig. 4.18. Also, calculate the impedance and current at resonance.*

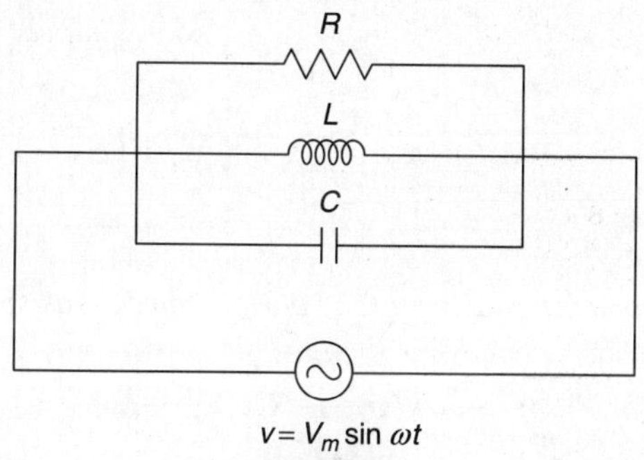


Fig. 4.18

**Solution** $\mathbf{Z}_1 = R, \quad \mathbf{Z}_2 = jX_L, \quad \mathbf{Z}_3 = -jX_C$

(a) Resonant frequency of the circuit
For a parallel circuit,

$$\frac{1}{\mathbf{Z}} = \frac{1}{\mathbf{Z}_1} + \frac{1}{\mathbf{Z}_2} + \frac{1}{\mathbf{Z}_3}$$

$$\mathbf{Y} = \frac{1}{R} + \frac{1}{jX_L} + \frac{1}{-jX_C} = \frac{1}{R} - j\frac{1}{X_L} + j\frac{1}{X_C} = \frac{1}{R} - j\left(\frac{1}{X_L} - \frac{1}{X_C}\right)$$

At resonance, the circuit is purely resistive. Hence, the condition for resonance is

$$\frac{1}{X_L} - \frac{1}{X_C} = 0$$

$$X_L = X_C$$

$$\omega_0 L = \frac{1}{\omega_0 C}$$

$$\omega_0^2 = \frac{1}{LC}$$

$$\omega_0 = \frac{1}{\sqrt{LC}}$$

$$f_0 = \frac{1}{2\pi\sqrt{LC}}$$

where $f_0$ is called the resonant frequency of the circuit.

(b) Impedance at resonance
At resonance, the circuit is purely resistive. Hence, the imaginary part of **Y** is zero.

$$Y_D = \frac{1}{R}$$

$$Z_D = R$$

(c) Current at resonance

$$I_0 = \frac{V}{Z_D} = \frac{V}{R}$$

## EXAMPLE 4.26

*Derive the expression for the resonant frequency of the parallel circuit, as shown in Fig. 4.19.*

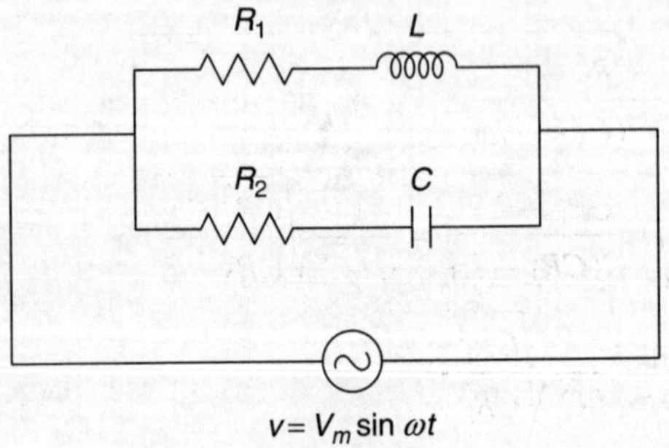


Fig. 4.19

**Solution**

$$\mathbf{Z}_1 = R_1 + jX_L$$

$$\mathbf{Z}_2 = R_2 - jX_C$$

For a parallel circuit,

$$\frac{1}{\mathbf{Z}} = \frac{1}{\mathbf{Z}_1} + \frac{1}{\mathbf{Z}_2}$$

$$\mathbf{Y}=\frac{1}{R_1+jX_L}+\frac{1}{R_2-jX_C}=\frac{R_1-jX_L}{R_1^2+X_L^2}+\frac{R_2+jX_C}{R_2^2+X_C^2}=\frac{R_1}{R_1^2+X_L^2}+\frac{R_2}{R_2^2+X_C^2}-j\left(\frac{X_L}{R_1^2+X_L^2}-\frac{X_C}{R_2^2+X_C^2}\right)$$

At resonance, the circuit is purely resistive. Hence, the condition for resonance is

$$\frac{X_L}{R_1^2+X_L^2}-\frac{X_C}{R_2^2+X_C^2}=0$$

$$\frac{X_L}{R_1^2+X_L^2}=\frac{X_C}{R_2^2+X_C^2}$$

$$\frac{\omega_0 L}{R_1^2+\omega_0^2L^2}=\frac{\frac{1}{\omega_0 C}}{R_2^2+\frac{1}{\omega_0^2C^2}}$$

$$\frac{\omega_0^2 LC}{R_1^2+\omega_0^2L^2}=\frac{\omega_0^2C^2}{R_2^2\omega_0^2C^2+1}$$

$$LC(R_2^2\omega_0^2C^2+1)=C^2(R_1^2+\omega_0^2L^2)$$

$$\omega_0^2R_2^2LC^3+LC=C^2R_1^2+\omega_0^2L^2C^2$$

$$\omega_0^2R_2^2LC^3-\omega_0^2L^2C^2=C^2R_1^2-LC$$

$$\omega_0^2LC^2(CR_2^2-L)=C(CR_1^2-L)$$

$$\omega_0^2LC(CR_2^2-L)=CR_1^2-L$$

$$\omega_0^2=\frac{CR_1^2-L}{LC(CR_2^2-L)}$$

$$\omega_0=\sqrt{\frac{CR_1^2-L}{LC(CR_2^2-L)}}=\frac{1}{\sqrt{LC}}\sqrt{\frac{CR_1^2-L}{CR_2^2-L}}$$

$$f_0=\frac{1}{2\pi\sqrt{LC}}\sqrt{\frac{CR_1^2-L}{CR_2^2-L}}$$

where $f_0$ is called the resonant frequency of the circuit.

## EXAMPLE 4.27

*Derive the expression for resonant frequency for the parallel circuit shown in Fig. 4.20.*

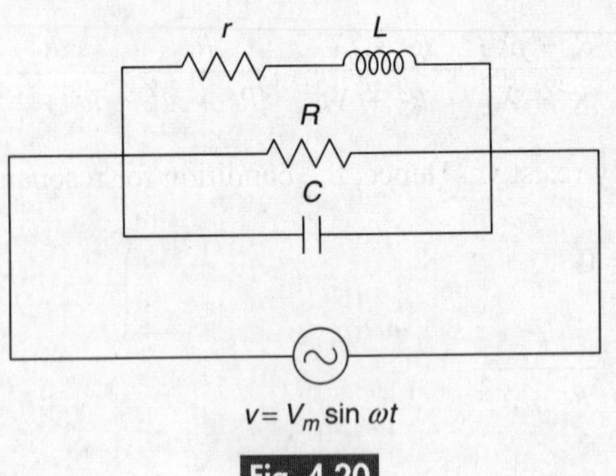


Fig. 4.20

**Solution** $\mathbf{Z}_1 = r + jX_L, \quad \mathbf{Z}_2 = R, \quad \mathbf{Z}_3 = -jX_C$

For a parallel circuit,

$$\frac{1}{\mathbf{Z}} = \frac{1}{\mathbf{Z}_1} + \frac{1}{\mathbf{Z}_2} + \frac{1}{\mathbf{Z}_3}$$

$$\mathbf{Y} = \frac{1}{r + jX_L} + \frac{1}{R} + \frac{1}{-jX_C} = \frac{r - jX_L}{r^2 + X_L^2} + \frac{1}{R} + j\frac{1}{X_C} = \left(\frac{r}{r^2 + X_L^2} + \frac{1}{R}\right) + j\left(\frac{1}{X_C} - \frac{X_L}{r^2 + X_L^2}\right)$$

At resonance, the circuit is purely resistive, i.e., the imaginary part of **Y** is equal to zero.

$$\frac{1}{X_C} - \frac{X_L}{r^2 + X_L^2} = 0$$

$$\frac{1}{X_C} = \frac{X_L}{r^2 + X_L^2}$$

$$X_L\, X_C = r^2 + X_L^2$$

$$\omega_0 L \frac{1}{\omega_0 C} = r^2 + \omega_0^2 L^2$$

$$\frac{L}{C} = r^2 + \omega_0^2 L^2$$

$$\omega_0^2 L^2 = \frac{L}{C} - r^2$$

$$\omega_0^2 = \frac{1}{LC} - \frac{r^2}{L^2}$$

$$\omega_0 = \sqrt{\frac{1}{LC} - \frac{r^2}{L^2}}$$

$$f_0 = \frac{1}{2\pi}\sqrt{\frac{1}{LC} - \frac{r^2}{L^2}}$$

where $f_0$ is called the resonant frequency of the circuit.

## EXAMPLE 4.28

*Find the value of R in the circuit shown in Fig. 4.21 to achieve resonance.*

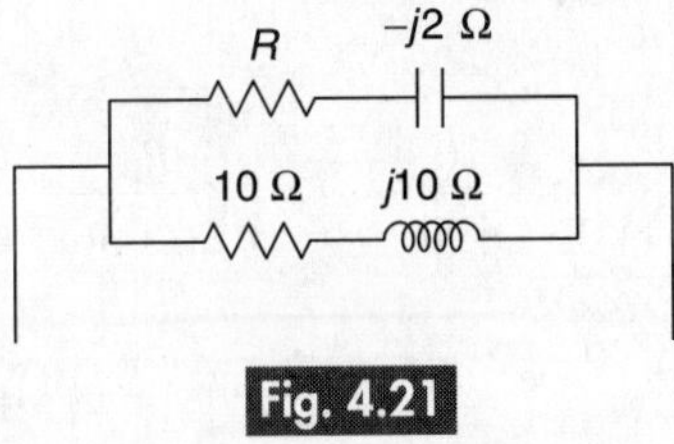


Fig. 4.21

**Solution**

$$\mathbf{Z}_1 = 10 + j10\ \Omega, \quad \mathbf{Z}_2 = R - j2\ \Omega$$

For a parallel circuit,

$$\frac{1}{\mathbf{Z}} = \frac{1}{\mathbf{Z}_1} + \frac{1}{\mathbf{Z}_2}$$

$$\mathbf{Y} = \frac{1}{10+j10} + \frac{1}{R-j2} = \frac{10-j10}{100+100} + \frac{R+j2}{R^2+4} = \left(\frac{10}{200} + \frac{R}{R^2+4}\right) - j\left(\frac{10}{200} - \frac{2}{R^2+4}\right)$$

At resonance, the circuit is purely resistive, i.e., the imaginary part of **Y** is equal to zero.

$$\frac{10}{200} - \frac{2}{R^2+4} = 0$$

$$\frac{2}{R^2+4} = \frac{1}{20}$$

$$R^2 + 4 = 40$$

$$R^2 = 36$$

$$R = 6\ \Omega$$

## EXAMPLE 4.29

*Find the value of $R_1$ such that the circuit given in Fig. 4.22 is in resonance.*

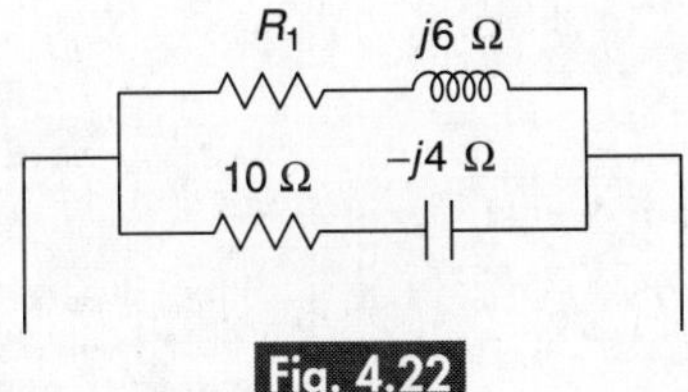


Fig. 4.22

**Solution**

$$\mathbf{Z}_1 = R_1 + j6\ \Omega, \quad \mathbf{Z}_2 = 10 - j4\ \Omega$$

For a parallel circuit,

$$\frac{1}{\mathbf{Z}} = \frac{1}{\mathbf{Z}_1} + \frac{1}{\mathbf{Z}_2}$$

$$\mathbf{Y} = \frac{1}{R_1 + j6} + \frac{1}{10 - j4} = \frac{R_1 - j6}{R_1^2 + 36} + \frac{10 + j4}{100 + 16} = \left(\frac{R_1}{R_1^2 + 36} + \frac{10}{116}\right) - j\left(\frac{6}{R_1^2 + 36} - \frac{4}{116}\right)$$

At resonance, the circuit is purely resistive, i.e., the imaginary part of **Y** is equal to zero.

$$\frac{6}{R_1^2 + 36} - \frac{4}{116} = 0$$

$$\frac{6}{R_1^2 + 36} = \frac{4}{116}$$

$$R_1^2 + 36 = \frac{116 \times 6}{4} = 174$$

$$R_1^2 = 138$$

$$R_1 = 11.75\ \Omega$$

**EXAMPLE 4.30**

*Find the value of C in the circuit shown in Fig. 4.23 to give resonance.*

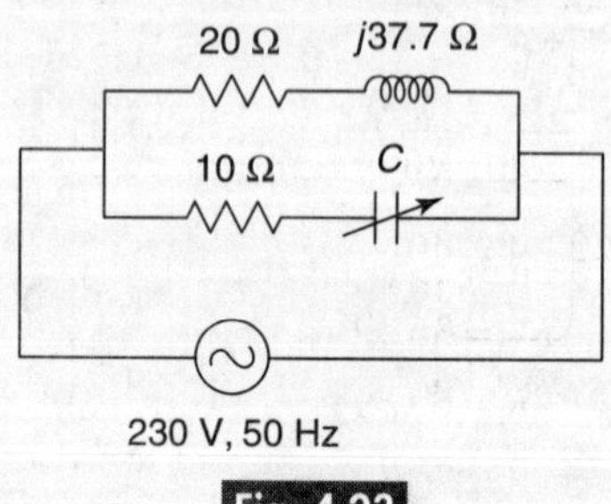


Fig. 4.23

**Solution**

$$\mathbf{Z}_1 = 20 + j37.7\ \Omega, \quad \mathbf{Z}_2 = 10 - jX_C$$

For a parallel circuit,

$$\frac{1}{\mathbf{Z}} = \frac{1}{\mathbf{Z}_1} + \frac{1}{\mathbf{Z}_2}$$

$$\mathbf{Y} = \frac{1}{20 + j37.7} + \frac{1}{10 - jX_C} = \frac{20 - j37.7}{400 + 1421.29} + \frac{10 + jX_C}{100 + X_C^2}$$

$$= \left(\frac{20}{1821.29} + \frac{10}{100 + X_C^2}\right) - j\left(\frac{37.7}{1821.29} - \frac{X_C}{100 + X_C^2}\right)$$

At resonance, the circuit is purely resistive, i.e., the imaginary part of **Y** is equal to zero.

$$\frac{37.7}{1821.29} - \frac{X_C}{100 + X_C^2} = 0$$

$$\frac{X_C}{100 + X_C^2} = 0.021$$

$$0.021\, X_C^2 - X_C + 2.1 = 0$$

Solving the quadratic equation,

$$X_C = 45.41\ \Omega \qquad \text{or} \qquad X_C = 2.2\ \Omega$$

$$\frac{1}{2\pi \times 50 \times C} = 45.41 \qquad \text{or} \qquad \frac{1}{2\pi \times 50 \times C} = 2.2$$

$$C = 70.1\ \mu\text{F} \qquad \text{or} \qquad C = 1.44\ \text{mF}$$

## EXAMPLE 4.31

*Find the value of L at which the circuit resonates at a frequency of 1000 rad/s in the circuit shown in Fig. 4.24.*

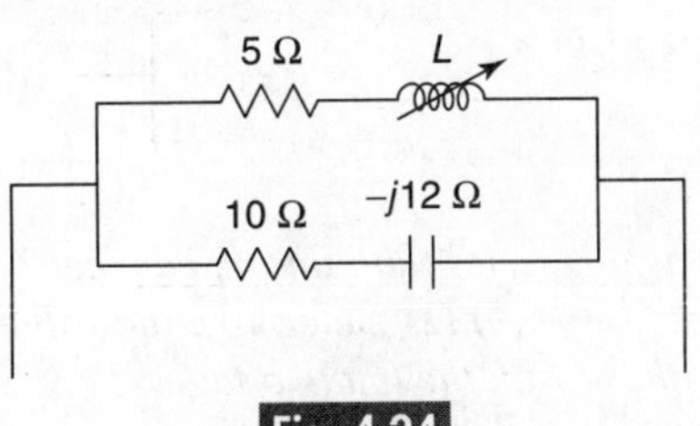


Fig. 4.24

**Solution**

$$\mathbf{Z}_1 = 5 + jX_L\ \Omega, \quad \mathbf{Z}_2 = 10 - j12\ \Omega$$

For a parallel circuit,

$$\frac{1}{\mathbf{Z}} = \frac{1}{\mathbf{Z}_1} + \frac{1}{\mathbf{Z}_2}$$

$$\mathbf{Y} = \frac{1}{5 + jX_L} + \frac{1}{10 - j12} = \frac{5 - jX_L}{25 + X_L^2} + \frac{10 + j12}{100 + 144} = \left(\frac{5}{25 + X_L^2} + \frac{10}{244}\right) - j\left(\frac{X_L}{25 + X_L^2} - \frac{12}{244}\right)$$

At resonance, the circuit is purely resistive, i.e., the imaginary part of **Y** is equal to zero.

$$\frac{X_L}{25+X_L^2}-\frac{12}{244}=0$$

$$\frac{X_L}{25+X_L^2}=\frac{12}{244}$$

$$12X_L^2-244X_L+300=0$$

Solving the quadratic equation,

$$X_L = 19.01 \quad \text{or} \quad X_L = 1.31\,\Omega$$

$$2\pi\times 50\times L = 19.01 \quad \text{or} \quad 2\pi\times 50\times L = 1.31$$

$$L = 19.01 \text{ mH} \quad \text{or} \quad L = 1.31 \text{ mH}$$

## EXAMPLE 4.32

*Two impedances $Z_1 = (20 + j10)\ \Omega$ and $Z_2 = (10 - j30)\ \Omega$ are connected in parallel and this combination is connected in series with $Z_3 = (30 + jX)\ \Omega$. Find the value of X which will produce resonance.*

**Solution**

$$\mathbf{Z}_1 = 20 + j10\,\Omega,\quad \mathbf{Z}_2 = 10 - j30\,\Omega,\quad \mathbf{Z}_3 = 30 + jX\,\Omega$$

$$\mathbf{Z}=\frac{\mathbf{Z}_1\mathbf{Z}_2}{\mathbf{Z}_1+\mathbf{Z}_2}+\mathbf{Z}_3=\frac{(20+j10)\,(10-j30)}{20+j10+10-j30}+(30+jX)=19.23-j3.85+30+jX=49.23+j(X-3.85)$$

At resonance, the circuit is purely resistive, i.e., imaginary part of **Z** is equal to zero.

$$X-3.85=0$$

$$X=3.85\,\Omega$$

## EXAMPLE 4.33

*Impedances $Z_2$ and $Z_3$ in parallel are in series with an impedance $Z_1$ across a 100 V, 50 Hz ac supply. $Z_1 = (6.25 + j1.25)\,\Omega, Z_2 = 5\,\Omega, Z_3 = (5 - jX_C)\,\Omega$. Determine the value of capacitance of $X_C$ such that the total current of the circuit will be in phase with the total voltage.*

**Solution**

$$\mathbf{Z}_1 = 6.25 + j1.25\,\Omega,\quad \mathbf{Z}_2 = 5\,\Omega,\quad \mathbf{Z}_3 = 5 - jX_C\,\Omega$$

$$\mathbf{Z}=\frac{\mathbf{Z}_2\mathbf{Z}_3}{\mathbf{Z}_2+\mathbf{Z}_3}+\mathbf{Z}_1=\frac{5(5-jX_C)}{5+5-jX_C}+(6.25+j1.25)$$

$$=\frac{25-j5X_C}{10-jX_C}+6.25+j1.25=\frac{25-j5X_C}{10-jX_C}\times\frac{10+jX_C}{10+jX_C}+6.25+j1.25$$

$$=\frac{250+5X_C{}^2}{100+X_C{}^2}-j\frac{25X_C}{100+X_C{}^2}+6.25+j1.25=\left(6.25+\frac{250+5X_C^2}{100+X_C^2}\right)-j\left(\frac{25X_C}{100+X_C^2}-1.25\right)$$

At resonance, the circuit is purely resistive, i.e., the imaginary part of **Z** is equal to zero.

$$\frac{25X_C}{100+X_C^2}-1.25=0$$

$$\frac{25X_C}{100+X_C^2}=1.25$$

$$1.25\,X_C^2-25X_C+125=0$$

$$X_C^2-20X_C+100=0$$

$$X_c=10$$

$$\frac{1}{2\pi\times 50\times C}=10$$

$$C=318.31\ \mu\text{F}$$

## EXAMPLE 4.34

*Find the frequency at which the circuit shown in Fig. 4.25 will be at resonance. If the capacitor and inductors are interchanged, what would be the value of resonant frequency?*

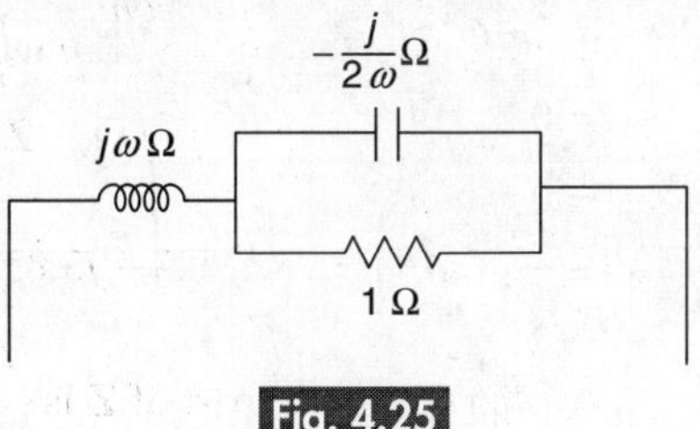


Fig. 4.25

**Solution**

$$\mathbf{Z}_1=j\omega\ \Omega,\quad \mathbf{Z}_2=-\frac{j}{2\omega}\ \Omega,\quad \mathbf{Z}_3=1\ \Omega$$

$$\mathbf{Z}=\mathbf{Z}_1+\frac{\mathbf{Z}_2\mathbf{Z}_3}{\mathbf{Z}_2+\mathbf{Z}_3}=j\omega+\frac{\left(-\frac{j}{2\omega}\right)(1)}{-\frac{j}{2\omega}+1}=j\omega-\frac{j}{2\omega-j}=j\omega-\frac{j(2\omega+j)}{4\omega^2+1}=\frac{1}{4\omega^2+1}+j\left(\omega-\frac{2\omega}{4\omega^2+1}\right)$$

At resonance, the circuit is purely resistive, i.e., imaginary part of **Z** is equal to zero.

$$\omega-\frac{2\omega}{4\omega^2+1}=0$$

$$\omega=\frac{2\omega}{4\omega^2+1}$$

$$\frac{1}{2}=\frac{1}{4\omega^2+1}$$

$$4\omega^2 + 1 = 2$$
$$4\omega^2 - 1 = 0$$
$$\omega = \pm 0.5 \text{ rad/s}$$

Considering positive values of $\omega$,

$$\omega = 0.5 \text{ rad/s}$$

If the capacitor and inductor are interchanged,

$$\mathbf{Z} = -\frac{j}{2\omega} + \frac{(1)(j\omega)}{1+j\omega} = -\frac{j}{2\omega} + \frac{j\omega(1-j\omega)}{1+\omega^2} = -\frac{j}{2\omega} + \frac{(\omega^2 + j\omega)}{1+\omega^2} = \frac{\omega^2}{1+\omega^2} - j\left(\frac{1}{2\omega} - \frac{\omega}{1+\omega^2}\right)$$

At resonance, the circuit is purely resistive, i.e., the imaginary part of **Z** is equal to zero.

$$\frac{1}{2\omega} - \frac{\omega}{1+\omega^2} = 0$$
$$\frac{1}{2\omega} = \frac{\omega}{1+\omega^2}$$
$$2\omega^2 - \omega^2 - 1 = 0$$
$$\omega^2 - 1 = 0$$
$$\omega = \pm 1 \text{ rad/s}$$

Considering positive values of $\omega$,

$$\omega = 1 \text{ rad/s}$$

## EXAMPLE 4.35

*A 400 V, 50 Hz supply feeds energy to a parallel circuit consisting of $10\angle 30°\ \Omega$ branch and $10\angle -60°\ \Omega$ branch. Determine the impedance of a circuit element such that if connected in series with the source, the system comes at resonance.*

**Solution**

$$\mathbf{Z}_p = \frac{(10\angle 30°)\,(10\angle -60°)}{10\angle 30° + 10\angle -60°} = 7.07\ \angle -15° = 6.83 - j1.83\ \Omega$$
$$\mathbf{Z}_{\text{eq}} = \mathbf{Z} + \mathbf{Z}_p = \mathbf{Z} + 6.83 - j1.83$$

At resonance, the circuit is purely resistive, i.e., the imaginary part of **Z** is equal to zero. Hence, **Z** must be equal to $j1.83\ \Omega$.

$$\mathbf{Z} = j1.83\ \Omega = jX_L$$
$$X_L = 1.83$$
$$2\pi \times 50 \times L = 1.83$$
$$L = 5.82 \text{ mH}$$

## EXAMPLE 4.36

*A coil of 400 Ω resistance and 318 μH inductance is connected in parallel with a capacitor and the circuit resonates at 1 MHz. If a second capacitor of 23.5 pF capacitance is connected in parallel with the first capacitor, find the frequency at which the circuit resonates.*

**Solution** $R = 400\ \Omega,\quad L = 318\ \mu\text{H},\quad f_0 = 1\ \text{MHz},\quad C_2 = 23.5\ \text{pF}$

$$f_0 = \frac{1}{2\pi}\sqrt{\frac{1}{LC_1} - \frac{R^2}{L^2}}$$

$$10^6 = \frac{1}{2\pi}\sqrt{\frac{1}{318\times10^{-6}\times C_1} - \frac{(400)^2}{(318\times10^{-6})^2}}$$

$$C_1 = 76.59\ \text{pF}$$

When capacitor of 23.5 pF is connected in parallel with $C_1 = 76.59$ pF,

$$C_T = C_1 + C_2 = 76.59 + 23.5 = 100.09\ \text{pF}$$

The new resonant frequency $f_0' = \frac{1}{2\pi}\sqrt{\frac{1}{LC_T} - \frac{R^2}{L^2}} = \frac{1}{2\pi}\sqrt{\frac{1}{318\times10^{-6}\times100.09\times10^{-12}} - \frac{(400)^2}{(318\times10^{-6})^2}}$

$$= 869.34\ \text{kHz}$$

## EXAMPLE 4.37

*A series circuit consisting of a 12 Ω resistor, 0.3 H inductor and a variable capacitor is connected across a 100 V, 50 Hz ac supply, as shown in Fig. 4.26. The capacitance value is adjusted to obtain maximum current. Find the capacitance value. Now, the supply frequency is raised to 60 Hz, the voltage remaining same at 100 V. Find the value of the capacitance $C_2$ to be connected across the above series circuit so that current drawn from the supply is minimum.*

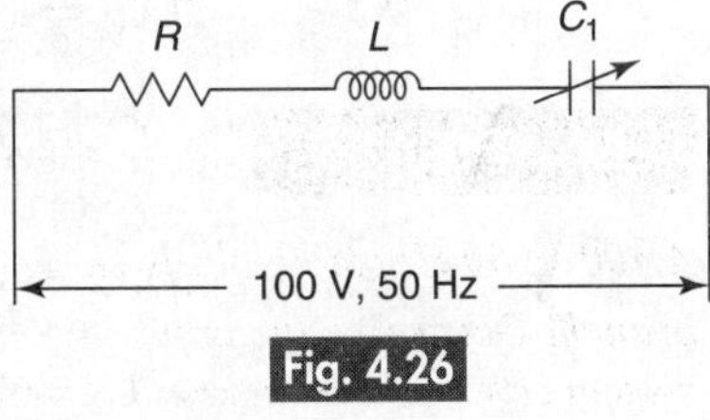


Fig. 4.26

**Solution** $R = 12\ \Omega,\quad L = 0.3\ \text{H},\quad V = 100\ \text{V},\quad f = 50\ \text{Hz}$

(a) Value of capacitance $C_1$

The resonance occurs at $f = 50$ Hz

$$f_0 = \frac{1}{2\pi\sqrt{LC_1}}$$

$$50 = \frac{1}{2\pi\sqrt{0.3\times C_1}}$$

$$C_1 = 33.77\ \mu\text{F}$$

(b) Value of capacitance $C_2$

The resonance occurs at 60 Hz for the circuit shown in Fig. 4.27.

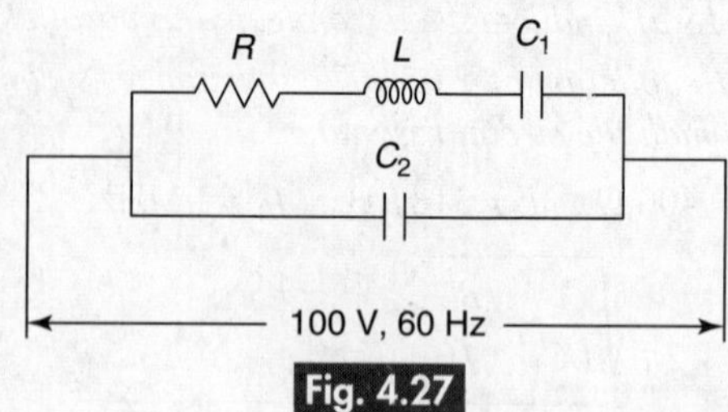


Fig. 4.27

$$X_L = 2\pi f_0 L = 2\pi \times 60 \times 0.3 = 113.1\,\Omega$$

$$X_{C_1} = \frac{1}{2\pi f_0 C_1} = \frac{1}{2\pi \times 60 \times 33.77 \times 10^{-6}} = 78.55\,\Omega$$

$$\mathbf{Z}_1 = 12 + j113.1 - j78.55 = 36.57\angle 70.85°\,\Omega$$

$$\mathbf{Y}_1 = \frac{1}{Z_1} = \frac{1}{36.57\angle 70.85°} = 0.027\angle 70.85° = 8.86 \times 10^{-3} - j0.0255\,℧$$

$$\mathbf{Y}_{\text{req}} = \mathbf{Y}_1 + \mathbf{Y}_2 = 8.86 \times 10^{-3} - j0.0255 + \mathbf{Y}_2$$

At resonance, the imaginary part of $\mathbf{Y}_{\text{req}}$ becomes zero.

$$\mathbf{Y}_2 = j0.0255\,℧$$

$$\mathbf{Y}_2 = \frac{1}{X_{C_2}} = 0.0255\,℧$$

$$X_{C_2} = 39.22\,\Omega$$

$$X_{C_2} = \frac{1}{2\pi f_0 C_2}$$

$$39.22 = \frac{1}{2\pi \times 60 \times C_2}$$

$$C_2 = 67.63\,\mu\text{F}$$

**EXAMPLE 4.38**

*Find active and reactive components of the current taken by a series circuit consisting of a coil of inductance 0.1 H and a resistance of 8 Ω and a capacitor of 120 μF connected to a 240 V, 50 Hz supply. Find the value of the capacitor that has to be connected in parallel with the above series circuit so that the pf of the entire circuit is unity.*

**Solution**

$$L = 0.1\text{ H},\quad R = 8\,\Omega,\quad C = 120\,\mu\text{F},\quad V = 240\text{ V},\quad f = 50\text{ Hz}$$

$$X_L = 2\pi f L = 2\pi \times 50 \times 0.1 = 31.42\,\Omega$$

$$X_C = \frac{1}{2\pi f C} = \frac{1}{2\pi \times 50 \times 120 \times 10^{-6}} = 26.53\,\Omega$$

$$\mathbf{Z}_1 = R + jX_L - jX_C = 8 + j31.42 - j26.53 = 9.38\angle 31.44°\ \Omega$$

$$I = \frac{V}{Z_1} = \frac{240}{9.43} = 25.45\text{ A}$$

Active component of current = $I\cos\phi = 25.45\cos(31.44°) = 21.71$ A

Reactive component of current = $I\sin\phi = 25.45\sin(31.44°) = 13.27$ A

When a capacitor is connected in parallel with the above series circuit, to make pf of the entire circuit unity,

$$\mathbf{Z}_1 = R + jX_L - jX_C = 8 + j31.42 - j26.53 = 8 + j4.89\ \Omega$$

$$\mathbf{Z}_2 = -jX_C$$

For a parallel circuit,

$$\frac{1}{\mathbf{Z}} = \frac{1}{\mathbf{Z}_1} + \frac{1}{\mathbf{Z}_2}$$

$$\mathbf{Y} = \frac{1}{8 + j4.89} + \frac{1}{-jX_C} = \frac{8 - j4.89}{64 + 23.91} + j\frac{1}{X_C} = \frac{8}{87.91} + j\left(\frac{1}{X_C} - \frac{4.89}{87.91}\right)$$

At resonance, pf is unity and the imaginary part of **Y** is equal to zero.

$$\frac{1}{X_C} - \frac{4.89}{87.91} = 0$$

$$\frac{1}{X_C} = 0.056$$

$$X_C = 17.86$$

$$\frac{1}{2\pi \times 50 \times C} = 17.86$$

$$C = 178.23\ \mu\text{F}$$

## EXAMPLE 4.39

*A coil of 10 Ω resistance and 0.5 H inductance is connected in series with a capacitor. On applying a sinusoidal voltage the current is maximum when the frequency is 50 Hz. A second capacitor is connected in parallel with the circuit. What capacitance should it have so that the combination acts as a non-inductive resistor at 100 Hz?*

**Solution**

$$R = 10\ \Omega,\quad L = 0.5\text{ H},\quad f_0 = 50\text{ Hz}$$

$$f_0 = \frac{1}{2\pi\sqrt{LC}}$$

$$50 = \frac{1}{2\pi\sqrt{0.5 \times C}}$$

$$C = 20.26\ \mu\text{F}$$

When a second capacitor is connected in parallel with the circuit so that the combination acts as a non-inductive resistor at 100 Hz,

$$X_L = 2\pi \times 100 \times 0.5 = 314.16\ \Omega$$

$$X_C = \frac{1}{2\pi \times 100 \times 20.26 \times 10^{-6}} = 78.56\ \Omega$$

$$\mathbf{Z}_1 = 10 + j314.16 - j78.56 = 10 + j235.6\ \Omega$$

$$\mathbf{Z}_2 = -jX_C$$

For a parallel circuit,

$$\frac{1}{\mathbf{Z}} = \frac{1}{\mathbf{Z}_1} + \frac{1}{\mathbf{Z}_2}$$

$$\mathbf{Y} = \frac{1}{10 + j235.6} + \frac{1}{-jX_C} = \frac{10 - j235.6}{100 + 55507.36} + j\frac{1}{X_C} = \frac{10}{55607.36} + j\left(\frac{1}{X_C} - \frac{235.6}{55607.36}\right)$$

At resonance, the circuit acts as a non-inductive resistor, i.e., the imaginary part of $\mathbf{Y}$ is equal to zero.

$$\frac{1}{X_C} - \frac{235.6}{55607.36} = 0$$

$$X_C = 236.02$$

$$\frac{1}{2\pi \times 100 \times C} = 236.02$$

$$C = 6.7\ \mu\text{F}$$

## EXAMPLE 4.40

*A coil having a resistance and inductance of 15 Ω and 8 mH respectively is connected in parallel with another coil having a resistance and inductance of 4 Ω and 18 mH, as shown in Fig. 4.28. If this parallel combination is to be replaced by a single coil, calculate the value of resistance and inductance of that coil. What value of capacitance should be connected in parallel with this coil in order to get unity power factor? Assume operating frequency to be 50 Hz.*

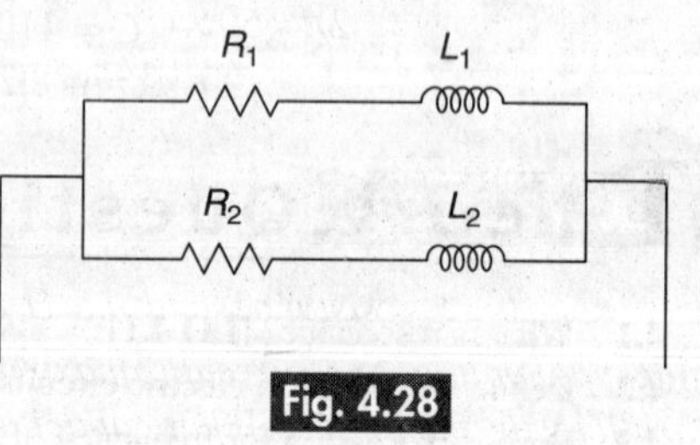

Fig. 4.28

**Solution** $R_1 = 15\ \Omega,\quad L_1 = 8\text{ mH},\quad R_2 = 4\ \Omega,\quad L_2 = 18\text{ mH},\quad f = 50\text{ Hz}$

(a) Value of resistance and inductance of the coil

$$X_{L_1} = 2\pi f L_1 = 2\pi \times 50 \times 8 \times 10^{-3} = 2.51\ \Omega$$

$$X_{L_2} = 2\pi f L_2 = 2\pi \times 50 \times 18 \times 10^{-3} = 5.65\ \Omega$$

$$\mathbf{Z}_1 = R_1 + jX_{L_1} = 15 + j2.51 = 15.21\ \angle 9.5^\circ\ \Omega$$

$$\mathbf{Z}_2 = R_2 + jX_{L_2} = 4 + j5.65 = 6.92\ \angle 54.7^\circ\ \Omega$$

$$\mathbf{Z} = \frac{\mathbf{Z}_1 \mathbf{Z}_2}{\mathbf{Z}_1 + \mathbf{Z}_2} = \frac{(15.21 \angle 9.5^\circ)(6.92 \angle 54.7^\circ)}{15.21 \angle 9.5^\circ + 6.92 \angle 54.7^\circ} = 5.09 \angle 40.96^\circ \ \Omega = 3.84 + j3.34 \ \Omega$$

$$R = 3.84 \ \Omega$$

$$X_L = 3.34 \ \Omega$$

$$X_L = 2\pi f L$$

$$3.34 = 2\pi \times 50 \times L$$

$$L = 10.63 \text{ mH}$$

(b) Value of capacitance

When a capacitance $C$ is connected in parallel with this coil, as shown in Fig. 4.29, power factor becomes unity. Hence, the circuit behaves like a parallel resonant circuit at 50 Hz.

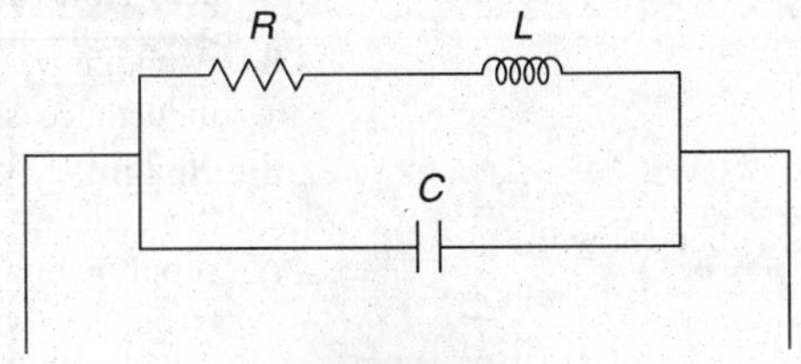


Fig. 4.29

$$f_0 = \frac{1}{2\pi}\sqrt{\frac{1}{LC} - \frac{R^2}{L^2}}$$

$$50 = \frac{1}{2\pi}\sqrt{\frac{1}{10.63 \times 10^{-3} \times C} - \frac{(3.84)^2}{(10.63 \times 10^{-3})^2}}$$

$$C = 410.46 \ \mu\text{F}$$

# Theory Questions

**4.1** What is resonance? **[LO 4.1]** ●○○

**4.2** Define resonance in electric circuits. **[LO 4.1]** ●○○

**4.3** Derive expression for frequency of resonance of a series RLC circuit. **[LO 4.1]** ●○○

**4.4** Draw variations of reactances against frequency in series RLC circuit. **[LO 4.1]** ●○○

**4.5** Define and explain Q-factor of resonating circuit. **[LO 4.1]** ○●○

**4.6** Derive the equation for quality factor of series RLC circuit. **[LO 4.1]** ○●○

**4.7** Derive expression for bandwidth of series resonant circuit. **[LO 4.1]** ○●○

**4.8** Show that the resonant frequency $\omega_0$ of series RLC circuit is the geometric mean of $\omega_1$ and $\omega_2$, the lower and upper half-power frequencies respectively. **[LO 4.1]** ○●○

**4.9** Derive the expression for resonant frequency of a parallel RLC circuit. **[LO 4.2]** ○●○

**4.10** Derive and explain following terms with reference to parallel resonant circuit. **[LO 4.2]** ○●○
(i) Bandwidth (ii) Selectivity

**4.11** Compare series and parallel resonant circuits. **[LO 4.3]** ●○○

# Practice Problems

**4.1** A series *RLC* circuit has the following parameter values:
$R = 10\ \Omega$, $L = 0.014$ H, $C = 100\ \mu$F. Compute the following.
(i) resonant frequency in rad/s
(ii) quality factor of the circuit
(iii) bandwidth
(iv) lower and upper frequency points of the bandwidth ●○○

**4.2** A series *RLC* circuit as $R = 500\ \Omega$, $L = 60$ mH and $C = 0.053\ \mu$F. Estimate
(i) circuit impedance at 50 Hz
(ii) resonance frequency in rad/s
(iii) quality factor of the circuit
(iv) bandwidth
(v) current at resonance frequency with an applied voltage of 30 V ●○○

**4.3** A choking coil of 10 Ω resistance and 0.1 H inductance is connected in series with a capacitor of 200 μF capacitance across a supply voltage of 230 V, 50 Hz ac. Find the following w.r.t. the resonant circuit.
(i) Neat circuit diagram indicating all the relevant parameters
(ii) At what frequency will the circuit resonate?
(iii) Value of reactances at resonance condition
(iv) Impedance of the coil at resonance condition
(v) Voltage across the coil and voltage across the capacitance
(vi) Half-power frequencies $f_1$ and $f_2$
(vii) $Q$ factor of the circuit
(vii) Power and power factor ●○○

**4.4** A coil of 40 Ω resistance and 0.75 H inductance forms part of a series circuit for which the resonant frequency is 55 Hz. If the supply is 250 V, 50 Hz, find
(i) the line current
(ii) the power factor
(iii) the voltage across the coil ●○○

**4.5** An *RLC* series circuit of 10 Ω resistance should be designed to have a bandwidth of 100 Hz. Determine the values of $L$ and $C$ so that the circuit resonates at 250 Hz. ●○○

**4.6** A resistor and capacitor are connected in series with a variable inductor. When the circuit is connected to a 220 V, 50 Hz supply, the maximum current obtained by varying the inductance is 0.314 A. The voltage across the capacitor is 800 V. Calculate the resistance, inductance and capacitance of the circuit. ●○○

**4.7** A coil of 2 Ω resistance and 0.01 H inductance is connected in series with a capacitor across 230 V mains. What must be the capacitance, in order that maximum current occurs at a frequency of 50 Hz? Find also the current and the voltage across the capacitor. ●○○

**4.8** A choking coil of 10-ohm resistance and 0.1 H inductance is connected in series with a capacitor of 200 μF capacitance. Calculate the current, the coil voltage and the capacitor voltage. The supply voltage is 230 V at 50 Hz. At what frequency will the circuit resonate? Calculate the voltages at resonant frequency across the coil and capacitor. For this, assume that supply voltage is 230 V of variable frequency. ○●○

**4.9** An inductive coil having an inductance of 0.04 H and a resistance of 25 Ω has been connected in series with another inductive coil of 0.2 H inductance and 15 Ω resistance. The whole circuit has been energised from 230 V, 50 Hz mains. Calculate power dissipation in each coil and power factor of the whole circuit. Draw the phasor diagram. Suggest a suitable capacitor for the above circuit to resonate at 50 Hz. ○●○

**4.10** A voltage $v(t) = 10\sqrt{2}\sin \omega t$ is applied to a series *RLC* circuit. At resonant frequency, voltage across the capacitor is found to be 500 V. The bandwidth of the circuit is known to be 400 rad/s and impedance at resonance, is 10 Ω. Determine resonant frequency, upper and lower cut-off frequencies, $L$ and $C$. ○●○

**4.11** An inductive coil having a resistance of 20 Ω and an inductance of 0.2 H is connected in parallel with a 20 μF capacitor with variable frequency, 230 V supply. Find the resonant frequency at which the total current taken from the supply is in phase with the supply voltage. Also, find the value of this current. ●○○

## ANSWERS TO PRACTICE PROBLEMS

**4.1** 845.2 rad/s, 1.185, 714.3 rad/s, 487.9 rad/s, 1202.1 rad/s

**4.2** 0.0041 Ω, 17733 rad/s 2.128, 8333.33 rad/s 60 mA

**4.3** 35.59 Hz, 22.36 Ω, 10 Ω, 744.28 V, 514.28 V, 27.63 Hz, 43.55 Hz, 2.24, 5.29 kW, 1

**4.4** 3.85 A, 0.616 (leading), 920.07 V

**4.5** 0.0159 H, 25 μF

**4.6** 700.63 Ω, 1.25 μF, 8.10 H

**4.7** 1 mF, 115 A, 361.28 V

**4.8** 12.47 A, 411.17, 198.47 V, 35.6 Hz, 563.3 V, 514.2 V

**4.9** 181.57 W, 108.95 W, 0.468 (lagging), 42.22 μF

**4.10** 3.183 kHz, 3.151 kHz, 3.214 kHz, 0.025 H, 0.1 μF

**4.11** 19.49 Hz, 4.6 A

# Objective-Type Questions

**From GATE and Other Competitive Examinations**

**4.1** For a series *RLC* resonant circuit, the total reactance at the lower half power frequency is ○●○

(a) $\sqrt{2}R\angle 45°$ (b) $\sqrt{2}R\angle -45°$
(c) $R$ (d) $-R$

**4.2** In a series *RLC* high *Q* circuit, the current peaks at a frequency ●○○

(a) equal to the resonant frequency
(b) greater than the resonant frequency
(c) less than the resonant frequency
(d) none of the above.

**4.3** In a series *RLC* circuit, $R = 2\text{k}\,\Omega, L = 1\,\text{H}$, $C = \dfrac{1}{400}\,\mu\text{F}$. The resonant frequency is ●○○

(a) $2\times10^4\,\text{Hz}$ (b) $\dfrac{1}{\pi}\times10^4\,\text{Hz}$
(c) $10^4\,\text{Hz}$ (d) $2\pi\times10^4\,\text{Hz}$

**4.4** For a series resonant circuit at low frequency, circuit impedance is ______ and at high frequency circuit impedance is ______. ●○○

(a) capacitive, inductive
(b) inductive, capacitive
(c) resistive, inductive
(d) capacitive, resistive

**4.5** A circuit with a resistor, inductor and capacitor in series in resonant of $f_0$ Hz. If all the component values are now doubled, the new resonant frequency is ○●○

(a) $2f_0$ (b) $f_0$
(c) $\dfrac{f_0}{4}$ (d) $\dfrac{f_0}{2}$

**4.6** In a series *RLC* circuit at resonance, the magnitude of the voltage developed across the capacitor ○●○

(a) is always zero
(b) can never be greater than the input voltage
(c) can be greater than the input voltage; however, it is 90° out of phase with the input voltage
(d) can be greater than the input voltage and is in phase with the input voltage

**4.7** The power in a series *RLC* circuit will be half of that at resonance when the magnitude of the current is equal to ○●○

(a) $\dfrac{V}{2R}$ (b) $\dfrac{V}{\sqrt{3}R}$
(c) $\dfrac{V}{\sqrt{2}R}$ (d) $\dfrac{\sqrt{2}V}{R}$

**4.8** A series *RLC* circuit has a resonance frequency of 1 kHz and a quality factor *Q* of 100. If each of *R*, *L* and *C* is doubled from its original value, the new *Q* of the circuit is ○●○

(a) 25 (b) 50
(c) 100 (d) 200

**4.9** A series $RLC$ circuit has a $Q$ of 100 and an impedance of $(100 + j0)\ \Omega$ at its resonant angular frequency of $10^7$ rad/s. The values of $R$ and $L$ are ○●○

(a) $100\ \Omega, 10^3$ H (b) $100\ \Omega, 10^{-3}$ H
(c) $10\ \Omega, 10$ H (d) $10\ \Omega, 0.1$ H

**4.10** The following circuit in Fig. 4.30 resonates at ○●○

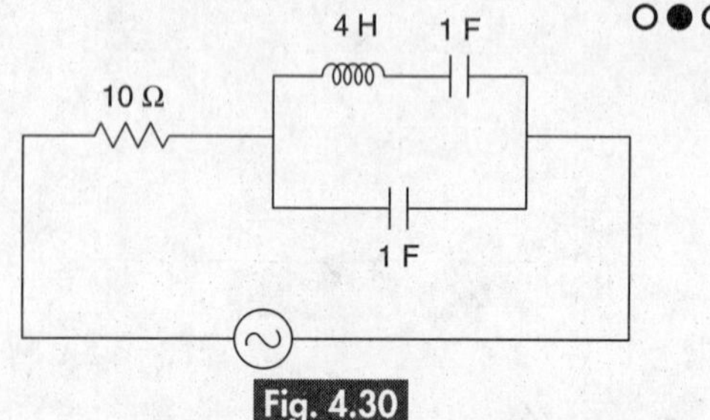


Fig. 4.30

(a) all frequencies (b) 0.5 rad/s
(c) 5 rad/s (d) 1 rad/s

**4.11** At resonance, the parallel circuit shown in Fig. 4.31 behaves like ○●○

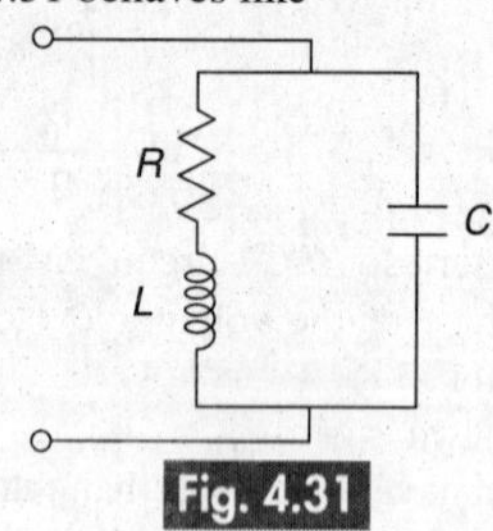


Fig. 4.31

(a) an open circuit
(b) a short circuit
(c) a pure resistor of value $R$
(d) a pure resistor of value much higher than $R$

**4.12** For a parallel RLC circuit, which one of the following statements is not correct? ●○○

(a) The bandwidth of the circuit decreases if $R$ is increased.
(b) The bandwidth of the circuit remains same if $L$ is increased.
(c) At resonance, the input impedance is a real quantity.
(d) At resonance, the magnitude of input impedance attains its minimum value.

**4.13** In the circuit shown in Fig. 4.32, the angular frequency $\omega$ (in rad/second) at which the Norton equivalent impedance as seen from terminal $b$-$b'$ is purely resistive is ○●○

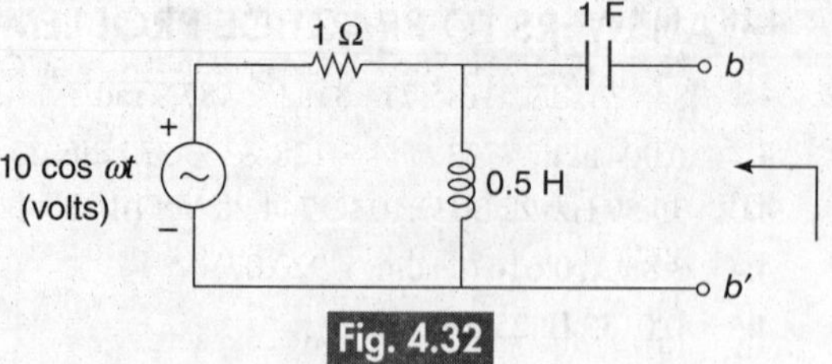


Fig. 4.32

(a) 1 (b) 2
(c) 1.2 (d) 3

**4.14** In the circuit shown in Fig. 4.33, at resonance, the amplitude of the sinusoidal voltage (in volts) across the capacitor is ○●○

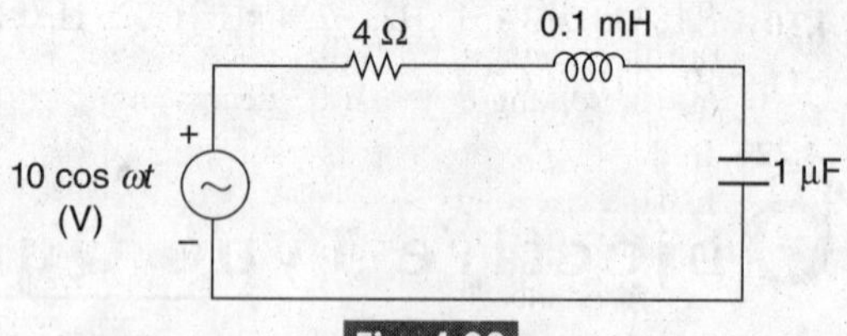


Fig. 4.33

(a) 25 b) 2.5
(c) 0.25 (d) 2

**4.15** An LC tank circuit consists of an ideal capacitor $C$ connected in parallel with a coil of inductance $L$ having an internal resistance $R$. The resonant frequency of the tank circuit is ○○●

(a) $\dfrac{1}{2\pi\sqrt{LC}}$

(b) $\dfrac{1}{2\pi\sqrt{LC}}\sqrt{1-\dfrac{R^2C}{L}}$

(c) $\dfrac{1}{2\pi\sqrt{LC}}\sqrt{1-\dfrac{L}{R^2C}}$

(d) $\dfrac{1}{2\pi\sqrt{LC}}\sqrt{1+\dfrac{R^2C}{L}}$

**4.16** The total reactance of series RLC circuit at resonance is ●○○

(a) equal to $X_L$ (b) equal to $X_C$
(c) equal to $R$ (d) zero

**4.17** In a series resonance circuit, which of the following statements are true? ●○○

(i) pf is unity
(ii) voltage magnification takes place
(iii) current magnification takes place
(iv) resonant frequency depends on resistance

(a) (i) and (ii) (b) (ii) and (iv)
(c) (i), (ii) and (iv) (d) (i) and (iii)

**4.18** In a series RLC circuit, for frequencies less than the resonant frequency, the circuit is ●○○

(a) inductive (b) capacitive

(c) resistive (d) none of these

**4.19** In a parallel resonant circuit, for frequencies greater than the resonant frequency, the circuit is ●○○

(a) inductive (b) capacitive

(c) resistive (d) none of these

**4.20** The $Q$ of a circuit can be increased by ●○○

(a) increasing the $BW$ (b) decreasing the $BW$

(c) increasing $R$ (d) none of these

**4.21** In an RLC circuit, the bandwidth is increased by ●○○

(a) decreasing $L$ (b) decreasing $C$

(c) increasing $R$ (d) decreasing $R$

**4.22** In an RLC circuit series resonant circuit, at the half-power points ●○○

(a) the current is half of the current at resonance

(b) the impedance is half of the impedance at resonance

(c) the resistance is equal to the resultant reactance

(d) none of these

**4.23** Which of the following statements are true?

(i) The higher the value of $Q$, the more selective will be the circuit and lesser will be bandwidth

(ii) Impedance of parallel resonant circuit is maximum at resonance ●○○

(a) (i) and (ii) (b) (i) only

(c) (ii) only (d) both are false

**4.24** Consider the following statements S1 and S2:

S1: At the resonant frequency, the impedance of a series RLC circuit is zero.

S2: In a parallel GLC circuit, increasing the conductance $G$ results in increase in its $Q$ factor. ○●○

Which one of the following statement is correct?

(a) S1 is FALSE and S2 is TRUE

(b) Both S1 and S2 are TRUE

(c) S1 is TRUE and S2 is FALSE

(d) Both S1 and S2 are FALSE

**4.25** A series LCR circuit is operated at a frequency different from its resonant frequency. The operating frequency is such that the current leads the supply voltage. The magnitude of current is half the value at resonance. If the values of $L$, $C$ and $R$ are 1 H, 1 F and 1 Ω respectively, the operating angular frequency (in rad/s) is ○○●

(a) 0.2 (b) 0.4

(c) 0.45 (d) 0.5

**4.26** In the circuit shown in Fig. 4.34, **V** is a sinusoidal voltage source. The current **I** is in phase with voltage **V**. The ratio ○○●

$$\frac{\text{amplitude of voltage across the capacitor}}{\text{amplitude of voltage across the resistor}} \text{ is}$$

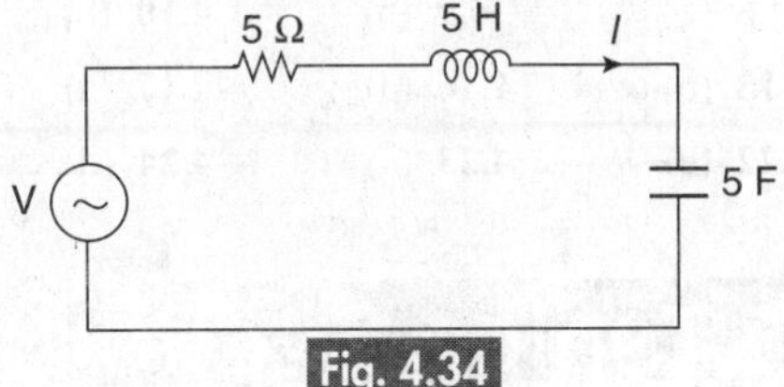


Fig. 4.34

(a) 0.1 (b) 0.3

(c) 0.2 (d) 0.4

**4.27** Two magnetically uncoupled inductive coils have $Q$ factors $q_1$ and $q_2$ at the chosen operating frequency. Their respective resistances are $R_1$ and $R_2$. When connected in series, their effective $Q$ factor at the same operating frequency is ○○●

(a) $q_1 + q_2$ (b) $\frac{1}{q_1} + \frac{1}{q_2}$

(c) $\frac{q_1R_1 + q_2R_2}{R_1 + R_2}$ (d) $\frac{q_1R_2 + q_2R_1}{R_1 + R_2}$

**4.28** Two series resonant circuits are shown in Fig. 4.35. Let the 3-dB bandwidth of circuit 1 be $B_1$ and that of circuit 2 be $B_2$. The value of $\frac{B_1}{B_2}$ is ○○●

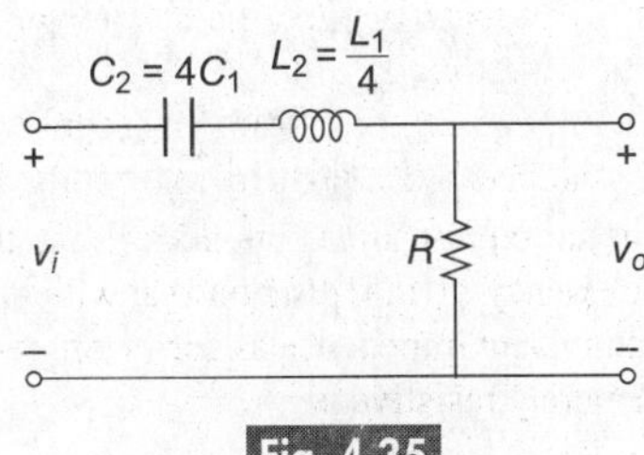


Fig. 4.35

(a) 4 (b) 1

(c) $\frac{1}{2}$ (d) $\frac{1}{4}$

## ANSWERS TO OBJECTIVE-TYPE QUESTIONS

| | | | | | | |
|---|---|---|---|---|---|---|
| **4.1** (d) | **4.2** (a) | **4.3** (b) | **4.4** (a) | **4.5** (d) | **4.6** (c) | **4.7** (c) |
| **4.8** (b) | **4.9** (b) | **4.10** (b) | **4.11** (d) | **4.12** (d) | **4.13** (b) | **4.14** (a) |
| **4.15** (b) | **4.16** (d) | **4.17** (a) | **4.18** (b) | **4.19** (b) | **4.20** (b) | **4.21** (a) |
| **4.22** (c) | **4.23** (a) | **4.24** (d) | **4.25** (c) | **4.26** (c) | **4.27** (c) | **4.28** (d) |

# LTspice Section

## EXAMPLE 4.1

*An RLC series circuit with a resistance of 10 Ω, inductance of 0.2 H and a capacitance of 40 μF is supplied with a 100 V supply at variable frequency. Find the frequency at which resonance takes place and current. Plot resonance curve.*

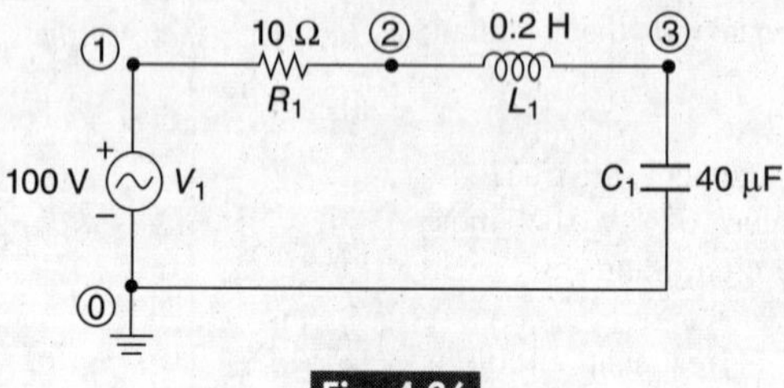


**Fig. 4.36**

**Solution**

```
*Plotting of series resonance curve

V1 1 0 AC 100 0
R1 1 2 10
L1 2 3 0.2
C1 3 0 40U
.AC LIN 1000 5 100
.PROBE
.END
```

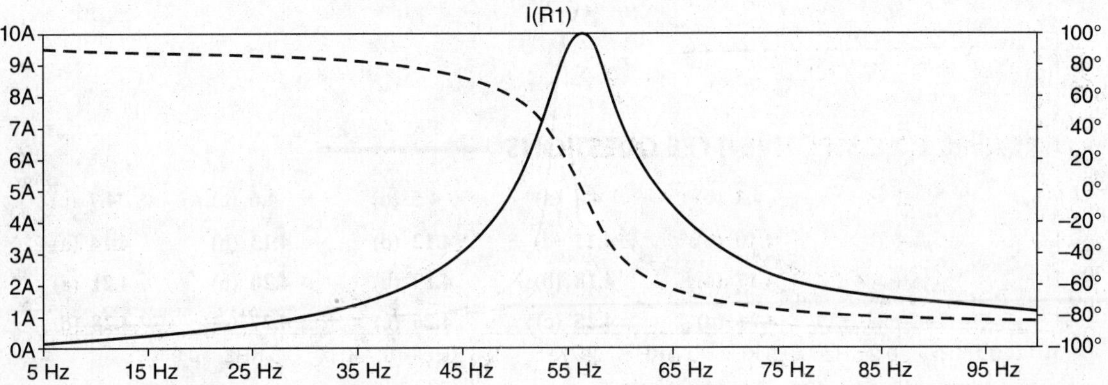


**Result**

$f_0 = 56.245$ Hz

$I_0 = 10$ A

## EXAMPLE 4.2

*A resistor of 100 Ω, an inductor of 1 mH and a capacitor of 100 μF is connected in parallel with a 1A current source at variable frequency. Find the frequency at which resonance takes place. Plot resonance curve.*

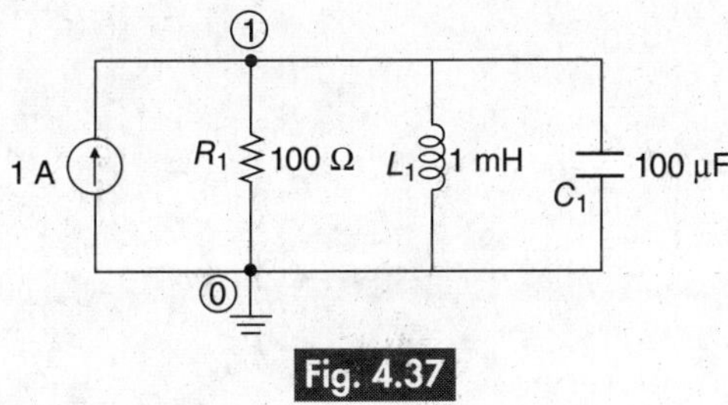


Fig. 4.37

**Solution**

```
*Plotting of parallel resonant curve

I1 1 0 AC 1 0
R1 1 0 100
L1 1 0 1M
C1 1 0 100U
.AC LIN 500 1 1000
.PROBE
.END
```

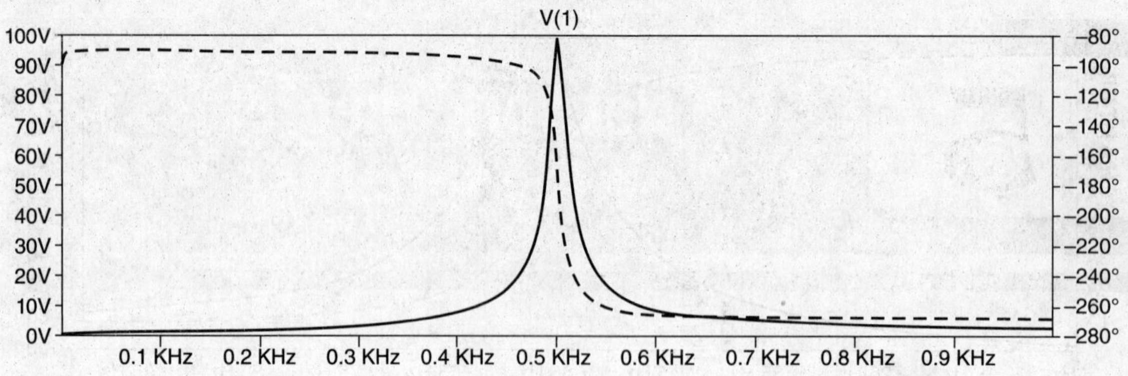


**Result**

$f_0 = 503.255$ Hz

$V_0 = 100$ V

CHAPTER 5

# Network Theorems (ac Circuits)

## LEARNING OBJECTIVES

**After studying this chapter, you should be able to:**

- **LO 5.1** Explain mesh and node analysis
- **LO 5.2** Analyse the networks using superposition theorem
- **LO 5.3** Analyse the networks using Thevenin's and Norton's theorems
- **LO 5.4** Analyse the networks using maximum power transfer theorem
- **LO 5.5** Explain reciprocity theorem
- **LO 5.6** Explain Millman's and Tellegen's theorems
- **LO 5.7** Explain substitution and compensation theorems

## INTRODUCTION

We have discussed the network theorems with reference to resistive load and dc sources. Now, all the theorems will be discussed when a network consists of ac sources, resistors, inductors and capacitors. All the theorems are also valid for ac sources.

The difference is that in ac circuits the impedances are used instead of resistances as done in dc circuits and the variables like currents and voltages have phasors instead of scalar currents and voltages.

## 5.1 | MESH ANALYSIS

LO 5.1

Explain mesh and node analysis

Mesh analysis is useful if a network has a large number of voltage sources. In this method, currents are assigned in each mesh. We can write mesh equations by Kirchhoff's voltage law in terms of unknown mesh currents.

### EXAMPLE 5.1

●○○

*Find mesh currents $\mathbf{I}_1$ and $\mathbf{I}_2$ in the network of Fig. 5.1.*

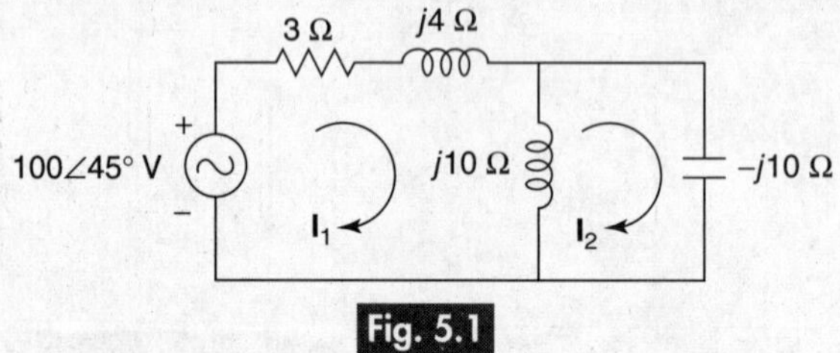


Fig. 5.1

**Solution** Applying KVL to mesh 1,

$$100\angle 45^\circ - (3+j4)\mathbf{I}_1 - j10(\mathbf{I}_1 - \mathbf{I}_2) = 0$$

$$(3+j14)\mathbf{I}_1 - j10\mathbf{I}_2 = 100\angle 45^\circ \quad \text{...(i)}$$

Applying KVL to mesh 2,

$$-j10(\mathbf{I}_2 - \mathbf{I}_1) + j10(\mathbf{I}_2) = 0$$

$$j10\mathbf{I}_1 = 0 \quad \text{...(ii)}$$

$$\mathbf{I}_1 = 0$$

Substituting $\mathbf{I}_1$ in Eq. (i),

$$-j10\mathbf{I}_2 = 100\angle 45^\circ$$

$$\mathbf{I}_2 = \frac{100\angle 45^\circ}{-j10} = 10\angle 135^\circ \text{ A}$$

### EXAMPLE 5.2

○●○

*Find mesh current $\mathbf{I}_1$, $\mathbf{I}_2$ and $\mathbf{I}_3$ in the network of Fig. 5.2.*

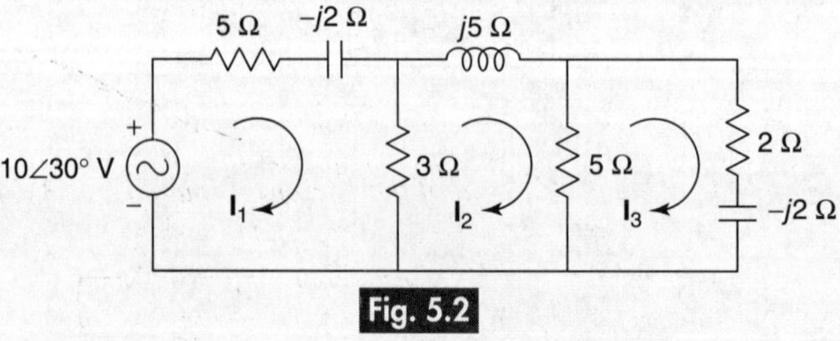


Fig. 5.2

**Note** Difficulty Level ●○○ — Easy; ○●○ — Medium; ○○● — Difficult

**Solution** Applying KVL to mesh 1,

$$10\angle 30° - (5 - j2)\,\mathbf{I}_1 - 3(\mathbf{I}_1 - \mathbf{I}_2) = 0$$

$$(8 - j2)\,\mathbf{I}_1 - 3\mathbf{I}_2 = 10\angle 30° \qquad \ldots \text{(i)}$$

Applying KVL to mesh 2,

$$-3(\mathbf{I}_2 - \mathbf{I}_1) - j5\mathbf{I}_2 - 5(\mathbf{I}_2 - \mathbf{I}_3) = 0$$

$$-3\mathbf{I}_1 + (8 + j5)\,\mathbf{I}_2 - 5\mathbf{I}_3 = 0 \qquad \ldots \text{(ii)}$$

Applying KVL to mesh 3,

$$-5(\mathbf{I}_3 - \mathbf{I}_2) - (2 - j2)\,\mathbf{I}_3 = 0$$

$$-5\mathbf{I}_2 + (7 - j2)\,\mathbf{I}_3 = 0 \qquad \ldots \text{(iii)}$$

Writing Eqs (i), (ii) and (iii),

$$\begin{bmatrix} 8-j2 & -3 & 0 \\ -3 & 8+j5 & -5 \\ 0 & -5 & 7-j2 \end{bmatrix} \begin{bmatrix} \mathbf{I}_1 \\ \mathbf{I}_2 \\ \mathbf{I}_3 \end{bmatrix} = \begin{bmatrix} 10\angle 30° \\ 0 \\ 0 \end{bmatrix}$$

By Cramer's rule,

$$\mathbf{I}_1 = \frac{\begin{vmatrix} 10\angle 30° & -3 & 0 \\ 0 & 8+j5 & -5 \\ 0 & -5 & 7-j2 \end{vmatrix}}{\begin{vmatrix} 8-j2 & -3 & 0 \\ -3 & 8+j5 & -5 \\ 0 & -5 & 7-j2 \end{vmatrix}} = 1.43\angle 38.7° \text{ A}$$

$$\mathbf{I}_2 = \frac{\begin{vmatrix} 8-j2 & 10\angle 30° & 0 \\ -3 & 0 & -5 \\ 0 & 0 & 7-j2 \end{vmatrix}}{\begin{vmatrix} 8-j2 & -3 & 0 \\ -3 & 8+j5 & -5 \\ 0 & -5 & 7-j2 \end{vmatrix}} = 0.693\angle -2.2° \text{ A}$$

$$\mathbf{I}_3 = \frac{\begin{vmatrix} 8-j2 & -3 & 10\angle 30° \\ -3 & 8+j5 & 0 \\ 0 & -5 & 0 \end{vmatrix}}{\begin{vmatrix} 8-j2 & -3 & 0 \\ -3 & 8+j5 & -5 \\ 0 & -5 & 7-j2 \end{vmatrix}} = 0.476\angle 13.8° \text{ A}$$

## EXAMPLE 5.3

*In the network of Fig. 5.3, find the value of $\mathbf{V}_2$ so that the current through (2 + j3) ohm impedance is zero.*

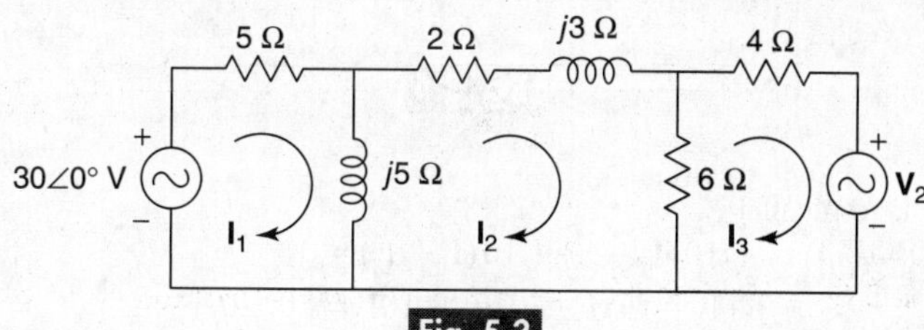


Fig. 5.3

**Solution** Applying KVL to mesh 1,

$$30\angle 0° - 5\mathbf{I}_1 - j5(\mathbf{I}_1 - \mathbf{I}_2) = 0$$

$$(5 + j5)\mathbf{I}_1 - j5\mathbf{I}_2 = 30\angle 0° \qquad \text{...(i)}$$

Applying KVL to mesh 2,

$$-j5(\mathbf{I}_2 - \mathbf{I}_1) - (2 + j3)\mathbf{I}_2 - 6(\mathbf{I}_2 - \mathbf{I}_3) = 0$$

$$-j5\mathbf{I}_1 + (8 + j8)\mathbf{I}_2 - 6\mathbf{I}_3 = 0 \qquad \text{...(ii)}$$

Applying KVL to mesh 3,

$$-6(\mathbf{I}_3 - \mathbf{I}_2) - 4\mathbf{I}_3 - \mathbf{V}_2 = 0$$

$$-6\mathbf{I}_2 + 10\mathbf{I}_3 = -\mathbf{V}_2 \qquad \text{...(iii)}$$

Writing Eqs (i), (ii) and (iii) in matrix form,

$$\begin{bmatrix} 5+j5 & -j5 & 0 \\ -j5 & 8+j8 & -6 \\ 0 & -6 & 10 \end{bmatrix} \begin{bmatrix} \mathbf{I}_1 \\ \mathbf{I}_2 \\ \mathbf{I}_3 \end{bmatrix} = \begin{bmatrix} 30\angle 0° \\ 0 \\ -\mathbf{V}_2 \end{bmatrix}$$

By Cramer's rule,

$$\mathbf{I}_2 = \frac{\begin{vmatrix} 5+j5 & 30\angle 0° & 0 \\ -j5 & 0 & -6 \\ 0 & -\mathbf{V}_2 & 10 \end{vmatrix}}{\begin{vmatrix} 5+j5 & -j5 & 0 \\ -j5 & 8+j8 & -6 \\ 0 & -6 & 10 \end{vmatrix}} = 0$$

$$(5+j5)(-6\mathbf{V}_2) - (30)(-j50) = 0$$

$$\mathbf{V}_2 = \frac{j1500}{30+j30} = 35.36\angle 45° \text{ V}$$

## EXAMPLE 5.4

*Find the value of the current $\mathbf{I}_3$ in the network shown in Fig. 5.4.*

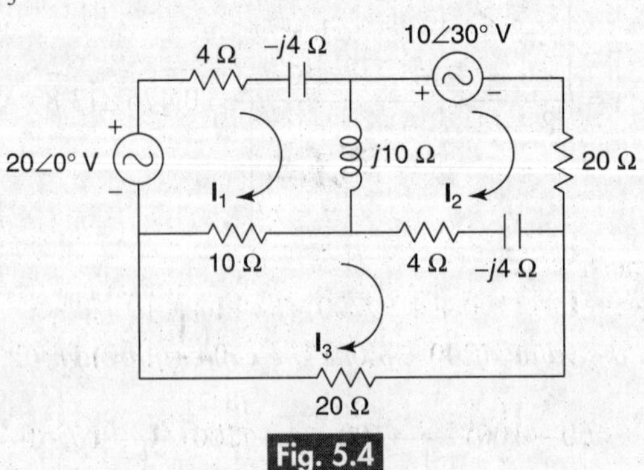


Fig. 5.4

**Solution** Applying KVL to mesh 1,

$$20\angle 0° - (4 - j4)\mathbf{I}_1 - j10(\mathbf{I}_1 - \mathbf{I}_2) - 10(\mathbf{I}_1 - \mathbf{I}_3) = 0$$

$$(14 + j6)\mathbf{I}_1 - j10\mathbf{I}_2 - 10\mathbf{I}_3 = 20\angle 0° \qquad \text{... (i)}$$

Applying KVL to mesh 2,

$$-j10(\mathbf{I}_2 - \mathbf{I}_1) - 10\angle 30^\circ - 20\mathbf{I}_2 - (4 - j4)(\mathbf{I}_2 - \mathbf{I}_3) = 0$$

$$-j10\mathbf{I}_1 + (24 + j6)\mathbf{I}_2 - (4 - j4)\mathbf{I}_3 = -10\angle 30^\circ \qquad \text{... (ii)}$$

Applying KVL to mesh 3,

$$-10(\mathbf{I}_3 - \mathbf{I}_1) - (4 - j4)(\mathbf{I}_3 - \mathbf{I}_2) - 20\mathbf{I}_3 = 0$$

$$-10\mathbf{I}_1 - (4 - j4)\mathbf{I}_2 + (34 - j4)\mathbf{I}_3 = 0 \qquad \text{... (iii)}$$

Writing Eqs (i), (ii) and (iii) in matrix form,

$$\begin{bmatrix} 14+j6 & -j10 & -10 \\ -j10 & 24+j6 & -(4-j4) \\ -10 & -(4-j4) & 34-j4 \end{bmatrix} \begin{bmatrix} \mathbf{I}_1 \\ \mathbf{I}_2 \\ \mathbf{I}_3 \end{bmatrix} = \begin{bmatrix} 20\angle 0^\circ \\ -10\angle 30^\circ \\ 0 \end{bmatrix}$$

By Cramer's rule,

$$\mathbf{I}_3 = \frac{\begin{vmatrix} 14+j6 & -j10 & 20\angle 0^\circ \\ -j10 & 24+j6 & -10\angle 30^\circ \\ -10 & -(4-j4) & 0 \end{vmatrix}}{\begin{vmatrix} 14+j6 & -10 & -10 \\ -j10 & 24+j6 & -(4-j4) \\ -10 & -(4-j4) & 34-j4 \end{vmatrix}} = 0.44\angle -14^\circ \text{ A}$$

## EXAMPLE 5.5

*Find the voltage $V_{AB}$ in the network of Fig. 5.5.*

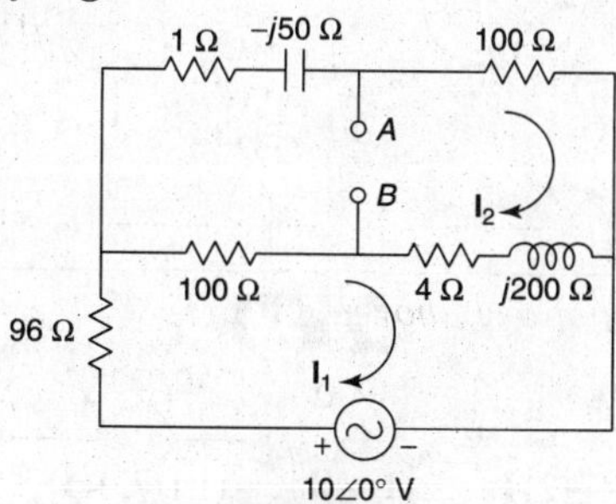


Fig. 5.5

**Solution** Applying KVL to mesh 1,

$$-96\,\mathbf{I}_1 - (100 + 4 + j200)\,(\mathbf{I}_1 - \mathbf{I}_2) + 10\,\angle 0^\circ = 0$$

$$(200 + j200)\,\mathbf{I}_1 - (104 + j200)\,\mathbf{I}_2 = 10\,\angle 0^\circ \qquad \text{...(i)}$$

Applying KVL to mesh 2,

$$-(1 - j50 - 100)\,\mathbf{I}_2 - (100 + 4 + j200)\,(\mathbf{I}_2 - \mathbf{I}_1) = 0$$

$$-(104 + j200)\,\mathbf{I}_1 + (205 + j150)\,\mathbf{I}_2 = 0 \qquad \text{...(ii)}$$

Writing Eqs (i) and (ii) in matrix form,

$$\begin{bmatrix} 200+j200 & -(104+j200) \\ -(104+j200) & 205+j150 \end{bmatrix} \begin{bmatrix} \mathbf{I}_1 \\ \mathbf{I}_2 \end{bmatrix} = \begin{bmatrix} 10\angle 0^\circ \\ 0 \end{bmatrix}$$

By Cramer's rule,

$$\mathbf{I}_1 = \frac{\begin{vmatrix} 10\angle 0° & -(104+j200) \\ 0 & 205+j150 \end{vmatrix}}{\begin{vmatrix} 200+j200 & -(104+j200) \\ -(104+j200) & 205+j150 \end{vmatrix}} = 0.051\angle 2.72\times 10^{-3}\,°\text{A}$$

$$\mathbf{I}_2 = \frac{\begin{vmatrix} 200+j200 & 10\angle 0° \\ -(104+j200) & 0 \end{vmatrix}}{\begin{vmatrix} 200+j200 & -(104+j200) \\ -(104+j200) & 205+j150 \end{vmatrix}} = 0.045\angle 26.34°\ \text{A}$$

$$\begin{aligned}\mathbf{V}_{AB} &= 100\mathbf{I}_2 - (4+j200)(\mathbf{I}_1 - \mathbf{I}_2) \\ &= 100(0.045\angle 26.34°) - (4+j200)(0.051\angle 2.72\times 10^{-3}\,° - 0.045\angle 26.34°) \\ &= 0.058\angle -92.65°\ \text{V}\end{aligned}$$

## EXAMPLE 5.6

*For the network shown in Fig. 5.6, find the voltage across the capacitor.*

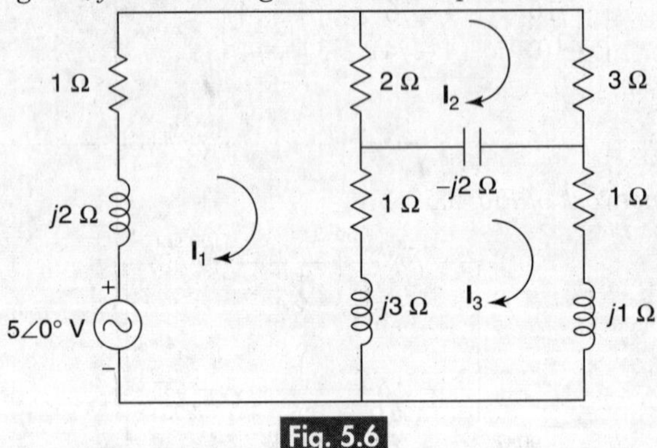


Fig. 5.6

**Solution** Applying KVL to mesh 1,

$$5\angle 0° - (1+j2)\mathbf{I}_1 - 2(\mathbf{I}_1 - \mathbf{I}_2) - (1+j3)(\mathbf{I}_1 - \mathbf{I}_3) = 0$$

$$(4+j5)\mathbf{I}_1 - 2\mathbf{I}_2 - (1+j3)\mathbf{I}_3 = 5\angle 0° \qquad \text{...(i)}$$

Applying KVL to mesh 2,

$$-2(\mathbf{I}_2 - \mathbf{I}_1) - 3\mathbf{I}_2 + j2(\mathbf{I}_2 - \mathbf{I}_3) = 0$$

$$-2\mathbf{I}_1 + (5-j2)\mathbf{I}_2 + j2\mathbf{I}_3 = 0 \qquad \text{...(ii)}$$

Applying KVL to mesh 3,

$$-(1+j3)(\mathbf{I}_3 - \mathbf{I}_1) + j2(\mathbf{I}_3 - \mathbf{I}_2) - (1+j1)\mathbf{I}_3 = 0$$

$$-(1+j3)\mathbf{I}_1 + j2\mathbf{I}_2 + (2+j2)\mathbf{I}_3 = 0 \qquad \text{...(iii)}$$

Writing Eqs (i), (ii) and (iii) in matrix form,

$$\begin{bmatrix} 4+j5 & -2 & -(1+j3) \\ -2 & 5-j2 & j2 \\ -(1+j3) & j2 & 2+j2 \end{bmatrix} \begin{bmatrix} \mathbf{I}_1 \\ \mathbf{I}_2 \\ \mathbf{I}_3 \end{bmatrix} = \begin{bmatrix} 5\angle 0° \\ 0 \\ 0 \end{bmatrix}$$

By Cramer's rule,

$$\mathbf{I}_2 = \frac{\begin{vmatrix} 4+j5 & 5\angle 0^\circ & -(1+j3) \\ -2 & 0 & j2 \\ -(1+j3) & 0 & 2+j2 \end{vmatrix}}{\begin{vmatrix} 4+j5 & -2 & -(1+j3) \\ -2 & 5-j2 & j2 \\ -(1+j3) & j2 & 2+j2 \end{vmatrix}} = 0.65\angle 130.51^\circ \text{ A}$$

$$\mathbf{I}_3 = \frac{\begin{vmatrix} 4+j5 & -2 & 5\angle 0^\circ \\ -2 & 5-j2 & 0 \\ -(1+j3) & j2 & 0 \end{vmatrix}}{\begin{vmatrix} 4+j5 & -2 & -(1+j3) \\ -2 & 5-j2 & j2 \\ -(1+j3) & j2 & 2+j2 \end{vmatrix}} = 0.91\angle -21.51^\circ \text{ A}$$

$$\mathbf{V}_c = (-j2)(\mathbf{I}_3 - \mathbf{I}_2) = (-j2)(0.91\angle -21.51^\circ - 0.65\angle 130.51^\circ) = 3.03\angle -123.12^\circ \text{ V}$$

## EXAMPLE 5.7

*Find the voltage across the 2 Ω resistor in the network of Fig. 5.7.*

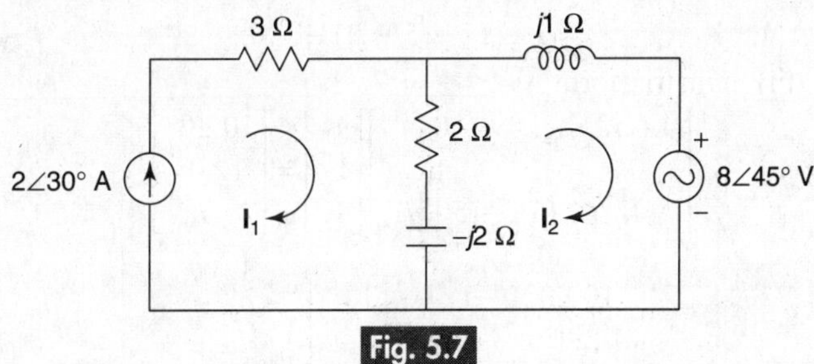

Fig. 5.7

**Solution** For mesh 1,

$$\mathbf{I}_1 = 2\angle 30^\circ \qquad \text{...(i)}$$

Applying KVL to mesh 2,

$$-(2-j2)(\mathbf{I}_2 - \mathbf{I}_1) - j1\mathbf{I}_2 - 8\angle 45^\circ = 0$$

$$(2-j2)\mathbf{I}_1 - (2-j1)\mathbf{I}_2 = 8\angle 45^\circ \qquad \text{...(ii)}$$

Substituting $\mathbf{I}_1$ in Eq. (i),

$$(2-j2)(2\angle 30^\circ) - (2-j1)\mathbf{I}_2 = 8\angle 45^\circ$$

$$\mathbf{I}_2 = \frac{-(8\angle 45^\circ) + (2-j2)(2\angle 30^\circ)}{2-j1} = 3.19\angle -65^\circ \text{ A}$$

$$\mathbf{V}_{2\,\Omega} = 2(\mathbf{I}_1 - \mathbf{I}_2) = 2(2\angle 30^\circ - 3.19\angle -65^\circ) = 7.82\angle 84.37^\circ \text{ V}$$

## EXAMPLE 5.8

*Find the current through 3 Ω resistor in the network of Fig. 5.8.*

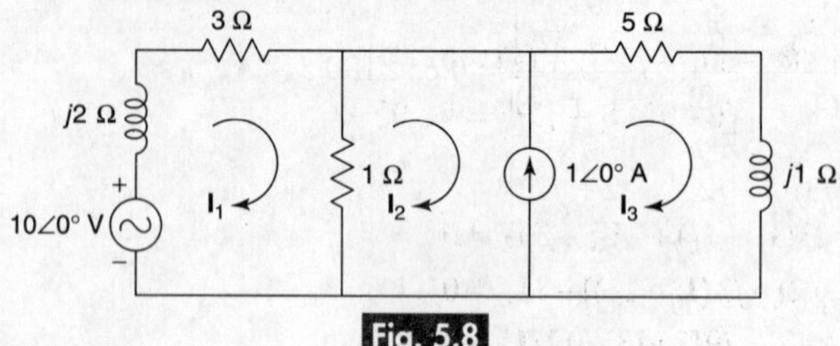


Fig. 5.8

**Solution** Applying KVL to mesh 1,

$$10\angle 0° - j2\mathbf{I}_1 - 3\mathbf{I}_1 - 1(\mathbf{I}_1 - \mathbf{I}_2) = 0$$

$$(4 + j2)\mathbf{I}_1 - \mathbf{I}_2 = 10\angle 0° \qquad \text{...(i)}$$

Meshes 2 and 3 will form a supermesh.
Writing current equation for the supermesh,

$$\mathbf{I}_3 - \mathbf{I}_2 = 1\angle 0° \qquad \text{...(ii)}$$

Applying KVL to the outer path of the supermesh,

$$-1(\mathbf{I}_2 - \mathbf{I}_1) - 5\mathbf{I}_3 - j1\mathbf{I}_3 = 0$$

$$\mathbf{I}_1 - \mathbf{I}_2 - (5 + j1)\mathbf{I}_3 = 0 \qquad \text{...(iii)}$$

Writing Eqs (i), (ii) and (iii) in matrix form,

$$\begin{bmatrix} 4+j2 & -1 & 0 \\ 0 & -1 & 1 \\ 1 & -1 & -(5+j1) \end{bmatrix} \begin{bmatrix} \mathbf{I}_1 \\ \mathbf{I}_2 \\ \mathbf{I}_3 \end{bmatrix} = \begin{bmatrix} 10\angle 0° \\ 1\angle 0° \\ 0 \end{bmatrix}$$

By Cramer's rule,

$$\mathbf{I}_1 = \frac{\begin{vmatrix} 10\angle 0° & -1 & 0 \\ 1\angle 0° & -1 & 1 \\ 0 & -1 & -(5+j1) \end{vmatrix}}{\begin{vmatrix} 4+j2 & -1 & 0 \\ 0 & -1 & 1 \\ 1 & -1 & -(5+j1) \end{vmatrix}} = 2.11\angle -28.01° \text{ A}$$

$$\mathbf{I}_{3\Omega} = \mathbf{I}_1 = 2.11\angle -28.01° \text{ A}$$

## EXAMPLE 5.9

*Find the currents $\mathbf{I}_1$ and $\mathbf{I}_2$ in the network of Fig. 5.9.*

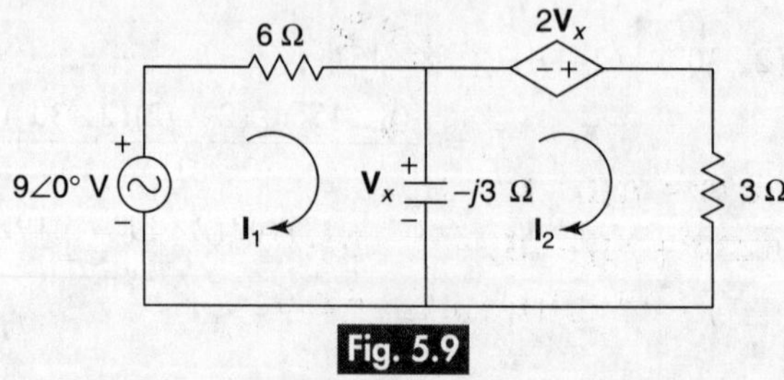


Fig. 5.9

**Solution** From Fig. 5.9,

$$\mathbf{V}_x = -j3(\mathbf{I}_1 - \mathbf{I}_2) \qquad \text{...(i)}$$

Applying KVL to mesh 1,

$$9\angle 0° - 6\,\mathbf{I}_1 + j3(\mathbf{I}_1 - \mathbf{I}_2) = 0$$

$$(6 - j3)\,\mathbf{I}_1 + j3\mathbf{I}_2 = 9\angle 0° \qquad \text{...(ii)}$$

Applying KVL to mesh 2,

$$j3(\mathbf{I}_2 - \mathbf{I}_1) + 2\mathbf{V}_x - 3\,\mathbf{I}_2 = 0$$

$$j3\mathbf{I}_2 - j3\mathbf{I}_1 + 2[-j3(\mathbf{I}_1 - \mathbf{I}_2)] - 3\,\mathbf{I}_2 = 0$$

$$j9\mathbf{I}_1 + (3 - j9)\,\mathbf{I}_2 = 0 \qquad \text{...(iii)}$$

Writing Eqs (ii) and (iii) in matrix form,

$$\begin{bmatrix} 6-j3 & j3 \\ j9 & 3-j9 \end{bmatrix}\begin{bmatrix} \mathbf{I}_1 \\ \mathbf{I}_2 \end{bmatrix} = \begin{bmatrix} 9\angle 0° \\ 0 \end{bmatrix}$$

By Cramer's rule,

$$\mathbf{I}_1 = \frac{\begin{vmatrix} 9\angle 0° & j3 \\ 0 & 3-j9 \end{vmatrix}}{\begin{vmatrix} 6-j3 & j3 \\ j9 & 3-j9 \end{vmatrix}} = 1.3\angle 2.49° \text{ A}$$

$$\mathbf{I}_2 = \frac{\begin{vmatrix} 6-j3 & 9\angle 0° \\ j9 & 0 \end{vmatrix}}{\begin{vmatrix} 6-j3 & j3 \\ j9 & 3-j9 \end{vmatrix}} = 1.24\angle -15.95° \text{ A}$$

## EXAMPLE 5.10

*Find the voltage across the 4 Ω resistor in the network of Fig. 5.10.*

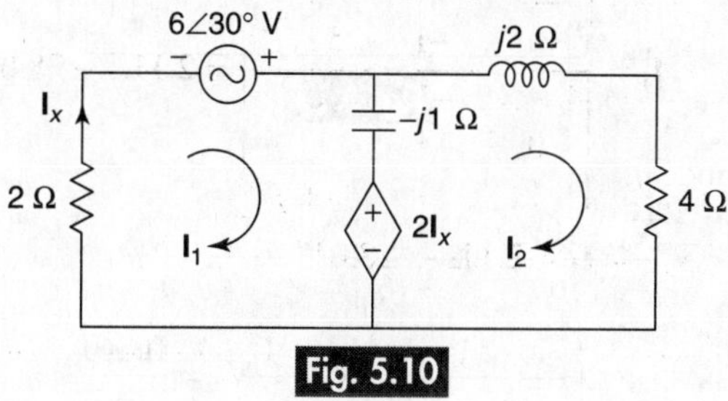


Fig. 5.10

**Solution** From Fig. 5.10,

$$\mathbf{I}_x = \mathbf{I}_1 \qquad \text{...(i)}$$

Applying KVL to mesh 1,

$$-2\mathbf{I}_1 + 6\angle 30° + j1(\mathbf{I}_1 - \mathbf{I}_2) - 2\mathbf{I}_x = 0$$

$$-2\mathbf{I}_1 + 6\angle 30° + j1\mathbf{I}_1 - j1\mathbf{I}_2 - 2\mathbf{I}_1 = 0$$

$$(4 - j1)\,\mathbf{I}_1 + j1\mathbf{I}_2 = 6\angle 30° \qquad \text{...(ii)}$$

Applying KVL to mesh 2,

$$2\mathbf{I}_x + j1(\mathbf{I}_2 - \mathbf{I}_1) - j2\mathbf{I}_2 - 4\mathbf{I}_2 = 0$$

$$2\mathbf{I}_1 + j1\mathbf{I}_2 - j1\,\mathbf{I}_1 - j2\mathbf{I}_2 - 4\mathbf{I}_2 = 0$$

$$(2 - j1)\mathbf{I}_1 - (4 + j1)\mathbf{I}_2 = 0 \qquad \ldots\text{(iii)}$$

Writing Eqs (ii) and (iii) in matrix form,

$$\begin{bmatrix} 4 - j1 & j1 \\ 2 - j1 & -(4 + j1) \end{bmatrix} \begin{bmatrix} \mathbf{I}_1 \\ \mathbf{I}_2 \end{bmatrix} = \begin{bmatrix} 6\angle 30^\circ \\ 0 \end{bmatrix}$$

By Cramer's rule,

$$\mathbf{I}_2 = \frac{\begin{vmatrix} 4 - j1 & 6\angle 30^\circ \\ 2 - j1 & 0 \end{vmatrix}}{\begin{vmatrix} 4 - j1 & j1 \\ 2 - j1 & -(4 + j1) \end{vmatrix}} = 0.74\angle -2.91^\circ \text{ A}$$

$$V_{4\Omega} = 4\mathbf{I}_2 = 4(0.74\angle -2.91^\circ) = 2.96\angle -2.91^\circ \text{ V}$$

## 5.2 NODE ANALYSIS

LO 5.1

Node analysis uses Kirchhoff's current law for finding currents and voltages in a network. For ac networks, Kirchhoff's current law states that the phasor sum of currents meeting at a point is equal to zero.

### EXAMPLE 5.11

*In the network shown in Fig. 5.11, determine $\mathbf{V}_a$ and $\mathbf{V}_b$.*

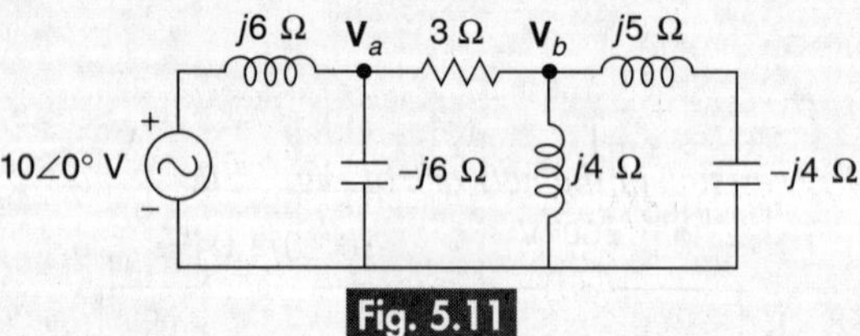


Fig. 5.11

**Solution** Applying KCL at node *a*,

$$\frac{\mathbf{V}_a - 10\angle 0^\circ}{j6} + \frac{\mathbf{V}_a}{-j6} + \frac{\mathbf{V}_a - \mathbf{V}_b}{3} = 0$$

$$\left(\frac{1}{j6} - \frac{1}{j6} + \frac{1}{3}\right)\mathbf{V}_a - \frac{1}{3}\mathbf{V}_b = \frac{10\angle 0^\circ}{j6}$$

$$0.33\mathbf{V}_a - 0.33\mathbf{V}_b = 1.67\angle -90^\circ \qquad \ldots\text{(i)}$$

Applying KCL at node *b*,

$$\frac{\mathbf{V}_b - \mathbf{V}_a}{3} + \frac{\mathbf{V}_b}{j4} + \frac{\mathbf{V}_b}{j1} = 0$$

$$-\frac{1}{3}\mathbf{V}_a + \left(\frac{1}{3} + \frac{1}{j4} + \frac{1}{j1}\right)\mathbf{V}_b = 0$$

$$-0.33\mathbf{V}_a + (0.33 - j1.25)\mathbf{V}_b = 0 \quad \text{...(ii)}$$

Adding Eqs (i) and (ii),

$$-j1.25\mathbf{V}_b = 1.67\angle{-90°}$$

$$\mathbf{V}_b = \frac{1.67\angle{-90°}}{-j1.25} = 1.34\angle 0° \text{ V}$$

Substituting $\mathbf{V}_b$ in Eq. (i),

$$0.33\mathbf{V}_a - 0.33(1.34\angle 0°) = 1.67\angle{-90°}$$

$$\mathbf{V}_a = \frac{1.73\angle 75.17°}{0.33} = 5.24\angle{-75.17°} \text{ V}$$

## EXAMPLE 5.12

*For the network shown in Fig. 5.12, find the voltages $V_1$ and $V_2$.*

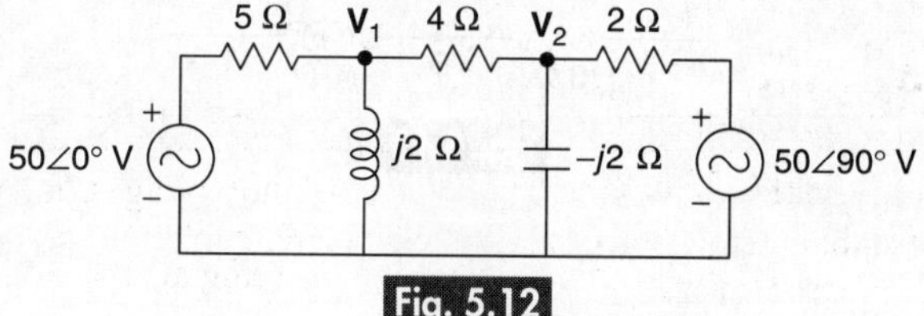


Fig. 5.12

Applying KCL at node 1,

$$\frac{\mathbf{V}_1 - 50\angle 0°}{5} + \frac{\mathbf{V}_1}{j2} + \frac{\mathbf{V}_1 - \mathbf{V}_2}{4} = 0$$

$$\left(\frac{1}{5} + \frac{1}{j2} + \frac{1}{4}\right)\mathbf{V}_1 - \frac{1}{4}\mathbf{V}_2 = 10\angle 0°$$

$$(0.45 - j0.5)\mathbf{V}_1 - 0.25\mathbf{V}_2 = 10\angle 0° \quad \text{...(i)}$$

Applying KCL at node 2,

$$\frac{\mathbf{V}_2 - \mathbf{V}_1}{4} + \frac{\mathbf{V}_2}{-j2} + \frac{\mathbf{V}_2 - 50\angle 90°}{2} = 0$$

$$-\frac{1}{4}\mathbf{V}_1 + \left(\frac{1}{4} + \frac{1}{-j2} + \frac{1}{2}\right)\mathbf{V}_2 = 25\angle 90°$$

$$-0.25\mathbf{V}_1 + (0.75 + j0.5)\mathbf{V}_2 = 25\angle 90° \quad \text{...(ii)}$$

Writing Eqs (i) and (ii) in matrix form,

$$\begin{bmatrix} 0.45 - j0.5 & -0.25 \\ -0.25 & 0.75 + j0.5 \end{bmatrix}\begin{bmatrix} \mathbf{V}_1 \\ \mathbf{V}_2 \end{bmatrix} = \begin{bmatrix} 10\angle 0° \\ 25\angle 90° \end{bmatrix}$$

By Cramer's rule,

$$\mathbf{V}_1 = \frac{\begin{vmatrix} 10\angle 0° & -0.25 \\ j25 & 0.75 + j0.5 \end{vmatrix}}{\begin{vmatrix} 0.45 - j0.5 & -0.25 \\ -0.25 & 0.75 + j0.5 \end{vmatrix}} = 24.7\angle 72.25° \text{ V}$$

$$\mathbf{V}_2 = \frac{\begin{vmatrix} 0.45 - j0.5 & 10\angle 0^\circ \\ -0.25 & 25\angle 90^\circ \end{vmatrix}}{\begin{vmatrix} 0.45 - j0.5 & -0.25 \\ -0.25 & 0.75 + j0.5 \end{vmatrix}} = 34.34\angle 52.82^\circ \text{ V}$$

## EXAMPLE 5.13

*Find the voltage $\mathbf{V}_{AB}$ in the network of Fig. 5.13.*

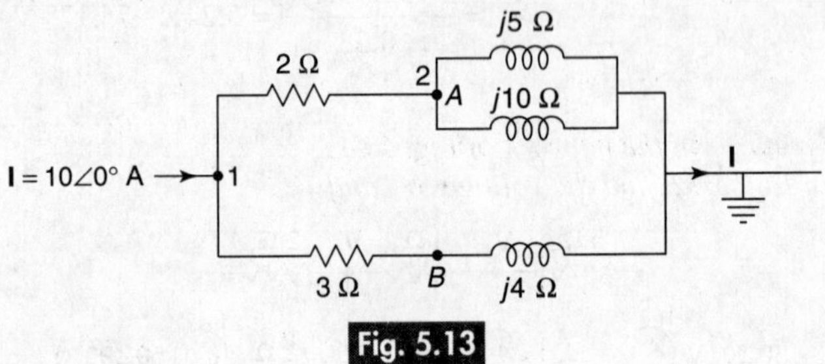


Fig. 5.13

**Solution** Applying KCL at node 1,

$$10\angle 0^\circ = \frac{\mathbf{V}_1 - \mathbf{V}_2}{2} + \frac{\mathbf{V}_1}{3 + j4}$$

$$\left(\frac{1}{2} + \frac{1}{3 + j4}\right)\mathbf{V}_1 - \frac{1}{2}\mathbf{V}_2 = 10\angle 0^\circ$$

$$(0.62 - j0.16)\mathbf{V}_1 - 0.5\mathbf{V}_2 = 10\angle 0^\circ \qquad \text{...(i)}$$

Applying KCL at node 2,

$$\frac{\mathbf{V}_2 - \mathbf{V}_1}{2} + \frac{\mathbf{V}_2}{j5} + \frac{\mathbf{V}_2}{j10} = 0$$

$$-\frac{1}{2}\mathbf{V}_1 + \left(\frac{1}{2} + \frac{1}{j5} + \frac{1}{j10}\right)\mathbf{V}_2 = 0$$

$$-0.5\mathbf{V}_1 + (0.5 - j0.3)\mathbf{V}_2 = 0 \qquad \text{...(ii)}$$

Writing Eqs (i) and (ii) in matrix form,

$$\begin{bmatrix} 0.62 - j0.16 & -0.5 \\ -0.5 & 0.5 - j0.3 \end{bmatrix}\begin{bmatrix} \mathbf{V}_1 \\ \mathbf{V}_2 \end{bmatrix} = \begin{bmatrix} 10\angle 0^\circ \\ 0 \end{bmatrix}$$

By Cramer's rule,

$$\mathbf{V}_1 = \frac{\begin{vmatrix} 10\angle 0^\circ & -0.5 \\ 0 & 0.5 - j0.3 \end{vmatrix}}{\begin{vmatrix} 0.62 - j0.16 & -0.5 \\ -0.5 & 0.5 - j0.3 \end{vmatrix}} = 21.8\angle 56.42^\circ \text{ V}$$

$$\mathbf{V}_2 = \frac{\begin{vmatrix} 0.62 - j0.16 & 10\angle 0° \\ -0.5 & 0 \end{vmatrix}}{\begin{vmatrix} 0.62 - j0.16 & -0.5 \\ -0.5 & 0.5 - j0.3 \end{vmatrix}} = 18.7\angle 87.42° \text{ V}$$

$$\mathbf{V}_A = \mathbf{V}_2 = 18.7\angle 87.42° \text{ V}$$

$$\mathbf{V}_B = \frac{\mathbf{V}_1}{3 + j4}(j4) = \frac{21.8\angle 56.42°}{3 + j4}(j4) = 17.45\angle 93.32° \text{ V}$$

$$\mathbf{V}_{AB} = \mathbf{V}_A - \mathbf{V}_B = (18.7\angle 87.42°) - (17.45\angle 93.32°) = 2.23\angle 34.1° \text{ V}$$

## EXAMPLE 5.14

*Find the node voltages $V_1$ and $V_2$ in the network of Fig. 5.14.*

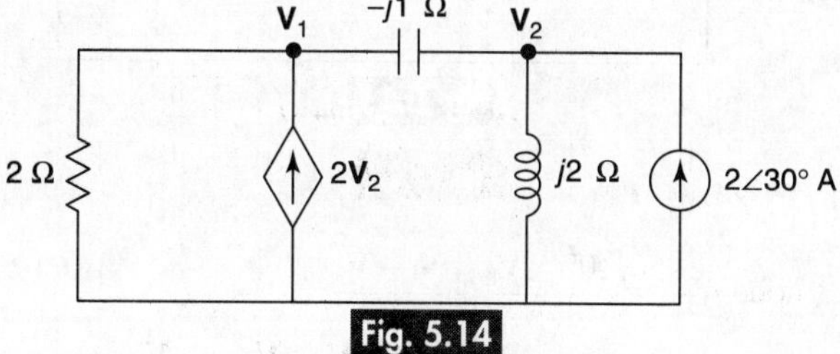


Fig. 5.14

**Solution** Applying KCL at node 1,

$$\frac{\mathbf{V}_1}{2} + \frac{\mathbf{V}_1 - \mathbf{V}_2}{-j1} = 2\mathbf{V}_2$$

$$\left(\frac{1}{2} + \frac{1}{-j1}\right)\mathbf{V}_1 - \left(2 - \frac{1}{j1}\right)\mathbf{V}_2 = 0$$

$$(0.5 + j1)\,\mathbf{V}_1 - (2 + j1)\mathbf{V}_2 = 0 \qquad \text{...(i)}$$

Applying KCL at node 2,

$$\frac{\mathbf{V}_2 - \mathbf{V}_1}{-j1} + \frac{\mathbf{V}_2}{j2} = 2\angle 30°$$

$$\frac{1}{j1}\mathbf{V}_1 + \left(\frac{1}{-j1} + \frac{1}{j2}\right)\mathbf{V}_2 = 2\angle 30°$$

$$-j1\,\mathbf{V}_1 + j\,0.5\,\mathbf{V}_2 = 2\angle 30° \qquad \text{...(ii)}$$

Writing Eqs (i) and (ii) in matrix form,

$$\begin{bmatrix} 0.5 + j1 & -(2 + j1) \\ -j1 & j0.5 \end{bmatrix}\begin{bmatrix} \mathbf{V}_1 \\ \mathbf{V}_2 \end{bmatrix} = \begin{bmatrix} 0 \\ 2\angle 30° \end{bmatrix}$$

By Cramer's rule,

$$\mathbf{V}_1 = \frac{\begin{vmatrix} 0 & -(2 + j1) \\ 2\angle 30° & j0.5 \end{vmatrix}}{\begin{vmatrix} 0.5 + j1 & -(2 + j1) \\ -j1 & j0.5 \end{vmatrix}} = 2.46\angle 130.62° \text{ V}$$

$$\mathbf{V}_2 = \frac{\begin{vmatrix} 0.5+j1 & 0 \\ -j1 & 2\angle 30^\circ \end{vmatrix}}{\begin{vmatrix} 0.5+j1 & -(2+j1) \\ -j1 & j0.5 \end{vmatrix}} = 1.23\angle 167.49^\circ \text{ V}$$

## EXAMPLE 5.15

*In the network of Fig. 5.15, find the voltage $\mathbf{V}_2$ which results in zero current through 4 Ω resistor.*

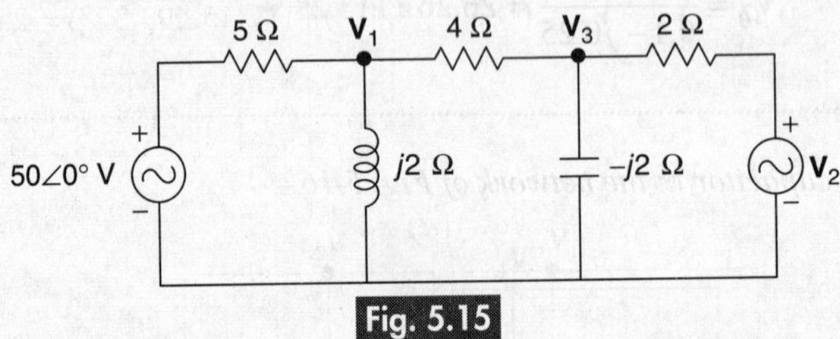


Fig. 5.15

**Solution** Applying KCL at node 1,

$$\frac{\mathbf{V}_1 - 50\angle 0^\circ}{5} + \frac{\mathbf{V}_1}{j2} + \frac{\mathbf{V}_1 - \mathbf{V}_3}{4} = 0$$

$$\left(\frac{1}{5} + \frac{1}{j2} + \frac{1}{4}\right)\mathbf{V}_1 - \frac{1}{4}\mathbf{V}_3 = 10\angle 0^\circ$$

$$(0.45 - j0.5)\mathbf{V}_1 - 0.25\mathbf{V}_3 = 10\angle 0^\circ \qquad \text{...(i)}$$

Applying KCL at node 3,

$$\frac{\mathbf{V}_3 - \mathbf{V}_1}{4} + \frac{\mathbf{V}_3}{-j2} + \frac{\mathbf{V}_3 - \mathbf{V}_2}{2} = 0$$

$$-\frac{1}{4}\mathbf{V}_1 + \left(\frac{1}{4} + \frac{1}{-j2} + \frac{1}{2}\right)\mathbf{V}_3 = 0.5\mathbf{V}_2$$

$$-0.25\mathbf{V}_1 + (0.75 + j0.5)\,\mathbf{V}_3 = 0.5\mathbf{V}_2 \qquad \text{...(ii)}$$

Writing Eqs (i) and (ii) in matrix form,

$$\begin{bmatrix} 0.45 - j0.5 & -0.25 \\ -0.25 & 0.75 + j0.5 \end{bmatrix}\begin{bmatrix} \mathbf{V}_1 \\ \mathbf{V}_3 \end{bmatrix} = \begin{bmatrix} 10\angle 0^\circ \\ 0.5\mathbf{V}_2 \end{bmatrix}$$

By Cramer's rule,

$$\mathbf{V}_1 = \frac{\begin{vmatrix} 10\angle 0^\circ & -0.25 \\ 0.5\mathbf{V}_2 & 0.75 + j0.5 \end{vmatrix}}{\begin{vmatrix} 0.45 - j0.5 & -0.25 \\ -0.25 & 0.75 + j0.5 \end{vmatrix}} = \frac{10(0.75 + j0.5) + 0.125\,\mathbf{V}_2}{0.55\angle -15.95^\circ}$$

$$\mathbf{V}_3 = \frac{\begin{vmatrix} 0.45 - j\,0.5 & 10\angle 0^\circ \\ -0.25 & 0.5\mathbf{V}_2 \end{vmatrix}}{\begin{vmatrix} 0.45 - j0.5 & -0.25 \\ -0.25 & 0.75 + j0.5 \end{vmatrix}} = \frac{0.5\,\mathbf{V}_2(0.45 - j0.5) + 2.5}{0.55\angle -15.95^\circ}$$

$$\mathbf{I}_{4\,\Omega} = \frac{\mathbf{V}_1 - \mathbf{V}_3}{4} = 0$$

$$\mathbf{V}_1 = \mathbf{V}_3$$

$$\frac{10(0.75 + j0.5) + 0.125\mathbf{V}_2}{0.55\angle -15.95^\circ} = \frac{0.5\mathbf{V}_2(0.45 - j0.5) + 2.5}{0.55\angle -15.95^\circ}$$

$$7.5 + 0.125\mathbf{V}_2 - j\,5 = 2.5 + 0.225\mathbf{V}_2 - j0.25\mathbf{V}_2$$

$$5 + j\,5 = \mathbf{V}_2(0.1 - j0.25)$$

$$\mathbf{V}_2 = \frac{5 + j5}{0.1 - j0.25} = 26.26\angle 113.2^\circ \text{ V}$$

## EXAMPLE 5.16

*Find the voltage across the capacitor in the network of Fig. 5.16.*

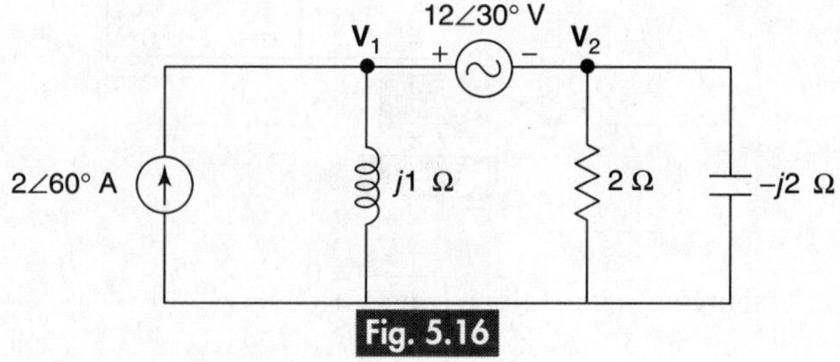


Fig. 5.16

**Solution** Nodes 1 and 2 will form a supernode.

Writing the voltage equation for the supernode,

$$\mathbf{V}_1 - \mathbf{V}_2 = 12\angle 30^\circ \qquad \text{...(i)}$$

Applying KCL to the supernode,

$$\frac{\mathbf{V}_1}{j1} + \frac{\mathbf{V}_2}{2} + \frac{\mathbf{V}_2}{-j2} = 2\angle 60^\circ$$

$$(-j1)\,\mathbf{V}_1 + (0.5 + j0.5)\,\mathbf{V}_2 = 2\angle 60^\circ \qquad \text{...(ii)}$$

Writing Eqs (i) and (ii) in matrix form,

$$\begin{bmatrix} 1 & -1 \\ -j1 & 0.5 + j0.5 \end{bmatrix} \begin{bmatrix} \mathbf{V}_1 \\ \mathbf{V}_2 \end{bmatrix} = \begin{bmatrix} 12\angle 30^\circ \\ 2\angle 60^\circ \end{bmatrix}$$

By Cramer's rule,

$$\mathbf{V}_2 = \frac{\begin{vmatrix} 1 & 12\angle 30^\circ \\ -j1 & 2\angle 60^\circ \end{vmatrix}}{\begin{vmatrix} 1 & -1 \\ -j1 & 0.5 + j0.5 \end{vmatrix}} = 18.55\angle 157.42^\circ \text{ V}$$

$$\mathbf{V}_c = \mathbf{V}_2 = 18.55\angle 157.42^\circ \text{ V}$$

## 5.3 SUPERPOSITION THEOREM

LO 5.2

Analyse the networks using superposition theorem

The superposition theorem can be used to analyse an ac network containing more than one source. The superposition theorem states that *in a network containing more than one voltage source or current source, the total current or voltage in any branch of the network is the phasor sum of currents or voltages produced in that branch by each source acting separately*. As each source is considered, all of the other sources are replaced by their internal impedances. This theorem is valid only for linear systems.

**EXAMPLE 5.17**

*Find the current through the 3 + j4 ohm impedance of Fig. 5.17.*

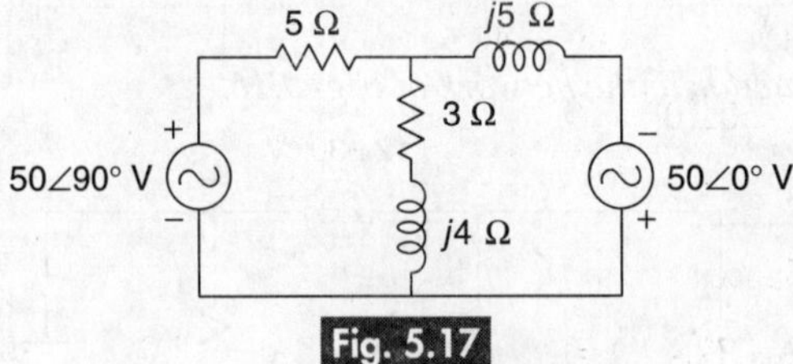


Fig. 5.17

**Solution**

***Step I*** When the 50 ∠90° V source is acting alone (Fig. 5.18)

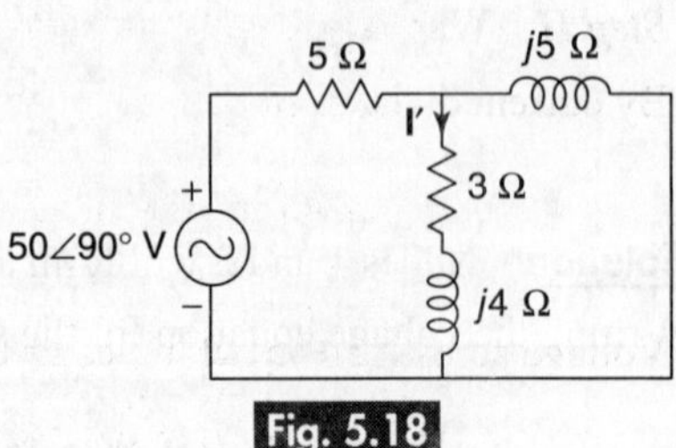


Fig. 5.18

$$\mathbf{Z}_T = 5 + \frac{(3+j4)(j5)}{3+j9} = 6.35\angle 23.2° \ \Omega$$

$$\mathbf{I}_T = \frac{50\angle 90°}{6.35\angle 23.2°} = 7.87\angle 66.8° \text{ A}$$

By current division rule,

$$\mathbf{I}' = (7.87\angle 66.8°)\left(\frac{j5}{3+j9}\right) = 4.15\angle 85.3° \text{ A}(\downarrow)$$

***Step II*** When the 50∠0° V source is acting alone (Fig. 5.19)

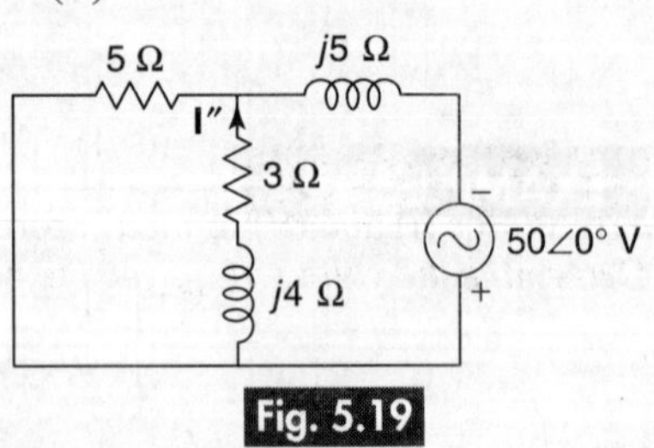


Fig. 5.19

$$\mathbf{Z}_T = j5 + \frac{5(3+j4)}{8+j4} = 6.74\angle 68.2° \ \Omega$$

$$\mathbf{I}_T = \frac{50\angle 0°}{6.74\angle 68.2°} = 7.42\angle -68.2° \text{ A}$$

By current division rule,

$$\mathbf{I}'' = (7.42\angle -68.2°)\left(\frac{5}{8+j4}\right) = 4.15\angle -94.77° \text{ A}(\uparrow) = 4.15\angle 85.3° \text{ A}(\downarrow)$$

***Step III*** By superposition theorem,

$$\mathbf{I} = \mathbf{I}' + \mathbf{I}'' = 4.15\ \angle 85.3° + 4.15\ \angle 85.3° = 8.31\ \angle 85.3° \text{A}\ (\downarrow)$$

## EXAMPLE 5.18

*Determine the voltage across the (2 + j5) ohm impedance for the network shown in Fig. 5.20.*

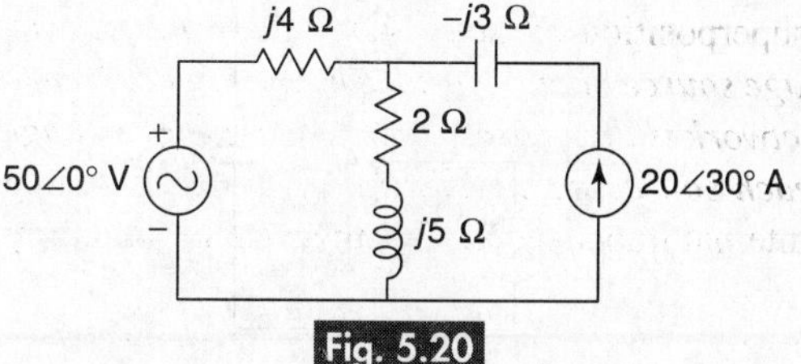


Fig. 5.20

### Solution

***Step I*** When the 50∠0° V source is acting alone (Fig. 5.21)

$$\mathbf{I} = \frac{50\angle 0^\circ}{2 + j4 + j5} = 5.42\angle -77.47^\circ \text{ A}$$

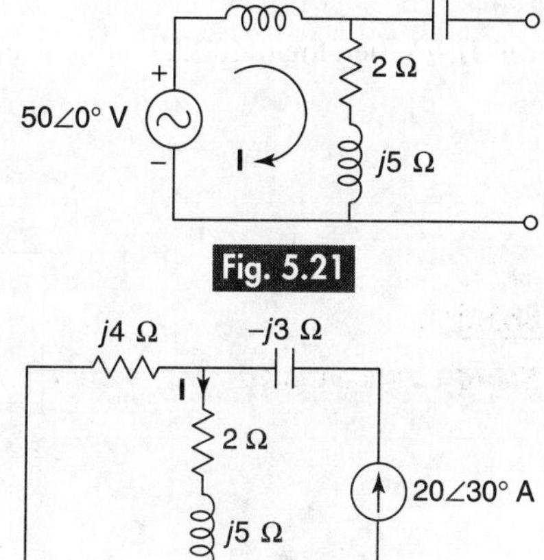


Fig. 5.21

Fig. 5.22

Voltage cross (2 + *j*5) Ω impedance

$$\mathbf{V'} = (2 + j5)\,(5.42\ \angle -77.47^\circ) = 29.16\ \angle -9.28^\circ \text{ V}$$

***Step II*** When the 20∠30° A source is acting alone (Fig. 5.22)

By current division rule,

$$\mathbf{I} = (20\angle 30^\circ)\left(\frac{j4}{2 + j9}\right) = 8.68\angle 42.53^\circ \text{ A}$$

Voltage across (2 + *j*5) Ω impedance

$$\mathbf{V''} = (2 + j5)\,(8.68\ \angle 42.53^\circ) = 46.69\ \angle 110.72^\circ \text{ V}$$

***Step III*** By superposition theorem,

$$\mathbf{V} = \mathbf{V'} + \mathbf{V''} = 29.16\ \angle -9.28^\circ + 46.69\ \angle 110.72^\circ = 40.85\ \angle 72.53^\circ \text{ V}$$

## EXAMPLE 5.19

*Determine the voltage $V_{AB}$ for the network shown in Fig. 5.23.*

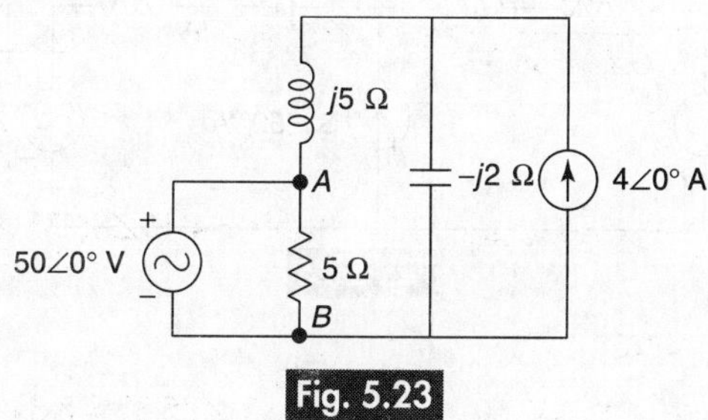


Fig. 5.23

**Solution**

***Step I*** When the $50\angle 0°$ V source is acting alone (Fig. 5.24)

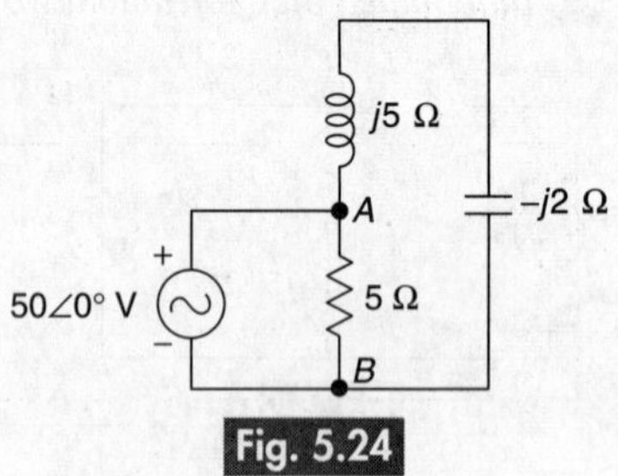


Fig. 5.24

$$\mathbf{V}'_{AB} = 50\angle 0° \text{ V}$$

***Step II*** When the $4\angle 0°$ A source is acting alone (Fig. 5.25)

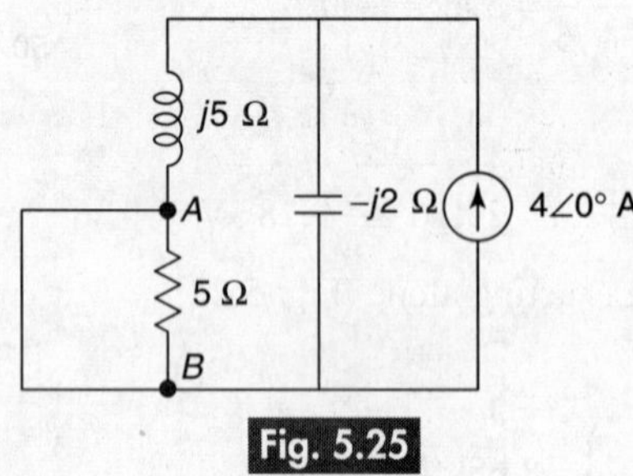


Fig. 5.25

$$\mathbf{V}''_{AB} = 0$$

***Step III*** By superposition theorem,

$$\mathbf{V}_{AB} = \mathbf{V}'_{AB} + \mathbf{V}''_{AB} = 50\angle 0° + 0 = 50\angle 0° \text{ V}$$

## EXAMPLE 5.20

*Find the current **I** in the network shown in Fig. 5.26.*

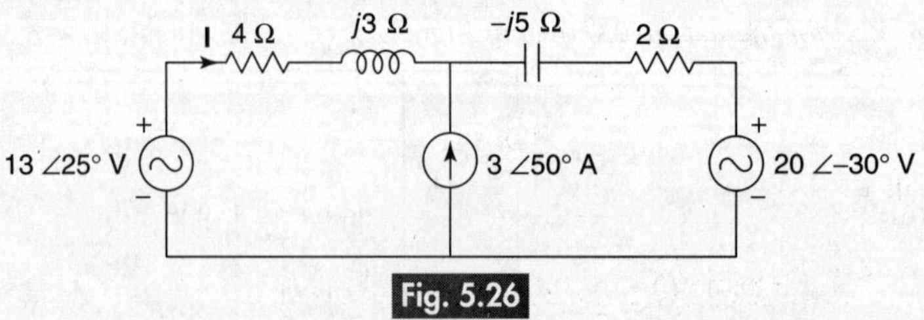


Fig. 5.26

**Solution**

***Step I*** When the $13\angle 25°$ V source is acting alone (Fig. 5.27)

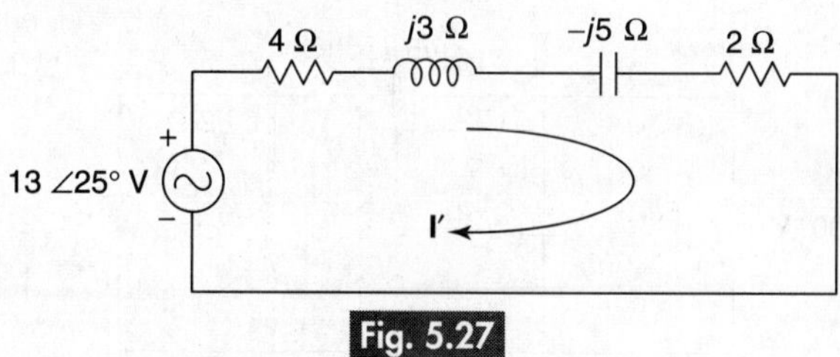


Fig. 5.27

$$\mathbf{I'} = \frac{13\angle 25°}{6 - j2} = 2.057\angle 43.43° \text{ A} \quad (\rightarrow)$$

***Step II*** When the $20\angle{-30°}$ V source is acting alone (Fig. 5.28)

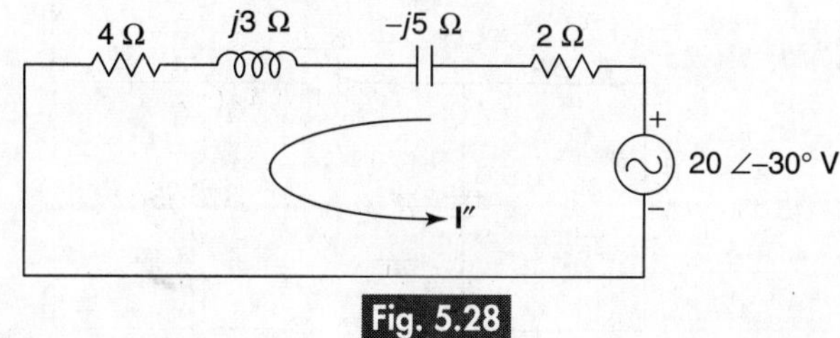


Fig. 5.28

$$\mathbf{I''} = \frac{20\angle -30° \text{ V}}{6 - j2} = 3.16\angle -11.57° \text{ A}(\leftarrow) = 3.16\angle 168.43° \text{ A}(\rightarrow)$$

***Step III*** When the $3\angle 50°$ A source is acting alone (Fig. 5.29)

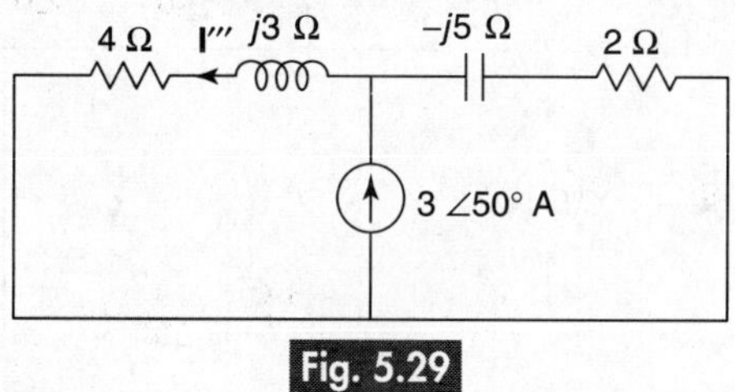


Fig. 5.29

By current division rule,

$$\mathbf{I'''} = 3\angle 50° \times \frac{2 - j5}{6 - j2} = 2.56\angle 0.23° \text{ A}(\leftarrow) = 2.56\angle -179.77° \text{ A}(\rightarrow)$$

***Step IV*** By superposition theorem,

$$\mathbf{I} = \mathbf{I'} + \mathbf{I''} + \mathbf{I'''} = 2.057\ \angle 43.13° + 3.16\ \angle 168.43° + 2.56\ \angle{-179.77°} \text{ A} = 4.62\ \angle 153.99° \text{ A } (\rightarrow)$$

## EXAMPLE 5.21

*Find the current through the j3 Ω reactance in the network of Fig. 5.30.*

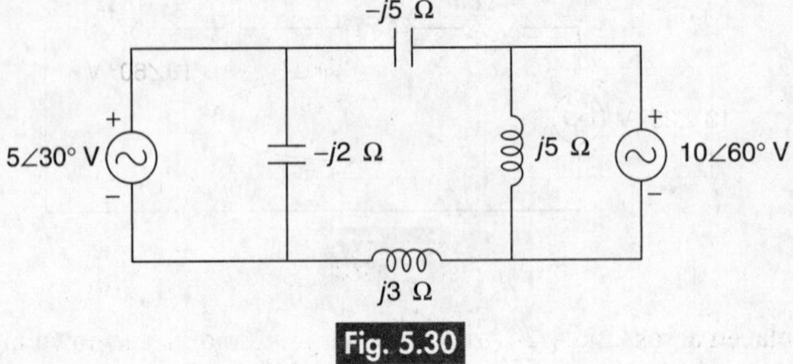


Fig. 5.30

**Solution**

***Step I*** When the 5∠30° V source is acting alone (Fig. 5.31)

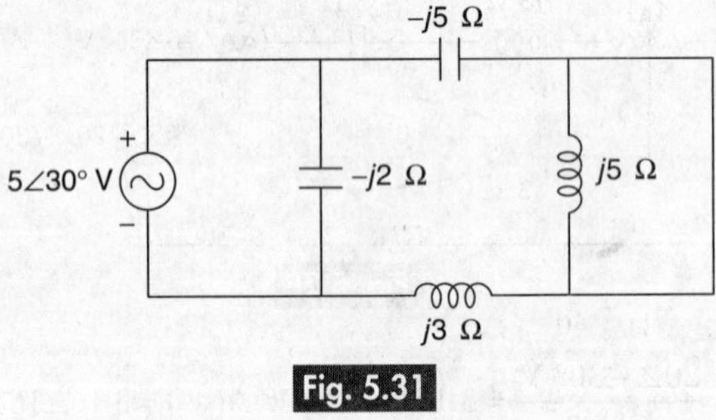


Fig. 5.31

When a short circuit is placed across $j15\ \Omega$ reactance, it gets shorted, as shown in Fig. 5.32.

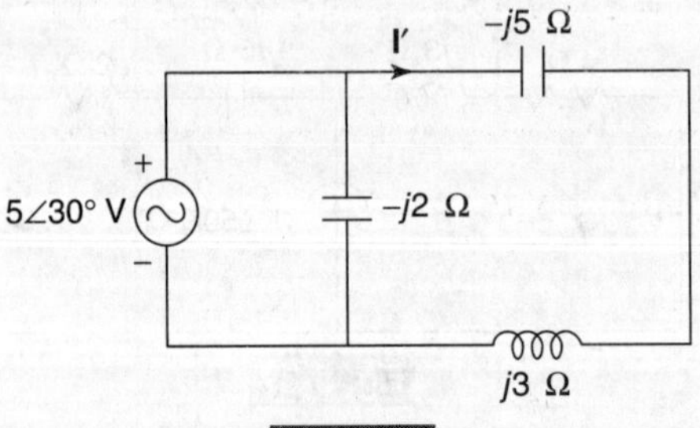


Fig. 5.32

$$\mathbf{I}' = \frac{5\angle 30^\circ}{-j5 + j3} = 2.5\angle 120^\circ \text{ A}(\leftarrow)$$

***Step II*** When the $10\angle 60°$ V source is acting alone (Fig. 5.33)

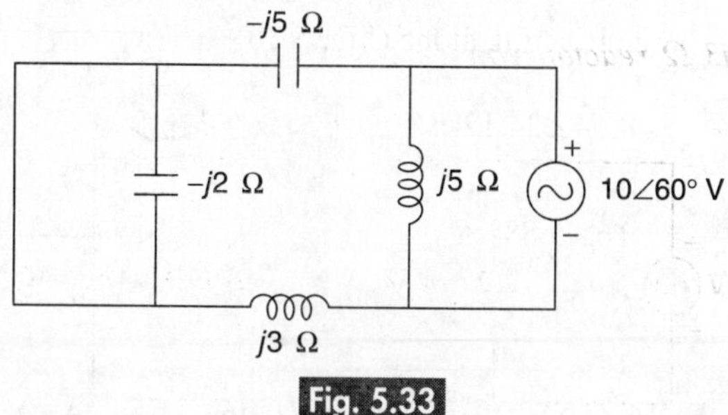


Fig. 5.33

When a short circuit is placed across the $-j2\ \Omega$ reactance, it gets shorted, as shown in Fig. 5.34

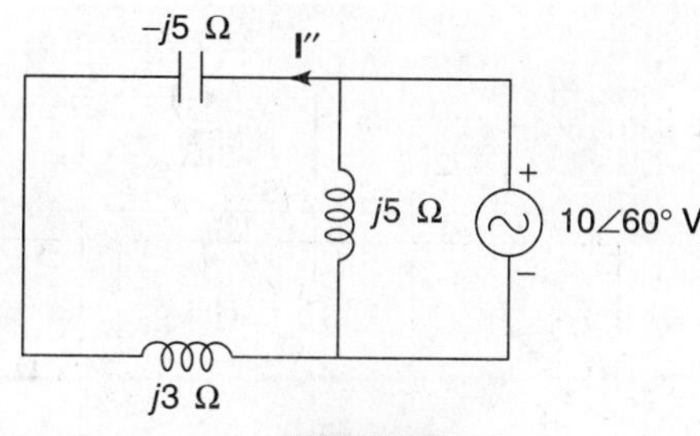


Fig. 5.34

$$\mathbf{I}'' = \frac{10\angle 60°}{-j5 + j3} = 5\angle 150°\ \text{A}\ (\rightarrow) = 5\angle -30°\ \text{A}\ (\leftarrow)$$

***Step III*** By superposition theorem,

$$\mathbf{I} = \mathbf{I}' + \mathbf{I}'' = 2.5\angle 120° + 5\angle -30° = 3.1\angle -6.21°\ \text{A}\quad (\leftarrow)$$

## EXAMPLE 5.22

*Find the current $\mathbf{I}_0$ in the network of Fig. 5.35.*

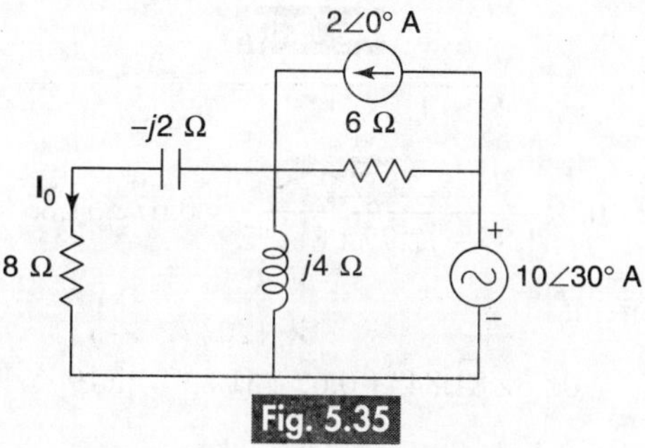


Fig. 5.35

**Solution**

***Step I*** When the $10\angle 30°$ V source is acting alone (Fig. 5.36)

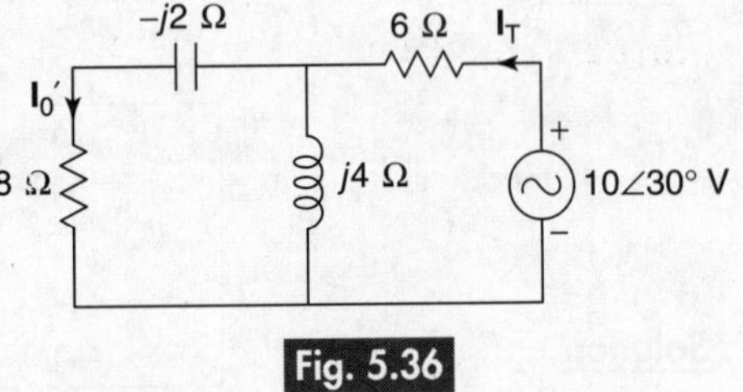

Fig. 5.36

$$\mathbf{Z}_T = 6 + \frac{j4(8-j2)}{j4+8-j2} = 8.64\angle 24.12°\ \Omega$$

$$\mathbf{I}_T = \frac{10\angle 30°}{8.64\angle 24.12°} = 1.16\angle 5.88°\ \text{A}$$

By current division rule,

$$\mathbf{I}_0' = 1.16\angle 5.88° \times \frac{j4}{8-j2+j4} = 0.56\angle 81.84°\ \text{A}\quad (\downarrow)$$

***Step II*** When the $2\angle 0°$ A source is acting alone (Fig. 5.37)

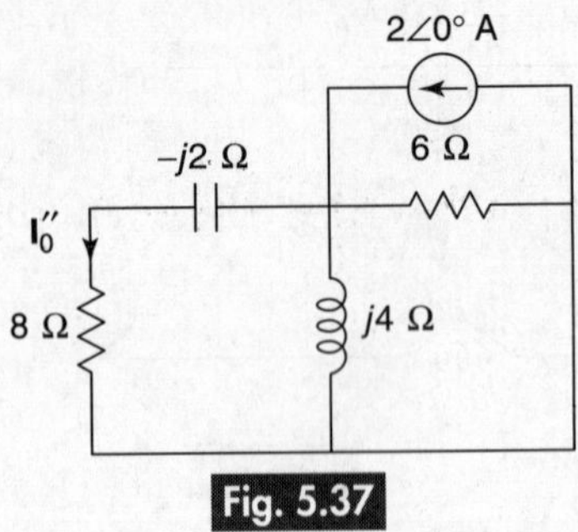

Fig. 5.37

The network can be redrawn, as shown in Fig. 5.38.

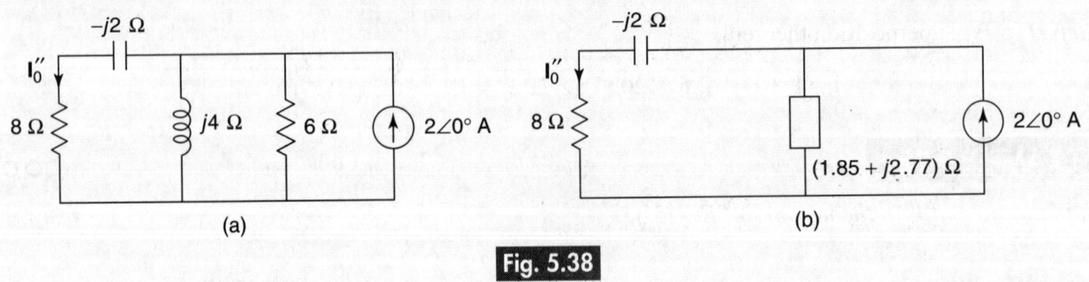

Fig. 5.38

By current division rule,

$$\mathbf{I}_0'' = 2\angle 0° \times \frac{1.85+j2.77}{1.85+j2.77+8-j2} = 0.67\angle 51.83°\ \text{A}\ (\downarrow)$$

***Step III*** By superposition theorem,

$$\mathbf{I}_0 = \mathbf{I}_0' + \mathbf{I}_0'' = 0.56\angle 81.84° + 0.67\angle 51.83° = 1.19\angle 65.46°\ \text{A}\ (\downarrow)$$

## EXAMPLE 5.23

*Find the current through the j5 Ω branch for the network shown in Fig. 5.39.*

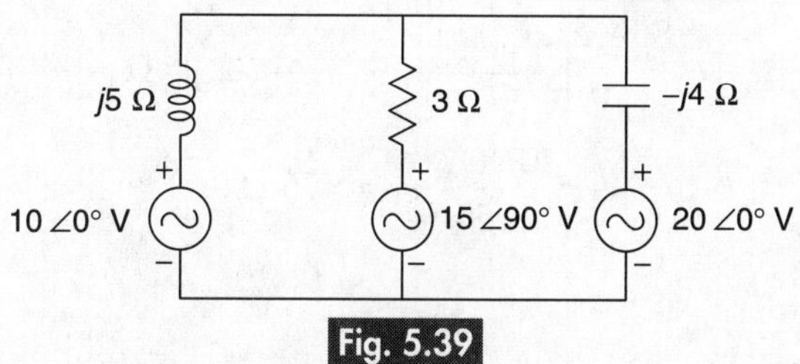


Fig. 5.39

## Solution

***Step I*** When the $10\angle 0°$ V source is acting alone (Fig. 5.40)

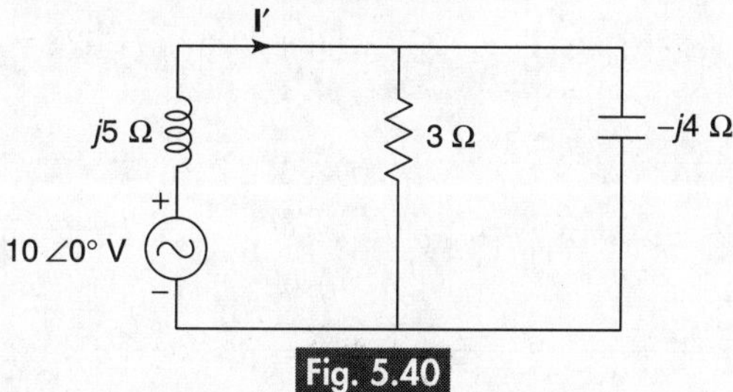


Fig. 5.40

$$\mathbf{Z}_T = j5 + \frac{3(-j4)}{3-j4} = 4.04\angle 61.66°\ \Omega$$

$$\mathbf{I}' = \frac{10\angle 0°}{4.04\angle 61.66°} = 2.48\angle -61.66° \text{A} \quad (\rightarrow)$$

***Step II*** When the $15\angle 90°$ V source is acting alone (Fig. 5.41)

$$\mathbf{Z}_T = 3 + \frac{(j5)(-j4)}{j5-j4} = 20.22\angle -81.47°\ \Omega$$

$$\mathbf{I}_T = \frac{15\angle 90°}{20.22\angle -81.47°} = 0.74\angle 171.47° \text{ A}$$

Fig. 5.41

By current division rule,

$$\mathbf{I}'' = 0.74\angle 171.47° \times \frac{-j4}{-j4+j5} = 2.96\angle -8.53° \text{ A } (\leftarrow) = 2.96\angle 171.47° \text{ A} \quad (\rightarrow)$$

***Step III*** When the $20\ \angle 0°$ V source is acting alone (Fig. 5.42)

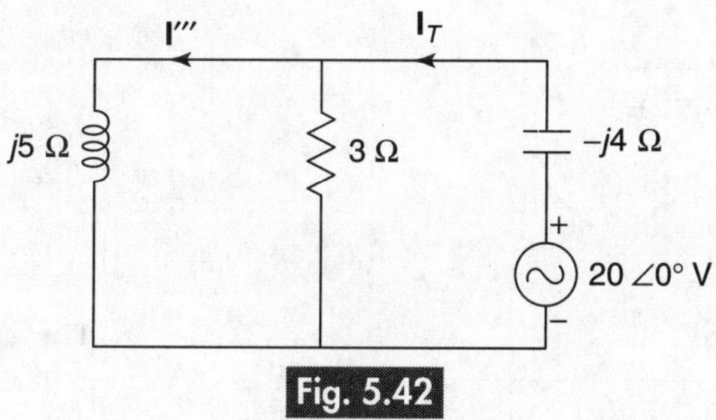


Fig. 5.42

$$\mathbf{Z}_T = -j4 + \frac{3(j5)}{3+j5} = 3.47\angle -50.51^\circ\ \Omega$$

$$\mathbf{I}_T = \frac{20\angle 0^\circ}{3.47\angle -50.51^\circ} = 5.76\angle 50.51^\circ\ \text{A}$$

By current division rule,

$$\mathbf{I}''' = 5.76\angle 50.51^\circ \times \frac{3}{3+j5} = 2.96\angle -8.53^\circ\ \text{A}\ (\leftarrow) = 2.96\angle 171.47^\circ\ \text{A}\ (\rightarrow)$$

***Step IV*** By superposition theorem,

$$\mathbf{I} = \mathbf{I}' + \mathbf{I}'' + \mathbf{I}''' = 2.48\angle -61.66^\circ + 2.96\angle 171.47^\circ + 2.96\angle 171.47^\circ = 4.86\angle -164.41^\circ\ \text{A}$$

## EXAMPLE 5.24

*Find the voltage drop across the capacitor for the network shown in Fig. 5.43.*

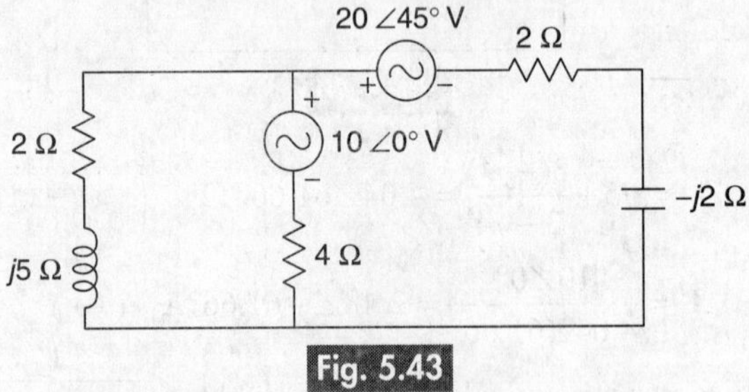


Fig. 5.43

### Solution

***Step I*** When the 10∠0° V source is acting alone (Fig. 5.44)

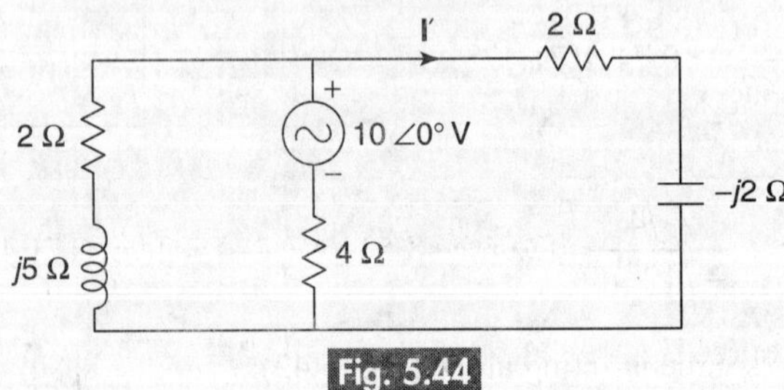


Fig. 5.44

$$\mathbf{Z}_T = 4 + \frac{(2+j5)(2-j2)}{2+j5+2-j2} = 7\angle -5.91^\circ\ \Omega$$

$$\mathbf{I}_T = \frac{10\angle 0^\circ}{7\angle -5.91^\circ} = 1.43\angle 5.91^\circ\ \text{A}$$

By current division rule,

$$\mathbf{I}' = (1.43\angle 5.91^\circ)\left(\frac{2+j5}{2+j5+2-j2}\right) = 1.54\angle 37.24^\circ\ \text{A}\quad (\rightarrow)$$

***Step II*** When the $20\angle 45°$ V source is acting alone (Fig. 5.45)

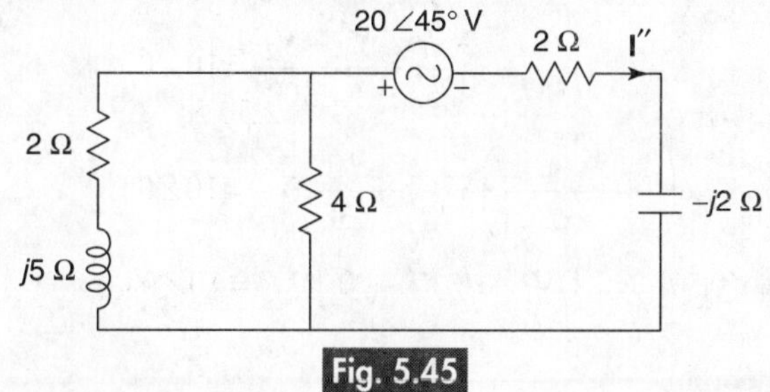


Fig. 5.45

$$\mathbf{Z}_T = (2 - j2) + \frac{4(2 + j5)}{4 + 2 + j5} = 4.48\angle -8.84°\ \Omega$$

$$\mathbf{I}'' = \frac{20\angle 45°}{4.48\angle -8.84°} = 4.46\angle 53.84°\ \text{A}\quad (\leftarrow) = -4.46\angle 53.84°\ \text{A}\quad (\rightarrow)$$

***Step III*** By superposition theorem,

$$\mathbf{I} = \mathbf{I}' + \mathbf{I}'' = 1.54\angle 37.24 - 4.46\angle 53.84° = 3.01\angle -117.78°\ \text{A}$$

$$\mathbf{V}_c = (-j2)\mathbf{I} = (-j2)\ (3.01\angle -117.78°) = 6.02\angle 152.22°\ \text{V}$$

## EXAMPLE 5.25

*Find the node voltage $V_2$ in the network of Fig. 5.46.*

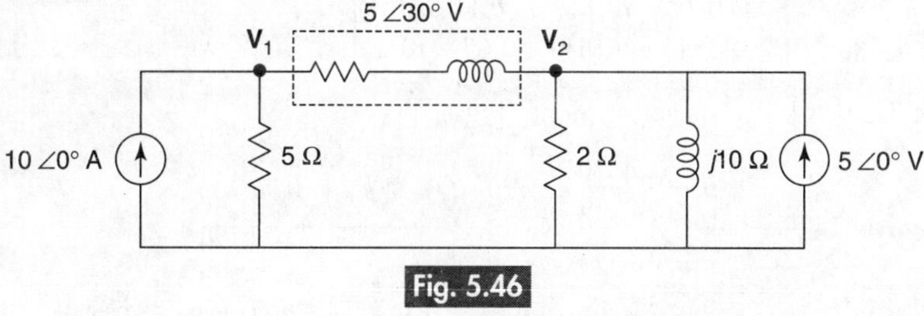


Fig. 5.46

### Solution

***Step I*** When the $10\angle 0°$A source is acting alone (Fig. 5.47)

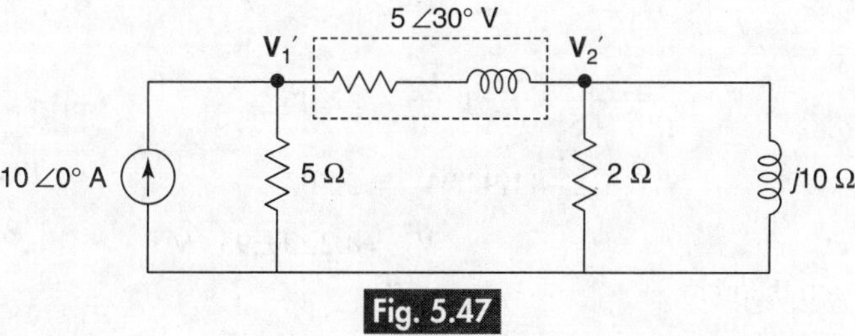


Fig. 5.47

Applying KCL at node 1,

$$\frac{\mathbf{V}_1'}{5}+\frac{\mathbf{V}_1'-\mathbf{V}_2'}{5\angle 30^\circ}=10\angle 0^\circ$$

$$\left(\frac{1}{5}+\frac{1}{5\angle 30^\circ}\right)\mathbf{V}_1'-\frac{1}{5\angle 30^\circ}\mathbf{V}_2'=10\angle 0^\circ$$

$$(0.37-j0.1)\mathbf{V}_1'-(0.17-j0.1)\mathbf{V}_2'=10\angle 0^\circ \qquad \text{...(i)}$$

Applying KCL at node 2,

$$\frac{\mathbf{V}_2'-\mathbf{V}_1'}{5\angle 30^\circ}+\frac{\mathbf{V}_2'}{2}+\frac{\mathbf{V}_2'}{j10}=0$$

$$-\frac{1}{5\angle 30^\circ}\mathbf{V}_1'+\left(\frac{1}{5\angle 30^\circ}+\frac{1}{2}+\frac{1}{j10}\right)\mathbf{V}_2'=0$$

$$-(0.17-j0.1)\mathbf{V}_1'+(0.67-j0.2)\mathbf{V}_2'=0 \qquad \text{...(ii)}$$

Writing Eqs (i) and (ii) in matrix form,

$$\begin{bmatrix} 0.37-j0.1 & -(0.17-j0.1) \\ -(0.17-j0.1) & 0.67-j0.2 \end{bmatrix}\begin{bmatrix} \mathbf{V}_1' \\ \mathbf{V}_2' \end{bmatrix}=\begin{bmatrix} 10\angle 0^\circ \\ 0 \end{bmatrix}$$

By Cramer's rule,

$$\mathbf{V}_2'=\frac{\begin{vmatrix} 0.37-j0.1 & 10\angle 0^\circ \\ -(0.17-j0.1) & 0 \end{vmatrix}}{\begin{vmatrix} 0.37-j0.1 & -(0.17-j0.1) \\ -(0.17-j0.1) & 0.67-j0.2 \end{vmatrix}}=8.57\angle -3.36^\circ \text{ V}$$

***Step II*** When the $5\angle 0^\circ$ A source is acting alone (Fig. 5.48)

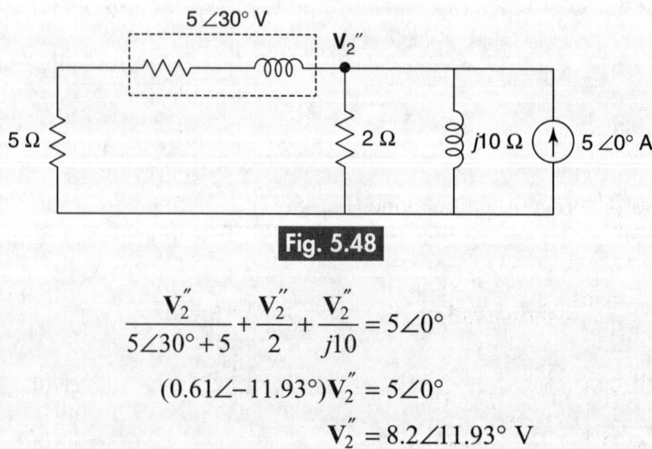


Fig. 5.48

$$\frac{\mathbf{V}_2''}{5\angle 30^\circ+5}+\frac{\mathbf{V}_2''}{2}+\frac{\mathbf{V}_2''}{j10}=5\angle 0^\circ$$

$$(0.61\angle -11.93^\circ)\mathbf{V}_2''=5\angle 0^\circ$$

$$\mathbf{V}_2''=8.2\angle 11.93^\circ \text{ V}$$

***Step III*** By superposition theorem,

$$\mathbf{V}_2=\mathbf{V}_2'+\mathbf{V}_2''=8.57\angle -3.36^\circ+8.2\angle 11.93^\circ=16.62\angle 4.12^\circ \text{ V}$$

## EXAMPLE 5.26

*Find current through inductor in the network of Fig. 5.49.*

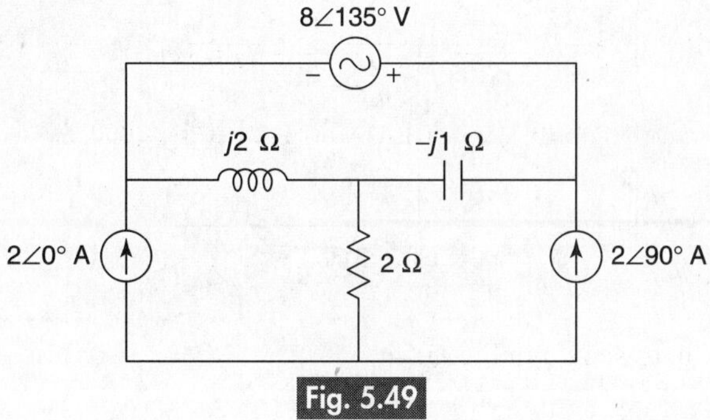


Fig. 5.49

### Solution

***Step I*** When the $8\angle 135°$ V source is acting alone (Fig. 5.50)

Applying KVL to the mesh,

$$8\angle 135° - (-j1)\mathbf{I}' - j2\mathbf{I}' = 0$$

$$\mathbf{I}' = \frac{8\angle 135°}{j1} = 8\angle 45° \text{ A } (\leftarrow) = 8\angle -135° \text{ A } (\rightarrow)$$

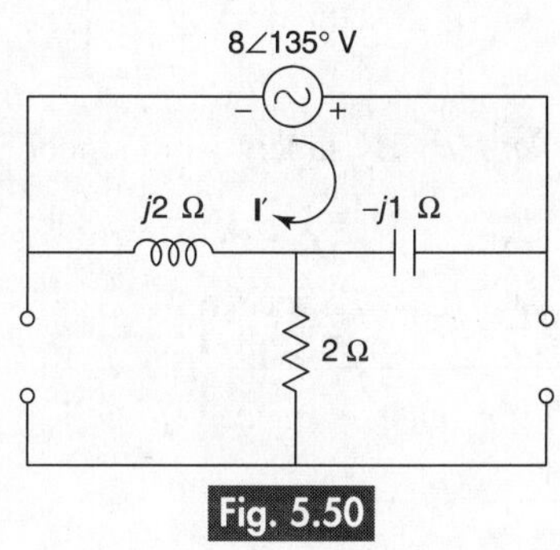


Fig. 5.50

***Step II*** When the $2\angle 0°$ A source is acting alone (Fig. 5.51)

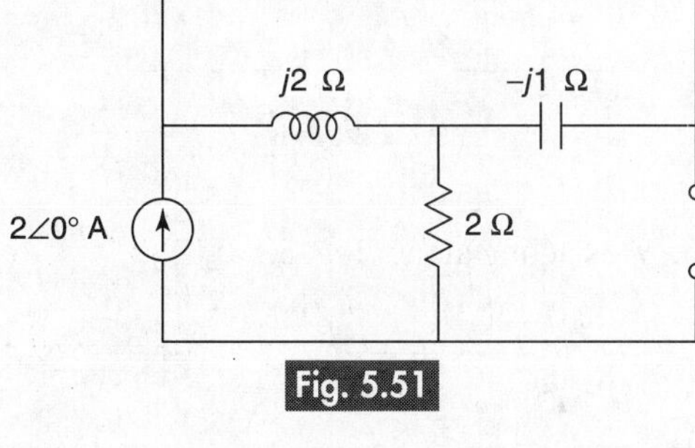


Fig. 5.51

The network can be redrawn, as shown in Fig. 5.52.

By current division rule,

$$\mathbf{I}'' = 2\angle 0° \left( \frac{-j1}{-j1 + j2} \right) = 2\angle 0° \left( \frac{-j1}{j1} \right) = 2\angle 180° \text{ A}(\rightarrow)$$

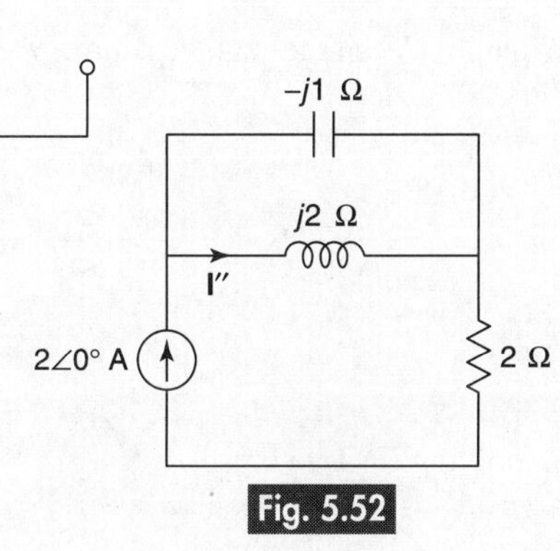


Fig. 5.52

***Step III*** When the $2\angle 90°$ A source is acting alone (Fig. 5.53)

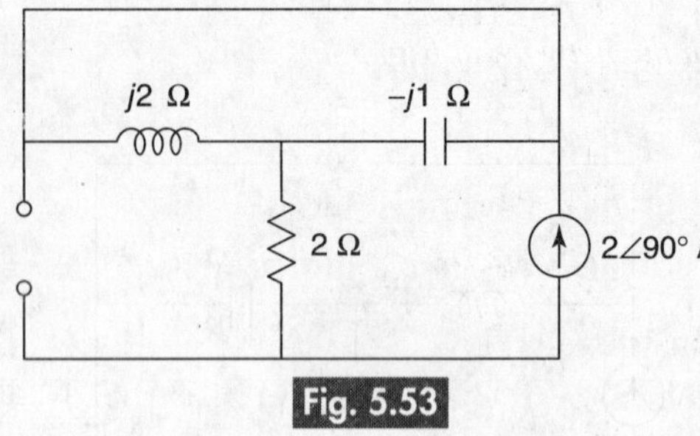


Fig. 5.53

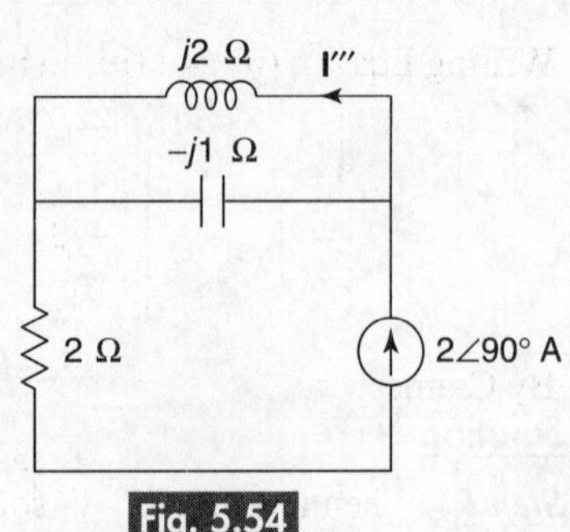


Fig. 5.54

The network can be redrawn, as shown in Fig. 5.54.

By current division rule,

$$\mathbf{I}''' = 2\angle 90°\left(\frac{-j1}{-j1+j2}\right) = 2\angle -90°\text{ A } (\leftarrow) = 2\angle 90°\text{ A } (\rightarrow)$$

***Step III*** By superposition theorem,

$$\mathbf{I} = \mathbf{I}' + \mathbf{I}'' + \mathbf{I}''' = 8\angle -135° + 2\angle 180° + 2\angle 90° = 8.49\angle -154.47°\text{A}$$

## EXAMPLE 5.27

*Determine the source voltage $V_S$ so that the current through 2 Ω resistor is zero in the network of Fig. 5.55.*

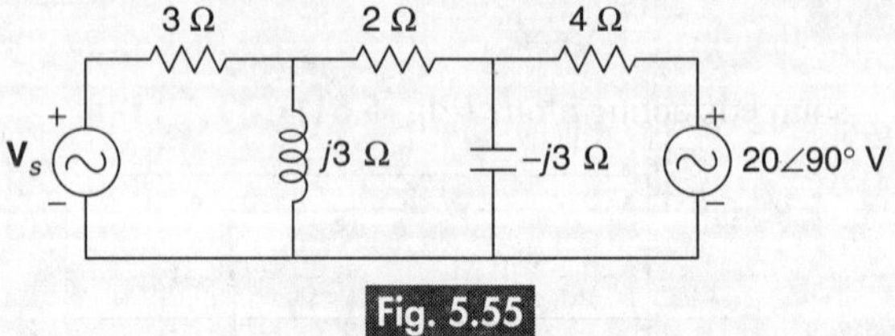


Fig. 5.55

**Solution**

***Step I*** When the voltage source $\mathbf{V}_s$ is acting alone (Fig. 5.56)

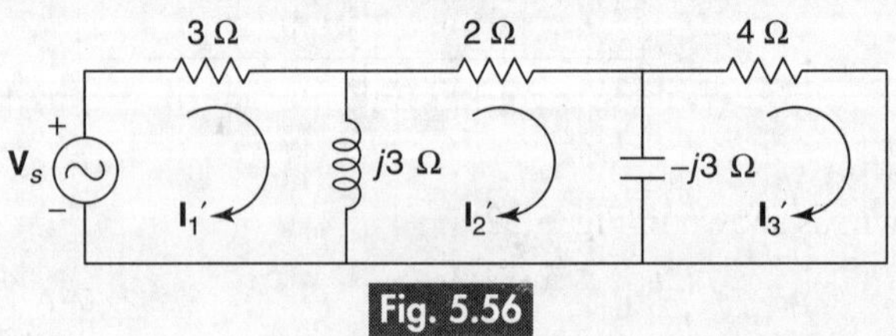


Fig. 5.56

Applying KVL to mesh 1,

$$\mathbf{V}_s - 3\mathbf{I}_1' - j3(\mathbf{I}_1' - \mathbf{I}_2') = 0$$

$$(3 + j3)\mathbf{I}_1' - j3\mathbf{I}_2' = \mathbf{V}_s \qquad \text{...(i)}$$

Appling KVL to mesh 2,

$$-j3(\mathbf{I}_2' - \mathbf{I}_1') - 2\mathbf{I}_2' + j3(\mathbf{I}_2' - \mathbf{I}_3') = 0$$

$$-j3\mathbf{I}_1' + 2\mathbf{I}_2' + j3\mathbf{I}_3' = 0 \qquad \text{...(ii)}$$

Applying KVL to mesh 3,

$$-j3(\mathbf{I}_3' - \mathbf{I}_2') - 4\mathbf{I}_3' = 0$$

$$j3\mathbf{I}_2' + (4 - j3)\mathbf{I}_3' = 0 \qquad \text{...(iii)}$$

Writing Eqs (i), (ii) and (iii) in matrix form,

$$\begin{bmatrix} 3+j3 & -j3 & 0 \\ -j3 & 2 & j3 \\ 0 & j3 & 4-j3 \end{bmatrix} \begin{bmatrix} \mathbf{I}_1' \\ \mathbf{I}_2' \\ \mathbf{I}_3' \end{bmatrix} = \begin{bmatrix} \mathbf{V}_s \\ 0 \\ 0 \end{bmatrix}$$

By Cramer's rule,

$$\mathbf{I}_2' = \frac{\begin{vmatrix} 3+j3 & \mathbf{V}_s & 0 \\ -j3 & 0 & j3 \\ 0 & 0 & 4-j3 \end{vmatrix}}{\begin{vmatrix} 3+j3 & -j3 & 0 \\ -j3 & 2 & j3 \\ 0 & j3 & 4-j3 \end{vmatrix}} = \frac{(9+j12)\mathbf{V}_s}{\Delta}$$

***Step II*** When the 20 ∠90° V source is acting alone (Fig. 5.57)

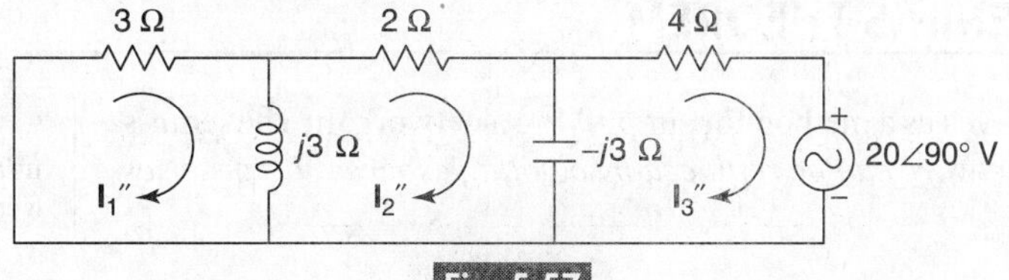


Fig. 5.57

Applying KVL to mesh 1,

$$-3\mathbf{I}_1'' - j3(\mathbf{I}_1'' - \mathbf{I}_2'') = 0$$

$$(3 + j3)\mathbf{I}_1'' - j3\mathbf{I}_2'' = 0 \qquad \text{...(i)}$$

Applying KVL to mesh 2,

$$-j3(\mathbf{I}_2'' - \mathbf{I}_1'') - 2\mathbf{I}_2'' + j3(\mathbf{I}_2'' - \mathbf{I}_3'') = 0$$

$$-j3\mathbf{I}_1'' + 2\mathbf{I}_2'' + j3\mathbf{I}_3'' = 0 \qquad \text{...(ii)}$$

Applying KVL to mesh 3,

$$j3(\mathbf{I}_3'' - \mathbf{I}_2'') - 4\mathbf{I}_3'' - 20\angle 90° = 0$$

$$j3\mathbf{I}_2'' + (4 - j3)\mathbf{I}_3'' = -20\angle 90° \qquad \text{...(iii)}$$

Writing Eqs (i), (ii) and (iii) in matrix form,

$$\begin{bmatrix} 3+j3 & -j3 & 0 \\ -j3 & 2 & j3 \\ 0 & j3 & 4-j3 \end{bmatrix} \begin{bmatrix} \mathbf{I}_1'' \\ \mathbf{I}_2'' \\ \mathbf{I}_3'' \end{bmatrix} = \begin{bmatrix} 0 \\ 0 \\ -20\angle 90° \end{bmatrix}$$

By Cramer's rule,

$$\mathbf{I}_2'' = \frac{\begin{vmatrix} 3+j3 & 0 & 0 \\ -j3 & 0 & j3 \\ 0 & -20\angle 90° & 4-j3 \end{vmatrix}}{\begin{vmatrix} 3+j3 & -j3 & 0 \\ -j3 & 2 & j3 \\ 0 & j3 & 4-j3 \end{vmatrix}} = \frac{-180 - j180}{\Delta}$$

***Step III*** By superposition theorem,

$$\mathbf{I}_2 = \mathbf{I}_2' + \mathbf{I}_2'' = \frac{(9+j12)\mathbf{V}_s + (-180 - j180)}{\Delta} = 0$$

$$(9+j12)\mathbf{V}_s + (-180 - j180) = 0$$

$$(9+j12)\mathbf{V}_s = 180 + j180$$

$$\mathbf{V}_s = 16.97\angle -8.13° \text{ V}$$

## 5.4 THEVENIN'S THEOREM

LO 5.3

Analyse the networks using Thevenin's and Norton's theorems

Thevenin's theorem gives us a method for simplifying a network. In Thevenin's theorem, *any linear network can be replaced by a voltage source* $\mathbf{V}_{\text{Th}}$ *in series with an impedance* $\mathbf{Z}_{\text{Th}}$.

**EXAMPLE 5.28**

*Obtain Thevenin's equivalent network for the terminals A and B in Fig. 5.58.*

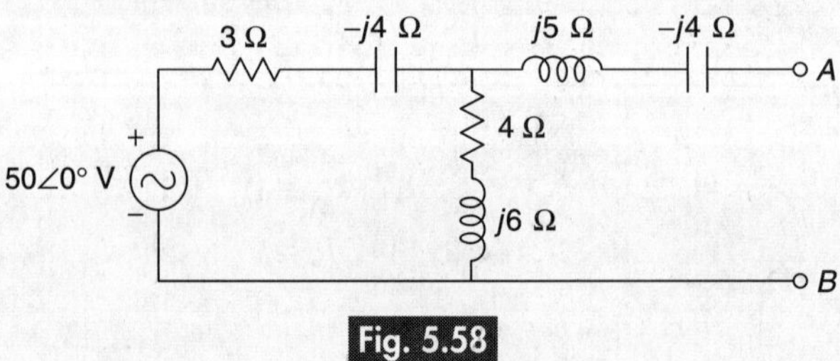


Fig. 5.58

## Solution

***Step I*** Calculation of $\mathbf{V}_{Th}$ (Fig. 5.59)

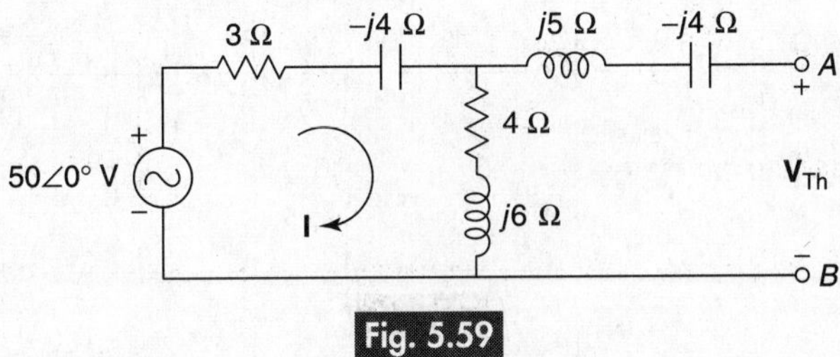


Fig. 5.59

Applying KVL to the mesh,

$$50\angle 0° - (3 - j4)\,\mathbf{I} - (4 + j6)\,\mathbf{I} = 0$$

$$\mathbf{I} = \frac{50\angle 0°}{(3 - j4) + (4 + j6)} = 6.87\angle -15.95° \text{ A}$$

$$\mathbf{V}_{Th} = (4 + j6)\,\mathbf{I} = (4 + j6)\,(6.87\angle -15.95°) = 49.5\angle 40.35° \text{ V}$$

***Step II*** Calculation of $\mathbf{Z}_{Th}$ (Fig. 5.60)

$$\mathbf{Z}_{Th} = (j5 - j4) + \frac{(3 - j4)(4 + j6)}{(3 - j4) + (4 + j6)} = 4.83\angle -1.13° \ \Omega$$

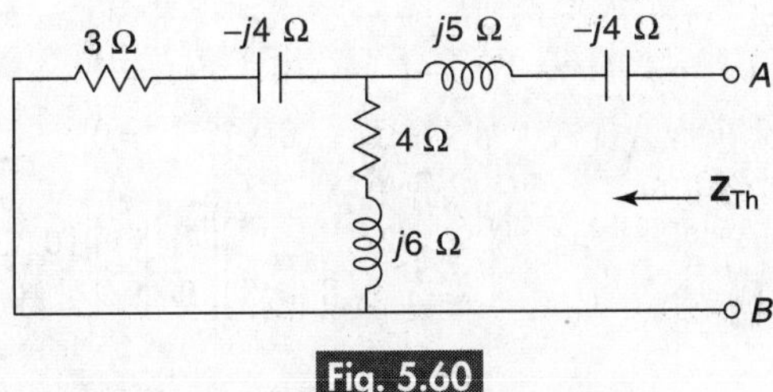


Fig. 5.60

***Step III*** Thevenin's Equivalent Network (Fig. 5.61)

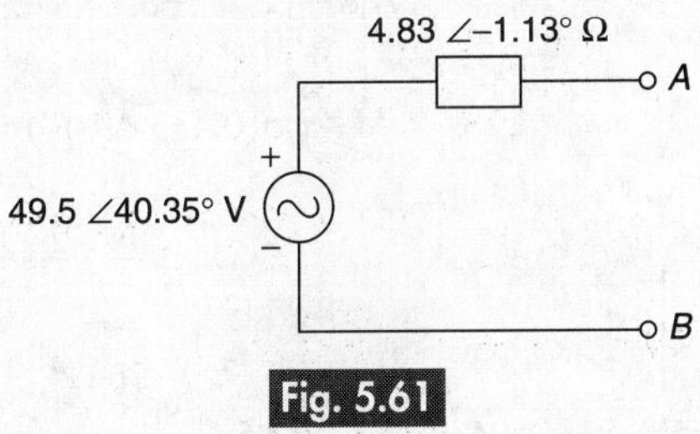


Fig. 5.61

## EXAMPLE 5.29

*Find Thevenin's equivalent network for Fig. 5.62.*

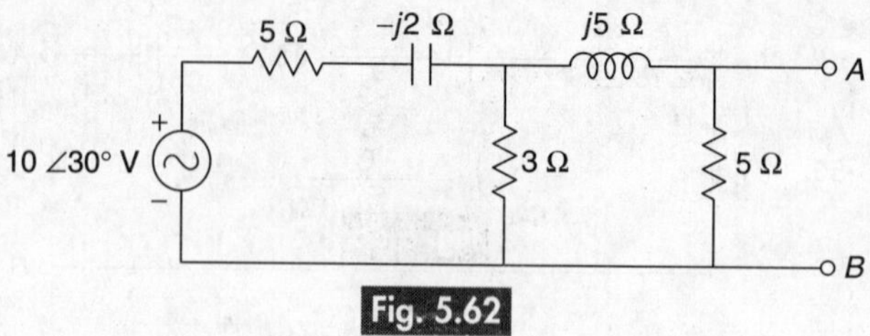


Fig. 5.62

### Solution

***Step I*** Calculation of $\mathbf{V}_{Th}$ (Fig. 5.63)

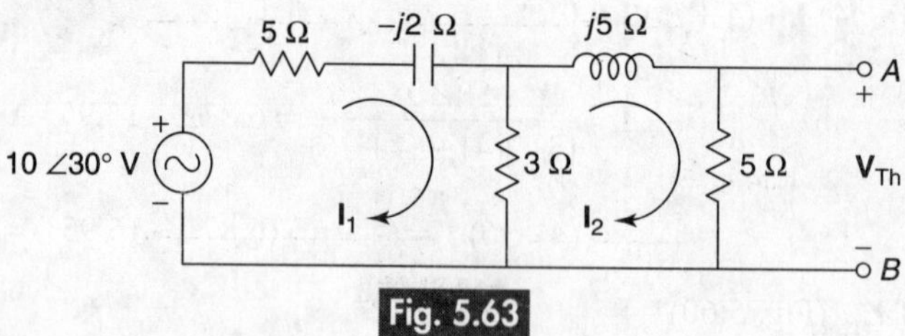


Fig. 5.63

Applying KVL to mesh 1,

$$10\angle 30° - (5 - j2)\,\mathbf{I}_1 - 3(\mathbf{I}_1 - \mathbf{I}_2) = 0$$

$$(8 - j2)\,\mathbf{I}_1 - 3\mathbf{I}_2 = 10\angle 30° \qquad \ldots\text{(i)}$$

Applying KVL to mesh 2,

$$-3(\mathbf{I}_2 - \mathbf{I}_1) - j5\,\mathbf{I}_2 - 5\,\mathbf{I}_2 = 0$$

$$-3\mathbf{I}_1 + (8 + j5)\mathbf{I}_2 = 0 \qquad \ldots\text{(ii)}$$

Writing Eqs (i) and (ii) in matrix form,

$$\begin{bmatrix} 8-j2 & -3 \\ -3 & 8+j5 \end{bmatrix}\begin{bmatrix} \mathbf{I}_1 \\ \mathbf{I}_2 \end{bmatrix} = \begin{bmatrix} 10\angle 30° \\ 0 \end{bmatrix}$$

By Cramer's rule,

$$\mathbf{I}_2 = \frac{\begin{vmatrix} 8-j2 & 10\angle 30° \\ -3 & 0 \end{vmatrix}}{\begin{vmatrix} 8-j2 & -3 \\ -3 & 8+j5 \end{vmatrix}} = 0.433\angle 9.7° \text{ A}$$

$$\mathbf{V}_{Th} = 5\mathbf{I}_2 = 5(0.433\angle 9.7°) = 2.16\angle 9.7° \text{ V}$$

***Step II*** Calculation of $\mathbf{Z}_{Th}$ (Fig. 5.64)

$$\mathbf{Z}_{Th} = \left[\left\{\frac{(5-j2)3}{5-j2+3}\right\} + j5\right] \| 5$$

$$= [1.94 - j0.265 + j5] \| 5 = (1.94 + j4.735) \| 5$$

$$= \frac{(1.94 + j4.735)5}{6.94 + j4.735} = 3.04\angle 33.4° \ \Omega$$

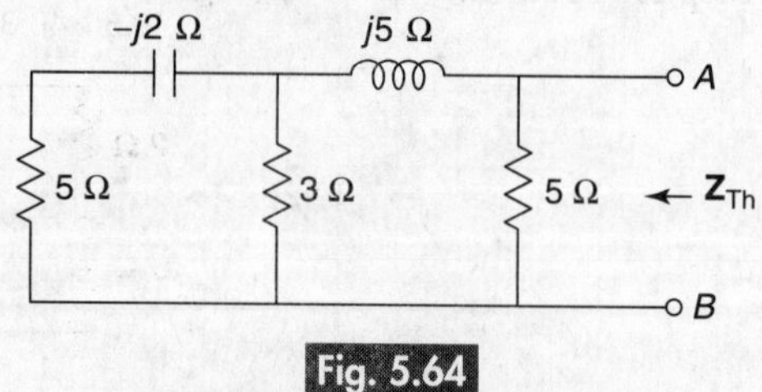


Fig. 5.64

***Step III*** Thevenin's equivalent Network (Fig. 5.65)

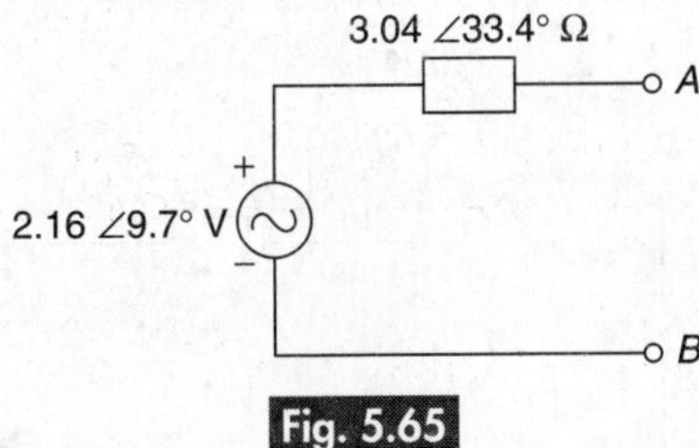


Fig. 5.65

## EXAMPLE 5.30

*Obtain Thevenin's equivalent network for Fig. 5.66.*

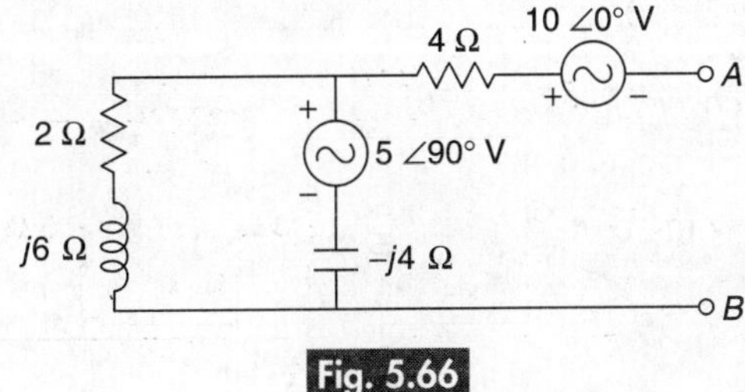


Fig. 5.66

### Solution

***Step I*** Calculation of $\mathbf{V}_{\text{Th}}$ (Fig. 5.67)

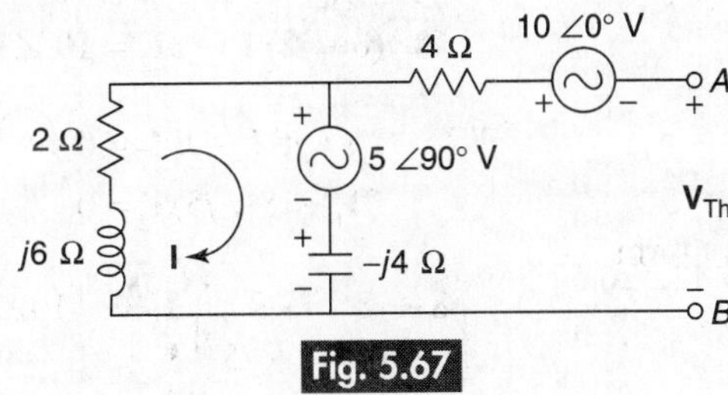


Fig. 5.67

Applying KVL to the mesh,

$$(2 + j6 - j4)\mathbf{I} - 5\angle 90° = 0$$

$$\mathbf{I} = \frac{5\angle 90°}{2 + j2} = 1.77\angle 45° \text{ A}$$

$$\mathbf{V}_{\text{Th}} = (-j4)\,\mathbf{I} + 5\angle 90° - 10\angle 0° = (4\angle -90°)(1.77\angle 45°) + 5\angle 90° - 10\angle 0° = 18\angle 146.31° \text{ V}$$

***Step II*** Calculation of $\mathbf{Z}_{\text{Th}}$ (Fig. 5.68)

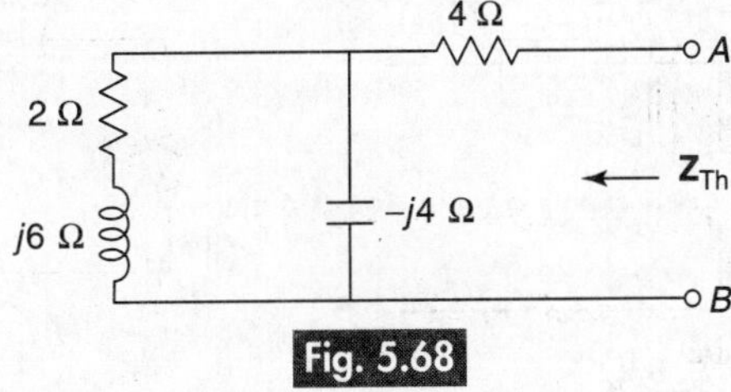


Fig. 5.68

$$\mathbf{Z}_{\text{Th}} = 4 + \frac{(2+j6)(-j4)}{2+j2} = 11.3\angle -44.93°\ \Omega$$

***Step III*** Thevenin's Equivalent Network (Fig. 5.69)

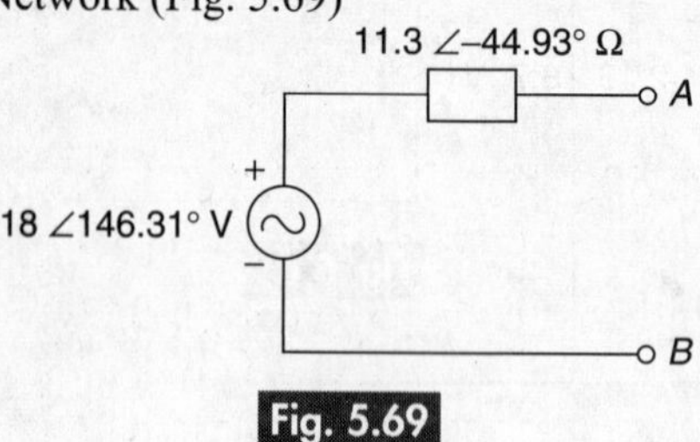


Fig. 5.69

## EXAMPLE 5.31

*Obtain Thevenin's equivalent network for Fig. 5.70.*

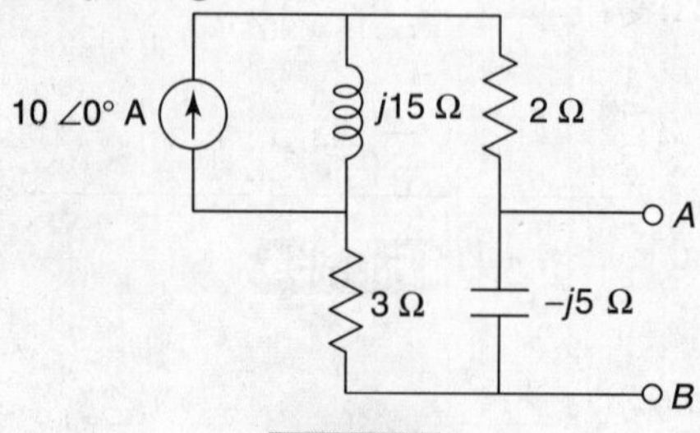


Fig. 5.70

**Solution**

***Step I*** Calculation of $\mathbf{V}_{\text{Th}}$ (Fig. 5.71)

By current division rule,

$$\mathbf{I} = \frac{(10\angle 0°)(j15)}{5 - j5 + j15} = 13.42\angle 26.57°\ \text{A}$$

$$\begin{aligned}\mathbf{V}_{\text{Th}} &= (-j5)\,\mathbf{I} \\ &= (5\angle -90°)\,(13.42\angle 26.57°) \\ &= 67.08\angle -63.43°\ \text{V}\end{aligned}$$

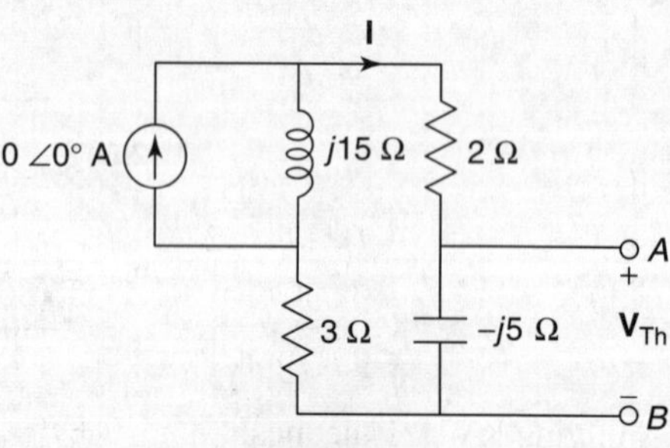


Fig. 5.71

***Step II*** Calculation of $\mathbf{Z}_{\text{Th}}$ (Fig. 5.72)

$$\mathbf{Z}_{\text{Th}} = \frac{(-j5)(5+j15)}{-j5+5+j15} = 7.07\angle -81.86°\ \Omega$$

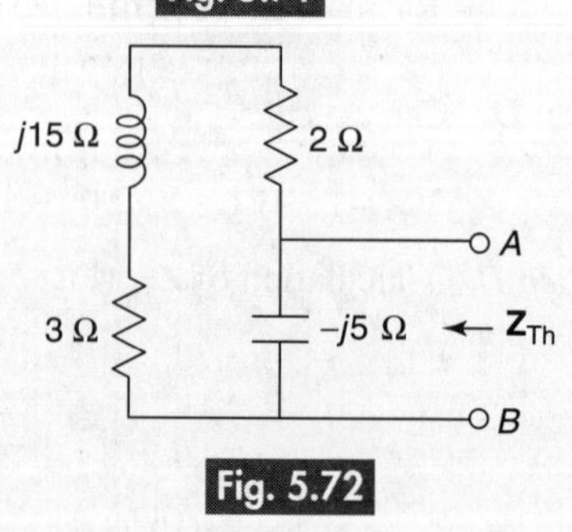


Fig. 5.72

***Step III*** Thevenin's Equivalent Network (Fig. 5.73)

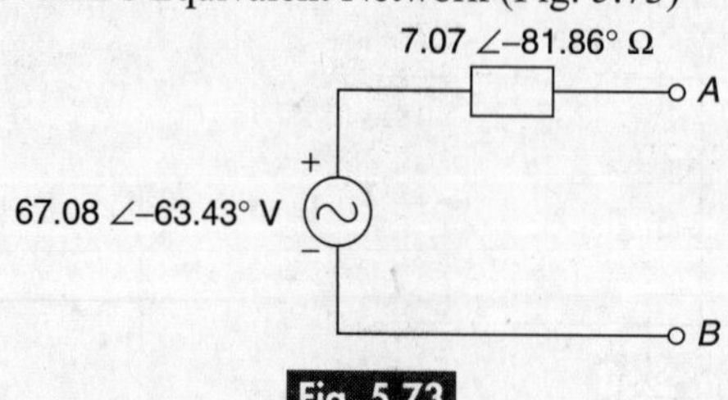


Fig. 5.73

## EXAMPLE 5.32

*Obtain Thevenin's equivalent network for Fig. 5.74.*

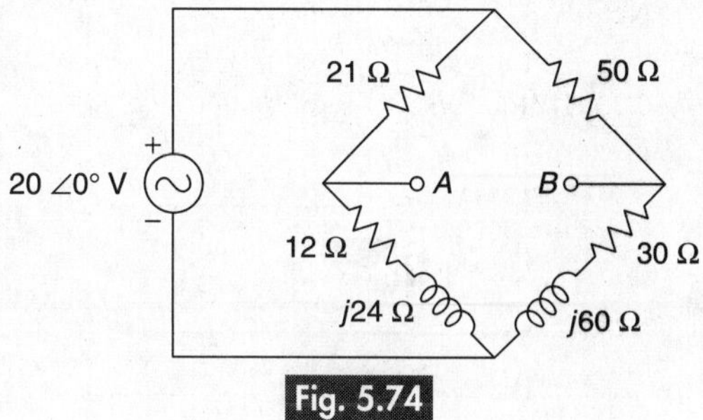


Fig. 5.74

### Solution

***Step I*** Calculation of $\mathbf{V}_{\text{Th}}$ (Fig. 5.75)

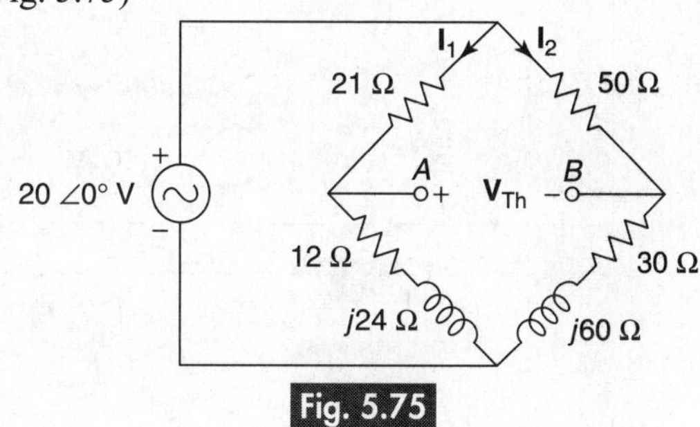


Fig. 5.75

$$\mathbf{I}_1 = \frac{20\angle 0^\circ}{21+12+j24} = 0.49\angle -36.02^\circ \text{ A}$$

$$\mathbf{I}_2 = \frac{20\angle 0^\circ}{80+j60} = 0.2\angle -36.86^\circ \text{ A}$$

$$\begin{aligned}\mathbf{V}_{\text{Th}} &= (12+j24)\,\mathbf{I}_1 - (30+j60)\,\mathbf{I}_2 \\ &= (26.83\angle 63.43^\circ)(0.49\angle -36.02^\circ) - (67.08\angle 63.43^\circ)(0.2\angle -36.86^\circ) \\ &= 0.33\angle 171.12^\circ \text{ V}\end{aligned}$$

***Step II*** Calculation of $\mathbf{Z}_{\text{Th}}$ (Fig. 5.76)

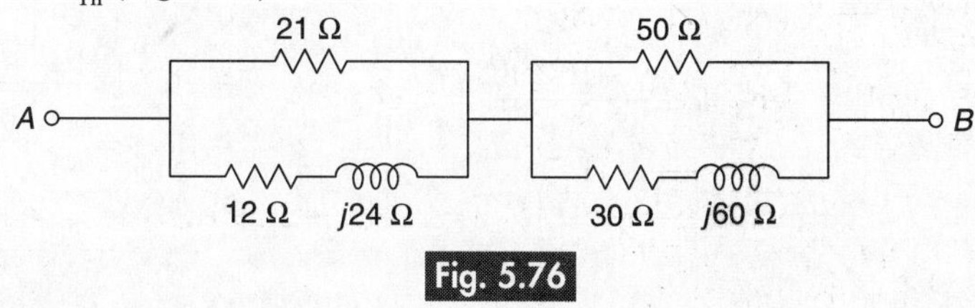


Fig. 5.76

$$\mathbf{Z}_{\text{Th}} = \frac{21(12+j24)}{33+j24} + \frac{50(30+j60)}{80+j60} = 47.4\angle 26.8^\circ \ \Omega$$

***Step III*** Thevenin's Equivalent Network (Fig. 5.77)

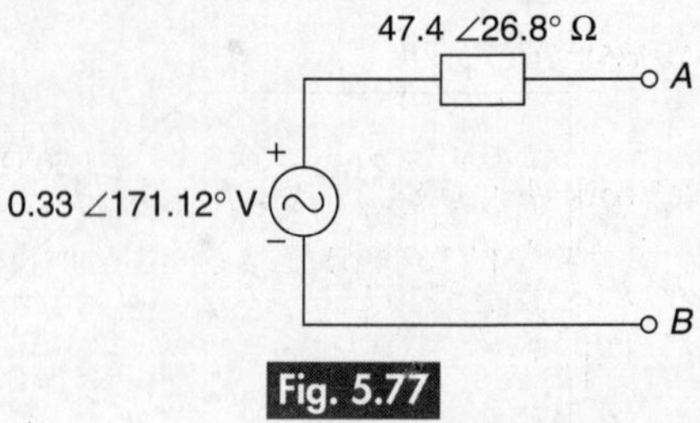


Fig. 5.77

## EXAMPLE 5.33

*Find Thevenin's equivalent network across terminals A and B for Fig. 5.78.*

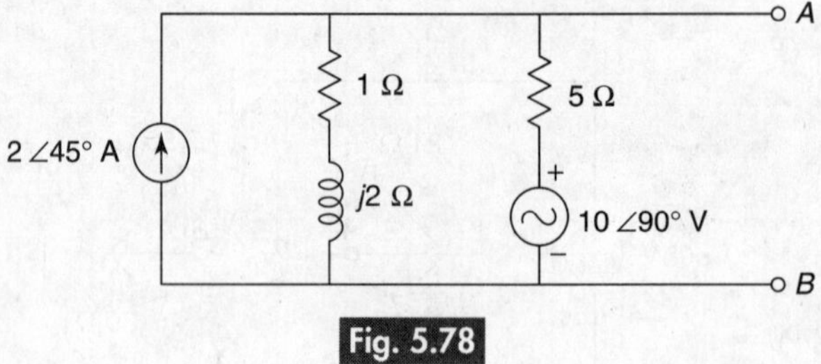


Fig. 5.78

### Solution

***Step I*** Calculation of $\mathbf{V}_{Th}$ (Fig. 5.79)

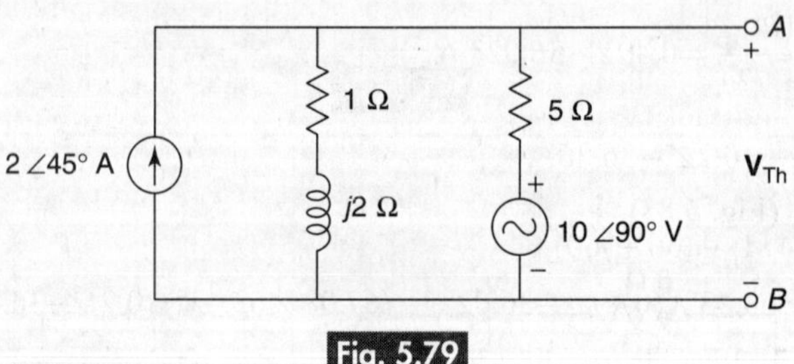


Fig. 5.79

Applying KCL at the node,

$$\frac{\mathbf{V}_{Th}}{1+j2}+\frac{\mathbf{V}_{Th}-10\angle 90°}{5}=2\angle 45°$$

$$\left(\frac{1}{1+j2}+\frac{1}{5}\right)\mathbf{V}_{Th}=2\angle 45°+2\angle 90°$$

$$(0.57\angle -45°)\mathbf{V}_{Th}=3.7\angle 67.5°$$

$$\mathbf{V}_{Th}=6.49\angle 112.5°\text{ V}$$

***Step II*** Calculation of $\mathbf{Z}_{\text{Th}}$ (Fig. 5.80)

$$\mathbf{Z}_{\text{Th}} = \frac{5(1+j2)}{5+1+j2} = 1.77\angle 45°\ \Omega$$

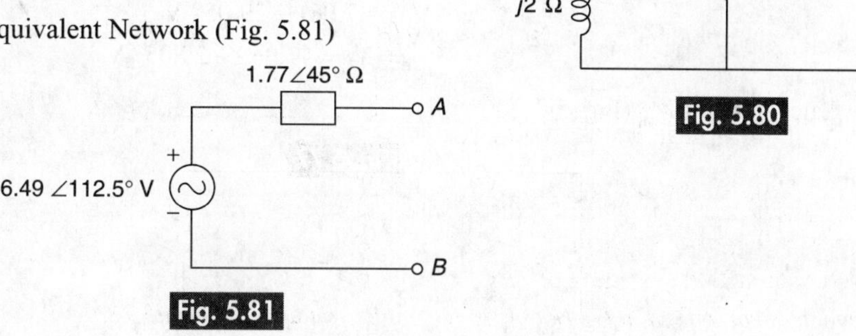


Fig. 5.80

***Step III*** Thevenin's Equivalent Network (Fig. 5.81)



Fig. 5.81

## EXAMPLE 5.34

*Find the current through the $(5+j2)\ \Omega$ impedance in the network of Fig. 5.82.*

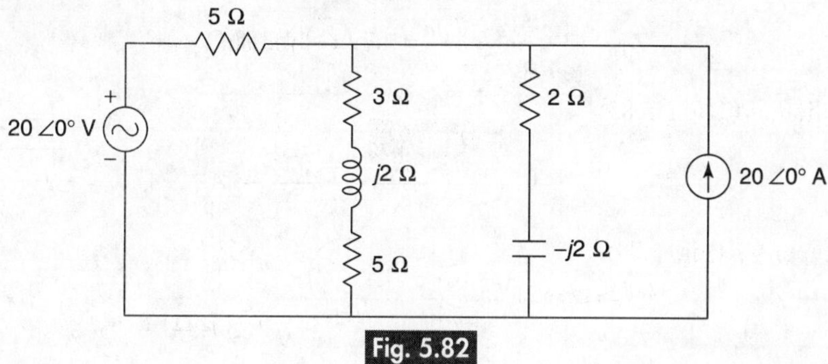


Fig. 5.82

**Solution**

***Step I*** Calculation of $\mathbf{V}_{\text{Th}}$ (Fig. 5.83)

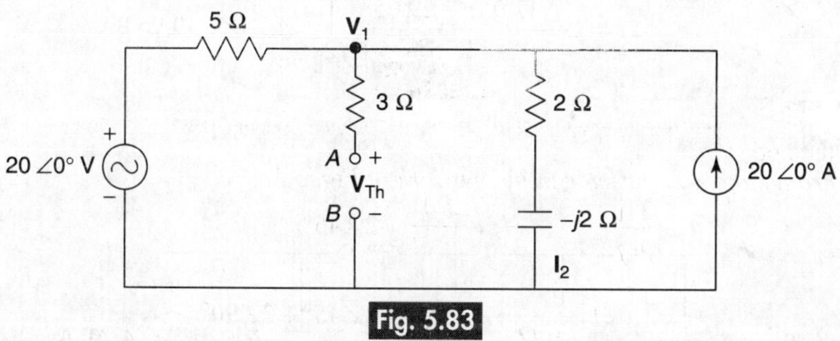


Fig. 5.83

Applying KCL at the node,

$$\frac{\mathbf{V}_1 - 20\angle 0°}{5} + \frac{\mathbf{V}_1}{2-j2} = 20\angle 0°$$

$$\left(\frac{1}{5}+\frac{1}{2-j2}\right)\mathbf{V}_1 = 20\angle 0° + 4\angle 0°$$

$$0.51\angle 29.05°\ \mathbf{V}_1 = 24\angle 0°$$

$$\mathbf{V}_1 = 47.06\angle -29.05°\ \text{V}$$

$$\mathbf{V}_{\text{Th}} = \mathbf{V}_1 = 47.06\angle -29.05°\ \text{V}$$

***Step II*** Calculation of $\mathbf{Z}_{\text{Th}}$ (Fig. 5.84)

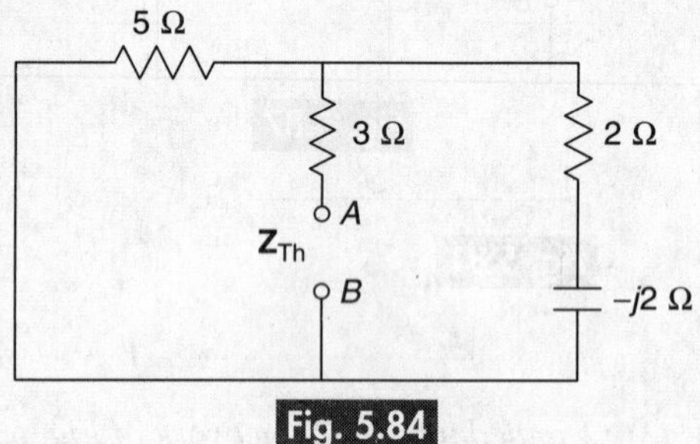


Fig. 5.84

$$\mathbf{Z}_{\text{Th}} = 3 + \frac{5(2-j2)}{5+2-j2} = 4.79\angle -11.35°\ \Omega$$

***Step III*** Calculation of $\mathbf{I}_L$ (Fig. 5.85)

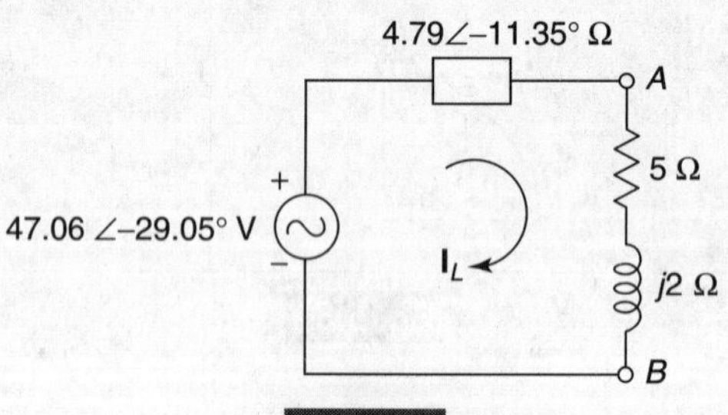


Fig. 5.85

$$\mathbf{I}_L = \frac{47.06\angle -29.05°}{4.79\angle -11.35° + 5 + j2} = 4.73\angle -39.96°\ \text{A}$$

## EXAMPLE 5.35

*Find the current through the 5 Ω resistor in the network of Fig. 5.86.*

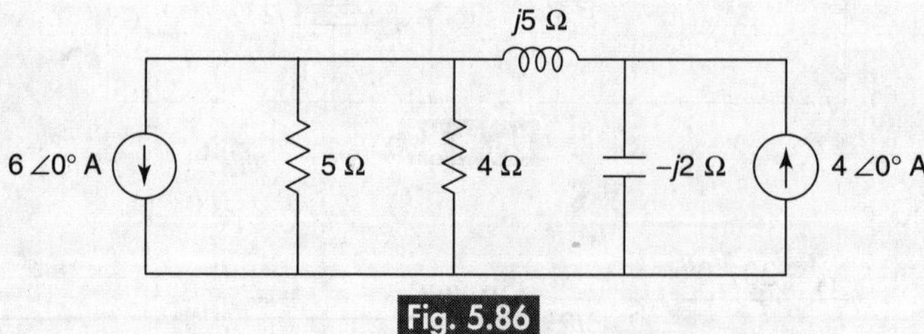


Fig. 5.86

## Solution

***Step I*** Calculation of $\mathbf{V}_{Th}$ (Fig. 5.87)

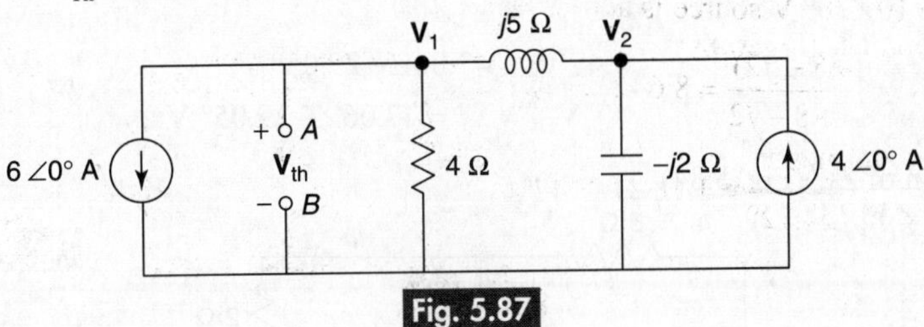


Fig. 5.87

Applying KCL at node 1,

$$\frac{\mathbf{V}_1}{4}+\frac{\mathbf{V}_1-\mathbf{V}_2}{j5}+6\angle 0^\circ=0$$

$$\left(\frac{1}{4}+\frac{1}{j5}\right)\mathbf{V}_1-\frac{1}{j5}\mathbf{V}_2=-6\angle 0^\circ$$

$$(0.25-j0.2)\mathbf{V}_1+j0.2\mathbf{V}_2=-6\angle 0^\circ \qquad \text{...(i)}$$

Applying KCL at node 2,

$$\frac{\mathbf{V}_2-\mathbf{V}_1}{j5}+\frac{\mathbf{V}_2}{-j2}=4\angle 0^\circ$$

$$\left(-\frac{1}{j5}\right)\mathbf{V}_1+\left(\frac{1}{j5}-\frac{1}{j2}\right)\mathbf{V}_2=4\angle 0^\circ$$

$$j0.2\,\mathbf{V}_1+j0.3\,\mathbf{V}_2=4\angle 0^\circ \qquad \text{...(ii)}$$

Writing Eqs (i) and (ii) in matrix form,

$$\begin{bmatrix}0.25-j0.2 & j0.2\\ j0.2 & j0.3\end{bmatrix}\begin{bmatrix}\mathbf{V}_1\\ \mathbf{V}_2\end{bmatrix}=\begin{bmatrix}-6\angle 0^\circ\\ 4\angle 0^\circ\end{bmatrix}$$

By Cramer's rule,

$$\mathbf{V}_1=\frac{\begin{vmatrix}-6\angle 0^\circ & j0.2\\ 4\angle 0^\circ & j0.3\end{vmatrix}}{\begin{vmatrix}0.25-j0.2 & j0.2\\ j0.2 & j0.3\end{vmatrix}}=20.8\angle -126.87^\circ\text{ V}$$

$$\mathbf{V}_{Th}=\mathbf{V}_1=20.8\angle -126.87^\circ\text{ V}$$

***Step II*** Calculation of $\mathbf{Z}_{Th}$ (Fig. 5.88)

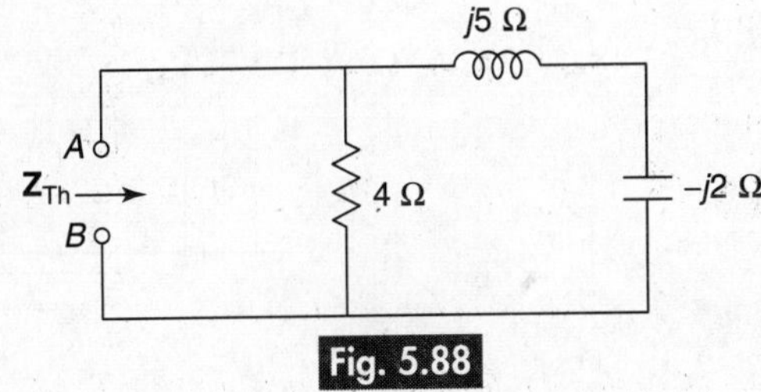


Fig. 5.88

$$\mathbf{Z}_{\text{Th}} = \frac{4(-j2+j5)}{4-j2+j5} = 2.4\angle 53.13°\ \Omega$$

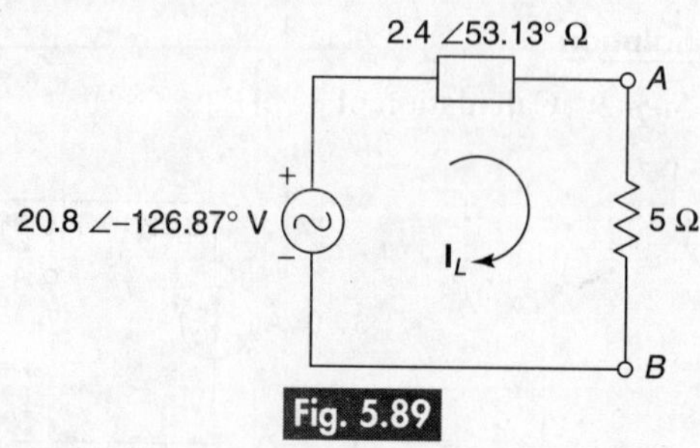

Fig. 5.89

***Step III*** Calculation of $\mathbf{I}_L$ (Fig. 5.89)

$$\mathbf{I}_L = \frac{20.8\angle -126.87°}{2.4\angle 53.13° + 5} = 3.1\angle -143.47°\ \text{A}$$

## EXAMPLE 5.36

*In the network of Fig. 5.90, find the current through the 10 Ω resistor.*

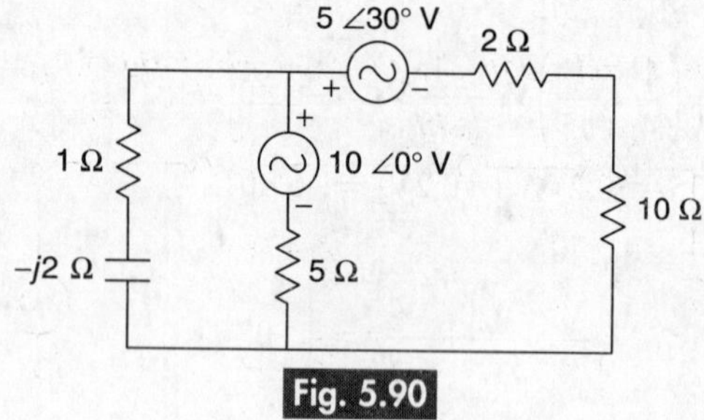

Fig. 5.90

**Solution**

***Step I*** Calculation of $\mathbf{V}_{\text{Th}}$ (Fig. 5.91)

Applying KVL to the mesh,

$$j2\mathbf{I} - 1\mathbf{I} - 10\angle 0° - 5\mathbf{I} = 0$$

$$(j2-6)\mathbf{I} = 10\angle 0°$$

$$\mathbf{I} = 1.58\angle -161.57°\ \text{A}$$

Writing $\mathbf{V}_{\text{Th}}$ equation,

$$5\mathbf{I} + 10\angle 0° - 5\angle 30° - 0 - \mathbf{V}_{\text{Th}} = 0$$

$$5(1.58\angle -161.57°) - 10\angle 0° - 5\angle 30° - \mathbf{V}_{\text{Th}} = 0$$

$$\mathbf{V}_{\text{Th}} = 5.32\angle -110.06°\ \text{V}$$

Fig. 5.91

***Step II*** Calculation of $\mathbf{Z}_{\text{Th}}$ (Fig. 5.92)

$$\mathbf{Z}_{\text{Th}} = 2 + \frac{5(1-j2)}{5+1-j2} = 3.48\angle -21.04°\ \Omega$$

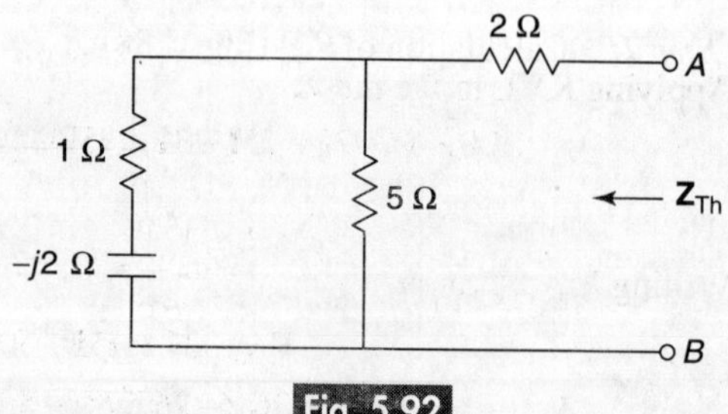

Fig. 5.92

***Step III*** Calculation of $\mathbf{I}_L$ (Fig. 5.93)

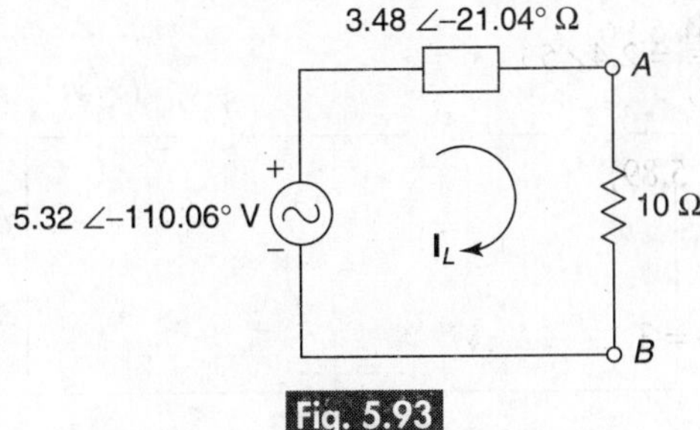


Fig. 5.93

$$\mathbf{I}_L = \frac{5.32\angle-110.06^\circ}{3.48\angle-21.04^\circ+10} = 0.4\angle-104.67^\circ \text{ A}$$

## EXAMPLE 5.37

*Find the current through (4 + j6) Ω impedance in the network of Fig. 5.94.*

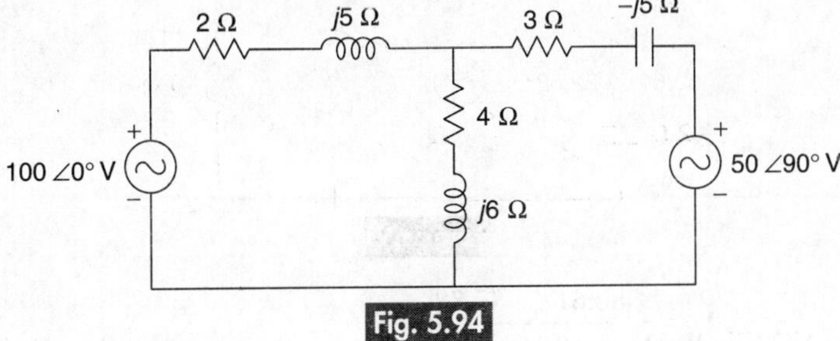


Fig. 5.94

**Solution**

***Step I*** Calculation of $\mathbf{V}_{\text{Th}}$ (Fig. 5.95)

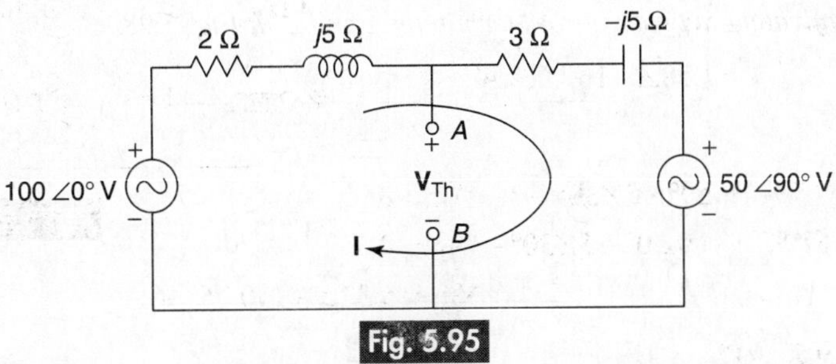


Fig. 5.95

Applying KVL to the mesh,

$$100\angle0^\circ - 2\mathbf{I} - j5\mathbf{I} - 3\mathbf{I} + j5\mathbf{I} - 50\angle90^\circ = 0$$

$$\mathbf{I} = 22.36\angle-26.57^\circ \text{ A}$$

Writing $\mathbf{V}_{\text{Th}}$ equation,

$$\mathbf{V}_{\text{Th}} - 3\mathbf{I} + j5\mathbf{I} - 50\angle90^\circ = 0$$

$$\mathbf{V}_{\text{Th}} - (3 - j5)(22.36\angle-26.57^\circ) - 50\angle90^\circ = 0$$

$$\mathbf{V}_{\text{Th}} = 80.61\angle-82.88^\circ \text{ V}$$

***Step II*** Calculation of $\mathbf{Z}_{\text{Th}}$ (Fig. 5.96)

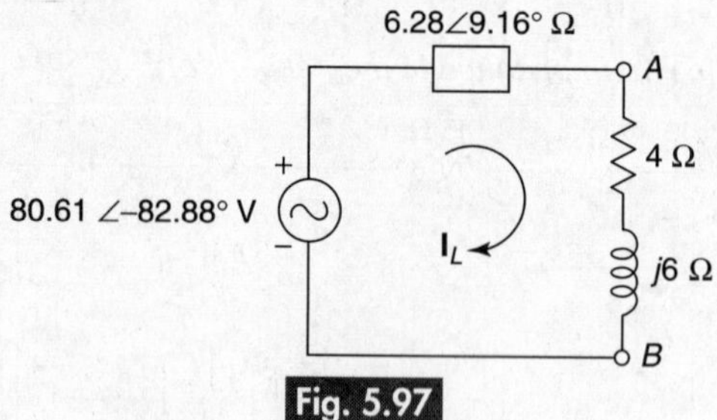


Fig. 5.96

$$\mathbf{Z}_{\text{Th}} = \frac{(2+j5)(3-j5)}{2+j5+3-j5} = 6.28\angle 9.16°\ \Omega$$

***Step III*** Calculation of $\mathbf{I}_L$ (Fig. 5.97)

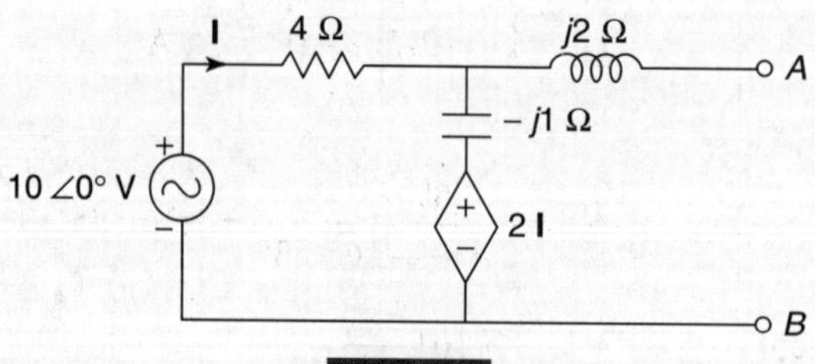


Fig. 5.97

$$\mathbf{I}_L = \frac{80.61\angle -82.88°}{6.28\angle 9.16° + 4 + j6} = 6.52\angle -117.34°\ \text{A}$$

## EXAMPLE 5.38

*Obtain Thevenin's equivalent network across terminals A and B in Fig. 5.98.*



Fig. 5.98

**Solution**

***Step I*** Calculation of $\mathbf{V}_{\text{Th}}$ (Fig. 5.99)

Applying KVL to the mesh,

$$10\angle 0° - 4\mathbf{I} + j1\mathbf{I} - 2\mathbf{I} = 0$$

$$\mathbf{I} = 1.64\angle 9.46°\ \text{A}$$

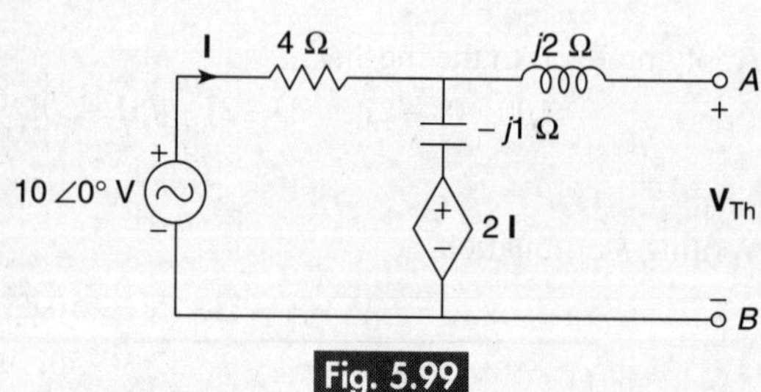


Fig. 5.99

Writing $\mathbf{V}_{\text{Th}}$ equation,

$$10\angle 0° - 4\mathbf{I} - 0 - \mathbf{V}_{\text{Th}} = 0$$

$$10\angle 0° - 4(1.64\angle 9.46°) - \mathbf{V}_{\text{Th}} = 0$$

$$\mathbf{V}_{\text{Th}} = 3.69\angle -17° \text{ V}$$

***Step II*** Calculation of $\mathbf{I}_N$ (Fig. 5.100)

From Fig. 5.100,

$$\mathbf{I} = \mathbf{I}_1$$

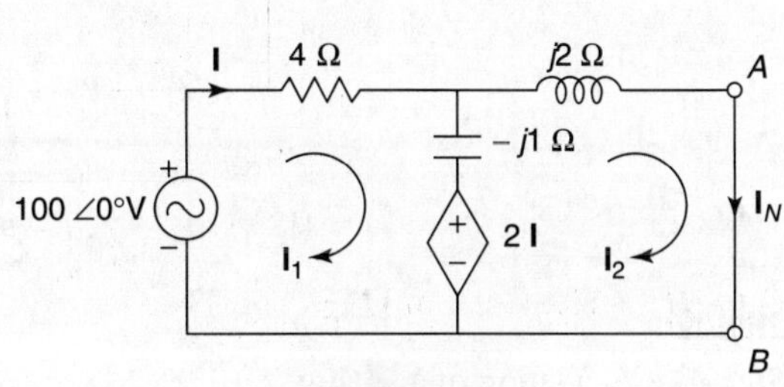


Fig. 5.100

Applying KVL to mesh 1,

$$10\angle 0° - 4\mathbf{I}_1 + j1(\mathbf{I}_1 - \mathbf{I}_2) - 2\mathbf{I} = 0$$

$$10\angle 0° - 4\mathbf{I}_1 + j1\mathbf{I}_1 - j1\mathbf{I}_2 - 2\mathbf{I}_1 = 0$$

$$(6 - j1)\,\mathbf{I}_1 + j1\mathbf{I}_2 = 10\angle 0° \quad \text{...(i)}$$

Applying KVL to mesh 2,

$$2\mathbf{I} + j1(\mathbf{I}_2 - \mathbf{I}_1) - j2\mathbf{I}_2 = 0$$

$$2\mathbf{I}_1 + j1\mathbf{I}_2 - j1\mathbf{I}_1 - j_2\mathbf{I}_2 = 0$$

$$(2 - j1)\mathbf{I}_1 - j1\mathbf{I}_2 = 0 \quad \text{...(ii)}$$

Writing Eqs (i) and (ii) in matrix form,

$$\begin{bmatrix} 6 - j1 & j1 \\ 2 - j1 & -j1 \end{bmatrix} \begin{bmatrix} \mathbf{I}_1 \\ \mathbf{I}_2 \end{bmatrix} = \begin{bmatrix} 10\angle 0° \\ 0 \end{bmatrix}$$

By Cramer's rule,

$$\mathbf{I}_2 = \frac{\begin{vmatrix} 6 - j1 & 10\angle 0° \\ 2 - j1 & 0 \end{vmatrix}}{\begin{vmatrix} 6 - j1 & j1 \\ 2 - j1 & -j1 \end{vmatrix}} = 2.71\angle -102.53° \text{ A}$$

$$\mathbf{I}_N = \mathbf{I}_2 = 2.71\angle -102.53° \text{ A}$$

***Step III*** Calculation of $\mathbf{Z}_{\text{Th}}$

$$\mathbf{Z}_{\text{Th}} = \frac{\mathbf{V}_{\text{Th}}}{\mathbf{I}_N} = \frac{3.69\angle -17°}{2.71\angle -102.53°} = 1.36\angle 85.53° \ \Omega$$

***Step IV*** Thevenin's Equivalent Network (Fig. 5.101)

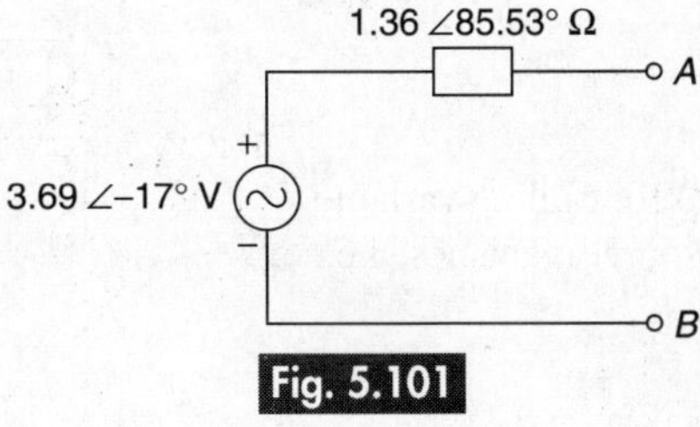


Fig. 5.101

## EXAMPLE 5.39

*Find Thevenin's equivalent network across terminals A and B for Fig. 5.102.*

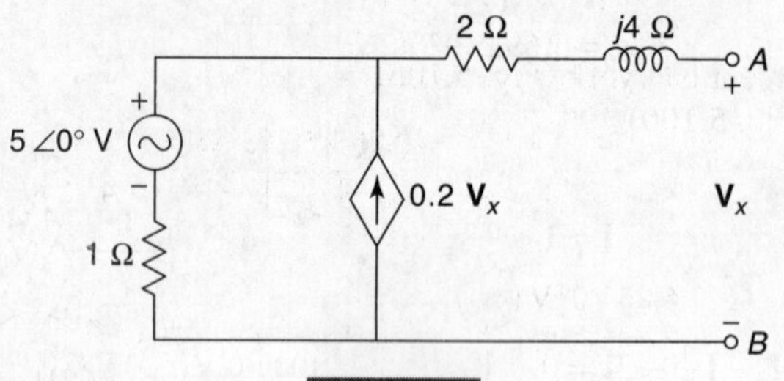


Fig. 5.102

**Solution**

***Step I*** Calculation of $\mathbf{V}_{\text{Th}}$ (Fig. 5.103)

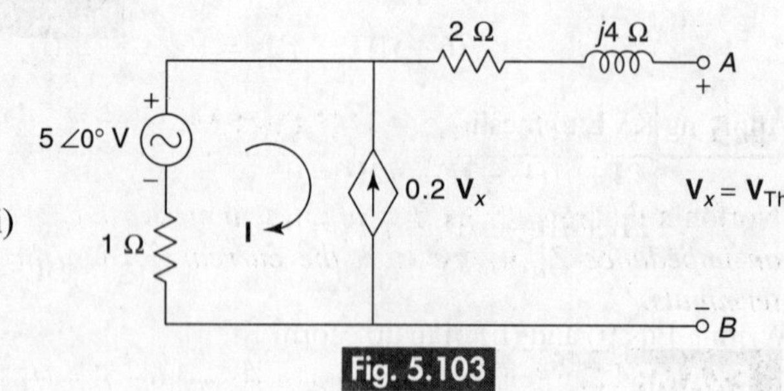


Fig. 5.103

From Fig. 5.103,

$$\mathbf{I} = -0.2\,\mathbf{V}_x \qquad \text{... (i)}$$

Writing $\mathbf{V}_{\text{Th}}$ equation,

$$-\mathbf{I} + 5\angle 0° - 0 - \mathbf{V}_x = 0$$

$$0.2\mathbf{V}_x + 5\angle 0° - \mathbf{V}_x = 0$$

$$\mathbf{V}_x = 6.25\angle 0° \text{ V}$$

$$\mathbf{V}_{\text{Th}} = \mathbf{V}_x = 6.25\angle 0° \text{ V}$$

***Step II*** Calculation of $\mathbf{I}_N$ (Fig. 5.104)

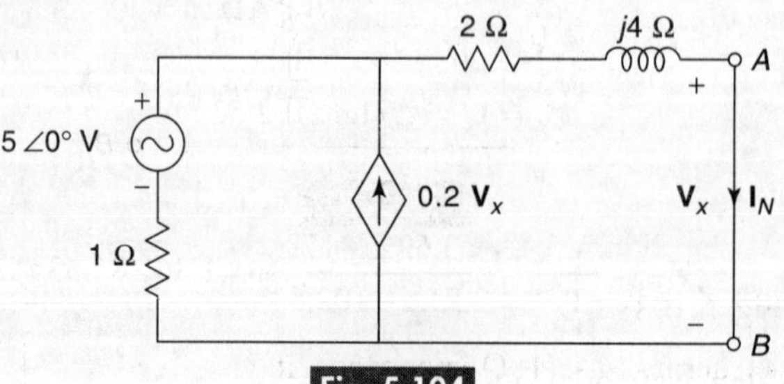


Fig. 5.104

From Fig. 5.104,

$$\mathbf{V}_x = 0$$

The dependent source depends on the controlling variable $\mathbf{V}_x$. When $\mathbf{V}_x = 0$, the dependent source vanishes, i.e., $0.2\,\mathbf{V}_x = 0$, as shown in Fig. 5.105.

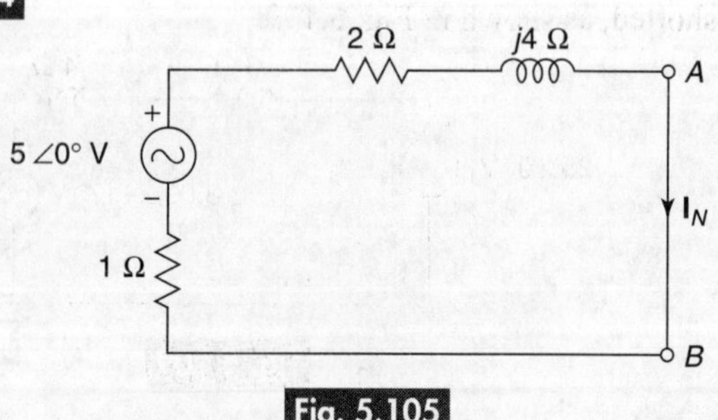


Fig. 5.105

$$\mathbf{I}_N = \frac{5\angle 0°}{1+2+j4} = 1\angle -53.13° \text{ A}$$

***Step III*** Calculation of $\mathbf{Z}_{\text{Th}}$

$$\mathbf{Z}_{\text{Th}} = \frac{\mathbf{V}_{\text{Th}}}{\mathbf{I}_N} = \frac{6.25\angle 0°}{1\angle -53.13°} = 6.25\angle 53.13°\ \Omega$$

***Step IV*** Thevenin's Equivalent Network (Fig. 5.106)

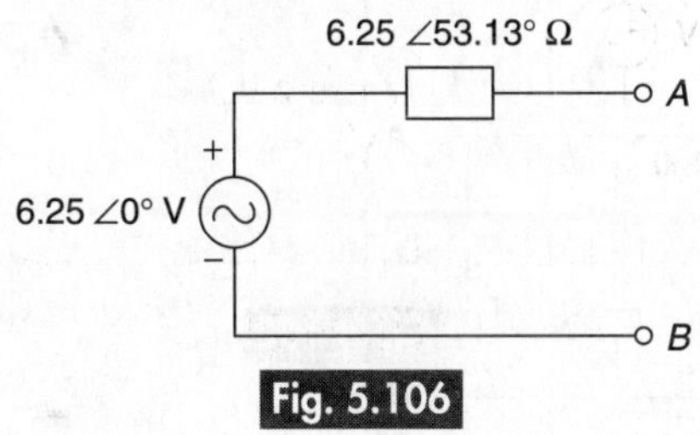


Fig. 5.106

## 5.5 NORTON'S THEOREM

LO 5.3

Norton's theorem states that *any linear network can be replaced by a current source* $\mathbf{I}_N$ *parallel with an impedance* $\mathbf{Z}_N$ *where* $\mathbf{I}_N$ *is the current flowing through the short-circuited path placed across the terminals.*

### EXAMPLE 5.40

*Obtain Norton's equivalent network between terminals A and B, as shown in Fig. 5.107.*

Fig. 5.107

**Solution**

***Step I*** Calculation of $\mathbf{I}_N$ (Fig. 5.108)

When a short circuit is placed across $(4 - j4)\ \Omega$ impedance, it gets shorted, as shown in Fig. 5.109.

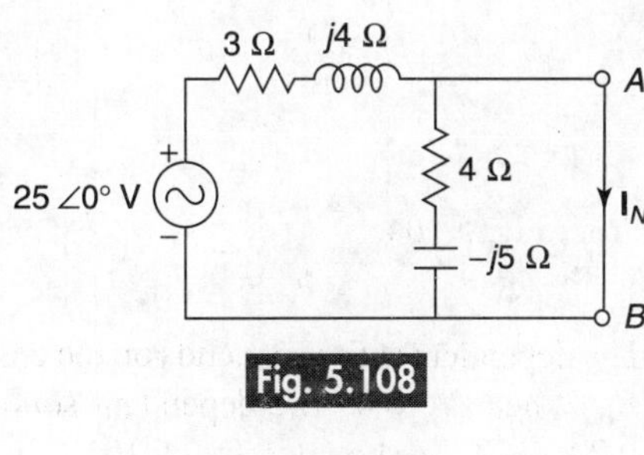


Fig. 5.108

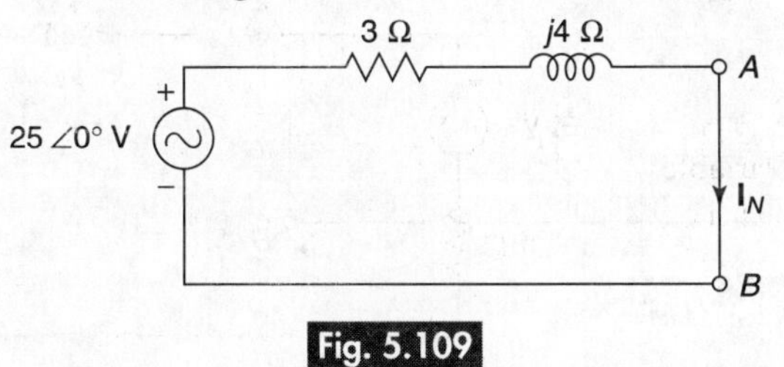


Fig. 5.109

$$\mathbf{I}_N = \frac{25\angle 0°}{3 + j4} = 5\angle -53.13° \text{ A}$$

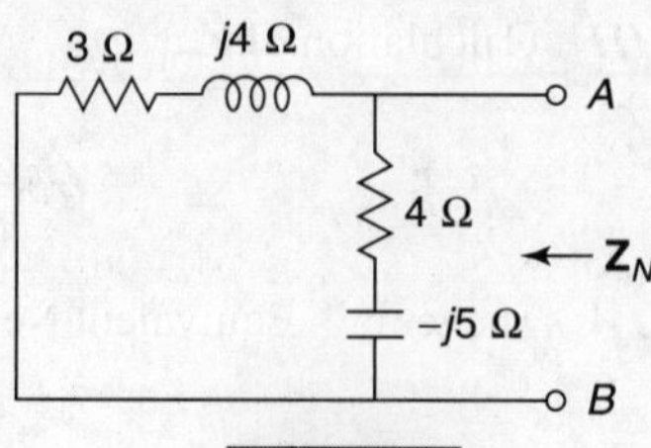

Fig. 5.110

***Step II*** Calculation of $\mathbf{Z}_N$ (Fig. 5.110)

$$\mathbf{Z}_N = \frac{(3 + j4)(4 - j5)}{3 + j4 + 4 - j5} = 4.53\angle 9.92° \ \Omega$$

***Step III*** Norton's Equivalent Network (Fig. 5.111)

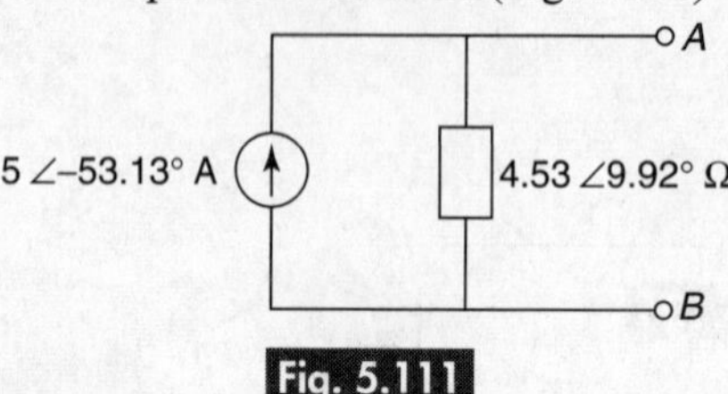

Fig. 5.111

## EXAMPLE 5.41

*Obtain Norton's equivalent network at the terminals A and B in Fig. 5.112.*

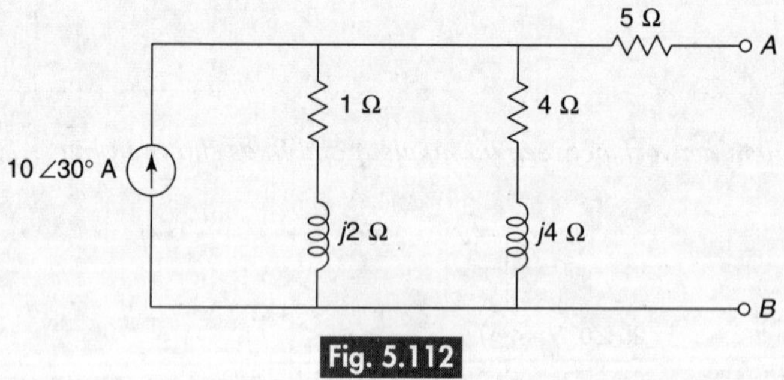

Fig. 5.112

**Solution**

***Step I*** Calculation of $\mathbf{I}_N$ (Fig. 5.113)

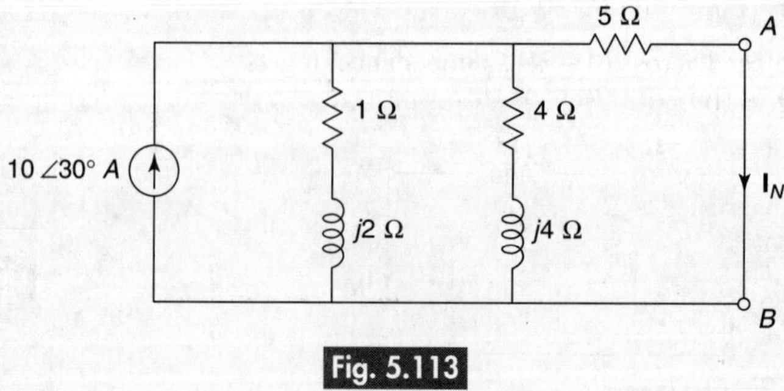

Fig. 5.113

By series–parallel reduction technique (Fig. 5.114)

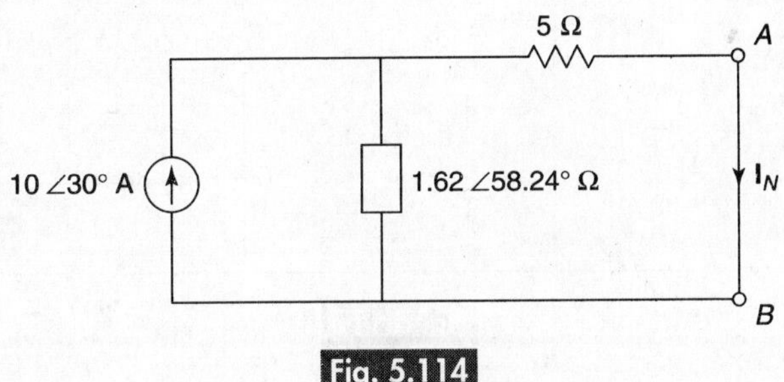


Fig. 5.114

$$\mathbf{I}_N = (10\angle 30°)\left(\frac{1.62\angle 58.24°}{1.62\angle 58.24° + 5}\right) = 2.69\angle 75°\ \text{A}$$

***Step II*** Calculation of $\mathbf{Z}_N$ (Fig. 5.115)

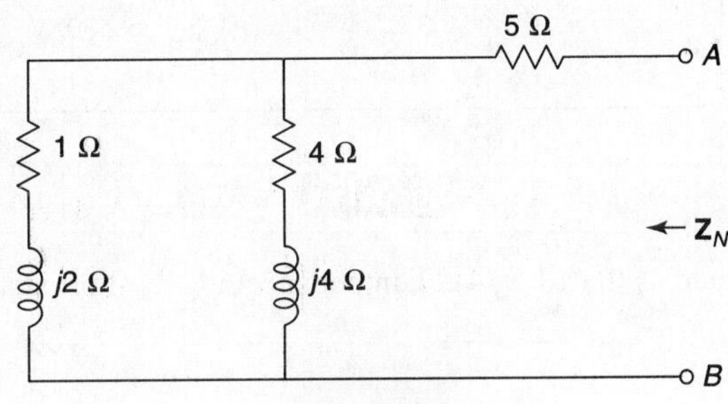


Fig. 5.115

$$\mathbf{Z}_N = 5 + \frac{(1+j2)(4+j4)}{1+j2+4+j4} = 6.01\angle 13.24°\ \Omega$$

***Step III*** Norton's Equivalent Network (Fig. 5.116)

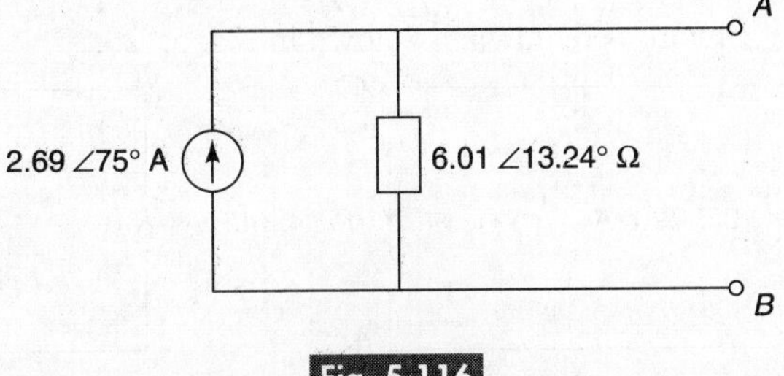


Fig. 5.116

## EXAMPLE 5.42

*Find Norton's equivalent network across terminals A and B in Fig. 5.117.*

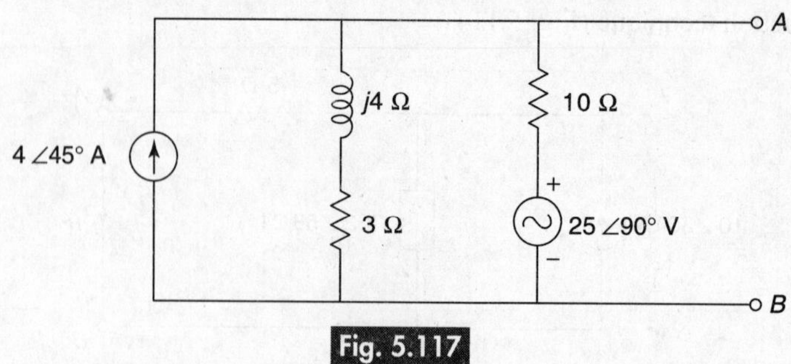


Fig. 5.117

**Solution**

***Step I*** Calculation of $\mathbf{I}_N$ (Fig. 5.118)

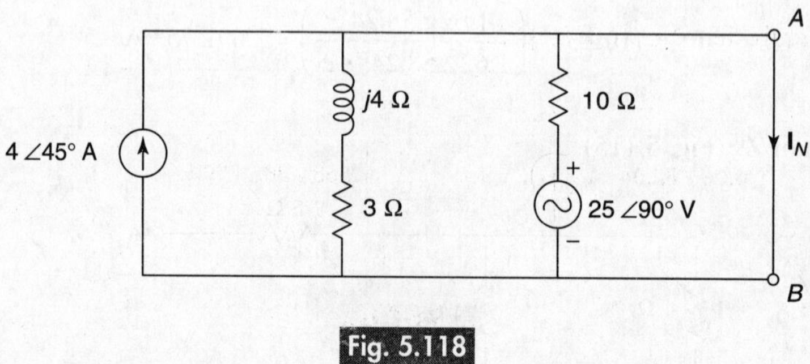


Fig. 5.118

When a short circuit is placed across the $(3+j4)\ \Omega$ impedance, it gets shorted, as shown in Fig. 5.119.

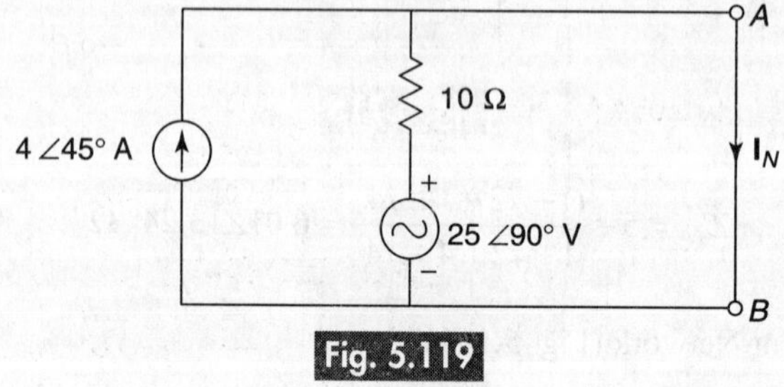


Fig. 5.119

By source transformation, the network is redrawn, as shown in Fig. 5.120.

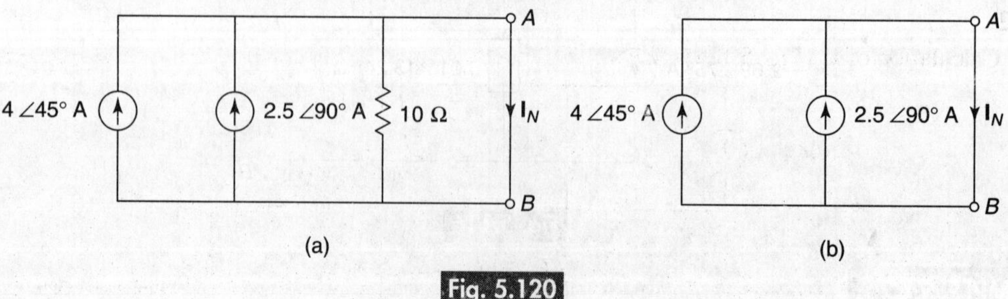


Fig. 5.120

$$I_N = 4\angle 45° + 2.5\angle 90° = 6.03\angle 62.04°\ \text{A}$$

***Step II*** Calculation of $\mathbf{Z}_N$ (Fig. 5.121)

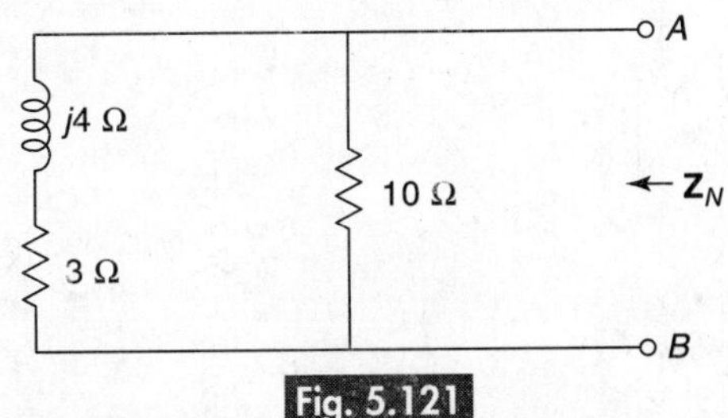


Fig. 5.121

$$\mathbf{Z}_N = \frac{10(3+j4)}{10+3+j4} = 3.68\angle 36.03° \ \Omega$$

***Step III*** Norton's Equivalent Network (Fig. 5.122)

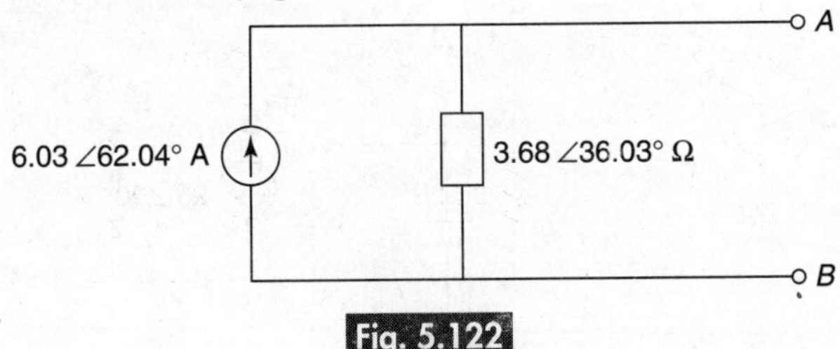


Fig. 5.122

## EXAMPLE 5.43

*Obtain the Norton's equivalent network for Fig. 5.123.*

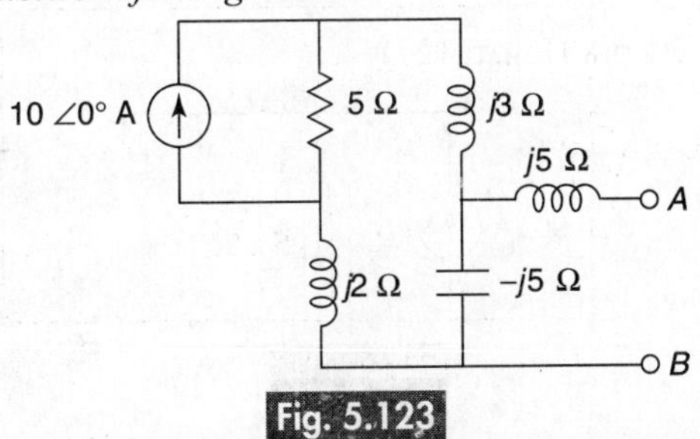


Fig. 5.123

**Solution**

***Step I*** Calculation of $\mathbf{I}_N$ (Fig. 5.124)

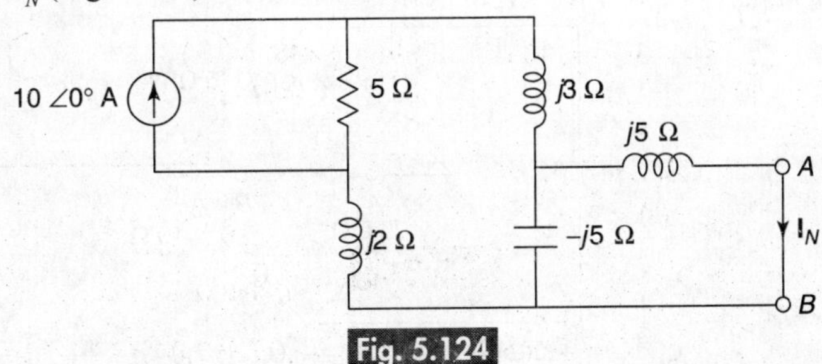


Fig. 5.124

By source transformation, the network can be redrawn, as shown in Fig. 5.125.

Writing KVL equations in matrix form,

$$\begin{bmatrix} 5 & j5 \\ j5 & 0 \end{bmatrix}\begin{bmatrix} \mathbf{I}_1 \\ \mathbf{I}_2 \end{bmatrix} = \begin{bmatrix} 50\angle 0^\circ \\ 0 \end{bmatrix}$$

Fig. 5.125

By Cramer's rule,

$$\mathbf{I}_2 = \frac{\begin{vmatrix} 5 & 50\angle 0^\circ \\ j5 & 0 \end{vmatrix}}{\begin{vmatrix} 5 & j5 \\ j5 & 0 \end{vmatrix}} = 10\angle -90^\circ \text{ A}$$

$$\mathbf{I}_N = \mathbf{I}_2 = 10\angle -90^\circ \text{ A}$$

***Step II*** Calculation of $\mathbf{Z}_N$ (Fig. 5.126)

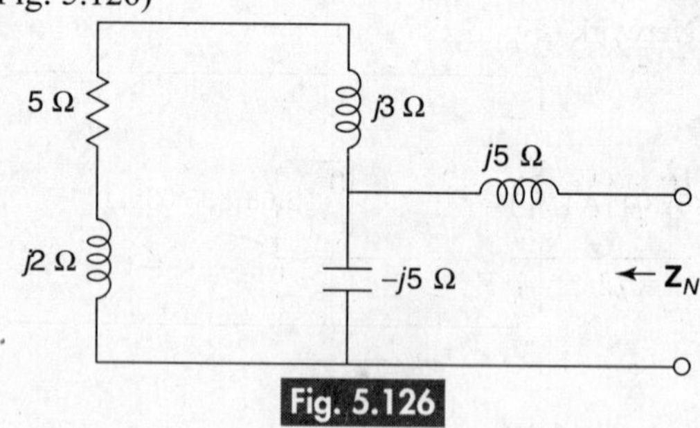


Fig. 5.126

$$\mathbf{Z}_N = j5 + \frac{(5+j5)(-j5)}{5+j5-j5} = 5\ \Omega$$

***Step III*** Norton's Equivalent Network (Fig. 5.127)

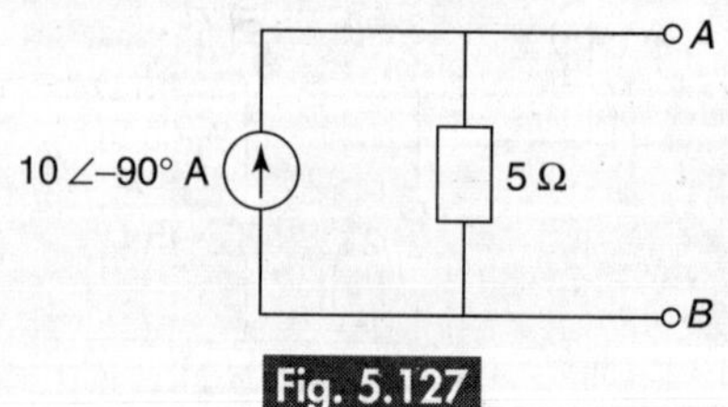


Fig. 5.127

## EXAMPLE 5.44

*Obtain Norton's equivalent network for Fig. 5.128.*

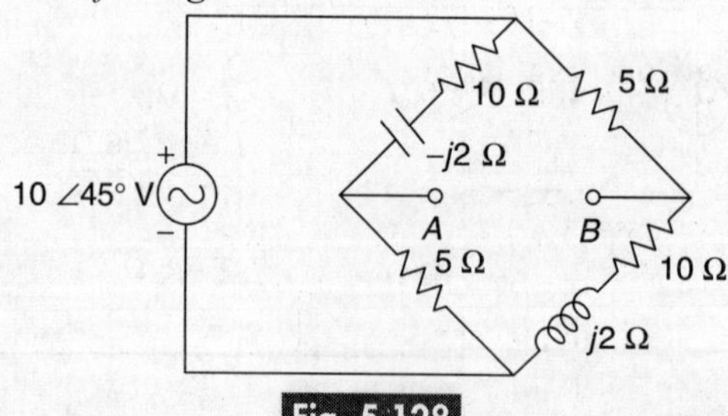


Fig. 5.128

## Solution

***Step I*** Calculation of $\mathbf{I}_N$ (Fig. 5.129)

Writing KVL equations in matrix form,

$$\begin{bmatrix} 15-j2 & -10+j2 & -5 \\ -10+j2 & 15-j2 & 0 \\ -5 & 0 & 15+j2 \end{bmatrix}\begin{bmatrix} \mathbf{I}_1 \\ \mathbf{I}_2 \\ \mathbf{I}_3 \end{bmatrix} = \begin{bmatrix} 10\angle 45^\circ \\ 0 \\ 0 \end{bmatrix}$$

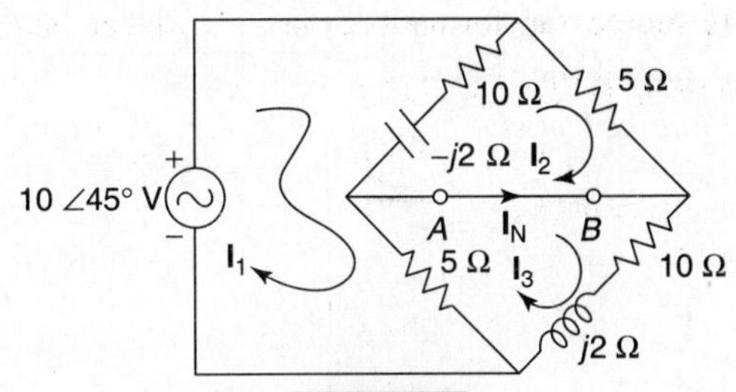


Fig. 5.129

By Cramer's rule,

$$\mathbf{I}_2 = \frac{\begin{vmatrix} 15-j2 & 10\angle 45^\circ & -5 \\ -10+j2 & 0 & 0 \\ -5 & 0 & 15+j2 \end{vmatrix}}{\begin{vmatrix} 15-j2 & -10+j2 & -5 \\ -10+j2 & 15-j2 & 0 \\ -5 & 0 & 15+j2 \end{vmatrix}} = 1\angle 41.28^\circ \text{ A}$$

$$\mathbf{I}_3 = \frac{\begin{vmatrix} 15-j2 & -10+j2 & 10\angle 45^\circ \\ -10+j2 & 15-j2 & 0 \\ -5 & 0 & 0 \end{vmatrix}}{\begin{vmatrix} 15-j2 & -10+j2 & -5 \\ -10+j2 & 15-j2 & 0 \\ -5 & 0 & 15+j2 \end{vmatrix}} = 0.49\angle 37.41^\circ \text{ A}$$

$$\mathbf{I}_N = \mathbf{I}_3 - \mathbf{I}_2 = 0.49\angle 37.41 - 1\angle 41.28^\circ = 0.51\angle -135^\circ \text{ A}$$

***Step II*** Calculation of $\mathbf{Z}_N$ (Fig. 5.130)

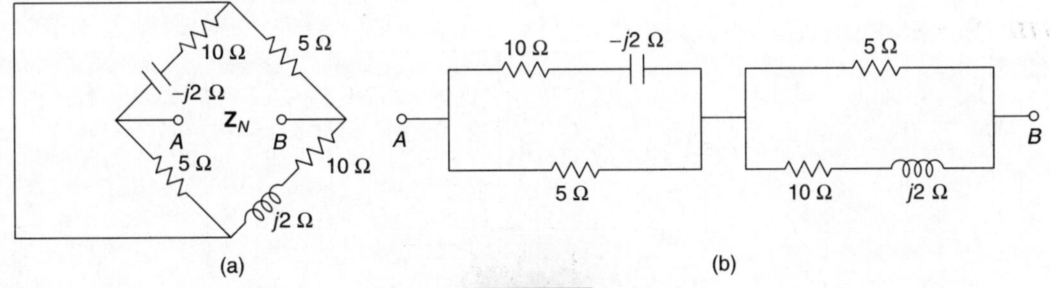


Fig. 5.130

$$\mathbf{Z}_N = \frac{5(10-j2)}{5+10-j2} + \frac{5(10+j2)}{5+10+j2} = 6.72\ \Omega$$

***Step III*** Norton's Equivalent Network (Fig. 5.131)

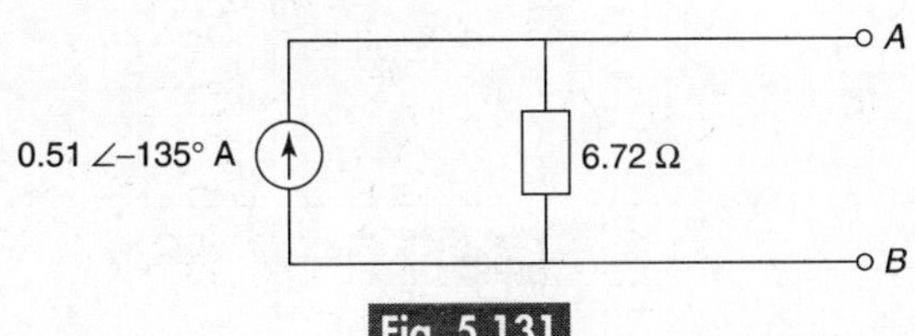


Fig. 5.131

## EXAMPLE 5.45

*Find the current through the 8 Ω resistor in the network of Fig. 5.132.*

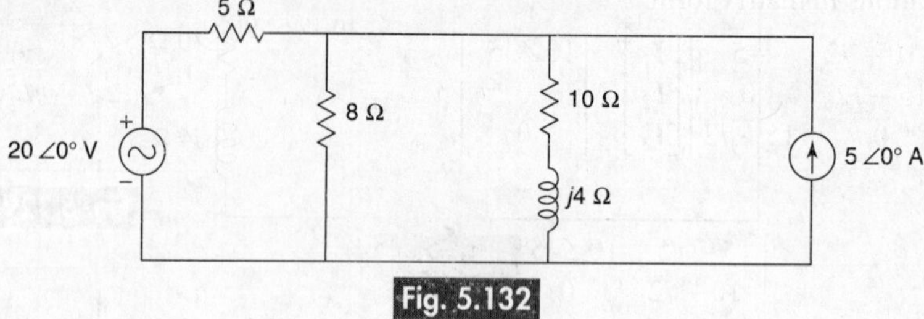


Fig. 5.132

**Solution**

***Step I*** Calculation of $\mathbf{I}_N$ (Fig. 5.133)

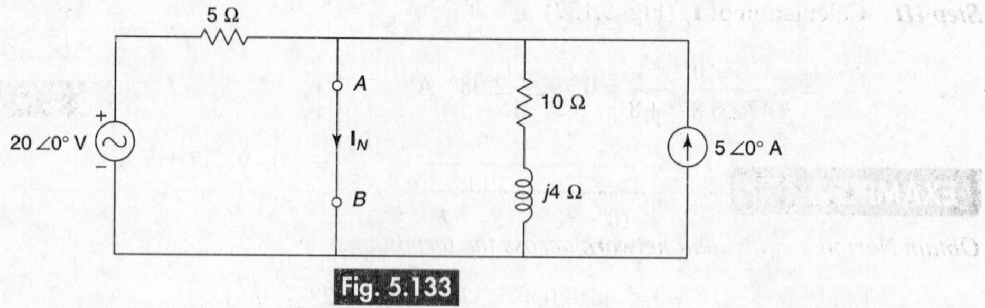


Fig. 5.133

When a short circuit is placed across the $(10 + j4)$ Ω impedance, it gets shorted, as shown in Fig. 5.134.

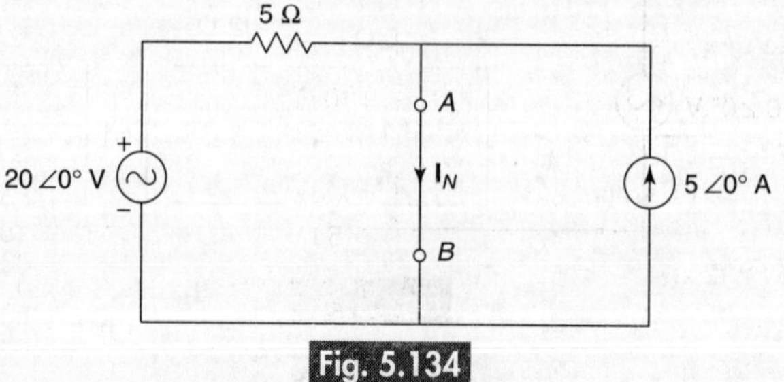


Fig. 5.134

By source transformation, the network is redrawn, as shown in Fig. 5.135.

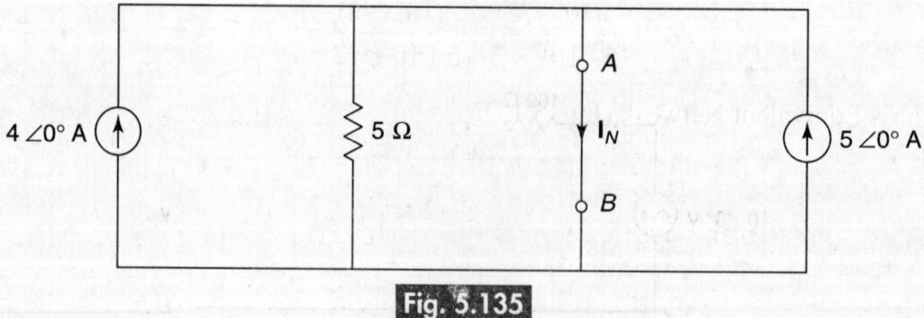


Fig. 5.135

$$\mathbf{I}_N = 4\angle 0° + 5\angle 0° = 9\angle 0° \text{ A}$$

***Step II*** Calculation of $\mathbf{Z}_N$ (Fig. 5.136)

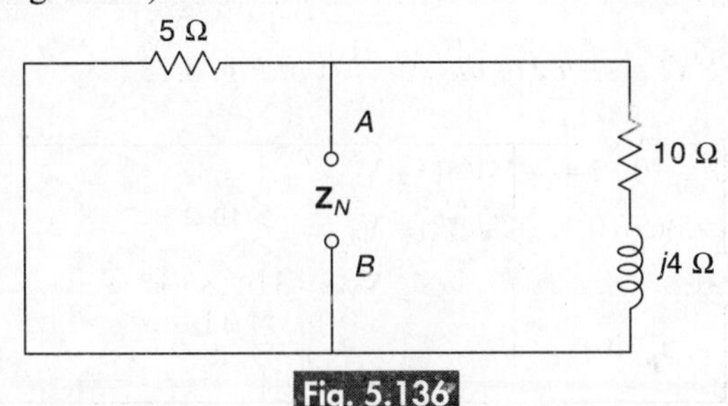

Fig. 5.136

$$\mathbf{Z}_N = \frac{5(10+j4)}{5+10+j4} = 3.47\angle 6.87°\ \Omega$$

***Step III*** Calculation of $\mathbf{I}_L$ (Fig. 5.137)

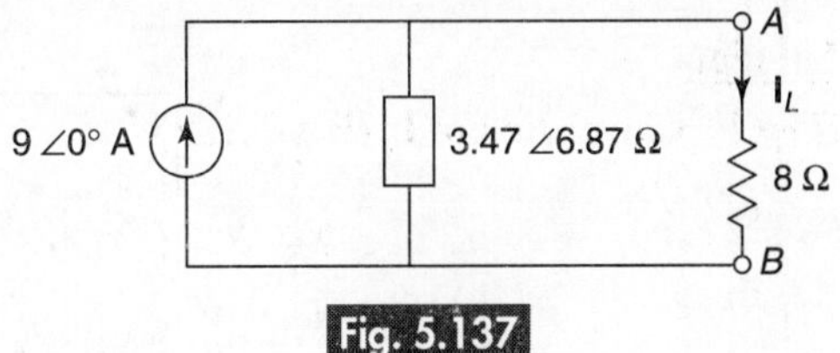

Fig. 5.137

$$\mathbf{I}_L = \frac{9\angle 0°}{3.47\angle 6.87° + 8} = 0.79\angle -2.08°\ \text{A}$$

## EXAMPLE 5.46

*Obtain Norton's equivalent network across the terminals A and B in Fig. 5.138.*

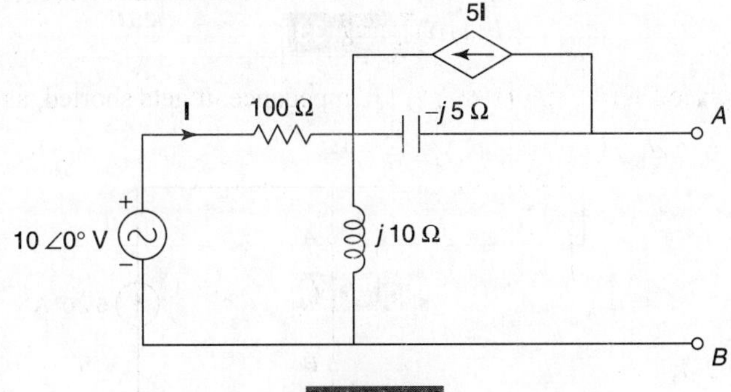

Fig. 5.138

**Solution**

***Step I*** Calculation of $\mathbf{V}_{\text{Th}}$ (Fig. 5.139)

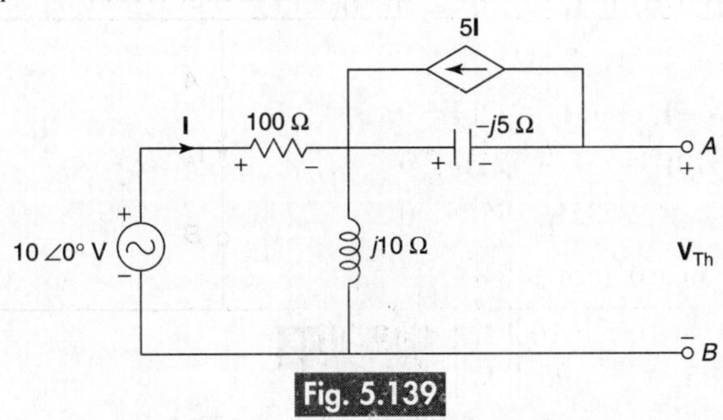

Fig. 5.139

$$\mathbf{I} = \frac{10\angle 0^\circ}{100 + j10} = 0.1\angle -5.71^\circ \text{ A}$$

Writing $\mathbf{V}_{\text{Th}}$ equation,

$$10\angle 0^\circ - 100\,\mathbf{I} - (-j5)(5\mathbf{I}) - \mathbf{V}_{\text{Th}} = 0$$

$$10\angle 0^\circ - 100(0.1\angle -5.71^\circ) + (j5)(5)(0.1\angle -5.71^\circ) - \mathbf{V}_{\text{Th}} = 0$$

$$\mathbf{V}_{\text{Th}} = 3.5\angle 85.1^\circ \text{ V}$$

***Step II*** Calculation of $\mathbf{I}_N$ (Fig. 5.140)

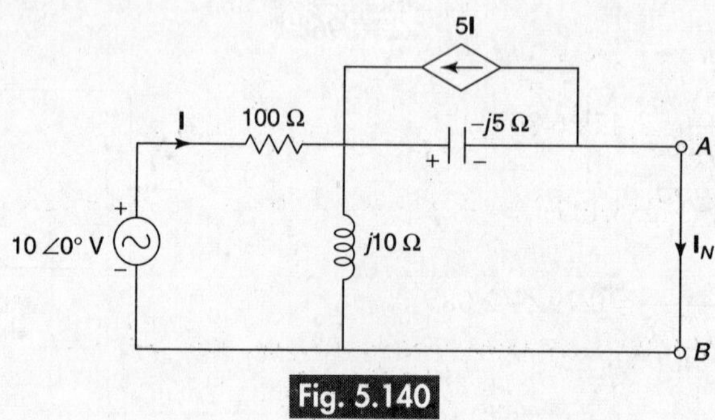


Fig. 5.140

By source transformation, the network is redrawn, as shown in Fig. 5.141.

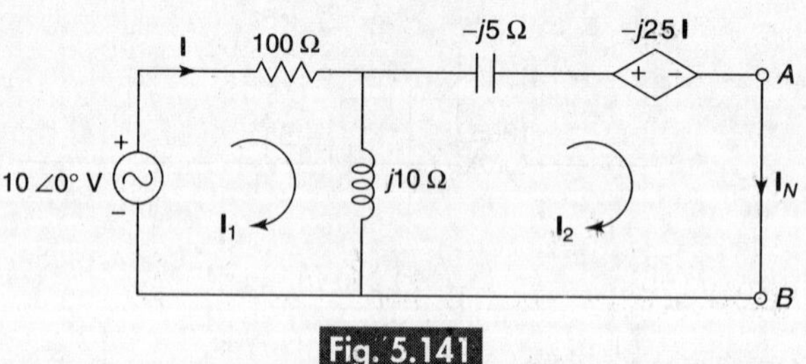


Fig. 5.141

From Fig. 5.141,

$$\mathbf{I} = \mathbf{I}_1 \qquad \text{...(i)}$$

Applying KVL to mesh 1,

$$10\angle 0^\circ - 100\,\mathbf{I}_1 - j10(\mathbf{I}_1 - \mathbf{I}_2) = 0$$

$$(100 + j10)\,\mathbf{I}_1 - j10\mathbf{I}_2 = 10\angle 0^\circ \qquad \text{...(ii)}$$

Applying KVL to mesh 2,

$$-j10(\mathbf{I}_2 - \mathbf{I}_1) + j5\mathbf{I}_2 + j25\mathbf{I} = 0$$

$$-j10\mathbf{I}_2 + j10\mathbf{I}_1 + j5\mathbf{I}_2 + j25\mathbf{I}_1 = 0$$

$$j35\mathbf{I}_1 - j5\mathbf{I}_2 = 0 \qquad \text{...(iii)}$$

Writing Eqs (ii) and (iii) in matrix form,

$$\begin{bmatrix} 100 + j10 & -j10 \\ j35 & -j5 \end{bmatrix} \begin{bmatrix} \mathbf{I}_1 \\ \mathbf{I}_2 \end{bmatrix} = \begin{bmatrix} 10\angle 0^\circ \\ 0 \end{bmatrix}$$

By Cramer's rule,

$$\mathbf{I}_2 = \frac{\begin{vmatrix} 100 + j10 & 10\angle 0° \\ j35 & 0 \end{vmatrix}}{\begin{vmatrix} 100 + j10 & -j10 \\ j35 & -j5 \end{vmatrix}} = 0.6\angle 30.96° \text{ A}$$

$$\mathbf{I}_N = \mathbf{I}_2 = 0.6\angle 30.96° \text{ A}$$

***Step III*** Calculation of $\mathbf{Z}_N$

$$\mathbf{Z}_N = \frac{\mathbf{V}_{\text{Th}}}{\mathbf{I}_N} = \frac{3.5\angle 85.1°}{0.6\angle 30.96°} = 5.83\angle 54.14° \ \Omega$$

***Step IV*** Norton's Equivalent Network (Fig. 5.142)

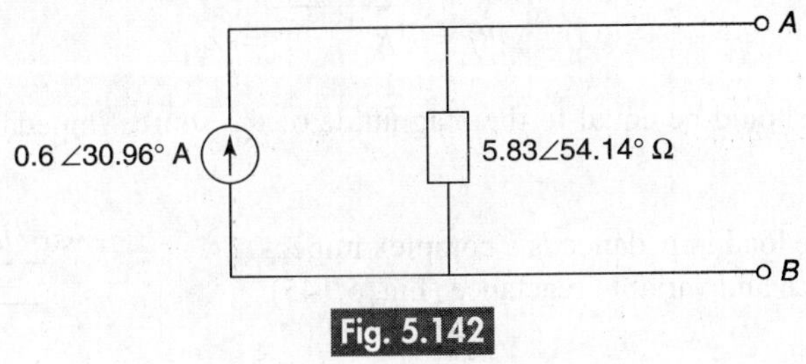


Fig. 5.142

## 5.6 MAXIMUM POWER TRANSFER THEOREM

LO 5.4

Analyse the networks using maximum power transfer theorem

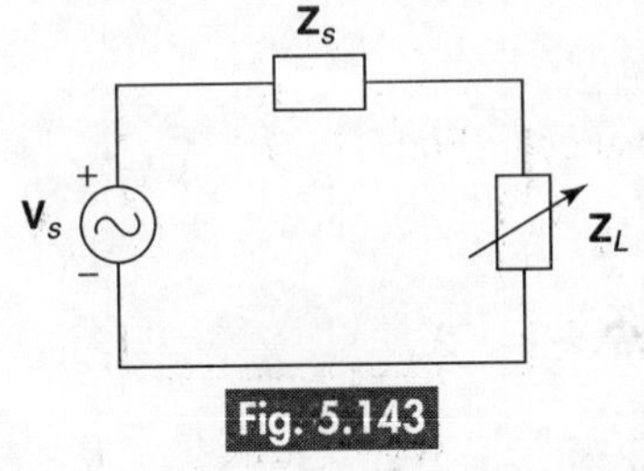


Fig. 5.143

This theorem is used to determine the value of load impedance for which the source will transfer maximum power.

Consider a simple network, as shown in Fig. 5.143. There are three possible cases for load impedance $\mathbf{Z}_L$.

➤ ***Case (i)*** When the load impedance is variable resistance (Fig. 5.144)

$$\mathbf{I}_L = \frac{\mathbf{V}_s}{\mathbf{Z}_s + \mathbf{Z}_L} = \frac{\mathbf{V}_s}{R_s + jX_s + R_L}$$

$$|\mathbf{I}_L| = \frac{|\mathbf{V}_s|}{\sqrt{(R_s + R_L)^2 + X_s^2}}$$

$\mathbf{Z}_S = R_S + jX_S$ · $\mathbf{V}_S$ · $\mathbf{Z}_L = R_L$ · $\mathbf{I}_L$

Fig. 5.144 *Purely resistive load*

The power delivered to the load is

$$P_L = |\mathbf{I}_L|^2 R_L = \frac{|\mathbf{V}_s|^2 R_L}{\sqrt{(R_s + R_L)^2 + X_s{}^2}}$$

For power to be maximum,

$$\frac{dP_L}{dR_L} = 0$$

$$|\mathbf{V}_s|^2 \left[ \frac{\{(R_s + R_L)^2 + X_s^2\} - 2R_L(R_s + R_L)}{[(R_s + R_L)^2 + X_s^2]^2} \right] = 0$$

$$(R_s + R_L)^2 + X_s^2 - 2R_L(R_s + R_L) = 0$$

$$R_s^2 + 2R_sR_L + R_L^2 + X_s^2 - 2R_LR_s - 2R_L^2 = 0$$

$$R_s^2 + X_s^2 - R_L^2 = 0$$

$$R_L^2 = R_s^2 + X_s^2$$

$$R_L = \sqrt{R_s^2 + X_s^2} = |Z_s|$$

Hence, load resistance $R_L$ should be equal to the magnitude of the source impedance for maximum power transfer.

➤ ***Case (ii)*** When the load impedance is a complex impedance with variable resistance and variable reactance (Fig. 5.145)

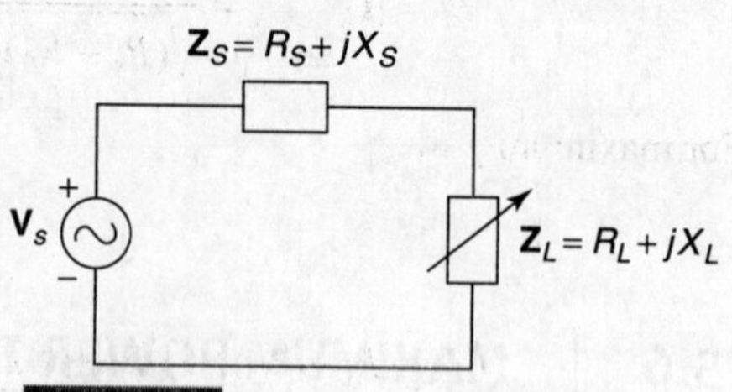


**Fig. 5.145** *Complex impedance load*

$$\mathbf{I}_L = \frac{\mathbf{V}_s}{\mathbf{Z}_s + \mathbf{Z}_L}$$

$$|\mathbf{I}_L| = \frac{|\mathbf{V}_s|}{\sqrt{(R_s + R_L)^2 + (X_s + X_L)^2}}$$

The power delivered to the load is

$$P_L = |\mathbf{I}_L|^2 R_L = \frac{|\mathbf{V}_S|^2 R_L}{(R_s + R_L)^2 + (X_s + X_L)^2}$$

For maximum value of $P_L$, denominator of the equation should be small, i.e., $X_L = -X_s$.

$$P_L = \frac{|\mathbf{V}_S|^2 R_L}{(R_s + R_L)^2}$$

Differentiating the above equation w.r.t. $R_L$ and equating to zero,

$$\frac{dP_L}{dR_L} = |\mathbf{V}_s|^2 \left[ \frac{(R_s + R_L)^2 - 2\,R_L\,(R_s + R_L)}{(R_s + R_L)^2} \right] = 0$$

$$(R_s + R_L)^2 - 2\,R_L\,(R_s + R_L) = 0$$

$$R_s^2 + 2\,R_sR_L + R_L^2 - 2\,R_LR_s - 2R_L^2 = 0$$

$$R_s^2 - R_L^2 = 0$$

$$R_L^2 = R_s^2$$

$$R_L = R_s$$

Hence, load resistance $R_L$ should be equal to source resistance $R_L$ and load reactance $X_L$ should be equal to negative value of source reactance for maximum power transfer.

$$\mathbf{Z}_L = \mathbf{Z}_s^* = R_s - jX_s$$

i.e., load impedance should be a complex conjugate of source impedance.

➤ ***Case (iii)*** When the load impedance is a complex impedance with variable resistance and fixed reactance (Fig. 5.146)

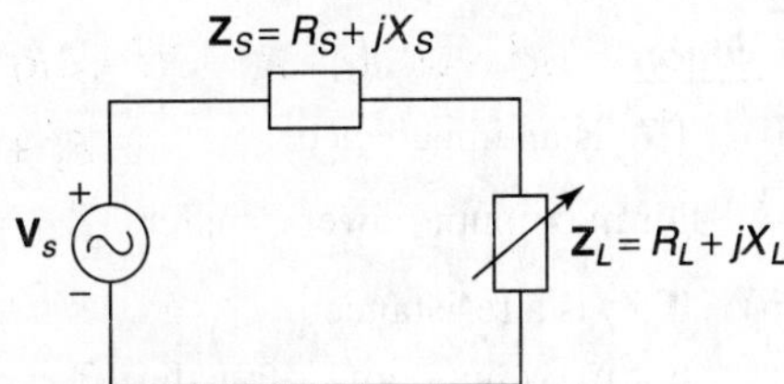


**Fig. 5.146** *Complex impedance load*

$$\mathbf{I}_L = \frac{\mathbf{V}_s}{\mathbf{Z}_s + \mathbf{Z}_L}$$

$$|\mathbf{I}_L| = \frac{|\mathbf{V}_s|}{\sqrt{(R_s + R_L)^2 + (X_s + X_L)^2}}$$

The power delivered to the load is

$$P_L = |\mathbf{I}_L|^2 R_L = \frac{|\mathbf{V}_s|^2 R_L}{\sqrt{(R_s + R_L)^2 + (X_s + X_L)^2}}$$

For maximum power,

$$\frac{dP_L}{dR_L} = 0$$

$$|\mathbf{V}_s|^2 \left[\frac{(R_s + R_L)^2 + (X_s + X_L)^2 - 2\,R_L(R_s + R_L)}{\{(R_s + R_L)^2 + (X_s + X_L)^2\}^2}\right] = 0$$

$$(R_s + R_L)^2 + (X_s + X_L)^2 - 2\,R_L(R_s + R_L) = 0$$

$$R_s^2 + 2\,R_s\,R_L + R_L^2 + (X_s + X_L)^2 - 2\,R_L R_s - 2\,R_L^2 = 0$$

$$R_s^2 + (X_s + X_L)^2 - R_L^2 = 0$$

$$R_L^2 = R_s^2 + (X_s + X_L)^2$$

$$R_L = \sqrt{R_s^2 + (X_s + X_L)^2}$$

$$= |R_s + j(X_s + X_L)|$$

$$= |R_s + jX_s + jX_L|$$

$$= |Z_s + jX_L|$$

Hence, load resistance $R_L$ should be equal to the magnitude of the impedance $\mathbf{Z}_s + jX_L$, i.e., $|\mathbf{Z}_s + jX_L|$ for maximum power transfer.

## EXAMPLE 5.47

*For maximum power transfer, find the value of* $\mathbf{Z}_L$ *in the network of Fig. 5.147 if (i)* $\mathbf{Z}_L$ *is an impedance, and (ii)* $\mathbf{Z}_L$ *is pure resistance.*

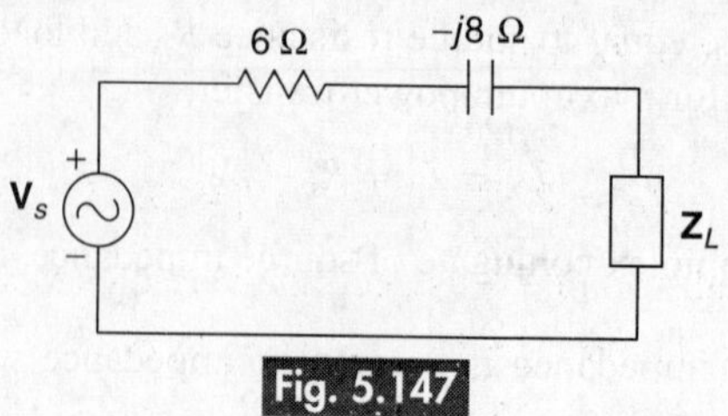


Fig. 5.147

**Solution** $\quad \mathbf{Z}_s = (6 - j8)\ \Omega$

(i) If $\mathbf{Z}_L$ is an impedance

For maximum power transfer, $\mathbf{Z}_L = \mathbf{Z}_s^* = (6 + j8)\ \Omega$

(ii) If $\mathbf{Z}_L$ is a resistance

For maximum power transfer, $\mathbf{Z}_L = |\mathbf{Z}_S| = |6 + j8| = 10\ \Omega$

## EXAMPLE 5.48

*For the maximum power transfer, find the value of* $\mathbf{Z}_L$ *in the network of Fig. 5.148 for the following cases: (i)* $\mathbf{Z}_L$ *is variable resistance, (ii)* $\mathbf{Z}_L$ *is complex impedance, with variable resistance and variable reactance, and (iii)* $\mathbf{Z}_L$ *is complex impedance with variable resistance and fixed reactance of j5 Ω.*

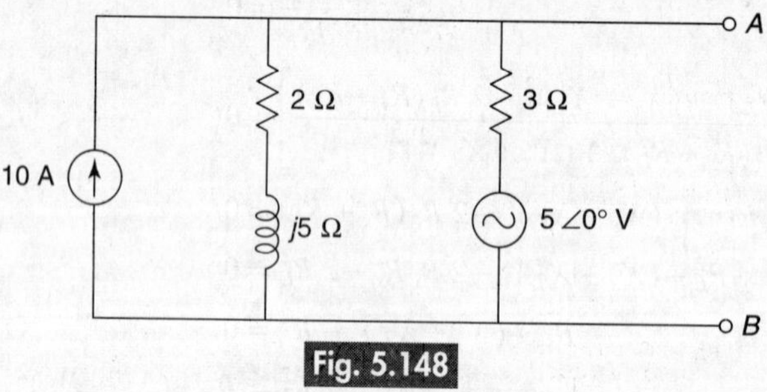


Fig. 5.148

**Solution** Thevenin's impedance can be calculated by replacing voltage source by a short circuit and current source by an open circuit.

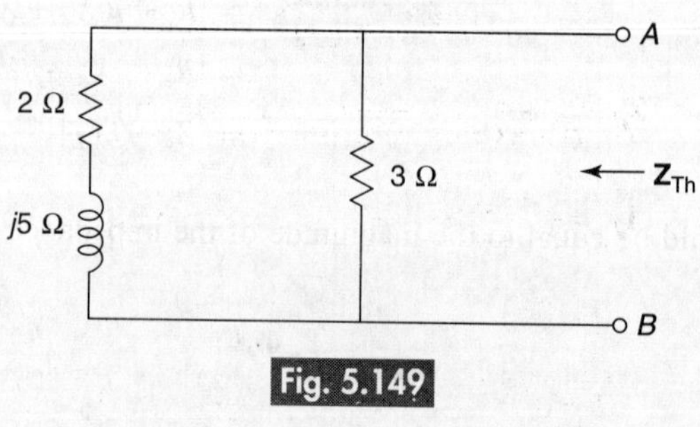


Fig. 5.149

$$\mathbf{Z}_{\text{Th}} = \frac{3(2 + j5)}{3 + 2 + j5} = (2.1 + j0.9)\ \Omega$$

For maximum power transfer, value of $\mathbf{Z}_L$ will be,

(i) $\mathbf{Z}_L$ is variable resistance

$$\mathbf{Z}_L = |\mathbf{Z}_{\text{Th}}| = |2.1 + j0.9| = 2.28\ \Omega$$

(ii) $\mathbf{Z}_L$ is complex impedance with variable resistance and variable reactance

$$\mathbf{Z}_L = \mathbf{Z}^*_{\text{Th}} = (2.1 - j0.9)\ \Omega$$

(iii) $\mathbf{Z}_L$ is complex impedance with variable resistance and fixed reactance of $j5\ \Omega$

$$\mathbf{Z}_L = |\mathbf{Z}_{\text{Th}} + j5| = |2.1 + j0.9 + j5| = 6.26\ \Omega$$

## EXAMPLE 5.49

*Find the impedance $\mathbf{Z}_L$ so that maximum power can be transferred to it in the network of Fig. 5.150. Find maximum power.*

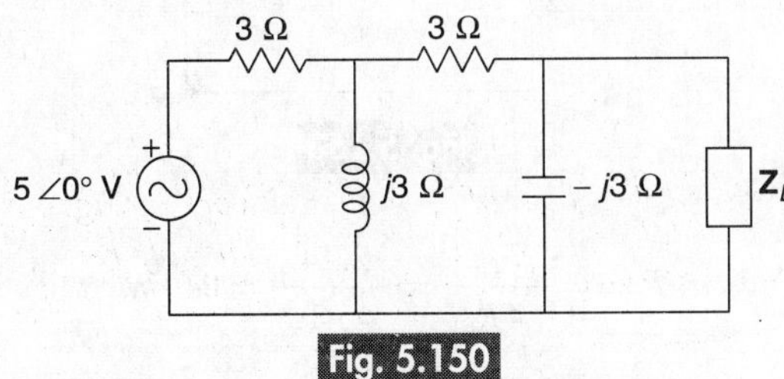


Fig. 5.150

### Solution

***Step I*** Calculation of $\mathbf{V}_{\text{Th}}$ (Fig. 5.151)

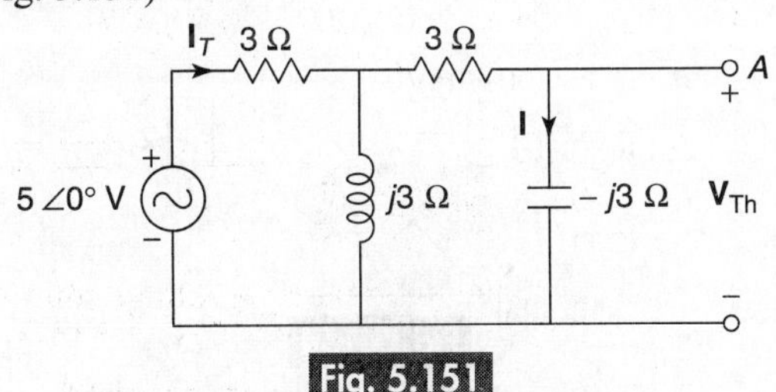


Fig. 5.151

$$\mathbf{Z}_T = 3 + \frac{j3(3 - j3)}{3 + j3 - j3} = 6.71\angle 26.57^\circ\ \Omega$$

$$\mathbf{I}_T = \frac{5\angle 0^\circ}{6.71\angle 26.57^\circ} = 0.75\angle -26.57^\circ\ \text{A}$$

By current division rule,

$$\mathbf{I} = 0.75\angle -26.57^\circ \times \frac{j3}{3 + j3 - j3} = 0.75\angle 63.43^\circ\ \text{A}$$

$$\mathbf{V}_{\text{Th}} = (-j3)(0.75\angle 63.43^\circ) = 2.24\angle -26.57^\circ\ \text{V}$$

***Step II*** Calculation of $\mathbf{Z}_{Th}$ (Fig. 5.152)

$$\mathbf{Z}_{Th} = [(3 \parallel j3) + 3] \parallel (-j3)$$
$$= 3\angle -53.12^\circ\ \Omega$$
$$= (1.8 - j2.4)\ \Omega$$

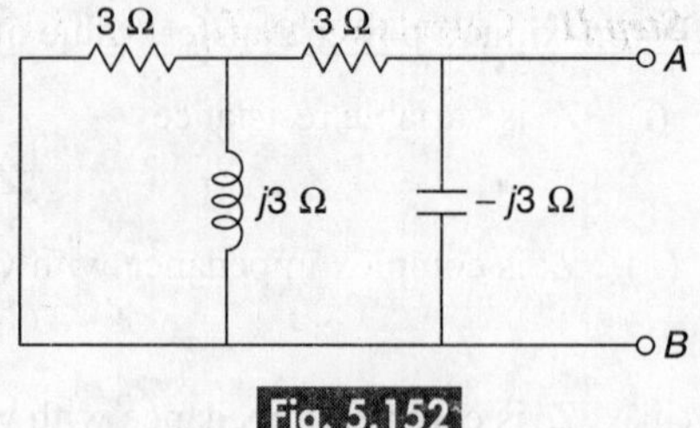

Fig. 5.152

***Step III*** Calculation of $\mathbf{Z}_L$

For maximum power transfer, the load impedance should be a complex conjugate of the source impedance.

$$\mathbf{Z}_L = (1.8 + j2.4)\ \Omega$$

***Step IV*** Calculation of $P_{max}$ (Fig. 5.153)

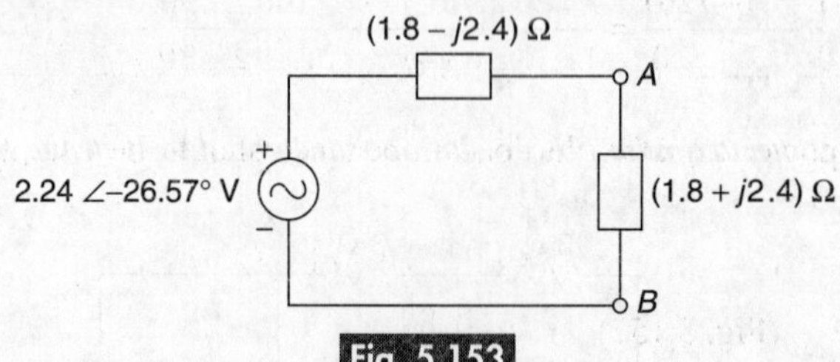

Fig. 5.153

$$P_{max} = \frac{|\mathbf{V}_{Th}|^2}{4R_L} = \frac{|2.24|^2}{4 \times 1.8} = 0.7\ \text{W}$$

## EXAMPLE 5.50

*Find the value of $\mathbf{Z}_L$ for maximum power transfer in the network shown and find maximum power.*

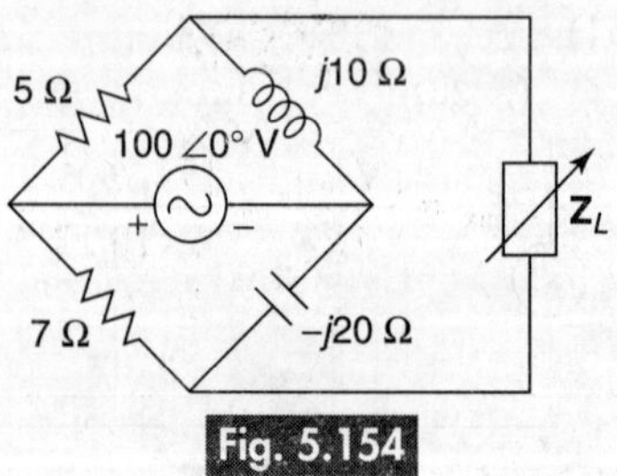

Fig. 5.154

**Solution**

***Step I*** Calculation of $\mathbf{V}_{Th}$ (Fig. 5.155)

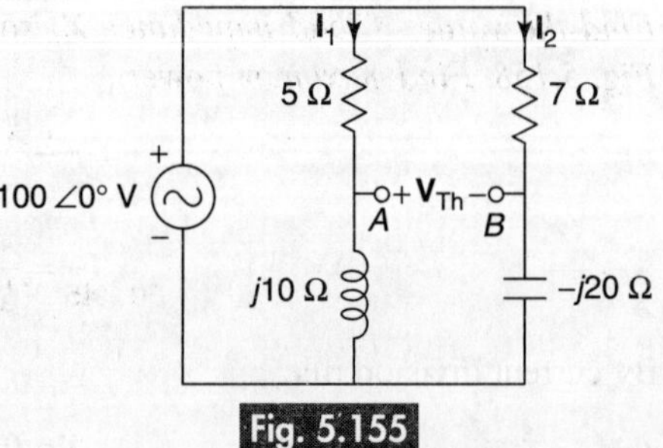

Fig. 5.155

$$\mathbf{I}_1 = \frac{100\angle 0^\circ}{5 + j10} = 8.94\angle -63.43^\circ\ \text{A}$$

$$\mathbf{I}_2 = \frac{100\angle 0^\circ}{7 - j20} = 4.72\angle 70.7^\circ\ \text{A}$$

$$\mathbf{V}_{Th} = \mathbf{V}_A - \mathbf{V}_B = (8.94\angle -63.43^\circ)(j10) - (4.72\angle 70.7^\circ)(-j20) = 71.76\angle 97.3^\circ\ \text{V}$$

***Step II*** Calculation of $\mathbf{Z}_{\text{Th}}$ (Fig. 5.156)

Fig. 5.156

$$\mathbf{Z}_{\text{Th}} = \frac{5(j10)}{5+j10} + \frac{7(-j20)}{7-j20} = \frac{50\angle 90^\circ}{11.18\angle 63.43^\circ} + \frac{140\angle -90^\circ}{21.19\angle -70.7^\circ} = (10.23 - j0.18)\ \Omega$$

***Step III*** For maximum power transfer, the load impedance should be complex conjugate of the source impedance.

$$\mathbf{Z}_L = (10.23 + j0.18)\ \Omega$$

***Step IV*** Calculation of $P_{\text{max}}$ (Fig. 5.157)

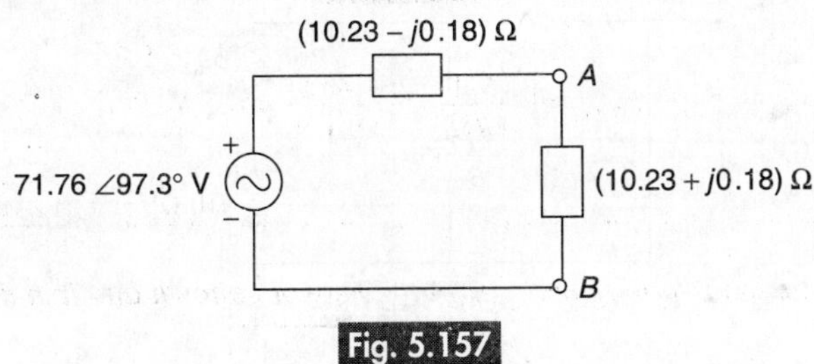


Fig. 5.157

$$P_{\text{max}} = \frac{|\mathbf{V}_{\text{Th}}|^2}{4R_L} = \frac{|71.76|^2}{4\times 10.23} = 125.84\ \text{W}$$

## EXAMPLE 5.51

*Find the value of load impedance $\mathbf{Z}_L$ so that maximum power can be transferred to it in the network of Fig. 5.158. Find maximum power.*

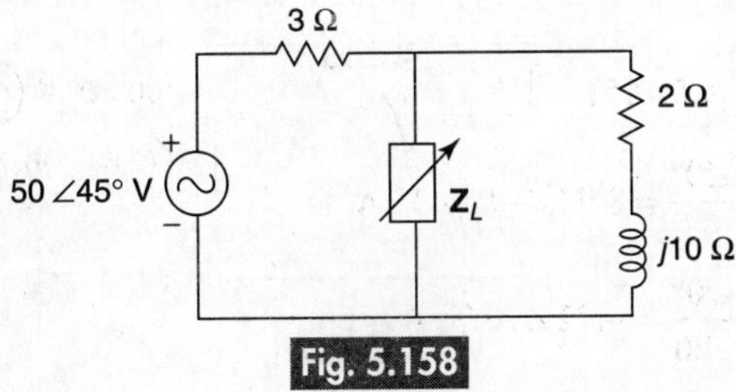


Fig. 5.158

## Solution

***Step I*** Calculation of $\mathbf{V}_{\text{Th}}$ (Fig. 5.159)

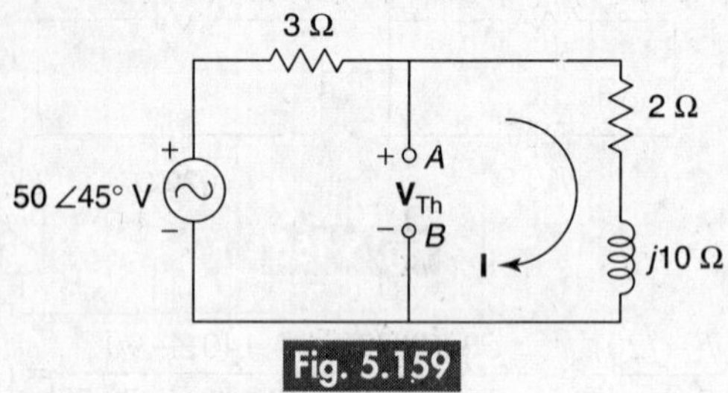


Fig. 5.159

$$\mathbf{I} = \frac{50\angle 45^\circ}{3+2+j10} = 4.47\angle{-18.43^\circ}\text{ A}$$

$$\mathbf{V}_{\text{Th}} = (2+j10)\,\mathbf{I} = (2+j10)(4.47\angle{-18.43^\circ}) = 45.6\angle 60.26^\circ\text{ V}$$

***Step II*** Calculation of $\mathbf{Z}_{\text{Th}}$ (Fig. 5.160)

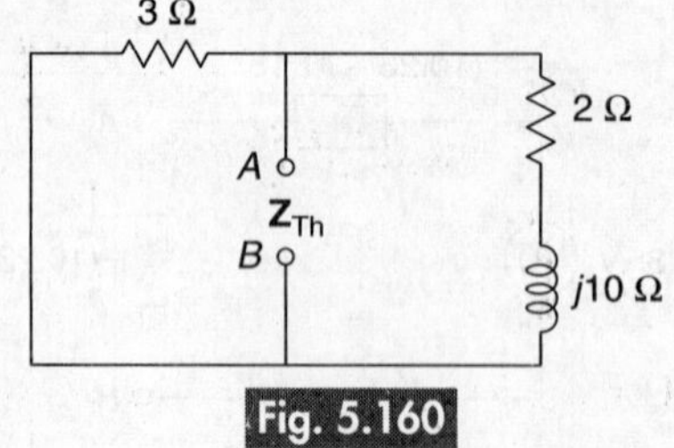


Fig. 5.160

$$\mathbf{Z}_{\text{Th}} = \frac{3(2+j10)}{3+2+j10} = (2.64+j0.72)\ \Omega$$

***Step III*** Calculation of $\mathbf{Z}_L$

For maximum power transfer, the load impedance should be complex conjugate of the source impedance.

$$\mathbf{Z}_L = (2.64 - j0.72)\ \Omega$$

***Step IV*** Calculation of $P_{\text{max}}$ (Fig. 5.161)

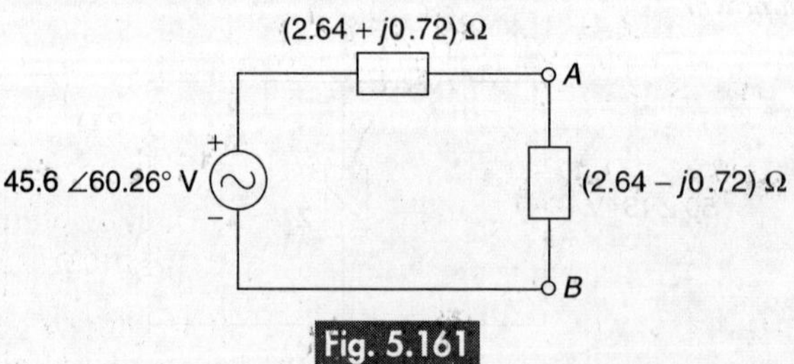


Fig. 5.161

$$P_{\text{max}} = \frac{|\mathbf{V}_{\text{Th}}|^2}{4R_L} = \frac{|45.6|^2}{4\times 2.64} = 196.91\text{ W}$$

## EXAMPLE 5.52

*Determine the load $\mathbf{Z}_L$ required to be connected in the network of Fig. 5.162 for maximum power transfer. Determine the maximum power drawn.*

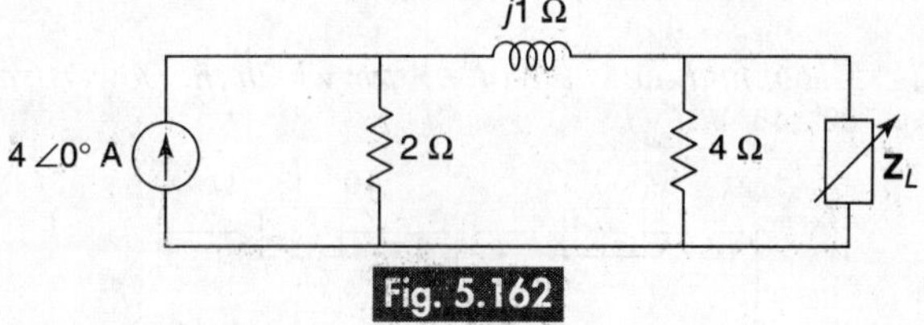


Fig. 5.162

### Solution

***Step I*** Calculation of $\mathbf{V}_{Th}$ (Fig. 5.163)

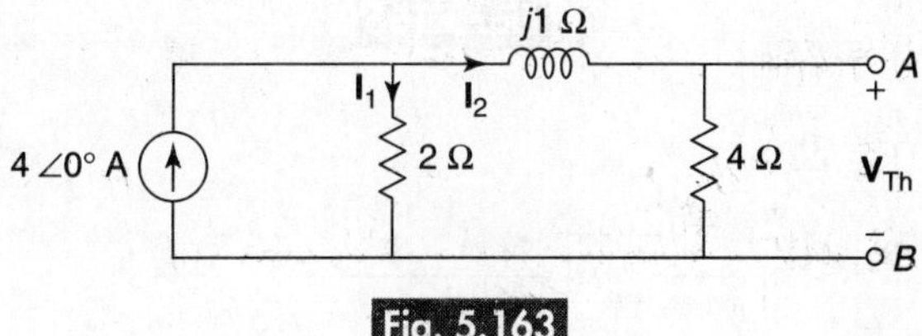


Fig. 5.163

$$\mathbf{I}_2 = 4\angle 0° \times \frac{2}{6+j1} = 1.315\angle -9.46° \text{ A}$$

$$\mathbf{V}_{Th} = 4\mathbf{I}_2 = 4(1.315\angle -9.46°) = 5.26\angle -9.46° \text{ V}$$

***Step II*** Calculation of $\mathbf{Z}_{Th}$ (Fig. 5.164)

$$\mathbf{Z}_{Th} = \frac{4(2+j1)}{4+2+j1} = 1.47\angle 17.1° = (1.41 + j0.43)\ \Omega$$

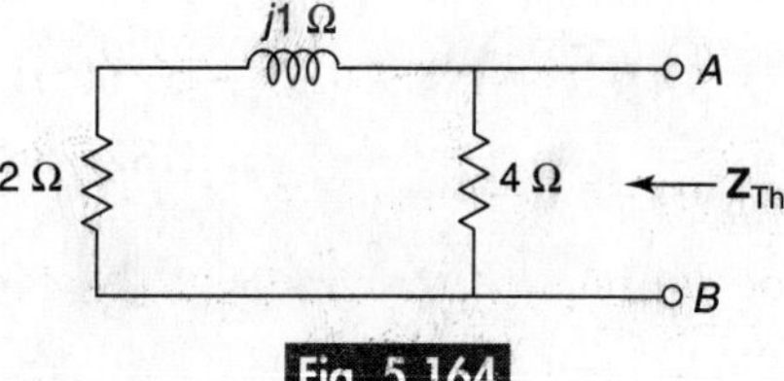


Fig. 5.164

***Step III*** Calculation of $\mathbf{Z}_L$

For maximum power transfer, the load impedance should be the complex conjugate of the source impedance.

$$\mathbf{Z}_L = (1.41 - j0.43)\ \Omega$$

***Step IV*** Calculation of $P_{max}$ (Fig. 5.165)

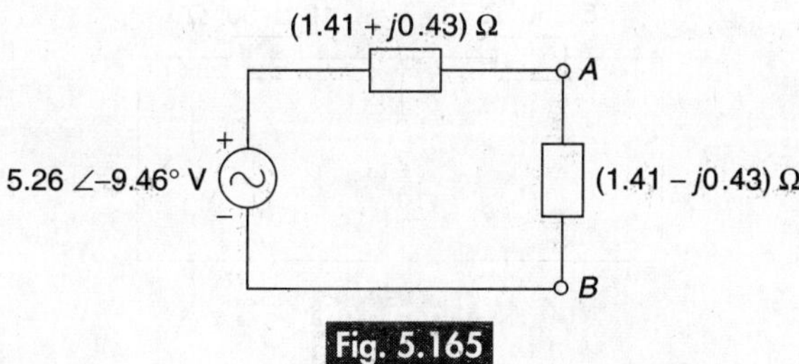


Fig. 5.165

$$P_{\max} = \frac{|\mathbf{V}_{\text{Th}}|^2}{4R_L} = \frac{|5.26|^2}{4 \times 1.41} = 4.91 \text{ W}$$

## EXAMPLE 5.53

*In the network shown in Fig. 5.166, find the value of $\mathbf{Z}_L$ for which the power transferred will be maximum. Also, find maximum power.*

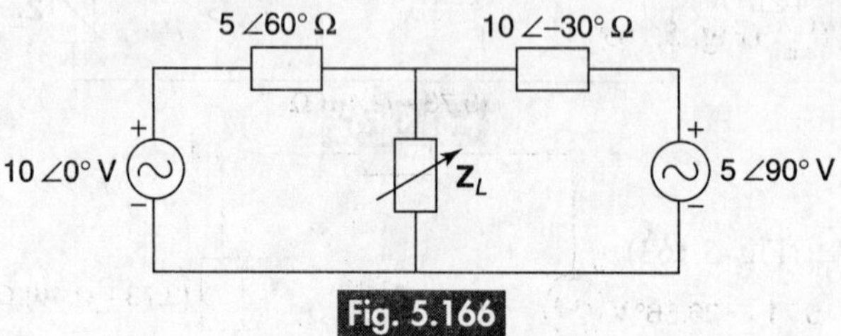


Fig. 5.166

**Solution**

***Step I*** Calculation of $\mathbf{V}_{\text{Th}}$ (Fig. 5.167)

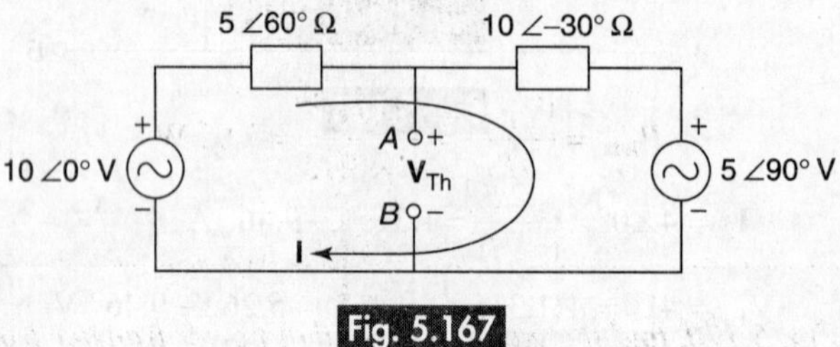


Fig. 5.167

Applying KVL to the mesh,

$$10\angle 0° - (5\angle 60°)\mathbf{I} - (10\angle -30°)\mathbf{I} - 5\angle 90° = 0$$

$$11.18\angle -26.57° - (11.18\angle -3.43°)\mathbf{I} = 0$$

$$\mathbf{I} = 1\angle -23.14° \text{ A}$$

Writing $\mathbf{V}_{\text{Th}}$ equation,

$$10\angle 0° - (5\angle 60°)\mathbf{I} - \mathbf{V}_{\text{Th}} = 0$$

$$10\angle 0° - (5\angle 60°)(1\angle -23.14°) - \mathbf{V}_{\text{Th}} = 0$$

$$\mathbf{V}_{\text{Th}} = 6.71\angle -26.56° \text{ V}$$

***Step II*** Calculation of $\mathbf{Z}_{\text{Th}}$ (Fig. 5.168)

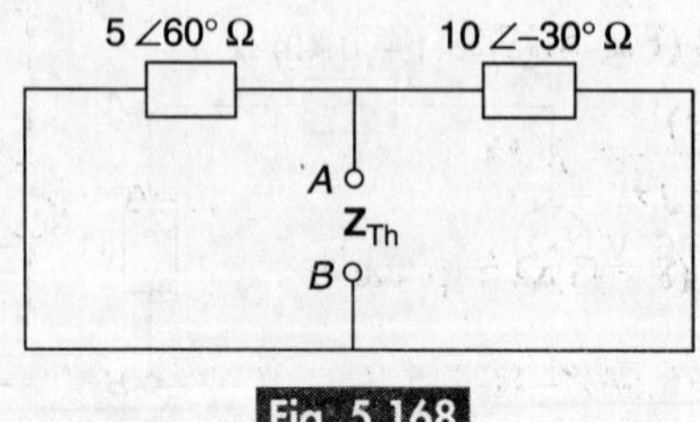


Fig. 5.168

$$\mathbf{Z}_{\text{Th}} = \frac{(5\angle 60°)(10\angle -30°)}{5\angle 60° + 10\angle -30°} = 4.47\angle 33.43°\ \Omega = (3.73 + j2.46)\ \Omega$$

***Step III*** Calculation of $\mathbf{Z}_L$

For maximum power transfer, the load impedance should be the complex conjugate of the source impedance.

$$Z_L = Z_{\text{Th}}^* = (3.73 - j2.46)\ \Omega$$

***Step IV*** Calculation of $P_{\text{max}}$ (Fig. 5.169)

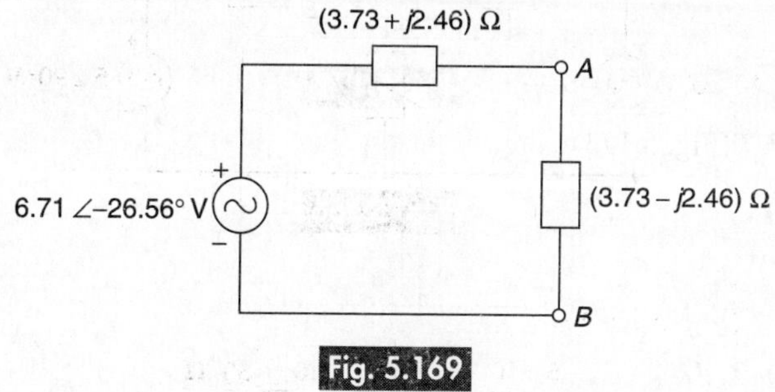


Fig. 5.169

$$P_{\text{max}} = \frac{|\mathbf{V}_{\text{Th}}|^2}{4R_L} = \frac{(6.71)^2}{4 \times 3.73} = 3.02\ \text{W}$$

## EXAMPLE 5.54

*In the network shown in Fig. 5.170, find the value of $\mathbf{Z}_L$ so that power transfer from the source is maximum. Also, find maximum power.*

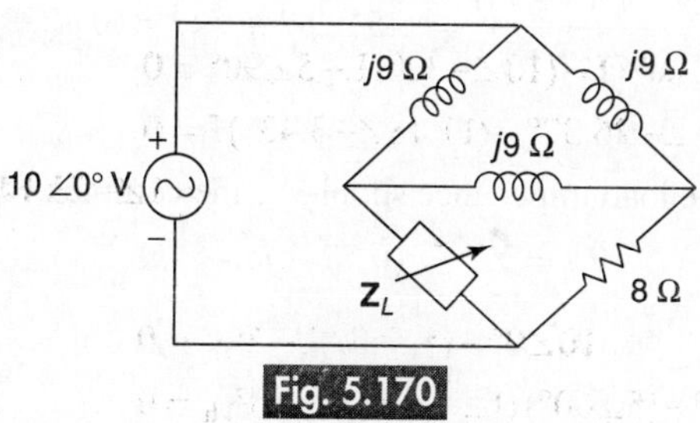


Fig. 5.170

### Solution

***Step I*** Calculation of $\mathbf{V}_{\text{Th}}$ (Fig. 5.171)

Applying Star–delta transformation (Fig. 5.172)

$$\mathbf{Z}_1 = \mathbf{Z}_2 = \mathbf{Z}_3 = \frac{(j9)(j9)}{j9 + j9 + j9} = j3\ \Omega$$

$\mathbf{V}_{\text{Th}}$ = Voltage drop across $(8 + j3)\Omega$ impedance

$$= (8 + j3)\frac{10\angle 0°}{8 + j3 + j3} = 8.54\angle -16.31°\ \text{V}$$

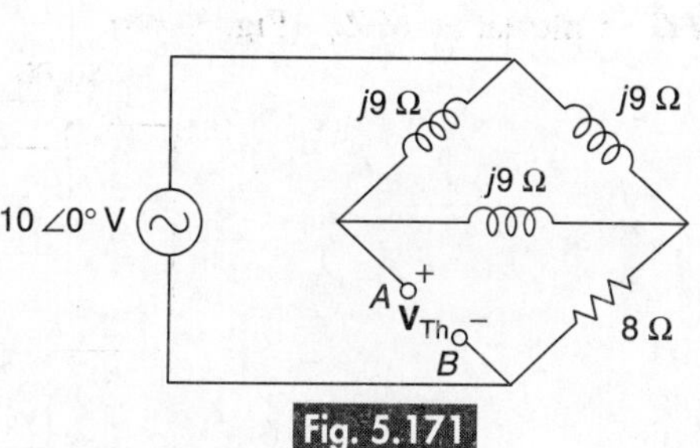


Fig. 5.171

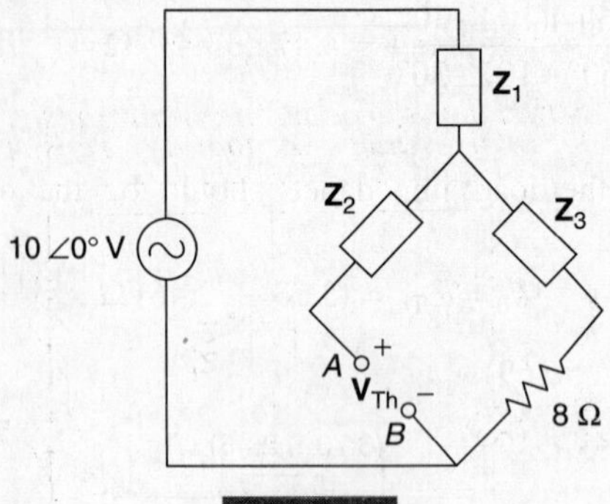


Fig. 5.172

*Step II* Calculation of $\mathbf{Z}_{Th}$ (Fig. 5.173)

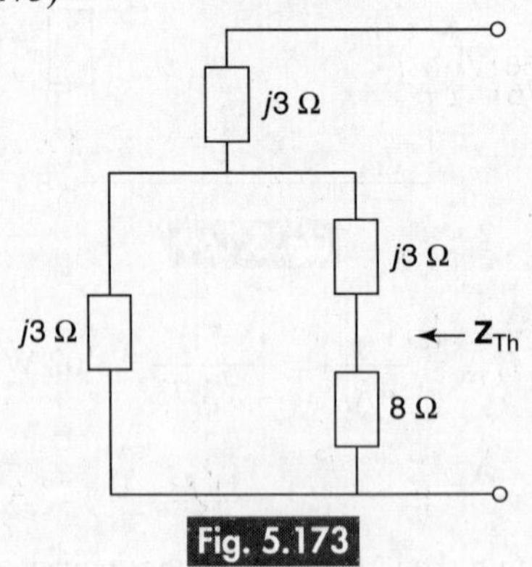


Fig. 5.173

$$\mathbf{Z}_{Th} = j3 + \frac{j3(8 + j3)}{j3 + 8 + j3)} = 5.51\angle 82.49^\circ\ \Omega = (0.72 + j5.46)\ \Omega$$

*Step III* Calculation of $\mathbf{Z}_L$

For maximum power transfer, the load impedance should be the complex conjugate of the source impedance.

$$\mathbf{Z}_L = \mathbf{Z}_{Th}^* = (0.72 - j5.46)\ \Omega$$

*Step IV* Calculation of $P_{max}$ (Fig. 5.174)

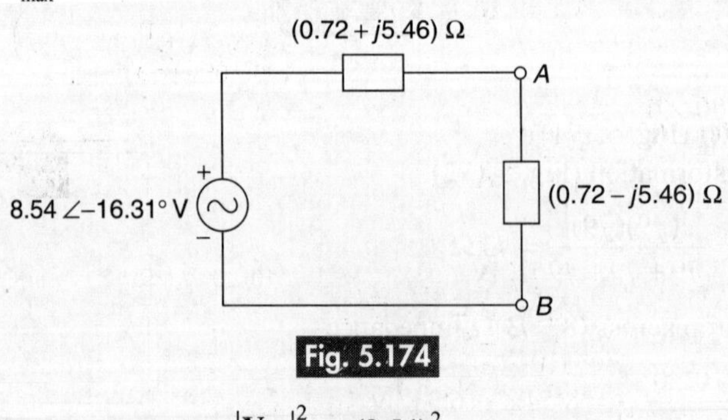


Fig. 5.174

$$P_{max} = \frac{|\mathbf{V}_{Th}|^2}{4R_L} = \frac{(8.54)^2}{4 \times 0.72} = 25.32\ \text{W}$$

## EXAMPLE 5.55

*For the network shown in Fig. 5.175, find the value of* $\mathbf{Z}_L$ *that will transfer maximum power from the source. Also, find maximum power.*

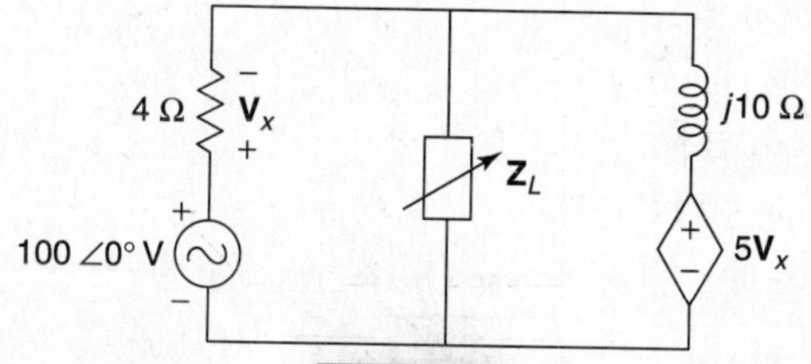


Fig. 5.175

**Solution**

***Step I*** Calculation of $\mathbf{V}_{\text{Th}}$ (Fig. 5.176)

From Fig. 5.176,

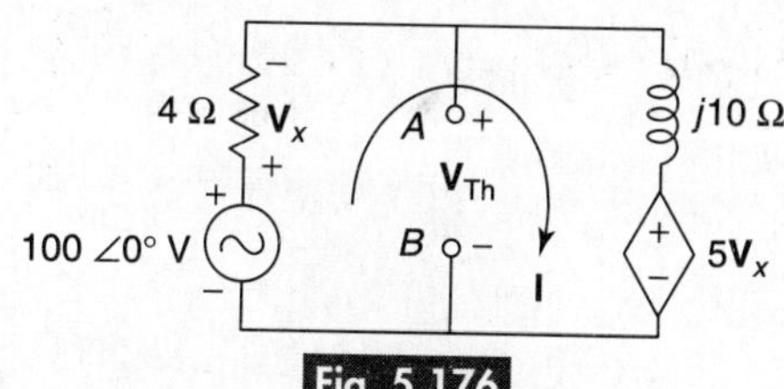


Fig. 5.176

$$\mathbf{V}_x = 4\mathbf{I}$$

Applying KVL to the mesh,

$$100\angle 0° - 4\mathbf{I} - j\,10\,\mathbf{I} - 5\mathbf{V}_x = 0$$
$$100\angle 0° - (4 + j10)\,\mathbf{I} - 5(4\mathbf{I}) = 0$$
$$\mathbf{I} = \frac{100\angle 0°}{24 + j10} = 3.85\angle -22.62° \text{ A}$$

Writing $\mathbf{V}_{\text{Th}}$ equation,

$$100\angle 0° - 4\mathbf{I} - \mathbf{V}_{\text{Th}} = 0$$
$$100\angle 0° - 4(3.85\angle -22.62°) - \mathbf{V}_{\text{Th}} = 0$$
$$\mathbf{V}_{\text{Th}} = 86\angle 3.95° \text{ V}$$

***Step II*** Calculation of $\mathbf{I}_N$ (Fig. 5.177)

From Fig. 5.177,

Fig. 5.177

$$\mathbf{V}_x = 4\mathbf{I}_1$$

Applying KVL to mesh 1,

$$100\angle 0° - 4\mathbf{I}_1 = 0$$
$$\mathbf{I}_1 = 25 \text{ A}$$

Applying KVL to mesh 2,

$$-j10\mathbf{I}_2 - 5\mathbf{V}_x = 0$$
$$-j10\mathbf{I}_2 - 5(4\mathbf{I}_1) = 0$$
$$-j10\mathbf{I}_2 - 5(100) = 0$$
$$\mathbf{I}_2 = 50\angle 90° \text{A}$$
$$\mathbf{I}_N = \mathbf{I}_1 - \mathbf{I}_2 = 25 - 50\angle 90° = 55.9\angle -63.43° \text{A}$$

***Step III*** Calculation of $\mathbf{Z}_{\text{Th}}$

$$\mathbf{Z}_{\text{Th}} = \frac{\mathbf{V}_{\text{Th}}}{\mathbf{I}_N} = \frac{86\angle 3.95°}{55.9\angle -63.43°} = 1.54\angle 67.38°\ \Omega = (0.59 + j1.42)\ \Omega$$

***Step IV*** Calculation of $\mathbf{Z}_L$

For maximum power transfer, $\mathbf{Z}_L = \mathbf{Z}^*_{\text{Th}} = (0.59 - j1.42)\ \Omega$

***Step V*** Calculation of $P_{\max}$ (Fig. 5.178)

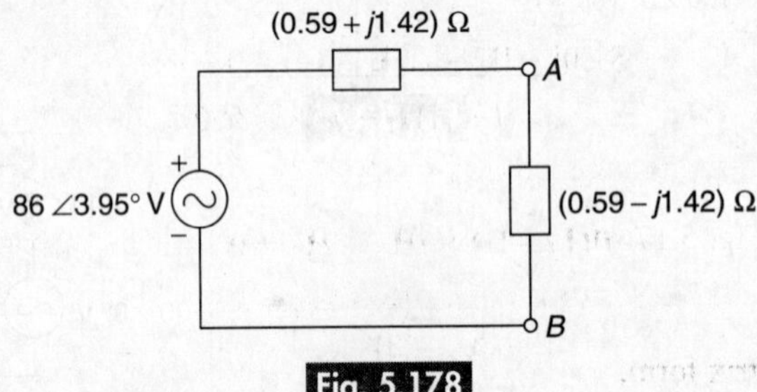


Fig. 5.178

$$P_{\max} = \frac{|\mathbf{V}_{\text{Th}}|^2}{4R_L} = \frac{(86)^2}{4 \times 0.59} = 3133.9\ \text{W}$$

## 5.7 RECIPROCITY THEOREM

LO 5.5

Explain reciprocity theorem

Reciprocity theorem states that *In a linear, bilateral, active, single-source network, the ratio of excitation to response remains same when the positions of excitation and response are interchanged.*

**EXAMPLE 5.56**

*Find the current through the 6 Ω resistor of Fig.5.179 and verify the reciprocity theorem.*

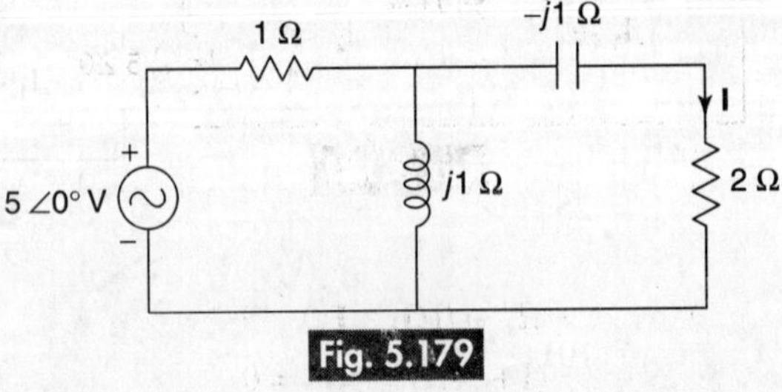


Fig. 5.179

**Solution**

***Case I*** Calculation of current **I** when excitation and response are not interchanged (Fig. 5.180)

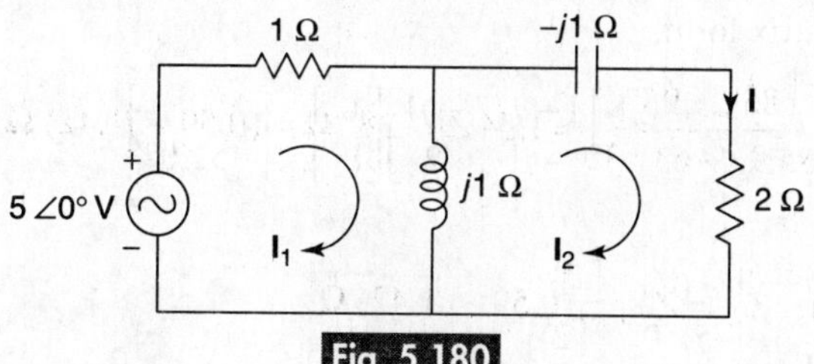


Fig. 5.180

Applying KVL to mesh 1,

$$5\angle 0° - 1\mathbf{I}_1 - j1(\mathbf{I}_1 - \mathbf{I}_2) = 0$$

$$(1 + j1)\mathbf{I}_1 - j1\mathbf{I}_2 = 5\angle 0° \quad \text{...(i)}$$

Applying KVL to mesh 2,

$$-j1(\mathbf{I}_2 - \mathbf{I}_1) + j1\mathbf{I}_2 - 2\mathbf{I}_2 = 0$$

$$-j1\mathbf{I}_1 + 2\mathbf{I}_2 = 0 \quad \text{...(ii)}$$

Writing Eqs (i) and (ii) in matrix form,

$$\begin{bmatrix} 1 + j1 & -j1 \\ -j1 & 2 \end{bmatrix} \begin{bmatrix} \mathbf{I}_1 \\ \mathbf{I}_2 \end{bmatrix} = \begin{bmatrix} 5\angle 0° \\ 0 \end{bmatrix}$$

By Cramer's rule,

$$\mathbf{I}_2 = \frac{\begin{vmatrix} 1 + j1 & 5\angle 0° \\ -j1 & 0 \end{vmatrix}}{\begin{vmatrix} 1 + j1 & -j1 \\ -j1 & 2 \end{vmatrix}} = 1.39\angle 56.31° \text{ A}$$

$$\mathbf{I} = \mathbf{I}_2 = 1.39\angle 56.31° \text{ A}$$

***Case II*** **Calculation of current I when excitation and response are interchanged (Fig. 5.181)**

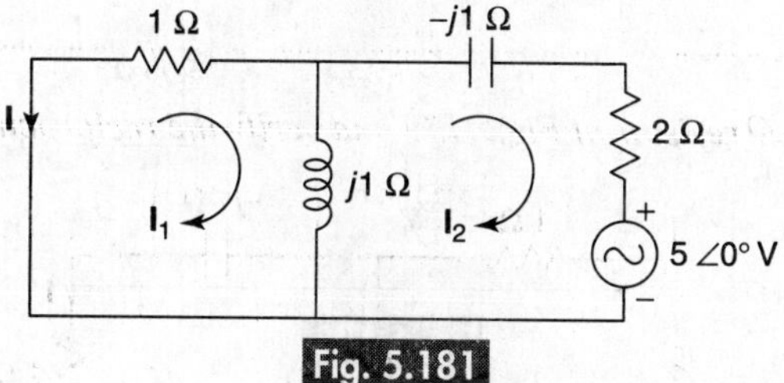


Fig. 5.181

Applying KVL to mesh 1,

$$-1\mathbf{I}_1 - j1(\mathbf{I}_1 - \mathbf{I}_2) = 0$$

$$(1 + j1)\mathbf{I}_1 - j1\mathbf{I}_2 = 0 \quad \text{...(i)}$$

Applying KVL to mesh 2,

$$-j1(\mathbf{I}_2 - \mathbf{I}_1) + j1\mathbf{I}_2 - 2\mathbf{I}_2 - 5\angle 0° = 0$$

$$-j1\mathbf{I}_1 + 2\mathbf{I}_2 = -5\angle 0° \quad \text{...(ii)}$$

Writing Eqs (i) and (ii) in matrix form,

$$\begin{bmatrix} 1+j1 & -j1 \\ -j1 & 2 \end{bmatrix}\begin{bmatrix} \mathbf{I}_1 \\ \mathbf{I}_2 \end{bmatrix} = \begin{bmatrix} 0 \\ -5\angle 0^\circ \end{bmatrix}$$

By Cramer's rule,

$$\mathbf{I}_1 = \frac{\begin{vmatrix} 0 & -j1 \\ -5\angle 0^\circ & 2 \end{vmatrix}}{\begin{vmatrix} 1+j1 & -j1 \\ -j1 & 2 \end{vmatrix}} = 1.38\angle -123.69^\circ \text{ A}$$

$$\mathbf{I} = -\mathbf{I}_1 = 1.39\angle 56.31^\circ \text{ A}$$

Since the current **I** is same in both the cases, reciprocity theorem is verified.

## EXAMPLE 5.57

*In the network of Fig. 5.182, find the voltage $\mathbf{V}_x$ and verify the reciprocity theorem.*

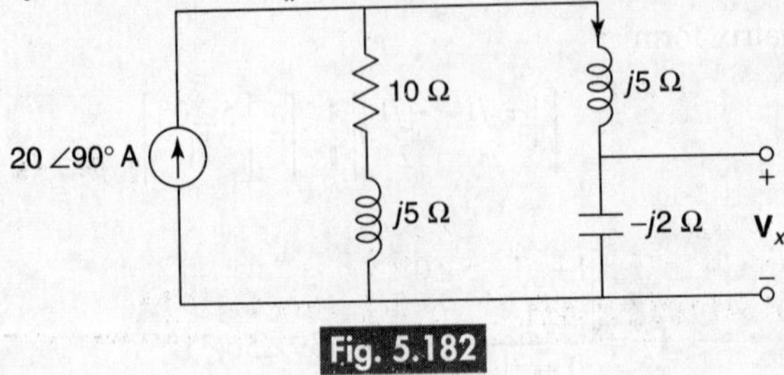


Fig. 5.182

### Solution

***Case I*** Calculation of voltage $\mathbf{V}_x$ when excitation and response are interchanged. (Fig. 5.183)

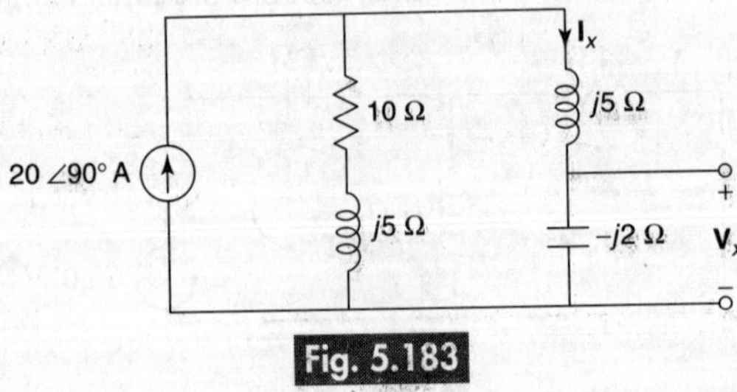


Fig. 5.183

By current division rule,

$$\mathbf{I}_x = (20\angle 90^\circ)\frac{(10+j5)}{(10+j5)+(j5-j2)} = 17.46\angle 77.91^\circ \text{ A}$$

$$\mathbf{V}_x = (-j2)\mathbf{I}_x = (-j2)(17.46\angle 77.91^\circ) = 34.92\ \angle -12.09^\circ \text{ V}$$

***Case II*** Calculation of voltage $\mathbf{V}_x$ when excitation and response are interchanged (Fig. 5.184)

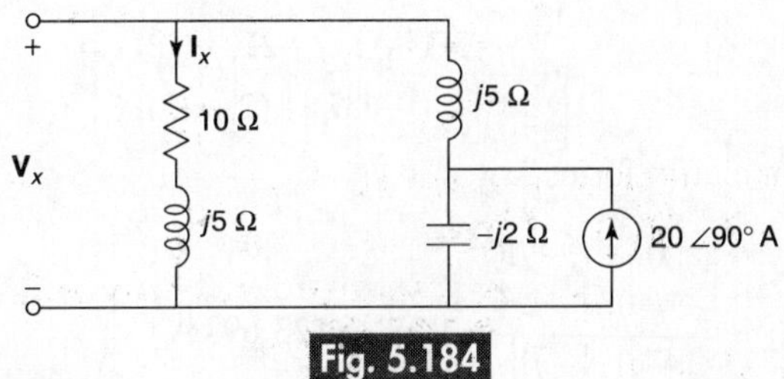


Fig. 5.184

$$\mathbf{I}_x = (20\angle 90°)\frac{(-j2)}{(-j2)+(10+j5+j5)} = 3.12\angle -38.66° \text{A}$$

$$\mathbf{V}_x = (10+j5)\mathbf{I}_x = (10+j5)(3.12\angle -38.66°) = 34.88\angle -12.09° \text{V}$$

Since the voltage $\mathbf{V}_x$ is same in both the cases, reciprocity theorem is verified.

## EXAMPLE 5.58

*Find **I** and verify the reciprocity theorem for the network shown in Fig. 5.185.*

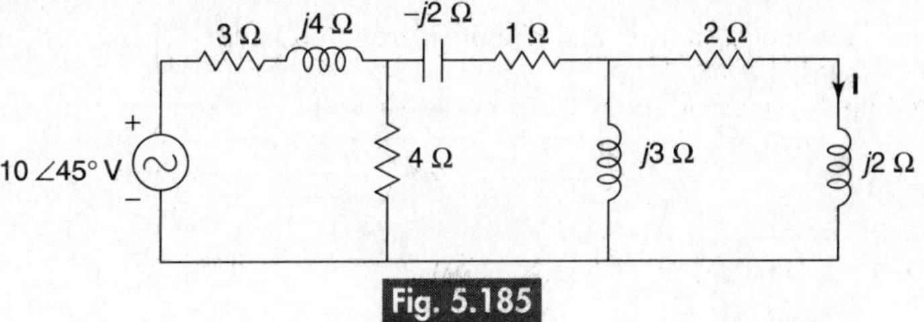


Fig. 5.185

## Solution

***Case I*** Calculation of **I** when excitation and response are not interchanged (Fig. 5.186)

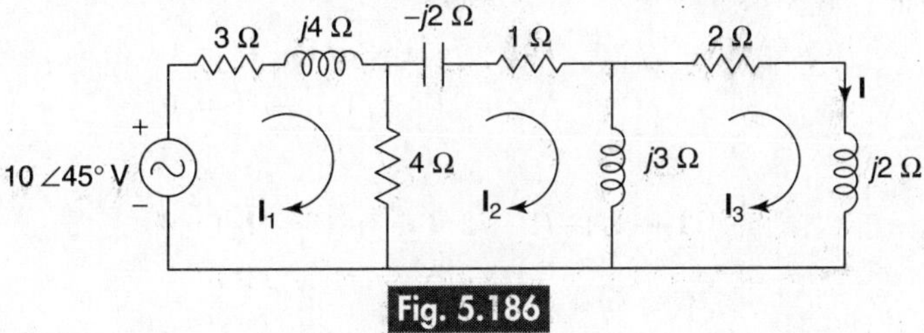


Fig. 5.186

Applying KVL to mesh 1,

$$10\angle 45° - (3+j4)\mathbf{I}_1 - 4(\mathbf{I}_1 - \mathbf{I}_2) = 0$$

$$(7+j4)\mathbf{I}_1 - 4\mathbf{I}_2 = 10\angle 45° \quad \text{...(i)}$$

Applying KVL to mesh 2,

$$-4(\mathbf{I}_2 - \mathbf{I}_1) - (1-j2)\,\mathbf{I}_2 - j3(\mathbf{I}_2 - \mathbf{I}_3) = 0$$

$$-4\mathbf{I}_1 + (5+j1)\mathbf{I}_2 - j3\mathbf{I}_3 = 0 \quad \text{...(ii)}$$

Applying KVL to mesh 3,

$$-j3(\mathbf{I}_3 - \mathbf{I}_2) - 2\mathbf{I}_3 - j2\mathbf{I}_3 = 0$$

$$-j3\mathbf{I}_2 + (2 + j5)\mathbf{I}_3 = 0 \qquad \ldots\text{(iii)}$$

Writing Eqs (i), (ii) and (iii) in matrix form,

$$\begin{bmatrix} 7+j4 & -4 & 0 \\ -4 & 5+j1 & -j3 \\ 0 & -j3 & 2+j5 \end{bmatrix} \begin{bmatrix} \mathbf{I}_1 \\ \mathbf{I}_2 \\ \mathbf{I}_3 \end{bmatrix} = \begin{bmatrix} 10\angle 45^\circ \\ 0 \\ 0 \end{bmatrix}$$

By Cramer's rule,

$$\mathbf{I}_3 = \frac{\begin{vmatrix} 7+j4 & -4 & 10\angle 45^\circ \\ -4 & 5+j1 & 0 \\ 0 & -j3 & 0 \end{vmatrix}}{\begin{vmatrix} 7+j4 & -4 & 0 \\ -4 & 5+j1 & -j3 \\ 0 & -j3 & 2+j5 \end{vmatrix}} = 0.704\angle 30.72^\circ \text{ A}$$

$$\mathbf{I} = \mathbf{I}_3 = 0.704\angle 30.72^\circ\text{A}$$

***Case II*** Calculation of **I** when excitation and response are interchanged (Fig. 5.187)

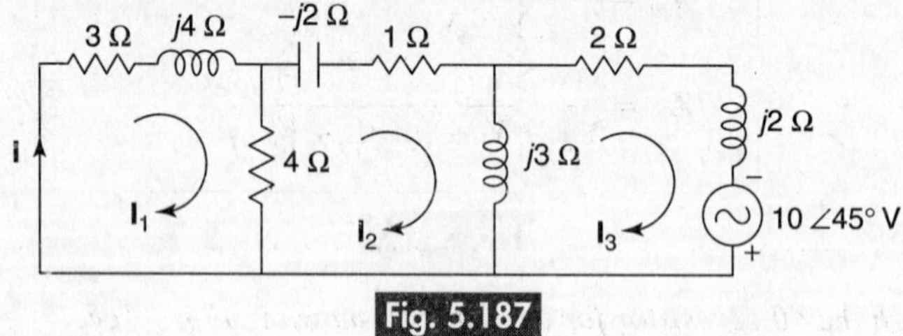


Fig. 5.187

Applying KVL to mesh 1,

$$-(3 + j4)\mathbf{I}_1 - 4(\mathbf{I}_1 - \mathbf{I}_2) = 0$$

$$(7 + j4)\mathbf{I}_1 - 4\mathbf{I}_2 = 0 \qquad \ldots\text{(i)}$$

Applying KVL to mesh 2,

$$-4(\mathbf{I}_2 - \mathbf{I}_1) - (1 - j2)\,\mathbf{I}_2 - j3(\mathbf{I}_2 - \mathbf{I}_3) = 0$$

$$-4\mathbf{I}_1 + (5 + j1)\mathbf{I}_2 - j3\mathbf{I}_3 = 0 \qquad \ldots\text{(ii)}$$

Applying KVL to mesh 3,

$$-j3(\mathbf{I}_3 - \mathbf{I}_2) - 2\mathbf{I}_3 - j2\mathbf{I}_3 + 10\angle 45^\circ = 0$$

$$-j3\mathbf{I}_2 + (2 + j5)\mathbf{I}_3 = 10\angle 45^\circ \qquad \ldots\text{(iii)}$$

Writing Eqs (i), (ii) and (iii) in matrix form,

$$\begin{bmatrix} 7+j4 & -4 & 0 \\ -4 & 5+j1 & -j3 \\ 0 & -j3 & 2+j5 \end{bmatrix} \begin{bmatrix} \mathbf{I}_1 \\ \mathbf{I}_2 \\ \mathbf{I}_3 \end{bmatrix} = \begin{bmatrix} 0 \\ 0 \\ 10\angle 45^\circ \end{bmatrix}$$

By Cramer's rule,

$$\mathbf{I}_1 = \frac{\begin{vmatrix} 0 & -4 & 0 \\ 0 & 5+j1 & -j3 \\ 10\angle 45^\circ & -j3 & 2+j5 \end{vmatrix}}{\begin{vmatrix} 7+j4 & -4 & 0 \\ -4 & 5+j1 & -j3 \\ 0 & -j3 & 2+j5 \end{vmatrix}} = 0.704\angle 30.72^\circ \text{A}$$

$$\mathbf{I} = \mathbf{I}_1 = 0.704\angle 30.72^\circ \text{A}$$

Since the current **I** is same in both the cases, the reciprocity theorem, is verified.

## 5.8 MILLMAN'S THEOREM

LO 5.6

Explain Millman's and Tellegen's theorems

Millman's theorem states that *If there are n voltage sources $V_1$, $V_2$, ... $V_n$ with internal impedances $Z_1$, $Z_2$, ... $Z_n$ respectively connected in parallel then these voltage sources can be replaced by a single voltage source $V_m$ and a single series impedance $Z_m$.*

$$\mathbf{V}_m = \frac{\mathbf{V}_1\,\mathbf{Y}_1 + \mathbf{V}_2\,\mathbf{Y}_2 + \ldots + \mathbf{V}_n\,\mathbf{Y}_n}{\mathbf{Y}_1 + \mathbf{Y}_2 + \ldots + \mathbf{Y}_n}$$

$$\mathbf{Z}_m = \frac{1}{\mathbf{Y}_m} = \frac{1}{\mathbf{Y}_1 + \mathbf{Y}_2 + \ldots + \mathbf{Y}_n}$$

**EXAMPLE 5.59**

*Find the current through the 40 Ω resistor for the network shown in Fig. 5.188.*

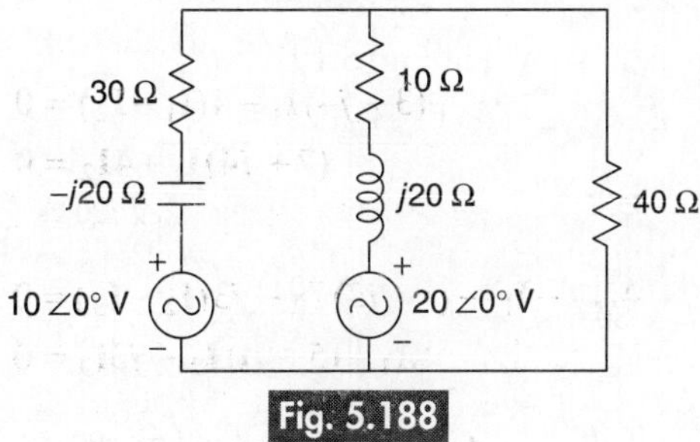


Fig. 5.188

**Solution**

***Step I*** Calculation of $\mathbf{V}_m$

$$\mathbf{V}_m = \frac{\mathbf{V}_1\mathbf{Y}_1 + \mathbf{V}_2\mathbf{Y}_2}{\mathbf{Y}_1 + \mathbf{Y}_2} = \frac{(10\angle 0^\circ)\left(\frac{1}{30 - j20}\right) + (20\angle 0^\circ)\left(\frac{1}{10 + j20}\right)}{\frac{1}{30 - j20} + \frac{1}{10 + j20}} = 18.2\angle -15.95^\circ \text{V}$$

***Step II*** Calculation of $\mathbf{Z}_m$

$$\mathbf{Z}_m = \frac{1}{\mathbf{Y}_m} = \frac{1}{\mathbf{Y}_1 + \mathbf{Y}_2} = \frac{1}{\dfrac{1}{30 - j20} + \dfrac{1}{10 + j20}} = 20.15\angle 29.74^\circ\ \Omega$$

***Step III*** Calculation of $\mathbf{I}_L$ (Fig. 5.189)

Fig. 5.189

$$\mathbf{I}_L = \frac{18.2\angle -15.95^\circ}{20.15\angle 29.74^\circ + 40} = 0.31\angle -25.81^\circ\ \text{A}$$

## EXAMPLE 5.60

*Find the current **I** in the network shown in Fig. 5.190.*

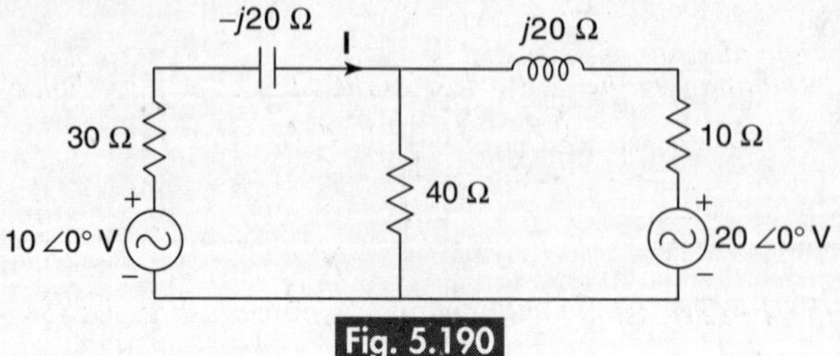


Fig. 5.190

**Solution** The network is redrawn, as shown in Fig. 5.191.

Fig. 5.191

***Step I*** Calculation of $\mathbf{V}_m$

$$\mathbf{V}_m = \frac{\mathbf{V}_1\mathbf{Y}_1 + \mathbf{V}_2\mathbf{Y}_2}{\mathbf{Y}_1 + \mathbf{Y}_2} = \frac{0\left(\dfrac{1}{40}\right) + (20\angle 0^\circ)\left(\dfrac{1}{10 + j20}\right)}{\dfrac{1}{40} + \dfrac{1}{10 + j20}} = 14.86\angle -21.8^\circ\ \text{V}$$

***Step II*** Calculation of $\mathbf{Z}_m$

$$\mathbf{Z}_m = \frac{1}{\mathbf{Y}_m} = \frac{1}{\mathbf{Y}_1 + \mathbf{Y}_2} = \frac{1}{\frac{1}{40} + \frac{1}{10 + j20}} = 16.61\angle 41.63^\circ\ \Omega$$

***Step III*** Calculation of **I** (Fig. 5.192)

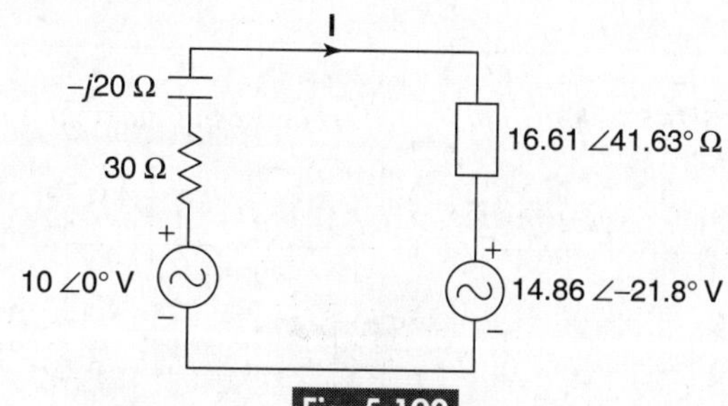


Fig. 5.192

$$\mathbf{I} = \frac{10 - 14.86\angle -21.8^\circ}{30 - j20 + 16.61\angle 41.63^\circ} = 0.15\angle 136.47^\circ\ \text{A}$$

## EXAMPLE 5.61

*Apply the dual Millman theorem and find the power loss in the (2 + j2) Ω impedance of Fig.5.193.*

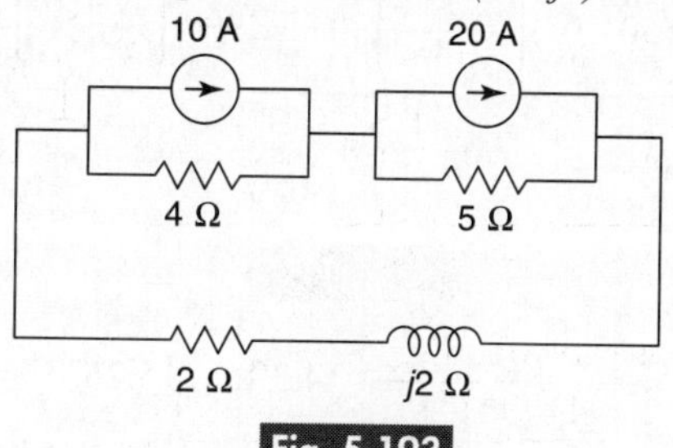


Fig. 5.193

**Solution**

***Step I*** Calculation of $\mathbf{I}_m$

$$\mathbf{I}_m = \frac{\mathbf{I}_1\mathbf{Z}_1 + \mathbf{I}_2\mathbf{Z}_2}{\mathbf{Z}_1 + \mathbf{Z}_2} = \frac{(10)(4) + (20)(5)}{4 + 5} = 15.56\ \text{A}$$

***Step II*** Calculation of $\mathbf{Z}_m$

$$\mathbf{Z}_m = \mathbf{Z}_1 + \mathbf{Z}_2 = 4 + 5 = 9\ \Omega$$

***Step III*** Calculation of *P* (Fig. 5.194)

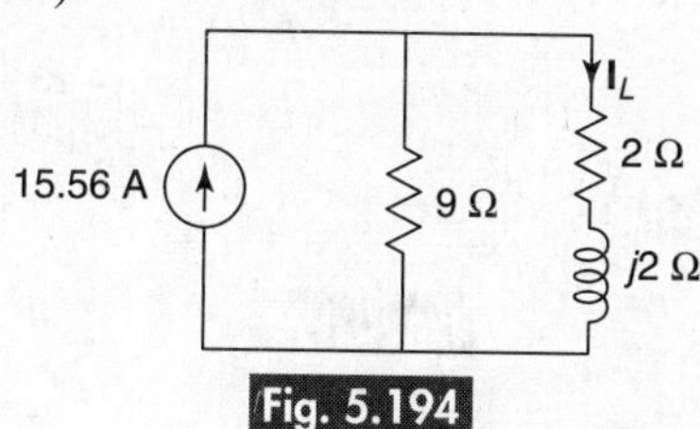


Fig. 5.194

By current division rule,

$$\mathbf{I}_L = 15.56 \times \frac{9}{9+2+j2} = 12.53\angle -10.3^\circ \text{ A}$$

$$P = \mathbf{I}_L^2 R_L = (12.53)^2 \times 2 = 314 \text{ W}$$

## EXAMPLE 5.62

*In the network shown in Fig. 5.195, what load $Z_L$ will receive the maximum power? Also, find maximum power.*

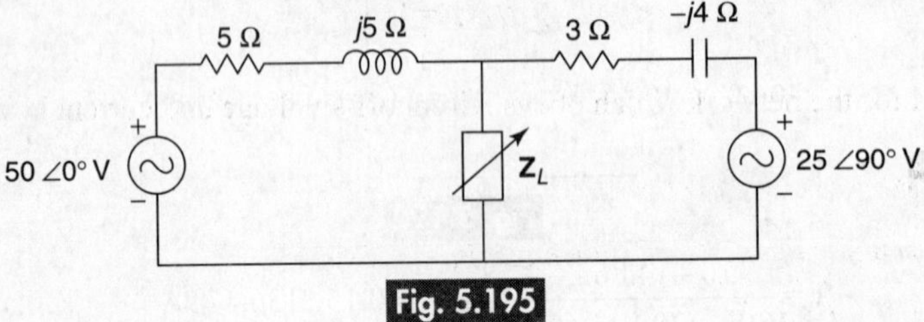


Fig. 5.195

**Solution**

***Step I*** Calculation of $\mathbf{V}_m$

$$\mathbf{V}_m = \frac{\mathbf{V}_1\mathbf{Y}_1 + \mathbf{V}_2\mathbf{Y}_2}{\mathbf{Y}_1 + \mathbf{Y}_2} = \frac{(50\angle 0^\circ)\left(\frac{1}{5+j5}\right) + (25\angle 90^\circ)\left(\frac{1}{3-j4}\right)}{\frac{1}{5+j5} + \frac{1}{3-j4}} = 9.81\angle -78.69^\circ \text{V}$$

***Step II*** Calculation of $\mathbf{Z}_m$

$$\mathbf{Z}_m = \frac{1}{\mathbf{Y}_m} = \frac{1}{\mathbf{Y}_1 + \mathbf{Y}_2} = \frac{1}{\frac{1}{5+j5} + \frac{1}{3-j4}} = 4.39\angle -15.26^\circ\ \Omega = (4.23 - j1.15)\ \Omega$$

***Step III*** Calculation of $\mathbf{Z}_L$

For maximum power transfer $\quad \mathbf{Z}_L = \mathbf{Z}_{\text{Th}}^* = (4.23 + j1.15)\ \Omega$

***Step IV*** Calculation of $P_{\max}$ (Fig. 5.196)

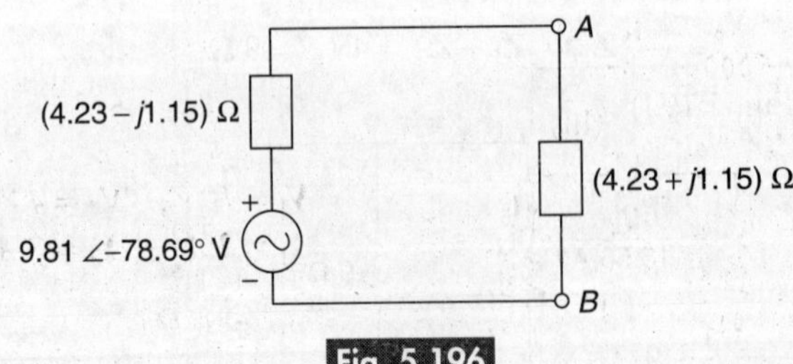


Fig. 5.196

$$P_{\max} = \frac{|\mathbf{V}_m|^2}{4R_L} = \frac{(9.81)^2}{4 \times 4.23} = 5.69 \text{ W}$$

## 5.9 TELLEGEN'S THEOREM

LO 5.5

Tellegen's theorem states that *The algebraic sum of the powers in all branches of the network at any instant is zero.*

$$\sum_{k=1}^{n} \mathbf{V}_k \mathbf{I}_k = 0$$

This condition is valid for the network which obeys Kirchhoff's voltage and current laws.

**EXAMPLE 5.63**

*Verify Tellegen's theorem for the network shown in Fig. 5.197.*

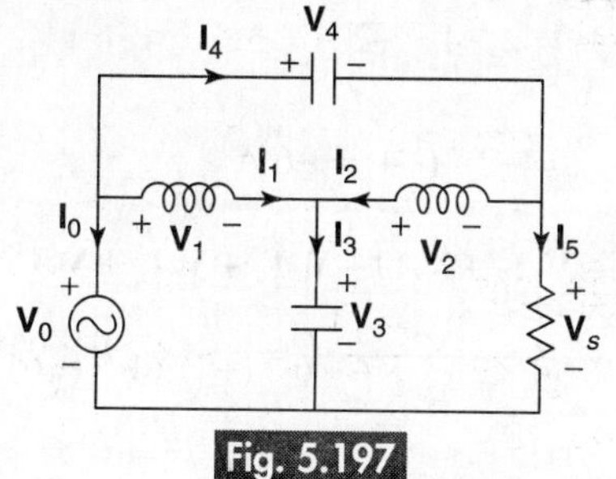


Fig. 5.197

$V_0 = 20\ V,\quad V_1 = 16\ V$

$V_2 = 2\ V,\quad V_3 = 4\ V$

$V_4 = 14\ V,\quad V_5 = 6\ V$

$V_0 = -16\ A\quad I_1 = 12\ A$

$I_2 = 2\ A,\quad I_3 = 14\ A$

$I_4 = 4\ A,\quad I_5 = 2\ A$

**Solution**

$$\sum_{b=0}^{5} \mathbf{V}_b \mathbf{I}_b = \mathbf{V}_0\mathbf{I}_0 + \mathbf{V}_1\mathbf{I}_1 + \mathbf{V}_2\mathbf{I}_2 + \mathbf{V}_3\mathbf{I}_3 + \mathbf{V}_4\mathbf{I}_4 + \mathbf{V}_5\mathbf{I}_5$$

$$= 20(-16) + 16 \times 12 + 2 \times 2 + 4 \times 14 + 14 \times 4 + 6 \times 2 = 0$$

Hence, Tellegen's theorem is verified.

**EXAMPLE 5.64**

*In the network shown in Fig. 5.198, check the validity of Tellegen's theorem.*

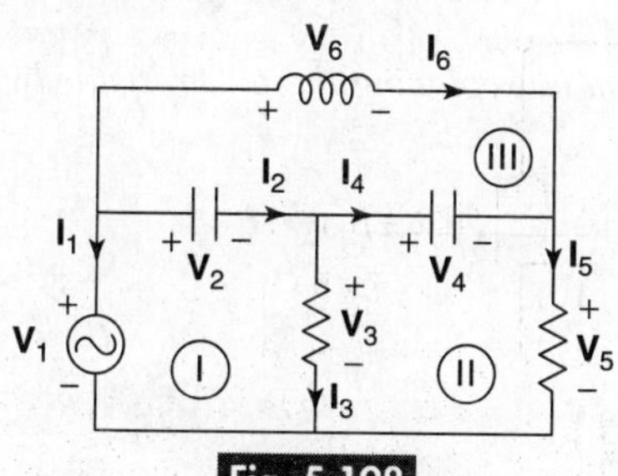


Fig. 5.198

$\mathbf{V}_1 = 10\ V,\quad \mathbf{V}_2 = 4\ V,\quad \mathbf{V}_4 = 6\ V$

$\mathbf{I}_1 = 2\ A,\quad \mathbf{I}_2 = 2\ A,\quad \mathbf{I}_3 = 4\ A$

**Solution** Applying KVL to mesh 1,

$$V_1 - V_2 - V_3 = 0$$
$$V_3 = V_1 - V_2 = 10 - 4 = 6\text{ V}$$

Applying KVL to mesh 2,

$$V_3 - V_4 - V_5 = 0$$
$$V_5 = V_3 - V_4 = 6 - 6 = 0$$

Applying KVL to mesh 3,

$$-V_6 + V_4 + V_2 = 0$$
$$V_6 = V_2 + V_4 = 4 + 6 = 10\text{ V}$$

Applying KCL at node 1,

$$I_1 + I_2 + I_6 = 0$$
$$I_6 = -I_1 - I_2 = -2 - 2 = -4\text{ A}$$

Applying KCL at node 2,

$$I_2 = I_3 + I_4$$
$$I_4 = I_2 - I_3 = 2 - 4 = -2\text{ A}$$

Applying KCL at node 3,

$$I_5 = I_4 + I_6 = -2 + (-4) = -6\text{ A}$$

$$\sum_{b=1}^{6} V_b I_b = V_1I_1 + V_2I_2 + V_3I_3 + V_4I_4 + V_5I_5 + V_6I_6$$
$$= 10\times2 + 4\times2 + 6\times4 + 6\times(-2) + 0\times(-6) + 10\times(-4)$$
$$= 0$$

Hence, Tellegen's theorem is verified.

## 5.10 SUBSTITUTION THEOREM

LO 5.7

Explain substitution and compensation theorems

The substitution theorem states that *Any branch in a network can be substituted by a different branch without disturbing the voltages and currents in the entire network, provided the new branch has the same set of terminal voltage and current as the original network.*

**EXAMPLE 5.65**

*In the network of Fig. 5.199, verify the substitution theorem by replacing the 6 Ω resistor by (a) a voltage source (b) a current source.*

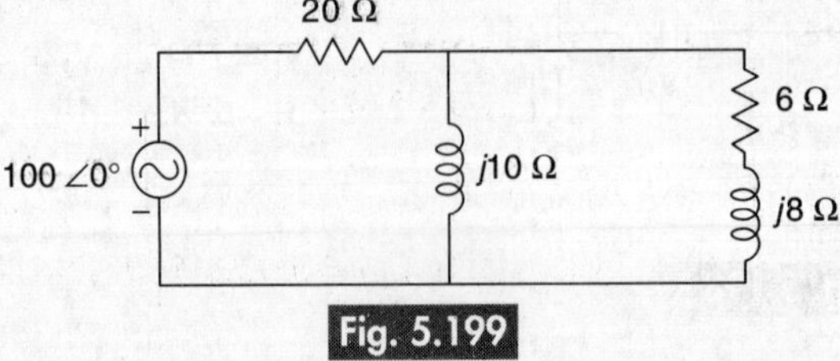


Fig. 5.199

**Solution**

***Step I*** Calculation of current through and voltage across the 6 Ω resistor (Fig. 5.200)

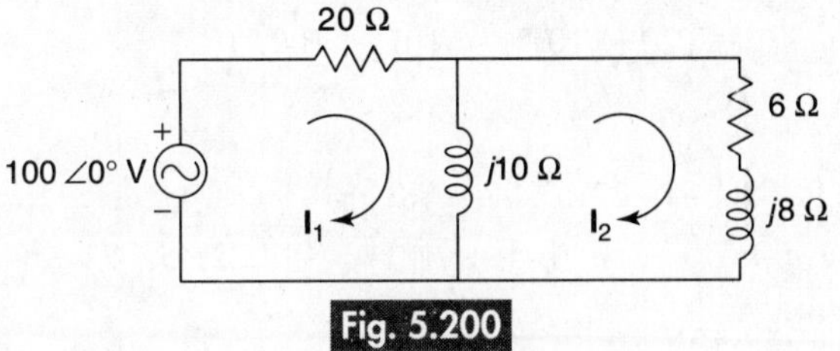


Fig. 5.200

Applying KVL to mesh 1,

$$100\angle 0° - 20\mathbf{I}_1 - j10(\mathbf{I}_1 - \mathbf{I}_2) = 0$$

$$(20 + j10)\mathbf{I}_1 - j10\mathbf{I}_2 = 100\angle 0° \qquad \text{...(i)}$$

Applying KVL to mesh 2,

$$-j10(\mathbf{I}_2 - \mathbf{I}_1) - (6 + j8)\mathbf{I}_2 = 0$$

$$-j10\mathbf{I}_1 + (6 + j18)\mathbf{I}_2 = 0 \qquad \text{...(ii)}$$

Writing Eqs (i) and (ii) in matrix form,

$$\begin{bmatrix} 20 + j10 & -j10 \\ -j10 & 6 + j18 \end{bmatrix} \begin{bmatrix} \mathbf{I}_1 \\ \mathbf{I}_2 \end{bmatrix} = \begin{bmatrix} 100\angle 0° \\ 0 \end{bmatrix}$$

By Cramer's rule,

$$\mathbf{I}_1 = \frac{\begin{vmatrix} 100\angle 0° & -j10 \\ 0 & 6 + j18 \end{vmatrix}}{\begin{vmatrix} 20 + j10 & -j10 \\ -j10 & 6 + j18 \end{vmatrix}} = 4.5\angle -13° \text{ A}$$

$$\mathbf{I}_2 = \frac{\begin{vmatrix} 20 + j10 & 100\angle 0° \\ -j10 & 0 \end{vmatrix}}{\begin{vmatrix} 20 + j10 & -j10 \\ -j10 & 6 + j18 \end{vmatrix}} = 2.37\angle 5.44° \text{ A}$$

$$\mathbf{I}_{6\Omega} = \mathbf{I}_2 = 2.37\angle 5.44° \text{ A}$$

$$\mathbf{V}_{6\Omega} = 6\mathbf{I}_2 = 6(2.37\angle 5.44°) = 14.22\angle 5.44° \text{ V}$$

***Step II*** When 6 Ω resistor is replaced by voltage source of 14.22∠5.44° V (Fig. 5.201)

Fig. 5.201

Applying KVL to mesh 1,

$$100\angle 0° - 20\mathbf{I}_1 - j10(\mathbf{I}_1 - \mathbf{I}_2) = 0$$

$$(20 + j10)\mathbf{I}_1 - j10\mathbf{I}_2 = 100\angle 0° \quad \text{...(i)}$$

Applying KVL to mesh 2,

$$-j10(\mathbf{I}_2 - \mathbf{I}_1) - 14.22\angle 5.44° - j8\mathbf{I}_2 = 0$$

$$-j10\mathbf{I}_1 + j18\mathbf{I}_2 = -14.22\angle 5.44° \quad \text{...(ii)}$$

Writing Eqs (i) and (ii) in matrix form,

$$\begin{bmatrix} 20 + j10 & -j10 \\ -j10 & j18 \end{bmatrix} \begin{bmatrix} \mathbf{I}_1 \\ \mathbf{I}_2 \end{bmatrix} = \begin{bmatrix} 100\angle 0° \\ -14.22\angle 5.44° \end{bmatrix}$$

By Cramer's rule,

$$\mathbf{I}_1 = \frac{\begin{vmatrix} 100\angle 0° & -j10 \\ -14.22\angle 5.44° & j18 \end{vmatrix}}{\begin{vmatrix} 20 + j10 & -j10 \\ -j10 & j18 \end{vmatrix}} = 4.5\angle -13° \text{ A}$$

$$\mathbf{I}_2 = \frac{\begin{vmatrix} 20 + j10 & 100\angle 0° \\ -j10 & -14.22\angle 5.44° \end{vmatrix}}{\begin{vmatrix} 20 + j10 & -j10 \\ -j10 & j18 \end{vmatrix}} = 2.37\angle 5.44° \text{ A}$$

Since currents $\mathbf{I}_1$ and $\mathbf{I}_2$ remain the same, substitution theorem is verified.

***Step III*** When the 6 Ω resistor is replaced by a current source of 2.37∠5.44° A (Fig. 5.202)

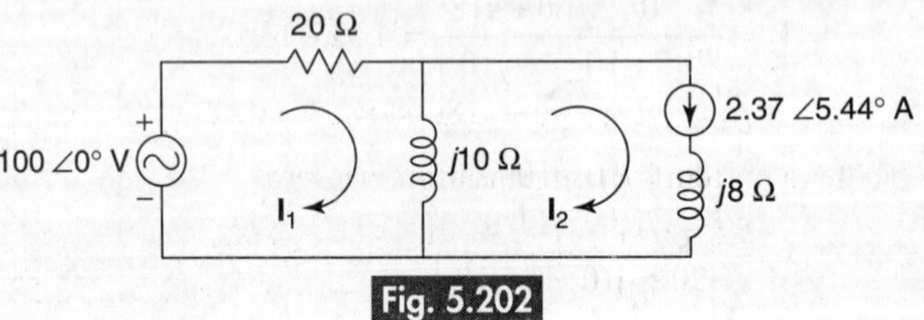


Fig. 5.202

Applying KVL to mesh 1,

$$100\angle 0° - 20\mathbf{I}_1 - j10(\mathbf{I}_1 - \mathbf{I}_2) = 0$$

$$(20 + j10)\mathbf{I}_1 - j10\mathbf{I}_2 = 100\angle 0° \quad \text{...(i)}$$

For mesh 2,

$$\mathbf{I}_2 = 2.37\angle 5.44° \text{ A} \quad \text{...(ii)}$$

Solving Eqs (i) and (ii),

$$\mathbf{I}_1 = 4.5\angle -13° \text{ A}$$

Since currents $\mathbf{I}_1$ and $\mathbf{I}_2$ remain the same, substitution theorem is verified.

## 5.11 COMPENSATION THEOREM

LO 5.7

The compensation theorem states that '*In any linear bilateral active network, if any branch carrying a current* **I** *has its impedance* **Z** *changed by an amount* δ**Z**, *the resulting changes that occur in the other branches are the same as those which would have been provided by an opposing voltage source of value* $\mathbf{V}_C$ **(I δZ)** *introduced into the modified branch.*'

### EXAMPLE 5.66

*In the network of Fig. 5.203, the impedance (3+j2) Ω is changed to (5+j3) Ω. Determine the change in current drawn from the source by direct calculation and then verify the result by compensation theorem.*

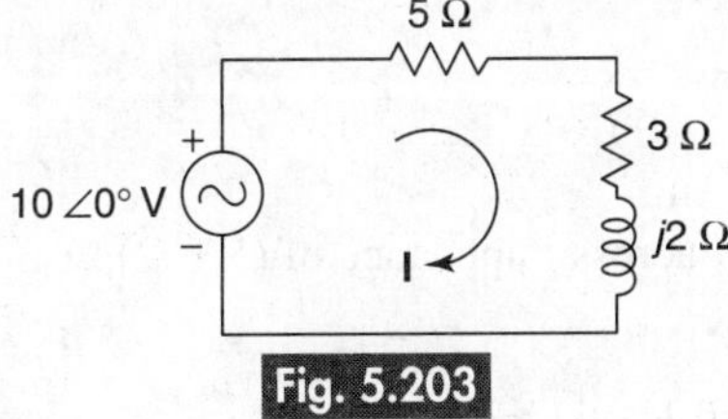


Fig. 5.203

**Solution**

***Step I*** Calculation of change in current

$$\mathbf{I} = \frac{10\angle 0^\circ}{5+3+j2} = 1.21\angle{-14.04^\circ} \text{ A}$$

When impedance (3 + *j*2) Ω is changed to (5+*j*3) Ω,

$$\mathbf{I}' = \frac{10\angle 0^\circ}{5+5+j3} = 0.96\angle{-16.7^\circ} \text{ A}$$

$$\delta\mathbf{I} = \mathbf{I}' - \mathbf{I} = 0.96\angle{-16.7^\circ} - 1.21\angle{-14.04^\circ} = 0.25\angle 176.02^\circ \text{ A}$$

***Step II*** Calculation of change in current by compensation theorem

$$\delta\mathbf{Z} = (5+j3) - (3+j2) = (2+j1)\ \Omega$$

$$\mathbf{V}_c = \delta\mathbf{Z}\mathbf{I} = (2+j1)(1.21\angle{-14.04^\circ}) = 2.71\angle 12.53^\circ \text{ V}$$

The compensating network is shown in Fig. 5.204.

$$\delta\mathbf{I} = -\frac{2.71\angle 12.53^\circ}{5+3+j2+2+j1}$$

$$= 0.26\angle 175.83^\circ \text{ A}$$

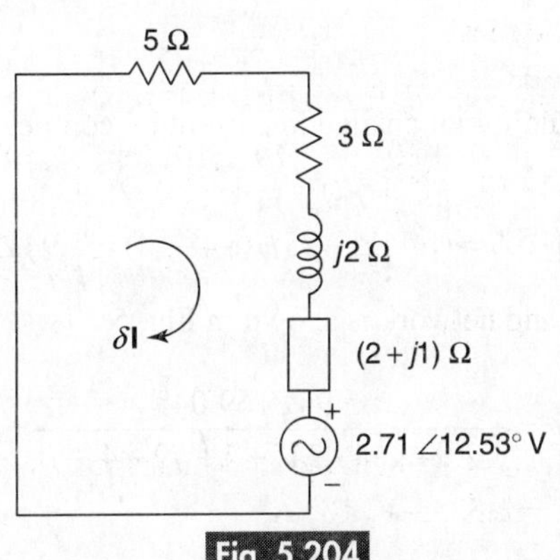


Fig. 5.204

## EXAMPLE 5.67

*In the network of Fig. 5.205, the impedance (5 + j2) Ω is changed to (1 + j1) Ω. Find the change in current drawn from the supply by direct calculation and then verify by the compensation theorem.*

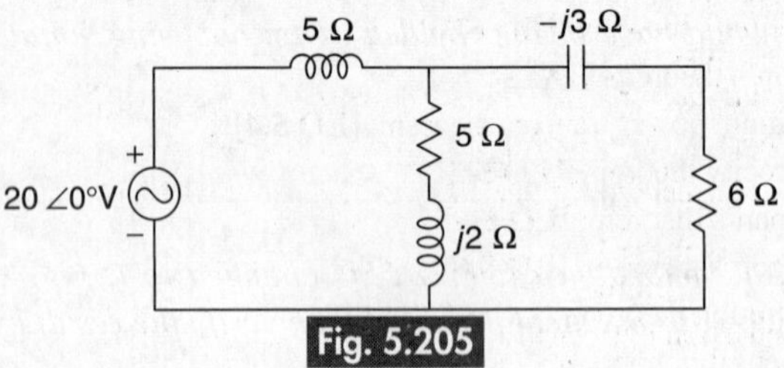


Fig. 5.205

### Solution

***Step I*** Calculation of change in current

Finding Thevenin's equivalent circuit across impedance of (5 + *j*2) Ω (Fig. 5.206)

$$\mathbf{Z}_{\text{Th}} = \frac{5(6-j3)}{5+6-j3} = 2.94\angle{-11.31°}\ \Omega$$

$$\mathbf{I} = \frac{20\angle 0°}{5+6-j3} = 1.75\angle 15.26°\ \text{A}$$

$$\mathbf{V}_{\text{Th}} = (6-j3)\mathbf{I} = (6-j3)(1.75\angle 15.26°) = 11.74\angle{-11.31°}\ \text{V}$$

Fig. 5.206

Thevenin's equivalent network is shown in Fig. 5. 207.

$$\mathbf{I}_L = \frac{11.74\angle{-11.31°}}{2.94\angle{-11.31°}+5+j2} = 1.47\angle{-21.55°}\ \text{A}$$

When impedance (5 + *j*2) Ω is changed to (1 + *j*1) Ω,

$$\mathbf{I}'_L = \frac{11.74\angle{-11.31°}}{2.94\angle{-11.31°}+1+j1} = 3\angle{-17.53°}\ \text{A}$$

Fig. 5.207

$$\delta\mathbf{I}_L = \mathbf{I}'_L - \mathbf{I}_L = 3\angle{-17.53°} - 1.44\angle{-25°} = 1.53\angle{-13.69°}\ \text{A}$$

***Step II*** Calculation of change in current by compensation theorem

$$\delta\mathbf{Z} = (1+j1)-(5+j2) = (-4-j1)\ \Omega$$

$$\mathbf{V}_c = \mathbf{I}_L\delta\mathbf{Z} = (1.44\angle{-25°})(-4-j1) = 5.94\angle 169.04°\ \text{V}$$

The compensating network is shown in Fig. 5.208.

$$\delta\mathbf{I}_L = -\frac{5.94\angle 169.04°}{2.94\angle{-11.31°}+5+j2-4-j1}$$

$$= 1.52\angle{-17.18°}\ \text{A}$$

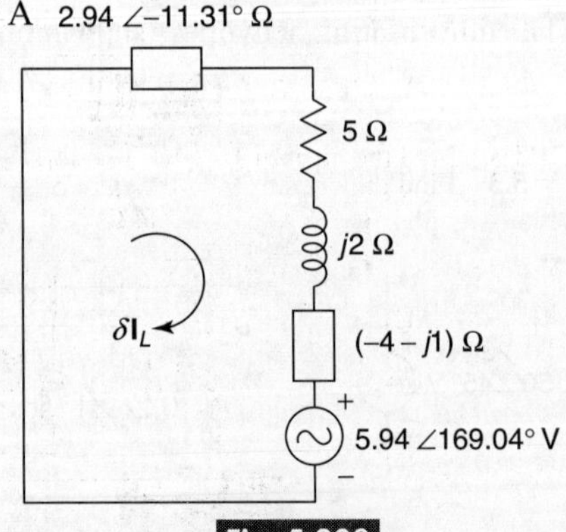


Fig. 5.208

## Theory Questions

5.1 State and explain superposition theorem. **[LO 5.2]** ○●○
5.2 State and explain Thevenin's theorem. **[LO 5.3]** ○●○
5.3 State and explain Norton's theorem. **[LO 5.3]** ○●○
5.4 State and explain maximum power transfer theorem. **[LO 5.4]** ○●○
5.5 State and explain reciprocity theorem. **[LO 5.5]** ○●○
5.6 State and explain Millman's theorem. **[LO 5.6]** ○●○
5.7 State and explain Tellegen's theorem. **[LO 5.6]** ○●○
5.8 State and explain substitution theorem. **[LO 5.7]** ○●○
5.9 State and explain compensation theorem. **[LO 5.7]** ○●○

## Practice Problems

### Mesh Analysis

5.1 Find the current through the $3 + j4\ \Omega$ impedance in Fig. 5.209. ○●○

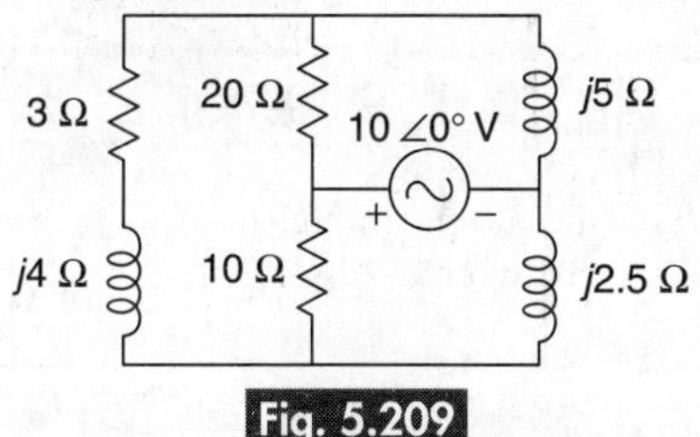


Fig. 5.209

5.2 In the network of Fig. 5.210, find $\mathbf{V}_0$. ○●○

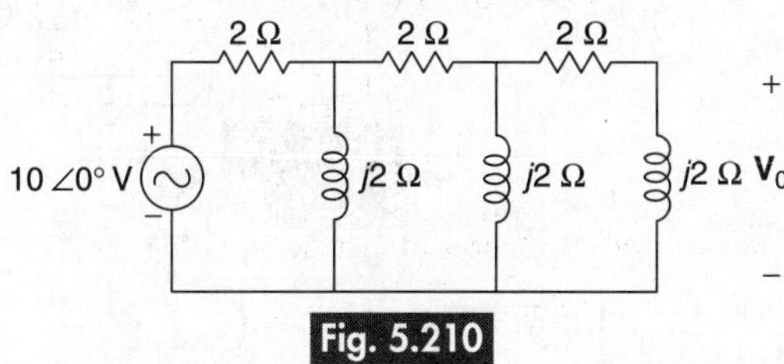


Fig. 5.210

5.3 Find the current $\mathbf{I}_3$ in the network of Fig. 5.211. ○●○

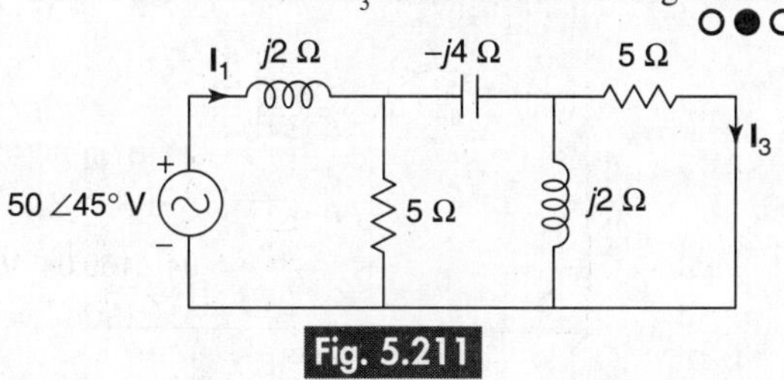


Fig. 5.211

5.4 In the network of Fig. 5.212, find $\mathbf{V}_2$ which results in zero current through the $4\ \Omega$ resistor. ○○●

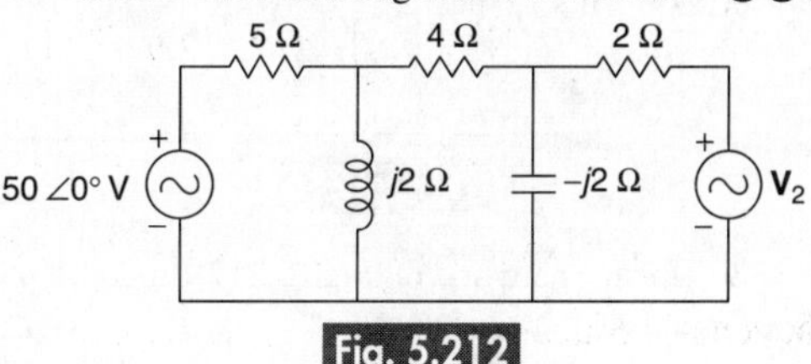


Fig. 5.212

### Node Analysis

5.5 For the network shown in Fig. 5.213, find the voltage $\mathbf{V}_{AB}$. ○●○

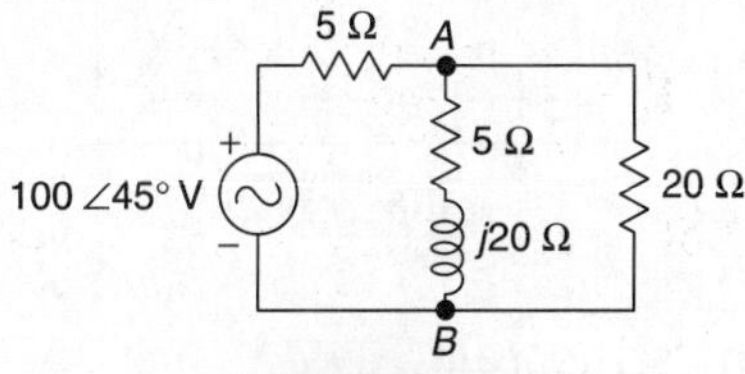


Fig. 5.213

5.6 Find the voltages at nodes 1 and 2 in the network of Fig. 5.214. ○●○

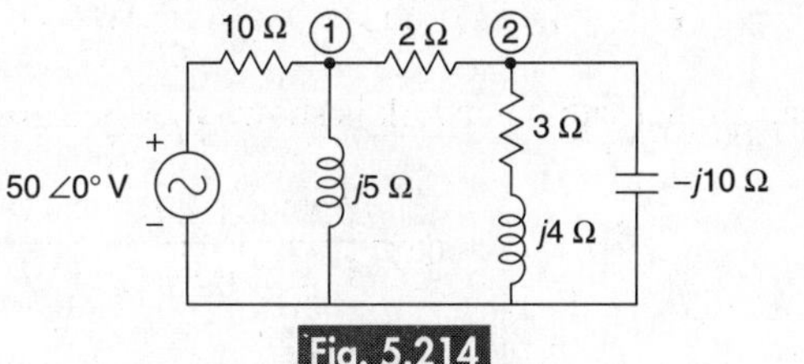


Fig. 5.214

**5.7** In the network of Fig. 5.215, find the current in the 10 ∠30° V source. ○●○

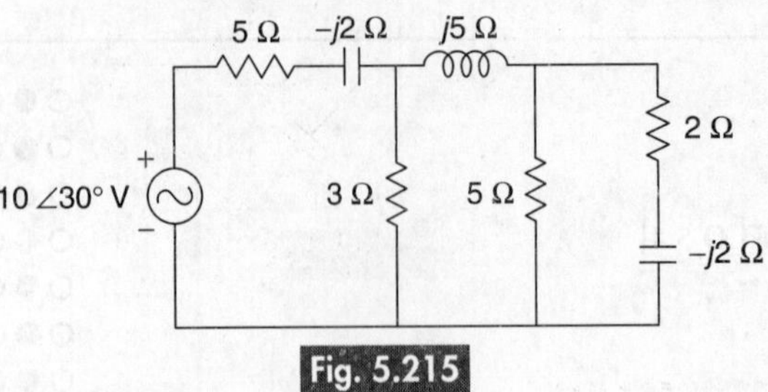


Fig. 5.215

## Superposition Theorem

**5.8** For the network shown in Fig. 5.216, find the current in the 10 Ω resistor. ○○●

Fig. 5.216

**5.9** In the network of Fig. 5.217, find the current through capacitance. ○○●

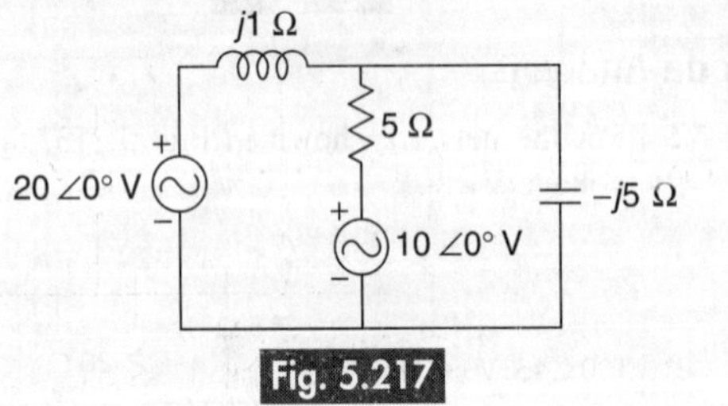


Fig. 5.217

## Thevenin's Theorem

**5.10** Obtain Thevenin's equivalent network for the network shown in Fig. 5.218. ○●○

Fig. 5.218

**5.11** Obtain Thevenin's equivalent network for Fig. 5.219. ○●○

Fig. 5.219

## Norton's Theorem

**5.12** Find Norton's equivalent network for Fig. 5.220. ○●○

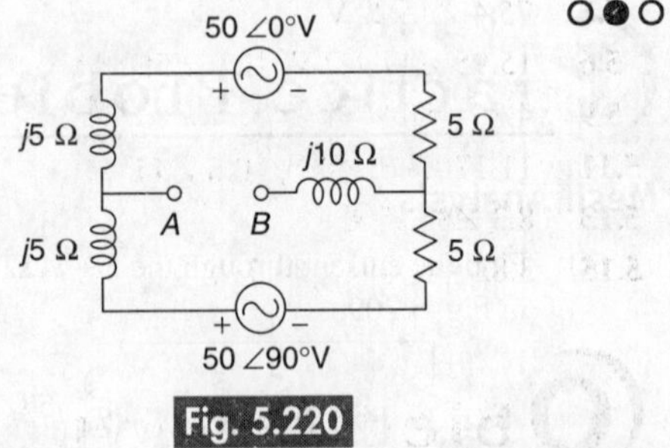


Fig. 5.220

**5.13** Find the current through the $(3 + j4)\ \Omega$ impedance in the network of Fig. 5.221. ○●○

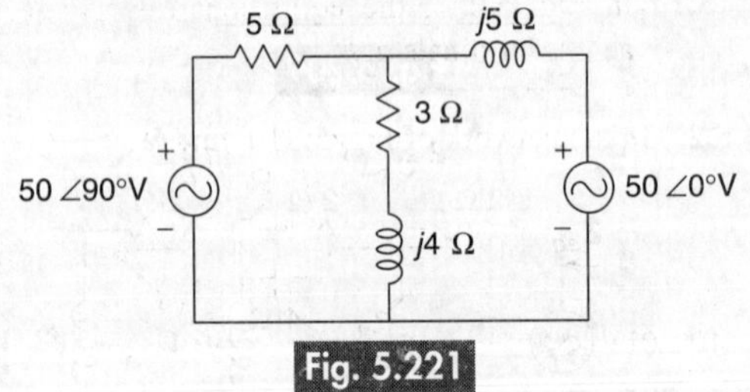


Fig. 5.221

## Maximum Power Transfer Theorem

**5.14** Determine the maximum power delivered to the load in the network shown in Fig. 5.222. ○●○

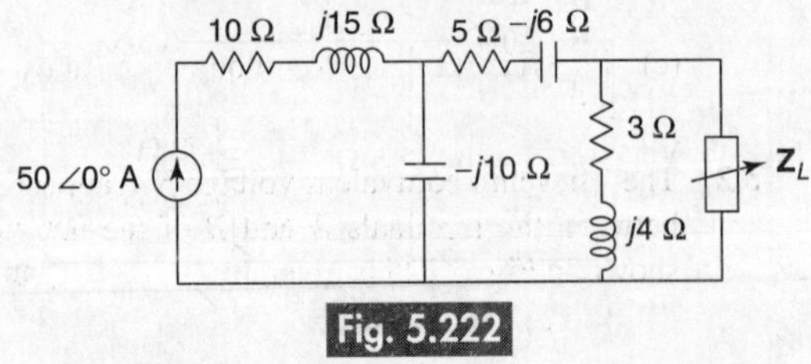


Fig. 5.222

**5.15** For the network shown in Fig. 5.223, find the value of $\mathbf{Z}_L$ that will receive the maximum power. Also, determine this power. ○●○

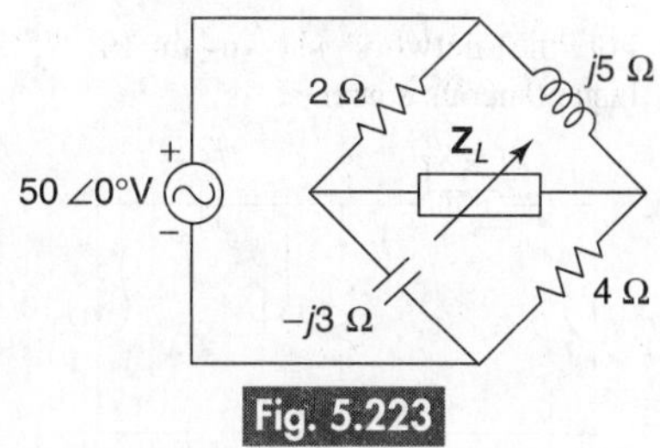


Fig. 5.223

## ANSWERS TO PRACTICE PROBLEMS

| | | | |
|---|---|---|---|
| **5.1** | 0 | **5.2** | 1.56 ∠128.7° V |
| **5.3** | 11.6 ∠113.2° A | **5.4** | 26.3 ∠113.2° V |
| **5.5** | 75.4 ∠55.2° V | **5.7** | 1.44 ∠38.8° A |
| **5.6** | 15.95 ∠49.94° V, 12.9 ∠55.5° V | **5.8** | 73.4 ∠−21.84° A |
| **5.9** | 4.86 ∠80.8° A | **5.10** | 0.192 ∠−43.4° V, 88.7 ∠11.55° Ω |
| **5.11** | 11.17 ∠−63.4° V, 10.6 ∠45° Ω | **5.12** | 2.77 ∠−33.7° A, 2.5 + $j$12.5 Ω |
| **5.13** | 8.3 ∠85.2° A | **5.14** | 1032.35 W |
| **5.15** | 3.82 − $j$1.03 Ω, 54.5 W | | |

# Objective-Type Questions

## From GATE and Other Competitive Examinations

**5.1** In Fig. 5.224, the equivalent impedance seen across terminals $a$, $b$, is ○●○

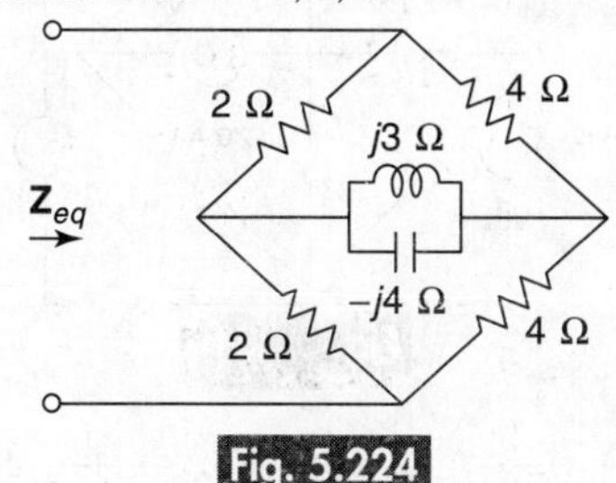


Fig. 5.224

(a) $\frac{16}{3}$ Ω (b) $\frac{8}{3}$ Ω

(c) $\left(\frac{8}{3}+j12\right)$ Ω (d) none of the above

**5.2** The Thevenin equivalent voltage $\mathbf{V}_{\text{Th}}$ appearing between the terminals $A$ and $B$ of the network shown in Fig. 5.225 is given by ○●○

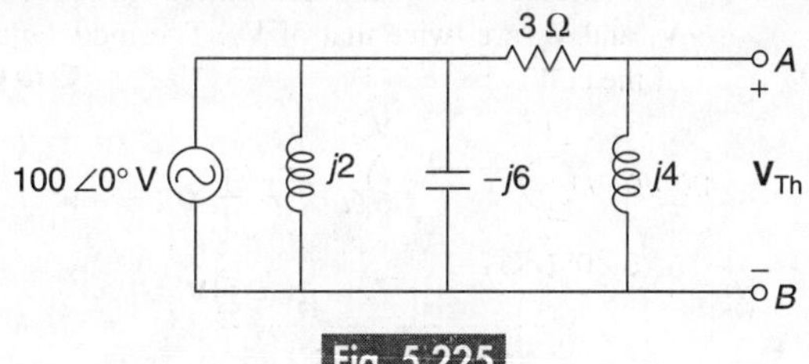


Fig. 5.225

(a) $j16(3 - j4)$ (b) $j16(3 + j4)$

(c) $16(3 + j4)$ (d) $16\,(3 - j4)$

**5.3** A source of angular frequency of 1 rad/s has a source impedance consisting of a 1 Ω resistance in series with a 1 H inductance. The load that will obtain the maximum power transfer is ○●○

(a) 1 Ω resistance

(b) 1 Ω resistance in parallel with 1 H inductance

(c) 1 Ω resistance in series with 1 F capacitance

(d) 1 Ω resistance in parallel with 1 F capacitance

**5.4** For the network shown in Fig. 5.226, the instantaneous current $I_1$ is ●○○

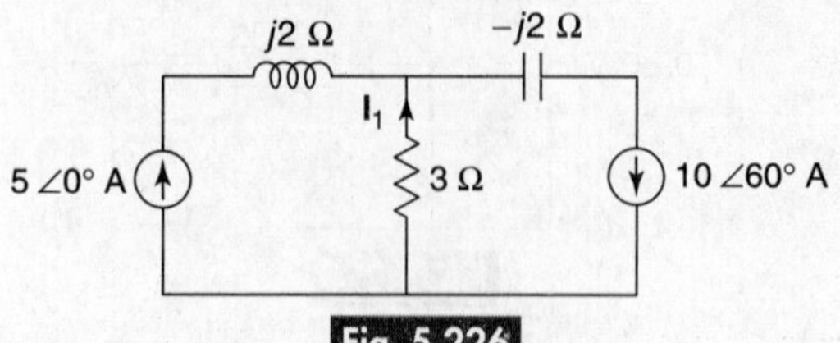


Fig. 5.226

(a) $\frac{10\sqrt{3}}{2}\angle 90°$ A (b) $\frac{10\sqrt{3}}{2}\angle -90°$ A

(c) 5 ∠60° A (d) 5∠−60° A

**5.5** In the network shown in Fig. 5.227, the current supplied by the sinusoidal current source **I** is ●○○

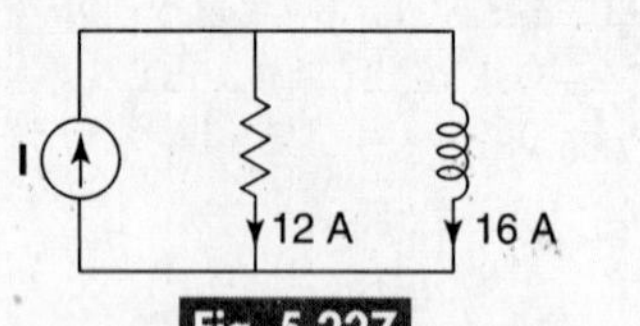


Fig. 5.227

(a) 28 A (b) 4 A

(c) 20 A (d) cannot be determined

**5.6** In the network of Fig. 5.228, the magnitudes of $\mathbf{V}_L$ and $\mathbf{V}_C$ are twice that of $\mathbf{V}_R$. The inductance of the coil is ○●○

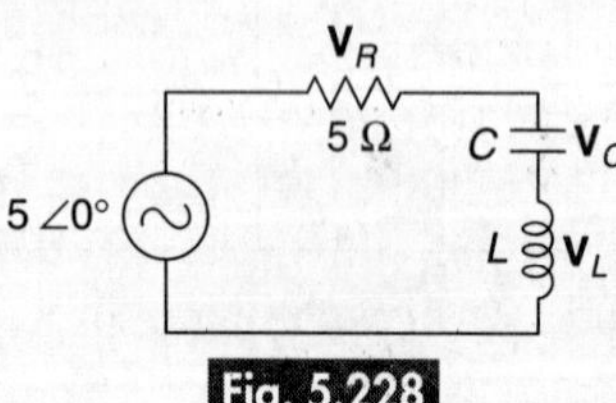


Fig. 5.228

(a) 2.14 mH (b) 5.3 H

(c) 31.8 mH (d) 1.32 H

**5.7** Phase angle of the current I with respect to the voltage $\mathbf{V}_1$ in the circuit shown in Fig. 5.229. ○●○

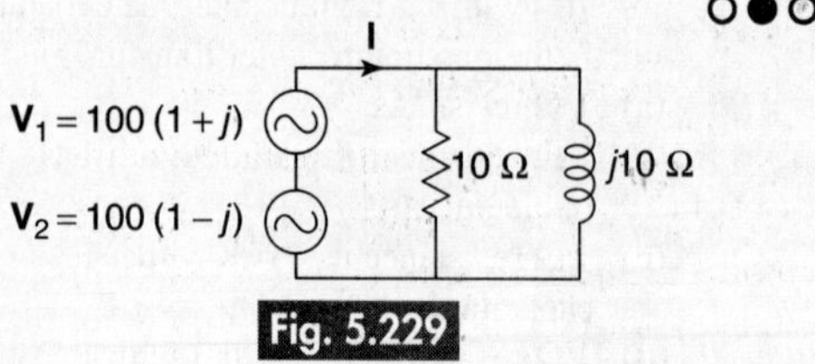


Fig. 5.229

(a) 0° (b) 45°

(c) −45° (d) −90°

**5.8** A source $V_s(t) = V \cos 100\,\pi t$ has an internal impedance of (4 + j3) Ω. If a purely resistive load connected to this source has to extract the maximum power out of the source, its value in Ω should be ○●○

(a) 3 (b) 4

(c) 5 (d) 7

**5.9** In the circuit shown in Fig. 5.230, if the source voltage $\mathbf{V}_s = 100\angle 53.13°$ V then the Thevenin's equivalent voltage in volts, as seen by the load resistance $R_L$ is ○○●

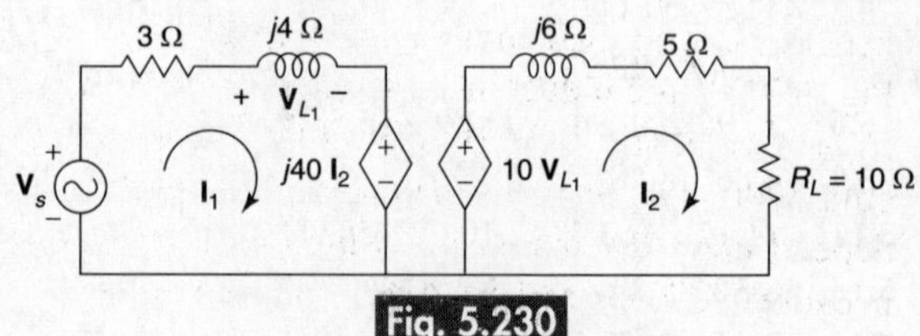


Fig. 5.230

(a) 100 ∠ 90° (b) 800 ∠ 0°

(c) 800 ∠ 90° (d) 100 ∠ 60°

**5.10** In the circuit shown in Fig. 5.231, the current through the inductor is ○○●

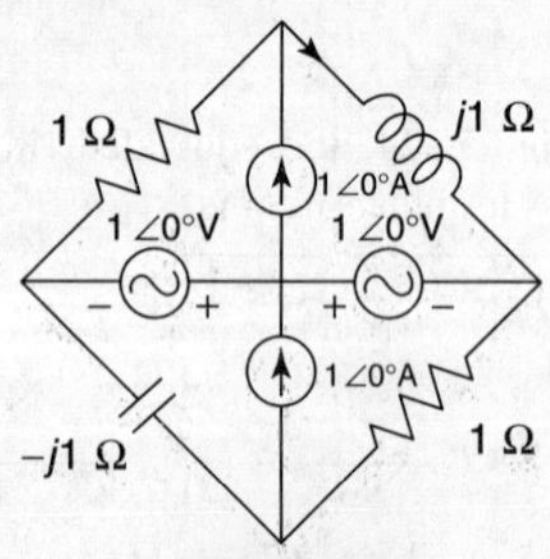


Fig. 5.231

(a) $\frac{2}{1+j}$ A (b) $-\frac{1}{1+j}$ A

(c) $\frac{1}{1+j}$ A (d) 0 A

**5.11** Assuming both the voltage sources are in phase, the value of R for which maximum power is transferred from circuit A to circuit B is ○●○

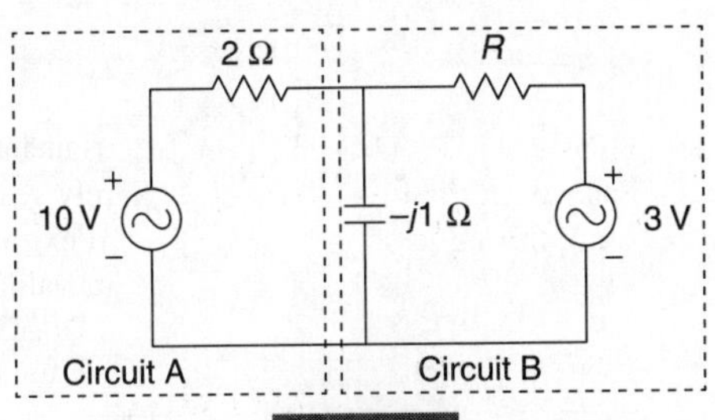

Fig. 5.232

(a) 0.8 Ω (b) 1.4 Ω
(c) 2 Ω (d) 2.8 Ω

**5.12** In the circuit shown in Fig. 5.233, the Norton equivalent current in amperes w.r.t. terminals $P$ and $Q$ is ○●○

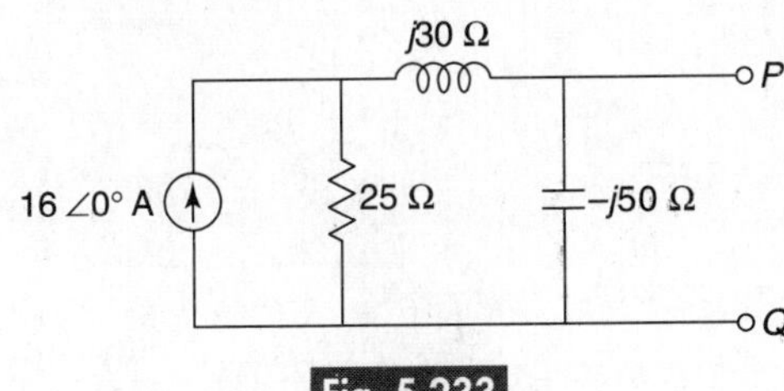

Fig. 5.233

(a) 6.4 − j4.8 (b) 6.56 − j7.87
(c) 10 + j0 (d) 16 + j0

**5.13** In the circuit shown in Fig. 5.234, the current **I** is equal to ○●○

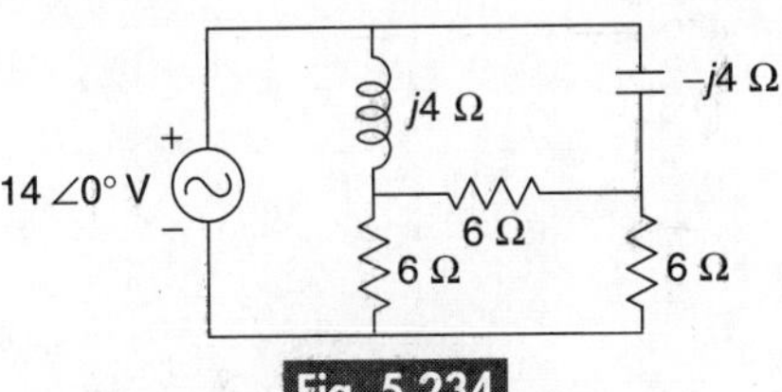

Fig. 5.234

(a) 1.4 ∠ 0° A (b) 2.0 ∠ 0° A
(c) 2.8 ∠ 0° A (d) 3.2 ∠ 0° A

**5.14** The current **I** in the circuit shown in Fig. 5.235 ○●○

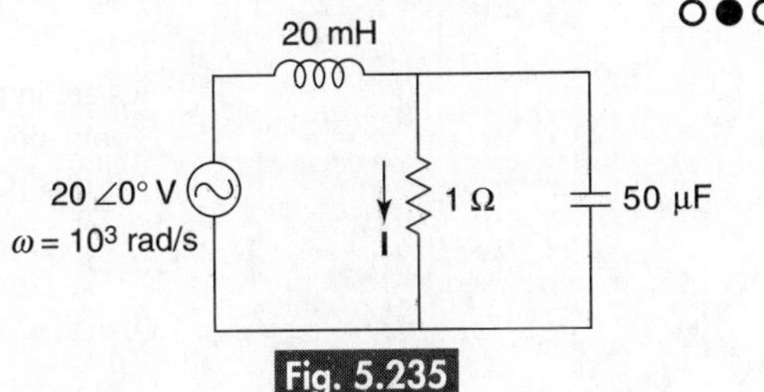

Fig. 5.235

(a) −j1 A (b) j1 A
(c) 0 A (d) 20 A

**5.15** An independent voltage source in series with an impedance $\mathbf{Z}_s = R_s + jX_s$ delivers a maximum average power to a load impedance $\mathbf{Z}_L$ when ●○○

(a) $\mathbf{Z}_L = R_s + jX_s$ (b) $\mathbf{Z}_L = R_s$
(c) $\mathbf{Z}_L = jX_s$ (d) $\mathbf{Z}_L = R_s - jX_s$

**5.16** If each branch of delta circuit has impedance of $\sqrt{3}Z$ then each branch of the equivalent wye circuit has impedance ●○○

(a) $\frac{Z}{\sqrt{3}}$ (b) 3Z
(c) $3\sqrt{3}Z$ (d) $\frac{Z}{3}$

**5.17** In the Fig. 5.236, the value of the load resistor $R_L$ which maximises the power delivered to it is ○●○

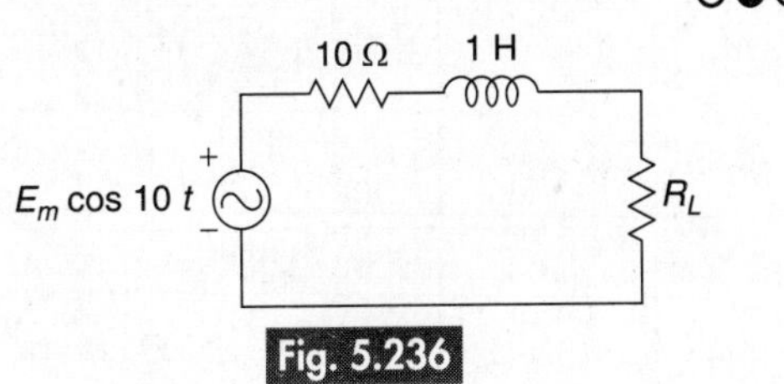

Fig. 5.236

(a) 14.14 Ω (b) 10 Ω
(c) 200 Ω (d) 28.28 Ω

**5.18** In the circuit of Fig. 5.237, the maximum power (in watts) that can be transferred to the load $R_L$ is ○●○

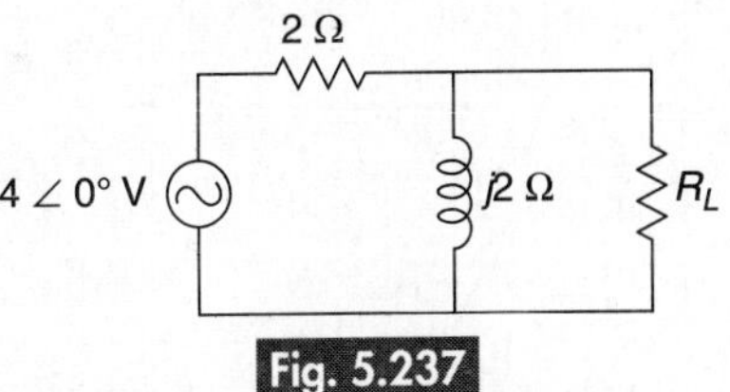

Fig. 5.237

(a) 1.649 (b) 1.469
(c) 1.5 (d) 1.2

**5.19** In the circuit shown in Fig. 5.238, the current $I$ flowing through 50 Ω resistor will be zero if the value of capacitor $C$ (in µF) is ○●○

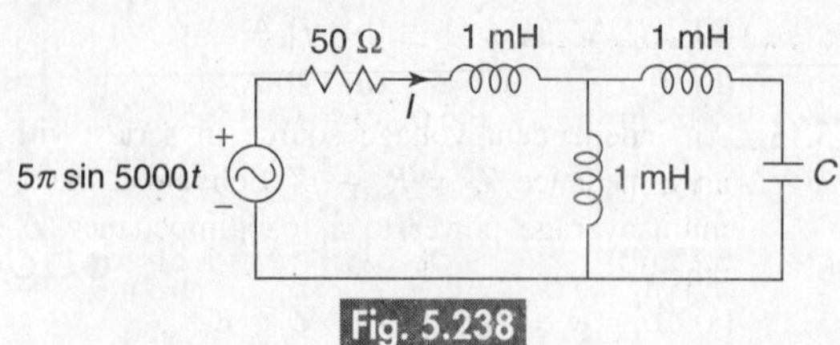


Fig. 5.238

(a) 10 (b) 20

(c) 1 (d) 5

**5.20** Norton's theorem states that a complex network connected to a load can be replaced with an equivalent impedance________. ●○○

(a) in series with a current source

(b) in parallel with a voltage source

(c) in series with a voltage source

(d) in parallel with a current source

**5.21** In the circuit shown in Fig. 5.239, the value of node voltage $V_2$ is ○●○

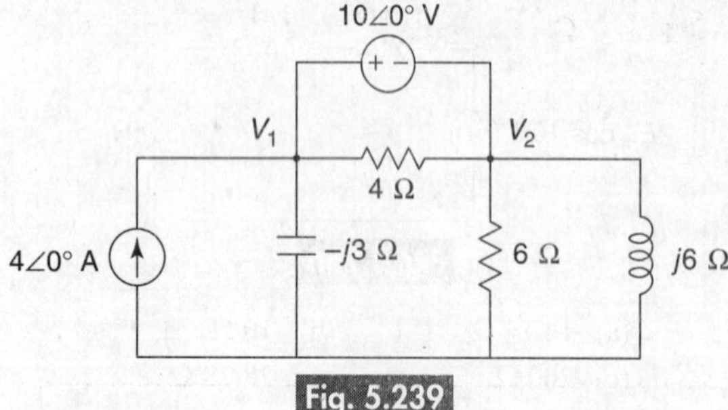


Fig. 5.239

(a) $22 + j2$ V (b) $2 + j22$ V

(c) $22 - j2$ V (d) $2 - j22$ V

**5.22** In the circuit shown in Fig. 5.240, the angular frequency $\omega$ (in rad/s), at which the Nortan equivalent impedance as seen from terminals $b$-$b'$ is purely resistive, is ○●○

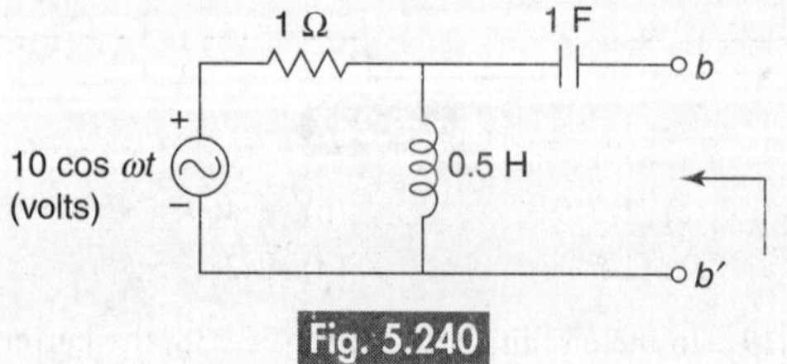


Fig. 5.240

(a) 2.5 (b) 2

(c) 3.1 (d) 1

**5.23** In the *RLC* circuit shown in Fig. 5.241, the input voltage is given by $v_i(t) = 2\cos(200t) + 4\sin(500t)$. The output voltage $v_o(t)$ is ○○●

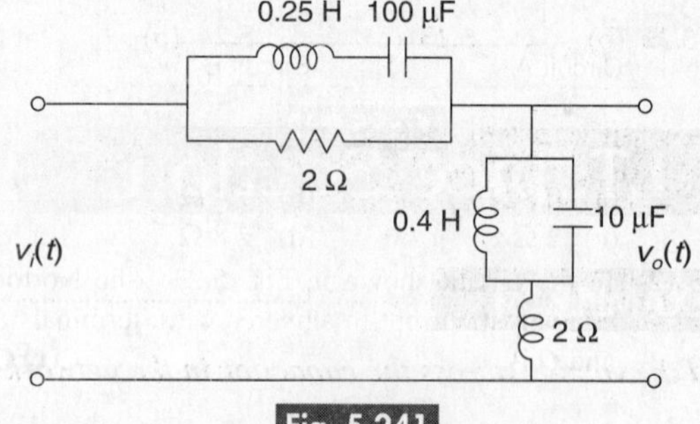


Fig. 5.241

(a) $\cos(200t) + 2\sin(500t)$

(b) $2\cos(200t) + 4\sin(500t)$

(c) $\sin(200t) + 2\cos(500t)$

(d) $2\sin(200t) + 4\cos(500t)$

**5.24** The steady state output of the circuit shown in Fig. 5.242 is given by $y(t) = A\omega \sin(\omega t - \phi(\omega))$. If the amplitude $|A\omega| = 0.25$ then the frequency $\omega$ is ○○●

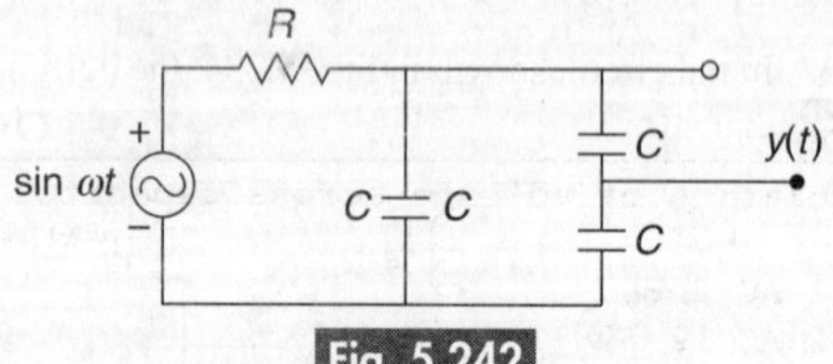


Fig. 5.242

(a) $\dfrac{1}{\sqrt{3}RC}$ (b) $\dfrac{2}{\sqrt{3}RC}$

(c) $\dfrac{1}{RC}$ (d) $\dfrac{2}{RC}$

## ANSWERS TO OBJECTIVE-TYPE QUESTIONS

| | | | | | | |
|---|---|---|---|---|---|---|
| 5.1 (b) | 5.2 (d) | 5.3 (c) | 5.4 (a) | 5.5 (c) | 5.6 (c) | 5.7 (d) |
| 5.8 (c) | 5.9 (c) | 5.10 (c) | 5.11 (a) | 5.12 (a) | 5.13 (b) | 5.14 (a) |
| 5.15 (d) | 5.16 (a) | 5.17 (a) | 5.18 (a) | 5.19 (b) | 5.20 (d) | 5.21 (d) |
| 5.22 (b) | 5.23 (b) | 5.24 (b) | | | | |

# LTspice Section

## EXAMPLE 5.1

*Find the voltage across the capacitor in the network of Fig. 5.243.*

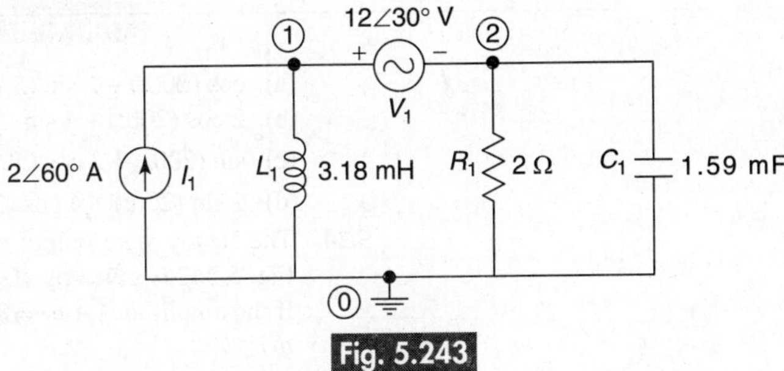


Fig. 5.243

### Solution

```
*Calculation of voltage across capacitor

I1 0 1 AC 2 60
V1 1 2 AC 12 30
R1 2 0 2
L1 1 0 3.18M
C1 2 0 1.59M
.AC LIN 1 50 50
.PRINT AC V(2)
.END
```

```
                         AC Analysis
frequency:      50                     Hz
V(2):           mag:             18.5158   phase:  157.496°        voltage
```

**Result**

$$V_C = V(2) = 18.5158 \angle 157.496° \text{ V}$$

## EXAMPLE 5.2

*Find the voltage across the 4 Ω resistor in the network of Fig. 5.244.*

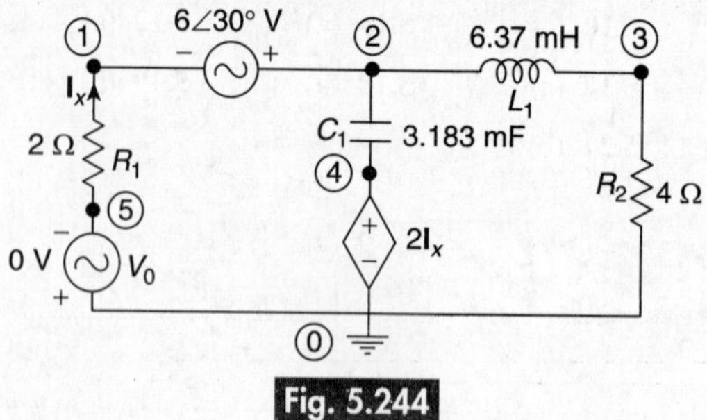


Fig. 5.244

**Solution**

```
*Calculation of voltage across 4 ohm resistor

V1 2 1 AC 6 30
R1 1 5 2
L1 2 3 6.37M
C1 2 4 3.183M
R2 3 0 4
H 4 0 V0 2
V0 0 5 0
.AC LIN 1 50 50
.PRINT AC V(3)
.END
```

```
                              AC Analysis
frequency:          50                  Hz
V(3):               mag:          2.96229   phase:   -2.91541°        voltage
```

**Result**

$$\mathbf{V}_{4\Omega} = \mathbf{V}(3) = 2.96229 \angle -2.91541° \text{ V}$$

## EXAMPLE 5.3

*Obtain Thevenin's equivalent network for Fig. 5.245.*

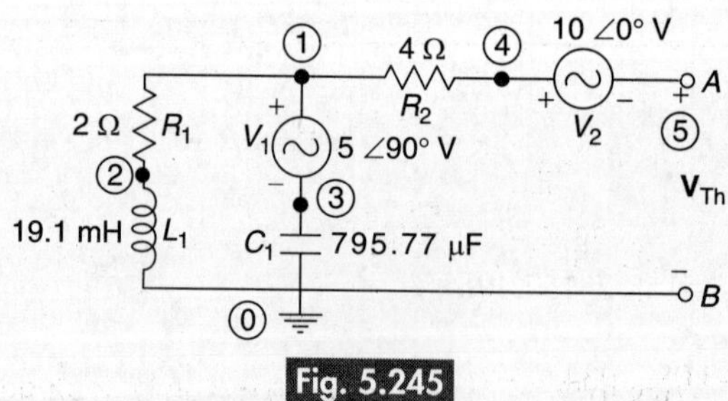


Fig. 5.245

**Solution**

(a) Calculation of Thevenin's voltage $\mathbf{V}_{Th}$ (Fig. 5.245)

```
*Calculation of Thevenin's voltage VTh

V1 1 3 AC 5 90
V2 4 5 AC 10 0
R1 1 2 2
R2 1 4 4
L1 2 0 19.1M
C1 3 0 795.77U
.AC LIN 1 50 50
.PRINT AC V(5)
.END
```

```
                              AC Analysis
frequency:        50                    Hz
V(5):             mag:         18.0255   phase:  146.315°        voltage
```

**Result**

$$\mathbf{V}_{Th} = \mathbf{V}(5) = 18.0255 \angle 146.315° \text{ V}$$

(b) Calculation of Thevenin's resistance $R_{Th}$ (Fig. 5.246)

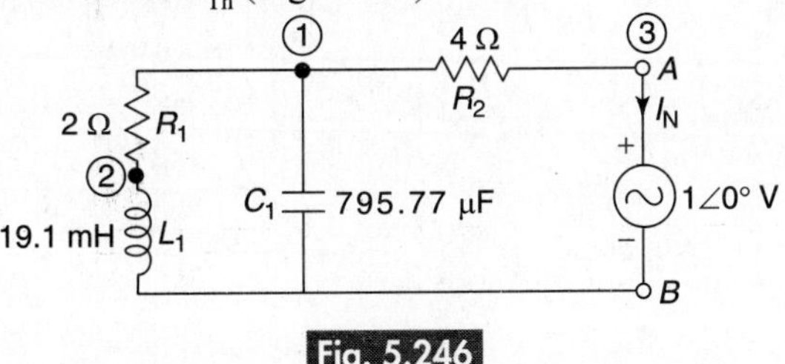


Fig. 5.246

```
*Calculation of Thevenin's resistance RTh

V1 3 0 AC 1 0
R1 1 2 2
R2 1 3 4
L1 2 0 19.1M
C1 1 0 795.77U
.AC LIN 1 50 50
.PRINT AC I(R2) V(3)
.END
```

```
                              AC Analysis
frequency:     50                  Hz
V(3):          mag:                1   phase:            0°      voltage
I(R2):         mag:        0.0884034   phase:     -135.004°      device_current
```

**Result**

$$\mathbf{I}_N = -\mathbf{I}(R_2) = -0.0884034 \angle -135.004° \text{A} = 0.0884034 \angle 44.996° \text{A}$$

$$\mathbf{Z}_{\text{Th}} = \frac{1\angle 0^\circ}{\mathbf{I}_N} = \frac{1\angle 0^\circ}{0.0884034\angle 44.996^\circ} = 11.3117\angle -44.996^\circ\ \Omega$$

Thevenin's Equivalent Network

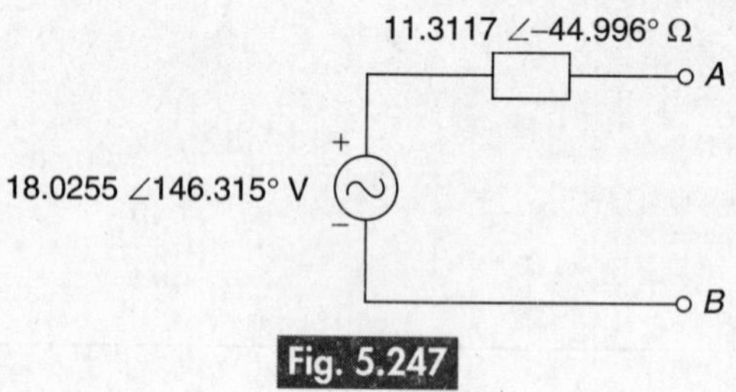


Fig. 5.247

CHAPTER

# 6 Coupled Circuits

## LEARNING OBJECTIVES

**After studying this chapter, you should be able to:**

- **LO 6.1** Explain the concepts of self-inductance and mutual inductance
- **LO 6.2** Derive the expression for coefficient of coupling between two coils
- **LO 6.3** Derive the expressions for inductances in series and parallel, for cumulative and differential couplings
- **LO 6.4** Describe dot convention
- **LO 6.5** Analyse coupled circuits using dot convention
- **LO 6.6** Explain conductively coupled equivalent circuits
- **LO 6.7** Discuss tuned circuits, their types and uses
- **LO 6.8** Explain the concept of an ideal transformer

## INTRODUCTION

Two circuits are said to be coupled circuits when energy transfer takes place from one circuit to the other without having any electrical connection between them. A changing current through the first circuit creates a changing magnetic field around it. The changing magnetic field induces an electromotive force in the second circuit by electromagnetic induction. The amount of inductive coupling between two circuits is measured by their mutual inductance. Such coupled circuits are frequently used in network analysis and synthesis. Common examples of coupled circuits are transformers, gyrators, etc. In this chapter, we will discuss self and mutual inductance, magnetically coupled circuits, dot conventions and tuned circuits.

## 6.1 SELF-INDUCTANCE

LO 6.1

Explain the concepts of self-inductance and mutual inductance

Consider a coil of $N$ turns carrying a current $i$, as shown in Fig. 6.1.

When current flows through the coil, a flux $\phi$ is produced in the coil. The flux produced by the coil links with the coil itself. If the current flowing through the coil changes, the flux linking the coil also changes. Hence, an emf is induced in the coil. This is known as self-induced emf. The direction of this emf is given by *Lenz's law*.

Fig. 6.1 *Coil carrying current*

We know that

$$\phi \propto i$$

$$\frac{\phi}{i} = k, \text{ a constant}$$

$$\phi = k\,i$$

Hence, rate of change of flux = $k \times$ rate of change of current

$$\frac{d\phi}{dt} = k\frac{di}{dt}$$

According to Faraday's laws of electromagnetic induction, a self-induced emf can be expressed as

$$v = -N\frac{d\phi}{dt} = -Nk\frac{di}{dt} = -N\frac{\phi}{i}\frac{di}{dt} = -L\frac{di}{dt}$$

where $L = \dfrac{N\phi}{i}$ and is called coefficient of self-inductance.

The property of a coil that opposes any change in the current flowing through it is called self-inductance or inductance of the coil. If the current in the coil is increasing, the self-induced emf is set up in such a direction so as to oppose the rise in current, i.e., the direction of self-induced emf is opposite to that of the applied voltage. Similarly, if the current in the coil is decreasing, the self-induced emf will be in the same direction as the applied voltage. Self-inductance does not prevent the current from changing, it serves only to delay the change.

## 6.2 MUTUAL INDUCTANCE

LO 6.1

If the flux produced by one coil links with the other coil, placed closed to the first coil, an emf is induced in the second coil due to change in the flux produced by the first coil. This is known as mutually induced emf.

Consider two coils 1 and 2 placed adjacent to each other, as shown in Fig. 6.2. Let coil 1 have $N_1$ turns while Coil 2 have $N_2$ turns.

If a current $i_1$ flows in coil 1, flux is produced and a part of this flux links coil 2. The emf induced in coil 2 is called mutually induced emf.

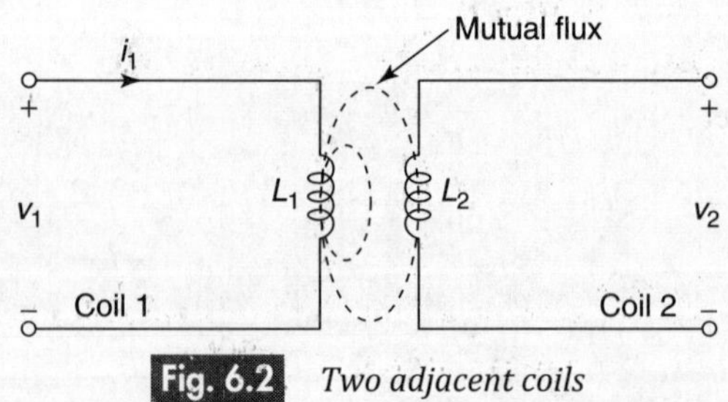


Fig. 6.2 *Two adjacent coils*

We know that

$$\phi_2 \propto i_1$$

$$\frac{\phi_2}{i_1} = k, \text{ a constant}$$

$$\phi_2 = k\, i_1$$

Hence, rate of change of flux = $k \times$ rate of change of current $i_1$

$$\frac{d\phi_2}{dt} = k \frac{di_1}{dt}$$

According to Faraday's law of electromagnetic induction, the induced emf is expressed as

$$v_2 = -N_2 \frac{d\phi_2}{dt} = -N_2\, k \frac{di_1}{dt} = -N_2 \frac{\phi_2}{i_1} \frac{di_1}{dt} = -M \frac{di_1}{dt}$$

where $M = \dfrac{N_2\, \phi_2}{i_1}$ and is called *coefficient of mutual inductance.*

## 6.3 COEFFICIENT OF COUPLING ($k$)

LO 6.2

Derive the expression for coefficient of coupling between two coils

The coefficient of coupling ($k$) between coils is defined as a fraction of magnetic flux produced by the current in one coil that links the other.

Consider two coils having number of turns $N_1$ and $N_2$ respectively. When a current $i_1$ is flowing in coil 1 and is changing, an emf is induced in coil 2.

$$M = \frac{N_2\, \phi_2}{i_1}$$

Let

$$k_1 = \frac{\phi_2}{\phi_1}$$

$$\phi_2 = k_1\, \phi_1$$

$$M = \frac{N_2\, k_1\, \phi_1}{i_1} \qquad \ldots(6.1)$$

If the current $i_2$ is flowing in coil 2 and is changing, an emf is induced in coil 1,

$$M = \frac{N_1\, \phi_1}{i_2}$$

Let

$$k_2 = \frac{\phi_1}{\phi_2}$$

$$\phi_1 = k_2\, \phi_2$$

$$M = \frac{N_1\, k_2\, \phi_2}{i_2} \qquad \ldots(6.2)$$

Multiplying Eqs (6.1) and (6.2),

$$M^2 = k_1 k_2 \times \frac{N_1 \phi_1}{i_1} \times \frac{N_2 \phi_2}{i_2} = k^2 L_1 L_2$$

$$M = k\sqrt{L_1 L_2}$$

where $$k = \sqrt{k_1 k_2}$$

## 6.4 | INDUCTANCES IN SERIES

LO 6.3

Derive the expressions for inductances in series and parallel, for cumulative and differential couplings

***1. Cumulative Coupling*** Figure 6.3 shows two coils 1 and 2 connected in series, so that currents through the two coils are in the same direction in order to produce flux in the same direction. Such a connection of two coils is known as *cumulative coupling*.

Let $L_1$ = coefficient of self-inductance of coil 1

$L_2$ = coefficient of self-inductance of coil 2

$M$ = coefficient of mutual inductance

**Fig. 6.3** *Cumulative coupling*

If the current in the coil increases by *di* amperes in *dt* seconds, then

Self-induced emf in coil 1 $= -L_1 \dfrac{di}{dt}$

Self-induced emf in coil 2 $= -L_2 \dfrac{di}{dt}$

Mutually induced emf in coil 1 due to change of current in coil 2 $= -M \dfrac{di}{dt}$

Mutually induced emf in coil 2 due to change of current in coil 1 $= -M \dfrac{di}{dt}$

Total induced emf $$v = -(L_1 + L_2 + 2M)\frac{di}{dt} \qquad \ldots(6.3)$$

If $L$ is the equivalent inductance then total induced emf in that single coil would have been

$$v = -L\frac{di}{dt} \qquad \ldots(6.4)$$

Equating Eqs (6.3) and (6.4),

$$L = L_1 + L_2 + 2M$$

***2. Differential Coupling*** Figure 6.4 shows the coils connected in series but the direction of current in coil 2 is now opposite to that in 1. Such a connection of two coils is known as *differential coupling*.

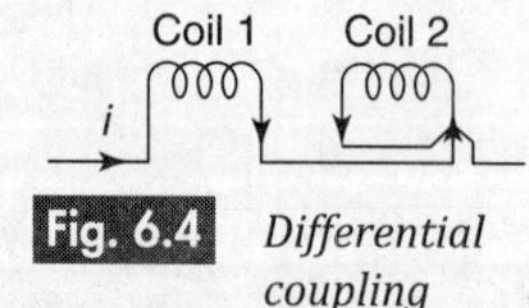


**Fig. 6.4** *Differential coupling*

Hence, total induced emf in coils 1 and 2 is

$$v = -L_1 \frac{di}{dt} - L_2 \frac{di}{dt} + 2M \frac{di}{dt} = -(L_1 + L_2 - 2M) \frac{di}{dt}$$

Coils 1 and 2 connected in series can be considered as a single coil with equivalent inductance $L$. The induced emf in the equivalent single coil with same rate of change of current is given by

$$v = -L \frac{di}{dt}$$

$$-L \frac{di}{dt} = -(L_1 + L_2 - 2M) \frac{di}{dt}$$

$$L = L_1 + L_2 - 2M$$

## 6.5 INDUCTANCES IN PARALLEL

LO 6.3

***1. Cumulative Coupling*** Figure 6.5 shows two coils 1 and 2 connected in parallel such that fluxes produced by the coils act in the same direction. Such a connection of two coils is known as cumulative coupling.

Let $L_1$ = coefficient of self-inductance of coil 1

$L_2$ = coefficient of self-inductance of coil 2

$M$ = coefficient of mutual inductance

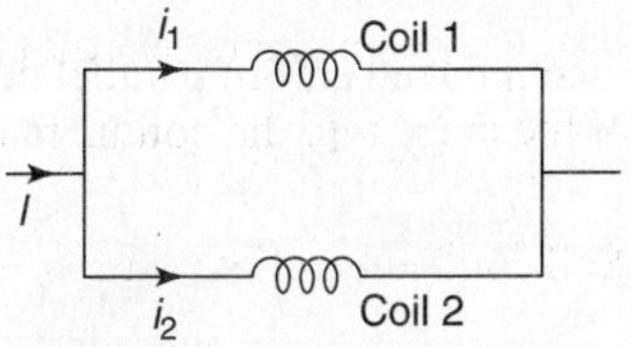

If the current in the coils changes by $di$ amperes in $dt$ seconds, then

Fig. 6.5 *Cumulative coupling*

Self-induced emf in coil 1 $= -L_1 \frac{di_1}{dt}$

Self-induced emf in coil 2 $= -L_2 \frac{di_2}{dt}$

Mutually induced emf in coil 1 due to change of current in coil 2 $= -M \frac{di_2}{dt}$

Mutually induced emf in coil 2 due to change of current in coil 1 $= -M \frac{di_1}{dt}$

Total induced emf in coil 1 $= -L_1 \frac{di_1}{dt} - M \frac{di_2}{dt}$

Total induced emf in coil 2 $= -L_2 \frac{di_2}{dt} - M \frac{di_1}{dt}$

As both the coils are connected in parallel, the emf induced in both the coils must be equal.

$$-L_1 \frac{di_1}{dt} - M \frac{di_2}{dt} = -L_2 \frac{di_2}{dt} - M \frac{di_1}{dt}$$

$$L_1 \frac{di_1}{dt} - M \frac{di_1}{dt} = L_2 \frac{di_2}{dt} - M \frac{di_2}{dt}$$

$$(L_1 - M) \frac{di_1}{dt} = (L_2 - M) \frac{di_2}{dt}$$

$$\frac{di_1}{dt} = \left(\frac{L_2 - M}{L_1 - M}\right)\frac{di_2}{dt} \qquad \text{...(6.5)}$$

Now,

$$i = i_1 + i_2$$

$$\frac{di}{dt} = \frac{di_1}{dt} + \frac{di_2}{dt}$$

$$= \left(\frac{L_2 - M}{L_1 - M}\right)\frac{di_2}{dt} + \frac{di_2}{dt}$$

$$= \left(\frac{L_2 - M}{L_1 - M} + 1\right)\frac{di_2}{dt}$$

$$= \left(\frac{L_1 + L_2 - 2M}{L_1 - M}\right)\frac{di_2}{dt} \qquad \text{...(6.6)}$$

If $L$ is the equivalent inductance of the parallel combination then the induced emf is given by

$$v = -L\frac{di}{dt}$$

Since induced emf in parallel combination is same as induced emf in any one coil,

$$L\frac{di}{dt} = L_1\frac{di_1}{dt} + M\frac{di_2}{dt}$$

$$\frac{di}{dt} = \frac{1}{L}\left(L_1\frac{di_1}{dt} + M\frac{di_2}{dt}\right)$$

$$= \frac{1}{L}\left[L_1\left(\frac{L_2 - M}{L_1 - M}\right)\frac{di_2}{dt} + M\frac{di_2}{dt}\right]$$

$$= \frac{1}{L}\left[L_1\left(\frac{L_2 - M}{L_1 - M}\right) + M\right]\frac{di_2}{dt} \qquad \text{...(6.7)}$$

Substituting Eq. (6.6) in Eq. (6.7),

$$\left(\frac{L_1 + L_2 - 2M}{L_1 - M}\right)\frac{di_2}{dt} = \frac{1}{L}\left[L_1\left(\frac{L_2 - M}{L_1 - M}\right) + M\right]\frac{di_2}{dt}$$

$$L = \frac{L_1\left(\frac{L_2 - M}{L_1 - M}\right) + M}{\frac{L_1 + L_2 - 2M}{L_1 - M}}$$

$$= \frac{L_1L_2 - L_1M + L_1M - M^2}{L_1 + L_2 - 2M}$$

$$= \frac{L_1L_2 - M^2}{L_1 + L_2 - 2M}$$

**2. *Differential Coupling*** Figure 6.6 shows two coils 1 and 2 connected in parallel such that fluxes produced by the coils act in the opposite direction. Such a connection of two coils is known as differential coupling.

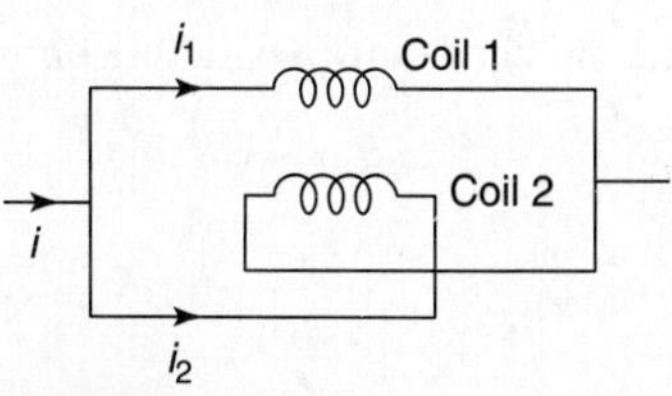


**Fig. 6.6** *Differential coupling*

Self-induced emf in coil 1 $= -L_1 \dfrac{di_1}{dt}$

Self-induced emf in coil 2 $= -L_2 \dfrac{di_2}{dt}$

Mutually induced emf in coil 1 due to change of current in coil 2 $= M \dfrac{di_2}{dt}$

Mutually induced emf in coil 2 due to change of current in coil 1 $= M \dfrac{di_1}{dt}$

Total induced emf in coil 1 $= -L_1 \dfrac{di_1}{dt} + M \dfrac{di_2}{dt}$

Total induced emf in coil 2 $= -L_2 \dfrac{di_2}{dt} + M \dfrac{di_1}{dt}$

As both the coils are connected in parallel, the emf induced in the coils must be equal.

$$-L_1 \frac{di_1}{dt} + M \frac{di_2}{dt} = -L_2 \frac{di_2}{dt} + M \frac{di_1}{dt}$$

$$L_1 \frac{di_1}{dt} + M \frac{di_1}{dt} = L_2 \frac{di_2}{dt} + M \frac{di_2}{dt}$$

$$(L_1 + M)\frac{di_1}{dt} = (L_2 + M)\frac{di_2}{dt}$$

$$\frac{di_1}{dt} = \left(\frac{L_2 + M}{L_1 + M}\right)\frac{di_2}{dt} \qquad \text{...(6.8)}$$

Now,

$$i = i_1 + i_2$$

$$\frac{di}{dt} = \frac{di_1}{dt} + \frac{di_2}{dt}$$

$$= \left(\frac{L_2 + M}{L_1 + M}\right)\frac{di_2}{dt} + \frac{di_2}{dt}$$

$$= \left(\frac{L_2 + M}{L_1 + M} + 1\right)\frac{di_2}{dt}$$

$$= \left(\frac{L_1 + L_2 + 2M}{L_1 + M}\right)\frac{di_2}{dt} \qquad \text{...(6.9)}$$

If $L$ is the equivalent inductance of the parallel combination then the induced emf is given by

$$v = -L\frac{di}{dt}$$

Since induced emf in parallel combination is same as induced emf in any one coil,

$$L\frac{di}{dt} = L_1\frac{di_1}{dt} - M\frac{di_2}{dt}$$

$$\frac{di}{dt} = \frac{1}{L}\left(L_1\frac{di_1}{dt} - M\frac{di_2}{dt}\right)$$

$$= \frac{1}{L}\left[L_1\left(\frac{L_2+M}{L_1+M}\right)\frac{di_2}{dt} - M\frac{di_2}{dt}\right]$$

$$= \frac{1}{L}\left[L_1\left(\frac{L_2+M}{L_1+M}\right) - M\right]\frac{di_2}{dt} \qquad \text{...(6.10)}$$

Substituting Eq. (6.9) in Eq. (6.10),

$$\left(\frac{L_1+L_2+2M}{L_1+M}\right)\frac{di_2}{dt} = \frac{1}{L}\left[L_1\left(\frac{L_2+M}{L_1+M}\right) - M\right]\frac{di_2}{dt}$$

$$L = \frac{L_1\left(\frac{L_2+M}{L_1+M}\right) - M}{\frac{L_1+L_2+2M}{L_1+M}}$$

$$= \frac{L_1L_2 + L_1M - L_1M - M^2}{L_1+L_2+2M}$$

$$= \frac{L_1L_2 - M^2}{L_1+L_2+2M}$$

## EXAMPLE 6.1

●○○

*The combined inductance of two coils connected in series is 0.6 H or 0.1 H depending on relative directions of currents in the two coils. If one of the coils has a self-inductance of 0.2 H, find (a) mutual inductance, and (b) coefficient of coupling.*

**Solution** $L_1 = 0.2\,\text{H}, \quad L_{\text{diff}} = 0.1\,\text{H}, \quad L_{\text{cum}} = 0.6\,\text{H}$

(a) Mutual inductance

$$L_{\text{cum}} = L_1 + L_2 + 2M = 0.6 \qquad \text{...(i)}$$

$$L_{\text{diff}} = L_1 + L_2 - 2M = 0.1 \qquad \text{...(ii)}$$

Adding Eqs (i) and (ii),

**Note** Difficulty Level ●○○— Easy; ○●○— Medium; ○○●— Difficult

$$2(L_1 + L_2) = 0.7$$
$$L_1 + L_2 = 0.35$$
$$L_2 = 0.35 - 0.2 = 0.15 \text{ H}$$

Subtracting Eqs (ii) from Eqs (i),

$$4M = 0.5$$
$$M = 0.125 \text{ H}$$

(b) Coefficient of coupling

$$k = \frac{M}{\sqrt{L_1 L_2}} = \frac{0.125}{\sqrt{0.2 \times 0.15}} = 0.72$$

## EXAMPLE 6.2

*Two coils with a coefficient of coupling of 0.6 between them are connected in series so as to magnetise in (a) same direction, and (b) opposite direction. The total inductance in the same direction is 1.5 H and in the opposite direction is 0.5 H. Find the self-inductance of the coils.*

**Solution**

$$k = 0.6, \quad L_{\text{diff}} = 0.5 \text{ H}, \quad L_{\text{cum}} = 1.5 \text{ H}$$

$$L_{\text{diff}} = L_1 + L_2 - 2M = 0.5 \quad \text{...(i)}$$
$$L_{\text{cum}} = L_1 + L_2 + 2M = 1.5 \quad \text{...(ii)}$$

Subtracting Eq. (i) from Eq. (ii),

$$4M = 1$$
$$M = 0.25 \text{ H}$$

Adding Eq. (i) and (ii),

$$2(L_1 + L_2) = 2$$
$$L_1 + L_2 = 1 \quad \text{...(iii)}$$
$$k = \frac{M}{\sqrt{L_1 L_2}}$$
$$0.6 = \frac{0.25}{\sqrt{L_1 L_2}}$$
$$L_1 L_2 = 0.1736 \quad \text{...(iv)}$$

Solving Eqs (iii) and (iv),

$$L_1 = 0.22 \text{ H}$$
$$L_2 = 0.78 \text{ H}$$

## EXAMPLE 6.3

*Two coils having self-inductances of 4 mH and 7 mH respectively are connected in parallel. If the mutual inductance between them is 5 mH, find the equivalent inductance.*

**Solution**

$$L_1 = 4 \text{ mH}, \quad L_2 = 7 \text{ mH}, \quad M = 5 \text{ mH}$$

For cumulative coupling,

$$L = \frac{L_1 L_2 - M^2}{L_1 + L_2 - 2M} = \frac{4 \times 7 - (5)^2}{4 + 7 - 2(5)} = 3 \text{ mH}$$

For differential coupling,

$$L = \frac{L_1 L_2 - M^2}{L_1 + L_2 + 2M} = \frac{4 \times 7 - (5)^2}{4 + 7 + 2(5)} = 0.143 \text{ mH}$$

**EXAMPLE 6.4**

*Two inductors are connected in parallel. Their equivalent inductance when the mutual inductance aids the self-inductance is 6 mH and it is 2 mH when the mutual inductance opposes the self-inductance. If the ratio of the self- inductances is 1:3 and the mutual inductance between the coils is 4 mH, find the self-inductances.*

**Solution**

$$L_{\text{cum}} = 6 \text{ mH}, \quad L_{\text{diff}} = 2 \text{ mH}, \quad \frac{L_1}{L_2} = 1.3, \quad M = 4 \text{ mH}$$

For cumulative coupling,

$$L = \frac{L_1 L_2 - M^2}{L_1 + L_2 - 2M}$$

$$6 = \frac{L_1 L_2 - (4)^2}{L_1 + L_2 - 2(4)}$$

$$6 = \frac{L_1 L_2 - 16}{L_1 + L_2 - 8} \qquad \text{...(i)}$$

For differential coupling,

$$L = \frac{L_1 L_2 - M^2}{L_1 + L_2 + 2M}$$

$$2 = \frac{L_1 L_2 - (4)^2}{L_1 + L_2 + 8}$$

$$2 = \frac{L_1 L_2 - 16}{L_1 + L_2 + 8} \qquad \text{...(ii)}$$

From Eqs (i) and (ii),

$$2(L_1 + L_2 + 8) = 6(L_1 + L_2 - 8)$$

$$L_1 + L_2 + 8 = 3L_1 + 3L_2 - 24$$

$$L_1 + L_2 = 16$$

But

$$\frac{L_1}{L_2} = 1.3$$

$$1.3\,L_2 + L_2 = 16$$

$$2.3\,L_2 = 16$$

$$L_2 = 6.95 \text{ mH}$$

$$L_1 = 1.3\,L_2 = 9.035 \text{ mH}$$

## 6.6 DOT CONVENTION

LO 6.4

Describe dot convention

Consider two coils of inductances $L_1$ and $L_2$ respectively connected in series, as shown in Fig. 6.7. Each coil will contribute the same mutual flux (since it is in a series connection, the same current flows through $L_1$ and $L_2$) and hence, same mutual inductance ($M$). If the mutual fluxes of the two coils aid each other, as shown in Fig. 6.7 (a), the inductances of each coil will be increased by $M$, i.e., the inductance of coils will become $(L_1 + M)$ and $(L_2 + M)$. If the mutual fluxes oppose each other, as shown in Fig. 6.7 (b), inductance of the coils will become $(L_1 - M)$ and $(L_2 - M)$. Whether the two mutual fluxes aid each other or oppose will depend upon the manner in which coils are wound. The method described above is very inconvenient because we have to include the pictures of the coils in the circuit. There is another simple method of defining the directions of currents in the coils. This is known as dot convention.

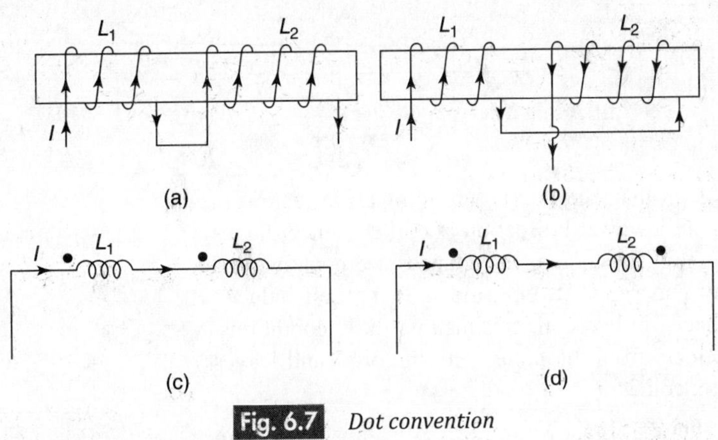


Fig. 6.7 *Dot convention*

Figure 6.7 shows the schematic connection of the two coils. It is not possible to state from Fig. 6.7(a) and Fig. 6.7(b) whether the mutual fluxes are additive or in opposition. However, dot convention removes this confusion.

If the current enters from both the dotted ends of coil 1 and coil 2, the mutual fluxes of the two coils aid each other, as shown in Fig. 6.7(c). If the current enters from the dotted end of coil 1 and leaves from the dotted end of coil 2, the mutual fluxes of the two coils oppose each other, as shown in Fig. 6.7(d).

When two mutual fluxes aid each other, the mutual inductance is positive and polarity of the mutually induced emf is same as that of the self-induced emf. When two mutual fluxes oppose each other, the mutual inductance is negative and polarity of the mutually induced emf is opposite to that of the self-induced emf.

## EXAMPLE 6.5

*Obtain the dotted equivalent circuit for Fig. 6.8.*

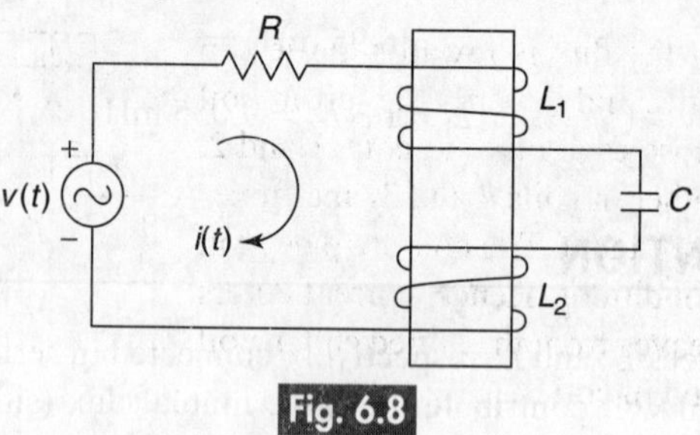


Fig. 6.8

**Solution** The current in the two coils is shown in Fig. 6.9. The corresponding flux due to current in each coil is also drawn with the help of right-hand thumb rule.

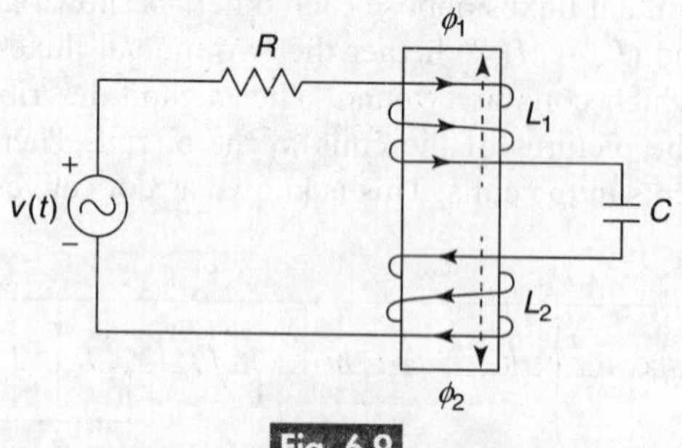


Fig. 6.9

From Fig. 6.9, it is seen that, the flux $\phi_1$ is in upward direction in coil 1, and flux $\phi_2$ is in downward direction in coil 2. Hence, fluxes are opposing each other. The mutual inductances are negative and mutually induced emfs have opposite polarities as that of self-induced emf. The dots are placed in two coils to illustrate these conditions. Hence, current $i(t)$ enters from the dotted end in coil 1 and leaves from the dotted end in coil 2.

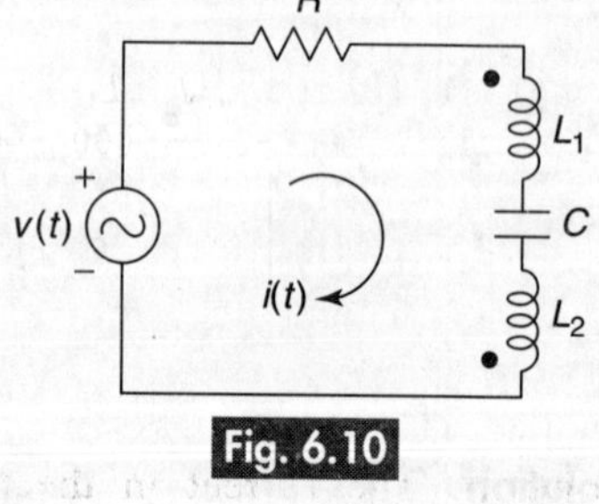


Fig. 6.10

The dotted equivalent circuit is shown in Fig. 6.10.

## EXAMPLE 6.6

*Obtain the dotted equivalent circuit for the circuit of Fig. 6.11.*

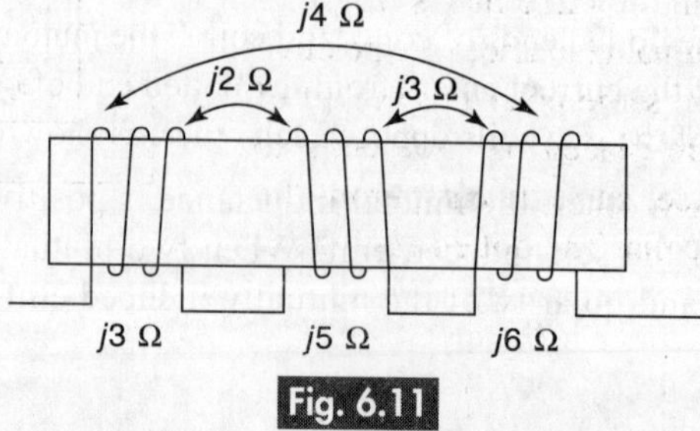


Fig. 6.11

**Solution** The current in the three coils is shown in Fig. 6.12. The corresponding flux due to current in each coil is also drawn with the help of right-hand thumb rule.

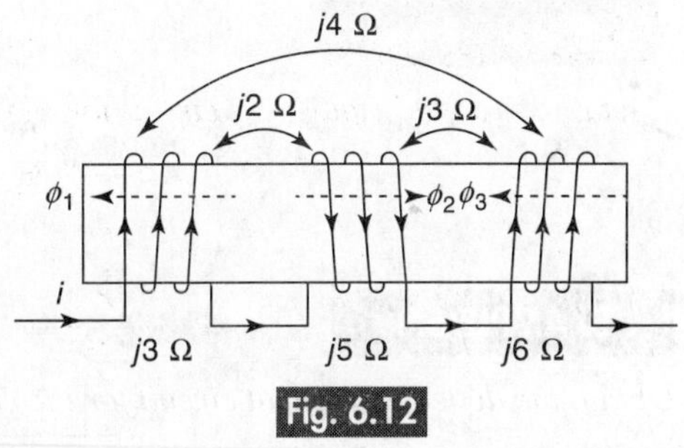

Fig. 6.12

From Fig. 6.12, it is seen that the flux is towards the left in coil 1, towards the right in coil 2 and towards the left in coil 3. Hence, fluxes $\phi_1$ and $\phi_2$ oppose each other in coils 1 and 2, fluxes $\phi_2$ and $\phi_3$ oppose each other in coils 2 and 3, and fluxes $\phi_1$ and $\phi_3$ aid each other in coils 1 and 3. The dots are placed in three coils to illustrate these conditions. Hence, current enters from the dotted end in coil 1, leaves from the dotted end in coil 2 and enters from the dotted end in coil 3.

The dotted equivalent circuit is shown in Fig. 6.13.

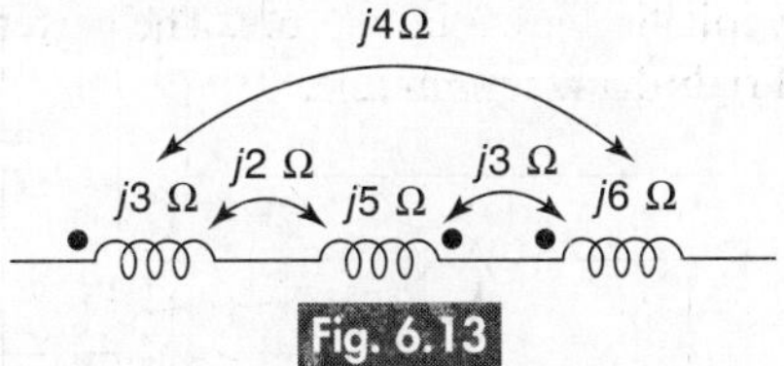

Fig. 6.13

## EXAMPLE 6.7

*Obtain the dotted equivalent circuit for the circuit shown in Fig. 6.14.*

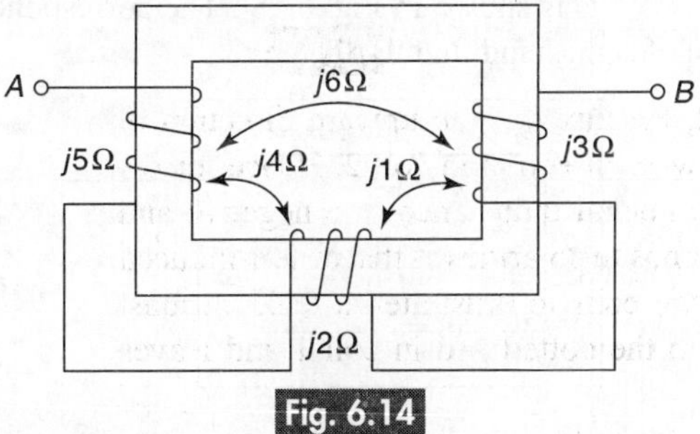

Fig. 6.14

**Solution** The current in the three coils is shown in Fig. 6.15. The corresponding flux due to current in each coil is also drawn with the help of right-hand thumb rule.

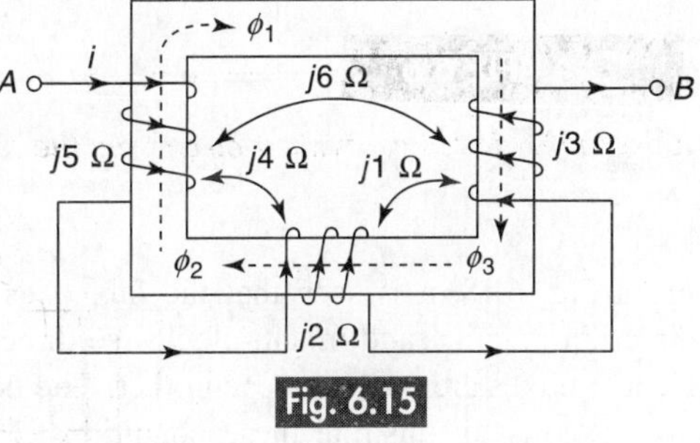

Fig. 6.15

From Fig. 6.15, it is seen that all the three fluxes $\phi_1$, $\phi_2$, $\phi_3$ aid each other. Hence, all the mutual reactances are positive and mutually induced emfs have same polarities as that of self-induced emfs. The dots are placed in three coils to illustrate these conditions. Hence, currents enter from the dotted end in each of the three coils. The dotted equivalent circuit is shown in Fig. 6.16.

Fig. 6.16

## EXAMPLE 6.8

*Obtain the dotted equivalent circuit for the coupled circuit of Fig. 6.17.*

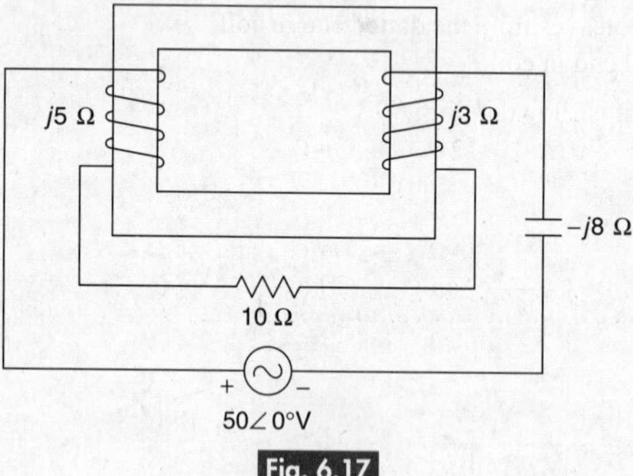


Fig. 6.17

**Solution** The current in the two coils is shown in Fig. 6.18 . The corresponding flux due to current in each coil is also drawn with the help of right-hand thumb rule.

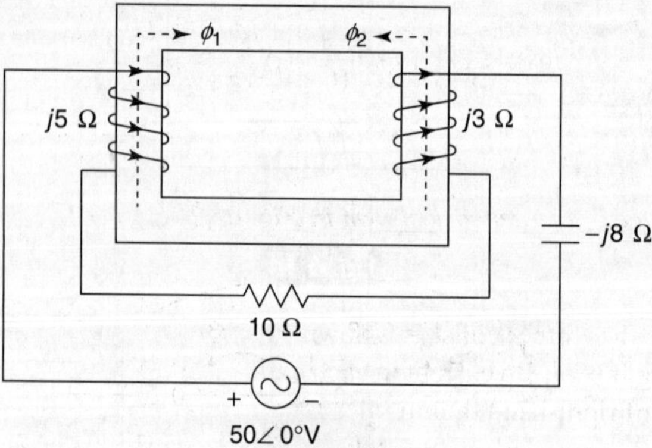


Fig. 6.18

From Fig. 6.18, it is seen that the flux $\phi_1$ is in clockwise direction in coil 1 and in anti-clockwise direction in coil 2. Hence, fluxes are opposing each other. The dots are placed in two coils to illustrate these conditions. Hence, current enters from the dotted end in coil 1 and leaves from the dotted end in coil 2. The dotted equivalent circuit is shown in Fig. 6.19.

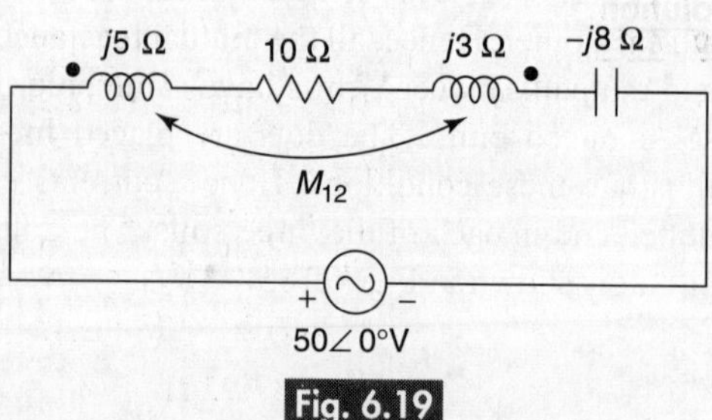


Fig. 6.19

## EXAMPLE 6.9

*Find the equivalent inductance of the network shown in Fig. 6.20.*

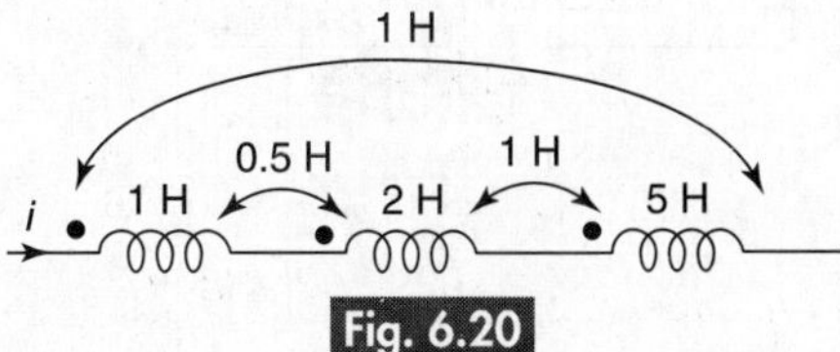


Fig. 6.20

**Solution**

$$\begin{aligned}L &= (L_1 + M_{12} + M_{13}) + (L_2 + M_{23} + M_{21}) + (L_3 + M_{31} + M_{32})\\ &= (1+0.5+1) + (2+1+0.5) + (5+1+1)\\ &= 13 \text{ H}\end{aligned}$$

## EXAMPLE 6.10

*Find the equivalent inductance of the network shown in Fig. 6.21.*

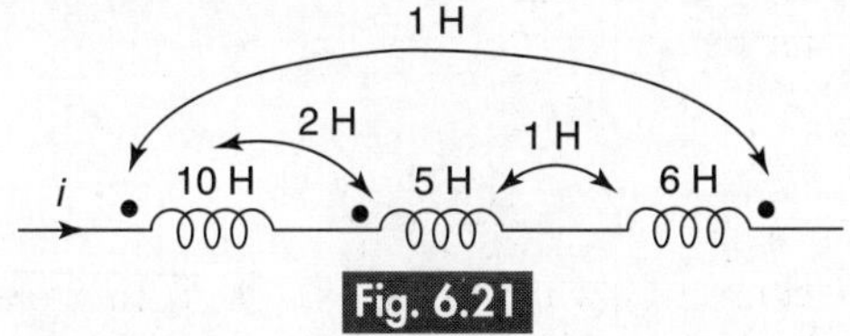


Fig. 6.21

**Solution**

$$\begin{aligned}L &= (L_1 + M_{12} - M_{13}) + (L_2 - M_{23} + M_{21}) + (L_3 - M_{31} - M_{23})\\ &= (10+2-1) + (5-1+2) + (6-1-1) = 21 \text{ H}\end{aligned}$$

## EXAMPLE 6.11

*Find the equivalent inductance of the network shown in Fig. 6.22.*

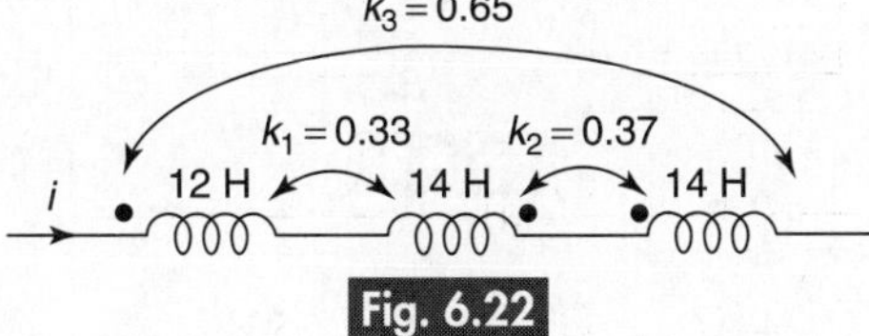


Fig. 6.22

**Solution**

$$M_{12} = M_{21} = k_1\sqrt{L_1L_2} = 0.33\sqrt{(12)(14)} = 4.28 \text{ H}$$

$$M_{23} = M_{32} = k_2\sqrt{L_2L_3} = 0.37\sqrt{(14)(14)} = 5.18 \text{ H}$$

$$M_{31} = M_{13} = k_3\sqrt{L_3L_1} = 0.65\sqrt{(12)(14)} = 8.42 \text{ H}$$

$$\begin{aligned}L &= (L_1 - M_{12} + M_{13}) + (L_2 - M_{23} - M_{21}) + (L_3 + M_{31} - M_{32})\\ &= (12-4.28+8.42) + (14-5.18-4.28) + (14+8.42-5.18)\\ &= 37.92 \text{ H}\end{aligned}$$

## EXAMPLE 6.12

*Find the equivalent inductance of the network shown in Fig. 6.23.*

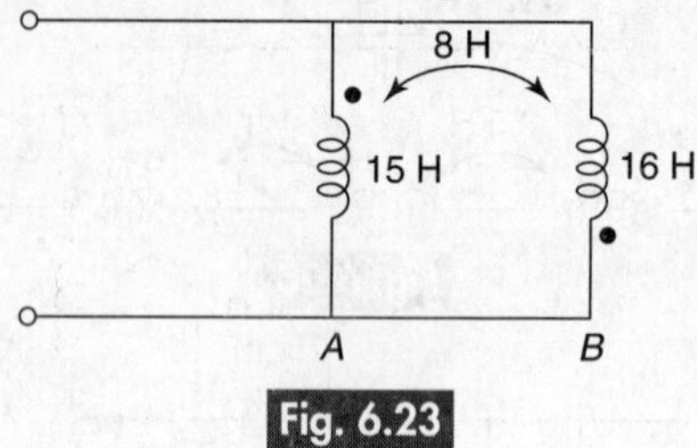


Fig. 6.23

**Solution** For coil $A$,

$$L_A = L_1 - M_{12} = 15 - 8 = 7 \text{ H}$$

For coil $B$,

$$L_B = L_2 - M_{12} = 16 - 8 = 8 \text{ H}$$

$$\frac{1}{L} = \frac{1}{L_A} + \frac{1}{L_B} = \frac{1}{7} + \frac{1}{8} = \frac{15}{56}$$

$$L = \frac{56}{15} = 3.73 \text{ H}$$

## EXAMPLE 6.13

*Find the equivalent inductance of the network shown in Fig. 6.24.*

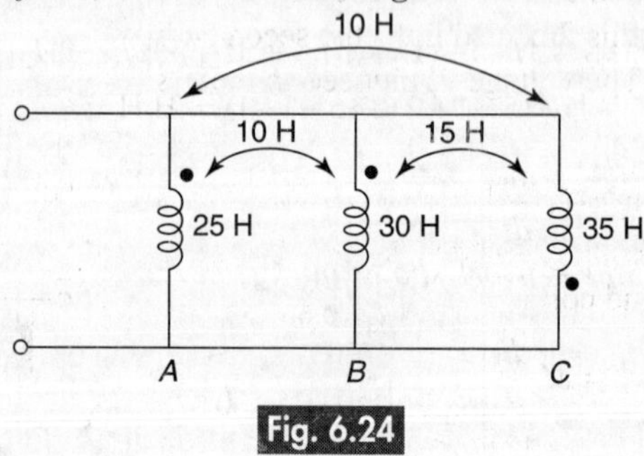


Fig. 6.24

**Solution** For coil $A$,

$$L_A = L_1 + M_{12} - M_{13} = 25 + 10 - 10 = 25 \text{ H}$$

For coil $B$,

$$L_B = L_2 - M_{23} + M_{21} = 35 - 15 + 10 = 25 \text{ H}$$

For coil $C$,

$$L_C = L_3 - M_{32} - M_{31} = 35 - 15 - 10 = 10 \text{ H}$$

$$\frac{1}{L} = \frac{1}{L_A} + \frac{1}{L_B} + \frac{1}{L_C} = \frac{1}{25} + \frac{1}{25} + \frac{1}{10} = \frac{9}{50}$$

$$L = \frac{50}{9} = 5.55 \text{ H}$$

**EXAMPLE 6.14**

*Find the equivalent impedance across the terminals A and B in Fig. 6.25.*

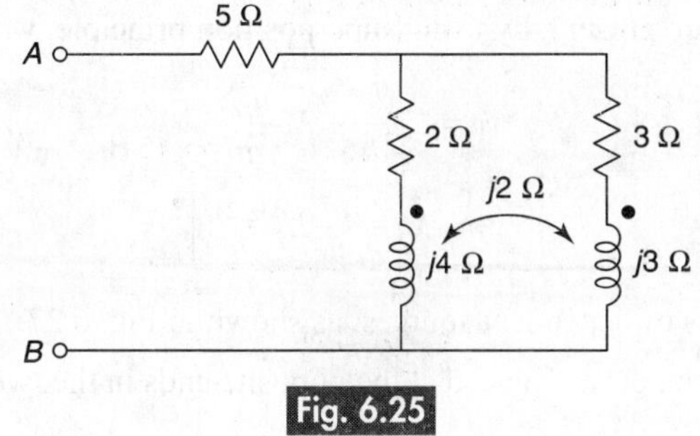


Fig. 6.25

**Solution**

$$\mathbf{Z}_1 = 5\,\Omega,\quad \mathbf{Z}_2 = (2 + j4)\,\Omega,\quad \mathbf{Z}_3 = (3 + j3)\,\Omega,\quad \mathbf{Z}_M = j2\,\Omega$$

$$\mathbf{Z} = \mathbf{Z}_1 + \frac{\mathbf{Z}_2\mathbf{Z}_3 - \mathbf{Z}_M^2}{\mathbf{Z}_2 + \mathbf{Z}_3 - 2\mathbf{Z}_M} = 5 + \frac{(2+j4)(3+j3) - (j2)^2}{2 + j4 + 3 + j3 - 2(j2)} = 6.9\angle 24.16^\circ\,\Omega$$

## 6.7 COUPLED CIRCUITS

LO 6.5

Analyse coupled circuits using dot convention

Consider two coils located physically close to one another, as shown in Fig. 6.26. When current $i_1$ flows in the first coil and $i_2 = 0$ in the second coil, flux $\phi_1$ is produced in the coil. A fraction of this flux also links the second coil and induces a voltage in this coil. The voltage $v_1$ induced in the first coil is

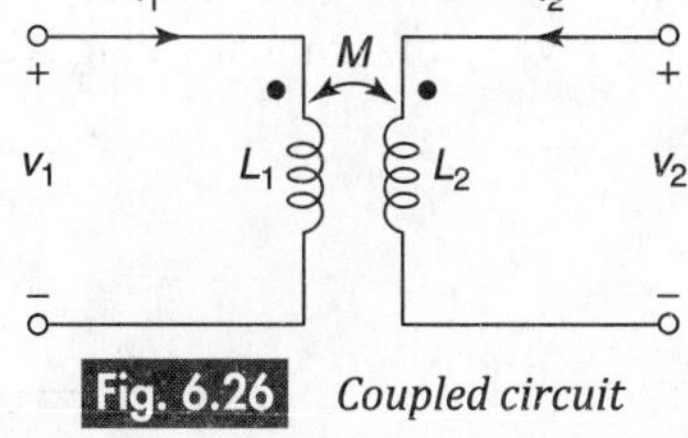


Fig. 6.26 *Coupled circuit*

$$v_1 = L_1 \left.\frac{di_1}{dt}\right|_{i_2 = 0}$$

The voltage $v_2$ induced in the second coil is

$$v_2 = M \left.\frac{di_1}{dt}\right|_{i_2 = 0}$$

The polarity of the voltage induced in the second coil depends on the way the coils are wound and it is usually indicated by dots. The dots signify that the induced voltages in the two coils (due to single current) have the same polarities at the dotted ends of the coils. Thus, due to $i_1$, the induced voltage $v_1$ must be positive at the dotted end of coil 1. The voltage $v_2$ is also positive at the dotted end in coil 2.

The same reasoning applies if a current $i_2$ flows in coil 2 and $i_1 = 0$ in coil 1. The induced voltages $v_2$ and $v_1$ are

$$v_2 = L_2 \left.\frac{di_2}{dt}\right|_{i_1 = 0}$$

and

$$v_1 = M \left.\frac{di_2}{dt}\right|_{i_1 = 0}$$

The polarities of $v_1$ and $v_2$ follow the dot convention. The voltage polarity is positive at the dotted end of inductor $L_2$ when the current direction for $i_2$ is shown in Fig. 6.26. Therefore, the voltage induced in coil 1 must be positive at the dotted end also.

Now, if both currents $i_1$ and $i_2$ are present, by using superposition principle, we can write

$$v_1 = L_1 \frac{di_1}{dt} + M \frac{di_2}{dt}$$

$$v_2 = M \frac{di_1}{dt} + L_2 \frac{di_2}{dt}$$

This can be represented in terms of dependent sources, as shown in Fig. 6.27.

Now, consider the case when the dots are placed at the opposite ends in the two coils, as shown in Fig. 6.28.

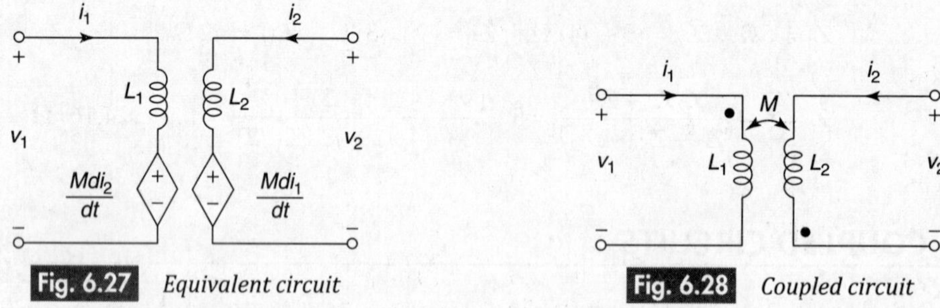


**Fig. 6.27** *Equivalent circuit*

**Fig. 6.28** *Coupled circuit*

Due to $i_1$, with $i_2 = 0$, the dotted end in coil 1 is positive, so the induced voltage in coil 2 is positive at the dot, which is the reverse of the designated polarity for $v_2$. Similarly, due to $i_2$, with $i_1 = 0$, the dotted ends have negative polarities for the induced voltages. The mutually induced voltages in both cases have polarities that are the reverse of terminal voltages and the equations are

$$v_1 = L_1 \frac{di_1}{dt} - M \frac{di_2}{dt}$$

$$v_2 = -M \frac{di_1}{dt} + L_2 \frac{di_2}{dt}$$

This can be repressed in terms of dependent sources, as shown in Fig. 6.29.

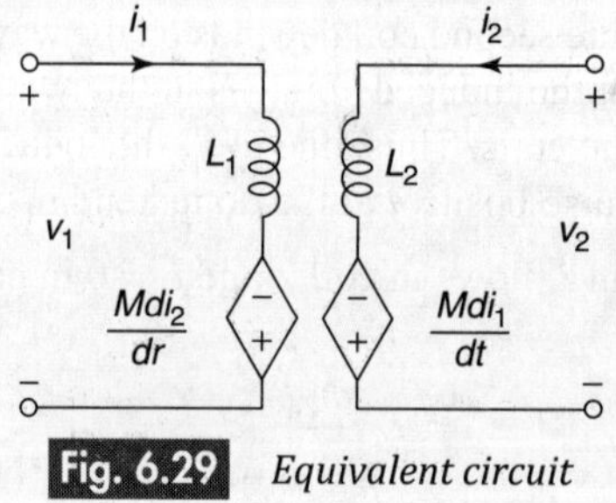


**Fig. 6.29** *Equivalent circuit*

The various cases are summarised in the table shown in Fig. 6.30.

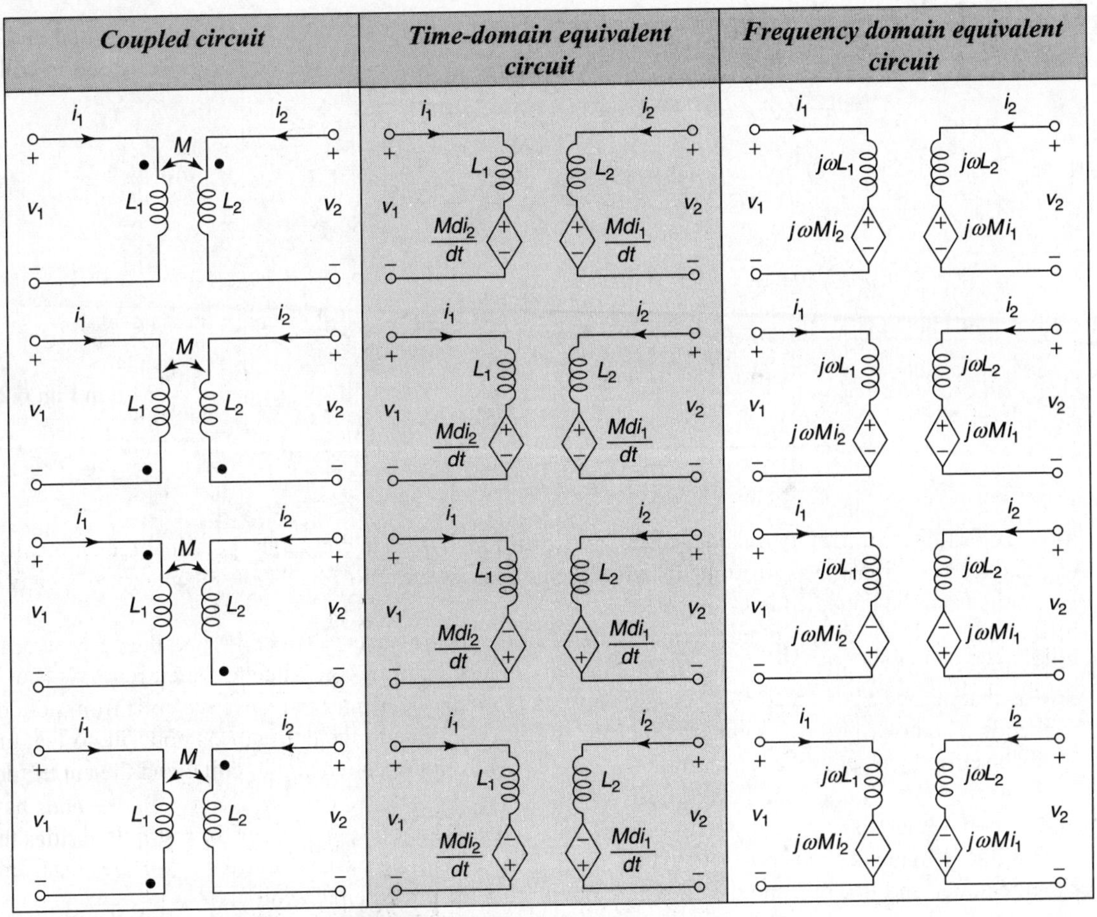

| *Coupled circuit* | *Time-domain equivalent circuit* | *Frequency domain equivalent circuit* |
|---|---|---|

Fig. 6.30 *Coupled circuits for various cases*

## EXAMPLE 6.15

*Write mesh equations for the network shown in Fig. 6.31.*

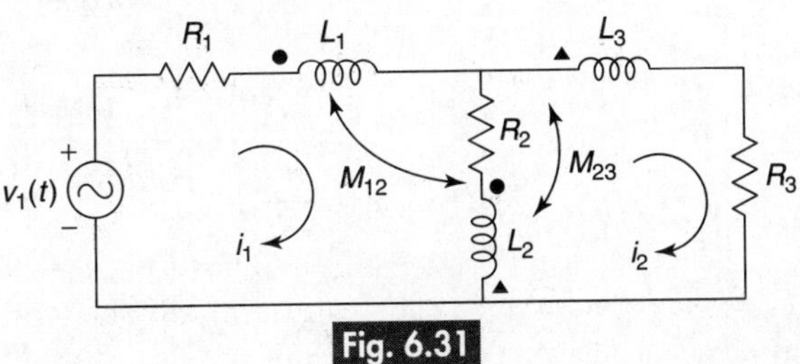


Fig. 6.31

**Solution** Coil 1 is magnetically coupled to coil 2. Similarly, coil 2 is magnetically coupled with coil 1 and coil 3. By applying dot convention, the equivalent circuit is drawn with the dependent sources.

The equivalent circuit in terms of dependent sources is shown in Fig. 6.32.

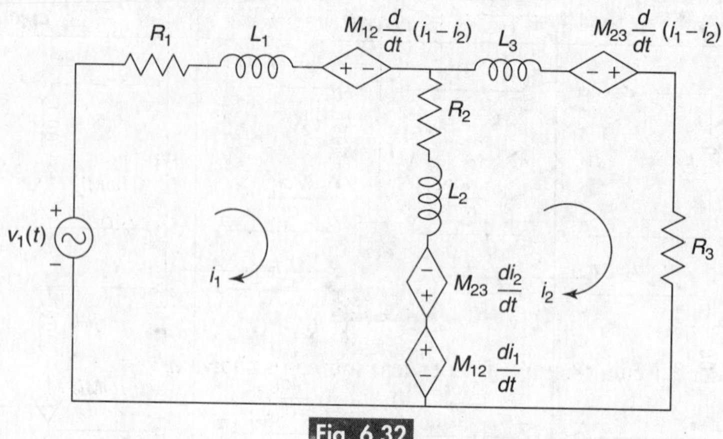

Fig. 6.32

(a) In coil 1, there is a mutually induced emf due to current $(i_1 - i_2)$ in coil 2. The polarity of the mutually induced emf is same as that of self-induced emf because currents $i_1$ and $(i_1 - i_2)$ enter in respective coils from the dotted ends.

(b) In coil 2, there are two mutually induced emfs, one due to current $i_1$ in coil 1 and the other due to current $i_2$ in coil 3. The polarity of the mutually induced emf in coil 2 due to the current $i_1$ is same as that of the self-induced emf because currents $i_1$ and $(i_1 - i_2)$ enter in respective coils from dotted ends. The polarity of the mutually induced emf in coil 2 due to the current $i_2$ is opposite to that of the self-induced emf because current $(i_1 - i_2)$ leaves from the dotted end in coil 2 and the current $i_2$ enters from the dotted end in coil 3.

(c) In coil 3, there is a mutually induced emf due to the current $(i_1 - i_2)$ in coil 2. The polarity of the mutually induced emf is opposite to that of self-induced emf because the current $(i_1 - i_2)$ leaves from the dotted end in coil 2 and the current $i_2$ enters from the dotted end in coil 3.

Applying KVL to mesh 1,

$$v_1(t) - R_1\, i_1 - L_1\frac{di_1}{dt} - M_{12}\frac{d}{dt}(i_1 - i_2) - R_2(i_1 - i_2) - L_2\frac{d}{dt}(i_1 - i_2) + M_{23}\frac{di_2}{dt} - M_{12}\frac{di_1}{dt} = 0$$

$$(R_1 + R_2)\, i_1 + (L_1 + L_2 + 2M_{12})\frac{di_1}{dt} - R_2 i_2 - (L_2 + M_{12} + M_{23})\frac{di_2}{dt} = v_1(t) \qquad \text{...(i)}$$

Applying KVL to mesh 2,

$$M_{12}\frac{di_1}{dt} - M_{23}\frac{di_2}{dt} - L_2\frac{d}{dt}(i_2 - i_1) - R_2(i_2 - i_1) - L_3\frac{di_2}{dt} + M_{23}\frac{d}{dt}(i_1 - i_2) - R_3 i_2 = 0$$

$$-R_2\, i_1 - (L_2 + M_{12} + M_{23})\frac{di_1}{dt} + (R_2 + R_3)\, i_2 + (L_2 + L_3 + 2M_{23})\frac{di_2}{dt} = 0 \qquad \text{...(ii)}$$

**EXAMPLE 6.16**

*Write KVL equations for the circuit shown in Fig. 6.33.*

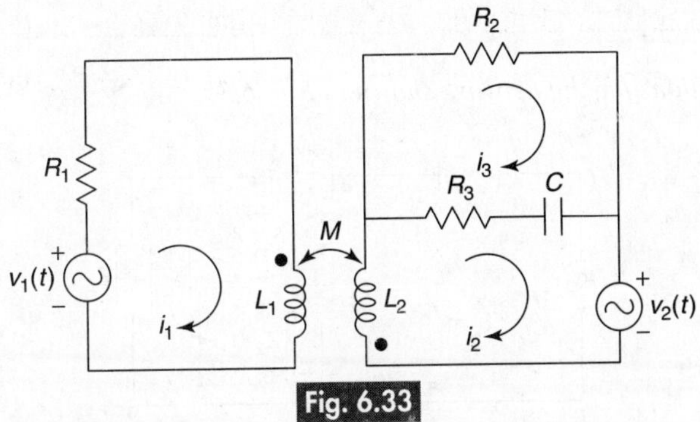


Fig. 6.33

**Solution** The equivalent circuit in terms of dependent sources is shown in Fig. 6.34.

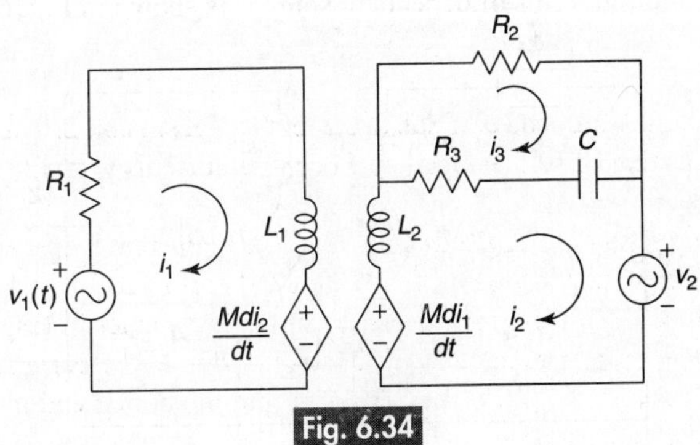


Fig. 6.34

Applying KVL to mesh 1,

$$v_1(t) - R_1\, i_1 - L_1 \frac{di_1}{dt} - M\frac{di_2}{dt} = 0$$

$$R_1\, i_1 + L_1 \frac{di_1}{dt} + M\frac{di_2}{dt} = v_1(t) \quad \text{...(i)}$$

Applying KVL to mesh 2,

$$M\frac{di_1}{dt} - L_2 \frac{di_2}{dt} - R_3(i_2 - i_3) - \frac{1}{C}\int_0^t (i_2 - i_3)\, dt - v_2(t) = 0$$

$$M\frac{di_1}{dt} - L_2 \frac{di_2}{dt} - R_3(i_2 - i_3) - \frac{1}{C}\int_0^t (i_2 - i_3)\, dt = v_2(t) \quad \text{...(ii)}$$

Applying KVL to mesh 3,

$$-R_2 i_3 - \frac{1}{C}\int_0^t (i_3 - i_2) dt - R_3(i_3 - i_2) = 0 \quad \text{...(iii)}$$

## EXAMPLE 6.17

*Write down the mesh equations for the network shown in Fig. 6.35.*

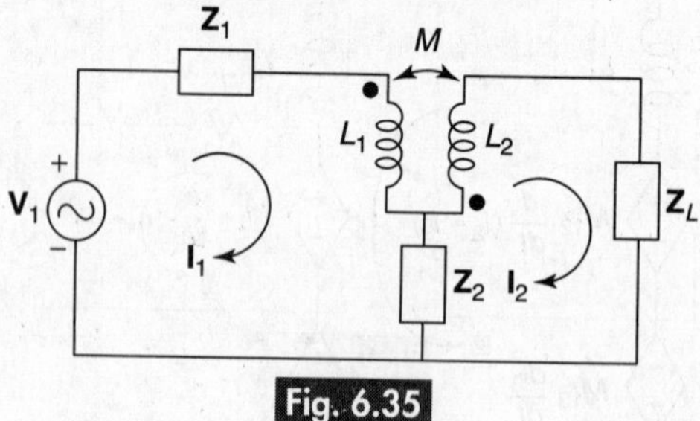


Fig. 6.35

**Solution** The equivalent circuit in terms of dependent sources is shown in Fig. 6.36.

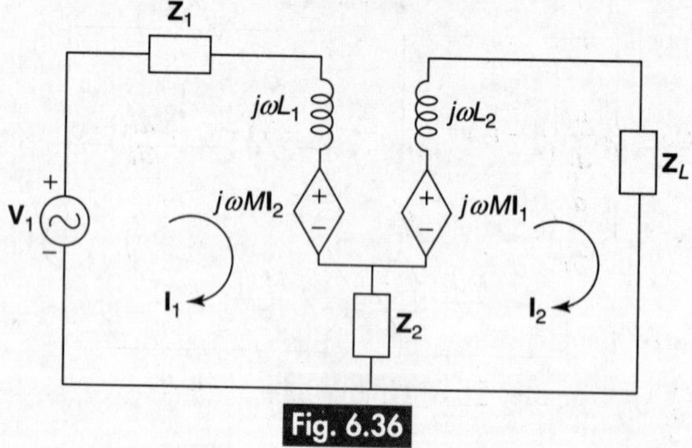


Fig. 6.36

Applying KVL to mesh 1,

$$\mathbf{V}_1 - \mathbf{Z}_1\mathbf{I}_1 - j\omega L_1\mathbf{I}_1 - j\omega M\mathbf{I}_2 - \mathbf{Z}_2(\mathbf{I}_1 - \mathbf{I}_2) = 0$$

$$(\mathbf{Z}_1 + j\omega L_1 + \mathbf{Z}_2)\,\mathbf{I}_1 - (\mathbf{Z}_2 - j\omega M)\,\mathbf{I}_2 = \mathbf{V}_1 \qquad \text{...(i)}$$

Applying KVL to mesh 2,

$$-\mathbf{Z}_2(\mathbf{I}_2 - \mathbf{I}_1) + j\omega M\mathbf{I}_1 - j\omega L_2\mathbf{I}_2 - \mathbf{Z}_L\mathbf{I}_2 = 0$$

$$-(\mathbf{Z}_2 - j\omega M)\,\mathbf{I}_1 + (\mathbf{Z}_2 + j\omega L_2 + \mathbf{Z}_L)\,\mathbf{I}_2 = 0 \qquad \text{...(ii)}$$

## EXAMPLE 6.18

*Write mesh equations for the network shown in Fig. 6.37.*

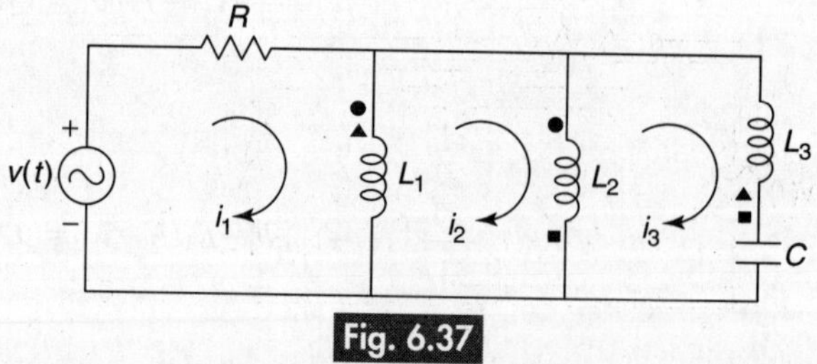


Fig. 6.37

**Solution** The equivalent circuit in terms of dependent sources is shown in Fig. 6.38.

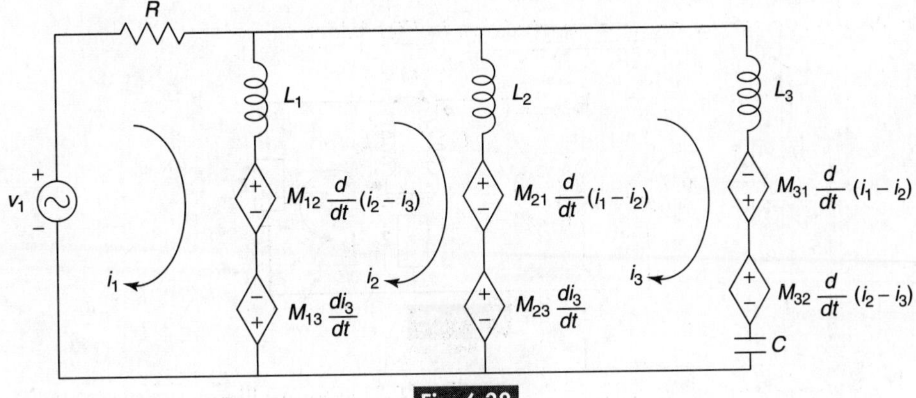


Fig. 6.38

Applying KVL to mesh 1,

$$v(t) - Ri_1 - L_1\frac{d}{dt}(i_1 - i_2) - M_{12}\frac{d}{dt}(i_2 - i_3) + M_{13}\frac{di_3}{dt} = 0$$

$$Ri_1 + L_1\frac{d}{dt}(i_1 - i_2) + M_{12}\frac{d}{dt}(i_2 - i_3) - M_{13}\frac{di_3}{dt} = v(t) \quad \text{...(i)}$$

Applying KVL to mesh 2,

$$-M_{13}\frac{di_3}{dt} + M_{12}\frac{d}{dt}(i_2 - i_3) - L_1\frac{d}{dt}(i_2 - i_1) - L_2\frac{d}{dt}(i_2 - i_3) - M_{21}\frac{d}{dt}(i_1 - i_2) - M_{23}\frac{di_3}{dt} = 0$$

$$M_{13}\frac{di_3}{dt} - M_{12}\frac{d}{dt}(i_2 - i_3) + L_1\frac{d}{dt}(i_2 - i_1) + L_2\frac{d}{dt}(i_2 - i_3) + M_{21}\frac{d}{dt}(i_1 - i_2) + M_{23}\frac{di_3}{dt} = 0 \quad \text{...(ii)}$$

Applying KVL to mesh 3,

$$M_{23}\frac{di_3}{dt} + M_{21}\frac{d}{dt}(i_1 - i_2) - L_2\frac{d}{dt}(i_3 - i_2) - L_3\frac{di_3}{dt} + M_{31}\frac{d}{dt}(i_1 - i_2) - M_{32}\frac{d}{dt}(i_2 - i_3) - \frac{1}{C}\int i_3\, dt = 0$$

$$-M_{23}\frac{di_3}{dt} - M_{21}\frac{d}{dt}(i_1 - i_2) + L_2\frac{d}{dt}(i_3 - i_2) + L_3\frac{di_3}{dt} - M_{31}\frac{d}{dt}(i_1 - i_2) + M_{32}\frac{d}{dt}(i_2 - i_3) + \frac{1}{C}\int i_3\, dt = 0 \quad \text{...(iii)}$$

## EXAMPLE 6.19

*Write KVL equations for the network shown in Fig. 6.39.*

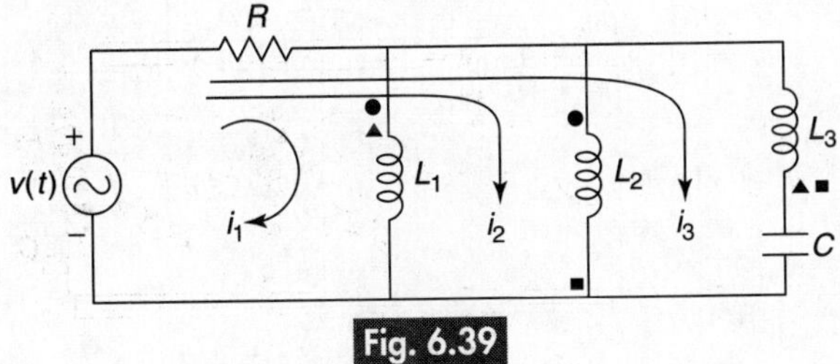


Fig. 6.39

**Solution** The equivalent circuit in terms of dependent sources is shown in Fig. 6.40.

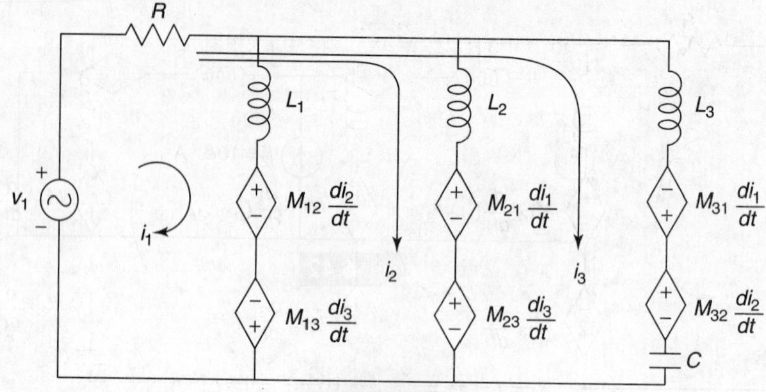


Fig. 6.40

Applying KVL to Loop 1,

$$v(t) - R(i_1 + i_2 + i_3) - L_1 \frac{di_1}{dt} - M_{12} \frac{di_2}{dt} + M_{13} \frac{di_3}{dt} = 0$$

$$R(i_1 + i_2 + i_3) + L_1 \frac{di_1}{dt} + M_{12} \frac{di_2}{dt} - M_{13} \frac{di_3}{dt} = v(t) \qquad \text{...(i)}$$

Applying KVL to Loop 2,

$$v(t) - R(i_1 + i_2 + i_3) - L_2 \frac{di_2}{dt} - M_{21} \frac{di_1}{dt} - M_{23} \frac{di_3}{dt} = 0$$

$$R(i_1 + i_2 + i_3) + L_2 \frac{di_2}{dt} + M_{21} \frac{di_1}{dt} + M_{23} \frac{di_3}{dt} = v(t) \qquad \text{...(ii)}$$

Applying KVL to Loop 3,

$$v(t) - R(i_1 + i_2 + i_3) - L_3 \frac{di_3}{dt} + M_{31} \frac{di_1}{dt} - M_{32} \frac{di_2}{dt} - \frac{1}{C}\int i_3 \, dt = 0$$

$$R(i_1 + i_2 + i_3) + L_3 \frac{di_3}{dt} - M_{31} \frac{di_1}{dt} + M_{32} \frac{di_2}{dt} + \frac{1}{C}\int i_3 \, dt = v(t) \qquad \text{...(iii)}$$

**EXAMPLE 6.20**

*In the network shown in Fig. 6.41, find the voltages $V_1$ and $V_2$.*

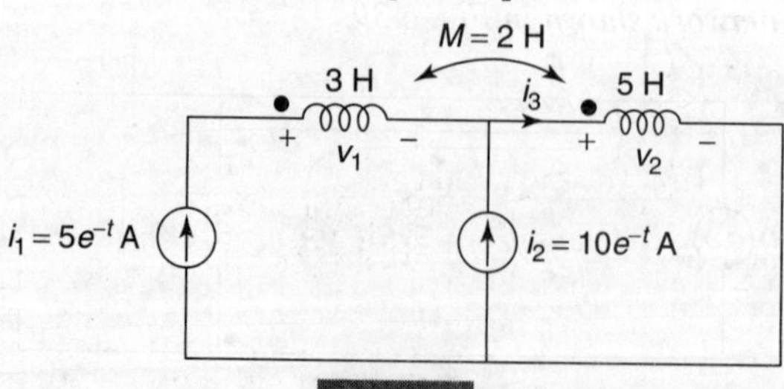


Fig. 6.41

**Solution** The equivalent circuit in terms of dependent sources is shown in Fig. 6.42.

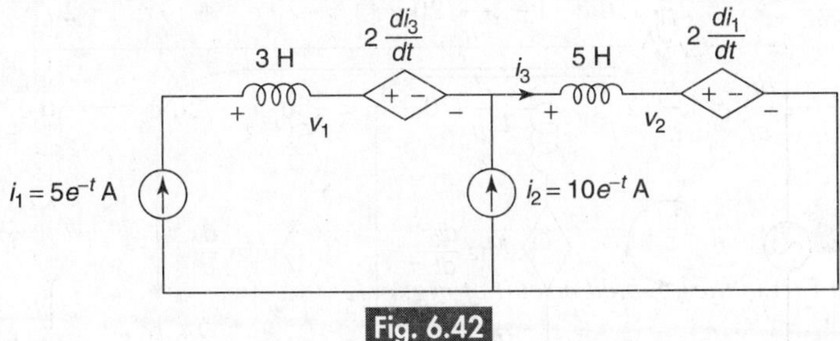


Fig. 6.42

From Fig. 6.42,

$$i_3 = i_1 + i_2 = 5\,e^{-t} + 10\,e^{-t} = 15\,e^{-t}\text{ A}$$

$$v_1 = 3\frac{di_1}{dt} + 2\frac{di_3}{dt} = 3\frac{d}{dt}(5\,e^{-t}) + 2\frac{d}{dt}(15\,e^{-t}) = -15\,e^{-t} - 30\,e^{-t} = -45\,e^{-t}\text{V}$$

$$v_2 = 5\frac{di_3}{dt} + 2\frac{di_1}{dt} = 5\frac{d}{dt}(15\,e^{-t}) + 2\frac{d}{dt}(5\,e^{-t}) = -75\,e^{-t} - 10\,e^{-t} = -85\,e^{-t}\text{V}$$

**EXAMPLE 6.21**

*In the network shown in Fig. 6.43, find the voltages $V_1$ and $V_2$.*

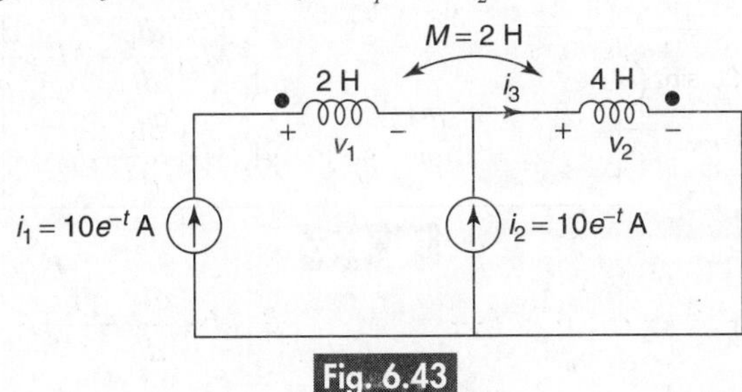


Fig. 6.43

**Solution** The equivalent circuit in terms of dependent sources is shown in Fig. 6.44.

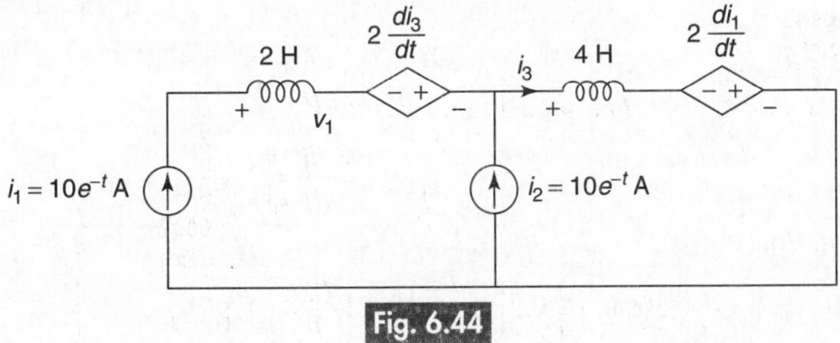


Fig. 6.44

From Fig. 6.44,

$$i_3 = i_1 + i_2 = 10\,e^{-t} + 10\,e^{-t} = 20\,e^{-t}\text{A}$$

$$v_1 = 2\frac{di_1}{dt} - 2\frac{di_3}{dt} = 2\frac{d}{dt}(10\,e^{-t}) - 2\frac{d}{dt}(20\,e^{-t}) = -20\,e^{-t} + 40\,e^{-t} = 20\,e^{-t}\,\text{A}$$

$$v_2 = 4\frac{di_3}{dt} - 2\frac{di_1}{dt} = 4\frac{d}{dt}(20\,e^{-t}) - 2\frac{d}{dt}(10\,e^{-t}) = -80\,e^{-t} + 20\,e^{-t} = -60\,e^{-t}\,\text{A}$$

## EXAMPLE 6.22

*Calculate the current $i_2(t)$ in the coupled circuit of Fig. 6.45.*

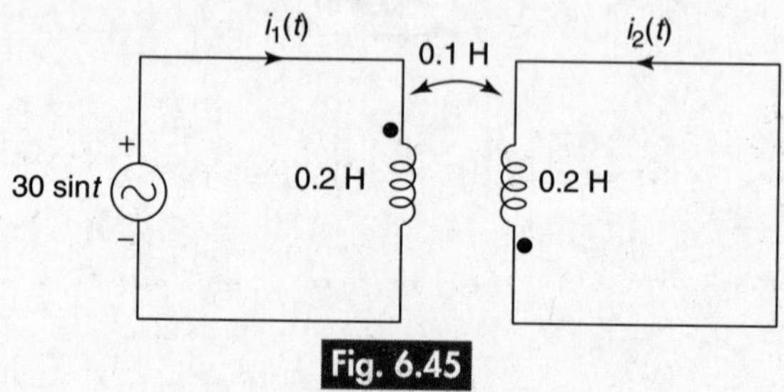


Fig. 6.45

**Solution** The equivalent circuit in terms of dependent sources is shown in Fig. 6.46.

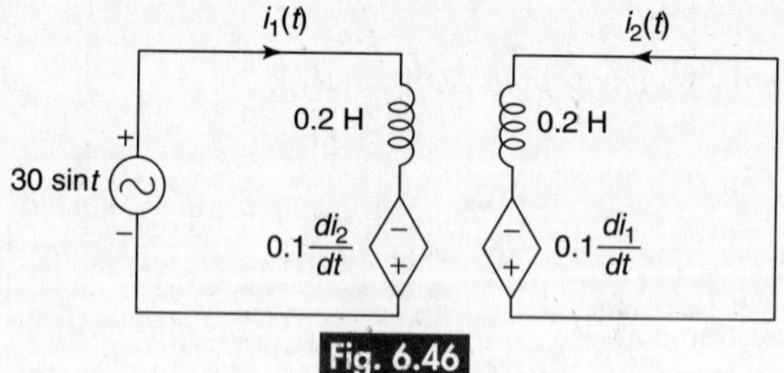


Fig. 6.46

Applying KVL to mesh 1,

$$30\sin t - 0.2\frac{di_1}{dt} + 0.1\frac{di_2}{dt} = 0 \quad \text{...(i)}$$

Applying KVL to mesh 2,

$$-0.2\frac{di_2}{dt} + 0.1\frac{di_1}{dt} = 0$$

$$\frac{di_1}{dt} = 2\frac{di_2}{dt} \quad \text{...(ii)}$$

Substituting Eq. (ii) in Eq. (i),

$$30\sin t - 0.2\left(2\frac{di_2}{dt}\right) + 0.1\frac{di_2}{dt} = 0$$

$$0.3\frac{di_2}{dt} = 30\sin t$$

$$\frac{di_2}{dt} = 100 \sin t$$

$$di_2 = 100 \sin t\, dt$$

Integrating both the sides,

$$i_2(t) = 100\int_0^t \sin t\, dt$$

$$= 100[-\cos t]_0^t$$

$$= 100\,(1 - \cos t)$$

**EXAMPLE 6.23**

*Find the voltage $V_2$ in the circuit shown in Fig. 6.47 such that the current in the left-hand loop (Loop 1) is zero.*

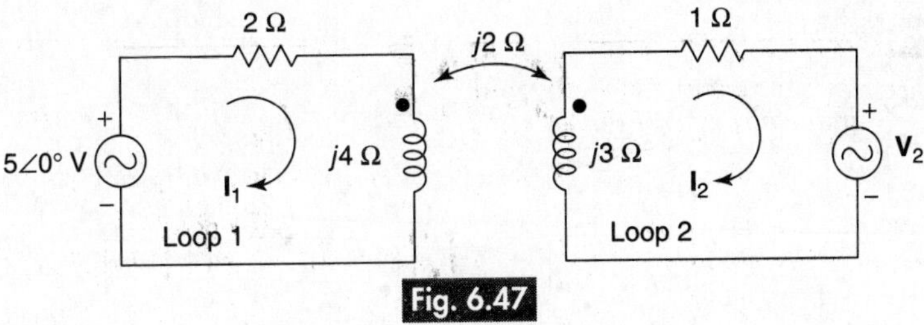


Fig. 6.47

**Solution** The equivalent circuit in terms of dependent sources is shown in Fig. 6.48.

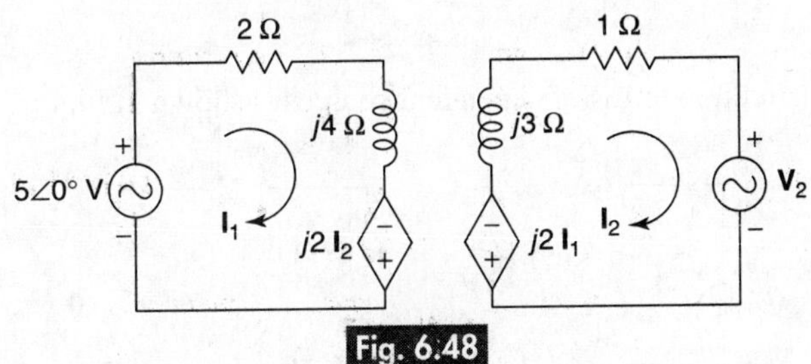


Fig. 6.48

Applying KVL to Loop 1,

$$5\angle 0° - 2\,\mathbf{I}_1 - j4\mathbf{I}_1 + j2\mathbf{I}_2 = 0$$

$$(2 + j4)\,\mathbf{I}_1 - j2\mathbf{I}_2 = 5\angle 0° \qquad \text{...(i)}$$

Applying KVL to Loop 2,

$$-j2\mathbf{I}_1 - j3\mathbf{I}_2 - 1\mathbf{I}_2 - \mathbf{V}_2 = 0$$

$$-j2\mathbf{I}_1 - (1 + j3)\,\mathbf{I}_2 = \mathbf{V}_2 \qquad \text{...(ii)}$$

Writing Eqs (i) and (ii) in matrix form,

$$\begin{bmatrix} 2+j4 & -j2 \\ -j2 & -(1+j3) \end{bmatrix} \begin{bmatrix} \mathbf{I}_1 \\ \mathbf{I}_2 \end{bmatrix} = \begin{bmatrix} 5\angle 0^\circ \\ \mathbf{V}_2 \end{bmatrix}$$

By Cramer's rule,

$$\mathbf{I}_1 = \frac{\begin{vmatrix} 5\angle 0^\circ & -j2 \\ \mathbf{V}_2 & -(1+j3) \end{vmatrix}}{\begin{vmatrix} 2+j4 & -j2 \\ -j2 & -(1+j3) \end{vmatrix}}$$

But $\mathbf{I}_1 = 0$.

$$\therefore -(5\angle 0^\circ)(1+j3) + j2\,\mathbf{V}_2 = 0$$

$$\mathbf{V}_2 = \frac{(5\angle 0^\circ)(1+j3)}{j2} = 7.91\angle -18.43^\circ \text{ V}$$

## EXAMPLE 6.24

*Determine the ratio* $\frac{\mathbf{V}_2}{\mathbf{V}_1}$ *in the circuit of Fig. 6.49, if* $\mathbf{I}_1 = 0$.

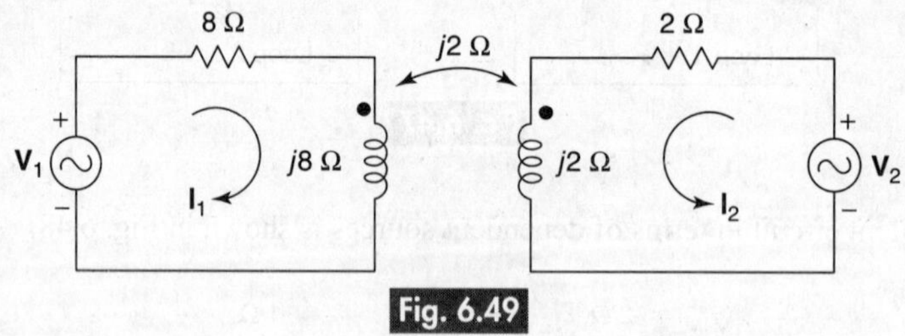


Fig. 6.49

**Solution** The equivalent circuit in terms of dependent sources is shown in Fig. 6.50.

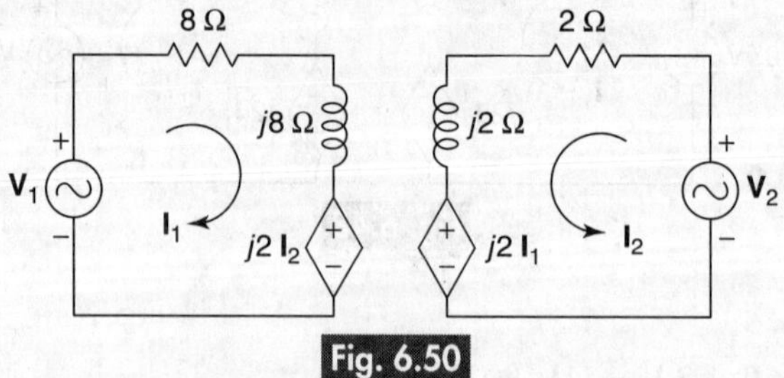


Fig. 6.50

Applying KVL to mesh 1,

$$\mathbf{V}_1 - 8\mathbf{I}_1 - j8\mathbf{I}_1 - j2\mathbf{I}_2 = 0$$

$$(8+j8)\,\mathbf{I}_1 + j2\mathbf{I}_2 = \mathbf{V}_1 \qquad \text{...(i)}$$

Putting $\mathbf{I}_1 = 0$ in Eq (i),

$$j2\,\mathbf{I}_2 = \mathbf{V}_1 \qquad \text{...(ii)}$$

Applying KVL to mesh 2,

$$\mathbf{V}_2 - 2\mathbf{I}_2 - j2\mathbf{I}_2 - j2\mathbf{I}_1 = 0$$

$$j2\mathbf{I}_1 + (2 + j2)\,\mathbf{I}_2 = \mathbf{V}_2 \qquad \text{...(iii)}$$

Putting $\mathbf{I}_1 = 0$ in Eq (iii),

$$(2 + j2)\,\mathbf{I}_2 = \mathbf{V}_2 \qquad \text{...(iv)}$$

From Eqs (ii) and (iv),

$$\frac{\mathbf{V}_2}{\mathbf{V}_1} = \frac{(2 + j2)\mathbf{I}_2}{j2\mathbf{I}_2} = \frac{2 + j2}{j2} = 1.41 \angle -45^\circ \text{ V}$$

## EXAMPLE 6.25

*For the coupled circuit shown in Fig. 6.51, find input impedance at terminals A and B.*

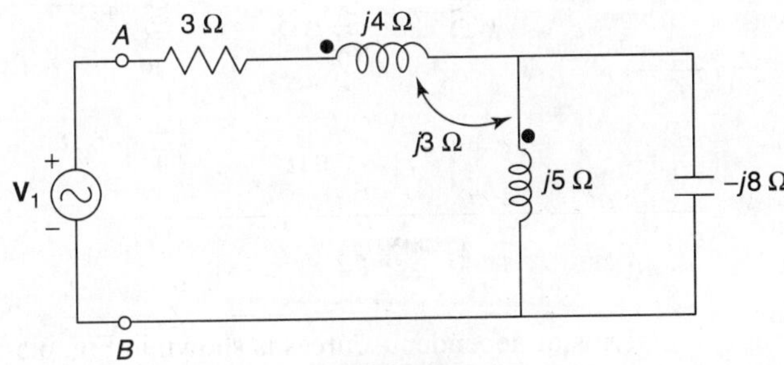


Fig. 6.51

**Solution** The equivalent circuit in terms of dependent sources is shown in Fig. 6.52.

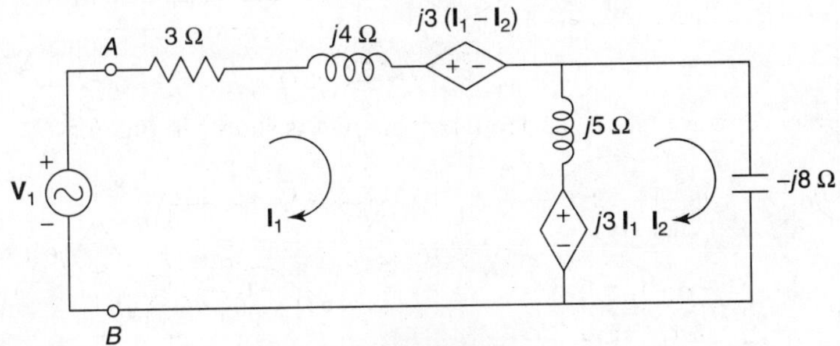


Fig. 6.52

Applying KVL to mesh 1,

$$\mathbf{V}_1 - 3\mathbf{I}_1 - j4\mathbf{I}_1 - j3\,(\mathbf{I}_1 - \mathbf{I}_2) - j5\,(\mathbf{I}_1 - \mathbf{I}_2) - j3\mathbf{I}_1 = 0$$

$$(3 + j15)\,\mathbf{I}_1 - j8\,\mathbf{I}_2 = \mathbf{V}_1 \qquad \text{...(i)}$$

Applying KVL to mesh 2,

$$j3\,\mathbf{I}_1 - j5\,(\mathbf{I}_2 - \mathbf{I}_1) + j8\,\mathbf{I}_2 = 0$$

$$j8\,\mathbf{I}_1 + j3\,\mathbf{I}_2 = 0$$

$$\mathbf{I}_2 = -\frac{j8}{j3}\mathbf{I}_1 = -2.67\,\mathbf{I}_1 \qquad \text{...(ii)}$$

Substituting Eq (ii) in Eq (i),

$$(3+j15)\mathbf{I}_1 - j8(-2.67\,\mathbf{I}_1) = \mathbf{V}_1$$

$$(3+j\,36.36)\,\mathbf{I}_1 = \mathbf{V}_1$$

$$\mathbf{Z}_i = \frac{\mathbf{V}_1}{\mathbf{I}_1} = (3+j\,36.36)\,\Omega = 36.48\angle 85.28°\,\Omega$$

## EXAMPLE 6.26

*Find equivalent impedance of the network shown in Fig. 6.53.*

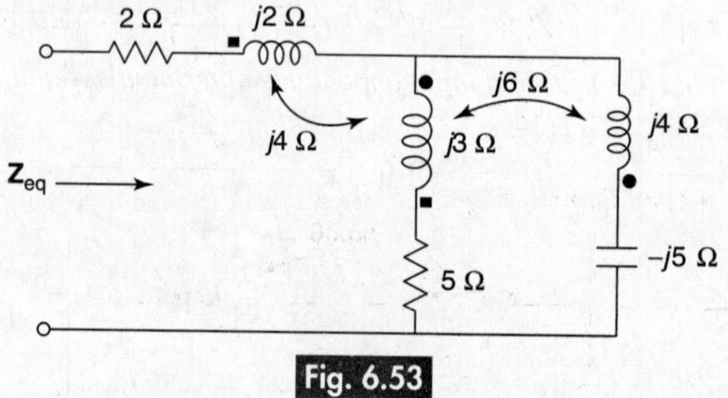


Fig. 6.53

**Solution** The equivalent circuit in terms of dependent sources is shown in Fig. 6.54.

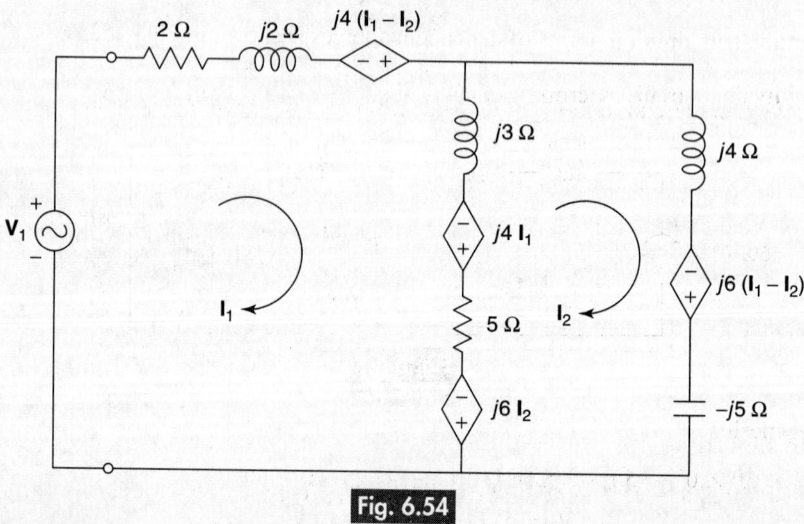


Fig. 6.54

Applying KVL to mesh 1,

$$\mathbf{V}_1 - 2\mathbf{I}_1 - j2\mathbf{I}_1 + j4(\mathbf{I}_1 - \mathbf{I}_2) - j3(\mathbf{I}_1 - \mathbf{I}_2) + j4\,\mathbf{I}_1 - 5(\mathbf{I}_1 - \mathbf{I}_2) + j6\mathbf{I}_2 = 0$$

$$(7 - j3)\,\mathbf{I}_1 - (5 + j5)\,\mathbf{I}_2 = \mathbf{V}_1 \qquad \text{...(i)}$$

Applying KVL to mesh 2,

$$-j6\mathbf{I}_2 - 5(\mathbf{I}_2 - \mathbf{I}_1) - j4\mathbf{I}_1 - j3(\mathbf{I}_2 - \mathbf{I}_1) - j4\mathbf{I}_2 + j6(\mathbf{I}_1 - \mathbf{I}_2) + j5\mathbf{I}_2 = 0$$

$$(5 + j5)\mathbf{I}_1 = (5 + j4)\,\mathbf{I}_2$$

$$\mathbf{I}_2 = \left(\frac{5 + j5}{5 + j4}\right)\mathbf{I}_1 \qquad \text{...(ii)}$$

Substituting Eq. (ii) in Eq. (i),

$$(7 - j3)\mathbf{I}_1 - (5 + j5)\left(\frac{5 + j5}{5 + j4}\right)\mathbf{I}_1 = \mathbf{V}_1$$

$$\mathbf{Z}_i = \frac{\mathbf{V}_1}{\mathbf{I}_1} = 7 - j3 - \frac{(5 + j5)(5 + j5)}{5 + j4} = 5.63\angle -47.15^\circ\ \Omega$$

## EXAMPLE 6.27

*Find the voltage across the 5 Ω resistor in Fig. 6.55 using mesh analysis.*

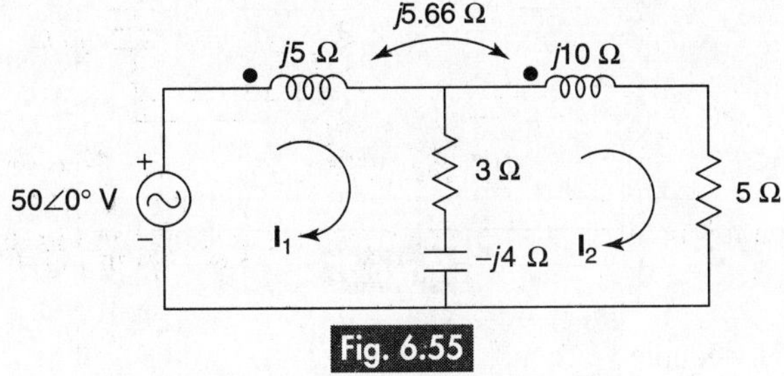


Fig. 6.55

**Solution** The equivalent circuit in terms of dependent sources is shown in Fig. 6.56.

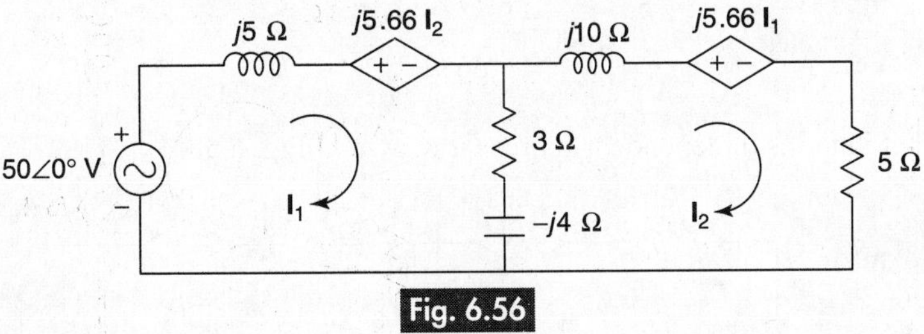


Fig. 6.56

Applying KVL to mesh 1,

$$50\angle 0^\circ - j5\,\mathbf{I}_1 - j\,5.66\,\mathbf{I}_2 - (3 - j4)(\mathbf{I}_1 - \mathbf{I}_2) = 0$$

$$(3 + j\,1)\,\mathbf{I}_1 - (3 - j\,9.66)\,\mathbf{I}_2 = 50\angle 0^\circ \qquad \text{...(i)}$$

Applying KVL to mesh 2,

$$-(3 - j4)(\mathbf{I}_2 - \mathbf{I}_1) - j\,10\mathbf{I}_2 - j\,5.66\,\mathbf{I}_1 - 5\mathbf{I}_2 = 0$$

$$-(3 - j\,9.66)\,\mathbf{I}_1 + (8 + j6)\,\mathbf{I}_2 = 0 \qquad \text{...(ii)}$$

Writing Eqs (i) and (ii) in matrix form,

$$\begin{bmatrix} 3+j1 & -(3-j9.66) \\ -(3-j9.66) & 8+j6 \end{bmatrix}\begin{bmatrix} \mathbf{I}_1 \\ \mathbf{I}_2 \end{bmatrix} = \begin{bmatrix} 50\angle 0° \\ 0 \end{bmatrix}$$

By Cramer's rule,

$$\mathbf{I}_2 = \frac{\begin{vmatrix} 3+j1 & 50\angle 0° \\ -(3-j9.66) & 0 \end{vmatrix}}{\begin{vmatrix} 3+j1 & -(3-j9.66) \\ -(3-j9.66) & 8+j6 \end{vmatrix}} = 3.82\angle -112.14° \text{ A}$$

$$\mathbf{V}_{5\,\Omega} = 5\,\mathbf{I}_2 = 5\,(3.82\angle -112.14°) = 19.1\angle -112.14° \text{ V}$$

## EXAMPLE 6.28

*Find the voltage across the 5 Ω resistor in Fig. 6.57 using mesh analysis.*

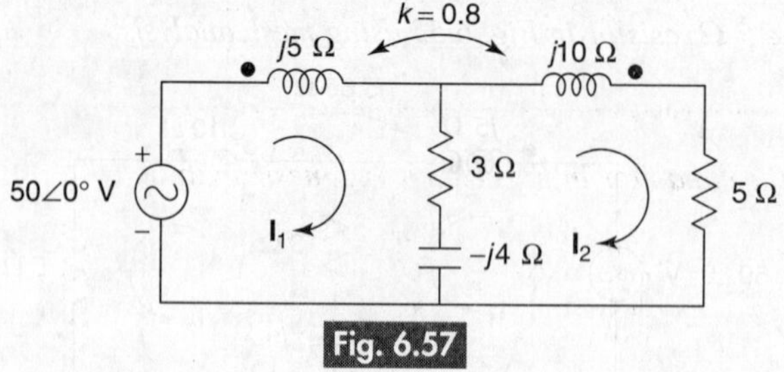


Fig. 6.57

**Solution** For a magnetically coupled circuit,

$$\begin{aligned} X_M &= k\sqrt{X_{L_1} X_{L_2}} \\ &= 0.8\sqrt{(5)(10)} \\ &= 5.66\ \Omega \end{aligned}$$

The equivalent circuit in terms of dependent sources is shown in Fig. 6.58.

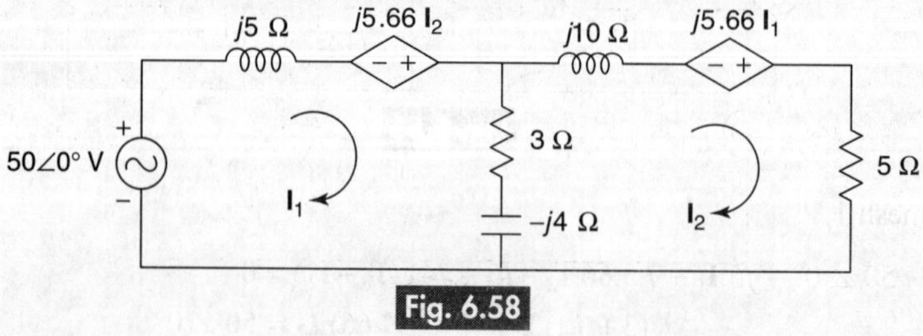


Fig. 6.58

Applying KVL to mesh 1,

$$50\angle 0° - j5\,\mathbf{I}_1 + j\,5.66\,\mathbf{I}_2 - (3-j4)\,(\mathbf{I}_1 - \mathbf{I}_2) = 0$$

$$(3+j1)\,\mathbf{I}_1 - (3+j\,1.66)\,\mathbf{I}_2 = 50\angle 0° \qquad \text{...(i)}$$

Applying KVL to mesh 2,

$$-(3-j4)(\mathbf{I}_2-\mathbf{I}_1)-j\,10\mathbf{I}_2+j\,5.66\,\mathbf{I}_1-5\mathbf{I}_2=0$$

$$-(3+j\,1.66)\,\mathbf{I}_1+(8+j6)\,\mathbf{I}_2=0 \qquad \text{...(ii)}$$

Writing Eqs (i) and (ii) in matrix form,

$$\begin{bmatrix} 3+j\,1 & -(3+j\,1.66) \\ -(3+j\,1.66) & 8+j\,6 \end{bmatrix}\begin{bmatrix} \mathbf{I}_1 \\ \mathbf{I}_2 \end{bmatrix}=\begin{bmatrix} 50\angle 0^\circ \\ 0 \end{bmatrix}$$

By Cramer's rule,

$$\mathbf{I}_2=\frac{\begin{vmatrix} 3+j\,1 & 50\angle 0^\circ \\ -(3+j\,1.66) & 0 \end{vmatrix}}{\begin{vmatrix} 3+j\,1 & -(3+j\,1.66) \\ -(3+j\,1.66) & 8+j6 \end{vmatrix}}=8.62\angle -24.79^\circ\text{ A}$$

$$\mathbf{V}_{5\,\Omega}=5\,\mathbf{I}_2=5\,(8.62\angle -24.79^\circ)=43.1\angle -24.79^\circ\text{ A}$$

## EXAMPLE 6.29

*Find the current through the capacitor in Fig. 6.59 using mesh analysis.*

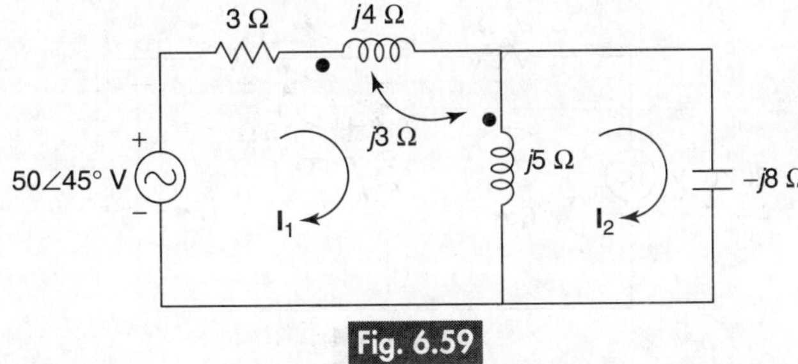


Fig. 6.59

**Solution** The equivalent circuit in terms of dependent sources is shown in Fig. 6.60.

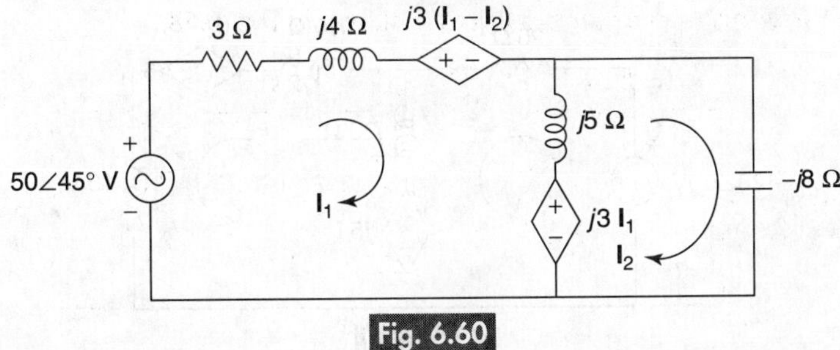


Fig. 6.60

Applying KVL to mesh 1,

$$50\angle 45^\circ-(3+j4)\,\mathbf{I}_1-j3(\mathbf{I}_1-\mathbf{I}_2)-j5\,(\mathbf{I}_1-\mathbf{I}_2)-j3\,\mathbf{I}_1=0$$

$$(3+j\,15)\,\mathbf{I}_1-j\,8\,\mathbf{I}_2=50\angle 45^\circ \qquad \text{...(i)}$$

Applying KVL to mesh 2,

$$j3\,\mathbf{I}_1 - j5\,(\mathbf{I}_2 - \mathbf{I}_1) + j8\,\mathbf{I}_2 = 0$$

$$-j8\,\mathbf{I}_1 - j3\,\mathbf{I}_2 = 0 \qquad \text{...(ii)}$$

Writing Eqs (i) and (ii) in matrix form,

$$\begin{bmatrix} 3+j15 & -j8 \\ -j8 & -j3 \end{bmatrix} \begin{bmatrix} \mathbf{I}_1 \\ \mathbf{I}_2 \end{bmatrix} = \begin{bmatrix} 50\angle 45^\circ \\ 0 \end{bmatrix}$$

By Cramer's rule,

$$\mathbf{I}_2 = \frac{\begin{vmatrix} 3+j15 & 50\angle 45^\circ \\ -j8 & 0 \end{vmatrix}}{\begin{vmatrix} 3+j15 & -j8 \\ -j8 & -j3 \end{vmatrix}} = 3.66\angle -310.33^\circ \text{ A}$$

$$\mathbf{I}_C = \mathbf{I}_2 = 3.66\angle -310.33^\circ \text{A}$$

## EXAMPLE 6.30

*Find the voltage across the 15 Ω resistor in Fig. 6.61 using mesh analysis.*

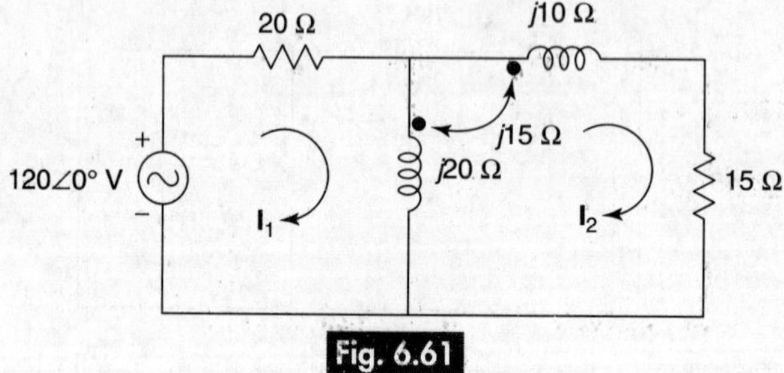


Fig. 6.61

**Solution** The equivalent circuit in terms of dependent sources is shown in Fig. 6.62.

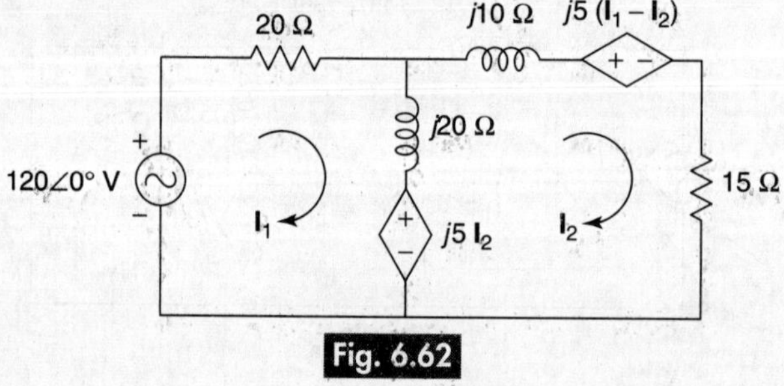


Fig. 6.62

Applying KVL to mesh 1,

$$120\angle 0^\circ - 20\,\mathbf{I}_1 - j20(\mathbf{I}_1 - \mathbf{I}_2) - j5\,\mathbf{I}_2 = 0$$

$$(20 + j\,20)\,\mathbf{I}_1 - j\,15\,\mathbf{I}_2 = 120\angle 0^\circ \qquad \text{...(i)}$$

Applying KVL to mesh 2,

$$j5\,\mathbf{I}_2 - j\,20\,(\mathbf{I}_2 - \mathbf{I}_1) - j10\,\mathbf{I}_2 - j5\,(\mathbf{I}_1 - \mathbf{I}_2) - 15\,\mathbf{I}_2 = 0$$

$$-j15\,\mathbf{I}_1 + (15 + j20)\,\mathbf{I}_2 = 0 \qquad \text{...(ii)}$$

Writing Eqs (i) and (ii) in matrix form,

$$\begin{bmatrix} 20 + j\,20 & -j15 \\ -j15 & 15 + j\,20 \end{bmatrix}\begin{bmatrix} \mathbf{I}_1 \\ \mathbf{I}_2 \end{bmatrix} = \begin{bmatrix} 120 \angle 0° \\ 0 \end{bmatrix}$$

By Cramer's rule,

$$\mathbf{I}_2 = \frac{\begin{vmatrix} 20 + j\,20 & 120 \angle 0° \\ -j15 & 0 \end{vmatrix}}{\begin{vmatrix} 20 + j\,20 & -j15 \\ -j15 & 15 + j\,20 \end{vmatrix}} = 2.53 \angle 10.12° \text{A}$$

$$\mathbf{V}_{15\,\Omega} = 15\,\mathbf{I}_2 = 15\,(2.53 \angle 10.12°) = 37.95 \angle 10.12° \text{V}$$

## EXAMPLE 6.31

*Find the current through the 6 Ω resistor in Fig. 6.63 using mesh analysis.*

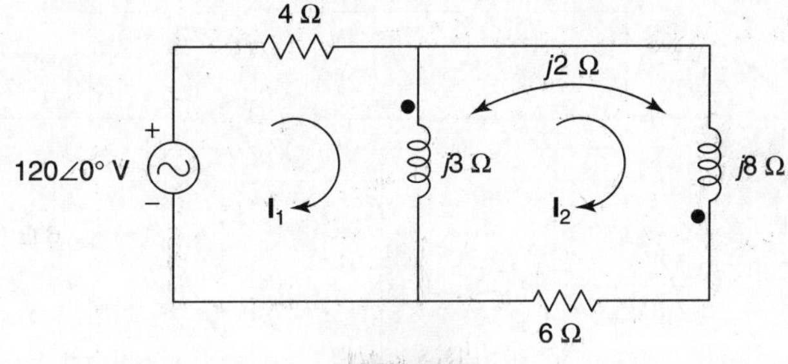


Fig. 6.63

**Solution** The equivalent circuit in terms of dependent sources is shown in Fig. 6.64.

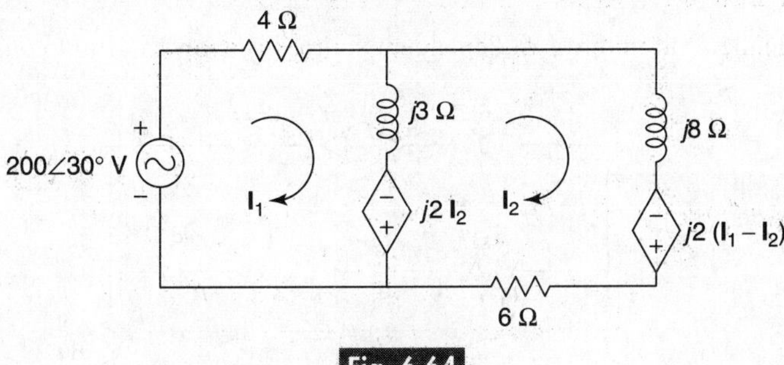


Fig. 6.64

Applying KVL to mesh 1,

$$120 \angle 0° - 4\,\mathbf{I}_1 - j3(\mathbf{I}_1 - \mathbf{I}_2) + j2\,\mathbf{I}_2 = 0$$

$$(4 + j\,3)\,\mathbf{I}_1 - j\,5\,\mathbf{I}_2 = 120 \angle 0° \qquad \text{...(i)}$$

Applying KVL to mesh 2,

$$-j\,2\,\mathbf{I}_2 - j\,3\,(\mathbf{I}_2 - \mathbf{I}_1) - j8\,\mathbf{I}_2 + j2\,(\mathbf{I}_1 - \mathbf{I}_2) - 6\,\mathbf{I}_2 = 0$$

$$-j5\,\mathbf{I}_1 + (6 + j15)\,\mathbf{I}_2 = 0 \qquad \ldots\text{(ii)}$$

Writing Eqs (i) and (ii) in matrix form,

$$\begin{bmatrix} 4+j\,3 & -j5 \\ -j5 & 6+j\,15 \end{bmatrix}\begin{bmatrix} \mathbf{I}_1 \\ \mathbf{I}_2 \end{bmatrix} = \begin{bmatrix} 120\angle 0° \\ 0 \end{bmatrix}$$

By Cramer's rule,

$$\mathbf{I}_2 = \frac{\begin{vmatrix} 4+j\,3 & 120\angle 0° \\ -j5 & 0 \end{vmatrix}}{\begin{vmatrix} 4+j\,3 & -j5 \\ -j5 & 6+j\,15 \end{vmatrix}} = 7.68\angle 2.94°\text{A}$$

## EXAMPLE 6.32

*Determine the mesh current $\mathbf{I}_3$ in the network of Fig. 6.65.*

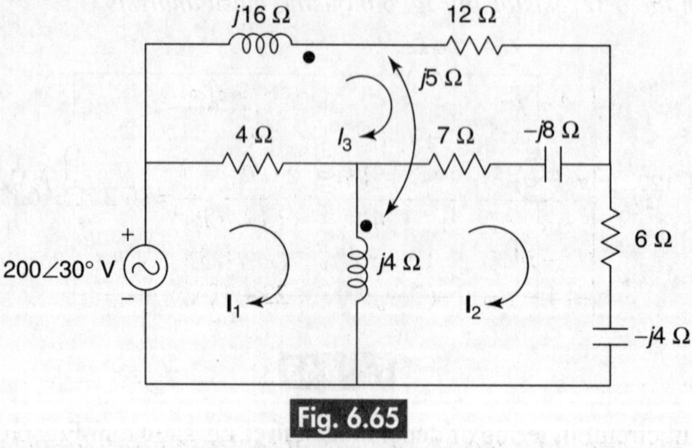


Fig. 6.65

**Solution** The equivalent circuit in terms of dependent sources is shown in Fig. 6.66.

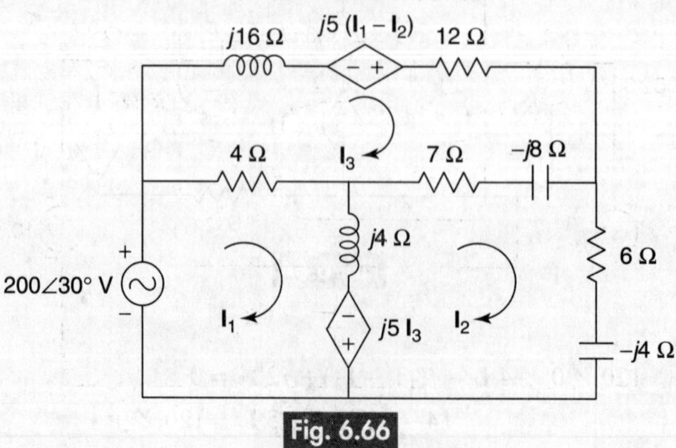


Fig. 6.66

Applying KVL to mesh 1,

$$200\angle 30° - 4(\mathbf{I}_1 - \mathbf{I}_3) - j4(\mathbf{I}_1 - \mathbf{I}_2) + j5\,\mathbf{I}_3 = 0$$

$$(4 + j4)\,\mathbf{I}_1 - j4\,\mathbf{I}_2 - (4 + j5)\,\mathbf{I}_3 = 200\angle 30° \qquad \ldots\text{(i)}$$

Applying KVL to mesh 2,

$$-j5\,\mathbf{I}_3 - j4(\mathbf{I}_2 - \mathbf{I}_1) - (7 - j8)(\mathbf{I}_2 - \mathbf{I}_3) - (6 - j4)\,\mathbf{I}_2 = 0$$

$$-j4\,\mathbf{I}_1 + (13 - j8)\,\mathbf{I}_2 - (7 - j13)\,\mathbf{I}_3 = 0 \qquad \ldots\text{(ii)}$$

Applying KVL to mesh 3,

$$-j16\,\mathbf{I}_3 + j5(\mathbf{I}_1 - \mathbf{I}_2) - 12\,\mathbf{I}_3 - (7 - j8)(\mathbf{I}_3 - \mathbf{I}_2) - 4(\mathbf{I}_3 - \mathbf{I}_1) = 0$$

$$-(4 + j5)\,\mathbf{I}_1 - (7 - j13)\,\mathbf{I}_2 + (23 + j8)\,\mathbf{I}_3 = 0 \qquad \ldots\text{(iii)}$$

Writing Eqs. (i), (ii) and (iii) in matrix form,

$$\begin{bmatrix} 4 + j4 & -j4 & -(4 + j5) \\ -j4 & 13 - j8 & -(7 - j13) \\ -(4 + j5) & -(7 - j13) & 23 + j8 \end{bmatrix}\begin{bmatrix} \mathbf{I}_1 \\ \mathbf{I}_2 \\ \mathbf{I}_3 \end{bmatrix} = \begin{bmatrix} 200\angle 30° \\ 0 \\ 0 \end{bmatrix}$$

By Cramer's rule,

$$\mathbf{I}_3 = \frac{\begin{vmatrix} 4 + j4 & -j4 & 200\angle 30° \\ -j4 & 13 - j8 & 0 \\ -(4 + j5) & -(7 - j13) & 0 \end{vmatrix}}{\begin{vmatrix} 4 + j4 & -j4 & -(4 + j5) \\ -j4 & 13 - j8 & -(7 - j13) \\ -(4 + j5) & -(7 - j13) & 23 + j8 \end{vmatrix}} = 16.28\angle 16.87°\text{A}$$

## EXAMPLE 6.33

*Obtain the dotted equivalent circuit for the coupled circuit shown in Fig. 6.67 and find mesh currents. Also, find the voltage across the capacitor.*

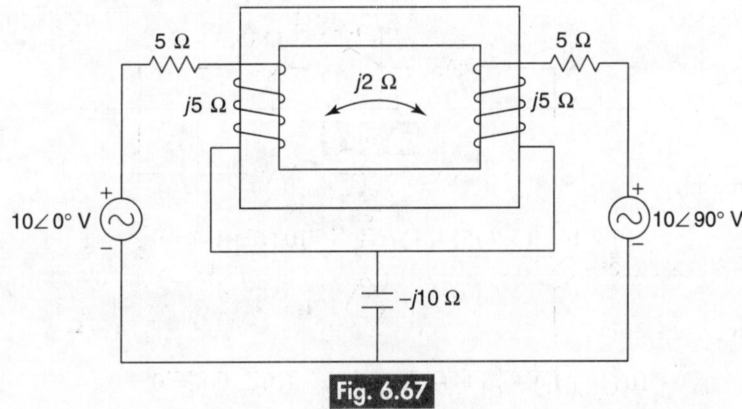


Fig. 6.67

**Solution** The currents in the coils are shown in Fig. 6.68. The corresponding flux due to current in each coil is also drawn with the help of right-hand thumb rule.

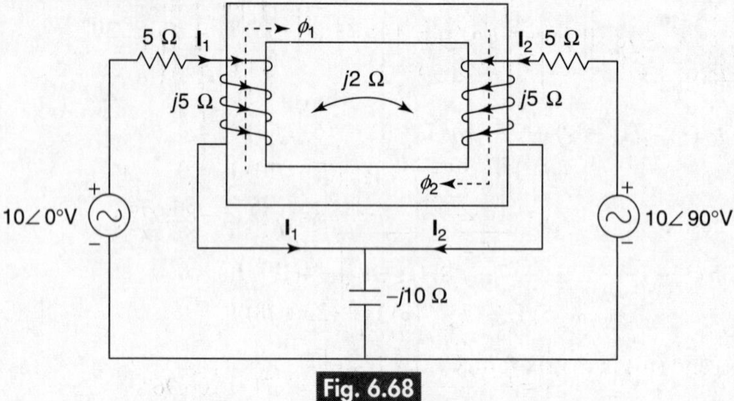


Fig. 6.68

From Fig. 6.68, it is seen that two fluxes $\phi_1$ and $\phi_2$ aid each other. Hence, dots are placed at the two coils, as shown in Fig. 6.69.

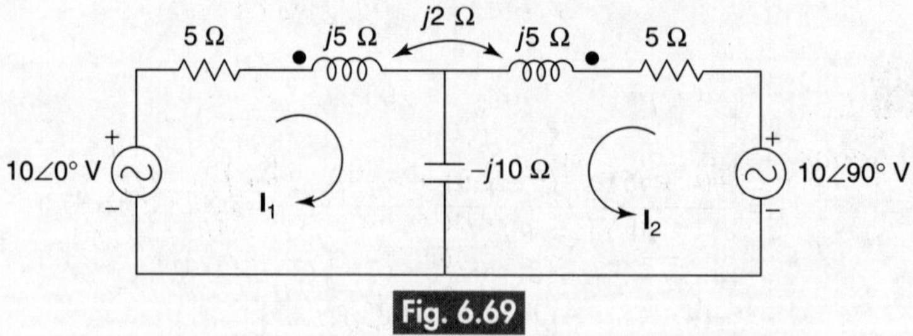


Fig. 6.69

The equivalent circuit in terms of dependent sources is shown in Fig. 6.70.

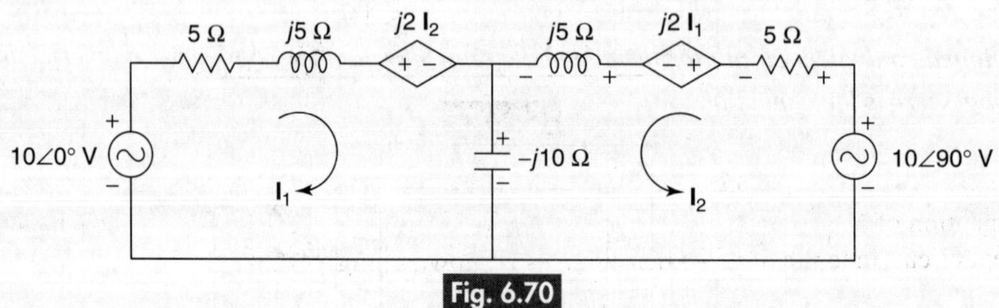


Fig. 6.70

Applying KVL to mesh 1,

$$10\angle 0° - (5 + j5)\,\mathbf{I}_1 - j2\,\mathbf{I}_2 + j10\,(\mathbf{I}_1 + \mathbf{I}_2) = 0$$

$$(5 - j\,5)\,\mathbf{I}_1 - j\,8\,\mathbf{I}_2 = 10\angle 0° \qquad \text{...(i)}$$

Applying KVL to mesh 2,

$$-j10\,(\mathbf{I}_2 + \mathbf{I}_1) + j5\,\mathbf{I}_2 - j2\,\mathbf{I}_1 + 5\,\mathbf{I}_2 - 10\angle 90° = 0$$

$$-j\,8\,\mathbf{I}_1 + (5 - j5)\,\mathbf{I}_2 = 10\angle 90° \qquad \text{...(ii)}$$

Writing Eqs. (i) and (ii) in matrix form,

$$\begin{bmatrix} 5-j5 & -j8 \\ -j8 & 5-j5 \end{bmatrix}\begin{bmatrix} \mathbf{I}_1 \\ \mathbf{I}_2 \end{bmatrix}=\begin{bmatrix} 10\angle 0^\circ \\ 10\angle 90^\circ \end{bmatrix}$$

By Cramer's rule,

$$\mathbf{I}_1=\frac{\begin{vmatrix} 10\angle 0^\circ & -j8 \\ 10\angle 90^\circ & 5-j5 \end{vmatrix}}{\begin{vmatrix} 5-j5 & -j8 \\ -j8 & 5-j5 \end{vmatrix}}=0.72\angle -82.97^\circ \text{A}$$

$$\mathbf{I}_2=\frac{\begin{vmatrix} 5-j5 & 10\angle 0^\circ \\ -j8 & 10\angle 90^\circ \end{vmatrix}}{\begin{vmatrix} 5-j5 & -j8 \\ -j8 & 5-j5 \end{vmatrix}}=1.71\angle 106.96^\circ \text{A}$$

$$\begin{aligned} \mathbf{V}_C &= -j10(\mathbf{I}_1+\mathbf{I}_2)=(-j10)(0.72\angle -82.97^\circ+1.71\angle 106.96^\circ \text{ A}) \\ &= 10.08\angle 24.03^\circ \text{V} \end{aligned}$$

## EXAMPLE 6.34

*Find Thevenin's and Norton's equivalent network at terminals A-B for Fig. 6.71.*

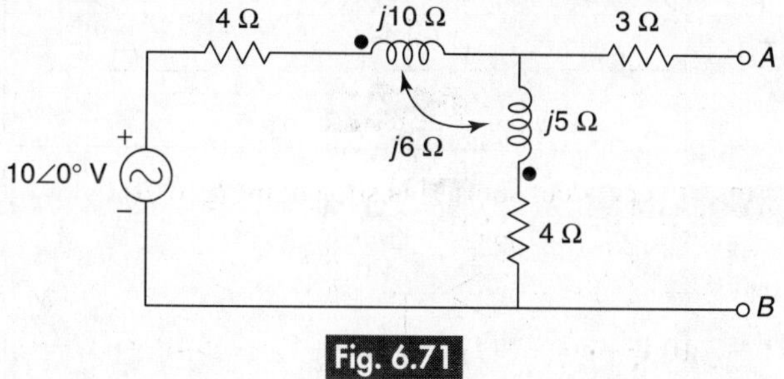


Fig. 6.71

**Solution**

***Step I*** Calculation of $\mathbf{V}_{Th}$

The equivalent circuit in terms of dependent sources is shown in Fig. 6.72.

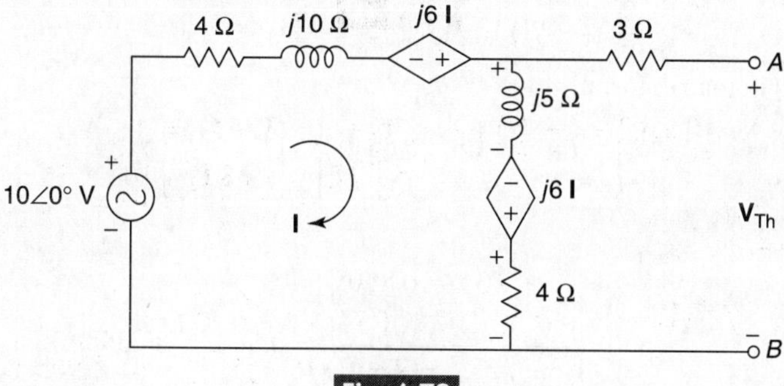


Fig. 6.72

Applying KVL to Mesh,

$$10\angle 0° - 4\mathbf{I} - j10\,\mathbf{I} + j6\,\mathbf{I} - j5\,\mathbf{I} + j6\,\mathbf{I} - 4\mathbf{I} = 0$$

$$10\angle 0° - (8 + j3)\,\mathbf{I} = 0$$

$$\mathbf{I} = \frac{10\angle 0°}{8 + j3} = 1.17\angle -20.56° \text{A}$$

Writing the $\mathbf{V}_{\text{Th}}$ equation,

$$4\mathbf{I} - j6\,\mathbf{I} + j5\,\mathbf{I} - 0 - \mathbf{V}_{\text{Th}} = 0$$

$$(4 - j1)\,\mathbf{I} - \mathbf{V}_{\text{Th}} = 0$$

$$\mathbf{V}_{\text{Th}} = (4 - j1)\,(1.17\angle -20.56°)$$

$$= 4.82\angle -34.6° \text{V}$$

***Step II*** Calculation of $\mathbf{I}_N$

The equivalent circuit in terms of dependent sources is shown in Fig. 6.73.

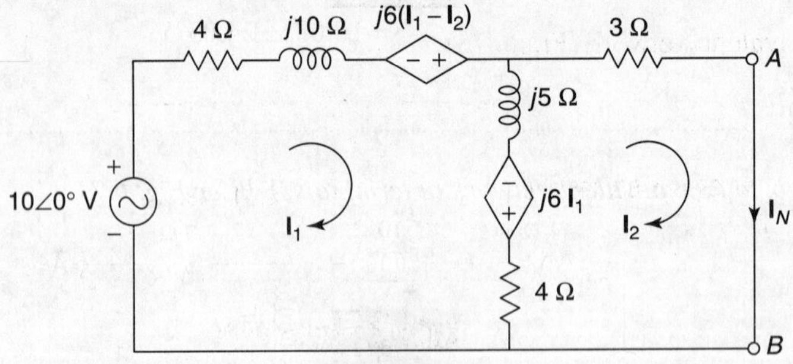


Fig. 6.73

Applying KVL to mesh 1,

$$10\angle 0° - 4\mathbf{I}_1 - j10\,\mathbf{I}_1 + j6\,(\mathbf{I}_1 - \mathbf{I}_2) - j5(\mathbf{I}_1 - \mathbf{I}_2) + j6\,\mathbf{I}_1 - 4(\mathbf{I}_1 - \mathbf{I}_2) = 0$$

$$(8 + j3)\,\mathbf{I}_1 - (4 - j1)\,\mathbf{I}_2 = 10\angle 0° \qquad \ldots\text{(i)}$$

Applying KVL to mesh 2,

$$-4(\mathbf{I}_2 - \mathbf{I}_1) - j6\,\mathbf{I}_1 - j5(\mathbf{I}_2 - \mathbf{I}_1) - 3\mathbf{I}_2 = 0$$

$$-(4 - j1)\,\mathbf{I}_1 + (7 + j5)\,\mathbf{I}_2 = 0 \qquad \ldots\text{(ii)}$$

Writing Eqs. (i) and (ii) in matrix form,

$$\begin{bmatrix} 8 + j3 & -(4 - j1) \\ -(4 - j1) & 7 + j5 \end{bmatrix} \begin{bmatrix} \mathbf{I}_1 \\ \mathbf{I}_2 \end{bmatrix} = \begin{bmatrix} 10\angle 0° \\ 0 \end{bmatrix}$$

By Cramer's rule,

$$\mathbf{I}_2 = \frac{\begin{vmatrix} 8 + j3 & 10\angle 0° \\ -(4 - j1) & 0 \end{vmatrix}}{\begin{vmatrix} 8 + j3 & -(4 - j1) \\ -(4 - j1) & 7 + j5 \end{vmatrix}} = 0.56\angle -83.39° \text{A}$$

$$\mathbf{I}_N = \mathbf{I}_2 = 0.56\angle -83.39°\text{A}$$

***Step III*** Calculation of $\mathbf{Z}_{\text{Th}}$

$$\mathbf{Z}_{\text{Th}} = \frac{\mathbf{V}_{\text{Th}}}{\mathbf{I}_N} = \frac{4.82\angle -34.6°}{0.56\angle -83.39°} = 8.61\angle 48.79°\ \Omega$$

***Step IV*** Thevenin's Equivalent Network (Fig. 6.74)

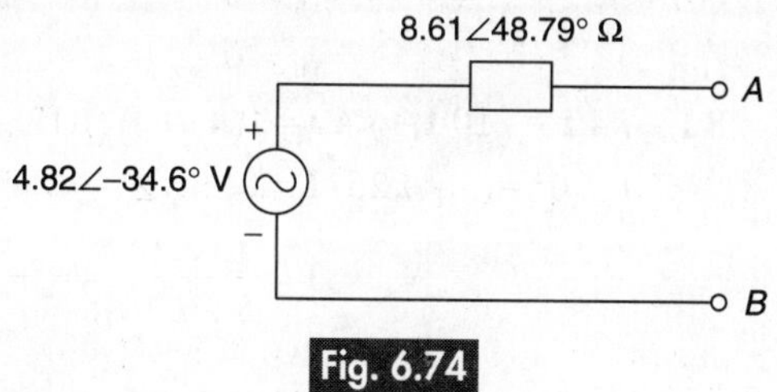


Fig. 6.74

***Step V*** Norton's Equivalent Network (Fig. 6.75)

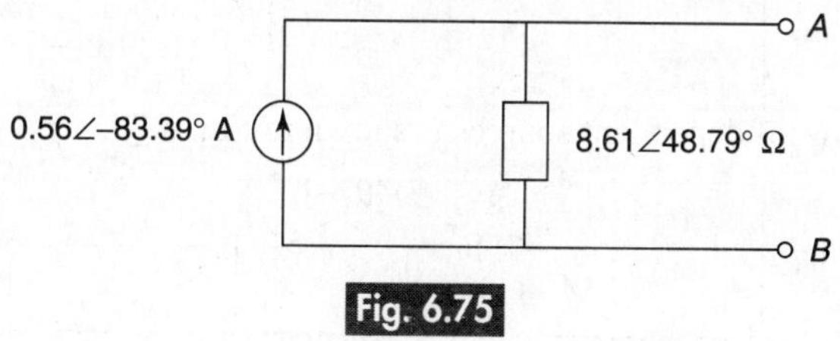


Fig. 6.75

## EXAMPLE 6.35

*Find the value of $Z_L$ connected across terminals A and B in Fig. 6. 76 to receive the maximum power when (a) $Z_L$ is complex impedance, and (b) $Z_L$ is pure resistance.*

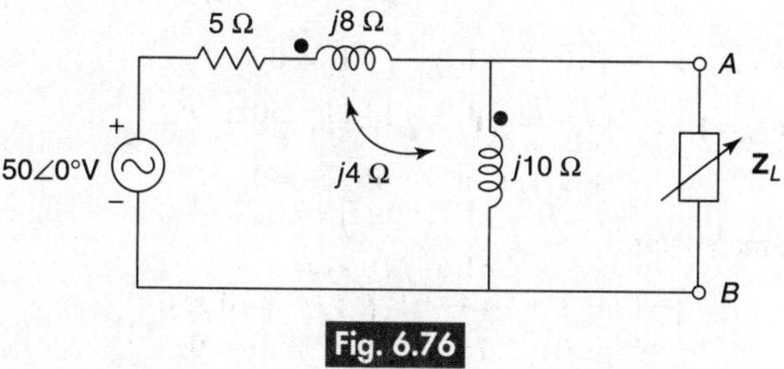


Fig. 6.76

**Solution**

***Step I*** Calculation of $\mathbf{V}_{\text{Th}}$

The equivalent circuit in terms of dependent sources is shown in Fig. 6.77.

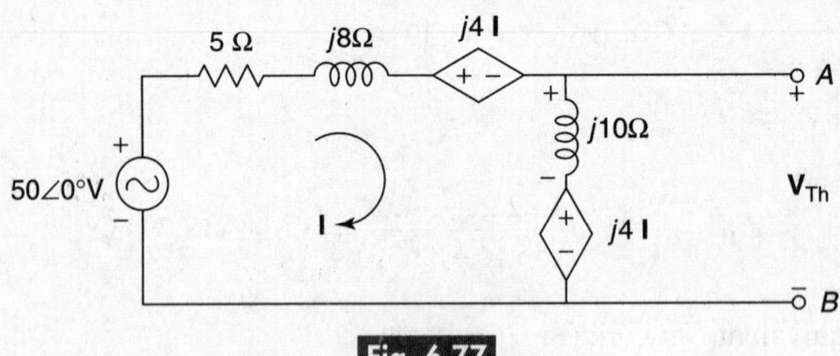


Fig. 6.77

Applying KVL to the mesh,

$$50\angle 0° - 5\mathbf{I} - j8\,\mathbf{I} - j4\,\mathbf{I} - j10\,\mathbf{I} - j4\,\mathbf{I} = 0$$

$$50\angle 0° - (5 + j26)\,\mathbf{I} = 0$$

$$\mathbf{I} = \frac{50\angle 0°}{5 + j26} = 1.89\angle -79.11° \text{ A}$$

Writing the $\mathbf{V}_{\text{Th}}$ equation,

$$j4\,\mathbf{I} + j10\,\mathbf{I} - \mathbf{V}_{\text{Th}} = 0$$

$$j14\,\mathbf{I} - \mathbf{V}_{\text{Th}} = 0$$

$$\mathbf{V}_{\text{Th}} = (j14)(1.89\angle -79.11°) = 26.46\angle 10.89° \text{ V}$$

***Step II*** Calculation of $\mathbf{I}_N$

The equivalent circuit in terms of dependent sources is shown in Fig. 6.78.

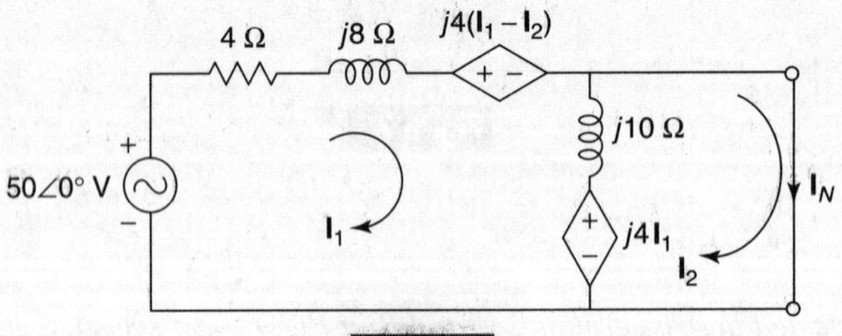


Fig. 6.78

Applying KVL to mesh 1,

$$50\angle 0° - 5\mathbf{I}_1 - j8\,\mathbf{I}_1 - j4\,(\mathbf{I}_1 - \mathbf{I}_2) - j10\,(\mathbf{I}_1 - \mathbf{I}_2) - j4\,\mathbf{I}_1 = 0$$

$$(5 + j26)\,\mathbf{I}_1 - j14\,\mathbf{I}_2 = 50\angle 0° \quad \text{...(i)}$$

Applying KVL to mesh 2,

$$j4\,\mathbf{I}_1 - j10\,(\mathbf{I}_2 - \mathbf{I}_1) = 0$$

$$\mathbf{I}_1 - j10\,\mathbf{I}_2 = 0$$

$$\mathbf{I}_1 = 0.71\,\mathbf{I}_2 \quad \text{...(ii)}$$

Substituting Eq. (ii) in Eq. (i),

$$(5 + j26)(0.71\,\mathbf{I}_2) - j14\,\mathbf{I}_2 = 50\angle 0$$

$$(5.7\angle 51.48°)\,\mathbf{I}_2 = 50\angle 0°$$

$$\mathbf{I}_2 = 8.77\angle -51.48° \text{ A}$$

$$\mathbf{I}_N = \mathbf{I}_2 = 8.77\angle -51.48° \text{ A}$$

***Step III*** Calculation of $\mathbf{Z}_{Th}$

$$\mathbf{Z}_{Th} = \frac{\mathbf{V}_{Th}}{\mathbf{I}_N} = \frac{26.46 \angle 10.89}{5.7 \angle -51.48} = 3.02 \angle 62.37° \ \Omega = (1.4 + j\,2.67)\ \Omega$$

***Step IV*** Calculation of $\mathbf{Z}_L$

(i) When $\mathbf{Z}_L$ is complex impedance

For maximum power transfer, $\mathbf{Z}_L = \mathbf{Z}_{Th}^* = (1.4 - j\,2.67)\ \Omega$

(ii) When $\mathbf{Z}_L$ is pure resistance

For maximum power transfer, $\mathbf{Z}_L = |\mathbf{Z}_{Th}| = |1.4 + j\,2.67| = 3.02\ \Omega$

## 6.8 CONDUCTIVELY COUPLED EQUIVALENT CIRCUITS

LO 6.6

Explain conductively coupled equivalent circuits

For simplifying circuit analysis, it is desirable to replace a magnetically coupled circuit with an equivalent circuit called conductively coupled circuit. In this circuit, no magnetic coupling is involved. The dot convention is also not needed in the conductively coupled circuit.

Consider a coupled circuit, as shown in Fig. 6.79.

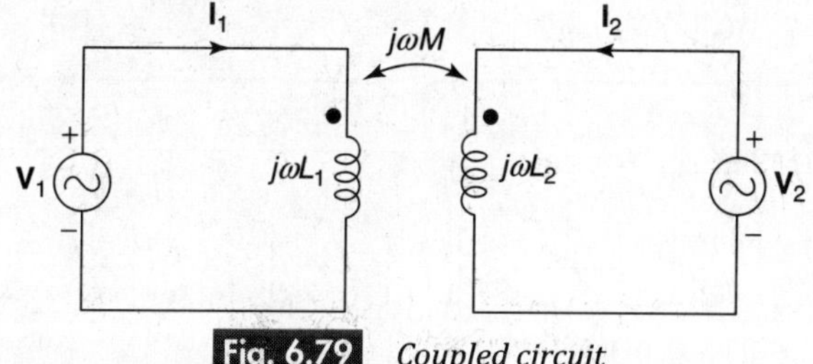


**Fig. 6.79** *Coupled circuit*

The equivalent circuit in terms of dependent sources is shown in Fig. 6.80.

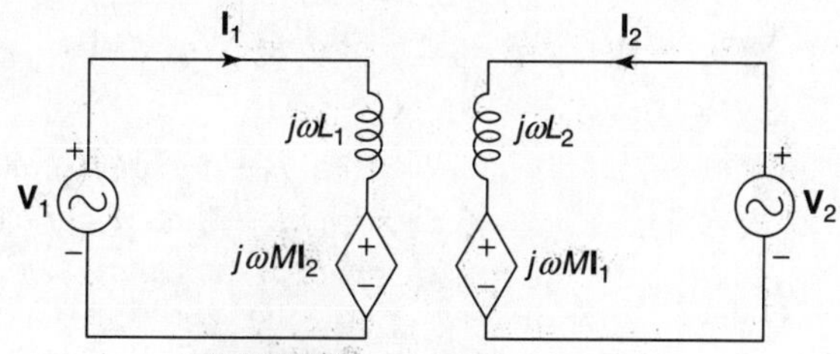


**Fig. 6.80** *Equivalent circuit*

Applying KVL to mesh 1,

$$\mathbf{V}_1 - j\omega L_1\,\mathbf{I}_1 - j\omega M\,\mathbf{I}_2 = 0$$

$$j\omega L_1\,\mathbf{I}_1 + j\omega M\,\mathbf{I}_2 = \mathbf{V}_1 \qquad \ldots(6.11)$$

Applying KVL to mesh 2,

$$\mathbf{V}_2 - j\omega L_2\,\mathbf{I}_2 - j\omega M\,\mathbf{I}_1 = 0$$

$$j\omega M\,\mathbf{I}_1 + j\omega L_2\,\mathbf{I}_2 = \mathbf{V}_2 \qquad \ldots(6.12)$$

Writing Eqs (6.11) and (6.12) in matrix form,

$$\begin{bmatrix} j\omega L_1 & j\omega M \\ j\omega M & j\omega L_2 \end{bmatrix} \begin{bmatrix} \mathbf{I}_1 \\ \mathbf{I}_2 \end{bmatrix} = \begin{bmatrix} \mathbf{V}_1 \\ \mathbf{V}_2 \end{bmatrix} \qquad \text{...(6.13)}$$

Consider a T-network, as shown in Fig. 6.81.

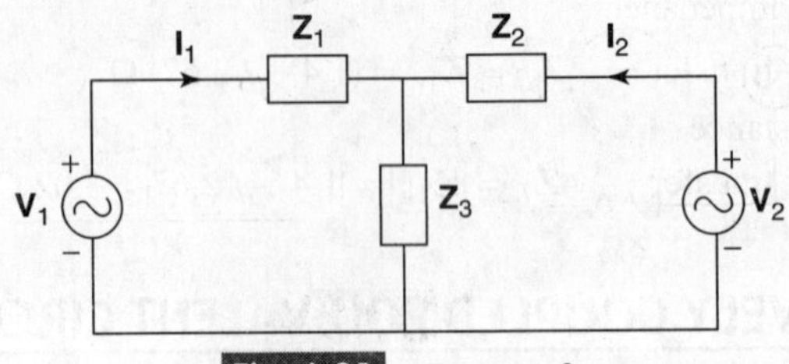


Fig. 6.81 *T-network*

Applying KVL to mesh 1,

$$\mathbf{V}_1 - \mathbf{Z}_1\,\mathbf{I}_1 - \mathbf{Z}_3(\mathbf{I}_1 + \mathbf{I}_2) = 0$$

$$(\mathbf{Z}_1 + \mathbf{Z}_3)\,\mathbf{I}_1 + \mathbf{Z}_3\,\mathbf{I}_2 = \mathbf{V}_1 \qquad \text{... (6.14)}$$

Applying KVL to mesh 2,

$$\mathbf{V}_2 - \mathbf{Z}_2\,\mathbf{I}_2 - \mathbf{Z}_3(\mathbf{I}_2 + \mathbf{I}_1) = 0$$

$$\mathbf{Z}_3\,\mathbf{I}_1 + (\mathbf{Z}_2 + \mathbf{Z}_3)\,\mathbf{I}_2 = \mathbf{V}_2 \qquad \text{... (6.15)}$$

Writing Eqs (6.14) and (6.15) in matrix form,

$$\begin{bmatrix} \mathbf{Z}_1 + \mathbf{Z}_3 & \mathbf{Z}_3 \\ \mathbf{Z}_3 & \mathbf{Z}_2 + \mathbf{Z}_3 \end{bmatrix} \begin{bmatrix} \mathbf{I}_1 \\ \mathbf{I}_2 \end{bmatrix} = \begin{bmatrix} \mathbf{V}_1 \\ \mathbf{V}_2 \end{bmatrix}$$

Comparing matrix equations,

$$\mathbf{Z}_1 + \mathbf{Z}_3 = j\,\omega\,L_1$$

$$\mathbf{Z}_3 = j\,\omega\,M$$

$$\mathbf{Z}_2 + \mathbf{Z}_3 = j\,\omega\,L_2$$

Solving these equations,

$$\mathbf{Z}_1 = j\,\omega\,L_1 - j\,\omega\,M = j\,\omega(L_1 - M)$$

$$\mathbf{Z}_2 = j\,\omega\,L_2 - j\,\omega\,M = j\,\omega(L_2 - M)$$

$$\mathbf{Z}_3 = j\,\omega\,M$$

Hence, the conductively coupled circuit of a magnetically coupled circuit is shown in Fig. 6.82.

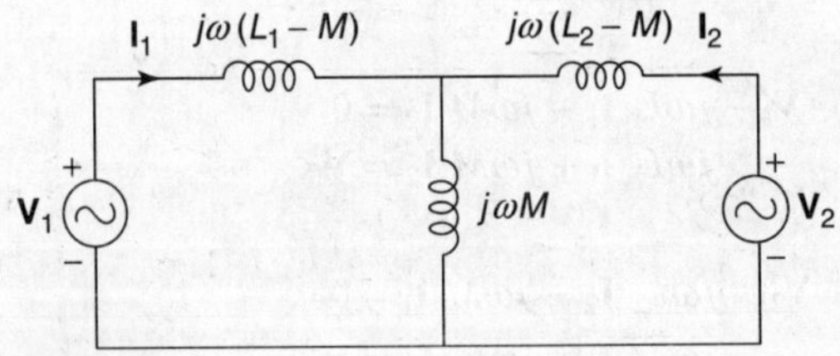


Fig. 6.82 *Conductively coupled equivalent circuit*

## EXAMPLE 6.36

*Find the conductively coupled equivalent circuit for the network shown in Fig. 6.83.*

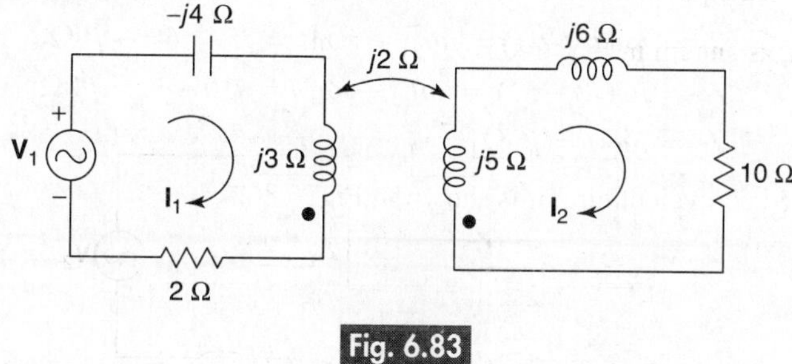


Fig. 6.83

**Solution** The current $\mathbf{I}_1$ leaves from the dotted end and $\mathbf{I}_2$ enters from the dotted end. Hence, mutual inductance $M$ is negative.

In the conductively coupled equivalent circuit,

$$\mathbf{Z}_1 = j\omega(L_1 - M) = j\omega L_1 - j\omega M = j3 - j2 = j1\,\Omega$$

$$\mathbf{Z}_2 = j\omega(L_2 - M) = j\omega L_2 - j\omega M = j5 - j2 = j3\,\Omega$$

$$\mathbf{Z}_3 = j\omega M = j2\,\Omega$$

The conductively coupled equivalent circuit is shown in Fig. 6.84.

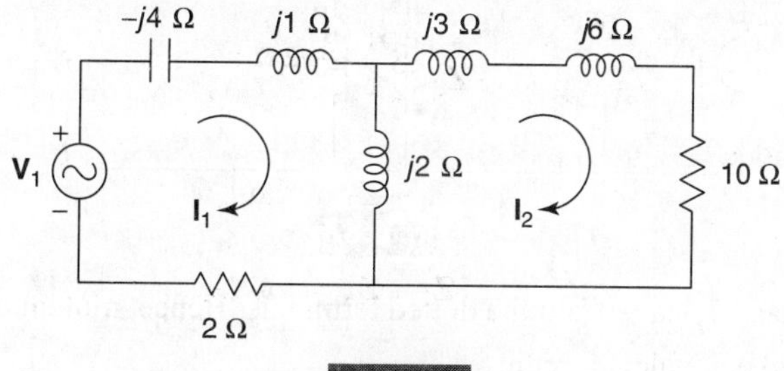


Fig. 6.84

## EXAMPLE 6.37

*Draw the conductively coupled equivalent circuit of Fig. 6.85.*

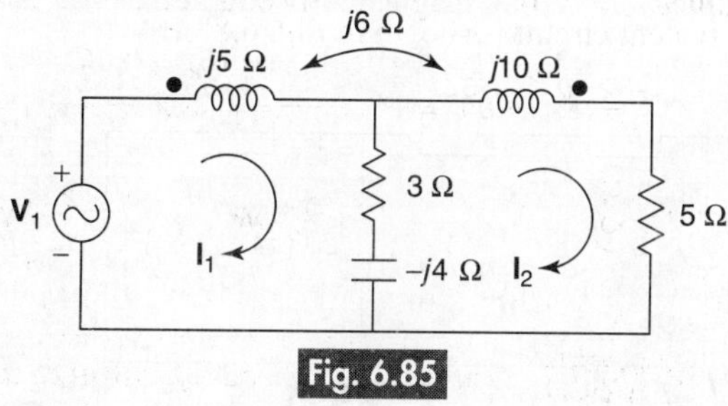


Fig. 6.85

**Solution** The current $\mathbf{I}_1$ enters from the dotted end and $\mathbf{I}_2$ leaves from the dotted end. Hence, the mutual inductance $M$ is negative.

In the conductively coupled equivalent circuit,

$$\mathbf{Z}_1 = j\omega(L_1 - M) = j\omega L_1 - j\omega M = j5 - j6 = -j1\,\Omega$$
$$\mathbf{Z}_2 = j\omega(L_2 - M) = j\omega L_2 - j\omega M = j10 - j6 = j4\,\Omega$$
$$\mathbf{Z}_3 = j\omega M = j6\,\Omega$$

The conductively coupled equivalent circuit is shown in Fig. 6.86.

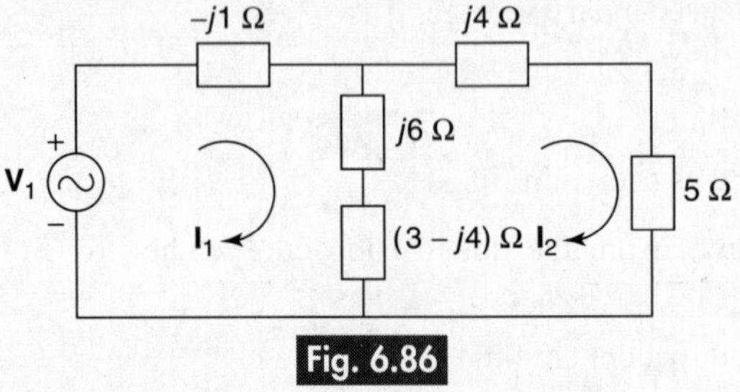


Fig. 6.86

## EXAMPLE 6.38

*Find the conductively coupled equivalent circuit of the network in Fig. 6.87.*

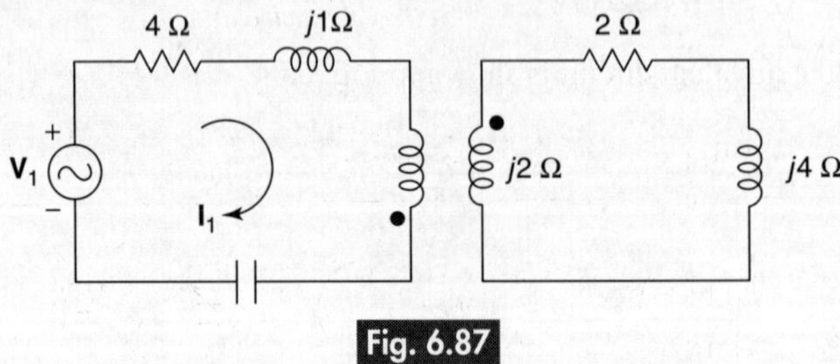


Fig. 6.87

**Solution** The currents $\mathbf{I}_1$ and $\mathbf{I}_2$ leave from the dotted terminals. Hence, mutual inductance is positive.

In the conductively coupled equivalent circuit,

$$\mathbf{Z}_1 = j\omega(L_1 + M) = j\omega L_1 + j\omega M = j4 + j2 = j6\,\Omega$$
$$\mathbf{Z}_2 = j\omega(L_2 + M) = j\omega L_2 + j\omega M = j2 + j2 = j4\,\Omega$$
$$\mathbf{Z}_3 = -j\omega M = -j2\,\Omega$$

The conductively coupled equivalent circuit is shown in Fig. 6.88.

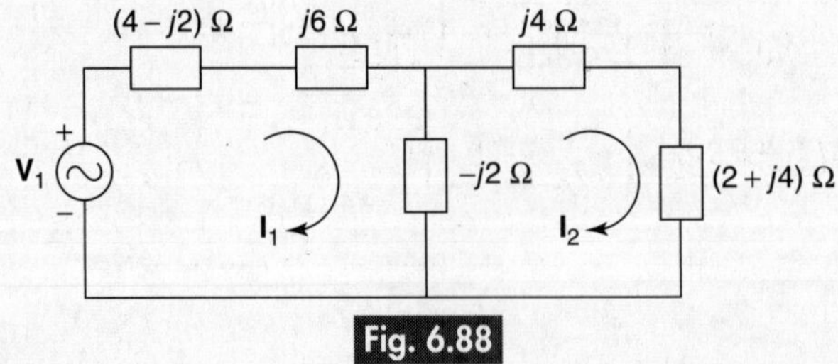


Fig. 6.88

## 6.9 TUNED CIRCUITS

LO 6.7

Discuss tuned circuits, their types and uses

At radio frequencies, the amplification of signals is done by tuned circuits. There are two types of tuned circuits – single-tuned circuit and double-tuned circuit. In the single-tuned circuit, only the secondary is tuned. In the double-tuned circuits, both primary and secondary of the coupled circuits are tuned. The tuned circuits are used in TV receivers to couple the antenna to the RF stage. In RF circuit design, the tuned circuits are generally employed for obtaining maximum power transfer to the load connected to secondary or for obtaining maximum possible value of the secondary voltage.

### 6.9.1 Single-Tuned Circuit

Consider a single-tuned circuit, as shown in Fig. 6.89.

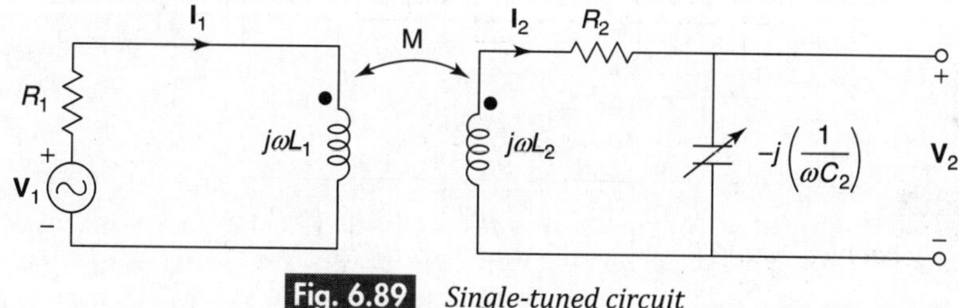


**Fig. 6.89** *Single-tuned circuit*

The conductively coupled equivalent circuit is shown in Fig. 6.90.

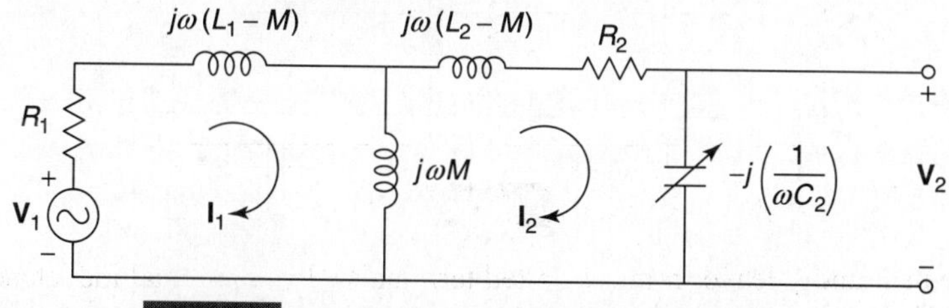


**Fig. 6.90** *Conductively coupled equivalent circuit*

Applying KVL to mesh 1,

$$\mathbf{V}_1 - R_1\mathbf{I}_1 - j\omega(L_1 - M)\mathbf{I}_1 - j\omega M(\mathbf{I}_1 - \mathbf{I}_2) = 0$$

$$(R_1 + j\omega L_1)\mathbf{I}_1 - j\omega M\,\mathbf{I}_2 = \mathbf{V}_1 \qquad \ldots(6.16)$$

Applying KVL to mesh 2,

$$-j\omega M(\mathbf{I}_2 - \mathbf{I}_1) - j\omega(L_2 - M)\mathbf{I}_2 - R_2\mathbf{I}_2 + j\frac{1}{\omega C_2}\mathbf{I}_2 = 0$$

$$-j\omega M\mathbf{I}_1 + \left[R_2 + j\left(\omega L_2 - \frac{1}{\omega C_2}\right)\right]\mathbf{I}_2 = 0 \qquad \ldots(6.17)$$

From Eq. (6.17),

$$\mathbf{I}_1 = \frac{R_2 + j\left(\omega L_2 - \dfrac{1}{\omega C_2}\right)}{j\omega M}\mathbf{I}_2 \qquad \text{...(6.18)}$$

Substituting Eq. (6.18) in Eq. (6.16),

$$(R_1 + j\omega L_1)\left[\frac{R_2 + j\left(\omega L_2 - \dfrac{1}{\omega C_2}\right)}{j\omega M}\right]\mathbf{I}_2 - j\omega M\mathbf{I}_2 = \mathbf{V}_1$$

$$\mathbf{I}_2\left\{\frac{(R_1 + j\omega L_1)\left[R_2 + j\left(\omega L_2 - \dfrac{1}{\omega C_2}\right)\right] + \omega^2 M^2}{j\omega M}\right\} = \mathbf{V}_1$$

$$\mathbf{I}_2 = \frac{j\omega M\,\mathbf{V}_1}{(R_1 + j\omega L_1)\left[R_2 + j\left(\omega L_2 - \dfrac{1}{\omega C_2}\right)\right] + \omega^2 M^2}$$

**1. Output Voltage**

$$\mathbf{V}_2 = -j\left(\frac{1}{\omega C_2}\right)\mathbf{I}_2 = \frac{1}{j\omega C_2}\mathbf{I}_2$$

$$= \frac{MV_1}{C_2\left\{(R_1 + j\omega L_1)\left[R_2 + j\left(\omega L_2 - \dfrac{1}{\omega C_2}\right)\right] + \omega^2 M^2\right\}}$$

**2. Voltage Amplification**

$$A = \frac{\mathbf{V}_2}{\mathbf{V}_1} = \frac{M}{C_2\left\{(R_1 + j\omega L_1)\left[R_2 + j\left(\omega L_2 - \dfrac{1}{\omega C_2}\right)\right] + \omega^2 M^2\right\}}$$

If $R_1 >> j\omega L_1$ and secondary circuit resonates at

$$\omega_0 = \frac{1}{\sqrt{L_2 C_2}}$$

then, at the resonant frequency $\omega_0$,

$$I_2 = \frac{\omega_0 M V_1}{R_1 R_2 + \omega_0^2 M^2}$$

$$V_2 = \frac{M V_1}{C_2(R_1 R_2 + \omega_0^2 M^2)}$$

$$A = \frac{M}{C_2(R_1R_2 + \omega_0^2 M^2)}$$

Output current, output voltage and voltage amplification depends on the mutual inductance $M$ at resonant frequency. The maximum amplification or maximum output voltage can be obtained by

$$\frac{dA}{dM} = 0$$

$$\frac{C_2(R_1R_2 + \omega_0^2 M^2) - 2C_2\omega_0^2 M^2}{\left[C_2(R_1R_2 + \omega_0^2 M^2)\right]^2} = 0$$

$$R_1R_2 + \omega_0^2 M^2 - 2\omega_0^2 M^2 = 0$$

$$\omega_0^2 M^2 = R_1R_2$$

$$M = \frac{\sqrt{R_1R_2}}{\omega_0}$$

where $M = \frac{\sqrt{R_1R_2}}{\omega_0}$ is the critical value of mutual inductance.

Hence, maximum value of $I_2$, $V_2$ and $A$ is

$$I_{2_{\max}} = \frac{V_1}{2\sqrt{R_1R_2}}$$

$$V_{2_{\max}} = \frac{V_1}{2\omega_0 C_2\sqrt{R_1R_2}}$$

$$A_{\max} = \frac{1}{2\omega_0 C_2\sqrt{R_1R_2}}$$

The variation of output voltage $V_0$ with angular frequency $\omega$ for different values of coefficient of coupling $k$ is shown in Fig. 6.91.

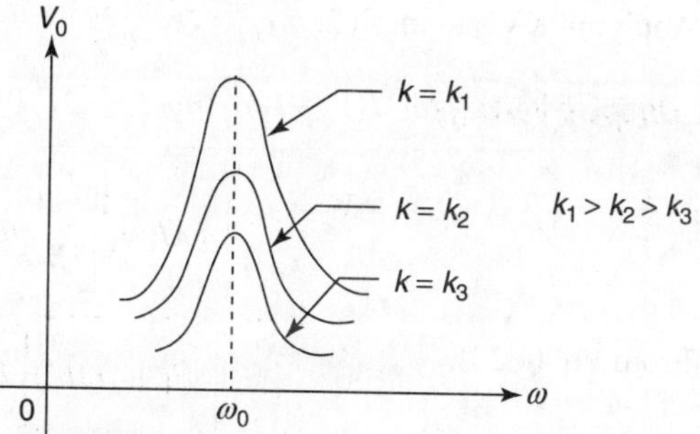


**Fig. 6.91** *Variation of $V_0$ with $\omega$ for different values of k*

### 6.9.2 Double-Tuned Circuit

Consider a double-tuned circuit with tuning capacitors placed both in primary and secondary circuits, as shown in Fig. 6.92.

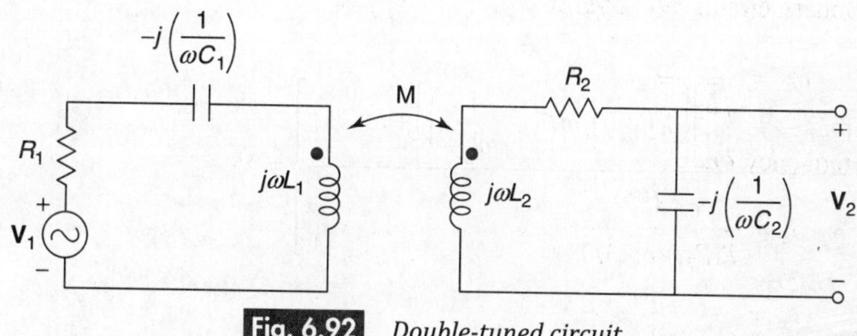


**Fig. 6.92** *Double-tuned circuit*

The conductively coupled equivalent circuit is shown in Fig. 6.93.

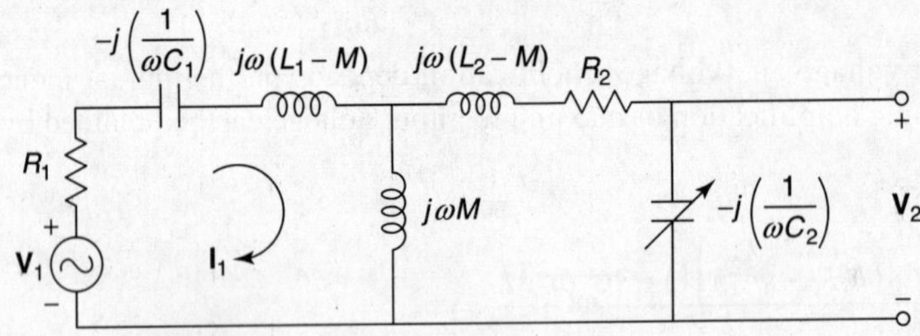


Fig. 6.93 Conductively coupled equivalent circuit

Applying KVL to mesh 1,

$$\mathbf{V}_1 - R_1\mathbf{I}_1 + j\frac{1}{\omega C_2}\mathbf{I}_1 - j\omega(L_1 - M)\mathbf{I}_1 - j\omega M(\mathbf{I}_1 - \mathbf{I}_2) = 0$$

$$\left(R_1 + j\omega L_1 - j\frac{1}{\omega C_1}\right)\mathbf{I}_1 - j\omega M\mathbf{I}_2 = \mathbf{V}_1 \qquad \text{...(6.19)}$$

Applying KVL to mesh 2,

$$-j\omega M(\mathbf{I}_2 - \mathbf{I}_1) - j\omega(L_2 - M)\mathbf{I}_2 - R_2\mathbf{I}_2 + j\frac{1}{\omega C_2}\mathbf{I}_2 = 0$$

$$-j\omega M\mathbf{I}_1 + \left[R_2 + j\left(\omega L_2 - \frac{1}{\omega C_2}\right)\right]\mathbf{I}_2 = 0 \qquad \text{...(6.20)}$$

From Eq. (6.20),

$$\mathbf{I}_1 = \frac{R_2 + j\left(\omega L_2 - \dfrac{1}{\omega C_2}\right)}{j\omega M}\mathbf{I}_2 \qquad \text{...(6.21)}$$

Substituting Eq. (6.21) in Eq. (6.19),

$$\left(R_1 + j\omega L_1 - j\frac{1}{\omega C_2}\right)\left[\frac{R_2 + j\left(\omega L_2 - \dfrac{1}{\omega C_2}\right)}{j\omega M}\right]\mathbf{I}_2 - j\omega M\mathbf{I}_2 = \mathbf{V}_1$$

$$\mathbf{I}_2\left\{\frac{\left[R_1 + j\left(\omega L_1 - \dfrac{1}{\omega C_2}\right)\right]\left[R_2 + j\left(\omega L_2 - \dfrac{1}{\omega C_2}\right)\right] + \omega^2 M^2}{j\omega M}\right\} = \mathbf{V}_1$$

$$\mathbf{I}_2 = \frac{j\omega M \mathbf{V}_1}{\left[R_1 + j\left(\omega L_1 - \frac{1}{\omega C_2}\right)\right]\left[R_2 + j\left(\omega L_2 - \frac{1}{\omega C_2}\right) + \omega^2 M^2\right]}$$

### 1. Output Voltage

$$\mathbf{V}_2 = -j\left(\frac{1}{\omega C_2}\right)\mathbf{I}_2 = \frac{1}{j\omega C_2}\mathbf{I}_2$$

$$= \frac{M\mathbf{V}_1}{C_2\left\{\left[R_1 + j\left(\omega L_1 - \frac{1}{\omega C_2}\right)\right]\left[R_2 + j\left(\omega L_2 - \frac{1}{\omega C_2}\right)\right] + \omega^2 M^2\right\}}$$

### 2. Voltage Amplification

$$A = \frac{\mathbf{V}_2}{\mathbf{V}_1} = \frac{M}{C_2\left\{\left[R_1 + j\left(\omega L_1 - \frac{1}{\omega C_2}\right)\right]\left[R_2 + j\left(\omega L_2 - \frac{1}{\omega C_2}\right)\right] + \omega^2 M^2\right\}}$$

If the primary and secondary circuits resonate at the same frequency $\omega_0$,

$$\omega_0 = \frac{1}{\sqrt{L_1 C_1}} = \frac{1}{\sqrt{L_2 C_2}}$$

Then, at the resonant frequency $\omega_0$,

$$I_2 = \frac{\omega_0 M V_1}{R_1 R_2 + \omega_0^2 M^2}$$

$$V_2 = \frac{M V_1}{C_2(R_1 R_2 + \omega_0^2 M^2)}$$

$$A = \frac{M}{C_2(R_1 R_2 + \omega_0^2 M^2)}$$

The maximum amplification or maximum output voltage can be obtained by,

$$\frac{dA}{dM} = 0$$

$$\frac{C_2(R_1 R_2 + \omega_0^2 M^2) - 2C_2\omega_0^2 M^2}{\left[C_2(R_1 R_2 + \omega_0^2 M^2)\right]^2} = 0$$

$$\left(R_1 R_2 + \omega_0^2 M^2\right) - 2\omega_0^2 M^2 = 0$$

$$\omega_0^2 M^2 = R_1 R_2$$

$$M = \frac{\sqrt{R_1 R_2}}{\omega_0}$$

where $M = \dfrac{\sqrt{R_1 R_2}}{\omega_0}$ is the critical value of mutual inductance.

Hence, maximum value of $I_2$, $V_2$ and $A$ is

$$I_{2_{\max}} = \frac{V_1}{2\sqrt{R_1 R_2}}$$

$$V_{2_{\max}} = \frac{V_1}{2\omega_0 C_2 \sqrt{R_1 R_2}}$$

$$A_{\max} = \frac{1}{2\omega_0 C_2 \sqrt{R_1 R_2}}$$

The variation of the output voltage $V_0$ with the angular frequency $\omega$ for different values of coefficient of coupling $k$ is shown in Fig. 6.94.

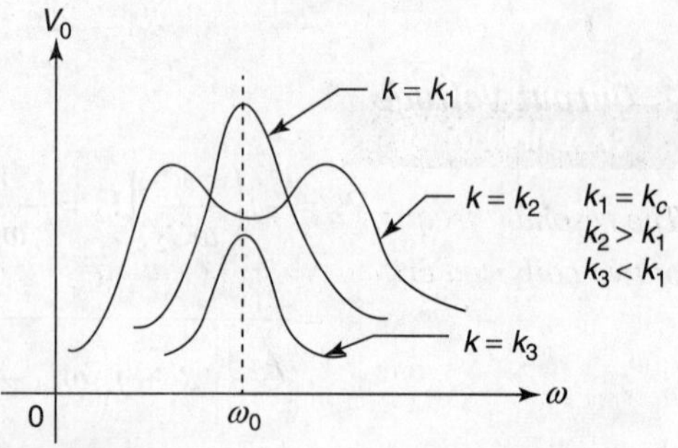


**Fig. 6.94** *Variation of $V_0$ with $\omega$ for different values of $k$*

## EXAMPLE 6.39

*For the single-tuned circuit shown in Fig. 6.95, determine (a) the resonant frequency, (b) output voltage at resonance, and (c) maximum output voltage. Assume $R_1 >> \omega_0 L_1$ and $k = 0.8$.*

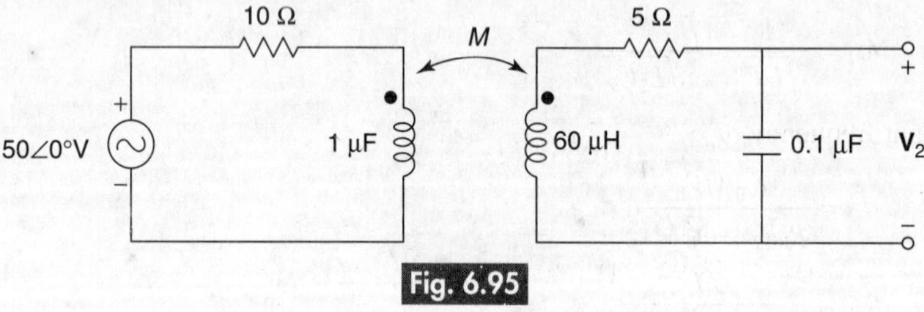


**Fig. 6.95**

**Solution**

$$M = k\sqrt{L_1 L_2} = 0.8\sqrt{(1\times10^{-6})(60\times10^{-6})} = 6.2\ \mu\text{H}$$

(a) Resonant frequency

$$\omega_0 = \frac{1}{\sqrt{L_2 C_2}} = \frac{1}{\sqrt{(60\times10^{-6})(0.1\times10^{-6})}} = 0.41\times10^6\ \text{rad/s}$$

$$f_0 = \frac{\omega_0}{2\pi} = \frac{0.41\times10^6}{2\pi} = 0.0653\ \text{MHz} = 65.3\ \text{kHz}$$

(b) Output voltage at resonance

$$V_0 = \frac{MV_1}{C_2\left(R_1 R_2 + \omega_0^2 M^2\right)} = \frac{6.2\times10^{-6}\times50}{0.1\times10^{-6}\left[(10\times5)+\left(0.42\times10^6\right)^2\left(6.2\times10^{-6}\right)^2\right]} = 54.6\ \text{V}$$

(c) Maximum output voltage

$$V_{2_{\max}} = \frac{V_1}{2\omega_0 C_2\sqrt{R_1 R_2}} = \frac{50}{2(0.42\times10^6)(0.1\times10^{-6})\sqrt{10\times5}} = 84.18 \text{ V}$$

**EXAMPLE 6.40**

*The resonant frequency of the tuned circuit shown in Fig. 6.96 is 1000 rad/s. Calculate the self-inductances of two coils and critical value of mutual inductance.*

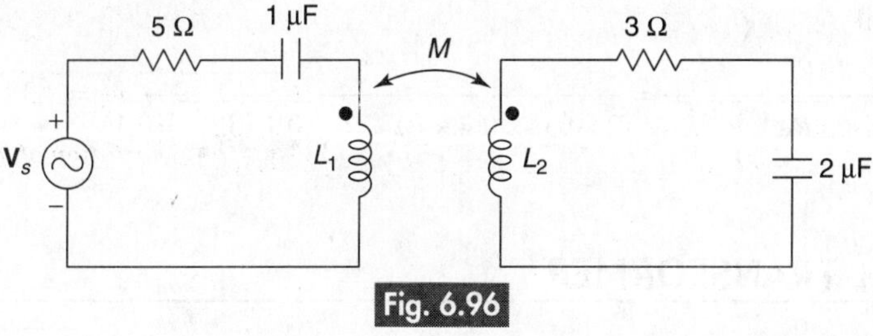


Fig. 6.96

**Solution**

$$\omega_0 = \frac{1}{\sqrt{L_1 C_1}} = \frac{1}{\sqrt{L_2 C_2}}$$

$$L_1 = \frac{1}{\omega_0^2 C_1} = \frac{1}{(1000)^2 \left(1\times10^{-6}\right)} = 1 \text{ H}$$

$$L_2 = \frac{1}{\omega_0^2 C_2} = \frac{1}{(1000)^2 \left(2\times10^{-6}\right)} = 0.5 \text{ H}$$

$$M_c = \frac{\sqrt{R_1 R_2}}{\omega_0} = \frac{\sqrt{5\times3}}{1000} = 3.87 \text{ mH}$$

**EXAMPLE 6.41**

*The tuned frequency of a double-tuned circuit shown in Fig. 6.97 is $10^4$ rad/s. If the source voltage is 2 V and has a resistance of 0.1 Ω, calculate the maximum output voltage.*

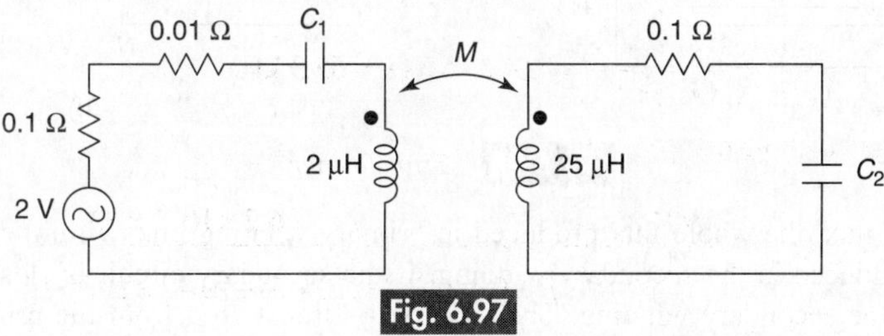


Fig. 6.97

**Solution**

$$M_C = \frac{\sqrt{(R_1 + R_S)R_2}}{\omega_0} = \frac{\sqrt{(0.01+0.1)(0.1)}}{10^4} = 10.49\ \mu\text{H}$$

$$\omega_0 = \frac{1}{\sqrt{L_2 C_2}}$$

$$10^4 = \frac{1}{\sqrt{(25\times10^{-6})C_2}}$$

$$C_2 = 0.4\ \text{mF}$$

$$V_{0_{max}} = \frac{V_1}{2\omega_0 C_2\sqrt{(R_S + R_1)R_2}} = \frac{2}{2\times10^4 \times 0.4\times10^{-3} \times \sqrt{(0.1+0.01)(0.1)}} = 2.38\ \text{V}$$

## 6.10 IDEAL TRANSFORMER

LO 6.8

Explain the concept of an ideal transformer

A transformer is a static device which can transfer electrical energy from one circuit to another circuit without change of frequency. It can increase or decrease the voltage but with a corresponding decrease or increase in current. It works on the principle of mutual induction. A transformer mainly consists of two coils or windings placed on a common core. A transformer consists of two coils, called *windings*, which are wrapped around the core. The winding in which electrical energy is fed is called the *primary winding*. The winding which is connected to the load is called the *secondary winding*.

An ideal transformer is a transformer with no losses in core and windings and having a core with infinite permeability, which results in perfect coupling with no leakage flux.

When an alternating voltage $V_1$ is applied to a primary winding, an alternating current $I_1$ flows in it producing an alternating flux in the core. As per Faraday's laws of electromagnetic induction, an emf $e_1$ is induced in the primary winding.

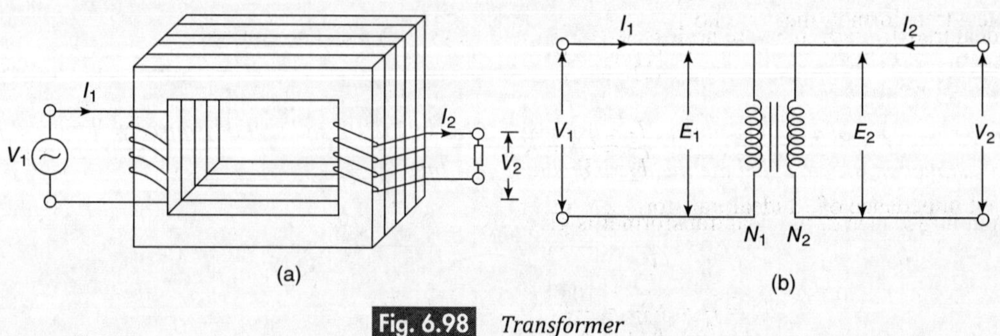


Fig. 6.98 *Transformer*

Assuming no leakage flux, the whole flux produced in primary winding links with the secondary winding. Hence, an emf $e_2$ is induced in the secondary winding. If the secondary circuit is closed through the load, a current $I_2$ flows in the secondary winding. Thus, energy is transferred from the primary winding to the secondary winding.

As the primary winding is excited by a sinusoidal alternating voltage, an alternating current flows in the winding, producing a sinusoidally varying flux $\phi$ in the core.

$$\phi = \phi_m \sin \omega t$$

As per Faraday's laws of electromagnetic induction, an emf $e_1$ is induced in the primary winding.

$$\begin{aligned} e_1 &= -N_1 \frac{d\phi}{dt} \\ &= -N_1 \frac{d}{dt}(\phi_m \sin \omega t) \\ &= -N_1 \phi_m \omega \cos \omega t \\ &= N_1 \phi_m \omega \sin(\omega t - 90°) \\ &= 2\pi f \phi_m N_1 \sin(\omega t - 90°) \end{aligned}$$

Maximum value of induced emf $= 2\pi f \phi_m N_1$

Hence, rms value of induced emf in primary winding is given by

$$E_1 = \frac{E_{\max}}{\sqrt{2}} = \frac{2\pi f \phi_m N_1}{\sqrt{2}} = 4.44 f \phi_m N_1$$

Similarly, rms value of induced emf in the secondary winding is given by

$$E_2 = 4.44 f \phi_m N_2$$

$$\frac{E_2}{E_1} = \frac{N_2}{N_1} = K$$

where $K$ is called the *transformation ratio.*

For an ideal transformer,

$$\begin{aligned} V_1 &= E_1 \\ V_2 &= E_2 \\ \frac{E_2}{E_1} &= \frac{V_2}{V_1} = \frac{N_2}{N_1} = K \end{aligned}$$

In an ideal transformer, there are no losses. Hence, input and output can be equated.

$$V_1 I_1 = V_2 I_2$$

$$\frac{I_1}{I_2} = \frac{V_2}{V_1} = K$$

The input impedance of an ideal transformer is given by

$$Z_{in} = \frac{V_1}{I_1} = \frac{\frac{V_2}{K}}{K I_2} = \frac{1}{K^2}\left(\frac{V_2}{I_2}\right) = \frac{1}{K^2} Z_L = \left(\frac{N_1}{N_2}\right)^2 Z_L$$

where load impedance of secondary $Z_L = \dfrac{V_2}{I_2}$.

Thus, ideal transformer changes the impedance of a load and can be used to match circuits with different impedances in order to achieve maximum power transfer.

## Theory Questions

6.1 Define and explain self-inductance. **[LO 6.1]** ●○○

6.2 Define and explain mutual conductance. **[LO 6.1]** ●○○

6.3 Derive the expression for coefficient of coupling between two coils. **[LO 6.2]** ○●○

6.4 Derive the expression for equivalent inductance of two coils connected in series with cumulative coupling connection. **[LO 6.3]** ○●○

6.5 Derive the expression for equivalent inductance of two coils connected in series with differential coupling connection. **[LO 6.3]** ○●○

6.6 Derive the expression for equivalent inductance of two coils connected in parallel with cumulative coupling connection. **[LO 6.3]** ○●○

6.7 Derive the expression for equivalent inductance of two coils connected in parallel with differential coupling connection. **[LO 6.3]** ○●○

6.8 Explain dot convention for coupled circuits. **[LO 6.4]** ●○○

6.9 Obtain the conductively coupled equivalent circuit for magnetically coupled circuits. **[LO 6.6]** ●○○

6.10 Explain the concept of single-tuned circuit. **[LO 6.7]** ○●○

6.11 Explain the concept of double-tuned circuit. **[LO 6.7]** ○●○

6.12 Explain the concept of an ideal transformer and derive the expressions for its emf equation and transformation ratio. **[LO 6.8]** ○●○

## Practice Problems

6.1 Two coupled coils have inductances of 0.8 H and 0.2 H. The coefficient of coupling is 0.90. Find the mutual inductance and the turns ratio $\frac{N_1}{N_2}$. ●○○

6.2 Two coils with coefficient of coupling 0.5 are connected in such a way that they magnetise (i) in the same direction, and (ii) in opposite directions. The corresponding equivalent inductances are 1.9 H and 0.7 H. Find self-inductances of the two coils and the mutual inductance between them. ●○○

6.3 Two coils having 3000 and 2000 turns are wound on a magnetic ring. 60% of the flux produced in the first coil links with the second coil. A current of 3 A produce a flux of 0.5 mwb in the first coil and 0.3 mwb in the second coil. Determine the mutual inductance and coefficient of coupling. ●○○

6.4 Find the equivalent inductance of the network shown in Fig. 6.99. ●○○

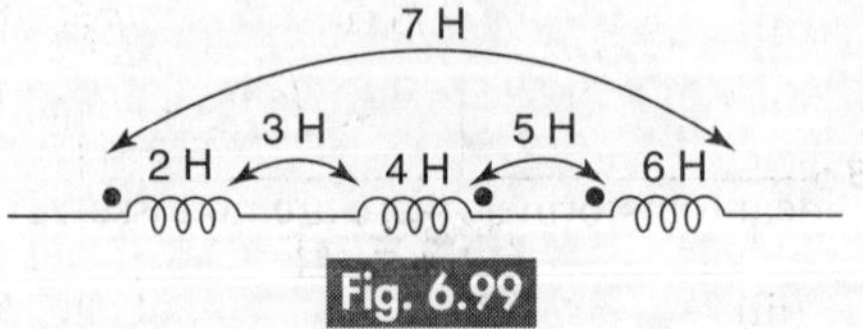


Fig. 6.99

6.5 Find the effective inductance of the network shown in Fig. 6.100. ●○○

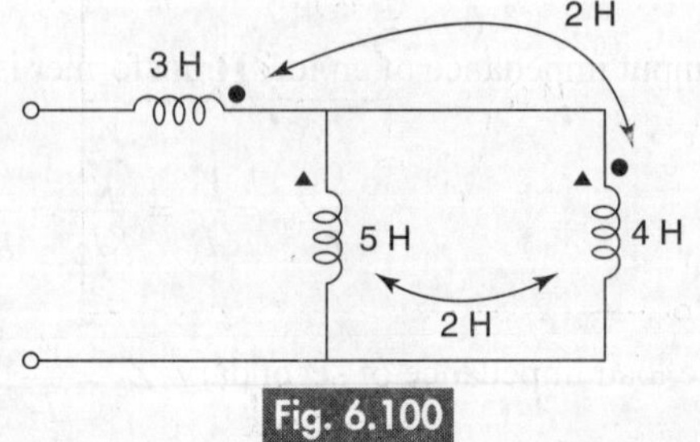


Fig. 6.100

**6.6** Write mesh equations of the network shown in Fig. 6.101. ○●○

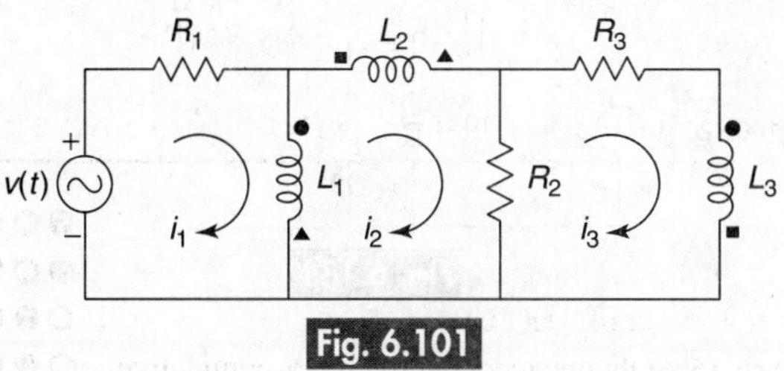


Fig. 6.101

**6.7** Find the input impedance at terminals *AB* of the coupled circuits shown in Fig. 6.102 to 6.104. ○●○

(i)

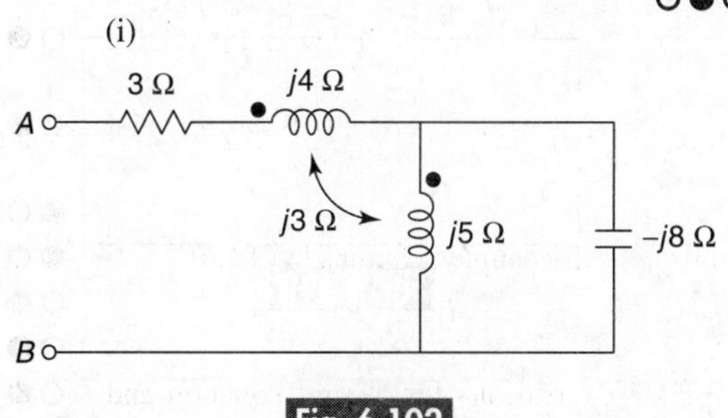


Fig. 6.102

(ii)

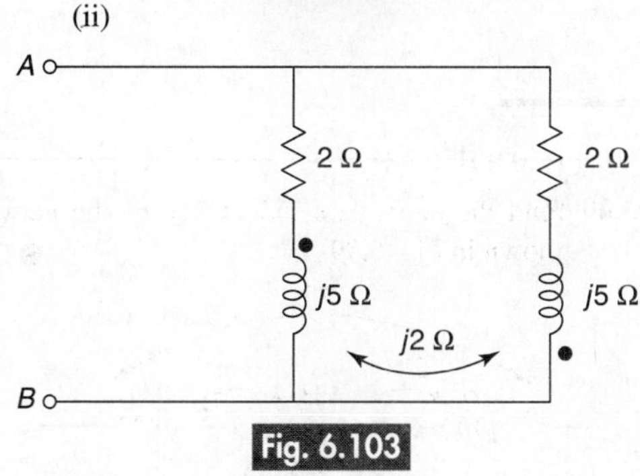


Fig. 6.103

(iii)

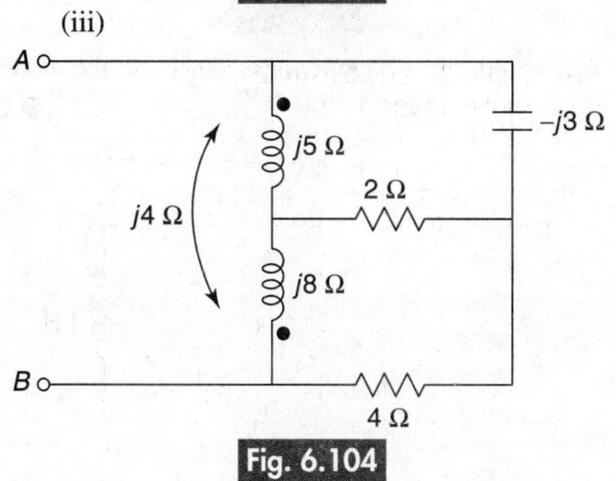


Fig. 6.104

**6.8** In the coupled circuit shown in Fig. 6.105, find $\mathbf{V}_2$ for which $\mathbf{I}_1 = 0$. What voltage appears at the 8 Ω inductive reactance under this condition? ○○●

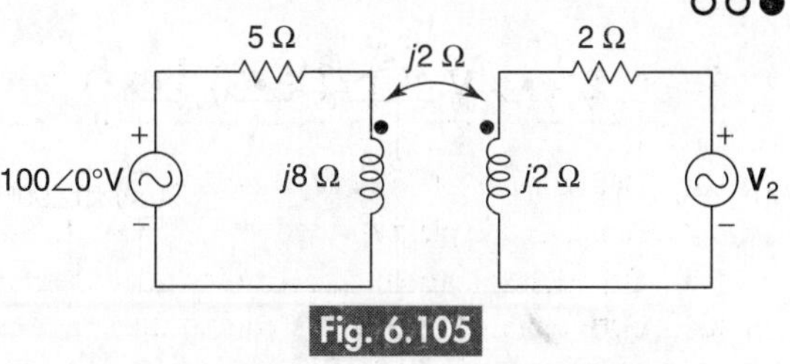


Fig. 6.105

**6.9** For the coupled circuit shown in Fig. 6.106, find the components of the current $\mathbf{I}_2$ resulting from each source $\mathbf{V}_1$ and $\mathbf{V}_2$. ○○●

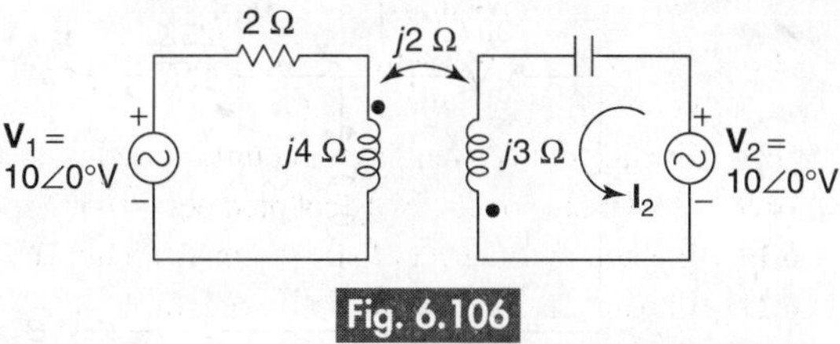


Fig. 6.106

**6.10** Find the voltage across the 5 Ω resistor in the network shown in Fig. 6.107. ○○●

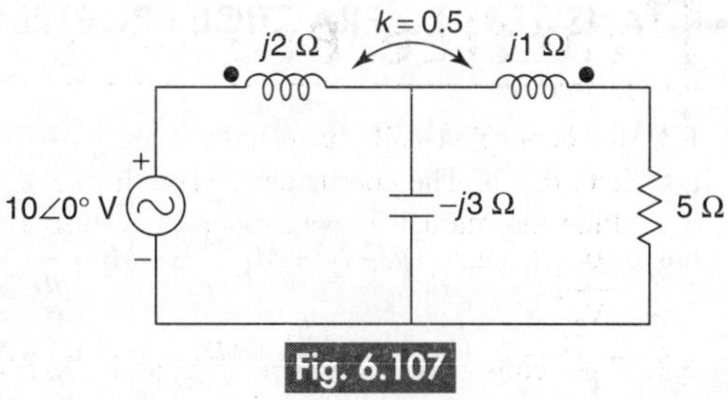


Fig. 6.107

**6.11** Find the power dissipated in the 5 Ω resistor in the network of Fig. 6.108. ○○●

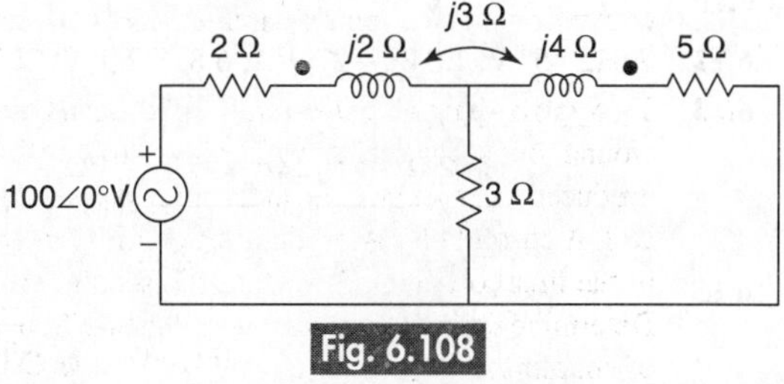


Fig. 6.108

**6.12** Obtain Thevenin's and Norton's equivalent network at terminals *AB* of the coupled circuit shown in Fig. 6.109. ○○●

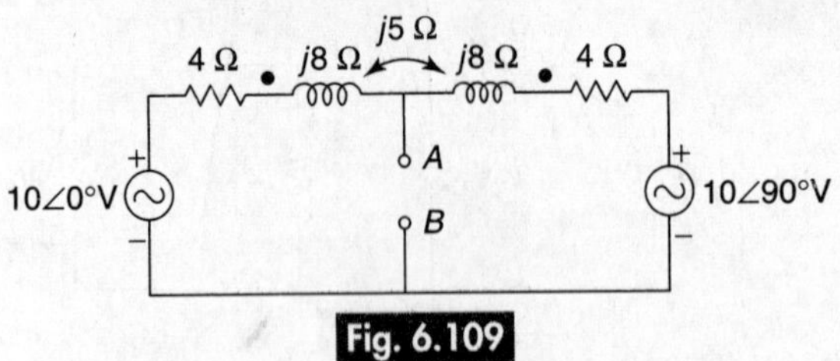


Fig. 6.109

**6.13** For the circuit shown in Fig. 6.110, what load connected to terminals *A* and *B* absorbs maximum power and what is this power? ○○●

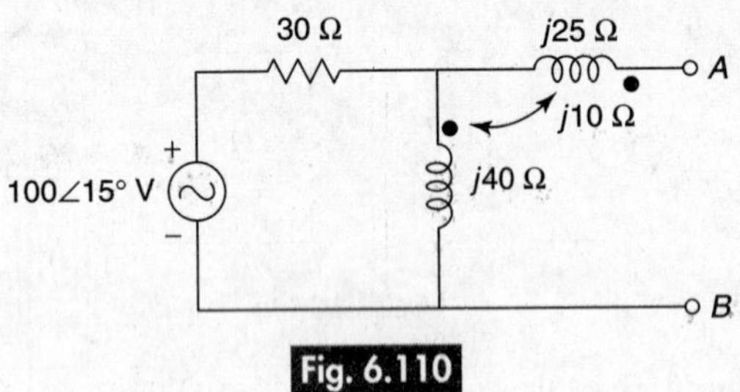


Fig. 6.110

**6.14** Find the current I in the circuit of Fig. 6.111. ○○●

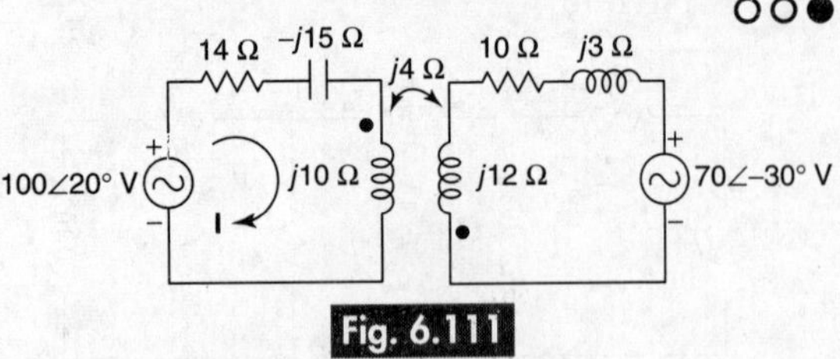


Fig. 6.111

**6.15** Obtain a conductively coupled circuit for the circuit shown in Fig. 6.112. ○●○

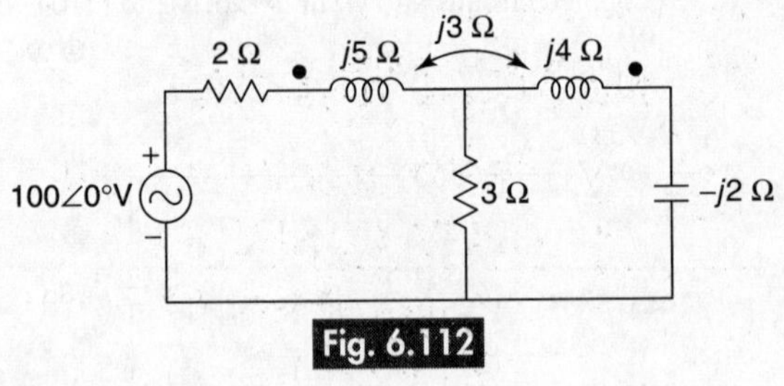


Fig. 6.112

## ANSWERS TO PRACTICE PROBLEMS

**6.1** 0.36 H, 2

**6.2** 0.4 H, 0.9 H, 0.3 H

**6.3** 0.2 H, 0.63

**6.4** 10 H

**6.5** 4.8 H

**6.6** $v = i_1R_1 + L_1\frac{d}{dt}(i_1 - i_2) + M_{12}\frac{di_2}{dt} + M_{13}\frac{di_3}{dt}$

$$R_2(i_3 - i_2) + R_3 i_3 + L_3\frac{di_3}{dt} + M_{13}\frac{d}{dt}(i_1 - i_2) - M_{23}\frac{di_2}{dt} = 0$$

**6.7** (a) $(3 + j36.3)\Omega$ (b) $(1 + j1.5)\Omega$ (c) $(6.22 + j4.65)\Omega$

**6.8** $141.5\angle -45°$V, $100\angle 0°$V

**6.9** $0.77\angle 112.6°$A, $1.72\angle 86.05°$A

**6.10** $19.2\angle -33.02°$V

**6.11** 668.16 W

**6.12** $7.07\angle 45°$ V, $1.04\angle -27.9°$A, $6.8\angle 72.9°\ \Omega$

**6.13** $54.1\angle -56.3°\ \Omega$, 83.3 W

**6.14** $7.38\angle 39.4°$ A

**6.15**

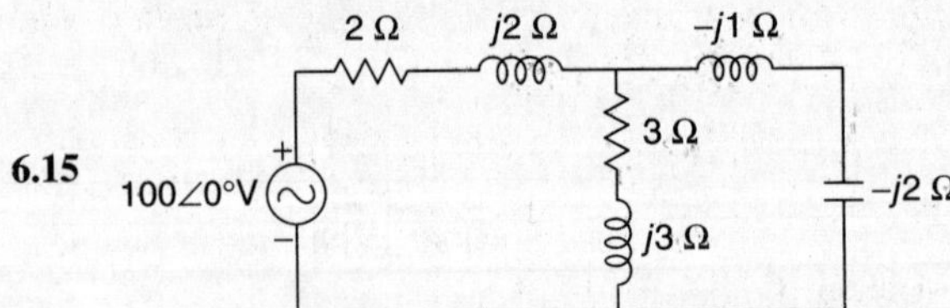

# Objective-Type Questions

## From GATE and Other Competitive Examinations

**6.1** Two coils are wound on a common magnetic core. The sign of mutual inductance $M$ for finding out effective inductance of each coil is positive if the ●○○

(a) two coils are wound in the same sense.
(b) fluxes produced by the two coils are equal.
(c) fluxes produced by the coils act in the same direction.
(d) fluxes produced by the two coils act in opposition.

**6.2** When two coils having self-inductances of $L_1$ and $L_2$ are coupled through a mutual inductance $M$, the coefficient of coupling $k$ is given by ●○○

(a) $k = \dfrac{M}{\sqrt{2L_1L_2}}$ (b) $k = \dfrac{M}{\sqrt{L_1L_2}}$

(c) $k = \dfrac{2M}{\sqrt{L_1L_2}}$ (d) $k = \dfrac{L_1L_2}{M}$

**6.3** The overall inductance of two coils connected in series, with mutual inductance aiding self-inductance is $L_1$; with mutual inductance opposing self-inductance, the overall inductance is $L_2$. The mutual inductance $M$ is given by ●○○

(a) $L_1 + L_2$ (b) $L_1 - L_2$

(c) $\dfrac{1}{4}(L_1 - L_2)$ (d) $\dfrac{1}{2}(L_1 + L_2)$

**6.4** Consider the following statements:
The coefficient of coupling between two oils depends upon

1. Orientation of the coils
2. Core material
3. Number of turns on the two coils
4. Self-inductance of the two coils ○●○

of these statements,

(a) 1, 2 and 3 are correct
(b) 1 and 2 are correct
(c) 3 and 4 are correct
(d) 1, 2 and 4 are correct

**6.5** Two coupled coils connected in series have an equivalent inductance of 16 mH or 8 mH depending on the inter connection. Then the mutual inductance $M$ between the coils is ●○○

(a) 12 mH (b) $8\sqrt{2}$ mH
(c) 4 mH (d) 2 mH

**6.6** Two coupled coils with $L_1 = L_2 = 0.6$ H have a coupling coefficient of $k = 0.8$. The turns ratio $\dfrac{N_1}{N_2}$ is ○●○

(a) 4 (b) 2
(c) 1 (d) 0.5

**6.7** The coupling between two magnetically coupled coils is said to be ideal if the coefficient of coupling is ●○○

(a) zero (b) 0.5
(c) 1 (d) 2

**6.8** The mutual inductance between two coupled coils is 10 mH. If the turns in one coil are doubled and that in the other are halved then the mutual inductance will be ○●○

(a) 5 mH (b) 10 mH
(c) 14 mH (d) 20 mH

**6.9** Two perfectly coupled coils, each of 1 H self-inductance, are connected in parallel so as to aid each other. The overall inductance in henrys is ●○○

(a) 2 (b) 1
(c) $\dfrac{1}{2}$ (d) Zero

**6.10** The impedance $Z$, as shown in Fig. 6.113 is ●○○

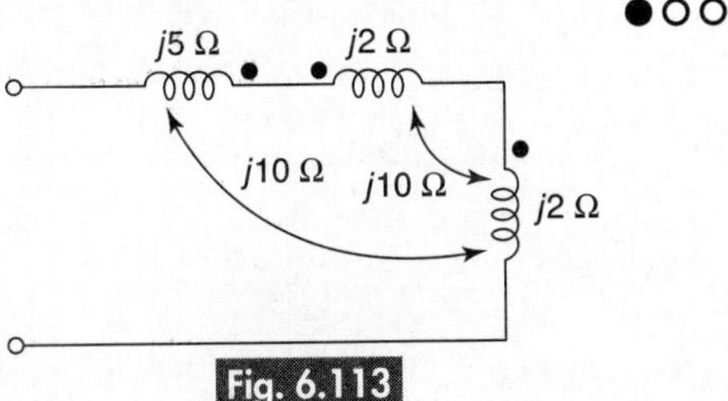


Fig. 6.113

(a) $j\,29\ \Omega$ (b) $j9\ \Omega$
(c) $j19\ \Omega$ (d) $j39\ \Omega$

**6.11** The equivalent inductance measured between the terminals 1 and 2 for the circuit shown in Fig. 6.113 is ●○○

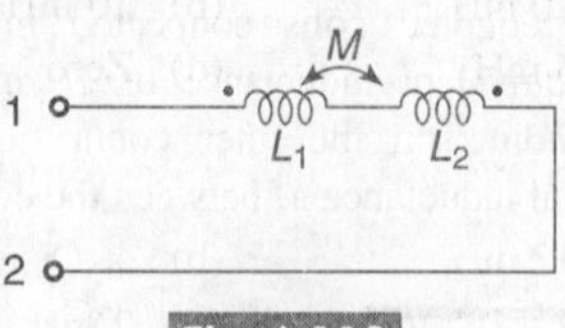

Fig. 6.113

(a) $L_1 + L_2 + M$ (b) $L_1 + L_2 - M$
(c) $L_1 + L_2 + 2M$ (d) $L_1 + L_2 - 2M$

**6.12** In the magnetically coupled circuit shown in Fig. 6.114, 56% of the total flux emanating from one coil links the other coil. The value of the mutual inductance (in H) is ○○●

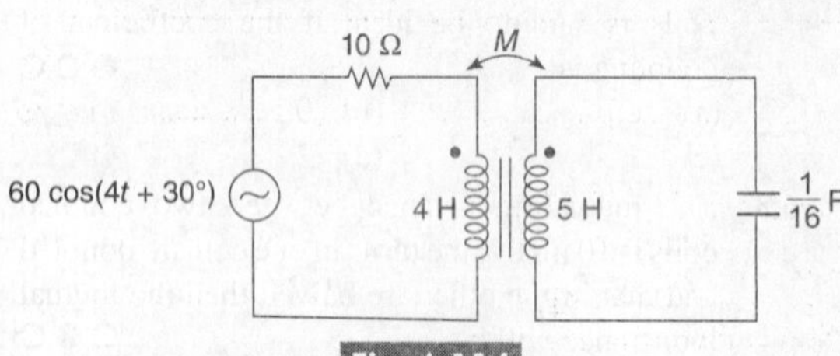

Fig. 6.114

(a) 2.5 (b) 25
(c) 0.25 (d) 2

**6.13** For the circuit shown in Fig. 6.115, the correct loop equation for Loop 1 is ○●○

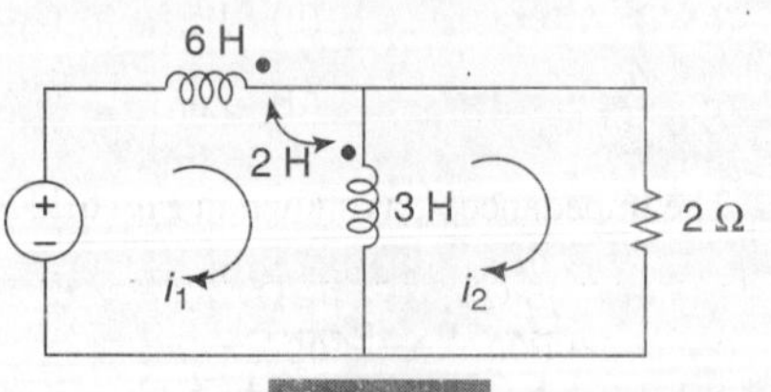

Fig. 6.115

(a) $5 + 13\dfrac{di_1}{dt} - 5\dfrac{di_2}{dt} = 0$

(b) $5 + 5\dfrac{di_1}{dt} - \dfrac{di_2}{dt} = 0$

(c) $5 - 13\dfrac{di_1}{dt} + 5\dfrac{di_2}{dt} = 0$

(d) $5 - 5\dfrac{di_1}{dt} + \dfrac{di_2}{dt} = 0$

**6.14** For the circuit shown in Fig. 6.116, the equivalent impedance is ○●○

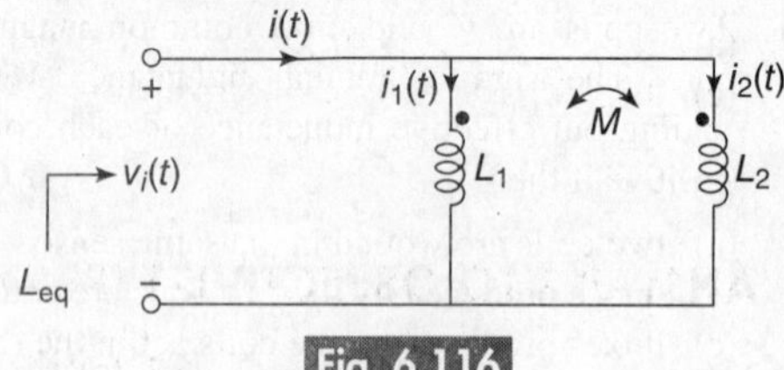

Fig. 6.116

(a) $\dfrac{L_1L_2 - M^2}{L_1 + L_2 + 2M}$ (b) $\dfrac{L_1L_2 + M^2}{L_1 + L_2 + 2M}$

(c) $\dfrac{L_1L_2 - M^2}{L_1 + L_2 - 2M}$ (d) $\dfrac{L_1L_2 + M^2}{L_1 + L_2 - 2M}$

**6.15** Given two coupled inductors $L_1$ and $L_2$, their mutual inductance $M$ satisfies ○●○

(a) $M = \sqrt{L_1^2 + L_2}$ (b) $M > \dfrac{L_1 + L_2}{2}$

(c) $M > \sqrt{L_1L_2}$ (d) $M \le \sqrt{L_1L_2}$

**6.16** Two coils have self-inductances of 0.09H and 0.01H and a mutual inductance of 0.015H. The coefficient of coupling between the coils is ●○○

(a) 0.06 (b) 0.5
(c) 1.0 (d) 0.05

**6.17** The effective inductance of the circuit across the terminals $A$, $B$ in the Fig. 6.117 shown is ●○○

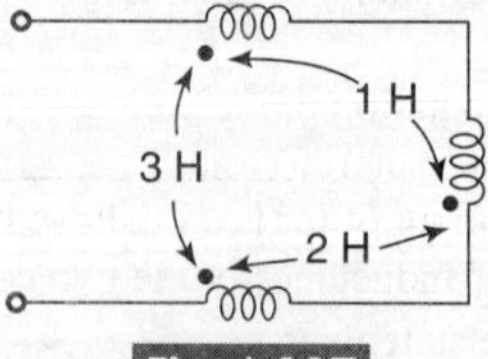

Fig. 6.117

(a) 9 H (b) 21 H
(c) 11 H (d) 6 H

**6.18** Two 2H inductance coils are connected in series and are also magnetically coupled to each other, the coefficient of coupling being 0.1. The total inductance of the combination can be ●○○

(a) 0.4 H (b) 3.2 H
(c) 4.0 H (d) 4.4 H

**6.19** In case all the flux from the current in coil 1 links with coil 2, the coefficient of coupling will be ●○○

(a) 2.0 (b) 1.0
(c) 0.5 (d) Zero

**6.20** Two coils having self-inductance of 10 mH and 15 mH and effective inductance of 40 mH are connected in series aiding. If the coils are connected in series opposing, the equivalent inductance will be ●○○

(a) 20 mH (b) 10 mH
(c) 5 mH (d) Zero

## ANSWERS TO OBJECTIVE-TYPE QUESTIONS

| | | | | | | |
|---|---|---|---|---|---|---|
| **6.1** (c) | **6.2** (b) | **6.3** (c) | **6.4** (d) | **6.5** (d) | **6.6** (c) | **6.7** (c) |
| **6.8** (b) | **6.9** (b) | **6.10** (b) | **6.11** (d) | **6.12** (a) | **6.13** (d) | **6.14** (c) |
| **6.15** (d) | **6.16** (b) | **6.17** (c) | **6.18** (d) | **6.19** (b) | **6.20** (b) | |

# LTspice Section

## EXAMPLE 6.1 ○○●

*Calculate the currents through $R_1$ and $R_2$ in the coupled circuit of Fig. 6.118.*

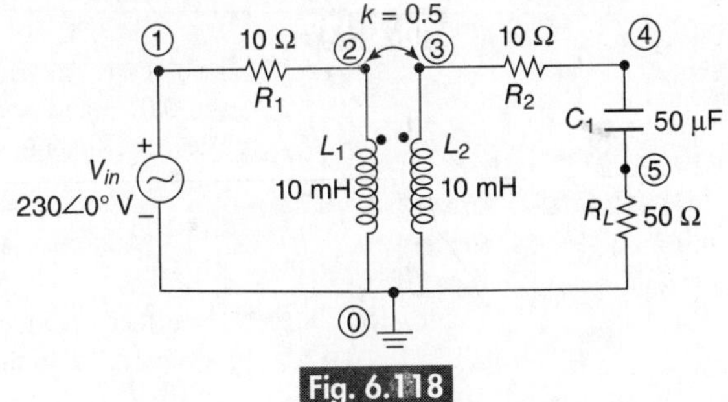


Fig. 6.118

### Solution

```
*Calculation of currents through R1 and R2

VIN 1 0 AC 230 0
R1 1 2 10
L1 2 0 10M
R2 3 4 10
L2 3 0 10M
C1 4 5 50U
RL 5 0 50
K L1 L2 0.5
.AC LIN 1 50 50
.PRINT AC I(R1) I(R2)
.END
```

```
                                AC Analysis
frequency:     50              Hz
I(R2):         mag:      0.403459    phase:      117.733°        device_current
I(R1):         mag:       21.8892    phase:     -17.5142°        device_current
```

**Result**

$$\mathbf{I}\,(R_1) = 21.8892 \angle -17.5142° \text{ A}$$

$$\mathbf{I}\,(R_2) = 0.403459 \angle 117.733° \text{ A}$$

## EXAMPLE 6.2

*Find the voltage across the 5Ω resistor in Fig. 6.119.*

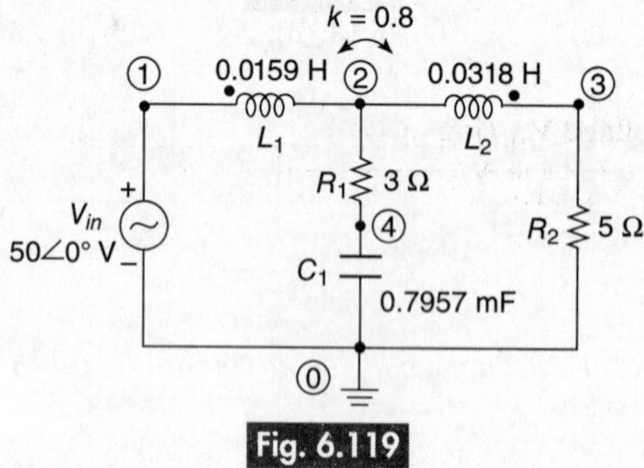


Fig. 6.119

**Solution**

```
*Calculation of voltage across 5 ohm resistor

VIN 1 0 AC 50 0
L1 1 2 0.0159
L2 2 3 0.0318
R1 2 4 3
C1 4 0 0.7957M
R2 3 0 5
K  L1 L2 -0.8
.AC LIN 1 50 50
.PRINT AC V(R2)
.END
```

```
                                AC Analysis
frequency:     50              Hz
V(3):          mag:       43.0644    phase:     -24.8797°        voltage
```

**Result**

$$\mathbf{V}_{5\Omega} = \mathbf{V}(3) = 43.0644 \angle -24.8797° \text{ A}$$

## EXAMPLE 6.3

*Find Thevenin's and Norton's equivalent network terminal AB for Fig. 6.120.*

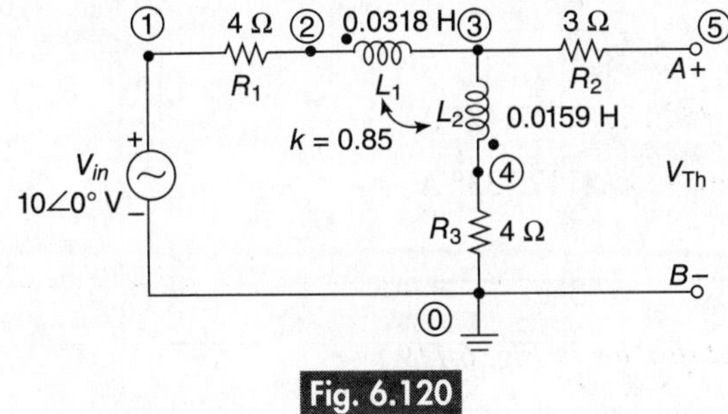


Fig. 6.120

**Solution**

(a) Calculation of Thevenin's voltage $\mathbf{V}_{Th}$ (Fig. 6.120)

```
*Calculation of Thevenin's voltage VTh

VIN 1 0 AC 10 0
R1 1 2 4
R2 3 5 3
L1 2 3 0.0318
L2 3 4 0.0159
R3 4 0 4
K L1 L2 -0.85
.AC LIN 1 50 50
.PRINT AC V(5)
.END
```

```
                              AC Analysis
frequency:          50                  Hz
V(5):               mag:         4.83311   phase:  -34.5702°        voltage
```

**Result**

$$\mathbf{V}_{Th} = \mathbf{V}(5) = 4.83311 \angle -34.5702° \text{ V}$$

(b) Calculation of Norton's current $\mathbf{I}_N$ (Fig. 6.121)

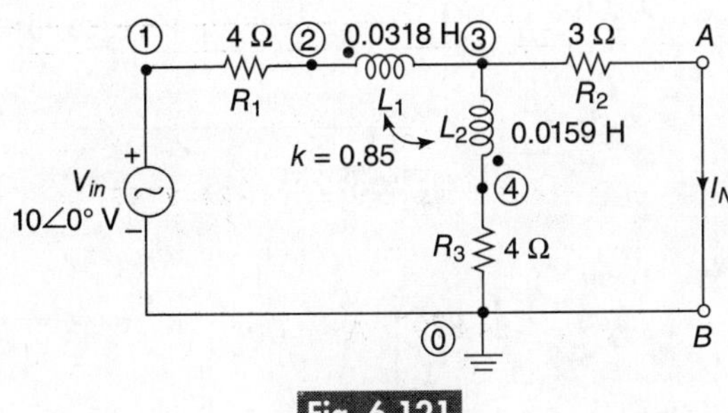


Fig. 6.121

## Solution

```
*Calculation of Norton's current IN

VIN 1 0 AC 10 0
R1 1 2 4
R2 3 0 3
L1 2 3 0.0318
L2 3 4 0.0159
R3 4 0 4
K L1 L2 -0.85
.AC LIN 1 50 50
.PRINT AC I(R2)
.END
```

```
                              AC Analysis
frequency:     50               Hz
I(R2):         mag:      0.559994    phase:        -83.3701°     device_current
```

**Result**

$$\mathbf{I}_N = \mathbf{I}(R2) = 0.559994\angle -83.3701°\text{A}$$

$$\mathbf{Z}_{\text{Th}} = \frac{\mathbf{V}_{Th}}{\mathbf{I}_N} = \frac{4.83311\angle -34.5702°}{0.559994\angle -83.3701°} = 8.63\angle 48.79°\ \Omega$$

Thevenin's Equivalent Network

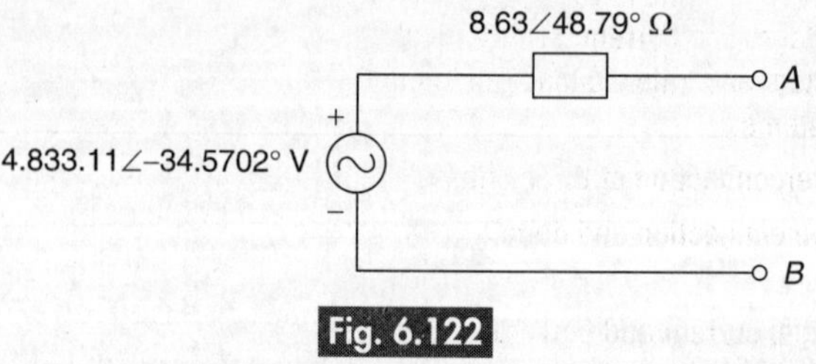


Fig. 6.122

Norton's Equivalent Network

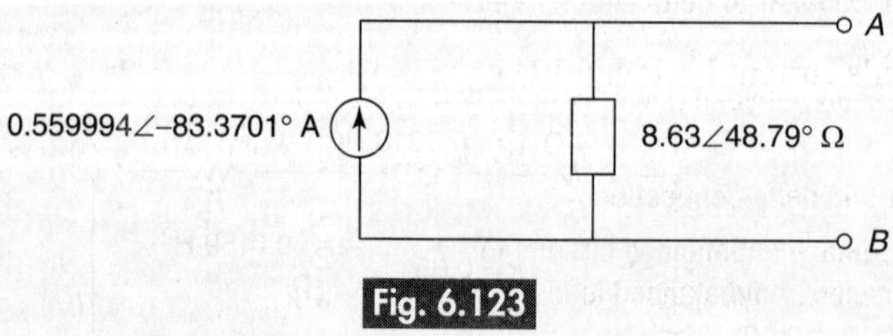


Fig. 6.123

CHAPTER 7

# Three-Phase Circuits

## LEARNING OBJECTIVES

**After studying this chapter, you should be able to:**

- **LO 7.1** Explain a three-phase system and its advantages
- **LO 7.2** Define phase sequence, phase voltage, phase current, line voltage, line current, symmetrical or balanced system and balance load related to three-phase systems
- **LO 7.3** Describe the interconnection of three phases
- **LO 7.4** Discuss star/wye connection and delta/mesh connection
- **LO 7.5** Determine voltage, current and power in balanced star-connected and delta-connected loads
- **LO 7.6** Describe balanced star to delta and delta to star conversion
- **LO 7.7** Derive the relation between power in delta and star systems
- **LO 7.8** Compare star and delta connections
- **LO 7.9** Analyse three-phase unbalanced circuits for the different cases of unbalanced loads
- **LO 7.10** Describe the measurement of three-phase power using one, two and three-wattmeters methods

## INTRODUCTION

A system which generates a single alternating voltage and current is termed a *single-phase system*. It utilises only one winding. A *polyphase system* utilises more than one winding. It will produce as many induced voltages as the number of windings.

There are two types of systems available in electric circuit, single phase and three phase system. In single phase system, there is only one phase, i.e., the current flows through only one wire and there is one return path called neutral line to complete the circuit. In three phase system, more than one phase can be used for generating, transmitting and for load system. The three phase system can act as three single phase systems. The three phase generation and single phase generation are same in the generator except the arrangement of coil in the generator to get 120° phase difference. The conductor needed in three phase system is 75% that of conductor needed in single phase system. In three phase system the net power from all the phases gives a continuous power to the load.

## 7.1 THREE-PHASE SYSTEM

LO 7.1

Explain a three-phase system and its advantages

A three-phase system consists of three separate but identical windings displaced by 120 electrical degrees from each other, as shown in Fig. 7.1. When these three windings are rotated in an anticlockwise direction with constant angular velocity in a uniform magnetic field, the emfs induced in each winding have the same magnitude and frequency but are displaced 120° from one another.

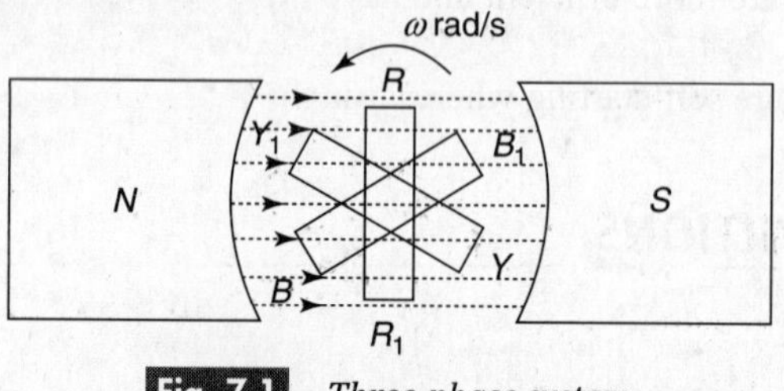


**Fig. 7.1** *Three-phase system*

The instantaneous values of generated voltage in windings $RR_1$, $YY_1$ and $BB_1$ are given by

$$e_R = E_m \sin\theta$$
$$e_Y = E_m \sin(\theta - 120°)$$
$$e_B = E_m \sin(\theta - 240°)$$

where $E_m$ is the maximum value of the induced voltage in each winding. The waveforms of these three voltages are shown in Fig. 7.2.

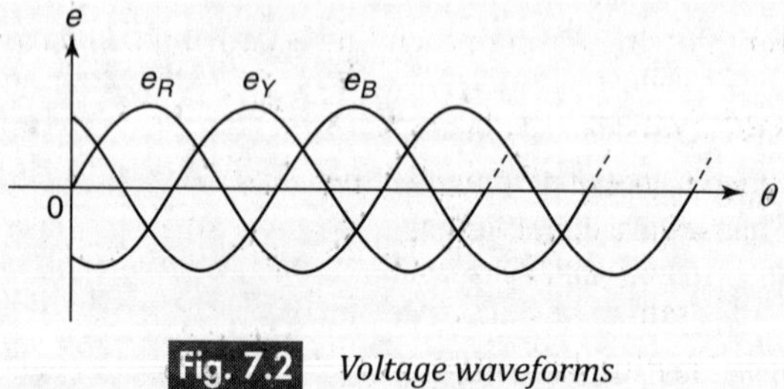


**Fig. 7.2** *Voltage waveforms*

Figure 7.3 shows the phasor diagram of these three induced voltages.

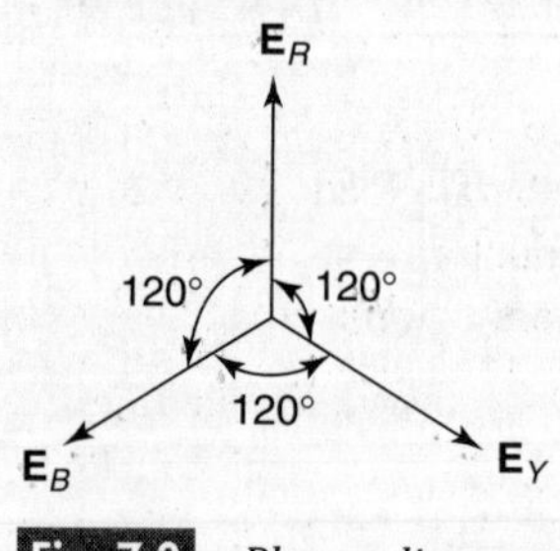


**Fig. 7.3** *Phasor diagram*

## 7.2 ADVANTAGES OF A THREE-PHASE SYSTEM

LO 7.1

1. In a single-phase system, the instantaneous power is fluctuating in nature. However, in a three-phase system, it is constant at all times.
2. The output of a three-phase system is greater than that of a single-phase system.
3. Transmission and distribution of a three-phase system is cheaper than that of a single-phase system.
4. Three-phase motors are more efficient and have higher power factors than single-phase motors of the same frequency.
5. Three-phase motors are self-starting whereas single-phase motors are not self-starting.

## 7.3 SOME DEFINITIONS

LO 7.2

Define phase sequence, phase voltage, phase current, line voltage, line current, symmetrical or balanced system and balance load related to three-phase systems

***1. Phase Sequence*** The sequence in which the voltages in the three phases reach the maximum positive value is called the *phase sequence* or *phase order*. From the phasor diagram of a three-phase system, it is clear that the voltage in the coil *R* attains maximum positive value first, next in the coil *Y* and then in the coil *B*. Hence, the phase sequence is *R-Y-B*.

***2. Phase Voltage*** The voltage induced in each winding is called the *phase voltage*.

***3. Phase Current*** The current flowing through each winding is called the *phase current*.

***4. Line Voltage*** The voltage available between any pair of terminals or lines is called the *line voltage*.

***5. Line Current*** The current flowing through each line is called the *line current*.

***6. Symmetrical or Balanced System*** A three-phase system is said to be balanced if the

(a) voltages in the three phases are equal in magnitude and differ in phase from one another by 120°, and
(b) currents in the three phases are equal in magnitude and differ in phase from one another by 120°.

***7. Balanced Load*** The load is said to be balanced if loads connected across the three phases are identical, i.e., all the loads have the same magnitude and power factor.

## 7.4 INTERCONNECTION OF THREE PHASES

LO 7.3

Describe the interconnection of three phases

In a three-phase system, there are three windings. Each winding has two terminals, viz., 'start' and 'finish'. If a separate load is connected across each winding, as shown in Fig. 7.4, six conductors are required to transmit and distribute power. This will make the system complicated and expensive.

In order to reduce the number of conductors, the three windings are connected in the following two ways:

1. Star, or Wye, connection
2. Delta, or Mesh, connection

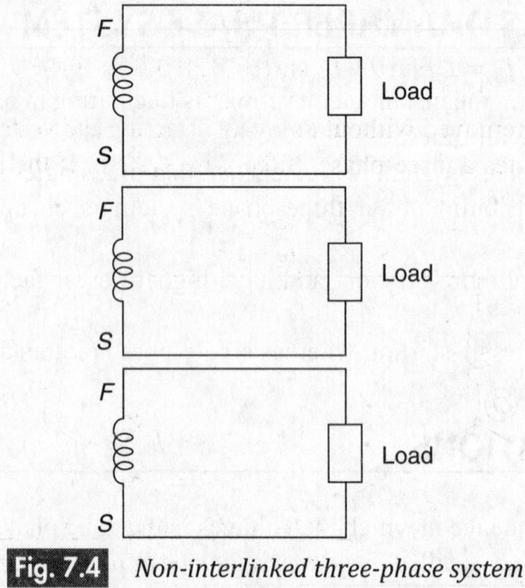


Fig. 7.4 *Non-interlinked three-phase system*

## 7.5 | STAR, OR WYE, CONNECTION

LO 7.4

Discuss star/wye connection and delta/mesh connection

In this method, similar terminals (start or finish) of the three windings are joined together, as shown in Fig. 7.5. The common point is called star or *neutral point*.

Figure 7.6 shows a three-phase system in star connection.

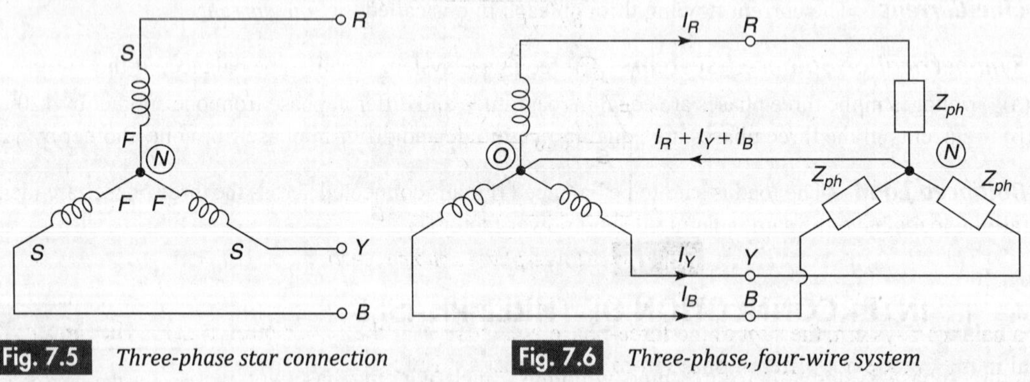


Fig. 7.5 *Three-phase star connection*

Fig. 7.6 *Three-phase, four-wire system*

This system is called a three-phase, four-wire system. If three identical loads are connected to each phase, the current flowing through the neutral wire is the sum of the three currents – $I_R$, $I_Y$ and $I_B$. Since the impedances are identical, the three currents are equal in magnitude but differ in phase from one another by 120°.

$$i_R = I_m \sin\theta$$

$$i_Y = I_m \sin(\theta - 120°)$$

$$i_B = I_m \sin(\theta - 240°)$$

$$i_R + i_Y + i_B = I_m \sin\theta + I_m \sin(\theta - 120°) + I_m \sin(\theta - 240°) = 0$$

Hence, the neutral wire can be removed without any way affecting the voltages or currents in the circuit, as shown in Fig. 7.7. This constitutes a three-phase, three-wire system. If the load is not balanced, the neutral wire carries some current.

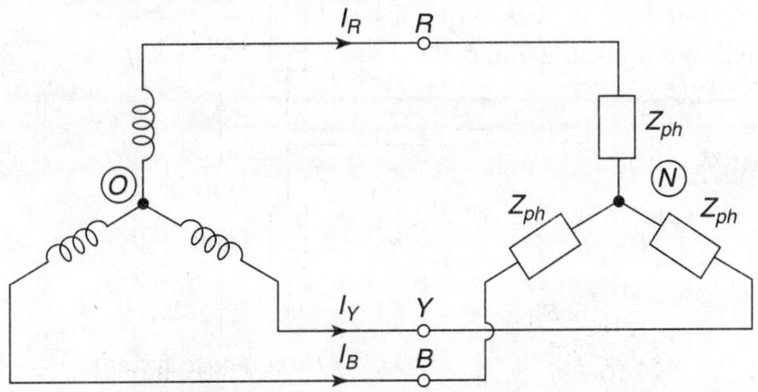


Fig. 7.7 *Three-phase, three-wire system*

## 7.6 DELTA, OR MESH, CONNECTION

LO 7.4

In this method, dissimilar terminals of the three windings are joined together, i.e., the 'finish' terminal of one winding is connected to the 'start' terminal of the other winding, and so on, as shown in Fig. 7.8. This system is also called a three-phase, three-wire system.

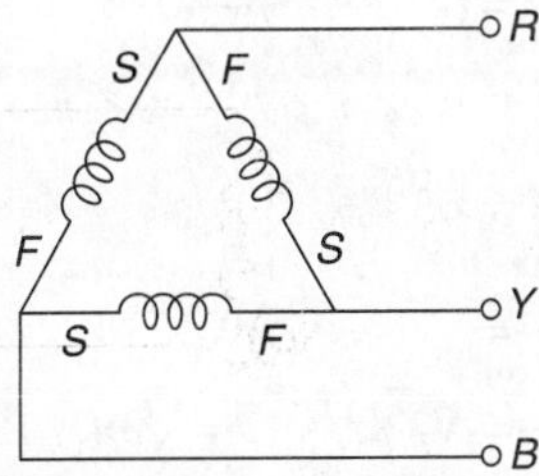


Fig. 7.8 *Three-phase delta connection*

For a balanced system, the sum of the three-phase voltages round the closed mesh is zero. The three emfs are equal in magnitude but differ in phase from one another by 120°.

$$e_R = E_m \sin\theta$$

$$e_Y = E_m \sin(\theta - 120°)$$

$$e_B = E_m \sin(\theta - 240°)$$

$$e_R + e_Y + e_B = E_m \sin\theta + E_m \sin(\theta - 120°) + E_m \sin(\theta - 240°) = 0$$

# 7.7 VOLTAGE, CURRENT AND POWER RELATIONS IN A BALANCED STAR-CONNECTED LOAD

LO 7.5

Determine voltage, current and power in balanced star-connected and delta-connected loads

## 7.7.1 Relation between Line Voltage and Phase Voltage

Figure 7.9 shows a balanced star-connected load.

Since the system is balanced, the three-phase voltages $V_{RN}$, $V_{YN}$, and $V_{BN}$ are equal in magnitude and differ in phase from one another by 120°.

Let $$V_{RN} = V_{YN} = V_{BN} = V_{ph}$$

where $V_{ph}$ indicates the rms value of phase voltage.

$$\mathbf{V}_{RN} = V_{ph}\angle 0°$$
$$\mathbf{V}_{YN} = V_{ph}\angle -120°$$
$$\mathbf{V}_{BN} = V_{ph}\angle -240°$$

Let $$V_{RY} = V_{YB} = V_{BR} = V_L$$

where $V_L$ indicates the rms value of line voltage.

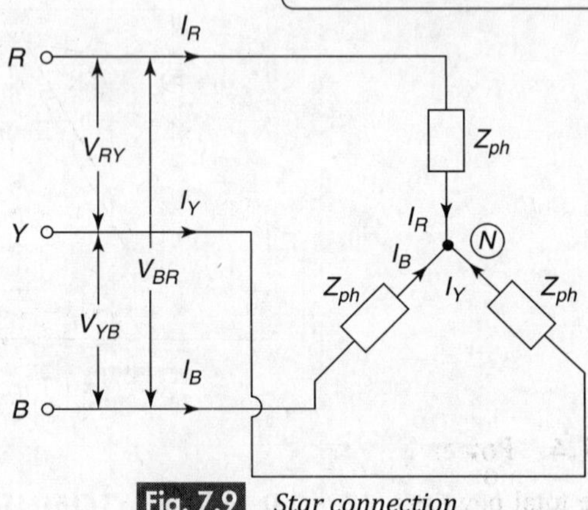


**Fig. 7.9** *Star connection*

Applying Kirchhoff's voltage law,

$$\begin{aligned}\mathbf{V}_{RY} &= \mathbf{V}_{RN} + \mathbf{V}_{NY}\\ &= \mathbf{V}_{RN} - \mathbf{V}_{YN}\\ &= V_{ph}\angle 0° - V_{ph}\angle -120°\\ &= (V_{ph} + j0) - (-0.5\,V_{ph} - j0.866\,V_{ph})\\ &= 1.5\,V_{ph} + j0.866\,V_{ph}\\ &= \sqrt{3}\,V_{ph}\angle 30°\end{aligned}$$

Similarly, $$\mathbf{V}_{YB} = \mathbf{V}_{YN} + \mathbf{V}_{NB} = \sqrt{3}\,V_{ph}\angle 30°$$

$$\mathbf{V}_{BR} = \mathbf{V}_{BN} + \mathbf{V}_{NR} = \sqrt{3}\,V_{ph}\angle 30°$$

Thus, in a star-connected, three-phase system, $V_L = \sqrt{3}\,V_{ph}$ and line voltages lead respective phase voltages by 30°.

## 7.7.2 Relation between Line Current and Phase Current

From Fig. 7.9, it is clear that line current is equal to the phase current.

$$I_L = I_{ph}$$

## 7.7.3 Phasor Diagram (Lagging Power Factor)

Figure 7.10 shows the phasor diagram of a balanced star-connected inductive load.

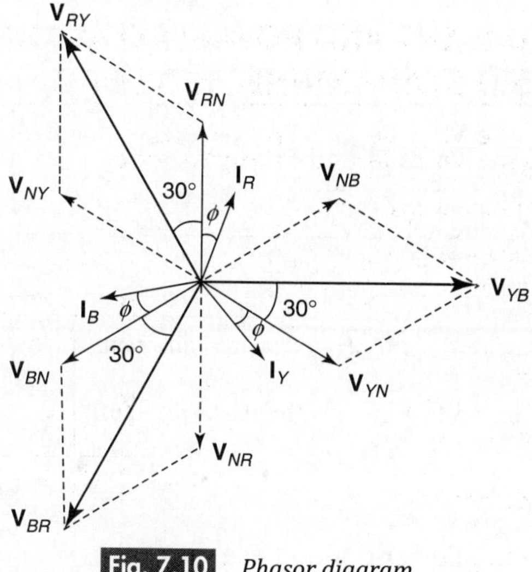


Fig. 7.10 *Phasor diagram*

### 7.7.4 Power

The total power in a three-phase system is the sum of powers in the three phases. For a balanced load, the power consumed in each load phase is the same.

Total active power $P = 3 \times$ power in each phase $= 3\ V_{ph}\ I_{ph} \cos \phi$

In a star-connected three-phase system,

$$V_{ph} = \frac{V_L}{\sqrt{3}}$$

$$I_{ph} = I_L$$

$$P = 3 \times \frac{V_L}{\sqrt{3}} \times I_L \times \cos \phi = \sqrt{3}\ V_L\ I_L \cos \phi$$

where $\phi$ is the phase difference between phase voltage and corresponding phase current.

Similarly, total reactive power $Q = 3 V_{ph}\ I_{ph} \sin \phi = \sqrt{3}\ V_L I_L \sin \phi$

Total apparent power $S = 3 V_{ph} I_{ph} = \sqrt{3}\ V_L I_L$

## 7.8 VOLTAGE, CURRENT AND POWER RELATIONS IN A BALANCED DELTA-CONNECTED LOAD

LO 7.5

### 7.8.1 Relation between Line Voltage and Phase Voltage

Figure 7.11 shows a balanced delta-connected load.

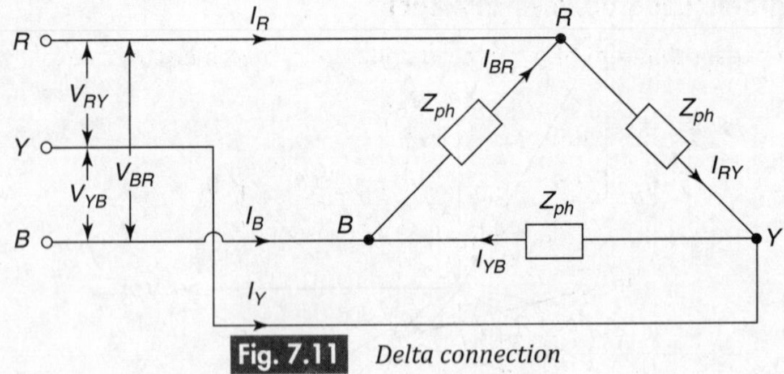


**Fig. 7.11** *Delta connection*

From Fig. 7.11, it is clear that line voltage is equal to phase voltage.

$$V_L = V_{ph}$$

### 7.8.2 Relation between Line Current and Phase Current

Since the system is balanced, the three-phase currents $I_{RY}$, $I_{YB}$, and $I_{BR}$ are equal in magnitude but differ in phase from one another by 120°.

Let $$I_{RY} = I_{YB} = I_{BR} = I_{ph}$$

where $I_{ph}$ indicates rms value of the phase current.

$$\mathbf{I}_{RY} = I_{ph}\angle 0^\circ$$
$$\mathbf{I}_{YB} = I_{ph}\angle -120^\circ$$
$$\mathbf{I}_{BR} = I_{ph}\angle -240^\circ$$

Let $$I_R = I_Y = I_B = I_L$$

where $I_L$ indicates rms value of the line current.

Applying Kirchhoff's current law,

$$\mathbf{I}_R + \mathbf{I}_{BR} = \mathbf{I}_{RY}$$
$$\mathbf{I}_R = \mathbf{I}_{RY} - \mathbf{I}_{BR}$$
$$= I_{ph}\angle 0^\circ - I_{ph}\angle -240^\circ$$
$$= (I_{ph} + j0) - (-0.5 I_{ph} + j0.866 I_{ph})$$
$$= 1.5 I_{ph} - j0.866 I_{ph}$$
$$= \sqrt{3} I_{ph}\angle -30^\circ$$

Similarly, $$\mathbf{I}_Y = \mathbf{I}_{YB} - \mathbf{I}_{RY} = \sqrt{3} I_{ph}\angle -30^\circ$$
$$\mathbf{I}_B = \mathbf{I}_{BR} - \mathbf{I}_{YB} = \sqrt{3} I_{ph}\angle -30^\circ$$

Thus, in a delta-connected, three-phase system, $I_L = \sqrt{3} I_{ph}$ and line currents lag behind the respective phase currents by 30°.

### 7.8.3 Phasor Diagram (Lagging Power Factor)

Figure 7.12 shows the phasor diagram of a balanced delta-connected inductive load.

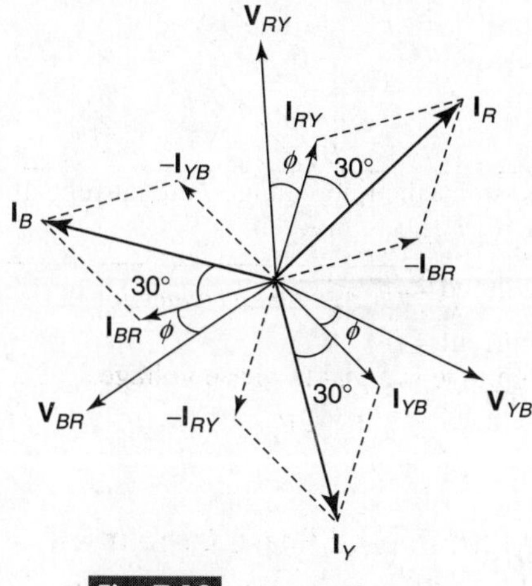


Fig. 7.12 Phasor diagram

### 7.8.4 Power

$$P = 3V_{ph}I_{ph}\cos\phi$$

In a delta-connected three-phase system,

$$V_{ph} = V_L$$

$$I_{ph} = \frac{I_L}{\sqrt{3}}$$

$$P = 3\times V_L \times \frac{I_L}{\sqrt{3}} \times \cos\phi = \sqrt{3}\, V_L I_L \cos\phi$$

Total reactive power $Q = 3\,V_{ph}I_{ph}\sin\phi = \sqrt{3}\,V_L I_L \sin\phi$

Total apparent power $S = 3\,V_{ph}I_{ph} = \sqrt{3}\,V_L I_L$

## 7.9 BALANCED Y/Δ AND Δ/Y CONVERSIONS

LO 7.6

Describe balanced star to delta and delta to star conversion

Any balanced star-connected system can be converted into the equivalent delta-connected system and vice versa.

For a balanced star-connected load,

$$\text{Line voltage} = V_L$$

$$\text{Line current} = I_L$$

$$\text{Impedance/phase} = Z_Y$$

$$V_{ph} = \frac{V_L}{\sqrt{3}}$$

$$I_{ph} = I_L$$

$$Z_Y = \frac{V_{ph}}{I_{ph}} = \frac{V_L}{\sqrt{3}\, I_L}$$

For an equivalent delta-connected system, the line voltages and currents must have the same values as in the star-connected system, i.e.,

$$\text{Line voltage} = V_L$$

$$\text{Line current} = I_L$$

$$\text{Impedance/phase} = Z_\Delta$$

$$V_{ph} = V_L$$

$$I_{ph} = \frac{I_L}{\sqrt{3}}$$

$$Z_\Delta = \frac{V_{ph}}{I_{ph}} = \frac{V_L}{\frac{I_L}{\sqrt{3}}} = \sqrt{3}\frac{V_L}{I_L} = 3Z_Y$$

$$Z_Y = \frac{1}{3} Z_\Delta$$

Thus, when three equal phase impedances are connected in delta, the equivalent star impedance is one-third of the delta impedance.

## 7.10 RELATION BETWEEN POWER IN DELTA AND STAR SYSTEMS

LO 7.7

Derive the relation between power in delta and star systems

Let a balanced load be connected in star having impedance per phase as $Z_{ph}$.

For a star-connected load,

$$V_{ph} = \frac{V_L}{\sqrt{3}}$$

$$I_{ph} = \frac{V_{ph}}{Z_{ph}} = \frac{V_L}{\sqrt{3}\, Z_{ph}}$$

$$I_L = I_{ph} = \frac{V_L}{\sqrt{3}\, Z_{ph}}$$

Now,

$$P_Y = \sqrt{3}\, V_L I_L \cos\phi = \sqrt{3} \times V_L \times \frac{V_L}{\sqrt{3} Z_{ph}} \times \cos\phi = \frac{V_L^2}{Z_{ph}} \cos\phi$$

For a delta-connected load,

$$V_{ph} = V_L$$

$$I_{ph} = \frac{V_{ph}}{Z_{ph}} = \frac{V_L}{Z_{ph}}$$

$$I_L = \sqrt{3}\, I_{ph} = \sqrt{3}\frac{V_L}{Z_{ph}}$$

Now,
$$P_\Delta = \sqrt{3}\, V_L I_L \cos\phi = \sqrt{3} \times V_L \times \sqrt{3}\frac{V_L}{Z_{ph}} \times \cos\phi = 3\frac{V_L^2}{Z_{ph}}\cos\phi = 3\, P_Y$$

$$P_Y = \frac{1}{3}P_\Delta$$

Thus, power consumed by a balanced star-connected load is one-third of that in the case of a delta-connected load.

## 7.11 COMPARISON BETWEEN STAR AND DELTA CONNECTIONS

LO 7.8

Compare star and delta connections

| *Star Connection* | *Delta Connection* |
|---|---|
| 1. $V_L = \sqrt{3}\, V_{ph}$ | 1. $V_L = V_{ph}$ |
| 2. $I_L = I_{ph}$ | 2. $I_L = \sqrt{3}\, I_{ph}$ |
| 3. Line voltage leads the respective phase voltage by 30°. | 3. Line current lags behind the respective phase current by 30° |
| 4. Power in star connection is one-third of power in delta connection. | 4. Power in delta connection is three times of the power in star connection. |
| 5. Three-phase, three-wire and three-phase, four-wire systems are possible. | 5. Only three-phase, three-wire system is possible. |
| 6. The phasor sum of all the phase currents is zero. | 6. The phasor sum of all the phase voltages is zero. |

**EXAMPLE 7.1** ●○○

*Three equal impedances, each of (8 + j10) ohms, are connected in star. This is further connected to a 440 V, 50 Hz, three-phase supply. Calculate (a) phase voltage, (b) phase angle, (c) phase current, (d) line current, (e) active power, and (f) reactive power.*

**Note** Difficulty Level ●○○— Easy; ○●○— Medium; ○○●— Difficult

**Solution** $\mathbf{Z}_{ph} = (8 + j10)\ \Omega, \quad V_L = 440\text{ V}, \quad f = 50\text{ Hz}$

For a star-connected load,

(a) Phase voltage

$$V_{ph} = \frac{V_L}{\sqrt{3}} = \frac{440}{\sqrt{3}} = 254.03\text{ V}$$

(b) Phase angle

$$\mathbf{Z}_{ph} = 8 + j10 = 12.81\angle 51.34^\circ\ \Omega$$
$$Z_{ph} = 12.81\ \Omega$$
$$\phi = 51.34^\circ$$

(c) Phase current

$$I_{ph} = \frac{V_{ph}}{Z_{ph}} = \frac{254.03}{12.81} = 19.83\text{ A}$$

(d) Line current

$$I_L = I_{ph} = 19.83\text{ A}$$

(e) Active power

$$P = \sqrt{3}V_L I_L \cos\phi = \sqrt{3}\times 440\times 19.83\times\cos(51.34^\circ) = 9.44\text{ kW}$$

(f) Reactive power

$$Q = \sqrt{3}V_L I_L \sin\phi = \sqrt{3}\times 440\times 19.83\times\sin(51.34^\circ) = 11.81\text{ kVAR}$$

### EXAMPLE 7.2

*A balanced delta-connected load of impedance (8 − j6) ohms per phase is connected to a three-phase, 230 V, 50 Hz supply. Calculate (a) power factor, (b) line current, and (c) reactive power.*

**Solution** $\mathbf{Z}_{ph} = (8 - j6)\ \Omega, \quad V_L = 230\text{ V}, \quad f = 50\text{ Hz}$

For a delta-connected load,

(a) Power factor

$$\mathbf{Z}_{ph} = 8 - j6 = 10\angle -36.87^\circ\ \Omega$$
$$Z_{ph} = 10\ \Omega$$
$$\phi = 36.87^\circ$$
$$\text{pf} = \cos\phi = \cos(36.87^\circ) = 0.8\text{ (leading)}$$

(b) Line current

$$V_{ph} = V_L = 230\text{ V}$$
$$I_{ph} = \frac{V_{ph}}{Z_{ph}} = \frac{230}{10} = 23\text{ A}$$
$$I_L = \sqrt{3}I_{ph} = \sqrt{3}\times 23 = 39.84\text{ A}$$

(c) Reactive power

$$Q = \sqrt{3} V_L \, I_L \sin\phi = \sqrt{3} \times 230 \times 39.84 \times \sin(36.87°) = 9.52 \text{ kVAR}$$

## EXAMPLE 7.3

*Three coils, each having a resistance and an inductance of 8 Ω and 0.02 H respectively, are connected in star across a three-phase, 230 V, 50 Hz supply. Find the (a) power factor, (b) line current, (c) power, (d) reactive volt-amperes, and (e) total volt-amperes.*

**Solution** $R = 8\ \Omega, \quad L = 0.02 \text{ H}, \quad V_L = 230 \text{ V}, \quad f = 50 \text{ Hz}$

For a star-connected load,

(a) Power factor

$$X_L = 2\pi fL = 2\pi \times 50 \times 0.02 = 6.28\ \Omega$$

$$\mathbf{Z}_{ph} = R + jX_L = 8 + j6.28 = 10.17 \angle 38.13°\ \Omega$$

$$Z_{ph} = 10.17\ \Omega$$

$$\phi = 38.13°$$

$$\text{pf} = \cos\phi = \cos(38.13°) = 0.786 \text{ (lagging)}$$

(b) Line current

$$V_{ph} = \frac{V_L}{\sqrt{3}} = \frac{230}{\sqrt{3}} = 132.79 \text{ V}$$

$$I_{ph} = \frac{V_{ph}}{Z_{ph}} = \frac{132.79}{10.17} = 13.05 \text{ A}$$

$$I_L = I_{ph} = 13.05 \text{ A}$$

(c) Power

$$P = \sqrt{3} V_L \, I_L \cos\phi = \sqrt{3} \times 230 \times 13.05 \times 0.786 = 4.088 \text{ kW}$$

(d) Reactive volt-amperes

$$Q = \sqrt{3} V_L \, I_L \sin\phi = \sqrt{3} \times 230 \times 13.05 \times \sin(38.13°) = 3.21 \text{ kVAR}$$

(e) Total volt-amperes

$$S = \sqrt{3} V_L \, I_L = \sqrt{3} \times 230 \times 13.05 = 5.198 \text{ kVA}$$

## EXAMPLE 7.4

*Three coils, each having a resistance of 8 Ω and an inductance of 0.02 H, are connected in delta to a three-phase, 400 V, 50 Hz supply. Calculate the (a) line current, and (b) power absorbed.*

**Solution** $R = 8\ \Omega, \quad L = 0.02 \text{ H}, \quad V_L = 400 \text{ V}, \quad f = 50 \text{ Hz}$

For a delta-connected load,

(a) Line current

$$V_L = V_{ph} = 400 \text{ V}$$

$$X_L = 2\pi fL = 2\pi \times 50 \times 0.02 = 6.28\ \Omega$$

$$\mathbf{Z}_{ph} = R + jX_L = 8 + j6.28 = 10.17\angle 38.13°\ \Omega$$

$$Z_{ph} = 10.17\ \Omega$$

$$\phi = 38.13°$$

$$I_{ph} = \frac{V_{ph}}{Z_{ph}} = \frac{400}{10.17} = 39.33\text{ A}$$

$$I_L = \sqrt{3}\,I_{ph} = \sqrt{3}\times 39.33 = 68.12\text{ A}$$

(b) Power absorbed

$$P = \sqrt{3}\,V_L\ I_L\cos\phi = \sqrt{3}\times 400\times 68.12\times\cos(38.13°) = 37.12\text{ kW}$$

## EXAMPLE 7.5

●○○

*The three equal impedances of each of $10\angle 60°\,\Omega$, are connected in star across a three-phase, 400 V, 50 Hz supply. Calculate the (a) line voltage and phase voltage, (b) power factor and active power consumed. (c) If the same three impedances are connected in delta to the same source of supply, what is the active power consumed?*

**Solution** $\mathbf{Z}_{ph} = 10\angle 60°\ \Omega,\quad V_L = 400\text{ V},\quad f = 50\text{ Hz}$

For a star-connected load,

(a) Line voltage and phase voltage

$$V_L = 400\text{ V}$$

$$V_{ph} = \frac{V_L}{\sqrt{3}} = \frac{400}{\sqrt{3}} = 230.94\text{ V}$$

(b) Power factor and active power consumed

$$\phi = 60°$$

$$\text{pf} = \cos\phi = \cos(60°) = 0.5\text{ (lagging)}$$

$$I_{ph} = \frac{V_{ph}}{Z_{ph}} = \frac{230.94}{10} = 23.094\text{ A}$$

$$I_L = I_{ph} = 23.094\text{ A}$$

$$P = \sqrt{3}\,V_L I_L\cos\phi = \sqrt{3}\times 400\times 23.094\times 0.5 = 8\text{ kW}$$

(c) Active power consumed for delta-connected load

$$V_L = 400\text{ V}$$

$$Z_{ph} = 10\ \Omega$$

$$V_{ph} = V_L = 400\text{ V}$$

$$I_{ph} = \frac{V_{ph}}{Z_{ph}} = \frac{400}{10} = 40\text{ A}$$

$$I_L = \sqrt{3}\,I_{ph} = \sqrt{3}\times 40 = 69.28\text{ A}$$

$$P = \sqrt{3}\,V_L I_L\cos\phi = \sqrt{3}\times 400\times 69.28\times\cos(60°) = 24\text{ kW}$$

## EXAMPLE 7.6

*Three similar coils A,B, and C are available. Each coil has a 9 Ω resistance and a 12 Ω reactance. They are connected in delta to a three-phase, 440 V, 50 Hz supply. Calculate for this load, the (a) phase current, (b) line current, (c) power factor, (d) total kVA, (e) active power, and (f) reactive power. If these coils are connected in star across the same supply, calculate all the above quantities.*

**Solution** $R = 9\ \Omega,\quad X_L = 12\ \Omega,\quad V_L = 440\ \text{V},\quad f = 50\ \text{Hz}$

For a delta-connected load,

(a) Phase current

$$V_L = V_{ph} = 440\ \text{V}$$

$$\mathbf{Z}_{ph} = R + jX_L = 9 + j12 = 15\ \angle 53.13°\ \Omega$$

$$Z_{ph} = 15\ \Omega$$

$$\phi = 53.13°$$

$$I_{ph} = \frac{V_{ph}}{Z_{ph}} = \frac{440}{15} = 29.33\ \text{A}$$

(b) Line current

$$I_L = \sqrt{3}\, I_{ph} = \sqrt{3} \times 29.33 = 50.8\ \text{A}$$

(c) Power factor

$$\text{pf} = \cos\phi = \cos(53.13°) = 0.6\ \text{(lagging)}$$

(d) Total kVA

$$S = \sqrt{3}\, V_L I_L = \sqrt{3} \times 440 \times 50.8 = 38.71\ \text{kVA}$$

(e) Active power

$$P = \sqrt{3}\, V_L I_L \cos\phi = \sqrt{3} \times 440 \times 50.8 \times 0.6 = 23.23\ \text{kW}$$

(f) Reactive power

$$Q = \sqrt{3}\, V_L I_L \sin\phi = \sqrt{3} \times 440 \times 50.8 \times \sin(53.13°) = 30.97\ \text{kVAR}$$

If these coils are connected in star across the same supply,

(a) Phase current

$$V_L = 440\ \text{V}$$

$$Z_{ph} = 15\ \Omega$$

$$V_{ph} = \frac{V_L}{\sqrt{3}} = \frac{440}{\sqrt{3}} = 254.03\ \text{V}$$

$$I_{ph} = \frac{V_{ph}}{Z_{ph}} = \frac{254.03}{15} = 16.94\ \text{A}$$

(b) Line current

$$I_L = I_{ph} = 16.94\ \text{A}$$

(c) Power factor

$$pf = 0.6 \text{ (lagging)}$$

(d) Total kVA

$$S = \sqrt{3}\, V_L I_L = \sqrt{3} \times 440 \times 16.94 = 12.91 \text{ kVA}$$

(e) Active power

$$P = \sqrt{3}\, V_L I_L \cos\phi = \sqrt{3} \times 440 \times 16.94 \times 0.6 = 7.74 \text{ kW}$$

(f) Reactive power

$$Q = \sqrt{3}\, V_L I_L \sin\phi = \sqrt{3} \times 440 \times 16.94 \times \sin(53.13°) = 12.33 \text{ kVAR}$$

## EXAMPLE 7.7

*A 415 V, 50 Hz, three-phase voltage is applied to three star-connected identical impedances. Each impedance consists of a resistance of 15 Ω, a capacitance of 177 μF and an inductance of 0.1 henry in series. Find the (a) power factor, (b) phase current, (c) line current, (d) active power, (e) reactive power, and (f) total VA. Draw a neat phasor diagram. If the same impedances are connected in delta, find the (a) line current, and (b) power consumed.*

**Solution**

$$V_L = 415 \text{ V}, \quad f = 50 \text{ Hz}, \quad R = 15\ \Omega, \quad C = 177\ \mu\text{F}, \quad L = 0.1 \text{ H}$$

For a star-connected load,

(a) Power factor

$$X_L = 2\pi f L = 2\pi \times 50 \times 0.1 = 31.42\ \Omega$$

$$X_C = \frac{1}{2\pi f C} = \frac{1}{2\pi \times 50 \times 177 \times 10^{-6}} = 17.98\ \Omega$$

$$\mathbf{Z}_{ph} = R + jX_L - jX_C = 15 + j31.42 - j17.98 = 15 + j13.44 = 20.14\angle 41.86°\ \Omega$$

$$Z_{ph} = 20.14\ \Omega$$

$$\phi = 41.86°$$

$$pf = \cos\phi = \cos(41.86°) = 0.744 \text{ (lagging)}$$

(b) Phase current

$$V_{ph} = \frac{V_L}{\sqrt{3}} = \frac{415}{\sqrt{3}} = 239.6 \text{ V}$$

$$I_{ph} = \frac{V_{ph}}{Z_{ph}} = \frac{239.6}{20.14} = 11.9 \text{ A}$$

(c) Line current

$$I_L = I_{ph} = 11.9 \text{ A}$$

(d) Active power

$$P = \sqrt{3}\, V_L I_L \cos\phi = \sqrt{3} \times 415 \times 11.9 \times 0.744 = 6.36 \text{ kW}$$

(e) Reactive power

$$Q = \sqrt{3}\, V_L I_L \sin\phi = \sqrt{3} \times 415 \times 11.9 \times \sin(41.86°) = 5.71 \text{ kVAR}$$

(f) Total VA

$$S = \sqrt{3}\, V_L I_L = \sqrt{3} \times 415 \times 11.9 = 8.55 \text{ kVA}$$

The phasor diagram is shown in Fig. 7.13.

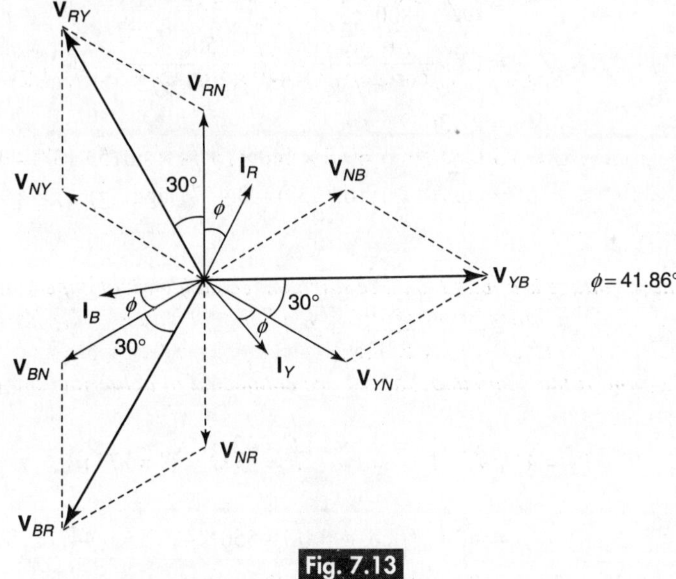


Fig. 7.13

If the same impedances are connected in delta,

(a) Line current

$$V_L = V_{ph} = 415 \text{ V}$$

$$Z_{ph} = 20.14\ \Omega$$

$$I_{ph} = \frac{V_{ph}}{Z_{ph}} = \frac{415}{20.14} = 20.61 \text{ A}$$

$$I_L = \sqrt{3}\, I_{ph} = \sqrt{3} \times 20.61 = 35.69 \text{ A}$$

(b) Power consumed

$$P = \sqrt{3}\, V_L I_L \cos\phi = \sqrt{3} \times 415 \times 35.69 \times 0.774 = 19.09 \text{ kW}$$

## EXAMPLE 7.8

*Each phase of a delta-connected load consists of a 50 mH inductor in series with a parallel combination of a 50 Ω resistor and a 50 μF capacitor. The load is connected to a three-phase, 550 V, 800 rad/s ac supply. Find the (a) power factor, (b) phase current, (c) the line current, (d) power drawn, (e) reactive power, and (f) kVA rating of the load.*

**Solution**

$$L = 50 \text{ mH}, \quad R = 50\ \Omega, \quad C = 50\ \mu\text{F}, \quad V_L = 550 \text{ V}, \quad \omega = 800 \text{ rad/s}$$

For a delta-connected load,

(a) Power factor

$$X_L = \omega L = 800 \times 50 \times 10^{-3} = 40\ \Omega$$

$$X_C = \frac{1}{\omega C} = \frac{1}{800 \times 50 \times 10^{-6}} = 25\ \Omega$$

$$\mathbf{Z}_{ph} = jX_L + \frac{R(-jX_C)}{R - jX_C} = j40 + \frac{50(-j25)}{50 - j25} = 10 + j20 = 22.36\ \angle 63.43°\ \Omega$$

$$\mathbf{Z}_{ph} = 22.36\ \Omega$$

$$\phi = 63.43°$$

$$\text{pf} = \cos\phi = \cos\,(63.43°) = 0.447\ \text{(lagging)}$$

(b) Phase current

$$V_L = V_{ph} = 550\ \text{V}$$

$$I_{ph} = \frac{V_{ph}}{Z_{ph}} = \frac{550}{22.36} = 24.6\ \text{A}$$

(c) Line current

$$I_L = \sqrt{3}\, I_{ph} = \sqrt{3} \times 24.6 = 42.61\ \text{A}$$

(d) Power drawn

$$P = \sqrt{3}\, V_L I_L \cos\phi = \sqrt{3} \times 550 \times 42.61 \times 0.447 = 18.14\ \text{kW}$$

(e) Reactive power

$$Q = \sqrt{3}\, V_L I_L \sin\phi = \sqrt{3} \times 550 \times 42.61 \times \sin\,(63.43°) = 36.3\ \text{kVAR}$$

(f) kVA rating of the load

$$S = \sqrt{3}\, V_L I_L = \sqrt{3} \times 550 \times 42.61 = 40.59\ \text{kVA}$$

## EXAMPLE 7.9

●○○

*A balanced star-connected load is supplied from a symmetrical three-phase 400 volts, 50 Hz system. The current in each phase is 30 A and lags 30° behind the phase voltage. Find the (a) phase voltage, (b) resistance and reactance per phase, (c) load inductance per phase, and (d) total power consumed.*

**Solution**

$$V_L = 400\ \text{V}, \quad f = 50\ \text{Hz}, \quad I_{ph} = 30\ \text{A}, \quad \phi = 30°$$

For a star-connected load,

(a) Phase voltage

$$V_{ph} = \frac{V_L}{\sqrt{3}} = \frac{400}{\sqrt{3}} = 230.94\ \text{V}$$

(b) Resistance and reactance per phase

$$Z_{ph} = \frac{V_{ph}}{I_{ph}} = \frac{230.94}{30} = 7.7\ \Omega$$

$$\mathbf{Z}_{ph} = Z_{ph} \angle \phi = 7.7 \angle 30° = (6.67 + j3.85)\ \Omega$$

$$R_{ph} = 6.67\ \Omega$$
$$X_{ph} = 3.85\ \Omega$$

(c) Load inductance per phase

$$X_{ph} = 2\pi f L_{ph}$$
$$3.85 = 2\pi \times 50 \times L_{ph}$$
$$L_{ph} = 0.01225\ \text{H}$$

(d) Total power consumed

$$P = 3V_{ph} I_{ph} \cos\phi = 3 \times 230.94 \times 30 \times \cos(30°) = 18\ \text{kW}$$

## EXAMPLE 7.10

*A symmetrical three-phase 400 V system supplies a basic load of 0.8 lagging power factor and is connected in star. If the line current is 34.64 A, find the (a) impedance, (b) resistance and reactance per phase, (c) total power, and (d) total reactive voltamperes.*

**Solution**

$$V_L = 400\ \text{V}, \quad \text{pf} = 0.8\ \text{(lagging)}, \quad I_L = 34.64\ \text{A}$$

For a star-connected load,

(a) Impedance

$$V_{ph} = \frac{V_L}{\sqrt{3}} = \frac{400}{\sqrt{3}} = 230.94\ \text{V}$$
$$I_{ph} = I_L = 34.64\ \text{A}$$
$$Z_{ph} = \frac{V_{ph}}{I_{ph}} = \frac{230.94}{34.64} = 6.67\ \Omega$$

(b) Resistance and reactance per phase

$$\text{pf} = \cos\phi = 0.8\ \text{(lagging)}$$
$$\phi = \cos^{-1}(0.8) = 36.87°$$
$$Z_{ph} = Z_{ph}\angle\phi = 6.67\angle 36.87° = (5.33 + j4)\ \Omega$$
$$R_{ph} = 5.33\ \Omega$$
$$X_{ph} = 4\ \Omega$$

(c) Total power

$$P = \sqrt{3}\, V_L I_L \cos\phi = \sqrt{3} \times 400 \times 34.64 \times 0.8 = 19.19\ \text{kW}$$

(d) Total reactive volt-amperes

$$Q = \sqrt{3}\, V_L I_L \sin\phi = \sqrt{3} \times 400 \times 34.64 \times \sin(36.87°) = 14.4\ \text{kVAR}$$

## EXAMPLE 7.11

*A balanced star-connected load is supplied by a 415 V, 50 Hz three-phase system. Current in each phase is 20 A and lags 30° behind its phase voltage. Find the (a) phase voltage, (b) power, and (c) circuit parameters. Also, find power consumed when the same load is connected in delta across the same supply.*

**Solution** $V_L = 415\text{ V},\quad f = 50\text{ Hz},\quad I_{ph} = 20\text{ A},\quad \phi = 30°$

For a star-connected load,

(a) Phase voltage

$$V_{ph} = \frac{V_L}{\sqrt{3}} = \frac{415}{\sqrt{3}} = 239.6\text{ V}$$

(b) Power

$$I_L = I_{ph} = 20\text{ A}$$

$$P = \sqrt{3}\,V_L I_L \cos\phi = \sqrt{3}\times 415\times 20\times \cos(30°) = 12.45\text{ kW}$$

(c) Circuit parameters

$$Z_{ph} = \frac{V_{ph}}{I_{ph}} = \frac{239.6}{20} = 11.98\,\Omega$$

$$\mathbf{Z}_{ph} = Z_{ph}\angle\phi = 11.98\angle 30° = (10.37 + j6)\,\Omega$$

$$R_{ph} = 10.37\,\Omega$$

$$X_{ph} = 6\,\Omega$$

Since

$$X_{ph} = 2\pi f L_{ph}$$

$$6 = 2\pi\times 50\times L_{ph}$$

$$L_{ph} = 19.1\text{ mH}$$

(d) Power consumed by same delta load across the same supply

$$P_\Delta = 3P_Y = 3\times 12.45\times 10^3 = 37.35\text{ kW}$$

## EXAMPLE 7.12

*Three identical coils connected in delta to a 440 V, three-phase supply take a total power of 50 kW and a line current of 90 A. Find the (a) phase current, (b) power factor, and (c) apparent power taken by the coils.*

**Solution** $V_L = 440\text{ V},\quad P = 50\text{ kW},\quad I_L = 90\text{ A}$

For a delta-connected load,

(a) Phase current

$$I_{ph} = \frac{I_L}{\sqrt{3}} = \frac{90}{\sqrt{3}} = 51.96\text{ A}$$

(b) Power factor

$$P = \sqrt{3}\,V_L I_L \cos\phi$$

$$50\times 10^3 = \sqrt{3}\times 440\times 90\times \cos\phi$$

$$\text{pf} = \cos\phi = 0.73\text{ (lagging)}$$

(c) Apparent power

$$S = \sqrt{3}\, V_L I_L = \sqrt{3} \times 440 \times 90 = 68.59 \text{ kVA}$$

**EXAMPLE 7.13**

*Three similar choke coils are connected in star to a three-phase supply. If the line current is 15 A, the total power consumed is 11 kW and the volt-ampere input is 15 kVA, find the line and phase voltages, the VAR input and the reactance and resistance of each coil. If these coils are now connected in delta to the same supply, calculate phase and line currents, active and reactive power.*

**Solution** $I_L = 15 \text{ A}, \quad P = 11 \text{ kW}, \quad S = 15 \text{ kVA}$

For a star-connected load,

(a) Line voltage

$$S = \sqrt{3}\, V_L I_L$$

$$15 \times 10^3 = \sqrt{3} \times V_L \times 15$$

$$V_L = 577.35 \text{ V}$$

(b) Phase voltage

$$V_{ph} = \frac{V_L}{\sqrt{3}} = \frac{577.35}{\sqrt{3}} = 333.33 \text{ V}$$

(c) VAR input

$$\cos\phi = \frac{P}{S} = \frac{11 \times 10^3}{15 \times 10^3} = 0.733$$

$$\phi = 42.86°$$

$$Q = \sqrt{3}\, V_L I_L \sin\phi = \sqrt{3} \times 577.35 \times 15 \times \sin(42.86°) = 10.2 \text{ kVAR}$$

(d) Reactance and resistance of coil

$$I_{ph} = I_L = 15 \text{ A}$$

$$Z_{ph} = \frac{V_{ph}}{I_{ph}} = \frac{333.33}{15} = 22.22\ \Omega$$

$$R = Z_{ph} \cos\phi = 22.22 \times 0.733 = 16.29\ \Omega$$

$$X_L = Z_{ph} \sin\phi = 22.22 \times \sin(42.86°) = 15.11\ \Omega$$

If these coils are now connected in delta,

(a) Phase current

$$V_{ph} = V_L = 577.35 \text{ V}$$

$$Z_{ph} = 22.22\ \Omega$$

$$I_{ph} = \frac{V_{ph}}{Z_{ph}} = \frac{577.35}{22.22} = 25.98 \text{ A}$$

(b) Line current

$$I_L = \sqrt{3}\, I_{ph} = \sqrt{3} \times 25.98 = 45 \text{ A}$$

(c) Active power

$$P = \sqrt{3}\, V_L I_L \cos\phi = \sqrt{3} \times 577.35 \times 45 \times 0.733 = 32.98 \text{ kW}$$

(d) Reactive power

$$Q = \sqrt{3}\, V_L I_L \sin\phi = \sqrt{3} \times 577.35 \times 45 \times \sin(42.86°) = 30.61 \text{ kVAR}$$

## EXAMPLE 7.14

*A balanced, three-phase, star-connected load of 100 kW takes a leading current of 80 A, when connected across a three-phase, 1100 V, 50 Hz supply. Find the circuit constants of the load per phase.*

**Solution**

$$P = 100 \text{ kW}, \quad I_L = 80 \text{ A}, \quad V_L = 1100 \text{ V}, \quad f = 50 \text{ Hz}$$

For a star-connected load,

$$V_{ph} = \frac{V_L}{\sqrt{3}} = \frac{1100}{\sqrt{3}} = 635.08 \text{ V}$$

$$I_{ph} = I_L = 80 \text{ A}$$

$$Z_{ph} = \frac{V_{ph}}{I_{ph}} = \frac{635.08}{80} = 7.94 \ \Omega$$

$$P = \sqrt{3}\, V_L I_L \cos\phi$$

$$100 \times 10^3 = \sqrt{3} \times 1100 \times 80 \times \cos\phi$$

$$\cos\phi = 0.656 \text{ (leading)}$$

$$\phi = 49°$$

$$R_{ph} = Z_{ph} \cos\phi = 7.94 \times 0.656 = 5.21 \ \Omega$$

$$X_{ph} = Z_{ph} \sin\phi = 7.94 \times \sin(49°) = 6 \ \Omega$$

This reactance will be capacitive in nature as the current is leading.

$$X_C = \frac{1}{2\pi f C}$$

$$6 = \frac{1}{2\pi \times 50 \times C}$$

$$C = 530.52 \ \mu\text{F}$$

## EXAMPLE 7.15

*Three identical impedances are connected in delta to a three-phase supply of 400 V. The line current is 34.65 A, and the total power taken from the supply is 14.4 kW. Calculate the resistance and reactance values of each impedance.*

**Solution** $V_L = 400 \text{ V}, \quad I_L = 34.65 \text{ A}, \quad P = 14.4 \text{ kW}$

For a delta-connected load,

$$V_L = V_{ph} = 400 \text{ V}$$
$$I_{ph} = \frac{I_L}{\sqrt{3}} = \frac{34.65}{\sqrt{3}} = 20 \text{ A}$$
$$Z_{ph} = \frac{V_{ph}}{I_{ph}} = \frac{400}{20} = 20 \ \Omega$$
$$P = \sqrt{3}\, V_L I_L \cos\phi$$
$$14.4 \times 10^3 = \sqrt{3} \times 400 \times 34.65 \times \cos\phi$$
$$\cos\phi = 0.6$$
$$\phi = 53.13°$$
$$R_{ph} = Z_{ph}\cos\phi = 20 \times 0.6 = 12 \ \Omega$$
$$X_{ph} = Z_{ph}\sin\phi = 20 \times \sin(53.13°) = 16 \ \Omega$$

## EXAMPLE 7.16

*A balanced, three-phase load connected in delta draws a power of 10.44 kW at 200 V at a power factor of 0.5 lead. Find the values of the circuit elements and the reactive volt-amperes drawn.*

**Solution** $P = 10.44 \text{ kW}, \quad V_L = 200 \text{ V}, \quad \text{pf} = 0.5 \text{ (leading)}$

For a delta-connected load,

(a) Values of circuit elements

$$V_L = V_{ph} = 200 \text{ V}$$
$$P = \sqrt{3}\, V_L I_L \cos\phi$$
$$10.44 \times 10^3 = \sqrt{3} \times 200 \times I_L \times 0.5$$
$$I_L = 60.28 \text{ A}$$
$$I_{ph} = \frac{I_L}{\sqrt{3}} = \frac{60.28}{\sqrt{3}} = 34.8 \text{ A}$$
$$Z_{ph} = \frac{V_{ph}}{I_{ph}} = \frac{200}{34.8} = 5.75 \ \Omega$$
$$R_{ph} = Z_{ph}\cos\phi = 5.75 \times 0.5 = 2.875 \ \Omega$$
$$X_{ph} = Z_{ph}\sin\phi = 5.75 \times \sin(\cos^{-1} 0.5) = 5.747 \times 0.866 = 4.98 \ \Omega$$

(b) Reactive volt-amperes drawn

$$Q = \sqrt{3}\, V_L I_L \sin\phi = \sqrt{3} \times 200 \times 60.28 \times 0.866 = 18.08 \text{ kVAR}$$

## EXAMPLE 7.17

*Three similar resistors are connected in star across 400 V, three-phase lines. The line current is 5 A. Calculate the value of each resistor. To what value should the line voltage be changed to obtain the same line current with the resistors connected in delta?*

**Solution** $V_L = 400 \text{ V}, \quad I_L = 5 \text{ A}$

For a star-connected load,

$$V_{ph} = \frac{V_L}{\sqrt{3}} = \frac{400}{\sqrt{3}} = 230.94 \text{ V}$$

$$I_{ph} = I_L = 5 \text{ A}$$

$$Z_{ph} = R_{ph} = \frac{V_{ph}}{I_{ph}} = \frac{230.94}{5} = 46.19 \ \Omega$$

For a delta-connected load,

$$I_L = 5 \text{ A}$$

$$R_{ph} = 46.19 \ \Omega$$

$$I_{ph} = \frac{I_L}{\sqrt{3}} = \frac{5}{\sqrt{3}} \text{ A}$$

$$V_{ph} = I_{ph} \ R_{ph} = \frac{5}{\sqrt{3}} \times 46.19 = 133.33 \text{ V}$$

$$V_L = 133.33 \text{ V}$$

Voltage needed is one-third of the star value.

## EXAMPLE 7.18

*Three 100 Ω, non-inductive resistors are connected in (a) star, and (b) delta across a 400 V, 50 Hz, three-phase supply. Calculate the power taken from the supply in each case. If one of the resistors is open-circuited, what would be the value of total power taken from the mains in each of the two cases?*

**Solution** $V_L = 400 \text{ V}, \quad Z_{ph} = 100 \ \Omega$

For a star-connected load,

$$V_{ph} = \frac{V_L}{\sqrt{3}} = \frac{400}{\sqrt{3}} = 230.94 \text{ V}$$

$$I_{ph} = \frac{V_{ph}}{Z_{ph}} = \frac{230.94}{100} = 2.31 \text{ A}$$

$$I_L = I_{ph} = 2.31 \text{ A}$$

$$\cos \phi = 1 \qquad \text{(For pure resistor, pf = 1)}$$

$$P = \sqrt{3} \ V_L I_L \cos \phi = \sqrt{3} \times 400 \times 2.31 \times 1 = 1600.41 \text{ W}$$

For a delta-connected load,

$$V_{ph} = V_L = 400 \text{ V}$$

$$I_{ph} = \frac{V_{ph}}{Z_{ph}} = \frac{400}{100} = 4 \text{ A}$$

$$I_L = \sqrt{3}\, I_{ph} = \sqrt{3} \times 4 = 6.93 \text{ A}$$

$$P = \sqrt{3}\, V_L I_L \cos\phi = \sqrt{3} \times 400 \times 6.93 \times 1 = 4801.24 \text{ W}$$

### When One of the Resistors is Open-circuited

***1. Star Connection*** The circuit consists of two 100 Ω resistors in series across a 400 V supply, as shown in Fig. 7.14.

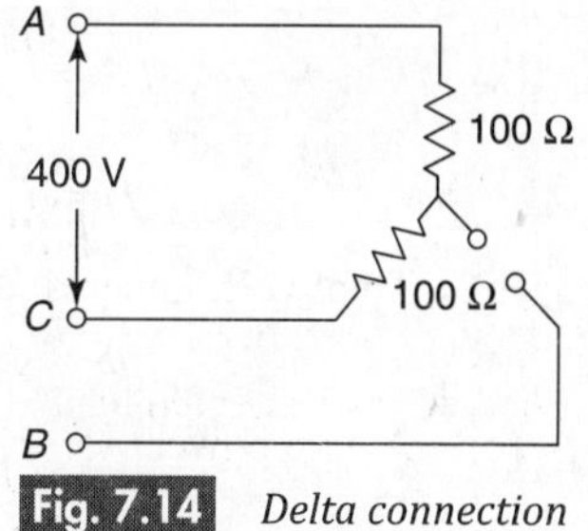


Fig. 7.14 *Delta connection*

$$\text{Currents in lines } A \text{ and } C = \frac{400}{200} = 2 \text{ A}$$

$$\text{Power taken from the mains} = 400 \times 2 = 800 \text{ W}$$

Hence, when one of the resistors is open-circuited, the power consumption is reduced by half.

***2. Delta Connection*** In this case, currents in A and C remains as usual 120° out of phase with each other, as shown in Fig. 7.15.

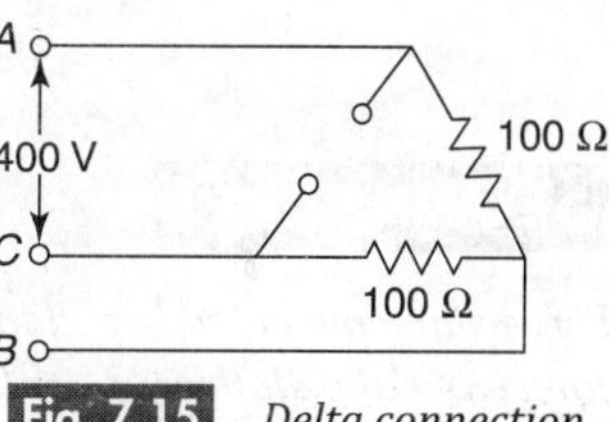


Fig. 7.15 *Delta connection*

$$\text{Currents in each phase} = \frac{400}{100} = 4 \text{ A}$$

$$\text{Power taken from the mains} = 2 \times 4 \times 400 = 3200 \text{ W}$$

Hence, when one of the resistors is open-circuited, the power consumption is reduced by one-third.

**EXAMPLE 7.19**

*Three identical impedances of $10\angle 30°\ \Omega$ each are connected in star and another set of three identical impedances of $18\angle 60°\ \Omega$ are connected in delta. If both the sets of impedances are connected across a balanced, three-phase 400 V supply, find the line current, total volt-amperes, active power and reactive power.*

**Solution**

$$\mathbf{Z}_Y = 10\angle 30°\ \Omega, \quad \mathbf{Z}_\Delta = 18\angle 60°\ \Omega, \quad V_L = 400 \text{ V}$$

Three identical delta impedances can be converted into equivalent star impedances.

$$\mathbf{Z}'_Y = \frac{\mathbf{Z}_\Delta}{3} = \frac{18\angle 60°}{3} = 6\angle 60°\ \Omega$$

Now, two star-connected impedances of $10\angle 30°\ \Omega$ and $6\angle 60°\ \Omega$ are connected in parallel across a three-phase supply.

$$\mathbf{Z}_{eq} = \frac{(10\angle 30°)(6\angle 60°)}{10\angle 30° + 6\angle 60°} = 3.87\angle 48.83°\ \Omega$$

For a star-connected load,

(a) Line current

$$V_{ph} = \frac{V_L}{\sqrt{3}} = \frac{400}{\sqrt{3}} = 230.94\ \text{V}$$

$$I_{ph} = \frac{V_{ph}}{Z_{ph}} = \frac{V_{ph}}{Z_{eq}} = \frac{230.94}{3.87} = 59.67\ \text{A}$$

$$I_L = I_{ph} = 59.67\ \text{A}$$

(b) Total volt-amperes

$$S = \sqrt{3}V_L I_L = \sqrt{3} \times 400 \times 59.67 = 41.34\ \text{kVA}$$

(c) Active power

$$P = \sqrt{3}V_L I_L \cos\phi = \sqrt{3} \times 400 \times 59.67 \times \cos(48.83°) = 27.21\ \text{kW}$$

(d) Reactive power

$$Q = \sqrt{3}V_L I_L \sin\phi = \sqrt{3} \times 400 \times 59.67 \times \sin(48.83°) = 31.12\ \text{kVAR}$$

## EXAMPLE 7.20

*Three star-connected impedances $\mathbf{Z}_Y = (20 + j37.7)\ \Omega$ per phase are connected in parallel with three delta-connected impedances $\mathbf{Z}_\Delta = (30 - j159.3)\ \Omega$ per phase. The line voltage is 398 V. Find the line current, pf, active and reactive power taken by the combination.*

**Solution** $\mathbf{Z}_Y = 20 + j37.7 = 42.68\angle 62.05°\ \Omega$, $\mathbf{Z}_\Delta = 30 - j159.3 = 162.1\angle -79.3°\ \Omega$, $V_L = 398$ V

Three identical delta-connected impedances can be converted into equivalent star impedances.

$$\mathbf{Z'}_Y = \frac{162.1\angle -79.3°}{3} = 54.03\angle -79.3°\ \Omega$$

Now, two star-connected impedances of $42.68\angle 62.05°\ \Omega$ and $54.03\angle -79.3°\ \Omega$ are connected in parallel across the three-phase supply.

$$\mathbf{Z}_{eq} = \frac{(42.68\angle 62.05°)(54.03\angle -79.3°)}{42.68\angle 62.05° + 54.03\angle -79.3°} = 68.33\ \angle 9.88°\ \Omega$$

For a star-connected load,

(a) Line current

$$V_{ph} = \frac{V_L}{\sqrt{3}} = \frac{398}{\sqrt{3}} = 229.79\ \text{V}$$

$$I_{ph} = \frac{V_{ph}}{Z_{ph}} = \frac{V_{ph}}{Z_{eq}} = \frac{229.79}{68.33} = 3.36\ \text{A}$$

$$I_L = I_{ph} = 3.36\ \text{A}$$

(b) Power factor

$$\text{pf} = \cos\phi = \cos(9.88°) = 0.99 \text{ (lagging)}$$

(c) Active power

$$P = \sqrt{3}V_L I_L \cos\phi = \sqrt{3}\times 398\times 3.36\times 0.99 = 2.29 \text{ kW}$$

(d) Reactive power

$$Q = \sqrt{3}V_L I_L \sin\phi = \sqrt{3}\times 398\times 3.36\times \sin(9.88°) = 397.43 \text{ VAR}$$

## EXAMPLE 7.21

*Three coils, each having a resistance of 20 Ω and a reactance of 15 Ω, are connected in star to a 400 V, three-phase, 50 Hz supply. Calculate (a) line current, (b) power supplied, and (c) power factor. If three capacitors, each of same capacitance, are connected in delta to the same supply so as to form a parallel circuit with the above coils, calculate the capacitance of each capacitor to obtain a resultant power factor of 0.95 lagging.*

**Solution**

$$R_{ph} = 20\ \Omega,\quad X_{ph} = 15\ \Omega,\quad V_L = 400 \text{ V}$$

For a star-connected load,

(a) Line current

$$\mathbf{Z}_{ph} = R_{ph} + jX_{ph} = 20 + j15 = 25\angle 36.87°\ \Omega$$

$$V_{ph} = \frac{V_L}{\sqrt{3}} = \frac{400}{\sqrt{3}} = 230.94 \text{ V}$$

$$I_{ph} = \frac{V_{ph}}{Z_{ph}} = \frac{230.94}{25} = 9.24 \text{ A}$$

$$I_L = I_{ph} = 9.24 \text{ A}$$

(b) Power supplied

$$P_1 = \sqrt{3}V_L I_L \cos\phi_1 = \sqrt{3}\times 400\times 9.24\times \cos(36.87°) = 5.12 \text{ kW}$$

(c) Power factor

$$\text{pf} = \cos\phi_1 = \cos(36.87°) = 0.8 \text{ (lagging)}$$

(d) Value of capacitance of each capacitor

$$Q_1 = \sqrt{3}V_L I_L \sin\phi_1 = \sqrt{3}\times 400\times 9.24\times \sin(36.87°) = 3.84 \text{ kVAR}$$

When capacitors are connected in delta to the same supply,

$$\text{pf} = 0.95$$

$$\phi_2 = \cos^{-1}(0.95) = 18.19°$$

$$\tan\phi_2 = \tan(18.19°) = 0.33$$

Since capacitors do not absorb any power, power remains the same even when capacitors are connected. But reactive power changes.

$$P_2 = 5.12 \text{ kW}$$
$$Q_2 = P_2 \tan\phi_2 = 5.12 \times 0.33 = 1.69 \text{ kVAR}$$

Difference in reactive power is supplied by three capacitors.

From Fig. 7.16,

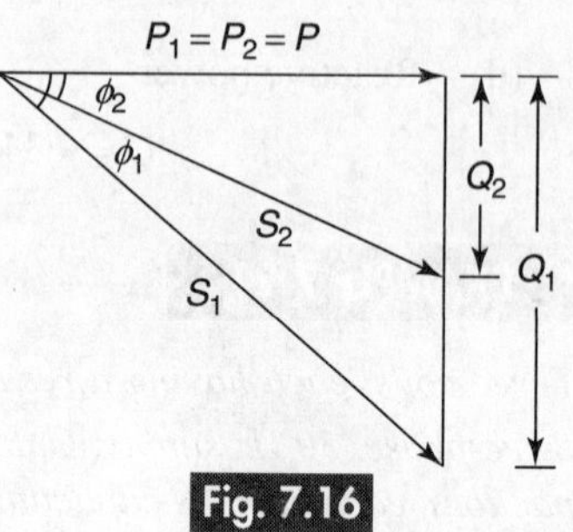


Fig. 7.16

$$Q = Q_1 - Q_2 = 3.84 - 1.69 = 2.15 \text{ kVAR}$$
$$Q = \sqrt{3}\, V_L I_L \sin\phi$$
$$2.15 \times 10^3 = \sqrt{3} \times 400 \times I_L \times \sin(90°)$$
$$I_L = 3.1 \text{ A}$$
$$I_{ph} = \frac{I_L}{\sqrt{3}} = 1.79 \text{ A}$$
$$I_{ph} = \frac{V_{ph}}{X_C} = V_{ph} \times 2\pi fC$$
$$C = \frac{I_{ph}}{V_{ph} \times 2\pi f} = \frac{1.79}{400 \times 2\pi \times 50} = 14.24 \text{ µF}$$

## 7.12 THREE-PHASE UNBALANCED CIRCUITS

LO 7.9

Analyse three-phase unbalanced circuits for the different cases of unbalanced loads

If the loads connected across the three phases are not identical to each other, i.e., the loads have different magnitude and power factors, the loads are said to be unbalanced. The phase currents in delta and phase or line current in star connection differ in unbalanced loading, giving rise to flow of current, in a neutral wire.

$$I_N = I_R + I_Y + I_B$$

There may be three cases of unbalanced loads:

(i) Unbalanced delta-connected load
(ii) Unbalanced three-wire star-connected load
(iii) Unbalanced four-wire star-connected load

### 7.12.1 Unbalanced Delta-connected Load

Figure 7.17 shows an unbalanced delta-connected load connected to a balanced three-phase supply.

For a delta-connected load,

Let $$V_L = V_{ph}$$
$$\mathbf{V}_{RY} = V_{ph}\angle 0°$$

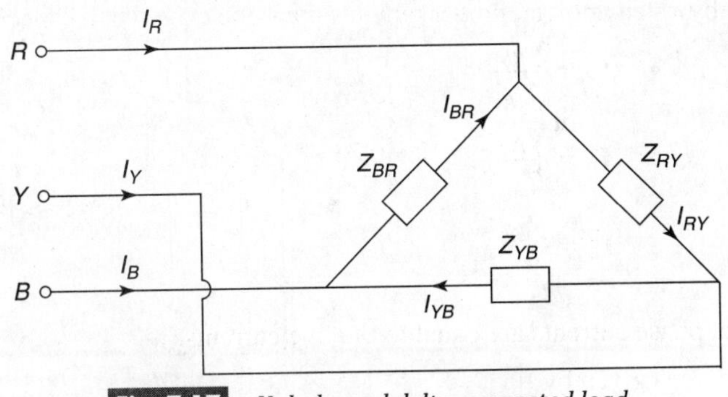


Fig. 7.17 Unbalanced delta-connected load

$$\mathbf{V}_{YB} = V_{ph} \angle -120^\circ$$

$$\mathbf{V}_{BR} = V_{ph} \angle -240^\circ$$

Phase currents are given by

$$\mathbf{I}_{RY} = \frac{\mathbf{V}_{RY}}{\mathbf{Z}_{RY}}$$

$$\mathbf{I}_{YB} = \frac{\mathbf{V}_{YB}}{\mathbf{Z}_{YB}}$$

$$\mathbf{I}_{BR} = \frac{\mathbf{V}_{BR}}{\mathbf{Z}_{BR}}$$

Line currents are given by

$$\mathbf{I}_R = \mathbf{I}_{RY} - \mathbf{I}_{BR}$$

$$\mathbf{I}_Y = \mathbf{I}_{YB} - \mathbf{I}_{RY}$$

$$\mathbf{I}_B = \mathbf{I}_{BR} - \mathbf{I}_{YB}$$

### 7.12.2 Unbalanced Four-wire Star-connected Load

Figure 7.18 shows an unbalanced star-connected load connected to a balanced three-phase, four-wire supply. The neutral point *N* of the load is connected to the neutral point *O* of the supply. Hence, voltage across the three load impedances is equal to the phase voltage of the supply.

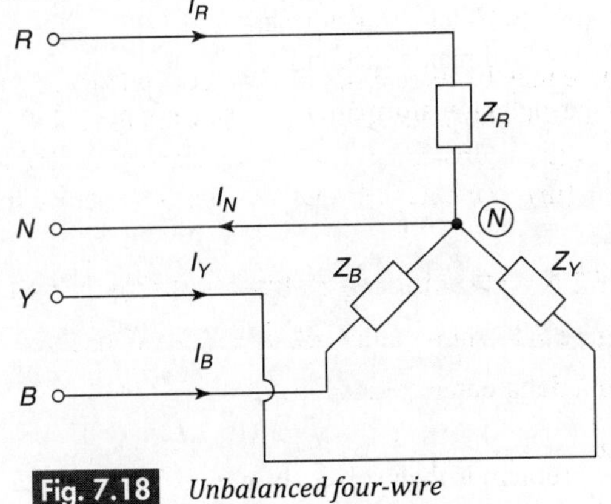


Fig. 7.18 Unbalanced four-wire star-connected load

For a star-connected load,

$$V_L = \sqrt{3}\, V_{ph}$$

Let

$$\mathbf{V}_{RN} = V_{ph} \angle 0^\circ$$

$$\mathbf{V}_{YN} = V_{ph} \angle -120^\circ$$

$$\mathbf{V}_{BN} = V_{ph} \angle -240^\circ$$

Phase currents are given by

$$\mathbf{I}_R = \frac{\mathbf{V}_{RN}}{\mathbf{Z}_R}$$

$$\mathbf{I}_Y = \frac{\mathbf{V}_{YN}}{\mathbf{Z}_Y}$$

$$\mathbf{I}_B = \frac{\mathbf{V}_{BN}}{\mathbf{Z}_B}$$

For a star-connected load, phase currents are equal to the line currents.

The current in a neutral wire is given by

$$\mathbf{I}_N = \mathbf{I}_R + \mathbf{I}_Y + \mathbf{I}_B$$

### 7.12.3 Unbalanced Three-wire Star-connected Load

Figure 7.19 shows an unbalanced three-wire star-connected load.

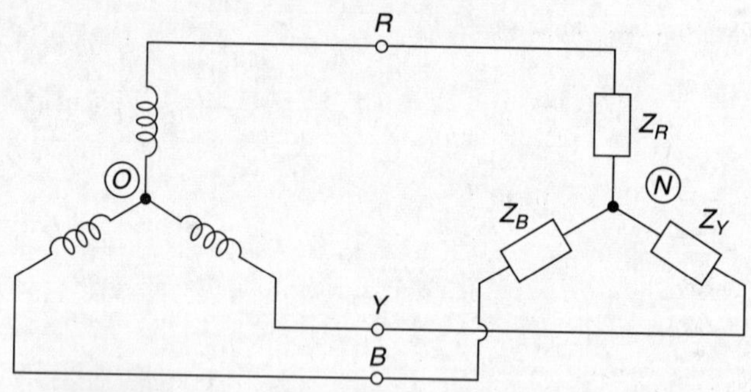


Fig. 7.19 *Unbalanced three-wire star-connected load*

If the neutral point *N* of the load is not connected to the neutral point *O* of the supply, there exists a voltage between the supply neutral point and the load neutral point. The load phase voltage is not the same as the supply phase voltage. There are many methods to solve such unbalanced star-connected loads. Two most commonly used methods are

(i) Star-delta transformation
(ii) Millman's theorem

In star-delta transformation, the star-connected loads are replaced by an equivalent delta-connected load.

$$\mathbf{Z}_{RY} = \mathbf{Z}_R + \mathbf{Z}_Y + \frac{\mathbf{Z}_R\mathbf{Z}_Y}{\mathbf{Z}_B}$$

$$\mathbf{Z}_{YB} = \mathbf{Z}_Y + \mathbf{Z}_B + \frac{\mathbf{Z}_Y\mathbf{Z}_B}{\mathbf{Z}_R}$$

$$\mathbf{Z}_{BR} = \mathbf{Z}_B + \mathbf{Z}_R + \frac{\mathbf{Z}_B\mathbf{Z}_R}{\mathbf{Z}_Y}$$

The problem is then solved as an unbalanced delta-connected load. The line currents so calculated are equal to the line currents of the original star-connected load.

An unbalanced three-wire star-connected load can also be solved by Millman's theorem. Let $V_{RO}$, $V_{YO}$ and $V_{BO}$ be the phase voltages of the supply, which are equal in magnitude but differ in phase from one another by 120°. Let $V_{RN}$, $V_{YN}$ and $V_{BN}$ be the load phase voltages, which are unequal in magnitude as well as differ in phase by unequal angles. The voltage between the neutral points, *N* and *O*, i.e, $V_{NO}$, is calculated using Millman's theorem.

$$\mathbf{V}_{NO} = \frac{\mathbf{V}_{RO}\,\mathbf{Y}_R + \mathbf{V}_{YO}\,\mathbf{Y}_Y + \mathbf{V}_{BO}\,\mathbf{Y}_B}{\mathbf{Y}_R + \mathbf{Y}_Y + \mathbf{Y}_B}$$

where $Y_R$, $Y_Y$ and $Y_B$ are the admittances of the branches of the unbalanced star-connected load. The voltage across phase impedance, i.e., load phase voltage can be calculated as,

$$\mathbf{V}_{RN} = \mathbf{V}_{RO} - \mathbf{V}_{NO}$$
$$\mathbf{V}_{YN} = \mathbf{V}_{YO} - \mathbf{V}_{NO}$$
$$\mathbf{V}_{BN} = \mathbf{V}_{BO} - \mathbf{V}_{NO}$$

The phase currents in the load are given by

$$\mathbf{I}_R = \frac{\mathbf{V}_{RN}}{\mathbf{Z}_R}$$

$$\mathbf{I}_Y = \frac{\mathbf{V}_{YN}}{\mathbf{Z}_Y}$$

$$\mathbf{I}_B = \frac{\mathbf{V}_{BR}}{\mathbf{Z}_B}$$

The line currents are equal to the phase currents for a star-connected load.

## EXAMPLE 7.22

*A three-phase supply with a line voltage of 250 V has an unbalanced delta-connected load, as shown in Fig. 7.20.*

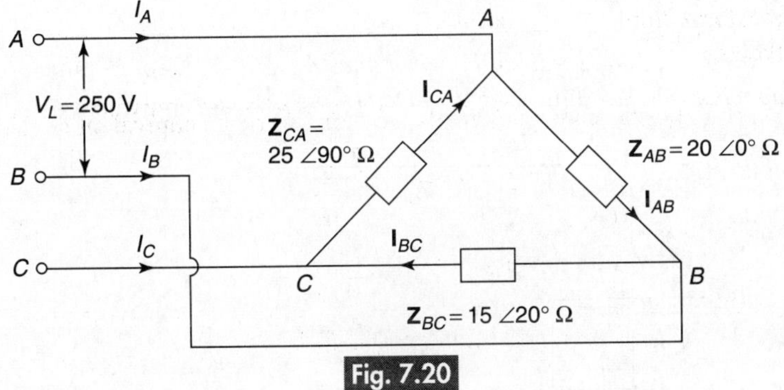


Fig. 7.20

*Determine (a) phase currents, (b) line currents, (c) total active power and (d) total reactive power, if phase sequence is ABC.*

**Solution** Let $\mathbf{V}_{AB} = 250\angle 0°$ V, $\mathbf{V}_{BC} = 250\angle -120°$ V, $\mathbf{V}_{CA} = 250\angle -240°$ V,

$\mathbf{Z}_{AB} = 20\angle 0°\ \Omega$, $\mathbf{Z}_{BC} = 15\angle 20°\ \Omega$, $\mathbf{Z}_{CA} = 25\angle 90°\ \Omega$

(a) Phase currents

$$\mathbf{I}_{AB} = \frac{\mathbf{V}_{AB}}{\mathbf{Z}_{AB}} = \frac{250\angle 0°}{20\angle 0°} = 12.5\angle 0° \text{A}$$

$$\mathbf{I}_{BC} = \frac{\mathbf{V}_{BC}}{\mathbf{Z}_{BC}} = \frac{250\angle -120°}{15\angle 20°} = 16.67\angle -140° \text{A}$$

$$\mathbf{I}_{CA} = \frac{\mathbf{V}_{CA}}{\mathbf{Z}_{CA}} = \frac{250\angle -240°}{25\angle 90°} = 10\angle 30° \text{A}$$

(b) Line currents

$$\mathbf{I}_A = \mathbf{I}_{AB} - \mathbf{I}_{CA} = 12.5\angle 0° - 10\angle 30° = 6.3\angle -52.48° \text{A}$$
$$\mathbf{I}_B = \mathbf{I}_{BC} - \mathbf{I}_{AB} = 16.67\angle -140° - 12.5\angle 0° = 27.45\angle -157.02° \text{A}$$
$$\mathbf{I}_C = \mathbf{I}_{CA} - \mathbf{I}_{BC} = 10\angle 30° - 16.67\angle -140° = 26.57\angle 36.25° \text{A}$$

(c) Total active power

$$P_{AB} = V_{AB}\, I_{AB} \cos\phi_{AB} = 250 \times 12.5 \times \cos(0°) = 3.13 \text{ kW}$$
$$P_{BC} = V_{BC}\, I_{BC} \cos\phi_{BC} = 250 \times 16.67 \times \cos(20°) = 3.92 \text{ kW}$$
$$P_{CA} = V_{CA}\, I_{CA} \cos\phi_{CA} = 250 \times 25 \times \cos(90°) = 0$$
$$P = P_{AB} + P_{BC} + P_{CA} = 3.13 + 3.92 + 0 = 7.05 \text{ kW}$$

(d) Total reactive power

$$Q_{AB} = V_{AB}\, I_{AB} \sin\phi_{AB} = 250 \times 12.5 \times \sin(0°) = 0$$
$$Q_{BC} = V_{BC}\, I_{BC} \sin\phi_{BC} = 250 \times 16.67 \times \sin(20°) = 1.43 \text{ kVAR}$$
$$Q_{CA} = V_{CA}\, I_{CA} \sin\phi_{CA} = 250 \times 25 \times \sin(90°) = 6.25 \text{ kVAR}$$
$$Q = Q_{AB} + Q_{BC} + Q_{CA} = 0 + 1.43 + 6.25 = 7.68 \text{ kVAR}$$

## EXAMPLE 7.23

*In the circuit of Fig. 7.21, a 400 V, 50 Hz, three-phase supply of phase sequence ABC is supplied to a delta-connected load consisting of a 100 Ω resistor between lines A and B, a 378 mH inductor between lines B and C, and a 37.8 μF capacitor between lines C and A. Determine phase and line currents.*

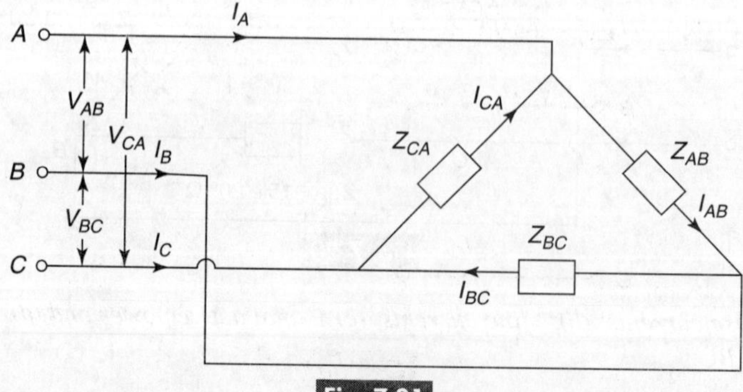


Fig. 7.21

**Solution** $V_L = 400\text{ V}, \quad f = 50\text{ Hz}, \quad R = 100\,\Omega, \quad L = 318\text{ mH}, \quad C = 31.8\,\mu\text{F}$

Let

$$\mathbf{V}_{AB} = 400\angle 0°\text{ V}$$
$$\mathbf{V}_{BC} = 400\angle -120°\text{ V}$$
$$\mathbf{V}_{CA} = 400\angle -240°\text{ V}$$
$$X_L = 2\pi fL = 2\pi \times 50 \times 318 \times 10^{-3} = 99.9\,\Omega$$
$$X_C = \frac{1}{2\pi fC} = \frac{1}{2\pi \times 50 \times 31.8 \times 10^{-6}} = 103.35\,\Omega$$
$$\mathbf{Z}_{AB} = R = 100\angle 0°\,\Omega$$
$$\mathbf{Z}_{BC} = jX_L = j99.9 = 99.9\angle 90°\,\Omega$$
$$\mathbf{Z}_{CA} = -jX_C = -j103.35 = 103.35\angle -90°\,\Omega$$

(a) Phase currents

$$\mathbf{I}_{AB} = \frac{\mathbf{V}_{AB}}{\mathbf{Z}_{AB}} = \frac{400\angle 0°}{100\angle 0°} = 4\angle 0°\text{A}$$
$$\mathbf{I}_{BC} = \frac{\mathbf{V}_{BC}}{\mathbf{Z}_{BC}} = \frac{400\angle -120°}{99.9\angle 90°} = 4\angle 150°\text{A}$$
$$\mathbf{I}_{CA} = \frac{\mathbf{V}_{CA}}{\mathbf{Z}_{CA}} = \frac{400\angle -240°}{103.35\angle -90°} = 3.87\angle -150°\text{A}$$

(b) Line currents

$$\mathbf{I}_A = \mathbf{I}_{AB} - \mathbf{I}_{CA} = 4\angle 0° - 3.87\angle -150° = 7.6\angle 14.75°\text{A}$$
$$\mathbf{I}_B = \mathbf{I}_{BC} - \mathbf{I}_{AB} = 4\angle 150° - 4\angle 0° = 7.73\angle 165°\text{A}$$
$$\mathbf{I}_C = \mathbf{I}_{CA} - \mathbf{I}_{BC} = 3.87\angle -150° - 4\angle 150° = 3.94\angle -88.36°\text{A}$$

## EXAMPLE 7.24

*A three-phase, 400 V, four-wire system of Fig. 7.22 has a star-connected load with* $\mathbf{Z}_A = (10 + j0)\,\Omega$, $\mathbf{Z}_B = (15 + j10)\,\Omega$, $\mathbf{Z}_C = (0 + j5)\,\Omega$. *Find the line currents and current through neutral conductor.*

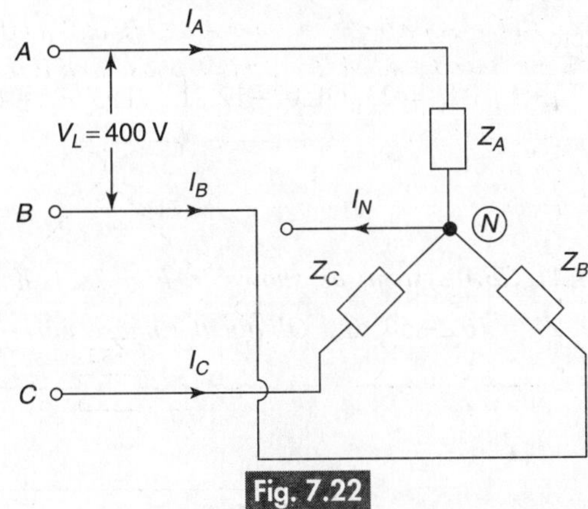


Fig. 7.22

**Solution**

$$V_L = 400 \text{ V}$$
$$\mathbf{Z}_A = (10 + j10)\ \Omega = 10\angle 0°\ \Omega$$
$$\mathbf{Z}_B = (15 + j10)\ \Omega = 18.03\angle 33.69\ \Omega$$
$$\mathbf{Z}_C = (0 + j5)\ \Omega = 5\angle 90°\ \Omega$$

For a star-connected load,

$$V_{ph} = \frac{V_L}{\sqrt{3}} = \frac{400}{\sqrt{3}} = 230.94 \text{ V}$$

The phase sequence is assumed as *A-B-C*.

$$\mathbf{V}_{AN} = 230.94\angle 0° \text{ V}$$
$$\mathbf{V}_{BN} = 230.94\angle -120° \text{ V}$$
$$\mathbf{V}_{CN} = 230.94\angle -240° \text{ V}$$

Phase currents

$$\mathbf{I}_A = \frac{\mathbf{V}_{AN}}{\mathbf{Z}_A} = \frac{230.94\angle 0°}{10\angle 0°} = 23.09\angle 0° \text{A}$$
$$\mathbf{I}_B = \frac{\mathbf{V}_{BN}}{\mathbf{Z}_B} = \frac{230.94\angle -120°}{18.03\angle 33.69°} = 12.81\angle -153.69° \text{A}$$
$$\mathbf{I}_C = \frac{\mathbf{V}_{CN}}{\mathbf{Z}_C} = \frac{230.94\angle -240°}{5\angle 90°} = 46.19\angle 30° \text{A}$$

Line currents are equal to the phase currents in a star-connected load.

$$\mathbf{I}_{L_1} = \mathbf{I}_A = 23.09\angle 0° \text{A}$$
$$\mathbf{I}_{L_2} = \mathbf{I}_B = 12.81\angle -153.69° \text{A}$$
$$\mathbf{I}_{L_3} = \mathbf{I}_C = 46.19\angle 30° \text{A}$$

Current through neutral conductor

$$\mathbf{I}_N = \mathbf{I}_A + \mathbf{I}_B + \mathbf{I}_C = 23.09\angle 0° + 12.81\angle -153.69° + 46.19\angle 30° = 54.47\angle 18.65° \text{A}$$

**EXAMPLE 7.25**

*A three-phase, four-wire, 208 V, CBA system, as shown in Fig. 7.23, has a star-connected load with $\mathbf{Z}_A = 5\angle 0°\ \Omega$, $\mathbf{Z}_B = 5\angle 30°\ \Omega$, $\mathbf{Z}_C = 10\angle -60°\ \Omega$. Obtain the phase currents, line currents and current through neutral wire.*

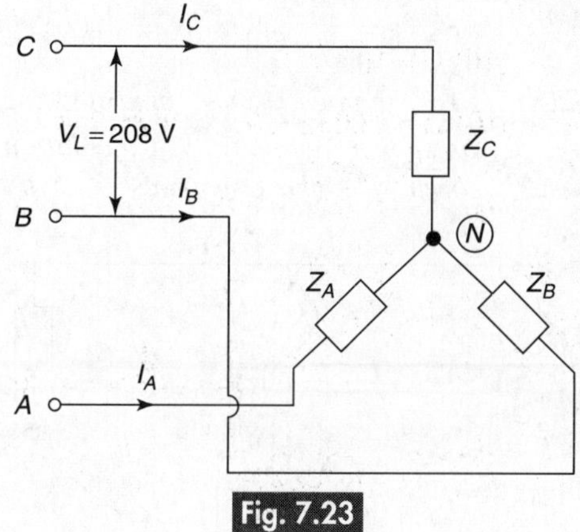


Fig. 7.23

**Solution** $V_L = 208$ V, $\mathbf{Z}_A = 5\angle 0°\ \Omega$, $\mathbf{Z}_B = 5\angle 30°\ \Omega$, $\mathbf{Z}_C = 10\angle -60°\ \Omega$

For a star-connected load,

$$V_{ph} = \frac{V_L}{\sqrt{3}} = \frac{208}{\sqrt{3}} = 120.09 \text{ V}$$

$$\mathbf{V}_{CN} = 120.09\angle 0° \text{V}$$

$$\mathbf{V}_{BN} = 120.09\angle -120° \text{ V}$$

$$\mathbf{V}_{CN} = 120.09\angle -240° \text{ V}$$

(a) Phase currents

$$\mathbf{I}_C = \frac{\mathbf{V}_{CN}}{\mathbf{Z}_C} = \frac{120.09\angle 0°}{10\angle -60°} = 12\angle 60° \text{ A}$$

$$\mathbf{I}_B = \frac{\mathbf{V}_{BN}}{\mathbf{Z}_B} = \frac{120.09\angle -120°}{5\angle 30°} = 24.02\angle -150° \text{ A}$$

$$\mathbf{I}_A = \frac{\mathbf{V}_{AN}}{\mathbf{Z}_A} = \frac{120.09\angle -240°}{5\angle 0°} = 24.02\angle 120° \text{ A}$$

(b) Line currents are equal to the phase currents in a star-connected load.

$$\mathbf{I}_{L_1} = \mathbf{I}_C = 12\angle 60° \text{A}$$

$$\mathbf{I}_{L_2} = \mathbf{I}_B = 24.02\angle -150° \text{A}$$

$$\mathbf{I}_{L_3} = \mathbf{I}_A = 24.02\angle 120° \text{A}$$

(c) Current through neutral wire

$$\mathbf{I}_N = \mathbf{I}_C + \mathbf{I}_B + \mathbf{I}_A = 12\angle 60° + 24.02\angle -150° + 24.02\angle 120° = 32.97\angle 144.42° \text{ A}$$

## EXAMPLE 7.26

*A symmetrical 440 V, three-phase system supplied a star-connected load with the branch impedances $\mathbf{Z}_R = 10\ \Omega$, $\mathbf{Z}_Y = j5\ \Omega$, $\mathbf{Z}_B = -j5\ \Omega$, as shown in Fig. 7.24. Calculate line currents and voltage across each phase impedance by Millman's theorem. The phase sequence is RYB.*

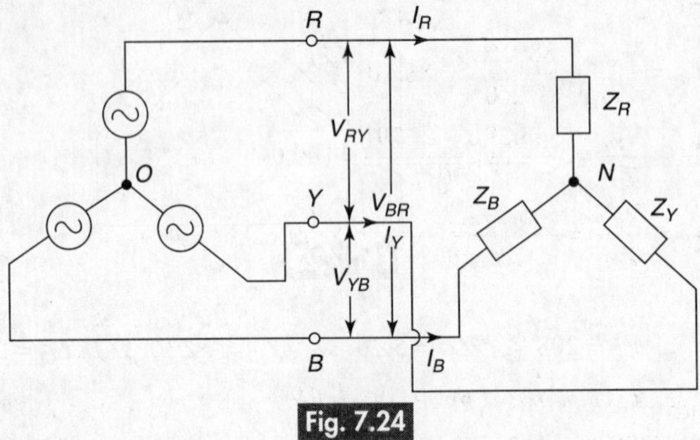


Fig. 7.24

**Solution** $\quad V_L = 440\text{ V},\quad \mathbf{Z}_R = 10\ \Omega,\quad \mathbf{Z}_Y = j5\ \Omega,\quad \mathbf{Z}_B = -j5\ \Omega$

For a star-connected load,

$$V_{ph=}\frac{V_L}{\sqrt{3}} = \frac{440}{\sqrt{3}} = 254.03\text{ V}$$

Let $O$ be the neutral point of the supply system.

Let

$$V_{RO} = 254.03\angle 0^\circ\text{ V}$$

$$V_{YO} = 254.03\angle -120^\circ\text{ V}$$

$$V_{BO} = 254.03\angle -240^\circ\text{ V}$$

$$\mathbf{Y}_R = \frac{1}{\mathbf{Z}_R} = \frac{1}{10} = \frac{1}{10\angle 0^\circ} = 0.1\angle 0^\circ\ \mho$$

$$\mathbf{Y}_Y = \frac{1}{\mathbf{Z}_Y} = \frac{1}{j5} = \frac{1}{5\angle 90^\circ} = 0.2\angle -90^\circ\ \mho$$

$$\mathbf{Y}_B = \frac{1}{\mathbf{Z}_B} = \frac{1}{-j5} = \frac{1}{5\angle -90^\circ} = 0.2\angle 90^\circ\ \mho$$

By Millman's theorem,

$$\mathbf{V}_{NO} = \frac{\mathbf{V}_{RO}\ \mathbf{Y}_R + \mathbf{V}_{YO}\ \mathbf{Y}_Y + \mathbf{Y}_{BO}\mathbf{Y}_B}{\mathbf{Y}_R + \mathbf{Y}_Y + \mathbf{Y}_B}$$

$$= \frac{(254.03\angle 0^\circ)(0.1\angle 0^\circ) + (254.03\angle -120^\circ)(0.2\angle -90^\circ) + (254.03\angle -240^\circ)(0.2\angle 90^\circ)}{0.1\angle 0^\circ + 0.2\angle -90^\circ + 0.2\angle 90^\circ}$$

$$= 625.96\angle 180^\circ\text{ V}$$

Voltage across phase impedance

$$\mathbf{V}_{RN} = \mathbf{V}_{RO} - \mathbf{V}_{NO} = 254.03\angle 0° - 625.96\angle 180° = 880\angle 0° \text{ V}$$
$$\mathbf{V}_{YN} = \mathbf{V}_{YO} - \mathbf{V}_{NO} = 254.03\angle -120° - 625.96\angle 180° = 545.29\angle -23.79° \text{ V}$$
$$\mathbf{V}_{BN} = \mathbf{V}_{BO} - \mathbf{V}_{NO} = 254.03\angle -240° - 625.96\angle 180° = 545.29\angle 23.79° \text{ V}$$

Phase currents/ line currents

$$\mathbf{I}_R = \frac{\mathbf{V}_{RN}}{\mathbf{Z}_R} = \frac{880\angle 0°}{10\angle 0°} = 88\angle 0° \text{ A}$$
$$\mathbf{I}_Y = \frac{\mathbf{V}_{YN}}{\mathbf{Z}_Y} = \frac{545.29\angle -23.79°}{5\angle 90°} = 109.06\angle -113.79° \text{ A}$$
$$\mathbf{I}_B = \frac{\mathbf{V}_{BN}}{\mathbf{Z}_B} = \frac{545.29\angle 23.79°}{5\angle -90°} = 109.06\angle 113.79° \text{ A}$$

**EXAMPLE 7.27**

*In the circuit of Fig. 7.25, a symmetrical three-phase 100 V, three-wire supply feeds an unbalanced star-connected load, with impedances of the load as* $\mathbf{Z}_R = 5\angle 0°\ \Omega$, $\mathbf{Z}_Y = 2\angle 90°\ \Omega$ *and* $\mathbf{Z}_B = 4\angle -90°\ \Omega$. *Find the line currents and voltage across the impedance using star-delta transformation method.*

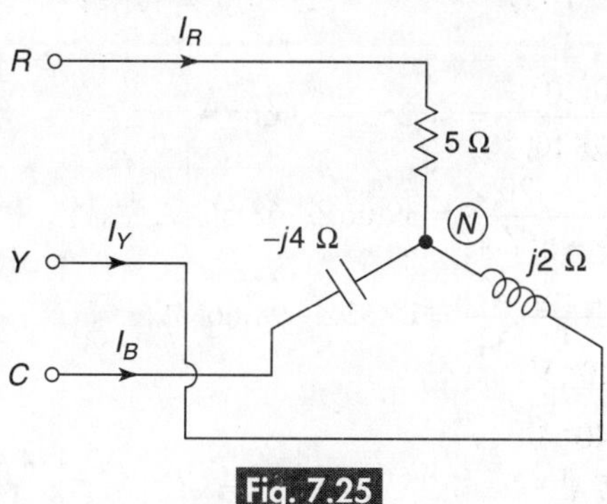


Fig. 7.25

**Solution** $V_L = 100 \text{ V}, \quad \mathbf{Z}_R = 5\angle 0°\ \Omega, \quad \mathbf{Z}_Y = 2\angle 90°\ \Omega, \quad \mathbf{Z}_B = 4\angle -90°\ \Omega$

The unbalanced star-connected load can be converted into equivalent delta-connected load by star-delta transformation technique.

$$\mathbf{Z}_{RY} = \mathbf{Z}_R + \mathbf{Z}_Y + \frac{\mathbf{Z}_R\mathbf{Z}_Y}{\mathbf{Z}_B} = 5\angle 0° + 2\angle 90° + \frac{(5\angle 0°)(2\angle 90°)}{4\angle -90°} = 3.2\angle 38.66°\ \Omega$$
$$\mathbf{Z}_{YB} = \mathbf{Z}_Y + \mathbf{Z}_B + \frac{\mathbf{Z}_Y\mathbf{Z}_B}{\mathbf{Z}_R} = 2\angle 90° + 4\angle -90° + \frac{(2\angle 90°)(4\angle -90°)}{5\angle 0°} = 2.56\angle -51.34°\ \Omega$$
$$\mathbf{Z}_{BR} = \mathbf{Z}_B + \mathbf{Z}_R + \frac{\mathbf{Z}_B\mathbf{Z}_R}{\mathbf{Z}_Y} = 4\angle -90° + 5\angle 0° + \frac{(4\angle -90°)(5\angle 0°)}{2\angle 90°} = 6.4\angle -141.34°\ \Omega$$

The equivalent delta-connected load is shown in Fig. 7.26.

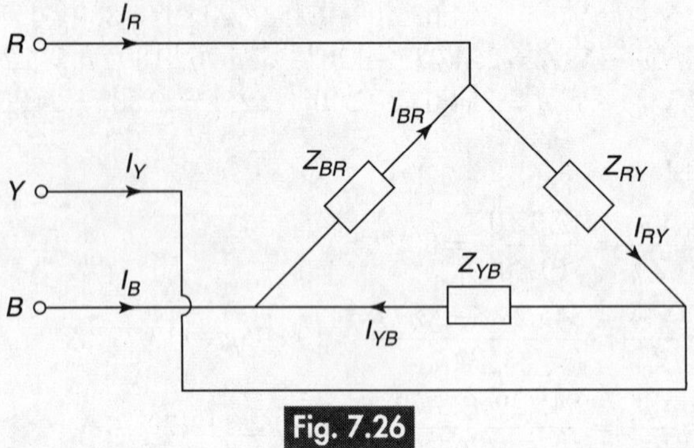


Fig. 7.26

For a delta-connected load,

$$V_{ph} = V_L = 100 \text{ V}$$

Let $\mathbf{V}_{RY} = 100\angle 0° \text{ V}$

$$\mathbf{V}_{YB} = 100\angle -120° \text{ V}$$
$$\mathbf{V}_{BR} = 100\angle -240° \text{ V}$$

Phase currents

$$\mathbf{I}_{RY} = \frac{\mathbf{V}_{RY}}{\mathbf{Z}_{RY}} = \frac{100\angle 0°}{3.2\angle 38.66°} = 31.25\angle -38.66° \text{ A}$$
$$\mathbf{I}_{YB} = \frac{\mathbf{V}_{YB}}{\mathbf{Z}_{YB}} = \frac{100\angle -120°}{2.56\angle -51.34°} = 39.06\angle -68.66° \text{ A}$$
$$\mathbf{I}_{BR} = \frac{\mathbf{V}_{BR}}{\mathbf{Z}_{BR}} = \frac{100\angle -240°}{6.4\angle -141.34°} = 15.63\angle -98.66° \text{ A}$$

Line currents

$$\mathbf{I}_R = \mathbf{I}_{RY} - \mathbf{I}_{BR} = 31.25\angle -38.66° - 15.63\angle -98.66° = 27.06\angle -8.65° \text{ A}$$
$$\mathbf{I}_Y = \mathbf{I}_{YB} - \mathbf{I}_{RY} = 39.06\angle -68.66° - 31.25\angle -38.66° = 19.7\angle -121.14° \text{ A}$$
$$\mathbf{I}_B = \mathbf{I}_{BR} - \mathbf{I}_{YB} = 15.63\angle -98.66° - 39.06\angle -68.66° = 26.69\angle 128.36° \text{ A}$$

These line currents are equal to the line currents of the original star-connected load.

For a star-connected load,

$$I_{ph} = I_L$$
$$\mathbf{I}_{RN} = 27.06\angle -8.65° \text{ A}$$
$$\mathbf{I}_{YN} = 19.7\angle -121.14° \text{ A}$$
$$\mathbf{I}_{BN} = 26.69\angle 128.36° \text{ A}$$
$$\mathbf{V}_{RN} = \mathbf{Z}_R\, \mathbf{I}_{RN} = (5\angle 0°)(27.06\angle -8.65°) = 135.3\angle -8.65° \text{ V}$$
$$\mathbf{V}_{YN} = \mathbf{Z}_Y\, \mathbf{I}_{YN} = (2\angle 90°)(19.7\angle -121.14°) = 39.4\angle -31.14° \text{ V}$$
$$\mathbf{V}_{BN} = \mathbf{Z}_B\, \mathbf{I}_{BN} = (4\angle -90°)(26.69\angle 128.36°) = 106.76\angle 38.36° \text{ V}$$

**EXAMPLE 7.28**

*A three-phase three-wire unbalanced load is star-connected, as shown in Fig. 7.27. The phase voltage of two of the arms are* $V_{RN} = 100\angle{-10^\circ}$ V *and* $V_{YN} = 150\angle 100^\circ$ V. *Calculate voltage between star point of the load and the supply neutral.*

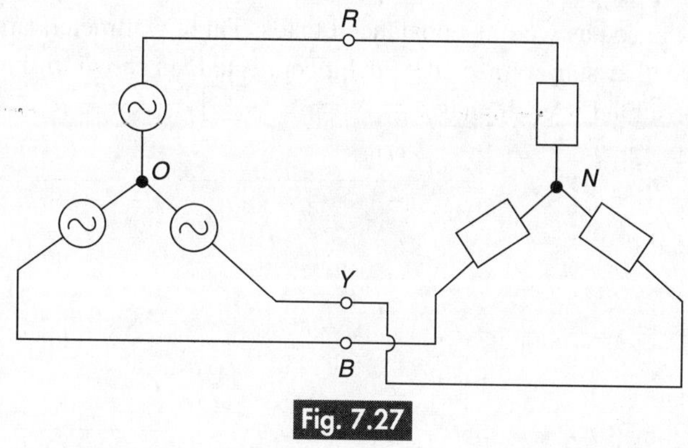


Fig. 7.27

**Solution** $\mathbf{V}_{RN} = 100\angle{-10^\circ}$ V, $\mathbf{V}_{YN} = 150\angle 100^\circ$ V

Let $\mathbf{V}_{RO} = V\angle 0^\circ$

$\mathbf{V}_{YO} = V\angle{-120^\circ}$

From Fig. 7.27,

$$\mathbf{V}_{RO} = \mathbf{V}_{RN} + \mathbf{V}_{NO}$$

$$\mathbf{V}_{NO} = \mathbf{V}_{RO} - \mathbf{V}_{RN} = V\angle 0^\circ - 100^\circ\angle{-10^\circ} \qquad \ldots\text{(i)}$$

Similarly,

$$\mathbf{V}_{NO} = \mathbf{V}_{YO} - \mathbf{V}_{YN} = V\angle{-120^\circ} - 150\angle 100^\circ \qquad \ldots\text{(ii)}$$

From Eqs (i) and (ii),

$$V\angle 0^\circ - 100\angle{-10^\circ} = V\angle{-120^\circ} - 150\angle 100^\circ$$

$$V\angle 0^\circ - V\angle{-120^\circ} = 100\angle{-10^\circ} - 150\angle 100^\circ$$

$$\sqrt{3}\, V\angle 30^\circ = 206.79\angle{-52.97^\circ}$$

$$V = 119.39\angle{-82.97}$$

$$\mathbf{V}_{NO} = 119.39\angle{-82.97} - 100\angle{-10} = 131.88\angle{-129.67^\circ}\text{ V}$$

## 7.13 MEASUREMENT OF THREE-PHASE POWER

LO 7.10

Describe the measurement of three-phase power using one, two and three-wattmeters methods

In a three-phase system, total power is the sum of powers in three phases. The power is measured by wattmeter. It consists of two coils: (i) Current coil, and (ii) Voltage coil. Current coil is connected in series with the load and it senses current. Voltage coil is connected across supply terminals and it senses voltages.

There are three methods to measure three-phase power:

1. Three-wattmeter method
2. Two-wattmeter method
3. One-wattmeter method

### 7.13.1 Three-Wattmeter Method

This method is used for balanced as well as unbalanced loads. Three wattmeters are inserted in each of the three phases of the load whether star connected or delta connected, as shown in Fig. 7.28. Each wattmeter will measure the power consumed in each phase.

For balanced load, $W_1 = W_2 = W_3$

For unbalanced load, $W_1 \neq W_2 \neq W_3$

Total power $P = W_1 + W_2 + W_3$

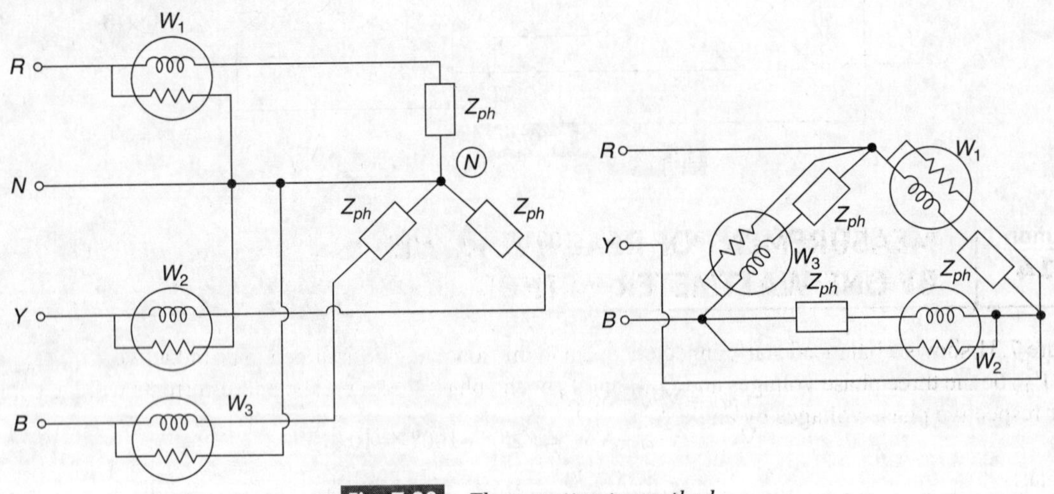


**Fig. 7.28** *Three-wattmeter method*

### 7.13.2 Two-Wattmeter Method

This method is used for balanced as well as unbalanced loads. The current coils of the two wattmeters are inserted in any two lines and the voltage coil of each wattmeter is joined to a third line. The load may be star or delta connected, as shown in Fig. 7.29. The sum of the two wattmeter readings gives three-phase power.

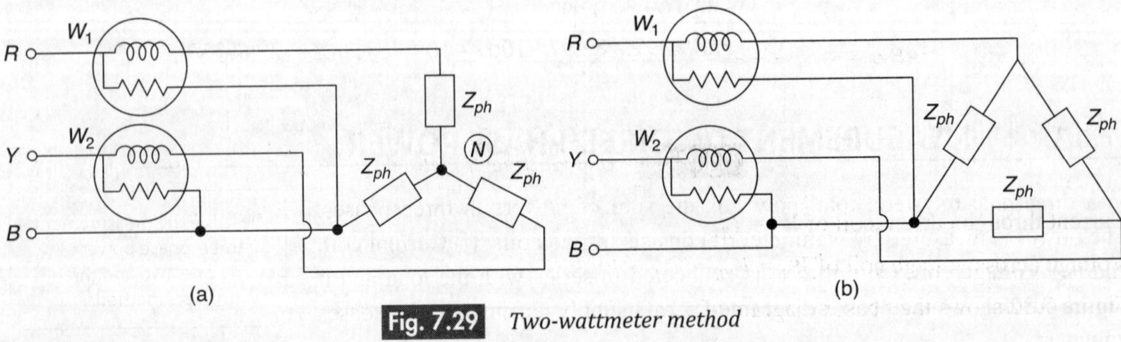


**Fig. 7.29** *Two-wattmeter method*

Total power $P = W_1 + W_2$

### 7.13.3 One-Wattmeter Method

This method is used for balanced loads only. When the load is balanced, total power is given by

$$P = 3\,V_{ph} I_{ph} \cos\phi$$

Hence, one wattmeter is used to measure power in one phase. The wattmeter reading is then multiplied by three to obtain three-phase power. The load may be star or delta connected, as shown in Fig. 7.30.

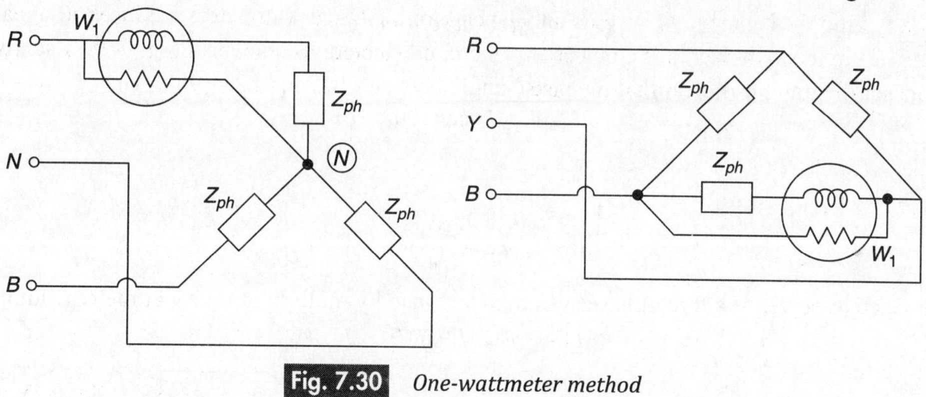


**Fig. 7.30** *One-wattmeter method*

## 7.14 MEASUREMENT OF REACTIVE POWER BY ONE-WATTMETER METHOD

LO 7.10

Figure 7.31 shows a balanced star-connected load and this load may be assumed to be inductive. Let $V_{RN}$, $V_{YN}$ and $V_{BN}$ be the three phase voltages and $I_R$, $I_Y$ and $I_B$ be the phase currents. The phase currents will lag behind their respective phase voltages by angle $\phi$.

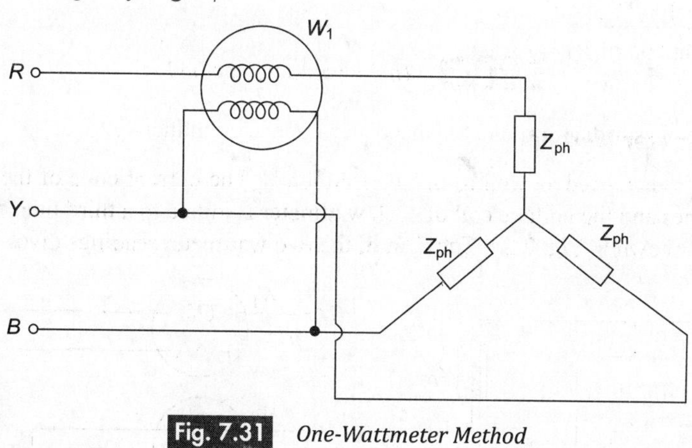


**Fig. 7.31** *One-Wattmeter Method*

Current through current coil of $W_1 = I_R$

Voltage across voltage coil of $W_1 = V_{YB} = V_{YN} + V_{NB}$

Figure 7.32 shows the phasor diagram of a balanced star-connected inductive load.

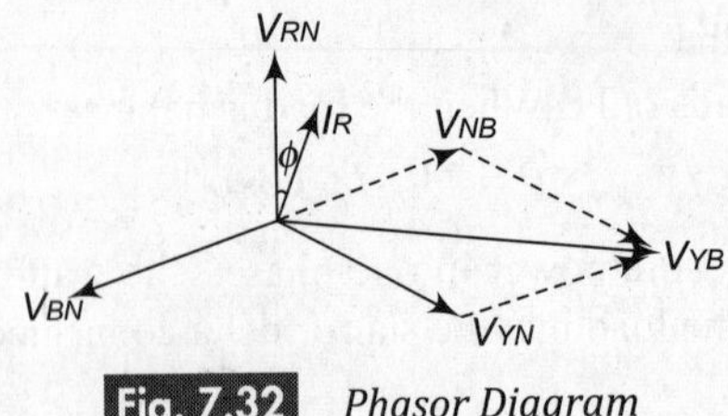


Fig. 7.32 *Phasor Diagram*

From the phasor diagram, it is clear that the phase angle between $V_{YB}$ and $I_R$ is $(90° - \phi)$.

$$W_1 = V_{YB} I_R \cos(90° - \phi)$$

But,

$$I_R = I_L$$

$$V_{YB} = V_L$$

$$W_1 = V_L I_L \cos(90° - \phi) = V_L I_L \sin\phi$$

Thus, total reactive power of a three-phase system is obtained by multiplying the wattmeter reading by $\sqrt{3}$.

$$Q = \sqrt{3}\, V_L I_L \sin\theta = \sqrt{3}\, W_1$$

## 7.15 MEASUREMENT OF ACTIVE POWER, REACTIVE POWER AND POWER FACTOR BY TWO-WATTMETER METHOD

LO 7.10

### 7.15.1 Measurement of Active Power by Two-Wattmeter Method

Figure 7.29 shows a balanced star-connected load and this load may be assumed to be inductive. Let $V_{RN}$, $V_{YN}$ and $V_{BN}$ be the three phase voltages and $I_R$, $I_Y$ and $I_B$ be the phase currents. The phase currents will lag behind their respective phase voltages by angle $\phi$.

Current through current coil of $W_1 = I_R$

Voltage across voltage coil of $W_1 = V_{RB} = V_{RN} + V_{NB} = V_{RN} - V_{BN}$

Figure 7.33 shows the phasor diagram of a balanced star-connected inductive load.

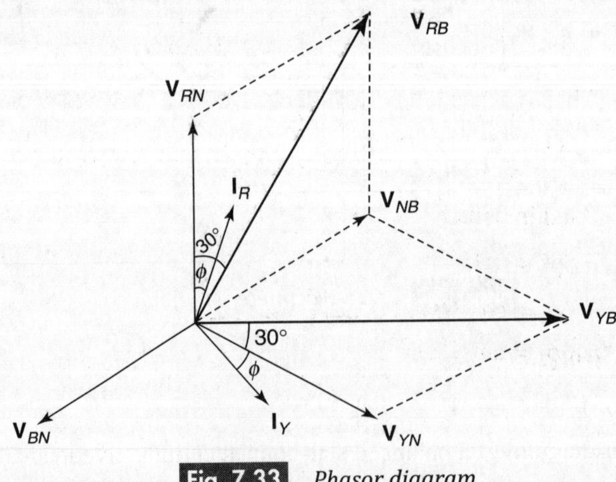


Fig. 7.33 *Phasor diagram*

From the phasor diagram, it is clear that the phase angle between $V_{RB}$ and $I_R$ is $(30° - \phi)$.

$$W_1 = V_{RB} I_R \cos(30° - \phi)$$

Current through current coil of $W_2 = I_Y$

Voltage across voltage coil of $W_2 = V_{YB} = V_{YN} + V_{NB} = V_{YN} - V_{BN}$

From the phasor diagram, it is clear that phase angle between $V_{YB}$ and $I_Y$ is $(30° + \phi)$.

$$W_2 = V_{YB}\, I_Y \cos(30° + \phi)$$

But,

$$I_R = I_Y = I_L$$

$$V_{RB} = V_{YB} = V_L$$

$$W_1 = V_L I_L \cos(30° - \phi)$$

$$W_2 = V_L I_L \cos(30° + \phi)$$

$$W_1 + W_2 = V_L I_L [\cos(30° + \phi) + \cos(30° - \phi)] = V_L I_L (2\cos 30° \cos\phi) = \sqrt{3} V_L I_L \cos\phi$$

Thus, the sum of two wattmeter readings gives three-phase power.

### 7.15.2 Measurement of Reactive Power by Two-Wattmeter Method

We know that

$$W_1 - W_2 = V_L I_L \sin\phi$$

The total reactive power in a three-phase system is given by

$$Q = \sqrt{3}\, V_L I_L \sin\phi = \sqrt{3}\,(W_1 - W_2)$$

Thus, total reactive power of a three-phase system is obtained by multiplying the difference of two-wattmeter readings by $\sqrt{3}$.

### 7.15.3 Measurement of Power Factor by Two-Wattmeter Method

#### *1. Lagging Power Factor*

$$W_1 = V_L I_L \cos(30° - \phi)$$

$$W_2 = V_L I_L \cos(30° + \phi)$$

$$\therefore W_1 > W_2$$

$$W_1 + W_2 = \sqrt{3} V_L I_L \cos\phi$$

$$W_1 - W_2 = V_L I_L [\cos(30° - \phi) - \cos(30° + \phi) = V_L I_L \sin\phi$$

$$\frac{W_1 - W_2}{W_1 + W_2} = \frac{V_L I_L \sin\phi}{\sqrt{3} V_L I_L \cos\phi}$$

$$\tan\phi = \sqrt{3}\frac{W_1 - W_2}{W_1 + W_2}$$

$$\phi = \tan^{-1}\left(\sqrt{3}\frac{W_1 - W_2}{W_1 + W_2}\right)$$

$$\text{pf} = \cos\phi = \cos\left\{\tan^{-1}\left(\sqrt{3}\frac{W_1 - W_2}{W_1 + W_2}\right)\right\}$$

### 2. Leading Power Factor

Figure 7.34 shows the phasor diagram of a balanced star-connected capacitive load.

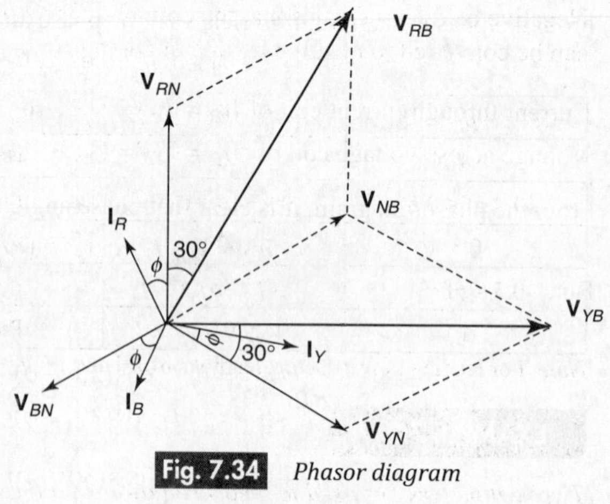


Fig. 7.34 Phasor diagram

$$W_1 = V_L I_L \cos (30° + \phi)$$

$$W_2 = V_L I_L \cos (30° - \phi)$$

$$\therefore W_1 < W_2$$

$$W_1 + W_2 = \sqrt{3} V_L I_L \cos \phi$$

$$W_1 - W_2 = -V_L I_L \sin \phi$$

$$\tan \phi = -\sqrt{3}\frac{(W_1 - W_2)}{(W_1 + W_2)}$$

$$\phi = \tan^{-1}\left(-\sqrt{3}\frac{(W_1 - W_2)}{(W_1 + W_2)}\right)$$

$$\text{pf} = \cos \phi = \cos\left\{\tan^{-1}\left(-\sqrt{3}\frac{W_1 - W_2}{W_1 + W_2}\right)\right\}$$

## 7.16 EFFECT OF POWER FACTOR ON WATTMETER READINGS IN TWO WATTMETER METHOD

LO 7.10

For a lagging power factor load,

$$W_1 = V_L I_L \cos (30° - \phi)$$

$$W_2 = V_L I_L \cos (30° + \phi)$$

***Case I:*** $\phi = 0°, \quad pf = \cos \phi = 1$

$$W_1 = V_L I_L \cos 30°$$

$$W_2 = V_L I_L \cos 30°$$

Hence, both wattmeter readings are equal and positive. For all power factors between 0.5 to 1, both wattmeter readings are positive.

***Case II:*** $\phi = 60°, \quad pf = \cos \phi = 0.5 \text{ (lagging)}$

$$W_1 = V_L I_L \cos (30° - 60°) = V_L I_L \cos 30° \qquad [\because \cos(-\theta) = \cos\theta]$$

$$W_2 = V_L I_L \cos (30° + 60°) = 0$$

Hence, wattmeter $W_1$ reading is positive and wattmeter $W_2$ reading is zero.

For all power factors between 0 to 0.5 (lagging), wattmeter $W_1$ reading is positive and wattmeter $W_2$ reading is negative.

***Case III:*** $\phi = 90°, \text{pf} = \cos \phi = 0$

$$W_1 = V_L I_L \cos (30° - 90°) = 0.5\, V_L I_L$$

$$W_2 = V_L I_L \cos (30° + 90°) = -0.5\, V_L I_L$$

Hence, $W_1 = -W_2$

Negative reading indicates that the pointer deflects in negative direction i.e., to the left of zero. The readings can be converted to positive by interchanging either current coil or voltage coil terminals.

| *pf* | $\phi$ | $W_1$ *Reading* | $W_2$ *Reading* | *Remark* |
|---|---|---|---|---|
| 0 | 90° | Positive | Negative | $W_1 = -W_2$ |
| $0 < \text{pf} < 0.5$ | $90° < \phi < 60°$ | Positive | Negative | |
| 0.5 | 60° | Positive | 0 | |
| $0.5 < \text{pf} < 1$ | $60° < \phi < 0°$ | Positive | Positive | |
| 1 | 0° | Positive | Positive | $W_1 = W_2$ |

***Note*** For leading power factor, readings of $W_1$ and $W_2$ are interchanged.

## EXAMPLE 7.29

*Two wattmeters are used to measure power in a three-phase balanced load. Find the power factor if (a) two readings are equal and positive, (b) two readings are equal and opposite, and (c) one wattmeter reads zero.*

**Solution**

(a) Power factor if two readings are equal and positive

$$W_1 = W_2$$

$$\tan\phi = \sqrt{3}\,\frac{W_1 - W_2}{W_1 + W_2} = \sqrt{3}\,(0) = 0$$

$$\phi = 0°$$

$$\text{Power factor} = \cos\phi = \cos(0°) = 1$$

(b) Power factor if two readings are equal and opposite

$$W_1 = -W_2$$

$$\tan\phi = \sqrt{3}\,\frac{W_1 - W_2}{W_1 + W_2} = \infty$$

$$\phi = 90°$$

$$\text{Power factor} = \cos\phi = \cos(90°) = 0$$

(c) Power factor if one wattmeter reads zero

$$W_2 = 0$$

$$\tan\phi = \sqrt{3}\,\frac{W_1 - W_2}{W_1 + W_2} = \sqrt{3}\left(\frac{W_1}{W_1}\right) = \sqrt{3}$$

$$\phi = 60°$$

$$\text{Power factor} = \cos\phi = \cos(60°) = 0.5$$

## EXAMPLE 7.30

*What will be the relation between readings on the wattmeter connected to measure power in a three-phase balanced circuit with (a) unity power factor, (b) zero power factor, and (c) power factor = 0.5.*

**Solution**

(a) Relation between wattmeter readings with power factor = 1

$$\cos\phi = 1$$
$$\phi = 0°$$
$$\tan\phi = \tan(0°) = 0$$
$$\tan\phi = \sqrt{3}\frac{W_1 - W_2}{W_1 + W_2}$$
$$0 = \sqrt{3}\frac{W_1 - W_2}{W_1 + W_2}$$
$$W_1 = W_2$$

(b) Relation between wattmeter readings with power factor = 0

$$\cos\phi = 0$$
$$\phi = 90°$$
$$\tan\phi = \tan(90°) = \infty$$
$$\tan\phi = \sqrt{3}\frac{W_1 - W_2}{W_1 + W_2}$$
$$W_1 + W_2 = 0$$
$$W_1 = -W_2$$

(c) Relation between wattmeter readings with power factor = 0.5

$$\cos\phi = 60°$$
$$\tan\phi = \tan(60°) = 1.732$$
$$\tan\phi = \sqrt{3}\frac{W_1 - W_2}{W_1 + W_2}$$
$$1.732 = \sqrt{3}\frac{W_1 - W_2}{W_1 + W_2}$$
$$W_1 - W_2 = W_1 + W_2$$
$$W_2 = 0$$

**EXAMPLE 7.31**

*In a balanced three-phase system, the power is measured by two-wattmeter method and the ratio of two-wattmeter readings is 4:1. The load is inductive. Determine the load power factor.*

**Solution**

$$\frac{W_1}{W_2} = \frac{4}{1}$$

Load power factor

$$W_1 = 4\,W_2$$
$$\tan\phi = \sqrt{3}\frac{W_1 - W_2}{W_1 + W_2} = \sqrt{3}\frac{(3W_2)}{(5W_2)} = \sqrt{3}\left(\frac{3}{5}\right) = 1.039$$

$$\phi = 46.1°$$

$$\text{pf} = \cos\phi = \cos(46.1°) = 0.0693 \text{ (lagging)}$$

## EXAMPLE 7.32

*Find the power and power factor of the balanced circuit in which the wattmeter readings are 5 kW and 0.5 kW, the latter being obtained after the reversal of the current coil terminals of the wattmeter.*

**Solution**

$$W_1 = 5 \text{ kW}, \quad W_2 = 0.5 \text{ kW}$$

(a) Power

When the latter reading is obtained after the reversal of the current coil terminals of the wattmeter,

$$W_1 = 5 \text{ kW}$$

$$W_2 = -0.5 \text{ kW}$$

$$\text{Power} = W_1 + W_2 = 5 + (-0.5) = 4.5 \text{ kW}$$

(b) Power factor

$$\tan\phi = \sqrt{3}\frac{W_1 - W_2}{W_1 + W_2} = \sqrt{3}\frac{(5+0.5)}{(5-0.5)} = 2.12$$

$$\phi = 64.72°$$

$$\text{Power factor} = \cos\phi = \cos(64.72°) = 0.43$$

## EXAMPLE 7.33

*Two wattmeters connected to measure the input to a balanced, three-phase circuit indicate 2000 W and 500 W respectively. Find the power factor of the circuit (a) when both readings are positive and (b) when the latter is obtained after reversing the connection to the current coil of one instrument.*

**Solution**

$$W_1 = 2000 \text{ W}, \quad W_2 = 500 \text{ W}$$

(a) Power factor of the circuit when both readings are positive

$$W_1 = 2000 \text{ W}$$

$$W_2 = 500 \text{ W}$$

$$\tan\phi = \sqrt{3}\frac{W_1 - W_2}{W_1 + W_2} = \sqrt{3}\frac{(2000-500)}{(2000+500)} = 1.039$$

$$\phi = 46.102°$$

$$\text{Power factor} = \cos\phi = \cos(46.102°) = 0.693$$

(b) Power factor of the circuit when the latter reading is obtained after reversing the connection to the current coil of one instrument

$$W_1 = 2000 \text{ W}$$

$$W_2 = -500 \text{ W}$$

$$\tan\phi = \sqrt{3}\frac{W_1 - W_2}{W_1 + W_2} = \sqrt{3}\frac{(2000+500)}{(2000-500)} = 2.887$$

$$\phi = 70.89°$$

$$\text{Power factor} = \cos\phi = \cos(70.89°) = 0.33$$

**EXAMPLE 7.34**

*A three-phase, 10 kVA load has a power factor of 0.342. The power is measured by the two-wattmeter method. Find the reading of each wattmeter when the (a) power factor is leading, and the (b) power factor is lagging.*

**Solution**

$$S = 10 \text{ kVA}, \quad \text{pf} = 0.342$$

$$S = \sqrt{3}\, V_L I_L$$

$$10 \times 10^3 = \sqrt{3}\, V_L I_L$$

$$V_L I_L = 5.77 \text{ kVA}$$

$$\cos\phi = 0.342$$

$$\phi = 72^\circ$$

(a) Reading of each wattmeter when the power factor is leading

$$W_1 = V_L I_L \cos(30^\circ + \phi) = 5.77 \times 10^3 \cos(30^\circ + 70^\circ) = -1 \text{ kW}$$

$$W_2 = V_L I_L \cos(30^\circ - \phi) = 5.77 \times 10^3 \cos(30^\circ - 70^\circ) = 4.42 \text{ kW}$$

(b) Reading of each wattmeter when the power factor is lagging

$$W_1 = V_L I_L \cos(30^\circ - \phi) = 4.42 \text{ kW}$$

$$W_2 = V_L I_L \cos(30^\circ + \phi) = -1 \text{ kW}$$

**EXAMPLE 7.35**

*A three-phase, star-connected load draws a line current of 20 A. The load kVA and kW are 20 and 11 respectively. Find the readings on each of the two wattmeters used to measure the three-phase power.*

**Solution**

$$I_L = 20 \text{ A}, \quad S = 20 \text{ kVA}, \quad P = 11 \text{ kW}$$

$$S = \sqrt{3}\, V_L I_L$$

$$20 \times 10^3 = \sqrt{3}\, V_L I_L$$

$$V_L I_L = 11.55 \text{ kVA}$$

$$P = \sqrt{3}\, V_L I_L \cos\phi$$

$$11 \times 10^3 = 20 \times 10^3 \times \cos\phi$$

$$\cos\phi = 0.55$$

$$\phi = 56.63^\circ$$

$$W_1 = V_L I_L \cos(30^\circ - \phi) = 11.55 \times 10^3 \times \cos(30^\circ - 56.63^\circ) = 10.32 \text{ kW}$$

$$W_2 = V_L I_L \cos(30^\circ + \phi) = 11.55 \times 10^3 \times \cos(30^\circ + 56.63^\circ) = 0.68 \text{ kW}$$

**EXAMPLE 7.36**

*Calculate the total power and readings of the two wattmeters connected to measure power in three-phase balanced load, if the reactive power is 15 kVAR and load pf is 0.8 lagging.*

**Solution**

$$Q = 15 \text{ kVAR}, \quad \text{pf} = 0.8 \text{ (lagging)}$$

(a) Reading of the two wattmeters

$$\cos\phi = 0.8$$
$$\phi = 36.87°$$
$$Q = \sqrt{3}\, V_L I_L \sin\phi$$
$$15\times10^3 = \sqrt{3}\, V_L I_L \sin(36.87°)$$
$$V_L I_L = 14.43 \text{ kVA}$$
$$W_1 = V_L I_L \cos(30° - \phi) = 14.43\times10^3 \times \cos(30° - 36.87°) = 14.03 \text{ kW}$$
$$W_2 = V_L I_L \cos(30° + \phi) = 14.43\times10^3 \times \cos(30° + 36.87°) = 5.67 \text{ kW}$$

(b) Total power

$$P = W_1 + W_2 = 14.03 + 5.67 = 19.7 \text{ kW}$$

## EXAMPLE 7.37

●○○

*Two wattmeters are connected to measure power in a three-phase circuit. The reading of one of the wattmeters is 5 kW when the load power factor is unity. If the power factor of the load is changed to 0.707 lagging without changing the total input power, calculate the readings of the two wattmeters.*

**Solution**

$$W_1 = 5 \text{ kW}$$

(a) When the power factor is unity,

$$W_1 = W_2 = 5 \text{ kW}$$
$$\text{Power} = W_1 + W_2 = 5 + 5 = 10 \text{ kW} \quad \ldots\text{(i)}$$

(b) When the power factor is changed to 0.707 lagging,

$$\text{pf} = \cos\phi = 0.707 \text{ (lagging)}$$
$$\phi = 45°$$
$$\tan\phi = \tan(45°) = 1$$
$$\tan\phi = \sqrt{3}\,\frac{W_1 - W_2}{W_1 + W_2}$$
$$1 = \sqrt{3}\,\frac{W_1 - W_2}{10}$$
$$W_1 - W_2 = \frac{10}{\sqrt{3}} = 5.77 \text{ kW} \quad \ldots\text{(ii)}$$

Solving Eq. (i) and (ii),

$$W_1 = 7.89 \text{ kW}$$
$$W_2 = 2.11 \text{ kW}$$

## EXAMPLE 7.38

●○○

*Three coils, each with a resistance of 10 Ω and reactance of 10 Ω, are connected in star across a three-phase, 50 Hz, 400 V supply. Calculate (a) line current, and (b) readings on the two wattmeters connected to measure the power.*

**Solution**

$$R = 10\ \Omega, \quad X_L = 10\ \Omega, \quad V_L = 400 \text{ V}$$

For a star-connected load,

(a) Line current

$$V_{ph} = \frac{V_L}{\sqrt{3}} = \frac{400}{\sqrt{3}} = 230.94 \text{ V}$$

$$\mathbf{Z}_{ph} = R + jX_L = 10 + j10 = 14.14 \angle 45° \ \Omega$$

$$Z_{ph} = 14.14 \ \Omega$$

$$\phi = 45°$$

$$\text{Power factor} = \cos\phi = \cos(45°) = 0.707 \text{ (lagging)}$$

$$I_{ph} = \frac{V_{ph}}{Z_{ph}} = \frac{230.94}{14.14} = 16.33 \text{ A}$$

$$I_L = I_{ph} = 16.33 \text{ A}$$

(b) Readings on the two wattmeters

$$P = \sqrt{3}\, V_L I_L \cos\phi = \sqrt{3} \times 400 \times 16.33 \times 0.707 = 7998.83 \text{ W}$$

$$W_1 + W_2 = 7998.83 \text{ W} \qquad \text{...(i)}$$

Also,

$$\tan\phi = \sqrt{3}\frac{W_1 - W_2}{W_1 + W_2}$$

$$\tan 45° = \sqrt{3}\frac{W_1 - W_2}{7998.83}$$

$$W_1 - W_2 = 4618.13 \text{ W} \qquad \text{...(ii)}$$

Solving Eqs (i) and (ii),

$$W_1 = 6308.48 \text{ W}$$

$$W_2 = 1690.35 \text{ W}$$

**EXAMPLE 7.39**

*Three coils, each having a resistance of 20 Ω and reactance of 15 Ω, are connected in (a) star, and (b) delta, across a three-phase, 400 V, 50 Hz supply. Calculate in each case, the readings on two wattmeters connected to measure the power input.*

**Solution**

$$R = 20 \ \Omega, \quad X_L = 15 \ \Omega, \quad V_L = 400 \text{ V}$$

(a) Readings on two wattmeters for a star-connected load

$$V_{ph} = \frac{V_L}{\sqrt{3}} = \frac{400}{\sqrt{3}} = 230.94 \text{ V}$$

$$\mathbf{Z}_{ph} = 20 + j\,15 = 25 \angle 36.87° \ \Omega$$

$$Z_{ph} = 25 \ \Omega$$

$$\phi = 36.87°$$

$$I_{ph} = \frac{V_{ph}}{Z_{ph}} = \frac{230.94}{25} = 9.24 \text{ A}$$

$$I_L = I_{ph} = 9.24 \text{ A}$$

$$W_1 = V_L\, I_L \cos(30° - \phi) = 400 \times 9.24 \times \cos(30° - 36.87°) = 3669.46 \text{ W}$$
$$W_2 = V_L\, I_L \cos(30° + \phi) = 400 \times 9.24 \times \cos(30° + 36.87°) = 1451.86 \text{ W}$$

(b) Readings on two wattmeters for a delta-connected load

$$V_{ph} = V_L = 400 \text{ V}$$
$$Z_{ph} = 25\ \Omega$$
$$\phi = 36.87°$$
$$I_{ph} = \frac{V_{ph}}{Z_{ph}} = \frac{400}{25} = 16 \text{ A}$$
$$I_L = \sqrt{3}\, I_{ph} = \sqrt{3} \times 16 = 27.72 \text{ A}$$
$$W_1 = V_L I_L \cos(30° - \phi) = 400 \times 27.72 \times \cos(30° - 36.87°) = 11008.39 \text{ W}$$
$$W_2 = V_L I_L \cos(30° + \phi) = 400 \times 27.72 \times \cos(30° + 36.87°) = 4355.57 \text{ W}$$

**EXAMPLE 7.40**

*Two wattmeters connected to measure three-phase power for star-connected load read 3 kW and 1 kW. The line current is 10 A. Calculate (a) line and phase voltages (b) resistance and reactance per phase.*

**Solution**

$$W_1 = 3 \text{ kW}, \quad W_2 = 1 \text{ kW}, \quad I_L = 10 \text{ A}$$

(a) Line and phase voltages

$$\tan\phi = \sqrt{3}\frac{W_1 - W_2}{W_1 + W_2} = \sqrt{3}\frac{(3-1)}{(3+1)} = 0.866$$
$$\phi = 40.89°$$
$$\text{Power factor} = \cos\phi = \cos(40.89°) = 0.756$$
$$P = W_1 + W_2 = 3 + 1 = 4 \text{ kW}$$
$$P = \sqrt{3}\, V_L I_L \cos\phi$$
$$4 \times 10^3 = \sqrt{3} \times V_L \times 10 \times 0.756$$
$$V_L = 305.48 \text{ V}$$

For a star-connected load,

$$V_{ph} = \frac{V_L}{\sqrt{3}} = \frac{305.48}{\sqrt{3}} = 176.37 \text{ V}$$

(b) Resistance and reactance per phase

$$I_{ph} = I_L = 10 \text{ A}$$
$$Z_{ph} = \frac{V_{ph}}{I_{ph}} = \frac{176.37}{10} = 17.637\ \Omega$$
$$R = Z_{ph}\cos\phi = 17.637 \times 0.756 = 13.33\ \Omega$$
$$X_L = Z_{ph}\sin\phi = 17.637 \times \sin(40.89°) = 11.55\ \Omega$$

## EXAMPLE 7.41

*The power input to a 2000 V, 50 Hz, three-phase motor running on full load at an efficiency of 90% is measured by two wattmeters which indicate 300 kW and 100 kW respectively. Calculate the (a) input power, (b) power factor, and (c) line current.*

**Solution**

$$V_L = 2000\text{ V},\quad \eta = 90\%,\quad W_1 = 300\text{ kW},\quad W_2 = 100\text{ kW}$$

(a) Input power

$$P = W_1 + W_2 = 300 + 100 = 400\,\text{kW}$$

(b) Power factor

$$\tan\phi = \sqrt{3}\,\frac{W_1 - W_2}{W_1 + W_2} = \sqrt{3}\,\frac{(300-100)}{(300+100)} = 0.866$$

$$\phi = 40.89°$$

$$\text{pf} = \cos\phi = \cos(40.89°) = 0.76\text{ (lagging)}$$

(c) Line current

$$P = \sqrt{3}\,V_L I_L \cos\phi$$

$$400\times10^3 = \sqrt{3}\times2000\times I_L\times0.76$$

$$I_L = 151.93\text{ A}$$

## EXAMPLE 7.42

*A three-phase, 400 V, 50 Hz induction motor has a full load output of 14.9 kW at which the efficiency and power factor are 0.88 and 0.8 respectively. What is the line current? Find the readings on the two wattmeters connected to measure the power input to the motor.*

**Solution**

$$V_L = 400\text{ V},\quad f = 50\text{ Hz},\quad P_o = 14.9\text{ kW},\quad \text{pf} = 0.8,\quad \eta = 0.88$$

(a) Line current

$$\eta = \frac{P_o}{P_i}$$

$$0.88 = \frac{14.9\times10^3}{P_i}$$

$$P_i = 16.93\text{ kW}$$

$$\text{pf} = \cos\phi = 0.8$$

$$\phi = 36.87°$$

$$P_i = \sqrt{3}\,V_L I_L \cos\phi$$

$$16.93\times10^3 = \sqrt{3}\times400\times I_L\times0.8$$

$$I_L = 30.55\text{ A}$$

(b) Readings on the two wattmeters

$$W_1 = V_L I_L \cos(30° - \phi) = 400\times30.55\times\cos(30° - 36.87°) = 12.13\,\text{kW}$$

$$W_2 = V_L I_L \cos(30° + \phi) = 400\times30.55\times\cos(30° + 36.87°) = 4.8\text{ kW}$$

## EXAMPLE 7.43

*A three-phase, 220 V, 50 Hz, 11.2 kW induction motor has a full load efficiency of 88% and draws a line current of 38 A under full load, when connected to a three-phase, 220 V supply. Determine power factor at which the motor is operating. Find the reading on two wattmeters connected in the circuit to measure the input to the motor.*

**Solution** $V_L = 220 \text{ V}, \quad P_o = 11.2 \text{ kW}, \quad \eta = 88\%, \quad I_L = 38 \text{ A}$

(a) Power factor at which the motor is operating

$$\eta = \frac{P_o}{P_i}$$

$$0.88 = \frac{11.2 \times 10^3}{P_i}$$

$$P_i = 12.73 \text{ kW}$$

But

$$P_i = \sqrt{3}\, V_L I_L \cos\phi$$

$$12.73 \times 10^3 = \sqrt{3} \times 220 \times 38 \times \cos\phi$$

$$\text{pf} = \cos\phi = 0.88 \text{ (lagging)}$$

(b) Reading on two wattmeters

$$\phi = 28.36°$$

$$W_1 = V_L I_L \cos(30° - \phi) = 220 \times 38 \times \cos(30° - 28.36°) = 8356.58 \text{ W}$$

$$W_2 = V_L I_L \cos(30° + \phi) = 220 \times 38 \times \cos(30° + 28.36°) = 4385.49 \text{ W}$$

## EXAMPLE 7.44

*Find the reading of a wattmeter when the network shown in Fig. 7.35 is connected to a symmetrical 440 V, three-phase supply. The phase sequence is RYB.*

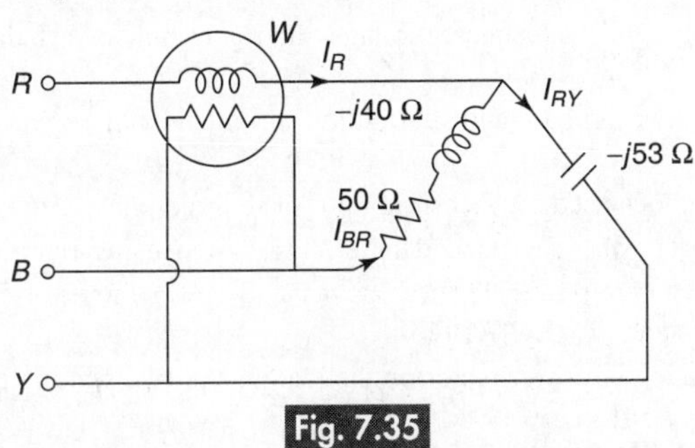


Fig. 7.35

**Solution**

$$V_L = 440 \text{ V}$$

Let

$$\mathbf{V}_{RY} = 440\angle 0° \text{V}$$

$$\mathbf{V}_{YB} = 440\angle -120° \text{V}$$

$$\mathbf{V}_{BR} = 440\angle -240° \text{V}$$

$$\mathbf{Z}_{RY} = -j53 = 53\angle -90°\ \Omega$$

$$\mathbf{Z}_{BR} = 50 + j40 = 64.03\angle 38.66°\ \Omega$$

$$\mathbf{I}_{RY} = \frac{\mathbf{V}_{RY}}{\mathbf{Z}_{RY}} = \frac{440\angle 0°}{53\angle -90°} = 8.3\angle 90°\ \text{A}$$

$$\mathbf{I}_{BR} = \frac{\mathbf{V}_{BR}}{\mathbf{Z}_{BR}} = \frac{440\angle -240°}{64.03\angle 38.66°} = 6.87\angle 81.34°\ \text{A}$$

$$\mathbf{I}_R = \mathbf{I}_{RY} - \mathbf{I}_{BR} = 8.3\angle 90° - 6.87\angle 81.34° = 1.83\angle 124.44°\ \text{A}$$

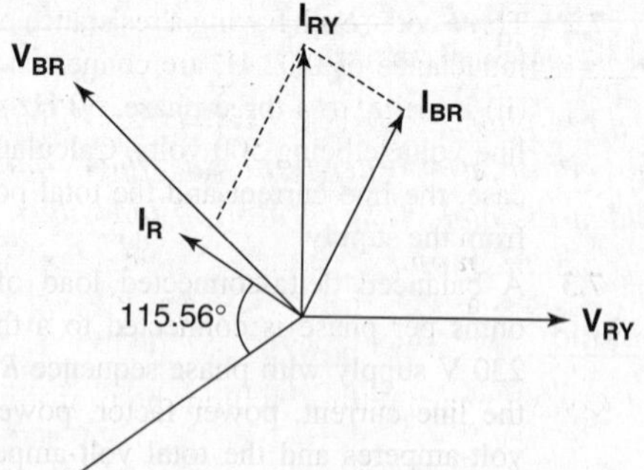

Fig. 7.36

The phasor diagram of the system is shown in Fig. 7.34.

From the phasor diagram, it is clear that angle between $V_{YB}$ and $I_R$ is 115.56°

$$W = V_{YB}\ I_R \cos(115.56°) = 440 \times 1.83 \times \cos(115.56°) = 347.41\ \text{W}$$

# Theory Questions

**7.1** What are the advantages of a polyphase system over a single-phase system? **[LO 7.1]** ●○○

**7.2** Define phase sequence. **[LO 7.2]** ●○○

**7.3** What is balanced supply and balanced load? **[LO 7.2]** ●○○

**7.4** Prove that current through neutral wire is zero in balanced star-connected load. **[LO 7.4]** ●○○

**7.5** Prove that sum of three induced emfs in balanced supply is zero. **[LO 7.4]** ●○○

**7.6** Write the relation between line and phase currents and voltages for balanced star-connected load. **[LO 7.5]** ●○○

**7.7** Derive the relation between line and phase voltages and currents for a balanced star-connected system. **[LO 7.5]** ○●○

**7.8** Write the relation between line and phase currents and voltages for balanced delta-connected load. **[LO 7.5]** ●○○

**7.9** Derive the relation between line and phase voltages and currents for a balanced delta-connected system. **[LO 7.5]** ○●○

**7.10** What is the relationship between phase and neutral line currents in a three-phase unbalanced system? **[LO 7.9]** ○●○

**7.11** What are the different methods used for measuring power in three-phase circuits? **[LO 7.10]** ●○○

**7.12** Explain the measurement of power in a balanced three-phase system using a single wattmeter. **[LO 7.10]** ○●○

**7.13** How do you measure the active power, reactive power and power factor of a balanced three-phase load using two wattmeter method? **[LO 7.10]** ○●○

**7.14** Discuss the effect of variation of power factor on the readings of two wattmeters used in three-phase power measurement. **[LO 7.10]** ○●○

# Practice Problems

**7.1** Three coils, each of 5 Ω resistance, and 6 Ω inductive reactance are connected in closed delta and supplied from a 440 V, three-phase system. Calculate the line and phase currents, the power factor of the system and the intake in watts. ●○○

**7.2** Three coils, each having a resistance of 10 Ω and inductance of 0.02 H, are connected (i) in star, (ii) in delta, to a three-phase, 50 Hz supply, the line voltage being 500 volts. Calculate, for each case, the line current and the total power taken from the supply. ●○○

**7.3** A balanced delta-connected load of (8 + *j*6) ohms per phase is connected to a three-phase, 230 V supply with phase sequence *R-Y-B*. Find the line current, power factor, power, reactive volt-amperes and the total volt-amperes. Draw the phasor diagram. ●○○

**7.4** A balanced star-connected load with (6 + *j*8) Ω per phase is connected to a three-phase, 440 V supply. Find the line current, power factor, power, reactive volt-amperes and volt-amperes total. ●○○

**7.5** Calculate the active and reactive components of the current in each phase of a star-connected 5000 V, three-phase, alternator supplying 3000 kW at a power factor of 0.8. ●○○

**7.6** Three similar coils, connected in star, take a total power of 1.5 kW at a power factor of 0.2 lagging from a three-phase, 440 V, 50 Hz supply. Calculate the resistance and inductance of each coil. ●○○

**7.7** A balanced three-phase load connected in delta draws a power of 10 kW at 440 V at a power factor of 0.6 lead. Find the values of the circuit elements and the reactive volt-amperes drawn. ●○○

**7.8** A balanced star-connected load, connected to a 400 V, 50 Hz, three-phase ac supply draws a phase current of 50 A at 0.6 power factor lagging. Calculate (a) phase voltage, (b) total power, and (c) parameters in the star-connected load. ●○○

**7.9** Three equal star-connected inductors consume 8 kW power at 0.8 power factor when connected to 415 V, three-phase, three-wire, 50 Hz supply. Estimate the load parameters per phase and determine the line currents. ●○○

**7.10** A balanced three-phase, star-connected load of 150 kW takes a leading current of 100 A with a line voltage of 1100 V, 50 Hz. Find the circuit constant of the load per phase. ●○○

**7.11** Three pure elements connected in star draw *x* kVAR. What will be the value of elements that will draw the same kVAR, when connected in delta across the same supply? ●○○

**7.12** A balanced wye-connected load with (10 + *j*20) ohms per phase is connected to a three-phase, 400 V supply. Determine the voltage across, current through and power dissipated in each resistor. Also, determine the total power. ●○○

**7.13** A delta-connected three-phase load is supplied from a 3- phase, 400 volts balanced supply system. The line current is 20 A and power taken by the load is 10 kW. Find (a) impedance in each branch, (b) line current, power factor and power consumed if the same load is connected in star. ●○○

**7.14** A balanced star-connected load is supplied from a symmetrical three-phase, 400 V system. The current in each phase is 30 A and lags 30° behind the phase voltage. Find (a) phase voltage, (b) the circuit elements, and (c) draw the vector diagram showing the currents and the voltages. ●○○

**7.15** A three-phase, delta-connected load having a (3 + *j*4) ohms per phase is connected across a 230 V, three-phase source. Calculate the magnitude of the line current. ●○○

**7.16** A 220 V, three-phase voltage is applied to a balanced delta-connected load. The rms value of the phase current is $20\angle{-30^\circ}$ A. Determine

(i) magnitude and phase of the line current

(ii) total power received by the three-phase load

(iii) value of the resistive portion of the phase impedance

Also, draw the phasor diagram showing clearly the line voltages, phase current and line currents. ○●○

**7.17** A three-phase, 37.3 kW, 440 V, 50 Hz induction motor operates on full load with an efficiency of 89% and at a power factor of 0.85 lagging. Calculate total kVA rating of capacitance required to raise power factor at 0.95 lagging. What will be the value of capacitance/phase if capacitors are (a) delta-connected (b) star-connected? ○○●

**7.18** Three coils, each having impedance (4 + *j*3) ohms, are connected in star to a 440 V, three-phase, 50 Hz supply. Calculate the line current and active power. Now, if three pure capacitors, each of *C* farads, connected in delta, are connected across the same supply, it is found that the total power factor of the circuit becomes 0.96 lag. Find the value of *C*. Also, find the total line current. ○○●

**7.19** Three identical coils, each having a resistance of 8 Ω and inductance of 0.02 H, are connected in (i) star, and (ii) delta, across a three-phase, 400 V, 50 Hz supply. Draw a neat phasor diagram and calculate the reading of two wattmeters connected to measure power. Also, calculate pf of the circuit. ●○○

**7.20** Three identical coils, each having a reactance of 20 Ω and resistance of 10 Ω, are connected in (i) star, (ii) delta across a 440 V, three-phase line. Calculate, for each method of connection, the line current and readings of each of the two wattmeters connected. ●○○

**7.21** A three-phase motor load has a pf of 0.397 lagging. Two wattmeters connected to measure power show the input as 30 kW. Find the reading on each wattmeter. ●○○

**7.22** Each of the wattmeters connected to measure the input to a three-phase induction motor reads 10 kW. If the power factor of the motor be changed to 0.866 lagging, determine the readings of the two wattmeters, the total input power remaining unchanged. ●○○

**7.23** A three-phase, star-connected load draws a line current of 25 A. The load kVA and kW are 20 and 16 respectively. Find the readings on each of the two wattmeters used to measure the three-phase power. ●○○

**7.24** Three similar coils are star-connected to a three-phase, 50 Hz supply. The line current taken is 25 A and the two wattmeters connected to measure the input indicate 5.185 kW and 10.37 kW respectively. Calculate (a) the line and phase voltages, and (b) the resistance and reactance of each coil. ●○○

**7.25** A three-phase, 500 V motor load has a power factor of 0.4. Two wattmeters connected to measure power show the input to be 30 kW. Find the reading on each instrument. ●○○

**7.26** The power in a three-phase circuit is measured by two wattmeters. If the total power is 100 kW and power factor is 0.66 leading, what will be the reading of each wattmeter? ●○○

**7.27** Two wattmeters are connected to measure the input to a 400 V, three-phase connected motor outputting 24.4 kW at a power factor of 0.4 lag and 80% efficiency. Calculate (i) resistance and reactance of motor per phase, (ii) reading of each wattmeter. ○●○

**7.28** In a balanced three-phase, 400 V circuit, the line current is 115.5 A. When power is measured by the two wattmeter method, one meter reads 40 kW and the other, zero. What is the power factor of the load? If the power factor were unity and the line current the same, what would be the reading of each wattmeter? ○●○

**7.29** A 440 V, three-phase, delta-connected induction motor has an output of 14.92 kW at pf of 0.82 and efficiency of 85%. Calculate the readings on each of the two wattmeters connected to measure the input. If another star-connected load of 10 kW at 0.85 pf lagging is added in parallel to the motor, what will be the current drawn from the line and the power taken from the line? ○●○

**7.30** Balanced delta-connected impedances, each of $10\angle 30^\circ$ Ω, are connected across three-phase 400 V mains. Determine the two-wattmeter readings if the current coils of the two wattmeters are connected in lines *R* and *Y* and the pressure coils are connected between *R* and *B* and *Y* and *B* lines respectively. ○●○

**7.31** A balanced star-connected load, each phase having a resistance of 10 Ω and the inductive reactance of 30 Ω, is connected to 400 V, 50 Hz supply. The phase rotation is *R*, *Y* and *B*. Wattmeters connected to read total power have their currents coils in the red and blue lines respectively. Calculate the reading on each wattmeter. ○●○

**7.32** A balanced star-connected load is supplied from a symmetrical three-phase 400 V, 50 Hz supply system. The current in each phase is 20 A and lags behind its phase voltage by an angle of $2\pi/9$ radians. Calculate line voltage, phase voltage, current in each phase, load parameter, power in each phase, total power, readings of the wattmeters connected in the load circuit to measure the total power. Draw a neat circuit diagram and vector/phase diagram. ○●○

## ANSWERS TO PRACTICE PROBLEMS

**7.1** 97.58 A, 56.33 A, 0.64 (lagging), 47.61 kW

**7.2** (a) star : 24.46 A, 17.94 kW, (b) delta : 73.39 A, 53.83 kW

**7.3** 39.85 A, 0.8 (lagging), 12.74 kW, 9.52 kVAR, 15.86 kVA

**7.4** 25.404 A, 0.6 (lagging), 11.616 kW, 15.488 kVAR, 19.360 kVA

**7.5** 250 A, 150 A

**7.6** 5.16 Ω, 0.08 H

**7.7** 20.91 Ω, 27.88 Ω, 13.33 kVAR

**7.8** 230.94 V, 20.84 kW, $(2.77 + j3.7)\ \Omega$

**7.9** 6.2 Ω, 0.0386 H, 13.83 A

**7.10** 5 Ω, 813 μF

**7.11** $Z_\Delta = 3Z_Y$

**7.12** 103.2 V, 10.32 V, 1067 W, 3201 W

**7.13** $(24.95 + j24.05)\ \Omega$, 6.66 A, 0.72 (lagging), 3323.21 W

**7.14** 230.94 V, 6.67 Ω, 3.849 Ω

**7.15** 76.21 A

**7.16** $34.65\angle{-60°}$ A, 11.43 kW, 9.53 Ω

**7.17** 12.19 kVA, 66.8 μF, 200.4 μF

**7.18** 50.8 A, 30.976 kW, 77.75 μF, 42.34 A

**7.19** 8.99 kW, 3.3 kW, 0.7866 (lagging), 26.98 kW, 10.14 kW, 0.786 (lagging)

**7.20** 11.36 A, 4.17 kW, – 299.07 W, 34.08 A, 12.52 kW, – 897.14 W

**7.21** 35 kW, – 5 kW

**7.22** 6.67 kW, 13.33 kW

**7.23** 11.46 kW, 4.54 kW

**7.24** 415 V, 240 V, 5.31 Ω, 4.8 Ω

**7.25** 35 kW, – 5 kW

**7.26** 17.26 kW, 82.74 kW

**7.27** 2.55 Ω, 5.58 Ω, 34915 W, – 4850 W

**7.28** 0.5, 40 kW, 40 kW

**7.29** 12.35 kW, 5.26 kW, 43.56 A, 27.6 kW

**7.30** 27.7 kW, 13.86 kW

**7.31** 2190 W, – 583 W

**7.32** 440 V, 254.034 V, 20 A, 9.73 Ω, 0.026 H, 3.892 kW, 11.676 kW, 8.666 kW, 3.009 kW

# Objective-Type Questions

## From GATE and Other Competitive Examinations

**7.1** In a three-phase system, voltages differ in phase by ●○○

(a) 30° (b) 60°
(c) 90° (d) 120°

**7.2** The rated voltage of a three-phase power system is given as ●○○

(a) rms phase voltage
(b) peak phase voltage
(c) rms line to line voltage
(d) peak line to line voltage

**7.3** Total instantaneous power supplied by a three-phase ac supply to a balanced *R-C* load is ●○○

(a) zero
(b) constant
(c) pulsating with zero average
(d) pulsating with non-zero average

**7.4** Which of the following equations is valid for a three-phase, balanced star-connected system? ●○○

(a) $I_R + I_Y + I_B = 0$ (b) $I_R + I_B = I_Y$
(c) $I_R + I_Y - I_B = 0$ (d) $\dfrac{V_R + V_B + V_Y}{Z} = I_N$

**7.5** A three-phase load is balanced if all the three phases have the same ●○○

(a) impedance
(b) power factor
(c) impedance and power factor
(d) none of the above

**7.6** The phase sequence of a three-phase system shown in Fig. 7.37 is ●○○

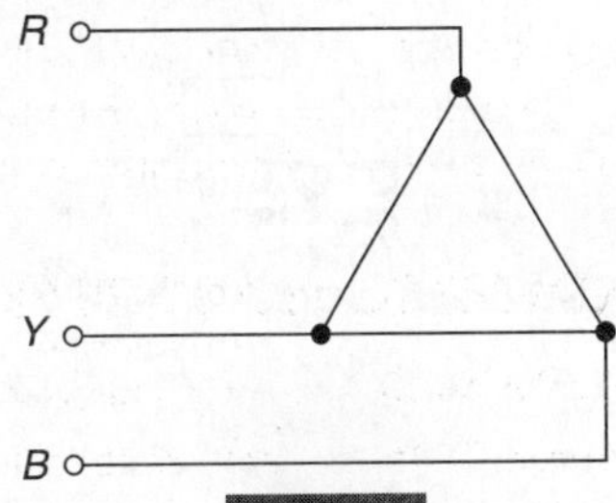


Fig. 7.37

(a) *RYB* (b) *RBY*
(c) *BRY* (d) *YBR*

**7.7** In a three-phase system, $\mathbf{V}_{YN} = 100\angle -120°$ V and $\mathbf{V}_{BN} = 100\angle 120°$ V. Then $\mathbf{V}_{YB}$ will be ●○○
(a) $170\angle 120°$ V
(b) $173\angle 90°$ V
(c) $200\angle 60°$ V
(d) none of the above

**7.8** If a balanced delta load has an impedance of $(6 + j9)$ ohms per phase, then the impedance of each phase in the equivalent star load is ●○○
(a) $(6 + j9)$ ohms (b) $(2 + j3)$ ohms
(c) $(2 + j8)$ ohms (d) $(3 + j4.5)$ ohms

**7.9** Three equal impedances are first connected in delta across a three-phase balanced supply. If the same impedances are connected in star across the same supply ●○○
(a) phase current will be one-third
(b) line current will be one-third
(c) power consumed will be one-third
(d) none of the above

**7.10** Three identical resistors connected in star carry a line current of 12 A. If the same resistors are connected in delta across the same supply, the line current will be ●○○
(a) 12 A (b) 4 A
(c) 8 A (d) 36 A

**7.11** Three delta-connected resistors absorb 60 kW when connected to a three-phase line. If the resistors are connected in star, the power absorbed is ●○○
(a) 60 kW (b) 20 kW
(c) 40 kW (d) 180 kW

**7.12** The power consumed in the star-connected load shown in Fig. 7.38 is 690 W. The line current is ○●○

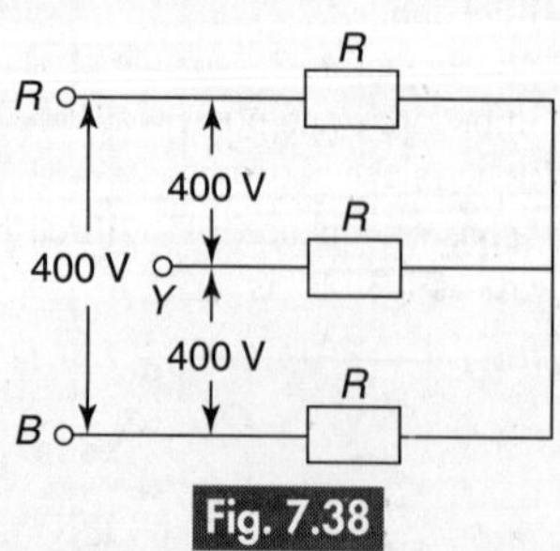


Fig. 7.38

(a) 2.5 A (b) 1 A
(c) 1.725 A (d) none of the above

**7.13** If the three-phase balanced source in Fig. 7.39 delivers 1500 W at a leading power factor of 0.844 then the value of $Z_L$ (in ohms) is approximately ○○●

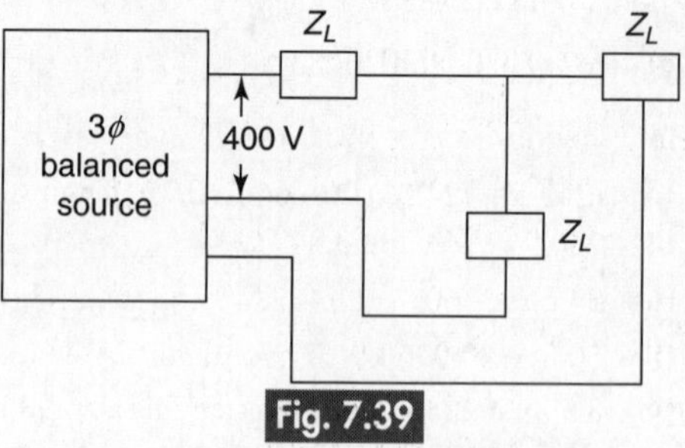


Fig. 7.39

(a) $90\angle 32.44°$ (b) $80\angle 32.44°$
(c) $80\angle -32.44°$ (d) $90\angle -32.44°$

**7.14** If one of the resistors in Fig. 7.40 is open-circuited, power consumed in the circuit is ○○●

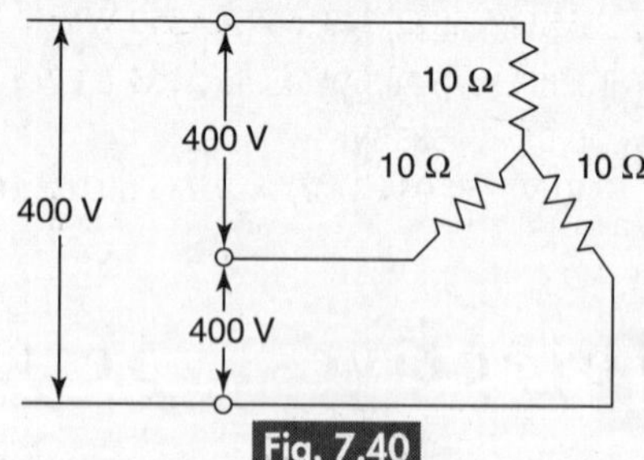


Fig. 7.40

(a) 8000 W (b) 4000 W
(c) 16000 W (d) none of the above

**7.15** For the three-phase circuit shown in Fig. 7.41, the ratio of the currents $I_R : I_Y : I_B$ is given by ○○●

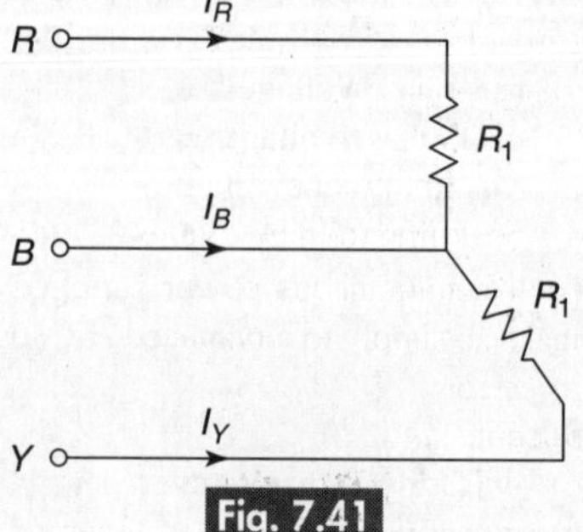


Fig. 7.41

(a) $1:1:\sqrt{3}$ (b) $1:1:2$

(c) 1:1:0 (d) $1:1:\sqrt{\frac{3}{2}}$

**7.16** The phase sequence *RYB* denotes that ●○○
(a) emf of phase *Y* lags behind that of phase *R* by 120°
(b) emf of phase *Y* leads that of phase *R* by 120°
(c) emf of phase *Y* and phase *R* are in phase
(d) none of the above

**7.17** In the two wattmeter method of measurement, if one of the wattmeters reads zero, then power factor will be ●○○
(a) zero (b) unity
(c) 0.5 (d) 0.866

**7.18** Two wattmeters, which are connected to measure the total power on a three-phase system, supplying a balanced load, read 10.5 kW and –2.5 kW, respectively. The total power and the power factor, respectively are ●○○
(a) 13 kW, 0.334
(b) 13 kW, 0.684
(c) 8 kW, 0.52
(d) 8 kW, 0.334

**7.19** The minimum number of wattmeter(s) required to measure three-phase, three-wire balanced or unbalanced power is ●○○
(a) 1 (b) 2
(c) 3 (d) 4

**7.20** One of the two wattmeters has read zero in the two-wattmeter method of power measurement. This indicated that the load phase angle is ●○○
(a) 0° (b) 30°
(c) 60° (d) 90°

## ANSWERS TO OBJECTIVE-TYPE QUESTIONS

| | | | | | | |
|---|---|---|---|---|---|---|
| **7.1** (d) | **7.2** (c) | **7.3** (b) | **7.4** (a) | **7.5** (c) | **7.6** (b) | **7.7** (b) |
| **7.8** (b) | **7.9** (c) | **7.10** (d) | **7.11** (b) | **7.12** (b) | **7.13** (d) | **7.14** (a) |
| **7.15** (a) | **7.16** (a) | **7.17** (c) | **7.18** (d) | **7.19** (b) | **7.20** (c) | |

# LTspice Section

## EXAMPLE 7.1 ●○○

*Three coils, each having a resistance and an inductance of 8 Ω and 0.02 H respectively, are connected in star across a three-phase, 230 V, 50 Hz supply. Find line currents and active power.*

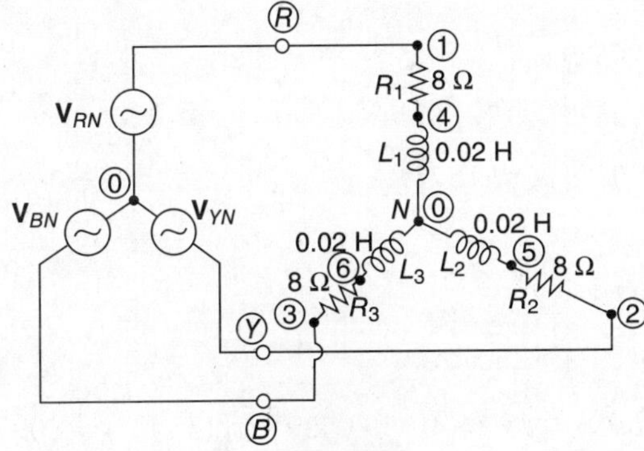


**Fig. 7.42**

## Solution

```
* Calculation of line currents and active power in 3 phase star connected load

VRN 1 0 AC 132.79 -30
VYN 2 0 AC 132.79 -150
VBN 3 0 AC 132.79 90
R1 1 4 8
L1 4 0 0.02
R2 2 5 8
L2 5 0 0.02
R3 3 6 8
L3 6 0 0.02
.AC LIN 1 50 50
.PRINT AC I(R1) I(R2) I(R3)
.END
```

```
                                    AC Analysis
frequency:    50                     Hz
I(R3):        mag:              13.0529   phase:        51.8575°          device_current
I(R2):        mag:              13.0529   phase:        171.857°          device_current
I(R1):        mag:              13.0529   phase:        -68.1425°         device_current
```

**Result**

$$\mathbf{Z}_{ph} = 10.17 \angle 38.13° \ \Omega$$

$$V_L = 230 \text{ V}$$

$$V_{ph} = \frac{230}{\sqrt{3}} = 132.79° \text{ V}$$

For star connected-source,

$$\mathbf{V}_{RN} = 132.79 \angle -30° \text{ V}$$

$$\mathbf{V}_{YN} = 132.79 \angle -150° \text{ V}$$

$$\mathbf{V}_{BN} = 132.79 \angle 90° \text{ V}$$

For star- connected-load,

$$\mathbf{I}_{RN} = \mathbf{I}(R1) = 13.0529 \angle -68.1425° \text{ A}$$

$$\mathbf{I}_{YN} = \mathbf{I}(R2) = 13.0529 \angle 171.857° \text{ A}$$

$$\mathbf{I}_{BN} = \mathbf{I}(R3) = 13.0529 \angle 51.8575° \text{ A}$$

$$\mathbf{I}_R = \mathbf{I}_{RN} = 13.0529 \angle -68.1425° \text{ A}$$

$$\mathbf{I}_Y = \mathbf{I}_{YN} = 13.0529 \angle 171.857° \text{ A}$$

$$\mathbf{I}_B = \mathbf{I}_{BN} = 13.0529 \angle 51.8575° \text{ A}$$

$$P = \sqrt{3}\, V_L\, I_L \cos\phi = \sqrt{3} \times 230 \times 13.0529 \times \cos(38.13°) = 4.09 \text{ kW}$$

## EXAMPLE 7.2

*Three coils, each having a resistance of 8 Ω and an inductance of 0.02 H, are connected in delta to a three-phase, 400 V, 50 Hz supply. Calculate the line current and power absorbed.*

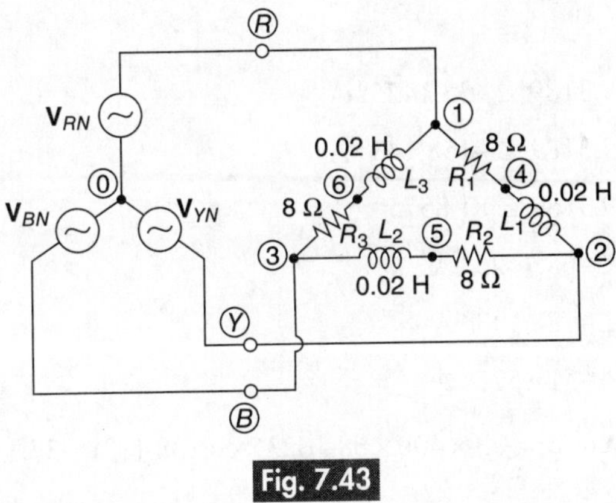


Fig. 7.43

## Solution

```
* Calculation of line currents and power absorbed in 3 phase delta connected load

VRN 1 0 AC 230.94 -30
VYN 2 0 AC 230.94 -150
VBN 3 0 AC 230.94 90
R1 1 4 8
L1 4 2 0.02
R2 2 5 8
L2 5 3 0.02
R3 3 6 8
L3 6 1 0.02
.AC LIN 1 50 50
.PRINT AC I(R1) I(R2) I(R3)
.END
```

```
                                AC Analysis

frequency:   50                 Hz
I(R3):       mag:         39.3189   phase:      81.8575°      device_current
I(R2):       mag:         39.3189   phase:    -158.143°       device_current
I(R1):       mag:         39.3189   phase:     -38.1425°      device_current
```

**Result**

$$\mathbf{Z}_{ph} = 10.17 \angle 38.13° \ \Omega$$

$$V_L = 400 \text{ V}$$

For star connected source,

$$\mathbf{V}_{RN} = 230.94 \angle -30° \text{ V}$$

$$\mathbf{V}_{YN} = 230.94 \angle -150° \text{ V}$$

$$\mathbf{V}_{BN} = 230.94 \angle 90° \text{ V}$$

For delta-connected-load,

$$\mathbf{I}_{RY} = \mathbf{I}(R1) = 39.3189 \angle -38.1425° \text{ A}$$

$$\mathbf{I}_{YB} = \mathbf{I}(R2) = 39.3189 \angle -158.143° \text{ A}$$

$$\mathbf{I}_{BR} = \mathbf{I}(R3) = 39.3189 \angle 81.8575° \text{ A}$$

$$\mathbf{I}_{R} = 68.1023 \angle -68.1425° \text{ A}$$

$$\mathbf{I}_{Y} = 68.1023 \angle -188.143° \text{ A}$$

$$\mathbf{I}_{B} = 68.1023 \angle -51.8575° \text{ A}$$

$$P = \sqrt{3}\, V_L\, I_L \cos\phi = \sqrt{3} \times 400 \times 68.1023 \times \cos(38.13°) = 37.1144 \text{ kW}$$

## EXAMPLE 7.3

*A symmetrical 440 V, three-phase system supplied a star-connected load with the branch impedances $\mathbf{Z}_R = 10\ \Omega$, $\mathbf{Z}_Y = j5\ \Omega$, $\mathbf{Z}_B = -j5\ \Omega$, as shown in Fig. 7.44. Calculate line currents. The phase sequence is RYB.*

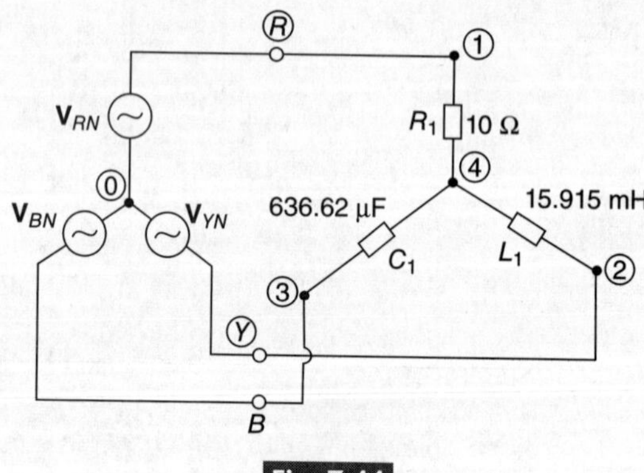


Fig. 7.44

## Solution

```
* Calculation of line currents in unbalanced 3 phase star connected load

VRN 1 0 AC 254.03 0
VYN 2 0 AC 254.03 -120
VBN 3 0 AC 254.03 -240
R1 1 4 10
L1 2 4 15.915M
C1 3 4 636.62U
.AC LIN 1 50 50
.PRINT AC I(R1) I(L1) I(C1)
.END
```

```
                              AC Analysis
frequency:   50           Hz
I(C1):       mag:     109.033    phase:       113.813°      device_current
I(L1):       mag:     109.018    phase:      -113.779°      device_current
I(R1):       mag:       87.98    phase:    0.00711989°      device_current
```

**Result**

$$\mathbf{I}_R = \mathbf{I}(R1) = 87.98 \angle 0.0071° \text{ A}$$

$$\mathbf{I}_Y = \mathbf{I}(L1) = 109.018 \angle -113.779° \text{ A}$$

$$\mathbf{I}_B = \mathbf{I}(C1) = 109.018 \angle 113.813° \text{ A}$$

CHAPTER 8

# Network Topology

## LEARNING OBJECTIVES

**After studying this chapter, you should be able to:**

- **LO 8.1** Explain the concept of graph of a network
- **LO 8.2** Define planar graph, non-planar graph, sub-graph, path, connected graph, rank of a graph, loop or circuit, tree and co-tree associated with a graph
- **LO 8.3** Write incidence matrix for a given network or graph
- **LO 8.4** Write loop matrix or circuit matrix for a given network or graph
- **LO 8.5** Write cutset matrix for a given network or graph
- **LO 8.6** Discuss relationship of submatrices of *A*, *B* and *Q*
- **LO 8.7** Express *KVL* in terms of *f*-circuit matrix
- **LO 8.8** Express *KCL* in terms of incidence and *f*-cutset matrices
- **LO 8.9** Describe the relation between branch voltage matrix $V_b$, twig voltage matrix $V_t$ and node voltage matrix $V_n$
- **LO 8.10** Describe the relation between current matrix $I_b$ and loop current matrix $I_l$
- **LO 8.11** Derive and explain network equilibrium equations
- **LO 8.12** Explain the concept of duality

## INTRODUCTION

The purpose of network analysis is to find voltage across and current through all the elements. When the network is complicated and has a large number of nodes and closed paths, network analysis can be done conveniently by using 'Network Topology'. This theory does not make any distinction between different types of physical elements of the network but makes the study based on a geometric pattern of the network. Topology is a branch of geometry which is concerned with the properties of a geometrical figure, which are not changed when the figure is physically distorted, provided that, no parts of the figure are cut open or joined together. Network topology is a graphical representation of electric circuits. It is useful for analyzing complex electric circuits by converting them into network graphs. Network topology is also called as Graph theory. The basic elements of this theory are nodes, branches, loops and meshes.

## 8.1 GRAPH OF A NETWORK

LO 8.1

Explain the concept of graph of a network

A linear graph is a collection of nodes and branches. The nodes are joined together by branches.

The graph of a network is drawn by first marking the nodes and then joining these nodes by lines, which correspond to the network elements of each branch. All the voltage and current sources are replaced by their internal impedances. The voltage sources are replaced by short circuits as their internal impedances are zero, whereas current sources are replaced by open circuits as their internal impedances are infinite. Nodes and branches are numbered. Figure 8.1 shows a network and its associated graphs.

Each branch of a graph may be given an orientation or a direction with the help of an arrow head, which represents the assigned reference direction for current. Such a graph is then referred to as a directed or oriented graph.

Branches whose ends fall on a node are said to be incident at that node. Degree of a node is defined as the number of branches incident to it. Branches 2, 3 and 4 are incident at Node 2 in Fig. 8.1(c). Hence, the degree of Node 2 is 3.

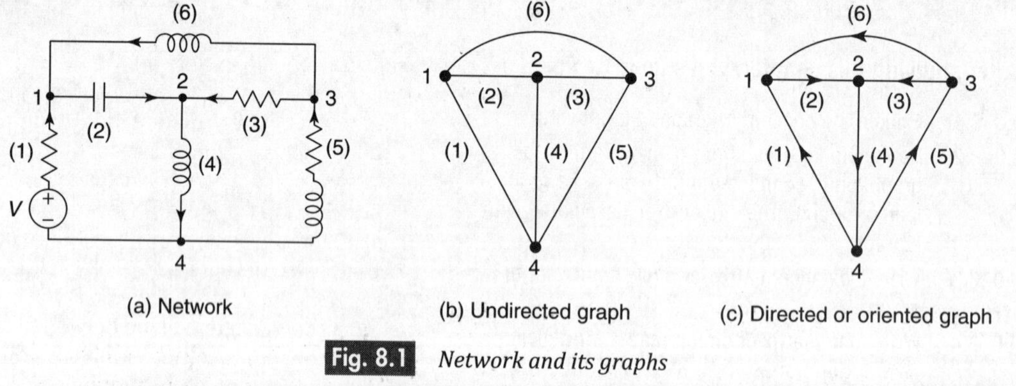


Fig. 8.1 *Network and its graphs*

## 8.2 DEFINITIONS ASSOCIATED WITH A GRAPH

LO 8.2

Define planar graph, non-planar graph, sub-graph, path, connected graph, rank of a graph, loop or circuit, tree and co-tree associated with a graph

***1. Planar Graph*** A graph drawn on a two-dimensional plane is said to be planar if two branches do not intersect or cross at a point, which is other than a node. Figure 8.2 shows such graphs.

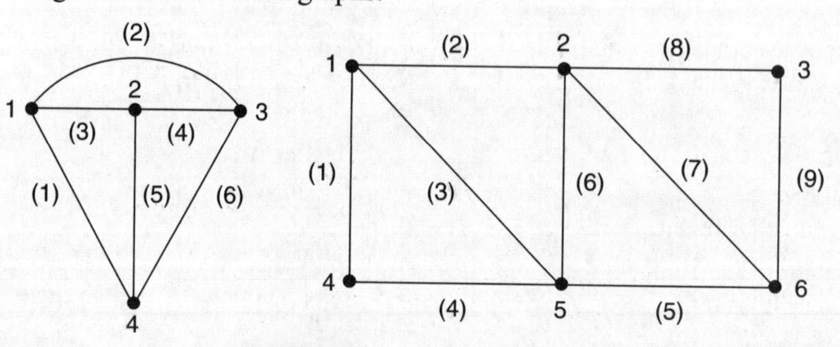


Fig. 8.2 *Planar graphs*

**2. Non-planar Graph** A graph drawn on a two-dimensional plane is said to be non-planar if there is intersection of two or more branches at another point which is not a node. Figure 8.3 shows non-planar graphs.

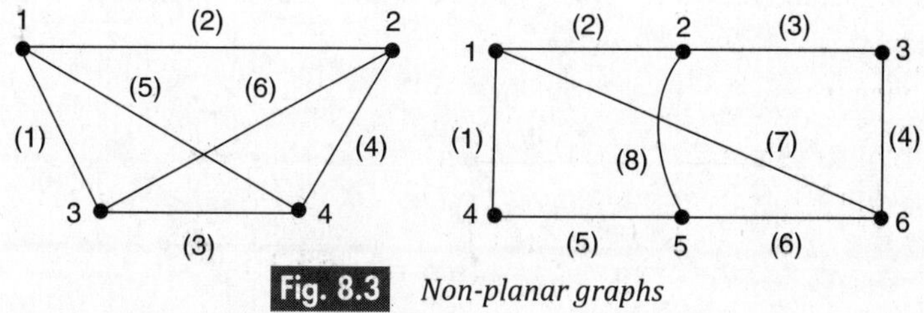


**Fig. 8.3** *Non-planar graphs*

**3. Sub-graph** It is a subset of branches and nodes of a graph. It is a proper sub-graph if it contains branches and nodes less than those on a graph. A sub-graph can be just a node or only one branch of the graph. Figure 8.4 shows a graph and its proper sub-graph.

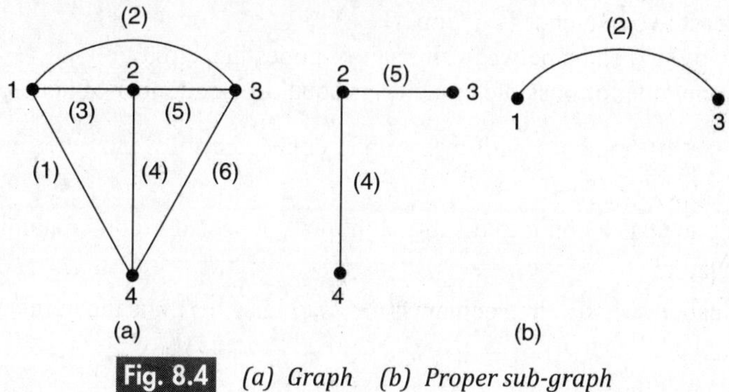


**Fig. 8.4** *(a) Graph (b) Proper sub-graph*

**4. Path** It is an improper sub-graph having the following properties:

1. At two of its nodes called terminal nodes, there is incident only one branch of sub-graph.
2. At all remaining nodes called internal nodes, there are incident two branches of a graph.

In Fig. 8.5, branches 2, 5 and 6 together with all the four nodes, constitute a path.

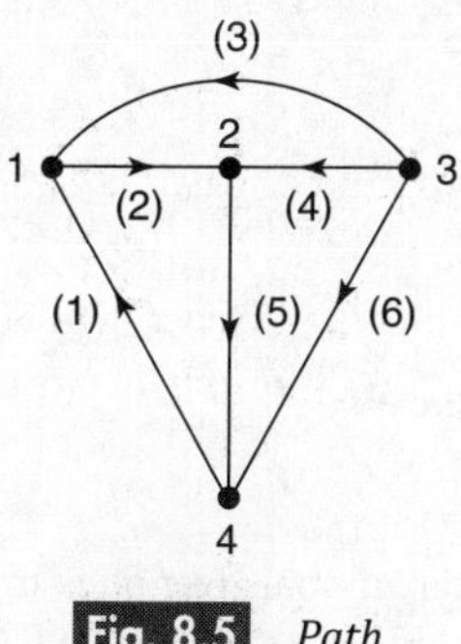


**Fig. 8.5** *Path*

**5. Connected Graph** A graph is said to be connected if there exists a path between any pair of nodes. Otherwise, the graph is disconnected.

***6. Rank of a Graph*** If there are $n$ nodes in a graph, the rank of the graph is $(n - 1)$.

***7. Loop or Circuit*** A loop is a connected sub-graph of a connected graph at each node of which are incident exactly two branches. If two terminals of a path are made to coincide, it will result in a loop or circuit.

Figure 8.6 shows two loops.

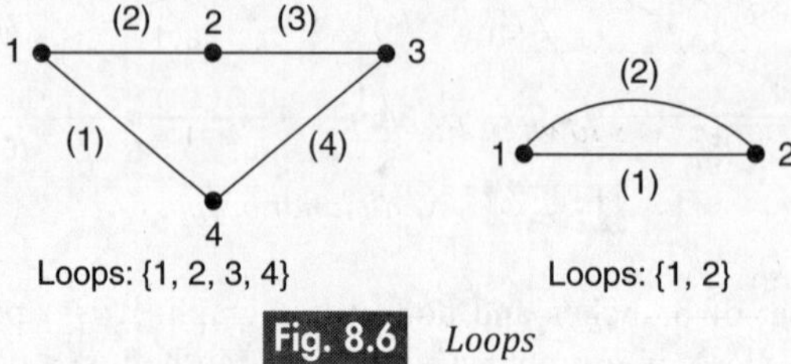


**Fig. 8.6** *Loops*

Loops of a graph have the following properties:

1. There are at least two branches in a loop.
2. There are exactly two paths between any pair of nodes in a circuit.
3. The maximum number of possible branches is equal to the number of nodes.

***8. Tree*** A tree is a set of branches with every node connected to every other node in such a way that removal of any branch changes this property.

Alternately, a tree is defined as a connected sub-graph of a connected graph containing all the nodes of the graph but not containing any loops.

Branches of a tree are called twigs. A tree contains $(n - 1)$ twigs where $n$ is the number of nodes in the graph. Figure 8.7 shows a graph and its trees.

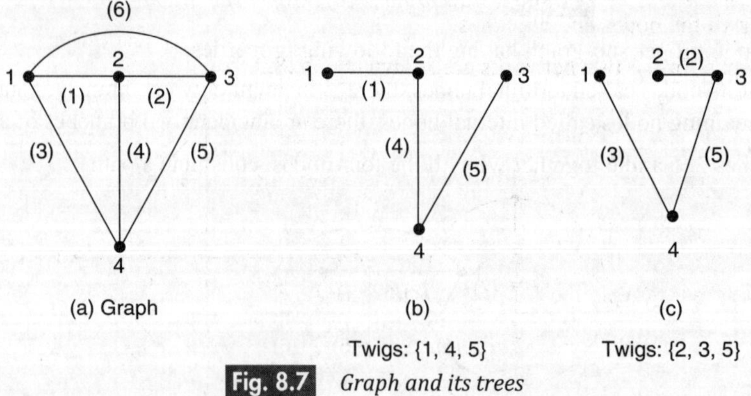


**Fig. 8.7** *Graph and its trees*

Trees have the following properties:

1. There exists only one path between any pair of nodes in a tree.
2. A tree contains all nodes of the graph.
3. If $n$ is the number of nodes of the graph, there are $(n - 1)$ branches in the tree.
4. Trees do not contain any loops.
5. Every connected graph has at least one tree.
6. The minimum terminal nodes in a tree are two.

### 9. Co-tree

Branches which are not on a tree are called links or chords. All links of a tree together constitute the compliment of the corresponding tree and is called the co-tree.

A co-tree contains $b - (n - 1)$ links, where $b$ is the number of branches of the graph.

In Fig. 8.7 (b) and (c), the links are {2, 3, 6} and {1, 4, 6} respectively.

**EXAMPLE 8.1** ●○○

*Draw directed graph of the networks shown in Fig. 8.8.*

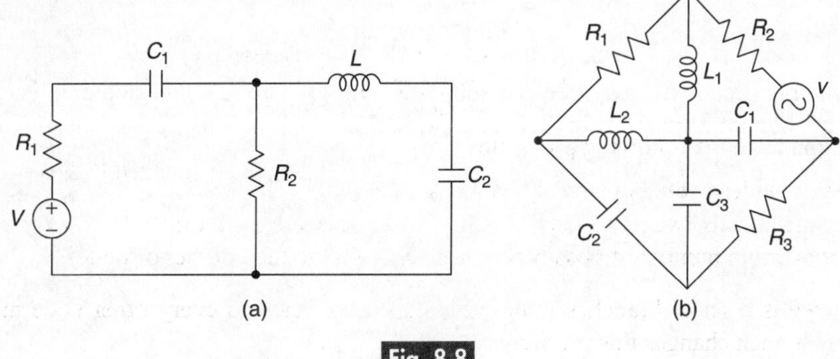


Fig. 8.8

**Solution** For drawing the directed graph,

1. replace all resistors, inductors and capacitors by line segments,
2. replace the voltage source by a short-circuit,
3. assume directions of branch currents, and
4. number all the nodes and branches.

The directed graphs for the two networks are shown in Fig. 8.9.

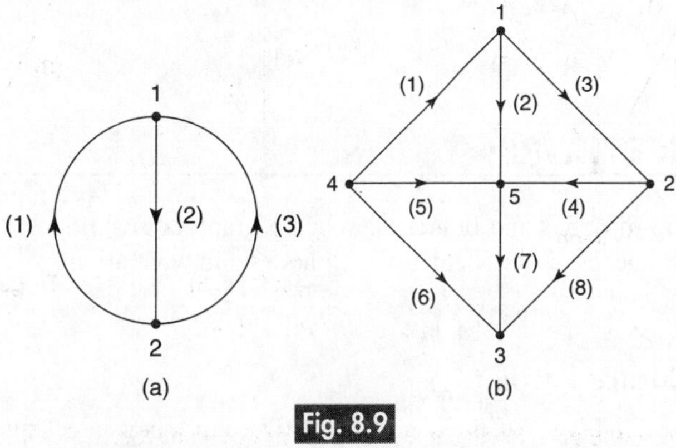


Fig. 8.9

**Note** Difficulty Level ●○○ — Easy; ○●○ — Medium; ○○● — Difficult

**EXAMPLE 8.2**

*Figure 8.10 shows a graph of the network. Show all the trees of this graph.*

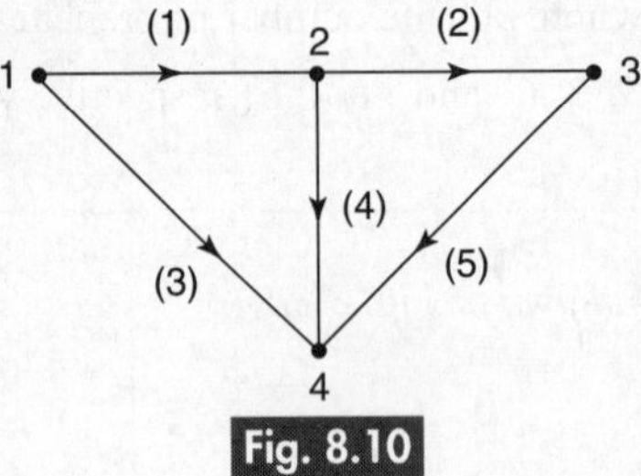


Fig. 8.10

**Solution** A graph has many trees. A tree is a connected sub-graph of a connected graph containing all the nodes of the graph but not containing any loops. Figure 8.11 shows various trees of the given graph.

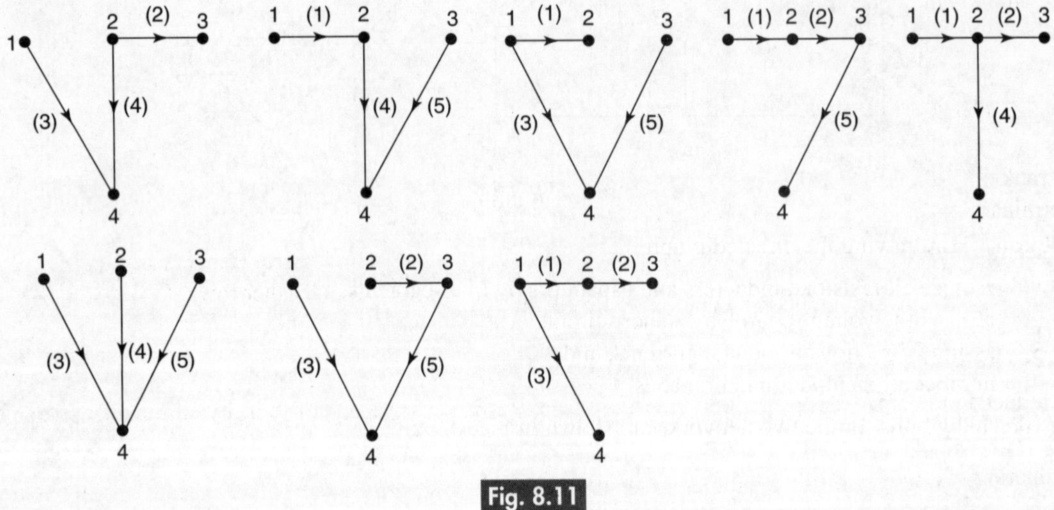

Fig. 8.11

## 8.3 INCIDENCE MATRIX

LO 8.3

Write incidence matrix for a given network or graph

A linear graph is made up of nodes and branches. When a graph is given, it is possible to tell which branches are incident at which nodes and what are its orientations relative to the nodes.

### 8.3.1 Complete Incidence Matrix ($A_a$)

For a graph with $n$ nodes and $b$ branches, the complete incidence matrix is a rectangular matrix of order $n \times b$. Elements of this matrix have the following values:

$a_{ij} = 1$, if branch $j$ is incident at node $i$ and is oriented away from node $i$.

$= -1$, if branch $j$ is incident at node $i$ and is oriented towards node $i$.

$= 0$, if branch $j$ is not incident at node $i$.

For the graph shown in Fig. 8.12, branch 1 is incident at nodes 1 and 4. It is oriented away from Node 1 and oriented towards Node 4. Hence, $a_{11} = 1$ and $a_{41} = -1$. Since branch 1 is not incident at nodes 2 and 3, $a_{21} = 0$ and $a_{31} = 0$. Similarly, other elements of the complete incidence matrix are written.

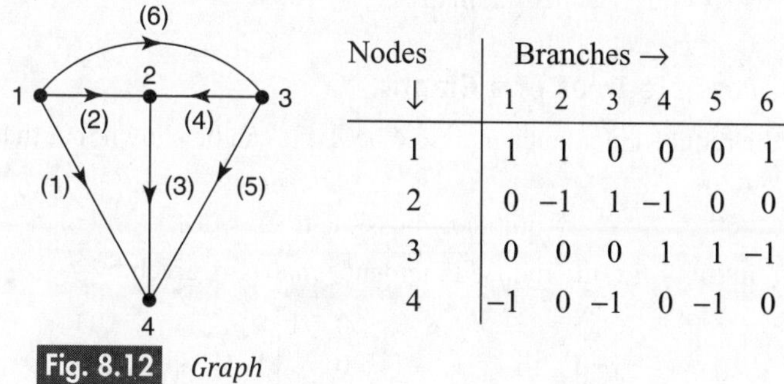


| Nodes ↓ | Branches → 1 | 2 | 3 | 4 | 5 | 6 |
|---|---|---|---|---|---|---|
| 1 | 1 | 1 | 0 | 0 | 0 | 1 |
| 2 | 0 | −1 | 1 | −1 | 0 | 0 |
| 3 | 0 | 0 | 0 | 1 | 1 | −1 |
| 4 | −1 | 0 | −1 | 0 | −1 | 0 |

**Fig. 8.12** *Graph*

The complete incidence matrix is

$$A_a = \begin{bmatrix} 1 & 1 & 0 & 0 & 0 & 1 \\ 0 & -1 & 1 & -1 & 0 & 0 \\ 0 & 0 & 0 & 1 & 1 & -1 \\ -1 & 0 & -1 & 0 & -1 & 0 \end{bmatrix}$$

The rank of the complete incidence matrix of a connected graph is $n - 1$ where $n$ is the number of nodes. The determinant of the complete incidence matrix of a closed loop is zero.

It is seen from the matrix $A_a$ that the sum of the elements in any column is zero. Hence, any one row of the complete incidence matrix can be obtained by the algebraic manipulation of other rows.

### 8.3.2 Reduced Incidence Matrix (*A*)

The reduced incidence matrix $A$ is obtained from the complete incidence matrix $A_a$ by eliminating one of the rows. It is also called *incidence matrix*. It is of order $(n - 1) \times b$.

Eliminating the third row of matrix $A_a$,

$$A = \begin{bmatrix} 1 & 1 & 0 & 0 & 0 & 1 \\ 0 & -1 & 1 & -1 & 0 & 0 \\ -1 & 0 & -1 & 0 & -1 & 0 \end{bmatrix}$$

When a tree is selected for the graph, as shown in Fig. 8.13, the incidence matrix is obtained by arranging a column such that the first $(n - 1)$ columns correspond to twigs of the tree and the last $b - (n - 1)$ branches correspond to the links of the selected tree.

1 —(2)→ 2 ←(4)— 3; 2 —(3)→ 4

Twigs: {2, 3, 4}
Links: {1, 5, 6}

**Fig. 8.13** *Tree*

Twigs: 2 3 4    Links: 1 5 6

$$A = \begin{bmatrix} 1 & 0 & 0 & 1 & 0 & 1 \\ -1 & 1 & -1 & 0 & 0 & 0 \\ 0 & -1 & 0 & -1 & -1 & 0 \end{bmatrix}$$

Matrix $A$ can be subdivided into submatrices $A_t$ and $A_l$.

$$A = [A_t : A_l]$$

where $A_t$ the is twig matrix and $A_l$ is the link matrix.

### 8.3.3 Number of Possible Trees of a Graph

Let the transpose of the reduced incidence matrix $A$ be $A^T$. It can be shown that the number of possible trees of a graph will be given by

$$\text{Number of possible trees} = |AA^T|$$

For the graphs shown in Fig. 8.12, the reduced incidence matrix is given by

$$A = \begin{bmatrix} 1 & 1 & 0 & 0 & 0 & 1 \\ 0 & -1 & 1 & -1 & 0 & 0 \\ -1 & 0 & -1 & 0 & -1 & 0 \end{bmatrix}$$

Then transpose of this matrix will be

$$A^T = \begin{bmatrix} 1 & 0 & -1 \\ 1 & -1 & 0 \\ 0 & 1 & -1 \\ 0 & -1 & 0 \\ 0 & 0 & -1 \\ 1 & 0 & 0 \end{bmatrix}$$

Hence, number of all possible trees of the graph

$$AA^T = \begin{bmatrix} 1 & 1 & 0 & 0 & 0 & 1 \\ 0 & -1 & 1 & -1 & 0 & 0 \\ -1 & 0 & -1 & 0 & -1 & 0 \end{bmatrix} \begin{bmatrix} 1 & 0 & -1 \\ 1 & -1 & 0 \\ 0 & 1 & -1 \\ 0 & -1 & 0 \\ 0 & 0 & -1 \\ 1 & 0 & 0 \end{bmatrix} = \begin{bmatrix} 3 & -1 & -1 \\ -1 & 3 & -1 \\ -1 & -1 & 3 \end{bmatrix}$$

$$|AA^T| = \begin{vmatrix} 3 & -1 & -1 \\ -1 & 3 & -1 \\ -1 & -1 & 3 \end{vmatrix} = 3(9-1)+(1)(-3-1)-1(1+3) = 16$$

Thus, 16 different trees can be drawn.

## 8.4 LOOP MATRIX OR CIRCUIT MATRIX

LO 8.4

Write loop matrix or circuit matrix for a given network or graph

When a graph is given, it is possible to tell which branches constitute which loop or circuit. Alternately, if a loop matrix or circuit matrix is given, we can reconstruct the graph.

For a graph having $n$ nodes and $b$ branches, the loop matrix $B_a$ is a rectangular matrix of order $b$ columns and as many rows as there are loops.

Its elements have the following values:

$b_{ij} = 1$, if branch $j$ is in loop $i$ and their orientations coincide.

$= -1$, if branch $j$ is in loop $i$ and their orientations do not coincide.

$= 0$, if branch $j$ is not in loop $i$.

A graph and its loops are shown in Fig. 8.14.

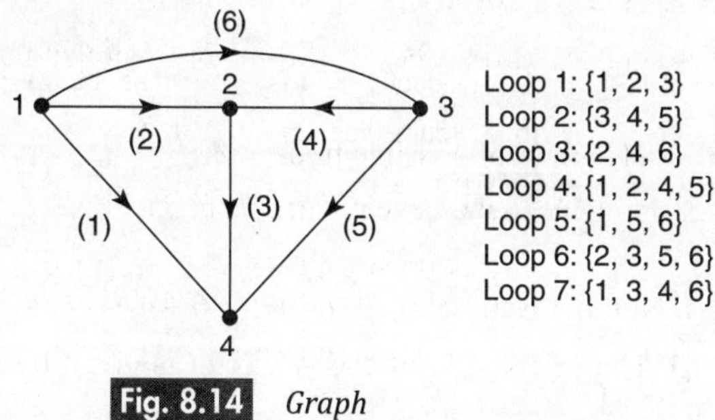


**Fig. 8.14** *Graph*

All the loop currents are assumed to be flowing in a clockwise direction.

| Loops ↓ \ Branches → | 1 | 2 | 3 | 4 | 5 | 6 |
|---|---|---|---|---|---|---|
| 1 | –1 | 1 | 1 | 0 | 0 | 0 |
| 2 | 0 | 0 | –1 | –1 | 1 | 0 |
| 3 | 0 | –1 | 0 | 1 | 0 | 1 |
| 4 | –1 | 1 | 0 | –1 | 1 | 0 |
| 5 | –1 | 0 | 0 | 0 | 1 | 1 |
| 6 | 0 | –1 | –1 | 0 | 1 | 1 |
| 7 | –1 | 0 | 1 | 1 | 0 | 1 |

$$B_a = \begin{bmatrix} -1 & 1 & 1 & 0 & 0 & 0 \\ 0 & 0 & -1 & -1 & 1 & 0 \\ 0 & -1 & 0 & 1 & 0 & 1 \\ -1 & 1 & 0 & -1 & 1 & 0 \\ -1 & 0 & 0 & 0 & 1 & 1 \\ 0 & -1 & -1 & 0 & 1 & 1 \\ -1 & 0 & 1 & 1 & 0 & 1 \end{bmatrix}$$

### 8.4.1 Fundamental Circuit (Tieset) and Fundamental Circuit Matrix

When a graph is given, first select a tree and remove all the links. When a link is replaced, a closed loop or circuit is formed. Circuits formed in this way are called fundamental circuits or *f*-circuits or tiesets.

Orientation of an *f*-circuit is given by the orientation of the connecting link. The number of *f*-circuits is same as the number of links for a graph. In a graph having $b$ branches and $n$ nodes, the number of *f*-circuits or tiesets will be $(b - n + 1)$. Figure 8.15 shows a tree and *f*-circuits (tiesets) for the graph shown in Fig. 8.14.

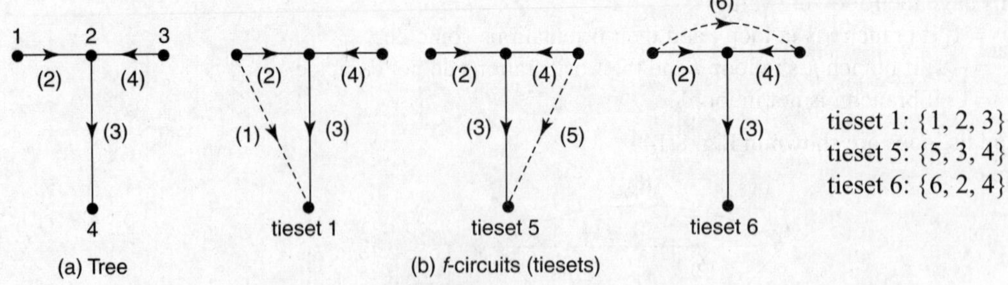


Fig. 8.15 *Tree and f-circuits*

Here, $b = 6$ and $n = 4$.

$$\text{Number of tiesets} = b - n + 1 = 6 - 4 + 1 = 3$$

*f*-circuits are shown in Fig. 8.15. The orientation of each *f*-circuit is given by the orientation of the corresponding connecting link.

Branches 1, 2 and 3 are in the tieset 1. Orientation of tieset 1 is given by orientation of branch 1. Since the orientation of branch 1 coincides with orientation of tieset 1, $b_{11} = 1$. The orientations of branches 2 and 3 do not coincide with the orientation of tieset 1. Hence, $b_{12} = -1$ and $b_{13} = -1$. Branches 4, 5 and 6 are not in tieset 1. Hence, $b_{14} = 0$, $b_{15} = 0$ and $b_{16} = 0$. Similarly, other elements of the tieset matrix are written.

Then, the tieset schedule will be written as

| Tiesets ↓ | Branches → | | | | | |
|---|---|---|---|---|---|---|
| | 1 | 2 | 3 | 4 | 5 | 6 |
| 1 | 1 | −1 | −1 | 0 | 0 | 0 |
| 5 | 0 | 0 | −1 | −1 | 1 | 0 |
| 6 | 0 | −1 | 0 | 1 | 0 | 1 |

Hence, an *f*-circuit matrix or tieset matrix will be given as

$$B = \begin{bmatrix} 1 & -1 & -1 & 0 & 0 & 0 \\ 0 & 0 & -1 & -1 & 1 & 0 \\ 0 & -1 & 0 & 1 & 0 & 1 \end{bmatrix}$$

Usually, the *f*-circuit matrix $B$ is rearranged so that the first $(n - 1)$ columns correspond to the twigs and $b - (n - 1)$ columns to the links of the selected tree.

$$\begin{array}{ccc} & \text{Twigs} & \text{Links} \\ & \begin{array}{cccccc} 2 & 3 & 4 & 1 & 5 & 6 \end{array} & \end{array}$$

$$B = \begin{bmatrix} -1 & -1 & 0 & 1 & 0 & 0 \\ 0 & -1 & -1 & 0 & 1 & 0 \\ -1 & 0 & 1 & 0 & 0 & 1 \end{bmatrix}$$

The matrix $B$ can be partitioned into two matrices $B_t$ and $B_l$.

$$B = [B_t : B_l] = [B_t : U]$$

where $B_t$ is the twig matrix, $B_l$ is the link matrix and $U$ is the unit matrix.

The rank of the tieset matrix is $b - n + 1$, same as number of links.

### 8.4.2 Orthogonal Relationship between Matrix *A* and Matrix *B*

For a linear graph, if the columns of the two matrices $A_a$ and $B_a$ are arranged in the same order, it can be shown that

$$A_a\, B_a^{\,T} = 0$$

or

$$B_a A_a^{\,T} = 0$$

The above equations describe the orthogonal relationship between the matrices $A_a$ and $B_a$.

If the reduced incidence matrix *A* and the *f*-circuit matrix *B* are written for the same tree, it can be shown that

$$A\,B^T = 0$$

or

$$B\,A^T = 0$$

These two equations show the orthogonal relationship between matrices *A* and *B*.

## 8.5 CUTSET MATRIX

LO 8.5

Write cutset matrix for a given network or graph

Consider a linear graph. By removing a set of branches without affecting the nodes, two connected sub-graphs are obtained and the original graph becomes unconnected. The removal of this set of branches, which results in cutting the graph into two parts, are known as a *cutset*. The cutset separates the nodes of the graph into two groups, each being in one of the two groups.

Figure 8.16 shows a graph.

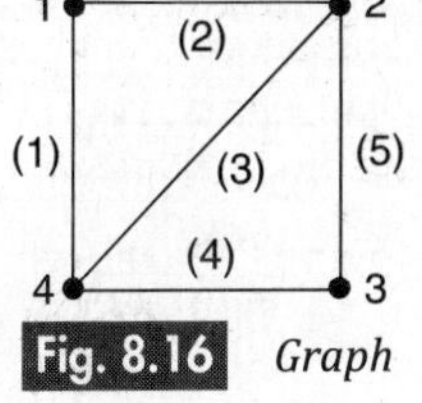

Fig. 8.16 *Graph*

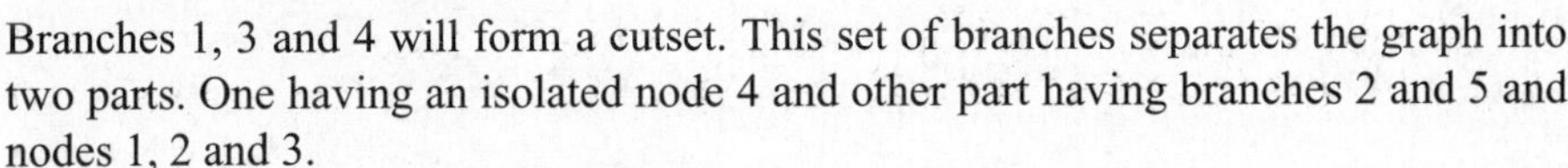
Branches 1, 3 and 4 will form a cutset. This set of branches separates the graph into two parts. One having an isolated node 4 and other part having branches 2 and 5 and nodes 1, 2 and 3.

Similarly, branches 1 and 2 will form a cutset. Each branch of the cutset has one of its terminals incident at a node in one part and its other end incident at other nodes in the other parts. The orientation of a cutset is made to coincide with the orientation of defining branch.

For a graph having *n* nodes and *b* branches, the cutset matrix $Q_a$ is a rectangular matrix of order *b* columns and as many rows as there are cutsets. Its elements have the following values:

$q_{ij} = 1$, if the branch *j* is in the cutset *i* and the orientation coincide.

$= -1$, if the branch *j* is in the cutset *i* and the orientations do not coincide.

$= 0$, if the branch *j* is not in the cutset *i*.

Figure 8.17 shows a directed graph and its cutsets.

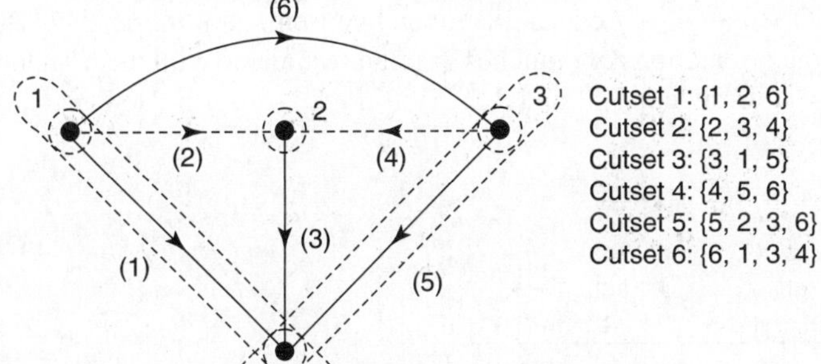


| Cutsets ↓ | Branches → 1 | 2 | 3 | 4 | 5 | 6 |
|---|---|---|---|---|---|---|
| 1 | 1 | 1 | 0 | 0 | 0 | 1 |
| 2 | 0 | 1 | −1 | 1 | 0 | 0 |
| 3 | 1 | 0 | 1 | 0 | 1 | 0 |
| 4 | 0 | 0 | 0 | 1 | 1 | −1 |
| 5 | 0 | −1 | 1 | 0 | 1 | −1 |
| 6 | 1 | 0 | 1 | −1 | 0 | 1 |

Fig. 8.17 *Directed graph*

For the cutset 2, which cuts branches 2, 3 and 4 and is shown by a dotted circle, the entry in the cutset schedule for branch 2 is 1, since the orientation of this cutset is given by the orientation of branch 2 and hence, it coincides. The entry for branch 3 is –1, as orientation of branch 3 is opposite to that of cutset 2, i.e., branch 2 goes into cutset while branch 3 goes out of cutset. The entry for branch 4 is 1 as branch 2 and branch 4 go into the cutset. Thus, their orientations coincide.

Hence, the cutset matrix $Q_a$ is given as

$$Q_a = \begin{bmatrix} 1 & 1 & 0 & 0 & 0 & 1 \\ 0 & 1 & -1 & 1 & 0 & 0 \\ 1 & 0 & 1 & 0 & 1 & 0 \\ 0 & 0 & 0 & 1 & 1 & -1 \\ 0 & -1 & 1 & 0 & 1 & -1 \\ 1 & 0 & 1 & -1 & 0 & 1 \end{bmatrix}$$

### 8.5.1 Fundamental Cutset and Fundamental Cutset Matrix

When a graph is given, first select a tree and note down its twigs. When a twig is removed from the tree, it separates a tree into two parts (one of the separated part may be an isolated node). Now, all the branches connecting one part of the disconnected tree to the other along with the twig removed, constitutes a cutset. This set of branches is called a fundamental cutset or *f*-cutset. A matrix formed by these *f*-cutsets is called an *f*-cutset matrix. The orientation of the *f*-cutset is made to coincide with the orientation of the defining branch, i.e., twig. The number of *f*-cutsets is the same as the number of twigs for a graph.

Figure 8.18 shows a graph, selected tree and *f*-cutsets corresponding to the selected tree.

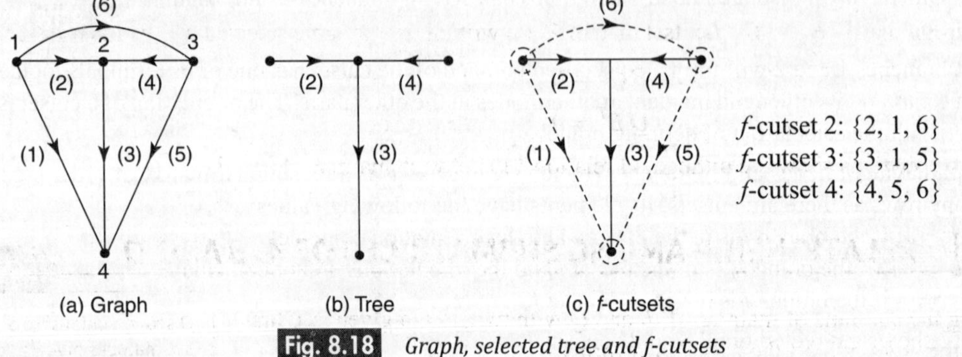


**Fig. 8.18** *Graph, selected tree and f-cutsets*

Branches 2, 1, and 6 are in the *f*-cutset 2. Orientation of *f*-cutset 2 is given by orientation of branch 2 which is moving away from the *f*-cutset 2. Since the orientations of branches 2, 1 and 6 coincide with the orientation of the *f*-cutset 2, $q_{11} = 1$, $q_{12} = 1$ and $q_{16} = 0$. Branches 3, 4 and 5 are not in the *f*-cutset 2. Hence, $q_{13} = 0$, $q_{14} = 0$ and $q_{15} = 0$.

Similarly, other elements of the *f*-cutset matrix are written.

The cutset schedule is

| *f*-cutsets ↓ | Branches → 1 | 2 | 3 | 4 | 5 | 6 |
|---|---|---|---|---|---|---|
| 2 | 1 | 1 | 0 | 0 | 0 | 1 |
| 3 | 1 | 0 | 1 | 0 | 1 | 0 |
| 4 | 0 | 0 | 0 | 1 | 1 | –1 |

Hence, the *f*-cutset matrix $Q$ is given by

$$Q = \begin{bmatrix} 1 & 1 & 0 & 0 & 0 & 1 \\ 1 & 0 & 1 & 0 & 1 & 0 \\ 0 & 0 & 0 & 1 & 1 & -1 \end{bmatrix}$$

The *f*-cutset matrix $Q$ is rearranged so that the first $(n - 1)$ columns correspond to twigs and $b - (n - 1)$ columns to links of the selected tree.

$$\begin{array}{c} \quad\quad \text{Twigs} \quad\quad\quad \text{Links} \\ \quad\quad 2 \quad 3 \quad 4 \quad\ 1 \quad 5 \quad 6 \end{array}$$

$$Q = \begin{bmatrix} 1 & 0 & 0 & 1 & 0 & 1 \\ 0 & 1 & 0 & 1 & 1 & 0 \\ 0 & 0 & 1 & 0 & 1 & -1 \end{bmatrix}$$

The matrix $Q$ can be subdivided into matrices $Q_t$ and $Q_l$.

$$Q = [Q_t : Q_l] = [U : Q_l]$$

where $Q_t$ is the twig matrix, $Q_l$ is the link matrix and $U$ is the unit matrix.

The rank of the *f*-cutset matrix is $n - 1$, same as number of *f*-cutsets.

### 8.5.2 Orthogonal Relationship between Matrix *B* and Matrix *Q*

For a linear graph, if the columns of two matrices $B_a$ and $Q_a$ are arranged in the same order, it can be shown that

$$Q_a B_a^T = 0$$

or

$$B_a Q_a^T = 0$$

If the *f*-circuit matrix $B$ and the *f*-cutset matrix $Q$ are written for the same selected tree, it can be shown that

$$B Q^T = 0$$

or

$$Q B^T = 0$$

These two equations show the orthogonal relationship between matrices $A$ and $B$.

## 8.6 RELATIONSHIP AMONG SUBMATRICES OF *A*, *B* AND *Q*

LO 8.6

Discuss relationship of submatrices of *A*, *B* and *Q*

Arranging the columns of matrices $A$, $B$ and $Q$ with twigs for a given tree first and then the links, we get the partitioned forms as

$$A = [A_t : A_l]$$
$$B = [B_t : B_l] = [B_t : U]$$
$$Q = [Q_t : Q_l] = [U : Q_l]$$

From the orthogonal relation, $AB^T = 0$,

$$AB^T = [A_t : A_l] \begin{bmatrix} B_t^T \\ \cdots \\ B_l^T \end{bmatrix}$$

$$A_t B_t^T + A_l B_l^T = 0$$

$$A_t B_t^T = -A_l B_l^T$$

Since $A_t$ is non-singular, i.e., $|A| \neq 0$, $A_t^{-1}$ exists.

Premultiplying with $A_t^{-1}$,

$$B_t^T = -A_t^{-1} A_l B_l^T$$

$$B_t = -B_l (A_t^{-1}.A_l)^T$$

Since $B_l$ is a unit matrix

$$B_t = -(A_t^{-1}\cdot A_l)^T$$

Hence, matrix $B$ is written as

$$B = [-(A_t^{-1}\cdot A_l)^T : U] \qquad \text{...(8.1)}$$

We know that

$$AB^T = 0$$

$$A_l B_l^T = -A_t B_t^T$$

Postmultiplying with $(B_l^T)^{-1}$,

$$A_l = -A_t B_t^T (B_l^T)^{-1} = -A_t B_t^T (B_l^{-1})^T = -A_t (B_l^{-1}\cdot B_t)^T$$

Hence, matrix $A$ can be written as

$$A = [A_t : -A_t (B_l^{-1}\cdot B_t)^T]$$

$$= A_t [U : -(B_l^{-1}\cdot B_t)^T] \qquad \text{...(8.2)}$$

Similarly, we can prove that

$$Q = [U : -(B_l^{-1}\cdot B_t)^T] \qquad \text{...(8.3)}$$

From Eqs (8.2) and (8.3), we can write

$$A = A_t\, Q$$

$$Q = A_t^{-1} A = A_t^{-1} [A_t : A_l] = [U : A_t^{-1} A_l]$$

We have shown that

$$B_t = -(A_t^{-1}\cdot A_l)^T$$

$$B_t^T = -(A_t^{-1}\cdot A_l)$$

Hence, $Q$ can be written as

$$Q = [U : -B_t^T]$$

$$Q_l = -B_t^T$$

**EXAMPLE 8.3**

*For the circuit shown in Fig. 8.19, draw the oriented graph and write the (a) incidence matrix, (b) tieset matrix, and (c) f-cutset matrix.*

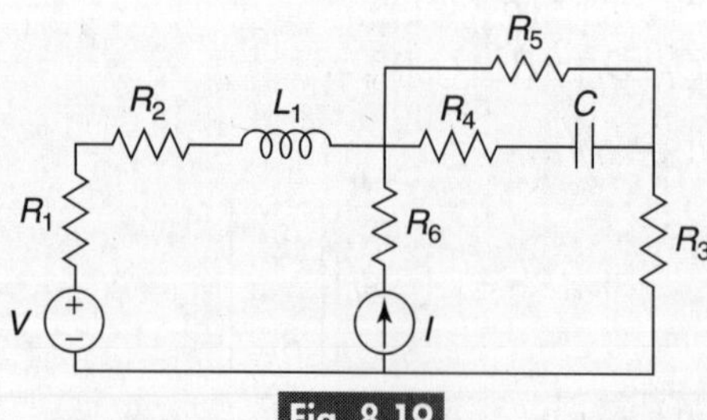


Fig. 8.19

**Solution** For drawing the oriented graph,

1. replace all resistors, inductors and capacitors by line segments,
2. replace the voltage source by short circuit and the current source by an open circuit,
3. assume the directions of branch currents arbitrarily, and
4. number all the nodes and branches.

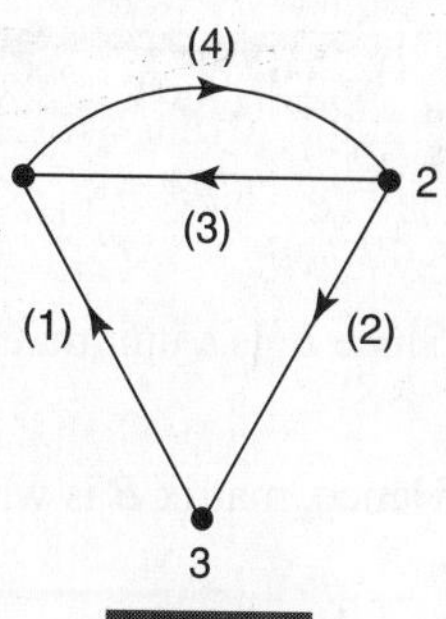

Fig. 8.20

The oriented graph is shown in Fig. 8.20.

(a) Incidence Matrix ($A$)

| Nodes ↓ | Branches → 1 | 2 | 3 | 4 |
|---|---|---|---|---|
| 1 | −1 | 0 | −1 | 1 |
| 2 | 0 | 1 | 1 | −1 |
| 3 | 1 | −1 | 0 | 0 |

$$A_a = \begin{bmatrix} -1 & 0 & -1 & 1 \\ 0 & 1 & 1 & -1 \\ 1 & -1 & 0 & 0 \end{bmatrix}$$

Eliminating the third row from the matrix $A_a$, we get the incidence matrix $A$.

$$A = \begin{bmatrix} -1 & 0 & -1 & 1 \\ 0 & 1 & 1 & -1 \end{bmatrix}$$

(b) Tieset Matrix ($B$)

The oriented graph, selected tree and tiesets are shown in Fig. 8.21.

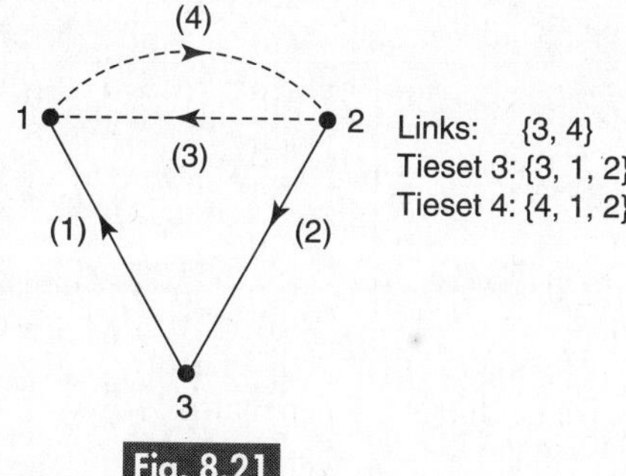

Fig. 8.21

$$B = \begin{matrix} & \begin{matrix} 1 & 2 & 3 & 4 \end{matrix} \\ \begin{matrix} 3 \\ 4 \end{matrix} & \begin{bmatrix} -1 & -1 & 1 & 0 \\ 1 & 1 & 0 & 1 \end{bmatrix} \end{matrix}$$

(c) $f$-cutset Matrix ($Q$)

The oriented graph, selected tree and $f$-cutsets are shown in Fig. 8.22.

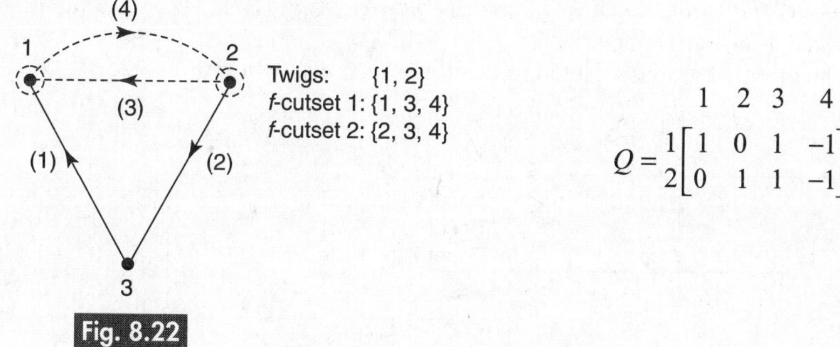


$$Q = \begin{matrix} & \begin{matrix} 1 & 2 & 3 & 4 \end{matrix} \\ \begin{matrix} 1 \\ 2 \end{matrix} & \begin{bmatrix} 1 & 0 & 1 & -1 \\ 0 & 1 & 1 & -1 \end{bmatrix} \end{matrix}$$

Fig. 8.22

## EXAMPLE 8.4

*For the network shown in Fig. 8.23, draw the oriented graph and write the (a) incidence matrix, (b) tieset matrix, and (c) f-cutset matrix.*

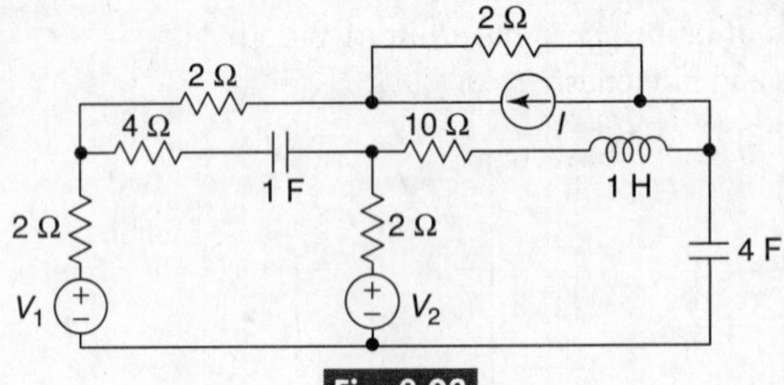


Fig. 8.23

**Solution** For drawing the oriented graph,

1. replace all resistors, inductors and capacitors by line segments,
2. replace all voltage sources by short circuits and current source by an open circuit,
3. assume directions of branch currents arbitrarily, and
4. number all the nodes and branches.

Fig. 8.24

The oriented graph is shown in Fig. 8.24.

(a) Incidence Matrix ($A$)

| Nodes ↓ \ Branches → | 1 | 2 | 3 | 4 | 5 | 6 | 7 |
|---|---|---|---|---|---|---|---|
| 1 | 1 | 0 | 0 | 1 | 0 | 1 | 0 |
| 2 | −1 | −1 | 1 | 0 | 0 | 0 | 0 |
| 3 | 0 | 1 | 0 | 0 | 1 | 0 | 1 |
| 4 | 0 | 0 | −1 | −1 | −1 | 0 | 0 |
| 5 | 0 | 0 | 0 | 0 | 0 | −1 | −1 |

$$A_a = \begin{bmatrix} 1 & 0 & 0 & 1 & 0 & 1 & 0 \\ -1 & -1 & 1 & 0 & 0 & 0 & 0 \\ 0 & 1 & 0 & 0 & 1 & 0 & 1 \\ 0 & 0 & -1 & -1 & -1 & 0 & 0 \\ 0 & 0 & 0 & 0 & 0 & -1 & -1 \end{bmatrix}$$

Eliminating the last row from the matrix $A_a$, we get the incidence matrix $A$.

$$A = \begin{bmatrix} 1 & 0 & 0 & 1 & 0 & 1 & 0 \\ -1 & -1 & 1 & 0 & 0 & 0 & 0 \\ 0 & 1 & 0 & 0 & 1 & 0 & 1 \\ 0 & 0 & -1 & -1 & -1 & 0 & 0 \end{bmatrix}$$

(b) Tieset Matrix ($B$)

The oriented graph, selected tree and tiesets are shown in Fig. 8.25.

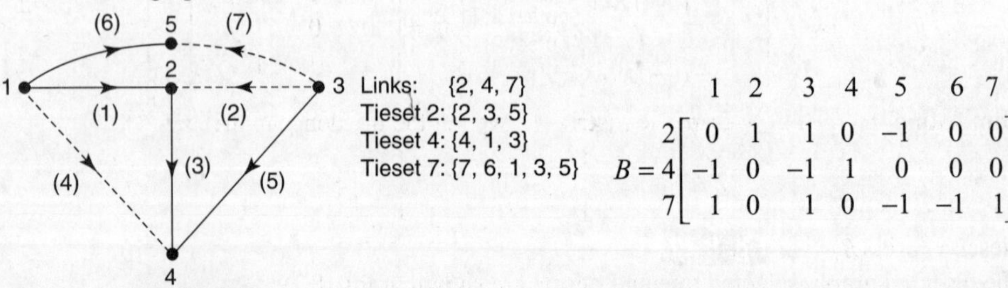

Links: {2, 4, 7}
Tieset 2: {2, 3, 5}
Tieset 4: {4, 1, 3}
Tieset 7: {7, 6, 1, 3, 5}

$$B = \begin{array}{c} \\ 2 \\ 4 \\ 7 \end{array} \begin{array}{c} \begin{matrix} 1 & 2 & 3 & 4 & 5 & 6 & 7 \end{matrix} \\ \begin{bmatrix} 0 & 1 & 1 & 0 & -1 & 0 & 0 \\ -1 & 0 & -1 & 1 & 0 & 0 & 0 \\ 1 & 0 & 1 & 0 & -1 & -1 & 1 \end{bmatrix} \end{array}$$

Fig. 8.25

(c) *f*-cutset Matrix ($Q$)

The oriented graph, selected tree and *f*-cutsets are shown in Fig. 8.26.

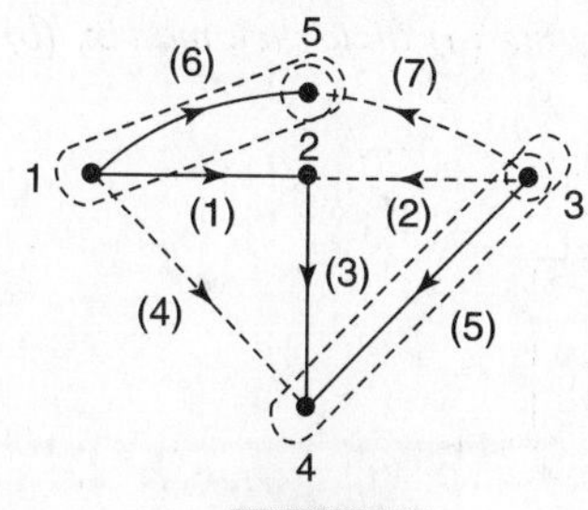


Twigs: {1, 3, 5, 6}
*f*-cutset 1: {1, 4, 7}
*f*-cutset 3: {3, 4, 7, 2}
*f*-cutset 5: {5, 2, 7}
*f*-cutset 6: {6, 7}

$$Q = \begin{array}{c} \\ 1 \\ 3 \\ 5 \\ 6 \end{array}\begin{array}{c} \begin{array}{ccccccc} 1 & 2 & 3 & 4 & 5 & 6 & 7 \end{array} \\ \begin{bmatrix} 1 & 0 & 0 & 1 & 0 & 0 & -1 \\ 0 & -1 & 1 & 1 & 0 & 0 & -1 \\ 0 & 1 & 0 & 0 & 1 & 0 & 1 \\ 0 & 0 & 0 & 0 & 0 & 1 & 1 \end{bmatrix} \end{array}$$

Fig. 8.26

## EXAMPLE 8.5

*For the circuit shown in Fig. 8.27, draw the oriented graph and write (a) incidence matrix, (b) tieset matrix, and (c) cutset matrix.*

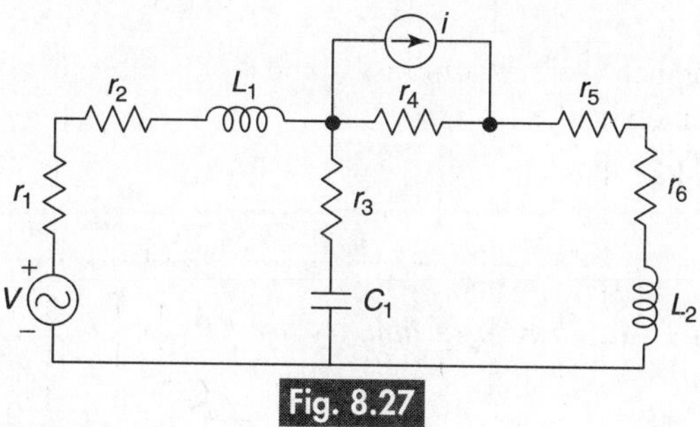


Fig. 8.27

**Solution** For drawing the oriented graph,

1. replace all resistors, inductors and capacitors by line segments,
2. replace voltage source by short circuit and current source by an open circuit,
3. assume directions of branch currents arbitrarily, and
4. number the nodes and branches.

The oriented graph is shown in Fig. 8.28.

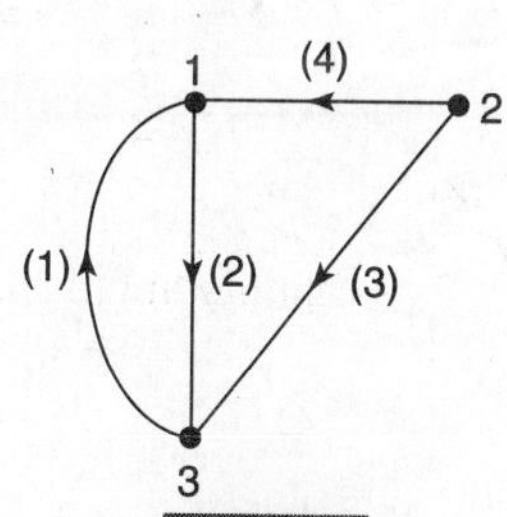


Fig. 8.28

(a) Incidence Matrix ($A$)

| Nodes ↓ | Branches → 1 | 2 | 3 | 4 |
|---|---|---|---|---|
| 1 | −1 | 1 | 0 | −1 |
| 2 | 0 | 0 | 1 | 1 |
| 3 | 1 | −1 | −1 | 0 |

$$A_a = \begin{bmatrix} -1 & 1 & 0 & -1 \\ 0 & 0 & 1 & 1 \\ 1 & -1 & -1 & 0 \end{bmatrix}$$

Eliminating the third row from the matrix $A_a$, we get the incidence matrix $A$.

$$A = \begin{bmatrix} -1 & 1 & 0 & -1 \\ 0 & 0 & 1 & 1 \end{bmatrix}$$

(b) Tieset Matrix ($B$)

The oriented graph, selected tree and tiesets are shown in Fig. 8.29.

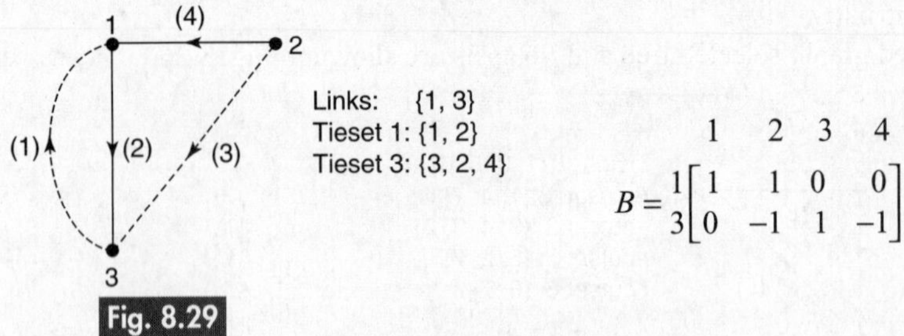


$$B = \begin{matrix} & \begin{matrix} 1 & 2 & 3 & 4 \end{matrix} \\ \begin{matrix} 1 \\ 3 \end{matrix} & \begin{bmatrix} 1 & 1 & 0 & 0 \\ 0 & -1 & 1 & -1 \end{bmatrix} \end{matrix}$$

Fig. 8.29

(c) *f*-cutset Matrix ($Q$)

The oriented graph, selected tree and *f*-cutsets are shown in Fig. 8.30.

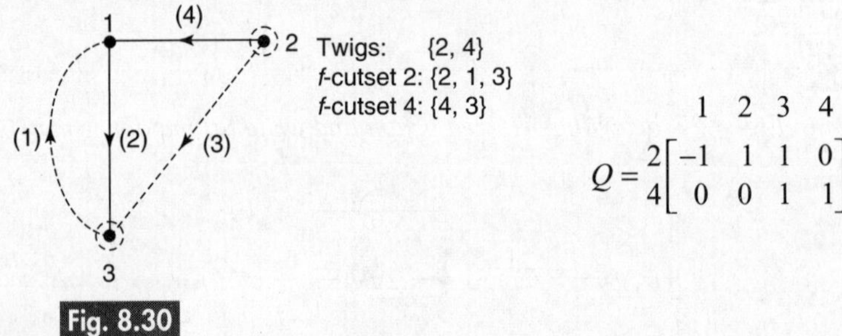


$$Q = \begin{matrix} & \begin{matrix} 1 & 2 & 3 & 4 \end{matrix} \\ \begin{matrix} 2 \\ 4 \end{matrix} & \begin{bmatrix} -1 & 1 & 1 & 0 \\ 0 & 0 & 1 & 1 \end{bmatrix} \end{matrix}$$

Fig. 8.30

## EXAMPLE 8.6

*For the circuit shown in Fig. 8.31, (a) draw its graph, (b) draw its tree, and (c) write the fundamental cutset matrix.*

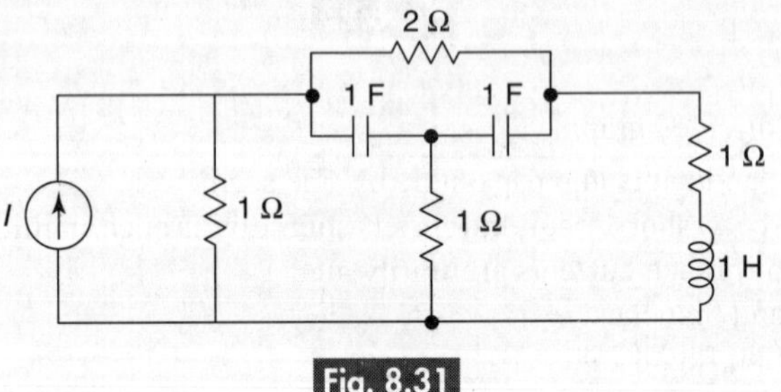


Fig. 8.31

**Solution**

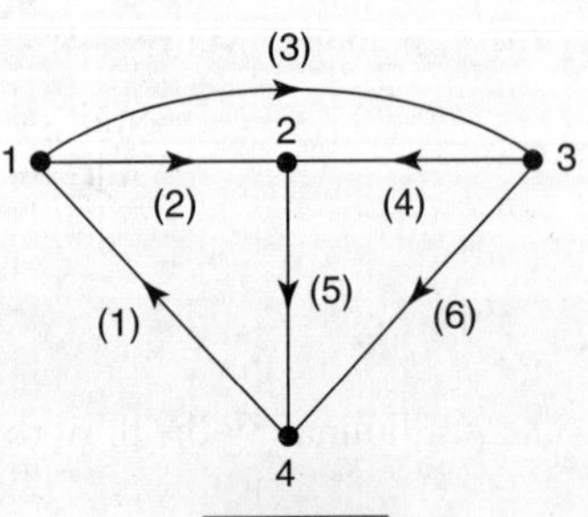


Fig. 8.32

(a) For drawing the oriented graph,

1. replace all resistors, inductors and capacitors by line segments,
2. replace the current source by an open circuit,
3. assume directions of branch currents, and
4. number all the nodes and branches.

The oriented graph is shown in Fig. 8.32.

(b) Tree

The oriented graph and its selected tree are shown in Fig. 8.33.

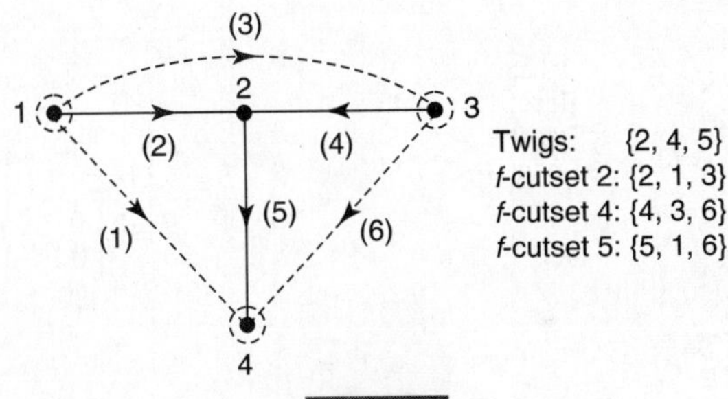


Fig. 8.33

(c) Fundamental Cutset Matrix ($Q$)

$$Q = \begin{matrix} & 1 & 2 & 3 & 4 & 5 & 6 \\ 2 & 1 & 1 & 1 & 0 & 0 & 0 \\ 4 & 0 & 0 & -1 & 1 & 0 & 1 \\ 5 & 1 & 0 & 0 & 0 & 1 & 1 \end{matrix}$$

## EXAMPLE 8.7

*The graph of a network is shown in Fig. 8.34. Write the (a) incidence matrix, (b) tieset matrix, and (c) f-cutset matrix.*

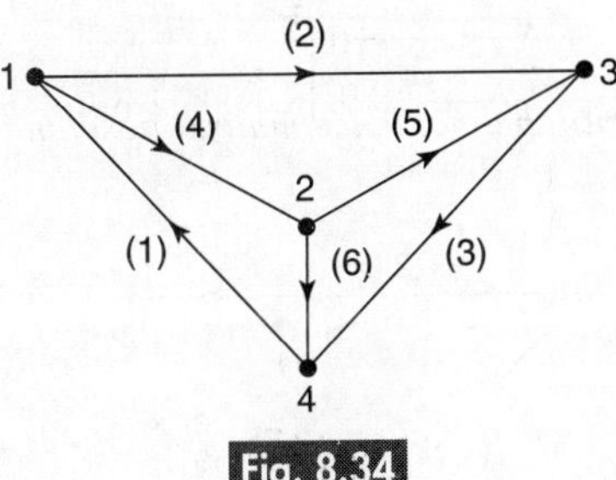


Fig. 8.34

**Solution**

(a) Incidence Matrix ($A$)

$$A_a = \begin{matrix} & 1 & 2 & 3 & 4 & 5 & 6 \\ 1 & -1 & 1 & 0 & 1 & 0 & 0 \\ 2 & 0 & 0 & 0 & -1 & 1 & 1 \\ 3 & 0 & -1 & 1 & 0 & -1 & 0 \\ 4 & 1 & 0 & -1 & 0 & 0 & -1 \end{matrix}$$

The incidence matrix $A$ is obtained by eliminating any row from the matrix $A_a$.

$$A = \begin{bmatrix} -1 & 1 & 0 & 1 & 0 & 0 \\ 0 & 0 & 0 & -1 & 1 & 1 \\ 0 & -1 & 1 & 0 & -1 & 0 \end{bmatrix}$$

(b) Tieset, Matrix ($B$)

The oriented graph, selected tree and tiesets are shown in Fig. 8.35.

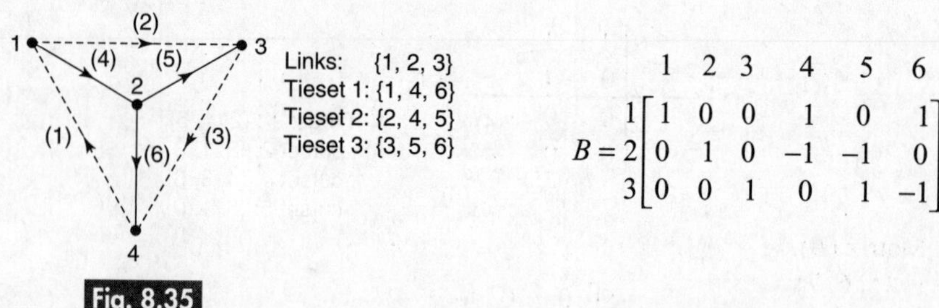


$$B = \begin{array}{c} \\ 1 \\ 2 \\ 3 \end{array}\begin{array}{c} \begin{array}{cccccc} 1 & 2 & 3 & 4 & 5 & 6 \end{array} \\ \begin{bmatrix} 1 & 0 & 0 & 1 & 0 & 1 \\ 0 & 1 & 0 & -1 & -1 & 0 \\ 0 & 0 & 1 & 0 & 1 & -1 \end{bmatrix} \end{array}$$

Fig. 8.35

(c) *f*-cutset Matrix ($Q$)

The oriented graph, selected tree and *f*-cutsets are shown in Fig. 8.36.

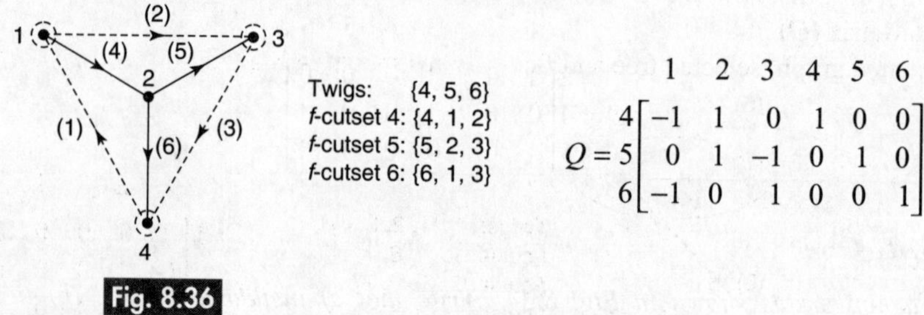


$$Q = \begin{array}{c} \\ 4 \\ 5 \\ 6 \end{array}\begin{array}{c} \begin{array}{cccccc} 1 & 2 & 3 & 4 & 5 & 6 \end{array} \\ \begin{bmatrix} -1 & 1 & 0 & 1 & 0 & 0 \\ 0 & 1 & -1 & 0 & 1 & 0 \\ -1 & 0 & 1 & 0 & 0 & 1 \end{bmatrix} \end{array}$$

Fig. 8.36

**EXAMPLE 8.8**

*For the graph shown in Fig. 8.37, write the incidence matrix, tieset matrix and f-cutset matrix.*

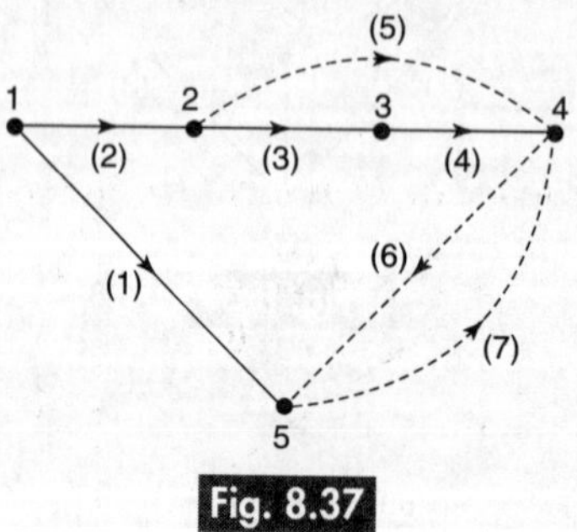

Fig. 8.37

**Solution**

(a) Incidence Matrix ($A$)

$$A_a = \begin{array}{c} \\ 1 \\ 2 \\ 3 \\ 4 \\ 5 \end{array}\begin{array}{c} \begin{array}{ccccccc} 1 & 2 & 3 & 4 & 5 & 6 & 7 \end{array} \\ \begin{bmatrix} 1 & 1 & 0 & 0 & 0 & 0 & 0 \\ 0 & -1 & 1 & 0 & 1 & 0 & 0 \\ 0 & 0 & -1 & 1 & 0 & 0 & 0 \\ 0 & 0 & 0 & -1 & -1 & 1 & -1 \\ -1 & 0 & 0 & 0 & 0 & -1 & 1 \end{bmatrix} \end{array}$$

The incidence matrix $A$ is obtained by eliminating any row from the matrix $A_a$.

$$A = \begin{bmatrix} 1 & 1 & 0 & 0 & 0 & 0 & 0 \\ 0 & -1 & 1 & 0 & 1 & 0 & 0 \\ 0 & 0 & -1 & 1 & 0 & 0 & 0 \\ 0 & 0 & 0 & -1 & -1 & 1 & -1 \end{bmatrix}$$

(b) Tieset Matrix ($B$)

Links: {5, 6, 7}

Tieset 5: {5, 3, 4}

Tieset 6: {6, 1, 2, 3, 4}

Tieset 7: {7, 1, 2, 3, 4}

$$B = \begin{matrix} & 1 & 2 & 3 & 4 & 5 & 6 & 7 \\ 5 & 0 & 0 & -1 & -1 & 1 & 0 & 0 \\ 6 & -1 & 1 & 1 & 1 & 0 & 1 & 0 \\ 7 & 1 & -1 & -1 & -1 & 0 & 0 & 1 \end{matrix}$$

(c) $f$-cutset Matrix ($Q$)

The oriented graph, selected tree and $f$-cutsets are shown in Fig. 8.38.

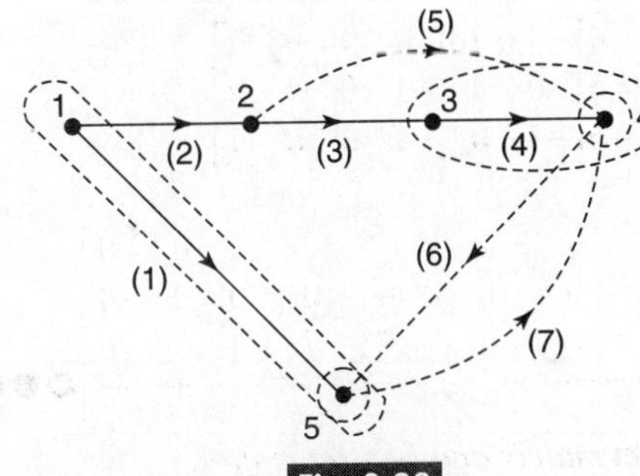


Twigs: {1, 2, 3, 4}

$f$-cutset 1: {1, 6, 7}

$f$-cutset 2: {2, 6, 7}

$f$-cutset 3: {3, 5, 6, 7}

$f$-cutset 4: {4, 5, 6, 7}

$$Q = \begin{matrix} & 1 & 2 & 3 & 4 & 5 & 6 & 7 \\ 1 & 1 & 0 & 0 & 0 & 0 & 1 & -1 \\ 2 & 0 & 1 & 0 & 0 & 0 & -1 & 1 \\ 3 & 0 & 0 & 1 & 0 & 1 & -1 & 1 \\ 4 & 0 & 0 & 0 & 1 & 1 & -1 & 1 \end{matrix}$$

Fig. 8.38

## EXAMPLE 8.9

*For the graph shown in Fig. 8.39, write the incidence matrix, tieset matrix and f-cutset matrix.*

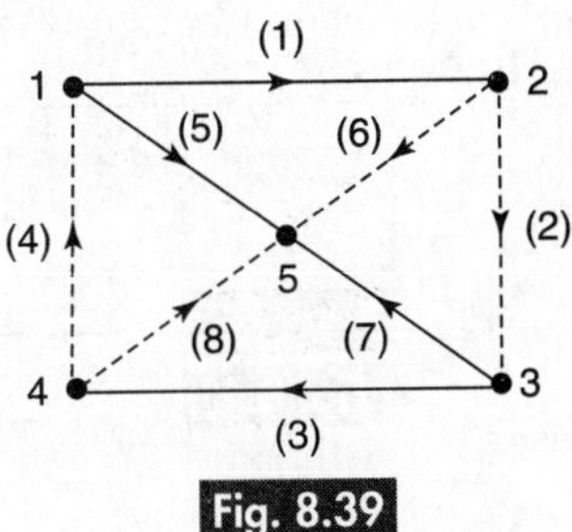


Fig. 8.39

**Solution**

(a) Incidence Matrix ($A$)

$$A_a = \begin{matrix} & 1 & 2 & 3 & 4 & 5 & 6 & 7 & 8 \\ 1 & 1 & 0 & 0 & -1 & 1 & 0 & 0 & 0 \\ 2 & -1 & 1 & 0 & 0 & 0 & 1 & 0 & 0 \\ 3 & 0 & -1 & 1 & 0 & 0 & 0 & 1 & 0 \\ 4 & 0 & 0 & -1 & 1 & 0 & 0 & 0 & 1 \\ 5 & 0 & 0 & 0 & 0 & -1 & -1 & -1 & -1 \end{matrix}$$

The incidence matrix is obtained by eliminating any one row.

$$A = \begin{bmatrix} 1 & 0 & 0 & -1 & 1 & 0 & 0 & 0 \\ -1 & 1 & 0 & 0 & 0 & 1 & 0 & 0 \\ 0 & -1 & 1 & 0 & 0 & 0 & 1 & 0 \\ 0 & 0 & -1 & 1 & 0 & 0 & 0 & 1 \end{bmatrix}$$

(b) Tieset Matrix ($B$)

Links: {2, 4, 6, 8}

Tieset 2: {2, 7, 5, 1}

Tieset 4: {4, 5, 7, 3}

Tieset 6: {6, 5, 1}

Tieset 8: {8, 7, 3}

$$B = \begin{array}{c} \\ 2 \\ 4 \\ 6 \\ 8 \end{array} \begin{array}{c} \begin{matrix} 1 & 2 & 3 & 4 & 5 & 6 & 7 & 8 \end{matrix} \\ \begin{bmatrix} 1 & 1 & 0 & 0 & -1 & 0 & 1 & 0 \\ 0 & 0 & 1 & 1 & 1 & 0 & -1 & 0 \\ 1 & 0 & 0 & 0 & -1 & 1 & 0 & 0 \\ 0 & 0 & 1 & 0 & 0 & 0 & -1 & 1 \end{bmatrix} \end{array}$$

(c) $f$-cutset Matrix ($Q$)

The oriented graph, selected tree and $f$-cutsets are shown in Fig. 8.40.

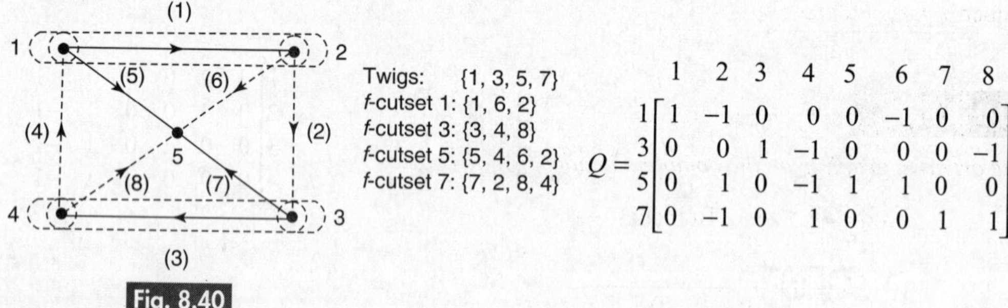


Twigs: {1, 3, 5, 7}

$f$-cutset 1: {1, 6, 2}

$f$-cutset 3: {3, 4, 8}

$f$-cutset 5: {5, 4, 6, 2}

$f$-cutset 7: {7, 2, 8, 4}

$$Q = \begin{array}{c} \\ 1 \\ 3 \\ 5 \\ 7 \end{array} \begin{array}{c} \begin{matrix} 1 & 2 & 3 & 4 & 5 & 6 & 7 & 8 \end{matrix} \\ \begin{bmatrix} 1 & -1 & 0 & 0 & 0 & -1 & 0 & 0 \\ 0 & 0 & 1 & -1 & 0 & 0 & 0 & -1 \\ 0 & 1 & 0 & -1 & 1 & 1 & 0 & 0 \\ 0 & -1 & 0 & 1 & 0 & 0 & 1 & 1 \end{bmatrix} \end{array}$$

Fig. 8.40

## EXAMPLE 8.10

*How many trees are possible for the graph of the network of Fig. 8.41.*

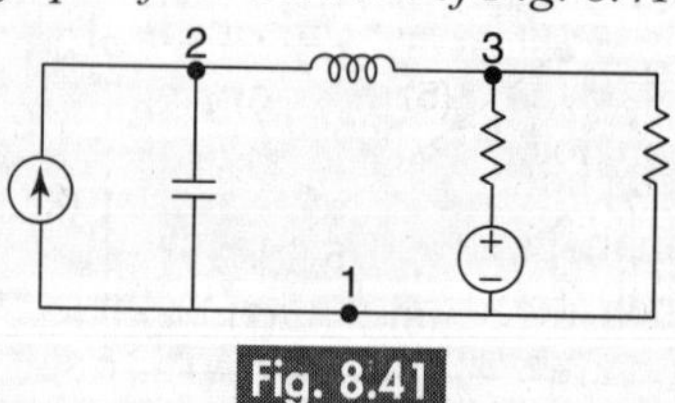


Fig. 8.41

**Solution** To draw the graph,

1. replace all resistors, inductors and capacitors by line segments,
2. replace voltage source by short circuit and current source by an open circuit,
3. assume directions of branch currents arbitrarily, and
4. number all the nodes and branches.

The oriented graph is shown in Fig. 8.42.

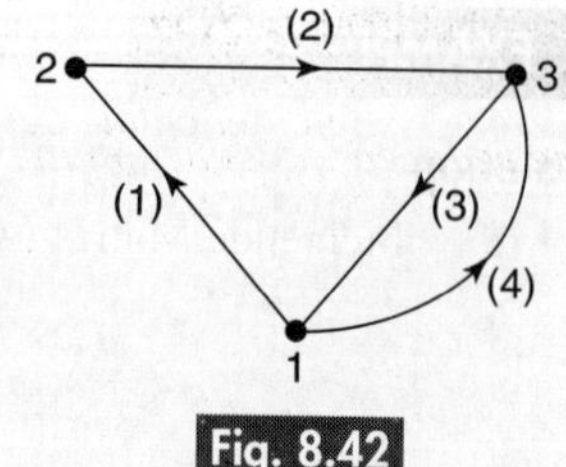


Fig. 8.42

The complete incidence matrix ($A_a$) is written as

$$A_a = \begin{matrix} & \begin{matrix} 1 & 2 & 3 & 4 \end{matrix} \\ \begin{matrix} 1 \\ 2 \\ 3 \end{matrix} & \begin{bmatrix} 1 & 0 & -1 & 1 \\ -1 & 1 & 0 & 0 \\ 0 & -1 & 1 & -1 \end{bmatrix} \end{matrix}$$

The reduced incidence matrix $A$ is obtained by eliminating the last row from matrix $A_a$.

$$A = \begin{bmatrix} 1 & 0 & -1 & 1 \\ -1 & 1 & 0 & 0 \end{bmatrix}$$

$$AA^T = \begin{bmatrix} 1 & 0 & -1 & 1 \\ -1 & 1 & 0 & 0 \end{bmatrix} \begin{bmatrix} 1 & -1 \\ 0 & 1 \\ -1 & 0 \\ 1 & 0 \end{bmatrix} = \begin{bmatrix} 3 & -1 \\ -1 & 2 \end{bmatrix}$$

The number of possible trees $= \left|AA^T\right| = \begin{vmatrix} 3 & -1 \\ -1 & 2 \end{vmatrix} = 6 - 1 = 5.$

## EXAMPLE 8.11

*Draw the oriented graph from the complete incidence matrix given below;*

| Nodes ↓ | Branches → 1 | 2 | 3 | 4 | 5 | 6 | 7 | 8 |
|---|---|---|---|---|---|---|---|---|
| 1 | 1 | 0 | 0 | 0 | 1 | 0 | 0 | 1 |
| 2 | 0 | 1 | 0 | 0 | −1 | 1 | 0 | 0 |
| 3 | 0 | 0 | 1 | 0 | 0 | −1 | 1 | −1 |
| 4 | 0 | 0 | 0 | 1 | 0 | 0 | −1 | 0 |
| 5 | −1 | −1 | −1 | −1 | 0 | 0 | 0 | 0 |

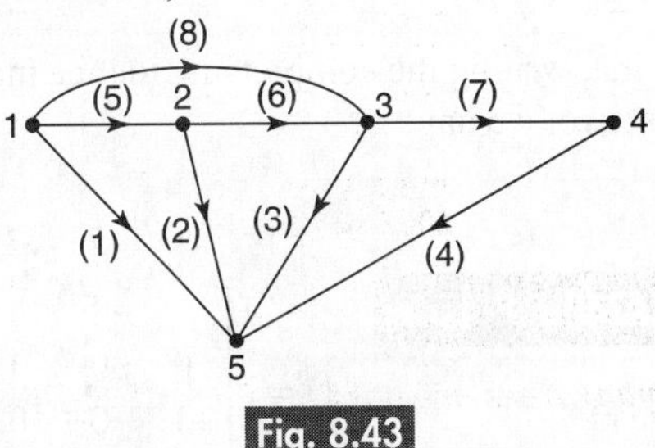

Fig. 8.43

**Solution** First, note down the nodes 1, 2, 3, 4, 5, as shown in Fig. 8.43. From the complete incidence matrix, it is clear that branch 1 is between nodes 1 and 5 and it is going away from node 1 and towards node 5, as the entry against node 1 is 1 and that against 5 is −1. Hence, connect the nodes 1 and 5 by a line, point the arrow towards 5 and call it branch 1, as shown in Fig. 8.43. Similarly, draw the other oriented branches.

## EXAMPLE 8.12

*The reduced incidence matrix of an oriented graph is given below. Draw the graph.*

$$A = \begin{bmatrix} 0 & -1 & 1 & 1 & 0 \\ 0 & 0 & -1 & -1 & -1 \\ -1 & 0 & 0 & 0 & 1 \end{bmatrix}$$

**Solution** First, writing the complete incidence matrix from the matrix $A$ such that the sum of all entries in each column of $A_a$ will be zero, we have

$$A_a = \begin{array}{c} \\ 1 \\ 2 \\ 3 \\ 4 \end{array}\begin{array}{c} \begin{array}{ccccc} 1 & 2 & 3 & 4 & 5 \end{array} \\ \begin{bmatrix} 0 & -1 & 1 & 1 & 0 \\ 0 & 0 & -1 & -1 & -1 \\ -1 & 0 & 0 & 0 & 1 \\ 1 & 1 & 0 & 0 & 0 \end{bmatrix} \end{array}$$

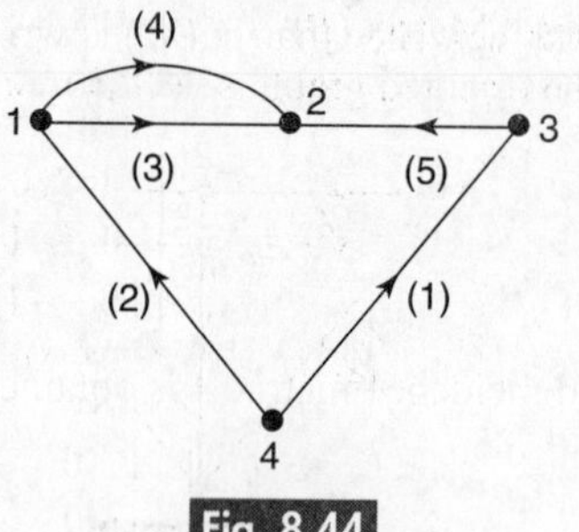


Fig. 8.44

Now, the oriented graph can be drawn with matrix $A_a$, as shown in Fig. 8.44.

## EXAMPLE 8.13

*The reduced incidence matrix of an oriented graph is*

$$A = \begin{bmatrix} 0 & -1 & 1 & 0 & 0 \\ 0 & 0 & -1 & -1 & -1 \\ -1 & 0 & 0 & 0 & 1 \end{bmatrix}$$

*(a) Draw the graph. (b) How many trees are possible for this graph? (c) Write the tieset and cutset matrices.*

**Solution**

(a) First, writing the complete incidence matrix $A_a$ such that the sum of all the entries in each column of $A_a$ is zero, we have

$$A_a = \begin{array}{c} \\ 1 \\ 2 \\ 3 \\ 4 \end{array}\begin{array}{c} \begin{array}{ccccc} 1 & 2 & 3 & 4 & 5 \end{array} \\ \begin{bmatrix} 0 & -1 & 1 & 0 & 0 \\ 0 & 0 & -1 & -1 & -1 \\ -1 & 0 & 0 & 0 & 1 \\ 1 & 1 & 0 & 1 & 0 \end{bmatrix} \end{array}$$

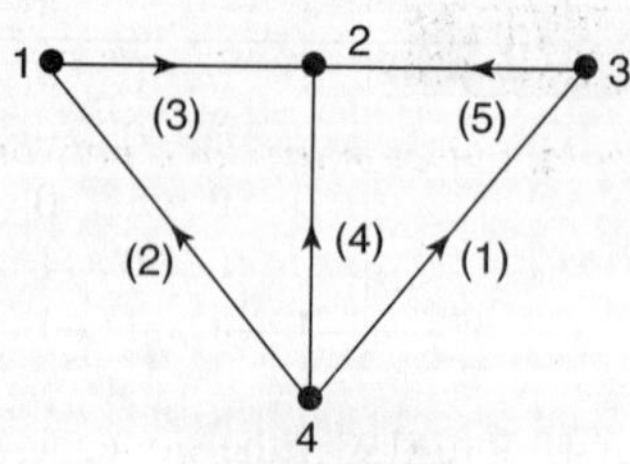


Fig. 8.45

Now, the oriented graph can be drawn with the matrix $A_a$, as shown in Fig. 8.45.

(b) The number of possible trees = $|AA^T|$

$$AA^T = \begin{bmatrix} 0 & -1 & 1 & 0 & 0 \\ 0 & 0 & -1 & -1 & -1 \\ -1 & 0 & 0 & 0 & 1 \end{bmatrix}\begin{bmatrix} 0 & 0 & -1 \\ -1 & 0 & 0 \\ 1 & -1 & 0 \\ 0 & -1 & 0 \\ 0 & -1 & 1 \end{bmatrix} = \begin{bmatrix} 2 & -1 & 0 \\ -1 & 3 & -1 \\ 0 & -1 & 2 \end{bmatrix}$$

$$\left|AA^T\right| = \begin{vmatrix} 2 & -1 & 0 \\ -1 & 3 & -1 \\ 0 & -1 & 2 \end{vmatrix} = 2(6-1)+1(-2) = 8$$

The number of possible trees = 8.

(c) Tieset Matrix ($B$)

The oriented graph, selected tree and tiesets are shown in Fig. 8.46.

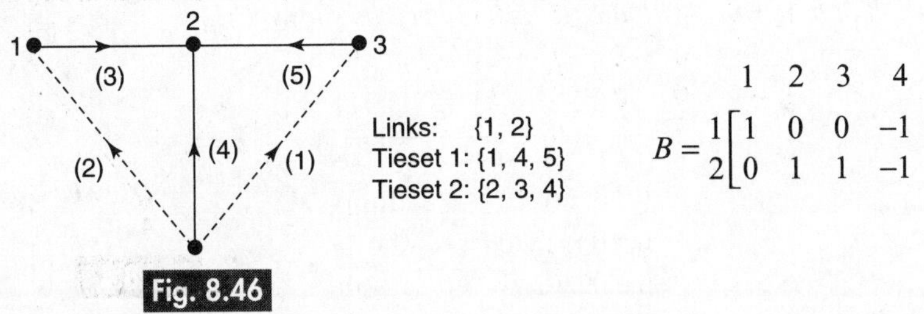


$$B = \begin{array}{c} \\ 1 \\ 2 \end{array} \overset{\begin{array}{ccccc} 1 & 2 & 3 & 4 & 5 \end{array}}{\begin{bmatrix} 1 & 0 & 0 & -1 & 1 \\ 0 & 1 & 1 & -1 & 0 \end{bmatrix}}$$

Fig. 8.46

$f$-cutset Matrix ($Q$)

The oriented graph, selected tree and $f$-cutsets are shown in Fig. 8.47.

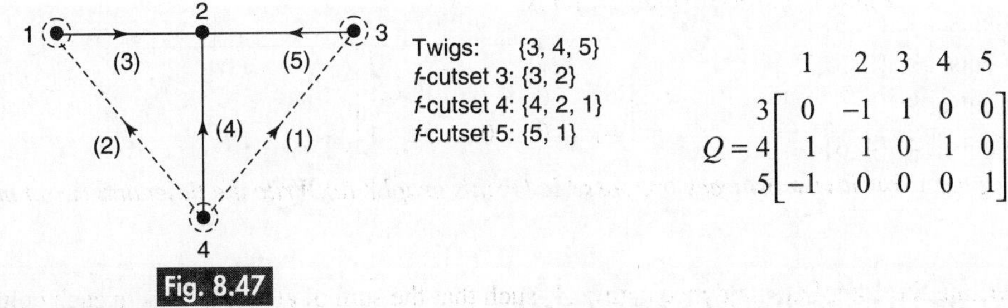


$$Q = \begin{array}{c} 3 \\ 4 \\ 5 \end{array} \overset{\begin{array}{ccccc} 1 & 2 & 3 & 4 & 5 \end{array}}{\begin{bmatrix} 0 & -1 & 1 & 0 & 0 \\ 1 & 1 & 0 & 1 & 0 \\ -1 & 0 & 0 & 0 & 1 \end{bmatrix}}$$

Fig. 8.47

## EXAMPLE 8.14

*The fundamental cutset matrix of a network is given as follows;*

| *Twigs* | | | *Links* | | |
|---|---|---|---|---|---|
| $a$ | $c$ | $e$ | $b$ | $d$ | $f$ |
| 1 | 0 | 0 | 1 | 0 | 1 |
| 0 | 1 | 0 | 0 | 1 | 1 |
| 0 | 0 | 1 | 1 | 1 | 1 |

*Draw the oriented graph.*

**Solution** No. of links $l = b - n + 1$

No. of nodes $n = b - l + 1 = 6 - 3 + 1 = 4$

$f$-cutsets are written as

$f$-cutsets $a$: $\{a, b, f\}$

$f$-cutsets $c$: $\{c, d, f\}$

$f$-cutsets $e$: $\{e, b, d, f\}$

The oriented graph is drawn, as shown in Fig. 8.48.

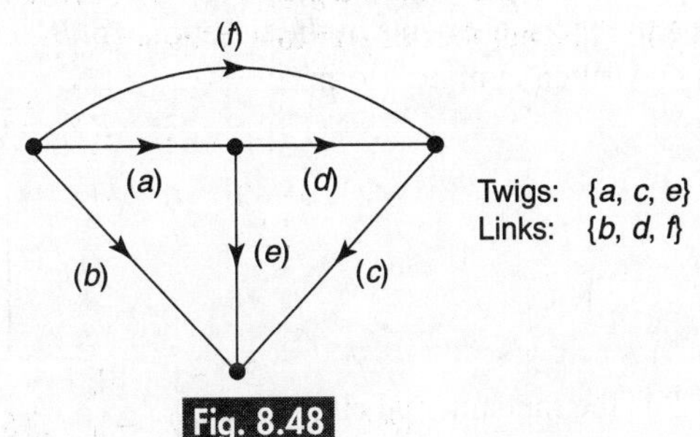


Fig. 8.48

## EXAMPLE 8.15

*Draw the oriented graph of a network with the f-cutset matrix, as shown below:*

| *Twigs* | | | | *Links* | | |
|---|---|---|---|---|---|---|
| 1 | 2 | 3 | 4 | 5 | 6 | 7 |
| 1 | 0 | 0 | 0 | −1 | 0 | 0 |
| 0 | 1 | 0 | 0 | 1 | 0 | 1 |
| 0 | 0 | 1 | 0 | 0 | 1 | 1 |
| 0 | 0 | 0 | 1 | 0 | 1 | 0 |

**Solution** No. of links $l = b - n + 1$

No. of nodes $n = b - l + 1 = 7 - 3 + 1 = 5$

*f*-cutsets are written as

*f*-cutset 1: {1, 5}

*f*-cutset 2: {2, 5, 7}

*f*-cutset 3: {3, 6, 7}

*f*-cutset 4: {4, 6}

Then oriented graph can be drawn, as shown in Fig. 8.49.

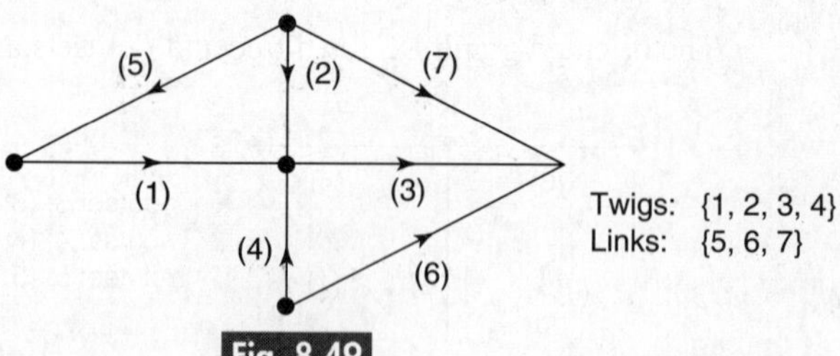


Fig. 8.49

## 8.7 KIRCHHOFF'S VOLTAGE LAW

LO 8.7

Express *KVL* in terms of *f*-circuit matrix

KVL states that if $v_k$ is the voltage drop across the $k^{th}$ branch, then

$$\sum v_k = 0$$

the sum being taken over all the branches in a given loop. If *l* is the number of loops or *f*-circuits, then there will be *l* number of KVL equations, one for each loop. The KVL equation for the *f*-circuit or loop '*l*' can be written as

$$\sum_{k=1}^{b} b_{ik}\, v_k = 0 \qquad (i = 1, 2, \ldots, l)$$

where $b_{ik}$ is the elements of the tieset matrix *B*, *b* being the number of branches. The set of *l* KVL equations can be written in matrix form.

$$BV_b = 0$$

where $V_b = \begin{bmatrix} v_1 \\ v_2 \\ \vdots \\ v_b \end{bmatrix}$ is a column vector of branch voltages.

and *B* is the fundamental circuit matrix.

## 8.8 KIRCHHOFF'S CURRENT LAW

LO 8.8

Express *KCL* in terms of incidence and *f*-cutset matrices

KCL states that if $i_k$ is the current in the $k^{\text{th}}$ branch then at a given node

$$\sum i_k = 0$$

the sum being taken over all the branches incident at a given node. If there are '$n$' nodes, there will '$n$' such equations, one for each node

$$\sum_{k=1}^{b} a_{ik}\, i_k = 0 \qquad (i = 1, 2, \ldots, n)$$

so that set of $n$ equations can be written in matrix form.

$$A_a\, I_b = 0 \qquad \ldots(8.4)$$

where $I_b = \begin{bmatrix} i_1 \\ i_2 \\ \vdots \\ i_b \end{bmatrix}$ is a column vector of branch currents.

and $A_a$ is the complete incidence matrix.

If one node is taken as reference node or datum node, we can write Eq. (8.4) as

$$AI_b = 0 \qquad \ldots(8.5)$$

where $A$ is the incidence matrix of order $(n - 1) \times b$.

We know that $A = A_t\, Q$

Equation (8.5) can be written as

$$A_t\, QI_b = 0$$

Premultiplying with $A_t^{-1}$,

$$A_t^{-1} A_t\, Q\, I_b = A_t^{-1} \cdot 0$$

$$I\, Q\, I_b = 0$$

$$Q\, I_b = 0$$

where $Q$ is the $f$-cutset matrix.

## 8.9 RELATION BETWEEN BRANCH VOLTAGE MATRIX $V_b$, TWIG VOLTAGE MATRIX $V_t$ AND NODE VOLTAGE MATRIX $V_n$

LO 8.9

Describe the relation between branch voltage matrix $V_b$, twig voltage matrix $V_t$ and node voltage matrix $V_n$

We know that $B V_b = 0$

$$[B_t : B_l]\begin{bmatrix} V_t \\ \cdots \\ V_l \end{bmatrix} = 0$$

$$B_t\, V_t + B_l\, V_l = 0$$

$$B_l\, V_l = -B_t\, V_t$$

Premultiplying with $B_l^{-1}$,

$$V_l = -B_l^{-1} B_t V_t = -(B_l^{-1} B_t) V_t$$

Now,

$$V_b = \begin{bmatrix} V_t \\ \cdots \\ V_l \end{bmatrix}$$

$$= \begin{bmatrix} V_t \\ \cdots \\ -\left(B_l^{-1} B_t\right) V_t \end{bmatrix} = \begin{bmatrix} U \\ \cdots \\ -\left(B_l^{-1} B_t\right) \end{bmatrix} \cdot V_t \qquad \ldots(8.6)$$

Also,

$$V_b = Q^T V_t$$

$$Q = A_t^{-1} A$$

$$Q^T = A^T (A_t^{-1})^T = A^T (A_t^T)^{-1}$$

Hence, Eq. (8.6) can be written as

$$V_b = A^T (A_t^T)^{-1} V_t = A^T \left\{ (A_t^T)^{-1} V_t \right\} = A^T V_n$$

where $V_n = (A_t^T)^{-1} V_t$ is node voltage matrix.

## 8.10 RELATION BETWEEN BRANCH CURRENT MATRIX $I_b$ AND LOOP CURRENT MATRIX $I_l$

LO 8.10

Describe the relation between current matrix $I_b$ and loop current matrix $I_l$

We know that

$$A I_b = 0$$

$$[A_t : A_l] \begin{bmatrix} I_t \\ \cdots \\ I_l \end{bmatrix} = 0$$

$$A_t I_t + A_l I_l = 0$$

$$A_t I_t = -A_l I_l$$

Premultiplying with $A_t^{-1}$,

$$I_t = -A_t^{-1} A_l I_l = -(A_t^{-1} A_l) I_l$$

Now,

$$I_b = \begin{bmatrix} I_t \\ \cdots \\ I_l \end{bmatrix} = \begin{bmatrix} -(A_t^{-1} A_l) I_l \\ \cdots \\ I_l \end{bmatrix} = \begin{bmatrix} -(A_t^{-1} A_l) \\ \cdots \\ U \end{bmatrix} \cdot I_l$$

$$I_b = B^T I_l$$

## 8.11 NETWORK EQUILIBRIUM EQUATIONS

LO 8.11

Derive and explain network equilibrium equations

### 8.11.1 KVL Equation

1. If there is a voltage source $v_{sk}$ in branch $k$, having impedance $z_k$ and carrying current $i_k$, as shown in Fig. 8.50,

$$v_k = z_k\, i_k - v_{sk} \qquad (k = 1, 2, \ldots, b)$$

In matrix form,

$$V_b = Z_b\, I_b - V_s$$

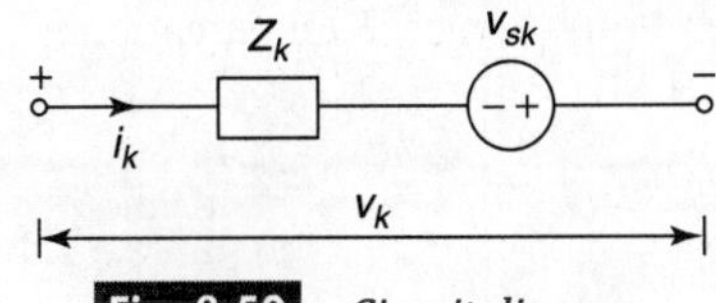


Fig. 8.50 *Circuit diagram*

where $Z_b$ is the branch impedance matrix, $I_b$ is the column vector of branch currents and $V_s$ is the column vector of source voltages. Hence, KVL equation can be written as

$$B V_b = 0$$

$$B(Z_b\, I_b - V_s) = 0$$

$$B\, Z_b\, I_b = B V_s$$

Also, $$I_b = B^T I_l$$

$$B\, Z_b\, B^T\, I_l = B V_s$$

$$Z I_l = E$$

where $$E = B V_s$$

and $$Z = B\, Z_b\, B^T$$

The matrix $Z$ is called *loop impedance matrix*.

2. If there is a voltage source in series with an impedance and a current source in parallel with the combination, as shown in Fig. 8.51,

$$i_k = \frac{(v_k + v_{sk})}{zk} - i_{sk}$$

$$v_k = z_k\, i_k + z_k\, i_{sk} - v_{sk}$$

In matrix form,

$$V_b = Z_b\, I_b + Z_b\, I_s - V_s$$

Fig. 8.51 *Circuit diagram*

KVL equation is $B V_b = 0$.

$$B V_b = B(Z_b\, I_b + Z_b\, I_s - V_s) = 0$$

$$B\, Z_b\, I_b = B V_s - B\, Z_b\, I_s$$

Now, $$I_b = B^T I_l$$

$$B\, Z_b B^T I_l = B V_s - B\, Z_b\, I_s$$

$$Z I_l = B V_s - B\, Z_b\, I_s$$

where $Z = B\, Z_b\, B^T$ is the loop impedance matrix. This is the generalised KVL equation.

### 8.11.2 KCL Equation

1. If the branch $k$ contains an input current source $i_{sk}$ and an admittance $y_k$, as shown in Fig. 8.52,

$$i_k = y_k v_k - i_{sk} \qquad (k = 1, 2,\ldots, b)$$

In the matrix form,

$$I_b = Y_b V_b - I_s$$

where $Y_b$ is the branch admittance matrix.
Hence, KCL equation is given by

$$A I_b = 0$$
$$A(Y_b V_b - I_s) = 0$$
$$A Y_b V_b = A I_s$$

Also,
$$V_b = A^T V_n$$
$$A Y_b A^T V_n = A I_s$$
$$Y V_n = I$$

where
$$Y = A Y_b A^T$$

and
$$I = A I_s$$

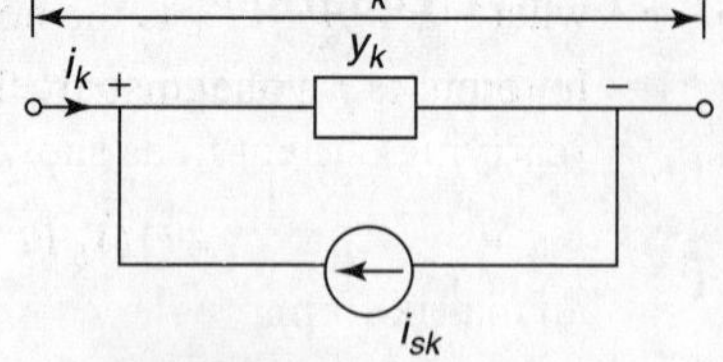


Fig. 8.52 *Circuit diagram*

The matrix $Y$ is called *admittance matrix*. This is the KCL equation in matrix form.
In terms of *f*-cutset matrix, the KCL equation can be written as

$$Q I_b = 0$$
$$Q(Y_b V_b - V_s) = 0$$
$$Q Y_b V_b = Q I_s$$

Also,
$$V_b = Q^T V_t$$
$$Q Y_b Q^T V_t = Q I_s$$
$$Y V_t = I$$

where
$$Y = Q Y_b Q^T$$

and
$$I = Q I_s$$

This is the KCL equation in matrix form.

2. If there is a voltage source in series with an impedance and a current source in parallel with the combination, as shown in Fig. 8.53,

$$y_k = \frac{1}{z_k}$$
$$i_k = y_k v_k + y_k v_{sk} - i_{sk}$$

In matrix form,

$$I_b = Y_b V_b + Y_b V_s - I_s$$

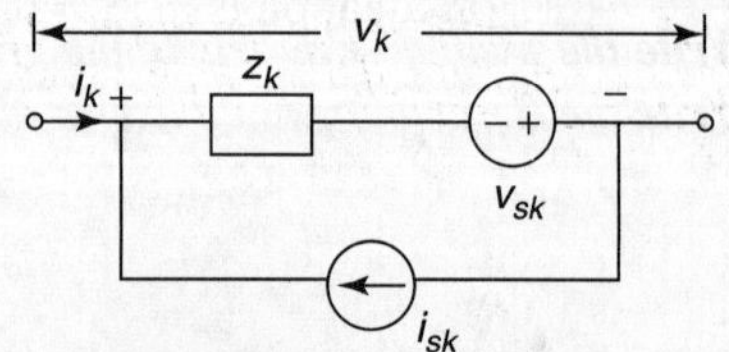


Fig. 8.53 *Circuit diagram*

KCL equation will be given by

$$A I_b = 0$$
$$A(Y_b V_b + Y_b V_s - I_s) = 0$$
$$A Y_b V_b = A I_s - A Y_b V_s$$

Also,
$$V_b = A^T V_n$$

$$A Y_b A^T V_n = A I_s - A Y_b V_s$$
$$Y V_n = A I_s - A V_b V_s$$

where $Y = A Y_b A^T$ is the node admittance matrix. This is a generalised KCL equation.

In terms of *f*-cutset matrix, the KCL equation can be written as

$$Q I_b = 0$$
$$Q(Y_b V_b + Y_b V_s - I_s) = 0$$
$$Q Y_b V_b = Q I_s - Q Y_b V_s$$

Also,
$$V_b = Q^T V_t$$
$$Q Y_b Q^T V_t = Q I_s - Q Y_b V_s$$
$$Y V_t = Q I_s - Q Y_b V_s$$

This is a generalised KCL equation.

### ➤ *Note*

(i) For a graph having $b$ branches, branch impedance matrix $Z_b$ is a square matrix of order $b$, having branch impedances as diagonal elements and the mutual impedances between the branches as non-diagonal elements. For a network having no mutual impedances, only diagonal elements will be present in the branch impedance matrix.

(ii) For a graph having $b$ branches, branch admittance matrix $Y_b$ is a square matrix of order $b$, having branch admittances as diagonal elements and the mutual admittances between the branches as non-diagonal elements. For a network having no mutual admittances, only diagonal elements will be present in the branch admittance matrix.

(iii) For a graph having $b$ branches, the voltage source matrix or vector $V_s$ is a rectangular matrix of order $b \times 1$, having the value of the voltage source in the particular branch. The value will be positive if there is a voltage rise in the direction of current and will be negative if there is a voltage fall in the direction of current.

(iv) For a graph having $b$ branches, the current source matrix or vector $I_s$ is a rectangular matrix of order $b \times 1$, having the value of the current source in the particular parallel branch. The value will be positive if the direction of the current source and the corresponding parallel branch current are not same. The value will be negative if the directions of the current source and corresponding parallel branch current are same.

## EXAMPLE 8.16

*Write the incidence matrix of the graph of Fig. 8.54 and express branch voltages in terms of node voltages. Write the tieset matrix and express branch currents in terms of loop currents.*

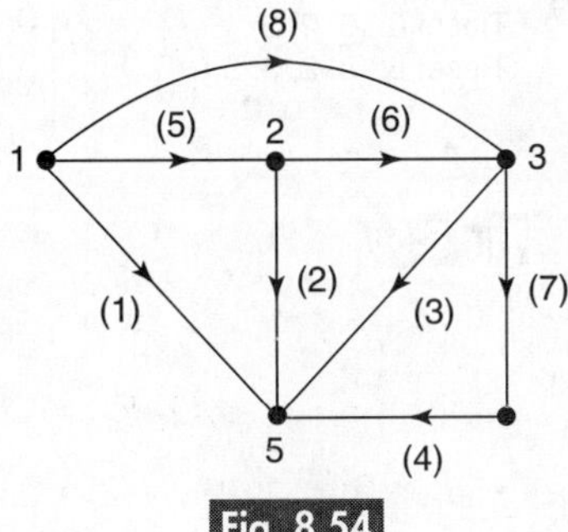


Fig. 8.54

## Solution

(a) Incidence Matrix

$$A_a = \begin{array}{c} \\ 1 \\ 2 \\ 3 \\ 4 \\ 5 \end{array} \begin{array}{c} \begin{array}{cccccccc} 1 & 2 & 3 & 4 & 5 & 6 & 7 & 8 \end{array} \\ \begin{bmatrix} 1 & 0 & 0 & 0 & 1 & 0 & 0 & 1 \\ 0 & 1 & 0 & 0 & -1 & 1 & 0 & 0 \\ 0 & 0 & 1 & 0 & 0 & -1 & 1 & -1 \\ 0 & 0 & 0 & 1 & 0 & 0 & -1 & 0 \\ -1 & -1 & -1 & -1 & 0 & 0 & 0 & 0 \end{bmatrix} \end{array}$$

The incidence matrix is obtained by eliminating any one row.

$$A = \begin{bmatrix} 1 & 0 & 0 & 0 & 1 & 0 & 0 & 1 \\ 0 & 1 & 0 & 0 & -1 & 1 & 0 & 0 \\ 0 & 0 & 1 & 0 & 0 & -1 & 1 & -1 \\ 0 & 0 & 0 & 1 & 0 & 0 & -1 & 0 \end{bmatrix}$$

(b) Branch voltages in terms of node voltages

$$V_b = A^T V_n$$

$$\begin{bmatrix} V_1 \\ V_2 \\ V_3 \\ V_4 \\ V_5 \\ V_6 \\ V_7 \\ V_8 \end{bmatrix} = \begin{bmatrix} 1 & 0 & 0 & 0 \\ 0 & 1 & 0 & 0 \\ 0 & 0 & 1 & 0 \\ 0 & 0 & 0 & 1 \\ 1 & -1 & 0 & 0 \\ 0 & 1 & -1 & 0 \\ 0 & 0 & 1 & -1 \\ 1 & 0 & -1 & 0 \end{bmatrix} \begin{bmatrix} V_{n_1} \\ V_{n_2} \\ V_{n_3} \\ V_{n_4} \end{bmatrix}$$

(c) Tieset Matrix

Selected tree and tiesets are shown in Fig. 8.55.

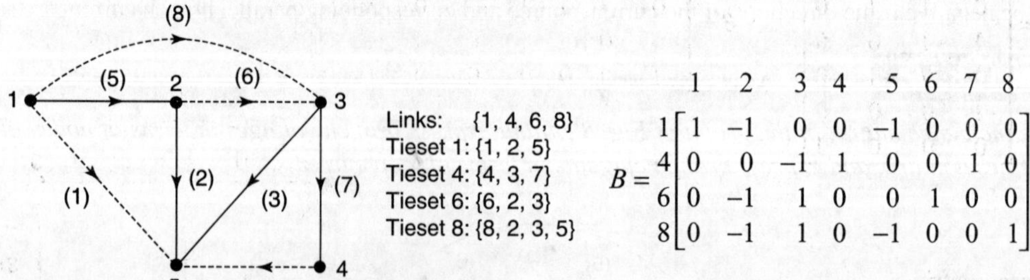


$$B = \begin{array}{c} \\ 1 \\ 4 \\ 6 \\ 8 \end{array} \begin{array}{c} \begin{array}{cccccccc} 1 & 2 & 3 & 4 & 5 & 6 & 7 & 8 \end{array} \\ \begin{bmatrix} 1 & -1 & 0 & 0 & -1 & 0 & 0 & 0 \\ 0 & 0 & -1 & 1 & 0 & 0 & 1 & 0 \\ 0 & -1 & 1 & 0 & 0 & 1 & 0 & 0 \\ 0 & -1 & 1 & 0 & -1 & 0 & 0 & 1 \end{bmatrix} \end{array}$$

Fig. 8.55

(d) Branch currents in terms of loop currents

$$I_b = B^T I_l$$

$$\begin{bmatrix} I_1 \\ I_2 \\ I_3 \\ I_4 \\ I_5 \\ I_6 \\ I_7 \\ I_8 \end{bmatrix} = \begin{bmatrix} 1 & 0 & 0 & 0 \\ -1 & 0 & -1 & -1 \\ 0 & -1 & 1 & 1 \\ 0 & 1 & 0 & 0 \\ -1 & 0 & 0 & -1 \\ 0 & 0 & 1 & 0 \\ 0 & 1 & 0 & 0 \\ 0 & 0 & 0 & 1 \end{bmatrix} \begin{bmatrix} I_{l_1} \\ I_{l_4} \\ I_{l_6} \\ I_{l_8} \end{bmatrix}$$

**EXAMPLE 8.17**

*Branch current and loop-current relationships are expressed in matrix form as*

$$\begin{bmatrix} I_1 \\ I_2 \\ I_3 \\ I_4 \\ I_5 \\ I_6 \\ I_7 \\ I_8 \end{bmatrix} = \begin{bmatrix} 1 & 0 & 0 & -1 \\ 0 & 1 & 0 & -1 \\ 0 & 1 & 1 & 0 \\ 0 & 1 & 1 & 0 \\ 1 & -1 & 0 & 0 \\ 0 & 0 & -1 & 0 \\ -1 & 0 & 0 & 0 \\ 0 & 0 & 0 & 1 \end{bmatrix} \begin{bmatrix} I_{l_1} \\ I_{l_2} \\ I_{l_3} \\ I_{l_4} \end{bmatrix}$$

*Draw the oriented graph.*

**Solution** Writing the equation in matrix form,

$$I_b = B^T I_l$$

$$B^T = \begin{bmatrix} 1 & 0 & 0 & -1 \\ 0 & 1 & 0 & -1 \\ 0 & 1 & 1 & 0 \\ 0 & 1 & 1 & 0 \\ 1 & -1 & 0 & 0 \\ 0 & 0 & -1 & 0 \\ -1 & 0 & 0 & 0 \\ 0 & 0 & 0 & 1 \end{bmatrix} \qquad \therefore B = \begin{array}{c} \begin{matrix} 1 & 2 & 3 & 4 & 5 & 6 & 7 & 8 \end{matrix} \\ \begin{bmatrix} 1 & 0 & 0 & 0 & 1 & 0 & -1 & 0 \\ 0 & 1 & 1 & 1 & -1 & 0 & 0 & 0 \\ 0 & 0 & 1 & 1 & 0 & -1 & 0 & 0 \\ -1 & -1 & 0 & 0 & 0 & 0 & 0 & 1 \end{bmatrix} \end{array}$$

From tieset matrix,

No. of links $l = 4$

No. of branches $b = 8$

No. of nodes $n = b - l + 1 = 8 - 4 + 1 = 5$

The oriented graph is shown in Fig. 8.56.

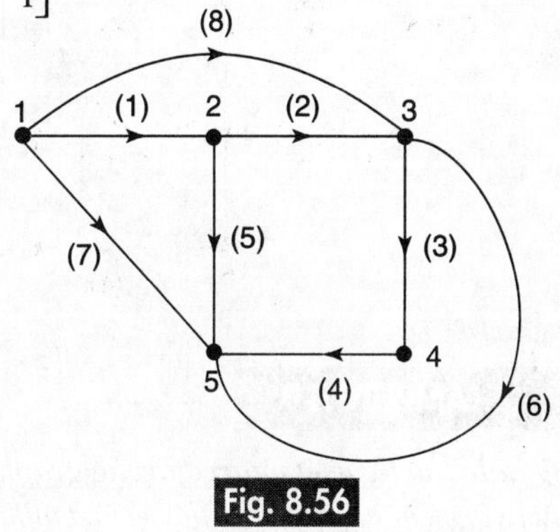

Fig. 8.56

## EXAMPLE 8.18

*For the given graph shown in Fig. 8.57, write down the basic tieset matrix and taking a tree of branches 2, 4, 5, write down KVL equations from the matrix.*

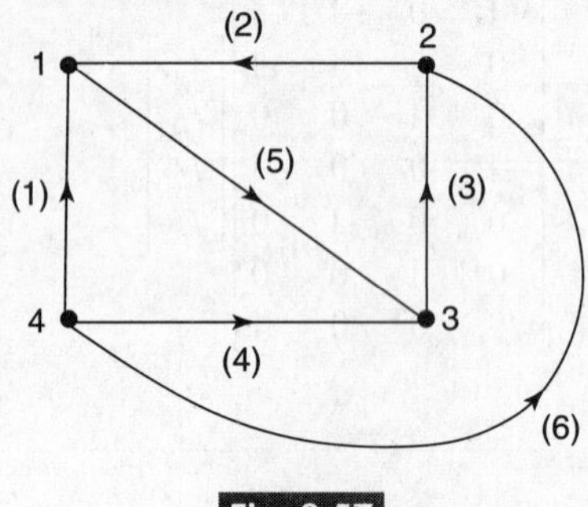


Fig. 8.57

**Solution** Selecting branches 2, 4, and 5, as the tree, as shown in Fig. 8.58,

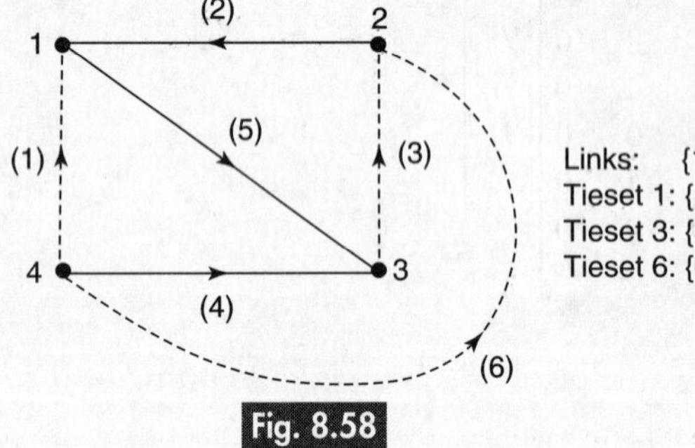


Fig. 8.58

Links: {1, 3, 6}
Tieset 1: {1, 5, 4}
Tieset 3: {3, 2, 5}
Tieset 6: {6, 2, 5, 4}

$$B = \begin{matrix} \\ 1 \\ 3 \\ 6 \end{matrix} \begin{matrix} \begin{matrix} 1 & 2 & 3 & 4 & 5 & 6 \end{matrix} \\ \begin{bmatrix} 1 & 0 & 0 & -1 & 1 & 0 \\ 0 & 1 & 1 & 0 & 1 & 0 \\ 0 & 1 & 0 & -1 & 1 & 1 \end{bmatrix} \end{matrix}$$

The KVL equation in matrix form is given by

$$BV_b = 0$$

$$\begin{bmatrix} 1 & 0 & 0 & -1 & 1 & 0 \\ 0 & 1 & 1 & 0 & 1 & 0 \\ 0 & 1 & 0 & -1 & 1 & 1 \end{bmatrix} \begin{bmatrix} V_1 \\ V_2 \\ V_3 \\ V_4 \\ V_5 \\ V_6 \end{bmatrix} = 0$$

$$V_1 - V_4 + V_5 = 0$$

$$V_2 + V_3 + V_5 = 0$$

$$V_2 - V_4 + V_5 + V_6 = 0$$

## EXAMPLE 8.19

*Obtain the f-cutset matrix for the graph shown in Fig. 8.59, taking 1, 2, 3, 4 as tree branches. Write down the network equations from the f-cutset matrix.*

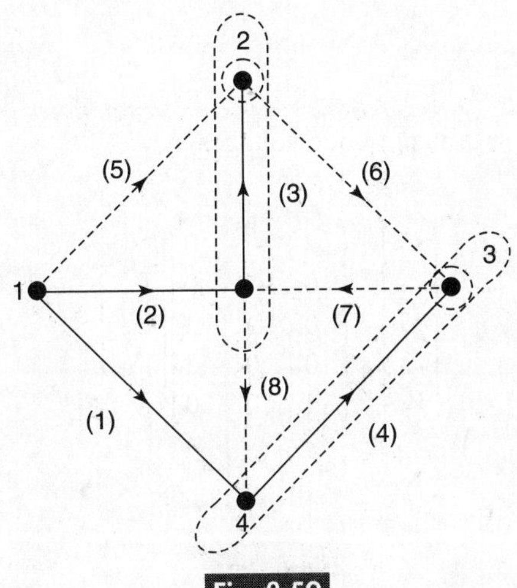


Fig. 8.59

**Solution** Twigs: {1, 2, 3, 4}

*f*-cutset 1 : {1, 6, 7, 8}

*f*-cutset 2 : {2, 5, 6, 7, 8}

*f*-cutset 3 : {3, 5, 6}

*f*-cutset 4 : {4, 6, 7}

$$Q = \begin{array}{c} \\ 1 \\ 2 \\ 3 \\ 4 \end{array} \begin{array}{c} \begin{array}{cccccccc} 1 & 2 & 3 & 4 & 5 & 6 & 7 & 8 \end{array} \\ \begin{bmatrix} 1 & 0 & 0 & 0 & 0 & 1 & -1 & 1 \\ 0 & 1 & 0 & 0 & 1 & -1 & 1 & -1 \\ 0 & 0 & 1 & 0 & 1 & -1 & 0 & 0 \\ 0 & 0 & 0 & 1 & 0 & 1 & -1 & 0 \end{bmatrix} \end{array}$$

The KCL equation in matrix form is given by

$$Q I_b = 0$$

$$\begin{bmatrix} 1 & 0 & 0 & 0 & 0 & 1 & -1 & 1 \\ 0 & 1 & 0 & 0 & 1 & -1 & 1 & -1 \\ 0 & 0 & 1 & 0 & 1 & -1 & 0 & 0 \\ 0 & 0 & 0 & 1 & 0 & 1 & -1 & 0 \end{bmatrix} \begin{bmatrix} I_1 \\ I_2 \\ I_3 \\ I_4 \\ I_5 \\ I_6 \\ I_7 \\ I_8 \end{bmatrix} = 0$$

$$I_1 + I_6 - I_7 + I_8 = 0$$

$$I_2 + I_5 - I_6 + I_7 - I_8 = 0$$

$$I_3 + I_5 - I_6 = 0$$

$$I_4 + I_6 - I_7 = 0$$

## EXAMPLE 8.20

*The reduced incidence matrix of a graph is given as*

$$A = \begin{bmatrix} 1 & 0 & 0 & 0 & -1 \\ -1 & -1 & -1 & 0 & 0 \\ 0 & 0 & 1 & -1 & 0 \end{bmatrix}$$

*Express branch voltages in terms of node voltages.*

**Solution** For the given graph,

No. of branches $b = 5$

No. of nodes $n = 3$

Branch voltages can be expressed in terms of node voltages by

$$V_b = A^T V_n$$

$$\begin{bmatrix} V_1 \\ V_2 \\ V_3 \\ V_4 \\ V_5 \end{bmatrix} = \begin{bmatrix} 1 & -1 & 0 \\ 0 & -1 & 0 \\ 0 & -1 & 1 \\ 0 & 0 & -1 \\ -1 & 0 & 0 \end{bmatrix} \begin{bmatrix} V_{n_1} \\ V_{n_2} \\ V_{n_3} \end{bmatrix}$$

$$V_1 = V_{n_1} - V_{n_2}$$

$$V_2 = -V_{n_2}$$

$$V_3 = -V_{n_2} + V_{n_3}$$

$$V_4 = -V_{n_3}$$

$$V_5 = -V_{n_1}$$

**EXAMPLE 8.21**

*The fundamental cutset matrix of a graph is given as*

$$Q = \begin{bmatrix} -1 & 1 & 0 & 0 & -1 \\ 0 & 0 & 1 & 0 & -1 \\ 1 & 0 & 0 & 1 & 0 \end{bmatrix}$$

*Express branch voltages in terms of twig voltages.*

**Solution** For the given graph,

No. of branches $b = 5$

No. of twigs = 3

Branch voltages are expressed in terms of twig voltages by

$$V_b = Q^T V_t$$

$$\begin{bmatrix} V_1 \\ V_2 \\ V_3 \\ V_4 \\ V_5 \end{bmatrix} = \begin{bmatrix} -1 & 0 & 1 \\ 1 & 0 & 0 \\ 0 & 1 & 0 \\ 0 & 0 & 1 \\ -1 & -1 & 0 \end{bmatrix} \begin{bmatrix} V_{t_1} \\ V_{t_2} \\ V_{t_3} \end{bmatrix}$$

$$V_1 = -V_{t_1} + V_{t_3}$$

$$V_2 = V_{t_1}$$

$$V_3 = V_{t_2}$$

$$V_4 = V_{t_3}$$

$$V_5 = -V_{t_1} - V_{t_2}$$

## EXAMPLE 8.22

*For this network shown in Fig. 8.60, write down the tieset matrix and obtain the network equilibrium equation in matrix form using KVL. Calculate the loop currents and branch currents.*

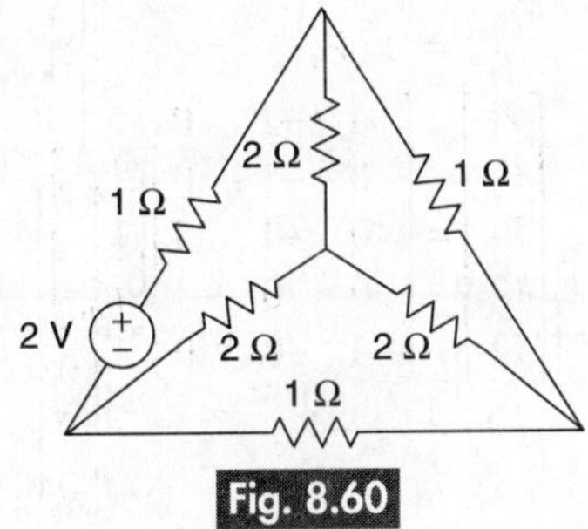


Fig. 8.60

**Solution** The oriented graph and one of its trees are shown in Fig. 8.61.

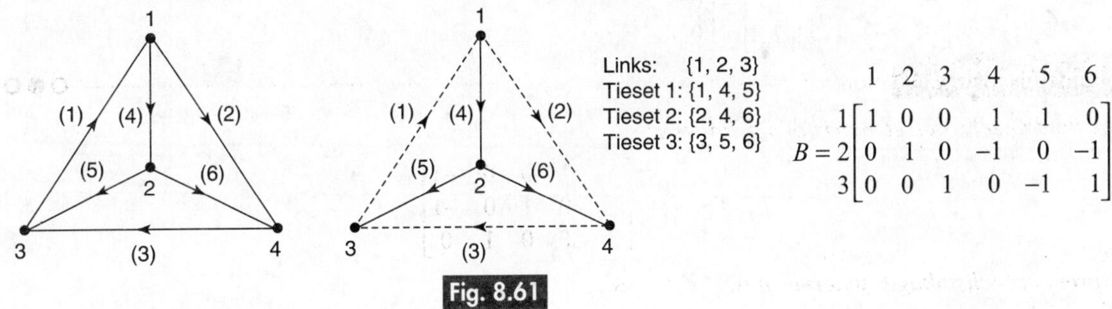


Links: {1, 2, 3}
Tieset 1: {1, 4, 5}
Tieset 2: {2, 4, 6}
Tieset 3: {3, 5, 6}

$$B = \begin{array}{c} \\ 1 \\ 2 \\ 3 \end{array}\begin{array}{c} \begin{array}{cccccc} 1 & 2 & 3 & 4 & 5 & 6 \end{array} \\ \begin{bmatrix} 1 & 0 & 0 & 1 & 1 & 0 \\ 0 & 1 & 0 & -1 & 0 & -1 \\ 0 & 0 & 1 & 0 & -1 & 1 \end{bmatrix} \end{array}$$

Fig. 8.61

The KVL equation in matrix form is given by

$$B\, Z_b\, B^T\, I_l = B\, V_s - B\, Z_b\, I_s$$

Here, $I_s = 0$,

$$B\, Z_b\, B^T\, I_l = B\, V_s$$

$$Z_b = \begin{bmatrix} 1 & 0 & 0 & 0 & 0 & 0 \\ 0 & 1 & 0 & 0 & 0 & 0 \\ 0 & 0 & 1 & 0 & 0 & 0 \\ 0 & 0 & 0 & 2 & 0 & 0 \\ 0 & 0 & 0 & 0 & 2 & 0 \\ 0 & 0 & 0 & 0 & 0 & 2 \end{bmatrix};\ B^T = \begin{bmatrix} 1 & 0 & 0 \\ 0 & 1 & 0 \\ 0 & 0 & 1 \\ 1 & -1 & 0 \\ 1 & 0 & -1 \\ 0 & -1 & 1 \end{bmatrix};\ V_s = \begin{bmatrix} 2 \\ 0 \\ 0 \\ 0 \\ 0 \\ 0 \end{bmatrix}$$

$$B\, Z_b = \begin{bmatrix} 1 & 0 & 0 & 1 & 1 & 0 \\ 0 & 1 & 0 & -1 & 0 & -1 \\ 0 & 0 & 1 & 0 & -1 & 1 \end{bmatrix} \begin{bmatrix} 1 & 0 & 0 & 0 & 0 & 0 \\ 0 & 1 & 0 & 0 & 0 & 0 \\ 0 & 0 & 1 & 0 & 0 & 0 \\ 0 & 0 & 0 & 2 & 0 & 0 \\ 0 & 0 & 0 & 0 & 2 & 0 \\ 0 & 0 & 0 & 0 & 0 & 2 \end{bmatrix} = \begin{bmatrix} 1 & 0 & 0 & 2 & 2 & 0 \\ 0 & 1 & 0 & -2 & 0 & -2 \\ 0 & 0 & 1 & 0 & -2 & 2 \end{bmatrix}$$

$$B\,Z_b\,B^T = \begin{bmatrix} 1 & 0 & 0 & 2 & 2 & 0 \\ 0 & 1 & 0 & -2 & 0 & -2 \\ 0 & 0 & 1 & 0 & -2 & 2 \end{bmatrix} \begin{bmatrix} 1 & 0 & 0 \\ 0 & 1 & 0 \\ 0 & 0 & 1 \\ 1 & -1 & 0 \\ 1 & 0 & -1 \\ 0 & -1 & 1 \end{bmatrix} = \begin{bmatrix} 5 & -2 & -2 \\ -2 & 5 & -2 \\ -2 & -2 & 5 \end{bmatrix}$$

$$BV_s = \begin{bmatrix} 1 & 0 & 0 & 1 & 1 & 0 \\ 0 & 1 & 0 & -1 & 0 & -1 \\ 0 & 0 & 1 & 0 & -1 & 1 \end{bmatrix} \begin{bmatrix} 2 \\ 0 \\ 0 \\ 0 \\ 0 \\ 0 \end{bmatrix} = \begin{bmatrix} 2 \\ 0 \\ 0 \end{bmatrix}$$

The KVL equation in matrix form is given by

$$\begin{bmatrix} 5 & -2 & -2 \\ -2 & 5 & -2 \\ -2 & -2 & 5 \end{bmatrix} \begin{bmatrix} I_{l_1} \\ I_{l_2} \\ I_{l_3} \end{bmatrix} = \begin{bmatrix} 2 \\ 0 \\ 0 \end{bmatrix}$$

Solving this matrix equation,

$$I_{l_1} = \frac{6}{7}\,\text{A}$$

$$I_{l_2} = \frac{4}{7}\,\text{A}$$

$$I_{l_3} = \frac{4}{7}\,\text{A}$$

The branch currents are given by

$$I_b = B^T\, I_l$$

$$\begin{bmatrix} I_1 \\ I_2 \\ I_3 \\ I_4 \\ I_5 \\ I_6 \end{bmatrix} = \begin{bmatrix} 1 & 0 & 0 \\ 0 & 1 & 0 \\ 0 & 0 & 1 \\ 1 & -1 & 0 \\ 1 & 0 & -1 \\ 0 & -1 & 1 \end{bmatrix} \begin{bmatrix} \frac{6}{7} \\ \frac{4}{7} \\ \frac{4}{7} \end{bmatrix} = \begin{bmatrix} \frac{6}{7} \\ \frac{4}{7} \\ \frac{4}{7} \\ \frac{2}{7} \\ \frac{2}{7} \\ 0 \end{bmatrix}$$

**EXAMPLE 8.23**

*For the network shown in Fig. 8.62, write down the tieset matrix and obtain the network equilibrium equation in matrix form using KVL. Calculate loop currents.*

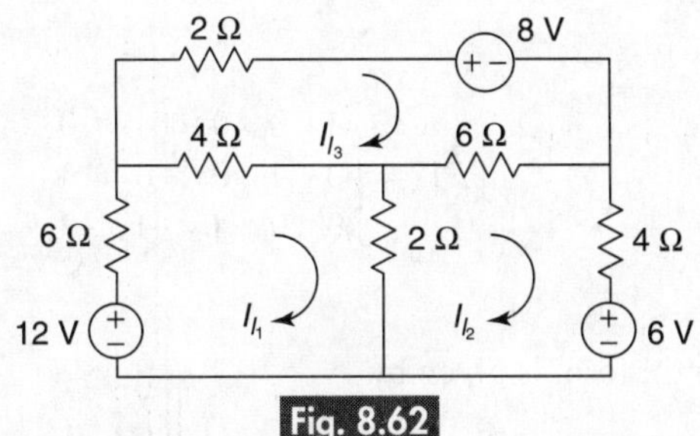


Fig. 8.62

**Solution** The oriented graph and its selected tree are shown in Fig. 8.63.

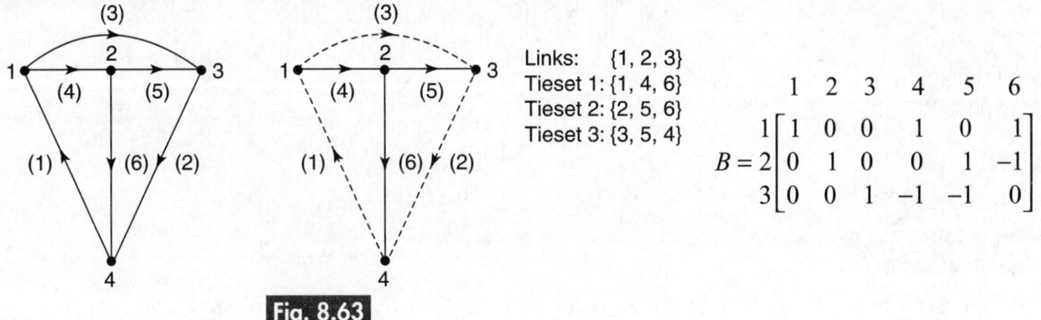


$$B = \begin{array}{c} \\ 1 \\ 2 \\ 3 \end{array}\begin{array}{c} \begin{array}{cccccc} 1 & 2 & 3 & 4 & 5 & 6 \end{array} \\ \begin{bmatrix} 1 & 0 & 0 & 1 & 0 & 1 \\ 0 & 1 & 0 & 0 & 1 & -1 \\ 0 & 0 & 1 & -1 & -1 & 0 \end{bmatrix} \end{array}$$

Fig. 8.63

The KVL equation in matrix form is given by

$$B\,Z_b\,B^T\,I_l = B\,V_s - B\,Z_b\,I_s$$

Here, $I_s = 0$,

$$B\,Z_b\,B^T\,I_l = B\,V_s$$

$$Z_b = \begin{bmatrix} 6 & 0 & 0 & 0 & 0 & 0 \\ 0 & 4 & 0 & 0 & 0 & 0 \\ 0 & 0 & 2 & 0 & 0 & 0 \\ 0 & 0 & 0 & 4 & 0 & 0 \\ 0 & 0 & 0 & 0 & 6 & 0 \\ 0 & 0 & 0 & 0 & 0 & 2 \end{bmatrix};\ B^T = \begin{bmatrix} 1 & 0 & 0 \\ 0 & 1 & 0 \\ 0 & 0 & 1 \\ 1 & 0 & -1 \\ 0 & 1 & -1 \\ 1 & -1 & 0 \end{bmatrix};\ V_s = \begin{bmatrix} 12 \\ -6 \\ -8 \\ 0 \\ 0 \\ 0 \end{bmatrix}$$

$$B\,Z_b = \begin{bmatrix} 1 & 0 & 0 & 1 & 0 & 1 \\ 0 & 1 & 0 & 0 & 1 & -1 \\ 0 & 0 & 1 & -1 & -1 & 0 \end{bmatrix}\begin{bmatrix} 6 & 0 & 0 & 0 & 0 & 0 \\ 0 & 4 & 0 & 0 & 0 & 0 \\ 0 & 0 & 2 & 0 & 0 & 0 \\ 0 & 0 & 0 & 4 & 0 & 0 \\ 0 & 0 & 0 & 0 & 6 & 0 \\ 0 & 0 & 0 & 0 & 0 & 2 \end{bmatrix} = \begin{bmatrix} 6 & 0 & 0 & 4 & 0 & 2 \\ 0 & 4 & 0 & 0 & 6 & -2 \\ 0 & 0 & 2 & -4 & -6 & 0 \end{bmatrix}$$

$$BZ_b\,B^T = \begin{bmatrix} 6 & 0 & 0 & 4 & 0 & 2 \\ 0 & 4 & 0 & 0 & 6 & -2 \\ 0 & 0 & 2 & -4 & -6 & 0 \end{bmatrix}\begin{bmatrix} 1 & 0 & 0 \\ 0 & 1 & 0 \\ 0 & 0 & 1 \\ 1 & 0 & -1 \\ 0 & 1 & -1 \\ 1 & -1 & 0 \end{bmatrix} = \begin{bmatrix} 12 & -2 & -4 \\ -1 & 12 & -6 \\ -4 & -6 & 12 \end{bmatrix}$$

$$BV_s = \begin{bmatrix} 1 & 0 & 0 & 1 & 0 & 1 \\ 0 & 1 & 0 & 0 & 1 & -1 \\ 0 & 0 & 1 & -1 & -1 & 0 \end{bmatrix} \begin{bmatrix} 12 \\ -6 \\ -8 \\ 0 \\ 0 \\ 0 \end{bmatrix} = \begin{bmatrix} 12 \\ -6 \\ -8 \end{bmatrix}$$

Hence, the KVL equation in matrix form is given by

$$\begin{bmatrix} 12 & -2 & -4 \\ -2 & 12 & -6 \\ -4 & -6 & 12 \end{bmatrix} \begin{bmatrix} I_{l_1} \\ I_{l_2} \\ I_{l_3} \end{bmatrix} = \begin{bmatrix} 12 \\ -6 \\ -8 \end{bmatrix}$$

Solving this matrix equation,

$$I_{l_1} = 0.55\text{A}$$
$$I_{l_2} = -0.866\text{A}$$
$$I_{l_3} = -0.916\text{A}$$

## EXAMPLE 8.24

*For the network shown in Fig. 8.64, draw the oriented graph. Write the tieset schedule and hence, obtain the equilibrium equation on loop basis. Calculate the values of branch currents and branch voltages.*

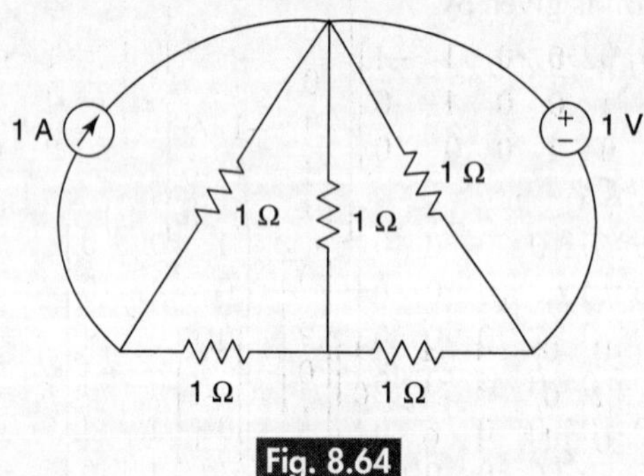


Fig. 8.64

**Solution** The oriented graph and one of its trees are shown in Fig. 8.65.

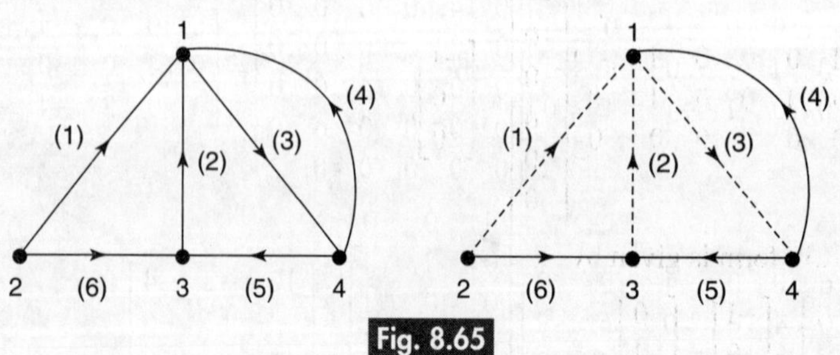


Fig. 8.65

$$B = \begin{matrix} & \begin{matrix} 1 & 2 & 3 & 4 & 5 & 6 \end{matrix} \\ \begin{matrix} 1 \\ 2 \\ 3 \end{matrix} & \begin{bmatrix} 1 & 0 & 0 & -1 & 1 & -1 \\ 0 & 1 & 0 & -1 & 1 & 0 \\ 0 & 0 & 1 & 1 & 0 & 0 \end{bmatrix} \end{matrix}$$

The KVL equation in matrix form is given by

$$B\,Z_b\,B^T\,I_l = B\,V_s - B\,Z_b\,I_s$$

$$Z_b = \begin{bmatrix} 1 & 0 & 0 & 0 & 0 & 0 \\ 0 & 1 & 0 & 0 & 0 & 0 \\ 0 & 0 & 1 & 0 & 0 & 0 \\ 0 & 0 & 0 & 0 & 0 & 0 \\ 0 & 0 & 0 & 0 & 1 & 0 \\ 0 & 0 & 0 & 0 & 0 & 1 \end{bmatrix}; B^T = \begin{bmatrix} 1 & 0 & 0 \\ 0 & 1 & 0 \\ 0 & 0 & 1 \\ -1 & -1 & 1 \\ 1 & 1 & 0 \\ -1 & 0 & 0 \end{bmatrix}; V_s = \begin{bmatrix} 0 \\ 0 \\ 0 \\ 1 \\ 0 \\ 0 \end{bmatrix}; I_s = \begin{bmatrix} -1 \\ 0 \\ 0 \\ 0 \\ 0 \\ 0 \end{bmatrix}$$

$$B\,Z_b = \begin{bmatrix} 1 & 0 & 0 & -1 & 1 & -1 \\ 0 & 1 & 0 & -1 & 1 & 0 \\ 0 & 0 & 1 & 1 & 0 & 0 \end{bmatrix} \begin{bmatrix} 1 & 0 & 0 & 0 & 0 & 0 \\ 0 & 1 & 0 & 0 & 0 & 0 \\ 0 & 0 & 1 & 0 & 0 & 0 \\ 0 & 0 & 0 & 0 & 0 & 0 \\ 0 & 0 & 0 & 0 & 1 & 0 \\ 0 & 0 & 0 & 0 & 0 & 1 \end{bmatrix} = \begin{bmatrix} 1 & 0 & 0 & 0 & 1 & -1 \\ 0 & 1 & 0 & 0 & 1 & 0 \\ 0 & 0 & 1 & 0 & 0 & 0 \end{bmatrix}$$

$$BZ_b\,B^T = \begin{bmatrix} 1 & 0 & 0 & 0 & 1 & -1 \\ 0 & 1 & 0 & 0 & 1 & 0 \\ 0 & 0 & 1 & 0 & 0 & 0 \end{bmatrix} \begin{bmatrix} 1 & 0 & 0 \\ 0 & 1 & 0 \\ 0 & 0 & 1 \\ -1 & -1 & 1 \\ 1 & 1 & 0 \\ -1 & 0 & 0 \end{bmatrix} = \begin{bmatrix} 3 & 1 & 0 \\ 1 & 2 & 0 \\ 0 & 0 & 1 \end{bmatrix}$$

$$B\,V_s = \begin{bmatrix} 1 & 0 & 0 & -1 & 1 & -1 \\ 0 & 1 & 0 & -1 & 1 & 0 \\ 0 & 0 & 1 & 1 & 0 & 0 \end{bmatrix} \begin{bmatrix} 0 \\ 0 \\ 0 \\ 1 \\ 0 \\ 0 \end{bmatrix} = \begin{bmatrix} -1 \\ -1 \\ 1 \end{bmatrix}$$

$$B\,Z_b\,I_s = \begin{bmatrix} 1 & 0 & 0 & 0 & 1 & -1 \\ 0 & 1 & 0 & 0 & 1 & 0 \\ 0 & 0 & 1 & 0 & 0 & 0 \end{bmatrix} \begin{bmatrix} -1 \\ 0 \\ 0 \\ 0 \\ 0 \\ 0 \end{bmatrix} = \begin{bmatrix} -1 \\ 0 \\ 0 \end{bmatrix}$$

Hence, the KVL equation in matrix form is given by

$$\begin{bmatrix} 3 & 1 & 0 \\ 1 & 2 & 0 \\ 0 & 0 & 1 \end{bmatrix} \begin{bmatrix} I_{l_1} \\ I_{l_2} \\ I_{l_3} \end{bmatrix} = \begin{bmatrix} -1 \\ -1 \\ 1 \end{bmatrix} - \begin{bmatrix} -1 \\ 0 \\ 0 \end{bmatrix} = \begin{bmatrix} 0 \\ -1 \\ 1 \end{bmatrix}$$

Solving this matrix equation,

$$I_{l_1} = \frac{1}{5}\text{A}$$

$$I_{l_2} = -\frac{3}{5}\text{A}$$

$$I_{l_3} = 1\text{A}$$

The branch currents are given by

$$I_b = B^T I_l + I_s$$

$$\begin{bmatrix} I_1 \\ I_2 \\ I_3 \\ I_4 \\ I_5 \\ I_6 \end{bmatrix} = \begin{bmatrix} 1 & 0 & 0 \\ 0 & 1 & 0 \\ 0 & 0 & 1 \\ -1 & -1 & 1 \\ 1 & 1 & 0 \\ -1 & 0 & 0 \end{bmatrix} \begin{bmatrix} \frac{1}{5} \\ -\frac{3}{5} \\ 1 \end{bmatrix} + \begin{bmatrix} -1 \\ 0 \\ 0 \\ 0 \\ 0 \\ 0 \end{bmatrix} = \begin{bmatrix} -\frac{4}{5} \\ -\frac{3}{5} \\ 1 \\ \frac{7}{5} \\ -\frac{2}{5} \\ -\frac{1}{5} \end{bmatrix}$$

The branch voltages are given by

$$V_b = Z_b I_b - V_s$$

$$\begin{bmatrix} V_1 \\ V_2 \\ V_3 \\ V_4 \\ V_5 \\ V_6 \end{bmatrix} = \begin{bmatrix} 1 & 0 & 0 & 0 & 0 & 0 \\ 0 & 1 & 0 & 0 & 0 & 0 \\ 0 & 0 & 1 & 0 & 0 & 0 \\ 0 & 0 & 0 & 0 & 0 & 0 \\ 0 & 0 & 0 & 0 & 1 & 0 \\ 0 & 0 & 0 & 0 & 0 & 1 \end{bmatrix} \begin{bmatrix} -\frac{4}{5} \\ -\frac{3}{5} \\ 1 \\ \frac{7}{5} \\ -\frac{2}{5} \\ -\frac{1}{5} \end{bmatrix} - \begin{bmatrix} 0 \\ 0 \\ 0 \\ 1 \\ 0 \\ 0 \end{bmatrix} = \begin{bmatrix} -\frac{4}{5} \\ -\frac{3}{5} \\ 1 \\ -1 \\ -\frac{2}{5} \\ -\frac{1}{5} \end{bmatrix}$$

**EXAMPLE 8.25**

*For the network shown in Fig. 8.66, obtain the loop equation in matrix form.*

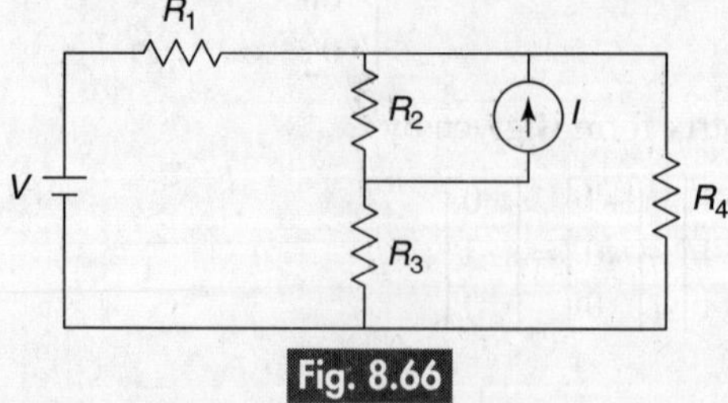


Fig. 8.66

**Solution** The oriented graph and one of its trees are shown in Fig. 8.67.

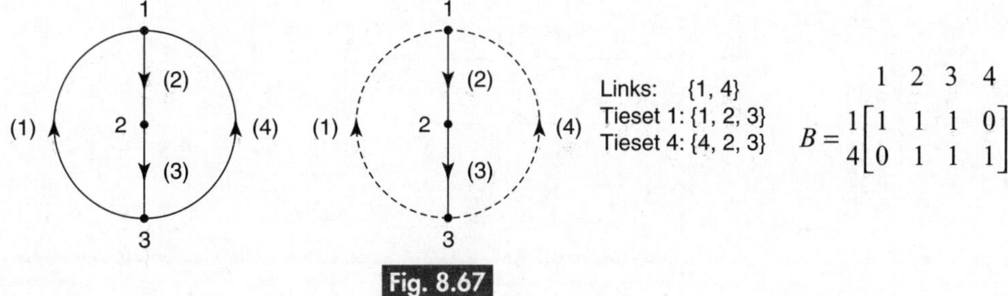


$$B = \begin{matrix} & \begin{matrix} 1 & 2 & 3 & 4 \end{matrix} \\ \begin{matrix} 1 \\ 4 \end{matrix} & \begin{bmatrix} 1 & 1 & 1 & 0 \\ 0 & 1 & 1 & 1 \end{bmatrix} \end{matrix}$$

Fig. 8.67

The KVL equation in matrix form is given by

$$B\,Z_b\,B^T\,I_l = BV_s - B\,Z_b I_s$$

$$Z_b = \begin{bmatrix} R_1 & 0 & 0 & 0 \\ 0 & R_2 & 0 & 0 \\ 0 & 0 & R_3 & 0 \\ 0 & 0 & 0 & R_4 \end{bmatrix};\ B^T = \begin{bmatrix} 1 & 0 \\ 1 & 1 \\ 1 & 1 \\ 0 & 1 \end{bmatrix};\ V_s = \begin{bmatrix} V \\ 0 \\ 0 \\ 0 \end{bmatrix};\ I_s = \begin{bmatrix} 0 \\ I \\ 0 \\ 0 \end{bmatrix}$$

$$B\,Z_b = \begin{bmatrix} 1 & 1 & 1 & 0 \\ 0 & 1 & 1 & 1 \end{bmatrix} \begin{bmatrix} R_1 & 0 & 0 & 0 \\ 0 & R_2 & 0 & 0 \\ 0 & 0 & R_3 & 0 \\ 0 & 0 & 0 & R_4 \end{bmatrix} = \begin{bmatrix} R_1 & R_2 & R_3 & 0 \\ 0 & R_2 & R_3 & R_4 \end{bmatrix}$$

$$B\,Z_b\,B^T = \begin{bmatrix} R_1 & R_2 & R_3 & 0 \\ 0 & R_2 & R_3 & R_4 \end{bmatrix} \begin{bmatrix} 1 & 0 \\ 1 & 1 \\ 1 & 1 \\ 0 & 1 \end{bmatrix} = \begin{bmatrix} R_1 + R_2 + R_3 & R_2 + R_3 \\ R_2 + R_3 & R_2 + R_3 + R_4 \end{bmatrix}$$

$$BV_s = \begin{bmatrix} 1 & 1 & 1 & 0 \\ 0 & 1 & 1 & 1 \end{bmatrix} \begin{bmatrix} V \\ 0 \\ 0 \\ 0 \end{bmatrix} = \begin{bmatrix} V \\ 0 \end{bmatrix}$$

$$B\,Z_b\,I_s = \begin{bmatrix} R_1 & R_2 & R_3 & 0 \\ 0 & R_2 & R_3 & R_4 \end{bmatrix} \begin{bmatrix} 0 \\ I \\ 0 \\ 0 \end{bmatrix} = \begin{bmatrix} R_2 I \\ R_2 I \end{bmatrix}$$

Hence, the KVL equation in matrix form is given by

$$\begin{bmatrix} R_1 + R_2 + R_3 & R_2 + R_3 \\ R_2 + R_3 & R_2 + R_3 + R_4 \end{bmatrix} \begin{bmatrix} I_{l_1} \\ I_{l_4} \end{bmatrix} = \begin{bmatrix} V \\ 0 \end{bmatrix} - \begin{bmatrix} R_2 & I \\ R_2 & I \end{bmatrix} = \begin{bmatrix} V - R_2 I \\ -R_2 I \end{bmatrix}$$

## EXAMPLE 8.26

*For the network shown in Fig. 8.68, write down the tieset matrix and obtain the network equilibrium equation in matrix form using KVL.*

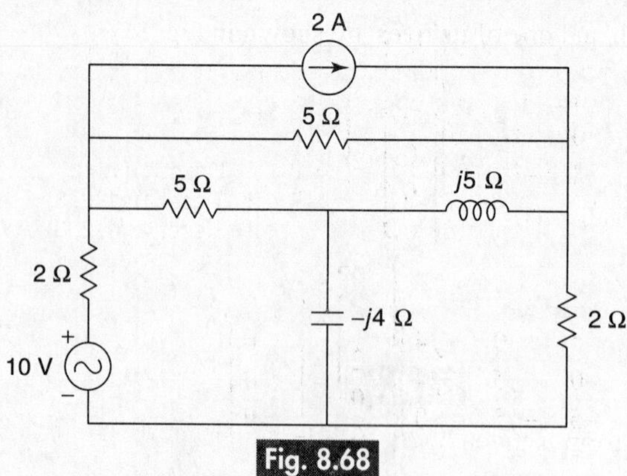


Fig. 8.68

**Solution** The oriented graph and its selected tree are shown in Fig. 8.69.

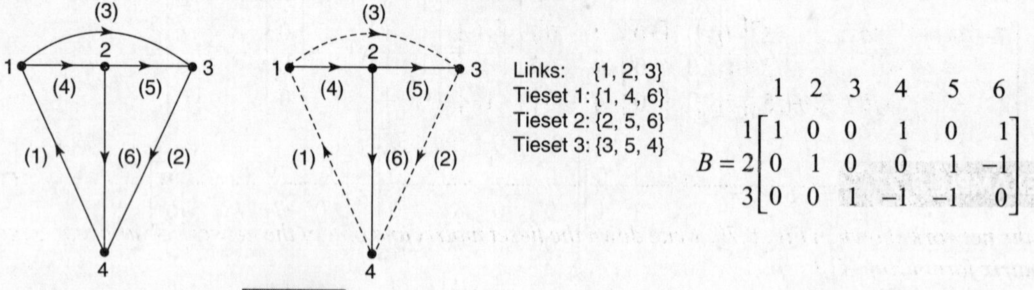


$$B = \begin{array}{c} \\ 1 \\ 2 \\ 3 \end{array} \begin{array}{c} \begin{matrix} 1 & 2 & 3 & 4 & 5 & 6 \end{matrix} \\ \begin{bmatrix} 1 & 0 & 0 & 1 & 0 & 1 \\ 0 & 1 & 0 & 0 & 1 & -1 \\ 0 & 0 & 1 & -1 & -1 & 0 \end{bmatrix} \end{array}$$

Fig. 8.69

The KVL equation in matrix form is given by

$$B\,Z_b\,B^T\,I_l = B V_s - B Z_b I_s$$

$$Z_b = \begin{bmatrix} 2 & 0 & 0 & 0 & 0 & 0 \\ 0 & 2 & 0 & 0 & 0 & 0 \\ 0 & 0 & 5 & 0 & 0 & 0 \\ 0 & 0 & 0 & 5 & 0 & 0 \\ 0 & 0 & 0 & 0 & j5 & 0 \\ 0 & 0 & 0 & 0 & 0 & -j4 \end{bmatrix};\; B^T = \begin{bmatrix} 1 & 0 & 0 \\ 0 & 1 & 0 \\ 0 & 0 & 1 \\ 1 & 0 & -1 \\ 0 & 1 & -1 \\ 1 & -1 & 0 \end{bmatrix};\; V_s = \begin{bmatrix} 10 \\ 0 \\ 0 \\ 0 \\ 0 \\ 0 \end{bmatrix};\; I_s = \begin{bmatrix} 0 \\ 0 \\ -2 \\ 0 \\ 0 \\ 0 \end{bmatrix}$$

$$B\,Z_b = \begin{bmatrix} 1 & 0 & 0 & 1 & 0 & 1 \\ 0 & 1 & 0 & 0 & 1 & -1 \\ 0 & 0 & 1 & -1 & -1 & 0 \end{bmatrix} \begin{bmatrix} 2 & 0 & 0 & 0 & 0 & 0 \\ 0 & 2 & 0 & 0 & 0 & 0 \\ 0 & 0 & 5 & 0 & 0 & 0 \\ 0 & 0 & 0 & 5 & 0 & 0 \\ 0 & 0 & 0 & 0 & j5 & 0 \\ 0 & 0 & 0 & 0 & 0 & -j4 \end{bmatrix} = \begin{bmatrix} 2 & 0 & 0 & 5 & 0 & -j4 \\ 0 & 2 & 0 & 0 & j5 & j4 \\ 0 & 0 & 5 & -5 & -j5 & 0 \end{bmatrix}$$

$$B\,Z_b\,B^T = \begin{bmatrix} 2 & 0 & 0 & 5 & 0 & -j4 \\ 0 & 2 & 0 & 0 & j5 & j4 \\ 0 & 0 & 5 & -5 & -j5 & 0 \end{bmatrix} \begin{bmatrix} 1 & 0 & 0 \\ 0 & 1 & 0 \\ 0 & 0 & 1 \\ 1 & 0 & -1 \\ 0 & 1 & -1 \\ 1 & -1 & 0 \end{bmatrix} = \begin{bmatrix} 7-j4 & j4 & -5 \\ j4 & 2+j1 & -j5 \\ -5 & -j5 & 10+j5 \end{bmatrix}$$

$$BV_s = \begin{bmatrix} 1 & 0 & 0 & 1 & 0 & 1 \\ 0 & 1 & 0 & 0 & 1 & -1 \\ 0 & 0 & 1 & -1 & -1 & 0 \end{bmatrix} \begin{bmatrix} 10 \\ 0 \\ 0 \\ 0 \\ 0 \\ 0 \end{bmatrix} = \begin{bmatrix} 10 \\ 0 \\ 0 \end{bmatrix}$$

$$BZ_b I_s = \begin{bmatrix} 2 & 0 & 0 & 5 & 0 & -j4 \\ 0 & 2 & 0 & 0 & j5 & j4 \\ 0 & 0 & 5 & -5 & -j5 & 0 \end{bmatrix} \begin{bmatrix} 0 \\ 0 \\ -2 \\ 0 \\ 0 \\ 0 \end{bmatrix} = \begin{bmatrix} 0 \\ 0 \\ -10 \end{bmatrix}$$

Hence, the KCL equation in matrix form is given by

$$\begin{bmatrix} 7-j4 & j4 & -5 \\ j4 & 2+j1 & -j5 \\ -5 & -j5 & 10+j5 \end{bmatrix} \begin{bmatrix} I_{l_1} \\ I_{l_2} \\ I_{l_3} \end{bmatrix} = \begin{bmatrix} 10 \\ 0 \\ 0 \end{bmatrix} - \begin{bmatrix} 0 \\ 0 \\ -10 \end{bmatrix} = \begin{bmatrix} 10 \\ 0 \\ 10 \end{bmatrix}$$

## EXAMPLE 8.27

*For the network shown in Fig. 8.70, write down the tieset matrix and obtain the network equilibrium equation in matrix form using KVL.*

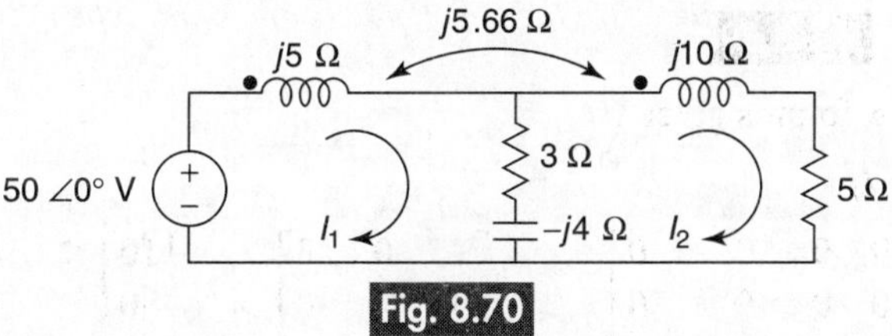

Fig. 8.70

**Solution** The branch currents are so chosen that they assume the direction out of the dotted terminals. Because of this choice of current direction, the mutual inductance is positive. The oriented graph and its selected tree are shown in Fig. 8.71.

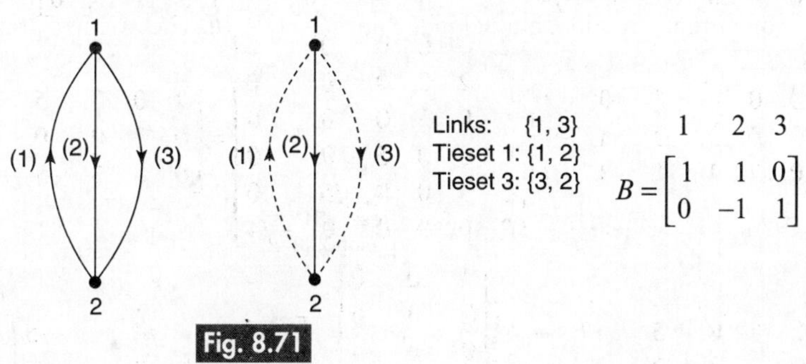


$$B = \begin{matrix} & \begin{matrix} 1 & 2 & 3 \end{matrix} \\ & \begin{bmatrix} 1 & 1 & 0 \\ 0 & -1 & 1 \end{bmatrix} \end{matrix}$$

Fig. 8.71

The KVL equation in matrix form is given by

$$BZ_b B^T I_l = BV_s - BZ_b I_s$$

Here, $I_s = 0$,

$$B Z_b B^T I_l = B V_s$$

$$Z_b = \begin{bmatrix} j5 & 0 & j5.66 \\ 0 & 3-j4 & 0 \\ j5.66 & 0 & 5+j10 \end{bmatrix}; B^T = \begin{bmatrix} 1 & 0 \\ 1 & -1 \\ 0 & 1 \end{bmatrix}; V_s = \begin{bmatrix} 50\angle 0° \\ 0 \\ 0 \end{bmatrix}$$

$$B Z_b = \begin{bmatrix} 1 & 1 & 0 \\ 0 & -1 & 1 \end{bmatrix} \begin{bmatrix} j5 & 0 & j5.66 \\ 0 & 3-j4 & 0 \\ j5.66 & 0 & 5+j10 \end{bmatrix} = \begin{bmatrix} j5 & 3-j4 & j5.66 \\ j5.66 & -3+j4 & 5+j10 \end{bmatrix}$$

$$B Z_b B^T = \begin{bmatrix} j5 & 3-j4 & j5.66 \\ j5.66 & -3+j4 & 5+j10 \end{bmatrix} \begin{bmatrix} 1 & 0 \\ 1 & -1 \\ 0 & 1 \end{bmatrix} = \begin{bmatrix} 3+j1 & -3+j9.66 \\ -3+j9.66 & 8+j6 \end{bmatrix}$$

$$B V_s = \begin{bmatrix} 1 & 1 & 0 \\ 0 & -1 & 1 \end{bmatrix} \begin{bmatrix} 50\angle 0° \\ 0 \\ 0 \end{bmatrix} = \begin{bmatrix} 50\angle 0° \\ 0 \end{bmatrix}$$

Hence, the KVL equation in matrix form is given by

$$\begin{bmatrix} 3+j1 & -3+j9.66 \\ -3+j9.66 & 8.j6 \end{bmatrix} \begin{bmatrix} I_{l_1} \\ I_{l_2} \end{bmatrix} = \begin{bmatrix} 50\angle 0° \\ 0 \end{bmatrix}$$

## EXAMPLE 8.28

*For the network shown in Fig. 8.72, write down the tieset matrix and obtain the network equilibrium equation in matrix form using KVL.*

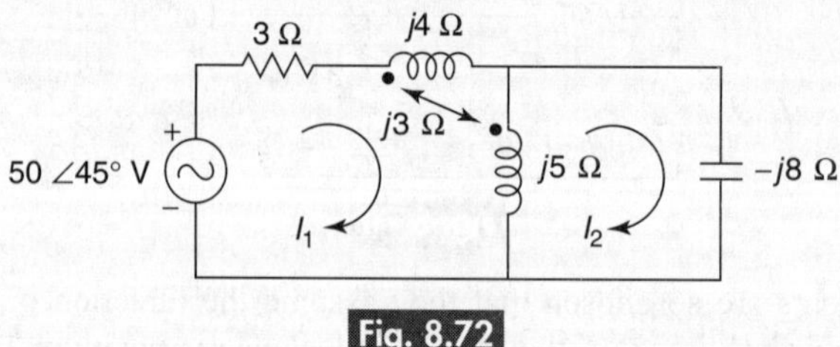


Fig. 8.72

**Solution** The branch currents are so chosen that they assume the direction out of the dotted terminals. Because of this choice of current direction, mutual inductance is positive. The oriented graph and its selected tree are shown in Fig. 8.73.

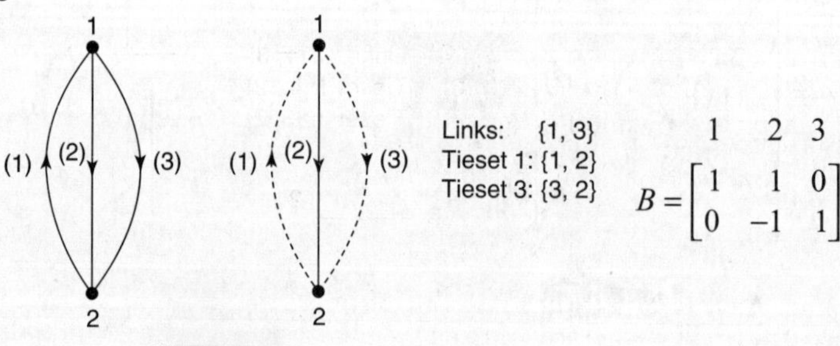


$$B = \begin{matrix} & \begin{matrix} 1 & 2 & 3 \end{matrix} \\ & \begin{bmatrix} 1 & 1 & 0 \\ 0 & -1 & 1 \end{bmatrix} \end{matrix}$$

Fig. 8.73

The KVL equation in matrix form is given by

$$B\,Z_b\,B^T\,I_l = B\,V_s - B\,Z_b\,I_s$$

Here, $$I_s = 0$$

$$B\,Z_b\,B^T\,I_l = B\,V_s$$

$$Z_b = \begin{bmatrix} 3+j4 & j3 & 0 \\ j3 & j5 & 0 \\ 0 & 0 & -j8 \end{bmatrix};\ B^T = \begin{bmatrix} 1 & 0 \\ 1 & -1 \\ 0 & 1 \end{bmatrix};\ V_s = \begin{bmatrix} 50\angle 45^\circ \\ 0 \\ 0 \end{bmatrix}$$

$$B\,Z_b = \begin{bmatrix} 1 & 1 & 0 \\ 0 & -1 & 1 \end{bmatrix}\begin{bmatrix} 3+j4 & j3 & 0 \\ j3 & j5 & 0 \\ 0 & 0 & -j8 \end{bmatrix} = \begin{bmatrix} 3+j7 & j8 & 0 \\ -j3 & -j5 & -j8 \end{bmatrix}$$

$$B\,Z_b\,B^T = \begin{bmatrix} 3+j7 & j8 & 0 \\ -j3 & -j5 & -j8 \end{bmatrix}\begin{bmatrix} 1 & 0 \\ 1 & -1 \\ 0 & 1 \end{bmatrix} = \begin{bmatrix} 3+j15 & -j8 \\ -j8 & -j3 \end{bmatrix}$$

$$B\,V_s = \begin{bmatrix} 1 & 1 & 0 \\ 0 & -1 & 1 \end{bmatrix}\begin{bmatrix} 50\angle 45^\circ \\ 0 \\ 0 \end{bmatrix} = \begin{bmatrix} 50\angle 45^\circ \\ 0 \end{bmatrix}$$

Hence, the KVL equation in matrix form is given by

$$\begin{bmatrix} 3+j15 & -j8 \\ -j8 & -j3 \end{bmatrix}\begin{bmatrix} I_{l_1} \\ I_{l_3} \end{bmatrix} = \begin{bmatrix} 50\angle 45^\circ \\ 0 \end{bmatrix}$$

## EXAMPLE 8.29

*For the network shown in Fig. 8.74, obtain branch voltages using KCL equation on node basis.*

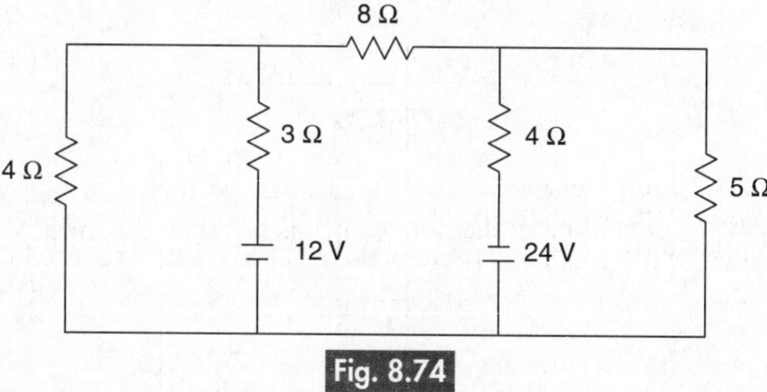


Fig. 8.74

**Solution** The oriented graph is shown in Fig. 8.75.

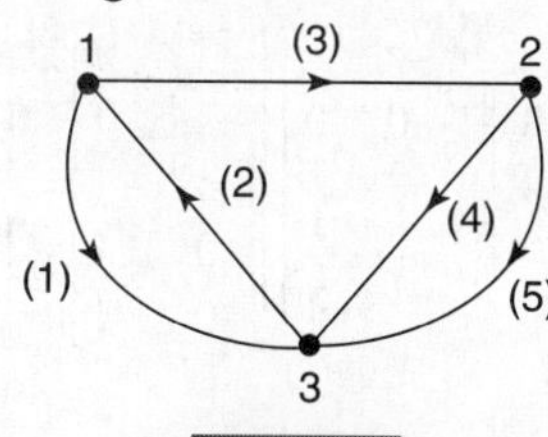


Fig. 8.75

The complete incidence matrix for the graph is

$$A_a = \begin{array}{c} \\ 1 \\ 2 \\ 3 \end{array}\!\!\begin{array}{c} \begin{array}{ccccc} 1 & 2 & 3 & 4 & 5 \end{array} \\ \begin{bmatrix} 1 & -1 & 1 & 0 & 0 \\ 0 & 0 & -1 & 1 & 1 \\ -1 & 1 & 0 & -1 & -1 \end{bmatrix} \end{array}$$

Eliminating the last row from the matrix $A_a$, we get the incidence matrix $A$.

$$A = \begin{array}{c} \\ 1 \\ 2 \end{array}\!\!\begin{array}{c} \begin{array}{ccccc} 1 & 2 & 3 & 4 & 5 \end{array} \\ \begin{bmatrix} 1 & -1 & 1 & 0 & 0 \\ 0 & 0 & -1 & 1 & 1 \end{bmatrix} \end{array}$$

The KCL equation in matrix form is given by

$$AY_b A^T V_n = AI_s - AY_b V_s$$

Here, $\quad I_s = 0$

$$AY_b A^T V_n = -AY_b V_s$$

$$Y_b = \begin{bmatrix} \frac{1}{4} & 0 & 0 & 0 & 0 \\ 0 & \frac{1}{3} & 0 & 0 & 0 \\ 0 & 0 & \frac{1}{8} & 0 & 0 \\ 0 & 0 & 0 & \frac{1}{4} & 0 \\ 0 & 0 & 0 & 0 & \frac{1}{5} \end{bmatrix}; A^T = \begin{bmatrix} 1 & 0 \\ -1 & 0 \\ 1 & -1 \\ 0 & 1 \\ 0 & 1 \end{bmatrix}; V_s = \begin{bmatrix} 0 \\ 12 \\ 0 \\ 24 \\ 0 \end{bmatrix}$$

$$AY_b = \begin{bmatrix} 1 & -1 & 1 & 0 & 0 \\ 0 & 0 & -1 & 1 & 1 \end{bmatrix} \begin{bmatrix} \frac{1}{4} & 0 & 0 & 0 & 0 \\ 0 & \frac{1}{3} & 0 & 0 & 0 \\ 0 & 0 & \frac{1}{8} & 0 & 0 \\ 0 & 0 & 0 & \frac{1}{4} & 0 \\ 0 & 0 & 0 & 0 & \frac{1}{5} \end{bmatrix} = \begin{bmatrix} \frac{1}{4} & -\frac{1}{3} & \frac{1}{8} & 0 & 0 \\ 0 & 0 & -\frac{1}{8} & \frac{1}{4} & \frac{1}{5} \end{bmatrix}$$

$$AY_b A^T = \begin{bmatrix} \frac{1}{4} & -\frac{1}{3} & \frac{1}{8} & 0 & 0 \\ 0 & 0 & -\frac{1}{8} & \frac{1}{4} & \frac{1}{5} \end{bmatrix} \begin{bmatrix} 1 & 0 \\ -1 & 0 \\ 1 & -1 \\ 0 & 1 \\ 0 & 1 \end{bmatrix} = \begin{bmatrix} \frac{17}{24} & -\frac{1}{8} \\ -\frac{1}{8} & \frac{23}{40} \end{bmatrix}$$

$$AY_bV_s = \begin{bmatrix} \frac{1}{4} & -\frac{1}{3} & \frac{1}{8} & 0 & 0 \\ 0 & 0 & -\frac{1}{8} & \frac{1}{4} & \frac{1}{5} \end{bmatrix} \begin{bmatrix} 0 \\ 12 \\ 0 \\ 24 \\ 0 \end{bmatrix} = \begin{bmatrix} -4 \\ 6 \end{bmatrix}$$

Hence, the KCL equation in matrix form is given by

$$\begin{bmatrix} \frac{17}{24} & -\frac{1}{8} \\ -\frac{1}{8} & \frac{23}{40} \end{bmatrix} \begin{bmatrix} V_{n_1} \\ V_{n_2} \end{bmatrix} = -\begin{bmatrix} -4 \\ 6 \end{bmatrix} = \begin{bmatrix} 4 \\ -6 \end{bmatrix}$$

Solving this matrix equation,

$$V_{n_1} = 3.96 \text{ V}$$
$$V_{n_2} = -9.57 \text{ V}$$

Branch voltages are given by

$$V_b = A^T V_n$$

$$\begin{bmatrix} V_1 \\ V_2 \\ V_3 \\ V_4 \\ V_5 \end{bmatrix} = \begin{bmatrix} 1 & 0 \\ -1 & 0 \\ 1 & -1 \\ 0 & 1 \\ 0 & 1 \end{bmatrix} \begin{bmatrix} 3.96 \\ -9.57 \end{bmatrix} = \begin{bmatrix} 3.96 \\ -3.96 \\ 13.53 \\ -9.57 \\ -9.57 \end{bmatrix}$$

**EXAMPLE 8.30**

*For the network shown in Fig. 8.76, write down the f-cutset matrix and obtain the network equilibrium equation in matrix form using KCL.*

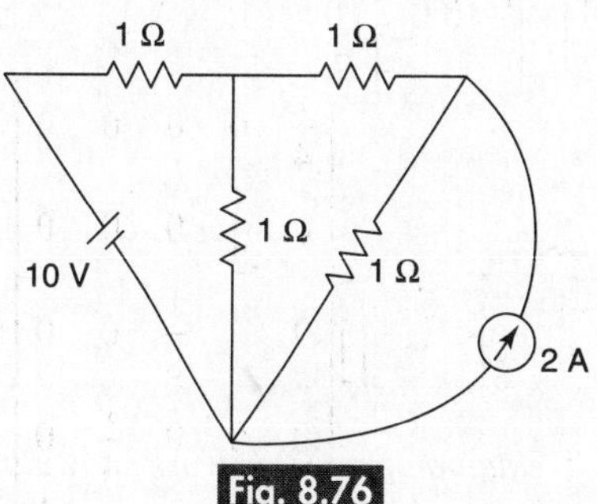


Fig. 8.76

**Solution** The oriented graph and its selected tree are shown in Fig. 8.77.

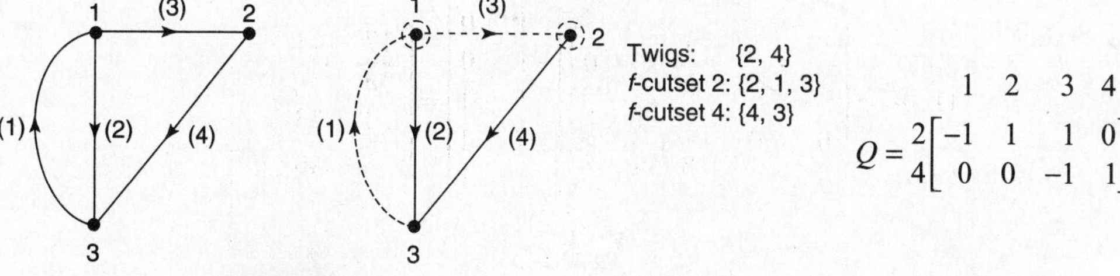


Fig. 8.77

The KCL equation in matrix form is given by

$$Q Y_b Q^T V_t = Q I_s - Q Y_b V_s$$

$$Y_b = \begin{bmatrix} 1 & 0 & 0 & 0 \\ 0 & 1 & 0 & 0 \\ 0 & 0 & 1 & 0 \\ 0 & 0 & 0 & 1 \end{bmatrix}; I_s = \begin{bmatrix} 0 \\ 0 \\ 0 \\ 2 \end{bmatrix}; V_s = \begin{bmatrix} 10 \\ 0 \\ 0 \\ 0 \end{bmatrix}; Q^T = \begin{bmatrix} -1 & 0 \\ 1 & 0 \\ 1 & -1 \\ 0 & 1 \end{bmatrix}$$

$$Q Y_b = \begin{bmatrix} -1 & 1 & 1 & 0 \\ 0 & 0 & -1 & 1 \end{bmatrix} \begin{bmatrix} 1 & 0 & 0 & 0 \\ 0 & 1 & 0 & 0 \\ 0 & 0 & 1 & 0 \\ 0 & 0 & 0 & 1 \end{bmatrix} = \begin{bmatrix} -1 & 1 & 1 & 0 \\ 0 & 0 & -1 & 1 \end{bmatrix}$$

$$Q Y_b Q^T = \begin{bmatrix} -1 & 1 & 1 & 0 \\ 0 & 0 & -1 & 1 \end{bmatrix} \begin{bmatrix} -1 & 0 \\ 1 & 0 \\ 1 & -1 \\ 0 & 1 \end{bmatrix} = \begin{bmatrix} 3 & -1 \\ -1 & 2 \end{bmatrix}$$

$$Q I_s = \begin{bmatrix} -1 & 1 & 1 & 0 \\ 0 & 0 & -1 & 1 \end{bmatrix} \begin{bmatrix} 0 \\ 0 \\ 0 \\ 2 \end{bmatrix} = \begin{bmatrix} 0 \\ 2 \end{bmatrix}$$

$$Q Y_b V_s = \begin{bmatrix} -1 & 1 & 1 & 0 \\ 0 & 0 & -1 & 1 \end{bmatrix} \begin{bmatrix} 10 \\ 0 \\ 0 \\ 0 \end{bmatrix} = \begin{bmatrix} -10 \\ 0 \end{bmatrix}$$

Hence, the KCL equation is given by

$$\begin{bmatrix} 3 & -1 \\ -1 & 2 \end{bmatrix} \begin{bmatrix} V_{t_2} \\ V_{t_4} \end{bmatrix} = \begin{bmatrix} 0 \\ 2 \end{bmatrix} - \begin{bmatrix} -10 \\ 0 \end{bmatrix} = \begin{bmatrix} 10 \\ 2 \end{bmatrix}$$

Solving this matrix equation,

$$V_{t_2} = 4.4 \text{ V}$$

$$V_{t_4} = 3.2 \text{ V}$$

**EXAMPLE 8.31**

*Calculate the twig voltages using KCL equation for the network shown in Fig. 8.78.*

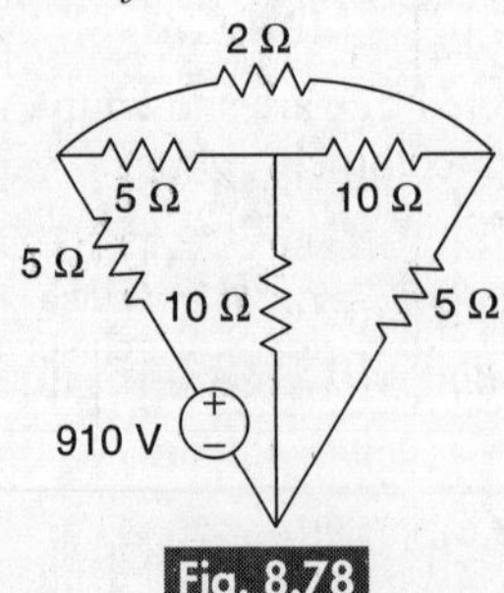


Fig. 8.78

**Solution** The oriented graph and one of the trees are shown in Fig. 8.79.

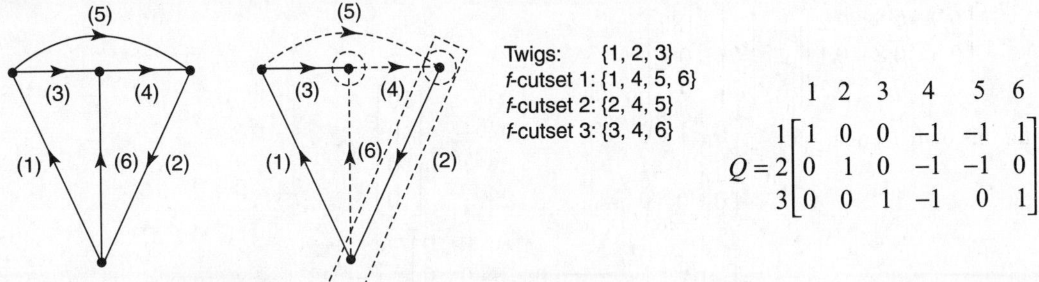


$$Q = \begin{array}{c} \\ 1 \\ 2 \\ 3 \end{array}\begin{array}{c} \begin{array}{cccccc} 1 & 2 & 3 & 4 & 5 & 6 \end{array} \\ \begin{bmatrix} 1 & 0 & 0 & -1 & -1 & 1 \\ 0 & 1 & 0 & -1 & -1 & 0 \\ 0 & 0 & 1 & -1 & 0 & 1 \end{bmatrix} \end{array}$$

Fig. 8.79

The network equilibrium equation on node basis can be written as

$$Q Y_b Q^T V_t = QI_s - QY_b V_s$$

Here, $$I_s = 0$$

$$Q Y_b Q^T V_t = -Q Y_b V_s$$

$$Y_b = \begin{bmatrix} 0.2 & 0 & 0 & 0 & 0 & 0 \\ 0 & 0.2 & 0 & 0 & 0 & 0 \\ 0 & 0 & 0.2 & 0 & 0 & 0 \\ 0 & 0 & 0 & 0.1 & 0 & 0 \\ 0 & 0 & 0 & 0 & 0.5 & 0 \\ 0 & 0 & 0 & 0 & 0 & 0.1 \end{bmatrix}; Q^T = \begin{bmatrix} 1 & 0 & 0 \\ 0 & 1 & 0 \\ 0 & 0 & 1 \\ -1 & -1 & -1 \\ -1 & -1 & 0 \\ 1 & 0 & 1 \end{bmatrix}; V_s = \begin{bmatrix} 910 \\ 0 \\ 0 \\ 0 \\ 0 \\ 0 \end{bmatrix}$$

$$Q Y_b = \begin{bmatrix} 1 & 0 & 0 & -1 & -1 & 1 \\ 0 & 1 & 0 & -1 & -1 & 0 \\ 0 & 0 & 1 & -1 & 0 & 1 \end{bmatrix} \begin{bmatrix} 0.2 & 0 & 0 & 0 & 0 & 0 \\ 0 & 0.2 & 0 & 0 & 0 & 0 \\ 0 & 0 & 0.2 & 0 & 0 & 0 \\ 0 & 0 & 0 & 0.1 & 0 & 0 \\ 0 & 0 & 0 & 0 & 0.5 & 0 \\ 0 & 0 & 0 & 0 & 0 & 0.1 \end{bmatrix} = \begin{bmatrix} 0.2 & 0 & 0 & -0.1 & -0.5 & 0.1 \\ 0 & 0.2 & 0 & -0.1 & -0.5 & 0 \\ 0 & 0 & 0.2 & -0.1 & 0 & 0.1 \end{bmatrix}$$

$$Q Y_b Q^T = \begin{bmatrix} 0.2 & 0 & 0 & -0.1 & -0.5 & 0.1 \\ 0 & 0.2 & 0 & -0.1 & -0.5 & 0 \\ 0 & 0 & 0.2 & -0.1 & 0 & 0.1 \end{bmatrix} \begin{bmatrix} 1 & 0 & 0 \\ 0 & 1 & 0 \\ 0 & 0 & 1 \\ -1 & -1 & -1 \\ -1 & -1 & 0 \\ 1 & 0 & 1 \end{bmatrix} = \begin{bmatrix} 0.9 & 0.6 & 0.2 \\ 0.6 & 0.8 & 0.1 \\ 0.2 & 0.1 & 0.3 \end{bmatrix}$$

$$Q Y_b V_s = \begin{bmatrix} 0.2 & 0 & 0 & -0.1 & -0.5 & 0.1 \\ 0 & 0.2 & 0 & -0.1 & -0.5 & 0 \\ 0 & 0 & 0.2 & -0.1 & 0 & 0.1 \end{bmatrix} \begin{bmatrix} 910 \\ 0 \\ 0 \\ 0 \\ 0 \\ 0 \end{bmatrix} = \begin{bmatrix} 182 \\ 0 \\ 0 \end{bmatrix}$$

Hence, KCL equation can be written as,

$$\begin{bmatrix} 0.9 & 0.6 & 0.2 \\ 0.6 & 0.8 & 0.1 \\ 0.2 & 0.1 & 0.3 \end{bmatrix}\begin{bmatrix} v_{t_1} \\ v_{t_2} \\ v_{t_3} \end{bmatrix} = \begin{bmatrix} -182 \\ 0 \\ 0 \end{bmatrix}$$

Solving this matrix equation,

$$v_{t_1} = -444.26\,\text{V}$$
$$v_{t_2} = 315.28\,\text{V}$$
$$v_{t_3} = 143.31\,\text{V}$$

## EXAMPLE 8.32

*For the network shown in Fig. 8.80, obtain equilibrium equation on node basis.*

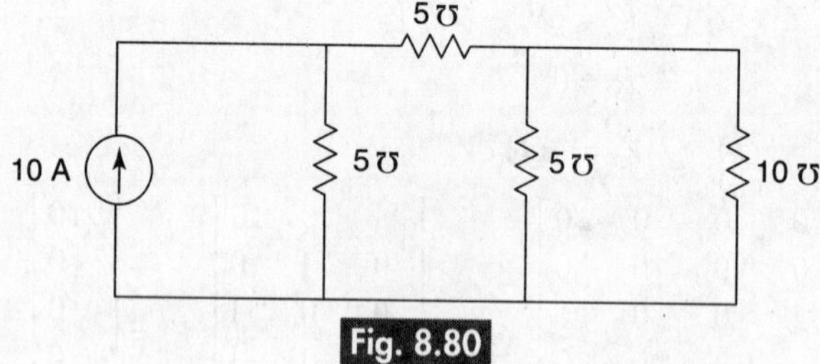


Fig. 8.80

**Solution** The oriented graph and its selected tree are shown in Fig. 8.81.

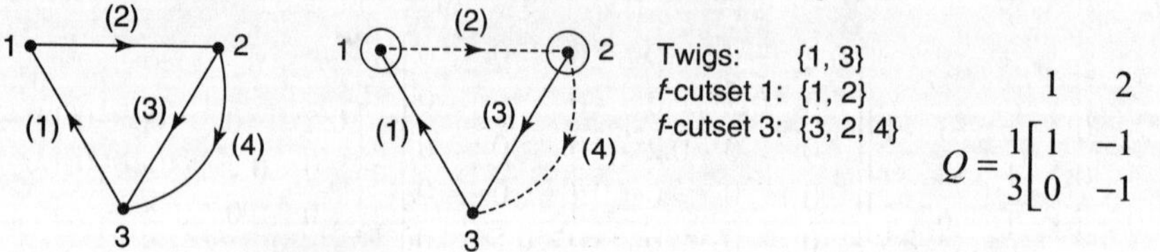


$$Q = \begin{matrix} & \begin{matrix} 1 & 2 & 3 & 4 \end{matrix} \\ \begin{matrix} 1 \\ 3 \end{matrix} & \begin{bmatrix} 1 & -1 & 0 & 0 \\ 0 & -1 & 1 & 1 \end{bmatrix} \end{matrix}$$

Fig. 8.81

The KCL equation in matrix form is given by

$$Q Y_b Q^T V_t = Q I_s - Q Y_b V_s$$

Here,

$$V_s = 0$$
$$Q Y_b Q^T V_t = Q I_s$$

$$Y_b = \begin{bmatrix} 5 & 0 & 0 & 0 \\ 0 & 5 & 0 & 0 \\ 0 & 0 & 5 & 0 \\ 0 & 0 & 0 & 10 \end{bmatrix}; Q^T = \begin{bmatrix} 1 & 0 \\ -1 & -1 \\ 0 & 1 \\ 0 & 1 \end{bmatrix}; I_s = \begin{bmatrix} -10 \\ 0 \\ 0 \\ 0 \end{bmatrix}$$

$$Q Y_b = \begin{bmatrix} 1 & -1 & 0 & 0 \\ 0 & -1 & 1 & 1 \end{bmatrix}\begin{bmatrix} 5 & 0 & 0 & 0 \\ 0 & 5 & 0 & 0 \\ 0 & 0 & 5 & 0 \\ 0 & 0 & 0 & 10 \end{bmatrix} = \begin{bmatrix} 5 & -5 & 0 & 0 \\ 0 & -5 & 5 & 10 \end{bmatrix}$$

$$QY_bQ^T = \begin{bmatrix} 5 & -5 & 0 & 0 \\ 0 & -5 & 5 & 10 \end{bmatrix} \begin{bmatrix} 1 & 0 \\ -1 & -1 \\ 0 & 1 \\ 0 & 1 \end{bmatrix} = \begin{bmatrix} 10 & 5 \\ 5 & 20 \end{bmatrix}$$

$$QI_s = \begin{bmatrix} 1 & -1 & 0 & 0 \\ 0 & -1 & 1 & 1 \end{bmatrix} \begin{bmatrix} -10 \\ 0 \\ 0 \\ 0 \end{bmatrix} = \begin{bmatrix} -10 \\ 0 \end{bmatrix}$$

Hence, KCL equation will be written as

$$\begin{bmatrix} 10 & 5 \\ 5 & 20 \end{bmatrix} \begin{bmatrix} v_{t_1} \\ v_{t_3} \end{bmatrix} = \begin{bmatrix} -10 \\ 0 \end{bmatrix}$$

Solving this matrix equation,

$$v_{t_1} = -\frac{8}{7}\text{ V}$$

$$v_{t_3} = \frac{2}{7}\text{ V}$$

## EXAMPLE 8.33

*For the network shown in Fig. 8.82, write down the f-cutset matrix and obtain the network equilibrium equation in matrix form using KCL and calculate v.*

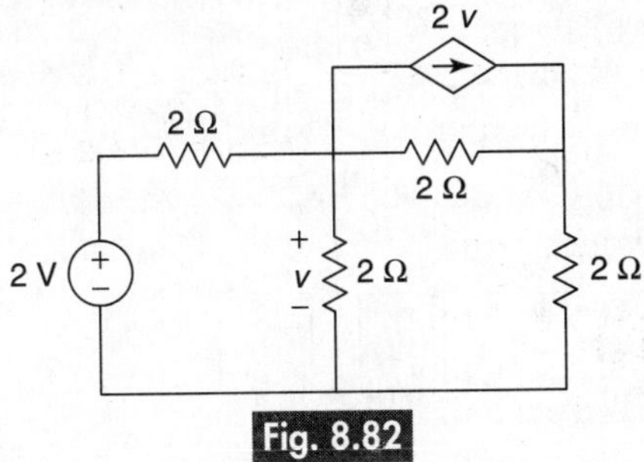


Fig. 8.82

**Solution** The oriented graph and its selected tree are shown in Fig. 8.83.

Since voltage $v$ is to be determined, branch 2 is chosen as twig.

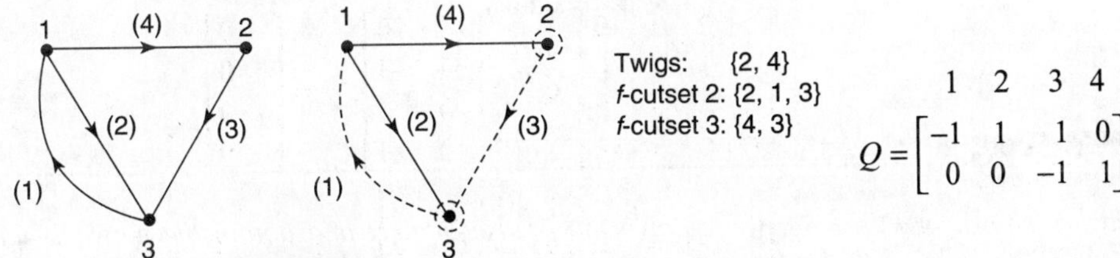


Fig. 8.83

The KCL equation in matrix form is given by

$$QY_b Q^T V_t = QI_s - QY_b V_s$$

$$Y_b = \begin{bmatrix} 0.5 & 0 & 0 & 0 \\ 0 & 0.5 & 0 & 0 \\ 0 & 0 & 0.5 & 0 \\ 0 & 0 & 0 & 0.5 \end{bmatrix}; Q^T = \begin{bmatrix} -1 & 0 \\ 1 & 0 \\ 1 & -1 \\ 0 & 1 \end{bmatrix}; I_s = \begin{bmatrix} 0 \\ 0 \\ 0 \\ -2v \end{bmatrix}; V_s = \begin{bmatrix} 2 \\ 0 \\ 0 \\ 0 \end{bmatrix}$$

$$QY_b = \begin{bmatrix} -1 & 1 & 1 & 0 \\ 0 & 0 & -1 & 1 \end{bmatrix} \begin{bmatrix} 0.5 & 0 & 0 & 0 \\ 0 & 0.5 & 0 & 0 \\ 0 & 0 & 0.5 & 0 \\ 0 & 0 & 0 & 0.5 \end{bmatrix} = \begin{bmatrix} -0.5 & 0.5 & 0.5 & 0 \\ 0 & 0 & -0.5 & 0.5 \end{bmatrix}$$

$$QY_b Q^T = \begin{bmatrix} -0.5 & 0.5 & 0.5 & 0 \\ 0 & 0 & -0.5 & 0.5 \end{bmatrix} \begin{bmatrix} -1 & 0 \\ 1 & 0 \\ 1 & -1 \\ 0 & 1 \end{bmatrix} = \begin{bmatrix} 1.5 & -0.5 \\ -0.5 & 1 \end{bmatrix}$$

$$QI_s = \begin{bmatrix} -1 & 1 & 1 & 0 \\ 0 & 0 & -1 & 1 \end{bmatrix} \begin{bmatrix} 0 \\ 0 \\ 0 \\ -2v \end{bmatrix} = \begin{bmatrix} 0 \\ -2v \end{bmatrix}$$

$$QY_b V_s = \begin{bmatrix} -0.5 & 0.5 & 0.5 & 0 \\ 0 & 0 & -0.5 & 0.5 \end{bmatrix} \begin{bmatrix} 2 \\ 0 \\ 0 \\ 0 \end{bmatrix} = \begin{bmatrix} -1 \\ 0 \end{bmatrix}$$

$$QI_s - QY_b V_s = \begin{bmatrix} 1 \\ -2v \end{bmatrix}$$

Hence, the KCL equation can be written as

$$\begin{bmatrix} 1.5 & -0.5 \\ -0.5 & 1 \end{bmatrix} \begin{bmatrix} v_{t_2} \\ v_{t_4} \end{bmatrix} = \begin{bmatrix} 1 \\ -2v \end{bmatrix}$$

From Fig. 8.82, $v_{t_2} = v$

Solving this matrix equation,

$$v_{t_2} = 0.44 \text{ V}$$

$$v_{t_4} = 0.66 \text{ V}$$

$$v = v_{t_2} = 0.44 \text{ V}$$

## EXAMPLE 8.34

*For the network shown in Fig. 8.84, write down the f-cutset matrix and obtain the network equilibrium equation in matrix form using KCL and calculate v.*

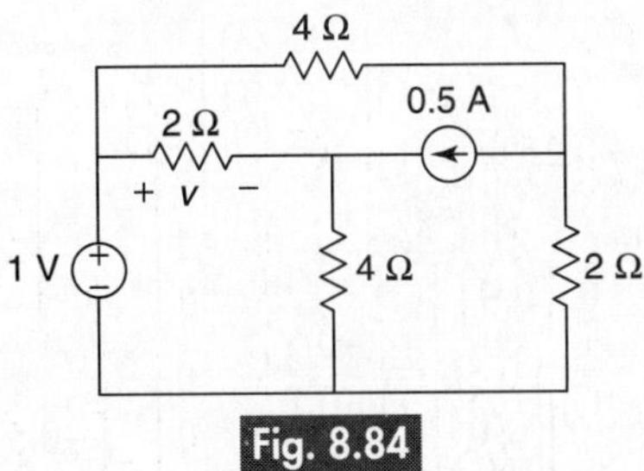

Fig. 8.84

**Solution** The voltage and current sources are converted into accompanied sources by source-shifting method, as shown in Fig. 8.85.

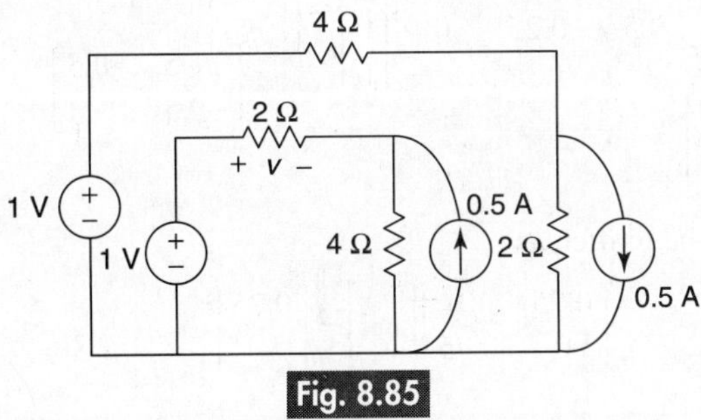

Fig. 8.85

The oriented graph and its selected tree are shown in Fig. 8.86.

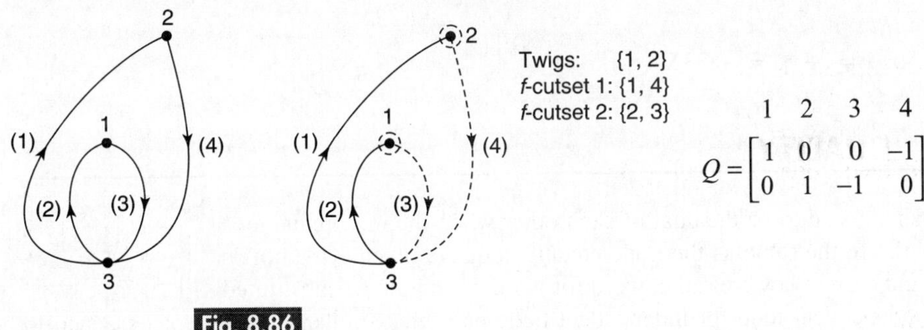


$$Q = \begin{bmatrix} 1 & 0 & 0 & -1 \\ 0 & 1 & -1 & 0 \end{bmatrix}$$

(columns 1, 2, 3, 4)

Fig. 8.86

The KCL equation in the matrix form is given by

$$Q\,Y_b\,Q^T\,V_t = Q\,I_s - Q\,Y_b\,V_s$$

$$Y_b = \begin{bmatrix} 0.25 & 0 & 0 & 0 \\ 0 & 0.5 & 0 & 0 \\ 0 & 0 & 0.25 & 0 \\ 0 & 0 & 0 & 0.5 \end{bmatrix}; Q^T = \begin{bmatrix} 1 & 0 \\ 0 & 1 \\ 0 & -1 \\ -1 & 0 \end{bmatrix}; \; I_s = \begin{bmatrix} 0 \\ 0 \\ 0.5 \\ -0.5 \end{bmatrix}; V_s = \begin{bmatrix} 1 \\ 1 \\ 0 \\ 0 \end{bmatrix}$$

$$Q\,Y_b = \begin{bmatrix} 1 & 0 & 0 & -1 \\ 0 & 1 & -1 & 0 \end{bmatrix} \begin{bmatrix} 0.25 & 0 & 0 & 0 \\ 0 & 0.5 & 0 & 0 \\ 0 & 0 & 0.25 & 0 \\ 0 & 0 & 0 & 0.5 \end{bmatrix} = \begin{bmatrix} 0.25 & 0 & 0 & -0.5 \\ 0 & 0.5 & -0.25 & 0 \end{bmatrix}$$

$$Q\,Y_b\,Q^T = \begin{bmatrix} 0.25 & 0 & 0 & -0.5 \\ 0 & 0.5 & -0.25 & 0 \end{bmatrix} \begin{bmatrix} 1 & 0 \\ 0 & 1 \\ 0 & -1 \\ -1 & 0 \end{bmatrix} = \begin{bmatrix} 0.75 & 0 \\ 0 & 0.75 \end{bmatrix}$$

$$Q\,I_s = \begin{bmatrix} 1 & 0 & 0 & -1 \\ 0 & 1 & -1 & 0 \end{bmatrix} \begin{bmatrix} 0 \\ 0 \\ 0.5 \\ -0.5 \end{bmatrix} = \begin{bmatrix} 0.5 \\ -0.5 \end{bmatrix}$$

$$Q\,Y_b\,V_s = \begin{bmatrix} 0.25 & 0 & 0 & -0.5 \\ 0 & 0.5 & -0.25 & 0 \end{bmatrix} \begin{bmatrix} 1 \\ 1 \\ 0 \\ 0 \end{bmatrix} = \begin{bmatrix} 0.25 \\ 0.5 \end{bmatrix}$$

$$Q\,I_s - Q\,Y_b\,V_s = \begin{bmatrix} 0.25 \\ -1 \end{bmatrix}$$

Hence, the KCL equation can be written as

$$\begin{bmatrix} 0.75 & 0 \\ 0 & 0.75 \end{bmatrix} \begin{bmatrix} v_{t_1} \\ v_{t_2} \end{bmatrix} = \begin{bmatrix} 0.25 \\ -1 \end{bmatrix}$$

Solving this matrix equation,

$$v_{t_1} = 0.33\text{ V}$$

$$v_{t_2} = -1.33\text{ V}$$

From Fig. 8.85, $v = 1 + v_{t_2} = -0.33\text{ V}$

## 8.12 DUALITY

LO 8.12

Explain the concept of duality

Two networks are said to be the dual of each other when the mesh equations of one network are the same as the node equations of the other. Kirchhoff's voltage law and current law are same, word for word, with voltage substituted for current, independent loop for independent node pair, etc. Similarly, two graphs are said to be dual of each other if the incidence matrix of any one of them is equal to the circuit matrix of the other. Only planar networks have duals.

**TABLE 8.1** Conversion for dual electrical circuits

| *Loop basis* | *Node basis* |
|---|---|
| Current | Voltage |
| Resistance | Conductance |
| Inductance | Capacitance |
| Branch current | Branch voltage |
| Mesh | Node |
| Short circuit | Open circuit |
| Parallel path | Series path |

The following steps are involved in constructing the dual of a network:

1. Place a node inside each mesh of the given network. These internal nodes correspond to the independent nodes in the dual network.
2. Place a node outside the given network. The external node corresponds to the datum node in the dual network.
3. Connect all internal nodes in the adjacent mesh by dashed lines crossing the common branches. Elements which are the duals of the common branches will form the branches connecting the corresponding independent node in the dual network.
4. Connect all internal nodes to the external node by dashed lines corresponding to all external branches. Duals of these external branches will form the branches connecting independent nodes and the datum node.
5. A clockwise current in a mesh corresponds to a positive polarity (with respect to the datum node) at the dual independent node.
6. A voltage rise in the direction of a clockwise mesh current corresponds to a current flowing towards the dual independent node.

## EXAMPLE 8.35

*Draw the dual of the network shown in Fig. 8.87.*

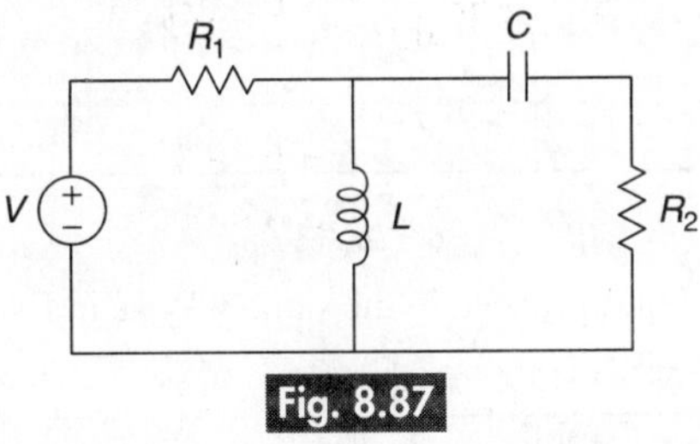


Fig. 8.87

**Solution** The following steps are involved in constructing the dual of the network, as shown in Fig. 8.88.

1. Place a node inside each mesh.
2. Place a node outside the mesh which will correspond to the datum node.
3. Connect two internal nodes through a dashed line. The element which is dual of the common branch (here capacitance) will form the branch connecting the corresponding independent node in the dual network.
4. Connect all internal nodes to the external node by dashed lines crossing all the branches. The dual of these branches will form the branches connecting the independent node and datum.

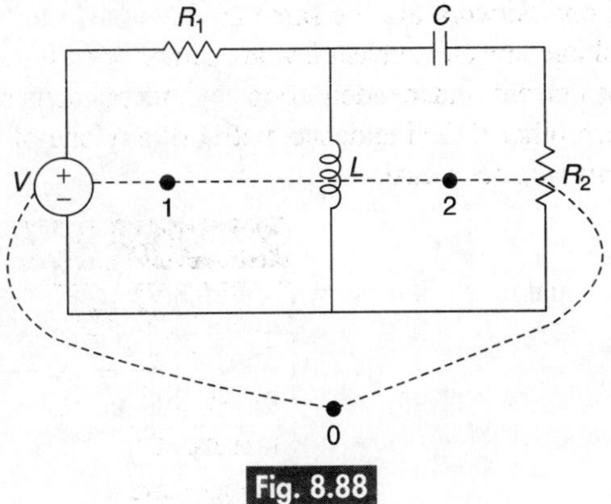


Fig. 8.88

The dual network is shown in Fig. 8.89.

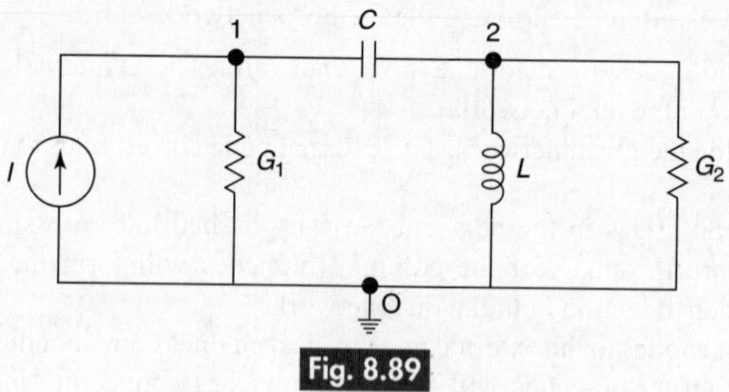


Fig. 8.89

## EXAMPLE 8.36

*Draw the dual of the network of Fig. 8.90.*

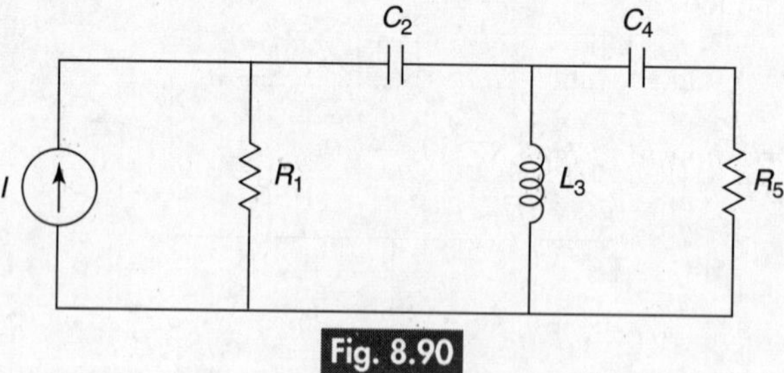


Fig. 8.90

**Solution** For drawing the dual network, proceed in the same way as in Example 8.35, as shown in Fig. 8.91.

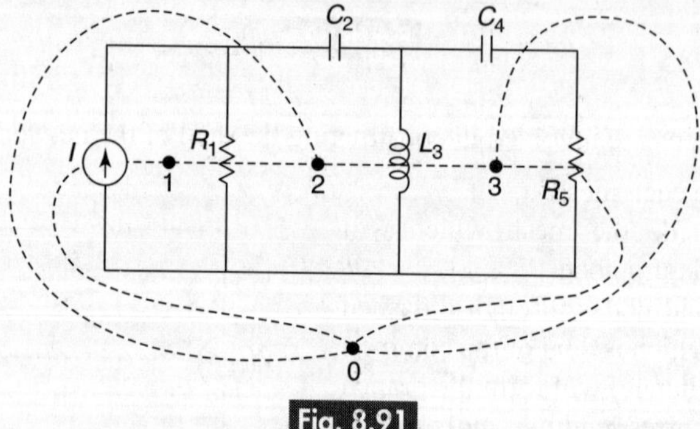


Fig. 8.91

The dual network is shown in Fig. 8.92.

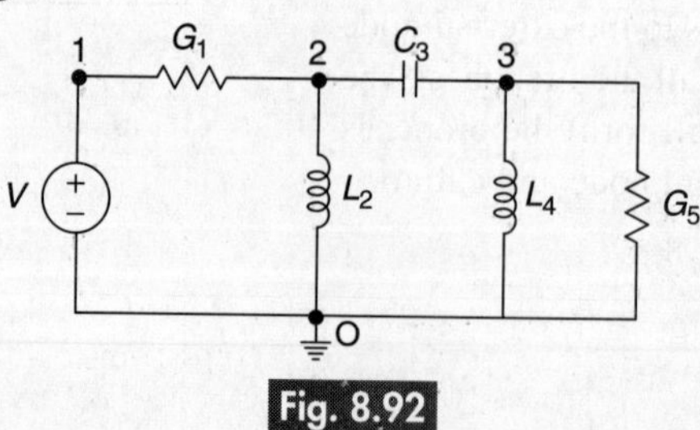


Fig. 8.92

## EXAMPLE 8.37

*Draw the dual of the network shown in Fig. 8.93.*

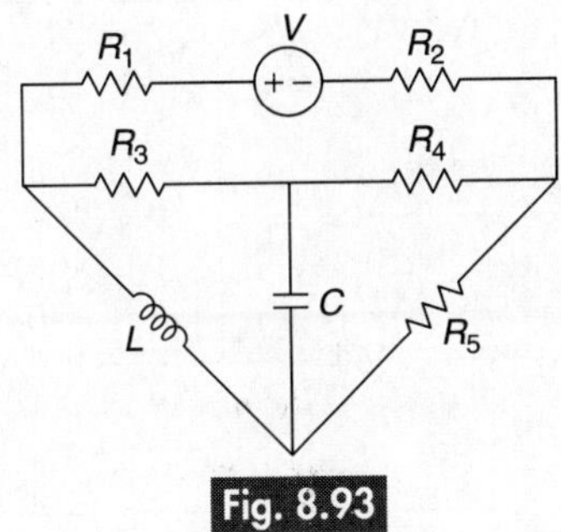


Fig. 8.93

**Solution** For drawing the dual network, proceed in the same way as in Example 8.35, as shown in Fig. 8.94.

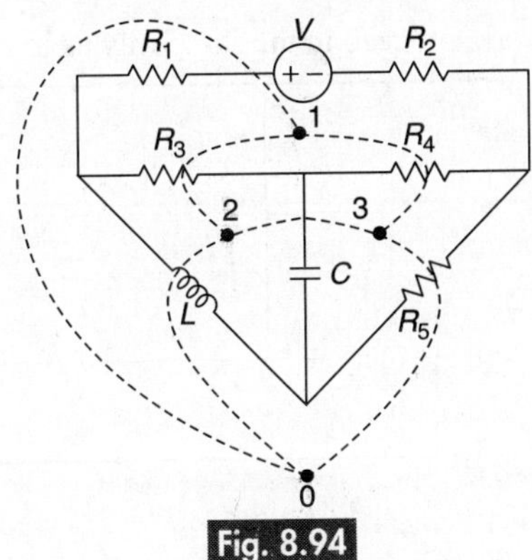


Fig. 8.94

The dual network is shown in Fig. 8.95.

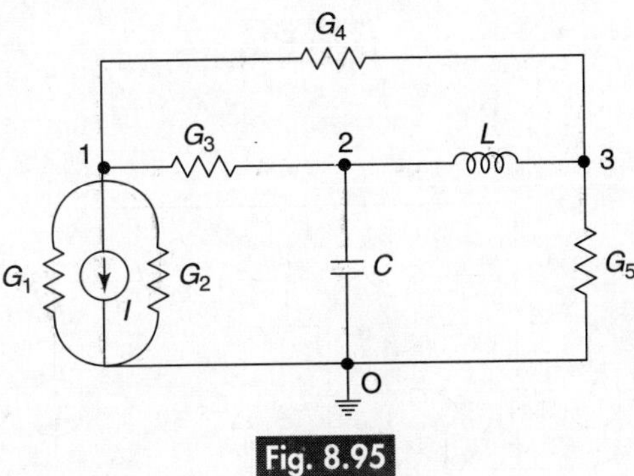


Fig. 8.95

## EXAMPLE 8.38

*Draw the dual of the network shown in Fig. 8.96.*

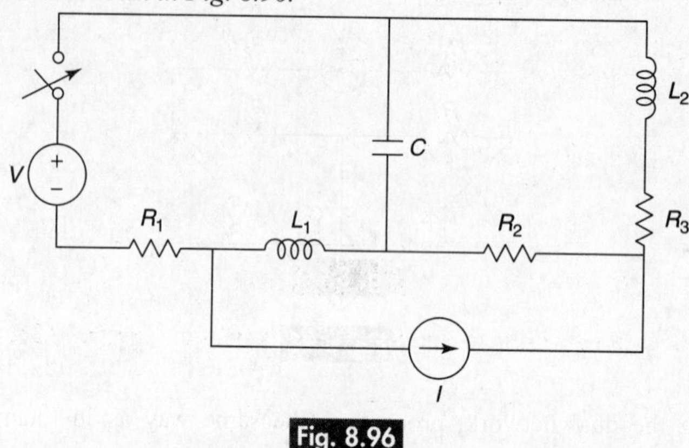


Fig. 8.96

**Solution** For drawing the dual network, proceed in the same way as in Example 8.35, as shown in Fig. 8.97.

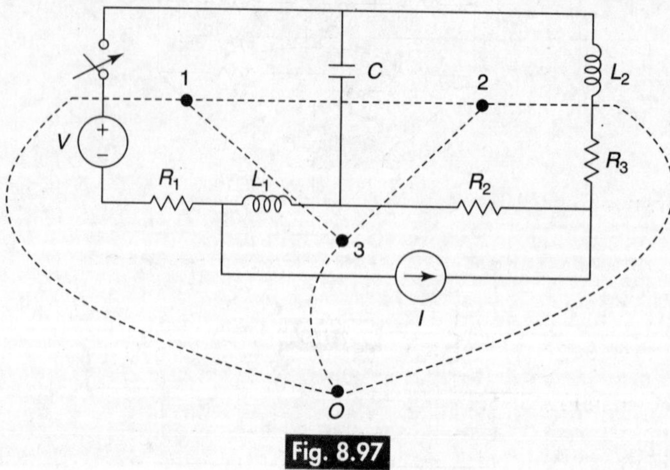


Fig. 8.97

The dual network is shown in Fig. 8.98.

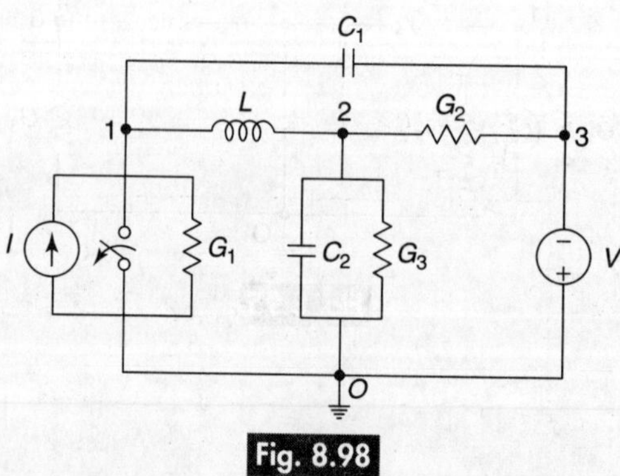


Fig. 8.98

## EXAMPLE 8.39

*Draw the dual of the network shown in Fig. 8.99.*

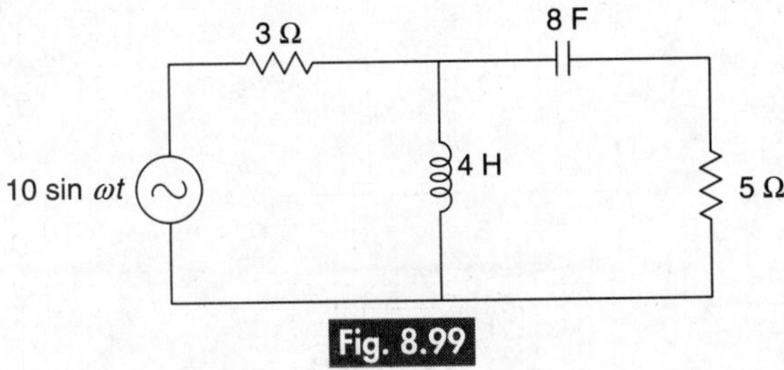


Fig. 8.99

**Solution** For drawing the dual network, proceed in the same way as in Example 8.35, as shown in Fig. 8.100.

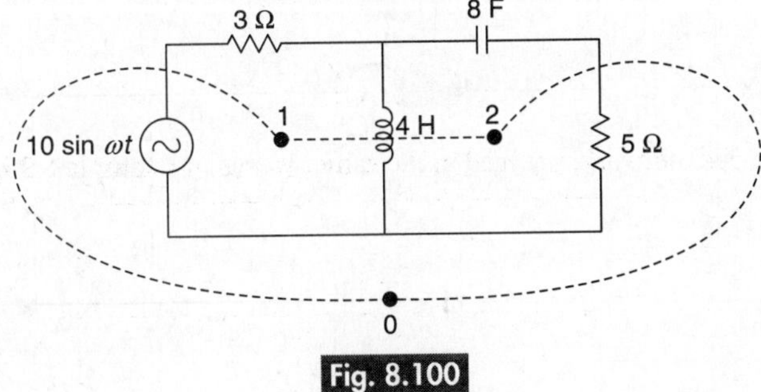


Fig. 8.100

The dual network is shown in Fig. 8.101.

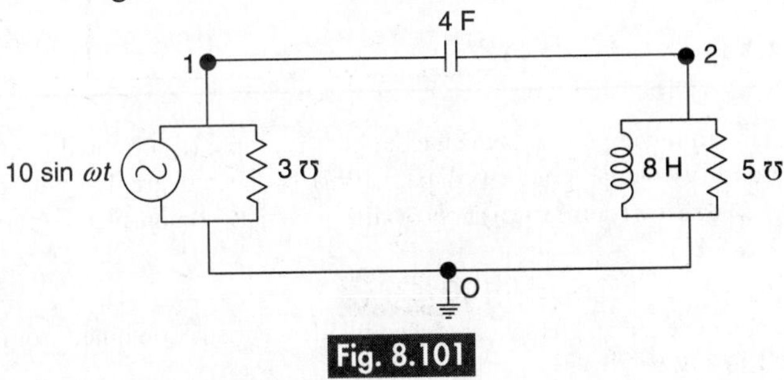


Fig. 8.101

## EXAMPLE 8.40

*Draw the dual of the network shown in Fig. 8.102.*

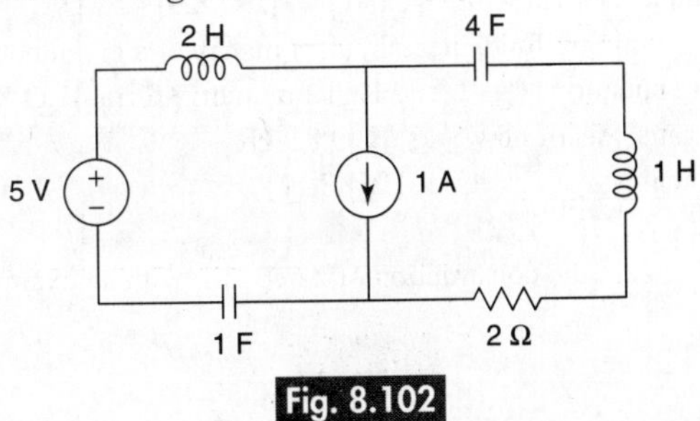


Fig. 8.102

**Solution** For drawing the dual network, proceed in the same way as in Example 8.35, as shown in Fig. 8.103.

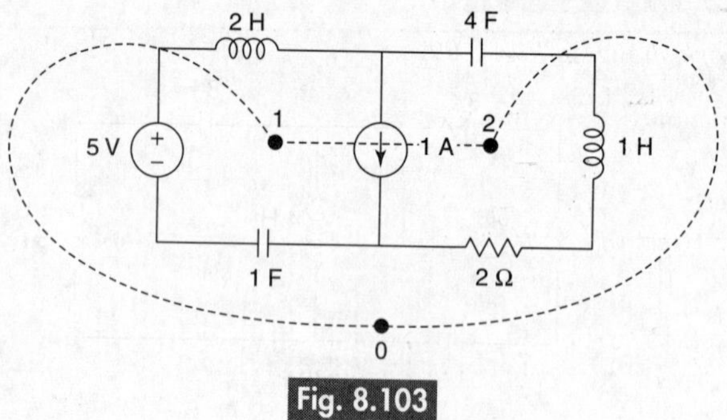


Fig. 8.103

The dual network is shown in Fig. 8.104.

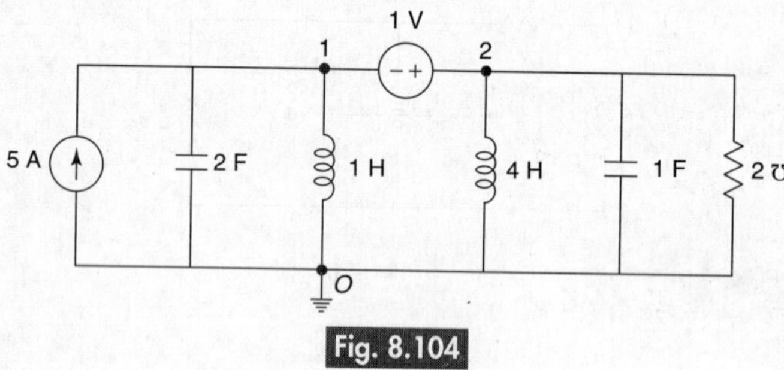


Fig. 8.104

# Theory Questions

**8.1** Define and explain the following terms with an example. (i) graph, (ii) oriented graph, (iii) subgraph, (iv) degree of a node (v) planar graph, (vi) path, (vii) connected graph, (viii) rank of a graph, (ix) loop or circuit, (x) tree, (xi) cotree, (xii) node, (xiii) branch, (xiv) non-planar graph, (xv) twig, and (xvi) link. **[LO 8.1 & 8.2]** ●○○

**8.2** Write the properties of a tree in the graph. **[LO 8.2]** ●○○

**8.3** What is complete incidence matrix? How is reduced incidence matrix obtained from it? Explain with suitable example. **[LO 8.3]** ○●○

**8.4** State the properties of complete incidence matrix. **[LO 8.3]** ●○○

**8.5** Define and illustrate with an example: tieset and *f*-tieset. **[LO 8.4]** ●○○

**8.6** Explain the procedure for obtaining fundamental tieset matrix of a given network. **[LO 8.4]** ○○●

**8.7** Define and explain cutset and f-cutset with an example. **[LO 8.5]** ○●○

**8.8** Explain the procedure for obtaining fundamental cutset matrix of a given network. **[LO 8.5]** ○○●

**8.9** Write network equilibrium equations (KVL and KCL) in matrix form. **[LO 8.11]** ○●○

**8.10** Explain nodal method for analysis of networks. **[LO 8.11]** ○○●

**8.11** Explain loop method for analysis of networks. **[LO 8.11]** ○○●

**8.12** Explain the concept of duality. **[LO 8.12]** ○●○

**8.13** What is a dual network? Explain the construction of a network with an example. **[LO 8.12]** ○○●

# Practice Problems

**8.1** For the networks shown in Fig. 8.105–8.108, write the incidence matrix, tieset matrix and *f*-cutset matrix.

(i)

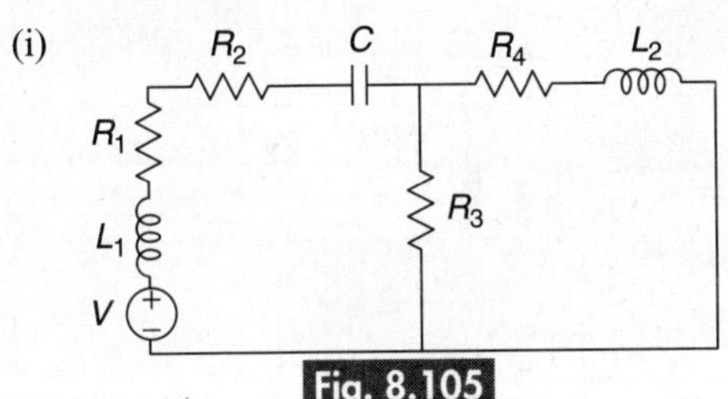


Fig. 8.105

(ii)

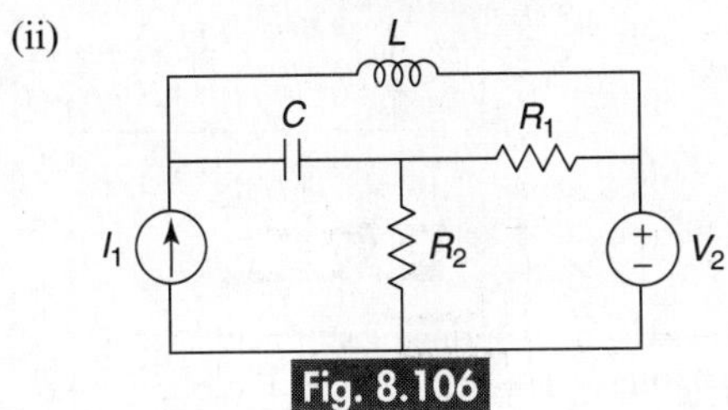


Fig. 8.106

(iii)

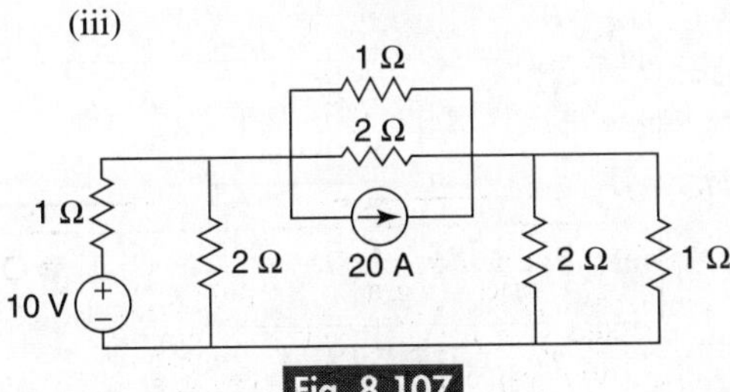


Fig. 8.107

(iv)

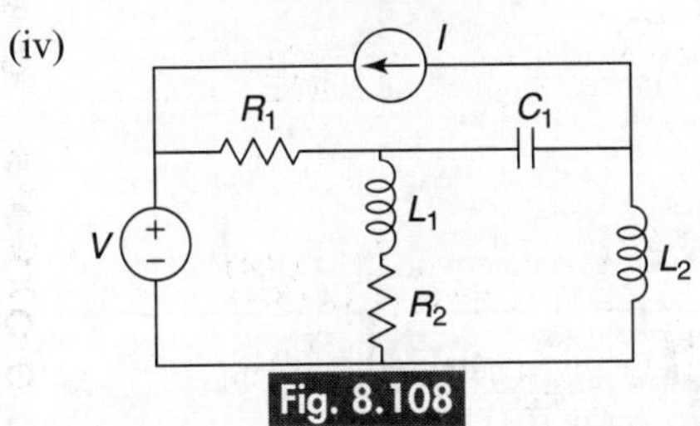


Fig. 8.108

**8.2** For the graph shown in Fig. 8.109, write the incidence matrix, tieset matrix and *f*-cutset matrix.

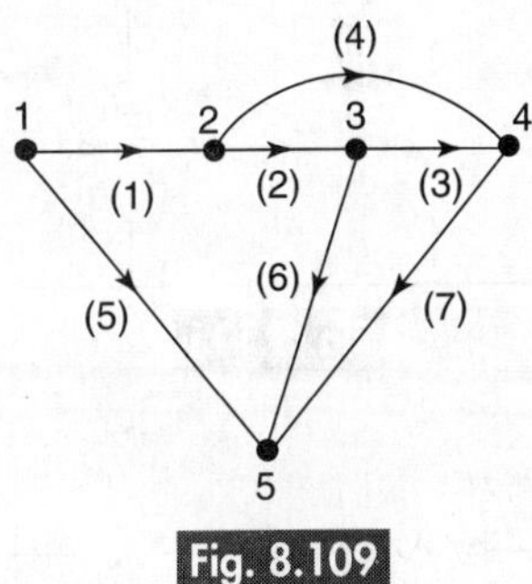


Fig. 8.109

**8.3** The incidence matrix is given as follows:

Branches →

| 1 | 2 | 3 | 4 | 5 | 6 | 7 | 8 |
|---|---|---|---|---|---|---|---|
| –1 | –1 | 0 | 0 | 0 | 0 | 1 | 0 |
| 0 | 1 | 1 | 0 | 1 | 0 | 0 | 0 |
| 0 | 0 | –1 | –1 | 0 | 1 | 0 | 0 |
| 1 | 0 | 0 | 1 | 0 | 0 | 0 | 1 |

Draw oriented graph and write tieset matrix.

**8.4** The incidence matrix is given below:

Branches →

| 1 | 2 | 3 | 4 | 5 | 6 | 7 | 8 | 9 | 10 |
|---|---|---|---|---|---|---|---|---|---|
| 0 | 0 | 1 | 1 | 1 | 1 | 0 | 1 | 0 | 0 |
| 0 | –1 | –1 | 0 | 0 | 0 | –1 | 0 | 0 | –1 |
| –1 | 1 | 0 | 0 | 0 | 0 | 0 | –1 | –1 | 1 |
| 1 | 0 | 0 | 0 | –1 | –1 | 1 | 0 | 0 | 0 |

Draw the oriented graph.

**8.5** For the network shown in Fig. 8.110, draw the oriented graph and obtain the tieset matrix. Use this matrix to calculate the current *i*.

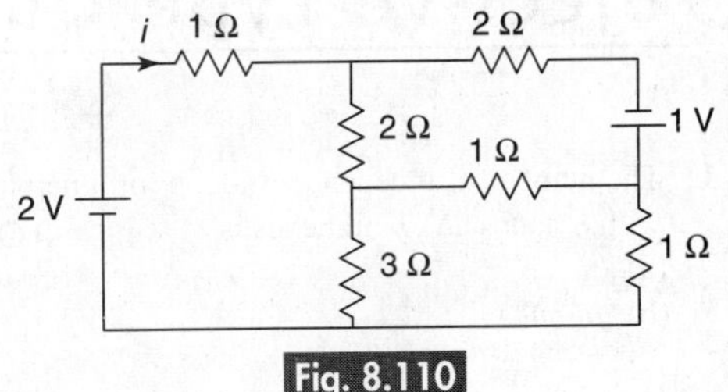


Fig. 8.110

**8.6** Draw the dual networks for the circuits shown in Fig. 8.111–8.115. ○●○

(i)

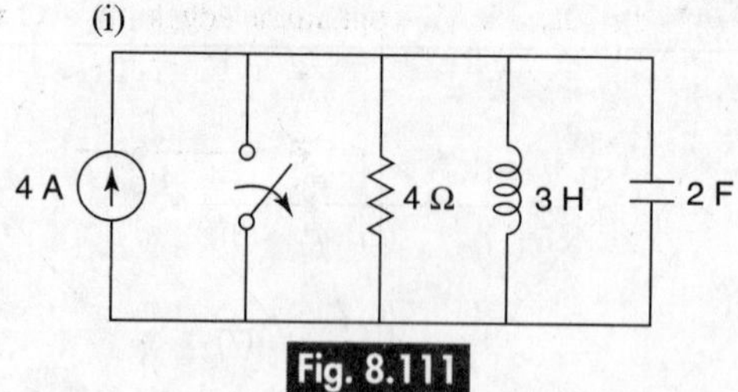


Fig. 8.111

(ii)

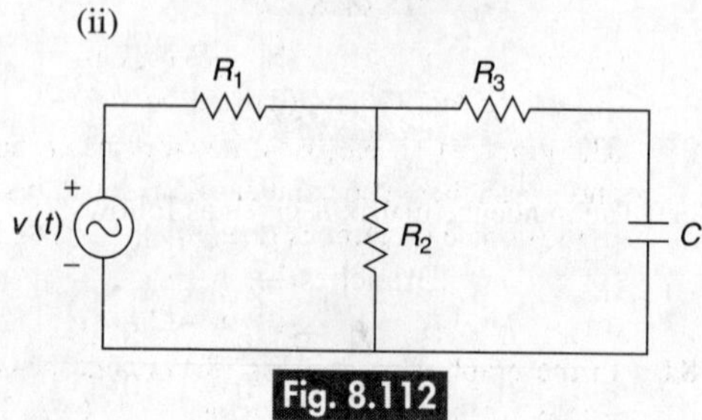


Fig. 8.112

(iii)

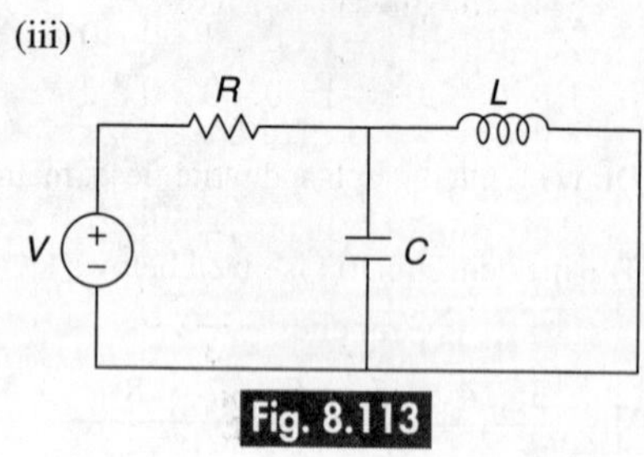


Fig. 8.113

(iv)

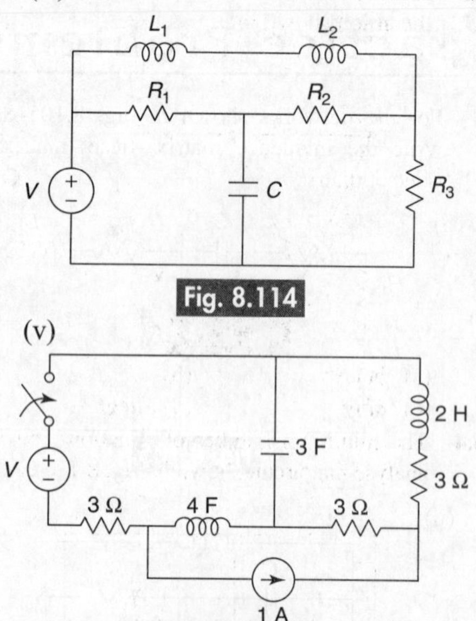


Fig. 8.114

(v)



Fig. 8.115

**8.7** Using the principles of network topology, write the node equation in matrix form for the network shown in Fig. 8.116. ○○●

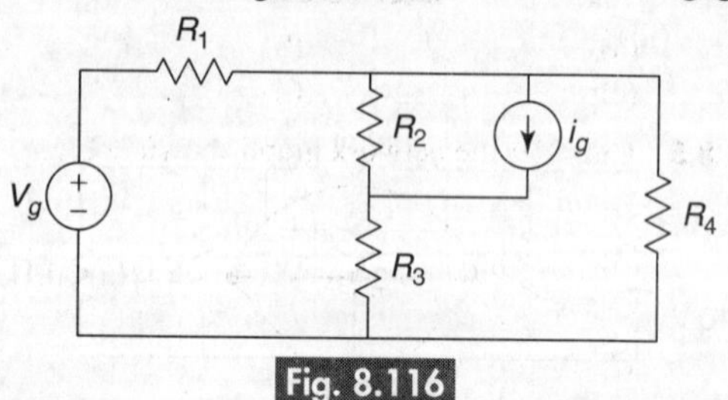


Fig. 8.116

## ANSWERS TO PRACTICE PROBLEMS

**8.5** 0.91 A

# Objective-Type Questions

## From GATE and Other Competitive Examinations

**8.1** The number of independent loops for a network with $n$ nodes and $b$ branches is ●○○

(a) $n - 1$

(b) $b - n$

(c) $b - n + 1$

(d) independent of the number of nodes

**8.2** A network has 7 nodes and 5 independent loops. The number of branches in the network is ●○○

(a) 13 (b) 12

(c) 11 (d) 10

**8.3** Identify which of the following is NOT a tree of the graph shown in Fig. 8.117. ○●○

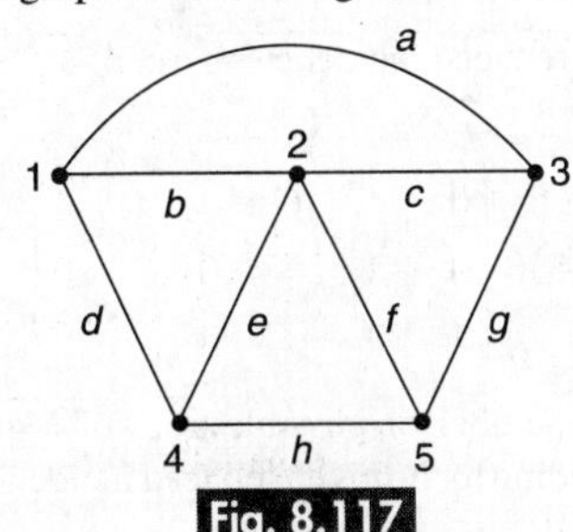


Fig. 8.117

(a) *begh* (b) *defg*
(c) *abfg* (d) *aegh*

**8.4** The minimum number of equations required to analyse the circuit shown in Fig. 8.118 is ○●○

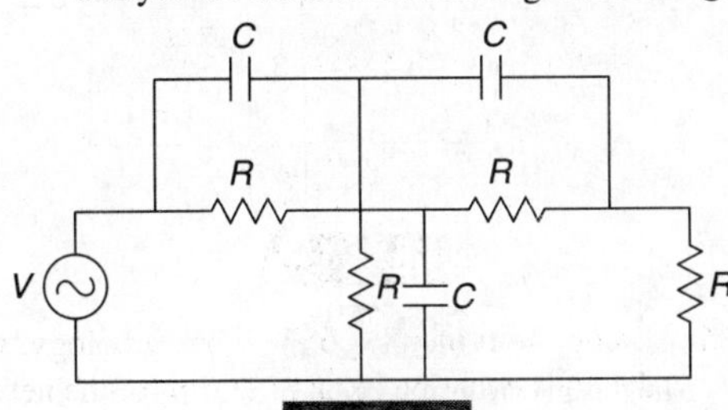


Fig. 8.118

(a) 3 (b) 4
(c) 6 (d) 7

**8.5** Consider the network graph shown in Fig. 8.119.

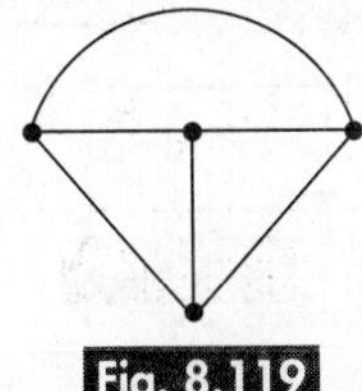

Fig. 8.119

Which one of the following is NOT a tree of this graph? ●○○

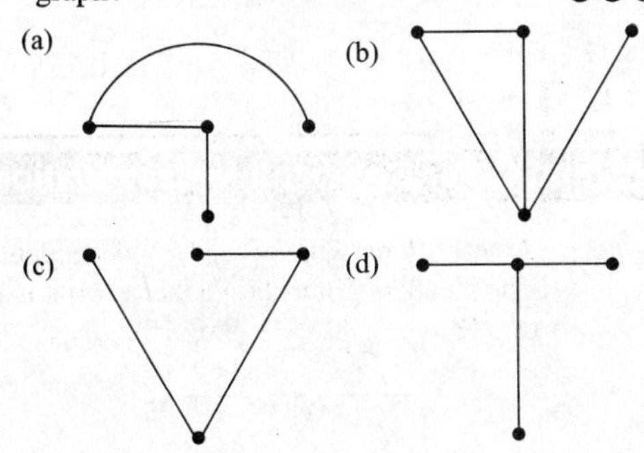


**8.6** Figure 8.120 shows a network and its graph is drawn aside. A proper tree chosen for analysing the network will contain the edges. ○●○

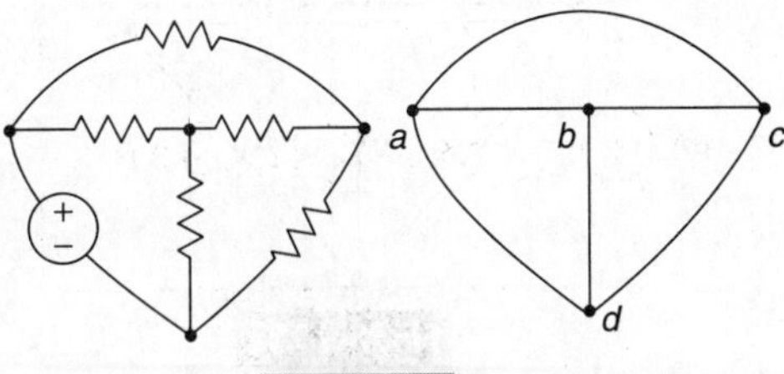


Fig. 8.120

(a) *ab, bc, ad* (b) *ab, bc, ca*
(c) *ab, bd, ca?* (d) *ac, bd, ad*

**8.7** The graph of an electrical network has *n* nodes and *b* branches. The number of links with respect to the choice of a tree is given by ●○○

(a) $b - n + 1$ (b) $b + n$
(c) $n - b + 1$ (d) $n - 2b - 1$.

**8.8** In the graph shown in Fig. 8.121, one possible tree is formed by the branches 4, 5, 6, 7. Then one possible fundamental cutset is ○●○

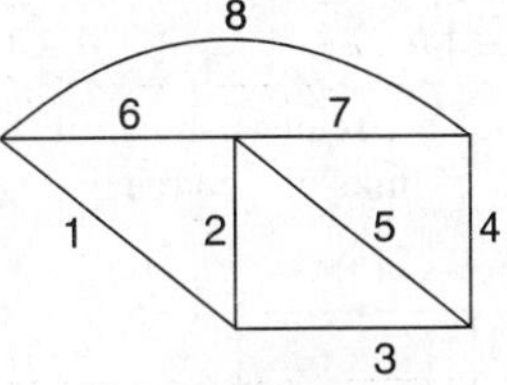


Fig. 8.121

(a) 1, 2, 3, 8 (b) 1, 2, 5, 6
(c) 1, 5, 6, 8 (d) 1, 2, 3, 7, 8

**8.9** Which one of the following represents the total number of trees in the graph given in Fig. 8.122? ○●○

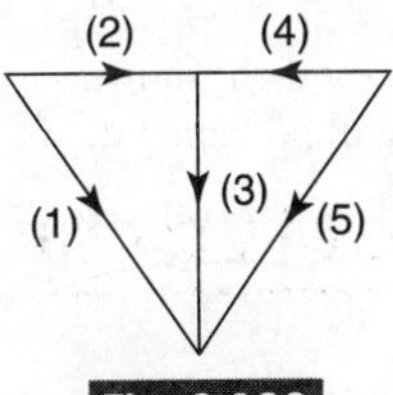


Fig. 8.122

(a) 4 (b) *C*
(c) 5 (d) 8

**8.10** Which one of the following is a cutset of the graph shown in Fig. 8.123? ○●○

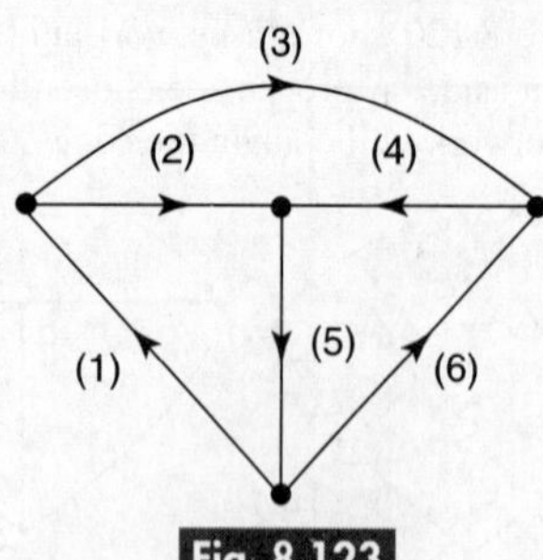

Fig. 8.123

(a) 1, 2, 3 and 4 (b) 2, 3, 4 and 6
(c) 1, 4, 5 and 6 (d) 1, 2, 4 and 5

**8.11** In the graph shown in Fig. 8.124, the number of trees ($P$) and the number of cutset ($Q$) are ●○○

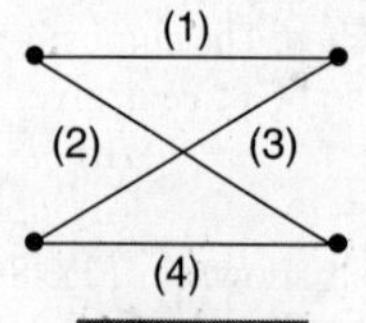

Fig. 8.124

(a) $P = 2, Q = 2$ (b) $P = 2, Q = 6$
(c) $P = 4, Q = 6$ (d) $P = 4, Q = 10$

**8.12** Graph of a circuit is shown in Fig. 8.125. The number of links of a cotree is ●○○

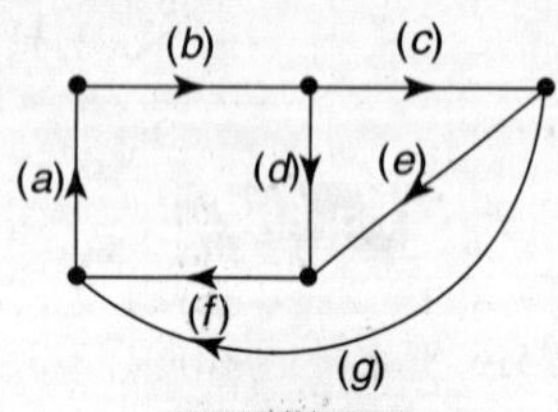

Fig. 8.125

(a) 2 (b) 3
(c) 4 (d) 5

**8.13** Consider a graph shown in Fig. 8.126. The number of all possible trees is ○●○

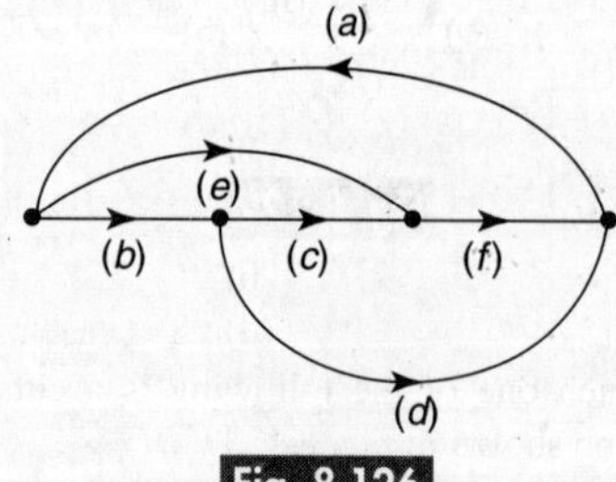

Fig. 8.126

(a) 10 (b) 12
(c) 16 (d) 20

**8.14** The reduced incidence matrix of a graph is given by ○●○

$$A_a = \begin{bmatrix} 0 & 1 & 0 & -1 & -1 & 1 \\ 0 & -1 & 1 & 0 & 1 & 0 \\ 1 & 0 & -1 & 0 & 0 & 0 \end{bmatrix}$$

The number of possible trees of a graph corresponding to the given reduced incidence matrix is

(a) 10 (b) 12
(c) 16 (d) 20

**8.15** Consider a graph shown in Fig. 8.127.

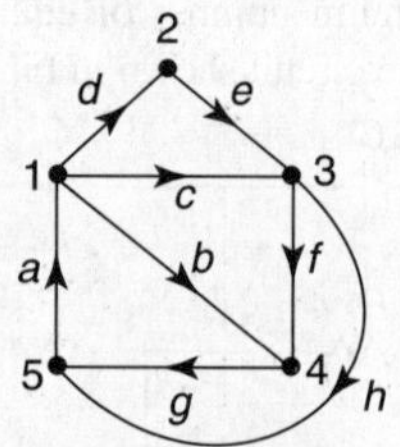

Fig. 8.127

In the given graph, which one of the following subgraph is not a tree? ○●○

(a) $\{a, c, g, h\}$ (b) $\{b, d, f, h\}$
(c) $\{a, c, d, h\}$ (d) $\{a, b, d, g\}$

**8.16** For the graph shown in Fig. 8.128, the number of cutset is ●○○

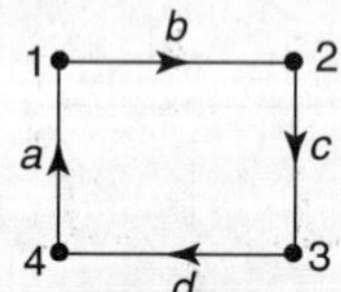

Fig. 8.128

(a) 2 (b) 4
(c) 6 (d) 8

**8.17** For the graph shown in Fig. 8.129, the number of $f$-cutset is ●○○

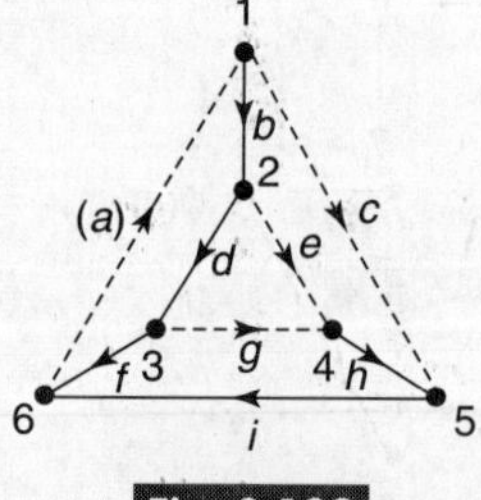

Fig. 8.129

(a) 3 (b) 4
(c) 5 (d) 6

**8.18** The oriented graph is shown in Fig. 8.130. The number of fundamental tieset is ●○○

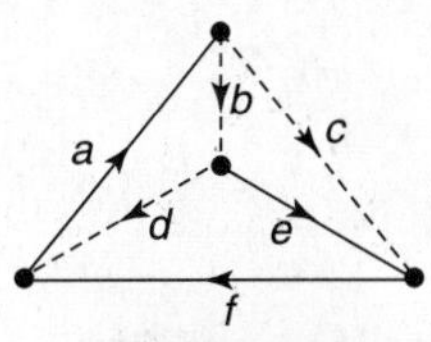


Fig. 8.130

(a) 1 (b) 2
(c) 3 (d) 4

**8.19** If $B$ is tieset matrix and $I_l$ is loop current matrix then branch current $I_b$ is given by ●○○

(a) $I_b = BI_l$ (b) $I_b = I_lB^T$
(c) $I_b = B^TI_l$ (d) $I_b = B^TI_l^T$

**8.20** For the graph shown in Fig. 8.131, the order of the $f$-tieset matrix is ○●○

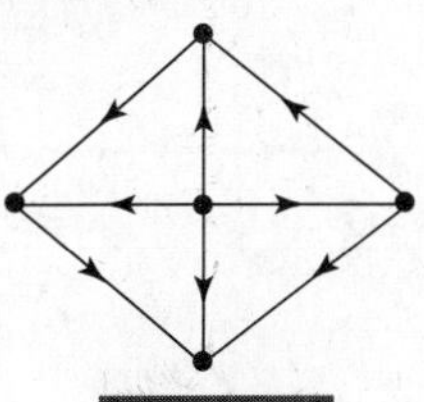

Fig. 8.131

(a) $4 \times 4$ (b) $4 \times 8$
(c) $8 \times 4$ (d) $8 \times 8$

**8.21** A planar graph has five nodes and nine branches. The number of meshes in the dual graph is ●○○

(a) 5 (b) 4
(c) 14 (d) none of these

**8.22** From the following graph in Fig. 8.132, which of them is non-planar? ●○○

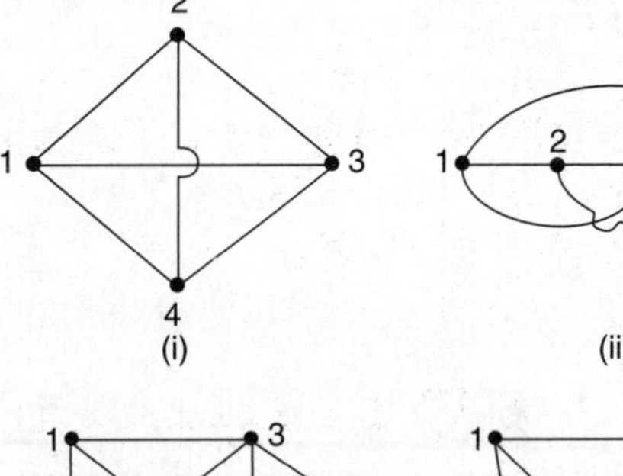


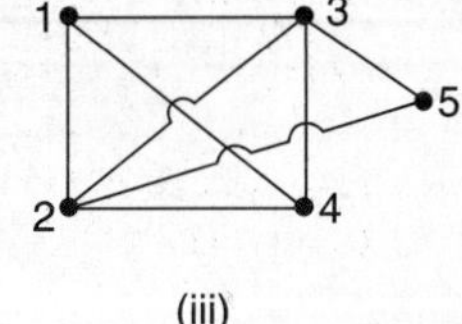


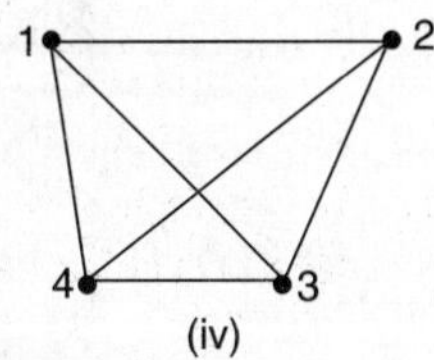


Fig. 8.132

(a) (i) and (ii) (b) (ii) and (iii)
(c) (iii) only (d) (iv) only

**8.23** If $V_b$, $Q$ and $V_t$ represent branch voltage matrix, $f$-cutset matrix and twig voltage matrix, then the relationship between them is given by ●○○

(a) $V_b = QV_t^T$ (b) $V_b = Q^TV_t^T$
(c) $V_b = V_tQ$ (d) $V_b = Q^TV_t$

**8.24** If the number of branches in a network is '$b$', the number of nodes is '$n$' and the number of dependent loops is '$l$' then the number of independent node equation will be ●○○

(a) $n + l - 1$ (b) $b - 1$
(c) $b - n$ (d) $n - 1$

**8.25** Number of fundamental cutsets of any graph will be ●○○

(a) same as the number of twigs
(b) same as the number of trees
(c) same as the number of nodes
(d) equal to one

## ANSWERS TO OBJECTIVE-TYPE QUESTIONS

| | | | | | | |
|---|---|---|---|---|---|---|
| **8.1** (c) | **8.2** (c) | **8.3** (c) | **8.4** (b) | **8.5** (b) | **8.6** (d) | **8.7** (a) |
| **8.8** (d) | **8.9** (d) | **8.10** (d) | **8.11** (c) | **8.12** (b) | **8.13** (c) | **8.14** (b) |
| **8.15** (c) | **8.16** (c) | **8.17** (c) | **8.18** (c) | **8.19** (c) | **8.20** (b) | **8.21** (a) |
| **8.22** (d) | **8.23** (d) | **8.24** (d) | **8.25** (a) | | | |

CHAPTER 9

# Transient Analysis

## LEARNING OBJECTIVES

**After studying this chapter, you should be able to:**

**LO 9.1** Explain the initial conditions for solving differential equations

**LO 9.2** Discuss the transient response of *RL* circuit for dc excitation

**LO 9.3** Discuss the transient response of *RL* circuit for sinusoidal excitation

**LO 9.4** Discuss the transient response of *RC* circuit for dc excitation

**LO 9.5** Discuss the transient response of *RC* circuit for sinusoidal excitation

**LO 9.6** Discuss the transient response of *RLC* circuit for dc excitation

**LO 9.7** Discuss the transient response of *RLC* circuit for sinusoidal excitation

## INTRODUCTION

Whenever a network containing energy storage elements such as an inductor or a capacitor is switched from one condition to another, either by change in applied source or change in network elements, the response current and voltage change from one state to the other state. The time taken to change from an initial steady state to the final steady state is known as the *transient period*. This response is known as *transient response* or *transients*. The response of the network after it attains a final steady value is independent of time and is called the steady-state response. The complete response of the network is determined with the help of a differential equation.

## 9.1 INITIAL CONDITIONS

LO 9.1

Explain the initial conditions for solving differential equations

In solving the differential equations in the network, we get some arbitrary constant. Initial conditions are used to determine these arbitrary constants. It helps us to know the behaviour of elements at the instant of switching.

To differentiate between the time immediately before and immediately after the switching, the signs '–' and '+' are used. The conditions existing just before switching are denoted as $i(0^-)$, $v(0^-)$, etc. Conditions just after switching are denoted as $i(0^+)$, $v(0^+)$.

Sometimes, conditions at $t = \infty$ are used in the evaluation of arbitrary constants. These are known as *final conditions*.

In solving the problems for initial conditions in the network, we divide the time period in the following ways:

1. Just before switching (from $t = -\infty$ to $t = 0^-$)
2. Just after switching (at $t = 0^+$)
3. After switching (for $t > 0$)

If the network remains in one condition for a long time without any switching action, it is said to be under steady-state condition.

***1. Initial Conditions for the Resistor*** For a resistor, current and voltage are related by $v(t) = Ri(t)$. The current through a resistor will change instantaneously if the voltage changes instantaneously. Similarly, the voltage will change instantaneously if the current changes instantaneously.

***2. Initial Conditions for the Inductor*** For an inductor, current and voltage are related by

$$v(t) = L\frac{di}{dt}$$

Voltage across the inductor is proportional to the rate of change of current. It is impossible to change the current through an inductor by a finite amount in zero time. This requires an infinite voltage across the inductor. An inductor does not allow an abrupt change in the current through it.

The current through the inductor is given by

$$i(t) = \frac{1}{L}\int_0^t v(t)dt + i(0)$$

where $i(0)$ is the initial current through the inductor.

If there is no current flowing through the inductor at $t = 0^-$, the inductor will act as an open circuit at $t = 0^+$. If a current of value $I_0$ flows through the inductor at $t = 0^-$, the inductor can be regarded as a current source of $I_0$ ampere at $t = 0^+$.

***3. Initial Conditions for the Capacitor*** For the capacitor, current and voltage are related by

$$i(t) = C\frac{dv(t)}{dt}$$

Current through a capacitor is proportional to the rate of change of voltage. It is impossible to change the voltage across a capacitor by a finite amount in zero time. This requires an infinite current through the capacitor. A capacitor does not allow an abrupt change in voltage across it.

The voltage across the capacitor is given by

$$v(t) = \frac{1}{C}\int_0^t i(t)dt + v(0)$$

where $v(0)$ is the initial voltage across the capacitor.

If there is no voltage across the capacitor at $t = 0^-$, the capacitor will act as a short circuit at $t = 0^+$. If the capacitor is charged to a voltage $V_0$ at $t = 0^-$, it can be regarded as a voltage source of $V_0$ volt at $t = 0^+$. These conditions are summarised in Fig. 9.1.

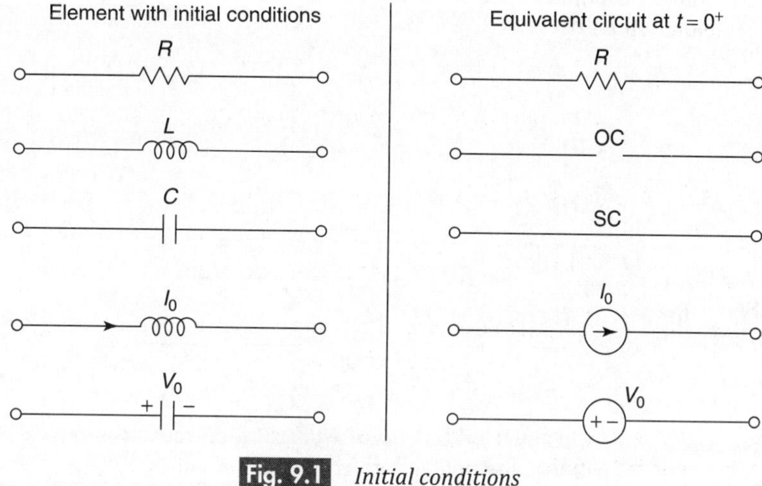


**Fig. 9.1** *Initial conditions*

Similarly, we can draw the chart for final conditions, as shown in Fig. 9.2.

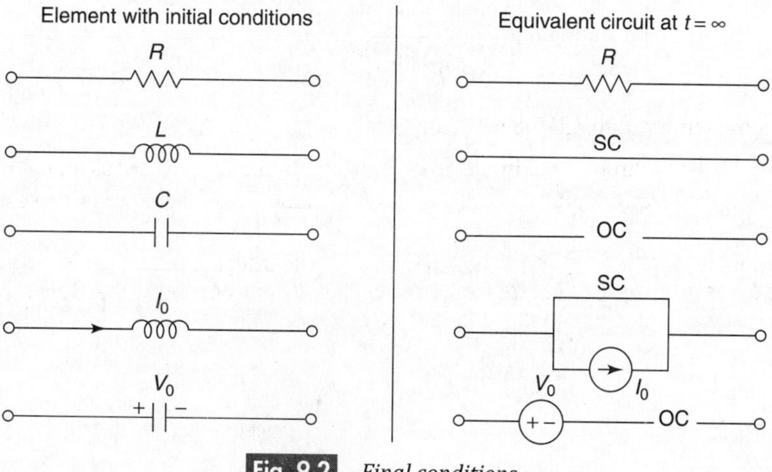


**Fig. 9.2** *Final conditions*

### 4. Procedure for Evaluating Initial Conditions

(i) Draw the equivalent network at $t = 0^-$. Before switching action takes place, i.e., for $t = -\infty$ to $t = 0^-$, the network is under steady-state conditions. Hence, find the current flowing through the inductors $i_L(0^-)$ and voltage across the capacitor $v_C(0^-)$.

(ii) Draw the equivalent network at $t = 0^+$, i.e., immediately after switching. Replace all the inductors with open circuits or with current sources $i_L(0^+)$ and replace all capacitors by short circuits or voltage sources $v_C(0^+)$. Resistors are kept as it is in the network. Initial voltages or currents in the network are determined from the equivalent network at $t = 0^+$.

(iii) Initial conditions, i.e., $\frac{di}{dt}(0^+), \frac{dv}{dt}(0^+), \frac{d^2i}{dt^2}(0^+), \frac{d^2v}{dt^2}(0^+)$ are determined by writing integro-differential equations for the network for $t > 0$, i.e., after the switching action by making use of initial condition.

**EXAMPLE 9.1** ●○○

*In the given network of Fig. 9.3, the switch is closed at t = 0. With zero current in the inductor, find i, $\frac{di}{dt}$ and $\frac{d^2i}{dt^2}$ at $t = 0^+$.*

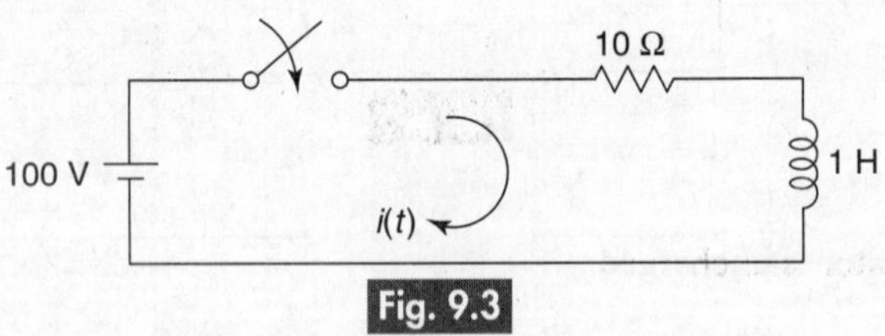


Fig. 9.3

**Solution**

(i) At $t = 0^-$, no current flows through the inductor.

$$i(0^-) = 0$$

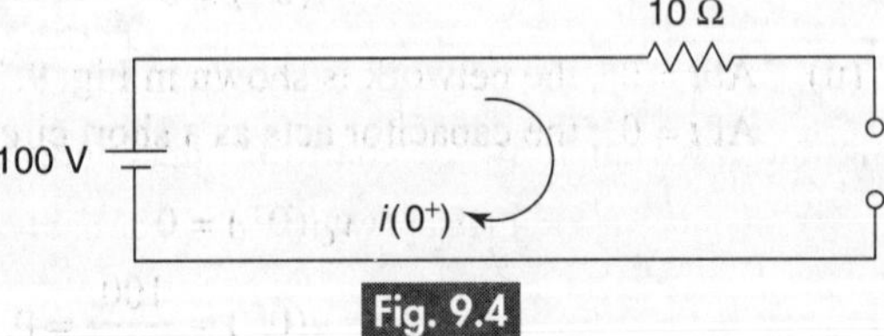


Fig. 9.4

(ii) At $t = 0^+$, the network is shown in Fig. 9.4.
At $t = 0^+$, the inductor acts as an open circuit.

$$i(0^+) = 0$$

(iii) For $t > 0$, the network is shown in Fig. 9.5.

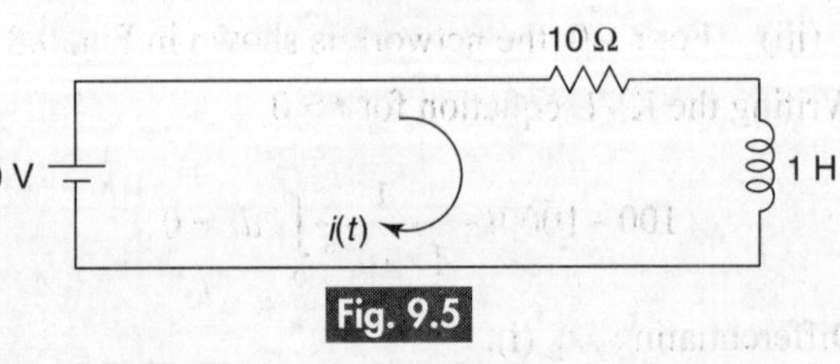


Fig. 9.5

Writing the KVL equation for $t > 0$,

$$100 - 10i - 1\frac{di}{dt} = 0 \qquad \ldots\text{(i)}$$

$$\frac{di}{dt} = 100 - 10i \qquad \ldots\text{(ii)}$$

**Note** Difficulty Level ●○○— Easy; ○●○— Medium; ○○●— Difficult

At $t = 0^+$, $$\frac{di}{dt}(0^+) = 100 - 10i(0^+) = 100 - 10(0) = 100 \text{ A/s}$$

Differentiating Eq. (ii),

$$\frac{d^2i}{dt^2} = -10\frac{di}{dt}$$

At $t = 0^+$, $$\frac{d^2i}{dt^2}(0^+) = -10\frac{di}{dt}(0^+) = -10(100) = -1000 \text{ A/s}^2$$

**EXAMPLE 9.2**

*In the network of Fig. 9.6, the switch is closed at t = 0. With the capacitor uncharged, find value for $i$, $\frac{di}{dt}$ and $\frac{d^2i}{dt^2}$ at $t = 0^+$.*

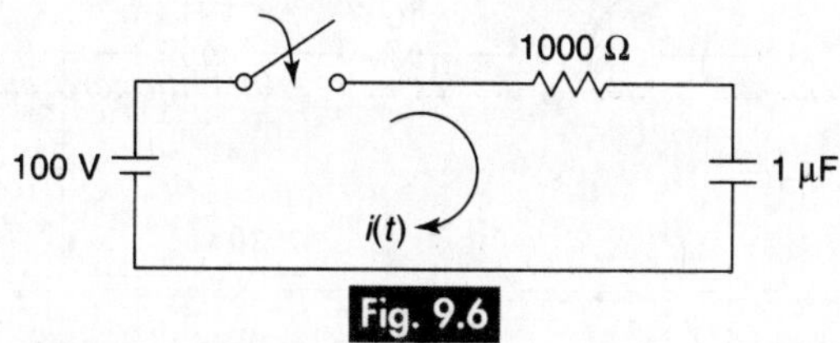


Fig. 9.6

**Solution**

(i) At $t = 0^-$, the capacitor is uncharged.

$$v_C(0^-) = 0$$

$$i(0^-) = 0$$

(ii) At $t = 0^+$, the network is shown in Fig. 9.7.
At $t = 0^+$, the capacitor acts as a short circuit.

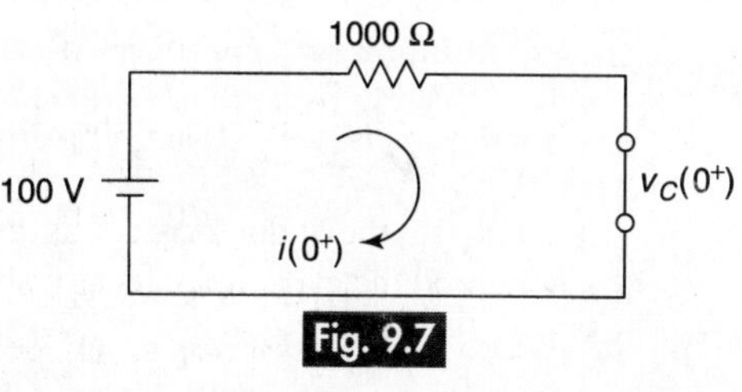


Fig. 9.7

$$v_C(0^+) = 0$$

$$i(0^+) = \frac{100}{1000} = 0.1 \text{ A}$$

(iii) For $t > 0$, the network is shown in Fig. 9.8.

Writing the KVL equation for $t > 0$,

$$100 - 1000i - \frac{1}{1 \times 10^{-6}}\int_0^t i\,dt = 0 \qquad \text{...(i)}$$

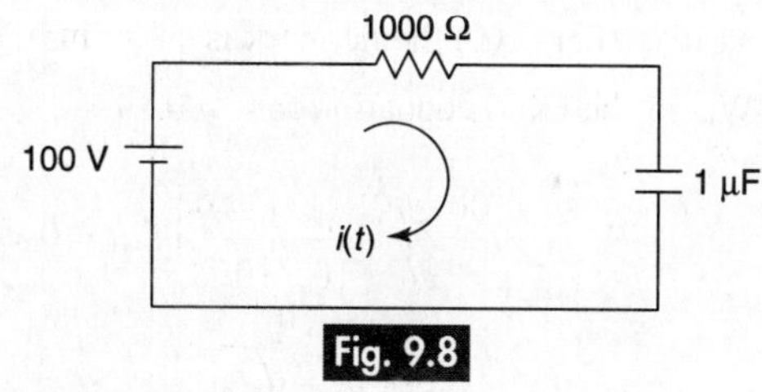


Fig. 9.8

Differentiating Eq. (i),

$$0 - 1000\frac{di}{dt} - 10^6 i = 0$$

$$\frac{di}{dt} = -\frac{10^6}{1000}i \qquad \text{...(ii)}$$

At $t = 0^+$, $$\frac{di}{dt}(0^+) = -\frac{10^6}{1000}i(0^+) = -\frac{10^6}{1000}(0.1) = -100 \text{ A/s}$$

Differentiating Eq. (ii),

$$\frac{d^2i}{dt^2} = -\frac{10^6}{1000}\frac{di}{dt}$$

At $t = 0^+$, $$\frac{d^2i}{dt^2}(0^+) = -\frac{10^6}{1000}\frac{di}{dt}(0^+) = -\frac{10^6}{1000}(-100) = 10^5 \text{ A/s}^2$$

## EXAMPLE 9.3

*In the network shown in Fig. 9.9, the switch is closed. Assuming all initial conditions as zero, find $i$, $\frac{di}{dt}$ and $\frac{d^2i}{dt^2}$ at $t = 0^+$.*

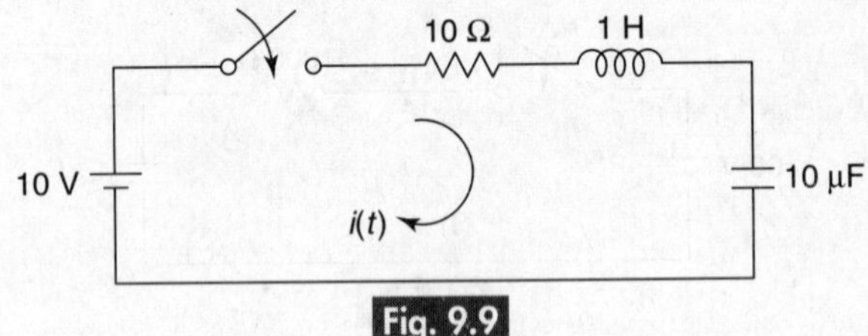


Fig. 9.9

**Solution**

(i) At $t = 0^-$,

$$i(0^-) = 0$$
$$v_C(0^-) = 0$$

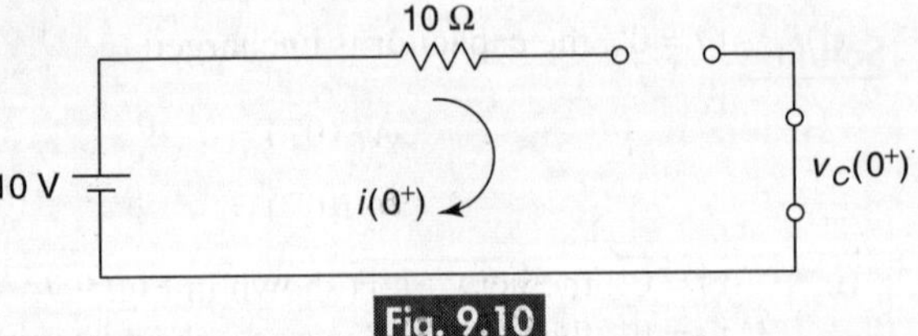


Fig. 9.10

(ii) At $t = 0^+$, the network is shown in Fig. 9.10.
At $t = 0^+$, the inductor acts as an open circuit and the capacitor acts as a short circuit.

$$i(0^+) = 0$$
$$v_C(0^+) = 0$$

(iii) For $t > 0$, the network is shown in Fig. 9.11.

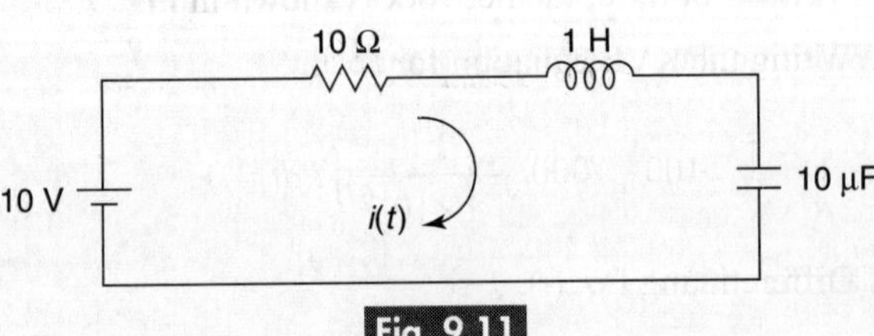


Fig. 9.11

Writing the KVL equation for $t > 0$,

$$10 - 10i - 1\frac{di}{dt} - \frac{1}{10 \times 10^{-6}}\int_0^t i\,dt = 0 \quad \ldots\text{(i)}$$

At $t = 0^+$, $$10 - 10i(0^+) - \frac{di}{dt}(0^+) - 0 = 0$$

$$\frac{di}{dt}(0^+) = 10 \text{A/s}$$

Differentiating Eq. (i),

$$0-10\frac{di}{dt}-\frac{d^2i}{dt^2}-\frac{1}{10\times10^{-6}}i=0$$

At $t = 0^+$,

$$0-10\frac{di}{dt}(0^+)-\frac{d^2i}{dt^2}(0^+)-\frac{1}{10^{-5}}i(0^+)=0$$

$$\frac{d^2i}{dt^2}(0^+)=-10\times10=-100\text{ A/s}^2$$

## EXAMPLE 9.4

*In the network shown in Fig. 9.12, at t = 0, the switch is opened. Calculate* $v, \frac{dv}{dt}$ *and* $\frac{d^2v}{dt^2}$ *at* $t = 0^+$.

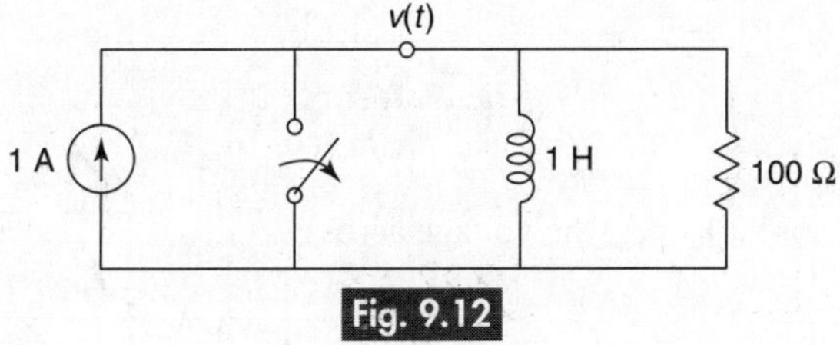


Fig. 9.12

**Solution**

(i) At $t = 0^-$, the switch is closed. Hence, no current flows through the inductor.

$$i_L(0^-)=0$$

(ii) At $t = 0^+$, the network is shown in Fig. 9.13.
At $t = 0^+$, the inductor acts as an open circuit.

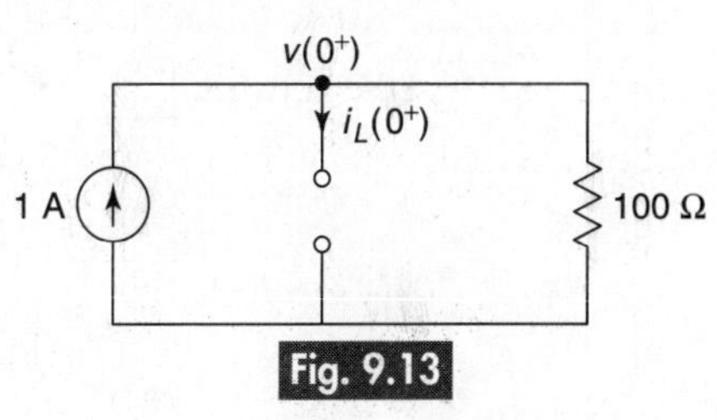


Fig. 9.13

$$i_L(0^+)=0$$

$$v(0^+)=100\times1=100\text{ V}$$

(iii) For $t > 0$, the network is shown in Fig. 9.14.

Writing the KCL equation for $t > 0$,

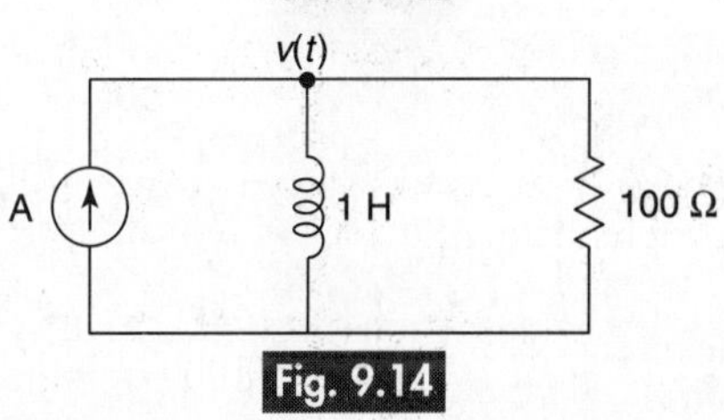


Fig. 9.14

$$\frac{v}{100}+\frac{1}{1}\int_0^t v\,dt=1 \qquad \ldots\text{(i)}$$

Differentiating Eq. (i),

$$\frac{1}{100}\frac{dv}{dt}+v=0 \qquad \ldots\text{(ii)}$$

At $t = 0^+$,

$$\frac{dv}{dt}(0^+)=-100v(0^+)=-100\times100=-10000\text{ V/s}$$

Differentiating Eq. (ii),

$$\frac{1}{100}\frac{d^2v}{dt^2}+\frac{dv}{dt}=0$$

At $t = 0^+$,
$$\frac{d^2v}{dt^2}(0^+)=-100\frac{dv}{dt}(0^+)=-100\times(-10^4)=10^6\text{ V/s}^2$$

## EXAMPLE 9.5

*In the given network of Fig. 9.15, the switch is opened at t = 0. Solve for v, $\frac{dv}{dt}$ and $\frac{d^2v}{dt^2}$ at t = 0⁺.*

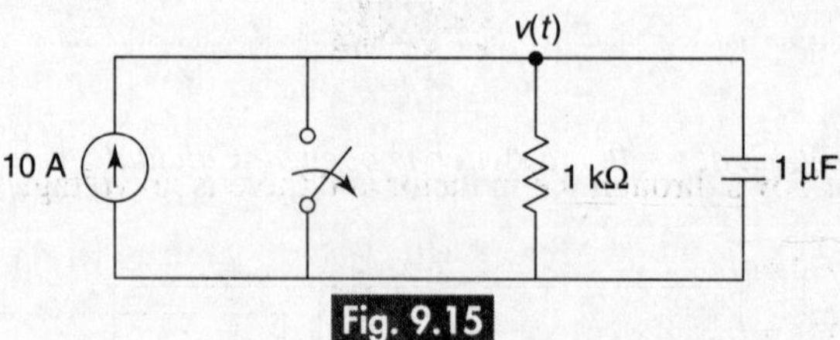


Fig. 9.15

### Solution

(i) At $t = 0^-$, switch is closed. Hence, the voltage across the capacitor is zero.

$$v(0^-)=v_C(0^-)=0$$

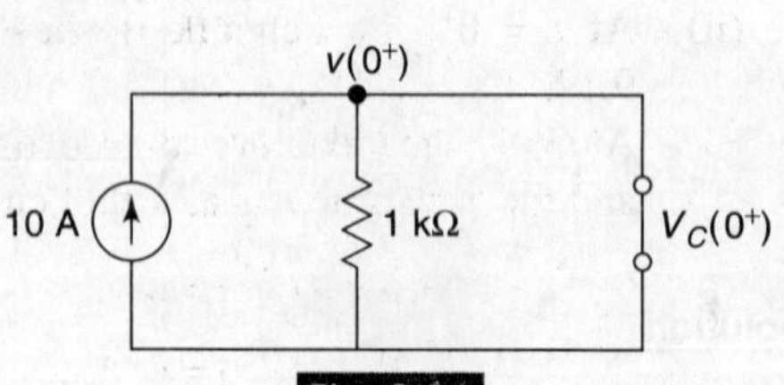


Fig. 9.16

(ii) At $t = 0^+$, the network is shown in Fig. 9.16.
At $t = 0^+$, the capacitor acts as a short circuit.

$$v(0^+)=v_C(0^+)=0$$

(iii) For $t > 0$, the network is shown in Fig. 9.17.

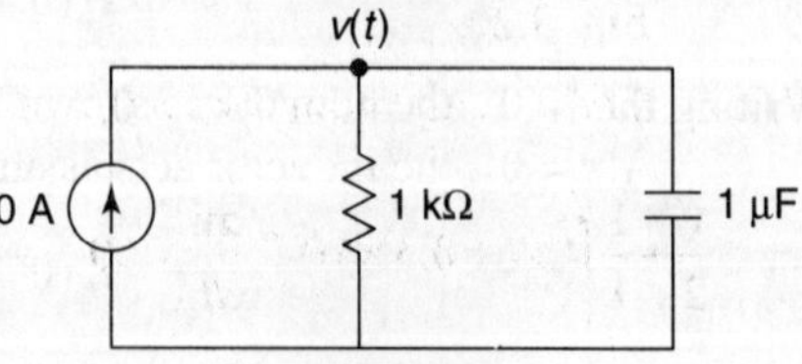


Fig. 9.17

Writing the KCL equation for $t > 0$,

$$\frac{v}{1000}+10^{-6}\frac{dv}{dt}=10 \qquad \ldots\text{(i)}$$

At $t = 0^+$,
$$\frac{v(0^+)}{1000}+10^{-6}\frac{dv}{dt}(0^+)=10$$

$$\frac{dv}{dt}(0^+)=\frac{10}{10^{-6}}=10\times10^6\text{ V/s}$$

Differentiating Eq. (i),

$$\frac{1}{1000}\frac{dv}{dt}+10^{-6}\frac{d^2v}{dt^2}=0$$

At $t = 0^+$,
$$\frac{1}{1000}\frac{dv}{dt}(0^+)+10^{-6}\frac{d^2v}{dt^2}(0^+)=0$$

$$\frac{d^2v}{dt^2}(0^+)=-\frac{1}{1000\times10^{-6}}\times10\times10^6=-10\times10^9\text{ V/s}^2$$

## EXAMPLE 9.6

*For the network shown in Fig. 9.18, the switch is closed at t = 0, determine v,* $\frac{dv}{dt}$ *and* $\frac{d^2v}{dt^2}$ *at t = 0⁺.*

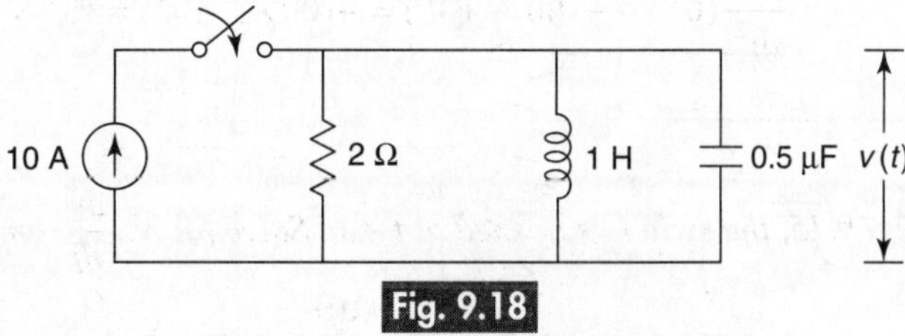


Fig. 9.18

**Solution**

(i) At $t = 0^-$, no current flows through the inductor and there is no voltage across the capacitor.

$$i_L(0^-) = 0$$

$$v(0^-) = 0$$

(ii) At $t = 0^+$, the network is shown in Fig. 9.19.
At $t = 0^+$, the inductor acts as an open circuit and the capacitor acts as a shot circuit.

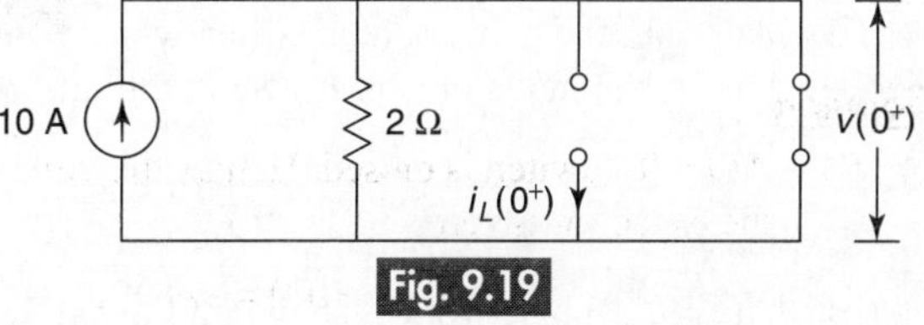


Fig. 9.19

$$i_L(0^+) = 0$$

$$v(0^+) = 0$$

(iii) For $t > 0$, the network is shown in Fig. 9.20.

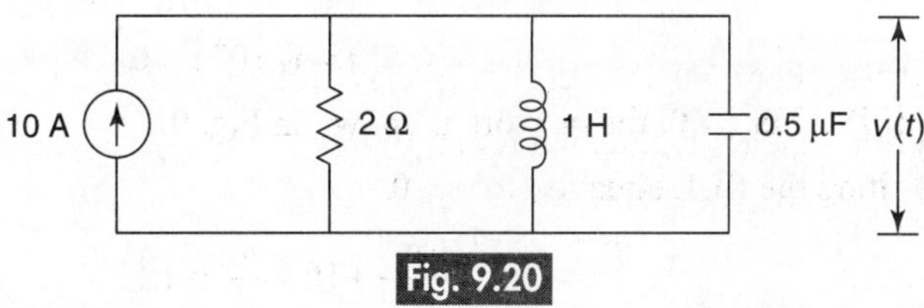


Fig. 9.20

Writing the KCL equation for $t > 0$,

$$\frac{v}{2} + \frac{1}{1}\int_1^t v\,dt + 0.5\times10^{-6}\frac{dv}{dt} = 10 \qquad \dots\text{(i)}$$

At $t = 0^+$,

$$\frac{v(0^+)}{2} + 0 + 0.5\times10^{-6}\frac{dv}{dt}(0^+) = 10$$

$$\frac{dv}{dt}(0^+) = 20\times10^6 \text{ V/s}$$

Differentiating Eq. (i),

$$\frac{1}{2}\frac{dv}{dt} + v + 0.5\times10^{-6}\frac{d^2v}{dt^2} = 0$$

At $t = 0^+$,

$$\frac{1}{2}\frac{dv}{dt}(0^+) + v(0^+) + 0.5\times10^{-6}\frac{d^2v}{dt^2}(0^+) = 0$$

$$\frac{d^2v}{dt^2}(0^+) = -20\times10^{12} \text{ V/s}^2$$

## EXAMPLE 9.7

*In the network shown in Fig. 9.21, the switch is changed from position 1 to position 2 at t = 0, steady condition having reached before switching. Find the values of i, $\frac{di}{dt}$ and $\frac{d^2i}{dt^2}$ at t = 0⁺.*

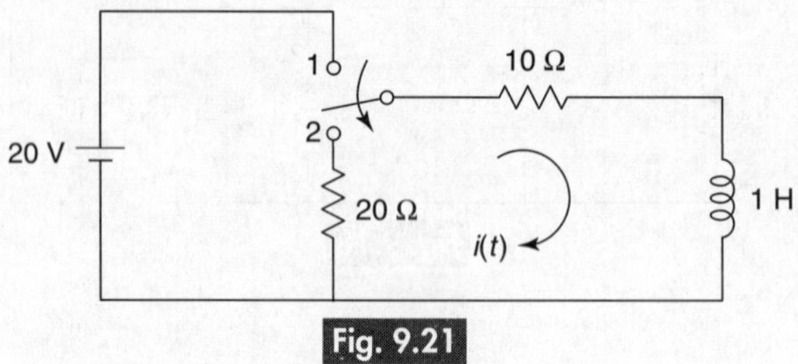


Fig. 9.21

**Solution**

(i) At $t = 0^-$, the network attains steady-state condition. Hence, the inductor acts as a short circuit.

$$i(0^-) = \frac{20}{10} = 2 \text{ A}$$

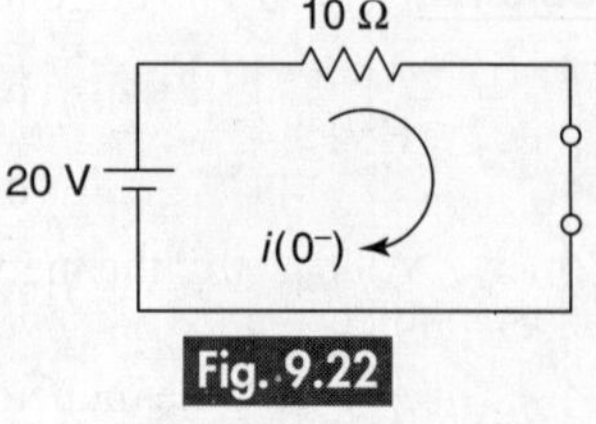


Fig. 9.22

(ii) At $t = 0^+$, the network is shown in Fig. 9.23. At $t = 0^+$, the inductor acts as a current source of 2 A.

$$i(0^+) = 2 \text{ A}$$

Fig. 9.23

(iii) For $t > 0$, the network is shown in Fig. 9.24.

Writing the KVL equation for $t > 0$,

$$-20i - 10i - 1\frac{di}{dt} = 0 \qquad \text{...(i)}$$

At $t = 0^+$,

$$-30i(0^+) - \frac{di}{dt}(0^+) = 0$$

$$\frac{di}{dt}(0^+) = -30 \times 2 = -60 \text{ A/s}$$

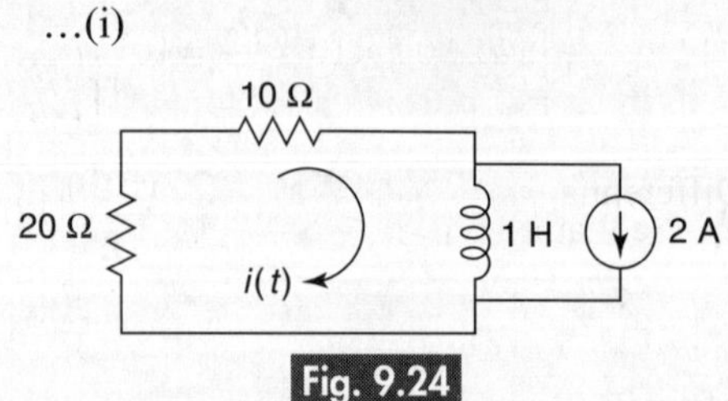


Fig. 9.24

Differentiating Eq. (i),

$$-30\frac{di}{dt} - \frac{d^2i}{dt^2} = 0$$

At $t = 0^+$,

$$-30\frac{di}{dt}(0^+) - \frac{d^2i}{dt^2}(0^+) = 0$$

$$\frac{d^2i}{dt^2}(0^+) = 1800 \text{ A/s}^2$$

## EXAMPLE 9.8

*In the network shown in Fig.4.25, the switch is changed from position 1 to position 2 at t = 0, steady condition having reached before switching. Find the values of i, $\frac{di}{dt}$ and $\frac{d^2i}{dt^2}$ at t = 0⁺.*

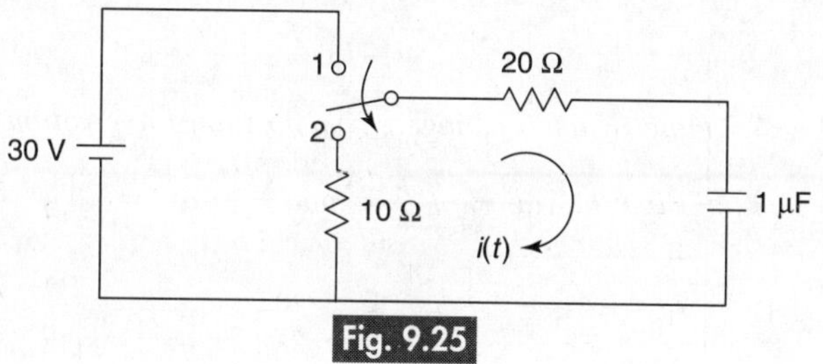


Fig. 9.25

**Solution**

(i) At $t = 0^-$, the network attains steady-state condition. Hence, the capacitor acts as an open circuit.

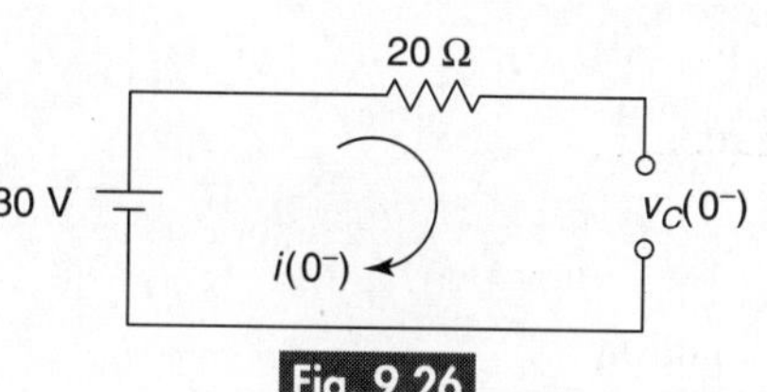


Fig. 9.26

$$v_C(0^-) = 30 \text{ V}$$

$$i(0^-) = 0$$

(ii) At $t = 0^+$, the network is shown in Fig. 9.27.
At $t = 0^+$, the capacitor acts as a voltage source of 30 V.

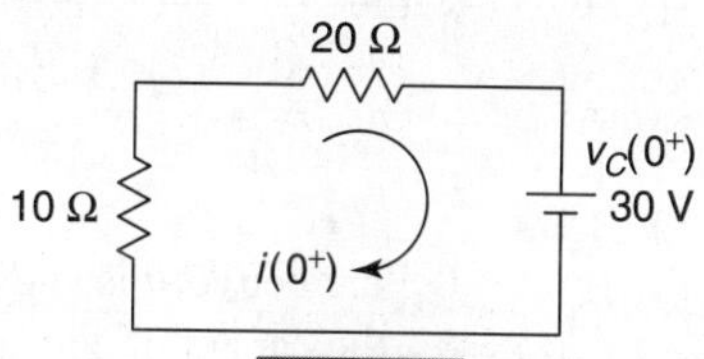


Fig. 9.27

$$v_C(0^+) = 30 \text{ V}$$

$$i(0^+) = -\frac{30}{30} = -1 \text{ A}$$

(iii) For $t > 0$, the network is shown in Fig. 9.28.
Writing the KVL equation for $t > 0$,

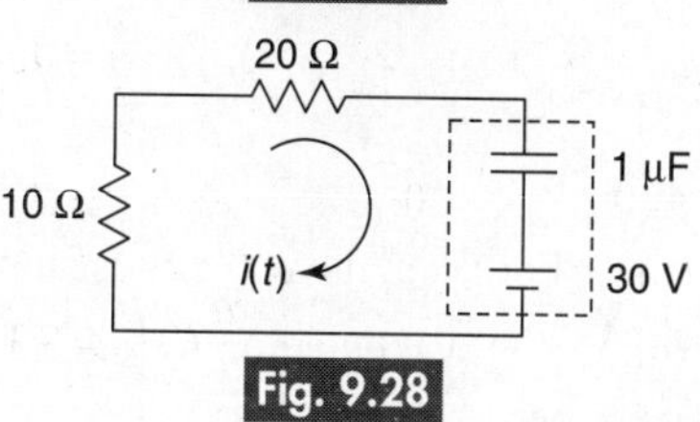


Fig. 9.28

$$-10i - 20i - \frac{1}{1 \times 10^{-6}} \int_0^t i \, dt - 30 = 0 \quad \text{...(i)}$$

Differentiating Eq. (i),

$$-30\frac{di}{dt} - 10^6 i = 0 \quad \text{...(ii)}$$

At $t = 0^+$,

$$-30\frac{di}{dt}(0^+) - 10^6 i(0^+) = 0$$

$$\frac{di}{dt}(0^+) = \frac{10^6(-1)}{30} = 0.33 \times 10^5 \text{ A/s}$$

Differentiating Eq. (ii),

$$-30\frac{d^2i}{dt^2} - 10^6 \frac{di}{dt} = 0$$

At $t = 0^+$, $$-30\frac{d^2i}{dt^2}(0^+) - 10^6\frac{di}{dt}(0^+) = 0$$

$$\frac{d^2i}{dt^3}(0^+) = -\frac{10^6 \times 0.33\times10^5}{30} = -1.1\times10^9 \text{ A/s}^2$$

## EXAMPLE 9.9

*In the network shown in Fig. 9.29, the switch is changed from position 1 to position 2 at $t = 0$, steady condition having reached before switching. Find the values of $i$, $\frac{di}{dt}$ and $\frac{d^2i}{dt^2}$ at $t = 0^+$.*

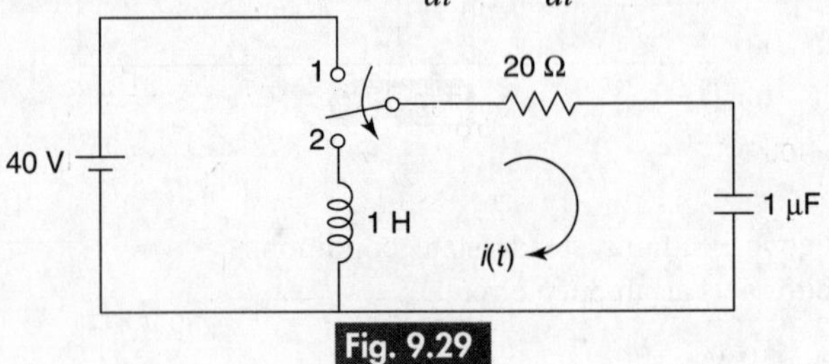


Fig. 9.29

**Solution**

(i) At $t = 0^-$, the network attains steady state. Hence, the capacitor acts as an open circuit.

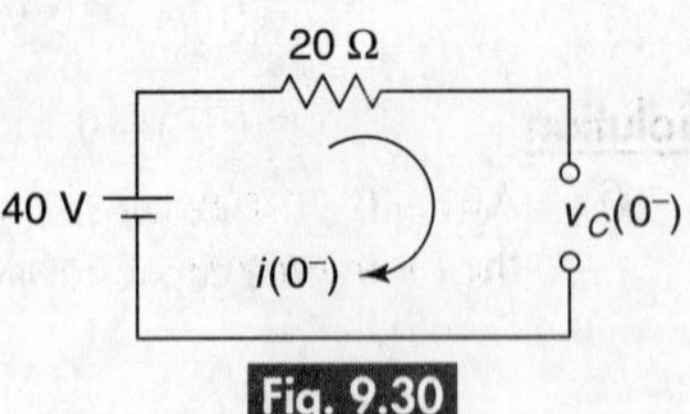


Fig. 9.30

$$v_C(0^-) = 40 \text{ V}$$

$$i(0^-) = 0$$

(ii) At $t = 0^+$, the network is shown in Fig. 9.31.
At $t = 0^+$, the capacitor acts as a voltage source of 40 V and the inductor acts as an open circuit.

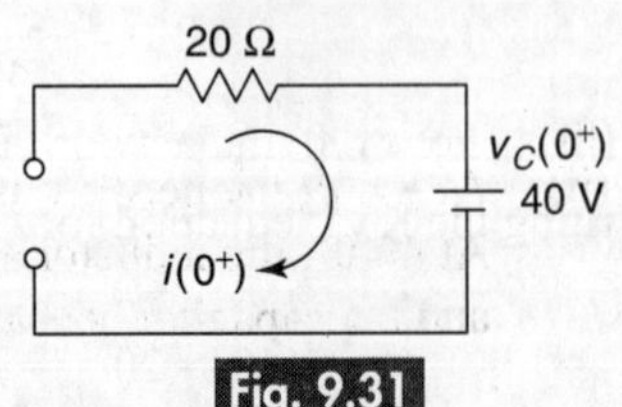


Fig. 9.31

$$v_C(0^+) = 40 \text{ V}$$

$$i(0^+) = 0$$

(iii) For $t > 0$, the network is shown in Fig. 9.32.

Writing the KVL equation for $t > 0$,

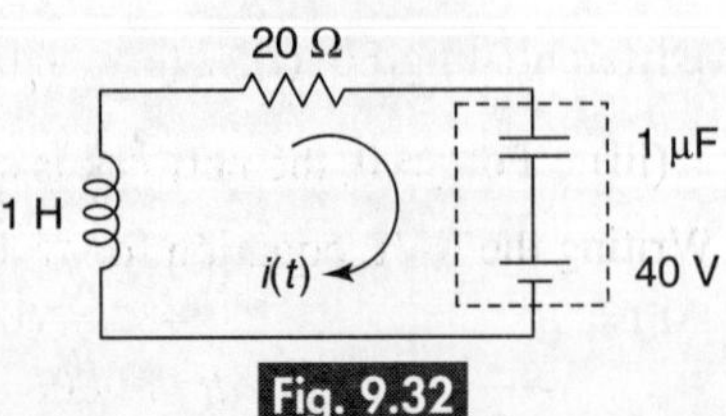


Fig. 9.32

$$-1\frac{di}{dt} - 20i - \frac{1}{1\times10^{-6}}\int_0^t i\,dt - 40 = 0 \qquad \ldots\text{(i)}$$

At $t = 0^+$, $$-\frac{di}{dt}(0^+) - 20i(0^+) - 0 - 40 = 0$$

$$\frac{di}{dt}(0^+) = -40 \text{ A/s}$$

Differentiating Eq. (i),

$$-\frac{d^2i}{dt^2} - 20\frac{di}{dt} - 10^6 i - 0 = 0$$

At $t = 0^+$,
$$-\frac{d^2i}{dt^2}(0^+) - 20\frac{di}{dt}(0^+) - 10^6 i(0^+) = 0$$

$$\frac{d^2i}{dt^2}(0^+) = 800 \text{ A/s}^2$$

## EXAMPLE 9.10

*In the network of Fig. 9.33, the switch is changed from position 'a' to 'b' at t = 0. Solve for i, $\frac{di}{dt}$ and $\frac{d^2i}{dt^2}$ at t = 0*$^+$.

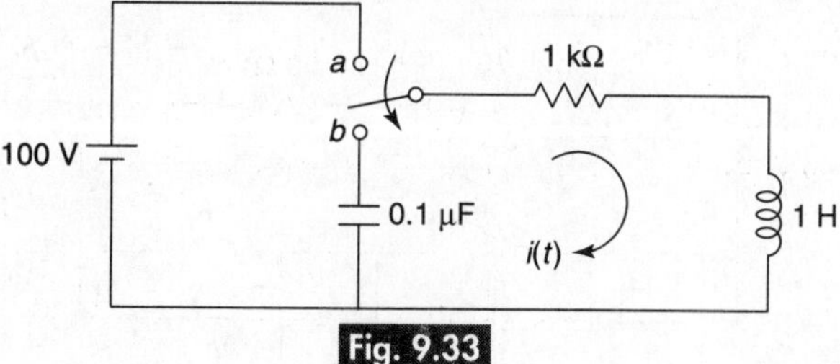

Fig. 9.33

### Solution

(i) At $t = 0^-$, the network attains steady condition. Hence, the inductor acts as a short circuit.

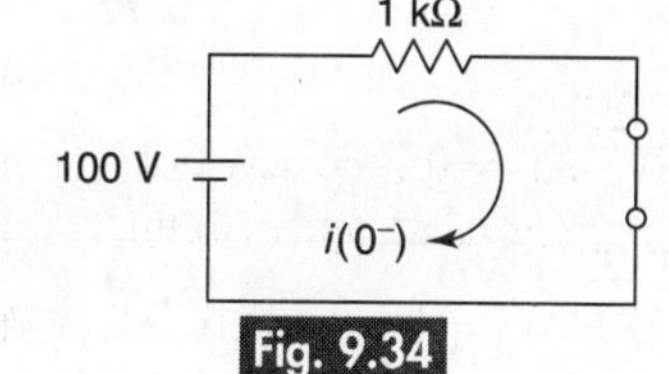

Fig. 9.34

$$i(0^-) = \frac{100}{1000} = 0.1 \text{ A}$$

$$v_C(0^-) = 0$$

(ii) At $t = 0^+$, the network is shown in Fig. 9.35.
At $t = 0^+$, the inductor acts as a current source of 0.1 A and the capacitor acts as a short circuit.

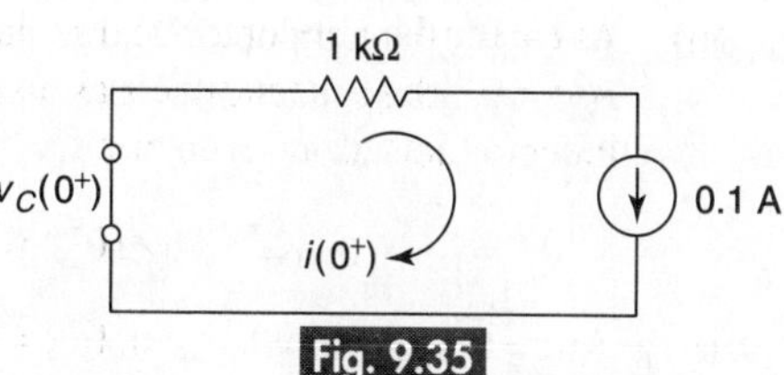

Fig. 9.35

$$i(0^+) = 0.1 \text{ A}$$

$$v_C(0^+) = 0$$

(iii) For $t > 0$, the network is shown in Fig. 9.36.

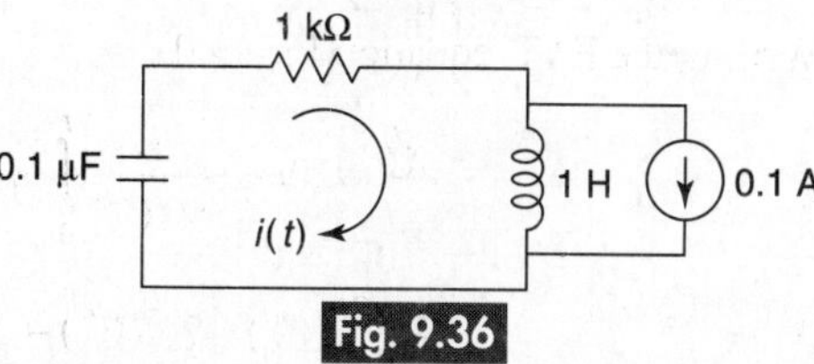

Fig. 9.36

Writing the KVL equation for $t > 0$,

$$-\frac{1}{0.1\times 10^{-6}}\int_0^t i\,dt - 1000i - 1\frac{di}{dt} = 0 \qquad \ldots\text{(i)}$$

At $t = 0^+$,
$$-0 - 1000i(0^+) - \frac{di}{dt}(0^+) = 0$$

$$\frac{di}{dt}(0^+) = -1000\,i(0^+) = -1000\times 0.1 = -100 \text{ A/s}$$

Differentiating Eq. (i),

$$-\frac{1}{10^{-7}}i - 1000\frac{di}{dt} - \frac{d^2i}{dt^2} = 0$$

At $t = 0^+$, $$-10^7 i(0^+) - 1000\frac{di}{dt}(0^+) - \frac{d^2i}{dt^2}(0^+) = 0$$

$$\frac{d^2i}{dt^2}(0^+) = -10^7(0.1) - 1000(-100) = -9\times10^5 \text{ A/s}^2$$

**EXAMPLE 9.11**

*The network of Fig. 9.37 attains steady-state with the switch closed. At t = 0, the switch is opened. Find the voltage across the switch $v_K$ and $\frac{dv_K}{dt}$ at $t = 0^+$.*

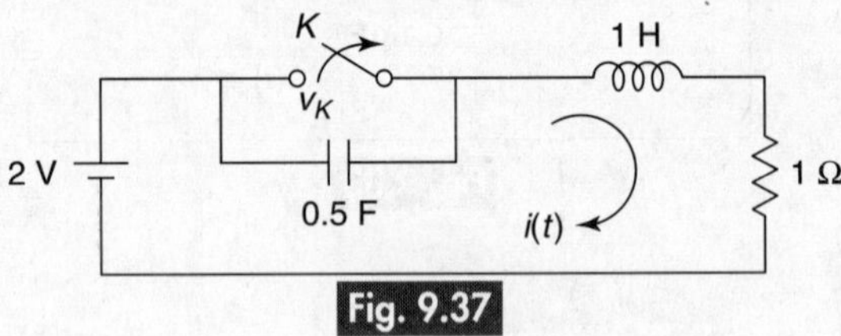


Fig. 9.37

**Solution**

(i) At $t = 0^-$, the network is shown in Fig. 4.38. At $t = 0^-$, the network attains steady-state condition. The capacitor acts as an open circuit and the inductor acts as a short circuit.

$$i(0^-) = \frac{2}{1} = 2 \text{ A}$$

$$v_C(0^-) = 0$$

Fig. 9.38

(ii) At $t = 0^+$, the network is shown in Fig. 9.39. At $t = 0^+$, the capacitor acts as a short circuit and the inductor acts as a current source of 2 A.

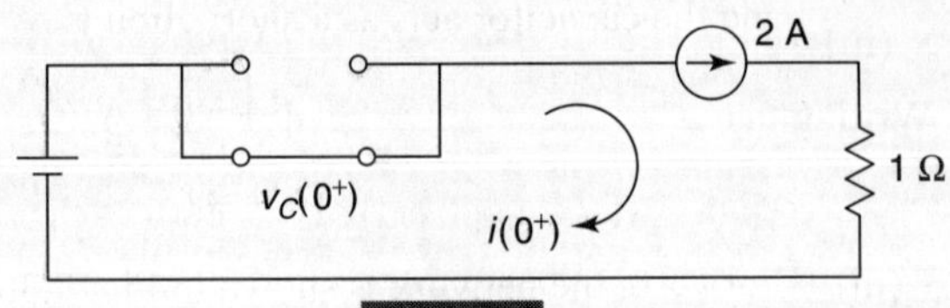


Fig. 9.39

$$i(0^+) = 2 \text{ A}$$

$$v_C(0^+) = 0$$

$$v_K(0^+) = 0$$

Also, $$v_K = \frac{1}{C}\int i\,dt$$

$$\frac{dv_K}{dt} = \frac{i}{C}$$

At $t = 0^+$, $$\frac{dv_K}{dt}(0^+) = \frac{i(0^+)}{C} = \frac{2}{0.5} = 4 \text{ A/s}$$

## EXAMPLE 9.12

*In the network shown in Fig. 9.40, assuming all initial conditions as zero, find* $i_1(0^+), i_2(0^+), \frac{di_1}{dt}(0^+), \frac{di_2}{dt}(0^+), \frac{d^2i_1}{dt^2}(0^+)$ *and* $\frac{d^2i_2}{dt^2}(0^+)$.

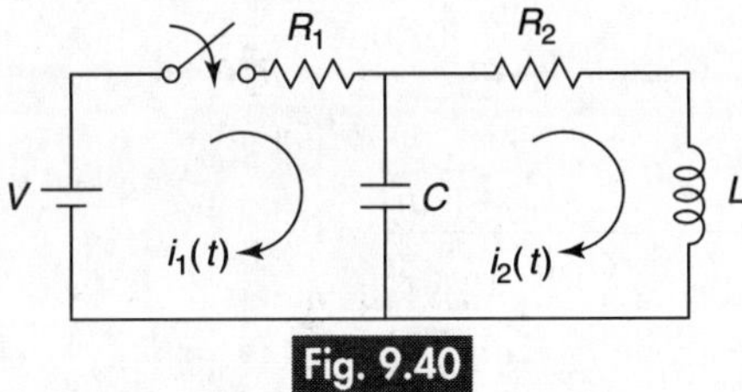


Fig. 9.40

**Solution**

(i) At $t = 0^-$, all initial conditions are zero.

$$v_C(0^-) = 0$$
$$i_1(0^-) = 0$$
$$i_2(0^-) = 0$$

(ii) At $t = 0^+$, the network is shown in Fig. 9.41.
At $t = 0^+$, the inductor acts as an open circuit and the capacitor acts as a short circuit.

$$i_1(0^+) = \frac{V}{R_1}$$
$$i_2(0^+) = 0$$
$$v_C(0^+) = 0$$

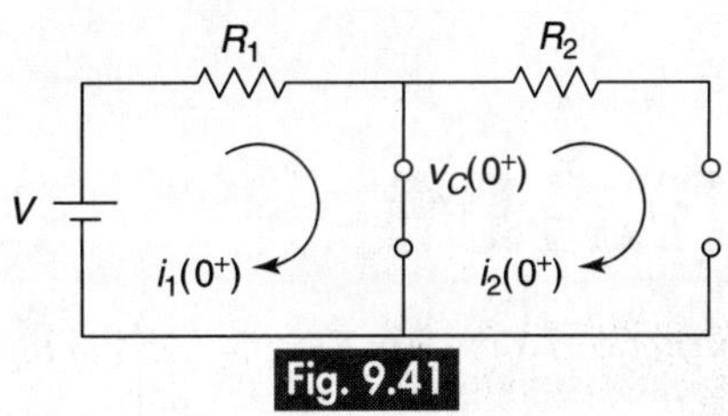


Fig. 9.41

(iii) For $t > 0$, the network is shown in Fig. 9.42.

Writing the KVL equations for two meshes for $t > 0$,

$$V - R_1 i_1 - \frac{1}{C}\int_0^t (i_1 - i_2)dt = 0 \qquad \ldots\text{(i)}$$

and $$-\frac{1}{C}\int (i_2 - i_1)dt - R_2 i_2 - L\frac{di_2}{dt} = 0 \qquad \ldots\text{(ii)}$$

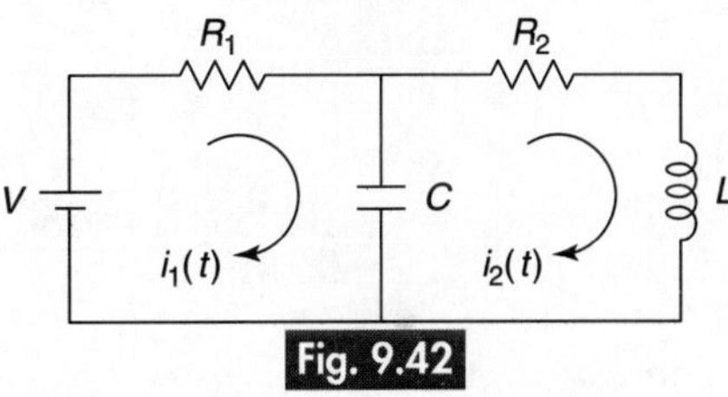


Fig. 9.42

From Eq. (ii), at $t = 0^+$,

$$-\frac{1}{C}\int_0^{0^+} (i_2 - i_1)dt - R_2 i_2(0^+) - L\frac{di_2}{dt}(0^+) = 0$$

$$\frac{di_2}{dt}(0^+) = 0$$

Differentiating Eq. (i),

$$0 - R_1\frac{di_1}{dt} - \frac{1}{C}(i_1 - i_2) = 0 \qquad \text{...(iii)}$$

At $t = 0^+$,
$$0 - R_1\frac{di_1}{dt}(0^+) - \frac{1}{C}i_1(0^+) + \frac{1}{C}i_2(0^+) = 0$$

$$R_1\frac{di_1}{dt}(0^+) + \frac{1}{C}\frac{V}{R_1} = 0$$

$$\frac{di_1}{dt}(0^+) = -\frac{V}{R_1^2 C}$$

Differentiating Eq. (iii),

$$-R_1\frac{d^2i_1}{dt^2} - \frac{1}{C}\frac{di_1}{dt} + \frac{1}{C}\frac{di_2}{dt} = 0$$

At $t = 0^+$,
$$-R_1\frac{d^2i_1}{dt^2}(0^+) - \frac{1}{C}\frac{di_1}{dt}(0^+) + \frac{1}{C}\frac{di_2}{dt}(0^+) = 0$$

$$\frac{d^2i_1}{dt^2}(0^+) = \frac{V}{R_1^3 C^2}$$

Differentiating Eq. (ii),

$$-\frac{1}{C}(i_2 - i_1) - R_2\frac{di_2}{dt} - L\frac{d^2i_2}{dt^2} = 0$$

At $t = 0^+$,
$$\frac{d^2i_2}{dt^2}(0^+) = -\frac{R_2}{L}\frac{di_2}{dt}(0^+) - \frac{1}{LC}[i_2(0^+) - i_1(0^+)] = \frac{V}{R_1 LC}$$

**EXAMPLE 9.13**

*In the network shown in Fig. 9.43, assuming all initial conditions as zero, find* $i_1, i_2\ \frac{di_1}{dt}, \frac{di_2}{dt}, \frac{d^2i_1}{dt^2}$ *and* $\frac{d^2i_2}{dt^2}$ *at* $t = 0^+$.

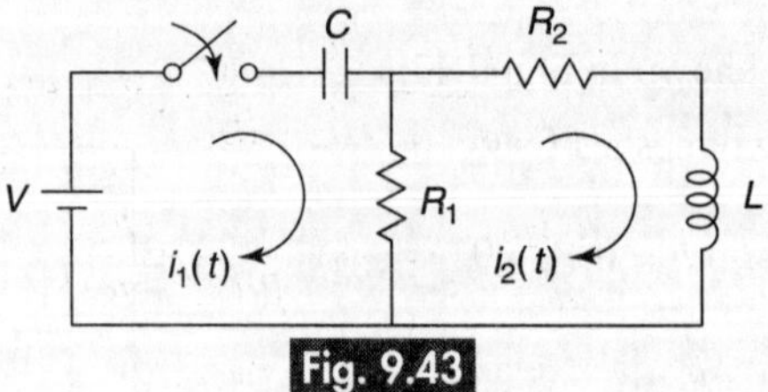


Fig. 9.43

**Solution**

(i) At $t = 0^-$, all initial conditions are zero.

$$v_C(0^-) = 0$$
$$i_1(0^-) = 0$$
$$i_2(0^-) = 0$$

(ii) At $t = 0^+$, the network is shown in Fig. 9.44.

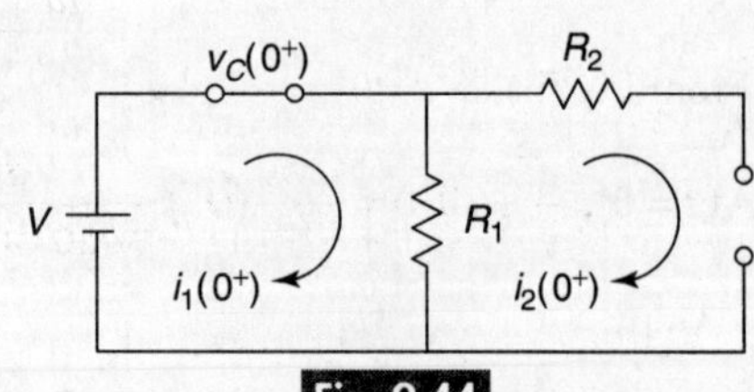


Fig. 9.44

At $t = 0^+$, the capacitor acts as a short circuit and the inductor acts as an open circuit.

$$i_1(0^+) = \frac{V}{R_1}$$

$$i_2(0^+) = 0$$

$$v_C(0^+) = 0$$

(iii) For $t > 0$, the network is shown in Fig. 9.45.

Writing the KVL equation for $t > 0$,

$$V - \frac{1}{C}\int_0^t i_1\, dt - R_1(i_1 - i_2) = 0 \qquad \ldots\text{(i)}$$

and $$-R_1(i_2 - i_1) - R_2 i_2 - L\frac{di_2}{dt} = 0 \qquad \ldots\text{(ii)}$$

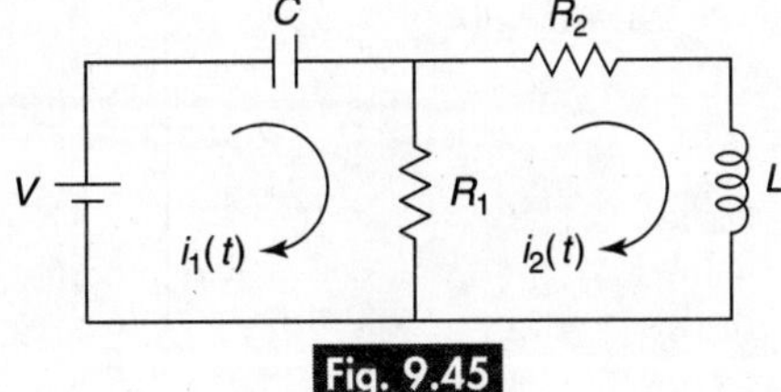

Fig. 9.45

From Eq. (ii),

$$\frac{di_2}{dt} = \frac{1}{L}[R_1 i_1 - (R_1 + R_2)i_2] \qquad \ldots\text{(iii)}$$

At $t = 0^+$,
$$\frac{di_2}{dt}(0^+) = \frac{1}{L}[R_1 i_1(0^+) - (R_1 + R_2)i_2(0^+)] = \frac{1}{L}\left[R_1\frac{V}{R_1} - (R_1 + R_2)0\right] = \frac{V}{L}$$

Differentiating Eq. (i),

$$0 - \frac{i_1}{C} - R_1\frac{di_1}{dt} + R_1\frac{di_2}{dt} = 0$$

$$\frac{di_1}{dt} = \frac{di_2}{dt} - \frac{i_1}{R_1 C} \qquad \ldots\text{(iv)}$$

At $t = 0^+$,
$$\frac{di_1}{dt}(0^+) = \frac{di_2}{dt}(0^+) - \frac{i_1(0^+)}{R_1 C} = \frac{V}{L} - \frac{V}{R_1^2 C}$$

Differentiating Eq. (iii),

$$\frac{d^2 i_2}{dt^2} = \frac{1}{L}\left[R_1\frac{di_1}{dt} - (R_1 + R_2)\frac{di_2}{dt}\right]$$

At $t = 0^+$,
$$\frac{d^2 i_2}{dt^2}(0^+) = -V\left(\frac{1}{R_1 LC} + \frac{R_2}{L^2}\right)$$

Differentiating Eq. (iv),

$$\frac{d^2 i_1}{dt^2} = \frac{d^2 i_2}{dt^2} - \frac{1}{R_1 C}\frac{di_1}{dt}$$

At $t = 0^+$,
$$\frac{d^2 i_1}{dt^2}(0^+) = \frac{d^2 i_2}{dt^2}(0^+) - \frac{1}{R_1 C}\frac{di_1}{dt}(0^+) = -\frac{V}{R_1 LC} - \frac{VR_2}{L^2} - \frac{1}{R_1 C}\left(\frac{V}{L} - \frac{V}{R_1^2 C}\right) = \frac{V}{R_1^3 C^2} - \frac{2V}{R_1 LC} - \frac{VR_2}{L^2}$$

## EXAMPLE 9.14

*In the network shown in Fig. 9.46, a steady state is reached with the switch open. At t = 0, the switch is closed. For the element values given, determine the value of $v_a(0^-)$, $v_b(0^-)$, $v_a(0^+)$ and $v_b(0^+)$.*

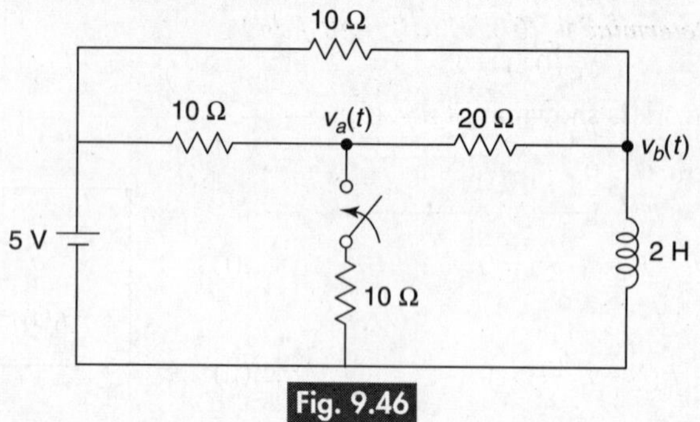


Fig. 9.46

### Solution

(i) At $t = 0^-$, the network is shown in Fig. 9.47. At $t = 0^-$, the network attains steady-state condition. Hence, the inductor acts as a short circuit.

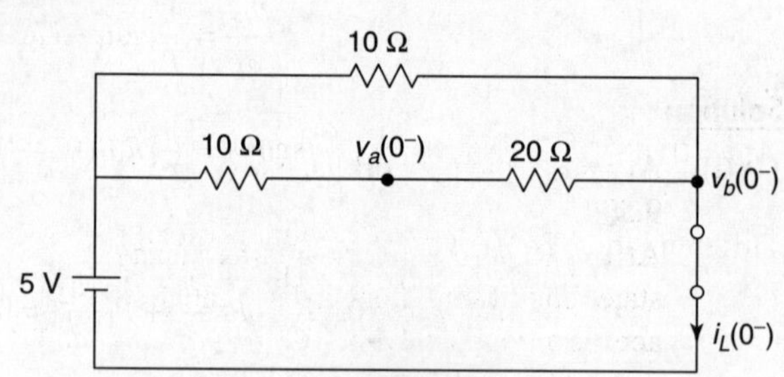


Fig. 9.47

$$i_L(0^-) = \frac{5}{(10 \parallel 30)} = \frac{5}{7.5} = \frac{2}{3} \text{ A}$$

$$v_b(0^-) = 0$$

$$v_a(0^-) = 5 \times \frac{20}{30} = 3.33 \text{ V}$$

(ii) At $t = 0^+$, the network is shown in Fig. 9.48. At $t = 0^+$, the inductor acts as a current source of $\frac{2}{3}$ A.

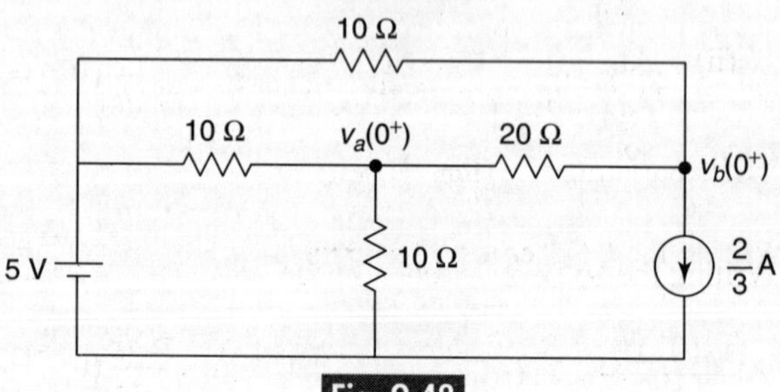


Fig. 9.48

$$i_L(0^+) = \frac{2}{3} \text{ A}$$

Writing the KCL equations at $t = 0^+$,

$$\frac{v_a(0^+) - 5}{10} + \frac{v_a(0^+)}{10} + \frac{v_a(0^+) - v_b(0^+)}{20} = 0$$

and
$$\frac{v_b(0^+) - v_a(0^+)}{20} + \frac{v_b(0^+) - 5}{10} + \frac{2}{3} = 0$$

Solving these two equations,

$$v_a(0^+) = 1.9 \text{ V}$$

$$v_b(0^+) = -0.477 \text{ V}$$

## EXAMPLE 9.15

*In the accompanying Fig. 9.49 is shown a network in which a steady state is reached with switch open. At t = 0, switch is closed. Determine* $v_a(0^-)$, $v_a(0^+)$, $v_b(0^-)$ *and* $v_b(0^+)$.

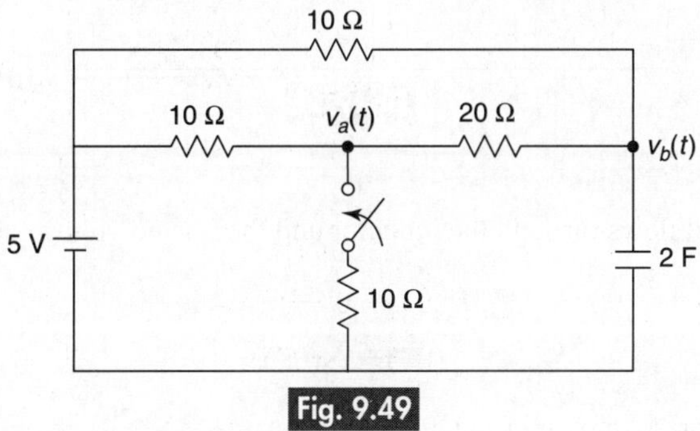


Fig. 9.49

**Solution**

(i) At $t = 0^-$, the network is shown in Fig. 9.50.

At $t = 0^-$, the network attains steady-state condition. Hence, the capacitor acts as an open circuit.

$$v_a(0^-) = 5 \text{ V}$$

$$v_b(0^-) = 5 \text{ V}$$

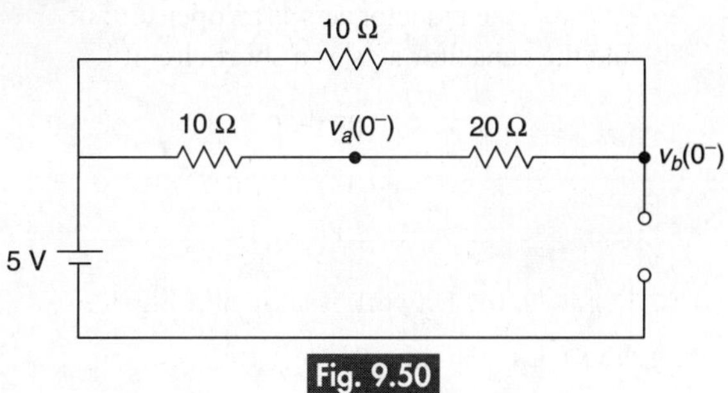


Fig. 9.50

(ii) At $t = 0^+$, the network is shown in Fig. 9.51.

At $t = 0^+$, the capacitor acts as a voltage source of 5 V.

$$v_b(0^+) = 5 \text{ V}$$

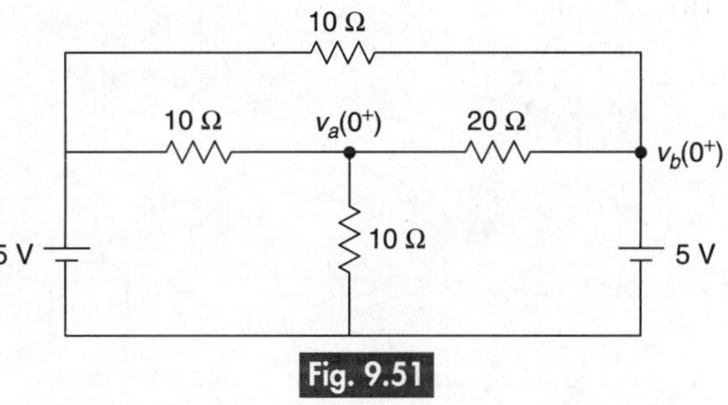


Fig. 9.51

Writing the KCL equation at $t = 0^+$,

$$\frac{v_a(0^+) - 5}{10} + \frac{v_a(0^+)}{10} + \frac{v_a(0^+) - 5}{20} = 0$$

$$0.25 v_a(0^+) = 0.75$$

$$v_a(0^+) = 3 \text{ V}$$

## EXAMPLE 9.16

*The network shown in Fig. 9.52 has two independent node pairs. If the switch is opened at t = 0. Find* $v_1, v_2, \dfrac{dv_1}{dt}$ *and* $\dfrac{dv_2}{dt}$ *at* $t = 0^+$.

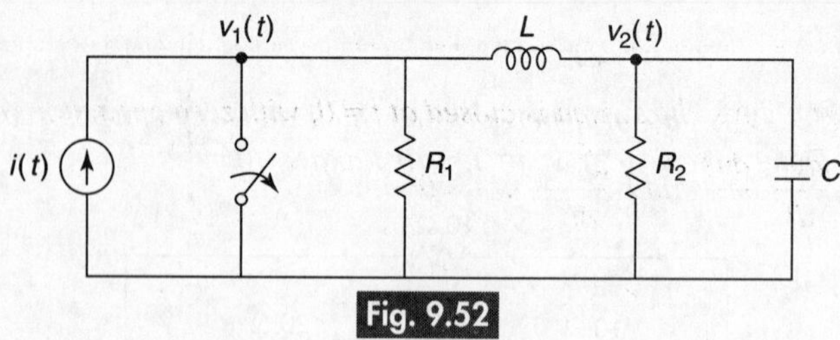


Fig. 9.52

## Solution

(i) At $t = 0^-$, no current flows through the inductor and there is no voltage across the capacitor.

$$i_L(0^-) = 0$$

$$v_C(0^-) = v_2(0^-) = 0$$

(ii) At $t = 0^+$, the network is shown in Fig. 9.53. At $t = 0^+$, the inductor acts as an open circuit and the capacitor acts as a short circuit.

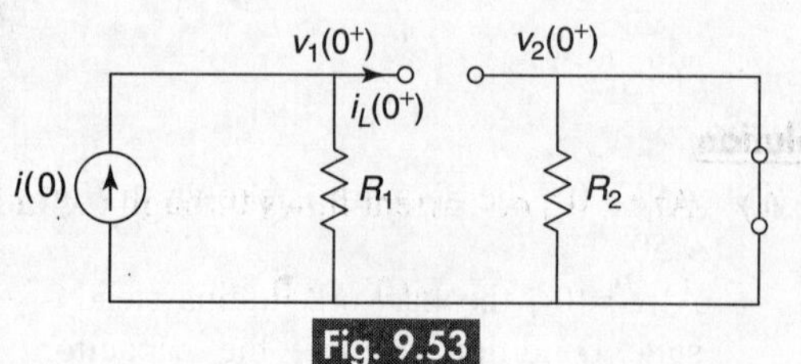


Fig. 9.53

$$i_L(0^+) = 0$$

$$v_1(0^+) = R_1\, i(0^+)$$

$$v_2(0^+) = 0$$

(iii) For $t > 0$, the network is shown in Fig. 9.54.

Fig. 9.54

Writing the KCL equation at Node 1 for $t > 0$,

$$\frac{v_1}{R_1} + \frac{1}{L}\int_0^t (v_1 - v_2)dt = i(t) \qquad \ldots(i)$$

Differentiating Eq. (i),

$$\frac{1}{R_1}\frac{dv_1}{dt} + \frac{1}{L}(v_1 - v_2) = \frac{di}{dt}$$

At $t = 0^+$,

$$\frac{dv_1}{dt}(0^+) = R_1\left[\frac{di}{dt}(0^+) - \frac{1}{L}R_1 i(0^+)\right]$$

Writing the KCL equation at Node 2 for $t > 0$,

$$\frac{1}{L}\int_0^t (v_2 - v_1)dt + \frac{v_2}{R_2} + C\frac{dv_2}{dt} = 0 \qquad \ldots(ii)$$

At $t = 0^+$,

$$0 + \frac{v_2(0^+)}{R_2} + C\frac{dv_2}{dt}(0^+) = 0$$

$$\frac{dv_2}{dt}(0^+) = 0$$

## EXAMPLE 9.17

*In the network shown in Fig. 9.55, the switch is closed at $t = 0$, with zero capacitor voltage and zero inductor current. Solve for $v_1, v_2, \frac{dv_1}{dt}, \frac{dv_2}{dt}$ and $\frac{d^2v_2}{dt^2}$ at $t = 0^+$.*

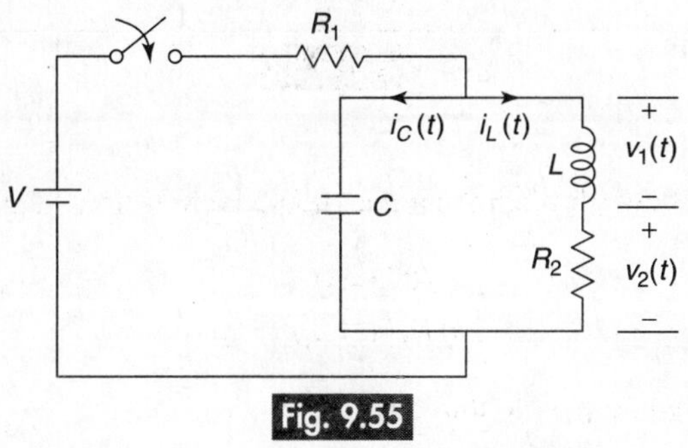


Fig. 9.55

**Solution**

(i) At $t = 0^-$, no current flows through the inductor and there is no voltage across the capacitor.

$$v_C(0^-) = 0$$

$$v_1(0^-) = 0$$

$$v_2(0^-) = 0$$

$$i_L(0^-) = 0$$

$$i_C(0^-) = 0$$

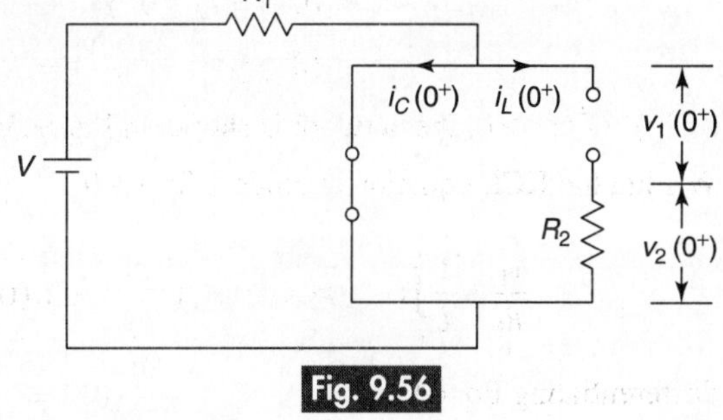


Fig. 9.56

(ii) At $t = 0^+$, the network is shown in Fig. 9.56.
At $t = 0^+$, the inductor acts as an open circuit and the capacitor acts as a short circuit.

$$v_C(0^+) = 0$$

$$v_1(0^+) = 0$$

$$v_2(0^+) = 0$$

$$i_L(0^+) = 0$$

$$i_C(0^+) = \frac{V}{R_1}$$

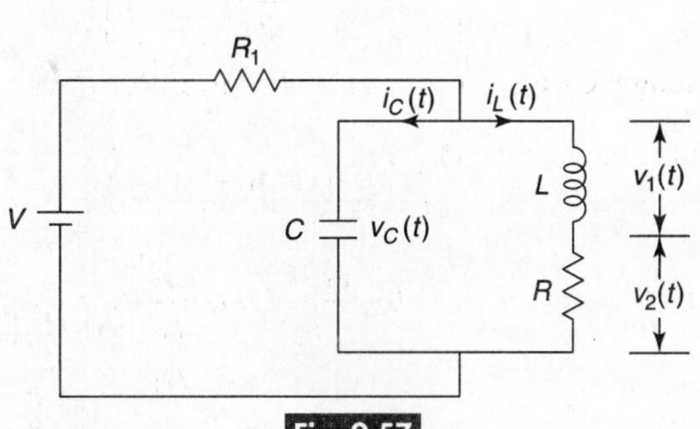


Fig. 9.57

(iii) For $t > 0$, the network is shown in Fig. 9.57.

Writing the KVL equation for $t > 0$,

$$v_C(t) = v_1(t) + v_2(t) \qquad \ldots\text{(i)}$$

Differentiating Eq. (i),

$$\frac{dv_C}{dt} = \frac{dv_1}{dt} + \frac{dv_2}{dt} \qquad \text{...(ii)}$$

Now,

$$v_C = \frac{1}{C}\int_0^t i_C \, dt \qquad \text{...(iii)}$$

$$\frac{dv_C}{dt} = \frac{i_C}{C}$$

At $t = 0^+$,

$$\frac{dv_C}{dt}(0^+) = \frac{i_C(0^+)}{C} = \frac{V}{R_1 C} \text{ V/s}$$

Also,

$$v_1 = L\frac{di_L}{dt} \qquad \text{...(iv)}$$

$$\frac{di_L}{dt} = \frac{v_1}{L} \qquad \text{...(v)}$$

At $t = 0^+$,

$$\frac{di_L}{dt}(0^+) = \frac{v_1(0^+)}{L} = 0$$

Also,

$$v_2 = R_2 i_L \qquad \text{...(vi)}$$

$$\frac{dv_2}{dt} = R_2 \frac{di_L}{dt} \qquad \text{...(vii)}$$

At $t = 0^+$,

$$\frac{dv_2}{dt}(0^+) = R_2 \frac{di_L}{dt}(0^+) = 0$$

$$\frac{dv_C}{dt}(0^+) = \frac{dv_1}{dt}(0^+) + \frac{dv_2}{dt}(0^+)$$

$$\frac{dv_1}{dt}(0^+) = \frac{V}{R_1 C} \text{ V/s}$$

Differentiating Eq. (vii),

$$\frac{d^2 v_2}{dt^2} = R_2 \frac{d^2 i_L}{dt^2}$$

At $t = 0^+$,

$$\frac{d^2 v_2}{dt^2}(0^+) = R_2 \frac{d^2 i_L}{dt}(0^+)$$

Differentiating Eq. (v),

$$\frac{d^2 i_L}{dt^2} = \frac{1}{L}\frac{dv_1}{dt}$$

At $t = 0^+$,

$$\frac{d^2 i_L}{dt^2}(0^+) = \frac{1}{L}\frac{dv_1}{dt}(0^+) = \frac{1}{L}\frac{V}{R_1 C}$$

$$\frac{d^2 v_2}{dt^2}(0^+) = \frac{R_2 V}{R_1 L C} \text{ V/s}^2$$

## EXAMPLE 9.18

*In the network shown in Fig. 9.58, a steady state is reached with switch open. At $t = 0$, switch is closed. Find the three loop currents at $t = 0^+$.*

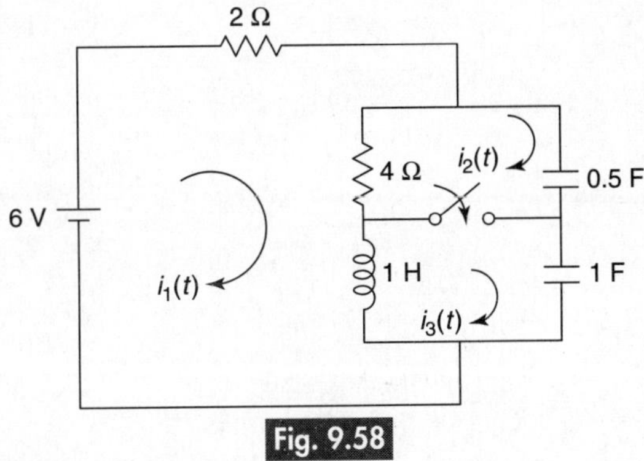


Fig. 9.58

**Solution**

(i) At $t = 0^-$, the network is shown in Fig. 9.59.
At $t = 0^-$, the network attains steady-state condition. Hence, the inductor acts as a short circuit and the capacitors act as open circuits.

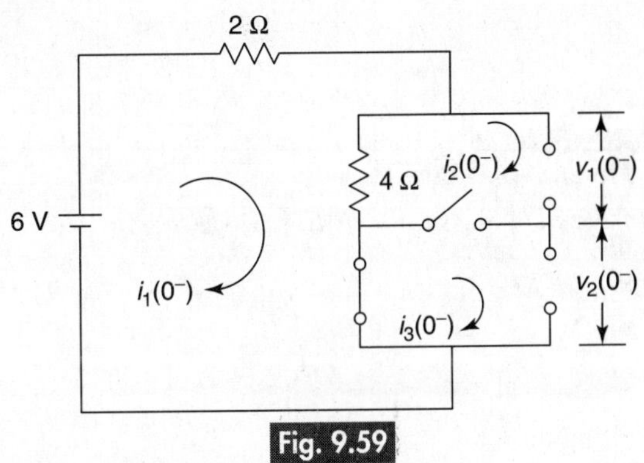


Fig. 9.59

$$i_{4\Omega}(0^-) = i_1(0^-) = \frac{6}{6} = 1\text{ A}$$

$$i_2(0^-) = 0$$

$$i_3(0^-) = 0$$

$$v_1(0^-) + v_2(0^-) = 6 \times \frac{4}{6} = 4\text{ V}$$

Since the charges on capacitors are equal when connected in series,

$$Q_1 = Q_2$$

$$C_1 v_1 = C_2 v_2$$

$$\frac{v_1(0^-)}{v_2(0^-)} = \frac{C_2}{C_1} = \frac{1}{0.5} = 2$$

$$v_1(0^-) = \frac{8}{3}\text{ V}$$

and $$v_2(0^-) = \frac{4}{3}\text{ V}$$

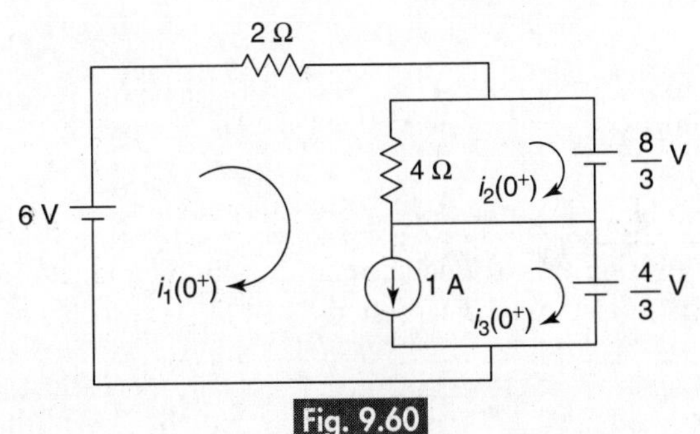


Fig. 9.60

(ii) At $t = 0^+$, the network is shown in Fig. 9.60.
At $t = 0^+$, the inductor is replaced by a current source of 1 A and the capacitors are replaced by a voltage source of $\frac{8}{3}$ V and $\frac{4}{3}$ V respectively.

$$v_1(0^+) = \frac{8}{3}\text{ V}$$

$$v_2(0^+) = \frac{4}{3}\text{ V}$$

At $t = 0^+$,
$$6 - 2i_1(0^+) - \frac{8}{3} - \frac{4}{3} = 0$$

$$i_1(0^+) = 1\text{ A}$$

Now,
$$i_1(0^+) - i_3(0^+) = 1$$

$$i_3(0^+) = 0$$

Writing the KVL equation for mesh 2,

$$-4[i_2(0^+) - i_1(0^+)] - \frac{8}{3} = 0$$

$$-4i_2(0^+) + 4 - \frac{8}{3} = 0$$

$$i_2(0^+) = \frac{1}{3}\text{ A}$$

**EXAMPLE 9.19**

*In the network shown in Fig. 9.61, the switch K is closed at t = 0 connecting a voltage $V_0 \sin \omega t$ to the parallel RL-RC circuit. Find (a) $i_1(0^+)$ and $i_2(0^+)$ (b) $\frac{di_1}{dt}(0^+)$ and $\frac{di_2}{dt}(0^+)$.*

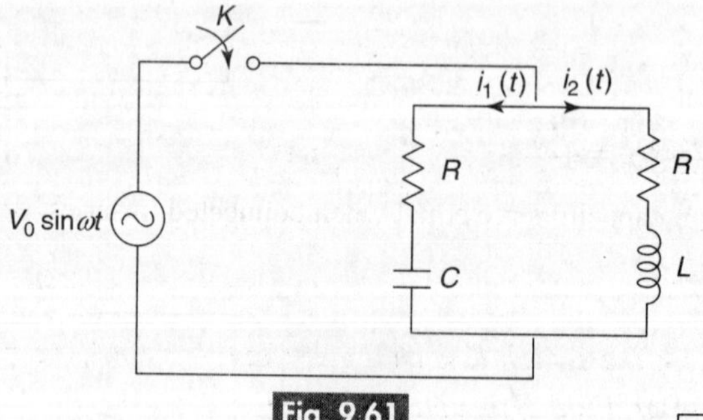


Fig. 9.61

**Solution**

(i) At $t = 0^-$, no current flows in the inductor and there is no voltage across the capacitor.

$$v_C(0^-) = 0$$

$$i_1(0^-) = 0$$

$$i_2(0^-) = 0$$

(ii) At $t = 0^+$, the network is shown in Fig. 9.62.

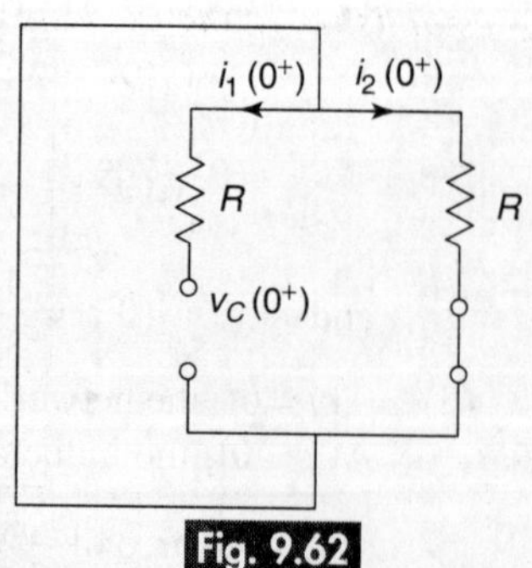


Fig. 9.62

At $t = 0^+$, the inductor acts as an open circuit and the capacitor acts as a short circuit. The voltage source $V_0 \sin \omega t$ acts as a short circuit.

$$i_1(0^+) = 0$$

$$i_2(0^+) = 0$$

$$v_C(0^+) = 0$$

(iii) For $t > 0$, the network is shown in Fig. 9.63.

Fig. 9.63

Writing the KVL equation for $t > 0$,

$$V_0 \sin \omega t - R\, i_1 - \frac{1}{C}\int i_1\, dt = 0 \qquad \text{...(i)}$$

and

$$V_0 \sin \omega t - R\, i_2 - L\frac{di_2}{dt} = 0 \qquad \text{...(ii)}$$

Differentiating Eq. (i),

$$V_0\, \omega \cos \omega t - R\frac{di_1}{dt} - \frac{i_1}{C} = 0$$

$$\frac{di_1}{dt} = \frac{V_0 \omega}{R}\cos \omega t - \frac{i_1}{RC} \qquad \text{...(iii)}$$

At $t = 0^+$,

$$\frac{di_1}{dt}(0^+) = \frac{V_0 \omega}{R}\cos \omega t\Big|_{t=0^+} - \frac{i_1(0^+)}{RC} = \frac{V_0 \omega}{R}$$

From Eq. (ii),

$$\frac{di_2}{dt} = \frac{V_0}{L}\sin \omega t - \frac{R}{L}i_2$$

At $t = 0^+$,

$$\frac{di_2}{dt}(0^+) = \frac{V_0}{L}\sin \omega t\Big|_{t=0^+} - \frac{R}{L}i_2(0^+) = 0$$

## EXAMPLE 9.20

*In the network of Fig. 9.64, the switch K is changed from 'a' to 'b' at t = 0 (a steady state having been established at the position a). Find $i_1, i_2$ and $i_3$ at $t = 0^+$.*

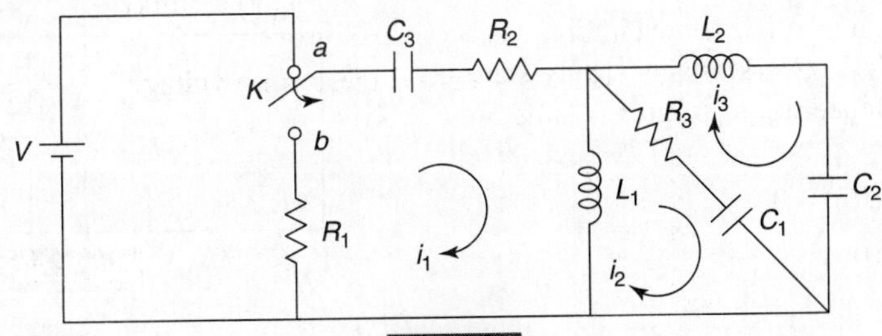


Fig. 9.64

**Solution**

(i) At $t = 0^-$, the network is shown in Fig. 9.65.
At $t = 0^-$, the network attains steady-state condition. Hence, the capacitors act as open circuits and inductors act as short circuits.

$$i_1(0^-) = 0$$
$$i_2(0^-) = 0$$
$$i_3(0^-) = 0$$
$$v_{C_3}(0^-) = V$$
$$v_{C_2}(0^-) = 0$$
$$v_{C_1}(0^-) = 0$$

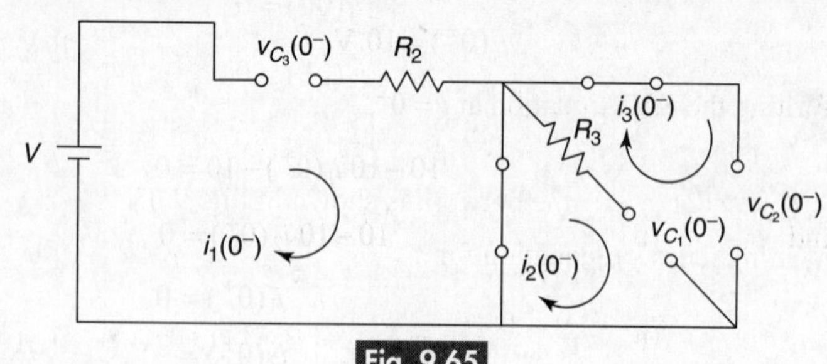

Fig. 9.65

(ii) At $t=0^+$, the network is shown in Fig. 9.66. At $t=0^+$, the capacitor $C_3$ acts as a voltage source of $V$ volts and capacitors $C_1$ and $C_2$ act as short circuits. The inductors act as open circuits.

$$i_1(0^+) = i_2(0^+) = -\frac{V}{R_1 + R_2 + R_3}$$
$$i_3(0^+) = 0$$

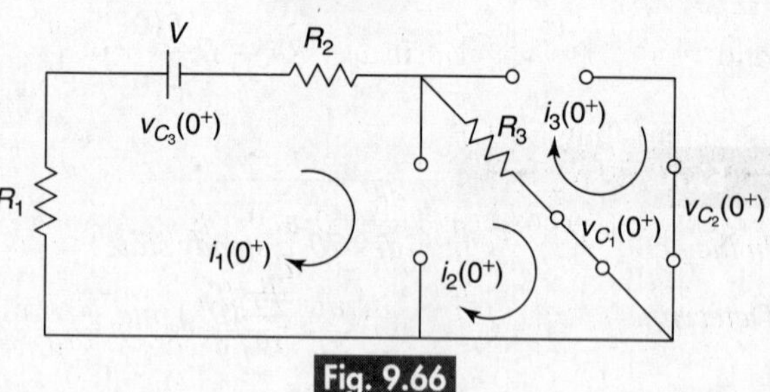

Fig. 9.66

## EXAMPLE 9.21

*In the network of Fig. 9. 67, the switch $K_1$ has been closed for a long time prior to $t = 0$. At $t = 0$, the switch $K_2$ is closed. Find $v_C(0^+)$ and $i_C(0^+)$.*

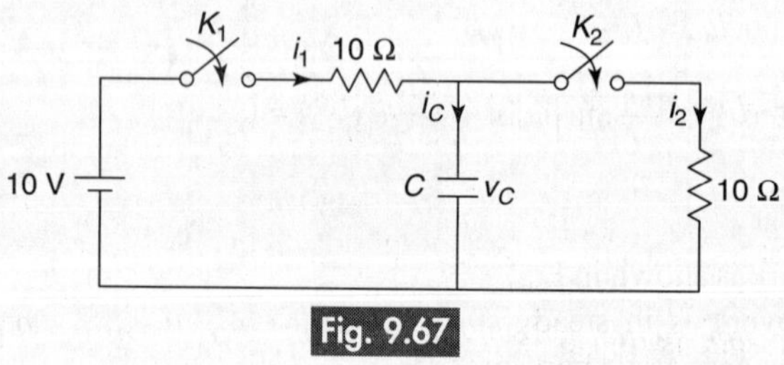

Fig. 9.67

**Solution**

(i) At $t = 0^-$, the network is shown in Fig. 9.68.
At $t = 0^-$, the network attains steady-state condition. Hence, the capacitor acts as an open circuit.

$$i_1(0^-) = 0$$
$$i_2(0^-) = 0$$
$$i_C(0^-) = 0$$
$$v_C(0^-) = 10 \text{ V}$$

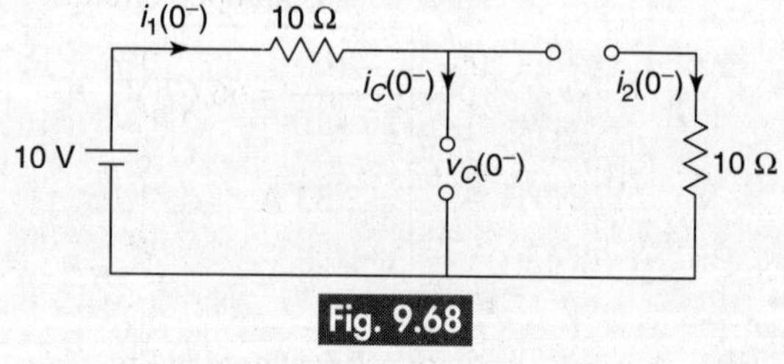

Fig. 9.68

(ii) At $t = 0^+$, the network is shown in Fig. 9.69.
At $t = 0^+$, the capacitor acts as a voltage source of voltage $V$.

$$v_C(0^+) = 10 \text{ V}$$

Fig. 9.69

Writing the KVL equation at $t = 0^+$,

$$10 - 10\, i_1(0^+) - 10 = 0$$

and

$$10 - 10\, i_2(0^+) = 0$$

$$i_1(0^+) = 0$$

$$i_2(0^+) = -1 \text{ A}$$

$$i_1(0^+) = i_C(0^+) + i_2(0^+)$$

$$i_C(0^+) = 1 \text{ A}$$

## EXAMPLE 9.22

*In the network shown in Fig. 9.70, a steady state is reached with the switch open. At t = 0, the switch is closed. Determine* $v_C(0^-), i_1(0^+), i_2(0^+), \frac{di_1}{dt}(0^+)$ *and* $\frac{di_2}{dt}(0^+)$.

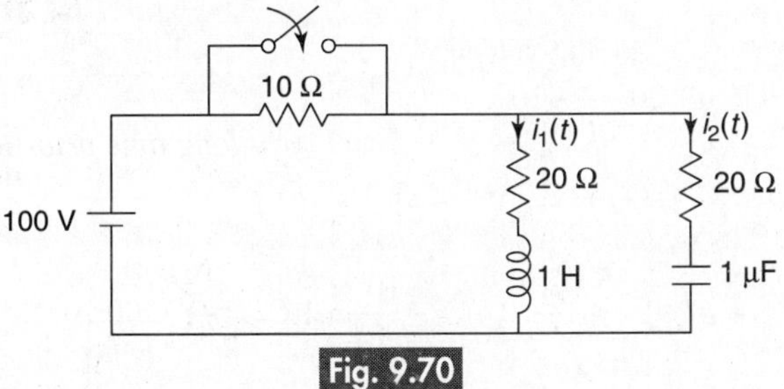


Fig. 9.70

**Solution**

(i) At $t = 0^-$, the network is shown in Fig. 9.71.
At $t = 0^-$, the network is in steady-state. Hence, the inductor acts as a short circuit and the capacitor acts as an open circuit.

$$v_C(0^-) = 100 \times \frac{20}{20+10} = 66.67 \text{ V}$$

$$i_1(0^-) = \frac{66.67}{20} = 3.33 \text{ A}$$

$$i_2(0^-) = 0$$

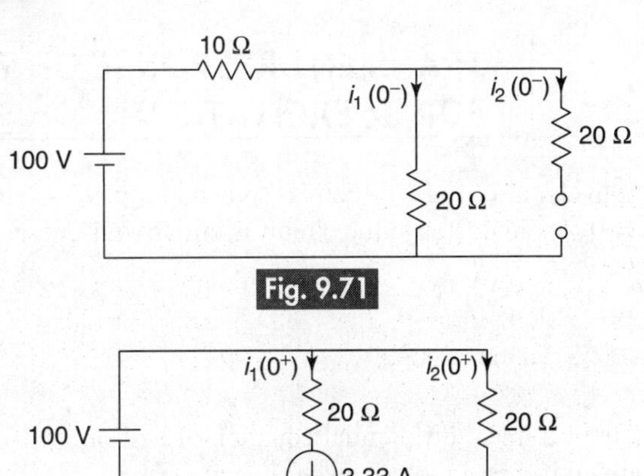


Fig. 9.71

Fig. 9.72

(ii) At $t = 0^+$, the network is shown in Fig. 9.72.

At $t = 0^+$, the inductor acts as a current source of 3.33 A and the capacitor acts as a voltage source of 66.67 V.

$$v_C(0^+) = 66.67 \text{ V}$$

$$i_1(0^+) = 3.33 \text{ A}$$

$$i_2(0^+) = \frac{100 - 66.67}{20} = 1.67 \text{ A}$$

(iii) For $t = 0^-$, the network is shown in Fig. 9.73.

Fig. 9.73

Writing the KVL equations for $t > 0$,

$$100 - 20i_1 - 1\frac{di_1}{dt} = 0 \qquad \ldots\text{(i)}$$

and

$$100 - 20\, i_2 - \frac{1}{10^{-6}}\int i_2\, dt - 66.67 = 0 \qquad \ldots\text{(ii)}$$

At $t = 0^+$, $\quad \frac{di_1}{dt}(0^+) = 100 - 20i_1(0^+) = 100 - 20\,(3.33) = 33.3 \text{ A/s}$

Differentiating Eq. (ii),

$$0 - 20\frac{di_2}{dt} - 10^6\, i_2 = 0$$

At $t = 0^+$, $\quad 20\frac{di_2}{dt}(0^+) = -10^6\, i_2(0^+)$

$$\frac{di_2}{dt}(0^+) = -\frac{10^6}{20} \times 1.67 = -83500 \text{ A/s}^2$$

## 9.2 TRANSIENT RESPONSE OF *RL* CIRCUIT FOR dc EXCITATION

LO 9.2

Discuss the transient response of *RL* circuit for dc excitation

Consider a series *RL* circuit, as shown in Fig. 9.74. The switch is closed at time $t = 0$. The inductor in the circuit is initially un-energised.

Applying KVL to the circuit for $t > 0$,

$$V - Ri - L\frac{di}{dt} = 0$$

This is a linear differential equation of first order. It can be solved if the variables can be separated.

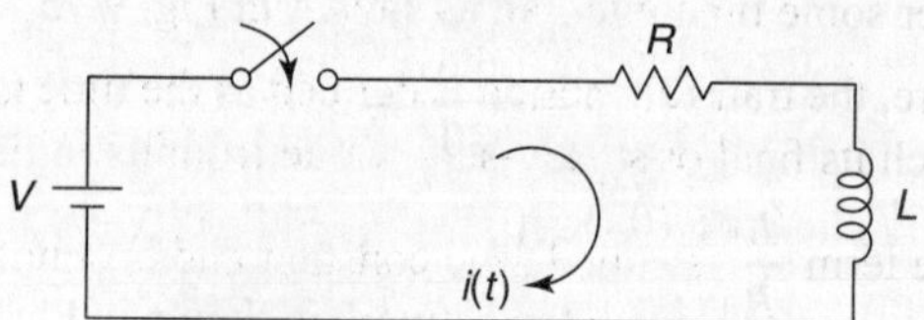


Fig. 9.74 *Series RL circuit*

$$(V - Ri)\,dt = L\,di$$

$$\frac{L\,di}{V - Ri} = dt$$

Integrating both the sides,

$$-\frac{L}{R} l_n (V - Ri) = t + k$$

where $l_n$ denotes that the logarithm is of base $e$ and $k$ is an arbitrary constant. $k$ can be evaluated from the initial condition. In the circuit, the switch is closed at $t = 0$, i.e., just before closing the switch, the current in the inductor is zero. Since the inductor does not allow sudden change in current, at $t = 0^+$, just after the switch is closed, the current remains zero.

Setting $i = 0$ at $t = 0$,

$$-\frac{L}{R} l_n V = k$$

$$-\frac{L}{R} l_n (V - Ri) = t - \frac{L}{R} l_n V$$

$$-\frac{L}{R}\left[l_n (V - Ri) - l_n V\right] = t$$

$$\frac{V - Ri}{V} = e^{-\frac{R}{L}t}$$

$$V - Ri = Ve^{-\frac{R}{L}t}$$

$$Ri = V - Ve^{-\frac{R}{t}t}$$

$$i = \frac{V}{R} - \frac{V}{R} e^{-\frac{R}{L}t} \qquad \text{for } t > 0$$

The complete response is composed of two parts, the steady-state response or forced response or zero state response $\frac{V}{R}$ and transient response or natural response or zero input response $\frac{V}{R}e^{-\frac{R}{L}t}$.

The natural response is a characteristic of the circuit. Its form may be found by considering the source-free circuit. The forced response has the characteristics of forcing function, i.e., applied voltage. Thus, when the switch is closed, response reaches the steady-state value after some time interval, as shown in Fig. 9.75.

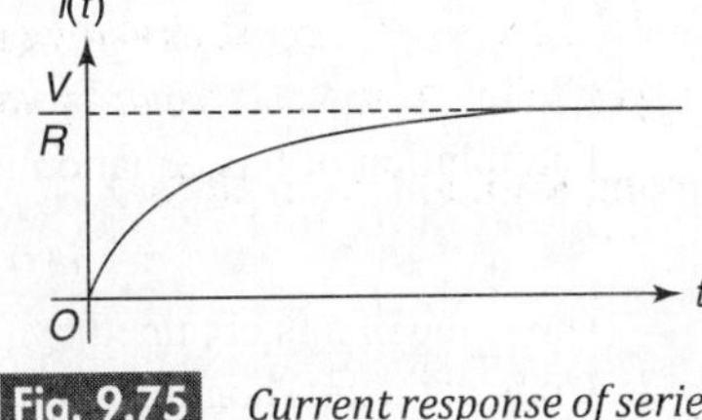


**Fig. 9.75** *Current response of series RL circuit*

Here, the transient period is defined as the time taken for the current to reach its final or steady-state value from its initial value.

The term $\frac{L}{R}$ is called time constant and is denoted by $T$.

Time constant is defined as the time taken by the current to reach 63.2 per cent of its final value in R-L circuit.

$$T = \frac{L}{R}$$

At one time constant, the current reaches 63.2 per cent of its final value $\frac{V}{R}$.

$$i(T) = \frac{V}{R} - \frac{V}{R} e^{-\frac{1}{T}t} = \frac{V}{R} - \frac{V}{R} e^{-1} = \frac{V}{R} - 0.368\frac{V}{R} = 0.632\frac{V}{R}$$

Similarly,

$$i(2T) = \frac{V}{R} - \frac{V}{R} e^{-2} = \frac{V}{R} - 0.135\frac{V}{R} = 0.865\frac{V}{R}$$

$$i(3T) = \frac{V}{R} - \frac{V}{R} e^{-3} = \frac{V}{R} - 0.0498\frac{V}{R} = 0.950\frac{V}{R}$$

$$i(5T) = \frac{V}{R} - \frac{V}{R} e^{-5} = \frac{V}{R} - 0.0067\frac{V}{R} = 0.993\frac{V}{R}$$

After 5 time constants, the current reaches 99.33 per cent of its final value. The voltage across resistor is

$$v_R = Ri = R \times \frac{V}{R}\left(1 - e^{-\frac{R}{L}t}\right)$$

$$= V\left(1 - e^{-\frac{R}{L}t}\right) \qquad \text{for } t > 0$$

Similarly, voltage across inductor is

$$v_L = \frac{di}{dt} = L\frac{V}{R}\frac{d}{dt}\left(1 - e^{-\frac{R}{L}t}\right)$$

$$= Ve^{-\frac{R}{L}t} \qquad \text{for } t > 0$$

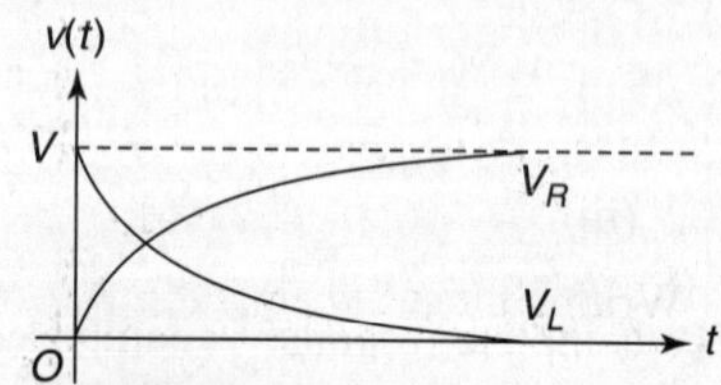


Fig. 9.76 *Voltage response of series RL circuit*

**Note**

1. Consider a homogeneous equation,

$$\frac{di}{dt} + Pi = 0 \qquad \text{where } P \text{ is a constant.}$$

The solution of this equation is given by

$$i(t) = ke^{-Pt}$$

The value of $k$ is obtained by putting $t = 0$ in the equation for $i(t)$.

2. Consider a non-homogeneous equation,

$$\frac{di}{dt} + Pi = Q$$

where $P$ is a constant and $Q$ may be a function of the independent variable $t$ or a constant.

The solution of this equation is given by

$$i(t) = e^{-Pt} \int Q\, e^{Pt}\, dt + k e^{-Pt}$$

The value of $k$ is obtained by putting $t = 0$ in the equation of $i(t)$.

## EXAMPLE 9.23

*In the network of Fig. 9.77, the switch is initially at the position 1. On the steady state having reached, the switch is changed to the position 2. Find current i(t).*

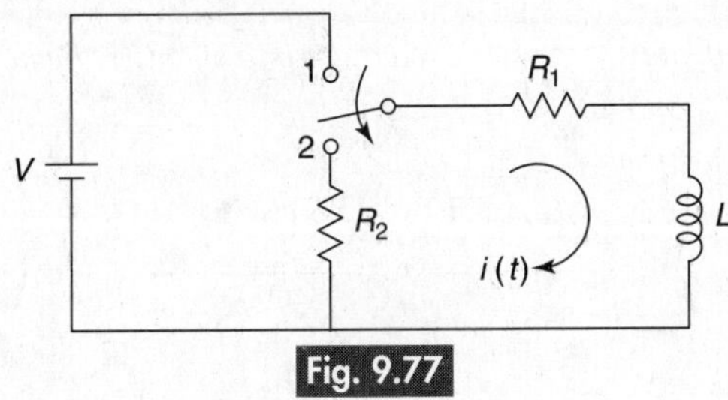


Fig. 9.77

**Solution**

(i) At $t = 0^-$, the network is shown in Fig. 9.78.
At $t = 0^-$, the network has attained steady-state condition. Hence, the inductor acts as a short circuit.

$$i(0^-) = \frac{V}{R_1}$$

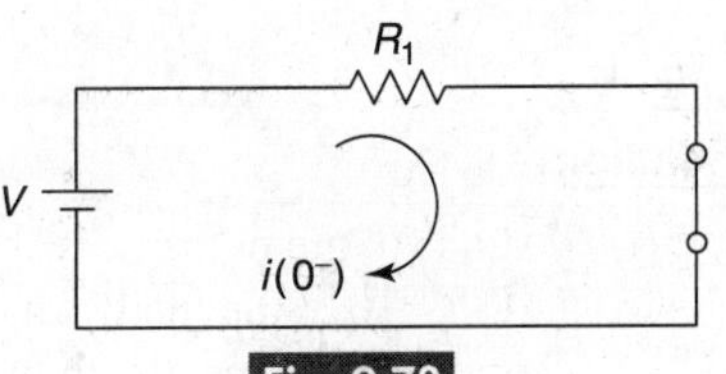


Fig. 9.78

(ii) Since the inductor does not allow sudden change in current,

$$i(0^+) = \frac{V}{R_1}$$

(iii) For $t > 0$, the network is shown in Fig. 9.79.

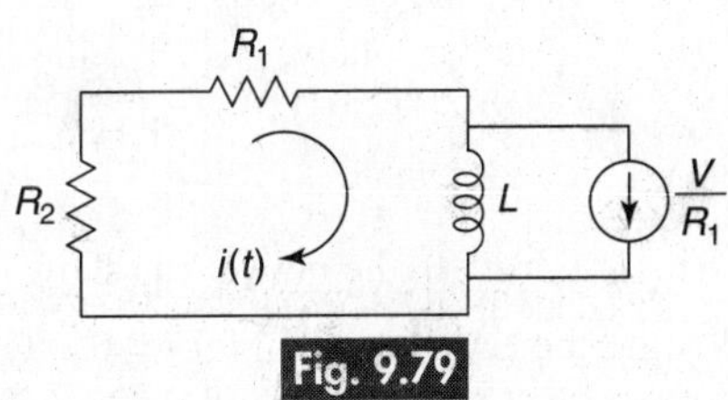


Fig. 9.79

Writing the KVL equation for $t > 0$,

$$-R_2 i - R_1 i - L\frac{di}{dt} = 0$$

$$\frac{di}{dt} + \frac{(R_1 + R_2)}{L} i = 0$$

Comparing with the differential equation $\dfrac{di}{dt} + Pi = 0$,

$$P = \frac{R_1 + R_2}{L}$$

The solution of this differential equation is given by

$$i(t) = k e^{-Pt}$$

$$i(t) = k e^{-\left(\frac{R_1 + R_2}{L}\right)t}$$

At $t = 0$, $i(0) = \dfrac{V}{R_1}$

$$\frac{V}{R_1} = k\,e^0 = k$$

$$i(t) = \frac{V}{R_1} e^{-\left(\frac{R_1+R_2}{L}\right)t} \qquad \text{for } t > 0$$

**EXAMPLE 9.24**

*In the network shown in Fig. 9.80, the switch is closed at t = 0, a steady state having previously been attained. Find the current i (t).*

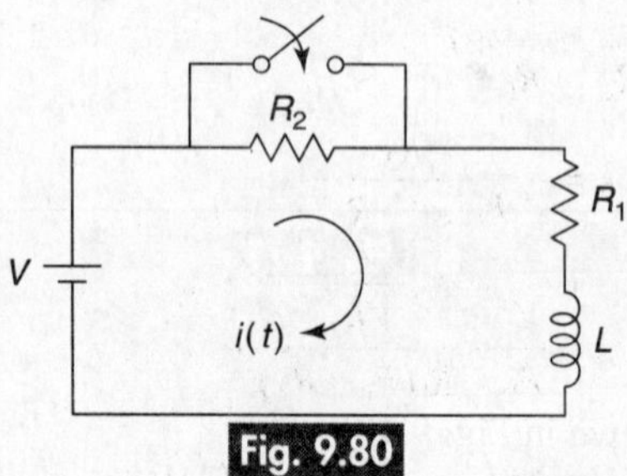


Fig. 9.80

**Solution**

(i) At $t = 0^-$, the network is shown in Fig. 9.81.
At $t = 0^-$, the network has attained steady-state condition. Hence, the inductor acts as a short circuit.

$$i(0^-) = \frac{V}{R_1 + R_2}$$

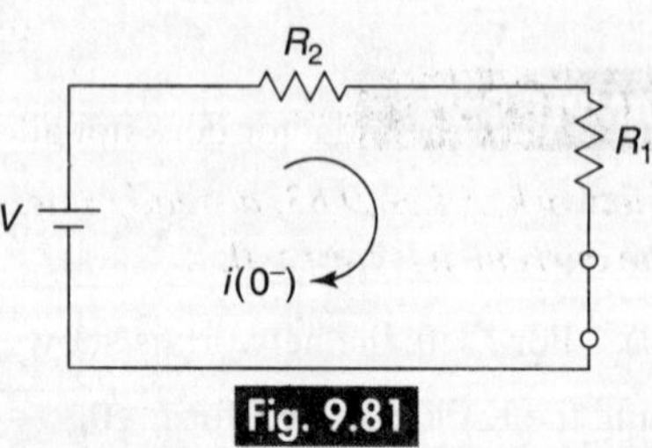


Fig. 9.81

(ii) Since the current through the inductor cannot change instantaneously,

$$i(0^+) = \frac{V}{R_1 + R_2}$$

(iii) For $t > 0$, the network is shown in Fig. 9.82.

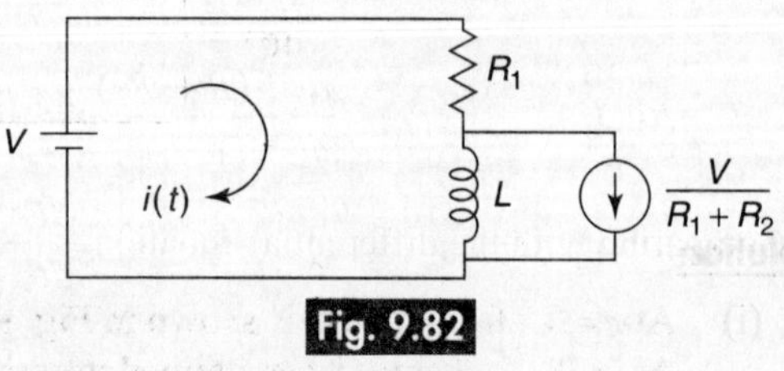


Fig. 9.82

Writing the KVL equation for $t > 0$,

$$V - R_1 i - L\frac{di}{dt} = 0$$

$$\frac{di}{dt} + \frac{R_1}{L} i = \frac{V}{L}$$

Comparing with the differential equation $\dfrac{di}{dt} + Pi = Q$,

$$P = \frac{R_1}{L},\ Q = \frac{V}{L}$$

The solution of this differential equation is given by

$$i(t) = e^{-Pt}\int Qe^{Pt}\,dt + k\,e^{-Pt}$$

$$= e^{-\frac{R_1}{L}t}\int \frac{V}{L}e^{\frac{R_1}{L}t}\,dt + k\,e^{-\frac{R_1}{L}t}$$

$$= \frac{V}{R_1} + k\,e^{-\frac{R_1}{L}t}$$

At $t = 0$, $i(0) = \dfrac{V}{R_1 + R_2}$

$$\frac{V}{R_1 + R_2} = \frac{V}{R_1} + k$$

$$k = -\frac{VR_2}{R_1(R_1 + R_2)}$$

$$i(t) = \frac{V}{R_1} - \frac{VR_2}{R_1(R_1 + R_2)}\,e^{-\frac{R_1}{L}t}$$

$$= \frac{V}{R_1}\left(1 - \frac{R_2}{R_1 + R_2}\,e^{-\frac{R_1}{L}t}\right) \quad \text{for } t > 0$$

**EXAMPLE 9.25**

*In the network of Fig. 9.83, a steady state is reached with the switch K open. At t = 0, the switch K is closed. Find the current i(t) for t > 0.*

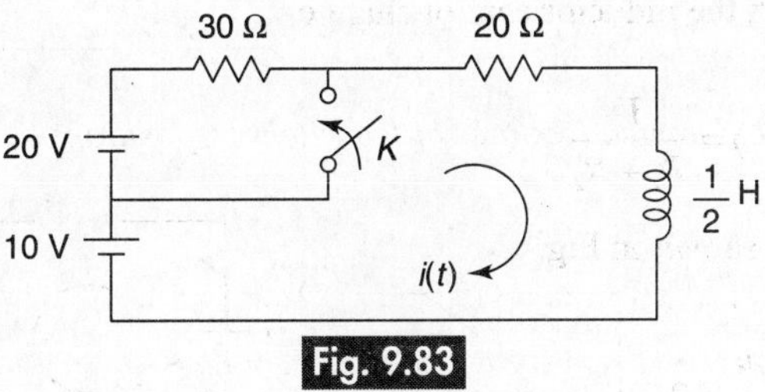


Fig. 9.83

**Solution**

(i) At $t = 0^-$, the network is shown in Fig. 9.84.
At $t = 0^-$, the network has attained steady-state condition. Hence, the inductor acts as a short circuit

$$i(0^-) = \frac{20 + 10}{30 + 20} = 0.6 \text{ A}$$

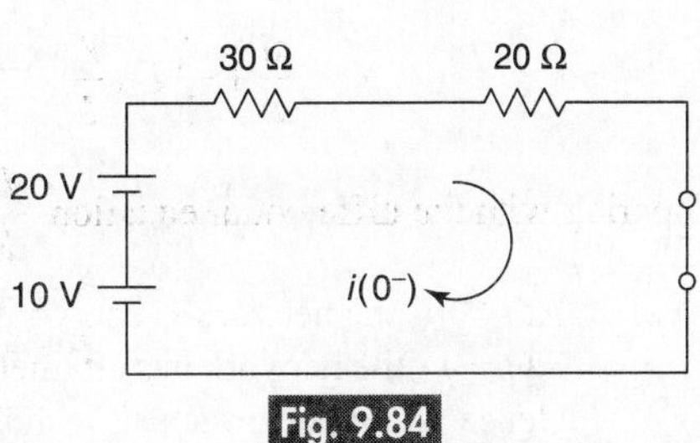


Fig. 9.84

(ii) Since the current through the inductor cannot change instantaneously,

$$i(0^+) = 0.6 \text{ A}$$

(iii) For $t > 0$, the network is shown in Fig. 9.85.

Writing the KVL equation for $t > 0$.

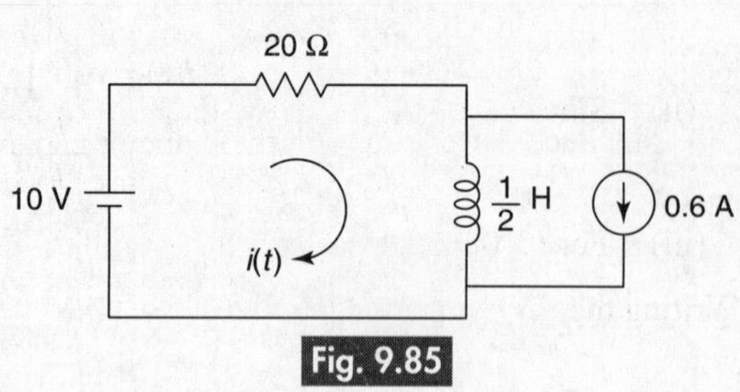


Fig. 9.85

$$10 - 20i - \frac{1}{2}\frac{di}{dt} = 0$$

$$\frac{di}{dt} + 40i = 20$$

Comparing with the differential equation $\frac{di}{dt} + Pi = Q$,

$$P = 40, \quad Q = 20$$

The solution of this differential equation is given by

$$\begin{aligned} i(t) &= e^{-Pt} \int Q\, e^{Pt}\, dt + k\, e^{-Pt} \\ &= e^{-40t} \int 20\, e^{40t}\, dt + k\, e^{-40t} \\ &= \frac{20}{40} + k\, e^{-40t} \\ &= 0.5 + k\, e^{-40t} \end{aligned}$$

At $t = 0$, $i(0) = 0.6$ A

$$0.6 = 0.5 + k$$

$$k = 0.1$$

$$i(t) = 0.5 + 0.1\, e^{-40t} \qquad \text{for } t > 0$$

## EXAMPLE 9.26

*The network of Fig. 9.86 is under steady state with switch at position 1. At t = 0, switch is moved to position 2. Find i (t).*

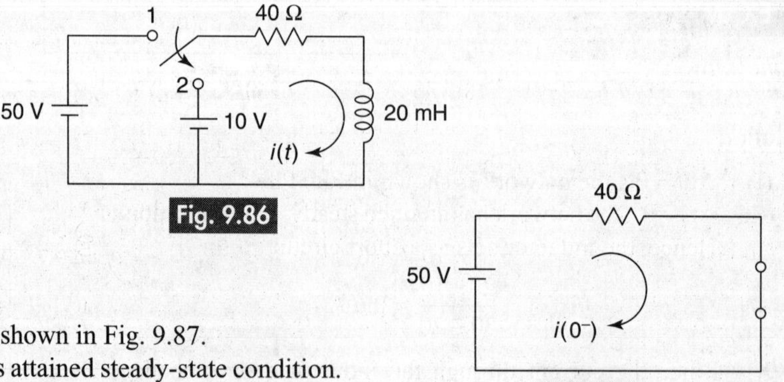


Fig. 9.86

Fig. 9.87

**Solution**

(i) At $t = 0^-$, the network is shown in Fig. 9.87.
At $t = 0^-$, the network has attained steady-state condition.
Hence, the inductor acts as a short circuit.

$$i(0^-) = \frac{50}{40} = 1.25 \text{ A}$$

(ii) Since current through the inductor cannot change instantaneously,

$$i(0^+) = 1.25 \text{ A}$$

(iii) For $t > 0$, the network is shown in Fig. 9.88.

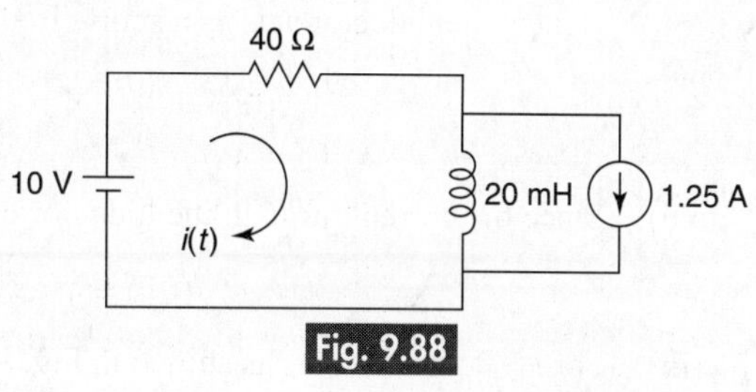

Fig. 9.88

Writing the KVL equation for $t > 0$,

$$10 - 40i - 20\times10^{-3}\frac{di}{dt} = 0$$

$$\frac{di}{dt} + 2000i = 500$$

Comparing with the differential equation $\frac{di}{dt} + Pi = Q$,

$$P = 2000, \quad Q = 500$$

The solution of this differential equation is given by

$$i(t) = e^{-Pt}\int Q\,e^{Pt}\,dt + k\,e^{-Pt}$$

$$= e^{-2000t}\int 500\,e^{2000t} + k\,e^{-2000t}$$

$$= \frac{500}{2000} + k\,e^{-2000t}$$

$$= 0.25 + k\,e^{-2000t}$$

At $t = 0$, $i(0) = 1.25$ A

$$1.25 = 0.25 + k$$

$$k = 1$$

$$i(t) = 0.25 + e^{-2000t} \qquad \text{for } t > 0$$

**EXAMPLE 9.27**

*In the network of Fig. 9.89, the switch is moved from 1 to 2 at t = 0. Determine i(t).*

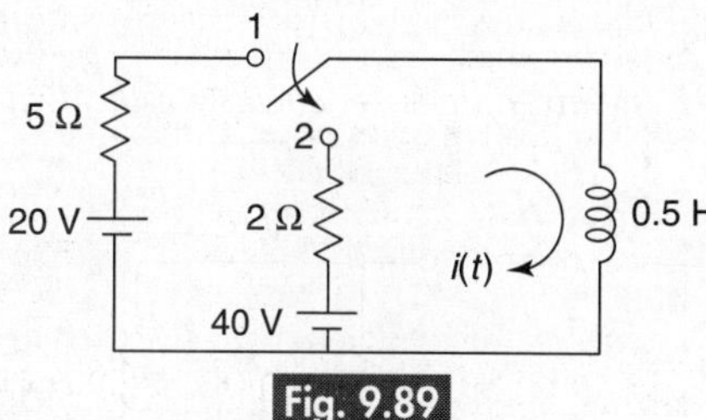

Fig. 9.89

**Solution**

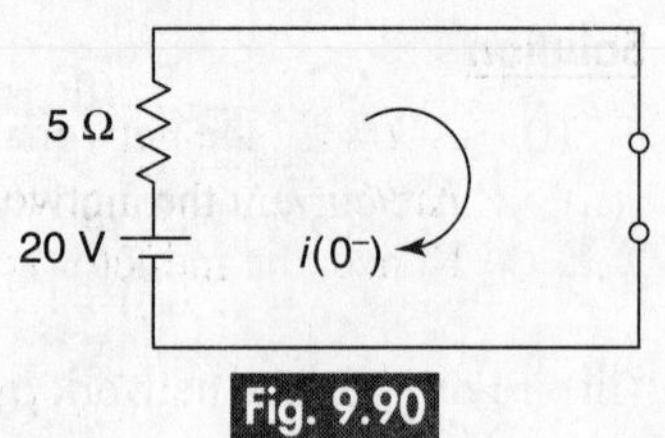

Fig. 9.90

(i) At $t = 0^-$, the network is shown in Fig. 9.90.
At $t = 0^-$, the network has attained steady-state condition. Hence, the inductor acts as a short circuit.

$$i(0^-) = \frac{20}{5} = 4 \text{ A}$$

(ii) Since the current through the inductor cannot change instantaneously,

$$i(0^+) = 4 \text{ A}$$

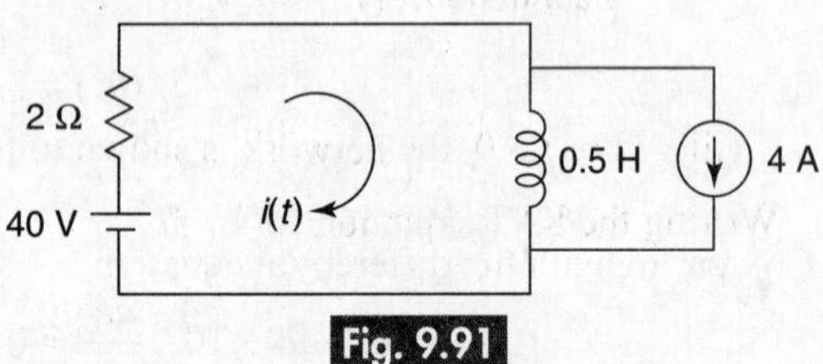

Fig. 9.91

(iii) For $t > 0$, the network is shown in Fig. 9.91.

Writing the KVL equation for $t > 0$,

$$40 - 2i - 0.5\frac{di}{dt} = 0$$

$$\frac{di}{dt} + 4i = 80$$

Comparing with the differential equation $\frac{di}{dt} + Pi = Q$,

$$P = 4, \quad Q = 80$$

The solution of this differential equation is given by

$$i(t) = e^{-Pt}\int Q\, e^{Pt}\, dt + k\, e^{-Pt}$$

$$= e^{-4t}\int 80\, e^{4t}\, dt + k\, e^{-4t}$$

$$= \frac{80}{4} + k\, e^{-4t}$$

$$= 20 + k\, e^{-4t}$$

At $t = 0$, $i(0) = 4$ A

$$4 = 20 + k$$

$$k = -16$$

$$i(t) = 20 - 16\, e^{-4t} \qquad \text{for } t > 0$$

## EXAMPLE 9.28

*For the network shown in Fig. 9.92, steady state is reached with the switch closed. The switch is opened at $t = 0$. Obtain expressions for $i_L(t)$ and $v_L(t)$.*

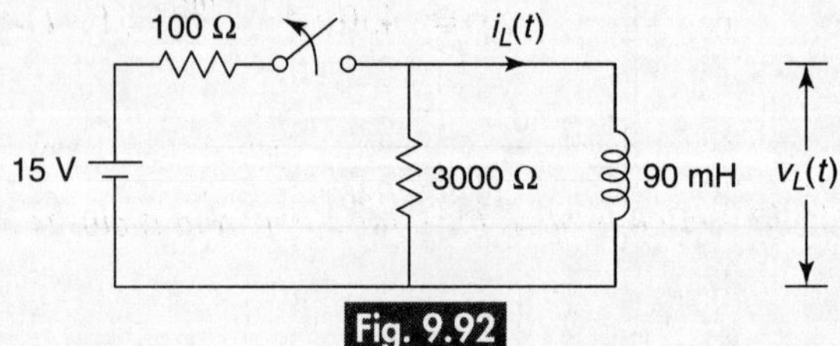

Fig. 9.92

## Solution

(i) At $t = 0^-$, the network is shown in Fig. 9.93.
At $t = 0^-$, the network has attained steady-state condition. Hence, the inductor acts as a short circuit.

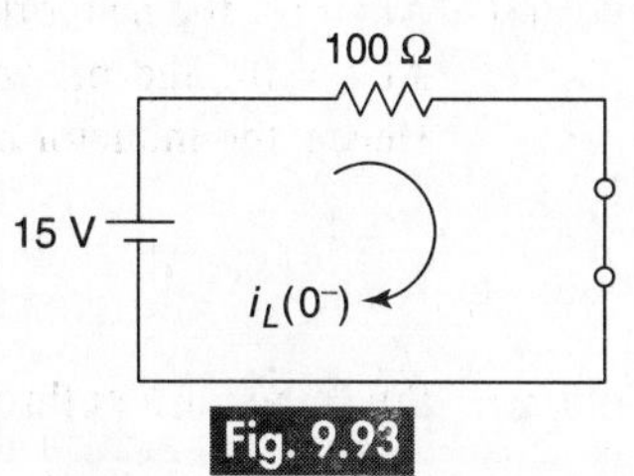

Fig. 9.93

$$i_L(0^-) = \frac{15}{100} = 0.15 \text{ A}$$

(ii) Since current through the inductor cannot change instantaneously,

$$i_L(0^+) = 0.15 \text{ A}$$

(iii) For $t > 0$, the network is shown in Fig. 9.94.

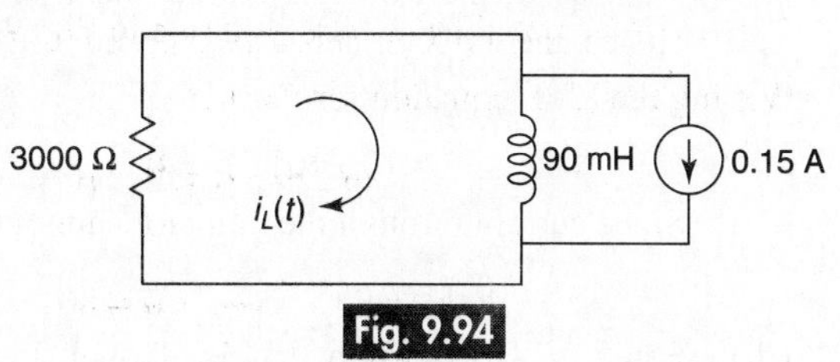

Fig. 9.94

Writing the KVL equation for $t > 0$,

$$-3000 i_L - 90\times10^{-3}\frac{di_L}{dt} = 0$$

$$\frac{di_L}{dt} + 33.33\times10^3\, i_L = 0$$

Comparing with the differential equation $\frac{di}{dt} + Pi = 0$,

$$P = 33.33\times10^3$$

The solution of this differential equation is given by

$$i_L(t) = k\,e^{-Pt}$$

$$i_L(t) = k\,e^{-33.33\times10^3 t}$$

At $t = 0,\ i_L(0) = 0.15$ A

$$0.15 = k$$

$$i_L(t) = 0.15 e^{-33.33\times10^3 t} \quad \text{for } t > 0$$

Also,
$$v_L(t) = L\frac{di_L}{dt}$$

$$= 90\times10^{-3}\frac{d}{dt}(0.15 e^{-33.33\times10^3 t})$$

$$= -90\times10^{-3}\times0.15\times33.33\times10^3\times e^{-33.33\times10^3 t}$$

$$= -450\, e^{-33.33\times10^3 t} \quad \text{for } t > 0$$

### EXAMPLE 9.29

*In the network of Fig. 9.95, the switch is open for a long time and it closes at t = 0. Find i(t).*

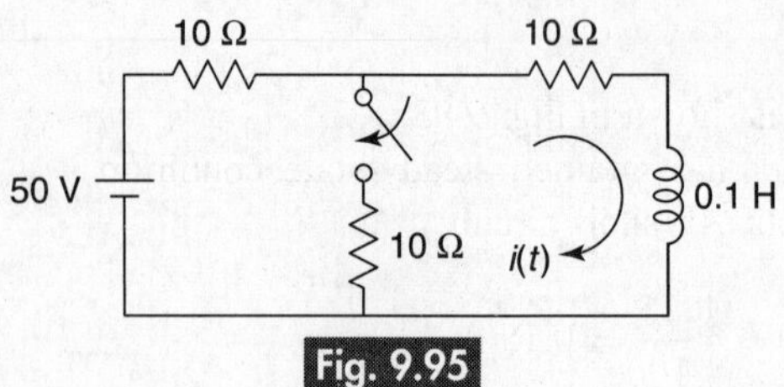


Fig. 9.95

## Solution

(i) At $t = 0^-$, the network is shown in Fig. 9.96.
At $t = 0^-$, the network has attained steady-state condition. Hence, the inductor acts as a short circuit.

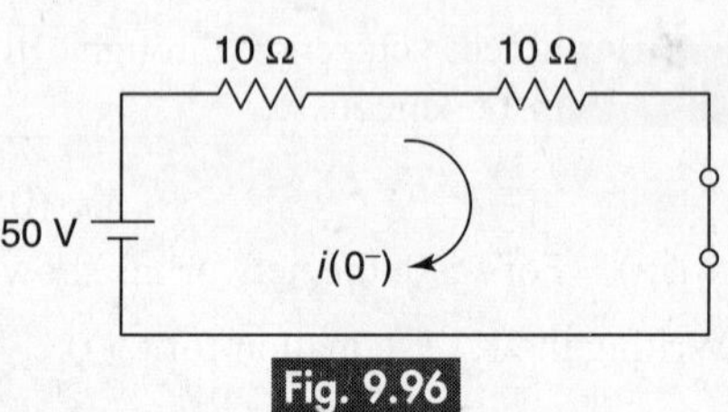


Fig. 9.96

$$i(0^-) = \frac{50}{10+10} = 2.5 \text{ A}$$

(ii) Since current through the inductor cannot change instantaneously,

$$i\,(0^+) = 2.5 \text{ A}$$

(iii) For $t > 0$, the network is shown in Fig. 9.97.
For $t > 0$, representing the network to the left of the inductor by Thevenin's equivalent network,

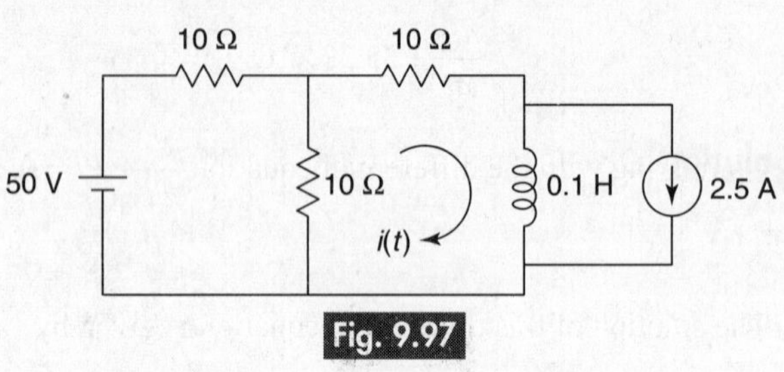


Fig. 9.97

$$V_{\text{eq}} = 50 \times \frac{10}{10+10} = 25 \text{ V}$$

$$R_{\text{eq}} = (10 \,||\, 10) + 10 = 15\ \Omega$$

For $t > 0$, Thevenin's equivalent network is shown in Fig. 9.98.

Writing the KVL equation for $t > 0$,

$$25 - 15i - 0.1\frac{di}{dt} = 0$$

$$\frac{di}{dt} + 150i = 250$$

Fig. 9.98

Comparing with the differential equation $\frac{di}{dt} + Pi = Q$,

$$P = 150, \quad Q = 250$$

The solution of this differential equation is given by

$$i(t) = e^{-Pt}\int Q\, e^{Pt}\, dt + k\,e^{-Pt}$$

$$= e^{-150t}\int 250\, e^{150t}\, dt + k\,e^{-Pt}$$

$$= \frac{250}{150} + k\,e^{-150t}$$

$$= 1.667 + k\,e^{-150t}$$

At $t = 0$, $i(0) = 2.5$ A

$$2.5 = 1.667 + k$$

$$k = 0.833$$

$$i(t) = 1.667 + 0.833\, e^{-150t} \qquad \text{for } t > 0$$

## EXAMPLE 9.30

*In Fig. 9.99, the switch is closed at t = 0. Find i (t) for t > 0.*

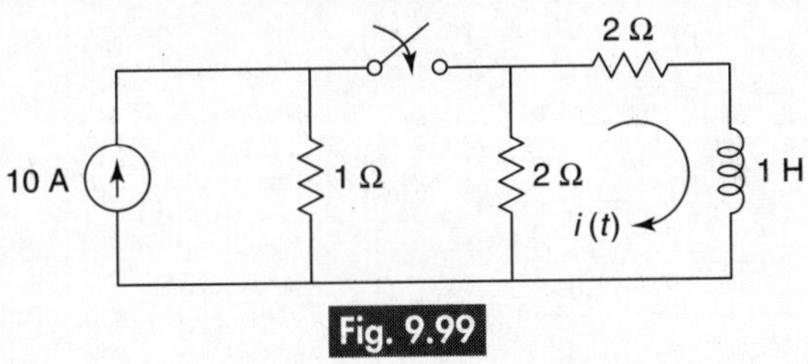


Fig. 9.99

## Solution

(i) At $t = 0^-$, $\qquad i(0^-) = 0$

(ii) Since current through inductor cannot change instantaneously,

$$i(0^+) = 0$$

(iii) For $t > 0$, simplifying the network by source-transformation technique, as shown in Fig. 9.100.

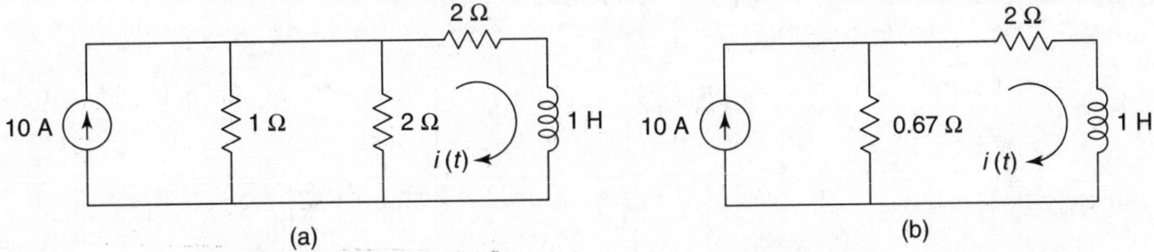


Writing the KVL equation for $t > 0$,

$$6.67 - 2.67i - 1\frac{di}{dt} = 0$$

$$\frac{di}{dt} + 2.67i = 6.67$$

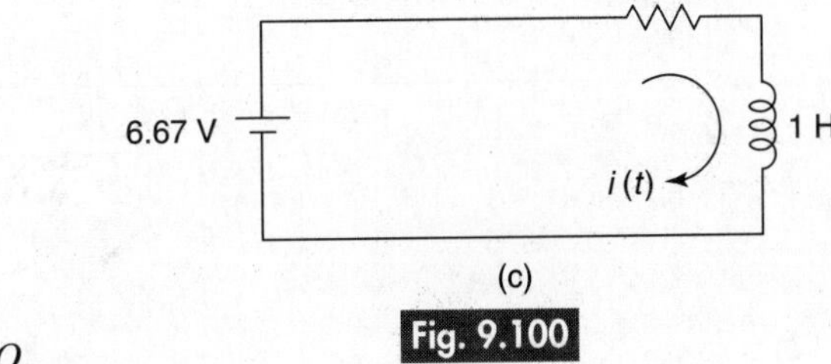


Fig. 9.100

Comparing with the differential equation $\dfrac{di}{dt} + Pi = Q$,

$$P = 2.67,\ Q = 6.67$$

The solution of this differential equation is given by

$$i(t) = e^{-Pt}\int Q\,e^{Pt}\,dt + k\,e^{-Pt}$$

$$= e^{-2.67t}\int 6.67\,e^{2.67t}\,dt + k\,e^{-2.67t}$$

$$= \frac{6.67}{2.67} + k\,e^{-2.67t}$$

$$= 2.5 + k\,e^{-2.67t}$$

At $t = 0$, $i\,(0) = 0$

$$0 = 2.5 + k$$

$$k = -2.5$$

$$i(t) = 2.5 - 2.5\,e^{-2.67t}$$

$$= 2.5(1 - e^{-2.67t}) \qquad \text{for } t > 0$$

## EXAMPLE 9.31

*Find the current i (t) for t > 0.*

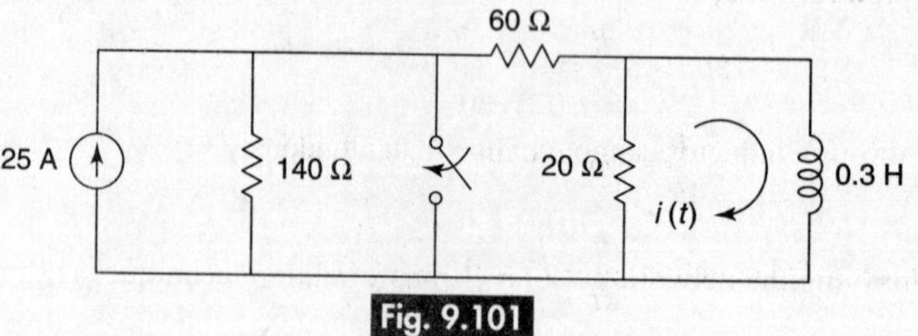


Fig. 9.101

**Solution**

(i) At $t = 0^-$, the inductor acts as a short circuit. Simplifying the network, as shown in Fig. 9.102.

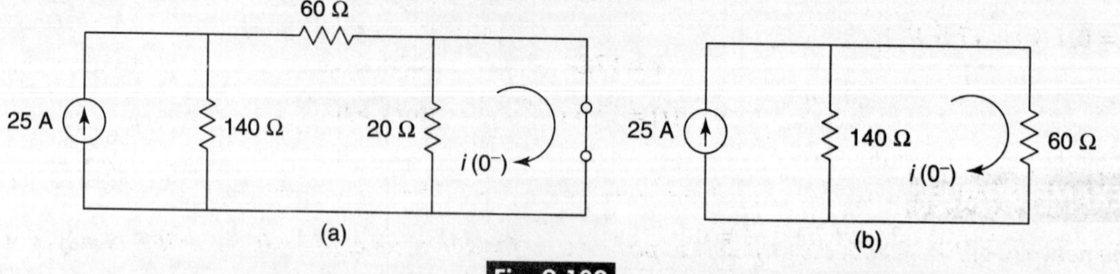


Fig. 9.102

$$i(0^-) = 25 \times \frac{140}{140 + 60} = 17.5 \text{ A}$$

(ii) Since current through the inductor cannot change instantaneously,

$$i(0^+) = 17.5 \text{ A}$$

(iii) For $t > 0$, the network is shown in Fig. 9.103.

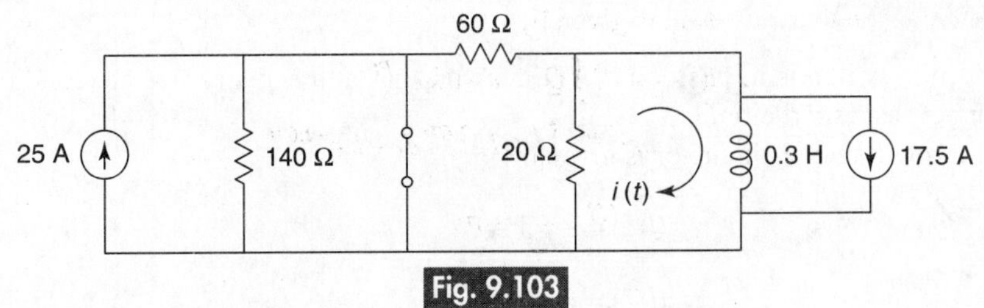


Fig. 9.103

Simplifying the network by source transformation, as shown in Fig. 9.104,

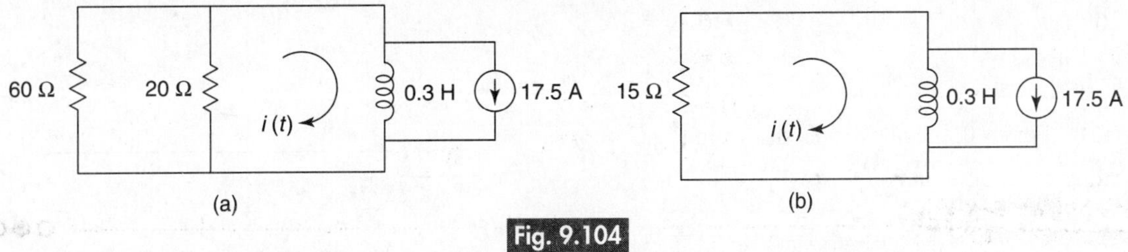


Fig. 9.104

Writing the KVL equation for $t > 0$,

$$-15i - 0.3\frac{di}{dt} = 0$$

$$\frac{di}{dt} + 50i = 0$$

Comparing with the differential equation $\frac{di}{dt} + Pi = 0$,

$$P = 50$$

The solution of this differential equation is given by

$$i(t) = k\,e^{-Pt} = k\,e^{-50t}$$

At $t = 0$, $i(0) = 17.5$ A

$$k = 17.5$$

$$i(t) = 17.5\,e^{-50t} \qquad \text{for } t > 0$$

## EXAMPLE 9.32

*In the network of Fig. 9.105, the switch is in position 'a' for a long time. At t = 0, the switch is moved from a to b. Find $v_2$ (t). Assume that the initial current in the 2 H inductor is zero.*

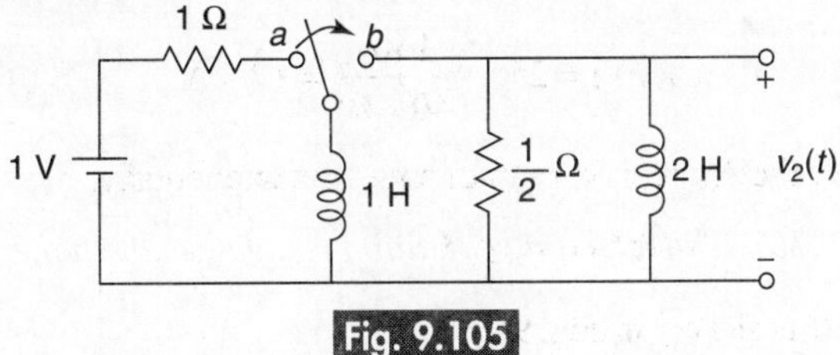


Fig. 9.105

## Solution

(i) At $t = 0^-$, the switch is in position $a$. The network has attained steady-state condition. Hence, the inductor acts as a short circuit.
Current through the 1 H inductor is given by

$$i(0^-) = \frac{1}{1} = 1\text{ A}$$

$$v_2(0^-) = 0$$

(ii) Since current through the inductor cannot change instantaneously,

$$i(0^+) = 1\text{ A}$$

$$v_2(0^+) = -1 \times \frac{1}{2} = -0.5\text{ V}$$

(iii) For $t > 0$, the network is shown in Fig. 9.106.

Writing the KCL equation for $t > 0$,

$$\frac{1}{1}\int_0^t v_2 dt + 1 + \frac{v_2}{\frac{1}{2}} + \frac{1}{2}\int_0^t v_2 dt = 0 \qquad \text{...(i)}$$

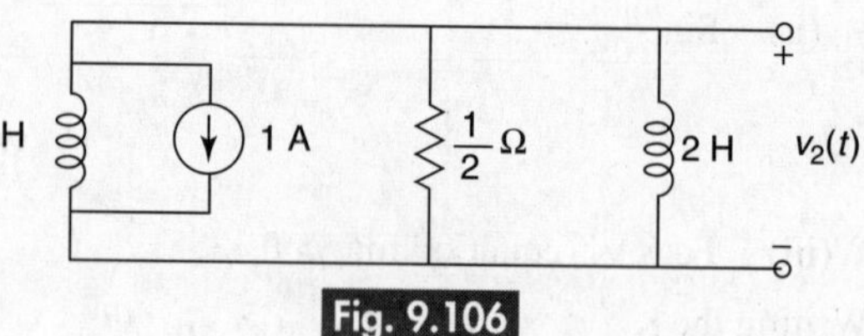


Fig. 9.106

Differentiating Eq. (i),

$$v_2 + 2\frac{dv_2}{dt} + \frac{1}{2}v_2 = 0$$

$$\frac{dv_2}{dt} + \frac{3}{4}v_2 = 0$$

Comparing with the differential equation $\frac{dv}{dt} + Pv = 0$,

$$P = \frac{3}{4}$$

The solution of this differential equation is given by

$$v_2(t) = k e^{-Pt} = k e^{-\frac{3}{4}t}$$

At $t = 0$, $v_2(0) = -0.5$ V

$$-0.5 = k e^{\circ}$$

$$k = -0.5$$

$$v_2(t) = -0.5\, e^{-\frac{3}{4}t} \qquad \text{for } t > 0$$

## EXAMPLE 9.33

*In the network shown in Fig. 9.107, a steady-state condition is achieved with the switch open. At t = 0, switch is closed. Find $v_a(t)$.*

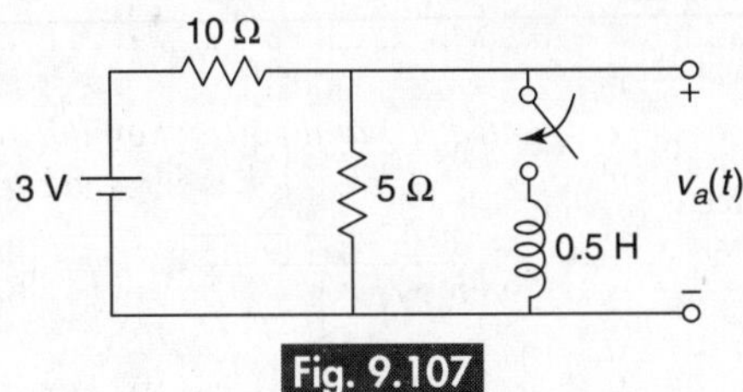


Fig. 9.107

**Solution**

(i) At $t = 0^-$, the network has attained steady-state condition. Hence, the inductor acts as a short circuit.

$$i_L(0^-) = 0$$

$$v_a(0^-) = 3 \times \frac{5}{10+5} = 1 \text{ V}$$

(ii) Since current through inductor cannot change instantaneously,

$$i_L(0^+) = 0$$

$$v_a(0^+) = 1 \text{ V}$$

(iii) For $t > 0$, the network is shown in Fig. 9.108.

Writing the KCL equation for $t > 0$,

$$\frac{1}{0.5}\int_0^t v_a \, dt + \frac{v_a}{5} + \frac{v_a - 3}{10} = 0$$

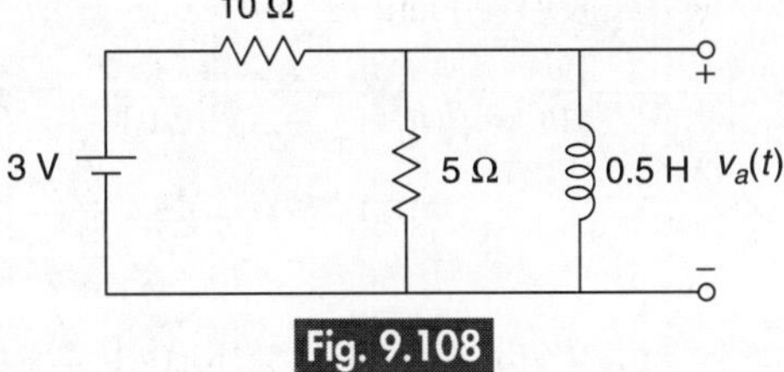


Fig. 9.108

Differentiating Eq. (i),

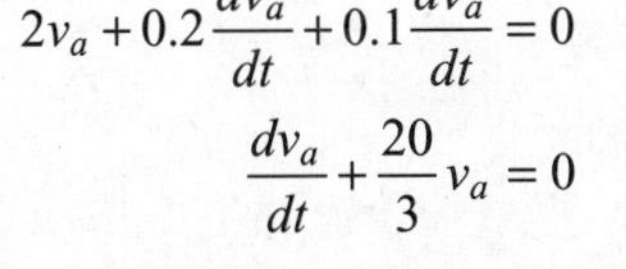

$$2v_a + 0.2\frac{dv_a}{dt} + 0.1\frac{dv_a}{dt} = 0$$

$$\frac{dv_a}{dt} + \frac{20}{3}v_a = 0$$

Comparing with the differential equation $\dfrac{dv}{dt} + Pv = 0$,

$$P = \frac{20}{3}$$

The solution of this differential equation is given by

$$v_a(t) = k\,e^{-Pt} = k\,e^{-\frac{20}{3}t}$$

At $t = 0$, $v_a(0) = 1$ V

$$1 = k$$

$$v_a(t) = e^{-\frac{20}{3}t} \qquad \text{for } t > 0$$

**EXAMPLE 9.34**

*In the network of Fig. 9.109, determine currents $i_1(t)$ and $i_2(t)$ when the switch is closed at $t = 0$.*

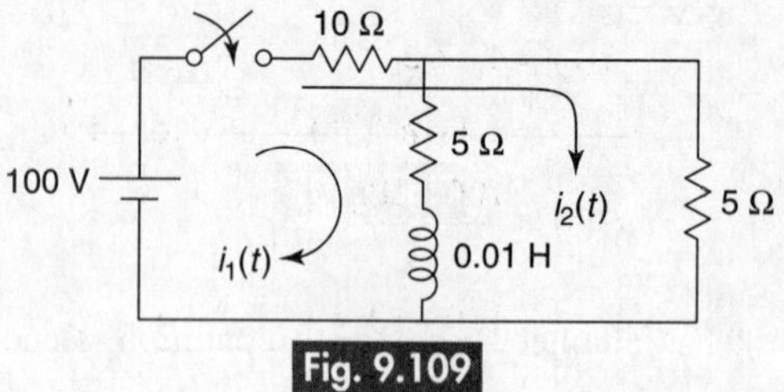


Fig. 9.109

**Solution**

(i) At $t = 0^-$, $\qquad i_1(0^-) = i_2(0^-) = 0$

(ii) At $t = 0^+$,

$$i_1(0^+) = 0$$

$$i_2(0^+) = \frac{100}{15} = 6.67 \text{ A}$$

(iii) For $t > 0$, the network is shown in Fig. 9.110.

Writing the KVL equations for $t > 0$,

$$100 - 10(i_1 + i_2) - 5i_1 - 0.01\frac{di_1}{dt} = 0 \qquad \ldots\text{(i)}$$

and
$$100 - 10(i_1 + i_2) - 5i_2 = 0 \qquad \ldots\text{(ii)}$$

Fig. 9.110

From Eq. (ii),

$$i_2 = \frac{100 - 10i_1}{15}$$

Substituting in Eq. (i),

$$\frac{di_1}{dt} + 833i_1 = 3333$$

Comparing with the differential equation $\frac{di}{dt} + Pi = Q$,

$$P = 833,\ Q = 3333$$

The solution of this differential equation is given by

$$i_1(t) = e^{-Pt}\int Q\,e^{Pt}\,dt + k\,e^{-Pt}$$

$$= e^{-833t}\int 3333\,e^{833t}\,dt + k\,e^{-833t}$$

$$= \frac{3333}{833} + k\,e^{-833t}$$

$$= 4 + k\,e^{-833t}$$

At $t = 0$, $i_1(0) = 0$

$$0 = 4 + k$$
$$k = -4$$
$$i_1(t) = 4 - 4e^{-833t}$$
$$= 4(1 - e^{-833t}) \qquad \text{for } t > 0$$
$$i_2(t) = \frac{100 - 10i_1}{15}$$
$$= \frac{100 - 10(4 - 4e^{-833t})}{15}$$
$$= 4 + 2.67e^{-833t} \qquad \text{for } t > 0$$

## EXAMPLE 9.35

*The switch in the network shown in Fig. 9.111 is closed at $t = 0$. Find $v_2(t)$ for all $t > 0$. Assume zero initial current in the inductor.*

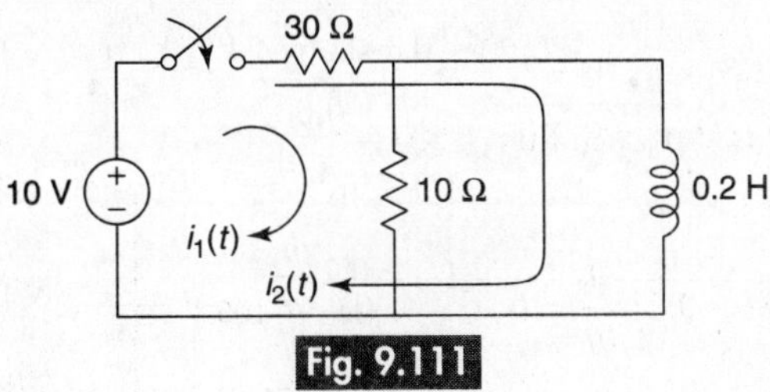


Fig. 9.111

**Solution**

(i) At $t = 0^-$,
$$i_1(0^-) = 0$$
$$i_2(0^-) = 0$$

(ii) Since current through the inductor cannot change instantaneously,
$$i_2(0^+) = 0$$
$$i_1(0^+) = \frac{10}{30 + 10} = 0.25 \text{ A}$$

(iii) For $t > 0$, the network is shown in Fig. 9.112.

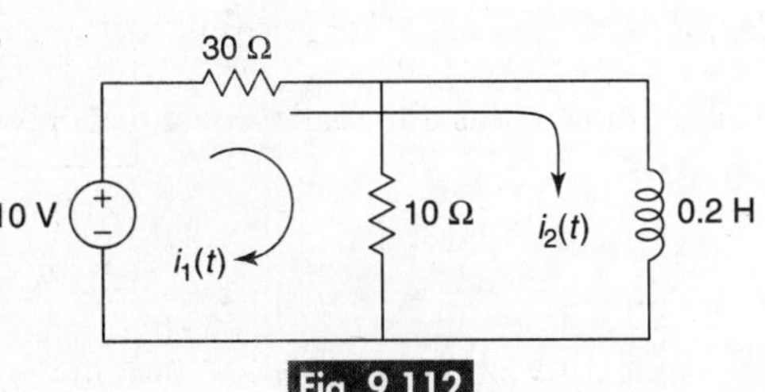


Fig. 9.112

Writing the KVL equations for $t > 0$,
$$10 - 30(i_1 + i_2) - 10i_1 = 0 \qquad \text{...(i)}$$
and
$$10 - 30(i_1 + i_2) - 0.2\frac{di_2}{dt} = 0 \qquad \text{...(ii)}$$

From Eq. (i),
$$i_1 = \frac{10 - 30\,i_2}{40} = 0.25 - 0.75\,i_2 \qquad \text{...(iii)}$$

Substituting Eq. (iii) into Eq. (ii),

$$\frac{di_2}{dt}+37.5\,i_2=2.5$$

Comparing with the differential equation $\frac{di}{dt}+Pi=Q$,

$$P=37.5,\ Q=2.5$$

The solution of this differential equation is given by

$$\begin{aligned}i_2(t)&=e^{-Pt}\int Q\,e^{Pt}\,dt+k\,e^{-Pt}\\&=e^{-37.5t}\int 2.5\,e^{37.5t}\,dt+k\,e^{-37.5t}\\&=\frac{2.5}{37.5}+k\,e^{-37.5t}\\&=0.067+k\,e^{-37.5t}\end{aligned}$$

At $t=0,\ i_2(0)=0$

$$0=0.067+k$$

$$k=-0.067$$

$$\begin{aligned}i_2(t)&=0.067-0.067\,e^{-37.5t}\\v_2(t)&=0.2\frac{di_2}{dt}\\&=0.2\frac{d}{dt}(0.067-0.067\,e^{-37.5t})\\&=0.5e^{-37.5t}\qquad\text{for } t>0\end{aligned}$$

## EXAMPLE 9.36

*For the network shown in Fig. 9.113, find the current i(t) when the switch is changed from position 1 to 2 at t = 0.*

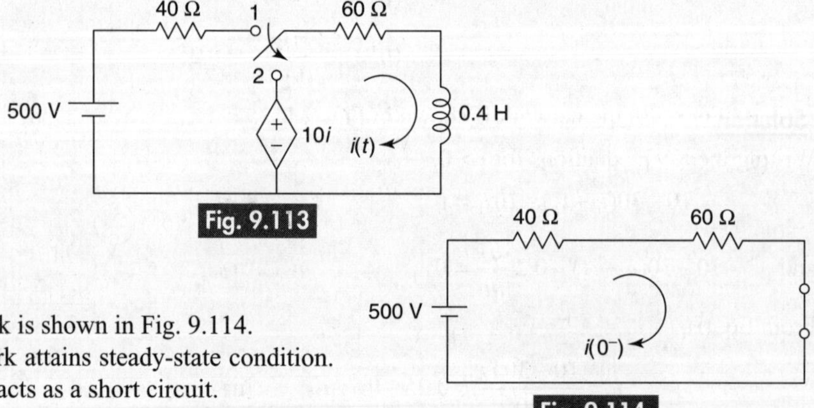


Fig. 9.113

Fig. 9.114

**Solution**

(i) At $t = 0^-$, the network is shown in Fig. 9.114.
At $t = 0^-$, the network attains steady-state condition.
Hence, the inductor acts as a short circuit.

$$i(0^-) = \frac{500}{40+60} = 5 \text{ A}$$

(ii) Since current through the inductor cannot change instantaneously,

$$i(0^+) = 5 \text{ A}$$

(iii) For $t > 0$, the network is shown in Fig. 9.115.

Writing the KVL equation for $t > 0$,

$$10i - 60i - 0.4\frac{di}{dt} = 0$$

$$\frac{di}{dt} + 125i = 0$$

Fig. 9.115

Comparing with the differential equation $\frac{di}{dt} + Pi = 0$,

$$P = 125$$

The solution of this differential equation is given by

$$i(t) = k\,e^{-Pt} = k\,e^{-125t}$$

At $t = 0$, $i(0) = 5$ A

$$5 = k$$

$$i(t) = 5e^{-125t} \qquad \text{for } t > 0$$

## EXAMPLE 9.37

*For the network shown in Fig. 9.116, find the current in the 20 Ω resistor when the switch is opened at t = 0.*

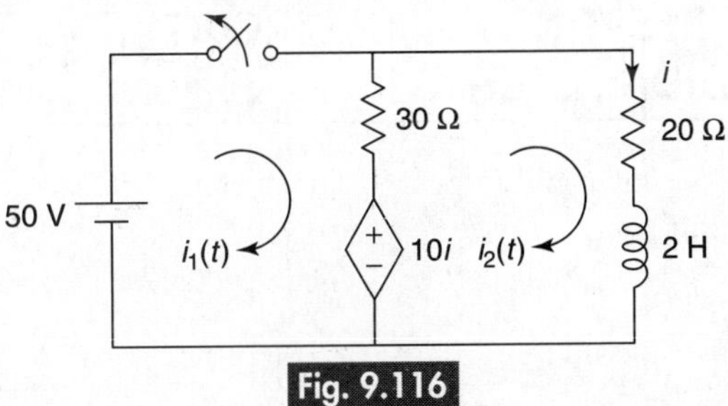


Fig. 9.116

**Solution**

(i) At $t = 0^-$, the network is shown in Fig. 9.117.
At $t = 0^-$, the network attains steady-state condition. Hence, the inductor acts as a short circuit.

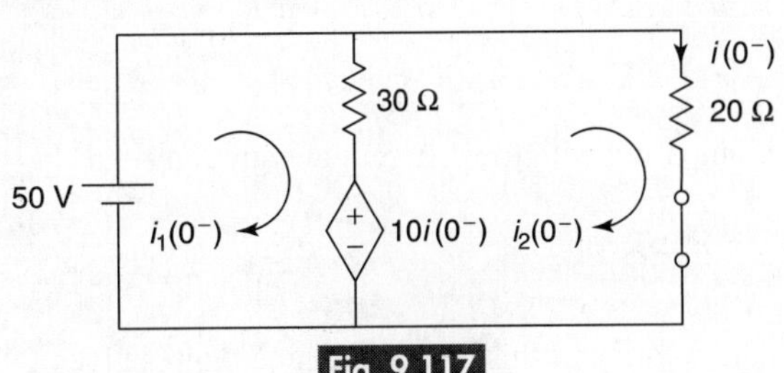


Fig. 9.117

$$i(0^-) = i_2(0^-)$$

Writing the KVL equations at $t = 0^-$,

$$50 - 30(i_1 - i_2) - 10i_2 = 0$$

$$10i_2 - 30(i_2 - i_1) - 20i_2 = 0$$

Solving these equations,

$$i_1(0^-) = 3.33 \text{ A}$$

$$i_2(0^-) = 2.5 \text{ A}$$

(ii) Since the current through the inductor cannot change instantaneously,

$$i_2(0^+) = 2.5 \text{ A}$$

(iii) For $t > 0$, the network is shown in Fig. 9.118.

Writing the KVL equation for $t > 0$,

$$10i_2 - 30i_2 - 20i_2 - 2\frac{di_2}{dt} = 0$$

$$\frac{di_2}{dt} + 20i_2 = 0$$

**Fig. 9.118**

Comparing with the differential equation $\frac{di}{dt} + Pi = 0$,

$$P = 20$$

The solution of this differential equation is given by

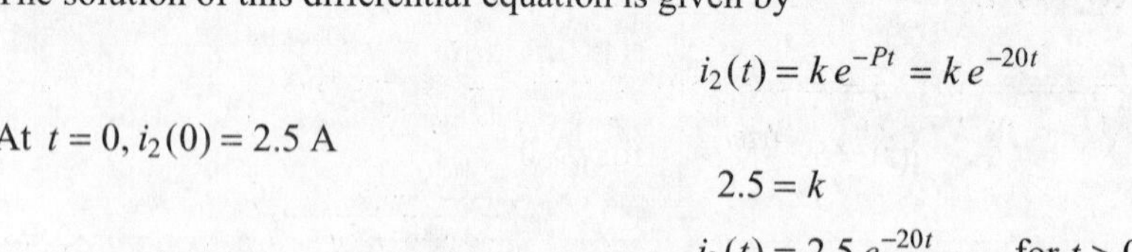

$$i_2(t) = k\,e^{-Pt} = k\,e^{-20t}$$

At $t = 0, i_2(0) = 2.5$ A

$$2.5 = k$$

$$i_2(t) = 2.5\,e^{-20t} \qquad \text{for } t > 0$$

## 9.3 TRANSIENT RESPONSE OF *RL* CIRCUIT FOR SINUSOIDAL EXCITATION

**LO 9.3** Discuss the transient response of *RL* circuit for sinusoidal excitation

Consider a series RL circuit, as shown in Fig. 9.119. The switch is closed at time $t = 0$. The inductor is initially un-energised.

Applying KVL to the circuit for $t > 0$,

$$V_m \sin \omega t - Ri - L\frac{di}{dt} = 0$$

$$\frac{di}{dt} + \frac{R}{L}i = \frac{V_m}{L}\sin \omega t$$

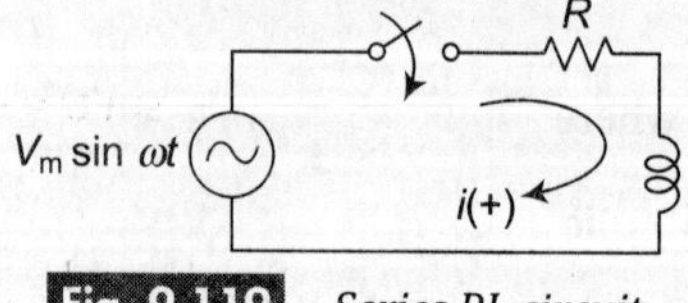


**Fig. 9.119** *Series RL circuit*

Comparing with the differential equation $\frac{di}{dt} + Pi = Q$,

$$P = \frac{R}{L}, \quad Q = \frac{V_m}{L}\sin \omega t$$

The solution of this differential equation is given by

$$i(t) = e^{-Pt}\int Qe^{Pt}\,dt + Ke^{-Pt}$$

$$= e^{-\frac{R}{L}t}\int \frac{V_m}{L}\sin \omega t \, e^{\frac{R}{L}t}\,dt + k\,e^{-\frac{R}{L}t}$$

$$= \frac{V_m}{L}e^{-\frac{R}{L}t}\left[\frac{e^{\frac{R}{L}t}}{\left(\frac{R}{L}\right)^2+\omega^2}\left\{\frac{R}{L}\sin \omega t - \omega \cos \omega t\right\}\right] + k\,e^{-\frac{R}{L}t}$$

$$= \frac{V_m R}{R^2+\omega^2L^2}\sin \omega t - \frac{V_m \omega L}{R^2+\omega^2L^2}\cos \omega t + k\,e^{-\frac{R}{L}t}$$

At $t = 0$, $i(0) = 0$

$$0 = 0 - \frac{V_m \omega L}{R^2+\omega^2L^2} + k$$

$$k = \frac{V_m \omega L}{R^2+\omega^2L^2}$$

$$i(t) = \frac{V_m R}{R^2+\omega^2L^2}\sin \omega t - \frac{V_m \omega L}{R^2+\omega^2L^2}\cos \omega t + \frac{V_m \omega L}{R^2+\omega^2L^2}e^{-\frac{R}{L}t}$$

$$= \frac{V_m}{\sqrt{R^2+\omega^2L^2}}\left(\frac{R}{\sqrt{R^2+\omega^2L^2}}\sin \omega t - \frac{\omega L}{\sqrt{R^2+\omega^2L^2}}\cos \omega t\right) + \frac{V_m \omega L}{R^2+\omega^2L^2}e^{-\frac{R}{L}t}$$

$$= \frac{V_m}{\sqrt{R^2+\omega^2L^2}}(\cos \theta \sin \omega t - \sin \theta \cos \omega t) + \frac{V_m \omega L}{R^2+\omega^2L^2}e^{-\frac{R}{L}t}$$

$$= \frac{V_m}{\sqrt{R^2+\omega^2L^2}}(\sin \omega t \cos \theta - \cos \omega t \sin \theta) + \frac{V_m \omega L}{R^2+\omega^2L^2}e^{-\frac{R}{L}t}$$

$$= \frac{V_m}{\sqrt{R^2+\omega^2L^2}}\sin(\omega t - \theta) + \frac{V_m \omega L}{R^2+\omega^2L^2}e^{-\frac{R}{L}t}$$

where

$$\sin \theta = \frac{\omega L}{\sqrt{R^2+\omega^2L^2}}$$

$$\cos \theta = \frac{R}{\sqrt{R^2+\omega^2L^2}}$$

$$\tan \theta = \frac{\omega L}{R}$$

$$\theta = \tan^{-1}\left(\frac{\omega L}{R}\right)$$

## EXAMPLE 9.38

*For the network shown in Fig. 9.120, a sinusoidal voltage source $v = 150\sin(500t + \theta)$ volts is applied at a time when $\theta = 0$. Find the expression for the current i(t).*

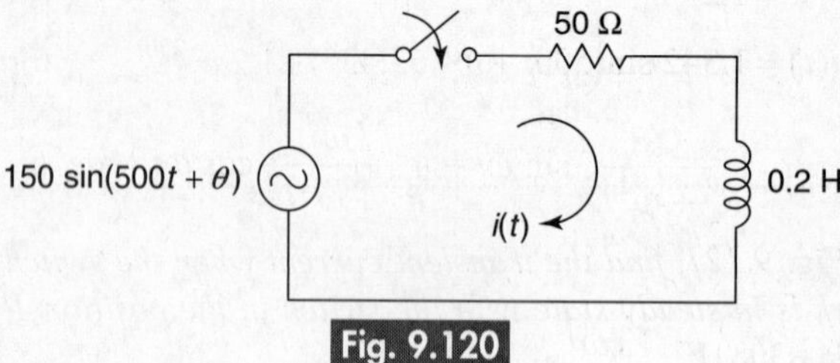


Fig. 9.120

**Solution** Writing the KVL equation for $t > 0$,

$$150\sin(500t+\theta) - 50i - 0.2\frac{di}{dt} = 0$$

$$\frac{di}{dt} + 250i = 750\sin(500t+\theta)$$

Comparing with the differential equation $\frac{di}{dt} + Pi = Q$,

$$P = 250, \quad Q = 750\sin(500t+\theta)$$

The solution of this differential equation is given by

$$i(t) = e^{-Pt}\int Q e^{Pt}\,dt + k\,e^{-Pt}$$

$$= e^{-250t}\int 750\sin(500t+\theta)\,e^{250t}\,dt + k\,e^{-250t}$$

$$= 750\,e^{-250t}\left[\frac{e^{250t}}{(250)^2+(500)^2}\{250\sin(500t+\theta) - 500\cos(500t+\theta)\}\right] + k\,e^{-250t}$$

$$= 0.6\sin(500t+\theta) - 1.2\cos(500t+\theta) + k\,e^{-250t}$$

Let $A\cos\phi = 0.6$

and $A\sin\phi = 1.2$

$$A^2\cos^2\phi + A^2\sin^2\phi = (0.6)^2 + (1.2)^2 = 1.8$$

$$A = 1.342$$

and $\phi = \tan^{-1}\left(\frac{1.2}{0.6}\right) = 63.43°$

$$i(t) = 1.342\cos(63.43°)\sin(500t+\theta) - 1.342\sin(63.43°)\cos(500t+\theta) + k\,e^{-250t}$$

$$i(t) = 1.342\sin(500t+\theta-63.43°) + k\,e^{-250t}$$

At $t = 0, \theta = 0, i(0) = 0$

$$0 = 1.342 \sin(-63.43°) + k$$
$$k = 1.2$$
$$i(t) = 1.342 \sin(500t + \theta - 63.43°) + 1.2\, e^{-250t} \qquad \text{for } t > 0$$

## EXAMPLE 9.39

*For the network shown in Fig. 9.121, find the transient current when the switch is moved from the position 1 to 2 at t = 0. The network is in steady state with the switch in the position 1. The voltage applied to the network is $v = 150 \cos(200t + 30°)$ V.*

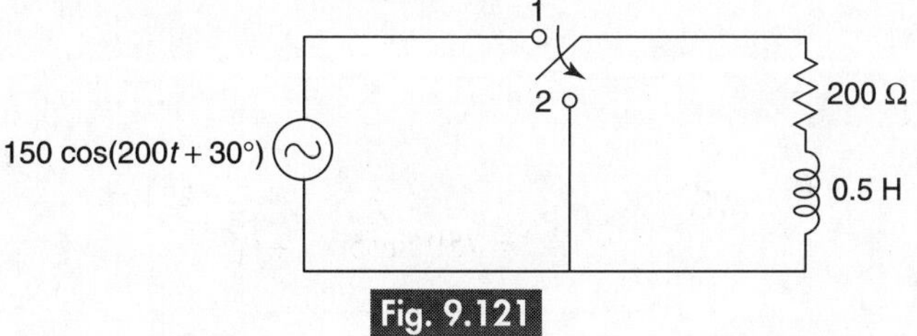


Fig. 9.121

**Solution**

(i) At $t = 0^-$, the network is shown in Fig 4.122.

At $t = 0^-$ the network attains steady-state condition.

Fig. 9.122

$$\mathbf{I} = \frac{\mathbf{V}}{\mathbf{Z}} = \frac{150\angle 30°}{200 + j \times 200 \times 0.5} = 0.67\angle 3.43° \text{ A}$$

The steady-state current passing through the network when the switch is in the position 1 is

$$i(t) = 0.67 \cos(200t + 3.43°) \qquad \ldots \text{(i)}$$

(ii) For $t > 0$, the network is shown in Fig. 9.123.

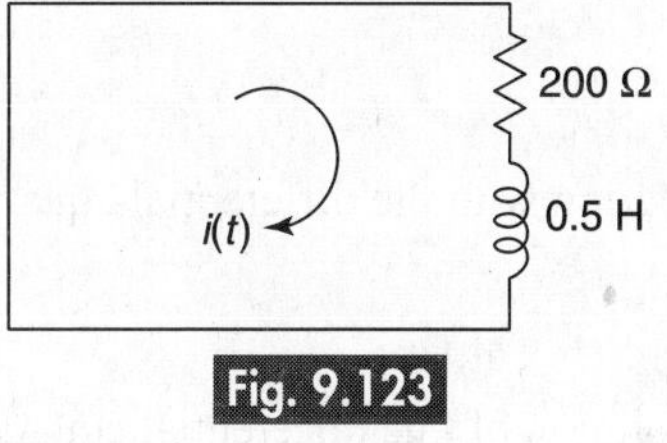


Fig. 9.123

Writing the KVL equation for $t > 0$,

$$-200i - 0.5\frac{di}{dt} = 0$$

$$\frac{di}{dt} + 400i = 0$$

Comparing with the differential equation $\frac{di}{dt} + Pi = 0$,

$$P = 400$$

The solution of this differential equation is given by

$$i(t) = k e^{-pt} = k e^{-400t} \qquad \ldots \text{(ii)}$$

From Eqs (i) and (ii),

$$0.67\cos(200t + 3.43°) = k\,e^{-400t}$$

$$0.67\cos(3.43°) = k$$

At $t = 0$,

$$k = 6.67$$

$$i(t) = 0.67\,e^{-400t} \qquad \text{for } t > 0$$

**EXAMPLE 9.40**

*In the network of Fig. 9.124, an exponential voltage $v(t) = 4\,e^{-3t}$ is applied at $t = 0$. Find the expression for current $i(t)$. Assume zero current through inductor at $t = 0$.*

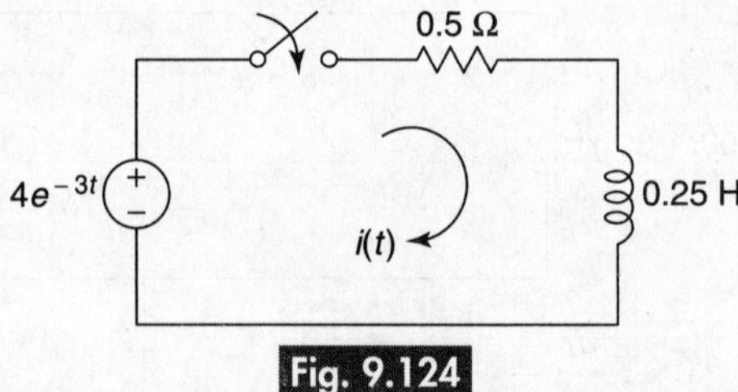


Fig. 9.124

**Solution** (i) At $t = 0^-$,

$$i(0^-) = 0$$

(ii) Since current through the inductor cannot change instantaneously,

$$i(0^+) = 0$$

(iii) Writing the KVL equation for $t > 0$,

$$4\,e^{-3t} - 0.5i - 0.25\frac{di}{dt} = 0$$

$$\frac{di}{dt} + 2i = 16\,e^{-3t}$$

Comparing with the differential equation $\frac{di}{dt} + Pi = Q$,

$$P = 2, \quad Q = 16\,e^{-3t}$$

The solution of this differential equation is given by

$$i(t) = e^{-Pt}\int Q\,e^{Pt}\,dt + k\,e^{-Pt}$$

$$= e^{-2t}\int 16\,e^{-3t}\,e^{2t}\,dt + +k\,e^{-2t}$$

$$= 16\,e^{-2t}\int e^{-t}\,dt + k\,e^{-2t}$$

$$= -16\,e^{-3t} + k\,e^{-2t}$$

At $t = 0$, $i(0) = 0$

$$0 = -16 + k$$

$$k = 16$$

$$i(t) = -16\,e^{-3t} + 16\,e^{-2t} \qquad \text{for } t > 0$$

## 9.4 TRANSIENT RESPONSE OF *RC* CIRCUIT FOR dc EXCITATION

LO 9.4

Discuss the transient response of *RC* circuit for dc excitation

Consider a series *RC* circuit, as shown in Fig. 9.125. The switch is closed at time $t = 0$. The capacitor is initially uncharged.

Applying KVL to the circuit for $t > 0$,

$$V - Ri - \frac{1}{C}\int_0^1 i\,dt = 0$$

Differentiating the above equation,

$$0 - R\frac{di}{dt} - \frac{i}{C} = 0$$

$$\frac{di}{dt} + \frac{1}{RC}i = 0$$

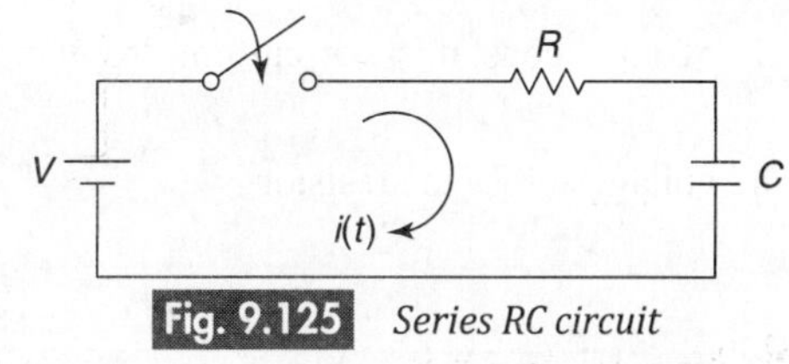


Fig. 9.125 *Series RC circuit*

This is a linear differential equation of first order. The variables may be separated to solve the equation.

$$\frac{di}{i} = -\frac{dt}{RC}$$

Integrating both the sides,

$$l_n i = -\frac{1}{RC}t + k$$

The constant $k$ can be evaluated from initial condition. In the circuit shown, the switch is closed at $t = 0$. Since the capacitor never allows sudden change in voltage, it will act as short circuit at $t = 0^+$. Hence, current in the circuit at $t = 0^+$ is $\frac{V}{R}$.

Setting $i = \frac{V}{R}$ at $t = 0$,

$$l_n \frac{V}{R} = k$$

$$l_n i = -\frac{1}{RC}t + l_n \frac{V}{R}$$

$$l_n i - l_n \frac{V}{R} = -\frac{1}{RC}t$$

$$l_n \frac{i}{\left(\frac{V}{R}\right)} = -\frac{1}{RC}t$$

$$\frac{i}{\frac{V}{R}} = e^{-\frac{1}{RC}t}$$

$$i = \frac{V}{R}e^{-\frac{1}{RC}t} \quad \text{for } t > 0$$

When the switch is closed, the response decays with time, as shown in Fig. 9.126.

The term $RC$ is called time constant and is denoted by $T$.

$$T = RC$$

Time constant is defined as the time taken by the current to drop to 36.8 percent of its initial value in $RC$ circuit.

After 5 time constants, the current drops to 99 percent of its initial value.



Fig. 9.126 *Current response of series RC circuit*

The voltage across the resistor is

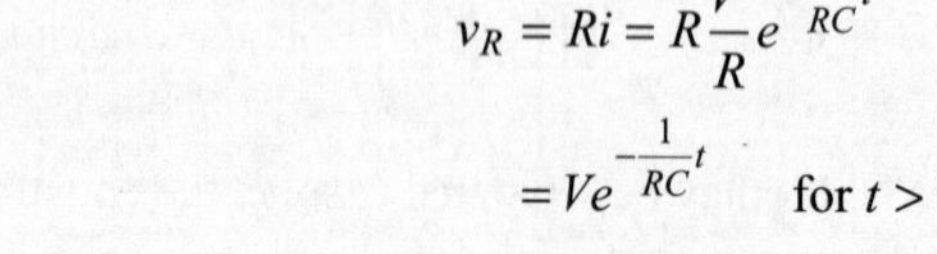

$$v_R = Ri = R\frac{V}{R}e^{-\frac{1}{RC}t}$$

$$= Ve^{-\frac{1}{RC}t} \quad \text{for } t > 0$$

Similarly, the voltage across the capacitor is

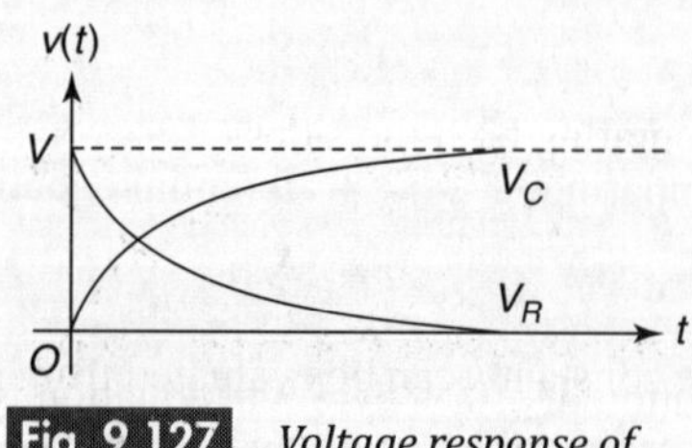


Fig. 9.127 *Voltage response of series RC circuit*

$$v_C = \frac{1}{C}\int_0^t i\,dt$$

$$= \frac{1}{C}\int_0^t \frac{V}{R}e^{-\frac{1}{RC}t}$$

$$= -Ve^{-\frac{1}{RC}t} + k$$

At $t = 0$, $v_C(0) = 0$

$$k = V$$

Hence,
$$v_C = V\left(1 - e^{-\frac{1}{RC}t}\right) \quad \text{for } t > 0$$

Time constant is also defined as the time taken by the capacitor voltage to rise to 63.8 percent of its final value in $RC$ circuit.

## EXAMPLE 9.41

*The switch in the circuit of Fig. 9.128 is moved from position 1 to 2 at t = 0. Find $v_C(t)$.*

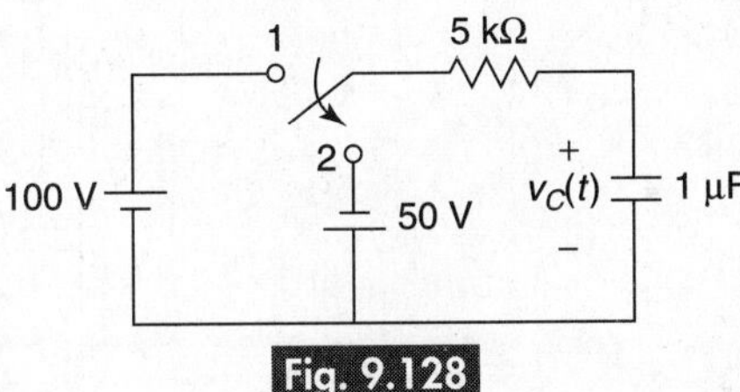


Fig. 9.128

**Solution**

(i) At $t = 0^-$, the network is shown in Fig. 9.129.
At $t = 0^-$, the network has attained steady-state condition. Hence, the capacitor acts as an open circuit.

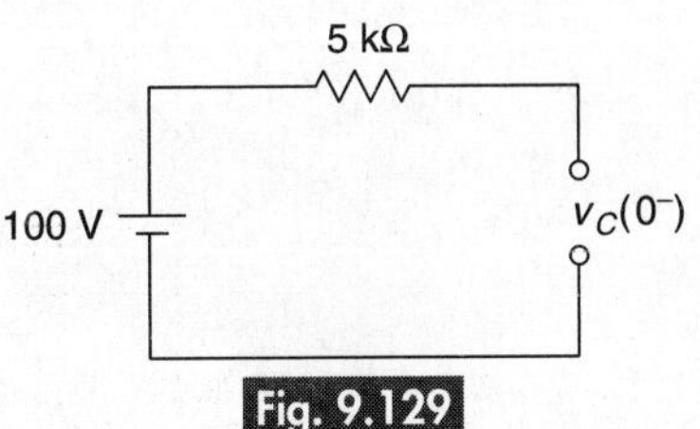


Fig. 9.129

$$v_C(0^-) = 100 \text{ V}$$

(ii) Since the voltage across the capacitor cannot change instantaneously,

$$v_C(0^+) = 100 \text{ V}$$

(iii) For $t > 0$, the network is shown in Fig. 9.130.

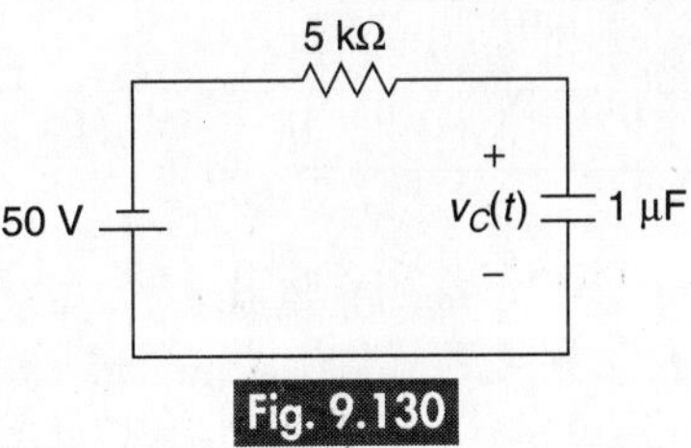


Fig. 9.130

Writing the KCL equation for $t > 0$,

$$1\times10^{-6}\frac{dv_C}{dt} + \frac{v_C + 50}{5000} = 0$$

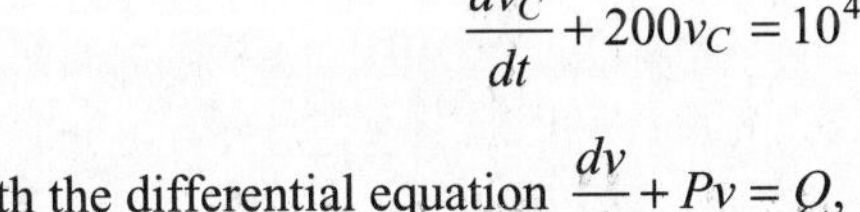

$$\frac{dv_C}{dt} + 200 v_C = 10^4$$

Comparing with the differential equation $\frac{dv}{dt} + Pv = Q$,

$$P = 200, \quad Q = 10^4$$

Solution of this differential equation is given by

$$v_C(t) = e^{-Pt}\int Q\, e^{Pt}\, dt + k\, e^{-Pt}$$

$$= e^{-200t}\int 10^4\, e^{200t}\, dt + k\, e^{-200t}$$

$$= \frac{10^4}{200} + k\, e^{-200t}$$

$$= -50 + k\, e^{-200t}$$

At $t = 0$, $v_C(0) = 100$ V

$$100 = -50 + k$$

$$k = 150$$

$$v_C(t) = -50 + 150\, e^{-200t} \qquad \text{for } t > 0$$

## EXAMPLE 9.42

*In the network shown in Fig. 9.131, the switch closes at $t = 0$. The capacitor is initially uncharged. Find $v_C(t)$ and $i_C(t)$.*

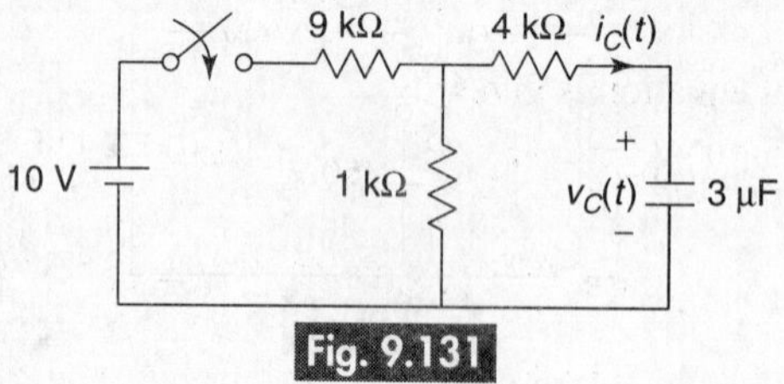


Fig. 9.131

### Solution

(i) At $t = 0^-$, the capacitor is uncharged. Hence, it acts as a short circuit.

$$v_C(0^-) = 0$$

$$i_C(0^-) = 0$$

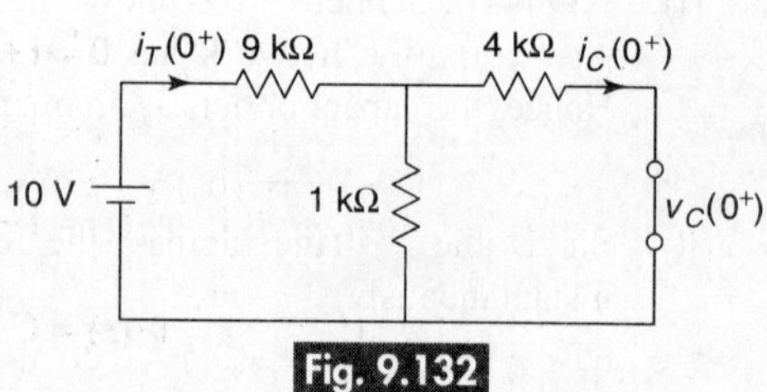


Fig. 9.132

(ii) At $t = 0^+$, the network is shown in Fig. 9.132. Since voltage across the capacitor cannot change instantaneously,

$$v_C(0^+) = 0$$

At $t = 0^+$, $\quad i_T(0^+) = \left[\dfrac{10}{9\text{ k} + (4\text{ k} \,||\, 1\text{ k})}\right] = \dfrac{10}{9.8\text{ k}} = 1.02\text{ mA}$

$$i_C(0^+) = 1.02\text{ m} \times \frac{1\text{ k}}{1\text{ k} + 4\text{ k}} = 0.204\text{ mA}$$

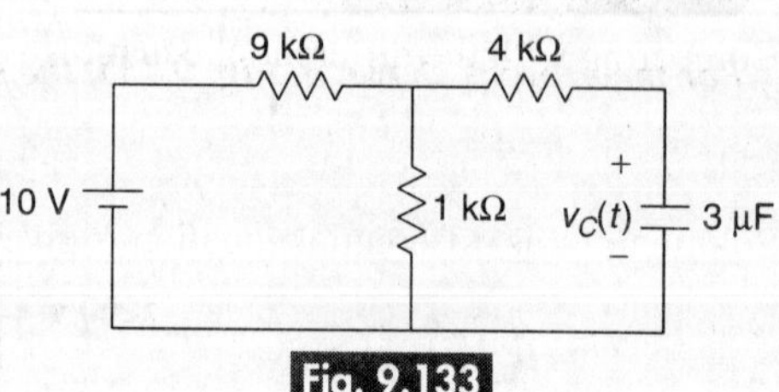


Fig. 9.133

(iii) For $t > 0$, the network is shown in Fig. 9.133. For $t > 0$, representing the network to the left of the capacitor by Thevenin's equivalent network,

$$V_{eq} = 10 \times \frac{1\text{ k}}{9\text{ k} + 1\text{ k}} = 1\text{ V}$$

$$R_{eq} = (9\text{ k} \,||\, 1\text{ k}) + 4\text{ k} = 4.9\text{ k}\Omega$$

For $t > 0$, Thevenin's equivalent network is shown in Fig. 9.134.

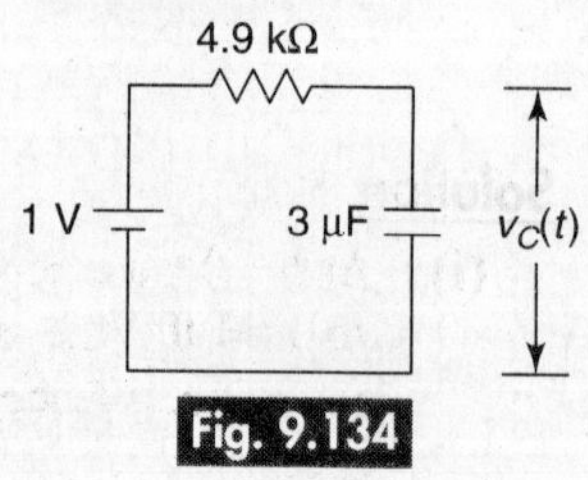


Fig. 9.134

Writing the KCL equation for $t > 0$,

$$3 \times 10^{-6} \frac{dv_C}{dt} + \frac{v_C - 1}{4.9 \times 10^3} = 0$$

$$\frac{dv_C}{dt} + 68.02\, v_C = 68.02$$

Comparing with the differential equation $\frac{dv}{dt} + Pv = Q$,

$$P = 68.02, \quad Q = 68.02$$

The solution of this differential equation is given by

$$v_C(t) = e^{-Pt}\int Q\, e^{Pt}\, dt + k\, e^{-Pt}$$

$$= e^{-68.02t}\int 68.02\, e^{68.02t}\, dt + k\, e^{-68.02t}$$

$$= 1 + k\, e^{-68.02t}$$

At $t = 0, v_C(0) = 0$

$$0 = 1 + k$$

$$k = -1$$

$$v_C(t) = 1 - e^{-68.02t} \qquad \text{for } t > 0$$

$$i_C(t) = C\frac{dv_C}{dt}$$

$$= 3\times10^{-6}\frac{d}{dt}(1 - e^{-68.02t})$$

$$= 3\times10^{-6}\times 68.02 e^{-68.02t}$$

$$= 204.06\times10^{-6} e^{-68.02t} \qquad \text{for } t > 0$$

**EXAMPLE 9.43**

*For the network shown in Fig. 9.135, the switch is open for a long time and closes at t = 0. Determine $v_C(t)$.*

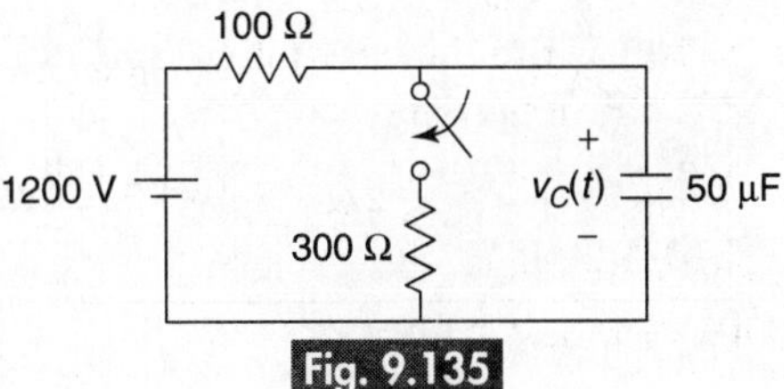


Fig. 9.135

**Solution**

(i) At $t = 0^-$, the network is shown in Fig. 9.136.
At $t = 0^-$, the network has attained steady-state condition. Hence, the capacitor acts as an open circuit.

$$v_C(0^-) = 1200 \text{ V}$$

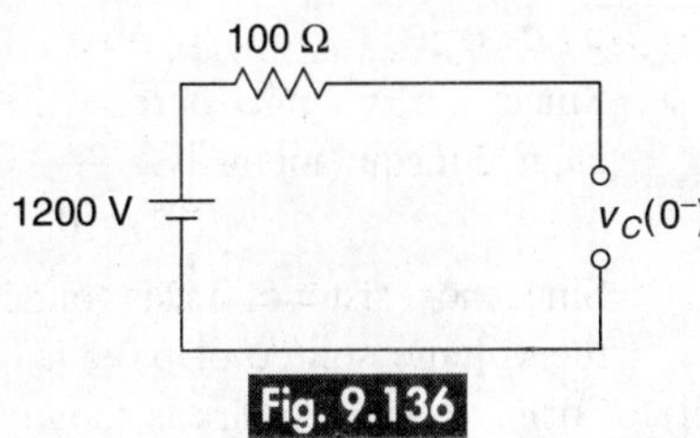


Fig. 9.136

(ii) Since the voltage across the capacitor cannot change instantaneously,

$$v_C(0^+) = 1200 \text{ V}$$

(iii) For $t > 0$, the network is shown in Fig. 9.137.

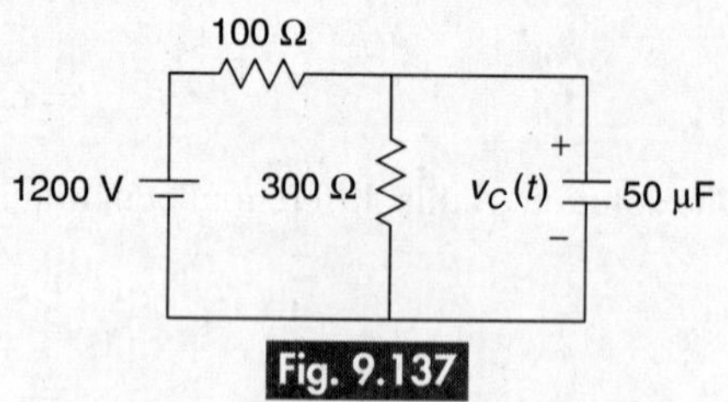


Fig. 9.137

Writing the KCL equation for $t > 0$,

$$50 \times 10^{-6} \frac{dv_C}{dt} + \frac{v_C}{300} + \frac{v_C - 1200}{100} = 0$$

$$\frac{dv_C}{dt} + 266.67\, v_C = 0.24 \times 10^6$$

Comparing with the differential equation $\frac{dv}{dt} + Pv = Q$,

$$P = 266.67, \quad Q = 0.24 \times 10^6$$

The solution of this differential equation is given by

$$v_C(t) = e^{-Pt} \int Q\, e^{Pt}\, dt + k\, e^{-Pt}$$

$$= e^{-266.67t} \int 0.24 \times 10^6\, e^{266.67t}\, dt + k\, e^{-266.67t}$$

$$= \frac{0.24 \times 10^6}{266.67} + k\, e^{-266.67t}$$

$$= 900 + k\, e^{-266.67t}$$

At $t = 0, v_C(0) = 1200$ V

$$1200 = 900 + k$$

$$k = 300$$

$$v_C(t) = 900 + 300\, e^{-266.67t} \quad \text{for } t > 0$$

## EXAMPLE 9.44

*In Fig. 9.138, the switch is closed at t = 0 Find $v_C(t)$ for $t > 0$.*

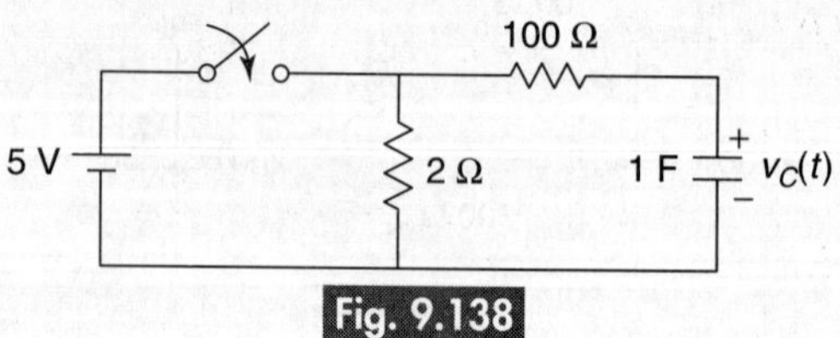


Fig. 9.138

### Solution

(i) At $t = 0^-$, $\quad v_C(0^-) = 0$

(ii) Since the voltage across the capacitor cannot change instantaneously,

$$v_C(0^+) = 0$$

Since the resistor of 2 Ω is connected in parallel with the voltage source of 5 V, it becomes redundant.

(iii) For $t > 0$, the network is shown in Fig. 9.139.

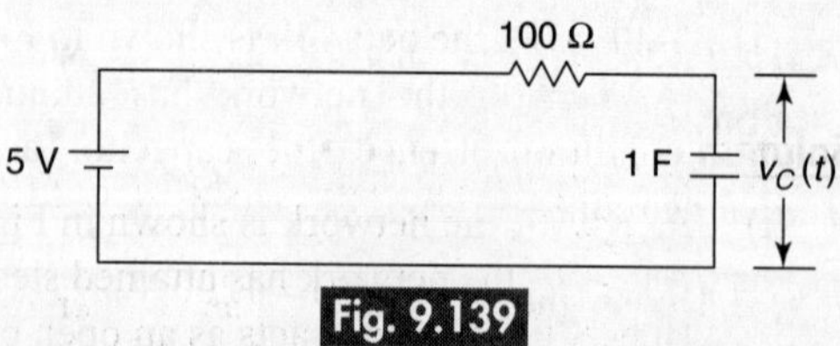


Fig. 9.139

Writing KCL equation for $t > 0$,

$$\frac{v_C - 5}{100} + 1\frac{dv_C}{dt} = 0$$

$$100\frac{dv_C}{dt} + v_C = 5$$

$$\frac{dv_C}{dt} + 0.01v_C = 0.05$$

Comparing with the differential equation $\frac{dv}{dt} + Pv = Q$,

$$P = 0.01, \quad Q = 0.05$$

The solution of this differential equation is given by

$$v_C(t) = e^{-Pt}\int Q e^{Pt}\, dt + k e^{-Pt}$$

$$= e^{-0.01}\int 0.05\, e^{0.01t}\, dt + k e^{-0.01t}$$

$$= \frac{0.05}{0.01} + k e^{-0.01t}$$

$$= 5 + k e^{-0.01t}$$

At $t = 0, v_C(0) = 0$

$$0 = 5 + k$$

$$k = -5$$

$$v_C(t) = 5 - 5e^{-0.01t}$$

$$= 5(1 - e^{-0.01t}) \quad \text{for } t > 0$$

## EXAMPLE 9.45

*In the network shown, the switch is shifted to position b at $t = 0$. Find v (t) for $t > 0$.*

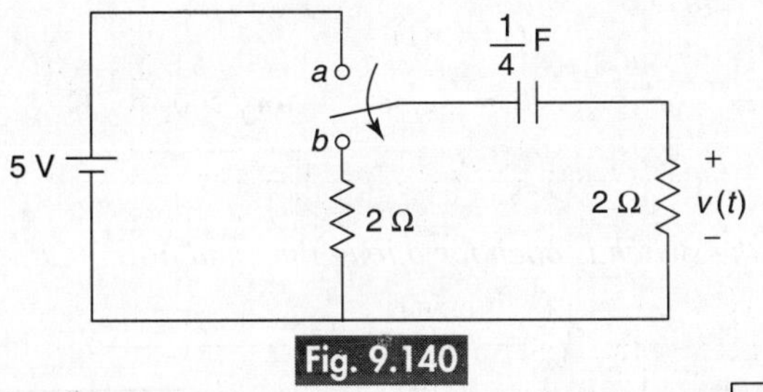


Fig. 9.140

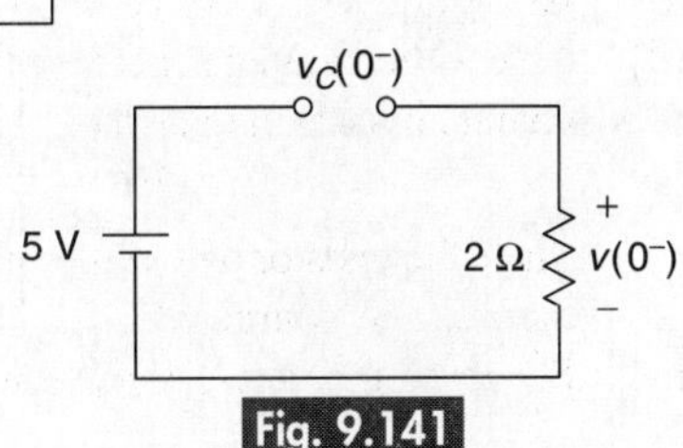


Fig. 9.141

**Solution**

(i) At $t = 0^-$, the network is shown in Fig. 9.141.
At $t = 0^-$, the network has attained steady-state condition.
Hence, the capacitor acts as an open circuit.

$$v_C(0^-) = 5 \text{ V}$$

$$v(0^-) = 0$$

(ii) At $t = 0^+$, the network is shown in Fig. 9.142.

At $t = 0^+$, the capacitor acts as a voltage source of 5 V.

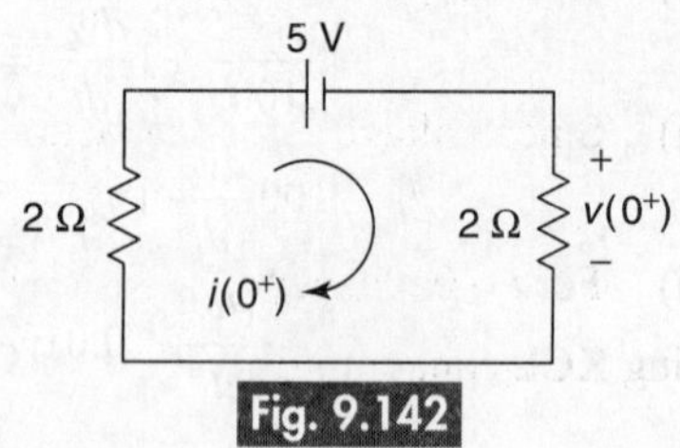

Fig. 9.142

$$i(0^+) = -\frac{5}{4} = -1.25 \text{ A}$$

$$v(0^+) = -1.25 \times 2 = -2.5 \text{ V}$$

(iii) For $t > 0$, the network is shown in Fig. 9.143.

Writing the KVL equation for $t > 0$,

$$-2i - 5 - \frac{1}{\frac{1}{4}}\int_0^t i\,dt - 2i = 0 \qquad \text{...(i)}$$

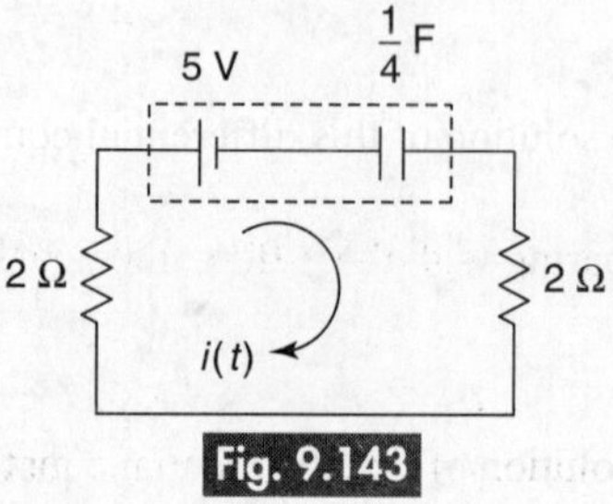

Fig. 9.143

Differentiating Eq. (i),

$$-4\frac{di}{dt} - 4i = 0$$

$$\frac{di}{dt} + i = 0$$

Comparing with the differential equation $\frac{di}{dt} + Pi = 0$,

$$P = 1$$

The solution of this differential equation is given by

$$i(t) = k\,e^{-Pt} = k\,e^{-t}$$

At $t = 0, i(0) = -1.25$ A

$$k = -1.25$$

$$i(t) = -1.25\,e^{-t} \quad \text{for } t > 0$$

$$v(t) = 2i(t)$$

$$= -2.5e^{-t} \quad \text{for } t > 0$$

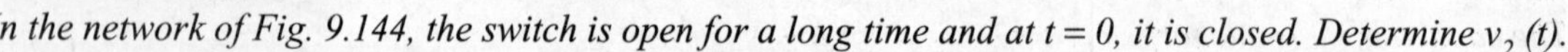

## EXAMPLE 9.46

*In the network of Fig. 9.144, the switch is open for a long time and at $t = 0$, it is closed. Determine $v_2(t)$.*

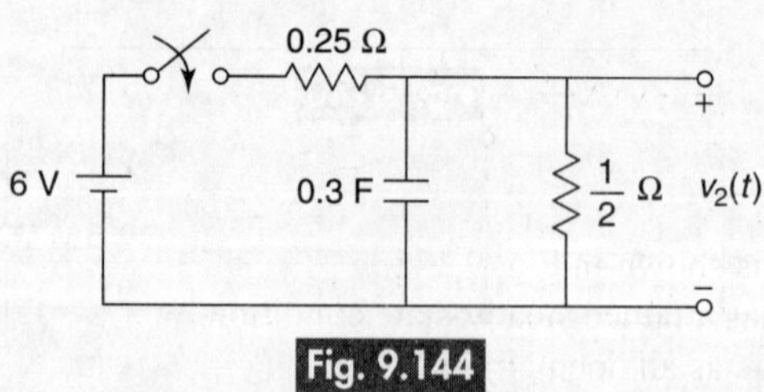

Fig. 9.144

**Solution**

(i) At $t = 0^-$, the switch is open.

$$v_2(0^-) = 0$$

(ii) Since voltage across capacitor cannot change instantaneously,

$$v_2(0^+) = 0$$

(iii) For $t > 0$, the network is shown in Fig. 9.145.

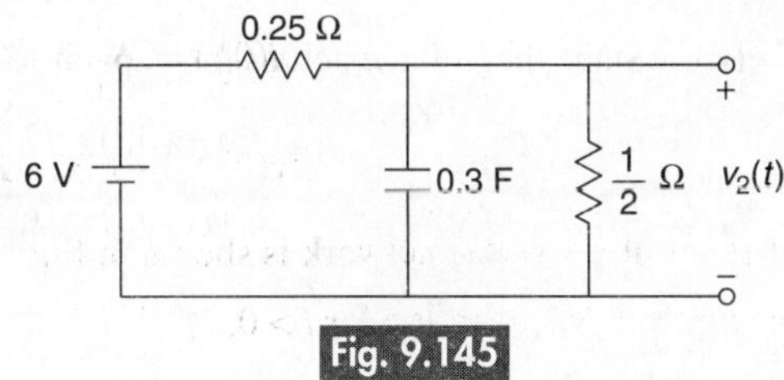


Fig. 9.145

Writing KCL equation for $t > 0$,

$$\frac{v_2}{\frac{1}{2}} + 0.3\frac{dv_2}{dt} + \frac{v_2 - 6}{0.25} = 0$$

$$\frac{dv_2}{dt} + 20v_2 = 80$$

Comparing with the differential equation $\frac{dv}{dt} + Pv = Q$,

$$P = 20, \quad Q = 80$$

The solution of this differential equation is given by

$$v(t) = e^{-Pt}\int Q\, e^{Pt}\, dt + k\, e^{-Pt}$$

$$= e^{-20t}\int 80\, e^{20t}\, dt + k\, e^{-20t}$$

$$= \frac{80}{20} + k\, e^{-20t}$$

$$v_2 t = 4 + k\, e^{-20t}$$

At $t = 0, v_2(0) = 0$

$$0 = 4 + k$$

$$k = -4$$

$$v_2(t) = 4 - 4e^{-20t}$$

$$= 4(1 - e^{-20t}) \quad \text{for } t > 0.$$

**EXAMPLE 9.47**

*The switch is moved from position a to b at t = 0, having been in position a for a long time before t = 0. The capacitor $C_2$ is uncharged at t = 0. Find i(t) and $v_2(t)$ for t > 0.*

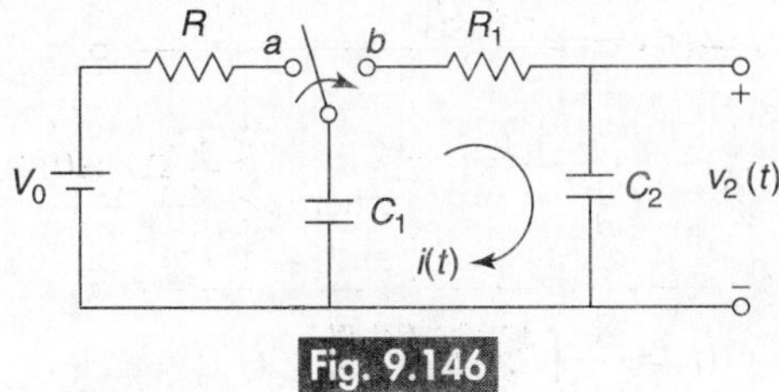


Fig. 9.146

**Solution**

(i) At $t = 0^-$, the network has attained steady-state condition. Hence, the capacitor $C_1$ acts as an open circuit and it will charge to $V_0$ volt.

$$v_{C_1}(0^-) = V_0$$

$$v_{C_2}(0^-) = 0$$

(ii) Since the voltage across the capacitor cannot change instantaneously,

$$v_{C_1}(0^+) = V_0$$

$$v_{C_2}(0^+) = 0$$

$$i(0^+) = \frac{V_0}{R_1}$$

(iii) For $t > 0$, the network is shown in Fig. 9.147.

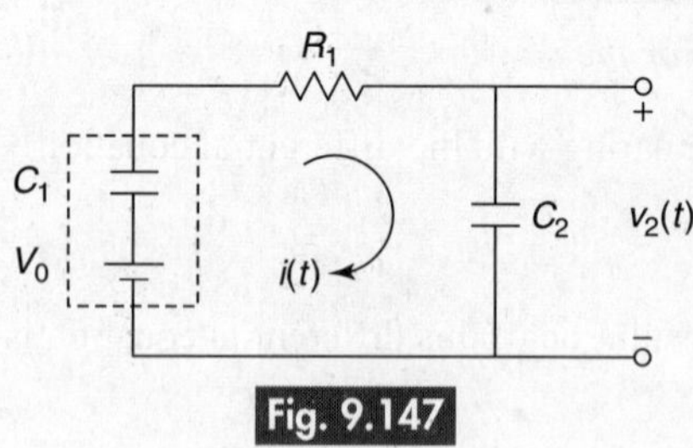


Fig. 9.147

Writing the KVL equation for $t > 0$,

$$V_0 - \frac{1}{C_1}\int_0^t i\,dt - R_1 i - \frac{1}{C_2}\int_0^t i\,dt = 0 \qquad \text{...(i)}$$

Differentiating Eq. (i),

$$-\frac{i}{C_1} - R_1\frac{di}{dt} - \frac{i}{C_2} = 0$$

$$\frac{di}{dt} + \frac{1}{R_1}\left(\frac{C_1 + C_2}{C_1 C_2}\right)i = 0$$

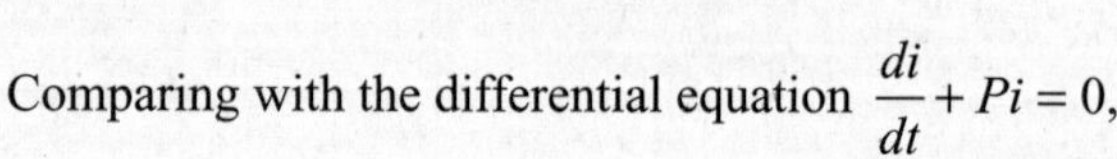

Comparing with the differential equation $\frac{di}{dt} + Pi = 0$,

$$P = \frac{1}{R_1}\left(\frac{C_1 + C_2}{C_1 C_2}\right)$$

The solution of this differential equation is given by

$$i(t) = k\,e^{-Pt} = k\,e^{-\frac{1}{R_1}\left(\frac{C_1+C_2}{C_1 C_2}\right)t}$$

At $t = 0$, $i(0) = \frac{V_0}{R_1}$

$$k = \frac{V_0}{R_1}$$

$$i(t) = \frac{V_0}{R_1}e^{-\frac{1}{R_1}\left(\frac{C_1+C_2}{C_1 C_2}\right)t}$$

$$= \frac{V_0}{R_1}e^{-\frac{1}{R_1 C}t} \qquad \text{where } C = \frac{C_1 C_2}{C_1 + C_2}$$

$$v_2(t) = \frac{1}{C_2}\int_0^t i\,dt$$

$$= \frac{1}{C_2}\int_0^t \frac{V_0}{R_1} e^{-\frac{t}{R_1 C}} dt$$

$$= \frac{V_0}{R_1 C_2} R_1 C \left(1 - e^{-\frac{1}{R_1 C}t}\right)$$

$$= \frac{V_0 C_1}{C_1 + C_2}\left(1 - e^{-\frac{t}{R_1 C}t}\right) \qquad \text{for } t > 0$$

**EXAMPLE 9.48**

*For the network shown in Fig. 9.148, the switch is opened at $t = 0$. Find $v(t)$ for $t > 0$.*

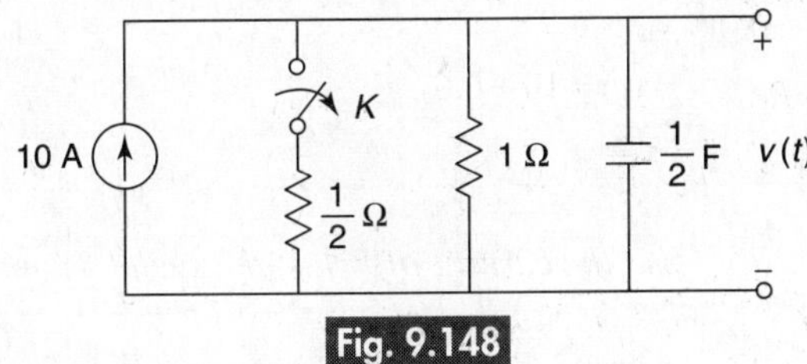


Fig. 9.148

**Solution**

(i) At $t = 0^-$, the network is shown in Fig. 9.149. At $t = 0^-$, the network attains steady-state condition. Hence, the capacitor acts as an open circuit.

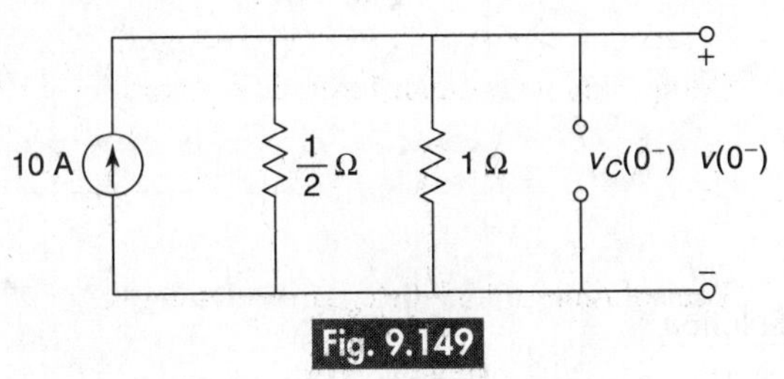


Fig. 9.149

$$v_C(0^-) = 0$$

Writing the KCL equation at $t = 0^-$,

$$\frac{v(0^-)}{1} + \frac{v(0^-)}{\frac{1}{2}} = 10$$

$$3v(0^-) = 10$$

$$v(0^-) = 3.33 \text{ V}$$

(ii) Since the voltage across the capacitor cannot change instantaneously,

$$v_C(0^+) = v(0^+) = 3.33 \text{ V}$$

(iii) For $t > 0$, the network is shown in Fig. 9.150.

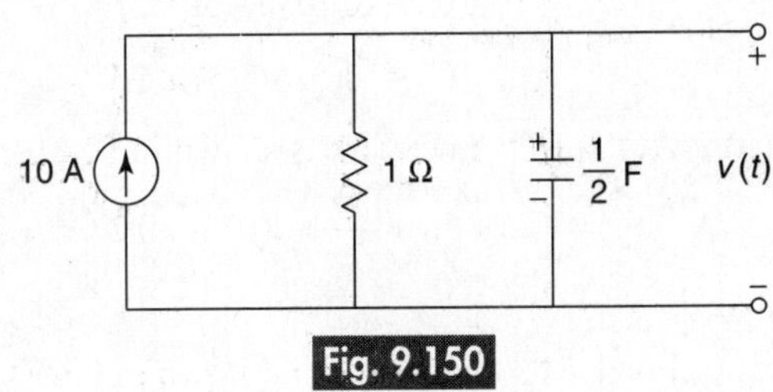


Fig. 9.150

Writing the KCL equation for $t > 0$,

$$\frac{1}{2}\frac{dv}{dt} + \frac{v}{1} = 10$$

$$\frac{dv}{dt} + 2v = 20$$

Comparing with the differential equation $\frac{dv}{dt} + Pv = Q$,

$$P = 2, \quad Q = 20$$

The solution of this differential equation is given by

$$v(t) = e^{-Pt} \int Q\, e^{Pt}\, dt + k\, e^{-Pt}$$

$$= e^{-2t} \int 20\, e^{-2t}\, dt + k\, e^{-2t}$$

$$= \frac{20}{2} + k\, e^{-2t}$$

$$= 10 + k\, e^{-2t}$$

At $t = 0$, $v(0) = 3.33$ V

$$3.33 = 10 + k$$

$$k = 6.67$$

$$v(t) = 10 + 6.67\, e^{-2t}$$

## EXAMPLE 9.49

*For the network shown in Fig. 9.151, find the current i(t) when the switch is opened at t = 0.*

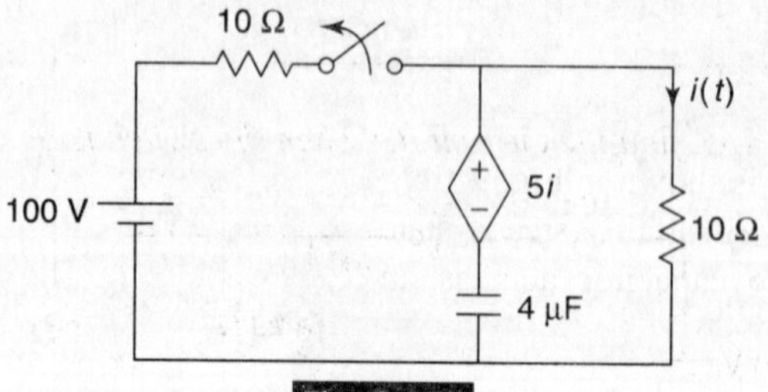


Fig. 9.151

**Solution**

(i) At $t = 0^-$, the network is shown in Fig. 9.152.
At $t = 0^-$, the network attains steady-state condition. Hence, the capacitor acts as open circuit.

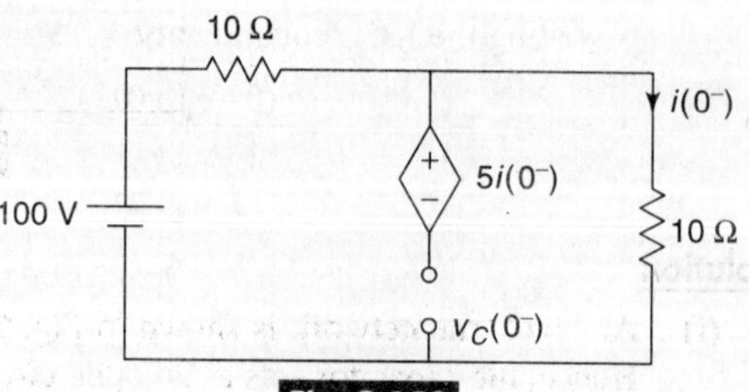


Fig. 9.152

$$i(0^-) = \frac{100}{10+10} = 5 \text{ A}$$

$$v_C(0^-) = 100 - 10i(0^-) - 5i(0^-)$$

$$= 100 - 10(5) - 5(5) = 25 \text{ V}$$

(ii) At $t = 0^+$, the network is shown in Fig. 9.153.

$$25 + 5i(0^-) - 10i(0^+) = 0$$

$$i(0^+) = 5 \text{ A}$$

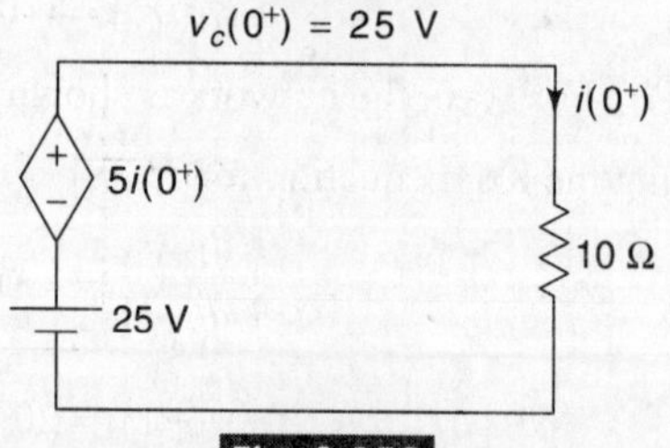


Fig. 9.153

(iii) For $t > 0$, the network is shown in Fig. 9.154.

$$25 - \frac{1}{4\times10^{-6}}\int_0^t i\,dt + 5i - 10i = 0 \qquad \ldots\text{(i)}$$

Differentiating Eq. (i),

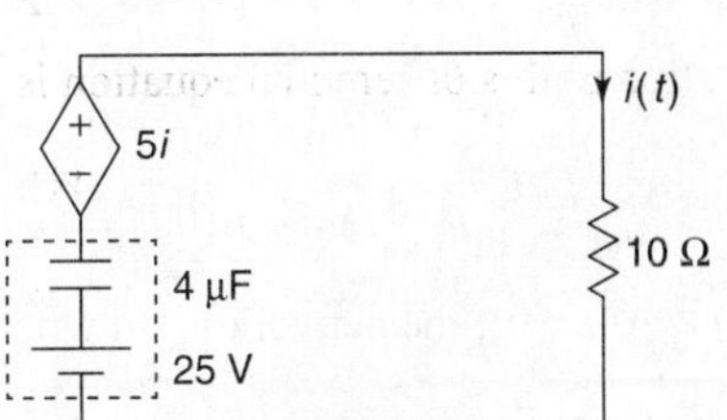

Fig. 9.154

$$0 - 0.25\times10^{6}\, i + 5\frac{di}{dt} - 10\frac{di}{dt} = 0$$

$$\frac{di}{dt} + 50000\, i = 0$$

Comparing with the differential equation $\frac{di}{dt} + Pi = 0$,

$$P = 50000$$

The solution of this differential equation is given by

$$i(t) = k\,e^{-Pt} = k\,e^{-50000t}$$

At $t = 0$, $i(0) = 5$ A

$$5 = k$$

$$i(t) = 5e^{-50000t} \qquad \text{for } t > 0$$

## EXAMPLE 9.50

*For the network shown in Fig. 9.155, find the current i(t) when the switch is opened at t = 0.*

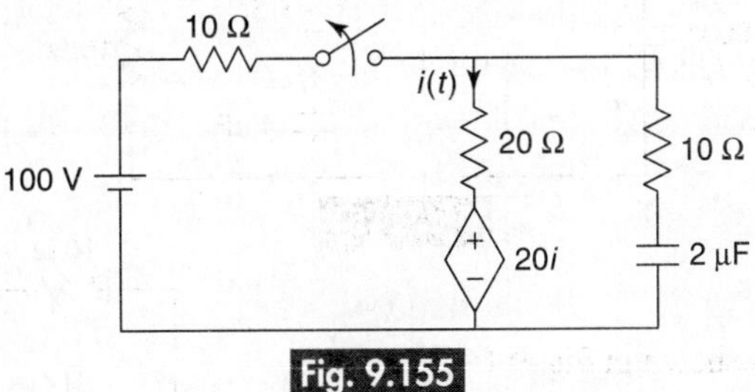

Fig. 9.155

**Solution**

(i) At $t = 0^-$, the network is shown in Fig. 9.156. At $t = 0^-$, the network attains steady-state condition. Hence, the capacitor acts as an open circuit.

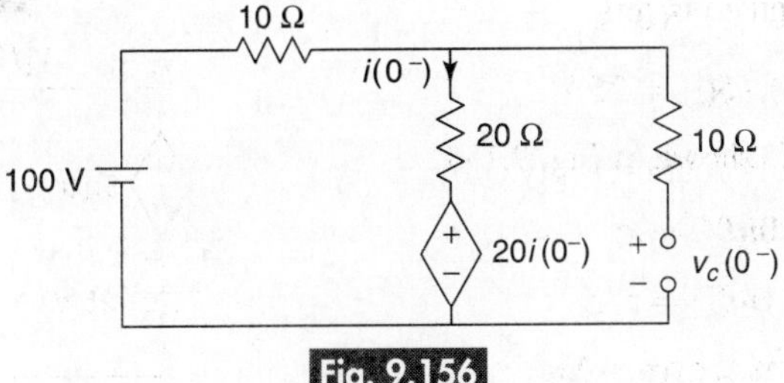

Fig. 9.156

Writing the KVL equation at $t = 0^-$,

$$100 - 10\,i(0^-) - 20\,i(0^-) - 20\,i(0^-) = 0$$

$$i(0^-) = 2\text{ A}$$

Also, $20\,i(0^-) + 20\,i(0^-) - 0 - v_C(0^-) = 0$

$$v_C(0^-) = 40\,i(0^-) = 40(2) = 80\text{ V}$$

(ii) At $t = 0^+$, the network is shown in Fig. 9.157.

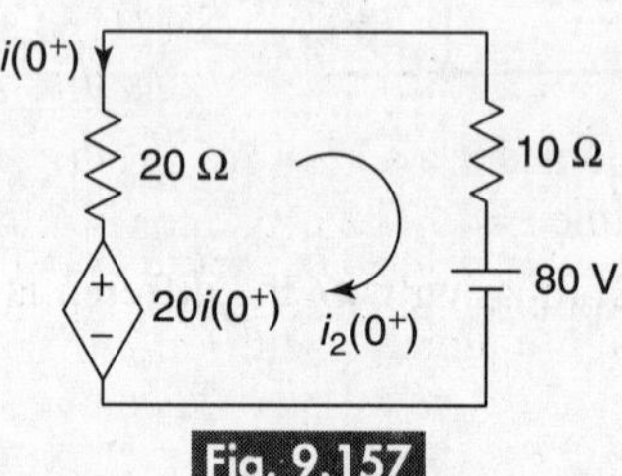


Fig. 9.157

From Fig. 9.157, $i(0^+) = -i_2(0^+)$

$$20\,i(0^+) - 20\,i_2(0^+) - 10\,i_2(0^+) - 80 = 0$$

$$20\,i(0^+) + 20\,i(0^+) + 10\,i(0^+) - 80 = 0$$

$$i(0^+) = 1.6\text{ A}$$

$$v_C(0^+) = 80\text{ V}$$

(iii) For $t > 0$, the network is shown in Fig. 9.158.

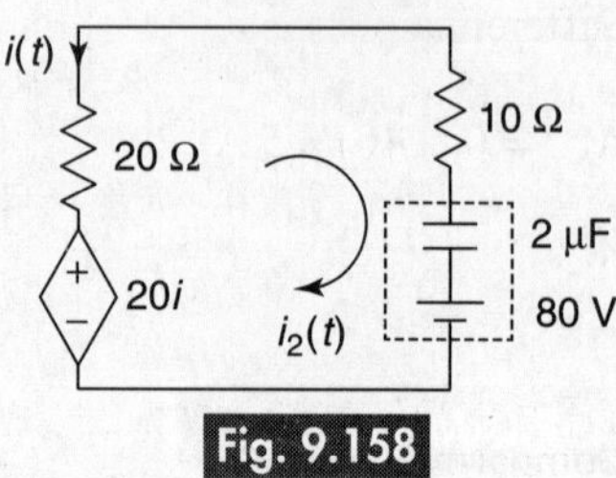


Fig. 9.158

From Fig. 9.158, $i(t) = -i_2(t)$

Writing the KVL equation for $t > 0$,

$$20i - 20i_2 - 10i_2 - \frac{1}{2\times10^{-6}}\int_0^t i_2\,dt - 80 = 0$$

$$20i + 20i_2 + 10i_2 + \frac{1}{2\times10^{-6}}\int_0^t i\,dt - 80 = 0$$

$$50i + \frac{1}{2\times10^{-6}}\int i\,dt - 80 = 0 \qquad \text{...(i)}$$

Differentiating Eq. (i),

$$50\frac{di}{dt} + 5\times10^5 i = 0$$

$$\frac{di}{dt} + 1\times10^4 i = 0$$

Comparing with the differential equation $\frac{di}{dt} + Pi = 0$,

$$P = 1\times10^4$$

The solution of this differential equation is given by

$$i(t) = k\,e^{-Pt} = k\,e^{-1\times10^4 t}$$

At $t = 0$, $i(0) = 1.6$ A

$$1.6 = k$$

$$i(t) = 1.6\, e^{-1\times 10^4 t} \qquad \text{for } t > 0$$

## 9.5 TRANSIENT RESPONSE OF *RC* CIRCUIT FOR SINUSOIDAL EXCITATION

LO 9.5

Discuss the transient response of *RC* circuit for sinusoidal excitation

Consider a series *RC* circuit, as shown in Fig. 9.159. The switch is closed at time $t = 0$. The capacitor is initially uncharged.

Applying KVL to the circuit for $t > 0$,

$$V_m \sin \omega t - Ri - \frac{1}{C}\int i\, dt = 0$$



Fig. 9.159 Series RC circuit

Differentiating the above equation,

$$V_m \omega \cos \omega t - R\frac{di}{dt} - \frac{i}{C} = 0$$

$$\frac{di}{dt} + \frac{1}{RC} i = \frac{V_m \omega}{R}\cos \omega t$$

Comparing with the differential equation $\dfrac{di}{dt} + Pi = Q$,

$$P = \frac{1}{RC}, \quad Q = \frac{V_m \omega}{R}\cos \omega t$$

The solution of this differential equation is given by

$$i(t) = e^{-Pt}\int Q\, e^{Pt}\, dt + k\, e^{-Pt}$$

$$= e^{-\frac{1}{RC}t}\int \frac{V_m \omega}{R}\cos \omega t\, e^{\frac{1}{RC}t}\, dt + k\, e^{-\frac{1}{RC}t}$$

$$= \frac{V_m \omega}{R} e^{-\frac{1}{RC}t}\left[\frac{e^{\frac{1}{RC}t}}{\left(\frac{1}{RC}\right)^2 + \omega^2}\left\{\frac{1}{RC}\cos \omega t + \omega \sin \omega t\right\}\right] + k\, e^{-\frac{1}{RC}t}$$

$$= \frac{V_m \omega C}{1 + \omega^2 R^2 C^2}\cos \omega t + \frac{V_m \omega^2 RC^2}{1 + \omega^2 R^2 C^2}\sin \omega t + k\, e^{-\frac{1}{RC}t}$$

At $t = 0$, $i(0) = 0$

$$0 = \frac{V_m \omega C}{1 + \omega^2 R^2 C^2} + k$$

$$k = -\frac{V_m \omega C}{1 + \omega^2 R^2 C^2}$$

$$i(t) = \frac{V_m \omega C}{1+\omega^2 R^2 C^2}\cos \omega t + \frac{V_m \omega^2 RC^2}{1+\omega^2 R^2 C^2}\sin \omega t - \frac{V_m \omega C}{1+\omega^2 R^2 C^2} e^{-\frac{1}{RC}t}$$

$$= \frac{V_m \omega C}{\sqrt{1+\omega^2 R^2 C^2}}\left(\frac{1}{\sqrt{1+\omega^2 R^2 C^2}}\cos \omega t + \frac{\omega RC}{\sqrt{1+\omega^2 R^2 C^2}}\sin \omega t\right) - \frac{V_m \omega C}{1+\omega^2 R^2 C^2} e^{-\frac{1}{RC}t}$$

$$= \frac{V_m \omega C}{\sqrt{1+\omega^2 R^2 C^2}}(\sin\theta \cos \omega t + \cos\theta \sin \omega t) - \frac{V_m \omega C}{1+\omega^2 R^2 C^2} e^{-\frac{1}{RC}t}$$

$$= \frac{V_m \omega C}{\sqrt{1+\omega^2 R^2 C^2}}(\sin \omega t \cos\theta + \sin\theta \cos \omega t) - \frac{V_m \omega C}{1+\omega^2 R^2 C^2} e^{-\frac{1}{RC}t}$$

$$= \frac{V_m \omega C}{\sqrt{1+\omega^2 R^2 L^2}}\sin(\omega t+\theta) - \frac{V_m \omega C}{1+\omega^2 R^2 C^2} e^{-\frac{1}{RC}t} \text{ for } t > 0$$

where
$$\sin\theta = \frac{1}{\sqrt{1+\omega^2 R^2 C^2}}$$

$$\cos\theta = \frac{\omega RC}{\sqrt{1+\omega^2 R^2 C^2}}$$

$$\tan\theta = \frac{1}{\omega RC}$$

$$\theta = \tan^{-1}\left(\frac{1}{\omega RC}\right)$$

**EXAMPLE 9.51**

*In the network shown in Fig. 9.160, a sinusoidal voltage $v = 100 \sin(500t+\theta)$ volts is applied to the circuit at a time corresponding to $\theta = 45°$. Obtain the expression for the current i(t).*

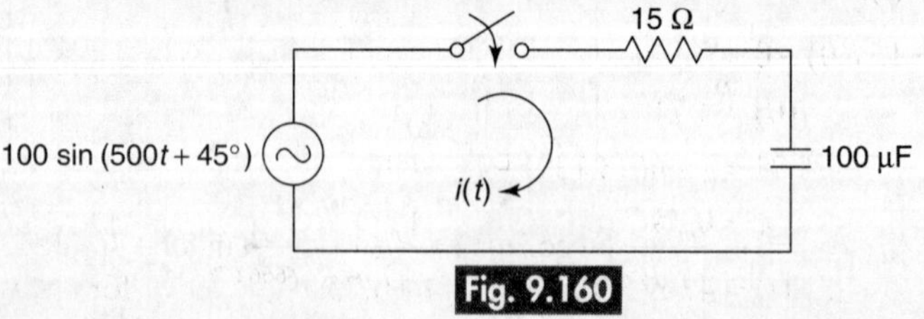


Fig. 9.160

**Solution**

Writing the KVL equation for $t > 0$,

$$100\sin(500t+45°) - 15i - \frac{1}{100\times10^{-6}}\int_0^t i\,dt = 0 \quad \text{...(i)}$$

Differentiating Eq. (i),

$$(100)(500)\cos(500t+45°)-15\frac{di}{dt}-10^4 i=0$$

$$\frac{di}{dt}+666.67i=3333.33\cos(500t+45°)$$

Comparing with the differential equation $\frac{di}{dt}+Pi=Q$,

$$P=666.67,\ Q=3333.33\cos(500t+45°)$$

The solution of this differential equation is given by

$$i(t)=e^{-Pt}\int Qe^{Pt}dt+ke^{-Pt}$$

$$=e^{-666.67t}\int 3333.33\cos(500t+45°)e^{666.67t}+ke^{-666.67t}$$

$$=3333.33\,e^{-666.67t}\left[\frac{e^{666.67t}}{(666.67)^2+(500)^2}\{666.67\cos(500t+45°)+500\sin(500t+45°)\}\right]+ke^{-666.67t}$$

$$=3.2\cos(500t+45°)+2.4\sin(500t+45°)+ke^{-666.67t}$$

Let $A\sin\phi=3.2$

and $A\cos\phi=2.4$

$$A^2\sin^2\phi+A^2\cos^2\phi=(3.2)^2+(2.4)^2=16$$

$$A=4$$

and $\phi=\tan^{-1}\left(\frac{3.2}{2.4}\right)=53.13°$

$$i(t)=4\sin(53.13°)\cos(500t+45°)+4\cos(53.13°)\sin(500t+45°)+ke^{-666.67t}$$

$$=4\sin(500t+98.13°)+ke^{-666.67t}$$

Putting $t=0$, in Eq. (i),

$$100\sin(45°)-15\,i(0)-0=0$$

$$i(0)=4.71$$

$$4.71=4\sin(98.13°)+k$$

$$k=0.75$$

$$i(t)=4\sin(500t+98.13°)+0.75\,e^{-666.67t}\quad \text{for } t>0$$

**EXAMPLE 9.52**

*In the network of Fig. 9.161, the switch is moved from position 1 to 2 at t = 0. The switch is in position 1 for a long time. Initial charge on the capacitor is $7\times10^{-4}$ coulombs. Determine the current expression i(t), when $\omega = 1000$ rad/s.*

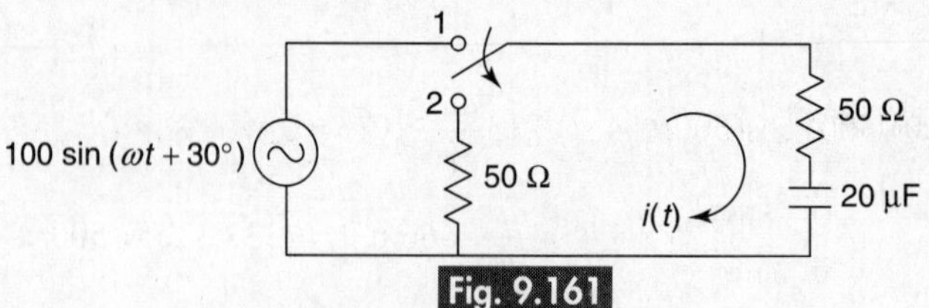


Fig. 9.161

**Solution**

(i) At $t = 0^-$, the network is shown in Fig. 9.162.

At $t = 0^-$, the network attains steady-state condition.

Fig. 9.162

$$\mathbf{I} = \frac{\mathbf{V}}{\mathbf{Z}} = \frac{100\angle 30^\circ}{50 - j\dfrac{1}{1000 \times 20 \times 10^{-6}}} = 1.41\angle 75^\circ \text{ A}$$

The steady-state current passing through the network when the switch is in position 1 is

$$i = 1.41 \sin(1000t + 75^\circ) \qquad \ldots\text{(i)}$$

(ii) For $t > 0$, the network is shown in Fig. 9.163.

Writing the KVL equation for $t > 0$,

$$-50i - 50i - \frac{1}{20 \times 10^{-6}} \int_0^t i\, dt - v_C(0) = 0 \qquad \ldots\text{(ii)}$$

Differentiating Eq. (ii),

$$-50\frac{di}{dt} - 50\frac{di}{dt} - \frac{1}{20 \times 10^{-6}} i = 0$$

$$\frac{di}{dt} + 500i = 0$$

Fig. 9.163

Comparing with differential equation $\dfrac{di}{dt} + Pi = 0$,

$$P = 500$$

The solution of this differential equation is given by

$$i(t) = k\,e^{-Pt} = k\,e^{-500t} \qquad \ldots\text{(iii)}$$

From Eqs (i) and (ii),

$$1.41 \sin(1000t + 75^\circ) = k\,e^{-500t}$$

At $t = 0$,

$$1.41 \sin(75^\circ) = k$$

$$k = 1.36$$

$$i(t) = 1.36\,e^{-500t} \quad \text{for } t > 0$$

## EXAMPLE 9.53

*In the network of Fig. 9.164, an exponential voltage $4e^{-5t}$ is applied at time $t = 0$. Find the expression for current $i(t)$. Assume zero voltage across the capacitor at $t = 0$.*

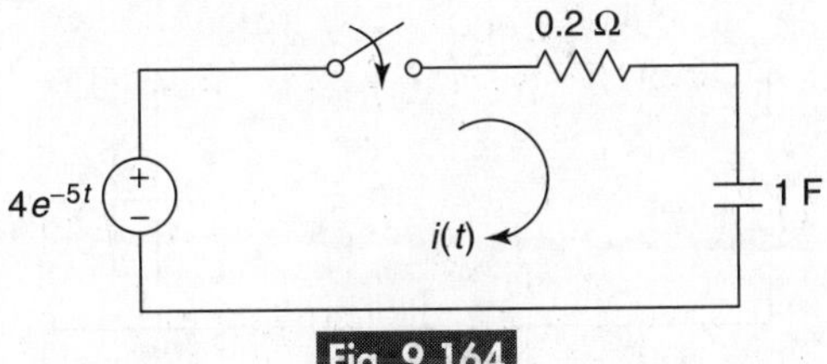


Fig. 9.164

**Solution** (i) At $t = 0^-$,

$$v_C(0^-) = 0$$

$$i(0^-) = 0$$

(ii) At $t = 0^+$, the network is shown in Fig. 9.165.
Since voltage across the capacitor cannot change instantaneously,

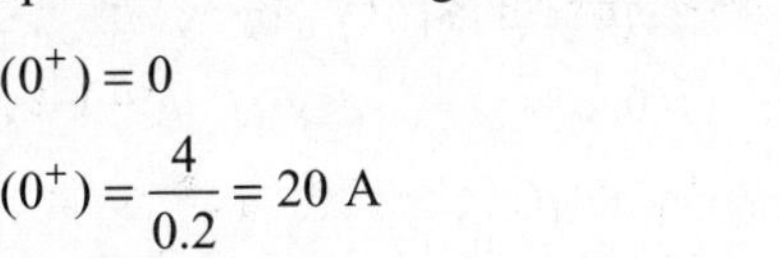

$$v_C(0^+) = 0$$

$$i(0^+) = \frac{4}{0.2} = 20 \text{ A}$$

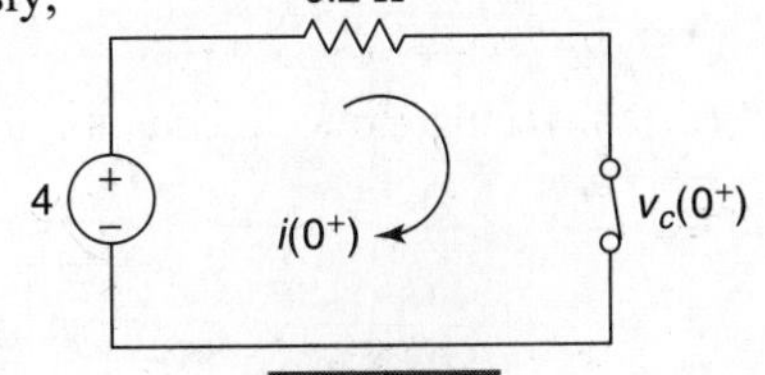


Fig. 9.165

(iii) Writing the KVL equation for $t > 0$,

$$4e^{-5t} - 0.2i - \frac{1}{1}\int_0^t i\, dt = 0 \qquad \ldots\text{(i)}$$

Differentiating Eq. (i),

$$-20e^{-5t} - 0.2\frac{di}{dt} - i = 0$$

$$\frac{di}{dt} + 5i = -100e^{-5t}$$

Comparing with the differential equation $\frac{di}{dt} + Pi = Q$,

$$P = 5, \quad Q = -100e^{-5t}$$

The solution of this differential equation is given by

$$i(t) = e^{-Pt}\int Q\, e^{Pt}\, dt + k e^{-Pt}$$

$$= e^{-5t}\int -100e^{-5t} e^{5t}\, dt + k e^{-5t}$$

$$= -100t e^{-5t} + k e^{-5t}$$

At $t = 0$, $i(0) = 20$ A

$$20 = k$$

$$i(t) = -100t e^{-5t} + 20e^{-5t} \qquad \text{for } t > 0$$

**EXAMPLE 9.54**

*In the network shown in Fig. 9.166, the switch is closed at $t = 0$ connecting a source $e^{-t}$ to the network. At $t = 0$, $v_C(0) = 0.5\,V$. Determine $v(t)$.*

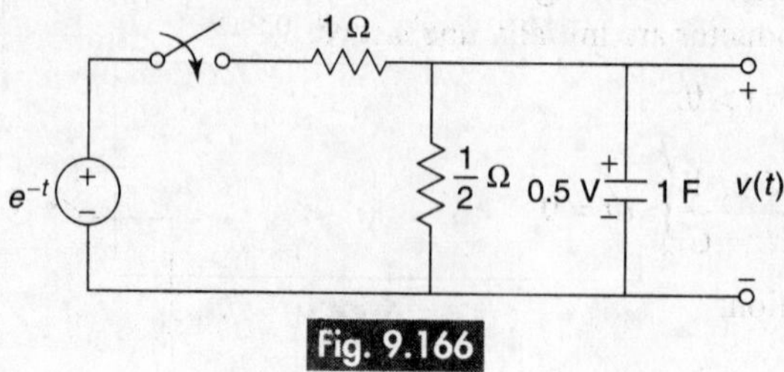


Fig. 9.166

**Solution**

(i) At $t = 0^-$, $$v(0) = v_C(0^-) = 0.5 \text{ V}$$

(ii) Since voltage across the capacitor cannot change instantaneously,

$$v(0^+) = v_C(0^+) = 0.5 \text{ V}$$

(iii) Writing the KCL equation for $t > 0$,

$$\frac{v - e^{-t}}{1} + \frac{v}{\frac{1}{2}} + 1\frac{dv}{dt} = 0$$

$$\frac{dv}{dt} + 3v = e^{-t}$$

Comparing with the differential equation $\dfrac{dv}{dt} + Pv = Q$,

$$P = 3, \quad Q = e^{-t}$$

The solution of this differential equation is given by

$$v(t) = e^{-Pt}\int Q\, e^{Pt}\, dt + k\, e^{-Pt}$$

$$= e^{-3t}\int e^{-t}\, e^{3t}\, dt + k\, e^{-3t}$$

$$= e^{-3t}\int e^{2t}\, dt + k\, e^{-3t}$$

$$= \frac{1}{2}e^{-t} + k\, e^{-3t}$$

At $t = 0$, $\quad v(0) = 0.5$ V

$$0.5 = \frac{1}{2} + k$$

$$k = 0$$

$$v(t) = 0.5e^{-t}$$

## 9.6 TRANSIENT RESPONSE OF *RLC* CIRCUIT FOR dc EXCITATION

LO 9.6

Discuss the transient response of *RLC* circuit for dc excitation

Consider a series *RLC* circuit, as shown in Fig. 9.167. The switch is closed at time $t = 0$. The capacitor and inductor are initially uncharged.

Applying KVL to the circuit for $t > 0$,

$$V - Ri - L\frac{di}{dt} - \frac{1}{C}\int_0^t i\, dt = 0$$

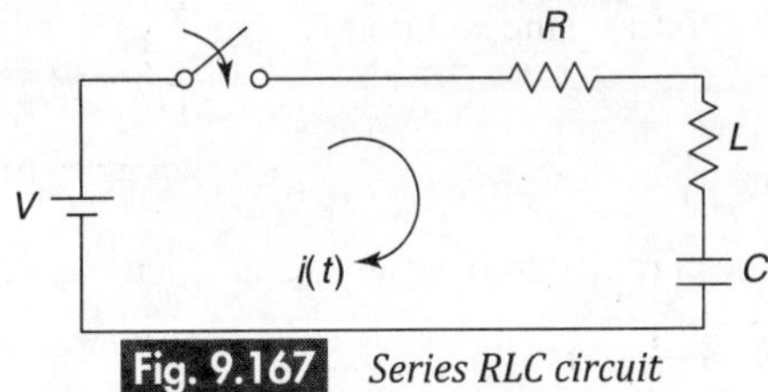


Fig. 9.167 *Series RLC circuit*

Differentiating the above equation,

$$0 - R\frac{di}{dt} - L\frac{d^2i}{dt^2} - \frac{1}{C}i = 0$$

$$\frac{d^2i}{dt^2} + \frac{R}{L}\frac{di}{dt} + \frac{1}{LC}i = 0$$

This is a second-order differential equation. The auxiliary equation or characteristic equation is given by

$$s^2 + \left(\frac{R}{L}\right)s + \left(\frac{1}{LC}\right) = 0$$

Let $s_1$ and $s_2$ be the roots of the equation.

$$s_1 = -\frac{R}{2L} + \sqrt{\left(\frac{R}{2L}\right)^2 - \frac{1}{LC}} = -\alpha + \sqrt{\alpha^2 - \omega_0^2} = -\alpha + \beta$$

$$s_2 = -\frac{R}{2L} - \sqrt{\left(\frac{R}{2L}\right)^2 - \frac{1}{LC}} = -\alpha - \sqrt{\alpha^2 - \omega_0^2} = -\alpha - \beta$$

where $\alpha = \dfrac{R}{2L}$

and is called damping factor of the circuit.

$$\omega_0 = \frac{1}{\sqrt{LC}}$$

and is called resonant frequency or undamped natural frequency of the circuit.

and $\beta = \sqrt{\alpha^2 - \omega_0^2}$

The solution of the above second-order differential equation is given by

$$i(t) = k_1 e^{s_1 t} + k_2 e^{s_2 t}$$

where $k_1$ and $k_2$ are constants to be determined and $s_1$ and $s_2$ are the roots of the equation.

Now, depending upon the values of $\alpha$ and $\omega_0$, we have three cases of the response.

### ➤ *Case I* *When $\alpha > \omega_0$*

i.e.,
$$\frac{R}{2L} > \frac{1}{\sqrt{LC}}$$

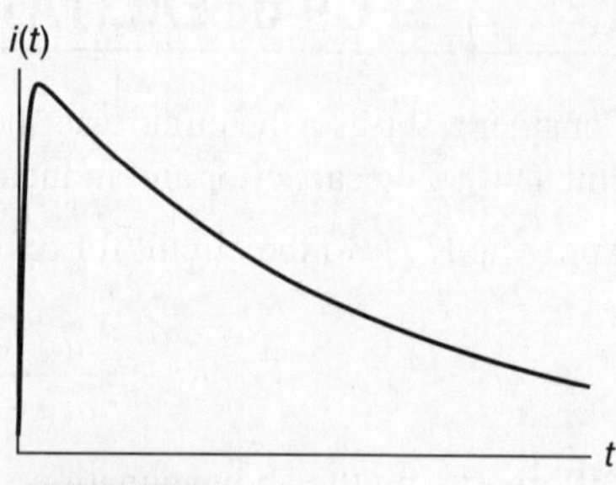


**Fig. 9.168** *Overdamped response*

The roots are real and unequal and it gives an overdamped response.

In this case, the solution is given by

$$i = e^{-\alpha t}\,(k_1\, e^{\beta t} + k_2\, e^{-\beta t})$$

or
$$i = k_1\, e^{s_1 t} + k_2\, e^{s_2 t} \qquad \text{for } t > 0$$

The current curve for an overdamped case is shown in Fig. 9.168.

### ➤ *Case II* *When $\alpha = \omega_0$*

i.e.,
$$\frac{R}{2L} = \frac{1}{\sqrt{LC}}$$

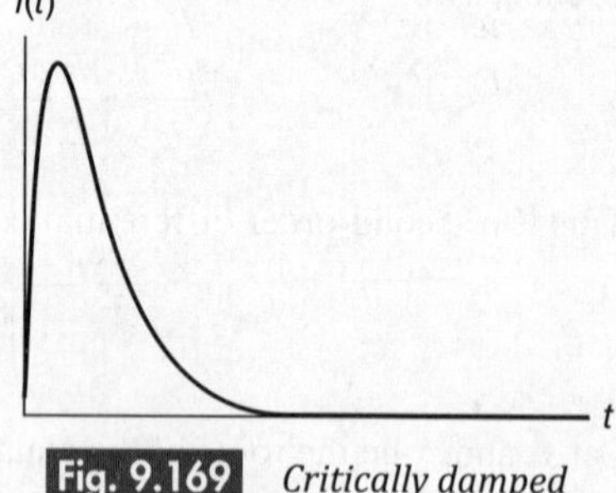


**Fig. 9.169** *Critically damped response*

The roots are real and equal and it gives a critically damped response.

In this case, the solution is given by

$$i = e^{-\alpha t}\,(k_1 + k_2 t) \quad \text{for } t > 0$$

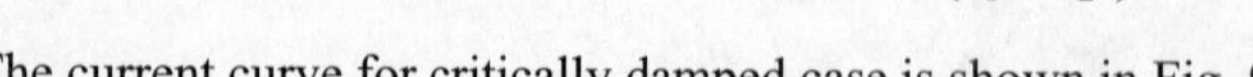

The current curve for critically damped case is shown in Fig. 9.169.

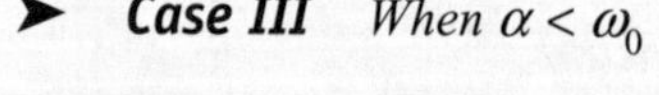

### ➤ *Case III* *When $\alpha < \omega_0$*

i.e.,
$$\frac{R}{2L} < \frac{1}{\sqrt{LC}}$$

The roots are complex conjugate and it gives an underdamped response.

In this case, the solution is given by

$$i(t) = k_1 e^{s_1 t} + k_2 e^{s_2 t}$$

where
$$s_{1,2} = -\alpha \pm \sqrt{\alpha^2 - \omega_0^2}$$

Let
$$\sqrt{\alpha^2 - \omega_0^2} = \sqrt{-1}\sqrt{\omega_0^2 - \alpha^2} = j\omega_d$$

where
$$j = \sqrt{-1}$$

and
$$\omega_d = \sqrt{\omega_0^2 - \alpha^2}$$

Hence,
$$i(t) = e^{-\alpha t}\,(k_1 e^{j\omega_d t} + k_2 e^{-j\omega_d t})$$

$$= e^{-\alpha t}\left\{(k_1 + k_2)\left[\frac{e^{j\omega_d t} + e^{-j\omega_d t}}{2}\right] + j(k_1 - k_2)\left[\frac{e^{j\omega_d t} - e^{-j\omega_d t}}{j2}\right]\right\}$$

$$= e^{-\alpha t}\left[(k_1 + k_2)\cos\omega_d t + j(k_1 - k_2)\sin\omega_d t\right] \quad \text{for } t > 0$$

The current curve for an underdamped case is shown in Fig. 9.170.

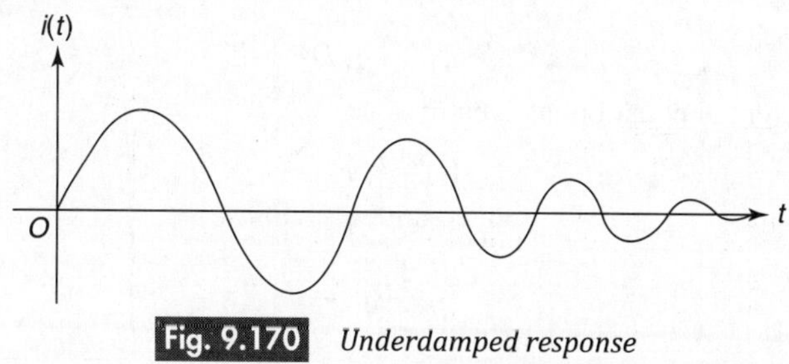


Fig. 9.170 *Underdamped response*

## EXAMPLE 9.55

*In the network of Fig. 9.171, the switch is closed at $t = 0$. Obtain the expression for current $i(t)$ for $t > 0$.*

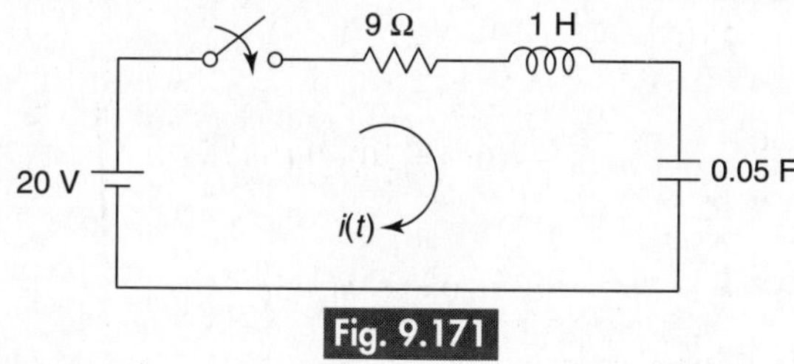


Fig. 9.171

**Solution**

(i) At $t = 0^-$, the switch is open.

$$i(0^-) = 0$$

$$v_C(0^-) = 0$$

(ii) Since current through the inductor and voltage across the capacitor cannot change instantaneously,

$$i(0^+) = 0$$

$$v_C(0^+) = 0$$

(iii) For $t > 0$, the network is shown in Fig. 9.172.

Writing the KVL equation for $t > 0$,

$$20 - 9i - 1\frac{di}{dt} - \frac{1}{0.05}\int_0^t i\, dt = 0 \qquad \ldots\text{(i)}$$

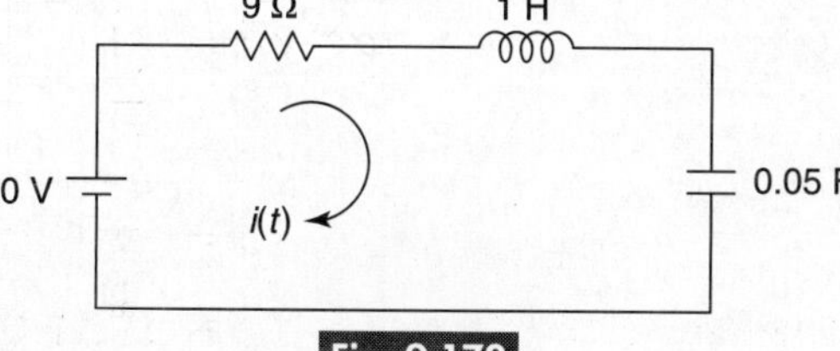


Fig. 9.172

Differentiating Eq. (i),

$$0 - 9\frac{di}{dt} - \frac{d^2i}{dt^2} - 20i = 0$$

$$\frac{d^2i}{dt^2} + 9\frac{di}{dt} + 20i = 0$$

$$(D^2 + 9D + 20)i = 0$$

$$D_1 = -4, D_2 = -5$$

The solution of this differential equation is given by

$$i(t) = k_1 e^{-4t} + k_2 e^{-5t} \quad \text{...(ii)}$$

Differentiating Eq. (ii),

$$\frac{di}{dt} = -4k_1 e^{-4t} - 5k_2 e^{-5t} \quad \text{...(iii)}$$

At $t = 0$, $i(0) = 0$

$$0 = k_1 + k_2 \quad \text{...(iv)}$$

$$\frac{di}{dt}(0) = -4k_1 - 5k_2 \quad \text{...(v)}$$

Putting $t = 0$ in Eq. (i),

$$20 - 9i(0^+) - \frac{di}{dt}(0^+) - 0 = 0$$

$$\frac{di}{dt}(0^+) = 20 - 9i(0^+) = 20 \text{ A/s}$$

From Eq. (v),

$$20 = -4k_1 - 5k_2 \quad \text{...(vi)}$$

Solving Eqs (iv) and (vi),

$$k_1 = 20$$

$$k_2 = 20$$

$$i(t) = 20e^{-4t} - 20e^{-5t} \quad \text{for } t > 0$$

## EXAMPLE 9.56

*In the network shown in Fig. 9.173, the switch is moved from position 1 to 2 at t = 0. The switch is in position 1 for a long time. Determine the expression for the current i(t).*

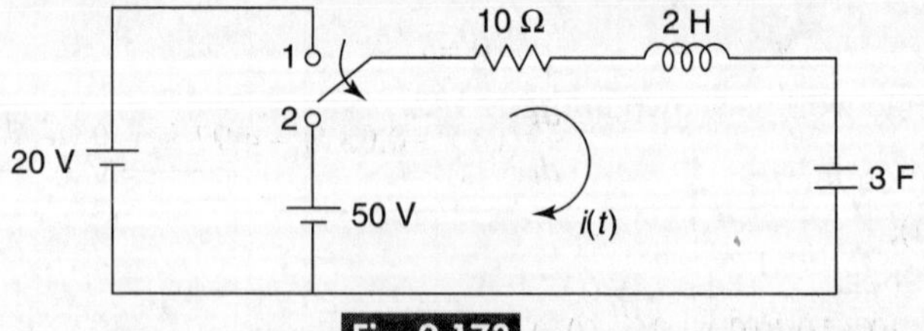


Fig. 9.173

**Solution**

(i) At $t = 0^-$, the network is shown in Fig. 9.174.

At $t = 0^-$, the network attains steady-state condition. Hence, the inductor acts as a short circuit and the capacitor acts as an open circuit.

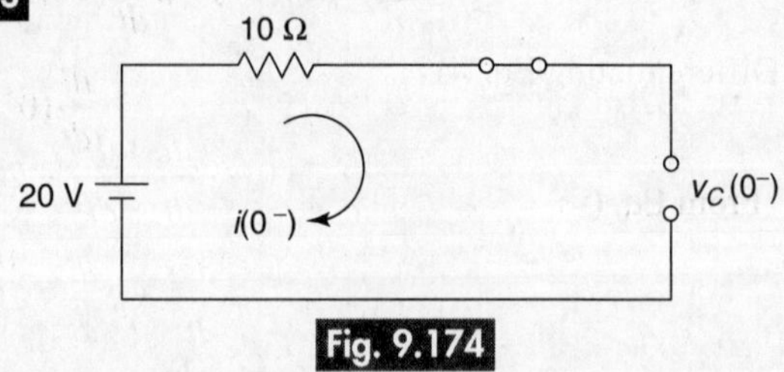


Fig. 9.174

$$v_C(0^-) = 20 \text{ V}$$

$$i(0^-) = 0$$

(ii) Since the current through the inductor and the voltage across the capacitor cannot change instantaneously,

$$v_C(0^+) = 20 \text{ V}$$

$$i(0^+) = 0$$

(iii) For $t > 0$, the network is shown in Fig. 9.175.

Writing the KVL equation for $t > 0$,

$$50 - 10i - 2\frac{di}{dt} - \frac{1}{3}\int_0^t i\,dt - 20 = 0 \qquad \ldots\text{(i)}$$

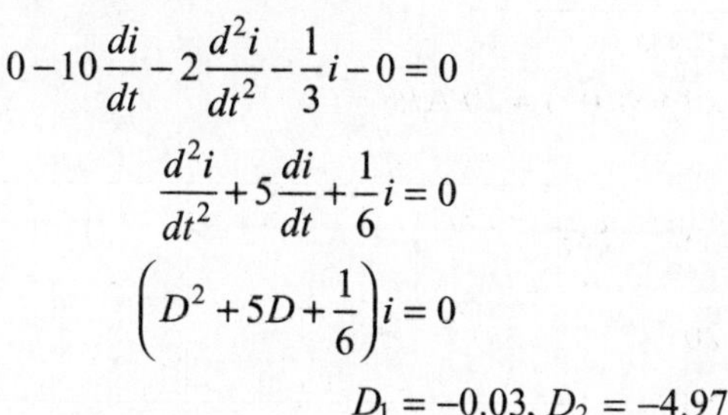


Fig. 9.175

Differentiating Eq. (i),

$$0 - 10\frac{di}{dt} - 2\frac{d^2i}{dt^2} - \frac{1}{3}i - 0 = 0$$

$$\frac{d^2i}{dt^2} + 5\frac{di}{dt} + \frac{1}{6}i = 0$$

$$\left(D^2 + 5D + \frac{1}{6}\right)i = 0$$

$$D_1 = -0.03, D_2 = -4.97$$

The solution of this differential equation is given by

$$i(t) = k_1\,e^{-0.03t} + k_2\,e^{-4.97t} \qquad \ldots\text{(ii)}$$

Differentiating Eq. (ii),

$$\frac{di}{dt} = -0.03k_1\,e^{-0.03t} - 4.97k_2\,e^{-4.97t} \qquad \ldots\text{(iii)}$$

At $t = 0$, $i(0) = 0$

$$0 = k_1 + k_2 \qquad \ldots\text{(iv)}$$

$$\frac{di}{dt}(0) = -0.03\,k_1 - 4.97\,k_2 \qquad \ldots\text{(v)}$$

Putting $t = 0$, in Eq. (i),

$$20 - 10\,i(0^+) - 2\frac{di}{dt}(0^+) - 0 = 0$$

$$\frac{di}{dt}(0^+) = \frac{20 - 10\,i(0^+)}{2} = 10 \text{ A/s}$$

From Eq. (v),

$$10 = -0.03\,k_1 - 4.97\,k_2 \qquad \ldots\text{(vi)}$$

Solving Eqs (iv) and (vi),

$$k_1 = 2.02$$

$$k_2 = 2.02$$

$$i(t) = 2.02\, e^{-0.03t} - 2.02\, e^{-4.97t} \qquad \text{for } t > 0$$

## EXAMPLE 9.57

*In the network of Fig. 9.176, the switch is closed and a steady state is reached in the network. At t = 0, the switch is opened. Find the expression for the current $i_2(t)$ in the inductor.*

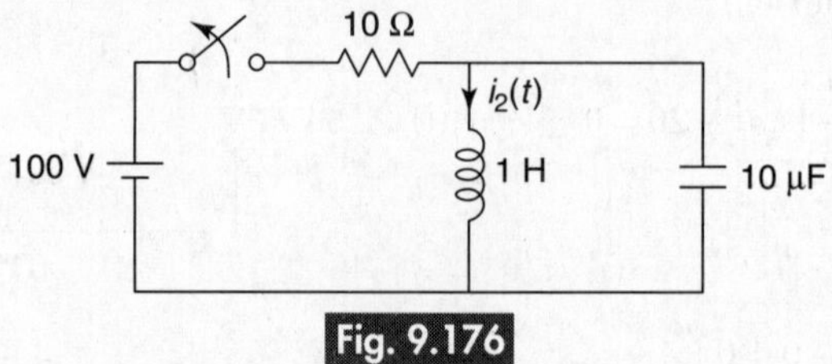


Fig. 9.176

**Solution**

(i) At $t = 0^-$, the network is shown in Fig. 9.177. At $t = 0^-$, the network attains steady-state condition. Hence, the inductor acts as a short circuit and the capacitor acts as an open circuit.

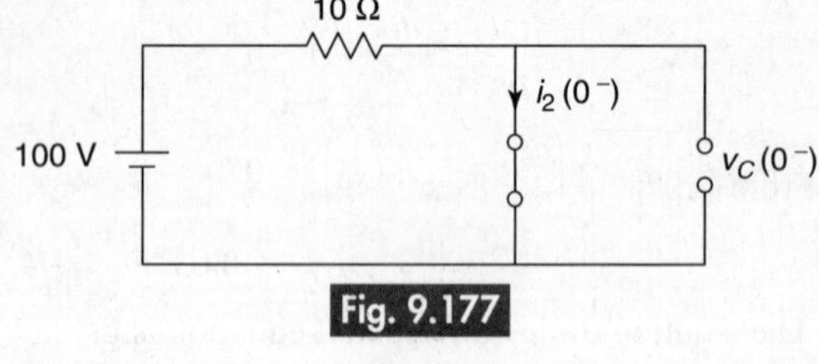


Fig. 9.177

$$i_2(0^-) = \frac{100}{10} = 10 \text{ A}$$

$$v_C(0^-) = 0$$

(ii) Since current through the inductor and voltage across capacitor cannot change instantaneously,

$$i_2(0^+) = 10 \text{ A}$$

$$v_C(0^+) = 0$$

(iii) For $t > 0$, the network is shown in Fig. 9.178.

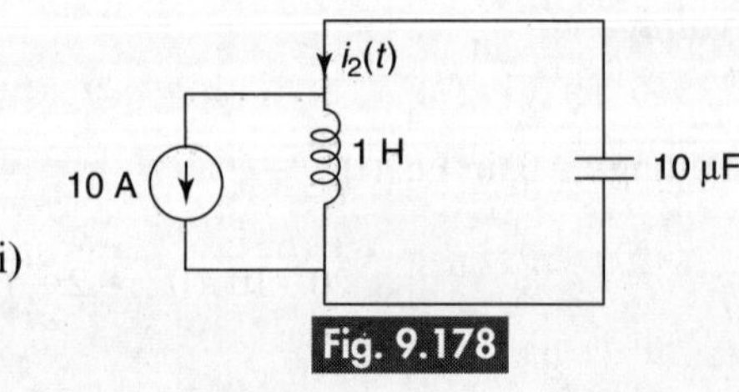


Fig. 9.178

Writing the KVL equation for $t > 0$,

$$-1\frac{di_2}{dt} - \frac{1}{10 \times 10^{-6}} \int_0^t i\, dt = 0 \qquad \text{...(i)}$$

Differentiating Eq. (i),

$$-\frac{d^2 i_2}{dt^2} - 10^5 i = 0$$

$$\frac{d^2 i_2}{dt^2} + 10^5 i = 0$$

$$(D^2 + 10^5)i = 0$$

$$D_1 = j\,316,\, D_2 = -j\,316$$

The solution of this differential equation is given by

$$i_2(t) = k_1 \cos 316t + k_2 \sin 316t \qquad \ldots\text{(ii)}$$

Differentiating Eq. (ii),

$$\frac{di_2}{dt} = -316\,k_1 \sin 316t + 316\,k_2 \cos 316t \qquad \ldots\text{(iii)}$$

At $t = 0,\, i_2(0) = 10$ A

$$10 = k_1 \qquad \ldots\text{(iv)}$$

$$\frac{di_2}{dt}(0) = 316\,k_2 \qquad \ldots\text{(v)}$$

Putting $t = 0$ in Eq. (i),

$$-\frac{di}{dt}(0^+) - 0 = 0$$

$$\frac{di}{dt}(0^+) = 0$$

From Eq. (v),

$$0 = 316\,k_2$$

$$k_2 = 0$$

$$i_2(t) = 10\cos 316t \quad \text{for } t > 0$$

## EXAMPLE 9.58

*In the network of Fig. 9.179, capacitor C has an initial voltage $v_c(0^-)$ of 10 V and at the same instant, current in the inductor L is zero. The switch is closed at time t = 0. Obtain the expression for the voltage v(t) across the inductor L.*

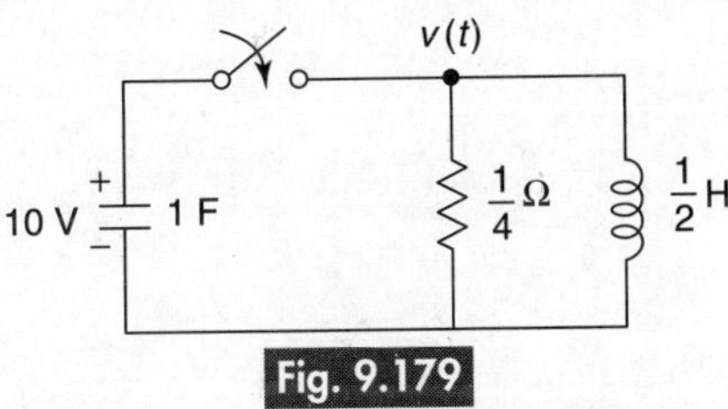


Fig. 9.179

**Solution**

(i) At $t = 0^-$,

$$i_L(0^-) = 0$$

$$v(0^-) = v_C(0^-) = 10 \text{ V}$$

(ii) Since current through the inductor and voltage across capacitor cannot change instantaneously,

$$i_L(0^+) = 0$$

$$v(0^+) = v_C(0^+) = 10 \text{ V}$$

(iii) For $t > 0$, the network is shown in Fig. 9.180.

Writing the KCL equation for $t > 0$,

$$1\frac{dv}{dt} + \frac{v}{\frac{1}{4}} + \frac{1}{\frac{1}{2}}\int_0^t v\, dt = 0 \qquad \ldots\text{(i)}$$

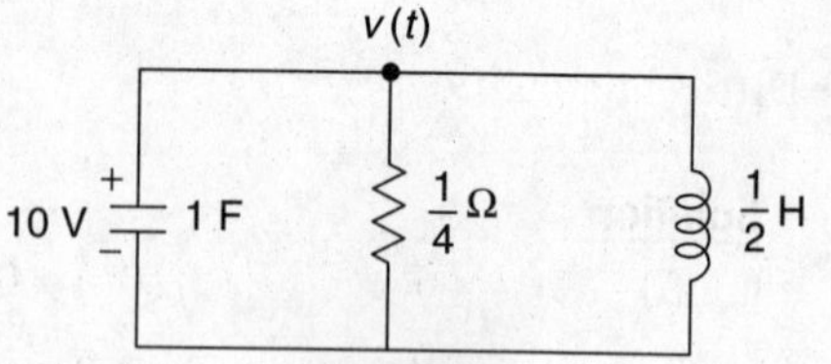

Fig. 9.180

Differentiating Eq. (i),

$$\frac{d^2v}{dt^2} + 4\frac{dv}{dt} + 2v = 0$$

$$(D^2 + 4D + 2)v = 0$$

$$D_1 = -1, D_2 = -3$$

The solution of this differential equation is given by

$$v(t) = k_1 e^{-t} + k_2 e^{-3t} \qquad \ldots\text{(ii)}$$

Differentiating Eq. (iii),

$$\frac{dv}{dt} = -k_1 e^{-t} - 3k_2 e^{-3t} \qquad \ldots\text{(iii)}$$

At $t = 0$, $v(0) = 10$ V

$$10 = k_1 + k_2 \qquad \ldots\text{(iv)}$$

$$\frac{dv}{dt}(0) = -k_1 - 3\,k_2 \qquad \ldots\text{(v)}$$

Putting $t = 0$ in Eq. (i),

$$\frac{dv}{dt}(0^+) + 4v(0) + 0 = 0$$

$$\frac{dv}{dt}(0^+) = -40 \text{ V/s}$$

From Eq. (v),

$$-40 = -k_1 - 3\,k_2 \qquad \ldots\text{(vi)}$$

Solving Eqs (iv) and (vi),

$$k_1 = -5$$

$$k_2 = 15$$

$$v(t) = -5\,e^{-t} + 15\,e^{-3t} \qquad \text{for } t > 0$$

## EXAMPLE 9.59

*In the network of Fig. 9.181, the switch is opened at $t = 0$. Obtain the expression for $v(t)$. Assume zero initial conditions.*

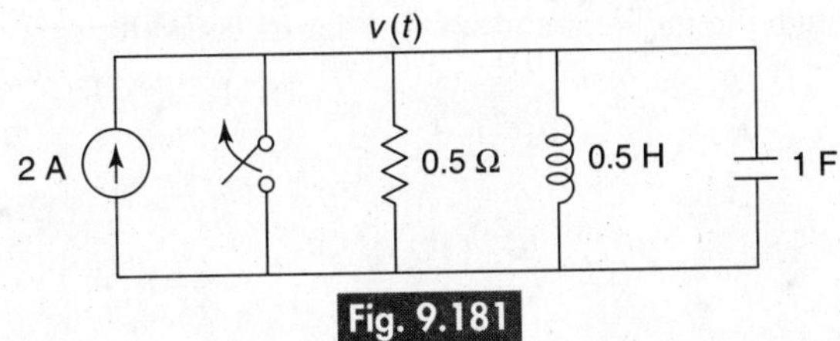

Fig. 9.181

**Solution**

(i) At $t = 0^-$, $i_L(0^-) = 0$

$$v(0^-) = v_C(0^-) = 0$$

(ii) Since current through the inductor and voltage across the capacitor cannot change instantaneously,

$$i_L(0^+) = 0$$

$$v(0^+) = v_C(0^+) = 0$$

(iii) For $t > 0$, the network is shown in Fig. 9.182.

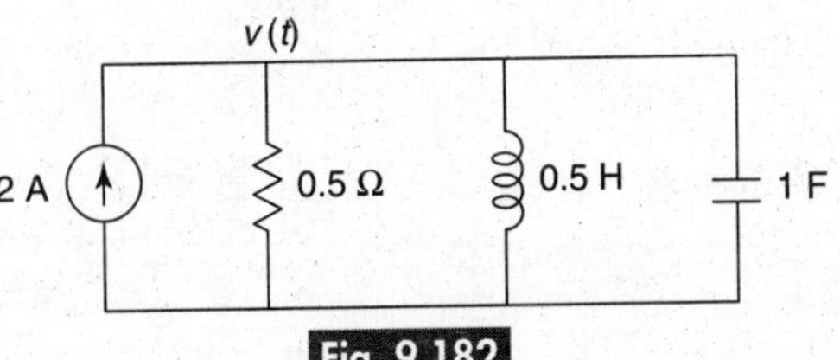

Fig. 9.182

Writing the KCL equation for $t > 0$,

$$\frac{v}{0.5} + \frac{1}{0.5}\int_0^t v\,dt + 1\frac{dv}{dt} = 2 \qquad \ldots\text{(i)}$$

Differentiating Eq. (i),

$$2\frac{dv}{dt} + 2v + \frac{d^2v}{dt^2} = 0$$

$$\frac{d^2v}{dt^2} + 2\frac{dv}{dt} + 2v = 0$$

$$(D^2 + 2D + 2)v = 0$$

$$D_1 = -1 + j1, \quad D_2 = -1 - j1$$

The solution of this differential equation is given by

$$v(t) = e^{-t}(k_1 \cos t + k_2 \sin t) \qquad \ldots\text{(ii)}$$

Differentiating Eq. (ii),

$$\frac{dv}{dt} = -e^{-t}(k_1 \cos t + k_2 \sin t) + e^{-t}(-k_1 \sin t + k_2 \cos t)$$

$$= e^{-t}[-k_1(\cos t + \sin t) + k_2(\cos t - \sin t)] \qquad \ldots\text{(iii)}$$

At $t = 0$, $v(0) = 0$

$$0 = k_1 \qquad \ldots\text{(iv)}$$

$$\frac{dv}{dt}(0) = -k_1 + k_2 \qquad \ldots\text{(v)}$$

Putting $t = 0$ in Eq. (i),

$$2v(0) + 0 + \frac{dv}{dt}(0) = 2$$

$$\frac{dv}{dt}(0) = 2\ V/s$$

From Eq. (v),

$$2 = -k_1 + k_2 \qquad \text{...(vi)}$$

Solving Eq. (iv) and (vi),

$$k_1 = 0$$
$$k_2 = 2$$
$$v(t) = 2\,e^{-t}\sin t \qquad \text{for } t > 0$$

## 9.7 TRANSIENT RESPONSE OF *RLC* CIRCUIT FOR SINUSOIDAL EXCITATION

LO 9.7

Discuss the transient response of *RLC* circuit for sinusoidal excitation

Consider a series *RLC* circuit, as shown in Fig. 9.183. The switch is closed at time $t = 0$. The inductor is initially unenergised and the capacitor is initially uncharged.

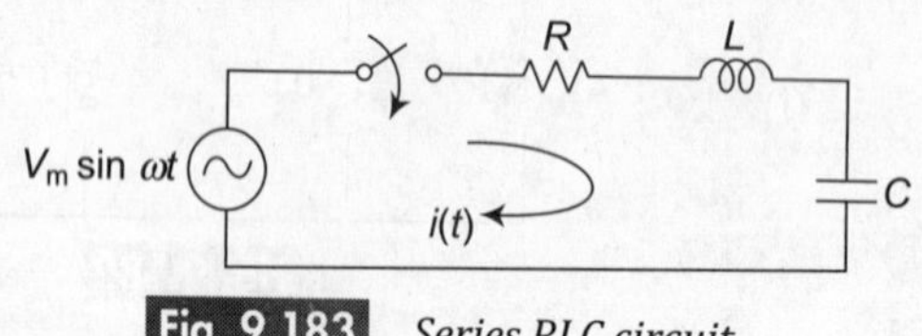


**Fig. 9.183** *Series RLC circuit*

Applying KVL to the circuit for $t > 0$,

$$V_m \sin \omega t - Ri - L\frac{di}{dt} - \frac{1}{C}\int i\,dt = 0$$

Differentiating the above equation,

$$V_m\omega \cos \omega t - R\frac{di}{dt} - L\frac{d^2 i}{dt^2} - \frac{i}{C} = 0$$

$$\frac{d^2 i}{dt^2} + \frac{R}{L}\frac{di}{dt} + \frac{1}{LC}i = \frac{V_m\omega}{L}\cos \omega t$$

This is a second-order differential equation. The solution consists of two parts, complementary function and particular integral.

The particular solution can be obtained by using method of undetermined coefficients. Let the particular integral be

$$i_{PI} = A\cos \omega t + B\sin \omega t$$

$$i'_{PI} = -A\omega \sin \omega t + B\omega \cos \omega t$$

$$i''_{PI} = -A\omega^2 \cos \omega t - B\omega^2 \sin \omega t$$

Substituting these derivates in the given differential equation,

$$(-A\omega^2 \cos \omega t - B\omega^2 \sin \omega t) + \frac{R}{L}(-A\omega \sin \omega t + B\omega \cos \omega t)$$

$$+ \frac{1}{LC}(A \cos \omega t + B \sin \omega t) = \frac{V_m\omega}{L} \cos \omega t$$

Comparing coefficients of cos $\omega t$ and sin $\omega t$ on both the sides,

$$- B\omega^2 - \frac{A\omega R}{L} + \frac{B}{LC} = 0$$

or
$$A\left(\frac{\omega R}{L}\right) + B\left(\omega^2 - \frac{1}{LC}\right) = 0$$

and
$$-A\omega^2 + \frac{B\omega R}{L} + \frac{A}{LC} = \frac{V_m\omega}{L}$$

or
$$A\left(-\omega^2 + \frac{1}{LC}\right) + B\left(\frac{\omega R}{L}\right) = \frac{V_m\omega}{L}$$

Solving these equations,

$$A = \frac{V_m\omega\left(\frac{1}{LC} - \omega^2\right)}{L\left[\left(\frac{\text{i}}{LC} - \omega^2\right)^2 + \frac{\omega^2 R^2}{L^2}\right]}$$

$$B = \frac{V_m \frac{\omega^2 R}{L^2}}{\left[\left(\frac{1}{LC} - \omega^2\right)^2 + \frac{\omega^2 R^2}{L^2}\right]}$$

Substituting the values of $A$ and $B$, the particular solution is

$$i_{PI} = \frac{V_m\omega\left(\frac{1}{LC} - \omega^2\right)}{L\left[\left(\frac{1}{LC} - \omega^2\right)^2 + \frac{\omega^2 R^2}{L^2}\right]} \cos \omega t + \frac{V_m \frac{\omega^2 R}{L^2}}{\left[\left(\frac{1}{LC} - \omega^2\right)^2 + \frac{\omega^2 R^2}{L^2}\right]} \sin \omega t$$

Let
$$M \sin \theta = \frac{V_m\omega\left(\frac{1}{LC} - \omega^2\right)}{L\left[\left(\frac{1}{LC} - \omega^2\right) + \frac{\omega^2 R^2}{L^2}\right]}$$

and
$$M \cos \theta = \frac{V_m \frac{\omega^2 R}{L^2}}{\left[\left(\frac{1}{LC} - \omega^2\right)^2 + \frac{\omega^2 R^2}{L^2}\right]}$$

$$\tan\theta = \frac{M\sin\theta}{M\cos\theta} = \frac{\frac{V_m\omega}{L}\left(\frac{1}{LC}-\omega^2\right)}{V_m\frac{\omega^2 R}{L^2}} = \frac{L}{\omega R}\left(\frac{1}{LC}-\omega^2\right) = \frac{1}{R}\left(\frac{1}{\omega C}-\omega L\right)$$

$$\theta = \tan^{-1}\left[\frac{1}{R}\left(\frac{1}{\omega C}-\omega L\right)\right]$$

Also,
$$M = \sqrt{M^2\cos^2\theta + M^2\sin^2\theta}$$
$$= \frac{V_m}{\sqrt{R^2+\left(\frac{1}{\omega C}-\omega L\right)^2}}$$

Hence,
$$i_{PI} = M\sin\theta\cos\omega t + M\cos\theta\sin\omega t$$
$$= M(\sin\omega t\cos\theta + \sin\theta\cos\omega t)$$
$$= M\sin(\omega t+\theta)$$
$$= \frac{V_m}{\sqrt{R^2+\left(\frac{1}{\omega C}-\omega L\right)^2}}\sin\left[\omega t + \tan^{-1}\left\{\frac{1}{R}\left(\frac{1}{\omega C}-\omega L\right)\right\}\right]$$

The complementary function can be obtained by the auxiliary or characteristic equation,

$$s^2 + \left(\frac{R}{L}\right)s + \frac{1}{LC} = 0$$

Let $s_1$ and $s_2$ be the roots of the equation.

$$s_1 = -\frac{R}{2L} + \sqrt{\left(\frac{R}{2L}\right)^2 - \frac{1}{LC}} = -\alpha + \sqrt{\alpha^2-\omega_0^2} = -\alpha + \beta$$

$$s_2 = -\frac{R}{2L} - \sqrt{\left(\frac{R}{2L}\right)^2 - \frac{1}{LC}} = -\alpha - \sqrt{\alpha^2-\omega_0^2} = -\alpha - \beta$$

where
$$\alpha = \frac{R}{2L}$$
$$\omega_0 = \frac{1}{LC}$$

and
$$\beta = \sqrt{\alpha^2-\omega_0^2}$$

Depending upon the values of $\alpha$ and $\omega_0$, there are three cases of the response.

➤ ***Case I*** When $\alpha > \omega_0$ i.e., $\frac{R}{2L} > \frac{1}{\sqrt{LC}}$

The roots are real and unequal and the system gives overdamped response. The complementary function is given by

$$i_{CF} = e^{-\alpha t}(k_1 e^{\beta t} + k_2 e^{-\beta t})$$

Hence, the complete solution is given by

$$i = e^{-\alpha t}(k_1 e^{\beta t} + k_2 e^{-\beta t}) + \frac{V_m}{\sqrt{R^2 + \left(\frac{1}{\omega C} - \omega L\right)^2}} \sin\left[\omega t + \tan^{-1}\left\{\frac{1}{R}\left(\frac{1}{\omega C} - \omega L\right)\right\}\right] \quad \text{for } t > 0$$

➤ ***Case II*** When $\alpha = \omega_0$ i.e., $\frac{R}{2L} = \frac{1}{\sqrt{LC}}$

The roots are real and equal and the system gives a critically damped response. The complementary function is given by

$$i_{CF} = e^{-\alpha t}(k_1 + k_2 t)$$

Hence, the complete solution is given by

$$i = e^{-\alpha t}(k_1 + k_2 t) + \frac{V_m}{\sqrt{R^2 + \left(\frac{1}{\omega C} - \omega L\right)^2}} \sin\left[\omega t + \tan^{-1}\left\{\frac{1}{R}\left(\frac{1}{\omega C} - \omega L\right)\right\}\right] \quad \text{for } t > 0$$

➤ ***Case III*** When $\alpha < \omega_0$ i.e., $\frac{R}{2L} < \frac{1}{\sqrt{LC}}$

The roots are complex conjugate and the system gives an underdamped response. The complementary function is given by

$$i_{CF} = e^{-\alpha t}[(k_1 + k_2)\cos \omega_d t + j(k_1 - k_2)\sin \omega_d t]$$

where $\omega_d = \sqrt{\omega_0^2 - \alpha^2}$

Hence, the complete solution is given by

$$i = e^{-\alpha t}[(k_1 + k_2)\cos \omega_d t + j(k_1 - k_2)\sin \omega_d t]$$
$$+ \frac{V_m}{\sqrt{R^2 + \left(\frac{1}{\omega C} - \omega L\right)^2}} \sin\left[\omega t + \tan^{-1}\left\{\frac{1}{R}\left(\frac{1}{\omega C} - \omega L\right)\right\}\right] \quad \text{for } t > 0$$

**EXAMPLE 9.60**

*In the network shown in Fig. 9.184, a sinusoidal voltage $v = 150 \sin(200t + \phi)$ is applied at $\phi = 30°$. Determine the current i(t).*

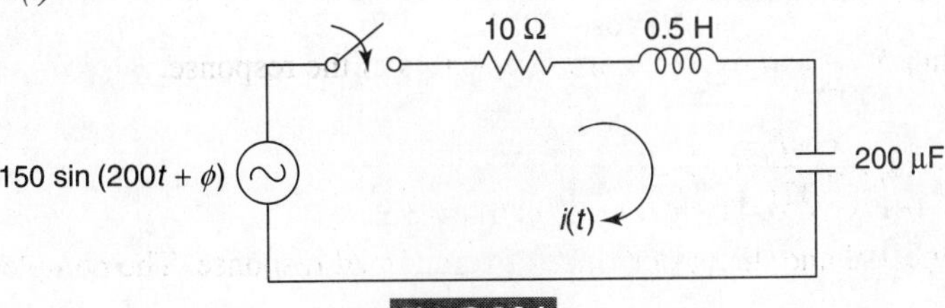


Fig. 9.184

**Solution** Writing the KVL equation for $t > 0$,

$$150 \sin(200t + 30°) - 10i - 0.5\frac{di}{dt} - \frac{1}{200 \times 10^{-6}}\int_0^t i\,dt = 0 \qquad \ldots\text{(i)}$$

Differentiating Eq. (i),

$$30000 \cos(200t + 30°) - 10\frac{di}{dt} - 0.5\frac{d^2i}{dt^2} - 5000i = 0$$

$$\frac{d^2i}{dt^2} + 20\frac{di}{dt} + 10000i = 60000 \cos(200t + 30°)$$

$$(D^2 + 20D + 10000)i = 60000 \cos(200t + 30°) \qquad \ldots\text{(ii)}$$

The roots of the characteristic equation are

$$D_1 = -10 + j\,99.5, \quad D_2 = -10 - j\,99.5$$

The complimentary function is

$$i_C = e^{-10t}(K_1 \cos 99.5t + K_2 \sin 99.5t)$$

Let the particular function be

$$i_P = A\cos(200t + 30°) + B\sin(200t + 30°)$$

$$i_P' = -200A\sin(200t + 30°) + 200B\cos(200t + 30°)$$

$$i_P'' = -40000A\cos(200t + 30°) - 40000B\sin(200t + 30°)$$

Substituting these values in Eq. (ii),

$$-40000\,A\cos(200t + 30°) - 40000\,B\sin(200t + 30°) + 20[-200\,A\sin(200t + 30°) + 200\,B\cos(200t + 30°)]$$
$$+10000[A\cos(200t + 30°) + B\sin(200t + 30°)] = 60000\cos(200t + 30°)$$

$$(-40000\,B - 4000\,A + 10000\,B)\sin(200\text{t} + 30°) + (-40000\,A + 4000\,B + 10000\,A)\cos(200t + 30°)$$
$$= 60000\cos(200t + 30°)$$

Equating the coefficients,

$$-40000\,B - 4000\,A + 10000\,B = 0$$

$$-40000\,A + 4000\,B + 10000\,A = 60000$$

Solving these equations,

$$A = -1.97$$

$$B = 0.26$$

$$i_P = -1.97\cos(200t + 30°) + 0.26\sin(200t + 30°)$$

Let $\qquad A\sin\phi = -1.97$

and $\qquad A\cos\phi = 0.26$

$$A^2\sin^2\phi + A^2\cos^2\phi = (-1.97)^2 + (0.26)^2 = 3.95$$

$$A = 1.987$$

and $\qquad \phi = \tan^{-1}\left(\frac{-1.97}{0.26}\right) = -82.48°$

$$
\begin{aligned}
i_P &= 1.987\sin(-82.48°)\cos(200t+30°)+1.987\cos(-82.48°)\sin(200t+30°)\\
&= 1.987\sin(200t+30°-82.48°)\\
&= 1.987\sin(200t-52.48°)
\end{aligned}
$$

The solution of the differential equation is given by

$$i(t) = e^{-10t}(k_1\cos 99.5t + k_2\sin 99.5t) + 1.987\sin(200t-52.48°) \qquad \text{...(iii)}$$

Differentiating Eq. (iii),

$$
\begin{aligned}
\frac{di}{dt} &= e^{-10t}(-99.5\,k_1\sin 99.5t + 99.5\,k_2\cos 99.5t)\\
&\quad -10\,e^{-10t}(k_1\cos 99.5t + k_2\sin 99.5t) + (1.987)(200)\cos(200t-52.48°)
\end{aligned}
$$

At $t=0$, $i(0)=0$

$$
\begin{aligned}
0 &= k_1 + 1.987\sin(-52.48°)\\
k_1 &= 1.58 \qquad \text{...(iv)}
\end{aligned}
$$

$$
\begin{aligned}
\frac{di}{dt}(0) &= 99.5\,k_2 - 10\,k_1 + (1.987)(200)\cos(-52.48°)\\
&= 99.5\,k_2 - 10(1.58) + 242.03\\
&= 99.5\,k_2 + 226.23 \qquad \text{...(v)}
\end{aligned}
$$

Putting $t=0$ in Eq. (i),

$$150\sin(30°) - 10(0) - 0.5\frac{di}{dt}(0) - 0 = 0$$

$$\frac{di}{dt}(0) = 150 \text{ A/s}$$

From Eq. (v),

$$
\begin{aligned}
150 &= 99.5\,k_2 + 226.23\\
k_2 &= -0.77
\end{aligned}
$$

$$i(t) = e^{-10t}(1.58\cos 99.5t - 0.77\sin 99.5t) + 1.987\sin(200t-52.48°) \quad \text{for } t>0$$

## EXAMPLE 9.61

*The switch in the network of Fig. 9.185 is opened at t = 0. Find i (t) for t > 0 if,*

*(a)* $L = \frac{1}{2}$ *H and C = 1 F* *(b) L = 1 H and C = 1 F* *(c) L = 5 H and C = 1 F*

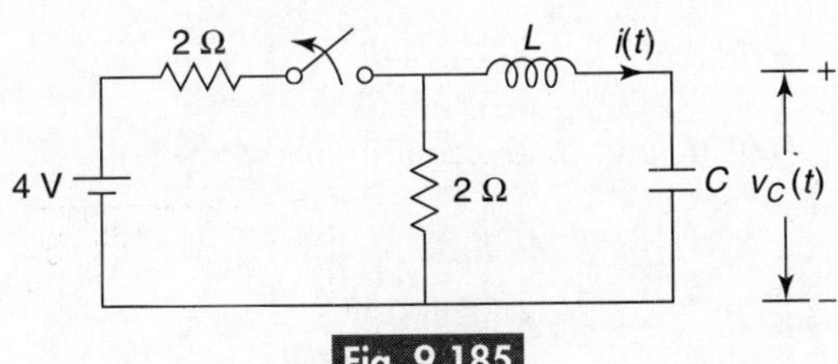


Fig. 9.185

**Solution** At $t = 0^-$, the network has attained steady-state condition. Hence, the inductor acts as a short circuit and the capacitor acts as an pen circuit.

$$v_C(0^-) = 4 \times \frac{2}{2+2} = 2 \text{ V}$$

$$i(0^-) = 0$$

Since current through the inductor and voltage across the capacitor cannot change instantaneously,

$$v_C(0^+) = 2 \text{ V}$$

$$i(0^+) = 0$$

***Case I*** *When* $R = 2\ \Omega,\ L = \frac{1}{2} H,\ C = 1\ F$

$$\alpha = \frac{R}{2L} = \frac{2}{2 \times \frac{1}{2}} = 2$$

$$\omega_0 = \frac{1}{\sqrt{LC}} = \frac{1}{\sqrt{\frac{1}{2} \times 1}} = \frac{1}{\sqrt{0.5}} = 1.414$$

$$\alpha > \omega_0$$

This indicates an overdamped case.

$$i(t) = A_1 e^{s_1 t} - A_2 e^{s_2 t}$$

where $$s_1 = -\alpha - \sqrt{\alpha^2 - \omega_0^2} = -2 - \sqrt{4-2} = -2 - \sqrt{2} = -3.414$$

and $$s_2 = -\alpha + \sqrt{\alpha^2 - \omega_0^2} = -2 + \sqrt{2} = -0.586$$

$$i(t) = k_1 e^{-3.414t} + k_2 e^{-0.586t}$$

At $t = 0$, $i(0) = 0$

$$k_1 + k_2 = 0 \qquad \ldots\text{(i)}$$

Also, $$v_L(0^+) + v_C(0^+) + v_R(0^+) = 0$$

$$v_L(0^+) = -v_R(0^+) - v_C(0^+) = -2i(0^+) - v_C(0^+) = -2 \text{ V} \qquad \ldots\text{(ii)}$$

$$v_L(0^+) = L\frac{di}{dt}(0^+)$$

$$\frac{di}{dt}(0^+) = \frac{v_L(0^+)}{L} = -\frac{2}{0.5} = -4 \text{ A/s}$$

Differentiating the equation of $i(t)$ and putting the condition at $t = 0$,

$$-3.414\, k_1 - 0.586\, k_2 = -4 \qquad \ldots\text{(iii)}$$

Solving Eqs (i) and (iii),

$$k_1 = 1.414 \quad \text{and} \quad k_2 = -1.414$$

$$i(t) = 1.414(e^{-3.414t} - e^{-0.586t}) \qquad \text{for } t > 0$$

***Case II*** *When* $R = 2\ \Omega$, $L = 1\ H$, $C = 1\ F$

$$\alpha = \frac{R}{2L} = \frac{2}{2 \times 1} = \frac{2}{2} = 1$$

$$\omega_0 = \frac{1}{\sqrt{LC}} = \frac{1}{\sqrt{1}} = 1$$

$$\alpha = \omega_0$$

This indicates a critically damped case.

$$i(t) = e^{-\alpha t}(k_1 + k_2 t) = e^{-t}(k_1 + k_2 t)$$

At $t = 0$, $i(0) = 0$

$$k_1 = 0$$

Also,

$$v_L(0^+) = L\frac{di}{dt}(0^+)$$

$$\frac{di}{dt}(0^+) = \frac{v_L(0^+)}{L} = -\frac{2}{1} = -2\ \text{A/s}$$

Differentiating the equation of $i(t)$ and putting the condition at $t = 0$,

$$\left.\frac{di}{dt}\right|_{t=0} = -k_1 + k_2 = -2$$

$$k_2 = -2$$

$$i(t) = -2t\,e^{-t} \qquad \text{for } t > 0$$

***Case III*** *When* $R = 2\ \Omega$, $L = 5\ H$, $C = 1\ F$

$$\alpha = \frac{R}{2L} = \frac{2}{10} = 0.2$$

$$\omega_0 = \frac{1}{\sqrt{LC}} = \frac{1}{\sqrt{5}} = 0.447$$

$$\alpha < \omega_0$$

This indicates an underdamped case.

$$i(t) = e^{-\alpha t}(B_1 \cos \omega_d t + B_2 \sin \omega_d t)$$

where

$$\omega_d = \sqrt{\omega_o^2 - \alpha^2} = \sqrt{(0.447)^2 - (0.2)^2} = 0.4$$

$$s_{1,2} = -\alpha \pm j\omega_d = -0.2 \pm j0.4$$

$$i(t) = e^{-0.2t}(B_1 \cos 0.4t + B_2 \sin 0.4t)$$

Applying the initial condition,

$$i(0^+) = 0$$

and

$$\frac{di}{dt}(0^+) = -\frac{v_L(0^+)}{L} = -\frac{2}{5}$$

$$B_1 = i(0) = 0$$

$$B_2 = -1$$

$$i(t) = -e^{-0.2t} \sin 0.4t \qquad \text{for } t > 0$$

# Theory Questions

**9.1** Explain why the current in inductor does not change in zero time. **[LO 9.1]** ●○○

**9.2** Explain why the voltage in capacitor does not change in zero time. **[LO 9.1]** ●○○

**9.3** Write a short note on the procedure employed to evaluate initial conditions. **[LO 9.1]** ○●○

**9.4** Explain steady-state or forced response. **[LO 9.1]** ●○○

**9.5** Explain the transient analysis of series *RL* circuit with dc excitation. **[LO 9.2]** ○●○

**9.6** How do you interpret time constant in transient analysis? **[LO 9.2]** ●○○

**9.7** Define the term time constant in *RL* circuit. **[LO 9.2]** ●○○

**9.8** Sketch the dc response of *RL* circuit and response curve. **[LO 9.2]** ●○○

**9.9** Draw the time response of inductor current in a series *RL* circuit excited by dc supply. **[LO 9.2]** ●○○

**9.10** Explain the transient analysis of series *RL* circuit with sinusoidal excitation. **[LO 9.3]** ○○●

**9.11** Explain the transient analysis of series *RC* circuit with dc excitation. Draw the voltage waveform across *R* & *C*. **[LO 9.4]** ○●○

**9.12** Define the term time constant in *RC* circuit. **[LO 9.4]** ●○○

**9.13** Sketch the dc response of *RC* circuit and response curve. **[LO 9.4]** ●○○

**9.14** Draw the time response of capacitor voltage in a series *RC* circuit excited by dc supply. **[LO 9.4]** ●○○

**9.15** Explain the transient analysis of series *RC* circuit with sinusoidal excitation. **[LO 9.5]** ○○●

**9.16** What is the condition for the response of a series *RLC* circuit excited by dc supply to have critically damped, overdamped and underdamped response? **[LO 9.6]** ●○○

**9.17** What is damping ratio? **[LO 9.6]** ●○○

**9.18** Obtain the expression for $i(t)$ in a series *RLC* circuit with dc excitation. Discuss the three cases of overdamped, underdamped and critically damped conditions. Sketch the voltage variation across each element. **[LO 9.6]** ○●○

**9.19** Derive the transient response of *RLC* series circuit with sinusoidal input. **[LO 9.7]** ○○●

# Practice Problems

**9.1** The switch in Fig. 9.186 is moved from position *a* to *b* at $t = 0$, the network having been in steady state in position *a*. Determine $i_1(0^+)$, $i_2(0^+)$, $i_3(0^+)$, $\frac{di_2}{dt}(0^+)$ and $\frac{di_3}{dt}(0^+)$. ○●○

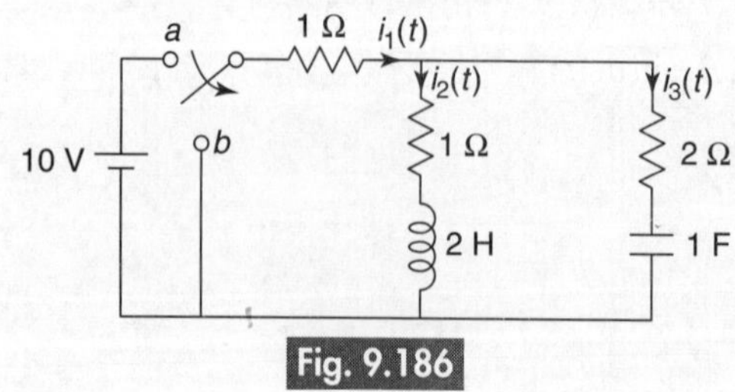


Fig. 9.186

**9.2** The switch *K* is closed at $t = 0$ in the network shown in Fig. 9.187. Determine $i(0^+)$, $\frac{di}{dt}(0^+)$ and $\frac{d^2i}{dt^2}(0^+)$. ○●○

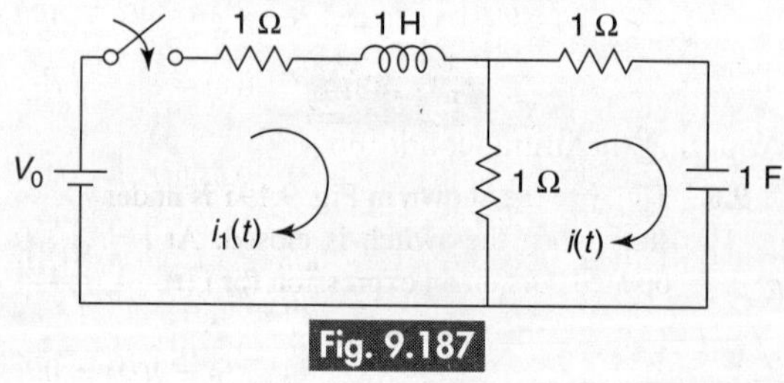


Fig. 9.187

**9.3** In the network of Fig. 9.188, the switch $K$ is closed at $t = 0$. At $t = 0^-$, all capacitor voltages and inductor currents are zero. Find

$v_1, \frac{dv_1}{dt}, v_2, \frac{dv_2}{dt}, v_3$ and $\frac{dv_3}{dt}$ at $t = 0^+$. ○○●

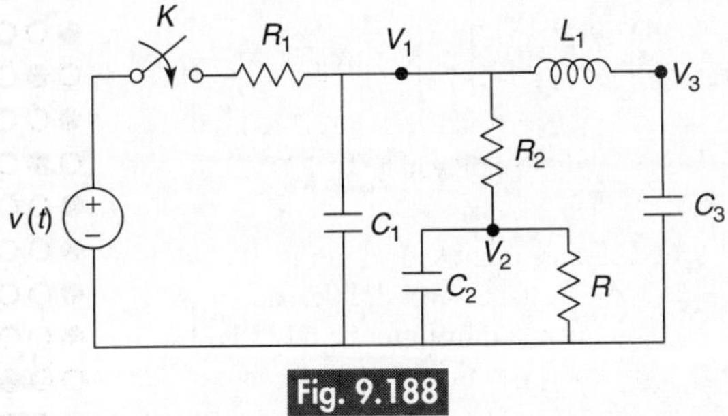


Fig. 9.188

**9.4** In the network at Fig. 9.189, the capacitor $C_1$ is charged to voltage 1000 V and the switch $K$ is closed at $t = 0$. Find $\frac{d^2 i_2}{dt^2}$ at $t = 0^+$. ○●○

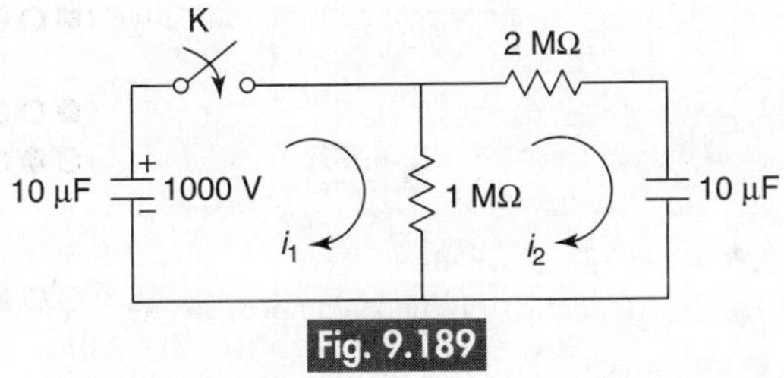


Fig. 9.189

**9.5** In the network shown in Fig. 9.190, switch is closed at $t = 0$. Obtain the current $i_2(t)$. ○●○

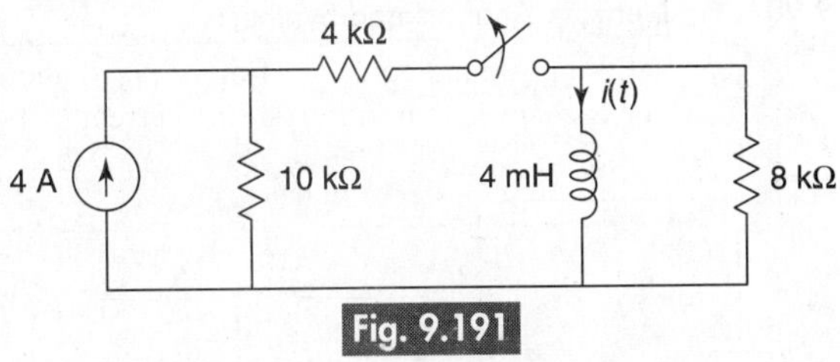


Fig. 9.190

**9.6** The network shown in Fig. 9.191 is under steady-state when the switch is closed. At $t = 0$, it is opened. Obtain an expression for $i(t)$. ○●○

Fig. 9.191

**9.7** The switch in Fig. 9.192 is open for a long time and closes at $t = 0$. Determine $i(t)$ for $t > 0$. ○●○

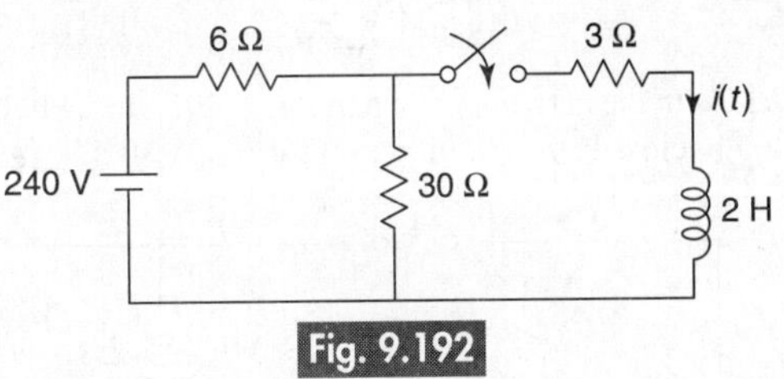


Fig. 9.192

**9.8** In the network shown in Fig. 9.193, the steady state is reached with the switch open. At $t = 0$, the switch is closed. Find $v_C(t)$ for $t > 0$. ○●○

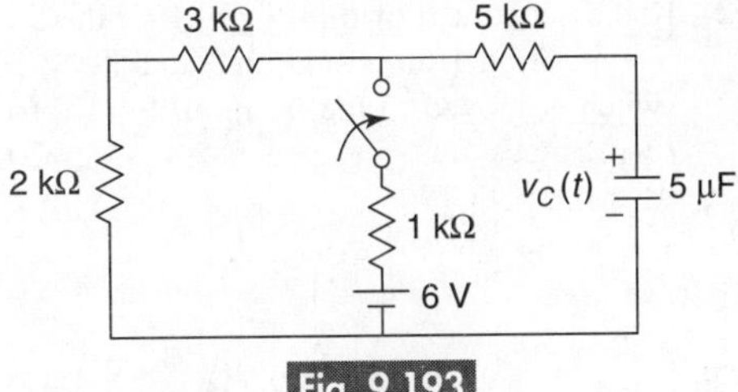


Fig. 9.193

**9.9** The circuit shown in Fig. 9.194 has acquired steady state before switching at $t = 0$. ○●○

(i) Obtain $v_C(0^+)$, $v_C(0^-)$, $i(0^+)$ and $i(0^-)$.

(ii) Obtain time constant for $t > 0$.

(iii) Find current $i(t)$ for $t > 0$.

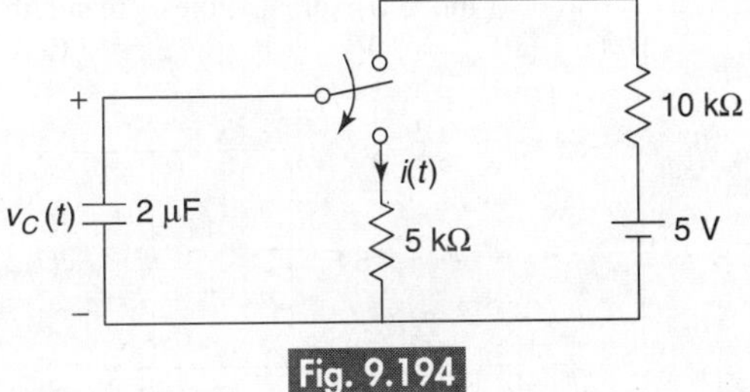


Fig. 9.194

**9.10** In the network shown in Fig. 9.195, the switch is initially at position 1 for a long time. At $t = 0$, the switch is changed to position 2. Find current $i(t)$ for $t > 0$.

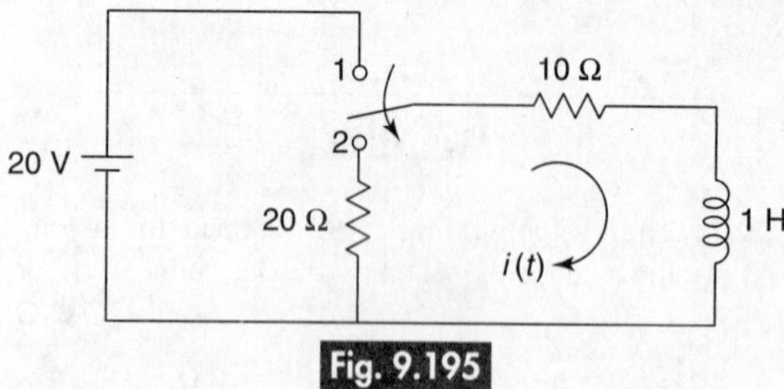


Fig. 9.195

**9.11** In the network shown in Fig. 9.196, the switch is closed at $t = 0$. Find $v(t)$ for $t > 0$.

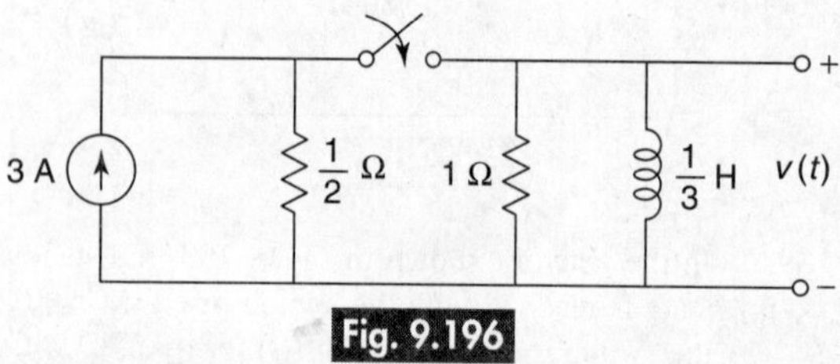


Fig. 9.196

**9.12** In the network shown in Fig. 9.197, the switch is in position 1 for a long time and at $t = 0$, the switch is moved to the position. Find $v(t)$ for $t > 0$.

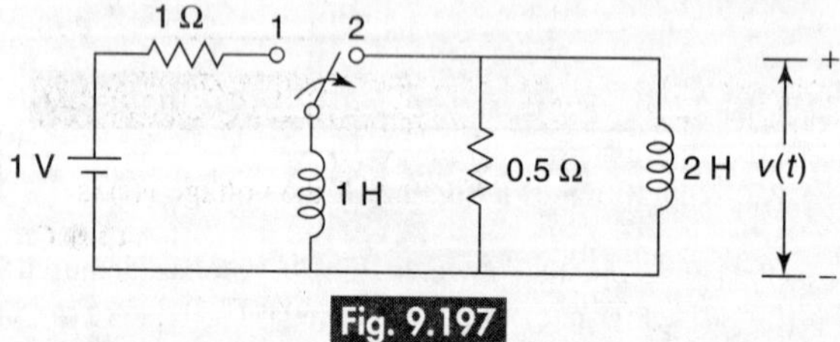


Fig. 9.197

**9.13** In Fig. 9.198, the switch is open until time $t = 100$ seconds and is closed for all times thereafter. Find $v(t)$ for all times greater than 100 if $v(100) = -3$ V.

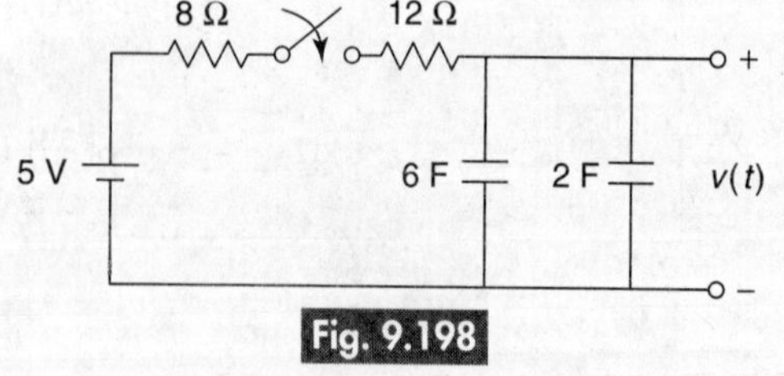


Fig. 9.198

**9.14** A series *RL* circuit shown in Fig. 9.199 has a constant voltage *V* applied at $t = 0$. At what time does $v_R = v_L$.

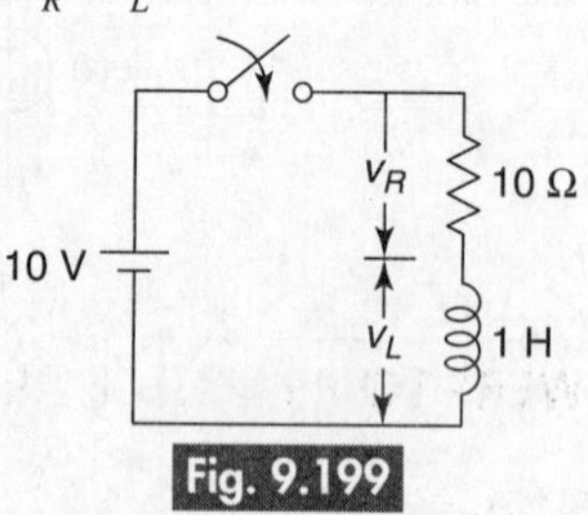


Fig. 9.199

**9.15** In the circuit shown in Fig. 9.200, at time $t = 0$, the voltage across the capacitor is zero and the switch is moved to the position *y*. The switch is kept at position *y* for 20 seconds and then moved to position *z* and kept in that position thereafter. Find the voltage across the capacitor at $t = 30$ seconds.

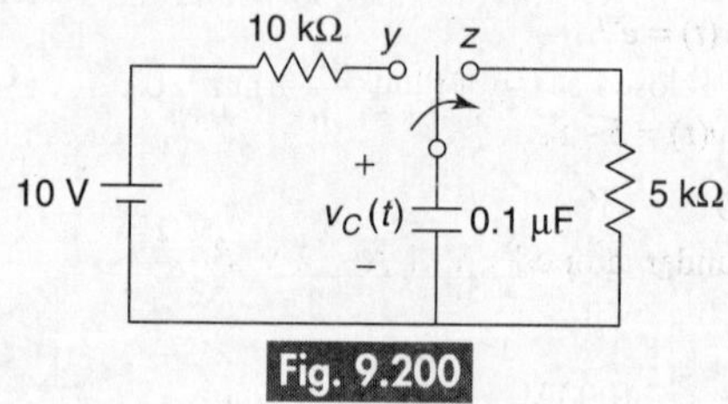


Fig. 9.200

**9.16** Determine whether *RLC* series circuit shown in Fig. 9.201 is underdamped, overdamped or critically damped. Also, find $v_L(0^+)$, $\frac{di}{dt}(0^+)$ and $i(\infty)$.

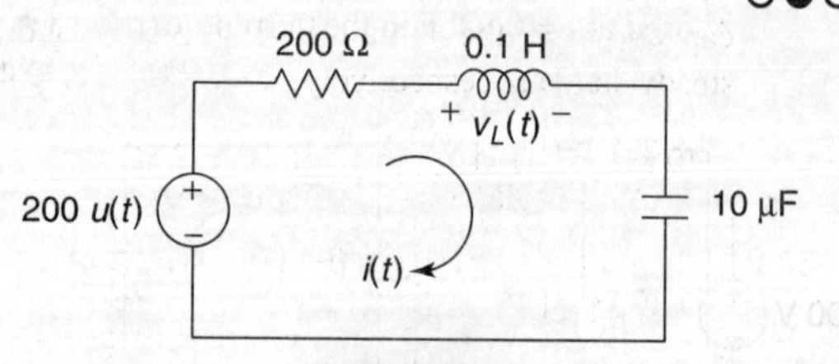


Fig. 9.201

**9.17** Determine whether *RLC* circuit of Fig. 9.202 is underdamped, overdamped or critically damped. Also, find $v_L(0^+)$, $\frac{di}{dt}(0^+)$, $\frac{d^2v}{dt^2}(0^+)$ if $v(t) = u(t)$.

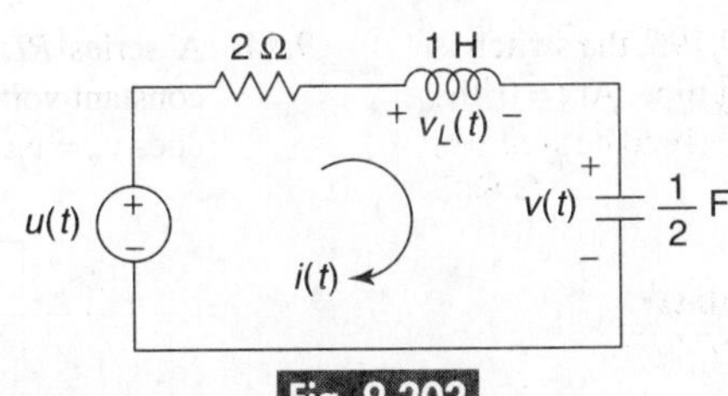


Fig. 9.202

## ANSWERS TO PRACTICE PROBLEMS

**9.1** 1.66 A, 5 A, −3.33 A, −3.33 A/s, 2.22 A/s

**9.2** $0, \frac{1}{2}V_0, -V_0$

**9.3** $0, \frac{1}{C}\frac{v(0^+)}{R_1}, 0, 0, 0, 0$

**9.4** $\frac{17}{400000}$ A/s$^2$

**9.5** $i_2(t) = 5\,e^{-100000t}$

**9.6** $i(t) = 2.857\,e^{-2\times10^6\,t}$

**9.7** $i(t) = 25(1 - e^{-4t})$

**9.8** $v_C(t) = 5e^{-20t}$

**9.9** (i) 5 V, 5 V, 1 mA, 0, (ii) 0.01 s, (iii) $e^{-100\,t}$ mA

**9.10** $i\,(t) = 2\,e^{-30t}$

**9.11** $v(t) = e^{-t}$

**9.12** $v\,(t) = -0.5\,e^{-\frac{3}{4}t}$

**9.13** $v(t) = 5 - 8e^{-\frac{(t-100)}{160}}$

**9.14** 0.0693 s

**9.15** 0

**9.16** critically damped, 200 V, 2000 A/s, 0

**9.17** underdamped 1 V, 1 A/s, 2 V/s$^2$

# Objective-Type Questions

## From GATE and Other Competitive Examinations

**9.1** The voltages $v_{C_1}, v_{C_2}$ and $v_{C_3}$ across the capacitors in the circuit in Fig. 9.203 under steady state are respectively ○○●

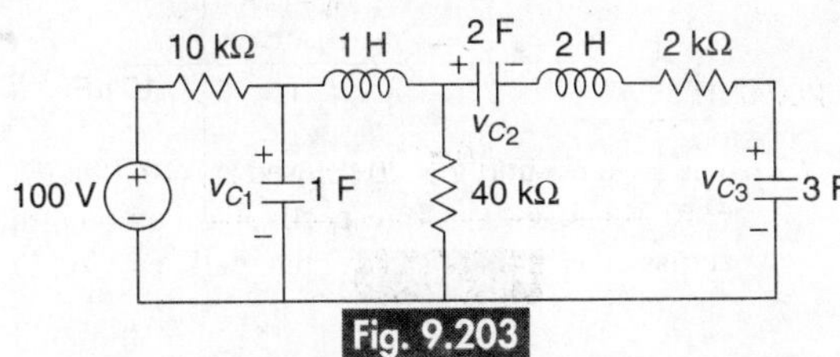


Fig. 9.203

(a) 80 V, 32 V, 48 V (b) 80 V, 48 V, 32 V
(c) 20 V, 8 V, 12 V (d) 20 V, 12 V, 8 V

**9.2** In the circuit of Fig. 9.204, the voltage $v(t)$ is ○●○

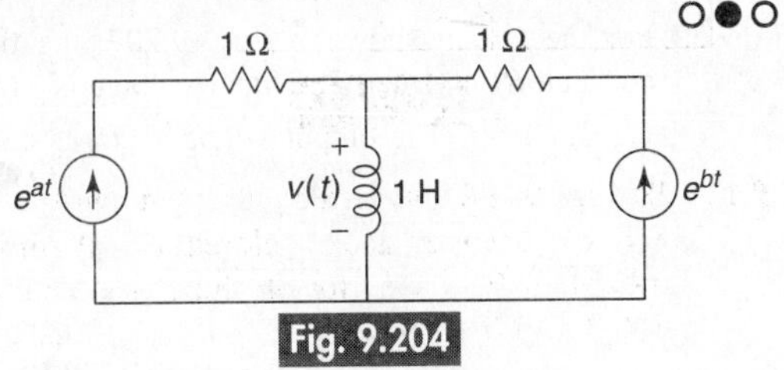


Fig. 9.204

(a) $e^{at} - e^{bt}$ (b) $e^{at} + e^{bt}$
(c) $ae^{dt} - be^{bt}$ (d) $ae^{at} + be^{bt}$

**9.3** The differential equation for the current $i(t)$ in the circuit of Fig. 9.205 is ○●○

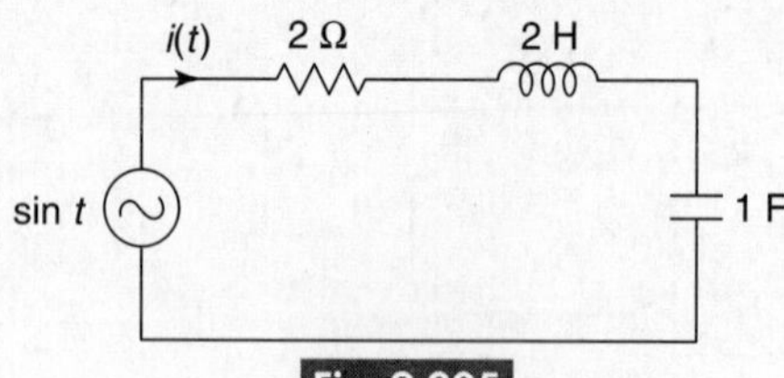


Fig. 9.205

(a) $2\dfrac{d^2i}{dt^2}+2\dfrac{di}{dt}+i(t)=\sin t$

(b) $\dfrac{d^2i}{dt^2}+2\dfrac{di}{dt}+2i(t)=\cos t$

(c) $2\dfrac{d^2i}{dt^2}+2\dfrac{di}{dt}+i(t)=\cos t$

(d) $\dfrac{d^2i}{dt^2}+2\dfrac{di}{dt}+2i(t)=\sin t$

**9.4** At $t = 0^+$, the current $i_1$ in Fig. 9.206 is ○●○

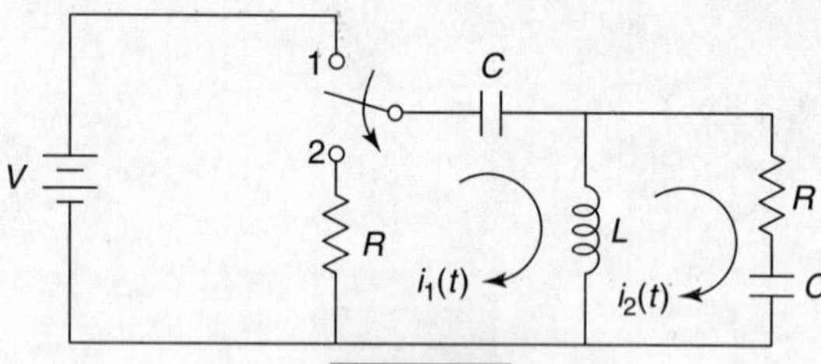


Fig. 9.206

(a) $-\dfrac{V}{2R}$ (b) $-\dfrac{V}{R}$

(c) $-\dfrac{V}{4R}$ (d) zero

**9.5** For the circuit shown in Fig. 9.207, the time constant $RC = 1$ ms. The input voltage is $v_i(t) = \sqrt{2}\sin 10^3 t$. The output voltage $v_0(t)$ is equal to ○●○

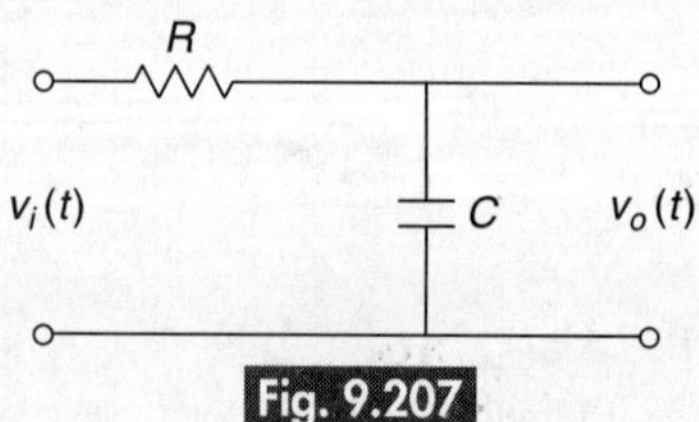


Fig. 9.207

(a) $\sin(10^3 - 45°)$ (b) $\sin(10^3 t + 45°)$
(c) $\sin(10^3 t - 53)$ (d) $\sin(10^3 t + 53°)$

**9.6** For the *RL* circuit shown in Fig. 9.208, the input voltage $v_i(t) = 1$ V. The current $i(t)$ is ○●○

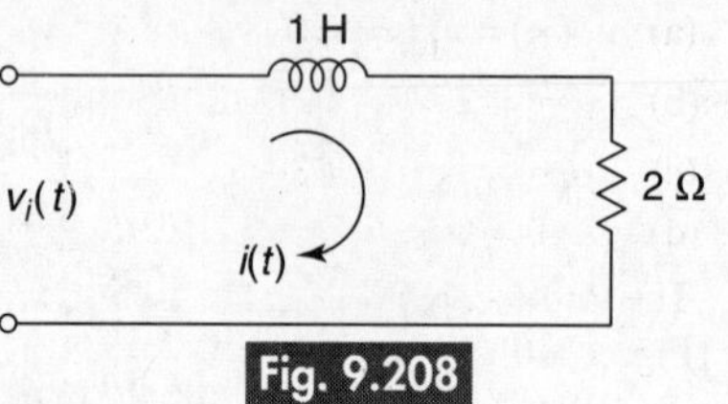


Fig. 9.208

(a)

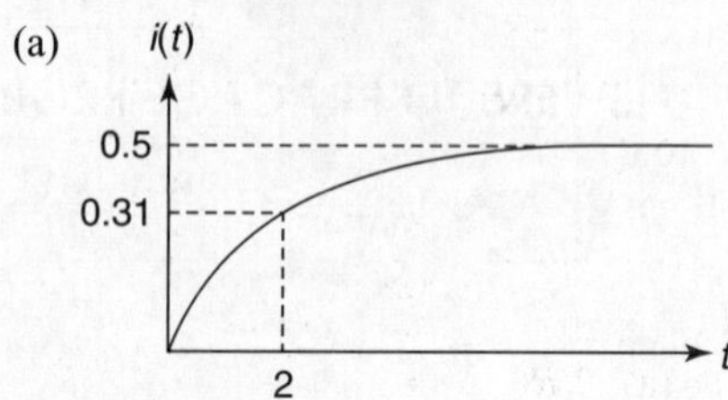


(b)

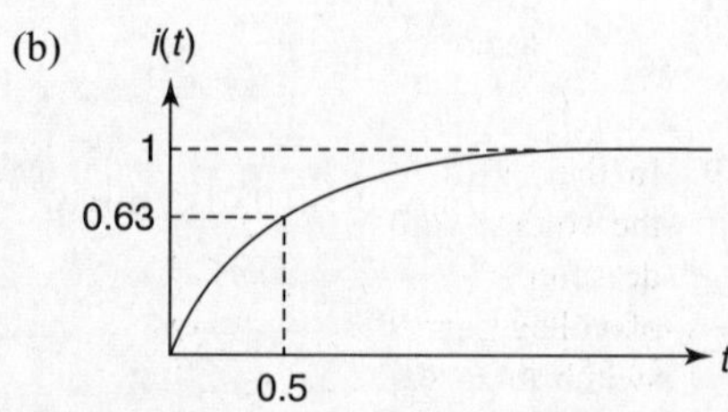


(c)

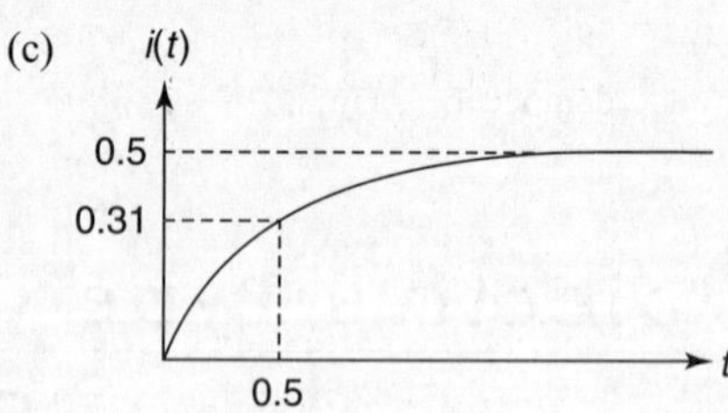


(d)

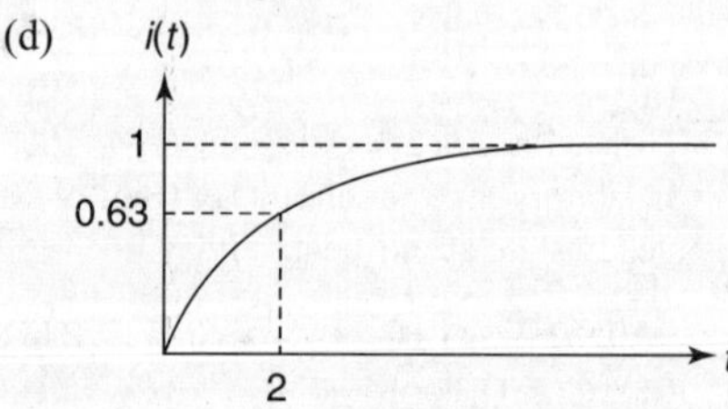


**9.7** The switch *S* in Fig. 9.209 closed at $t = 0$. If $v_2(0) = 10$ V and $v_1(0) = 0$ respectively, the voltages across capacitors in steady state will be ○●○

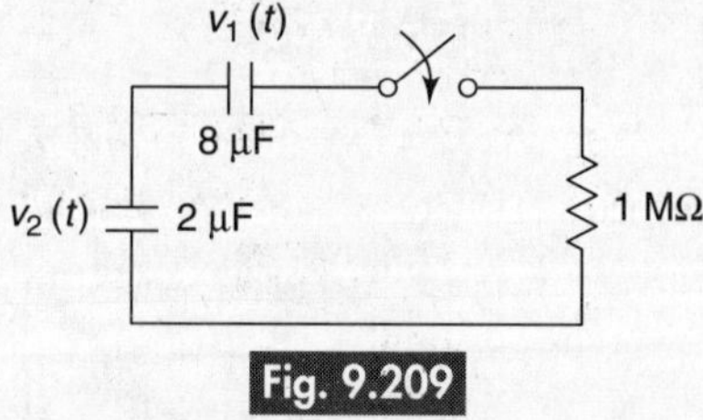


Fig. 9.209

(a) $v_2(\infty) = v_1(\infty) = 0$
(b) $v_2(\infty) = 2$ V, $v_1(\infty) = 8$ V
(c) $v_2(\infty) = v_1(\infty) = 8$ V
(d) $v_2(\infty) = 8$ V, $v_1(\infty) = 2$ V

**9.8** The time constant of the network shown in Fig. 9.210 is ○●○

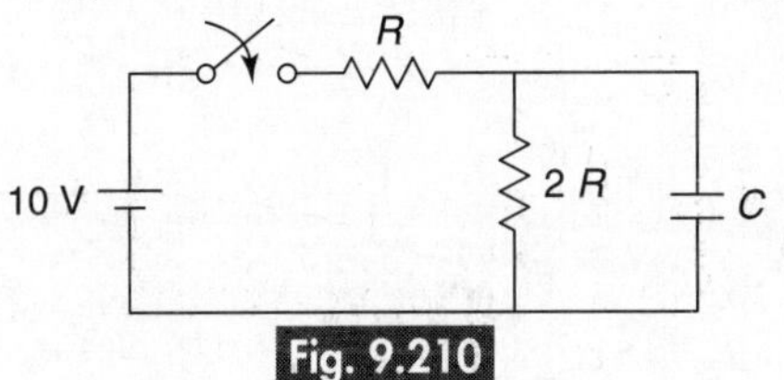


Fig. 9.210

(a) 2 *RC* (b) 3 *RC*
(c) $\frac{1}{2}RC$ (d) $\frac{2}{3}RC$

**9.9** In the series *RC* circuit shown in Fig. 9.211, the voltage across *C* starts increasing when the dc source is switched on. The rate of increase of voltage across *C* at the instant just after the switch is closed i.e., at $t = 0^+$ will be ○●○

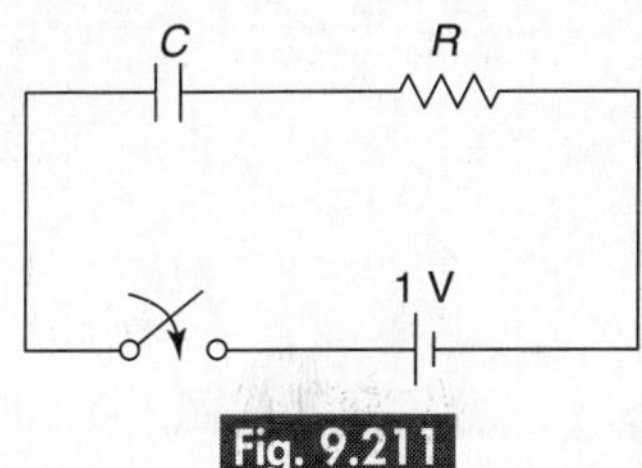


Fig. 9.211

(a) zero (b) infinity
(c) *RC* (d) $\frac{1}{RC}$

**9.10** The $v - i$ characteristic as seen from the terminal pair ($A$ – $B$) of the network of Fig. 9.212 is shown in Fig. 9.213. If an inductance of value 6 mH is connected across the terminal pair, the time constant of the system will be ○○●

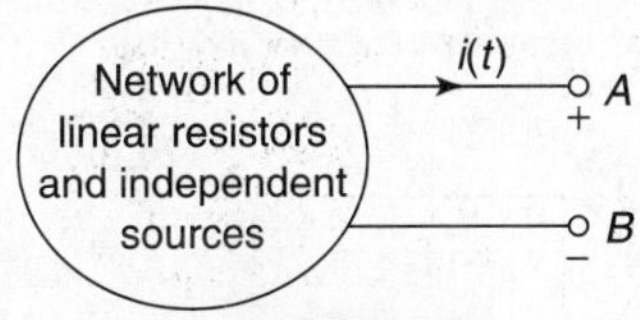


Fig. 9.212

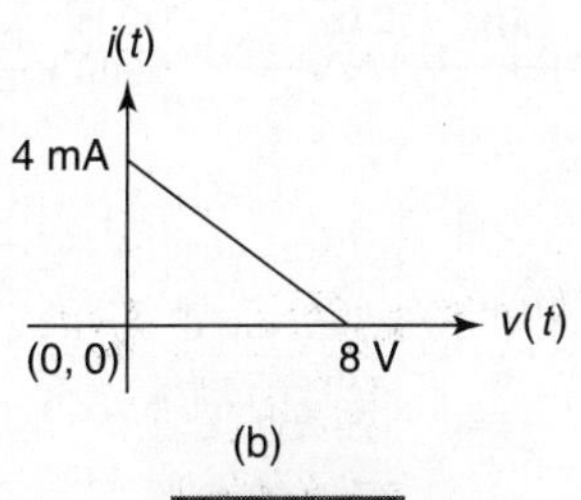


Fig. 9.213

(a) 3 μs (b) 12 s
(c) 32 s (d) unknown, unless actual network is specified

**9.11** In the network shown in Fig. 9.214, the circuit was initially in the steady-state condition with the switch *K* closed. At the instant when the switch is opened, the rate of decay of current through inductance will be ○●○

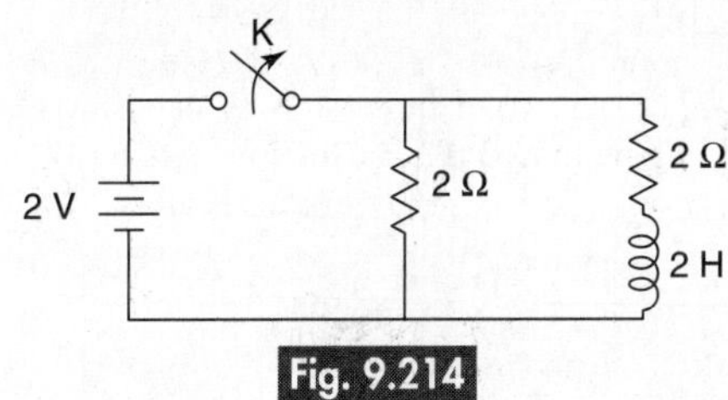


Fig. 9.214

(a) zero (b) 0.5 A/s
(c) 1 A/s (d) 2 A/s

**9.12** A step function voltage is applied to an *RLC* series circuit having $R = 2\ \Omega$, $L = 1$ H and $C = 1$ F. The transient current response of the circuit would be ○●○

(a) overdamped (b) critically damped
(c) underdamped (d) none of these

**9.13** Assume that the switch *S* is in position 1 for a long time and thrown to position 2 at $t = 0$. At $t = 0^+$, the current $i_1$ is ○●○

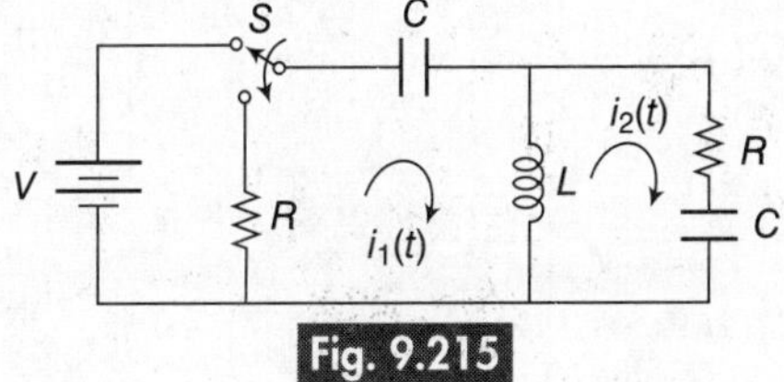


Fig. 9.215

(a) $-\frac{V}{2R}$ (b) $-\frac{V}{R}$

(c) $-\frac{V}{4R}$ (d) zero

**9.14** In the following circuit, the switch $S$ is closed at $t = 0$. The rate of change of current $\frac{di}{dt}(0^+)$ is given by

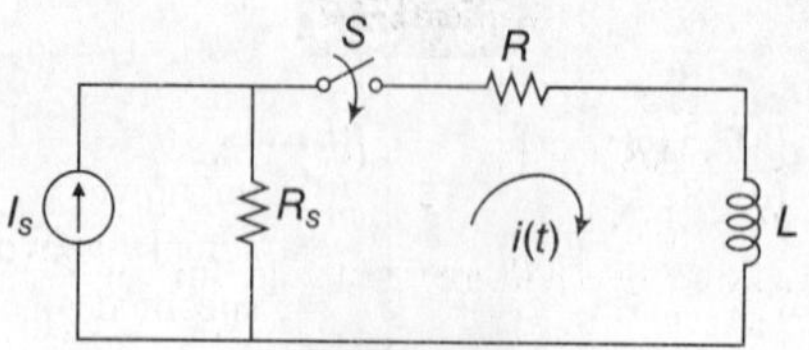


Fig. 9.216

(a) 0 (b) $\frac{R_s I_s}{L}$

(c) $\frac{(R+R_s)I_s}{L}$ (d) ∞

**9.15** The switch $S$ in the circuit was on position '$a$' for a long time and is moved to position '$b$' at time $t = 0$. The current $i(t)$ for $t > 0$ is given by

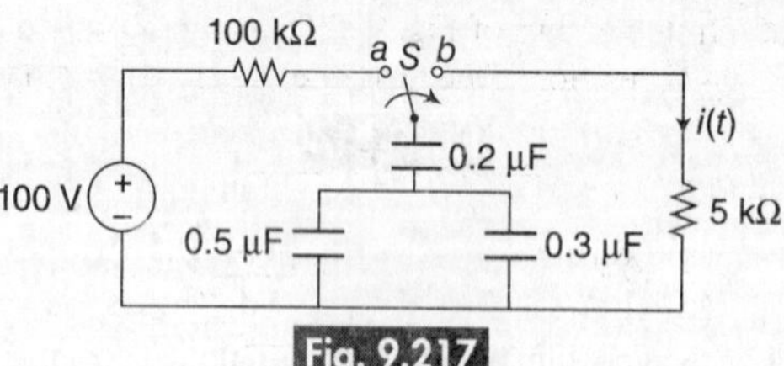


Fig. 9.217

(a) $0.2\,e^{-125t}$ mA (b) $20\,e^{-1250t}$ mA

(c) $0.2\,e^{-1250t}$ mA (d) $20\,e^{-1000t}$ mA

**9.16** In the circuit shown in Fig. 9.218, the switch $S$ is open for a long time and is closed at $t = 0$. The current $i(t)$ for $t \geq 0$ is

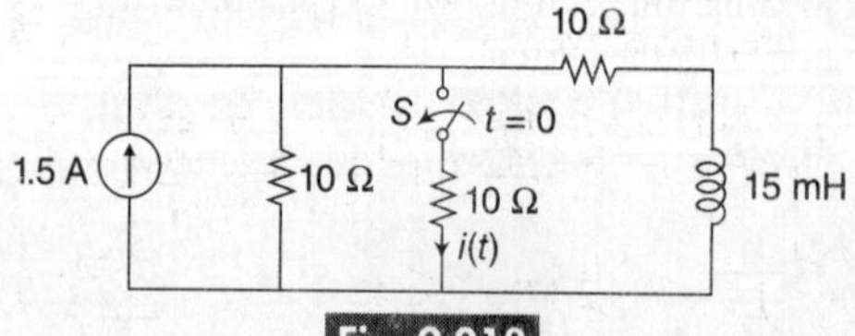


Fig. 9.218

(a) $0.5 - 0.125\,e^{-1000t}$ (b) $1.5 - 0.125\,e^{-1000t}$

(c) $0.5 - 0.5\,e^{-1000t}$ (d) $0.375\,e^{-1000t}$

**9.17** In the circuit shown in Fig. 9.219, the initial charge on the capacitor is 2.5 mC with the voltage polarity as indicated. The switch is closed at time $t = 0$. The current $i(t)$ at a time $t$ after the switch is closed is

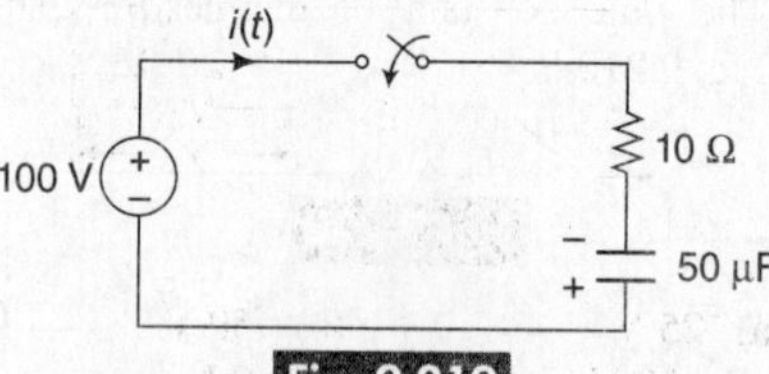


Fig. 9.219

(a) $15\,e^{-2\times10^3 t}$ A (b) $5\,e^{-2\times10^3 t}$ A

(c) $10\,e^{-2\times10^3 t}$ A (d) $-5\,e^{-2\times10^3 t}$ A

**9.18** In the Fig. 9.220, the ideal switch has been opened for a long time.

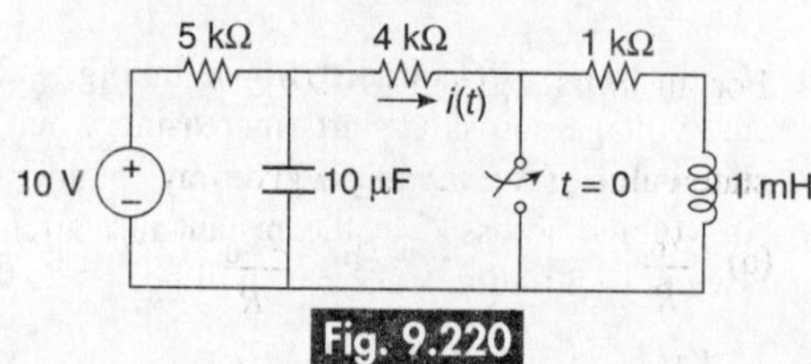


Fig. 9.220

If it is closed at $t = 0$ then the magnitude of the current (in mA) through the 4 kΩ resistor at $t = 0^+$ is

(a) 1.25 (b) 2.5

(c) 2 (d) 1

**9.19** In the circuit shown in Fig. 9.221, switch is closed at $t = 0$. Assuming zero initial conditions, the value at $v_c(t)$ (in volts) at $t = 1$ second is

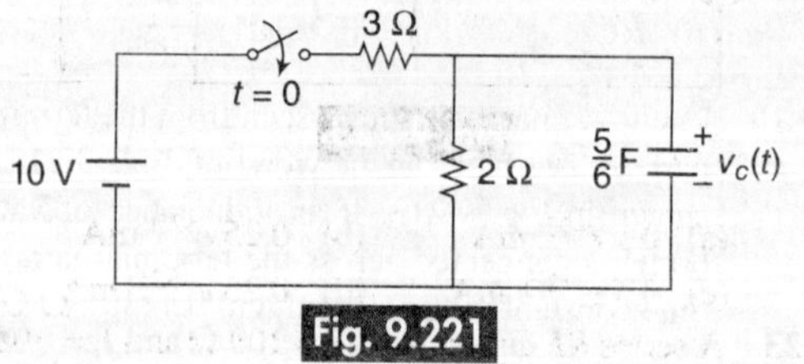


Fig. 9.221

(a) 0.25 (b) 2.528

(c) 2 (d) 25

**9.20** In the Fig. 9.222, the switch was closed for a long time before opening at $t = 0$. The voltage $v_x$ at $t = 0^+$

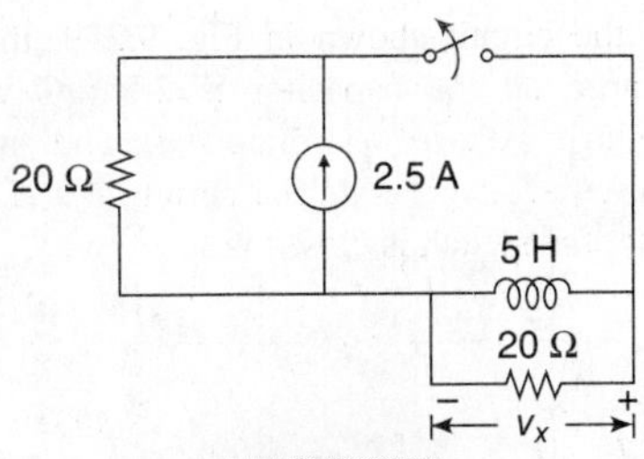

Fig. 9.222

(a) 25 V (b) 50 V
(c) –50 V (d) 0 V

**9.21** The time-domain behaviour of an *RL* circuit is represented by

$$L\frac{di}{dt}+Ri=V_o\left(1+Be^{-\frac{R}{L}t}\sin t\right)$$

For an initial current of $i(0)=\frac{V_0}{R}$, the steady state value of the current is given by ○○●

(a) $\frac{V_0}{R}$ (b) $\frac{2V_0}{R}$

(c) $\frac{V_0}{R}(1+B)$ (d) $\frac{2V_0}{R}(1+B)$

**9.22** In the circuit shown in Fig. 9.223, $v_c(t)$ is 0 volt at $t = 0$ second. For $t > 0$, the capacitor current $i_c(t)$ where $t$ is in seconds is given by ○●○

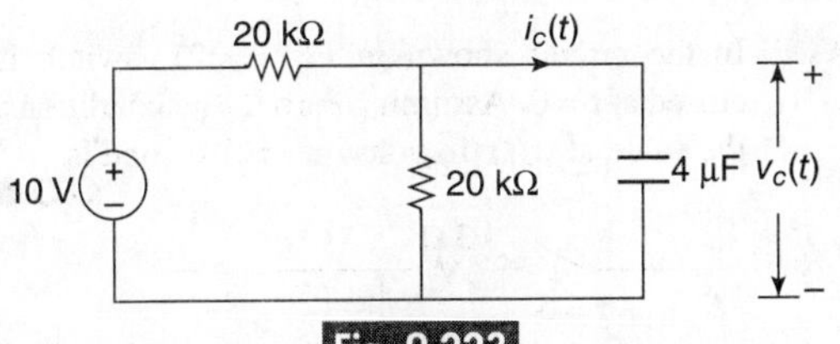

Fig. 9.223

(a) $0.5\,e^{-25t}$ mA (b) $0.25\,e^{-25t}$ mA
(c) $0.5\,e^{-12.5t}$ mA (d) $0.25\,e^{-6.25t}$ mA

**9.23** A series *RL* circuit with $R = 100\ \Omega$ and $L = 50$ H is supplied to a dc source of 100 V. The time taken for the current to rise 70% of its steady-state value is ○○●

(a) 0.3 s (b) 0.6 s
(c) 2.4 s (d) 70% of time required to reach steady state

**9.24** In the network shown in Fig. 9.224, the circuit was initially in the steady state with the switch closed. At the instant when the switch is opened, the rate of decay of current through the inductor will be ○●○

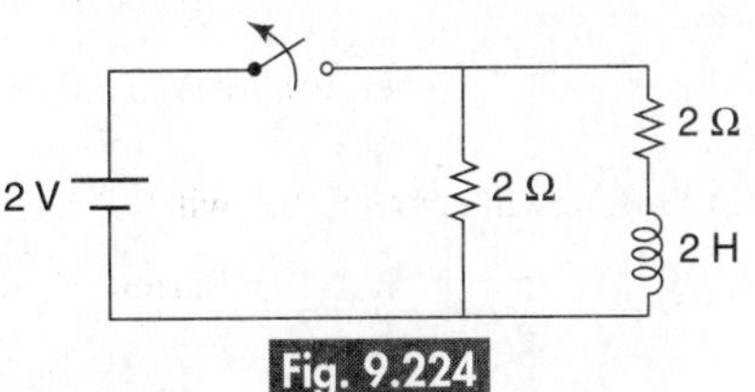

Fig. 9.224

(a) zero (b) 0.5 A/s
(c) 1 A/s (d) 2 A/s

**9.25** In the given circuit shown in Fig. 9.225, the value of *R* that will give critical damping is ○●○

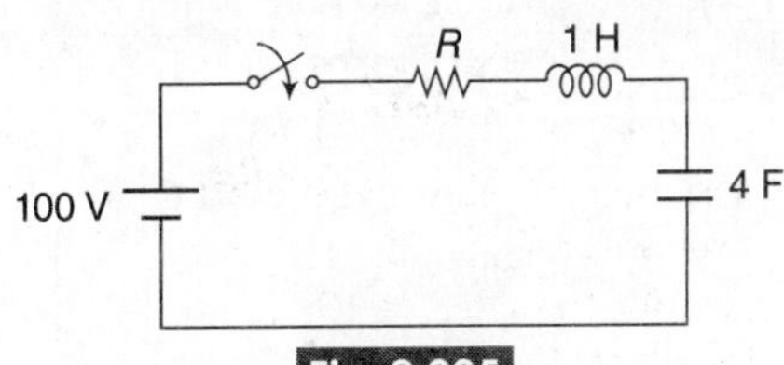

Fig. 9.225

(a) 1 Ω (b) 2 Ω
(c) 4 Ω (d) 10 Ω

**9.26** In the circuit of Fig. 9.226, energy absorbed by 4 Ω resistor in the time interval (0, ∞) is ○●○

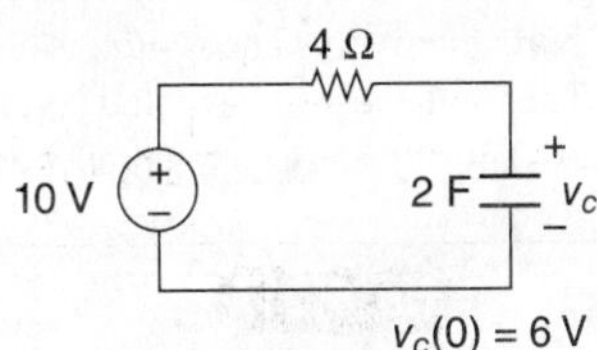

Fig. 9.226

(a) 36 J (b) 16 J
(c) 256 J (d) none of these

**9.27** The voltage $v_{C_1}, v_{C_2}$ and $v_{C_3}$ across the capacitors in the Fig. 9.227, under steady state are, respectively ○●○

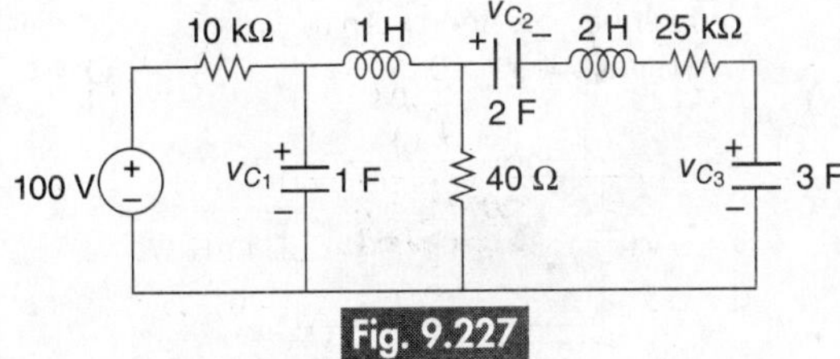

Fig. 9.227

(a) 80 V, 32 V, 48 V (b) 80 V, 48 V, 32 V

(c) 20 V, 8 V, 12 V (d) 20 V, 12 V, 8 V

**9.28** In the circuit shown in Fig. 9.228, the switch SW is thrown from position *A* to position *B* at time $t = 0$. The energy (in μJ) taken from 3 V source to charge to 0.1 μF capacitor from 0 V to 3 V is ○●○

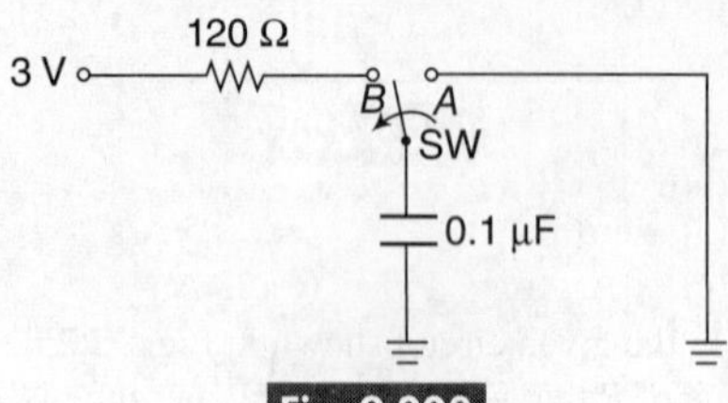


Fig. 9.228

(a) 0.3 (b) 0.45

(c) 0.9 (d) 3

**9.29** The damping ratio of a series *RLC* circuit can be expressed as ○●○

(a) $\dfrac{R^2C}{2L}$ (b) $\dfrac{2L}{R^2C}$

(c) $\dfrac{R}{2}\sqrt{\dfrac{C}{L}}$ (d) $\dfrac{2}{R}\sqrt{\dfrac{L}{C}}$

**9.30** In the circuit shown in Fig. 9.229, the initial voltages across the capacitors $C_1$ and $C_2$ are 1 V and 3 V respectively. The switch is closed at time $t = 0$. The total energy dissipated (in Joules) in the resistor *R* until steady state is reached is ○●○

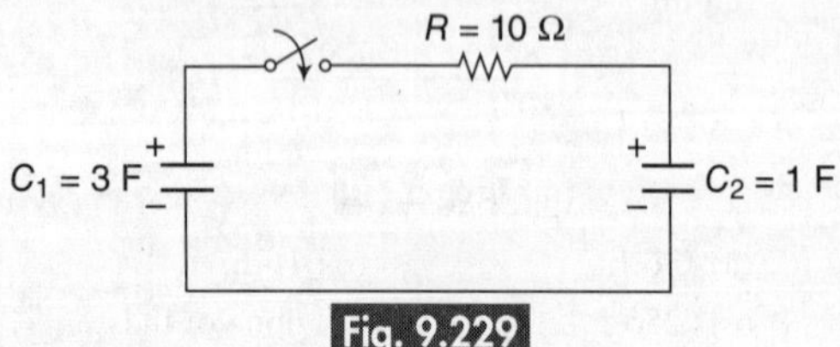


Fig. 9.229

(a) 1 (b) 1.5

(c) 3 (d) 2

**9.31** In Fig. 9.230, the capacitor is initially uncharged. Which one the following describes the current *i*(*t*) (in mA) for $t > 0$? ○●○

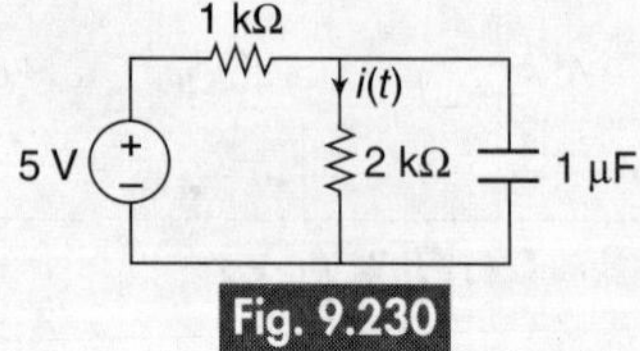


Fig. 9.230

(a) $\dfrac{5}{3}\left(1 - e^{-\frac{t}{\tau}}\right), \tau = \dfrac{2}{3}$ ms

(b) $\dfrac{5}{2}\left(1 - e^{-\frac{t}{\tau}}\right), \tau = \dfrac{2}{3}$ ms

(c) $\dfrac{5}{3}\left(1 - e^{-\frac{t}{\tau}}\right), \tau = 3$ ms

(d) $\dfrac{5}{2}\left(1 - e^{-\frac{t}{\tau}}\right), \tau = 3$ ms

**9.32** The switch has been in position 1 for a long time and abruptly changes to position 2 at $t = 0$.

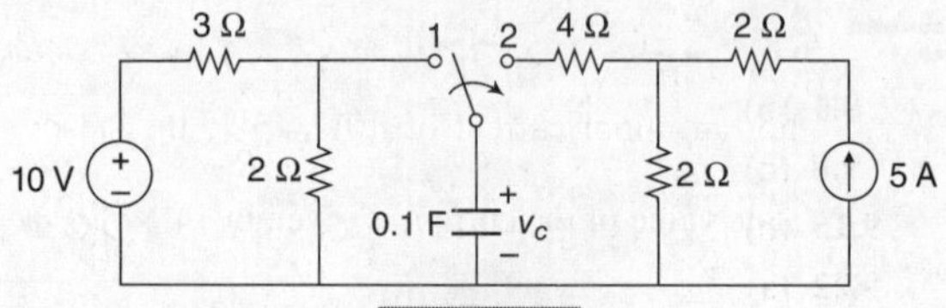


Fig. 9.231

If time *t* is in seconds, the capacitor voltage $v_c$ (in volts) for $t > 0$ is given by ○●○

(a) $4\left(1 - e^{-\frac{t}{0.5}}\right)$ (b) $10 - 6e^{-\frac{t}{0.5}}$

(c) $4\left(1 - e^{-\frac{t}{0.6}}\right)$ (d) $10 - 6e^{-\frac{t}{0.6}}$

**9.33** In the circuit shown in Fig. 9.232, the voltage $v_{in}(t)$ is described by

$$v_{in} = \begin{cases} 0 & \text{for } t < 0 \\ 15\text{ V} & \text{for } t \geq 0 \end{cases}$$

where *t* is in seconds. The time (in seconds) in which the current *i* in the circuit will reach the value 2 amperes is ○○●

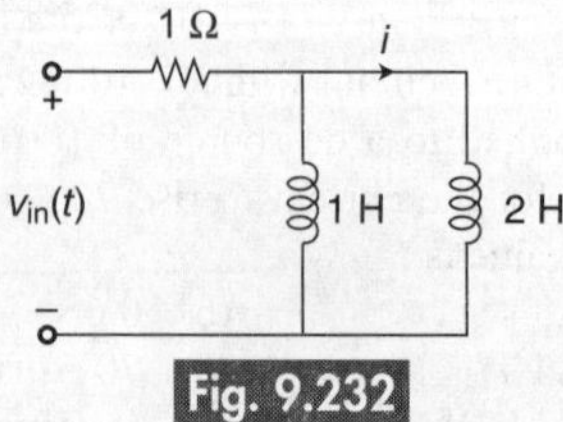


Fig. 9.232

(a) 0.4 (b) 0.34

(c) 0.1 (d) 1

**9.34** The switch in the circuit shown in Fig. 9.233 was open for a long time and is closed at $t = 0$. The current $i(t)$ (in amperes) at $t = 0.5$ second is

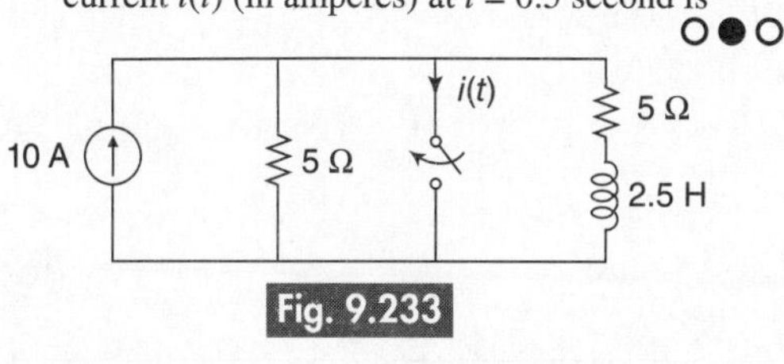


Fig. 9.233

(a) 8.16 (b) 9
(c) 5 (d) 12

**9.35** For the circuit shown in Fig. 9.234, the magnitude of the loop current (in amperes) 0.5 second after closing the switch is

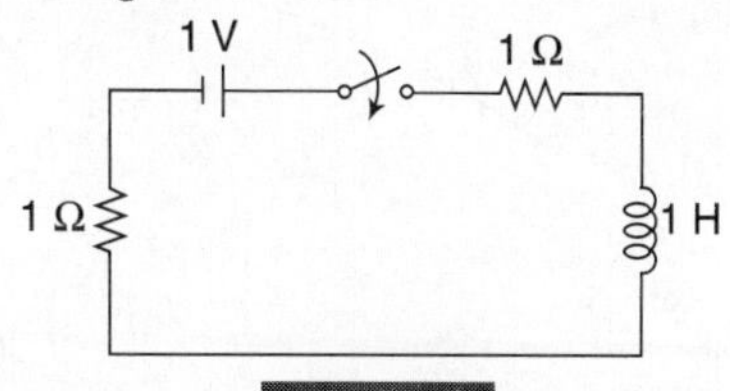


Fig. 9.234

(a) 0.316 (b) 0.42
(c) 0.5 (d) 0.6

## ANSWERS TO OBJECTIVE-TYPE QUESTIONS

| | | | | | | |
|---|---|---|---|---|---|---|
| **9.1** (b) | **9.2** (d) | **9.3** (c) | **9.4** (d) | **9.5** (a) | **9.6** (b) | **9.7** (d) |
| **9.8** (d) | **9.9** (d) | **9.10** (a) | **9.11** (d) | **9.12** (b) | **9.13** (a) | **9.14** (b) |
| **9.15** (b) | **9.16** (a) | **9.17** (a) | **9.18** (a) | **9.19** (b) | **9.20** (c) | **9.21** (a) |
| **9.22** (a) | **9.23** (b) | **9.24** (d) | **9.25** (a) | **9.26** (b) | **9.27** (b) | **9.28** (b) |
| **9.29** (c) | **9.30** (b) | **9.31** (a) | **9.32** (d) | **9.33** (b) | **9.34** (a) | **9.35** (a) |

# LTspice Section

## EXAMPLE 9.1

*In the network of Fig. 9.235, the switch is moved from 1 to 2 at t = 0. Sketch i(t) for t > 0.*

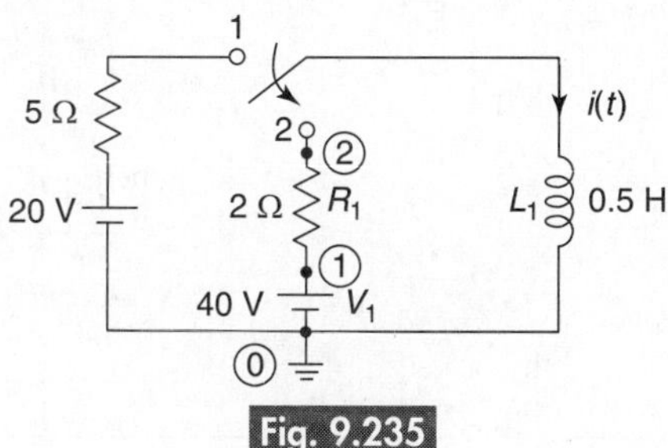


Fig. 9.235

**Solution**

```
*Plotting of i(t)

V1 1 0 40
R1 1 2 2
L1 2 0 0.5
.IC I(L1) 4
.TRAN 0 1.5
.PROBE
.END
```

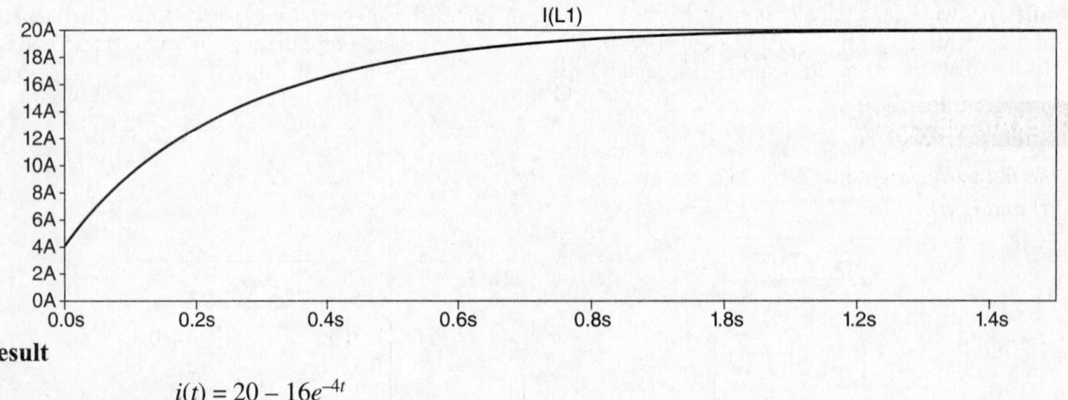


**Result**

$$i(t) = 20 - 16e^{-4t}$$

## EXAMPLE 9.2

*In Fig. 9.236, the switch is closed at t = 0. Sketch i(t) for t > 0.*

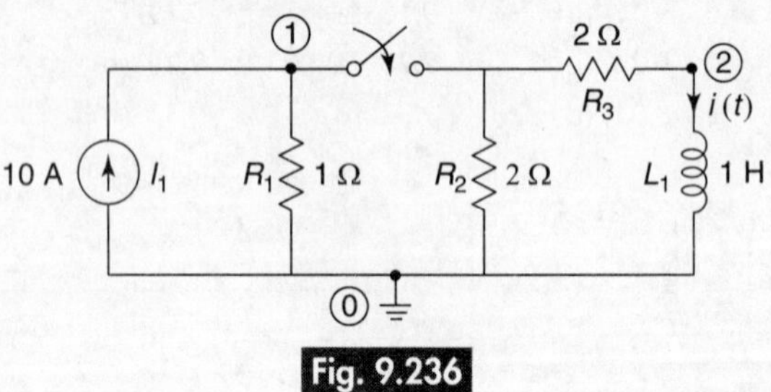


Fig. 9.236

**Solution**

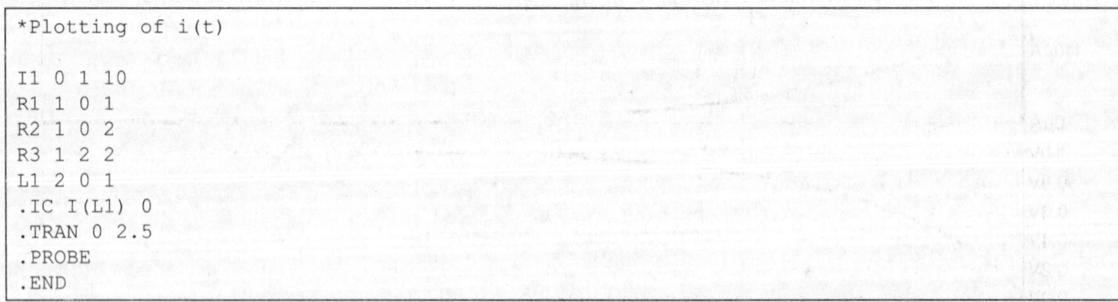

```
*Plotting of i(t)

I1 0 1 10
R1 1 0 1
R2 1 0 2
R3 1 2 2
L1 2 0 1
.IC I(L1) 0
.TRAN 0 2.5
.PROBE
.END
```

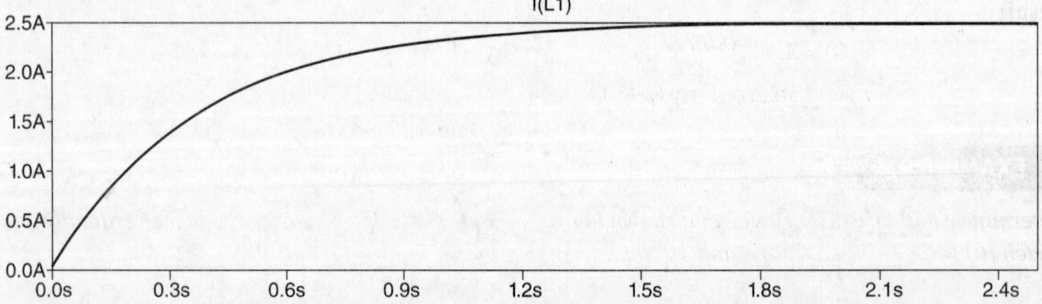

**Result**

$$i(t) = 2.5(1 - e^{-2.67t})$$

## EXAMPLE 9.3

*In the network shown in Fig. 9.237, the switch closes at t = 0. The capacitor is initially uncharged. Sketch $v_C(t)$ and $i_C(t)$.*

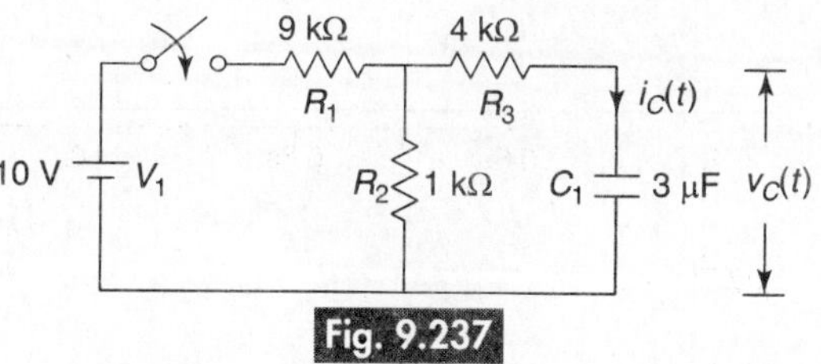


Fig. 9.237

**Solution**

```
*Plotting of vc(t) and ic(t)

V1 1 0 10
R1 1 2 9K
R2 2 0 1K
R3 2 3 4K
C1 3 0 3U
.IC V(3) 0
.TRAN 100M
.PROBE
.END
```

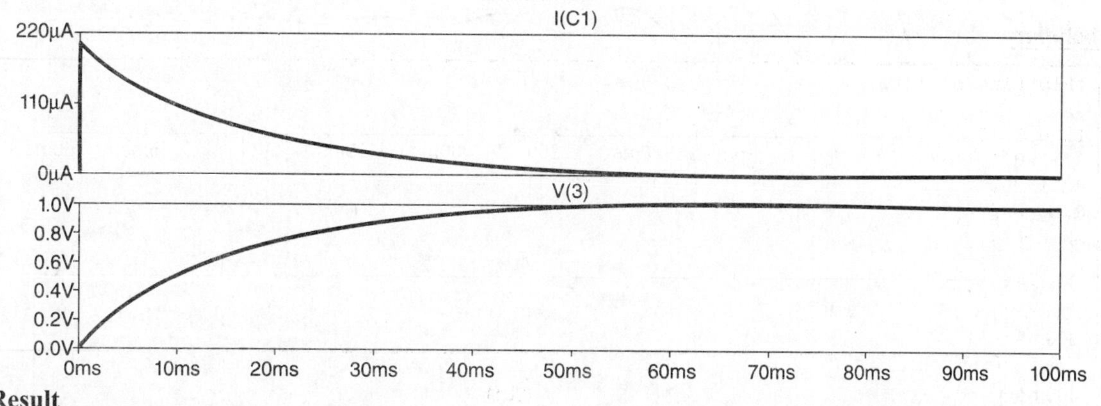


**Result**

$$v_C(t) = 1 - e^{-68.02t}$$

$$i_C(t) = 204.06 \times 10^{-6} e^{-68.02t}$$

## EXAMPLE 9.4

*Determine whether RLC series circuit shown in Fig. 9.238 is underdamped, overdamped or critically damped. Sketch i(t) for R = 20 Ω, 200 Ω and 1000 Ω.*

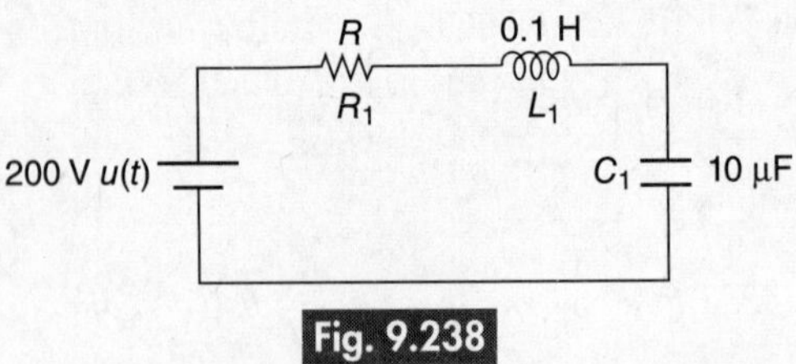


Fig. 9.238

## Solution

```
*Plotting of i(t)

V1 1 0 200
R1 1 2 {R}
L1 2 3 0.1
C1 3 0 10U
.IC I(L1) 0
.IC V(3) 0
.STEP PARAM R LIST 20 200 1000
.TRAN 1M 50M
.PROBE
.END
```

For $R = 20\ \Omega$

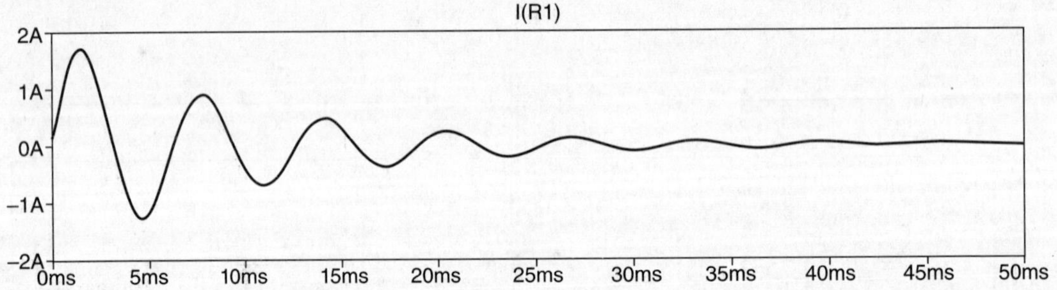


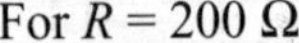
For $R = 200\ \Omega$

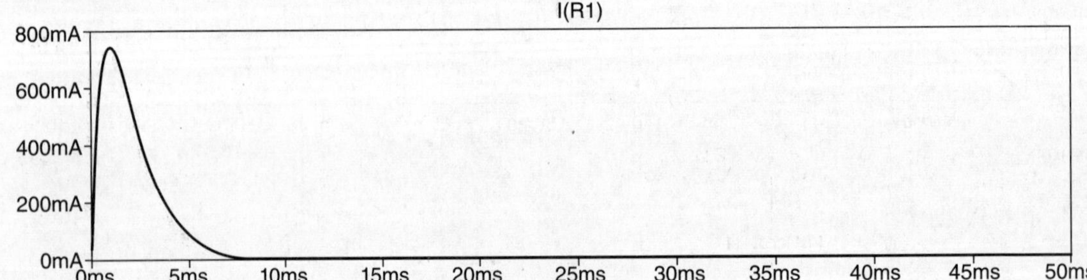

For $R = 1000\ \Omega$

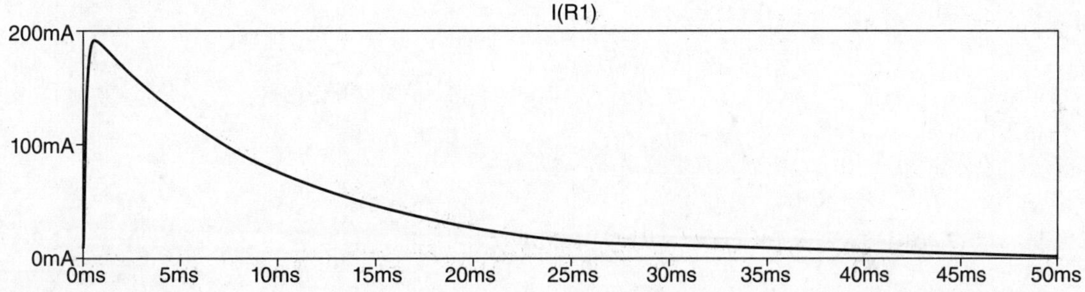


**Result**

For $R = 20\ \Omega$, *RLC* series circuit is underdamped.

For $R = 200\ \Omega$, *RLC* series circuit is critically damped.

For $R = 1000\ \Omega$, *RLC* series circuit is overdamped.

CHAPTER

# 10 Application of Laplace Transform in Network Analysis

## LEARNING OBJECTIVES

**After studying this chapter, you should be able to:**

**LO 10.1** Explain Laplace transformation

**LO 10.2** Discuss Laplace transformations of some important functions

**LO 10.3** Describe and prove the properties of Laplace transform

**LO 10.4** Discuss Laplace transform of periodic functions

**LO 10.5** Describe waveform synthesis

**LO 10.6** Find inverse Laplace transform

**LO 10.7** Use Laplace transform in obtaining solution of differential equations with constant coefficients

**LO 10.8** Discuss the transformed circuit

**LO 10.9** Discuss the transient responses of *RL*, *RC*, and *RLC* circuits to dc excitation

**LO 10.10** Explain the response of *RL* and *RC* circuits to various functions

## INTRODUCTION

Time-domain analysis is the conventional method of analysing a network. For a simple network with first-order differential equation of network variable, this method is very useful. As the order of network variable equation increases, this method of analysis becomes very tedious. For such applications, frequency domain analysis using Laplace transform is very convenient. The Laplace transform method has the following advantages:

1. Solution of differential equations is a systematic procedure.
2. Initial conditions are automatically incorporated.
3. It gives the complete solution, i.e., both complementary and particular solution in one step.

It has many important applications in mathematics, physics, optics, electrical engineering, control engineering, signal processing and probability theory.

## 10.1 LAPLACE TRANSFORMATION

LO 10.1

Explain Laplace transformation

The Laplace transform of a function $f(t)$ is defined as

$$F(s) = L\{f(t)\} = \int_0^\infty f(t)e^{-st}\, dt$$

where $s$ is the complex frequency variable.

$$s = \sigma + j\omega$$

The function $f(t)$ must satisfy the following condition to possess a Laplace transform,

$$\int_0^\infty |f(t)|e^{-\sigma t}\, dt < \infty$$

where $\sigma$ is real and positive.

The inverse Laplace transform $L^{-1}\{F(s)\}$ is

$$f(t) = \frac{1}{2\pi j}\int_{\sigma - j\infty}^{\sigma + j\infty} F(s)e^{st}\, ds$$

## 10.2 LAPLACE TRANSFORMS OF SOME IMPORTANT FUNCTIONS

LO 10.2

Discuss Laplace transformations of some important functions

**1. *Constant Function k*** The Laplace transform of a constant function is

$$L\{k\} = \int_0^\infty ke^{-st}\, dt = k\left[\frac{e^{-st}}{-s}\right]_0^\infty = \frac{k}{s}$$

**2. *Function $t^n$*** The Laplace transform of $f(t)$ is

$$L\{t^n\} = \int_0^\infty t^n e^{-st}\, dt$$

Putting $st = x$, $\quad dt = \dfrac{dx}{s}$

$$L\{t^n\} = \int_0^\infty \left(\frac{x}{s}\right)^n e^{-x}\frac{dx}{s} = \frac{1}{s^{n+1}}\int_0^\infty x^n e^{-x}\, dx = \frac{\sqrt{n+1}}{s^{n+1}},\ s > 0,\ n+1 > 0$$

If $n$ is a positive integer, $\sqrt{n+1} = n!$

$$L\{t^n\} = \frac{n!}{s^{n+1}}$$

**3. Unit-Step Function** The unit-step function (Fig. 10.1) is defined by the equation,

$$u(t) = 1 \qquad t > 0$$
$$= 0 \qquad t < 0$$

The Laplace transform of unit step function is

$$L\{u(t)\} = \int_0^\infty 1 \cdot e^{-st}\, dt = \left[-\frac{e^{-st}}{s}\right]_0^\infty = \frac{1}{s}$$

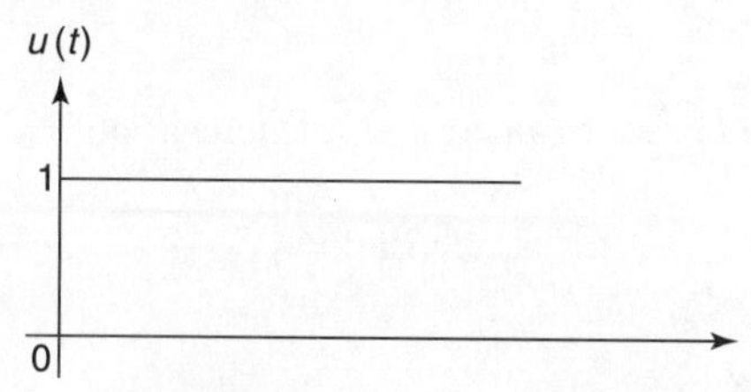


Fig. 10.1 *Unit-step function*

**4. Delayed or Shifted Unit-Step Function** The delayed or shifted unit-step function (Fig. 10.2) is defined by the equation

$$u\,(t-a) = 1 \qquad t > a$$
$$= 0 \qquad t < a$$

The Laplace transform of $u\,(t-a)$ is

$$L\{u(t-a)\} = \int_a^\infty 1 \cdot e^{-st}\, dt = \left[-\frac{e^{-st}}{s}\right]_a^\infty = \frac{e^{-as}}{s}$$

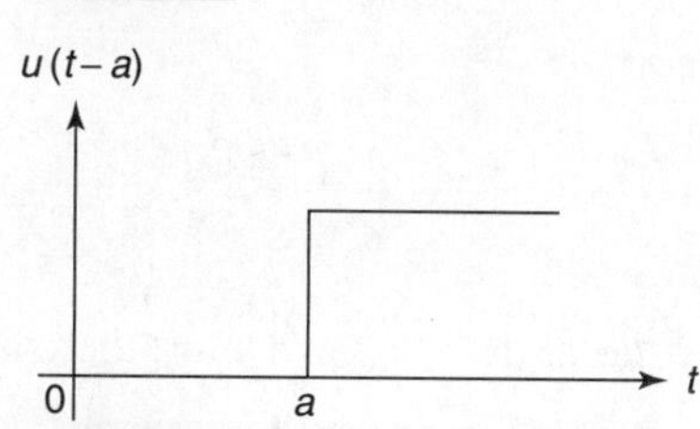


Fig. 10.2 *Shifted unit-step function*

**5. Unit-Ramp Function** The unit-ramp function (Fig. 10.3) is defined by the equation

$$r(t) = t \qquad t > 0$$
$$= 0 \qquad t < 0$$

The Laplace transform of the unit-ramp function is

$$L\{r(t)\} = \int_0^\infty t\, e^{-st} = \frac{1}{s^2}$$

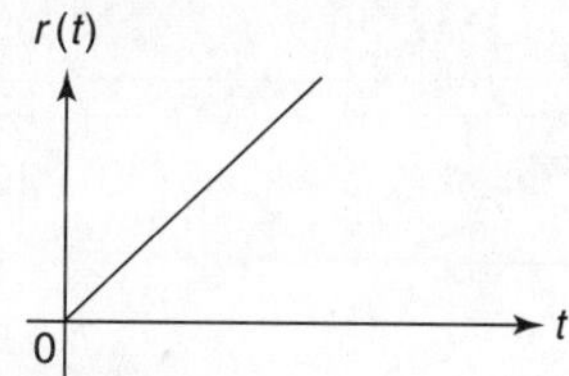


Fig. 10.3 *Unit-ramp function*

**6. Delayed Unit-Ramp Function** The delayed unit-ramp function (Fig. 10.4) is defined by the equation

$$r\,(t-a) = t \qquad t > a$$
$$= 0 \qquad t < a$$

The Laplace transform of $r\,(t-a)$ is

$$L\{r(t-a)\} = \int_a^\infty t\, e^{-st}\, dt = \frac{e^{-as}}{s^2}$$

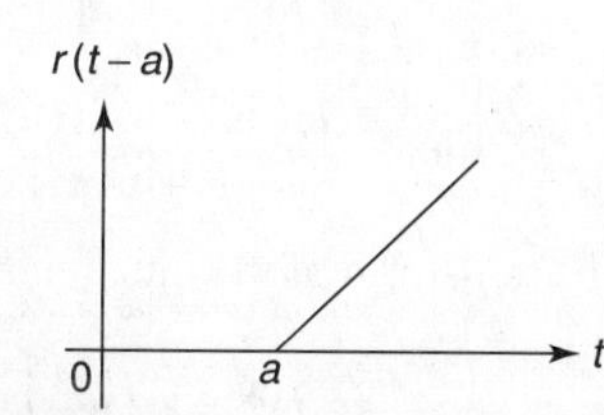


Fig. 10.4 *Delayed unit-ramp function*

***7. Unit-Impulse Function*** The unit-impulse function (Fig. 10.5) is defined by the equation

$$\delta(t) = 0 \qquad t \neq 0$$

and

$$\int_{-\infty}^{\infty} \delta(t)\,dt = 1 \qquad t = 0$$

Fig. 10.5 *Unit-impulse function*

The Laplace transform of the unit-impulse function is

$$L\{\delta(t)\} = \int_{0}^{\infty} \delta(t) e^{-st}\,dt = 1$$

***8. Exponential Function ($e^{at}$)*** The Laplace transform of the exponential function (Fig. 10.6) is

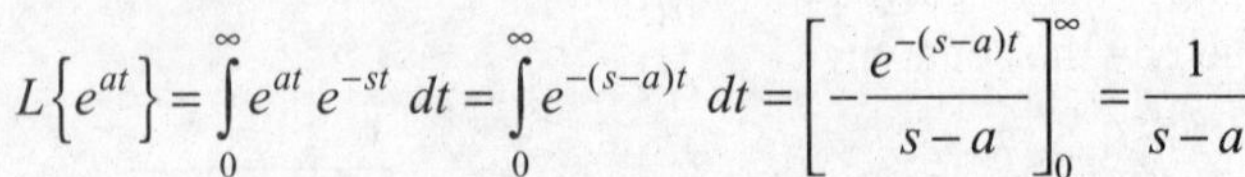

$$L\{e^{at}\} = \int_{0}^{\infty} e^{at} e^{-st}\,dt = \int_{0}^{\infty} e^{-(s-a)t}\,dt = \left[-\frac{e^{-(s-a)t}}{s-a}\right]_{0}^{\infty} = \frac{1}{s-a}$$

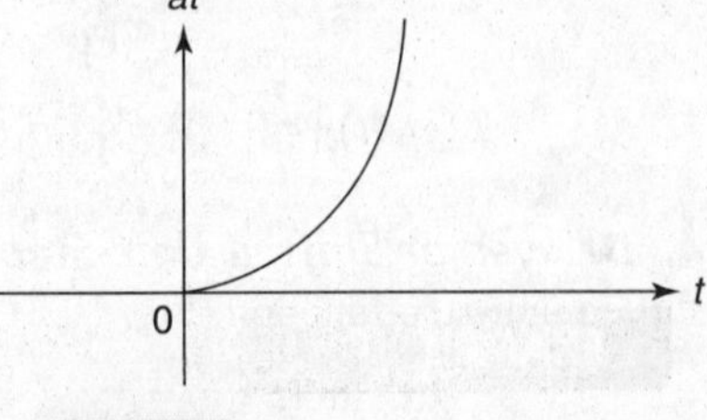


Fig. 10.6 *Exponential function*

***9. Sine Function*** We know that $\sin \omega t = \frac{1}{2j}\left[e^{j\omega t} - e^{-j\omega t}\right]$.

The Laplace transform of the sine function is

$$L\{\sin \omega t\} = L\left\{\frac{1}{2j}(e^{j\omega t} - e^{-j\omega t})\right\} = \frac{1}{2j}\left[L\{e^{j\omega t}\} - L\{e^{-j\omega t}\}\right] = \frac{1}{2j}\left[\frac{1}{s-j\omega} - \frac{1}{s+j\omega}\right] = \frac{\omega}{s^2+\omega^2}$$

***10. Cosine Function*** We know that $\cos \omega t = \frac{1}{2}\left[e^{j\omega t} + e^{-j\omega t}\right]$.

The Laplace transform of the cosine function is

$$L\{\cos \omega t\} = L\left\{\frac{1}{2}(e^{j\omega t} + e^{-j\omega t})\right\} = \frac{1}{2}\left[L\{e^{j\omega t}\} + L\{e^{-j\omega t}\}\right] = \frac{1}{2}\left[\frac{1}{s-j\omega} + \frac{1}{s+j\omega}\right] = \frac{s}{s^2+\omega^2}$$

***11. Exponentially Damped Function*** Laplace transform of an exponentially damped function $e^{-at} f(t)$ is

$$L\{e^{-at} f(t)\,dt\} = \int_{0^-}^{\infty} f(t) e^{-at} e^{-st}\,dt = \int_{0^-}^{\infty} f(t) e^{-(s+a)t}\,dt = F(s+a)$$

Thus, the transform of the function $e^{-at} f(t)$ is obtained by putting $(s + a)$ in place of $s$ in the transform of $f(t)$.

$$L\{e^{-at} \sin \omega t\} = \frac{\omega}{(s+a)^2 + \omega^2}$$

$$L\{e^{-at} \cos \omega t\} = \frac{s+a}{(s+a)^2 + \omega^2}$$

## 10.3 | PROPERTIES OF LAPLACE TRANSFORM

LO 10.3

Describe and prove the properties of Laplace transform

### 10.3.1 Linearity

If $L\{f_1(t)\} = F_1(s)$ and $L\{f_2(t)\} = F_2(s)$ then

$L\{af_1(t) + bf_2(t)\} = aF_1(s) + bF_2(s)$

where $a$ and $b$ are constants.

***Proof***

$$L\{f(t)\} = \int_0^\infty f(t)\, e^{-st}\, dt$$

$$L\{af_1(t) + bf_2(t)\} = \int_0^\infty \{af_1(t) + bf_2(t)\}e^{-st} dt = a\int_0^\infty f_1(t)e^{-st} dt + b\int_0^\infty f_2(t)e^{-st}\, dt = aF_1(s) + bF_2(s)$$

**EXAMPLE 10.1** ●○○

*Find the Laplace transform of* $4t^2 + \sin 3t + e^{2t}$.

**Solution** $L\{4t^2 + \sin 3t + e^{2t}\} = 4L\{t^2\} + L\{\sin 3t\} + L\{e^{2t}\} = 4\cdot\frac{2}{s^3} + \frac{3}{s^2+9} + \frac{1}{s-2} = \frac{8}{s^3} + \frac{3}{s^2+9} + \frac{1}{s-2}$

**EXAMPLE 10.2** ●○○

*Find the Laplace transform of* $t^2 - e^{-2t} + \cosh^2 3t$ .

**Solution** $L\{t^2 - e^{-2t} + \cosh^2 3t\} = L\{t^2\} - L\{e^{-2t}\} + L\{\cosh^2 3t\} = L\{t^2\} - L\{e^{-2t}\} + \frac{1}{2}L\{1 + \cosh 6t\}$

$$= \frac{2}{s^3} - \frac{1}{s+2} + \frac{1}{2s} + \frac{s}{2(s^2-36)}$$

**EXAMPLE 10.3** ●○○

*Find the Laplace transform of* $(\sin 2t - \cos 2t)^2$.

**Solution** $L\{(\sin 2t - \cos 2t)^2\} = L\{\sin^2 2t + \cos^2 2t - 2\cos 2t \sin 2t\} = L\{1 - \sin 4t\} = L\{1\} - L\{\sin 4t\}$

$$= \frac{1}{s} - \frac{4}{s^2+16}$$

**Note** Difficulty Level ●○○— Easy; ○●○— Medium; ○○●— Difficult

**EXAMPLE 10.4**

*Find the Laplace transform of* $\cos(\omega t + b)$.

**Solution** $L\{\cos(\omega t+b)\} = L\{\cos\omega t\cos b - \sin\omega t\sin b\} = \cos b L\{\cos\omega t\} - \sin b L\{\sin\omega t\}$

$$= \cos b \cdot \frac{s}{s^2+\omega^2} - \sin b \cdot \frac{\omega}{s^2+\omega^2}$$

### 10.3.2 Time Scaling

If $L\{f(t)\} = F(s)$ then $L\{f(at)\} = \frac{1}{a}F\left(\frac{s}{a}\right)$

***Proof***

$$L\{f(t)\} = \int_0^\infty f(t)\, e^{-st}\, dt$$

$$L\{f(at)\} = \int_0^\infty f(at) e^{-st}\, dt$$

Putting $at = x$, $dt = \frac{dx}{a}$

$$L\{(f(at)\} = \int_0^\infty f(x)\, e^{-s\left(\frac{x}{a}\right)} \frac{dx}{a} = \frac{1}{a}\int_0^\infty f(x)\, e^{-\left(\frac{s}{a}\right)x}\, dx = \frac{1}{a}F\left(\frac{s}{a}\right)$$

**EXAMPLE 10.5**

*If* $L\{f(t)\} = \log\left(\frac{s+3}{s+1}\right)$, *find* $L\{f(2t)\}$.

**Solution**

$$L\{f(t)\} = \log\left(\frac{s+3}{s+1}\right)$$

By time-scaling property,

$$L\{f(2t)\} = \frac{1}{2}\log\left(\frac{\frac{s}{2}+3}{\frac{s}{2}+1}\right) = \frac{1}{2}\log\left(\frac{s+6}{s+2}\right)$$

**EXAMPLE 10.6**

*If* $L\{f(t)\} = \frac{2}{s^3}e^{-s}$, *find* $L\{f(3t)\}$.

**Solution** $$L\{f(t)\} = \frac{2}{s^3}e^{-s}$$

By time-shifting property,

$$L\{f(3t)\} = \frac{1}{3}\frac{2}{\left(\frac{s}{3}\right)^3}e^{-\frac{s}{3}} = \frac{1}{3}\frac{54}{s^3}e^{-\frac{s}{3}} = \frac{18}{s^3}e^{-\frac{s}{3}}$$

### 10.3.3 Frequency-Shifting Theorem

If $L\{f(t)\} = F(s)$ then $L\{e^{-at} f(t)\} = F(s+a)$

***Proof*** $$L\{f(t)\} = \int_0^\infty f(t)t\, e^{-st}\, d$$

$$L\{e^{-at} f(t)\} = \int_0^\infty e^{-at} f(t) e^{-st}\, dt = \int_0^\infty f(t) e^{-(s+a)t}\, dt = F(s+a)$$

**EXAMPLE 10.7**

*Find the Laplace transform of* $e^{-3t}t^4$.

**Solution** $$L\{t^4\} = \frac{4!}{s^5}$$

By frequency-shifting theorem,

$$L\{e^{-3t}t^4\} = \frac{4!}{(s+3)^5}$$

**EXAMPLE 10.8**

*Find the Laplace transform of* $(t+1)^2 e^t$.

**Solution** $$L\{(t+1)^2\} = L\{t^2 + 2t + 1\} = \frac{2}{s^3} + \frac{2}{s^2} + \frac{1}{s}$$

By frequency-shifting theorem,

$$L\{(t+1)^2 e^t\} = \frac{2}{(s-1)^3} + \frac{2}{(s-1)^2} + \frac{1}{s-1}$$

**EXAMPLE 10.9**

*Find the Laplace transform of* $e^{4t}\sin^3 t$.

$$L\{\sin^3 t\} = \frac{1}{4}L\{3\sin t - \sin 3t\} = \frac{3}{4(s^2+1)} - \frac{3}{4(s^2+9)}$$

**Solution** By frequency-shifting theorem,

$$L\{e^{4t}\sin^3 t\} = \frac{3}{4[(s-4)^2+1]} - \frac{3}{4[(s-4)^2+9]} = \frac{3}{4(s^2-8s+17)} - \frac{3}{4(s^2-8s+25)} = \frac{6}{(s^2-8s+7)(s^2-8s+25)}$$

**EXAMPLE 10.10**

*Find the Laplace transform of cosh at cos at.*

**Solution**

$$\cosh at \cos at = \left(\frac{e^{at}+e^{-at}}{2}\right)\cos at = \frac{1}{2}(e^{at}\cos at + e^{-at}\cos at)$$

$$L\{\cos at\} = \frac{s}{s^2+a^2}$$

$$L\{\cosh at \cos at\} = \frac{1}{2}L\{e^{at}\cos at + e^{-at}\cos at\}$$

By frequency-shifting theorem,

$$L\{\cosh at \cos at\} = \frac{1}{2}\left[\frac{s-a}{(s-a)^2+a^2} + \frac{s+a}{(s+a)^2+a^2}\right] = \frac{1}{2}\left[\frac{s-a}{s^2+2a^2-2as} + \frac{s+a}{s^2+2a^2+2as}\right]$$

$$= \frac{1}{2}\left[\frac{(s-a)(s^2+2a^2+2as)+(s+a)(s^2+2a^2-2as)}{(s^2+2a^2)^2-4a^2s^2}\right] = \frac{s^3}{s^4+4a^4}$$

### 10.3.4 Time-Shifting Theorem

If $L\{f(t)\} = F(s)$ then $L\{f(t-a)\} = e^{-as}F(s)$

***Proof***

$$L\{f(t)\} = \int_0^\infty f(t)e^{-st}\,dt$$

$$L\{f(t-a)\} = \int_0^\infty f(t-a)\,e^{-st}\,dt$$

Putting $t-a = x, \quad dt = dx$

When $t = a, \quad x = 0$

$t \to \infty, \quad x \to \infty$

$$L\{f(t-a)\} = \int_0^\infty f(x)e^{-s(a+x)}\,dx = e^{-as}\int_0^\infty f(x)e^{-sx}\,dx = e^{-as}\int_0^\infty f(t)\,e^{-st}\,dt = e^{-as}F(s)$$

**EXAMPLE 10.11**

*Find the Laplace transform of* $\cos(t-a) \quad t > a$.

**Solution** Let

$$f(t) = \cos t$$

$$L\{f(t)\} = F(s) = \frac{s}{s^2+1}$$

By time-shifting theorem,

$$L\{\cos(t-a)\} = e^{-as}\frac{s}{s^2+1}$$

**EXAMPLE 10.12**

*Find the Laplace transform of* $e^{t-a} \quad t > a$.

**Solution** Let

$$f(t) = e^t$$

$$L\{f(t)\} = F(s) = \frac{1}{s-1}$$

By time-shifting theorem,

$$L\{e^{t-a}\} = e^{-as}\frac{1}{s-1}$$

**EXAMPLE 10.13**

*Find the Laplace transform of* $\sin\left(t-\frac{\pi}{4}\right) \quad t > \frac{\pi}{4}$.

**Solution** Let

$$f(t) = \sin t$$

$$L\{f(t)\} = F(s) = \frac{1}{s^2+1}$$

By time-shifting theorem,

$$L\left\{\sin\left(t-\frac{\pi}{4}\right)\right\} = e^{-\frac{\pi s}{4}}\frac{1}{s^2+1}$$

**EXAMPLE 10.13**

*Find the Laplace transform of* $(t-1)^3 \quad t > 1$.

**Solution** Let

$$f(t) = t^3$$

$$L\{f(t)\} = F(s) = \frac{3!}{s^4}$$

By time-shifting theorem,

$$L\left\{(t-1)^3\right\} = e^{-s}\frac{3!}{s^4}$$

### 10.3.5 Multiplication by *t* (Frequency-Differentiation Theorem)

If $L\{f(t)\} = F(s)$ then $L\{t\, f(t)\} = -\dfrac{d}{ds}F(s)$

***Proof***

$$L\{f(t)\} = F(s) = \int_0^\infty f(t)e^{-st}\, dt$$

Differentiating both the sides w.r.t $s$ using DUIS,

$$\frac{d}{ds}F(s) = \frac{d}{ds}\int_0^\infty f(t)e^{-st}dt = \int_0^\infty \frac{\partial}{\partial s} f(t)e^{-st}\, dt$$

$$= \int_0^\infty (-t)\, f(t)e^{-st}\, dt = \int_0^\infty \{-t\, f(t)\}e^{-st} dt = -L\{t\, f(t)\}$$

$$L\{t\, f(t)\} = (-1)\frac{d}{ds}F(s)$$

**EXAMPLE 10.15**

*Find the Laplace transform of t sin at.*

**Solution**

$$L\{\sin at\} = \frac{a}{s^2 + a^2}$$

$$L\{t \sin at\} = -\frac{d}{ds}L\{\sin at\} = -\frac{d}{ds}\left(\frac{a}{s^2 + a^2}\right) = \frac{2as}{(s^2 + a^2)^2}$$

**EXAMPLE 10.16**

*Find the Laplace transform of $t\cos^2 t$.*

**Solution**

$$L\{\cos^2 t\} = L\left\{\frac{1 + \cos 2t}{2}\right\} = \frac{1}{2}L\{1 + \cos 2t\} = \frac{1}{2}\left(\frac{1}{s} + \frac{s}{s^2 + 4}\right)$$

$$L\{t\cos^2 t\} = -\frac{d}{ds}L\{\cos^2 t\} = -\frac{1}{2}\frac{d}{ds}\left(\frac{1}{s} + \frac{s}{s^2 + 4}\right) = -\frac{1}{2}\left[-\frac{1}{s^2} + \frac{(s^2+4)\cdot 1 - s\cdot 2s}{(s^2+4)^2}\right] = \frac{1}{2s^2} + \frac{s^2 - 4}{2(s^2+4)^2}$$

**EXAMPLE 10.17**

*Find the Laplace transform of $t\sin^3 t$.*

**Solution**

$$L\{\sin^3 t\} = L\left\{\frac{3\sin t - \sin 3t}{4}\right\} = \frac{1}{4}\left(\frac{3}{s^2+1} - \frac{1}{s^2+9}\right) = \frac{3}{4}\left(\frac{1}{s^2+1} - \frac{1}{s^2+9}\right)$$

$$L\{t\sin^3 t\} = -\frac{d}{ds}L\{\sin^3 t\} = -\frac{3}{4}\frac{d}{ds}\left(\frac{1}{s^2+1} - \frac{1}{s^2+9}\right) = -\frac{3}{4}\left[\frac{-2s}{(s^2+1)^2} + \frac{2s}{(s^2+9)^2}\right] = \frac{3s}{2}\left[\frac{(s^2+9)^2 - (s^2+1)^2}{(s^2+1)^2(s^2+9)^2}\right]$$

$$= \frac{3s}{2}\left[\frac{s^4 + 18s^2 + 81 - s^4 - 2s^2 - 1}{(s^2+1)^2(s^2+9)^2}\right] = \frac{3s}{2}\cdot\frac{16(s^2+5)}{(s^2+1)^2(s^2+9)^2} = \frac{24s(s^2+5)}{(s^2+1)^2(s^2+9)^2}$$

**EXAMPLE 10.18**

*Find the Laplace transform of t sin 2t cosh t .*

**Solution** $L\{\sin 2t \cosh t\} = L\left\{\sin 2t\left(\dfrac{e^t + e^{-t}}{2}\right)\right\} = \dfrac{1}{2}L\{e^t \sin 2t + e^{-t}\sin 2t\}$

$$= \frac{1}{2}\left[\frac{2}{(s-1)^2+4} + \frac{2}{(s+1)^2+4}\right] = \frac{1}{s^2-2s+5} + \frac{1}{s^2+2s+5}$$

$$L\{t\sin 2t \cosh t\} = -\frac{d}{ds}L\{\sin 2t\cosh t\} = -\frac{d}{ds}\left(\frac{1}{s^2-2s+5}+\frac{1}{s^2+2s+5}\right) = \frac{2s-2}{(s^2-2s+5)^2} + \frac{2s+2}{(s^2+2s+5)^2}$$

### 10.3.6 Division by *t* (Frequency-Integration Theorem)

If $L\{f(t)\} = F(s)$, then $L\left\{\dfrac{f(t)}{t}\right\} = \int_s^{\infty} F(s)\, ds$

***Proof*** $L\{f(t)\} = F(s) = \int_0^{\infty} f(t)\, e^{-st}\, dt$

Integrating both the sides w.r.t *s* from *s* to ∞,

$$\int_s^{\infty} F(s)\, ds = \int_s^{\infty}\int_0^{\infty} f(t) e^{-st} dt\, ds$$

Since *s* and *t* are independent variables, interchanging the order of integration,

$$\int_s^{\infty} F(s) ds = \int_0^{\infty}\left[\int_s^{\infty} f(t) e^{-st} ds\right] dt = \int_0^{\infty}\left[\frac{1}{-t} f(t) e^{-st}\right]_s^{\infty} dt = \int_0^{\infty} \frac{f(t)}{t} e^{-st} dt$$

$$L\left\{\frac{f(t)}{t}\right\} = \int_s^{\infty} F(s) ds$$

**EXAMPLE 10.19**

*Find the Laplace transform of* $\dfrac{1-e^{-t}}{t}$.

**Solution** $L\{1-e^{-t}\} = \dfrac{1}{s} - \dfrac{1}{s+1}$

$$L\left\{\frac{1-e^{-t}}{t}\right\}=\int_s^{\infty} L\{1-e^{-t}\}ds=\int_s^{\infty}\left(\frac{1}{s}-\frac{1}{s+1}\right)ds=\left|\log s-\log(s+1)\right|_s^{\infty}$$

$$=\left[\log\frac{s}{s+1}\right]_s^{\infty}=\log\left[\frac{1}{1+\frac{1}{s}}\right]_s^{\infty}=\log 1-\log\left(\frac{1}{1+\frac{1}{s}}\right)=-\log\frac{s}{s+1}=\log\frac{s+1}{s}$$

**EXAMPLE 10.20**

*Find the Laplace transform of* $\dfrac{e^{-at}-e^{-bt}}{t}$.

**Solution** $L\{e^{-at}-e^{-bt}\}=\dfrac{1}{s+a}-\dfrac{1}{s+b}$

$$L\left\{\frac{e^{-at}-e^{-bt}}{t}\right\}=\int_s^{\infty} L\{e^{-at}-e^{-bt}\}\,ds=\int_s^{\infty}\left(\frac{1}{s+a}-\frac{1}{s+b}\right)ds=\left[\log(s+a)-\log(s+b)\right]_s^{\infty}$$

$$=\left[\log\frac{s+a}{s+b}\right]_s^{\infty}=\left[\log\frac{1+\frac{a}{s}}{1+\frac{b}{s}}\right]_s^{\infty}=\log 1-\log\frac{1+\frac{a}{s}}{1+\frac{b}{s}}=-\log\frac{s+a}{s+b}=\log\frac{s+b}{s+a}$$

**EXAMPLE 10.21**

*Find the Laplace transform of* $\dfrac{\sinh t}{t}$.

**Solution** $L\{\sinh t\}=L\left\{\dfrac{e^{t}-e^{-t}}{2}\right\}=\dfrac{1}{2}\left(\dfrac{1}{s-1}-\dfrac{1}{s+1}\right)$

$$L\left\{\frac{\sinh t}{t}\right\}=\int_s^{\infty} L\{\sinh t\}\,ds=\frac{1}{2}\int_s^{\infty}\left(\frac{1}{s-1}-\frac{1}{s+1}\right)ds=\frac{1}{2}\left[\log(s-1)-\log(s+1)\right]_s^{\infty}=\frac{1}{2}\left[\log\frac{s-1}{s+1}\right]_s^{\infty}$$

$$=\frac{1}{2}\left[\log\frac{1-\frac{1}{s}}{1+\frac{1}{s}}\right]_s^{\infty}=\frac{1}{2}\left(\log 1-\log\frac{1-\frac{1}{s}}{1+\frac{1}{s}}\right)=-\frac{1}{2}\log\frac{s-1}{s+1}=\frac{1}{2}\log\frac{s+1}{s-1}$$

**EXAMPLE 10.22**

*Find the Laplace transform of* $\dfrac{\cos h2t\ \sin 2t}{t}$.

**Solution**
$$L\left\{\frac{\cosh 2t \sin 2t}{t}\right\} = L\left\{\left(\frac{e^{2t}+e^{-2t}}{2t}\right)\sin 2t\right\} = \frac{1}{2}\left[L\left\{\frac{e^{2t}\sin 2t}{t}\right\} + L\left\{\frac{e^{-2t}\sin 2t}{t}\right\}\right]$$

$$L\{\sin 2t\} = \frac{2}{s^2+4}$$

$$L\left\{\frac{\sin 2t}{t}\right\} = \int_s^\infty L\{\sin 2t\}ds = \int_s^\infty \frac{2}{s^2+4}ds = \left[\tan^{-1}\frac{s}{2}\right]_s^\infty = \frac{\pi}{2} - \tan^{-1}\frac{s}{2} = \cot^{-1}\frac{s}{2}$$

By first shifting theorem,

$$L\left\{\frac{\cosh 2t \sin 2t}{t}\right\} = \frac{1}{2}\left[L\left\{\frac{e^{2t}\sin 2t}{t}\right\} + L\left\{\frac{e^{-2t}\sin 2t}{t}\right\}\right] = \frac{1}{2}\left[\cot^{-1}\left(\frac{s-2}{2}\right) + \cot^{-1}\left(\frac{s+2}{2}\right)\right]$$

### 10.3.7 Time-Differentiation Theorem: Laplace Transform of Derivatives

If $L\{f(t)\} = F(s)$ then

$$L\{f'(t)\} = sF(s) - f(0)$$
$$L\{f''(t)\} = s^2F(s) - sf(0) - f'(0)$$

In general,

$$L\{f''(t)\} = s''F(s) - s^{n-1}f(0) - s^{n-2}f'(0) - s^{n-3}f''(0)\ldots - f^{(n-1)}(0)$$

***Proof***

$$L\{f'(t)\} = \int_0^\infty f'(t)\,e^{-st}\,dt$$

Integrating by parts,

$$L\{f'(t)\} = \left[f(t)e^{-st}\right]_0^\infty - \int_0^\infty (-s)f(t)e^{-st}dt = -f(0) + s\int_0^\infty f(t)e^{-st}dt = -f(0) + sL\{f(t)\}$$

Similarly,

$$L\{f''\ t\} = -f' + sL\{f'\ t\} = -f'(0) + s[-f(0) + sL\{f(t)\}] = -f'(0) - sf(0) + s^2L\{f(t)\}$$

In general, $\quad L\{f^n(t)\} = s^nF(s) - s^{n-1}f(0) - s^{n-2}f'(0) - s^{n-3}f''(0)\ldots - f^{n-1}(0)$

**EXAMPLE 10.23**

*Find $L\{f(t)\}$ and $L\{f'(t)\}$ of $f(t) = \dfrac{\sin t}{t}$.*

**Solution**

$$L\{f(t)\} = F(s) = L\left\{\frac{\sin t}{t}\right\} = \int_s^\infty L\{\sin t\}ds = \int_s^\infty \frac{1}{s^2+1}ds = \left[\tan^{-1}s\right]_s^\infty = \frac{\pi}{2} - \tan^{-1}s = \cot^{-1}s$$

$$L\{f'(t)\} = sF(s) - f(0) = s\cot^{-1}s - \lim_{t\to 0}\frac{\sin t}{t} = s\cot^{-1}s^{-1}$$

**EXAMPLE 10.24**

*Find $L\{f(t)\}$ and $L\{f'(t)\}$ of the following function:*

$$f(t) = 3 \qquad 0 \le t < 5$$
$$= 0 \qquad t > 5.$$

**Solution** $$L\{f(t)\} = F(s) = \int_s^{\infty} e^{-st} f(t)dt = \int_0^5 e^{-st}\cdot 3dt + \int_5^{\infty} 0\cdot dt = 3\left[\frac{e^{-st}}{-s}\right]_0^5 + 0 = \frac{-3}{s}(e^{-5s}-1) = \frac{3}{s}(1-e^{-5s})$$

$$L\{f'(t)\} = sF(s) - f(0) = s\cdot\frac{3}{s}(1-e^{-5s}) - 3 = -3e^{-5s}$$

**EXAMPLE 10.25**

*Find $L\{f(t)\}$ and $L\{f'(t)\}$ of $f(t) = e^{-5t}\sin t$.*

**Solution** $$L\{f(t)\} = F(s) = L\{e^{-5t}\sin t\} = \frac{1}{(s+5)^2+1}$$

$$L\{f'(t)\} = sF(s) - f(0) = s\cdot\frac{1}{s^2+10s+26} - e^0\sin 0 = \frac{s}{s^2+10s+26}$$

**EXAMPLE 10.26**

*Find $L\{f(t)\}$ and $L\{f'(t)\}$ of the following function:*

$$f(t) = t \qquad 0 \le t < 3$$
$$= 6 \qquad t > 3.$$

**Solution** $$L\{f(t)\} = F(s) = \int_0^{\infty} e^{-st} f(t)dt = \int_0^3 e^{-st}t\,dt + \int_3^{\infty} e^{-st}\cdot 6\,dt = \left[\frac{e^{-st}}{-s}\cdot t\right]_0^3 - \left[\frac{e^{-st}}{s^2}\right]_0^3 + 6\left[\frac{e^{-st}}{-s}\right]_3^{\infty}$$

$$= -\frac{3e^{-3s}}{s} - \frac{e^{-3s}}{s^2} + \frac{1}{s^2} + \frac{6}{s}e^{-3s} = \frac{1}{s^2} + e^{-3s}\left(\frac{3}{s} - \frac{1}{s^2}\right)$$

$$L'\{f(t)\} = sF(s) = f(0) = \frac{1}{s} + e^{-3s}\left(3 - \frac{1}{s}\right)$$

### 10.3.8 Time-Integration Theorem: Laplace Transform of Integral

If $L\{f(t)\} = F(s)$ then $L\left\{\int_0^t f(t)dt\right\} = \frac{F(s)}{s}$

***Proof*** $$L\left\{\int_0^t f(t)dt\right\} = \int_0^{\infty}\left\{\int_0^t f(t)\,dt\right\}e^{-st}dt$$

Integrating by parts,

$$L\left\{\int_0^t f(t)dt\right\} = \left[\int_0^t f(t)dt\left(\frac{e^{-st}}{-s}\right)\right]_0^\infty - \int_0^\infty\left[\left(\frac{e^{-st}}{-s}\right)\left(\frac{d}{dt}\int_0^t f(t)dt\right)\right]dt = \int_0^\infty \frac{1}{s}f(t)e^{-st}dt = \frac{1}{s}L\{f(t)\} = \frac{F(s)}{s}$$

**EXAMPLE 10.27**

*Find the Laplace transform of* $\int_0^t e^{-2t}t^3 dt$.

**Solution**

$$L\{e^{-2t}t^3\} = \frac{3!}{(s+2)^4} = \frac{6}{(s+2)^4}$$

$$L\left\{\int_0^t e^{-2t}t^3 dt\right\} = \frac{1}{s}L\left\{e^{-2t}t^3\right\} = \frac{6}{s(s+2)^4}$$

**EXAMPLE 10.28**

*Find the Laplace transform of* $\int_0^t t \cosh t\, dt$.

**Solution** $L\{t\cosh t\} = L\left\{t\left(\frac{e^t+e^{-t}}{2}\right)\right\} = \frac{1}{2}L\{te^t+te^{-t}\} = \frac{1}{2}\left[\frac{1}{(s-1)^2}+\frac{1}{(s+1)^2}\right] = \frac{1}{2}\cdot\frac{2(s^2+1)}{(s^2-1)^2} = \frac{s^2+1}{(s^2-1)^2}$

$$L\left\{\int_0^t t\cosh t\, dt\right\} = \frac{1}{s}L\{t\cosh t\} = \frac{s^2+1}{s(s^2-1)^2}$$

**EXAMPLE 10.29**

*Find the Laplace transform of* $\int_0^t te^{-4t}\sin 3t\, dt$.

**Solution**

$$L\{t\sin 3t\} = -\frac{d}{ds}L\{\sin 3t\} = -\frac{d}{ds}\left(\frac{3}{s^2+9}\right) = \frac{6s}{(s^2+9)^2}$$

$$L\{te^{-4t}\sin 3t\} = \frac{6(s+4)}{[(s+4)^2+9]^2} = \frac{6(s+4)}{(s^2+8s+25)^2}$$

$$L\left\{\int_0^t te^{-4t}\sin 3t\, dt\right\} = \frac{1}{s}L\{te^{-4t}\sin 3t\} = \frac{6(s+4)}{s(s^2+8s+25)^2}$$

**EXAMPLE 10.30**

*Find the Laplace transform of* $e^{-4t}\int_0^t t \sin 3t\, dt$.

**Solution**

$$L\{t\sin 3t\} = -\frac{d}{ds}L\{\sin 3t\} = -\frac{d}{ds}\left(\frac{3}{s^2+9}\right) = \frac{6s}{(s^2+9)^2}$$

$$L\left\{\int_0^t t\sin 3t\right\} = \frac{1}{s}L\{t\sin 3t\} = \frac{6}{(s^2+9)^2}$$

$$L\left\{e^{-4t}\int_0^t t\sin 3t\right\} = \frac{6}{[(s+4)^2+9]^2} = \frac{6}{(s^2+8s+25)^2}$$

### 10.3.9 Initial Value Theorem

If $L\{f(t)\} = F(s)$ then $\lim_{t\to 0} f(t) = \lim_{s\to\infty} sF(s)$

***Proof*** We know that

$$L\{f'(t)\} = sF(s) - f(0)$$

$$sF(s) = L\{f'(t)\} + f(0) = \int_0^\infty f'(t)\, e^{-st}\, dt + f(0)$$

$$\lim_{s\to\infty} sF(s) = \lim_{s\to\infty}\int_0^\infty f'(t)e^{-st}dt + f(0) = \int_0^\infty \lim_{s\to\infty}[f'(t)e^{-st}]dt + f(0) = 0 + f(0) = f(0) = \lim_{t\to 0} f(t)$$

### 10.3.10 Final Value Theorem

If $L\{f(t)\} = F(s)$ then $\lim_{t\to\infty} f(t) = \lim_{s\to\infty} sF(s)$

***Proof*** We know that

$$L\{f'(t)\} = sF(s) - f(0)$$

$$sF(s) = L\{f'(t)\} + f(0) = \int_0^\infty f'(t)\, e^{-st}\, dt + f(0)$$

$$\lim_{s\to\infty} sF(s) = \lim_{s\to 0}\int_0^\infty f'(t)\, e^{-st}\, dt + f(0) = \int_0^\infty \lim_{s\to 0}\left[f'(t)e^{-st}\right]dt + f(0) = \int_0^\infty f'(t)dt + f(0)$$

$$= \left|f(t)\right|_0^\infty + f(0) = \lim_{t\to\infty} f(t) - f(0) + f(0) = \lim_{t\to\infty} f(t)$$

## EXAMPLE 10.31

*Verify the initial and final value theorems for $e^{-t}(t+1)^2$.*

**Solution**

$$f(t) = e^{-t}(t+1)^2 = e^{-t}(t^2+2t+1)$$

$$F(s) = \frac{2}{(s+1)^3} + \frac{2}{(s+1)^2} + \frac{1}{s+1}$$

$$sF(s) = \frac{2s}{(s+1)^3} + \frac{2s}{(s+1)^2} + \frac{s}{s+1}$$

$$\lim_{t\to 0} f(t) = 1$$

$$\lim_{s\to\infty} sF(s) = \lim_{s\to\infty}\left[\frac{\frac{2}{s^2}}{\left(1+\frac{1}{s}\right)^3} + \frac{\frac{2}{s}}{\left(1+\frac{1}{s}\right)^2} + \frac{1}{1+\frac{1}{s}}\right] = 1$$

Hence, the initial value theorem is verified.

$$\lim_{t\to\infty} f(t) = 0$$

$$\lim_{s\to 0} sF(s) = 0$$

Hence, the final value theorem is verified.

## EXAMPLE 10.32

*Verify the initial and final value theorems for $e^{-t}(t^2 + \cos 3t)$.*

**Solution**

$$f(t) = e^{-t}(t^2 + \cos 3t)$$

$$F(s) = \frac{2}{(s+1)^3} + \frac{s+1}{(s+1)^2+9}$$

$$sF(s) = \frac{2s}{(s+1)^3} + \frac{s(s+1)}{(s+1)^2+9}$$

$$\lim_{t\to 0} f(t) = 1$$

$$\lim_{s\to\infty} sF(s) = \lim_{s\to\infty}\left[\frac{\frac{2}{s^2}}{\left(1+\frac{1}{s}\right)^3} + \frac{\left(1+\frac{1}{s}\right)}{\left(1+\frac{1}{s}\right)^2 + \frac{9}{s^2}}\right] = 1$$

Hence, the initial value theorem is verified.

$$\lim_{t\to\infty} f(t) = \lim_{t\to\infty}(t^2 + \cos 3t)e^{-t} = 0$$

$$\lim_{s\to 0} sF(s) = \lim_{s\to 0}\left[\frac{2s}{(s+1)^3} + \frac{s(s+1)}{(s+1)^2+9}\right] = 0$$

Hence, the final value theorem is verified.

**EXAMPLE 10.33**

*Find the initial and final values of the function whose Laplace transform is*

$$F(s) = \frac{2s+1}{s^3+6s^2+11s+6}.$$

**Solution**

$$F(s) = \frac{2s+1}{s^3+6s^2+11s+6}$$

$$f(0) = \lim_{s\to\infty} sF(s) = \lim_{s\to\infty} \frac{2s^2+s}{s^3+6s^2+11s+6} = \lim_{s\to\infty} \frac{\frac{2}{s}+\frac{1}{s^2}}{1+\frac{6}{s}+\frac{11}{s^2}+\frac{6}{s^3}} = 0$$

$$f(\infty) = \lim_{s\to 0} sF(s) = \lim_{s\to 0} \frac{2s^2+s}{s^3+6s^2+11s+6} = 0$$

**EXAMPLE 10.34**

*Find the final value of the function whose Laplace transform is* $I(s) = \frac{s+6}{s(s+3)}$.

**Solution**

$$I(s) = \frac{s+6}{s(s+3)}$$

$$I(\infty) = \lim_{s\to 0} s\,I(s) = \lim_{s\to 0} \frac{s+6}{s+3} = 2$$

## 10.4 LAPLACE TRANSFORM OF PERIODIC FUNCTIONS

LO 10.4

Discuss Laplace transform of periodic functions

A function $f(t)$ is said to be periodic if there exists a constant $T (T > 0)$ such that $f(t+T) = f(t)$, for all values of $t$.

$$f(t+2T) = f(t+T+T) = f(t+T) = f(t)$$

In general, $f(t+nT) = f(t)$ for all $t$, where $n$ is an integer (positive or negative) and $T$ is the period of the function.

If $f(t)$ is a piecewise continuous periodic function with period $T$ then

$$L\{f(t)\} = \frac{1}{1-e^{-Ts}} \int_0^T f(t)e^{-st}\,dt$$

***Proof***

$$L\{f(t)\} = \int_0^\infty f(t)\,e^{-st}dt = \int_0^T f(t)e^{-st}dt + \int_T^\infty f(t)e^{-st}dt$$

In the second integral, putting $t = x+T$, $dt = dx$

When

$$t = T, \quad x = 0$$

$$t \to \infty, \quad x \to \infty$$

$$L\{f(t)\} = \int_0^T f(t)e^{-st}\,dt + \int_0^\infty f(x+T)e^{-s(x+T)}\,dx$$

$$= \int_0^T f(t)e^{-st}\,dt + e^{-Ts}\int_0^\infty f(x)e^{-sx}\,dx$$

$$= \int_0^T f(t)e^{-st}\,dt + e^{-Ts}\int_0^\infty f(t)e^{-st}\,dt$$

$$= \int_0^T f(t)e^{-st}\,dt + e^{-Ts}L\{f(t)\}$$

$$(1-e^{-Ts})L\{f(t)\} = \int_0^T f(t)e^{-st}\,dt$$

$$L\{f(t)\} = \frac{1}{1-e^{-Ts}}\int_0^T f(t)e^{-st}\,dt$$

**EXAMPLE 10.35**

*Find the Laplace transform of the waveform shown in Fig. 10.7.*

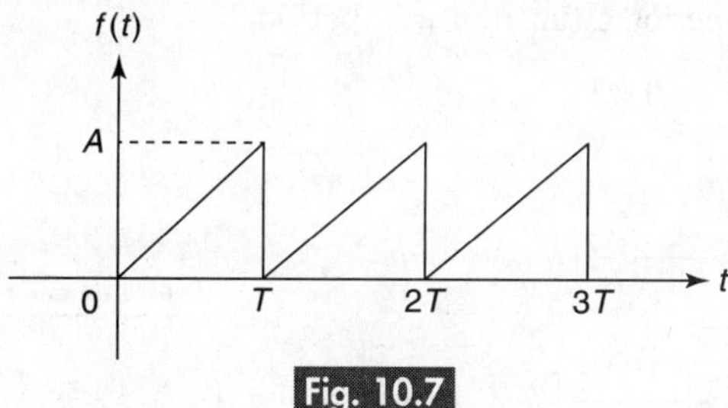


Fig. 10.7

**Solution** The function $f(t)$ is a periodic function with period T.

$$f(t) = \frac{At}{T} \qquad 0<t<t$$

$$L\{f(t)\} = \frac{1}{1-e^{-Ts}}\int_0^T f(t)e^{-st}\,dt$$

$$= \frac{1}{1-e^{-Ts}}\int_0^T \frac{At}{T}e^{-st}\,dt$$

$$= \frac{1}{1-e^{-Ts}}\frac{A}{T}\int_0^T te^{-st}\,dt$$

$$= \frac{A}{T(1-e^{-Ts})}\left[t\frac{e^{-st}}{-s} - \frac{e^{-st}}{s^2}\right]_0^T$$

$$= \frac{A}{T(1-e^{-Ts})}\left(-T\frac{e^{-Ts}}{s} - \frac{e^{-Ts}}{s^2} + \frac{1}{s^2}\right)$$

$$= \frac{A}{T(1-e^{-Ts})}\left[-\frac{Te^{-Ts}}{s} + \frac{1}{s^2}(1-e^{-Ts})\right]$$

$$= \frac{A}{Ts^2} - \frac{Ae^{-Ts}}{s(1-e^{-Ts})}$$

**EXAMPLE 10.36**

*Find the Laplace transform of the waveform shown in Fig. 10.8.*

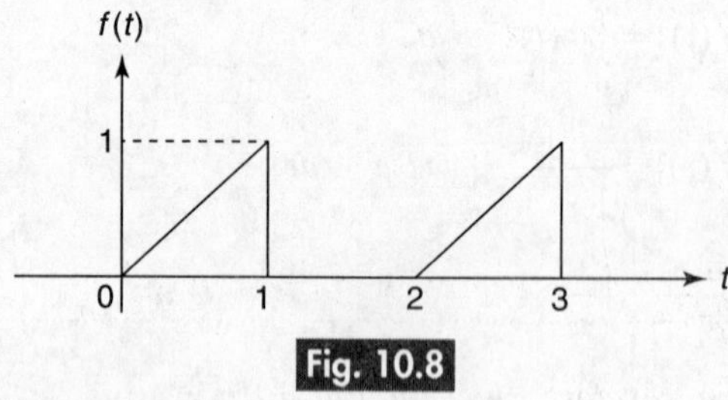


Fig. 10.8

**Solution** The function $f(t)$ is a periodic function with period 2.

$$f(t) = t \quad 0 < t < 1$$
$$= 0 \quad 1 < t < 2$$

$$L\{f(t)\} = \frac{1}{1-e^{-2s}}\int_0^2 f(t)e^{-st}\, dt$$

$$= \frac{1}{1-e^{-2s}}\left[\int_0^1 te^{-st}\, dt + \int_1^2 0\cdot e^{-st} dt\right]$$

$$= \frac{1}{1-e^{-2s}}\left[\frac{e^{-st}}{-s}t - \frac{e^{-st}}{s^2}\right]_0^1$$

$$= \frac{1}{1-e^{-2s}}\left(\frac{e^{-s}}{-s} - \frac{e^{-s}}{s^2} + \frac{1}{s^2}\right)$$

$$= \frac{1}{s^2(1-e^{-2s})}(1-e^{-s}-se^{-s})$$

**EXAMPLE 10.37**

*Find the Laplace transform of the waveform shown in Fig. 10.9.*

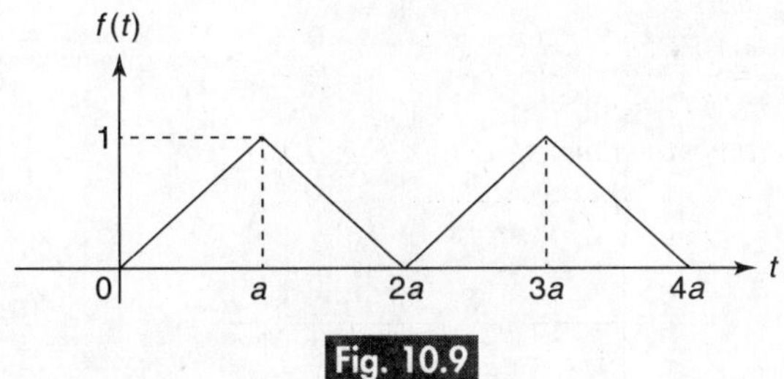


Fig. 10.9

**Solution** The function $f(t)$ is a periodic function with period $2a$.

$$f(t) = \frac{t}{a} \qquad 0 < t < a$$

$$= \frac{1}{a}(2a - t) \qquad a < t < 2a$$

$$L\{f(t)\} = \frac{1}{1-e^{-2as}} \int_0^{2a} f(t) e^{-st}\, dt$$

$$= \frac{1}{1-e^{-2as}} \left[ \int_a^{a} \frac{t}{a} e^{-st} dt + \int_a^{2a} \frac{1}{a}(2a-t) e^{-st}\, dt \right]$$

$$= \frac{1}{a(1-e^{-2as})} \left\{ \left[ \frac{e^{-st}}{-s} t - \frac{e^{-st}}{s^2} \right]_0^a + \left[ \frac{e^{-st}}{-s}(2a-t) + \frac{e^{-st}}{s^2} \right]_a^{2a} \right\}$$

$$= \frac{1}{a(1-e^{-2as})} \left( -\frac{e^{-as}}{s^2} + \frac{1}{s^2} + \frac{e^{-2as}}{s^2} - \frac{e^{-as}}{s^2} \right)$$

$$= \frac{-2e^{-as} + 1 + e^{-2as}}{as^2(1-e^{-2as})}$$

$$= \frac{(1-e^{-as})^2}{as^2(1-e^{-as})(1+e^{-as})}$$

$$= \frac{1-e^{-as}}{as^2(1+e^{-as})}$$

$$= \frac{e^{\frac{as}{2}} - e^{\frac{-as}{2}}}{as^2\left( e^{\frac{as}{2}} + e^{\frac{-as}{2}} \right)}$$

$$= \frac{\tanh\left(\frac{as}{2}\right)}{as^2}$$

## EXAMPLE 10.38

*Find the Laplace transform of the waveform shown in Fig. 10.10.*

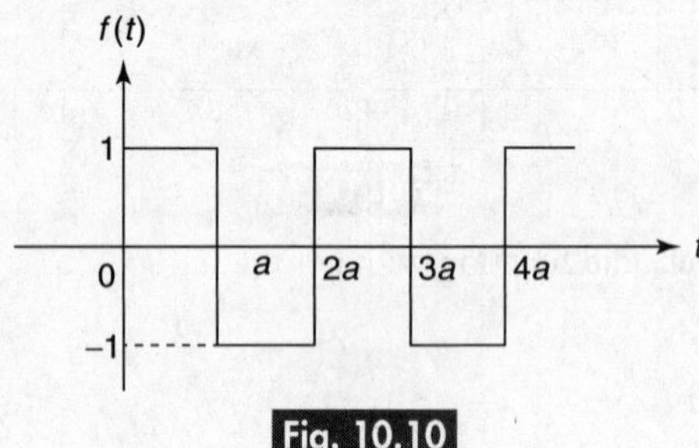


Fig. 10.10

**Solution** The function $f(t)$ is periodic with period with period $2a$.

$$f(t) = 1 \qquad 0 < t < a$$
$$= -1 \qquad a < t < 2a$$

$$L\{f(t)\} = \frac{1}{1-e^{-2as}} \int_0^{2a} f(t)e^{-st}\, dt$$

$$= \frac{1}{1-e^{-2as}} \left[ \int_0^a e^{-st}\, dt + \int_a^{2a} e^{-st}(-1)\, dt \right]$$

$$= \frac{1}{1-e^{-2as}} \left\{ \left[ \frac{e^{-st}}{-s} \right]_0^a + \left[ \frac{e^{-st}}{s} \right]_a^{2a} \right\}$$

$$= \frac{1}{1-e^{-2as}} \left( -\frac{e^{-as}}{-s} + \frac{1}{s} + \frac{e^{-2as}}{s} - \frac{e^{-as}}{s} \right)$$

$$= \frac{(1-e^{-as})^2}{s(1+e^{-as})(1-e^{-as})}$$

$$= \frac{1-e^{-as}}{s(1+e^{-as})}$$

$$= \frac{1}{s} \cdot \frac{e^{\frac{as}{2}} - e^{-\frac{as}{2}}}{\left( e^{\frac{as}{2}} + e^{-\frac{as}{2}} \right)}$$

$$= \frac{1}{s} \tanh\left( \frac{as}{2} \right)$$

**EXAMPLE 10.39**

*Find the Laplace transform of the waveform shown in Fig. 10.11.*

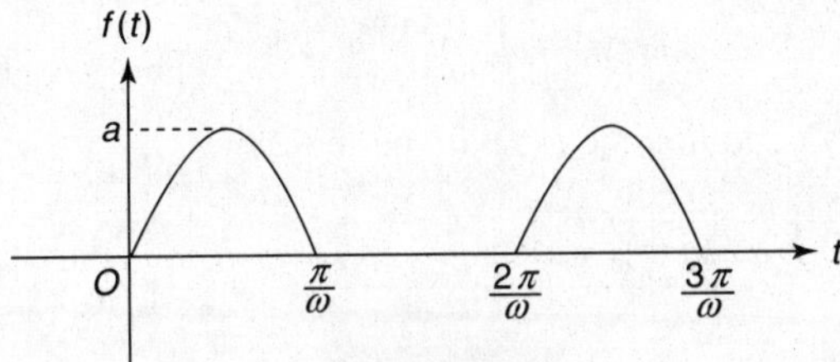


Fig. 10.11

**Solution** The function $f(t)$ is known as a half-sine wave rectifier function with period $\frac{2\pi}{\omega}$.

$$f(t) = a\sin\omega t \quad 0 < t < \frac{\pi}{\omega}$$

$$= 0 \quad \frac{\pi}{\omega} < t < \frac{2\pi}{\omega}$$

The function $f(t)$ is a periodic function.

$$L\{f(t)\} = \frac{1}{1-e^{-\left(\frac{2\pi}{\omega}\right)s}} \int_0^{\frac{2\pi}{\omega}} f(t)e^{-st}\, dt$$

$$= \frac{1}{1-e^{-\frac{2\pi s}{\omega}}} \left( \int_0^{\frac{\pi}{\omega}} a\sin\omega t\, e^{-st} dt + \int_{\frac{\pi}{\omega}}^{\frac{2\pi}{\omega}} 0 \cdot e^{-st}\, dt \right)$$

$$= \frac{a}{1-e^{-\frac{2\pi s}{\omega}}} \left[ \frac{1}{s^2+\omega^2} \cdot e^{-st}(-s\sin\omega t - \omega\cos\omega t) \right]_0^{\frac{\pi}{\omega}}$$

$$= \frac{a}{1-e^{-\frac{2\pi s}{\omega}}} \cdot \frac{1}{s^2+\omega^2} \left[ e^{-\frac{\pi s}{\omega}}(\omega) + \omega \right]$$

$$= \frac{a\omega\left(1+e^{\frac{-\pi s}{\omega}}\right)}{\left(1+e^{\frac{-\pi s}{\omega}}\right)\left(1-e^{\frac{-\pi s}{\omega}}\right)} \cdot \frac{1}{s^2+\omega^2}$$

$$= \frac{a\omega}{\left(1-e^{\frac{-\pi s}{\omega}}\right)} \cdot \frac{1}{s^2+\omega^2}$$

**EXAMPLE 10.40**

*Find the Laplace transform of*

$$f(t) = t^2 \qquad 0 < t < 2$$

if $$f(t) = f(t+2).$$

**Solution** The function $f(t)$ is a periodic function with period 2.

$$L\{f(t)\} = \frac{1}{1-e^{-2s}}\int_0^2 e^{-st} f(t)\,dt = \frac{1}{1-e^{-2s}}\int_0^2 e^{-st}\cdot t^2\,dt$$

$$= \frac{1}{1-e^{-2s}}\left[t^2\cdot\left(\frac{e^{-st}}{-s}\right) - 2t\left(\frac{e^{-st}}{s^2}\right) + 2\left(\frac{e^{-st}}{-s^3}\right)\right]_0^2$$

$$= \frac{1}{1-e^{-2s}}\left(-4\frac{e^{-2s}}{s} - 4\frac{e^{-2s}}{s^2} - 2\frac{e^{-2s}}{s^3} + \frac{2}{s^3}\right)$$

$$= \frac{1}{\left(1-e^{-2s}\right)s^3}\left(2 - 2e^{-2s} - 4se^{-2s} - 4s^2e^{-2s}\right)$$

**EXAMPLE 10.41**

*Find the Laplace transform of*

$$f(t) = e^t \qquad 0 < t < 2\pi$$

if $$f(t) = f(t+2\pi).$$

**Solution** The function $f(t)$ is a periodic function with period $2\pi$.

$$L\{f(t)\} = \frac{1}{1-e^{-2\pi s}}\int_0^{2\pi} e^{-st} f(t)\,dt$$

$$= \frac{1}{1-e^{-2\pi s}}\int_0^{2\pi} e^{-st} e^t\,dt$$

$$= \frac{1}{1-e^{-2\pi s}}\int_0^{2\pi} e^{(1-s)t}\,dt$$

$$= \frac{1}{1-e^{-2\pi s}}\left[\frac{e^{(1-s)t}}{1-s}\right]_0^{2\pi}$$

$$= \frac{1}{1-e^{-2\pi s}}\left[\frac{e^{(1-s)2\pi}}{1-s} - \frac{1}{1-s}\right]$$

$$= \frac{e^{(1-s)2\pi} - 1}{(1-e^{-2\pi s})(1-s)}$$

**EXAMPLE 10.42**

*Find the Laplace transform of the function shown in Fig. 10.12.*

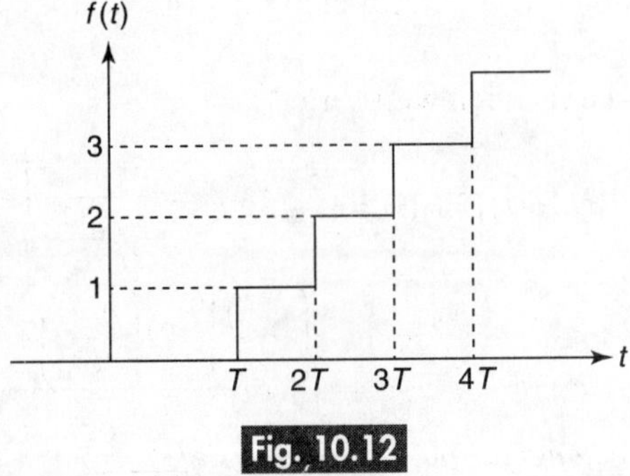


Fig. 10.12

**Solution** The function $f(t)$ can be represented in terms of Heaviside unit step function.

$$f(t) = [u(t-T) - u(t-2T)] + 2[u(t-2T) - u(t-3T) + 3[u(t-3T) - u(t-4t)] + \dots\infty$$

$$= u(t-T) + u(t-2T) + u(t-3T) + \dots\infty$$

$$L\{f(t)\} = L\{u(t-T) + u(t-2T) + u(t-3T) + \dots\}$$

$$= \frac{1}{s}e^{-Ts} + \frac{1}{s}e^{-2Ts} + \frac{1}{s}e^{-3Ts} + \dots$$

$$= \frac{1}{s}\left[e^{-Ts} + e^{-2Ts} + e^{-3Ts} + \dots\right]$$

$$= \frac{e^{-Ts}}{s(1-e^{-Ts})}$$

## 10.5 WAVEFORM SYNTHESIS

LO 10.5

Describe waveform synthesis

Any waveform can be constructed with unit step, unit ramp and unit impulse functions, etc. We know the Laplace transforms of these special functions. Hence, we can find the Laplace transform of any function in terms of these functions.

There is another way of synthesising the waveforms. Any function can be expressed in terms of a gate function. The gate function is shown in Fig. 10.13.

This function can be expressed in terms of unit-step functions.

$$f(t) = Au(t) - Au(t-T)$$

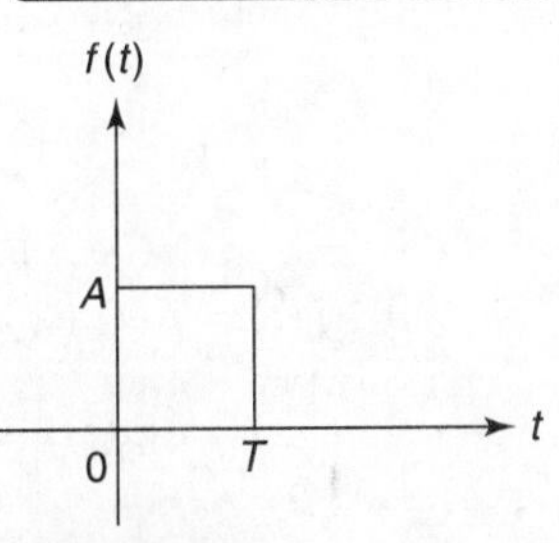


Fig. 10.13 *Gate function*

**EXAMPLE 10.43**

*Find the Laplace transform of the unit-doublet function.*

**Solution** The unit-doublet function $\delta'(t)$ is shown in Fig. 10.14.

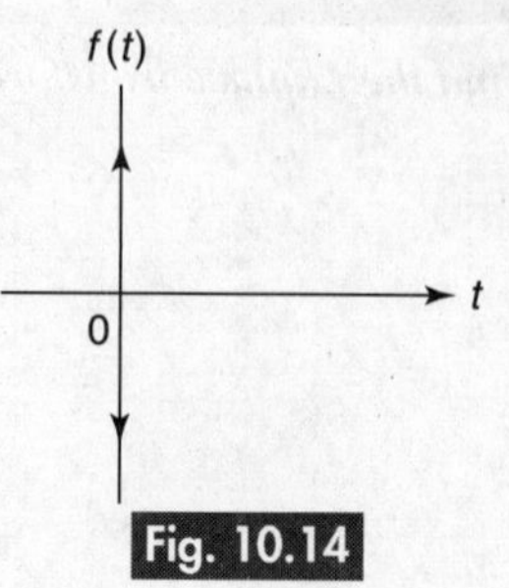

Fig. 10.14

$$\delta'(t) = \frac{d}{dt}\delta(t)$$

$$L\{\delta'(t)\} = L\left\{\frac{d}{dt}\delta(t)\right\} = sL\{\delta(t)\} = s(1) = s$$

**EXAMPLE 10.44**

*Find the Laplace transform of a rectangular pulse shown in Fig. 10.15.*

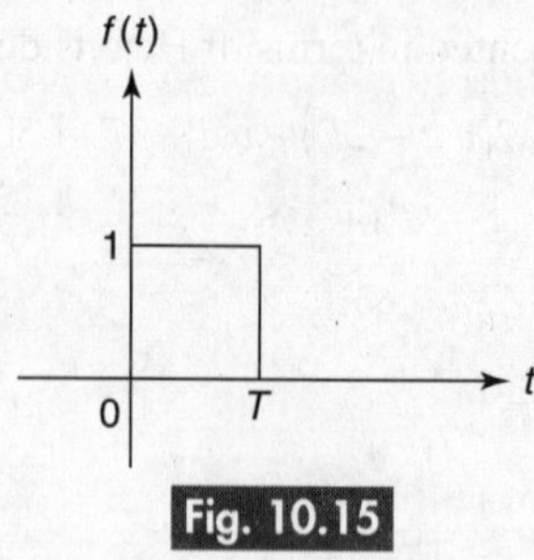

Fig. 10.15

**Solution** The rectangular pulse can be constructed from two functions, as shown in Fig. 10.16. This function is known as gate function.

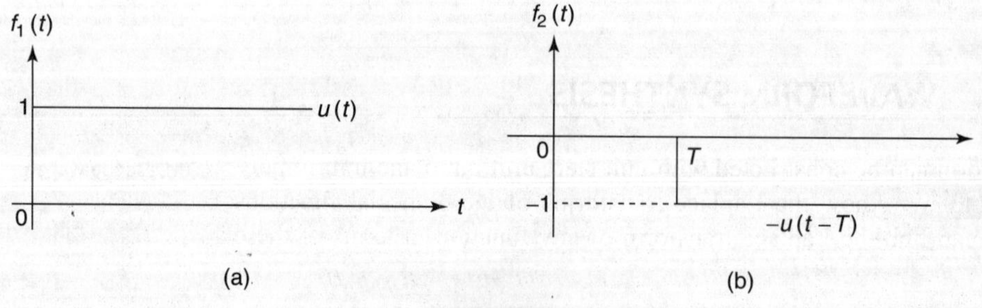

Fig. 10.16

$$f(t) = f_1(t) + f_2(t) = u(t) - u(t-T)$$

$$F(s) = L\{u(t)\} - L\{u(t-T)\} = \frac{1}{s} - \frac{1}{s}e^{-Ts} = \frac{1}{s}(1 - e^{-Ts})$$

## EXAMPLE 10.45

*Find the Laplace transform of a sawtooth waveform shown in Fig. 10.17.*

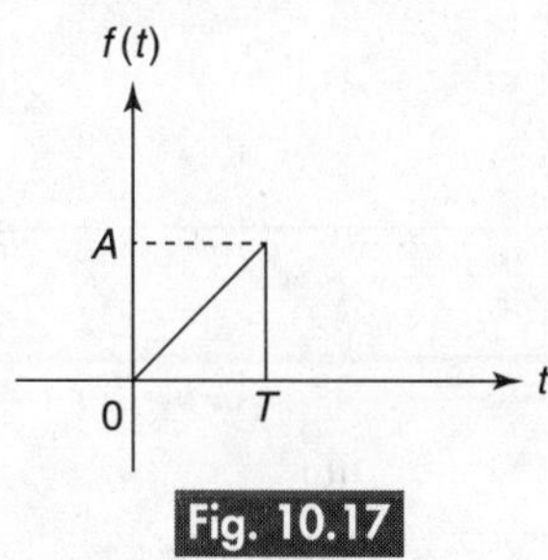


Fig. 10.17

**Solution** The sawtooth waveform can be constructed from three functions, as shown in Fig. 10.18.

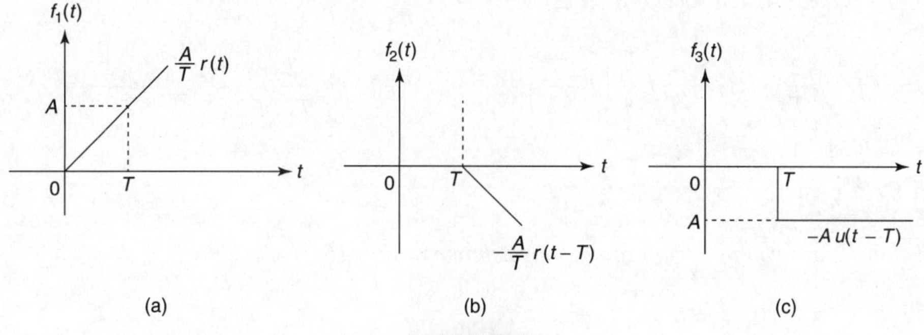


Fig. 10.18

$$f(t) = f_1(t) + f_2(t) + f_3(t) = \frac{A}{T}r(t) - \frac{A}{T}r(t-T) - Au(t-T)$$

$$F(s) = \frac{A}{T}L\{r(t)\} - \frac{A}{T}L\{r(t-T)\} - AL\{u(t-T)\} = \frac{A}{Ts^2} - \frac{A}{T}\frac{1}{s^2}e^{-Ts} - \frac{A}{s}e^{-Ts}$$

## EXAMPLE 10.46

*Find the Laplace transform of a triangular waveform shown in Fig. 10.19.*

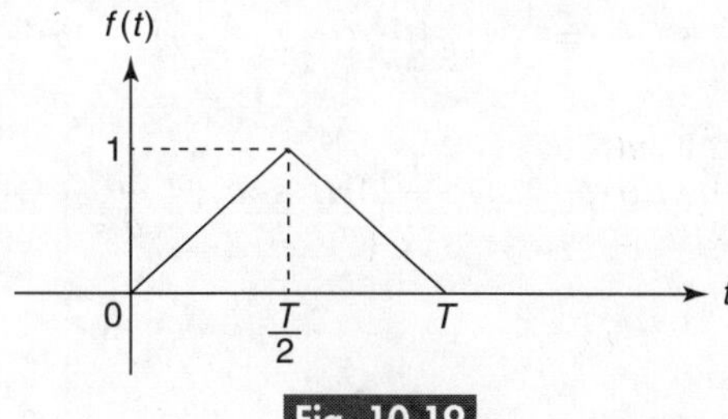


Fig. 10.19

**Solution** The triangular waveform can be constructed from three ramp functions, as shown in Fig. 10.20.

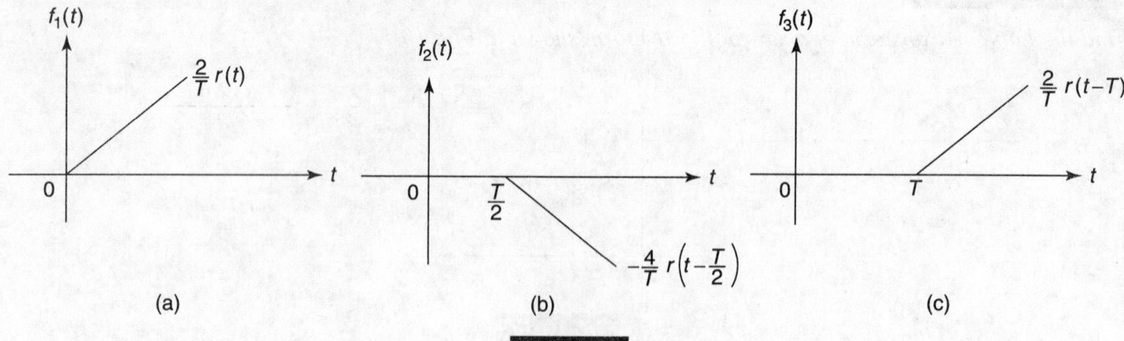


Fig. 10.20

$$f(t) = f_1(t) + f_2(t) + f_3(t) = \frac{2}{T}r(t) - \frac{4}{T}r\left(t - \frac{T}{2}\right) + \frac{2}{T}r(t-T)$$

$$F(s) = \frac{2}{T}L\{r(t)\} - \frac{4}{T}L\left\{r\left(t - \frac{T}{2}\right)\right\} + \frac{2}{T}L\{r(t-T)\} = \frac{2}{Ts^2} - \frac{4}{Ts^2}e^{-\frac{Ts}{2}} + \frac{2}{Ts^2}e^{-Ts}$$

**EXAMPLE 10.47**

*Find the Laplace transform of a trapezoidal pulse shown in Fig. 10.21.*

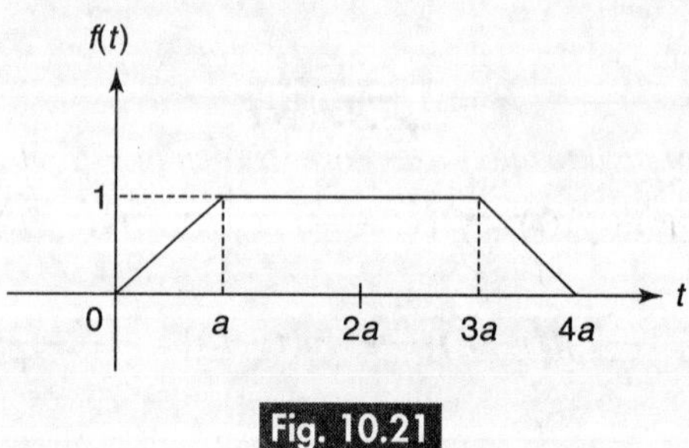


Fig. 10.21

**Solution** The trapezoidal waveform can be constructed from four ramp functions, as shown in Fig. 10.22.

$$f(t) = f_1(t) + f_2(t) + f_3(t) + f_4(t) = \frac{1}{a}r(t) - \frac{1}{a}r(t-a) - \frac{1}{a}r(t-3a) + \frac{1}{a}r(t-4a)$$

$$F(s) = \frac{1}{a}L\{r(t)\} - \frac{1}{a}L\{r(t-a)\} - \frac{1}{a}L\{r(t-3a)\} + \frac{1}{a}L\{r(t-4a)\} = \frac{1}{a}\frac{1}{s^2} - \frac{1}{a}\frac{1}{s^2}e^{-as} - \frac{1}{a}\frac{1}{s^2}e^{-3as} + \frac{1}{a}\frac{1}{s^2}e^{-4s}$$

$$= \frac{1}{as^2}(1 - e^{-as} - e^{-3as} + e^{-4as})$$

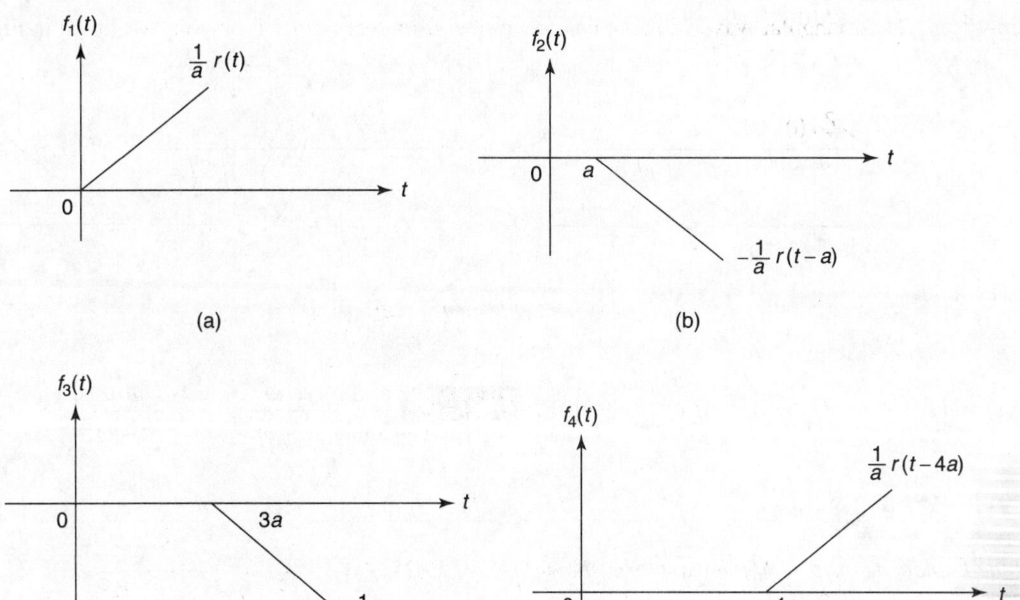


Fig. 10.22

## EXAMPLE 10.48

*Find the Laplace transform of a sinusoidal waveform shown in Fig. 10.23.*

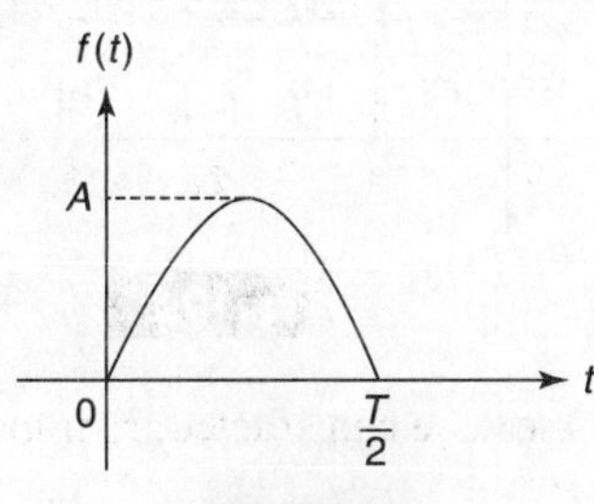


Fig. 10.23

**Solution** The waveform can be constructed from two functions, as shown in Fig. 10.24.

$$f(t) = f_1(t) + f_2(t) = A\sin\omega t\ u(t) + A\sin\omega t\left(t - \frac{T}{2}\right)u\left(t - \frac{T}{2}\right)$$

where $$\omega = \frac{2\pi}{T}$$

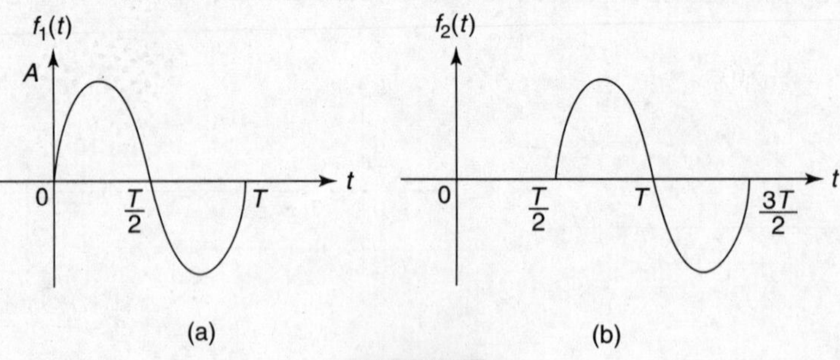


Fig. 10.24

$$F(s) = A\,L\{\sin\omega t\, u(t)\} + AL\left\{\sin\omega t\left(t-\frac{T}{2}\right)u\left(t-\frac{T}{2}\right)\right\} = \frac{A\omega}{s^2+\omega^2} + \frac{A\omega}{s^2+\omega^2}e^{-\frac{Ts}{2}} = \frac{A\omega}{s^2+\omega^2}\left(1+e^{-\frac{Ts}{2}}\right)$$

## EXAMPLE 10.49

*Find the Laplace transform of the waveform shown in Fig. 10.25.*

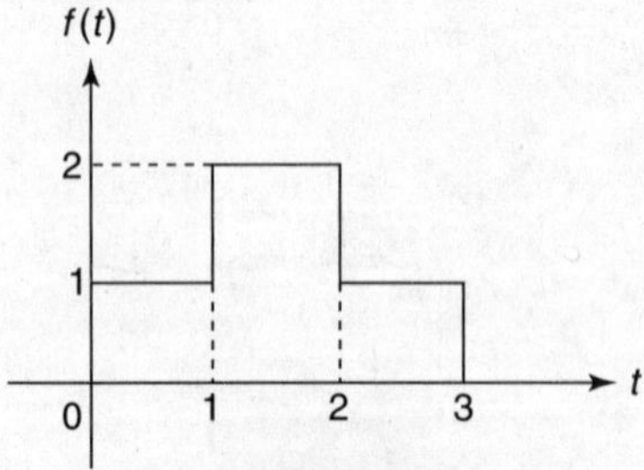


Fig. 10.25

**Solution** The function $f(t)$ can be expressed as sum of four step-functions.

$$f(t) = u(t) + u(t-1) - u(t-2) - u(t-3)$$

$$F(s) = L\{u(t)\} + L\{u(t-1)\} - L\{u(t-2)\} - L\{u(t-3)\} = \frac{1}{s} + \frac{1}{s}e^{-s} - \frac{1}{s}e^{-2s} - \frac{1}{s}e^{-3s} = \frac{1}{s}\left(1 + e^{-s} - e^{-2s} - e^{-3s}\right)$$

## EXAMPLE 10.50

*Determine the Laplace transform of the waveform shown in Fig. 10.26.*

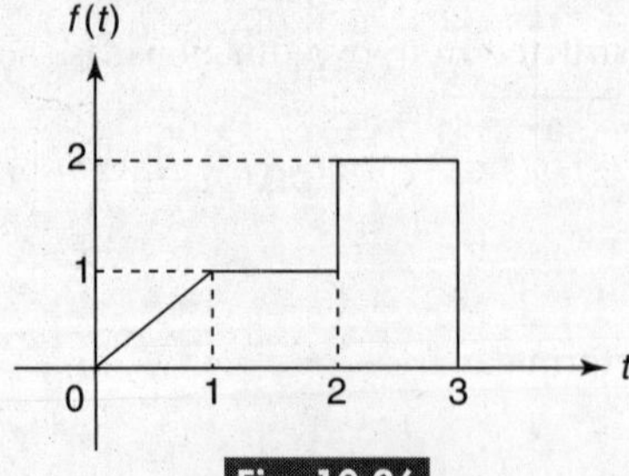


Fig. 10.26

**Solution** The function $f(t)$ can be expressed as sum of four functions, as shown in Fig. 10.27.

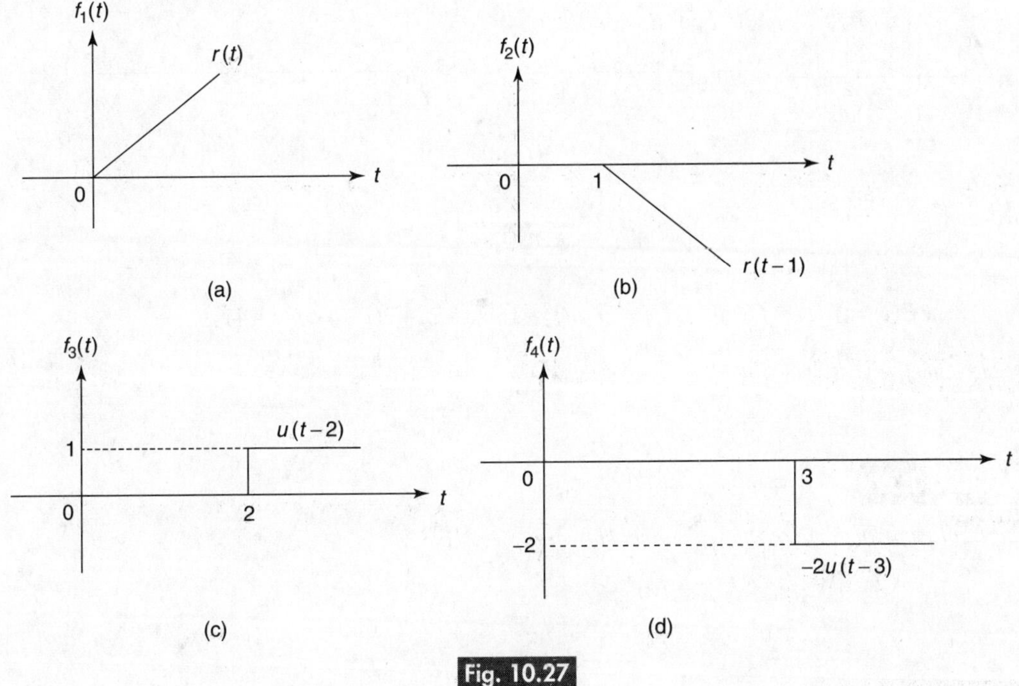


Fig. 10.27

$$f(t)=f_1(t)+f_2(t)+f_3(t)+f_4(t)=r(t)+r(t-1)+u(t-2)-2u(t-3)$$

$$F(s)=L\{r(t)\}+L\{r(t-1)\}+L\{u(t-2)\}-2L\{u(t-3)\}=\frac{1}{s^2}+\frac{1}{s^2}e^{-s}+\frac{1}{s}e^{-2s}-\frac{2}{s}e^{-3s}$$

## EXAMPLE 10.51

*Find the Laplace transform of the waveform shown in Fig. 10.28.*

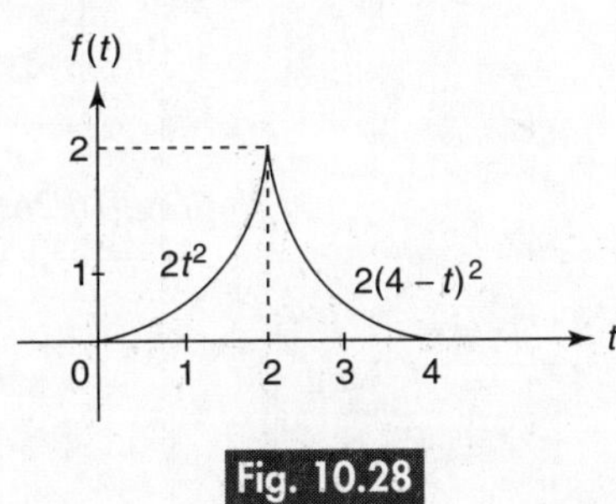


Fig. 10.28

**Solution** The given parabolic waveform can be constructed from three functions, as shown in Fig. 10.29.

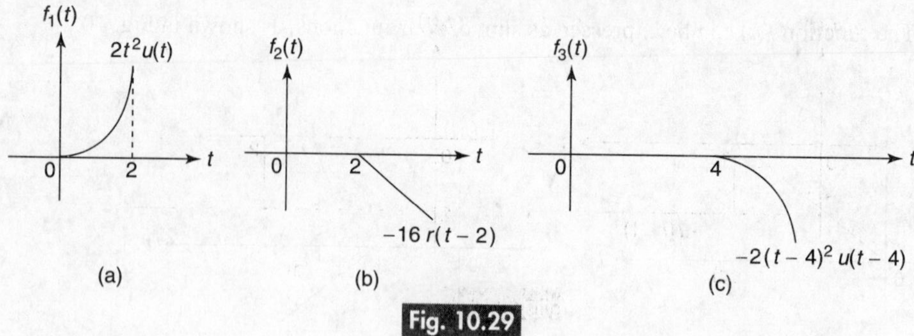


Fig. 10.29

$$F(t) = f_1(t) + f_2(t) + f_3(t) = 2t^2u(t) - 16r(t-2) - 2(t-4)^2u(t-4)$$

$$F(s) = 2L\{t^2u(t)\} - 16L\{r(t-2)\} - 2L\{(t-4)^2u(t-4)\} = 2\frac{2}{s^3} - 16\frac{1}{s^2}e^{-2s} - 2\frac{2}{s^3}e^{-4s} = \frac{4}{s^3}(1-e^{-4s}) - \frac{16}{s^2}e^{-2s}$$

## EXAMPLE 10.52

*Find the Laplace transform of the waveform shown in Fig. 10.30.*

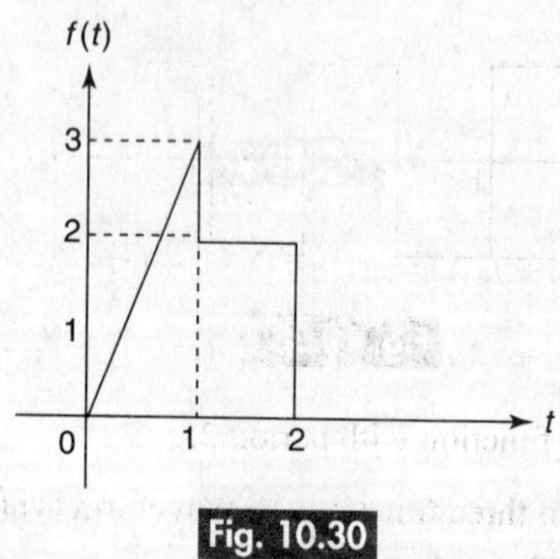


Fig. 10.30

**Solution** The given waveform can be constructed from four functions, as shown in Fig. 10.31.

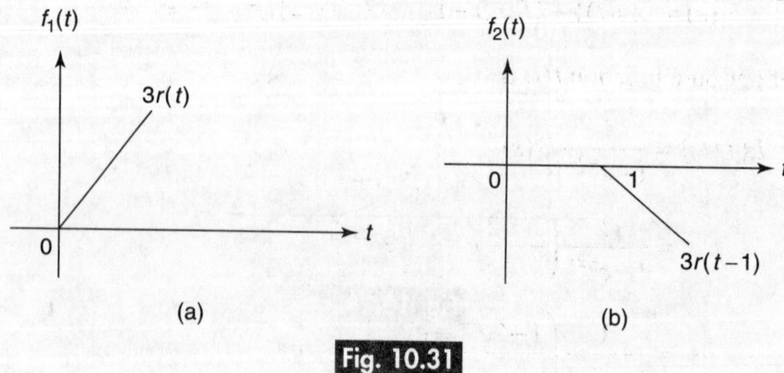


Fig. 10.31

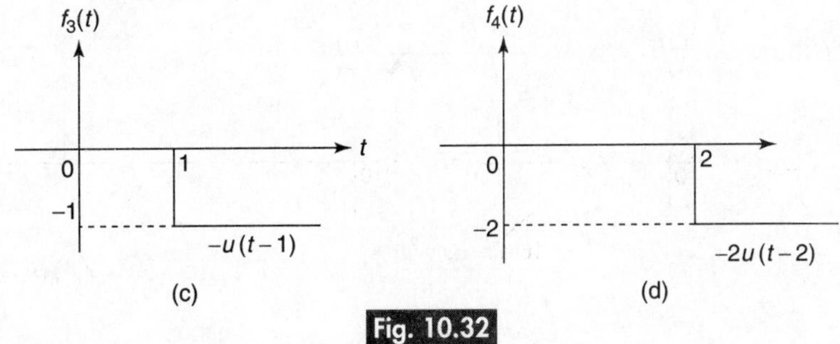


Fig. 10.32

$$f(t) = f_1(t) + f_2(t) + f_3(t) + f_4(t) = 3r(t) - 3r(t-1) - u(t-1) - 2u(t-2)$$

$$F(s) = 3L\{r(t)\} - 3L\{r(t-1)\} - L\{u(t-1)\} - 2L\{u(t-2)\} = \frac{3}{s^2} - \frac{3}{s^2}e^{-s} - \frac{1}{s}e^{-s} - \frac{2}{s}e^{-2s}$$

**EXAMPLE 10.53**

*Find the Laplace transform of the periodic waveform shown in Fig. 10.33.*

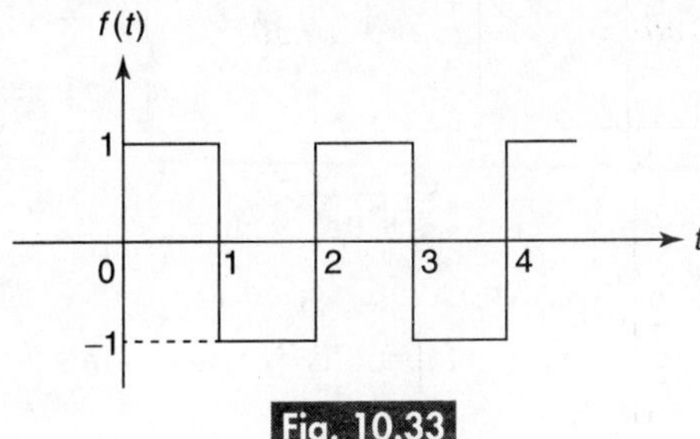


Fig. 10.33

**Solution** The function $f(t)$ is a periodic function with period 2.

The function $f_1(t)$ can be constructed from three functions by waveform synthesis.

$$f_1(t) = u(t) - 2u(t-1) + u(t-2)$$

$$F_1(s) = L\{u(t)\} - 2L\{u(t-1)\} + L\{u(t-2)\} = \frac{1}{s} - \frac{2}{s}e^{-s} + \frac{1}{s}e^{-2s}$$

The Laplace transform of periodic function $f(t)$ is

$$L\{f(t)\} = \frac{1}{1-e^{-2s}} F_1(s)$$

$$= \frac{1}{1-e^{-2s}}\left(\frac{1}{s} - \frac{2}{s}e^{-s} + \frac{1}{s}e^{-2s}\right)$$

$$= \frac{1}{1-e^{-2s}}\left(\frac{1-2e^{-s}+e^{-2s}}{s}\right)$$

$$= \frac{(1-e^{-s})^2}{s(1-e^{-s})(1+e^{-s})}$$

$$= \frac{1}{s}\frac{1-e^{-s}}{1+e^{-s}}$$

$$= \frac{1}{s}\frac{e^{\frac{s}{2}} - e^{-\frac{s}{2}}}{e^{\frac{s}{2}} + e^{-\frac{s}{2}}}$$

$$= \frac{1}{s}\tanh\left(\frac{s}{2}\right)$$

**EXAMPLE 10.54**

*Find the Laplace transform of the waveform shown in Fig. 10.34.*

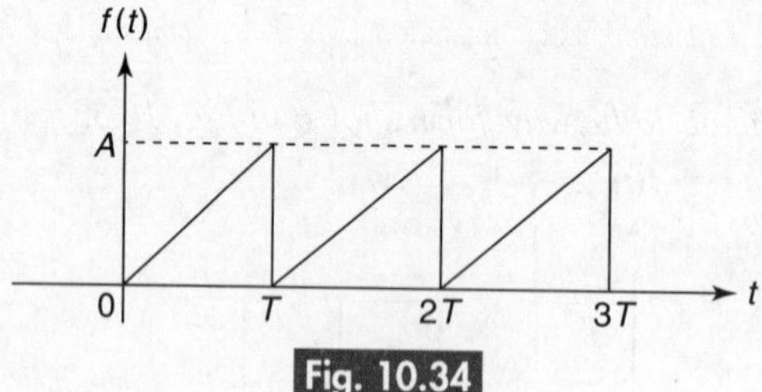


Fig. 10.34

**Solution** The function $f(t)$ is a periodic function with period $T$.

The function $f_1(t)$ can be constructed from three functions by waveform synthesis.

$$f_1(t) = \frac{A}{T}r(t) - \frac{A}{T}r(t-T) - Au(t-T)$$

$$F_1(s) = \frac{A}{T}L\{r(t)\} - \frac{A}{T}L\{r(t-T)\} - A\,L\{u(t-T)\} = \frac{A}{Ts^2} - \frac{A}{T}\frac{1}{s^2}e^{-Ts} - \frac{A}{s}e^{-Ts}$$

The Laplace transform of the periodic function $f(t)$ is

$$L\{f(t)\} = \frac{1}{1-e^{-Ts}}F_1(s) = \frac{1}{1-e^{-Ts}}\left(\frac{A}{Ts^2} - \frac{A}{T}e^{-Ts} - \frac{A}{s}e^{-Ts}\right)$$

**EXAMPLE 10.55**

*Find the Laplace transform of periodic waveform shown in Fig. 10.35.*

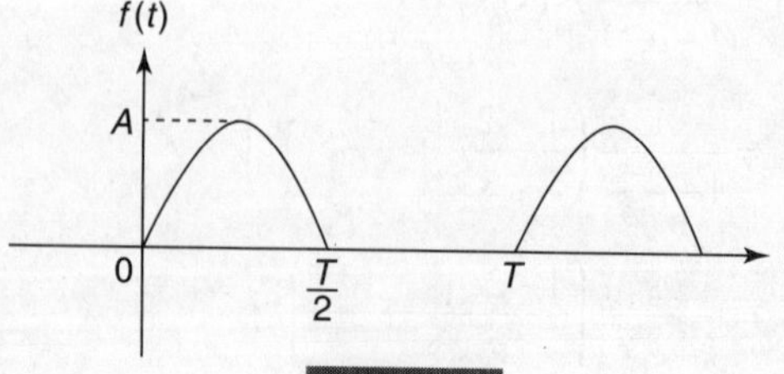


Fig. 10.35

**Solution** The function $f(t)$ is a periodic function with period $T$.

The function $f_1(t)$ can be constructed from two functions by waveform synthesis.

$$f_1(t) = A\sin\omega t\, u(t) + A\sin\omega\left(t - \frac{T}{2}\right)u\left(t - \frac{T}{2}\right)$$

$$F_1(s) = AL\{\sin\omega t\, u(t)\} + AL\left\{\sin\omega\left(t - \frac{T}{2}\right)u\left(t - \frac{T}{2}\right)\right\} = A\frac{\omega}{s^2+\omega^2} + A\frac{\omega}{s^2+\omega^2}e^{-\frac{Ts}{2}} = \frac{A\omega}{s^2+\omega^2}\left(1+e^{-\frac{Ts}{2}}\right)$$

The Laplace transform of the periodic function $f(t)$ is

$$\begin{aligned}
L\{f(t)\} &= \frac{1}{1-e^{-Ts}}F_1(s) \\
&= \frac{1}{1-e^{-Ts}}\frac{A\omega}{s^2+\omega^2}\left(1+e^{-\frac{Ts}{2}}\right) \\
&= \frac{A\omega}{s^2+\omega^2}\frac{1+e^{-\frac{Ts}{2}}}{\left(1-e^{-\frac{Ts}{2}}\right)\left(1+e^{-\frac{Ts}{2}}\right)} \\
&= \frac{A\omega}{s^2+\omega^2}\frac{1}{1-e^{-\frac{Ts}{2}}}
\end{aligned}$$

## 10.6 INVERSE LAPLACE TRANSFORM

LO 10.6

Find inverse Laplace transform

If $L\{f(t)\} = F(s)$ then $f(t)$ is called inverse Laplace transform of $F(s)$ and symbolically written as

$$f(t) = L^{-1}\{F(s)\}$$

where $L^{-1}$ is called the inverse Laplace transform operator.

Inverse Laplace transform can be found by the following methods:

(i) Standard results
(ii) Partial fraction expansion
(iii) Convolution theorem

### 10.6.1 Standard Results

Inverse Laplace transforms of some simple functions can be found by standard results and properties of Laplace transform.

## EXAMPLE 10.56

*Find the inverse Laplace transform of* $\dfrac{s^2-3s+4}{s^3}$.

**Solution**

$$F(s)=\frac{s^2-3s+4}{s^3}=\frac{1}{s}-\frac{3}{s^2}+\frac{4}{s^3}$$

$$L^{-1}\{F(s)\}=1-3t+2t^2$$

## EXAMPLE 10.57

*Find the inverse Laplace transform of* $\dfrac{3s+4}{s^2+9}$.

**Solution**

$$F(s)=\frac{3s+4}{s^2+9}=\frac{3s}{s^2+9}+\frac{4}{s^2+9}$$

$$L^{-1}\{F(s)\}=3\cos 3t+\frac{4}{3}\sin 3t$$

## EXAMPLE 10.58

*Find the inverse Laplace transform of* $\dfrac{4s+15}{16s^2-25}$.

**Solution**

$$F(s)=\frac{4s+15}{16s^2-25}=\frac{4s+15}{16\left(s^2-\frac{25}{16}\right)}=\frac{1}{4}\frac{s}{s^2-\frac{25}{16}}+\frac{15}{16}\frac{1}{s^2-\frac{25}{16}}$$

$$L^{-1}\{F(s)\}=\frac{1}{4}\cosh\frac{5}{4}t+\frac{3}{4}\sinh\frac{5}{4}t$$

## EXAMPLE 10.59

*Find the inverse Laplace transform of* $\dfrac{2s+2}{s^2+2s+10}$.

**Solution**

$$F(s)=\frac{2s+2}{s^2+2s+10}=\frac{2(s+1)}{(s+1)^2+9}$$

$$L^{-1}\{F(s)\}=2e^{-t}L^{-1}\left\{\frac{s}{s^2+9}\right\}=2e^{-t}\cos 3t$$

## EXAMPLE 10.60

*Find the inverse Laplace transform of* $\dfrac{3s+7}{s^2-2s-3}$.

**Solution**

$$F(s)=\frac{3s+7}{s^2-2s-3}=\frac{3(s-1)+10}{(s-1)^2-4}=3\frac{(s-1)}{(s-1)^2-4}+10\frac{1}{(s-1)^2-4}$$

$$L^{-1}\{F(s)\}=3e^t L^{-1}\left\{\frac{s}{s^2-4}\right\}+10e^t L^{-1}\left\{\frac{1}{s^2-4}\right\}=3e^t\cosh 2t+5e^t\sinh 2t$$

### 10.6.2 Partial Fraction Expansion

Any function $F(s)$ can be written as $\frac{P(s)}{Q(s)}$ where $P(s)$ and $Q(s)$ are polynomials in $s$. For performing partial fraction expansion, the degree of $P(s)$ must be less than the degree of $Q(s)$. If not, $P(s)$ must be divided by $Q(s)$, so that the degree of $P(s)$ becomes less than that of $Q(s)$. Assuming that the degree of $P(s)$ is less than that of $Q(s)$, four possible cases arise depending upon the factors of $Q(s)$.

***Case I*** Factors are linear and distinct,

$$F(s)=\frac{P(s)}{(s+a)(s+b)}$$

By partial-fraction expansion,

$$F(s)=\frac{A}{s+a}+\frac{B}{s+b}$$

***Case II*** Factors are linear and repeated,

$$F(s)=\frac{P(s)}{(s+a)(s+b)^n}$$

By partial-fraction expansion,

$$F(s)=\frac{A}{s+a}+\frac{B_1}{s+b}+\frac{B_2}{(s+b)^2}+\ldots+\frac{B_n}{(s+b)^n}$$

***Case III*** Factors are quadratic and distinct,

$$F(s)=\frac{P(s)}{(s^2+as+b)(s^2+cs+d)}$$

By partial-fraction expansion,

$$F(s)=\frac{As+B}{s^2+as+b}+\frac{Cs+D}{s^2+cs+d}$$

***Case IV*** Factors are quadratic are repeated,

$$F(s)=\frac{P(s)}{(s^2+as+b)(s^2+cs+d)^n}$$

By partial-fraction expansion,

$$F(s)=\frac{As+B}{s^2+as+b}+\frac{C_1s+D_1}{s^2+cs+d}+\frac{C_2s+D_2}{(s^2+cs+d)^2}+\ldots+\frac{C_ns+D_n}{(s^2+cs+d)^n}$$

**EXAMPLE 10.61**

*Find the inverse Laplace transform of* $\dfrac{s+2}{s(s+1)(s+3)}$.

**Solution**

$$F(s)=\frac{s+2}{s(s+1)(s+3)}$$

By partial-fraction expansion,

$$F(s)=\frac{A}{s}+\frac{B}{s+1}+\frac{C}{s+3}$$

$$A=sF(s)\Big|_{s=0}=\left.\frac{s+2}{(s+1)(s+3)}\right|_{s=0}=\frac{2}{3}$$

$$B=(s+1)F(s)\Big|_{s=-1}=\left.\frac{s+2}{s(s+3)}\right|_{s=-1}=-\frac{1}{2}$$

$$C=(s+3)F(s)\Big|_{s=-3}=\left.\frac{s+2}{s(s+1)}\right|_{s=-3}=-\frac{1}{6}$$

$$F(s)=\frac{2}{3}\cdot\frac{1}{s}-\frac{1}{2}\cdot\frac{1}{s+1}-\frac{1}{6}\cdot\frac{1}{s+3}$$

$$L^{-1}\{F(s)\}=\frac{2}{3}L^{-1}\left\{\frac{1}{s}\right\}-\frac{1}{2}L^{-1}\left\{\frac{1}{s+1}\right\}-\frac{1}{6}L^{-1}\left\{\frac{1}{s+3}\right\}=\frac{2}{3}-\frac{1}{2}e^{-t}-\frac{1}{6}e^{-3t}$$

**EXAMPLE 10.62**

*Find the inverse Laplace transform of* $\dfrac{s+2}{s^2(s+3)}$.

**Solution**

$$F(s)=\frac{s+2}{s^2(s+3)}$$

By partial-fraction expansion,

$$F(s)=\frac{A}{s}+\frac{B}{s^2}+\frac{C}{s+3}$$

$$\begin{aligned}s+2&=As(s+3)+B(s+3)+Cs^2\\&=As^2+3As+Bs+3B+Cs^2\\&=(A+C)s^2+(3A+B)s+3B\end{aligned}$$

Comparing coefficients of $s^2, s^1$ and $s^0$,

$$\begin{aligned}A+C&=0\\3A+B&=1\\3B&=2\end{aligned}$$

Solving these equations,

$$A=\frac{1}{9},\ B=\frac{2}{3},\ C=-\frac{1}{9}$$

$$F(s)=\frac{1}{9}\cdot\frac{1}{s}+\frac{2}{3}\cdot\frac{1}{s^2}-\frac{1}{9}\cdot\frac{1}{s+3}$$

$$L^{-1}\{F(s)\}=\frac{1}{9}L^{-1}\left\{\frac{1}{s}\right\}+\frac{2}{3}L^{-1}\left\{\frac{1}{s^2}\right\}-\frac{1}{9}L^{-1}\left\{\frac{1}{s+3}\right\}=\frac{1}{9}+\frac{2}{3}t-\frac{1}{9}e^{-3t}$$

## EXAMPLE 10.63

*Find the inverse Laplace transform of* $\dfrac{s^2-15s-11}{(s+1)(s-2)^2}$.

**Solution**

$$F(s)=\frac{5s^2-15s-11}{(s+1)(s-2)^2}$$

By partial-fraction expansion,

$$F(s)=\frac{A}{s+1}+\frac{B}{s-2}+\frac{C}{(s-2)^2}$$

$$\begin{aligned}5s^2-15s-11&=A(s-2)^2+B(s+1)(s-2)+C(s+1)\\&=A(s^2-4s+4)+B(s^2-s-2)+C(s+1)\\&=As^2-4As+4A+Bs^2-Bs-2B+Cs+c\\&=(A+B)s^2-(4A+B-C)s+(4A-2B+C)\end{aligned}$$

Comparing coefficients of $s^2$, $s^1$ and $s^0$,

$$\begin{aligned}A+B&=5\\4A+B-C&=15\\4A-2B+C&=-11\end{aligned}$$

Solving these equations,

$$\begin{aligned}A&=1\\B&=4\\C&=-7\end{aligned}$$

$$F(s)=\frac{1}{s+1}+\frac{4}{s-2}-\frac{7}{(s-2)^2}$$

$$L^{-1}\{F(s)\}=L^{-1}\left\{\frac{1}{s+1}\right\}+4L^{-1}\left\{\frac{1}{s-2}\right\}-7L^{-1}\left\{\frac{1}{(s-2)^2}\right\}=e^{-t}+4e^{2t}-7te^{2t}$$

**EXAMPLE 10.64**

*Find the inverse Laplace transform of* $\dfrac{3s+1}{(s+1)(s^2+2)}$.

**Solution**

$$F(s)=\frac{3s+1}{(s+1)(s^2+2)}$$

By partial-fraction expansion,

$$F(s)=\frac{A}{s+1}+\frac{Bs+C}{s^2+2}$$

$$\begin{aligned}3s+1&=A(s^2+2)+(Bs+C)(s+1)\\&=As^2+2A+Bs^2+Bs+Cs+C\\&=(A+B)s^2+(B+C)s+(2A+C)\end{aligned}$$

Comparing coefficients of $s^2, s^1$ and $s^0$,

$$\begin{aligned}A+B&=0\\B+C&=3\\2A+C&=1\end{aligned}$$

Solving these equations,

$$A=-\frac{2}{3},\; B=\frac{2}{3},\; C=\frac{7}{3}$$

$$F(s)=-\frac{2}{3}\cdot\frac{1}{s+1}+\frac{2}{3}\cdot\frac{s}{s^2+2}+\frac{7}{3}\cdot\frac{1}{s^2+2}$$

$$L^{-1}\{F(s)\}=-\frac{2}{3}L^{-1}\left\{\frac{1}{s+1}\right\}+\frac{2}{3}L^{-1}\left\{\frac{s}{s^2+2}\right\}+\frac{7}{3}L^{-1}\left\{\frac{1}{s^2+2}\right\}=-\frac{2}{3}e^{-t}+\frac{2}{3}\cos\sqrt{2}t+\frac{7}{3\sqrt{2}}\sin\sqrt{2}t$$

**EXAMPLE 10.65**

*Find the inverse Laplace transform of* $\dfrac{s}{(s^2+1)(s^2+4)}$.

**Solution**

$$F(s)=\frac{s}{(s^2+1)(s^2+4)}=\frac{s}{3}\left[\frac{s^2+4-s^2-1}{(s^2+1)(s^2+4)}\right]=\frac{1}{3}\left[\frac{s}{s^2+1}-\frac{s}{s^2+4}\right]$$

$$L^{-1}\{F(s)\}=\frac{1}{3}\left[L^{-1}\left\{\frac{s}{s^2+1}\right\}-L^{-1}\left\{\frac{s}{s^2+4}\right\}\right]=\frac{1}{3}[\cos t-\cos 2t]$$

### 10.6.3 Convolution Theorem

If $L^{-1}\{F_1(s)\}=f_1(t)$ and $L^{-1}\{F_2(s)\}=f_2(t)$ then $L^{-1}\{F_1(s)\cdot F_2(s)\}=\int_0^t f_1(u)f_2(t-u)du$

where $\int_0^t f_1(u)f_2(t-u)du=f_1(t)*f_2(t)$

**Proof** $$F_1(s)\cdot F_2(s) = L\{f_1(t)\}\cdot L\{f_2(t)\} = \int_0^\infty e^{-su} f_1(u)du \cdot \int_0^\infty e^{-sv} f_2(v)dv = \int_0^\infty\int_0^\infty e^{-s(u+v)} f_1(u) f_2(v)du\,dv$$

$$= \int_0^\infty f_1(u)\left[\int_0^\infty e^{-s(u+v)} f_2(v)dv\right]du$$

Putting $u+v=t$, $\quad dv = dt$

When $\quad v=0,\quad t=u$

$\quad v\to\infty,\quad t\to\infty$

$$F_1(s)\cdot F_2(s) = \int_0^\infty f_1(u)\left[\int_u^\infty e^{-st} f_2(t-u)dt\right]du = \int_0^\infty\int_0^\infty e^{-st} f_1(u) f_2(t-u)dt\,du$$

The region of integration is bounded by the lines $u=0$ and $u=t$. To change the order of integration, draw a vertical strip which starts from line $u=0$ and terminates on the line $u=t$. Hence, $u$ varies from 0 to $t$ and $t$ varies from 0 to $\infty$.

$$F_1(s)\cdot F_2(s) = \int_0^\infty e^{-st}\int_0^t f_1(u) f_2(t-u)\,du\,dt = L\left\{\int_0^t f_1(u) f_2(t-u)\,du\right\}$$

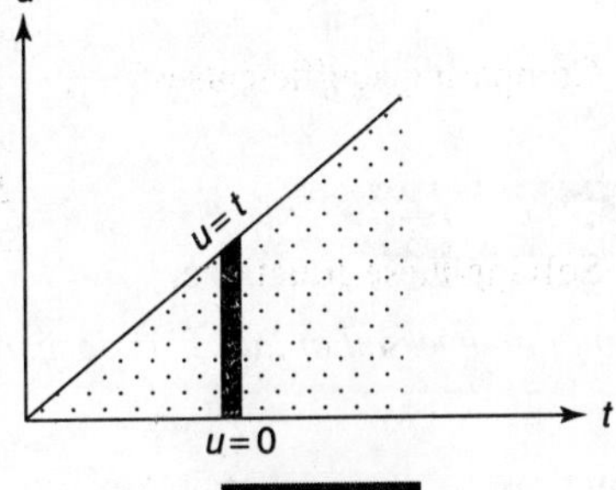

Fig. 10.36

Hence, $\quad L^{-1}\{F_1(s)\cdot F_2(s)\} = \int_0^t f_1(u) f_2(t-u)du$

**Note** Convolution operation is commutative, i.e.,

$$L\left\{\int_0^t f_1(u) f_2(t-u)du\right\} = L\left\{\int_0^t f_1(t-u) f_2(u)du\right\}$$

## EXAMPLE 10.66

*Find the inverse Laplace transform of* $\dfrac{1}{(s+2)(s-1)}$.

**Solution** $$F(s) = \frac{1}{(s+2)(s-1)}$$

Let $\quad F_1(s) = \dfrac{1}{s+2} \qquad F_2(s) = \dfrac{1}{s-1}$

$\quad f_1(t) = e^{-2t} \qquad f_2(t) = e^t$

By convolution theorem,

$$L^{-1}\{F(s)\} = \int_0^t e^{-2u} e^{t-u} du = e^t\int_0^t e^{-3u} du = e^t\left[\frac{e^{-3u}}{-3}\right]_0^t = \frac{e^t}{3}(1-e^{-3t})$$

## EXAMPLE 10.67

*Find the inverse Laplace transform of* $\dfrac{1}{s^2(s+1)^2}$.

**Solution**

$$F(s)=\frac{1}{s^2(s+1)^2}$$

Let

$$F(s)=\frac{1}{(s+1)^2} \qquad F_2(s)=\frac{1}{s^2}$$

$$f_1(t)=te^{-t} \qquad f_2(t)=t$$

By convolution theorem,

$$L^{-1}\{F(s)\}=\int_0^t ue^{-u}(t-u)\,du=\int_0^t (ut-u^2)e^{-u}\,du=\left[(ut-u^2)(-e^{-u})-(t-2u)(e^{-u})+(-2)(-e^{-u})\right]_0^t$$

$$=te^{-t}+2e^{-t}+t-2$$

## EXAMPLE 10.68

*Find the inverse Laplace transform of* $\dfrac{1}{(s-2)(s+2)^2}$.

**Solution**

$$F(s)=\frac{1}{(s-2)(s+2)^2}$$

Let

$$F_1(s)=\frac{1}{(s+2)^2} \qquad F_2(s)=\frac{1}{s-2}$$

$$f_1(t)=te^{-2t} \qquad f_2(t)=e^{2t}$$

By convolution theorem,

$$L^{-1}\{F(s)\}=\int_0^t ue^{-2u}\,e^{2(t-u)}\int_0^t du=e^{2t}\int_0^t ue-4u\,du=e^{2t}\left[\frac{ue^{-4u}}{-4}-\frac{e^{-4u}}{16}\right]_0^t=e^{2t}\left(\frac{-te^{-4t}}{4}-\frac{e^{-4t}}{16}+\frac{1}{16}\right)$$

$$=\frac{e^{2t}}{16}-\frac{te^{-2t}}{4}-\frac{e^{-2t}}{16}=\frac{1}{16}\left(e^{2t}-e^{-2t}-4te^{-2t}\right)$$

## EXAMPLE 10.69

*Find the inverse Laplace transform of* $\dfrac{1}{s^2(s^2+1)}$.

**Solution**

$$F(s)=\frac{1}{s^2(s^2+1)}$$

Let

$$F_1(s)=\frac{1}{s^2+1} \qquad F_2(s)=\frac{1}{s^2}$$

$$f_1(t)=\sin t \qquad f_2(t)=t$$

By convolution theorem,

$$L^{-1}\{F(s)\} = \int_0^t \sin u\,(t-u)\,du = \left[(t-u)(-\cos u) - \sin u\right]_0^t = t - \sin t$$

**EXAMPLE 10.70** ●○○

*Find the inverse Laplace transform of* $\dfrac{1}{(s+1)(s^2+1)}$.

**Solution**

$$F(s) = \frac{1}{(s+1)(s^2+1)}$$

Let

$$F_1(s) = \frac{1}{s^2+1} \qquad F_2(s) = \frac{1}{s+1}$$

$$f_1(t) = \sin t \qquad f_2(t) = e^{-t}$$

By convolution theorem,

$$L^{-1}\{F(s)\} = \int_0^t \sin u\, e^{-(t-u)}\,du = \int_1^t e^{u-t} \sin u\, du = e^{-t}\left[\frac{e^u}{2}(\sin u - \cos u)\right]_0^t = \frac{e^{-t}}{2}[e^t(\sin t - \cos t) + 1]$$

$$= \frac{1}{2}(\sin t - \cos t) + \frac{1}{2}e^{-t}$$

## 10.7 SOLUTION OF DIFFERENTIAL EQUATIONS WITH CONSTANT COEFFICIENTS

LO 10.7

Use Laplace transform in obtaining solution of differential equations with constant coefficients

The Laplace transform is useful in solving linear differential equations with given initial conditions by using algebraic methods. Initial conditions are included from the very beginning of the solution.

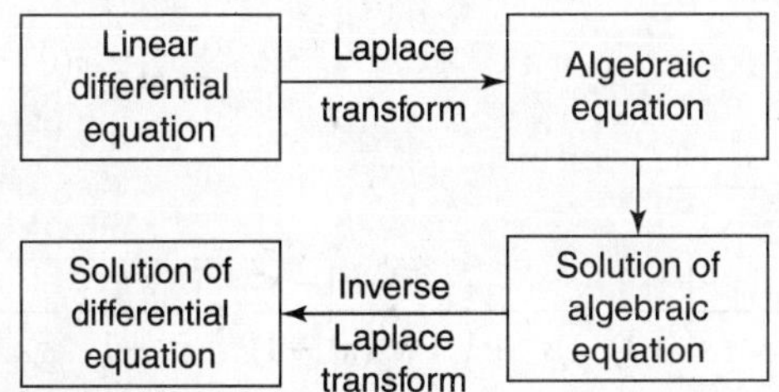


**EXAMPLE 10.71** ○●○

*Solve* $\dfrac{dy}{dt} + 2y = e^{-3t}$, $y(0) = 1$.

**Solution** Taking Laplace transform of both the sides,

$$sY(s)-y(0)+2Y(s)=\frac{1}{s+3}$$

$$sY(s)-1+2Y(s)=\frac{1}{s+3} \qquad [\because y(0)=1]$$

$$(s+2)Y(s)=\frac{1}{s+3}+1=\frac{s+4}{s+3}$$

$$Y(s)=\frac{s+4}{(s+2)(s+3)}$$

By partial-fraction expansion,

$$Y(s)=\frac{A}{s+2}+\frac{B}{s+3}$$

$$A=(s+2)Y(s)\big|_{s=-2}=\left.\frac{s+4}{s+3}\right|_{s=-2}=2$$

$$B=(s+3)Y(s)\big|_{s=-3}=\left.\frac{s+4}{s+2}\right|_{s=-3}=-1$$

$$Y(s)=\frac{2}{s+2}-\frac{1}{s+3}$$

Taking inverse Laplace transform of both the sides.

$$y(t)=2e^{-2t}-e^{-3t}$$

**EXAMPLE 10.72**

*Solve* $y''+y=t,\ y(0)=1,\ y'(0)=0$.

**Solution** Taking Laplace transform of both the sides,

$$[s^2Y(s)-sy(0)-y'(0)]+Y(s)=\frac{1}{s^2}$$

$$s^2Y(s)-s+Y(s)=\frac{1}{s^2} \qquad [\because y(0)=1,\ y'(0)=0]$$

$$(s^2+1)Y(s)=\frac{1}{s^2}+s=\frac{s^3+1}{s^2}$$

$$Y(s)=\frac{s^3+1}{s^2(s^2+1)}=\frac{s}{s^2+1}+\frac{1}{s^2(s^2+1)}=\frac{s}{s^2+1}+\frac{s^2+1-s^2}{s^2(s^2+1)}=\frac{s}{s^2+1}+\frac{1}{s^2}-\frac{1}{s^2+1}$$

Taking inverse Laplace transform of both the sides,

$$y(t)=\cos t+t-\sin t$$

**EXAMPLE 10.73**

*Solve* $y''+y=t^2+2t,\ y(0)=4,\ y'(0)=-2$.

**Solution** Taking Laplace transform of both sides,

$$\left[s^2Y(s)-sy(0)-y'(0)\right]+\left[sY(s)-y(0)\right]=\frac{2}{s^3}+\frac{2}{s^2}$$

$$s^2Y(s)-4s+2+sY(s)-4=\frac{2}{s^3}+\frac{2}{s^2}$$

$$(s^2+s)\,Y(s)=\frac{2}{s^3}+\frac{2}{s^2}+4s+2=\frac{2(1+s)}{s^3}+4s+2$$

$$Y(s)=\frac{2(1+s)}{s^3(s^2+s)}+\frac{4s}{s^2+s}+\frac{2}{s^2+s}=\frac{2}{s^4}+\frac{4}{s+1}+\frac{2}{s}-\frac{2}{s+1}=\frac{2}{s^4}+\frac{2}{s}-\frac{2}{s+1}$$

Taking inverse Laplace transform of both the sides,

$$y(t)=\frac{t^3}{3}+2+2e^{-t}$$

## EXAMPLE 10.74

*Solve* $y''+4y=\delta(t)$, $y(0)=0$, $y'(0)=0$.

**Solution** Taking Laplace transform of both the sides,

$$s^2Y(s)-sy(0)-y'(0)+4Y(s)=1$$

$$s^2\,Y(s)+4Y(s)=1 \qquad [\because y(0)=0,\ y'(0)=0]$$

$$(s^2+4)\,Y(s)=1$$

$$Y(s)=\frac{1}{s^2+4}$$

Taking inverse Laplace transform of both the sides,

$$y(t)=\frac{1}{2}\sin 2t$$

## EXAMPLE 10.75

*Solve* $y''+3y'+2y=t\delta(t-1)$, $y(0)=0$, $y'(0)=0$.

**Solution** Taking Laplace transform of both the sides,

$$\left[s^2Y(s)-sy(0)-y'(0)\right]+3\left[sY(s)-y(0)\right]+2Y(s)=e^{-s}$$

$$s^2Y(s)+3s\,Y(s)+2Y(s)=e^{-s} \qquad [\because y(0)=0,\ y'(0)=0]$$

$$(s^2+3s+2)\,Y(s)=e^{-s}$$

$$Y(s)=\frac{e^{-s}}{s^2+3s+2}=\frac{e^{-s}}{(s+1)(s+2)}=e^{-s}\left(\frac{1}{s+1}-\frac{1}{s+2}\right)$$

Taking inverse Laplace transform of both the sides,

$$y(t)=e^{-(t-1)}u(t-1)-e^{-2(t-1)}u(t-1)$$

**EXAMPLE 10.76**

*Solve* $y'' + 4y = u(t-2)$, $y(0) = 0$, $y'(0) = 1$.

**Solution** Taking Laplace transform of both the sides,

$$\left[s^2 Y(s) - sy(0) - y'(0)\right] + 4Y(s) = \frac{e^{-2s}}{s}$$

$$s^2 Y(s) - 1 + 4Y(s) = \frac{e^{-2s}}{s} \qquad [\because y(0) = 0, \ y'(0) = 1]$$

$$(s^2 + 4)Y(s) = \frac{e^{-2s}}{s} + 1$$

$$Y(s) = \frac{e^{-2s}}{s(s^2+4)} + \frac{1}{s^2+4} = \frac{e^{-2s}}{4}\left(\frac{1}{s} - \frac{s}{s^2+4}\right) + \frac{1}{s^2+4}$$

Taking inverse Laplace transform of both the sides,

$$y(t) = \frac{1}{4}u(t-2) - \frac{1}{4}\cos 2(t-2)u(t-2) + \frac{1}{2}\sin 2t$$

## 10.8 THE TRANSFORMED CIRCUIT

LO 10.8

Discuss the transformed circuit

Voltage–current relationships of network elements can also be represented in the frequency domain.

**1. *Resistor*** For the resistor, the *v–i* relationship in time domain is

$$v(t) = R\,i(t)$$

The corresponding frequency-domain relation is given as

$$V(s) = RI(s)$$

The transformed network is shown in Fig. 10.37.

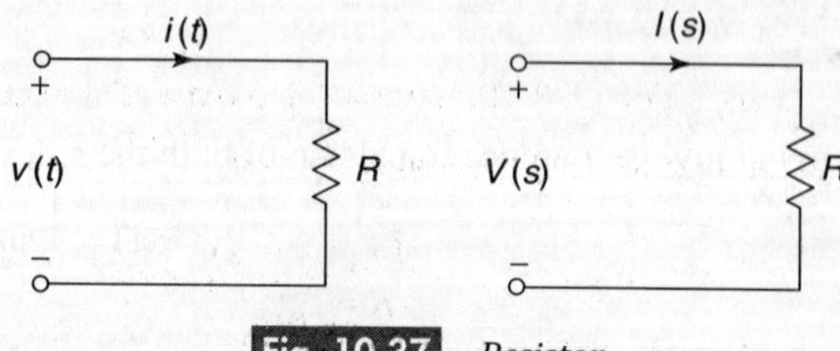


Fig. 10.37 *Resistor*

**2. *Inductor*** For the inductor, the *v–i* relationships in time domain are

$$v(t) = L\frac{di}{dt}$$

$$i(t) = \frac{1}{L}\int_0^t v(t)\,dt + i(0)$$

The corresponding frequency-domain relations are given as

$$V(s) = Ls\,I(s) - L\,i(0)$$

$$I(s) = \frac{1}{Ls}V(s) + \frac{i(0)}{s}$$

The transformed network is shown in Fig. 10.38.

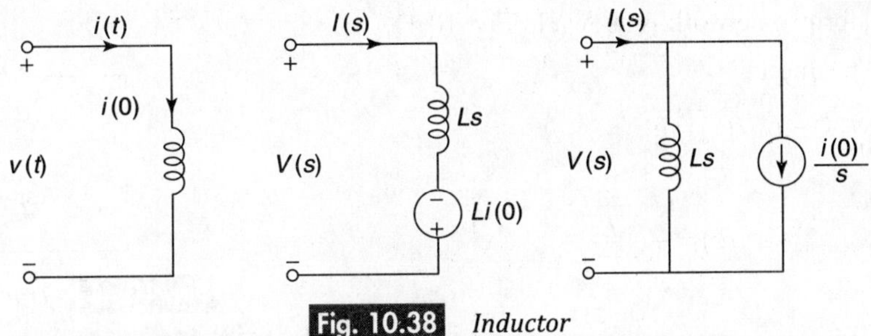


Fig. 10.38 *Inductor*

**3. Capacitor** For capacitor, the *v–i* relationships in time domain are

$$v(t) = \frac{1}{C}\int_0^t i(t)\,dt + v(0)$$

$$i(t) = C\frac{dv}{dt}$$

The corresponding frequency–domain relations are given as

$$V(s) = \frac{1}{Cs}I(s) + \frac{v(0)}{s}$$

$$I(s) = CsV(s) - Cv(0)$$

The transformed network is shown in Fig. 10.39.

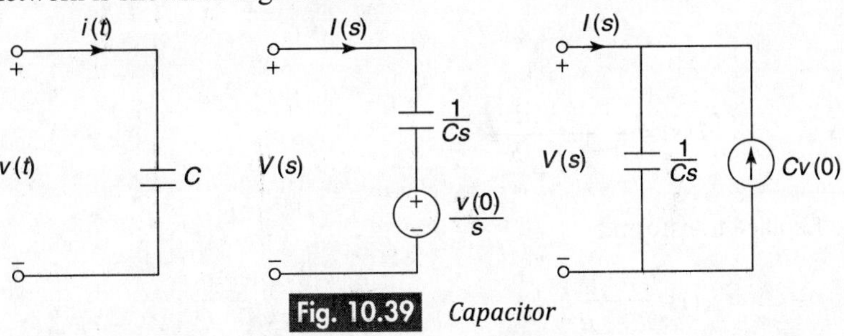


Fig. 10.39 *Capacitor*

## 10.9 TRANSIENT RESPONSE OF *RL* CIRCUIT TO dc EXCITATION

LO 10.9

Discuss the transient responses of *RL*, *RC*, and *RLC* circuits to dc excitation

Consider a series *RL* circuit, as shown in Fig. 10.40. The switch is closed at time $t = 0$.

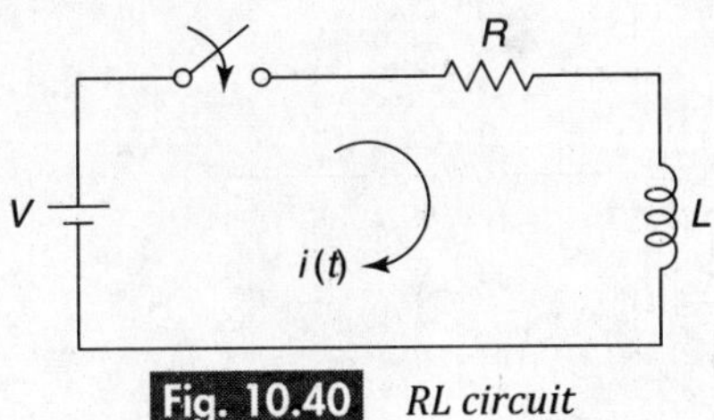


Fig. 10.40 *RL circuit*

For $t > 0$, the transformed network is shown in Fig. 10.41.

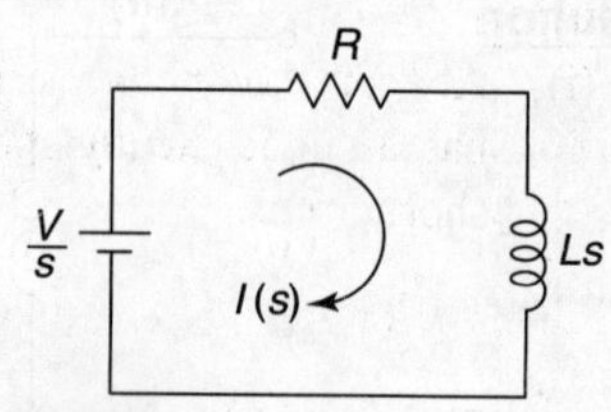


**Fig. 10.41** *Transformed network*

Applying KVL to the mesh,

$$\frac{V}{s} - RI(s) - Ls\, I(s) = 0$$

$$I(s) = \frac{\frac{V}{L}}{s\left(s+\frac{R}{L}\right)}$$

By partial-fraction expansion,

$$I(s) = \frac{A}{s} + \frac{B}{s+\frac{R}{L}}$$

$$A = sI(s)\big|_{s=0} = s \times \left.\frac{\frac{V}{L}}{s\left(s+\frac{R}{L}\right)}\right|_{s=0} = \frac{V}{R}$$

$$B = \left(s+\frac{R}{L}\right)I(s)\bigg|_{s=-\frac{R}{L}} = \left(s+\frac{R}{L}\right) \times \left.\frac{\frac{V}{L}}{s\left(s+\frac{R}{L}\right)}\right|_{s=-\frac{R}{L}} = -\frac{V}{R}$$

$$I(s) = \frac{\frac{V}{R}}{s} + \frac{\left(-\frac{V}{R}\right)}{s+\frac{R}{L}}$$

Taking the inverse Laplace transform,

$$i(t) = \frac{V}{R} - \frac{V}{R}e^{-\frac{R}{L}t}$$

$$= \frac{V}{R}\left[1 - e^{-\frac{R}{L}t}\right] \quad \text{for } t > 0$$

**EXAMPLE 10.77**

*In the network of Fig. 10.42, the switch is moved from position 1 to 2 at t = 0, steady-state condition having been established at position 1. Determine i (t) for t > 0.*

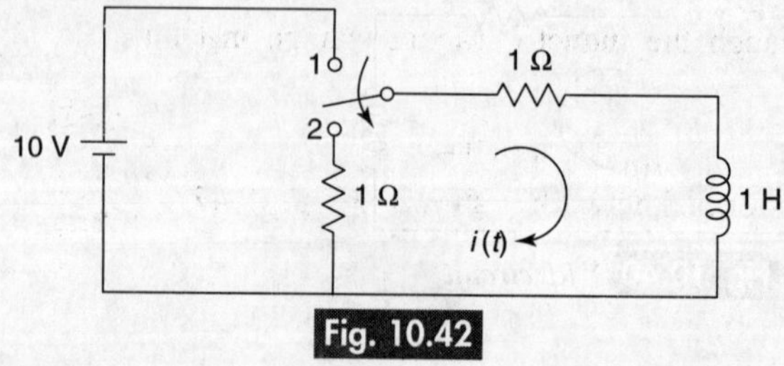


**Fig. 10.42**

## Solution

(i) At $t = 0^-$, the network is shown in Fig. 10.43. At $t = 0^-$, the network has attained steady-state condition. Hence, the inductor acts as a short circuit.

$$i(0^-) = \frac{10}{1} = 10 \text{ A}$$

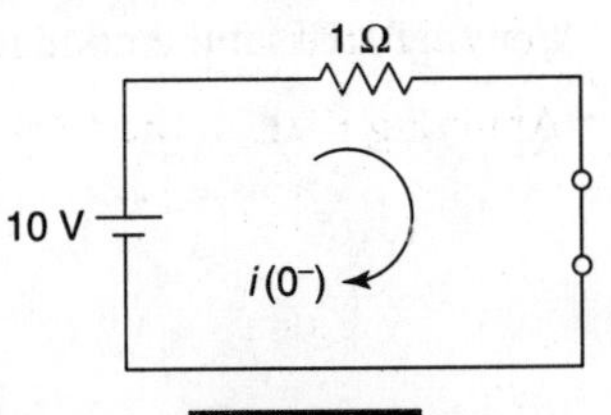


Fig. 10.43

(ii) Since the current through the inductor cannot change instantaneously,

$$i\,(0^+) = 10 \text{ A}$$

(iii) For $t > 0$, the transformed network is shown in Fig. 10.44.

Applying KVL to the mesh for $t > 0$,

$$-I(s) - I(s) - sI(s) + 10 = 0$$

$$I(s)(s+2) = 10$$

$$I(s) = \frac{10}{s+2}$$

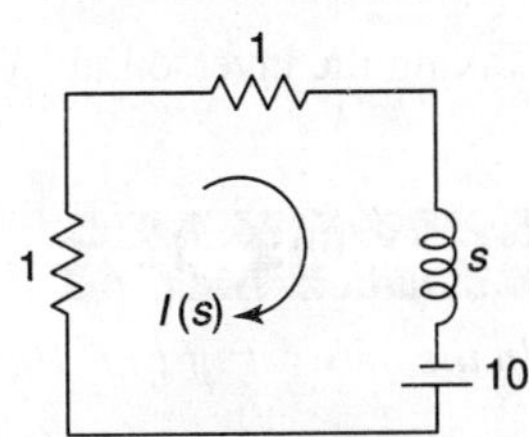


Fig. 10.44

Taking inverse Laplace transform,

$$i(t) = 10e^{-2t} \quad \text{for } t > 0$$

## EXAMPLE 10.78

*The network of Fig. 10.45 was initially in the steady state with the switch in the position a. At t = 0, the switch goes from a to b. Find an expression for voltage v (t) for t > 0.*

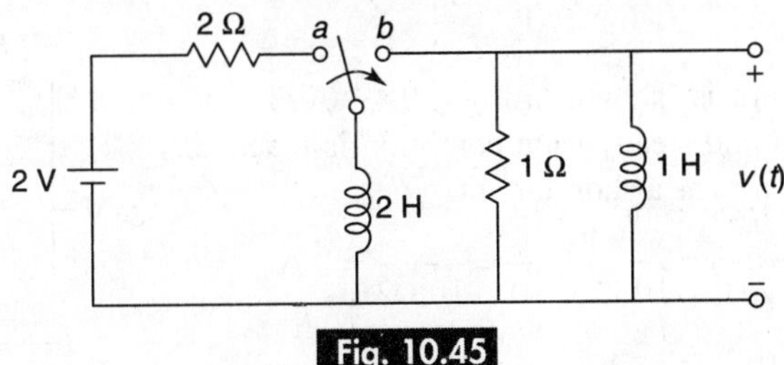


Fig. 10.45

## Solution

(i) At $t = 0^-$, the network is shown in Fig. 10.46. At $t = 0^-$, the network has attained steady-state condition. Hence, the inductor of 2H acts as a short circuit.

$$i(0^-) = \frac{2}{2} = 1 \text{ A}$$

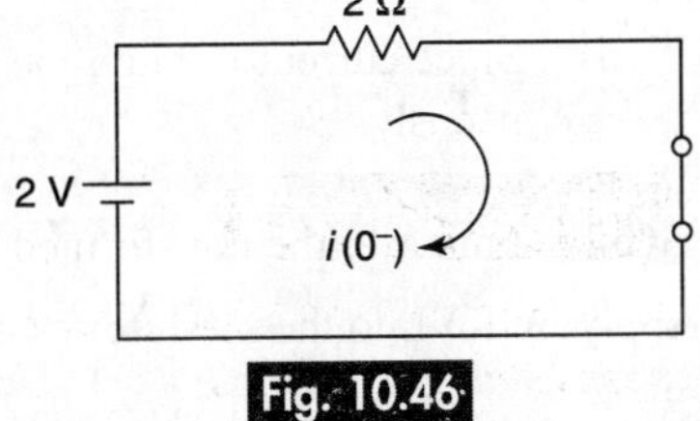


Fig. 10.46

(ii) Since current through the inductor cannot change instantaneously,

$$i\,(0^+) = 1 \text{ A}$$

(iii) For $t > 0$, the transformed network is shown in Fig. 10.47.

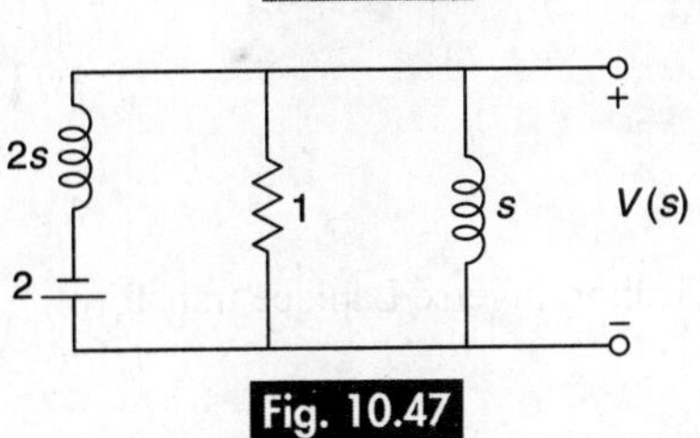


Fig. 10.47

Applying KCL at the node for $t > 0$,

$$\frac{V(s)+2}{2s}+\frac{V(s)}{1}+\frac{V(s)}{s}=0$$

$$V(s)\left(1+\frac{3}{2s}\right)=-\frac{1}{s}$$

$$V(s)=\frac{-\frac{1}{s}}{\frac{2s+3}{2s}}=-\frac{2}{2s+3}=-\frac{1}{s+1.5}$$

Taking the inverse Laplace transform,

$$v(t)=-e^{-1.5t} \qquad \text{for } t>0$$

## EXAMPLE 10.79

*In the network of Fig. 10.48, the switch is opened at t = 0. Find i(t).*

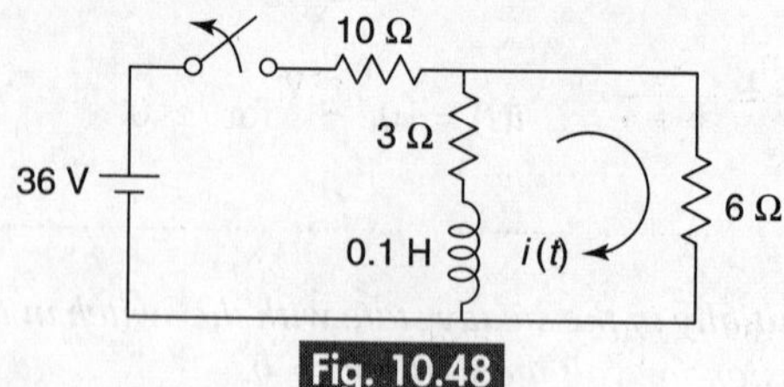


Fig. 10.48

**Solution**

(i) At $t = 0^-$, the network is shown in Fig. 10.49. At $t = 0^-$, the switch is closed and steady-state condition is reached. Hence, the inductor acts as a short circuit.

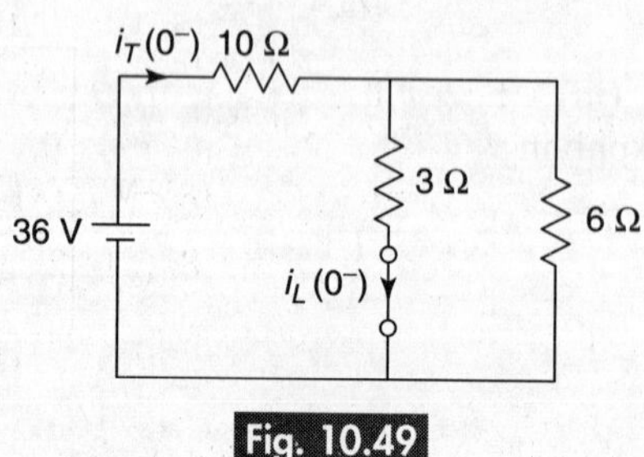


Fig. 10.49

$$i_T(0^-)=\frac{36}{10+(3\,||\,6)}=\frac{36}{10+2}=3\text{ A}$$

$$i_L(0^-)=3\times\frac{6}{6+3}=2\text{ A}$$

(ii) Since current through the inductor cannot change instantaneously,

$$i_L(0^+)=2\text{ A}$$

(iii) For $t > 0$, the transformed network is shown in Fig. 10.50.

Applying KVL to the mesh for $t > 0$,

$$-0.2-0.1s\,I(s)-3I(s)-6I(s)=0$$

$$0.1sI(s)+9I(s)=-0.2$$

$$I(s)=\frac{-0.2}{0.1s+9}=\frac{-2}{s+90}$$

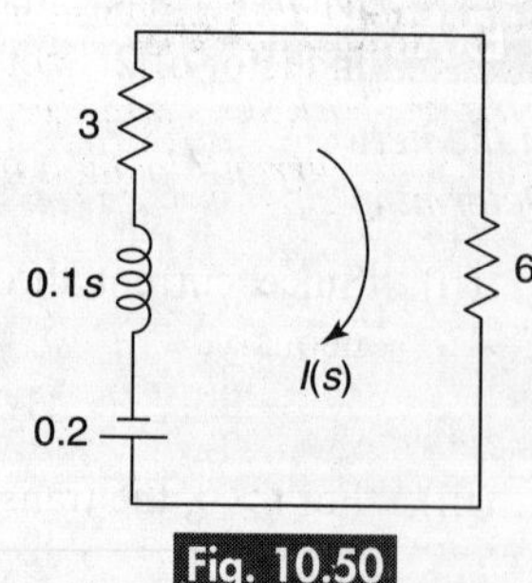


Fig. 10.50

Taking inverse Laplace transform,

$$i(t)=-2e^{-90t} \qquad \text{for } t>0$$

## EXAMPLE 10.80

*The network shown in Fig. 10.51 has acquired steady-state with the switch closed for t < 0. At t = 0, the switch is opened. Obtain i (t) for t > 0.*

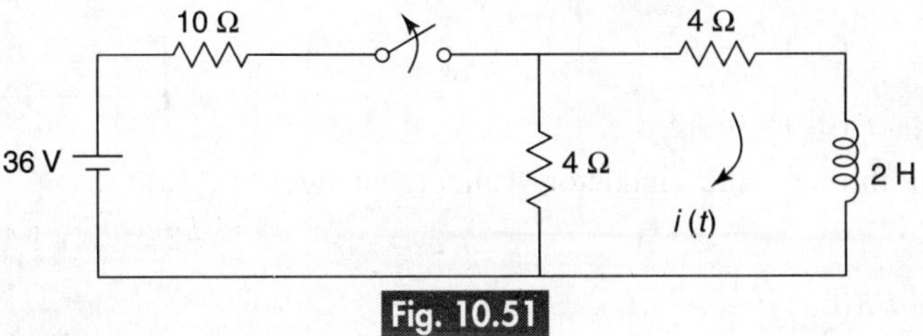


Fig. 10.51

### Solution

(i) At $t = 0^-$, the network is shown in Fig. 10.52.
At $t = 0^-$, the switch is closed and the network has acquired steady-state. Hence, the inductor acts as a short circuit.

$$i_T(0^-) = \frac{36}{10 + (4 \parallel 4)} = \frac{36}{10+2} = 3 \text{ A}$$

$$i(0^-) = 3 \times \frac{4}{4+4} = 1.5 \text{ A}$$

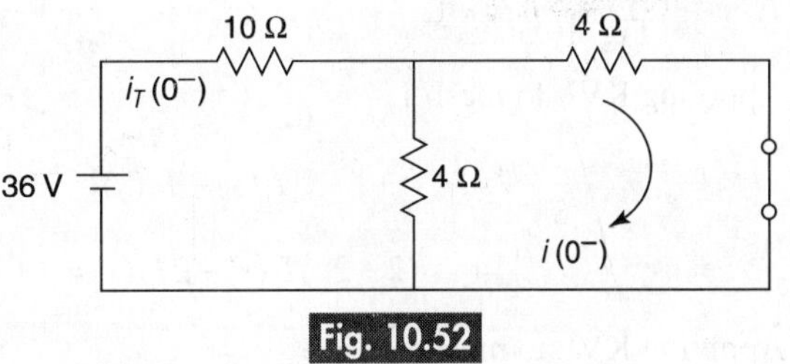


Fig. 10.52

(ii) Since current through the inductor cannot change instantaneously,

$$i(0^+) = 1.5 \text{ A}$$

(iii) For $t > 0$, the transformed network is shown in Fig. 10.53.
Applying KVL to the mesh for $t > 0$,

$$-4I(s) - 4I(s) - 2sI(s) + 3 = 0$$

$$8I(s) + 2sI(s) = 3$$

$$I(s) = \frac{3}{2s+8} = \frac{1.5}{s+4}$$

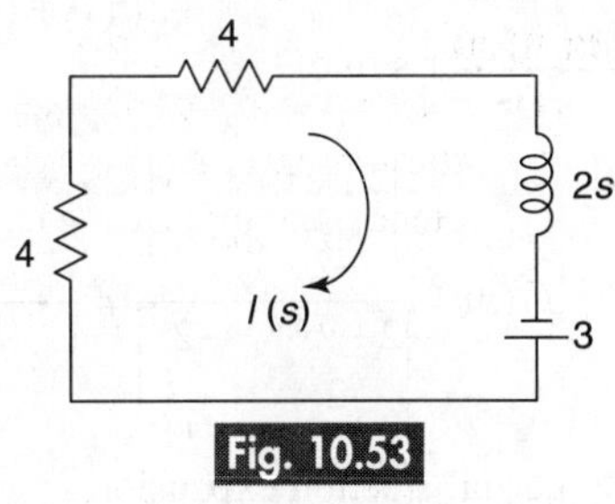


Fig. 10.53

Taking the inverse Laplace transform,

$$i(t) = 1.5e^{-4t} \qquad \text{for } t > 0$$

## EXAMPLE 10.81

*In the network shown in Fig. 10.54, the switch is closed at t = 0, the steady-state being reached before t = 0. Determine current through inductor of 3 H.*

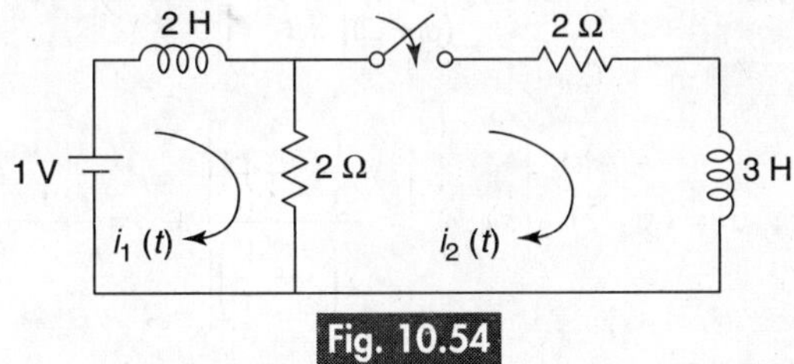


Fig. 10.54

## Solution

(i) At $t = 0^-$, the network is shown in Fig. 10.55. At $t = 0^-$, steady-state condition is reached. Hence, the inductor of 2 H acts as a short circuit.

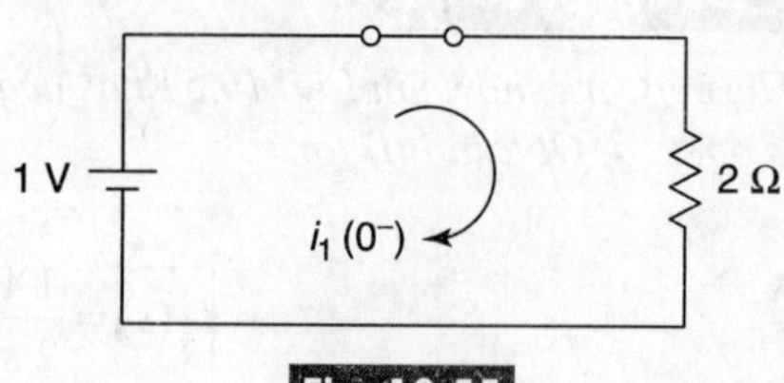

Fig. 10.55

$$i_1(0^-) = \frac{1}{2} \text{ A}$$

$$i_2(0^-) = 0$$

(ii) Since current through the inductor cannot change instantaneously,

$$i_1(0^+) = \frac{1}{2} \text{ A}$$

$$i_2(0^+) = 0$$

(iii) For $t > 0$, the transformed network is shown in Fig. 10.56.

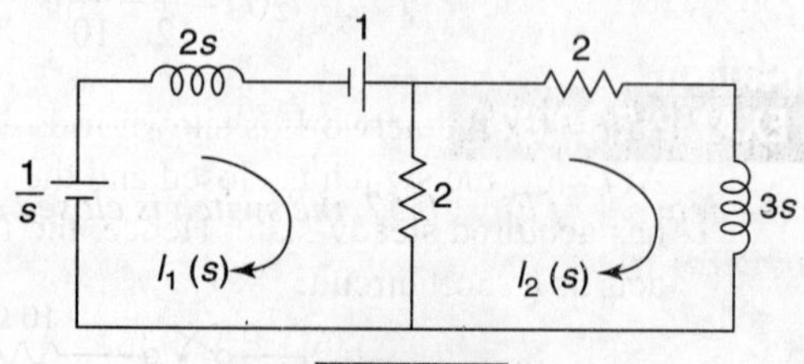

Fig. 10.56

Applying KVL to mesh 1,

$$\frac{1}{s} - 2s\, I_1(s) + 1 - 2[I_1(s) - I_2(s)] = 0$$

$$(2+2s)\, I_1(s) - 2I_2(s) = 1 + \frac{1}{s}$$

Applying KVL to mesh 2,

$$-2\,[I_2(s) - I_1(s)] - 2I_2(s) - 3s\, I_2\,(s) = 0$$

$$-2I_1(s) + (4+3s)\, I_2(s) = 0$$

By Cramer's rule,

$$I_2(s) = \frac{\begin{vmatrix} 2+2s & 1+\frac{1}{s} \\ -2 & 0 \end{vmatrix}}{\begin{vmatrix} 2+2s & -2 \\ -2 & 4+3s \end{vmatrix}} = \frac{\frac{2}{s}(s+1)}{(2+2s)(4+3s)-4} = \frac{s+1}{s(3s^2+7s+2)} = \frac{s+1}{3s\left(s+\frac{1}{3}\right)(s+2)} = \frac{\frac{1}{3}(s+1)}{s(s+2)\left(s+\frac{1}{3}\right)}$$

By partial-fraction expansion,

$$I_2(s) = \frac{A}{s} + \frac{B}{s+2} + \frac{C}{s+\frac{1}{3}}$$

$$A = s\, I_2(s)\big|_{s=0} = \left.\frac{\frac{1}{3}(s+1)}{(s+2)\left(s+\frac{1}{3}\right)}\right|_{s=0} = \frac{1}{2}$$

$$B = (s+2) I_2(s)\big|_{S=-2} = \left.\frac{\frac{1}{3}(s+1)}{s\left(s+\frac{1}{3}\right)}\right|_{s=-2} = -\frac{1}{10}$$

$$C = \left(s+\frac{1}{3}\right) I_2(s)\Big|_{s=-\frac{1}{3}} = \left.\frac{\frac{1}{3}(s+1)}{s(s+2)}\right|_{s=-\frac{1}{3}} = -\frac{2}{5}$$

$$I_2(s) = \frac{1}{2}\frac{1}{s} - \frac{1}{10}\frac{1}{s+2} - \frac{2}{5}\frac{1}{s+\frac{1}{3}}$$

Taking inverse Laplace transform

$$i_2(t) = \frac{1}{2} - \frac{1}{10}e^{-2t} - \frac{2}{5}e^{-\frac{1}{3}t} \quad \text{for } t > 0$$

## EXAMPLE 10.82

*In the network of Fig. 10.57, the switch is closed at t = 0 with the network previously unenergised. Determine currents $i_1(t)$.*

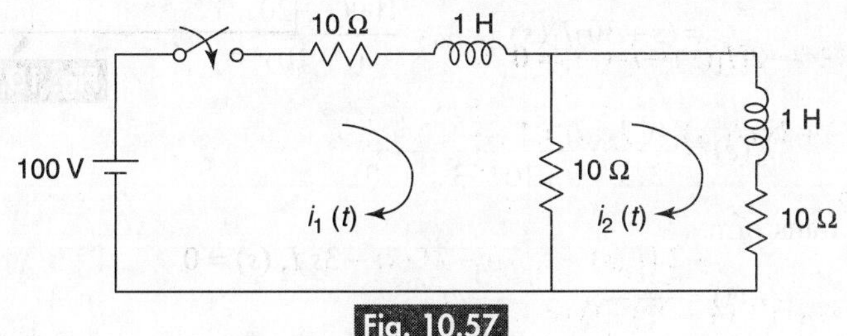


Fig. 10.57

**Solution**

(i) At $t = 0^-$,

$$i_1(0^-) = 0$$
$$i_2(0^-) = 0$$

(ii) Since current through the inductor cannot change instantaneously,

$$i_1(0^+) = 0$$
$$i_2(0^+) = 0$$

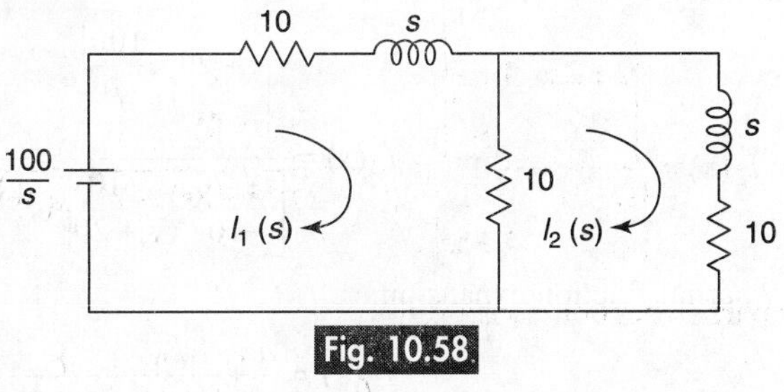


Fig. 10.58

(iii) For $t > 0$, the transformed network is shown in Fig. 10.58.

Applying KVL to mesh 1,

$$\frac{100}{s} - 10I_1(s) - sI_1(s) - 10\left[I_1(s) - I_2(s)\right] = 0$$

$$(s+20)I_1(s) - 10I_2(s) = \frac{100}{s}$$

Applying KVL to mesh 2,

$$-10\left[I_2(s) - I_1(s)\right] - s\, I_2(s) - 10\, I_2(s) = 0$$

$$-10\, I_1(s) + (s+20)I_2(s) = 0$$

By Cramer's rule,

$$I_1(s)=\frac{\begin{vmatrix}\frac{100}{s} & -10\\ 0 & s+20\end{vmatrix}}{\begin{vmatrix}s+20 & -10\\ -10 & s+20\end{vmatrix}}=\frac{\frac{100}{s}(s+20)}{(s+20)^2-100}=\frac{100(s+20)}{s(s^2+40s+300)}=\frac{100(s+20)}{s(s+10)(s+30)}$$

By partial-fraction expansion,

$$I_1(s)=\frac{A}{s}+\frac{B}{s+10}+\frac{C}{s+30}$$

$$A=s\,I_1(s)\,|_{s=0}=\left.\frac{100(s+20)}{(s+10)(s+30)}\right|_{s=0}=\frac{20}{3}$$

$$B=(s+10)I_1(s)\,|_{s=-10}=\left.\frac{100(s+20)}{s(s+30)}\right|_{s=-10}=-5$$

$$C=(s+30)I_1(s)\,|_{s=-30}=\left.\frac{100(s+20)}{s(s+10)}\right|_{s=-30}=-\frac{5}{3}$$

$$I_1(s)=\frac{20}{3}\frac{1}{s}-\frac{5}{s+10}-\frac{5}{3}\frac{1}{s+30}$$

Taking inverse Laplace transform,

$$i_1(t)=\frac{20}{3}-5e^{-10t}-\frac{5}{3}e^{-30t}$$

Similarly,

$$I_2(s)=\frac{\begin{vmatrix}s+20 & \frac{100}{s}\\ -10 & 0\end{vmatrix}}{\begin{vmatrix}s+20 & -10\\ -10 & s+20\end{vmatrix}}=\frac{\frac{1000}{s}}{(s+20)^2-100}=\frac{1000}{s(s^2+40s+300)}=\frac{1000}{s(s+10)(s+30)}$$

By partial-fraction expansion,

$$I_2(s)=\frac{A}{s}+\frac{B}{s+10}+\frac{C}{s+30}$$

$$A=sI_2(s)\,|_{s=0}=\left.\frac{1000}{(s+10)(s+30)}\right|_{s=0}=\frac{10}{3}$$

$$B=(s+10)I_2(s)\,|_{s=-10}=\left.\frac{1000}{s(s+30)}\right|_{s=-10}=-5$$

$$C=(s+30)I_2(s)\,|_{s=-30}=\left.\frac{1000}{s(s+10)}\right|_{s=-30}=\frac{5}{3}$$

$$I_2(s)=\frac{10}{3}\frac{1}{s}-\frac{5}{s+10}+\frac{5}{3}\frac{1}{s+30}$$

Taking inverse Laplace transform,

$$i_2(t) = \frac{10}{3} - 5e^{-10t} + \frac{5}{3}e^{-30t} \qquad \text{for } t > 0$$

## 10.10 TRANSIENT RESPONSE OF *RC* CIRCUIT TO dc EXCITATION

LO 10.9

Consider a series *RC* circuit, as shown in Fig. 10.59. The switch is closed at time $t = 0$.

For $t > 0$, the transformed network is shown in Fig. 10.60.

Applying KVL to the mesh,

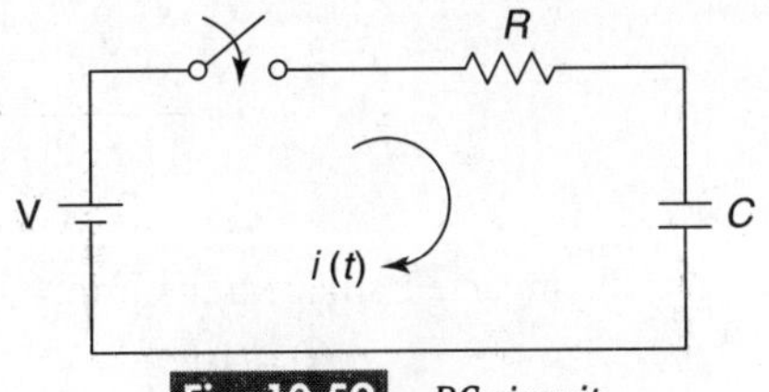


**Fig. 10.59** *RC circuit*

$$\frac{V}{s} - RI(s) - \frac{1}{Cs}I(s) = 0$$

$$\left(R + \frac{1}{Cs}\right)I(s) = \frac{V}{s}$$

$$I(s) = \frac{\frac{V}{s}}{R + \frac{1}{Cs}} = \frac{\frac{V}{s}}{\frac{RCs+1}{Cs}} = \frac{\frac{V}{R}}{s + \frac{1}{RC}}$$

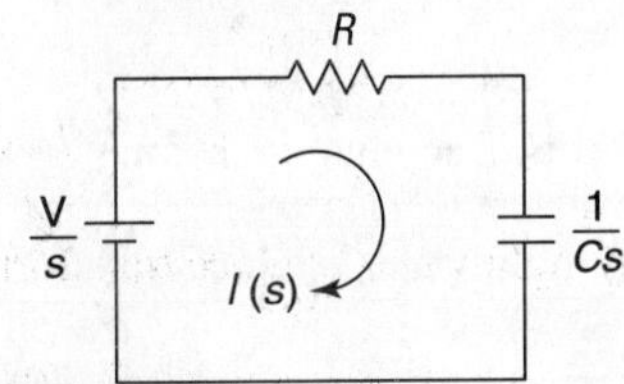


**Fig. 10.60** *Transformed network*

Taking the inverse Laplace transform,

$$i(t) = \frac{V}{R}e^{-\frac{1}{RC}t} \qquad \text{for } t > 0$$

**EXAMPLE 10.83** 

*In the network of Fig. 10.61, the switch is moved from a to b at t = 0. Determine i(t) and $v_c(t)$.*

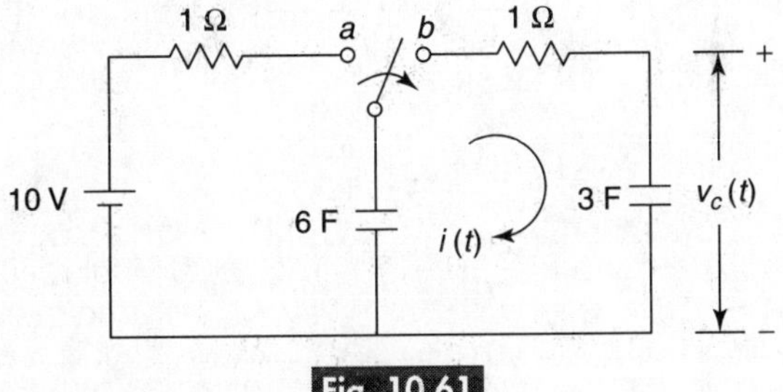


**Fig. 10.61**

**Solution**

(i) At $t = 0^-$, the network is shown in Fig. 10.62. At $t = 0^-$, the network has attained steady-state condition. Hence, the capacitor of 6 F acts as an open circuit.

$$v_{6\text{ F}}(0^-) = 10 \text{ V}$$
$$i(0^-) = 0$$
$$v_{3\text{ F}}(0^-) = 0$$

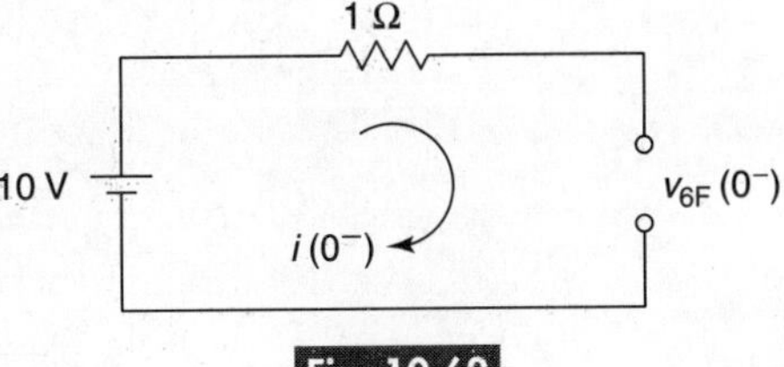


**Fig. 10.62**

(ii) Since voltage across the capacitor cannot change instantaneously,

$$v_{6\,F}(0^+) = 10 \text{ V}$$

$$v_{3\,F}(0^+) = 0$$

(iii) For $t > 0$, the transformed network is shown in Fig. 10.63.

Fig. 10.63

Applying KVL to the mesh for $t > 0$,

$$\frac{10}{s} - \frac{1}{6s}I(s) - I(s) - \frac{1}{3s}I(s) = 0$$

$$\frac{1}{6s}I(s) + I(s) + \frac{1}{3s}I(s) = \frac{10}{s}$$

$$I(s) = \frac{10}{s\left(1 + \frac{1}{6s} + \frac{1}{3s}\right)} = \frac{60}{6s+3} = \frac{10}{s+0.5}$$

Taking the inverse Laplace transform,

$$i(t) = 10e^{-0.5t} \qquad \text{for } t > 0$$

Voltage across the 3 F capacitor is given by

$$V_c(s) = \frac{1}{3s}I(s) = \frac{10}{3s(s+0.5)}$$

By partial-fraction expansion,

$$V_c(s) = \frac{A}{s} + \frac{B}{s+0.5}$$

$$A = sV_c(s)\Big|_{s=0} = \frac{10}{3(s+0.5)}\Bigg|_{s=0} = \frac{20}{3}$$

$$B = (s+0.5)V_c(s)\Big|_{s=-0.5} = \frac{10}{3s}\Bigg|_{s=-0.5} = -\frac{20}{3}$$

$$V_c(s) = \frac{20}{3}\frac{1}{s} - \frac{20}{3}\frac{1}{s+0.5}$$

Taking the inverse Laplace transform,

$$v_c(t) = \frac{20}{3} - \frac{20}{3}e^{-0.5t}$$

$$= \frac{20}{3}(1 - e^{-0.5t}) \qquad \text{for } t > 0$$

**EXAMPLE 10.84**

*The switch in the network shown in Fig. 10.64 is closed at t = 0. Determine the voltage cross the capacitor.*

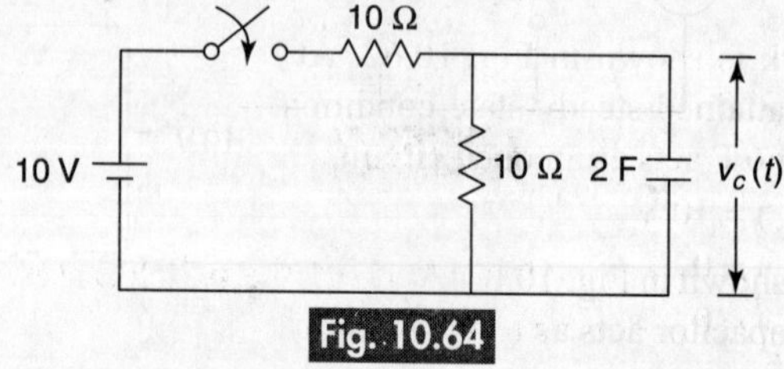


Fig. 10.64

## Solution

(i) At $t = 0^-$, the capacitor is uncharged.

$$v_c(0^-) = 0$$

(ii) Since the voltage across the capacitor cannot change instantaneously,

$$v_c(0^+) = 0$$

(iii) For $t > 0$, the transformed network is shown in Fig. 10.65.

Applying KCL at the node for $t > 0$,

$$\frac{V_C(s) - \frac{10}{s}}{10} + \frac{V_C(s)}{10} + \frac{V_C(s)}{\frac{1}{2s}} = 0$$

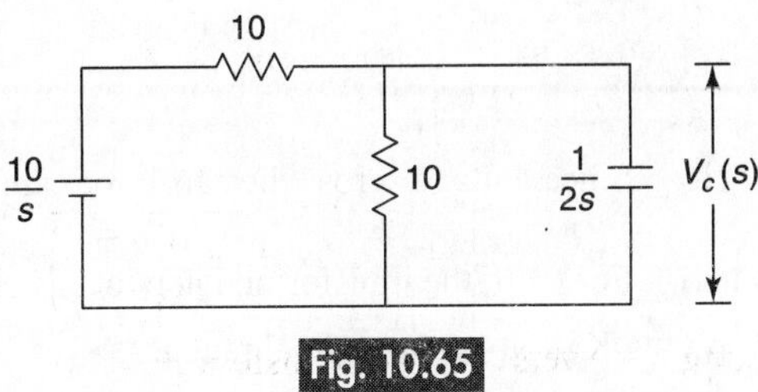


Fig. 10.65

$$2sV_C(s) + 0.2V_C(s) = \frac{1}{s}$$

$$V_C(s) = \frac{1}{s(2s+0.2)} = \frac{0.5}{s(s+0.1)}$$

By partial-fraction expansion,

$$V_C(s) = \frac{A}{s} + \frac{B}{s+0.1}$$

$$A = sV_C(s)\big|_{s=0} = \left.\frac{0.5}{s+0.1}\right|_{s=0} = \frac{0.5}{0.1} = 5$$

$$B = (s+0.1)V_C(s)\big|_{s=-0.1} = \left.\frac{0.5}{s}\right|_{s=-0.1} = -\frac{0.5}{0.1} = -5$$

$$V_C(s) = \frac{5}{s} - \frac{5}{s+0.1}$$

Taking inverse Laplace transform,

$$v_C(t) = 5 - 5e^{-0.1t} \qquad \text{for } t > 0$$

## EXAMPLE 10.85

*In the network of Fig. 10.66, the switch is closed for a long time and at t = 0, the switch is opened. Determine the current through the capacitor.*

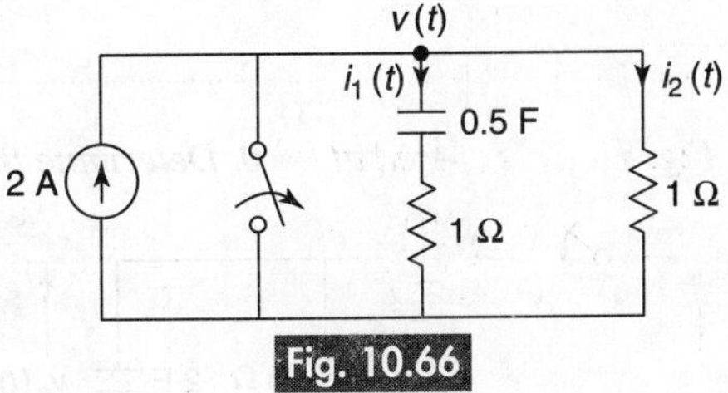


Fig. 10.66

## Solution

(i) At $t = 0^-$, the network is shown in Fig. 10.67. At $t = 0^-$, the switch is closed and steady-state condition is reached. Hence, the capacitor acts as an open circuit.

$$v_c(0^-) = 0$$

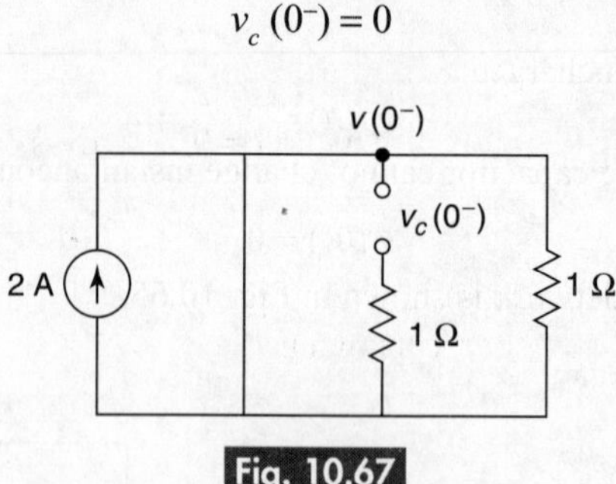


Fig. 10.67

(ii) Since voltage across the capacitor cannot change instantaneously,

$$v_c(0^+) = 0$$

(iii) For $t > 0$, the transformed network is shown in Fig. 10.68.

Applying KVL to two parallel branches,

$$\frac{2}{s}I_1(s) + I_1(s) = I_2(s)$$

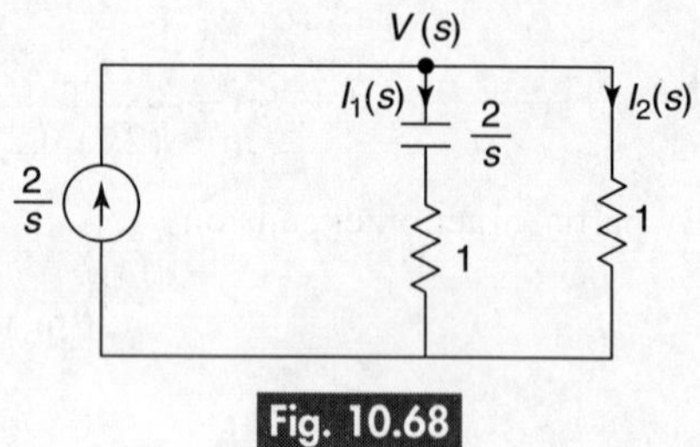


Fig. 10.68

Applying KCL at the node for $t > 0$,

$$\frac{2}{s} = I_1(s) + I_2(s)$$

$$\frac{2}{s}I_1(s) + I_1(s) = \frac{2}{s} - I_1(s)$$

$$\frac{2}{s}I_1(s) + 2I_1(s) = \frac{2}{s}$$

$$I_1(s) = \frac{\frac{2}{s}}{\frac{2}{s}+2} = \frac{1}{s+1}$$

Taking the inverse Laplace transform,

$$i_1(t) = e^{-t} \qquad \text{for } t > 0$$

**EXAMPLE 10.86**

*In the network of Fig. 10.69, the switch is moved from a to b, at t = 0. Find v(t).*

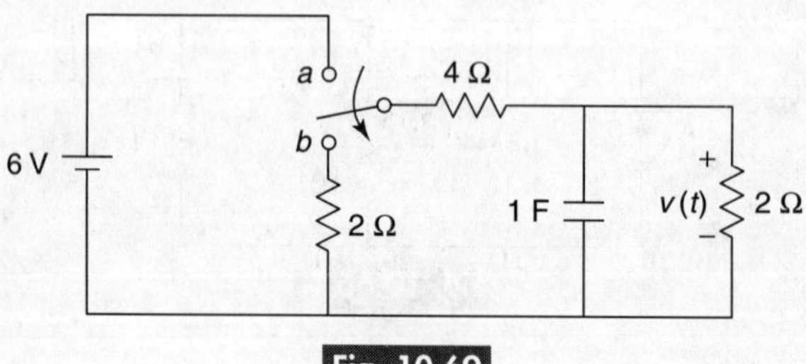


Fig. 10.69

## Solution

(i) At $t = 0^-$, the network is shown in Fig. 10.70. At $t = 0^-$, steady-state condition is reached. Hence, the capacitor acts as an open circuit.

$$v(0^-) = 6 \times \frac{2}{4+2} = 2 \text{ V}$$

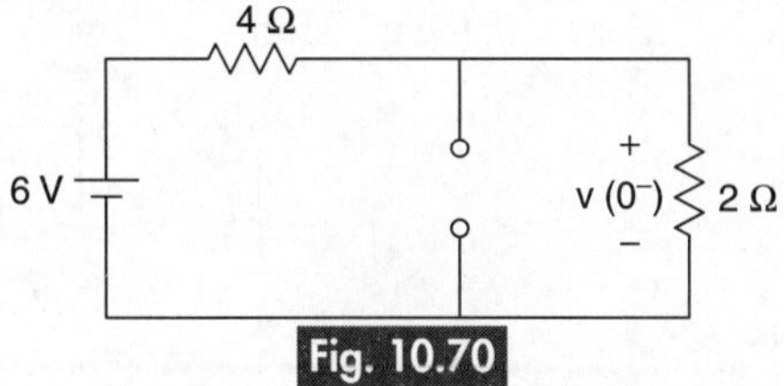


Fig. 10.70

(ii) Since voltage across the capacitor cannot change instantaneously,

$$v(0^+) = 2 \text{ V}$$

(iii) For $t > 0$, the transformed network is shown in Fig. 10.71.

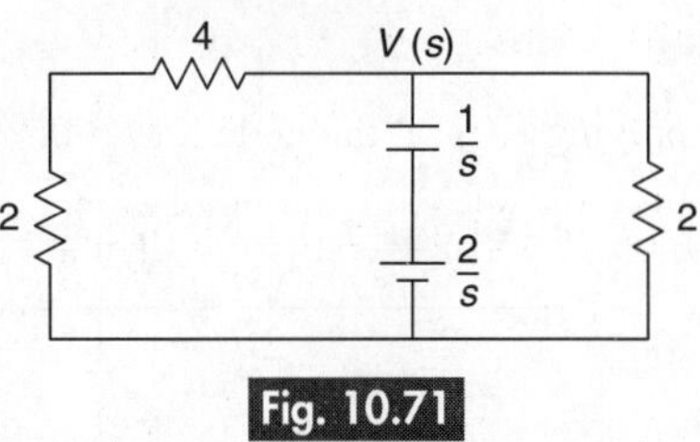


Fig. 10.71

Applying KCL at the node for $t > 0$,

$$\frac{V(s)}{6} + \frac{V(s) - \frac{2}{s}}{\frac{1}{s}} + \frac{V(s)}{2} = 0$$

$$V(s)\left(\frac{2}{3} + s\right) = 2$$

$$V(s) = \frac{2}{s + \frac{2}{3}}$$

Taking the inverse Laplace transform,

$$v(t) = 2e^{-\frac{2}{3}t} \qquad \text{for } t > 0$$

## EXAMPLE 10.87

*The network shown in Fig. 10.72 has acquired steady-state at t < 0 with the switch open. The switch is closed at t = 0. Determine v (t).*

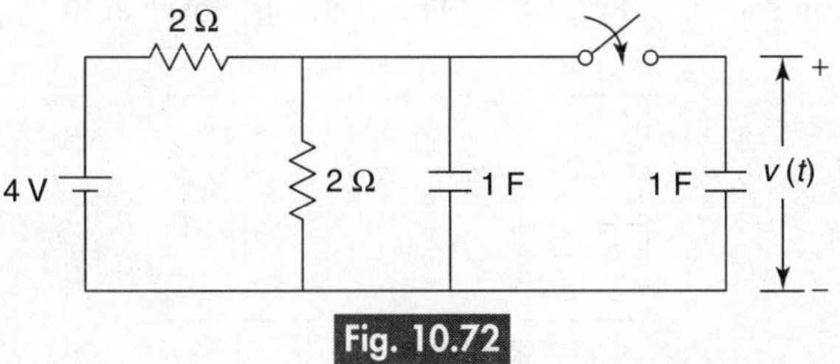


Fig. 10.72

## Solution

(i) At $t = 0^-$, the network is shown in Fig. 10.73. At $t = 0^-$, steady-state condition is reached. Hence, the capacitor of 1 F acts as an open circuit.

$$v(0^-) = 4 \times \frac{2}{2+2} = 2 \text{ V}$$

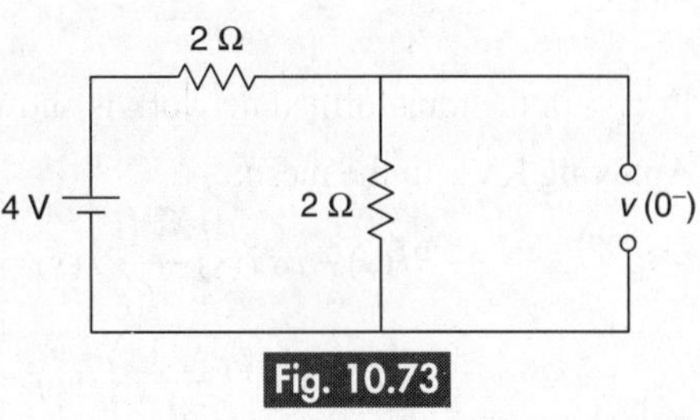


Fig. 10.73

(ii) Since voltage across the capacitor cannot change instantaneously,

$$v(0^+) = 2\text{ V}$$

(iii) For $t > 0$, the transformed network is shown in Fig. 10.74.

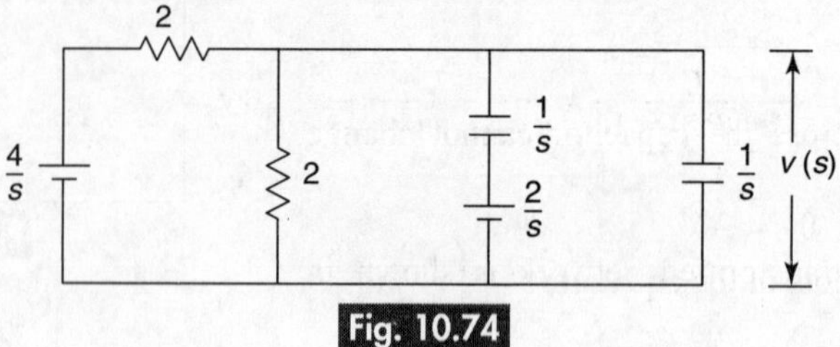


Fig. 10.74

Applying KCL at the node for $t > 0$,

$$\frac{V(s)-\frac{4}{s}}{2}+\frac{V(s)}{2}+\frac{V(s)-\frac{2}{s}}{\frac{1}{s}}+\frac{V(s)}{\frac{1}{s}}=0$$

$$2sV(s)+V(s)=\frac{2}{s}+2$$

$$V(s)=\frac{\frac{2}{s}+2}{2s+1}=\frac{2s+2}{s(2s+1)}=\frac{2}{s}-\frac{2}{2s+1}=\frac{2}{s}-\frac{1}{s+0.5}$$

Taking the inverse Laplace transform,

$$v(t)=2-e^{-0.5t} \qquad \text{for } t>0$$

## 10.11 TRANSIENT RESPONSE OF *RLC* CIRCUIT TO dc EXCITATION

LO 10.9

Consider a series *RLC* circuit shown in Fig. 10.75. The switch is closed at time $t = 0$.

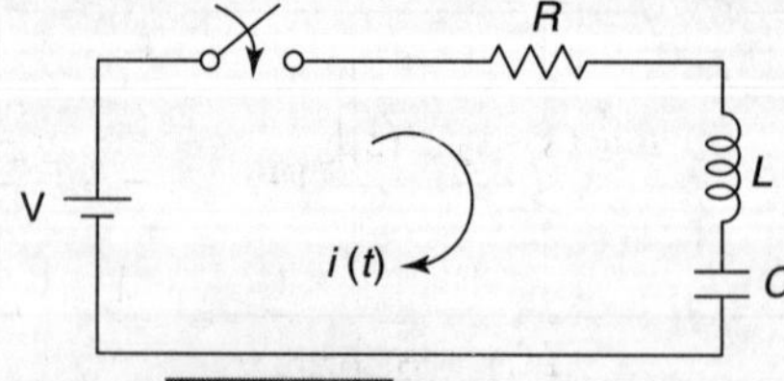


Fig. 10.75 *RLC circuit*

For $t > 0$, the transformed network is shown in Fig. 10.76.

Applying KVL to the mesh,

$$\frac{V}{s}-RI(s)-LsI(s)-\frac{1}{Cs}I(s)=0$$

$$\left(R+Ls+\frac{1}{Cs}\right)I(s)=\frac{V}{s}$$

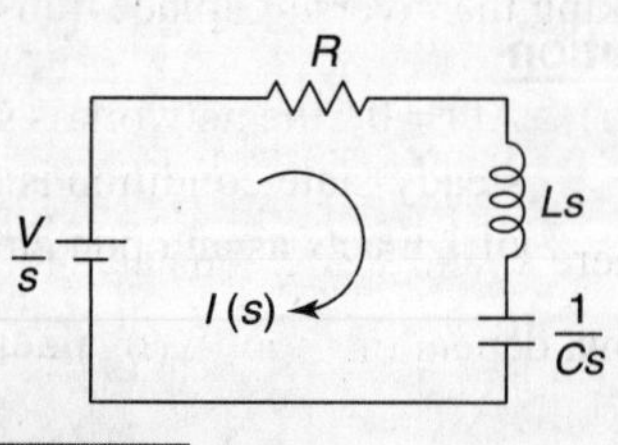


Fig. 10.76 *Transformed network*

$$\left(\frac{LCs^2 + RCs + 1}{Cs}\right) I(s) = \frac{V}{s}$$

$$I(s) = \frac{\frac{V}{s}}{\frac{LCs^2 + RCs + 1}{Cs}} = \frac{\frac{V}{L}}{s^2 + \frac{R}{L}s + \frac{1}{LC}} = \frac{\frac{V}{L}}{(s - s_1)(s - s_2)}$$

where $s_1$ and $s_2$ are the roots of the equation $s^2 + \left(\frac{R}{L}\right)s + \left(\frac{1}{LC}\right) = 0.$

$$s_1 = -\frac{R}{2L} + \sqrt{\left(\frac{R}{2L}\right)^2 - \frac{1}{LC}} = -\alpha + \sqrt{\alpha^2 - \omega_0^2} = -\alpha + \beta$$

$$s_2 = -\frac{R}{2L} - \sqrt{\left(\frac{R}{2L}\right)^2 - \frac{1}{LC}} = -\alpha - \sqrt{\alpha^2 - \omega_0^2} = -\alpha - \beta$$

where $\alpha = \frac{R}{2L}$

$$\omega_0 = \frac{1}{\sqrt{LC}}$$

and $\beta = \sqrt{\alpha^2 - \omega_0^2}$

By partial-fraction expansion, of $I(s)$,

$$I(s) = \frac{A}{s - s_1} + \frac{B}{s - s_2}$$

$$A = (s - s_1) I(s)\Big|_{s=s_1} = \frac{\frac{V}{L}}{s_1 - s_2}$$

$$B = (s - s_2) I(s)\Big|_{s=s_2} = \frac{\frac{V}{L}}{s_2 - s_1} = -\frac{\frac{V}{L}}{s_1 - s_2}$$

$$I(s) = \frac{V}{L(s_1 - s_2)}\left[\frac{1}{s - s_1} - \frac{1}{s - s_2}\right]$$

Taking the inverse Laplace transform,

$$i(t) = \frac{V}{L(s_1 - s_2)}\left[e^{s_1 t} - e^{s_2 t}\right] = k_1 e^{s_1 t} + k_2 e^{s_2 t}$$

where $k_1$ and $k_2$ are constants to be determined and $s_1$ and $s_2$ are the roots of the equation.

Now, depending upon the values of $s_1$ and $s_2$, we have three cases of the response.

***Case I*** When the roots are real and unequal, it gives an overdamped response.

$$\frac{R}{2L} > \frac{1}{\sqrt{LC}}$$

$$\alpha > \omega_0$$

In this case, the solution is given by

$$i(t) = e^{-\alpha t}\left(k_1 e^{\beta t} + k_2 e^{-\beta t}\right)$$

or

$$i(t) = k_1\, e^{s_1 t} + k_2\, e^{s_2 t} \qquad \text{for } t > 0$$

***Case II*** When the roots are real and equal, it gives a critically damped response.

$$\frac{R}{2L} = \frac{1}{\sqrt{LC}}$$

$$\alpha = \omega_0$$

In this case, the solution is given by

$$i(t) = e^{-\alpha t}\,(k_1 + k_2\, t) \qquad \text{for } t > 0$$

***Case III*** When the roots are complex conjugate, it gives an underdamped response.

$$\frac{R}{2L} < \frac{1}{\sqrt{LC}}$$

$$\alpha < \omega_0$$

In this case, the solution is given by

$$i(t) = k_1\, e^{s_1 t} + k_2\, e^{s_2 t}$$

where

$$s_{1,2} = -\alpha \pm \sqrt{\alpha^2 - \omega_0^2}$$

Let

$$\sqrt{\alpha^2 - \omega_0^2} = \sqrt{-1}\sqrt{\omega_0^2 - \alpha^2} = j\omega_d$$

where

$$j = \sqrt{-1}$$

and

$$\omega_d = \sqrt{\omega_0^2 - \alpha^2}$$

Hence,

$$i(t) = e^{-\alpha t}\left(k_1\, e^{j\omega_d t} + k_2\, e^{-j\omega_d t}\right)$$

$$= e^{-\alpha t}\left[(k_1 + k_2)\left\{\frac{e^{j\omega_d t} + e^{-j\omega_d t}}{2}\right\} + j(k_1 - k_2)\left\{\frac{e^{j\omega_d t} - e^{-j\omega_d t}}{2j}\right\}\right]$$

$$= e^{-\alpha t}\left[(k_1 + k_2)\cos\omega_d t + j(k_1 - k_2)\sin\omega_d t\right] \qquad \text{for } t > 0$$

**EXAMPLE 10.88**

*The switch in Fig. 10.77 is opened at time t = 0. Determine the voltage v(t) for t > 0.*

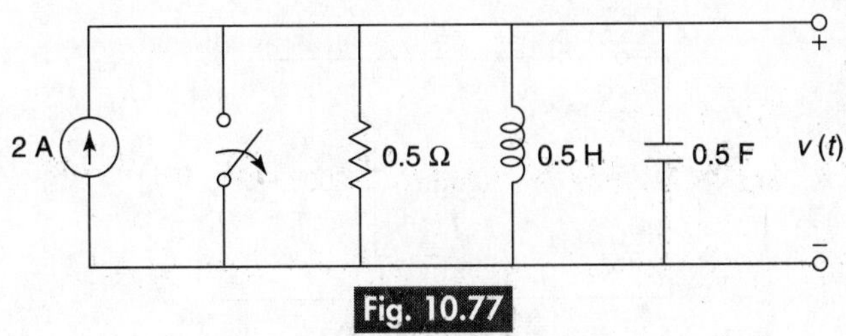


Fig. 10.77

## Solution

(i) At $t = 0^-$, the network is shown in Fig. 10.78. At $t = 0^-$, the network has attained steady-state condition. Hence, the inductor acts as a short circuit and the capacitor acts as an open circuit.

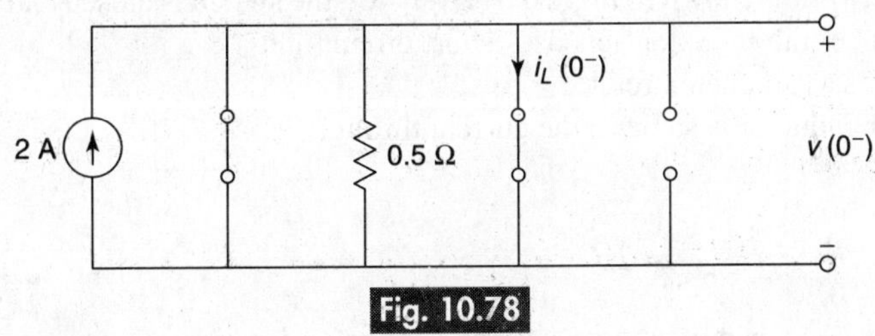


Fig. 10.78

$$i_L(0^-) = 0$$

$$v(0^-) = 0$$

(ii) Since current through the inductor and voltage across the capacitor cannot change instantaneously,

$$i_L(0^+) = 0$$

$$v(0^+) = 0$$

(iii) For $t > 0$, the transformed network is shown in Fig. 10.79.

Applying KCL at the node for $t > 0$,

$$\frac{V(s)}{0.5} + \frac{V(s)}{0.5s} + \frac{V(s)}{\frac{1}{0.5s}} = \frac{2}{s}$$

$$2V(s) + \frac{2}{s}V(s) + 0.5sV(s) = \frac{2}{s}$$

Fig. 10.79

$$V(s) = \frac{\frac{2}{s}}{\frac{2}{s} + 0.5s + 2} = \frac{4}{s^2 + 4s + 4} = \frac{4}{(s+2)^2}$$

Taking inverse Laplace transform,

$$v(t) = 4t\,e^{-2t} \qquad \text{for } t > 0$$

## EXAMPLE 10.89

*In the network of Fig. 10.80, the switch is closed and steady-state is attained. At t = 0, switch is opened. Determine the current through the inductor.*

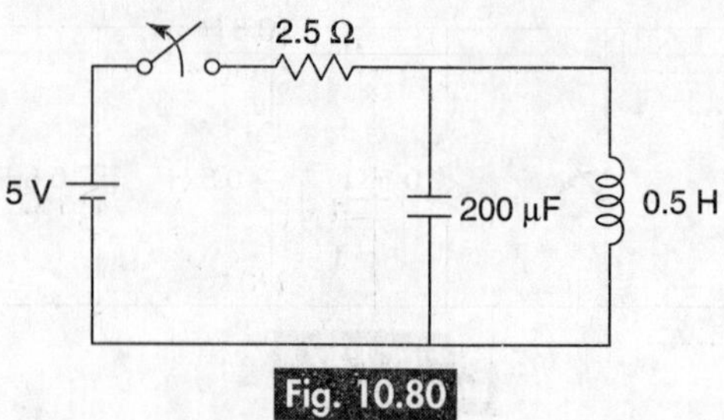


Fig. 10.80

## Solution

(i) At $t = 0^-$, the network is shown in Fig. 10.81. At $t = 0^-$, the switch is closed and steady-state condition is attained. Hence, the inductor acts as a short circuit and the capacitor acts as an open circuit.

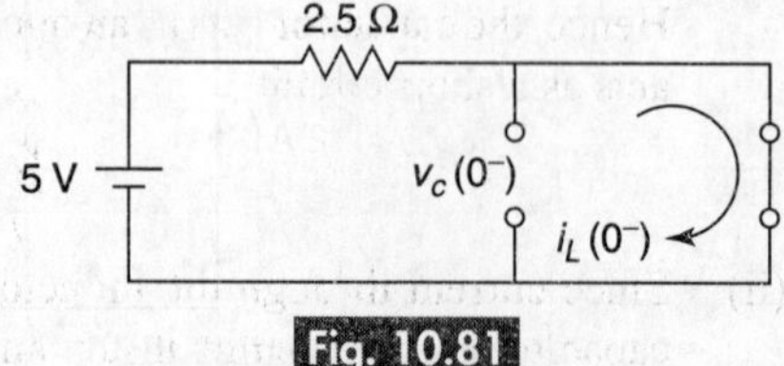


Fig. 10.81

Current through inductor is same as the current through the resistor.

$$i_L(0^-) = \frac{5}{2.5} = 2 \text{ A}$$

Voltage across the capacitor is zero as it is connected in parallel with a short.

$$v_c(0^-) = 0$$

(ii) Since voltage across the capacitor and current through the inductor cannot change instantaneously,

$$i_L(0^+) = 2 \text{ A}$$

$$v_c(0^+) = 0$$

(iii) For $t > 0$, the transformed network is shown in Fig. 10.82.

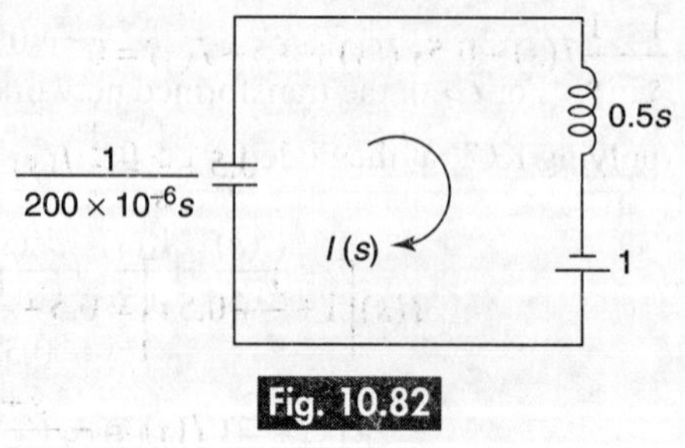


Fig. 10.82

Applying KVL to the mesh for $t > 0$,

$$-\frac{1}{200 \times 10^{-6} s} I(s) - 0.5s\, I(s) + 1 = 0$$

$$0.5s\, I(s) - 1 + 5000 \frac{I(s)}{s} = 0$$

$$I(s) = \frac{1}{0.5s + \dfrac{5000}{s}} = \frac{2s}{s^2 + 10000}$$

Taking inverse Laplace transform,

$$i(t) = 2 \cos 100t \qquad \text{for } t > 0$$

## EXAMPLE 10.90

*In the network shown in Fig. 10.83, the switch is opened at t = 0. Steady-state condition is achieved before t = 0. Find i(t).*

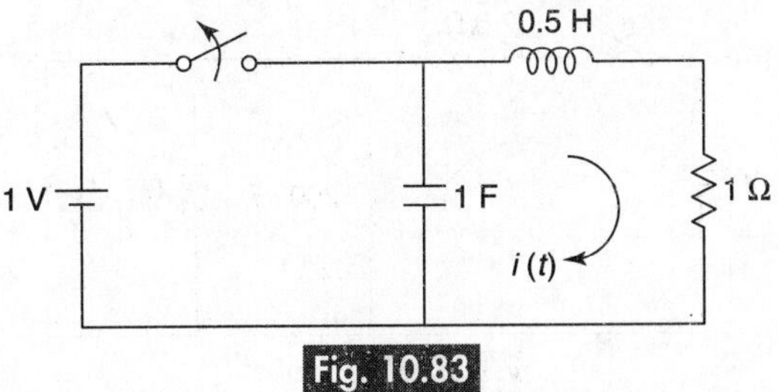


Fig. 10.83

## Solution

(i) At $t = 0^-$, the network is shown in Fig. 10.84. At $t = 0^-$, the switch is closed and steady-state condition is achieved. Hence, the capacitor acts as an open circuit and the inductor acts as a short circuit.

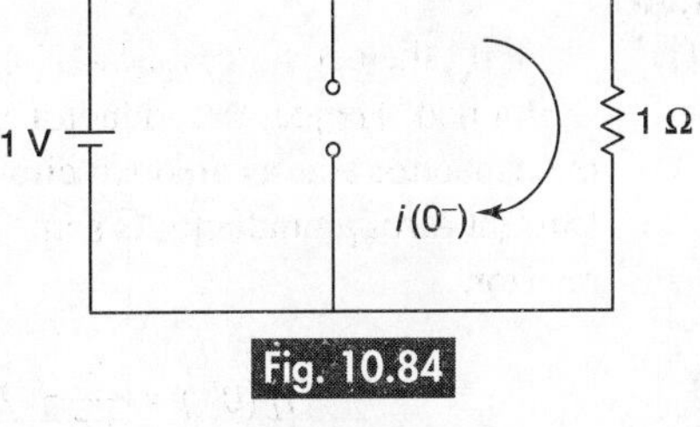


Fig. 10.84

$$v_c(0^-) = 1 \text{ V}$$

$$i(0^-) = 1 \text{ A}$$

(ii) Since current through the inductor and voltage across the capacitor cannot change instantaneously,

$$v_c(0^+) = 1 \text{ V}$$

$$i(0^+) = 1 \text{ A}$$

(iii) For $t > 0$, the transformed network is shown in Fig. 10.85.

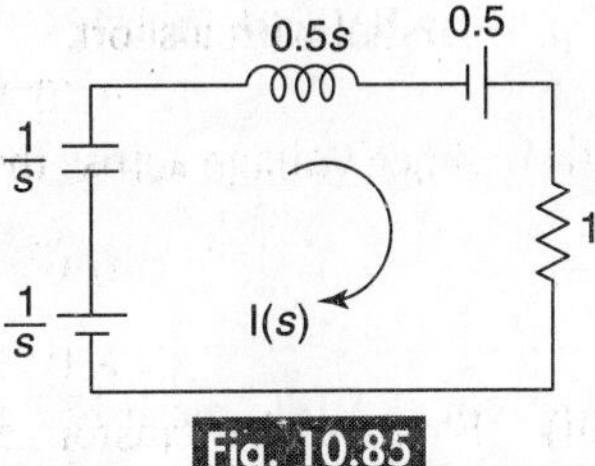


Fig. 10.85

Applying KVL to the mesh for $t > 0$,

$$\frac{1}{s} - \frac{1}{s} I(s) - 0.5s\, I(s) + 0.5 - I(s) = 0$$

$$0.5 + \frac{1}{s} = \frac{1}{s} I(s) + 0.5\, s\, I(s) + I(s)$$

$$I(s)\left[1 + \frac{1}{s} + 0.5s\right] = 0.5 + \frac{1}{s}$$

$$I(s) = \frac{s+2}{s^2+2s+2} = \frac{(s+1)+1}{(s+1)^2+1} = \frac{s+1}{(s+1)^2+1} + \frac{1}{(s+1)^2+1}$$

Taking the inverse Laplace transform,

$$i(t) = e^{-t}\cos t + e^{-t}\sin t \qquad \text{for } t > 0$$

## EXAMPLE 10.91

*In the network shown in Fig. 10.86, the switch is closed at $t = 0$. Find the currents $i_1(t)$ and $i_2(t)$ when initial current through the inductor is zero and initial voltage on the capacitor is 4 V.*

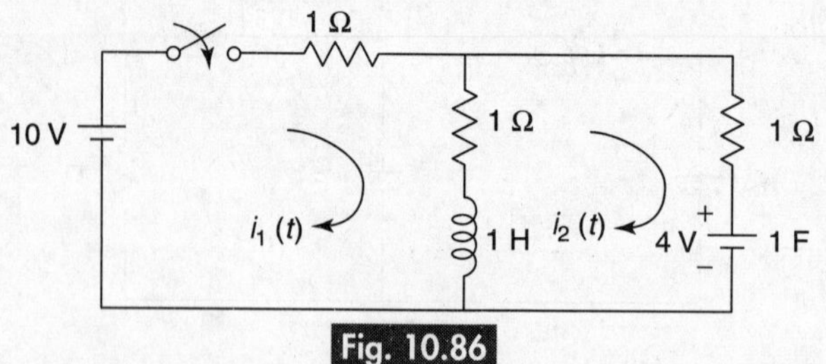


Fig. 10.86

**Solution** For $t > 0$, the transformed network is shown in Fig. 10.87.

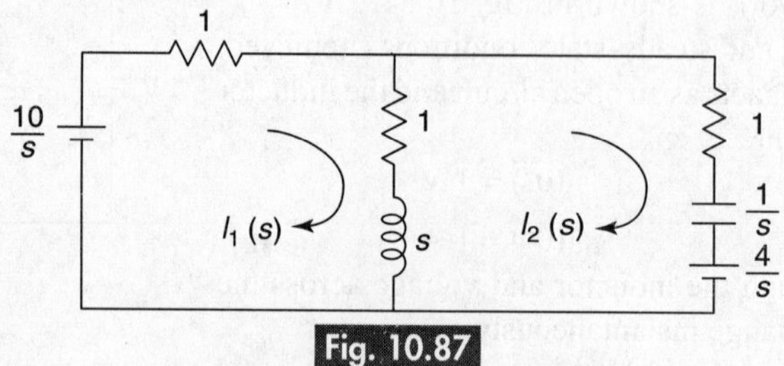


Fig. 10.87

Applying KVL to mesh 1,

$$\frac{10}{s} - I_1(s) - (1+s)[I_1(s) - I_2(s)] = 0$$

$$(s+2)I_1(s) - (s+1)I_2(s) = \frac{10}{s}$$

Applying KVL to mesh 2,

$$-(s+1)[I_2(s) - I_1(s)] - I_2(s) - \frac{1}{s}I_2(s) - \frac{4}{s} = 0$$

$$-(s+1)I_1(s) + \left(s+2+\frac{1}{s}\right)I_2(s) = -\frac{4}{s}$$

By Cramer's rule,

$$I_1(s) = \frac{\begin{vmatrix} \frac{10}{s} & -(s+1) \\ -\frac{4}{s} & s+2+\frac{1}{s} \end{vmatrix}}{\begin{vmatrix} s+2 & -(s+1) \\ -(s+1) & s+2+\frac{1}{s} \end{vmatrix}} = \frac{\left(\frac{10}{s}\right)\left(\frac{s^2+2s+1}{s}\right) - (s+1)\left(\frac{4}{s}\right)}{(s+2)\left(\frac{s^2+2s+1}{s}\right) - (s+1)^2} = \frac{\frac{10}{s^2}(s+1)^2 - (s+1)\frac{4}{s}}{(s+2)\frac{(s+1)^2}{s} - (s+1)^2}$$

$$= \frac{\frac{10}{s^2}(s+1) - \frac{4}{s}}{(s+2)\frac{(s+1)}{s} - (s+1)} = \frac{3s+5}{s(s+1)}$$

By partial-fraction expansion,

$$I_1(s) = \frac{A}{s} + \frac{B}{s+1}$$

$$A = sI_1(s)\big|_{s=0} = \left.\frac{3s+5}{s+1}\right|_{s=0} = 5$$

$$B = (s+1)I_1(s)\big|_{s=-1} = \left.\frac{3s+5}{s}\right|_{s=-1} = -2$$

$$I_1(s) = \frac{5}{s} - \frac{2}{s+1}$$

Taking inverse Laplace transform,

$$i_1(t) = 5 - 2e^{-t} \qquad \text{for } t > 0$$

Similarly,

$$I_2(s) = \frac{\begin{vmatrix} s+2 & \frac{10}{s} \\ -(s+1) & -\frac{4}{s} \end{vmatrix}}{\begin{vmatrix} s+2 & -(s+1) \\ -(s+1) & s+2+\frac{1}{s} \end{vmatrix}} = \frac{3s+1}{(s+1)^2} = \frac{3s+3-2}{(s+1)^2} = \frac{3(s+1)-2}{(s+1)^2} = \frac{3}{s+1} - \frac{2}{(s+1)^2}$$

Taking inverse Laplace transform,

$$i_2(t) = 3e^{-t} - 2te^{-t} \qquad \text{for } t > 0$$

## 10.12 RESPONSE OF *RL* CIRCUIT TO VARIOUS FUNCTIONS

LO 10.10

Explain the response of *RL* and *RC* circuits to various functions

Consider a series *RL* circuit shown in Fig. 10.88. When the switch is closed at $t = 0,\ i(0^-) = i(0^+) = 0$.

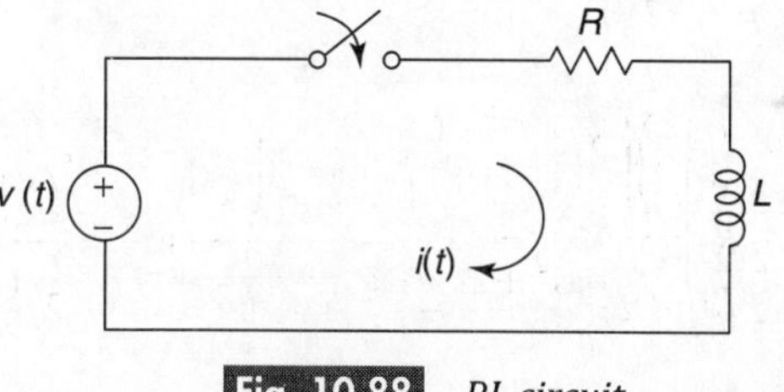


Fig. 10.88 *RL circuit*

For $t > 0$, the transformed network is shown in Fig. 10.89.

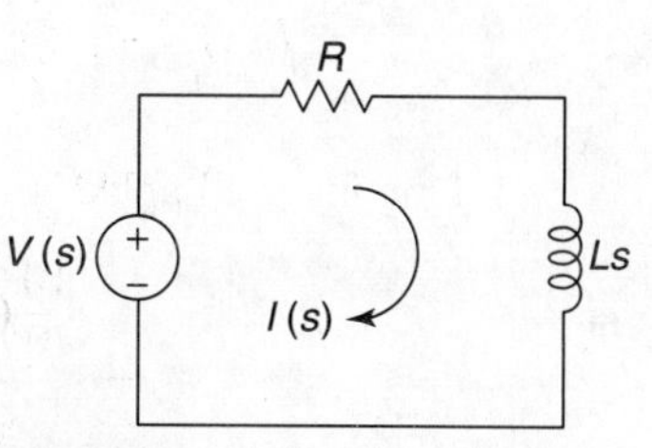


Fig. 10.89 *Transformed network*

Applying KVL to the mesh,

$$V(s) - RI(s) - Ls\,I(s) = 0$$

$$I(s) = \frac{V(s)}{R+Ls} = \frac{1}{L}\frac{V(s)}{s+\frac{R}{L}}$$

(a) When the unit step signal is applied,

$$v(t) = u(t)$$

Taking Laplace transform,

$$V(s) = \frac{1}{s}$$

$$I(s) = \frac{1}{L}\frac{\frac{1}{s}}{s+\frac{R}{L}}$$

$$= \frac{1}{L}\frac{1}{s\left(s+\frac{R}{L}\right)}$$

By partial-fraction expansion,

$$I(s) = \frac{1}{L}\left(\frac{A}{s}+\frac{B}{s+\frac{R}{L}}\right)$$

$$A = s\,I(s)\big|_{s=0} = \frac{1}{s+\frac{R}{L}}\Bigg|_{s=0} = \frac{L}{R}$$

$$B = \left(s+\frac{R}{L}\right)I(s)\bigg|_{s=-\frac{R}{L}} = \frac{1}{s}\bigg|_{s=-\frac{R}{L}} = -\frac{L}{R}$$

$$I(s) = \frac{1}{L}\left(\frac{L}{R}\frac{1}{s}-\frac{L}{R}\frac{1}{s+\frac{R}{L}}\right)$$

$$= \frac{1}{R}\left(\frac{1}{s}-\frac{1}{s+\frac{R}{L}}\right)$$

Taking inverse Laplace transform,

$$i(t) = \frac{1}{R}[1-e^{-\left(\frac{R}{L}\right)t}] \qquad \text{for } t>0$$

(b) When unit ramp signal is applied,

$$v(t) = r(t) = t \qquad \text{for } t>0$$

Taking Laplace transform,

$$V(s) = \frac{1}{s^2}$$

$$I(s) = \frac{1}{L}\frac{1}{s^2\left(s+\frac{R}{L}\right)}$$

By partial-faction expansion,

$$\frac{1}{L}\frac{1}{s^2\left(s+\frac{R}{L}\right)} = \frac{A}{s}+\frac{B}{s^2}+\frac{C}{s+\frac{R}{L}}$$

$$\frac{1}{L} = As\left(s+\frac{R}{L}\right)+B\left(s+\frac{R}{L}\right)+Cs^2$$

Putting $s = 0$,

$$B = \frac{1}{R}$$

Putting $s = -\frac{R}{L}$,

$$C = \frac{L}{R^2}$$

Comparing coefficients of $s^2$,

$$A+C = 0$$

$$A = -C = -\frac{L}{R^2}$$

$$I(s) = -\frac{L}{R^2}\frac{1}{s}+\frac{1}{R}\frac{1}{s^2}+\frac{L}{R^2}\frac{1}{s+\frac{R}{L}}$$

Taking inverse Laplace transform,

$$i(t) = -\frac{L}{R^2}+\frac{1}{R}t+\frac{L}{R^2}e^{-\left(\frac{R}{L}\right)t}$$

$$= \frac{1}{R}t-\frac{L}{R^2}[1-e^{-\left(\frac{R}{L}\right)t}] \qquad \text{for } t > 0$$

(c) When unit impulse signal is applied,

$$v(t) = \delta(t)$$

Taking Laplace transform,

$$V(s) = 1$$

$$I(s) = \frac{1}{L}\frac{1}{s+\frac{R}{L}}$$

Taking inverse Laplace transform,

$$i(t) = \frac{1}{L} e^{-\left(\frac{R}{L}\right)t} \qquad \text{for } t > 0$$

(d) When the sinusoidal signal is applied,

$$v(t) = V_m \sin \omega t$$

Taking Laplace transform,

$$V(s) = \frac{V_m \omega}{s^2 + \omega^2}$$

$$I(s) = \frac{V_m \omega}{L\left(s + \frac{R}{L}\right)(s^2 + \omega^2)}$$

By partial-fraction expansion,

$$I(s) = \frac{A}{s + \frac{R}{L}} + \frac{Bs + C}{s^2 + \omega^2}$$

$$\frac{V_m \omega}{L} = A(s^2 + \omega^2) + (Bs + C)\left(s + \frac{R}{L}\right)$$

$$= (A + B)s^2 + \left(\frac{BR}{L} + C\right)s + \left(A\omega^2 + \frac{CR}{L}\right)$$

Comparing coefficients,

$$A + B = 0$$

$$\frac{BR}{L} + C = 0$$

$$A\omega^2 + \frac{CR}{L} = \frac{V_m \omega}{L}$$

Solving the equations,

$$A = \frac{V_m \omega L}{R^2 + \omega^2 L^2}$$

$$B = -\frac{V_m \omega L}{R^2 + \omega^2 L^2}$$

$$C = \frac{V_m \omega R}{R^2 + \omega^2 L^2}$$

$$I(s) = \frac{V_m \omega L}{R^2 + \omega^2 L^2} \frac{1}{s + \frac{R}{L}} - \frac{V_m \omega L}{R^2 + \omega^2 L^2} \frac{s}{s^2 + \omega^2} + \frac{V_m \omega R}{R^2 + \omega^2 L^2} \frac{1}{s^2 + \omega^2}$$

$$= \frac{V_m \omega L}{R^2 + \omega^2 L^2} \frac{1}{s + \frac{R}{L}} - \frac{V_m \omega L}{R^2 + \omega^2 L^2} \left(\frac{s}{s^2 + \omega^2} - \frac{R}{L} \frac{1}{s^2 + \omega^2}\right)$$

$$= \frac{V_m \omega L}{R^2 + \omega^2 L^2} \frac{1}{s + \frac{R}{L}} - \frac{V_m \omega L}{R^2 + \omega^2 L^2} \left( \frac{s}{s^2 + \omega^2} - \frac{R}{\omega L} \frac{\omega}{s^2 + \omega^2} \right)$$

Taking inverse Laplace transform,

$$i(t) = \frac{V_m \omega L}{R^2 + \omega^2 L^2} e^{-\frac{R}{L}t} - \frac{V_m \omega L}{R^2 + \omega^2 L^2} \left( \cos \omega t - \frac{R}{\omega L} \sin \omega t \right)$$

$$= \frac{V_m \omega L}{R^2 + \omega^2 L^2} e^{-\frac{R}{L}t} - \frac{V_m}{\sqrt{R^2 + \omega^2 L^2}} \left( \frac{\omega L}{\sqrt{R^2 + \omega^2 L^2}} \cos \omega t - \frac{R}{\omega L} \frac{\omega L}{\sqrt{R^2 + \omega^2 L^2}} \sin \omega t \right)$$

$$= \frac{V_m \omega L}{R^2 + \omega^2 L^2} e^{-\frac{R}{L}t} - \frac{V_m}{\sqrt{R^2 + \omega^2 L^2}} \left( \frac{\omega L}{\sqrt{R^2 + \omega^2 L^2}} \cos \omega t - \frac{R}{\sqrt{R^2 + \omega^2 L^2}} \sin \omega t \right)$$

$$= \frac{V_m \omega t}{R^2 + \omega^2 L^2} e^{-\frac{R}{L}t} - \frac{V_m}{\sqrt{R^2 + \omega^2 L^2}} (\sin \theta \cos \omega t - \cos \theta \sin \omega t)$$

$$= \frac{V_m \omega L}{R^2 + \omega^2 L^2} e^{-\frac{R}{L}t} + \frac{V_m}{\sqrt{R^2 + \omega^2 L^2}} (\sin \omega t \cos \theta - \sin \theta \cos \omega t)$$

$$= \frac{V_m \omega L}{R^2 + \omega^2 L^2} e^{-\frac{R}{L}t} + \frac{V_m}{\sqrt{R^2 + \omega^2 L^2}} \sin(\omega t - \theta) \qquad \text{for } t > 0$$

where $\sin \theta = \dfrac{\omega L}{\sqrt{R^2 + \omega^2 L^2}}$

$$\cos \theta = \frac{R}{\sqrt{R^2 + \omega^2 L^2}}$$

$$\tan \theta = \frac{\omega L}{R}$$

$$\theta = \tan^{-1} \left( \frac{\omega L}{R} \right)$$

**EXAMPLE 10.92**

*At t = 0, unit pulse voltage of unit width is applied to a series RL circuit, as shown in Fig. 10.90. Obtain an expression for i(t).*

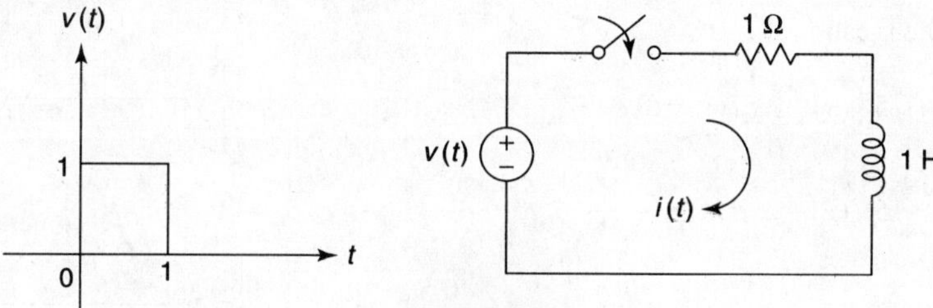


Fig. 10.90

**Solution**

$$v(t) = u(t) - u(t-1)$$

$$V(s) = \frac{1}{s} - \frac{e^{-s}}{s} = \frac{1-e^{-s}}{s}$$

For $t > 0$, the transformed network is shown in Fig. 10.91.

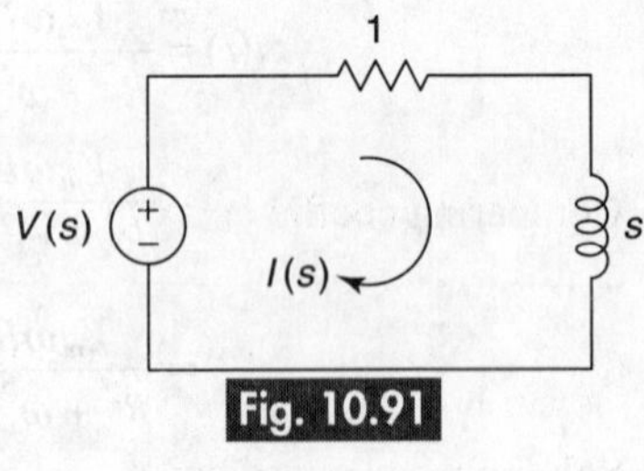

Fig. 10.91

Applying KVL to the mesh,

$$V(s) - I(s) - sI(s) = 0$$

$$I(s) = \frac{V(s)}{s+1}$$

$$= \frac{1-e^{-s}}{s(s+1)}$$

$$= \frac{1}{s(s+1)} - \frac{e^{-s}}{s(s+1)}$$

$$= \frac{1}{s} - \frac{1}{s+1} - \frac{e^{-s}}{s} + \frac{e^{-s}}{s+1}$$

Taking inverse Laplace transform,

$$i(t) = u(t) - e^{-t}u(t) - u(t-1) + e^{-(t-1)}u(t-1)$$

$$= (1-e^{-t})u(t) - [1-e^{-(t-1)}]u(t-1) \qquad \text{for } t > 0$$

**EXAMPLE 10.93**

*For the network shown in Fig. 10.92, determine the current i(t) when the switch is closed at t = 0. Assume that initial current in the inductor is zero.*

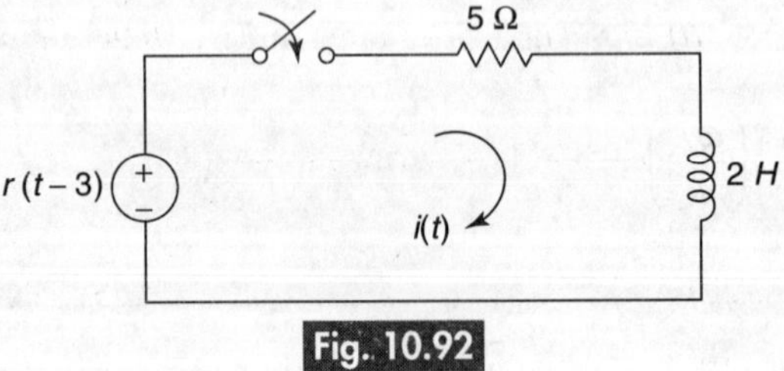

Fig. 10.92

**Solution** For $t > 0$, the transformed network is shown in Fig. 10.93.

Applying KVL to the mesh for $t > 0$,

$$\frac{e^{-3s}}{s^2} - 5\,I(s) - 2s\,I(s) = 0$$

$$5\,I(s) + 2s\,I(s) = \frac{e^{-3s}}{s^2}$$

$$I(s) = \frac{e^{-3s}}{s^2(2s+5)} = \frac{0.5\,e^{-3s}}{s^2(s+2.5)}$$

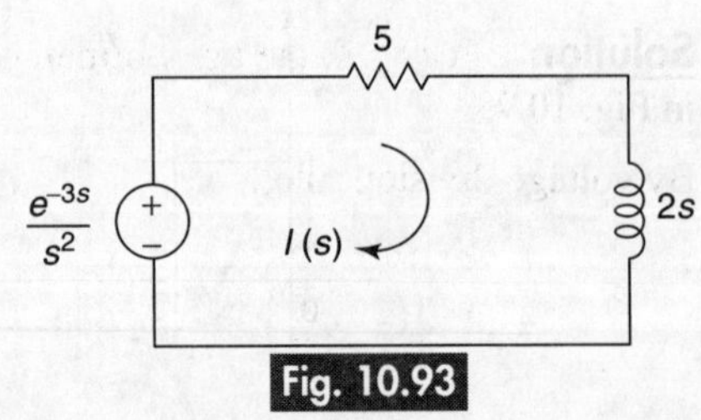

Fig. 10.93

By partial-fraction expansion,

$$\frac{0.5}{s^2(s+2.5)} = \frac{A}{s} + \frac{B}{s^2} + \frac{C}{s+2.5}$$

$$0.5 = As(s+2.5) + B(s+2.5) + Cs^2$$

$$= As^2 + 2.5As + Bs + 2.5B + Cs^2$$

$$= (A+C)s^2 + (2.5A+B)s + 2.5\,B$$

Comparing coefficients of $s^2$, $s$ and $s^0$,

$$A + C = 0$$

$$2.5A + B = 0$$

$$2.5B = 0.5$$

Solving these equations,

$$A = -0.08$$

$$B = 0.2$$

$$C = 0.08$$

$$I(s) = e^{-3s}\left(-\frac{0.08}{s} + \frac{0.2}{s^2} + \frac{0.08}{s+2.5}\right)$$

$$= -0.08\frac{e^{-3s}}{s} + 0.2\frac{e^{-3s}}{s^2} + 0.08\frac{e^{-3s}}{s+2.5}$$

Taking inverse Laplace transform,

$$i(t) = -0.08u(t-3) + 0.2r(t-3) + 0.08e^{-2.5(t-3)}u(t-3)$$

**EXAMPLE 10.94**

*Determine the expression for $v_L(t)$ in the network shown in Fig. 10.94. Find $v_L(t)$ when (i) $v_s(t) = \delta(t)$, and (ii) $v_s(t) = e^{-t}u(t)$.*

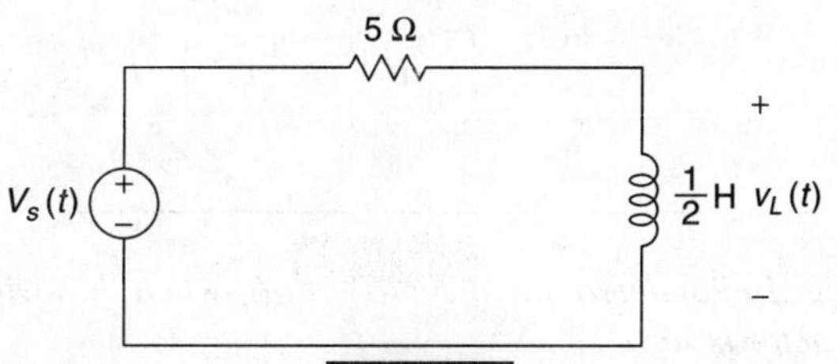


Fig. 10.94

**Solution** For $t > 0$, the transformed network is shown in Fig. 10.95.

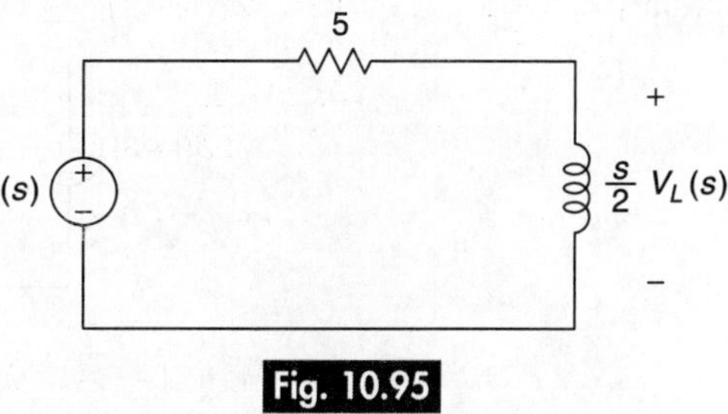


Fig. 10.95

By voltage-division rule,

$$V_L(s) = V_s(s) \times \frac{\frac{s}{2}}{\frac{s}{2}+5} = \frac{s}{s+10}V_s(s)$$

(a) For impulse input,

$$V_s(s) = 1$$

$$V_L(s) = \frac{s}{s+10} = \frac{s+10-10}{s+10} = 1 - \frac{10}{s+10}$$

Taking inverse Laplace transform,

$$V_L(t) = \delta(t) - 10e^{-10t}u(t) \qquad \text{for } t > 0$$

(b) For $v_s(t) = e^{-t}u(t)$,

$$V_s(s) = \frac{1}{s+1}$$

$$V_L(s) = \frac{s}{(s+10)(s+1)}$$

By partial-fraction expansion,

$$V_L(s) = \frac{A}{s+10} + \frac{B}{s+1}$$

$$A = (s+10)V_L(s)\big|_{s=-10} = \frac{s}{s+1}\bigg|_{s=-10} = \frac{10}{9}$$

$$B = (s+1)V_L(s)\big|_{s=-1} = \frac{s}{s+10}\bigg|_{s=-1} = -\frac{1}{9}$$

$$V_L(s) = \frac{10}{9}\frac{1}{s+10} - \frac{1}{9}\frac{1}{s+1}$$

Taking inverse Laplace transform,

$$v_L(t) = \frac{10}{9}e^{-10t}u(t) - \frac{1}{9}e^{-t}u(t)$$

$$= \left(\frac{10}{9}e^{-10t} - \frac{1}{9}e^{-t}\right)u(t) \qquad \text{for } t > 0$$

**EXAMPLE 10.95**

*For the network shown in Fig. 10.96, determine the current i (t) when the switch is closed at t = 0. Assume that initial current in the inductor is zero.*

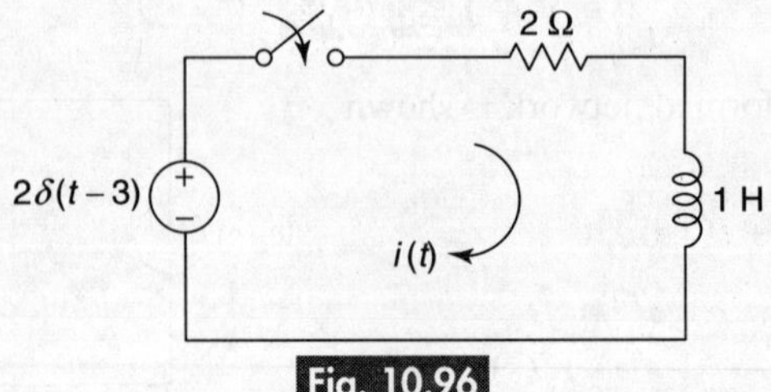


Fig. 10.96

**Solution** For $t > 0$, the transformed network is shown in Fig. 10.97.

Applying KVL to the mesh for $t > 0$,

$$2e^{-3s} - 2I(s) - sI(s) = 0$$

$$2I(s) + sI(s) = 2e^{-3s}$$

$$I(s) = \frac{2e^{-3s}}{s+2}$$

Fig. 10.97

Taking inverse Laplace transform,

$$i(t) = 2e^{-2(t-3)}u(t-3) \qquad \text{for } t > 0$$

## EXAMPLE 10.96

*Determine the current i(t) in the network shown in Fig. 10.98, when the switch is closed at t = 0.*

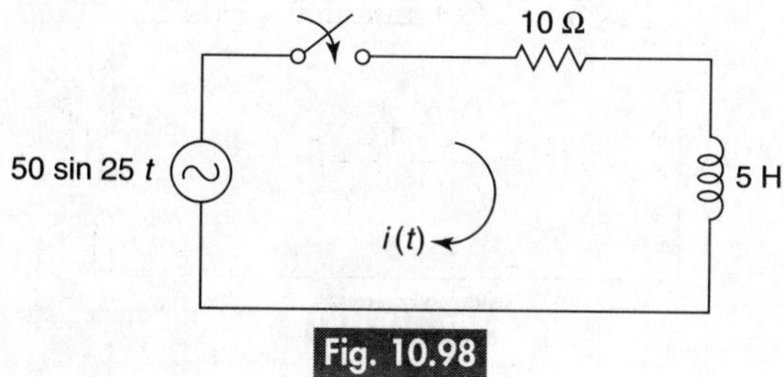


Fig. 10.98

**Solution** For $t > 0$, the transformed network is shown in Fig. 10.99.

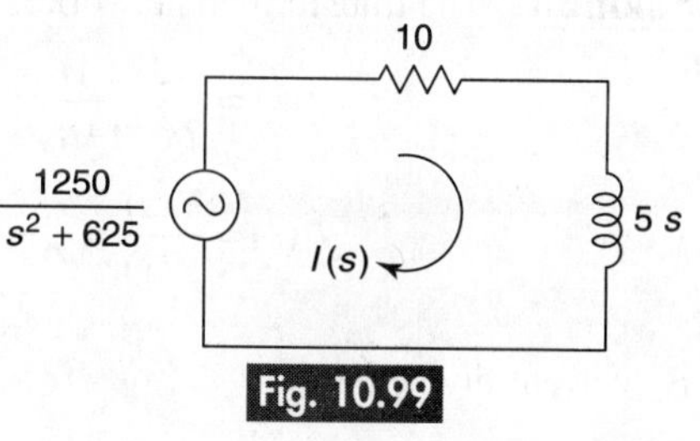


Fig. 10.99

Applying KVL to the mesh for $t > 0$,

$$\frac{1250}{s^2+625} - 10I(s) - 5sI(s) = 0$$

$$I(s) = \frac{250}{(s^2+625)(s+2)}$$

By partial-fraction expansion,

$$I(s) = \frac{As+B}{s^2+625} + \frac{C}{s+2}$$

$$250 = (As+B)(s+2) + C(s^2+625)$$

$$= (A+C)s^2 + (2A+B)s + (2B+625C)$$

Comparing coefficients,

$$A + C = 0$$

$$2A + B = 0$$

$$2B + 625C = 250$$

Solving the equations,

$$A = -0.397$$
$$B = 0.795$$
$$C = 0.397$$

$$I(s) = \frac{-0.397s + 0.795}{s^2 + 625} + \frac{0.397}{s+2} = -\frac{0.397s}{s^2 + 625} + \frac{0.795}{s^2 + 625} + \frac{0.397}{s+2}$$

Taking the inverse Laplace transform,

$$i(t) = -0.397\cos 25t + 0.032\sin 25t + 0.397e^{-2t} \qquad \text{for } t > 0$$

## EXAMPLE 10.97

*Find impulse response of the current i(t) in the network shown in Fig. 10.100.*

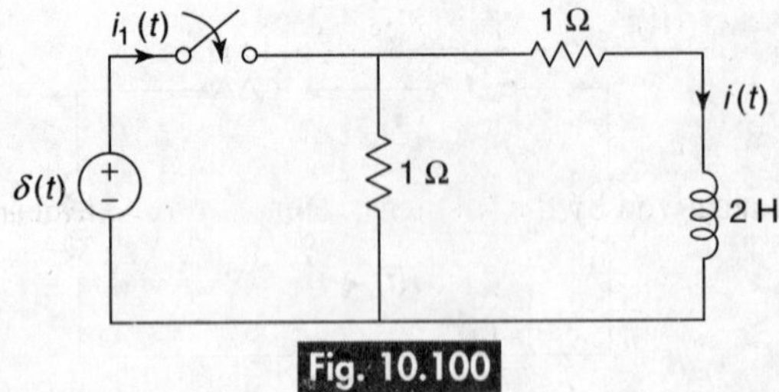


Fig. 10.100

**Solution** The transformed network is shown in Fig. 10.101.

$$Z(s) = \frac{1(2s+1)}{2s+1+1} = \frac{2s+1}{2s+2}$$

$$I_1(s) = \frac{V(s)}{Z(s)} = \frac{1}{\frac{2s+1}{2s+2}} = \frac{2s+2}{2s+1}$$

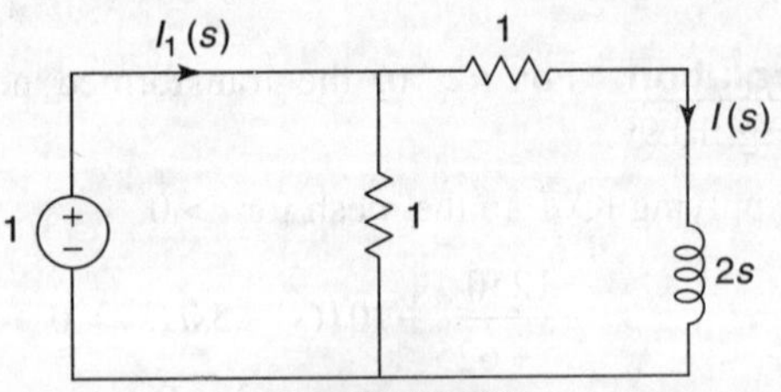


Fig. 10.101

By current-division rule,

$$I(s) = I_1(s) \times \frac{1}{2s+2} = \frac{1}{2s+2} \times \frac{2s+2}{2s+1} = \frac{1}{2s+1} = \frac{1}{2}\frac{1}{s+0.5}$$

Taking inverse Laplace transform,

$$i(t) = \frac{1}{2}e^{-0.5t}u(t) \qquad \text{for } t > 0$$

## EXAMPLE 10.98

*The network shown in Fig. 10.102 is at rest for $t < 0$. If the voltage $v(t) = u(t)\cos t + A\delta(t)$ is applied to the network, determine the value of A so that there is no transient term in the current response i(t).*

$$v(t) = u(t)\cos t + A\delta(t)$$

$$V(s) = \frac{s}{s^2+1} + A$$

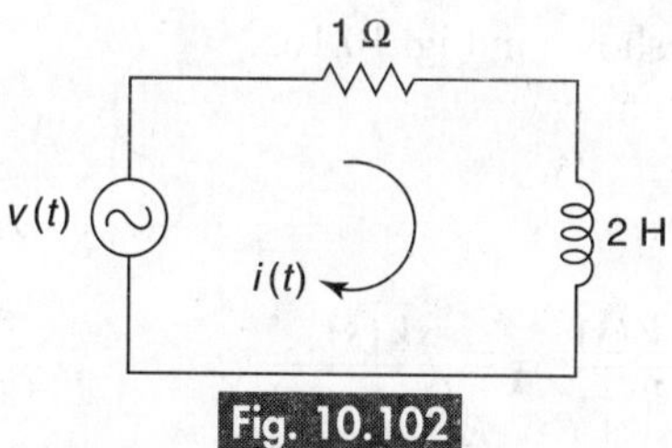

Fig. 10.102

**Solution** For $t > 0$, the transformed network is shown in Fig. 10.103.

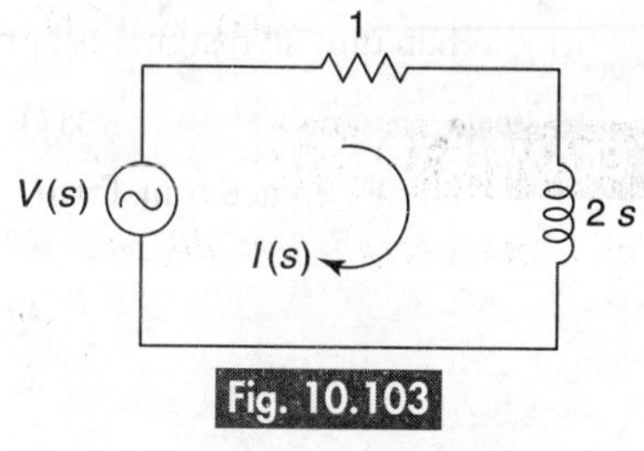

Fig. 10.103

Applying KVL to the mesh for $t > 0$,

$$V(s) = 2sI(s) + I(s) = \frac{s}{s^2+1} + A$$

$$I(s) = \frac{s + A(s^2+1)}{2\left(s+\frac{1}{2}\right)(s^2+1)} = \frac{K_1}{s+\frac{1}{2}} + \frac{K_2 s + K_3}{s^2+1}$$

The transient part of the response is given by the first term. Hence, for the transient term to vanish, $K_1 = 0$.

$$K_1 = \left(s+\frac{1}{2}\right)I(s)\Big|_{s=-\frac{1}{2}} = \frac{\frac{-1}{2} + A\left(\frac{5}{4}\right)}{2\left(\frac{5}{4}\right)}$$

When $\quad K_1 = 0$

$$\frac{5}{4}A = \frac{1}{2}$$

$$A = \frac{2}{5} = 0.4$$

## 10.13 RESPONSE OF *RC* CIRCUIT TO VARIOUS FUNCTIONS

LO 10.10

Consider a series *RC* circuits, as shown in Fig. 10.104.

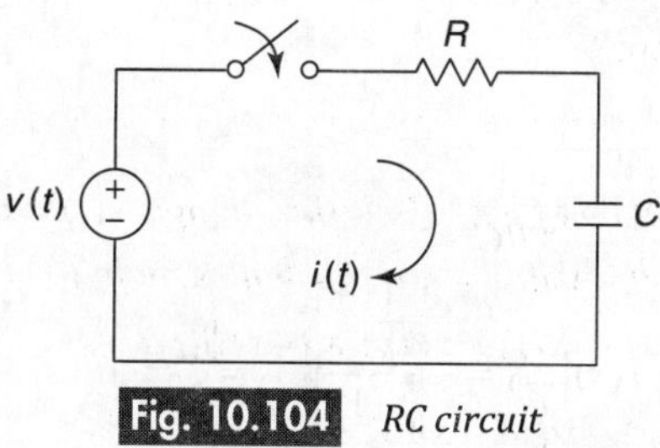

Fig. 10.104 *RC circuit*

For $t > 0$, the transformed network is shown in Fig. 10.105.

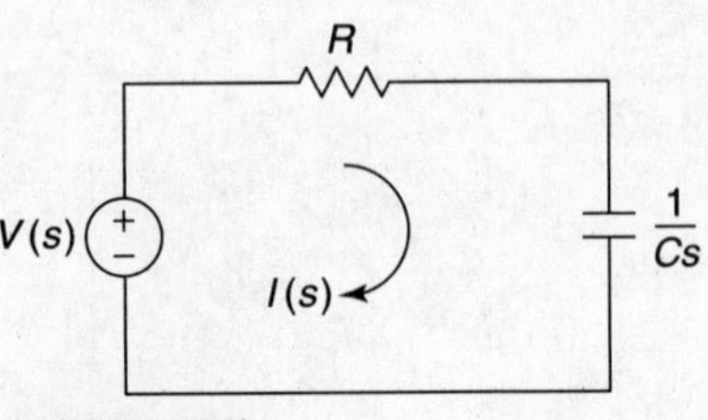


Fig. 10.105 *Transformed network*

Applying KVL to the mesh,

$$V(s) - RI(s) - \frac{1}{Cs}I(s) = 0$$

$$I(s) = \frac{V(s)}{\frac{1}{Cs} + R} = \frac{sV(s)}{R\left(s + \frac{1}{RC}\right)}$$

(a) When unit step signal is applied,

$$v(t) = u(t)$$

Taking Laplace transform,

$$V(s) = \frac{1}{s}$$

$$I(s) = \frac{s \times \frac{1}{s}}{R\left(s + \frac{1}{RC}\right)} = \frac{1}{R\left(s + \frac{1}{RC}\right)}$$

Taking inverse Laplace transform,

$$i(t) = \frac{1}{R}e^{-\frac{1}{RC}t} \qquad \text{for } t > 0$$

(b) When unit ramp signal is applied,

$$v(t) = r(t) = t$$

Taking Laplace transform,

$$V(s) = \frac{1}{s^2}$$

$$I(s) = \frac{s \times \frac{1}{s^2}}{R\left(s + \frac{1}{RC}\right)} = \frac{\frac{1}{R}}{s\left(s + \frac{1}{RC}\right)}$$

By partial-fraction expansion,

$$I(s) = \frac{A}{s} + \frac{B}{s + \frac{1}{RC}}$$

$$A = s\,I(s)\Big|_{s=0} = \left.\frac{\frac{1}{R}}{s + \frac{1}{RC}}\right|_{s=0} = C$$

$$B = \left(s + \frac{1}{RC}\right) I(s)\Big|_{s=-\frac{1}{RC}} = \left.\frac{\frac{1}{R}}{s}\right|_{s=-\frac{1}{RC}} = -C$$

$$I(s) = \frac{C}{s} - \frac{C}{s + \frac{1}{RC}}$$

Taking inverse Laplace transform,

$$i(t) = C - Ce^{-\frac{1}{RC}t} \qquad \text{for } t > 0$$

(c) When unit inpulse signal is applied,

$$v(t) = \delta(t)$$

Taking Laplace transform,

$$V(s) = 1$$

$$I(s) = \frac{s}{R\left(s + \frac{1}{RC}\right)} = \frac{s + \frac{1}{RC} - \frac{1}{RC}}{R\left(s + \frac{1}{RC}\right)} = \frac{1}{R}\left(1 - \frac{\frac{1}{RC}}{s + \frac{1}{RC}}\right)$$

Taking inverse Laplace transform,

$$i(t) = \frac{1}{R}\left[\delta(t) - \frac{1}{RC}e^{-\frac{1}{RC}t}\right] \qquad \text{for } t > 0$$

(d) When the sinusoidal signal is applied.

$$v(t) = V_m \sin \omega t$$

Taking Laplace transform,

$$V(s) = \frac{V_m \omega}{s^2 + \omega^2}$$

$$I(s) = \frac{sV_m\omega}{R\left(s + \frac{1}{RC}\right)(s^2 + \omega^2)}$$

By partial-fraction expansion,

$$I(s) = \frac{A}{s + \frac{1}{RC}} + \frac{Bs + C'}{s^2 + \omega^2}$$

$$\frac{sV_m\omega}{R} = A(s^2 + \omega^2) + (Bs + C')\left(s + \frac{1}{RC}\right)$$

$$= (A + B)s^2 + \left(\frac{B}{RC} + C'\right)s + \left(A\omega^2 + \frac{C'}{RC}\right)$$

Comparing coefficients,

$$A + B = 0$$

$$\frac{B}{RC} + C' = \frac{V_m \omega}{R}$$

$$A\omega^2 + \frac{C'}{RC} = 0$$

Solving the equations,

$$A = -\frac{V_m \omega C}{1+\omega^2 R^2 C^2}$$

$$B = \frac{V_m \omega C}{1+\omega^2 R^2 C^2}$$

$$C' = \frac{V_m \omega^3 RC^2}{1+\omega^2 R^2 C^2}$$

$$I(s) = -\frac{V_m \omega C}{1+\omega^2 R^2 C^2} \frac{1}{s+\frac{1}{RC}} + \frac{V_m \omega C}{1+\omega^2 R^2 C^2} \frac{s}{s^2+\omega^2} + \frac{V_m \omega^3 RC^2}{1+\omega^2 R^2 C^2} \frac{1}{s^2+\omega^2}$$

$$= -\frac{V_m \omega C}{1+\omega^2 R^2 C^2} \frac{1}{s+\frac{1}{RC}} + \frac{V_m \omega C}{1+\omega^2 R^2 C^2} \left( \frac{s}{s^2+\omega^2} + \frac{\omega^2 RC}{s^2+\omega^2} \right)$$

$$= -\frac{V_m \omega C}{1+\omega^2 R^2 C^2} \frac{1}{s+\frac{1}{RC}} + \frac{V_m \omega C}{1+\omega^2 R^2 C^2} \left( \frac{s}{s^2+\omega^2} + \omega RC \frac{\omega}{s^2+\omega^2} \right)$$

Taking inverse Laplace transform,

$$i(t) = -\frac{V_m \omega C}{1+\omega^2 R^2 C^2} e^{-\frac{1}{RC}t} + \frac{V_m \omega C}{1+\omega^2 R^2 C^2} (\cos \omega t + \omega RC \sin \omega t)$$

$$= -\frac{V_m \omega C}{1+\omega^2 R^2 C^2} e^{-\frac{1}{RC}t} + \frac{V_m \omega C}{\sqrt{1+\omega^2 R^2 C^2}} \left( \frac{1}{\sqrt{1+\omega^2 R^2 C^2}} \cos \omega t + \frac{\omega RC}{\sqrt{1+\omega^2 R^2 C^2}} \sin \omega t \right)$$

$$= -\frac{V_m \omega C}{1+\omega^2 R^2 C^2} e^{-\frac{1}{RC}t} + \frac{V_m \omega C}{\sqrt{1+\omega^2 R^2 C^2}} (\cos \omega t \sin \theta + \sin \omega t \cos \theta)$$

$$= -\frac{V_m \omega C}{1+\omega^2 R^2 C^2} e^{-\frac{1}{RC}t} + \frac{V_m \omega C}{\sqrt{1+\omega^2 R^2 C^2}} (\sin \omega t \cos \theta + \sin \theta \cos \omega t)$$

$$= -\frac{V_m \omega C}{1+\omega^2 R^2 C^2} e^{-\frac{1}{RC}t} + \frac{V_m \omega C}{\sqrt{1+\omega^2 R^2 C^2}} \sin(\omega t + \theta) \qquad \text{for } t > C$$

where
$$\sin\theta = \frac{1}{\sqrt{1+\omega^2R^2C^2}}$$
$$\cos\theta = \frac{\omega RC}{\sqrt{1+\omega^2R^2C^2}}$$
$$\tan\theta = \frac{1}{\omega RC}$$
$$\theta = \tan^{-1}\left(\frac{1}{\omega RC}\right)$$

**EXAMPLE 10.99**

*A rectangular voltage pulse of unit height and T-seconds duration is applied to a series RC network at t = 0. Obtain the expression for the current i(t). Assume the capacitor to be initially uncharged.*

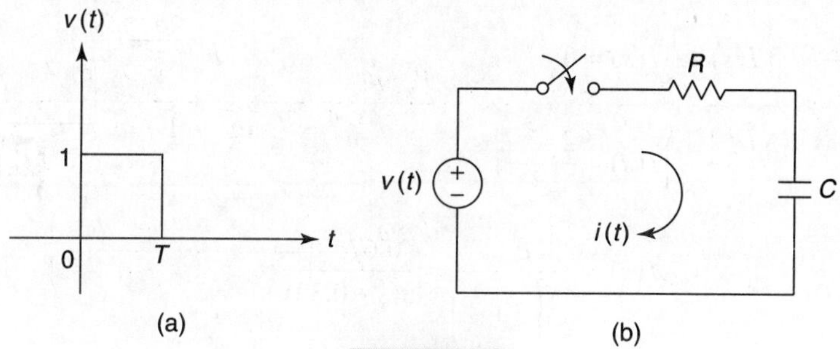


Fig. 10.106

**Solution**

$$v(t) = u(t) - u(t-T)$$
$$V(s) = \frac{1}{s} - \frac{e^{-sT}}{s} = \frac{1-e^{-sT}}{s}$$

For $t > 0$, the transformed network is shown in Fig. 10.107.

Fig. 10.107

Applying KVL to the mesh for $t > 0$,
$$V(s) - RI(s) - \frac{1}{Cs}I(s) = 0$$
$$I(s) = \frac{V(s)}{R+\frac{1}{Cs}} = \frac{\frac{1}{R}s}{s+\frac{1}{RC}}V(s) = \frac{1-e^{-sT}}{R\left(s+\frac{1}{RC}\right)} = \frac{1}{R}\left[\frac{1}{s+\frac{1}{RC}} - \frac{e^{-sT}}{s+\frac{1}{RC}}\right]$$

Taking inverse Laplace transform,
$$i(t) = \frac{1}{R}\left[e^{-\left(\frac{1}{RC}\right)t}u(t) - e^{-\left(\frac{1}{RC}\right)(t-T)}u(t-T)\right] \qquad \text{for } t > 0$$

**EXAMPLE 10.100**

*For the network shown in Fig. 10.108, determine the current i(t) when the switch is closed at t = 0 with zero initial conditions.*

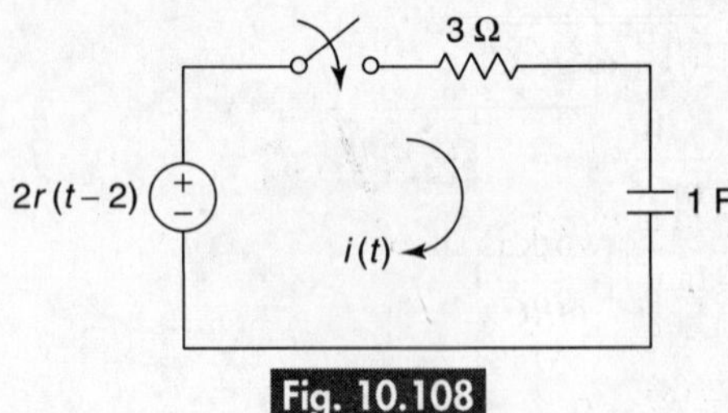


Fig. 10.108

**Solution** For $t > 0$, the transformed network is shown in Fig. 10.109.

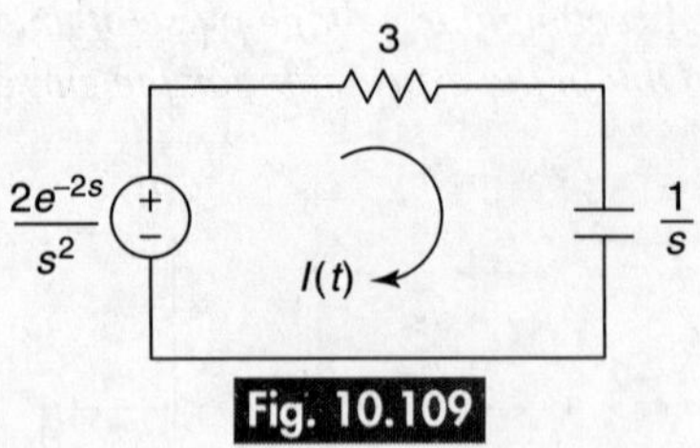


Fig. 10.109

Applying KVL to the mesh for $t > 0$,

$$\frac{2e^{-2s}}{s^2} - 3\,I(s) - \frac{1}{s}I(s) = 0$$

$$\left(3 + \frac{1}{s}\right)I(s) = \frac{2e^{-2s}}{s^2}$$

$$I(s) = \frac{2e^{-2s}}{s^2\left(3 + \frac{1}{s}\right)} = \frac{0.67e^{-2s}}{s(s+0.33)}$$

By partial-fraction expansion,

$$\frac{0.67}{s(s+0.33)} = \frac{A}{s} + \frac{B}{s+0.33}$$

$$A = \left.\frac{0.67}{s+0.33}\right|_{s=0} = 2$$

$$B = \left.\frac{0.67}{s}\right|_{s=-0.33} = -2$$

$$I(s) = e^{-2s}\left(\frac{2}{s} - \frac{2}{s+0.33}\right) = 2\frac{e^{-2s}}{s} - 2\frac{e^{-2s}}{s+0.33}$$

Taking inverse Laplace transform,

$$i(t) = 2u(t-2) - 2e^{-0.33(t-2)}u(t-2) \qquad \text{for } t > 0$$

**EXAMPLE 10.101**

*For the network shown in Fig. 10.110, determine the current i(t) when the switch is closed at t = 0 with zero initial conditions.*

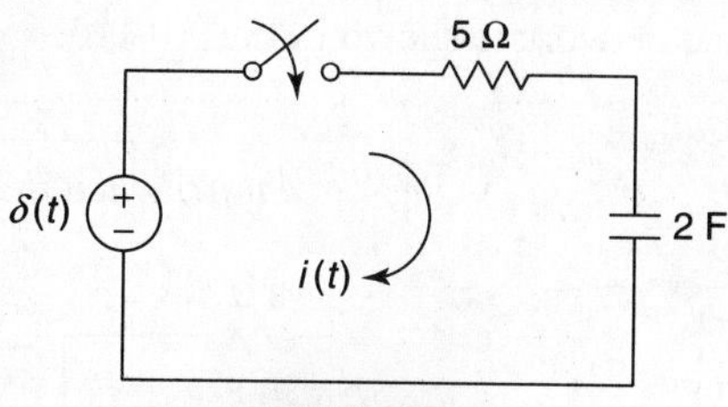


Fig. 10.110

**Solution** For $t > 0$, the transformed network is shown in Fig. 10.111.

Applying KVL to the mesh for $t > 0$,

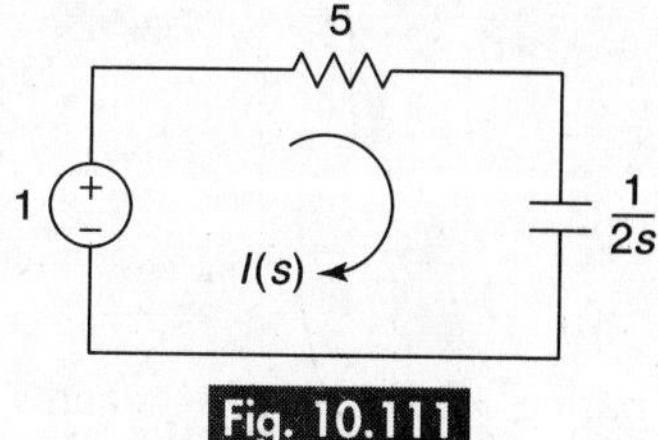


Fig. 10.111

$$1 - 5\,I(s) - \frac{1}{2s} I(s) = 0$$

$$\left(5 + \frac{1}{2s}\right) I(s) = 1$$

$$I(s) = \frac{1}{5 + \frac{1}{2s}}$$

$$= \frac{2s}{10s + 1}$$

$$= \frac{0.2s}{s + 0.1}$$

$$= \frac{0.2(s + 0.1 - 0.1)}{s + 0.1}$$

$$= 0.2\left(1 - \frac{0.1}{s + 0.1}\right)$$

$$= 0.2 - \frac{0.02}{s + 0.1}$$

Taking inverse Laplace transform,

$$i(t) = 0.2\delta(t) - 0.02\, e^{-0.1t} u(t)$$

## EXAMPLE 10.102

*For the network shown in Fig. 10.112, find the response $v_0\,(t)$.*

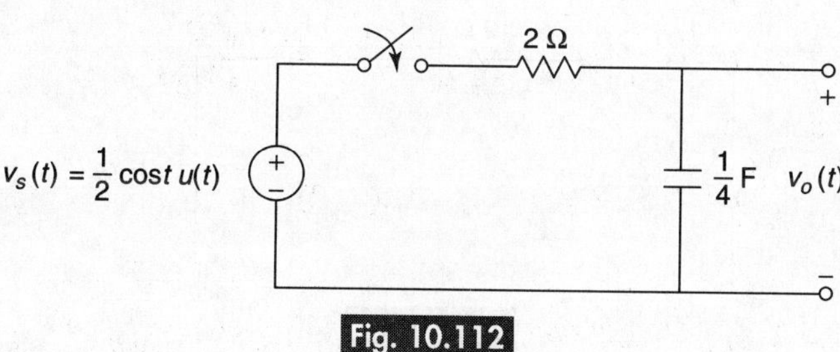


Fig. 10.112

**Solution** For $t > 0$, the transformed network is shown in Fig. 10.113.

$$V_s(s) = \frac{1}{2}\frac{s}{s^2+1}$$

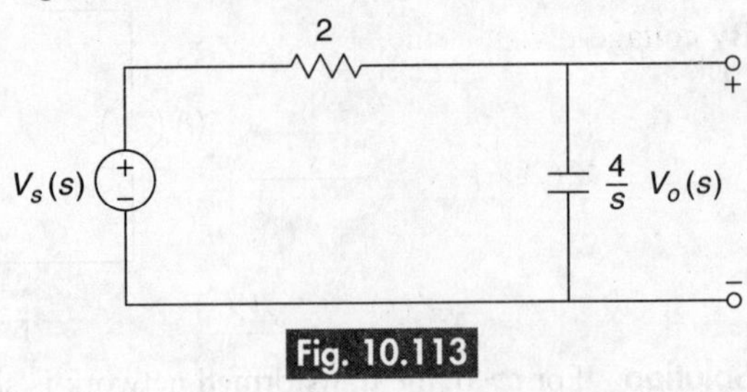


Fig. 10.113

By voltage-division rule,

$$V_o(s) = V_s(s) \times \frac{\frac{4}{s}}{2+\frac{4}{s}} = \frac{2V_s(s)}{s+2} = \frac{s}{(s^2+1)(s+2)}$$

By partial-fraction expansion,

$$V_o(s) = \frac{As+B}{s^2+1} + \frac{C}{s+2}$$

$$s = (As+B)(s+2) + c(s^2+1)$$

$$s = (A+C)s^2 + (2A+B)s + (2B+C)$$

Comparing coefficient of $s^2$, $s$ and $s^0$,

$$A + C = 0$$
$$2A + B = 1$$
$$2B + C = 0$$

Solving the equations,

$$A = 0.4$$
$$B = 0.2$$
$$C = -0.4$$

$$V_o(s) = \frac{0.4s+0.2}{s^2+1} - \frac{0.4}{s+2} = \frac{0.4s}{s^2+1} + \frac{0.2}{s^2+1} - \frac{0.4}{s+2}$$

Taking the inverse Laplace transform,

$$i(t) = 0.4\cos t + 0.2\sin t - 0.4e^{-2t} \qquad \text{for } t > 0$$

**EXAMPLE 10.103**

*Find the impulse response of the voltage across the capacitor in the network shown in Fig. 10.114. Also, determine response $v_c(t)$ for step input.*

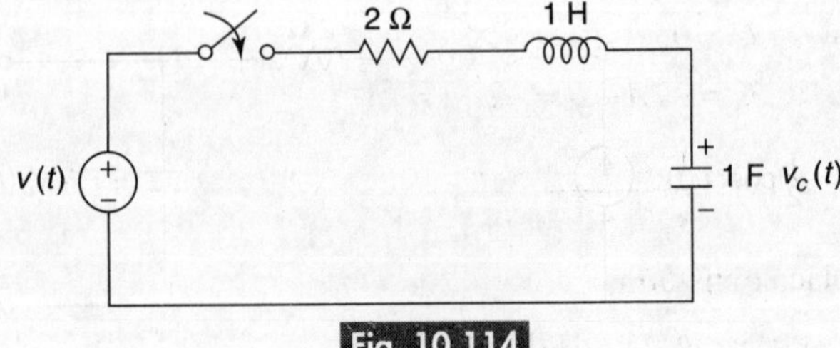


Fig. 10.114

**Solution** For $t > 0$, the transformed network is shown in Fig. 10.115.

By voltage-division rule,

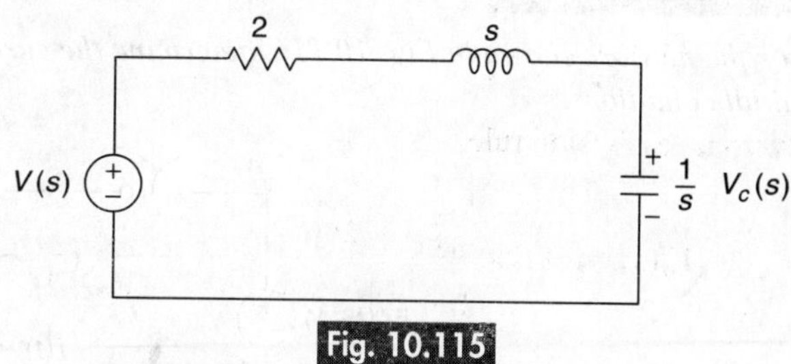

Fig. 10.115

$$V_c(s) = V(s) \times \frac{\frac{1}{s}}{2+s+\frac{1}{s}}$$

$$= \frac{V(s)}{s^2+2s+1} = \frac{V(s)}{(s+1)^2}$$

(a) For impulse input,

$$V(s) = 1$$

$$V_c(s) = \frac{1}{(s+1)^2}$$

Taking inverse Laplace transform,

$$v_c(t) = te^{-t}u(t) \qquad \text{for } t > 0$$

(b) For step input,

$$V(s) = \frac{1}{s}$$

$$V_c(s) = \frac{1}{s(s+1)^2}$$

By partial-fraction expansion,

$$V_c(s) = \frac{A}{s} + \frac{B}{s+1} + \frac{C}{(s+1)^2}$$

$$1 = A(s+1)^2 + Bs(s+1) + Cs$$

$$= A(s^2+2s+1) + B(s^2+s) + Cs$$

$$= (A+B)s^2 + (2A+B+C)s + A$$

Comparing coefficient of $s^2$, $s^1$ and $s^0$,

$$A = 1$$

$$A + B = 0$$

$$B = -A = -1$$

$$2A + B + C = 0$$

$$C = -2A - B = -2 + 1 = -1$$

$$V_c(s) = \frac{1}{s} - \frac{1}{s+1} - \frac{1}{(s+1)^2}$$

Taking inverse Laplace transform,

$$v_c(t) = u(t) - e^{-t}u(t) - te^{-t}u(t)$$

$$= (1 - e^{-t} - te^{-t})u(t) \qquad \text{for } t > 0$$

## EXAMPLE 10.104

*For the network shown in Fig. 10.116, determine the current i(t) when the switch is closed at t = 0 with zero initial conditions.*

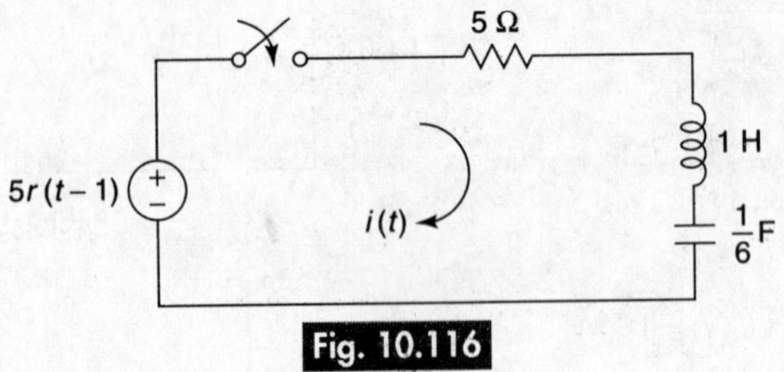


Fig. 10.116

**Solution** For $t > 0$, the transformed network is shown in Fig. 10.117.

Applying KVL to the mesh for $t > 0$,

$$\frac{5e^{-s}}{s^2} - 5I(s) - sI(s) - \frac{6}{s}I(s) = 0$$

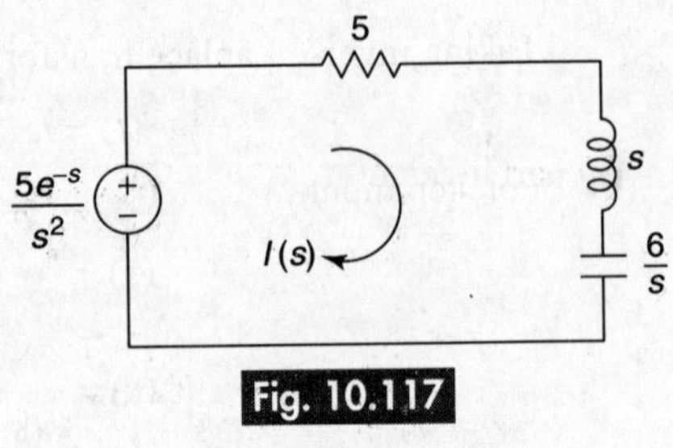


Fig. 10.117

$$5I(s) + sI(s) + \frac{6}{s}I(s) = \frac{5e^{-s}}{s^2}$$

$$I(s) = \frac{5e^{-s}}{s(s^2+5s+6)} = \frac{5e^{-s}}{s(s+3)(s+2)}$$

By partial-fraction expansion,

$$\frac{1}{s(s+3)(s+2)} = \frac{A}{s} + \frac{B}{s+3} + \frac{C}{s+2}$$

$$A = \left.\frac{1}{(s+3)(s+2)}\right|_{s=0} = \frac{1}{6}$$

$$B = \left.\frac{1}{s(s+2)}\right|_{s=-3} = \frac{1}{3}$$

$$C = \left.\frac{1}{s(s+3)}\right|_{s=-2} = -\frac{1}{2}$$

$$I(s) = 5e^{-s}\left[\frac{1}{6s} + \frac{1}{3(s+3)} - \frac{1}{2(s+2)}\right] = \frac{5}{6}\frac{e^{-s}}{s} + \frac{5}{3}\frac{e^{-s}}{s+3} - \frac{5}{2}\frac{e^{-s}}{s+2}$$

Taking inverse Laplace transform,

$$i(t) = \frac{5}{6}u(t-1) + \frac{5}{3}e^{-3(t-1)}u(t-1) - \frac{5}{2}e^{-2(t-1)}u(t-1) \qquad \text{for } t > 0$$

## EXAMPLE 10.105

*For the network shown in Fig. 10.118, the switch is closed at t = 0. Determine the current i(t) assuming zero initial conditions.*

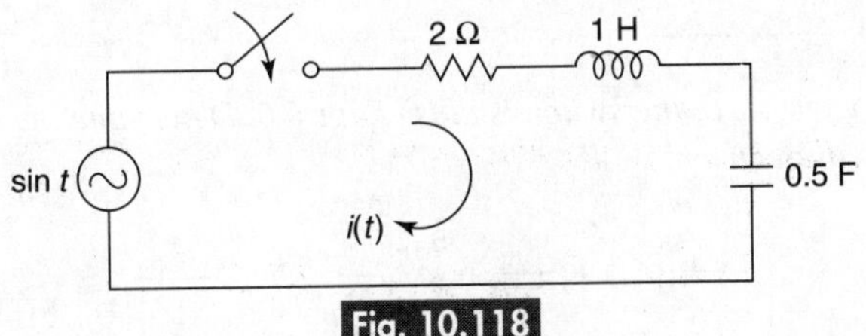

Fig. 10.118

**Solution** For $t > 0$, the transformed network is shown in Fig. 10.119.

Applying KVL to the mesh for $t > 0$,

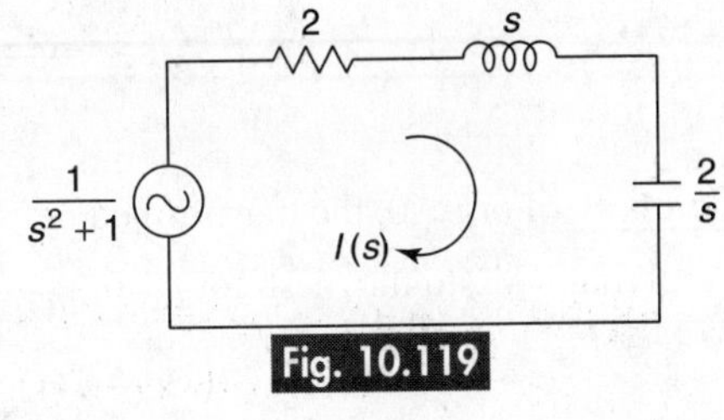

Fig. 10.119

$$\frac{1}{s^2+1} - 2I(s) - s\,I(s) - \frac{2}{s}I(s) = 0$$

$$\left(2 + s + \frac{2}{s}\right)I(s) = \frac{1}{s^2+1}$$

$$I(s) = \frac{s}{(s^2+1)(s^2+2s+2)}$$

By partial-fraction expansion,

$$I(s) = \frac{As+B}{s^2+1} + \frac{Cs+D}{s^2+2s+2}$$

$$s = (As+B)(s^2+2s+2) + (Cs+D)(s^2+1)$$

$$= As^3 + 2As^2 + 2As + Bs^2 + 2Bs + 2B + Cs^3 + Cs + Ds^2 + D$$

$$= (A+C)s^3 + (2A+B+D)s^2 + (2A+2B+C)s + (2B+D)$$

Comparing coefficients of $s^3$, $s^2$, $s^1$ and $s^0$,

$$A + C = 0$$

$$2A + B + D = 0$$

$$2A + 2B + C = 1$$

$$2B + D = 0$$

Solving these equations,

$$A = 0.2,\ B = 0.4,\ C = -0.2,\ D = -0.8$$

$$I(s) = \frac{0.2s+0.4}{s^2+1} - \frac{0.2s+0.8}{s^2+2s+2}$$

$$= \frac{0.2s}{s^2+1} + \frac{0.4}{s^2+1} - \frac{0.2s+0.2+0.6}{(s+1)^2+(1)^2}$$

$$= \frac{0.2s}{s^2+1} + \frac{0.4}{s^2+1} - \frac{0.2(s+1)}{(s+1)^2+1} - \frac{0.6}{(s+1)^2+1}$$

Taking inverse Laplace transform,

$$i(t) = 0.2\cos t + 0.4\sin t - 0.2\,e^{-t}\cos t - 0.6\,e^{-t}\sin t$$

$$= 0.2\cos t + 0.4\sin t - e^{-t}(0.2\cos t + 0.6\sin t) \qquad \text{for } t > 0$$

## EXAMPLE 10.106

*For the network shown in Fig. 10.120, the switch is closed at t = 0. Determine the current i(t) assuming zero initial conditions in the network elements.*

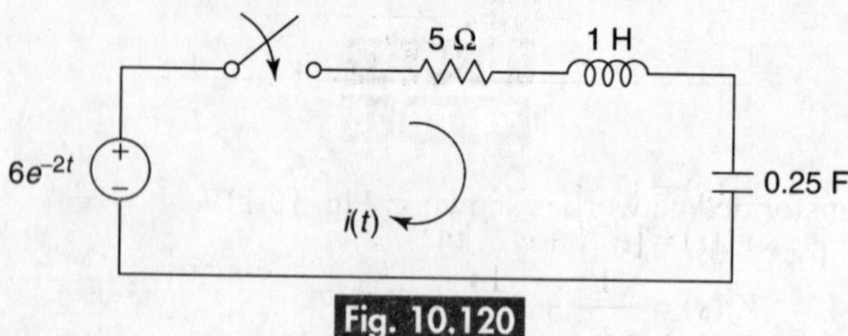


Fig. 10.120

**Solution** For $t > 0$, the transformed network is shown in Fig. 10.121.

Applying KVL to the mesh for $t > 0$,

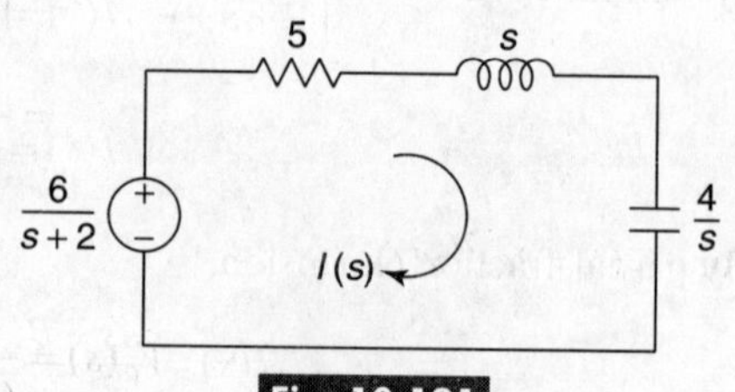


Fig. 10.121

$$\frac{6}{s+2} - 5I(s) - s\,I(s) - \frac{4}{s}I(s) = 0$$

$$\left(5 + s + \frac{4}{s}\right)I(s) = \frac{6}{s+2}$$

$$I(s) = \frac{6s}{(s+2)(s^2+5s+4)}$$

$$= \frac{6s}{(s+2)(s+1)(s+4)}$$

By partial-fraction expansion,

$$I(s) = \frac{A}{s+2} + \frac{B}{s+1} + \frac{C}{s+4}$$

$$A = (s+2)I(s)\big|_{s=-2} = \left.\frac{6s}{(s+1)(s+4)}\right|_{s=-2} = 6$$

$$B = (s+1)I(s)\big|_{s=-1} = \left.\frac{6s}{(s+2)(s+4)}\right|_{s=-1} = -2$$

$$C = (s+4)I(s)\big|_{s=-4} = \left.\frac{6s}{(s+2)(s+1)}\right|_{s=-4} = -4$$

$$I(s) = \frac{6}{s+2} - \frac{2}{s+1} - \frac{4}{s+4}$$

Taking inverse Laplace transform,

$$i(t) = 6e^{-2t}u(t) - 2e^{-t}u(t) - 4\,e^{-4t}u(t) \qquad \text{for } t > 0$$

## EXAMPLE 10.107

*The network shown has zero initial conditions. A voltage $v_i(t) = \delta(t)$ applied to two terminal network produces voltage $v_o(t) = [e^{-2t} + e^{-3t}]\,u(t)$. What should be $v_i(t)$ to give $v_o(t) = t\,e^{-2t}\,u(t)$?*

Fig. 10.122

**Solution** For $v_i(t) = \delta(t)$,

$$V_i(s) = 1$$

$$v_o(t) = [e^{-2t} + e^{-3t}]u(t)$$

$$V_o(s) = \frac{1}{s+2} + \frac{1}{s+3}$$

System function

$$H(s) = \frac{V_o(s)}{V_i(s)}$$

$$= \frac{1}{s+2} + \frac{1}{s+3} = \frac{2s+5}{(s+2)(s+3)} \qquad \text{...(i)}$$

For $v_o(t) = te^{-2t}u(t)$,

$$V_o(s) = \frac{1}{(s+2)^2}$$

From Eq. (i),

$$V_i(s) = \frac{V_o(s)}{H(s)} = \frac{1}{(s+2)^2} \times \frac{(s+2)(s+3)}{2s+5} = \frac{(s+3)}{2(s+2.5)(s+2)}$$

By partial-fraction expansion,

$$V_i(s) = \frac{A}{s+2} + \frac{B}{s+2.5}$$

$$A = 1$$

$$B = -0.5$$

$$V_i(s) = \frac{1}{s+2} - \frac{0.5}{s+2.5}$$

Taking inverse Laplace transform,

$$v_i(t) = e^{-2t} - 0.5e^{-2.5t} \qquad \text{for } t > 0$$

**EXAMPLE 10.108**

*A unit impulse applied to a two-terminal black box produces a voltage $v_o(t) = 2e^{-t} - e^{-3t}$. Determine the terminal voltage when a current pulse of 1 A height and a duration of 2 seconds is applied at the terminal.*

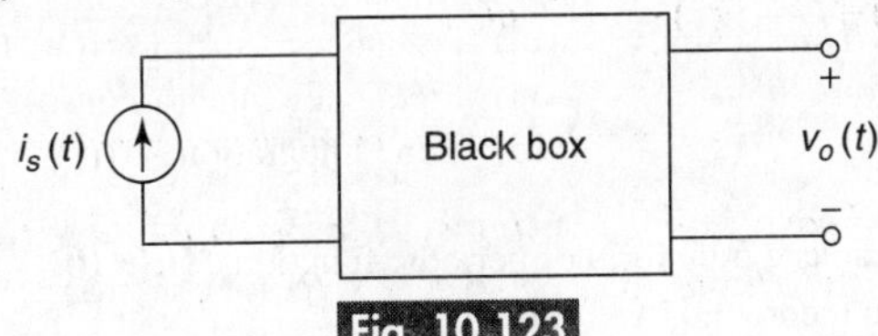

Fig. 10.123

**Solution**

$$v_o(t) = 2e^{-t} - e^{-3t}$$

$$V_o(s) = \frac{2}{s+1} - \frac{1}{s+3}$$

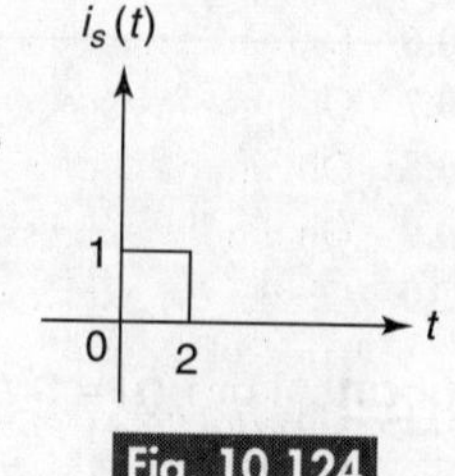

Fig. 10.124

When $i_s(t) = \delta(t)$,

$$I_s(s) = 1$$

$$V_o(s) = Z(s)\, I_s(s) \qquad \ldots\text{(i)}$$

$$Z(s) = \frac{V_o(s)}{I_s(s)} = \frac{2}{s+1} - \frac{1}{s+3}$$

When $i_s(t)$ is a pulse of 1 A height and a duration of 2 seconds then,

$$i_s(t) = u(t) - u(t-2)$$

$$I_s(s) = \frac{1}{s} - \frac{e^{-2s}}{s}$$

From Eq. (i),

$$V_o(s) = \left[\frac{2}{s+1} - \frac{1}{s+3}\right]\left[\frac{1}{s} - \frac{e^{-2s}}{s}\right]$$

$$= \frac{2}{s(s+1)} - \frac{1}{s(s+3)} - \frac{2e^{-2s}}{s(s+1)} + \frac{e^{-2s}}{s(s+3)}$$

$$= 2\left[\frac{1}{s} - \frac{1}{s+1}\right] - \frac{1}{3}\left[\frac{1}{s} - \frac{1}{s+3}\right] - 2e^{-2s}\left[\frac{1}{s} - \frac{1}{s+1}\right] + \frac{e^{-2s}}{3}\left[\frac{1}{s} - \frac{1}{s+3}\right]$$

Taking the inverse Laplace transform,

$$v(t) = 2[u(t) - e^{-t}u(t)] - \frac{1}{3}[u(t) - e^{-3t}u(t)] - 2[u(t-2) - e^{-(t-2)}u(t-2)] + \frac{1}{3}[u(t-2) - e^{-3(t-2)}u(t-2)]$$

for $t > 0$

# Theory Questions

**10.1** Define Laplace transform and inverse Laplace transform. **[LO 10.1]** ●○○

**10.2** Derive Laplace transform of the following functions: **[LO 10.2]** ●○○

(i) $K$ (ii) $t^n$ (iii) $u(t)$ (iv) $r(t)$
(v) $\delta(t)$ (vi) $e^{at}$ (vii) $\sin \omega t$ (viii) $\cos \omega t$
(ix) $\sinh \omega t$ (x) $\cosh \omega t$

**10.3** State and prove the following properties of Laplace transform: **[LO 10.3]** ○●○

(i) Linearity (ii) Time scaling (iii) Frequency shifting (iv) Time shifting
(v) Frequency differentiation (vi) Frequency integration
(vii) Time differentiation (viii) Time integration (ix) Initial value theorem
(x) Final value theorem

**10.4** Derive the expression for Laplace transform of periodic functions. **[LO 10.4]** ○●○

**10.5** State and prove convolution theorem. **[LO 10.6]** ○●○

**10.6** Draw the frequency-domain equivalent circuits for resistor, inductor and capacitor. **[LO 10.8]** ●○○

**10.7** Obtain the expression for transient current in series RL circuit with dc excitation. **[LO 10.9]** ○●○

**10.8** Obtain the expression for transient current in series RC circuit with dc excitation. **[LO 10.9]** ○●○

**10.9** Obtain the expression for transient current in series RLC circuit with dc excitation. **[LO 10.9]** ○●○

**10.10** Obtain the expression for transient current in series RL circuit with following functions: **[LO 10.10]** ○●○
(i) Unit step (ii) Unit ramp (iii) Unit impulse (iv) Sinusoidal

**10.11** Obtain the expression for transient current in series RC circuit with following functions: **[LO 10.10]** ○●○
(i) Unit step (ii) Unit ramp (iii) Unit impulse (iv) Sinusoidal

# Practice Problems

**10.1** Find $L\{f'(t)\}$ of $f(t)=\left(\dfrac{1-\cos 2t}{t}\right)$ ●○○

**10.2** Find Laplace transform of the following function: ●○○

$$f(t)=t+1 \quad 0 \le t \le 2$$
$$=3 \quad t>2$$

**10.3** For the network shown in Fig. 10.125, the switch is closed at $t = 0$. Find the current $i_1(t)$ for $t > 0$. ○●○

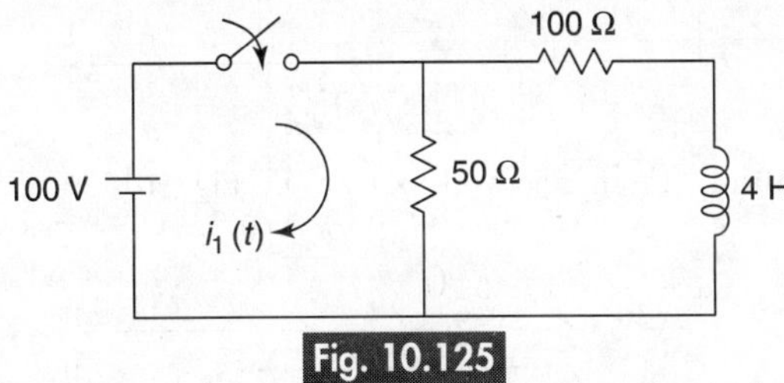


Fig. 10.125

**10.4** Determine the current $i(t)$ in the network of Fig. 10.126, when the switch is closed at $t = 0$. The inductor is initially unenergised. ○●○

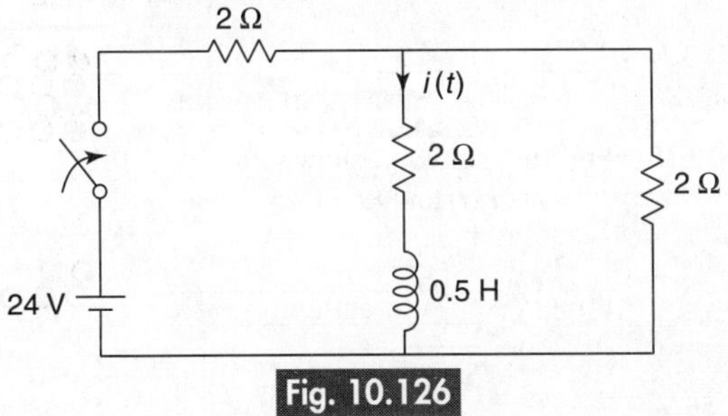


Fig. 10.126

**10.5** In the network of Fig. 10.127, after the switch has been in the open position for a long time, it is closed at $t = 0$. Find the voltage across the capacitor. ○●○

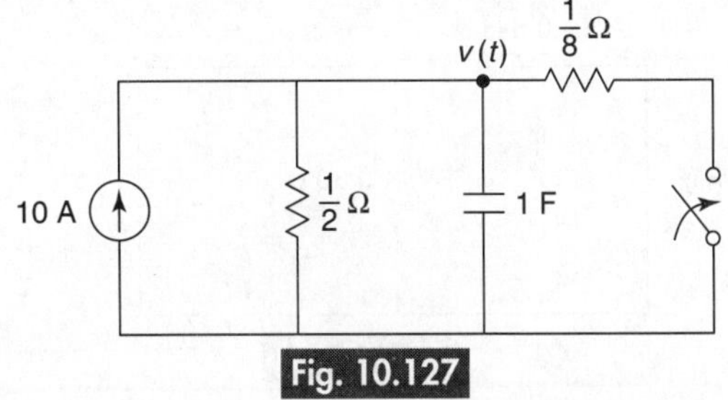


Fig. 10.127

**10.6** The circuit of Fig. 10.128, has been in the condition shown for a long time. At $t = 0$, switch is closed. Find $v(t)$ for $t > 0$. ○●○

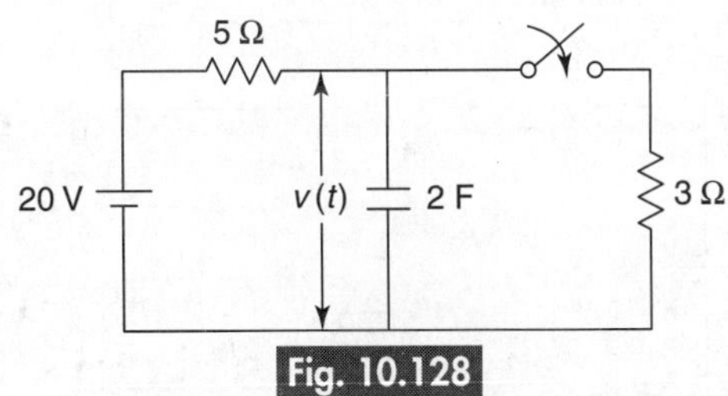


Fig. 10.128

**10.7** Figure 10.129 shows a circuit which is in the steady-state with the switch open. At $t = 0$, the switch is closed. Determine the current $i(t)$. Find its value at $t = 0.114$ μ seconds. ○●○

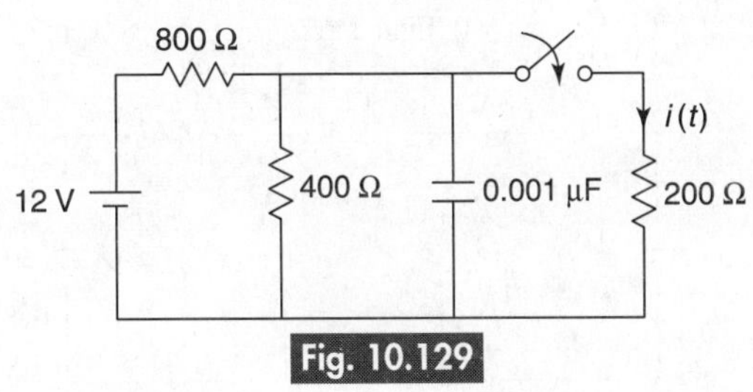


Fig. 10.129

**10.8** Find $i(t)$ for the network shown in Fig. 10.130. ○●○

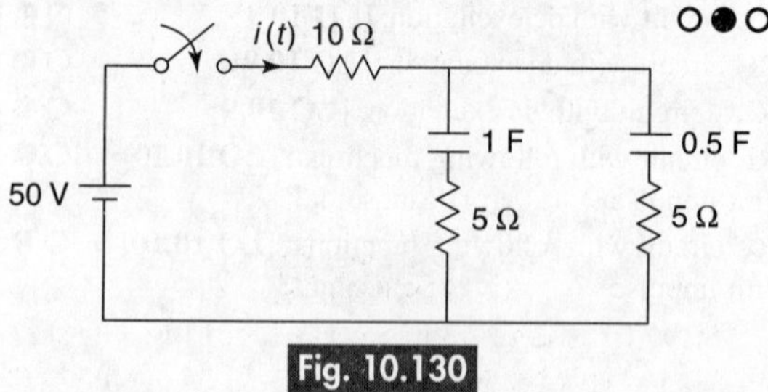


Fig. 10.130

**10.9** Determine $v(t)$ in the network of Fig. 10.131 where $i_L(0^-) = 15$ A and $v_c(0^-) = 5$ V. ○●○

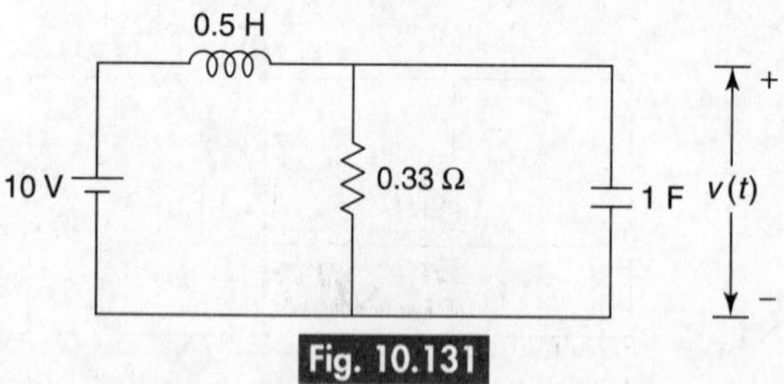


Fig. 10.131

**10.10** The network shown in Fig. 10.132 has acquired steady state with the switch at position 1 for $t < 0$. At $t = 0$, the switch is thrown to the position 2. Find $v(t)$ for $t > 0$. ○○●

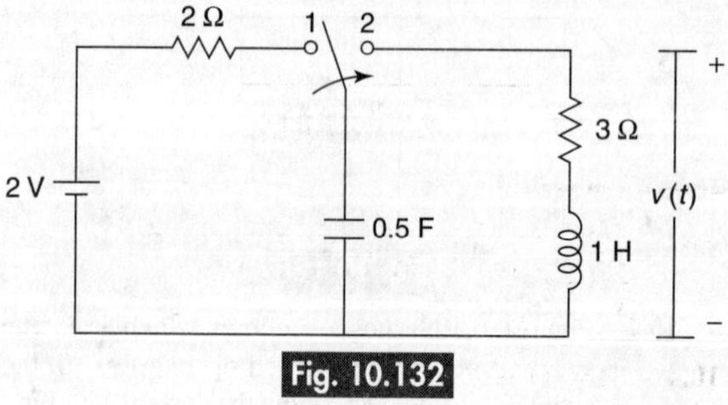


Fig. 10.132

**10.11** In the network shown in Fig. 10.133, the switch is closed at $t = 0$. Find current $i_1(t)$ for $t > 0$. ○○●

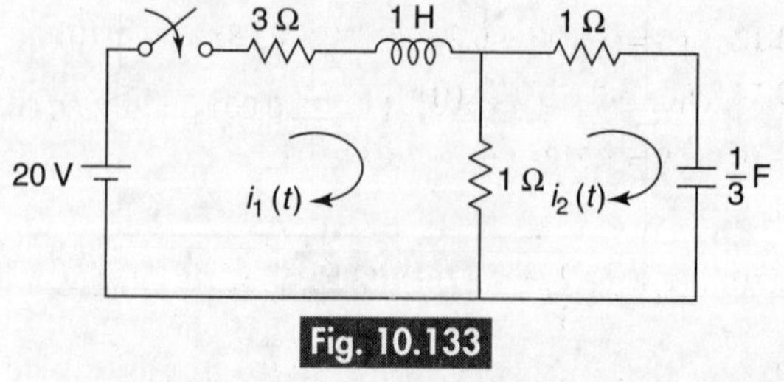


Fig. 10.133

**10.12** In the network shown in Fig. 10.134, the switch is closed at $t = 0$. Find the current through the 30 Ω resistor. ○○●

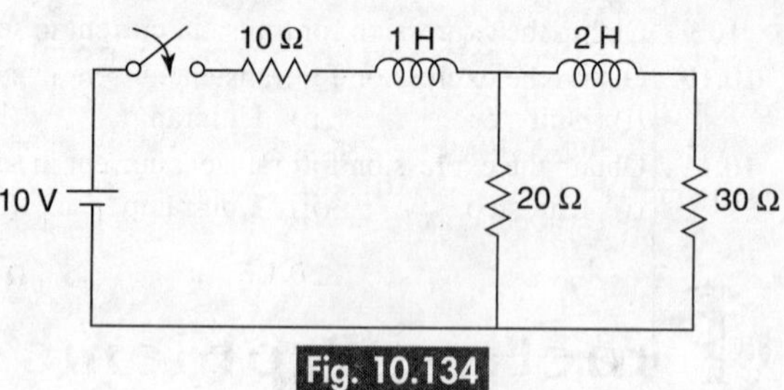


Fig. 10.134

**10.13** The network shown in Fig. 10.135 is in steady state with $s_1$ closed and $s_2$ open. At $t = 0$, $s_1$ is opened and $s_2$ is closed. Find the current through the capacitor. ○○●

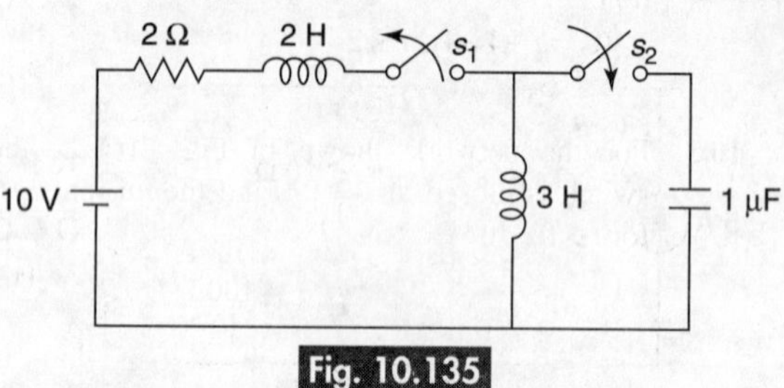


Fig. 10.135

**10.14** In the network shown in Fig. 10.136, find currents $i_1(t)$ and $i_2(t)$ for $t > 0$. ○○●

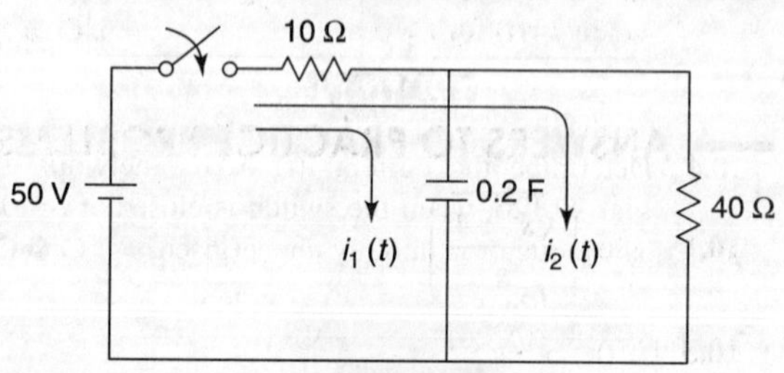


Fig. 10.136

**10.15** For the network shown in Fig. 10.137, find currents $i_1(t)$ and $i_2(t)$ for $t > 0$. ○○●

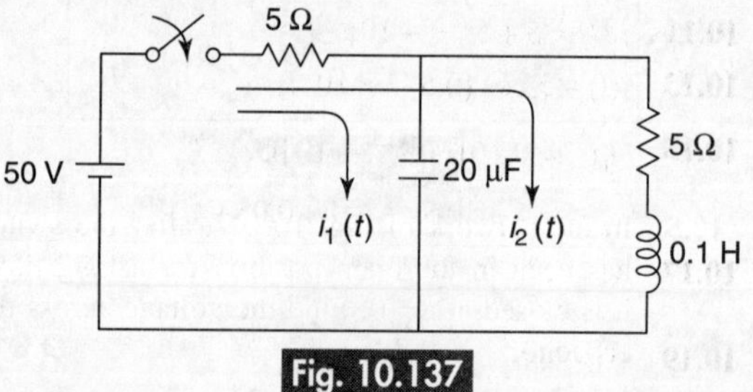


Fig. 10.137

**10.16** In the network shown in Fig. 10.138, the switch is opened at $t = 0$, the steady state having been established previously. Find $i(t)$ for $t > 0$. ○○●

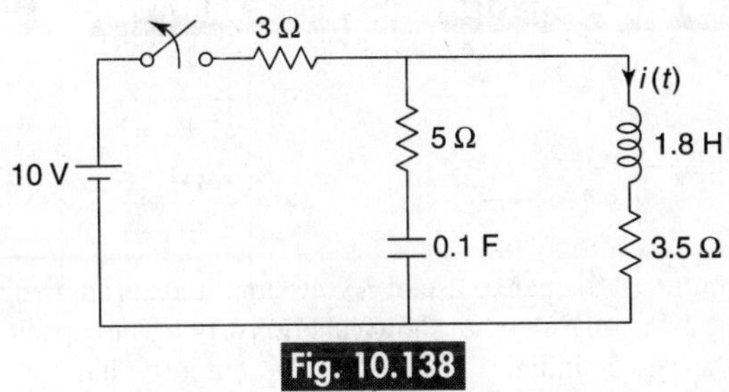

Fig. 10.138

**10.17** Find the current $i(t)$ in the network of Fig. 10.139, if the switch is closed at $t = 0$. Assume initial conditions to be zero. ○○●

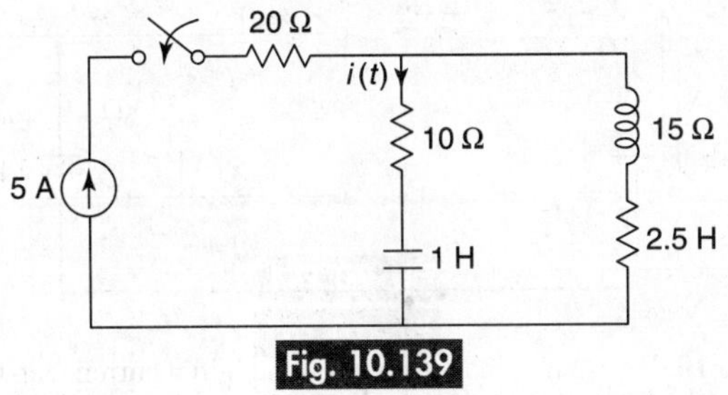

Fig. 10.139

**10.18** In the network shown in Fig. 10.140, find the voltage $v(t)$ for $t > 0$. ○●○

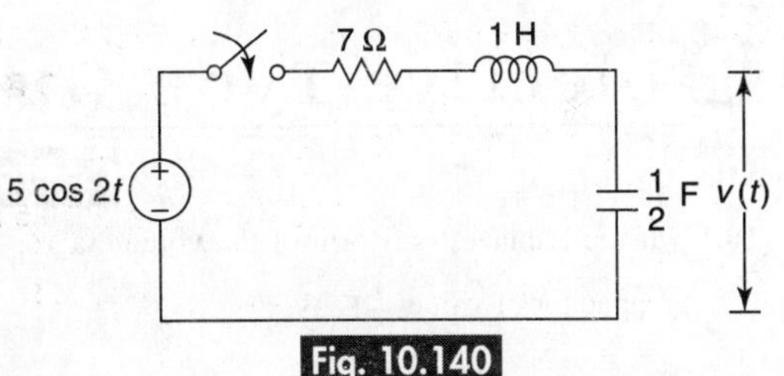

Fig. 10.140

**10.19** For the network shown in Fig. 10.141, determine $v(t)$ when the input is ○●○

(i) an impulse function

(ii) $i(t) = 4e^{-t}\, u(t)$

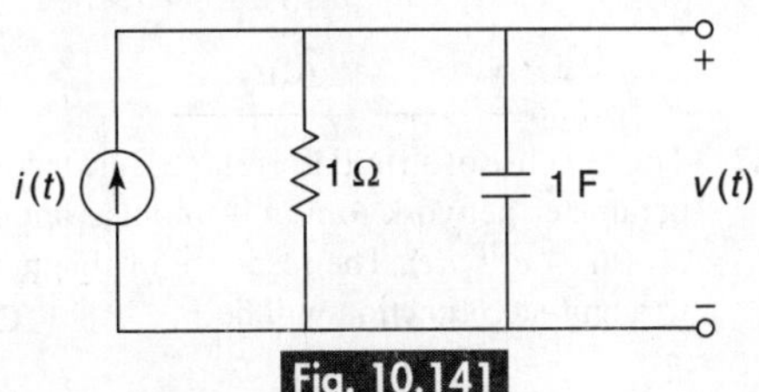

Fig. 10.141

**10.20** For a unit-ramp input shown in Fig. 10.142, find the response $v_c(t)$ for $t > 0$. ○●○

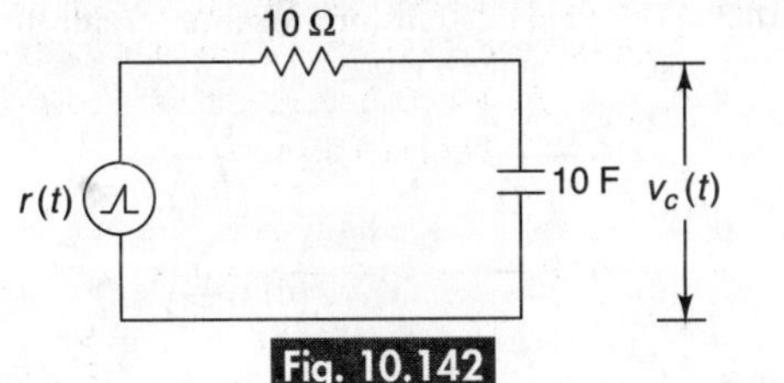

Fig. 10.142

## ANSWERS TO PRACTICE PROBLEMS

**10.1** $s \log\left(\dfrac{\sqrt{s^2+4}}{s}\right)$

**10.2** $\dfrac{1}{s}(1-e^{-2s})$

**10.3** $i_1(t) = 3 - e^{-25t}$

**10.4** $i(t) = 4(1 - e^{-6t})$

**10.5** $v(t) = 1 + 4\,e^{-10t}$

**10.6** $v(t) = 7.5 + 12.5\,e^{-(4/15)t}$

**10.7** $i(t) = 0.00857 + 0.01143\,e^{-8.75 \times 10^6 t}$, 0.013 A

**10.8** $i(t) = 0.125\,e^{-0.308t} + 3.875\,e^{-0.052t}$

**10.9** $v(t) = 10 - 10e^{-t} + 5e^{-2t}$

**10.10** $v(t) = 4e^{-t} - 2\,e^{-2t}$

**10.11** $i_1(t) = 5 + 5e^{-2t} - 10e^{-3t}$

**10.12** $i(t) = 0.1818 - 0.265\,e^{-13.14t} + 0.083\,e^{-41.86t}$

**10.13** $i(t) = 5\cos(0.577 \times 10^3\, t)$

**10.14** $i_1(t) = 5\,e^{-0.625t}$, $i_2(t) = 1 - e^{-0.625t}$

**10.15** $i_1(t) = 0.101e^{-100.5t} + 10.05e^{-9949.5t}$

$i_2(t) = 5 - 5.05e^{-100.5t} + 0.05e^{-9949.5t}$

**10.16** $i(t) = 1.5124e^{-2.22t} + 3.049e^{-2.5t}$

**10.17** $i(t) = 3 + 0.57e^{-7.14t}$

**10.18** $v(t) = -\dfrac{6}{5}e^{-t} + \dfrac{9}{10}e^{-6t} + \dfrac{3}{10}\cos 2t + \dfrac{21}{10}\sin 2t$

**10.19** (i) $e^{-t}\, u(t)$, (ii) $4t\, e^{-t}\, u(t)$

**10.20** $v_c(t) = -100\, u(t) + 100e^{-0.01t}\, u(t) + tu(t)$

# Objective-Type Questions

## From GATE and Other Competitive Examinations

**10.1** If the Laplace transform of the voltage across a capacitor of value $\frac{1}{2}$F is

$$V_c(s) = \frac{1}{s^2+1}$$

the value of the current through the capacitor at $t = 0^+$ is ○●○

(a) 0 (b) 2 A

(c) $\frac{1}{2}$ A (d) 1 A

**10.2** The response of an initially relaxed linear constant parameter network to a unit impulse applied at $t = 0$ is $4\,e^{-2t}\,u(t)$. The response of this network to a unit-step function will be ○○●

(a) $2[1 - e^{-2t}]\,u(t)$

(b) $4[e^{-t} - e^{-2t}]\,u(t)$

(c) $\sin 2t$

(d) $(1 - 4\,e^{-4t})\,u(t)$

**10.3** The Laplace transform of a unit-ramp function starting at $t = a$ is ○●○

(a) $\frac{1}{(s+a)^2}$ (b) $\frac{e^{-as}}{(s+a)^2}$

(c) $\frac{e^{-as}}{s^2}$ (d) $\frac{a}{s^2}$

**10.4** The Laplace transform of $e^{at}\cos \alpha t$ is equal to ●○○

(a) $\frac{s-\alpha}{(s-\alpha)^2+\alpha^2}$ (b) $\frac{s+\alpha}{(s-\alpha)^2+\alpha^2}$

(c) $\frac{1}{(s-\alpha)^2}$ (d) none of the above

**10.5** The circuit shown in Fig. 10.143 has initial current $i(0^-) = 1$ A through the inductor and an initial voltage $v_c(0^-) = -1$ V across the capacitor. For input $v(t) = u(t)$, the Laplace transform of the current $i(t)$ for $t \geq 0$ is ○●○

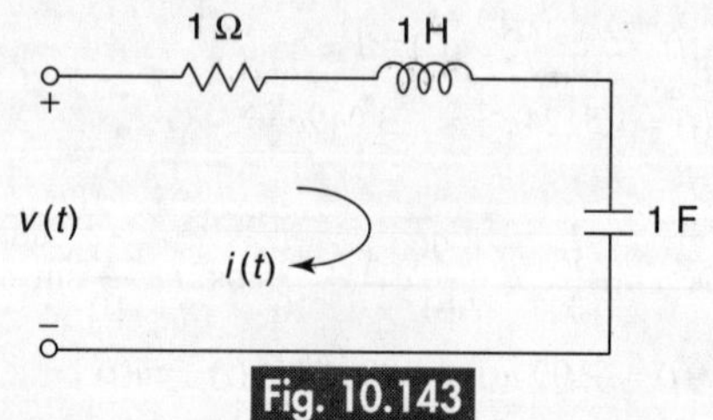


Fig. 10.143

(a) $\frac{s}{s^2+s+1}$ (b) $\frac{s+2}{s^2+s+1}$

(c) $\frac{s-2}{s^2+s+1}$ (d) $\frac{s-2}{s^2+s+1}$

**10.6** A square pulse of 3 volts amplitude is applied to an $RC$ circuit shown in Fig. 10.144. The capacitor is initially uncharged. The output voltage $v_0$ at time $t = 2$ seconds is ○○●

(a) 3 V (b) −3 V

(c) 4 V (d) −4 V

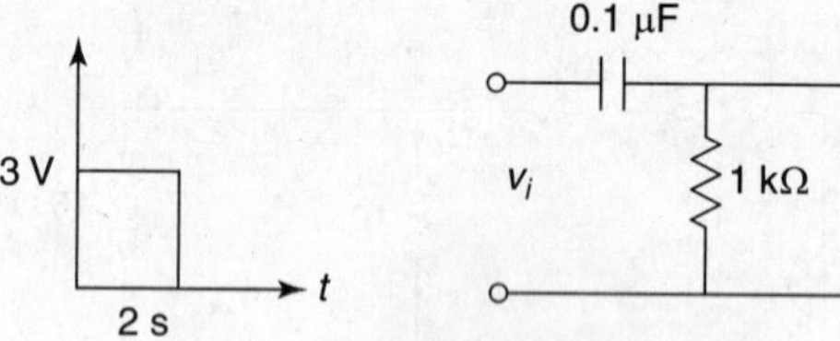


Fig. 10.144

**10.7** A 2 mH inductor with some initial current can be represented, as shown in Fig. 10.145. The value of the initial current is ○●○

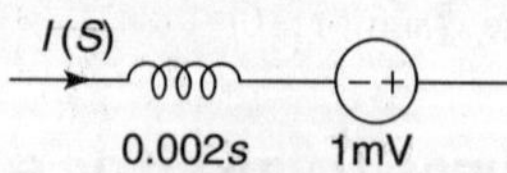


Fig. 10.145

(a) 0.5 A (b) 2 A

(c) 1 A (d) 0

**10.8** A current impulse $5\,\delta(t)$ is forced through a capacitor $C$. The voltage $v_c(t)$ across the capacitor is given by ○●○

(a) $5\,t$ (b) $5\,u(t) - C$

(c) $\frac{5}{C}t$ (d) $\frac{5u(t)}{C}$

**10.9** In Fig. 10.146, $C_1$ and $C_2$ are ideal capacitors. $C_1$ has been charged to 12 V before the ideal switch $S$ is closed at $t = 0$. The current $i(t)$ for all $t$ is ○●○

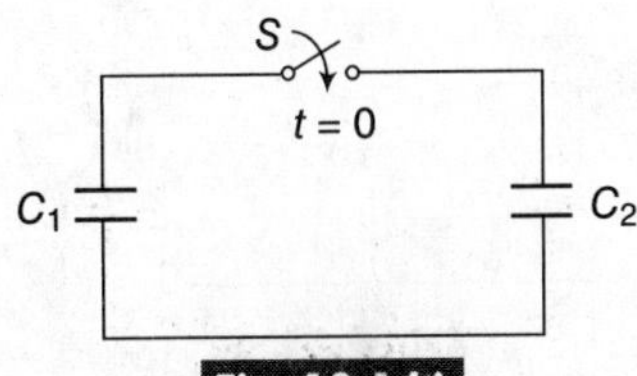

Fig. 10.146

(a) zero
(b) a step function
(c) an exponentially decaying function
(d) an impulse function

**10.10** The series *RLC* circuit with zero conditions is excited by a unit impulse functions $\delta(t)$. For $t > 0$, the output voltage $v_c(t)$ is ○●○

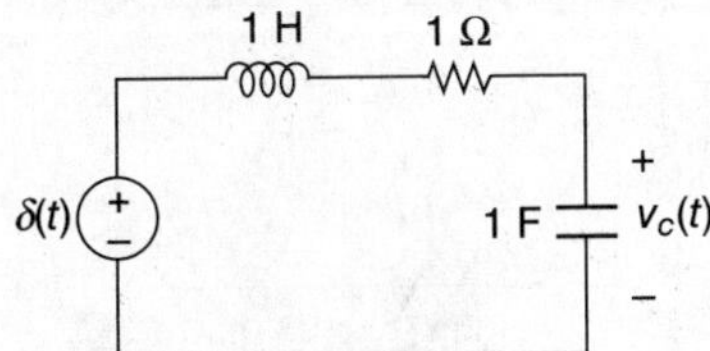

Fig. 10.147

(a) $\frac{2}{\sqrt{3}}\left(e^{-\frac{1}{2}t} - e^{-\frac{\sqrt{3}}{2}t}\right)$

(b) $\frac{2}{\sqrt{3}} te^{-\frac{1}{2}t}$

(c) $\frac{2}{\sqrt{3}} e^{-\frac{1}{2}t} \cos\left(\frac{\sqrt{3}}{2}t\right)$

(d) $\frac{2}{\sqrt{3}} e^{-\frac{1}{2}t} \sin\left(\frac{\sqrt{3}}{2}t\right)$

**10.11** If the Laplace transform of the voltage across a capacitor of $\frac{1}{2}$F is

$$V_c(s) = \frac{s+1}{s^3 + s^2 + s + 1}$$

The value of the current through the capacitor at $t = 0^+$ is ○○●

(a) 0 A (b) $\frac{1}{2}$ A
(c) 2 A (d) 1 A

**10.12** A ramp voltage $v(t) = 100t$ volts is applied to an *RC* differentiating circuit with $R = 5$ kΩ and $C = 4$ μF. The maximum output voltage is ○○●

(a) 0.2 V (b) 2 V
(c) 10 V (d) 5 V

**10.13** A series *RL* circuit is initially relaxed. A step voltage is applied to the circuit. If $\tau$ is the time constant of the circuit, the voltage across *R* and *L* will be the same at time *t* equal to ○○●

(a) $\tau \log 2$ (b) $\tau \log\left(\frac{1}{2}\right)$

(c) $\frac{1}{\tau \log 2}$ (d) $\frac{1}{\tau \log\left(\frac{1}{2}\right)}$

**10.14** If a unit step voltage is applied at $t = 0$ to a series *RL* circuit with zero initial conditions, ○○●

(a) it is possible for the current to be oscillatory
(b) the voltage across the resistor at $t = 0^+$ is zero
(c) the energy stored in the inductor in the steady state is zero
(d) the resistor current eventually falls to zero

**10.15** A series *RL* circuit is to be connected to an ac source $v(t) = V_m \sin(\omega t + \phi)$ volt. Which one of the following is correct? The transient current will be absent if the source is connected at a time $t_0$ such that ○○●

(a) $\omega t_0 = 0$

(b) $\omega t_0 = \frac{\pi}{2}$

(c) $\omega t_0 = \tan^{-1}\left(\frac{\omega L}{R}\right)$

(d) $\omega t_0$ has any arbitrary value

**10.16** The voltage applied to an *RL* circuit at $t = 0$ when switch is closed is 100 cos (100*t* + 30°). The circuit resistance is 80 Ω and inductance is 0.6H (in which initial current is zero). What is the maximum amplitude of current flowing through the circuit? ○○●

(a) 1 A (b) 2 A
(c) 5 A (d) 10 A

**10.17** An initially relaxed *RC* series network with $R = 2$ MΩ and $C = 1$ μF is switched on to a 10 V step input. The voltage across the capacitor after 2 seconds will be ○●○

(a) zero (b) 3.68 V
(c) 6.32 V (d) 10 V

**10.18** The steady-state current in the *RC* series circuit, on the application of step voltage of magnitude *E* will be ○●○

(a) zero (b) $\frac{E}{R}$

(c) $\frac{E}{R}e^{-\frac{1}{RC}t}$ (d) $\frac{E}{RC}e^{-t}$

**10.19** For the following circuit shown in Fig. 10.148, a source of $v_1(t) = e^{-2t}$ is applied. The resulting response $v_2(t)$ is given by ○○●

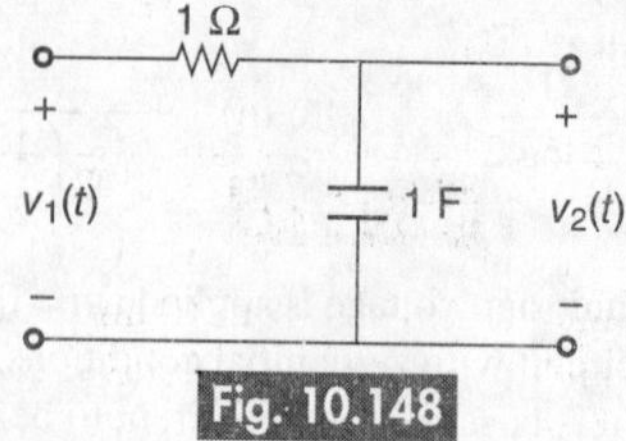


Fig. 10.148

(a) $e^{-2t} + e^{-t}$ (b) $e^{-t}$

(c) $e^{-t} - e^{-2t}$ (d) $\frac{e^{-2t}}{2}$

**10.20** In the circuit shown in Fig. 10.149, the response current *i*(*t*) is ○●○

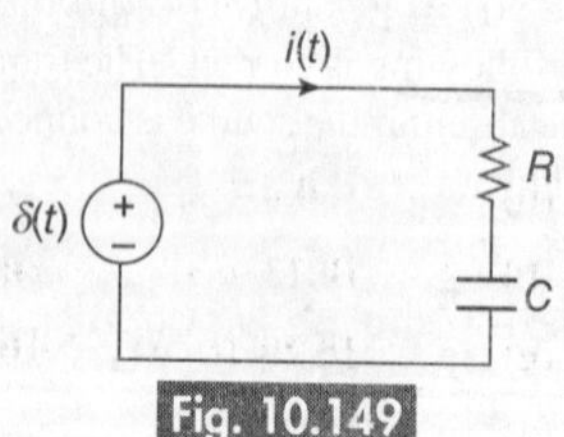


Fig. 10.149

(a) $\frac{1}{R}e^{-\frac{1}{RC}t}$

(b) $\frac{1}{R}\delta(t)$

(c) $\frac{1}{R}\left[\delta(t) - \frac{1}{RC}e^{-\frac{1}{RC}t}\right]$

(d) $\frac{1}{R}\left[\delta(t) - e^{-\frac{1}{RC}t}\right]$

**10.21** In the circuit shown in Fig. 10.150, the initial voltage across the capacitor is 2 V and *I* is a unit-step current source. The voltage across the capacitor for $t > 0$ is ○●○

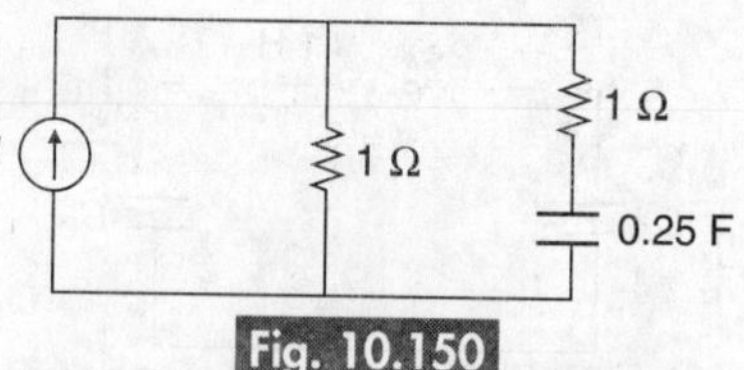


Fig. 10.150

(a) $(2 - e^{-2t})\, u(t)$ (b) $(2 + e^{2t})\, u(t)$

(c) $(1 - e^{-2t})\, u(t)$ (d) $(1 + e^{-2t})\, u(t)$

**10.22** For the circuit shown in Fig. 10.151, the time constant $RC = 1$ ms. The input voltage is $v_i(t) = \sqrt{2}\sin 10^3 t$. The output voltage $v_o(t)$ is equal to ○●○

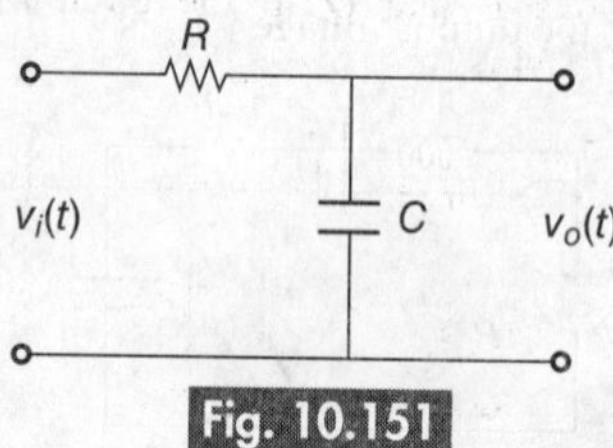


Fig. 10.151

(a) $\sin(10^3 t - 45°)$ (b) $\sin(10^3 t + 45°)$

(c) $\sin(10^3 t - 53°)$ (d) $\sin(10^3 t + 53°)$

**10.23** In the circuit shown in Fig. 10.152, the values of $i(0^+)$ and $i(\infty)$ will be respectively ○●○

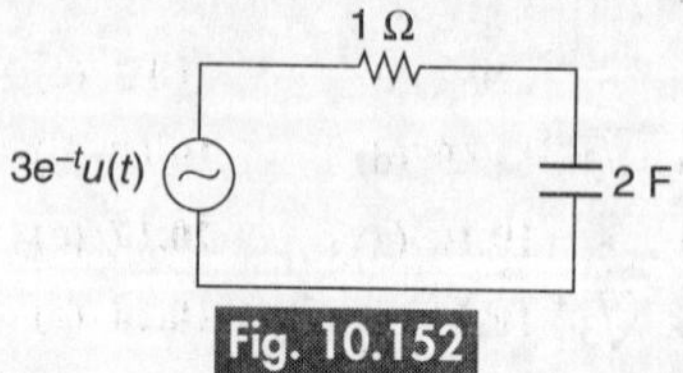


Fig. 10.152

(a) zero and 1.5 A (b) 1.5 A and 3 A

(c) 3 A and zero (d) 3 A and 1.5 A

**10.24** A series *RLC* circuit is switched on to a step voltage *V* at $t = 0$. What are the initial and final values of the current in the circuit respectively? ○●○

(a) $\frac{V}{R}, \frac{V}{R}$ (b) zero, infinity

(c) zero, zero (d) zero, $\frac{V}{R}$

**10.25** A step voltage is applied to the circuit shown in Fig. 10.153, what is the transient current response of the circuit? ●○○

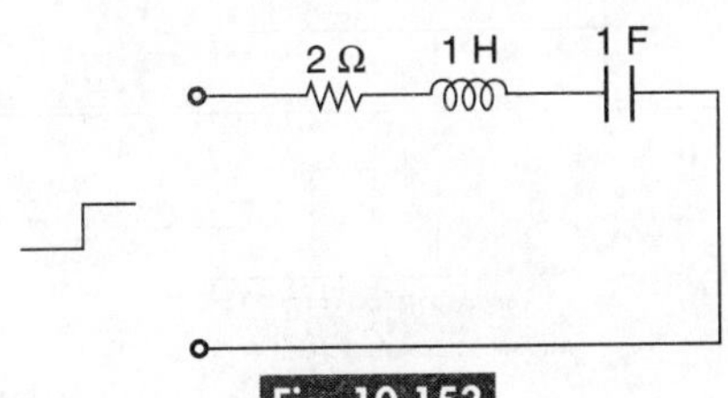


Fig. 10.153

(a) Undamped sinusoidal
(b) Underdamped
(c) Overdamped
(d) Critically damped

**10.26** The Thevenin equivalent impedance $Z_{Th}$ between the nodes $P$ and $Q$ in the circuit shown in Fig. 10.154 is ○○●

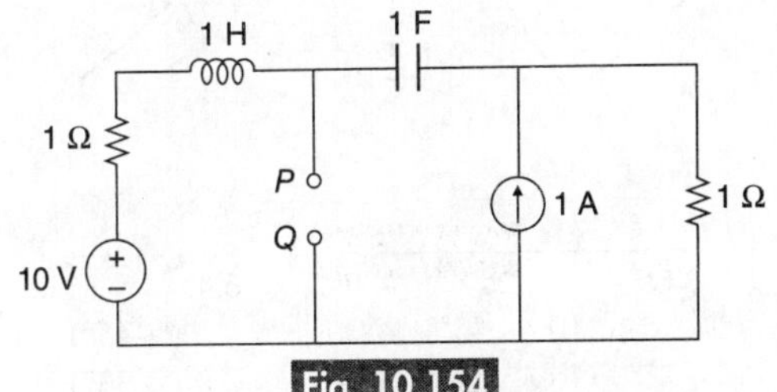


Fig. 10.154

(a) 1
(b) $1+s+\frac{1}{s}$
(c) $2+s+\frac{1}{s}$
(d) $\frac{s^2+s+1}{s^2+2s+1}$

**10.27** In the circuit shown in Fig. 10.155, the value of capacitor $C$ (in mF) needed to have critically damped response $i(t)$ is ●○○

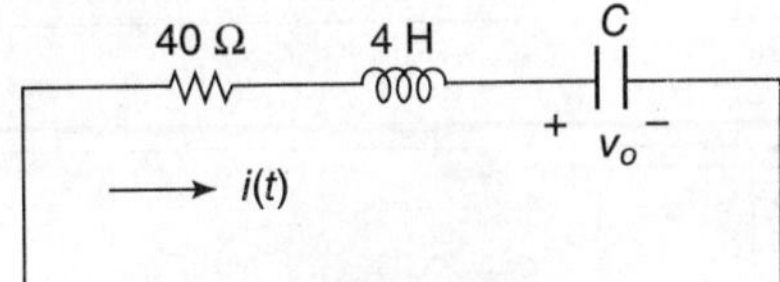


Fig. 10.155

(a) 1 mF
(b) 10 mF
(c) 5 mF
(d) 2 mF

## ANSWERS TO OBJECTIVE-TYPE QUESTIONS

| | | | | | | |
|---|---|---|---|---|---|---|
| **10.1** (c) | **10.2** (a) | **10.3** (c) | **10.4** (a) | **10.5** (b) | **10.6** (b) | **10.7** (a) |
| **10.8** (d) | **10.9** (d) | **10.10** (d) | **10.11** (b) | **10.12** (b) | **10.13** (a) | **10.14** (b) |
| **10.15** (c) | **10.16** (a) | **10.17** (c) | **10.18** (a) | **10.19** (c) | **10.20** (c) | **10.21** (d) |
| **10.22** (a) | **10.23** (c) | **10.24** (c) | **10.25** (d) | **10.26** (a) | **10.27** (b) | |

# LTspice Section

### EXAMPLE 10.1 ○○●

*At t = 0, unit pulse voltage is applied to a series RL circuit, as shown in Fig. 10.156. Sketch the current i(t).*

Fig. 10.156

## Solution

```
*Plotting of i(t)

V1 1 0 PULSE(0 1 0 0.0001 0.0001 1 2)
R1 1 2 1
L1 2 0 1
.TRAN 0 6
.PROBE
.END
```

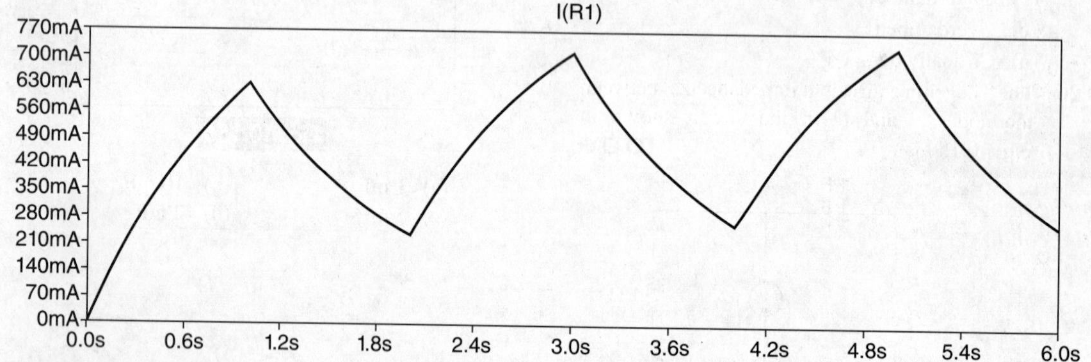


### EXAMPLE 10.2

*A voltage pulse is applied to a series RC circuit at t = 0. Sketch the voltage $v_C(t)$.*

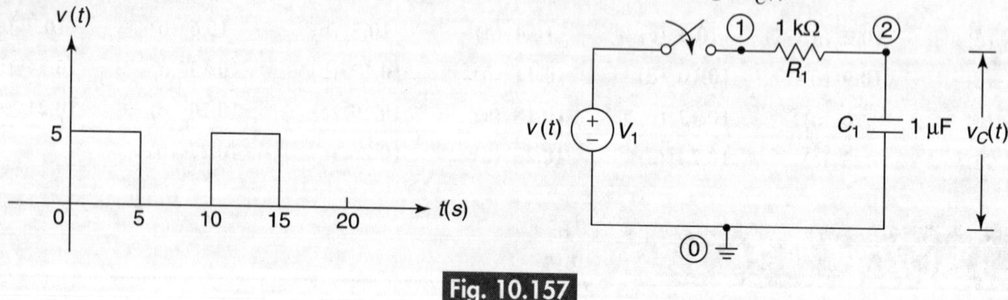


Fig. 10.157

## Solution

```
*Plotting of vc(t)

V1 1 0 PULSE(0 5 0 1ns 1ns 5ms 10ms)
R1 1 2 1K
C1 2 0 1U
.TRAN 0 20M
.PROBE
.END
```

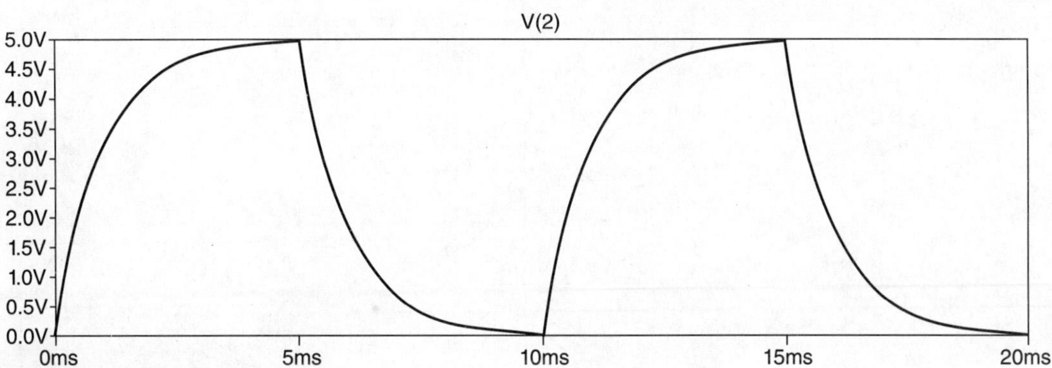


## EXAMPLE 10.3

*For the network shown in Fig. 10.158, sketch the current i(t) when the switch is closed at t = 0 with zero initial conditions.*

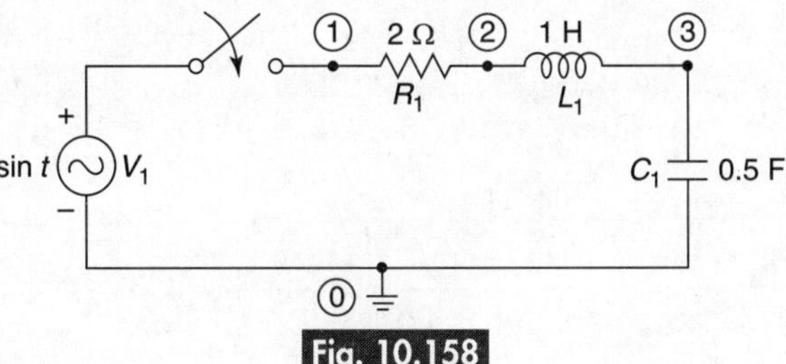


Fig. 10.158

### Solution

```
*Series RLC Circuit

V1 1 0 SINE(0 1 0.159 0 0 0)
R1 1 2 2
L1 2 3 1
C1 3 0 0.5
.TRAN 0 18.84
.PROBE
.END
```

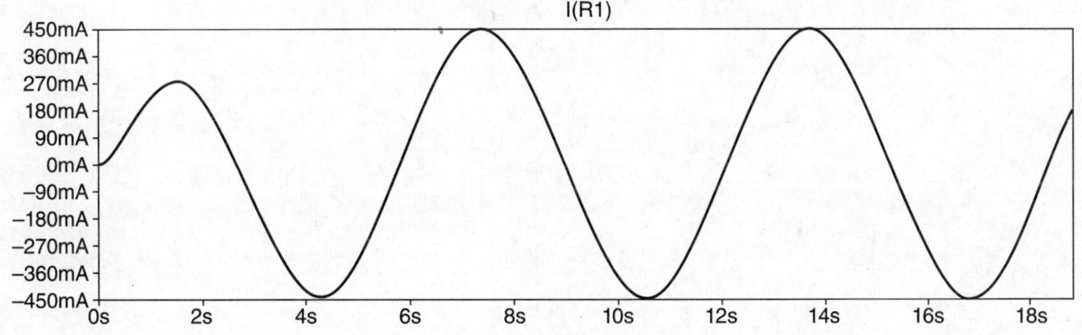

CHAPTER 11

# Network Functions

## LEARNING OBJECTIVES

**After studying this chapter, you should be able to:**

**LO 11.1** Explain the concept of complex frequency

**LO 11.2** Explain terminal pairs/ports

**LO 11.3** Discuss different forms of driving-point functions and transfer functions

**LO 11.4** Analyse ladder and non-ladder networks

**LO 11.5** Explain poles and zeros of network functions

**LO 11.6** Discuss the necessary conditions for driving-point and transfer functions

**LO 11.7** Determine the time-domain behaviour of a system from the pole-zero plot

**LO 11.8** Describe the graphical method for determination of residue

**LO 11.9** Draw the Bode plots for network functions

## INTRODUCTION

All the networks are designed to produce a particular output or response when the input or excitation is applied to it. The relation between input (excitation) and output (response) is given in terms of network function. The network function is a characteristic of the system and is not dependent on input or output. The output changes according to the input. Mathematically, a network function is defined as the ratio of Laplace transform of output (response) of the network to the Laplace transform of input (excitation), with all initial conditions as zero.

Network function is broadly classified as driving-point and transfer function.

## 11.1 CONCEPT OF COMPLEX FREQUENCY

LO 11.1

Explain the concept of complex frequency

In time-domain analysis, the general solution of a differential equation is given as

$$i(t) = k_n e^{s_n t}$$

where $s_n$ is a complex number, which is root of the characteristic equation and is expressed as

$$s_n = \sigma_n + j\omega_n$$

The complex number $s_n$ has two parts – the real part $\sigma_n$ and the imaginary part $\omega_n$. The real part $\sigma_n$ decides the amplitude variation and appears as an exponential power in the time domain as $e^{\sigma_n t}$. It is called *neper frequency* and is expressed in neper/second. The imaginarily part $\omega_n$ decides the oscillatory terms in the time domain in the form sin $\omega_n t$ or cos $\omega_n t$. It is called *radian frequency* and is expressed in radians/second.

The complex sum $s_n = \sigma_n + j\omega_n$ is called the *complex frequency*. It depends upon the two parameters which control the magnitude and rotation of the signal.

### 11.1.1 Physical Interpretation of Complex Frequency

The complex frequency appears in the exponential form $e^{s_n t}$. There are three special cases for the values of $s_n$.

➤ **Case (i)** $s_n = \sigma_n + j0$

The general solution becomes $i(t) = k_n e^{s_n t} = k_n e^{\sigma_n t}$. This exponential function increases exponential for $\sigma_n > 0$ and decreases exponentially for $\sigma_n < 0$. For $\sigma_n = 0$, the function reduces to $k_n$ and represents a constant valued function such as dc current. Figure 11.1 shows the variation of $i(t)$ with time $t$ for $\sigma > 0$, $\sigma < 0$ and $\sigma = 0$.

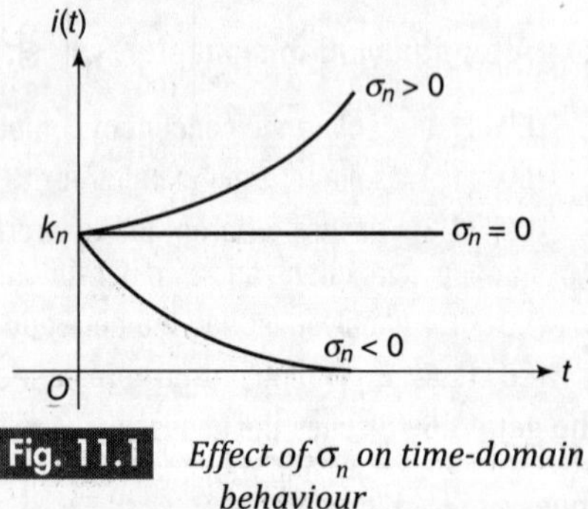


**Fig. 11.1** *Effect of $\sigma_n$ on time-domain behaviour*

➤ **Case (ii)** $s_n = 0 \pm j\omega_n$

The general solution becomes $i(t) = k_n e^{\pm j\omega_n t} = k_n(\cos\omega_n t \pm j\sin\omega_n t)$. This exponential term $e^{\pm j\omega_n t}$ can be represented in polar form as a rotating phasor of unit length.

$$e^{\pm j\omega_n t} = 1\angle \pm \omega_n t$$

The $e^{j\omega_n t}$ term represents the anticlockwise or positive rotation of the phasor while the $e^{-j\omega_n t}$ term represents the clockwise or negative rotation of phasor.

For positive or anticlockwise rotation, the real part of $e^{j\omega_n t}$ or the projection on the real axis is cos $\omega_n t$ while the imaginary part of $e^{j\omega_n t}$ or the projection on the imaginary axis is sin $\omega_n t$.

Thus, $e^{\pm j\omega_n t}$ term represents sinusoidal behaviour in time domain. Figure 11.2 shows the time-domain behaviour of $e^{\pm j\omega_n t}$ term.

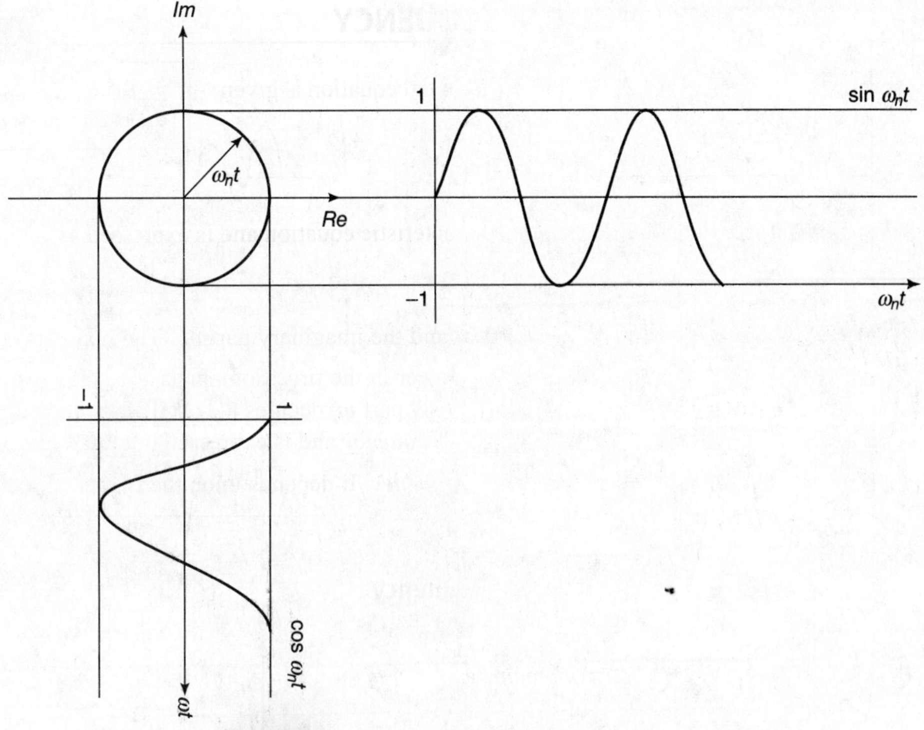


**Fig. 11.2** *Time-domain behaviour of $e^{\pm j\omega_n t}$ term*

### ➤ Case (ii) $s_n = \sigma_n + j\omega_n$

The general solution becomes $i(t) = k_n e^{s_n t} = k_n e^{(\sigma_n + j\omega_n)t} = k_n e^{\sigma_n t} e^{j\omega_n t}$

Thus, *i*(*t*) is the product of two terms, one corresponding to $e^{\sigma_n t}$ and other corresponding to $e^{j\omega_n t}$. The time behaviour of $e^{\sigma_n t}$ is purely exponential and that of $e^{j\omega_n t}$ is purely sinusoidal, which is either sin $\omega_n t$ or cos $\omega_n t$. The real and imaginary projections of the phasor are

$$Re(e^{S_n t}) = e^{\sigma_n t} \cos \omega_n t$$

$$Im(e^{S_n t}) = e^{\sigma_n t} \sin \omega_n t$$

If $\sigma_n > 0$, the term $e^{\sigma_n t} \cos \omega_n t$ or $e^{\sigma_n t} \sin \omega_n t$ produces a sinusoidal behaviour, whose amplitude increases exponentially due to the term $e^{\sigma_n t}$.

If $\sigma_n < 0$, the term $e^{\sigma_n t} \cos \omega_n t$ or $e^{\sigma_n t} \sin \omega_n t$ produces a sinusoidal behaviour, whose amplitude decreases exponentially due to the term $e^{\sigma_n t}$. These oscillations are called *damped oscillations*.

Figure 11.3 shows the various cases of time domain functions which may be produced due to general complex frequency $s_n = \sigma_n + j\omega_n$.

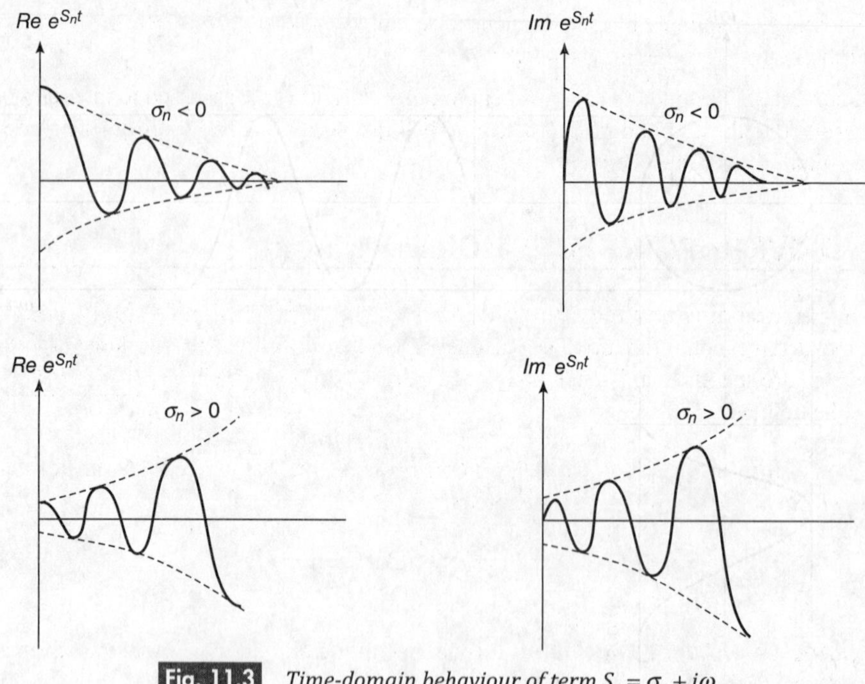


**Fig. 11.3** *Time-domain behaviour of term $S_n = \sigma_n + j\omega_n$*

It can be seen that the imaginary part of the complex frequency governs the sinusoidal oscillations and the real part of the complex frequency governs the exponential decay or rise. Thus, the roles of two types of frequencies are similar but the variations caused by them are different.

## 11.2 TERMINAL PAIRS OR PORTS

LO 11.2

Explain terminal pairs/ports

Any network may be represented schematically by a rectangular box. Terminals are needed to connect any network to any other network or for taking some measurements. Two such associated terminals are called *terminal pair* or *port*. If there is only one pair of terminals in the network, it is called a one-port network. If there are two pairs of terminals, it is called a two-port network. The port to which energy source is connected is called the *input port*. The port to which load is connected is known as the *output port*. One such network having only one pair of terminals (1 – 1′) is shown in Fig. 11.4 and is called *one-port network.* Figure 11.5 shows a two-port network with two pairs of terminals. The terminals 1 – 1′ together constitute a port. Similarly, the terminals 2 – 2′ constitute another port.

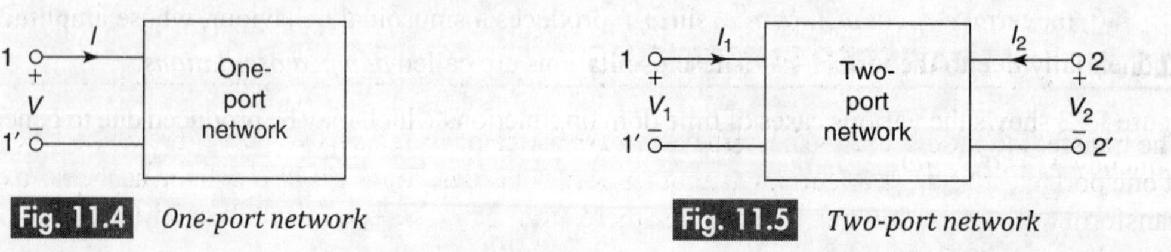


**Fig. 11.4** *One-port network*

**Fig. 11.5** *Two-port network*

Two ports containing no sources in their branches are called *passive ports* whereas two ports containing sources in their branches are called *active ports*.

A voltage and current are assigned to each of the two ports. $V_1$ and $I_1$ are assigned to the input port, whereas $V_2$ and $I_2$ are assigned to the output port. It is also assumed that currents $I_1$ and $I_2$ are entering into the network at the upper terminals 1 and 2 respectively.

## 11.3 DRIVING-POINT FUNCTIONS

LO 11.3

Discuss different forms of driving-point functions and transfer functions

If excitation and response are measured at the same ports, the network function is known as the driving-point function. For a one-port network, only one voltage and current are specified and hence, only one network function (and its reciprocal) can be defined.

**1. *Driving-point Impedance Function*** It is defined as the ratio of the voltage transform at one port to the current transform at the same port. It is denoted by $Z(s)$.

$$Z(s) = \frac{V(s)}{I(s)}$$

**2. *Driving-point Admittance Function*** It is defined as the ratio of the current transform at one port to the voltage transform at the same port. It is denoted by $Y(s)$.

$$Y(s) = \frac{I(s)}{V(s)}$$

For a two-port network, the driving-point impedance function and driving-point admittance function at port 1 are

$$Z_{11}(s) = \frac{V_1(s)}{I_1(s)}$$

$$Y_{11}(s) = \frac{I_1(s)}{V_1(s)}$$

Similarly, at port 2,

$$Z_{22}(s) = \frac{V_2(s)}{I_2(s)}$$

$$Y_{22}(s) = \frac{I_2(s)}{V_2(s)}$$

## 11.4 TRANSFER FUNCTIONS

LO 11.3

The transfer function is used to describe networks which have at least two ports. It relates a voltage or current at one port to the voltage or current at another port. These functions are also defined as the ratio of a response transform to an excitation transform. Thus, there are four possible forms of transfer functions.

**1. *Voltage Transfer Function*** It is defined as the ratio of the voltage transform at one port to the voltage transform at another port. It is denoted by $G(s)$.

$$G_{12}(s) = \frac{V_2(s)}{V_1(s)}$$

$$G_{21}(s) = \frac{V_1(s)}{V_2(s)}$$

**2. *Current Transfer Function*** It is defined as the ratio of the current transform at one port to the current transform at another port. It is denoted by $\alpha(s)$.

$$\alpha_{12}(s) = \frac{I_2(s)}{I_1(s)}$$

$$\alpha_{21}(s) = \frac{I_1(s)}{I_2(s)}$$

**3. *Transfer Impedance Function*** It is defined as the ratio of the voltage transform at one port to the current transform at another port. It is denoted by $Z(s)$.

$$Z_{12}(s) = \frac{V_2(s)}{I_1(s)}$$

$$Z_{21}(s) = \frac{V_1(s)}{I_2(s)}$$

**4. *Transfer Admittance Function*** It is defined as the ratio of the current transform at one port to the voltage transform at another port. It denoted by $Y(s)$.

$$Y_{12}(s) = \frac{I_2(s)}{V_1(s)}$$

$$Y_{21}(s) = \frac{I_1(s)}{V_2(s)}$$

**EXAMPLE 11.1** ●○○

*Determine the driving-point impedance function of a one-port network shown in Fig. 11.6.*

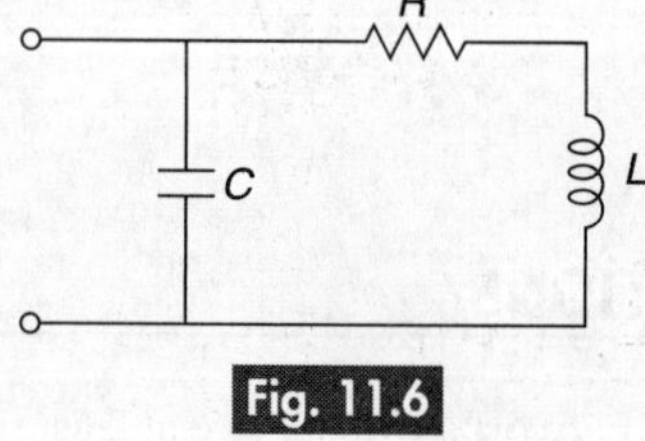


Fig. 11.6

**Note** Difficulty Level ●○○— Easy; ○●○— Medium; ○○●— Difficult

**Solution** The transformed network is shown in Fig. 11.7.

$$Z(s)=\frac{\frac{1}{Cs}(R+Ls)}{\frac{1}{Cs}+(R+Ls)}=\frac{R+Ls}{LCs^2+RCs+1}=\frac{1}{C}\frac{s+\frac{R}{L}}{s^2+\frac{R}{L}s+\frac{1}{LC}}$$

Fig. 11.7

## EXAMPLE 11.2

*Determine the driving-point impedance of the network shown in Fig. 11.8.*

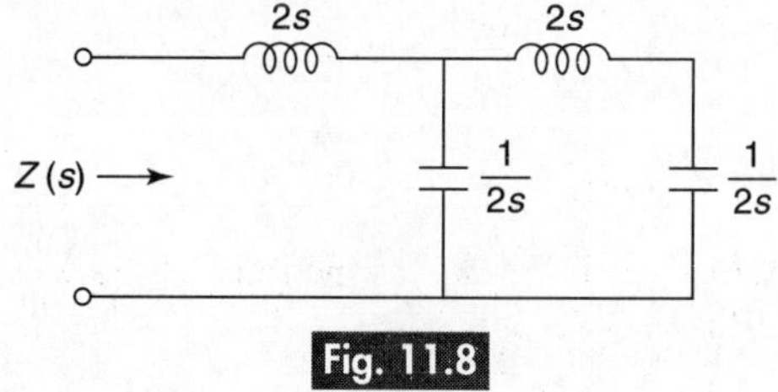


Fig. 11.8

**Solution**

$$Z(s)=2s+\frac{\frac{1}{2s}\left(2s+\frac{1}{2s}\right)}{\frac{1}{2s}+2s+\frac{1}{2s}}=2s+\frac{\frac{1}{2s}\left(2s+\frac{1}{2s}\right)}{\frac{2+4s^2}{2s}}=2s+\frac{2s+\frac{1}{2s}}{2+4s^2}=\frac{4s+8s^3+2s+\frac{1}{2s}}{2+4s^2}=\frac{16s^4+12s^2+1}{8s^3+4s}$$

## EXAMPLE 11.3

*Determine the driving-point impedance of the network shown in Fig. 11.9.*

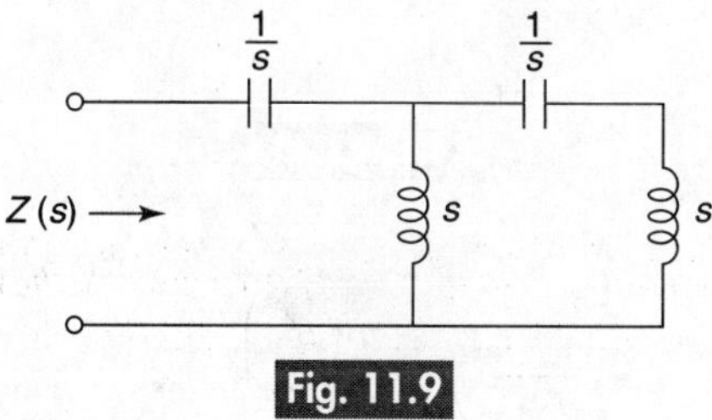


Fig. 11.9

**Solution**

$$Z(s)=\frac{1}{s}+\frac{s\left(\frac{1}{s}+s\right)}{s+\frac{1}{s}+s}=\frac{1}{s}+\frac{(1+s^2)s}{2s^2+1}=\frac{1}{s}+\frac{s+s^3}{2s^2+1}=\frac{s^4+3s^2+1}{2s^3+s}$$

## EXAMPLE 11.4

*Find the driving-point admittance function of the network shown in Fig. 11.10.*

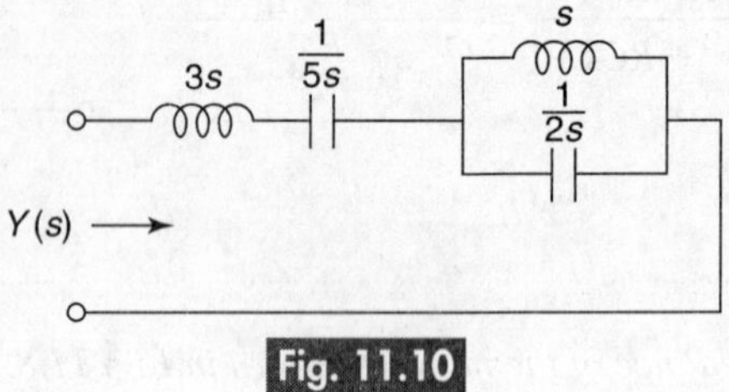


Fig. 11.10

**Solution**

$$Z(s) = 3s + \frac{1}{5s} + \frac{s\left(\frac{1}{2s}\right)}{s + \frac{1}{2s}} = 3s + \frac{1}{5s} + \frac{s}{2s^2+1} = \frac{30s^4 + 15s^2 + 2s^2 + 1 + 5s^2}{5s\,(2s^2+1)} = \frac{30s^4 + 22s^2 + 1}{5s\,(2s^2+1)}$$

$$Y(s) = \frac{1}{Z(s)} = \frac{5s\,(2s^2+1)}{30s^4 + 22s^2 + 1}$$

## EXAMPLE 11.5

*Find the transfer impedance function $Z_{12}(s)$ for the network shown in Fig. 11.11.*

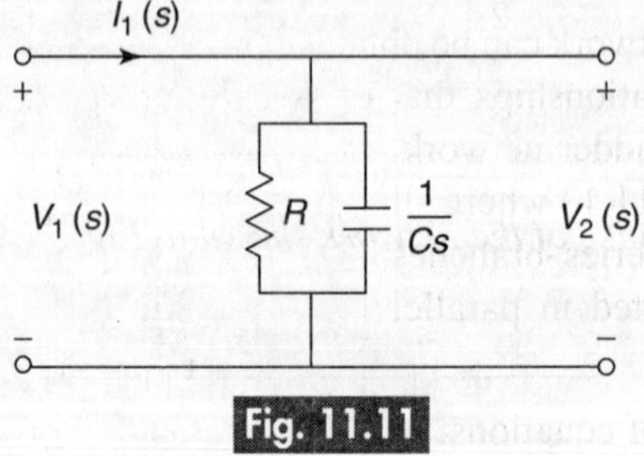


Fig. 11.11

**Solution**

$$V_2(s) = I_1(s)\frac{R\left(\frac{1}{Cs}\right)}{R + \frac{1}{Cs}}$$

$$\frac{V_2(s)}{I_1(s)} = \frac{R}{RCs+1}$$

$$Z_{12}(s) = \frac{V_2(s)}{I_1(s)} = \frac{1}{C\left(s + \frac{1}{RC}\right)}$$

**EXAMPLE 11.6**

*Find voltage transfer function of the two-port network shown in Fig. 11.12.*

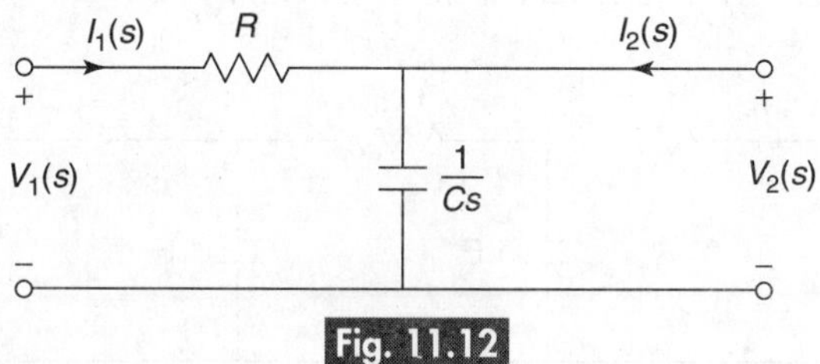


Fig. 11.12

**Solution** By voltage division rule,

$$V_2(s) = V_1(s)\frac{\frac{1}{Cs}}{R+\frac{1}{Cs}} = V_1(s)\frac{1}{RCs+1} = V_1(s)\frac{\frac{1}{RC}}{s+\frac{1}{RC}}$$

Voltage transfer function

$$\frac{V_2(s)}{V_1(s)} = \frac{\frac{1}{RC}}{s+\frac{1}{RC}}$$

## 11.5 ANALYSIS OF LADDER NETWORKS

LO 11.4

Analyse ladder and non-ladder networks

The network functions of a ladder network can be obtained by a simple method. This method depends upon the relationships that exist between the branch currents and node voltages of the ladder network. Consider the network shown in Fig. 11.13 where all the impedances are connected in series branches and all the admittances are connected in parallel branches.

Analysis is done by writing the set of equations. In writing these equations, we begin at Port 2 of the ladder and work towards Port 1.

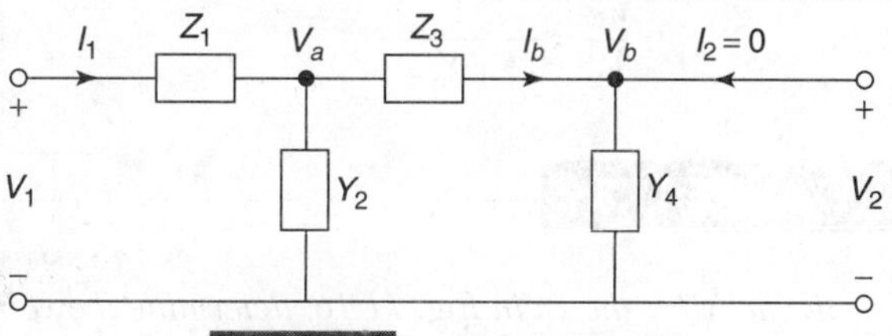


Fig. 11.13 *Ladder network*

$$V_b = V_2$$
$$I_b = Y_4 V_2$$
$$V_a = Z_3 I_b + V_2 = (Z_3 Y_4 + 1) V_2$$
$$I_1 = Y_2 V_a + I_b = [Y_2 (Z_3 Y_4 + 1) + Y_4] V_2$$
$$V_1 = Z_1 I_1 + V_a = [Z_1 \{Y_2 (Z_3 Y_4 + 1) + Y_4\} + (Z_3 Y_4 + 1)] V_2$$

Thus, each succeeding equation takes into account one new impedance or admittance. Except the first two equations, each subsequent equation is obtained by multiplying the equation just preceding it by immittance (either impedance or admittance) that is next down the line and then adding to this product the equation twice preceding it. After writing these equations, we can obtain any network function.

## EXAMPLE 11.7

*For the network shown in Fig. 11.14, determine transfer function* $\dfrac{V_2}{V_1}$.

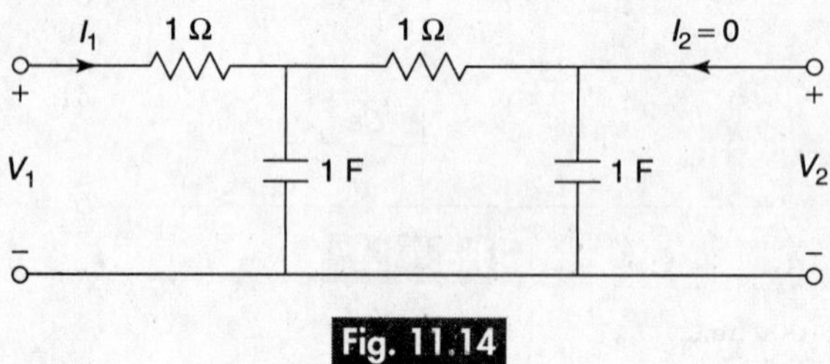


Fig. 11.14

**Solution** The transformed network is shown in Fig. 11.15.

$$V_b = V_2$$

$$I_b = \frac{V_2}{\frac{1}{s}} = sV_2$$

$$V_a = 1I_b + V_2$$

$$= sV_2 + V_2 = (s+1)V_2$$

Fig. 11.15

$$I_1 = \frac{V_a}{\frac{1}{s}} + I_b = sV_a + I_b = s(s+1)V_2 + sV_2 = (s^2 + 2s)V_2$$

$$V_1 = 1I_1 + V_a = (s^2 + 2s)V_2 + (s+1)V_2 = (s^2 + 3s + 1)V_2$$

Hence, $$\frac{V_2}{V_1} = \frac{1}{s^2 + 3s + 1}$$

## EXAMPLE 11.8

*For the network shown in Fig. 11.16, determine the voltage transfer function* $\dfrac{V_2}{V_1}$.

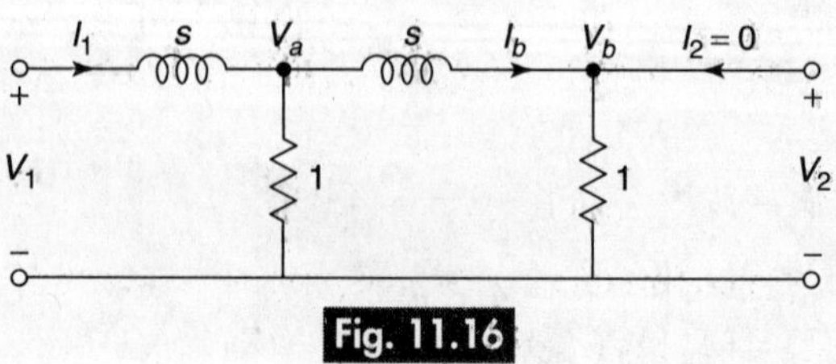


Fig. 11.16

**Solution**

$$V_b = V_2$$

$$I_b = \frac{V_2}{1} = V_2$$

$$V_a = sI_b + V_2 = sV_2 + V_2 = (s+1)V_2$$

$$I_1 = \frac{V_a}{1} + I_b = (s+1)V_2 + V_2 = (s+2)V_2$$

$$V_1 = sI_1 + V_a = s(s+2)V_2 + (s+1)V_2 = (s^2+3s+1)V_2$$

Hence,
$$\frac{V_2}{V_1} = \frac{1}{s^2+3s+1}$$

## EXAMPLE 11.9

*Find the network functions* $\frac{V_1}{I_1}, \frac{V_2}{V_1}$ *and* $\frac{V_2}{I_1}$ *for the network shown in Fig. 11.17.*

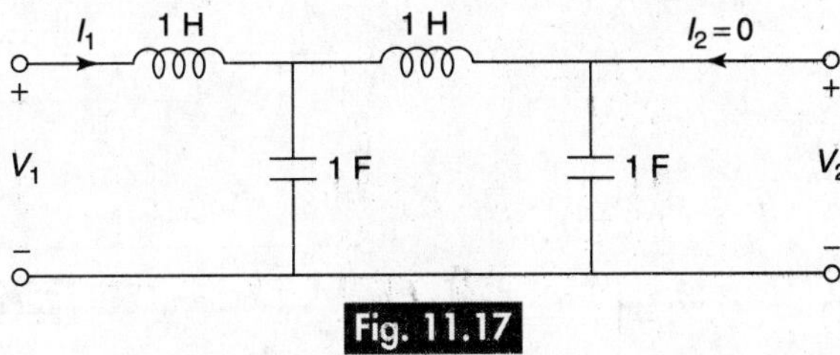


Fig. 11.17

**Solution** The transformed network is shown in Fig. 11.18.

$$V_b = V_2$$

$$I_b = \frac{V_2}{\frac{1}{s}} = sV_2$$

$$V_a = sI_b + V_2 = s(sV_2) + V_2 = (s^2+1)V_2$$

Fig. 11.18

$$I_1 = \frac{V_a}{\frac{1}{s}} + I_b = sV_a + I_b = s(s^2+1)V_2 + sV_2 = (s^3+2s)V_2$$

$$V_1 = sI_1 + V_a = s(s^3+2s)V_2 + (s^2+1)V_2 = (s^4+2s^2+s^2+1)V_2 = (s^4+3s^2+1)V_2$$

Hence,
$$\frac{V_1}{I_1} = \frac{s^4+3s^2+1}{s^3+2s}$$

$$\frac{V_2}{V_1} = \frac{1}{s^4+3s^2+1}$$

$$\frac{V_2}{I_1} = \frac{1}{s^3+2s}$$

## EXAMPLE 11.10

*Find the network functions* $\dfrac{V_1}{I_1}, \dfrac{V_2}{V_1}$, *and* $\dfrac{V_2}{I_1}$ *for the network in Fig. 11.19.*

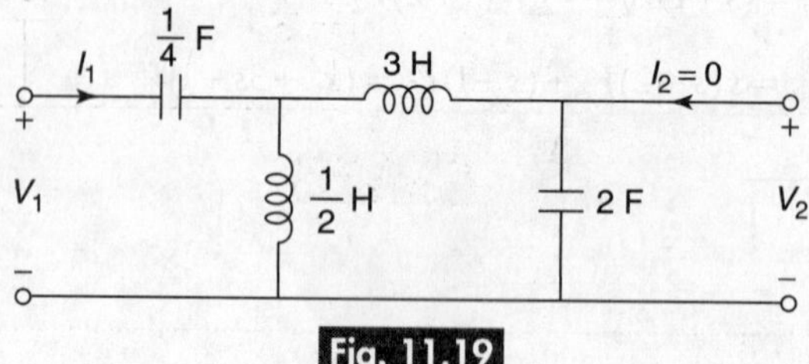


Fig. 11.19

**Solution** The transformed network is shown in Fig. 11.20.

$$V_b = V_2$$

$$I_b = \frac{V_2}{\frac{1}{2s}} = 2sV_2$$

$$V_a = 3sI_b + V_2 = 3s(2sV_2) + V_2 = (6s^2+1)V_2$$

$$I_1 = \frac{V_a}{\frac{s}{2}} + I_b = \frac{2}{s}(6s^2+1)V_2 + 2sV_2 = \left(\frac{14s^2+2}{s}\right)V_2$$

Fig. 11.20

$$V_1 = \frac{4}{s}I_1 + V_a = \frac{4}{s}\left(\frac{14s^2+2}{s}\right)V_2 + (6s^2+1)V_2 = \left(\frac{6s^4+57s^2+8}{s^2}\right)V_2$$

Hence,
$$\frac{V_1}{I_1} = \frac{6s^4+57s^2+8}{14s^3+2s}$$

$$\frac{V_2}{V_1} = \frac{s^2}{6s^4+57s^2+8}$$

$$\frac{V_2}{I_1} = \frac{s}{14s^2+2}$$

## EXAMPLE 11.11

*For the ladder network of Fig. 11.21, find the driving-point impedance at the 1 – 1′ terminal with 2 – 2′ open.*

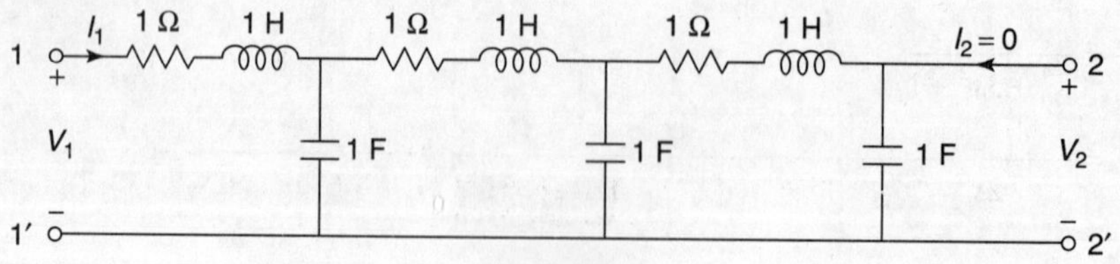


Fig. 11.21

**Solution** The transformed network is shown in Fig. 11.22.

Fig. 11.22

$$V_c = V_2$$

$$I_b = \frac{V_2}{\frac{1}{s}} = s\,V_2$$

$$V_b = (s+1)\,I_b + V_2 = (s+1)\,sV_2 + V_2 = (s^2+s+1)V_2$$

$$I_a = \frac{V_b}{\frac{1}{s}} + I_b = sV_b + I_b = s(s^2+s+1)V_2 + sV_2 = (s^3+s^2+2s)V_2$$

$$V_a = (s+1)\,I_a + V_b = (s+1)(s^3+s^2+2s)V_2 + (s^2+s+1)V_2 = (s^4+2s^3+4s^2+3s+1)V_2$$

$$I_1 = \frac{V_a}{\frac{1}{s}} + I_a = sV_a + I_a = s(s^4+2s^3+4s^2+3s+1)V_2 + (s^3+s^2+2s)V_2$$

$$= (s^5+2s^4+5s^3+4s^2+3s)V_2$$

$$V_1 = (s+1)\,I_1 + V_a = (s+1)(s^5+2s^4+5s^3+4s^2+3s)V_2 + (s^4+2s^3+4s^2+3s+1)V_2$$

$$= (s^6+3s^5+8s^4+11s^3+11s^2+6s+1)V_2$$

Hence, $$Z_{11} = \frac{V_1}{I_1} = \frac{s^6+3s^5+8s^4+11s^3+11s^2+6s+1}{s^5+2s^4+5s^3+4s^2+3s}$$

**EXAMPLE 11.12**

*Determine the voltage transfer function* $\frac{V_2}{V_1}$ *for the network shown in Fig. 11.23.*

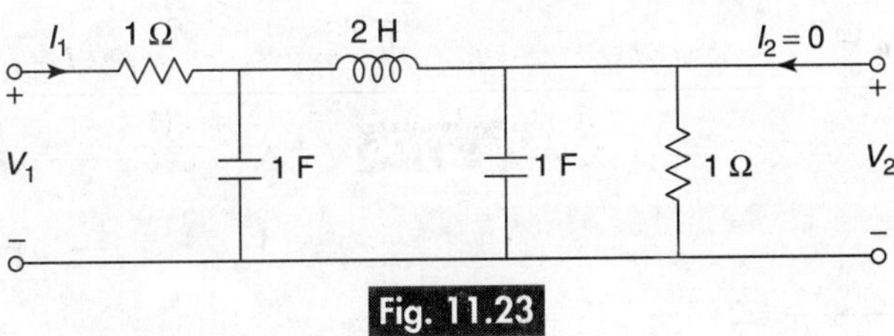


Fig. 11.23

**Solution** The transformed network is shown in Fig. 11.24.

$$V_c = V_b = V_2$$

$$I_a = I_b + I_c = \frac{V_2}{\frac{1}{s}} + \frac{V_2}{1} = s V_2 + V_2 = (s+1)V_2$$

$$V_a = 2s I_a + V_2 = 2s(s+1)V_2 + V_2$$

$$= (2s^2 + 2s + 1)V_2$$

Fig. 11.24

$$I_1 = \frac{V_a}{\frac{1}{s}} + I_a = sV_a + I_a = s(2s^2 + 2s + 1)V_2 + (s+1)V_2 = (2s^3 + 2s^2 + 2s + 1)V_2$$

$$V_1 = 1I_1 + V_a = (2s^3 + 2s^2 + 2s + 1)V_2 + (2s^2 + 2s + 1)V_2 = (2s^3 + 4s^2 + 4s + 2)V_2$$

Hence, $$\frac{V_2}{V_1} = \frac{1}{2s^3 + 4s^2 + 4s + 2}$$

## EXAMPLE 11.13

*For the network shown in Fig. 11.25, determine the transfer function* $\frac{I_2}{V_1}$.

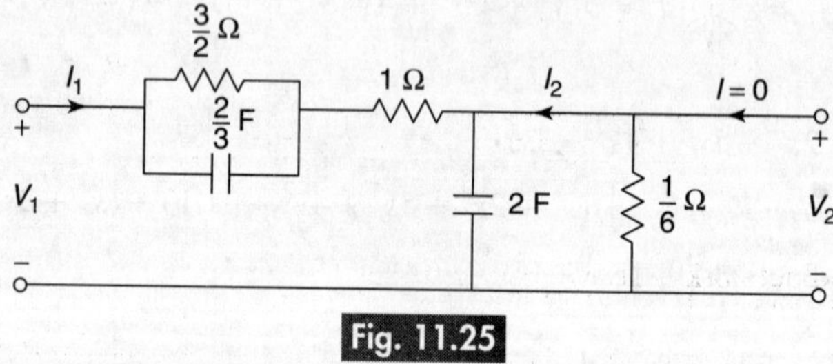


Fig. 11.25

**Solution** The transformed network is shown in Fig. 11.25.

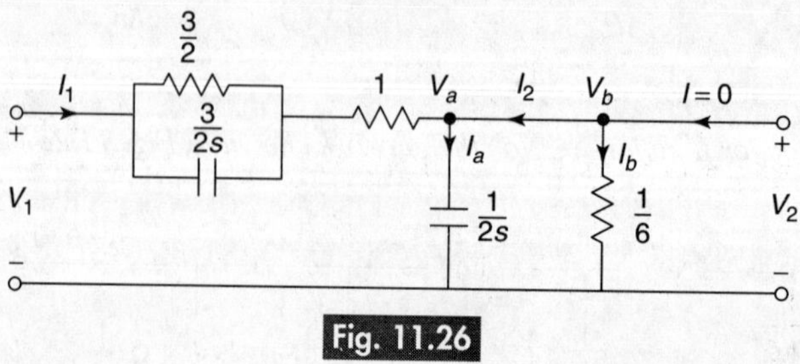


Fig. 11.26

$$V_b = V_a = V_2$$

$$I_1 = I_a + I_b = \frac{V_2}{\frac{1}{2s}} + \frac{V_2}{\frac{1}{6}} = 2sV_2 + 6V_2 = (2s+6)V_2$$

$$V_1=\left(\frac{\frac{3}{2}\times\frac{3}{2s}}{\frac{3}{2}+\frac{3}{2s}}+1\right)I_1+V_2=\left(\frac{9}{6s+6}+1\right)I_1+V_2=\frac{(6s+15)}{6s+6}(2s+6)V_2+V_2=\left[\frac{(2s+5)(s+3)}{(s+1)}+1\right]V_2$$

$$=\left[\frac{(2s+5)(s+3)+(s+1)}{s+1}\right]V_2=\left(\frac{2s^2+6s+5s+15+s+1}{s+1}\right)V_2=\left(\frac{2s^2+12s+16}{s+1}\right)V_2$$

$$=\frac{2(s^2+6s+8)}{s+1}V_2=\frac{2(s+4)(s+2)}{s+1}V_2$$

Also, $I_2=-I_b=-6\,V_2$

$$\frac{I_2}{V_1}=-\frac{3(s+1)}{(s+4)(s+2)}$$

## EXAMPLE 11.14

*For the network shown in Fig. 11.27, compute* $\alpha_{12}\,(s)=\dfrac{I_2}{I_1}$ *and* $Z_{12}(s)=\dfrac{V_2}{I_1}$.

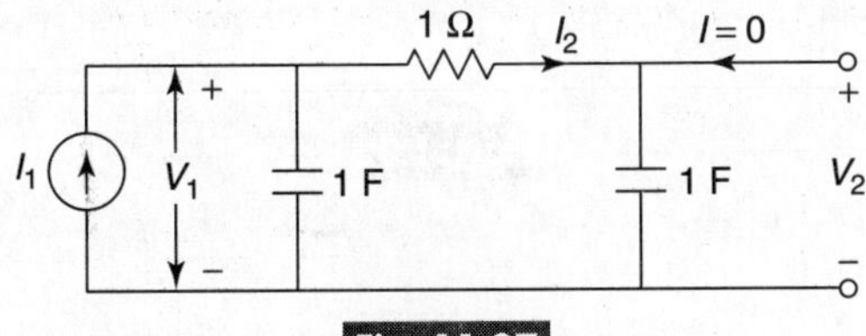


Fig. 11.27

**Solution** The transformed network is shown in Fig. 11.28.

$$V_a=V_2$$

$$I_2=\frac{V_2}{\frac{1}{s}}=sV_2$$

$$V_1=1I_2+V_a=\;sV_2+V_2=\;(s+1)V_2$$

$$I_1=\frac{V_1}{\frac{1}{s}}+I_2=sV_1+I_2=s(s+1)V_2+sV_2=(s^2+2s)V_2$$

Fig. 11.28

Hence, $\alpha_{12}(s)=\dfrac{I_2}{I_1}=\dfrac{1}{s+2}$

and $Z_{12}(s)=\dfrac{V_2}{I_1}=\dfrac{1}{s^2+2s}$

## EXAMPLE 11.15

*Determine the voltage ratio* $\dfrac{V_2}{V_1}$, *current ratio* $\dfrac{I_2}{I_1}$, *transfer impedance* $\dfrac{V_2}{I_1}$ *and driving-point impedance* $\dfrac{V_1}{I_1}$ *for the network shown in Fig. 11.29.*

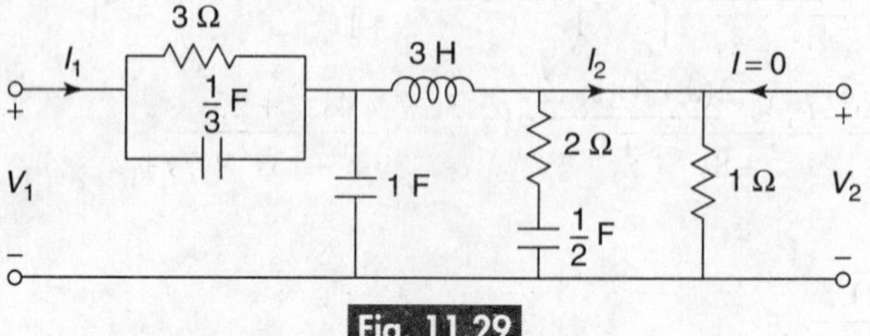


Fig. 11.29

**Solution** The transformed network is shown in Fig. 11.30.

Fig. 11.30

$$V_c = V_b = V_2$$

$$I_2 = \frac{V_2}{1} = V_2$$

$$I_a = I_b + I_2 = \frac{V_2}{2+\frac{2}{s}} + \frac{V_2}{1} = \frac{s}{2s+2}V_2 + V_2 = \left(\frac{3s+2}{2s+2}\right)V_2$$

$$V_a = 3s\,I_a + V_2 = \frac{3s(3s+2)}{2s+2}V_2 + V_2 = \left(\frac{9s^2+8s+2}{2s+2}\right)V_2$$

$$I_1 = \frac{V_a}{\frac{1}{s}} + I_a = sV_a + I_a = \frac{s(9s^2+8s+2)}{2s+2}V_2 + \left(\frac{3s+2}{2s+2}\right)V_2 = \left(\frac{9s^3+8s^2+5s+2}{2s+2}\right)V_2$$

$$V_1 = \left(\frac{3\times\frac{3}{s}}{3+\frac{3}{s}}\right)I_1 + V_a = \left(\frac{3}{s+1}\right)I_1 + V_a = \left(\frac{3}{s+1}\right)\left(\frac{9s^3+8s^2+5s+2}{2s+2}\right)V_2 + \left(\frac{9s^2+8s+2}{2s+2}\right)V_2$$

$$= \left[\frac{27s^3+24s^2+15s+6+9s^3+8s^2+2s+9s^2+8s+2}{(s+1)(2s+2)}\right]V_2 = \frac{(36s^3+41s^2+25s+8)}{(s+1)(2s+2)}V_2$$

$$= \left(\frac{36s^3+41s^2+25s+8}{2s^2+4s+2}\right)V_2$$

Hence,
$$\frac{V_2}{V_1} = \frac{2s^2+4s+2}{36s^3+41s^2+25s+8}$$
$$\frac{I_2}{I_1} = \frac{2s+2}{9s^3+8s^2+5s+2}$$
$$\frac{V_2}{I_1} = \frac{2s+2}{9s^3+8s^2+5s+2}$$
$$\frac{V_1}{I_1} = \frac{36s^3+41s^2+25s+8}{(s+1)(9s^3+8s^2+5s+2)} = \frac{36s^3+41s^2+25s+8}{9s^4+17s^3+13s^2+7s+2}$$

**EXAMPLE 11.16**

*For the resistive two-port network of Fig. 11.31, find* $\frac{V_2}{V_1}, \frac{V_2}{I_1}, \frac{I_2}{V_1}$ *and* $\frac{I_2}{I_1}$.

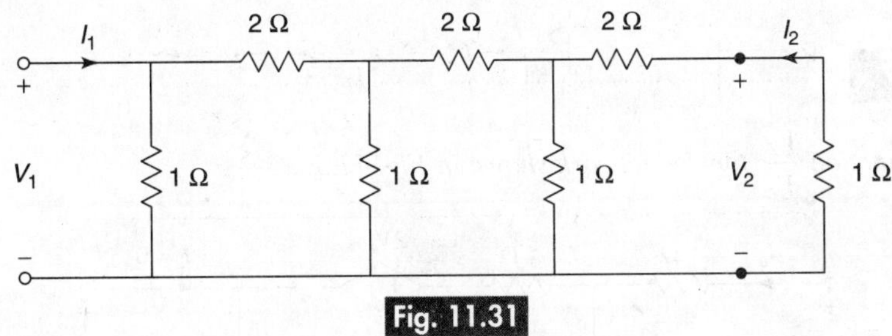


Fig. 11.31

**Solution** The network is redrawn, as shown in Fig. 11.32.

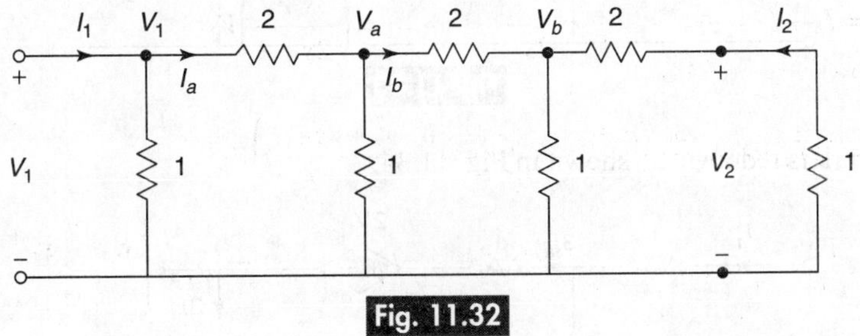


Fig. 11.32

$$I_2 = -\frac{V_2}{1} = -V_2$$
$$V_b = -3I_2 = 3V_2$$
$$I_b = \frac{V_b}{1} + \frac{V_b}{3} = \frac{4}{3}V_b = 4V_2$$
$$V_a = 2I_b + V_b = 8V_2 + 3V_2 = 11V_2$$

$$I_a = \frac{V_a}{1} + I_b = 11\,V_2 + 4\,V_2 = 15\,V_2$$

$$V_1 = 2\,I_a + V_a = 30\,V_2 + 11\,V_2 = 41\,V_2$$

$$I_1 = \frac{V_1}{1} + I_a = 41\,V_2 + 15\,V_2 = 56\,V_2$$

Hence,

$$\frac{V_2}{V_1} = \frac{1}{41}$$

$$\frac{V_2}{I_1} = \frac{1}{56}\ \Omega$$

$$\frac{I_2}{V_1} = -\frac{1}{41}\ \mho$$

$$\frac{I_2}{I_1} = -\frac{1}{56}$$

## EXAMPLE 11.17

*Find the network function $\frac{V_2}{V_1}$ for the network shown in Fig. 11.33.*

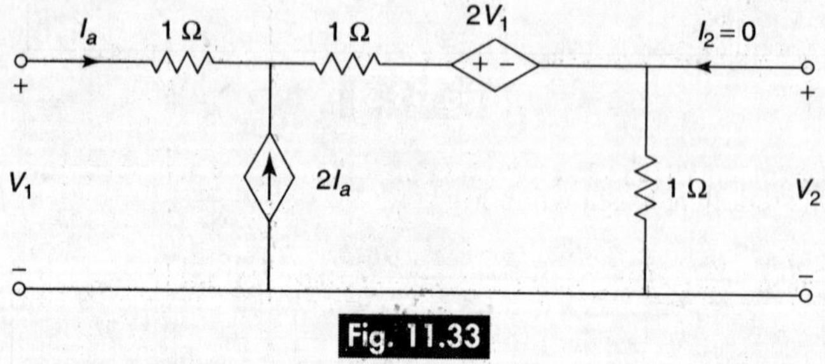


Fig. 11.33

**Solution** The network is redrawn, as shown in Fig. 11.34.

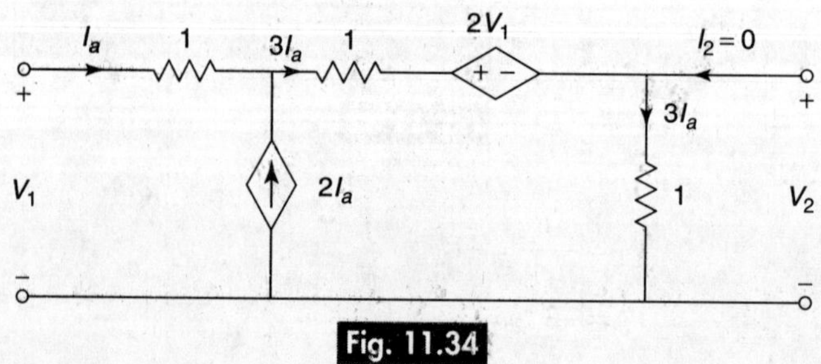


Fig. 11.34

From Fig. 11.34,

$$V_2 = 1\,(3\,I_a) = 3\,I_a$$

Applying KVL to the outermost loop,

$$V_1 - 1\,(I_a) - 1\,(3I_a) - 2\,V_1 - 1\,(3I_a) = 0$$

$$V_1 = -7I_a$$

Hence,

$$\frac{V_2}{V_1} = -\frac{3}{7}$$

## EXAMPLE 11.18

*Find the network function* $\frac{I_2}{I_1}$ *for the network shown in Fig. 11.35.*

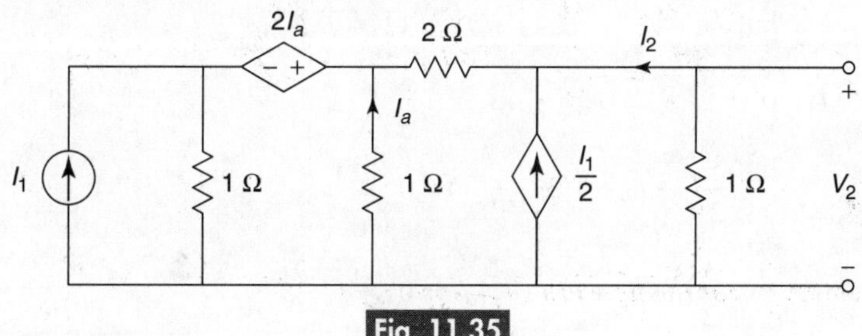


Fig. 11.35

**Solution** The network is redrawn, as shown in Fig. 11.36.

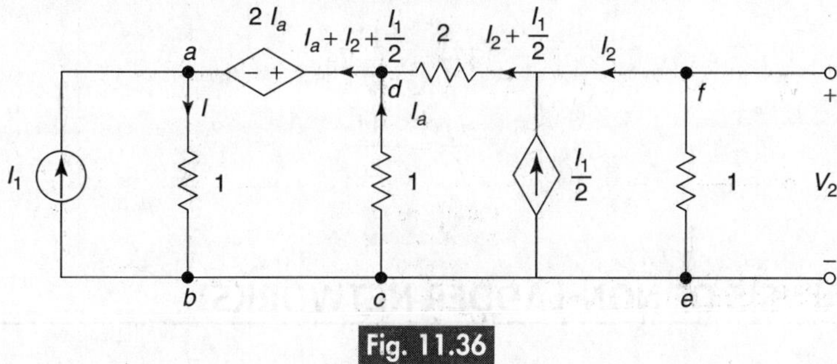


Fig. 11.36

From Fig. 11.36,

$$I = I_1 + I_a + I_2 + \frac{I_1}{2}$$

$$= \frac{3}{2}I_1 + I_a + I_2 \qquad \text{...(i)}$$

Applying KVL to the loop *abcda*,

$$-1I - 1I_a - 2I_a = 0$$

$$-I - 3I_a = 0$$

$$I + 3I_a = 0 \qquad \text{...(ii)}$$

Substituting Eq. (i) in Eq. (ii),

$$\frac{3}{2}I_1 + I_a + I_2 + 3I_a = 0$$

$$\frac{3}{2}I_1 + I_2 + 4I_a = 0 \qquad \text{...(iii)}$$

Applying KVL to the loop *dcefd,*

$$1I_a - 1I_2 - 2\left(I_2 + \frac{I_1}{2}\right) = 0$$

$$I_a - 3I_2 - I_1 = 0$$

$$I_a = 3I_2 + I_1 \qquad \text{...(iv)}$$

Substituting Eq. (iv) in Eq. (iii),

$$\frac{3}{2}I_1 + I_2 + 4(3I_2 + I_1) = 0$$

$$\frac{3}{2}I_1 + I_2 + 12I_2 + 4I_1 = 0$$

$$\frac{11}{2}I_1 + 13I_2 = 0$$

$$13I_2 = -\frac{11}{2}I_1$$

Hence,

$$\frac{I_2}{I_1} = -\frac{11}{26}$$

## 11.6 ANALYSIS OF NON-LADDER NETWORKS

LO 11.4

The above method is applicable for ladder networks. There are other network configurations to which the technique described is not applicable. Figure 12.37 shows one such network.

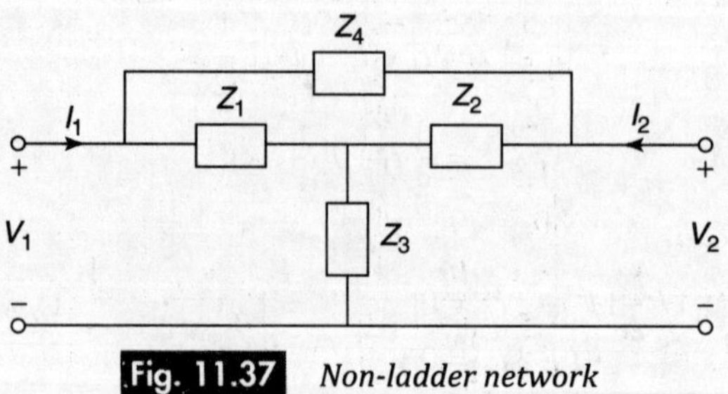


**Fig. 11.37** *Non-ladder network*

For such a type of network, it is necessary to express the network functions as a quotient of determinants, formulated on KVL and KCL basis.

## EXAMPLE 11.19

*For the resistive bridged T-network shown in Fig. 11.38, find* $\frac{V_2}{V_1}, \frac{V_2}{I_1}, \frac{I_2}{V_1}$ *and* $\frac{I_2}{I_1}$.

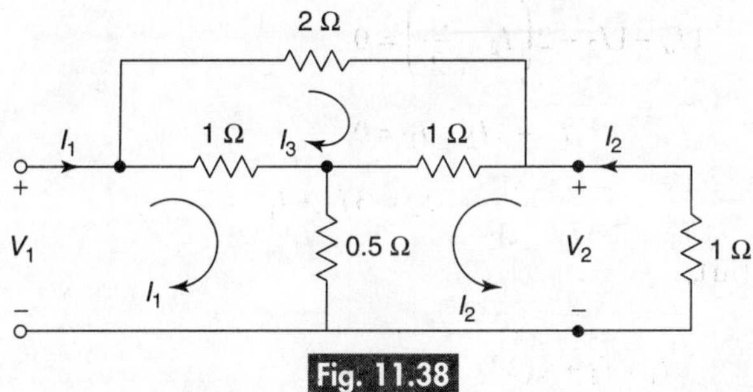


Fig. 11.38

**Solution** Applying KVL to mesh 1,

$$V_1 = 1.5I_1 + 0.5I_2 - I_3 \qquad \text{...(i)}$$

Applying KVL to mesh 2,

$$0 = 0.5I_1 + 2.5I_2 + I_3 \qquad \text{...(ii)}$$

Applying KVL to mesh 3,

$$0 = -I_1 + I_2 + 4I_3 \qquad \text{...(iii)}$$

Writing these equations in matrix form,

$$\begin{bmatrix} V_1 \\ 0 \\ 0 \end{bmatrix} = \begin{bmatrix} 1.5 & 0.5 & -1 \\ 0.5 & 2.5 & 1 \\ -1 & 1 & 4 \end{bmatrix} \begin{bmatrix} I_1 \\ I_2 \\ I_3 \end{bmatrix} \qquad \text{...(iv)}$$

$$I_1 = \frac{\Delta_1}{\Delta} = \frac{\begin{vmatrix} V_1 & 0.5 & -1 \\ 0 & 2.5 & 1 \\ 0 & 1 & 4 \end{vmatrix}}{\begin{vmatrix} 1.5 & 0.5 & -1 \\ 0.5 & 2.5 & 1 \\ -1 & 1 & 4 \end{vmatrix}} = \frac{V_1(10-1)}{9} = V_1 \qquad \text{...(iv)}$$

$$I_2 = \frac{\Delta_2}{\Delta} = \frac{\begin{vmatrix} 1.5 & V_1 & -1 \\ 0.5 & 0 & 1 \\ -1 & 0 & 4 \end{vmatrix}}{\begin{vmatrix} 1.5 & 0.5 & -1 \\ 0.5 & 2.5 & 1 \\ -1 & 1 & 4 \end{vmatrix}} = \frac{-V_1(2+1)}{9} = -\frac{1}{3}V_1 \qquad \text{...(v)}$$

From Fig. 11.38, $V_2 = -1(I_2) = -I_2$

From Eq. (v), $V_1 = -3I_2$

From Eqs (iv) and (v), $I_2 = -\frac{1}{3}V_1 = -\frac{1}{3}I_1$

$$I_1 = -3I_2$$

Hence, $\frac{I_2}{V_1} = -\frac{1}{3}\,\mho$

$$\frac{I_2}{I_1} = \frac{-\frac{1}{3}V_1}{V_1} = -\frac{1}{3}$$

$$\frac{V_2}{V_1} = \frac{-I_2}{-3I_2} = \frac{1}{3}$$

$$\frac{V_2}{I_1} = \frac{-I_2}{-3I_2} = \frac{1}{3}\,\Omega$$

## EXAMPLE 11.20

*For the network of Fig. 11.39, find $Z_{11}$, $Z_{12}$ and $G_{12}$.*

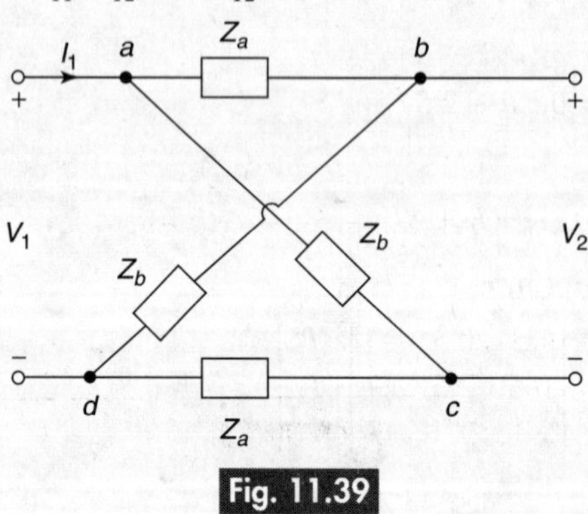


Fig. 11.39

**Solution** The network can be redrawn, as shown in Fig. 11.40. Since the network consists of two identical impedances connected in parallel, the current in $I_1$ divides equally in each branch.

$$V_1 = (Z_a + Z_b)\frac{I_1}{2}$$

$$Z_{11} = \frac{V_1}{I_1} = \frac{Z_a + Z_b}{2}$$

$$V_2 = Z_b\frac{I_1}{2} - Z_a\left(\frac{I_1}{2}\right) = (Z_b - Z_a)\frac{I_1}{2}$$

$$Z_{12} = \frac{V_2}{I_1} = \frac{Z_b - Z_a}{2}$$

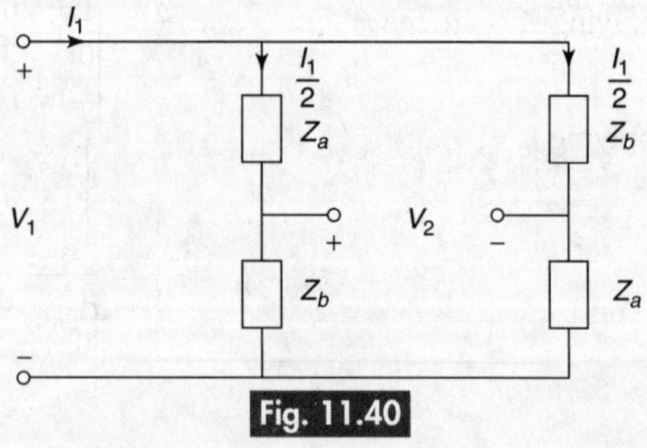


Fig. 11.40

By voltage-division rule,

$$V_2 = \frac{Z_b}{Z_a + Z_b} V_1 - \frac{Z_a}{Z_a + Z_b} V_1 = \frac{Z_b - Z_a}{Z_a + Z_b} V_1$$

$$G_{12} = \frac{V_2}{V_1} = \frac{Z_b - Z_a}{Z_a + Z_b}$$

**EXAMPLE 11.21**

*For the network shown in Fig. 11.41, determine $Z_{11}(s)$, $G_{12}(s)$ and $Z_{12}(s)$.*

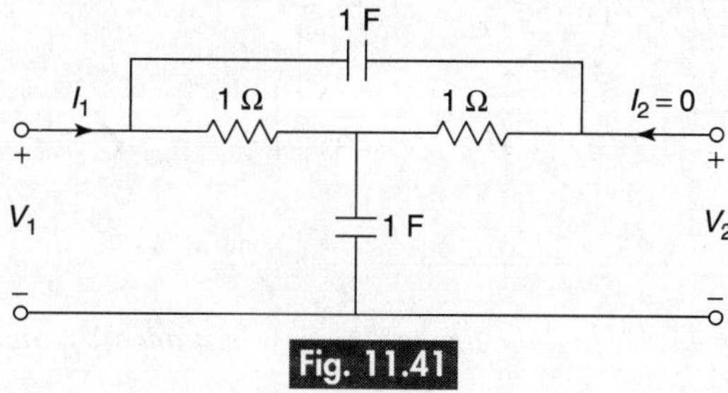


Fig. 11.41

**Solution** The transformed network is shown in Fig. 11.42.

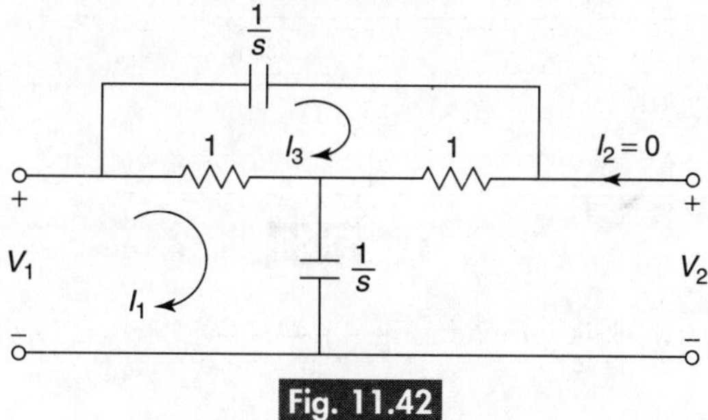


Fig. 11.42

Applying KVL to mesh 1,

$$V_1 = \left(1 + \frac{1}{s}\right) I_1 - I_3 \qquad \text{...(i)}$$

Applying KVL to mesh 2,

$$V_2 = \frac{1}{s} I_1 + I_3 \qquad \text{...(ii)}$$

Applying KVL to mesh 3,

$$-I_1 + \left(2 + \frac{1}{s}\right) I_3 = 0$$

$$I_3 = \left(\frac{s}{2s+1}\right) I_1 \qquad \text{...(iii)}$$

Substituting Eq. (iii) in Eqs (i) and (ii),

$$V_1 = \left(1+\frac{1}{s}\right)I_1 - \left(\frac{s}{2s+1}\right)I_1 = \left(\frac{s+1}{s} - \frac{s}{2s+1}\right)I_1 = \left[\frac{s^2+3s+1}{s(2s+1)}\right]I_1$$

$$V_2 = \frac{1}{s}I_1 + \frac{s}{2s+1}I_1 = \left[\frac{s^2+2s+1}{s(2s+1)}\right]I_1$$

Hence,

$$Z_{11}(s) = \frac{V_1}{I_1} = \frac{s^2+3s+1}{s(2s+1)}$$

$$Z_{12}(s) = \frac{V_2}{I_1} = \frac{s^2+2s+1}{s(2s+1)}$$

$$G_{12}(s) = \frac{V_2}{V_1} = \frac{s^2+2s+1}{s^2+3s+1}$$

## EXAMPLE 11.22

*For the network shown in Fig. 11.43, find the driving-point admittance $Y_{11}$ and transfer admittance $Y_{12}$.*

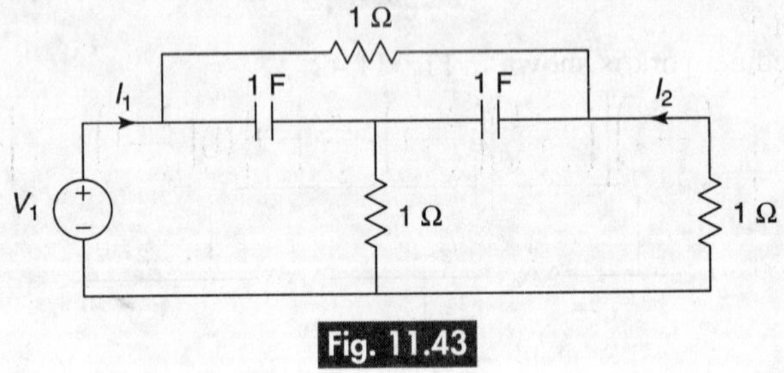


Fig. 11.43

**Solution** The transformed network is shown in Fig. 11.44.

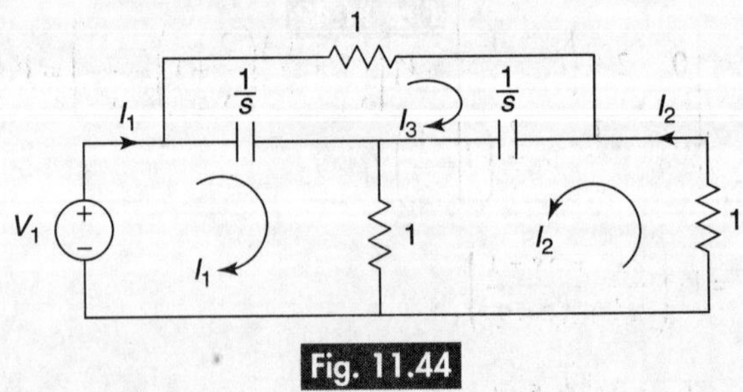


Fig. 11.44

Applying KVL to mesh 1,

$$V_1 = \left(\frac{1}{s}+1\right)I_1 + I_2 - \frac{1}{s}I_3 \qquad \text{...(i)}$$

Applying KVL to mesh 2,

$$0 = I_1 + \left(2+\frac{1}{s}\right) I_2 + \frac{1}{s} I_3 \qquad \text{...(ii)}$$

Applying KVL to mesh 3,

$$0 = -\frac{1}{s} I_1 + \frac{1}{s} I_2 + \left(\frac{2}{s}+1\right) I_3 \qquad \text{...(iii)}$$

Writing these equations in matrix from,

$$\begin{bmatrix} V_1 \\ 0 \\ 0 \end{bmatrix} = \begin{bmatrix} \frac{1}{s}+1 & 1 & -\frac{1}{s} \\ 1 & 2+\frac{1}{s} & \frac{1}{s} \\ -\frac{1}{s} & \frac{1}{s} & \frac{2}{s}+1 \end{bmatrix} \begin{bmatrix} I_1 \\ I_2 \\ I_3 \end{bmatrix}$$

$$I_1 = \frac{\Delta_1}{\Delta}$$

$$\Delta = \begin{vmatrix} \frac{1}{s}+1 & 1 & -\frac{1}{s} \\ 1 & 2+\frac{1}{s} & \frac{1}{s} \\ -\frac{1}{s} & \frac{1}{s} & \frac{2}{s}+1 \end{vmatrix} = \left(\frac{1}{s}+1\right)\left[\left(2+\frac{1}{s}\right)\left(\frac{2}{s}+1\right)-\frac{1}{s^2}\right]-1\left[(1)\left(\frac{2}{s}+1\right)+\frac{1}{s^2}\right]-\frac{1}{s}\left[(1)\left(\frac{1}{s}\right)+\left(\frac{1}{s}\right)\left(2+\frac{1}{s}\right)\right]$$

$$= \frac{s^2+5s+2}{s^2}$$

$$\Delta_1 = \begin{vmatrix} V_1 & 1 & -\frac{1}{s} \\ 0 & 2+\frac{1}{s} & \frac{1}{s} \\ 0 & \frac{1}{s} & \frac{2}{s}+1 \end{vmatrix} = V_1\left[\left(2+\frac{1}{s}\right)\left(\frac{2}{s}+1\right)-\frac{1}{s^2}\right] = V_1\left(\frac{2s^2+5s+1}{s^2}\right)$$

$$I_1 = V_1\left(\frac{2s^2+5s+1}{s^2+5s+2}\right)$$

Hence,

$$Y_{11} = \frac{I_1}{V_1} = \frac{2s^2+5s+1}{s^2+5s+2}$$

$$I_2 = \frac{\Delta_2}{\Delta}$$

$$\Delta_2 = \begin{vmatrix} \frac{1}{s}+1 & V_1 & -\frac{1}{s} \\ 1 & 0 & \frac{1}{s} \\ -\frac{1}{s} & 0 & \frac{2}{s}+1 \end{vmatrix} = -V_1\left(\frac{2}{s}+1+\frac{1}{s^2}\right) = -V_1\left(\frac{s^2+2s+1}{s^2}\right)$$

$$I_2 = -V_1\left(\frac{s^2+2s+1}{s^2+5s+2}\right)$$

Hence,
$$Y_{12} = \frac{I_2}{V_1} = -\frac{s^2+2s+1}{s^2+5s+2}$$

## 11.7 POLES AND ZEROS OF NETWORK FUNCTIONS

LO 11.5

Explain poles and zeros of network functions

The network function $F(s)$ can be written as a ratio of two polynomials.

$$F(s) = \frac{N(s)}{D(s)} = \frac{a_n s^n + a_{n-1}\, s^{n-1} + \ldots + a_1\, s + a_0}{b_m s^m + b_{m-1}\, s^{m-1} + \ldots + b_1\, s + b_0}$$

where $a_0, a_1, \ldots, a_n$ and $b_0, b_1, \ldots, b_m$ are the coefficients of the polynomials $N(s)$ and $D(s)$. These are real and positive for networks of passive elements. Let $N(s) = 0$ have $n$ roots, as $z_1, z_2, \ldots\ldots, z_n$ and $D(s) = 0$ have m roots as $p_1, p_2, \ldots\ldots, p_m$. Then, $F(s)$ can be written as

$$F(s) = H\frac{(s-z_1)(s-z_2)\ldots(s-z_n)}{(s-p_1)(s-p_2)\ldots(s-p_m)}$$

where $\frac{a_n}{b_m}$ is a constant called *scale factor* and $z_1, z_2, \ldots, z_n, p_1, p_2, \ldots, p_m$ are complex frequencies. When the variable $s$ has the values $z_1, z_2, \ldots, z_n$, the network function becomes zero; such complex frequencies are known as the zeros of the network function. When the variable $s$ has values $p_1, p_2, \ldots, p_m$, the network function becomes infinite; such complex frequencies are known as the poles of the network function. A network function is completely specified by its poles, zeros and the scale factor.

If the poles or zeros are not repeated, then the function is said to be having simple poles or simple zeros. If the poles or zeros are repeated, then the function is said to be having multiple poles or multiple zeros. When $n > m$, then $(n - m)$ zeros are at $s = \infty$, and for $m > n$, $(m - n)$ poles are at $s = \infty$.

The total number of zeros is equal to the total number of poles. For any network function, poles and zeros at zero and infinity are taken into account in addition to finite poles and zeros.

Poles and zeros are critical frequencies. The network function becomes infinite at poles, while the network function becomes zero at zeros. The network function has a finite, non-zero value at other frequencies.

Poles and zeros provide a representation of a network function, as shown in Fig. 11.45. The zeros are shown by circles and the poles by crosses. This diagram is referred to as pole-zero plot.

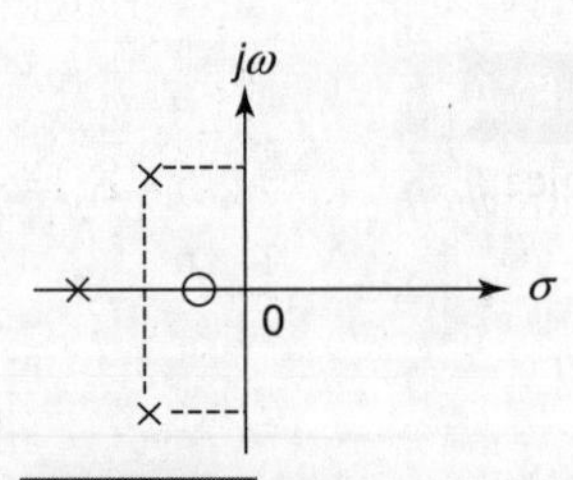


**Fig. 11.45** *Pole-zero plot*

## 11.8 NECESSARY CONDITIONS FOR DRIVING-POINT FUNCTIONS

LO 11.6

Discuss the necessary conditions for driving-point and transfer functions

The necessary conditions for a network function to be a driving-point function with common factors in numerator polynomial $N(s)$ and denominator polynomial $D(s)$ cancelled are as follows:

1. The coefficients in the polynomials $N(s)$ and $D(s)$ must be real and positive.
2. The poles and zeros, if complex or imaginary, must occur in conjugate pairs.
3. The real part of all poles and zeros must be negative or zero, i.e., the poles and zeros must lie in left half of $s$-plane.
4. If the real part of pole or zero is zero, then that pole or zero must be simple.
5. The polynomials $N(s)$ and $D(s)$ may not have missing terms between those of highest and lowest degree, unless all even or all odd terms are missing.
6. The degree of $N(s)$ and $D(s)$ may differ by either zero or one only. This condition prevents multiple poles and zeros at $s = \infty$.
7. The terms of lowest degree in $N(s)$ and $D(s)$ may differ in degree by one at most. This condition prevents multiple poles and zeros at $s = 0$.

## 11.9 NECESSARY CONDITIONS FOR TRANSFER FUNCTIONS

LO 11.6

The necessary conditions for a network function to be a transfer function with common factors in numerator polynomial $N(s)$ and denominator polynomial $D(s)$ cancelled are as follows:

1. The coefficients in the polynomials $N(s)$ and $D(s)$ must be real, and those for $D(s)$ must be positive.
2. The poles and zeros, if complex or imaginary, must occur in conjugate pairs.
3. The real part of poles must be negative or zero. If the real part is zero, then that pole must be simple.
4. The polynomial $D(s)$ may not have any missing terms between that of highest and lowest degree, unless all even or all odd terms are missing.
5. The polynomial $N(s)$ may have missing terms between the terms of lowest and highest degree, and some of the coefficients may be negative.
6. The degree of $N(s)$ may be as small as zero, independent of the degree of $D(s)$.
7. For voltage and current transfer functions, the maximum degree of $N(s)$ is the degree of $D(s)$.
8. For transfer impedance and admittance functions, the maximum degree of $N(s)$ is the degree of $D(s)$ plus one.

**EXAMPLE 11.23** ●○○

*Test whether the following represent driving-point immittance functions.*

(a) $\dfrac{5s^4 + 3s^2 - 2s + 1}{s^3 + 6s + 20}$ (b) $\dfrac{s^3 + s^2 + 5s + 2}{s^4 + 6s^3 + 9s^2}$ (c) $\dfrac{s^2 + 3s + 2}{s^2 + 6s + 2}$

**Solution**

(a) The numerator and denominator polynomials have a missing term between those of highest and lowest degree and one of the coefficient is negative in numerator polynomial. Hence, the function does not represent a driving-point immittance function.

(b) The term of lowest degree in numerator and denominator polynomials differ in degree by two. Hence, the function does not represent a driving-point immittance function.

(c) The function satisfies all the necessary conditions. Hence, it represents a driving-point immittance function.

## EXAMPLE 11.24

*Test whether the following represent transfer functions.*

(a) $G_{21} = \dfrac{3s+2}{5s^3+4s^2+1}$ (b) $\alpha_{12} = \dfrac{2s^2+5s+1}{s+7}$ (c) $Z_{21} = \dfrac{1}{s^3+2s}$

**Solution**

(a) The polynomial $D(s)$ has a missing term between that of highest and lowest degree. Hence, the function does not represent a transfer function.

(b) The degree of $N(s)$ is greater than $D(s)$. Hence, the function does not represent a transfer function.

(c) The function satisfies all the necessary conditions. Hence, it represents a transfer function.

## EXAMPLE 11.25

*Obtain the pole-zero plot of the following functions.*

(a) $F(s) = \dfrac{s(s+2)}{(s+1)(s+3)}$ (b) $F(s) = \dfrac{s(s+1)}{(s+2)^2(s+3)}$

(c) $F(s) = \dfrac{s(s+2)}{(s+1+j1)(s+1-j1)}$ (d) $F(s) = \dfrac{(s+1)^2(s+5)}{(s+2)(s+3+j2)(s+3-j2)}$

(e) $F(s) = \dfrac{s^2+4}{(s+2)(s^2+9)}$

**Solution**

(a) The function $F(s)$ has zeros at $s = 0$ and $s = -2$ and poles at $s = -1$ and $s = -3$. The pole-zero plot is shown in Fig. 11.46.

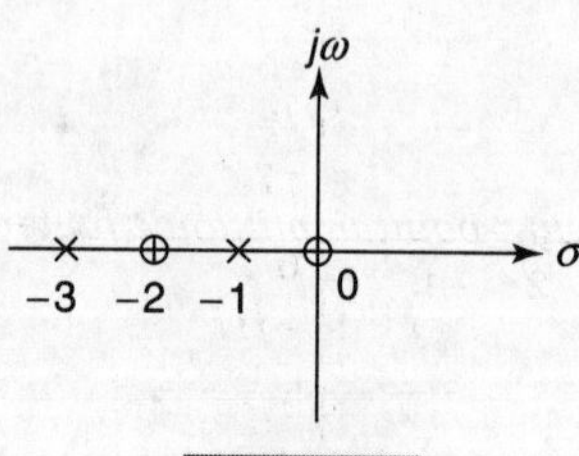


Fig. 11.46

(b) The function $F(s)$ has zeros at $s = 0$ and $s = -1$ and poles at $s = -2, -2$ and $s = -3$. The pole-zero plot is shown in Fig. 11.47.

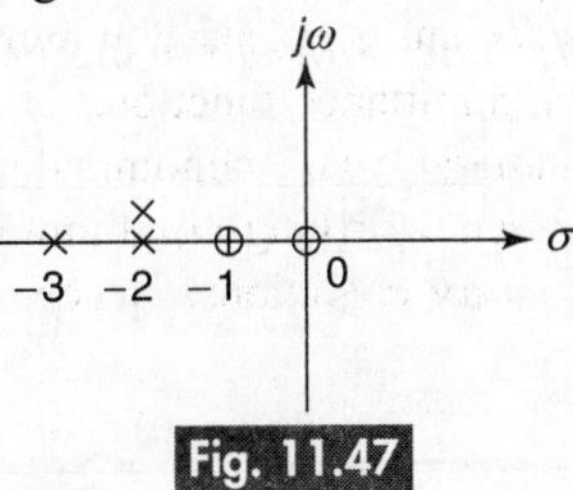


Fig. 11.47

(c) The function $F(s)$ has zeros at $s = 0$ and $s = -2$ and poles at $s = -1 - j1$ and $s = -1 + j1$. The pole-zero plot is shown in Fig. 11.48.

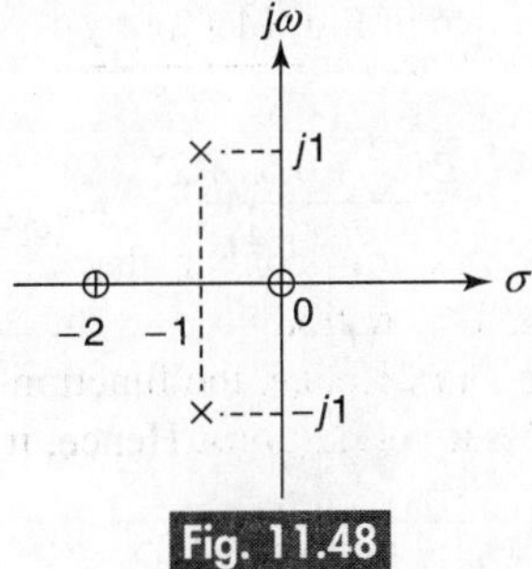


Fig. 11.48

(d) The function $F(s)$ has zeros at $s = -1, -1$ and $s = -5$ and poles at $s = -2$, $s = -3 + j2$ and $s = -3 - j2$. The pole-zero plot is shown in Fig. 11.49.

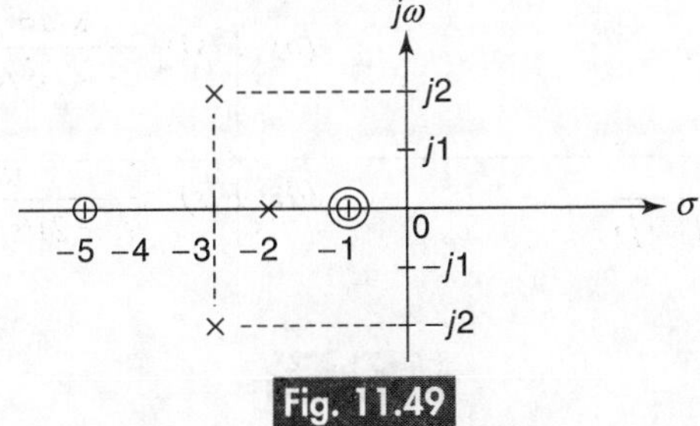


Fig. 11.49

(e) The function $F(s)$ has zeros at $s = j2$ and $s = -j2$ and poles at $s = -2$, $s = j3$ and $s = -j3$. The pole-zero plot is shown in Fig. 11.50.

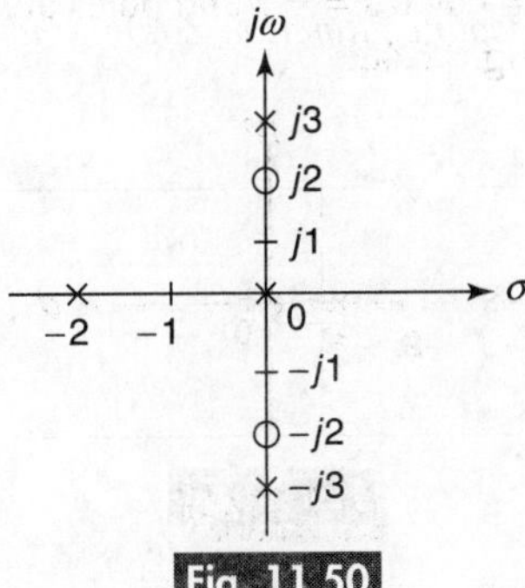


Fig. 11.50

**EXAMPLE 11.26**

*Find poles and zeros of the impedance of the network shown in Fig. 11.51 and plot them on the s-plane.*

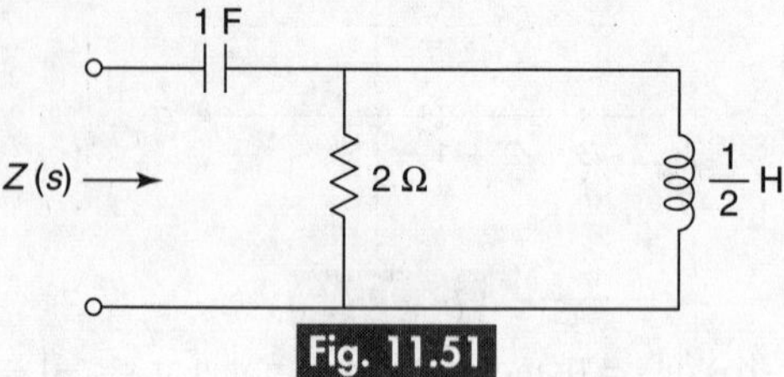


Fig. 11.51

**Solution** The transformed network is shown in Fig. 11.52.

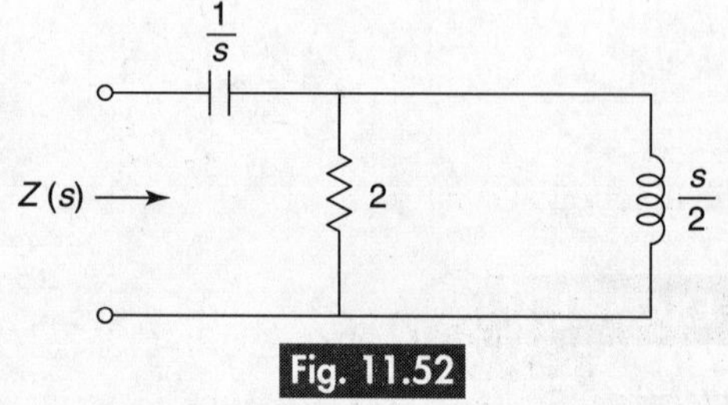


Fig. 11.52

$$Z(s) = \frac{1}{s} + \frac{\frac{s}{2} \times 2}{\frac{s}{2} + 2} = \frac{1}{s} + \frac{2s}{s+4} = \frac{2s^2 + s + 4}{s(s+4)} = \frac{2(s^2 + 0.5s + 2)}{s(s+4)}$$

$$= \frac{2(s + 0.25 + j1.4)(s + 0.25 - j1.4)}{s(s+4)}$$

The function $Z(s)$ has zeros at $s = -0.25 + j1.4$ and $s = -0.25 - j1.4$ and poles at $s = 0$ and $s = -4$, as shown in Fig. 11.53.

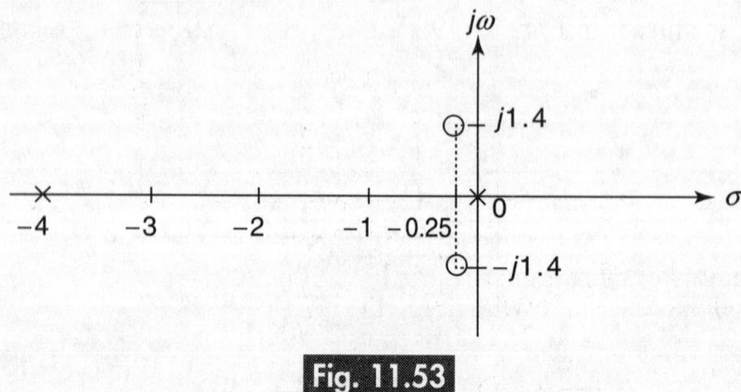


Fig. 11.53

**EXAMPLE 11.27**

*Determine the poles and zeros of the impedance function Z (s) in the network shown in Fig. 11.54.*

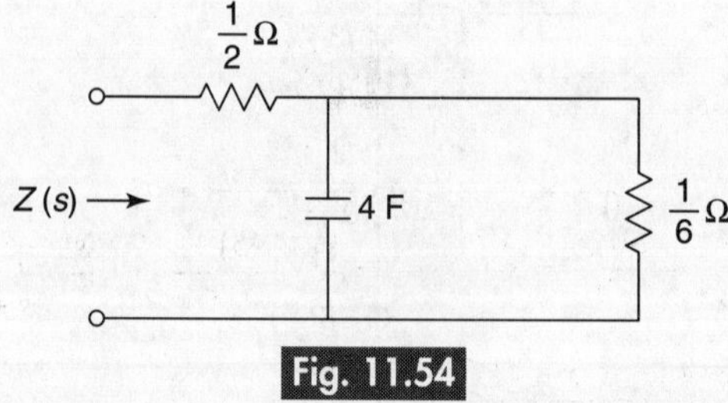


Fig. 11.54

**Solution** The transformed network is shown in Fig. 11.55.

Fig. 11.55

$$Z(s)=\frac{1}{2}+\frac{\frac{1}{4s}\times\frac{1}{6}}{\frac{1}{4s}+\frac{1}{6}}=\frac{1}{2}+\frac{1}{4s+6}=\frac{4s+8}{2(4s+6)}=\frac{s+2}{2s+3}=\frac{0.5(s+2)}{s+1.5}$$

The function $Z(s)$ has zero at $s=-2$ and pole at $s=-1.5$.

## EXAMPLE 11.28

*Determine Z(s) in the network shown in Fig. 11.56. Find poles and zeros of Z(s) and plot them on s-plane.*

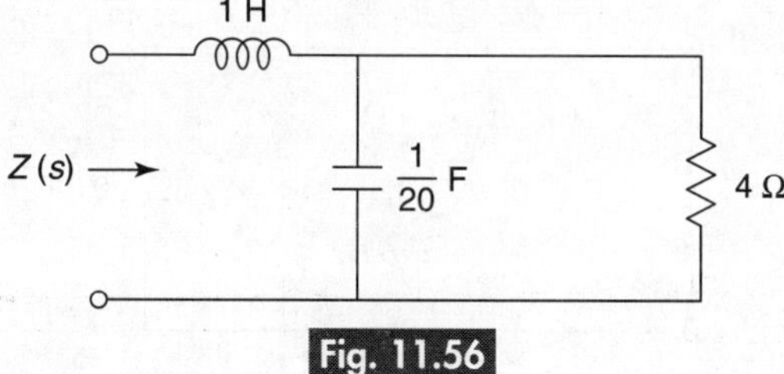


Fig. 11.56

**Solution** The transformed network is shown in Fig. 11.57.

Fig. 11.57

$$Z(s)=s+\frac{\frac{20}{s}\times 4}{\frac{20}{s}+4}=s+\frac{80}{4s+20}=s+\frac{20}{s+5}=\frac{s(s+5)+20}{s+5}=\frac{s^2+5s+20}{s+5}$$

$$=\frac{(s+2.5+j3.71)(s+2.5-j3.71)}{s+5}$$

The function $Z(s)$ has zeros at $s = -2.5 + j3.71$ and $s = -2.5 - j3.71$ and pole at $s = -5$.

The pole-zero diagram is shown in Fig. 11.58.

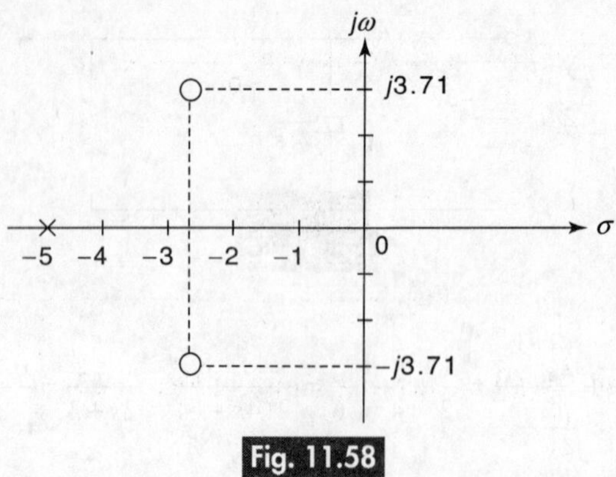


Fig. 11.58

## EXAMPLE 11.29

*For the network shown in Fig. 11.59, plot poles and zeros of function* $\dfrac{I_0}{I_i}$.

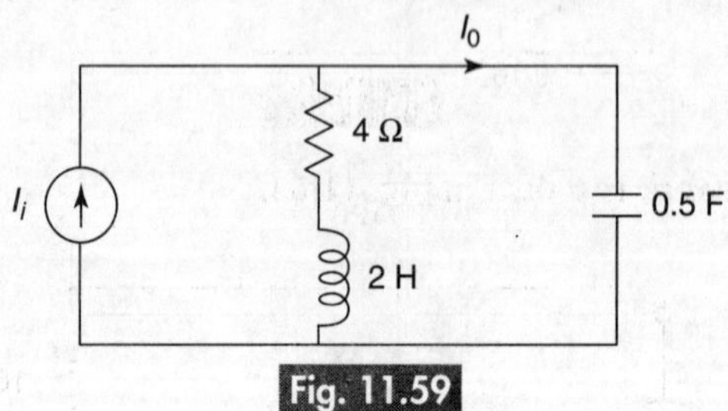


Fig. 11.59

**Solution** The transformed network is shown in Fig. 11.60.

By current-division rule,

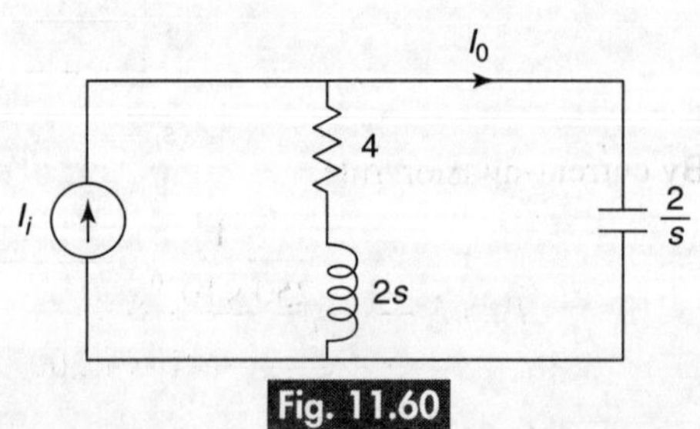


Fig. 11.60

$$I_0 = I_i \left( \frac{4+2s}{4+2s+\dfrac{2}{s}} \right)$$

$$\frac{I_0}{I_i} = \frac{s(4+2s)}{4s+2s^2+2} = \frac{s(s+2)}{s^2+2s+1} = \frac{s(s+2)}{(s+1)(s+1)}$$

The function has zeros at $s = 0$ and $s = -2$ and double poles at $s = -1$.

The pole-zero diagram is shown in Fig. 11.61.

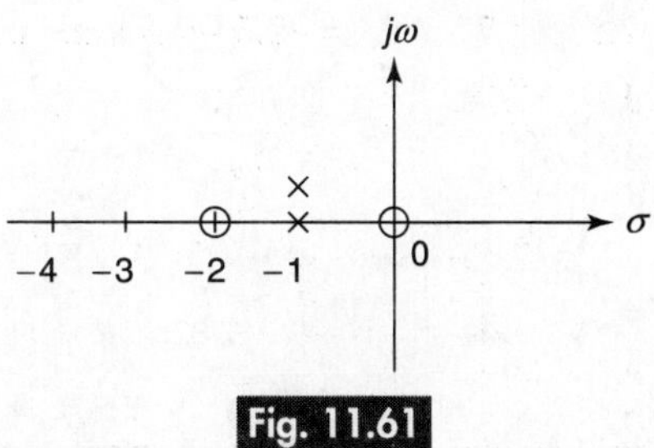

Fig. 11.61

**EXAMPLE 11.30**

*Draw the pole-zero diagram of* $\frac{I_2}{I_1}$ *for the network shown in Fig. 11.62.*

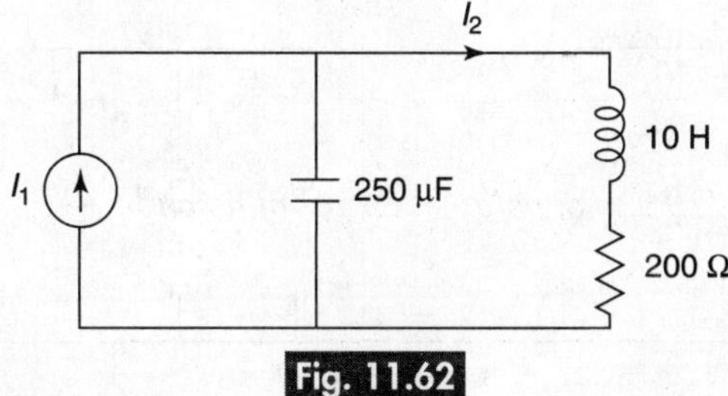

Fig. 11.62

**Solution** The transformed network is shown in Fig. 11.63.

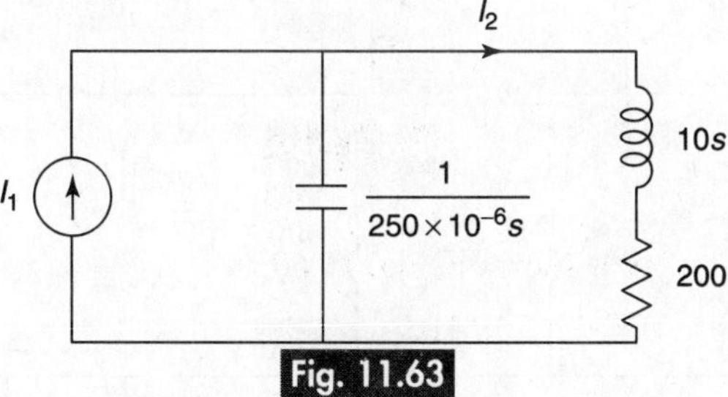

Fig. 11.63

By current-division rule,

$$I_2 = I_1 \frac{\dfrac{1}{250\times10^{-6}s}}{\dfrac{1}{250\times10^{-6}s}+10s+200}$$

$$\frac{I_2}{I_1} = \frac{400}{s^2+20s+400} = \frac{400}{(s+10-j17.32)(s+10+j17.32)}$$

The function has no zero and poles at $s = -10 + j17.32$ and $s = -10 - j17.32$.

The pole-zero diagram is shown in Fig. 11.64.

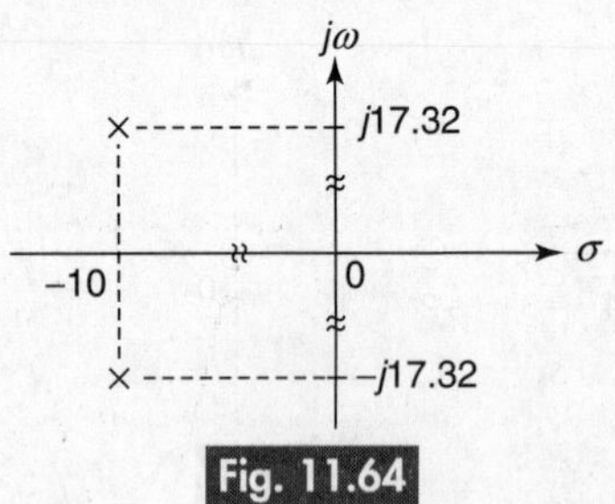


Fig. 11.64

## EXAMPLE 11.31

*For the network shown in Fig. 11.65, draw pole-zero plot of* $\frac{V_c}{V_1}$.

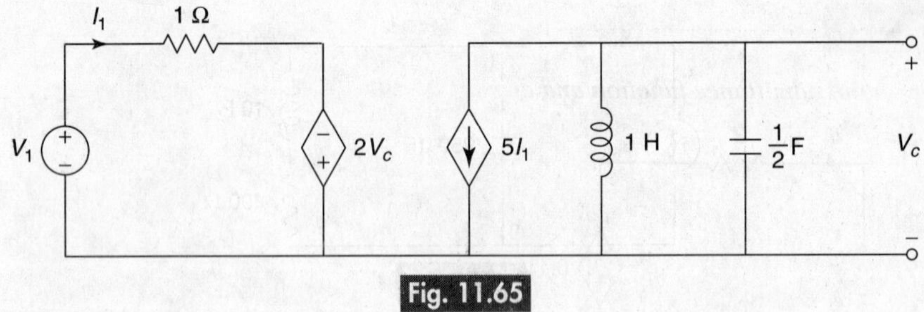


Fig. 11.65

**Solution** The transformed network is shown in Fig. 11.66.

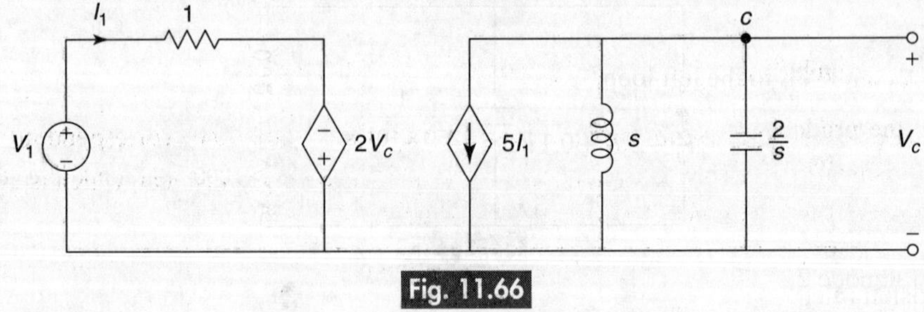


Fig. 11.66

Applying KVL to the left loop,

$$V_1 - 1I_1 + 2V_c = 0$$

$$I_1 = V_1 + 2V_c$$

Applying KCL at node $C$,

$$5I_1 + \frac{V_c}{s} + \frac{V_c}{\frac{2}{s}} = 0$$

$$5(V_1 + 2V_c) + \frac{V_c}{s} + \frac{s}{2}V_c = 0$$

$$5V_1 + 10V_c + \frac{V_c}{s} + \frac{s}{2}V_c = 0$$

$$V_c\left(\frac{20s + 2 + s^2}{2s}\right) = -5V_1$$

$$\frac{V_c}{V_1} = -\frac{10s}{s^2 + 20s + 2}$$

$$= -\frac{10s}{(s + 0.1)(s + 19.9)}$$

The function has zero at $s = 0$ and poles at $s = -0.1$ and $s = -19.9$.

The pole-zero diagram is shown in Fig. 11.67.

Fig. 11.67

## EXAMPLE 11.32

*Find the driving-point admittance function and draw pole-zero plot for the network shown in Fig. 11.68.*

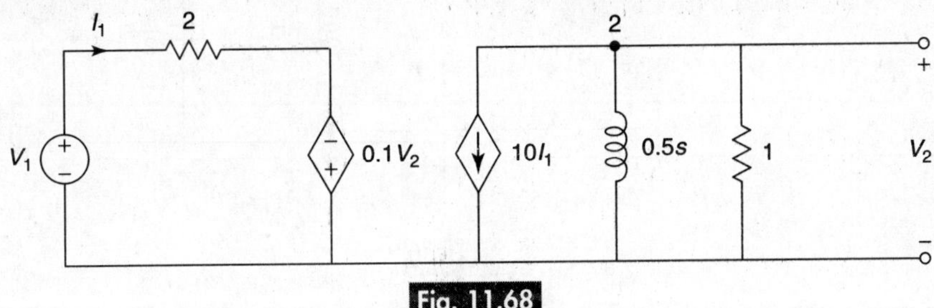


Fig. 11.68

**Solution** Applying KVL to the left loop,

$$V_1 - 2\,I_1 + 0.1\,V_2 = 0$$

$$I_1 = \frac{V_1 + 0.1\,V_2}{2} \qquad \text{...(i)}$$

Applying KCL at node 2,

$$10\,I_1 + \frac{V_2}{0.5s} + \frac{V_2}{1} = 0$$

$$10\,I_1 + \frac{2}{s}V_2 + V_2 = 0$$

$$10\,I_1 + \left(\frac{2}{s} + 1\right)V_2 = 0$$

$$10\,I_1 + \left(\frac{2 + s}{s}\right)V_2 = 0$$

$$\left(\frac{s+2}{s}\right)V_2 = -10\, I_1$$

$$V_2 = -\frac{10s}{s+2} I_1 \qquad \text{...(ii)}$$

Substituting Eq. (ii) in Eq. (i),

$$I_1 = \frac{V_1 + 0.1\left(-\frac{10s}{s+2}\right)I_1}{2} = 0.5V_1 + 0.05\left(-\frac{10s}{s+2}\right)I_1$$

$$I_1\left(1 + \frac{0.5s}{s+2}\right) = 0.5V_1$$

Hence,
$$Y_{11} = \frac{I_1}{V_1} = \frac{0.5}{1+\frac{0.5s}{s+2}} = \frac{0.5\,(s+2)}{s+0.5s+2} = \frac{0.5s+1}{1.5s+2}$$

The function has zero at $s = -2$ and pole at $s = -1.33$. The pole-zero diagram is shown in Fig. 11.69.

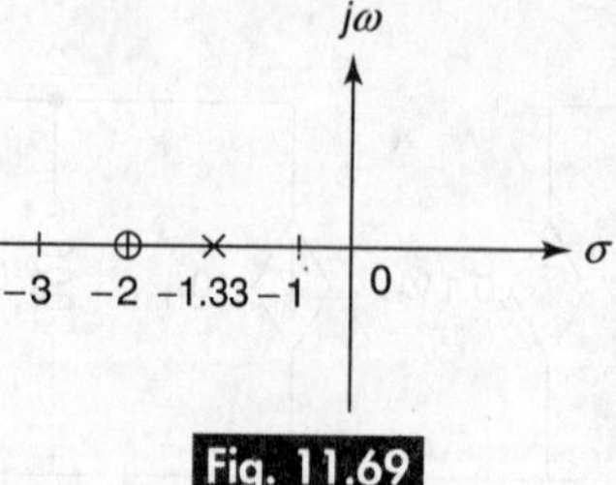


Fig. 11.69

## EXAMPLE 11.33

*For the network shown in Fig. 11.70, determine* $\frac{V_2}{I_g}$*. Plot the pole-zero diagram of* $\frac{V_2}{I_g}$*.*

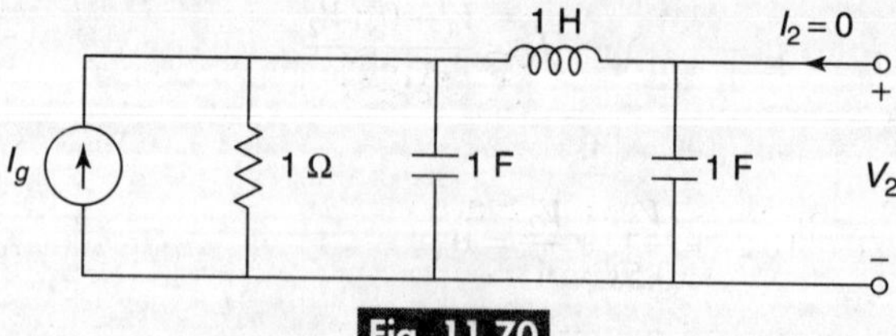


Fig. 11.70

**Solution** The transformed network is shown in Fig. 11.71.

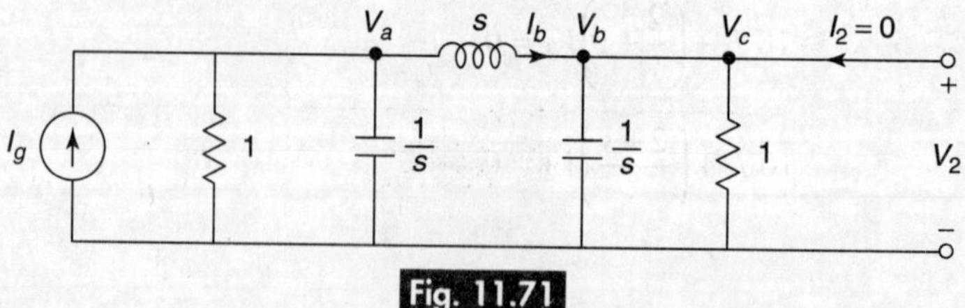


Fig. 11.71

$$V_c = V_b = V_2$$

$$I_b = \frac{V_b}{\frac{1}{s}} + \frac{V_c}{1} = sV_2 + V_2 = (s+1)V_2$$

$$V_a = sI_b + V_b = s(s+1)V_2 + V_2 = (s^2+s+1)V_2$$

$$I_g = \frac{V_a}{1} + \frac{V_a}{\frac{1}{s}} + I_b = (s^2+s+1)V_2 + s(s^2+s+1)V_2 + (s+1)V_2 = (s^3+2s^2+3s+2)V_2$$

Hence, $$\frac{V_2}{I_g} = \frac{1}{s^3+2s^2+3s+2}$$

The function has no zeros. It has poles at $s = -1$, $s = -0.5 + j1.32$ and $s = -0.5 - j1.32$,

The pole-zero diagram is shown in Fig. 11.72.

$j\omega$, $j1.32$, $\sigma$, $-2$, $-1$, $-0.5$, $0$, $-j1.32$

Fig. 11.72

## EXAMPLE 11.34

*For the transfer function* $H(s) = \frac{V_0}{V_i} = \frac{10}{s^2+3s+10}$, *realise the function using the network shown in Fig. 11.73. Find L and C when R* = 5 Ω.

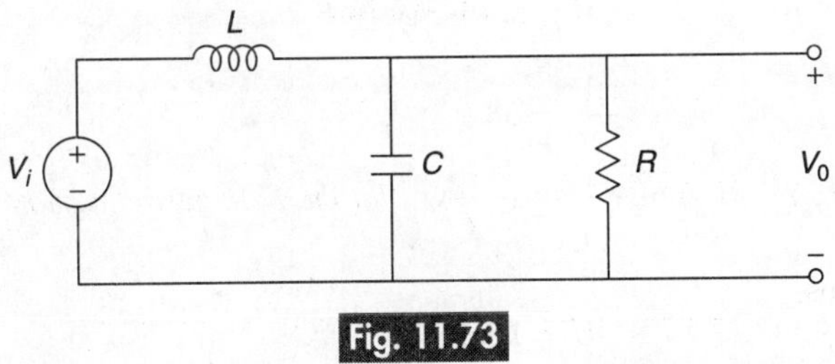


Fig. 11.73

**Solution** The transformed network is shown in Fig. 11.74.

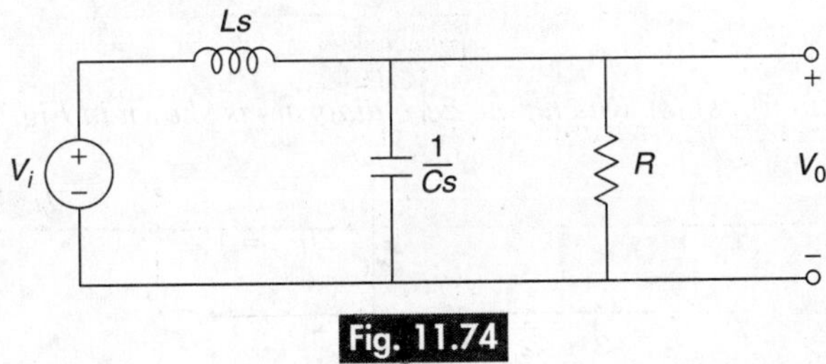


Fig. 11.74

Simplifying the network, as shown in Fig. 11.75,

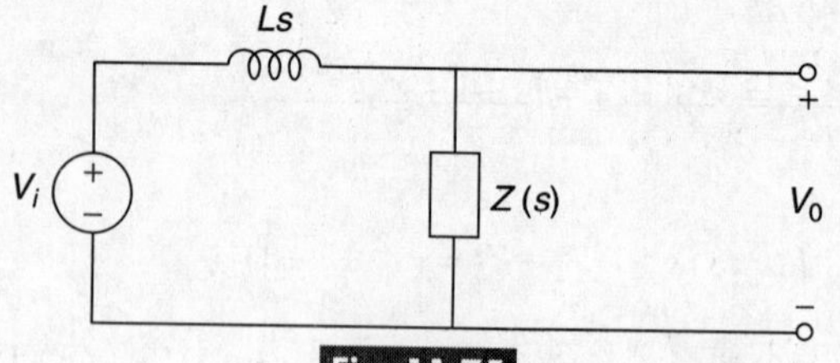


Fig. 11.75

$$Z(s)=\frac{R\times\frac{1}{Cs}}{R+\frac{1}{Cs}}=\frac{R}{RCs+1}$$

$$V_0=V_i\frac{\frac{R}{RCs+1}}{Ls+\frac{R}{RCs+1}}$$

$$\frac{V_0}{V_i}=\frac{R}{RLC\,s^2+Ls+R}=\frac{\frac{1}{LC}}{s^2+\frac{1}{RC}s+\frac{1}{LC}} \qquad \text{...(i)}$$

But
$$\frac{V_0}{V_i}=\frac{10}{s^2+3s+10} \qquad \text{...(ii)}$$

and
$$R=5\ \Omega$$

Comparing Eq. (ii) with Eq. (i),

$$\frac{1}{RC}=3$$

$$\frac{1}{LC}=10$$

Solving the above equations,

$$L=1.5\text{ H}$$

$$C=\frac{1}{15}\text{F}$$

## EXAMPLE 11.35

*Obtain the impedance function Z(s) for which pole-zero diagram is shown in Fig. 11.76.*

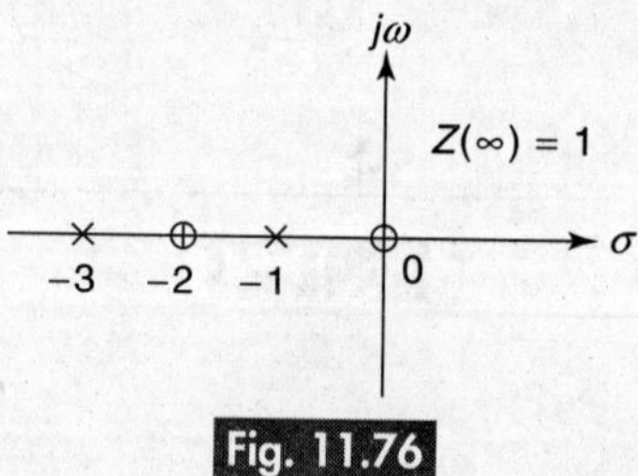


Fig. 11.76

**Solution** The function $Z(s)$ has poles at $s = -1$ and $s = -3$ and zeros at $s = 0$ and $s = -2$.

$$Z(s) = H\frac{s(s+2)}{(s+1)(s+3)} = H\frac{s^2\left(1+\frac{2}{s}\right)}{s^2\left(1+\frac{1}{s}\right)\left(1+\frac{3}{s}\right)}$$

For $s = \infty$,

$$Z(\infty) = H\frac{1}{(1)(1)} = H$$

When $Z(\infty) = 1$,

$$H = 1$$

$$Z(s) = \frac{s(s+2)}{(s+1)(s+3)}$$

## EXAMPLE 11.36

*Obtain the admittance function Y(s) for which the pole-zero diagram is shown in Fig. 11.77.*

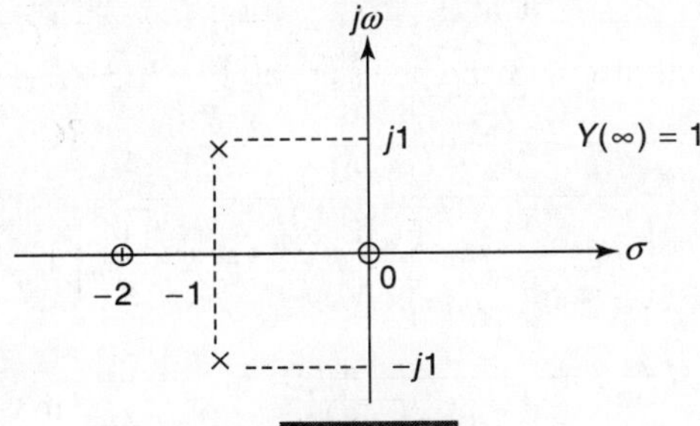


Fig. 11.77

**Solution** The function $Y(s)$ has poles at $s = -1 + j1$ and $s = -1 - j1$ and zeros at $s = 0$ and $s = -2$.

$$Y(s) = H\frac{s(s+2)}{(s+1+j1)(s+1-j1)} = H\frac{s(s+2)}{(s+1)^2-(j1)^2} = H\frac{s(s+2)}{s^2+2s+2} = H\frac{s^2\left(1+\frac{2}{s}\right)}{s^2\left(1+\frac{2}{s}+\frac{2}{s^2}\right)}$$

For $s = \infty$,

$$Y(\infty) = H\frac{(1)}{(1)} = H$$

When $Y(\infty) = 1$,

$$H = 1$$

$$Y(s) = \frac{s(s+2)}{s^2+2s+2}$$

**EXAMPLE 11.37**

*A network and its pole-zero configuration are shown in Fig. 11.78. Determine the values of R, L and C if Z (j0) = 1.*

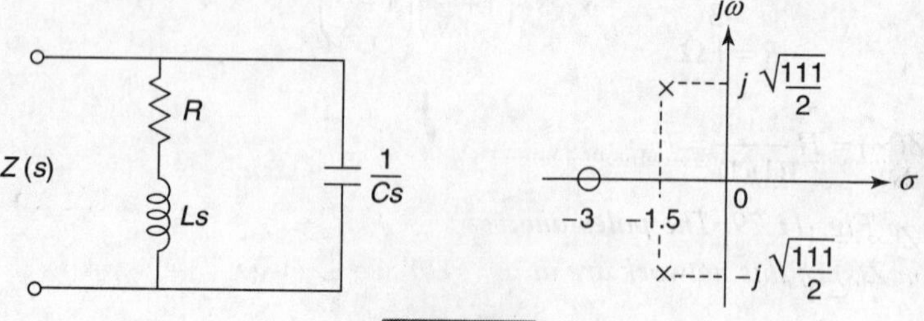


Fig. 11.78

**Solution**

$$Z(s)=\frac{(Ls+R)\frac{1}{Cs}}{(Ls+R)+\frac{1}{Cs}}=\frac{Ls+R}{LCs^2+RCs+1}=\frac{\frac{1}{C}\left(s+\frac{R}{L}\right)}{s^2+\frac{R}{L}s+\frac{1}{LC}} \quad \text{...(i)}$$

From the pole-zero diagram, zero is at $s=-3$ and poles are at $s=-1.5+j\frac{\sqrt{111}}{2}$ and $s=-1.5-j\frac{\sqrt{111}}{2}$

$$Z(s)=H\frac{s+3}{\left(s+1.5+j\frac{\sqrt{111}}{2}\right)\left(s+1.5-j\frac{\sqrt{111}}{2}\right)}$$

$$Z(s)=H\frac{s+3}{(s+1.5)^2-\left(j\frac{\sqrt{111}}{2}\right)^2}=H\frac{s+3}{s^2+3s+30}$$

When $Z(j0)=1$,

$$1=H\left(\frac{3}{30}\right)$$

$$H=10$$

$$Z(s)=\frac{10(s+3)}{s^2+3s+30} \quad \text{...(ii)}$$

Comparing Eq. (ii) with Eq. (i),

$$\frac{R}{L}=3$$

$$\frac{1}{C}=10$$

$$\frac{1}{LC}=30$$

Solving the above equations,

$$C = \frac{1}{10}\text{ F}$$

$$L = \frac{1}{3}\text{ H}$$

$$R = 1\,\Omega$$

## EXAMPLE 11.38

*A network is shown in Fig. 11.79. The poles and zeros of the driving-point function Z(s) of this network are at the following places:*

*Poles at* $-\frac{1}{2} \pm j\frac{\sqrt{3}}{2}$

*Zero at –1*

*If Z (j0) = 1, determine the values of R, L and C.*

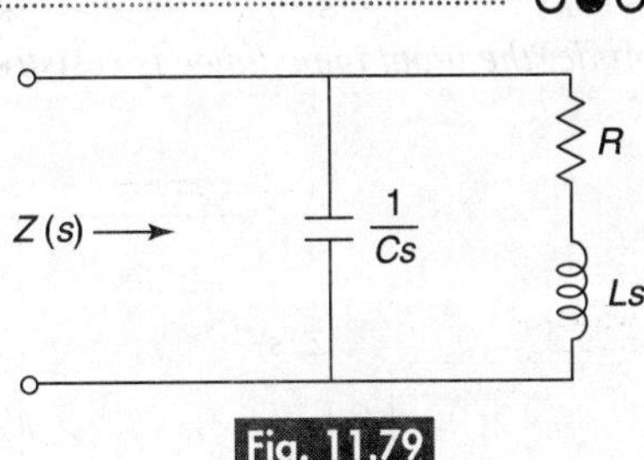


Fig. 11.79

**Solution**

$$Z(s) = \frac{(Ls+R)\frac{1}{Cs}}{Ls+R+\frac{1}{Cs}} = \frac{Ls+R}{LCs^2+RCs+1} = \frac{\frac{1}{C}\left(s+\frac{R}{L}\right)}{s^2+\frac{R}{L}s+\frac{1}{LC}} \qquad \text{...(i)}$$

The poles are at $-\frac{1}{2} \pm j\frac{\sqrt{3}}{2}$ and zero is at –1.

$$Z(s) = H\frac{s+1}{\left(s+\frac{1}{2}+j\frac{\sqrt{3}}{2}\right)\left(s+\frac{1}{2}-j\frac{\sqrt{3}}{2}\right)} = H\frac{s+1}{\left(s+\frac{1}{2}\right)^2-\left(j\frac{\sqrt{3}}{2}\right)^2} = H\frac{s+1}{s^2+s+1}$$

When $\qquad Z(j0) = 1,$

$$1 = H\frac{(1)}{(1)}$$

$$H = 1$$

$$Z(s) = \frac{s+1}{s^2+s+1} \qquad \text{...(ii)}$$

Comparing Eq. (ii) with Eq. (i),

$$C = 1$$

$$\frac{R}{L} = 1$$

$$\frac{1}{LC} = 1$$

Solving the above equations,

$$C = 1\ \text{F}$$
$$L = 1\ \text{H}$$
$$R = 1\ \Omega$$

**EXAMPLE 11.39**

*The pole-zero diagram of the driving-point impedance function of the network of Fig. 11.80 is shown below. At dc, the input impedance is resistive and equal to 2 Ω. Determine the values of R, L and C.*

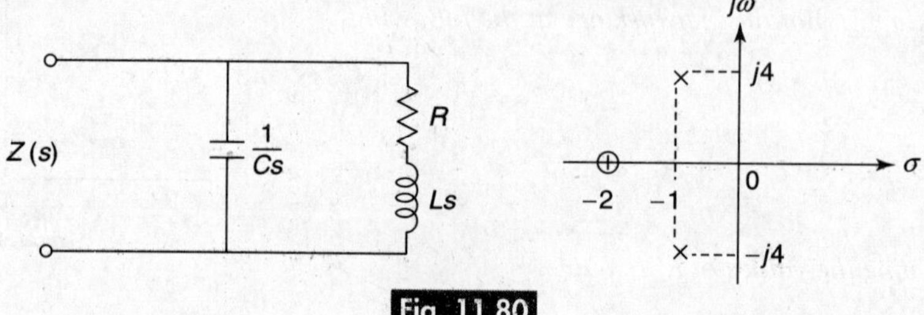


Fig. 11.80

**Solution**

$$Z(s) = \frac{(Ls+R)\frac{1}{Cs}}{Ls+R+\frac{1}{Cs}} = \frac{Ls+R}{LCs^2+RCs+1} = \frac{\frac{1}{C}\left(s+\frac{R}{L}\right)}{s^2+\frac{R}{L}s+\frac{1}{LC}} \quad \text{...(i)}$$

From the pole-zero diagram, zero is at $s = -2$ and poles are at $s = -1 + j4$ and $s = -1 - j4$.

$$Z(s) = H\frac{s+2}{(s+1+j4)(s+1-j4)} = H\frac{s+2}{(s+1)^2-(j4)^2} = H\frac{s+2}{s^2+2s+17}$$

At dc, i.e., $\omega = 0,\ Z(j0) = 2$

$$2 = H\frac{2}{17}$$
$$H = 17$$
$$Z(s) = 17\frac{s+2}{s^2+2s+17} \quad \text{...(ii)}$$

Comparing Eq. (ii) with Eq. (i),

$$\frac{1}{C} = 17$$
$$\frac{R}{L} = 2$$
$$\frac{1}{LC} = 17$$

Solving the above equations,

$$C = \frac{1}{17}\,\text{F}$$
$$L = 1\,\text{H}$$
$$R = 2\,\Omega$$

**EXAMPLE 11.40**

*The network shown in Fig. 11.81 has the driving-point admittance Y (s) of the form*

$$Y(s) = H\frac{(s-s_1)(s-s_2)}{(s-s_3)}$$

*(a) Express $s_1$, $s_2$, $s_3$ in terms of R, L and C.*

*(b) When $s_1 = -10 + j10^4$, $s_2 = -10 - j10^4$ and $Y(j0) = 10^{-1}$ mho, find the values of R, L and C and determine the value of $s_3$.*

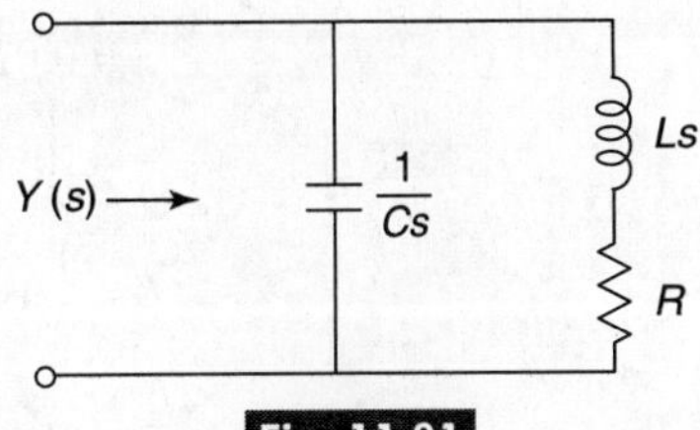


Fig. 11.81

**Solution**

(a) $$Y(s) = Cs + \frac{1}{Ls+R} = \frac{(Ls+R)\,Cs+1}{Ls+R} = \frac{LCs^2+RCs+1}{Ls+R} = \frac{C\left(s^2+\frac{R}{L}s+\frac{1}{LC}\right)}{s+\frac{R}{L}} \quad \text{...(i)}$$

But $$Y(s) = \frac{H(s-s_1)(s-s_2)}{(s-s_3)}$$

where $$s_1, s_2 = \frac{-\frac{R}{L} \pm \sqrt{\left(\frac{R}{L}\right)^2 - \frac{4}{LC}}}{2} = -\frac{R}{2L} \pm \sqrt{\left(\frac{R}{2L}\right)^2 - \frac{1}{LC}}$$

$$s_3 = -\frac{R}{L}$$

(b) When $$s_1 = -10 + j10^4$$
$$s_2 = -10 - j10^4$$

$$Y(s) = H\frac{(s+10-j10^4)(s+10+j10^4)}{s-s_3} = H\frac{s^2+20s+10^8}{s-s_3} \quad \text{...(ii)}$$

Comparing Eq. (ii) with Eq. (i),

$$\frac{R}{L} = 20$$
$$s_3 = -20$$
$$Y(s) = H\frac{(s^2+20s+10^8)}{(s+20)}$$

At $s = j0$,

$$Y(j0) = H\frac{(10^8)}{20} = 10^{-1}$$

$$H = 0.02 \times 10^{-6}$$

$$Y(s) = 0.02 \times 10^{-6}\frac{(s^2 + 20s + 10^8)}{(s+20)} \qquad \text{...(iii)}$$

Comparing Eq. (iii) with Eq. (i),

$$C = 0.02 \times 10^{-6}\text{ F} = 0.02\ \mu\text{F}$$

$$\frac{1}{LC} = 10^8$$

$$L = \frac{1}{2}\text{ H}$$

$$\frac{R}{L} = 20$$

$$R = 10\ \Omega$$

**EXAMPLE 11.41**

*A network and pole-zero diagram for driving-point impedance Z(s) are shown in Fig. 11.82. Calculate the values of the parameters R, L, G and C if Z(j0) = 1.*

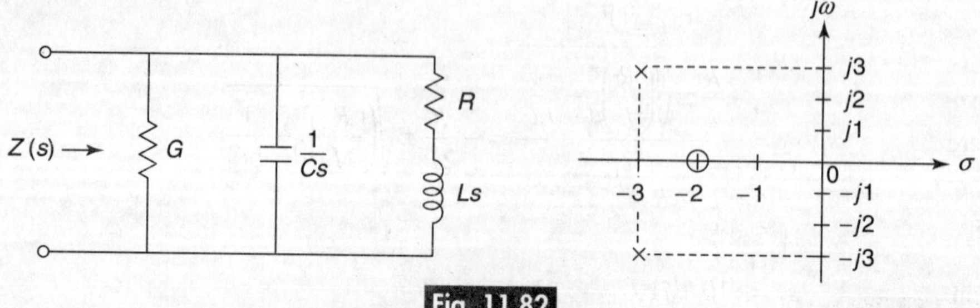


Fig. 11.82

**Solution** It is easier to calculate $Y(s)$ and then invert it to obtain $Z(s)$.

$$Y(s) = G + Cs + \frac{1}{Ls + R} = \frac{(G + Cs)(Ls + R) + 1}{Ls + R} = \frac{LCs^2 + (GL + RC)\,s + 1 + GR}{Ls + R}$$

$$Z(s) = \frac{1}{Y(s)} = \frac{Ls + R}{LCs^2 + (GL + RC)\,s + 1 + GR} = \frac{\frac{1}{C}\left(s + \frac{R}{L}\right)}{s^2 + \left(\frac{G}{C} + \frac{R}{L}\right)s + \left(\frac{1 + GR}{LC}\right)} \qquad \text{...(i)}$$

From the pole-zero diagram, zero is at $s = -2$ and poles are at $s = -3 \pm j3$.

$$Z(s) = H\frac{(s+2)}{(s+3-j3)(s+3+j3)} = H\frac{(s+2)}{(s+3)^2 - (j3)^2} = H\frac{s+2}{s^2 + 6s + 18}$$

When $Z(j0) = 1,$

$$1 = H\frac{2}{18}$$

$$H = 9$$

$$Z(s) = \frac{9\,(s+2)}{(s^2+6s+18)} \quad \text{...(ii)}$$

Comparing Eq. (ii) with Eq. (i),

$$\frac{1}{C} = 9$$

$$\frac{R}{L} = 2$$

$$\frac{G}{C} + \frac{R}{L} = 6$$

$$\frac{1+GR}{LC} = 18$$

Solving the above equation,

$$C = \frac{1}{9}\text{ F}$$

$$L = \frac{9}{10}\text{ H}$$

$$G = \frac{4}{9}\,\mho$$

$$R = \frac{9}{5}\,\Omega$$

**EXAMPLE 11.42**

*A series R-L-C circuit has its driving-point admittance and pole-zero diagram is shown in Fig. 11.83. Find the values of R, L and C.*

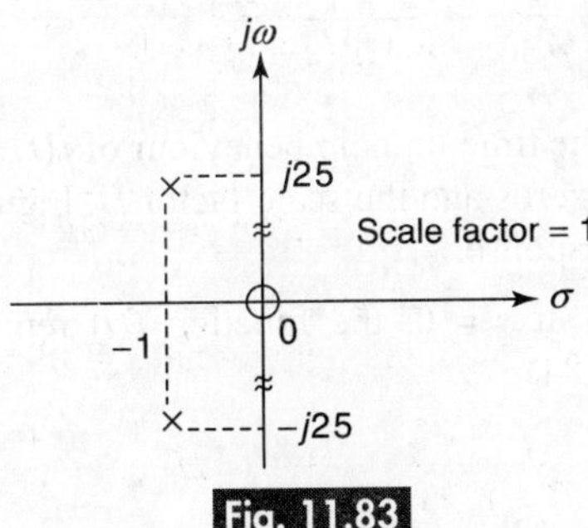


Fig. 11.83

**Solution** The function $Y(s)$ has poles at $s = -1 + j25$ and $s = -1 - j25$ and zero at $s = 0$.

$$Y(s) = H\frac{s}{(s+1+j25)(s+1-j25)} = H\frac{s}{(s+1)^2 - (j25)^2} = H\frac{s}{s^2+2s+626}$$

Scale factor $\qquad H = 1$

$$Y(s) = \frac{s}{s^2+2s+626} \qquad \text{...(i)}$$

For a series *RLC* circuit,

$$Z(s) = R + Ls + \frac{1}{Cs} = \frac{LCs^2 + RCs + 1}{Cs} = \frac{L\left(s^2 + \frac{R}{L}s + \frac{1}{LC}\right)}{s}$$

$$Y(s) = \frac{1}{Z(s)} = \frac{s}{L\left(s^2 + \frac{R}{L}s + \frac{1}{LC}\right)} \qquad \text{...(ii)}$$

Comparing Eq. (i) with Eq. (ii),

$$L = 1\text{ H}$$

$$\frac{1}{LC} = 626$$

$$C = \frac{1}{626}\text{ F}$$

$$\frac{R}{L} = 2$$

$$R = 2\ \Omega$$

## 11.10 TIME-DOMAIN BEHAVIOUR FROM THE POLE-ZERO PLOT

LO 11.7

Determine the time-domain behaviour of a system from the pole-zero plot

The time-domain behaviour of a system can be determined from the pole-zero plot. Consider a network function

$$F(s) = H\frac{(s-z_1)(s-z_2)\dots(s-z_n)}{(s-p_1)(s-p_2)\dots(s-p_m)}$$

The poles of this function determine the time-domain behaviour of $f(t)$. The function $f(t)$ can be determined from the knowledge of the poles, the zeros and the scale factor $H$. Figure 11.84 shows some pole locations and the corresponding time-domain response.

(i) When pole is at origin, i.e., at $s = 0$, the function $f(t)$ represents steady-state response of the circuit i.e., dc value. (Fig. 11.84)

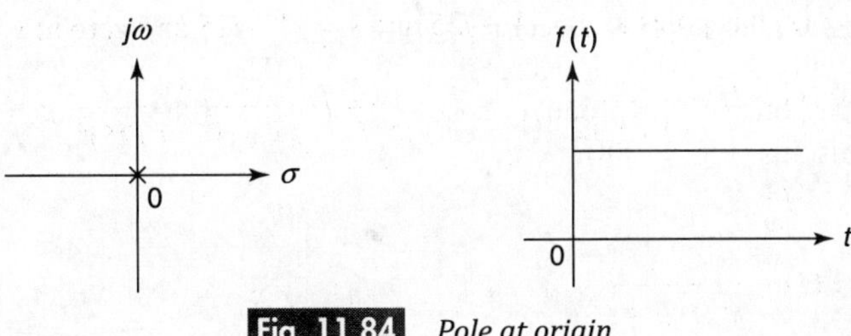


Fig. 11.84 *Pole at origin*

(ii) When pole lies in the left half of the *s*-planc, thc rcsponse decreases exponentially. (Fig. 11.85)

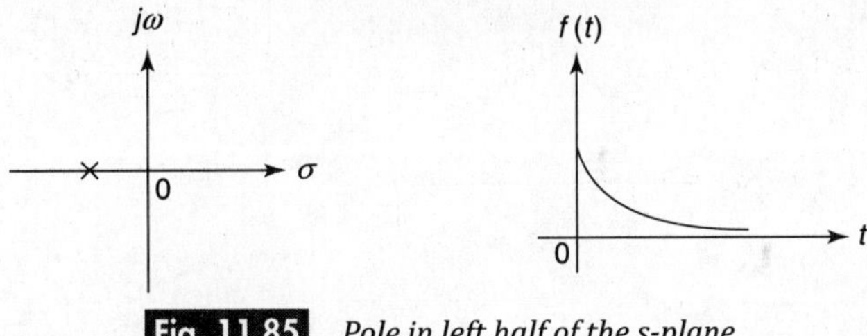


Fig. 11.85 *Pole in left half of the s-plane*

(iii) When pole lies in the right half of the *s*-plane, the response increases exponentially. A pole in the right-half plane gives rise to unbounded response and unstable system. (Fig. 11.86)

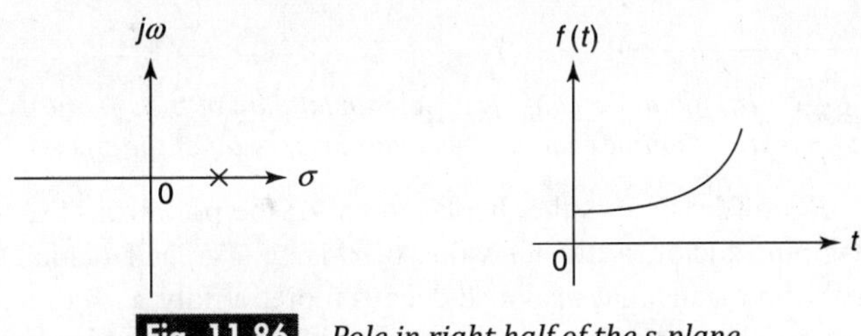


Fig. 11.86 *Pole in right half of the s-plane*

(iv) For $s = 0 \pm j\omega_n$, the response becomes $f(t) = Ae^{\pm j\omega_n t} = A(\cos \omega_n t \pm j \sin \omega_n t)$. The exponential response $e^{\pm j\omega_n t}$ may be interpreted as a rotating phasor of unit length. A positive sign of exponential $e^{j\omega_n t}$ indicates counterclockwise rotation, while a negative sign of exponential $e^{-j\omega_n t}$ indicates clockwise rotation. The variation of exponential function $e^{j\omega_n t}$ with time is sinusoidal and hence, constitutes the case of sinusoidal steady state. (Fig. 11.87)

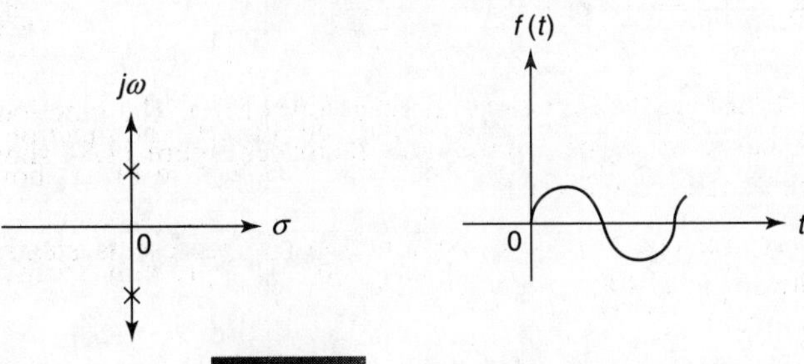


Fig. 11.87 *Poles on jω-axis*

(v) For $s = \sigma_n + j\omega_n$, the response becomes $f(t) = Ae^{st} = Ae^{(\sigma_n + j\omega_n t)} = Ae^{\sigma_n t}\, e^{j\omega_n t}$. The response $e^{\sigma_n t}$ is an exponentially increasing or decreasing function. The response $e^{j\omega_n t}$ is a sinusoidal function. Hence, the response of the product of these responses will be over-damped sinusoids or under-damped sinusoids (Fig. 11.88).

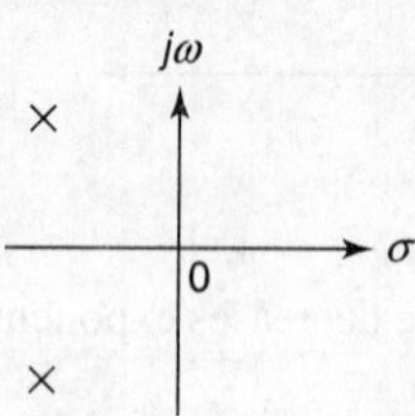

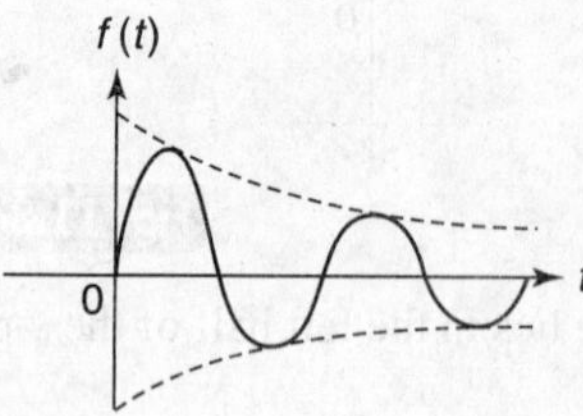


(a)

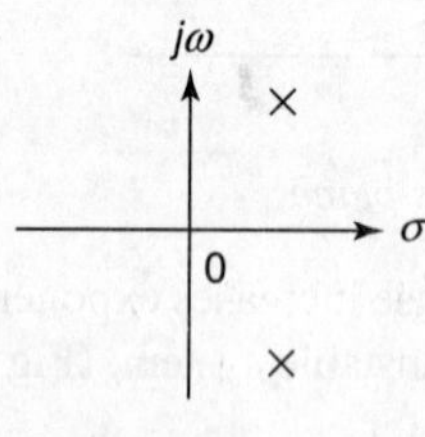

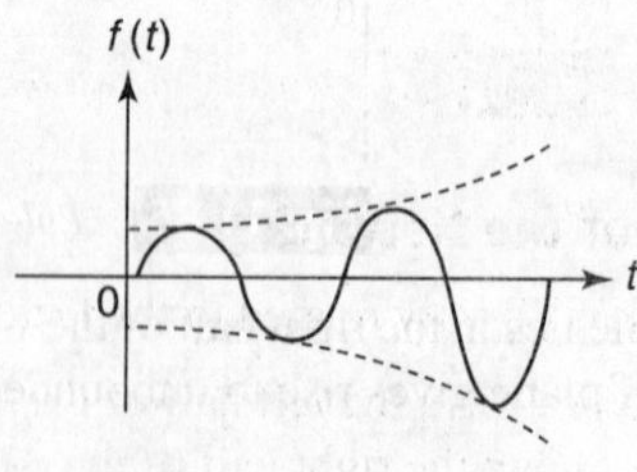


(b)

**Fig. 11.88** *(a) Complex conjugate poles in left half of the s-plane*
*(b) Complex conjugate poles in right half of the s-plane*

(vi) The real part of $s$ of the pole is the displacement of the pole from the imaginary axis. Since $\sigma$ is also the damping factor, a greater value of $\sigma$ (i.e., a greater displacement of the pole from the imaginary axis) means that response decays more rapidly with time. The poles with greater displacement from the real axis correspond to higher frequency of oscillation (Fig. 11.89).

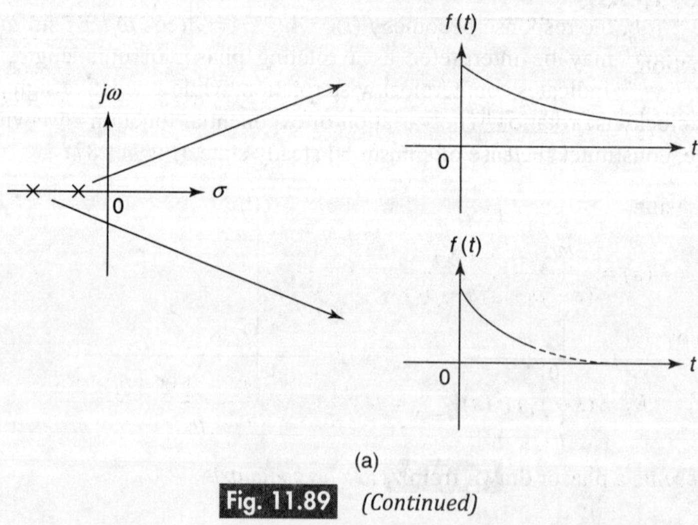


(a)

**Fig. 11.89** *(Continued)*

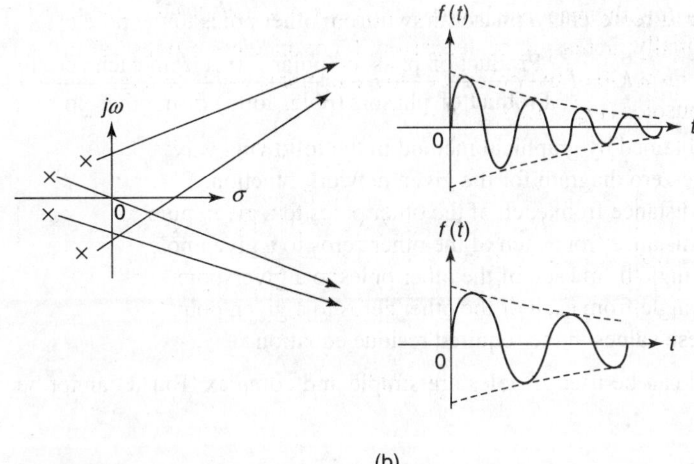


(b)

**Fig. 11.89** *Nature of response with different positions of poles*

### 11.10.1 Stability of the Network

Stability of the network is directly related to the location of poles in the $s$-plane.

(i) When all the poles lie in the left half of the $s$-plane, the network is said to be stable.

(ii) When the poles lie in the right half of the $s$-plane, the network is said to be unstable.

(iii) When the poles lie on the $j\omega$-axis, the network is said to be marginally stable.

(iv) When there are multiple poles on the $j\omega$-axis, the network is said to be unstable.

(v) When the poles move away from $j\omega$-axis towards the left half of the $s$-plane, the relative stability of the network improves.

## 11.11 GRAPHICAL METHOD FOR DETERMINATION OF RESIDUE

LO 11.8

Describe the graphical method for determination of residue

Consider a network function,

$$F(s) = H\frac{(s-z_1)(s-z_2)\cdots(s-z_n)}{(s-p_1)(s-p_2)\cdots(s-p_m)}$$

By partial fraction expansion,

$$F(s) = \frac{K_1}{(s-p_1)} + \frac{K_2}{(s-p_2)} + \cdots + \frac{K_m}{(s-p_m)}$$

The residue $K_i$ is given by

$$K_i = (s-p_i)F(s)\big|_{s\to p_i} = H\frac{(p_i-z_1)(p_i-z_2)\cdots(p_i-z_n)}{(p_i-p_1)(p_i-p_2)\cdots(p_i-p_m)}$$

Each term $(p_i - z_i)$ represents a phasor drawn from zero $z_i$ to pole $p_i$.

Each term $(p_i - p_k)$, $i \neq k$, represents a phasor drawn from other poles to the pole $p_i$.

$$K_i = H\frac{\text{Product of phasors (polar form) from each zero to } p_i}{\text{Product of phasors (polar form) from other poles to } p_i}$$

The residues can be obtained by graphical method in the following way:

1. Draw the pole-zero diagram for the given network function.
2. Measure the distance from each of the other poles to a given pole.
3. Measure the distance from each of the other zeros to a given pole.
4. Measure the angle from each of the other poles to a given pole.
5. Measure the angle from each of the other zeros to a given pole.
6. Substitute these values in the required residue equation.

The graphical method can be used if poles are simple and complex. But it cannot be used when there are multiple poles.

## EXAMPLE 11.43

*The current I(s) in a network is given by* $I(s) = \dfrac{2s}{(s+1)(s+2)}$. *Plot the pole-zero pattern in the s-plane and hence, obtain i(t).*

**Solution** Poles are at $s = -1$ and $s = -2$ and zero is at $s = 0$. The pole-zero plot is shown in Fig. 11.90.

Fig. 11.90

By partial-fraction expansion,

$$I(s) = \frac{K_1}{s+1} + \frac{K_2}{s+2}$$

The coefficients $K_1$ and $K_2$, often referred as residues, can be evaluated from he pole-zero diagram. From Fig. 11.91,

$$K_1 = H\frac{\text{Phasor from zero at origin to pole at } A}{\text{Phasor from pole at } B \text{ to pole at } A} = 2\left(\frac{1\angle 180^\circ}{1\angle 0^\circ}\right) = 2\angle 180^\circ = -2$$

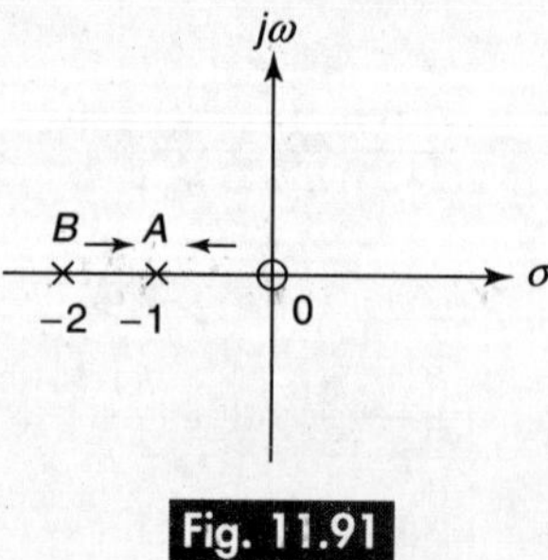


Fig. 11.91

From Fig. 11.92,

$$K_2 = H\frac{\text{Phasor from zero at origin to pole at } B}{\text{Phasor from pole at } A \text{ to pole at } B} = 2\left(\frac{2\angle 180^\circ}{1\angle 180^\circ}\right) = 4$$

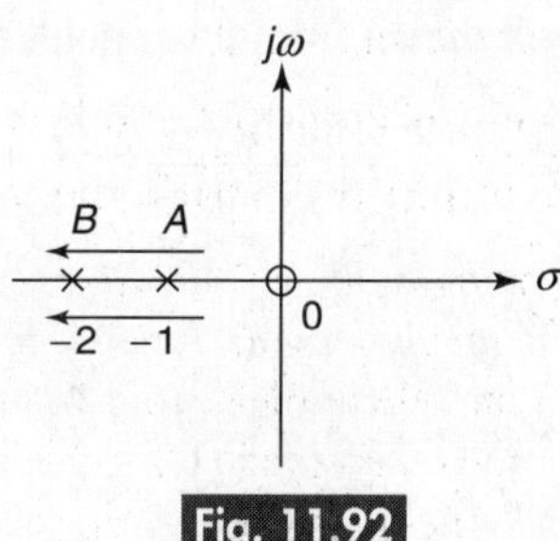

Fig. 11.92

$$I(s) = -\frac{2}{s+1} + \frac{4}{s+2}$$

Taking inverse Laplace transform,

$$i(t) = -2e^{-t} + 4e^{-2t}$$

**EXAMPLE 11.44**

*The voltage V(s) of a network is given by*

$$V(s) = \frac{3s}{(s+2)(s^2+2s+2)}$$

*Plot its pole-zero diagram and hence, obtain v (t).*

**Solution**

$$V(s) = \frac{3s}{(s+2)(s^2+2s+2)} = \frac{3s}{(s+2)(s+1+j1)(s+1-j1)}$$

Poles are at $s = -2$ and $s = -1 \pm j1$ and zero is at $s = 0$, as shown in Fig. 11.93.

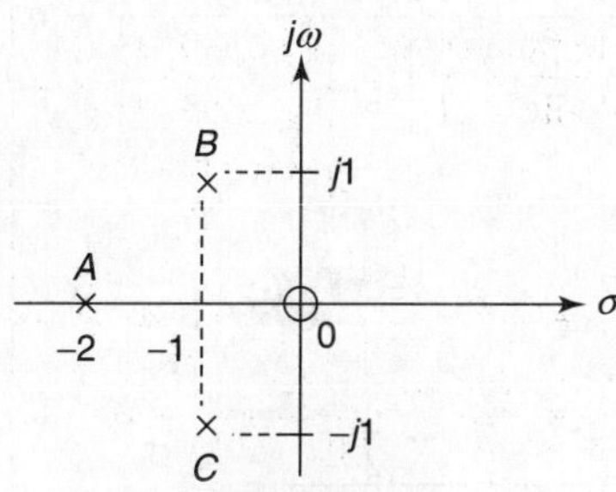

Fig. 11.93

By partial-fraction expansion,

$$V(s) = \frac{K_1}{s+2} + \frac{K_2}{s+1-j1} + \frac{K_2^*}{s+1+j1}$$

The coefficients $K_1$, $K_2$ and $K_2^*$ can be evaluated from the pole-zero diagram.

From Fig. 11.94,

$$K_1 = \frac{3\,(\overline{OA})}{(\overline{BA})\,(\overline{CA})} = 3\left[\frac{2\angle 180°}{(\sqrt{2}\angle -135°)\,(\sqrt{2}\angle 135°)}\right] = 3\sqrt{180°} = -3$$

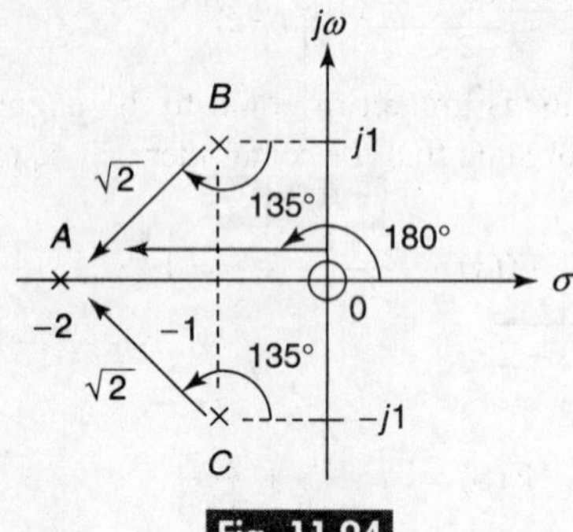


Fig. 11.94

From Fig. 11.95,

$$K_2 = \frac{3\,(\overline{OB})}{(\overline{AB})\,(\overline{CB})} = 3\left[\frac{(\sqrt{2}\angle 135°)}{(\sqrt{2}\angle 45°)\,(2\angle 90°)}\right] = \frac{3}{2}$$

$$K_2^* = \frac{3}{2}$$

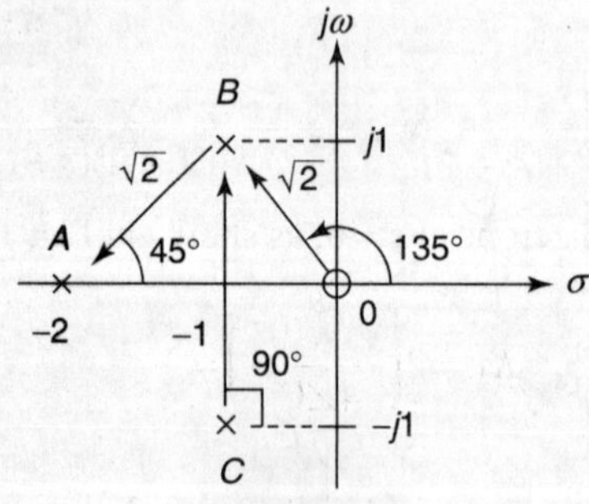


Fig. 11.95

$$V(s) = -\frac{3}{(s+2)} + \frac{\frac{3}{2}}{(s+1-j1)} + \frac{\frac{3}{2}}{(s+1+j1)}$$

Taking inverse Laplace transform,

$$v(t) = -3e^{-2t} + \frac{3}{2}\left[e^{(-1+j1)t} + e^{(-1-j1)t}\right] = -3e^{-2t} + 2\times\frac{3}{2}e^{-t}\left(\frac{e^{j1}+e^{-j1}}{2}\right) = -3e^{-2t} + 3e^{-t}\cos t$$

## EXAMPLE 11.45

*Find the function v(t) using the pole-zero plot of following function:*

$$V(s) = \frac{(s+2)(s+6)}{(s+1)(s+5)}$$

**Solution** If the degree of the numerator is greater or equal to the degree of the denominator, we have to divide the numerator by the denominator such that the remainder can be expanded into partial fractions.

$$V(s) = \frac{s^2+8s+12}{s^2+6s+5} = 1 + \frac{2s+7}{s^2+6s+5} = 1 + \frac{2(s+3.5)}{(s+1)(s+5)}$$

By partial fraction expansion,

$$V(s) = 1 + \frac{K_1}{s+1} + \frac{K_2}{s+5}$$

$K_1$ and $K_2$ can be evaluated from the pole-zero diagram shown in Fig. 11.96 and Fig. 11.97.

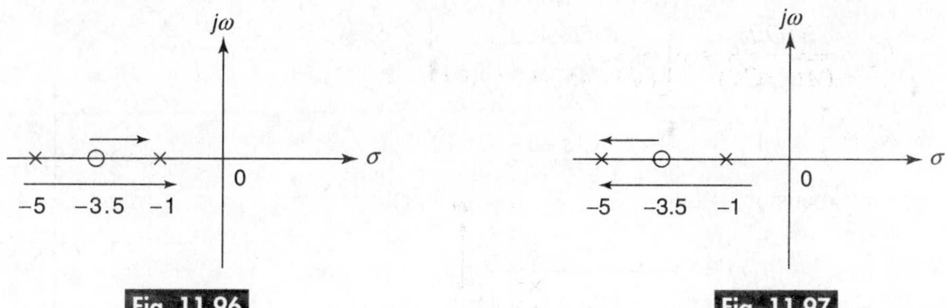


Fig. 11.96 Fig. 11.97

From Fig. 11.96

$$K_1 = 2\left(\frac{2.5\angle 0°}{4\angle 0°}\right) = \frac{5}{4}$$

From Fig. 11.97

$$K_2 = 2\left(\frac{1.5\angle 180°}{4\angle 180°}\right) = \frac{3}{4}$$

$$V(s) = 1 + \frac{\frac{5}{4}}{s+1} + \frac{\frac{3}{4}}{s+5}$$

Taking inverse Laplace transform,

$$v(t) = \delta(t) + \frac{5}{4}e^{-t} + \frac{3}{4}e^{-5t}$$

## EXAMPLE 11.46

*The pole-zero plot of the current I(s) of a network is shown in Fig. 11.98. Find the time-domain response.*

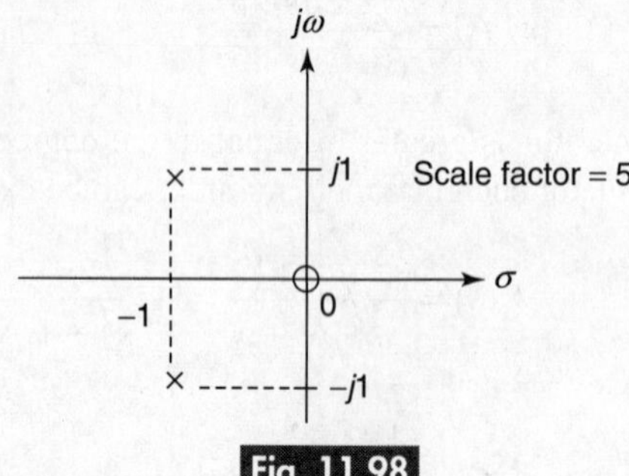


Fig. 11.98

**Solution** The function $I(s)$ has poles at $s = -1 + j1$ and $s = -1 - j1$ and zero at $s = 0$.

$$I(s) = H\frac{s}{(s+1+j1)(s+1-j1)}$$

Scale factor $\qquad H = 5$

$$I(s) = \frac{5s}{(s+1+j1)(s+1-j1)}$$

By partial fraction expansion,

$$I(s) = \frac{K_1}{s+1+j1} + \frac{K_1^*}{s+1-j1}$$

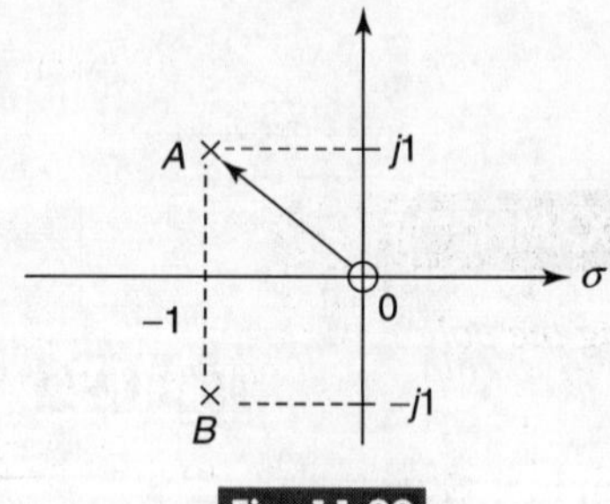


Fig. 11.99

The coefficients $K_1$ and $K_1^*$ can be evaluated from the pole-zero diagram. From Fig. 11.99,

$$K_1 = \frac{5\,(\overline{OA})}{(\overline{BA})} = \frac{5\,(\sqrt{2}\angle 135°)}{2\angle 90°} = 3.54\angle 45°$$

$$K_1^* = 3.54\angle -45°$$

$$I(s) = \frac{3.54\angle 45°}{s+1+j1} + \frac{3.54\angle -45°}{s+1-j1}$$

Taking inverse Laplace transform,

$$i(t) = 3.54\angle 45°\, e^{(-1-j1)t} + 3.54\angle -45° e^{(-1+j1)t}$$

## EXAMPLE 11.47

*Evaluate amplitude and phase of the network function* $F(s) = \dfrac{4s}{s^2 + 2s + 2}$ *from the pole-zero plot at* $s = j2$.

**Solution**

$$F(s) = \frac{4s}{s^2 + 2s + 2} = \frac{4s}{(s+1+j1)(s+1-j1)}$$

The pole-zero plot is shown in Fig. 11.100.

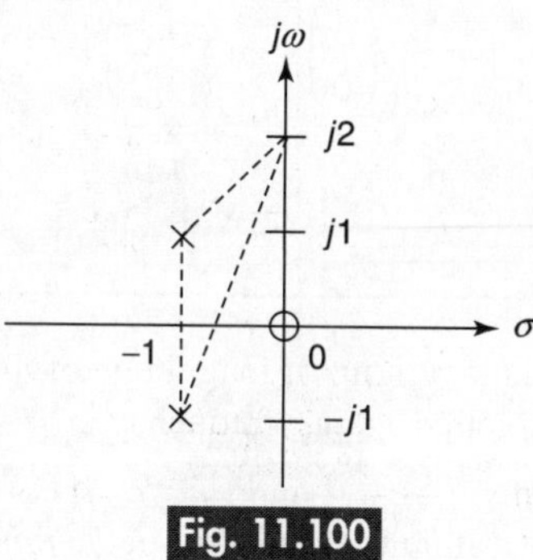


Fig. 11.100

At $s = j2$,

$$|F(j2)| = \frac{\text{Product of phasor magnitudes from all zero to } j2}{\text{Product of phasor magnitudes from all poles to } j2} = \frac{2}{(\sqrt{2})(\sqrt{10})} = 0.447$$

$$\phi(\omega) = \tan^{-1}\left(\frac{2}{0}\right) - \tan^{-1}\left(\frac{3}{1}\right) - \tan^{-1}\left(\frac{1}{1}\right) = 90° - 71.56° - 45° = -26.56°$$

**EXAMPLE 11.48**

*Using the pole-zero plot, find magnitude and phase of the function*

$$F(s) = \frac{(s+1)(s+3)}{s(s+2)} \text{ at } s = j4.$$

**Solution**

$$F(s) = \frac{(s+1)(s+3)}{s(s+2)}$$

The pole-zero plot is shown in Fig. 11.101.

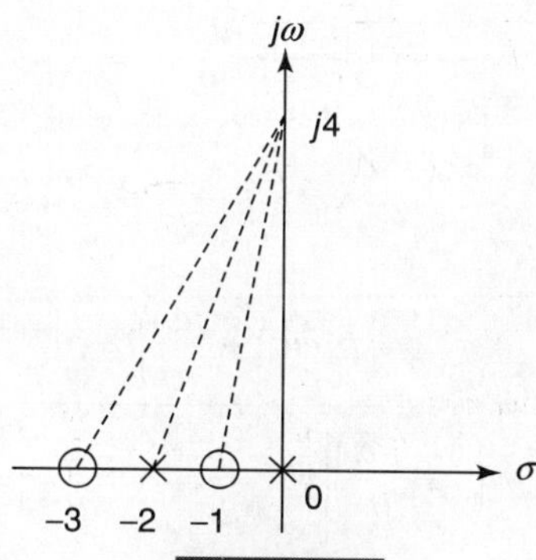


Fig. 11.101

At $s = j4$,

$$|F(j4)| = \frac{\text{Product of phasor magnitudes from all zeros to } j4}{\text{product of phasor magnitudes from all poles to } j4} = \frac{(5)(\sqrt{17})}{(\sqrt{20})(4)} = 1.15$$

$$\phi(\omega) = \tan^{-1}\left(\frac{4}{1}\right) + \tan^{-1}\left(\frac{4}{3}\right) - \tan^{1}\left(\frac{4}{0}\right) - \tan^{-1}\left(\frac{4}{2}\right) = 75.96° + 53.13° - 90° - 63.43° = -24.34°$$

## 11.12 BODE PLOT

LO 11.9

Draw the Bode plots for network functions

Bode plot consists of two graphs, one is logarithm of magnitude of $F(j\omega)$ and the other is phase angle of $F(j\omega)$, both plotted against frequency in logarithmic scale.

The standard representation of the logarithmic magnitude of $F(j\omega)$ is 20 log $|F(j\omega)|$, where the base of logarithm is 10. The unit of magnitude 20 log $|F(j\omega)|$ is decibel, abbreviated as db. The curves are normally drawn on semilog paper using log scale for frequency and linear scale for magnitude in db and phase in degrees. The main advantage of using logarithmic plot is that multiplication of magnitudes can be converted into addition.

In Bode plot, frequency ratios are expressed in terms of octaves or decades. An octal is a frequency band from $\omega_1$ to $2\omega_1$, where $\omega_1$ is any frequency. A decade is a frequency band from $\omega_1$ to 10 $\omega_1$. On the logarithmic scale of semilog paper, any given frequency ratio can be represented by same horizontal distance. For example, the horizontal distances from $\omega = 1$ to $\omega = 10$ is equal to that from $\omega = 5$ to $\omega = 50$.

Consider a transfer function $F(s)$ given by

$$F(s) = \frac{Hs(s+a)}{(s+b)(s^2+\alpha s+\beta^2)}$$

$$= \frac{H \cdot a \cdot s\left(1+\frac{s}{a}\right)}{b \cdot \beta^2 \cdot \left(1+\frac{s}{b}\right)\left(1+\frac{\alpha}{\beta^2}s+\frac{1}{\beta^2}s^2\right)}$$

$$= \frac{Ks\left(1+\frac{s}{a}\right)}{\left(1+\frac{s}{b}\right)\left(1+\frac{\alpha}{\beta^2}s+\frac{1}{\beta^2}s^2\right)}$$

Putting $s = j\omega$,

$$F(j\omega) = \frac{Kj\omega\left(1+\frac{j\omega}{a}\right)}{\left(1+\frac{j\omega}{b}\right)\left[\left(1-\frac{\omega^2}{\beta^2}\right)+j\frac{\alpha\omega}{\beta^2}\right]}$$

The magnitude of $F(j\omega)$ in db is written as

$$20 \log|F(j\omega)| = 20 \log K + 20 \log|j\omega| + 20 \log\left|1+\frac{j\omega}{a}\right| - 20 \log\left|1+\frac{j\omega}{b}\right| - 20 \log\left|\left(\frac{1-\omega^2}{\beta^2}\right)+j\frac{\alpha\omega}{\beta^2}\right|$$

The phase angle of $F(j\omega)$ is written as

$$\phi(\omega) = \angle F(j\omega) = \angle K + \angle j\omega + \angle\left(1+\frac{j\omega}{a}\right) - \angle\left(1+\frac{j\omega}{b}\right) - \angle\left[\left(1-\frac{\omega^2}{\beta^2}\right)+j\frac{\alpha\omega}{\beta^2}\right]$$

The basic factors that frequently occur in any function $F(j\omega)$ are

(a) Constant $K$

(b) Root at the origin, $j\omega$

(c) Simple real root, $1+\dfrac{j\omega}{a}$

(d) Complex conjugate root $\left[\left(1-\dfrac{\omega^2}{\beta^2}\right)+j\dfrac{\alpha\omega}{\beta^2}\right]$

If these factors are in the numerator, their magnitudes in db and phase angle in degrees carry positive signs. If these factors belong to the denominator, their magnitudes in db and phase angle in degrees carry negative signs.

1. Constant $K$: $F(j\omega) = K$
   The magnitude of $K$ in db is given by
   $$20 \log |F(j\omega)| = 20 \log K = M \text{ db}$$
   M is positive if $K > 1$ and negative if $K < 1$. Thus, the magnitude plot for constant $K$ is a straight line at the magnitude of $20 \log K$ db.
   The phase angle $\phi(\omega)$ is either 0° or −180°, depending on whether $K$ is positive or negative. The magnitude and phase for constant $K$ are shown in Fig. 11.102(a).

2. Factor $j\omega$: $F(j\omega) = j\omega$
   The magnitude of $j\omega$ in db is given by
   $$20 \log | F(j\omega)| = 20 \log | j\omega | = 20 \log \omega \text{ db}$$
   Thus, the magnitude plot for $j\omega$ is a straight line with slope of 20 db/decade passing through 0 db at $\omega = 1$. The phase angle $\phi(\omega)$ of $j\omega$ is given by
   $$\phi(\omega) = 90°$$
   For factor $(j\omega)^n$, magnitude in db is given by
   $$20 \log | (j\omega)^n | = n \times 20 \log | j\omega | = 20\, n \log \omega \text{ db}$$
   Thus, magnitude plot of $(j\omega)^n$ is a straight line with slope of $20\,n$ db/decade passing through 0 db at $\omega = 1$. The phase angle of $(j\omega)^n$ is equal to $90°\, n$ for all $\omega$. The magnitude plot and phase plots for $(j\omega)^n$ are shown in Fig. 11.102(b).

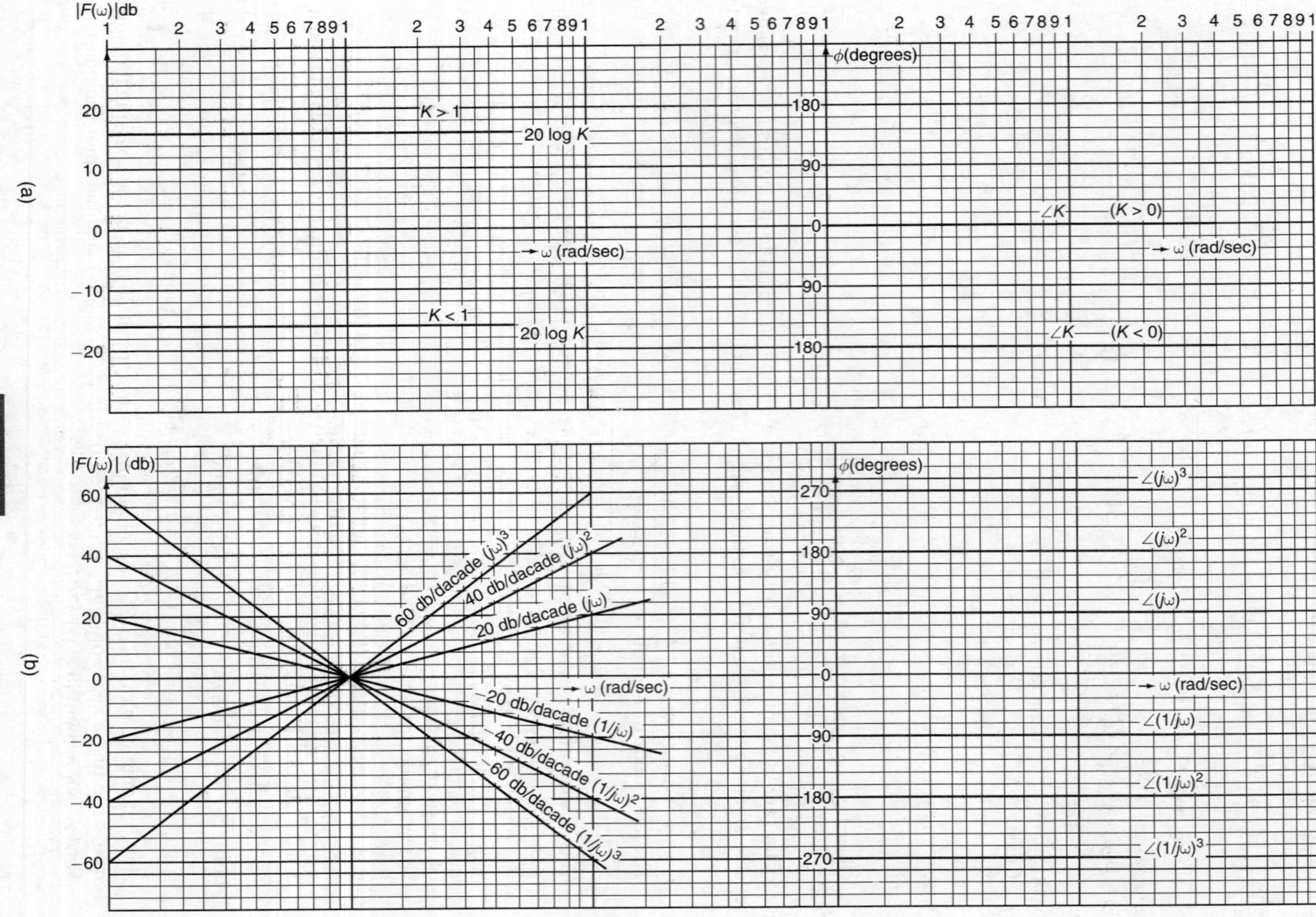
|F(ω)|db
20
10
0
−10
−20
K > 1
20 log K
K < 1
20 log K
→ ω (rad/sec)
φ(degrees)
180
90
0
90
180
∠K (K > 0)
∠K (K < 0)
→ ω (rad/sec)
(a)
|F(jω)| (db)
60
40
20
0
−20
−40
−60
60 db/dacade (jω)^3
40 db/dacade (jω)^2
20 db/dacade (jω)
→ ω (rad/sec)
−20 db/dacade (1/jω)
−40 db/dacade (1/jω)^2
−60 db/dacade (1/jω)^3
φ(degrees)
270
180
90
0
90
180
270
∠(jω)^3
∠(jω)^2
∠(jω)
→ ω (rad/sec)
∠(1/jω)
∠(1/jω)^2
∠(1/jω)^3
(b)

Fig. 11.102

3. Factor $\left(1+\frac{j\omega}{a}\right)$: $F(j\omega)=1+\frac{j\omega}{a}$

The magnitude of $F(j\omega)$ in db is given by

$$20 \log |F(j\omega)| = 20\log\left|1+\frac{j\omega}{a}\right| = 20\log\sqrt{1+\frac{\omega^2}{a^2}} \text{ db}$$

For low frequencies, i.e., $\frac{\omega}{a} << 1$,

$$20 \log |F(j\omega)| = 20 \log 1 = 0 \text{ db}$$

For high frequencies, i.e., $\frac{\omega}{a} >> 1$,

$$20 \log F(j\omega) = 20 \log \frac{\omega}{a} \text{ db}$$

Thus, magnitude plot can be approximated by two straight-line asymptotes, one a straight-line at 0 db for the frequency range $0 < \omega < a$ and other a straight line with slope of 20 db/dec for frequency range $a < \omega < \infty$. The frequency at which the two asymptotes meet is called corner or break frequency.

The phase angle of $\left(1+\frac{j\omega}{a}\right)$ is given by

$$\phi(\omega) = \tan^{-1}\frac{\omega}{a}$$

At zero frequency, the phase angle is 0°. At the corner frequency, i.e., at $\omega = a$, $\phi(\omega) = \tan^{-1}\frac{\omega}{a} =$ 45°. At infinity, the phase angle is 90°. Thus, phase angle varies from 0° to 90°.

Similarly, for the factor $\left(1+\frac{j\omega}{a}\right)^n$, the magnitude plot can be approximated by two straight-line asymptotes, one a straight line at 0 db for $0 < \omega < a$ and other a straight line with slope of 20 $n$ db/decade for frequency range $a < \omega < \infty$. The phase angle will be $n$ times $\tan^{-1}\frac{\omega}{a}$.

The magnitude and phase plots for function $(1+j\omega)$ and $\frac{1}{(1+j\omega)}$ shown in Fig. 11.103.

4. Quadratic factor $\left[\left(1-\frac{\omega^2}{\beta^2}\right)+j\frac{\alpha\omega}{\beta^2}\right]$: $F(\omega)=1-\frac{\omega^2}{\beta^2}+j\frac{\alpha\omega}{\beta^2}$

The magnitude of $F(j\omega)$ in db is given by

$$20\log|F(j\omega)| = 20\log\left|1-\frac{\omega^2}{\beta^2}+j\frac{\alpha\omega}{\beta^2}\right| = 20\log\sqrt{\left(1-\frac{\omega^2}{\beta^2}\right)^2+\left(\frac{\alpha\omega}{\beta^2}\right)^2}$$

For low frequencies, i.e., $\frac{\omega}{\beta} <<1$,

$$20 \log |F(j\omega)| = 20 \log 1 = 0 \text{ db}$$

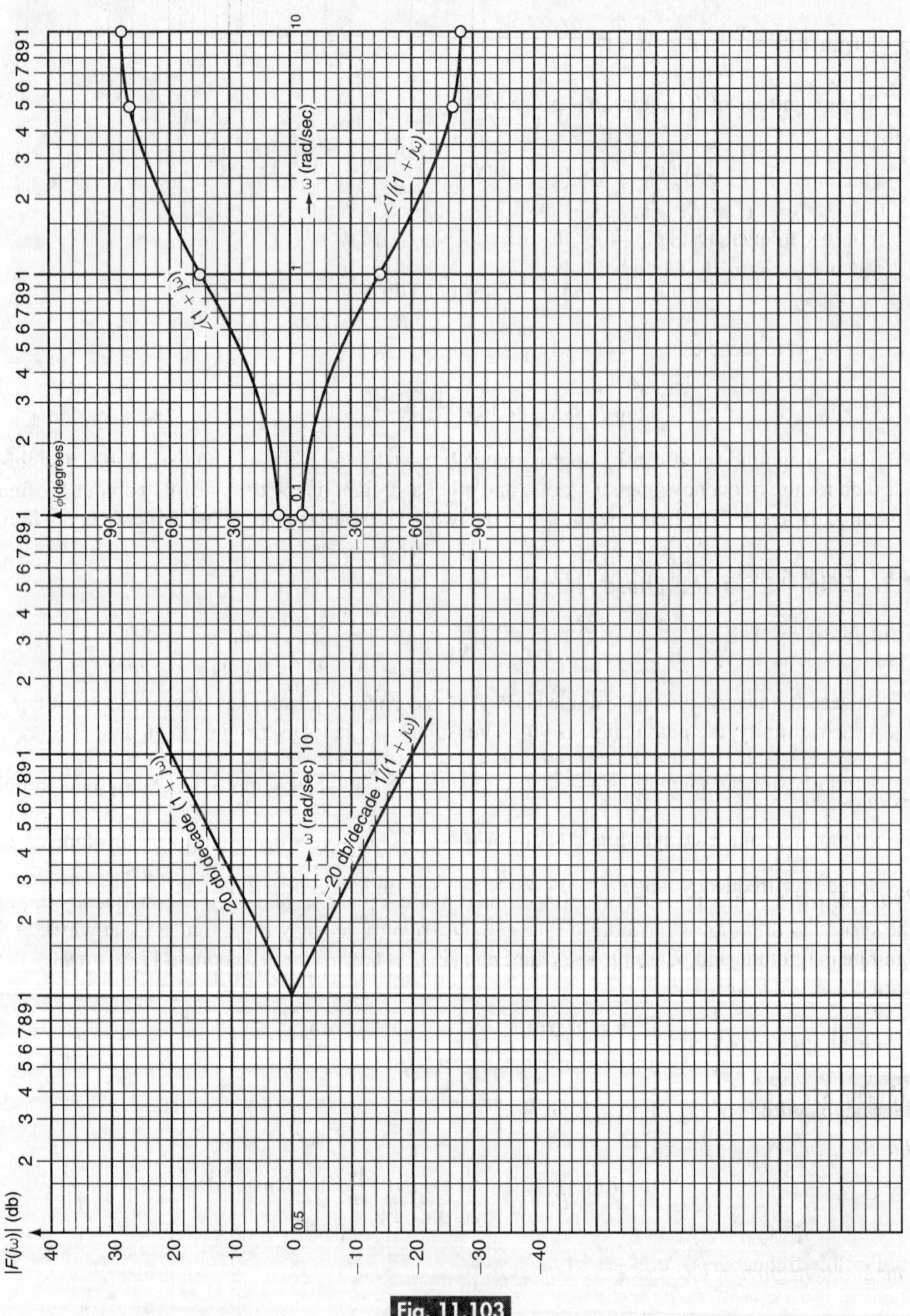
|F(jω)| (db)
φ(degrees)
→ ω (rad/sec)
20 db/decade (1 + jω)
–20 db/decade 1/(1 + jω)
∠(1 + jω)
∠1/(1 + jω)

Fig. 11.103

For high frequencies, i.e., $\frac{\omega}{\beta} >> 1$,

$$20 \log |F(j\omega)| = 20 \log \frac{\omega^2}{\beta^2} = 40 \log \frac{\omega}{\beta} \text{ db}$$

Thus, magnitude plot can be approximated by two straight-line asymptotes, one a straight line at 0 db for the frequency range $0 < \omega < \beta$ and other a straight line with slope of 40 db/decade. For frequency range $\beta < \omega < \infty$, the corner frequency is at $\omega = \beta$.
The phase angle of $F(j\omega)$ is given by

$$\phi(\omega) = \tan^{-1} \frac{\frac{\alpha\omega}{\beta^2}}{1 - \frac{\omega^2}{\beta^2}}$$

$$= \tan^{-1}\left(\frac{\alpha\omega}{\beta^2 - \omega^2}\right)$$

### 11.12.1 Gain Margin and Phase Margin

➤ ***Gain Margin*** It is the factor by which the gain can be increased to bring the system to the verge of instability. Gain margin is defined as the reciprocal of the gain at the frequency at which the phase angle becomes −180°. The frequency at which the phase angle is −180° is called phase crossover frequency.

$$\text{Gain margin} = \frac{1}{|F(j\omega)|}$$

In terms of decibel,

$$\text{Gain margin (db)} = -20 \log |F(j\omega)|$$

➤ ***Phase Margin*** It is that amount of additional phase lag at the gain crossover frequency required to bring the system to the verge of instability. The gain crossover frequency is the frequency at which $|F(j\omega)|$, the magnitude of the function, is unity. The phase margin is 180° plus the phase angle of the transfer function at the gain crossover frequency.

$$\text{Phase margin} = 180° + \phi$$

**EXAMPLE 11.49**

*Draw the Bode plot for the function*

$$F(s) = \frac{10(s+10)}{s(s+2)(s+5)}$$

*Calculate gain margin and phase margin.*

## Solution

***Step 1:*** Write $F(s)$ in standard form.

$$F(s)=\frac{10\times10\left(1+\frac{s}{10}\right)}{2\times5\times s\left(1+\frac{s}{2}\right)\left(1+\frac{s}{5}\right)}$$

$$=\frac{10\left(1+\frac{s}{10}\right)}{s\left(1+\frac{s}{2}\right)\left(1+\frac{s}{5}\right)}$$

Putting $s=j\omega$,

$$F(j\omega)=\frac{10\left(1+\frac{j\omega}{10}\right)}{j\omega\left(1+\frac{j\omega}{2}\right)\left(1+\frac{j\omega}{5}\right)}$$

$$20\log|F(j\omega)|=20\log10-20\log|j\omega|-20\log\left|1+\frac{j\omega}{2}\right|-20\log\left|1+\frac{j\omega}{5}\right|+20\log\left|1+\frac{j\omega}{10}\right|$$

***Step 2:*** Write down each factor in order of their occurrence as frequency increase in the table.

| *No.* | *Factor* | *Corner frequency* | *Magnitude characteristic* |
|---|---|---|---|
| 1 | 10 | – | Straight line of magnitude 20 log 10 = 20 db |
| 2 | $\frac{1}{j\omega}$ | – | Straight line of slope −20 db/decade passing through 0 db at $\omega = 1$. |
| 3 | $\frac{1}{1+\frac{j\omega}{2}}$ | 2 | Straight line of 0 db for $\omega < 2$, straight line of slope −20 db/decade for $\omega > 2$. |
| 4 | $\frac{1}{1+\frac{j\omega}{5}}$ | 5 | Straight line of 0 db for $\omega < 5$, straight line of slope −20 db/decade for $\omega > 5$. |
| 5 | $1+\frac{j\omega}{10}$ | 10 | Straight line of 0 db for $\omega < 10$, straight line of slope 20 db/decade for $\omega > 10$. |

***Step 3:*** Draw all the factors clearly on semilog paper.

***Step 4:*** Add all the factors in following manner given below.

(i) We start the with left-most point. The factor 10 raises the magnitude curve of factor $\frac{1}{j\omega}$ by the amount 20 log 10 = 20 db. It shifts the plot of $\frac{1}{j\omega}$ to 40 db with same slope − 20 db/dec.

(ii) Let us now add the plot of the factor $\frac{1}{\left(1+\frac{j\omega}{2}\right)}$ corresponding to the lowest corner frequency $\omega = 2$. Since this factor contributes 0 db for $\omega < 2$, the resultant plot upto $\omega = 2$ is same as that of the combination of 10 and $\frac{1}{j\omega}$. From $\omega > 2$, this factor contributes –20 db/decade such that the resultant plot of these three factors is the straight line of slope (–20) + (–20) = − 40 db/decade upto next corner frequency $\omega = 5$.

(iii) Above $\omega = 5$, the factor $\frac{1}{\left(1+\frac{j\omega}{5}\right)}$ is effective. This gives rise to a straight line of slope − 20 db/decade for $\omega > 5$, which when added results in a straight line with a slope of (− 40) + (− 20) = − 60 db/decade from $\omega = 5$ to next corner frequency $\omega = 10$.

(iv) Above $\omega = \frac{5}{10}$, the plot of $\left(1+\frac{j\omega}{10}\right)$ is to be added. This factor gives rise to a straight line of slope 20 db/decade for $\omega > 10$, which when added results in a straight line having a slope of (–60) + 20 = –40 db/decade from $\omega = 10$ to $\omega = \infty$.

***Step 5:*** Draw the phase plot with the help of table drawn for phase angle $\phi(\omega)$.

$$\phi(\omega) = 0 - 90° - \tan^{-1}\frac{\omega}{2} - \tan^{-1}\frac{\omega}{5} + \tan^{-1}\frac{\omega}{10}$$

$$= \tan^{-1}\frac{\omega}{10} - \left(\tan^{-1}\frac{\omega}{2} + \tan^{-1}\frac{\omega}{5} + 90°\right)$$

Magnitude and phase plots, drawn on semilog paper is shown in Fig. 11.104.

***Phase Margin:*** Unity gain occurs at $\omega = 4.6$ rad/sec. This is gain crossover frequency. Phase corresponding to $\omega = 4.6$ rad/sec is –171°.

$$\text{Phase margin} = 180° + \phi = 180° - 171° = 9°$$

***Gain Margin:*** Phase plot has phase of –180° at $\omega = 6$ rad/sec

At $\omega_p = 6$ rad/sec, gain margin = 6 db

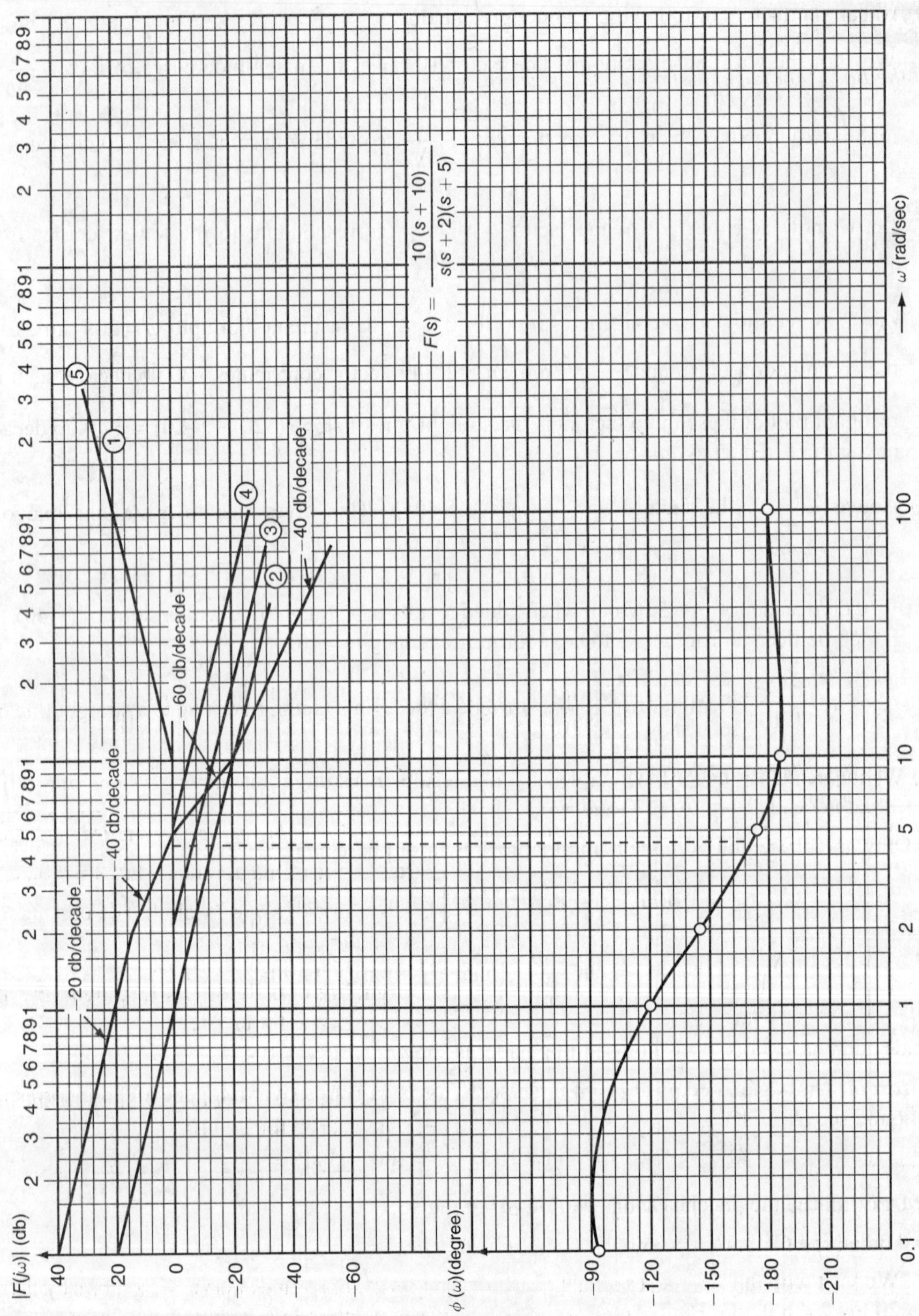

$F(s) = \dfrac{10(s+10)}{s(s+2)(s+5)}$
|F(jω)| (db)
ϕ (ω)(degree)
ω (rad/sec)
–20 db/decade
–40 db/decade
–60 db/decade
–40 db/decade
1
2
3
4
5


Fig. 11.104

## EXAMPLE 11.50

*Sketch the Bode plot for the following transfer function,*

$$F(s) = \frac{20s}{(s+1)(s+10)}$$

**Solution**

***Step 1:*** Write $F(s)$ in standard form.

$$F(s) = \frac{20s}{10(1+s)\left(1+\frac{s}{10}\right)}$$

$$= \frac{2s}{(1+s)\left(1+\frac{s}{10}\right)}$$

Putting $s = j\omega$,

$$F(j\omega) = \frac{2j\omega}{(1+j\omega)\left(1+\frac{j\omega}{10}\right)}$$

$$20\log|F(j\omega)| = 20\log 2 + 20\log|j\omega| - 20\log|1+j\omega| - 20\log\left|\left(1+\frac{j\omega}{10}\right)\right|$$

***Step 2:*** Write down each factor in the table.

| *No.* | *Factor* | *Corner frequency* | *Magnitude characteristic* |
|---|---|---|---|
| 1 | 2 | – | Straight line of magnitude 20 log 2 = 6.02 db |
| 2 | $j\omega$ | – | Straight line of slope 20 db/decade passing through 0 db at $\omega = 1$. |
| 3 | $\frac{1}{1+j\omega}$ | 1 | Straight line of 0 db for $\omega < 1$, straight line of slope –20 db/decade for $\omega > 1$. |
| 4 | $\frac{1}{1+\frac{j\omega}{10}}$ | 10 | Straight line of 0 db for $\omega < 10$, straight line of slope –20 db/decade for $\omega > 10$. |

***Step 3:*** Draw all the factors clearly on semilog paper.

***Step 4:*** Add all the factors in following manner given below.

(i) We start with the left-most point. The factor 2 raises the magnitude curve of factor $j\omega$ by the amount 20 log 2 = 6.02 db. Hence, plot of $j\omega$ starts with the point −14 db approximately having same slope 20 db/decade.

(ii) Now, plot of the factor $\frac{1}{1+j\omega}$ corresponding to corner frequency $\omega = 1$ is added. Since this factor contributes 0 db for $\omega < 1$, the resultant plot upto $\omega = 1$ is same as that of the combination of 2 and $j\omega$. From $\omega = 1$, this factor contributes −20 db/decade such that resultant plot of these three factors is the straight line of slope (−20) + 20 = 0 db/decade upto next corner frequency $\omega = 10$.

(iii) Above $\omega = 10$, the plot of $\frac{1}{1+\frac{j\omega}{10}}$ is to be added. This factor gives rise to a straight line of slope −20 db/decade for $\omega > 10$, which when added results in a straight line having a slope of 0 + (− 20) = −20 db/decade from $\omega = 10$ to $\omega = \infty$.

***Step 5:*** Draw the phase plot with the help of table for $\phi(\omega)$. For any arbitrary value of $\omega$,

$$\phi(\omega) = 0 + 90° - \tan^{-1}\omega - \tan^{-1}\frac{\omega}{10}$$

$$= 90° - \tan^{-1}\omega - \tan^{-1}\frac{\omega}{10}$$

Magnitude and phase plots are shown in Fig. 11.105.

## EXAMPLE 11.51

*Draw the Bode plot for the function*

$$F(s) = \frac{4\left(1+\frac{s}{2}\right)}{s^2\left(1+\frac{s}{8}\right)\left(1+\frac{s}{10}\right)}$$

*Calculate gain margin and phase margin.*

**Solution**

***Step 1:*** Write $F(s)$ in standard form.

$$F(s) = \frac{4\left(1+\frac{s}{2}\right)}{s^2\left(1+\frac{s}{8}\right)\left(1+\frac{s}{10}\right)}$$

Putting $s = j\omega$,

$$F(j\omega) = \frac{4\left(1+\frac{j\omega}{2}\right)}{(j\omega)^2 + \left(1+\frac{j\omega}{8}\right)\left(1+\frac{j\omega}{10}\right)}$$

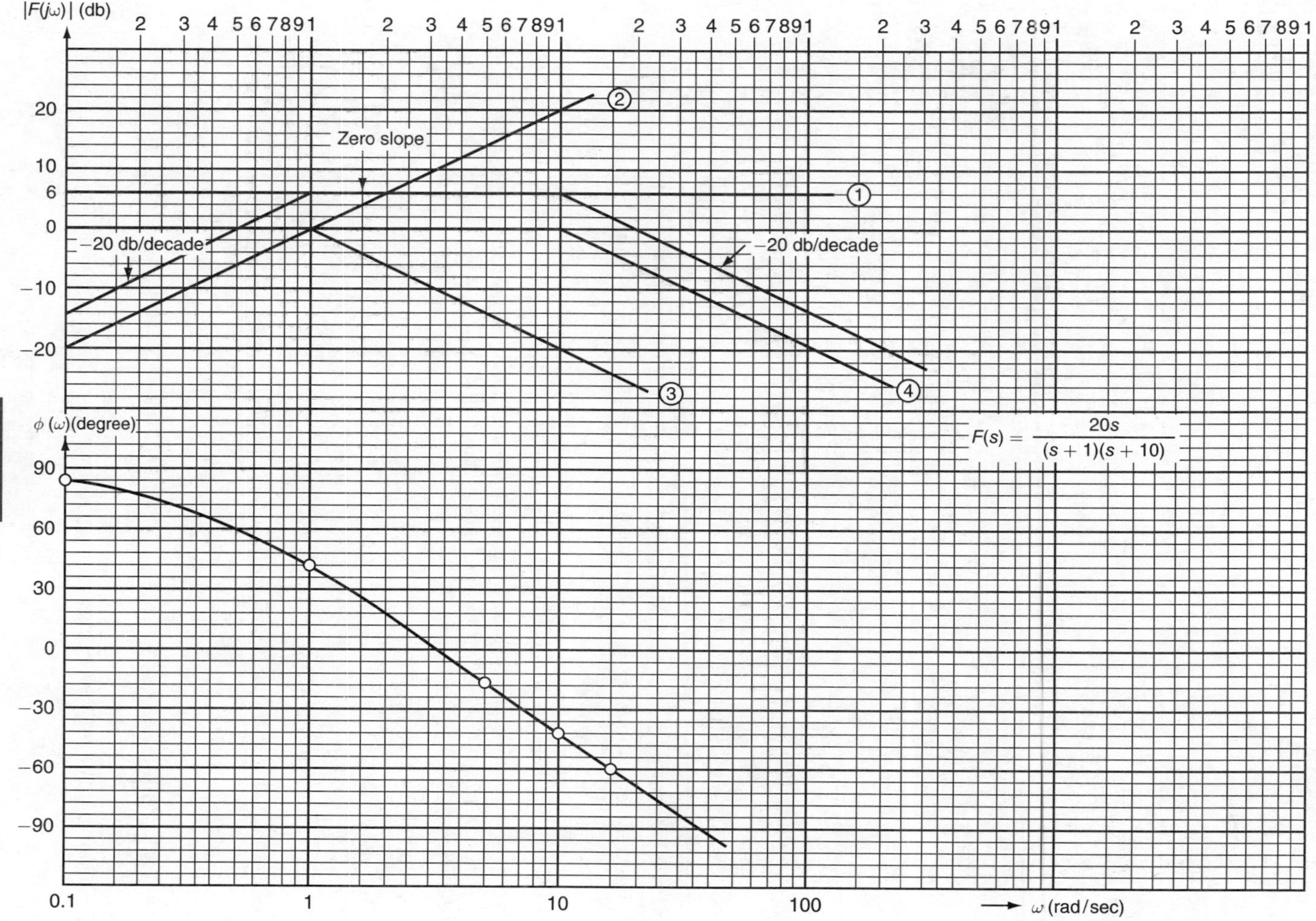

|F(jω)| (db)
20
10
6
0
–10
–20
Zero slope
–20 db/decade
–20 db/decade
1
2
3
4
φ (ω)(degree)
90
60
30
0
–30
–60
–90
F(s) = 20s/((s + 1)(s + 10))
0.1
1
10
100
ω (rad/sec)


Fig. 11.105

$$20\log|F(j\omega)| = 20\log 4 - 20\log|(j\omega)^2| + 20\log\left|\left(1+\frac{j\omega}{2}\right)\right| - 20\log\left|\left(1+\frac{j\omega}{8}\right)\right| - 20\log\left|\left(1+\frac{j\omega}{10}\right)\right|$$

***Step 2:*** Write down each factor in the table.

| *No.* | *Factor* | *Corner frequency* | *Magnitude characteristic* |
|---|---|---|---|
| 1 | 4 | – | Straight line of magnitude 20 log 4 = 12.02 db. |
| 2 | $\frac{1}{(j\omega)^2}$ | – | Straight line of slope –40 db/decade passing through 0 db at $\omega = 1$. |
| 3 | $1+\frac{j\omega}{2}$ | 2 | Straight line of 0 db for $\omega < 2$, straight line of 20 db/decade for $\omega > 2$. |
| 4 | $\frac{1}{1+\frac{j\omega}{8}}$ | 8 | Straight line of db for $\omega < 8$, straight line of –20 db/decade for $\omega > 8$. |
| 5 | $\frac{1}{1+\frac{j\omega}{10}}$ | 10 | Straight line of 0 db for $\omega < 10$, straight line of –20 db/decade for $\omega > 10$. |

***Step 3:*** Draw all the factors clearly.

***Step 4:*** Add all the factors in the same manner as done in the previous problems to get magnitude plot.

***Step 5:*** Draw the phase plot with the help of table for $\phi(\omega)$ for any arbitrary values of $\omega$.

$$\phi(\omega) = -180° + \tan^{-1}\frac{\omega}{2} - \tan^{-1}\frac{\omega}{8} - \tan^{-1}\frac{\omega}{10}$$

Magnitude and phase plots are shown in Fig. 11.106.

***Phase Margin:*** Unity gain occurs at $\omega = 2$ rad/sec. This is gain crossover frequency. Corresponding phase at $\omega = 2$ is −166.28°.

$$\text{Phase margin} = 180 + \phi = 180° + (-166.28°) = 13.72°$$

***Gain Margin:*** Phase plot has phase of −180° at $\omega = 6.6$ rad/sec. This is phase crossover frequency.

$$\text{Gain margin} = 10 \text{ db.}$$

## EXAMPLE 11.52

*Sketch the Bode plot for following function,*

$$F(s) = \frac{200(s+2)}{s(s^2+10s+100)}$$

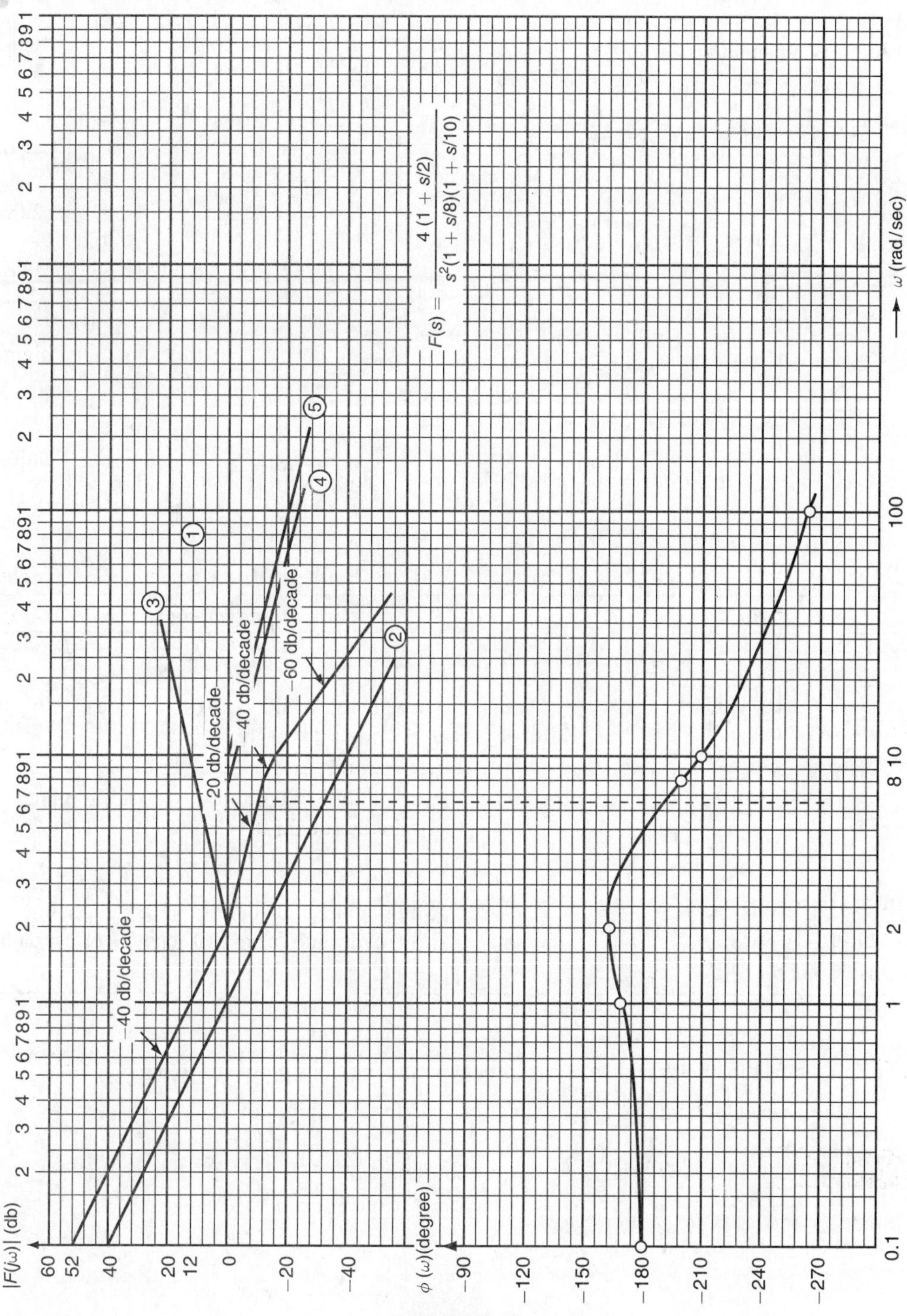
|F(jω)| (db)
60
52
40
20
12
0
−20
−40
φ (ω)(degree)
−90
−120
−150
−180
−210
−240
−270
−40 db/decade
−20 db/decade
−40 db/decade
−60 db/decade
−40 db/decade
1
2
3
4
5
F(s) = 4 (1 + s/2) / s²(1 + s/8)(1 + s/10)
0.1
1
2
8 10
100
→ ω (rad/sec)

Fig. 11.106

## Solution

***Step 1:*** Write $F(s)$ in standard form.

$$F(s)=\frac{200\times 2\left(1+\frac{s}{2}\right)}{100\times s\left(1+\frac{s}{10}+\frac{s^2}{100}\right)}$$

Putting $s=j\omega$,

$$F(j\omega)=\frac{4\left(1+\frac{j\omega}{2}\right)}{j\omega\left[\left(1-\frac{\omega^2}{100}\right)+\frac{j\omega}{10}\right]}$$

$$20\log|F(j\omega)|=20\log 4-20\log|j\omega|+20\log\left|1+\frac{j\omega}{2}\right|-20\log\left|\left(1-\frac{\omega^2}{100}\right)+\frac{j\omega}{10}\right|$$

***Step 2:*** Write down each factor in the table.

| *No.* | *Factor* | *Corner frequency* | *Magnitude characteristic* |
|---|---|---|---|
| 1 | $4$ | – | Straight line of magnitude 20 log 4 = 6.02 db. |
| 2 | $\frac{1}{j\omega}$ | – | Straight line of slope –20 db/decade passing through 0 db at $\omega = 1$. |
| 3 | $1+\frac{j\omega}{2}$ | 2 | Straight line of 0 db for $\omega < 2$, straight line of slope 20 db/decade for $\omega > 2$. |
| 4 | $\frac{1}{\left(1-\frac{\omega^2}{100}\right)+\frac{j\omega}{10}}$ | 10 | Straight line of 0 db for $\omega < 10$, straight line of slope –40 db/decade for $\omega > 10$. |

***Step 3:*** Draw all the factors clearly.

***Step 4:*** Add all the factors in the same manner as done in the previous problems to get magnitude plot.

***Step 5:*** Draw the phase plot with the help of table for $\phi(\omega)$ for any values of $\omega$.

$$\phi(\omega)=0-90^\circ+\tan^{-1}\frac{\omega}{2}-\tan^{-1}\frac{0.1\omega}{1-\frac{\omega^2}{100}}$$

$$=-90^\circ+\tan^{-1}\frac{\omega}{2}-\tan^{-1}\left(\frac{10\omega}{100-\omega^2}\right)$$

Magnitude and phase plots are shown in Fig. 11.107.

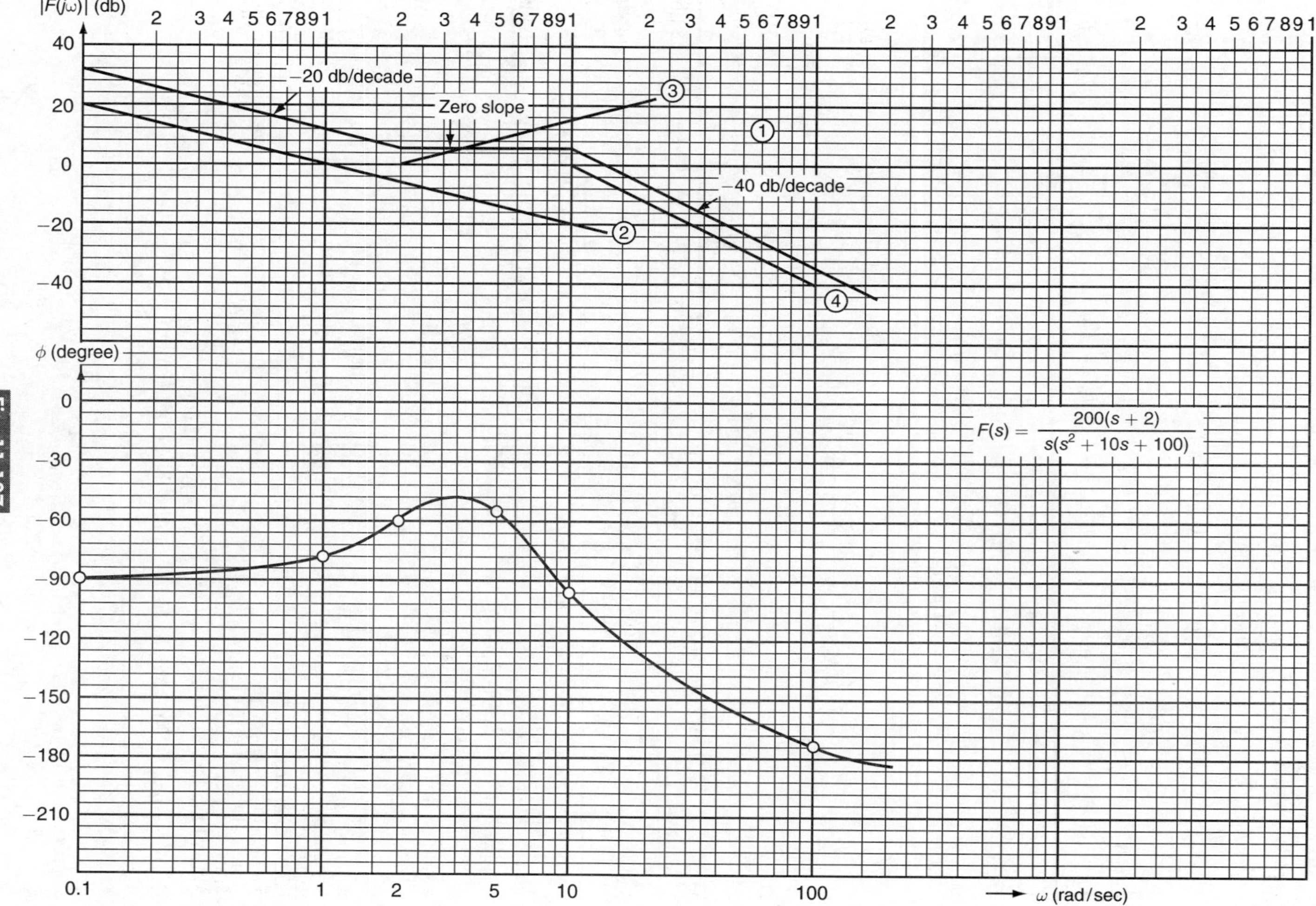

|F(jω)| (db)
40
20
0
−20
−40
−20 db/decade
Zero slope
−40 db/decade
①
②
③
④
φ (degree)
0
−30
−60
−90
−120
−150
−180
−210
F(s) = 200(s + 2) / s(s² + 10s + 100)
0.1
1
2
5
10
100
ω (rad/sec)


Fig. 11.107

## EXAMPLE 11.53

*Construct the Bode plot for the function*

$$F(s) = \frac{4}{(1+s)\left(1+\frac{s}{3}\right)^2}$$

**Solution**

***Step 1:*** Write $F(s)$ in standard form.

$$F(s) = \frac{4}{(1+s)\left(1+\frac{s}{3}\right)^2}$$

Putting $s = j\omega$,

$$F(j\omega) = \frac{4}{(1+j\omega)\left(1+\frac{j\omega}{3}\right)^2}$$

$$20\log|F(j\omega)| = 20\log 4 - 20\log|1+j\omega| - 20\log\left|\left(1+\frac{j\omega}{2}\right)^2\right|$$

***Step 2:*** Write down each factor in the table.

| No. | Factor | Corner frequency | Magnitude characteristic |
|---|---|---|---|
| 1 | $4$ | – | Straight line of magnitude 20 log 4 = 12.04 db. |
| 2 | $\frac{1}{1+j\omega}$ | 1 | Straight line of 0 db for $\omega < 1$, straight line of slope –20 db/decade for $\omega > 1$. |
| 3 | $\frac{1}{\left(1+\frac{j\omega}{3}\right)^2}$ | 3 | Straight line of 0 db for $\omega < 3$, straight line of slope –40db/decade for $\omega > 3$. |

***Step 3:*** Draw all the factors clearly.

***Step 4:*** Add all the factors to get magnitude plot.

***Step 5:*** Draw the phase plot with the help of table for $\phi(\omega)$ for any value of $\omega$.

$$\phi(\omega) = \phi \tan^{-1}\omega - 2\tan^{-1}\frac{\omega}{3}$$

Magnitude and phase plots are shown in Fig. 11.108.

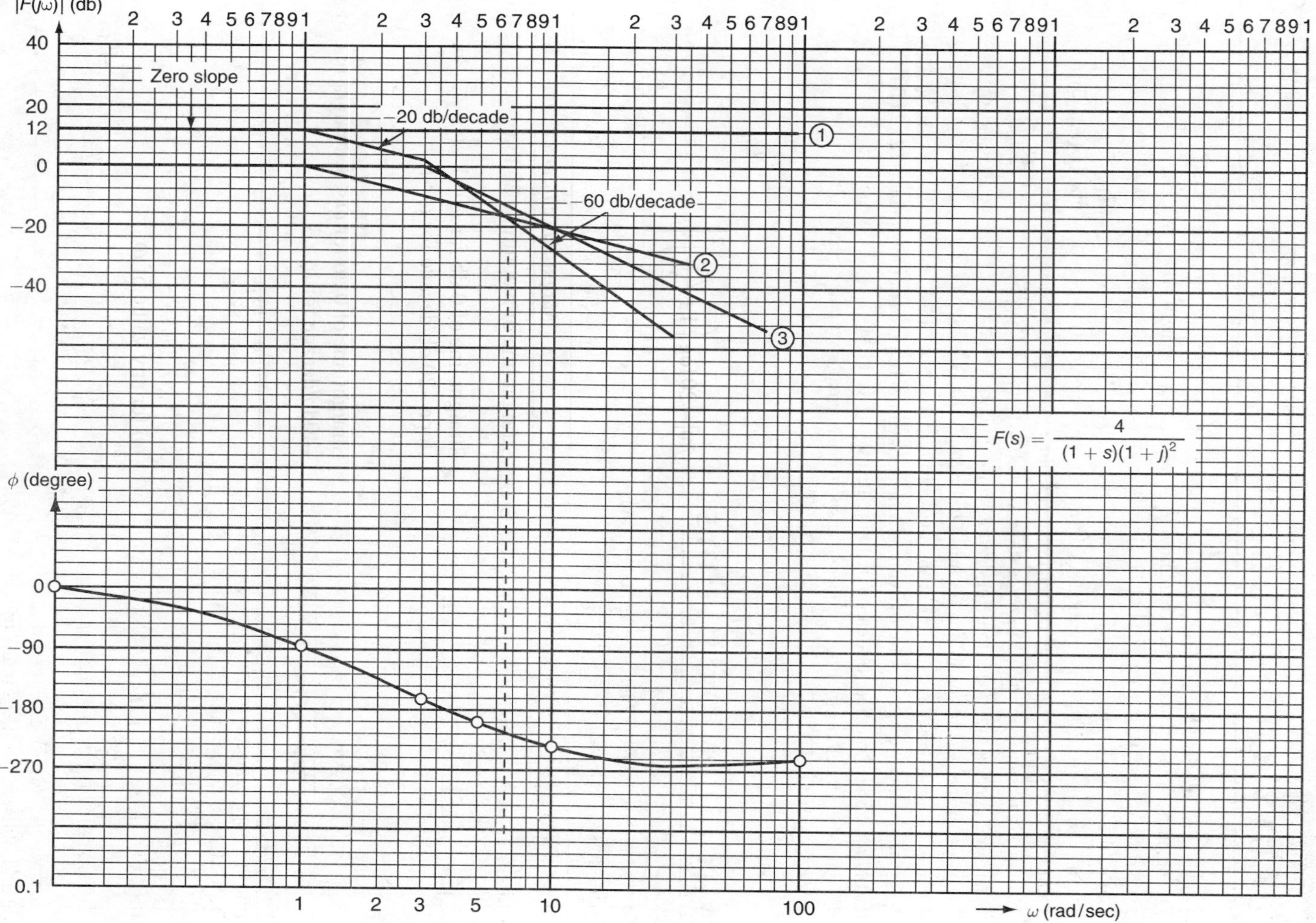
$|F(j\omega)|$ (db)
Zero slope
−20 db/decade
−60 db/decade
$F(s) = \frac{4}{(1+s)(1+j)^2}$
$\phi$ (degree)
$\omega$ (rad/sec)
40
20
12
0
−20
−40
0
−90
−180
−270
0.1
1
2
3
5
10
100

Fig. 11.108

## Theory Questions

**11.1** Explain the concept of complex frequency. Also, explain its interpretation. **[LO 11.1]** ○○●

**11.2** Define parts of a network. Hence, explain one-port and two-port networks. **[LO 11.2]** ●○○

**11.3** Define active and passive ports. **[LO 11.2]** ●○○

**11.4** Define the network functions of one-port network. **[LO 11.3]** ●○○

**11.5** Define various driving-point functions and transfer functions for two-port network. **[LO 11.3]** ●○○

**11.6** Define poles and zeros of network functions. **[LO 11.5]** ●○○

**11.7** Explain significance of poles and zeros of network functions. **[LO 11.5]** ○●○

**11.8** What are the necessary conditions for driving-point functions? **[LO 11.6]** ○●○

**11.9** What are the necessary conditions for transfer functions? **[LO 11.6]** ○●○

**11.10** Explain the time domain behaviour from pole-zero plot. **[LO 11.7]** ○●○

**11.11** Explain the stability of the network with reframe to location of poles in the $s$-plane. **[LO 11.7]** ○●○

**11.12** Explain graphical method for determination of residue. **[LO 11.8]** ○●○

**11.13** Explain the procedure to draw frequency response, i.e., magnitude and phase plot with the help of Bode Plot. **[LO 11.9]** ○●○

## Practice Problems

**11.1** Determine the driving-point impedance $\frac{V_1}{I_1}$, transfer impedance $\frac{V_2}{I_1}$ and voltage transfer ratio $\frac{V_2}{V_1}$ for the network shown in Fig. 11.109. ●○○

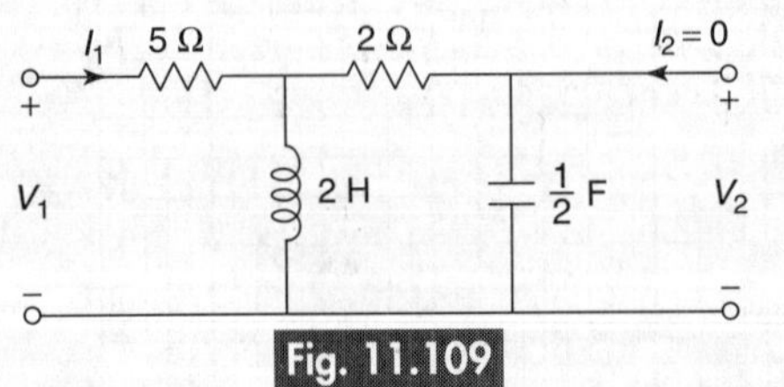


Fig. 11.109

**11.2** For the network shown in Fig. 11.110, determine $\frac{V_2}{V_1}$ and $\frac{V_2}{I_1}$. ○●○

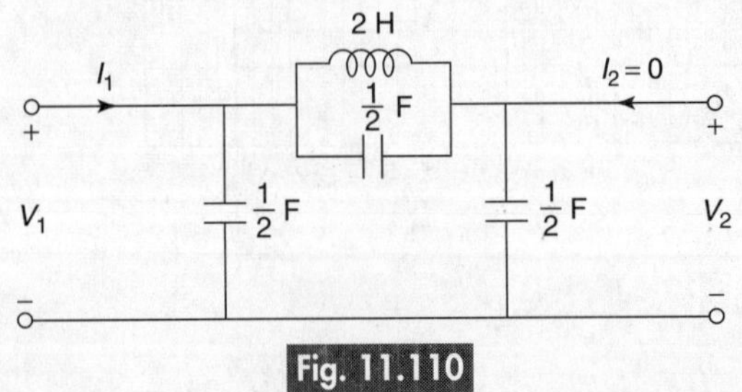


Fig. 11.110

**11.3** Find the open-circuit transfer impedance $Z_{21}$ and open-circuit voltage ratio $G_{21}$ for the ladder network shown in Fig. 11.111. ○●○

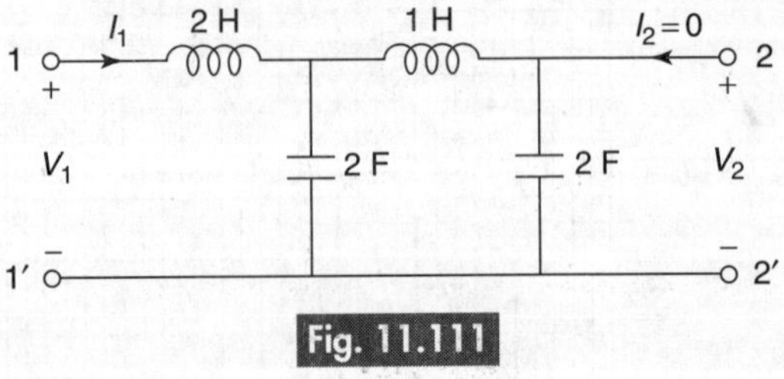


Fig. 11.111

**11.4** For the two-port network shown in Fig. 11.112, determine $Z_{11}$, $Z_{21}$ and voltage transfer ratio $G_{21}(s)$. ○●○

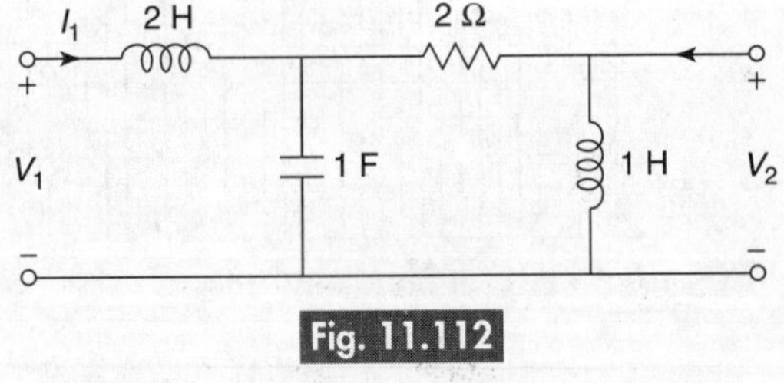


Fig. 11.112

**11.5** Draw the pole-zero diagram of the following network functions: ●○○

(i) $F(s)=\dfrac{s^2+4}{s^2+6s+4}$

(ii) $F(s)=\dfrac{5s-12}{s^2+4s+13}$

(iii) $F(s)=\dfrac{s+1}{(s^2+2s+2)^2}$

(iv) $F(s)=\dfrac{s(s^2+5)}{s^4+2s^2+1}$

(v) $F(s)=\dfrac{s^2+s+2}{s^4+5s^3+6s^2}$

(vi) $F(s)=\dfrac{s^2-s}{s^3+2s^2-s-2}$

(vii) $F(s)=\dfrac{s^2+3s+2}{s^2+3s}$

(viii) $F(s)=\dfrac{(s^2+4)(s+1)}{(s^2+1)(s^2+2s+5)}$

**11.6** For the network shown in Fig. 11.113, draw the pole-zero plot of the impedance function $Z(s)$. ●○○

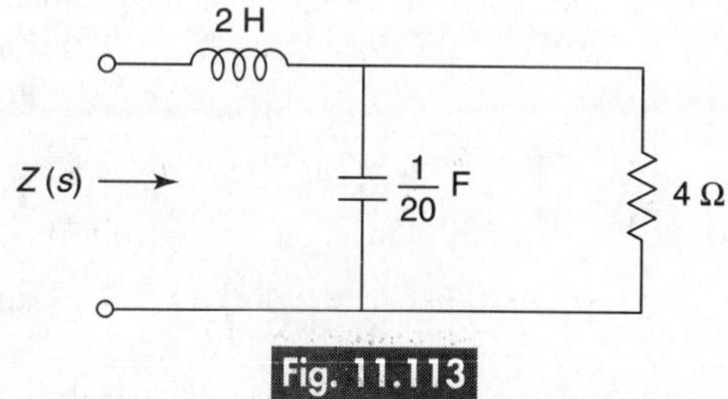


Fig. 11.113

**11.7** For the network shown in Fig. 11.114, draw the pole-zero plot of driving-point impedance function $Z(s)$. ●○○

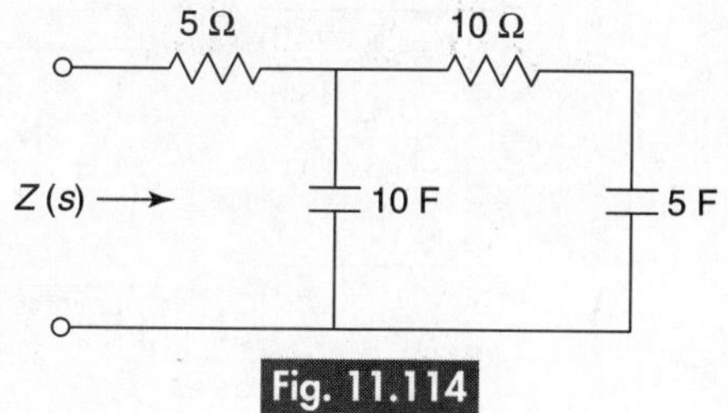


Fig. 11.114

**11.8** Find the driving-point impedance of the network shown in Fig. 11.115. Also, find poles and zeros. ○●○

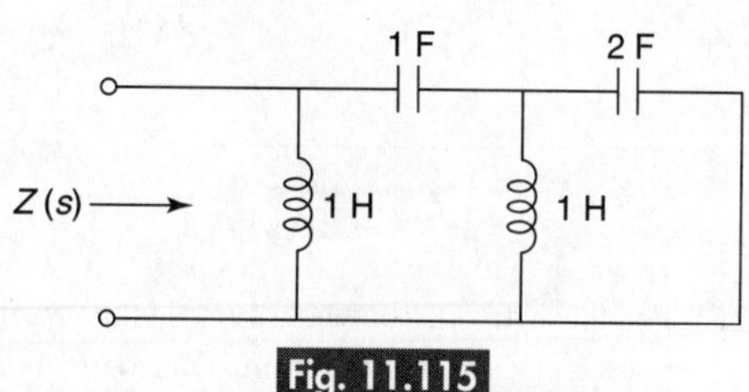


Fig. 11.115

**11.9** Find network functions $\dfrac{V_2}{V_1}$ and $\dfrac{V_1}{I_1}$ for the network shown in Fig. 11.116 and plot poles and zeros of $\dfrac{V_2(s)}{V_1(s)}$. ○●○

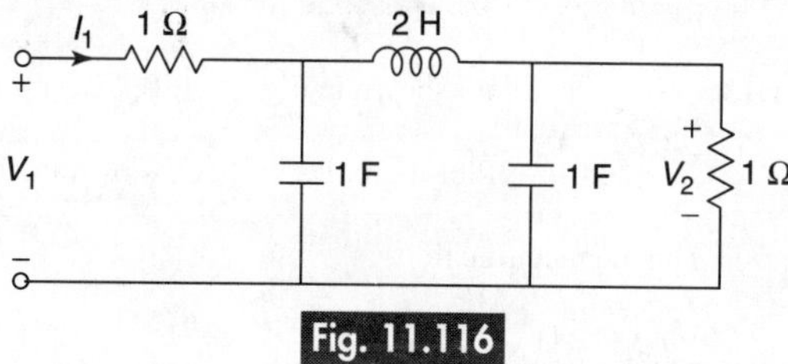


Fig. 11.116

**11.10** For the network shown in Fig. 11.117, determine $\dfrac{V_1}{I_1}$ and $\dfrac{V_2}{I_1}$. Plot the poles and zeros of $\dfrac{V_2}{I_1}$. ○●○

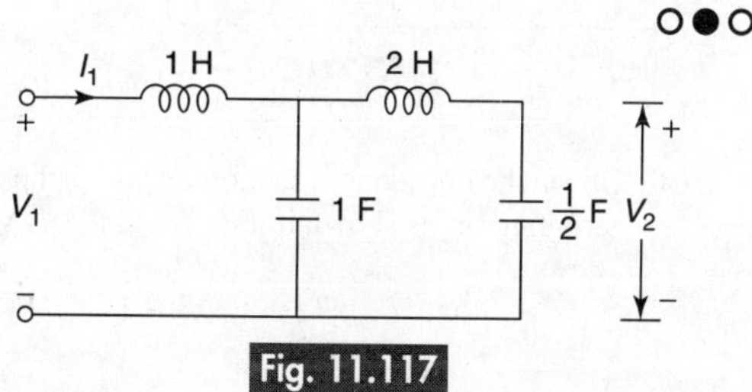


Fig. 11.117

**11.11** For the network shown in Fig. 11.118, determine $\dfrac{V_1}{I_1}$ and $\dfrac{V_2}{V_1}$. Plot the pole and zeros for $\dfrac{V_2}{V_1}$. ○●○

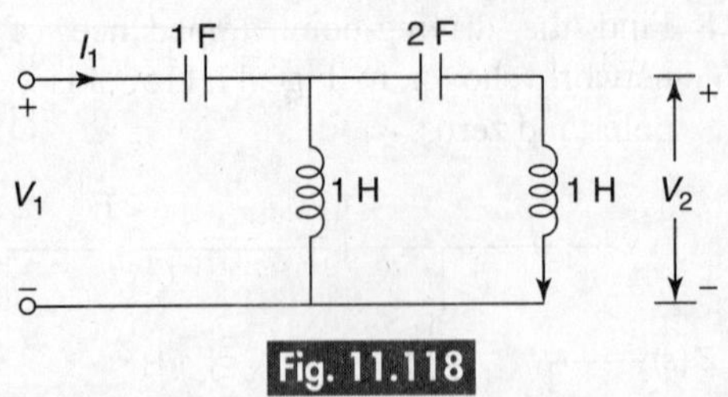


Fig. 11.118

**11.12** For the network shown in Fig. 11.119, plot the poles and zeros of transfer impedance function.

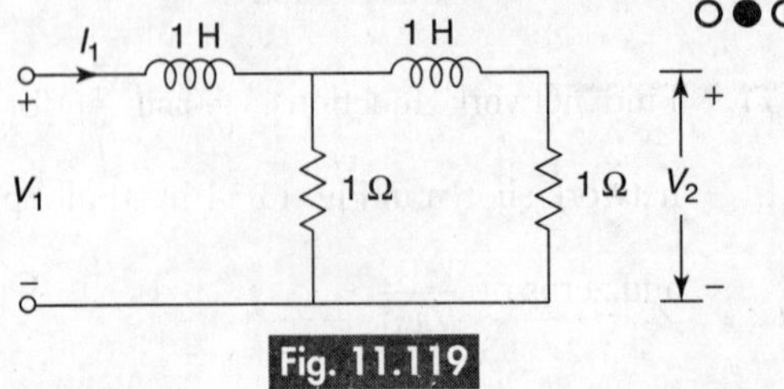


Fig. 11.119

**11.13** For the network shown in Fig. 11.120, determine $\frac{V_1}{I_1}$ and $\frac{V_2}{V_1}$. Plot the poles and zeros of transfer impedance function.

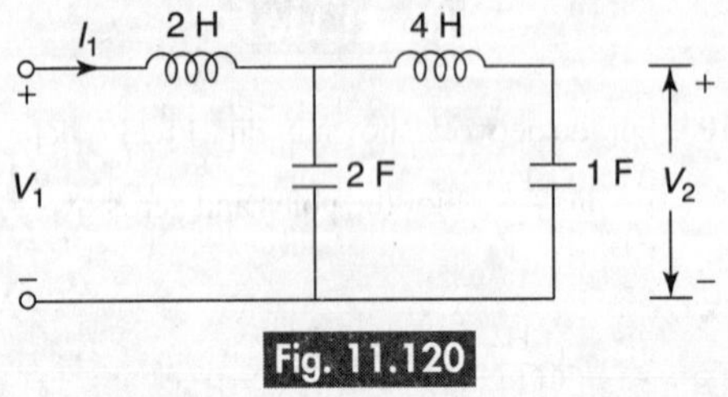


Fig. 11.120

**11.14** Obtain the impedance function for which the pole-zero diagram is shown in Fig. 11.121.

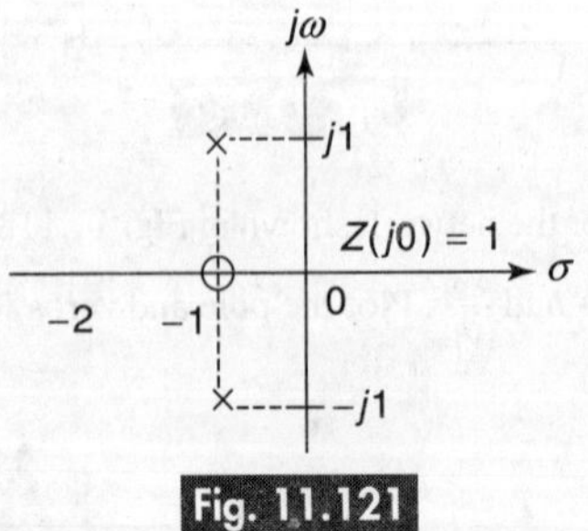


Fig. 11.121

**11.15** For the network shown in Fig. 11.122, poles and zeros of driving-point function $Z(s)$ are,

Poles: $(-1 \pm j4)$; zero: $-2$

If $Z(j0) = 1$, find the values of $R$, $L$ and $C$.

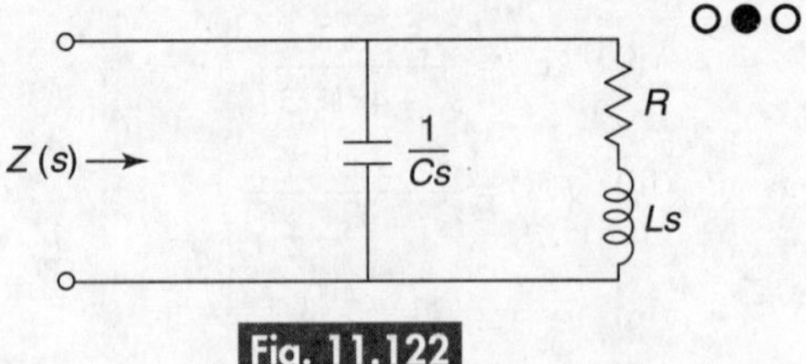


Fig. 11.122

**11.16** For the two-port network shown in Fig. 11.123, find $R_1$, $R_2$ and $C$. $\frac{V_2}{V_1} = \frac{0.2}{s^2 + 3s + 2}$

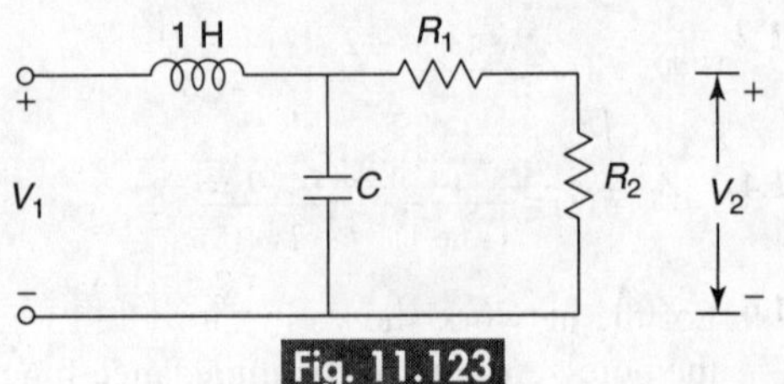


Fig. 11.123

**11.17** For the given network function, draw the pole-zero diagram and hence, obtain the time-domain voltage.

$$V(s) = \frac{5(s+5)}{(s+2)(s+7)}$$

**11.18** A transfer function is given by $Y(s) = \frac{10s}{(s+5+j15)(s+5-j15)}$. Find time-domain response using graphical method.

**11.19** Draw the Bode plot of the system with following transfer function and determine the gain and phase margin

(i) $F(s) = \frac{20}{s(s+2)(s+10)}$

(ii) $F(s) = \frac{0.3s}{(s+1)(3s+1)}$

(iii) $Z(s) = \frac{100(1+0.6s)}{s(s+10)(s+3)}$

(iv) $F(s) = \frac{10^4(s+1)}{(s+10)(s+100)}$

(v) $F(s)=\dfrac{2(s+0.25)}{s^2(s+1)(s+0.5)}$

(vi) $H(s)=\dfrac{100\left(1+\dfrac{s}{10}\right)}{s(1+s^2)\left(1+\dfrac{s}{100}\right)}$

(vii) $Z(s)=\dfrac{200(s+2)}{s(s^2+10s+100)}$

(viii) $G(j\omega)=\dfrac{2}{j\omega\left(1+\dfrac{j\omega}{2}\right)\left(1+\dfrac{j\omega}{5}\right)}$

(ix) $H(\omega)=\dfrac{200\,j\omega}{(j\omega+2)(j\omega+107)}$

## ANSWERS TO PRACTICE PROBLEMS

**11.1** $\dfrac{V_1}{I_1}=\dfrac{7s^2+7s+5}{s2+s+1};\dfrac{V_2}{I_1}=\dfrac{2s}{s^2+s+1};\dfrac{V_2}{V_1}=\dfrac{2s}{7s^2+7s+5}$

**11.2** $\dfrac{V_2}{V_1}=\dfrac{s^2+1}{2s^2+1};\dfrac{V_2}{I_1}=\dfrac{2s^2+2}{s(3s^2+2)}$

**11.3** $Z_{21}=\dfrac{1}{2s^3+3s},G_{21}=\dfrac{1}{4s^4+7s^2+1}$

**11.4** $Z_{11}=\dfrac{2s^3+4s^2+3s+2}{s^2+2s+1},Z_{21}=\dfrac{s}{s^2+2s+1},G_{21}=\dfrac{s}{2s^3+4s^2+3s+2}$

**11.6** $Z(s)=\left[\dfrac{(s+2.5-j1.94)(s+2.5+j1.94)}{s+5}\right]$

**11.7** $Z(s)=\dfrac{5(s+0.01)(s+0.04)}{s(s+0.03)}$

**11.8** $Z(s)=\dfrac{1.5s(s^2+0.33)}{(s^2+1.707)(s^2+0.293)}$

**11.9** $\dfrac{V_2}{V_1}=\dfrac{1}{2(s^3+2s^2+2s+1)},\dfrac{V_1}{I_1}=\dfrac{2(s^3+2s^2+2s+1)}{2s^3+2s^2+2s+1}$

**11.10** $\dfrac{V_1}{I_1}=\dfrac{2s^4+5s^2+2}{2s^3+3s},\dfrac{V_2}{I_1}=\dfrac{2}{2s^3+3s}$

**11.11** $\dfrac{V_1}{I_1}=\dfrac{s^4+3s^2+1}{2s^3+s}$

**11.12** $\dfrac{V_2}{I_1}=\dfrac{1}{s+2}$

**11.13** $\dfrac{V_1}{I_1}=\dfrac{16s^4+10s^2+1}{8s^3+3s},\dfrac{V_2}{I_1}=\dfrac{1}{8s^3+3s},\dfrac{V_2}{V_1}=\dfrac{1}{16s^4+10s^2+1}$

**11.14** $Z(s)=\dfrac{2\,(s+1)}{s^2+2s+2}$

**11.15** $1\,\Omega, 0.5\text{ H}, \dfrac{2}{17}\text{ F}$

**11.16** $\dfrac{3}{5}\,\Omega,\dfrac{1}{15}\,\Omega, 0.5\text{ F}$

**11.17** $[v(t)=3e^{-2t}+2e^{-7t}]$

**11.18** $5.26\angle 18.4^\circ\, e^{-(5+j15)t}+5.26\angle -18.4^\circ\, e^{-(5-j15)t}$

# Objective-Type Questions

**From GATE and Other Competitive Examinations**

**11.1** The driving-point impedance $Z(s)$ of a network has the pole-zero locations, as shown in Fig. 11.124. If $Z(0) = 3$, then $Z(s)$ is ○●○

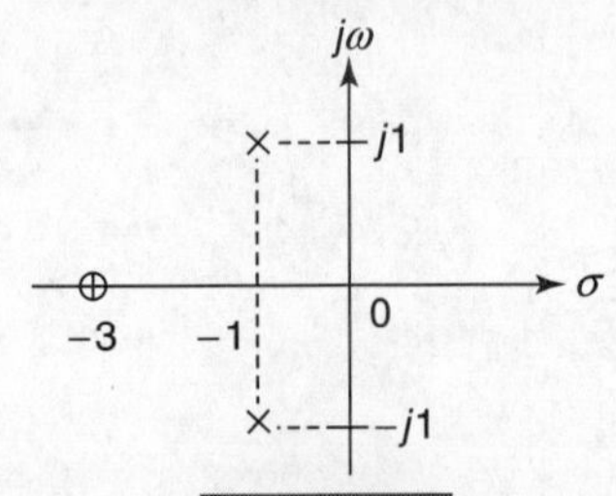


Fig. 11.124

(a) $\dfrac{3(s+3)}{s^2+2s+3}$ (b) $\dfrac{2(s+3)}{s^2+2s+2}$

(c) $\dfrac{3(s-3)}{s^2-2s-2}$ (d) $\dfrac{2(s-3)}{s^2-2s-3}$

**11.2** For the circuit shown in Fig. 11.125, the initial conditions are zero. Its transfer function $H(s) = \dfrac{V_0(s)}{V_1(s)}$ is ○●○

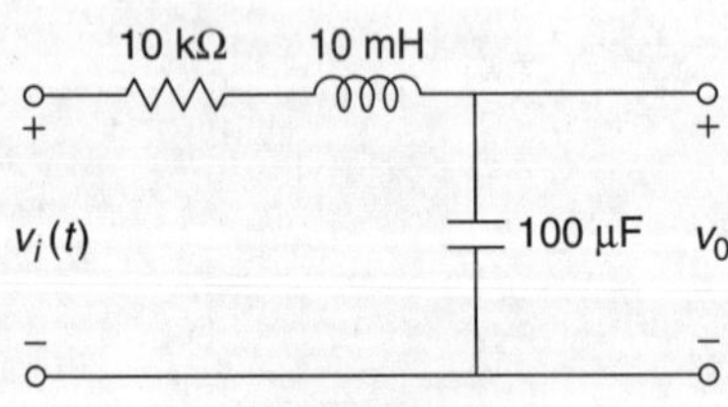


Fig. 11.125

(a) $\dfrac{1}{s^2+10^6 s+10^6}$ (b) $\dfrac{10^6}{s^2+10^3 s+10^6}$

(c) $\dfrac{10^3}{s^2+10^3 s+10^6}$ (d) $\dfrac{10^6}{s^2+10^6 s+10^6}$

**11.3** A system is represented by the transfer function $\dfrac{10}{(s+1)(s+2)}$. The dc gain of this system is ●○○

(a) 1 (b) 2

(c) 5 (d) 10

**11.4** Which one of the following is the ratio $\dfrac{V_{24}}{V_{13}}$ of the network shown in Fig. 11.126? ○●○

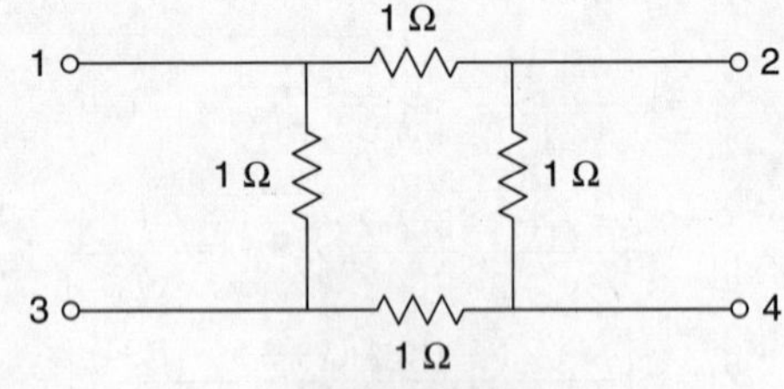


Fig. 11.126

(a) $\dfrac{1}{3}$ (b) $\dfrac{2}{3}$

(c) $\dfrac{3}{4}$ (d) $\dfrac{4}{3}$

**11.5** A network has response with time, as shown in Fig. 11.127. Which one of the following diagrams represents the location of the poles of this network? ○●○

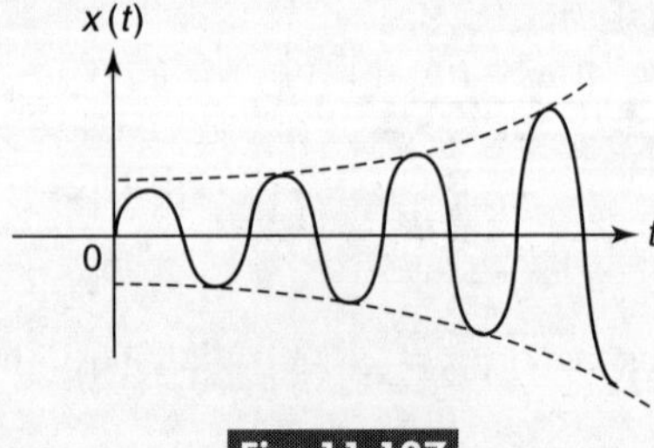


Fig. 11.127

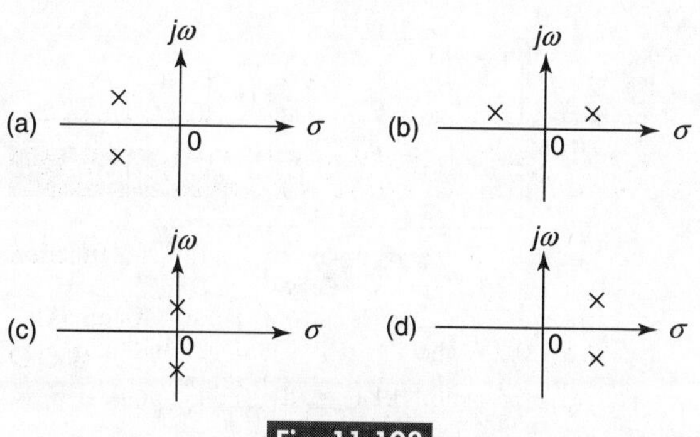


Fig. 11.128

**11.6** The driving-point admittance function of the network shown in Fig. 11.129 has a ○●○

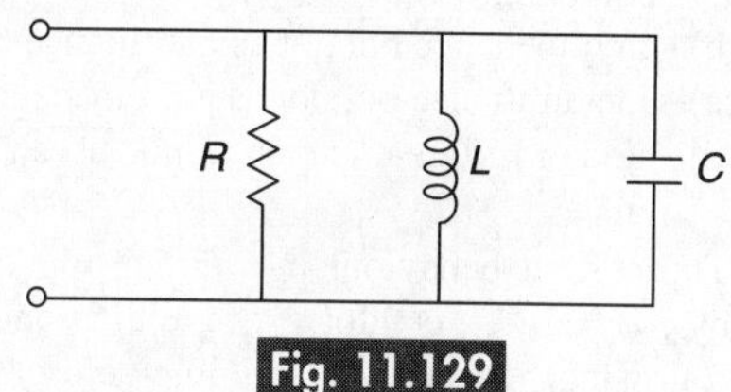


Fig. 11.129

(a) pole at $s = 0$ and zero at $s = \infty$
(b) pole at $s = 0$ and pole at $s = \infty$
(c) pole at $s = \infty$ and zero at $s = 0$
(d) pole at $s = \infty$ and zero at $s = \infty$

**11.7** The transfer function $Y_{12}(s) = \dfrac{I_2(s)}{V_1(s)}$ for the network shown in Fig. 11.130 is ○●○

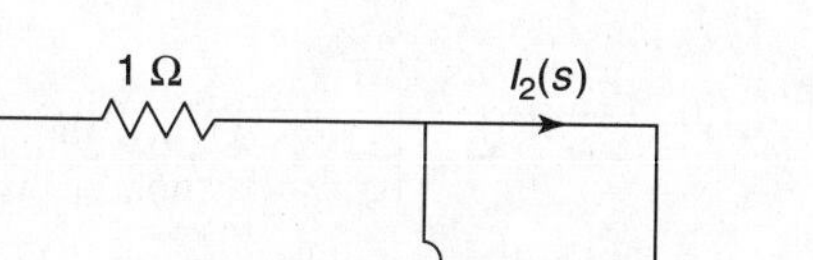


Fig. 11.130

(a) $\dfrac{s^2}{s^2+s+1}$ (b) $\dfrac{s}{s+1}$

(c) $\dfrac{1}{s+1}$ (d) $\dfrac{s+1}{s^2+1}$

**11.8** As the poles of a network shift away from the $x$ axis, the response ●○○
(a) remains constant
(b) becomes less oscillating
(c) becomes more oscillating
(d) none of these

**11.9** The transfer function $\dfrac{V_2(s)}{V_1(s)}$ of the circuit shown in Fig. 11.131 is ○●○

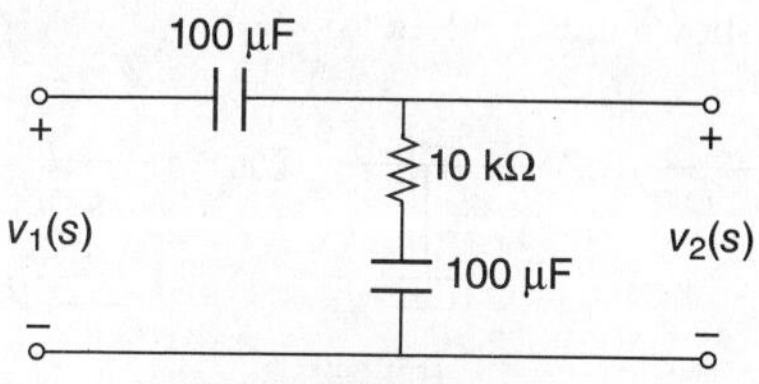


Fig. 11.131

(a) $\dfrac{0.5s+1}{s+1}$ (b) $\dfrac{3s+6}{s+2}$

(c) $\dfrac{s+2}{s+1}$ (d) $\dfrac{s+1}{s+2}$

**11.10** If the transfer function of the following network is ○●○

$$\frac{V_o(s)}{V_i(s)} = \frac{1}{2+sCR}$$

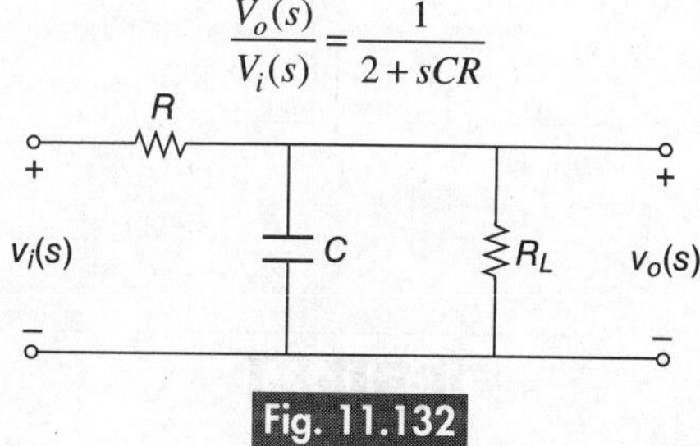


Fig. 11.132

The value of the load resistance $R_L$ is

(a) $\dfrac{R}{4}$ (b) $\dfrac{R}{2}$

(c) $R$ (d) $2R$

**11.11** The driving-point impedance of the following network is given, as shown in Fig. 11.133. The component values are ○●○

$$Z(s) = \frac{0.2s}{s^2+0.1s+2}$$

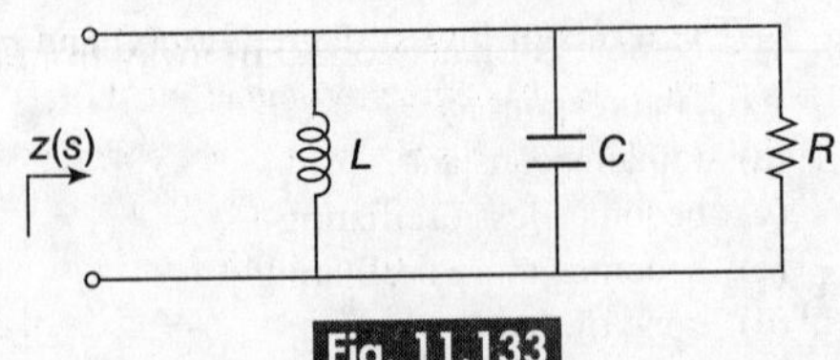


Fig. 11.133

(a) 5 H, 0.5 Ω, 0.1 F (b) 0.1 H, 0.5 Ω, 5 F

(c) 5 H, 2 Ω, 0.1 F (d) 0.1 H, 2 Ω, 5 F

**11.12** The driving-point impedance of the network shown in Fig. 11.134 is ○●○

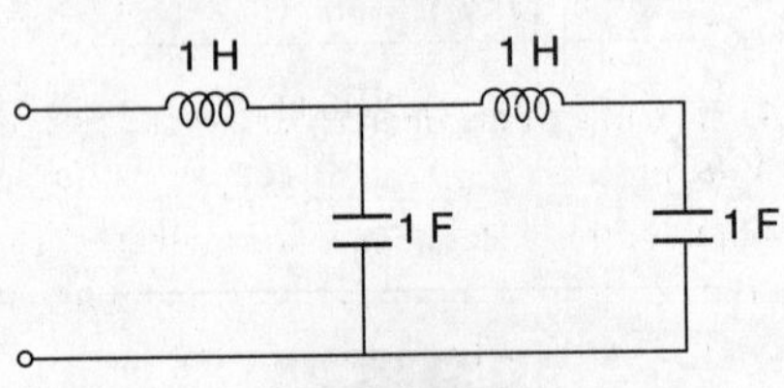


Fig. 11.134

(a) $\dfrac{s^4+3s^2+1}{s^3+2s}$ (b) $\dfrac{s^2+1}{s(s^2+2)}$

(c) $\dfrac{s^4+3s^3+2s^2+1}{s^3+2s}$ (d) $\dfrac{s^2+1}{s+1}$

**11.13** The driving-point impedance of the network shown in Fig. 11.135 is ○●○

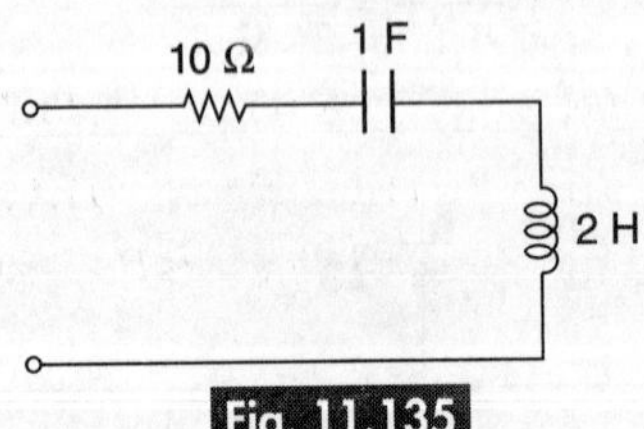


Fig. 11.135

(a) $10+2s$ (b) $10+2s+\dfrac{1}{s}$

(c) 10 (d) $\dfrac{1}{s}$

**11.14** For the network shown in Fig. 11.136, $\dfrac{V_o(s)}{V_i(s)} = \dfrac{4s}{s^2+4s+20}$ when $R = 2\ \Omega$. The value of $L$ and $C$ are ○●○

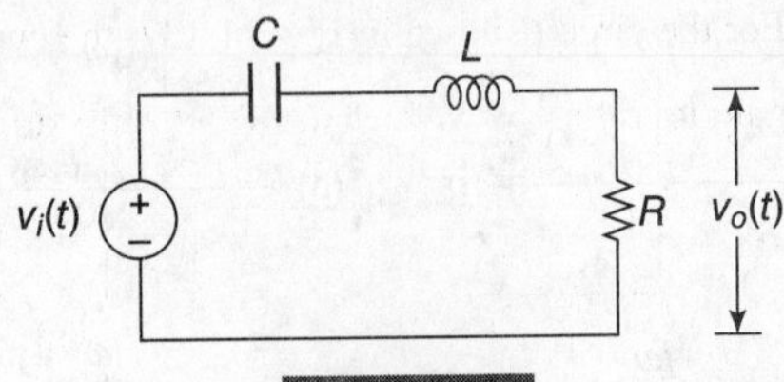


Fig. 11.136

(a) 0.3 H and 1 F (b) 0.4 H and 0.5 F

(c) 0.5 H and 0.1 F (d) 0.5 H and 0.01 F

**11.15** The function $s + 2 + \dfrac{3}{s}$ can be realised as ○●○

(a) both driving-point impedance and driving-point admittance

(b) an impedance but not as admittance

(c) an admittance but not as an impedance

(d) neither as an impedance nor as an admittance

**11.16** The current behaviour in a circuit is expressed by $i(t) = 2e^{-t} - e^{-5t}$ for $t \geq 0$. Which one of the following figures show the pole-zero pattern of $I(s)$? ○●○

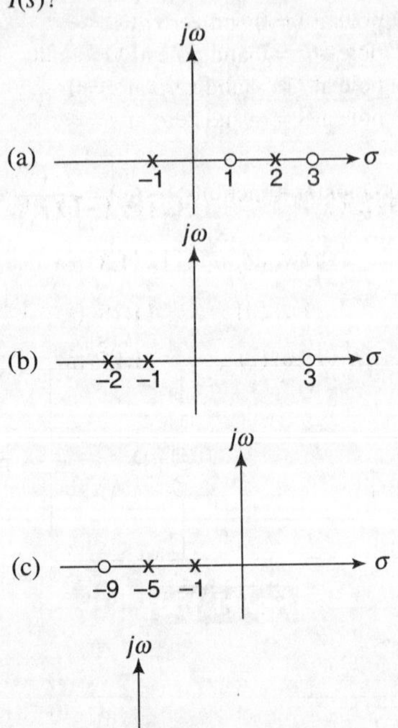

**11.17** For the circuit shown in Fig. 11.137, the current gain function $\frac{I_o(s)}{I_i(s)}$ has poles and zeros at ○●○

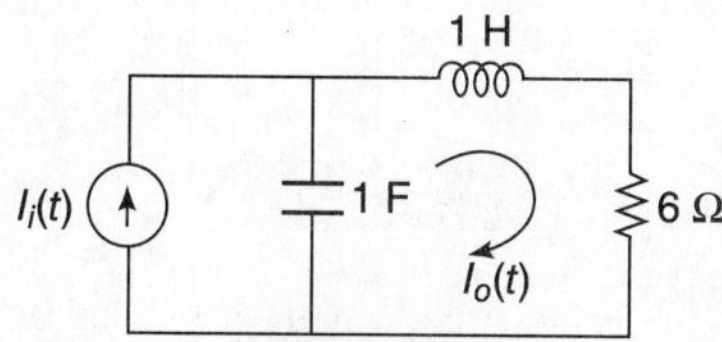


Fig. 11.137

(a) No zeros, $P_{1,2} = -3 \pm 2\sqrt{2}$

(b) $Z_1 = 0,\ Z_2 = 2,\ P_1 = \pm 3 \pm 2\sqrt{2}$

(c) No zeros, $P_{1,2} = 1$

(d) $Z_{1,2} = 1,\ P_{1,2} = 3 + j2\sqrt{2}$

**11.18** Consider the following statements:

The necessary conditions for driving-point functions with common factors in $p(s)$ and $q(s)$ cancelled:

1. The coefficients of the polynomial in $p(s)$ and $q(s)$ must be real.
2. Poles and zero must be conjugate pairs if imaginary or complex.
3. The terms of lowest degree in $p(s)$ and $q(s)$ may differ in degree by one at most.

Which of the above statement is/are correct? ○●○

(a) 1, 2 and 3 (b) 1 only
(c) 1 and 2 only (d) 2 and 3 only

**11.19** For a network transfer function $H(s) = \frac{P(s)}{Q(s)}$, where $P(s)$ and $Q(s)$ are polynomials in $s$.

1. The degree of $P(s)$ and $Q(s)$ are same.
2. The degree of $P(s)$ is always greater than the degree of $Q(s)$.
3. The degree $P(s)$ is independent of the degree of $Q(s)$.
4. The maximum degree of $P(s)$ and $Q(s)$ differ at most by one.

Which of these statements are correct? ○●○

(a) 1, 2, 3 and 4 (b) 1, 2 and 3 only
(c) 1, 2 and 4 only (d) 3 only

**11.20** The transfer function $H(s) = \frac{V_o(s)}{V_i(s)}$ of an *RLC* circuit is given by

$$H(s) = \frac{10^6}{s^2 + 20s + 10^6}$$

The quality factor of this circuit is ○●○

(a) 25 (b) 50
(c) 100 (d) 5000

## ANSWERS TO OBJECTIVE-TYPE QUESTIONS

| | | | | | | |
|---|---|---|---|---|---|---|
| **11.1** (b) | **11.2** (d) | **11.3** (c) | **11.4** (a) | **11.5** (d) | **11.6** (a) | **11.7** (a) |
| **11.8** (c) | **11.9** (d) | **11.10** (c) | **11.11** (d) | **11.12** (a) | **11.13** (b) | **11.14** (c) |
| **11.15** (a) | **11.16** (c) | **11.17** (a) | **11.18** (a) | **11.19** (d) | **11.20** (b) | |

CHAPTER **12**

# Two-Port Networks

## LEARNING OBJECTIVES

**After studying this chapter, you should be able to:**

**LO 12.1** Explain two-port networks

**LO 12.2** Describe open-circuit impedance parameters (*Z* parameters)

**LO 12.3** Describe short-circuit admittance parameters (*Y* parameters)

**LO 12.4** Discuss transmission and inverse-transmission parameters

**LO 12.5** Explain hybrid parameters (*h* parameters) and inverse-hybrid parameters (*g* parameters)

**LO 12.6** Determine interrelationships between the parameters

**LO 12.7** Discuss interconnection of two-port network

**LO 12.8** Explain *T*-network, *Pi*-network and lattice network

**LO 12.9** Discuss terminated two-port networks

**LO 12.10** Explain image parameters

## INTRODUCTION

Basic network elements such as resistors, capacitors, inductors and independent sources form the most elementary kind of one-port networks. A one-port network can have any number of positive elements, independent and dependent sources and nodes. Some devices such as bipolar junction resistors (BJT), metal-oxide semiconductor field-effect transistors (MOSFETs), operational amplifiers (OP-AMPs), etc., have more than two terminals. In such cases, it is impossible to represent them as one-port networks. These devices are represented as two-port networks. A two-port network is an electrical network with two pairs of terminals to connect to external circuits. Examples of networks analysed as two-ports are filters, matching networks, transmission lines, transformers and small-signal models for transistors, etc.

## 12.1 TWO-PORT NETWORK

LO 12.1

Explain two-port networks

A two-port network has two pairs of terminals, one pair at the input known as *input port* and one pair at the output known as *output port,* as shown in Fig. 12.1. There are four variables – $V_1$, $V_2$, $I_1$ and $I_2$ – associated with a two-port network. Two of these variables can be expressed in terms of the other two variables. Thus, there will be two dependent variables and two independent variables. The number of possible combinations generated by four variables, taken two at a time is ${}^4C_2$, i.e., six. There are six possible sets of equations describing a two-port network.

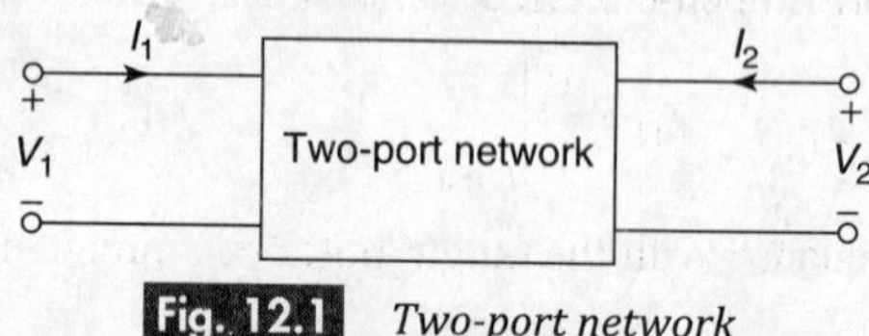


**Fig. 12.1** *Two-port network*

**TABLE 12.1 Two–port parameters**

| ***Parameter*** | ***Variables*** | | ***Equation*** |
|---|---|---|---|
| | ***Express*** | ***In terms of*** | |
| Open-Circuit Impedance | $V_1, V_2$ | $I_1, I_2$ | $V_1 = Z_{11} I_1 + Z_{12} I_2$<br>$V_2 = Z_{21} I_1 + Z_{22} I_2$ |
| Short-Circuit Admittance | $I_1, I_2$ | $V_1, V_2$ | $I_1 = Y_{11} V_1 + Y_{12} V_2$<br>$I_2 = Y_{21} V_1 + Y_{22} V_2$ |
| Transmission | $V_1, I_1$ | $V_2, I_2$ | $V_1 = AV_2 - BI_2$<br>$I_1 = CV_2 - DI_2$ |
| Inverse Transmission | $V_2, I_2$ | $V_1, I_1$ | $V_2 = A' V_1 - B' I_1$<br>$I_2 = C' V_1 - D' I_1$ |
| Hybrid | $V_1, I_2$ | $I_1, V_2$ | $V_1 = h_{11} I_1 + h_{12} V_2$<br>$I_2 = h_{21} I_1 + h_{22} V_2$ |
| Inverse Hybrid | $I_1, V_2$ | $V_1, I_2$ | $I_1 = g_{11} V_1 + g_{12} I_2$<br>$V_2 = g_{21} V_1 + g_{22} I_2$ |

## 12.2 OPEN-CIRCUIT IMPEDANCE PARAMETERS (*Z* PARAMETERS)

LO 12.2

Describe open-circuit impedance parameters (*Z* parameters)

The *Z* parameters of a two-port network may be defined by expressing two-port voltages $V_1$ and $V_2$ in terms of two-port currents $I_1$ and $I_2$.

$$(V_1, V_2) = f(I_1, I_2)$$

$$V_1 = Z_{11} I_1 + Z_{12} I_2$$

$$V_2 = Z_{21} I_1 + Z_{22} I_2$$

In matrix form, we can write

$$\begin{bmatrix} V_1 \\ V_2 \end{bmatrix} = \begin{bmatrix} Z_{11} & Z_{12} \\ Z_{21} & Z_{22} \end{bmatrix} \begin{bmatrix} I_1 \\ I_2 \end{bmatrix}$$

$$[V] = [Z][I]$$

The individual $Z$ parameters for a given network can be defined by setting each of the port currents equal to zero.

➤ ***Case 1*** When the output port is open-circuited, i.e., $I_2 = 0$

$$Z_{11} = \left. \frac{V_1}{I_1} \right|_{I_2 = 0}$$

where $Z_{11}$ is the driving-point impedance with the output port open-circuited. It is also called *open-circuit input impedance.*

Similarly,

$$Z_{21} = \left. \frac{V_2}{I_1} \right|_{I_2 = 0}$$

where $Z_{21}$ is the transfer impedance with the output port open-circuited. It is also called *open-circuit forward transfer impedance.*

➤ ***Case 2*** When input port is open-circuited, i.e., $I_1 = 0$

$$Z_{12} = \left. \frac{V_1}{I_2} \right|_{I_1 = 0}$$

where $Z_{12}$ is the transfer impedance with the input port open-circuited. It is also called *open-circuit reverse transfer impedance.*

Similarly,

$$Z_{22} = \left. \frac{V_2}{I_2} \right|_{I_1 = 0}$$

where $Z_{22}$ is the open-circuit driving-point impedance with the input port open-circuited. It is also called *open-circuit output impedance.*

As these impedance parameters are measured with either the input or output port open-circuited, these are called *open-circuit impedance parameters.*

The equivalent circuit of the two-port network in terms of $Z$ parameters is shown in Fig. 12.2.

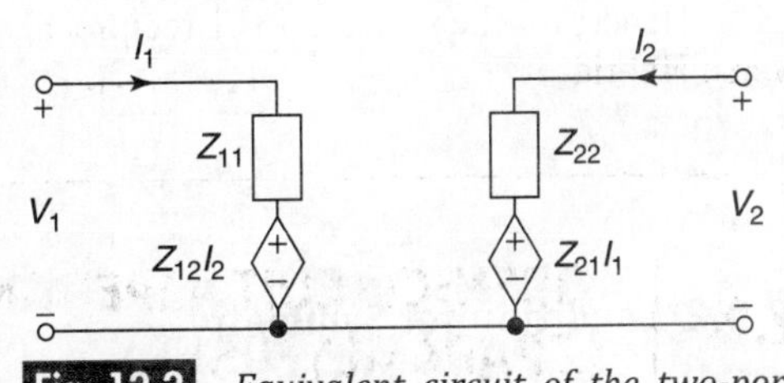


**Fig. 12.2** *Equivalent circuit of the two-port network in terms of Z parameter*

### 12.2.1 Condition for Reciprocity

A network is said to be reciprocal if the ratio of excitation at one port to response at the other port is same if excitation and response are interchanged.

(a) As shown in Fig. 12.3, voltage $V_s$ is applied at the input port with the output port short-circuited.

i.e.,

$$V_1 = V_s$$
$$V_2 = 0$$
$$I_2 = -I_2'$$

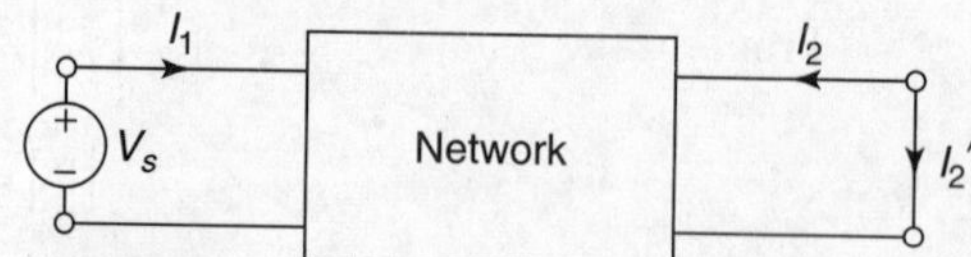


**Fig. 12.3** *Network for deriving condition for reciprocity*

From the $Z$ parameter equations,

$$V_s = Z_{11}\, I_1 - Z_{12}\, I_2'$$
$$0 = Z_{21}\, I_1 - Z_{22}\, I_2'$$
$$I_1 = \frac{Z_{22}}{Z_{21}}\, I_2'$$
$$V_s = Z_{11}\frac{Z_{22}}{Z_{21}} I_2' - Z_{12}\, I_2'$$
$$\frac{V_s}{I_2'} = \frac{Z_{11}\, Z_{22} - Z_{12}\, Z_{21}}{Z_{21}}$$

(b) As shown in Fig. 12.4, voltage $V_s$ is applied at the output port with the input port short-circuited.

i.e.,

$$V_2 = V_s$$
$$V_1 = 0$$
$$I_1 = -I_1'$$

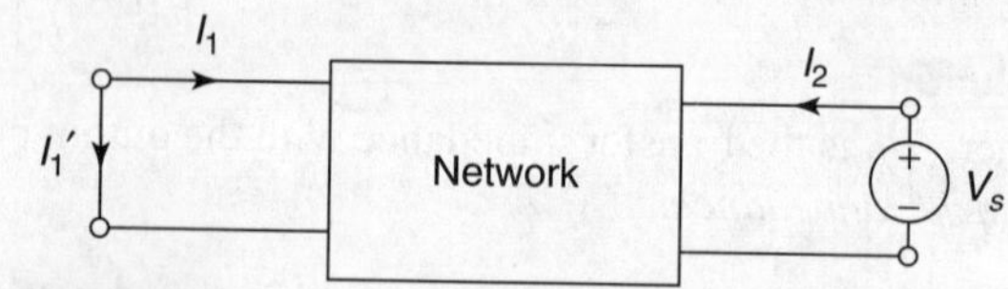


**Fig. 12.4** *Network for deriving condition for reciprocity*

From the $Z$ parameter equations,

$$0 = -Z_{11}\, I_1' + Z_{12}\, I_2$$
$$V_s = -Z_{21}\, I_1' + Z_{22}\, I_2$$
$$I_2 = \frac{Z_{11}}{Z_{12}}\, I_1'$$
$$V_s = -Z_{21}I_1' + Z_{22}\frac{Z_{11}}{Z_{12}}\, I_1'$$
$$\frac{V_s}{I_1'} = \frac{Z_{11}Z_{22} - Z_{12}Z_{21}}{Z_{12}}$$

Hence, for the network to be reciprocal,

$$\frac{V_s}{I_1'} = \frac{V_s}{I_2'}$$

i.e.,

$$Z_{12} = Z_{21}$$

### 12.2.2 Condition for Symmetry

For a network to be symmetrical, the voltage-to-current ratio at one port should be the same as the voltage-to-current ratio at the other port with one of the ports open-circuited.

(a) When the output port is open-circuited, i.e., $I_2 = 0$

From the $Z$ parameter equation,

$$V_s = Z_{11}\, I_1$$
$$\frac{V_s}{I_1} = Z_{11}$$

(b) When the input port is open-circuited, i.e., $I_1 = 0$

From the $Z$ parameter equation,

$$V_s = Z_{22}\, I_2$$

$$\frac{V_s}{I_2} = Z_{22}$$

Hence, for the network to be symmetrical,

$$\frac{V_s}{I_1} = \frac{V_s}{I_2}$$

i.e.,

$$Z_{11} = Z_{22}$$

## EXAMPLE 12.1

●○○

*Test results for a two-port network are (a) $I_1 = 0.1\angle 0°$ A, $V_1 = 5.2\angle 50°$ V, $V_2 = 4.1\angle -25°$ V with port 2 open-circuited (b) $I_2 = 0.1\angle 0°$ A, $V_1 = 3.1\angle -80°$ V, $V_2 = 4.2\angle 60°$ V, with port 1 open-circuited. Find Z parameters.*

**Solution**

$$Z_{11} = \left.\frac{V_1}{I_1}\right|_{I_2=0} = \frac{5.2\angle 50°}{0.1\angle 0°} = 52\angle 50°\ \Omega, \qquad Z_{12} = \left.\frac{V_1}{I_2}\right|_{I_1=0} = \frac{3.1\angle -80°}{0.1\angle 0°} = 31\angle -80°\ \Omega$$

$$Z_{21} = \left.\frac{V_2}{I_1}\right|_{I_2=0} = \frac{4.1\angle -25°}{0.1\angle 0°} = 41\angle -25°\ \Omega, \qquad Z_{22} = \left.\frac{V_2}{I_2}\right|_{I_1=0} = \frac{4.2\angle 60°}{0.1\angle 0°} = 42\angle 60°\ \Omega$$

Hence, the $Z$ parameters are

$$\begin{bmatrix} Z_{11} & Z_{12} \\ Z_{21} & Z_{22} \end{bmatrix} = \begin{bmatrix} 52\angle 50° & 31\angle -80° \\ 41\angle -25° & 42\angle 60° \end{bmatrix}$$

## EXAMPLE 12.2

●○○

*Find the Z parameters for the network shown in Fig. 12.5.*

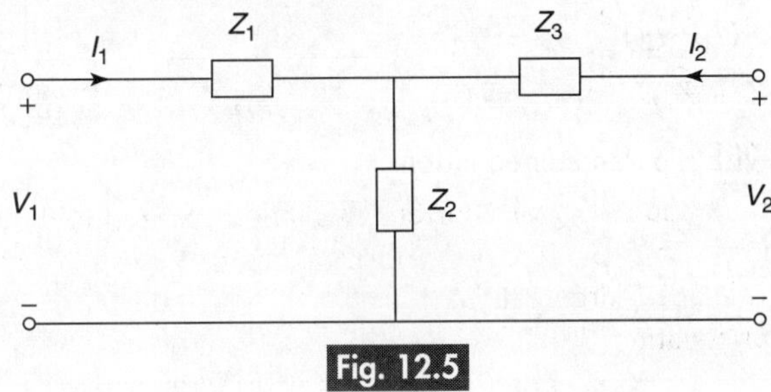


Fig. 12.5

**Note** Difficulty Level ●○○— Easy; ○●○— Medium; ○○●— Difficult

**Solution**

**First Method**

*Case 1* When the output port is open-circuited, i.e., $I_2 = 0$.

Applying KVL to mesh 1,

$$V_1 = (Z_1 + Z_2)\, I_1$$

$$Z_{11} = \left.\frac{V_1}{I_1}\right|_{I_2=0} = Z_1 + Z_2$$

Also,

$$V_2 = Z_2\, I_1$$

$$Z_{21} = \left.\frac{V_2}{I_1}\right|_{I_2=0} = Z_2$$

*Case 2* When the input port is open-circuited, i.e., $I_1 = 0$.

Applying KVL to mesh 2,

$$V_2 = (Z_2 + Z_3)\, I_2$$

$$Z_{22} = \left.\frac{V_2}{I_2}\right|_{I_1=0} = Z_2 + Z_3$$

Also,

$$V_1 = Z_2\, I_2$$

$$Z_{12} = \left.\frac{V_1}{I_2}\right|_{I_1=0} = Z_2$$

Hence, the $Z$ parameters are

$$\begin{bmatrix} Z_{11} & Z_{12} \\ Z_{21} & Z_{22} \end{bmatrix} = \begin{bmatrix} Z_1 + Z_2 & Z_2 \\ Z_2 & Z_2 + Z_3 \end{bmatrix}$$

**Second Method**

The network is redrawn, as shown in Fig. 12.6.

Applying KVL to mesh 1,

$$V_1 = Z_1 I_1 + Z_2 (I_1 + I_2)$$

$$= (Z_1 + Z_2) I_1 + Z_2 I_2 \qquad \text{...(i)}$$

Applying KVL to mesh 2,

$$V_2 = Z_3 I_2 + Z_2 (I_1 + I_2)$$

$$= Z_2 I_1 + (Z_2 + Z_3) I_2 \qquad \text{...(ii)}$$

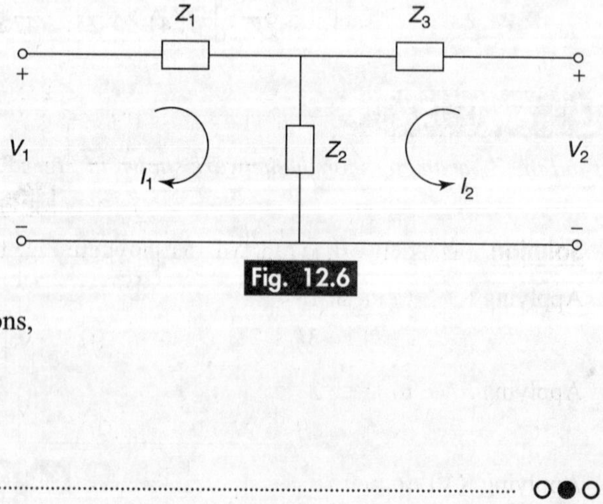

Fig. 12.6

Comparing Eqs (i) and (ii) with $Z$ parameter equations,

$$\begin{bmatrix} Z_{11} & Z_{12} \\ Z_{21} & Z_{22} \end{bmatrix} = \begin{bmatrix} Z_1 + Z_2 & Z_2 \\ Z_2 & Z_2 + Z_3 \end{bmatrix}$$

## EXAMPLE 12.3

*Find Z parameter for the network shown in Fig. 12.7.*

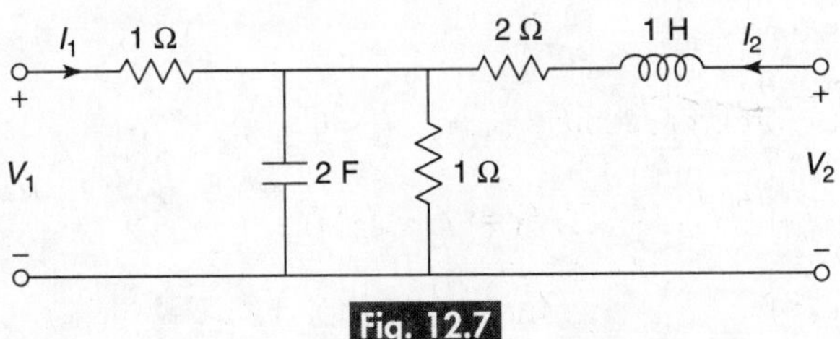


Fig. 12.7

**Solution** The transformed network is shown in Fig. 12.8.

$$Z_1 = 1$$

$$Z_2 = \frac{\left(\frac{1}{2s}\right)(1)}{\frac{1}{2s}+1} = \frac{1}{2s+1}$$

$$Z_3 = s+2$$

Fig. 12.8

From definition of $Z$ parameters,

$$Z_{11} = \left.\frac{V_1}{I_1}\right|_{I_2=0} = Z_1 + Z_2 = 1 + \frac{1}{2s+1} = \frac{2s+2}{2s+1}, \qquad Z_{12} = \left.\frac{V_1}{I_2}\right|_{I_1=0} = Z_2 = \frac{1}{2s+1}$$

$$Z_{21} = \left.\frac{V_2}{I_1}\right|_{I_2=0} = Z_2 = \frac{1}{2s+1}, \qquad Z_{22} = \left.\frac{V_2}{I_2}\right|_{I_1=0} = Z_2 + Z_3 = \frac{1}{2s+1} + s + 2 = \frac{2s^2+5s+3}{2s+1}$$

**EXAMPLE 12.4**

*Find Z parameters for the network shown in Fig. 12.9.*

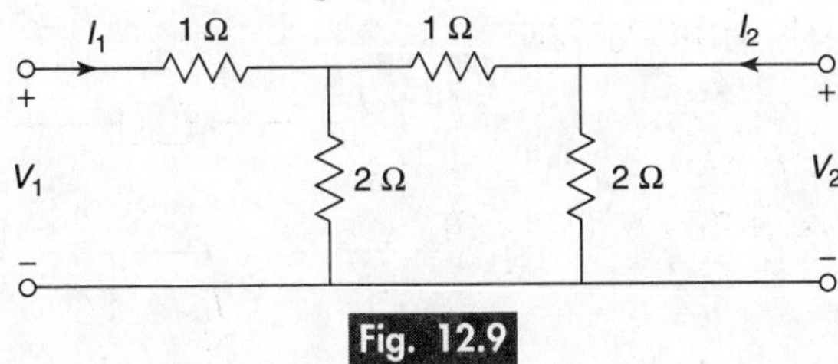


Fig. 12.9

**Solution** The network is redrawn, as shown in Fig. 12.10.

Applying KVL to mesh 1,

$$V_1 = 3I_1 - 2I_3 \qquad \ldots\text{(i)}$$

Applying KVL to mesh 2,

$$V_2 = 2I_2 + 2I_3 \qquad \ldots\text{(ii)}$$

Applying KVL to mesh 3,

$$-2I_1 + 2I_2 + 5I_3 = 0$$

$$I_3 = \frac{2}{5}I_1 - \frac{2}{5}I_2 \qquad \ldots\text{(iii)}$$

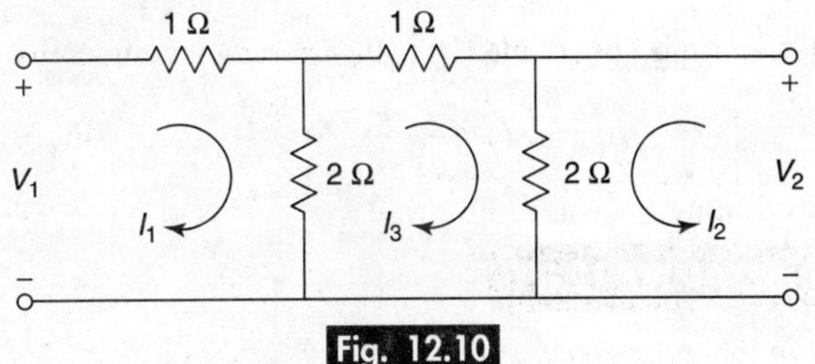


Fig. 12.10

Substituting Eq. (iii) in Eq. (i),

$$V_1 = 3I_1 - \frac{4}{5}I_1 + \frac{4}{5}I_2$$

$$= \frac{11}{5}I_1 + \frac{4}{5}I_2 \quad \ldots\text{(iv)}$$

Substituting Eq. (iii) in Eq. (ii),

$$V_2 = 2I_2 + \frac{4}{5}I_1 - \frac{4}{5}I_2$$

$$= \frac{4}{5}I_1 + \frac{6}{5}I_2 \quad \ldots\text{(v)}$$

Comparing Eqs (iv) and (v) with $Z$ parameter equations,

$$\begin{bmatrix} Z_{11} & Z_{12} \\ Z_{21} & Z_{22} \end{bmatrix} = \begin{bmatrix} \frac{11}{5} & \frac{4}{5} \\ \frac{4}{5} & \frac{6}{5} \end{bmatrix}$$

## EXAMPLE 12.5

*Find the Z parameters for the network shown in Fig. 12.11.*

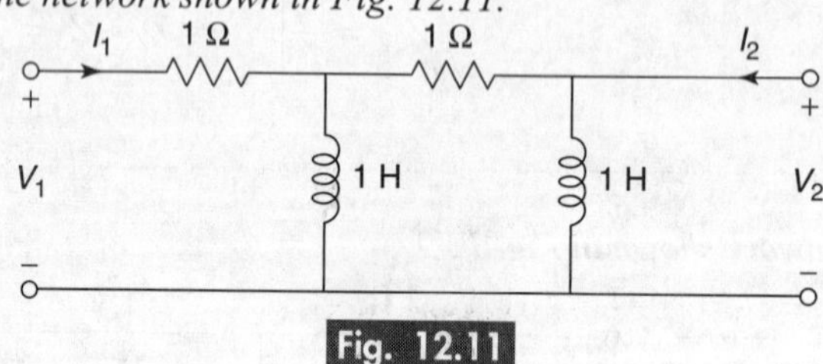


Fig. 12.11

**Solution** The transformed network is shown in Fig. 12.12.

Applying KVL to mesh 1,

$$V_1 = (s+1)I_1 - sI_3 \quad \ldots\text{(i)}$$

Applying KVL to mesh 2,

$$V_2 = sI_2 + sI_3 \quad \ldots\text{(ii)}$$

Applying KVL to mesh 3,

$$-sI_1 + sI_2 + (2s+1)I_3 = 0$$

$$I_3 = \frac{s}{2s+1}I_1 - \frac{s}{2s+1}I_2 \quad \ldots\text{(iii)}$$

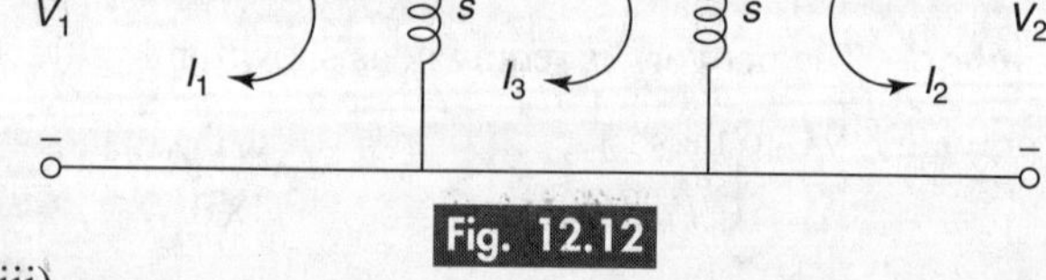


Fig. 12.12

Substituting Eq. (iii) in Eq. (i),

$$V_1 = (s+1)I_1 - s\left(\frac{s}{2s+1}I_1 - \frac{s}{2s+1}I_2\right)$$

$$= \left(\frac{s^2+3s+1}{2s+1}\right)I_1 + \left(\frac{s^2}{2s+1}\right)I_2 \quad \ldots\text{(iv)}$$

Substituting Eq. (iii) in Eq. (ii),

$$V_2 = sI_2 + s\left(\frac{s}{2s+1}I_1 - \frac{s}{2s+1}I_2\right)$$

$$= \left(\frac{s^2}{2s+1}\right)I_1 + \left(\frac{s^2+s}{2s+1}\right)I_2 \qquad \text{...(v)}$$

Comparing Eqs (iv) and (v) with $Z$ parameter equations,

$$\begin{bmatrix} Z_{11} & Z_{12} \\ Z_{21} & Z_{22} \end{bmatrix} = \begin{bmatrix} \frac{s^2+3s+1}{2s+1} & \frac{s^2}{2s+1} \\ \frac{s^2}{2s+1} & \frac{s^2+s}{2s+1} \end{bmatrix}$$

**EXAMPLE 12.6**

*Find the open-circuit impedance parameters for the network shown in Fig. 12.13. Determine whether the network is symmetrical and reciprocal.*

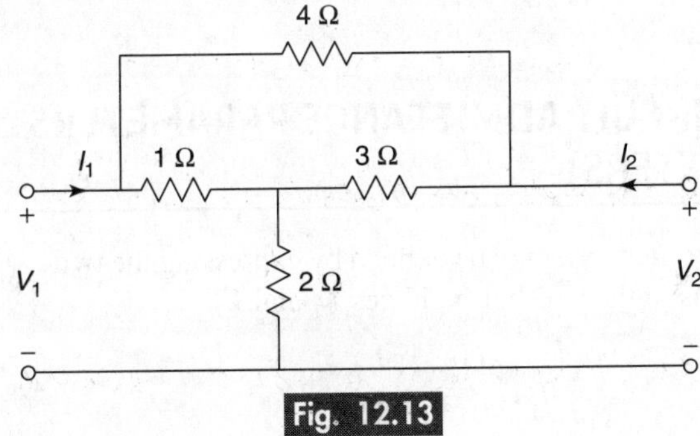


Fig. 12.13

**Solution** The network is redrawn, as shown in Fig. 12.14.

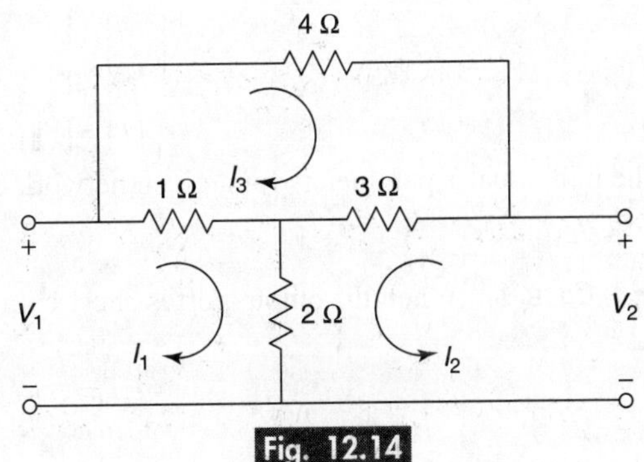


Fig. 12.14

Applying KVL to mesh 1,

$$V_1 - 1(I_1 - I_3) - 2(I_1 + I_2) = 0$$

$$V_1 = 3I_1 + 2I_2 - I_3 \qquad \text{...(i)}$$

Applying KVL to mesh 2,

$$V_2 - 3(I_2 + I_3) - 2(I_1 + I_2) = 0$$

$$V_2 = 2I_1 + 5I_2 + 3I_3 \qquad \text{...(ii)}$$

Applying KVL to mesh 3,

$$-4I_3 - 3(I_2 + I_3) - 1(I_3 - I_1) = 0$$

$$I_1 - 3I_2 + 8I_3 = 0$$

$$I_3 = \frac{1}{8}I_1 - \frac{3}{8}I_2 \qquad \text{...(iii)}$$

Substituting Eq. (iii) in Eq. (i),

$$V_1 = 3I_1 + 2I_2 - \left(\frac{1}{8}I_1 - \frac{3}{8}I_2\right)$$

$$= \frac{23}{8}I_1 + \frac{19}{8}I_2 \qquad \ldots\text{(iv)}$$

Substituting Eq. (iii) in Eq. (ii),

$$V_2 = 2I_1 + 5I_2 + 3\left(\frac{1}{8}I_1 - \frac{3}{8}I_2\right)$$

$$= \frac{19}{8}I_1 + \frac{31}{8}I_2 \qquad \ldots\text{(v)}$$

Comparing Eqs (iv) and (v) with $Z$ parameter equations,

$$\begin{bmatrix} Z_{11} & Z_{12} \\ Z_{21} & Z_{22} \end{bmatrix} = \begin{bmatrix} \frac{23}{8} & \frac{19}{8} \\ \frac{19}{8} & \frac{31}{8} \end{bmatrix}$$

Since $Z_{11} \neq Z_{22}$, the network is not symmetrical.
Since $Z_{12} = Z_{21}$, the network is reciprocal.

## 12.3 SHORT-CIRCUIT ADMITTANCE PARAMETERS (*Y* PARAMETERS)

LO 12.3

Describe short-circuit admittance parameters (*Y* parameters)

The *Y* parameters of a two-port network may be defined by expressing the two-port currents $I_1$ and $I_2$ in terms of the two-port voltages $V_1$ and $V_2$.

$$(I_1, I_2) = f(V_1, V_2)$$

$$I_1 = Y_{11}\,V_1 + Y_{12}\,V_2$$

$$I_2 = Y_{21}\,V_1 + Y_{22}\,V_2$$

In matrix form, we can write

$$\begin{bmatrix} I_1 \\ I_2 \end{bmatrix} = \begin{bmatrix} Y_{11} & Y_{12} \\ Y_{21} & Y_{22} \end{bmatrix} \begin{bmatrix} V_1 \\ V_2 \end{bmatrix}$$

$$[I] = [Y]\,[V]$$

The individual *Y* parameters for a given network can be defined by setting each of the port voltages equal to zero.

➤ ***Case 1*** When the output port is short-circuited, i.e., $V_2 = 0$

$$Y_{11} = \left.\frac{I_1}{V_1}\right|_{V_2=0}$$

where $Y_{11}$ is the driving-point admittance with the output port short-circuited. It is also called *short-circuit input admittance*.

Similarly,

$$Y_{21} = \left.\frac{I_2}{V_1}\right|_{V_2=0}$$

where $Y_{21}$ is the transfer admittance with the output port short-circuited. It is also called *short-circuit forward transfer admittance.*

➤ ***Case 2*** When the input port is short-circuited, i.e., $V_1 = 0$

$$Y_{12} = \left.\frac{I_1}{V_2}\right|_{V_1=0}$$

where $Y_{12}$ is the transfer admittance with the input port short-circuited. It is also called *short-circuit reverse transfer admittance.*

Similarly,

$$Y_{22} = \left.\frac{I_2}{V_2}\right|_{V_1=0}$$

where $Y_{22}$ is the short-circuit driving-point admittance with the input port short-circuited. It is also called the *short circuit output admittance.*

As these admittance parameters are measured with either input or output port short-circuited, these are called *short-circuit admittance parameters.*

The equivalent circuit of the two-port network in terms of $Y$ parameters is shown in Fig. 12.15.

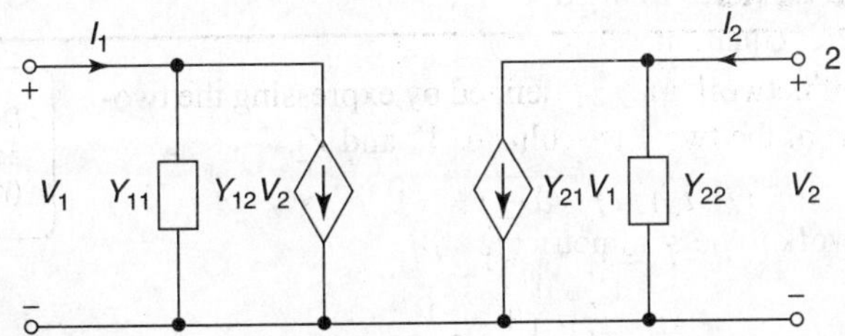


**Fig. 12.15** *Equivalent circuit of the two-port network in terms of Y parameters*

### 12.3.1 Condition for Reciprocity

(a) As shown in Fig. 12.16, voltage $V_s$ is applied at input port with the output port short-circuited.

i.e.,

$$V_1 = V_s$$
$$V_2 = 0$$
$$I_2 = -I_2'$$

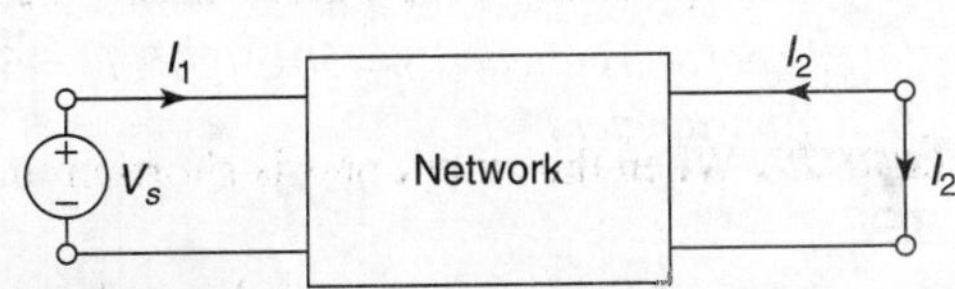


**Fig. 12.16** *Network for deriving condition for reciprocity*

From the $Y$ parameter equation,

$$-I_2' = Y_{21}\, V_s$$

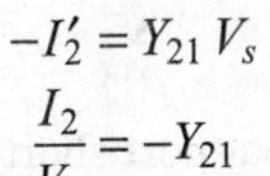

$$\frac{I_2}{V_s} = -Y_{21}$$

(b) As shown in Fig. 12.17, voltage $V_s$ is applied at output port with the input port short-circuited.

i.e.,

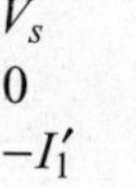

$$V_2 = V_s$$
$$V_1 = 0$$
$$I_1 = -I_1'$$

From the $Y$ parameter equation,

$$-I_1' = Y_{12} V_s$$

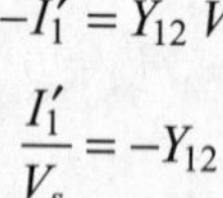

$$\frac{I_1'}{V_s} = -Y_{12}$$

**Fig. 12.17** *Network for deriving condition for reciprocity*

Hence, for the network to be reciprocal,

$$\frac{I_2'}{V_s} = \frac{I_1'}{V_s}$$

i.e.,
$$Y_{12} = Y_{21}$$

### 12.3.2 Condition for Symmetry

(a) When the output port is short-circuited, i.e., $V_2 = 0$.
From the $Y$ parameter equation,

$$I_1 = Y_{11} V_s$$
$$\frac{V_s}{I_1} = \frac{1}{Y_{11}}$$

(b) When the input port is short-circuited, i.e., $V_1 = 0$.
From the $Y$ parameter equation,

$$I_2 = Y_{22} V_s$$
$$\frac{V_s}{I_2} = \frac{1}{Y_{22}}$$

Hence, for the network to be symmetrical,

$$\frac{V_s}{I_1} = \frac{V_s}{I_2}$$

i.e.,
$$Y_{11} = Y_{22}$$

**EXAMPLE 12.7**

*Test results for a two-port network are*
*(a) Port 2 short-circuited:* $V_1 = 50\angle 0°\ V, I_1 = 2.1\angle -30°\ A, I_2 = -1.1\angle -20°\ A$
*(b) Port 1 short-circuited:* $V_2 = 50\angle 0°\ V, I_2 = 3\angle -15°\ A, I_1 = -1.1\angle -20°\ A.$
*Find Y parameters.*

**Solution**

$$Y_{11} = \left.\frac{I_1}{V_1}\right|_{V_2=0} = \frac{2.1\angle -30°}{50\angle 0°} = 0.042\angle -30°\ \mho, \qquad Y_{12} = \left.\frac{I_1}{V_2}\right|_{V_1=0} = \frac{-1.1\angle -20°}{50\angle 0°} = -0.022\angle -20°\ \mho$$

$$Y_{21} = \left.\frac{I_2}{V_1}\right|_{V_2=0} = \frac{-1.1\angle -20°}{50\angle 0°} = -0.022\angle -20°\ \mho, \qquad Y_{22} = \left.\frac{I_2}{V_2}\right|_{V_1=0} = \frac{3\angle -15°}{50\angle 0°} = 0.06\angle -15°\ \mho$$

Hence, the $Y$ parameters are

$$\begin{bmatrix} Y_{11} & Y_{12} \\ Y_{21} & Y_{22} \end{bmatrix} = \begin{bmatrix} 0.042\angle -30° & -0.022\angle -20° \\ -0.022\angle -20° & 0.06\angle -15° \end{bmatrix}$$

**EXAMPLE 12.8**

*Find Y parameters for the network shown in Fig. 12.18.*

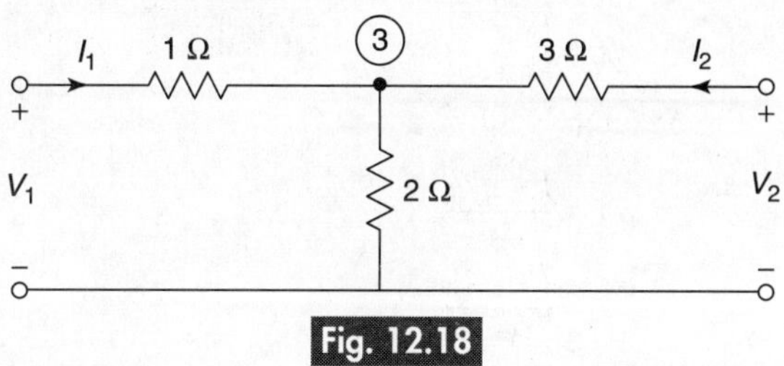


Fig. 12.18

**Solution**

**First Method**

***Case 1*** When the output port is short-circuited, i.e., $V_2 = 0$, as shown in Fig. 12.19,

$$R_{eq} = 1 + \frac{2 \times 3}{2+3} = 1 + \frac{6}{5} = \frac{11}{5}\ \Omega$$

Now,

$$V_1 = \frac{11}{5} I_1$$

$$Y_{11} = \left.\frac{I_1}{V_1}\right|_{V_2=0} = \frac{5}{11}\ \mho$$

Also,

$$I_2 = \frac{2}{5}(-I_1) = -\frac{2}{5} \times \frac{5}{11} V_1 = -\frac{2}{11} V_1$$

$$Y_{21} = \left.\frac{I_2}{V_1}\right|_{V_2=0} = -\frac{2}{11}\ \mho$$

Fig. 12.19

***Case 2*** When the input port is short-circuited, i.e., $V_1 = 0$, as shown in Fig. 12.20,

$$R_{eq} = 3 + \frac{1 \times 2}{1+2} = 3 + \frac{2}{3} = \frac{11}{3}\ \Omega$$

Now,

$$V_2 = \frac{11}{3} I_2$$

$$Y_{22} = \left.\frac{I_2}{V_2}\right|_{V_1=0} = \frac{3}{11}\ \mho$$

Also,

$$I_1 = \frac{2}{3}(-I_2) = -\frac{2}{3} \times \frac{3}{11} V_2 = -\frac{2}{11} V_2$$

$$Y_{12} = \left.\frac{I_1}{V_2}\right|_{V_1=0} = -\frac{2}{11}\ \mho$$

Fig. 12.20

Hence, the $Y$ parameters are

$$\begin{bmatrix} Y_{11} & Y_{12} \\ Y_{21} & Y_{22} \end{bmatrix} = \begin{bmatrix} \frac{5}{11} & -\frac{2}{11} \\ -\frac{2}{11} & \frac{3}{11} \end{bmatrix}$$

**Second Method** (Refer Fig. 12.18)

$$I_1 = \frac{V_1 - V_3}{1}$$

$$= V_1 - V_3 \quad \text{...(i)}$$

$$I_2 = \frac{V_2 - V_3}{3}$$

$$= \frac{V_2}{3} - \frac{V_3}{3} \quad \text{...(ii)}$$

Applying KCL at node 3,

$$I_1 + I_2 = \frac{V_3}{2} \quad \text{...(iii)}$$

Substituting Eqs (i) and (ii) in Eq. (iii),

$$V_1 - V_3 + \frac{V_2}{3} - \frac{V_3}{3} = \frac{V_3}{2}$$

$$V_1 + \frac{V_2}{3} = \frac{11}{6} V_3$$

$$V_3 = \frac{6}{11} V_1 + \frac{2}{11} V_2 \quad \text{...(iv)}$$

Substituting Eq. (iv) in Eq. (i),

$$I_1 = V_1 - \frac{6}{11} V_1 - \frac{2}{11} V_2$$

$$= \frac{5}{11} V_1 - \frac{2}{11} V_2 \quad \text{...(v)}$$

Substituting Eq. (iv) in Eq. (ii),

$$I_2 = \frac{V_2}{3} - \frac{1}{3}\left(\frac{6}{11} V_1 + \frac{2}{11} V_2\right)$$

$$= -\frac{2}{11} V_1 + \frac{3}{11} V_2 \quad \text{...(vi)}$$

Comparing Eqs (v) and (vi) with $Y$ parameter equations,

$$\begin{bmatrix} Y_{11} & Y_{12} \\ Y_{21} & Y_{22} \end{bmatrix} = \begin{bmatrix} \frac{5}{11} & -\frac{2}{11} \\ -\frac{2}{11} & \frac{3}{11} \end{bmatrix}$$

## EXAMPLE 12.9

*Find Y parameters of the network shown in Fig. 12.21.*

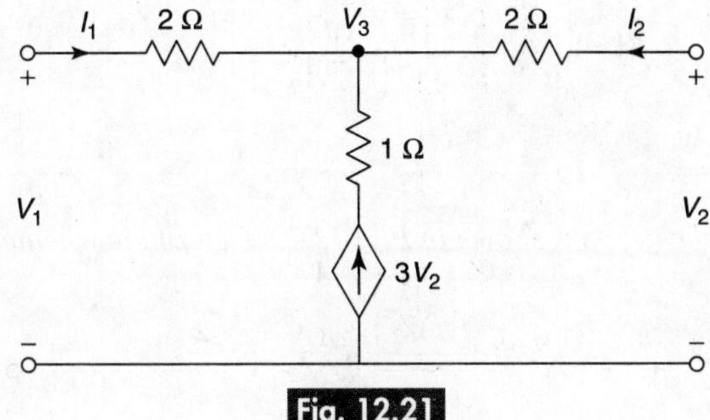


Fig. 12.21

**Solution** From Fig. 12.21,

$$I_1 = \frac{V_1 - V_3}{2}$$

$$= \frac{1}{2}V_1 - \frac{1}{2}V_3 \qquad \text{...(i)}$$

$$I_2 = \frac{V_2 - V_3}{2}$$

$$= \frac{1}{2}V_2 - \frac{1}{2}V_3 \qquad \text{...(ii)}$$

Applying KCL at node 3,

$$I_1 + I_2 + 3V_2 = 0 \qquad \text{...(iii)}$$

Substituting Eqs (i) and (ii) in Eq. (iii),

$$\frac{V_1 - V_3}{2} + \frac{V_2 - V_3}{2} + 3V_2 = 0$$

$$2V_3 = V_1 + 7V_2$$

$$V_3 = \frac{1}{2}V_1 + \frac{7}{2}V_2 \qquad \text{...(iv)}$$

Substituting Eq. (iv) in Eq. (i),

$$I_1 = \frac{1}{2}V_1 - \frac{1}{2}\left(\frac{1}{2}V_1 + \frac{7}{2}V_2\right)$$

$$= \frac{1}{4}V_1 - \frac{7}{4}V_2 \qquad \text{...(v)}$$

Substituting Eq. (iv) in Eq. (ii),

$$I_2 = \frac{1}{2}V_2 - \frac{1}{2}\left(\frac{1}{2}V_1 + \frac{7}{2}V_2\right)$$

$$= -\frac{1}{4}V_1 - \frac{5}{4}V_2 \qquad \text{...(vi)}$$

Comparing Eqs (v) and (vi) with *Y* parameter equations,

$$\begin{bmatrix} Y_{11} & Y_{12} \\ Y_{21} & Y_{22} \end{bmatrix} = \begin{bmatrix} \frac{1}{4} & -\frac{7}{4} \\ -\frac{1}{4} & -\frac{5}{4} \end{bmatrix}$$

## EXAMPLE 12.10

*Determine Y parameters for the network shown in Fig. 12.22. Determine whether the network is symmetrical and reciprocal.*

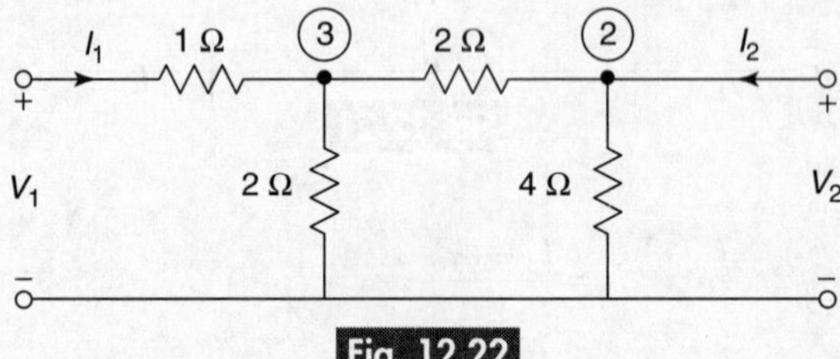


Fig. 12.22

**Solution** From Fig. 12.31,

$$I_1 = \frac{V_1 - V_3}{1}$$

$$= V_1 - V_3 \qquad \ldots\text{(i)}$$

Applying KCL at node 3,

$$I_1 = \frac{V_3}{2} + \frac{V_3 - V_2}{2}$$

$$= V_3 - \frac{V_2}{2} \qquad \ldots\text{(ii)}$$

Applying KCL at node 2,

$$I_2 = \frac{V_2}{4} + \frac{V_2 - V_3}{2}$$

$$= \frac{3}{4}V_2 - \frac{V_3}{2} \qquad \ldots\text{(iii)}$$

Substituting Eq. (i) in Eq. (ii),

$$V_1 - V_3 = V_3 - \frac{V_2}{2}$$

$$V_3 = \frac{V_1}{2} + \frac{V_2}{4} \qquad \ldots\text{(iv)}$$

Substituting Eq. (iv) in Eq. (ii),

$$I_1 = \frac{V_1}{2} + \frac{V_2}{4} - \frac{V_2}{2}$$

$$= \frac{V_1}{2} - \frac{V_2}{4} \qquad \ldots\text{(v)}$$

Substituting Eq. (iv) in Eq. (iii),

$$I_2 = \frac{3}{4}V_2 - \frac{1}{2}\left(\frac{V_1}{2} + \frac{V_2}{4}\right)$$

$$= -\frac{V_1}{4} + \frac{5V_2}{8} \quad \text{...(vi)}$$

Comparing Eqs (v) and (vi) with $Y$ parameter equations,

$$\begin{bmatrix} Y_{11} & Y_{12} \\ Y_{21} & Y_{22} \end{bmatrix} = \begin{bmatrix} \frac{1}{2} & -\frac{1}{4} \\ -\frac{1}{4} & \frac{5}{8} \end{bmatrix}$$

Since $Y_{11} \neq Y_{22}$, the network is not symmetrical.
Since $Y_{12} = Y_{21}$, the network is reciprocal.

**EXAMPLE 12.11**

*Determine the short-circuit admittance parameters for the network shown in Fig. 12.23.*

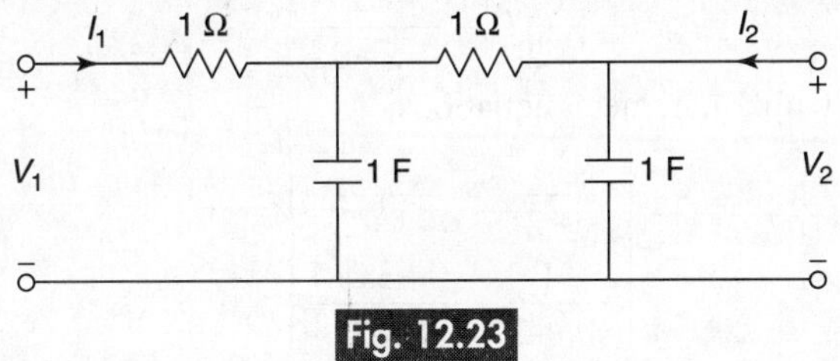


Fig. 12.23

**Solution** The transformed network is shown in Fig. 12.24.

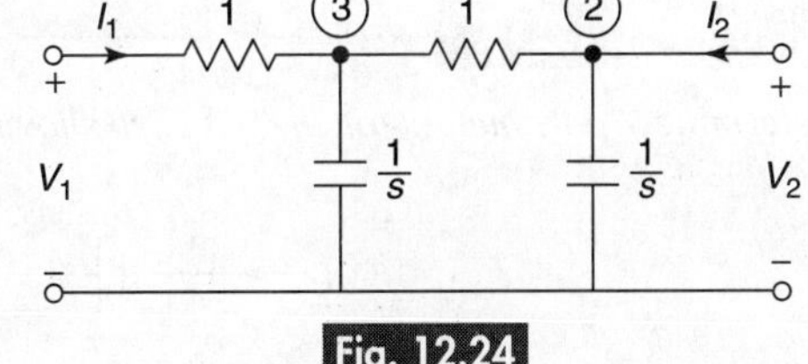


Fig. 12.24

From Fig. 12.24,

$$I_1 = \frac{V_1 - V_3}{1}$$

$$= V_1 - V_3 \quad \text{...(i)}$$

Applying KCL at node 3,

$$I_1 = \frac{V_3}{\frac{1}{s}} + \frac{(V_3 - V_2)}{1}$$

$$= (s+1)V_3 - V_2 \quad \text{...(ii)}$$

Applying KCL at node 2,

$$I_2 = \frac{V_2}{\frac{1}{s}} + \frac{(V_2 - V_3)}{1}$$

$$= (s+1)V_2 - V_3 \quad \text{...(iii)}$$

Substituting Eq. (i) in Eq. (ii),

$$V_1 - V_3 = (s+1)\,V_3 - V_2$$

$$(s+2)\,V_3 = V_1 + V_2$$

$$V_3 = \frac{1}{s+2}V_1 + \frac{1}{s+2}V_2 \qquad \text{...(iv)}$$

Substituting Eq. (iv) in Eq. (ii),

$$I_1 = (s+1)\left(\frac{1}{s+2}V_1 + \frac{1}{s+2}V_2\right) - V_2$$

$$= \frac{s+1}{s+2}V_1 - \frac{1}{s+2}V_2 \qquad \text{...(v)}$$

Substituting Eq. (iv) in Eq. (iii),

$$I_2 = (s+1)\,V_2 - \left(\frac{1}{s+2}V_1 + \frac{1}{s+2}V_2\right)$$

$$= -\frac{1}{s+2}V_1 + \frac{s^2+3s+1}{s+2}V_2 \qquad \text{...(vi)}$$

Comparing Eqs (v) and (vi) with $Y$ parameter equations,

$$\begin{bmatrix} Y_{11} & Y_{12} \\ Y_{21} & Y_{22} \end{bmatrix} = \begin{bmatrix} \dfrac{s+1}{s+2} & -\dfrac{1}{s+2} \\ -\dfrac{1}{s+2} & \dfrac{s^2+3s+1}{s+2} \end{bmatrix}$$

**EXAMPLE 12.12**

*Determine Y parameters for the network shown in Fig. 12.25.*

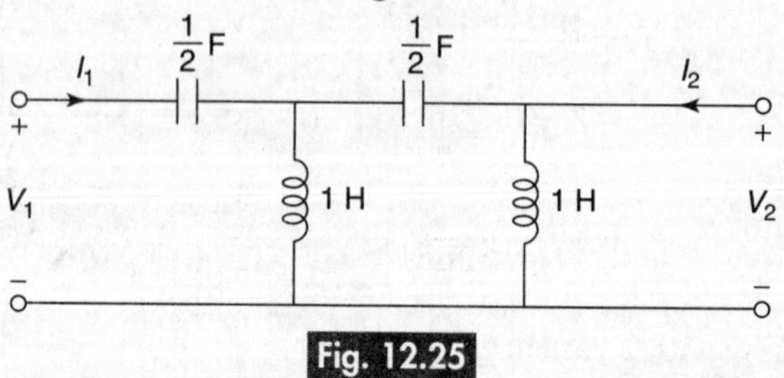


Fig. 12.25

**Solution** The transformed network is shown in Fig. 12.26.
From Fig. 12.26,

$$I_1 = \frac{V_1 - V_3}{\frac{2}{s}}$$

$$= \frac{s}{2}V_1 - \frac{s}{2}V_3 \qquad \text{...(i)}$$

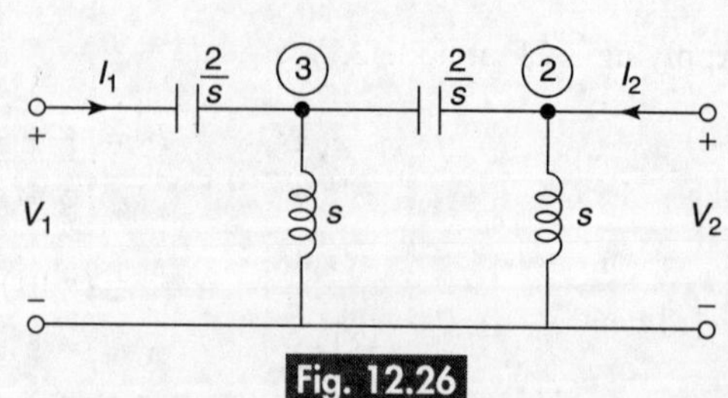


Fig. 12.26

Applying KCL at node 3,

$$\frac{s}{2}(V_1 - V_3) = \frac{V_3}{s} + \frac{s}{2}(V_3 - V_2)$$

$$\frac{s}{2}V_3 + \frac{1}{s}V_3 + \frac{s}{2}V_3 = \frac{s}{2}V_1 + \frac{s}{2}V_2$$

$$V_3 = \frac{s^2}{2(s^2+1)}V_1 + \frac{s^2}{2(s^2+1)}V_2 \qquad \text{...(ii)}$$

Substituting Eq. (ii) in Eq. (i),

$$I_1 = \frac{s}{2}V_1 - \frac{s}{2}\left[\frac{s^2}{2(s^2+1)}V_1 + \frac{s^2}{2(s^2+1)}V_2\right]$$

$$= \left[\frac{s}{2} - \frac{s^3}{4(s^2+1)}\right]V_1 - \frac{s^3}{4(s^2+1)}V_2$$

$$= \frac{s^3+2s}{4(s^2+1)}V_1 - \frac{s^3}{4(s^2+1)}V_2 \qquad \text{...(iii)}$$

Applying KCL at node 2,

$$I_2 = \frac{V_2}{s} + \frac{s}{2}(V_2 - V_3)$$

$$= \frac{s^2+2}{2s}V_2 - \frac{s}{2}V_3 \qquad \text{...(iv)}$$

Substituting Eq. (ii) in Eq. (iv),

$$I_2 = \frac{s^2+2}{2s}V_2 - \frac{s}{2}\left[\frac{s^2}{2(s^2+1)}V_1 + \frac{s^2}{2(s^2+1)}V_2\right]$$

$$= -\frac{s^3}{4(s^2+1)}V_1 + \left[\frac{s^2+2}{2s} - \frac{s^3}{4(s^2+1)}\right]V_2$$

$$= -\frac{s^3}{4(s^2+1)}V_1 + \frac{s^4+6s^2+4}{4s(s^2+1)}V_2 \qquad \text{...(v)}$$

Comparing Eqs (iii) and (v) with $Y$ parameter equation,

$$\begin{bmatrix} Y_{11} & Y_{12} \\ Y_{21} & Y_{22} \end{bmatrix} = \begin{bmatrix} \dfrac{s^3+2s}{4(s^2+1)} & -\dfrac{s^3}{4(s^2+1)} \\ -\dfrac{s^3}{4(s^2+1)} & \dfrac{s^4+6s^2+4}{4s(s^2+1)} \end{bmatrix}$$

## EXAMPLE 12.13

*Obtain Y parameters of the network shown in Fig. 12.27.*

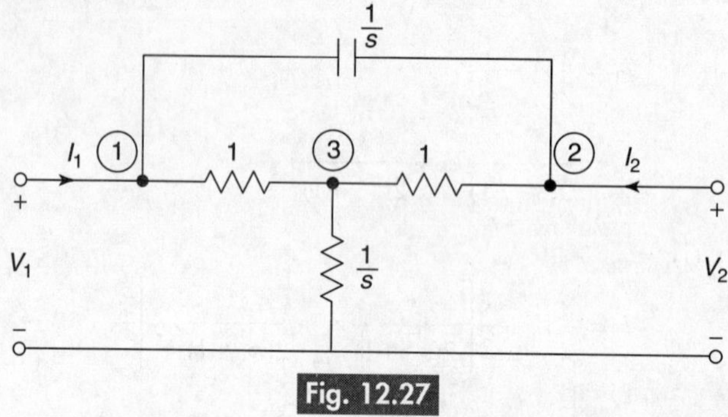


Fig. 12.27

**Solution**

Applying KCL at node 1,

$$I_1 = \frac{V_1 - V_3}{1} + \frac{V_1 - V_2}{\frac{1}{s}}$$

$$= (s+1)\,V_1 - s\,V_2 - V_3 \qquad \text{...(i)}$$

Applying KCL at node 2,

$$I_2 = \frac{V_2 - V_3}{1} + \frac{V_2 - V_1}{\frac{1}{s}}$$

$$= (s+1)\,V_2 - s\,V_1 - V_3 \qquad \text{...(ii)}$$

Applying KCL at node 3,

$$\frac{V_3}{\frac{1}{s}} + \frac{V_3 - V_1}{1} + \frac{V_3 - V_2}{1} = 0$$

$$(s+2)\,V_3 - V_1 - V_2 = 0$$

$$V_3 = \frac{1}{s+2}V_1 + \frac{1}{s+2}V_2 \qquad \text{...(iii)}$$

Substituting Eq. (iii) in Eq. (i),

$$I_1 = (s+1)\,V_1 - sV_2 - \left(\frac{1}{s+2}V_1 + \frac{1}{s+2}V_2\right)$$

$$= \left[\frac{(s+1)(s+2)-1}{(s+2)}\right]V_1 - \left[\frac{s(s+2)+1}{(s+2)}\right]V_2$$

$$= \left(\frac{s^2+3s+1}{s+2}\right)V_1 - \left(\frac{s^2+2s+1}{s+2}\right)V_2 \qquad \text{...(iv)}$$

Substituting Eq. (iii) in Eq. (ii),

$$I_2 = (s+1)V_2 - sV_1 - \left(\frac{1}{s+2}V_1 + \frac{1}{s+2}V_2\right)$$

$$= -\left[\frac{s(s+2)+1}{(s+2)}\right]V_1 + \left[\frac{(s+1)(s+2)-1}{(s+2)}\right]V_2$$

$$= -\left(\frac{s^2+2s+1}{s+2}\right)V_1 + \left(\frac{s^2+3s+1}{s+2}\right)V_2 \qquad \ldots\text{(v)}$$

Comparing Eqs (iv) and (v) with *Y* parameter equations,

$$\begin{bmatrix} Y_{11} & Y_{12} \\ Y_{21} & Y_{22} \end{bmatrix} = \begin{bmatrix} \dfrac{s^2+3s+1}{s+2} & -\dfrac{(s^2+2s+1)}{s+2} \\ -\dfrac{(s^2+2s+1)}{s+2} & \dfrac{s^2+3s+1}{s+2} \end{bmatrix}$$

## 12.4 TRANSMISSION PARAMETERS (*ABCD* PARAMETERS)

LO 12.4

Discuss transmission and inverse-transmission parameters

The transmission parameters or chain parameters or *ABCD* parameters serve to relate the voltage and current at the input port to voltage and current at the output port. In equation form,

$$(V_1, I_1) = f(V_2, -I_2)$$

$$V_1 = AV_2 - BI_2$$

$$I_1 = CV_2 - DI_2$$

Here, the negative sign is used with $I_2$ and not for parameters *B* and *D*. The reason the current $I_2$ carries a negative sign is that in transmission field, the output current is assumed to be coming out of the output port instead of going into the port.

In matrix form, we can write

$$\begin{bmatrix} V_1 \\ I_1 \end{bmatrix} = \begin{bmatrix} A & B \\ C & D \end{bmatrix}\begin{bmatrix} V_2 \\ -I_2 \end{bmatrix}$$

where matrix $\begin{bmatrix} A & B \\ C & D \end{bmatrix}$ is called transmission matrix.

For a given network, these parameters are determined as follows:

➤ ***Case 1*** When the output port is open-circuited, i.e., $I_2 = 0$

$$A = \left.\frac{V_1}{V_2}\right|_{I_2=0}$$

where *A* is the reverse voltage gain with the output port open-circuited.

Similarly,

$$C = \left.\frac{I_1}{V_2}\right|_{I_2=0}$$

where *C* is the transfer admittance with the output port open-circuited.

➤ ***Case 2*** When output port is short-circuited, i.e., $V_2 = 0$

$$B = -\left.\frac{V_1}{I_2}\right|_{V_2=0}$$

where $B$ is the transfer impedance with the output port short-circuited.

Similarly,
$$D = -\left.\frac{I_1}{I_2}\right|_{V_2=0}$$

where $D$ is the reverse current gain with the output port short-circuited.

### 12.4.1 Condition for Reciprocity

(a) As shown in Fig. 12.28, voltage $V_s$ is applied at the input port with the output port short-circuited.

i.e.,

$$V_1 = V_s$$
$$V_2 = 0$$
$$I_2' = -I_2$$

From the transmission parameter equations,

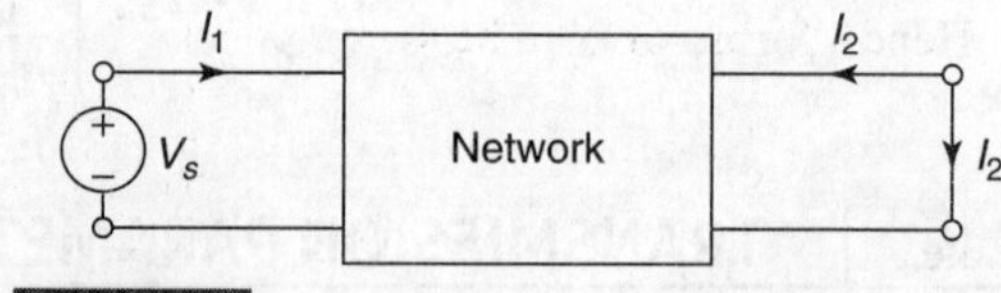


**Fig. 12.28** *Network for deriving condition for reciprocity*

$$V_s = B I_2'$$
$$\frac{V_s}{I_2'} = B$$

(b) As shown in Fig. 12.29, voltage $V_s$ is applied at the output port with the input port short-circuited.

i.e.,

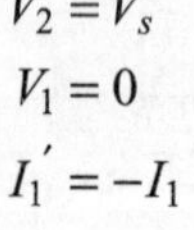

$$V_2 = V_s$$
$$V_1 = 0$$
$$I_1' = -I_1$$

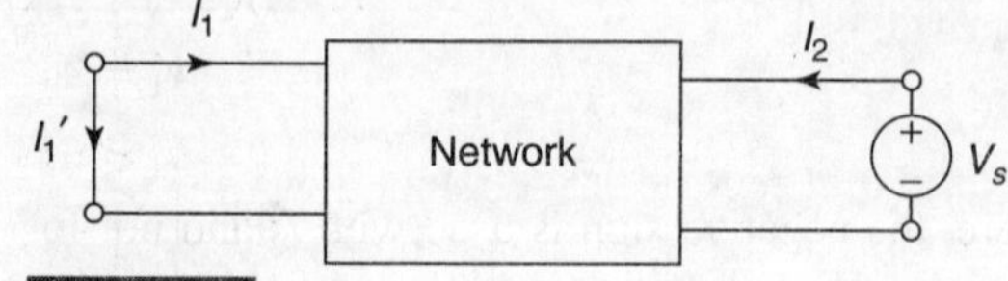


**Fig. 12.29** *Network for deriving condition for reciprocity*

From the transmission parameter equations,

$$0 = AV_s - BI_2$$
$$-I_1' = CV_s - DI_2$$
$$I_2 = \frac{A}{B} V_s$$
$$-I_1' = CV_s - \frac{AD}{B} V_s$$
$$\frac{V_s}{I_1'} = \frac{B}{AD - BC}$$

Hence, for the network to be reciprocal,

$$\frac{V_s}{I_2'} = \frac{V_s}{I_1'}$$

i.e.,
$$B = \frac{B}{AD - BC}$$

i.e.,
$$AD - BC = 1$$

### 12.4.2 Condition for Symmetry

(a) When the output port is open-circuited, i.e., $I_2 = 0$.
From the transmission-parameter equations,

$$V_s = AV_2$$
$$I_1 = CV_2$$
$$\frac{V_s}{I_1} = \frac{A}{C}$$

(b) When the input port is open-circuited, i.e., $I_1 = 0$.
From the transmission parameter equation,

$$CV_s = DI_2$$
$$\frac{V_s}{I_2} = \frac{D}{C}$$

Hence, for network to be symmetrical,

$$\frac{V_s}{I_1} = \frac{V_s}{I_2}$$

i.e., $$A = D$$

**EXAMPLE 12.14**

*Find the transmission parameters for the network shown in Fig. 12.30.*

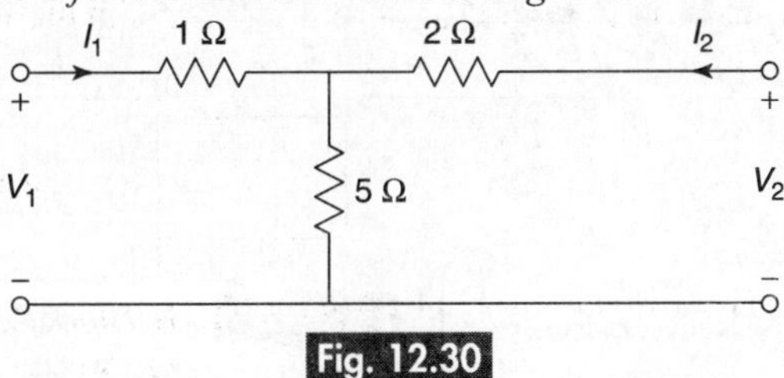

Fig. 12.30

**Solution**

**First Method**

*Case 1* When the output port is open-circuited, i.e., $I_2 = 0$.

$$V_1 = 6I_1$$

and $$V_2 = 5I_1$$

$$A = \left.\frac{V_1}{V_2}\right|_{I_2=0} = \frac{6I_1}{5I_1} = \frac{6}{5}$$

$$C = \left.\frac{I_1}{V_2}\right|_{I_2=0} = \frac{1}{5}\ \mho$$

*Case 2* When the output port is short-circuited, i.e., $V_2 = 0$, as shown in Fig. 12.31,

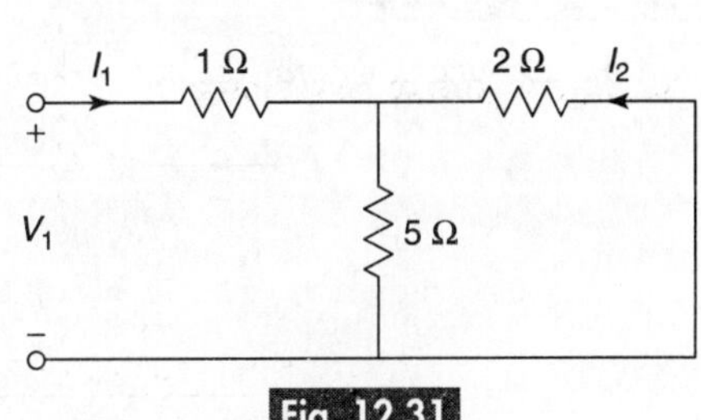

Fig. 12.31

$$R_{eq} = 1 + \frac{5 \times 2}{5+2} = 1 + \frac{10}{7} = \frac{17}{7}\ \Omega$$

Now, $$V_1 = \frac{17}{7} I_1$$

and $$I_2 = \frac{5}{7}(-I_1) = -\frac{5}{7}I_1$$

$$B = -\left.\frac{V_1}{I_2}\right|_{V_2=0} = -\frac{\frac{17}{7}I_1}{-\frac{5}{7}I_1} = \frac{17}{5}\ \Omega$$

$$D = -\left.\frac{I_1}{I_2}\right|_{V_2=0} = \frac{7}{5}$$

Hence, the transmission parameters are

$$\begin{bmatrix} A & B \\ C & D \end{bmatrix} = \begin{bmatrix} \frac{6}{5} & \frac{17}{5} \\ \frac{1}{5} & \frac{7}{5} \end{bmatrix}$$

**Second Method** (Refer Fig. 12.37)
Applying KVL to mesh 1,

$$V_1 = 6I_1 + 5I_2 \qquad \text{...(i)}$$

Applying KVL to mesh 2,

$$V_2 = 5I_1 + 7I_2 \qquad \text{...(ii)}$$

Hence,

$$5I_1 = V_2 - 7I_2$$

$$I_1 = \frac{1}{5}V_2 - \frac{7}{5}I_2 \qquad \text{...(iii)}$$

Substituting Eq. (iii) in Eq. (i),

$$V_1 = 6\left(\frac{1}{5}V_2 - \frac{7}{5}I_2\right) + 5I_2$$

$$= \frac{6}{5}V_2 - \frac{17}{5}I_2 \qquad \text{...(iv)}$$

Comparing Eqs (iii) and (iv) with transmission parameter equations,

$$\begin{bmatrix} A & B \\ C & D \end{bmatrix} = \begin{bmatrix} \frac{6}{5} & \frac{17}{5} \\ \frac{1}{5} & \frac{7}{5} \end{bmatrix}$$

## EXAMPLE 12.15

*Obtain ABCD parameters for the network shown in Fig. 12.32.*

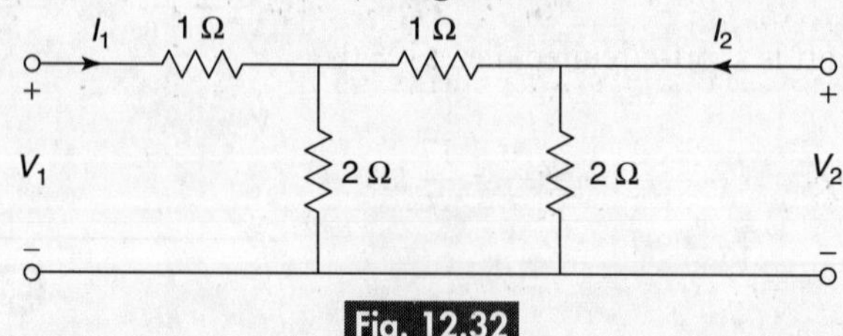


Fig. 12.32

**Solution** The network is redrawn, as shown in Fig. 12.33.

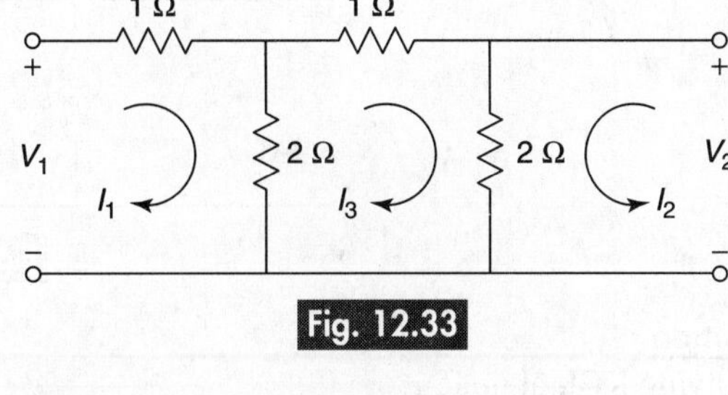


Fig. 12.33

Applying KVL to mesh 1,

$$V_1 = 3I_1 - 2I_3 \qquad \text{...(i)}$$

Applying KVL to mesh 2,

$$V_2 = 2I_2 + 2I_3 \qquad \text{...(ii)}$$

Applying KVL to mesh 3,

$$-2(I_3 - I_1) - I_3 - 2(I_3 + I_2) = 0$$

$$5I_3 = 2I_1 - 2I_2$$

$$I_3 = \frac{2}{5}I_1 - \frac{2}{5}I_2 \qquad \text{...(iii)}$$

Substituting Eq. (iii) in Eq. (i),

$$V_1 = 3I_1 - 2\left(\frac{2}{5}I_1 - \frac{2}{5}I_2\right)$$

$$= \frac{11}{5}I_1 + \frac{4}{5}I_2 \qquad \text{...(iv)}$$

Substituting Eq. (iii) in Eq. (ii),

$$V_2 = 2I_2 + 2\left(\frac{2}{5}I_1 - \frac{2}{5}I_2\right)$$

$$= \frac{4}{5}I_1 + \frac{6}{5}I_2$$

$$\frac{4}{5}I_1 = V_2 - \frac{6}{5}I_2$$

$$I_1 = \frac{5}{4}V_2 - \frac{3}{2}I_2 \qquad \text{...(v)}$$

Substituting Eq. (v) in Eq. (iv),

$$V_1 = \frac{11}{5}\left(\frac{5}{4}V_2 - \frac{3}{2}I_2\right) + \frac{4}{5}I_2$$

$$= \frac{11}{4}V_2 - \frac{5}{2}I_2 \qquad \text{...(vi)}$$

Comparing Eqs (v) and (vi) with *ABCD* parameter equations,

$$\begin{bmatrix} A & B \\ C & D \end{bmatrix} = \begin{bmatrix} \frac{11}{4} & \frac{5}{2} \\ \frac{5}{4} & \frac{3}{2} \end{bmatrix}$$

**EXAMPLE 12.16**

*Determine the transmission parameters for the network shown in Fig. 12.34.*

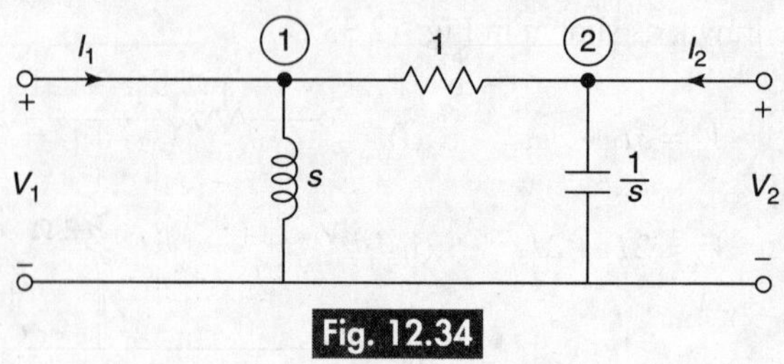

Fig. 12.34

**Solution**

Applying KCL at node 1,

$$I_1 = \frac{V_1}{s} + (V_1 - V_2)$$

$$= \frac{s+1}{s} V_1 - V_2 \qquad \text{...(i)}$$

Applying KCL at node 2,

$$I_2 = \frac{V_2}{\frac{1}{s}} + (V_2 - V_1)$$

$$= (s+1)\, V_2 - V_1$$

$$V_1 = (s+1)\, V_2 - I_2 \qquad \text{...(ii)}$$

Substituting Eq. (ii) in Eq. (i),

$$I_1 = \frac{s+1}{s}[(s+1)\, V_2 - I_2] - V_2$$

$$= \left[\frac{(s+1)^2}{s} - 1\right] V_2 - \frac{s+1}{s} I_2$$

$$= \left(\frac{s^2+s+1}{s}\right) V_2 - \left(\frac{s+1}{s}\right) I_2 \qquad \text{...(iii)}$$

Comparing Eqs (ii) and (iii) with *ABCD* parameter equations,

$$\begin{bmatrix} A & B \\ C & D \end{bmatrix} = \begin{bmatrix} s+1 & 1 \\ \frac{s^2+s+1}{s} & \frac{s+1}{s} \end{bmatrix}$$

**EXAMPLE 12.17**

*Find transmission parameters for the two-port network shown in Fig. 12.35.*

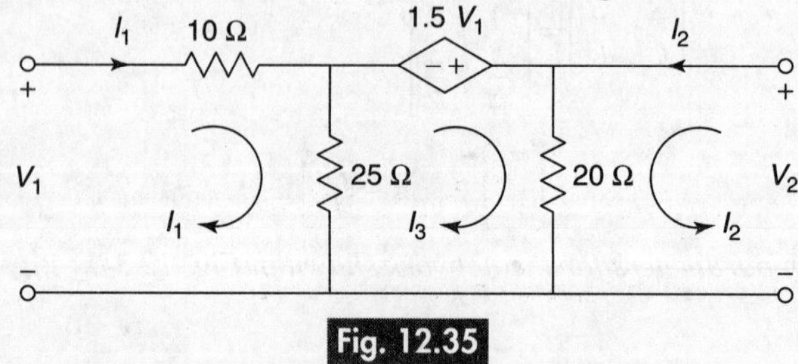

Fig. 12.35

**Solution** Applying KVL to mesh 1,

$$V_1 = 10I_1 + 25(I_1 - I_3)$$
$$= 35I_1 - 25I_3 \quad \text{...(i)}$$

Applying KVL to mesh 2,

$$V_2 = 20(I_2 + I_3)$$
$$= 20I_2 + 20I_3 \quad \text{...(ii)}$$

Applying KVL to mesh 3,

$$-25(I_3 - I_1) + 1.5\,V_1 - 20(I_2 + I_3) = 0$$
$$-25I_3 + 25I_1 + 1.5\,(35I_1 - 25I_3) - 20I_2 - 20I_3 = 0$$
$$-25I_3 + 25I_1 + 52.5I_1 - 37.5I_3 - 20I_2 - 20I_3 = 0$$
$$82.5I_3 = 77.5I_1 - 20I_2$$
$$I_3 = 0.94I_1 - 0.24I_2 \quad \text{...(iii)}$$

Substituting Eq. (iii) in Eq. (i),

$$V_1 = 35I_1 - 25(0.94I_1 - 0.24I_2)$$
$$= 11.5I_1 + 6I_2 \quad \text{...(iv)}$$

Substituting Eq. (iii) in Eq. (ii),

$$V_2 = 20I_2 + 20(0.94I_1 - 0.24I_2)$$
$$= 18.8I_1 + 15.2I_2 \quad \text{...(v)}$$

From Eq. (v),

$$I_1 = 0.053\,V_2 - 0.81I_2 \quad \text{...(vi)}$$

Substituting Eq. (vi) in Eq. (iv),

$$V_1 = 11.5(0.053\,V_2 - 0.81I_2) + 6I_2$$
$$= 0.61\,V_2 - 3.32I_2 \quad \text{...(vii)}$$

Comparing Eqs (vi) and (vii) with *ABCD* parameter equations,

$$\begin{bmatrix} A & B \\ C & D \end{bmatrix} = \begin{bmatrix} 0.61 & 3.32 \\ 0.053 & 0.81 \end{bmatrix}$$

## 12.5 INVERSE TRANSMISSION PARAMETERS (*A′B′C′D′* PARAMETERS)

LO 12.4

The inverse transmission parameters serve to relate the voltage and current at the output port to the voltage and current at the input port. In equation form,

$$(V_2, I_2) = f(V_1, -I_1)$$
$$V_2 = A'\,V_1 - B'I_1$$
$$I_2 = C'\,V_1 - D'I_1$$

In matrix form, we can write

$$\begin{bmatrix} V_2 \\ I_2 \end{bmatrix} = \begin{bmatrix} A' & B' \\ C' & D' \end{bmatrix} \begin{bmatrix} V_1 \\ -I_1 \end{bmatrix}$$

where matrix $\begin{bmatrix} A' & B' \\ C' & D' \end{bmatrix}$ is called the *inverse transmission matrix.*

For a given network, these parameters are determined as follows:

➤ ***Case 1*** When the input port is open-circuited, i.e., $I_1 = 0$

$$A' = \left.\frac{V_2}{V_1}\right|_{I_1=0}$$

where $A'$ is the forward voltage gain with the input port open-circuited.

Similarly,
$$C' = \left.\frac{I_2}{V_1}\right|_{I_1=0}$$

where $C'$ is the transfer admittance with the input port open-circuited.

➤ ***Case 2*** When the input port is short-circuited, i.e., $V_1 = 0$

$$B' = -\left.\frac{V_2}{I_1}\right|_{V_1=0}$$

where $B'$ is the transfer impedance with the input port short-circuited.
Similarly,

$$D' = -\left.\frac{I_2}{I_1}\right|_{V_1=0}$$

where $D'$ is the forward current gain with the input port short-circuited.

### 12.5.1 Condition for Reciprocity

(a) As shown in Fig. 12.36, voltage $V_s$ is applied at input port with the output port short-circuited.

i.e.,
$$V_1 = V_s$$
$$V_2 = 0$$
$$I_2 = -I_2'$$

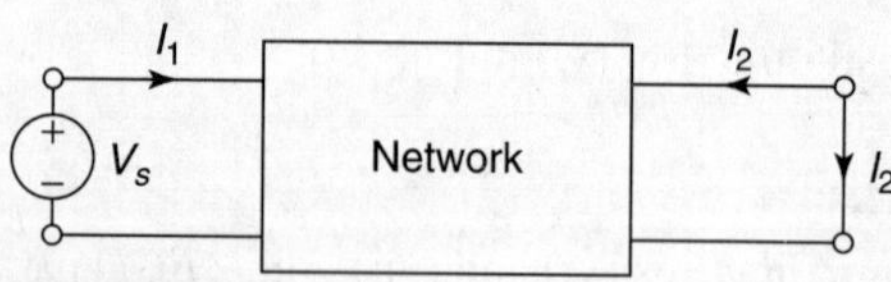


**Fig. 12.36** *Network for deriving condition for reciprocity*

From the inverse transmission parameter equations,

$$0 = A'V_s - B'I_1$$
$$-I_2' = C'V_s - D'I_1$$
$$\frac{I_2'}{V_s} = \frac{A'D' - B'C'}{B'}$$

(b) As shown in Fig. 12.37, voltage $V_s$ is applied at the output port with the input port short-circuited.

i.e.,
$$V_2 = V_s$$
$$V_1 = 0$$
$$I_1 = -I_1'$$

From the inverse transmission parameter equations,

$$V_s = B'I_1'$$
$$I_2 = \frac{A'}{B'}V_s$$
$$\frac{I_1'}{V_s} = \frac{1}{B'}$$

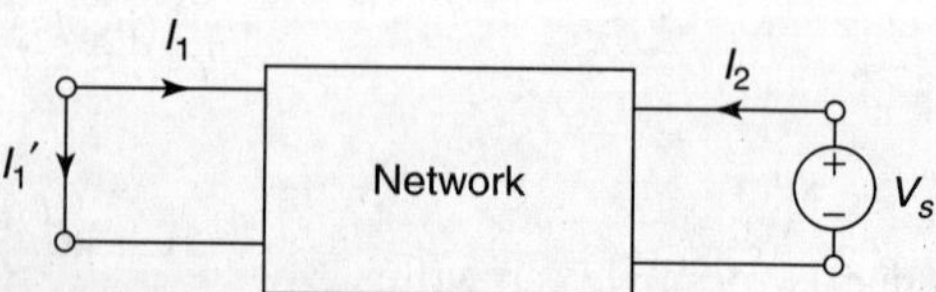


**Fig. 12.37** *Network for deriving condition for reciprocity*

Hence, for the network to be reciprocal,

$$\frac{I_2'}{V_s} = \frac{I_1'}{V_s}$$

i.e., $$A'D' - B'C' = 1$$

### 12.5.2 Condition for Symmetry

The condition for symmetry is obtained from the $Z$ parameters.

$$Z_{11} = \left.\frac{V_1}{I_1}\right|_{I_2=0} = 0 = \frac{D'}{C'}$$

Similarly,

$$Z_{22} = \left.\frac{V_2}{I_2}\right|_{I_1=0} = 0 = \frac{A'}{C'}$$

For symmetrical network

$$Z_{11} = Z_{22}$$

$$A' = D'$$

**EXAMPLE 12.18**

*Find the inverse transmission parameters for the network shown in Fig. 12.38.*

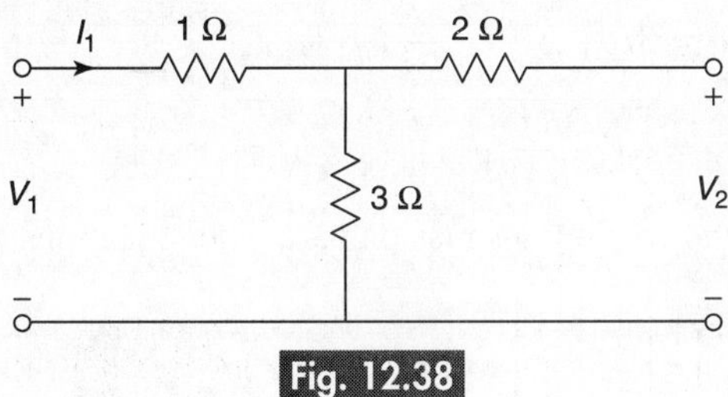


Fig. 12.38

**Solution**

**First method**

***Case 1*** When the input port is open-circuited, i.e., $I_1 = 0$

$$V_1 = 3I_2$$

$$V_2 = 5I_2$$

$$A' = \left.\frac{V_2}{V_1}\right|_{I_1=0} = \frac{5}{3}$$

$$C' = \left.\frac{I_2}{V_1}\right|_{I_1=0} = \frac{1}{3} \mho$$

***Case 2*** When the input port is short-circuited, i.e., $V_1 = 0$, as shown in Fig. 12.39.

By current division rule,

$$I_1 = -\frac{3}{4} I_2$$

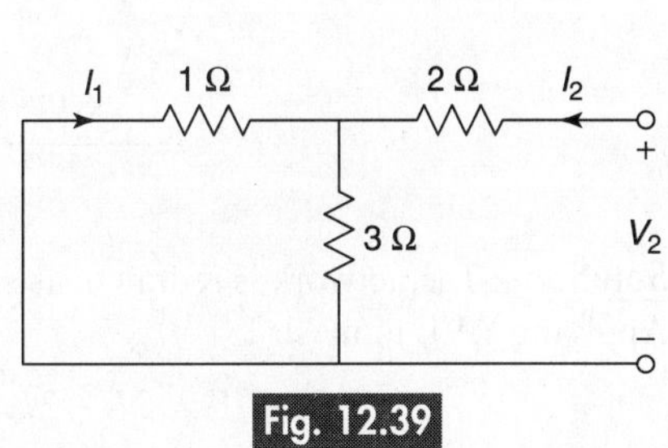


Fig. 12.39

$$D' = -\left.\frac{I_2}{I_1}\right|_{V_1=0} = \frac{4}{3}$$

$$R_{eq} = 2 + \frac{3\times1}{3+1} = 2 + \frac{3}{4} = \frac{11}{4}\,\Omega$$

$$V_2 = \frac{11}{4}I_2 = \frac{11}{4}\left(-\frac{4}{3}\right)I_1 = -\frac{11}{3}I_1$$

$$B' = -\left.\frac{V_2}{I_1}\right|_{V_1=0} = \frac{11}{3}\,\Omega$$

**Second Method** Refer Fig. 12.38.

Applying KVL to mesh 1,

$$V_1 = 4I_1 + 3I_2 \quad \text{...(i)}$$

Applying KVL to mesh 2,

$$V_2 = 3I_1 + 5I_2 \quad \text{...(ii)}$$

Hence,

$$3I_2 = V_1 - 4I_1$$

$$I_2 = \frac{1}{3}V_1 - \frac{4}{3}I_1 \quad \text{...(iii)}$$

Substituting Eq. (iii) in Eq. (ii),

$$V_2 = 3I_1 + 5\left(\frac{1}{3}V_1 - \frac{4}{3}I_1\right)$$

$$= \frac{5}{3}V_1 - \frac{11}{3}I_1 \quad \text{...(iv)}$$

Comparing Eqs (iii) and (iv) with inverse transmission parameter equations,

$$\begin{bmatrix} A' & B' \\ C' & D' \end{bmatrix} = \begin{bmatrix} \frac{5}{3} & \frac{11}{3} \\ \frac{1}{3} & \frac{4}{3} \end{bmatrix}$$

**EXAMPLE 12.19**

*Find the inverse transmission parameters for the network shown in Fig. 12.40*

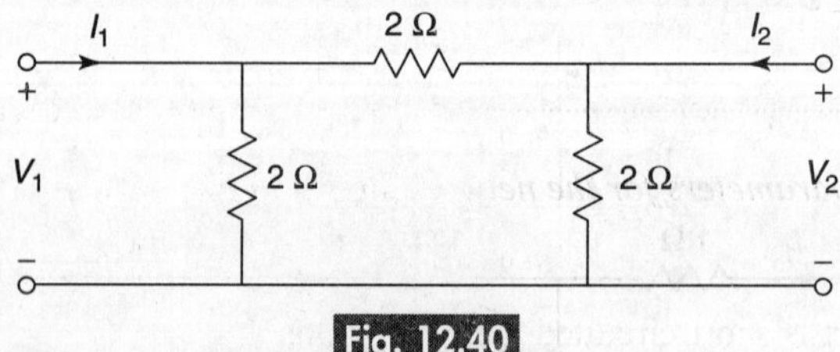


Fig. 12.40

**Solution** The network is redrawn, as shown in Fig. 12.41.

Applying KVL to mesh 1,

$$V_1 = 2I_1 - 2I_3 \quad \text{...(i)}$$

Applying KVL to mesh 2,

$$V_2 = 2I_2 + 2I_3 \quad \text{...(ii)}$$

Applying KVL to mesh 3,

$$-2I_1 + 2I_2 + 6I_3 = 0$$

$$I_3 = \frac{1}{3}I_1 - \frac{1}{3}I_2 \quad \text{...(iii)}$$

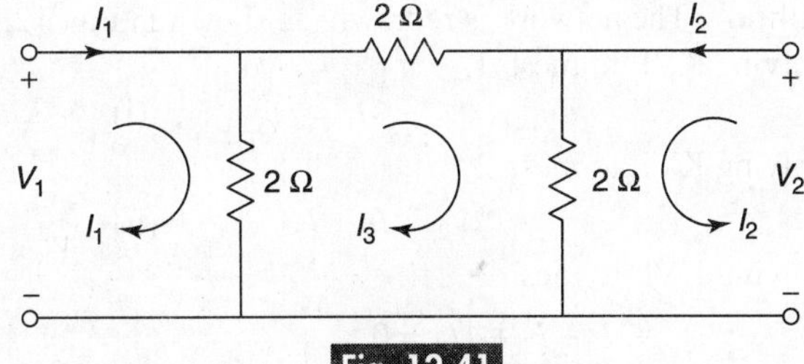


Fig. 12.41

Substituting Eq. (iii) in Eq. (i),

$$V_1 = 2I_1 - 2\left(\frac{1}{3}I_1 - \frac{1}{3}I_2\right)$$

$$= \frac{4}{3}I_1 + \frac{2}{3}I_2 \quad \text{...(iv)}$$

Substituting Eq. (iii) in Eq. (ii),

$$V_2 = 2I_2 + 2\left(\frac{1}{3}I_1 - \frac{1}{3}I_2\right)$$

$$= \frac{2}{3}I_1 + \frac{4}{3}I_2 \quad \text{...(v)}$$

Rewriting Eq. (iv),

$$\frac{2}{3}I_2 = V_1 - \frac{4}{3}I_1$$

$$I_2 = \frac{3}{2}V_1 - 2I_1 \quad \text{...(vi)}$$

Substituting Eq. (vi) in Eq. (v),

$$V_2 = \frac{2}{3}I_1 + \frac{4}{3}\left(\frac{3}{2}V_1 - 2I_1\right)$$

$$= 2V_1 - 2I_1 \quad \text{...(vii)}$$

Comparing Eq. (vi) and (vii) with inverse transmission parameter equations,

$$\begin{bmatrix} A' & B' \\ C' & D' \end{bmatrix} = \begin{bmatrix} 2 & 2 \\ \frac{3}{2} & 2 \end{bmatrix}$$

## EXAMPLE 12.20

*Find the inverse transmission parameters for the network shown in Fig. 12.42.*

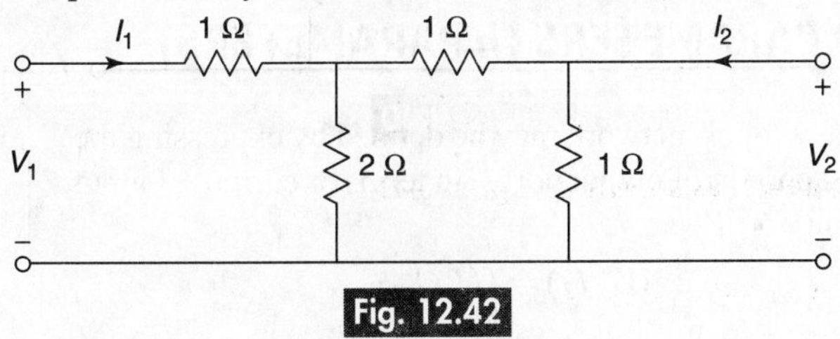


Fig. 12.42

**Solution** The network is redrawn, as shown in Fig. 12.43.

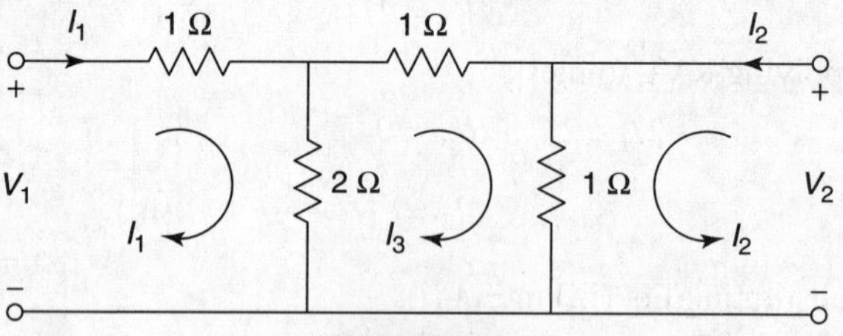

Applying KVL to mesh 1,

$$V_1 = 3I_1 - 2I_3 \quad \text{...(i)}$$

Applying KVL to mesh 2,

$$V_2 = I_2 + I_3 \quad \text{...(ii)}$$

Applying KVL to mesh 3,

$$-2I_1 + I_2 + 4I_3 = 0$$

$$I_3 = \frac{1}{2}I_1 - \frac{1}{4}I_2 \quad \text{...(iii)}$$

Fig. 12.43

Substituting Eq. (iii) in Eq. (i),

$$V_1 = 3I_1 - 2\left(\frac{1}{2}I_1 - \frac{1}{4}I_2\right)$$

$$= 2I_1 + \frac{1}{2}I_2 \quad \text{...(iv)}$$

Substituting Eq. (iii) in Eq. (ii),

$$V_2 = I_2 + \frac{1}{2}I_1 - \frac{1}{4}I_2$$

$$= \frac{1}{2}I_1 + \frac{3}{4}I_2 \quad \text{...(v)}$$

Rewriting Eq. (iv),

$$\frac{1}{2}I_2 = V_1 - 2I_1$$

$$I_2 = 2V_1 - 4I_1 \quad \text{...(vi)}$$

Substituting the Eq. (vi) in Eq. (v),

$$V_2 = \frac{1}{2}I_1 + \frac{3}{4}(2V_1 - 4I_1)$$

$$= \frac{3}{2}V_1 - \frac{5}{2}I_1 \quad \text{...(vii)}$$

Comparing Eqs (vi) and (vii) with inverse transmission-parameter equations,

$$\begin{bmatrix} A' & B' \\ C' & D' \end{bmatrix} = \begin{bmatrix} \frac{3}{2} & \frac{5}{2} \\ 2 & 4 \end{bmatrix}$$

## 12.6 HYBRID PARAMETERS (*h* PARAMETERS)

LO 12.5

Explain hybrid parameters (*h* parameters) and inverse-hybrid parameters (*g* parameters)

The hybrid parameters of a two-port network may be defined by expressing the voltage of input port $V_1$ and current of output port $I_2$ in terms of current of input port $I_1$ and voltage of output port $V_2$.

$$(V_1, I_2) = f(I_1, V_2)$$

$$V_1 = h_{11}\, I_1 + h_{12}\, V_2$$
$$I_2 = h_{21}\, I_1 + h_{22}\, V_2$$

In matrix form, we can write

$$\begin{bmatrix} V_1 \\ I_2 \end{bmatrix} = \begin{bmatrix} h_{11} & h_{12} \\ h_{21} & h_{22} \end{bmatrix} \begin{bmatrix} I_1 \\ V_2 \end{bmatrix}$$

The individual $h$ parameters can be defined by setting $I_1 = 0$ and $V_2 = 0$.

➤ ***Case 1*** When the output port is short-circuited i.e., $V_2 = 0$

$$h_{11} = \left.\frac{V_1}{I_1}\right|_{V_2=0}$$

where $h_{11}$ is the short-circuit input impedance.

$$h_{21} = \left.\frac{I_2}{I_1}\right|_{V_2=0}$$

where $h_{21}$ is the short-circuit forward current gain.

➤ ***Case 2*** When the input port is open-circuited, i.e., $I_1 = 0$

$$h_{12} = \left.\frac{V_1}{V_2}\right|_{I_1=0}$$

where $h_{12}$ is the open-circuit reverse voltage gain.

$$h_{22} = \left.\frac{I_2}{V_2}\right|_{I_1=0}$$

where $h_{22}$ is the open-circuit output admittance.

Since $h$ parameters represent dimensionally an impedance, an admittance, a voltage gain and a current gain, these are called *hybrid parameters*.

The equivalent circuit of a two-port network in terms of hybrid parameters is shown in Fig. 12.44.

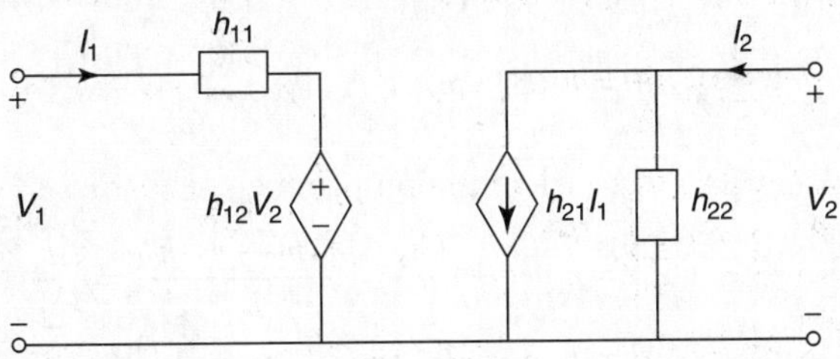


**Fig. 12.44** *Equivalent circuit of the two-port network in terms of h parameters*

### 12.6.1 Condition for Reciprocity

(a) As shown in Fig. 12.45, voltage $V_s$ is applied at the input port and the output port is short-circuited. i.e.,

$$V_1 = V_s$$
$$V_2 = 0$$
$$I_2{}' = -I_2$$

From the $h$ parameter equations,

$$V_s = h_{11} I_1$$
$$-I_2' = h_{21} I_1$$
$$\frac{V_s}{I_2'} = -\frac{h_{11}}{h_{21}}$$

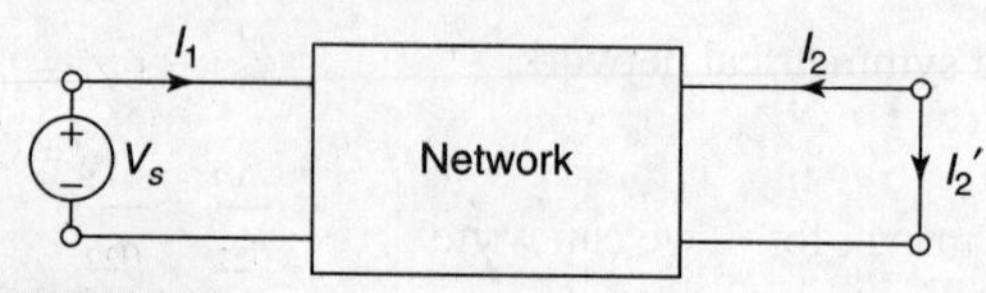

Fig. 12.45 *Network for deriving condition for reciprocity*

(b) As shown in Fig. 12.46, voltage $V_s$ is applied at the output port with the input port short-circuited.

i.e.,

$$V_1 = 0$$
$$V_2 = V_s$$
$$I_1 = -I_1'$$

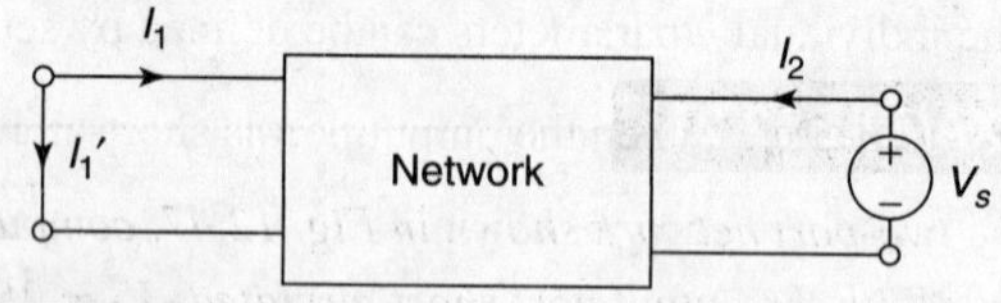

Fig. 12.46 *Network for deriving condition for reciprocity*

From the $h$ parameter equations,

$$0 = h_{11}I_1 + h_{12} V_s$$
$$h_{12} V_s = -h_{11} I_1 = h_{11} I_1'$$
$$\frac{V_s}{I_1'} = \frac{h_{11}}{h_{12}}$$

Hence, for the network to be reciprocal,

$$\frac{V_s}{I_2'} = \frac{V_s}{I_1'}$$

i.e.,

$$h_{21} = -h_{12}$$

### 12.6.2 Condition for Symmetry

The condition for symmetry is obtained from the $Z$ parameters.

$$Z_{11} = \left.\frac{V_1}{I_1}\right|_{I_2=0} = \left.\frac{h_{11}I_1 + h_{12}V_2}{I_1}\right|_{I_2=0} = h_{11} + h_{12}\frac{V_2}{I_1}$$

But with $I_2 = 0$,

$$0 = h_{21} I_1 + h_{22} V_2$$
$$\frac{V_2}{I_1} = -\frac{h_{21}}{h_{22}}$$
$$Z_{11} = h_{11} - \frac{h_{12}h_{21}}{h_{22}} = \frac{h_{11}h_{22} - h_{12}h_{21}}{h_{22}} = \frac{\Delta h}{h_{22}}$$

where

$$\Delta h = h_{11}h_{22} - h_{12}h_{21}$$

Similarly,

$$Z_{22} = \left.\frac{V_2}{I_2}\right|_{I_1=0}$$

With $I_1 = 0$,

$$I_2 = h_{22} V_2$$
$$Z_{22} = \left.\frac{V_2}{I_2}\right|_{I_1=0} = \frac{1}{h_{22}}$$

For a symmetrical network, $Z_{11} = Z_{22}$

i.e., $$\frac{\Delta h}{h_{22}} = \frac{1}{h_{22}}$$

i.e., $$\Delta h = 1$$

i.e., $$h_{11}\, h_{22} - h_{12}\, h_{21} = 1$$

**EXAMPLE 12.21**

*In the two-port network shown in Fig. 12.47, compute h parameters from the following data:*

*(a) With the output port short-circuited: $V_1 = 25\ V, I_1 = 1\ A, I_2 = 2\ A$*

*(b) With the input port open-circuited: $V_1 = 10\ V, V_2 = 50\ V, I_2 = 2\ A$*

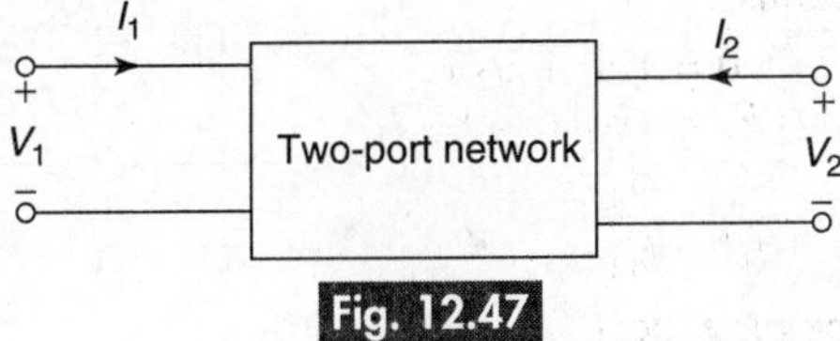


Fig. 12.47

**Solution**

$$h_{11} = \left.\frac{V_1}{I_1}\right|_{V_2=0} = \frac{25}{1} = 25\ \Omega, \qquad h_{12} = \left.\frac{V_1}{V_2}\right|_{I_1=0} = \frac{10}{50} = 0.2$$

$$h_{21} = \left.\frac{I_2}{I_1}\right|_{V_2=0} = \frac{2}{1} = 2, \qquad h_{22} = \left.\frac{I_2}{V_2}\right|_{I_1=0} = \frac{2}{50} = 0.04\ \mho$$

Hence, the $h$ parameters are

$$\begin{bmatrix} h_{11} & h_{12} \\ h_{21} & h_{22} \end{bmatrix} = \begin{bmatrix} 25 & 0.2 \\ 2 & 0.04 \end{bmatrix}$$

**EXAMPLE 12.22**

*Determine hybrid parameters for the network of Fig. 12.48. Determine whether the network is reciprocal.*

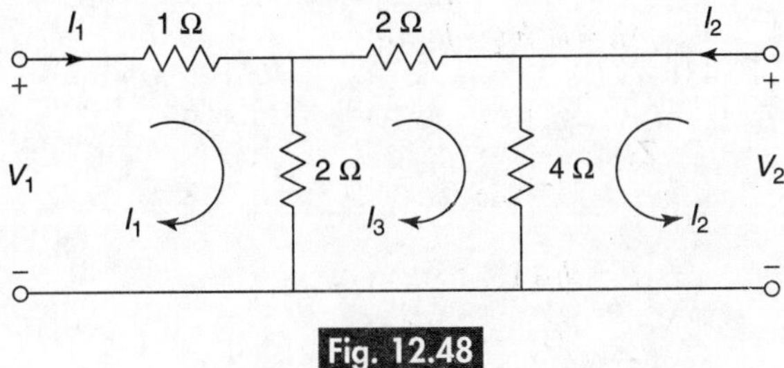


Fig. 12.48

## Solution

**First Method**

***Case 1*** When port 2 is short-circuited, i.e., $V_2 = 0$, as shown in Fig. 12.49,

$$R_{eq} = 1 + \frac{2 \times 2}{2+2} = 2\ \Omega$$

Now,

$$V_1 = 2I_1$$

$$h_{11} = \left.\frac{V_1}{I_1}\right|_{V_2=0} = 2\ \Omega$$

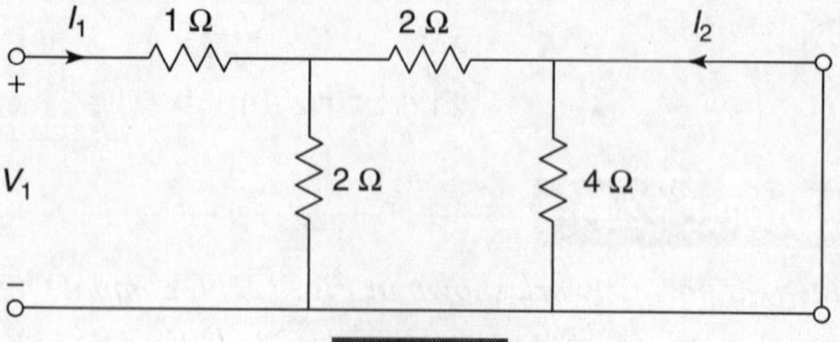

Also,

$$I_2 = -I_1 \times \frac{2}{2+2} = -\frac{I_1}{2}$$

$$h_{21} = \left.\frac{I_2}{I_1}\right|_{V_2=0} = -\frac{1}{2}$$

Fig. 12.49

***Case 2*** When port 1 is open-circuited, i.e., $I_1 = 0$, as shown in Fig. 12.50,

$$R_{eq} = \frac{(2+2)\times 4}{2+2+4} = 2\ \Omega$$

$$V_1 = 2I_y$$

$$I_y = \frac{I_2}{2}$$

$$V_2 = 4I_x$$

$$I_x = \frac{I_2}{2}$$

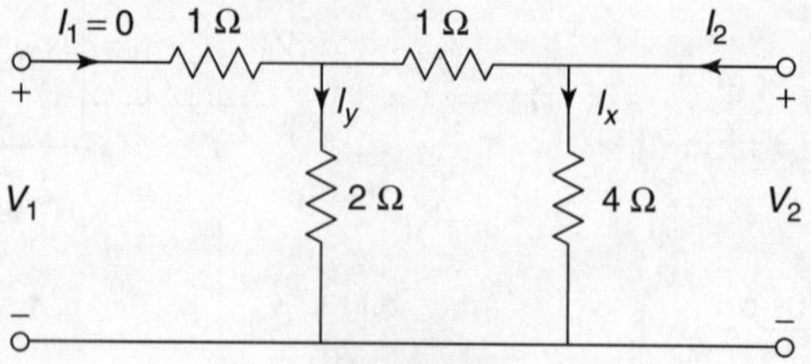

Fig. 12.50

$$h_{12} = \left.\frac{V_1}{V_2}\right|_{I_1=0} = \frac{2I_y}{4I_x} = \frac{2 \times \frac{I_2}{2}}{4 \times \frac{I_2}{2}} = \frac{1}{2}$$

$$h_{22} = \left.\frac{I_2}{V_2}\right|_{I_1=0} = \frac{2I_x}{4I_x} = \frac{1}{2}\ \mho$$

Hence, the $h$ parameters are

$$\begin{bmatrix} h_{11} & h_{12} \\ h_{21} & h_{22} \end{bmatrix} = \begin{bmatrix} 2 & \frac{1}{2} \\ -\frac{1}{2} & \frac{1}{2} \end{bmatrix}$$

**Second Method** (Refer Fig. 12.48)

Applying KVL to mesh 1,

$$V_1 = 3I_1 - 2I_3 \qquad \text{...(i)}$$

Applying KVL to mesh 2,

$$V_2 = 4I_2 + 4I_3 \qquad \text{...(ii)}$$

Applying KVL to mesh 3,

$$-2(I_3 - I_1) - 2I_3 - 4(I_3 + I_2) = 0$$

$$8I_3 = 2I_1 - 4I_2$$

$$I_3 = \frac{I_1}{4} - \frac{I_2}{2} \qquad \text{...(iii)}$$

Substituting Eq. (iii) in Eq. (i),

$$V_1 = 3I_1 - 2\left(\frac{I_1}{4} - \frac{I_2}{2}\right)$$

$$= \frac{5}{2}I_1 + I_2 \qquad \text{...(iv)}$$

Substituting Eq. (iii) in Eq. (ii),

$$V_2 = 4I_2 + 4\left(\frac{I_1}{4} - \frac{I_2}{2}\right)$$

$$= 4I_2 + I_1 - 2I_2$$

$$= I_1 + 2I_2$$

$$I_2 = -\frac{1}{2}I_1 + \frac{1}{2}V_2 \qquad \text{...(v)}$$

Substituting Eq. (v) in Eq. (iv),

$$V_1 = \frac{5}{2}I_1 - \frac{1}{2}I_1 + \frac{1}{2}V_2$$

$$= 2I_1 + \frac{1}{2}V_2 \qquad \text{...(vi)}$$

Comparing Eqs (v) and (vi) with $h$ parameter equations,

$$\begin{bmatrix} h_{11} & h_{12} \\ h_{21} & h_{22} \end{bmatrix} = \begin{bmatrix} 2 & \frac{1}{2} \\ -\frac{1}{2} & \frac{1}{2} \end{bmatrix}$$

Since $h_{12} = -h_{21}$, the network is reciprocal.

**EXAMPLE 12.23**

*Find h parameters for the network shown in Fig. 12.51.*

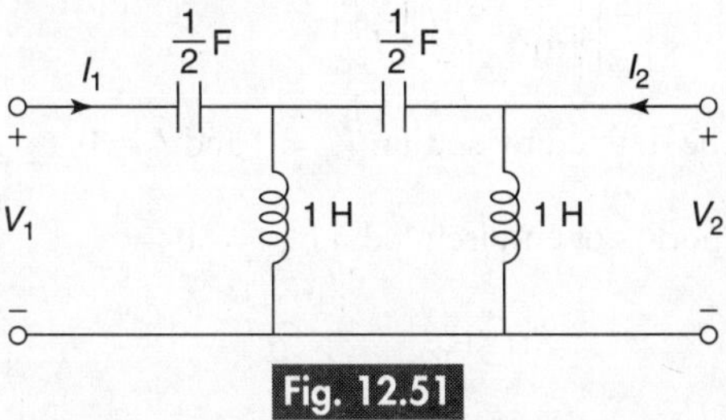


Fig. 12.51

**Solution** As solved in Example 12.12, derive the equations for $I_1$ and $I_2$ in terms of $V_1$ and $V_2$.

$$I_1 = \frac{s^3 + 2s}{4(s^2+1)}V_1 - \frac{s^3}{4(s^2+1)}V_2 \qquad \text{...(i)}$$

$$I_2 = -\frac{s^3}{4(s^2+1)}V_1 + \frac{s^4+6s^2+4}{4s(s^2+1)}V_2 \qquad \text{...(ii)}$$

From Eq. (i),

$$V_1 = \frac{4(s^2+1)}{s(s^2+2)}I_1 + \frac{s^2}{s^2+2}V_2 \qquad \text{...(iii)}$$

Substituting Eq. (iii) in Eq (ii),

$$I_2 = -\frac{s^3}{4(s^2+1)}\left[\frac{4(s^2+1)}{s(s^2+2)}I_1 + \frac{s^2}{s^2+2}V_2\right] + \frac{s^4+6s^2+4}{4s(s^2+1)}V_2$$

$$= -\frac{s^2}{s^2+2}I_1 + \frac{2(s^2+1)}{s(s^2+2)}V_2 \qquad \text{...(iv)}$$

Comparing Eqs (iii) and (iv) with $h$ parameter equations,

$$\begin{bmatrix} h_{11} & h_{12} \\ h_{21} & h_{22} \end{bmatrix} = \begin{bmatrix} \dfrac{4(s^2+1)}{s(s^2+2)} & \dfrac{s^2}{s^2+2} \\ -\dfrac{s^2}{s^2+2} & \dfrac{2(s^2+1)}{s(s^2+2)} \end{bmatrix}$$

## 12.7 INVERSE HYBRID PARAMETERS ($g$ PARAMETERS)

LO 12.5

The inverse hybrid parameters of a two-port network may be defined by expressing the current of the input port $I_1$ and voltage of the output port $V_2$ in terms of the voltage of the input port $V_1$ and the current of the output port $I_2$.

$$(I_1, V_2) = f(V_1, I_2)$$

$$I_1 = g_{11}V_1 + g_{12}I_2$$

$$V_2 = g_{21}V_1 + g_{22}I_2$$

In matrix form, we can write

$$\begin{bmatrix} I_1 \\ V_2 \end{bmatrix} = \begin{bmatrix} g_{11} & g_{12} \\ g_{21} & g_{22} \end{bmatrix}\begin{bmatrix} V_1 \\ I_2 \end{bmatrix}$$

The individual $g$ parameters can be defined by setting $V_1 = 0$ and $I_2 = 0$.

➤ ***Case 1*** When the output port is open-circuited, i.e., $I_2 = 0$

$$g_{11} = \left.\frac{I_1}{V_1}\right|_{I_2=0}$$

where $g_{11}$ is the open-circuit input admittance.

$$g_{21} = \left.\frac{V_2}{V_1}\right|_{I_2=0}$$

where $g_{21}$ is the open-circuit forward voltage gain.

➤ ***Case 2*** When the input port is short-circuited, i.e., $V_1 = 0$

$$g_{12} = \left.\frac{I_1}{I_2}\right|_{V_1=0}$$

where $g_{12}$ is the short-circuit reverse current gain.

$$g_{22} = \left.\frac{V_2}{I_2}\right|_{V_1=0}$$

where $g_{22}$ is the short-circuit output impedance.

The equivalent circuit of a two-port network in terms of inverse hybrid parameters is shown in Fig. 12.52.

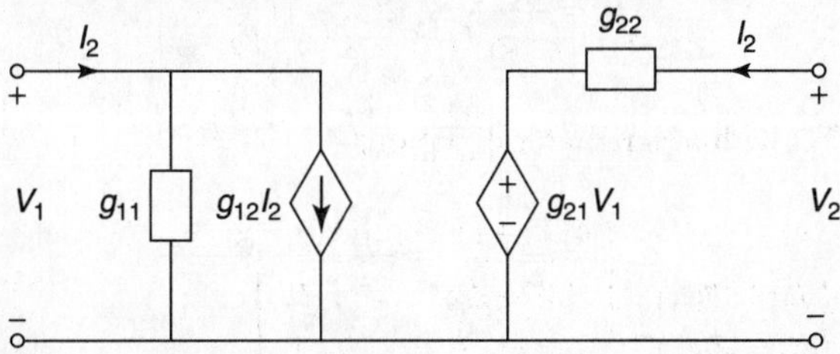


**Fig. 12.52** *Equivalent circuit of two-port network in terms of g parameters*

### 12.7.1 Condition for Reciprocity

(a) As shown in Fig. 12.53, voltage $V_s$ is applied at the input port and the output port is short-circuited, i.e.,

$$V_1 = V_s$$
$$V_2 = 0$$
$$I_2' = -I_2$$

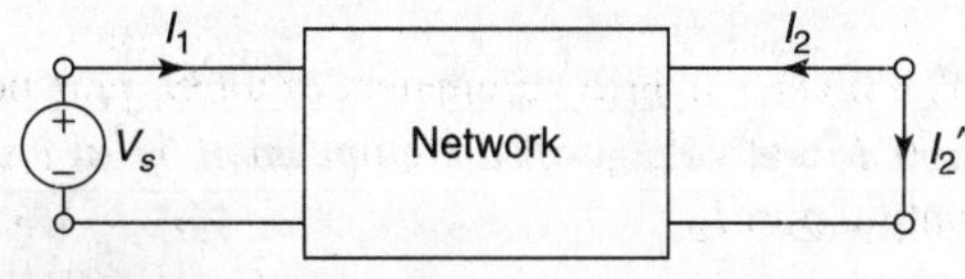


**Fig. 12.53** *Network for deriving condition for reciprocity*

From the g parameter equation,

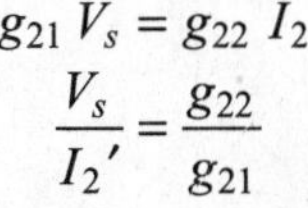

$$g_{21}\, V_s = g_{22}\, I_2'$$
$$\frac{V_s}{I_2'} = \frac{g_{22}}{g_{21}}$$

(b) As shown in Fig. 12.54, voltage $V_s$ is applied at the output port with the input port short-circuited, i.e.,

$$V_1 = 0$$
$$V_2 = V_s$$
$$I_1 = -I_1'$$

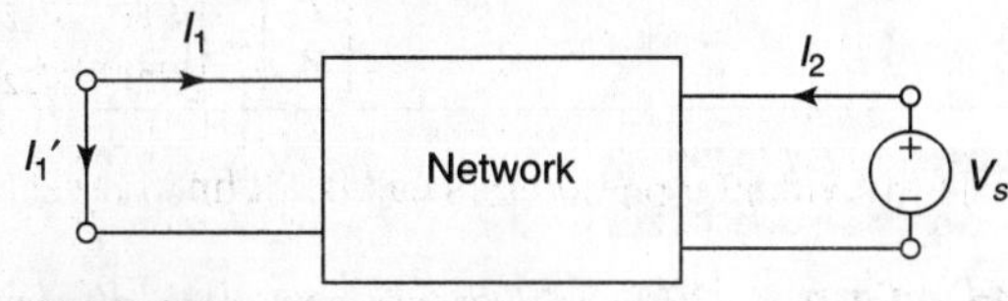


**Fig. 12.54** *Network for deriving condition for reciprocity*

From the g parameter equations,

$$-I_1' = g_{12}\, I_2$$
$$V_s = g_{22}\, I_2$$
$$\frac{V_s}{I_1'} = -\frac{g_{22}}{g_{12}}$$

Hence, for the network to be reciprocal,

$$\frac{V_s}{I_2'} = \frac{V_s}{I_1'}$$

i.e.,

$$g_{21} = -g_{12}$$

### 12.7.2 Condition for Symmetry

The condition for symmetry is obtained from the $Z$ parameters.

$$Z_{11} = \left.\frac{V_1}{I_1}\right|_{I_2=0} = \frac{1}{g_{11}}$$

Similarly,

$$Z_{22} = \left.\frac{V_2}{I_2}\right|_{I_1=0}$$

$$0 = g_{11} V_1 + g_{12} I_2$$

$$V_1 = -\frac{g_{12}}{g_{11}} I_2$$

$$V_2 = g_{21}\left(-\frac{g_{12}}{g_{11}}\right) I_2 + g_{22} I_2$$

$$Z_{22} = \left.\frac{V_2}{I_2}\right|_{I_1=0} = \frac{g_{11}g_{22} - g_{12}g_{21}}{g_{11}}$$

For a symmetrical network, $Z_{11} = Z_{22}$.

i.e., $$\frac{1}{g_{11}} = \frac{g_{11}g_{22} - g_{12}g_{21}}{g_{11}}$$

i.e., $$g_{11}g_{22} - g_{12}g_{21} = 1$$

**TABLE 12.2 Conditions for reciprocity and symmetry**

| *Parameter* | *Condition for Reciprocity* | *Condition for Symmetry* |
|---|---|---|
| $Z$ | $Z_{12} = Z_{21}$ | $Z_{11} = Z_{22}$ |
| $Y$ | $Y_{12} = Y_{21}$ | $Y_{11} = Y_{22}$ |
| $T$ | $AD - BC = 1$ | $A = D$ |
| $T'$ | $A'D' - B'C' = 1$ | $A' = D'$ |
| $h$ | $h_{12} = -h_{21}$ | $h_{11} h_{22} - h_{12} h_{21} = 1$ |
| $g$ | $g_{12} = -g_{21}$ | $g_{11} g_{22} - g_{12} g_{21} = 1$ |

**EXAMPLE 12.24**

*Find g parameters for the network shown in Fig. 12.55.*

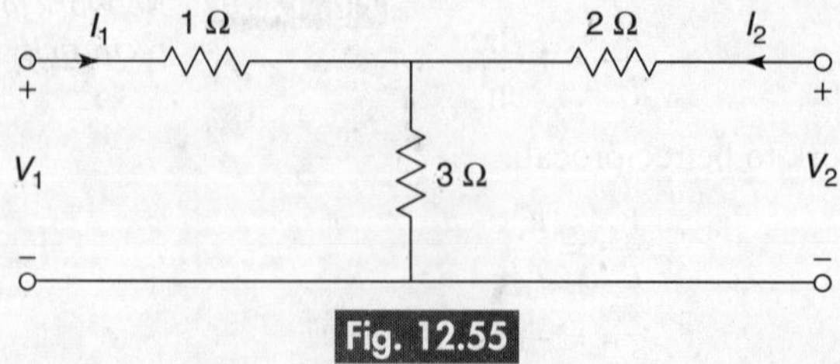


Fig. 12.55

## Solution

**First Method**

***Case 1*** When the output port is open-circuited, i.e., $I_2 = 0$

Applying KVL to mesh 1,

$$V_1 = 4\,I_1$$

$$g_{11} = \left.\frac{I_1}{V_1}\right|_{I_2=0} = \frac{1}{4}\ \mho$$

Also,

$$V_2 = 3\,I_1$$

$$g_{21} = \left.\frac{V_2}{V_1}\right|_{I_2=0} = \frac{3\,I_1}{4\,I_1} = \frac{3}{4}$$

***Case 2*** When the input port is short-circuited, i.e., $V_1 = 0$, as shown in Fig. 12.56.

By current division rule,

$$I_1 = -\frac{3}{4}\,I_2$$

$$g_{12} = \left.\frac{I_1}{I_2}\right|_{V_1=0} = -\frac{3}{4}$$

$$R_{eq} = 2 + \frac{3\times1}{3+1} = 2 + \frac{3}{4} = \frac{11}{4}\ \Omega$$

$$V_2 = \frac{11}{4}\,I_2$$

$$g_{22} = \left.\frac{V_2}{I_2}\right|_{V_1=0} = \frac{11}{4}\ \Omega$$

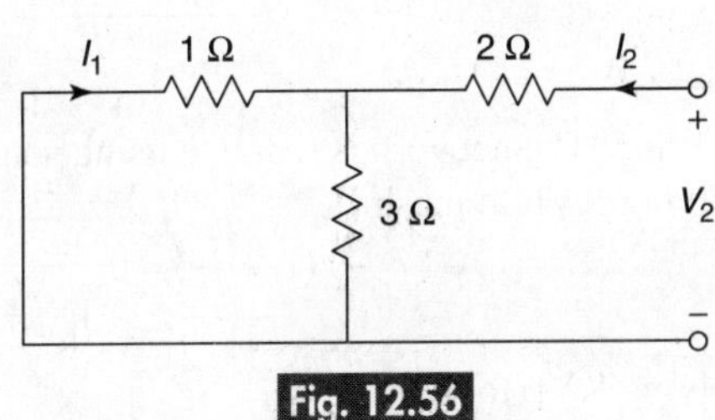


Fig. 12.56

**Second Method** (Refer Fig. 12.55).

Applying KVL to mesh 1,

$$V_1 = 4\,I_1 + 3\,I_2 \qquad \text{...(i)}$$

Applying KVL to mesh 2,

$$V_2 = 3\,I_1 + 5\,I_2 \qquad \text{...(ii)}$$

Hence,

$$4\,I_1 = V_1 - 3\,I_2$$

$$I_1 = \frac{1}{4}\,V_1 - \frac{3}{4}\,I_2 \qquad \text{...(iii)}$$

Substituting Eq. (iii) in Eq. (ii),

$$V_2 = 3\left(\frac{1}{4}\,V_1 - \frac{3}{4}\,I_2\right) + 5\,I_2$$

$$= \frac{3}{4}\,V_1 + \frac{11}{4}\,I_2 \qquad \text{...(iv)}$$

Comparing Eqs (iii) and (iv) with $g$ parameter equations,

$$\begin{bmatrix} g_{11} & g_{12} \\ g_{21} & g_{22} \end{bmatrix} = \begin{bmatrix} \frac{1}{4} & -\frac{3}{4} \\ \frac{3}{4} & \frac{11}{4} \end{bmatrix}$$

**EXAMPLE 12.25**

*Find g parameters for the network shown in Fig. 12.57.*

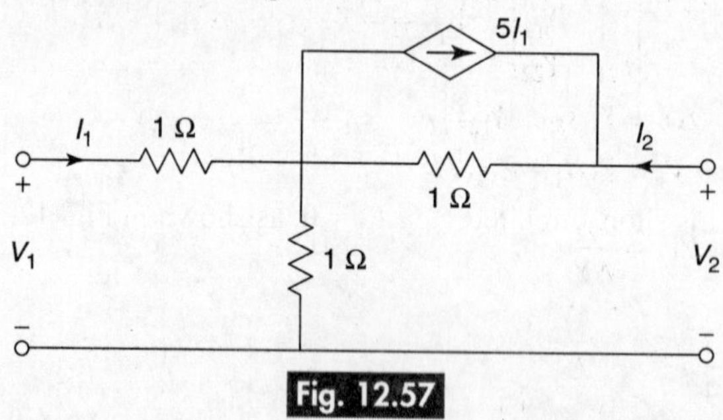


Fig. 12.57

**Solution** The network is redrawn using source transformation, as shown in Fig. 12.58.

Applying KVL to mesh 1,

$$V_1 - 1\,I_1 - 1\,(I_1 + I_2) = 0$$

$$V_1 = 2\,I_1 + I_2 \quad \text{...(i)}$$

Applying KVL to mesh 2,

$$V_2 - 5\,I_1 - 1\,I_2 - 1\,(I_2 + I_1) = 0$$

$$V_2 = 6\,I_1 + 2\,I_2 \quad \text{...(ii)}$$

Fig. 12.58

Hence,

$$2\,I_1 = V_1 - I_2$$

$$I_1 = \frac{1}{2}V_1 - \frac{1}{2}I_2 \quad \text{...(iii)}$$

Substituting Eq (iii) in Eq. (ii),

$$V_2 = 6\left(\frac{1}{2}V_1 - \frac{1}{2}I_2\right) + 2\,I_2$$

$$= 3\,V_1 - I_2 \quad \text{...(iv)}$$

Comparing Eqs (iii) and (iv) the $g$-parameter equations,

$$\begin{bmatrix} g_{11} & g_{12} \\ g_{21} & g_{22} \end{bmatrix} = \begin{bmatrix} \frac{1}{2} & -\frac{1}{2} \\ 3 & -1 \end{bmatrix}$$

## 12.8 INTERRELATIONSHIPS BETWEEN THE PARAMETERS

LO 12.6

Determine interrelationships between the parameters

When it is required to find out two or more parameters of a particular network, then finding each parameter will be tedious. But if we find a particular parameter, then the other parameters can be found if the interrelationship between them is known.

### 12.8.1 Z Parameters in Terms of Other Parameters

***1. Z Parameters in Terms of Y Parameters*** We know that

$$I_1 = Y_{11} V_1 + Y_{12} V_2$$
$$I_2 = Y_{21} V_1 + Y_{22} V_2$$

By Cramer's rule,

$$V_1 = \frac{\begin{vmatrix} I_1 & Y_{12} \\ I_2 & Y_{22} \end{vmatrix}}{\begin{vmatrix} Y_{11} & Y_{12} \\ Y_{21} & Y_{22} \end{vmatrix}} = \frac{Y_{22}I_1 - Y_{12}I_2}{Y_{11}Y_{22} - Y_{12}Y_{21}} = \frac{Y_{22}}{\Delta Y} I_1 - \frac{Y_{12}}{\Delta Y} I_2$$

where $\Delta Y = Y_{11}Y_{22} - Y_{12}Y_{21}$

Comparing with $V_1 = Z_{11}I_1 + Z_{12},I_2,$

$$Z_{11} = \frac{Y_{22}}{\Delta Y}$$

$$Z_{12} = -\frac{Y_{12}}{\Delta Y}$$

Also,

$$V_2 = \frac{\begin{vmatrix} Y_{11} & I_1 \\ Y_{21} & I_2 \end{vmatrix}}{\Delta Y} = \frac{Y_{11}}{\Delta Y} I_2 - \frac{Y_{21}}{\Delta Y} I_1$$

Comparing with $V_2 = Z_{21} I_1 + Z_{22} I_2,$

$$Z_{22} = \frac{Y_{11}}{\Delta Y}$$

$$Z_{21} = -\frac{Y_{21}}{\Delta Y}$$

***2. Z Parameters in Terms of ABCD Parameters*** We know that

$$V_1 = AV_2 - BI_2$$
$$I_1 = CV_2 - DI_2$$

Rewriting the second equation,

$$V_2 = \frac{1}{C} I_1 + \frac{D}{C} I_2$$

Comparing with $V_2 = Z_{21} I_1 + Z_{22} I_2,$

$$Z_{21} = \frac{1}{C}$$

$$Z_{22} = \frac{D}{C}$$

Also,

$$V_1 = A\left[\frac{1}{C} I_1 + \frac{D}{C} I_2\right] - BI_2 = \frac{A}{C} I_1 + \left[\frac{AD}{C} - B\right] I_2 = \frac{A}{C} I_1 + \left[\frac{AD - BC}{C}\right] I_2$$

Comparing with $V_1 = Z_{11} I_1 + Z_{12} I_2,$

$$Z_{11} = \frac{A}{C}$$

$$Z_{12} = \frac{AD - BC}{C}$$

**3. Z Parameters in Terms of A'B'C'D' Parameters** We know that

$$V_2 = A' V_1 - B' I_1$$
$$I_2 = C' V_1 - D' I_1$$

Rewriting the second equation,

$$V_1 = \frac{D'}{C'} I_1 + \frac{1}{C'} I_2$$

Comparing with

$$V_1 = Z_{11} I_1 + Z_{12} I_2,$$

$$Z_{11} = \frac{D'}{C'}$$

$$Z_{12} = \frac{1}{C'}$$

Also,

$$V_2 = A'\left[\frac{D'}{C'} I_1 + \frac{1}{C'} I_2\right] - B' I_1 = \left[\frac{A'D' - B'C'}{C'}\right] I_1 + \frac{A'}{C'} I_2$$

Comparing with

$$V_2 = Z_{21} I_1 + Z_{22} I_2,$$

$$Z_{21} = \frac{A'D' - B'C'}{C'} = \frac{\Delta T'}{C'}$$

$$Z_{22} = \frac{A'}{C'}$$

**4. Z Parameters in Terms of Hybrid Parameters** We know that

$$V_1 = h_{11} I_1 + h_{12} V_2$$
$$I_2 = h_{21} I_1 + h_{22} V_2$$

Rewriting the second equation,

$$V_2 = -\frac{h_{21}}{h_{22}} I_1 + \frac{1}{h_{22}} I_2$$

Comparing with

$$V_2 = Z_{21} I_1 + Z_{22} I_2,$$

$$Z_{21} = -\frac{h_{21}}{h_{22}}$$

$$Z_{22} = \frac{1}{h_{22}}$$

Also,

$$V_1 = h_{11} I_1 + h_{12}\left[-\frac{h_{21}}{h_{22}} I_1 + \frac{1}{h_{22}} I_2\right] = h_{11} I_1 + \frac{h_{12}}{h_{22}} I_2 - \frac{h_{12}h_{21}}{h_{22}} I_1 = \left[\frac{h_{11}h_{22} - h_{12}h_{21}}{h_{22}}\right] I_1 + \frac{h_{12}}{h_{22}} I_2$$

Comparing with

$$V_1 = Z_{11} I_1 + Z_{12} I_2,$$

$$Z_{11} = \frac{h_{11}h_{22} - h_{12}h_{21}}{h_{22}} = \frac{\Delta h}{h_{22}}$$

$$Z_{12} = \frac{h_{12}}{h_{22}}$$

***5. Z Parameters in Terms of Inverse Hybrid Parameters*** We know that

$$I_1 = g_{11} V_1 + g_{12} I_2$$

$$V_2 = g_{21} V_1 + g_{22} I_2$$

Rewriting the first equation,

$$V_1 = \frac{1}{g_{11}} I_1 - \frac{g_{12}}{g_{11}} I_2$$

Comparing with $V_1 = Z_{11} I_1 + Z_{12} I_2$,

$$Z_{11} = \frac{1}{g_{11}}$$

$$Z_{12} = -\frac{g_{12}}{g_{11}}$$

Also,

$$V_2 = g_{21}\left[\frac{1}{g_{11}} I_1 - \frac{g_{12}}{g_{11}} I_2\right] + g_{22} I_2 = \frac{g_{21}}{g_{11}} I_1 + \left[\frac{g_{11}g_{22} - g_{12}g_{21}}{g_{11}}\right] I_2$$

Comparing with $V_2 = Z_{21} I_1 + Z_{22} I_2$,

$$Z_{21} = \frac{g_{21}}{g_{11}}$$

$$Z_{22} = \frac{g_{11} g_{22} - g_{12} g_{21}}{g_{11}} = \frac{\Delta g}{g_{11}}$$

### 12.8.2 *Y* Parameters in Terms of Other Parameters

***1. Y Parameters in terms of Z Parameters*** We know that

$$V_1 = Z_{11} I_1 + Z_{12} I_2$$

$$V_2 = Z_{21} I_1 + Z_{22} I_2$$

By Cramer's rule,

$$I_1 = \frac{\begin{vmatrix} V_1 & Z_{12} \\ V_2 & Z_{22} \end{vmatrix}}{\begin{vmatrix} Z_{11} & Z_{12} \\ Z_{21} & Z_{22} \end{vmatrix}} = \frac{Z_{22} V_1 - Z_{12} V_2}{Z_{11} Z_{22} - Z_{12} Z_{21}} = \frac{Z_{22}}{\Delta Z} V_1 - \frac{Z_{12}}{\Delta Z} V_2$$

where $\Delta Z = Z_{11} Z_{22} - Z_{12} Z_{21}$

Comparing with $I_1 = Y_{11} V_1 + Y_{12} V_2$,

$$Y_{11} = \frac{Z_{22}}{\Delta Z}$$

$$Y_{12} = -\frac{Z_{12}}{\Delta Z}$$

Also, $$I_2 = \frac{\begin{vmatrix} Z_{11} & V_1 \\ Z_{21} & V_2 \end{vmatrix}}{\Delta Z} = \frac{Z_{11}V_2 - Z_{12}V_1}{\Delta Z} = -\frac{Z_{21}}{\Delta Z}V_1 + \frac{Z_{11}}{\Delta Z}V_2$$

Comparing with $$I_2 = Y_{21}\, V_1 + Y_{22}\, V_2,$$

$$Y_{21} = -\frac{Z_{21}}{\Delta Z}$$

$$Y_{22} = \frac{Z_{11}}{\Delta Z}$$

***2. Y Parameters in Terms of ABCD-Parameters*** We know that

$$V_1 = AV_2 - BI_2$$
$$I_1 = CV_2 - DI_2$$

Rewriting the first equation,

$$I_2 = -\frac{1}{B}V_1 + \frac{A}{B}V_2$$

Comparing with $$I_2 = Y_{21}\, V_1 + Y_{22}\, V_2,$$

$$Y_{21} = -\frac{1}{B}$$

$$Y_{22} = \frac{A}{B}$$

Also, $$I_1 = CV_2 - D\left[-\frac{1}{B}V_1 + \frac{A}{B}V_2\right] = \frac{D}{B}V_1 + \left[\frac{BC - AD}{B}\right]V_2$$

Comparing with $$I_1 = Y_{11}\, V_1 + Y_{12}\, V_2,$$

$$Y_{11} = \frac{D}{B}$$

$$Y_{12} = \frac{BC - AD}{B} = -\frac{AD - BC}{B} = -\frac{\Delta T}{B}$$

***3. Y Parameters in Terms of A′B′C′D′-Parameters*** We know that

$$V_2 = A'V_1 - B'I_1$$
$$I_2 = C'V_1 - D'I_1$$

Rewriting the first equation,

$$I_1 = \frac{A'}{B'}V_1 - \frac{1}{B'}V_2$$

Comparing with $$I_1 = Y_{11}\, V_1 + Y_{12}\, V_2,$$

$$Y_{11} = \frac{A'}{B'}$$

$$Y_{12} = -\frac{1}{B'}$$

Also,
$$I_2 = C'V_1 - D'\left[\frac{A'}{B'}V_1 - \frac{1}{B'}V_2\right] = -\left[\frac{A'D' - B'C'}{B'}\right]V_1 + \frac{D'}{B'}V_2$$

Comparing with
$$I_2 = Y_{21}V_1 + Y_{22}V_2,$$
$$Y_{21} = -\left[\frac{A'D' - B'C'}{B'}\right] = -\frac{\Delta T'}{B'}$$

and
$$Y_{22} = \frac{D'}{B'}$$

***4. Y Parameters in Terms of Hybrid-Parameters*** We know that
$$V_1 = h_{11}I_1 + h_{12}V_2$$
$$I_2 = h_{21}I_1 + h_{22}V_2$$

Rewriting the first equation,
$$I_1 = \frac{1}{h_{11}}V_1 - \frac{h_{12}}{h_{11}}V_2$$

Comparing with
$$I_1 = Y_{11}V_1 + Y_{12}V_2,$$
$$Y_{11} = \frac{1}{h_{11}}$$
$$Y_{12} = -\frac{h_{12}}{h_{11}}$$

Also,
$$I_2 = h_{21}\left[\frac{1}{h_{11}}V_1 - \frac{h_{12}}{h_{11}}V_2\right] + h_{22}V_2 = \frac{h_{21}}{h_{11}}V_1 + \left[\frac{h_{11}h_{22} - h_{12}h_{21}}{h_{11}}\right]V_2$$

Comparing with
$$I_2 = Y_{21}V_1 + Y_{22}V_2,$$
$$Y_{21} = \frac{h_{21}}{h_{11}}$$
$$Y_{22} = \frac{h_{11}h_{22} - h_{12}h_{21}}{h_{11}} = \frac{\Delta h}{h_{11}}$$

***5. Y Parameters in Terms of Inverse Hybrid Parameters*** We know that
$$I_1 = g_{11}V_1 + g_{12}I_2$$
$$V_2 = g_{21}V_1 + g_{22}I_2$$

Rewriting the second equation,
$$I_2 = -\frac{g_{21}}{g_{22}}V_1 + \frac{1}{g_{22}}V_2$$

Comparing with
$$I_2 = Y_{21}V_1 + Y_{22}V_2,$$
$$Y_{21} = -\frac{g_{21}}{g_{22}}$$
$$Y_{22} = \frac{1}{g_{22}}$$

Also, $$I_1 = g_{11} V_1 + g_{12}\left[-\frac{g_{21}}{g_{22}} V_1 + \frac{1}{g_{22}} V_2\right] = \left[\frac{g_{11}\, g_{22} - g_{12}\, g_{21}}{g_{22}}\right] V_1 + \frac{g_{12}}{g_{22}} V_2$$

Comparing with $$I_1 = Y_{11} V_1 + Y_{12} V_2,$$

$$Y_{11} = \frac{g_{11} g_{22} - g_{12} g_{21}}{g_{22}} = \frac{\Delta g}{g_{22}}$$

$$Y_{12} = \frac{g_{12}}{g_{22}}$$

### 12.8.3 *ABCD* Parameters in Terms of Other Parameters

***1. ABCD Parameters in Terms of Z Parameters*** We know that

$$V_1 = Z_{11} I_1 + Z_{12} I_2$$

$$V_2 = Z_{21} I_1 + Z_{22} I_2$$

Rewriting the second equation,

$$I_1 = \frac{1}{Z_{21}} V_2 - \frac{Z_{22}}{Z_{21}} I_2$$

Comparing with $$I_1 = CV_2 - DI_2,$$

$$C = \frac{1}{Z_{21}}$$

$$D = \frac{Z_{22}}{Z_{21}}$$

Also, $$V_1 = Z_{11}\left[\frac{1}{Z_{21}} V_2 - \frac{Z_{22}}{Z_{21}} I_2\right] + Z_{12}\, I_2 = \frac{Z_{11}}{Z_{21}} V_2 - \frac{Z_{22}\, Z_{11}}{Z_{21}} I_2 + Z_{12}\, I_2$$

$$= \frac{Z_{11}}{Z_{21}} V_2 - \left[\frac{Z_{11}\, Z_{22} - Z_{12}\, Z_{21}}{Z_{21}}\right] I_2$$

Comparing with $$V_1 = AV_2 - BI_2,$$

$$A = \frac{Z_{11}}{Z_{21}}$$

$$B = \frac{Z_{11} Z_{22} - Z_{12} Z_{21}}{Z_{21}} = \frac{\Delta Z}{Z_{21}}$$

***2. ABCD Parameters in Terms of Y Parameters*** We know that

$$I_1 = Y_{11} V_1 + Y_{12} V_2$$

$$I_2 = Y_{21} V_1 + Y_{22} V_2$$

Rewriting the second equation,

$$V_1 = -\frac{Y_{22}}{Y_{21}} V_2 + \frac{1}{Y_{21}} I_2$$

Comparing with $$V_1 = AV_2 - BI_2,$$

$$A = -\frac{Y_{22}}{Y_{21}}$$

$$B = -\frac{1}{Y_{21}}$$

Also,
$$I_1 = Y_{11}\left[-\frac{Y_{22}}{Y_{21}}V_2 + \frac{1}{Y_{21}}I_2\right] + Y_{12}\,V_2 = \left[\frac{Y_{12}\,Y_{21} - Y_{11}\,Y_{22}}{Y_{21}}\right]V_2 + \frac{Y_{11}}{Y_{21}}I_2$$

Comparing with
$$I_1 = CV_2 - DI_2,$$
$$C = \frac{Y_{12}\,Y_{21} - Y_{11}\,Y_{22}}{Y_{21}} = -\frac{\Delta Y}{Y_{21}}$$
$$D = \frac{Y_{11}}{Y_{21}}$$

***3. ABCD Parameters in terms of A′B′C′D′ Parameters*** We know that

$$V_2 = A'V_1 - B'I_1$$
$$I_2 = C'V_1 - D'I_1$$

By Cramer's rule,

$$V_1 = \frac{\begin{vmatrix} V_2 & B' \\ I_2 & D' \end{vmatrix}}{\begin{vmatrix} A' & B' \\ C' & D' \end{vmatrix}} = \frac{D'}{\Delta T'}V_2 - \frac{B'}{\Delta T'}I_2$$

where
$$\Delta T' = A'D' - B'C'$$

Comparing with
$$V_1 = AV_2 - BI_2,$$
$$A = \frac{D'}{\Delta T'}$$
$$B = \frac{B'}{\Delta T'}$$

Also,
$$-I_1 = \frac{\begin{vmatrix} A' & V_2 \\ C' & I_2 \end{vmatrix}}{\Delta T'} = -\frac{C'}{\Delta T'}V_2 + \frac{A'}{\Delta T'}I_2$$
$$I_1 = \frac{C'}{\Delta T'}V_2 - \frac{A'}{\Delta T'}I_2$$

Comparing with
$$I_1 = CV_2 - DI_2,$$
$$C = \frac{C'}{\Delta T'}$$
$$D = \frac{A'}{\Delta T'}$$

***4. ABCD Parameters in Terms of Hybrid Parameters*** We know that

$$V_1 = h_{11}\,I_1 + h_{12}\,V_2$$
$$I_2 = h_{21}\,I_1 + h_{22}\,V_2$$

Rewriting the second equation,

$$I_1 = -\frac{h_{22}}{h_{21}}V_2 + \frac{1}{h_{21}}I_2$$

Comparing with $I_1 = CV_2 - DI_2$,

$$C = -\frac{h_{22}}{h_{21}}$$

$$D = -\frac{1}{h_{21}}$$

Also, $$V_1 = h_{11}\left[\frac{1}{h_{21}}I_2 - \frac{h_{22}}{h_{21}}V_2\right] + h_{12}V_2 = \left[\frac{h_{12}h_{21} - h_{11}h_{22}}{h_{21}}\right]V_2 + \frac{h_{11}}{h_{21}}I_2$$

Comparing with $V_1 = AV_2 - BI_2$,

$$A = \frac{h_{12}h_{21} - h_{11}h_{22}}{h_{21}} = -\frac{\Delta h}{h_{21}}$$

$$B = -\frac{h_{11}}{h_{21}}$$

***5. ABCD Parameters in Terms of Inverse Hybrid Parameters*** We know that

$$I_1 = g_{11}V_1 + g_{12}I_2$$
$$V_2 = g_{21}V_1 + g_{22}I_2$$

Rewriting the second equation,

$$V_1 = \frac{1}{g_{21}}V_2 - \frac{g_{22}}{g_{21}}I_2$$

Comparing with $V_1 = AV_2 - BI_2$,

$$A = \frac{1}{g_{21}}$$

$$B = \frac{g_{22}}{g_{21}}$$

Also, $$I_1 = g_{11}\left[\frac{1}{g_{21}}V_2 - \frac{g_{22}}{g_{21}}I_2\right] + g_{12}I_2 = \frac{g_{11}}{g_{21}}V_2 - \left[\frac{g_{11}g_{22} - g_{12}g_{21}}{g_{21}}\right]I_2$$

Comparing with $I_1 = CV_2 - DI_2$,

$$C = \frac{g_{11}}{g_{21}}$$

$$D = \frac{g_{11}g_{22} - g_{12}g_{21}}{g_{21}} = \frac{\Delta g}{g_{21}}$$

### 12.8.4 *A′B′C′D′* Parameters in Terms of Other Parameters

***1. A′B′C′D′ Parameters in Terms of Z Parameters*** We know that

$$V_1 = Z_{11}I_1 + Z_{12}I_2$$
$$V_2 = Z_{21}I_1 + Z_{22}I_2$$

Rewriting the first equation,

$$I_2 = \frac{1}{Z_{12}}V_1 - \frac{Z_{11}}{Z_{12}}I_1$$

Comparing with $$I_2 = C'V_1 - D'I_1,$$

$$C' = \frac{1}{Z_{12}}$$

$$D' = \frac{Z_{11}}{Z_{12}}$$

Also, $$V_2 = Z_{21}I_1 + Z_{22}\left[\frac{1}{Z_{12}}V_1 - \frac{Z_{11}}{Z_{12}}I_1\right] = Z_{12}I_1 + \frac{Z_{22}}{Z_{12}}V_1 - \frac{Z_{22}Z_{11}}{Z_{12}}I_1$$

$$= \frac{Z_{22}}{Z_{12}}V_1 - \left[\frac{Z_{11}Z_{22} - Z_{12}Z_{21}}{Z_{12}}\right]I_1$$

Comparing with $$V_2 = A'V_1 - B'I_1,$$

$$A' = \frac{Z_{22}}{Z_{12}}$$

$$B' = \frac{Z_{11}Z_{22} - Z_{12}Z_{21}}{Z_{12}} = \frac{\Delta Z}{Z_{12}}$$

***2. A′B′C′D′ Parameters in Terms of Y Parameters*** We know that

$$I_1 = Y_{11}V_1 + Y_{12}V_2$$
$$I_2 = Y_{21}V_1 + Y_{22}V_2$$

Rewriting the first equation,

$$V_2 = -\frac{Y_{11}}{Y_{12}}V_1 + \frac{1}{Y_{12}}I_1$$

Comparing with $$V_2 = A'V_1 - B'I_1,$$

$$A' = -\frac{Y_{11}}{Y_{12}}$$

$$B' = -\frac{1}{Y_{12}}$$

Also, $$I_2 = Y_{21}V_1 + Y_{22}\left[-\frac{Y_{11}}{Y_{12}}V_1 + \frac{1}{Y_{12}}I_1\right] = \left[\frac{Y_{12}Y_{21} - Y_{11}Y_{22}}{Y_{12}}\right]V_1 + \frac{Y_{22}}{Y_{12}}I_1$$

Comparing with $$I_2 = C'V_1 - D'I_1,$$

$$C' = \frac{Y_{12}Y_{21} - Y_{11}Y_{22}}{Y_{12}} = -\frac{\Delta Y}{Y_{12}}$$

$$D' = -\frac{Y_{22}}{Y_{12}}$$

***3. A′B′C′D′ Parameters in Terms of ABCD Parameters*** We know that

$$V_1 = AV_2 - BI_2$$
$$I_1 = CV_2 - DI_2$$

By Cramer's rule,

$$V_2 = \frac{\begin{vmatrix} V_1 & B \\ I_1 & D \end{vmatrix}}{\begin{vmatrix} A & B \\ C & D \end{vmatrix}} = \frac{D}{\Delta T} V_2 - \frac{B}{\Delta T} I_2$$

where $\Delta T = AD - BC$

Comparing with $V_2 = A'V_1 - B'I_1$,

$$A' = \frac{D}{\Delta T}$$

$$B' = \frac{B}{\Delta T}$$

Also,

$$-I_2 = \frac{\begin{vmatrix} A & V_1 \\ C & I_1 \end{vmatrix}}{\Delta T} = -\frac{C}{\Delta T} V_1 + \frac{A}{\Delta T} I_1$$

$$I_2 = \frac{C}{\Delta T} V_1 - \frac{A}{\Delta T} I_1$$

Comparing with $I_2 = C'V_1 - D'I_1$,

$$C' = \frac{C}{\Delta T}$$

$$D' = \frac{A}{\Delta T}$$

***4. A′B′C′D′ Parameters in Terms of Hybrid Parameters*** We know that

$$V_1 = h_{11} I_1 + h_{12} V_2$$

$$I_2 = h_{21} I_1 + h_{22} V_2$$

Rewriting the first equation,

$$V_2 = \frac{1}{h_{12}} V_1 - \frac{h_{11}}{h_{12}} I_1$$

Comparing with $V_2 = A'V_1 - B'I_1$,

$$A' = \frac{1}{h_{12}}$$

$$B' = \frac{h_{11}}{h_{12}}$$

Also,

$$I_2 = h_{21} I_1 + h_{22} \left[ \frac{1}{h_{12}} V_1 - \frac{h_{11}}{h_{12}} I_1 \right] = \frac{h_{22}}{h_{12}} V_1 + \left[ \frac{h_{11} h_{22} - h_{12} h_{21}}{h_{12}} \right] I_1$$

Comparing with $I_2 = C'V_1 - D'I_1$,

$$C' = \frac{h_{22}}{h_{12}}$$

$$D' = \left[ \frac{h_{11} h_{22} - h_{12} h_{21}}{h_{12}} \right] = \frac{\Delta h}{h_{12}}$$

***5. A′B′C′D′ Parameters in Terms of Inverse Hybrid Parameters*** We know that

$$I_1 = g_{11} V_1 + g_{12} I_2$$
$$V_2 = g_{21} V_1 + g_{22} I_2$$

Rewriting the first equation,

$$I_2 = -\frac{g_{11}}{g_{12}} V_1 + \frac{1}{g_{12}} I_1$$

Comparing with $I_2 = C' V_1 - D' I_1$,

$$C = -\frac{g_{11}}{g_{12}}$$

$$D' = -\frac{1}{g_{12}}$$

Also, $$V_2 = g_{21} V_1 + g_{22}\left[-\frac{g_{11}}{g_{12}} V_1 + \frac{1}{g_{12}} I_1\right] = -\left[\frac{g_{11}\, g_{22} - g_{12}\, g_{21}}{g_{12}}\right] V_2 + \frac{g_{22}}{g_{12}} I_1$$

Comparing with $V_2 = A' V_1 - B' I_1$,

$$A' = -\left[\frac{g_{11}\, g_{22} - g_{12}\, g_{21}}{g_{12}}\right] = -\frac{\Delta g}{g_{12}}$$

$$B' = \frac{g_{22}}{g_{12}}$$

### 12.8.5 Hybrid Parameters in Terms of Other Parameters

***1. Hybrid Parameters in Terms of Z Parameters*** We know that

$$V_1 = Z_{11} I_1 + Z_{12} I_2$$
$$V_2 = Z_{21} I_1 + Z_{22} I_2$$

Rewriting the second equation,

$$I_2 = -\frac{Z_{21}}{Z_{22}} I_1 + \frac{1}{Z_{22}} V_2$$

Comparing with $I_2 = h_{21} I_1 + h_{22} V_2$,

$$h_{21} = -\frac{Z_{21}}{Z_{22}}$$

$$h_{22} = \frac{1}{Z_{22}}$$

Also, $$V_1 = Z_{11} I_1 + Z_{12}\left[-\frac{Z_{21}}{Z_{22}} I_1 + \frac{1}{Z_{22}} V_2\right] = \left[\frac{Z_{11}\, Z_{22} - Z_{12}\, Z_{21}}{Z_{22}}\right] I_1 + \frac{Z_{12}}{Z_{22}} V_2$$

Comparing with $V_1 = h_{11} I_1 + h_{12} V_2$,

$$h_{11} = \frac{Z_{11}\, Z_{22} - Z_{12}\, Z_{21}}{Z_{22}} = \frac{\Delta Z}{Z_{22}}$$

$$h_{12} = \frac{Z_{12}}{Z_{22}}$$

***2. Hybrid Parameters in Terms of Y Parameters*** We know that

$$I_1 = Y_{11} V_1 + Y_{12} V_2$$

$$I_2 = Y_{21} V_1 + Y_{22} V_2$$

Rewriting the first equation,

$$V_1 = \frac{1}{Y_{11}} I_1 - \frac{Y_{12}}{Y_{11}} V_2$$

Comparing with $V_1 = h_{11} I_1 + h_{12} V_2,$

$$h_{11} = \frac{1}{Y_{11}}$$

$$h_{12} = -\frac{Y_{12}}{Y_{11}}$$

Also,

$$I_2 = Y_{21}\left[\frac{1}{Y_{11}} I_1 - \frac{Y_{12}}{Y_{11}} V_2\right] + Y_{22} V_2 = \left[\frac{Y_{11} Y_{22} - Y_{12} Y_{21}}{Y_{11}}\right] V_2 + \frac{Y_{21}}{Y_{11}} I_1$$

Comparing with $I_2 = h_{21} I_1 + h_{22} V_2,$

$$h_{21} = \frac{Y_{22}}{Y_{11}}$$

$$h_{22} = \frac{Y_{11} Y_{22} - Y_{12} Y_{21}}{Y_{11}} = \frac{\Delta Y}{Y_{11}}$$

***3. Hybrid Parameters in Terms of ABCD-Parameters*** We know that

$$V_1 = AV_2 - BI_2$$

$$I_1 = CV_2 - DI_2$$

Rewriting the second equation,

$$I_2 = -\frac{1}{D} I_1 + \frac{C}{D} V_2$$

Comparing with $I_2 = h_{21} I_1 + h_{22} V_2,$

$$h_{21} = -\frac{1}{D}$$

$$h_{22} = \frac{C}{D}$$

Also,

$$V_1 = AV_2 - B\left[-\frac{1}{D} I_1 + \frac{C}{D} V_2\right] = \frac{B}{D} I_1 + \left[\frac{AD - BC}{D}\right] V_2$$

Comparing with $V_1 = h_{11} I_1 + h_{12} V_2,$

$$h_{11} = \frac{B}{D}$$

$$h_{12} = \frac{AD - BC}{D} = \frac{\Delta T}{D}$$

**4. Hybrid Parameters in Terms of A′B′C′D′ Parameters** We know that

$$V_2 = A'V_1 - B'I_1$$
$$I_2 = C'V_1 - D'I_1$$

Rewriting the first equation,

$$V_1 = \frac{B'}{A'}I_1 + \frac{1}{A'}V_2$$

Comparing with $V_1 = h_{11}I_1 + h_{12}V_2$,

$$h_{11} = \frac{B'}{A'}$$

$$h_{12} = \frac{1}{A'}$$

Also,

$$I_2 = C'\left[\frac{B'}{A'}I_1 + \frac{1}{A'}V_2\right] - D'I_1 = -\left[\frac{A'D' - B'C'}{A'}\right]I_1 + \frac{C'}{A'}V_2$$

Comparing with $I_2 = h_{21}I_1 + h_{22}V_2$,

$$h_{21} = -\left[\frac{A'D' - B'C'}{A'}\right] = -\frac{\Delta T'}{A'}$$

$$h_{22} = \frac{C'}{A'}$$

**5. Hybrid Parameters in Terms of Inverse Hybrid Parameters** We know that

$$I_1 = g_{11}V_1 + g_{12}I_2$$
$$V_2 = g_{21}V_1 + g_{22}I_2$$

By Cramer's rule,

$$V_1 = \frac{\begin{vmatrix} I_1 & g_{12} \\ V_2 & g_{22} \end{vmatrix}}{\begin{vmatrix} g_{11} & g_{12} \\ g_{21} & g_{22} \end{vmatrix}} = \frac{g_{22}}{\Delta g}I_1 - \frac{g_{12}}{\Delta g}V_2$$

where $\Delta g = g_{11}g_{22} - g_{12}g_{21}$

Comparing with $V_1 = h_{11}I_1 + h_{12}V_2$,

$$h_{11} = \frac{g_{22}}{\Delta g}$$

$$h_{12} = -\frac{g_{12}}{\Delta g}$$

Also,

$$I_2 = \frac{\begin{vmatrix} g_{11} & I_1 \\ g_{21} & V_2 \end{vmatrix}}{\Delta g} = -\frac{g_{21}}{\Delta g}I_1 + \frac{g_{11}}{\Delta g}V_2$$

Comparing with $$I_2 = h_{21} I_1 + h_{22} V_2,$$

$$h_{21} = -\frac{g_{21}}{\Delta g}$$

$$h_{22} = \frac{g_{11}}{\Delta g}$$

### 12.8.6 Inverse Hybrid Parameters in Terms of Other Parameters

***1. Inverse Hybrid Parameters in Terms of Z Parameters*** We know that

$$V_1 = Z_{11} I_1 + Z_{12} I_2$$
$$V_2 = Z_{21} I_1 + Z_{22} I_2$$

Rewriting the first equation,

$$I_1 = \frac{1}{Z_{11}} V_1 - \frac{Z_{12}}{Z_{11}} I_2$$

Comparing with $$I_1 = g_{11} V_1 + g_{12} I_2,$$

$$g_{11} = \frac{1}{Z_{11}}$$

$$g_{12} = -\frac{Z_{12}}{Z_{11}}$$

Also, $$V_2 = Z_{21}\left[\frac{1}{Z_{11}} V_1 - \frac{Z_{12}}{Z_{11}} I_2\right] + Z_{22} I_2 = \frac{Z_{21}}{Z_{11}} V_1 + \left[\frac{Z_{11} Z_{22} - Z_{12} Z_{21}}{Z_{11}}\right] I_2$$

Comparing with $$V_2 = g_{21} V_1 + g_{22} I_2,$$

$$g_{21} = \frac{Z_{21}}{Z_{11}}$$

$$g_{22} = \frac{Z_{11} Z_{22} - Z_{12} Z_{21}}{Z_{11}} = \frac{\Delta Z}{Z_{11}}$$

***2. Inverse Hybrid Parameters in Terms of Y Parameters*** We know that

$$I_1 = Y_{11} V_1 + Y_{12} V_2$$
$$I_2 = Y_{21} V_1 + Y_{22} V_2$$

Rewriting the second equation,

$$V_2 = -\frac{Y_{21}}{Y_{22}} V_1 + \frac{1}{Y_{22}} I_2$$

Comparing with $$V_2 = g_{21} V_1 + g_{22} I_2,$$

$$g_{21} = -\frac{Y_{21}}{Y_{22}}$$

$$g_{22} = \frac{1}{Y_{22}}$$

Also, $$I_1 = Y_{11}V_1 + Y_{12}\left[-\frac{Y_{21}}{Y_{22}}V_1 + \frac{1}{Y_{22}}I_2\right] = \left[\frac{Y_{11}Y_{22} - Y_{12}Y_{21}}{Y_{22}}\right]V_1 + \frac{Y_{12}}{Y_{22}}I_2$$

Comparing with $$I_1 = g_{11}V_1 + g_{12}I_2,$$

$$g_{11} = \frac{Y_{11}Y_{22} - Y_{12}Y_{21}}{Y_{22}} = \frac{\Delta Y}{Y_{22}}$$

$$g_{12} = \frac{Y_{12}}{Y_{22}}$$

**3. *Inverse Hybrid Parameters in Terms of ABCD Parameters*** We know that

$$V_1 = AV_2 - BI_2$$
$$I_1 = CV_2 - DI_2$$

Rewriting the first equation,

$$V_2 = \frac{1}{A}V_1 + \frac{B}{A}I_2$$

Comparing with $$V_2 = g_{21}V_1 + g_{22}I_2,$$

$$g_{21} = \frac{1}{A}$$

$$g_{22} = \frac{B}{A}$$

Also, $$I_1 = C\left[\frac{1}{A}V_1 + \frac{B}{A}I_2\right] - DI_2 = \frac{C}{A}V_1 - \left[\frac{AD - BC}{A}\right]I_2$$

Comparing with $$I_1 = g_{11}V_1 + g_{12}I_2,$$

$$g_{11} = \frac{C}{A}$$

$$g_{12} = -\left[\frac{AD - BC}{A}\right] = -\frac{\Delta T}{A}$$

**4. *Inverse Hybrid Parameters in Terms of A′B′C′D′ Parameters*** We know that

$$V_2 = A'V_1 - B'I_1$$
$$I_2 = C'V_1 - D'I_1$$

Rewriting the second equation,

$$I_1 = \frac{C'}{D'}V_1 - \frac{1}{D'}I_2$$

Comparing with $$I_1 = g_{11}V_1 + g_{12}I_2,$$

$$g_{11} = \frac{C'}{D'}$$

$$g_{12} = -\frac{1}{D'}$$

Also,
$$V_2 = A'V_1 - B'\left[\frac{C'}{D'}V_1 - \frac{1}{D'}I_2\right] = \left[\frac{A'D' - B'C'}{D'}\right]V_1 + \frac{B'}{D'}I_2$$

Comparing with
$$V_2 = g_{21}V_1 + g_{22}I_2,$$

$$g_{21} = \left[\frac{A'D' - B'C'}{D'}\right] = \frac{\Delta T'}{D'}$$

$$g_{22} = \frac{B'}{D'}$$

**5. *Inverse Hybrid Parameters in Terms of Hybrid Parameters*** We know that

$$V_1 = h_{11}I_1 + h_{12}V_2$$
$$I_2 = h_{21}I_1 + h_{22}V_2$$

By Cramer's rule,

$$I_1 = \frac{\begin{vmatrix} V_1 & h_{12} \\ I_2 & h_{22} \end{vmatrix}}{\begin{vmatrix} h_{11} & h_{12} \\ h_{21} & h_{22} \end{vmatrix}} = \frac{h_{22}}{\Delta h}V_1 - \frac{h_{12}}{\Delta h}I_2$$

where
$$\Delta h = h_{11}h_{22} - h_{12}h_{21}$$

Comparing with
$$I_1 = g_{11}V_1 + g_{12}I_2,$$

$$g_{11} = \frac{h_{22}}{\Delta h}$$

$$g_{12} = -\frac{h_{12}}{\Delta h}$$

Also,
$$V_2 = \frac{\begin{vmatrix} h_{11} & V_1 \\ h_{21} & I_2 \end{vmatrix}}{\Delta h} = -\frac{h_{21}}{\Delta h}V_1 + \frac{h_{11}}{\Delta h}I_2$$

Comparing with
$$V_2 = g_{21}V_1 + g_{22}I_2,$$

$$g_{21} = -\frac{h_{21}}{\Delta h}$$

$$g_{22} = \frac{h_{11}}{\Delta h}$$

**TABLE 12.3 Inter-relationship between parameters**
$\Delta X = X_{11}X_{22} - X_{12}X_{21}$

| | *In terms of* | | | | | |
|---|---|---|---|---|---|---|
| | **[Z]** | **[Y]** | **[T]** | **[T′]** | **[h]** | **[g]** |
| [Z] | $Z_{11}$ $Z_{12}$ | $\frac{Y_{22}}{\Delta Y}$ $-\frac{Y_{12}}{\Delta Y}$ | $\frac{A}{C}$ $\frac{\Delta T}{C}$ | $\frac{D'}{C'}$ $\frac{1}{C'}$ | $\frac{\Delta h}{h_{22}}$ $\frac{h_{12}}{h_{22}}$ | $\frac{1}{g_{11}}$ $-\frac{g_{12}}{g_{11}}$ |
| | $Z_{21}$ $Z_{22}$ | $-\frac{Y_{21}}{\Delta Y}$ $\frac{Y_{11}}{\Delta Y}$ | $\frac{1}{C}$ $\frac{D}{C}$ | $\frac{\Delta T'}{C'}$ $\frac{A'}{C'}$ | $-\frac{h_{21}}{h_{22}}$ $\frac{1}{h_{22}}$ | $\frac{g_{21}}{g_{11}}$ $\frac{\Delta g}{g_{11}}$ |
| [Y] | $\frac{Z_{22}}{\Delta Z}$ $-\frac{Z_{12}}{\Delta Z}$ | $Y_{11}$ $Y_{12}$ | $\frac{D}{B}$ $-\frac{\Delta T}{B}$ | $\frac{A'}{B'}$ $-\frac{1}{B'}$ | $\frac{1}{h_{11}}$ $-\frac{h_{12}}{h_{11}}$ | $\frac{\Delta g}{g_{22}}$ $\frac{g_{12}}{g_{22}}$ |
| | $-\frac{Z_{21}}{\Delta Z}$ $\frac{Z_{11}}{\Delta Z}$ | $Y_{21}$ $Y_{22}$ | $-\frac{1}{B}$ $\frac{A}{B}$ | $\frac{\Delta T'}{B'}$ $\frac{D'}{B'}$ | $\frac{h_{21}}{h_{11}}$ $\frac{\Delta h}{h_{11}}$ | $-\frac{g_{21}}{g_{22}}$ $\frac{1}{g_{22}}$ |
| [T] | $\frac{Z_{11}}{Z_{21}}$ $\frac{\Delta Z}{Z_{21}}$ | $-\frac{Y_{22}}{Y_{21}}$ $-\frac{1}{Y_{21}}$ | $A$ $B$ | $\frac{D'}{\Delta T'}$ $\frac{B'}{\Delta T'}$ | $-\frac{\Delta h}{h_{21}}$ $-\frac{h_{11}}{h_{21}}$ | $\frac{1}{g_{21}}$ $\frac{g_{22}}{g_{21}}$ |
| | $\frac{1}{Z_{21}}$ $\frac{Z_{22}}{Z_{21}}$ | $-\frac{\Delta Y}{Y_{21}}$ $-\frac{Y_{11}}{Y_{21}}$ | $C$ $D$ | $\frac{C'}{\Delta T'}$ $\frac{A'}{\Delta T'}$ | $-\frac{h_{22}}{h_{21}}$ $-\frac{1}{h_{21}}$ | $\frac{g_{11}}{g_{21}}$ $\frac{\Delta g}{g_{21}}$ |
| [T′] | $\frac{Z_{22}}{Z_{12}}$ $\frac{\Delta Z}{Z_{12}}$ | $-\frac{Y_{11}}{Y_{12}}$ $-\frac{1}{Y_{12}}$ | $\frac{D}{\Delta T}$ $\frac{B}{\Delta T}$ | $A'$ $B'$ | $\frac{1}{h_{12}}$ $\frac{h_{11}}{h_{12}}$ | $-\frac{\Delta g}{g_{12}}$ $-\frac{g_{22}}{g_{12}}$ |
| | $\frac{1}{Z_{12}}$ $\frac{Z_{11}}{Z_{12}}$ | $-\frac{\Delta Y}{Y_{12}}$ $-\frac{Y_{22}}{Y_{12}}$ | $\frac{C}{\Delta T}$ $\frac{A}{\Delta T}$ | $C'$ $D'$ | $\frac{h_{22}}{h_{12}}$ $\frac{\Delta h}{h_{12}}$ | $-\frac{g_{11}}{g_{12}}$ $-\frac{1}{g_{12}}$ |
| [h] | $\frac{\Delta Z}{Z_{22}}$ $\frac{Z_{12}}{Z_{22}}$ | $\frac{1}{Y_{11}}$ $-\frac{Y_{12}}{Y_{11}}$ | $\frac{B}{D}$ $\frac{\Delta T}{D}$ | $\frac{B'}{A'}$ $\frac{1}{A'}$ | $h_{11}$ $h_{12}$ | $\frac{g_{22}}{\Delta g}$ $-\frac{g_{12}}{\Delta g}$ |
| | $-\frac{Z_{21}}{Z_{22}}$ $\frac{1}{Z_{22}}$ | $\frac{Y_{21}}{Y_{11}}$ $\frac{\Delta Y}{Y_{11}}$ | $-\frac{1}{D}$ $\frac{C}{D}$ | $-\frac{\Delta T'}{A'}$ $\frac{C'}{A'}$ | $h_{21}$ $h_{22}$ | $-\frac{g_{21}}{\Delta g}$ $\frac{g_{11}}{\Delta g}$ |
| [g] | $\frac{1}{Z_{11}}$ $-\frac{Z_{12}}{Z_{11}}$ | $\frac{\Delta Y}{Y_{22}}$ $\frac{Y_{12}}{Y_{22}}$ | $\frac{C}{A}$ $-\frac{\Delta T}{A}$ | $\frac{C'}{D'}$ $-\frac{1}{D'}$ | $\frac{h_{22}}{\Delta h}$ $-\frac{h_{12}}{\Delta h}$ | $g_{11}$ $g_{12}$ |
| | $\frac{Z_{21}}{Z_{11}}$ $\frac{\Delta Z}{Z_{11}}$ | $-\frac{Y_{21}}{Y_{22}}$ $\frac{1}{Y_{22}}$ | $\frac{1}{A}$ $\frac{B}{A}$ | $\frac{\Delta T'}{D'}$ $\frac{B'}{D'}$ | $-\frac{h_{21}}{\Delta h}$ $\frac{h_{11}}{\Delta h}$ | $g_{21}$ $g_{22}$ |

## EXAMPLE 12.26

*The Z parameters of a two-port network are $Z_{11} = 20\ \Omega$, $Z_{22} = 30\ \Omega$, $Z_{12} = Z_{21} = 10\ \Omega$. Find Y and ABCD parameters.*

**Solution**

$$\Delta Z = Z_{11}Z_{22} - Z_{12}Z_{21} = (20)(30) - (10)(10) = 500$$

***Y* parameters**

$$Y_{11} = \frac{Z_{22}}{\Delta Z} = \frac{30}{500} = \frac{3}{50}\ \mho, \qquad Y_{12} = -\frac{Z_{12}}{\Delta Z} = -\frac{10}{500} = -\frac{1}{50}\ \mho$$

$$Y_{21} = -\frac{Z_{21}}{\Delta Z} = -\frac{10}{500} = -\frac{1}{50}\ \mho, \qquad Y_{22} = \frac{Z_{11}}{\Delta Z} = \frac{20}{500} = \frac{2}{50}\ \mho$$

Hence, the $Y$ parameters are

$$\begin{bmatrix} Y_{11} & Y_{12} \\ Y_{21} & Y_{22} \end{bmatrix} = \begin{bmatrix} \frac{3}{50} & -\frac{1}{50} \\ -\frac{1}{50} & \frac{2}{50} \end{bmatrix}$$

***ABCD* parameters**

$$A = \frac{Z_{11}}{Z_{21}} = \frac{20}{10} = 2, \qquad B = \frac{\Delta Z}{Z_{21}} = \frac{500}{10} = 50$$

$$C = \frac{1}{Z_{21}} = \frac{1}{10} = 0.1, \qquad D = \frac{Z_{22}}{Z_{21}} = \frac{30}{10} = 3$$

Hence, the $ABCD$ parameters are

$$\begin{bmatrix} A & B \\ C & D \end{bmatrix} = \begin{bmatrix} 2 & 50 \\ 0.1 & 3 \end{bmatrix}$$

## EXAMPLE 12.27

*Currents $I_1$ and $I_2$ entering at port 1 and port 2 respectively of a two-port network are given by the following equations:*

$$I_1 = 0.5V_1 - 0.2V_2$$
$$I_2 = -0.2V_1 + V_2$$

*Find Y, Z and ABCD parameters for the network.*

**Solution**

$$Y_{11} = \left.\frac{I_1}{V_1}\right|_{V_2=0} = 0.5\ \mho, \qquad Y_{12} = \left.\frac{I_1}{V_2}\right|_{V_1=0} = -0.2\ \mho$$

$$Y_{21} = \left.\frac{I_2}{V_1}\right|_{V_2=0} = -0.2\ \mho, \qquad Y_{22} = \left.\frac{I_2}{V_2}\right|_{V_1=0} = 1\ \mho$$

Hence, the $Y$ parameters are

$$\begin{bmatrix} Y_{11} & Y_{12} \\ Y_{21} & Y_{22} \end{bmatrix} = \begin{bmatrix} 0.5 & -0.2 \\ -0.2 & 1 \end{bmatrix}$$

***Z* parameters**

$$\Delta Y = Y_{11} Y_{22} - Y_{12} Y_{21} = (0.5)(1) - (-0.2)(-0.2) = 0.46$$

$$Z_{11} = \frac{Y_{22}}{\Delta Y} = \frac{1}{0.46} = 2.174\ \Omega, \qquad Z_{12} = -\frac{Y_{12}}{\Delta Y} = -\frac{(-0.2)}{0.46} = 0.434\ \Omega$$

$$Z_{21} = -\frac{Y_{21}}{\Delta Y} = -\frac{(-0.2)}{0.46} = 0.434\ \Omega, \qquad Z_{22} = \frac{Y_{11}}{\Delta Y} = \frac{0.5}{0.46} = 1.087\ \Omega$$

$$\begin{bmatrix} Z_{11} & Z_{12} \\ Z_{21} & Z_{22} \end{bmatrix} = \begin{bmatrix} 2.174 & 0.434 \\ 0.434 & 1.087 \end{bmatrix}$$

***ABCD* parameters**

$$A = -\frac{Y_{22}}{Y_{21}} = -\frac{1}{-0.2} = 5, \qquad B = -\frac{1}{Y_{21}} = -\frac{1}{-0.2} = 5$$

$$C = -\frac{\Delta Y}{Y_{21}} = -\frac{0.46}{-0.2} = 2.3, \qquad D = -\frac{Y_{11}}{Y_{21}} = -\frac{0.5}{-0.2} = 2.5$$

Hence, the *ABCD* parameters are

$$\begin{bmatrix} A & B \\ C & D \end{bmatrix} = \begin{bmatrix} 5 & 5 \\ 2.3 & 2.5 \end{bmatrix}$$

## EXAMPLE 12.28

*Using the relation $Y = Z^{-1}$, show that $|Z| = \frac{1}{2}\left(\frac{Z_{22}}{Y_{11}} + \frac{Z_{11}}{Y_{22}}\right)$.*

**Solution** We know that

$$Y = Z^{-1}$$

i.e.,

$$\begin{bmatrix} Y_{11} & Y_{12} \\ Y_{21} & Y_{22} \end{bmatrix} = \begin{bmatrix} \frac{Z_{22}}{\Delta Z} & -\frac{Z_{12}}{\Delta Z} \\ -\frac{Z_{21}}{\Delta Z} & \frac{Z_{11}}{\Delta Z} \end{bmatrix}$$

$$|Z| = Z_{11} Z_{22} - Z_{12} Z_{21}$$

$$\frac{1}{2}\left(\frac{Z_{22}}{Y_{11}} + \frac{Z_{11}}{Y_{22}}\right) = \frac{1}{2}\left(\frac{Z_{22}}{\frac{Z_{22}}{\Delta Z}} + \frac{Z_{11}}{\frac{Z_{11}}{\Delta Z}}\right) = \frac{1}{2}(\Delta Z + \Delta Z) = \frac{1}{2}(2\Delta Z) = \Delta Z = Z_{11} Z_{12} - Z_{12} Z_{21}$$

$$|Z| = \frac{1}{2}\left(\frac{Z_{22}}{Y_{11}} + \frac{Z_{11}}{Y_{22}}\right)$$

## EXAMPLE 12.29

*For the network shown in Fig. 12.59, find Z and Y parameters.*

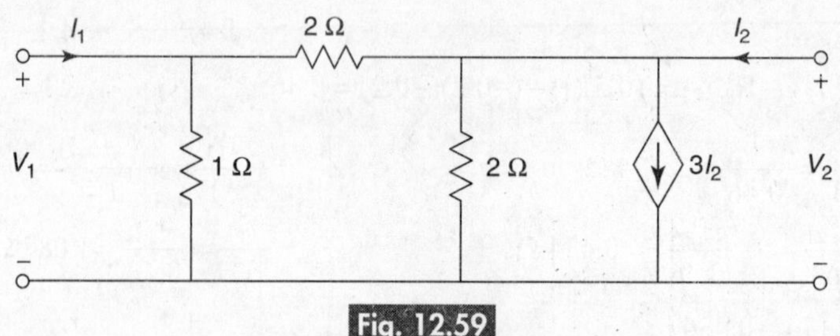


Fig. 12.59

**Solution** The network is redrawn by source transformation technique, as shown in Fig. 12.60.

Applying KVL to mesh 1,

$$V_1 = I_1 - I_3 \qquad \text{...(i)}$$

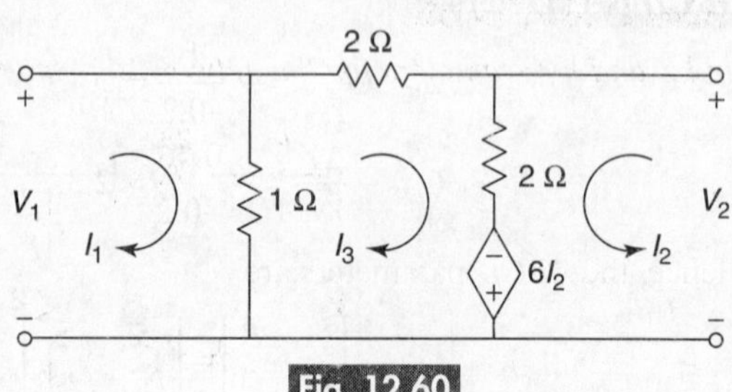


Fig. 12.60

Applying KVL to mesh 2,

$$V_2 = 2(I_2 + I_3) - 6I_2$$

$$= -4I_2 + 2I_3 \qquad \text{...(ii)}$$

Applying KVL to mesh 3,

$$-(I_3 - I_1) - 2I_3 - 2(I_2 + I_3) + 6I_2 = 0$$

$$5I_3 = I_1 + 4I_2$$

$$I_3 = \frac{1}{5}I_1 + \frac{4}{5}I_2 \qquad \text{...(iii)}$$

Substituting Eq. (iii) in Eq. (i),

$$V_1 = I_1 - \frac{1}{5}I_1 - \frac{4}{5}I_2$$

$$= \frac{4}{5}I_1 - \frac{4}{5}I_2 \qquad \text{...(iv)}$$

Substituting Eq. (iii) in Eq. (ii),

$$V_2 = -4I_2 + 2\left(\frac{1}{5}I_1 + \frac{4}{5}I_2\right)$$

$$= \frac{2}{5}I_1 - \frac{12}{5}I_2 \qquad \text{...(v)}$$

Comparing Eqs (iv) and (v) with Z parameter equations,

$$\begin{bmatrix} Z_{11} & Z_{12} \\ Z_{21} & Z_{22} \end{bmatrix} = \begin{bmatrix} \frac{4}{5} & -\frac{4}{5} \\ \frac{2}{5} & -\frac{12}{5} \end{bmatrix}$$

***Y* parameters**

$$\Delta Z = Z_{11}Z_{22} - Z_{12}Z_{21} = \left(\frac{4}{5}\right)\left(-\frac{12}{5}\right) - \left(-\frac{4}{5}\right)\left(\frac{2}{5}\right) = -\frac{40}{25} = -\frac{8}{5}$$

$$Y_{11} = \frac{Z_{22}}{\Delta Z} = \frac{-\frac{12}{5}}{-\frac{8}{5}} = \frac{3}{2}\ ℧, \qquad Y_{12} = -\frac{Z_{12}}{\Delta Z} = \frac{-\frac{4}{5}}{-\frac{8}{5}} = -\frac{1}{2}\ ℧$$

$$Y_{21} = -\frac{Z_{21}}{\Delta Z} = \frac{-\frac{2}{5}}{-\frac{8}{5}} = \frac{1}{4}\,\mho, \qquad Y_{22} = \frac{Z_{11}}{\Delta Z} = \frac{\frac{4}{5}}{-\frac{8}{5}} = -\frac{1}{2}\,\mho$$

Hence, the $Y$ parameters are

$$\begin{bmatrix} Y_{11} & Y_{12} \\ Y_{21} & Y_{22} \end{bmatrix} = \begin{bmatrix} \frac{3}{2} & -\frac{1}{2} \\ \frac{1}{4} & -\frac{1}{2} \end{bmatrix}$$

## EXAMPLE 12.30

*Find Z and h parameters for the network shown in Fig. 12.61.*

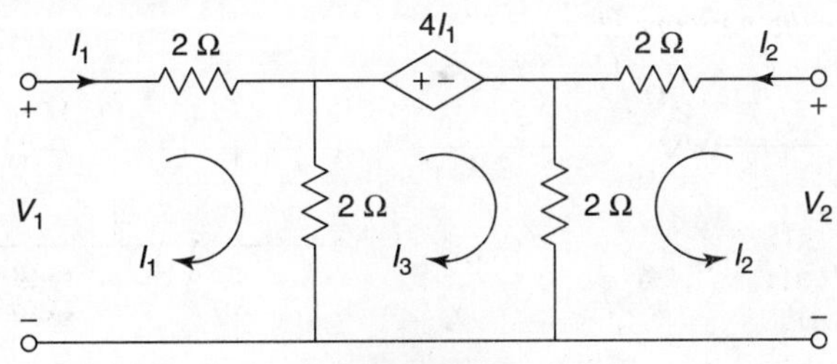


Fig. 12.61

**Solution** Applying KVL to mesh 1,

$$V_1 = 2I_1 + 2(I_1 - I_3)$$
$$= 4I_1 - 2I_3 \qquad \ldots\text{(i)}$$

Applying KVL to mesh 2,

$$V_2 = 2I_2 + 2(I_2 + I_3)$$
$$= 4I_2 + 2I_3 \qquad \ldots\text{(ii)}$$

Applying KVL to mesh 3,

$$-2(I_3 - I_1) - 4I_1 - 2(I_3 + I_2) = 0$$
$$I_1 + I_2 = -2I_3 \qquad \ldots\text{(iii)}$$

Substituting Eq. (iii) in Eq. (i),

$$V_1 = 4I_1 + I_1 + I_2$$
$$= 5I_1 + I_2 \qquad \ldots\text{(iv)}$$

Substituting Eq. (iii) in Eq. (ii),

$$V_2 = 4I_2 - I_1 - I_2$$
$$= -I_1 + 3I_2 \qquad \ldots\text{(v)}$$

Comparing Eqs (iv) and (v) with $Z$ parameter equations,

$$\begin{bmatrix} Z_{11} & Z_{12} \\ Z_{21} & Z_{22} \end{bmatrix} = \begin{bmatrix} 5 & 1 \\ -1 & 3 \end{bmatrix}$$

***h* parameters**

$$\Delta Z = Z_{11}Z_{22} - Z_{12}Z_{21} = (5)(3) - (1)(-1) = 15 + 1 = 16$$

$$h_{11} = \frac{\Delta Z}{Z_{22}} = \frac{16}{3}\ \Omega, \qquad h_{12} = \frac{Z_{12}}{Z_{22}} = \frac{1}{3}$$

$$h_{21} = -\frac{Z_{21}}{Z_{22}} = \frac{1}{3}, \qquad h_{22} = \frac{1}{Z_{22}} = \frac{1}{3}\ \mho$$

Hence, the $h$ parameters are

$$\begin{bmatrix} h_{11} & h_{12} \\ h_{22} & h_{22} \end{bmatrix} = \begin{bmatrix} \frac{16}{3} & \frac{1}{3} \\ \frac{1}{3} & \frac{1}{3} \end{bmatrix}$$

## EXAMPLE 12.31

*Find Y and Z parameters for the network shown in Fig. 12.62.*

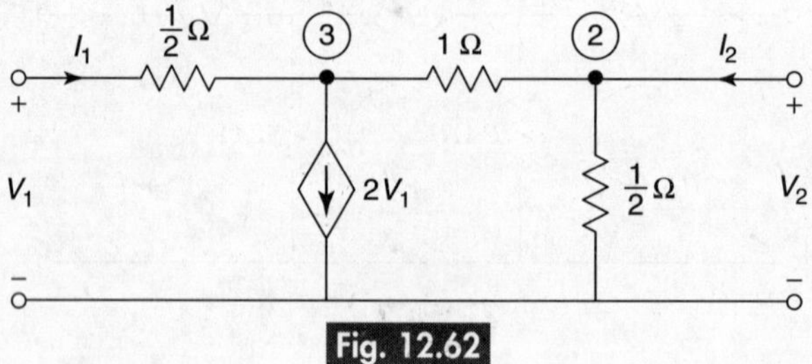


Fig. 12.62

**Solution** Applying KCL at node 3,

$$2(V_1 - V_3) = 2V_1 + (V_3 - V_2)$$

$$V_3 = \frac{V_2}{3} \qquad \text{...(i)}$$

Now,

$$I_1 = 2V_1 + (V_3 - V_2)$$

$$= 2V_1 + \frac{V_2}{3} - V_2$$

$$= 2V_1 - \frac{2}{3}V_2 \qquad \text{...(ii)}$$

$$I_2 = 2V_2 + (V_2 - V_3)$$

$$= 3V_2 - \frac{V_2}{3}$$

$$= \frac{8}{3}V_2 \qquad \text{...(iii)}$$

Comparing Eqs (ii) and (iii) with $Y$ parameter equations,

$$\begin{bmatrix} Y_{11} & Y_{12} \\ Y_{21} & Y_{22} \end{bmatrix} = \begin{bmatrix} 2 & -\frac{2}{3} \\ 0 & \frac{8}{3} \end{bmatrix}$$

**Z parameters**

$$\Delta Y = Y_{11}Y_{22} - Y_{12}Y_{21} = (2)\left(\frac{8}{3}\right) - 0 = \frac{16}{3}$$

$$Z_{11} = \frac{Y_{22}}{\Delta Y} = \frac{\frac{8}{3}}{\frac{16}{3}} = \frac{1}{2}\ \Omega, \qquad Z_{12} = -\frac{Y_{12}}{\Delta Y} = -\frac{\left(-\frac{2}{3}\right)}{\frac{16}{3}} = \frac{1}{8}\ \Omega$$

$$Z_{21} = -\frac{Y_{21}}{\Delta Y} = -\frac{0}{\frac{16}{3}} = 0, \qquad Z_{22} = \frac{Y_{11}}{\Delta Y} = \frac{2}{\frac{16}{3}} = \frac{3}{8}\ \Omega$$

Hence, the $Z$ parameters are

$$\begin{bmatrix} Z_{11} & Z_{12} \\ Z_{21} & Z_{22} \end{bmatrix} = \begin{bmatrix} \frac{1}{2} & \frac{1}{8} \\ 0 & \frac{3}{8} \end{bmatrix}$$

**EXAMPLE 12.32**

*For the network shown in Fig. 12.63, find Y and Z parameters.*

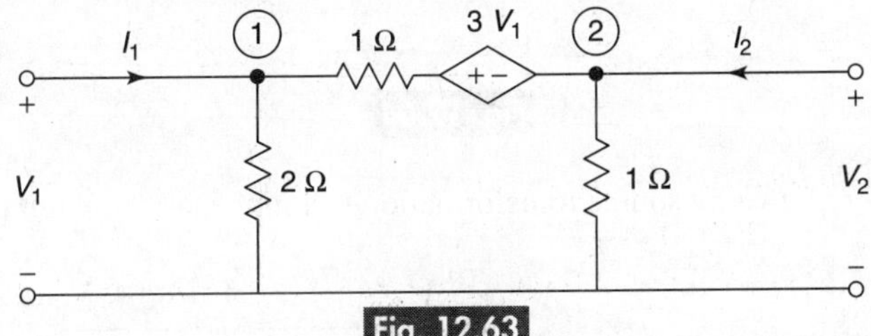


Fig. 12.63

**Solution** Applying KCL at node 1,

$$I_1 = \frac{V_1}{2} + \frac{V_1 - 3V_1 - V_2}{1}$$

$$= -\frac{3}{2}V_1 - V_2 \qquad \text{...(i)}$$

Applying KCL at node 2,

$$I_2 = \frac{V_2}{1} + \frac{V_2 + 3V_1 - V_1}{1} \qquad \text{...(ii)}$$

$$= 2V_1 + 2V_2$$

Comparing Eqs (i) and (ii) with $Y$ parameter equations,

$$\begin{bmatrix} Y_{11} & Y_{12} \\ Y_{21} & Y_{22} \end{bmatrix} = \begin{bmatrix} -\frac{3}{2} & -1 \\ 2 & 2 \end{bmatrix}$$

**Z parameters**

$$\Delta Y = Y_{11}Y_{22} - Y_{12}Y_{21} = \left(-\frac{3}{2}\right)(2) - (-1)(2) = -3 + 2 = -1$$

$$Z_{11} = \frac{Y_{22}}{\Delta Y} = \frac{2}{-1} = -2\ \Omega, \qquad Z_{12} = -\frac{Y_{12}}{\Delta Y} = -\frac{(-1)}{(-1)} = -1\ \Omega$$

$$Z_{21} = -\frac{Y_{21}}{\Delta Y} = -\frac{2}{(-1)} = 2\ \Omega, \qquad Z_{22} = \frac{Y_{11}}{\Delta Y} = \frac{-\frac{3}{2}}{-1} = \frac{3}{2}\ \Omega$$

Hence, the $Z$ parameters are

$$\begin{bmatrix} Z_{11} & Z_{12} \\ Z_{21} & Z_{22} \end{bmatrix} = \begin{bmatrix} -2 & -1 \\ 2 & \frac{3}{2} \end{bmatrix}$$

**EXAMPLE 12.33**

*Find Z parameters for the network shown in Fig. 12.64. Hence, find Y and h parameters.*

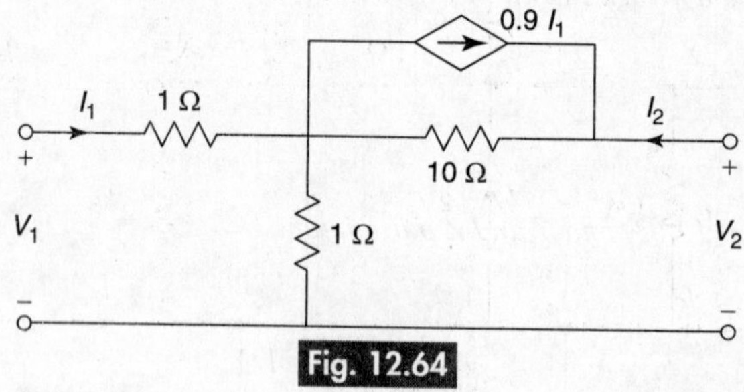


Fig. 12.64

**Solution** The network is redrawn by source transformation technique, as shown in Fig. 12.65.

Applying KVL to mesh 1,

$$V_1 = 2I_1 + I_2 \qquad \text{...(i)}$$

Applying KVL to mesh 2,

$$V_2 = 9I_1 + 10I_2 + 1(I_1 + I_2)$$
$$= 10I_1 + 11I_2 \qquad \text{...(ii)}$$

Comparing Eqs (i) and (ii) with $Z$ parameter equations,

$$\begin{bmatrix} Z_{11} & Z_{12} \\ Z_{21} & Z_{22} \end{bmatrix} = \begin{bmatrix} 2 & 1 \\ 10 & 11 \end{bmatrix}$$

Fig. 12.65

***Y* parameters**

$$\Delta Z = Z_{11}Z_{22} - Z_{12}Z_{21} = (2)(11) - (1)(10) = 22 - 10 = 12$$

$$Y_{11} = \frac{Z_{22}}{\Delta Z} = \frac{11}{12}\ \mho, \qquad Y_{12} = -\frac{Z_{12}}{\Delta Z} = -\frac{1}{12}\ \mho$$

$$Y_{21} = -\frac{Z_{21}}{\Delta Z} = -\frac{10}{12} = -\frac{5}{6}\ \mho, \qquad Y_{22} = \frac{Z_{11}}{\Delta Z} = \frac{2}{12} = \frac{1}{6}\ \mho$$

Hence, the $Y$ parameters are

$$\begin{bmatrix} Y_{11} & Y_{12} \\ Y_{21} & Y_{22} \end{bmatrix} = \begin{bmatrix} \frac{11}{12} & -\frac{1}{12} \\ -\frac{5}{6} & \frac{1}{6} \end{bmatrix}$$

***h* parameters**

$$h_{11} = \frac{\Delta Z}{Z_{22}} = \frac{12}{11}\ \Omega, \qquad h_{12} = \frac{Z_{12}}{Z_{22}} = \frac{1}{11}$$

$$h_{21} = -\frac{Z_{21}}{Z_{22}} = -\frac{10}{11}, \qquad h_{22} = \frac{1}{Z_{22}} = \frac{1}{11}\ \mho$$

Hence, *h* parameters are

$$\begin{bmatrix} h_{11} & h_{12} \\ h_{21} & h_{22} \end{bmatrix} = \begin{bmatrix} \frac{12}{11} & \frac{1}{11} \\ -\frac{10}{11} & \frac{1}{11} \end{bmatrix}$$

## EXAMPLE 12.34

*Find Y and Z parameters of the network shown in Fig. 12.66.*

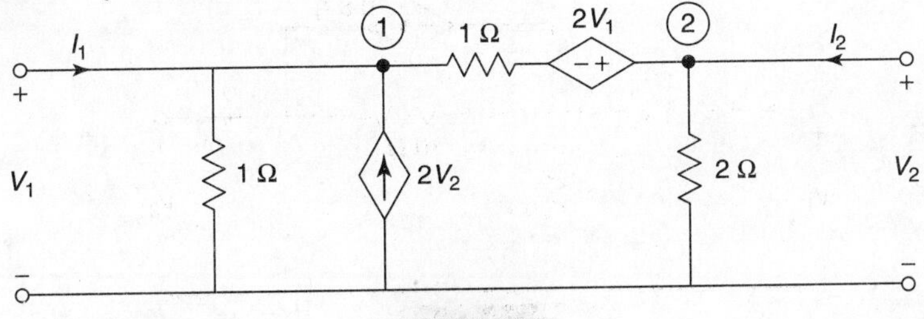


Fig. 12.66

**Solution** Applying KCL at node 1,

$$I_1 + 2V_2 = \frac{V_1}{1} + \frac{3V_1 - V_2}{1}$$

$$I_1 = 4V_1 - 3V_2 \qquad \ldots\text{(i)}$$

Applying KCL at node 2,

$$I_2 = \frac{V_2}{2} + \frac{V_2 - 2V_1 - V_1}{1}$$

$$= -3V_1 + 1.5V_2 \qquad \ldots\text{(ii)}$$

Comparing Eqs (i) and (ii) with *Y* parameter equations,

$$\begin{bmatrix} Y_{11} & Y_{12} \\ Y_{21} & Y_{22} \end{bmatrix} = \begin{bmatrix} 4 & -3 \\ -3 & 1.5 \end{bmatrix}$$

***Z* parameters**

$$\Delta Y = Y_{11}Y_{22} - Y_{12}Y_{21} = (4)(1.5) - (-3)(-3) = -3$$

$$Z_{11} = \frac{Y_{22}}{\Delta Y} = -\frac{1.5}{3} = -0.5\ \Omega, \qquad Z_{12} = -\frac{Y_{12}}{\Delta Y} = -\frac{(-3)}{-3} = -1\ \Omega$$

$$Z_{21} = -\frac{Y_{21}}{\Delta Y} = -\frac{(-3)}{-3} = -1\ \Omega, \qquad Z_{22} = \frac{Y_{11}}{\Delta Y} = -\frac{4}{3} = -\frac{4}{3}\ \Omega$$

Hence, the *Z* parameters are

$$\begin{bmatrix} Z_{11} & Z_{12} \\ Z_{21} & Z_{22} \end{bmatrix} = \begin{bmatrix} -0.5 & -1 \\ -1 & -\frac{4}{3} \end{bmatrix}$$

## EXAMPLE 12.35

*Determine Y and Z parameters for the network shown in Fig. 12.67.*

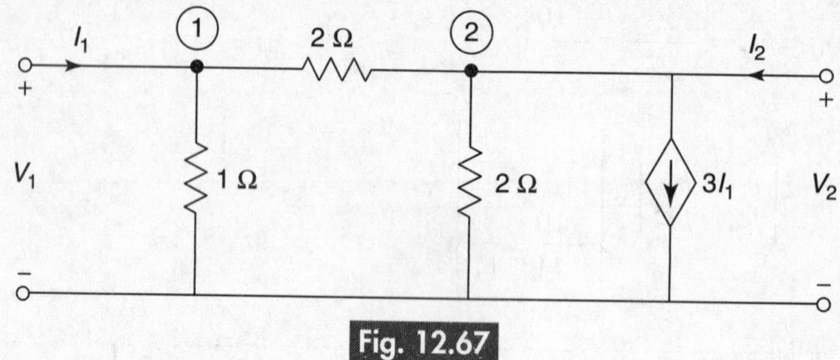


Fig. 12.67

**Solution** Applying KCL at node 1,

$$I_1 = \frac{V_1}{1} + \frac{V_1 - V_2}{2}$$
$$= 1.5V_1 - 0.5V_2 \quad \text{...(i)}$$

Applying KCL at node 2,

$$I_2 = \frac{V_2}{2} + 3I_1 + \frac{V_2 - V_1}{2}$$
$$= \frac{V_2}{2} + 3(1.5V_1 - 0.5V_2) + \frac{V_2 - V_1}{2}$$
$$= 0.5V_2 + 4.5V_1 - 1.5V_2 + 0.5V_2 - 0.5V_1$$
$$= 4V_1 - 0.5V_2 \quad \text{...(ii)}$$

Comparing Eqs (i) and (ii) with the $Y$ parameter equation,

$$\begin{bmatrix} Y_{11} & Y_{12} \\ Y_{21} & Y_{22} \end{bmatrix} = \begin{bmatrix} 1.5 & -0.5 \\ 4 & -0.5 \end{bmatrix}$$

***Z* parameters**

$$\Delta Y = Y_{11}Y_{22} - Y_{12}Y_{21} = (1.5)(-0.5) - (-0.5)(4) = 1.25$$

$$Z_{11} = \frac{Y_{22}}{\Delta Y} = -\frac{0.5}{1.25} = -0.4\ \Omega, \qquad Z_{12} = -\frac{Y_{12}}{\Delta Y} = \frac{0.5}{1.25} = 0.4\ \Omega$$

$$Z_{21} = -\frac{Y_{21}}{\Delta Y} = -\frac{4}{1.25} = -3.2\ \Omega, \qquad Z_{22} = \frac{Y_{11}}{\Delta Y} = \frac{1.5}{1.25} = 1.2\ \Omega$$

Hence, the $Z$ parameters are

$$\begin{bmatrix} Z_{11} & Z_{12} \\ Z_{21} & Z_{22} \end{bmatrix} = \begin{bmatrix} -0.4 & 0.4 \\ -3.2 & 1.2 \end{bmatrix}$$

## EXAMPLE 12.36

*Determine the Y and Z parameters for the network shown in Fig. 12.68.*

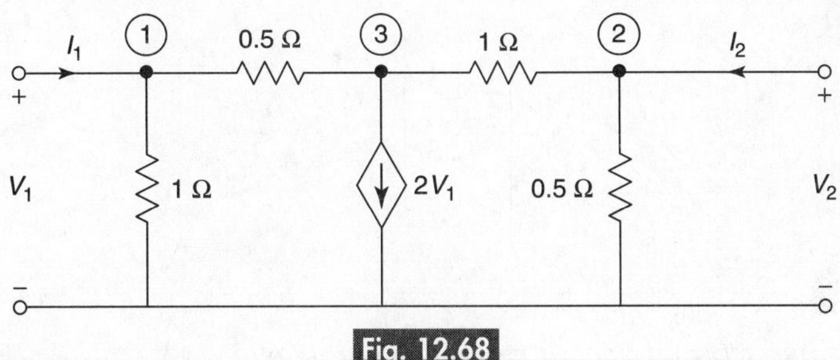


Fig. 12.68

**Solution** Applying KCL at node 1,

$$I_1 = \frac{V_1}{1} + \frac{V_1 - V_3}{0.5}$$
$$= 3V_1 - 2V_3 \quad \text{...(i)}$$

Applying KCL at node 2,

$$I_2 = \frac{V_2}{0.5} + \frac{V_2 - V_3}{1}$$
$$= 3V_2 - V_3 \quad \text{...(ii)}$$

Applying KCL at node 3,

$$\frac{V_3 - V_1}{0.5} + 2V_1 + \frac{V_3 - V_2}{1} = 0$$
$$V_3 = \frac{1}{3}V_2 \quad \text{...(iii)}$$

Substituting Eq. (iii) in Eqs (i) and (ii),

$$I_1 = 3V_1 - \frac{2}{3}V_2 \quad \text{...(iv)}$$
$$I_2 = 0V_1 + \frac{8}{3}V_2 \quad \text{...(v)}$$

Comparing Eqs (iv) and (v) with $Y$ parameter equations,

$$\begin{bmatrix} Y_{11} & Y_{12} \\ Y_{21} & Y_{22} \end{bmatrix} = \begin{bmatrix} 3 & -\frac{2}{3} \\ 0 & \frac{8}{3} \end{bmatrix}$$

***Z* parameters**

$$\Delta Y = Y_{11}Y_{22} - Y_{12}Y_{21} = (3)\left(\frac{8}{3}\right) - 0 = 8$$

$$Z_{11} = \frac{Y_{22}}{\Delta Y} = \frac{\frac{8}{3}}{8} = \frac{1}{3}\,\Omega, \qquad Z_{12} = -\frac{Y_{12}}{\Delta Y} = \frac{\frac{2}{3}}{8} = \frac{1}{12}\,\Omega$$

$$Z_{21} = -\frac{Y_{12}}{\Delta Y} = \frac{\frac{2}{3}}{8} = \frac{1}{12}\,\Omega, \qquad Z_{22} = \frac{Y_{11}}{Y\Delta} = \frac{3}{8}\,\Omega$$

Hence, the $Z$ parameters are

$$\begin{bmatrix} Z_{11} & Z_{12} \\ Z_{21} & Z_{22} \end{bmatrix} = \begin{bmatrix} \frac{1}{3} & \frac{1}{12} \\ 0 & \frac{3}{8} \end{bmatrix}$$

## EXAMPLE 12.37

*Determine Z and Y parameters of the network shown in Fig. 12.69.*

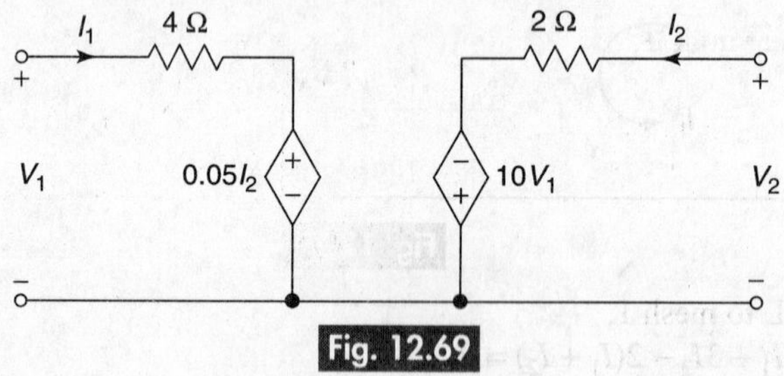


Fig. 12.69

**Solution** Applying KVL to mesh 1,

$$V_1 - 4I_1 - 0.05\,I_2 = 0$$

$$V_1 = 4I_1 + 0.05I_2 \qquad \text{...(i)}$$

Applying KVL to mesh 2,

$$V_2 - 2I_2 + 10V_1 = 0$$

$$V_2 = 2I_2 - 10V_1 \qquad \text{...(ii)}$$

Substituting Eq. (i) in Eq. (ii),

$$V_2 = 2I_2 - 40I_1 - 0.5I_2$$

$$= -40I_1 + 1.5I_2 \qquad \text{...(iii)}$$

Comparing Eqs (i) and (iii) with $Z$ parameter equations,

$$\begin{bmatrix} Z_{11} & Z_{12} \\ Z_{21} & Z_{22} \end{bmatrix} = \begin{bmatrix} 4 & 0.05 \\ -40 & 1.5 \end{bmatrix}$$

***Y* parameters**

$$\Delta Z = Z_{11}Z_{22} - Z_{12}Z_{21} = (4)(1.5) - (0.05)(-40) = 8$$

$$Y_{11} = \frac{Z_{22}}{\Delta Z} = \frac{1.5}{8}\,℧, \qquad Y_{12} = -\frac{Z_{12}}{\Delta Z} = -\frac{0.05}{8}\,℧$$

$$Y_{21} = -\frac{Z_{21}}{\Delta Z} = -\frac{(-40)}{8} = \frac{40}{8}\,℧, \qquad Y_{22} = \frac{Z_{11}}{\Delta Z} = \frac{4}{8}\,℧$$

Hence, the $Y$ parameters are

$$\begin{bmatrix} Y_{11} & Y_{12} \\ Y_{21} & Y_{22} \end{bmatrix} = \begin{bmatrix} \frac{1.5}{8} & -\frac{0.05}{8} \\ \frac{40}{8} & \frac{4}{8} \end{bmatrix}$$

## EXAMPLE 12.38

*Determine Z and Y parameters of the network shown in Fig. 12.70.*

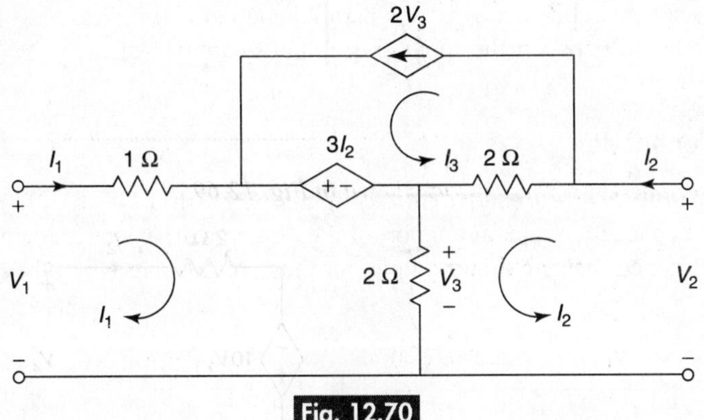


Fig. 12.70

**Solution** Applying KVL to mesh 1,

$$V_1 - 1I_1 - 3I_2 - 2(I_1 + I_2) = 0$$

$$V_1 = 3I_1 + 5I_2 \quad \text{...(i)}$$

Applying KVL to mesh 2,

$$V_2 - 2(I_2 - I_3) - 2(I_1 + I_2) = 0$$

$$V_2 - 2I_2 + 2I_3 - 2I_1 - 2I_2 = 0$$

$$V_2 = 2I_1 + 4I_2 - 2I_3 \quad \text{...(ii)}$$

Writing equation for mesh 3,

$$I_3 = 2V_3 \quad \text{...(iii)}$$

From Fig. 12.70,

$$V_3 = 2(I_1 + I_2)$$

$$I_3 = 2V_3 = 4I_1 + 4I_2 \quad \text{...(iv)}$$

Substituting Eq. (iv) in Eq. (ii),

$$V_2 = -6I_1 - 4I_2 \quad \text{...(v)}$$

Comparing Eqs (i) and (v) with $Z$ parameter equations,

$$\begin{bmatrix} Z_{11} & Z_{12} \\ Z_{21} & Z_{22} \end{bmatrix} = \begin{bmatrix} 3 & 5 \\ -6 & -4 \end{bmatrix}$$

***Y* parameters**

$$\Delta Z = Z_{11}Z_{22} - Z_{12}Z_{21} = (3)(-4) - (5)(-6) = 18$$

$$Y_{11} = \frac{Z_{22}}{\Delta Z} = -\frac{4}{18} = -\frac{2}{9}\ \mho, \qquad Y_{12} = -\frac{Z_{12}}{\Delta Z} = -\frac{5}{18}\ \mho$$

$$Y_{21} = -\frac{Z_{21}}{\Delta Z} = -\frac{(-6)}{18} = \frac{1}{3}\ \mho, \qquad Y_{22} = \frac{Z_{11}}{\Delta Z} = \frac{3}{18}\ \mho$$

Hence, $Y$ parameters are

$$\begin{bmatrix} Y_{11} & Y_{12} \\ Y_{21} & Y_{22} \end{bmatrix} = \begin{bmatrix} -\frac{2}{9} & -\frac{5}{18} \\ \frac{1}{3} & \frac{3}{18} \end{bmatrix}$$

## 12.9 INTERCONNECTION OF TWO-PORT NETWORKS

LO 12.7

Discuss interconnection of two-port network

We shall now discuss the various types of interconnections of two-port networks, namely, cascade, parallel, series, series-parallel and parallel-series. We shall derive the relation between the input and output quantities of the combined two-port networks.

### 12.9.1 Cascade Connection

***1. Transmission Parameter Representation*** Figure 12.71 shows two-port networks connected in cascade. In the cascade connection, the output port of the first network becomes the input port of the second network. Since it is assumed that input and output currents are positive when they enter the network, we have

$$I_1' = -I_2$$

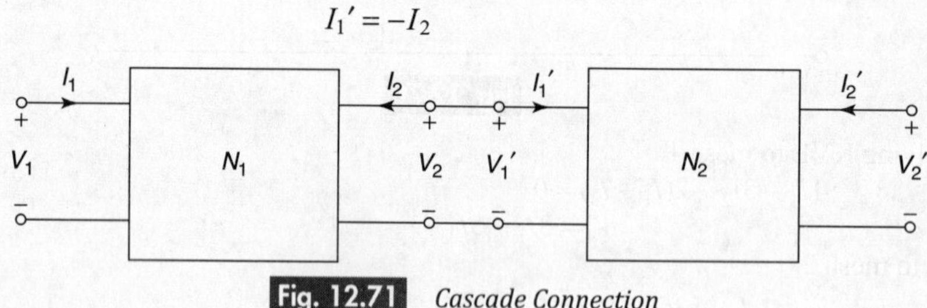


**Fig. 12.71** *Cascade Connection*

Let $A_1,B_1,C_1,D_1$ be the transmission parameters of the network $N_1$ and $A_2,B_2,C_2,D_2$ be the transmission parameters of the network $N_2$.

For the network $N_1$,

$$\begin{bmatrix} V_1 \\ I_1 \end{bmatrix} = \begin{bmatrix} A_1 & B_1 \\ C_1 & D_1 \end{bmatrix} \begin{bmatrix} V_2 \\ -I_2 \end{bmatrix} \qquad \text{...(12.1)}$$

For the network $N_2$,

$$\begin{bmatrix} V_1' \\ I_1' \end{bmatrix} = \begin{bmatrix} A_2 & B_2 \\ C_2 & D_2 \end{bmatrix} \begin{bmatrix} V_2' \\ -I_2' \end{bmatrix} \qquad \text{...(12.2)}$$

Since $V_1' = V_2$ and $I_2' = -I_2$, we can write

$$\begin{bmatrix} V_2 \\ -I_2 \end{bmatrix} = \begin{bmatrix} A_2 & B_2 \\ C_2 & D_2 \end{bmatrix} \begin{bmatrix} V_2' \\ -I_2' \end{bmatrix} \qquad \text{...(12.3)}$$

Combining Eqs (12.1) and (12.3),

$$\begin{bmatrix} V_1 \\ I_1 \end{bmatrix} = \begin{bmatrix} A_1 & B_1 \\ C_1 & D_1 \end{bmatrix} \begin{bmatrix} A_2 & B_2 \\ C_2 & D_2 \end{bmatrix} \begin{bmatrix} V_2' \\ -I_2' \end{bmatrix} = \begin{bmatrix} A & B \\ C & D \end{bmatrix} \begin{bmatrix} V_2' \\ -I_2' \end{bmatrix}$$

Hence,

$$\begin{bmatrix} A & B \\ C & D \end{bmatrix} = \begin{bmatrix} A_1 & B_1 \\ C_1 & D_1 \end{bmatrix} \begin{bmatrix} A_2 & B_2 \\ C_2 & D_2 \end{bmatrix} \qquad \text{...(12.4)}$$

Equation 12.4 shows that the resultant $ABCD$ matrix of the cascade connection is the product of the individual $ABCD$ matrices.

***2. Inverse Transmission Parameter Representation*** Figure 12.72 shows two-port networks connected in cascade. Since it is assumed that input and output currents are positive when they enter the network, we have

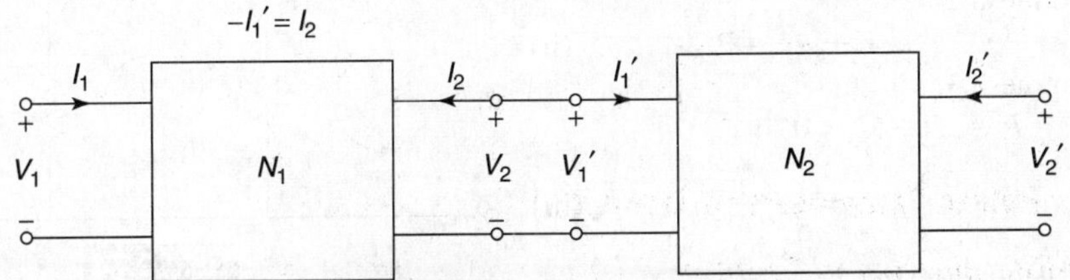


**Fig. 12.72** *Cascade connection*

Let $A_1', B_1', C_1', D_1'$ be the transmission parameters of the network $N_1$ and $A_2', B_2', C_2', D_2'$ be the transmission parameters of the network $N_2$.

For the network $N_1$,

$$\begin{bmatrix} V_2 \\ I_2 \end{bmatrix} = \begin{bmatrix} A_1' & B_1' \\ C_1' & D_1' \end{bmatrix} \begin{bmatrix} V_1 \\ -I_1 \end{bmatrix} \qquad \text{...(12.5)}$$

For the network $N_2$,

$$\begin{bmatrix} V_2' \\ I_2' \end{bmatrix} = \begin{bmatrix} A_2' & B_2' \\ C_2' & D_2' \end{bmatrix} \begin{bmatrix} V_2' \\ -I_1' \end{bmatrix} \qquad \text{...(12.6)}$$

Since $V_1' = V_2$ and $-I_1' = I_2$, we can write

$$\begin{bmatrix} V_2' \\ I_2' \end{bmatrix} = \begin{bmatrix} A_2' & B_2' \\ C_2' & D_2' \end{bmatrix} \begin{bmatrix} V_2 \\ I_2 \end{bmatrix} \qquad \text{...(12.7)}$$

Combining equations (12.5) and (12.7),

$$\begin{bmatrix} V_2' \\ I_2' \end{bmatrix} = \begin{bmatrix} A_2' & B_2' \\ C_2' & D_2' \end{bmatrix} \begin{bmatrix} A_1' & B_1' \\ C_1' & D_1' \end{bmatrix} \begin{bmatrix} V_1 \\ -I_1 \end{bmatrix} = \begin{bmatrix} A' & B' \\ C' & D' \end{bmatrix} \begin{bmatrix} V_1 \\ -I_1 \end{bmatrix}$$

Hence,

$$\begin{bmatrix} A' & B' \\ C' & D' \end{bmatrix} = \begin{bmatrix} A_2' & B_2' \\ C_2' & D_2' \end{bmatrix} \begin{bmatrix} A_1' & B_1' \\ C_1' & D_1' \end{bmatrix} \qquad \text{...(12.8)}$$

Equation 12.8 shows that the resultant $A'B'C'D'$ matrix of the cascade connection is the product of the individual $A'B'C'D'$ matrices.

## EXAMPLE 12.39

*Two identical sections of the network shown in Fig. 12.73 are connected in cascade. Obtain the transmission parameters of the overall connection.*

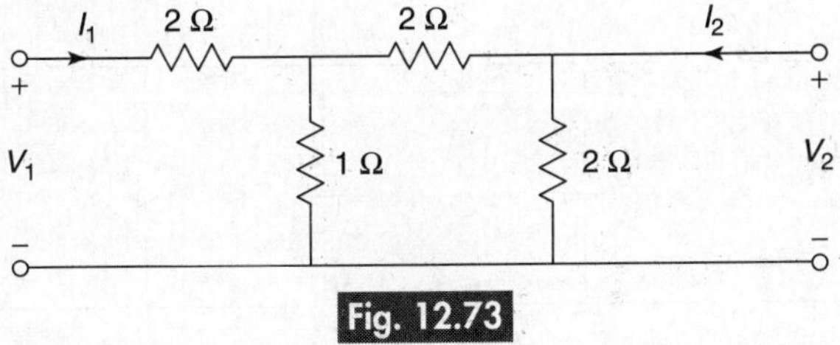


**Fig. 12.73**

**Solution** The network is redrawn, as shown in Fig. 12.74.

Applying KVL to mesh 1,

$$V_1 = 3I_1 - I_3 \quad \text{...(i)}$$

Applying KVL to mesh 2,

$$V_2 = 2I_2 + 2I_3 \quad \text{...(ii)}$$

Applying KVL to mesh 3,

$$-I_1 + 2I_2 + 5I_3 = 0$$

$$I_3 = \frac{1}{5}I_1 - \frac{2}{5}I_2 \quad \text{...(iii)}$$

Fig. 12.74

Substituting Eq. (iii) in Eq. (i),

$$V_1 = 3I_1 - \left(\frac{1}{5}I_1 - \frac{2}{5}I_2\right)$$

$$= \frac{14}{5}I_1 + \frac{2}{5}I_2 \quad \text{...(iv)}$$

Substituting Eq. (iii) in Eq. (ii),

$$V_2 = 2I_2 + 2\left(\frac{1}{5}I_1 - \frac{2}{5}I_2\right)$$

$$= \frac{2}{5}I_1 + \frac{6}{5}I_2$$

$$I_1 = \frac{5}{2}V_2 - 3I_2 \quad \text{...(v)}$$

Substituting Eq. (v) in Eq. (iv),

$$V_1 = \frac{14}{5}\left(\frac{5}{2}V_2 - 3I_2\right) + \frac{2}{5}I_2$$

$$= 7V_2 - 8I_2 \quad \text{...(vi)}$$

Comparing the Eqs (vi) and (v) with *ABCD*-parameter equations,

$$\begin{bmatrix} A_1 & B_1 \\ C_1 & D_1 \end{bmatrix} = \begin{bmatrix} 7 & 8 \\ 2.5 & 3 \end{bmatrix}$$

Hence, transmission parameters of the overall cascaded network are

$$\begin{bmatrix} A & B \\ C & D \end{bmatrix} = \begin{bmatrix} 7 & 8 \\ 2.5 & 3 \end{bmatrix}\begin{bmatrix} 7 & 8 \\ 2.5 & 3 \end{bmatrix} = \begin{bmatrix} 69 & 80 \\ 25 & 29 \end{bmatrix}$$

## EXAMPLE 12.40

*Determine ABCD-parameters for the ladder network shown in Fig. 12.75.*

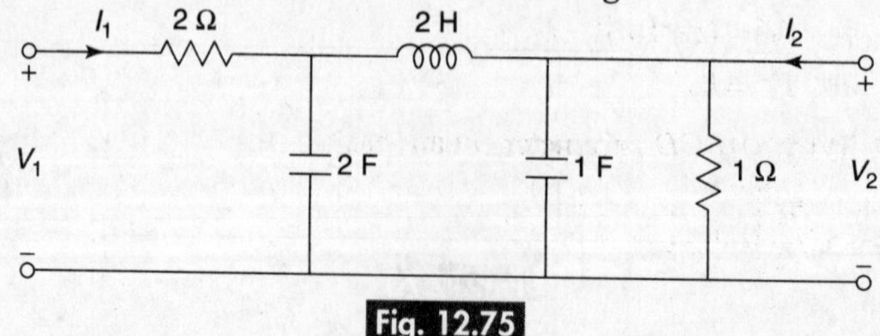


Fig. 12.75

**Solution** The above network can be considered as a cascade connection of two networks $N_1$ and $N_2$. The network $N_1$ is shown in Fig. 12.76.

Applying KVL to mesh 1,

$$V_1 = \left(2+\frac{1}{2s}\right)I_1 + \frac{1}{2s}I_2 \qquad \ldots\text{(i)}$$

Applying KVL to mesh 2,

$$V_2 = \frac{1}{2s}I_1 + \left(2s+\frac{1}{2s}\right)I_2 \qquad \ldots\text{(ii)}$$

Fig. 12.76

From Eq. (ii),

$$I_1 = 2s\,V_2 - (4s^2+1)\,I_2 \qquad \ldots\text{(iii)}$$

Substituting Eq. (iii) in Eq. (i),

$$V_1 = \left(2+\frac{1}{2s}\right)[2s\,V_2 - (4s^2+1)I_2] + \frac{1}{2s}I_2$$

$$= (4s+1)V_2 - (8s^2+2s+2)I_2 \qquad \ldots\text{(iv)}$$

Comparing Eqs (iv) and (iii) with *ABCD*-parameter equations,

$$\begin{bmatrix} A_1 & B_1 \\ C_1 & D_1 \end{bmatrix} = \begin{bmatrix} 4s+1 & 8s^2+2s+2 \\ 2s & 4s^2+1 \end{bmatrix}$$

The network $N_2$ is shown in Fig. 12.77.

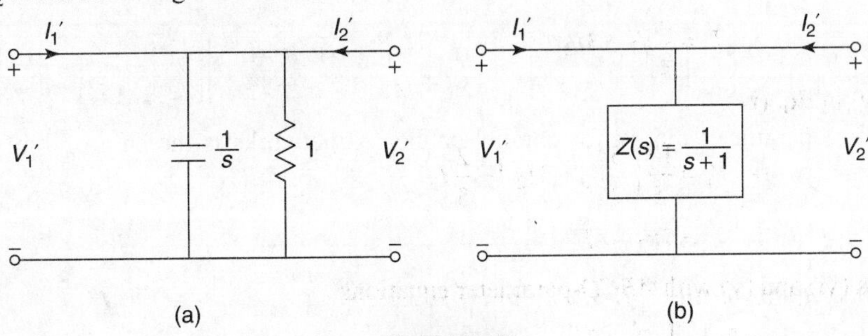


Fig. 12.77

Applying KVL to mesh 1,

$$V_1' = \frac{1}{s+1}I_1' + \frac{1}{s+1}I_2' \qquad \ldots\text{(i)}$$

Applying KVL to mesh 2,

$$V_2' = \frac{1}{s+1}I_1' + \frac{1}{s+1}I_2' \qquad \ldots\text{(ii)}$$

From Eq. (ii),

$$I_1' = (s+1)V_2' - I_2' \qquad \ldots\text{(iii)}$$

Also,

$$V_1' = V_2' \qquad \ldots\text{(iv)}$$

Comparing Eqs (iv) and (iii) with *ABCD*-parameter equations,

$$\begin{bmatrix} A_2 & B_2 \\ C_2 & D_2 \end{bmatrix} = \begin{bmatrix} 1 & 0 \\ s+1 & 1 \end{bmatrix}$$

Hence, overall $ABCD$-parameters are

$$\begin{bmatrix} A & B \\ C & D \end{bmatrix} = \begin{bmatrix} 4s+1 & 8s^2+2s+2 \\ 2s & 4s^2+1 \end{bmatrix} \begin{bmatrix} 1 & 0 \\ s+1 & 1 \end{bmatrix} = \begin{bmatrix} 8s^3+10s^2+8s+3 & 8s^2+2s+2 \\ 4s^3+4s^2+3s+1 & 4s^2+1 \end{bmatrix}$$

### 12.9.2 Parallel Connection

Figure12.78 shows two-port networks connected in parallel. In the parallel connection, the two networks have the same input voltages and the same output voltages.

Let $Y_{11}', Y_{12}', Y_{21}', Y_{22}'$ be the $Y$ parameters of the network $N_1$ and $Y_1'', Y_{12}'', Y_{21}'', Y_{22}''$ be the $Y$ parameters of the network $N_2$.

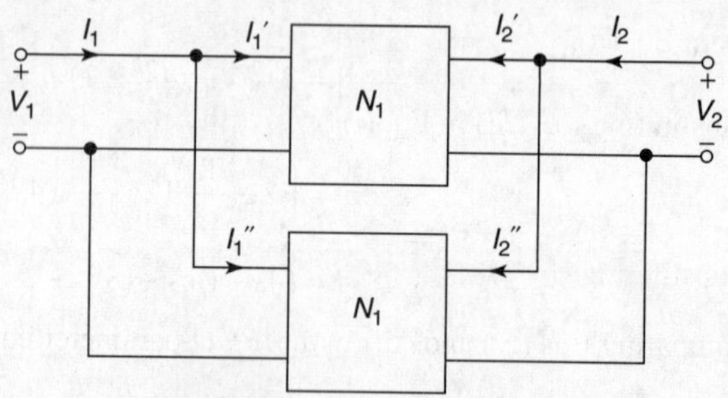

Fig. 12.78 Parallel connection

For the network $N_1$,

$$\begin{bmatrix} I_1' \\ I_2' \end{bmatrix} = \begin{bmatrix} Y_{11}' & Y_{12}' \\ Y_{21}' & Y_{22}' \end{bmatrix} \begin{bmatrix} V_1 \\ V_2 \end{bmatrix}$$

For the network $N_2$,

$$\begin{bmatrix} I_1'' \\ I_2'' \end{bmatrix} = \begin{bmatrix} Y_{11}'' & Y_{12}'' \\ Y_{21}'' & Y_{22}'' \end{bmatrix} \begin{bmatrix} V_1 \\ V_2 \end{bmatrix}$$

For the combined network, $\quad I_1 = I_1' + I_1''$ and $I_2 = I_2' + I_2''$.

Hence,

$$\begin{bmatrix} I_1 \\ I_2 \end{bmatrix} = \begin{bmatrix} I_1' + I_1'' \\ I_2' + I_2'' \end{bmatrix} = \begin{bmatrix} Y_{11}' + Y_{11}'' & Y_{12}' + Y_{12}'' \\ Y_{21}' + Y_{21}'' & Y_{22}' + Y_{22}'' \end{bmatrix} \begin{bmatrix} V_1 \\ V_2 \end{bmatrix} = \begin{bmatrix} Y_{11} & Y_{12} \\ Y_{21} & Y_{22} \end{bmatrix} \begin{bmatrix} V_1 \\ V_2 \end{bmatrix}$$

Thus, the resultant $Y$ parameter matrix for parallel connected networks is the sum of $Y$ matrices of each individual two-port networks.

**EXAMPLE 12.41**

*Determine Y parameters for the network shown in Fig. 12.79.*

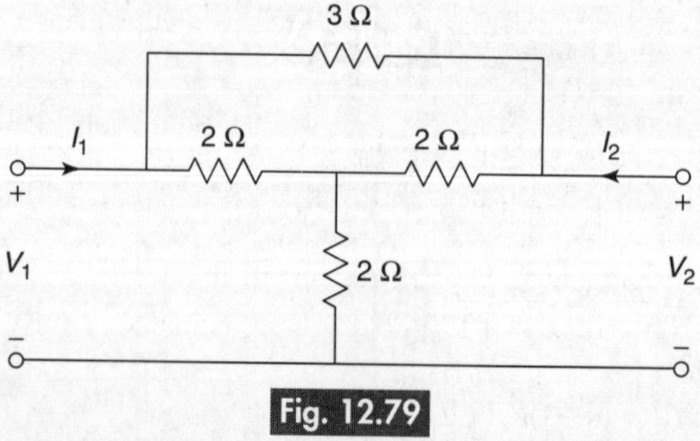

Fig. 12.79

**Solution** The above network can be considered as a parallel connection of two networks, $N_1$ and $N_2$. The network $N_1$ is shown in Fig. 12.80.

Applying KCL at node 3,

$$I_1' + I_2' = \frac{V_3}{2} \qquad \ldots\text{(i)}$$

From Fig. 12.80,

$$I_1' = \frac{V_1 - V_3}{2} \qquad \text{...(ii)}$$

$$I_2' = \frac{V_2 - V_3}{2} \qquad \text{...(iii)}$$

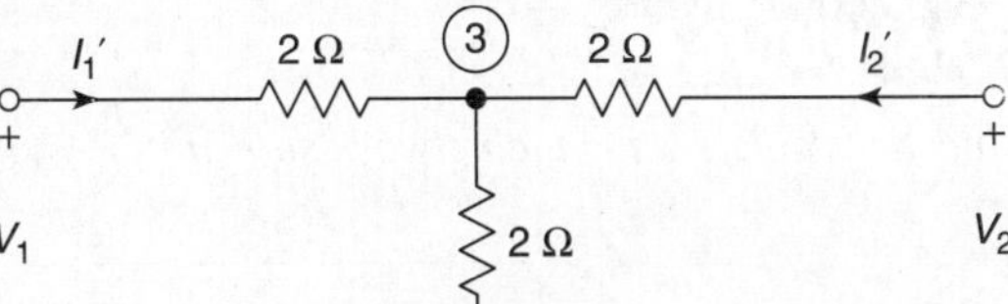


Fig. 12.80

Substituting Eqs (ii) and (iii) in Eq (i),

$$\frac{V_1 - V_3}{2} + \frac{V_2 - V_3}{2} = \frac{V_3}{2}$$

$$3V_3 = V_1 + V_2$$

$$V_3 = \frac{V_1}{3} + \frac{V_2}{3} \qquad \text{...(iv)}$$

Substituting Eq. (iv) in Eq. (ii),

$$I_1' = \frac{V_1}{2} - \frac{1}{2}\left(\frac{V_1}{3} + \frac{V_2}{3}\right)$$

$$= \frac{1}{3}V_1 - \frac{1}{6}V_2 \qquad \text{...(v)}$$

Substituting Eq. (iv) in Eq. (iii),

$$I_2' = \frac{V_2}{2} - \frac{1}{2}\left(\frac{V_1}{3} + \frac{V_2}{3}\right)$$

$$= -\frac{1}{6}V_1 + \frac{1}{3}V_2 \qquad \text{...(vi)}$$

Comparing Eqs (v) and (vi) with $Y$ parameter equations,

$$\begin{bmatrix} Y_{11}' & Y_{12}' \\ Y_{21}' & Y_{22}' \end{bmatrix} = \begin{bmatrix} \frac{1}{3} & -\frac{1}{6} \\ -\frac{1}{6} & \frac{1}{3} \end{bmatrix}$$

The network $N_2$ is shown in Fig. 12.81.

Fig. 12.81

$$I_1'' = -I_2'' = \frac{V_1 - V_2}{3} = \frac{1}{3}V_1 - \frac{1}{3}V_2$$

Hence, the $Y$ parameters are

$$\begin{bmatrix} Y_{11}'' & Y_{12}'' \\ Y_{21}'' & Y_{22}'' \end{bmatrix} = \begin{bmatrix} \frac{1}{3} & -\frac{1}{3} \\ -\frac{1}{3} & \frac{1}{3} \end{bmatrix}$$

The overall $Y$ parameters of the network are

$$\begin{bmatrix} Y_{11} & Y_{12} \\ Y_{21} & Y_{22} \end{bmatrix} = \begin{bmatrix} Y_{11}' + Y_{11}'' & Y_{12}' + Y_{12}'' \\ Y_{21}' + Y_{21}'' & Y_{22}' + Y_{22}'' \end{bmatrix} = \begin{bmatrix} \frac{1}{3} + \frac{1}{3} & -\frac{1}{6} - \frac{1}{3} \\ -\frac{1}{6} - \frac{1}{3} & \frac{1}{3} + \frac{1}{3} \end{bmatrix} = \begin{bmatrix} \frac{2}{3} & -\frac{1}{2} \\ -\frac{1}{2} & \frac{2}{3} \end{bmatrix}$$

**EXAMPLE 12.42**

*Find Y parameters for the network shown in Fig. 12.82*

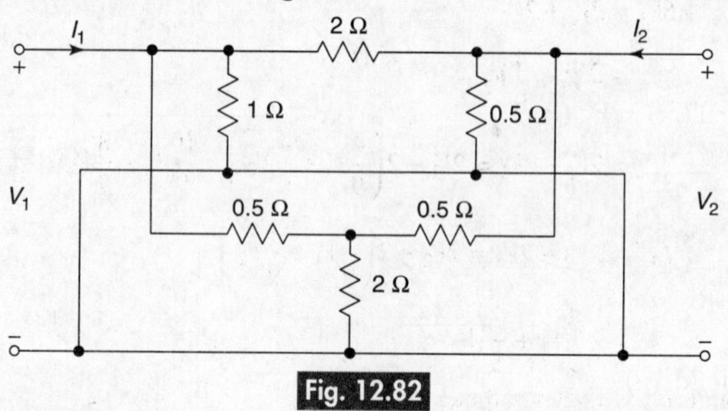


Fig. 12.82

**Solution** The above network can be considered as a parallel combination of two networks $N_1$ and $N_2$.

The network $N_1$ is shown in Fig. 12.83.

Applying KCL at node 1,

$$I_1' = \frac{V_1}{1} + \frac{V_1 - V_2}{2}$$

$$= \frac{3}{2}V_1 - \frac{1}{2}V_2 \qquad \ldots(i)$$

Fig. 12.83

Applying KCL at node 2,

$$I_2' = \frac{V_2}{0.5} + \frac{V_2 - V_1}{2}$$

$$= -\frac{1}{2}V_1 + \frac{5}{2}V_2 \qquad \ldots(ii)$$

Comparing Eqs (i) and (ii) with $Y$ parameter equation,

$$\begin{bmatrix} Y_{11}' & Y_{12}' \\ Y_{21}' & Y_{22}' \end{bmatrix} = \begin{bmatrix} \frac{3}{2} & -\frac{1}{2} \\ -\frac{1}{2} & \frac{5}{2} \end{bmatrix}$$

The network $N_2$ is shown in Fig. 12.84.

Applying KCL at node 3,

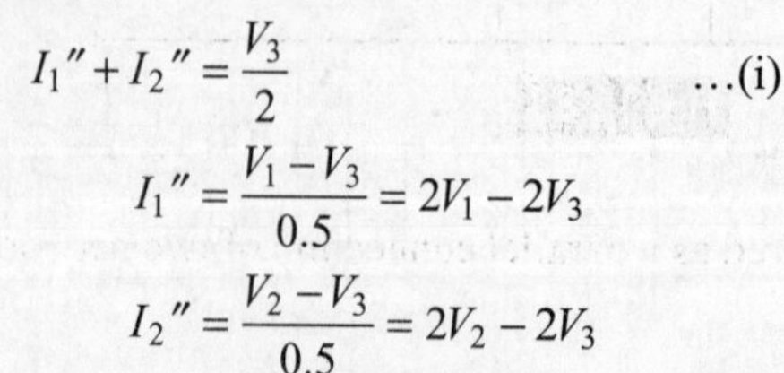

$$I_1'' + I_2'' = \frac{V_3}{2} \qquad \ldots(i)$$

where

$$I_1'' = \frac{V_1 - V_3}{0.5} = 2V_1 - 2V_3$$

$$I_2'' = \frac{V_2 - V_3}{0.5} = 2V_2 - 2V_3$$

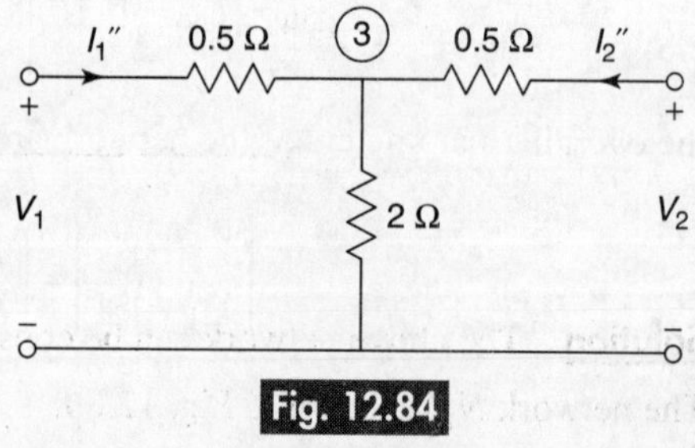


Fig. 12.84

Substituting $I_1''$ and $I_2''$ in Eq (i),

$$2V_1 - 2V_3 + 2V_2 - 2V_3 = 0.5V_3$$

$$4.5V_3 = 2V_1 + 2V_2$$

$$V_3 = \frac{4}{9}V_1 + \frac{4}{9}V_2 \qquad \text{...(ii)}$$

$$I_1'' = 2V_1 - 2V_3 = 2V_1 - 2\left(\frac{4}{9}V_1 + \frac{4}{9}V_2\right) = \frac{10}{9}V_1 - \frac{8}{9}V_2 \qquad \text{...(iii)}$$

and

$$I_2'' = 2V_2 - 2V_3 = 2V_2 - 2\left(\frac{4}{9}V_1 + \frac{4}{9}V_2\right)$$

$$= -\frac{8}{9}V_1 + \frac{10}{9}V_2 \qquad \text{...(iv)}$$

Comparing Eqs (iii) and (iv) with $Y$ parameter equations,

$$\begin{bmatrix} Y_{11}'' & Y_{12}'' \\ Y_{21}'' & Y_{22}'' \end{bmatrix} = \begin{bmatrix} \frac{10}{9} & -\frac{8}{9} \\ -\frac{8}{9} & \frac{10}{9} \end{bmatrix}$$

Hence, overall $Y$ parameters of the network are

$$\begin{bmatrix} Y_{11} & Y_{12} \\ Y_{21} & Y_{22} \end{bmatrix} = \begin{bmatrix} Y_{11}' + Y_{11}'' & Y_{12}' + Y_{12}'' \\ Y_{21}' + Y_{21}'' & Y_{22}' + Y_{22}'' \end{bmatrix} = \begin{bmatrix} \frac{3}{2} + \frac{10}{9} & -\frac{1}{2} - \frac{8}{9} \\ -\frac{1}{2} - \frac{8}{9} & \frac{5}{2} + \frac{10}{9} \end{bmatrix} = \begin{bmatrix} \frac{47}{18} & -\frac{25}{18} \\ -\frac{25}{18} & \frac{65}{18} \end{bmatrix}$$

## EXAMPLE 12.43

*Find Y parameters for the network shown in Fig. 12.85.*

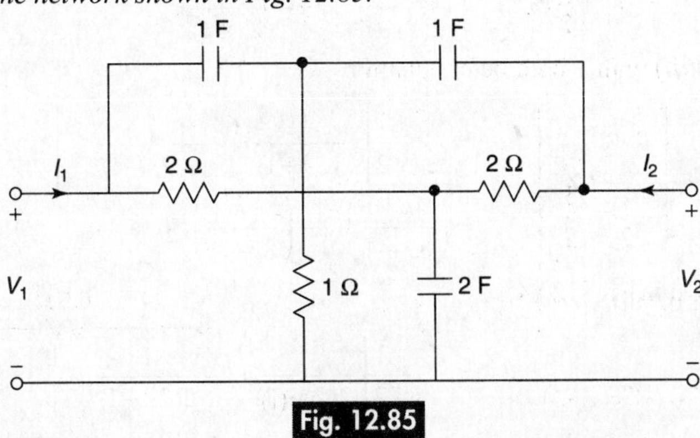


Fig. 12.85

**Solution** The above network can be considered as a parallel connection of two networks, $N_1$ and $N_2$. The network $N_1$ is shown in Fig. 12.86.

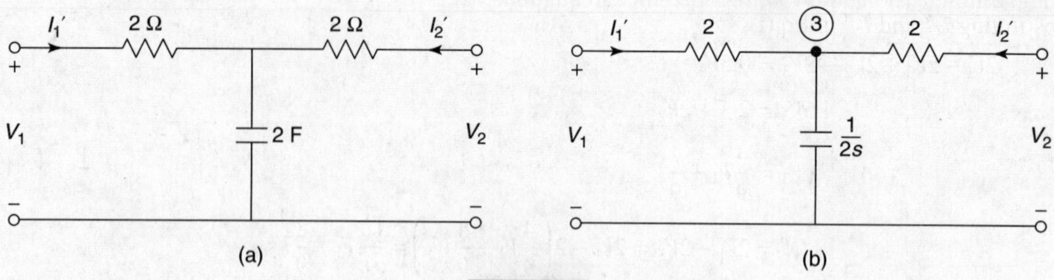


Fig. 12.86

Applying KCL at node 3,

$$I_1' + I_2' = 2s\, V_3 \quad \ldots\text{(i)}$$

From Fig. 12.86,

$$I_1' = \frac{V_1 - V_3}{2}$$

$$= \frac{1}{2}V_1 - \frac{1}{2}V_3 \quad \ldots\text{(ii)}$$

$$I_2' = \frac{V_2 - V_3}{2}$$

$$= \frac{1}{2}V_2 - \frac{1}{2}V_3 \quad \ldots\text{(iii)}$$

Substituting Eq. (ii) and Eq. (iii) in Eq. (i),

$$\frac{V_1}{2} - \frac{V_3}{2} + \frac{V_2}{2} - \frac{V_3}{2} = (2s)\, V_3$$

$$(2s+1)V_3 = \frac{V_1}{2} + \frac{V_2}{2}$$

$$V_3 = \frac{1}{2(2s+1)}V_1 + \frac{1}{2(2s+1)}V_2 \quad \ldots\text{(iv)}$$

Substituting Eq. (iv) in Eq. (ii),

$$I_1' = \frac{V_1}{2} - \frac{1}{2}\left[\frac{1}{2(2s+1)}V_1 + \frac{1}{2(2s+1)}V_2\right]$$

$$= \left(\frac{4s+1}{8s+4}\right)V_1 - \left(\frac{1}{8s+4}\right)V_2 \quad \ldots\text{(v)}$$

Substituting Eq. (iv) in Eq. (iii),

$$I_2' = \frac{V_2}{2} - \frac{1}{2}\left[\frac{1}{2(2s+1)}V_1 - \frac{1}{2(2s+1)}V_2\right]$$

$$= -\left(\frac{1}{8s+4}\right)V_1 + \left(\frac{4s+1}{8s+4}\right)V_2 \quad \ldots\text{(vi)}$$

Comparing Eqs (v) and (vi) with $Y$ parameter equations,

$$\begin{bmatrix} Y_{11}' & Y_{12}' \\ Y_{21}' & Y_{22}' \end{bmatrix} = \begin{bmatrix} \dfrac{4s+1}{8s+4} & -\dfrac{1}{8s+4} \\ -\dfrac{1}{8s+4} & \dfrac{4s+1}{8s+4} \end{bmatrix}$$

The network $N_2$ is shown in Fig. 12.87.

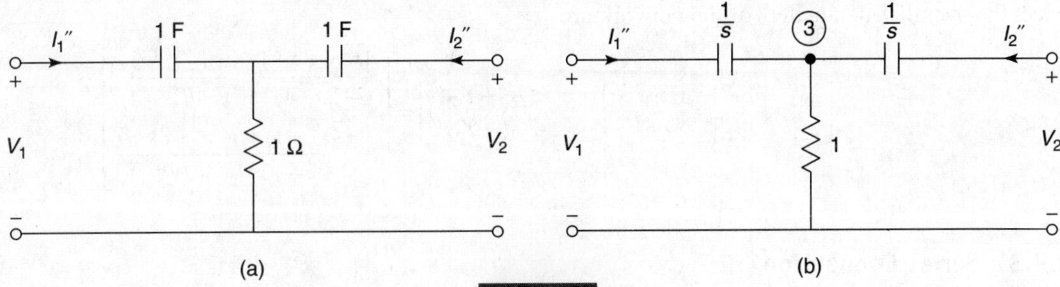


Fig. 12.87

Applying KCL at node 3,

$$I_1'' + I_2'' = V_3 \qquad \ldots\text{(i)}$$

From Fig. 12.87,

$$I_1'' = \frac{V_1 - V_3}{\frac{1}{s}}$$

$$= sV_1 - sV_3 \qquad \ldots\text{(ii)}$$

$$I_2' = \frac{V_2 - V_3}{\frac{1}{s}}$$

$$= sV_2 - sV_3 \qquad \ldots\text{(iii)}$$

Substituting Eqs (ii) and (iii) in Eq. (i),

$$sV_1 - sV_3 + sV_2 - sV_3 = V_3$$

$$(2s+1)V_3 = sV_1 + sV_2$$

$$V_3 = \left(\frac{s}{2s+1}\right)V_1 + \left(\frac{s}{2s+1}\right)V_2 \qquad \ldots\text{(iv)}$$

Substituting Eq. (iv) in Eq. (ii),

$$I_1'' = sV_1 - s\left[\left(\frac{s}{2s+1}\right)V_1 + \frac{s}{(2s+1)}V_2\right]$$

$$= \left[\frac{s(s+1)}{2s+1}\right]V_1 - \left(\frac{s^2}{2s+1}\right)V_2 \qquad \ldots\text{(v)}$$

Substituting Eq. (iv) in Eq. (iii),

$$I_2'' = sV_2 - s\left[\left(\frac{s}{2s+1}\right)V_1 + \left(\frac{s}{2s+1}\right)V_2\right]$$

$$= -\left(\frac{s^2}{2s+1}\right)V_1 + \left[\frac{s(s+1)}{2s+1}\right]V_2 \qquad \ldots\text{(vi)}$$

Comparing Eqs (v) and (vi) with $Y$ parameter equations,

$$\begin{bmatrix} Y_{11}'' & Y_{12}'' \\ Y_{21}'' & Y_{22}'' \end{bmatrix} = \begin{bmatrix} \dfrac{s(s+1)}{2s+1} & -\left(\dfrac{s^2}{2s+1}\right) \\ -\left(\dfrac{s^2}{2s+1}\right) & \dfrac{s(s+1)}{2s+1} \end{bmatrix}$$

Hence, the overall $Y$ parameters of the network are

$$\begin{bmatrix} Y_{11} & Y_{12} \\ Y_{21}' & Y_{22} \end{bmatrix} = \begin{bmatrix} Y_{11}'+Y_{11}'' & Y_{12}'+Y_{12}'' \\ Y_{21}'+Y_{21}'' & Y_{22}'+Y_{22}'' \end{bmatrix} = \begin{bmatrix} \dfrac{4s^2+8s+1}{4(2s+1)} & -\dfrac{(4s^2+1)}{4(2s+1)} \\ -\dfrac{(4s^2+1)}{4(2s+1)} & \dfrac{4s^2+8s+1}{4(2s+1)} \end{bmatrix}$$

## 12.9.3 Series Connection

Figure 12.88 shows two-port networks connected in series. In a series connection, both the networks carry the same input current. Their output currents are also equal.

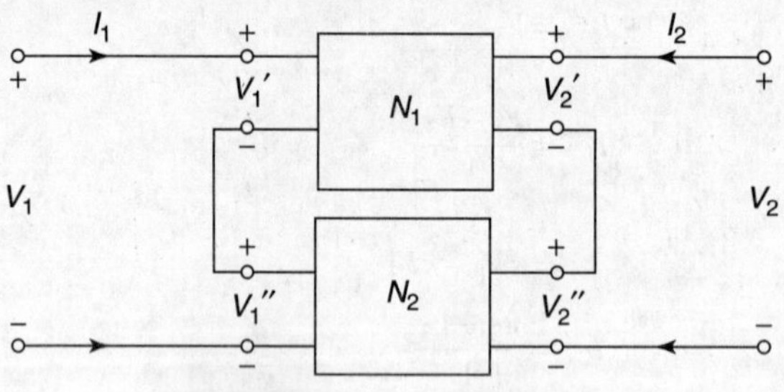


**Fig. 12.88** *Series connection*

Let $Z_{11}', Z_{12}', Z_{21}', Z_{22}'$ be the $Z$ parameters of the network $N_1$ and $Z_{11}'', Z_{12}'', Z_{21}'', Z_{22}''$ be the $Z$ parameters of the network $N_2$.

For the network $N_1$,

$$\begin{bmatrix} V_1' \\ V_2' \end{bmatrix} = \begin{bmatrix} Z_{11}' & Z_{12}'' \\ Z_{21}' & Z_{22}'' \end{bmatrix} \begin{bmatrix} I_1 \\ I_2 \end{bmatrix}$$

For the network $N_2$,

$$\begin{bmatrix} V_1'' \\ V_2'' \end{bmatrix} = \begin{bmatrix} Z_{11}' & Z_{12}'' \\ Z_{21}' & Z_{22}'' \end{bmatrix} \begin{bmatrix} I_1 \\ I_2 \end{bmatrix}$$

For the combined network $\quad V_1 = V_1' + V_1''$ and $V_2 = V_2' + V_2''$.

Hence,

$$\begin{bmatrix} V_1 \\ V_2 \end{bmatrix} = \begin{bmatrix} V_1'+V_1'' \\ V_2'+V_2'' \end{bmatrix} = \begin{bmatrix} Z_{11}'+Z_{11}'' & Z_{12}'+Z_{12}'' \\ Z_{21}'+Z_{21}'' & Z_{22}'+Z_{22}'' \end{bmatrix} \begin{bmatrix} I_1 \\ I_2 \end{bmatrix} = \begin{bmatrix} Z_{11} & Z_{12} \\ Z_{21} & Z_{22} \end{bmatrix} \begin{bmatrix} I_1 \\ I_2 \end{bmatrix}$$

Thus, the resultant $Z$ parameter matrix for the series-connected networks is the sum of $Z$ matrices of each individual two-port network.

## EXAMPLE 12.44

*Two identical sections of the network shown in Fig. 12.89 are connected in series. Obtain Z parameters of the overall connection.*

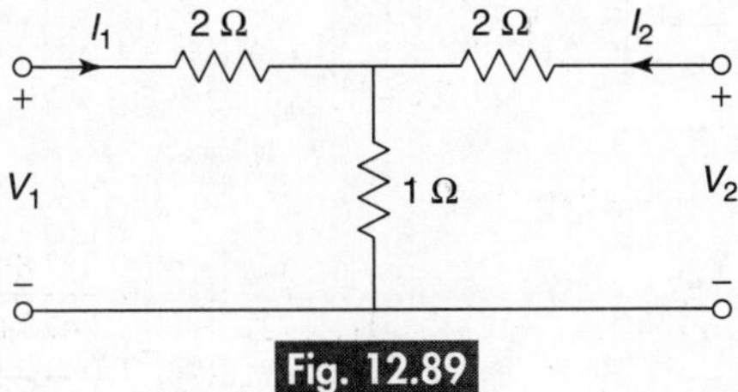


Fig. 12.89

**Solution**

Applying KVL to mesh 1,

$$V_1 = 3I_1 + I_2 \qquad \text{...(i)}$$

Applying KVL to mesh 2,

$$V_2 = I_1 + 3I_2 \qquad \text{...(ii)}$$

Comparing Eqs (i) and (ii) with $Z$ parameter equations,

$$\begin{bmatrix} Z_{11}'' & Z_{12}'' \\ Z_{21}'' & Z_{22}'' \end{bmatrix} = \begin{bmatrix} 3 & 1 \\ 1 & 3 \end{bmatrix}$$

Hence, $Z$ parameters of the overall connection are

$$\begin{bmatrix} Z_{11} & Z_{12} \\ Z_{21} & Z_{22} \end{bmatrix} = \begin{bmatrix} 3 & 1 \\ 1 & 3 \end{bmatrix} + \begin{bmatrix} 3 & 1 \\ 1 & 3 \end{bmatrix} = \begin{bmatrix} 6 & 2 \\ 2 & 6 \end{bmatrix}$$

## EXAMPLE 12.45

*Determine Z parameters for the network shown in Fig. 12.90.*

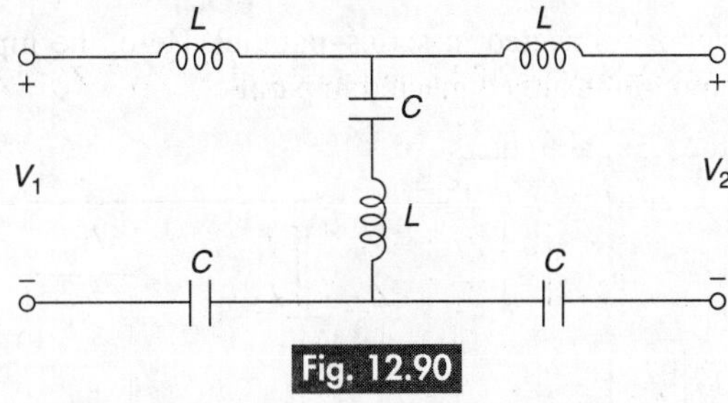


Fig. 12.90

**Solution** The above network can be considered as a series connection of two networks, $N_1$ and $N_2$. The network $N_1$ is shown in Fig. 12.91.

Applying KVL to mesh 1,

$$V_1' = \left(Ls + \frac{1}{Cs}\right)I_1 + \left(\frac{1}{Cs}\right)I_2 \qquad \text{...(i)}$$

Applying KVL to mesh 2,

$$V_2' = \left(\frac{1}{Cs}\right)I_1 + \left(Ls + \frac{1}{Cs}\right)I_2 \qquad \text{...(ii)}$$

Fig. 12.91

Comparing Eqs (i) and (ii) with $Z$ parameter equations,

$$\begin{bmatrix} Z_{11}' & Z_{12}' \\ Z_{21}' & Z_{22}' \end{bmatrix} = \begin{bmatrix} Ls+\dfrac{1}{Cs} & \dfrac{1}{Cs} \\ \dfrac{1}{Cs} & Ls+\dfrac{1}{Cs} \end{bmatrix}$$

The network $N_2$ is shown in Fig. 12.92.

Fig. 12.92

Applying KVL to mesh 1,

$$V_1'' = \left(Ls+\frac{1}{Cs}\right)I_1 + (Ls)I_2 \qquad \text{...(i)}$$

Applying KVL to mesh 2,

$$V_2'' = (Ls)I_1 + \left(Ls+\frac{1}{Cs}\right)I_2 \qquad \text{...(ii)}$$

Comparing Eqs (i) and (ii) with $Z$ parameter equations,

$$\begin{bmatrix} Z_{11}'' & Z_{12}'' \\ Z_{21}'' & Z_{22}'' \end{bmatrix} = \begin{bmatrix} Ls+\dfrac{1}{Cs} & Ls \\ Ls & Ls+\dfrac{1}{Cs} \end{bmatrix}$$

Hence, the overall $Z$ parameters of the network are

$$\begin{bmatrix} Z_{11} & Z_{12} \\ Z_{21} & Z_{22} \end{bmatrix} = \begin{bmatrix} Z_{11}'+Z_{11}'' & Z_{12}'+Z_{12}'' \\ Z_{21}'+Z_{21}'' & Z_{22}'+Z_{22}'' \end{bmatrix} = \begin{bmatrix} 2Ls+\dfrac{2}{Cs} & Ls+\dfrac{1}{Cs} \\ Ls+\dfrac{1}{Cs} & 2Ls+\dfrac{2}{Cs} \end{bmatrix} = \left(Ls+\frac{1}{Cs}\right)\begin{bmatrix} 2 & 1 \\ 1 & 2 \end{bmatrix}$$

### 12.9.4 Series–Parallel Connection

Figure 12.93 shows two networks connected in series–parallel. Here, the input ports of two networks are connected in series and the output ports are connected in parallel.

Let $h_{11}', h_{12}', h_{21}', h_{22}'$ be the $h$ parameters of the network $N_1$ and $h_{11}'', h_{12}'', h_{21}'', h_{22}''$ be the $h$ parameters of the network $N_2$.

For the network $N_1$,

$$\begin{bmatrix} V_1' \\ V_2' \end{bmatrix} = \begin{bmatrix} h_{11}' & h_{12}' \\ h_{21}' & h_{22}' \end{bmatrix}\begin{bmatrix} I_1 \\ V_2 \end{bmatrix}$$

For the network $N_2$,

$$\begin{bmatrix} V_1'' \\ I_2'' \end{bmatrix} = \begin{bmatrix} h_{11}'' & h_{12}'' \\ h_{21}'' & h_{22}'' \end{bmatrix}\begin{bmatrix} I_1 \\ V_2 \end{bmatrix}$$

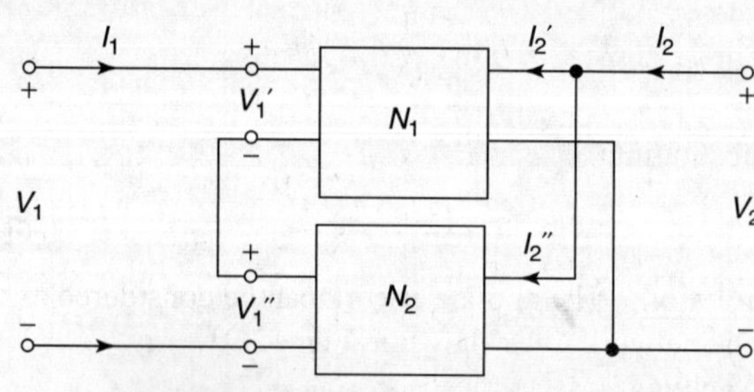

Fig. 12.93 Series–parallel connection

For the combined network, $V_1 = V_1' + V_1''$ and $I_2 = I_2' + I_2''$

Hence,

$$\begin{bmatrix} V_1 \\ I_2 \end{bmatrix} = \begin{bmatrix} V_1'+V_1'' \\ I_2'+I_2'' \end{bmatrix} = \begin{bmatrix} h_{11}'+h_{11}'' & h_{12}'+h_{12}'' \\ h_{21}'+h_{21}'' & h_{22}'+h_{22}'' \end{bmatrix}\begin{bmatrix} I_1 \\ V_2 \end{bmatrix} = \begin{bmatrix} h_{11} & h_{12} \\ h_{21} & h_{22} \end{bmatrix}\begin{bmatrix} I_1 \\ V_2 \end{bmatrix}$$

Thus, the resultant $h$ parameter matrix is the sum of $h$ parameter matrices of each individual two-port networks.

## EXAMPLE 12.46

*Determine h parameters for the network shown in Fig. 12.94.*

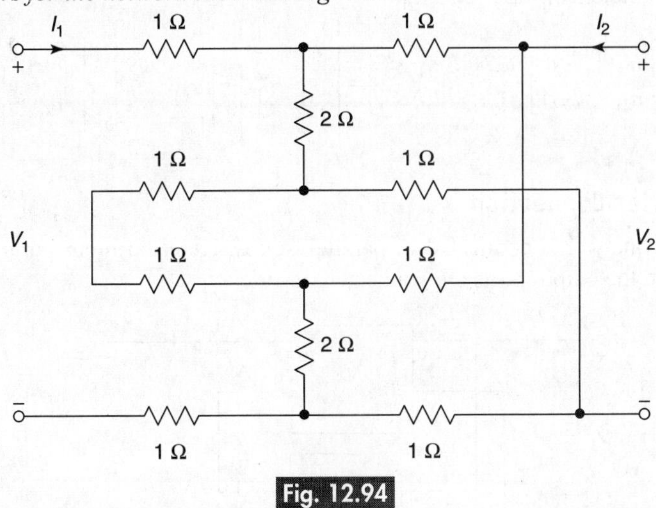


Fig. 12.94

**Solution** The above network can be considered as a series–parallel connection of two networks $N_1$ and $N_2$. The network $N_1$ is shown in Fig. 12.95.

Applying KVL to mesh 1,

$$V_1 = 4I_1 + 2I_2 \qquad \text{...(i)}$$

Applying KVL to mesh 2,

$$V_2 = 2I_1 + 4I_2 \qquad \text{...(ii)}$$

Rewriting Eq. (ii)

$$4I_2 = -2I_1 + V_2$$

$$I_2 = -\frac{1}{2}I_1 + \frac{1}{4}V_2 \qquad \text{...(iii)}$$

Fig. 12.95

Substituting Eq. (iii) in Eq. (i),

$$V_1 = 4I_1 + 2\left(-\frac{1}{2}I_1 + \frac{1}{4}V_2\right)$$

$$= 3I_1 + \frac{1}{2}V_2 \qquad \text{...(iv)}$$

Comparing Eqs (iii) and (iv) with $h$ parameters equations,

$$\begin{bmatrix} h_{11}' & h_{12}' \\ h_{21}' & h_{22}' \end{bmatrix} = \begin{bmatrix} 3 & \frac{1}{2} \\ -\frac{1}{2} & \frac{1}{4} \end{bmatrix}$$

For network $N_2$, $h$ parameters will be same as the two networks are identical.

$$\begin{bmatrix} h_{11}'' & h_{12}'' \\ h_{21}'' & h_{22}'' \end{bmatrix} = \begin{bmatrix} 3 & \frac{1}{2} \\ -\frac{1}{2} & \frac{1}{4} \end{bmatrix}$$

Hence, the overall $h$ parameters of the network are

$$\begin{bmatrix} h_{11} & h_{12} \\ h_{21} & h_{22} \end{bmatrix} = \begin{bmatrix} h_{11}' & h_{12}' \\ h_{21}' & h_{22}' \end{bmatrix} + \begin{bmatrix} h_{11}'' & h_{12}'' \\ h_{21}'' & h_{22}'' \end{bmatrix} = \begin{bmatrix} 3 & \frac{1}{2} \\ -\frac{1}{2} & \frac{1}{4} \end{bmatrix} + \begin{bmatrix} 3 & \frac{1}{2} \\ -\frac{1}{2} & \frac{1}{4} \end{bmatrix} = \begin{bmatrix} 6 & 1 \\ -1 & \frac{1}{2} \end{bmatrix}$$

### 12.9.5 Parallel–Series Connection

Figure 12.96 shows two networks connected in parallel–series. Here the input ports of two networks are connected in parallel and the output ports are connected in series.

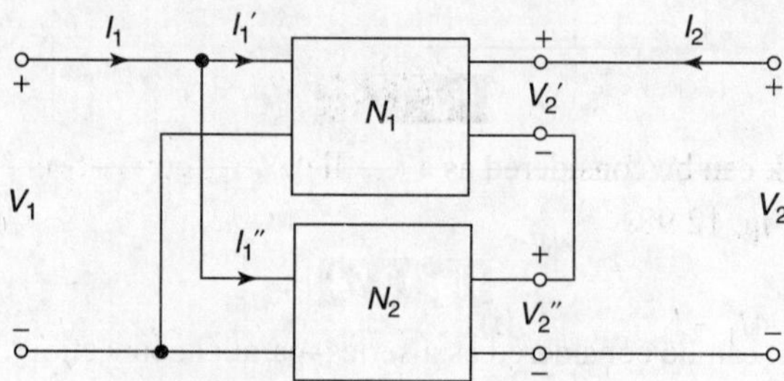


Fig. 12.96 Parallel–series connection

Let $g_{11}', g_{12}', g_{21}', g_{22}'$ be the $g$ parameters of the network $N_1$ and $g_{11}'', g_{12}'', g_{21}'', g_{22}''$ be the $g$ parameters of the network $N_2$,

For the network $N_1$,

$$\begin{bmatrix} I_1' \\ V_2' \end{bmatrix} = \begin{bmatrix} g_{11}' & g_{12}' \\ g_{21}' & g_{22}' \end{bmatrix} \begin{bmatrix} V_1 \\ I_2 \end{bmatrix}$$

For the network $N_2$,

$$\begin{bmatrix} I_1'' \\ V_2'' \end{bmatrix} = \begin{bmatrix} g_{11}'' & g_{12}'' \\ g_{21}'' & g_{22}'' \end{bmatrix} \begin{bmatrix} V_1 \\ I_2 \end{bmatrix}$$

For the combined network, $I_1 = I_1' + I_1''$ and $V_2 = V_2' + V_2''$

Hence,

$$\begin{bmatrix} I_1 \\ V_2 \end{bmatrix} = \begin{bmatrix} I_1' + I_1'' \\ V_2' + V_2'' \end{bmatrix} = \begin{bmatrix} g_{11}' + g_{11}'' & g_{12}' + g_{12}'' \\ g_{21}' + g_{21}'' & g_{22}' + g_{22}'' \end{bmatrix} \begin{bmatrix} V_1 \\ I_2 \end{bmatrix}$$

$$= \begin{bmatrix} g_{11} & g_{12} \\ g_{21} & g_{22} \end{bmatrix} \begin{bmatrix} V_1 \\ I_2 \end{bmatrix}$$

Thus, the resultant $g$ parameter matrix is the sum of the $g$ parameter matrices of each individual two-port network.

## EXAMPLE 12.47

*Determine the g parameters for the network shown in Fig. 12.97.*

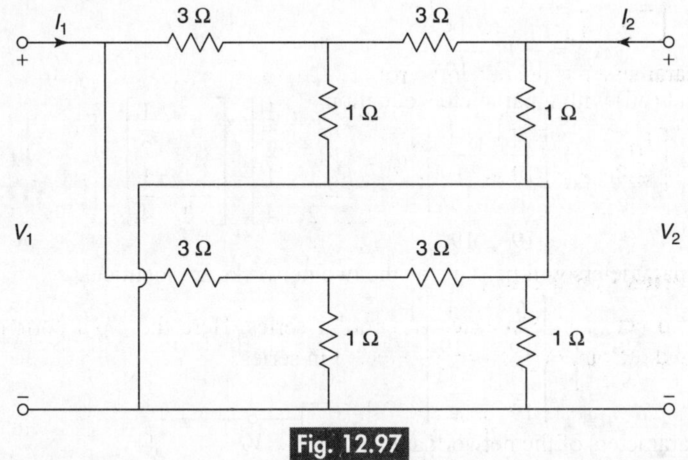


Fig. 12.97

**Solution** The above network can be considered as a parallel series connection of two networks $N_1$ and $N_2$. The network $N_1$ is shown in Fig. 12.98.

Applying KVL to mesh 1,

$$V_1 = 4I_1 - I_3 \qquad \ldots\text{(i)}$$

Applying KVL to mesh 2,

$$V_2 = I_2 + I_3 \qquad \ldots\text{(ii)}$$

Applying KVL to mesh 3,

$$-I_1 + I_2 + 5I_3 = 0$$

$$I_3 = \frac{1}{5}I_1 - \frac{1}{5}I_2 \qquad \ldots\text{(iii)}$$

Fig. 12.98

Substituting Eq (iii) in Eq (i),

$$V_1 = 4I_1 - \left(\frac{1}{5}I_1 - \frac{1}{5}I_2\right)$$

$$= \frac{19}{5}I_1 + \frac{1}{5}I_2 \qquad \ldots\text{(iv)}$$

Substituting Eq (iii) in Eq (ii),

$$V_2 = I_2 + \left(\frac{1}{5}I_1 - \frac{1}{5}I_2\right)$$

$$= \frac{1}{5}I_1 + \frac{4}{5}I_2 \qquad \ldots\text{(v)}$$

Rewriting Eq (iv),

$$\frac{19}{5}I_1 = V_1 - \frac{1}{5}I_2$$

$$I_1 = \frac{5}{19}V_1 - \frac{1}{19}I_2 \qquad \ldots\text{(vi)}$$

Substituting Eq (vi) in Eq (v),

$$V_2 = \frac{1}{5}\left(\frac{5}{19}V_1 - \frac{1}{19}I_2\right) + \frac{4}{5}I_2$$

$$= \frac{1}{19}V_1 + \frac{15}{19}I_2 \qquad \text{...(vii)}$$

Comparing Eqs (vi) and (vii) with $g$ parameters equation,

$$\begin{bmatrix} g_{11}' & g_{12}' \\ g_{21}' & g_{22}' \end{bmatrix} = \begin{bmatrix} \frac{5}{19} & -\frac{1}{19} \\ \frac{1}{19} & \frac{15}{19} \end{bmatrix}$$

For the network $N_2$, $g$ parameters will be same as the two networks are identical.

$$\begin{bmatrix} g_{11}'' & g_{12}'' \\ g_{21}'' & g_{22}'' \end{bmatrix} = \begin{bmatrix} \frac{5}{19} & -\frac{1}{19} \\ \frac{1}{19} & \frac{15}{19} \end{bmatrix}$$

Hence, the overall $g$ parameters of the network are

$$\begin{bmatrix} g_{11} & g_{12} \\ g_{21} & g_{22} \end{bmatrix} = \begin{bmatrix} g_{11}' & g_{12}' \\ g_{21}' & g_{22}' \end{bmatrix} + \begin{bmatrix} g_{11}'' & g_{12}'' \\ g_{21}'' & g_{22}'' \end{bmatrix} = \begin{bmatrix} \frac{5}{19} & -\frac{1}{19} \\ \frac{1}{19} & \frac{15}{19} \end{bmatrix} + \begin{bmatrix} \frac{5}{19} & -\frac{1}{19} \\ \frac{1}{19} & \frac{15}{19} \end{bmatrix} = \begin{bmatrix} \frac{10}{19} & -\frac{2}{19} \\ \frac{2}{19} & \frac{30}{19} \end{bmatrix}$$

## 12.10 *T*-NETWORK

LO 12.8

Explain *T*-network, *Pi*-network and lattice network

Any two-port network can be represented by an equivalent $T$ network, as shown in Fig. 12.99.

The elements of the equivalent $T$ network may be expressed in terms of $Z$ parameters.

Applying KVL to mesh 1,

$$V_1 = Z_A I_1 + Z_C(I_1 + I_2)$$

$$= (Z_A + Z_C)I_1 + Z_C I_2 \qquad \text{...(12.9)}$$

Applying KVL to mesh 2,

$$V_2 = Z_B I_2 + Z_C(I_2 + I_1)$$

$$= Z_C I_1 + (Z_B + Z_C)I_2 \qquad \text{...(12.10)}$$

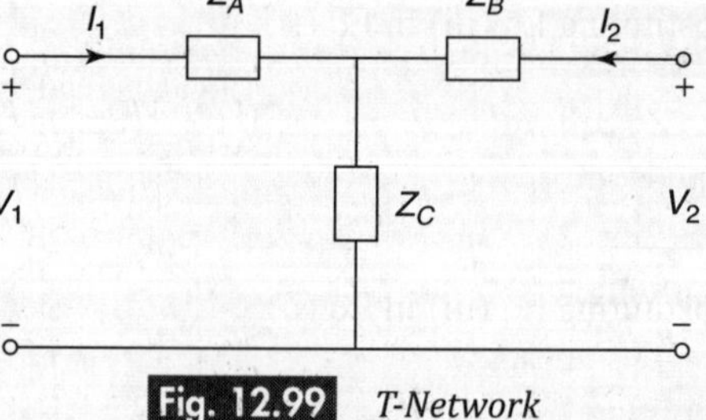


Fig. 12.99 *T-Network*

Comparing Eqs (12.9) and (12.10) with $Z$ parameter equations,

$$Z_{11} = Z_A + Z_C$$

$$Z_{12} = Z_C$$

$$Z_{21} = Z_C$$

$$Z_{22} = Z_B + Z_C$$

Solving the above equations,

$$Z_A = Z_{11} - Z_{12} = Z_{11} - Z_{21}$$
$$Z_B = Z_{22} - ZZ_{21} = Z_{22} - Z_{12}$$
$$Z_C = Z_{12} = Z_{21}$$

## 12.11 | PI (π)-NETWORK

LO 12.8

Any two-port network can be represented by an equivalent pi (π) network, as shown in Fig. 12.100.

Applying KCL at node 1,

$$I_1 = Y_A V_1 + Y_B (V_1 - V_2)$$
$$= (Y_A + Y_B) V_1 - Y_B V_2 \qquad ...(12.11)$$

Applying KCL at node 2,

$$I_2 = Y_C V_2 + Y_B (V_2 - V_1)$$
$$= -Y_B V_1 + (Y_B + Y_C) V_2 \qquad ...(12.12)$$

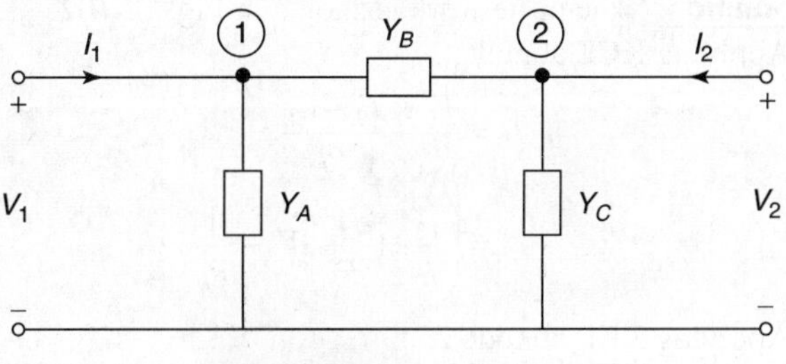


Fig. 12.100 π-network

Comparing Eqs (12.11) and (12.12) with Y parameter equations,

$$Y_{11} = Y_A + Y_B$$
$$Y_{12} = -Y_B$$
$$Y_{21} = -Y_B$$
$$Y_{22} = Y_B + Y_C$$

Solving the above equations,

$$Y_A = Y_{11} + Y_{12} = Y_{11} + Y_{21}$$
$$Y_B = -Y_{12} = -Y_{21}$$
$$Y_C = Y_{22} + Y_{12} = Y_{22} + Y_{21}$$

### EXAMPLE 12.48

*The Z parameters of a two-port network are: $Z_{11}$ = 10 Ω, $Z_{12}$ = $Z_{21}$ = 5 Ω, $Z_{22}$ = 20 Ω. Find the equivalent T-network.*

**Solution** The T-network is shown in Fig. 12.101

Applying KVL to mesh 1,

$$V_1 = (Z_1 + Z_2) I_1 + Z_2 I_2 \qquad \ldots(\text{i})$$

Applying KVL to mesh 2,

$$V_2 = Z_2 I_1 + (Z_2 + Z_3) I_2 \qquad \ldots(\text{ii})$$

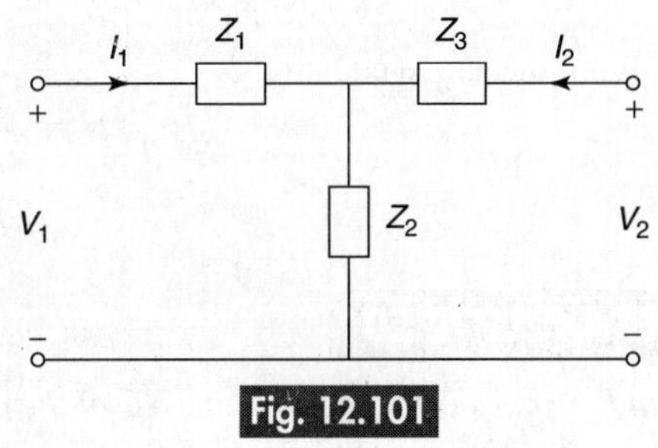


Fig. 12.101

Comparing Eqs (i) and (ii) with Z parameter equations,

$$Z_{11} = Z_1 + Z_2 = 10$$
$$Z_{12} = Z_2 = 5$$
$$Z_{21} = Z_2 = 5$$
$$Z_{22} = Z_2 + Z_3 = 20$$

Solving the above equations,

$$Z_1 = 5\ \Omega$$
$$Z_2 = 5\ \Omega$$
$$Z_3 = 15\ \Omega$$

## EXAMPLE 12.49

*Admittance parameters of a pi-network are $Y_{11} = 0.09$ ℧, $Y_{12} = Y_{21} = -0.05$ ℧ and $Y_{22} = 0.07$ ℧. Find the values of $R_a$, $R_b$ and $R_c$.*

**Solution** The pi-network is shown in Fig. 12.102.

Applying KCL at node, 1,

$$I_1 = \frac{V_1}{R_a} + \frac{V_1 - V_2}{R_b}$$

$$= \left(\frac{1}{R_a} + \frac{1}{R_b}\right)V_1 - \frac{1}{R_b}V_2 \qquad \ldots\text{(i)}$$

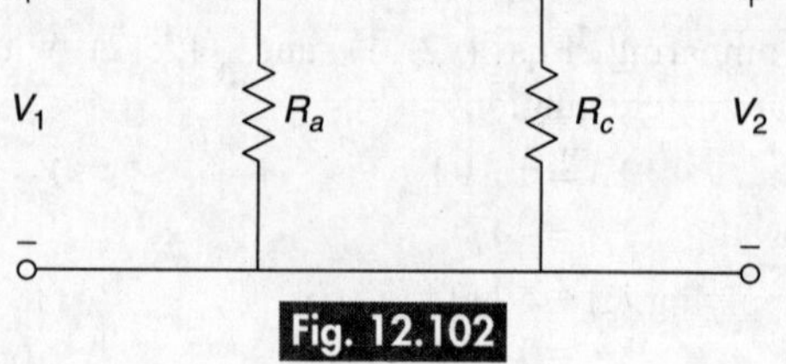

Fig. 12.102

Applying KCL at node 2,

$$I_2 = \frac{V_2}{R_c} + \frac{V_2 - V_1}{R_b}$$

$$= -\frac{1}{R_b}V_1 + \left(\frac{1}{R_B} + \frac{1}{R_c}\right)V_2 \qquad \ldots\text{(ii)}$$

Comparing Eqs (i) and (ii) with $Y$ parameter equations,

$$Y_{11} = \frac{1}{R_a} + \frac{1}{R_b} = 0.09$$

$$Y_{12} = -\frac{1}{R_b} = -0.05$$

$$Y_{21} = -\frac{1}{R_b} = -0.05$$

$$Y_{22} = \frac{1}{R_b} + \frac{1}{R_c} = 0.07$$

Solving the above equations,

$$R_a = 25\ \Omega$$
$$R_b = 20\ \Omega$$
$$R_c = 50\ \Omega$$

## EXAMPLE 12.50

*Find the parameters YA, YB and YC of the equivalent p network, as shown in Fig. 12.103 to represent a two-terminal pair network for which the following measurements were taken:*

(a) *With terminal 2 short-circuited, a voltage of $10 \angle 0°$ V applied at terminal pair I resulted in $I_1 = 2.5 \angle 0°$ A and $I_2 = -0.5 \angle 0°$ A.*

*(b) With terminal 1 short-circuited, the same voltage at terminal pair 2 resulted in $I_2 = 1.5 \angle 0°$ A and $I_1 = -1.1 \angle -20°$ A.*

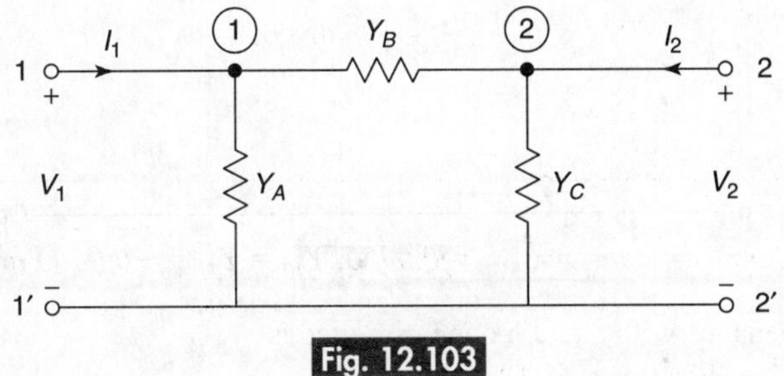


Fig. 12.103

**Solution** Since measurements were taken with either of the terminal pairs short-circuited, we have to calculate $Y$ parameters first.

$$Y_{11} = \left.\frac{I_1}{V_1}\right|_{V_2=0} = \frac{2.5\angle 0°}{10\angle 0°} = 0.25\ \mho$$

$$Y_{21} = \left.\frac{I_2}{V_1}\right|_{V_2=0} = \frac{-0.5\angle 0°}{10\angle 0°} = -0.05\ \mho$$

$$Y_{22} = \left.\frac{I_2}{V_2}\right|_{V_1=0} = \frac{1.5\angle 0°}{10\angle 0°} = 0.15\ \mho$$

Applying KCL at node 1,

$$I_1 = Y_A V_1 + Y_B(V_1 - V_2)$$

$$= (Y_A + Y_B)V_1 - Y_B V_2 \qquad \text{...(i)}$$

Applying KCL at node 2,

$$I_2 = Y_C V_2 + Y_B(V_2 - V_1)$$

$$= -Y_B V_1 + (Y_B + Y_C)V_2 \qquad \text{...(ii)}$$

Comparing Eqs (i) and (ii) with the $Y$ parameter equation,

$$Y_{11} = Y_A + Y_B = 0.25$$

$$Y_{12} = Y_{21} = -Y_B = -0.05$$

$$Y_{22} = Y_B + Y_C = 0.15$$

Solving the above equation,

$$Y_A = 0.20\ \mho$$

$$Y_B = 0.05\ \mho$$

$$Y_C = 0.10\ \mho$$

## EXAMPLE 12.51

*A network has two input terminals (a, b) and two output terminals (c, d), as shown in Fig. 12.104. The input impedance with c and d open-circuited is (250 + j100) ohms and with c and d short-circuited is (400 + j 300) ohms. The impedance across c and d with a and b open-circuited is 200 ohms. Determine the equivalent T-network parameters.*

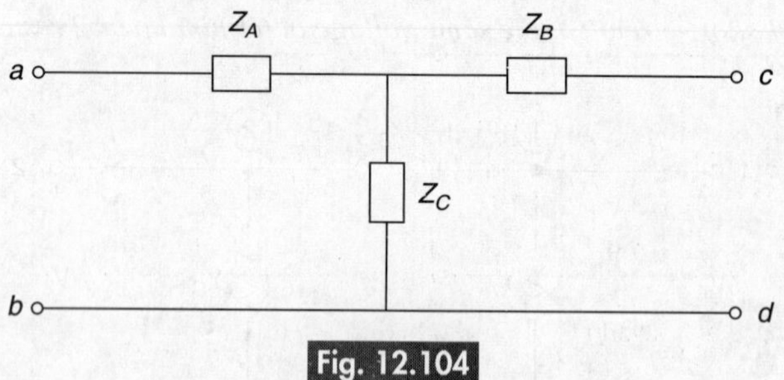


Fig. 12.104

**Solution** The input impedance with *c* and *d* open-circuited is

$$Z_A + Z_C = 250 + j100 \quad \text{...(i)}$$

The input impedance with *c* and *d* short-circuited is,

$$Z_A + \frac{Z_B Z_C}{Z_B + Z_C} = 400 + j300 \quad \text{...(ii)}$$

The impedance across *c* and *d* with *a* and *b* open-circuited is

$$Z_B + Z_C = 200 \quad \text{...(iii)}$$

Subtracting Eq. (i) from (ii),

$$\frac{Z_B Z_C}{Z_B + Z_C} - Z_C = 150 + j200 \quad \text{...(iv)}$$

From Eq. (iii),

$$Z_B = 200 - Z_C \quad \text{...(v)}$$

Subtracting the value of $Z_B$ in the equation (iv) and simplifying,

$$Z_C = (100 - j200)\ \Omega \quad \text{...(vi)}$$

From Eqs (i) and (vi),

$$Z_A = (150 + j300)\ \Omega$$

From Eqs (iii) and (vi),

$$Z_B = (100 + j200)\ \Omega$$

## EXAMPLE 12.52

*Find the equivalent π-network for the T-network shown in Fig. 12.105.*

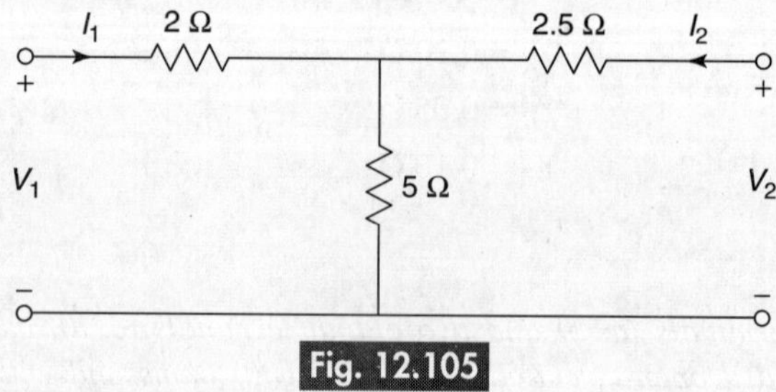


Fig. 12.105

**Solution** Figure 12.106 shows *T*-network and *π*-network.

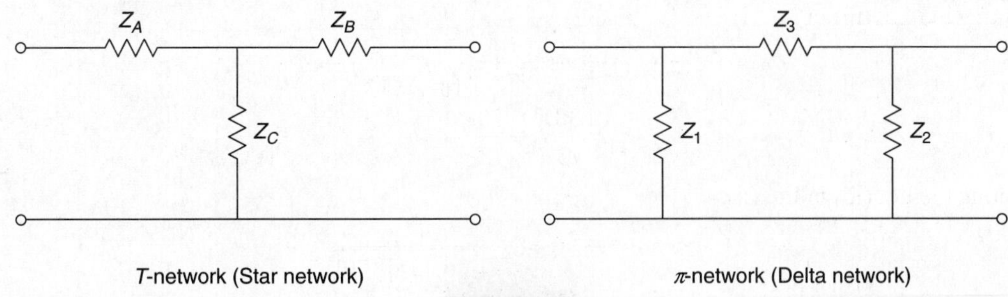


Fig. 12.106

For converting a $T$-network (star network) into an equivalent $\pi$-network (delta network), we can use star-delta transformation technique.

$$Z_1 = Z_A + Z_C + \frac{Z_A Z_C}{Z_B} = 2+5+\frac{2\times 5}{2.5} = 11\,\Omega$$

$$Z_3 = Z_A + Z_B + \frac{Z_A Z_B}{Z_C} = 2+2.5+\frac{2\times 2.5}{5} = 5.5\,\Omega$$

$$Z_2 = Z_B + Z_C + \frac{Z_B Z_C}{Z_A} = 2.5+5+\frac{2.5\times 5}{2} = 13.75\,\Omega$$

The equivalent $\pi$-network is shown in Fig. 12.107.

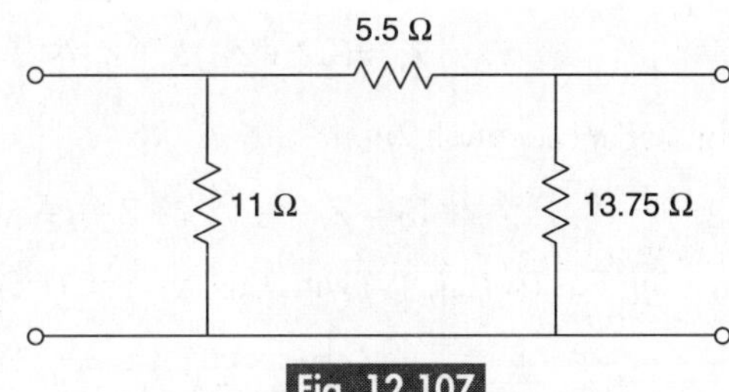


Fig. 12.107

## EXAMPLE 12.53

*For the network shown in Fig. 12.108. Find the equivalent T-network.*

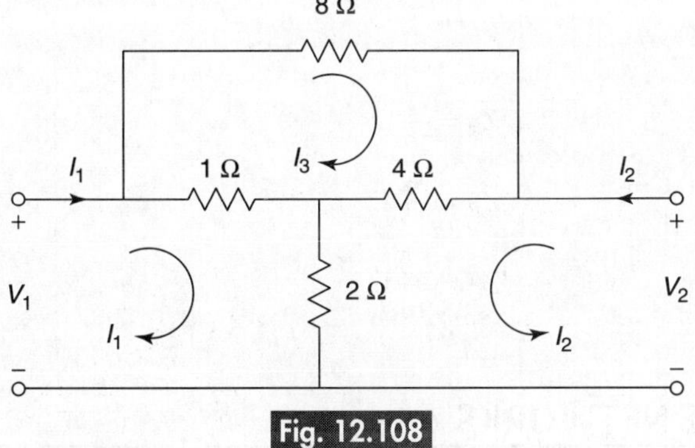


Fig. 12.108

**Solution** Applying KVL to mesh 1,

$$V_1 = 3I_1 + 2I_2 - I_3 \qquad \text{...(i)}$$

Applying KVL to mesh 2,

$$V_2 = 2I_1 + 6I_2 + 4I_3 \qquad \text{...(ii)}$$

Applying KVL to mesh 3,

$$13I_3 - I_1 + 4I_2 = 0$$

$$I_3 = \frac{1}{13}I_1 - \frac{4}{13}I_2 \qquad \text{...(iii)}$$

Substituting the Eq. (iii) in Eq. (i),

$$V_1 = 3I_1 + 2I_2 - \frac{1}{13}I_1 + \frac{4}{13}I_2$$

$$= \frac{38}{13}I_1 + \frac{30}{13}I_2 \qquad \text{...(iv)}$$

Substituting the Eq. (iii) in Eq. (ii),

$$V_2 = 2I_1 + 6I_2 + 4\left(\frac{1}{13}I_1 - \frac{4}{13}I_2\right)$$

$$= \frac{30}{13}I_1 + \frac{62}{13}I_2 \qquad \text{...(v)}$$

The *T*-network is shown in Fig. 12.109.

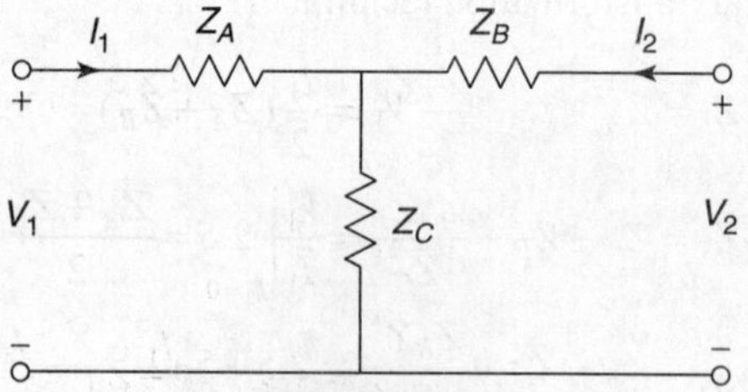

Applying KVL to mesh 1,

$$V_1 = (Z_A + Z_C)I_1 + Z_C I_2 \qquad \text{...(vi)}$$

Applying KVL to mesh 2,

$$V_2 = Z_C I_1 + (Z_B + Z_C)I_2 \qquad \text{...(vii)}$$



Fig. 12.109

Comparing Eqs (iv) and (v) with Eqs (vi) and (vii),

$$Z_A + Z_C = \frac{38}{13}$$

$$Z_C = \frac{30}{13}$$

$$Z_B + Z_C = \frac{62}{13}$$

Solving the above equations,

$$Z_A = \frac{8}{13}\,\Omega$$

$$Z_B = \frac{32}{13}\,\Omega$$

$$Z_C = \frac{30}{13}\,\Omega$$

## 12.12 LATTICE NETWORKS

LO 12.8

A lattice network is one of the common two-port networks, as shown in Fig. 12.110. It is used in filter sections and is also used as attenuator. This network can be represented in terms of *Z* parameters.

The lattice network can be redrawn as a bridge network, as shown in Fig. 12.111. This lattice network is symmetric and reciprocal. The current $I_1$ divides equally between the two arms of the bridge.

When the output port is open-circuited, i.e., $I_2 = 0$

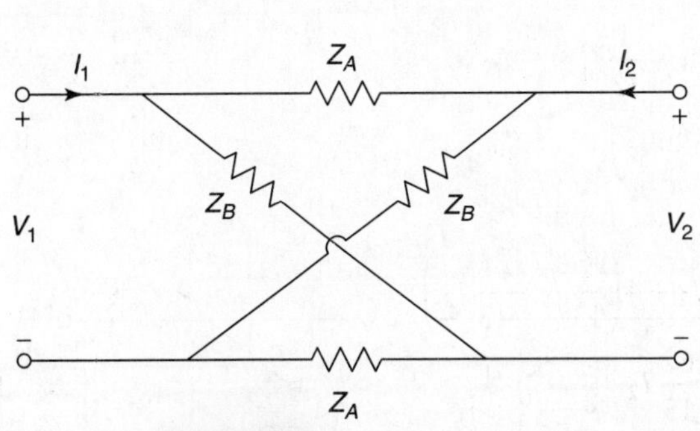


Fig. 12.110 *Lattice network*

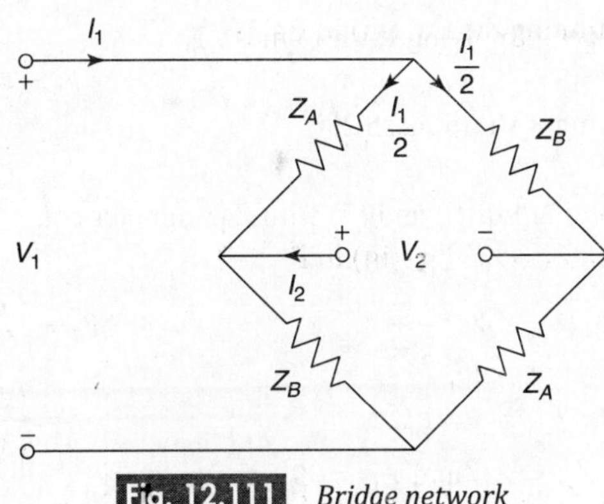


Fig. 12.111 *Bridge network*

$$V_1 = \frac{I_1}{2}(Z_A + Z_B)$$

$$Z_{11} = \left.\frac{V_1}{I_1}\right|_{I_2=0} = \frac{Z_A + Z_B}{2}$$

Also,
$$V_2 = \frac{I_1}{2}Z_B - \frac{I_1}{2}Z_A = \frac{I_1}{2}(Z_B - Z_A)$$

$$Z_{21} = \left.\frac{V_2}{I_1}\right|_{I_2=0} = \frac{Z_B - Z_A}{2}$$

Since the network is symmetric,

$$Z_{11} = Z_{22} = \frac{Z_A + Z_B}{2}$$

$$Z_{12} = Z_{21} = \frac{Z_B - Z_A}{2}$$

Solving the above equations,

$$Z_A = Z_{11} - Z_{12}$$
$$Z_B = Z_{11} + Z_{12}$$

The lattice network can be represented in terms of other two-port network parameters, with the help of inter-relationship formulae of various parameters.

## EXAMPLE 12.54

*Find the lattice equivalent of a symmetrical T network shown in Fig. 12.112.*

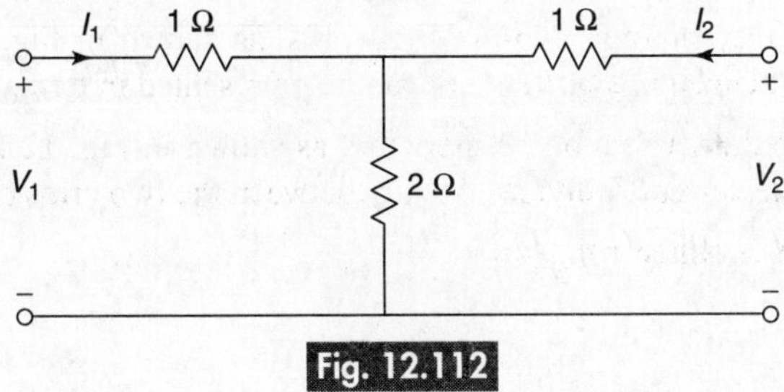


Fig. 12.112

**Solution** Applying KVL to mesh 1,

$$V_1 = 3I_1 + 2I_2 \quad \ldots(i)$$

Applying KVL to mesh 2,

$$V_2 = 2I_1 + 3I_2 \quad \ldots(ii)$$

Comparing Eqs (i) and (ii) with $Z$ parameter equations,

$$Z_{11} = 3\,\Omega$$
$$Z_{12} = 2\,\Omega$$
$$Z_{21} = 2\,\Omega$$
$$Z_{22} = 3\,\Omega$$

Since $Z_{11} = Z_{22}$ and $Z_{12} = Z_{21}$, the network is symmetric and reciprocal. The parameters of lattice network are

$$Z_A = Z_{11} - Z_{12} = 3 - 2 = 1\,\Omega$$
$$Z_B = Z_{11} + Z_{12} = 3 + 2 = 5\,\Omega$$

The lattice network is shown in Fig. 12.113.

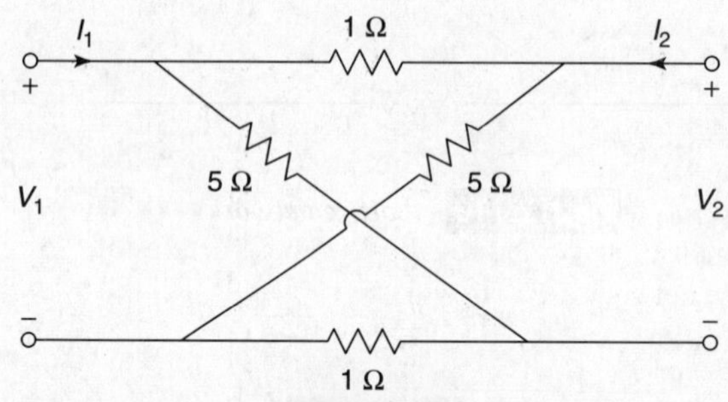

Fig. 12.113

## EXAMPLE 12.55

*Find the lattice equivalent of a symmetric π-network shown in Fig. 12.114.*

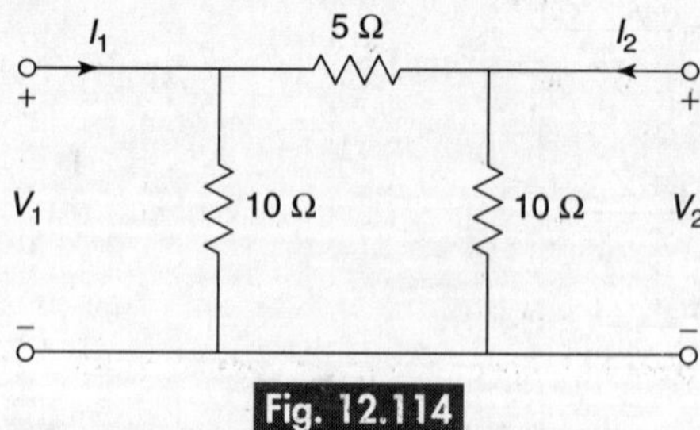

Fig. 12.114

**Solution** The network is redrawn, as shown in Fig. 12.115.

Applying KVL to mesh 1,

$$V_1 = 10I_1 - 10I_3 \quad \ldots(i)$$

Applying KVL to mesh 2,

$$V_2 = 10I_2 + 10I_3 \quad \ldots(ii)$$

Applying KVL to mesh 3,

$$-10I_1 + 10I_2 + 25I_3 = 0$$

$$I_3 = \frac{2}{5}I - \frac{2}{5}I_2 \quad \ldots(iii)$$

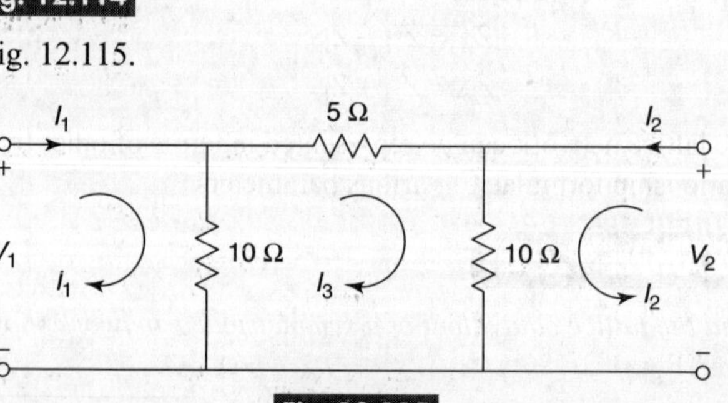

Fig. 12.115

Substituting Eq (iii) in Eq (i),

$$V_1 = 10I_1 - 10\left(\frac{2}{5}I_1 - \frac{2}{5}I_2\right)$$

$$= 6I_1 + 4I_2 \quad \ldots(iv)$$

Substituting Eq (iii) in Eq (ii),

$$V_2 = 10 I_2 + 10\left(\frac{2}{5} I_1 - \frac{2}{5} I_2\right)$$

$$= 4 I_1 - 6 I_2 \qquad \ldots \text{(v)}$$

Comparing the Eqs (iv) and (v) with $Z$ parameter equations,

$$Z_{11} = 6\ \Omega$$
$$Z_{12} = 4\ \Omega$$
$$Z_{21} = 4\ \Omega$$
$$Z_{22} = 6\ \Omega$$

Since $Z_{11} = Z_{22}$ and $Z_{12} = Z_{21}$, the network is symmetric and reciprocal. The parameters of lattice network are

$$Z_A = Z_{11} - Z_{12} = 6 - 4 = 2\ \Omega$$
$$Z_B = Z_{11} + Z_{12} = 6 + 4 = 10\ \Omega$$

The lattice network is shown in Fig. 12.116.

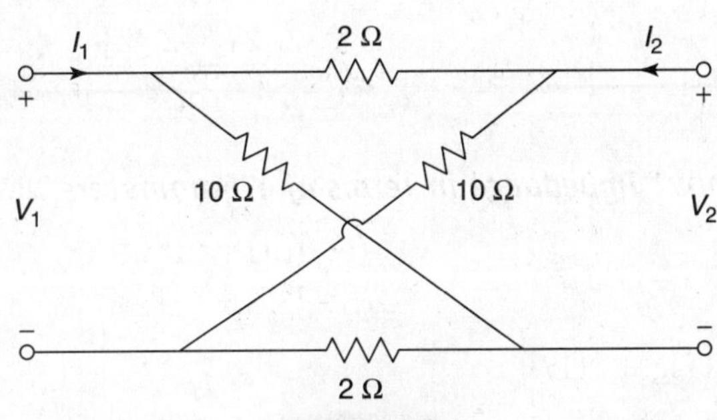

Fig. 12.116

## 12.13 TERMINATED TWO-PORT NETWORKS

LO 12.9

Discuss terminated two-port networks

### 12.13.1 Driving-Point Impedance at Input Port

A two-port network is shown in Fig. 12.117. The output port of the network is terminated in load impedance $Z_L$. The input impedance of this network can be expressed in terms of parameters of two-port network parameters.

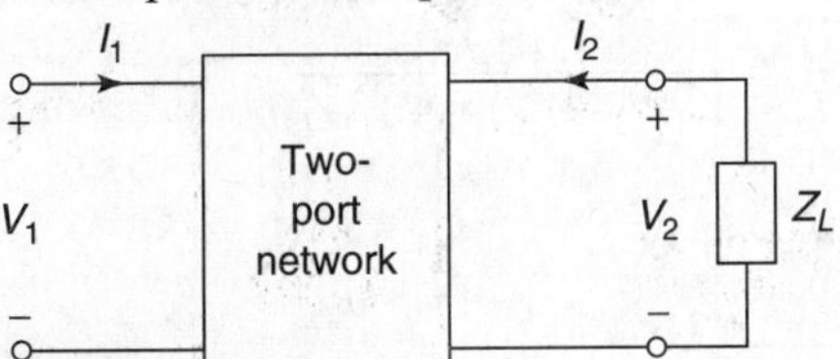

Fig. 12.117 *Terminated two-port network*

***1. Input Impedance in Terms of Z Parameters*** We know that

$$V_1 = Z_{11} I_1 + Z_{12} I_2$$
$$V_2 = Z_{21} I_1 + Z_{22} I_2$$

From Fig. 12.117,

$$V_2 = -Z_L I_2$$
$$-I_2 Z_L = Z_{21} I_1 + Z_{22} I_2$$
$$I_2 = -\frac{Z_{21}}{Z_{22} + Z_L} I_1$$
$$Z_{\text{in}} = \frac{V_1}{I_1} = Z_{11} + Z_{12}\left(-\frac{Z_{21}}{Z_{22} + Z_L}\right) = \frac{Z_{11}Z_{22} + Z_{11}Z_L - Z_{12}Z_{21}}{Z_{22} + Z_L}$$

If the output port is open-circuited, i.e., $Z_L = \infty$,

$$Z_{in} = \lim_{Z_L \to \infty} \frac{\frac{Z_{11}Z_{22} - Z_{12}Z_{21}}{Z_L} + Z_{11}}{\frac{Z_{22}}{Z_L} + 1} = Z$$

If the output port is short-circuited, i.e., $Z_L = 0$,

$$Z_{in} = \frac{Z_{11}Z_{22} - Z_{12}Z_{21}}{Z_{22}}$$

***2. Input Impedance in Terms of Y Parameters*** We know that

$$I_1 = Y_{11}V_1 + Y_{12}V_2$$
$$I_2 = Y_{21}V_1 + Y_{22}V_2$$

From Fig. 12.117,

$$V_2 = -Z_L I_2$$
$$I_2 = -\frac{V_2}{Z_L} = -Y_L V_2 \qquad \text{where } Y_L = \frac{1}{Z_L}$$
$$-Y_L V_2 = Y_{21}V_1 + Y_{22}V_2$$
$$V_2 = -\frac{Y_{21}}{Y_{22} + Y_L} V_1$$
$$I_1 = Y_{11}V_1 + Y_{12}\left(-\frac{Y_{21}}{Y_{22} + Y_L}\right)V_1 = Y_{11}V_1 - \frac{Y_{21}Y_{12}}{Y_{22} + Y_L}V_1 = \frac{Y_{11}Y_{22} - Y_{12}Y_{21} + Y_{11}Y_L}{Y_{22} + Y_L}V_1$$
$$Z_{in} = \frac{V_1}{I_1} = \frac{Y_{22} + Y_L}{Y_{11}Y_{22} - Y_{12}Y_{21} + Y_{11}Y_L}$$

When output port is open-circuited, i.e., $Y_L = 0$

$$Z_{in} = \frac{Y_{22}}{Y_{11}Y_{22} - Y_{12}Y_{21}}$$

When output port is short-circuited, i.e., $Y_L = \infty$,

$$Z_{in} = \lim_{Y_L \to \infty} \frac{\frac{Y_{22}}{Y_L} + 1}{\frac{Y_{11}Y_{22} - Y_{12}Y_{21}}{Y_L} + Y_{11}} = \frac{1}{Y_{11}}$$

***3. Input Impedance in Terms of Transmission Parameters*** We know that

$$V_1 = AV_2 - BV_2$$
$$I_1 = CV_2 - DI_2$$

From Fig. 12.117,

$$V_2 = -Z_L I_2$$

$$I_1 = -CZ_L I_2 - DI_2 = -(CZ_L + D)I_2$$

$$I_2 = -\frac{I_1}{CZ_L + D}$$

$$V_1 = AZ_L I_2 - B = \left(-\frac{I_1}{CZ_L + D}\right) = \left(\frac{AZ_L + B}{CZ_L + D}\right) I_1$$

$$Z_{in} = \frac{V_1}{I_1} = \frac{AZ_L + B}{CZ_L + D}$$

If the output port is open-circuited, i.e., $Z_L = \infty$,

$$Z_{in} = \frac{A}{C}$$

If the output port is short-circuited, i.e., $Z_L = 0$,

$$Z_{in} = \frac{B}{D}$$

***4. Input Impedance in Terms of Hybrid Parameters*** We know that

$$V_1 = h_{11} I_1 + h_{12} V_2$$

$$I_2 = h_{21} I_1 + h_{22} V_2$$

$$V_2 = -Z_L I_2$$

$$I_2 = h_{21} I_1 - h_{22} Z_L I_2$$

$$I_2 = \frac{h_{21}}{1 + h_{22} Z_L} I_L$$

$$V_2 = -\frac{h_{21} Z_L}{1 + h_{22} Z_L} I_1$$

Substituting the value of $V_2$ in $V_1$,

$$V_1 = h_{11} I_1 + h_{12} \left[\frac{-h_{21} Z_L}{1 + h_{22} Z_L} I_L\right] = \left[\frac{(h_{11} h_{22} - h_{12} h_{21}) Z_L + h_{11}}{1 + h_{22} Z_L}\right] I_1$$

$$Z_{in} = \frac{V_1}{I_1} = \frac{(h_{11} h_{22} - h_{12} h_{21}) Z_L + h_{11}}{1 + h_{22} Z_L}$$

If the output port is open-circuited, i.e., $Z_L = \infty$,

$$Z_{in} = \frac{h_{11} h_{22} - h_{12} h_{21}}{h_{22}}$$

If the output port is short-circuited, i.e., $Z_L = 0$,

$$Z_{in} = h_{11}$$

### 12.13.2 Driving-Point Impedance at Output Port

A two-port network is shown in Fig. 12.118. The input port is terminated in load impedance $Z_L$. The output impedance of this network can be expressed in terms of two-port network parameters.

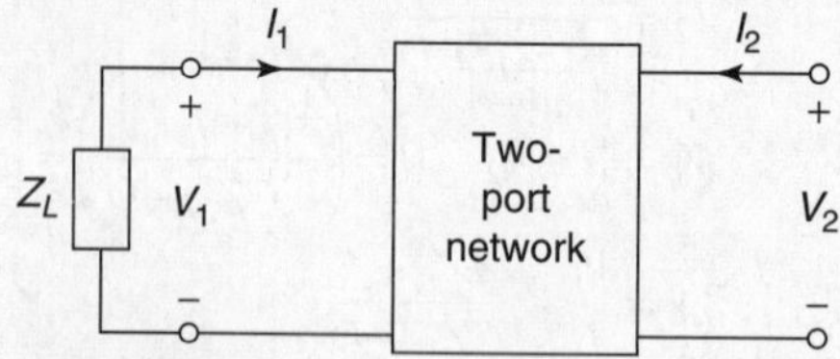


Fig. 12.118 *Terminated two-port network*

***1. Output Impedance in terms of Z parameters*** We know that

$$V_1 = Z_{11}I_1 + Z_{12}I_2$$
$$V_2 = Z_{21}I_1 + Z_{22}I_2$$

From Fig. 12.118,

$$V_1 = -Z_L I_1$$
$$-I_1 Z_1 = Z_{11}I_1 + Z_{12}I_2$$
$$I_1 = \left(-\frac{Z_{12}}{Z_L + Z_{11}}\right) I_2$$

$$V_2 = Z_{21}\left(-\frac{Z_{12}}{Z_L + Z_{11}}\right) I_2 + Z_{22}I_2 = I_2\left(Z_{22} - \frac{Z_{21}Z_{12}}{Z_L + Z_{11}}\right) = \left(\frac{Z_{11}Z_{22} - Z_{12}Z_{21} + Z_{22}Z_L}{Z_{11} + Z_L}\right) I_2$$

$$Z_0 = \frac{V_2}{I_2} = \frac{Z_{11}Z_{22} - Z_{12}Z_{21} + Z_{22}Z_L}{Z_{11} + Z_L}$$

If the input port is open-circuited, i.e., $Z_L = \infty$,

$$Z_0 = Z_{22}$$

If the input port is short-circuited, i.e., $Z_L = 0$,

$$Z_0 = \frac{Z_{11}Z_{22} - Z_{12}Z_{21}}{Z_{11}}$$

***2. Output Impedance in Terms of Y parameters*** We know that

$$I_1 = Y_{11}V_1 + Y_{12}V_2$$
$$I_2 = Y_{21}V_1 + Y_{22}V_2$$

From Fig. 12.118,

$$V_1 = -Z_L I_1$$
$$I_1 = -\frac{V_1}{Z_L} = -Y_L V_1$$

$$-Y_LV_1 = Y_{11}V_1 + Y_{12}V_2$$

$$V_1 = \left(-\frac{Y_{12}}{Y_L + Y_{11}}\right)V_2$$

$$I_2 = Y_{21}\left(-\frac{Y_{12}}{Y_L + Y_{11}}\right)V_2 + Y_{22}V_2 = V_2\left[Y_{22} - \frac{Y_{21}Y_{12}}{Y_L + Y_{11}}\right] = V_2\left[\frac{Y_{11}Y_{22} - Y_{12}Y_{21} + Y_LY_{22}}{Y_L + Y_{11}}\right]$$

$$Z_0 = \frac{V_2}{I_2} = \frac{Y_L + Y_{11}}{Y_{11}Y_{22} - Y_{12}Y_{21} + Y_LY_{22}}$$

If input port is open-circuited, i.e., $Y_L = 0$,

$$Z_0 = \frac{Y_{11}}{Y_{11}Y_{22} - Y_{12}Y_{21}}$$

If input port is short-circuited, i.e., $Y_L = \infty$,

$$Z_0 = \frac{1}{Y_{22}}$$

***3. Output Impedance in Terms of ABCD-Parameters*** We know that

$$V_1 = AV_2 - BI_2$$
$$I_1 = CV_2 - DI_2$$

From Fig. 12.118,

$$V_1 = -Z_LI_1$$

$$\frac{V_1}{I_1} = -Z_L = \frac{AV_2 - BI_2}{CV_2 - DI_2}$$

$$V_2(CZ_L + A) = I_2(DZ_L + B)$$

$$Z_0 = \frac{V_2}{I_2} = \frac{DZ_L + B}{CZ_L + A}$$

If input port is open-circuited, i.e., $Z_L = \infty$,

$$Z_0 = \frac{D}{C}$$

If input port is short-circuited, i.e., $Z_L = 0$,

$$Z_0 = \frac{B}{A}$$

***4. Output Impedance in Terms of h Parameters*** We know that

$$V_1 = h_{11}I_1 + h_{12}V_{12}$$
$$I_2 = h_{21}I_1 + h_{22}V_2$$

From Fig. 12.118,

$$V_1 = -Z_LI_1$$
$$-I_1Z_L = h_{11}I_1 + h_{22}V_2$$

$$I_1 = \left(-\frac{h_{12}}{h_{11}+Z_L}\right)V_2$$

$$I_2 = h_{21}\left(-\frac{h_{12}}{h_{11}+Z_L}\right)V_2 + h_{22}V_2 = V_2\left[\frac{h_{11}h_{22}-h_{12}h_{21}+h_{22}Z_L}{h_{11}+Z_L}\right]$$

$$Z_0 = \frac{V_2}{I_2} = \frac{h_{11}+Z_L}{h_{11}h_{22}-h_{12}h_{21}+h_{22}Z_L}$$

If input port is open-circuited, i.e., $Z_L = \infty$,

$$Z_0 = \frac{1}{h_{22}}$$

If input port is short-circuited i.e., $Z_L = 0$,

$$Z_0 = \frac{h_{11}}{h_{11}h_{22}-h_{12}h_{21}}$$

## EXAMPLE 12.56

*Measurements were made on a two-terminal network shown in Fig. 12.119.*

*(a) With terminal pair 2 open, a voltage of 100 ∠0° V applied to terminal pair 1 resulted in*

$$I_1 = 10\angle 0^\circ\ A, \quad V_2 = 25\angle 0^\circ\ V$$

*(b) With terminal pair 1 open, the same voltage applied to terminal pair 2 resulted in*

$$I_2 = 20\angle 0^\circ\ A, \quad V_1 = 50\angle 0^\circ\ V$$

*Write mesh equations for this network. What will be the voltage across a 10-Ω resistor connected across terminal pair 2 if a 100 ∠0° V is connected across terminal pair 1?*

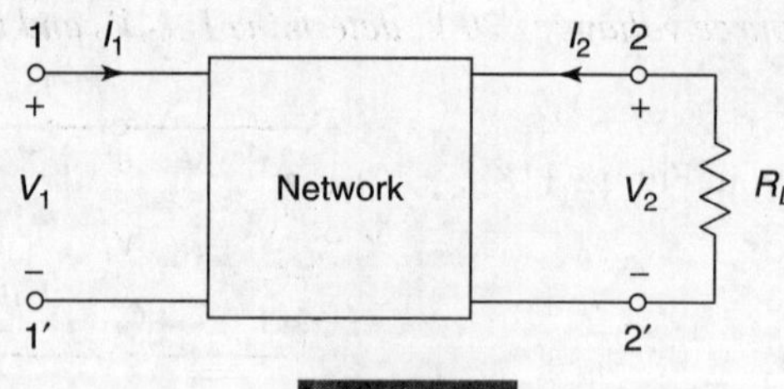


Fig. 12.119

**Solution** Since measurements were done with either of the terminal pairs open-circuited, we have to calculate $Z$ parameters first.

$$Z_{11} = \left.\frac{V_1}{I_1}\right|_{I_2=0} = \frac{100\angle 0^\circ}{10\angle 0^\circ} = 10\ \Omega$$

$$Z_{21} = \left.\frac{V_2}{I_1}\right|_{I_2=0} = \frac{25\angle 0^\circ}{10\angle 0^\circ} = 2.5\ \Omega$$

$$Z_{22} = \left.\frac{V_2}{I_2}\right|_{I_1=0} = \frac{100\angle 0^\circ}{20\angle 0^\circ} = 5\ \Omega$$

$$Z_{12} = \left.\frac{V_1}{I_2}\right|_{I_1=0} = \frac{50\angle 0^\circ}{20\angle 0^\circ} = 2.5\ \Omega$$

Putting these values in $Z$ parameter equations,

$$V_1 = 10I_1 + 2.5I_2 \qquad \ldots\text{(i)}$$

$$V_2 = 2.5I_1 + 5I_2 \qquad \ldots\text{(ii)}$$

When a 10-Ω resistor is connected across terminal pair 1,

$$V_1 = 100\angle 0°\ V$$

$$V_2 = -R_L I_2 = -10 I_2$$

Substituting values of $V_1$ and $V_2$ in Eqs (i) and (ii),

$$100 = 10 I_1 + 2.5 I_2$$

and

$$-10 I_2 = 2.5 I_1 + 5 I_2$$

$$2.5 I_1 = -15 I_2$$

$$I_1 = -6 I_2$$

$$100 = -60 I_2 + 2.5 I_2$$

$$I_2 = -\frac{100}{57.5} = -1.74\ \text{A}$$

$$\text{Voltage across the resistor} = -I_2 R_L = -10(-1.74) = 17.4\ \text{V}$$

**EXAMPLE 12.57**

*The Z parameters of a two-port network shown in Fig. 12.120 are $Z_{11} = Z_{22} = 10\ \Omega$, $Z_{21} = Z_{22} = 4\ \Omega$. If the source voltage is 20 V, determine $I_1, I_2, V_2$ and input impedance.*

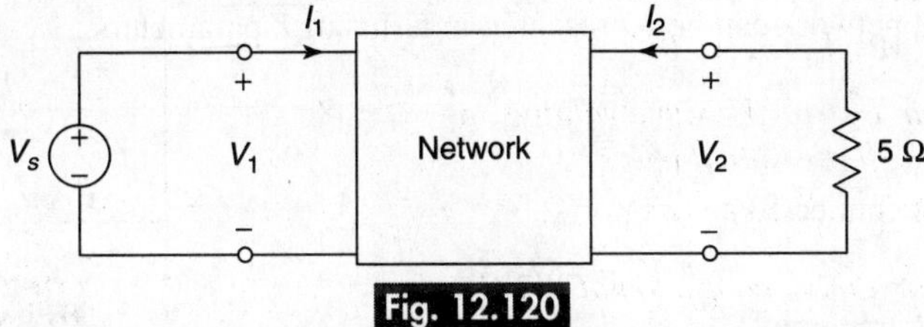


Fig. 12.120

**Solution**

$$V_1 = V_s = 20\ \text{V}$$

$$V_2 = -20 I_2$$

The two-port network can be represented in terms of $Z$ parameters.

$$V_1 = 10 I_1 + 4 I_2 \quad \text{...(i)}$$

$$V_2 = 4 I_1 + 10 I_2 \quad \text{...(ii)}$$

$$-20 I_2 = 4 I_1 + 10 I_2$$

$$4 I_1 = -30 I_2$$

$$I_1 = -7.5 I_2$$

Substituting the value of $I_1$ in Eq. (i),

$$V_1 = 10(-7.5 I_2) + 4 I_2 = -71 I_2$$

$$20 = -71 I_2$$

$$I_2 = -0.28\ \text{A}$$

$$I_1 = -7.5(-0.28) = 2.1 \text{ A}$$
$$V_2 = -20(-0.28) = 56 \text{ V}$$
$$\text{Input impedance } Z_i = \frac{V_1}{I_1} = \frac{20}{2.1} = 9.52\ \Omega$$

## EXAMPLE 12.58

*The Z parameters of a two-port network shown in Fig. 12.121 are $Z_{11} = 2\ \Omega$, $Z_{12} = 1\ \Omega$, $Z_{21} = 2\ \Omega$, $Z_{22} = 5\ \Omega$. Calculate the voltage ratio $\frac{V_2}{V_s}$, current ratio $-\frac{I_2}{I_1}$ and input impedance $\frac{V_1}{I_1}$.*

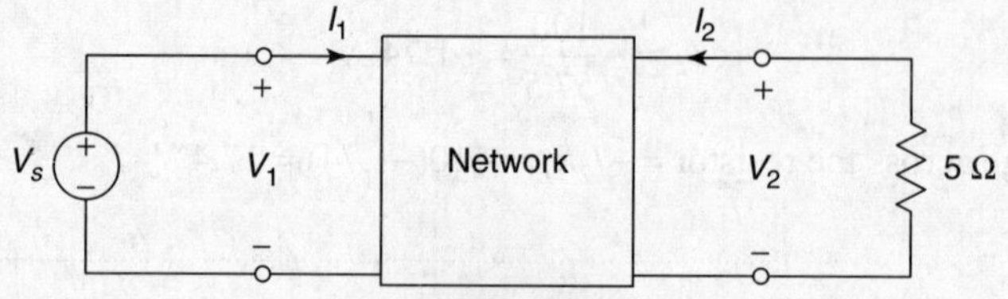


Fig. 12.121

**Solution** The two-port network can be represented in terms of $Z$ parameters.

$$V_1 = 2I_1 + I_2 \quad \ldots\text{(i)}$$
$$V_2 = 2I_1 + 5I_2 \quad \ldots\text{(ii)}$$

When the 5 Ω resistor is connected across port 2,

$$V_2 = -5I_2 \quad \ldots\text{(iii)}$$

Applying KVL to the input port,

$$V_s - 1I_1 - V_1 = 0$$
$$V_1 = V_s + I_1 \quad \ldots\text{(iv)}$$

Substituting values of $V_1$ and $V_2$ in Eqs (i) and (ii),

$$V_s - I_1 = 2I_1 + I_2$$
$$V_s = 3I_1 + I_2 \quad \ldots\text{(v)}$$

and

$$-5I_2 = 2I_1 + 5I_2$$
$$0 = 2I_1 + 10I_2 \quad \ldots\text{(vi)}$$

Solving Eqs (v) and (vi),

$$I_1 = \frac{\begin{vmatrix} V_s & 1 \\ 0 & 10 \end{vmatrix}}{\begin{vmatrix} 3 & 1 \\ 2 & 10 \end{vmatrix}} = \frac{5}{14} V_s$$

$$I_2 = \frac{\begin{vmatrix} 3 & V_s \\ 0 & 0 \end{vmatrix}}{\begin{vmatrix} 3 & 1 \\ 2 & 10 \end{vmatrix}} = -\frac{1}{14}V_s$$

$$-\frac{I_2}{I_1} = \frac{1}{5}$$

$$V_2 = 2I_1 + 5I_2 = 2\left(\frac{5}{14}V_s\right) + 5\left(-\frac{1}{14}V_s\right) = \frac{5}{14}V_s$$

$$\frac{V_2}{V_s} = \frac{5}{14}$$

$$V_1 = 2I_1 + I_2 = 2\left(\frac{5}{14}V_s\right) - \frac{1}{14}V_s = \frac{9}{14}V_s$$

$$\frac{V_1}{I_1} = \frac{9}{5}\,\Omega$$

## EXAMPLE 12.59

*The following equations give the voltages $V_1$ and $V_2$ at the two ports of a two-port network shown in Fig. 12.122.*

$$V_1 = 5I_1 + 2I_2$$
$$V_2 = 2I_1 + I_2$$

*A load resistor of 3 Ω is connected across port 2. Calculate the input impedance.*

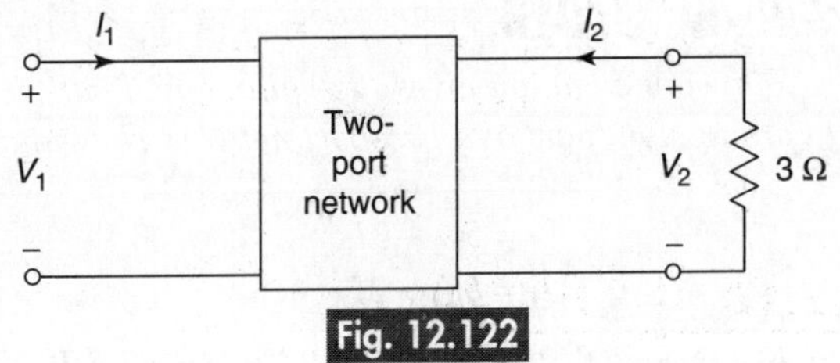

Fig. 12.122

**Solution** From Fig. 12.122,

$$V_2 = -3I_2 \qquad \text{...(i)}$$

Substituting Eq. (i) in the given equation,

$$-3I_2 = 2I_1 + I_2$$

$$I_2 = -\frac{I_1}{2} \qquad \text{(ii)}$$

Substituting the Eq. (ii) in the given equation.

$$V_1 = 5I_1 - I_1 = 4I_1$$

Input impedance
$$Z_i = \frac{V_1}{I_1} = 4\,\Omega$$

## EXAMPLE 12.60

*The Y parameters for a two-port network shown in Fig. 12.123 are given as, $Y_{11} = 4$ ℧, $Y_{22} = 5$ ℧, $Y_{12} = Y_{21} = 4$ ℧. If a resistor of 1 Ω is connected across port 1 of the network then find the output impedance.*

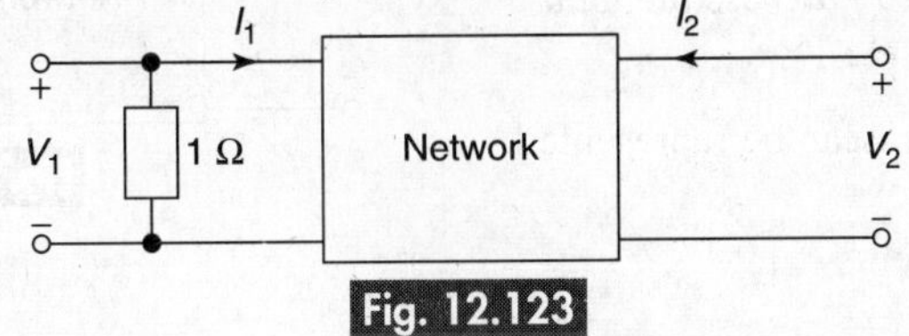

Fig. 12.123

**Solution** The two-port network can be represented in terms of $Y$ parameters.

$$I_1 = 4V_1 + 4V_2 \quad \ldots\text{(i)}$$

$$I_2 = 4V_1 + 5V_2 \quad \ldots\text{(ii)}$$

When the 1-Ω resistor is connected across port-1 of the network,

$$V_1 = -1I_1 = -I_1$$

$$I_1 = -V_1$$

Substituting value of $I_1$ in Eq (i),

$$-V_1 = 4V_1 + 4V_2$$

$$-5V_1 = 4V_2$$

$$V_1 = -\frac{4}{5}V_2$$

Substituting value of $V_1$ in Eq (ii),

$$I_2 = 4\left(-\frac{4}{5}V_2\right) + 5V_2 = \frac{9}{5}V_2$$

$$\text{Output impedance } Z_0 = \frac{V_2}{I_2} = \frac{5}{9}\,\Omega$$

## EXAMPLE 12.61

*The following equation gives the voltage and current at the input port of a two-port network shown in Fig. 12.124.*

$$V_1 = 5V_2 - 3I_2$$

$$I_1 = 6V_2 - 2I_2$$

*A load resistance of 5 Ω is connected across the output port. Calculate the input impedance.*

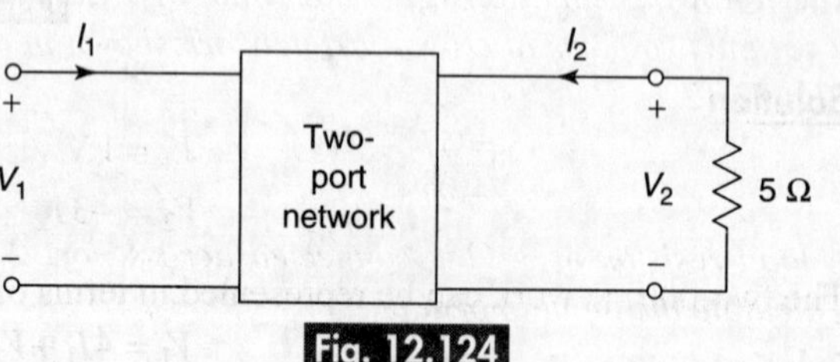

Fig. 12.124

**Solution** From Fig. 12.124,

$$V_2 = -5I_2$$

Substituting the value of $V_2$ in the given equations,

$$V_1 = 5(-5I_2) - 3I_2 = -28I_2$$

$$I_1 = 6(-5I_2) - 2I_2 = -32I_2$$

Input impedance

$$Z_i = \frac{V_1}{I_1} = \frac{-28I_2}{-32I_2} = \frac{7}{8}\,\Omega$$

## EXAMPLE 12.62

*The ABCD parameters of a two-port network shown in Fig. 12.125 are A = 2.5, B = 4 Ω, C = 1 ℧, D = 2. What must be the input voltage $V_1$ applied for the output voltage $V_2$ to be 10 V across the load of 10 Ω connected at port 2?*

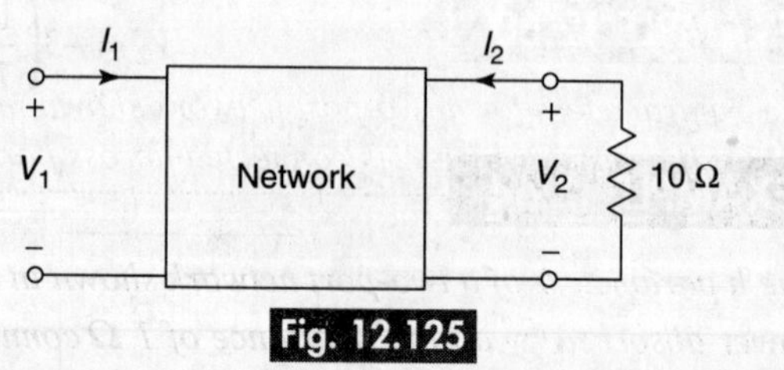

Fig. 12.125

**Solution** The two-port network can be represented in terms of *ABCD*-parameters.

$$V_1 = 2.5\,V_2 - 4I_2 \qquad \text{...(i)}$$
$$I_1 = V_2 - 2I_2 \qquad \text{...(ii)}$$

When the 10 Ω resistor is connected across port 2,

$$V_2 = -10I_2 = 10 \qquad \text{...(iii)}$$
$$I_2 = -1\text{A}$$
$$V_1 = 2.5(10) - 4(-1) = 29 \text{ V}$$

## EXAMPLE 12.63

*The h parameters of a two-port network shown in Fig. 12.126 are $h_{11} = 4\ \Omega$, $h_{12} = 1$, $h_{21} = 1$, $h_{22} = 0.5$ ℧. Calculate the output voltage $V_2$ when the output port is terminated in a 3 Ω resistance and a 1 V is applied at the input port.*

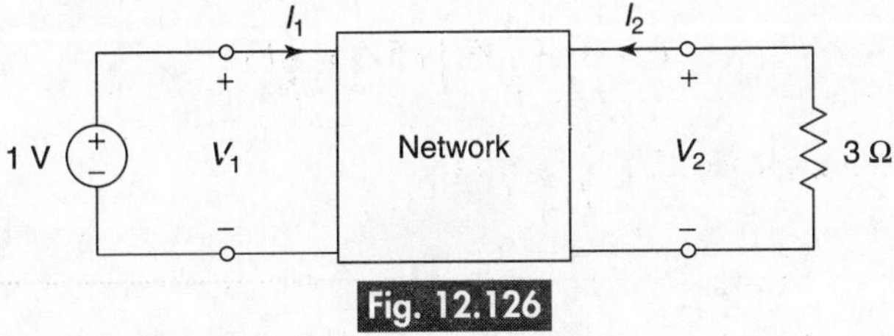


Fig. 12.126

**Solution**

$$V_1 = 1\text{ V}$$
$$V_2 = -3I_2$$

The two-port network can be represented in terms of $h$ parameters.

$$V_1 = 4I_1 + V_2 \qquad \text{...(i)}$$
$$I_2 = I_1 + 0.5\,V_2 \qquad \text{...(ii)}$$
$$I_2 = I_1 + 0.5(-3I_2)$$
$$2.5\,I_2 = I_1$$

Substituting the value of $V_1$ and $I_1$ in Eq (i),

$$1 = 4(2.5\,I_2) - 3\,I_2$$
$$1 = 7I_2$$
$$I_2 = \frac{1}{7}\text{A}$$
$$V_2 = -3\left(\frac{1}{7}\right) = -\frac{3}{7}\text{V}$$

## EXAMPLE 12.64

*The h parameters of a two-port network shown in Fig. 12.127 are $h_{11} = 1\ \Omega$, $h_{12} = -h_{21} = 2$, $h_{22} = 1$ ℧. The power absorbed by a load resistance of 1 Ω connected across port 2 is 100 W. The network is excited by a voltage source of generated voltage $V_s$ and internal resistance 2 Ω. Calculate the value of $V_s$.*

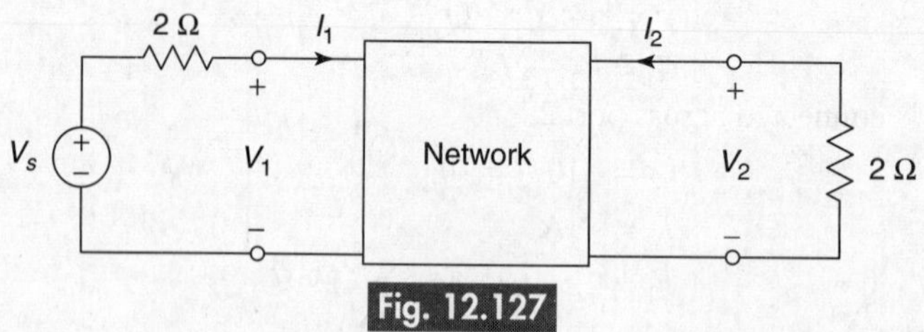


Fig. 12.127

**Solution** The two-port network can be represented in terms of $h$ parameters.

$$V_1 = I_1 + 2V_2 \quad \text{...(i)}$$

$$I_2 = -2I_1 + V_2 \quad \text{...(ii)}$$

When the 1 Ω resister is connected across port 2,

$$\frac{V_2^2}{1} = 100$$

$$V_2 = 10 \text{ V}$$

$$V_2 = -1I_2 = 10$$

$$I_2 = -10 \text{ A}$$

Substituting values of $I_2$ and $V_2$ in Eq (ii),

$$-10 = -2I_1 + 10$$

$$I_1 = 10 \text{ A}$$

Applying KVL to the input port,

$$V_s - 2I_1 - V_1 = 0$$

$$V_s - 2I_1 - (I_1 + 2V_2) = 0$$

$$V_s - 3I_1 - 2V_2 = 0$$

$$V_s = 3I_1 + 2V_2 = 3(10) + 2(10) = 50 \text{ V}$$

## 12.14 | IMAGE PARAMETERS

LO 12.10

Explain image parameters

If the driving-point impedance at port 1, with impedance $Z_{i2}$ connected across port 2, is $Z_{i1}$ and driving-point impedance at port 2, with impedance $Z_{i1}$ connected across the port 1, is $Z_{i2}$ then $Z_{i1}$ and $Z_{i2}$ are known as image impedances of the network. These are also known as image parameters.

The image parameters can be expressed in terms of *ABCD*-parameters. Figure 12.128 shows a two-port network terminated in $Z_{i2}$ at port 2.

$$V_1 = AV_2 - BI_2$$

$$I_1 = CV_2 - DI_2$$

$$V_2 = -Z_{i2}I_2$$

$$Z_{i1} = \frac{V_1}{I_1} = \frac{AV_2 - BI_2}{CV_2 - DI_2} = \frac{-AZ_{i2}I_2 - BI_2}{-CZ_{i2}I_2 - DI_2} = \frac{-AZ_{i2} - B}{-CZ_{i2} - D}$$

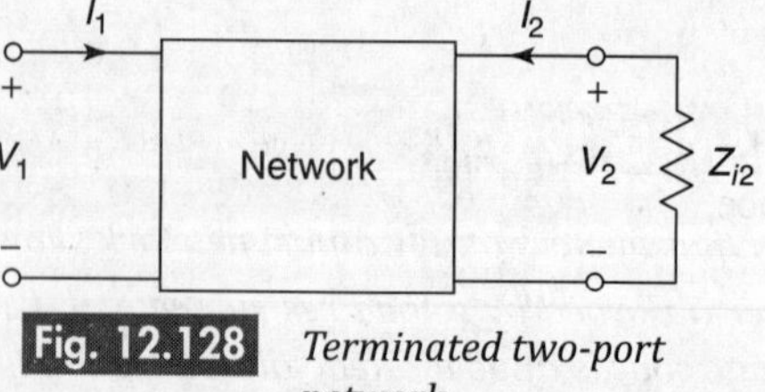


Fig. 12.128 *Terminated two-port network*

$$= \frac{A Z_{i2} + B}{C Z_{i2} + D} \qquad \text{...(12.13)}$$

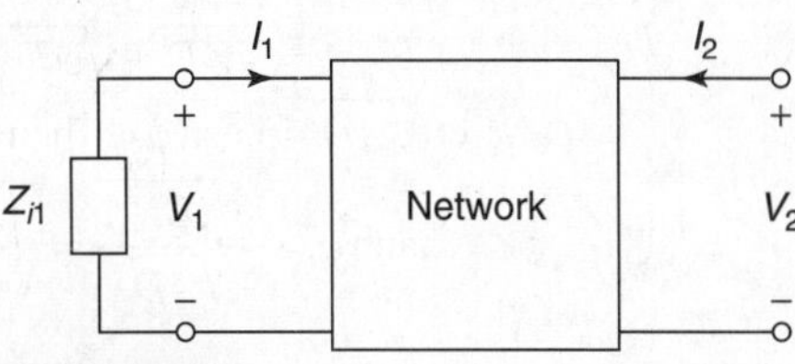

Fig. 12.129 *Terminated two-port network*

Similarly, if the two-port network is terminated in $Z_{i1}$ at port 1, as shown in Fig. 12.129, then

$$V_1 = -Z_{i1} I_1$$

$$Z_{i2} = \frac{V_2}{I_2} = \frac{V_1\left(\frac{D}{AD-BC}\right) - I_1\left(\frac{B}{AD-BC}\right)}{V_1\left(\frac{C}{AD-BC}\right) - I_1\left(\frac{A}{AD-BC}\right)} \qquad \text{...(from Cramer's rule)}$$

$$= \frac{-Z_{i1}I_1\left(\frac{D}{AD-BC}\right) - I_1\left(\frac{B}{AD-BC}\right)}{-Z_{i1}I_1\left(\frac{C}{AD-BC}\right) - I_1\left(\frac{A}{AD-BC}\right)} = \frac{-DZ_{i1} - B}{-CZ_{i1} - A}$$

$$= \frac{DZ_{i1} + B}{CZ_{i1} + A} \qquad \text{...(12.14)}$$

Solving Eqs (12.13) and (12.14),

$$Z_{i1} = \sqrt{\frac{AB}{CD}}$$

$$Z_{i2} = \sqrt{\frac{BD}{AC}}$$

The image impedances $Z_{i1}$ and $Z_{i2}$ do not define a network completely. A third parameter image transfer constant $\phi$ is also used to define the network. $\phi$ can also be expressed in terms of *ABCD* parameters. Let the network be terminated in impedance $Z_{i2}$ at port 2.

$$V_2 = -Z_{i2}\, I_2$$

$$V_1 = AV_2 - B\,I_2 = AV_2 - B\left(\frac{V_2}{-Z_{i2}}\right) = \left(A + \frac{B}{Z_{i2}}\right)V_2$$

$$I_1 = C\,V_2 - D\,I_2 = -C\,Z_{i2}\,I_2 - D\,I_2 = -(C\,Z_{i2} + D)I_2$$

$$\frac{V_1}{V_2} = A + \frac{B}{Z_{i2}} = A + B\sqrt{\frac{AC}{BD}} = A + \frac{\sqrt{ABCD}}{D} = \frac{AD + \sqrt{ABCD}}{D}$$

$$-\frac{I_1}{I_2} = C\,Z_{i2} + D = C\sqrt{\frac{BD}{AC}} + D = \frac{\sqrt{ABCD}}{A} + D = \frac{\sqrt{ABCD} + AD}{A} = \frac{AD + \sqrt{ABCD}}{A}$$

Hence,

$$-\frac{V_1}{V_2}\frac{I_1}{I_2} = \frac{(AD + \sqrt{ABCD})^2}{AD} = (\sqrt{AD} + \sqrt{BC})^2$$

$$\sqrt{-\frac{V_1}{V_2}\frac{I_1}{I_2}} = \sqrt{AD} + \sqrt{BC}$$

$$= \sqrt{AD} + \sqrt{AD-1} \qquad (\because AD - BC = 1)$$

$$\text{Let } \sqrt{AD} = \cosh\phi, \quad \text{then } \sqrt{AD-1} = \sinh\phi$$

$$\tanh\phi = \frac{\sqrt{AD-1}}{\sqrt{AD}} = \sqrt{\frac{BC}{AD}}$$

$$\phi = \tanh^{-1}\sqrt{\frac{BC}{AD}}$$

Also,
$$\sqrt{-\frac{V_1}{V_2}\frac{I_1}{I_2}} = \cosh\phi + \sinh\phi = e^{\phi}$$

$$\phi = \log_e\sqrt{-\frac{V_1}{V_2}\frac{I_1}{I_2}} = \frac{1}{2}\log_e\left(-\frac{V_1}{V_2}\frac{I_1}{I_2}\right)$$

### ➤ *Relationship between Image parameters and the Open-circuit and Short-circuit Impedances*

Open and short-circuit impedance parameters can be expressed in terms of *ABCD*-parameters.

$$V_1 = AV_2 - BI_2$$
$$I_1 = CV_2 - DI_2$$

When the output port is open-circuited, i.e., $I_2 = 0$,

$$V_1 = AV_2$$
$$I_1 = CV_2$$

Hence, the impedance measured at input port with output port open-circuited is

$$Z_{oc_1} = \frac{V_1}{I_1} = \frac{A}{C}$$

When the output port is short-circuited, i.e., $V_2 = 0$,

$$V_1 = -BI_2$$
$$I_1 = -DI_2$$

Hence, the impedance measured at input port with output port short-circuited is

$$Z_{sc_1} = \frac{V_1}{I_1} = \frac{B}{D}$$

Similarly, the impedance measured at output port with input port open-circuited and short-circuited are

$$Z_{oc_2} = \frac{D}{C}$$

$$Z_{sc_2} = \frac{B}{A}$$

The ratio of short-circuit to open-circuit impedance at the two ports is

$$\frac{Z_{sc_1}}{Z_{oc_1}} = \frac{Z_{sc_2}}{Z_{oc_2}} = \frac{BC}{AD}$$

The image parameters can also be expressed in terms of open circuit and short-circuit impedances.

$$Z_{i1} = \sqrt{\frac{AB}{CD}} = \sqrt{Z_{oc_1} Z_{sc_1}}$$

$$Z_{i2} = \sqrt{\frac{BD}{AC}} = \sqrt{Z_{oc_2} Z_{sc_2}}$$

$$\phi = \tanh^{-1}\sqrt{\frac{BC}{AD}} = \tanh^{-1}\sqrt{\frac{Z_{sc_1}}{Z_{oc_1}}} = \tanh^{-1}\sqrt{\frac{Z_{sc_2}}{Z_{oc_2}}}$$

## EXAMPLE 12.65

*The ABCD-parameters of a two-port network are given as,* $A = \frac{6}{5}, B = \frac{17}{5}, C = \frac{1}{5}, D = \frac{7}{5}$. *Find the image parameters.*

**Solution**

$$Z_{i1} = \sqrt{\frac{AB}{CD}} = \sqrt{\frac{\left(\frac{6}{5}\right)\left(\frac{17}{5}\right)}{\left(\frac{1}{5}\right)\left(\frac{7}{5}\right)}} = 3.82\ \Omega$$

$$Z_{i2} = \sqrt{\frac{BD}{AC}} = \sqrt{\frac{\left(\frac{17}{5}\right)\left(\frac{7}{5}\right)}{\left(\frac{6}{5}\right)\left(\frac{1}{5}\right)}} = 4.45\ \Omega$$

$$\phi = \tanh^{-1}\sqrt{\frac{BC}{AD}} = \tanh^{-1}\sqrt{\frac{\left(\frac{17}{5}\right)\left(\frac{1}{5}\right)}{\left(\frac{6}{5}\right)\left(\frac{7}{5}\right)}} = \tanh^{-1}\sqrt{\frac{17}{42}} = 0.75°$$

## EXAMPLE 12.66

*Find the image parameters of the network shown in Fig. 12.130.*

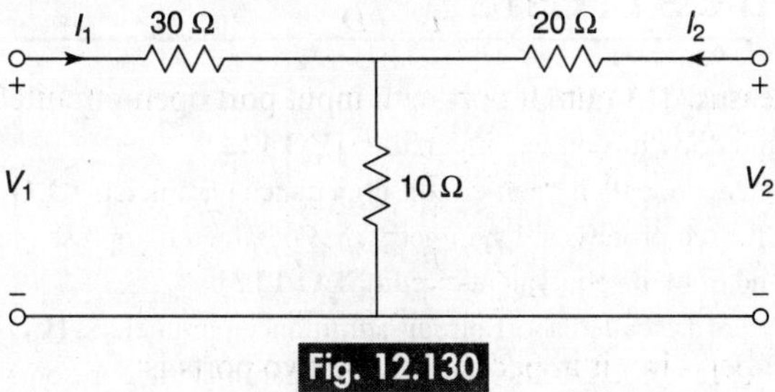


Fig. 12.130

**Solution**

$$Z_{oc_1} = 30 + 10 = 40\ \Omega$$

$$Z_{sc_1} = 30 + \frac{10 \times 20}{10 + 20} = 36.67\ \Omega$$

$$Z_{i1} = \sqrt{Z_{oc_1}\ Z_{sc_1}} = \sqrt{40 \times 36.67} = 38.3\ \Omega$$

$$Z_{oc_2} = 20+10 = 30\ \Omega$$
$$Z_{sc_2} = 20+\frac{10\times 30}{10+30} = 27.5\ \Omega$$
$$Z_{i2} = \sqrt{Z_{oc_2}\ Z_{sc_2}} = \sqrt{30\times 27.5} = 28.72\ \Omega$$
$$\phi = \tanh^{-1}\sqrt{\frac{Z_{sc_1}}{Z_{oc_1}}} = \tanh^{-1}\sqrt{\frac{36.67}{40}} = 1.91°$$

## EXAMPLE 12.67

●○○

*Find image parameters for the lattice two-port network shown in Fig. 12.131.*

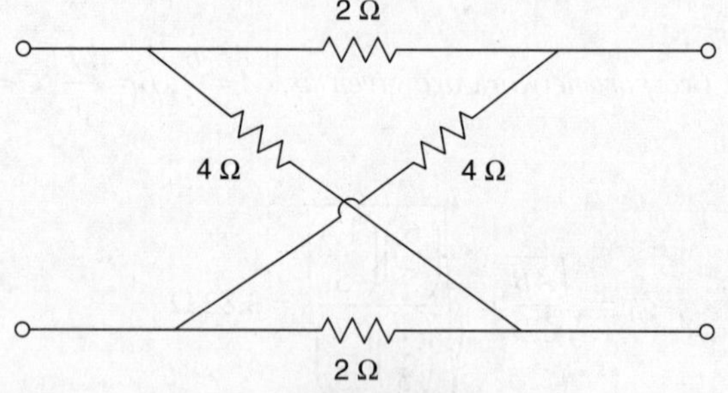


Fig. 12.131

**Solution** The network is redrawn, as shown in Fig. 12.132.

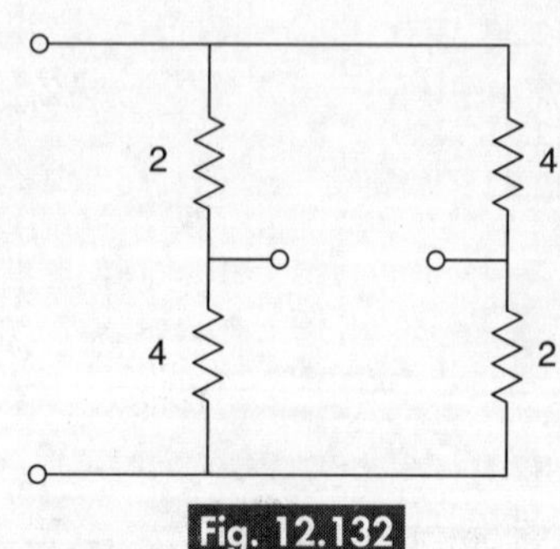


Fig. 12.132

$$Z_{oc_1} = Z_{oc_2} = (2+4)\,||\,(2+4) = 3\ \Omega$$
$$Z_{sc_1} = Z_{sc_2} = (2\,||\,4)+(2\,||\,4) = 2.67\ \Omega$$
$$Z_{i1} = \sqrt{Z_{oc_1}\ Z_{sc_1}} = \sqrt{(3)(2.67)} = 2.83\ \Omega$$
$$Z_{i2} = \sqrt{Z_{oc_2}\ Z_{sc_2}} = \sqrt{(3)(2.67)} = 2.83\ \Omega$$
$$\phi = \tanh^{-1}\sqrt{\frac{Z_{sc_1}}{Z_{oc_1}}} = \tanh^{-1}\sqrt{\frac{2.67}{3}} = 1.76°$$

# Theory Questions

**12.1** What is a two-port network? **[LO 12.1]** ●○○

**12.2** Define $Z$ parameters and draw its equivalent circuits. **[LO 12.2]** ●○○

**12.3** Explain why $Z$ parameters are called open-circuit impedance parameters. **[LO 12.2]** ●○○

**12.4** Derive the conditions for reciprocity and symmetry in $Z$ parameters representation. **[LO 12.2]** ○○●

**12.5** Define $Y$ parameters and draw its equivalent circuit. **[LO 12.3]** ●○○

**12.6** Explain why $Y$ parameters are called short-circuit admittance parameters. **[LO 12.3]** ●○○

**12.7** Derive the conditions for reciprocity and symmetry in $Y$ parameters representation. **[LO 12.3]** ○○●

**12.8** Define transmission parameters. Why *ABCD*-parameters are called transmission parameters? **[LO 12.4]** ●○○

**12.9** Derive the conditions for reciprocity and symmetry in transmission parameters presentation. **[LO 12.4]** ○○●

**12.10** Define inverse transmission parameters. **[LO 12.4]** ●○○

**12.11** Derive the conditions for reciprocity and symmetry in inverse transmission parameters presentation. **[LO 12.4]** ○○●

**12.12** Define $h$ parameters and draw its equivalent circuit. **[LO 12.5]** ●○○

**12.13** Why $h$ parameters are called hybrid parameters? **[LO 12.5]** ●○○

**12.14** Derive the conditions for reciprocity and symmetry in $h$ parameters presentation. **[LO 12.5]** ○○●

**12.15** Define inverse hybrid parameters and draw its equivalent circuit. **[LO 12.5]** ●○○

**12.16** Derive the conditions for reciprocity and symmetry in inverse hybrid parameters presentation. **[LO 12.5]** ○○●

**12.17** Express $Z$ parameters in terms of $Y$, $ABCD$, $h$, $g$ and $A'B'C'D'$ parameters. **[LO 12.6]** ○●○

**12.18** Express $Y$ parameters in terms of $Z$, $ABCD$, $h$, $g$ and $A'B'C'D'$ parameters. **[LO 12.6]** ○●○

**12.19** Obtain $ABCD$-parameters in terms of $Z$, $Y$ and $h$ parameters. **[LO 12.6]** ○●○

**12.20** Obtain $h$ parameters in terms of $Z$, $Y$ and $ABCD$ parameters. **[LO 12.6]** ○●○

**12.21** Obtain transmission parameters when two transmission networks having the transmission parameters $A_1$, $B_1$, $C_1$, $D_1$ and $A_2$, $B_2$, $C_2$, $D_2$ are connected in cascade. **[LO 12.7]** ○●○

**12.22** Derive expressions for impedance parameters of 2 two-port networks connected in series. **[LO 12.7]** ○●○

**12.23** Derive expressions for admittance parameters of 2 two-port networks connected in parallel. **[LO 12.7]** ○●○

**12.24** Write short-note of series–parallel connections of two-port networks. **[LO 12.7]** ○●○

**12.25** Write short-note of parallel–series connections of two-port networks. **[LO 12.7]** ○●○

**12.26** Express $T$-network in terms of $Z$ parameters. **[LO 12.8]** ○●○

**12.27** Express $\pi$-network in terms of $Y$ parameters. **[LO 12.8]** ○●○

**12.28** Express lattice network in terms of $Z$ parameters. **[LO 12.8]** ○○●

**12.29** Find input impedance of a two-port network terminated in load impedance $Z_L$ in terms of $Z$ parameters. **[LO 12.9]** ○○●

**12.30** Find output impedance of a two-port network terminated in load impedance $Z_L$ in terms of $Y$ parameters. **[LO 12.9]** ○○●

**12.31** Derive relationship between image parameters and open-circuit and short-circuit impedances. **[LO 12.10]** ○○●

**12.32** What are image parameters? Express image parameters in terms of $ABCD$ parameters. **[LO 12.10]** ○○●

# Practice Problems

**12.1** Determine $Z$ parameters for the network shown in Fig. 12.133. ○●○

Fig. 12.133

**12.2** Find $Z$ parameters for the network shown in Fig. 12.134. ○○●

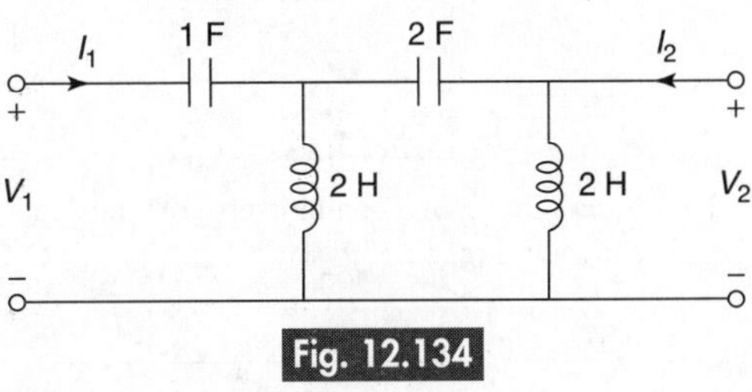


Fig. 12.134

**12.3** Find $Y$ parameters of the network shown in Fig. 12.135. ○●○

Fig. 12.135

**12.4** Find $Y$ parameters for the network shown in Fig. 12.136.

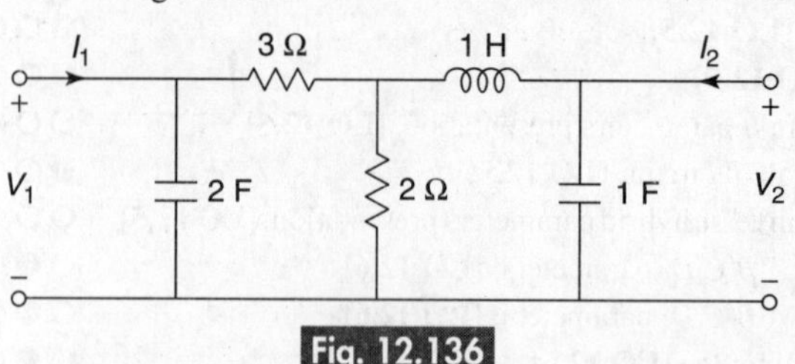

Fig. 12.136

**12.5** Find $Y$ parameters for the network shown in Fig. 12.137.

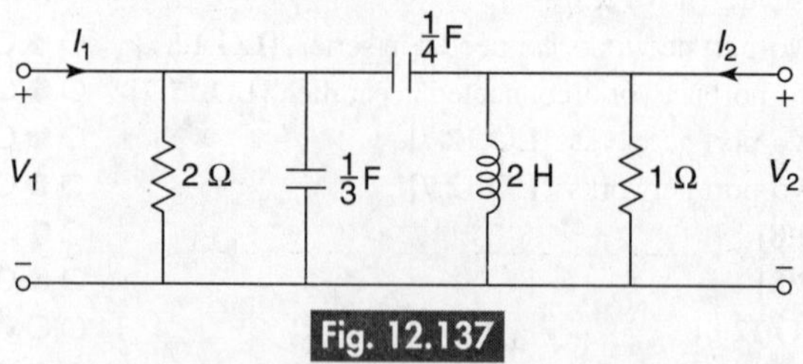

Fig. 12.137

**12.6** Find $Y$ parameters for the network shown in Fig. 12.138.

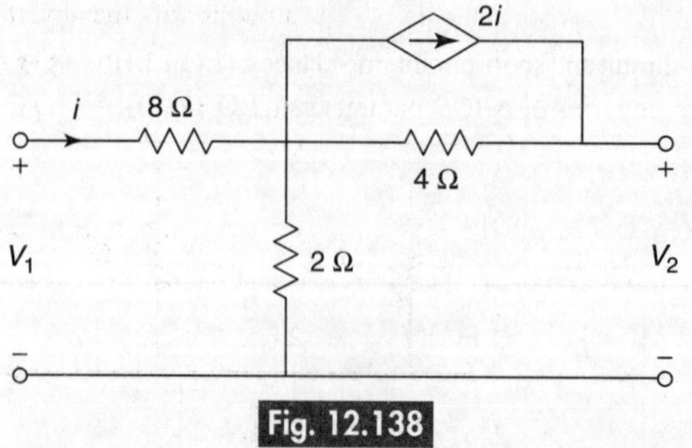

Fig. 12.138

**12.7** Show the *ABCD*-parameters of the network shown in Fig. 12.139.

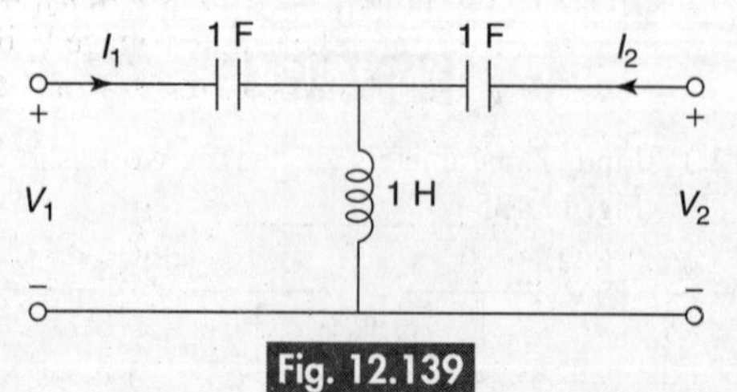

Fig. 12.139

**12.8** Find *ABCD* parameters for the network shown in Fig. 12.140.

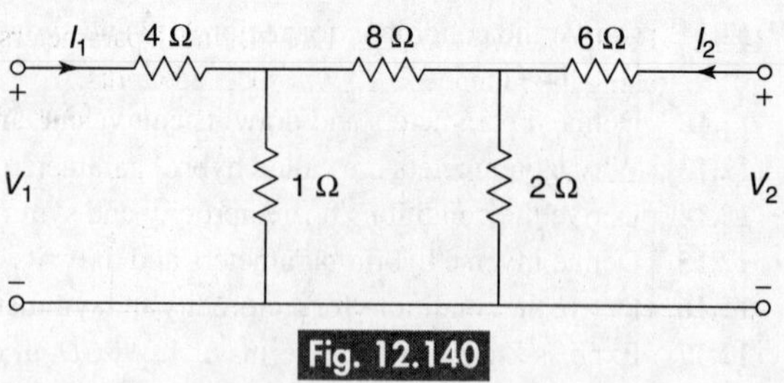

Fig. 12.140

**12.9** For the network shown in Fig. 12.141, determine parameter $h_{21}$.

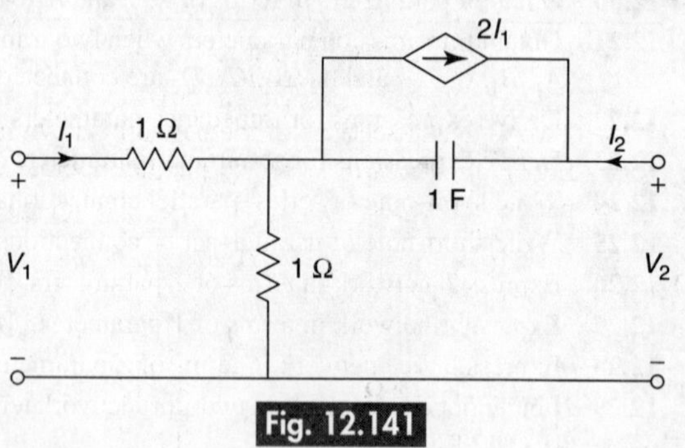

Fig. 12.141

**12.10** Determine $Y$ and $Z$ parameters for the network shown in Fig. 12.142.

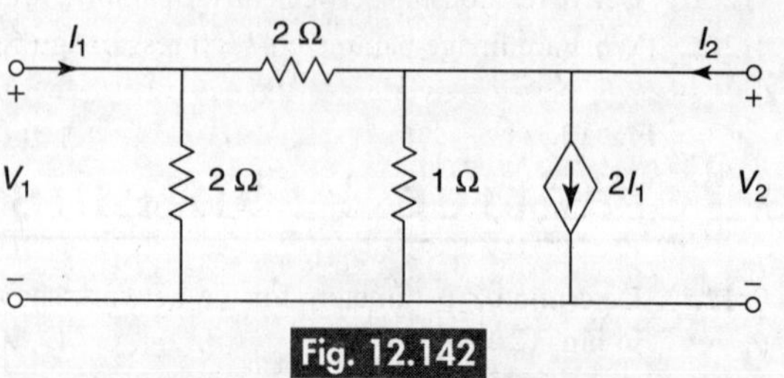

Fig. 12.142

**12.11** For the bridged $T$, $R$-$C$ network shown in Fig. 12.143 determine $Y$ parameters using interconnections of two-port networks.

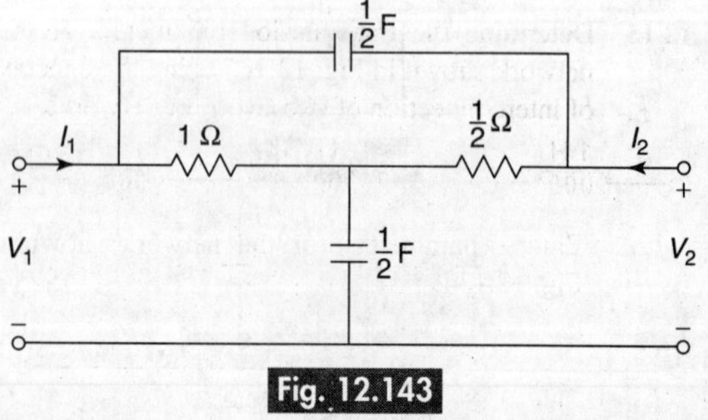

Fig. 12.143

**12.12** For the network of Fig. 12.144, find $Y$ parameters using interconnection of two-port networks.

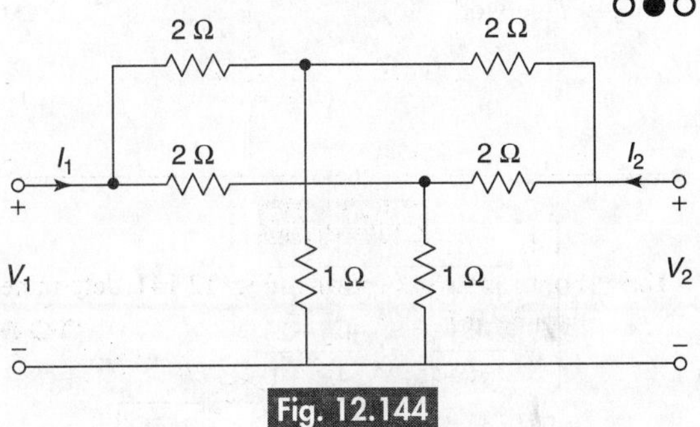


Fig. 12.144

**12.13** Two identical sections of the network shown in Fig. 12.145 are connected in parallel. Obtain $Y$ parameters of the connection.

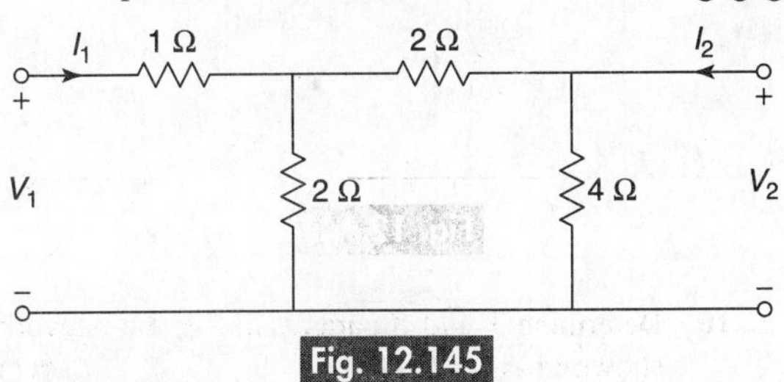


Fig. 12.145

**12.14** Determine $Y$ parameters using interconnection of two-port networks for the network shown in Fig. 12.146.

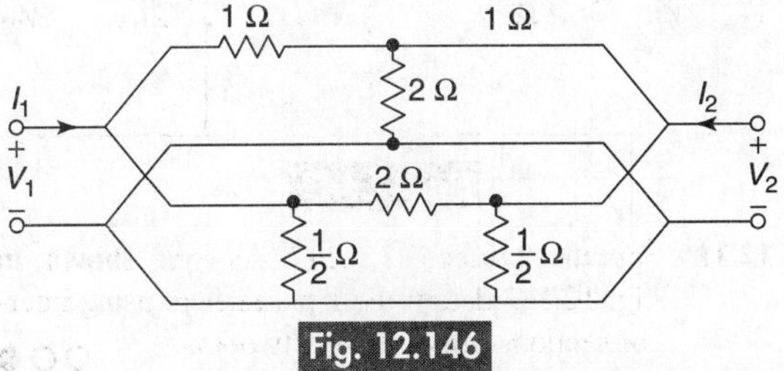


Fig. 12.146

**12.15** Determine the transmission parameters of the network shown in Fig. 12.147 using the concept of interconnection of two two-port networks.

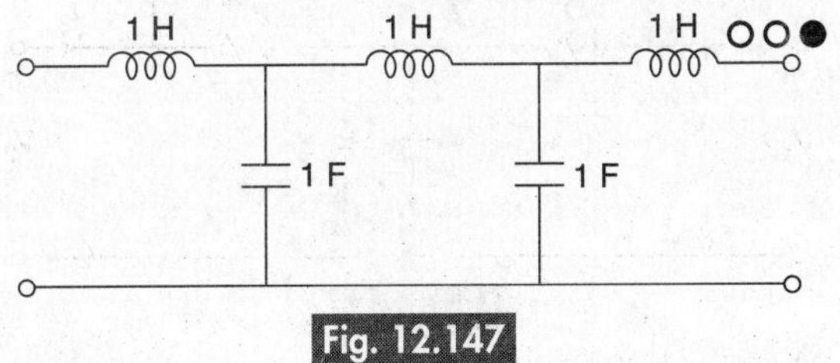


Fig. 12.147

**12.16** Two networks shown in Fig. 12.148 are connected in series. Obtain the $Z$ parameters of the resulting network.

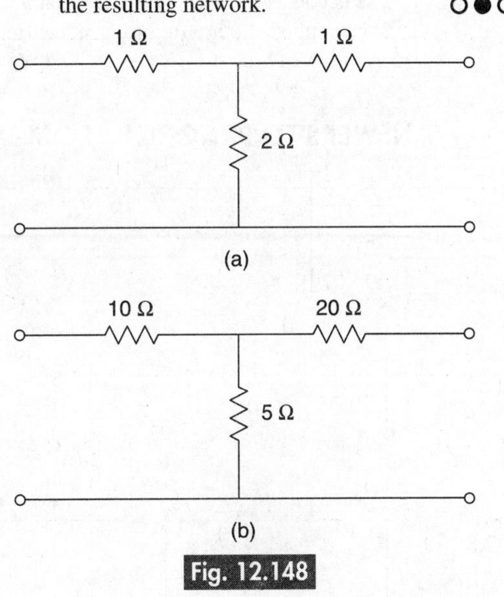


Fig. 12.148

**12.17** Two identical sections of the network shown in Fig. 12.149 are connected in series–parallel. Determine the $h$ parameters of the overall network.

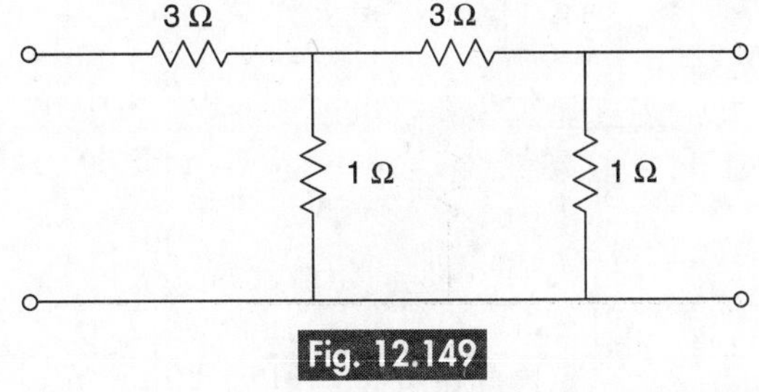


Fig. 12.149

**12.18** The $h$ parameters of a two-port network shown in Fig. 12.150 are $h_{11} = 2\ \Omega$, $h_{12} = 4$, $h_{21} = -5$, $h_{22} = 2\ \mho$. Determine the supply voltage $V_s$ if the power dissipated in the load resistor of 4 Ω is 25 W and $R_s = 2\ \Omega$.

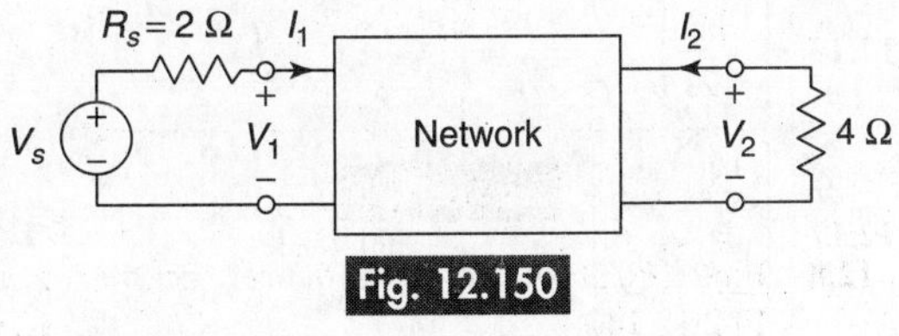


Fig. 12.150

**12.19** The $Z$ parameters of a two-port network are $Z_{11}$ = 2.1 Ω, $Z_{12} = Z_{21}$ = 0.6 Ω, $Z_{22}$ = 1.6 Ω. A resistor of 2 Ω is connected across port 2. What voltage must be applied at port 1 to produce a current of 0.5 A in the 2 Ω resistor. ○●○

**12.20** If a two-port network has $Z_{11}$ = 25 Ω, $Z_{12}$ = $Z_{21}$ = 20 Ω, $Z_{22}$ = 50 Ω, find the equivalent $T$-network. ○●○

## ANSWERS TO PRACTICE PROBLEMS

**12.1** $Z=\begin{bmatrix} \frac{13}{7} & \frac{2}{7} \\ \frac{2}{7} & \frac{3}{7} \end{bmatrix}$

**12.2** $Z=\begin{bmatrix} \frac{4s^4+6s^2+1}{4s^3+s} & \frac{4s^3}{4s^2+1} \\ \frac{4s^3}{4s^2+1} & \frac{4s^3+2s}{4s^2+1} \end{bmatrix}$

**12.3** $Y=\begin{bmatrix} 0.36 & -0.033 \\ -0.033 & -0.36 \end{bmatrix}$

**12.4** $Y=\begin{bmatrix} \frac{10s^2+13s+2}{5s+6} & -\frac{2}{5s+6} \\ -\frac{2}{5s+6} & \frac{5s^2+6s+5}{5s+6} \end{bmatrix}$

**12.5** $Y=\begin{bmatrix} \frac{7s+6}{12} & -\frac{s}{4} \\ -\frac{s}{4} & \frac{s^2+4s+2}{4s} \end{bmatrix}$

**12.6** $Y=\begin{bmatrix} \frac{3}{20} & -\frac{1}{20} \\ -\frac{1}{4} & \frac{1}{4} \end{bmatrix}$

**12.7** $\begin{bmatrix} A & B \\ C & D \end{bmatrix}=\begin{bmatrix} \frac{1+s^2}{s^2} & \frac{1+2s^2}{s^3} \\ \frac{1}{s} & \frac{1+s^2}{s^2} \end{bmatrix}$

**12.8** $\begin{bmatrix} A & B \\ C & D \end{bmatrix}=\begin{bmatrix} 27 & 206 \\ \frac{11}{2} & 42 \end{bmatrix}$

**12.9** $h_{21}=\frac{-(2+s)}{1+s}$

**12.10** $Y_{11}=1\,℧, Y_{12}=-0.5\,℧, Y_{21}=1.5\,℧, Y_{22}=0.5\,℧$

$Z_{11}=\frac{2}{5}\Omega, Z_{12}=\frac{2}{5}\Omega, Z_{21}=-\frac{6}{5}\Omega, Z_{22}=\frac{4}{5}\Omega$

**12.11** $Y=\begin{bmatrix} \frac{s^2+8s+8}{2(s+6)} & -\frac{(s^2+6s+8)}{2(s+6)} \\ -\frac{(s^2+6s+8)}{2(s+6)} & \frac{s^2+10s+8}{2(s+6)} \end{bmatrix}$

**12.12** $Y=\begin{bmatrix} \frac{3}{4} & -\frac{1}{4} \\ -\frac{1}{4} & \frac{3}{4} \end{bmatrix}$

**12.13** $Y=\begin{bmatrix} 1 & -\frac{1}{2} \\ -\frac{1}{2} & \frac{5}{4} \end{bmatrix}$

**12.14** $Y=\begin{bmatrix} 3.1 & -0.9 \\ -0.9 & 3.1 \end{bmatrix}$

**12.15** $\begin{bmatrix} 1+3s^2+s^4 & 3s+4s^3+s^5 \\ 2s+s^3 & 1+3s^2+s^4 \end{bmatrix}$

**12.16** $\begin{bmatrix} 18 & 7 \\ 7 & 28 \end{bmatrix}$

**12.17** $\begin{bmatrix} \frac{15}{2} & -\frac{1}{2} \\ -\frac{1}{2} & \frac{5}{2} \end{bmatrix}$

**12.18** 58 V

**12.19** 6 V

**12.20** 10 Ω, 30 Ω, 20 Ω

# Objective-Type Questions

## From GATE and Other Competitive Examinations

**12.1** The open-circuit impedance matrix of the two-port network shown in Fig. 12.151 is ○●○

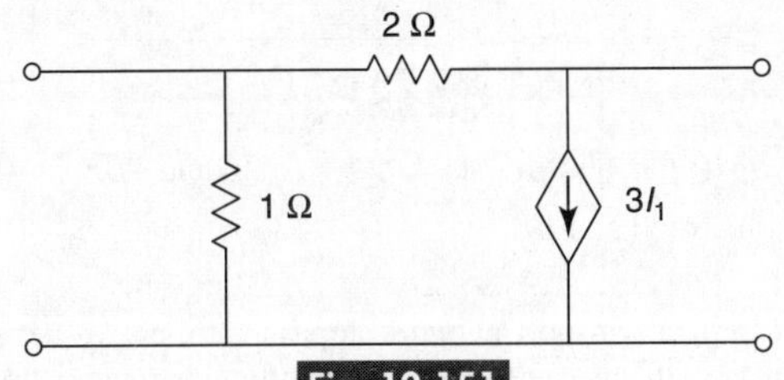


Fig. 12.151

(a) $\begin{bmatrix} -2 & 1 \\ -8 & 3 \end{bmatrix}$ (b) $\begin{bmatrix} -2 & -8 \\ 1 & 3 \end{bmatrix}$

(c) $\begin{bmatrix} 0 & 1 \\ 1 & 0 \end{bmatrix}$ (d) $\begin{bmatrix} 2 & -1 \\ -1 & 3 \end{bmatrix}$

**12.2** Two two-port networks are connected in cascade. The combination is to be represented as a single two-port network. The parameters are obtained by multiplying the individual ●○○

(a) $Z$ parameter matrix
(b) $h$ parameter matrix
(c) $Y$ parameter matrix
(d) $ABCD$-parameter matrix

**12.3** For a two-port network to be reciprocal ●○○

(a) $z_{11} = z_{22}$ (b) $y_{21} = y_{12}$
(c) $h_{21} = h_{12}$ (d) $AD - BC = 0$

**12.4** The short-circuit admittance matrix of a two-port network is $\begin{bmatrix} 0 & -\frac{1}{2} \\ \frac{1}{2} & 0 \end{bmatrix}$. The two-port network is ●○○

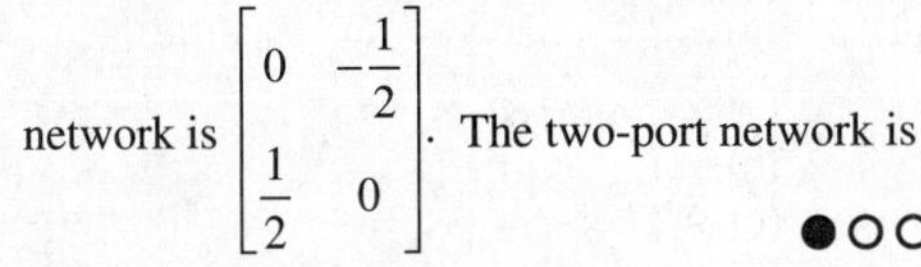

(a) non-reciprocal and passive
(b) non-reciprocal and active
(c) reciprocal and passive
(d) reciprocal and active

**12.5** A two-port network is shown in Fig. 12.152. The parameter $h_{21}$ for this network can be given by ○●○

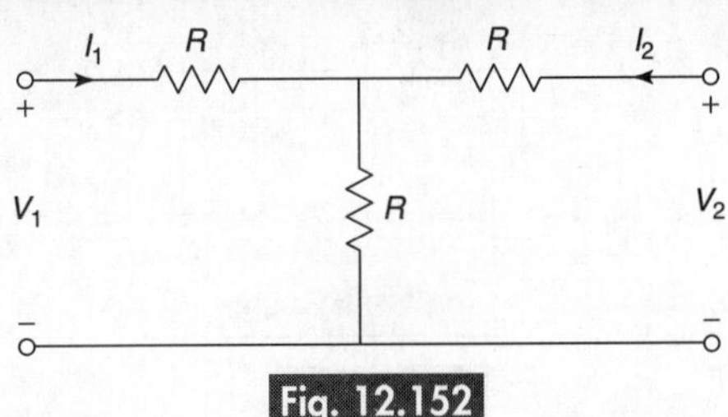


Fig. 12.152

(a) $-\frac{1}{2}$ (b) $\frac{1}{2}$

(c) $-\frac{3}{2}$ (d) $\frac{3}{2}$

**12.6** The admittance parameter $Y_{12}$ in the two-port network in Fig. 12.153 is ○●○

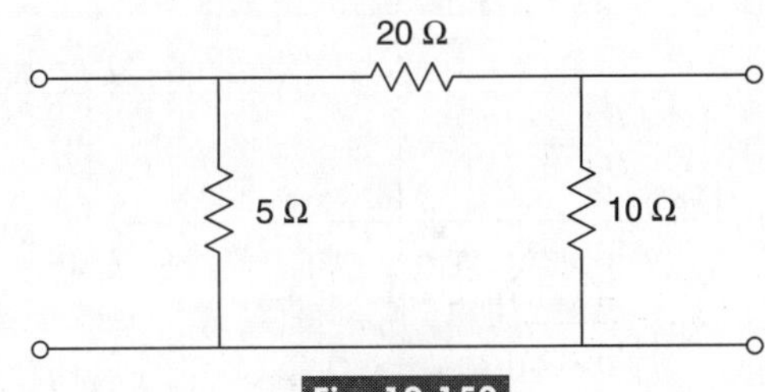


Fig. 12.153

(a) –0.2 mho (b) 0.1 mho
(c) –0.05 mho (d) 0.05 mho

**12.7** The Z parameters $Z_{11}$ and $Z_{21}$ for the two-port network in Fig. 12.154 are ○●○

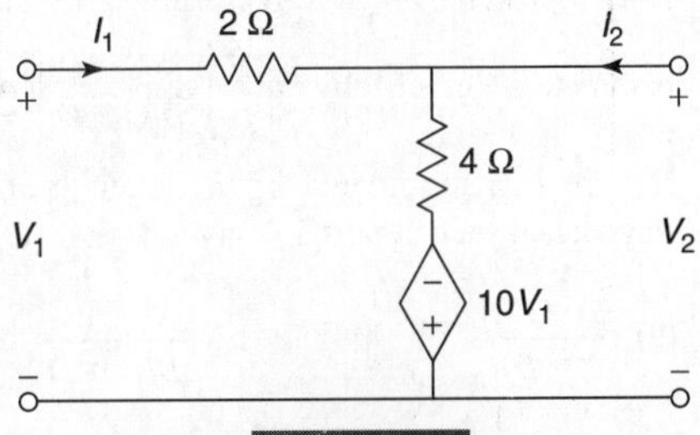


Fig. 12.154

(a) $-\frac{6}{11}\Omega, \frac{16}{11}\Omega$ (b) $\frac{6}{11}\Omega, \frac{4}{11}\Omega$

(c) $\frac{6}{11}\Omega, -\frac{16}{11}\Omega$ (d) $\frac{4}{11}\Omega, \frac{4}{11}\Omega$

**12.8** The impedance parameters $Z_{11}$ and $Z_{12}$ of a two-port network in Fig. 12.155 are ○●○

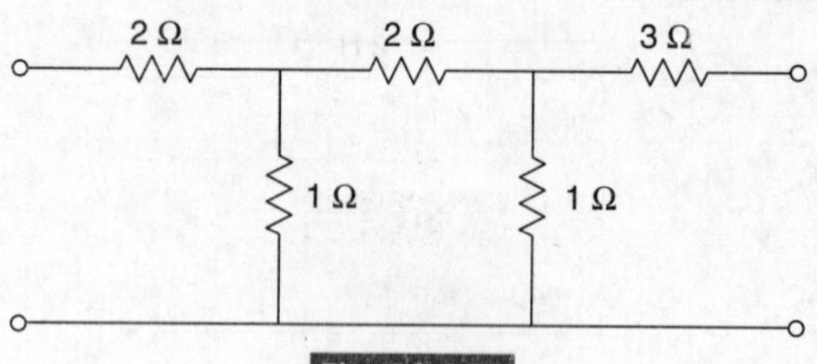


Fig. 12.155

(a) 2.75 Ω, 0.25 Ω (b) 3 Ω, 0.5 Ω
(c) 3 Ω, 0.25 Ω (d) 2.25 Ω, 0.5 Ω

**12.9** The $h$ parameters of the circuit shown in Fig. 12.156 is ○●○

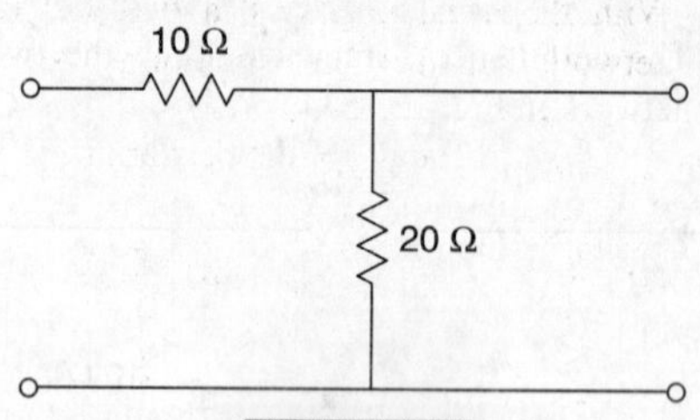


Fig. 12.156

(a) $\begin{bmatrix} 0.1 & 0.1 \\ -0.1 & 0.3 \end{bmatrix}$ (b) $\begin{bmatrix} 10 & -1 \\ 1 & 0.05 \end{bmatrix}$

(c) $\begin{bmatrix} 30 & 20 \\ 20 & 20 \end{bmatrix}$ (d) $\begin{bmatrix} 10 & 1 \\ -1 & 0.05 \end{bmatrix}$

**12.10** A two-port network is represented by $ABCD$ parameters given by $\begin{bmatrix} V_1 \\ I_1 \end{bmatrix} = \begin{bmatrix} A & B \\ C & D \end{bmatrix}\begin{bmatrix} V_2 \\ -I_2 \end{bmatrix}$.
If port 2 is terminated by $R_L$, then the input impedance seen at port 1 is given by ○○●

(a) $\frac{A+BR_L}{C+DR_L}$ (b) $\frac{AR_L+C}{BR_L+D}$

(c) $\frac{DR_L+A}{BR_L+C}$ (d) $\frac{B+AR_L}{D+CR_L}$

**12.11** In the two-port network shown in Fig. 12.157, $Z_{12}$ and $Z_{21}$ are respectively ○●○

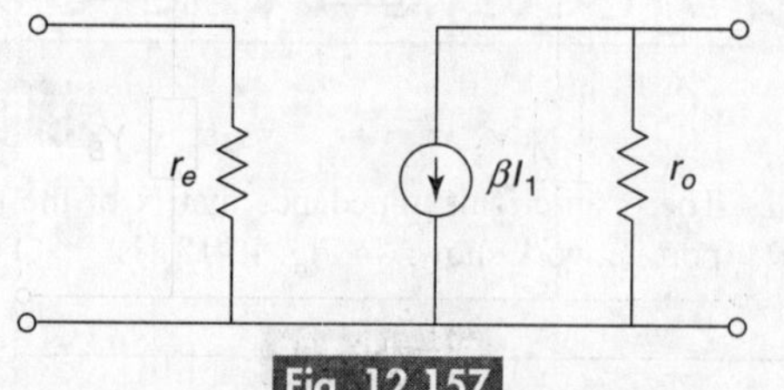


Fig. 12.157

(a) $r_e$ and $\beta r_0$ (b) 0 and $-\beta r_0$
(c) 0 and $\beta r_0$ (d) $r_e$ and $-\beta r_0$

**12.12** If a two-port network is passive, then we have, with the usual notation, the following relationship for symmetrical network ●○○

(a) $h_{12} = h_{21}$ (b) $h_{12} = -h_{21}$
(c) $h_{11} = h_{22}$ (d) $h_{11}h_{22} - h_{12}h_{21} = 1$

**12.13** A two-port network is defined by the following pair of equations $I_1 = 2V_1 + V_2$ and $I_2 = V_1 + V_2$. Its impedance parameters ($Z_{11}, Z_{12}, Z_{21}, Z_{22}$) are given by ●○○

(a) 2, 1, 1, 1 (b) 1, –1, –1, 2
(c) 1, 1, 1, 2 (d) 2, –1, –1, 1

**12.14** A two-port network has transmission parameters $\begin{bmatrix} A & B \\ C & D \end{bmatrix}$. The input impedance of the network at port 1 will be ○●○

(a) $\frac{A}{C}$ (b) $\frac{AD}{BC}$

(c) $\frac{AB}{DC}$ (d) $\frac{D}{C}$

**12.15** A two-port network is symmetrical if ●○○

(a) $Z_{11}Z_{22} - Z_{12}Z_{21} = 1$
(b) $AD - BC = 1$
(c) $h_{11}h_{22} - h_{12}h_{21} = 1$
(d) $Y_{11}Y_{22} - Y_{12}Y_{21} = 1$

**12.16** For the network shown in Fig. 12.158, admittance parameters are $Y_{11} = 8$ mho, $Y_{12} = Y_{21} = -6$ mho and $Y_{22} = 6$ mho. The value of $Y_A$, $Y_B$ and $Y_C$ (in mho) will be respectively ○●○

(a) 2, 6, –6 (b) 2,6,0
(c) 2,0,6 (d) 2,6,8

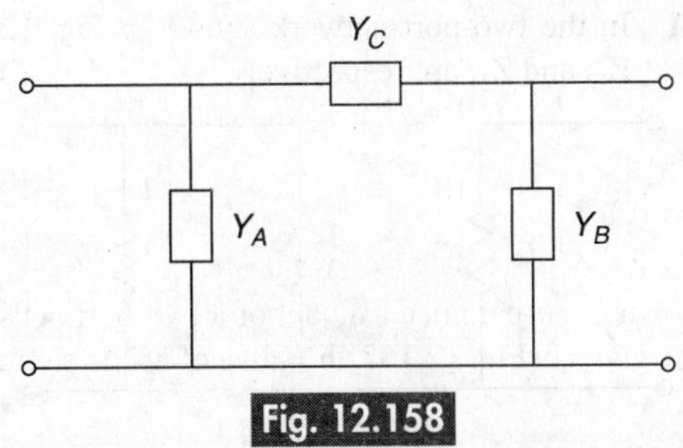

Fig. 12.158

**12.17** The impedance matrices of two two-port networks are given by $\begin{bmatrix} 3 & 2 \\ 2 & 3 \end{bmatrix}$ and $\begin{bmatrix} 15 & 5 \\ 3 & 25 \end{bmatrix}$. If these two networks are connected in series, the impedance matrix of the resulting two-port network will be ●○○

(a) $\begin{bmatrix} 3 & 5 \\ 2 & 25 \end{bmatrix}$ (b) $\begin{bmatrix} 18 & 7 \\ 7 & 28 \end{bmatrix}$

(c) $\begin{bmatrix} 15 & 2 \\ 5 & 3 \end{bmatrix}$ (d) indeterminate

**12.18** If the $\pi$-network and $T$-network are equivalent, then the values of $R_1$, $R_2$ and $R_3$ (in ohms) will be respectively ○●○

(a) 6, 6, 6 (b) 6, 6, 9
(c) 9, 6, 9 (d) 6, 9, 6

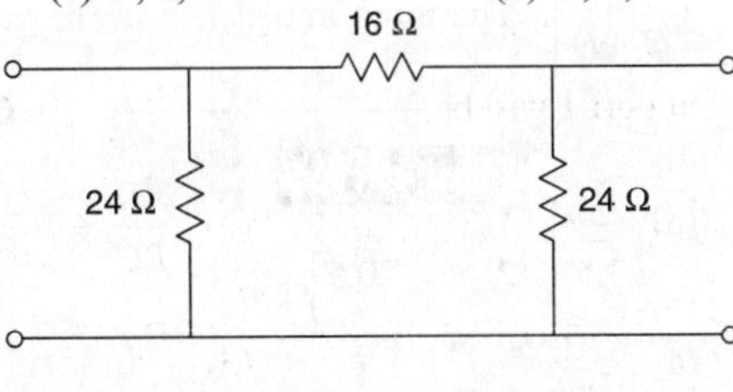


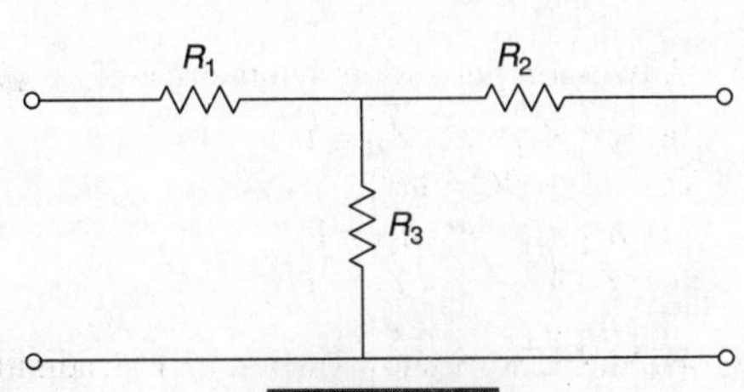

Fig. 12.159

**12.19** For a two-port symmetrical bilateral network, if $A = 3$ and $B = 1$, the value of the parameter $C$ will be ○●○

(a) 4 (b) 6
(c) 8 (d) 16

**12.20** The impedance matrix for the network shown in Fig. 12.160 is ○●○

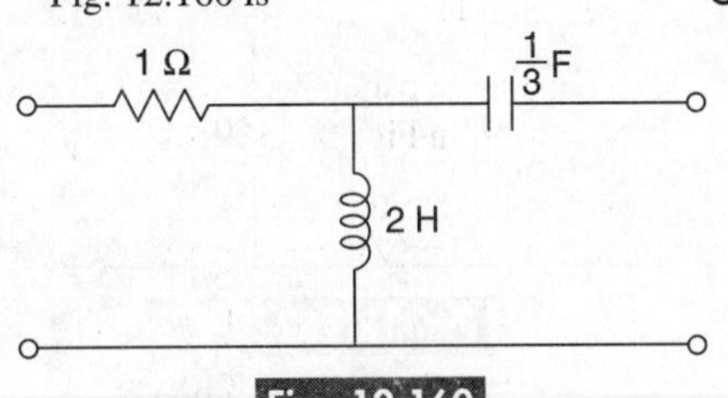

Fig. 12.160

(a) $\begin{bmatrix} 2s+1 & 2s \\ 2s & 2s+\frac{3}{s} \end{bmatrix}$ (b) $\begin{bmatrix} 2s+1 & -2s \\ -2s & 2s+\frac{3}{s} \end{bmatrix}$

(c) $\begin{bmatrix} 2s+1 & 2s \\ -2s & 2s+\frac{3}{s} \end{bmatrix}$ (d) $\begin{bmatrix} 2s+\frac{3}{2} & -2s \\ 2s & 2s+\frac{3}{s} \end{bmatrix}$

**12.21** With the usual notations, a two-port resistive network satisfies the conditions $A = D = \frac{3}{2}B = \frac{4}{3}C$. The $Z_{11}$ of the network is ○●○

(a) $\frac{5}{3}$ (b) $\frac{4}{3}$

(c) $\frac{2}{3}$ (d) $\frac{1}{3}$

**12.22** In the circuit shown in Fig. 12.161, the network N is described by the following $Y$ matrix:

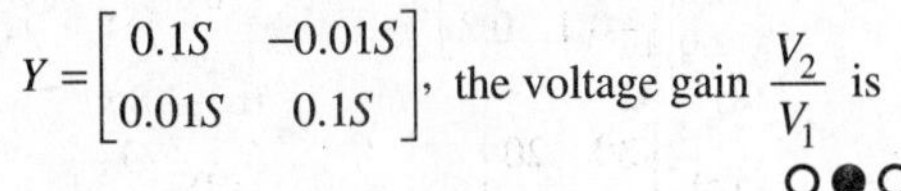

$$Y = \begin{bmatrix} 0.1S & -0.01S \\ 0.01S & 0.1S \end{bmatrix},$$ the voltage gain $\frac{V_2}{V_1}$ is ○●○

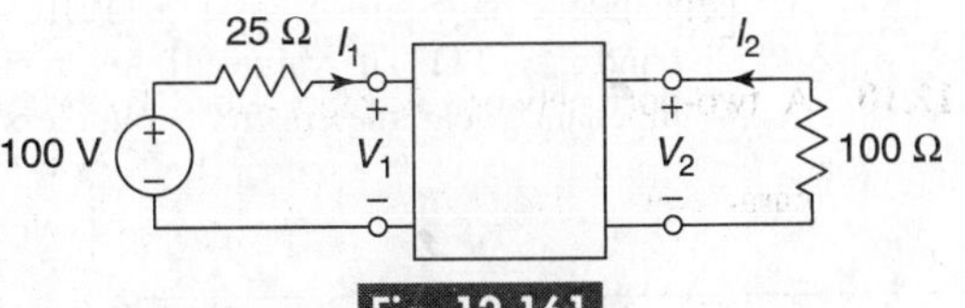

Fig. 12.161

(a) $\frac{1}{90}$ (b) $-\frac{1}{90}$

(c) $-\frac{1}{99}$ (d) $-\frac{1}{11}$

**12.23** For the two-port network shown in Fig. 12.162 the short-circuit admittance parameter matrix is: ○●○

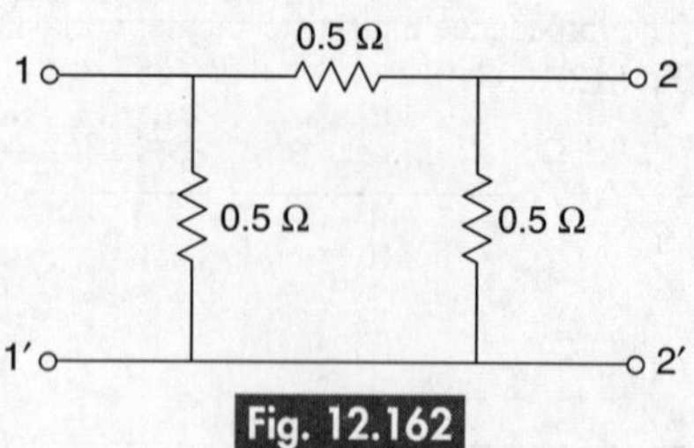

Fig. 12.162

(a) $\begin{bmatrix} 4 & -2 \\ -2 & 4 \end{bmatrix}$ (b) $\begin{bmatrix} 1 & -0.5 \\ -0.5 & 1 \end{bmatrix}$

(c) $\begin{bmatrix} 1 & 0.5 \\ 0.5 & 1 \end{bmatrix}$ (d) $\begin{bmatrix} 4 & 2 \\ 2 & 4 \end{bmatrix}$

**12.24** The *ABCD* matrix for a two-port network is defined by

$$\begin{bmatrix} V_1 \\ I_1 \end{bmatrix} = \begin{bmatrix} A & B \\ C & D \end{bmatrix} \begin{bmatrix} V_2 \\ -I_2 \end{bmatrix}$$

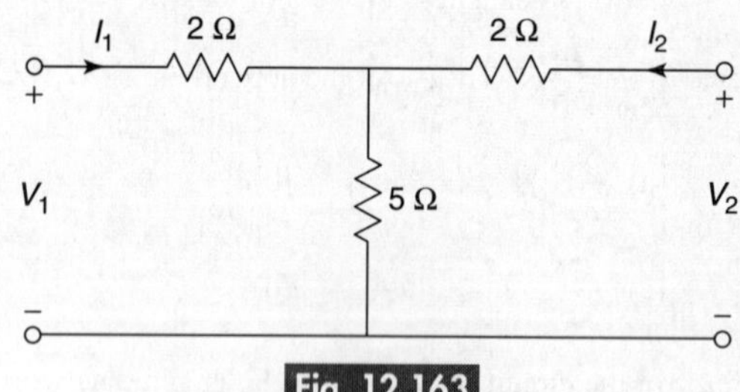

Fig. 12.163

The parameter *B* for the given two-port network (in ohms) is ○●○

(a) 3 Ω (b) 4.8 Ω
(c) 2 Ω (d) 4 Ω

**12.25** For the lattice circuit shown in Fig. 12.164, $Z_a = j2\ \Omega$ and $Z_b = 2\ \Omega$. The values of the open-circuit impedance parameters (*Z*-parameters) are: ○●○

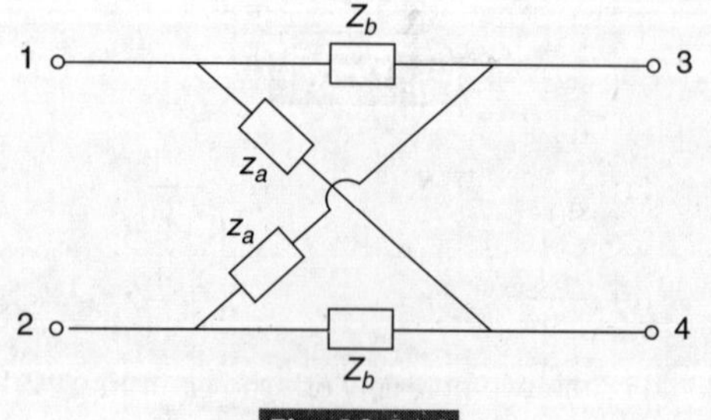

Fig. 12.164

(a) $\begin{bmatrix} 1-j & 1+j \\ 1+j & 1+j \end{bmatrix}$ (b) $\begin{bmatrix} 1-j & 1+j \\ -1+j & 1-j \end{bmatrix}$

(c) $\begin{bmatrix} 1+j & 1+j \\ 1-j & 1-j \end{bmatrix}$ (d) $\begin{bmatrix} 1+j & -1+j \\ -1+j & 1+j \end{bmatrix}$

**12.26** In the *h*-parameter model of a two-port network given in Fig. 12.165, the value of $h_{22}$ (in siemens) is ○●○

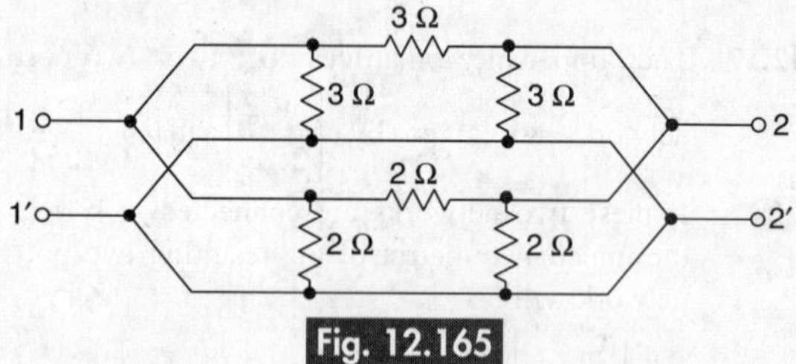

Fig. 12.165

(a) 2.5 (b) 25
(c) 1.24 (d) 0.25

**12.27** The *ABCD*-parameters of the following two-port network are: ○●○

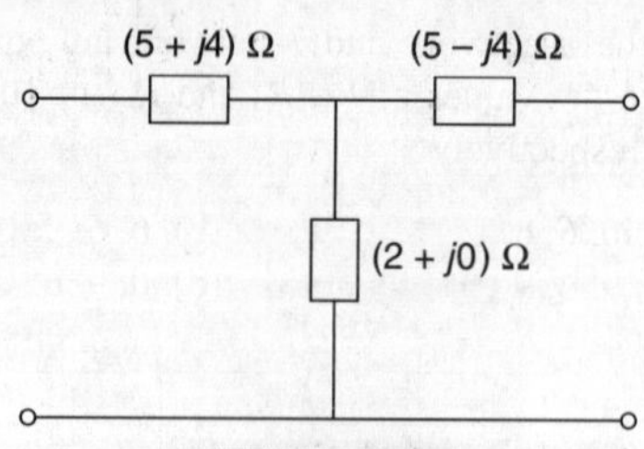

Fig. 12.166

(a) $\begin{bmatrix} 3.5+j2 & 20.5 \\ 20.5 & 3.5-j2 \end{bmatrix}$

(b) $\begin{bmatrix} 3.5+j2 & 0.5 \\ 0.5 & 3.5-j2 \end{bmatrix}$

(c) $\begin{bmatrix} 10 & 2+j0 \\ 2+j0 & 10 \end{bmatrix}$

(d) $\begin{bmatrix} 7+j4 & 0.5 \\ 0.5 & 7-j4 \end{bmatrix}$

**12.28** The two-port admittance matrix of the circuit shown in Fig. 12.167 is given by: ○●○

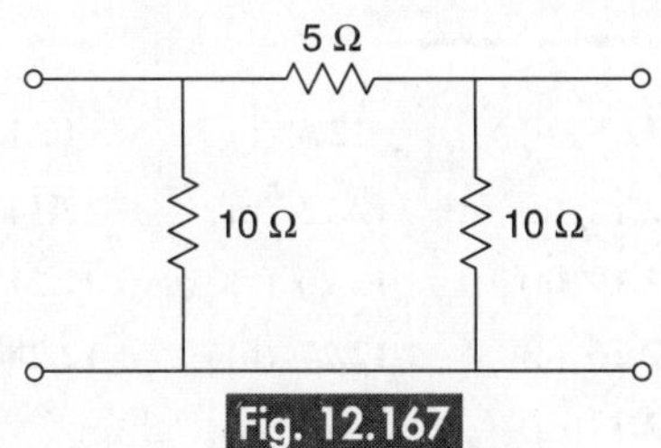

Fig. 12.167

(a) $\begin{bmatrix} 0.3 & -0.2 \\ -0.2 & 0.3 \end{bmatrix}$ (b) $\begin{bmatrix} 15 & 5 \\ 5 & 15 \end{bmatrix}$

(c) $\begin{bmatrix} 3.33 & 5 \\ 5 & 3.33 \end{bmatrix}$ (d) $\begin{bmatrix} 0.3 & 0.4 \\ 0.4 & 0.3 \end{bmatrix}$

**12.29** A two-port network shown in Fig. 12.168 is excited by external dc source. The voltage and the current are measured with voltmeters $V_1$, $V_2$ and ammeters. $A_1$, $A_2$, (all assumed to be ideal) as indicated

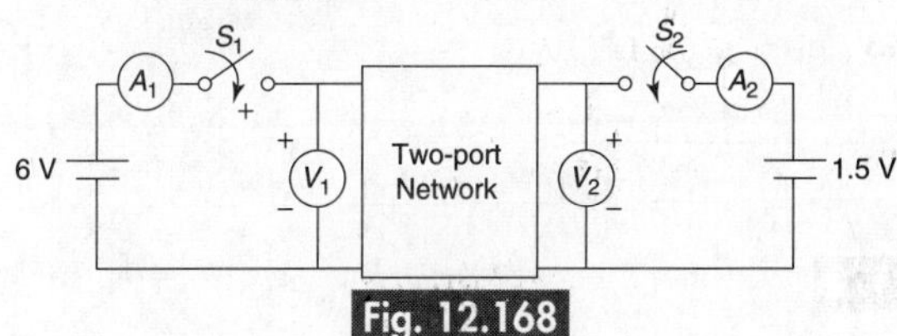

Fig. 12.168

Under following conditions, the readings obtained are

(1) $S_1$-open, $S_2$-closed, $A_1 = 0$, $V_1 = 4.5$ V, $V_2 = 1.5$ V, $A_2 = 1$ A

(2) $S_1$-open, $S_2$-closed, $A_1 = 4$ A, $V_1 = 6$ V, $V_2 = 6$ V, $A_2 = 0$

The $Z$-parameter matrix for this network is ○○●

(a) $\begin{bmatrix} 1.5 & 1.5 \\ 4.5 & 1.5 \end{bmatrix}$ (b) $\begin{bmatrix} 1.5 & 4.5 \\ 1.5 & 4.5 \end{bmatrix}$

(c) $\begin{bmatrix} 1.5 & 4.5 \\ 1.5 & 1.5 \end{bmatrix}$ (d) $\begin{bmatrix} 4.5 & 1.5 \\ 1.5 & 4.5 \end{bmatrix}$

**12.30** For the two-port network shown in Fig. 12.169, the impedance ($Z$) matrix (in Ω) is ○●○

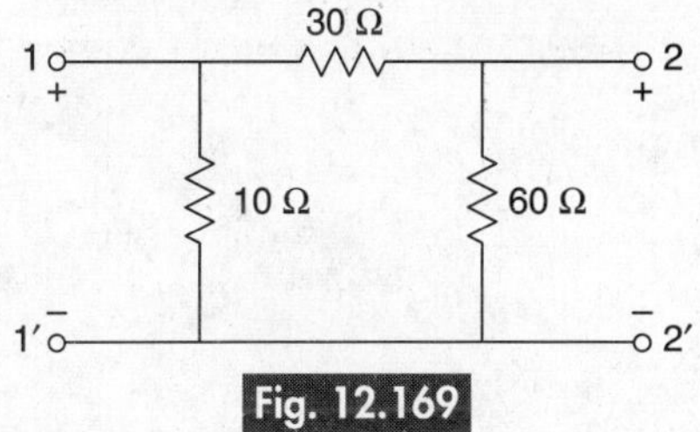

Fig. 12.169

(a) $\begin{bmatrix} 6 & 24 \\ 42 & 9 \end{bmatrix}$ (b) $\begin{bmatrix} 9 & 8 \\ 8 & 24 \end{bmatrix}$

(c) $\begin{bmatrix} 9 & 6 \\ 6 & 24 \end{bmatrix}$ (d) $\begin{bmatrix} 42 & 6 \\ 6 & 60 \end{bmatrix}$

**12.31** Consider a two-port network with the transmission matrix $T = \begin{bmatrix} A & B \\ C & D \end{bmatrix}$. If the network is reciprocal then ●○○

(a) $T^{-1} = T$ (b) $T^2 = T$

(c) Determinant $(T) = 0$

(d) Determinant $(T) = 1$

**12.32** The $Z$-parameter matrix for the two-port network shown in Fig. 12.170 is $\begin{bmatrix} 2j\omega & j\omega \\ j\omega & 3+2j\omega \end{bmatrix}$, where the entries are in Ω. Suppose $Z_b(j\omega) = R_b + j\omega$. Then the value of $R_b$ (in Ω) equals ○●○

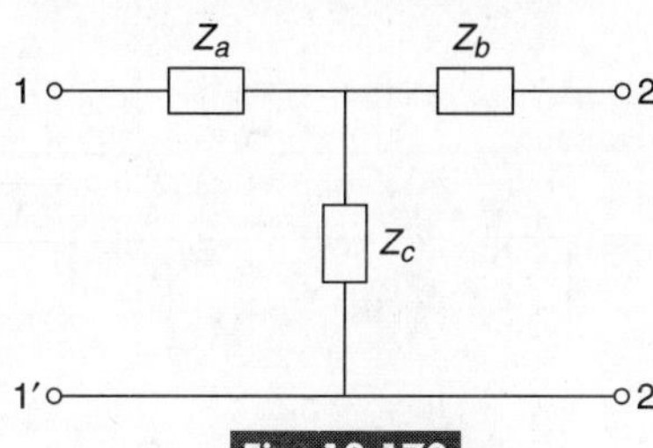

Fig. 12.170

(a) 3 (b) 2

(c) 1 (d) 4

**12.33** The $Z$-parameter matrix $\begin{bmatrix} Z_{11} & Z_{12} \\ Z_{21} & Z_{22} \end{bmatrix}$ for the two-port network shown in Fig. 12.171 is ○●○

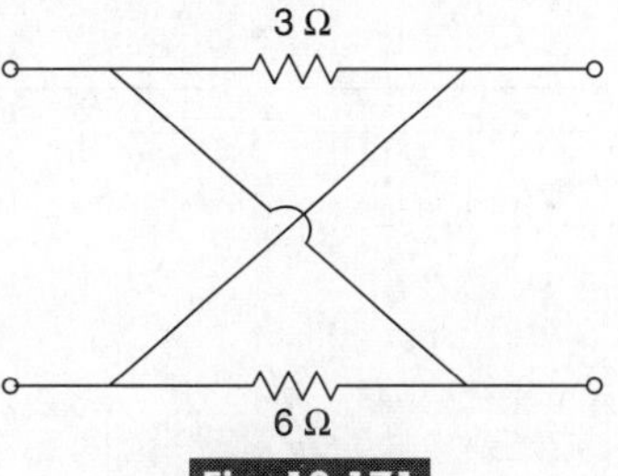

Fig. 12.171

(a) $\begin{bmatrix} 2 & -2 \\ -2 & 2 \end{bmatrix}$ (b) $\begin{bmatrix} 9 & -3 \\ 6 & 9 \end{bmatrix}$

(c) $\begin{bmatrix} 2 & 2 \\ 2 & 2 \end{bmatrix}$ (d) $\begin{bmatrix} 9 & 3 \\ 6 & 9 \end{bmatrix}$

## ANSWERS TO OBJECTIVE-TYPE QUESTIONS

| | | | | | | |
|---|---|---|---|---|---|---|
| **12.1** (a) | **12.2** (d) | **12.3** (b) | **12.4** (b) | **12.5** (a) | **12.6** (c) | **12.7** (c) |
| **12.8** (a) | **12.9** (d) | **12.10** (d) | **12.11** (b) | **12.12** (d) | **12.13** (b) | **12.14** (a) |
| **12.15** (c) | **12.16** (c) | **12.17** (b) | **12.18** (a) | **12.19** (c) | **12.20** (a) | **12.21** (b) |
| **12.22** (d) | **12.23** (a) | **12.24** (b) | **12.25** (d) | **12.26** (c) | **12.27** (b) | **12.28** (a) |
| **12.29** (c) | **12.30** (c) | **12.31** (c) | **12.32** (a) | **12.33** (a) | | |

# LTspice Section

## EXAMPLE 12.1

*Find Z parameters to the network shown in Fig. 12.172.*

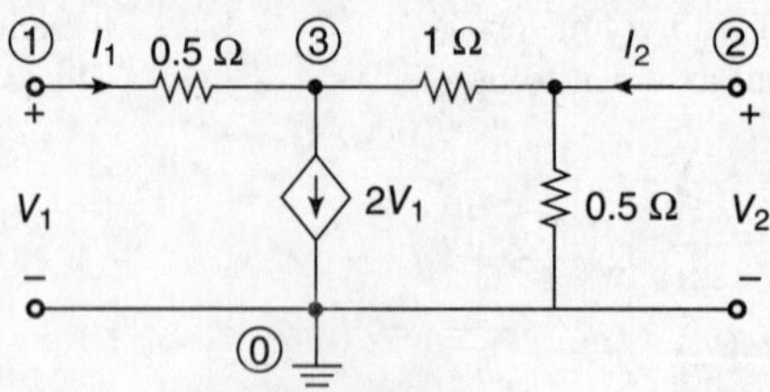


Fig. 12.172

**Solution**

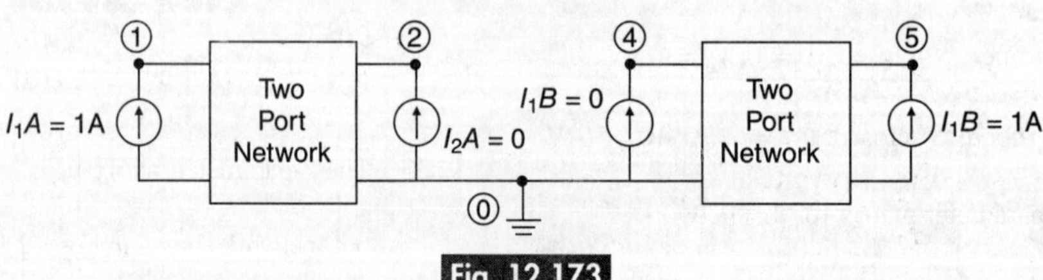


Fig. 12.173

```
* Calculation of Z parameters

.SUBCKT TWOPORT 1 2
R1 1 3 0.5
R2 3 2 1
R3 2 0 0.5
G 3 0 1 0 2
.ENDS
I1A 0 1 1
I2A 0 2 0
I1B 0 4 0
I2B 0 5 1
X1 1 2 TWOPORT
X2 4 5 TWOPORT
.OP
.END
```

```
                    Operating Point
V(1):                   0.5                      voltage
V(2):                   0                        voltage
V(4):                   0.125                    voltage
V(5):                   0.375                    voltage
I(I2b):                 1                        device_current
I(I1b):                 0                        device_current
I(I2a):                 0                        device_current
I(I1a):                 1                        device_current
Ix(1:1):                1                        subckt_current
Ix(1:2):                0                        subckt_current
Ix(2:1):                0                        subckt_current
Ix(2:2):                1                        subckt_current
```

**Result**

Subcircuit 1 is with the output port open circuited i.e., $I_2A = 0$.

$$V_1 = V(1) = 0.5 \text{ V}$$

$$V_2 = V(2) = 0$$

$$I_1 = I(I1a) = 1 \text{ A}$$

$$Z_{11} = \frac{V_1}{I_1} = \frac{0.5}{1} = 0.5\ \Omega$$

$$Z_{21} = \frac{V_2}{I_1} = \frac{0}{1} = 0$$

Subcircuit 2 is with the input port open-circuited i.e., $I_1B = 0$.

$$V_1 = V(4) = 0.125 \text{ V}$$

$$V_2 = V(5) = 0.375 \text{ V}$$

$$I_2 = I(I2b) = 1 \text{ A}$$

$$Z_{12} = \frac{V_1}{I_2} = \frac{0.125}{1} = 0.125\ \Omega$$

$$Z_{22} = \frac{V_2}{I_2} = \frac{0.375}{1} = 0.375\ \Omega$$

Hence, $Z$ parameters are

$$\begin{bmatrix} Z_{11} & Z_{12} \\ Z_{21} & Z_{22} \end{bmatrix} = \begin{bmatrix} 0.5 & 0.125 \\ 0 & 0.375 \end{bmatrix}$$

**EXAMPLE 12.2**

*Find Y parameters of the network shown in Fig. 12.174.*

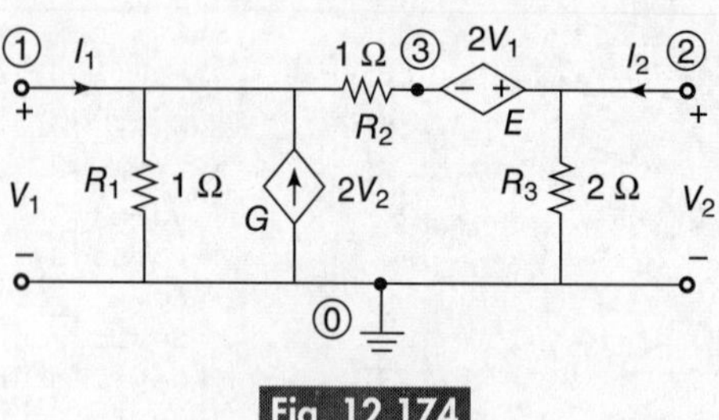


Fig. 12.174

**Solution**

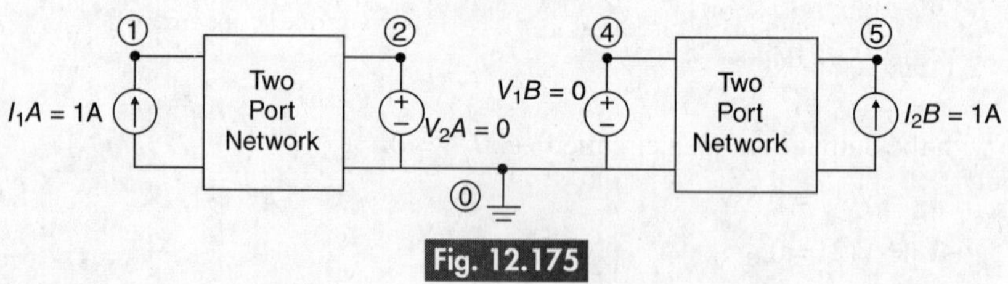


Fig. 12.175

```
* Calculation of Y parameters

.SUBCKT TWOPORT 1 2
R1 1 0 1
R2 1 3 1
R3 2 0 2
G 0 1 2 0 2
E 2 3 1 0 2
.ENDS
I1A 0 1 1
V2A 2 0 0
V1B 4 0 0
I2B 0 5 1
X1 1 2 TWOPORT
X2 4 5 TWOPORT
.OP
.END
```

```
                    Operating Point
V(1):                    0.25               voltage
V(2):                    0                  voltage
V(4):                    0                  voltage
V(5):                    0.666667           voltage
I(I2b):                  1                  device_current
I(I1a):                  1                  device_current
I(V1b):                  2                  device_current
I(V2a):                  0.75               device_current
Ix(1:1):                 1                  subckt_current
Ix(1:2):                -0.75               subckt_current
Ix(2:1):                -2                  subckt_current
Ix(2:2):                 1                  subckt_current
```

**Result**

Subcircuit 1 is with the output port short-circuited i.e., $V_2A = 0$.

$$V_1 = V(1) = 0.25\text{ V}$$
$$I_1 = I(I1a) = 1\text{ A}$$
$$I_2 = -I(V2a) = -0.75\text{ A}$$
$$Y_{11} = \frac{I_1}{V_1} = \frac{1}{0.25} = 4\ \mho$$
$$Y_{21} = \frac{I_2}{V_1} = \frac{-0.75}{0.25} = -3\ \mho$$

Subcircuit 2 is with the input port short-circuited i.e., $V_1B = 0$.

$$V_2 = V(5) = 0.666667\text{ V}$$
$$I_1 = -I(V1b) = -2\text{A}$$
$$I_2 = I(I2b) = 1\text{ A}$$
$$Y_{12} = \frac{I_1}{V_2} = \frac{-2}{0.666667} = -3\ \mho$$
$$Y_{22} = \frac{I_2}{V_2} = \frac{1}{0.666667} = 1.5\ \mho$$

Hence, the $Y$ parameters are

$$\begin{bmatrix} Y_{11} & Y_{12} \\ Y_{21} & Y_{22} \end{bmatrix} = \begin{bmatrix} 4 & -3 \\ -3 & 1.5 \end{bmatrix}$$

## EXAMPLE 12.3

*Find transmission parameters for the two-port network shown in Fig. 12.176.*

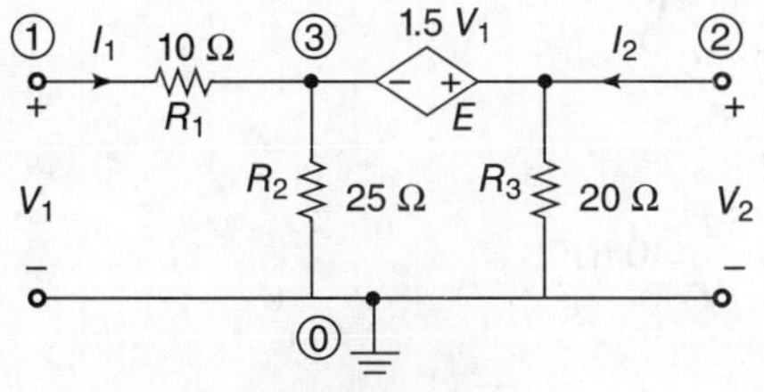


Fig. 12.176

**Solution**

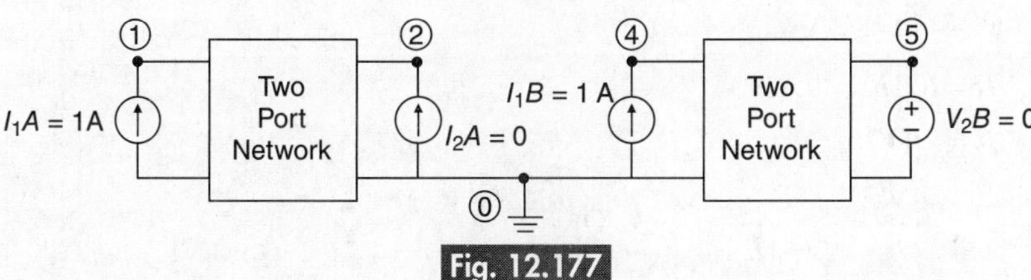


Fig. 12.177

```
* Calculation of transmission parameters

.SUBCKT TWOPORT 1 2
R1 1 3 10
R2 3 0 25
R3 2 0 20
E 2 3 1 0 1.5
.ENDS
I1A 0 1 1
I2A 0 2 0
I1B 0 4 1
V2B 5 0 0
X1 1 2 TWOPORT
X2 4 5 TWOPORT
.OP
.END
```

```
                    Operating Point
V(1):                  11.5152              voltage
V(2):                  18.7879              voltage
V(4):                   4                   voltage
V(5):                   0                   voltage
I(I1b):                 1                   device_current
I(I2a):                 0                   device_current
I(I1a):                 1                   device_current
I(V2b):                 1.24                device_current
Ix(1:1):                1                   subckt_current
Ix(1:2):                0                   subckt_current
Ix(2:1):                1                   subckt_current
Ix(2:2):               -1.24                subckt_current
```

**Result**

Subcircuit 1 is with the output port open-circuited i.e., $I_2A = 0$.

$$V_1 = V(1) = 11.5152 \text{ V}$$

$$V_2 = V(2) = 18.7879 \text{ V}$$

$$I_1 = I(I1a) = 1 \text{ A}$$

$$A = \frac{V_1}{V_2} = \frac{11.5152}{18.7879} = 0.6129$$

$$C = \frac{I_1}{V_2} = \frac{1}{18.7879} = 0.0532 \ \mho$$

Subcircuit 2 is with the output port short-circuited i.e., $V_2B = 0$.

$$V_1 = V(4) = 4 \text{ V}$$

$$I_1 = I(I1b) = 1 \text{ A}$$

$$I_2 = -I(V2b) = -1.24 \text{ A}$$

$$B = -\frac{V_1}{I_2} = -\frac{4}{(-1.24)} = 3.32 \ \Omega$$

$$D = -\frac{I_1}{I_2} = -\frac{1}{(-1.24)} = 0.8065$$

Hence, the transmission parameters are

$$\begin{bmatrix} A & B \\ C & D \end{bmatrix} = \begin{bmatrix} 0.6129 & 3.32 \\ 0.0532 & 0.8065 \end{bmatrix}$$

## EXAMPLE 12.4

*Determine hybrid parameters for the network of Fig. 12.178.*

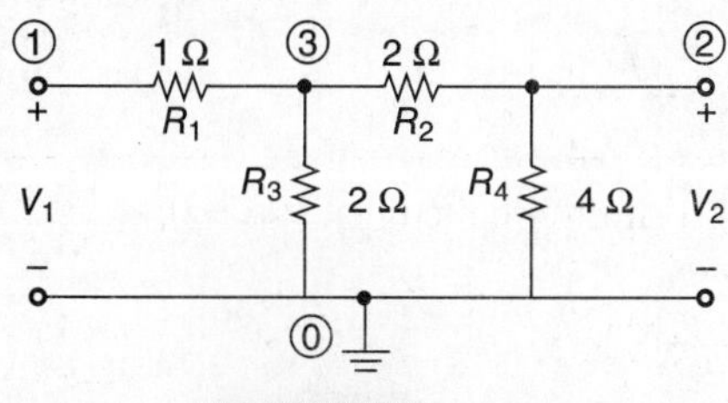


Fig. 12.178

**Solution**

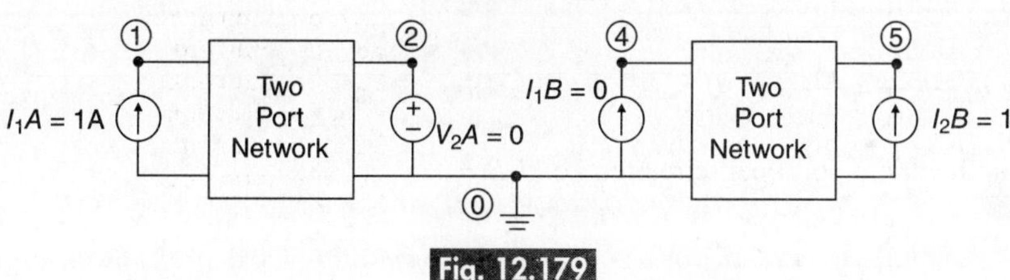


Fig. 12.179

```
* Calculation of h parameters

.SUBCKT TWOPORT 1 2
R1 1 3 1
R2 3 2 2
R3 3 0 2
R4 2 0 4
.ENDS
I1A 0 1 1
V2A 2 0 0
I1B 0 4 0
I2B 0 5 1
X1 1 2 TWOPORT
X2 4 5 TWOPORT
.OP
.END
```

```
                    Operating Point
V(1):                     2                    voltage
V(2):                     0                    voltage
V(4):                     1                    voltage
V(5):                     2                    voltage
I(I2b):                   1                    device_current
I(I1b):                   0                    device_current
I(I1a):                   1                    device_current
I(V2a):                   0.5                  device_current
Ix(1:1):                  1                    subckt_current
Ix(1:2):                 -0.5                  subckt_current
Ix(2:1):                  0                    subckt_current
Ix(2:2):                  1                    subckt_current
```

**Result**

Subcircuit 1 is with the output port short-circuited i.e., $V_2A = 0$.

$$V_1 = V(1) = 2 \text{ V}$$

$$I_1 = I(I1a) = 1 \text{ A}$$

$$I_2 = -I(V2a) = -0.5 \text{ A}$$

$$h_{11} = \frac{V_1}{I_1} = \frac{2}{1} = 2\,\Omega$$

$$h_{21} = \frac{I_2}{I_1} = \frac{-0.5}{1} = -0.5$$

Subcircuit 2 is with the input port open-circuited i.e., $I_1B = 0$.

$$V_1 = V(4) = 1 \text{ V}$$

$$V_2 = V(5) = 2 \text{ V}$$

$$I_2 = I(I2b) = 1 \text{ A}$$

$$h_{12} = \frac{V_1}{V_2} = \frac{1}{2} = 0.5$$

$$h_{22} = \frac{I_2}{V_2} = \frac{1}{2} = 0.5\,℧$$

Hence, the $h$ parameters are

$$\begin{bmatrix} h_{11} & h_{12} \\ h_{21} & h_{22} \end{bmatrix} = \begin{bmatrix} 2 & 0.5 \\ -0.5 & 0.5 \end{bmatrix}$$

CHAPTER

# 13 Fourier Analysis

## LEARNING OBJECTIVES

**After studying this chapter, you should be able to:**

- **LO 13.1** Discuss trigonometric Fourier Series
- **LO 13.2** Explain types of waveform symmetry
- **LO 13.3** Discuss exponential Fourier series
- **LO 13.4** Derive the expressions for average value and rms value of a periodic complex wave
- **LO 13.5** Derive the expression for power supplied by complex wave
- **LO 13.6** Explain Fourier transform
- **LO 13.7** Derive Fourier transforms of one-sided exponential function, two-sided exponential function, gate function, impulse function, constant function, signum function, unit step function, sine function, cosine function and exponential function
- **LO 13.8** Derive Fourier transforms of periodic functions
- **LO 13.9** Prove properties of Fourier transform
- **LO 13.10** Explain energy density spectrum

## INTRODUCTION

Any arbitrary periodic function can be represented by an infinite series of sinusoids of harmonically related frequencies. This representation is known as *Fourier-series representation*. The Fourier representation of periodic functions is extended to non-periodic functions by letting the fundamental period $T$ tend to infinity, and this Fourier method of representing non-periodic functions as a function of frequency is called *Fourier transform*. The Fourier representation of functions is also known as *frequency-domain representation*. The Fourier-series representation can be obtained only for periodic functions, but the Fourier-transform technique can be applied to both periodic and non-periodic functions to obtain the frequency-domain representation of functions. The information about magnitude and phase of various frequency components can be obtained by Fourier analysis. The plot of magnitude versus frequency is called *magnitude spectrum*, and the plot of phase versus frequency is called *phase spectrum*.

## 13.1 TRIGONOMETRIC FOURIER SERIES

LO 13.1

Discuss trigonometric Fourier Series

Any periodic function *f(t)* can be expressed in terms of an infinite trigonometric series if it satisfies the following conditions:

1. It is well defined and single valued, except possibly at a finite number of points.
2. It has a finite number of discontinuities in the period $T$.
3. It has a finite number of positive and negative maxima in the period $T$.

These conditions are known as *Dirichlet's conditions.*

Any function, *f(t)*, which is periodic and satisfies the Dirichlet's condition, can be represented in terms of sine and cosine functions.

$$f(t) = a_0 + a_1 \cos \omega t + a_2 \cos 2\omega t + \ldots + a_n \cos n\,\omega t + b_1 \sin \omega t + b_2 \sin 2\omega t + \ldots + b_n \sin n\,\omega t + \ldots$$

$$= a_0 + \sum_{n=1}^{\infty} a_n \cos n\,\omega t + \sum_{n=1}^{\infty} b_n \sin n\,\omega t \qquad \ldots(13.1)$$

where the coefficients $a_0$, $a_n$ and $b_n$ are given by

$$a_0 = \frac{1}{T}\int_0^T f(t)\,dt$$

$$a_n = \frac{2}{T}\int_0^T f(t)\cos n\,\omega t\,dt$$

$$b_n = \frac{2}{T}\int_0^T f(t)\sin n\,\omega t\,dt$$

### 13.1.1 Evaluation of Fourier Coefficients

**1. *Evaluation of $a_0$*** Integrating Eq. (13.1) w.r.t. $t$,

$$\int_0^T f(t)\,dt = a_0\int_0^T dt + \int_0^T\left(\sum_{n=1}^{\infty} a_n \cos n\,\omega t\right)dt + \int_0^T\left(\sum_{n=1}^{\infty} b_n \sin n\,\omega t\right)dt$$

$$= a_0\,T + 0 + 0$$

$$\left[\because \int_0^T \sin n\,\omega t\,dt = 0 \text{ for all } n \quad \text{and} \int_0^T \cos n\,\omega t\,dt = 0 \text{ for } n \neq 0\right]$$

$$a_0 = \frac{1}{T}\int_0^T f(t)\,dt$$

**2. *Evaluation of $a_n$*** Multiplying Eq. (13.1) by cos $n\,\omega t$ and integrating w.r.t $t$ between the limits 0 and $T$,

$$\int_0^T f(t)\cos n\,\omega t\,dt = \int_0^T a_0 \cos n\,\omega t\,dt + \int_0^T \cos n\,\omega t \sum_{n=1}^{\infty} a_n \cos n\,\omega t\,dt + \int_0^T \cos n\,\omega t \sum_{n=1}^{\infty} b_n \sin n\,\omega t\,dt$$

$$= 0 + \frac{T}{2} a_n + 0$$

$$a_n = \frac{2}{T}\int_0^T f(t)\cos n\,\omega t\,dt$$

**3. *Evaluation of $b_n$*** Multiplying Eq. (13.1) by sin $n\,\omega t$ and integrating w.r.t $t$ between the limits 0 and $T$,

$$\int_0^T f(t)\sin n\,\omega t\,dt = \int_0^T a_0 \sin n\,\omega t\,dt + \int_0^T \sin n\,\omega t \sum_{n=1}^{\infty} a_n \cos n\,\omega t\,dt + \int_0^T \sin n\,\omega t \sum_{n=1}^{\infty} b_n \sin n\,\omega t\,dt$$

$$= 0 + 0 + \frac{T}{2} b_n$$

$$b_n = \frac{2}{T}\int_0^T f(t)\sin n\,\omega t\,dt$$

### 13.1.2 Complex Fourier Spectrum

A Fourier series expansion of a periodic function is equivalent to resolving the function in terms of its components of various frequencies. A periodic function with period $T$ has frequency components of angular frequencies $\omega$, $2\omega$, $3\omega$,... $n\omega$ where $\omega = \frac{2\pi}{T}$. Thus, the periodic function $f(t)$ possesses its spectrum of frequencies, known as *line spectrum*.

The spectrum exists only at $\omega$, $2\omega$, $3\omega$,... etc. Thus, the spectrum is not a continuous curve but exists only at some discrete values of $\omega$. The line spectrum is the plot which shows the variation of magnitude and phase of the function w.r.t $n$.

***(i) Magnitude Spectrum*** It is a plot of magnitude $c_n$ versus $n\omega$ where $c_n = \sqrt{a_n^2 + b_n^2}$.

***(ii) Phase Spectrum*** It is a plot of phase angle $\phi_n$ versus $n\omega$ where $\phi_n = \tan^{-1}\frac{b_n}{a_n}$.

**EXAMPLE 13.1** ○●○

*Find the trigonometric Fourier series of the waveform shown in Fig. 13.1. Draw the magnitude and phase spectrum.*

**Note** Difficulty Level ●○○— Easy; ○●○— Medium; ○○●— Difficult

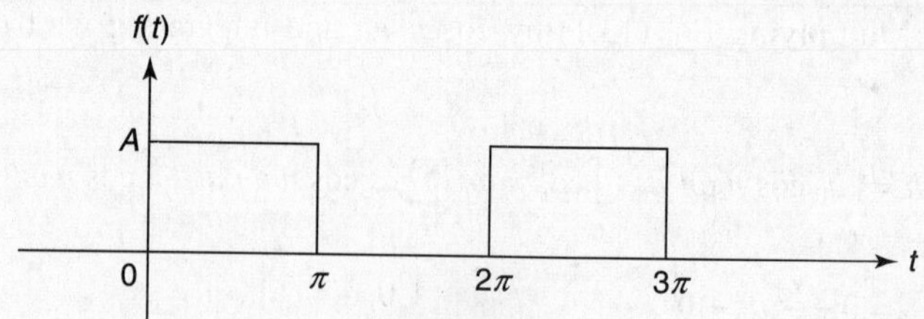


Fig. 13.1

**Solution**

$$T = 2\pi$$

$$\omega = \frac{2\pi}{T} = \frac{2\pi}{2\pi} = 1$$

$$f(t) = A \quad 0 < t < \pi$$
$$= 0 \quad \pi < t < 2\pi$$

The trigonometric Fourier series of $f(t)$ is

$$f(t) = a_0 + \sum_{n=1}^{\infty} a_n \cos n\,\omega\, t + \sum_{n=1}^{\infty} b_n \sin n\,\omega t$$

$$a_0 = \frac{1}{T}\int_0^T f(t)\,dt$$

$$= \frac{1}{2\pi}\left[\int_0^{\pi} A\,dt + \int_{\pi}^{2\pi} 0\,dt\right]$$

$$= \frac{A}{2\pi}[t]_0^{\pi}$$

$$= \frac{A}{2\pi}(\pi - 0)$$

$$= \frac{A}{2}$$

$$a_n = \frac{2}{T}\int_0^T f(t)\cos n\,\omega t\,dt$$

$$= \frac{2}{2\pi}\left[\int_0^{\pi} A\cos n\,t\,dt + \int_{\pi}^{2\pi} 0\,dt\right] \qquad [\because \omega = 1]$$

$$= \frac{A}{\pi}\left[\frac{\sin n\,t}{n}\right]_0^{\pi}$$

$$= \frac{A}{\pi}\left[\frac{1}{n}(\sin n\pi - \sin 0)\right]$$

$$= 0 \qquad [\because \sin n\pi = 0]$$

$$b_n = \frac{2}{T}\int_0^T f(t)\sin n\,\omega t\,dt$$

$$= \frac{2}{2\pi}\left[\int_0^{\pi} A\sin n\,t\,dt + \int_{\pi}^{2\pi} 0\,dt\right] \quad [\because \omega = 1]$$

$$= \frac{A}{\pi}\left[-\frac{\cos n\,t}{n}\right]_0^{\pi}$$

$$= \frac{A}{n\pi}[-\cos n\pi + \cos 0]$$

$$= \frac{A}{n\pi}[-(-1)^n + 1]$$

$$b_n = \begin{cases} 0 & \text{if } n \text{ is even} \\ \dfrac{2A}{n\pi} & \text{if } n \text{ is odd} \end{cases}$$

$$f(t) = \frac{A}{2} + \sum_{\substack{n=1 \\ n=odd}}^{\infty} \frac{2A}{n\pi}\sin n\,\omega t$$

$$= \frac{A}{2} + \frac{2A}{\pi}\sin \omega t + \frac{2A}{3\pi}\sin 3\,\omega t + \ldots\ldots$$

The magnitude and phase spectrum are shown in Fig. 13.2.

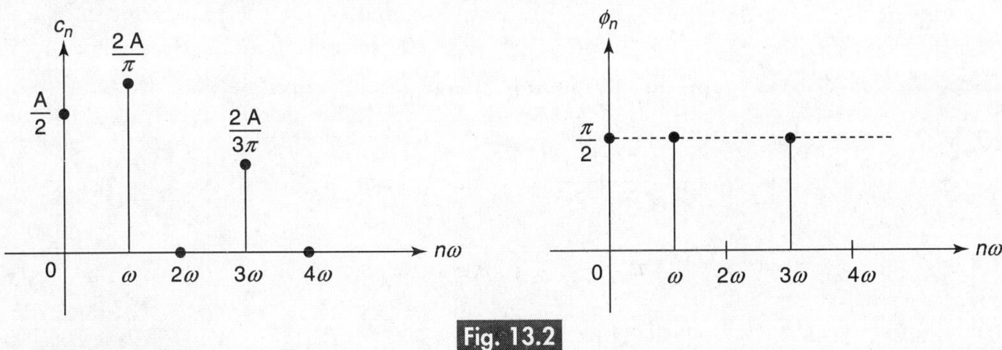


Fig. 13.2

## EXAMPLE 13.2

*Find the trigonometric Fourier series of the waveform shown in Fig. 13.3. Draw the magnitude and phase spectrum.*

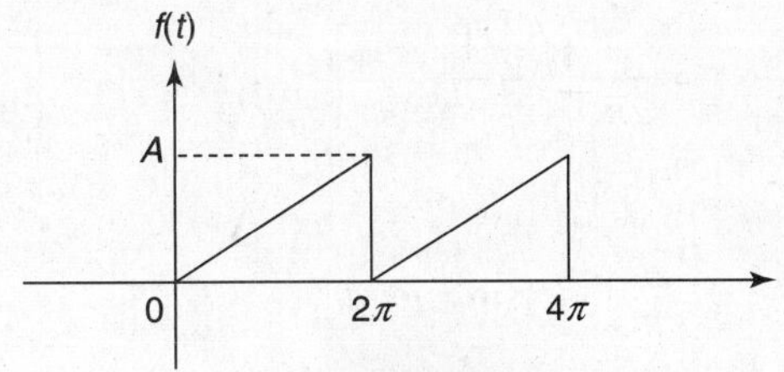


Fig. 13.3

**Solution**

$$T = 2\pi$$

$$\omega = \frac{2\pi}{T} = \frac{2\pi}{2\pi} = 1$$

$$f(t) = \frac{A}{2\pi}t \qquad 0 < t < 2\pi$$

The trigonometric Fourier series of $f(t)$ is

$$f(t) = a_0 + \sum_{n=1}^{\infty} a_n \cos n\,\omega\,t + \sum_{n=1}^{\infty} b_n \sin n\,\omega\,t$$

$$a_0 = \frac{1}{T}\int_0^T f(t)\,dt$$

$$= \frac{1}{2\pi}\int_0^{2\pi} \frac{A}{2\pi} t\,dt$$

$$= \frac{A}{4\pi^2}\left[\frac{t^2}{2}\right]_0^{2\pi}$$

$$= \frac{A}{4\pi^2}\left[\frac{4\pi^2}{2} - 0\right]$$

$$= \frac{A}{2}$$

$$a_n = \frac{2}{T}\int_0^T f(t)\cos n\,\omega t\,dt$$

$$= \frac{2}{2\pi}\int_0^{2\pi} \frac{A}{2\pi} t\cos nt\,dt \qquad [\because \omega = 1]$$

$$= \frac{A}{2\pi^2}\int_0^{2\pi} t\cos nt\,dt$$

$$= \frac{A}{2\pi^2}\left[t\left(\frac{\sin nt}{n}\right) - (1)\left(-\frac{\cos nt}{n^2}\right)\right]_0^{2\pi}$$

$$= \frac{A}{2\pi^2}\left[2\pi\left(\frac{\sin 2n\pi}{n}\right) + \frac{\cos 2n\pi}{n^2} - \frac{\cos 0}{n^2}\right]$$

$$= \frac{A}{2\pi^2}\left[0 + \frac{1}{n^2} - \frac{1}{n^2}\right] \qquad \left[\begin{matrix}\because \sin 2n\pi = 0 \\ \cos 2n\pi = 1\end{matrix}\right]$$

$$= 0$$

$$b_n = \frac{2}{T}\int_0^T f(t)\sin n\,\omega t\,dt$$

$$= \frac{2}{2\pi}\int_0^{2\pi} \frac{A}{2\pi} t \sin n\, dt \qquad [\because \omega = 1]$$

$$= \frac{A}{2\pi^2}\int_0^{2\pi} t \sin n\, t\, dt$$

$$= \frac{A}{2\pi^2}\left[t\left(-\frac{\cos n\, t}{n}\right) - (1)\left(-\frac{\sin n\, t}{n^2}\right)\right]_0^{2\pi}$$

$$= \frac{A}{2\pi^2}\left[-2\pi\left(\frac{\cos 2\, n\pi}{n}\right) + \frac{\sin 2\, n\pi}{n^2} - \frac{\sin 0}{n^2}\right]$$

$$= \frac{A}{2\pi^2}\left[-\frac{2\pi}{n}\right] \qquad \left[\begin{matrix}\because \cos 2\, n\pi = 1 \\ \sin 2\, n\pi = 0\end{matrix}\right]$$

$$= -\frac{A}{n\pi}$$

$$f(t) = \frac{A}{2} + \sum_{n=1}^{\infty} -\frac{A}{n\,\pi} \sin n\, \omega t$$

$$= \frac{A}{2} - \frac{A}{\pi} \sin \omega t - \frac{A}{2\pi} \sin 2\, \omega t - \ldots\ldots$$

The magnitude and phase spectrum are shown in Fig. 13.4.

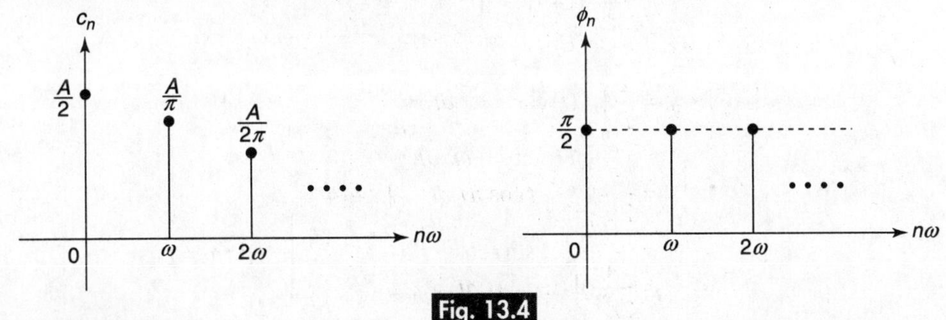


Fig. 13.4

## EXAMPLE 13.3

*Find the trigonometric Fourier series of the waveform shown in Fig. 13.5.*

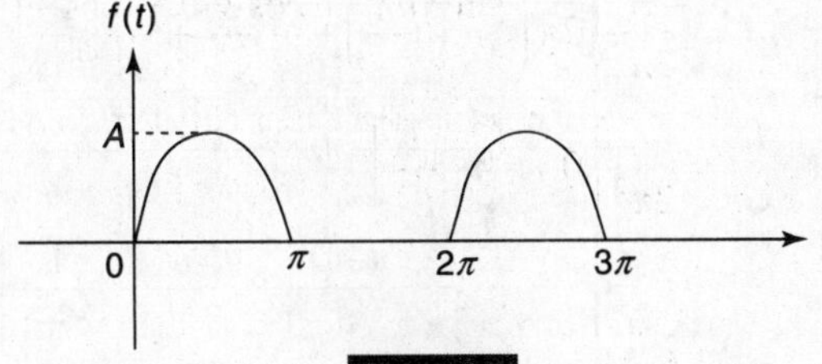


Fig. 13.5

**Solution**

$$T = 2\pi$$
$$\omega = \frac{2\pi}{T} = \frac{2\pi}{2\pi} = 1$$
$$f(t) = A\sin\omega t$$
$$\begin{aligned} f(t) &= A\sin t \qquad 0 < t < \pi \\ &= 0 \qquad \pi < t < 2\pi \end{aligned}$$

The trigonometric Fourier series of $f(t)$ is

$$f(t) = a_0 + \sum_{n=1}^{\infty} a_n \cos n\,\omega\, t + \sum_{n=1}^{\infty} b_n \sin n\,\omega\, t$$

$$\begin{aligned}
a_0 &= \frac{1}{T}\int_0^T f(t)\,dt \\
&= \frac{1}{2\pi}\left[\int_0^{\pi} A\sin t\,dt + \int_{\pi}^{2\pi} 0\,dt\right] \\
&= \frac{A}{2\pi}[-\cos t]_0^{\pi} \\
&= \frac{A}{2\pi}[-\cos\pi + \cos 0] \\
&= \frac{A}{2\pi}[1+1] \qquad [\because \cos\pi = -1] \\
&= \frac{A}{\pi}
\end{aligned}$$

$$\begin{aligned}
a_n &= \frac{2}{T}\int_0^T f(t)\cos n\,\omega t\,dt \\
&= \frac{2}{2\pi}\left[\int_0^{\pi} A\sin t\cos n\,t\,dt + \int_{\pi}^{2\pi} 0\,dt\right] \qquad [\because \omega = 1] \\
&= \frac{A}{2\pi}\left[\int_0^{\pi}\{\sin(n+1)\,t - \sin(n-1)\,t\}\,dt\right] \qquad \left[\begin{aligned}&\because 2\cos A\sin B \\ &= \sin(A+B) - \sin(A-B)\end{aligned}\right] \\
&= \frac{A}{2\pi}\left[-\frac{\cos(n+1)\,t}{n+1} + \frac{\cos(n-1)\,t}{n-1}\right]_0^{\pi} \\
&= \frac{A}{2\pi}\left[-\frac{\cos(n+1)\pi}{n+1} + \frac{\cos(n-1)\pi}{n-1} + \frac{\cos 0}{n+1} - \frac{\cos 0}{n-1}\right] \\
&= \frac{A}{2\pi}\left[-\frac{(-1)^{n+1}}{n+1} + \frac{(-1)^{n-1}}{n-1} + \frac{1}{n+1} - \frac{1}{n-1}\right]
\end{aligned}$$

$$= \frac{A}{2\pi}\left[-\frac{-(-1)^n}{n+1} + \frac{-(-1)^n}{n-1} + \frac{1}{n+1} - \frac{1}{n-1}\right] \qquad \begin{bmatrix}(-1)^1 & = -1\\(-1)^{-1} & = -1\end{bmatrix}$$

$$= \frac{A}{2\pi}\left[(-1)^n\left(\frac{1}{n+1} - \frac{1}{n-1}\right) + \left(\frac{1}{n+1} - \frac{1}{n-1}\right)\right]$$

$$= \frac{A}{2\pi}\left[(-1)^n\left(\frac{-2}{n^2-1}\right) + \left(\frac{-2}{n^2-1}\right)\right]$$

$$= \frac{A}{2\pi}\left(-\frac{2}{n^2-1}\right)\left[(-1)^n + 1\right]$$

$$= -\frac{A}{\pi(n^2-1)}\left[(-1)^n + 1\right]$$

$$a_n = \begin{cases} -\dfrac{2A}{\pi(n^2-1)} & \text{if } n \text{ is even}\\ 0 & \text{if } n \text{ is odd}\end{cases}$$

$$b_n = \frac{2}{T}\int_0^T f(t)\sin n\,\omega t\,dt$$

$$= \frac{2}{2\pi}\left[\int_0^\pi A\sin t\sin n\,t\,dt + \int_\pi^{2\pi} 0\,dt\right] \qquad [\because \omega = 1]$$

$$= \frac{A}{2\pi}\left[\int_0^\pi \{\cos(n-1)\,t - \cos(n+1)\,t\}\,dt\right]$$

$$= \frac{A}{2\pi}\left[\frac{\sin(n-1)t}{n-1} - \frac{\sin(n+1)t}{n+1}\right]_0^\pi$$

$$= \frac{A}{2\pi}\left[\frac{\sin(n-1)\pi}{n-1} - \frac{\sin(n+1)\pi}{n+1} - \frac{\sin 0}{n-1} + \frac{\sin 0}{n+1}\right]$$

$$= \frac{A}{2\pi}[0] \qquad n \neq 1 \qquad \begin{bmatrix}\sin(n-1)\pi & = 0\\ \sin(n+1)\pi & = 0\end{bmatrix}$$

$$= 0$$

For $n = 1$,

$$b_1 = \frac{2}{2\pi}\int_0^\pi A\sin t\sin t\,dt$$

$$= \frac{A}{\pi}\int_0^\pi \sin^2 t\,dt$$

$$= \frac{A}{\pi}\int_0^\pi \frac{1-\cos 2t}{2}\,dt$$

$$= \frac{A}{2\pi}\left[t - \frac{\sin 2t}{2}\right]_0^{\pi}$$

$$= \frac{A}{2\pi}\left[\pi - \frac{\sin 2\pi}{2} - 0 + \frac{\sin 0}{2}\right]$$

$$= \frac{A}{2\pi}[\pi] \qquad [\because \sin 2\pi = 0]$$

$$= \frac{A}{2}$$

$$f(t) = \frac{A}{\pi} + \sum_{\substack{n=1 \\ n=even}}^{\infty} \left\{-\frac{2A}{\pi(n^2-1)}\right\} \cos n\,\omega t + \frac{A}{2}\sin n\,\omega t$$

$$= \frac{A}{\pi} + \frac{A}{2}\sin \omega t - \frac{2A}{3\pi}\cos 2\,\omega t - \frac{2A}{15\pi}\cos 4\,\omega t - \ldots\ldots$$

## 13.2 WAVEFORM SYMMETRY

LO 13.2

Explain types of waveform symmetry

There are four types of waveform symmetry in any function:

(i) Even symmetry
(ii) Odd symmetry
(iii) Half-wave symmetry
(iv) Quarter-wave symmetry

### 13.2.1 Even Symmetry

A function is said to have even symmetry if $f(t) = f(-t)$, as shown in Fig. 13.6. Even functions are symmetrical about the vertical axis. Examples of even functions are $x^2$, cos $x$, cosh $x$, etc. The product of an even and odd function is an odd function, and the product of two even functions is an even function.

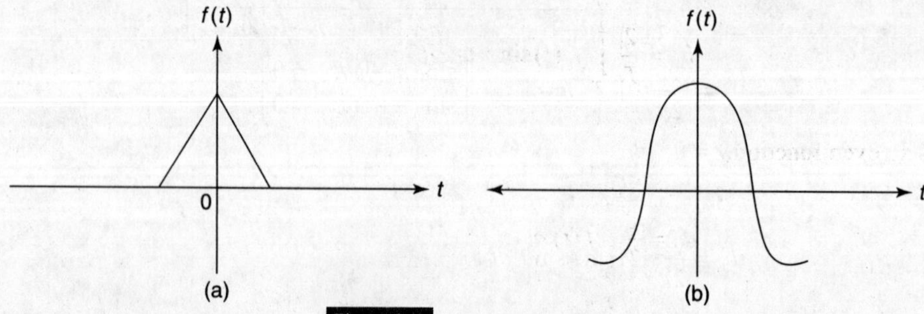


**Fig. 13.6** *Even functions*

For an even function,

$$f_e(t)\,dt = \int_{-T}^{0} f_e(t)\,dt + \int_{0}^{T} f_e(t)\,dt$$

Let $t = -x,$

$$\int_{-T}^{T} f_e(t)\, dt = \int_{0}^{T} f_e(-x)\, dx + \int_{0}^{T} f_e(t)\, dt$$

$$= \int_{0}^{T} f_e(x)\, dx + \int_{0}^{T} f_e(t)\, dt \qquad [\therefore f_e(-x) = f_e(x)]$$

$$= 2\int_{0}^{T} f_e(t)\, dt$$

Similarly, for an odd function,

$$\int_{-T}^{T} f_0\,(t)\, dt = \int_{-T}^{0} f_0\,(t) + \int_{0}^{T} f_0\,(t)\, dt$$

$$= -\int_{0}^{T} f_0\,(x)\, dx + \int_{0}^{T} f_0\,(t)\, dt$$

$$= -\int_{0}^{T} f_0\,(t)\, dt + \int_{0}^{T} f_0\,(t)\, dt$$

$$= 0$$

We know that

$$a_0 = \frac{1}{T}\int_{-\frac{T}{2}}^{\frac{T}{2}} f(t)\, dt$$

$$a_n = \frac{2}{T}\int_{-\frac{T}{2}}^{\frac{T}{2}} f\,(t)\cos n\,\omega t\, dt$$

$$b_n = \frac{2}{T}\int_{-\frac{T}{2}}^{\frac{T}{2}} f\,(t)\sin n\,\omega t\, dt$$

When $f(t)$ is an even function,

$$a_0 = \frac{2}{T}\int_{0}^{\frac{T}{2}} f(t)\, dt$$

$$a_n = \frac{4}{T}\int_{0}^{\frac{T}{2}} f(t)\cos n\,\omega t\, dt \quad [\because f\,(t) \text{ and } \cos n\,\omega t \text{ are even functions}]$$

$$b_n = 0 \quad [\because f\,(t) \text{ is an even function and } \sin n\,\omega t \text{ is an odd function}]$$

### 13.2.2 Odd Symmetry

A function is said to have odd symmetry if $f(t) = -f(-t)$, as shown in Fig. 13.7. Odd functions are symmetrical about the origin. Examples of odd functions are $x$, $x^3$, sin $x$, etc. The product of an even and an odd function is an odd function, and the product of two odd functions is an even function.

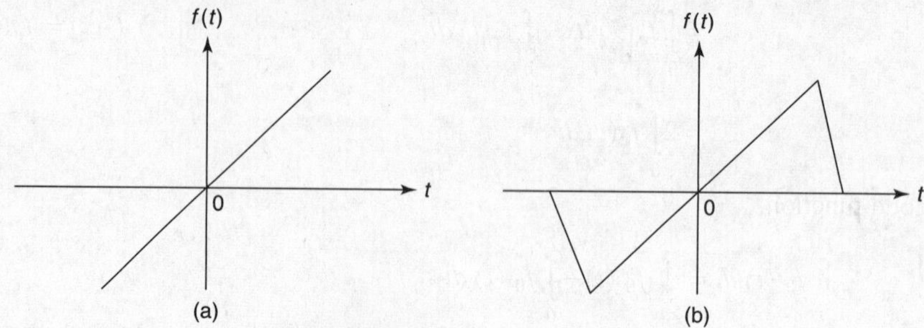


**Fig. 13.7** *Odd functions*

When *f(t)* is an odd function,

$$a_0 = 0$$

$$a_n = 0$$

$$b_n = \frac{4}{T}\int_0^{\frac{T}{2}} f(t)\sin n\,\omega t\,dt$$

### 13.2.3 Half-Wave Symmetry

A function is said to have half-wave symmetry if $f(t) = -f\left(t \pm \frac{T}{2}\right)$ as shown in Fig. 13.8. The values of *f(t)* are equal and opposite during the interval $0 < t < \frac{T}{2}$ and $\frac{T}{2} < t < T$. Similarly, the values of *f(t)* are also equal and opposite during the interval $-\frac{T}{2} < t < 0$ and $-T < t < -\frac{T}{2}$.

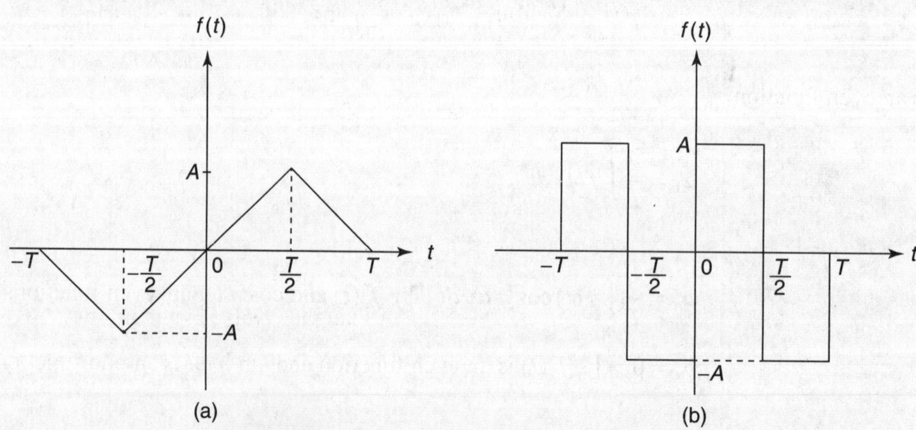


**Fig. 13.8** *Functions with half-wave symmetry*

When *f(t)* has half-wave symmetry,

$$a_0 = 0$$

$$a_n = 0 \qquad \text{if } n \text{ is even}$$

$$= \frac{4}{T}\int_0^{\frac{T}{2}} f(t)\cos n\,\omega t\,dt \qquad \text{if } n \text{ is odd}$$

$$b_n = 0 \qquad \text{if } n \text{ is even}$$

$$= \frac{4}{T}\int_0^{\frac{T}{2}} f(t)\sin n\,\omega t\,dt \qquad \text{if } n \text{ is odd}$$

### 13.2.4 Quarter-Wave Symmetry

A function is said to have quarter-wave symmetry if it is a combination of even, odd and half-wave symmetries, as shown in Fig. 13.9.

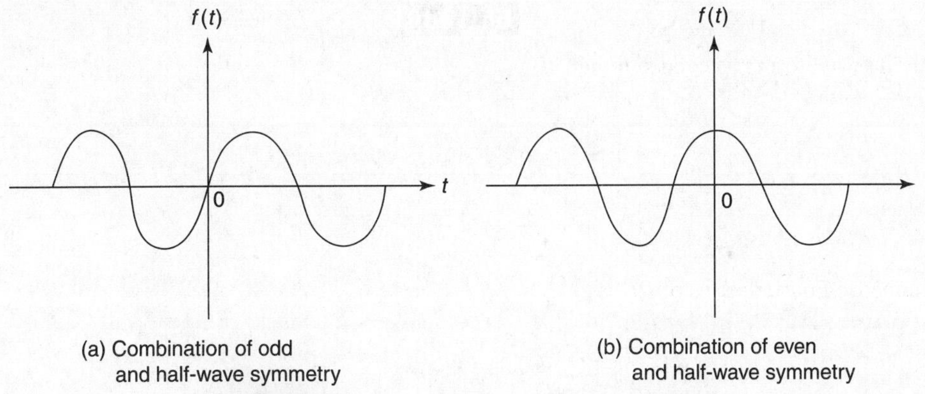


**Fig. 13.9** *Functions with quarter-wave symmetry*

When *f(t)* has quarter-wave symmetry (with combination of even and half-wave symmetries),

$$a_0 = 0$$

$$a_n = 0 \qquad \text{if } n \text{ is even}$$

$$= \frac{8}{T}\int_0^{\frac{T}{4}} f(t)\cos n\,\omega t\,dt \qquad \text{if } n \text{ is odd}$$

$$b_n = 0$$

When *f(t)* has quarter-wave symmetry (with combination of odd and half-wave symmetries),

$$a_0 = 0$$

$$a_n = 0$$

$$b_n = 0 \qquad \text{if } n \text{ is even}$$

$$= \frac{8}{T}\int_0^{\frac{T}{4}} f(t)\sin n\,\omega t\,dt \qquad \text{if } n \text{ is odd}$$

## EXAMPLE 13.4

*Find the trigonometric Fourier series of the waveform shown in Fig. 13.10.*

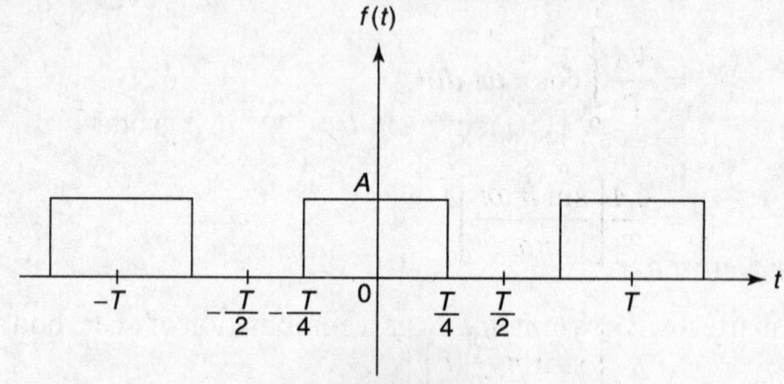


Fig. 13.10

**Solution** The waveform has even symmetry.

$$b_n = 0$$

$$f(t) = A \qquad 0 < t < \frac{T}{4}$$

$$= 0 \qquad \frac{T}{4} < t < \frac{T}{2}$$

The trigonometric Fourier series of *f(t)* is

$$f(t) = a_0 + \sum_{n=1}^{\infty} a_n \cos n\,\omega t$$

$$a_0 = \frac{2}{T}\int_0^{\frac{T}{2}} f(t)\,dt$$

$$= \frac{2}{T}\left[\int_0^{\frac{T}{4}} A\,dt + \int_{\frac{T}{4}}^{\frac{T}{2}} 0\,dt\right]$$

$$= \frac{2}{T}[At]_0^{\frac{T}{4}}$$

$$= \frac{2}{T}[A\frac{T}{4} - 0]$$

$$= \frac{A}{2}$$

$$a_n = \frac{4}{T}\int_0^{\frac{T}{2}} f(t)\cos n\,\omega t\,dt$$

$$= \frac{4}{T}\left[\int_0^{\frac{T}{4}} A\cos n\,\omega t\,dt + \int_{\frac{T}{4}}^{\frac{T}{2}} 0\cos n\,\omega t\,dt\right]$$

$$= \frac{4A}{T}\int_0^{\frac{T}{4}} \cos n\,\omega t\,dt$$

$$= \frac{4A}{T}\left[\frac{\sin n\,\omega t}{n\omega}\right]_0^{\frac{T}{4}}$$

$$= \frac{4A}{T}\left[\frac{\sin\left(n\frac{2\pi}{T}t\right)}{n\frac{2\pi}{T}}\right]_0^{\frac{T}{4}} \qquad \left[\because \omega = \frac{2\pi}{T}\right]$$

$$= \frac{4A}{T}\left[\frac{\sin\left(n\frac{2\pi}{T}\frac{T}{4}\right)}{n\frac{2\pi}{T}} - \frac{\sin 0}{n\frac{2\pi}{T}}\right]$$

$$= \frac{4A}{T}\left[\frac{T}{2n\pi}\sin\frac{n\pi}{2}\right] \qquad [\because \sin 0 = 0]$$

$$= \frac{2A}{n\pi}\sin\frac{n\pi}{2}$$

$$a_n = \begin{cases} \dfrac{2A}{n\pi} & \text{for } n = 1,5,9,\ldots \\ -\dfrac{2A}{n\pi} & \text{for } n = 3,7,11,\ldots \\ 0 & \text{for } n = 2,4,6 \end{cases}$$

$$f(t) = \frac{A}{2} + \sum_{n=1}^{\infty}\left(\frac{2A}{n\pi}\sin\frac{n\pi}{2}\right)\cos n\,\omega t$$

$$= \frac{A}{2} + \frac{2A}{\pi}\cos\omega t - \frac{2A}{3\pi}\cos 3\,\omega t + \frac{2A}{5\pi}\cos 5\,\omega t - \ldots$$

## EXAMPLE 13.5

*Find the trigonometric Fourier series of the waveform shown in Fig. 13.11.*

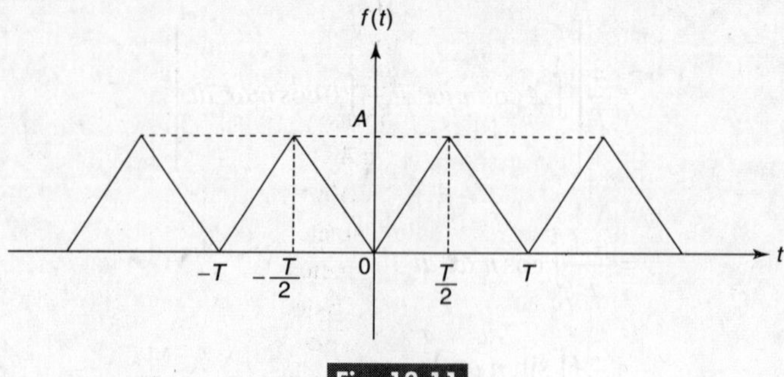


Fig. 13.11

**Solution** The waveform has even symmetry.

$$b_n = 0$$

$$f(t) = \frac{2A}{T}t \qquad 0 < t < \frac{T}{2}$$

The trigonometric Fourier series of *f(t)* is

$$f(t) = a_0 + \sum_{n=1}^{\infty} a_n \cos n\,\omega t$$

$$a_0 = \frac{2}{T}\int_0^{\frac{T}{2}} f(t)\,dt$$

$$= \frac{2}{T}\int_0^{\frac{T}{2}} \frac{2A}{T}t\,dt$$

$$= \frac{4A}{T^2}\left[\frac{t^2}{2}\right]_0^{\frac{T}{2}}$$

$$= \frac{4A}{T^2}\left[\frac{T^2}{8} - 0\right]$$

$$= \frac{A}{2}$$

$$a_n = \frac{4}{T}\int_0^{\frac{T}{2}} f(t)\cos n\,\omega t\,dt$$

$$= \frac{4}{T}\int_0^{\frac{T}{2}} \frac{2A}{T} t \cos n\,\omega t\, dt$$

$$= \frac{8\,A}{T^2}\int_0^{\frac{T}{2}} t \cos n\,\omega t\, dt$$

$$= \frac{8A}{T^2}\left[t\left(\frac{\sin n\,\omega t}{n\,\omega}\right) - (1)\left(-\frac{\cos n\,\omega t}{n^2\,\omega^2}\right)\right]_0^{\frac{T}{2}}$$

$$= \frac{8A}{T^2}\left[\frac{t\sin\left(n\frac{2\pi}{T}t\right)}{n\frac{2\pi}{T}} + \frac{\cos\left(n\frac{2\pi}{T}t\right)}{n^2\frac{4\pi^2}{T^2}}\right]_0^{\frac{T}{2}} \qquad \left[\because \omega = \frac{2\pi}{T}\right]$$

$$= \frac{8\,A}{T^2}\left[\frac{T}{2}\frac{\sin\left(n\frac{2\pi}{T}\frac{T}{2}\right)}{n\frac{2\pi}{T}} + \frac{\cos\left(n\frac{2\pi}{T}\frac{T}{2}\right)}{n^2\frac{4\pi^2}{T^2}} - \frac{1}{n^2\frac{4\pi^2}{T^2}}\right]$$

$$= \frac{8\,A}{T^2}\left[\frac{T^2}{4n\pi}\sin n\pi + \frac{T^2}{4n^2\pi^2}\cos n\pi - \frac{T^2}{4n^2\pi^2}\right]$$

$$= \frac{8\,A}{T^2}\left[0 + \frac{T^2}{4n^2\pi^2}(-1)^n - \frac{T^2}{4n^2\pi^2}\right] \qquad \left[\because \begin{array}{l}\sin n\pi = 0\\ \cos n\pi = (-1)^n\end{array}\right]$$

$$= \frac{8\,A}{T^2}\left[\frac{T^2}{4n^2\pi^2}\left\{(-1)^n - 1\right\}\right]$$

$$= \frac{2A}{n^2\pi^2}\left[(-1)^n - 1\right]$$

$$a_n = \begin{cases} 0 & \text{if } n \text{ is even} \\ -\dfrac{4A}{n^2\pi^2} & \text{if } n \text{ is odd} \end{cases}$$

$$f(t) = \frac{A}{2} + \sum_{\substack{n=1\\ n=odd}}^{\infty}\left(-\frac{4A}{n^2\pi^2}\right)\cos n\,\omega t$$

$$= \frac{A}{2} - \frac{4A}{\pi^2}\cos\omega t - \frac{4A}{9\pi^2}\cos 3\omega t - \ldots\ldots$$

## EXAMPLE 13.6

*Find the trigonometric Fourier series of the waveform shown in Fig. 13.12.*

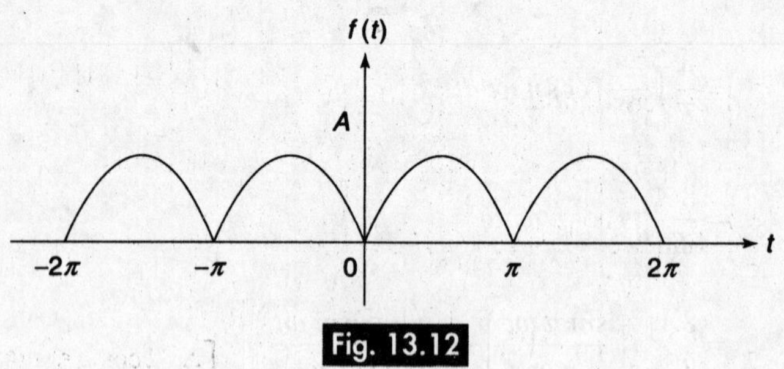


Fig. 13.12

**Solution** The waveform has even symmetry.

$$b_n = 0$$

$$T = \pi$$

$$\omega = \frac{2\pi}{T} = \frac{2\pi}{\pi} = 2$$

$$f(t) = A \sin \omega t$$
$$= A \sin 2t \quad 0 < t < \pi$$

The trigonometric Fourier series of $f(t)$ is

$$f(t) = a_0 + \sum_{n=1}^{\infty} a_n \cos n\,\omega t$$

$$a_0 = \frac{2}{T}\int_0^{\frac{T}{2}} f(t)\,dt$$

$$= \frac{2}{\pi}\int_0^{\frac{\pi}{2}} A \sin 2t\,dt$$

$$= \frac{2A}{\pi}\left[-\frac{\cos 2t}{2}\right]_0^{\frac{\pi}{2}}$$

$$= \frac{2A}{2\pi}\left[-\cos 2\frac{\pi}{2} + \cos 0\right]$$

$$= \frac{A}{\pi}(-\cos\pi + \cos 0) \qquad \begin{bmatrix} \therefore \cos\pi & = -1 \\ \cos 0 & = \phantom{-}1 \end{bmatrix}$$

$$= \frac{A}{\pi}[1+1]$$

$$= \frac{2A}{\pi}$$

$$a_n = \frac{4}{T}\int_0^{\frac{T}{2}} f(t)\cos n\,\omega t\,dt$$

$$= \frac{4}{\pi}\int_0^{\frac{\pi}{2}} A\sin 2t\cos 2n\,t\,dt$$

$$= \frac{2A}{\pi}\int_0^{\frac{\pi}{2}} \{\sin(2n+2)\,t - \sin(2n-2)\,t\}\,dt \qquad \left[\begin{aligned}\therefore\ & 2\cos A\sin B \\ & = \sin(A+B) - \sin(A-B)\end{aligned}\right]$$

$$= \frac{2A}{\pi}\left[-\frac{\cos(2n+2)\,t}{2n+2} + \frac{\cos(2n-2)\,t}{2n-2}\right]_0^{\frac{\pi}{2}}$$

$$= \frac{2A}{\pi}\left[-\frac{\cos\left\{(2n+2)\frac{\pi}{2}\right\}}{2n+2} + \frac{\cos\left\{(2n-2)\frac{\pi}{2}\right\}}{2n-2} + \frac{\cos 0}{2n+2} - \frac{\cos 0}{2n-2}\right]$$

$$= \frac{A}{\pi}\left[-\frac{\cos(n+1)\,\pi}{n+1} + \frac{\cos(n-1)\,\pi}{n-1} + \frac{1}{n+1} - \frac{1}{n-1}\right]$$

$$= \frac{A}{\pi}\left[-\frac{(-1)^{n+1}}{n+1} + \frac{(-1)^{n-1}}{n-1} + \frac{1}{n+1} - \frac{1}{n-1}\right]$$

$$= \frac{A}{\pi}\left[-\frac{-(-1)^n}{n+1} + \frac{-(-1)^n}{n-1} + \frac{1}{n+1} - \frac{1}{n-1}\right] \qquad \left[\begin{aligned}\because\ & (-1)^1 = -1 \\ & (-1)^{-1} = -1\end{aligned}\right]$$

$$= \frac{A}{\pi}\left[(-1)^n\left(\frac{1}{n+1} - \frac{1}{n-1}\right) + \left(\frac{1}{n+1} - \frac{1}{n-1}\right)\right]$$

$$= \frac{A}{\pi}\left[(-1)^n\left(-\frac{2}{n^2-1}\right) + \left(-\frac{2}{n^2-1}\right)\right]$$

$$= \frac{A}{\pi}\left(-\frac{2}{n^2-1}\right)[(-1)^n + 1]$$

$$= -\frac{2A}{\pi(n^2-1)}[(-1)^n + 1]$$

$$a_n = \begin{cases} -\dfrac{4A}{\pi(n^2-1)} & \text{if } n \text{ is even} \\ 0 & \text{if } n \text{ is odd}\end{cases}$$

$$f(t) = \frac{2A}{\pi} + \sum_{\substack{n=1 \\ n=\text{even}}}^{\infty}\left\{-\frac{4A}{\pi(n^2-1)}\right\}\cos 2n\,\omega t$$

$$= \frac{2A}{\pi} - \frac{4A}{3\pi}\cos 4\,\omega t - \frac{4A}{15\pi}\cos 8\,\omega t - \ldots\ldots$$

## EXAMPLE 13.7

*Find the trigonometric Fourier series of the waveform shown in Fig. 13.13.*

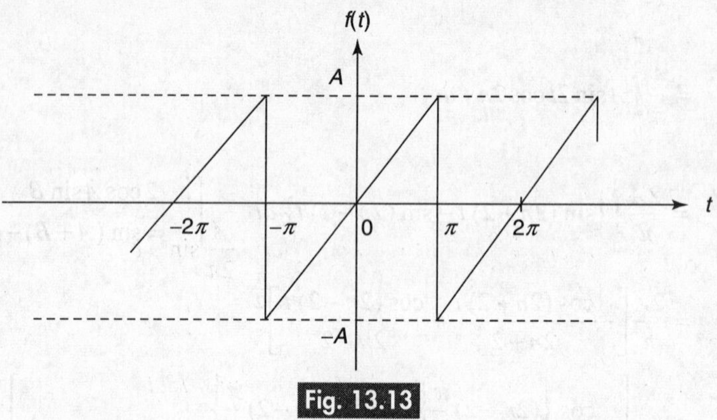


Fig. 13.13

**Solution** The waveform has odd symmetry.

$$a_0 = 0 \text{ and } a_n = 0$$

$$T = 2\pi$$

$$\omega = \frac{2\pi}{T} = \frac{2\pi}{2\pi} = 1$$

$$f(t) = \frac{A}{\pi}t \quad 0 < t < \pi$$

The trigonometric Fourier series is

$$f(t) = \sum_{n=1}^{\infty} b_n \sin n\,\omega t$$

$$b_n = \frac{4}{T}\int_0^{\frac{T}{2}} f(t)\sin n\,\omega t\,dt$$

$$= \frac{4}{2\pi}\int_0^{\pi} \frac{A}{\pi} t\sin n\,t\,dt \qquad [\because \omega = 1]$$

$$= \frac{2A}{\pi^2}\int_0^{\pi} t\sin n\,t\,dt$$

$$= \frac{2A}{\pi^2}\left[t\left(-\frac{\cos n\,t}{n}\right) - (1)\left(-\frac{\sin n\,t}{n^2}\right)\right]_0^{\pi}$$

$$= \frac{2A}{\pi^2}\left[-\pi\left(\frac{\cos n\pi}{n}\right) + \frac{\sin n\pi}{n^2} - \frac{\sin 0}{n^2}\right]$$

$$= \frac{2A}{\pi^2}\left[-\frac{\pi(-1)^n}{n}\right] \qquad [\because \sin n\pi = 0]$$

$$= \frac{2A}{n\pi}(-1)^n$$

$$= \begin{cases} \dfrac{2A}{n\pi} & \text{if } n \text{ is even} \\ -\dfrac{2A}{n\pi} & \text{if } n \text{ is odd} \end{cases}$$

$$f(t) = \sum_{n=1}^{\infty} \left\{ \frac{2A}{n\pi}(-1)^n \right\} \sin n\,\omega t$$

$$= \frac{2A}{\pi}\sin \omega t - \frac{A}{\pi}\sin 2\,\omega t + \frac{2A}{3\pi}\sin 3\,\omega t - \frac{A}{2\pi}\sin 4\,\omega t + \ldots\ldots$$

## EXAMPLE 13.8

*Find the trigonometric Fourier series of the waveform shown in Fig. 13.14.*

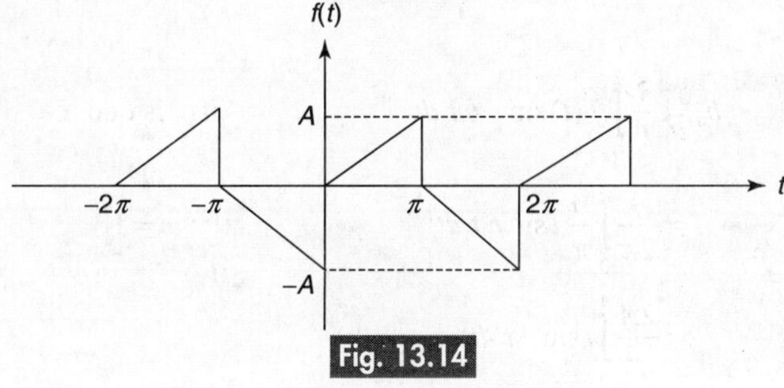


Fig. 13.14

**Solution** The waveform has half-wave symmetry.

$$a_0 = 0$$

$$T = 2\pi$$

$$\omega = \frac{2\pi}{T} = \frac{2\pi}{2\pi} = 1$$

$$f(t) = \frac{A}{\pi}t \qquad 0 < t < \pi$$

The trigonometric Fourier series of $f(t)$ is

$$f(t) = \sum_{n=1}^{\infty} a_n \cos n\,\omega t + \sum_{n=1}^{\infty} b_n \sin n\,\omega t$$

$$a_n = \frac{4}{T}\int_0^{\frac{T}{2}} f(t)\cos n\,\omega t\, dt, \text{ if } n \text{ is odd}$$

$$= \frac{4}{2\pi}\int_0^{\pi} \frac{A}{\pi}\, t\cos nt\, dt \qquad [\because \omega = 1]$$

$$= \frac{2A}{\pi^2}\int_0^{\pi} t\cos nt\, dt$$

$$= \frac{2A}{\pi^2}\left[t\left(\frac{\sin nt}{n}\right) - (1)\left(-\frac{\cos nt}{n^2}\right)\right]_0^{\pi}$$

$$= \frac{2A}{\pi^2}\left[\pi\left(\frac{\sin n\pi}{n}\right) + \frac{\cos n\pi}{n^2} - \frac{\cos 0}{n^2}\right]$$

$$= \frac{2A}{\pi^2}\left[0 + \frac{(-1)^n}{n^2} - \frac{1}{n^2}\right] \qquad \left[\begin{array}{l}\because \sin n\pi = 0\\ \cos n\pi = (-1)^n\end{array}\right]$$

$$= \frac{2A}{n^2\pi^2}\left[(-1)^n - 1\right]$$

$$a_n = -\frac{4A}{n^2\pi^2} \qquad \text{if } n \text{ is odd}$$

$$b_n = \frac{4}{T}\int_0^{\frac{T}{2}} f(t)\sin n\,\omega t\, dt \qquad \text{if } n \text{ is odd}$$

$$= \frac{4}{2\pi}\int_0^{\pi} \frac{A}{\pi}\, t\sin n\, t\, dt \qquad [\because \omega = 1]$$

$$= \frac{2A}{\pi^2}\int_0^{\pi} t\sin n\, t\, dt$$

$$= \frac{2A}{\pi^2}\left[t\left(-\frac{\cos n\, t}{n}\right) - (1)\left(-\frac{\sin n\, t}{n^2}\right)\right]_0^{\pi}$$

$$= \frac{2A}{\pi^2}\left[-\pi\left(\frac{\cos n\pi}{n}\right) + \frac{\sin n\pi}{n^2} - \frac{\sin 0}{n^2}\right]$$

$$= \frac{2A}{\pi^2}\left[-\pi\frac{(-1)^n}{n}\right]$$

$$= \frac{2A}{n\pi}(-1)^n$$

$$b_n = -\frac{2A}{n\pi} \qquad \text{if } n \text{ is odd}$$

$$f(t) = \sum_{\substack{n=1\\ n=odd}}^{\infty}\left[\frac{2A}{n^2\pi^2}\left\{(-1)^n - 1\right\}\right]\cos n\,\omega t + \sum_{\substack{n=1\\ n=odd}}^{\infty}\left\{\frac{2A}{n\pi}(-1)^n\right\}\sin n\,\omega t$$

$$= \left(-\frac{4A}{\pi^2}\cos\,\omega t - \frac{4A}{9\pi^2}\cos 2\,\omega t - \ldots\ldots\right) + \left(-\frac{2A}{\pi}\sin\,\omega t - \frac{2A}{3\pi}\sin 3\,\omega t - \ldots\ldots\right)$$

## EXAMPLE 13.9

*Find the trigonometric Fourier series of the waveform shown in Fig. 13.15.*

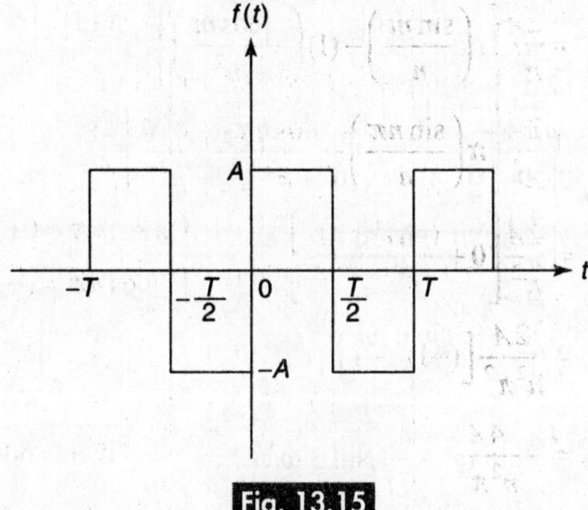


Fig. 13.15

**Solution** The waveform has odd symmetry, half-wave symmetry and quarter-wave symmetry.

$$a_0 = 0 \text{ and } a_n = 0$$

$$f(t) = A \quad 0 < t < \frac{T}{2}$$

The trigonometric Fourier series of $f(t)$ is

$$f(t) = \sum_{n=1}^{\infty} b_n \sin n\,\omega t$$

$$b_n = \frac{4}{T}\int_0^{\frac{T}{2}} f(t) \sin n\,\omega t\, dt$$

$$= \frac{4}{T}\int_0^{\frac{T}{2}} A \sin n\,\omega t\, dt$$

$$= \frac{4A}{T}\left[-\frac{\cos n\,\omega t}{n\omega}\right]_0^{\frac{T}{2}}$$

$$= \frac{4A}{T}\left[-\frac{\cos\left(n\frac{2\pi}{T}t\right)}{n\frac{2\pi}{T}}\right]_0^{\frac{T}{2}} \qquad \left[\because \omega = \frac{2\pi}{T}\right]$$

$$= \frac{4A}{T}\left[-\frac{1}{n\frac{2\pi}{T}}\left\{\cos\left(n\frac{2\pi}{T}\frac{T}{2}\right) - \cos 0\right\}\right]$$

$$= \frac{4A}{T}\left[-\frac{T}{2n\pi}(\cos n\pi - \cos 0)\right]$$

$$= -\frac{2A}{n\pi}\left[(-1)^n - 1\right] \qquad \left[\because \cos n\pi = (-1)^n\right]$$

$$= \frac{2A}{n\pi}\left[1-(-1)^n\right]$$

$$b_n = \begin{cases} 0 & \text{if } n \text{ is even} \\ \dfrac{4A}{n\pi} & \text{if } n \text{ is odd} \end{cases}$$

$$f(t) = \sum_{\substack{n=1 \\ n=odd}}^{\infty} \frac{4A}{n\pi} \sin n\,\omega t$$

$$= \frac{4A}{\pi}\sin \omega t + \frac{4A}{3\pi}\sin 3\,\omega t + \ldots$$

## EXAMPLE 13.10

*Find the trigonometric Fourier series of the waveform shown in Fig. 13.16.*

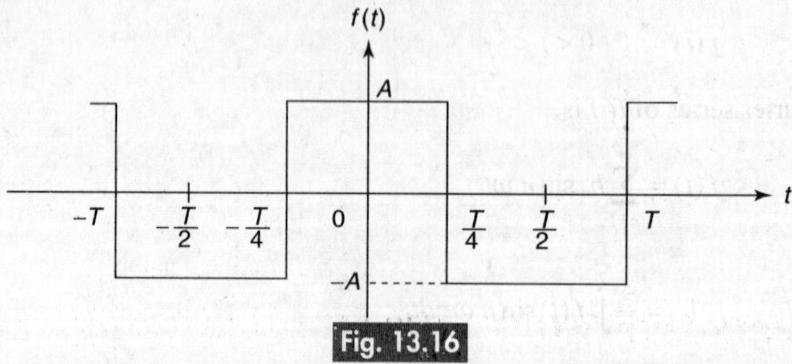


Fig. 13.16

**Solution** The waveform has even symmetry, half-wave symmetry and quarter-wave symmetry.

$$a_0 = 0 \quad \text{and} \quad b_n = 0$$

$$f(t) = A \qquad 0 < t < \frac{T}{4}$$

The trigonometric Fourier series of $f(t)$ is

$$f(t) = \sum_{n=1}^{\infty} a_n \cos n\,\omega t$$

$$a_n = \frac{8}{T}\int_0^{\frac{T}{4}} f(t)\cos n\,\omega t\,dt, \qquad \text{if } n \text{ is odd}$$

$$= \frac{8}{T}\int_0^{\frac{T}{4}} A\cos n\,\omega t\,dt$$

$$= \frac{8A}{T}\left[\frac{\sin n\,\omega t}{n\,\omega}\right]_0^{\frac{T}{4}}$$

$$= \frac{8A}{T}\left[\frac{\sin\left(n\frac{2\pi}{T}t\right)}{n\frac{2\pi}{T}}\right]_0^{\frac{T}{4}} \qquad \left[\because \omega = \frac{2\pi}{T}\right]$$

$$= \frac{8A}{T}\left[\frac{\sin\left(n\frac{2\pi}{T}\frac{T}{4}\right)}{n\frac{2\pi}{T}} - \frac{\sin 0}{n\frac{2\pi}{T}}\right]$$

$$= \frac{8A}{T}\left[\frac{T}{2n\pi}\sin\frac{n\pi}{2} - 0\right]$$

$$= \frac{4A}{n\pi}\sin\frac{n\pi}{2}$$

$$a_n = \begin{cases} \dfrac{4A}{n\pi} & \text{for } n = 1, 5, 9, \ldots\ldots\ldots \\ -\dfrac{4A}{n\pi} & \text{for } n = 3, 7, 11, \ldots\ldots\ldots \end{cases}$$

$$f(t) = \left(\sum_{n=1}^{\infty}\frac{4A}{n\pi}\sin n\frac{\pi}{2}\right)\cos n\,\omega t$$

$$= \frac{4A}{\pi}\cos\omega t - \frac{4A}{3\pi}\cos 3\,\omega t + \frac{4A}{5\pi}\cos 5\,\omega t - \ldots\ldots\ldots$$

## EXAMPLE 13.11

*Find the trigonometric Fourier series of the waveform shown in Fig. 13.17.*

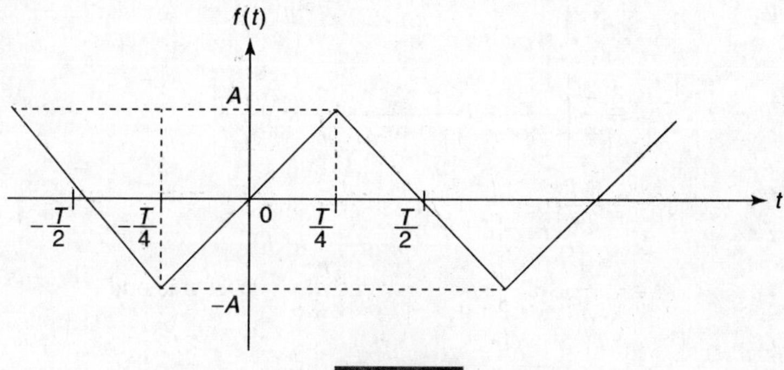


Fig. 13.17

**Solution** The waveform has odd symmetry, half-wave symmetry and quarter-wave symmetry.

$$a_0 = 0 \text{ and } a_n = 0$$

$$f(t) = \frac{4A}{T}t \quad 0 < t < \frac{T}{4}$$

The trigonometric Fourier series of $f(t)$ is

$$f(t) = \sum_{n=1}^{\infty} b_n \sin n\,\omega t$$

$$b_n = \frac{8}{T}\int_0^{\frac{T}{4}} f(t)\sin n\,\omega t\,dt, \qquad \text{if } n \text{ is odd}$$

$$= \frac{8}{T}\int_0^{\frac{T}{4}} \frac{4A}{T} t\sin n\,\omega t\,dt$$

$$= \frac{32A}{T^2}\int_0^{\frac{T}{4}} t\sin n\,\omega t\,dt$$

$$= \frac{32A}{T^2}\left[t\left(-\frac{\cos n\,\omega t}{n\,\omega}\right) - (1)\left(-\frac{\sin n\,\omega t}{n^2\,\omega^2}\right)\right]_0^{\frac{T}{4}}$$

$$= \frac{32A}{T^2}\left[-t\frac{\cos\left(n\frac{2\pi}{T}t\right)}{n\frac{2\pi}{T}} + \frac{\sin\left(n\frac{2\pi}{T}t\right)}{n^2\frac{4\pi^2}{T^2}}\right]_0^{\frac{T}{4}} \qquad \left[\because \omega = \frac{2\pi}{T}\right]$$

$$= \frac{32A}{T^2}\left[-\frac{T}{4}\frac{\cos\left(n\frac{2\pi}{T}\frac{T}{4}\right)}{n\frac{2\pi}{T}} + \frac{\sin\left(n\frac{2\pi}{T}\frac{T}{4}\right)}{n^2\frac{4\pi^2}{T^2}} + 0 - \frac{\sin 0}{n^2\frac{4\pi^2}{T^2}}\right]$$

$$= \frac{32A}{T^2}\left[-\frac{T^2}{8n\pi}\cos\frac{n\pi}{2} + \frac{T^2}{4n^2\pi^2}\sin\frac{n\pi}{2}\right]$$

$$= -\frac{4A}{n\pi}\cos\frac{n\pi}{2} + \frac{8A}{n^2\pi^2}\sin\frac{n\pi}{2}$$

$$= \frac{8A}{n^2\pi^2}\sin\frac{n\pi}{2} \qquad \left[\because \cos\frac{n\pi}{2} = 0 \quad \text{if } n \text{ is odd}\right]$$

$$b_n = \begin{cases} \dfrac{8A}{n^2\pi^2} & \text{for } n = 1, 5, 9, \ldots \\ -\dfrac{8A}{n^2\pi^2} & \text{for } n = 3, 7, 11, \ldots \end{cases}$$

$$f(t) = \sum_{n=1}^{\infty} \left( \frac{8A}{n^2\pi^2} \sin\frac{n\pi}{2} \right) \sin n\,\omega t$$

$$= \frac{8A}{\pi^2} \sin \omega t - \frac{8A}{9\pi^2} \sin 3\,\omega t + \frac{8A}{25\pi^2} \sin 5\,\omega t - \ldots$$

## 13.3 EXPONENTIAL FOURIER SERIES

LO 13.3

Discuss exponential Fourier series

Any periodic function *f(t)* can be expressed into an infinite series in terms of exponential functions.

$$f(t) = \sum_{n=-\infty}^{\infty} c_n\, e^{jn\omega t} \qquad \ldots(13.2)$$

where the coefficient $c_n$ is given by

$$c_n = \frac{1}{T} \int_{-\frac{T}{2}}^{\frac{T}{2}} f(t)\, e^{-jn\omega t}\, dt$$

$$\text{or } c_n = \frac{1}{T} \int_0^T f(t)\, e^{-jn\omega t}\, dt$$

➤ ***Evaluation of $c_n$*** Multiplying Eq. (13.2) by $e^{-jn\omega t}$ and integrating w.r.t $t$ between the limits 0 and $T$,

$$\int_0^T f(t)\, e^{-jn\omega t}\, dt = \int_0^T e^{-jn\omega t} \sum_{n=-\infty}^{\infty} c_n\, e^{jn\omega t}\, dt$$

$$= T\, c_n$$

$$c_n = \frac{1}{T} \int_0^T f(t)\, e^{-jn\omega t}\, dt$$

*Magnitude spectrum* is the plot of the magnitude $c_n$ versus $n\omega$, and *phase spectrum* is the plot of the phase angle $\phi_n$ versus $n\omega$.

**EXAMPLE 13.12**

*Find the exponential Fourier series of the waveform shown in Fig. 13.18. Draw the magnitude spectrum.*

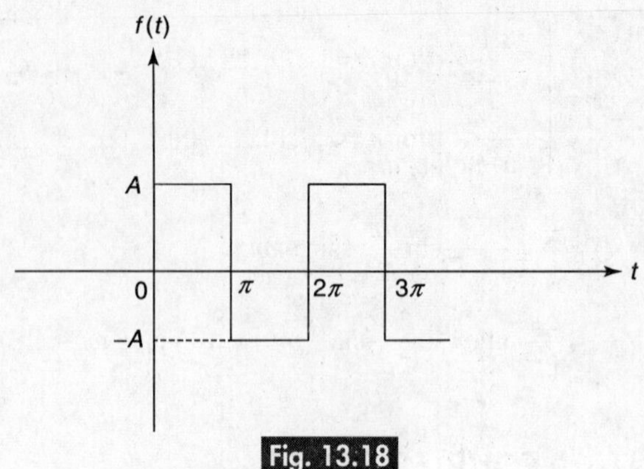


Fig. 13.18

**Solution**

$$T = 2\pi$$

$$\omega = \frac{2\pi}{T} = \frac{2\pi}{2\pi} = 1$$

$$f(t) = A \qquad 0 < t < \pi$$

$$= -A \quad \pi < t < 2\pi$$

The exponential Fourier series of $f(t)$ is

$$f(t) = \sum_{n=-\infty}^{\infty} c_n \, e^{jn\omega t}$$

$$c_n = \frac{1}{T}\int_0^T f(t)\, e^{-jn\omega t}\, dt$$

$$= \frac{1}{2\pi}\left[\int_0^{\pi} A\, e^{-jnt}\, dt + \int_{\pi}^{2\pi} (-A)\, e^{-jnt}\, dt\right] \quad [\because \omega = 1]$$

$$= \frac{A}{2\pi}\left[\frac{e^{-jnt}}{-jn}\right]_0^{\pi} - \frac{A}{2\pi}\left[\frac{e^{-jnt}}{-jn}\right]_{\pi}^{2\pi}$$

$$= \frac{A}{-j2n\pi}\left[e^{-jn\pi} - e^{0}\right] + \frac{A}{j2n\pi}\left[e^{-j2n\pi} - e^{-jn\pi}\right]$$

$$= \frac{A}{-j2n\pi}\left[(-1)^n - 1\right] + \frac{A}{j2n\pi}\left[1 - (-1)^n\right]$$

$$\left[\begin{aligned} \because e^{-jn\pi} &= (-1)^n \\ e^{-j2n\pi} &= 1 \end{aligned}\right]$$

$$= \frac{2A}{j2n\pi}\left[1 - (-1)^n\right]$$

$$= -j\frac{A}{n\pi}\left[1 - (-1)^n\right] \qquad n \neq 0$$

$$c_n = 0 \qquad \text{if } n \text{ is even}$$

$$= -j\frac{2A}{n\pi} \qquad \text{if } n \text{ is odd}$$

$$c_0 = \frac{1}{T}\int_0^T f(t)\,dt$$

$$= \frac{1}{2\pi}\left[\int_0^{\pi} A\,dt + \int_{\pi}^{2\pi} (-A)\,dt\right]$$

$$= \frac{A}{2\pi}[t]_0^{\pi} - \frac{A}{2\pi}[t]_{\pi}^{2\pi}$$

$$= \frac{A}{2\pi}[\pi - 0] - \frac{A}{2\pi}[2\pi - \pi]$$

$$= \frac{A}{2} - \frac{A}{2}$$

$$= 0$$

$$f(t) = \sum_{\substack{n=-\infty \\ n\ odd}}^{\infty} \left(-j\frac{2A}{n\pi}\right) e^{jn\omega t}$$

$$= \ldots + j\frac{2A}{3\pi}e^{-j3\omega t} + j\frac{2A}{\pi}e^{-j\omega t} - j\frac{2A}{\pi}e^{j\omega t} - j\frac{2A}{3\pi}e^{j3\omega t} \ldots$$

The magnitude spectrum is shown in Fig. 13.19.

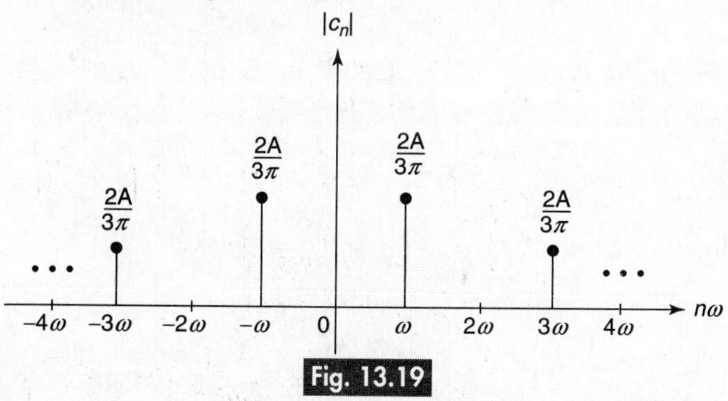


Fig. 13.19

**EXAMPLE 13.13**

*Find the exponential Fourier series of the waveform shown in Fig. 13.20. Draw the magnitude spectrum.*

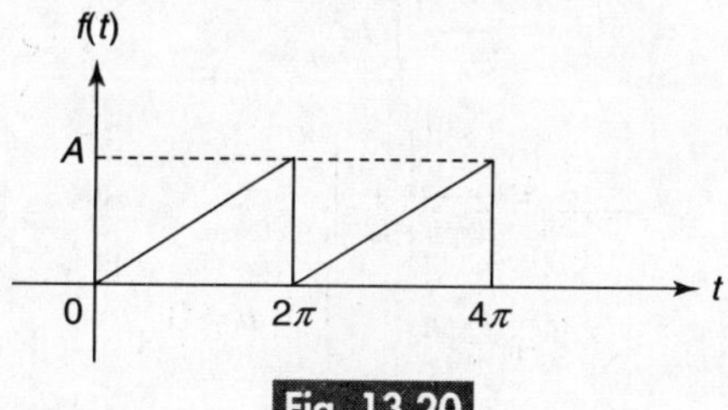


Fig. 13.20

**Solution**

$$T = 2\pi$$

$$\omega = \frac{2\pi}{T} = \frac{2\pi}{2\pi} = 1$$

$$f(t) = \frac{A}{2\pi} t \qquad 0 < t < 2\pi$$

The exponential Fourier series is

$$f(t) = \sum_{n=-\infty}^{\infty} c_n \, e^{jn\omega t}$$

$$c_n = \frac{1}{T}\int_0^T f(t)\, e^{-jn\omega t}\, dt$$

$$= \frac{1}{2\pi}\int_0^{2\pi} \frac{A}{2\pi} t \, e^{-jnt}\, dt \qquad [\because \omega = 1]$$

$$= \frac{A}{4\pi^2}\int_0^{2\pi} t\, e^{-jnt}\, dt$$

$$= \frac{A}{4\pi^2}\left[t\left(\frac{e^{-jnt}}{-jn}\right) - \left\{\frac{e^{-jnt}}{(-jn)^2}\right\}\right]_0^{2\pi}$$

$$= \frac{A}{4\pi^2}\left[2\pi\frac{e^{-j2n\pi}}{-jn} + \frac{e^{-j2n\pi}}{n^2} - 0 - \frac{1}{n^2}\right]$$

$$= \frac{A}{4\pi^2}\left[\frac{2\pi}{-jn} + \frac{1}{n^2} - \frac{1}{n^2}\right] \qquad \left[\because e^{-j2n\pi} = 1\right]$$

$$= \frac{A}{4\pi^2}\, j\frac{2\pi}{n}$$

$$= j\frac{A}{2\pi n} \qquad n \neq 0$$

$$c_0 = \frac{1}{T}\int_0^T f(t)\, dt$$

$$= \frac{1}{2\pi}\int_0^{2\pi} \frac{A}{2\pi} t\, dt$$

$$= \frac{A}{4\pi^2}\int_0^{2\pi} t\, dt$$

$$= \frac{A}{4\pi^2}\left[\frac{t^2}{2}\right]_0^{2\pi}$$

$$= \frac{A}{2}$$

$$f(t) = \frac{A}{2} + \sum_{\substack{n=-\infty \\ n\neq 0}}^{\infty} j\frac{A}{2\pi n} e^{jn\omega t}$$

$$= \ldots - j\frac{A}{2\pi} e^{-j2\omega t} - j\frac{A}{4\pi} e^{-j\omega t} + \frac{A}{2} + j\frac{A}{2\pi} e^{j\omega t} + j\frac{A}{4\pi} e^{j2\omega t} + \ldots$$

The magnitude spectrum is shown in Fig. 13.21.

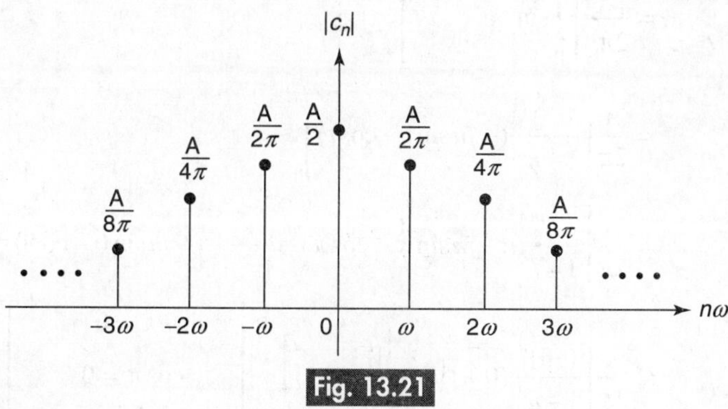


Fig. 13.21

## EXAMPLE 13.14

*Find the exponential Fourier series of the waveform shown in Fig. 13.22.*

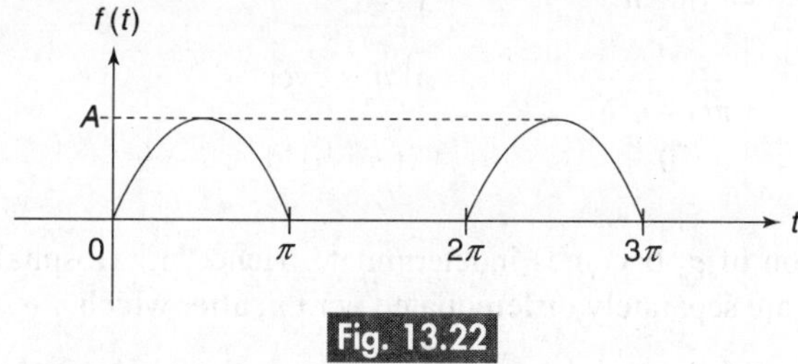


Fig. 13.22

**Solution**

$$T = 2\pi$$

$$\omega = \frac{2\pi}{T} = \frac{2\pi}{2\pi} = 1$$

$$f(t) = A\sin\omega t$$

$$f(t) = A\sin t \qquad 0 < t < \pi$$

$$= 0 \qquad \pi < t < 2\pi$$

The exponential Fourier series of $f(t)$ is

$$f(t) = \sum_{n=-\infty}^{\infty} c_n e^{jn\omega t}$$

$$c_n = \frac{1}{T}\int_0^T f(t)\, e^{-jn\omega t}\, dt$$

$$= \frac{1}{2\pi}\left[\int_0^{\pi} A \sin t\, e^{-jnt}\, dt + \int_{\pi}^{2\pi} 0\, dt\right] \qquad [\because \omega = 1]$$

$$= \frac{A}{2\pi}\left[\int_0^{\pi} \sin t\, e^{-jnt}\, dt\right]$$

$$= \frac{A}{2\pi}\left[\frac{e^{-jnt}}{1-n^2}(-jn\sin t - \cos t)\right]_0^{\pi}$$

$$= \frac{A}{2\pi}\left[\frac{e^{-jn\pi}}{1-n^2}(-jn\sin\pi - \cos\pi) - \frac{e^0}{1-n^2}(-jn\sin 0 - \cos 0)\right]$$

$$= \frac{A}{2\pi}\left[\frac{(-1)^n}{1-n^2}(0+1) - \frac{1}{1-n^2}(-1)\right] \qquad \left[\begin{array}{l}\because \sin n\pi = 0 \\ \cos\pi = 0 \\ e^{-jn\pi} = (-1)^n\end{array}\right]$$

$$= \frac{A}{2\pi}\left[\frac{1}{1-n^2}\left\{(-1)^n + 1\right\}\right], \qquad n \neq \pm 1$$

$$= \begin{cases} \dfrac{A}{\pi(1-n^2)} & \text{if } n \text{ is even} \\ 0 & \text{if } n \text{ is odd} \end{cases}$$

When $n = \pm 1$, the expression of $c_n$ becomes indeterminate. Hence, L' Hospital's rule is applied, i.e., the numerator and denominator are separately differentiated w.r.t $n$, after which $n$ is allowed to approach $\pm 1$.

$$c_n = \frac{A}{2\pi}\left[\frac{1}{1-n^2}(e^{-jn\pi} + 1)\right]$$

$$= \frac{A}{2\pi}\frac{(e^{-jn\pi} + 1)}{1-n^2}$$

$$= \frac{A}{2\pi}\left(\frac{-j\pi\, e^{-jn\pi}}{-2n}\right)$$

$$= j\frac{A}{4n}e^{-jn\pi}$$

when $n \to 1$, $c_1 = j\frac{A}{4}e^{-j\pi} = -j\frac{A}{4}$ $\qquad [\because e^{-j\pi} = -1]$

when $n \to -1$, $c_{-1} = -j\frac{A}{4}e^{j\pi} = j\frac{A}{4}$ $\qquad [\because e^{j\pi} = -1]$

When $n = 0$,

$$c_0 = \frac{1}{2\pi}\int_0^{\pi} A \sin t \, dt$$

$$= \frac{A}{2\pi}[-\cos t]_0^{\pi}$$

$$= \frac{A}{2\pi}[-\cos \pi + \cos 0]$$

$$= \frac{A}{2\pi}(1+1) \qquad [\because \cos \pi = (-1)]$$

$$= \frac{A}{\pi}$$

$$f(t) = \frac{A}{\pi} - j\frac{A}{4} + \sum_{\substack{n=-\infty \\ n=\text{even} \\ n\neq 0 \\ n\neq \pm 1}}^{\infty} \frac{A}{\pi(1-n^2)} e^{jn\omega t}$$

$$= \ldots - \frac{A}{3\pi} e^{-j2\omega t} + j\frac{A}{4} + \frac{A}{\pi} - j\frac{A}{4} - \frac{A}{3\pi} e^{j2\omega t} - \ldots$$

## EXAMPLE 13.15

*Find the exponential Fourier series of the waveform shown in Fig. 13.23.*

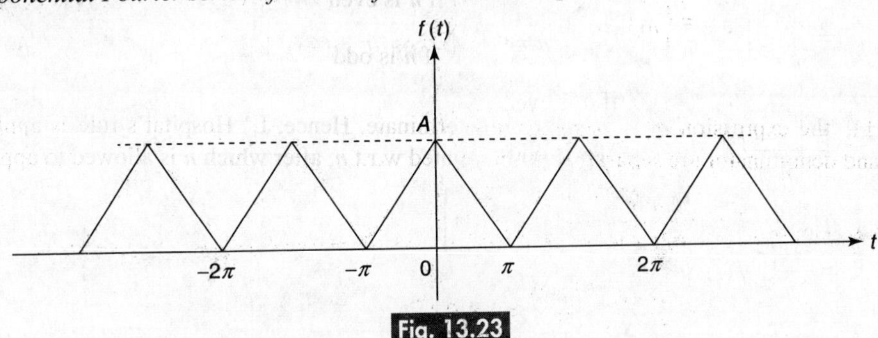


Fig. 13.23

**Solution**

$$T = 2\pi$$

$$\omega = \frac{2\pi}{T} = \frac{2\pi}{2\pi} = 1$$

$$f(t) = \frac{A}{\pi}t + A \qquad -\pi < t < 0$$

$$= -\frac{A}{\pi}t + A \qquad 0 < t < \pi$$

The exponential Fourier series of *f(t)* is

$$f(t) = \sum_{n=-\infty}^{\infty} c_n \, e^{jn\omega t}$$

$$c_n = \frac{1}{T}\int_{-\frac{T}{2}}^{\frac{T}{2}} f(t)e^{-jn\omega t}\, dt$$

$$= \frac{1}{2\pi}\int_{-\pi}^{\pi} f(t)\, e^{-jn\omega t}\, dt$$

$$= \frac{1}{2\pi}\left[\int_{-\pi}^{0}\left(\frac{A}{\pi}t + A\right)e^{-jnt}\, dt + \int_{0}^{\pi}\left(-\frac{A}{\pi}t + A\right)e^{-jnt}\, dt\right]$$

$$= \frac{A}{2\pi}\left[\left(\frac{t}{\pi}+1\right)\frac{e^{-jnt}}{-jn} - \frac{1}{\pi}\cdot\frac{e^{-jnt}}{(-jn)^2}\right]_{-\pi}^{0} + \frac{A}{2\pi}\left[\left(-\frac{t}{\pi}+1\right)\frac{e^{-jnt}}{-jn} - \left(-\frac{1}{\pi}\right)\frac{e^{-jnt}}{-jn^2}\right]_{0}^{\pi}$$

$$= \frac{A}{2\pi}\left[-\frac{1}{jn} + \frac{1}{\pi}\cdot\frac{1}{n^2} - \frac{1}{\pi}\cdot\frac{e^{jn\pi}}{n^2}\right] + \frac{A}{2\pi}\left[\frac{1}{jn} - \frac{1}{\pi}\frac{e^{-jn\pi}}{n^2} + \frac{1}{\pi}\frac{1}{n^2}\right]$$

$$= \frac{A}{2\pi}\left[\frac{2}{\pi n^2} - \frac{1}{\pi n^2}(e^{jn\pi} + e^{-jn\pi})\right]$$

$$= \frac{A}{2\pi}\left[\frac{2}{\pi n^2} - \frac{1}{\pi n^2}\cdot 2\cos n\pi\right]$$

$$= \frac{A}{n^2\pi^2}\left[1-(-1)^n\right], \qquad n \neq 0 \qquad [\because \cos n\pi = (-1)^n]$$

$$= \begin{cases} 0 & \text{if } n \text{ is even} \\ \dfrac{2A}{n^2\pi^2} & \text{if } n \text{ is odd} \end{cases}$$

For $n = 0$,

$$c_0 = \frac{1}{2\pi}\int_{-\pi}^{\pi} f(t)\, dt$$

$$= \frac{1}{2\pi}\left[\int_{-\pi}^{0}\left(\frac{A}{\pi}t + A\right)dt + \int_{0}^{\pi}\left(-\frac{A}{\pi}t + A\right)dt\right]$$

$$= \frac{1}{2\pi}\left[\frac{A}{\pi}\frac{t^2}{2} + At\right]_{-\pi}^{0} + \frac{1}{2\pi}\left[-\frac{A}{\pi}\frac{t^2}{2} + At\right]_{0}^{\pi}$$

$$= \frac{1}{2\pi}\left[-\frac{A}{\pi}\frac{\pi^2}{2} + A\pi\right] + \frac{1}{2\pi}\left[-\frac{A}{\pi}\frac{\pi^2}{2} + A\pi\right]$$

$$= \frac{1}{2\pi}\left[-\frac{A\pi}{2} + A\pi\right] + \frac{1}{2\pi}\left[-\frac{A\pi}{2} + A\pi\right]$$

$$= \frac{1}{2\pi}\left[\frac{A\pi}{2}\right] + \frac{1}{2\pi}\left[\frac{A\pi}{2}\right]$$

$$= \frac{A}{4} + \frac{A}{4}$$

$$= \frac{A}{2}$$

$$f(t) = \frac{A}{2} + \sum_{\substack{n=-\infty \\ n=\text{odd} \\ n\neq 0}}^{\infty} \frac{2A}{n^2\pi^2} e^{jn\omega t}$$

$$= \frac{A}{2} + \frac{2A}{\pi^2} e^{j\omega t} + \frac{2A}{9\pi^2} e^{j3\omega t} + \ldots$$

## 13.4 AVERAGE VALUE OF A PERIODIC COMPLEX WAVE

LO 13.4

Derive the expressions for average value and rms value of a periodic complex wave

Let the Fourier series representation of a periodic complex wave be,

$$v(t) = V_0 + \sum_{n=1}^{n} V_{nm} \sin(n\omega t + \phi_n)$$

$$= V_0 + V_{1m} \sin(\omega t + \phi_1) + V_{2m} \sin(2\omega t + \phi_2) + \ldots\ldots + V_{nm} \sin(n\omega t + \phi_n)$$

The average value of the periodic wave is given by

$$V_{\text{avg}} = \frac{1}{T}\int_0^T v(t)\, dt$$

Since the integration of any sine function between $T = 0$ to $T = 2\pi$ is zero,

$$V_{\text{avg}} = V_0 + 0 + 0 + \cdots$$

$$= V_0$$

Hence, the average value of any periodic complex wave is the constant term of the Fourier series representing the periodic wave.

## 13.5 rms VALUE OF PERIODIC COMPLEX WAVE

LO 13.4

Let the Fourier series representation of a periodic complex wave be,

$$v(t) = V_0 + \sum_{n=1}^{n} V_{nm} \sin(\omega t + \phi_n)$$

$$= V_0 + V_{1m} \sin(\omega t + \phi_1) + V_{2m} \sin(2\omega t + \phi_2) \ldots\ldots + V_{nm} \sin(n\omega t + \phi_n)$$

The rms value of the periodic wave is given by

$$V_{\text{rms}} = \sqrt{\frac{1}{T}\int_0^T v^2(t)\,dt}$$

$$= \sqrt{\frac{1}{2\pi}\int_0^{2\pi} [V_0 + V_{1m}\sin(\omega t+\phi_1) + V_{2m}\sin(\omega t+\phi_2) + \cdots + V_{nm}\sin(\omega t+\phi_n)]^2\,dt}$$

It can be proved that

$$V_{\text{rms}} = \sqrt{V_0^2 + \frac{V_{1m}^2}{2} + \frac{V_{2m}^2}{2} + \cdots + \frac{V_{nm}^2}{2}}$$

$$= \sqrt{V_0^2 + \left(\frac{V_{1m}}{\sqrt{2}}\right)^2 + \left(\frac{V_{2m}}{\sqrt{2}}\right)^2 + \cdots + \left(\frac{V_{nm}}{\sqrt{2}}\right)^2}$$

$$= \sqrt{V_0^2 + V_1^2 + V_2^2 + \ldots + V_n^2}$$

where $V_1, V_2, \ldots, V_n$ are the rms values of the harmonic components of the wave. Hence, the rms value of any periodic complex wave is the square root of sum of squares of rms values of each harmonic component and the square of constant terms.

## 13.6 POWER SUPPLIED BY COMPLEX WAVE

LO 13.5

Derive the expression for power supplied by complex wave

Let the complex voltage be represented by the equation

$$v(t) = V_0 + \sum_{n=1}^{n} V_{nm}\sin(n\omega t + \phi_n)$$

be applied to a circuit. Let the equation of the resultant current be

$$i(t) = I_0 + \sum_{n=1}^{n} I_{nm}\sin(n\omega t + \phi_n + \psi_n)$$

The average power of the complex wave is given by

$$P_{\text{avg}} = \frac{1}{2\pi}\int_0^{2\pi} v\cdot i\,dt$$

$$= \frac{1}{2\pi}\int_0^{2\pi}\left[\left\{V_0 + \sum_{n=1}^{n} V_{nm}\sin(n\omega t+\phi_n)\right\}\cdot\left\{I_0 + \sum_{n=1}^{n} I_{nm}\sin(n\omega t+\phi_n+\psi_n)\right\}\right]dt$$

$$= \frac{1}{2\pi}\int_0^{2\pi}\left[V_0 I_0 + V_0\sum_{n=1}^{n} I_{nm}\sin(n\omega t+\phi_n+\psi_n) + I_0\sum_{n=1}^{n} V_{nm}\sin(n\omega t+\phi_n)\right.$$

$$\left. + \left[\left\{\sum_{n=1}^{n} V_{nm}\sin(n\omega t+\phi_n)\right\}\left\{\sum_{n=1}^{n} I_{nm}\sin(n\omega t+\phi_n+\psi_n)\right\}\right]\right]dt$$

$$= V_0 I_0 + \frac{V_{1m} V_{1m}}{2} \cos\psi_1 + \frac{V_{2m} I_{2m}}{2} \cos\psi_2 + \ldots\ldots + \frac{V_{nm} I_{nm}}{2} \cos\psi_n$$

$$= V_0 I_0 + V_1 I_1 \cos\psi_1 + V_2 I_2 \cos\psi_2 + \ldots\ldots + V_n I_n \cos\psi_n$$

Hence, the average power supplied by a complex wave is the sum of the average power supplied by each harmonic component acting independently.

## EXAMPLE 13.16

*A complex wave is given by $i(t) = 10 + 100 \sin\omega t + 40 \sin 5\,\omega t$. Determine the average value and rms value of the complex wave.*

**Solution**

$$i(t) = 10 + 100 \sin\omega t + 40 \sin 5\omega t$$

$$I_{avg} = 10 \text{ A}$$

$$I_{rms} = \sqrt{(10)^2 + \left(\frac{100}{\sqrt{2}}\right)^2 + \left(\frac{40}{\sqrt{2}}\right)^2} = 76.81 \text{ A}$$

## EXAMPLE 13.17

*A complex wave of 240 V rms value has 20% third harmonic content, 5% fifth harmonic content and 2% seventh harmonic content. Find the rms value of the fundamental and each harmonic.*

**Solution** Let $V_1, V_3, V_5$ and $V_7$ be the rms values of the fundamental and harmonic voltages.

$$V_3 = 0.2\ V_1$$

$$V_5 = 0.05\ V_1$$

$$V_7 = 0.02\ V_1$$

$$V_{rms} = \sqrt{V_1^2 + V_3^2 + V_5^2 + V_7^2}$$

$$240 = \sqrt{V_1^2 + (0.2V_1)^2 + (0.05V_1)^2 + (0.02V_1)^2}$$

$$V_1 = 235.01 \text{ V}$$

$$V_3 = 0.2 \times 235.01 = 47 \text{ V}$$

$$V_5 = 0.05 \times 235.01 = 11.75 \text{ V}$$

$$V_7 = 0.02 \times 235.01 = 4.7 \text{ V}$$

## EXAMPLE 13.18

*Find the value of R if the average power dissipated in the resistor is 1000 W if the voltage has the following Fourier series:*

$$v(t) = 200 \sin\omega t + 100 \sin 3\omega t + 50 \sin 5\omega t$$

**Solution**

$$V_{rms} = \sqrt{\left(\frac{200}{\sqrt{2}}\right)^2 + \left(\frac{100}{\sqrt{2}}\right)^2 + \left(\frac{50}{\sqrt{2}}\right)^2} = 162.02 \text{ V}$$

$$P = \frac{V_{\text{rms}}^2}{R}$$

$$1000 = \frac{(162.02)^2}{R}$$

$$R = 26.25\ \Omega$$

## EXAMPLE 13.19

*If $v(t) = 10 + 6\cos(t + 45°) + 1.8\cos(2t - 10)°$ volts and $i(t) = 3 + 1.4\cos(t + 20°)$ $+0.5\cos 2t$ A, determine the effective value of the voltage and current. Also, calculate the average power.*

**Solution**

$$v(t) = 10 + 6\cos(t + 45°) + 1.8\cos(2t - 10)°$$

$$V_{\text{eff}} = \sqrt{V_{0m}^2 + \left(\frac{V_{1m}}{\sqrt{2}}\right)^2 + \left(\frac{V_{2m}}{\sqrt{2}}\right)^2} = \sqrt{(10)^2 + \left(\frac{6}{\sqrt{2}}\right)^2 + \left(\frac{1.8}{\sqrt{2}}\right)^2} = 10.94\ \text{V}$$

$$i(t) = 3 + 1.4\cos(t + 20°) + 0.5\cos 2t$$

$$I_{\text{eff}} = \sqrt{I_{om}^2 + \left(\frac{I_{1m}}{\sqrt{2}}\right)^2 + \left(\frac{I_{2m}}{\sqrt{2}}\right)^2} = \sqrt{(3)^2 + \left(\frac{1.4}{\sqrt{2}}\right)^2 + \left(\frac{0.5}{\sqrt{2}}\right)^2} = 3.18\ \text{A}$$

$$P_{\text{avg}} = V_{0m} I_{0m} + \frac{V_{1m} I_{1m}}{2}\cos\phi_1 + \frac{V_{2m} I_{2m}}{2}\cos\phi_2$$

$$= 10 \times 3 + \frac{6 \times 1.4}{2}\cos(45° - 20°) + \frac{1.8 \times 5}{2}\cos(-10°)$$

$$= 34.25\ \text{W}$$

## EXAMPLE 13.20

*A series RL circuit with $R = 10\ \Omega$ and $L = 5\ H$ contains a current $i(t) = 10\ \sin 1000\,t + 5\sin 3000\,t + 3\sin 5000t$. Find the effective value of voltage and the average power.*

**Solution**

$$i(t) = 10\sin 1000t + 5\sin 3000t + 3\sin 5000t$$

$$\omega = 1000\ \text{rad/s}$$

For fundamental harmonic,

$$R_1 = 10\ \Omega$$

$$X_{L_1} = \omega L = 1000 \times 5 = 5000\ \Omega$$

$$\mathbf{Z}_1 = 10 + j5000 = 5000\angle 89.89°\ \Omega$$

For third harmonic,

$$R_3 = 10\ \Omega$$

$$X_{L_3} = 3\omega L = 3 \times 1000 \times 5 = 15000\ \Omega$$

$$\mathbf{Z}_3 = 10 + j15000 = 15000\angle 89.96°\ \Omega$$

For fifth harmonic,

$$R_5 = 10\ \Omega$$

$$X_{L_5} = 5\omega L = 5\times 1000\times 5 = 25000\ \Omega$$

$$\mathbf{Z}_5 = 10 + j25000 = 25000\angle 89.98°\ \Omega$$

$$v(t) = (10)(5000)\sin(1000t + 89.89°) + (5)(15000)\sin(3000t + 89.96°)$$

$$+ 3(25000)\sin(5000t + 89.98°)$$

$$= 50000\sin(1000t + 89.89°) + 75000\sin(3000t + 89.96°)$$

$$+ 75000\sin(5000t + 89.98°)$$

$$V_{\text{eff}} = \sqrt{\left(\frac{V_{1m}}{\sqrt{2}}\right)^2 + \left(\frac{V_{2m}}{\sqrt{2}}\right)^2 + \left(\frac{V_{3m}}{\sqrt{2}}\right)^2} = \sqrt{\left(\frac{50000}{\sqrt{2}}\right)^2 + \left(\frac{75000}{\sqrt{2}}\right)^2 + \left(\frac{75000}{\sqrt{2}}\right)^2} = 82.92\ \text{kV}$$

$$P_{\text{avg}} = \frac{V_{1m}I_{1m}}{2}\cos\phi_1 + \frac{V_{2m}I_{2m}}{2}\cos\phi_2 + \frac{V_{3m}I_{3m}}{2}\cos\phi_3$$

$$= \frac{50000\times 10}{2}\cos(89.89°) + \frac{75000\times 5}{2}\cos(89.96°) + \frac{75000\times 3}{2}\cos(89.98°)$$

$$= 650.13\ \text{W}$$

**EXAMPLE 13.21**

*The voltage given by $v(t) = 100\cos 314t + 50\sin(1570t - 30°)$ is applied to a circuit consisting of a resistor of 10 Ω, an inductor of 0.02 H and a capacitor of 50 μF. Determine the instantaneous current through the circuit. Also, find the rms value of the voltage and current.*

**Solution** $v(t) = 100\cos 314t + 50\sin(1570t - 30°)$

$$\omega = 314\ \text{rad/s}$$

For fundamental harmonic,

$$R_1 = 10\ \Omega$$

$$X_{L_1} = \omega L = 314\times 0.02 = 6.28\ \Omega$$

$$X_{C_1} = \frac{1}{\omega C} = \frac{1}{314\times 50\times 10^{-6}} = 63.69\ \Omega$$

$$\mathbf{Z}_1 = 10 + j6.28 - j63.69 = 58.27\angle -80.12°\ \Omega$$

For fifth harmonic,

$$R_5 = 10\ \Omega$$

$$X_{L_5} = 5\omega L = 5\times 314\times 0.02 = 31.4\ \Omega$$

$$X_{C_5} = \frac{1}{5\omega C} = \frac{1}{5\times 314\times 50\times 10^{-6}} = 12.74\ \Omega$$

$$\mathbf{Z}_2 = 10 + j31.4 - j12.74 = 21.17\angle 61.81°\ \Omega$$

$$i(t) = \frac{100}{58.27}\cos(314t + 80.12°) + \frac{50}{21.17}\sin(1570t - 30° - 61.81°)$$

$$= 1.72\cos(314t + 80.12°) + 2.36\sin(1570t - 91.81°)$$

$$V_{\text{rms}} = \sqrt{\left(\frac{V_{1m}}{\sqrt{2}}\right)^2 + \left(\frac{V_{2m}}{\sqrt{2}}\right)^2} = \sqrt{\left(\frac{100}{\sqrt{2}}\right)^2 + \left(\frac{50}{\sqrt{2}}\right)^2} = 79.06 \text{ V}$$

$$I_{\text{rms}} = \sqrt{\left(\frac{I_{1m}}{\sqrt{2}}\right)^2 + \left(\frac{I_{2m}}{\sqrt{2}}\right)^2} = \sqrt{\left(\frac{1.72}{\sqrt{2}}\right)^2 + \left(\frac{2.36}{\sqrt{2}}\right)^2} = 2.06 \text{ A}$$

## 13.7 FOURIER TRANSFORM

LO 13.6

Explain Fourier transform

Any non-periodic signal can be viewed as a limiting case of a periodic signal where the period of the signal approaches infinity.

Consider a periodic signal $f(t)$ with period $T$. The Fourier series representation for this signal is

$$f(t) = \frac{1}{T}\sum_{n=-\infty}^{\infty} c_n\, e^{jn\omega t} \qquad \ldots(13.3)$$

where

$$c_n = \int_{-\frac{T}{2}}^{\frac{T}{2}} f(t)\, e^{-jn\omega t}\, dt$$

and

$$\omega = \frac{2\pi}{T}$$

A typical discrete magnitude spectrum is shown in Fig. 13.24.

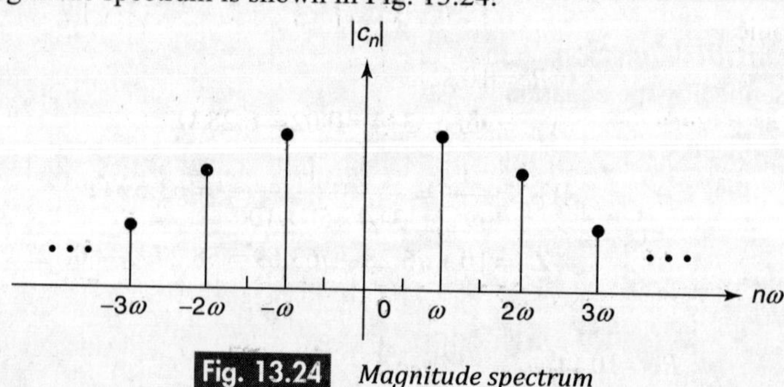


**Fig. 13.24** *Magnitude spectrum*

The spacing between successive harmonics is $\omega = \dfrac{2\pi}{T} = \Delta\omega$ (say)

$$\frac{1}{T} = \frac{\Delta\omega}{2\pi}$$

Hence, Eq. (13.3) can be written as

$$f(t) = \frac{1}{2\pi} \sum_{n=-\infty}^{\infty} c_n \, e^{jn\omega t} (\Delta\omega)$$

Considering the limiting case as $T \to \infty$, $\Delta\omega \to 0$, the discrete line in the spectrum merges to form a continuous spectrum. The infinite sum becomes an integral. $c_n$ is now defined for all frequencies, rather only for integral multiples of $\omega$. The integer $n$ has no significance now and in the limit as $T \to \infty$, $c_n$ becomes a continuous function.

$$F(\omega) = \lim_{T\to\infty} c_n$$

$$F(\omega) = \int_{-\infty}^{\infty} f(t)\, e^{-j\omega t}\, dt \qquad \text{...(13.4)}$$

The Fourier series for a periodic signal now becomes the Fourier integral representation for non-periodic signal over the entire interval given by

$$f(t) = \frac{1}{2\pi} \int_{-\infty}^{\infty} F(\omega) e^{j\omega t}\, d\omega \qquad \text{...(13.5)}$$

The above Eqs (13.4) and (13.5) represent a Fourier transform pair.

### Conditions for Existence of Fourier Transform

Fourier transform $F(\omega)$ exists if the function $f(t)$ satisfies the following Dirichlet's conditions:

(i) $f(t)$ is absolutely integrable.
(ii) $f(t)$ has a finite number of maxima and minima.
(iii) $f(t)$ has a finite number of discontinuities.

There are certain functions which are not absolutely intergrable. In such cases, we find the Fourier transform of the function as the limiting value of the Fourier transform of some other function.

## 13.8 FOURIER TRANSFORMS OF SOME USEFUL FUNCTIONS

LO 13.7

Derive Fourier transforms of one-sided exponential function, two-sided exponential function, gate function, impulse function, constant function, signum function, unit step function, sine function, cosine function and exponential function

***1. One-sided Exponential Function*** One-sided exponential function shown in Fig. 13.25 is defined by the equation

$$f(t) = e^{-at} \qquad 0 < t < \infty$$
$$= 0 \qquad t < 0$$

$$F(\omega) = \int_{-\infty}^{\infty} f(t) e^{-j\omega t}\, dt$$

$$= \int_{-\infty}^{\infty} e^{-at} e^{-j\omega t}\, dt$$

$$= \int_{-\infty}^{\infty} e^{-(a+j\omega)t}\, dt$$

$$= \left[ \frac{e^{-(a+j\omega)t}}{-(a+j\omega)} \right]_0^{\infty}$$

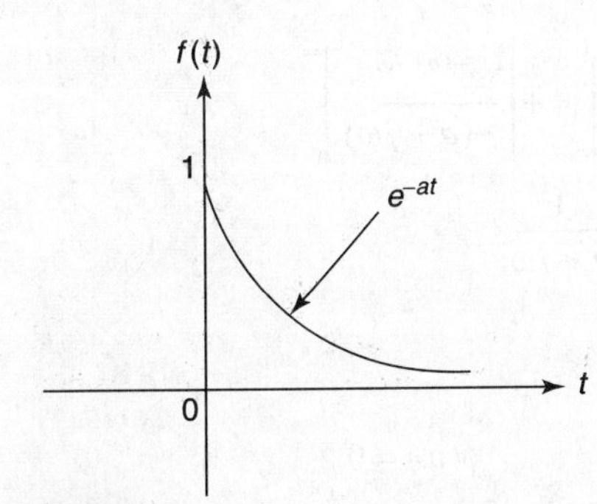

Fig. 13.25 *One-sided exponential function*

$$= \frac{1}{a + j\omega}$$

$$|F(\omega)| = \frac{1}{\sqrt{a^2 + \omega^2}}$$

The magnitude and phase spectrum are shown in Fig. 13.26.

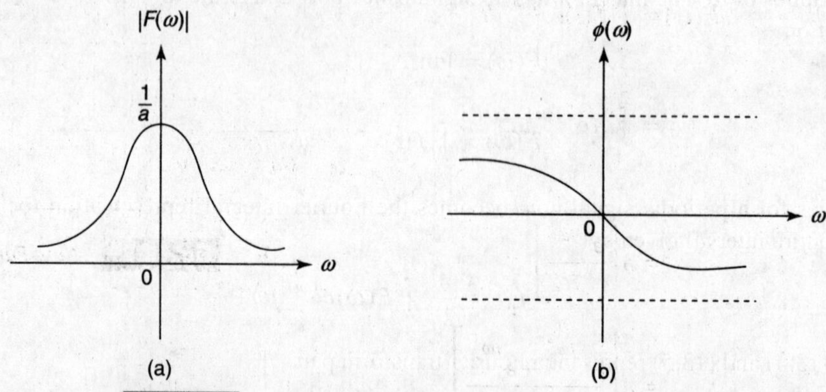


Fig. 13.26 *(a) Magnitude spectrum, (b) Phase spectrum*

***2. Two-sided Exponential Function*** Two-sided exponential function shown in Fig. 13.27 is defined by the equation

$$f(t) = e^{-at} \qquad t > 0$$

$$= e^{at} \qquad t < 0$$

$$F(\omega) = \int_{-\infty}^{\infty} f(t) e^{-j\omega t}\, dt$$

$$= \int_{-\infty}^{0} e^{at} e^{-j\omega t}\, dt + \int_{0}^{\infty} e^{-at} e^{-j\omega t}\, dt$$

$$= \int_{-\infty}^{0} e^{(a-j\omega)t}\, dt + \int_{0}^{\infty} e^{-(a+j\omega)t}\, dt$$

$$= \left[\frac{e^{(a-j\omega)t}}{(a - j\omega)}\right]_{-\infty}^{0} + \left[\frac{e^{-(a+j\omega)t}}{-(a + j\omega)}\right]_{0}^{\infty}$$

$$= \frac{1}{a - j\omega} + \frac{1}{a + j\omega}$$

$$= \frac{2a}{a^2 + \omega^2}$$

$$|F(\omega)| = \frac{2a}{a^2 + \omega^2}, \qquad \phi(\omega) = 0$$

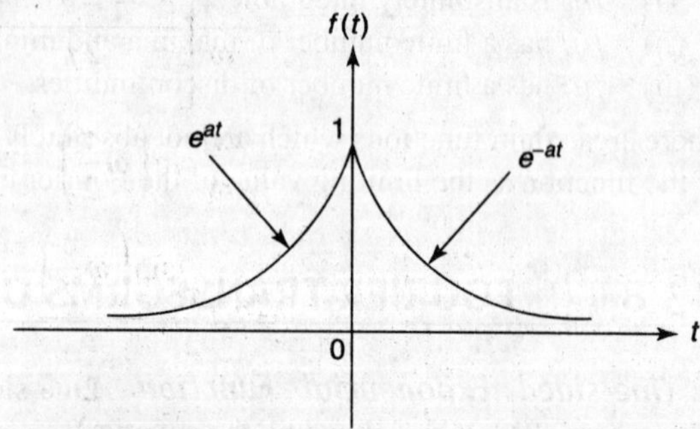


Fig. 13.27 *Two-sided exponential function*

The magnitude spectrum is shown in Fig. 13.28.

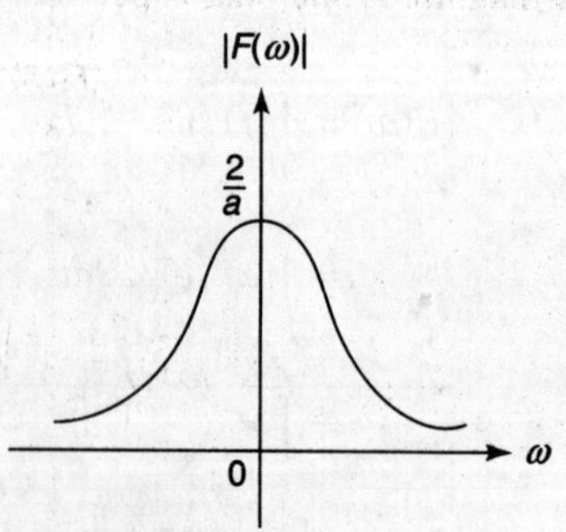


Fig. 13.28 *Magnitude Spectrum*

***3. Gate Function*** The gate function shown in Fig. 13.29 is defined by the equation

$$f(t) = A \qquad -\frac{\tau}{2} < t < \frac{\tau}{2}$$

$$= 0 \qquad |t| > \frac{\tau}{2}$$

$$F(\omega) = \int_{-\infty}^{\infty} f(t) e^{-j\omega t}\, dt$$

$$= \int_{-\frac{\tau}{2}}^{\frac{\tau}{2}} A e^{-j\omega t}\, dt$$

$$= A \left[ \frac{e^{-j\omega t}}{-j\omega} \right]_{-\frac{\tau}{2}}^{\frac{\tau}{2}}$$

$$= A \left[ \frac{e^{-j\omega\frac{\tau}{2}} - e^{j\omega\frac{\tau}{2}}}{-j\omega} \right]$$

$$= \frac{2A}{\omega} \left[ \frac{e^{j\omega\frac{\tau}{2}} - e^{-j\omega\frac{\tau}{2}}}{2j} \right]$$

$$= \frac{2A}{\omega} \sin\left( \omega \frac{\tau}{2} \right)$$

$$= 2A\frac{\tau}{2} \frac{\sin\left( \omega \frac{\tau}{2} \right)}{\omega \frac{\tau}{2}}$$

$$= A\tau \,\text{Sa}\left( \omega \frac{\tau}{2} \right)$$

**Fig. 13.29** *Gate Function*

The magnitude and phase spectrum are shown in Fig. 13.30.

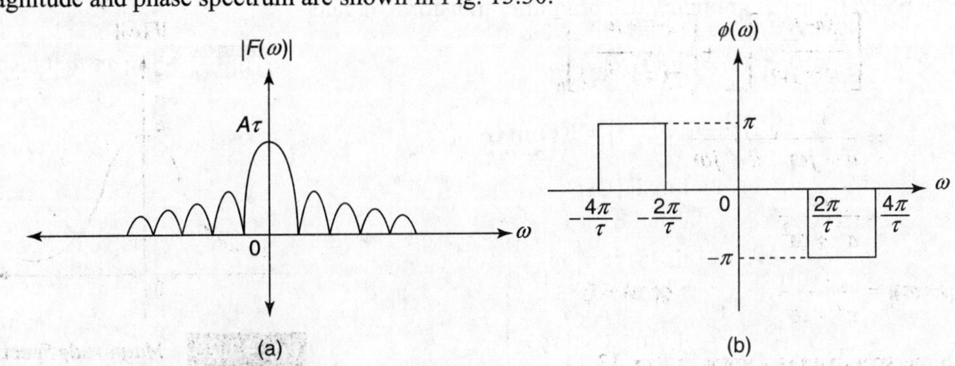


**Fig. 13.30** *(a) Magnitude spectrum (b) Phase spectrum*

**4. Impulse Function** The impulse function shown in Fig. 13.31 is defined by the equation

$$\delta(t) = 0 \qquad t \neq 0$$

$$\int_{-\infty}^{\infty} \delta(t)\, dt = 1 \qquad t = 0$$

$$F(\omega) = \int_{-\infty}^{\infty} f(t) e^{-j\omega t}\, dt$$

$$= \int_{-\infty}^{\infty} \delta(t) e^{-j\omega t}\, dt$$

$$= e^{-j\omega(0)} \int_{-\infty}^{\infty} \delta(t)\, dt \left\{ \begin{array}{l} \because \int_{-\infty}^{\infty} f(t)\delta(t) = f(0) \int_{-\infty}^{\infty} \delta(t) dt = f(0)1 = f(0) \\ \text{where } f(0) \text{ is the value of the function } f(t) \text{ at } t = 0. \end{array} \right\}$$

$$= 1$$

**Fig. 13.31** *Impulse function*

The magnitude spectrum is shown in Fig. 13.32.

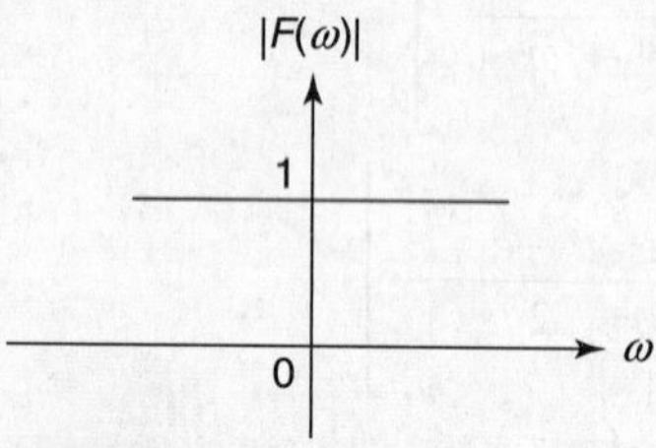


**Fig. 13.32** *Magnitude spectrum*

**5. Constant Function** The constant function shown in Fig. 13.33 is defined by the equation

$$f(t) = A \qquad -\infty < t < \infty$$

$$\int_{-\infty}^{\infty} A\, dt = \infty$$

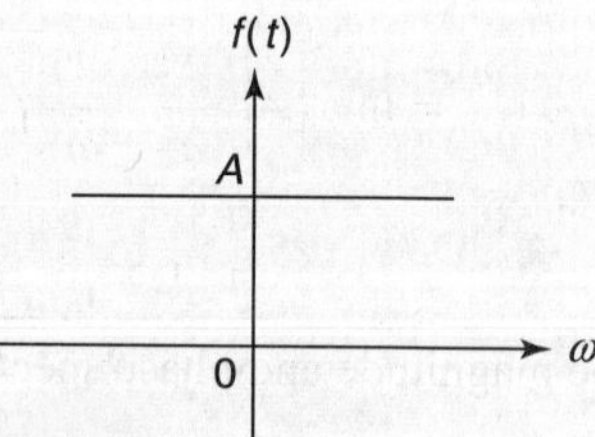


**Fig. 13.33** *Constant function*

The Fourier transform cannot be obtained directly. Hence, its Fourier transform can be evaluated as limiting value of Fourier transform of gate function.

$$f(t) = \lim_{\tau \to \infty} G(t)$$

$$F(\omega) = \mathbf{F}\{f(t)\} = \mathbf{F}\left\{\lim_{\tau \to \infty} G(t)\right\}$$

$$= \lim_{\tau \to \infty} \mathbf{F}\{G(t)\}$$

$$= \lim_{\tau \to \infty} A\tau \text{Sa}\left(\omega \frac{\tau}{2}\right)$$

$$= A \lim_{\tau \to \infty} \tau \text{Sa}\left(\omega \frac{\tau}{2}\right)$$

$$= 2\pi A \lim_{\frac{\tau}{2}\to\infty} \frac{\tau}{2\pi} Sa\left(\frac{\omega\tau}{2}\right)$$

$$= 2\pi A \lim_{\tau\to\infty} \frac{\tau}{2\pi} Sa\left(\frac{\omega\tau}{2}\right)$$

$$= 2\pi A\, \delta(\omega) \qquad \left[\because \lim_{K\to\infty} \frac{K}{\pi} \text{Sa}(Kt) = \delta(t)\right]$$

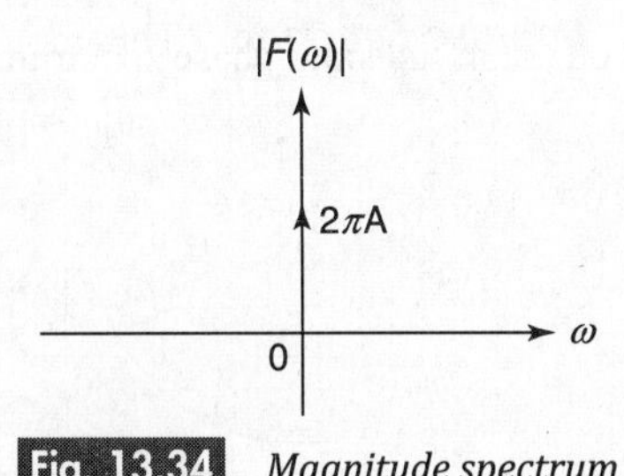

Fig. 13.34 *Magnitude spectrum*

The magnitude spectrum is shown in Fig. 13.34.

**6. Signum Function** The signum function shown in Fig. 13.35 is defined by the equation

$$f(t) = 1 \qquad t > 0$$
$$= -1 \qquad t < 0$$

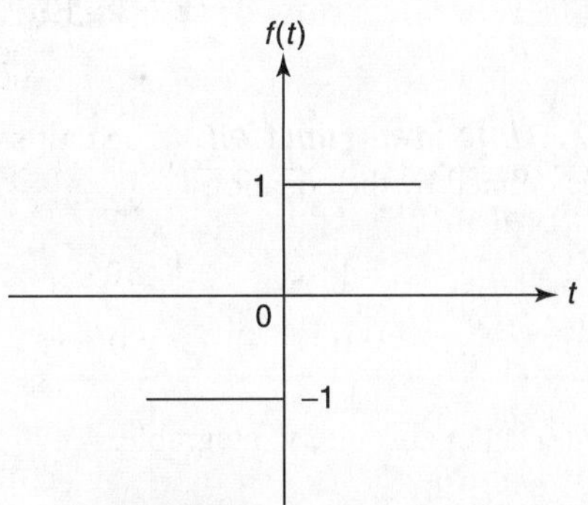

Fig. 13.35 *Signum function*

Since signum function is not absolutely integrable, its Fourier transform is evaluated as limiting value of Fourier transform of an exponential function.

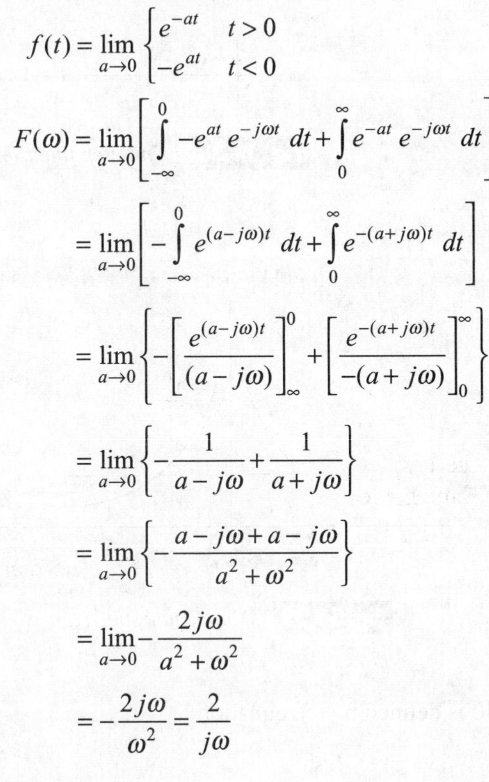

$$f(t) = \lim_{a\to 0} \begin{cases} e^{-at} & t > 0 \\ -e^{at} & t < 0 \end{cases}$$

$$F(\omega) = \lim_{a\to 0}\left[\int_{-\infty}^{0} -e^{at}\, e^{-j\omega t}\, dt + \int_{0}^{\infty} e^{-at}\, e^{-j\omega t}\, dt\right]$$

$$= \lim_{a\to 0}\left[-\int_{-\infty}^{0} e^{(a-j\omega)t}\, dt + \int_{0}^{\infty} e^{-(a+j\omega)t}\, dt\right]$$

$$= \lim_{a\to 0}\left\{-\left[\frac{e^{(a-j\omega)t}}{(a-j\omega)}\right]_{-\infty}^{0} + \left[\frac{e^{-(a+j\omega)t}}{-(a+j\omega)}\right]_{0}^{\infty}\right\}$$

$$= \lim_{a\to 0}\left\{-\frac{1}{a-j\omega} + \frac{1}{a+j\omega}\right\}$$

$$= \lim_{a\to 0}\left\{-\frac{a-j\omega+a-j\omega}{a^2+\omega^2}\right\}$$

$$= \lim_{a\to 0} -\frac{2j\omega}{a^2+\omega^2}$$

$$= -\frac{2j\omega}{\omega^2} = \frac{2}{j\omega}$$

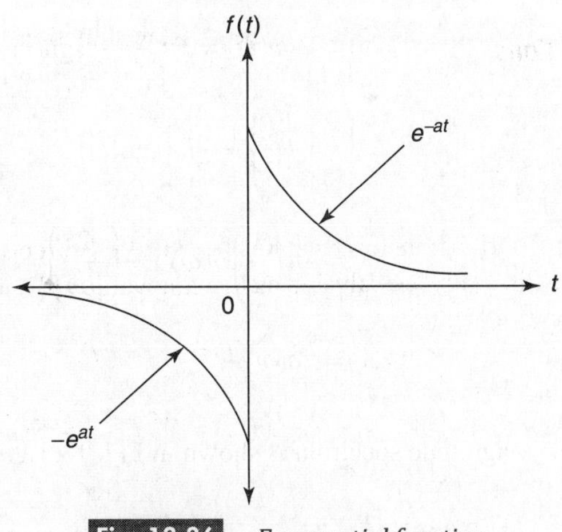

Fig. 13.36 *Exponential function*

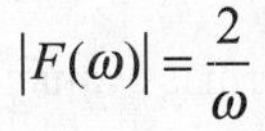

$$|F(\omega)| = \frac{2}{\omega}$$

The magnitude and phase spectrum are shown in Fig. 13.37.

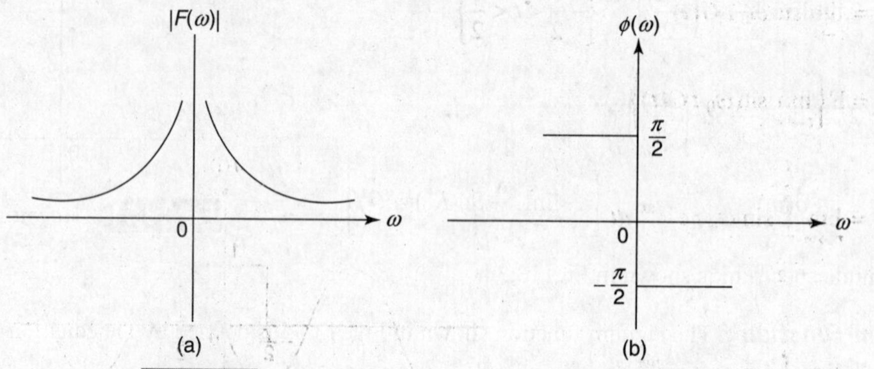


**Fig. 13.37** *(a) Magnitude spectrum (b) Phase spectrum*

***7. Unit Step Function*** The unit step function shown in Fig. 13.38 is defined by the equation

$$u(t) = 1 \qquad t \geq 0$$
$$= 0 \qquad t < 0$$

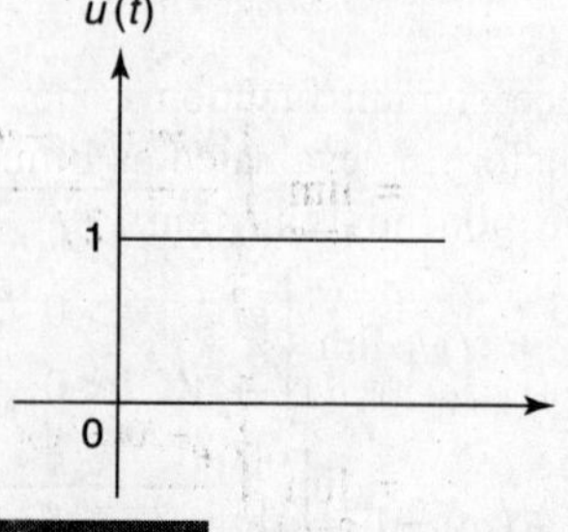


**Fig. 13.38** *Unit step function*

$u(t)$ is not absolutely integrable.

$$u(t) = \frac{1}{2}\{1 + \text{sgn}(t)\}$$

$$F(\omega) = \mathbf{F}\{u(t)\} = \mathbf{F}\left\{\frac{1}{2} + \frac{1}{2}\text{sgn}(t)\right\}$$

$$= \mathbf{F}\left\{\frac{1}{2}\right\} + \frac{1}{2}\mathbf{F}\{\text{sgn}(t)\}$$

$$= 2\pi\left(\frac{1}{2}\right)\delta(\omega) + \frac{1}{2}\left(\frac{2}{j\omega}\right)$$

$$= \pi\delta(\omega) + \frac{1}{j\omega}$$

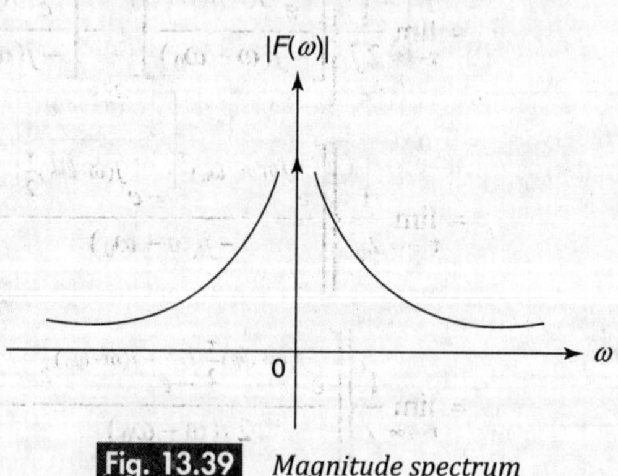


**Fig. 13.39** *Magnitude spectrum*

The magnitude spectrum is shown in Fig. 13.39.

***8. Sine Function*** The sine function shown in Fig. 13.40 is defined by the equation

$$f(t) = \sin \omega_0 t \qquad -\infty < t < \infty$$

The sine function is not absolutely integrable in the interval $(-\infty, \infty)$. Hence, its Fourier transform is evaluated as a limiting case of some other function.

$$f(t) = \lim_{\tau\to\infty} \sin\omega_0 t\, G(t) \qquad \left\{-\frac{\tau}{2} < t < \frac{\tau}{2}\right\}$$

$$F(\omega) = \mathbf{F}\left\{\lim_{\tau\to\infty} \sin\omega_0 t\, G(t)\right\}$$

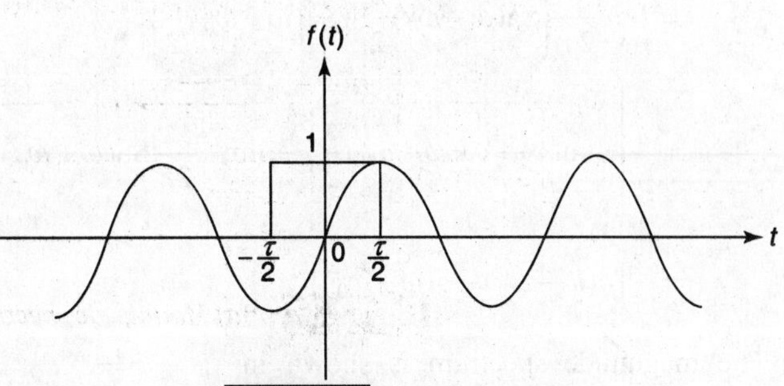


Fig. 13.40 *Sine function*

$$= \lim_{\tau\to\infty} \int_{-\frac{\tau}{2}}^{\frac{\tau}{2}} \sin\omega_0 t\, e^{-j\omega t}\, dt$$

$$= \lim_{\tau\to\infty} \int_{-\frac{\tau}{2}}^{\frac{\tau}{2}} \sin\omega_0 t\, e^{-j\omega t}\, dt$$

$$= \lim_{\tau\to\infty} \int_{-\frac{\tau}{2}}^{\frac{\tau}{2}} \frac{e^{j\omega_0 t} - e^{-j\omega_0 t}}{2j} e^{-j\omega t}\, dt$$

$$= \lim_{\tau\to\infty} \int_{-\frac{\tau}{2}}^{\frac{\tau}{2}} \frac{e^{-j(\omega-\omega_0)t} - e^{-j(\omega+\omega_0)t}}{2j}\, dt$$

$$= \lim_{\tau\to\infty} \frac{1}{2j}\left\{\left[\frac{e^{-j(\omega-\omega_0)t}}{-j(\omega-\omega_0)}\right]_{-\frac{\tau}{2}}^{\frac{\tau}{2}} - \left[\frac{e^{-j(\omega+\omega_0)t}}{-j(\omega+\omega_0)}\right]_{-\frac{\tau}{2}}^{\frac{\tau}{2}}\right\}$$

$$= \lim_{\tau\to\infty} \frac{1}{2j}\left\{\left[\frac{e^{-j(\omega-\omega_0)\frac{\tau}{2}} - e^{j(\omega-\omega_0)\frac{\tau}{2}}}{-j(\omega-\omega_0)} - \frac{e^{-j(\omega+\omega_0)\frac{\tau}{2}} - e^{j(\omega+\omega_0)\frac{\tau}{2}}}{-j(\omega+\omega_0)}\right]\right\}$$

$$= \lim_{\tau\to\infty} \frac{1}{j}\left\{\left[\frac{e^{j(\omega-\omega_0)\frac{\tau}{2}} - e^{-j(\omega-\omega_0)\frac{\tau}{2}}}{2j(\omega-\omega_0)} - \frac{e^{-j(\omega+\omega_0)\frac{\tau}{2}} - e^{j(\omega+\omega_0)\frac{\tau}{2}}}{2j(\omega+\omega_0)}\right]\right\}$$

$$= \lim_{\tau\to\infty} \frac{1}{j}\left\{\frac{\sin(\omega-\omega_0)\frac{\tau}{2}}{(\omega-\omega_0)} - \frac{\sin(\omega+\omega_0)\frac{\tau}{2}}{\omega+\omega_0}\right\}$$

$$= \lim_{\tau\to\infty} \frac{\tau}{2j}\left\{\frac{\sin(\omega-\omega_0)\frac{\tau}{2}}{(\omega-\omega_0)\frac{\tau}{2}} - \frac{\sin(\omega+\omega_0)\frac{\tau}{2}}{(\omega+\omega_0)\frac{\tau}{2}}\right\}$$

$$= \lim_{\tau\to\infty} \frac{\tau}{2j}\left\{\mathrm{Sa}(\omega-\omega_0)\frac{\tau}{2} - \mathrm{Sa}(\omega+\omega_0)\frac{\tau}{2}\right\}$$

$$= \frac{\pi}{j}\left[\lim_{\frac{\tau}{2}\to\infty}\left\{\frac{\tau}{2j}\mathrm{Sa}(\omega-\omega_0)\frac{\tau}{2}\right\} - \lim_{\frac{\tau}{2}\to\infty}\left\{\frac{\tau}{2\pi}\mathrm{Sa}(\omega+\omega_0)\frac{\tau}{2}\right\}\right]$$

$$= \frac{\pi}{j}[\delta(\omega-\omega_0) - \delta(\omega+\omega_0)]$$

The magnitude spectrum is shown in Fig. 13.41.

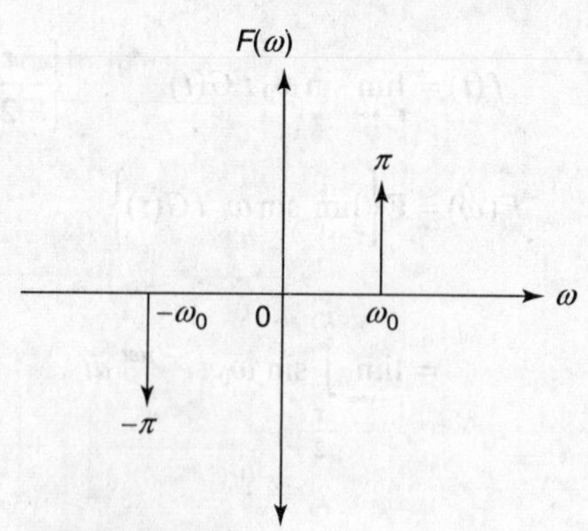


Fig. 13.41 *Magnitude spectrum*

***9. Cosine Function*** The cosine function shown in Fig. 13.42 is defined by the equation

$$f(t) = \cos\omega_0 t \qquad -\infty < t < \infty$$

The cosine function is not absolutely integrable in the interval $(-\infty, \infty)$. Hence, its Fourier transform is calculated as a limiting case of some other function.

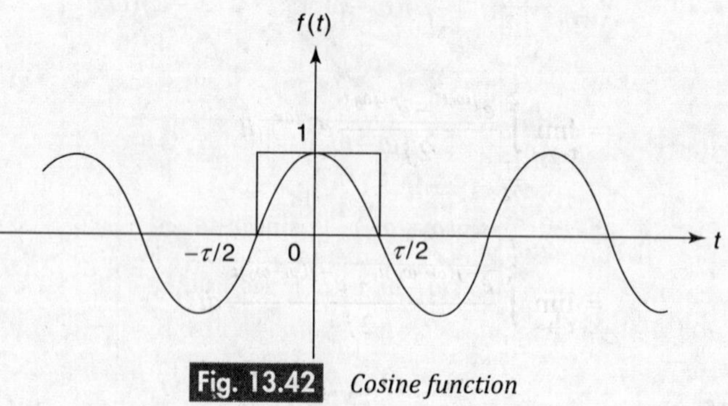


Fig. 13.42 *Cosine function*

$$f(t) = \lim_{\tau\to\infty} \cos\omega_0 t\, G(t) \quad \left(-\frac{\tau}{2} < t < \frac{\tau}{2}\right)$$

$$F(\omega) = \mathbf{F}\left\{\lim_{\tau\to\infty} \cos\omega_0 t\, G(t)\right\}$$

$$= \lim_{\tau\to\infty} \int_{-\frac{\tau}{2}}^{\frac{\tau}{2}} \cos\omega_0 t\, G(t) e^{-j\omega t}\, dt$$

$$= \lim_{\tau\to\infty} \int_{-\frac{\tau}{2}}^{\frac{\tau}{2}} \cos\omega_0 t\, e^{-j\omega t}\, dt$$

$$= \lim_{\tau\to\infty} \int_{-\frac{\tau}{2}}^{\frac{\tau}{2}} \frac{e^{j\omega_0 t} + e^{-j\omega_0 t}}{2} e^{-j\omega t}\, dt$$

$$= \lim_{\tau\to\infty} \int_{-\frac{\tau}{2}}^{\frac{\tau}{2}} \frac{e^{-j(\omega-\omega_0)t} + e^{-j(\omega+\omega_0)t}}{2} dt$$

$$= \lim_{\tau\to\infty} \int_{-\frac{\tau}{2}}^{\frac{\tau}{2}} \frac{e^{-j(\omega-\omega_0)t}}{2} dt \int_{-\frac{\tau}{2}}^{\frac{\tau}{2}} \frac{e^{-j(\omega+\omega_0)t}}{2} dt$$

$$= \lim_{\tau\to\infty} \left\{ \left[ \frac{e^{-j(\omega-\omega_0)t}}{-2j(\omega-\omega_0)} \right]_{-\frac{\tau}{2}}^{\frac{\tau}{2}} + \left[ \frac{e^{-j(\omega+\omega_0)t}}{-2j(\omega+\omega_0)} \right]_{-\frac{\tau}{2}}^{\frac{\tau}{2}} \right\}$$

$$= \lim_{\tau\to\infty} \left\{ \frac{e^{-j(\omega-\omega_0)\frac{\tau}{2}} - e^{j(\omega-\omega_0)\frac{\tau}{2}}}{-2j(\omega-\omega_0)} + \frac{e^{-j(\omega+\omega_0)\frac{\tau}{2}} - e^{j(\omega+\omega_0)\frac{\tau}{2}}}{-2j(\omega+\omega_0)} \right\}$$

$$= \lim_{\tau\to\infty} \left\{ \frac{e^{j(\omega-\omega_0)\frac{\tau}{2}} - e^{-j(\omega-\omega_0)\frac{\tau}{2}}}{2j(\omega-\omega_0)} + \frac{e^{j(\omega+\omega_0)\frac{\tau}{2}} - e^{-j(\omega+\omega_0)\frac{\tau}{2}}}{2j(\omega+\omega_0)} \right\}$$

$$= \lim_{\tau\to\infty} \left\{ \frac{\sin(\omega-\omega_0)\frac{\tau}{2}}{(\omega-\omega_0)} + \frac{\sin(\omega+\omega_0)\frac{\tau}{2}}{(\omega+\omega_0)} \right\}$$

$$= \lim_{\tau\to\infty} \frac{\tau}{2} \left\{ \frac{\sin(\omega-\omega_0)\frac{\tau}{2}}{(\omega-\omega_0)\frac{\tau}{2}} + \frac{\sin(\omega+\omega_0)\frac{\tau}{2}}{(\omega+\omega_0)\frac{\tau}{2}} \right\}$$

$$= \pi \lim_{\frac{\tau}{2}\to\infty} \frac{\tau}{2\pi} \left\{ \text{Sa}(\omega-\omega_0)\frac{\tau}{2} + \text{Sa}(\omega+\omega_0)\frac{\tau}{2} \right\}$$

$$= \pi\left[\delta(\omega-\omega_0) + \delta(\omega+\omega_0)\right]$$

**Fig. 13.43** *Magnitude spectrum*

The magnitude spectrum is shown in Fig. 13.43.

**9. Exponential Function $e^{j\omega_0 t}$** The exponential function $e^{j\omega_0 t}$ is not absolutely integrable.

We know that

$$e^{j\omega_0 t} = \cos\omega_0 t + j\sin\omega_0 t$$

$$F(\omega) = \mathbf{F}\left\{e^{j\omega_0 t}\right\}$$

$$= \mathbf{F}\left\{\cos\omega_0 t + j\sin\omega_0 t\right\}$$

$$= \mathbf{F}\left\{\cos\omega_0 t\right\} + j\,\mathbf{F}\left\{\sin\omega_0 t\right\}$$

$$= \pi\left[\delta(\omega-\omega_0) + \delta(\omega+\omega_0)\right] + j\frac{\pi}{j}\left[\delta(\omega-\omega_0) - \delta(\omega+\omega_0)\right]$$

$$= 2\pi\delta(\omega-\omega_0)$$

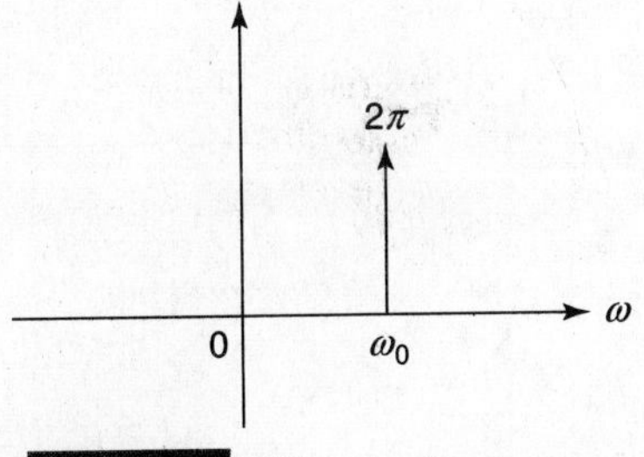


**Fig. 13.44** *Magnitude spectrum*

The magnitude spectrum is shown in Fig. 13.44.

## 13.9 FOURIER TRANSFORM OF PERIODIC FUNCTION

LO 13.8

Derive Fourier transforms of periodic functions

Periodic function exists from $-\infty$ to $\infty$.

$$\int_{-\infty}^{\infty} f(t)\,dt = \infty$$

i.e., $f(t)$ is not absolutely integrable. Strictly speaking, the Fourier transform of a periodic function does not exist. But its Fourier transform can be evaluated as a limiting value of Fourier transform of some other function. A periodic function $f(t)$ with angular frequency $\omega_0$ can be represented in exponential Fourier series as,

$$f(t) = \sum_{n=-\infty}^{\infty} c_n\, e^{jn\omega_0 t}$$

where

$$c_n = \frac{1}{T}\int_{-\frac{T}{2}}^{\frac{T}{2}} f(t)e^{-jn\omega_0 t}\,dt \text{ and } \omega_0 = \frac{2\pi}{T}$$

$$\mathbf{F}\{f(t)\} = \mathbf{F}\left\{\sum_{n=-\infty}^{\infty} c_n\, e^{jn\omega_0 t}\right\}$$

$$= \sum_{n=-\infty}^{\infty} c_n \mathbf{F}\left\{e^{jn\omega_0 t}\right\}$$

$$= \sum_{n=-\infty}^{\infty} c_n\, 2\pi\,\delta(\omega - n\omega_0)$$

$$= 2\pi \sum_{n=-\infty}^{\infty} c_n\, \delta(\omega - n\omega_0)$$

**EXAMPLE 13.22**

*Find the Fourier transform of periodic gate function shown in Fig. 13.45.*

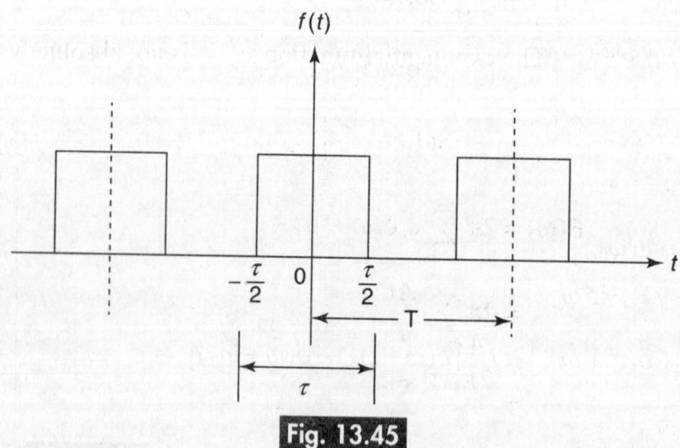


Fig. 13.45

**Solution**

$$f(t) = A \qquad -\frac{\tau}{2} < \tau < \frac{\tau}{2}$$

$$= 0 \qquad |t| > \frac{\tau}{2}$$

$$c_n = \frac{1}{T}\int_{-\frac{\tau}{2}}^{\frac{\tau}{2}} f(t)e^{-jn\omega_0 t}\, dt$$

$$= \frac{1}{T}\int_{-\frac{\tau}{2}}^{\frac{\tau}{2}} Ae^{-jn\omega_0 t}\, dt$$

$$= \frac{A}{T}\int_{-\frac{\tau}{2}}^{\frac{\tau}{2}} e^{-jn\omega_0 t}\, dt$$

$$= \frac{A}{T}\left[\frac{e^{-jn\omega_0 t}}{-jn\omega_0}\right]_{-\frac{\tau}{2}}^{\frac{\tau}{2}}$$

$$= \frac{A}{n\omega_0\tau}\left[\frac{e^{-jn\omega_0\frac{\tau}{2}} - e^{jn\omega_0\frac{\tau}{2}}}{-j}\right]$$

$$= \frac{2A}{n\omega_0\tau}\left[\frac{e^{jn\omega_0\frac{\tau}{2}} - e^{-jn\omega_0\frac{\tau}{2}}}{2j}\right]$$

$$= \frac{2A}{n\omega_0\tau}\sin n\omega_0\frac{\tau}{2}$$

$$= \frac{2A\frac{\tau}{2}}{T}\frac{\sin n\omega_0\frac{\tau}{2}}{n\omega_0\frac{\tau}{2}}$$

$$= \frac{A\tau}{T}\,\text{Sa}\left(n\omega_0\frac{\tau}{2}\right)$$

$$F(\omega) = 2\pi\sum_{n=-\infty}^{\infty} c_n\delta(\omega - n\omega_0)$$

$$= 2\pi\sum_{n=-\infty}^{\infty}\frac{A\tau}{T}\,\text{Sa}\left(n\omega_0\frac{\tau}{2}\right)\delta(\omega - n\omega_0)$$

$$= \frac{2\pi A\tau}{T}\sum_{n=-\infty}^{\infty}\text{Sa}\left(n\omega_0\frac{\tau}{2}\right)\delta(\omega - n\omega_0)$$

$$= \omega_0 A\tau \sum_{n=-\infty}^{\infty} \text{Sa}\left( n\omega_0 \frac{\tau}{2} \right) \delta(\omega - n\omega_0)$$

The Fourier transform is shown in Fig. 13.46.

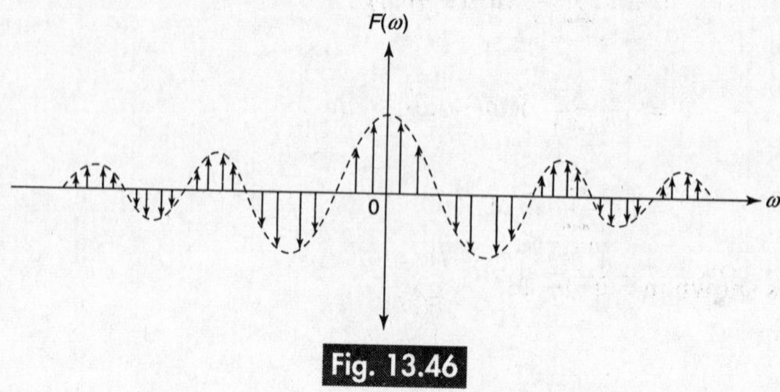


Fig. 13.46

## EXAMPLE 13.23

*Find the Fourier transform of an impulse train shown in Fig. 13.47.*

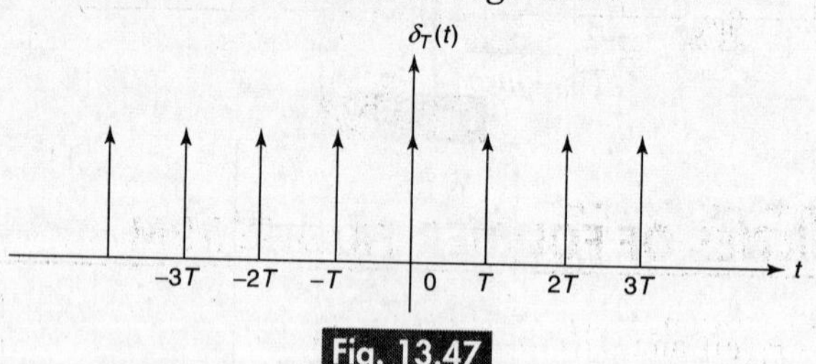


Fig. 13.47

**Solution**

$$\delta_T(t) = \sum_{n=-\infty}^{\infty} \delta(t - nT)$$

$$c_n = \frac{1}{T} \int_{t_0}^{t_0+T} f(t) e^{-jn\omega_0 t} \, dt$$

$$= \frac{1}{T} \int_{t_0}^{t_0+T} \delta_T(t) e^{-jn\omega_0 t} \, dt$$

$$= \frac{1}{T} \int_{-\frac{T}{2}}^{\frac{T}{2}} \delta(t) e^{-jn\omega_0 t} \, dt$$

$$= \frac{1}{T} e^{-jn\omega_0 (0)} \delta(0)$$

$$= \frac{1}{T}$$

$$F(\omega) = 2\pi \sum_{n=-\infty}^{\infty} c_n\, \delta(\omega - n\omega_0)$$

$$= 2\pi \sum_{n=-\infty}^{\infty} \frac{1}{T}\, \delta(\omega - n\omega_0)$$

$$= \frac{2\pi}{T} \sum_{n=-\infty}^{\infty} \delta(\omega - n\omega_0)$$

$$= \omega_0 \sum_{n=-\infty}^{\infty} \delta(\omega - n\omega_0)$$

The Fourier transform is shown in Fig. 13.48.

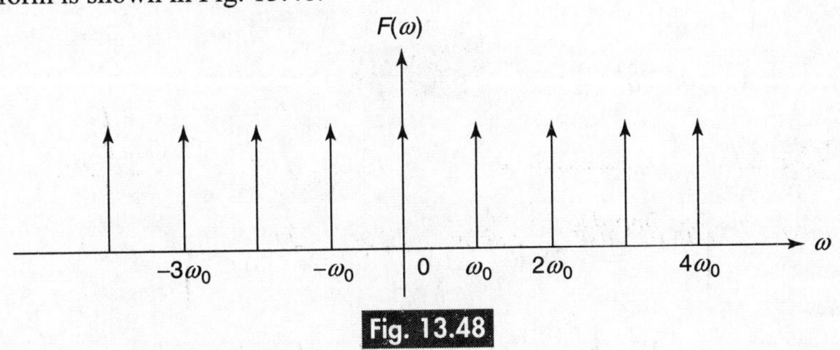


Fig. 13.48

## 13.10 PROPERTIES OF FOURIER TRANSFORM

LO 13.9

Prove properties of Fourier transform

**1. *Linearity*** If $f_1(t) \leftrightarrow F_1(\omega)$ and $f_2(t) \leftrightarrow F_2(\omega)$ then

$a_1\, f_1(t) + a_2\, f_2(t) \leftrightarrow a_1\, F_1(\omega) + a_2\, F_2(\omega)$

**Proof:**

$$\mathbf{F}\{a_1 f_1(t) + a_2 f_2(t)\} = \int_{-\infty}^{\infty} \{a_1 f_1(t) + a_2 f_2(t)\} e^{-j\omega t}\, dt$$

$$= a_1 \int_{-\infty}^{\infty} f_1(t)\, e^{-j\omega t}\, dt + a_2 \int_{-\infty}^{\infty} f_2(t)\, e^{-j\omega t}\, dt = a_1 F_1(\omega) + a_2 F_2(\omega)$$

**2. *Time Scaling*** If $f(t) \leftrightarrow F(\omega)$ then $f(at) \leftrightarrow \dfrac{1}{|a|} F\left(\dfrac{\omega}{a}\right)$

**Proof:**

(a) When $a > 0$

$$\mathbf{F}\{f(at)\} = \int_{-\infty}^{\infty} f(at)\, e^{-j\omega t}\, dt$$

Putting $at = \lambda,\ t = \dfrac{\lambda}{a},\ dt = \dfrac{d\lambda}{a}$

$$\mathbf{F}\{f(at)\} = \int_{-\infty}^{\infty} f(\lambda)\, e^{-j\left(\frac{\omega}{a}\right)\lambda}\, \frac{d\lambda}{a} = \frac{1}{a} F\left(\frac{\omega}{a}\right)$$

(b) When $a < 0$

$$\mathbf{F}\{f(at)\} = -\frac{1}{a}F\left(\frac{\omega}{a}\right)$$

Hence, $$f(at) \leftrightarrow \frac{1}{|a|}F\left(\frac{\omega}{a}\right)$$

The above proof shows that compression in time domain is equivalent to expansion in frequency domain and vice versa.

**3. *Time Shifting*** If $f(t) \leftrightarrow F(\omega)$ then $f(t-t_0) \leftrightarrow F(\omega)e^{-j\omega t_0}$

**Proof:** $$\mathbf{F}\{f(t-t_0)\} = \int_{-\infty}^{\infty} f(t-t_0)e^{-j\omega t}\, dt$$

Putting $t - t_0 = \lambda, t = \lambda + t_0, dt = d\lambda$

$$\mathbf{F}\{f(t-t_0)\} = \int_{-\infty}^{\infty} f(\lambda)e^{-j(\lambda+t_0)\omega}\, d\lambda = \int_{-\infty}^{\infty} f(\lambda)e^{-j\lambda\omega}\, e^{-j\omega t_0}\, d\lambda$$

$$= e^{-j\omega t_0}\int_{-\infty}^{\infty} f(\lambda)e^{-j\omega\lambda}\, d\lambda = F(\omega)\, e^{-j\omega t_0}$$

Similarly, $$f(t+t_0) \leftrightarrow F(\omega)\, e^{j\omega t_0}$$

The above proof shows that shifting in time domain introduces a phase lag $(-\omega t_0)$ in the frequency domain.

**EXAMPLE 13.24**

*Find the Fourier transform of the function shown in Fig. 13.49.*

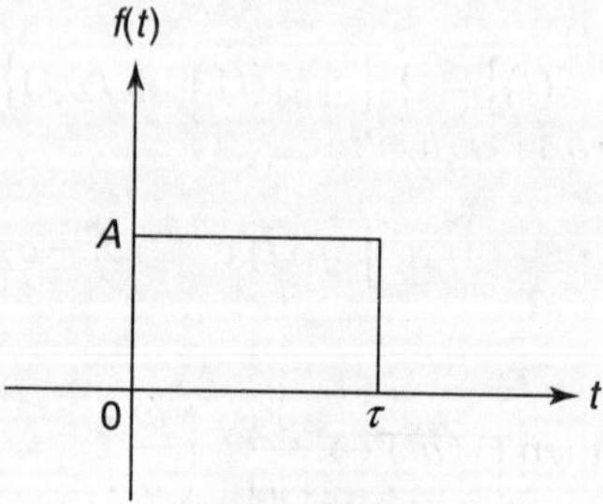


Fig. 13.49

**Solution** $$f(t) = G\left(t - \frac{\tau}{2}\right)$$

By time-shifting property, $f(t-t_0) \leftrightarrow F(\omega)e^{-j\omega t_0}$

$$\mathbf{F}\{G(t)\} = A\tau\, \text{Sa}\left(\frac{\omega\tau}{2}\right)$$

$$\mathbf{F}\{f(t)\} = A\tau \text{ Sa}\left(\frac{\omega\tau}{2}\right)e^{-j\omega\frac{\tau}{2}}$$

**EXAMPLE 13.25**

*Find the Fourier transform of the function shown in Fig. 13.50.*

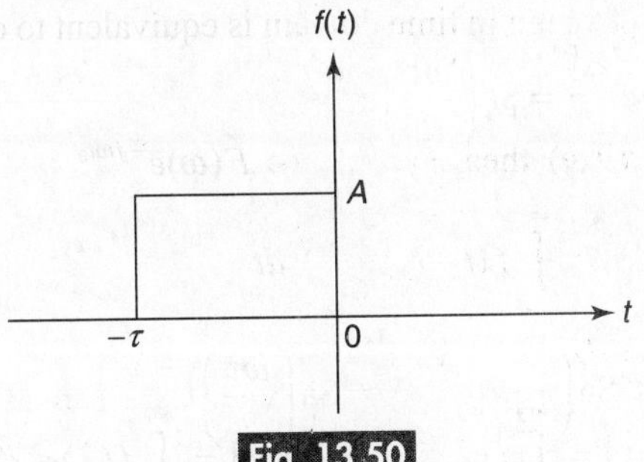


Fig. 13.50

**Solution**
$$f(t) = G\left(t + \frac{\tau}{2}\right)$$

By time-shifting property, $f(t+t_0) \leftrightarrow F(\omega)e^{-j\omega t_0}$

$$\mathbf{F}\{G(t)\} = A\tau \text{ Sa}\left(\frac{\omega\tau}{2}\right)$$

$$\mathbf{F}\{f(t)\} = A\tau \text{ Sa}\left(\frac{\omega\tau}{2}\right)e^{j\omega\frac{\tau}{2}}$$

**EXAMPLE 13.26**

*Find the Fourier transform of the function shown in Fig.13.51.*

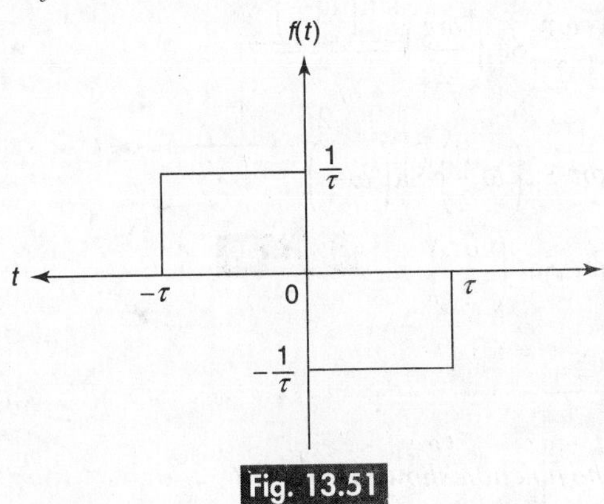


Fig. 13.51

**Solution** The function $f(t)$ can be viewed as a combination of two functions $f_1(t)$ and $f_2(t)$.

$$f(t) = f_1(t) - f_2(t)$$

$$f_1(t) = G\left(t + \frac{\tau}{2}\right)$$

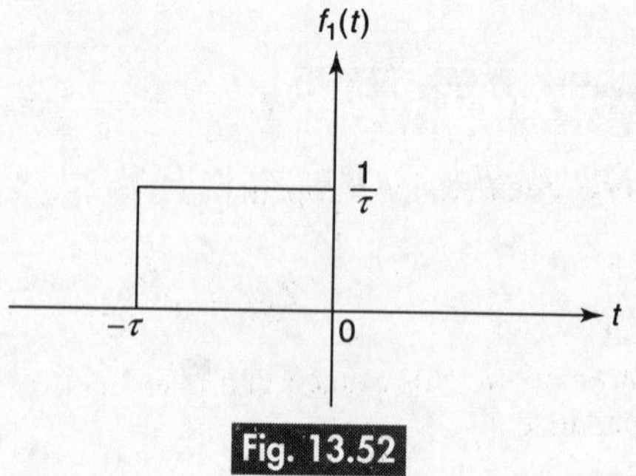

Fig. 13.52

By time-shifting property,

$$F_1(\omega) = \frac{1}{\tau} \times \tau \text{ Sa}\left(\frac{\omega\tau}{2}\right) e^{j\omega\frac{\tau}{2}} = \text{Sa}\left(\frac{\omega\tau}{2}\right) e^{j\omega\frac{\tau}{2}}$$

$$f_2(t) = G\left(t - \frac{\tau}{2}\right)$$

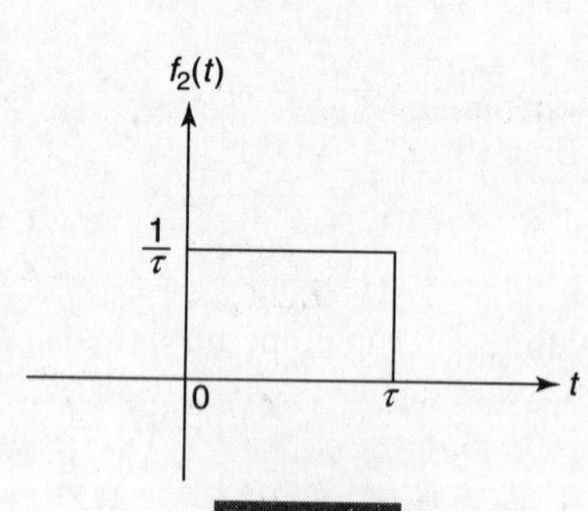

Fig. 13.53

$$F_2(\omega) = \frac{1}{\tau} \times \tau \text{ Sa}\left(\frac{\omega\tau}{2}\right) e^{-j\omega\frac{\tau}{2}} = \text{Sa}\left(\frac{\omega\tau}{2}\right) e^{-j\omega\frac{\tau}{2}}$$

$$F(\omega) = F_1(\omega) - F_2(\omega)$$

$$= \text{Sa}\left(\frac{\omega\tau}{2}\right) e^{j\omega\frac{\tau}{2}} - \text{Sa}\left(\frac{\omega\tau}{2}\right) e^{-j\omega\frac{\tau}{2}}$$

$$= \text{Sa}\left(\frac{\omega\tau}{2}\right)\left(e^{j\omega\frac{\tau}{2}} - e^{-j\omega\frac{\tau}{2}}\right)$$

$$= 2j \text{ Sa}\left(\frac{\omega\tau}{2}\right)\left(\frac{e^{j\omega\frac{\tau}{2}} - e^{-j\omega\frac{\tau}{2}}}{2j}\right)$$

$$= 2j \text{ Sa}\left(\frac{\omega\tau}{2}\right) \sin\left(\frac{\omega\tau}{2}\right)$$

$$= 2j\frac{\omega\tau}{2} \text{ Sa}\left(\frac{\omega\tau}{2}\right) \frac{\sin\left(\omega\frac{\tau}{2}\right)}{\omega\frac{\tau}{2}}$$

$$= j\omega\tau \text{ Sa}\left(\omega\frac{\tau}{2}\right) \text{Sa}\left(\omega\frac{\tau}{2}\right)$$

$$= j\omega\tau \text{ Sa}^2\left(\frac{\omega\tau}{2}\right)$$

**EXAMPLE 13.27**

*Find the Fourier transform of the function shown in Fig. 13.54.*

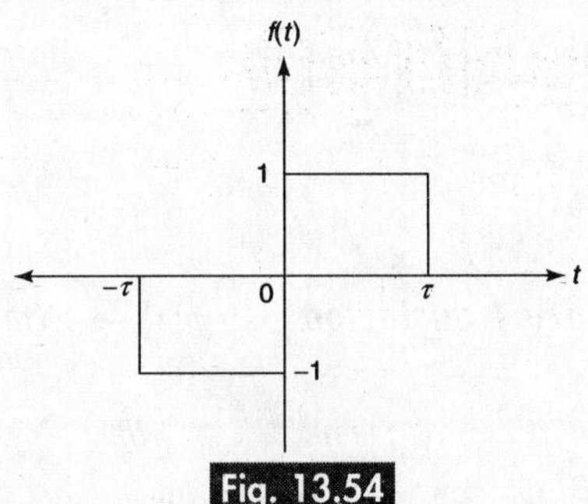

Fig. 13.54

**Solution** The function $f(t)$ is considered as a combination of two functions $f_1(t)$ and $f_2(t)$.

$$f(t) = f_2(t) - f_1(t)$$

Now,
$$f_2(t) = G\left(t - \frac{\tau}{2}\right)$$

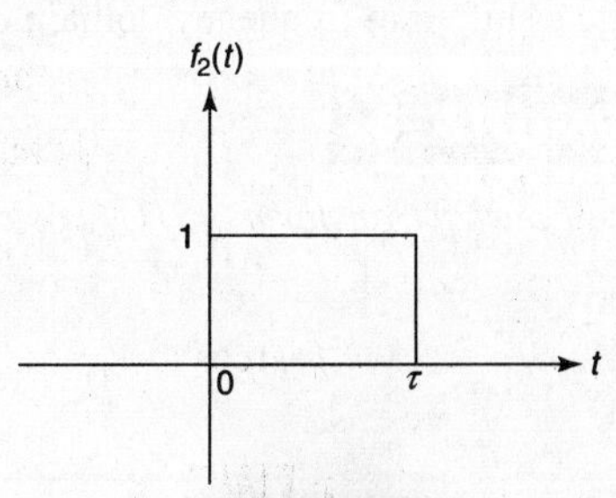

Fig. 13.55

By time-shifting property,

$$\mathbf{F}\{G(t)\} = A\tau \text{ Sa}\left(\frac{\omega\tau}{2}\right)$$

$$\mathbf{F}\{f_2(t)\} = F_2(\omega) = \tau \text{ Sa}\left(\frac{\omega\tau}{2}\right)e^{-j\omega\frac{\tau}{2}}$$

Also,
$$f_1(t) = G\left(t + \frac{\tau}{2}\right)$$

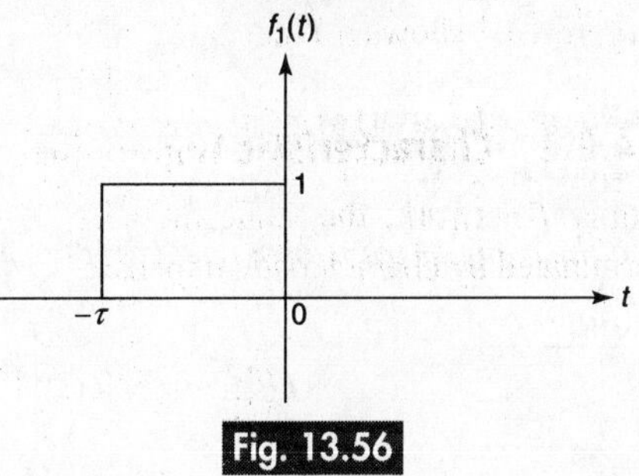

Fig. 13.56

$$F_1(\omega) = \tau \text{ Sa}\left(\frac{\omega\tau}{2}\right)e^{j\omega\frac{\tau}{2}}$$

$$F(\omega) = F_2(\omega) - F_1(\omega)$$

$$= \tau \text{ Sa}\left(\frac{\omega\tau}{2}\right)e^{-j\omega\frac{\tau}{2}} - \tau \text{ Sa}\left(\frac{\omega\tau}{2}\right)e^{j\omega\frac{\tau}{2}}$$

$$= \tau \text{ Sa}\left(\frac{\omega\tau}{2}\right)\left[e^{-j\omega\frac{\tau}{2}} - e^{j\omega\frac{\tau}{2}}\right]$$

$$= -\tau \text{ Sa}\left(\frac{\omega\tau}{2}\right)\left[\frac{e^{j\omega\frac{\tau}{2}} - e^{-j\omega\frac{\tau}{2}}}{2j}\right]$$

$$= 2j\tau \text{ Sa}\left(\frac{\omega\tau}{2}\right)\sin\left(\frac{\omega\tau}{2}\right)$$

$$= -2j\tau\frac{\omega\tau}{2} \text{ Sa}\left(\frac{\omega\tau}{2}\right)\frac{\sin\left(\omega\frac{\tau}{2}\right)}{\omega\frac{\tau}{2}}$$

$$= -j\omega\tau^2 \text{ Sa}\left(\frac{\omega\tau}{2}\right)\text{Sa}\left(\frac{\omega\tau}{2}\right)$$

$$= -j\omega\tau^2 \text{ Sa}^2\left(\frac{\omega\tau}{2}\right)$$

***4. Frequency Shifting or Frequency Translation*** If $f(t) \leftrightarrow F(\omega)$ then $f(t)\, e^{j\omega_0 t} \leftrightarrow F(\omega - \omega_0)$

**Proof:**

$$\mathbf{F}\left\{f(t)e^{j\omega_0 t}\right\} = \int_{-\infty}^{\infty} f(t)e^{j\omega_0 t}\, e^{-j\omega t}\, dt = \int_{-\infty}^{\infty} f(t)e^{-j(\omega-\omega_0)t}\, dt = F(\omega - \omega_0)$$

This proof shows that if the function *f(t)* is given a time lead $\omega_0$ in the time domains then the spectrum of the signal gets shifted in frequency domain by $\omega_0$.

**EXAMPLE 13.28**

*Find the Fourier transform of $f(t) \cos \omega_0 t$.*

**Solution**

$$f(t)\cos \omega_0 t = f(t)\left[\frac{e^{j\omega_0 t} + e^{-j\omega_0 t}}{2}\right] = \frac{1}{2} f(t)e^{j\omega_0 t} + \frac{1}{2} f(t)e^{-j\omega_0 t}$$

$$\mathbf{F}\{f(t)\cos \omega_0\, t\} = \frac{1}{2}\mathbf{F}\left\{f(t)e^{j\omega_0 t} + f(t)e^{-j\omega_0 t}\right\} = \frac{1}{2}[F(\omega - \omega_0) + F(\omega + \omega_0)]$$

**EXAMPLE 13.29**

*Find the Fourier transform of $f(t) \sin \omega_0 t$.*

**Solution**

$$f(t)\sin \omega_0 t = f(t)\left[\frac{e^{j\omega_0 t} - e^{-j\omega_0 t}}{2j}\right] = \frac{1}{2j}\left[f(t)\, e^{j\omega_0 t} - f(t)\, e^{-j\omega_0 t}\right]$$

$$\mathbf{F}\{f(t)\sin \omega_0 t\} = \frac{1}{2j}\mathbf{F}\left\{f(t)\, e^{j\omega_0 t} - f(t)\, e^{-j\omega_0 t}\right\} = \frac{1}{2j}[F(\omega - \omega_0) + F(\omega + \omega_0)]$$

**EXAMPLE 13.30**

*Find Fourier transform of periodic function $e^{j\omega_0 t}$. Hence, find Fourier transform of the periodic function (i) $\sin \omega_0 t$, and (ii) $\cos\omega_0 t$.*

**Solution**

$$e^{j\omega_0 t} = 1e^{j\omega_0 t}$$

$$\mathbf{F}\{1\} = 2\pi\, \delta(\omega)$$

By frequency-shifting property,

$$\mathbf{F}\left\{e^{j\omega_0 t}\right\} = 2\pi\, \delta(\omega - \omega_0)$$

Now,

$$\sin \omega_0 t = \frac{e^{j\omega_0 t} - e^{-j\omega_0 t}}{2j}$$

$$\mathbf{F}\{\sin \omega_0 t\} = \frac{1}{2j}\mathbf{F}\left\{e^{j\omega_0 t} - e^{-j\omega_0 t}\right\} = \frac{1}{2j}[2\pi\,\delta(\omega-\omega_0) - 2\pi\,\delta(\omega+\omega_0)] = \frac{\pi}{j}[\delta(\omega-\omega_0) - \delta(\omega+\omega_0)]$$

$$\cos \omega_0 t = \frac{e^{j\omega_0 t} + e^{-j\omega_0 t}}{2}$$

$$\mathbf{F}\{\cos \omega_0 t\} = \frac{1}{2}\mathbf{F}\left\{e^{j\omega_0 t} + e^{-j\omega_0 t}\right\} = \frac{1}{2}\mathbf{F}\left\{e^{j\omega_0 t} + e^{-j\omega_0 t}\right\} = \frac{1}{2}[2\pi\,\delta(\omega-\omega_0) + 2\pi\,\delta(\omega+\omega_0)]$$

$$= \pi[\delta(\omega-\omega_0) + \delta(\omega+\omega_0)]$$

**5. *Time Differentiation*** If $f(t) \leftrightarrow F(\omega)$ then $\frac{d}{dt}f(t) \leftrightarrow j\omega F(\omega)$

**Proof:**

$$f(t) = \frac{1}{2\pi}\int_{-\infty}^{\infty} F(\omega)e^{j\omega t}\, d\omega$$

$$\frac{d}{dt}f(t) = \frac{d}{dt}\left[\frac{1}{2\pi}\int_{-\infty}^{\infty} F(\omega)e^{j\omega t}\, d\omega\right] = \frac{1}{2\pi}\frac{d}{dt}\int_{-\infty}^{\infty} F(\omega)e^{j\omega t}\, d\omega = \frac{1}{2\pi}\int_{-\infty}^{\infty} F(\omega)\frac{d}{dt}e^{j\omega t}\, d\omega$$

$$= \frac{1}{2\pi}\int_{-\infty}^{\infty} j\omega\, F(\omega)e^{j\omega t}\, d\omega$$

Comparing with inverse Fourier transform equation,

$$\frac{d}{dt}f(t) \leftrightarrow j\omega F(\omega)$$

**EXAMPLE 13.31**

*Find the Fourier transform of the function shown in Fig. 13.57.*

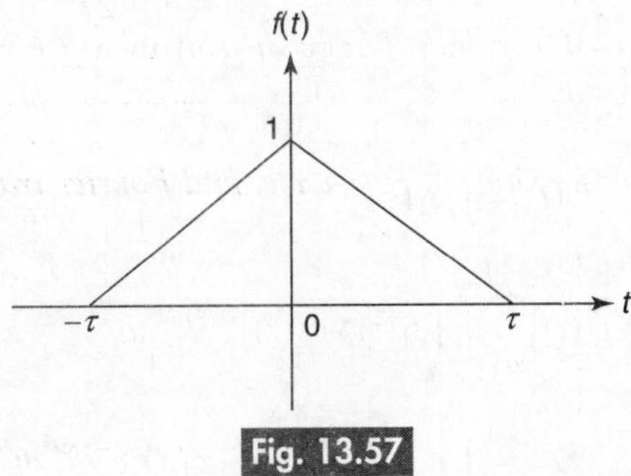


Fig. 13.57

**Solution**

$$f(t) = -\frac{1}{\tau}t + 1 \qquad 0 < t < \tau$$

$$= \frac{1}{\tau}t + 1 \qquad -\tau < t < 0$$

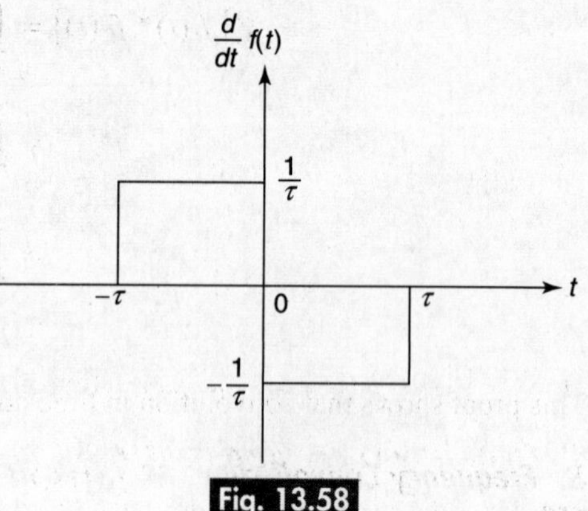


Fig. 13.58

Differentiating $f(t)$ w.r.t. $t$,

$$\frac{d}{dt}f(t) = -\frac{1}{\tau} \qquad 0 < t < \tau$$

$$= \frac{1}{\tau} \qquad -\tau < t < 0$$

$$\mathbf{F}\left\{\frac{d}{dt}f(t)\right\} = j\omega\tau\ \text{Sa}^2\left(\omega\frac{\tau}{2}\right)$$

By time-differentiation property,

$$\mathbf{F}\left\{\frac{d}{dt}f(t)\right\} = j\omega\, F(\omega)$$

$$F(\omega) = \tau\ \text{Sa}^2\left(\frac{\omega\tau}{2}\right)$$

***6. Frequency Differentiation*** If $f(t) \leftrightarrow F(\omega)$ then $\frac{d}{d\omega}F(\omega) \leftrightarrow -jt\, f(t)$

**Proof:** $$F(\omega) = \int_{-\infty}^{\infty} f(t)e^{-j\omega t}\, dt$$

Differentiating w.r.t $\omega$,

$$\frac{d}{d\omega}F(\omega) = \frac{d}{d\omega}\int_{-\infty}^{\infty} f(t)e^{-j\omega t}\, dt = \int_{-\infty}^{\infty} f(t)\frac{d}{d\omega}e^{-j\omega t}\, dt = \int_{-\infty}^{\infty} (-jt)\, f(t)e^{-j\omega t}\, dt$$

$$\frac{d}{d\omega}[F(\omega)] \leftrightarrow -jt\, f(t)$$

***7. Time Convolution*** If $f_1(t) \leftrightarrow F_1(\omega)$ and $f_2(t) \leftrightarrow F_2(\omega)$ then $f_1(t) * f_2(t) \leftrightarrow F_1(\omega)\cdot F_2(\omega)$

**Proof:** By definition of convolution,

$$f_1(t) * f_2(t) = \int_{-\infty}^{\infty} f_1(\tau)\, f_2(t-\tau)\, d\tau$$

$$\mathbf{F}\{f_1(t) * f_2(t)\} = \int_{-\infty}^{\infty} \{f_1(t) * f_2(t)\}e^{-j\omega t}\, dt$$

$$= \int_{-\infty}^{\infty}\int_{-\infty}^{\infty} f_1(\tau) f_2(t-\tau)\, d\tau\, e^{-j\omega t}\, dt$$

Putting $\quad t-\tau=\lambda, \quad t=\lambda+\tau, \quad dt=d\lambda$

$$\mathbf{F}\{f_1(t)*f_2(t)\}=\int_{-\infty}^{\infty}\int_{-\infty}^{\infty} f_1(\tau)f_2(\lambda)\,d\tau\, e^{-j\omega(\lambda+\tau)}\,d\lambda$$

$$=\int_{-\infty}^{\infty}\int_{-\infty}^{\infty} f_1(\tau)f_2(\lambda)\,d\tau\, e^{-j\omega\tau}\,e^{-j\omega t}\,d\lambda$$

$$=\int_{-\infty}^{\infty} f_1(\tau)e^{-j\omega\tau}d\tau\cdot\int_{-\infty}^{\infty} f_2(\lambda)e^{-j\omega\lambda}\,d\lambda$$

$$=F_1(\omega)\cdot F_2(\omega)$$

This proof shows that convolution in time domain is equivalent to multiplication in frequency domain.

***8. Frequency Convolution*** If $f_1(t)\leftrightarrow F_1(\omega)$ and $f_2(t)\leftrightarrow F_2(\omega)$ then $F_1(\omega)*F_2(\omega)\leftrightarrow 2\pi f_1(t)\cdot f_2(t)$

**Proof:** By definition of convolution,

$$F_1(\omega)*F_2(\omega)=\int_{-\infty}^{\infty} F_1(u)\,F_2(\omega-u)\,du$$

$$\mathbf{F}^{-1}\{F_1(\omega)*F_2(\omega)\}=\frac{1}{2\pi}\int_{-\infty}^{\infty}\int_{-\infty}^{\infty} F_1(u)F_2(\omega-u)\,du\,e^{j\omega t}\,d\omega$$

Putting $\quad \omega-u=\lambda, \quad \omega=\lambda+u, \quad d\omega=d\lambda$

$$\mathbf{F}^{-1}\{F_1(\omega)*f_2(\omega)\}=\frac{1}{2\pi}\int_{-\infty}^{\infty}\int_{-\infty}^{\infty} F_1(u)F_2(\lambda)\,du\,e^{j(\lambda+u)t}\,d\lambda$$

$$=\frac{1}{2\pi}\int_{-\infty}^{\infty}\int_{-\infty}^{\infty} F_1(u)F_2(\lambda)e^{j\lambda t}\,e^{jut}\,du\,d\lambda$$

$$=\frac{1}{2\pi}\int_{-\infty}^{\infty} F_1(u)e^{jut}du\cdot\int_{-\infty}^{\infty} F_2(\lambda)e^{j\lambda t}\,d\lambda$$

$$=f_1(t)\cdot 2\pi f_2(t)$$

$$=2\pi f_1(t)\cdot f_2(t)$$

This proof shows that convolution in the frequency domain is equivalent to multiplication in the time domain.

## 13.11 ENERGY DENSITY SPECTRUM

LO 13.10

Explain energy density spectrum

The energy of any function *f(t)* is given by

$$E=\int_{-\infty}^{\infty} f^2(t)\,dt$$

We know that

$$f(t) = \frac{1}{2\pi}\int_{-\infty}^{\infty} F(\omega)e^{j\omega t}\, d\omega$$

$$E = \int_{-\infty}^{\infty} f(t)\cdot f(t)\, dt$$

$$= \int_{-\infty}^{\infty} f(t)\left[\frac{1}{2\pi}\int_{-\infty}^{\infty} F(\omega)e^{j\omega t}\, d\omega\right] dt$$

$$= \frac{1}{2\pi}\int_{-\infty}^{\infty} F(\omega)\left[\int_{-\infty}^{\infty} f(t)e^{j\omega t}\, dt\right] d\omega$$

$$= \frac{1}{2\pi}\int_{-\infty}^{\infty} F(\omega)\cdot F(-\omega)\, d\omega$$

$$= \frac{1}{2\pi}\int_{-\infty}^{\infty} |F(\omega)|^2\, d\omega \text{ where } |F(\omega)|^2 = F(\omega)\cdot F(-\omega)$$

$|F(j\omega)|$ is even function of $\omega$.

$$E = \frac{1}{\pi}\int_{0}^{\infty} |F(\omega)|^2\, d\omega$$

**EXAMPLE 13.32**

*A low-pass brick-wall filter is given by*

$$H(\omega) = \begin{cases} 1 & |\omega| < W_1 \\ 0 & |\omega| > W_1 \end{cases}$$

*(a) Determine impulse response of the filter and sketch it as a function of time.*

*(b) It the bandwidth of the brick-wall filter is decreased to* $\frac{1}{2}W_1$*, sketch its impulse response.*

**Solution**

(a)

$$h(t) = \frac{1}{2\pi}\int_{-\infty}^{\infty} F_1(\omega)e^{j\omega t}\, d\omega$$

$$= \frac{1}{2\pi}\int_{-W_1}^{W_1} 1\cdot e^{j\omega t}\, d\omega$$

$$= \frac{1}{2\pi}\left[\frac{e^{j\omega t}}{jt}\right]_{-W_1}^{W_1}$$

$$= \frac{1}{\pi t}\left(\frac{e^{jW_1 t} - e^{-jW_1 t}}{2j}\right)$$

$$= \frac{1}{\pi t}\left(\sin W_1 t\right)$$

$$= \frac{W_1}{\pi}\left(\frac{\sin W_1 t}{W_1 t}\right)$$

$$= \frac{W_1}{\pi}\ \text{Sa}\ (W_1 t)$$

The impulse response is shown in Fig. 13.59.

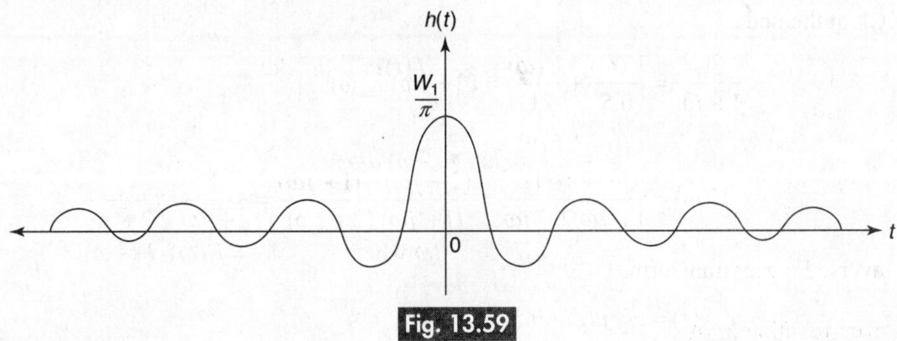


Fig. 13.59

(b) As we decrease the bandwidth of brick-wall filter, the function $h(t)$ becomes broader and vice versa.

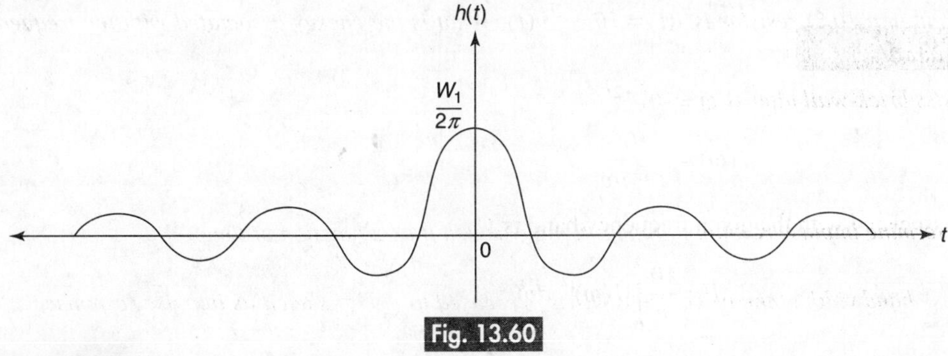


Fig. 13.60

## EXAMPLE 13.33

*Find the output voltage response for the network shown in Fig. 13.61.*

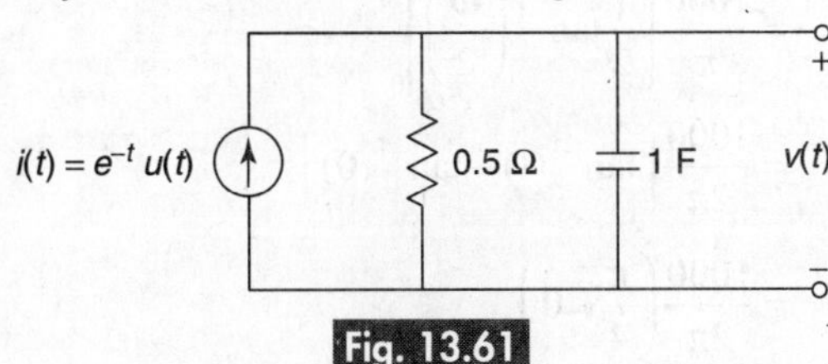


Fig. 13.61

**Solution** The transformed network is shown in Fig. 13.62.

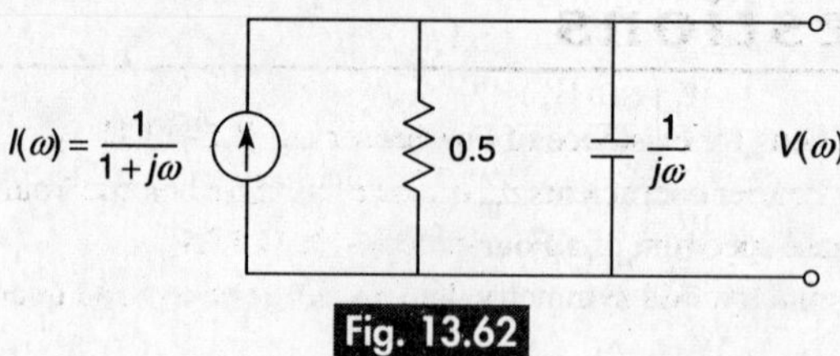


Fig. 13.62

Applying KCL at the node,

$$\frac{1}{1+j\omega}=\frac{V(\omega)}{0.5}+\frac{V(\omega)}{\frac{1}{j\omega}}=(2+j\omega)\,V(\omega)$$

$$V(\omega)=\frac{1}{1+j\omega}\frac{1}{2+j\omega}=\frac{(2+j\omega)-(1+j\omega)}{(1+j\omega)\,(2+j\omega)}=\frac{1}{1+j\omega}-\frac{1}{2+j\omega}$$

Taking the inverse Fourier transform,

$$v(t)=e^{-t}\,u(t)-0.5e^{-2t}$$

## EXAMPLE 13.34

*The current in a 10 Ω resistor is $i(t)=10\,e^{-2t}u(t)$. What is the energy associated with the frequency band $0\le\omega\le 2$ rad/s?*

**Solution**

$$i(t)=10\,e^{-2t}$$

$$I(\omega)=\frac{10}{2+j\omega}$$

Energy associated with the given frequency band is

$$E=\frac{10}{\pi}\int_0^2 |I(\omega)|^2\,d\omega$$

$$=\frac{10}{\pi}\int_0^2\frac{100}{4+\omega^2}\,d\omega$$

$$=\frac{1000}{\pi}\left[\frac{1}{2}\tan^{-1}\left(\frac{\omega}{2}\right)\right]_0^2$$

$$=\frac{1000}{2\pi}\left[\tan^{-1}(1)-\tan^{-1}(0)\right]$$

$$=\frac{1000}{2\pi}\left(\frac{\pi}{4}-0\right)$$

$$=125\text{ J}$$

# Theory Questions

13.1 What are Dirichlet's conditions for existence of Fourier series? **[LO 13.1]** ●○○

13.2 Derive the expressions for Fourier coefficients $a_0$, $a_n$ and $b_n$ in trigonometric Fourier series. **[LO 13.1]** ○○●

13.3 Explain magnitude and phase spectrum of a Fourier series. **[LO 13.1]** ○●○

13.4 Explain the terms even symmetry, odd symmetry, half-wave symmetry and quarter-wave symmetry. **[LO 13.2]** ○●○

13.5 Explain exponential Fourier series. **[LO 13.3]** ○●○

13.6 Write the expressions for average value and rms value and average power of a periodic complex wave. **[LO 13.4]** ●○○

13.7 What is a Fourier transform? Write the condition for existence of a Fourier transform. **[LO 13.5]** ●○○

13.8 Derive Fourier transforms for the following functions: **[LO 13.7]** ○●○

(i) One-sided exponential functions
(ii) Two-sided exponential functions
(iii) Gate function
(iv) Impulse function
(v) Constant function
(vi) Cosine function
(vii) Sine function
(viii) Exponential function

13.9 Derive the expression for Fourier transform of periodic functions. **[LO 13.8]** ○●○

13.10 Explain the various properties of Fourier transform. **[LO 13.9]** ○●○

# Practice Problems

13.1 Find the trigonometric Fourier series of the waveform shown in Fig. 13.63. ○●○

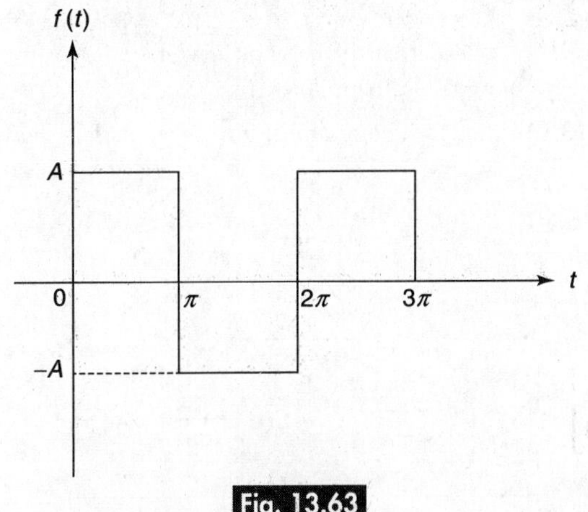


Fig. 13.63

13.2 Find the trigonometric Fourier series of the waveform shown in Fig. 13.64. ○●○

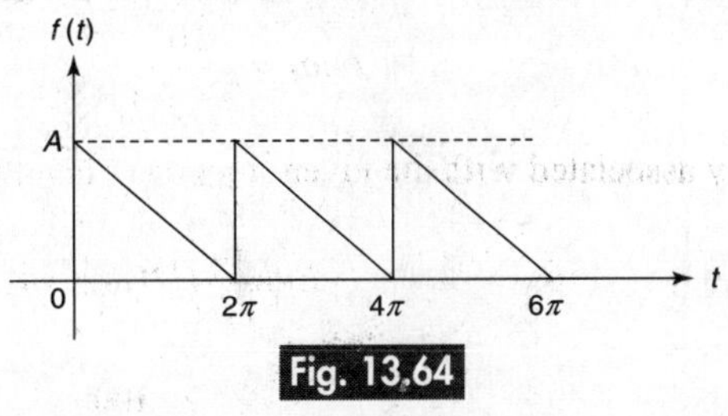


Fig. 13.64

13.3 Find the trigonometric Fourier series of the waveform shown in Fig. 13.65. ○○●

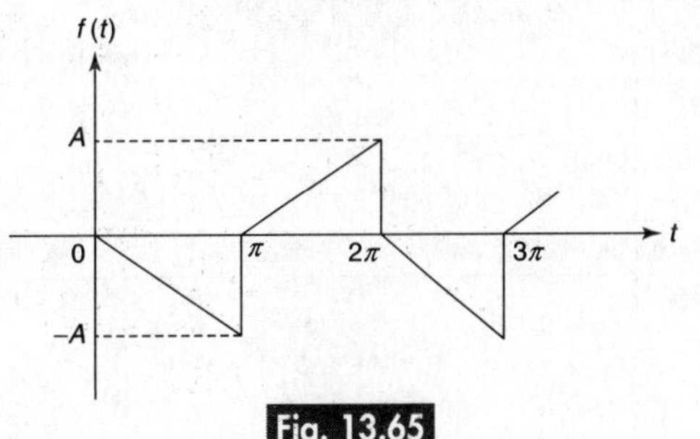


Fig. 13.65

**13.4** Find the trigonometric Fourier series of the waveform shown in Fig. 13.66. ○●○

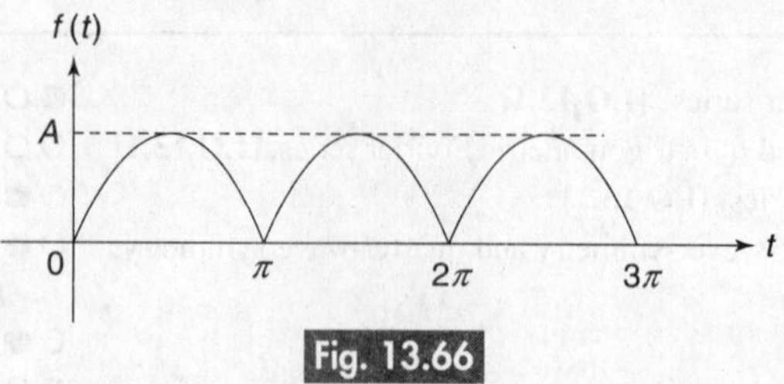


Fig. 13.66

**13.5** Find the trigonometric Fourier series of the waveform shown in Fig. 13.67. ○●○

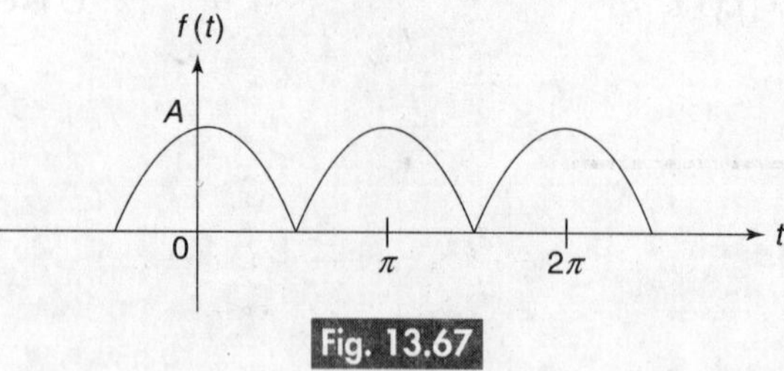


Fig. 13.67

**13.6** Find the trigonometric Fourier series of the waveform shown in Fig. 13.68. ○○●

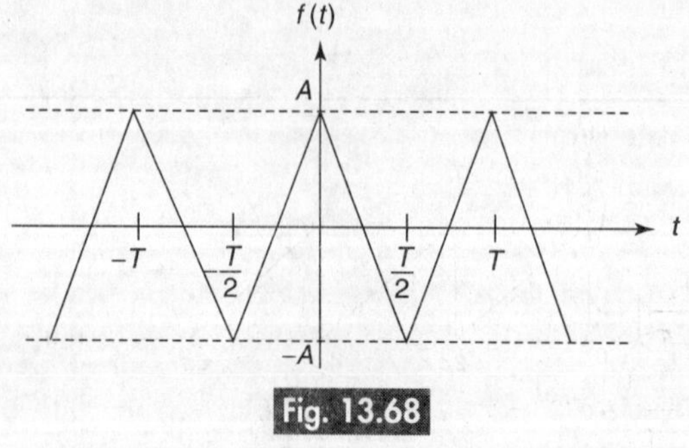


Fig. 13.68

**13.7** Find the exponential Fourier series of the waveform shown in Fig. 13.69. ○●○

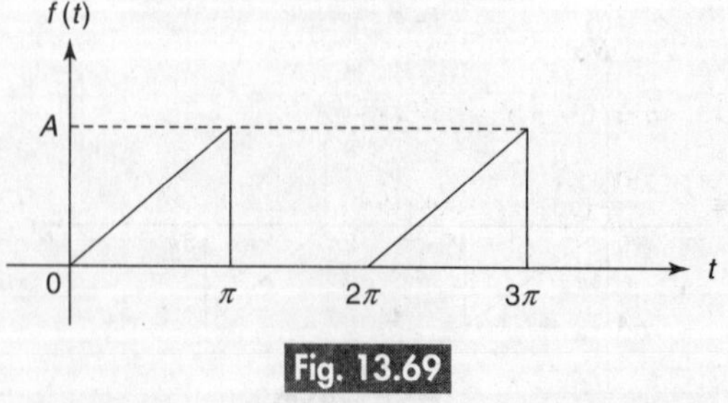


Fig. 13.69

**13.8** Find the exponential Fourier series of the waveform shown in Fig. 13.70. ○●○

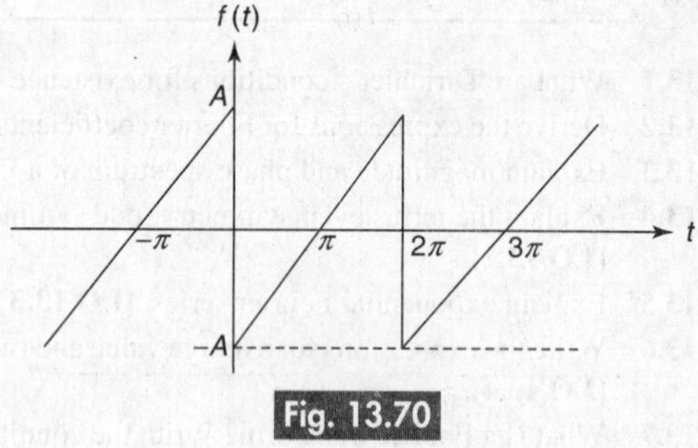


Fig. 13.70

**13.9** Find the effective voltage, effective current, and average power supplied to a passive network if the applied voltage is $v(t) = 200 + 100\cos(500t + 30°) + 75\cos(1500t + 60°)$ volts and the resulting current is $i(t) = 3.53\cos(500t + 75°) + 3.55\cos(1500t + 78.45°)$ amperes. ○●○

**13.10** A two-element series circuit with $R = 10\ \Omega$ and $L = 20$ mH has current $i = 5\sin 100t + 3\sin 300t + 2\sin 100t$. Find the effective applied voltage and the average power. ○●○

**13.11** A three-element series circuit with $R = 5\ \Omega$ $L = 5\ \mu$H and $C = 50\ \mu$F, has an applied voltage $v = 150\sin 1000t + 10\sin 200t + 75\sin 300t$. Find the effective current and the average power for the circuit. ○●○

**13.12** A three-element circuit consists of $R = 5\ \Omega$ in series with a parallel combination of $L$ and $C$. At $\omega = 500$ rad/s, $X_L = 2\ \Omega$, $X_C = 8\ \Omega$, find the total current if the applied voltage is given by $v = 50 + 20\sin 500t + 10\sin 1000t$. ○●○

**13.13** Find the Fourier transform of the function shown in Fig. 13.71. ○●○

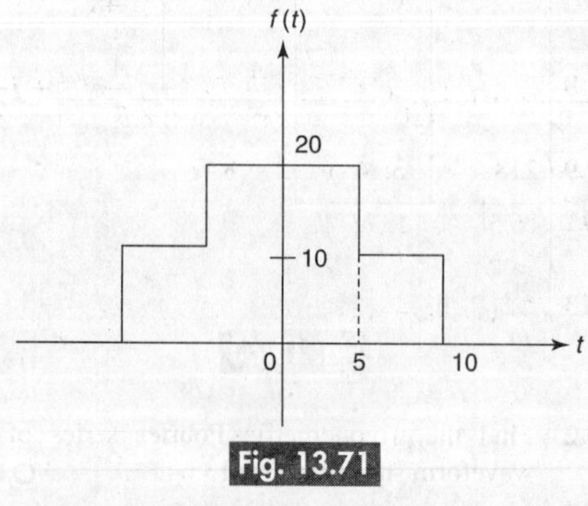


Fig. 13.71

**13.14** Find the Fourier transform of the function shown in Fig. 13.72. ○○●

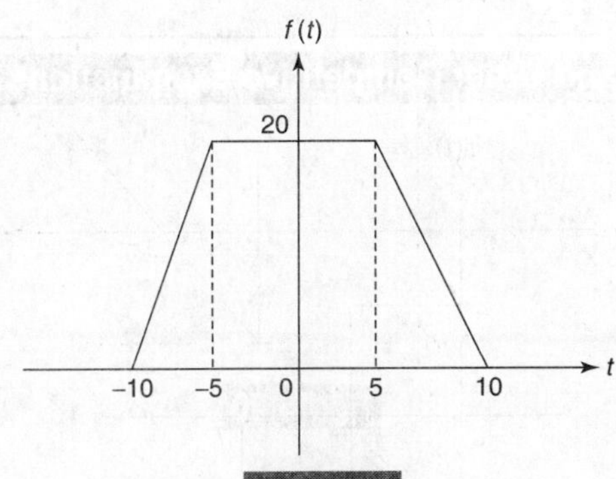


Fig. 13.72

## ANSWERS TO PRACTICE PROBLEMS

**13.1** $\frac{4A}{\pi}\sin\omega t+\frac{4A}{3\pi}\sin 3\omega t+\frac{4A}{5\pi}\sin 5\omega t+\ldots\ldots$

**13.2** $-\frac{2A}{\pi}\sin\omega t-\frac{A}{\pi}\sin 2\omega t-\frac{2A}{3\pi}\sin 3\omega t-\ldots\ldots$

**13.3** $\left(\frac{4A}{\pi^2}\cos\omega t-\frac{4A}{9\pi^2}\cos 3\omega t+\ldots\right)+\left(\frac{2A}{\pi}\sin\omega t-\frac{2A}{3\pi}\sin 3\omega t-\ldots\right)$

**13.4** $\frac{2A}{\pi}-\frac{4A}{3\pi}\cos 2\omega t-\frac{4A}{15\pi}\cos 4\omega t-\frac{4A}{35\pi}\cos 6\omega t-\ldots\ldots$

**13.5** $\frac{2A}{\pi}+\frac{4A}{3\pi}\cos 2\omega t-\frac{4A}{15\pi}\cos 4\omega t+\frac{4A}{35\pi}\cos 6\omega t-\ldots\ldots$

**13.6** $\frac{8A}{\pi^2}\cos\omega t+\frac{8A}{9\pi^2}\cos 3\omega t+\frac{8A}{25\pi^2}\cos 5\omega t+\ldots\ldots$

**13.7** $\ldots\ldots+\left(\frac{1}{9\pi^2}-j\frac{1}{6\pi}\right)A\,e^{-j3\omega t}-j\frac{A}{4\pi}e^{-j2\omega t}-\left(\frac{1}{\pi^2}-j\frac{1}{2\pi}\right)A\,e^{-j\omega t}$
$+\frac{1}{4}-\left(\frac{1}{\pi^2}+j\frac{1}{2\pi}\right)A\,e^{j\omega t}+j\frac{A}{4\pi}e^{j2\omega t}-\left(\frac{1}{9\pi^2}+j\frac{1}{6\pi}\right)A\,e^{j3\omega t}-\ldots\ldots$

**13.8** $\ldots\ldots-j\frac{A}{2\pi}e^{-j2\omega t}-j\frac{A}{\pi}e^{-j\omega t}+j\frac{A}{\pi}e^{j\omega t}+j\frac{A}{2\pi}e^{j2\omega t}+\ldots\ldots$

**13.9** 218.5 V, 3.54 A, 250.8 W

**13.10** 48 V, 190 W

**13.11** 16.58 A, 1374 W

**13.12** $i=10+3.53\sin(500t-28.1°)$

**13.13** $\frac{20}{\omega}(\sin 5\omega+\sin 10\omega)$

**13.14** $\frac{200}{\omega^2}(\cos 5\omega-\cos 10\omega)$

# Objective-Type Questions

## From GATE and Other Competitive Examinations

**13.1** A periodic function $f(t)$ with time period $T$ repeats itself after half time-period $\frac{T}{2}$. The Fourier series of $f(t)$ would contain ○●○

(a) cosine terms only
(b) odd harmonic terms only
(c) even harmonic terms only
(d) sine terms only

**13.2** The Fourier series expansion of a periodic function with half-wave symmetry contains only ●○○

(a) sine terms (b) cosine terms
(c) odd harmonics (d) even harmonics

**13.3** With regard to Fourier transform, tick the correct combination: ○●○

| Function | Transform |
|---|---|
| A Real and even | 1. Real and even |
| B Real and odd | 2. Real and odd |
| C. Real even plus imaginary odd | 3. Complex and even |
| D. Complex and even | 4. Real |
| | 5. Imaginary and odd |

| | A | B | C | D |
|---|---|---|---|---|
| (a) | 1 | 2 | 3 | 4 |
| (b) | 1 | 5 | 3 | 4 |
| (c) | 1 | 5 | 4 | 3 |
| (d) | 2 | 5 | 4 | 3 |

**13.4** Which of the following periodic waveforms will have only odd harmonics of sinusoidal waveforms? ○●○

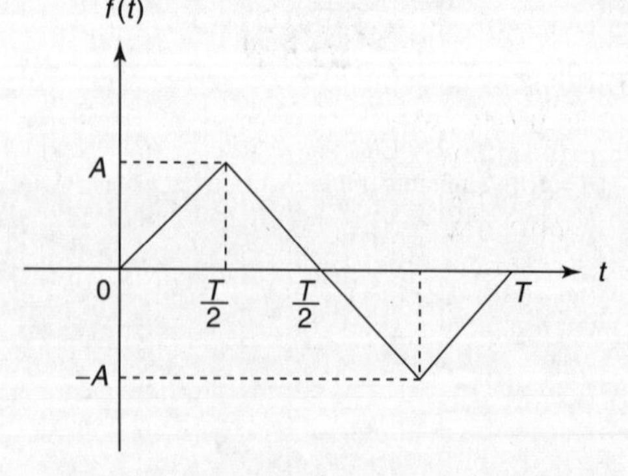


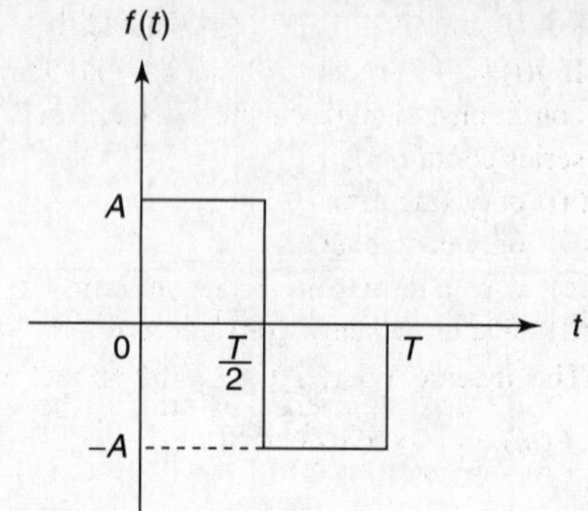


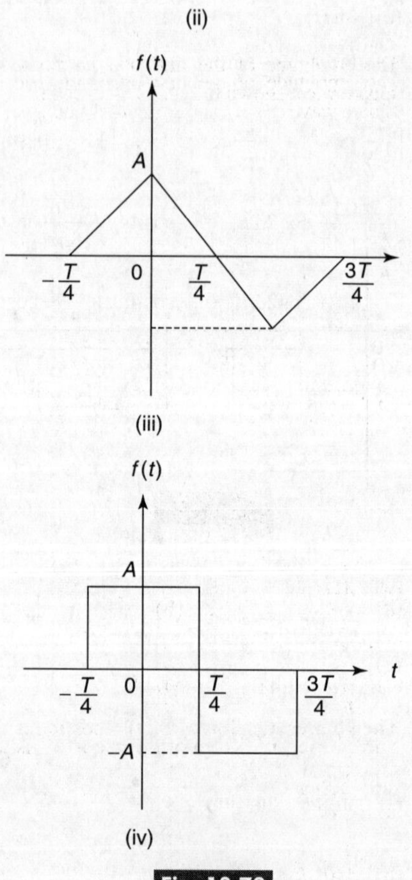


Fig. 13.73

Select the correct answer using the codes given below:

(a) (i) and (ii) (b) (i) and (iii)
(c) (i) and (iv) (d) (ii) and (iv)

**13.5** If $f(t) = -f(-t)$ and $f(t)$ satisfy the Dirichlet's conditions, then $f(t)$ can be expanded in a Fourier series containing ○●○

(a) only sine terms
(b) only cosine terms
(c) cosine terms and a constant term
(d) sine terms and a constant term

**13.6** The inverse Fourier transform of the function $F(\omega) = \frac{1}{j\omega} + \pi\,\delta(\omega)$ is ○●○

(a) $\sin \omega t$ (b) $\cos \omega t$
(c) $\sin (t)$ (d) $\mu(t)$

**13.7** The amplitude of the first odd harmonic of the square wave shown in Fig. 13.74 is equal to ○●○

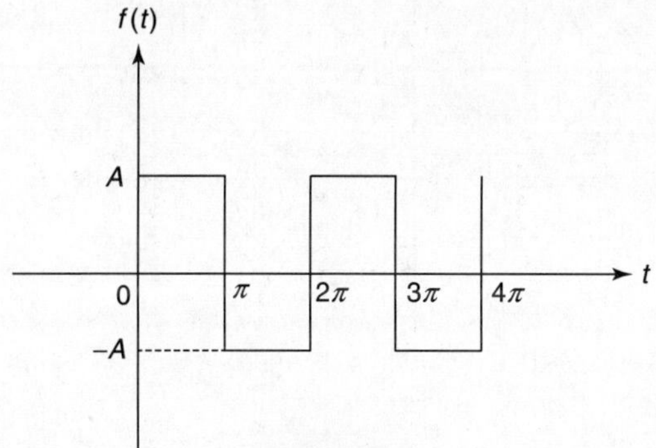


Fig. 13.74

(a) $\frac{4A}{\pi}$ (b) $\frac{2A}{3\pi}$

(c) $\frac{A}{\pi}$ (d) 0

**13.8** The Fourier transform of $f(t) = \cos \omega_0 t$ is ○●○

(a) $\frac{1}{2}\delta(f - f_0)$

(b) $\frac{1}{2}\delta(f + f_0)$

(c) $\frac{1}{2}[\delta(f - f_0) - \delta(f + f_0)]$

(d) $\frac{1}{2}[\delta(f - f_0) + \delta(f + f_0)]$

**13.9** A periodic function $f(t)$ is said to have a quarter-wave symmetry, if it possesses ○●○

(a) even symmetry at an interval of quarter of a wave
(b) even symmetry and half-wave symmetry only
(c) even or odd symmetry without half-wave symmetry
(d) even or odd symmetry with half-wave symmetry

**13.10** Periodic signal that obeys Dirichlet's condition can be represented by ●○○

(a) Fourier series
(b) Fourier transform
(c) inverse Fourier transform
(d) none of these

**13.11** The current waveform in a pure resistor of 10 Ω is shown in Fig. 13.75 power dissipated in the resistor is ○●○

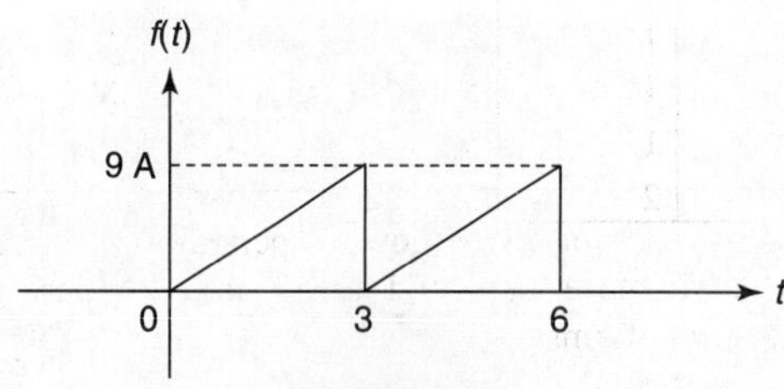


Fig. 13.75

(a) 7.29 W
(b) 52.4 W
(c) 135 W
(d) 270 W

## ANSWERS TO OBJECTIVE-TYPE QUESTIONS

| | | | | | | |
|---|---|---|---|---|---|---|
| **13.1** (c) | **13.2** (c) | **13.3** (c) | **13.4** (a) | **13.5** (a) | **13.6** (d) | **13.7** (a) |
| **13.8** (d) | **13.9** (d) | **13.10** (a) | **13.11** (d) | | | |

CHAPTER 14

# Filters and Attenuators

## LEARNING OBJECTIVES

**After studying this chapter, you should be able to:**

**LO 14.1** Explain classification of filters

**LO 14.2** Derive the expressions for characteristic impedance and propagation constant for *T* and *pi*-networks

**LO 14.3** Explain characteristics of filters

**LO 14.4** Design constant-*k* low-pass filters and constant-*k* high-pass filters

**LO 14.5** Design band-pass filters and band-stop filters

**LO 14.6** Explain *m*-derived filters, *m*-derived low-pass filters, and *m*-derived high-pass filters and their characteristics

**LO 14.7** Discuss terminating half-sections

**LO 14.8** Explain composite filters and their characteristics

**LO 14.9** Discuss attenuators and their types – lattice, *T*-type, *pi*-type, and ladder-type

## INTRODUCTION

Filters are frequency-selective networks that attenuate signals at some frequency and allow others to pass with or without attenuation. A filter is constructed from purely reactive elements. Ideally, filters should produce no attenuation in the desired band, called *pass band*, and should provide attenuation at all other frequencies called *attenuation band* or *stop band*. The frequency which separates the pass band and the stop band is called *cut-off frequency*. Filter networks are widely used in communication systems to separate various channels in carrier-frequency telephone circuits.

## 14.1 CLASSIFICATION OF FILTERS

LO 14.1

Explain classification of filters

On the basis of frequency characteristics, filters are classified into four categories:

(i) Low-pass filter
(ii) High-pass filter
(iii) Band-pass filter
(iv) Band-stop filter

A *low-pass filter* allows all the frequencies up to a certain cut-off frequency to pass through it and attenuates all the other frequencies above the cut-off frequency.

A *high-pass filter* attenuates all the frequencies below the cut-off frequency and allows all other frequencies above the cut-off frequency to pass through it.

A *band-pass filter* allows a limited band of frequencies to pass through it and attenuates all other frequencies below or above the frequency band.

A *band-stop filter* attenuates a limited band of frequencies but allows all other frequencies to pass through it.

## 14.2 *T*-NETWORK

LO 14.2

Derive the expressions for characteristic impedance and propagation constant for *T* and pi-networks

Figure 14.1 shows a *T*-network.

### 14.2.1 Characteristic Impedance

For a *T*-network, the value of input impedance when it is terminated by characteristic impedance $\mathbf{Z}_0$, is given by

$$\mathbf{Z}_{in} = \frac{\mathbf{Z}_1}{2} + \frac{\mathbf{Z}_2\left(\frac{\mathbf{Z}_1}{2} + \mathbf{Z}_0\right)}{\frac{\mathbf{Z}_1}{2} + \mathbf{Z}_2 + \mathbf{Z}_0}$$

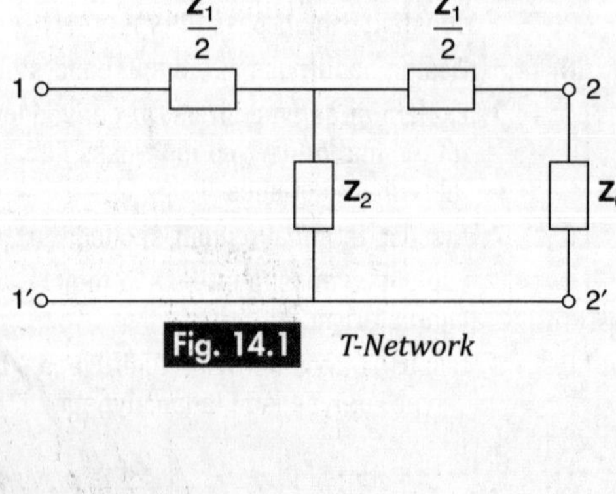

Fig. 14.1 *T-Network*

But $\mathbf{Z}_{in} = \mathbf{Z}_0$

$$\mathbf{Z}_0 = \frac{\mathbf{Z}_1}{2} + \frac{2\mathbf{Z}_2\left(\frac{\mathbf{Z}_1}{2} + \mathbf{Z}_0\right)}{\mathbf{Z}_1 + 2\mathbf{Z}_2 + 2\mathbf{Z}_0}$$

$$= \frac{\mathbf{Z}_1}{2} + \frac{\mathbf{Z}_1\mathbf{Z}_2 + 2\mathbf{Z}_2\mathbf{Z}_0}{\mathbf{Z}_1 + 2\mathbf{Z}_2 + 2\mathbf{Z}_0}$$

$$= \frac{\mathbf{Z}_1^2 + 2\mathbf{Z}_1\mathbf{Z}_2 + 2\mathbf{Z}_1\mathbf{Z}_0 + 2\mathbf{Z}_1\mathbf{Z}_2 + 4\mathbf{Z}_2\mathbf{Z}_0}{2(\mathbf{Z}_1 + 2\mathbf{Z}_2 + 2\mathbf{Z}_0)}$$

$$2\mathbf{Z}_1\mathbf{Z}_0 + 4\mathbf{Z}_2\mathbf{Z}_0 + 4{\mathbf{Z}_0}^2 = \mathbf{Z}_1^2 + 2\mathbf{Z}_1\mathbf{Z}_2 + 2\mathbf{Z}_1\mathbf{Z}_0 + 2\mathbf{Z}_1\mathbf{Z}_2 + 4\mathbf{Z}_2\mathbf{Z}_0$$

$$4\mathbf{Z}_0^2 = \mathbf{Z}_1^2 + 4\mathbf{Z}_1\mathbf{Z}_2$$

$$\mathbf{Z}_0^2 = \frac{\mathbf{Z}_1^2}{4} + \mathbf{Z}_1\mathbf{Z}_2$$

$$\mathbf{Z}_0 = \sqrt{\frac{\mathbf{Z}_1^2}{4} + \mathbf{Z}_1\mathbf{Z}_2}$$

Hence, characteristic impedance for symmetrical $T$ section is given by

$$\mathbf{Z}_{0T} = \sqrt{\frac{\mathbf{Z}_1^2}{4} + \mathbf{Z}_1\mathbf{Z}_2}$$

Characteristic impedance can also be expressed in terms of open-circuit impedance $\mathbf{Z}_{oc}$ and short-circuit impedance $\mathbf{Z}_{sc}$.

Open-circuit impedance $\mathbf{Z}_{oc} = \dfrac{\mathbf{Z}_1}{2} + \mathbf{Z}_2 = \dfrac{\mathbf{Z}_1 + 2Z_2}{2}$

Short-circuit impedance $\mathbf{Z}_{sc} = \dfrac{\mathbf{Z}_1}{2} + \dfrac{\dfrac{\mathbf{Z}_1}{2}\mathbf{Z}_2}{\dfrac{\mathbf{Z}_1}{2} + \mathbf{Z}_2} = \dfrac{\mathbf{Z}_1}{2} + \dfrac{\mathbf{Z}_1\mathbf{Z}_2}{\mathbf{Z}_1 + 2\mathbf{Z}_2} = \dfrac{\mathbf{Z}_1^2 + 4\mathbf{Z}_1\mathbf{Z}_2}{2\mathbf{Z}_1 + 4\mathbf{Z}_2}$

$$\mathbf{Z}_{oc}\mathbf{Z}_{sc} = \left(\frac{\mathbf{Z}_1 + 2\mathbf{Z}_2}{2}\right)\left(\frac{\mathbf{Z}_1^2 + 4\mathbf{Z}_1\mathbf{Z}_2}{2\mathbf{Z}_1 + 4\mathbf{Z}_2}\right) = \frac{\mathbf{Z}_1^2}{4} + \mathbf{Z}_1\mathbf{Z}_2 = \mathbf{Z}_{0T}^2$$

$$\mathbf{Z}_{0T} = \sqrt{\mathbf{Z}_{oc}\mathbf{Z}_{sc}}$$

### 14.2.2 Propagation Constant

The propagation constant $\gamma$ of the network in Fig. 14.2 is given by

$$\gamma = \log_e \frac{I_1}{I_2}$$

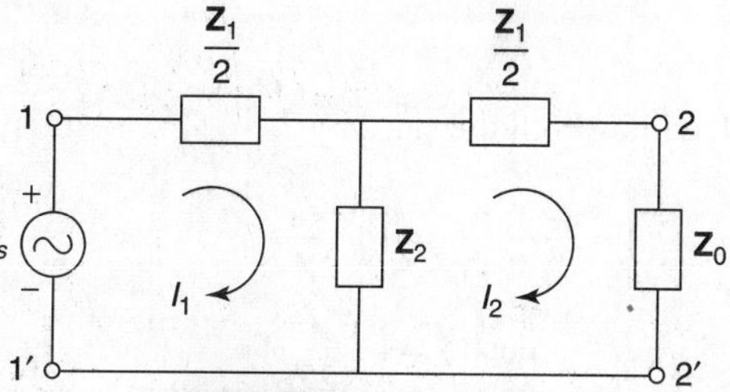

Applying KVL to mesh 1,

$$V_s - \frac{\mathbf{Z}_1}{2}I_1 - \mathbf{Z}_2(I_1 - I_2) = 0$$

$$V_s = \left(\frac{\mathbf{Z}_1}{2} + \mathbf{Z}_2\right)I_1 - \mathbf{Z}_2 I_2$$



Fig. 14.2 T-Network

Applying KVL to mesh 2,

$$-\mathbf{Z}_2(I_2 - I_1) - \frac{\mathbf{Z}_1}{2}I_2 - \mathbf{Z}_0 I_2 = 0$$

$$-\mathbf{Z}_2 I_1 + \left(\frac{\mathbf{Z}_1}{2} + \mathbf{Z}_2 + \mathbf{Z}_0\right)I_2 = 0$$

$$\mathbf{Z}_2 I_1 = \left(\frac{\mathbf{Z}_1}{2} + \mathbf{Z}_2 + \mathbf{Z}_0\right)I_2$$

$$\frac{I_1}{I_2} = \frac{\dfrac{\mathbf{Z}_1}{2} + \mathbf{Z}_2 + \mathbf{Z}_0}{\mathbf{Z}_2} = e^{\gamma}$$

$$\frac{\mathbf{Z}_1}{2}+\mathbf{Z}_2+\mathbf{Z}_0=\mathbf{Z}_2e^{\gamma}$$

$$\mathbf{Z}_0=\mathbf{Z}_2(e^{\gamma}-1)-\frac{\mathbf{Z}_1}{2}$$

The characteristic impedance of the $T$-network is given by

$$\mathbf{Z}_0=\sqrt{\frac{\mathbf{Z}_1^2}{4}+\mathbf{Z}_1\mathbf{Z}_2}$$

$$\sqrt{\frac{\mathbf{Z}_1^2}{4}+\mathbf{Z}_1\mathbf{Z}_2}=\mathbf{Z}_2(e^{\gamma}-1)-\frac{\mathbf{Z}_1}{2}$$

$$\frac{\mathbf{Z}_1^2}{4}+\mathbf{Z}_1\mathbf{Z}_2=\mathbf{Z}_2^2(e^{\gamma}-1)^2+\frac{\mathbf{Z}_1^2}{4}-\mathbf{Z}_1\mathbf{Z}_2(e^{\gamma}-1)$$

$$\mathbf{Z}_2^2(e^{\gamma}-1)^2-\mathbf{Z}_1\mathbf{Z}_2(1+e^{\gamma}-1)=0$$

$$\mathbf{Z}_2^2(e^{\gamma}-1)^2-\mathbf{Z}_1\mathbf{Z}_2e^{\gamma}=0$$

$$\mathbf{Z}_2(e^{\gamma}-1)^2-\mathbf{Z}_1e^{\gamma}=0$$

$$(e^{\gamma}-1)^2=\frac{\mathbf{Z}_1}{\mathbf{Z}_2}e^{\gamma}$$

$$e^{2\gamma}-2e^{\gamma}+1=\frac{\mathbf{Z}_1}{\mathbf{Z}_2e^{-\gamma}}$$

$$e^{-\gamma}(e^{2\gamma}-2e^{\gamma}+1)=\frac{\mathbf{Z}_1}{\mathbf{Z}_2}$$

$$e^{\gamma}+e^{-\gamma}-2=\frac{\mathbf{Z}_1}{\mathbf{Z}_2}$$

Dividing both the sides by 2,

$$\frac{e^{\gamma}+e^{-\gamma}}{2}=1+\frac{\mathbf{Z}_1}{2\mathbf{Z}_2}$$

$$\cosh\gamma=1+\frac{\mathbf{Z}_1}{2\mathbf{Z}_2}$$

$$\sinh\gamma=\sqrt{\cosh^2\gamma-1}=\sqrt{\left(1+\frac{\mathbf{Z}_1}{2\mathbf{Z}_2}\right)^2-1}=\sqrt{1+\frac{\mathbf{Z}_1}{\mathbf{Z}_2}+\frac{\mathbf{Z}_1^2}{4\mathbf{Z}_2^2}-1}=\sqrt{\frac{\mathbf{Z}_1}{\mathbf{Z}_2}+\left(\frac{\mathbf{Z}_1}{2\mathbf{Z}_2}\right)^2}$$

$$=\frac{1}{\mathbf{Z}_2}\sqrt{\mathbf{Z}_1\mathbf{Z}_2+\frac{\mathbf{Z}_1^2}{4}}=\frac{\mathbf{Z}_{0T}}{\mathbf{Z}_2}$$

$$\tanh\gamma=\frac{\sinh\gamma}{\cosh\gamma}=\frac{\mathbf{Z}_{0T}}{\mathbf{Z}_2\left(1+\frac{\mathbf{Z}_1}{2\mathbf{Z}_2}\right)}=\frac{\mathbf{Z}_{0T}}{\mathbf{Z}_2+\frac{\mathbf{Z}_1}{2}}$$

But $\quad \mathbf{Z}_{0T}=\sqrt{\mathbf{Z}_{oc}\mathbf{Z}_{sc}}$

and $$\mathbf{Z}_{oc} = \frac{\mathbf{Z}_1}{2} + \mathbf{Z}_2$$

$$\tanh\gamma = \sqrt{\frac{\mathbf{Z}_{sc}}{\mathbf{Z}_{oc}}}$$

Also, $$\sinh\frac{\gamma}{2} = \sqrt{\frac{1}{2}(\cosh\gamma - 1)} = \sqrt{\frac{1}{2}\left(1 + \frac{\mathbf{Z}_1}{2\mathbf{Z}_2} - 1\right)} = \sqrt{\frac{\mathbf{Z}_1}{4\mathbf{Z}_2}}$$

## 14.3 π-NETWORK

LO 14.2

Figure 14.3 shows a π-network.

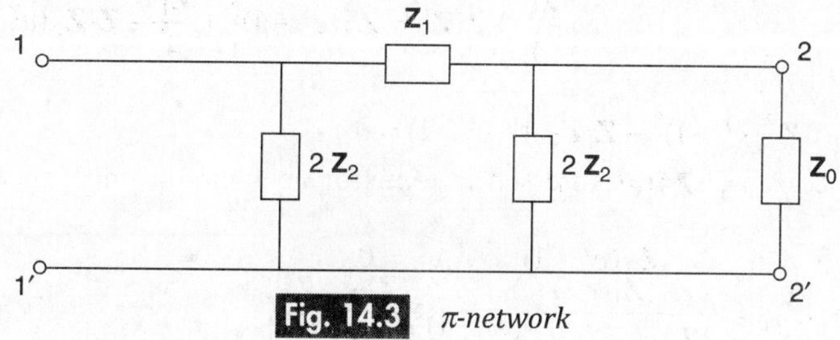


**Fig. 14.3** *π-network*

### 14.3.1 Characteristic Impedance

For a π-network, the value of input impedance when it is terminated by impedance $\mathbf{Z}_0$, is given by

$$\mathbf{Z}_{in} = \frac{2\mathbf{Z}_2\left(\mathbf{Z}_1 + \dfrac{2\mathbf{Z}_2\mathbf{Z}_0}{2\mathbf{Z}_2 + \mathbf{Z}_0}\right)}{\mathbf{Z}_1 + \dfrac{2\mathbf{Z}_2\mathbf{Z}_0}{2\mathbf{Z}_2 + \mathbf{Z}_0} + 2\mathbf{Z}_2}$$

But $$\mathbf{Z}_{in} = \mathbf{Z}_0$$

$$\mathbf{Z}_0 = \frac{2\mathbf{Z}_2\left(\mathbf{Z}_1 + \dfrac{2\mathbf{Z}_2\mathbf{Z}_0}{2\mathbf{Z}_2 + \mathbf{Z}_0}\right)}{\mathbf{Z}_1 + \dfrac{2\mathbf{Z}_2\mathbf{Z}_0}{2\mathbf{Z}_2 + \mathbf{Z}_0} + 2\mathbf{Z}_2}$$

$$\mathbf{Z}_0\mathbf{Z}_1 + \frac{2\mathbf{Z}_2\mathbf{Z}_0^2}{2\mathbf{Z}_2 + \mathbf{Z}_0} + 2\mathbf{Z}_0\mathbf{Z}_2 = \frac{2\mathbf{Z}_2(2\mathbf{Z}_1\mathbf{Z}_2 + \mathbf{Z}_0\mathbf{Z}_1 + 2\mathbf{Z}_0\mathbf{Z}_2)}{2\mathbf{Z}_2 + \mathbf{Z}_0}$$

$$2\mathbf{Z}_0\mathbf{Z}_1\mathbf{Z}_2 + \mathbf{Z}_1\mathbf{Z}_0^2 + 2\mathbf{Z}_0\mathbf{Z}_2^2 + 4\mathbf{Z}_2\mathbf{Z}_0^2 + 2\mathbf{Z}_2\mathbf{Z}_0^2 = 4\mathbf{Z}_1\mathbf{Z}_2^2 + 2\mathbf{Z}_0\mathbf{Z}_1\mathbf{Z}_2 + 4\mathbf{Z}_0\mathbf{Z}_2^2$$

$$\mathbf{Z}_1\mathbf{Z}_0^2 + 4\mathbf{Z}_2\mathbf{Z}_0^2 = 4\mathbf{Z}_1\mathbf{Z}_2^2$$

$$\mathbf{Z}_0^2(\mathbf{Z}_1 + 4\mathbf{Z}_2) = 4\mathbf{Z}_1\mathbf{Z}_2^2$$

$$\mathbf{Z}_0^2 = \frac{4\mathbf{Z}_1\mathbf{Z}_2^2}{\mathbf{Z}_1 + 4\mathbf{Z}_2}$$

$$\mathbf{Z}_0 = \sqrt{\frac{4\mathbf{Z}_1\mathbf{Z}_2^2}{\mathbf{Z}_1 + 4\mathbf{Z}_2}}$$

Dividing both the sides by $4Z_2$,

$$\mathbf{Z}_0 = \sqrt{\frac{\mathbf{Z}_1\mathbf{Z}_2}{1+\frac{\mathbf{Z}_1}{4\mathbf{Z}_2}}}$$

Hence, characteristic impedance of a symmetrical $\pi$ network is given by

$$\mathbf{Z}_{0\pi} = \sqrt{\frac{\mathbf{Z}_1\mathbf{Z}_2}{1+\frac{\mathbf{Z}_1}{4\mathbf{Z}_2}}} = \frac{\mathbf{Z}_1\mathbf{Z}_2}{\sqrt{\mathbf{Z}_1\mathbf{Z}_2+\frac{\mathbf{Z}_1^2}{4}}}$$

But

$$\mathbf{Z}_{0T} = \sqrt{\frac{\mathbf{Z}_1^2}{4}+\mathbf{Z}_1\mathbf{Z}_2}$$

$$\mathbf{Z}_{0\pi} = \frac{\mathbf{Z}_1\mathbf{Z}_2}{\mathbf{Z}_{0T}}$$

Characteristic impedance can also be expressed in terms of open-circuit impedance $\mathbf{Z}_{oc}$ and short-circuit impedance $\mathbf{Z}_{sc}$.

Open-circuit impedance $\mathbf{Z}_{oc} = \dfrac{2\mathbf{Z}_2(\mathbf{Z}_1+2\mathbf{Z}_2)}{2\mathbf{Z}_2+\mathbf{Z}_1+2\mathbf{Z}_2} = \dfrac{2\mathbf{Z}_2(\mathbf{Z}_1+2\mathbf{Z}_2)}{\mathbf{Z}_1+4\mathbf{Z}_2}$

Short-circuit impedance $\mathbf{Z}_{sc} = \dfrac{2\mathbf{Z}_1\mathbf{Z}_2}{2\mathbf{Z}_2+\mathbf{Z}_1}$

$$\mathbf{Z}_{oc}\mathbf{Z}_{sc} = \frac{4\mathbf{Z}_1\mathbf{Z}_2^2}{\mathbf{Z}_1+4\mathbf{Z}_2} = \frac{\mathbf{Z}_1\mathbf{Z}_2}{1+\frac{\mathbf{Z}_1}{4\mathbf{Z}_2}}$$

$$\mathbf{Z}_{0\pi} = \sqrt{\mathbf{Z}_{oc}\mathbf{Z}_{sc}}$$

### 14.3.2 Propagation Constant

The propagation constant of a symmetrical $\pi$ network is same as that of a symmetrical $T$ network.

## 14.4 CHARACTERISTIC OF FILTERS

LO 14.3

Explain characteristics of filters

A filter transmits or passes desired range of frequencies without loss and attenuates all undesired frequencies.

The propagation constant

$$\gamma = \alpha + j\beta$$

where $\alpha$ is attenuation constant and $\beta$ is the phase constant. We know that

$$\sinh\frac{\gamma}{2} = \sqrt{\frac{\mathbf{Z}_1}{4\mathbf{Z}_2}}$$

$$\sinh\left(\frac{\alpha+j\beta}{2}\right) = \sinh\frac{\alpha}{2}\cos\frac{\beta}{2} + j\cosh\frac{\alpha}{2}\sin\frac{\beta}{2} = \sqrt{\frac{\mathbf{Z}_1}{4\mathbf{Z}_2}}$$

Depending upon the type of $\mathbf{Z}_1$ and $\mathbf{Z}_2$, there are two cases:

➤ ***Case (i)*** If $\mathbf{Z}_1$ and $\mathbf{Z}_2$ are same type of reactances then $\frac{\mathbf{Z}_1}{4\mathbf{Z}_2}$ and $\sinh\frac{\gamma}{2}$ are real.

$$\cosh\frac{\alpha}{2}\sin\frac{\beta}{2} = 0$$

$$\sin\frac{\beta}{2} = 0 \qquad \text{if } \beta = 0 \text{ or } n\pi \text{ where } n = 0, 1, 2, \ldots \quad \left[\because \cosh\frac{\alpha}{2} \text{ cannot be zero}\right]$$

$$\cos\frac{\beta}{2} = 1$$

$$\sinh\frac{\alpha}{2} = \sqrt{\frac{\mathbf{Z}_1}{4\mathbf{Z}_2}}$$

$$\alpha = 2\sinh^{-1}\sqrt{\frac{\mathbf{Z}_1}{4\mathbf{Z}_2}}$$

➤ ***Case (ii)*** If $\mathbf{Z}_1$ and $\mathbf{Z}_2$ are opposite types of reactances then $\frac{\mathbf{Z}_1}{4\mathbf{Z}_2}$ is negative, i.e., $\frac{\mathbf{Z}_1}{4\mathbf{Z}_2} < 0$ and $\sqrt{\frac{\mathbf{Z}_1}{4\mathbf{Z}_2}}$ is purely imaginary.

$$\sinh\frac{\alpha}{2}\cos\frac{\beta}{2} = 0$$

$$j\cosh\frac{\alpha}{2}\sin\frac{\beta}{2} = j\sqrt{\frac{\mathbf{Z}_1}{4\mathbf{Z}_2}}$$

$$\cosh\frac{\alpha}{2}\sin\frac{\beta}{2} = \sqrt{\frac{\mathbf{Z}_1}{4\mathbf{Z}_2}}$$

The two conditions of operation of the filter, viz. the pass band and stop band are mathematically obtained from these equations. Both the above equations must be satisfied simultaneously by $\alpha$ and $\beta$. Two conditions may arise

(a) $\sinh\frac{\alpha}{2} = 0$ i.e $\alpha = 0$ when $\beta \neq 0$

Since $\frac{\mathbf{Z}_1}{4\mathbf{Z}_2}$ is negative and $\sin\frac{\beta}{2}$ is real,

$$\sin\frac{\beta}{2} = \left|\sqrt{\frac{\mathbf{Z}_1}{4\mathbf{Z}_2}}\right| \qquad \text{as } \cosh\frac{\alpha}{2} = 1$$

This signifies the region of zero attenuation or pass band, which is limited by the upper limit of sine terms.

$$\sin\frac{\beta}{2} = 1$$

$$-1 < \frac{\mathbf{Z}_1}{4\mathbf{Z}_2} < 0$$

The phase angle in the pass band is given by

$$\frac{\beta}{2} = \sin^{-1}\left|\sqrt{\frac{\mathbf{Z}_1}{4\mathbf{Z}_2}}\right|$$

$$\beta = 2\sin^{-1}\left|\sqrt{\frac{\mathbf{Z}_1}{4\mathbf{Z}_2}}\right|$$

(b)

$$\cos\frac{\beta}{2} = 0$$

$$\sin\frac{\beta}{2} = \pm 1$$

Since $\frac{\mathbf{Z}_1}{4\mathbf{Z}_2}$ is negative and $\cosh\frac{\alpha}{2}$ is real,

$$\cosh\frac{\alpha}{2} = \left|\sqrt{\frac{\mathbf{Z}_1}{\mathbf{Z}_2}}\right|$$

This signifies a stop band since $\alpha \neq 0$.

$$\frac{\alpha}{2} = \cosh^{-1}\left|\sqrt{\frac{\mathbf{Z}_1}{4\mathbf{Z}_2}}\right|$$

$$\alpha = 2\cosh^{-1}\left|\sqrt{\frac{\mathbf{Z}_1}{4\mathbf{Z}_2}}\right|$$

and

$$\frac{\mathbf{Z}_1}{4\mathbf{Z}_2} < -1$$

## 14.5 CONSTANT-$k$ LOW-PASS FILTER

LO 14.4

Design constant-$k$ low-pass filters and constant-$k$ high-pass filters

A $T$ or $\pi$-network is said to be of the constant-$k$ type if $\mathbf{Z}_1$ and $\mathbf{Z}_2$ are opposite types of reactances satisfying the relation

$$\mathbf{Z}_1\mathbf{Z}_2 = k^2$$

where $k$ is a constant, independent of frequency. $k$ is often referred to as *design impedance* or *nominal impedance* of the constant-$k$ filter. The constant-$k$, T or $\pi$-type filter is also known as the prototype filter because other complex networks can be derived from it. Figure 14.4 shows constant-$k$, T and $\pi$-section filters.

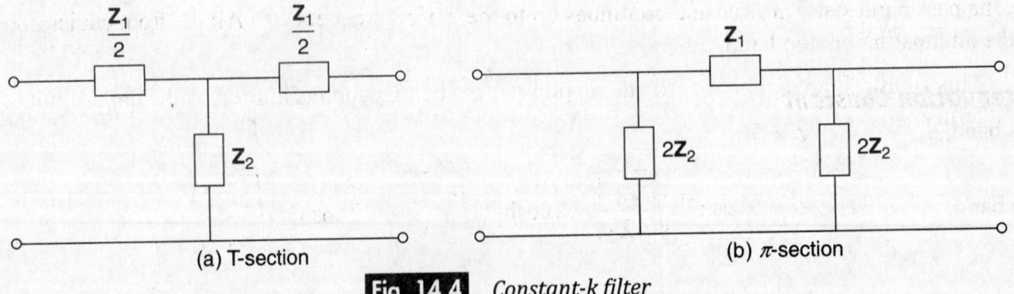


**Fig. 14.4** *Constant-k filter*

In constant-$k$ low-pass filter,

$$\mathbf{Z}_1 = j\omega L$$

$$\mathbf{Z}_2 = -j\frac{1}{\omega c} = \frac{1}{j\omega c}$$

### 1. Nominal Impedance

$$k = \sqrt{\mathbf{Z}_1\mathbf{Z}_2} = \sqrt{(j\omega L)\left(\frac{1}{j\omega c}\right)} = \sqrt{\frac{L}{C}}$$

### 2. Cut-off Frequency

The cut-off frequencies are obtained when $\frac{\mathbf{Z}_1}{4\mathbf{Z}_2} = 0$ and $\frac{\mathbf{Z}_1}{4\mathbf{Z}_2} = -1$

(i) When $\frac{\mathbf{Z}_1}{4\mathbf{Z}_2} = 0$

$$\mathbf{Z}_1 = 0$$

$$j\omega L = 0$$

$$\omega = 0$$

$$f = 0$$

(ii) When $\frac{\mathbf{Z}_1}{4\mathbf{Z}_2} = -1$

$$\mathbf{Z}_1 = -4\mathbf{Z}_2$$

$$j\omega L = \frac{4j}{\omega C}$$

$$\omega^2 LC = 4$$

$$\omega^2 = \frac{4}{LC}$$

$$\omega = \omega_c = \frac{2}{\sqrt{LC}}$$

$$f = f_c = \frac{1}{\pi\sqrt{LC}}$$

Hence, the pass band starts at $f = 0$ and continues up to the cut-off frequency $f_c$. All the frequencies above $f_c$ are in the attenuation or stop band.

### 3. Attenuation Constant

In pass band, $\alpha = 0$

In stop band, $\alpha = 2\cosh^{-1}\sqrt{\left|\frac{\mathbf{Z}_1}{4\mathbf{Z}_2}\right|} = 2\cosh^{-1}\sqrt{\frac{\omega^2 LC}{4}} = 2\cosh^{-1}\sqrt{\frac{\omega^2}{{\omega_c}^2}}$

$$= 2\cosh^{-1}\left(\frac{\omega}{\omega_c}\right) = 2\cosh^{-1}\left(\frac{f}{f_c}\right)$$

The attenuation constant $\alpha$ is zero throughout the pass band but increases gradually from the cut-off frequency.

The variation of $\alpha$ is plotted in Fig. 14.5.

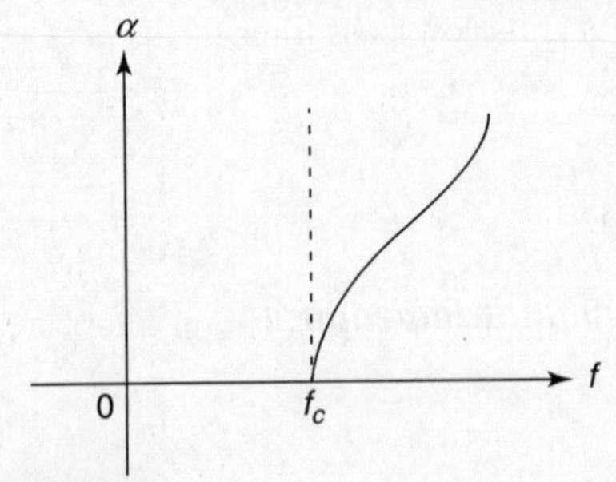


Fig. 14.5 *Variation of α with frequency*

### 4. Phase Constant

In pass band,

$$\beta = 2\sin^{-1}\sqrt{\left|\frac{\mathbf{Z}_1}{4\mathbf{Z}_2}\right|} = 2\sin^{-1}\left(\frac{f}{f_c}\right)$$

In stop band, $\beta = \pi$.

The phase constant $\beta$ is zero at zero frequency and increases gradually through the pass band, reaches $\pi$ at cut-off frequency $f_c$ and remains at $\pi$ for all frequency beyond $f_c$. The variation of $\beta$ is plotted in Fig. 14.6.

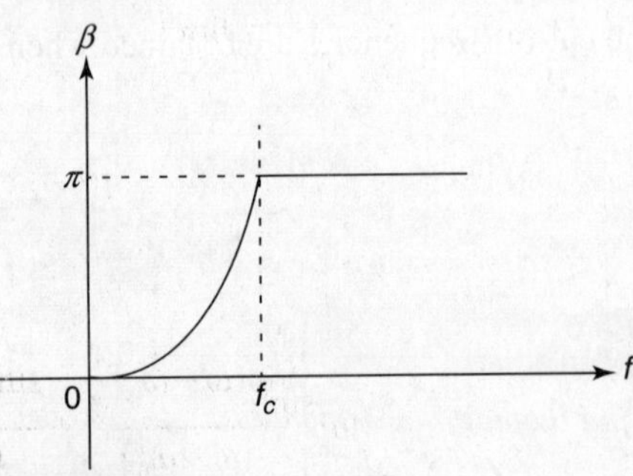


Fig. 14.6 *Variation of β with frequency*

### 5. Characteristic Impedance

$$\mathbf{Z}_{0T} = \sqrt{\frac{\mathbf{Z}_1^2}{4} + \mathbf{Z}_1\mathbf{Z}_2} = \sqrt{\mathbf{Z}_1\mathbf{Z}_2\left(1 + \frac{\mathbf{Z}_1}{4\mathbf{Z}_2}\right)}$$

$$= \sqrt{\frac{L}{C}\left(1 - \frac{\omega^2 LC}{4}\right)} = k\sqrt{1 - \left(\frac{\omega}{\omega_c}\right)^2} = k\sqrt{1 - \left(\frac{f}{f_c}\right)^2}$$

$$\mathbf{Z}_{0\pi} = \frac{\mathbf{Z}_1\mathbf{Z}_2}{\mathbf{Z}_{0T}} = \frac{k}{\sqrt{1 - \left(\frac{f}{f_c}\right)^2}}$$

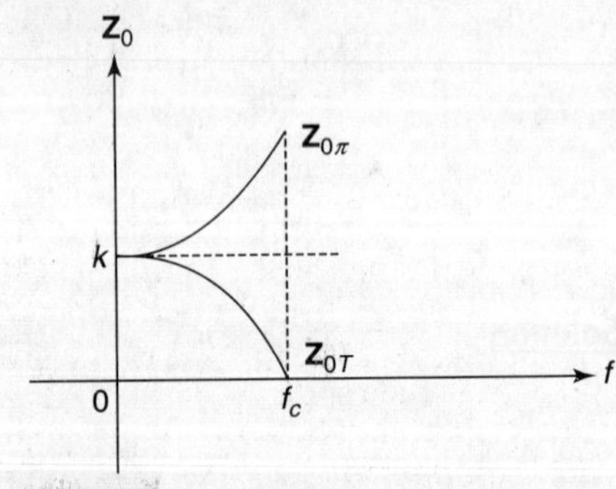


Fig. 14.7 *Variation of characteristic impedance with frequency*

The plot of characteristic impedance versus frequency is shown in Fig. 14.7.

The characteristic impedance $\mathbf{Z}_{0T}$ is real when $f < f_c$. At $f = f_c$, $\mathbf{Z}_{0T} = 0$. For $f > f_c$, $\mathbf{Z}_{0T}$ is imaginary in the stop band, rising to infinite reactance at infinite frequency. $\mathbf{Z}_{0\pi}$ is real when $f < f_c$. At $f = f_c$, $\mathbf{Z}_{0\pi}$ is infinite and for $f > f_c$, $\mathbf{Z}_{0\pi}$ is imaginary.

### 6. Design of Filter

$$k = \sqrt{\frac{L}{C}}$$

$$f_c = \frac{1}{\pi\sqrt{LC}}$$

Solving these two equations,

$$L = \frac{k}{\pi f_c}$$

$$C = \frac{1}{\pi f_c k}$$

The constant-$k$, $T$ and $\pi$-section filters are shown in Fig. 14.8.

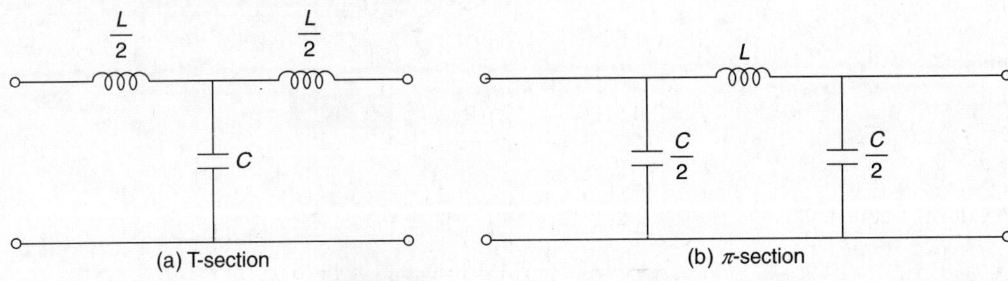


**Fig. 14.8** *Constant-k low-pass filter*

**EXAMPLE 14.1** ●○○

*Find the nominal impedance, cut-off frequency and pass band for the network shown in Fig. 14.9.*

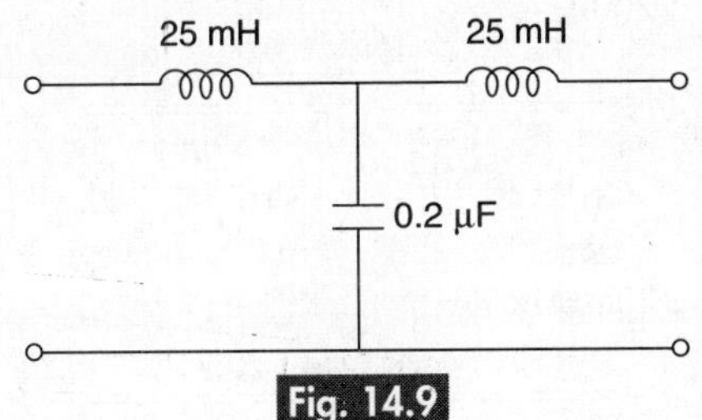


**Fig. 14.9**

**Solution** The network is a low-pass filter.

$$\frac{L}{2} = 25 \text{ mH}, \quad C = 0.2 \text{ μF}$$

$$L = 50 \text{ mH}$$

(a) Nominal impedance

$$k = \sqrt{\frac{L}{C}} = \sqrt{\frac{50 \times 10^{-3}}{0.2 \times 10^{-6}}} = 500 \ \Omega$$

(b) Cut-off frequency

$$f_c = \frac{1}{\pi\sqrt{LC}} = \frac{1}{\pi\sqrt{50 \times 10^{-3} \times 0.2 \times 10^{-6}}} = 3.18 \text{ kHz}$$

**Note** Difficulty Level ●○○ — Easy; ○●○ — Medium; ○○● — Difficult

(c) Pass band
The pass band is from zero to 3.18 kHz.

## EXAMPLE 14.2

*A low-pass filter is composed of a symmetrical π-section. Each series branch is a 0.02 H inductor and shunt branch is a 2 μF capacitor. Find (a) cut-off frequency, (b) nominal impedance, (c) characteristic impedance at 200 Hz and 2000 Hz, (d) attenuation at 200 Hz and 2000 Hz, and (e) phase-shift constant at 200 Hz and 2000 Hz.*

**Solution**

$$L = 0.02\text{ H}, \quad \frac{C}{2} = 2\ \mu\text{F}$$

$$C = 4\ \mu\text{F}$$

(a) Cut-off frequency

$$f_c = \frac{1}{\pi\sqrt{LC}} = \frac{1}{\pi\sqrt{0.02\times 4\times 10^{-6}}} = 1125.4\text{ Hz}$$

(b) Nominal impedance

$$k = \sqrt{\frac{L}{C}} = \sqrt{\frac{0.02}{4\times 10^{-6}}} = 70.71\ \Omega$$

(c) Characteristic impedance at 200 Hz

$$\mathbf{Z}_0 = \frac{k}{\sqrt{1-\left(\frac{f}{f_c}\right)^2}} = \frac{70.71}{\sqrt{1-\left(\frac{200}{1125.4}\right)^2}} = 71.85\ \Omega$$

Characteristic impedance at 2000 Hz

$$\mathbf{Z}_0 = \frac{k}{\sqrt{1-\left(\frac{f}{f_c}\right)^2}} = \frac{70.71}{\sqrt{1-\left(\frac{2000}{1125.4}\right)^2}} = j48.13\ \Omega$$

(d) Attenuation at 200 Hz and 2000 Hz
The 200 Hz frequency lies in the pass band.

$$\alpha = 0$$

At 2000 Hz,

$$\alpha = 2\cosh^{-1}\left(\frac{f}{f_c}\right) = 2\cosh^{-1}\left(\frac{2000}{1125.4}\right) = 2.35$$

(e) Phase-shift constant at 200 Hz and 2000 Hz
At 200 Hz,

$$\beta = 2\sin^{-1}\left(\frac{f}{f_c}\right) = 2\sin^{-1}\left(\frac{200}{1125.4}\right) = 20.47°$$

2000 Hz frequency lies in the attenuation band.

$$\beta = 180°$$

## EXAMPLE 14.3

*A π-section filter network consists of a series arm inductor of 20 mH and two shunt-arm capacitors of 0.16 μF each. Calculate the cut-off frequency, and attenuation and phase shift at 15 kHz. What is the value of the nominal impedance in the pass band?*

**Solution**

$$L = 20 \text{ mH}, \quad \frac{C}{2} = 0.16 \text{ μF}$$

$$C = 0.32 \text{ μF}$$

(a) Cut-off frequency

$$f_c = \frac{1}{\pi\sqrt{LC}} = \frac{1}{\pi\sqrt{20\times10^{-3}\times0.32\times10^{-6}}} = 3.98 \text{ kHz}$$

(b) Attenuation at 15 kHz

$$\alpha = 2\cosh^{-1}\left(\frac{f}{f_c}\right) = 2\cosh^{-1}\left(\frac{15\times10^3}{3.98\times10^3}\right) = 4$$

(c) Phase shift at 15 kHz
15 kHz frequency lies in the attenuation band.

$$\beta = 180°$$

(d) Nominal impedance

$$k = \sqrt{\frac{L}{C}} = \sqrt{\frac{20\times10^{-3}}{0.32\times10^{-6}}} = 250 \ \Omega$$

## EXAMPLE 14.4

*Each of the two series elements of a T-section low-pass filter consists of an inductor of 60 mH having negligible resistance and a shunt element having a capacitance of 0.2 μF. Calculate (a) the cut-off frequency, (b) nominal impedance, and (c) characteristic impedance at frequencies of 1 kHz and 5 kHz.*

**Solution**

$$L = 60 \text{ mH}, \quad C = 0.2 \text{ μF}$$

(a) Cut-off frequency

$$f_c = \frac{1}{\pi\sqrt{LC}} = \frac{1}{\pi\sqrt{60\times10^{-3}\times0.2\times10^{-6}}} = 2.91 \text{ kHz}$$

(b) Nominal impedance

$$k = \sqrt{\frac{L}{C}} = \sqrt{\frac{60\times10^{-3}}{0.2\times10^{-6}}} = 547.72 \ \Omega$$

(c) Characteristic impedance at 1 kHz

$$\mathbf{Z}_0 = k\sqrt{1-\left(\frac{f}{f_c}\right)^2} = 547.72\sqrt{1-\left(\frac{1\times10^3}{2.91\times10^3}\right)^2} = 514.36\,\Omega$$

Characteristic impedance at 5 kHz

$$\mathbf{Z}_0 = k\sqrt{1-\left(\frac{f}{f_c}\right)^2} = 547.72\sqrt{1-\left(\frac{5\times10^3}{2.91\times10^3}\right)^2} = j765.29\ \Omega$$

**EXAMPLE 14.5**

*Design a constant-k low-pass T and π-section filters having cut-off frequency of 4 kHz and nominal characteristic impedance of 500 Ω.*

**Solution**

$$f_c = 4\text{ kHz},\quad k = 500\ \Omega$$

$$L = \frac{k}{\pi f_c} = \frac{500}{\pi\times4\times10^3} = 39.79\text{ mH}$$

$$C = \frac{1}{\pi f_c k} = \frac{1}{\pi\times4\times10^3\times500} = 0.16\ \mu\text{F}$$

The *T*-section consists of an inductor of $\frac{L}{2}$, i.e., 19.9 mH in each series branch and a capacitor of 0.16 μF in the shunt branch, as shown in Fig. 14.10 (a). The π-section consists of an inductor of 39.79 mH in the series branch and a capacitor of $\frac{C}{2}$, i.e., 0.08 μF in each shunt branch, as shown in Fig. 14.10 (b).

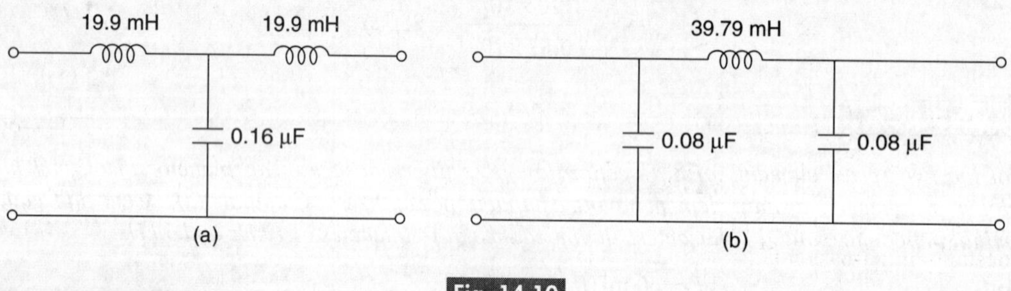


Fig. 14.10

**EXAMPLE 14.6**

*Design a constant-k, T-section low-pass filter having 2.5 kHz cut-off frequency and nominal impedance of 700 Ω. Also, find the frequency at which this filter produces an attenuation of 19.1 dB. Find its characteristic impedances and phase constant at pass band and stop or attenuation band.*

**Solution**

$$f_c = 2.5\text{ kHz},\quad k = 700\ \Omega$$

$$L = \frac{k}{\pi f_c} = \frac{700}{\pi\times2.5\times10^3} = 89.13\text{ mH}$$

$$C = \frac{1}{\pi f_c k} = \frac{1}{\pi\times2.5\times10^3\times700} = 0.18\ \mu\text{F}$$

The $T$-section filter consists of an inductor of $\frac{L}{2}$, i.e., 44.57 mH in each series arm and a capacitor of 0.18 μF in the shunt arm, as shown in Fig. 14.11.

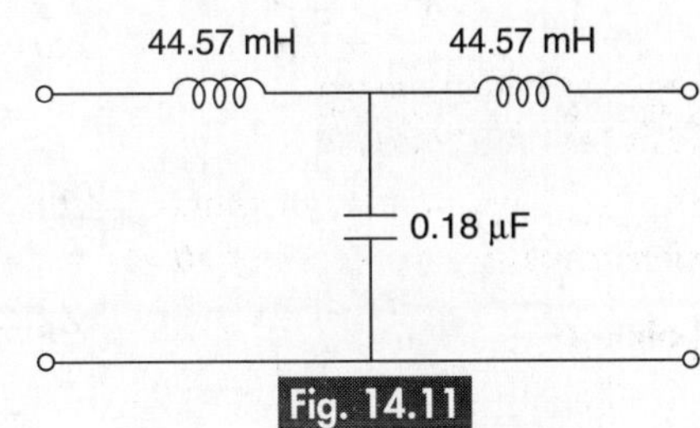


Fig. 14.11

$$\alpha = 19.1 \text{ dB} = 2.197 \text{ nepers}$$

$$\alpha = 2\cosh^{-1}\left(\frac{f}{f_c}\right)$$

$$2.197 = 2\cosh^{-1}\left(\frac{f}{2.5\times 10^3}\right)$$

$$f = 4.17 \text{ kHz}$$

$\beta$ is imaginary in pass band.

In attenuation band, $\beta = 180°$

## 14.6 CONSTANT-*k* HIGH-PASS FILTER

LO 14.4

A constant-$k$ high-pass filter is obtained by changing the positions of series and shunt arm of the constant-$k$ low-pass filter. Figure 14.12 shows a constant-$k$ $T$ and $\pi$-section high-pass filter.

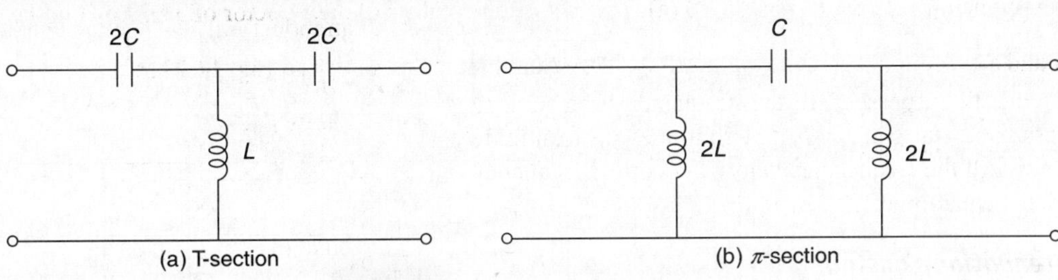


Fig. 14.12 *Constant-k high pass filter*

In a constant-$k$ high-pass filter

$$\mathbf{Z}_1 = -j\frac{1}{\omega C} = \frac{1}{j\omega C}$$

$$\mathbf{Z}_2 = j\omega L$$

### *1. Nominal Impedance*

$$k = \sqrt{\mathbf{Z}_1\mathbf{Z}_2} = \sqrt{\left(\frac{1}{j\omega C}\right)(j\omega L)} = \sqrt{\frac{L}{C}}$$

### *2. Cut-off Frequency*

The cut-off frequencies are obtained when $\frac{\mathbf{Z}_1}{4\mathbf{Z}_2} = 0$ and $\frac{\mathbf{Z}_1}{4\mathbf{Z}_2} = -1$

(i) When $\frac{\mathbf{Z}_1}{4\mathbf{Z}_2} = 0$

$$\mathbf{Z}_1 = 0$$

$$\frac{1}{j\omega C} = 0$$

$$\omega = \infty$$

$$f = \infty$$

(ii) When
$$\frac{\mathbf{Z}_1}{4\mathbf{Z}_2} = -1$$

$$\mathbf{Z}_1 = -4\mathbf{Z}_2$$

$$-j\frac{1}{\omega_c} = 4\,j\omega L$$

$$\omega^2 LC = \frac{1}{4}$$

$$\omega^2 = \frac{1}{4LC}$$

$$\omega = \omega_c = \frac{1}{2\sqrt{LC}}$$

$$f = f_c = \frac{1}{4\pi\sqrt{LC}}$$

Hence, the filter passes all the frequencies beyond $f_c$. The pass band starts at $f = f_c$ and continues up to infinite frequency. All the frequencies below the cut-off frequency lie in the attenuation or stop band.

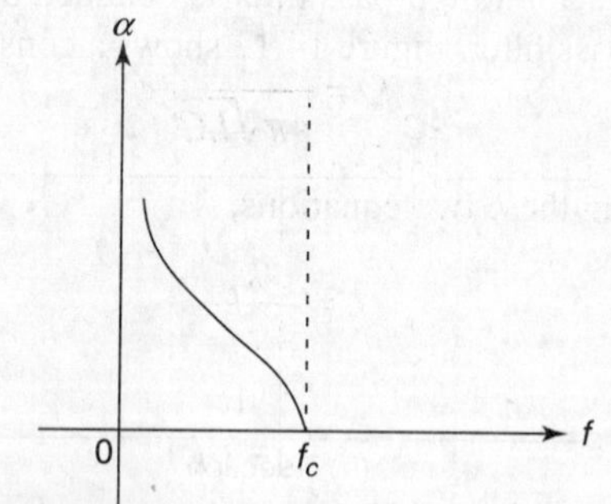


Fig. 14.13 *Variation of α with frequency*

### 3. Attenuation Constant

In pass band, $\alpha = 0$

In stop band, $\alpha = 2\cosh^{-1}\sqrt{\left|\frac{\mathbf{Z}_1}{4\mathbf{Z}_2}\right|} = 2\cosh^{-1}\left(\frac{f_c}{f}\right)$

The attenuation constant $\alpha$ decreases gradually to zero at the cut-off frequency and remains at zero through the pass band. The variation of $\alpha$ is plotted in Fig. 14.13.

### 4. Phase Constant

In pass band, $\beta = 2\sin^{-1}\sqrt{\left|\frac{\mathbf{Z}_1}{4\mathbf{Z}_2}\right|} = 2\sin^{-1}\left(\frac{f_c}{f}\right)$

In stop band, $\beta = \pi$ .

The phase constant $\beta$ remains at constant value $\pi$ in the stop band and decreases to $-\pi$ in at $f_c$ and reaches zero value gradually as $f$ increases in the pass band. The variation of $\beta$ is plotted in Fig. 14.14.

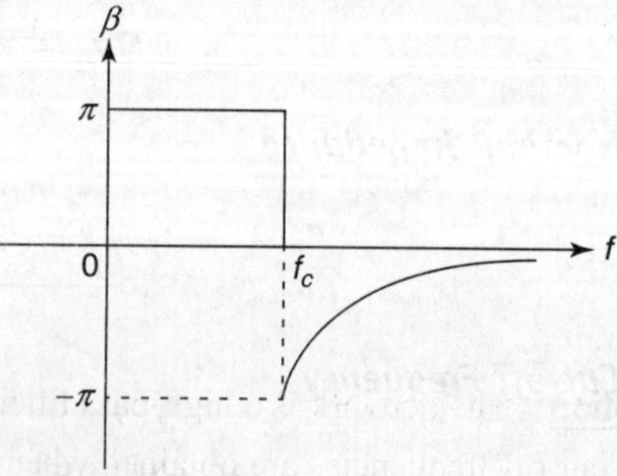


Fig. 14.14 *Variation of β with frequency*

### 5. Characteristic Impedance

$$\mathbf{Z}_{0T} = \sqrt{\frac{\mathbf{Z}_1^2}{4} + \mathbf{Z}_1\mathbf{Z}_2} = \sqrt{\mathbf{Z}_1\mathbf{Z}_2\left(1 + \frac{\mathbf{Z}_1}{4\mathbf{Z}_2}\right)}$$

$$= \sqrt{\frac{L}{C}\left(1 - \frac{1}{4\omega^2 LC}\right)} = k\sqrt{1 - \left(\frac{f_c}{f}\right)^2}$$

$$\mathbf{Z}_{0\pi} = \frac{\mathbf{Z}_1\mathbf{Z}_2}{\mathbf{Z}_{0T}} = \frac{k}{\sqrt{1 - \left(\frac{f_c}{f}\right)^2}}$$

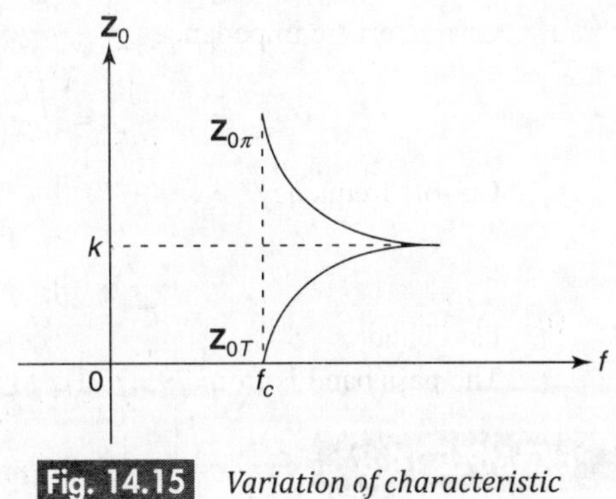


Fig. 14.15 *Variation of characteristic impedance with frequency*

The variation of characteristic impedance is plotted in Fig. 14.15.

### 6. Design of Filter

$$k = \sqrt{\frac{L}{C}}$$

$$f_c = \frac{1}{4\pi\sqrt{LC}}$$

Solving these two equations,

$$L = \frac{k}{4\pi f_c}$$

$$C = \frac{1}{4\pi f_c k}$$

## EXAMPLE 14.7

*Find the characteristic impedance, cut-off frequency and pass band for the network shown in Fig. 14.16.*

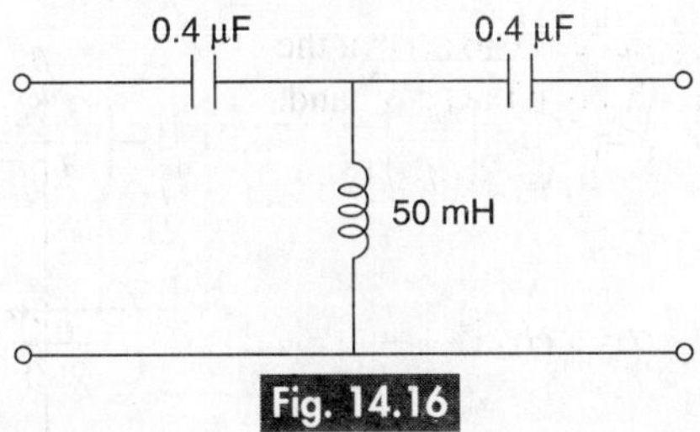


Fig. 14.16

**Solution** The network is a high-pass filter.

$$2C = 0.4\ \mu\text{F}, \quad L = 50\ \text{mH}$$

$$C = 0.2\ \mu\text{F}$$

(a) Characteristic impedance

$$k = \sqrt{\frac{L}{C}} = \sqrt{\frac{50 \times 10^{-3}}{0.2 \times 10^{-6}}} = 500\ \Omega$$

(b) Cut-off frequency

$$f_c = \frac{1}{4\pi\sqrt{LC}} = \frac{1}{4\pi\sqrt{50 \times 10^{-3} \times 0.2 \times 10^{-6}}} = 795.77 \text{ Hz}$$

(c) Pass band
The pass band is from 795.77 Hz to infinite frequency.

**EXAMPLE 14.8**

*A high-pass filter section is constructed from two capacitors of 1 μF each and a 15 mH inductance. Find (a) cut-off frequency, (b) infinite frequency characteristic impedance, (c) characteristic impedance at 200 Hz and 2000 Hz, (d) attenuation at 200 Hz and 2000 Hz, and (e) phase constant at 200 Hz and 2000 Hz.*

**Solution**

$$L = 15 \text{ mH}, \quad 2C = 1\ \mu\text{F}$$

$$C = 0.5\ \mu\text{F}$$

(a) Cut-off frequency

$$f_c = \frac{1}{4\pi\sqrt{LC}} = \frac{1}{4\pi\sqrt{15 \times 10^{-3} \times 0.5 \times 10^{-6}}} = 918.88 \text{ Hz}$$

(b) Infinite-frequency characteristic impedance

At $f = \infty$,

$$\mathbf{Z}_0 = k = \sqrt{\frac{L}{C}} = \sqrt{\frac{1.5 \times 10^{-3}}{0.5 \times 10^{-6}}} = 173.21\ \Omega$$

(c) Characteristic impedance at 200 Hz

$$\mathbf{Z}_{0T} = k\sqrt{1 - \left(\frac{f_c}{f}\right)^2} = 173.21\sqrt{1 - \left(\frac{918.88}{2000}\right)^2} = j776.72\ \Omega$$

Characteristic impedance at 2000 Hz

$$\mathbf{Z}_{0T} = k\sqrt{1 - \left(\frac{f_c}{f}\right)^2} = 173.21\sqrt{1 - \left(\frac{918.88}{2000}\right)^2} = 153.85\ \Omega$$

(d) Attenuation at 200 Hz

$$\alpha = 2\cosh^{-1}\left(\frac{f_c}{f}\right) = 2\cosh^{-1}\left(\frac{918.88}{200}\right) = 4.41$$

The frequency of 2000 Hz lies in the pass band.

$$\alpha = 0$$

(e) Phase constant
The frequency 200 Hz lies in the attenuation band.

$$\beta = \pi \text{ radians}$$

At 2000 Hz,

$$\beta = 2\sin^{-1}\left(\frac{f_c}{f}\right) = 2\sin^{-1}\left(\frac{918.88}{2000}\right) = 54.7°$$

## EXAMPLE 14.9

*Design a constant-k high-pass T and π-sections filters having a cut-off frequency of 2000 Hz and infinite frequency characteristic impedance of 300 Ω.*

**Solution**

$$f_c = 2000 \text{ Hz}, \quad k = 300\ \Omega$$

$$L = \frac{k}{4\pi f_c} = \frac{300}{4\pi \times 2000} = 11.94 \text{ mH}$$

$$C = \frac{1}{4\pi f_c k} = \frac{1}{4\pi \times 2000 \times 300} = 0.13\ \mu\text{F}$$

The *T*-section filter consists of a capacitor of 2*C*, i.e., 0.26 μF in each series arm and an inductor of 11.94 mH in shunt arm, as shown in Fig. 14.17 (a).

The *π*-section filter consists of a capacitor of 0.13 μF in the series arm and an inductor of 2*L*, i.e., 23.88 mH in each shunt arm, as shown in Fig. 14.17 (b).

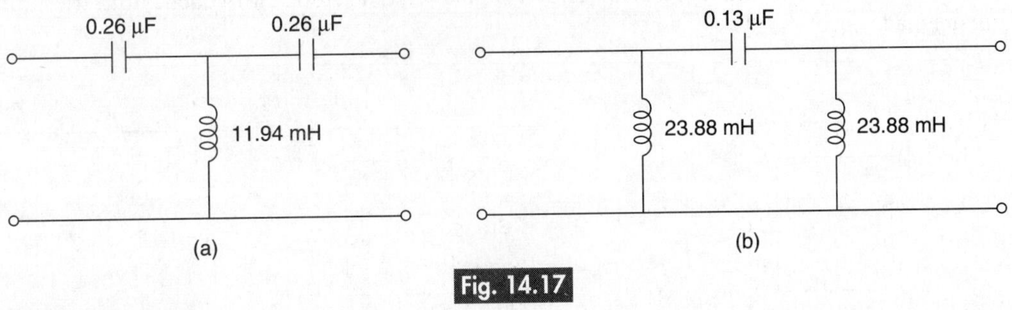


Fig. 14.17

## EXAMPLE 14.10

*Design a T-section constant-k high-pass filter having a cut-off frequency of 10 kHz and a design impedance of 600 Ω. Find its characteristic impedance and phase constant at 25 kHz.*

**Solution**

$$f_c = 10 \text{ kHz}, \quad k = 600\ \Omega$$

$$L = \frac{k}{4\pi f_c} = \frac{600}{4\pi \times 10 \times 10^3} = 4.77 \text{ mH}$$

$$C = \frac{1}{4\pi f_c k} = \frac{1}{4\pi \times 10 \times 10^3 \times 600} = 0.013\ \mu\text{F}$$

The *T*-section filter consists of a capacitor of 2*C*, i.e., 0.026 μF in each series arm and an inductor of 4.77 mH in shunt arm, as shown in Fig. 14.18.

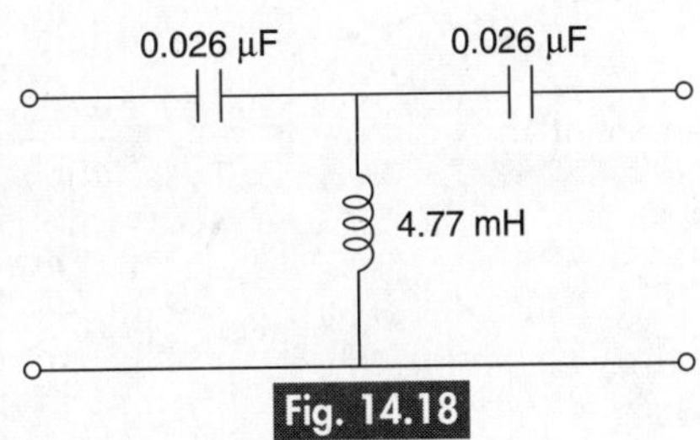


Fig. 14.18

(a) Characteristic impedance at 25 kHz

$$\mathbf{Z}_0 = k\sqrt{1-\left(\frac{f_c}{f}\right)^2} = 600\sqrt{1-\left(\frac{10\times10^3}{25\times10^3}\right)^2} = 549.91\ \Omega$$

(b) Phase constant at 25 kHz

$$\beta = 2\sin^{-1}\left(\frac{f_c}{f}\right) = 2\sin^{-1}\left(\frac{10\times10^3}{25\times10^3}\right) = 47.16°$$

The frequency of 25 kHz lies in the attenuation band.
In the attenuation band, $\beta = 180° = \pi$ radians

## 14.7 BAND-PASS FILTER

LO 14.5

Design band-pass filters and band-stop filters

A band-pass filter attenuates all the frequencies below a lower cut-off frequency and above an upper cut-off frequency. It passes a band of frequencies without attenuation. A band pass filter is obtained by using a low pass filter followed by a high-pass filter.

Figure 14.19 shows a band pass filter. The series arm is a series resonant circuit comprising $L_1$ and $C_1$ while its shunt arm is formed by a parallel resonant circuit $L_2$ and $C_2$. The resonant frequency of series arm and shunt arm are made equal.

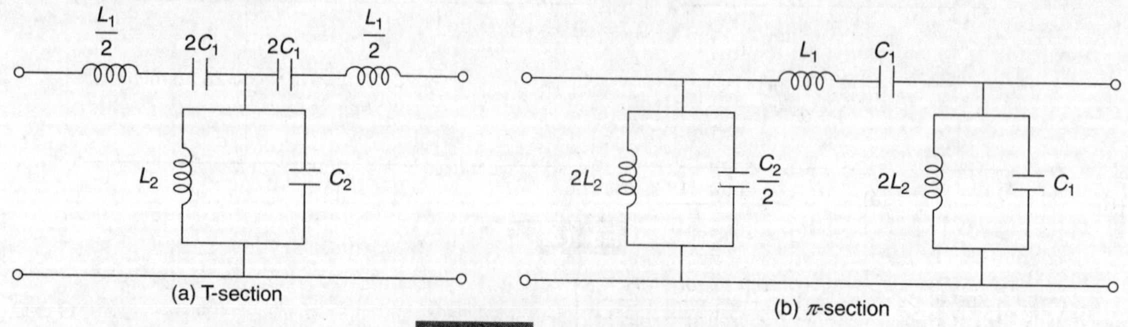


**Fig. 14.19** *Band-pass filter*

For series arm,

$$\omega_0 \frac{L_1}{2} = \frac{1}{2\omega_0 C_1}$$

$$\omega_0^2 = \frac{1}{L_1 C_1}$$

For shunt arm,

$$\frac{1}{\omega_0 C_2} = \omega_0 L_2$$

$$\omega_0^2 = \frac{1}{L_2 C_2}$$

$$L_1 C_1 = L_2 C_2$$

For series arm,

$$\mathbf{Z}_1 = j\omega L_1 - \frac{j}{\omega c_1} = j\left(\frac{\omega^2 L_1 C_1 - 1}{\omega c_1}\right)$$

For shunt arm,

$$\mathbf{Z}_2 = \frac{j\omega L_2 \dfrac{1}{j\omega c_2}}{j\omega L_2 + \dfrac{1}{j\omega c_2}} = \frac{j\omega L_2}{1-\omega^2 L_2 C_2}$$

$$\mathbf{Z}_1\mathbf{Z}_2 = j\left(\frac{\omega^2 L_1 C_1 - 1}{\omega c_1}\right)\left(\frac{j\omega L_2}{1-\omega^2 L_2 C_2}\right) = -\frac{L_2}{C_1}\left(\frac{\omega^2 L_1 C_1 - 1}{1-\omega^2 L_2 C_2}\right) = \frac{L_2}{C_1} = \frac{L_1}{C_2} = k^2$$

where $k$ is constant.

For constant-$k$ filter, at cut-off frequency,

$$\mathbf{Z}_1 = -4\mathbf{Z}_2$$

$$\mathbf{Z}_1^2 = -4\mathbf{Z}_1\mathbf{Z}_2 = -4k^2$$

$$\mathbf{Z}_1 = \pm j2k$$

i.e., the value of $\mathbf{Z}_1$ at lower cut-off frequency is equal to the negative value of $\mathbf{Z}_1$ at the upper cut-off frequency.

$$\frac{1}{j\omega_1 C_1} + j\omega_1 L_1 = -\left(\frac{1}{j\omega_2 C_1} + j\omega_2 L_1\right)$$

$$1-\omega_1^2 L_1 C_1 = \frac{\omega_1}{\omega_2}\left(\omega_2^2 L_1 C_1 - 1\right)$$

But

$$\omega_0^2 = \frac{1}{L_1 C_1}$$

$$1-\frac{\omega_1^2}{\omega_0^2} = \frac{\omega_1}{\omega_2}\left(\frac{\omega_2^2}{\omega_0^2} - 1\right)$$

$$(\omega_0^2 - \omega_1^2)\omega_2 = \omega_1(\omega_2^2 - \omega_0^2)$$

$$\omega_0^2\omega_2 - \omega_1^2\omega_2 = \omega_1\omega_2^2 - \omega_1\omega_0^2$$

$$\omega_0^2(\omega_1 + \omega_2) = \omega_1\omega_2(\omega_2 + \omega_1)$$

$$\omega_0^2 = \omega_1\omega_2$$

$$\omega_0 = \sqrt{\omega_1\omega_2}$$

$$f_0 = \sqrt{f_1 f_2}$$

Thus, resonant frequency is the geometric mean of the cut-off frequencies. The variation of attenuation, phase constant and characteristic impedance with frequency are shown in Fig. 14.20.

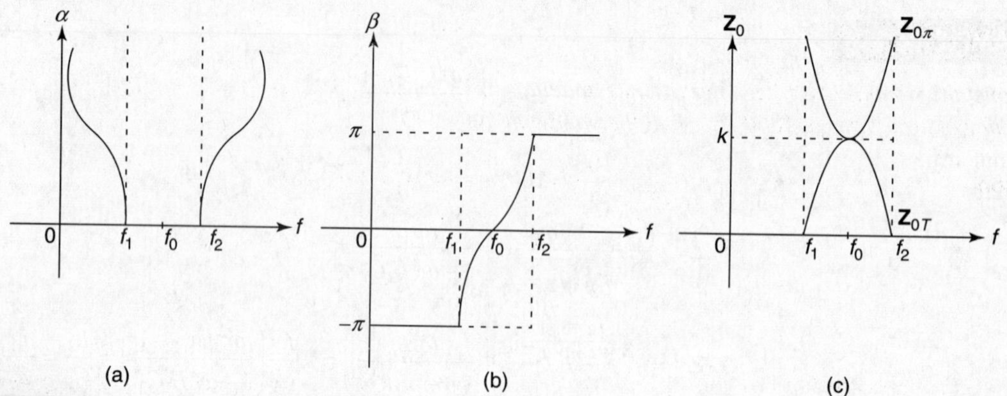


**Fig. 14.20** *Variation of (a) attenuation, (b) phase constant, and (c) characteristic impedance with frequency for constant–k band-pass filter*

➤ ***Design of Filter*** If the filter is terminated in a load resistance $R = k$ then at lower cut-off frequency,

$$\mathbf{Z}_1 = -2\,jk$$

$$\frac{1}{j\omega_1 C_1} + j\omega_1 L_1 = -2\,jk$$

$$\frac{1}{\omega_1 C_1} - \omega_1 L_1 = 2k$$

$$1 - \omega_1^2 L_1 C_1 = 2k\omega_1 C_1$$

$$1 - \frac{\omega_1^2}{\omega_0^2} = 2k\omega_1 C_1 \qquad \left(\because\ \omega_0^2 = \frac{1}{L_1 C_1}\right)$$

$$1 - \left(\frac{f_1}{f_0}\right)^2 = 4\pi k f_1 C_1$$

$$1 - \frac{f_1^2}{f_1 f_2} = 4\pi k f_1 C_1 \qquad \left(\because\ f_0 = \sqrt{f_1 f_2}\right)$$

$$f_2 - f_1 = 4\pi k f_1 f_2 C_1$$

$$C_1 = \frac{f_2 - f_1}{4\pi\, k f_1 f_2}$$

$$L_1 = \frac{1}{\omega_0^2 C_1} = \frac{4\pi\, k f_1 f_2}{\omega_0^2 (f_2 - f_1)} = \frac{4\pi\, k f_1 f_2}{4\pi^2\ f_0^2\,(f_2 - f_1)} = \frac{k}{\pi(f_2 - f_1)}$$

For shunt arm,

$$\mathbf{Z}_1\mathbf{Z}_2 = \frac{L_2}{C_1} = \frac{L_1}{C_2} = k^2$$

$$L_2 = C_1 k^2 = \frac{(f_2 - f_1)k}{4\pi\ f_1 f_2}$$

$$C_2 = \frac{L_1}{k^2} = \frac{1}{\pi(f_2 - f_1)k}$$

## EXAMPLE 14.11

*In a constant-k band-pass filter, the ratio of capacitances in the shunt and series arms is 100:1. The resonant frequency of both arms is 1000 Hz. Find the bandwidth.*

**Solution**

$$\frac{C_2}{C_1} = \frac{100}{1} = 100, \quad f_0 = 1000 \text{ Hz}$$

$$C_2 = \frac{1}{\pi k(f_2 - f_1)}$$

$$C_1 = \frac{f_2 - f_1}{4\pi k f_1 f_2}$$

$$\frac{C_2}{C_1} = \frac{1}{\pi k(f_2 - f_1)} \frac{4\pi k f_1 f_2}{f_2 - f_1}$$

$$100 = \frac{4 f_1 f_2}{(f_2 - f_1)^2}$$

$$100 = \frac{4 f_0^2}{(f_2 - f_1)^2}$$

$$f_2 - f_1 = \frac{2 f_0}{\sqrt{100}} = \frac{2 \times 1000}{\sqrt{100}} = 200$$

$$BW = f_2 - f_1 = 200 \text{ Hz}$$

## EXAMPLE 14.12

*Design a band-pass constant-k filter with cut-off frequency of 4 kHz and 10 kHz and nominal characteristic impedance of 500 Ω.*

**Solution**

$$f_1 = 4 \text{ kHz}, \quad f_2 = 10 \text{ kHz}, \quad k = 500 \ \Omega$$

$$L_1 = \frac{k}{\pi(f_2 - f_1)} = \frac{500}{\pi(10 \times 10^3 - 4 \times 10^3)} = 26.53 \text{ mH}$$

$$C_1 = \frac{f_2 - f_1}{4\pi k f_1 f_2} = \frac{10 \times 10^3 - 4 \times 10^3}{4\pi \times 500 \times 4 \times 10^3 \times 10 \times 10^3} = 0.024 \ \mu\text{F}$$

$$L_2 = \frac{(f_2 - f_1)k}{4\pi f_1 f_2} = \frac{(10 \times 10^3 - 4 \times 10^3)\, 500}{4\pi \times 4 \times 10^3 \times 10 \times 10^3} = 5.97 \text{ mH}$$

$$C_2 = \frac{1}{\pi(f_2 - f_1)k} = \frac{1}{\pi \times (10 \times 10^3 - 4 \times 10^3) \times 500} = 0.11 \ \mu\text{F}$$

The *T*-section filter consists of series combination of an inductor of $\frac{L_1}{2}$, i.e., 13.27 mH and a capacitor of 2 $C_1$, i.e., 0.048 μF in each series arm and a parallel combination of an inductor of 5.97 mH and a capacitor of 0.11 μF in shunt arm, as shown in Fig. 14.21.

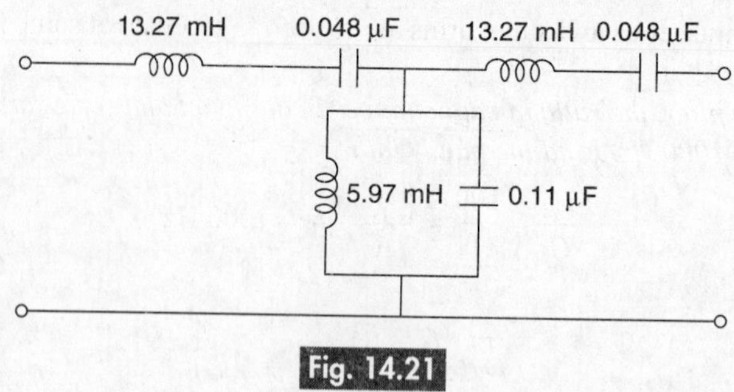


Fig. 14.21

The $\pi$-section filter consists of a series combination of an inductor 26.53 mH and a capacitor of 0.024 μF in the series arm and a parallel combination of an inductor of $2L_2$, i.e., 11.94 mH and a capacitor of $\frac{C_2}{2}$, i.e., 0.055 μF in each shunt arm, as shown in Fig. 14.22.

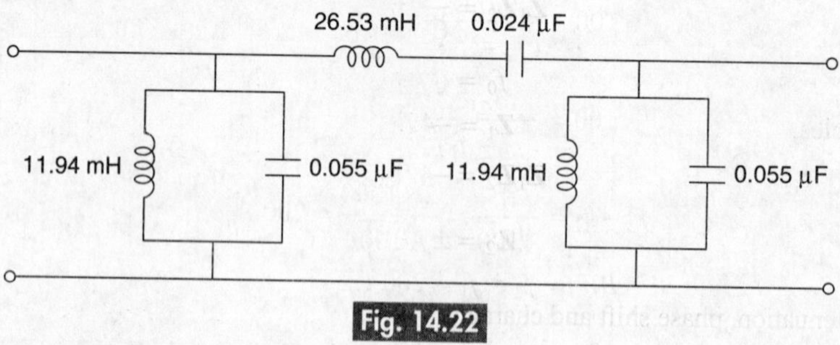


Fig. 14.22

## 14.8 BAND-STOP FILTER

LO 14.5

A band-stop filter attenuates a specified band of frequencies and allows all frequencies below and above this band. A band-stop filter is realised by connecting a low-pass filter in parallel with a high-pass filter. Figure 14.23 shows a band-stop filter.

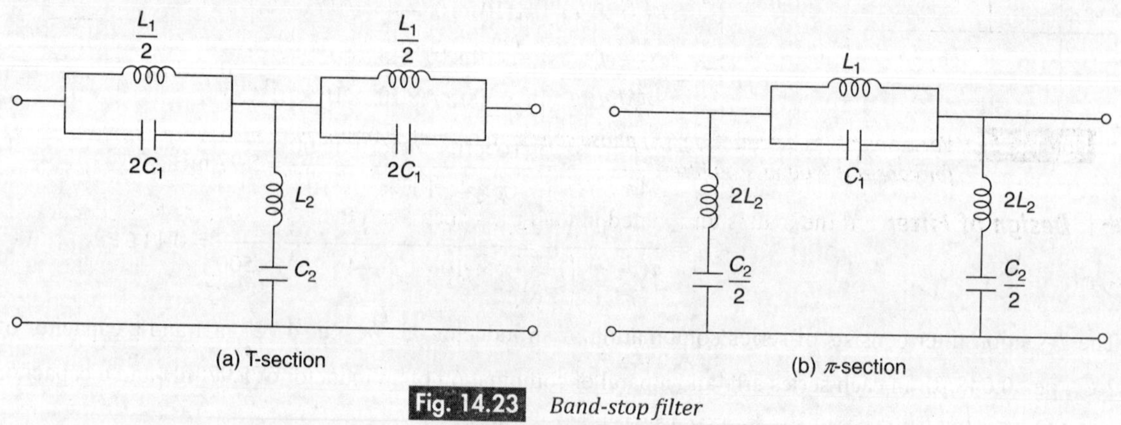


Fig. 14.23 *Band-stop filter*

As in the band-pass filter, the series and shunt arms are chosen to resonate at same frequency $\omega_0$.

For series arm,

$$\frac{\omega_0 L_1}{2} = \frac{1}{2\omega_0 C_1}$$

$$\omega_0^2 = \frac{1}{L_1 C_1}$$

For shunt arm,

$$\omega_0 L_2 = \frac{1}{\omega_0 C_2}$$

$$\omega_0^2 = \frac{1}{L_2 C_2}$$

$$L_1 C_1 = L_2 C_2$$

Similarly,

$$\mathbf{Z}_1 \mathbf{Z}_2 = \frac{L_1}{C_2} = \frac{L_2}{C_1} = k^2$$

and

$$f_0 = \sqrt{f_1 f_2}$$

At cut-off frequencies,

$$\mathbf{Z}_1 = -4\mathbf{Z}_2$$

$$\mathbf{Z}_1 \mathbf{Z}_2 = -4\mathbf{Z}_2^2 = k^2$$

$$\mathbf{Z}_2 = \pm j\frac{k}{2}$$

The variation of attenuation, phase shift and characteristic impedance with frequency are shown in Fig. 14.24.

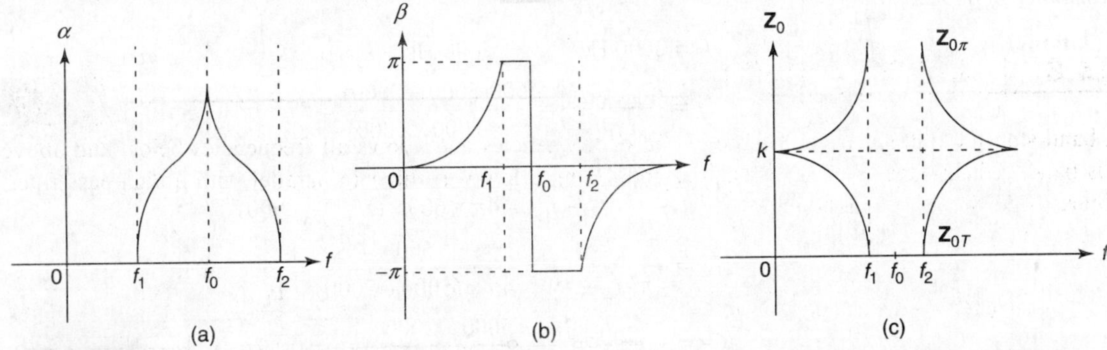


**Fig. 14.24** *Variation of (a) attenuation, (b) phase constant, and (c) characteristic impedance with frequency for constant-k band-stop filter.*

➤ ***Design of Filter*** If the load is terminated in load resistance $R = k$ then at lower cut-off frequency,

$$\mathbf{Z}_2 = j\left(\frac{1}{\omega_1 C_2} - \omega_1 L_2\right) = j\frac{k}{2}$$

$$\frac{1}{\omega_1 C_2} - \omega_1 L_2 = \frac{k}{2}$$

$$1 - \omega_1^2 L_2 C_2 = \omega_1 C_2 \frac{k}{2}$$

$$1-\frac{\omega_1^2}{\omega_0^2}=\frac{k}{2}\omega_1 C_2 \qquad \left(\because \omega_0^2=\frac{1}{L_2C_2}\right)$$

$$1-\left(\frac{f_1}{f_0}\right)^2=k\pi f_1 C_2$$

$$C_2=\frac{1}{k\pi f_1}\left[1-\left(\frac{f_1}{f_0}\right)^2\right]=\frac{1}{k\pi}\left(\frac{1}{f_1}-\frac{1}{f_2}\right)=\frac{1}{k\pi}\left(\frac{f_2-f_1}{f_1f_2}\right)=\frac{f_2-f_1}{\pi k\, f_1f_2}$$

$$L_2=\frac{1}{\omega_0^2C_2}=\frac{\pi kf_1f_2}{\omega_0^2(f_2-f_1)}=\frac{\pi kf_1f_2}{4\pi^2f_0^2(f_2-f_1)}=\frac{k}{4\pi(f_2-f_1)}$$

$$k^2=\frac{L_1}{C_2}=\frac{L_2}{C_1}$$

$$L_1=k^2C_2=\frac{k(f_2-f_1)}{\pi f_1f_2}$$

$$C_1=\frac{L_2}{k^2}=\frac{1}{4\pi\, k(f_2-f_1)}$$

**EXAMPLE 14.13**

*Design a constant-k band-stop filter having cut-off frequencies at 2000 Hz and 5000 Hz and characteristic resistance of 600 Ω.*

**Solution**

$$f_1=2000\text{ Hz},\quad f_2=5000\text{ Hz},\quad k=600\ \Omega$$

$$L_1=\frac{k(f_2-f_1)}{\pi f_1f_2}=\frac{600(5000-2000)}{\pi\times2000\times5000)}=57.3\text{ mH}$$

$$C_1=\frac{1}{4\pi k(f_2-f_1)}=\frac{1}{4\pi\times600\times(5000-2000)}=0.044\ \mu\text{F}$$

$$L_2=\frac{k}{4\pi(f_2-f_1)}=\frac{600}{4\pi\times(5000-2000)}=15.92\text{ mH}$$

$$C_2=\frac{f_2-f_1}{\pi kf_1f_2}=\frac{5000-2000}{\pi\times600\times2000\times5000}=0.16\ \mu\text{F}$$

The *T*-section filter consists of a parallel combination of $\frac{L_1}{2}$, i.e., 28.65 mH and a capacitor of 2 $C_1$, i.e., 0.088 μF in each series arm and a series combination of an inductor of 15.92 mH and a capacitor of 0.16 μF in shunt arm, as shown in Fig. 14.25.

The $\pi$-section filter consists of a parallel combination of an inductor of 57.3 mH and a capacitor of 0.044 μF in the series arm and a series combination of an inductor of $2L_2$, i.e., 31.84 mH and a capacitor of $\frac{C_2}{2}$, i.e., 0.08 μF in each shunt arm, as shown in Fig. 14.26.

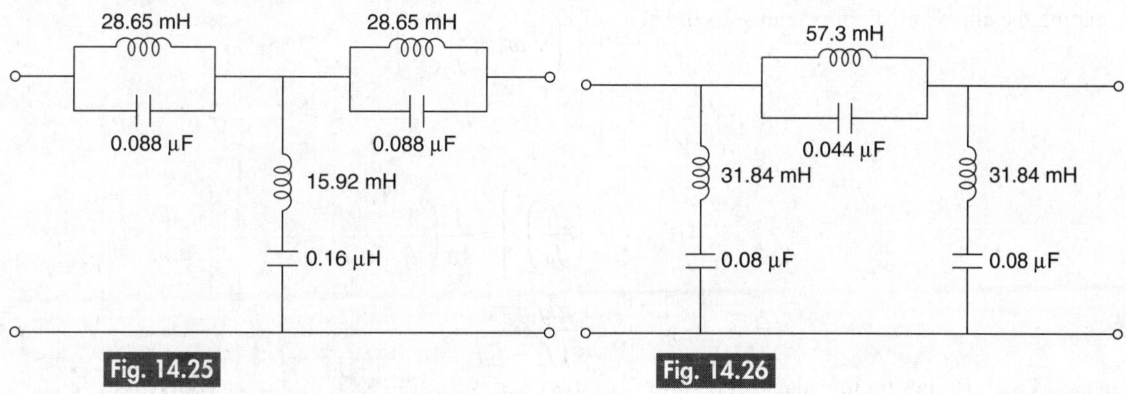


Fig. 14.25

Fig. 14.26

## 14.9 m-DERIVED FILTERS

LO 14.6

Explain *m*-derived filters, *m*-derived low-pass filters, and *m*-derived high-pass filters and their characteristics

There are two disadvantages of constant-*k* filters.

(i) The attenuation is not sharp in the stop band.
(ii) The characteristic impedance varies widely in the pass band.

If the constant-*k* filter is regarded as a prototype, it is possible to design a filter to have rapid attenuation in the stop band and the same characteristic impedance as the prototype throughout the pass band and the stop band. Such a filter is called an *m-derived filter*.

Constant-*k* and *m*-derived *T*-sections are shown in Fig. 14.27. The constant-*k* *T*-network is identical to that of the *m*-derived *T*-network except that the series arm is multiplier by *m*.

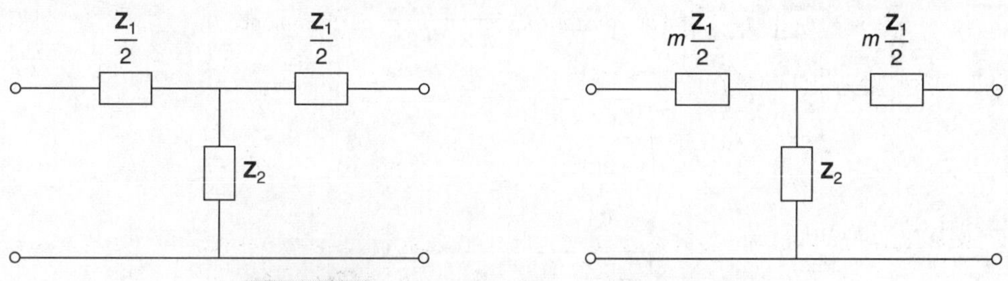


Fig. 14.27 *Constant-k and m-derived T-sections*

For the constant-*k* *T*-section,

$$\mathbf{Z}_{OT} = \sqrt{\frac{\mathbf{Z}_1^2}{4} + \mathbf{Z}_1\,\mathbf{Z}_2}$$

For the *m*-derived *T*-section,

$$\mathbf{Z}_{OT} = \sqrt{\frac{m^2\,\mathbf{Z}_1^2}{4} + m\,\mathbf{Z}_1\,\mathbf{Z}_2'}$$

Equating the characteristic impedance of the networks,

$$\sqrt{\frac{\mathbf{Z}_1^2}{4}+\mathbf{Z}_1\,\mathbf{Z}_2} = \sqrt{\frac{m^2\mathbf{Z}_1^2}{4}+m\mathbf{Z}_1\,\mathbf{Z}_2'}$$

$$\frac{\mathbf{Z}_1^2}{4}+\mathbf{Z}_1\,\mathbf{Z}_2 = \frac{m^2\mathbf{Z}_1^2}{4}+m\mathbf{Z}_1\,\mathbf{Z}_2'$$

$$m\mathbf{Z}_1\,\mathbf{Z}_2' = \frac{\mathbf{Z}_1^2}{4}(1-m^2)+\mathbf{Z}_1\,\mathbf{Z}_2$$

$$\mathbf{Z}_2' = \left(\frac{1-m^2}{4m}\right)\mathbf{Z}_1+\frac{\mathbf{Z}_2}{m}$$

Fig. 14.28 m-derived T-section filter

Hence, $\mathbf{Z}_2'$ must be an impedance composed of two series impedances $\left(\frac{1-m^2}{4m}\right)\mathbf{Z}_1$ and $\frac{\mathbf{Z}_2}{m}$. The term $\frac{1-m^2}{4m}$ should be positive to realise the impedance $\mathbf{Z}_2'$ physically, i.e., $0<m<1$. Thus, an *m*-derived filter can be obtained from constant-*k* filter by modifying its series and shunt impedances, as shown in Fig. 14.28.

Similarly, the constant-*k* $\pi$-section filter can be modified to *m*-derived $\pi$-section filter. A constant-*k* and *m*-derived $\pi$-sections are shown in Fig. 14.29.

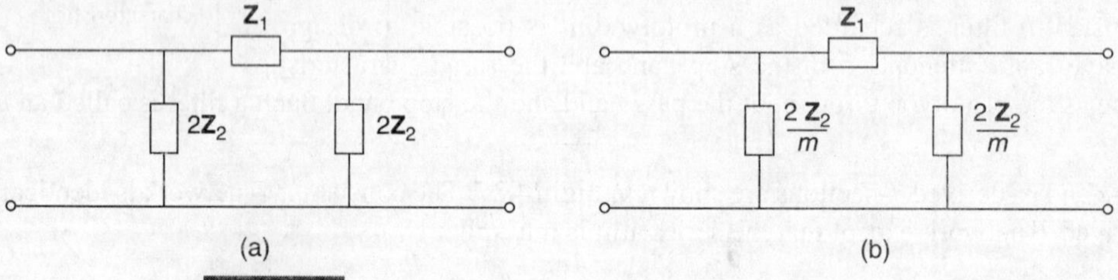


Fig. 14.29 (a) Constant-k section (b) m-derived π-section

For the constant-*k* $\pi$-section,

$$\mathbf{Z}_{O\pi} = \sqrt{\frac{\mathbf{Z}_1\,\mathbf{Z}_2}{1+\dfrac{\mathbf{Z}_1}{4\mathbf{Z}_2}}}$$

For the *m*-derived $\pi$-section,

$$\mathbf{Z}_{O\pi} = \sqrt{\frac{\mathbf{Z}_1'\,\dfrac{\mathbf{Z}_2}{m}}{1+\dfrac{\mathbf{Z}_1'}{4\dfrac{\mathbf{Z}_2}{m}}}}$$

Equating the characteristic impedance of the networks,

$$\sqrt{\frac{\mathbf{Z}_1\,\mathbf{Z}_2}{1+\dfrac{\mathbf{Z}_1}{4\mathbf{Z}_2}}} = \sqrt{\frac{\mathbf{Z}_1'\,\dfrac{\mathbf{Z}_2}{m}}{1+\dfrac{\mathbf{Z}_1'}{4\dfrac{\mathbf{Z}_2}{m}}}}$$

$$\frac{\mathbf{Z}_1 \mathbf{Z}_2}{1+\dfrac{\mathbf{Z}_1}{4\mathbf{Z}_2}} = \frac{\mathbf{Z}_1' \dfrac{\mathbf{Z}_2}{m}}{1+\dfrac{\mathbf{Z}_1'}{4\dfrac{\mathbf{Z}_2}{m}}}$$

$$\mathbf{Z}_1 \mathbf{Z}_2 \left(1+\frac{\mathbf{Z}_1'}{4\dfrac{\mathbf{Z}_2}{m}}\right) = \mathbf{Z}_1' \frac{\mathbf{Z}_2}{m}\left(1+\frac{\mathbf{Z}_1}{4\mathbf{Z}_2}\right)$$

$$\mathbf{Z}_1 \mathbf{Z}_2 + \frac{m\mathbf{Z}_1 \mathbf{Z}_1'}{4} = \frac{\mathbf{Z}_1' \mathbf{Z}_2}{m} + \frac{\mathbf{Z}_1 \mathbf{Z}_1'}{4m}$$

$$4\mathbf{Z}_1 \mathbf{Z}_2 + m\mathbf{Z}_1 \mathbf{Z}_1' = \frac{4\mathbf{Z}_1' \mathbf{Z}_2 + \mathbf{Z}_1 \mathbf{Z}_1'}{m}$$

$$\mathbf{Z}_1'\left(\frac{\mathbf{Z}_1}{m} + \frac{4\mathbf{Z}_2}{m} - m\mathbf{Z}_1\right) = 4\mathbf{Z}_1 \mathbf{Z}_2$$

$$\mathbf{Z}_1' = \frac{\mathbf{Z}_1 \mathbf{Z}_2}{\dfrac{\mathbf{Z}_1}{4m} + \dfrac{\mathbf{Z}_2}{4m} - \dfrac{m\mathbf{Z}_1}{4}}$$

$$= \frac{\mathbf{Z}_1 \mathbf{Z}_2}{\dfrac{\mathbf{Z}_1}{4m}(1-m^2) + \dfrac{\mathbf{Z}_2}{m}} = \frac{\mathbf{Z}_1 \mathbf{Z}_2 \dfrac{4m^2}{(1-m^2)}}{m\mathbf{Z}_1 + \dfrac{4m^2}{m(1-m)}\mathbf{Z}_2}$$

$$= \frac{m\mathbf{Z}_1 \dfrac{4m}{1-m^2}\mathbf{Z}_2}{m\mathbf{Z}_1 + \dfrac{4m}{1-m^2}\mathbf{Z}_2}$$

Hence, $\mathbf{Z}_1'$ must be an impedance composed of two parallel impedances $m\mathbf{Z}_1$ and $\left(\dfrac{4m}{1-m^2}\right)\mathbf{Z}_2$. Thus, an $m$-derived filter can be obtained from a constant-$k$ filter by modifying its series and shunt impedances, as shown in Fig. 14.30.

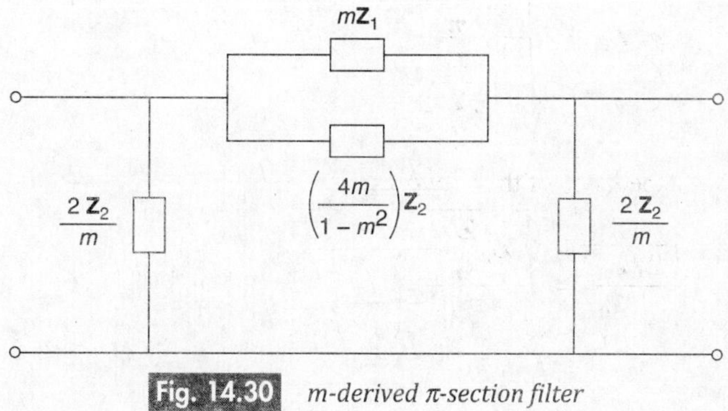


**Fig. 14.30** *m-derived π-section filter*

## 14.10 m-DERIVED LOW-PASS FILTER

LO 14.6

Figure 14.31 shows an $m$-derived low-pass $T$ and $\pi$-filter. At a particular frequency, the shunt arm of the $T$-section or series arm of the $\pi$-section will be in resonance, giving a short circuit to the input for the $T$-section and open circuit for the $\pi$-section, causing infinite attenuation.

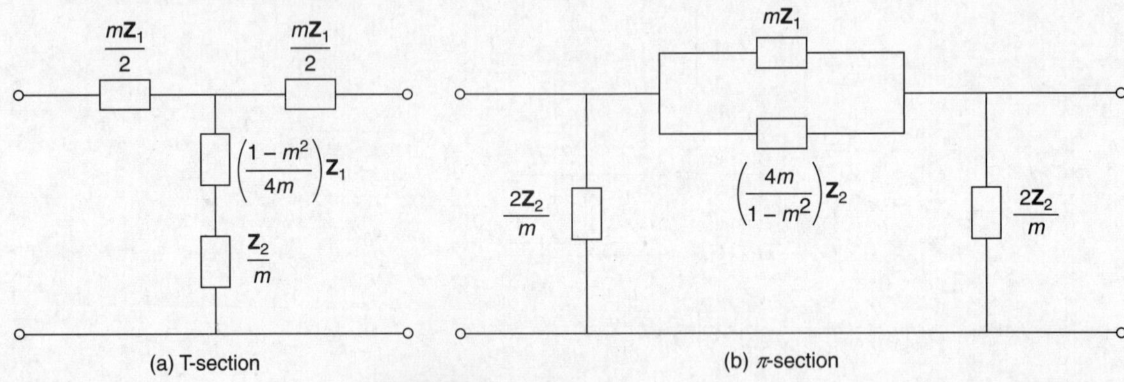


Fig. 14.31 m-derived low-pass filter

Let

$$\mathbf{Z}_1 = j\omega L$$

$$\mathbf{Z}_2 = \frac{1}{j\omega C} = \frac{-j}{\omega C}$$

At resonant frequency,

$$\left(\frac{1-m^2}{4m}\right)\omega_0 L = \frac{1}{m\,\omega_0 C}$$

$$\omega_0{}^2 = \frac{4}{(1-m^2)\,LC}$$

$$\omega_0 = \frac{2}{\sqrt{LC(1-m^2)}}$$

$$f_0 = \frac{1}{\pi\sqrt{LC(1-m^2)}} = f_\infty$$

For low-pass filter,

$$f_c = \frac{1}{\pi\sqrt{LC}}$$

$$f_\infty = \frac{f_c}{\sqrt{1-m^2}}$$

$$m = \sqrt{1-\left(\frac{f_c}{f_\infty}\right)^2}$$

For sharp cut-off, $f_\infty$ should be near to $f_C$. For smaller value of $m$, $f_\infty$ comes close to $f_c$. The $m$-derived $T$-section low-pass filter is shown in Fig. 14.32.

Similarly, for $m$-derived $\pi$-section, the inductance and capacitance in the series arm constitute a resonant circuit.

At resonant frequency,

$$m\,\omega_0 L = \frac{1}{\left(\frac{1-m^2}{4m}\right)\omega_0 C}$$

$$\omega_0^2 = \frac{4}{LC(1-m^2)}$$

$$\omega_0 = \frac{4}{\sqrt{LC(1-m^2)}}$$

$$f_0 = \frac{1}{\pi\sqrt{LC(1-m^2)}} = f_\infty$$

**Fig. 14.32** *m-derived T-section low-pass filter*

For low-pass filter,

$$f_c = \frac{1}{\pi\sqrt{LC}}$$

$$f_\infty = \frac{f_c}{\sqrt{1-m^2}}$$

For both $m$-derived low-pass networks, $f_\infty > f_c$ for positive values of $m$ $(0 < m < 1)$.

The $m$-derived $\pi$ section low-pass filter is shown in Fig. 14.33.

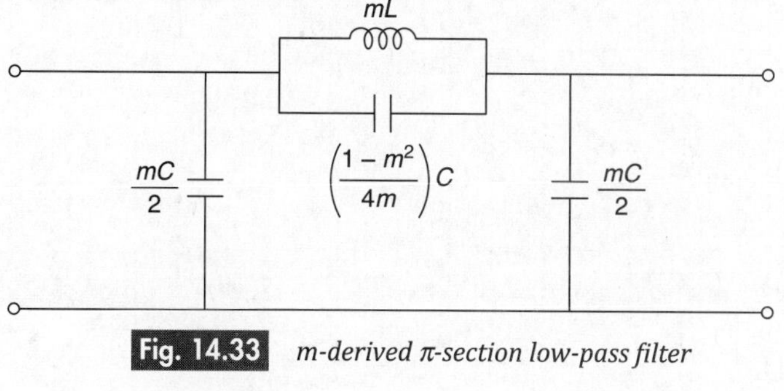


**Fig. 14.33** *m-derived π-section low-pass filter*

The variation of attenuation with frequency is shown in Fig. 14.34. It is seen that the attenuation rises abruptly becomes infinite at $f_\infty$ and then decreases for the $m$-derived filter.

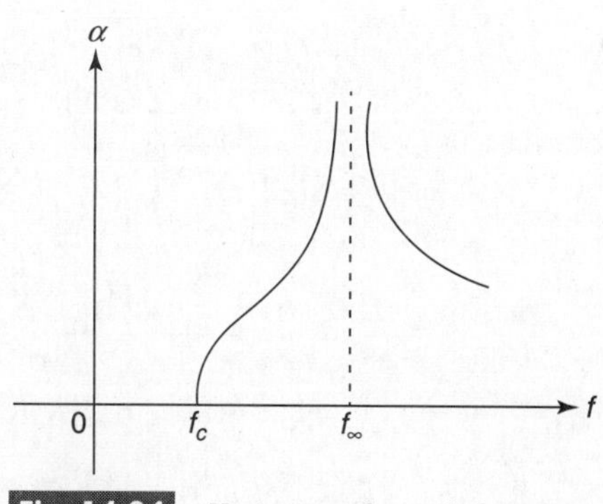


**Fig. 14.34** *Variation of α with frequency*

Thus, an $m$-derived filter gives a sharp cut-off. The decrease in attenuation for frequencies higher than $f_\infty$ can be avoided by connecting an $m$-derived filter and a constant-$k$ filter in cascade.

The variation of $\beta$ with frequency is shown in Fig. 14.35.

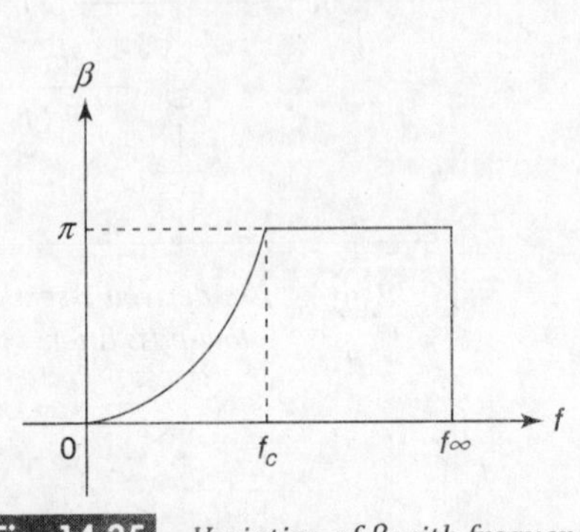


**Fig. 14.35** *Variation of β with frequency*

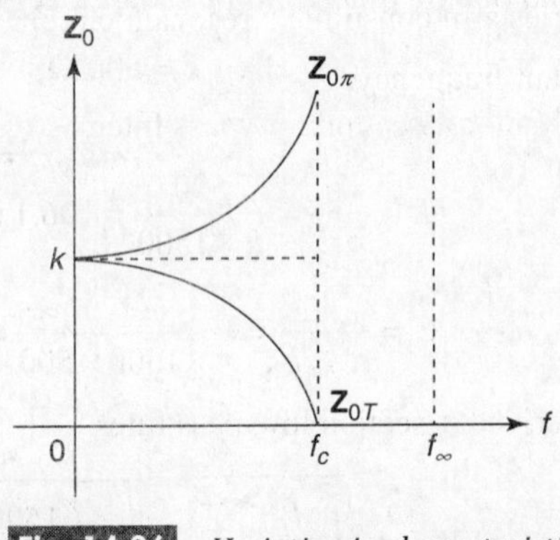


**Fig. 14.36** *Variation in characteristic impedance with frequency*

The variation of characteristic impedance with frequency is shown in Fig. 14.36. The characteristic impedance of an $m$-derived filter also varies with frequency. The impedance matching can be achieved by using half-section terminations.

## EXAMPLE 14.14

*Design an m-derived T-section low-pass filter having cut-off frequency of 800 Hz, design impedance of 500 Ω and frequency of attenuation of 1000 Hz.*

**Solution** $k = 500\ \Omega, \quad f_c = 800\text{ Hz}, \quad f_\infty = 1000\text{ Hz}$

For a constant-$k$ $T$-section low-pass filter

$$L = \frac{k}{\pi f_c} = \frac{500}{\pi \times 800} = 198.94\text{ mH}$$

$$C = \frac{1}{\pi f_c k} = \frac{1}{\pi \times 800 \times 500} = 0.8\ \mu\text{F}$$

For an $m$-derived $T$-section low-pass filter

$$m = \sqrt{1-\left(\frac{f_c}{f_\infty}\right)^2} = \sqrt{1-\left(\frac{800}{1000}\right)^2} = 0.6$$

$$\frac{mL}{2} = \frac{0.6 \times 198.94 \times 10^{-3}}{2} = 59.68\text{ mH}$$

$$mC = 0.6 \times 0.8 \times 10^{-6} = 0.48\ \mu\text{F}$$

$$\left(\frac{1-m^2}{4m}\right)L = \left[\frac{1-(0.6)^2}{4(0.6)}\right] \times 198.94 \times 10^{-3} = 53.05\text{ mH}$$

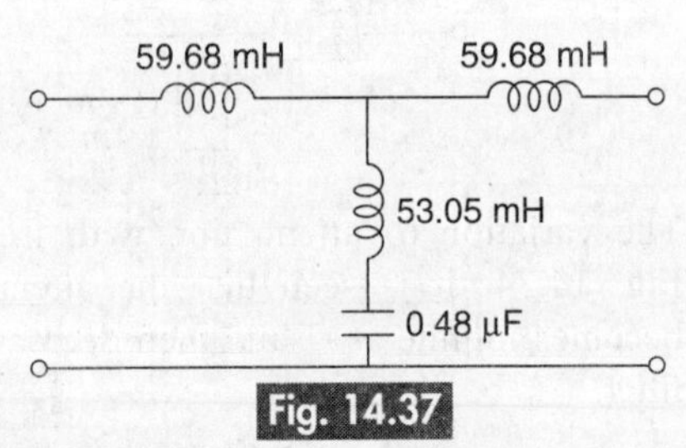


**Fig. 14.37**

The $m$-derived $T$-section low-pass filter is shown in Fig. 14.37.

**EXAMPLE 14.15**

*Design an m-derived π-section low-pass filter having cut-off frequency of 1500 Hz, design impedance of 500 Ω and infinite attenuation frequency of 2000 Hz.*

**Solution** $f_C = 1500$ Hz, $k = 500\ \Omega$, $f_\infty = 2000$ Hz

For constant-$k$ π-section low-pass filter,

$$L = \frac{k}{\pi f_c} = \frac{500}{\pi \times 1500} = 106.1 \text{ mH}$$

$$C = \frac{1}{\pi f_c k} = \frac{1}{\pi \times 1500 \times 500} = 0.424\ \mu\text{F}$$

For $m$-derived π-section low-pass filter,

$$m = \sqrt{1 - \left(\frac{f_c}{f_\infty}\right)^2} = \sqrt{1 - \left(\frac{1500}{2000}\right)^2} = 0.66$$

$$\frac{mC}{2} = \frac{0.66 \times 0.424 \times 10^{-6}}{2} = 0.14\ \mu\text{F}$$

$$mL = 0.66 \times 106.1 \times 10^{-3} = 70.03 \text{ mH}$$

$$\left(\frac{1 - m^2}{4m}\right) C = \frac{1 - (0.66)^2}{4 \times 0.66} \times 0.424 \times 10^{-6} = 0.09\ \mu\text{F}$$

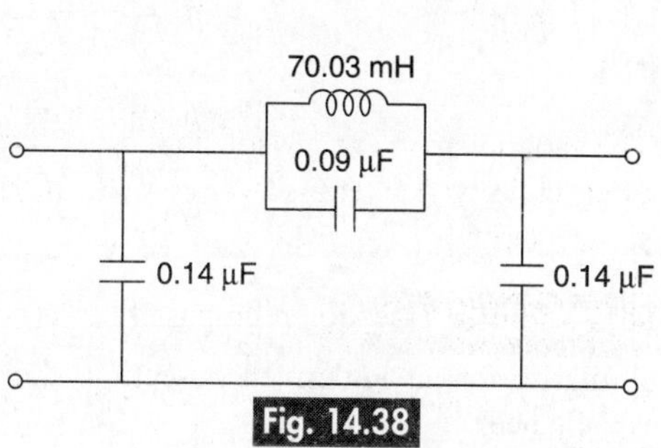


Fig. 14.38

The $m$-derived low-pass filter is shown in Fig. 14.38.

## 14.11 m-DERIVED HIGH-PASS FILTER

LO 14.6

Figure 14.39 shows $m$-derived high-pass $T$ and π-filter.

Let $$\mathbf{Z}_1 = \frac{1}{j\omega c}$$

$$\mathbf{Z}_2 = j\omega L$$

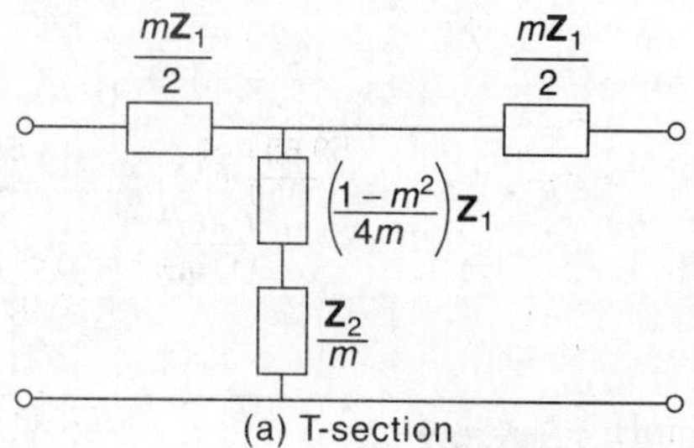


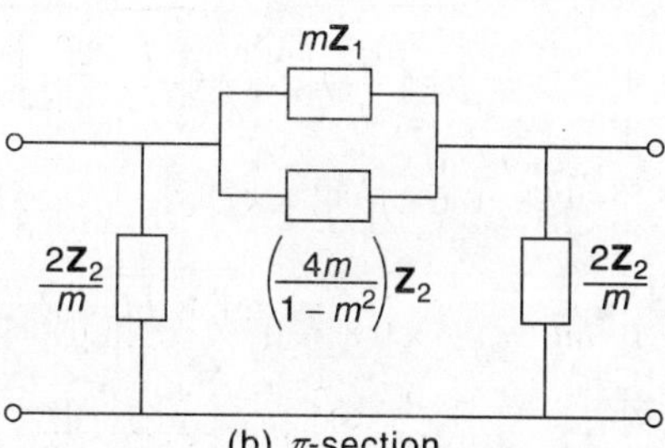


Fig. 14.39 *m-derived high-pass filter*

At resonant frequency,

$$\omega_0 \frac{L}{m} = \frac{1}{\omega_0 \left(\frac{4m}{1-m^2}\right) C}$$

$$\omega_0^2 = \frac{1}{\frac{L}{m}\left(\frac{4m}{1-m^2}\right) C} = \frac{1-m^2}{4LC}$$

$$\omega_0 = \frac{\sqrt{1-m^2}}{2\sqrt{LC}}$$

$$f_0 = \frac{\sqrt{1-m^2}}{4\pi\sqrt{LC}} = f_\infty$$

For a high-pass filter,

$$f_c = \frac{1}{4\pi\sqrt{LC}}$$

$$f_\infty = f_c\sqrt{1-m^2}$$

$$m = \sqrt{1-\left(\frac{f_\infty}{f_c}\right)^2}$$

Fig. 14.40 *m-derived T-section high-pass filter*

The *m*-derived *T*-section high-pass filter is shown in Fig. 14.40.

Similarly, for an *m*-derived $\pi$ section, the resonant circuit is formed by the series arm inductance and capacitance.

At resonant frequency,

$$\left(\frac{4m}{1-m^2}\right)\omega_0 L = \frac{1}{\omega_0 \frac{C}{m}}$$

$$\omega_0^2 = \frac{1-m^2}{4LC}$$

$$\omega_0 = \frac{\sqrt{1-m^2}}{2\sqrt{LC}}$$

$$f_0 = \frac{\sqrt{1-m^2}}{4\pi\sqrt{LC}} = f_\infty$$

For a high-pass filter,

$$f_c = \frac{1}{4\pi\sqrt{LC}}$$

$$f_\infty = f_c\sqrt{1-m^2}$$

$$m = \sqrt{1-\left(\frac{f_\infty}{f_c}\right)^2}$$

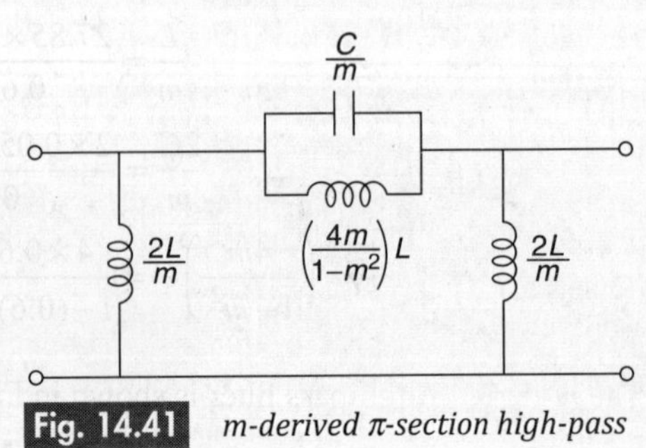


Fig. 14.41 *m-derived $\pi$-section high-pass filter*

The $m$-derived $\pi$-section high-pass filter is shown in Fig. 14.41. The variation of attenuation phase constant and characteristic impedance with frequency are shown in Fig. 14.42 for an $m$-derived high-pass filter. The attenuation rises abruptly, becomes infinite at $f_\infty$ and then decreases, thus giving a sharp cut-off.

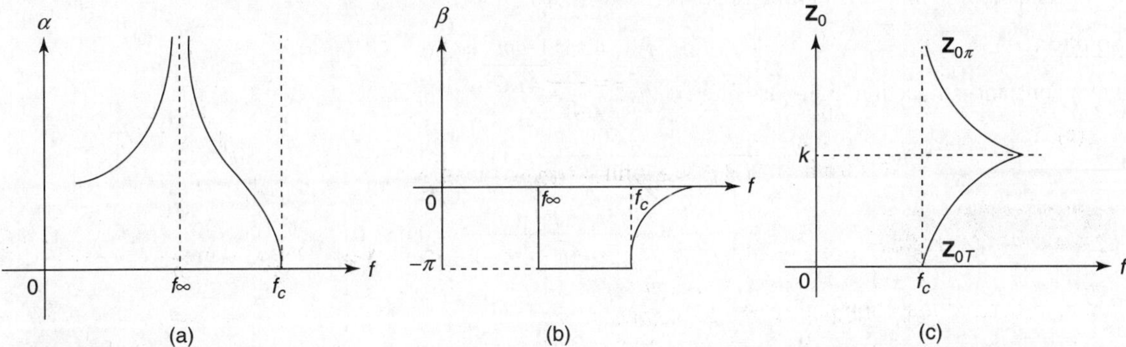


**Fig. 14.42** *Variation of (a) attenuation, (b) phase constant, (c) characteristic impedance of m-derived high-pass filter*

The use of $m$-derived and constant-$k$ high-pass filters in series gives a sharp cut-off and high attenuation in the entire stop band. The half-section termination provides impedance matching.

## EXAMPLE 14.16

*Design an m-derived T-section high-pass filter with a cut-off frequency of 2 kHz, design impedance of 700 Ω and m = 0.6.*

**Solution** $f_C = 2 \text{ kHz}, \quad k = 700\ \Omega, \quad m = 0.6$

For constant-$k$ $T$-section high-pass filter,

$$L = \frac{k}{4\pi f_c} = \frac{700}{4\pi \times 2 \times 10^3} = 27.85 \text{ mH}$$

$$C = \frac{1}{4\pi f_c k} = \frac{1}{4\pi \times 2000 \times 700} = 0.057\ \mu\text{F}$$

For an $m$-derived $T$-section high-pass filter,

$$\frac{L}{m} = \frac{27.85 \times 10^{-3}}{0.6} = 46.42 \text{ mH}$$

$$\frac{2C}{m} = \frac{2 \times 0.057 \times 10^{-6}}{0.6} = 0.19\ \mu\text{F}$$

$$\left(\frac{4m}{1-m^2}\right) C = \frac{4 \times 0.6}{1-(0.6)^2} \times 0.057 \times 10^{-6} = 0.21\ \mu\text{F}$$

0.19 μF  0.19 μF
0.21 μF
46.42 mH

**Fig. 14.43**

The $m$-derived high-pass filter is shown in Fig. 14.43.

**EXAMPLE 14.17**

*Design the π-section of an m-derived high-pass filter having a design impedance of 600 Ω, cut-off frequency of 4 kHz and an infinite attenuation at 3.6 kHz.*

**Solution**

$$k = 600\ \Omega, \quad f_c = 4\text{ kHz}, \quad f_\infty = 3.6\text{ kHz}$$

For a constant-$k$ π-section high-pass filter,

$$L = \frac{k}{4\pi f_c} = \frac{600}{4\pi \times 4 \times 10^3} = 11.94\text{ mH}$$

$$C = \frac{1}{4\pi f_c k} = \frac{1}{4\pi \times 4 \times 10^3 \times 600} = 0.033\ \mu\text{F}$$

For an $m$-derived π-section high-pass filter,

$$m = \sqrt{1 - \left(\frac{f_\infty}{f_c}\right)^2} = \sqrt{1 - \left(\frac{3.6 \times 10^3}{4 \times 10^3}\right)^2} = 0.436$$

$$\frac{2L}{m} = \frac{2 \times 11.94 \times 10^{-3}}{0.436} = 54.77\text{ mH}$$

$$\frac{C}{m} = \frac{0.033 \times 10^{-6}}{0.436} = 0.076\ \mu\text{F}$$

$$\left(\frac{4m}{1-m^2}\right)L = \frac{4 \times 0.436}{1-(0.436)^2} \times 11.94 \times 10^{-3} = 25.71\text{ mH}$$

The $m$-derived π-section high-pass filter is shown in Fig. 14.44.

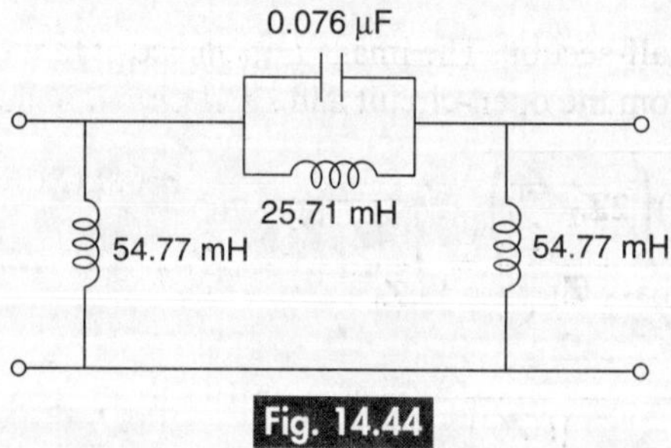


Fig. 14.44

## 14.12 TERMINATING HALF-SECTIONS

LO 14.7

Discuss terminating half-sections

A filter is composed of a number of sections. As the characteristic impedance of an equivalent $T$ or π-section does not match with each other, a half-section is used for impedance matching between $T$ and π-sections.

The input impedance of the half-section is same as the characteristic impedance of a $T$-section, while the output impedance of the half-section is same as the characteristic impedance of the π-section. Hence, matching can be obtained if a half-section is connected in between a $T$ and π-section.

### 14.12.1 Constant-*k* Half-sections

Figure 14.45(a) shows a constant-*k* *T*-section filter. If this section is bisected longitudinally, a half-section is obtained, as shown in Fig. 14.45 (b).

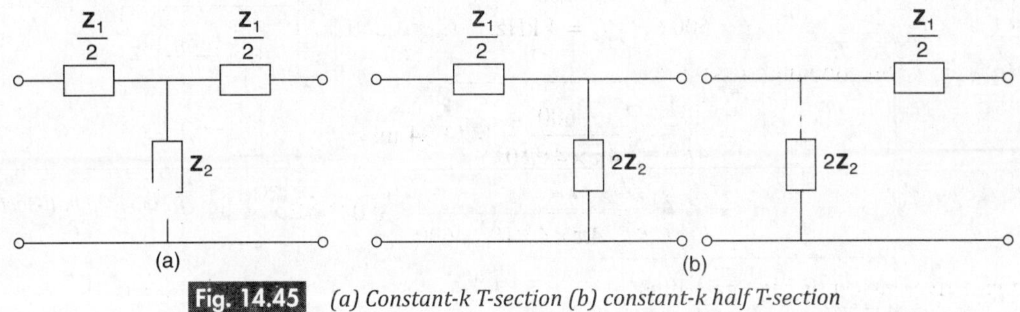


**Fig. 14.45** *(a) Constant-k T-section (b) constant-k half T-section*

Similarly, a constant-*k* $\pi$-section can be bisected into two half-sections, as shown in Fig. 14.46.

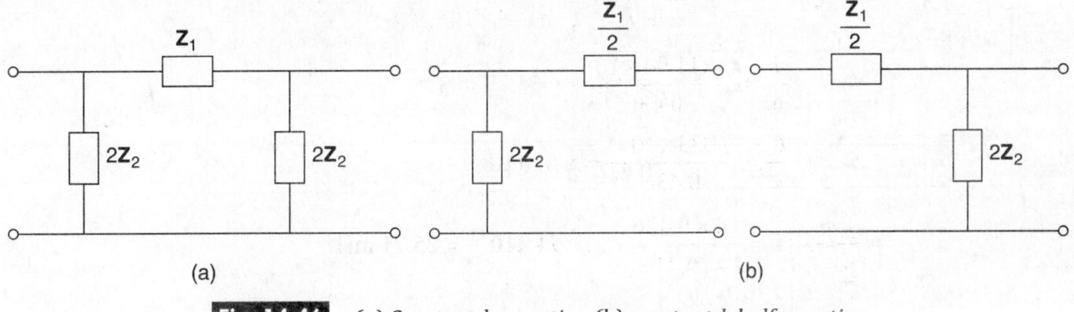


**Fig. 14.46** *(a) Constant-k $\pi$-section (b) constant-k half $\pi$-section*

Figure 14.47 shows a constant-*k* half-section. The image impedance of the section as seen from terminals 1-2 and terminals 3–4 can be found from the open-circuit and short-circuit impedances.

$$\mathbf{Z}_{12} = \sqrt{\mathbf{Z}_{oc}\,\mathbf{Z}_{sc}} = \sqrt{\frac{(2\mathbf{Z}_2)\left(2\mathbf{Z}_2\,\dfrac{\mathbf{Z}_1}{2}\right)}{2\mathbf{Z}_2 + \dfrac{\mathbf{Z}_1}{2}}} = \sqrt{\frac{4\mathbf{Z}_1\,\mathbf{Z}_2^2}{\mathbf{Z}_1 + 4\mathbf{Z}_2}} = \mathbf{Z}_{0\pi}$$

$$\mathbf{Z}_{34} = \sqrt{\mathbf{Z}_{oc}\,\mathbf{Z}_{sc}} = \sqrt{\left(\frac{\mathbf{Z}_1}{2} + 2\mathbf{Z}_2\right)\left(\frac{\mathbf{Z}_1}{2}\right)}$$

$$= \sqrt{\mathbf{Z}_1\,\mathbf{Z}_2\left(1 + \frac{\mathbf{Z}_1}{4\mathbf{Z}_2}\right)} = \mathbf{Z}_{0T}$$

**Fig. 14.47** *Constant-k half-section*

Thus, the half-section has the impedance characteristics of a $\pi$-section between terminals 1–2 and that of a *T*-section between terminals 3-4. Hence, this half-section can be used to match a $\pi$-section to a *T*-section. It can also be used to match a filter section to a terminating impedance, which differs from the characteristic impedance of a $\pi$-section.

### 14.12.2 *m*-derived Half-sections

Figure 14.48 shows and *m*-derived half-section. The image impedance of the section, as seen from terminals 1–2 and terminals 3–4 can be found from the open-circuit and short-circuit impedances.

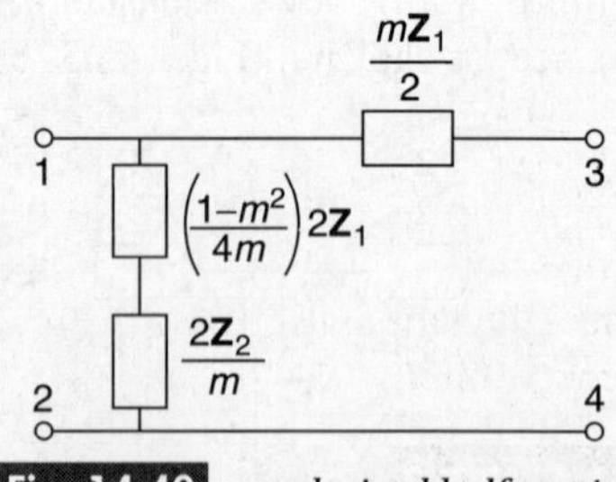


**Fig. 14.48** *m-derived half-section*

$$\mathbf{Z}_{12} = \sqrt{\mathbf{Z}_{oc}\,\mathbf{Z}_{sc}}$$

$$= \sqrt{\frac{\left(\frac{1-m^2}{2m}\mathbf{Z}_1 + \frac{2\mathbf{Z}_2}{m}\right)\left(\frac{1-m^2}{2m}\mathbf{Z}_1 + \frac{2\mathbf{Z}_2}{m}\right)\left(m\frac{\mathbf{Z}_1}{2}\right)}{\frac{1-m^2}{2m}\mathbf{Z}_1 + \frac{2\mathbf{Z}_2}{m} + \frac{m\mathbf{Z}_1}{2}}}$$

$$= \sqrt{\frac{\left(\frac{1-m^2}{2m}\mathbf{Z}_1 + \frac{2\mathbf{Z}_2}{m}\right)^2\left(\frac{m\mathbf{Z}_1}{2}\right)}{\frac{1-m^2}{2m}\mathbf{Z}_1 + \frac{2\mathbf{Z}_2}{m} + \frac{m\mathbf{Z}_1}{2}}}$$

$$= \sqrt{\frac{\left(\frac{1-m^2}{2m}\mathbf{Z}_1 + \frac{2\mathbf{Z}_2}{m}\right)^2\left(\frac{m\mathbf{Z}_1}{2}\right)^2}{\left(\frac{1-m^2}{2m}\mathbf{Z}_1 + \frac{2\mathbf{Z}_2}{m} + \frac{m\mathbf{Z}_1}{2}\right)\left(\frac{m\mathbf{Z}_1}{2}\right)}}$$

$$= \sqrt{\frac{\left[\left(\frac{1-m^2}{4}\right)\mathbf{Z}_1^2 + \mathbf{Z}_1\,\mathbf{Z}_2\right]^2}{\frac{\mathbf{Z}_1^2}{4} - \frac{m^2\mathbf{Z}_1^2}{4} + \mathbf{Z}_1\,\mathbf{Z}_2 + \frac{m^2\mathbf{Z}_1^2}{4}}}$$

$$= \frac{\mathbf{Z}_1\,\mathbf{Z}_2 + \frac{(1-m^2)}{4}\mathbf{Z}_1^2}{\sqrt{\mathbf{Z}_1\,\mathbf{Z}_2 + \frac{\mathbf{Z}_1^2}{4}}}$$

$$= \frac{\mathbf{Z}_1\,\mathbf{Z}_2}{\mathbf{Z}_{0T}}\left[1 + \frac{\mathbf{Z}_1}{4\mathbf{Z}_2}(1-m)^2\right]$$

$$= \mathbf{Z}_{0\pi}\left[1 + \frac{\mathbf{Z}_1}{4\mathbf{Z}_2}(1-m)^2\right]$$

$$\mathbf{Z}_{34} = \sqrt{\mathbf{Z}_{oc}\,\mathbf{Z}_{sc}}$$

$$= \sqrt{\left[\frac{m\mathbf{Z}_1}{2} + \left(\frac{1-m^2}{2m}\right)\mathbf{Z}_1 + \frac{2\mathbf{Z}_2}{m}\right]\left(\frac{m\mathbf{Z}_1}{2}\right)}$$

$$= \sqrt{\frac{m^2 \mathbf{Z}_1^2}{4} + \frac{\mathbf{Z}_1^2}{4} - \frac{m^2 \mathbf{Z}_1^2}{4} + \mathbf{Z}_1 \mathbf{Z}_2}$$

$$= \sqrt{\mathbf{Z}_1 \mathbf{Z}_2 \left(1 + \frac{\mathbf{Z}_1}{4\mathbf{Z}_2}\right)}$$

$$= \mathbf{Z}_{0T}$$

Hence, the terminals 3–4 of the *m*-derived half-section can be used to match the impedance of a constant-*k* *T*-section filter.

**EXAMPLE 14.18**

*Find the values of shunt and series element of each half-section of a constant-k T-section high-pass filter. The termination is 600 Ω and the filter is cut off below 20000 Hz.*

**Solution** $k = 600\ \Omega, \quad f_c = 20000\ \text{Hz}$

$$L = \frac{k}{4\pi f_c} = \frac{600}{4\pi \times 20000} = 2.39\ \text{mH}$$

$$C = \frac{1}{4\pi f_c k} = \frac{1}{4\pi \times 20000 \times 600} = 0.0066\ \mu\text{F}$$

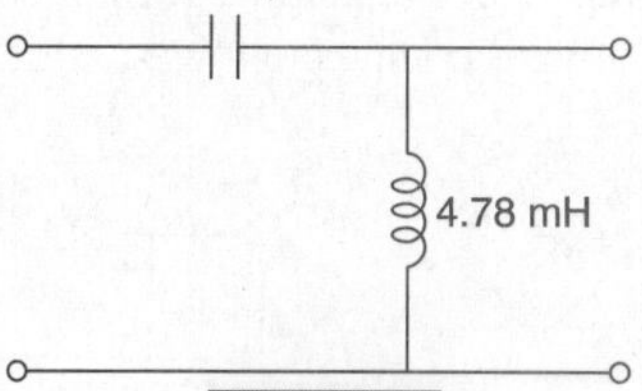

The half-section consists of a capacitor of $2C$, i.e., 0.0133 μF in the series branch and an inductor of $2L$, i.e., 4.78 mH in the shunt branch, as shown in Fig. 14.49.



Fig. 14.49

**EXAMPLE 14.19**

*A prototype high-pass filter with L = 4.77 mH and C = 0.0133 μF has a cut-off frequency of 10 kHz and design impedance of 600 Ω. Design a suitable terminating half-section with m = 0.6 such as to operate with same cut-off frequency.*

**Solution** $L = 4.77\ \text{mH}, \quad C = 0.0133\ \mu\text{F}, \quad f_c = 10\ \text{kHz}, \quad k = 600\ \Omega$

For *m*-derived *T*-section high-pass filter,

$$\frac{L}{m} = \frac{4.77 \times 10^{-3}}{0.6} = 7.95\ \text{mH}$$

$$\frac{2C}{m} = \frac{2 \times 0.0133 \times 10^{-6}}{0.6} = 0.044\ \mu\text{F}$$

$$\left(\frac{4m}{1-m^2}\right) C = \frac{4 \times 0.6}{1-(0.6)^2} \times 0.0133 \times 10^{-6} = 0.05\ \mu\text{F}$$

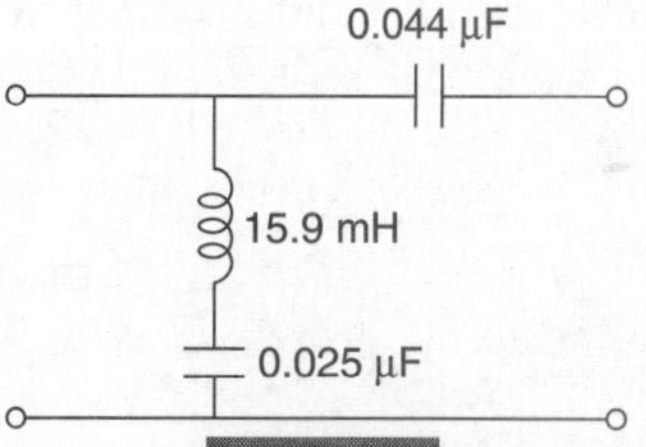

The *m*-derived *T*-half-section is shown in Fig. 14.50.



Fig. 14.50

For *m*-derived *π*-section high-pass filter,

$$\frac{2L}{m} = \frac{2 \times 4.77 \times 10^{-3}}{0.6} = 15.9\ \text{mH}$$

$$\frac{C}{m} = \frac{0.0133 \times 10^{-6}}{0.6} = 0.022\ \mu\text{F}$$

$$\left(\frac{4m}{1-m^2}\right)L = \frac{4 \times 0.6}{1-(0.6)^2} \times 4.77 \times 10^{-3} = 17.89\ \text{mH}$$

The $m$-derived $\pi$-half-section is shown in Fig. 14.51.

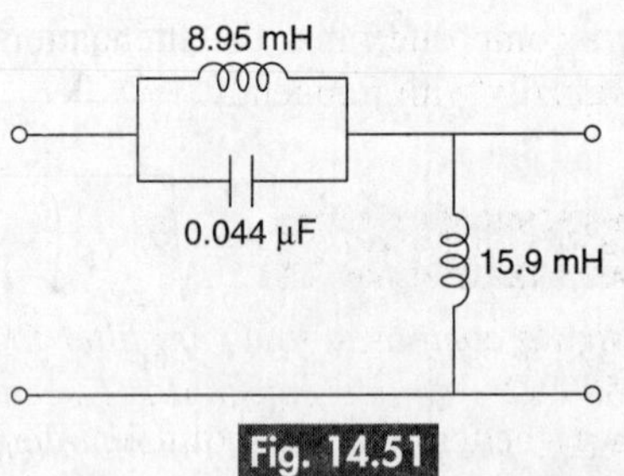


Fig. 14.51

## 14.13 COMPOSITE FILTER

LO 14.8 Explain composite filters and their characteristics

A constant-$k$ filter does not give a sharp cut-off. An $m$-derived filter section has a sharp cut off, but its attenuation decreases for frequencies beyond $f_\infty$. Moreover, two terminating half-sections, one at each end, are needed for impedance matching. A filter composed of all the above sections is known as a *composite filter*. Figure 14.52 shows a composite low-pass filter.

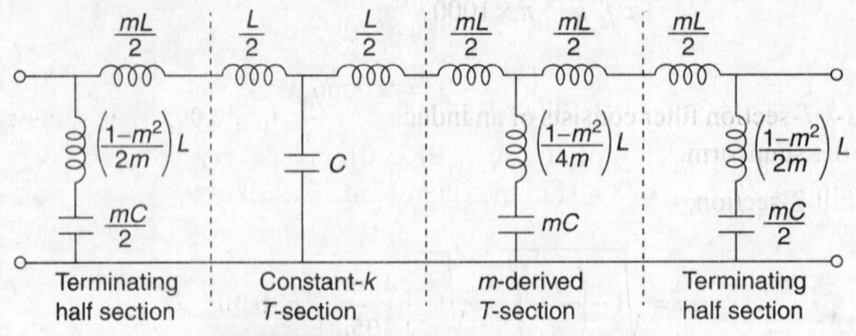


Fig. 14.52 *Composite low-pass filter*

A composite filter consists of the following components:

(i) One or more constant-$k$ sections to produce cut-off frequency, i.e., transition from pass band to the stop band at a specified frequency $f_c$.

(ii) One or more $m$-derived sections to give infinite attenuation at a frequency $f_\infty$ near to $f_c$.

(iii) Two terminating $m$-derived half-sections with $m = 0.6$ to provide matching with the source and the load.

Figure 14.53 shows the attenuation-versus-frequency characteristics of a constant-$k$ low-pass filter, $m$-derived low-pass filter and a composite filter.

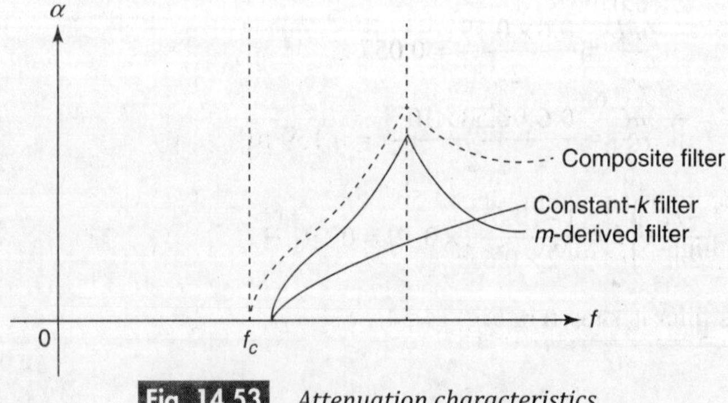


Fig. 14.53 *Attenuation characteristics*

For a composite filter, the attenuation rises very rapidly with frequency in the range $f_c$ to $f_\infty$ and falls only marginally with frequency.

**EXAMPLE 14.20**

*Design a composite low-pass filter to have a cut-off frequency of 1000 Hz and a characteristic impedance of 600 Ω. Use one constant-k T-section, one m-derived T-section and two terminating half-sections with m = 0.6. The frequency of infinite attenuation is 1050 Hz.*

**Solution** $f_c = 1000$ Hz, $k = 600\ \Omega$, $f_\infty = 1050$ Hz

For constant-$k$ $T$-section,

$$L = \frac{k}{\pi f_c} = \frac{600}{\pi \times 1000} = 0.19 \text{ H}$$

$$C = \frac{1}{\pi f_c k} = \frac{1}{\pi \times 1000 \times 600} = 0.53\ \mu\text{F}$$

Hence, the constant-$k$ $T$-section filter consists of an inductor of $\frac{L_1}{2}$, i.e., 0.095 H in series arm and a capacitor $C_1$, i.e., 0.53 μF in the shunt arm.

For the $m$-derived full $T$-section,

$$m = \sqrt{1 - \left(\frac{f_c}{f_\infty}\right)^2} = \sqrt{1 - \left(\frac{1000}{1050}\right)^2} = 0.305$$

$$\frac{mL}{2} = \frac{0.305 \times 0.19}{2} = 0.029 \text{ H}$$

$$mC = 0.305 \times 0.53 \times 10^{-6} = 0.162\ \mu\text{F}$$

$$\left(\frac{1-m^2}{4m}\right)L = \frac{1-(0.305)^2}{4 \times 0.305} \times 0.19 = 0.14 \text{ H}$$

For each terminating half-section with $m = 0.6$,

$$\frac{mL}{2} = \frac{0.6 \times 0.19}{2} = 0.057 \text{ H}$$

$$\frac{mC}{2} = \frac{0.6 \times 0.53 \times 10^{-6}}{2} = 0.159\ \mu\text{F}$$

$$\left(\frac{1-m^2}{2m}\right)L = \frac{1-(0.6)^2}{2 \times 0.6} \times 0.19 = 0.101 \text{ H}$$

The composite low-pass filter is shown in Fig. 14.54.

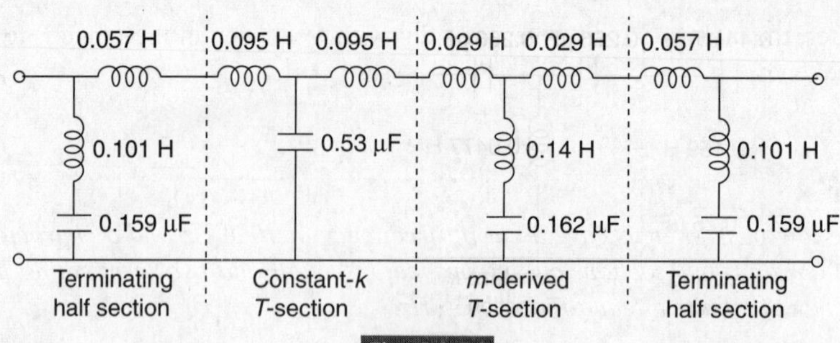


Fig. 14.54

## EXAMPLE 14.21

*Design a composite high-pass filter having a characteristic impedance of 600 Ω and a cut-off frequency of 1000 Hz. Use one a constant-k T-section, one m-derived T-section with m = 0.2 and two m-derived terminating half-sections with m = 0.6.*

**Solution**

$$k = 600\ \Omega, \quad f_c = 1000\text{ Hz}$$

For a constant-$k$ $T$-section,

$$L = \frac{k}{4\pi f_c} = \frac{600}{4\pi \times 1000} = 0.0477\text{ H}$$

$$C = \frac{1}{4\pi f_c k} = \frac{1}{4\pi \times 1000 \times 600} = 0.133\ \mu\text{F}$$

Hence, the constant-$k$ $T$-section filter consists of an inductor of 0.0477 H in the shunt branch and a capacitor of $2C$, i.e., 0.266 μF in each series branch.

For an $m$-derived $T$-section with $m = 0.2$,

$$\frac{2C}{m} = \frac{2 \times 0.133 \times 10^{-6}}{0.2} = 1.33\ \mu\text{F}$$

$$\frac{L}{m} = \frac{0.0477}{0.2} = 0.239\text{ H}$$

$$\left(\frac{4m}{1-m^2}\right)C = \frac{4 \times 0.2}{1-(0.2)^2} \times 0.133 \times 10^{-6} = 0.11\ \mu\text{F}$$

For each terminating half-section with $m = 0.6$,

$$\frac{2C}{m} = \frac{2 \times 0.133 \times 10^{-6}}{0.6} = 0.44\ \mu\text{F}$$

$$\frac{2L}{m} = \frac{2 \times 0.0477}{0.6} = 0.159\text{ H}$$

$$\left(\frac{2m}{1-m^2}\right)C = \frac{2 \times 0.6}{1-(0.6)^2} \times 0.133 \times 10^{-6} = 0.25\ \mu\text{F}$$

The composite high-pass filter is shown in Fig. 14.55.

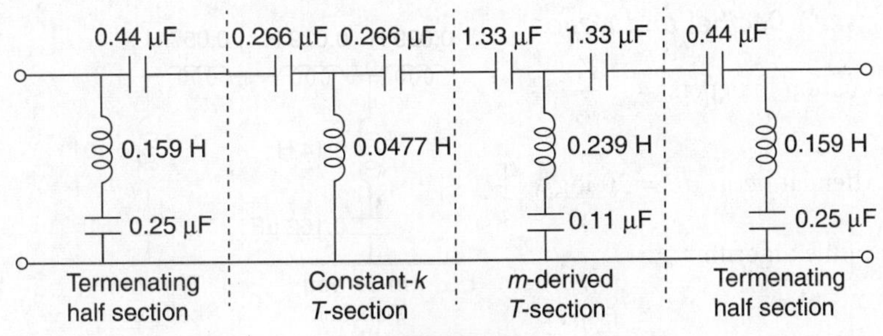


Fig. 14.55

## 14.14 ATTENUATOR

LO 14.9

Discuss attenuators and their types – lattice, T-type, pi-type, and ladder-type

An attenuator is a two-port resistive network. It is used to reduce the signal level when used between a generator and a load. Attenuators may be symmetrical or asymmetrical. They may provide fixed or variable attenuation. A fixed attenuator is also called a pad. The attenuation is expressed in decibels (dB).

$$\text{Attenuation in } dB = 10\log_{10}\frac{P_1}{P_2}$$

where $P_1$ is the input power and $P_2$ is the output power.

For a properly matched network,

$$P_1 = I_1^2 R_0 = \frac{V_1^2}{R_0}$$

$$P_2 = I_2^2 R_0 = \frac{V_2^2}{R_0}$$

where $R_0$ is the characteristic resistance of the network.

Hence, $$\text{attenuation in } dB = 20\log_{10}\frac{V_1}{V_2} = 20\log_{10}\frac{I_1}{I_2}$$

Attenuation is also expressed in nepers, as the natural logarithm of the voltage or current ratio.

$$\text{Attenuation in nepers} = \ln\frac{V_1}{V_2} = \ln\frac{I_1}{I_2} = \frac{1}{2}\ln\frac{P_1}{P_2}$$

If $\frac{V_1}{V_2} = \frac{I_1}{I_2} = N$ then $\frac{P_1}{P_2} = N^2$

$$\text{Attenuation in } dB = 20\log_{10} N$$

$$N = \text{antilog}\left(\frac{dB}{20}\right)$$

where $N$ is the attenuation in nepers.

### ➤ Relation between Decibel and Neper

$$\text{Attenuation in nepers} = \ln\frac{V_1}{v_2}$$

$$\text{Attenuation in } dB = 20\log_{10}\frac{V_1}{V_2}$$

Changing the base of the algorithm,

$$\text{attenuation in } dB = 20\frac{\ln\frac{V_1}{V_2}}{\ln 10} = \frac{20}{2.303}\ln\frac{V_1}{V_2} = 8.686 \text{ (attenuation in neper)}$$

$$\text{Attenuation in nepers} = \frac{1}{8.686}\text{ (attenuation in } dB) = 0.115 \text{ (attenuation in } dB)$$

## 14.15 LATTICE ATTENUATOR

LO 14.9

A lattice is a general type of symmetrical and balanced network. Any symmetrical balanced or unbalanced network can be transformed into an equivalent lattice network. Figure 14.56 shows a lattice network terminated through a characteristic resistance $R_0$.

The elements of a lattice attenuator can be specified in terms of characteristic impedance and propagation constant.

Fig. 14.56 Lattice attenuator

We know that $\quad Z_0 = \sqrt{Z_{oc}\,Z_{sc}}$

$$Z_{oc} = \frac{R_A + R_B}{2}$$

$$Z_{sc} = \frac{2R_A R_B}{R_A + R_B}$$

$$Z_0 = R_0 = \sqrt{Z_{oc}\,Z_{sc}} = \sqrt{\left(\frac{R_A + R_B}{2}\right)\left(\frac{2R_A R_B}{R_A + R_B}\right)} = \sqrt{R_A R_B}$$

Redrawing the network, as shown in Fig. 14.57,

Applying KVL to the loop,

$$V_1 = R_0 I_1 = R_A(I_1 - I) + R_0 I_2 + R_A(I + I_2)$$

$$R_0 I_1 = R_A(I_1 + I_2) + R_0 I_2$$

$$(R_0 - R_A)I_1 = (R_A + R_0)I_2$$

$$\frac{I_1}{I_2} = \frac{R_A + R_0}{R_0 - R_A} = \frac{1 + \frac{R_A}{R_0}}{1 - \frac{R_A}{R_0}}$$

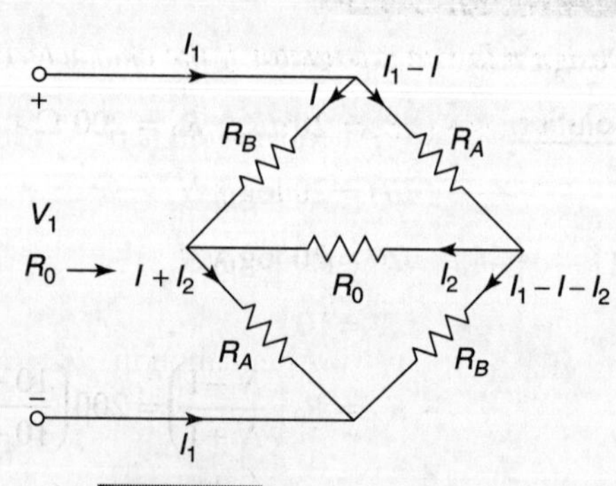


Fig. 14.57 Modified network

$$N = e^{\alpha} = \frac{I_1}{I_2} = \frac{1+\frac{R_A}{R_0}}{1-\frac{R_A}{R_0}} = \frac{1+\sqrt{\frac{R_A}{R_0}}}{1-\sqrt{\frac{R_A}{R_0}}}$$

$$\alpha = \log\left(\frac{1+\sqrt{\frac{R_A}{R_0}}}{1-\sqrt{\frac{R_A}{R_0}}}\right)$$

We can express $R_A$ and $R_B$ in terms of attenuation.

$$N\left(1-\frac{R_A}{R_0}\right) = 1+\frac{R_A}{R_0}$$

$$R_A = R_0\left(\frac{N-1}{N+1}\right)$$

Similarly, $$R_B = R_0\left(\frac{N+1}{N-1}\right)$$

These equations can be used to find the equivalent lattice network for $T$ and $\pi$-networks using the bisection theorem.

### Bisection Theorem

A network is said to have been bisected when the open-circuited and short-circuited input impedances of the two bisected networks are equivalent. Also, the square root of the product of these impedances is the characteristic impedance of the original whole network.

The bisection theorem states that *any symmetrical balanced or unbalanced network can be transformed into an equivalent lattice network. The series arm of the lattice is equal to the short-circuited impedance of the bisected network and the diagonal arm is equal to the open-circuited impedance of the bisected network.*

**EXAMPLE 14.22**

*Design a lattice attenuator if the characteristic resistance is 200 Ω and the attenuation is 20 dB.*

**Solution** $N(dB) = 20\,dB, \quad R_0 = 200\ \Omega$

$$N(dB) = 20\log_{10} N$$

$$20 = 20\log_{10} N$$

$$N = 10$$

$$R_A = R_0\left(\frac{N-1}{N+1}\right) = 200\left(\frac{10-1}{10+1}\right) = 163.6\ \Omega$$

$$R_B = R_0\left(\frac{N+1}{N-1}\right) = 200\left(\frac{10+1}{10-1}\right) = 244.5\ \Omega$$

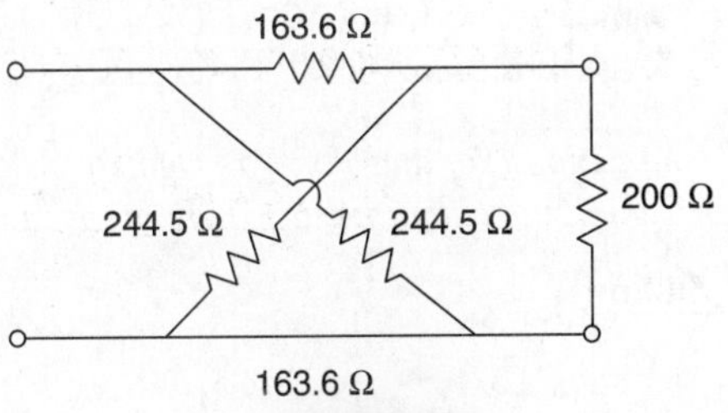

The lattice attenuator is shown in Fig. 14.58.



Fig. 14.58

## 14.16 T-TYPE ATTENUATOR

LO 14.9

A *T*-type attenuator is a symmetrical but unbalanced network and is shown in Fig. 14.59 (a). Its bisected network is shown in Fig. 14.59 (b).

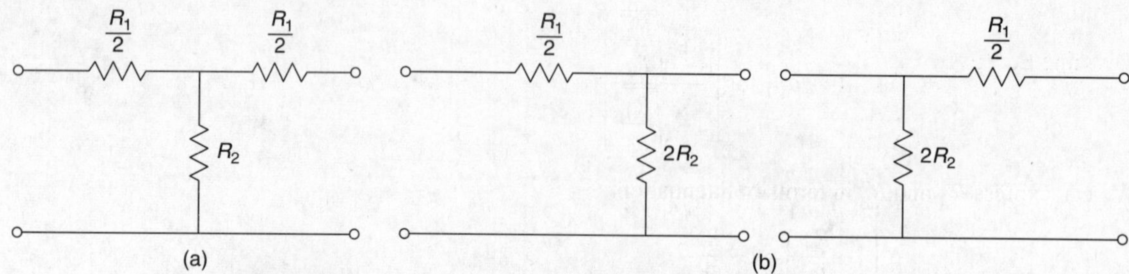


**Fig. 14.59** *(a) T-type attenuator (b) bisection of T-type attenuator*

From the bisection theorem, the series arm of the lattice network is equal to the short-circuited input resistance of the bisected network and the diagonal arm is equal to the open-circuited input resistance of the bisected network.

$$R_A = \frac{R_1}{2}$$

$$R_B = \frac{R_1}{2} + 2R_2$$

From lattice network,

$$R_A = R_0\left(\frac{N-1}{N+1}\right)$$

and

$$R_B = R_0\left(\frac{N+1}{N-1}\right)$$

Solving these equations,

$$R_1 = 2R_0\left(\frac{N-1}{N+1}\right)$$

$$2R_2 = R_0\left(\frac{N+1}{N-1} - \frac{N-1}{N+1}\right)$$

$$R_2 = \frac{R_0}{2}\left(\frac{4N}{N^2-1}\right) = \frac{2N\,R_0}{N^2-1}$$

**EXAMPLE 14.23**

*If the ratio of $R_1$ and $R_2$ of a symmetrical T network is $\frac{1}{4}$, find the ratio of the input current to the output current. Also, calculate the attenuation in dB.*

**Solution**

$$\frac{R_1}{R_2} = \frac{1}{4}$$

For a $T$-type attenuator,

$$R_1 = 2R_0\left(\frac{N-1}{N+1}\right) \tag{i}$$

$$R_2 = R_0\left(\frac{2N}{N^2-1}\right) \tag{ii}$$

Dividing Eq. (ii) by Eq. (i),

$$\frac{\dfrac{2N}{N^2-1}}{2\left(\dfrac{N-1}{N+1}\right)} = \frac{1}{4}$$

$$\frac{2N}{N^2-1} = \frac{1}{2}\left(\frac{N-1}{N+1}\right)$$

$$\frac{2N}{(N+1)(N-1)} = \frac{1}{2}\left(\frac{N-1}{N+1}\right)$$

$$4N = (N-1)^2$$

$$N^2 - 6N + 1 = 0$$

$$N = 5.83 \quad \text{or} \quad N = 0.172$$

$$N \text{ in } dB = 20\log_{10} 5.83 = 15.31\ dB$$

or

$$N \text{ in } dB = 20\log_{10} 0.172 = -15.29\ dB$$

Since attenuation cannot be negative,

$$N = 5.83 \text{ nepers} = 15.31\ dB$$

$$\frac{I_1}{I_2} = N = 5.83$$

## EXAMPLE 14.24

*An attenuator is composed of a symmetrical T-section having a series arm of 175 Ω and a shunt arm of 350 Ω. Find the characteristic impedance and attenuation in dB.*

**Solution**

$$\frac{R_1}{2} = 175\ \Omega, \quad R_1 = 350\ \Omega, \quad R_2 = 350\ \Omega$$

$$R_1 = 2R_0\left(\frac{N-1}{N+1}\right) = 350 \qquad \ldots\text{(i)}$$

$$R_2 = R_0\left(\frac{2N}{N^2-1}\right) = 350 \qquad \ldots\text{(ii)}$$

Dividing Eq. (ii) by Eq. (i),

$$\frac{\dfrac{2N}{N^2-1}}{2\left(\dfrac{N-1}{N+1}\right)} = 1$$

$$\frac{2N}{N^2-1} = 2\left(\frac{N-1}{N+1}\right)$$

$$\frac{N}{(N+1)(N-1)} = \frac{N-1}{N+1}$$

$$N = (N-1)^2$$

$$N^2 - 3N + 1 = 0$$

$$N = 2.618 \quad \text{or} \quad N = 0.3819$$

$$N \text{ in } dB = 20 \log_{10} 2.618 = 8.36\ dB$$

$$\text{or } N \text{ in } dB = 20 \log_{10} 0.3819 = -8.36\ dB$$

Since attenuation cannot be negative,

$$N = 2.618 \text{ nepers} = 8.36\ dB$$

Putting $N = 2.618$ in Eq. (i),

$$350 = 2R_0\left(\frac{2.618-1}{2.618+1}\right)$$

$$R_0 = 391.32\ \Omega$$

**EXAMPLE 14.25**

*Design a T-type attenuator to give an attenuation of 60 dB and characteristic resistance of 500 Ω.*

**Solution**

$$N(dB) = 60\ dB, \quad R_0 = 500\ \Omega$$

$$N(dB) = 20 \log_{10} N$$

$$60 = 20 \log_{10} N$$

$$N = 1000$$

$$R_1 = 2R_0\left(\frac{N-1}{N+1}\right) = 2\times 500\left(\frac{1000-1}{1000+1}\right) = 998\ \Omega$$

$$R_2 = R_0\left(\frac{2N}{N^2-1}\right) = 500\left[\frac{2\times 1000}{(1000)^2-1}\right] = 1\ \Omega$$

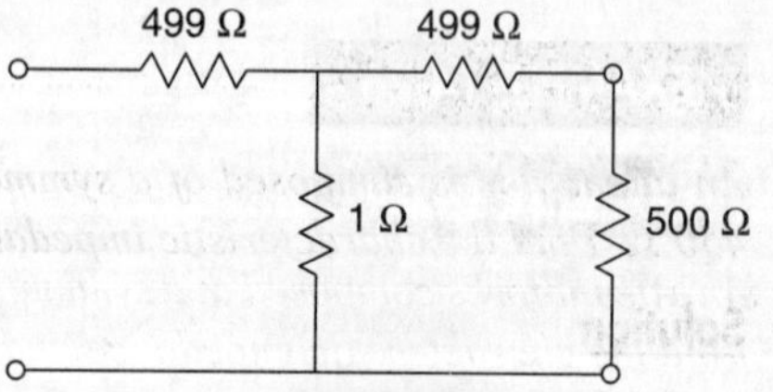

499 Ω 499 Ω 1 Ω 500 Ω

Fig. 14.60

The *T*-type attenuator is shown in Fig. 14.60.

## 14.17 π-TYPE ATTENUATOR

LO 14.9

A symmetrical π-type attenuator is shown in Fig. 14.61(a). Its bisected network is shown in Fig. 14.61(b). From the bisection theorem, the series arm of the lattice network is equal to the short-circuited input resistance of the bisected network and the diagonal arm is equal to the open-circuited input resistance of the bisected network.

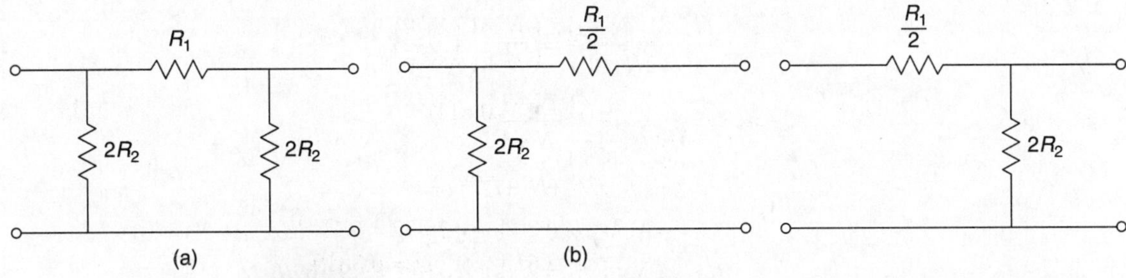


Fig. 14.61 *(a) π-attenuator (b) Bisection of π-type attenuator*

$$R_A = \frac{R_1 R_2}{\frac{R_1}{2} + 2R_2}$$

$$R_B = 2R_2$$

From lattice network,

$$R_A = R_0 \left( \frac{N-1}{N+1} \right)$$

$$R_B = R_0 \left( \frac{N+1}{N-1} \right)$$

Solving these equations,

$$R_1 = \frac{2 R_A R_B}{R_B - R_A} = R_0 \left( \frac{N^2 - 1}{2N} \right)$$

$$R_2 = \frac{R_B}{2} = \frac{R_0}{2} \left( \frac{N+1}{N-1} \right)$$

## EXAMPLE 14.26

*An attenuator is composed of a symmetrical π-section having series arm of 275 Ω and each shunt arm of 450 Ω. Find the characteristic impedance and attenuation in dB.*

**Solution**

$$R_1 = 275\ \Omega, \quad 2R_2 = 450\ \Omega, \quad R_2 = 225\ \Omega$$

$$R_1 = R_0 \left( \frac{N^2 - 1}{2N} \right) = 275 \qquad \text{...(i)}$$

$$R_2 = \frac{R_0}{2} \left( \frac{N+1}{N-1} \right) = 225 \qquad \text{...(ii)}$$

Dividing Eq. (ii) by Eq. (i),

$$\frac{\frac{N^2 - 1}{2N}}{\frac{1}{2}\left( \frac{N+1}{N-1} \right)} = \frac{275}{225}$$

$$\frac{(N+1)(N-1)}{2N} = 0.611\left(\frac{N+1}{N-1}\right)$$

$$(N-1)^2 = 2N(0.611)$$

$$N^2 - 3.222N + 1 = 0$$

$$N = 2.872 \quad \text{or} \quad N = 0.348$$

$$N \text{ in } dB = 20 \log_{10} 2.872 = 9.16\ dB$$

or

$$N \text{ in } dB = 20 \log_{10} 0.348 = -9.16\ dB$$

Since attenuation cannot be negative,

$$N = 2.872 \text{ neper} = 9.16\ dB$$

Putting $N = 2.872$ in Eq. (i),

$$275 = R_0\left[\frac{(2.872)^2 - 1}{2(2.872)}\right]$$

$$R_0 = 217.92\ \Omega$$

**EXAMPLE 14.27**

*Design a π-type attenuator to give attenuation of 20 dB and characteristic resistance of 500 Ω.*

**Solution** $N(dB) = 20\,dB, \quad R_0 = 500\ \Omega$

$$N(dB) = 20 \log_{10} N$$

$$20 = 20 \log_{10} N$$

$$N = 10$$

$$R_1 = R_0\left(\frac{N^2-1}{2N}\right) = 500\left[\frac{(10)^2 - 1}{2\times 10}\right] = 2475\ \Omega$$

$$R_2 = \frac{R_0}{2}\left(\frac{N+1}{N-1}\right) = \frac{500}{2}\left(\frac{10+1}{10-1}\right) = 305.5\ \Omega$$

The π-type attenuator is shown in Fig. 14.62.

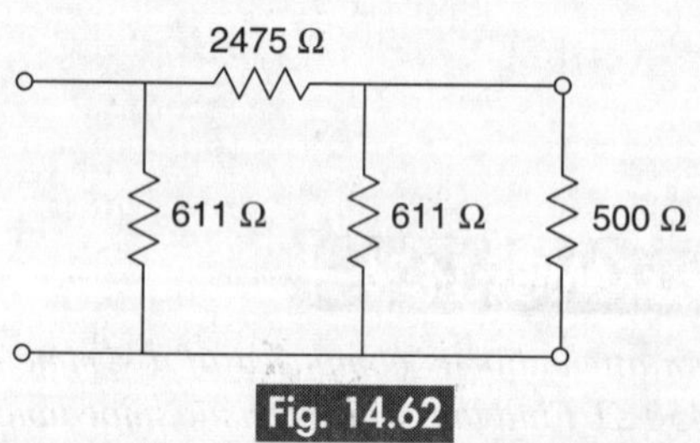

Fig. 14.62

## 14.18 LADDER-TYPE ATTENUATOR

LO 14.9

When a number of symmetrical *T*-or is π-type attenuators are connected in cascade to provide the attenuation in steps, the resultant network is termed ladder-type attenuator. Figure 14.63 shows a ladder-type attenuator with three identical and symmetrical π-sections connected in cascade.

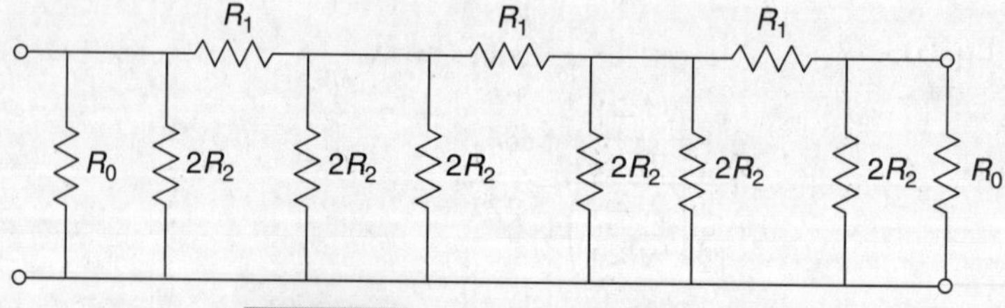

Fig. 14.63 *Ladder-type attenuator*

The output terminals are terminated with resistance $R_0$ which is the characteristic resistance of the network. The source-end also has resistance $R_0$ so that it is a matched network. The net attenuation is the sum of the attenuation of individual sections between the input and output terminals.

**EXAMPLE 14.28**

*Design a ladder-type attenuator for a load resistance of 500 Ω and an attenuation of 3 dB per step.*

**Solution**

$$N(dB) = 3\,dB, \quad R_0 = 500\ \Omega$$

$$N(dB) = 20\log_{10} N$$

$$3 = 20\log_{10} N$$

$$N = 1.413$$

$$R_1 = R_0\left(\frac{N^2-1}{2N}\right) = 500\left[\frac{(1.413)^2-1}{2\times 1.413}\right] = 176.32\ \Omega$$

$$R_2 = \frac{R_0}{2}\left(\frac{N+1}{N-1}\right) = \frac{500}{2}\left(\frac{1.413+1}{1.413-1}\right) = 1460.65\ \Omega$$

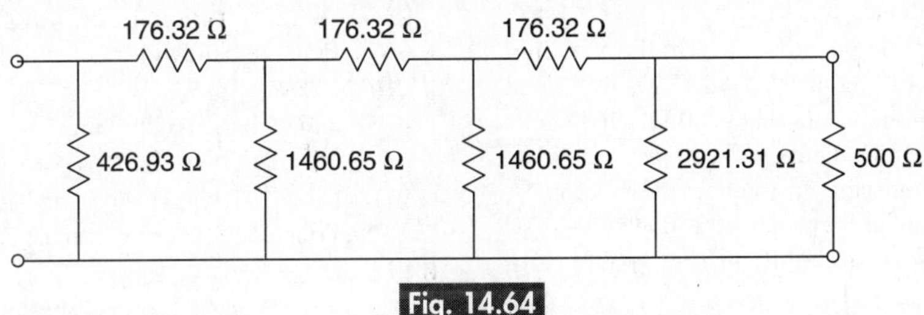


Fig. 14.64

## Theory Questions

14.1 What are different types of filters? **[LO 14.1]** ●○○

14.2 Derive the expressions for characteristic impedance and propagation constant of T network. **[LO 14.2]** ○○●

14.3 Derive the expressions for characteristic impedance and propagation constant of pi network. **[LO 14.3]** ○○●

14.4 Explain the general configuration and parameters of a constant-*k* low-pass filter. **[LO 14.4]** ○○●

14.5 What is a high-pass filter? Explain the general configuration and parameters of a constant-*k* high-pass filter. **[LO 14.4]** ○○●

14.6 Explain the design procedure of constant-*k* high-pass filters. **[LO 14.4]** ○○●

14.7 Draw the circuit diagram of a band-pass filter. Explain the design procedure of this filter in detail. **[LO 14.5]** ○○●

14.8 What is a band-pass filter? Explain the general configuration and various parameters of constant-*k* band-pass filter for *T* and $\pi$-sections. **[LO 14.5]** ○○●

14.9 What is an *m*-derived filter? Explain the general configuration and parameters of *m*-derived low-pass filter for *T* and $\pi$-sections **[LO 14.6]** ○○●

14.10 What are the steps involved in design of composite filter? **[LO 14.8]** ○●○

**14.11** Explain the design procedure of lattice attenuator. **[LO 14.9]** ○●○

**14.12** Explain the design procedure for *T*-type attenuator. **[LO 14.9]** ○●○

**14.13** Explain the design procedure for $\pi$-type attenuator. **[LO 14.9]** ○●○

## Practice Problems

**14.1** A *T*-section low-pass filter has a series inductance of 80 mH and a shunt capacitance of 0.022 μF. Find the cut-off frequency and nominal impedance. Also, design the equivalent $\pi$-section. ○●○

**14.2** Calculate the frequency of a constant-*k*, *T*-section low-pass filter having a cut-off frequency of 1000 Hz at which it has an attenuation of 10 *dB*. ●○○

**14.3** Design a low-pass constant-*k* (a) *T*-section, and (b) $\pi$-section filter with $f_c$ = 6 kHz and $R_O$ = 500 Ω. Calculate $\alpha$ and $\beta$ for the filters for $f$ = 10 kHz. Also, determine the frequency at which the attenuation is 10 *dB*. ○●○

**14.4** Design a $\pi$-section constant-*k* high-pass filter having a cut-off frequency $f_c$ = 8 kHz and nominal characteristic impedance $k$ = 600 Ω. Find (a) its characteristic impedance at a frequency of 12 kHz, (b) phase constant at frequency of 12 kHz, (c) attenuation at frequency of 800 Hz. ○●○

**14.5** Design a band-pass constant-*k* filter with $f_1$ = 2 kHz and $f_2$ = 3 kHz and $k$ = 500 Ω. ○●○

**14.6** Design a band-stop constant-*k* filter with cut-off frequencies of 8 kHz and 12 kHz and nominal characteristic impedance of 500 Ω. ○●○

**14.7** Design an *m*-derived *T*-section low-pass filter with cut-off frequency $f_c$ = 1 kHz, design impedance of 600 Ω and frequency of infinite attenuation of 1050 Hz. ○●○

**14.8** Design an *m*-derived high-pass *T*-section filter having a design impedance of 600 Ω, cut-off frequency of 5 kHz and $m$ = 0.35. Also, determine the frequency of infinite attenuation. ○●○

**14.9** In a constant-*k* band-pass filter, the ratio of capacitance in the shunt and series arms is 50:1 and the resonant frequency of both arms is 1000 Hz. Find the bandwidth of the filter. ○●○

**14.10** Design a symmetrical lattice attenuator to have characteristic impedance of 800 Ω and attenuation of 20 *dB*. ○●○

**14.11** Design a *T*-type attenuator to have a characteristic resistance of 200 Ω and attenuation of 20 *dB*. ○●○

**14.12** Design a $\pi$-type attenuator to give 20 *dB* attenuation and characteristic impedance of 100 Ω. ○●○

## ANSWERS TO PRACTICE PROBLEMS

**14.1** $f_c = 7.587$ kHz, $k = 1.907$ kΩ, $L = 80$ mH, $\frac{C}{2} = 0.011$ μF

**14.2** $f = 1170$ Hz

**14.3** $\alpha = 2.2$ neper, $\beta = 1.46$ radians, $\beta = \pi$ at 10 kHz $T \rightarrow \frac{L}{2} = 13.25$ mH, $C = 0.106$ μF $\pi \rightarrow L = 26.5$ mH, $\frac{C}{2} = 0.053$ μF, $f = 7$ kHz

**14.4** $L = 5.971$ mH, $C = 0.016$ μF, $Z_{O\pi} = 805$ Ω, $\beta = 83.6°$, $\alpha = 5$ nepers

**14.5** $L_1 = 159$ mH, $C_1 = 0.026$ μF, $L_2 = 20.8$ mH, $C_2 = 0.637$ μF

**14.6** $L_1 = 6.6$ mH, $C_1 = 0.0398$ μF, $L_2 = 9.9$ mH, $C_2 = 0.0265$ μF

**14.7** $L = 191.08$ mH, $C = 0.53$ μF, $m = 0.3$

**14.8** $\frac{2C}{m} = 0.148$ μF, $\frac{L}{m} = 27.28$ mH, $\frac{4m}{1-m^2}C = 0.0414$ μF, $f_\infty = 4.684$ kHz

**14.9** 282.84 Hz

**14.10** 654.55 Ω, 977.78 Ω

**14.11** 163.6 Ω, 40.4 Ω

**14.12** 495 Ω, 122.22 Ω

# Objective-Type Questions

## From GATE and Other Competitive Examinations

**14.1** A 500 Ω is resistance attenuator is to have an attenuation of 20 *dB*. The resistances of the series and shunt arms of the lattice network, respectively are ○●○

(a) 400 Ω, 500 Ω approx.
(b) 410 Ω, 510 Ω approx.
(c) 410 Ω, 610 Ω approx.
(d) none of the above

**14.2** For the design of low-pass prototype filter Fig. 14.65 of with load resistance $R_L = 1\ \Omega$ and angular frequency $\omega = 1$ rad/s the values of $L$ and $C$ would be ○●○

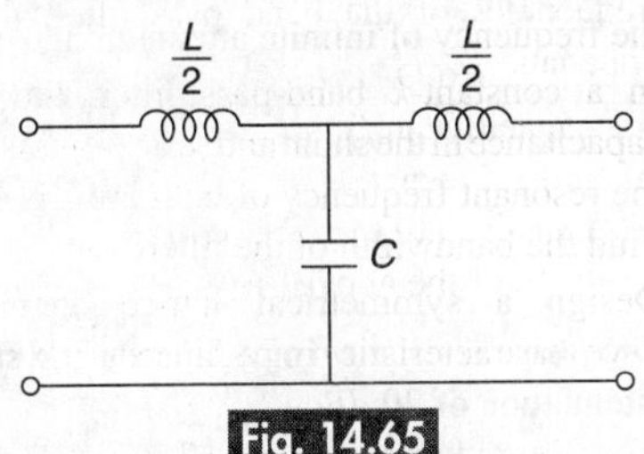

Fig. 14.65

(a) 1 H and I F (b) 1 H and 2 F
(c) 2 H and I F (d) 2 H and 2 F

**14.3** The passband of a typical filter network with $Z_1$ and $Z_2$ as the series and shunt-arm impedances is characterised by ○○●

(a) $-1 < \frac{Z_1}{4Z_2} < 0$ (b) $-1 < \frac{Z_1}{4Z_2} < 1$

(c) $0 < \frac{Z_1}{4Z_2} < 1$ (d) none of the above

**14.4** In an *m*-derived low-pass filter, the value of *m* is ○○●

(a) $\sqrt{1-\left(\frac{f_\infty}{f_c}\right)^2}$ (b) $\sqrt{1-\left(\frac{f_c}{f_\infty}\right)^2}$

(c) $\sqrt{1+\left(\frac{f_\infty}{f_c}\right)^2}$ (d) $\sqrt{1+\left(\frac{f_c}{f_\infty}\right)^2}$

**14.5** For the lattice-type attenuater shown in Fig. 14.66, the characteristic impedance $R_0$ is ○○●

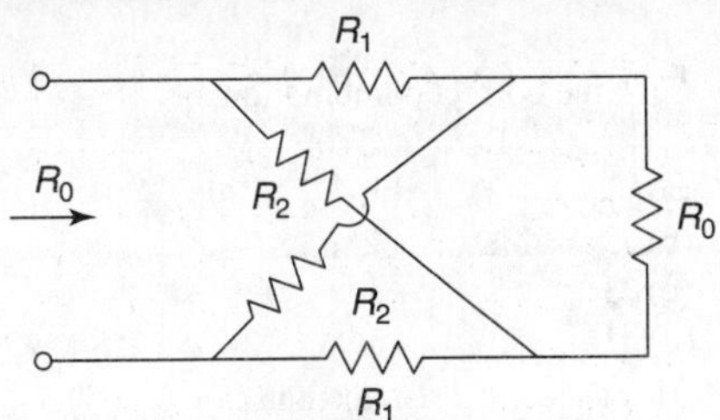

Fig. 14.66

(a) $\frac{R_1 + R_2}{2}$ (b) $\frac{2R_1R_2}{R_1 + R_2}$

(c) $\sqrt{R_1R_2}$ (d) $R_1 + \frac{R_2}{0}$

**14.6** A T-type attenuator is designed for an attenuation of 40 dB and terminating resistance of 75 ohms. Which of the following values represent full series arm $R_1$ and shunt arm $R_2$? ○○●

(a) $R_1 \simeq 147\ \Omega$ (b) $R_1 \simeq 153\ \Omega$

(c) $R \simeq 1.5\ \Omega$ (d) $R_2 \simeq 3750\ \Omega$

Select the correct answer from the codes given below:

(a) 1 and 3 (b) 1 and 4
(c) 2 and 3 (d) 2 and 4

**14.7** The application of the bisection theorem finds out an equivalent lattice network if the original network is ○●○

(a) symmetrical and balanced only
(b) unsymmetrical and balanced only
(c) symmetrical, balanced and unbalanced only
(d) symmetrical and unbalanced only

**14.8** The attenuation of an attenuator is 20 dB. Its attenuation constant *N* is ○●○

(a) 1 (b) 2
(c) 10 (d) 20

**14.9** $Z_1$ and $Z_2$ are the total series and shunt impedances of a T or π-filter. Consider the following zones of operation of filters and the conditions on the impedances ○●○

(a) Pass band 1. $\frac{Z_1}{4Z_2} < -1$

(b) Stop band 2. $\frac{Z_1}{4Z_2} = -1$

(c) Transition band 3. $-1 < \frac{Z_1}{4Z_2} < 0$

Tick the correct combination:

| | A | B | C |
|---|---|---|---|
| (a) | 1 | 2 | 3 |
| (b) | 3 | 1 | 2 |
| (c) | 3 | 2 | 1 |
| (d) | 2 | 3 | 1 |

**14.10** Tick the correct statement in case of a filter. ○●○

(a) Characteristic impedance is resistive in stop band.

(b) Characteristic impedance is reactive in pass band.

(c) Characteristic impedance is resistive in pass band.

(d) None of the above

**14.11** If $L$ is the total series inductance and $C$ the total shunt capacitance of a $T$ or $\pi$-type low-pass filter, the pass-band frequency range of the filter is given as ○○●

(a) 0 to $\frac{1}{2\pi\sqrt{L_C}}$ Hz

(b) 0 to $\frac{1}{\pi\sqrt{L_C}}$ Hz

(c) 0 to $\frac{2}{\pi\sqrt{L_C}}$ Hz

(d) 0 to $\frac{1}{4\pi\sqrt{L_C}}$ Hz

**14.12** If $C$ is the total series capacitance, $L$ is the total shunt inductance of a $T$ or $\pi$-type high-pass filter, the frequency range for the stop band of the filter is ○○●

(a) 0 to $\frac{1}{2\pi\sqrt{L_C}}$ Hz

(b) 0 to $\frac{1}{\pi\sqrt{L_C}}$ Hz

(c) 0 to $\frac{2}{\pi\sqrt{L_C}}$ Hz

(d) 0 to $\frac{2}{4\pi\sqrt{L_C}}$ Hz

**14.13** If $f_1$ and $f_2$ are the lower and upper cut-off frequencies of the band pass filter, the series impedance $Z_1$ is ○●○

(a) capacitive at $f_1$

(b) inductive at $f_1$

(c) resistive at $f_2$

(d) none of the above

**14.14** The phase constant $\beta$ of a filter during stop band is ○●○

(a) Zero radian (b) 2

(c) $\pi$ (d) $2\pi$

## ANSWERS TO OBJECTIVE-TYPE QUESTIONS

**14.1** (c) **14.2** (d) **14.3** (a) **14.4** (b) **14.5** (c) **14.6** (a) **14.7** (c)
**14.8** (c) **14.9** (b) **14.10** (c) **14.11** (b) **14.12** (d) **14.13** (a) **14.14** (c)

# LTspice Section

## EXAMPLE 14.1

*Determine the response of low pass filter shown in Fig. 14.67.*

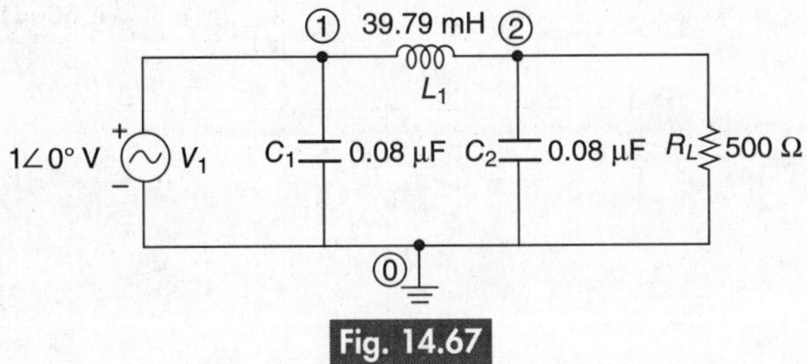


Fig. 14.67

**Solution**

```
*Low pass filter

V1 1 0 AC 1 0
C1 1 0 0.08U
L1 1 2 39.79M
C2 2 0 0.08U
RL 2 0 500
.AC DEC 500 1 10K
.PLOT AC V(2)
.END
```

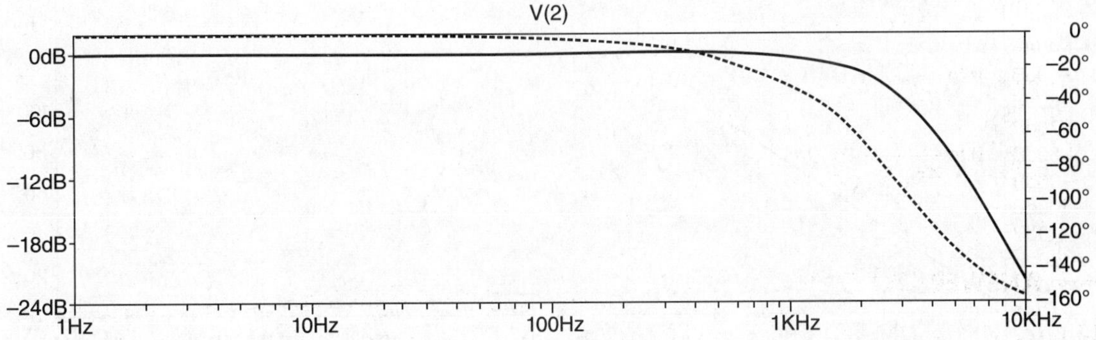

## EXAMPLE 14.2

*Determine the response of high pass filter shown in Fig. 14.68.*

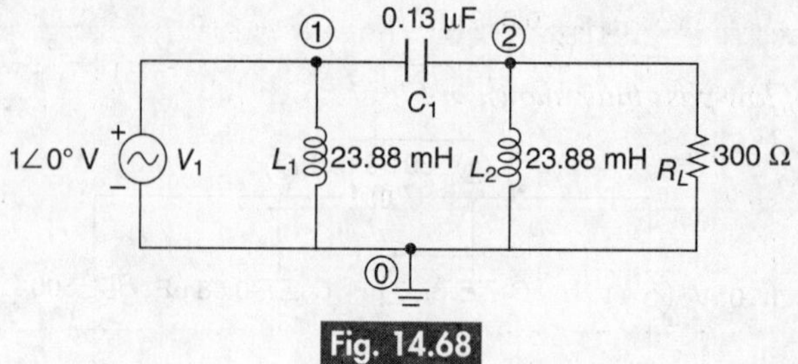


Fig. 14.68

**Solution**

```
*High pass filter

V1 1 0 AC 1 0
L1 1 0 23.88M
C1 1 2 0.13U
L2 2 0 23.88M
RL 2 0 300
.AC DEC 500 1 1000K
.PLOT AC V(2)
.END
```

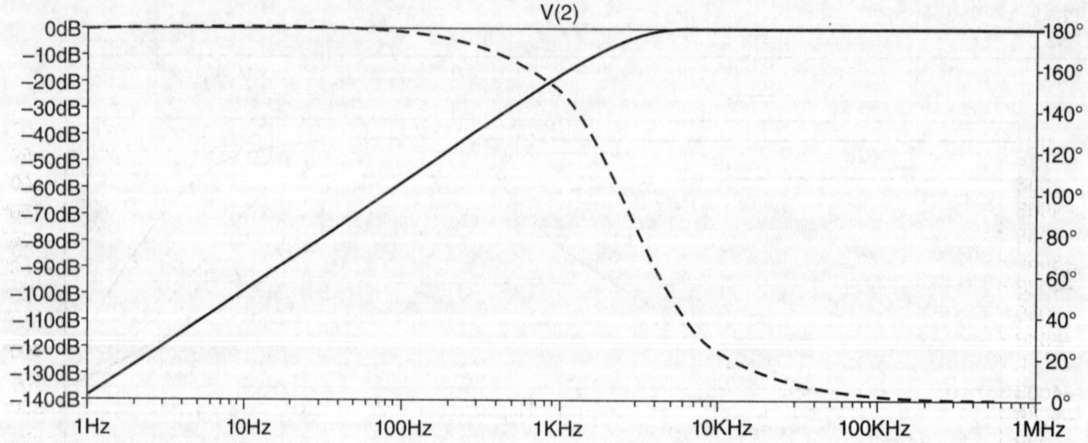

## EXAMPLE 14.3

*Determine the response of band-pass filter shown in Fig. 14.69.*

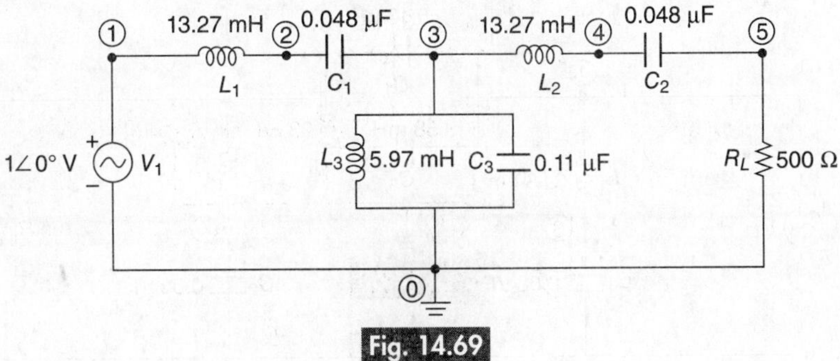


Fig. 14.69

**Solution**

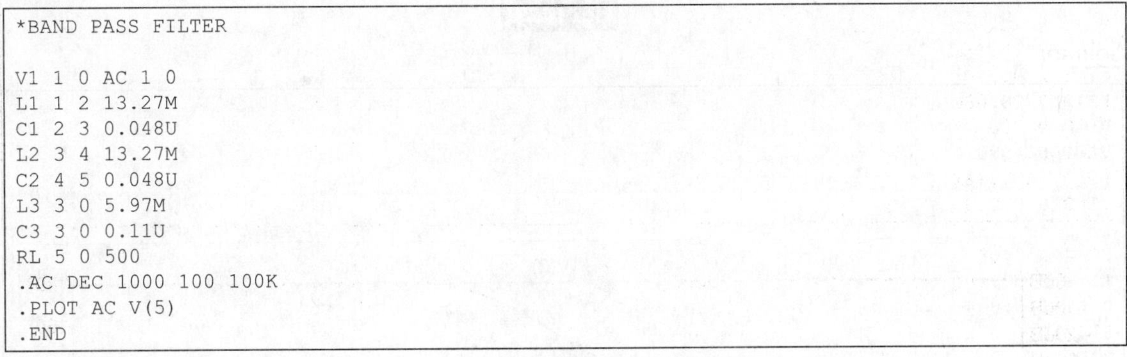

```
*BAND PASS FILTER

V1 1 0 AC 1 0
L1 1 2 13.27M
C1 2 3 0.048U
L2 3 4 13.27M
C2 4 5 0.048U
L3 3 0 5.97M
C3 3 0 0.11U
RL 5 0 500
.AC DEC 1000 100 100K
.PLOT AC V(5)
.END
```

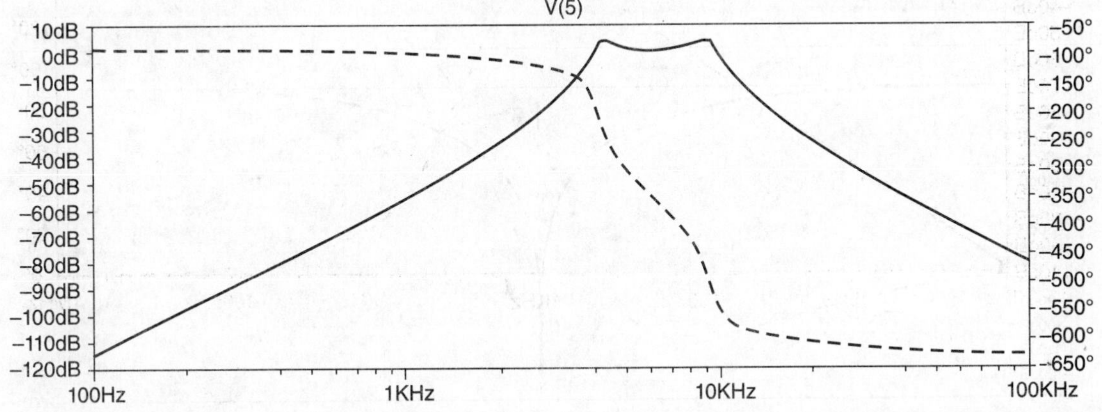

## EXAMPLE 14.4

*Determine the response of band-stop filter shown in Fig. 14.70.*

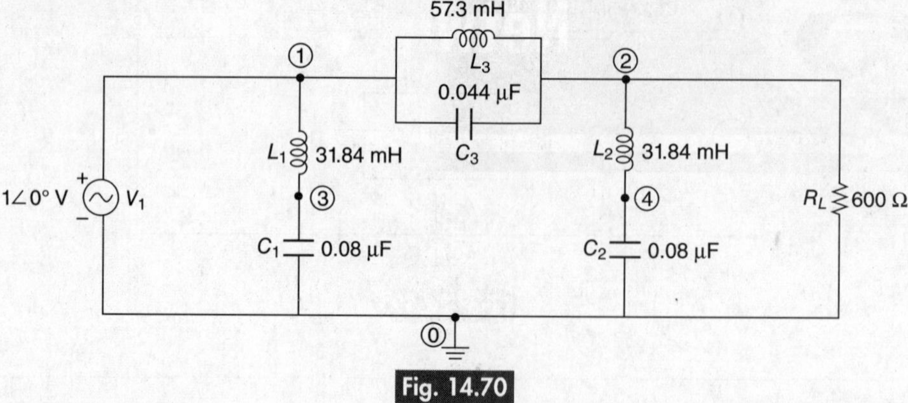


Fig. 14.70

### Solution

```
*BAND STOP FILTER

V1 1 0 AC 1 0
L1 1 3 31.84M
C1 3 0 0.08U
L2 2 4 31.84M
C2 4 0 0.08U
L3 1 2 57.3M
C3 1 2 0.044U
RL 2 0 600
.AC DEC 1000 1k 10K
.PLOT AC V(2)
.END
```

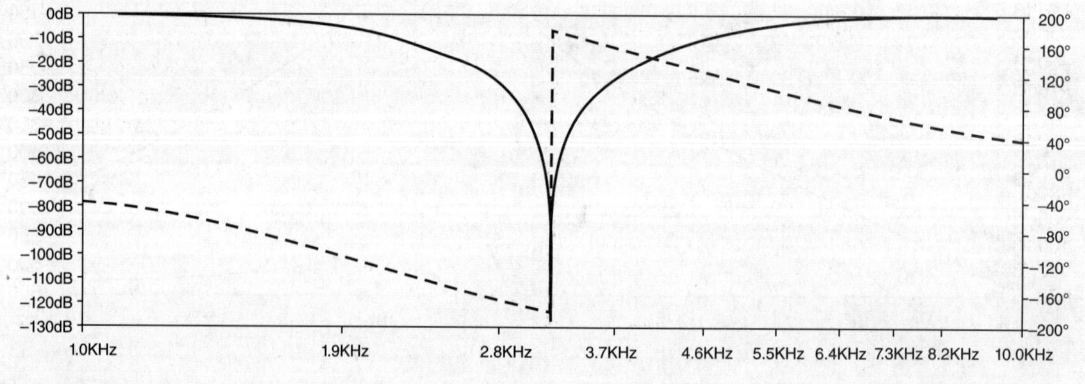

CHAPTER 15

# Network Synthesis

## LEARNING OBJECTIVES

**After studying this chapter, you should be able to:**

- **LO 15.1** Describe Hurwitz polynomials, their properties and conditions
- **LO 15.2** Explain positive real functions, their properties and conditions
- **LO 15.3** Discuss elementary synthesis concepts and explain four removal operations
- **LO 15.4** Explain Foster and Cauer forms of realising *LC* functions, and their properties
- **LO 15.5** Explain Foster and Cauer forms of realising *RC* functions, and their properties
- **LO 15.6** Explain Foster and Cauer forms of realising *RL* functions, and their properties

## INTRODUCTION

In the study of electrical networks, broadly there are two topics: 'Network Analysis' and 'Network Synthesis'. Any network consists of excitation, response and network functions. In network analysis, network and excitation are given, whereas the response has to be determined. In network synthesis, excitation and response are given, and the network has to be determined. Thus, in network synthesis, we are concerned with the realisation of a network for a given excitation–response characteristic. Also, there is one major difference between analysis and synthesis. In analysis, there is a unique solution to the problem. But in synthesis, the solution is not unique and many networks can be realised.

The first step in synthesis procedure is to determine whether the network function can be realised as a physical passive network.

## 15.1 HURWITZ POLYNOMIALS

LO 15.1

Describe Hurwitz polynomials, their properties and conditions

A polynomial $P(s)$ is said to be Hurwitz if the following conditions are satisfied:

(a) $P(s)$ is real when $s$ is real.

(b) The roots of $P(s)$ have real parts which are zero or negative.

### Properties of Hurwitz Polynomials

1. All the coefficients in the polynomial

$$P(s) = a_n s^n + a_{n-1} s^{n-1} + \cdots + a_1 s + a_0$$

are positive. A polynomial may not have any missing terms between the highest and the lowest order unless all even or all odd terms are missing.

2. The roots of odd and even parts of the polynomial $P(s)$ lie on the $j\omega$-axis only.
3. If the polynomial $P(s)$ is either even or odd, the roots of polynomial $P(s)$ lie on the $j\omega$-axis only.
4. All the quotients are positive in the continued fraction expansion of the ratio of odd to even parts or even to odd parts of the polynomial $P(s)$.
5. If the polynomial $P(s)$ is expressed as $W(s)\ P_1(s)$, then $P(s)$ is Hurwitz if $W(s)$ and $P_1(s)$ are Hurwitz.
6. If the ratio of the polynomial $P(s)$ and its derivative $P'(s)$ gives a continued fraction expansion with all positive coefficients then the polynomial $P(s)$ is Hurwitz.

This property helps in checking a polynomial for Hurwitz if the polynomial is an even or odd function because in such a case, it is not possible to obtain the continued fraction expansion.

**EXAMPLE 15.1** ●○○

*State for each case, whether the polynomial is Hurwitz or not. Give reasons in each case.*

*(a)* $s^4 + 4s^3 + 3s + 2$

*(b)* $s^6 + 5s^5 + 4s^4 - 3s^3 + 2s^2 + s + 3$

**Solution** (a) In the given polynomial, the term $s^2$ is missing and it is neither an even nor an odd polynomial. Hence, it is not Hurwitz.

(b) Polynomial $s^6 + 5s^5 + 4s^4 - 3s^3 + 2s^2 + s + 3$ is not Hurwitz as it has a term $(-3s^3)$ which has a negative coefficient.

**EXAMPLE 15.2** ○●○

*Test whether the polynomial* $P(s) = s^4 + s^3 + 5s^2 + 3s + 4$ *is Hurwitz.*

**Solution** Even part of $P(s) = m(s) = s^4 + 5s^2 + 4$

Odd part of $P(s) = n(s) = s^3 + 3s$

$$Q(s) = \frac{m(s)}{n(s)}$$

**Note** Difficulty Level ●○○ — Easy; ○●○ — Medium; ○○● — Difficult

By continued fraction expansion,

$$
\begin{array}{l}
s^3+3s\overline{)\,s^4+5s^2+4\,}\left(s\right. \\
\qquad\quad \underline{s^4+3s^2} \\
\qquad\quad 2s^2+4\overline{)\,s^3+3s\,}\left(\frac{1}{2}s\right. \\
\qquad\qquad\qquad \underline{s^3+2s} \\
\qquad\qquad\qquad\quad s\overline{)\,2s^2+4\,}\left(2s\right. \\
\qquad\qquad\qquad\qquad \underline{2s^2} \\
\qquad\qquad\qquad\qquad\quad 4\overline{)\,s\,}\left(\frac{1}{4}s\right. \\
\qquad\qquad\qquad\qquad\qquad \underline{s} \\
\qquad\qquad\qquad\qquad\qquad 0
\end{array}
$$

Since all the quotient terms are positive, $P(s)$ is Hurwitz.

## EXAMPLE 15.3

*Test whether the polynomial* $P(s) = s^3 + 4s^2 + 5s + 2$ *is Hurwitz.*

**Solution** Even part of $P(s) = m(s) = 4s^2 + 2$

Odd part of $P(s)$ $n(s) = s^3 + 5s$

The continued fraction expansion can be obtained by dividing $n(s)$ by $m(s)$ as $n(s)$ is of higher order than $m(s)$.

$$Q(s) = \frac{n(s)}{m(s)}$$

$$
\begin{array}{l}
4s^2+2\overline{)\,s^3+5s\,}\left(\frac{1}{4}s\right. \\
\qquad\quad \underline{s^3+\frac{2}{4}s} \\
\qquad\quad \frac{9}{2}s\overline{)\,4s^2+2\,}\left(\frac{8}{9}s\right. \\
\qquad\qquad\quad \underline{4s^2} \\
\qquad\qquad\quad 2\overline{)\,\frac{9}{2}s\,}\left(\frac{9}{4}s\right. \\
\qquad\qquad\qquad \underline{\frac{9}{2}s} \\
\qquad\qquad\qquad 0
\end{array}
$$

Since all the quotient terms are positive, $P(s)$ is Hurwitz.

**EXAMPLE 15.4**

*Test whether the polynomial* $P(s) = s^4 + s^3 + 3s^2 + 2s + 12$ *is Hurwitz.*

**Solution** Even part of $P(s) = m(s) = s^4 + 3s^2 + 12$

Odd part of $P(s) = n(s) = s^3 + 2s$

$$Q(s) = \frac{m(s)}{n(s)}$$

By continued fraction expansion,

$$
\begin{array}{l}
s^3 + 2s\,\big)\, s^4 + 3s^2 + 12\,\big(\, s \\
\qquad\quad s^4 + 2s^2 \\
\qquad\quad \overline{\qquad\qquad s^2 + 12\,\big)\, s^3 + 2s\,\big(\, s} \\
\qquad\qquad\qquad\qquad\quad s^3 + 12s \\
\qquad\qquad\qquad\qquad\quad \overline{\qquad -10s\,\big)\, s^2 + 12\,\big(\, -\frac{1}{10}s} \\
\qquad\qquad\qquad\qquad\qquad\qquad\quad s^2 \\
\qquad\qquad\qquad\qquad\qquad\qquad\quad \overline{\quad 12\,\big)\, -10s\,\big(\, -\frac{10}{12}s} \\
\qquad\qquad\qquad\qquad\qquad\qquad\qquad\qquad -10s \\
\qquad\qquad\qquad\qquad\qquad\qquad\qquad\qquad \overline{\qquad 0}
\end{array}
$$

Since two quotient terms are negative, $P(s)$ is not Hurwitz.

**EXAMPLE 15.5**

*Prove that polynomial* $P(s) = s^4 + s^3 + 2s^2 + 3s + 2$ *is not Hurwitz.*

**Solution** Even part of $P(s) = m(s) = s^4 + 2s^2 + 2$

Odd part of $P(s) = n(s) = s^3 + 3s$

$$Q(s) = \frac{m(s)}{n(s)}$$

By continued fraction expansion,

$$
\begin{array}{l}
s^3 + 3s)\, s^4 + 2s^2 + 2\ (s \\
\qquad\quad s^4 + 3s^2 \\
\qquad\quad \overline{\qquad\qquad -s^2 + 2)\, s^3 + 3s\,(-s} \\
\qquad\qquad\qquad\qquad\quad s^3 - 2s \\
\qquad\qquad\qquad\qquad\quad \overline{\qquad\qquad}
\end{array}
$$

$$5s\,\overline{)\,-s^2+2\,}\left(-\frac{1}{5}s\right.$$
$$\underline{-s^2}$$
$$2\,\overline{)\,5s\,}\left(\frac{5}{2}s\right.$$
$$\underline{5s}$$
$$0$$

Since two quotient terms are negative, $P(s)$ is not Hurwitz.

## EXAMPLE 15.6

*Prove that polynomial* $P(s) = 2s^4 + 5s^3 + 6s^2 + 3s + 1$ *is Hurwitz.*

**Solution** Even part of $P(s) = m(s) = 2s^4 + 6s^2 + 1$

Odd part of $P(s) = n(s) = 5s^3 + 3s$

$$Q(s) = \frac{m(s)}{n(s)}$$

By continued fraction expansion,

$$5s^3+3s\,\overline{)\,2s^4+6s^2+1\,}\left(\frac{2}{5}s\right.$$
$$\underline{2s^4+\frac{6}{5}s^2}$$
$$\frac{24}{5}s^2+1\,\overline{)\,5s^3+3s\,}\left(\frac{25}{24}s\right.$$
$$\underline{5s^3+\frac{25}{24}s}$$
$$\frac{47}{24}s\,\overline{)\,\frac{24}{5}s^2+1\,}\left(\frac{576}{235}s\right.$$
$$\underline{\frac{24}{5}s^2}$$
$$1\,\overline{)\,\frac{47}{24}s\,}\left(\frac{24}{47}s\right.$$
$$\underline{\frac{47}{24}s}$$
$$0$$

Since all the quotient terms are positive, the polynomial $P(s)$ is Hurwitz.

## EXAMPLE 15.7

*Test whether the polynomial* $P(s)=s^4+7s^3+6s^2+21s+8$ *is Hurwitz.*

**Solution** Even part of $P(s)=m(s)=s^4+6s^2+8$

Odd part of $P(s)=n(s)=7s^3+21s$

$$Q(s)=\frac{m(s)}{n(s)}$$

By continued fraction expansion,

$$7s^3+21s\,\overline{)\,s^4+6s^2+8\,}\left(\frac{1}{7}s\right.$$
$$\underline{s^4+3s^2}$$
$$3s^2+8\,\overline{)\,7s^3+21s\,}\left(\frac{7}{3}s\right.$$
$$\underline{7s^3+\frac{56}{3}s}$$
$$\frac{7}{3}s\,\overline{)\,3s^2+8\,}\left(\frac{9}{7}s\right.$$
$$\underline{3s^2}$$
$$8\,\overline{)\,\frac{7}{3}s\,}\left(\frac{7}{24}s\right.$$
$$\underline{\frac{7}{3}s}$$
$$0$$

Since all the quotient terms are positive, the polynomial $P(s)$ is Hurwitz.

## EXAMPLE 15.8

*Check whether* $P(s)=s^4+5s^3+5s^2+4s+10$ *is Hurwitz.*

**Solution** Even part of $P(s)=m(s)=s^4+5s^2+10$

Odd part of $P(s)=n(s)=5s^3+4s$

$$Q(s)=\frac{m(s)}{n(s)}$$

By continued fraction expansion,

$$5s^3+4s\,\overline{)\,s^4+5s^2+10\,}\left(\frac{1}{5}s\right.$$
$$\underline{s^4+\frac{4}{5}s^2}$$

$$\frac{21}{5}s^2+10\overline{\Big)\,5s^3+4s\Big(\frac{25}{21}s}$$
$$5s^3+\frac{250}{21}s$$
$$-\frac{166}{21}s\overline{\Big)\,\frac{21}{5}s^2+10\Big(-\frac{441}{830}s}$$
$$\frac{21}{5}s^2$$
$$10\overline{\Big)\,-\frac{166}{21}s\Big(-\frac{166}{210}s}$$
$$-\frac{166}{21}s$$
$$0$$

Since the last two quotient terms are negative, the polynomial $P(s)$ is not Hurwitz.

## EXAMPLE 15.9

*Test whether the polynomial $s^5+3s^3+2s$ is Hurwitz.*

**Solution** Since the given polynomial contains odd functions only, it is not possible to perform a continued fraction expansion.

$$P'(s)=\frac{d}{ds}P(s)=5s^4+9s^2+2$$

$$Q(s)=\frac{P(s)}{P'(s)}$$

By continued fraction expansion,

$$5s^4+9s^2+2\overline{\Big)\,s^5+3s^3+2s\Big(\frac{1}{5}s}$$
$$s^5+\frac{9}{5}s^3+\frac{2}{5}s$$
$$\frac{6}{5}s^3+\frac{8}{5}s\overline{\Big)\,5s^4+9s^2+2\Big(\frac{25}{6}s}$$
$$5s^4+\frac{20}{3}s^2$$
$$\frac{7}{3}s^2+2\overline{\Big)\,\frac{6}{5}s^3+\frac{8}{5}s\Big(\frac{18}{35}s}$$
$$\frac{6}{5}s^3+\frac{36}{35}s$$

$$\frac{20}{35}s\overline{\Big)\frac{7}{3}s^2+2}\Big(\frac{49}{12}s$$

$$\frac{7}{3}s^2$$

$$2\overline{\Big)\frac{20}{35}s}\Big(\frac{10}{35}s$$

$$\frac{20}{35}s$$

$$0$$

Since all the quotient terms are positive, the polynomial $P(s)$ is Hurwitz.

**EXAMPLE 15.10**

*Test whether the polynomial P(s) is Hurwitz.*

$$P(s) = s^5 + s^3 + s$$

**Solution** Since the given polynomial contains odd functions only, it is not possible to perform continued fraction expansion.

$$P'(s) = \frac{d}{ds}P(s) = 5s^4 + 3s^2 + 1$$

$$Q(s) = \frac{P(s)}{P'(s)}$$

By continued fraction expansion,

$$5s^4 + 3s^2 + 1\overline{\Big)s^5 + s^3 + s}\Big(\frac{1}{5}s$$

$$s^5 + \frac{3}{5}s^3 + \frac{1}{5}s$$

$$\frac{2}{5}s^3 + \frac{4}{5}s\overline{\Big)5s^4 + 3s^2 + 1}\Big(\frac{25}{2}s$$

$$5s^4 + 10s^2$$

$$-7s^2 + 1\overline{\Big)\frac{2}{5}s^3 + \frac{4}{5}s}\Big(-\frac{2}{35}s$$

$$\frac{2}{5}s^3 - \frac{2}{35}s$$

$$\frac{26}{35}s\overline{\Big)-7s^2 + 1}\Big(-\frac{245}{26}s$$

$$-7s^2$$

$$1\overline{)\frac{26}{35}s}\left(\frac{26}{35}s\right.$$

$$\frac{\frac{26}{35}s}{0}$$

Since the third and fourth quotient terms are negative, $P(s)$ is not Hurwitz.

## EXAMPLE 15.11

*Test the polynomial P(s) of Hurwitz property.*

$$P(s) = s^6 + 3s^5 + 8s^4 + 15s^3 + 17s^2 + 12s + 4$$

**Solution** Even part of $P(s) = m(s) = s^6 + 8s^4 + 17s^2 + 4$

Odd part of $P(s) = n(s) = 3s^5 + 15s^3 + 12s$

$$Q(s) = \frac{m(s)}{n(s)}$$

By continued fraction expansion,

$$3s^5 + 15s^3 + 12s\overline{)s^6 + 8s^4 + 17s^2 + 4}\left(\frac{1}{3}s\right.$$

$$\frac{s^6 + 5s^4 + 4s^2}{3s^4 + 13s^2 + 4\overline{)3s^5 + 15s^3 + 12s}\left(s\right.}$$

$$\frac{3s^5 + 13s^3 + 4s}{2s^3 + 8s\overline{)3s^4 + 13s^2 + 4}\left(\frac{3}{2}s\right.}$$

$$\frac{3s^4 + 12s^2}{s^2 + 4\overline{)2s^3 + 8s}\left(2s\right.}$$

$$\frac{2s^3 + 8s}{0}$$

The division has terminated abruptly (i.e., the number of partial quotients (that is four) is not equal to the order of polynomial (that is six) with common factor $(s^2 + 4)$.

$$P(s) = s^6 + 3s^5 + 8s^4 + 15s^3 + 17s^2 + 12s + 4 = (s^2 + 4)(s^4 + 3s^3 + 4s^2 + 3s + 1)$$

If both the factors are Hurwitz, $P(s)$ will be Hurwitz.

Let $$P_1(s) = s^2 + 4$$

Since it contains only even functions, we have to find the continued fraction expansion of $\frac{P_1(s)}{P_1'(s)}$.

$$P_1'(s) = 2s$$

$$\frac{P_1(s)}{P_1'(s)} = \frac{s^2+4}{2s} = \frac{s^2}{2s} + \frac{4}{2s} = \frac{s}{2} + \frac{1}{\frac{s}{2}}$$

Since all the quotient terms are positive, $P_1(s)$ is Hurwitz.

Now, let
$$P_2(s) = s^4 + 3s^3 + 4s^2 + 3s + 1$$
$$m_2(s) = s^4 + 4s^2 + 1$$
$$n_2(s) = 3s^3 + 3s$$

By continued fraction expansion,

$$3s^3 + 3s\,\big)\, s^4 + 4s^2 + 1\,\big(\, \frac{1}{3}s$$
$$\underline{s^4 + s^2}$$
$$3s^2 + 1\,)\, 3s^3 + 3s\,(\, s$$
$$\underline{3s^3 + s}$$
$$2s\,\big)\, 3s^2 + 1\,\big(\, \frac{3}{2}s$$
$$\underline{3s^2}$$
$$1)\, 2s\,(\, 2s$$
$$\underline{2s}$$
$$0$$

Since all the quotient terms are positive, $P_2(s)$ is Hurwitz.

Hence, $P(s) = (s^2+4)(s^4+3s^3+4s^2+3s+1)$ is Hurwitz.

**EXAMPLE 15.12**

*Test whether the polynomial* $P(s) = s^7 + 2s^6 + 2s^5 + s^4 + 4s^3 + 8s^2 + 8s + 4$ *is Hurwitz.*

**Solution** Even part of $P(s) = m(s) = 2s^6 + s^4 + 8s^2 + 4$

Odd part of $P(s) = n(s) = s^7 + 2s^5 + 4s^3 + 8s$

$$Q(s) = \frac{n(s)}{m(s)}$$

By continued fraction expansion,

$$2s^6+s^4+8s^2+4\overline{\big)\,s^7+2s^5+4s^3+8s\,}\Big(\frac{1}{2}s$$
$$\underline{s^7+\frac{1}{2}s^5+4s^3+2s}$$
$$\frac{3}{2}s^5\qquad+6s\,\overline{\big)\,2s^6+s^4+8s^2+4\,}\Big(\frac{4}{3}s$$
$$\underline{2s^6\qquad+8s^2}$$
$$s^4\qquad+4\,\overline{\big)\,\frac{3}{2}s^5+6s\,}\Big(\frac{3}{2}s$$
$$\underline{\frac{3}{2}s^5+6s}$$
$$0$$

Since the division has terminated abruptly it indicates a common factor $s^4+4$. The polynomial can be written as

$$P(s)=(s^4+4)(s^3+2s^2+2s+1)$$

If both the factor are Hurwitz, $P(s)$ will be Hurwitz.

In the polynomial $(s^4+4)$, the terms $s^3$, $s^2$ and $s$ are missing. Hence, it is not Hurwitz.

Therefore, $P(s)$ is not Hurwitz.

## EXAMPLE 15.13

*Test whether the polynomial $2s^6+s^5+13s^4+6s^3+56s^2+25s+25$ is Hurwitz.*

**Solution** Even part of $P(s)=m(s)=2s^6+13s^4+56s^2+25$

Odd part of $P(s)=n(s)=s^5+6s^3+25s$

$$Q(s)=\frac{m(s)}{n(s)}$$

By continued fraction expansion,

$$s^5+6s^3+25s)2s^6+13s^4+56s^2+25(2s$$
$$\underline{2s^6+12s^4+50s^2}$$
$$s^4+6s^2\ +25)s^5+6s^3+25s(s$$
$$\underline{s^5+6s^3+25s}$$
$$0$$

The division has terminated abruptly.

$$P(s)=2s^6+s^5+13s^4+6s^3+56s^2+25s+25=(s^4+6s^2+25)\,(2s^2+s+1)$$

Let $$P_1(s) = s^4 + 6s^2 + 25$$

Since $P_1(s)$ contains only even functions, we have to find the continued fraction expansion of $\dfrac{P_1(s)}{P_1'(s)}$.

$$P_1'(s) = 4s^3 + 12s$$

By continued fraction expansion,

$$\begin{array}{l}
4s^3 + 12s\,\big)\; s^4 + 6s^2 + 25 \;\big(\tfrac{1}{4}s \\
\qquad\qquad\quad \underline{s^4 + 3s^2} \\
\qquad\qquad\quad 3s^2 + 25\,\big)\; 4s^3 + 12s \;\big(\tfrac{4}{3}s \\
\qquad\qquad\qquad\qquad\quad \underline{4s^3 + \tfrac{100}{3}s} \\
\qquad\qquad\qquad\qquad\quad -\tfrac{64}{3}s\,\big)\; 3s^2 + 25 \;\big(-\tfrac{9}{64}s \\
\qquad\qquad\qquad\qquad\qquad\qquad \underline{3s^2} \\
\qquad\qquad\qquad\qquad\qquad\qquad 25\,\big)\; -\tfrac{64}{3}s \;\big(-\tfrac{64}{75}s \\
\qquad\qquad\qquad\qquad\qquad\qquad\quad \underline{-\tfrac{64}{3}s} \\
\qquad\qquad\qquad\qquad\qquad\qquad\qquad 0
\end{array}$$

Since two of the quotient terms are negative, $P_1(s)$ is not Hurwitz.

We need not test the other factor $(2s^2 + s + 1)$ for being Hurwitz.

Hence, $P(s)$ is not Hurwitz.

There is another method to test a Hurwitz polynomial. In this method, we construct the Routh–Hurwitz array for the required polynomial.

Let $$P(s) = a_n s^n + a_{n-1}s^{n-1} + a_{n-2}s^{n-2} + \ldots + a_1 s + a_0$$

The Routh–Hurwitz array is given by

$$\begin{array}{c|cccc}
s^n & a_n & a_{n-2} & a_{n-4} & \ldots \\
s^{n-1} & a_{n-1} & a_{n-3} & a_{n-5} & \ldots \\
s^{n-2} & b_n & b_{n-1} & b_{n-2} & \ldots \\
s^{n-3} & c_n & c_{n-1} & & \ldots \\
\cdot & \cdot & & & \\
\cdot & \cdot & & & \\
\cdot & \cdot & & & \\
\cdot & \cdot & & & \\
s^1 & \cdot & & & \\
s^0 & \cdot & & &
\end{array}$$

The coefficients of $s^n$ and $s^{n-1}$ rows are directly written from the given equation.

where
$$b_n = \frac{a_{n-1}a_{n-2} - a_n a_{n-3}}{a_{n-1}}$$

$$b_{n-1} = \frac{a_{n-1}a_{n-4} - a_n a_{n-5}}{a_{n-1}}$$

$$b_{n-2} = \frac{a_{n-1}a_{n-6} - a_n a_{n-7}}{a_{n-1}}$$

$$c_n = \frac{b_n a_{n-3} - a_{n-1}b_{n-1}}{b_n}$$

$$c_{n-1} = \frac{b_n a_{n-5} - a_{n-1}b_{n-2}}{b_n}$$

Hence, for polynomial $P(s)$ to be Hurwitz, there should not be any sign change in the first column of the array.

## EXAMPLE 15.14

*Test whether* $P(s) = s^4 + 7s^3 + 6s^2 + 21s + 8$ *is Hurwitz.*

**Solution** The Routh array is given by

$$\begin{array}{c|ccc} s^4 & 1 & 6 & 8 \\ s^3 & 7 & 21 & \\ s^2 & 3 & 8 & \\ s^1 & \frac{7}{3} & 0 & \\ s^0 & 8 & & \end{array}$$

Since all the elements in the first column are positive, the polynomial $P(s)$ is Hurwitz.

## EXAMPLE 15.15

*Determine whether* $P(s) = s^4 + s^3 + 2s^2 + 3s + 2$ *is Hurwitz.*

**Solution** The Routh array is given by

$$\begin{array}{c|ccc} s^4 & 1 & 2 & 2 \\ s^3 & 1 & 3 & \\ s^2 & -1 & 2 & \\ s^1 & 5 & 0 & \\ s^0 & 2 & & \end{array}$$

Since there is a sign change in the first column of the array, the polynomial $P(s)$ is not Hurwitz.

## EXAMPLE 15.16

*Test whether* $P(s) = s^5 + 2s^4 + 4s^3 + 6s^2 + 2s + 5$ *is Hurwitz.*

**Solution** The Routh array is given by

| | | | |
|---|---|---|---|
| $s^5$ | 1 | 4 | 2 |
| $s^4$ | 2 | 6 | 5 |
| $s^3$ | 1 | −0.5 | |
| $s^2$ | 7 | 5 | |
| $s^1$ | −1.21 | | |
| $s^0$ | 5 | | |

Since there is a sign change in the first column of the array, the polynomial is not Hurwitz.

## EXAMPLE 15.17

*Test whether the polynomial* $P(s) = s^5 + s^3 + s$ *is Hurwitz.*

**Solution** The given polynomial contains odd functions only.

$$P'(s) = 5s^4 + 3s^2 + 1$$

The Routh array is given by

| | | | |
|---|---|---|---|
| $s^5$ | 1 | 1 | 1 |
| $s^4$ | 5 | 3 | 1 |
| $s^3$ | 0.4 | 0.8 | |
| $s^2$ | −7 | 1 | |
| $s^1$ | 0.86 | | |
| $s^0$ | 1 | | |

Since there is a sign change in the first column of the array, the polynomial is not Hurwitz.

## EXAMPLE 15.18

*Test whether the polynomial* $P(s) = s^8 + 5s^6 + 2s^4 + 3s^2 + 1$ *is Hurwitz.*

**Solution** The given polynomial contains even functions only.

$$P'(s) = 8s^7 + 30s^5 + 8s^3 + 6s$$

The Routh array is given by

| | | | | | |
|---|---|---|---|---|---|
| $s^8$ | 1 | 5 | 2 | 3 | 1 |
| $s^7$ | 8 | 30 | 8 | 6 | 0 |
| $s^6$ | 1.25 | 1 | 2.25 | 1 | |
| $s^5$ | 23.6 | −6.4 | −0.4 | 0 | |
| $s^4$ | 1.33 | 2.27 | 1 | | |
| $s^3$ | −46.6 | −18.14 | 0 | | |
| $s^2$ | 1.75 | 1 | | | |
| $s^1$ | 8.49 | | | | |
| $s^0$ | 1 | | | | |

Since there is a sign change in the first column of the array, the polynomial is not Hurwitz.

## EXAMPLE 15.19

*Test whether $P(s) = s^5 + 12s^4 + 45s^3 + 60s^2 + 44s + 48$ is Hurwitz.*

**Solution** The Routh array is given by

| | | | |
|---|---|---|---|
| $s^5$ | 1 | 45 | 44 |
| $s^4$ | 12 | 60 | 48 |
| $s^3$ | 40 | 40 | |
| $s^2$ | 48 | 48 | |
| $s^1$ | 0 | 0 | |
| $s^0$ | | | |

**Notes:** When all the elements in any one row are zero, the following steps are followed:

(i) Write an auxiliary equation with the help of the coefficients of the row just above the row of zeros.
(ii) Differentiate the auxiliary equation and replace its coefficient in the row of zeros.
(iii) Proceed for the Routh test.

Auxiliary equation,

$$A(s) = 48s^2 + 48$$
$$A'(s) = 96s$$

| | | | |
|---|---|---|---|
| $s^5$ | 1 | 45 | 44 |
| $s^4$ | 12 | 60 | 48 |
| $s^3$ | 40 | 40 | |
| $s^2$ | 48 | 48 | |
| $s^1$ | 96 | 0 | |
| $s^0$ | 48 | | |

Since there is no sign change in the first column of the array, the polynomial $P(s)$ is Hurwitz.

## EXAMPLE 15.20

*Check whether $P(s) = 2s^6 + s^5 + 13s^4 + 6s^3 + 56s^2 + 25s + 25$ is Hurwitz.*

**Solution** The Routh array is given by

| | | | | |
|---|---|---|---|---|
| $s^6$ | 2 | 13 | 56 | 25 |
| $s^5$ | 1 | 6 | 25 | |
| $s^4$ | 1 | 6 | 25 | |
| $s^3$ | 0 | 0 | 0 | |
| $s^2$ | | | | |
| $s^1$ | | | | |
| $s^0$ | | | | |

$$A(s) = s^4 + 6s^2 + 25$$
$$A'(s) = 4s^3 + 12s$$

Now, the Routh array will be given by

$$\begin{array}{c|cccc} s^6 & 2 & 13 & 56 & 25 \\ s^5 & 1 & 6 & 25 & \\ s^4 & 1 & 6 & 25 & \\ s^3 & 4 & 12 & & \\ s^2 & 3 & 25 & & \\ s^1 & -21.3 & & & \\ s^0 & 25 & & & \end{array}$$

Since there is a sign change in the first column of the array, the polynomial $P(s)$ is not Hurwitz.

## EXAMPLE 15.21

*Determine the range of values of 'a' so that $P(s) = s^4 + s^3 + as^2 + 2s + 3$ is Hurwitz.*

**Solution** The Routh array is given by

$$\begin{array}{c|ccc} s^4 & 1 & a & 3 \\ s^3 & 1 & 2 & \\ s^2 & a-2 & 3 & \\ s^1 & \dfrac{2a-7}{a-2} & & \\ s^0 & 3 & & \end{array}$$

For the polynomial to be Hurwitz, all the terms in the first column of the array should be positive, i.e.,

$$a - 2 > 0$$
$$a > 2$$

and

$$\frac{2a-7}{a-2} > 0$$
$$a > \frac{7}{2}$$

Hence, $P(s)$ will be Hurwitz when $a > \frac{7}{2}$.

## EXAMPLE 15.22

*Determine the range of values of k so that the polynomial $P(s) = s^3 + 3s^2 + 2s + k$ is Hurwitz.*

**Solution** The Routh array is given by

$$\begin{array}{c|cc} s^3 & 1 & 2 \\ s^2 & 3 & k \\ s^1 & \dfrac{6-k}{3} & 0 \\ s^0 & k & \end{array}$$

For the polynomial to be Hurwitz, all the terms in the first column of the array should be positive,

i.e.,
$$\frac{6-k}{3} > 0$$
$$6-k > 0$$

i.e., $k < 6$ and $k > 0$

Hence, $P(s)$ will be Hurwitz for $0 < k < 6$.

## 15.2 POSITIVE REAL FUNCTIONS

LO 15.2

Explain positive real functions, their properties and conditions

A function $F(s)$ is positive real if the following conditions are satisfied:

(a) $F(s)$ is real for real $s$.

(b) The real part of $F(s)$ is greater than or equal to zero when the real part of $s$ is greater than or equal to zero, i.e.,
$\text{Re } F(s) \geq 0 \qquad \text{for } \text{Re}(s) \geq 0$

### 15.2.1 Properties of Positive Real Functions

1. If $F(s)$ is positive real then $\frac{1}{F(s)}$ is also positive real.
2. The sum of two positive real functions is positive real.
3. The poles and zeros of a positive real function cannot have positive real parts, i.e., they cannot be in the right half of the $s$-plane.
4. Only simple poles with real positive residues can exist on the $j\omega$-axis.
5. The poles and zeros of a positive real function are real or occur in conjugate pairs.
6. The highest powers of the numerator and denominator polynomials may differ at most by unity. This condition prevents the possibility of multiple poles and zeros at $s = \infty$.
7. The lowest powers of the denominator and numerator polynomials may differ at most by unity. Hence, a positive real function has neither multiple poles nor zeros at the origin.

### 15.2.2 Necessary and Sufficient Conditions for Positive Real Functions

The necessary and sufficient conditions for a function with real coefficients $F(s)$ to be positive real are the following:

1. $F(s)$ must have no poles and zeros in the right half of the $s$-plane.
2. The poles of $F(s)$ on the $j\omega$-axis must be simple and the residues evaluated at these poles must be real and positive.
3. $\text{Re } F(j\omega) \geq 0$ for all $\omega$.

➤ ***Testing of the Above Conditions*** Condition (1) requires that we test the numerator and denominator of $F(s)$ for roots in the right half of the $s$-plane, i.e., we must determine whether the numerator and denominator of $F(s)$ are Hurwitz. This is done through a continued fraction expansion of the odd to even or even to odd parts of the numerator and denominator.

Condition (2) is tested by making a partial fraction expansion of $F(s)$ and checking whether the residues of the poles on the $j\omega$-axis are positive and real. Thus, if $F(s)$ has a pair of poles at $s = \pm j\omega_0$, a partial fraction expansion gives terms of the form

$$\frac{K_1}{s - j\omega_0} + \frac{K_1^*}{s + j\omega_0}$$

Since residues of complex conjugate poles are themselves conjugate, $K_1 = K_1^*$ and should be positive and real.

Condition (3) requires that Re $F(j\omega)$ must be positive and real for all $\omega$.

Now, to compute Re $F(j\omega)$ from $F(s)$, the numerator and denominator polynomials are separated into even and odd parts.

$$F(s) = \frac{m_1(s) + n_1(s)}{m_2(s) + n_2(s)} = \frac{m_1 + n_1}{m_2 + n_2}$$

Multiplying $N(s)$ and $D(s)$ by $m_2 - n_2$,

$$F(s) = \frac{m_1 + n_1}{m_2 + n_2}\,\frac{m_2 - n_2}{m_2 - n_2} = \frac{m_1 m_2 - n_1 n_2}{m_2^2 - n_2^2} + \frac{m_2 n_1 - m_1 n_2}{m_2^2 - n_2^2}$$

But the product of two even functions or odd functions is itself an even function, while the product of an even and odd function is odd.

$$\text{Ev } F(s) = \frac{m_1 m_2 - n_1 n_2}{m_2^2 - n_2^2}$$

$$\text{Od } F(s) = \frac{m_2 n_1 - m_1 n_2}{m_2^2 - n_2^2}$$

Now, substituting $s = j\omega$ in the even polynomial gives the real part of $F(s)$ and substituting $s = j\omega$ into the odd polynomial gives the imaginary part of $F(s)$.

$$\text{Ev } F(s)\big|_{s=j\omega} = \text{Re } F(j\omega)$$
$$\text{Od } F(s)\big|_{s=j\omega} = j\,\text{Im } F(j\omega)$$

We have to test Re $F(j\omega) \geq 0$ for all $\omega$.

The denominator of Re $F(j\omega)$ is always a positive quantity because

$$m_2^2 - n_2^2\Big|_{s=j\omega} \geq 0$$

Hence, the condition that Ev $F(j\omega)$ should be positive requires

$$m_1 m_2 - n_1 n_2\big|_{s=j\omega} = A(\omega^2)$$

should be positive and real for all $\omega \geq 0$.

## EXAMPLE 15.23

*Test whether* $F(s)=\dfrac{s+3}{s+1}$ *is a positive real function.*

**Solution**

(a) $F(s)=\dfrac{N(s)}{D(s)}=\dfrac{s+3}{s+1}$

The function $F(s)$ has pole at $s=-1$ and zero at $s=-3$, as shown in Fig. 15.1.

Thus, pole and zero are in the left half of the $s$-plane.

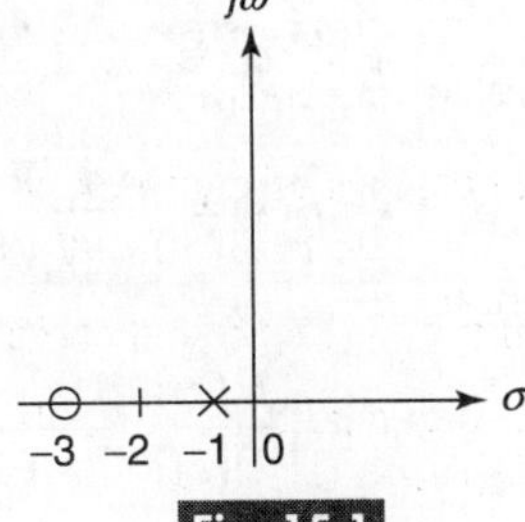

Fig. 15.1

(b) There is no pole on the $j\omega$ axis. Hence, the residue test is not carried out.

(c) Even part of $N(s)=m_1=3$

Odd part of $N(s)=n_1=s$

Even part of $D(s)=m_2=1$

Odd part of $D(s)=n_2=s$

$$A(\omega^2)=m_1m_2-n_1n_2\,|_{s=j\omega}=(3)(1)-(s)(s)\,|_{s=j\omega}=3-s^2\,|_{s=j\omega}=3+\omega^2$$

$A(\omega^2)$ is positive for all $\omega\geq 0$.

Since all the three conditions are satisfied, the function is positive real.

## EXAMPLE 15.24

*Test whether* $F(s)=\dfrac{s^2+6s+5}{s^2+9s+14}$ *is positive real function.*

**Solution**

(a) $F(s)=\dfrac{N(s)}{D(s)}=\dfrac{s^2+6s+5}{s^2+9s+14}=\dfrac{(s+5)(s+1)}{(s+7)(s+2)}$

The function $F(s)$ has poles at $s=-7$ and $s=-2$ and zeros at $s=-5$ an $s=-1$, as shown in Fig. 15.2.

Thus, all the poles and zeros are in the left half of the $s$-plane.

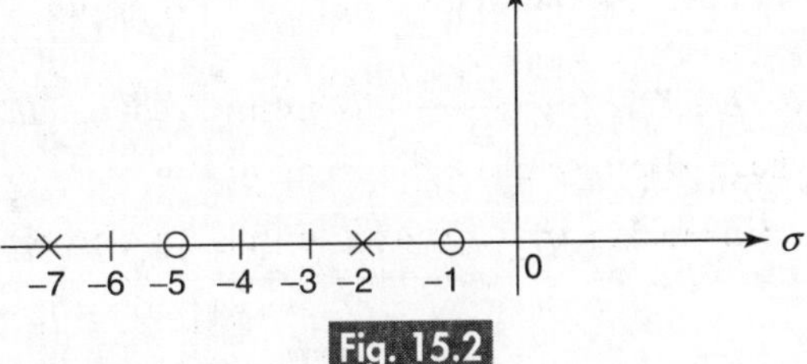

Fig. 15.2

(b) Since there is no pole on the $j\omega$ axis, the residue test is not carried out.

(c) Even part of $N(s)=m_1=s^2+5$

Odd part of $N(s)=n_1=6s$

Even part of $D(s)=m_2=s^2+14$

Odd part of $D(s)=n_2=9s$

$$A(\omega^2) = m_1m_2 - n_1n_2 \,|_{s=j\omega} = (s^2+5)\,(s^2+14) - (6s)(9s)\,|_{s=j\omega} = s^4 - 35s^2 + 70 \;|_{s=j\omega} = \omega^4 + 35\omega^2 + 70$$

$A(\omega^2)$ is positive for all $\omega \geq 0$.

Since all the three conditions are satisfied, the function is positive real.

## EXAMPLE 15.25

*Test whether* $F(s) = \dfrac{s(s+3)(s+5)}{(s+1)(s+4)}$ *is positive real function.*

**Solution**

(a) $F(s) = \dfrac{N(s)}{D(s)} = \dfrac{s(s+3)(s+5)}{(s+1)(s+4)} = \dfrac{s^3+8s^2+15s}{s^2+5s+4}$

The function $F(s)$ has poles at $s = -1$ and $s = -4$ and zeros at $s = 0$, $s = -3$ and $s = -5$, as shown in Fig. 15.3.

Thus, all the poles and zeros are in the left half of the $s$-plane.

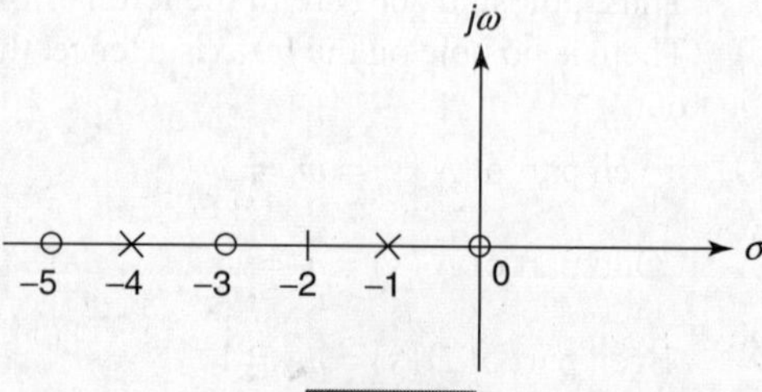

Fig. 15.3

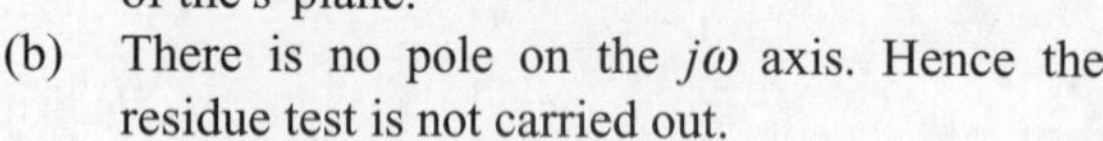

(b) There is no pole on the $j\omega$ axis. Hence the residue test is not carried out.

(c) Even part of $N(s) = m_1 = 8s^2$

Odd part of $N(s) = n_1 = s^3 + 15s$

Even part of $D(s) = m_2 = s^2 + 4$

Odd part of $D(s) = n_2 = 5s$

$$A(\omega^2) = m_1m_2 - n_1n_2 \,|_{s=j\omega} = (8s^2)(s^2+4) - (s^3+15s)(5s)\,|_{s=j\omega} = 3s^4 - 43s^2 \;|_{s=j\omega} = 3\omega^4 + 43\omega^2$$

$A(\omega^2)$ is positive for all $\omega \geq 0$.

Since all the three conditions are satisfied, the function is positive real.

## EXAMPLE 15.26

*Test whether* $F(s) = \dfrac{s^2+1}{s^3+4s}$ *is positive real function.*

**Solution**

(a) $F(s) = \dfrac{N(s)}{D(s)} = \dfrac{s^2+1}{s^3+4s} = \dfrac{(s+j1)(s-j1)}{s(s+j2)(s-j2)}$

The function $F(s)$ has poles at $s = 0$, $s = -j2$ and $s = j2$ and zeros at $s = -j1$ and $s = j1$, as shown in Fig. 15.4.

Thus, all the poles and zeros are on the $j\omega$ axis.

(b) The poles on the $j\omega$ axis are simple. Hence, residue test is carried out.

$$F(s) = \frac{s^2+1}{s^3+4s} = \frac{s^2+1}{s(s^2+4)}$$

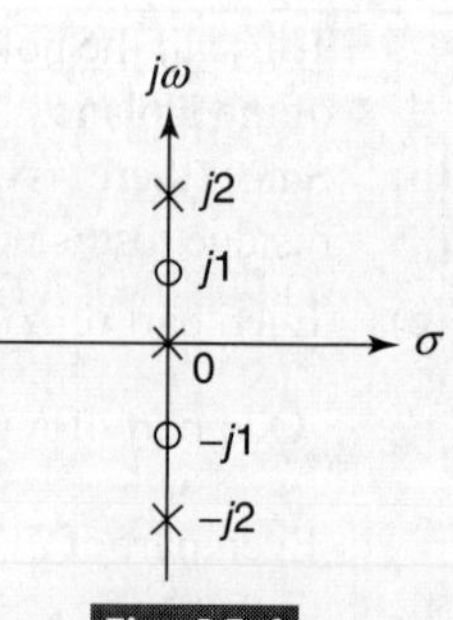

Fig. 15.4

By partial fraction expansion,

$$F(s)=\frac{K_1}{s}+\frac{K_2}{s+j2}+\frac{K_2^*}{s-j2}$$

The constants $K_1$, $K_2$ and $K_2$* are called residues.

$$K_1 = s\,F(s)\,|_{s=0} = \left.\frac{s^2+1}{s^2+4}\right|_{s=0} = \frac{1}{4}$$

$$K_2 = (s+j2)F(s)\,|_{s=-j2} = \left.\frac{s^2+1}{s(s-j2)}\right|_{s=-j2} = \frac{-4+1}{(-j2)(-j2-j2)} = \frac{3}{8}$$

$$K_2^* = K_2 = \frac{3}{8}$$

Thus, residues are real and positive.

(c) Even part of $N(s) = m_1 = s^2+1$

Odd part of $N(s) = n_1 = 0$

Even part of $D(s) = m_2 = 0$

Odd part of $D(s) = n_2 = s^3+4s$

$$A(\omega^2) = m_1 m_2 - n_1 n_2\,|_{s=j\omega} = (s^2+1)(0)-(0)(s^3+4s)\,|_{s=j\omega} = 0$$

$A(\omega^2)$ is zero for all $\omega \ge 0$.

Since all the three conditions are satisfied, the function is positive real.

## EXAMPLE 15.27

*Test whether* $F(s)=\dfrac{2s^3+2s^2+3s+2}{s^2+1}$ *is positive real function.*

**Solution**

(a) $$F(s)=\frac{N(s)}{D(s)}=\frac{2s^3+2s^2+3s+2}{s^2+1}=\frac{2s^3+2s^2+3s+2}{(s+j1)(s-j1)}$$

Since numerator polynomial cannot be easily factorised, we will prove whether $N(s)$ is Hurwitz.

Even part of $N(s) = m(s) = 2s^2+2$

Odd part of $N(s) = n(s) = 2s^3+3s$

By continued fraction expansion,

$$2s^2+2\,\overline{\big)\,2s^3+3s\,\big(\,s}$$
$$\underline{2s^3+2s}$$
$$s\,\overline{\big)\,2s^2+2s\,\big(\,2s}$$
$$\underline{2s^2}$$
$$2\,\overline{\big)\,s\,\big(\,\tfrac{1}{2}s}$$
$$\underline{s}$$
$$0$$

Since all the quotient terms are positive, $N(s)$ is Hurwitz. This indicates that zeros are in the left half of the $s$-plane.

The function $F(s)$ has poles at $s=-j1$ and $s=j1$.

Thus, all the poles and zeros are in the left half of the $s$-plane.

(b) The poles on the $j\omega$ axis are simple. Hence, residue test is carried out.

$$F(s)=\frac{2s^3+2s^2+3s+2}{s^2+1}$$

As the degree of the numerator is greater than that of the denominator, division is first carried out before partial fraction expansion.

$$s^2+1\,\overline{\big)\,2s^3+2s^2+3s+2\,\big(\,2s+2}$$
$$\underline{2s^3\qquad+2s}$$
$$2s^2+s+2$$
$$\underline{2s^2\qquad+2}$$
$$s$$

$$F(s)=2s+2+\frac{s}{s^2+1}$$

By partial fraction expansion,

$$F(s)=2s+2+\frac{K_1}{s+j1}+\frac{K_1^*}{s-j1}$$

$$K_1=(s+j1)F(s)\big|_{s=-j1}=\frac{-j1}{-j1-j1}=\frac{1}{2}$$

$$K_1^*=K_1=\frac{1}{2}$$

Thus, residues are real and positive.

(c) Even part of $N(s) = m_1 = 2s^2 + 2$

Odd part of $N(s) = n_1 = 2s^3 + 3s$

Even part of $D(s) = m_2 = s^2 + 1$

Odd part of $D(s) = n_2 = 0$

$$A(\omega^2) = m_1 m_2 - n_1 n_2 |_{s=j\omega} = (2s^2+2)(s^2+1) - (2s^3+3s)(0) |_{s=j\omega} = 2s^4 + 4s^2 + 2 \;|_{s=j\omega}$$
$$= 2(\omega^4 - 2\omega^2 + 1) = 2(\omega^2 - 1)^2$$

$A(\omega^2) \geq 0$ for all $\omega \geq 0$.

Since all the three conditions are satisfied, the function is positive real.

## EXAMPLE 15.28

*Test whether* $F(s) = \dfrac{s^3 + 6s^2 + 7s + 3}{s^2 + 2s + 1}$ *is positive real function.*

**Solution**

(a) $F(s) = \dfrac{N(s)}{D(s)} = \dfrac{s^3 + 6s^2 + 7s + 3}{s^2 + 2s + 1} = \dfrac{s^3 + 6s^2 + 7s + 3}{(s+1)(s+1)}$

Since a numerator polynomial cannot be easily factorised, we will test whether $N(s)$ is Hurwitz.

Even part of $N(s) = m(s) = 6s^2 + 3$

Odd part of $N(s) = n(s) = s^3 + 7s$

By continued fraction expansion,

$$
\begin{array}{l}
6s^2+3 \,\big)\, s^3 + 7s \,\big(\, \tfrac{1}{6}s \\
\qquad\quad \underline{s^3 + 0.5s} \\
\qquad\qquad 6.5s \,\big)\, 6s^2 + 3 \,\big(\, 0.92s \\
\qquad\qquad\qquad \underline{6s^2} \\
\qquad\qquad\qquad\quad 3 \,\big)\, 6.5s \,\big(\, 2.17s \\
\qquad\qquad\qquad\qquad \underline{6.5s} \\
\qquad\qquad\qquad\qquad\quad 0
\end{array}
$$

Since all the quotient terms are positive, $N(s)$ is Hurwitz. This indicates that the zeros are in the left half of the $s$-plane.

The function $F(s)$ has a double pole at $s = -1$.

Thus, all the poles and zeros are in the left half of the $s$-plane.

(b) There is no pole on the $j\omega$ axis. Hence, the residue test is not carried out.

(c) Even part of $N(s) = m_1 = 6s^2 + 3$

Odd part of $N(s) = n_1 = s^3 + 7s$

Even part of $D(s) = m_2 = s^2 + 1$

Odd part of $D(s) = n_2 = 2s$

$$A(\omega^2) = m_1 m_2 - n_1 n_2 \,|_{s=j\omega} = (6s^2+3)(s^2+1) - (s^3+7s)(2s)\,|_{s=j\omega} = 4s^4 - 5s^2 + 3\,|_{s=j\omega}$$
$$= 4\omega^4 + 5\omega^2 + 3$$

$A(\omega^2)$ is positive for all $\omega \geq 0$.

Since all the three conditions are satisfied, the function is positive real.

## EXAMPLE 15.29

*Test whether* $F(s) = \dfrac{s^2+s+6}{s^2+s+1}$ *is a positive real function.*

**Solution**

(a) $$F(s) = \frac{N(s)}{D(s)} = \frac{s^2+s+6}{s^2+s+1} = \frac{\left(s+\frac{1}{2}+j\frac{\sqrt{23}}{2}\right)\left(s+\frac{1}{2}-j\frac{\sqrt{23}}{2}\right)}{\left(s+\frac{1}{2}+j\frac{\sqrt{3}}{2}\right)\left(s+\frac{1}{2}-j\frac{\sqrt{3}}{2}\right)}$$

The function $F(s)$ has zeros at $s = -\frac{1}{2} \pm j\frac{\sqrt{23}}{2}$ and poles at $s = -\frac{1}{2} \pm j\frac{\sqrt{3}}{2}$.

(b) There is no pole on the $j\omega$ axis. Hence, the residue test is not carried out.

(c) Even part of $N(s) = m_1 = s^2 + 6$

Odd part of $N(s) = n_1 = s$

Even part of $D(s) = m_2 = s^2 + 1$

Odd part of $D(s) = n_2 = s$

$$A(\omega^2) = m_1 m_2 - n_1 n_2 \,|_{s=j\omega} = (s^2+6)(s^2+1) - (s)(s)\,|_{s=j\omega} = s^4 + 6s^2 + 6\,|_{s=j\omega} = \omega^4 - 6\omega^2 + 6$$

For $\omega = 2$, $A(\omega^2) = 16 - 24 + 6 = -2$

This condition is not satisfied.

Hence, the function $F(s)$ is not positive real.

## EXAMPLE 15.30

*Test whether* $F(s) = \dfrac{s^2+4}{s^3+3s^2+3s+1}$ *is positive real function.*

**Solution**

(a) $$F(s) = \frac{N(s)}{D(s)} = \frac{s^2+4}{s^3+3s^2+3s+1} = \frac{(s+j2)(s-j2)}{(s+1)^3}$$

The function $F(s)$ has two zeros at $s = \pm j2$ and three poles at $s = -1$.
Thus, all the poles and zeros are in the left half of the $s$-plane.

(b) There is no pole on the $j\omega$ axis. Hence, the residue test is not carried out.

(c) Even part of $N(s) = m_1 = s^2 + 4$

Odd part of $N(s) = n_1 = 0$

Even part of $D(s) = m_2 = 3s^2 + 1$

Odd part of $D(s) = n_2 = s^3 + 3s$

$$A(\omega^2) = m_1 m_2 - n_1 n_2 \,|_{s=j\omega} = (s^2+4)(3s^2+1) - (0)(s^3+3s)\,|_{s=j\omega} = 3s^4 + 13s^2 + 4\,|_{s=j\omega}$$

$$= 3\omega^4 - 13\omega^2 + 4$$

For $\omega = 1$, $A(\omega)^2 = 3 - 13 + 4 = -6$

This condition is not satisfied.

Hence, the function $F(s)$ is not positive real.

## EXAMPLE 15.31

*Test whether* $F(s) = \dfrac{s^3 + 5s}{s^4 + 2s^2 + 1}$ *is positive real function.*

**Solution**

(a) $$F(s) = \frac{N(s)}{D(s)} = \frac{s^3 + 5s}{s^4 + 2s^2 + 1} = \frac{s(s^2+5)}{(s^2+1)^2} = \frac{s(s + j\sqrt{5})(s - j\sqrt{5})}{(s \pm j1)(s \pm j1)}$$

The function $F(s)$ has zeros at $s = 0, s = \pm j\sqrt{5}$ and two poles at $s = j1$ and two poles at $s = -j1$.

Thus, poles on the $j\omega$ axis are not simple.
Hence, the function $F(s)$ is not positive real.

## EXAMPLE 15.32

*Test whether* $F(s) = \dfrac{s^4 + 3s^3 + s^2 + s + 2}{s^3 + s^2 + s + 1}$ *is positive real function.*

**Solution**

$$F(s) = \frac{N(s)}{D(s)} = \frac{s^4 + 3s^3 + s^2 + s + 2}{s^3 + s^2 + s + 1}$$

Here, it is easier to prove that $N(s)$ and $D(s)$ are Hurwitz.

By Routh array,

$$\begin{array}{c|ccc} s^4 & 1 & 1 & 2 \\ s^3 & 3 & 1 & \\ s^2 & \frac{2}{3} & 2 & \\ s^1 & -8 & & \\ s^0 & 2 & & \end{array}$$

Since there is a sign change in the first column of the array, $N(s)$ is not Hurwitz. Thus, all the zeros are not in the left half of the $s$-plane. The remaining two tests need not be carried out.
Hence, the function $F(s)$ is not positive real.

## 15.3 ELEMENTARY SYNTHESIS CONCEPTS

LO 15.3

Discuss elementary synthesis concepts and explain four removal operations

We know that impedances and admittances of passive networks are positive real functions. Hence, addition of impedances of the two passive networks gives a function which is also a positive real function. Thus, $Z(s) = Z_1(s) + Z_2(s)$ is a positive real function, if $Z_1(s)$ and $Z_2(s)$ are positive real functions. Similarly, $Y(s) = Y_1(s) + Y_2(s)$ is a positive real function, if $Y_1(s)$ and $Y_2(s)$ are positive real functions. There is a special terminology for synthesis procedure. We have,

$$Z(s) = Z_1(s) + Z_2(s)$$

$$Z_2(s) = Z(s) - Z_1(s)$$

Here, $Z_1(s)$ is said to have been removed from $Z(s)$ in forming the new function $Z_2(s)$, as shown in Fig. 15.5. If the removed network is associated with the pole or zero of the original network impedance then that pole or zero is also said to have been removed.

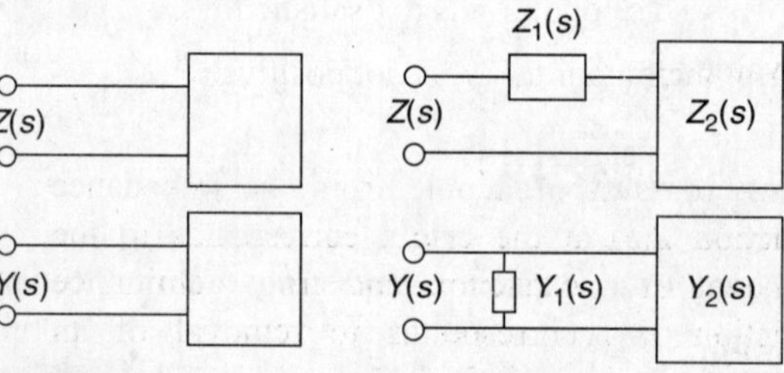


**Fig. 15.5** *Network interpretation of the removal of impedance and admittance*

There are four important removal operations.

### 15.3.1 Removal of a Pole at Infinity

Consider an impedance function $Z(s)$ having a pole at infinity, which means that the numerator polynomial is one degree greater than the degree of the denominator polynomial.

$$Z(s) = \frac{a_{n+1}s^{n+1} + a_n s^n + \ldots + a_1 s + a_0}{b_n s^n + b_{n-1}s^{n-1} + \ldots + b_1 s + b_0} = Hs + \frac{c_n s^n + c_{n-1}s^{n-1} + \ldots + c_1 s + c_0}{b_n s^n + b_{n-1}s^{n-1} + \ldots + b_1 s + b_0}$$

where $H = \dfrac{a_{n+1}}{b_n}$

Let $Z_1(s) = Hs$

and $Z_2(s) = \dfrac{c_n s^n + c_{n-1}s^{n-1} + \ldots + c_1 s + c_0}{b_n s^n + b_{n-1}s^{n-1} + \ldots + b_1 s + b_0} = Z(s) - Hs$

$Z_1(s) = Hs$ represents impedance of an inductor of value $H$. Hence, the removal of a pole at infinity corresponds to the removal of an inductor from the network of Fig. 15.6(a).

If the given function is an admittance function $Y(s)$, then $Y_1(s) = Hs$ represents the admittance of a capacitor $Y_C(s) = Cs$. The network for $Y_1(s)$ is a capacitor of value $C = H$, as shown in Fig. 15.6(b).

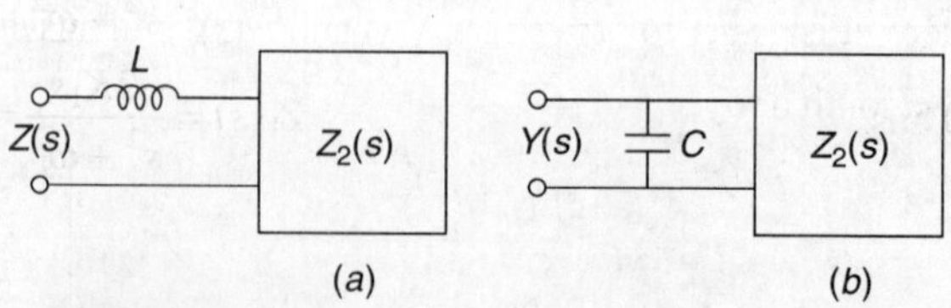


**Fig. 15.6** *Network interpretation of the removal of a pole at infinity*

### 15.3.2 Removal of a Pole at Origin

If $Z(s)$ has a pole at the origin then it may be written as

$$Z(s) = \frac{a_0 + a_1 s + \ldots + a_{n-1}s^{n-1} + a_n s^n}{b_1 s + b_2 s^2 + \ldots + b_m s^m} = \frac{K_0}{s} + \frac{d_1 + d_2 s + \ldots + d_n s^{n-1}}{b_1 + b_2 s + \ldots + b_m s^{m-1}} = Z_1(s) + Z_2(s)$$

where $K_0 = \dfrac{a_0}{b_1}$

$Z_1(s) = \dfrac{K_0}{s}$ represents the impedance of a capacitor of value $\dfrac{1}{K_0}$.

If the given function is an admittance function $Y(s)$ then removal of $Y_1(s) = \dfrac{K_0}{s}$ corresponds to an inductor of value $\dfrac{1}{K_0}$.

Thus, removal of a pole from the impedance function $Z(s)$ at the origin corresponds to the removal of a capacitor, and from admittance function $Y(s)$ corresponds to removal of an inductor, as shown in Fig. 15.7.

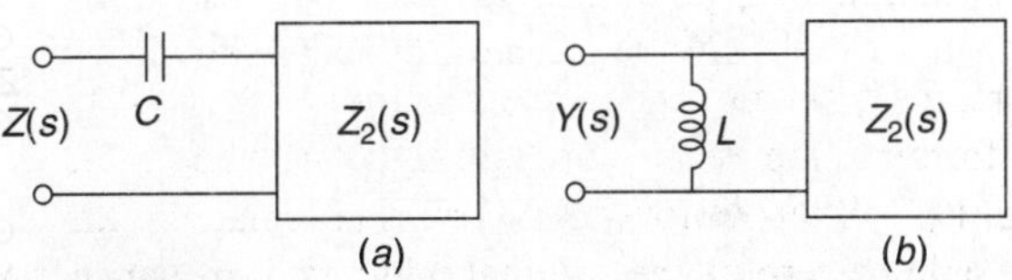


**Fig. 15.7** *Network interpretation of the removal of a pole at origin*

### 15.3.3 Removal of Conjugate Imaginary Poles

If $Z(s)$ contains poles on the imaginary axis, i.e., at $s = \pm j\omega_1$ then $Z(s)$ will have factors $(s + j\omega_1)(s - j\omega_1) = s^2 + \omega_1^2$ in the denominator polynomial

$$Z(s) = \frac{p(s)}{(s^2 + \omega_1^2)q_1(s)}$$

By partial fraction expansion,

$$Z(s) = \frac{K_1}{s + j\omega_1} + \frac{K_1^*}{s - j\omega_1} + Z_2(s)$$

For a positive real function, $j\omega$-axis poles must themselves be conjugate and must have equal, positive and real residues.

$$K_1 = K_1^*$$

Hence,

$$Z(s) = \frac{2K_1 s}{s^2 + \omega_1^2} + Z_2(s)$$

Thus,

$$Z_1(s) = \frac{2K_1 s}{s^2 + \omega_1^2} = \frac{1}{\dfrac{s}{2K_1} + \dfrac{\omega_1^2}{2K_1 s}} = \frac{1}{Y_a + Y_b}$$

where $Y_a = \dfrac{s}{2K_1}$ is the admittance of a capacitor of value $C = \dfrac{1}{2K_1}$

and $Y_b = \dfrac{\omega_1^2}{2K_1 s}$ is the admittance of an inductor of value $L = \dfrac{2K_1}{\omega_1^2}$

If the given function is an admittance function $Y(s)$ then

$$Y_1(s) = \frac{2K_1 s}{s^2 + \omega_1^2} = \frac{1}{Z_a + Z_b} = \frac{1}{\frac{s}{2K_1} + \frac{\omega_1^2}{2K_1 s}}$$

where $Z_a = \frac{s}{2K_1}$ is the impedance of an inductor of value $L = \frac{1}{2K_1}$ and $Z_b = \frac{\omega_1^2}{2K_1 s}$ is the impedance of a capacitor of value $C = \frac{2K_1}{\omega_1^2}$.

Thus, removal of conjugate imaginary poles from impedance function $Z(s)$ corresponds to the removal of the parallel combination of $L - C$ and from admittance function $Y(s)$ corresponds to removal of series combination of $L - C$, as shown in Fig. 15.8.

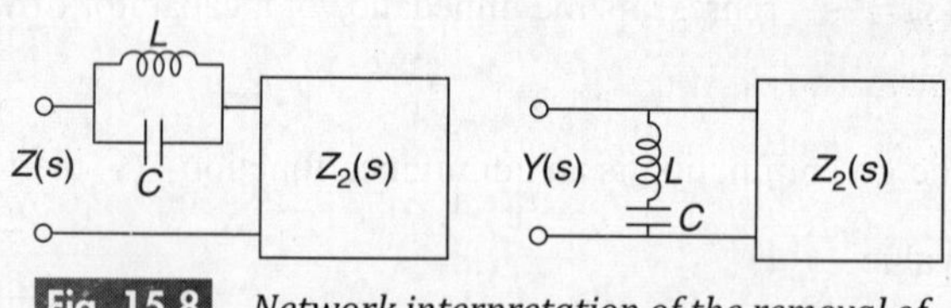


**Fig. 15.8** *Network interpretation of the removal of conjugate imaginary poles*

### 15.3.4 Removal of a Constant

If a real number $R_1$ is subtracted from $Z(s)$ such that

$$Z_2(s) = Z(s) - R_1$$
$$Z(s) = R_1 + Z_2(s)$$

then $R_1$ represents a resistor.

If the given function is an admittance function $Y(s)$, then removal of $Y_1(s) = R_1$ represents a conductance of value $R_1$.

Thus, removal of a constant from impedance function $Z(s)$ corresponds to the removal of a resistance, and from admittance function $Y(s)$ corresponds to removal of a conductance.

**EXAMPLE 15.33**

*Synthesise the impedance function* $Z(s) = \frac{s^3 + 4s}{s^2 + 2}$.

**Solution**

By long division of $Z(s)$,

$$s^2 + 2 \overline{)\, s^3 + 4s \,(} \; s$$
$$\underline{s^3 + 2s}$$
$$2s$$

$$Z(s) = s + \frac{2s}{s^2 + 2} = Z_1(s) + Z_2(s)$$

$Z_1(s) = s$ represents impedance of an inductor of value 1 H.

$$Y_2(s) = \frac{1}{Z_2(s)} = \frac{s^2 + 2}{2s} = \frac{s^2}{2s} + \frac{2}{2s} = \frac{1}{2}s + \frac{1}{s} = Y_3(s) + Y_4(s)$$

$Y_3(s) = \frac{1}{2}s$ represents the admittance of a capacitor of value $\frac{1}{2}$ F.

$Y_4(s) = \frac{1}{s}$ represents the admittance of an inductor of value 1 H.

The impedances are connected in the series branches whereas the admittances are connected in the parallel branches. The network is shown in Fig. 15.9.

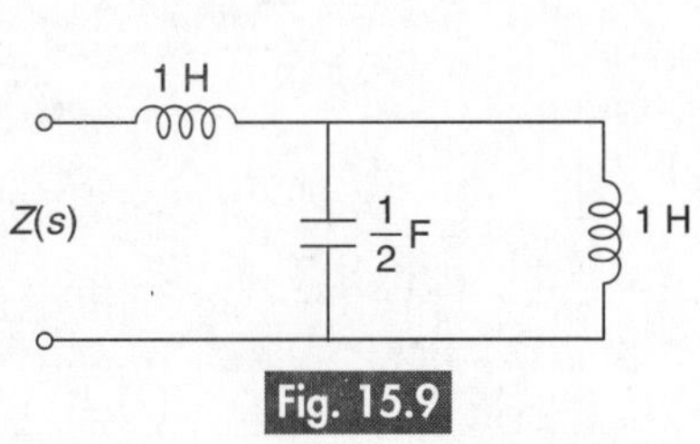


Fig. 15.9

## EXAMPLE 15.34

*Realise the network having impedance function*

$$Z(s) = \frac{s^2 + 2s + 10}{s(s+5)}$$

**Solution**

By long division of $Z(s)$,

$$s^2 + 5s \,\big)\, s^2 + 2s + 10 \,\Big(\, \frac{2}{s}$$

$$\frac{2s + 10}{s^2}$$

$$Z(s) = \frac{2}{s} + \frac{s^2}{s^2 + 5s} = \frac{2}{s} + \frac{s}{s+5} = Z_1(s) + Z_2(s)$$

$Z_1(s) = \frac{2}{s}$ represents the impedance of capacitor of value $\frac{1}{2}$ F.

$$Y_2(s) = \frac{1}{Z_2(s)} = \frac{s+5}{s} = 1 + \frac{5}{s} = Y_3(s) + Y_4(s)$$

$Y_3(s) = 1$ represents the admittance of a resistor of value 1 Ω.

$Y_4(s) = \frac{5}{s}$ represents the admittance of an inductor of value $\frac{1}{5}$ H.

The impedances are connected in the series branches whereas the admittances are connected in the parallel branches. The network is shown in Fig. 15.10.

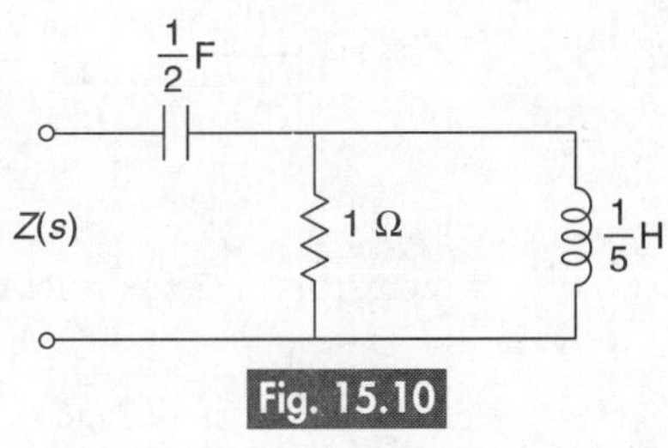


Fig. 15.10

## EXAMPLE 15.35

*Realise the network having impedance function* $Z(s) = \frac{6s^3 + 5s^2 + 6s + 4}{2s^3 + 2s}$.

**Solution** By long division of $Z(s)$,

$$2s^3+2s\,\overline{)\,6s^3+5s^2+6s+4\,}\,(\,3$$
$$\underline{6s^3\quad +6s}$$
$$5s^2\quad +4$$

$$Z(s)=3+\frac{5s^2+4}{2s^3+2s}=Z_1(s)+Z_2(s)$$

$Z_1(s)=3$ represents the impedance of a resistor of value 3 Ω.

$$Y_2(s)=\frac{1}{Z_2(s)}=\frac{2s^3+2s}{5s^2+4}$$

By long division of $Y_2(s)$,

$$5s^2+4\,\overline{)\,2s^3+2s\,}\,(\,\frac{2}{5}s$$
$$\underline{2s^3+\frac{8}{5}s}$$
$$\frac{2}{5}s$$

$$Y_2(s)=\frac{2}{5}s+\frac{\frac{2}{5}s}{5s^2+4}=Y_3(s)+Y_4(s)$$

$Y_3(s)=\frac{2}{5}s$ represents the admittance of a capacitor of value $\frac{2}{5}$ F.

$$Z_4(s)=\frac{1}{Y_4(s)}=\frac{5s^2+4}{\frac{2}{5}s}=\frac{25s^2+20}{2s}=\frac{25}{2}s+\frac{10}{s}=Z_5(s)+Z_6(s)$$

$Z_5(s)=\frac{25}{2}s$ represents the impedance of an inductor of value $\frac{25}{2}$ H.

$Z_6(s)=\frac{10}{s}$ represents the impedance of a capacitor of value $\frac{1}{10}$ F.

The impedances are connected in the series branches, whereas the admittances are connected in the parallel branches. The network is shown in Fig. 15.11.

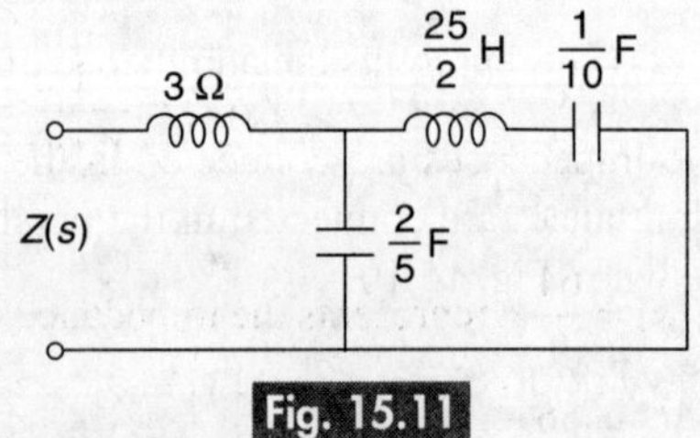


Fig. 15.11

## EXAMPLE 15.36

*Realise the network having impedance function*

$$Z(s)=\frac{s^4+10s^2+7}{s^3+2s}$$

**Solution** By long division of $Z(s)$,

$$\begin{array}{r|l} s^3+2s & s^4+10s^2+7 \;(\, s \\ & \underline{s^4+2s^2} \\ & \quad 8s^2+7 \end{array}$$

$$Z(s)=s+\frac{8s^2+7}{s^3+2s}=Z_1(s)+Z_2(s)$$

$Z_1(s)=s$ represents the impedance of an inductor of value 1 H.

$$Y_2(s)=\frac{1}{Z_2(s)}=\frac{s^3+2s}{8s^2+7}$$

By long division of $Y_2(s)$,

$$\begin{array}{r|l} 8s^2+7 & s^3+2s \;\left(\, \frac{1}{8}s \right. \\ & \underline{s^3+\frac{7}{8}s} \\ & \quad \frac{9}{8}s \end{array}$$

$$Y_2(s)=\frac{1}{8}s+\frac{\frac{9}{8}s}{8s^2+7}=Y_3(s)+Y_4(s)$$

$Y_3(s)=\frac{1}{8}s$ represents the admittance of a capacitor of value $\frac{1}{8}$ F.

$$Z_4(s)=\frac{1}{Y_4(s)}=\frac{8s^2+7}{\frac{9}{8}s}=\frac{64}{9}s+\frac{56}{9s}=Z_5(s)+Z_6(s)$$

$Z_5(s)=\frac{64}{9}s$ represents the impedance of an inductor of value $\frac{64}{9}$ H.

$Z_6(s)=\frac{56}{9s}$ represents the impedance of a capacitor of value $\frac{9}{56}$ F.

The impedances are connected in the series branches, whereas the admittances are connected in the parallel branches. The network is shown in Fig. 15.12.

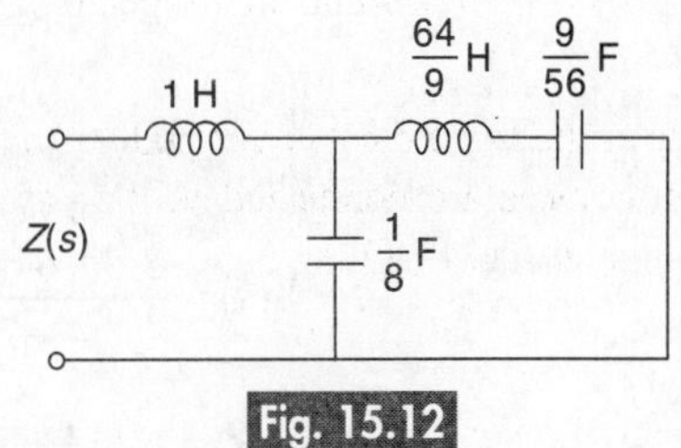


Fig. 15.12

## EXAMPLE 15.37

*Realise the network having admittance function* $Y(s)=\dfrac{4s^2+6s}{s+1}$.

**Solution** By long division of $Y(s)$,

$$s+1\overline{)\,4s^2+6s\,}\,(4s$$
$$\underline{4s^2+4s}$$
$$2s$$

$$Y(s)=4s+\frac{2s}{s+1}=Y_1(s)+Y_2(s)$$

$Y_1(s)=4s$ represents the admittance of a capacitor of value 4 F.

$$Z_2(s)=\frac{1}{Y_2(s)}=\frac{s+1}{2s}=\frac{1}{2}+\frac{1}{2s}=Z_3(s)+Z_4(s)$$

$Z_3(s)=\dfrac{1}{2}$ represents the impedance of a resistor of value $\dfrac{1}{2}\,\Omega$.

$Z_4(s)=\dfrac{1}{2s}$ represents the impedance of a capacitor of value 2 F.

The impedances are connected in the series branches, whereas the admittances are connected in the parallel branches. The network is shown in Fig. 15.13.

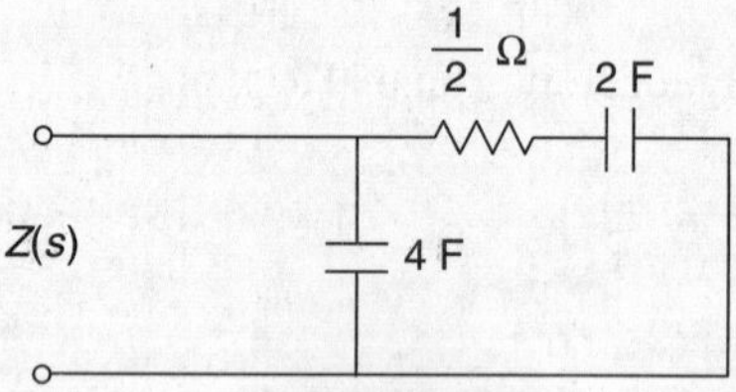

Fig. 15.13

## EXAMPLE 15.38

*Realise the admittance function* $Y(s)=\dfrac{3+5s}{4+2s}$.

**Solution** By long division,

$$4+2s\overline{)\,3+5s\,}\,\left(\frac{3}{4}\right.$$
$$\underline{3+\frac{3}{2}s}$$
$$\frac{7}{2}s$$

$$Y(s)=\frac{3}{4}+\frac{\frac{7}{2}s}{4+2s}=Y_1(s)+Y_2(s)$$

$Y_1(s)=\dfrac{3}{4}$ represents the admittance of a resistor of value $\dfrac{4}{3}\,\Omega$.

$$Z_2(s) = \frac{1}{Y_2(s)} = \frac{4+2s}{\frac{7}{2}s} = \frac{8+4s}{7s} = \frac{8}{7s} + \frac{4}{7} = Z_3(s) + Z_4(s)$$

$Z_3(s) = \frac{8}{7s}$ represents the impedance of a capacitor of value $\frac{7}{8}$ F.

$Z_4(s) = \frac{4}{7}$ represents the impedance of a resistor of value $\frac{4}{7}\ \Omega$.

The impedances are connected in the series branches, whereas the admittances are connected in the parallel branches. The network is shown in Fig. 15.14.

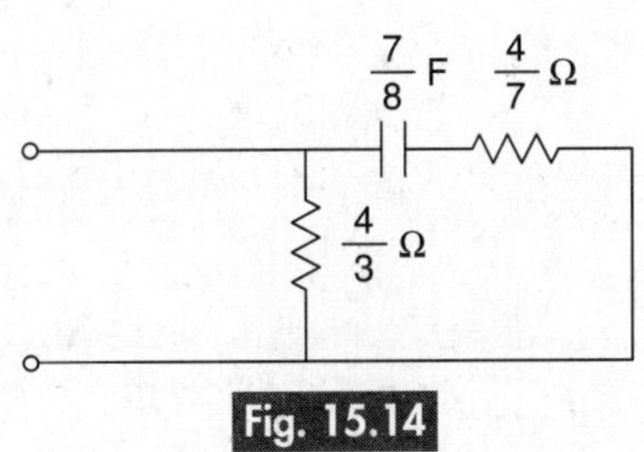


Fig. 15.14

## 15.4 REALISATION OF *LC* FUNCTIONS

LO 15.4

Explain Foster and Cauer forms of realising *LC* functions, and their properties

*LC* driving point immitance functions have the following properties.

1. It is the ratio of odd to even or even to odd polynomials.
2. The poles and zeros are simple and lie on the $j\omega$-axis.
3. The poles and zeros interlace on the $j\omega$-axis.
4. There must be either a zero or a pole at the origin and infinity.
5. The difference between any two successive powers of numerator and denominator polynomials is at most two. There cannot be any missing terms.
6. The highest powers of numerator and denominator polynomials must differ by unity; the lowest powers also differ by unity.

There are a number of methods of realising an *LC* function. But we will study only four basic forms – Foster I, Foster II, Cauer I, and Cauer II forms. The Foster forms are obtained by partial fraction expansion of $F(s)$, and the Cauer forms are obtained by continued fraction expansion of $F(s)$.

### 15.4.1 Foster Realisation

Consider a general *LC* function $F(s)$ given by

$$F(s) = \frac{H(s^2+\omega_1^2)(s^2+\omega_3^2)\ldots}{s(s^2+\omega_2^2)(s^2+\omega_4^2)\ldots}$$

where $0 \le \omega_1^2 < \omega_2^2 < \omega_3^2 \ldots$ and $H$ is positive.

By partial fraction expansion of $F(s)$,

$$F(s) = \frac{K_0}{s} + \frac{K_2}{s+j\omega_2} + \frac{K_2}{s-j\omega_2} + \ldots + K_\infty s$$

Combining terms with conjugate poles,

$$F(s) = \frac{K_0}{s} + \frac{2K_2 s}{s+\omega_2^2} \ldots + K_\infty s$$

where $K_0$, $K_i$ and $K_\infty$ are the residues of $F(s)$ at the origin, at $j\omega_i$ and at infinity respectively.

These residues are given by

$$K_0 = sF(s)\big|_{s=0}$$

$$K_i = \left.\frac{\left(s^2+\omega_i^2\right)F(s)}{2s}\right|_{s^2=-\omega_i^2}$$

$$K_\infty = \left.\frac{F(s)}{s}\right|_{s\to\infty}$$

➤ ***Foster I Form*** If $F(s)$ represents an impedance function, it gives a series connection of impedances.

$$F(s) = Z(s) = \frac{K_0}{s} + \frac{2K_2 s}{s^2+\omega_2^2} \dots + K_\infty s = Z_1(s) + Z_2(s) + \dots + Z_n(s)$$

The first term $\frac{K_0}{s}$ represents the impedance of a capacitor of $\frac{1}{K_0}$ farad.

The last term $K_\infty s$ represents the impedance of an inductor of $K_\infty$ henry.

The remaining terms, i.e., $\frac{2K_i s}{s^2+\omega_i^2}$ represent the impedance of a parallel combination of capacitor $C_i$ and inductor $L_i$. For parallel combination of $L_i$ and $C_i$,

$$Z(s) = \frac{1}{C_i s + \frac{1}{L_i s}} = \frac{\left(\frac{1}{C_i}\right)s}{s^2 + \frac{1}{L_i C_i}} = \frac{2K_i s}{s^2+\omega_i^2}$$

$$C_i = \frac{1}{2K_i} \quad \text{and} \quad L_i = \frac{2K_i}{\omega_i^2}$$

**TABLE 15.1 Realisation of Foster-I form of LC network**

| *Impedance function* | *Element* |
|---|---|
| $\frac{K_0}{s} = \frac{1}{C_0 s}$ | Capacitor; $C_0 = \frac{1}{K_0}$ |
| $\frac{2K_i s}{s^2+\omega_i^2} = \frac{\left(\frac{1}{C_i}\right)s}{s^2+\frac{1}{L_i C_i}}$ | $L_i = \frac{2K_i}{\omega_i^2}$; parallel inductor and capacitor; $C_i = \frac{1}{2K_i}$ |
| $K_\infty s = Ls$ | Inductor; $L_\infty = K_\infty$ |

The network corresponding to Foster I form is shown in Fig. 15.15.

If $Z(s)$ has no pole at the origin then capacitor $C_0$ is not present in the network. Similarly, if there is no pole at ∞, inductor $L_\infty$ is not present in the network.

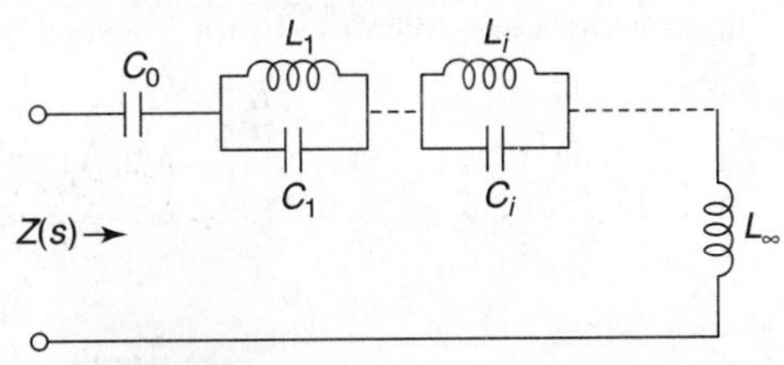


**Fig. 15.15** *Foster-I form of LC network*

➤ ***Foster II Form*** If $F(s)$ represents an admittance function, it gives the parallel combination of admittances.

$$F(s) = Y(s) = \frac{K_0}{s} + \frac{2K_2 s}{s^2 + \omega_2^2} + \ldots + K_\infty s = Y_1(s) + Y_2(s) + \ldots Y_n(s)$$

The first term $\frac{K_0}{s}$ represents the admittance of an inductor of $\frac{1}{K_0}$ henry.

The last term $K_\infty s$ represents the admittance of a capacitor of $K_\infty$ farad.

The remaining terms, i.e., $\frac{2K_i s}{s^2 + \omega_i^2}$ represent the admittance of a series combination of an inductor $L_i$ and a capacitor $C_i$.

For series combination of $L_i$ and $C_i$,

$$Y(s) = \frac{1}{L_i s + \frac{1}{C_i s}} = \frac{\left(\frac{1}{L_i}\right)s}{s^2 + \frac{1}{L_i C_i}} = \frac{2K_i s}{s^2 + \omega_i^2}$$

$$L_i = \frac{1}{2K_i} \quad \text{and} \quad C_i = \frac{2K_i}{\omega_i^2}$$

**TABLE 15.2** **Realisation of Foster-II form of LC network**

| *Admittance function* | *Element* |
|---|---|
| $\frac{K_0}{s} = \frac{1}{L_0 s}$ | $L_0 = \frac{1}{K_0}$ |
| $\frac{2K_i s}{s^2 + \omega_i^2} = \frac{\left(\frac{1}{L_i}\right)s}{s^2 + \frac{1}{L_i C_i}}$ | $L_i = \frac{1}{2K_i}$<br>$C_i = \frac{2K_i}{\omega_i^2}$ |
| $K_\infty s = Cs$ | $C_\infty = K_\infty$ |

The network corresponding to the Foster II form is shown in Fig. 15.16.

If $Y(s)$ has no pole at the origin then inductor $L_0$ is not present. Similarly, if there is no pole at infinity, capacitor $C_\infty$ is not present.

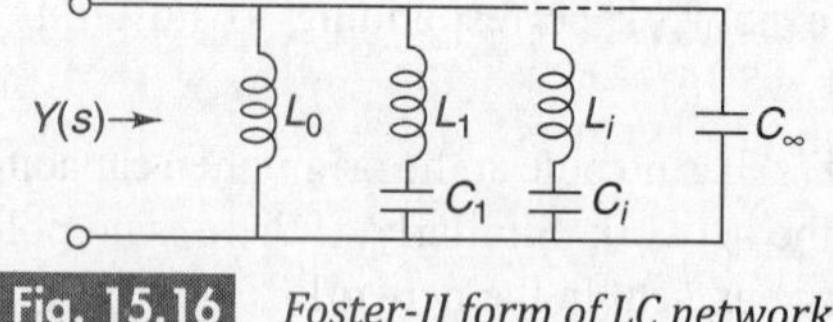


**Fig. 15.16** *Foster-II form of LC network*

### 15.4.2 Cauer Realisation or Ladder Realisation

➤ ***Cauer I Form*** Since the numerator and denominator polynomials of an $LC$ function always differ in degrees by unity, there is always a zero or a pole at $s = \infty$. The Cauer I Form is obtained by successive removal of a pole or a zero at infinity from the function.

Consider an impedance function $Z(s)$ having a pole at infinity.

By removing the pole at infinity, we get

$$Z_2(s) = Z(s) - L_1 s$$

Now, $Z_2(s)$ has a zero at $s = \infty$. If we invert $Z_2(s)$, $Y_2(s)$ will have a pole at $s = \infty$.

By removing this pole,

$$Y_3(s) = Y_2(s) - C_2 s$$

Now, $Y_3(s)$ has a zero at $s = \infty$, which we can invert and remove. This process continues until the remainder is zero. Each time we remove a pole, we remove an inductor or a capacitor depending on whether the function is an impedance or an admittance. The impedance $Z(s)$ can be written as a continued fraction expansion.

$$Z(s) = L_1 s + \cfrac{1}{C_2 s + \cfrac{1}{L_3 s + \cfrac{1}{C_4 s + \ldots}}}$$

Thus, the final structure is a ladder network whose series arms are inductors and shunt arms are capacitors. The Cauer I network is shown in Fig. 15.17.

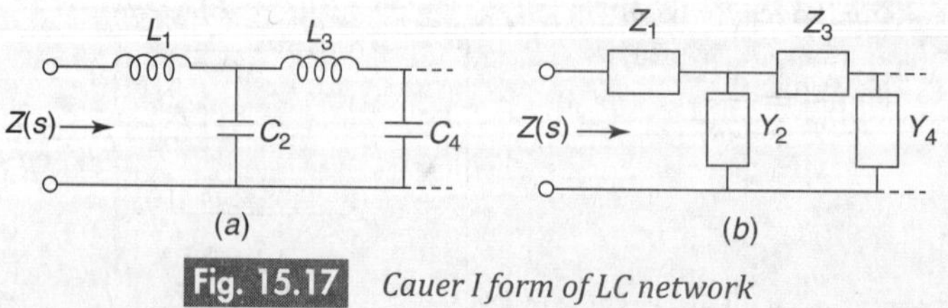


**Fig. 15.17** *Cauer I form of LC network*

If the impedance function has zero at infinity, i.e., if degree of numerator is less than that of its denominator by unity, the function is first inverted and continued fraction expansion proceeds as usual. In this case, the first element is a capacitor, as shown in Fig. 15.18.

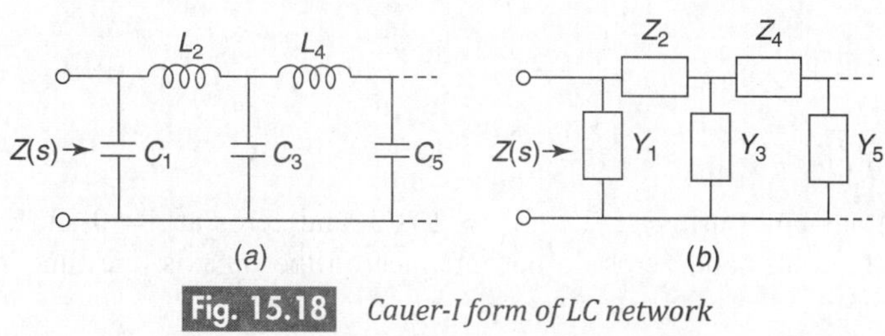


**Fig. 15.18** *Cauer-I form of LC network*

➤ ***Cauer II Form*** Since the lowest degrees of numerator and denominator polynomials of *LC* function must differ by unity, there is always a zero or a pole at $s = 0$. The Cauer II form is obtained by successive removal of a pole or a zero at $s = 0$ from the function.

In this method, continued fraction expansion of $Z(s)$ is carried out in terms of poles at the origin by removal of the pole at the origin, inverting the resultant function to create a pole at the origin, which is removed and this process is continued until the remainder is zero. To do this, we arrange both numerator and denominator polynomials in ascending order and divide the lowest power of the denominator into the lowest power of the numerator. Then we invert the remainder and divide again. The impedance $Z(s)$ can be written as a continued fraction expansion.

$$Z(s) = \frac{1}{C_1 s} + \cfrac{1}{\cfrac{1}{L_2 s} + \cfrac{1}{\cfrac{1}{C_3 s} + \cfrac{1}{\cfrac{1}{L_4 s} + \dots}}}$$

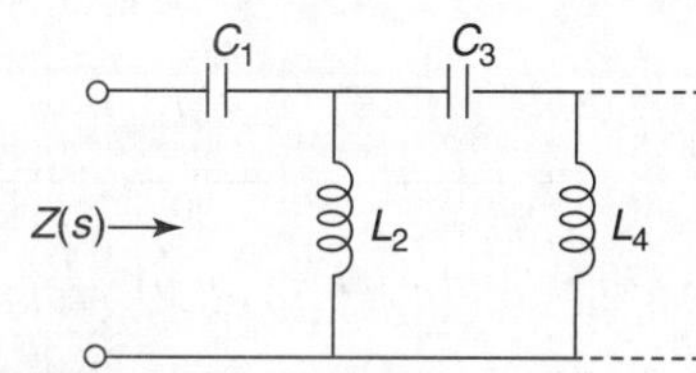


**Fig. 15.19** *Cauer-II form of LC network*

Thus, the final structure is a ladder network whose first element is a series capacitor and second element is a shunt inductor, as shown in Fig. 15.19.

If the impedance function has a zero at the origin then the first element is a shunt inductor and the second element is a series capacitor, as shown in Fig. 15.20.

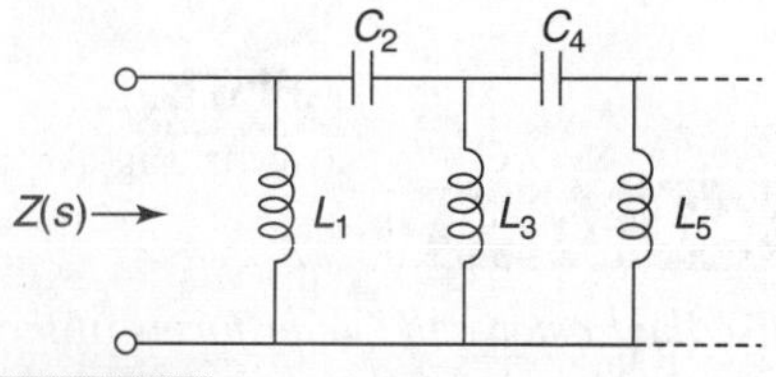


**Fig. 15.20** *Cauer–II form of LC network*

Thus, the *LC* function $F(s)$ can be realised in four different forms. All these forms have the same number of elements and the number is equal to the number of poles and zeros of $F(s)$ including any at infinity.

## EXAMPLE 15.39

*State whether the following functions are driving point immittance of LC networks are not:*

(a) $Z(s) = \dfrac{5s(s^2 + 4)}{(s^2 + 1)(s^2 + 3)}$ (b) $Z(s) = \dfrac{2(s^2 + 1)(s^2 + 9)}{s(s^2 + 2)}$

**Solution**

(a) $Z(s) = \dfrac{5s(s^2+4)}{(s^2+1)(s^2+3)}$

The function $Z(s)$ has poles at $s = \pm j1$ and $s = \pm j\sqrt{3}$ and zeros at $s = 0$ and $s = \pm j2$, as shown in Fig. 15.21. Since the poles and zeros do not interlace on the $j\omega$ axis, the function $Z(s)$ is not an $LC$ impedance function.

(b) $Z(s) = \dfrac{2(s^2+1)(s^2+9)}{s(s^2+2)}$

The function $Z(s)$ has poles at $s = 0$ and $s = \pm j\sqrt{2}$ and zeros at $s = \pm j1$ and $s = \pm j3$, as shown in Fig. 15.22. The poles and zeros are simple and lie on the $j\omega$-axis. The poles and zeros interlace on the $j\omega$ axis. Hence, the function $Z(s)$ is an $LC$ impedance function.

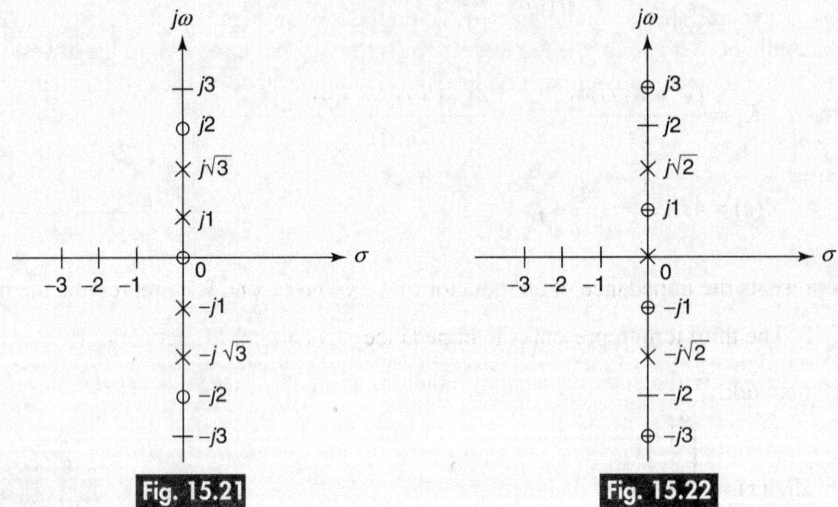


Fig. 15.21 Fig. 15.22

**EXAMPLE 15.40**

*Realise the Foster and Cauer forms of the following impedance function*

$$Z(s) = \frac{4(s^2+1)(s^2+9)}{s(s^2+4)}$$

**Solution** The function $Z(s)$ has poles at $s = 0$ and $s = \pm j2$ and zeros at $s = \pm j1$ and $s = \pm j3$, as shown in Fig. 15.23.

From the pole-zero diagram, it is clear that poles and zeros are simple and lie on the $j\omega$ axis. Poles and zeros are interlaced. Hence, the given function is an $LC$ function.

***Foster I Form*** The Foster I form is obtained by partial fraction expansion of the impedance function $Z(s)$. But degree of numerator is greater than degree of denominator. Hence, division is first carried out.

$$Z(s)=\frac{4(s^2+1)(s^2+9)}{s(s^2+4)}=\frac{4s^4+40s^2+36}{s^3+4s}$$

$$s^3+4s)\;4s^4+40s^2+36\;(4s$$
$$\underline{4s^4+16s^2}$$
$$24s^2+36$$

$$Z(s)=4s+\frac{24s^2+36}{s^3+4s}=4s+\frac{24s^2+36}{s(s^2+4)}$$

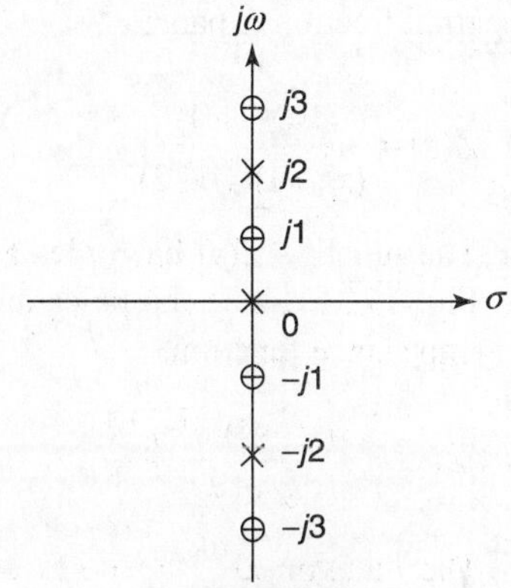

jω, j3, j2, j1, 0, σ, −j1, −j2, −j3

Fig. 15.23

By partial fraction expansion,

$$Z(s)=4s+\frac{K_0}{s}+\frac{K_1}{s+j2}+\frac{K_1^*}{s-j2}=4s+\frac{K_0}{s}+\frac{2K_1s}{s^2+4}$$

where $\quad K_0=sZ(s)\big|_{s=0}=\dfrac{4(1)(9)}{4}=9$

$$K_1=\left.\frac{(s^2+4)Z(s)}{2s}\right|_{s^2=-4}=\frac{4(-4+1)(-4+9)}{2(-4)}=\frac{15}{2}$$

$$Z(s)=4s+\frac{9}{s}+\frac{15s}{s^2+4}$$

The first term represents the impedance of an inductor of 4 H. The second term represents the impedance of a capacitor of $\frac{1}{9}$ F. The third term represents the impedance of a parallel $LC$ network.

For a parallel $LC$ network,

$$Z_{LC}(s)=\frac{\left(\frac{1}{C}\right)s}{s^2+\frac{1}{LC}}$$

By direct comparison,

$$C=\frac{1}{15}\text{F}$$

$$L=\frac{15}{4}\text{H}$$

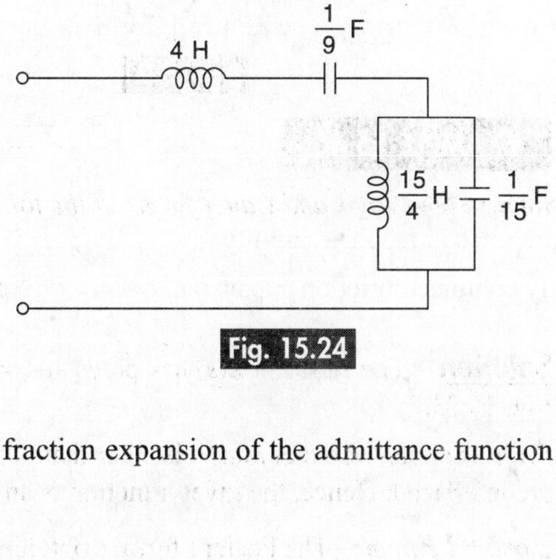

4 H, $\frac{1}{9}$ F, $\frac{15}{4}$ H, $\frac{1}{15}$ F

Fig. 15.24

The network is shown in Fig. 15.24.

***Foster II Form*** The Foster II form is obtained by partial fraction expansion of the admittance function $Y(s)$.

$$Y(s)=\frac{s(s^2+4)}{4(s^2+1)(s^2+9)}$$

By partial fraction expansion,

$$Y(s) = \frac{K_1}{s+j1} + \frac{K_1^*}{s-j1} + \frac{K_2}{s+j3} + \frac{K_2^*}{s-j3} = \frac{2K_1 s}{s^2+1} + \frac{2K_2 s}{s^2+9}$$

where

$$K_1 = \frac{(s^2+1)}{2s} Y(s)\bigg|_{s^2=-1} = \frac{(-1+4)}{8(-1+9)} = \frac{3}{64}$$

$$K_2 = \frac{(s^2+9)}{2s} Y(s)\bigg|_{s^2=-9} = \frac{(-9+4)}{8(-9+1)} = \frac{5}{64}$$

$$Y(s) = \frac{\left(\frac{3}{32}\right)s}{s^2+1} + \frac{\left(\frac{5}{32}\right)s}{s^2+9}$$

These two terms represent admittance of a series $LC$ network. For a series $LC$ network,

$$Y_{LC}(s) = \frac{\left(\frac{1}{L}\right)s}{s^2 + \frac{1}{LC}}$$

By direct comparison,

$$L_1 = \frac{32}{3}\text{ H} \qquad C_1 = \frac{3}{32}\text{ F}$$

$$L_2 = \frac{32}{5}\text{ H} \qquad C_2 = \frac{5}{288}\text{ F}$$

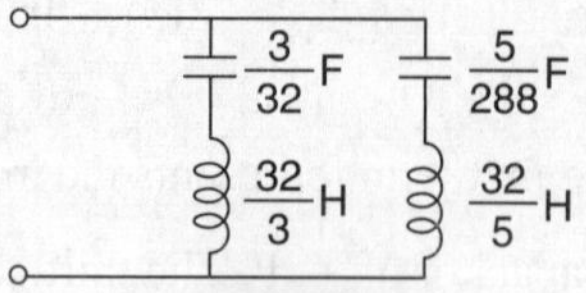

Fig. 15.25

The network is shown in Fig. 15.25.

***Cauer I Form*** The Cauer I form is obtained from continued fraction expansion about the pole at infinity.

$$Z(s) = \frac{4s^4 + 40s^2 + 36}{s^3 + 4s}$$

Since the degree of the numerator is greater than the degree of the denominator by one, it indicates the presence of a pole at infinity.

By continued fraction expansion,

$$\begin{array}{l} s^3+4s \overline{)\,4s^4+40s^2+36\,(}\; 4s \leftarrow Z \\ \qquad\quad\;\; \underline{4s^4+16s^2} \\ \qquad\qquad 24s^2+36 \overline{)\,s^3+4s\,(}\; \frac{1}{24}s \leftarrow Y \\ \qquad\qquad\qquad\quad\; \underline{s^3+\frac{3}{2}s} \end{array}$$

$$\frac{5}{2}s\Big)24s^2+36\Big(\frac{48}{5}s \leftarrow Z$$
$$\underline{24s^2}$$
$$36\Big)\frac{5}{2}s\Big(\frac{5}{72}s \leftarrow Y$$
$$\underline{\frac{5}{2}s}$$
$$0$$

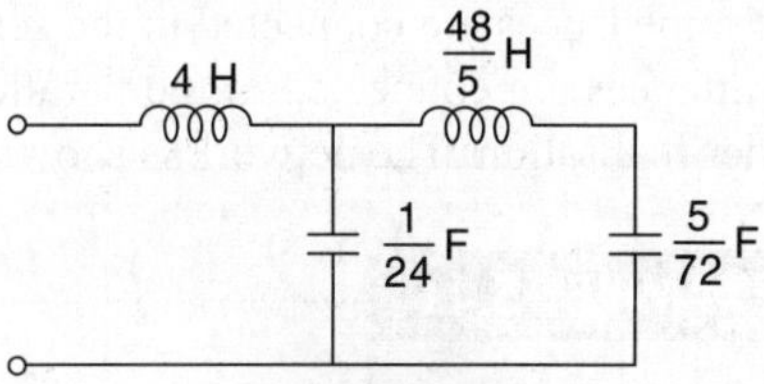

The impedances are connected in the series branches whereas the admittances are connected in the parallel branches in a Cauer or ladder realisation. The network is shown in Fig. 15.26.



Fig. 15.26

***Cauer II Form*** The Cauer II form is obtained from partial fraction expansion about pole at origin.

$$Z(s)=\frac{4(s^2+1)(s^2+9)}{s(s^2+4)}=\frac{4s^4+40s^2+36}{s^3+4s}$$

The function $Z(s)$ has a pole at origin. Arranging the numerator and denominator polynomials in ascending order of $s$,

$$Z(s)=\frac{36+40s^2+4s^4}{4s+s^3}$$

By continued fraction expansion,

$$4s+s^3\Big)36+40s^2+4s^4\Big(\frac{9}{s} \leftarrow Z$$
$$\underline{36+\ 9s^2}$$
$$31s^2+4s^4\Big)4s+s^3\Big(\frac{4}{31s} \leftarrow Y$$
$$\underline{4s+\frac{16}{31}s^3}$$
$$\frac{15}{31}s^3\Big)31s^2+4s^4\Big(\frac{961}{15s} \leftarrow Z$$
$$\underline{31s^2}$$

$$4s^4\Big)\frac{15}{31}s^3\Big(\frac{15}{124s} \leftarrow Y$$
$$\frac{\frac{15}{31}s^3}{0}$$

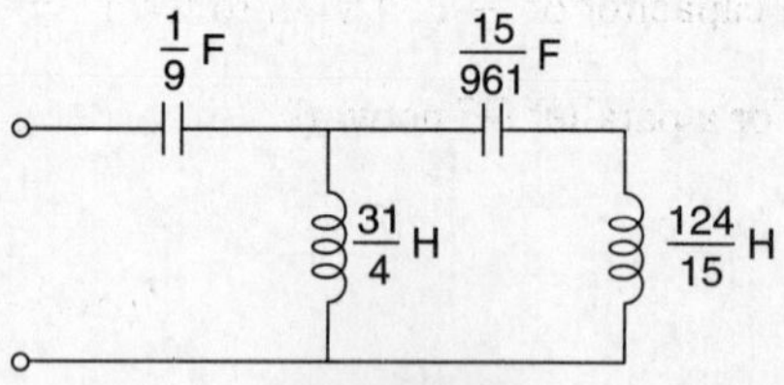

$\frac{1}{9}$ F $\quad \frac{15}{961}$ F $\quad \frac{31}{4}$ H $\quad \frac{124}{15}$ H

Fig. 15.27

The impedances are connected in the series branches whereas the admittances are connected in the parallel branches in a Cauer or ladder realisation. The network is shown in Fig. 15.27.

## EXAMPLE 15.41

*Realise Foster forms of the LC impedance function*

$$Z(s) = \frac{(s^2 + 1)(s^2 + 3)}{s(s^2 + 2)}$$

### Solution

***Foster I Form*** The Foster I form is obtained by partial fraction expansion of the impedance function $Z(s)$. Since the degree of the numerator is greater than the degree of the denominator, division is first carried out.

$$Z(s) = \frac{(s^2 + 1)(s^2 + 3)}{s(s^2 + 2)} = \frac{s^4 + 4s^2 + 3}{s^3 + 2s}$$

$$\begin{array}{r|l} s^3 + 2s \,\big) \; s^4 + 4s^2 + 3 & \big( s \\ s^4 + 2s^2 & \\ \hline 2s^2 + 3 & \end{array}$$

$$Z(s) = s + \frac{2s^2 + 3}{s^3 + 2s} = s + \frac{2s^2 + 3}{s(s^2 + 2)}$$

By partial fraction expansion,

$$Z(s) = s + \frac{K_0}{s} + \frac{K_1}{s + j2} + \frac{K_1^*}{s - j2} = s + \frac{K_0}{s} + \frac{2K_1 s}{s^2 + 2}$$

where
$$K_0 = sZ(s)|_{s=0} = \frac{(1)(3)}{2} = \frac{3}{2}$$

$$K_1 = \frac{(s^2 + 2)}{2s} Z(s)\bigg|_{s^2=-2} = \frac{(-2+1)(-2+3)}{2(-2)} = \frac{1}{4}$$

$$Z(s) = s + \frac{\left(\frac{3}{2}\right)}{s} + \frac{\left(\frac{1}{2}\right)s}{s^2 + 2}$$

The first term represents the impedance of an inductor of 1 H. The second term represents the impedance of a capacitor of $\frac{2}{3}$ F. The third term represents the impedance of a parallel $LC$ network.

For a parallel $LC$ network,

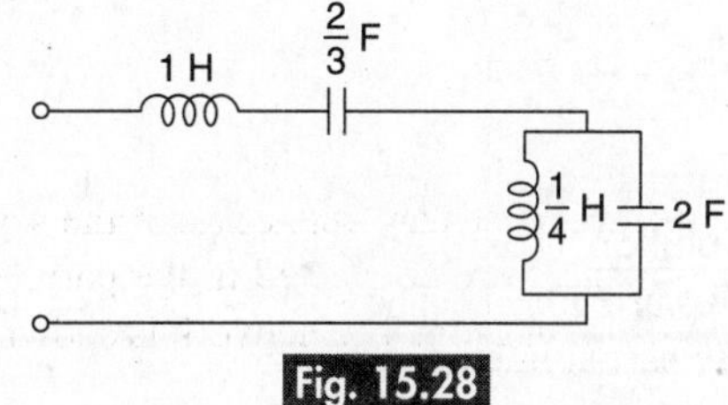

Fig. 15.28

$$Z_{LC}(s) = \frac{\left(\frac{1}{C}\right)s}{s^2 + \frac{1}{LC}}$$

By direct comparison,

$$C = 2\text{F}$$

$$L = \frac{1}{4}\text{H}$$

The network is shown in Fig. 15.28.

***Foster II Form*** The Foster II form is obtained by partial fraction expansion of the admittance function $Y(s)$.

$$Y(s) = \frac{s(s^2+2)}{(s^2+1)(s^2+3)}$$

By partial fraction expansion,

$$Y(s) = \frac{K_1}{s+j1} + \frac{K_1^*}{s-j1} + \frac{K_2}{s+j\sqrt{3}} + \frac{K_2^*}{s-j\sqrt{3}} = \frac{2K_1 s}{s^2+1} + \frac{2K_2 s}{s^2+3}$$

where

$$K_1 = \left.\frac{(s^2+1)}{2s} Y(s)\right|_{s^2=-1} = \frac{(-1+2)}{2(-1+3)} = \frac{1}{4}$$

$$K_2 = \left.\frac{(s^2+3)}{2s} Y(s)\right|_{s^2=-3} = \frac{-3+2}{2(-3+1)} = \frac{1}{4}$$

$$Y(s) = \frac{\left(\frac{1}{2}\right)s}{s^2+1} + \frac{\left(\frac{1}{2}\right)s}{s^2+3}$$

These two terms represent admittance of a series $LC$ network. For a series $LC$ network,

$$Y_{LC}(s) = \frac{\left(\frac{1}{L}\right)s}{s^2 + \frac{1}{LC}}$$

By direct comparison,

$$L_1 = 2\text{H}, \quad C_1 = \frac{1}{2}\text{F}$$

$$L_2 = 2\text{H}, \quad C_2 = \frac{1}{6}\text{F}$$

The network is shown in Fig. 15.29.

Fig. 15.29

**EXAMPLE 15.42**

*Realise Foster forms of the following LC impedance function:*

$$Z(s) = \frac{(s^2+1)(s^2+3)}{s(s^2+2)(s^2+4)}$$

**Solution**

***Foster I Form*** The Foster I form is obtained by partial fraction expansion of the impedance function $Z(s)$. By partial fraction expansion,

$$Z(s) = \frac{K_0}{s} + \frac{K_1}{s+j\sqrt{2}} + \frac{K_1^*}{s-j\sqrt{2}} + \frac{K_2}{s+j2} + \frac{K_2^*}{s-j2} = \frac{K_0}{s} + \frac{2K_1 s}{s^2+2} + \frac{2K_2 s}{s^2+4}$$

where $K_0 = sZ(s)\big|_{s=0} = \frac{(1)(3)}{(2)(4)} = \frac{3}{8}$

$$K_1 = \frac{(s^2+2)}{2s} Z(s)\bigg|_{s^2=-2} = \frac{(-2+1)(-2+3)}{2(-2)(-2+4)} = \frac{1}{8}$$

$$K_2 = \frac{(s^2+4)}{2s} Z(s)\bigg|_{s^2=-4} = \frac{(-4+1)(-4+3)}{2(-4)(-4+2)} = \frac{3}{16}$$

$$Z(s) = \frac{\frac{3}{8}}{s} + \frac{\left(\frac{1}{4}\right)s}{s^2+2} + \frac{\left(\frac{3}{8}\right)s}{s^2+4}$$

The first term represents the impedance of a capacitor of $\frac{8}{3}$ F. The other two terms represent the impedance of a parallel $LC$ network.

For a parallel $LC$ network,

$$Z_{LC}(s) = \frac{\left(\frac{1}{C}\right)s}{s^2 + \frac{1}{LC}}$$

By direct comparison,

$$C_1 = 4\text{F}, \quad L_1 = \frac{1}{8}\text{H}$$

$$C_2 = \frac{8}{3}\text{F}, \quad L_2 = \frac{3}{32}\text{H}$$

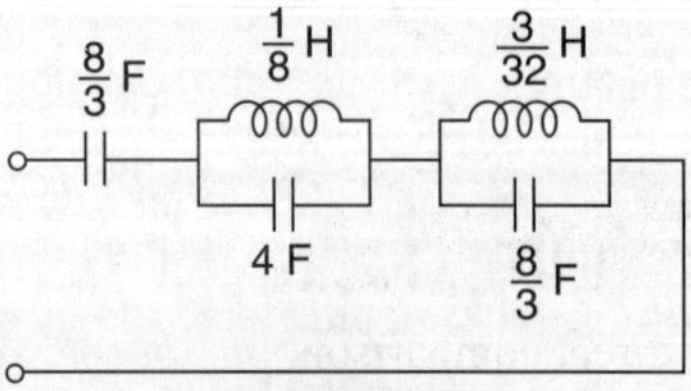

The network is shown in Fig. 15.30.



Fig. 15.30

***Foster II Form*** The Foster II form is obtained by partial fraction expansion of the admittance function $Y(s)$.

$$Y(s) = \frac{s(s^2+2)(s^2+4)}{(s^2+1)(s^2+3)} = \frac{s^5+6s^3+8s}{s^4+4s^2+3}$$

Since the degree of the numerator is greater than the degree of the denominator, division is first carried out.

$$s^4+4s^2+3)\,s^5+6s^3+8s\,(s$$
$$\underline{s^5+4s^3+3s}$$
$$2s^3+5s$$

$$Y(s)=s+\frac{2s^3+5s}{s^4+4s^2+3}=s+\frac{2s^3+5s}{(s^2+1)(s^2+3)}$$

By partial fraction expansion,

$$Y(s)=s+\frac{K_1}{s+j1}+\frac{K_1^*}{s-j1}+\frac{K_2}{s+j\sqrt{3}}+\frac{K_2^*}{s-j\sqrt{3}}=s+\frac{2K_1s}{s^2+1}+\frac{2K_2s}{s^2+3}$$

where

$$K_1=\frac{(s^2+1)}{2s}Y(s)\bigg|_{s^2=-1}=\frac{(-1+2)(-1+4)}{2(-1+3)}=\frac{3}{4}$$

$$K_2=\frac{(s^2+3)}{2s}Y(s)\bigg|_{s^2=-3}=\frac{(-3+2)(-3+4)}{2(-3+1)}=\frac{1}{4}$$

$$Y(s)=s+\frac{\left(\frac{3}{2}\right)s}{s^2+1}+\frac{\left(\frac{1}{2}\right)s}{s^2+3}$$

The first term represents the admittance of capacitor of 1 F. The other two terms represent admittance of a series $LC$ network. For a series $LC$ network,

$$Y_{LC}(s)=\frac{\left(\frac{1}{L}\right)s}{s^2+\frac{1}{LC}}$$

By direct comparison,

$$L_1=\frac{2}{3}\text{H},\quad C_1=\frac{3}{2}\text{F}$$

$$L_2=2\,\text{H},\quad C_2=\frac{1}{6}\text{F}$$

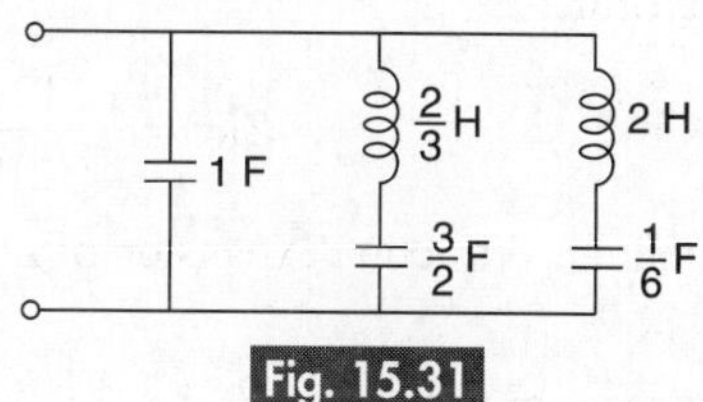

Fig. 15.31

The network is shown in Fig. 15.31.

## EXAMPLE 15.43

*Realise Cauer forms of the following LC impedance function:*

$$Z(s)=\frac{10s^4+12s^2+1}{2s^3+2s}$$

**Solution**

***Cauer I Form*** The Cauer I form is obtained from continued fraction expansion about the pole at infinity.

$$Z(s)=\frac{10s^4+12s^2+1}{2s^3+2s}$$

Since the degree of the numerator is greater than the degree of the denominator by one, it indicates the presence of a pole at infinity.

By continued fraction expansion,

$$2s^3+2s)\,10s^4+12s^2+1\,(5s \leftarrow Z$$
$$\underline{10s^4+10s^2}$$
$$2s^2+1)\,2s^3+2s\,(s \leftarrow Y$$
$$\underline{2s^3+s}$$
$$s)\,2s^2+1\,(2s \leftarrow Z$$
$$\underline{2s^2}$$
$$1)\,s\,(s \leftarrow Y$$
$$\underline{s}$$
$$0$$

The impedances are connected in the series branches whereas the admittances are connected in the parallel branches in a Cauer or ladder realisation. The network is shown in Fig. 15.32.

5 H, 2 H, 1 F, 1 F

Fig. 15.32

***Cauer II Form*** The Cauer II form is obtained from continued fraction expansion about the pole at the origin.

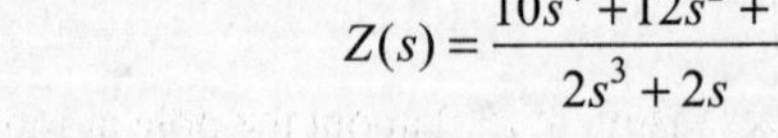

$$Z(s)=\frac{10s^4+12s^2+1}{2s^3+2s}$$

The function $Z(s)$ has a pole at the origin. Arranging the numerator and denominator polynomials in ascending order of $s$,

$$Z(s)=\frac{1+12s^2+10s^4}{2s+2s^3}$$

By continued fraction expansion of $Z(s)$,

$$2s+2s^3\Big)\,1+12s^2+10s^4\Big(\frac{1}{2s} \leftarrow Z$$
$$\underline{1+\ \ s^2}$$
$$11s^2+10s^4\Big)\,2s+2s^3\Big(\frac{2}{11s} \leftarrow Y$$
$$\underline{2s+\frac{20}{11}s^3}$$
$$\frac{2}{11}s^3\Big)\,11s^2+10s^4\Big(\frac{121}{2s} \leftarrow Z$$

$$\begin{array}{r} 11s^2 \\ \hline 10s^4 \overline{)\frac{2}{11}s^3}\left(\frac{2}{110s} \leftarrow Y \right. \\ \frac{2}{11}s^3 \\ \hline 0 \end{array}$$

The impedances are connected in the series branches whereas the admittances are connected in the parallel branches in Cauer or ladder realisation. The network is shown in Fig. 15.33.

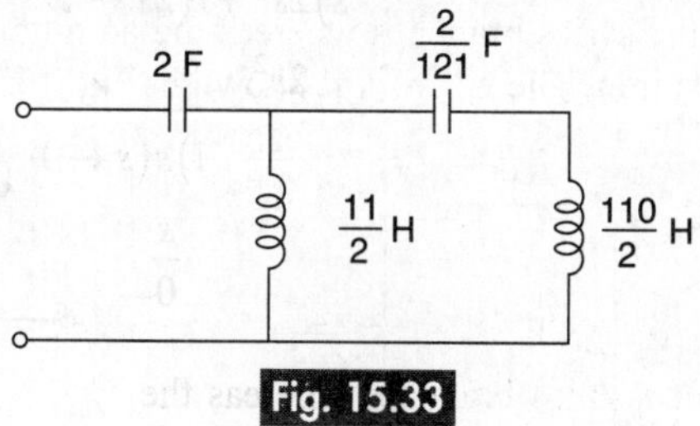


Fig. 15.33

**EXAMPLE 15.44**

*Realise the following network function in Cauer I form:*

$$Z(s) = \frac{6s^4 + 42s^2 + 48}{s^5 + 18s^3 + 48s}$$

**Solution** The Cauer I form is obtained by continued fraction expansion of $Z(s)$ about the pole at infinity. In the above function, the degree of the numerator is less than the degree of the denominator, which indicates the presence of a zero at infinity. The admittance function $Y(s)$ has a pole at infinity. Hence, the continued fraction expansion of $Y(s)$ is carried out.

$$Y(s) = \frac{s^5 + 18s^3 + 48s}{6s^4 + 42s^2 + 48}$$

By continued fraction expansion

$$6s^4 + 42s^2 + s^2 \overline{)s^5 + 18s^3 + 48s}\left(\frac{1}{6}s \leftarrow Y \right.$$

$$\underline{s^5 + 7s^3 + 8s}$$

$$11s^3 + 40s \overline{)6s^4 + 42s^2 + 48}\left(\frac{6}{11}s \leftarrow Z \right.$$

$$\underline{6s^4 + \frac{240}{11}s^2}$$

$$\frac{222}{11}s^2 + 30 \overline{)11s^3 + 40s}\left(\frac{121}{222}s \leftarrow Y \right.$$

$$\underline{11s^3 + \frac{5808}{222}s}$$

$$\frac{3072}{222}s\overline{\Big)\frac{222}{11}s^2+48}\Big(\frac{49284}{33792}s \leftarrow Z$$

$$\frac{222}{11}s^2$$

$$48\overline{\Big)\frac{3072}{222}s}\Big(\frac{128}{444}s \leftarrow Y$$

$$\frac{3072}{222}s$$

$$0$$

The impedances are connected in the series branches whereas the admittances are connected in the parallel branches in a Cauer or ladder realisation. The network is shown in Fig. 15.34.

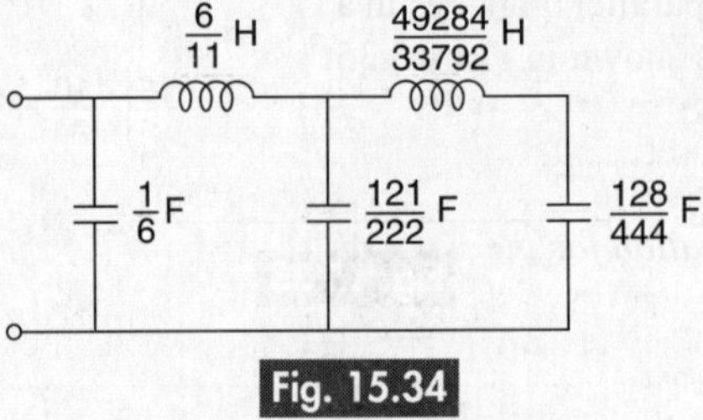


Fig. 15.34

## EXAMPLE 15.45

*Realise Cauer II form of the function:*

$$Z_{LC}(s)=\frac{s(s^4+3s^2+1)}{3s^4+4s^2+1}$$

**Solution** The Cauer II form is obtained by continued fraction expansion about the pole at the origin. The given function has a zero at the origin. The admittance function $Y(s)$ has a pole at origin. Hence, the continued fraction expansion of $Y(s)$ is carried out. Arranging the polynomials in ascending order of s,

$$Y_{LC}(s)=\frac{3s^4+4s^2+1}{s^5+3s^3+s}=\frac{1+4s^2+3s^4}{s+3s^3+s^5}$$

By continued fraction expansion of $Y(s)$, we have

$$s+3s^3+s^5\overline{\Big)1+4s^2+3s^4}\Big(\frac{1}{s}\leftarrow Y$$

$$1+3s^2+s^4$$

$$s^2+2s^4\overline{\Big)s+3s^3+s^5}\Big(\frac{1}{s}\leftarrow Z$$

$$s+2s^3$$

$$s^3+s^5\overline{\Big)s^2+2s^4}\Big(\frac{1}{s}\leftarrow Y$$

$$
\begin{array}{l}
s^2 + s^4 \\
\hline
s^4 \overline{)\, s^3 + s^5} \left( \frac{1}{s} \leftarrow Z \right. \\
\quad s^3 \\
\hline
s^5 \overline{)\, s^4} \left( \frac{1}{s} \leftarrow Y \right. \\
\quad s^4 \\
\hline
\quad 0
\end{array}
$$

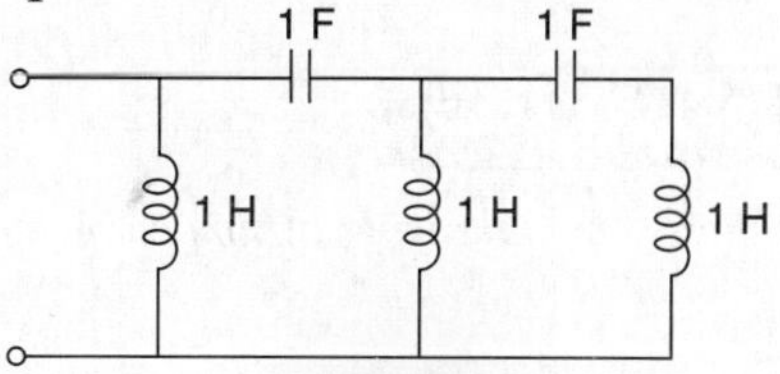

The impedances are connected in the series branches whereas the admittances are connected in the parallel branches in a Cauer or ladder realisation. The network is shown in Fig. 15.35.

1 F 1 F 1 H 1 H 1 H

Fig. 15.35

## EXAMPLE 15.46

*Obtain the Cauer I form of realisation for the function*

$$Z_{LC}(s) = \frac{s^5 + 7s^3 + 10s}{s^4 + 5s^2 + 4}$$

**Solution** The Cauer I form is obtained by continued fraction expansion of $Z_{LC}(s)$ about pole at infinity.

$$
\begin{array}{l}
s^4 + 5s^2 + 4 \overline{)\, s^5 + 7s^3 + 10s} \left( s \leftarrow Z \right. \\
\quad s^5 + 5s^3 + 4s \\
\hline
2s^3 + 6s \overline{)\, s^4 + 5s^2 + 4} \left( \frac{1}{2} s \leftarrow Y \right. \\
\quad s^4 + 3s^2 \\
\hline
2s^2 + 4 \overline{)\, 2s^3 + 6s} \left( s \leftarrow Z \right. \\
\quad 2s^3 + 4s \\
\hline
2s \overline{)\, 2s^2 + 4} \left( s \leftarrow Y \right. \\
\quad 2s^2 \\
\hline
4 \overline{)\, 2s} \left( \frac{1}{2} s \leftarrow Z \right. \\
\quad 2s \\
\hline
\quad 0
\end{array}
$$

The impedances are connected in the series branches, whereas the admittances are connected in the parallel branches in a Cauer or ladder realisation. The network is shown in Fig. 15.36.

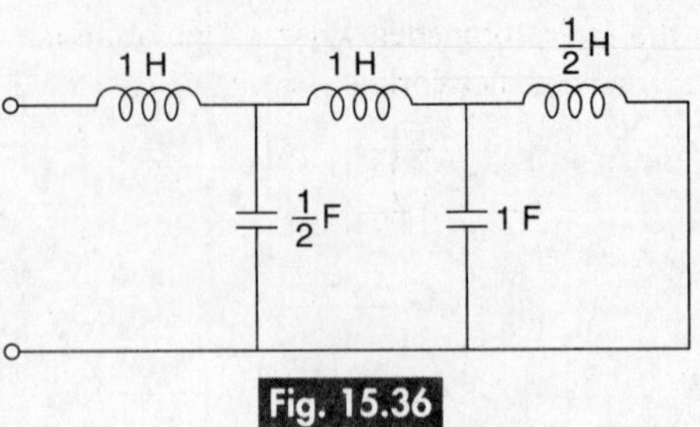


Fig. 15.36

**EXAMPLE 15.47**

*Synthesise the following LC impedance function in Cauer II form:*

$$Z(s) = \frac{s^3 + 2s}{s^4 + 4s^2 + 3}$$

**Solution** The Cauer II form is obtained by continued fraction expansion about the pole at the origin.

$$Z(s) = \frac{s(s^2 + 2)}{(s^2 + 3)(s^2 + 1)}$$

But $Z(s)$ has a zero at the origin. Hence, the continued fraction expansion of $Y(s)$ is carried out. Arranging the polynomials in ascending order of $s$,

$$Y(s) = \frac{3 + 4s^2 + s^4}{2s + s^3}$$

By continued fraction expansion of $Y(s)$,

$$2s + s^3 \overline{\big)\, 3 + 4s^2 + s^4 \,\big(} \frac{3}{2s} \leftarrow Y$$

$$\underline{3 + \frac{3}{2}s^2}$$

$$\frac{5}{2}s^2 + s^4 \overline{\big)\, 2s + s^3 \,\big(} \frac{4}{5s} \leftarrow Z$$

$$\underline{2s + \frac{4}{5}s^3}$$

$$\frac{s^3}{5} \overline{\big)\, \frac{5}{2}s^2 + s^4 \,\big(} \frac{25}{2s} \leftarrow Y$$

$$\underline{\frac{5}{2}s^2}$$

$$s^4 \overline{\big)\, \frac{1}{5}s^3 \,\big(} \frac{1}{5s} \leftarrow Z$$

$$\underline{\frac{1}{5}s^3}$$

$$0$$

The impedances are connected in the series branches whereas the admittances are connected in the parallel branches in a Cauer or ladder realisation. The network is shown in Fig. 15.37.

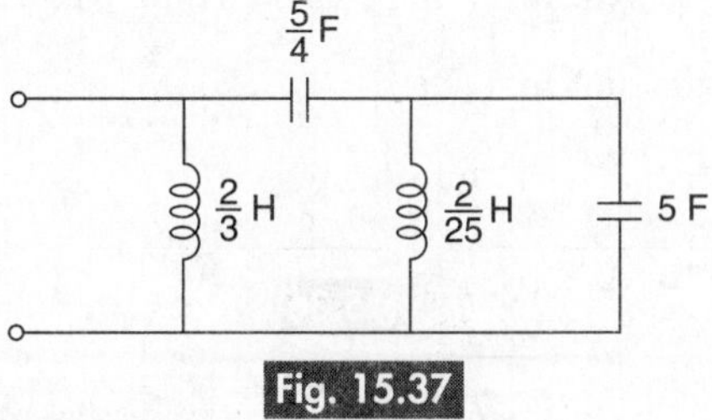


Fig. 15.37

## 15.5 REALISATION OF *RC* FUNCTIONS

LO 15.5

Explain Foster and Cauer forms of realising *RC* functions, and their properties

*RC* driving point immittance functions have following properties:

1. The poles and zeros are simple and are located on the negative real axis of the *s*-plane.
2. The poles and zeros are interlaced.
3. The lowest critical frequency nearest to the origin is a pole.
4. The highest critical frequency farthest to the origin is a zero.
5. Residues evaluated at the poles of $Z_{RC}(s)$ are real and positive.
6. The slope $\frac{d}{d\sigma} Z_{RC}$ is negative.
7. $Z_{RC}(\infty) < Z_{RC}(0)$.

RC functions can also be realised in four different ways. The impedance function of RC networks is given by

$$Z(s) = \frac{H(s+\sigma_1)(s+\sigma_3)...}{s(s+\sigma_2)...}$$

### 15.5.1 Foster Realisation

➤ ***Foster I Form*** The Foster I form is obtained by partial fraction expansion of $Z(s)$.

$$Z(s) = \frac{K_0}{s} + \frac{K_1}{s+\sigma_1} + \frac{K_2}{s+\sigma_2} + ... + K_\infty$$

where $K_0, K_1, K_2, \ldots K_\infty$ are residues of $Z(s)$.

$$K_o = sZ(s)\big|_{s=0}$$

$$K_i = (s+\sigma_i)Z(s)\big| s = -\sigma_i$$

$$K_\infty = \frac{Z(s)}{s}\bigg|_{s\to\infty}$$

The first term $\frac{K_0}{s}$ represents the impedance of a capacitor of $\frac{1}{K_o}$ farads.

The last term $K_\infty$ represents the impedance of a resistor of $K_\infty$ ohms.

The remaining terms, i.e., $\frac{K_i}{s+\sigma_i}$ represent the impedance of the parallel combination of resistor $R_i$ and capacitor $C_i$. For parallel combination of $R_i$ and $C_i$,

$$Z(s) = \frac{R_i\left(\frac{1}{C_i s}\right)}{R_i + \frac{1}{C_i s}} = \frac{K_i}{s+\sigma_i}$$

$$R_i = \frac{K_i}{\sigma_i} \text{ and } C_i = \frac{1}{K_i}$$

**TABLE 15.3 Realisation of Foster-II form of RC network**

| *Impedance function* | *Element* |
|---|---|
| $\frac{K_0}{s} = \frac{1}{C_0 s}$ | (capacitor) $C_0 = \frac{1}{K_0}$ |
| $\frac{K_i}{s+\sigma_i} = \frac{(R_i)\left(\frac{1}{C_i s}\right)}{R_i + \frac{1}{C_i s}}$ | $Ri = \frac{K_i}{\sigma_i}$ (resistor in parallel with capacitor) $C_i = \frac{1}{K_i}$ |
| $K_\infty = R_\infty$ | (resistor) $R_\infty = K_\infty$ |

The network corresponding to the Foster-I form is shown in Fig. 15.38.

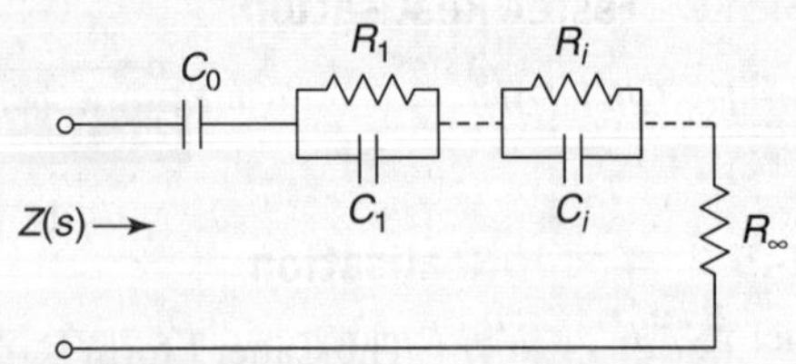


**Fig. 15.38** *Foster-I form of RC network*

➤ ***Foster II Form*** The Foster-II form is obtained by partial fraction expansion of $Y(s)$. Since $Y(s) = \frac{1}{Z(s)}$ has negative residue at its pole, Foster II form is obtained by expanding $\frac{Y(s)}{s}$.

$$\frac{Y(s)}{s} = \frac{K_o}{s} + \sum_{i=1}^{n} \frac{K_i}{(s+\sigma_i)} + K_\infty$$

Multiplying this equation by $s$,

$$Y(s) = K_o + \sum_{i=1}^{n} \frac{K_i s}{(s+\sigma_i)} + K_\infty s$$

The first term $K_o$ represents the conductance of a resistor of $\dfrac{1}{K_o}$ ohms.

The last term $K_\infty s$ represents the admittance of a capacitor of $K_\infty$ farads.

The remaining terms, i.e., $\dfrac{K_i s}{s+\sigma_i}$ represent the admittance of series combination of resistor $R_i$ and capacitor $C_i$ with $R_i = \dfrac{1}{K_i}$ ohms and $C_i = \dfrac{K_i}{\sigma_i}$ farads.

**TABLE 15.4 Realisation of Foster-II form of RC network**

| *Admittance function* | *Element* |
|---|---|
| $K_0 = \dfrac{1}{R_0}$ | $R_o = \dfrac{1}{K_o}$ |
| $\dfrac{K_i}{s+\omega_i} = \dfrac{\left(\dfrac{1}{R_i}\right)s}{s+\dfrac{1}{R_iC_i}}$ | $R_i = \dfrac{1}{K_i}$, $C_i = \dfrac{K_i}{\sigma_i}$ |
| $K_\infty s = C_\infty s$ | $C_\infty = K_\infty$ |

The network corresponding to the Foster II form is shown in Fig. 15.39.

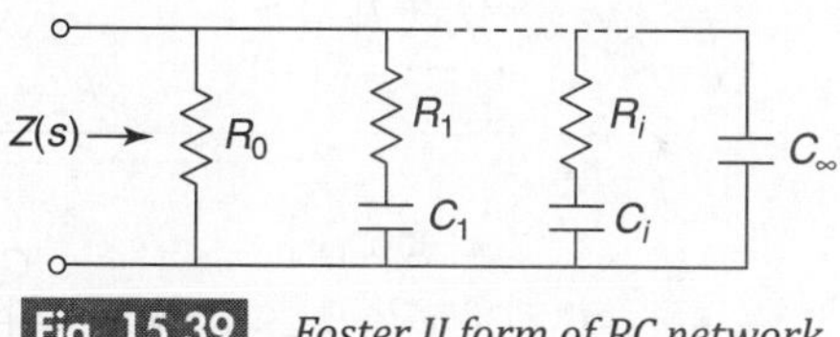


**Fig. 15.39** *Foster II form of RC network*

### 15.5.2 Cauer Realisation

➤ ***Cauer I Form*** The Cauer I form is obtained by removal of the pole from the impedance function $Z(s)$ at $s = \infty$. This is the same as a continued fraction expansion of the impedance function about infinity. The impedance $Z(s)$ can be written as a continued fraction expansion.

$$Z(s) = R_1 + \cfrac{1}{C_2 s + \cfrac{1}{R_3 + \cfrac{1}{C_4 s + \ldots}}}$$

The network is shown in Fig. 15.40.

**Fig. 15.40** *Cauer-I form of RC network*

In the network shown in Fig. 15.40, if $Z(s)$ has a zero at $s = \infty$, the first element is the capacitor $C_1$. If $Z(s)$ is a constant at $s = \infty$, the first element is $R_1$. If $Z(s)$ has a pole at $s = 0$, the last element is $C_n$. If $Z(s)$ is a constant at $s = 0$, the last element is $R_n$.

➤ ***Cauer II Form*** The Cauer II form is obtained by removal of the pole from the impedance function at the origin. This is the same as a continued fraction expansion of an impedance function about the origin. If the given impedance function has a pole at the origin, it is removed as a capacitor $C_1$. The reciprocal of the remainder function has a minimum value at $s = 0$, which is removed as a constant of resistor $R_2$. If the original impedance has no pole at the origin, then the first capacitor is absent and the process is repeated with the removal of the constant corresponding to the resistor $R_2$.

The impedance $Z(s)$ can be written as a continued fraction expansion.

$$Z(s) = \cfrac{1}{C_1 s} + \cfrac{1}{\cfrac{1}{R_2} + \cfrac{1}{\cfrac{1}{C_3 s} + \cfrac{1}{\cfrac{1}{R_4} + \dots}}}$$

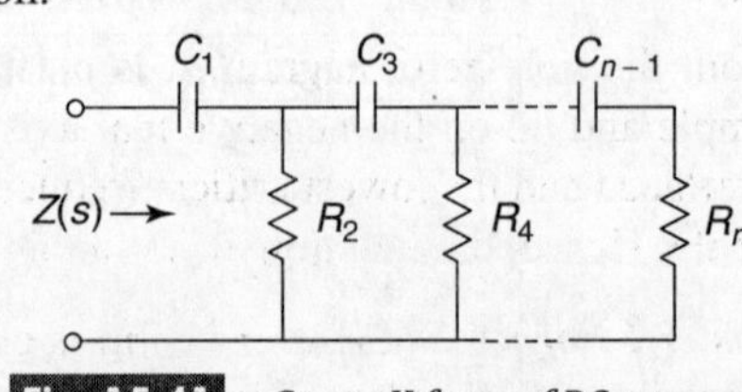

Fig. 15.41 *Cauer-II form of RC network*

The network is shown in Fig. 15.41.

In the network shown in Fig. 15.41, if $Z(s)$ has a pole at $s = 0$, the first element is $C_1$. If $Z(s)$ is a constant at $s = 0$, the first element is $R_2$. If $Z(s)$ has a zero at $s = \infty$, the last element is $C_n$. If $Z(s)$ is constant at $s = \infty$, the last element is $R_n$.

**EXAMPLE 15.48**

*Determine whether following functions are RC impedance function or not.*

*(a)* $Z(s) = \dfrac{3(s+2)(s+4)}{s(s+3)}$ *(b)* $\dfrac{2(s+1)(s+3)}{(s+2)(s+6)}$

**Solution**

(a) $Z(s) = \dfrac{3(s+2)(s+4)}{s(s+3)}$

The function $Z(s)$ has poles at $s = 0$ and $s = -3$ and zeros at $s = -2$ and $s = -4$, as shown in Fig. 15.42. The poles and zeros are simple and located on the negative real axis of the $s$-plane. The poles and zeros are interlaced. The lowest critical frequency nearest to the origin is a pole. Hence, the function $Z(s)$ is an $RC$ impedance function.

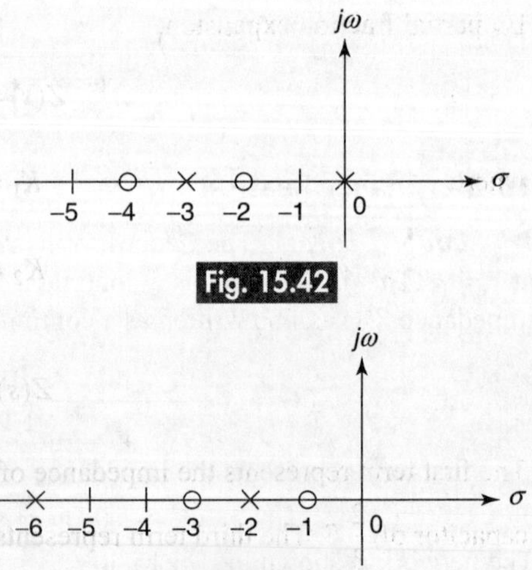

Fig. 15.42

Fig. 15.43

(b) $Z(s) = \dfrac{2(s+1)(s+3)}{(s+2)(s+6)}$

The function $Z(s)$ has poles at $s = -2$ and $s = -6$ and zeros at $s = -1$ and $s = -3$, as shown in Fig. 15.43. The poles and zeros are simple and located on the negative real axis of the $s$-plane. The poles and zeros are interlaced. But the lowest critical frequency nearest to the origin is not a pole, but zero. Hence, the function $Z(s)$ is not an $RC$ impedance function.

## EXAMPLE 15.49

*Realise the Foster and Cauer forms of the impedance function*

$$Z(s)=\frac{(s+1)(s+3)}{s(s+2)}$$

**Solution** The function $Z(s)$ has poles at $s = 0$ and $s = -2$ and zeros at $s = -1$ and $s = -3$, as shown in Fig. 15.44.

From the pole-zero diagram, it is clear that poles and zeros are simple and lie on the negative real axis. The poles and zeros are interlaced and the lowest critical frequency nearest to the origin is a pole. Hence, the function $Z(s)$ is an $RC$ function.

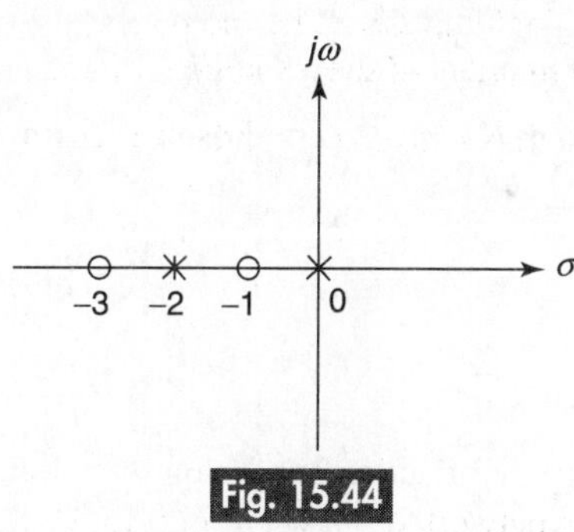

Fig. 15.44

***Foster I Form*** The Foster I form is obtained by partial fraction expansion of impedance function $Z(s)$. Since the degree of the numerator is greater than the degree of the denominator, division is first carried out.

$$Z(s)=\frac{s^2+4s+3}{s^2+2s}$$

$$s^2+2s\,\big)\,s^2+4s+3\,\big(\,1$$
$$\underline{s^2+2s}$$
$$2s+3$$

$$Z(s)=1+\frac{2s+3}{s^2+2s}=1+\frac{2s+3}{s(s+2)}$$

By partial fraction expansion,

$$Z(s)=1+\frac{K_1}{s}+\frac{K_2}{s+2}$$

where

$$K_1=sZ(s)\big|_{s=0}=\frac{(1)(3)}{2}=\frac{3}{2}$$

$$K_2=(s+2)Z(s)\big|_{s=-2}=\frac{(-2+1)(-2+3)}{-2}=\frac{1}{2}$$

$$Z(s)=1+\frac{\frac{3}{2}}{s}+\frac{\frac{1}{2}}{s+2}$$

The first term represents the impedance of a resistor of 1 Ω. The second term represents the impedance of a capacitor of $\frac{2}{3}$ F. The third term represents the impedance of parallel $RC$ circuit for which

$$Z_{RC}(s) = \frac{\frac{1}{C_i}}{s + \frac{1}{R_i C_i}}$$

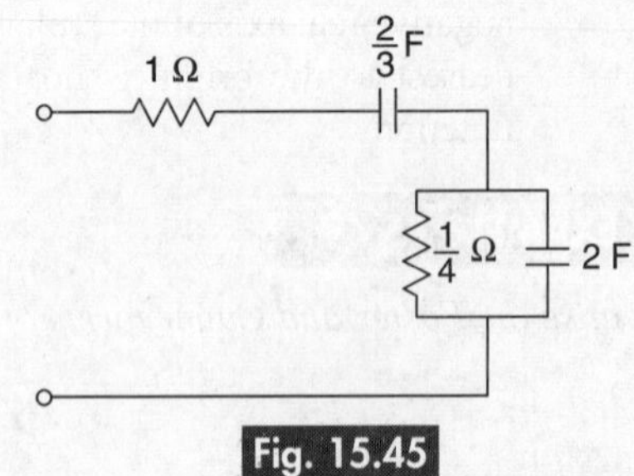

Fig. 15.45

By direct comparison,

$$R = \frac{1}{4}\,\Omega$$

$$C = 2\text{ F}$$

The network is shown in Fig. 15.45.

***Foster II Form*** The Foster II form is obtained by the partial fraction expansion of admittance function $\frac{Y(s)}{s}$.

$$Y(s) = \frac{1}{Z(s)} = \frac{s(s+2)}{(s+1)(s+3)}$$

$$\frac{Y(s)}{s} = \frac{s+2}{(s+1)(s+3)}$$

By partial fraction expansion,

$$\frac{Y(s)}{s} = \frac{K_1}{s+1} + \frac{K_2}{s+3}$$

where

$$K_1 = (s+1)\frac{Y(s)}{s}\bigg|_{s=-1} = \frac{(-1+2)}{(-1+3)} = \frac{1}{2}$$

$$K_2 = (s+3)\frac{Y(s)}{s}\bigg|_{s=-3} = \frac{(-3+2)}{(-3+1)} = \frac{1}{2}$$

$$\frac{Y(s)}{s} = \frac{\frac{1}{2}}{s+1} + \frac{\frac{1}{2}}{s+3}$$

$$Y(s) = \frac{\frac{1}{2}s}{s+1} + \frac{\frac{1}{2}s}{s+3}$$

These two terms represent the admittance of a series $RC$ circuit. For a series $RC$ circuit.

$$Y_{RC}(s) = \frac{\left(\frac{1}{R_i}\right)s}{s + \frac{1}{R_i C_i}}$$

By direct comparison,

$$R_1 = 2\,\Omega, \quad C_1 = \frac{1}{2}\text{ F}$$

$$R_2 = 2\,\Omega, \quad C_2 = \frac{1}{6}\text{ F}$$

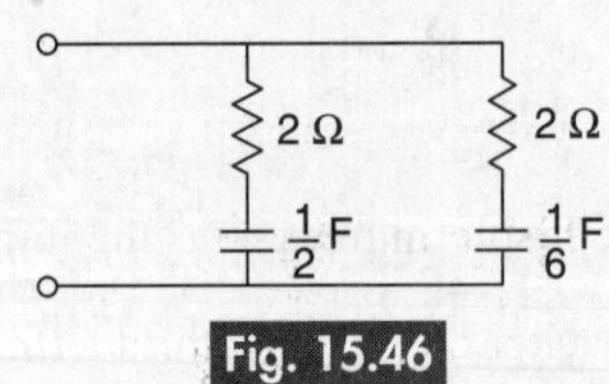

Fig. 15.46

The network is shown in Fig. 15.46.

***Cauer I Form*** The Cauer I form is obtained by continued fraction expansion about the pole at infinity.

$$Z(s)=\frac{s^2+4s+3}{s^2+2s}$$

By continued fraction expansion,

$$s^2+2s\overline{)\,s^2+4s+3\,}\left(1\leftarrow Z\right.$$
$$\underline{s^2+2s}$$
$$2s+3\overline{)\,s^2+2s\,}\left(\frac{1}{2}s\leftarrow Y\right.$$
$$\underline{s^2+\frac{3}{2}s}$$
$$\frac{1}{2}s\overline{)\,2s+3\,}\left(4\leftarrow Z\right.$$
$$\underline{2s}$$
$$3\overline{)\,\frac{1}{2}s\,}\left(\frac{1}{6}s\leftarrow Y\right.$$
$$\underline{\frac{1}{2}s}$$
$$0$$

1 Ω, 4 Ω, $\frac{1}{2}$ F, $\frac{1}{6}$ F

Fig. 15.47

The impedances are connected in the series branches whereas admittances are connected in the parallel branches. The network is shown in Fig. 15.47.

***Cauer II Form*** The Cauer II form is obtained from continued fraction expansion about the pole at the origin. Arranging the numerator and denominator polynomials of $Z(s)$ in ascending order of $s$,

$$Z(s)=\frac{3+4s+s^2}{2s+s^2}$$

By continued fraction expansion,

$$2s+s^2\overline{)\,3+4s+s^2\,}\left(\frac{3}{2s}\leftarrow Z\right.$$
$$\underline{3+\frac{3}{2}s}$$
$$\frac{5}{2}s+s^2\overline{)\,2s+s^2\,}\left(\frac{4}{5}\leftarrow Y\right.$$
$$\underline{2s+\frac{4}{5}s^2}$$

$$\begin{array}{l} \frac{1}{5}s^2 \Big) \frac{5}{2}s + s^2 \Big( \frac{25}{2s} \leftarrow Z \\ \qquad \frac{5}{2}s \\ \hline \qquad s^2 \Big) \frac{1}{5}s^2 \Big( \frac{1}{5} \leftarrow Y \\ \qquad\qquad \frac{1}{5}s^2 \\ \hline \qquad\qquad 0 \end{array}$$

The impedances are connected in the series branches whereas admittances are connected in the parallel branches. The network is shown in Fig. 15.48.

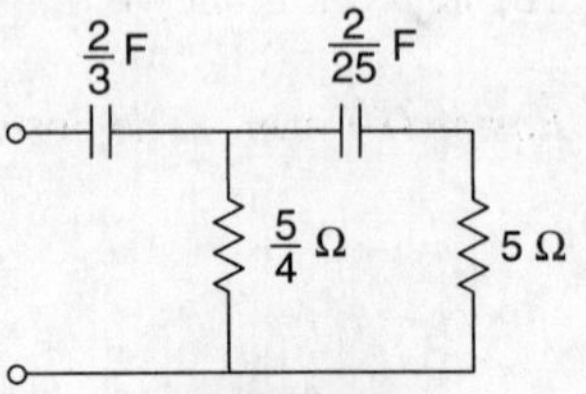

$\frac{2}{3}$ F, $\frac{2}{25}$ F, $\frac{5}{4}\ \Omega$, $5\ \Omega$

Fig. 15.48

## EXAMPLE 15.50

*Determine the Foster form of realisation of the RC impedance function.*

$$Z(s) = \frac{(s+1)(s+3)}{s(s+2)(s+4)}$$

**Solution**

***Foster I Form*** The Foster I form is obtained by the partial fraction expansion of the impedance function $Z(s)$.

By partial fraction expansion,

$$Z(s) = \frac{K_0}{s} + \frac{K_1}{s+2} + \frac{K_2}{s+4}$$

where
$$K_0 = sZ(s)\big|_{s=0} = \frac{(1)(3)}{(2)(4)} = \frac{3}{8}$$

$$K_1 = (s+2)Z(s)\big|_{s=-2} = \frac{(-2+1)(-2+3)}{(-2)(-2+4)} = \frac{(-1)(1)}{(-2)(2)} = \frac{1}{4}$$

$$K_2 = (s+4)Z(s)\big|_{s=-4} = \frac{(-4+1)(-4+3)}{(-4)(-4+2)} = \frac{(-3)(-1)}{(-4)(-2)} = \frac{3}{8}$$

$$Z(s) = \frac{\frac{3}{8}}{s} + \frac{\frac{1}{4}}{s+2} + \frac{\frac{3}{8}}{s+4}$$

The first term represents the impedance of a capacitor of $\frac{8}{3}$ F. The remaining terms represent the impedance of a parallel *RC* circuit for which

$$Z_{RC}(s) = \frac{\frac{1}{C_i}}{s + \frac{1}{R_i C_i}}$$

By direct comparison,

$$R_1 = \frac{1}{8}\,\Omega, \quad C_1 = 4\text{ F}$$

$$R_2 = \frac{3}{32}\,\Omega, \quad C_2 = \frac{8}{3}\text{ F}$$

The network is shown in Fig. 15.49.

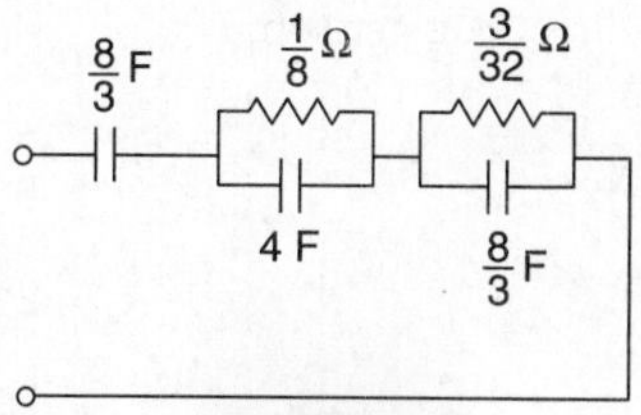

Fig. 15.49

***Foster II Form*** The Foster II form is obtained by partial fraction expansion of admittance function $\frac{Y(s)}{s}$.

$$Y(s) = \frac{s(s+2)(s+4)}{(s+1)(s+3)}$$

$$\frac{Y(s)}{s} = \frac{(s+2)(s+4)}{(s+1)(s+3)} = \frac{s^2+6s+8}{s^2+4s+3}$$

Since the degree of the numerator is equal to the degree of the denominator, division is carried out first.

$$s^2+4s+3\overline{)\,s^2+6s+8\,}(1$$

$$\underline{s^2+4s+3}$$

$$2s+5$$

$$\frac{Y(s)}{s} = 1 + \frac{2s+5}{s^2+4s+3} = 1 + \frac{2s+5}{(s+1)(s+3)}$$

By partial fraction expansion,

$$\frac{Y(s)}{s} = 1 + \frac{K_1}{s+1} + \frac{K_2}{s+3}$$

where

$$K_1 = (s+1)\frac{Y(s)}{s}\bigg|_{s=-1} = \frac{(-1+2)(-1+4)}{(-1+3)} = \frac{(1)(3)}{2} = \frac{3}{2}$$

$$K_2 = (s+3)\frac{Y(s)}{s}\bigg|_{s=-3} = \frac{(-3+2)(-3+4)}{(-3+1)} = \frac{(-1)(1)}{(-2)} = \frac{1}{2}$$

$$\frac{Y(s)}{s} = 1 + \frac{\frac{3}{2}}{s+1} + \frac{\frac{1}{2}}{s+3}$$

$$Y(s) = s + \frac{\frac{3}{2}s}{s+1} + \frac{\frac{1}{2}s}{s+3}$$

The first term represents the admittance of a capacitor of 1 F. The other two terms represent the admittance of a series $RC$ circuit. For a series $RC$ circuit,

$$Y_{RC}(s) = \frac{\left(\frac{1}{R_i}\right)s}{s + \frac{1}{R_i C_i}}$$

By direct comparison,

$$R_1 = \frac{2}{3}\ \Omega, \quad C_1 = \frac{3}{2}\ \text{F}$$

$$R_2 = 2\ \Omega, \quad C_2 = \frac{1}{6}\ \text{F}$$

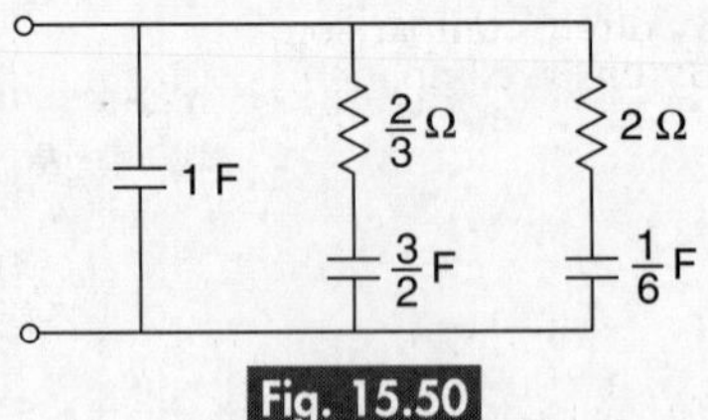


Fig. 15.50

The network is shown in Fig. 15.50.

## EXAMPLE 15.51

*Realise Foster forms of the following RC impedance function*

$$Z(s) = \frac{2(s+2)(s+4)}{(s+1)(s+3)}$$

**Solution**

***Foster I Form*** The Foster I form is obtained by the partial fraction expansion of the impedance function $Z(s)$. Since the degree of the numerator is equal to the degree of the denominator, division is carried out first.

$$Z(s) = \frac{2s^2+12s+16}{s^2+4s+3}$$

$$s^2+4s+3\,\overline{)\,2s^2+12s+16\,}\,(\,2$$
$$\underline{2s^2+8s+6}$$
$$4s+10$$

$$Z(s) = 2 + \frac{4s+10}{s^2+4s+3} = 2 + \frac{4s+10}{(s+1)(s+3)}$$

By partial fraction expansion,

$$Z(s) = 2 + \frac{K_1}{s+1} + \frac{K_2}{s+3}$$

where $$K_1 = (s+1)Z(s)\big|_{s=-1} = \frac{2(-1+2)(-1+4)}{(-1+3)} = 3$$

$$K_2 = (s+3)Z(s)\big|_{s=-3} = \frac{2(-3+2)(-3+4)}{(-3+1)} = 1$$

$$Z(s) = 2 + \frac{3}{s+1} + \frac{1}{s+3}$$

The first term represents the impedance of a resistor of 2 Ω. The remaining terms represent the impedance of a parallel $RC$ circuit for which

$$Z_{RC}(s) = \frac{\frac{1}{C_i}}{s + \frac{1}{R_i C_i}}$$

By direct comparison,

$$R_1 = 3\,\Omega, \quad C_1 = \frac{1}{3}\text{ F}$$

$$R_2 = \frac{1}{3}\,\Omega, \quad C_2 = 1\text{ F}$$

The network is shown in Fig. 15.51.

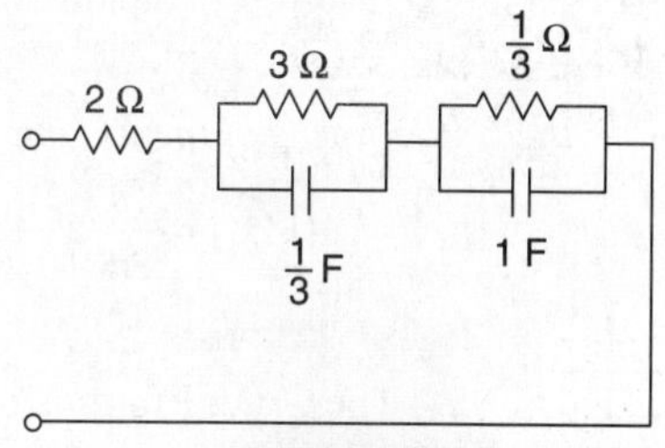


Fig. 15.51

***Foster II Form*** The Foster II form is obtained by partial fraction expansion of admittance function $\frac{Y(s)}{s}$.

$$Y(s) = \frac{(s+1)(s+3)}{2(s+2)(s+4)}$$

$$\frac{Y(s)}{s} = \frac{(s+1)(s+3)}{2s(s+2)(s+4)}$$

By partial fraction expansion,

$$\frac{Y(s)}{s} = \frac{K_0}{s} + \frac{K_1}{s+2} + \frac{K_2}{s+4}$$

where

$$K_0 = s\frac{Y(s)}{s}\bigg|_{s=0} = \frac{(1)(3)}{(2)(2)(4)} = \frac{3}{16}$$

$$K_1 = (s+2)\frac{Y(s)}{s}\bigg|_{s=-2} = \frac{(-2+1)(-2+3)}{2(-2)(-2+4)} = \frac{(-1)(1)}{2(-2)(2)} = \frac{1}{8}$$

$$K_2 = (s+4)\frac{Y(s)}{s}\bigg|_{s=-4} = \frac{(-4+1)(-4+3)}{2(-4)(-4+2)} = \frac{(-3)(-1)}{2(-4)(-2)} = \frac{3}{16}$$

$$\frac{Y(s)}{s} = \frac{\frac{3}{16}}{s} + \frac{\frac{1}{8}}{s+2} + \frac{\frac{3}{16}}{s+4}$$

$$Y(s) = \frac{3}{16} + \frac{\frac{1}{8}s}{s+2} + \frac{\frac{3}{16}s}{s+4}$$

The first term represents the admittance of a resistor of $\frac{16}{3}$ Ω. The other two terms represent the admittance of a series $RC$ circuit. For a series $RC$ circuit.

$$Y_{RC}(s) = \frac{\left(\frac{1}{R_i}\right)s}{s + \frac{1}{R_iC_i}}$$

By direct comparison,

$$R_1 = 8\,\Omega, \quad C_1 = \frac{1}{16}\text{ F}$$

$$R_2 = \frac{16}{3}\,\Omega, \quad C_2 = \frac{3}{64}\text{ F}$$

The network is shown in Fig. 15.52.

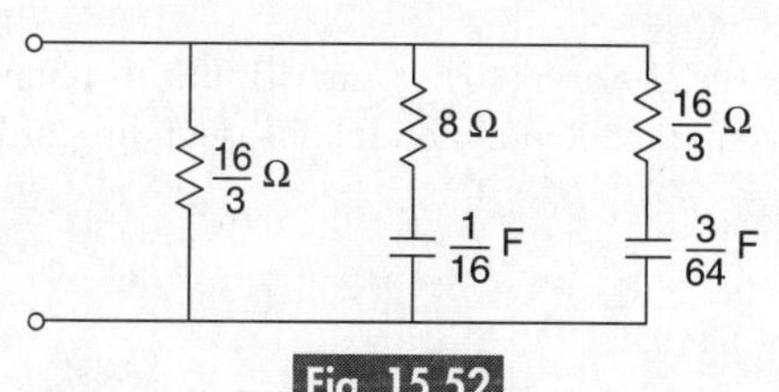


Fig. 15.52

**EXAMPLE 15.52**

*Obtain the Cauer forms of the RC impedance function*

$$Z(s) = \frac{(s+2)(s+6)}{2(s+1)(s+3)}$$

**Solution**

***Cauer I Form*** The Cauer I form is obtained by continued fraction expansion about the pole at infinity.

$$Z(s) = \frac{(s+2)(s+6)}{2(s+1)(s+3)} = \frac{s^2+8s+12}{2s^2+8s+6}$$

By continued fraction expansion,

$$2s^2+8s+6\,\big)\,s^2+8s+12\,\big(\,\frac{1}{2} \leftarrow Z$$
$$\underline{s^2+4s+3}$$
$$4s+9\,\big)\,2s^2+8s+6\,\big(\,\frac{1}{2}s \leftarrow Y$$
$$\underline{2s^2+\frac{9}{2}s}$$
$$\frac{7}{2}s+6\,\big)\,4s+9\,\big(\,\frac{8}{7} \leftarrow Z$$
$$\underline{4s+\frac{48}{7}}$$
$$\frac{15}{7}\,\big)\,\frac{7}{2}s+6\,\big(\,\frac{49}{30}s \leftarrow Y$$
$$\underline{\frac{7}{2}s}$$
$$6\,\big)\,\frac{15}{7}\,\big(\,\frac{5}{14} \leftarrow Z$$
$$\underline{\frac{15}{7}}$$
$$0$$

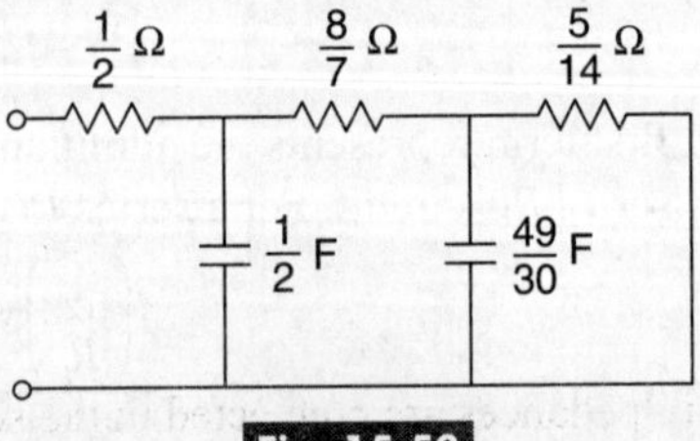

The impedances are connected in the series branches whereas the admittances are connected in the parallel branches. The network is shown in Fig. 15.53.



**Fig. 15.53**

***Cauer II Form*** The Cauer II form is obtained by continued fraction expansion about the pole at the origin. Arranging the polynomials in ascending order of *s*,

$$Z(s) = \frac{12+8s+s^2}{6+8s+2s^2}$$

By continued fraction expansion,

$$6+8s+2s^2\overline{\smash{\big)}\,12+8s+s^2\,}\big(\,2$$

$$\underline{12+16s+4s^2}$$

$$-8s-3s^2$$

Since negative term results, continued fraction expansion of $Y(s)$ is carried out.

$$Y(s)=\frac{6+8s+2s^2}{12+8s+s^2}$$

By continued fraction expansion,

$$12+8s+s^2\overline{\smash{\big)}\,6+8s+2s^2\,}\left(\frac{1}{2}\leftarrow Y\right.$$

$$\underline{6+4s+\frac{1}{2}s^2}$$

$$4s+\frac{3}{2}s^2\overline{\smash{\big)}\,12+8s+s^2\,}\left(\frac{3}{s}\leftarrow Z\right.$$

$$\underline{12+\frac{9}{2}s}$$

$$\frac{7}{2}s+s^2\overline{\smash{\big)}\,4s+\frac{3}{2}+s^2\,}\left(\frac{8}{7}\leftarrow Y\right.$$

$$\underline{4s+\frac{8}{7}s^2}$$

$$\frac{5}{14}s^2\overline{\smash{\big)}\,\frac{7}{2}s+s^2\,}\left(\frac{49}{5s}\leftarrow Z\right.$$

$$\underline{\frac{7}{2}s}$$

$$s^2\overline{\smash{\big)}\,\frac{5}{14}s^2\,}\left(\frac{5}{14}\leftarrow Y\right.$$

$$\underline{\frac{5}{14}s}$$

$$0$$

The impedances are connected in the series branches, whereas the admittances are connected in the parallel branches. The network is shown in Fig. 15.54.

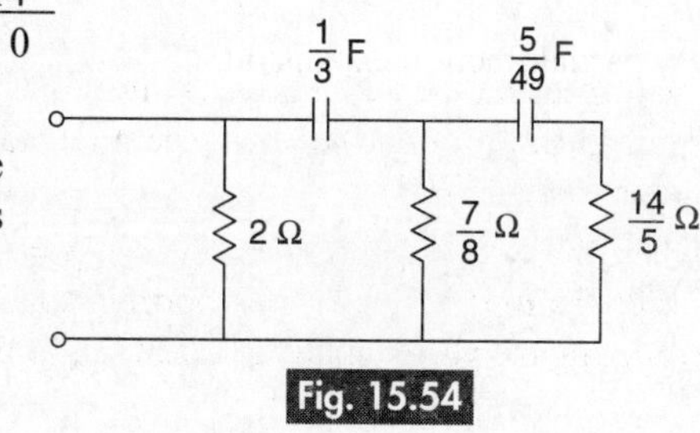


Fig. 15.54

**EXAMPLE 15.53**

*Realise the RC impedance in Cauer I and Foster I forms*

$$Z(s) = \frac{s+4}{(s+2)(s+6)}$$

**Solution**

***Cauer I Form*** The Cauer I form is obtained by continued fraction expansion of $Z(s)$ about the pole at infinity. In the above function, the degree of the numerator is less than the degree of the denominator, which indicates presence of a zero at infinity. Hence, the admittance function $Y(s)$ has a pole at infinity.

$$Y(s) = \frac{s^2+8s+12}{s+4}$$

By continued fraction expansion,

$$\begin{array}{l}
s+4\,\big)\,s^2+8s+12\,\big(\,s \leftarrow Y \\
\qquad\;\; \underline{s^2+4s} \\
\qquad\qquad 4s+12\,\big)\,s+4\,\big(\,\frac{1}{4} \leftarrow Z \\
\qquad\qquad\qquad\;\; \underline{s+3} \\
\qquad\qquad\qquad\qquad 1\,\big)\,4s+12\,\big(\,4s \leftarrow Y \\
\qquad\qquad\qquad\qquad\quad\;\; \underline{4s} \\
\qquad\qquad\qquad\qquad\qquad 12\,\big)\,1\,\big(\,\frac{1}{12} \leftarrow Z \\
\qquad\qquad\qquad\qquad\qquad\quad\;\; \underline{1} \\
\qquad\qquad\qquad\qquad\qquad\quad\;\; 0
\end{array}$$

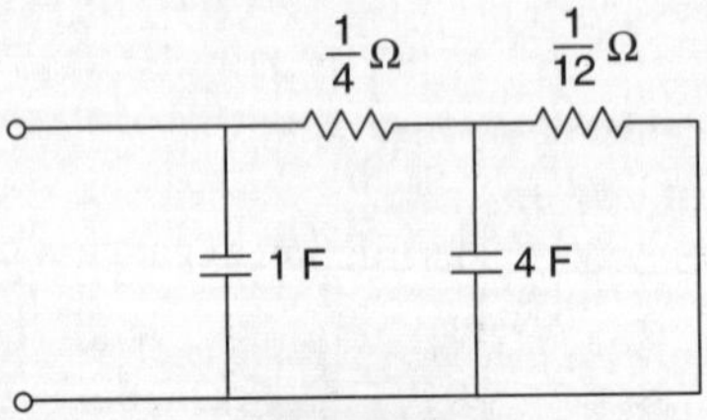

The impedances are connected in series branches, whereas the admittances are connected in parallel branches. The network is shown in Fig. 15.55.



Fig. 15.55

***Foster I Form*** The Foster I form is obtained by partial fraction expansion of $Z(s)$.

$$Z(s) = \frac{s+4}{(s+2)(s+6)}$$

By partial fraction expansion,

$$Z(s) = \frac{K_1}{s+2} + \frac{K_2}{s+6}$$

where
$$K_1 = (s+2)Z(s)\big|_{s=-2} = \frac{(-2+4)}{(-2+6)} = \frac{1}{2}$$

$$K_2 = (s+6)Z(s)\big|_{s=-6} = \frac{(-6+4)}{(-6+2)} = \frac{1}{2}$$

$$Z(s) = \frac{\frac{1}{2}}{s+2} + \frac{\frac{1}{2}}{s+6}$$

These two terms represent the impedance of a parallel $RC$ circuit for which

$$Z_{RC}(s) = \frac{\frac{1}{C_i}}{s + \frac{1}{R_i C_i}}$$

By direct comparison,

$$R_1 = \frac{1}{4}\ \Omega, \quad C_1 = 2\ \text{F}$$

$$R_2 = \frac{1}{12}\ \Omega, \quad C_2 = 2\ \text{F}$$

The network is shown in Fig. 15.56.

Fig. 15.56

**EXAMPLE 15.54**

*The RC driving-point impedance function is given as* $Z(s) = H\dfrac{(s+1)(s+4)}{s(s+3)}$. *Realise the impedance function in the ladder form, given* $Z(-2) = 1$.

**Solution** Putting $s = -2$,

$$Z(-2) = H\frac{(-2+1)(-2+4)}{(-2)(-2+3)} = H$$

$$H = 1$$

$$Z(s) = \frac{(s+1)(s+4)}{s(s+3)}$$

***Cauer I Form*** The Cauer I form is obtained by continued fraction expansion of $Z(s)$ about the pole at infinity.

By continued fraction expansion of $Z(s)$,

$$\begin{array}{l}
s^2+3s\,\big)\,s^2+5s+4\,\big(\,1 \leftarrow Z \\
\qquad\quad\;\; \underline{s^2+3s} \\
\qquad\quad 2s+4\,\big)\,s^2+3s\,\big(\,\frac{1}{2}s \leftarrow Y \\
\qquad\qquad\qquad\;\; \underline{s^2+2s} \\
\qquad\qquad\qquad\quad s\,\big)\,2s+4\,\big(\,2 \leftarrow Z \\
\qquad\qquad\qquad\qquad\;\; \underline{2s} \\
\qquad\qquad\qquad\qquad\; 4\,\big)\,s\,\big(\,\frac{1}{4}s \leftarrow Y \\
\qquad\qquad\qquad\qquad\qquad \underline{s} \\
\qquad\qquad\qquad\qquad\qquad 0
\end{array}$$

The impedances are connected in the series branches whereas admittances are connected in the parallel branches. The network is shown in Fig. 15.57.

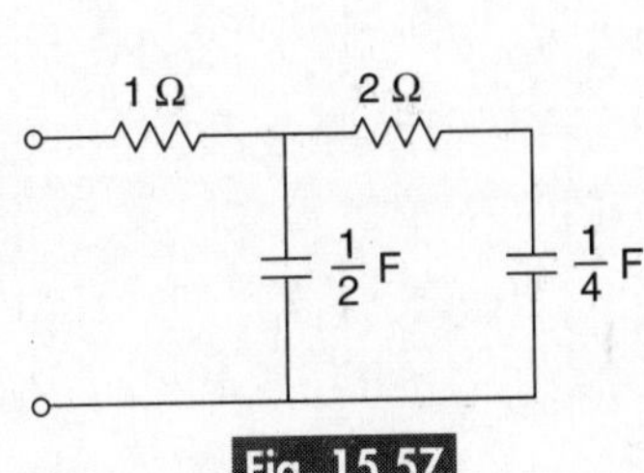


Fig. 15.57

***Cauer II Form*** The Cauer II form is obtained by continued fraction expansion about the pole at the origin. Arranging the polynomials in ascending order of $s$,

$$Z(s) = \frac{4+5s+s^2}{3s+s^2}$$

By continued fraction expansion,

$$3s+s^2\overline{\Big)\,4+5s+s^2\,\Big(}\frac{4}{3s} \leftarrow Z$$
$$\underline{4+\frac{4}{3}s}$$
$$\frac{11}{3}s+s^2\overline{\Big)\,3s+s^2\,\Big(}\frac{9}{11} \leftarrow Y$$
$$\underline{3s+\frac{9}{11}s^2}$$
$$\frac{2}{11}s^2\overline{\Big)\,\frac{11}{3}s+s^2\,\Big(}\frac{121}{6s} \leftarrow Z$$
$$\underline{\frac{11}{3}s}$$
$$s^2\overline{\Big)\,\frac{2}{11}s^2\,\Big(}\frac{2}{11} \leftarrow Y$$
$$\underline{\frac{2}{11}s^2}$$
$$0$$

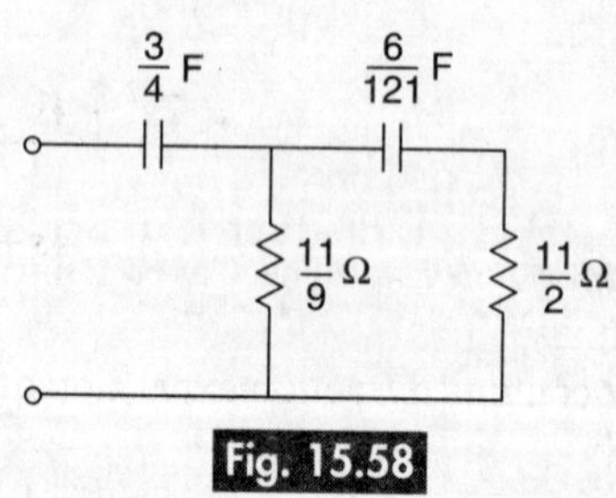

Fig. 15.58

The impedances are connected in the series branches whereas the admittances are connected in the parallel branches. The network is shown in Fig. 15.58.

## EXAMPLE 15.55

*An impedance function has the pole-zero diagram, as shown in Fig. 15.59. Find the impedance function such that $Z(-4) = \frac{3}{4}$ and realise in Cauer I and Foster II forms.*

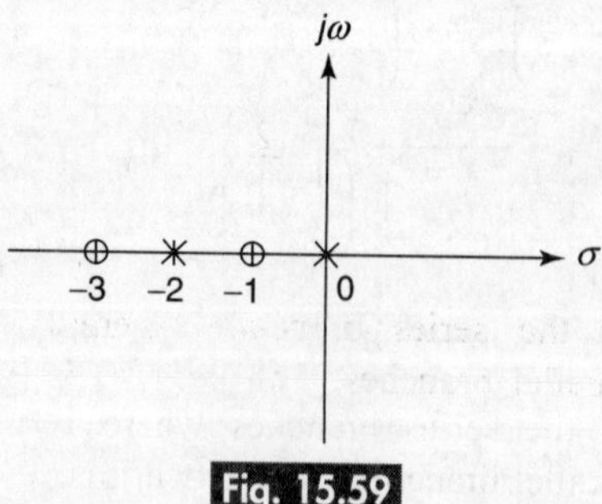

Fig. 15.59

**Solution** The function $Z(s)$ has poles at $s = 0$ and $s = -2$ and zeros at $s = -1$ and $s = -3$.

$$Z(s) = H\frac{(s+1)(s+3)}{s(s+2)}$$

Putting $s = -4$,

$$Z(-4) = H\frac{(-4+1)(-4+3)}{(-4)(-4+2)} = H\frac{(-3)(-1)}{(-4)(-2)} = \frac{3}{8}\text{H}$$

$$\frac{3}{4} = \frac{3}{8}\text{H}$$

$$H = 2$$

$$Z(s) = \frac{2(s+1)(s+3)}{s(s+2)} = \frac{2s^2+8s+6}{s^2+2s}$$

***Cauer I Form*** The Cauer I form is obtained by continued fraction expansion of $Z(s)$ about the pole at infinity.

By continued fraction expansion of $Z(s)$,

$$s^2+2s\overline{)\,2s^2+8s+6\,}\big(2 \leftarrow Z$$
$$\underline{2s^2+4s}$$
$$4s+6\overline{)\,s^2+2s\,}\Big(\frac{1}{4}s \leftarrow Y$$
$$\underline{s^2+\frac{3}{2}s}$$
$$\frac{1}{2}s\overline{)\,4s+6\,}\big(8 \leftarrow Z$$
$$\underline{4s}$$
$$6\overline{)\,\frac{1}{2}s\,}\Big(\frac{1}{12}s \leftarrow Y$$
$$\underline{\frac{1}{2}s}$$
$$0$$

The impedances are connected in the series branches whereas admittances are connected in the parallel branches. The network is shown in Fig. 15.60.

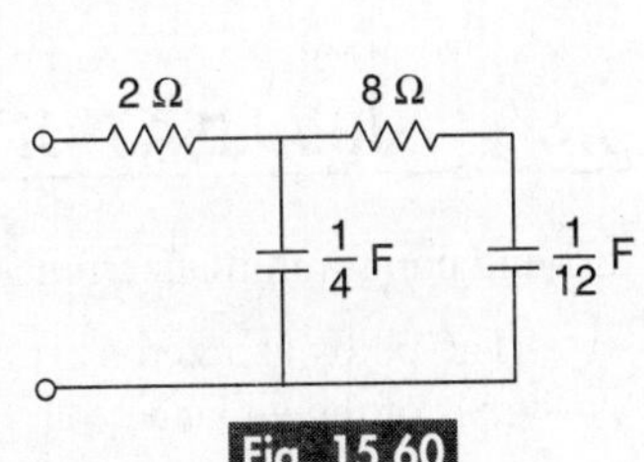


Fig. 15.60

***Foster II Form*** The Foster II form is obtained by partial fraction expansion of $\frac{Y(s)}{s}$.

$$\frac{Y(s)}{s} = \frac{s+2}{2(s+1)(s+3)}$$

By partial fraction expansion,

$$\frac{Y(s)}{s} = \frac{K_1}{s+1} + \frac{K_2}{s+3}$$

where
$$K_1 = (s+1)\frac{Y(s)}{s}\bigg|_{s=-1} = \frac{(-1+2)}{2(-1+3)} = \frac{1}{4}$$

$$K_2 = (s+3)\frac{Y(s)}{s}\bigg|_{s=-3} = \frac{(-3+2)}{2(-3+1)} = \frac{-1}{2(-2)} = \frac{1}{4}$$

$$\frac{Y(s)}{s} = \frac{\frac{1}{4}}{s+1} + \frac{\frac{1}{4}}{s+3}$$

$$Y(s) = \frac{\frac{1}{4}s}{s+1} + \frac{\frac{1}{4}s}{s+3}$$

Two terms represent the admittance of a series $RC$ circuit. For a series $RC$ circuit,

$$Y_{RC}(s) = \frac{\left(\frac{1}{R_i}\right)s}{s + \frac{1}{R_i C_i}}$$

By direct comparison,

$$R_1 = 4\ \Omega,\quad C_1 = \frac{1}{4}\text{ F}$$

$$R_2 = 4\ \Omega,\quad C_2 = \frac{1}{12}\text{ F}$$

The network is shown in Fig. 15.61.

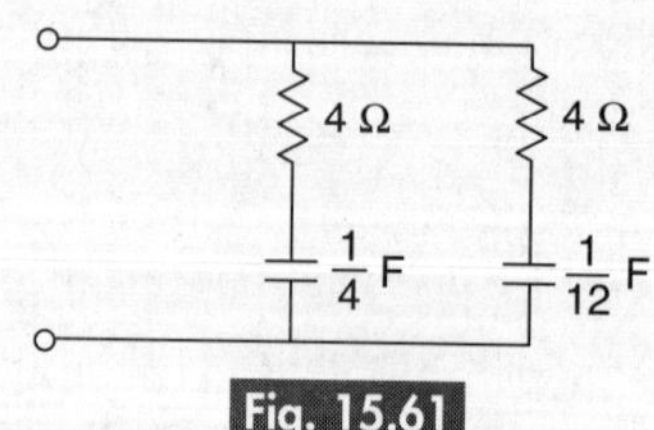


Fig. 15.61

## 15.6 REALISATION OF *RL* FUNCTIONS

LO 15.6

Explain Foster and Cauer forms of realising *RL* functions, and their properties

*RL* driving point immittance functions have following properties:

1. The poles and zeros are simple and are located on the negative real axis of the $s$-plane.
2. The poles and zeros are interlaced.
3. The lowest critical frequency is a zero which may be at $s = 0$.
4. The highest critical frequency is a pole which may be at infinity.

5. Residues evaluated at the poles of $Z_{RL}(s)$ are real and negative while that of $\frac{Z_{RL}(s)}{s}$ are real and positive.
6. The slope $\frac{d}{d\sigma} Z_{RL}$ is positive.
7. $Z_{RL}(0) < Z_{RL}(\infty)$.

The admittance of an inductor is similar to the impedance of a capacitor. Hence, properties of an *RL* admittance are identical to those of an *RC* impedance and vice-versa, i.e.,

$$Z_{RC}(s) = Y_{RL}(s)$$
$$Z_{RL}(s) = Y_{RC}(s)$$

An *RL* admittance can be considered as the dual of an *RC* impedance and vice-versa.

**EXAMPLE 15.56**

*Indicate which of the following functions are either RL, RC or LC impedance functions.*

(a) $Z(s) = \frac{4(s+1)(s+3)}{s(s+2)}$ (b) $Z(s) = \frac{s(s+4)(s+8)}{(s+1)(s+6)}$

(c) $Z(s) = \frac{(s+1)(s+4)}{s(s+2)}$ (d) $Z(s) = \frac{2(s+1)(s+3)}{(s+2)(s+16)}$

**Solution**

(a) $Z(s) = \frac{4(s+1)(s+3)}{s(s+2)}$

This is an *RC* impedance function since (i) poles and zeros are on the negative real axis, (ii) they are interlaced, and (iii) critical frequency nearest to the origin is a pole.

(b) $Z(s) = \frac{s(s+4)(s+8)}{(s+1)(s+6)}$

This is an *RL* impedance function as (i) poles and zeros are on the negative real axis, (ii) they are interlaced, and (iii) critical frequency nearest to the origin is a zero.

(c) $Z(s) = \frac{(s+1)(s+4)}{s(s+2)}$

This is an *RC* impedance function since (i) poles and zeros are on the negative real axis, (ii) they are interlaced, and (iii) critical frequency nearest to the origin is a pole.

(d) $Z(s) = \frac{2(s+1)(s+3)}{(s+2)(s+6)}$

This is an *RL* impedance function as (i) poles and zeros are on the negative real axis, (ii) they are interlaced, and (iii) critical frequency nearest to the origin is a zero.

**EXAMPLE 15.57**

*Realise following RL impedance function in Foster-I and Foster-II form.*

$$Z(s) = \frac{2(s+1)(s+3)}{(s+2)(s+6)}$$

**Solution**

***Foster I Form*** The Foster I form is obtained by partial fraction expansion of the impedance function $Z(s)$. By partial fraction expansion,

$$Z(s) = \frac{K_1}{s+2} + \frac{K_2}{s+6}$$

where

$$K_1 = (s+2)Z(s)\Big|_{s=-2} = \frac{2(-2+1)(-2+3)}{(-2+6)} = -\frac{1}{2}$$

$$K_2 = (s+6)Z(s)\Big|_{s=-6} = \frac{2(-6+1)(-6+3)}{(-6+2)} = -\frac{15}{2}$$

Since residues of $Z(s)$ are negative, partial fraction expansion of $\frac{Z(s)}{s}$ is carried out.

$$\frac{Z(s)}{s} = \frac{2(s+1)(s+3)}{s(s+2)(s+6)}$$

By partial fraction expansion,

$$\frac{Z(s)}{s} = \frac{K_0}{s} + \frac{K_1}{s+2} + \frac{K_2}{s+6}$$

where

$$K_0 = s\frac{Z(s)}{s}\Big|_{s=0} = \frac{2(1)(3)}{(2)(6)} = \frac{1}{2}$$

$$K_1 = (s+2)\frac{Z(s)}{s}\Big|_{s=-2} = \frac{2(-2+1)(-2+3)}{(2)(-2+6)} = \frac{1}{4}$$

$$K_2 = (s+6)\frac{Z(s)}{s}\Big|_{s=-6} = \frac{2(-6+1)(-6+3)}{(-6)(-6+2)} = \frac{5}{4}$$

$$\frac{Z(s)}{s} = \frac{\frac{1}{2}}{s} + \frac{\frac{1}{4}}{s+2} + \frac{\frac{5}{4}}{s+6}$$

$$Z(s) = \frac{1}{2} + \frac{\frac{1}{4}s}{s+2} + \frac{\frac{5}{4}s}{s+6}$$

The first term represents the impedance of the resistor of $\frac{1}{2}\,\Omega$. The other two terms represent the impedance of the parallel $RL$ circuit for which

$$Z_{RL}(s) = \frac{R_i s}{s + \frac{R_i}{L_i}}$$

By direct comparison,

$$R_1 = \frac{1}{4}\,\Omega, \quad L_1 = \frac{1}{8}\,\text{H}$$

$$R_2 = \frac{5}{4}\,\Omega, \quad L_2 = \frac{5}{24}\,\text{H}$$

The network is shown in Fig. 15.62.

Fig. 15.62

***Foster II Form*** The Foster II form is obtained by partial fraction expansion of $Y(s)$. Since the degree of the numerator is equal to the degree of the denominator, division is first carried out.

$$Y(s) = \frac{(s+2)(s+6)}{2(s+1)(s+3)} = \frac{s^2+8s+12}{2s^2+8s+6}$$

$$2s^2+8s+6 \overline{\big)\, s^2+8s+12 \,} \Big( \frac{1}{2}$$
$$\underline{s^2+4s+3}$$
$$4s+9$$

$$Y(s) = \frac{1}{2} + \frac{4s+9}{2s^2+8s+6} = \frac{1}{2} + \frac{4s+9}{2(s+1)(s+3)}$$

By partial fraction expansion,

$$Y_1(s) = \frac{4s+9}{2(s+1)(s+3)} = \frac{K_0}{s+1} + \frac{K_1}{s+3}$$

where

$$K_0 = (s+1)Y_1(s)\Big|_{s=-1} = \frac{(-4+9)}{2(-1+3)} = \frac{5}{4}$$

$$K_1 = (s+3)Y_1(s)\Big|_{s=-3} = \frac{(-12+9)}{2(-3+1)} = \frac{3}{4}$$

$$Y(s) = \frac{1}{2} + \frac{\frac{5}{4}}{s+1} + \frac{\frac{3}{4}}{s+3}$$

The first term represents the admittance of a resistor of 2 Ω. The other two terms represent the admittance of a series *RL* circuit. For a series *RL* circuit,

$$Y_{RL}(s) = \frac{\frac{1}{L_i}}{s + \frac{R_i}{L_i}}$$

By direct comparison,

$$R_1 = \frac{4}{5}\,\Omega, \quad L_1 = \frac{4}{5}\,\text{H}$$

$$R_2 = 4\,\Omega, \quad L_2 = \frac{4}{3}\,\text{H}$$

The network is shown in Fig. 15.63.

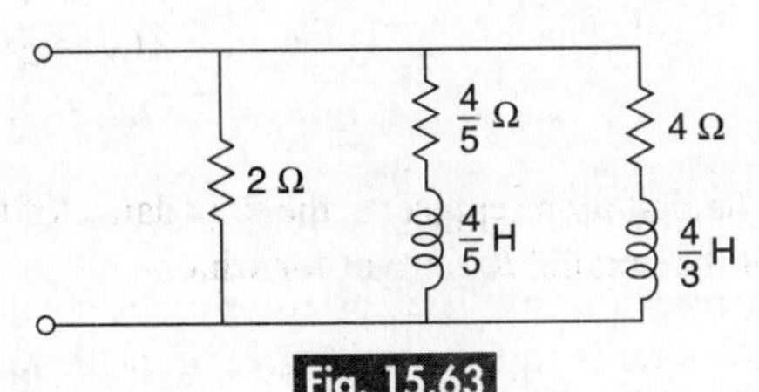

Fig. 15.63

**EXAMPLE 15.58**

*Find the Foster forms of the RL impedance function:*

$$Z(s)=\frac{(s+1)(s+4)}{(s+5)(s+3)}$$

**Solution**

***Foster I Form*** The Foster I form is obtained by partial fraction expansion of impedance function $\frac{Z(s)}{s}$.

$$\frac{Z(s)}{s}=\frac{(s+1)(s+4)}{s(s+5)(s+3)}$$

By partial-faction expansion,

$$\frac{Z(s)}{s}=\frac{K_0}{s}+\frac{K_1}{s+3}+\frac{K_2}{s+5}$$

where

$$K_0=s\frac{Z(s)}{s}\bigg|_{s=0}=\frac{(1)(4)}{(5)(3)}=\frac{4}{15}$$

$$K_1=(s+3)\frac{Z(s)}{s}\bigg|_{s=-3}=\frac{(-3+1)(-3+4)}{(-3)(-3+5)}=\frac{(-2)(1)}{(-3)(2)}=\frac{1}{3}$$

$$K_2=(s+5)\frac{Z(s)}{s}\bigg|_{s=-5}=\frac{(-5+1)(-5+4)}{(-5)(-5+3)}=\frac{(-4)(-1)}{(-5)(-2)}=\frac{2}{5}$$

$$\frac{Z(s)}{s}=\frac{\frac{4}{15}}{s}+\frac{\frac{1}{3}}{s+3}+\frac{\frac{2}{5}}{s+5}$$

$$Z(s)=\frac{4}{15}+\frac{\frac{1}{3}s}{s+3}+\frac{\frac{2}{5}s}{s+5}$$

The first term represents the impedance of the resistor of $\frac{4}{15}\,\Omega$. The other two terms represent the impedance of a parallel $RL$ circuit for which

$$Z_{RL}(s)=\frac{R_i s}{s+\frac{R_i}{L_i}}$$

By direct comparison,

$$R_1=\frac{1}{3}\,\Omega,\quad L_1=\frac{1}{9}\,\text{H}$$

$$R_2=\frac{2}{5}\,\Omega,\quad L_2=\frac{2}{25}\,\text{H}$$

The network is shown in Fig. 15.64.

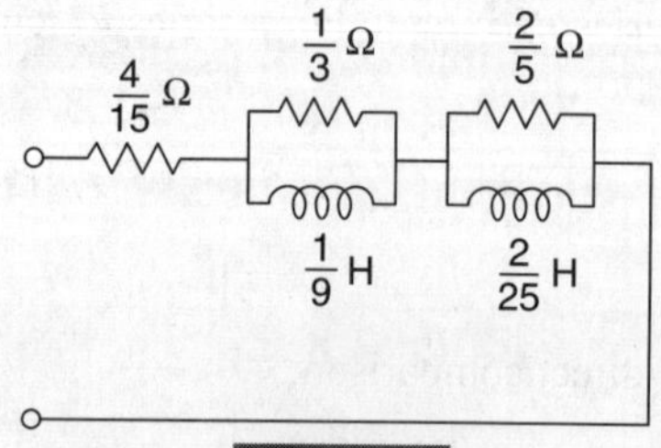


Fig. 15.64

***Foster II Form*** The Foster II form is obtained by partial fraction expansion of $Y(s)$. Since the degree of the numerator is equal to the degree of the denominator, division is first carried out.

$$Y(s) = \frac{(s+5)(s+3)}{(s+1)(s+4)} = \frac{s^2+8s+15}{s^2+5s+4}$$

$$s^2+5s+4)s^2+8s+15(1$$
$$\underline{s^2+5s+4}$$
$$3s+11$$

$$Y(s) = 1 + \frac{3s+11}{(s+1)(s+4)}$$

By partial fraction expansion,

$$Y_1(s) = \frac{K_0}{s+1} + \frac{K_1}{s+4}$$

where
$$K_0 = (s+1)Y_1(s)\big|_{s=-1} = \frac{(-3+11)}{(-1+4)} = \frac{8}{3}$$

$$K_1 = (s+4)Y_1(s)\big|_{s=-4} = \frac{(-12+11)}{(-4+1)} = \frac{1}{3}$$

$$Y_1(s) = \frac{\frac{8}{3}}{s+1} + \frac{\frac{1}{3}}{s+4}$$

$$Y(s) = 1 + \frac{\frac{8}{3}}{s+1} + \frac{\frac{1}{3}}{s+4}$$

The first term represents the admittance of a resistor of 1 Ω. The other two terms represent the admittance of a series *RL* circuit.

For a series *RL* circuit,

$$Y_{RL}(s) = \frac{\frac{1}{L_i}}{s + \frac{R_i}{L_i}}$$

By direct comparison,

$$R_1 = \frac{3}{8}\ \Omega, \quad L_1 = \frac{3}{8}\ \text{H}$$

$$R_2 = 12\ \Omega, \quad L_2 = 3\ \text{H}$$

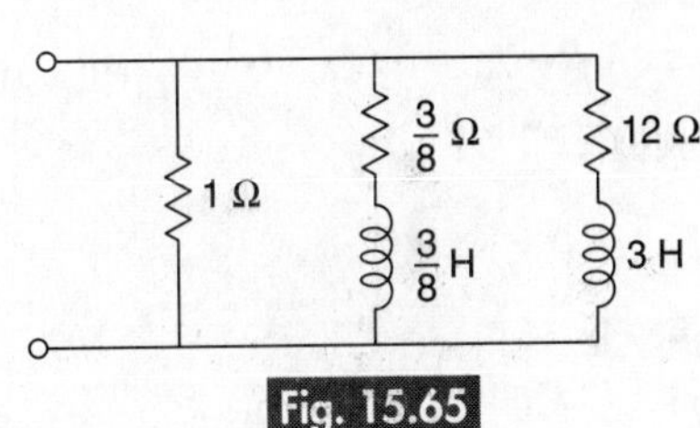

Fig. 15.65

The network is shown in Fig. 15.65.

## EXAMPLE 15.59

*Find the Cauer forms of the RL impedance function:*

$$Z(s) = \frac{2(s+1)(s+3)}{(s+2)(s+6)}$$

**Solution**

***Cauer I Form*** The Cauer I form is obtained by a continued fraction expansion of $Z(s)$ about the pole at infinity.

$$Z(s)=\frac{2(s+1)(s+3)}{(s+2)(s+6)}=\frac{2s^2+8s+6}{s^2+8s+12}$$

By continued fraction expansion,

$$\begin{array}{l} s^2+8s+12)2s^2+8s+6(2 \leftarrow Z \\ \underline{\quad 2s^2+16s+24} \\ \quad\quad -8s-18 \end{array}$$

Since a negative term results, continued fraction expansion of $Y(s)$ is carried out.

$$Y(s)=\frac{s^2+8s+12}{2s^2+8s+6}$$

By continued fraction expansion,

$$\begin{array}{l} 2s^2+8s+6\overline{\big)\,s^2+8s+12}\left(\frac{1}{2}\leftarrow Y\right. \\ \underline{\quad s^2+4s+3} \\ \quad 4s+9\overline{\big)\,2s^2+8s+6}\left(\frac{1}{2}s\leftarrow Z\right. \\ \quad\quad \underline{2s^2+\frac{9}{2}s} \\ \quad\quad \frac{7}{2}s+6\overline{\big)\,4s+9}\left(\frac{8}{7}\leftarrow Y\right. \\ \quad\quad\quad \underline{4s+\frac{48}{7}} \\ \quad\quad\quad \frac{15}{7}\overline{\big)\,\frac{7}{2}s+6}\left(\frac{49}{30}s\leftarrow Z\right. \\ \quad\quad\quad\quad \underline{\frac{7}{2}s} \\ \quad\quad\quad\quad 6\overline{\big)\,\frac{15}{7}}\left(\frac{15}{42}\leftarrow Y\right. \\ \quad\quad\quad\quad\quad \underline{\frac{15}{7}} \\ \quad\quad\quad\quad\quad 0 \end{array}$$

The impedances are connected in the series branches whereas the admittances are connected in the parallel branches. The network is shown in Fig. 15.66.

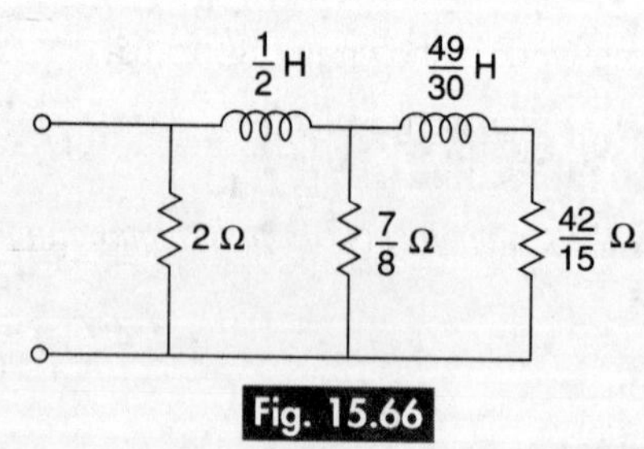

Fig. 15.66

***Cauer II Form*** The Cauer II form is obtained from a continued fraction expansion about the pole at the origin. Arranging the numerator and denominator polynomials of $Z(s)$ in ascending order of $s$,

$$Z(s)=\frac{6+8s+2s^2}{12+8s+s^2}$$

By continued fraction expansion,

$$12+8s+s^2\,\overline{\big)\,6+8s+2s^2\,}\left(\frac{1}{2}\leftarrow Z\right.$$

$$\underline{6+4s+\frac{1}{2}s^2}$$

$$4s+\frac{3}{2}s^2\,\overline{\big)\,12+8s+s^2\,}\left(\frac{3}{s}\leftarrow Y\right.$$

$$\underline{12+\frac{9}{2}s}$$

$$\frac{7}{2}s+s^2\,\overline{\big)\,4s+\frac{3}{2}s^2\,}\left(\frac{8}{7}\leftarrow Z\right.$$

$$\underline{4s+\frac{8}{7}s^2}$$

$$\frac{5}{14}s^2\,\overline{\big)\,\frac{7}{2}s+s^2\,}\left(\frac{98}{10s}\leftarrow Y\right.$$

$$\underline{\frac{7}{2}s}$$

$$s^2\,\overline{\big)\,\frac{5}{14}s^2\,}\left(\frac{5}{14}\leftarrow Z\right.$$

$$\underline{\frac{5}{14}s}$$

$$0$$

The impedances are connected in the series branches whereas the admittances are connected in the parallel branches. The network is shown in Fig. 15.67.

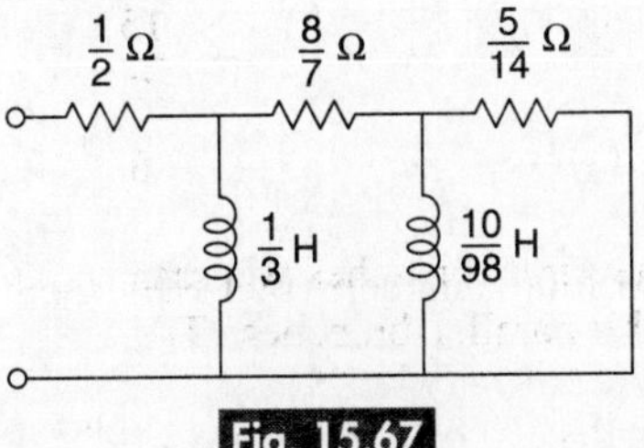

Fig. 15.67

## EXAMPLE 15.60

*Obtain the Foster I and Cauer I forms of the RL impedance function.*

$$Z(s) = \frac{s(s+4)(s+8)}{(s+1)(s+6)}$$

**Solution**

***Foster I Form*** The Foster I form is obtained by partial fraction expansion of $\frac{Z(s)}{s}$.

$$\frac{Z(s)}{s} = \frac{(s+4)(s+8)}{(s+1)(s+6)}$$

Since the degree of the numerator is equal to the degree of the denominator, division is first carried out.

$$s^2+7s+6)s^2+12s+32(1$$
$$\underline{s^2+7s+6}$$
$$5s+26$$

$$\frac{Z(s)}{s} = 1 + \frac{5s+26}{s^2+7s+6} = 1 + \frac{5s+26}{(s+1)(s+6)}$$

By partial fraction expansion,

$$\frac{Z(s)}{s} = 1 + \frac{K_0}{s+1} + \frac{K_1}{s+6}$$

where
$$K_0 = \left.\frac{5s+26}{s+6}\right|_{s=-1} = \frac{-5+26}{-1+6} = \frac{21}{5}$$

$$K_1 = \left.\frac{5s+26}{s+1}\right|_{s=-6} = \frac{-30+26}{-6+1} = \frac{4}{5}$$

$$\frac{Z(s)}{s} = 1 + \frac{\frac{21}{5}}{s+1} + \frac{\frac{24}{5}}{s+6}$$

$$Z(s) = s + \frac{\frac{21}{5}s}{s+1} + \frac{\frac{4}{5}s}{s+6}$$

The first term represents the impedance of the inductor of 1 H. The other two terms represent the impedance of a parallel *RL* circuit for which

$$Z_{RL}(s) = \frac{R_i s}{s + \frac{R_i}{L_i}}$$

By direct comparison,

$$R_1 = \frac{21}{5}\,\Omega, \quad L_1 = \frac{21}{5}\,\text{H}$$

$$R_2 = \frac{4}{5}\,\Omega, \quad L_2 = \frac{4}{30}\,\text{H}$$

The network is shown in Fig. 15.68.

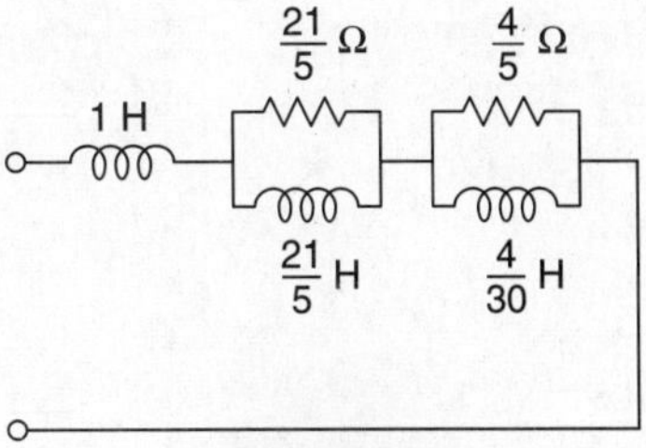

Fig. 15.68

***Cauer I Form*** The Cauer I form is obtained by continued fraction expansion of $Z(s)$ about the pole at infinity.

$$Z(s) = \frac{s^3 + 12s^2 + 32s}{s^2 + 7s + 6}$$

By continued fraction expansion,

$$s^2+7s+6\,\big)\,s^3+12s^2+32s\,\big(\,s \leftarrow Z$$
$$s^3+7s^2+6s$$
$$\overline{\quad 5s^2+26s\,\big)\,s^2+7s+6\,\big(\,\frac{1}{5} \leftarrow Y}$$
$$s^2+\frac{26}{5}s$$
$$\overline{\quad \frac{9}{5}s+6\,\big)\,5s^2+26s\,\big(\,\frac{25}{9}s \leftarrow Z}$$
$$5s^2+\frac{50}{3}s$$
$$\overline{\quad \frac{28}{3}s\,\big)\,\frac{9}{5}s+6\,\big(\,\frac{27}{140} \leftarrow Y}$$
$$\frac{9}{5}s$$
$$\overline{\quad 6\,\big)\,\frac{28}{3}s\,\big(\,\frac{28}{18}s \leftarrow Z}$$
$$\frac{28}{3}s$$
$$\overline{\quad 0}$$

The impedances are connected in the series branches, whereas the admittances are connected in the parallel branches. The network is shown in Fig. 15.69.

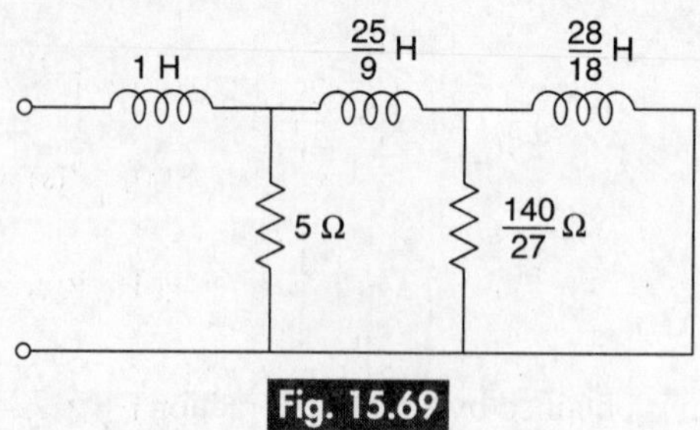


Fig. 15.69

# Theory Questions

**15.1** Define Hurwitz polynomial. What are the properties of Hurwitz polynomials? **[LO 15.1]** ●○○

**15.2** Define positive real function. What are the properties of positive real functions? **[LO 15.2]** ●○○

**15.3** What are the necessary and sufficient conditions for positive real functions? **[LO 15.2]** ●○○

**15.4** State the properties of LC driving point immitance functions. **[LO 15.4]** ●○○

**15.5** State the properties of RC driving point immitance functions. **[LO 15.5]** ●○○

**15.6** State the properties of RL driving point immitance functions. **[LO 15.6]** ●○○

**15.7** Draw the structure for Foster I , Foster II, Cauer I and Couer II form for LC functions. **[LO 15.4]** ●○○

**15.8** Draw the structure for Foster I , Foster II, Cauer I and Couer II form for RC functions. **[LO 15.5]** ●○○

**15.9** Draw the structure for Foster I , Foster II, Cauer I and Couer II form for RL functions. **[LO 15.6]** ●○○

# Practice Problems

**15.1** Test the following polynomials for Hurwitz property: ○●○

(i) $s^3 + s^2 + 2s + 2$

(ii) $s^4 + s^2 + s + 1$

(iii) $s^3 + 4s^2 + 5s + 2$

(iv) $s^4 + 7s^3 + 6s^2 + 21s + 8$

(v) $s^4 + s^3 + s + 1$

(vi) $s^7 + 3s^6 + 8s^5 + 15s^4 + 17s^3 + 12s^2 + 4s$

(vii) $s^7 + 2s^6 + 2s^5 + s^4 + 4s^3 + 8s^2 + 8s + 4$

(viii) $s^7 + 3s^5 + 2s^3 + s$

(ix) $s^5 + 2s^3 + s$

(x) $s^3 + 2s^2 + 4s + 2$

(xi) $s^4 + s^3 + 4s^2 + 2s + 3$

(xii) $s^5 + 8s^4 + 24s^3 + 28s^2 + 23s + 6$

(xiii) $s^7 - 2s^6 + 2s^5 + 9s^2 + 8s + 4$

(xiv) $s^7 + 3s^5 + 2s^3 + 3$

(xv) $s^5 + s^3 + s$

(xvi) $s^6 + 7s^4 + 5s^3 + s^2 + s$

(xvii) $s^4 + s^3 + 2s^2 + 3s + 2$

**15.2** Determine whether the following functions are positive real: ○●○

(i) $\dfrac{s^3 + 5s}{s^4 + 2s^2 + 1}$

(ii) $\dfrac{s(s+3)(s+5)}{(s+1)(s+4)}$

(iii) $\dfrac{2s^2 + 2s + 1}{s^3 + 2s^2 + s + 2}$

(iv) $\dfrac{s^4 + 3s^3 + s^2 + s + 2}{s^3 + s^2 + s + 1}$

(v) $\dfrac{2s^3 + 2s^2 + 3s + 2}{s^2 + 1}$

(vi) $\dfrac{s^2 + 2s + 1}{s^2 + 4s + 4}$

(vii) $\dfrac{s^3 + 2s^2 + 3s + 1}{s^3 + 2s^2 + s + 2}$

(viii) $\dfrac{s^3+2s^2+s+1}{s^2+s+1}$

(ix) $\dfrac{s+4}{s^2+2s+1}$

(x) $\dfrac{s^2+4s+3}{s^2+6s+8}$

(xi) $\dfrac{s^2+1}{s^3+4s}$

(xii) $\dfrac{s^4+2s^3+3s^2+1}{s^4+s^3+3s^2+2s+1}$

(xiii) $\dfrac{s^2+2s+4}{(s+1)(s+3)}$

(xiv) $\dfrac{2s+4}{s+5}$

(xv) $\dfrac{s^2+2s}{s^2+1}$

(xvi) $\dfrac{s^2+4}{s^3+3s^2+3s+1}$

**15.3** Determine whether the following functions are *LC*, *RC* or *RL* functions: ●○○

(i) $F(s)=\dfrac{2(s+1)(s+3)}{(s+2)(s+6)}$

(ii) $Z(s)=\dfrac{3(s+2)(s+4)}{s(s+3)}$

(iii) $Z(s)=\dfrac{(s+1)(s+8)}{(s+2)(s+4)}$

(iv) $Z(s)=\dfrac{Ks(s^2+4)}{(s^2+1)(s^2+3)}$

(v) $Z(s)=\dfrac{2(s^2+1)(s^2+9)}{s(s^2+2)}$

(vi) $Z(s)=\dfrac{4(s+1)(s+3)}{s(s+2)}$

(vii) $Z(s)=\dfrac{(s^2+1)(s^2+3)}{s(s^2+2)}$

(viii) $F(s)=\dfrac{(s+1)(s+2)}{s(s+3)}$

(ix) $Z(s)=\dfrac{(s+1)(s+3)}{(s+2)(s+4)}$

(x) $Z(s)=\dfrac{(s+2)(s+4)}{(s+1)}$

(xi) $Y(s)=\dfrac{4(s+3)}{(s+1)(s+5)}$

(xii) $Y(s)=\dfrac{2(s+1)(s+3)}{(s+2)(s+6)}$

(xiii) $Z(s)=\dfrac{s(s^2+4)(s^2+16)}{(s^2+9)(s^2+25)}$

(xiv) $Z(s)=\dfrac{(s^2+1)(s^2+8)}{s(s^2+4)}$

**15.4** Realise the following functions in Foster I form: ○●○

(i) $Z(s)=\dfrac{3(s+2)(s+4)}{s(s+3)}$

(ii) $Z(s)=\dfrac{2(s^2+1)(s^2+9)}{s(s^2+4)}$

(iii) $F(s)=\dfrac{4(s+1)(s+3)}{(s+2)(s+6)}$

(iv) $Z(s)=\dfrac{s+4}{(s+2)(s+6)}$

(v) $Z(s)=\dfrac{(s+1)(s+4)}{s(s+2)}$

(vi) $Y(s)=\dfrac{(s+2)(s+5)}{s(s+4)(s+6)}$

(vii) $Z(s)=\dfrac{s^2+2s+2}{s^2+s+1}$

**15.5** Realise the following functions in Foster II form: ○●○

(i) $Z(s)=\dfrac{3(s+2)(s+4)}{s(s+3)}$

(ii) $Z(s)=\dfrac{2(s^2+1)(s^2+9)}{s(s^2+4)}$

(iii) $Z(s)=\dfrac{4(s+1)(s+3)}{(s+2)(s+6)}$

(iv) $Y(s)=\dfrac{4(s^2+4)(s^2+25)}{s(s^2+16)}$

(v) $Z(s)=\dfrac{(s+2)(s+5)}{s(s+4)(s+6)}$

**15.6** Realise the following functions in Cauer I form: ○●○

(i) $F(s)=\dfrac{2(s+1)(s+3)}{(s+2)(s+6)}$

(ii) $Z(s)=\dfrac{(s^2+1)(s^2+3)}{s(s^2+2)}$

(iii) $Z(s)=\dfrac{(s+1)(s+3)}{(s+2)(s+4)}$

(iv) $Z(s)=\dfrac{2(s^2+1)(s^2+9)}{s(s^2+4)}$

(v) $F(s)=\dfrac{(s+1)(s+3)}{s(s+2)}$

(vi) $Z(s)=\dfrac{s+4}{(s+2)(s+6)}$

(vii) $Z(s)=\dfrac{6(s+2)(s+4)}{s(s+3)}$

(viii) $Z(s)=\dfrac{s^3+2s}{s^4+4s^2+3}$

(ix) $Z(s)=\dfrac{s(s^2+2)(s^2+5)}{(s^2+1)(s^2+3)}$

(x) $Z(s)=\dfrac{s^2+2s+2}{s^2+s+1}$

**15.7** Realise the following function in Cauer II form: ○●○

(i) $F(s)=\dfrac{(s^2+1)(s^2+3)}{s(s^2+2)}$

(ii) $Z(s)=\dfrac{(s+1)(s+3)}{(s+2)(s+4)}$

(iii) $Z(s)=\dfrac{2(s^2+1)(s^2+9)}{s(s^2+4)}$

(iv) $Z(s)=\dfrac{(s+1)(s+3)}{s(s+2)}$

(v) $F(s)=\dfrac{s^3+12s^2+32s}{s^2+7s+6}$

(vi) $Z(s)=\dfrac{2(s+1)(s+3)}{(s+2)(s+6)}$

(vii) $Z(s)=\dfrac{s(s^2+2)(s^2+5)}{(s^2+1)(s^2+3)}$

(viii) $Z(s)=\dfrac{s^2+2s+2}{s^2+s+1}$

**15.8** An impedance function has the pole-zero diagram, as shown in Fig. 15.70. If $Z(-2) = 3$, synthesise the impedance function in Foster and Cauer forms. ○○●

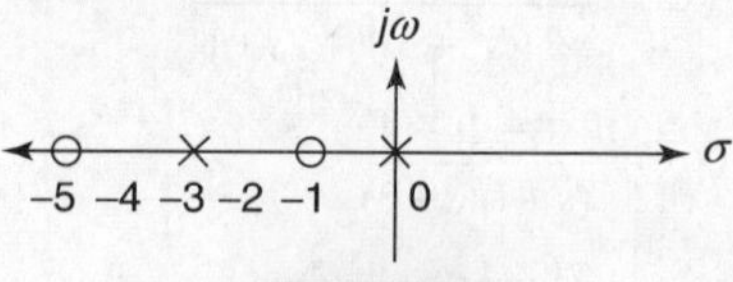


Fig. 15.70

**15.9** An impedance function has the pole-zero diagram, as shown in Fig. 15.71. Find the impedance function such that $Z(-4)=\dfrac{8}{3}$ and realise in Cauer forms. ○○●

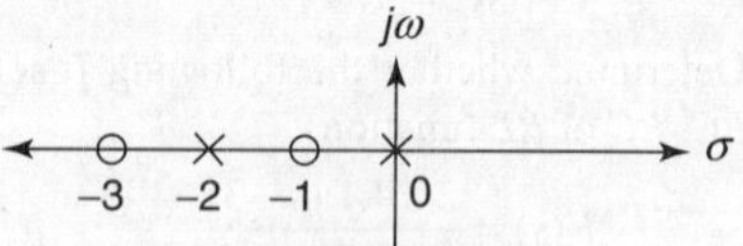


Fig. 15.71

**15.10** For the realisation of a given function $F(s)$.

$$F(s)=\frac{K_0}{s}+\sum_{i=1}^{n}\frac{sK_i}{(s^2+\omega_i^2)}+sK_\infty$$

where $K_0$, $K_i$ ($i$ = 1, 2, 3, … $n$) and $K_\infty$ are constants. ○○●

(i) Mention the type of function (*RC*, *RL* or *LC*)

(ii) Given that $K_0 = 6$, $K_1 = 8$, $\omega_1 = 4$, $K_2 = 10$, $\omega_2 = 8$, $K_\infty = 5$, find the component values of realised network for $F(s) = Z(s)$ and $F(s) = Y(s)$. Draw neat diagrams.

# Objective-Type Questions

## From GATE and Other Competitive Examinations

**15.1** The necessary and sufficient condition for a rational function $F(s)$ to be the driving-point impedance of an $RC$ network is that all poles and zeros should be ●○○
(a) simple and lie on the negative real axis in the $s$-plane
(b) complex and lie in the left half of $s$-plane
(c) complex and lie in the right-half of $s$-plane
(d) simple and lie on the positive real axis of the $s$-plane

**15.2** The number of roots of $s^3 + 5s^2 + 7s + 3 = 0$ in the left half of $s$-plane is ●○○
(a) zero (b) one
(c) two (d) three

**15.3** The first and the last critical frequencies of a driving-point impedance function of a passive network having two kinds of elements, are a pole and a zero respectively. The above property will be satisfied by ●○○
(a) $RL$ network only
(b) $RC$ network only
(c) $LC$ network only
(d) $RC$ as well as $RL$ network

**15.4** The pole-zero pattern of a particular network is shown in Fig. 15.72. It is that of an ●○○

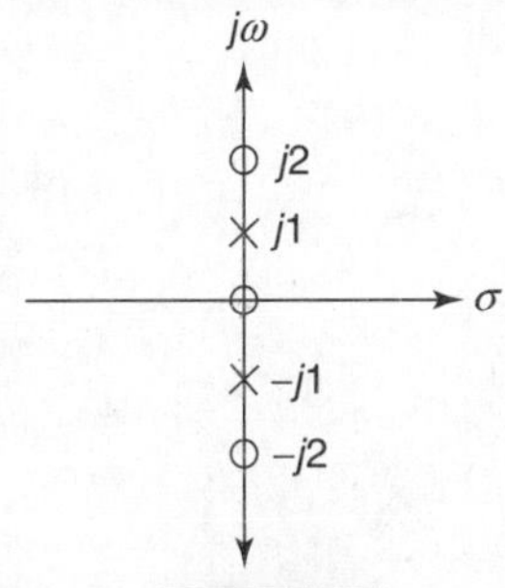


Fig. 15.72

(a) $LC$ network (b) $RC$ network
(c) $RL$ network (d) none of these

**15.5** The first critical frequency nearest to the origin of the complex frequency plane for an $RL$ driving-point impedance function will be ●○○
(a) a zero in the left-half plane
(b) a zero in the right-half plane
(c) a pole in the left-half plane
(d) a pole in the right-half plane

**15.6** Consider the following polynomials: ○●○
$P_1 = s^8 + 2s^6 + 4s^4$
$P_2 = s^6 - 3s^2 + 2s^2 + 1$
$P_3 = s^4 + 3s^3 + 3s^2 + 2s + 1$
$P_4 = s^7 + 2s^6 + 2s^4 + 4s^3 + 8s^2 + 8s + 4$
which one of these polymials is not Hurwitz?
(a) $P_1$ (b) $P_2$
(c) $P_3$ (d) $P_4$

**15.7** For very high frequencies, the driving-point admittance function, $Y(s) = \dfrac{4(s+1)(s+3)}{s(s+2)(s+4)}$ behaves as ○●○
(a) a resistance of $\dfrac{3}{2}\,\Omega$
(b) a capacitance of 4 F
(c) an inductance of $\dfrac{1}{4}$ H
(d) an inductance of 4 H

**15.8** The driving-point impedance $Z(s) = \dfrac{s+3}{s+4}$ behaves as ○●○
(a) a resistance of 0.75 Ω at low frequencies
(b) a resistance of 1 Ω at high frequencies
(c) both (a) and (b) above
(d) none of the above

**15.9** An $RC$ driving-point impedance function has zeros at $s = -2$ and $s = -5$. The admissible poles for the functions would be ○●○
(a) $s = 0, s = -6$ (b) $s = -1, s = -3$
(c) $s = 0, s = -1$ (d) $s = -3, s = -4$

**15.10** Consider the following from the point of view of possible realisation as driving-point impedances using passive elements: ○●○
1. $\dfrac{1}{s(s+5)}$ 2. $\dfrac{s+3}{s^2(s+5)}$
3. $\dfrac{s^2+3}{s^2(s^2+5)}$ 4. $\dfrac{s+5}{s(s+5)}$
Of these, the realisable are
(a) 1, 2 and 4 (b) 1, 2 and 3
(c) 3 and 4 (d) none of these

**15.11** The poles and zeros of a driving-point function of a network are simple and interlace on the negative real axis with a pole closest to the origin. It can be realised ○●○

(a) by an $LC$ network
(b) as an $RC$ driving-point impedance
(c) as an $RC$ driving-point admittance
(d) only by an $RLC$ network

**15.12** If $F_1(s)$ and $F_2(s)$ are two positive real functions then the function which is always positive real, is ○○●

(a) $F_1(s)\,F_2(s)$

(b) $\dfrac{F_1(s)}{F_2(s)}$

(c) $\dfrac{F_1(s)F_2(s)}{F_1(s)+F_2(s)}$

(d) $F_1(s) - F_2(s)$

**15.13** The circuit shown in Fig. 15.73 is ○●○

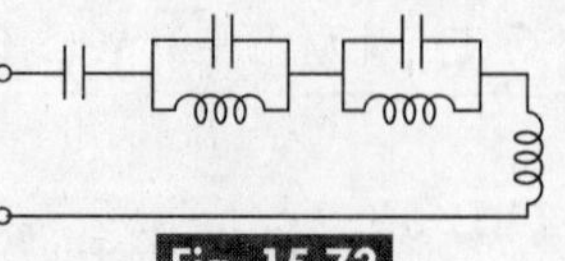

Fig. 15.73

(a) Cauer I form (b) Foster I form
(c) Cauer II form (d) Foster II form

**15.14** For an $RC$ driving-point impedance function, the poles and zeros ●○○

(a) should alternate on the real axis
(b) should alternate only on the negative real axis
(c) should alternate on the imaginary axis
(d) can lie anywhere on the left half-plane

## ANSWERS TO OBJECTIVE-TYPE QUESTIONS

| | | | | | | |
|---|---|---|---|---|---|---|
| **15.1** (a) | **15.2** (a) | **15.3** (b) | **15.4** (a) | **15.5** (a) | **15.6** (b) | **15.7** (c) |
| **15.8** (c) | **15.9** (b) | **15.10** (a) | **15.11** (b) | **15.12** (c) | **15.13** (b) | **15.14** (b) |

# Appendix LTspice Basics

LTspice XVII is a schematic-driven circuit simulation programme. LTspice is a registered trademark of Linear Technology Corporation. SPICE is an acronym for Simulation Program with Integrated Circuit Emphasis. This appendix introduces the basics of computer-aided circuit analysis using LTspice. It is freeware and supported on both Windows and Mac OS X. LTspice is intended to be used as a general-purpose SPICE simulator. New circuits can be drafted with the built-in schematic capture. Simulation commands and parameters are placed as text on the schematic using established SPICE syntax. Waveforms of circuit nodes and device currents can be plotted by clicking the mouse on the nodes in the schematic during or after simulation.

In LTspice, the circuit to be analysed is described by a text file called a netlist. The netlist consists of a list of circuit elements and their nodes, model definitions, and other SPICE commands. The first line in the netlist is ignored, that is, it is assumed to be a comment. The last line of the netlist is usually simply the line ".END", but this can be omitted. Any line after the line ".END" can be ignored. The order of the lines between the comment and end is irrelevant. Lines can be comments, circuit element declarations or simulation directives.

## CIRCUIT ELEMENTS

### Resistor

Syntax: RXXX N1 N2 <VALUE>
Example: R1 1 2 20

This statement places a resistor of 20 ohms between nodes 1 and 2.

### Inductor

Syntax: LXXX N+ N- <INDUCTANCE>
Example: L1 1 2 0.2

This statement places an inductor of 0.2 henry between nodes 1 and 2.

### Capacitor

Syntax: CXXX N1 N2 <CAPACITANCE>

Example: C1 1 2 20U

This statement places a capacitor of 20 microfarads between nodes 1 and 2.

## Mutual Inductance

Syntax: KXXX L1 L2 [L3 ...] <COEFFICIENT>

L1 and L2 are the names of inductors in the circuit. The mutual coupling coefficient must be in the range of -1 to 1.

Example: K1 L1 L2 0.5

This statement indicates coefficient of coupling of 0.5 between inductances L1 and L2.

## Voltage Source

Syntax: VXXX N+ N- <VOLTAGE> [AC=<AMPLITUDE>]

Example: V1 1 0 20

This statement places a voltage source of 20 volts between nodes 1 and 0.

## Current Source

Syntax: IXXX N+ N- <CURRENT> [AC=<AMPLITUDE>]

Example: I1 0 1 10

This statement places a current source of 10 amperes between nodes 0 and 1.

## Voltage-Controlled Voltage Source

Syntax: EXXX N+ N- NC+ NC- <GAIN>

Example: E 1 2 3 4 10

This statement places a voltage-controlled voltage source of gain 10 between the nodes 1 and 2 that depends on the input voltage between nodes 3 and 4.

## Current-Controlled Current Source

Syntax: FXXX N+ N- <VNAM> <GAIN>

Example: F 1 2 VIN 0.5

This statement places a current-controlled current source of gain 0.5 between nodes 1 and 2. The current applied is equal to the value of the gain times the current through the voltage source specified with independent voltage source VIN.

## Voltage-Controlled Current Source

Syntax: GXXX N+ N- NC+ NC- <GAIN>

Example: G 1 2 3 4 10

This statement places a voltage-controlled current source of gain 10 between nodes 1 and 2 that depends on the input voltage between nodes 3 and 4.

## Current-Controlled Voltage Source

Syntax: HXXX N+ N- <VNAM> <TRANSRESISTANCE>

Example: H1 1 2 VO 10

This statement places a current controlled voltage source of gain 10 between nodes 1 and 2. The voltage applied is equal to the value of the transresistance times the current through the zero voltage source VO.

## Subcircuit

Syntax: **X**XXX N1 N2 N3... <SUBCKT NAME>

Subcircuits allow circuitry to be defined and stored in a library for later retrieval by name. The end of a subcircuit definition must be a .ends directive.

Example: X1 1 2 TWOPORT

This statement defines and calls a subcircuit TWOPORT and invokes it in a circuit.

## Input Sources

### ➤ *Exponential*

Syntax: EXP (V1 V2 TD1 TR1 TD2 TR2)

This statement describes the exponential waveform with initial voltage (V1), peak voltage (V2) fall delay time (TD1), rise time constant (TR1), fall delay time (TD2) and fall time constants (TR2).

### ➤ *Pulse*

Syntax: PULSE (V1 V2 TD TR TF PW PER)

This statement describes the pulse form of voltage with initial voltage (V1), peak value of pulse (V2), delay time (TD), rise time (TR), fall time (TF), width of the pulse (PW) and period of the pulse (PER).

### ➤ *Piece wise linear*

Syntax: PWL (T1, V1 T2, V2 … TNVN)

This statement describes a piecewise linear waveform. The arguments in parenthesis represent time-voltage pairs at the corners of the waveform.

### ➤ *Single frequency FM*

Syntax: SFFM (VO VA FC MD FS)

This statement describes the single frequency, frequency modulated wave, with offset voltage (VO), peak amplitude (VA), carrier frequency (FC), modulation index (MD), and signal frequency (FS).

### ➤ *Sine wave*

Syntax: SIN (VO VA FREQ TD DF PHASE)

This statement describes the sinusoidal waveform with an offset voltage (VO), peak value (VA), frequency (FREQ), delay time (TD), damping factor (DF), and a phase angle (PHASE).

# SIMULATOR DIRECTIVES – DOT COMMANDS

## .END

This directive marks the end of the textual netlist. All lines after this one are ignored.

## .ENDS

This directive marks the end of a subcircuit definition.

## .PRINT

This statement consists of .PRINT followed by a space and DC/AC, another space, and the desired node voltage or node voltages separated by at least one space.

.PRINT DC V(1) V(2)

This statement prints the voltage at the node 1 and the node 2 with reference to zero node.

## .PROBE

This statement writes the results from dc, ac and transient analysis to a data file named PROBE.DAT for graphics analysis by postprocessor.

.PROBE

This statement writes all the node voltages and all the device currents to the data file.

.PROBE V (1) V (2, 3) I (R2)

This statement writes the voltage of node 1, voltage between nodes 2 and 3 and the current through R2 to the data file.

## .IC – Set Initial Conditions

The .ic directive allows initial conditions for transient analysis to be specified. Node voltages and inductor currents may be specified.

Syntax: .IC [V(<N1>)=<VOLTAGE>] [I(<INDUCTOR>)=<CURRENT>]

Example: .IC V(IN)=2 V(OUT)=5 V(VC)=1.8 I(L1)=300M

## .STEP – Parameter Sweeps

This command causes an analysis to be repeatedly performed while stepping the temperature, a model parameter, a global parameter, or an independent source. Steps may be linear, logarithmic, or specified as a list of values.

Example: .STEP OCT V1 1 20 5

Step-independent voltage source V1 from 1 to 20 logarithmically with 5 points per octave.

Example: .STEP I1 10U 100U 10U

Step-independent current source I1 from 10u to 100u in step increments of 10u.

Example: .STEP PARAM RLOAD LIST 5 10 15

Perform the simulation three times with global parameter Rload being 5, 10 and 15.

Example: .STEP TEMP -55 125 10

Step the temperature from -55°C to 125°C in 10-degree step. Step sweeps may be nested

## TYPES OF ANALYSIS

There are different types of analyses that can be performed, each with a different analysis command.

### .AC – Perform an Small Signal AC Analysis Linearized About the DC Operating Point

The statement begins with the specification .AC and continues with four additional terms. The first term indicates the type of frequency sweep (linear, octave and decade). The second term indicates the number of points in the sweep and the third and fourth terms indicate the start and end frequencies.

Syntax: .AC <OCT, DEC, LIN> <NPOINTS> <STARTFREQ> <ENDFREQ>

Example: .AC LIN 10 5 50

.AC LIN 10 5 50 statement provides results at the start and end frequencies and eight intermediate frequencies that are uniformly spaced 5, 10, 15, 20, 25, 30, 35, 40, 45, 50.

### .DC – Perform a DC Source Sweep Analysis

.DC statement gives a range to voltages/currents. This is called a sweep of voltage/current. This statement specifies the values used during the dc sweep. This statement specifies source value to be swept, the starting value, the end value and the amount of increment in each step.

Syntax: .DC <SRCNAM1> <VSTART1> <VSTOP1> <VINCR1>
+ [<SRCNAM2> <VSTART2> <VSTOP2> <VINCR2>]

The <srcnam> is either an independent voltage or current source that is to be swept from <Vstart> to <Vstop> in <Vincr> step sizes.

Example: .DC VIN 0 100 10

.DC statement specifies an independent voltage source VIN that is to be swept from 0 to 100 V in steps of 10 V.

### OP – Find the DC Operating Point

.OP statement performs a DC operating point solution with capacitances open circuited and inductances short circuited. The .OP statement is a control statement which instructs the computer to calculate the dc voltage between each node and the reference node.

Example: .OP

### .TRAN – Perform a Nonlinear Transient Analysis

.TRAN statement specifies the time interval over which the transient analysis takes place. This statement is followed by two values. The first value indicates the print-step (interval) value and the second value indicates the final value of time for the analysis.

Syntax: .TRAN <TSTEP> <TSTOP>

Example: .TRAN 2ms 15ms

.TRAN statement performs transient analysis with step interval of 2 ms and stop time of 15 ms.

# Index

## D



## E



## F



## G



## H

# I



# K



# L



# M

## N



## O



## P



## Q



## R